HEBREW WRITING: Consonantal alphabet which survives in modern Hebrew. (Fragment of Dead Sea Scrolls: c 100 B.C.)

THE READER'S DIGEST

GREAT
ENCYCLOPAEDIC
DICTIONARY

THE READER'S DIGEST GREAT ENCYCLOPAEDIC DICTIONARY

IN THREE VOLUMES

2

M-Z

THE READER'S DIGEST ASSOCIATION
LONDON, MONTREAL and CAPE TOWN

THIRD EDITION
December 1979

Published by
THE READER'S DIGEST ASSOCIATION LIMITED
25 BERKELEY SQUARE, LONDON, W.I
215 REDFERN AVENUE, MONTREAL
AND PARKADE, STRAND STREET, CAPE TOWN
and
OXFORD UNIVERSITY PRESS
ELY HOUSE, LONDON, W.I

All rights reserved. No part of this book may be
reproduced, stored in a retrieval system, or transmitted
in any form or by any means, electronic, mechanical,
photocopying, recording or otherwise without permission
in writing from the publishers.

© THE READER'S DIGEST ASSOCIATION LIMITED 1976
© OXFORD UNIVERSITY PRESS 1976

© READER'S DIGEST ASSOCIATION FAR EAST LIMITED 1978
PHILIPPINES © READER'S DIGEST ASSOCIATION FAR EAST LIMITED 1978

PRINTED IN GREAT BRITAIN AT THE UNIVERSITY PRESS, OXFORD
BY ERIC BUCKLEY, PRINTER TO THE UNIVERSITY

VOLUME TWO

M-Z

COMPILED BY
OXFORD
UNIVERSITY
PRESS

CONTENTS

Volume One:	A–L	19
Volume Two:	M–Z	537
	Addenda to Volumes One and Two	1013

Volume Three: THE ARTS
Classical and Contemporary Architecture — 1026
Literature — 1044
Music — 1054
Painting and Sculpture — 1070
Theatre — 1092

GOVERNMENT
Civics and Government — 1116
English and Scots Law — 1141

LANGUAGE
Foreign Phrases — 1198
General and Forces Slang — 1209
Idioms and Picturesque Phrases — 1238
Language of Food — 1250
Proverbs — 1259
Rhyming Slang — 1267
Underworld Slang — 1276

NAMES
Christian or Given Names — 1288
Nicknames — 1304
Surnames — 1310

MYTHOLOGY AND RELIGIONS
Classical Myths and Legends — 1334
Religions — 1349

THE SCIENCES
Archaeology — 1372
Astronomy — 1402
Biology (Botany and Zoology) — 1420
Chemistry and Physics — 1469
Cinema, Television, and Radio — 1538
Geography — 1552
Medicine — 1593
Physical Anthropology — 1636

SPORT
Fishing — 1652
Sports and Games — 1666

M

M, m (ĕm). 1. 13th letter of modern English and 12th of ancient Roman alphabet, representing a bilabial nasal (usu. voiced) consonant; the form of the letter is derived from Phoenician ᛩ (early Gk & L ᛩ, ⱲW, M). 2. Roman numeral symbol for 1,000. 3. (print.) = EM.
M. *abbrev.* Mega-; monsieur; motorway.
m. *abbrev.* Maiden (over); male; mark(s) (coin); married; masculine; metre(s); mile(s); milli-; million(s); minute(s).
ma (mah) *n.* (vulg.) = MAMMA[1].
M.A. *abbrev.* Master of Arts; Military Academy.
ma'am (mahm, măm, mam, m̐) *n.* Madam, used esp. in addressing Queen or royal princesses (pr. măm, mahm), or officers in the women's services (pr. măm), or by servants etc. addressing mistresses (pr. mam, m).
Maas : see MEUSE.
Măbĭnō'gĭon. Collection of ancient Welsh prose tales (*Mabinogi* pr. -ŏgĭ, = 'instruction for young bards') dealing with Celtic legends and mythology; four of them are contained in the 'Red Book of Hergest' which was compiled in the 14th and 15th centuries.
Mabūse (-z), Jan Gossaert (d. c 1535). Flemish painter, active also in Holland; painted in an Italian style.
măc *n.* (colloq.) = MACINTOSH.
maca'bre (-ahbr) *adj.* Grim, gruesome; *danse* ~, (Fr.) Dance of Death.
maca'cō[1] (-kah-) *n.* = MACAQUE; any of various S. Amer. monkeys. [Port., = 'monkey']
maca'cō[2] (-kah-) *n.* Any of several lemurs, esp. the black lemur, *Lemur macaco*.
măcă'dam *n.* (Material for) road surface made with successive layers of small broken stones rolled in with some binding material.
măcă'damize *v.t.* **măcădamĭzā'tion** *n.* [John Loudon *McAdam*, Scottish engineer (1756–1836)]
maca'que (-kahk) *n.* Monkey of genus *Macacus*, of Asia and N. Africa (ill. MONKEY).
măcarō'nĭ *n.* Pasta formed into long tubes; (hist.) 18th-c. dandy affecting continental manners and fashions.
măcarō'nic *adj.* (of verse) Of burlesque form containing Latin or other foreign words and vernacular words with Latin etc. terminations. **măcarō'nics** *n.pl.* Macaronic verse.
măcaroo'n *n.* Small cake or biscuit of ground almonds, white of egg, sugar, etc.
Macă'ssar *n.* (also ~ *oil*) Oil said to consist of ingredients obtained from Macassar, a port of Celebes, formerly used as a hairdressing; similar oil or preparation.
Macau'lay, Thomas Babington, 1st Baron Macaulay (1800–59). English historian and essayist.
macaw' *n.* Any of several large long-tailed brightly coloured parrots, mostly native to S. and Central America.
Măcbĕ'th (d. 1057). King of Scotland; seized the throne (to which he perhaps had some claim through his wife Gruach) after slaying the king, Duncan, in 1040; hero of a tragedy by Shakespeare.
Macc. *abbrev.* Maccabees (Apocr.).
Mă'ccabees (-z). Family of Jews, consisting of Mattathias and his 5 sons, Jochanan, Simon, Judas, Eleazar, and Jonathan, who led a revolt against the oppression of the Syrian king Antiochus Epiphanes (175–165 B.C.), and established a dynasty of priest-kings which ruled until the time of Herod (40 B.C.); (*Books of*) ~, four books of Jewish history and theology, of which the first two are included in the Apocrypha. **Măccabē'an** *adj.*
Macdŏ'nald[1], Flora (1722–90). Jacobite heroine, daughter of a farmer in the Hebrides; she helped Prince Charles Edward Stuart, the Young Pretender, to escape to Skye after his defeat at Culloden, 1746; for this she was imprisoned in the Tower of London, but released 1747.
MacDŏ'nald[2], James Ramsay (1866–1937). British Labour politician; prime minister in Labour Government 1924 and 1929–31, and of National Government 1931–5.
Măcdŭ'ff. Thane of Fife, a partly or wholly mythical personage who helped Duncan's son, Malcolm Canmore, against MACBETH.
māce[1] *n.* 1. (hist.) Heavy usu. metal-headed and spiked club. 2. Staff of office resembling this (*see illustration, p. 538*); *the M*~, the symbol of the Speaker's authority in the House of Commons, placed on the table when he is in the chair. 3. Flat-headed stick used in bagatelle.
māce[2] *n.* Dried outer covering of nutmeg, as spice.
mă'cėdoine (-dwahn) *n.* Mixed fruit or vegetables, esp. cut up small. [Fr. *Macédoine* Macedonia]
Mă'cėdon. (Gk hist.) Macedonia.
Măcėdō'nia. Mountainous Balkan country, N. of ancient Greece, now divided between Greece and Yugoslavia; under Philip II and his son Alexander III (the Great) it dominated Greece in the 4th c. B.C.; in 146 B.C. it became a Roman province, and when the Roman Empire was divided it was assigned to the eastern half; in the 5th c. A.D. Slavs began to invade

[537]

and colonize it and it became in turn an independent kingdom, a part of the Bulgarian and then of the Serbian Empire; from the end of the 14th c. until the Balkan war of 1912 it was under Turkish rule.
Măcĕdō′nian *adj.* & *n.*
mă′cerāte *v.* Make or become soft by soaking; become emaciated by fasting. **măcerā′tion** *n.*
McGi′ll (mag-), James (1744–1813). Scottish-born Canadian philanthropist; founded a college at Montreal which became ~ *University* (1821).
măch (-k; *or* mahk) *n.* (also ~ *number*) Ratio of the velocity of a body passing through a fluid medium to the velocity of sound in that medium. [E. *Mach* (1838–1916), Austrian physicist]
machair′ (-χ-) *n.* (geog.) Flat or low-lying strip of calcareous natural grassland usu. overlying shell sand.
mache′tè (-chä-) *n.* Broad heavy knife used in Central America and W. Indies as implement and weapon.
Măchiavĕ′lli (-k-), Niccolo di Bernardo dei (1469–1527). Florentine political philosopher, author of a famous and influential treatise on statecraft, 'The Prince' (*Il Principe*, 1513), advocating the principle that any political means, however unscrupulous, are justifiable if they strengthen the power of a State; hence, an unscrupulous schemer, one who practises duplicity in statecraft. **Măchiavĕ′llian** *adj.* & *n.* **Măchiavĕ′llianism, Măchiavĕ′llism** *ns.*
machicolā′tion *n.* Opening between supporting corbels for dropping stones etc. on assailants (ill. CASTLE). **machi′colāted** *adj.* Furnished with machicolations.
mă′chināte (-k-) *v.i.* Lay plots, intrigue. **măchinā′tion, mă′chinātor** *ns.*

A. WAR MACE, c 1480. B. CEREMONIAL MACE CARRIED BY THE SERJEANTS-AT-ARMS AT CORONATIONS, LATE 16TH C.

machi′ne (-shēn) *n.* Apparatus for applying mechanical power, having several parts each with definite function (the kind often being specified as *sewing-, printing-, ~*); bicycle, motor-cycle, etc.; aircraft; person who acts mechanically and without intelligence or with unfailing regularity; instrument directing application of, or transmitting, force; organized system for carrying out specific functions, as the *political, party ~*; ~*-gun*, belt-fed, water-cooled, single-barrelled gun, firing solid bullets from a fixed mounting, designed to utilize part of the energy of one explosion to extract the spent cartridge and load and fire the next round and capable of very high speeds of firing for hours on end; hence ~*-gunner*, ~*-tool*, cutting or shaping tool, worked by machinery, not by hand. ~ *v.t.* Make, operate on, print, sew, etc., with a machine.
machi′nery (-shēn-) *n.* Machines; mechanism; organization.
machi′nist (-shēn-) *n.* Maker of machinery; worker who operates a machine.
mă′chmēter (-k-; *or* mahk-) *n.* Instrument in aircraft for measuring mach number.
mă′cintŏsh, măck- *n.* Waterproof material of cloth and rubber; coat or cloak of this or of plastic or nylon material; waterproof sheet. [Charles *Macintosh* (1766–1843), inventor]
Mackĕ′nzie, Henry (1745–1831). Scottish novelist; author of 'The Man of Feeling' (1771); sometimes referred to as 'the Addison of the North'.
mă′ckerel *n.* Edible sea-fish, *Scomber scombrus*, of N. Atlantic, having a silvery belly and greenish back with dark-blue stripes; ~ *sky*, sky covered with clouds resembling the patterns on a mackerel's back (cirrocumulus).
McKi′nley (mak-), William (1843–1901). 25th president of U.S., 1897–1901; assassinated by an anarchist.
mackintosh: see MACINTOSH.
Macli′se (-ēz), Daniel (1806–70). Irish-born historical painter and illustrator.
Măc-Mähŏn, Marie Edmé Patrice Maurice de, Duke of Magenta (1808–93). French marshal and president of the Republic 1873–9.
Macmi′llan, Harold (1894–). British Conservative statesman; prime minister 1957–63.
Mâcon (mahkawṅ). *n.* Wine made near Mâcon, a city on the river Saône in central France.
Macphĕr′son, James (1736–96). Scottish poet; he claimed to have translated from the Gaelic two ancient epics by a poet called Ossian; after his death an investigating committee reported that he had used traditional Gaelic poems but edited them freely and added inventions of his own.

macramé (-ah′mĭ) *n.* Fringe or trimming of knotted thread or cord.
Macrea′dў (-rēdĭ), William Charles (1793–1873). English actor, famous for Shakespearian tragic parts.
măcro- *prefix.* Large (opp. *micro-*).
măcrocĕphă′lĭc *adj.* Long- or large-headed.
mă′crocŏsm *n.* Great world, universe (contrasted with *microcosm*); any great whole.
măcromŏ′lĕcūle *n.* Very large molecule like those in proteins, synthetic plastics, etc.
mă′cron *n.* Straight horizontal line (¯) over a vowel to indicate that it is long.
măcrophotŏ′graphў *n.* Photography of macroscopic objects.
măcroscŏ′pic *adj.* Visible to the naked eye (opp. *microscopic*).
măcroscŏ′pically *adv.*
mă′cūla *n.* (pl. *-ae*). Dark spot on sun or moon (ill. SUN); spot in mineral due to presence of particles of another mineral; spot, blemish, on the skin; (anat.) also ~ *lu′tĕa*) region of greatest visual acuity in the retina (ill. EYE).
mă′cūlar *adj.* **măcūlā′tion** *n.*
măd *adj.* Of disordered mind, insane; (of animals) rabid; wildly foolish; (colloq.) annoyed; ~ *about*, (colloq.) keen on; infatuated with; *ma′dcap*, wildly impulsive person; *ma′dhouse*, lunatic asylum; *ma′dman, ma′dwoman*. **mă′dlў** *adv.* **mă′dnĕss** *n.*
Mădagă′scar. Large island in India Ocean, off SE. coast of Africa; a republic within the French Community; capital, Tananarive.
mă′dam *n.* Polite formal address to woman; woman in charge of a brothel; (contempt.) minx. [OF *ma dame* my lady]
Madame (-ahm) *n.* (pl. *Mesdames*, pr. mādahm). Title of (corresp. to *Mrs.*) or form of address to French married woman. [Fr.]
mă′dden *v.* Make, become, mad; irritate.
mă′dder *n.* Herbaceous climbing plant (*Rubia tinctorum*) with yellowish flowers; red dye obtained from its root.
mād̆e *adj.*: see MAKE; (esp.) ~ *dish*, food prepared from several ingredients; ~ *man*, one who has attained success in life.
Madeir′a[1] (-ēra). Island in Atlantic Ocean, off W. coast of Africa, in Portuguese possession.
Madeir′a[2] (-ēra) *n.* 1. Fortified wine produced in Madeira, ambercoloured or brownish, varying in sweetness, and resembling sherry. 2. (also ~ *cake*) Kind of rich sweet cake without fruit.
Mademoiselle (mădmwăzĕl *or* măm-) *n.* (pl. *Mesdemoiselles*, pr. mădmwăzĕl). Title of (corresp. to *Miss*) or form of address to

[538]

French unmarried woman; *m~*, French governess in England. [Fr.]
Madhya Prade'sh (mah'dia, -āsh). State of central India formed in 1956; capital, Bhopal.
Măd'ison, James (1751-1836). 4th president of U.S., 1809-17.
madŏ'nna *n.* (Picture, statue, of) Virgin Mary; ~ *lily*, tall white lily (*Lilium candidum*), as often depicted in pictures of the Annunciation.
Madră's (*or* -ahs). Seaport on E. coast of India, capital of Tamil Nadu.
mă'drepore *n.* Perforate coral of genus *Madrepora*; animal producing this. [It. *madre* mother + *poro* coral-like but porous substance]
Madri'd. Capital city of Spain.
mă'drĭgal *n.* Short amatory poem; part-song for several voices in elaborate contrapuntal style, usu. without accompaniment.
Maeă'nder. Ancient name of a river of Phrygia, (now R. *Menderes*) remarkable for its winding course.
Maecē'năs (mi-), Gaius Cilnius (*c* 70-8 B.C.). Roman knight; patron of Virgil and Horace and friend and adviser of Augustus; celebrated for his patronage of learning and letters; hence, generous patron of literature or art.
mae'lstrom (māl-) *n.* Great whirlpool (also fig.). [f. *Maelström*, the whirlpool S. of the Lofoten Is. off W. coast of Norway]
mae'nad *n.* Bacchante. **maenă'dĭc** *adj.*
mae'strō (mī-) *n.* (pl. -*rī* pr. -rē). Eminent musical composer, teacher, or conductor.
Mae'terlinck (mā- *or* mah-), Maurice (1862-1949). Belgian poet and dramatist; Nobel Prize for literature 1911.
Mae West (mā). Inflatable lifejacket. [professional name of Amer. film actress (1892-)]
Mă'fĕking. Town in Cape Province, S. Africa; during the 2nd Boer War a small British force under Baden-Powell withstood a siege there for 7 months; its relief, in May 1900, caused riotous rejoicing (*mafficking*) in London.
mă'fficking *n.* See MAFEKING.
mafia (mah'fia) *n.* 1. (in Sicily) Spirit of hostility to the law and its ministers prevailing among a part of the population; also, those who share in this spirit (not, as often supposed, an organized secret society). 2. Secret international criminal organization.
măgazi'ne (-ēn) *n.* 1. Store for explosives, arms, or military provisions; receptacle for number of rounds loaded at one time in rifle and various types of automatic gun (ill. GUN); reservoir or supplychamber in a machine, store, battery, etc. 2. Periodical publication containing articles on various subjects by different writers. [Arab. *makhasin* storehouses]
Mă'gdalĕn, **Măgdalē'nĕ** (*or*

ma'gdalēn *or* -lĭn). Appellation of Mary of Magdala (Luke 8: 2), a disciple of Christ, commonly identified with the 'sinner' of Luke 7: 37 and traditionally represented as a prostitute restored to purity and sanctified by repentance and faith; hence, a reformed prostitute.
Măgdalē'nian *adj.* Of the palaeolithic culture which followed the Aurignacian and Solutrean and is characterized by weapons and tools of horn and bone. [f. rock-shelter of La *Madeleine*, Dordogne, France]
Mă'gdĕbūrg. City in E. Germany; ~ *hemispheres*, pair of copper hemispheres joined to form a hollow globe from which the air could be extracted, after which they were practically inseparable, devised by a German physicist, Otto von Guericke (1602-86), to demonstrate the effect of air pressure.
Magĕ'llan (-g-). Fernão de Magalhães (*c* 1470-1521), Portuguese navigator; the first European to pass through the strait that bears his name, between Tierra del Fuego and the S. American mainland; he undertook the first expedition round the world, but perished in the Philippines (only one of his ships completed the voyage).
Magĕ'nta[1]. Town in Lombardy near which the Austrians were defeated in 1859 by the French under Napoleon III and Mac-Mahon.
magĕ'nta[2] *n.* Brilliant crimson aniline dye (fuchsin), discovered in the year of the battle of Magenta; colour of this.
mă'ggot *n.* Grub or larva, esp. of bluebottle or cheese-fly; fad, whim. **mă'ggotў** *adj.*
Magi: see MAGUS.
mă'gic *n.* Pretended art of influencing events by occult control of nature or of spirits, witchcraft; mysterious agency or power; *black, white*, ~, magic performed by aid of demons, of benevolent spirits. ~ *adj.* Of, producing, produced by, magic; ~ *lantern*: see LANTERN; ~ *square*, square divided into smaller squares each containing a number, so arranged that the sums of the rows, vertical, horizontal, or diagonal, are the same. **mă'gical** *adj.* **mă'gicallў** *adv.*
magi'cian (-shn) *n.* One skilled in magic, wizard.
Mă'ginot line (-zhĭnō). Line of fortifications built in the years preceding the 1939-45 war along the eastern borders of France from Montmédy to Belfort; crossed by German forces in 1940. [André *Maginot* (1877-1932), French war minister]
măgĭstē'rial *adj.* Of a magistrate; dictatorial. **măgĭstē'riallў** *adv.*
mă'gĭstracў *n.* Magistrates; magisterial office.
mă'gĭstrāte *n.* Civil officer

administering law; in England and Wales, person appointed to try minor offences and small civil cases and conduct preliminary hearing of serious offences, either a layman (Justice of the Peace) or a paid judicial officer (*stipendiary* ~). **mă'gĭstrateship**, **mă'gĭstrature** *ns.*
mă'gma *n.* (geol.) Mixture of molten and crystalline materials which on cooling forms igneous rocks.
Mă'gna Chăr'ta (k-), **Căr'ta**. Great Charter of the liberties of England, granted by King John, under pressure from his barons, at Runnymede in 1215; among its chief provisions was that no freeman should be imprisoned or banished except by the law of the land and that supplies should not be exacted without the consent of the Common Council of the realm. [L *magna carta* great charter]
măgnă'nĭum *n.* Alloy of magnesium and aluminium combining lightness with rigidity.
măgnă'nĭmous *adj.* Forgiving, free from petty resentment. **măgnă'nĭmouslў** *adv.* **măgnani'mitў** *n.*
mă'gnāte *n.* Man of high position, wealth, authority, power, etc., often with reference to class or occupation, as *financial* ~.
măgnē'sia (-sha) *n.* (chem.) Magnesium oxide (MgO); *cream, milk, of* ~, suspension of magnesium hydroxide in water, used medicinally. **măgnē'sian** *adj.* [Gk *Magnēsia lithos* stone from Magnesia in Asia Minor]
măgnē'sium (-z- *or* -sh-) *n.* (chem.) Silvery-white metallic element, symbol Mg, at. no. 12, at. wt 24·305, burning with a bright white light; ~ *ribbon, wire*, thin strip or wire of magnesium, prepared for burning to produce bright light.
mă'gnĕt *n.* 1. Loadstone. 2. Piece of iron, steel, cobalt, nickel, or one of their alloys to which has been imparted, by contact, induction, or electric current, the property of attracting iron and of pointing north. 3. (fig.) Thing that attracts.
măgnē'tic *adj.* Of or like or acting as magnet; (fig.) very attractive; ~ *declination, deviation*, angular difference between true and magnetic meridians; ~ *dip*, magnetic inclination; ~ *equator*, imaginary line round the earth, at all points along which the magnetic inclination is zero; ~ *field*: see FIELD; ~ *inclination*, vertical angle between the horizontal and the direction of the earth's magnetic field at any point; ~ *mine*, seamine designed to be detonated by the magnetic field of a steel ship passing near it; ~ *moment*, torque exerted by a magnetic field on any magnetized object within it; ~ *needle*: see NEEDLE, 2; ~ *north*, magnetic pole some 6 degrees W. of

[539]

MAGNETISM

true north; ~ *pole*, either of the poles of a magnet; either of the two points on the earth's surface towards which the compass needle points and at which it dips vertically (ill. EARTH); ~ *storm*, erratic disturbance of earth's magnetism, probably due to solar electric activity; ~ *tape*, strip of usu. plastic material coated with magnetic oxide to make it sensitive to electromagnetism. **măgnĕ′tically** *adv*. **măgnĕ′tics** *n*. That branch of physics which deals with magnetic phenomena.
mă′gnĕtism *n*. 1. Magnetic phenomena; science of these; *terrestrial* ~, magnetic properties of the earth as a whole. 2. (fig.) Attraction, personal charm.
mă′gnĕtite *n*. Magnetic iron oxide (Fe₃O₄).
mă′gnĕtize *v.t*. Make into a magnet; attract as a magnet does. **măgnĕtĭzā′tion** *n*.
măgnĕ′tō *n*. Magneto-electric machine, esp. an alternating-current generator with permanent magnets used to generate the electric ignition spark in an internal combustion engine.
măgnē′tō-chĕ′mistrў (-k-) *n*. That branch of science which treats of the relation of magnetic to chemical phenomena. **măgnĕ′tō-chĕ′mical** *adj*.
măgnē′tō-ĕlĕctrĭ′citў *n*. Electricity generated by relative movement of electric conductors and magnets. **măgnē′tō-ĕlĕ′ctric** *adj*.
măgnĕtŏ′mĕter *n*. Instrument for the measurement of magnetic forces, esp. terrestrial magnetism.
măgnĕtōmō′tive *adj*. ~ *force*, (abbrev. m.m.f.) sum of the magnetizing forces in a magnetic circuit (the magnetic analogy of electromotive force).
măgnĕ′ton *n*. Unit of magnetic moment, used in measuring the magnetic moment of electrons and protons.
măgnĕtŏstă′tics *n*. Science of the properties of non-varying magnetic fields.
mă′gnĕtrŏn *n*. 1. Kind of thermionic vacuum tube in which the motion of the electrons is controlled by an externally applied magnetic field. 2. Electronic device utilizing an axial magnetic field for generating electromagnetic radiations of very short wavelength. [f. *magnet* and *electron*]
Măgnĭ′ficăt *n*. Hymn of Virgin Mary in Luke 1: 46–55, in the Vulgate beginning *Magnificat anima mea Dominum* (L, = 'my soul doth magnify the Lord') used as a canticle; musical setting for this; *m*~, song of praise.
măgnĭ′ficent *adj*. Splendid, sumptuous; imposing, stately; fine, excellent. **măgnĭ′ficentlў** *adv*. **măgnĭ′ficence** *n*.
mă′gnĭfў *v.t*. Increase apparent size of, as with lens, microscope, or concave mirror; exaggerate; (archaic) extol. **măgnĭfĭcā′tion** *n*.

angular ~, (optics) ratio of the angle subtended by the object.
măgnĭ′loquent *adj*. Lofty in expression; boastful. **măgnĭ′loquentlў** *adv*. **măgnĭ′loquence** *n*.
mă′gnĭtūde *n*. Largeness; size; importance; one of the classes into which the fixed stars have been arranged acc. to their brilliancy; *of the first* ~, (fig.) of great importance.
măgnō′lĭa *n*. Tree of genus *M*~, with conspicuous wax-like flowers and dark-green foliage, native in America and Asia. [Pierre *Magnol*, Fr. botanist (1638–1715)]
mă′gnum *n*. (Bottle containing) two quarts (of wine etc.).
Magog: see GOG AND MAGOG.
mă′gpĭe *n*. European bird (*Pica pica*) with long pointed tail and black-and-white plumage; idle chatterer; (shot hitting) circle on target between inner and outer circles.
mă′gus *n*. (pl. -*gī*). 1. Member of ancient Persian priestly caste; one skilled in Oriental magic and astrology; *Simon M*~: see SIMON. 2. *the Magi*, the (traditionally three) 'wise men' who came from the East bearing gifts to the infant Jesus Christ (Matt. 2: 1). **mā′gĭan** *adj*. & *n*. **mā′gĭanism** *n*. Doctrines, philosophy, of the Persian magi.
Mă′gyăr (-g-) *n*. Member, language, of a Mongoloid people predominant in Hungary; Hungarian. ~ *adj*. Of the Magyars; ~ *sleeve*, sleeve cut in one piece with body of garment (ill. SLEEVE).
Mahabharata (mah-hahbah′-rata). One of the two great epics (the other being the Ramayana) of the Hindus, supposed to have been composed c 500 B.C.
maharaja, -jah (mah-harah′ja) *n*. Title of some Indian princes.
mahara′ni, -nee *n*. Maharajah's wife. [Hind. *mahā* great, *rāja* king, *rānī* queen]
Măhără′shtra. State of W. India bordering on Arabian Sea, formed 1960 from SE. part of former Bombay State; capital, Bombay.
mahă′tma (ma-h-). In Buddhism, one of a class of persons with preternatural powers supposed to exist in India and Tibet; in theosophy, a sage or adept, reputed to have superior knowledge and powers. [Sansk. *mahātman* great-souled]
Mahaya′na (mah-hayah-) *n*. One of the two great schools of Buddhism, developed in China, Japan, and Tibet. [Sansk. *mahā* great, *yāna* vehicle]
Mah′dĭ *n*. Title of spiritual and temporal leader expected by Muslims; claimant of this title, esp. Muhammad Ahmed (1843–85), who besieged General Gordon in Khartoum and overthrew Egyptian power in the Sudan. **Mah′dĭsm**, **Mah′dĭst** *adjs*. [Arab. *mahdīy* he who is guided right, pass. part. of *hadā* guide]

MAIL

mah-jŏ′ngg, -jŏng *n*. Chinese game for 4 players played with 144 tiles, in which by discarding and drawing tiles each player attempts to obtain 4 sets of 3 tiles each together with one pair.
Mah′ler, Gustav (1860–1911). Austrian musician; composer of 9 symphonies for very large orchestra.
mah′lstĭck *n*. Long thin stick held by painter in one hand as support for the other, with padded ball at one end. [Du. *maalstok* (*malen* paint, *stok* stick)]
mahŏ′ganў (ma-h-) *n*. Reddish-brown wood esp. of a tropical Amer. tree (*Swietenia mahogani*), used for furniture etc. and taking high polish; tree producing this; colour of this wood.
Mahŏ′mĕt (ma-h-). Var. of MUHAMMAD.
mahou′t (ma-h-) *n*. Elephant-driver.
Mahră′tta (mar-) *n*. · Var. of MARATHA.
Maia (mī′a). 1. (Gk myth.) Daughter of Atlas and mother of Hermes. 2. (Rom. myth.) Goddess associated with Vulcan, and also (by confusion with 1 above) with Mercury. [Gk, = 'mother', 'nurse']
maid *n*. 1. Maiden, 1 (archaic & poet.); *the M*~ (*of Orleans*), Joan of Arc; *old* ~, elderly spinster; round game of cards; *M*~ *Marian*, legendary companion of Robin Hood; ~ *of honour*, unmarried woman attending queen or princess; chief bridesmaid (esp. U.S.); kind of tartlet. 2. Female servant.
mai′den *n*. 1. (archaic & poet.) Girl; spinster; virgin. 2. (hist.) One of two supports for bobbin in spinning wheel (ill. SPINNING). 3. (hist.) Kind of guillotine formerly used in Edinburgh. 4. Maiden horse. ~ *adj*. Unmarried (usu. in ~ *aunt, lady*); virgin (obs.); untried; with blank record; (of horse) that has never won a race; *maidenhair* (*fern*), kind of fern, genus *Adiantum*, with hair-like stalks and delicate fronds; *maidenhair tree*, GINKGO; *mai′denhead*, virginity; hymen; ~ *name*, woman's surname before marriage; ~ *over*, (cricket) one in which no runs are scored; ~ *speech*, one made in Parliament by a member speaking for the first time. **mai′denhōōd** *n*. **mai′denlў** *adv*.
maieu′tĭc (māū-) *adj*. (Of Socratic mode of inquiry) Serving to bring out person's latent ideas into clear consciousness. [Gk *maieuomai* act as midwife]
Maigret (-rā). Detective-superintendent in the crime stories of Georges Simenon.
mail[1] *n*. (hist.) Armour of rings or chain-work, or of metal plates (ill. ARMOUR). ~ *v.t*. (hist. & poet.) Clothe (as) with mail; *mailed fist*, (fig.) armed power.
mail[2] *n*. (Letter etc. conveyed

[540]

by) post; train or other vehicle carrying post; ∼-*boat*, boat carrying mail; ∼-*coach*, (hist.) stagecoach carrying mail; ∼ *order*, order for goods to be sent by post; ∼-*order* (attrib.); ∼-*train*, train conveying mail. ∼ *v.t.* Send by post.
maim *v.t.* Cripple, mutilate.
Maimŏ′nidēs (mi-, -z). Moses ben Maimon(1135-1204), Spanish-Jewish philosopher and Rabbinic scholar, much influenced by Greek, esp. Aristotelian, philosophy.
main[1] *adj*. Chief, principal; exerted to the full; ∼-*brace*, (naut.) brace of main yard (ill. SHIP); *splice the* ∼-*brace*, (hist.) serve out extra rum ration on special occasion, celebrate such occasion by drinking (said to be because splicing so thick a rope would justify a special reward); ∼ *chance*, opportunity for greatest (personal) advantage; *mai′nland*, country or continent without its adjacent islands; *mai′nmast*, principal mast of a ship (ill. SHIP); *mai′nsail* (or -sl), (in square-rigged vessel) lowest sail of mainmast (ill. SHIP); (in fore-and-aft rig) sail set on after part of mainmast; *mai′nspring*, chief spring of watch or clock (ill. CLOCK[1]) (also fig.); *mai′nstay*, stay running from top of mainmast to foot of foremast; (fig.) chief support; *mai′nstream*, (fig.) principal course or trend; ∼-*top*, platform at top of lower mainmast. **mai′nly** *adv*.
main[2] *n*. Physical force (only in *with might and* ∼); high sea (poet.); principal channel, duct, conductor, etc., for water, sewage, electricity, etc.; *Spanish M*∼: see SPANISH.
main[3] *n*. Number (from 5 to 9) called before dice are thrown, in hazard; match between fightingcocks.
Maine. North-eastern State of U.S., on the Atlantic coast; admitted to the Union in 1820; capital, Augusta.
maintai′n *v.t.* Carry on, keep up; support; assert as true.
mai′ntēnance *n*. 1. Maintaining; (provision of) means of subsistence. 2. (law) Offence of aiding a party in litigation without lawful cause.
Maintenon (măṅtenawṅ), Francoise d'Aubigné, Marquise de (1635-1719). Mistress and 2nd wife of Louis XIV of France.
maiolica: see MAJOLICA.
maisonně′tte, maisoně′tte (-z-) *n*. Small house; part of house let or used separately but not all on the same floor.
maize *n.* Amer. cereal plant (*Zea mays*); edible seed of this plant, Indian corn.
Maj. *abbrev*. Major.
majē′stic *adj*. Characterized by majesty, imposing, stately. **majē′stically** *adv*.
mǎ′jĕstỹ *n*. 1. Impressive stateliness; sovereign power; *Your*, *His*, *Her*, *M*∼, title used in speaking to or of sovereign. 2. Representation of God or Christ (or occas. Virgin Mary) enthroned within an aureole; so *Christ in M*∼.
mǎ′jlĭs *n*. Parliament of various countries, including Iran.
majŏ′lica, maio- (mayŏ′-) *n*. Italian earthenware coated with an opaque white enamel ornamented with metallic colours; modern imitation of this. [It., f. former name of *Majorca*, ships of which brought Spanish wares to Italy]
mǎ′jor[1] *n*. Army officer next in rank below lieutenant-colonel and above captain. [Fr., short for *sergent-major*]
mǎ′jor[2] *adj.* Greater of two things, classes, etc.; senior; (in schools) elder of the name (as *Jones* ∼); (mus.) of intervals, greater by a chromatic semitone than those called minor (ill. INTERVAL); normal or perfect; (of keys) in which the scale has a major third (ill. SCALE[3]); ∼ *premiss*, (logic) first of a syllogism, containing a statement of the general rule; ∼ *suit*, (bridge) spades or hearts; ∼ *term*, (logic) predicate of the conclusion of a syllogism. ∼ *n*. Person of full legal age; major premiss; (in U.S. universities) subject to which special attention is given in a course of study, whence ∼ (*v.i.*) take, or qualify in, such subject; ∼-*dō′mō*, chief official of Italian or Spanish princely household; house-steward; ∼-*general*, Army officer ranking next above a brigadier and below a lieutenant-general.
Majŏr′ca (*or* may-). (Span. *Mallorca*) Largest of the Balearic Islands.
majŏ′rĭtỹ *n*. 1. Greater number or part (*of*); *absolute* ∼, more than half number of electors or actual voters. 2. Number by which votes cast on one side exceed those on the other. 3. Full legal age. 4. Office of major in army.
mǎ′juscŭle *adj*. (palaeog.; of a letter) Large (whether capital or uncial); written in majuscule. ∼ *n.* Majuscule letter; formal script, orig. based on Roman monumental lettering, used in manuscripts until the development of the MINUSCULE from cursive writing (ill. SCRIPT).
majŭ′scŭlar *adj.*
māke[1] *v.* (past t. & past part. *māde*). Create, manufacture; cause to exist, bring about; amount to, constitute; bring total up to; represent as being or doing; acquire by effort, earn; win (trick at cards); score (runs at cricket etc.); produce by cookery; perform, execute; utter or record (remark etc.); ∼ *believe*, pretend; ∼-*believe* (*n.*) pretence; ∼ *do*, manage *with* what is available or inferior substitute; ∼ *for*, take direction of; ∼ *good*, fulfil (promise etc.), prove (statement); pay for, repair (damage etc.); succeed in an undertaking; ∼ *off*, depart hastily; ∼ *off with*, carry away, steal; ∼ *out*, draw up or write out (list etc.); prove; represent as; understand; (colloq.) succeed; ∼ *shift with*, use as temporary expedient or device, whence *ma′keshift* (*n. & adj.*) temporary (expedient); ∼ *up*, supply deficiency, complete; arrange; concoct; put an end to (a quarrel); adapt (face etc. of actor) for his part; apply cosmetics (to); ∼-*up* (*n.*) way actor etc. is made up; way type is made up into pages; fundamental qualities of person's nature; ∼ *up to*, curry favour with; ∼-*weight*, small quantity added to make up required weight; unimportant argument etc. to supply deficiency.
māke[2] *n*. Way thing is made; figure, shape; brand, sort; *on the* ∼, (slang) intent on gain.
mā′ker *n*. One who makes; esp. *M*∼, the Creator.
mā′king *n*. Creating, manufacturing, etc.; (pl.) what one earns; essential qualities, **as** *he has the* ∼*s. of a general*.
makū′ta *n. pl.*: see LIKUTA.
Mal. *abbrev*. Malachi (O.T.).
mal- *prefix*. 1. Bad(ly), as *maltreat*. 2. Un-, as *maladroit*.
Mǎ′labār. Coastal district of SW India; ∼ *Christians*, group of Christians of SW. India, tracing their origin to St. THOMAS[2] who traditionally landed in these parts.
Mala′cca. State of Malaysia, on W. coast of Malay Peninsula; its capital; *Strait of* ∼, strait *c*. 500 miles long between SW. end of Malay Peninsula and Sumatra; ∼ *cane*, rich-brown walking-cane made of the stem of a palm-tree (*Calamus scipionum*).
Mǎ′lachī (-kī). Prophetic book of the O.T., belonging to a period immediately before Ezra and Nehemiah; Malachi is prob. not a personal name. [Heb., = 'my messenger']
mǎ′lachīte (-k-) *n*. Hydrated copper carbonate, a bright-green mineral taking a high polish and used as decorative stone.
mǎladjū′stment *n*. Faulty adjustment; person's psychological inability to adjust himself, his wishes, etc., to his environment. **mǎladjŭ′stĕd** *adj.*
mǎladmĭnĭstrā′tion *n*. Faulty administration.
mǎ′ladroit *adj*. Bungling; tactless. **mǎ′ladroitlỹ** *adv*. **mǎ′l-adroitnĕss** *n*.
mǎ′ladỹ *n*. Ailment, disease.
Mǎ′laga[1]. Province of S. Spain, part of the ancient kingdom of Granada; its capital, a Mediterranean seaport.
Mǎ′laga[2] *n*. Dark sweet fortified wine produced near the city of Malaga.
Mǎlagǎ′sỹ *adj. & n.* (Native, language) of Madagascar.
mǎlai′se (-z) *n*. Feeling of uneasiness or discomfort.
malanders: see MALLENDERS.
Mǎ′laprŏp, Mrs. In Sheridan's play 'The Rivals' (1775), a lady

MALAPROPOS

who ludicrously misuses long words, as *illiterate him from your memory*. **mă'lapropism** *n*. Misapplication of a (long) word. **mălăpropo's** (-pō) *adv*. & *adj*. (Done, said, etc.) inopportunely. ~ *n*. Inopportune remark etc. **mā'lar** *adj*. & *n*. (Bone) of the cheek.
malār'ia *n*. Intermittent and remittent fever, caused by a microorganism (*Plasmodium*) which is transmitted by the bite of certain mosquitoes of the genus *Anopheles*. **malār'ial, malār'ious** *adjs*. [It. *mal' aria* bad air (because formerly attributed to unwholesome exhalations of marshes)]
Mala'wi (-lah-). Republic of central Africa; member State of the Commonwealth; formerly the British protectorate of Nyasaland, independent 1964; cap., Lilongwe.
Malay' *n*. Member of a light-brown people of mixed Caucasian and Mongolian stock, predominating in the Malay Peninsula and Archipelago; language of this people. ~ *adj*. Of Malays or their country or language; ~ *Archipelago*, very large group of islands, including Sumatra, Java, Borneo, the Philippines, and New Guinea, lying SE. of Asia and N. and NE. of Australia; ~ *Peninsula*, most southerly projection of the mainland of Asia, running southward from Siam.
Malay'a. Federation of States in the Malay Peninsula, forming part of Malaysia. **Malay'an** *adj*. & *n*.
Mălaya'lăm (-yah-) *n*. A Dravidian dialect, closely related to Tamil, spoken on the W. coast of S. India.
Malay'sia (-z- *or* -sha). Federation of States within the Commonwealth, formed in 1963, comprising Malaya, Sabah, and Sarawak; capital Kuala Lumpur. **Malay'sian** *adj*. & *n*.
mă'lcontĕnt *n*. Discontented person, one inclined to rebellion.
măl de mer (mār). Seasickness. [Fr.]
Mă'ldive I'slands (maw'ldiv ilandz). Chain of coral islands in the Indian Ocean, south-west of India, constituting an independent republic; capital, Malé. **Maldī'vĭan** *adj*. & *n*.
māle *adj*. Of the sex in human beings, other animals, and plants, which begets young by fecundating the female; (of part of machinery etc.) designed to enter or fill the corresponding female (hollow) part; ~ *screw*: see SCREW[1]; ~ *fern*, fern (*Dryopteris filixmas*), producing an oleo-resin used for expelling tapeworms. ~ *n*. Male person, animal, or plant.
Malebranche (mălbrahṅsh), Nicolas (1638–1715). French philosopher, a follower of Descartes and of St. Augustine.
mălĕdi'ction *n*. Curse. **mălĕdi'ctorў** *adj*.

mă'lĕfăctor *n*. Criminal, evil-doer. **mă'lĕfăction** *n*.
malĕ'fĭc *adj*. Harmful, baneful. **malĕ'fĭcent** *adj*. Hurtful; criminal. **malĕ'fĭcence** *n*.
malĕ'volent *adj*. Wishing ill to others. **malĕ'volentlў** *adv*. **malĕ'volence** *n*.
mălfea'sance (-ēz-) *n*. Official misconduct.
mălforma'tion *n*. Faulty formation. **mălfōr'med** (-md) *adj*.
Malherbe (mălārb), François de (1555–1628). French poet, prose writer, and critic.
Ma'lĭ (mah-). Republic in W. Africa; formerly the French colony of Soudan; capital, Bamako.
mā'lĭc *adj*. ~ *acid*, acid ($C_4H_6O_5$) present in many acid fruits such as unripe apples, grapes, and esp. mountain ash berries.
mă'lĭce *n*. Ill will; desire to do harm. **malĭ'cious** (-shŭs) *adj*. **malĭ'ciouslў** *adv*.
malĭ'gn (-īn) *adj*. Maleficent; (of disease) malignant. **malĭ'gnlў** *adv*. **malĭ'gn** *v.t*. Speak ill of, slander.
malĭ'gnant *adj*. 1. Feeling or showing intense ill will. 2. (path., of disease) Of the form which kills, as dist. from milder forms; (of tumour) cancerous, growing into surrounding tissue and destroying it and giving rise to secondary growths in other parts (opp. BENIGN). **malĭ'gnantlў** *adv*. **malĭ'gnancў** *n*. **Malĭ'gnant** *n*. (hist.) Supporter of Charles I against Parliament.
malĭ'gnĭtў *n*. Malignant character or feeling.
malĭ'nger (-ngg-) *v.i*. Pretend illness to escape duty. **malĭ'ngerer** *n*.
Măll, The. Avenue along the N. side of St. James's Park, London, originally a 'mall' or alley where the game of pall-mall was played.
mă'llard *n*. Wild duck (*Anas boscas*).
Mălla̅rmé (-mā), Stéphane (1842–98). French symbolist poet; author of 'L'Après-midi d'un Faune'.
mă'llĕable *adj*. (of metal etc.) That can be hammered, beaten, or rolled into a different form without a tendency to return to its original form or to fracture; adaptable, pliable. **mă'llĕabi'litў** *n*.
mă'llenders, mă'lan- (-z) *n.pl*. Dry eruption inside horse's knee (cf. SALLENDERS).
mălleō'lus *n*. (pl. -ī). (anat.) Bone of hammer-head shape, esp. ankle-bone (ill. FOOT).
mă'llĕt *n*. Hammer (usu. wooden); implement for striking croquet or polo ball.

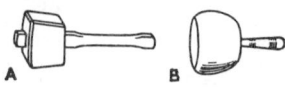

A. CARPENTER'S MALLET.
B. MASON'S MALLET.

MALTHUS

mă'llĕus *n*. (pl. *-ī*). Small bone of middle ear transmitting vibrations of tympanum to incus (ill. EAR[1]). [L, = 'hammer']
Mallorca: see MAJORCA.
mă'llow (-ō) *n*. Wild plant of genus *Malva*, esp. *common* ~, *M. sylvestris*, with hairy leaves and stem and rose-purple flowers.
malm (mahm) *n*. Soft chalky rock; loamy soil from disintegration of this.
mălmai'son (-z-) *n*. Variety of carnation. [name of palace of Empress Josephine]
malmsey (mah'mzĭ) *n*. Strong sweet wine made formerly in Greece, now also in Spain, Madeira, and the Azores. [Gk *Monembasia*, place in the Peloponnese]
mălnŭtri'tion *n*. Underfeeding; diet that does not include what is needful for health.
malō'dorous *adj*. Evil-smelling.
Mă'lorў, Sir Thomas (d. 1471). English author, his 'Le Morte Darthur', a collection of Arthurian stories, was one of the first books printed by Caxton (1485).
Mălpi'ghi (-ēgē), Marcello (1628–94). Italian physician and anatomist. **Mălpi'ghian** *adj*. (anat.) Of certain structures (esp. in the substance of the kidneys) discovered by Malpighi.
Mălplaquet (-kā). Village near Mons, France; scene of a victory (1709) of the allied British and Austrian troops under Marlborough and Prince Eugene over the French.
mălpra'ctĭce *n*. Wrong-doing; (law) improper treatment of patient by medical attendant; illegal action for one's own benefit while in position of trust.
malt (maw- *or* mŏ-) *n*. Barley or other grain for brewing, steeped in water, allowed to germinate and then dried slowly in a kiln; ~ *liquor*, made from fermented malt (e.g. beer), not by distillation. ~ *v.t*. Convert grain into malt.
Ma'lta G.C. (maw- *or* mŏ-). Island in the Mediterranean, south of Sicily; member State of the Commonwealth, independent 1964; capital, Valletta; occupied successively by Arabs (870), Sicily (1090), the Order of St. John (1530), France (1788), and Britain (1814); the island was awarded the George Cross for the gallantry of its population under air attack during the war of 1939–45; *Knights of* ~ : see HOSPITALLER.
Maltē'se (maw- *or* mŏ-; -z) *adj*. Of Malta; ~ *cross*, cross of the Knights of Malta, with four equal limbs broadened at the ends and indented (ill. CROSS). ~ *n*. Native, inhabitant, of Malta; its language, a dialect of Arabic, written in Roman characters.
Mă'lthus, Thomas Robert (1766–1835). English clergyman, author of an essay (1798) arguing that population increases faster than the means of subsistence and

[542]

urging that its increase should be checked, mainly by sexual restraint. **Mălthū'sian** (-z-) *adj.* & *n.* **Mălthū'sianism** *n.*

ma'ltōse (maw- *or* mŏ-) *n.* (chem.) Sugar obtained by hydrolysis of starch by enzymes present in malt.

mältrea't *v.t.* Ill-treat. **mältrea'tment** *n.*

ma'ltster (maw- *or* mŏ-) *n.* One who makes malt.

mălvā'ceous (-shus) *adj.* Of the genus *Malva* (mallow).

mălversā'tion *n.* Corrupt handling of public or trust funds.

mama' (-ah) *n.* Var. of MAMMA[1].

mă'mba *n.* Venomous African snake of genus *Dendraspis*.

mă'melon *n.* Small rounded hillock.

Mă'mèluke, Mă'mluk (-ook) *adj.* & *n.* (Member) of a body of Turkoman warriors who were brought to Egypt as slaves to act as bodyguard for the caliphs and sultans, and became powerful, ruling as sultans from 1250 to 1517, when the Ottoman Turks conquered Egypt, and locally as beys under a Turkish viceroy; Napoleon defeated them in the battle of the Pyramids, 1798, and the surviving Mamelukes were massacred by Muhammad Ali in 1811. [Arab. *mamlūk* slave]

mami'lla *n.* Nipple of female breast; nipple-shaped organ. **mă'millarў, mă'millate, mami'llifōrm** *adjs.*

Mamluk: see MAMELUKE.

mamma'[1] (-ah) *n.* (Child's name for) mother.

mă'mma[2] *n.* (pl. *-ae*). (anat.) Milk-secreting organ of female in mammals; corresponding rudimentary structure in males. **mă'marў, mammi'ferous, mă'mmifōrm** *adjs.*

mă'mmal *n.* Member of the Mammalia, class of animals having mammae. **mammā'lian** *adj.* & *n.* **mammăl'ogĭst, mammăl'ogў** *ns.* Student, study, of mammals. **mă'mmarў** *adj.* Of the mammae.

mă'mmato- *prefix.* (meteor.) Descriptive of clouds resembling rounded festoons, as ∼-*cirrus*, ∼-*cumulus*.

Mă'mmon. Aramaic word for 'riches' used in Matt. 6: 24 and Luke 16: 9–13, taken by medieval writers as the proper name of the devil of covetousness; this use was revived by Milton in 'Paradise Lost'; hence, as personification, term of opprobrium for wealth regarded as an idol or evil influence. [Aram. *māmôn*]

mă'mmoth *n.* Large extinct elephant with long hairy coat and curved tusks whose fossilized remains are found in N. America, Northern Europe, and Asia. ∼ *adj.* Huge.

mă'mmў *n.* (Child's word for) mother; (U.S.) coloured nurse of white children.

măn[1] *n.* (pl. *men*). Human being,

individual of the genus *Homo*, distinguished from other animals by superior mental development, power of articulate speech, and upright posture, etc.; person; human race; adult human male; husband; manservant; workman; one of a set of objects used in board-games; (pl.) soldiers, the rank and file, as dist. from officers; *as one* ∼, in unison; *to a* ∼, without exception; ∼-*at-arms*, (archaic) mounted, fully armed soldier; ∼-*eater*, cannibal; maneating shark or tiger; *ma'nhole*, opening in floor, sewer, etc. for man to pass through; ∼-*hour*, one hour's work by one man, as measure of output in industry etc.; ∼ *in the street*, average citizen, ordinary person; ∼-*of-war*, warship; *ma'npower*, amount of men available for military or other service; ∼-*tailored*, (of women's clothing) tailored in masculine style; ∼-*trap*, trap formerly set to catch trespassers, consisting of two iron half-hoops, hinged together, which closed when a spring was released. ∼ *v.t.* Furnish with men for service or defence; place men at (part of ship); fill (post); fortify spirits or courage of (esp. *oneself*).

Măn[2], Isle of. Island in the Irish Sea, a British crown possession enjoying home rule; it has its own legislature (the TYNWALD) and judicial system; capital, Douglas.

Man. *abbrev.* Manitoba.

mă'nacle *n.* (usu. pl.) & *v.t.* Fetter, handcuff.

mă'nage *v.* Handle, wield (tool etc.); conduct working of (business etc.); have effective control of (household, institution, etc.); subject (animal, person, etc.) to one's control; gain one's ends with (person etc.) by flattery etc.; contrive (*to* do), succeed in one's aim; cope with. **mă'nageable** (-ja-) *adj.* **mănageabi'litў, mă'nageableness** *ns.* **mă'nageablў** *adv.* **mă'nagement** (-ijm-) *n.* Act of managing; state of being managed; body of persons managing a business etc.; administration of business concern or public undertaking.

mă'nager (-nĭj-) *n.* (fem. *mă'nagerĕ'ss*) Person conducting a business, institution, etc. **managēr'ial** *adj.*

mă'nakin *n.* One of the small gaily-coloured birds of the passerine family Pipridae, inhabiting Central and S. America.

Manā'sseh (-ī *or* -e). Hebrew patriarch, first-born son of Joseph (Gen. 48: 19); tribe of Israel, traditionally descended from him.

Manā'ssēs (-z), Prayer of. Book of the Apocrypha consisting of a penitential prayer put into the mouth of Manasseh, king of Judah (2 Kings 21: 1–18).

mănatee' *n.* Large aquatic herbivorous mammal of W. African and American coasts, sea-cow.

Mă'nchèster. City in the metropolitan county of Greater Manchester, the chief centre of cotton manufacture in England; university, 1880; ∼ *School*, name first applied by Disraeli to Cobden and Bright and their followers, who, before the repeal of the Corn Laws, held their meetings at Manchester and advocated free trade and laissez-faire.

Mănchu' (-ōō) *adj.* & *n.* (Member) of a Tatar people who conquered China and founded the Ch'ing dynasty (1644–1912); (of) their language, written in a modified Mongolian script, at one time an official language of China, but now spoken only in parts of N. Manchuria.

Mănchūkuo (-kwō'): see MANCHURIA.

Mănchūr'ia. Region forming the NE. portion of China; in 1932 declared an independent State by Japan and renamed *Manchukuo*; restored to China in 1945.

mă'nciple *n.* Official who buys provisions for college etc.

Mancun. *abbrev.* (Bishop) of Manchester (replacing surname in his signature).

Măncū'nian *adj.* & *n.* (Native or inhabitant) of Manchester; (member) of Manchester Grammar School. [*Mancunium*, name of the Roman settlement]

Măndae'an *adj.* & *n.* (Member) of a Gnostic sect, of which a small community survives in Iraq, very hostile to Christianity since Byzantine times.

Măndalay'. City of central Burma, on the Irrawaddy river.

măndā'mus *n.* Judicial writ issued from King's (Queen's) Bench Division as command to inferior court. [L, = 'we command']

mă'ndarĭn[1] *n.* Chinese official in any of the nine grades; (transf.) pedantic official bureaucrat; nodding toy figure in Chinese costume; form of the Chinese language spoken by officials and educated persons and used in official documents; ∼ *collar*, upright collar not quite meeting at the front. [Sansk. *mantrin* counsellor]

mă'ndarĭn[2] *n.* 1. Small flattened deep-coloured Chinese orange, also cultivated in N. Africa. 2. Deep-orange dye obtained from coal-tar. [prob. f. MANDARIN[1], from the yellow silk robes of mandarins]

mă'ndatarў *n.* One to whom a MANDATE is given.

mă'ndāte *n.* Authoritative command from superior; commission to act for another, esp. one given by League of Nations to a State (the *mandatary*) to administer certain colonies of the defeated enemy powers in the war of 1914–18 for the benefit of the inhabitants; political instructions inferred from votes of electorate. **măndā'te** *v.t.* Commit (State etc.) *to* mandatary.

mă'ndatorў *adj.* Of, conveying, a command. ∼ *n.* = MANDATARY.

[543]

Mă'ndĕville, Sir John. Ostensible author of a 14th-c. book of travels and travellers' tales, written in French and much translated (actually compiled by an unknown hand from the works of several writers).

mă'ndĭble n. Lower jaw-bone (ill. HEAD); either part of bird's beak; either half of crushing organ in mouth parts of many arthropods (ill. INSECT). **măndĭ'bular, -arў** adjs.

măndō'la n. Large kind of mandolin.

mă'ndŏlĭne, -ĭn n. Musical instrument of lute kind with paired

MANDOLINE

metal strings stretched on deeply rounded body, played tremolo with a plectrum.

măndōr'a n. = MANDOLA.

măndōr'la n. Almond-shaped oval around figure in medieval sculpture and painting; vesica.

măndră'gora, mă'ndrāke n. Poisonous plant with emetic and narcotic properties, with root formerly thought to resemble human form and to shriek when plucked up from the ground.

mă'ndrel, -ĭl n. Axis on which material revolves in lathe; rod round which metal etc. is forged or shaped.

mă'ndrĭll n. Large and ferocious baboon (*Mandrillus sphinx*) of W. Africa with highly coloured patches and callosities on face and hindquarters.

mă'ndūcāte v.t. Chew. **măndūcā'tion** n. **mă'ndūcatorў** adj.

māne n. Long hair on neck of horse, lion, etc. (also fig. of person's hair).

manège, -ege (-ā'zh) n. Riding-school; movements of trained horse; horsemanship.

mā'nēs[1] (-z; or mah-) n. 1. (as pl.; Rom. myth.) Deified souls of departed ancestors. 2. (as sing.) Shade of dead person as object of reverence.

Mā'nēs[2] (-z) (c 215–75). (also *Mani, Manichaeus*) Founder of MANICHAEISM.

Mănet (-nā), Edouard (1832–83). French Impressionist painter.

mă'nful adj. Brave, resolute. **mă'nfullў** adv. **mă'nfulnĕss** n.

mă'ngabey (-nggabā) n. Small long-tailed W. African monkey of genus *Cercocebus*. [name of a region in Madagascar]

mă'nganēse (-ngg-, -z) n. (chem.) Grey brittle metallic element, used in making alloys of steel, symbol Mn, at. no. 25, at. wt 54·9380; ~ *dioxide*, black mineral (MnO$_2$) used as an oxidizing agent, esp. in glass-making, electric batteries, etc. [Fr. *manganèse*, corrupt. of MAGNESIA]

mānge (-j) n. Skin-disease caused by a parasite which destroys hairy coat of animals, occas. communicated to man.

mă'ngel-wŭr'zel (-ngg-) n. Large kind of beet used as cattle-food. [Ger. *mangold* beet, *wurzel* root]

mă'nger (-j-) n. Box or trough in stable etc. for horses or cattle to eat from.

mă'ngle[1] (-nggl) n. Machine of two or more cylinders between which washed clothes are rolled to press out the water. ~ v.t. Press (clothes) in mangle.

mă'ngle[2] (-nggl) v.t. Hack, cut about, mutilate; spoil, garble (text, pronunciation, etc.).

mă'ngo (-nggō) n. Fleshy fruit, eaten ripe or used green for pickles etc., of the Indian tree *Mangifera indica*; this tree; ~*-trick*, Indian juggling trick in which a mango-tree appears to grow from a seed and bear fruit in a few hours.

mă'ngold (-ngg-) n. (also ~*-wurzel*) Mangel-wurzel.

mă'ngosteen (-ngg-) n. Fruit of E. Indian tree *Garcinia mangostana*, with thick red rind and white juicy pulp; this tree.

mă'ngrōve (-ngg-) n. Tropical tree or shrub growing in mud at sea-shore with aerating roots above ground.

mā'ngy (-jĭ) adj. Having the mange; squalid, shabby. **mā'ngĭlў** adv. **mā'ngĭnĕss** n.

mă'nhăndle v.t. Move by man's strength without mechanical aid; treat roughly, pull or hustle about.

Mănhă'ttan[1]. Island at mouth of Hudson River, now part of New York city.

mănhă'ttan[2] n. Cocktail made of vermouth and whisky with a dash of bitters.

mă'nhŏod n. State of being a man; manliness, courage; men of a country etc.

Mani (mah'nē). = MANES[2].

mā'nia n. 1. Mental derangement marked by excitement, hallucination, and violence. 2. Excessive enthusiasm.

mā'niăc n. Person afflicted with mania. **manī'acal** adj. **mani'acallў** adv.

mā'nic adj. Of, affected with, mania; ~*-depressive*, (person) affected with mental disorder characterized by alternating mania and depression.

Mănichae'ism, -chē- (-k-) n. Dualistic ascetic religious system, regarding existence as a conflict between the powers of light and the demons of darkness, which was widely accepted from the 3rd to the 5th c., founded by MANES[2]. **Mănich(a)e'an** adj. & n. **Mă'nich(a)eanism** n. **Mănichee'** (or mă'-) n. Manichaean.

Mănichae'us (-k-). = MANES[2]. [L]

mă'nicūre n. Cosmetic care and treatment of hands and (esp.) finger-nails. ~ v.t. Apply manicure treatment to. **mă'nicūrist** n.

mă'nifĕst[1] n. List of ship's cargo for use of customs officials.

mă'nifĕst[2] adj. Clear to sight or mind. **mă'nifĕstlў** adv. **mă'nifĕst** v. Show plainly to eye or mind; be evidence of, prove; display, evince (quality, feeling) by one's acts; (of thing) reveal *itself*; (of ghost) appear. **mănifĕstā'tion** n. **mănifĕ'stative** adj.

mănifĕ'stō n. Public declaration by sovereign, State, or body of individuals, of principles and future policy.

mă'nifōld adj. Having various forms, applications, functions, etc.; many and various. ~ v.t. Mutiply copies of (letter etc.). ~ n. (mech.) Pipe or chamber with several openings. **mă'nifōldlў** adv. **mă'nifōldnĕss** n.

mă'nĭkĭn n. Little man, dwarf; artist's lay figure; anatomical model of the body..

Mani'la[1]. City on island of Luzon, capital of the Philippine Islands; ~ (or *Manilla*) *hemp*, a fibrous material, obtained from the leaves of *Musa textilis*, a tree native to the Philippines, and used for ropes, matting, textiles, etc.; ~ (or *Manilla*) *paper*, brown wrapping-paper orig. made from Manila hemp.

Mani'la[2], **Mani'lla** n. Manila hemp; Manila paper; cigar or cheroot made of Philippine tobacco.

mani'lle n. Second highest trump or honour in quadrille and ombre.

mă'niŏc n. = CASSAVA. [native Brazilian *mandioca*]

mă'niple n. 1. (Rom. antiq.) subdivision of a legion, containing 120 or 60 men. 2. One of the Eucharistic vestments, orig. a napkin, consisting now of a strip of stuff 2–4 ft in length, worn hanging from left arm (ill. VESTMENT).

mani'pūlāte v.t. Handle; deal skilfully with; manage craftily. **manipūlā'tion** n. **mani'pūlātor** n.

Mănitō'ba. Province of central Canada, with coastline on Hudson Bay; capital, Winnipeg.

mă'nitou (-ōō) n. (Amer. Ind.) Good or evil spirit, thing having supernatural power.

mănkīnd (-n-k-) n. 1. (-kī'-) Human species. 2. (mă'-) Male sex, males.

mă'nlīke adj. Like a man; (of woman) mannish.

mă'nlў adj. Having the qualities or bearing of a man; befitting a man. **mă'nlĭnĕss** n.

Mănn, Thomas (1875–1955). German novelist; author of 'Buddenbrooks', which describes the decline of a Lübeck merchant family.

mă'nna n. Substance miraculously supplied as food to Israelites in wilderness (Exod. 16); sweet juice from bark of ~-**ash** (*Fraxinus Ornus*) and other plants, used as gentle laxative.

mă'nnėquin (-kĭn) *n.* Woman employed to display clothes to customers by wearing them; lay figure for shop windows etc.

mă'nner *n.* Way a thing is done or happens; outward bearing; (pl.) behaviour in social intercourse; habits indicating good breeding.

mă'nnered (-e*r*d) *adj.* Showing mannerisms, affected; *ill-*, *well-*, *~*, having bad, good, manners.

mă'nnerlėss *adj.* Ill-mannered.

Mă'nnerheim line (-hīm). Finnish defensive system erected across the Karelian isthmus in the 1930s. [C. E. E. *Mannerheim* (1867-1951), Finnish marshal and statesman]

mă'nnerism *n.* 1. Trick of speech, gesture, or style; excessive addiction to a distinctive manner in art or literature. 2. Style of art which originated in Italy *c* 1530 and preceded the Baroque, characterized by contorted figures, startling light effects, etc. **mă'nnerist** *adj.* & *n.* (Exponent) of mannerism in art etc.

mă'nnerlў *adj.* Well-mannered, polite. **mă'nnerlinėss** *n.*

Mă'nning, Henry Edward (1808-92). English churchman; joined R.C. Church 1851, and became cardinal 1875.

mă'nnish *adj.* Characteristic of a man as opp. to a woman; (of woman) masculine. **mă'nnishnėss** *n.*

manœuvre (-ōō'ver) *n.* Strategical or tactical movement; skilful plan. *~ v.* Perform, make (troops, ships, or aircraft) perform, manœuvre(s); force, drive *into*, *out*, etc., by contrivance. **manœu'vrable** *adj.* Capable of being (easily) manœuvred, esp. of aircraft. **manœuvrabi'litў** *n.*

manŏ'mėter *n.* Instrument for measuring the pressure of gases and vapours by the difference in level which they produce in a liquid in a U-tube, one side of which may be open to the atmosphere or evacuated and sealed off.

mă'nor *n.* English territorial unit, orig. feudal, the lord's demesne and lands from whose holders he could exact certain fees etc.; *~ house*, house of lord of the manor. **manŏr'ial** *adj.*

mă'nsard *n.* Form of roof (usu. *~ roof*) in which each face has two slopes, the lower one steeper than the upper, usu. broken by projecting windows (ill. ROOF). [François *Mansart* (1598-1666), Fr. architect]

mănse *n.* Ecclesiastical residence, esp. that of Scottish Presbyterian minister.

mă'nsion (-shon) *n.* Large residence; (pl.) large building divided into flats; *~-house*, mansion, manor house; *M~ House*, official residence of Lord Mayor of London.

mă'nslaughter (-slawt-) *n.*

Slaughter of human beings; (law) unlawful killing of a human being without malice aforethought.

mă'nsuetūde (-swĭ-) *n.* Gentleness, meekness.

Măntegna (-tā'nya), Andrea (1431-1506). Italian painter and engraver.

mă'ntel *n.* Structure of wood, marble, etc., above and around fireplace (ill. FIRE); *ma'ntelpiece*, mantel; *~-shelf*, shelf above fireplace; *~-tree*, beam or stone over opening of fireplace.

mă'ntic *adj.* Of divination.

mănti'lla *n.* Lace veil worn by Spanish women over the head and shoulders.

mă'ntis *n.* Orthopterous insect, esp. the *praying ~, Mantis religiosa,* which holds its forelegs in a position suggesting hands folded in prayer. [Gk, = 'prophet']

mănti'ssa *n.* Decimal part of a logarithm. [L, = 'makeweight']

mă'ntle *n.* Loose sleeveless cloak (ill. CLOAK); fragile hood consisting usu. of oxides of thorium and cerium, fixed round gas-jet to give incandescent light (also *gas-~*); (zool.) covering or envelope, as that enclosing body of mollusc (ill. MOLLUSC); (ornith.) back, scapulars, and wing coverts of bird, esp. when of distinguishing colour; (geol.) region lying between crust and core of earth; (fig.) covering. *~ v.* Envelop, cover (as) with mantle; (of liquids) form a scum; (of blood) suffuse cheeks; blush.

mă'ntlėt *n.* Short mantle; bullet-proof screen for gunners.

mă'ntling *n.* (her.) Ornamental drapery or scrollwork behind and around an achievement (ill. HERALDRY).

Mă'ntūa. City of Lombardy, birthplace of Virgil. **Mă'ntūan** *adj.* & *n.* the *~*, Virgil.

mă'nūal *adj.* Of or done with the hands. **mă'nūallў** *adv.* **mă'nūal** *n.* 1. Handbook, textbook, primer. 2. Keyboard of organ (ill. ORGAN).

mănūfă'cture *n.* Making of articles by physical labour or machinery, esp. on large scale; branch of such an industry; anything manufactured from raw products. *~ v.t.* Produce by labour, esp. on large scale; invent, fabricate. **mănūfă'cturer** *n.*

mănūfă'ctorў *n.* Factory.

mănūmi't *v.t.* Give freedom to (slave). **mănūmi'ssion** *n.*

manūr'e *n.* Substance, esp. dung, used for fertilizing soil. *~ v.t.* Apply manure to.

mă'nus *n.* (zool.) That part of the forelimb of any tetrapod which corresponds to the human hand, esp. the bones within it.

mă'nūscript *adj.* & *n.* (Book, document) written by hand, not printed; (of) author's written or typed copy for printer (abbrev. MS., pl. MSS.).

Mănx *adj.* Of the Isle of MAN[2]; of the Celtic language spoken there;

~ cat, cat of tailless breed originating there. *~ n.* Manx language.

ma'nў (mĕ-) *adj.* & *n.* (Consisting of) a large number; *the ~*, the multitude; *~-sided*, having many sides; having a variety of interests, capabilities, etc.; *~-sidedness* (*n*).

Mănzō'ni (-ndz-), Alessandro (1785-1873). Italian Romantic novelist and poet.

Maori (mow'rĭ or mah'rĭ) *n.* (Member, language, of) aboriginal people of New Zealand, of Polynesian stock. *~ adj.*

Mao Tse-tung (mow tsĭ-tōō'ng) (1893-1976). Chinese revolutionary leader; became head of the Communist republic in Kiangsi province (SE. China), 1931; after defeat by Kuomintang forces, led his followers on the 'long march' of 1934-5 to Shensi province (N. China) where they established a new State; since 1936 chairman of central committee of Chinese Communist party; chairman of the People's Republic of China 1949-58; relinquished position as head of State but remained chairman of the Communist party.

măp *n.* Representation on paper etc. of earth's surface or part of it, showing physical and political features etc. (*illustration, p. 519*); similar representation of heavens showing position of stars etc.; *put on the ~*, establish position or vogue of. *~ v.t.* Make map of; *~ out*, plan out, arrange in detail.

mā'ple *n.* Tree or shrub of genus *Acer* grown for shade, ornament, wood, or sugar; *~ leaf*, leaf of maple, emblem of Canada; *~-sugar*, sugar got by evaporation of sap of a kind of maple.

maquĕ'tte (-kĕt) *n.* Small preliminary model for a statue.

mă'quis (-kē; or mah-) *n.* Dense scrubby forest of various dwarf trees and shrubs in Corsica etc.; *M~*, secret army of patriots in France during the German occupation (1940-5), so named from their being conceived as hiding in the undergrowth. **măquisar'd** (-zār) *n.* Member of the Maquis. [Fr., f. Corsican It. *macchia* thicket]

măr *v.t.* Spoil, impair the perfection of.

Mar. *abbrev.* March.

mă'rabou (-ōō) *n.* Large W. African stork, *Leptoptilus crumeniferus* (also *~ stork*); tuft of down from its wings or tail as trimming for hat etc.

mă'rabout (-ōōt) *n.* Muslim hermit or saint, esp. in N. Africa; shrine marking marabout's burialplace.

măraschi'nō (-skē-) *n.* Strong sweet liqueur made from the *marasca*, a small black cherry grown in Dalmatia.

mară'smus (-z-) *n.* (path.) Wasting away of the body. **mară'smic** *adj.*

Mărat (-rah), Jean Paul (1743-

MARATHA

93). French revolutionary leader, philosopher, and scientist; stabbed to death by Charlotte Corday.
Mara′tha (-ahta), **Mahrä′tta** (mar-) n. Member of a Hindu people of central and SW. India.
Mara′thi (-ahtĭ) n. Language of the Marathas.
Mă′rathon[1]. Plain on E. coast of Attica, Greece, where the invading Persian army was defeated by the Athenians and Plataeans under Miltiades (490 B.C.); the Athenian courier Pheidippides ran to Sparta to bring the news of the Persian landing and ask for help, and is said to have completed the distance (150 miles) in 2 days.

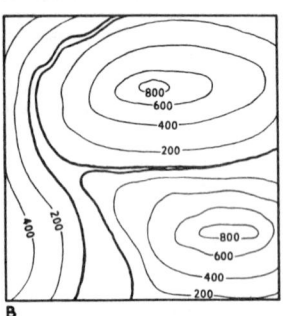

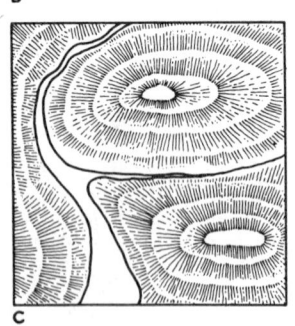

MAPS
A. OBLIQUE AIR VIEW. B. MAP WITH CONTOURS. C. MAP WITH HACHURES

mă′rathon[2] n. (also ~-race) Long-distance road race, esp. the race (26 miles 385 yards) which is a principal event of the modern Olympic Games (also attrib. of any lengthy feat of great endurance). [f. MARATHON[1], from the story (4th c. B.C.) of an unnamed man who fought at the battle, ran to Athens, announced the victory, and died]
marau′d v.i. Make raid, pillage.
marau′der n.
măr′ble n. Limestone in crystalline or granular state and capable of taking polish, used in sculpture etc.; (pl.) collection of sculptures; small ball of marble, glass, clay, etc., used as toy; M~ Arch, arch with three gateways erected (1827) in front of Buckingham Palace, London, and moved (1851) to present site at NE. corner of Hyde Park. ~ v.t. Stain, colour, to look like variegated marble.
Măr′burg. University town of central western Germany; scene of conference (1529) between Luther and Zwingli, and other divines, on the doctrine of transubstantiation.
marc n. Mass left after juice has been pressed from fruit.
Măr′can adj. Of St. Mark.
măr′casite n. Crystalline iron pyrites; piece of this used as ornament.
marcĕ′l n. (also ~ wave) Kind of deep-grooved artificial wave in hair. ~ v.t. Wave (hair) in marcel fashion. [f. name of Paris hairdresser]
Mărch[1]. 3rd month of Gregorian (1st of Julian) calendar, with 31 days. [L Martius (mensis) month of Mars]
march[2] v. (Cause to) walk in military manner or with regular paces; progress steadily. ~ n. Marching of troops; progress; distance covered in marching or walking; uniform step of troops etc.; piece of music meant to accompany march, usu. in $\frac{4}{4}$, $\frac{6}{8}$ or $\frac{2}{4}$ time; musical composition, or part of one, of similar character; steal a ~ on, gain advantage over, esp. surreptitiously; ~-past, parade past reviewing officer or sovereign etc.
march[3] n. (hist.) Boundary, limit, frontier, (often pl., esp. of borderland between England and Wales); tract of (often debatable) land between two countries. ~ v.i. Have common boundary with.
măr′chioness (-sho-) n. Wife, widow, of a marquis; lady holding in her own right rank equal to that of marquis.
măr′chpāne n. = MARZIPAN.
Mărcō′ni, Guglielmo (1874–1937). Italian electrical engineer; inventor of methods of communication by wireless telegraphy etc.; awarded the Nobel Prize for physics in 1909.
Marco Polo: see POLO.
Măr′cusAurē′liusAntonī′nus (ăn-). Marcus Annius Verus (121–180); nephew and adopted son of Antoninus Pius; Roman emperor, 161–180, and Stoic philosopher; author of twelve books of 'Meditations' in Greek.

MARIA THERESA

māre n. Female of horse or other equine animal; ~'s nest, illusory discovery; ~'s-tail, tall slender plant (Hippuris vulgaris) growing in marshy ground; long straight streaks of cirrus cloud.
Marĕ′ngō (-nggō). Village in N. Italy, scene of defeat of Austrians by Napoleon, 1800.
Măr′garĕt, Queen (d. 1093). Scottish saint and queen of Scotland.
Măr′garĕt of Anjou (ahnzhōō) (1430–82). Queen consort of Henry VI of England; a determined leader of her faction in Wars of the Roses.
margarī′ne (-ēn; or -j-) n. Edible fat made by the catalytic reduction of unsaturated acids in animal and vegetable oils and fats and freq. coloured to resemble butter.
măr′gay n. Small S. Amer. tiger-cat (Felis tigrina) related to the ocelot.
mărge[1] n. (poet.) Margin.
mărge[2] n. (colloq.) Margarine.
măr′gin n. Border; strip near edge of anything; plain space round printed page, picture, etc.; extra amount over what is necessary; difference between cost and selling-price; sum deposited with stockbroker to cover risk of loss on transaction.
măr′ginal adj. Of, written in, the margin; of, at, the edge; close to the limit (freq. fig.). **măr′ginally** adv.
mărginā′lia n.pl. Marginal notes.
măr′grāve n. (hist.) German title, orig. of ruler of a border province; later, hereditary title of some princes of the Holy Roman Empire. **măr′gravine** n. Margrave's wife.
mărguerī′te (-gerēt) n. Ox-eye daisy. [Gk margarītēs pearl]
Măr′ian adj. Of the Virgin Mary; of Mary I, Queen of England or Mary, Queen of Scots. ~ n. Adherent of Mary, Queen of Scots.
Mărīa′na (-ahna), Juan de (1536–1624). Spanish Jesuit priest and historian; remembered for a work defining the circumstances in which it was legitimate to get rid of a tyrannical prince.
Mărīa′na I′slands (-ahna ilandz). (also Marianas) Group of islands in the NW. Pacific administered (except for GUAM) by U.S. under trusteeship of U.N.
Mărĭănne. Sobriquet of the French Republic, from name of a secret society (perhaps called after Juan de MARIANA) formed c 1852 with the object of establishing the Republic.
Marī′a Therĕ′sa (or -rēa; ter-; or -āza) (1717–80). Queen of Hungary and Bohemia and archduchess of Austria; succeeded her father Charles VI as Empress of Germany in 1740. Her right to the throne was contested and gave rise

[546]

to the War of the Austrian Succession (1740-8); during her reign Austria was attacked by Frederick the Great and defeated in the Seven Years War (1756-63).
Mărie Antoinĕtte (ahṅtwah-) (1755-93). Daughter of MARIA THERESA and queen of Louis XVI of France; guillotined on 16 Oct. 1793.
Mărie de Médicis (mādēsēs) (1573-1642). Wife of Henry IV of France; regent of France 1610-17.
mă′rĭgōld n. 1. Any of several plants of genera *Calendula* and *Tagetes*, with bright-yellow or golden composite flowers; *fig-~*, species of *Mesembrianthemum*. 2. = MARSH marigold. [f. *Mary* (prob. the Virgin)+*gold*]
mărijua′na, -hua′na (-hwahna). n. Dried leaves of Indian hemp, used to make narcotic cigarettes (reefers); the plant itself.
mari′mba n. Primitive African xylophone; modern orchestral instrument evolved from this.
mari′na (-rē-) n. Pleasure-boat harbour.
mărinā′de n. Pickle of wine or vinegar with herbs and spices, in which fish or meat is steeped before cooking. ~ v.t. Steep in marinade.
mă′rināte v.t. Marinade.
mari′ne (-ēn) adj. Of, from, beside, the sea; for use at sea; of shipping; ~ *stores*, old ships' materials as merchandise; shop selling them. ~ n. Country's fleet of ships, naval or mercantile; member of body of troops trained to fight on land or sea; (pl.) this branch of armed forces (in U.K., Royal Marines).
mă′rĭner n. Sailor; *master ~*, captain of a merchant ship.
Mărinĕ′tti, Filippo Tommaso (1876-1944). Italian author; initiator of FUTURISM.
Mări′ni (-rē-), Giovanni Battista (1569-1625) Neapolitan poet, noted for the flamboyance of his style. **Mari′nism** n. Artificial affected style of writing. **Mari′nist** n.
Mărĭŏ′latrў n. Idolatrous worship of the Virgin Mary.
mărionĕ′tte n. Puppet worked with strings.
mă′rĭtal (or marī′-) adj. Of a husband; of or between husband and wife. **mă′rĭtallў** adv.
mă′rĭtīme adj. Of or connected with the sea or seafaring; situated near the sea.
Mār′ius, Gaius (155-86 B.C.). Roman general and consul; conqueror of Jugurtha in Africa and the Cimbri and Teutones; rival of Sulla, who outlawed him in 88 B.C.
Mărivaux (-ēvō), Pierre Carlet de Chamblain de (1688-1763). French author of comedies and romances marked by elaborate analysis of sentiment.
mār′joram n. Any of several aromatic herbs of genera *Origanum* and *Majorana*, used for flavouring.
mārk[1] n. 1. = DEUTSCHE MARK.

2. (abbrev. M.) Monetary unit of the German Democratic Republic, = 100 pfennig.
mārk[2] n. 1. Target, thing aimed at; *beside, wide of, the ~*, not hitting it, (fig.) not to the point. 2. Trace left by something; stain, scar, spot, dent. 3. Sign, indication, (of quality, character, etc.). 4. Affixed or impressed sign, seal, etc.; written symbol; cross etc. made by person who cannot write his name. 5. Unit in appraising merit of schoolchild's work in class, candidate's in examination, etc. 6. Line serving to indicate position, e.g. starting-point in race. 7. (boxing) Pit of stomach. 8. (Rugby footb.) Heel-mark on ground made by player who has obtained fair catch. 9. (hist.) Tract of land held by Teutonic village community, frontier district. 10. *M~ I, M~ II*, etc., designation of weapon or piece of equipment indicating first, second, etc., design, whence *M~ I*, (colloq.) primitive, antiquated. ~ v. Make a mark on; distinguish with a mark; characterize or serve as a mark of; assign marks of merit to; notice, observe, watch; keep close to (opposing player) in games; record as score or act as scorer in games; ~ *down*, note and remember (place etc.); (also) reduce price of; ~ *off*, separate by boundary, ~ *out*, trace out (boundary etc.); ~ *time*, move feet as in marching, but without advancing (often fig.); ~ *up*, raise price of.
Mārk[3], King. In Arthurian legend, king of Cornwall and husband of Iseult.
Mārk[4], St. Apostle, companion of Peter and Paul; traditional author of the 2nd Gospel (the earliest in date); commemorated 25 April; 2nd Gospel.
mārked (-kt) adj. (esp.) Noticeable, conspicuous. **mār′kĕdlў** adv.
mār′ker n. 1. Scorer at billiards. 2. Thing used to mark place (in book etc). 3. Anything used to indicate position on ground to aircraft, course at sea to boats, etc.
mār′kĕt n. Gathering of people for sale of provisions, livestock, etc.; time of this, space or building used for it; demand *for*; seat of trade; *buyer's ~*, state of purchasing favourable to buyer; so *seller's ~*; ~ *cross*, cross erected in market-place; ~-*day*, day on which market is held; ~ *garden*, garden in which vegetables are grown for market; ~-*gardener, -gardening* (ns.); ~ *place*, square, open place, where market is held; ~-*price*, prevailing price in ordinary conditions; ~ *town*, town where market is held on fixed days; ~ *value*, saleable value. ~ v. Buy, offer for sale, in market. **mār′kĕtable** adj. Fit for sale; sellable.
mār′king n. (esp.) Colouring of feathers, skin, etc.; ~-*ink*, indelible ink for marking linen.

mār′kka n. Principal monetary unit of Finland, = 100 penniä.
mār′ksman n. (pl. -*men*). One skilled at aiming at mark, esp. rifleman of certain standard of proficiency. **mār′ksmanship** n.
mārl n. Rock, freq. soft but sometimes hard, of mud and lime; soil consisting of this in broken or powdered state, used as fertilizer. ~ v.t. Apply marl to. **mār′lў** adj.
Mār′lăg n. German prison camp for sailors. [Ger., abbrev. of *M*arine navy, *Lag*er camp]
Marlborough[1] (maw′lboro), John Churchill, 1st Duke of (1650-1722). English soldier; in the War of the Spanish Succession he defeated the French and their allies at Blenheim, Ramillies, Oudenarde, and Malplaquet; married Sarah Jennings, favourite of Queen Anne; both later fell out of favour; ~ *House*, house in Pall Mall, London, designed c 1710 by Sir Christopher Wren for the 1st Duke of Marlborough; a royal residence 1863-1959; now a Commonwealth centre.
Marlborough[2] (maw′lboro). Short for ~ *College*, public school in Wiltshire, founded 1843.
mār′line n. (naut.) Small line of 2 strands used for binding shrouds etc.; ~-*spike*, pointed tool for

MARLINE-SPIKE

separating strands of rope in splicing.
mār′lite n. Variety of marl which does not become pulverized by the action of air.
Mār′lowe (-lō), Christopher (1564-93). English poet and playwright; author of 'Tamburlaine', 'The Jew of Malta', 'Edward II', and 'The Tragedy of Dr. Faustus'; became involved in political intrigues; was killed in obscure circumstances after a brawl in a Deptford tavern.
mār′malāde n. Preserve of oranges or other citrus fruit, cut up and boiled with the peel and sugar; orange-yellow colour, esp. of cats. [Port. *marmelada* f. *marmelo* quince]
Mār′mara, Sea of. Small inland sea lying between the Black Sea and the Aegean.
mărmōr′ĕal adj. Of or like marble.
mār′mosĕt (-z-) n. Small tropical Amer. monkey with bushy tail, of several genera in family Callithricidae (ill. MONKEY).
mār′mot n. Burrowing hibernating rodent of genus *Arctomys*, of squirrel family. [Fr. *marmotte* prob. ult. f. L *murem montis* mountain mouse (*mus* mouse)]
Marne. River of N. France, scene of two battles in 1914-18 war.
mă′rocain n. Dress-fabric with wavy texture, of silk etc. [Fr., = 'Moroccan']

[547]

Mar′onite n. One of a sect of Syrian Christians living in Lebanon, named after their founder Maron, who lived probably in the 4th c.

maroo′n[1] n. 1. Brownish-crimson colour. 2. Explosive device producing loud report. ~ adj. Maroon-coloured. [Fr. *marron* chestnut]

maroo′n[2] n. One of a group of Negroes, orig. fugitive slaves, living in mountains of W. Indies; marooned person ~ v.t. Put (person) ashore and leave on desolate island or coast as punishment; leave without means of getting away. [Fr. *marron*, perh. f. Span. *cimarron* wild]

Marot (mărō), Clément (1497–1544). French Protestant poet and translator of the Psalms.

Marprĕ′late, Martin. Pseudonym of author of several satirical pamphlets issued from a secret press in 1588–9, abusing the bishops and defending the Presbyterian system of discipline.

marque (-k) n. (hist.) *letters of* ~, licence given to private person to fit out armed vessel and employ it in capture of enemy's merchant shipping.

marquee′ (-kē) n. Large tent, esp. one used at fêtes, shows, etc.

Marque′sas I′slands (-kā-, ilandz). Group of islands in the Pacific, in French possession.

mar′quetry, -terie (-k-) n. Decoration of flat surface, as of furniture, by glueing together shaped pieces of wood, ivory, or other substance(s) so as to cover the whole surface; also, inlay; furniture etc. so decorated.

mar′quis, mar′quess n. Noble ranking below duke and above earl or count. **mar′quisate** n. [It. *marchese* ruler of MARCH[3]].

marqui′se (-kēz) n. 1. (of foreign nobility) Marchioness. 2. (also ~ *ring*) Finger-ring with head shaped like ~ *cut*, a boat-shaped brilliant cut. 3. (archaic) Marquee.

mar′quois (-kwoiz) n. ~ *scale*, apparatus for drawing equidistant parallel lines.

ma′rram n. Coarse, tough, binding grass (*Ammophila arenaria*) growing on dunes near sea-shore.

ma′rriage (-rĭj) n. Act, ceremony, or procedure by which a man and a woman are legally united for the purpose of living together; (fig.) intimate union; *communal* ~, (anthrop.) system by which within a small community all the men are regarded as married to all the women; *companionate* ~, (U.S.) probationary union of man and woman; ~ *articles*, agreement concerning rights of property, succession, etc., made before marriage; ~ *licence*, official permit for two persons to marry; ~ *lines*, certificate of marriage; ~ *portion*, dowry. **ma′rriageable** (-ja-) adj.

ma′rron glacé (-sā). Chestnut preserved in sugar as sweet.

ma′rrow (-rō) n. 1. Soft fatty substance in cavities of bones (ill. BONE); essential or best part of anything, essence; ~-*bone*, bone containing edible marrow; (pl. facet.) knees; *ma′rrowfat* (*pea*), kind of large rich pea; ~ *scoop*, narrow spoon-like utensil for extracting marrow. 2. (also *vegetable* ~) Kind of edible gourd, the fruit of *Cucurbita pepo*. **ma′rrowy** adj.

ma′rry v. Unite, give, or take in marriage; take a wife or husband; (fig.) unite intimately.

Ma′rryat, Captain Frederick (1792–1848). English naval captain; author of 'Peter Simple', 'Mr Midshipman Easy', 'Masterman Ready', and other novels and stories, mostly of sea life.

Mars (-z). 1. (Rom. myth.) God of war, identified with the Greek ARES. 2. (astron.) 4th planet in the order of distance from the sun, with an orbit lying between that of the earth and Jupiter (ill. PLANET). **Mar′tian** (-shan) adj. & n. (Supposed inhabitant) of the planet Mars.

Marsa′la (-sah-) n. Fortified wine produced at Marsala, a town on the W. coast of Sicily, orig. as imitation of sherry for English consumption.

Marseillai′se (-selāz), The. The French national anthem, composed by a young engineer officer, Rouget de Lisle, at Strasbourg in 1792, on the declaration of war against Austria, and first sung in Paris by Marseilles patriots.

Marsei′lles (-ālz). French seaport, on the Mediterranean coast, on site of an ancient Greek colony, Massilia.

marsh n. Low-lying land, more or less permanently waterlogged; bog, morass; ~-*gas*, methane; ~-*mallow*, shrubby herb (*Althaea officinalis*) growing near salt-marshes; *marshmallow*, soft sweet containing albumen and gum arabic or gelatine; ~ *marigold*, plant of family Ranunculus with bright golden flowers, growing in moist meadows. **mar′shy** adj. **mar′shiness** n.

mar′shal n. 1. Official of a royal household or court directing ceremonies, in England the *Earl M*~; (hist.) *knight* ~, officer of royal household with judicial functions. 2. Military officer of highest rank in some foreign armies, in the British Army, a *Field M*~. 3. Part of title of officers of high rank in the R.A.F., as *Air* (*Chief, Vice-*) *M*~. ~ v.t. Arrange in due order (persons at banquet etc., soldiers, facts, etc.); lead, conduct, with ceremony; (her.) put in due order quarterings etc. on an escutcheon (ill. HERALDRY); *marshalling yard*, railway yard in which trains are assembled and distributed.

Mar′shall, George Catlett (1880–1959). U.S. general and statesman; Nobel Prize for peace, 1953; ~ *Aid*, financial aid given to certain European countries under the ~ *Plan* (1948).

Mar′shall I′slands (ilandz). Group of islands in the NW. Pacific administered by U.S. under trusteeship of U.N.

Mar′shalsea. Debtors' prison in Southwark, under the control of the knight marshal, dating from the 14th c.; abolished 1842. [orig. *marshalcy*]

Mar′ston Moor. Battle (1644) fought 7 miles W. of York in which the Royalist army under Prince Rupert was decisively defeated by the Parliamentary army.

marsū′pial adj. & n. (Animal) of the class of mammals which are born in a very immature condition, as e.g. the kangaroo, wombat, and are carried in a pouch (*marsupium*) until able to fend for themselves.

Mar′syas. (Gk myth.) Satyr, who took to flute-playing; he challenged Apollo to a musical contest and was flayed alive when he lost.

mart n. Market-place; auction room; trade centre.

Martĕ′llō tow′er. One of a number of small circular forts with massive walls erected on the coasts of the British Isles against invasion in the Napoleonic wars.

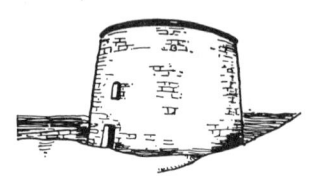

MARTELLO TOWER

[corrupt. of Cape *Mortella* in Corsica, where a tower of this kind was captured by the English fleet in 1794]

mar′ten n. Any of various carnivorous mammals of the genus *Martes*, resembling large weasels, with valuable fur.

Mar′tha. Sister of Lazarus and Mary and friend of Jesus Christ (Luke 10: 40); in Christian allegory she symbolizes the active life and her sister the contemplative life.

mar′tial[1] (-shal) adj. Of, suitable for, appropriate to, warfare; militant, ready, eager, to fight; ~ *law*, military government, during which ordinary law is suspended. **mar′tially** adv. **mar′tialize** v.t. Make suitable, prepare, for war; impart martial spirit to.

Mar′tial[2] (-shal). Marcus Valerius Martialis (*c* 40–*c* 104), Roman satiric poet and epigrammatist.

mar′tin[1] n. Name given to several birds of swallow family, esp. the house-martin (*Delichon urbica*), which builds a mud nest under eaves etc., and the sand-martin (*Riparia riparia*), nesting in sand. (*Illustration, p. 549*.)

[548]

HOUSE-MARTIN
Length 127 mm

Mār'tin², St. Bishop of Tours c 371; legend represents him as a Roman soldier who cut his cloak in two and gave half to a beggar; patron saint of tavern-keepers; commemorated 11 Nov. (MARTINMAS); *St. ~'s Summer*, period of fine mild weather often occurring about this date.

Mār'tineau (-nō). *Harriet ~* (1802–76), English Unitarian and writer of works on political economy and social reform; *James ~* (1805–1900), her brother; Unitarian divine and philosopher.

mārtině't *n.* Strict (esp. military) disciplinarian. **mārtině'ttish** *adj.* **mārtině'ttism** *n.* [name of French drillmaster in reign of Louis XIV]

mār'tingāle (-ngg-) *n.* 1. Strap fastened to bridle and girth of horse to prevent rearing etc. (ill. SADDLERY). 2. Gambling system of doubling stakes at each venture.

mārti'ni (-tē-) *n.* Cocktail of gin or vodka and vermouth. [perh. f. name of inventor]

Mārtinique' (-ēk). French W. Indian island, one of the Lesser Antilles; capital, Fort de France; the former capital, St. Pierre, was completely destroyed by an eruption of Mont Pelée in 1902.

Mār'tinmas, Mār'tlemas (-tlm-). Feast of St. Martin, 11 Nov.; formerly the usual time in England for hiring servants and for slaughtering cattle to be salted for the winter; one of the Scottish term days.

mār'tlet *n.* Swift; martin; (her.) footless bird (ill. HERALDRY).

mār'tyr (-er) *n.* Person who undergoes death or suffering for any great cause, specif. one who suffers death on account of his adherence to the Christian faith; *~ to*, constant sufferer from (ailment etc.). *~ v.t.* Put to death as martyr; torment. [Gk *martus* witness]

mār'tyrdom (-ter-) *n.* Sufferings and death of martyr; torment.

mār'tyrize *v.t.* (-ter-). Make martyr of.

mārtyrŏ'logy (-ter-) *n.* List, history, of (esp. Christian) martyrs. **mārtyrolŏ'gical** *adj.* **mārtyrŏ'logist** *n.*

mār'tyry (-terĭ) *n.* Shrine, church, erected in honour of martyr.

mār'vel *n.* Wonderful thing; wonderful example *of* (quality). *~ v.i.* Be surprised (*at, that*); wonder (*how, why*, etc.).

Mār'vell, Andrew (1621–78). English poet and political writer of Parliamentarian sympathies.

mār'vellous *adj.* Astonishing; extravagantly improbable. **mār'vellouslў** *adv.* **mār'vellousnèss** *n.*

Mārx, Karl (1818–83). German revolutionary writer; settled in England after 1849; wrote 'Das Kapital' (1867), criticizing the capitalistic system as permitting a diminishing number of capitalists to appropriate the benefits of improved industrial methods, while the labouring class were left in increasing dependency and misery; held the remedy to be total abolition of private property, to be effected by the class-war; when the community owned all means of production and all property, it would provide every individual with work and the means of subsistence. **Mār'xist, Mār'xian** *adjs. & ns.* **Mār'xism** *n.*

Mār'ў¹. (*Blessed*) *Virgin ~, ~ the Virgin*, mother of Jesus Christ; daughter of Joachim and Anne; was betrothed to Joseph of Nazareth at the time of the Annunciation.

Mār'ў². Name of 2 reigning queens of England: *Mary I* or Mary Tudor (1516–58), daughter of Henry VIII and Catherine of Aragon; reigned 1553–8; married Philip II of Spain, 1554; fervently Catholic; known as 'Bloody Mary' because of the religious persecutions of her reign; *Mary II* (1662–94), eldest child of James II; married William of Orange, 1677; was invited, with him, to take the throne of England and Scotland after the deposition of her father, and reigned 1689–94.

Mār'ў Cělě'ste. Amer. brig found in the N. Atlantic by a British barque on 5 Dec. 1872, in perfect condition but abandoned and without her boats; the fate of the crew was never discovered.

Mār'ўlănd (*or* mĕ'rĭland) State of eastern U.S., on Atlantic coast, one of the thirteen States of the Union (1788); capital, Annapolis. [named after Henrietta *Maria*, queen of Charles I]

Mā'rylebone (-relebon *or* -rĭb-; *or* mār'lib-). District of London N. of Oxford Street; *~ Cricket Club*, (abbrev. M.C.C.) cricket club founded towards the end of the 18th c., and now the legislative authority on the game. [orig. called TYBURN; altered to *Maryborne* f. church dedicated to St. Mary, and later to *Marylebone* as if = 'Mary the Good']

Mary Magdalene : see MAGDALEN.

Mār'ў, Queen of Scŏts (1542–87). Mary Stuart, daughter of James V of Scotland and great-granddaughter of Henry VII; married the dauphin (François II) of France; claimed English throne on Mary I's death, and returned to Scotland, 1560; married, 1565, her cousin the Earl of Darnley, by whom she had a son (James I); soon after Darnley's mysterious death she married the Earl of Bothwell, 1567; was imprisoned by Elizabeth I, 1567, and was forced to abdicate; was tried for conspiracy, 1586, and beheaded.

mārzipā'n *n.* Paste of ground almonds, sugar, and white of egg, eaten as sweet and in cakes.

Masă'cciō (-ăch-), Tommaso di Giovanni (1401–28), Italian painter of the early Renaissance.

Masai' (-sĭ) *n.* (Member of) warlike pastoral people of mixed Hamitic stock, inhabiting S. Kenya and N. Tanganyika.

Mă'sarўk (-z-), Thomas Garrigue (1850–1937). Czech statesman and philosopher; first president of Czechoslovakia, 1918–37.

Mascagni (-kă'nyĭ), Piero (1863–1945). Italian composer of operas, famous for his 'Cavalleria Rusticana'.

măscār'a *n.* Preparation for darkening eyelashes, eyebrows, etc., in make-up. [name of a town in Oran, Algiers]

mă'scle *n.* (her.) Charge in form of lozenge with lozenge-shaped opening (ill. HERALDRY).

mă'scŏn *n.* Massive concentration of dense matter with strong gravitational pull beneath surface of moon.

mă'scot *n.* Person, animal, thing, supposed to bring luck; talisman.

mă'sculine (*or* mah-) *adj.* 1. (gram.) Of the gender to which appellations of males belong; (of ending) proper to this gender. 2. Of men; manly; mannish. 3. (pros.) *~ caesura*, caesura immediately following stress; *~ ending*, ending of line of verse with stress on final syllable; *~ rhyme*, (in French verse) rhyme between words ending in stressed syllables, not *e* mute; hence, rhyme of stressed syllables. *~ n.* (gram.) (Word having) masculine gender. **mă'sculinenèss** (-n-n-), **măscūli'nitў** *ns.*

Mā'sefield (-sf-), John (1878–1967). English poet and novelist; poet laureate 1930–67.

mā'sĕr (-z-) *n.* Device for amplifying microwaves; *optical ~*, laser. [microwave amplification by stimulated emission of radiation]

măsh¹ *n.* Malt mixed with water for brewing; boiled grain, bran, etc., given warm to horses etc.; soft pulp made by crushing, mixing with water, etc.; (slang) mashed potatoes. *~ v.t.* Make into mash; crush, pound, to pulp; (dial.) steep (tea) in boiling water.

măsh² *v.t.* (obs. slang) Excite sentimental admiration in (one of opposite sex). **mă'sher** *n.* (obs. slang) Lady-killer, fop.

mă'shie, mă'shў *n.* Metal-headed golf-club with lofted face (no. 5 iron).

mask (mah-) *n.* 1. Covering for

MASOCHISM

concealing the face; (archaic) person wearing this at ball etc. 2. Covering of wire, gauze, etc., worn to protect (part of) face or to filter air inhaled or exhaled; respirator. 3. Reproduction of face on cloth etc. worn by actor to symbolize character; grotesque representation of a face worn on festive and other occasions to produce a humorous or terrifying effect; hollow figure of human head esp. as worn by Greek and Roman actors. 4. Likeness of person's face, esp. one made by taking mould from face during life or after death (*life-~, death-~*). 5. (photog.) Screen used to cover or shield part of an image. 6. Face, head, of fox. 7. (fig.) Disguise ~ *v.t.* Cover with mask; disguise or hide as with mask; *masked ball*, one at which masks are worn. ma′sker *n.* One who takes part in masque or masquerade.

mă′sochism (-k-; *or* măz-) *n.* Deriving of pleasure from one's pain or humiliation, esp. as a method of sexual gratification (opp. SADISM). mă′sochist *n.* măsochi′stic *adj.* [L. von Sacher-*Masoch* (1835-95), Austrian novelist who described it] mā′son *n.* 1. Worker in stone.

2. Freemason (see FREE). masŏ′nic *adj.* Of freemasons. mā′sonry *n.* 1. Stonework. 2. Freemasonry. Mā′son and Di′xon line. (also *Mason–Dixon Line*) Boundary between Maryland and Pennsylvania, partly surveyed (1763-7) by Charles Mason and Jeremiah Dixon, English astronomers; before the abolition of slavery pop. regarded as demarcation between free and slave States. Măsōr′ah, Măssōr′ah (-*a*) *n.* Critical notes and traditions relating to text of Hebrew Bible, compiled by Jewish scholars in 10th and preceding centuries. Mă′soretes (-ts) *n.pl.* Compilers of the Masorah. Măsorĕ′tic *adj.*

masque (mahsk) *n.* Amateur histrionic and musical performance, orig. in dumb-show, later with metrical dialogue etc.; dramatic composition for this. ma′squer *n.* Masker. masquerā′de (mahske-) *n.* Masked ball; false show, pretence. ~ *v.i.* Appear in disguise; ~ *as*, pretend to be. Măss[1] *n.* Celebration (esp. R.C.) of the Eucharist; liturgy, musical setting of liturgy, used in this; *High ~*, with incense, music and assistance of deacon and subdeacon; *Low ~*, without music and with minimum of ceremony. [Low L *messa*, possibly f. words of dismissal at end of service: *ite, missa est*]

măss[2] *n.* Coherent body of matter of indefinite shape; dense aggregation, large number, *of*; unbroken expanse *of* (light etc.); majority or main part (*of*); (phys.) quantity of matter a body contains, as determined by comparing the changes in the velocities that result when the body and a standard body impinge; *the masses*, the lower classes of society; *~-energy*: see ENERGY; *~ media*, means of communication, as television, radio, newspapers, etc., directed to or reaching the majority of people; *~ meeting*, large assembly of people; *~ observation*, study and record of the social habits of the masses of the people; *~ production*, production in large quantities of standardized article(s) by standardized mechanical means; hence, *~-produce*(*d*). ~ *v.* Gather into mass; (mil.) concentrate (troops). mă′ssў *adj.* Solid, bulky. **Mass.** *abbrev.* Massachusetts. Măssachu′sĕtts (-ōō-) *n.* New England State of U.S., one of the original thirteen States of the Union (1788); capital, Boston. mă′ssacre (-k*er*) *n.* Indiscriminate killing, esp. of unresisting persons. ~ *v.t.* Make a massacre of. măssa′ge (-ahzh; *or* mă′-) *n.* Kneading and rubbing of muscles, joints, etc., with hands, to stimulate their action. ~ *v.t.* Apply massage to. [Fr., f. L *massa* lump]

massé (măsă′) *n.* (billiards) Stroke made with cue held perpendicularly. Măssenet (-enă), Jules Émile Frédéric (1842-1912). French composer of operas and other music. măssĕ′ter *n.* Masticatory muscle (ill. HEAD). măsseur′ (-ĕr) *n.* (fem. *masseuse*, pr. -ĕrz) One whose profession is providing massage. mă′ssĭf *n.* Mountain heights forming compact group; *M~ Central* (măsēf sahṅtrahl), plateau in central France occupying about a fifth of the country and including the Cévennes, Auvergne, and Limousin mountains. Mă′ssinger (-j*er*), Philip (1583-1640). English poet and playwright. mă′ssive *adj.* Large and heavy or solid; (fig.) solid, substantial; (psychol.) of sensation etc.) having large volume or magnitude. mă′ssively *adv.* mă′ssiveness *n.* **Massorah**: see MASORAH.

mast[1] (mah-) *n.* Fruit of beech and other forest trees, esp. as food for swine.

mast[2] (mah-) *n.* Long pole of timber etc. set upright in ship to support sails etc.(ill. SHIP); long pole supporting flag, radio aerial, etc.; *before the ~*, as an ordinary seaman, so described because sailors are quartered in the forecastle; *half-~*: see HALF; *~-head*, highest part of mast, esp. lower mast, as place of observation or punishment; (*v.t.*) send (sailor) to this as punishment (now an obs.

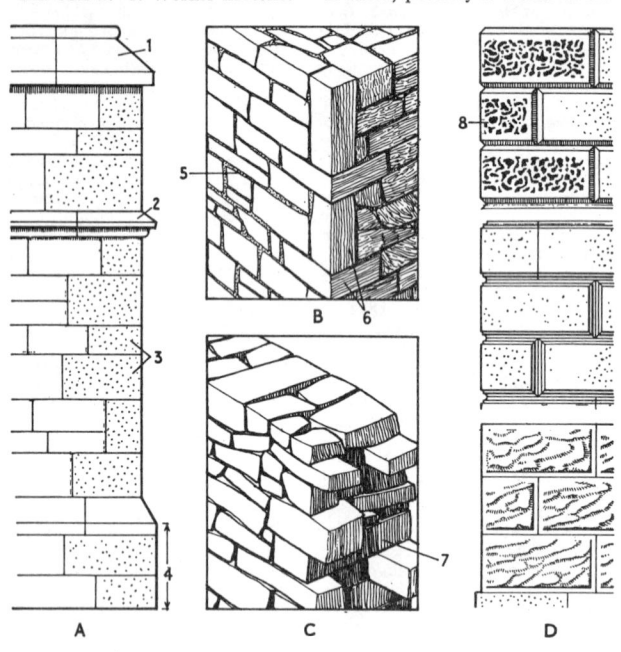

MASONRY

A. ASHLAR.   B. COURSED RUBBLE WALLING.   C. DRY WALLING.
D. RUSTICATED ASHLAR

1. Coping. 2. String-course. 3. Quoins. 4. Plinth. 5. Pointing. 6. Long-and-short work. 7. Binder or parpen. 8. Vermiculated rustication

[550]

practice); raise (sail) to its position. ~ v.t. Furnish with masts.
măˈstaba n. 1. (in Islamic countries) Fixed bench, esp. of stone, attached to a dwelling. 2. Ancient Egyptian tomb with sloping sides and flat roof.
maˈster (mah-) n. 1. Person having control; captain of merchant-vessel; employer; owner of dog etc.; male head of household; one with thorough knowledge of subject or facility in technique; one who has or gets the upper hand. 2. Teacher in school; teacher in philosophy etc. 3. Skilled workman or one in business on his own account. 4. Person eminently skilled in an art etc. 5. M~, title given to heads of certain colleges at Oxford and Cambridge, as ~ of Balliol; title given to eldest son and heir of some ancient Scottish baronies, as ~ of Lovat; title of boy or young man with no superior title. 6. One holding degree of Master of Arts or Science. 7. (in titles etc.) ~ at arms, police officer on warship or liner; M~ of Arts (M.A.), Science (M.Sc.), etc., holder of university degree ranking above bachelor, and orig. qualifying to teach in university; ~ of ceremonies, person presiding over arrangements at social gathering etc.; ~ of foxhounds (M.F.H.), person having control of a pack. 8. (attrib.) Commanding, superior (as ~ mind); principal (as ~ bedroom); ~-key, one made to open many locks, each also opened by separate key; maˈsterpiece, consummate piece of workmanship, best work; maˈstersinger: see MEISTERSINGER; ~ stroke, masterly action. ~ v.t. Overcome; reduce to subjection; acquire complete knowledge of or facility in.
maˈsterful (mah-) adj. Self-willed, imperious. **maˈsterfully** adv. **maˈsterfulness** n.
maˈsterly (mah-) adj. Worthy of a master, very skilful.
maˈstery (mah-) n. Sway; masterly skill, use or knowledge; upper hand.
măˈstic n. Gum or resin exuding from certain trees, growing esp. in the Levant, used in making varnish; trees yielding this; mastic colour, pale yellow; kind of cement made of mastic.
măˈsticāte v.t. Grind (food) with teeth, chew. **măsticāˈtion**, **măˈsticātor** ns. **măˈsticatory** adj. ~ n. Substance chewed to increase saliva.
măˈstiff (or mah-) n. Large strong dog with drooping ears and pendulous lips, valuable as a watch-dog (ill. DOG).
măstiˈtis n. Inflammation of the breast.
măˈstodŏn n. Any of several large extinct mammals esp. of genus Mammut, resembling elephants but having nipple-shaped tubercles on crowns of molar teeth.
măˈstoid adj. (anat.) Shaped like female breast; ~ process, conical prominence in temporal bone behind ear (ill. HEAD). ~ n. Mastoid process; (colloq.) mastoiditis. **măstoidiˈtis** n. Inflammation of mastoid process.
măsturbāˈtion n. Sexual stimulation so as to produce orgasm, achieved esp. by manipulation of the genitals, not by coition. **măˈsturbāte** v. Practise masturbation (on).
măt[1] n. Fabric of plaited or woven rushes, hemp, etc., or pliant material such as rubber; piece of this as protection or ornament on floor etc.; small rug; small piece of material as protection or ornament on surface of table etc.; thick pad on floor to cushion falls in gymnastics. ~ v. Entangle, become entangled, in thick mass.
mat[2] see MATT.
Mătabēˈlė n. (Member of) a S. African people, one of the main branches of the Zulu group of tribes; now settled in the W. part of S. Rhodesia.
măˈtador n. 1. Man appointed to kill bull in bullfight. 2. One of three chief cards in ombre and quadrille.
mătch[1] n. Person equal in some particular, person or thing exactly corresponding, to another; contest in which persons or teams are matched against each other; matrimonial alliance; person viewed in light of eligibility for marriage; maˈtchboard, board with tongue cut along one edge and groove along another, so as to fit into similar boards; maˈtchmaker, person fond of trying to arrange marriages; ~ point, state of game when one side needs only one point to win the match; the point itself. ~ v. Find or be a match for; place (person etc.) in competition with, in conflict against, another; be equal, correspond in colour, shape etc.
mătch[2] n. Short strip of wood (maˈtchstick) etc. with tip (~-head) covered with some combustible substance which ignites when rubbed on rough or (safety ~) specially prepared surface; fuse for firing cannon etc.; maˈtchbox, box for holding matches; maˈtchlock, (hist.) (gun with) lock in which match was placed for igniting powder (ill. MUSKET; maˈtchwood, wood of suitable size for making matches; (wood reduced to) minute splinters.
măˈtchet n. = MACHETE.
măˈtchless adj. Without an equal, peerless. **măˈtchlessly** adv.
māte[1] n. (chess) = CHECK-MATE; fool's ~, in which first player is mated at opponent's second move. ~ v.t. Checkmate.
māte[2] n. 1. Companion, fellow worker; (colloq.) friend (also used as form of address among equals). 2. Fitting partner in marriage; one of a pair, esp. of birds. 3. (naut.) Officer on merchant ship who sees to execution of master's commands and deputizes for him. 4. Assistant to some specialist, as gunner's ~, plumber's ~. ~ v. Associate as mate; copulate (with); cause (animals) to copulate for breeding. **māˈtey** adj. (colloq.) Companionable, sociable. **māˈteyness, -tiness** n.
maté (măˈtā) n. Paraguay tea (also yerba ~), infusion of leaves of S. Amer. shrub Ilex paraguayensis; vessel for this.
măˈtelōte n. Dish of fish stewed with wine, onions, etc.
māˈter n. (school slang) Mother. **matēˈrial** adj. Concerned with or composed of matter; unspiritual; concerned with bodily comfort, riches, etc.; important, essential. **matēˈrially** adv. **matēˈrial** n. Matter from which thing is made; elements; stuff, fabric; writing-~s, requisites for writing.
matēˈrialism n. Opinion that nothing exists but matter and its movements and modifications and that consciousness are and will are wholly due to material agency; (art) tendency to lay stress on material aspect of objects; desire for material rather than spiritual prosperity etc. **matēˈrialist** n. & adj. **matēriaˈlistic** adj. **matēriaˈlistically** adv.
matēˈrialize v. Make, represent as, material; appear, cause (spirit) to appear, in bodily form; make materialistic; become actual fact. **matērializāˈtion** n.
matēriă mēˈdica. Remedial substances used in practice of medicine; branch of science dealing with their origin and properties.
matériel (-tāriĕl) n. Stock of materials, equipment, etc., used in any complex operation (opp. PERSONNEL). [Fr.]
matēˈrnal adj. Of mothers; motherly; related on mother's side, as ~ uncle, mother's brother. **matēˈrnally** adv. **matēˈrnity** n. Motherhood; motherliness; ~ home, hospital, institution for care of women during (or immediately after) childbirth.
măth n. (U.S., colloq.) Mathematics.
măthēmăˈtics n.pl. (usu. treated as sing.) Abstract science of space and number (also pure ~); this applied to branches of physics etc. (also applied ~). **măthēmăˈtical** adj. Of mathematics; (of proof etc.) rigorously precise. **măthēmăˈtically** adv. **măthēmătiˈcian** (-shan) n.
măths n. (colloq.) Mathematics.
Matiˈlda (1102–67). Daughter and heir of Henry I of England; married Henry V of Germany and was crowned empress, 1114; on her father's death in 1135 her cousin Stephen was chosen as king; she returned to England 1139, captured Stephen, and was acknowledged in 1141 as 'Lady of England and Normandy', but was

eventually forced to withdraw to the Continent; her son became Henry II.

mă′tinée (-nā) *n.* Afternoon theatrical or musical performance, afternoon cinema show; ~ *coat*, *jacket*, baby's short coat; ~ *idol*, handsome actor.

Mă′tins, Mă′ttins (-z) *n.* 1. (R.C. Ch.) Canonical HOUR; service for this, a midnight office, but also recited at daybreak. 2. Morning Prayer in Church of England.

Mătisse (-ēs), Henri (1869–1954). French Post-Impressionist painter.

mă′trass *n.* Long-necked glass vessel with round or oval body, used in distilling etc.

mă′triărch (-k) *n.* Woman corresponding in status to patriarch. **mă′triărchal** *adj.*

mă′triărchў (-k-) *n.* Social organization in which the mother is head of the family and descent and relationship are reckoned through mothers.

matrī′c *n.* (colloq.) = MATRICULATION.

mă′tricīde *n.* Killing of one's own mother; person guilty of this. **mă′tricīdal** *adj.*

matrī′cūlate *v.* Admit, be admitted, to privileges of university. **matriculā′tion** *n.* Matriculating; examination qualifying for this.

mă′trimonў *n.* 1. Rite of marriage, state of being married. 2. Declaration of king and queen of trumps in some card-games. **mătrimō′nial** *adj.* **mătrimō′niallў** *adv.*

mā′trix *n.* (pl. *-ices* pr. -isēz, *-ixes*). Womb; place in which thing is developed; mass of rock etc. enclosing gems etc.; mould in which type etc. is cast or shaped; something to be mechanically reproduced; (physiol.) formative part of animal organ; (biol.) substance between cells; (math.) rectangular arrangement of quantities or symbols.

mā′tron *n.* Married woman; woman managing domestic affairs of schools etc.; woman in charge of nursing in hospital. [It. *matron-age*, **mā′tronhŏod, mā′tronship** *ns.* **mā′tronal** *adj.* **mā′tronlў** *adj.* Resembling a married woman in appearance and bearing; staid; portly.

mătt, măt[2] *adj.* Without lustre, ~ *v.t.* Make (surface etc.) matt; frost (glass). ~ *n.* Dull-gold border round framed picture; lustreless surface or appearance; roughened or frosted groundwork.

Matt. *abbrev.* Matthew.

mă′tter *n.* 1. Substance(s) of which a physical thing is made; grey ~, parts of central nervous system which appear grey owing to presence of massed groups of nerve-cells (also, joc., brain, intellectual power), as dist. from *white* ~, parts consisting mainly of nerve-fibre tracts. 2. Physical substance in general as dist. from spirit,

mind, etc. 3. Purulent discharge. 4. Content as dist. from form; material for thought or expression; substance of book, speech, etc. 5. Thing(s); material, as *printed* ~. 6. Affair, concern; *no* ~, it is unimportant; ~ *of fact*, what pertains to the sphere of fact (opp. to *opinion* etc.); *as a* ~ *of fact*, (law) part of a judicial inquiry concerned with truth of alleged facts (opp. to ~ *of law*); ~*-of-fact* (*adj.*) unimaginative, prosaic. ~ *v.i.* 1. Be of importance, signify. 2. Secrete or discharge pus.

Mă′tterhorn. Alpine peak (4478 m, 14,691 ft) on Italian-Swiss frontier, first climbed in 1865.

Matthew (mă′thū), St. Apostle, a tax-gatherer from Capernaum; traditionally but erroneously supposed to be the author of the 1st Gospel, which was written after A.D. 70, and based largely on St. Mark; commemorated 21 Sept.; 1st Gospel.

Matthew Paris: see PARIS.[3]

Matthew Walker knŏt (mă′-thū waw′ker n-). (naut.) Knot made in end of rope (ill. KNOT).

mă′tting *n.* Material for mats.

mă′ttock *n.* Tool shaped like pick, with adze and chisel edge as ends of head.

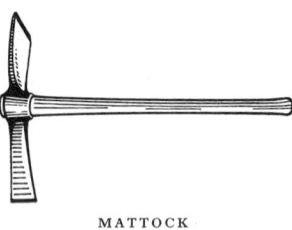

MATTOCK

mă′ttress *n.* Case of canvas or other strong material stuffed with hair, straw, wool, etc., as bed; series of wire springs stretched in frame as support for bed (also *spring* ~); series of wires (*wire* ~) stretched on frame to support mattress of hair etc. [It. *materasso* prob. f. Arab. *almatrah* place, cushion (*taraha* throw)]

mă′tūrate *v.i.* (med.) Attain full development, ripen. **mătūrā′tion** *n.* Final series of changes in the growth and formation of germ cells. **matūr′ative** *adj.* Causing maturation.

matūr′e *adj.* Fully developed; ripe; adult; (in finance, of bonds etc.) due for payment. **matūr′elў** *adv.* **matūr′eněss, matūr′itў** *ns.* **matūr′e** *v.* Bring to or reach mature state.

Mă′tūrin, Charles Robert (1782–1826). Irish playwright and author of novels of terror.

mătūti′nal (*or* matū′tī-) *adj.* Of, in, the morning, early.

maud *n.* (archaic) Scotch shepherd's grey striped woollen plaid; travelling-rug like this.

mau′dlin *adj.* Mawkishly sentimental, esp. of tearful and effusively affectionate stage of drunkenness. ~ *n.* Mawkish sentiment. [f. MAGDALEN]

Maugham (mawm), William Somerset (1874–1965). English writer of novels, plays, and short stories.

maul *n.* Heavy hammer, usu. of wood (ill. BEETLE[1]). ~ *v.t.* Beat and bruise; handle or paw roughly; lacerate; damage by criticism.

mau′lstick *n.* Var. of MAHLSTICK.

mau′nder *v.i.* Talk ramblingly; wander about vaguely and listlessly.

Mau′ndў *n.* (hist.) Ceremony of washing the feet of the poor, performed by royal or other eminent persons on the Thursday before Easter (~ *Thursday*) in commemoration of Christ's washing of the Apostles' feet, and commonly followed by almsgiving; it survives in England in the distribution of ~ *money* (silver coins minted for this), usu. at Westminster Abbey. [L *mandatum* commandment]

Maupassant (mōpăsahň), Guy de (1850–93). French novelist, famous as a writer of short stories.

Maurĕ′sque (-sk) *adj.* = MORESQUE.

Mauretā′nia. Ancient country and Roman province in N. Africa, corresponding roughly to N. Morocco and Algeria. [L, = 'country of the Moors' (*Mauri*)]

Mau′rist (mō-) *n.* Member of a congregation of French Benedictine monks, established in 1618 in order to reform the order, famous for scholarship and literary zeal. [f. MAURUS].

Mauritā′nia (mō-). Republic in NW Africa; independent since 1960; capital, Nouakchott. **Mauritā′nian** *adj. & n.*

Mauritius (mori′shus). Island in Indian Ocean E. of Madagascar; member State of the Commonwealth; formerly (1810–1968) a British colony; capital, Port Louis. **Mauri′tian** (-shan) *adj. & n.*

Mau′rus (mō-), St. (d. 565). Legendary founder of the Benedictine order in France.

Mauser (mowz-) *n.* Repeating rifle with interlocking bolt-head and box magazine; ~ *pistol*, self-loading pistol. [Peter Paul *Mauser* (1838–1917), German inventor]

mausolē′um *n.* Large, magnificent tomb, orig. that at Halicarnassus in Caria (formerly one of the Seven Wonders of the World) ordered for himself by *Mausō′lus*, king of Caria (d. 353 B.C.), and erected by his queen Artemisia (d. 351 B.C.).

mauve (mōv) *n.* Pale purple; delicate purple dye from coal-tar aniline. ~ *adj.* [L *malva* mallow]

mă′verick *n.* (U.S.) Unbranded calf etc.; unorthodox or undisciplined person.

mā′vis *n.* (poet.) Song-thrush.

[552]

maw n. Stomach (of animal); abomasum (ill. RUMINANT).
maw'kĭsh adj. Of faint sickly flavour; feebly sentimental. **maw'kĭshlȳ** adv. **maw'kĭshnĕss** n. [obs. *mawk* maggot]
maw'seed n. Seed of opium poppy.
măxĭ'lla n. Upper jaw in most vertebrates (ill. HEAD); component of mouth parts of many arthropods. **măxĭ'llarȳ**, **măxĭ'llĭfŏrm** adjs.
măxĭ'llĭpĕd n. Crustacean's fore-limb modified so as to assist in mastication (ill. LOBSTER).
mă'xĭm[1] n. General truth drawn from science or experience; principle, rule of conduct.
Mă'xĭm[2] n. Single-barrelled, rapid-firing, water-cooled machine-gun. [Sir H. S. *Maxim* (1840-1916), American-born inventor]
mă'xĭmal adj. Greatest possible in size, duration, etc.
mă'xĭmalist n. Person who holds out for maximum of his demands and rejects compromises (esp. member of section of Russian Socialist Revolutionary Party, distinguished for terrorist activities c 1905-7).
Măxĭmĭ'lian[1] (-lyan). Name of 2 Holy Roman Emperors: *Maximilian I* (1459-1519), reigned 1493-1519; *Maximilian II* (1527-76), reigned 1564-76.
Măxĭmĭ'lian[2] (-lyan) (1832-67). Emperor of Mexico; brother of Austrian Emperor Francis Joseph; was offered throne of Mexico 1863; French troops supported him, but after their withdrawal he was defeated by republican forces, captured, and shot.
mă'xĭmīze v.t. Increase, magnify, to the utmost; interpret (doctrine etc.) vigorously. **măxĭmīzā'tion** n.
mă'xĭmum n. (pl.-*ima*). Highest possible or highest recorded magnitude or quantity (freq. attrib.).
mă'xĭmus adj. (in schools) Eldest of the name (as *Jones* ~).
Mă'xwell[1], James Clerk (1831-79). Professor of experimental physics at Cambridge University; contributed to the theory of the conservation of energy and of electricity and magnetism; ~('s) **demon**, (physics) a hypothetical intelligent being imagined by him to illustrate limitations of the second law of thermodynamics.
mă'xwell[2] n. Unit of magnetic flux in c.g.s. system, equal to the flux of magnetic induction per square centimetre in a magnetic field whose intensity is one gauss (abbrev. Mx). [f. MAXWELL[1]]
may[1] v. auxil. (past t. *might* pr. mīt). Expressing possibility, permission, request, wish.
May[2]. 5th month of Gregorian (3rd of Julian) calendar, with 31 days; ~ **day**, 1 May, traditionally celebrated with dancing round a maypole, gathering garlands of flowers, and the choice of a May queen; since 1889, the international Labour holiday; **may'flower**, flower that blooms in May, used locally for cowslip, lady's smock, etc.; *Mayflower*, ship in which the Pilgrim Fathers sailed to America from Southampton in 1620; **may'fly**, insect of the order

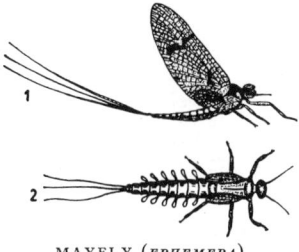

MAYFLY (*EPHEMERA*)
1. Adult. 2. Nymph

Ephemeroptera; imitation of this used by anglers; **may'pole**, gaily coloured pole decorated with flowers and ribbons, which is danced round on May day; ~ **queen**, girl or young woman chosen to be queen of the May and crowned with flowers; ~ **week**, week in late May or early June when boat races are held at Cambridge. [L *Maius*, perh. f. the Roman goddess *Maia*]
may[3] n. 1. Hawthorn blossom. 2. *Mays*, (Camb. Univ.) examinations held in May; boat races held during May week. [f. MAY[2]]
ma'ya[1] (mah-) n. (Hind. philos.) Illusion, esp. the material world regarded as deceptive and unreal.
Ma'ya[2] (mah-) n. Member, language, of an Amer. Indian people, remarkable for their art and knowledge of astronomy, who lived from c 300 in Guatemala (the 'Old Empire') in city states, and migrated in 9th c. to Yucatan in E. Mexico ('New Empire'), where their culture partially merged with that of the Toltecs, but disintegrated in mid-15th c. owing to civil wars, and was found in decay by the invading Spaniards in 1511. **Ma'yan** adj. & n.
Mayakovsky (mĭyakŏ'fskĭ), Vladimir Vladimirovich (1893-1930). Russian futurist poet.
may'bē adv. Perhaps.
mayday. International vocal radio-telephonic distress signal from aircraft or ship. [pron. of Fr. *m'aider* imp. infin. 'help me!']
May'fair. District N. of Piccadilly, London, very fashionable in 19th c. [so called from annual fair held there in May from Stuart times until end of 18th c.]
may'hĕm n. Crime of causing malicious personal injury; also fig.
May'ō. Western maritime county of Connacht.
mayonnai'se (-z) n. Sauce of yolk of eggs, oil, and vinegar used as dressing for salads, fish, etc.; dish with this dressing.
mayor (mār) n. Head of municipal corporation of city or borough (formerly, until 1 April 1974); head of district council having borough status (since 1 April 1974). **may'oral** adj. **may'oraltȳ** n. Mayor's (period of) office. **may'orĕss** n. Mayor's wife; lady who fulfils duties of mayor's wife.
mă'zard n. Small black cherry.
Măzarin (-ăṅ), Jules (1606-61). Italian papal legate in Paris, 1634; became cardinal, 1641, and succeeded Richelieu, 1642, as prime minister of France; ~ *Bible*, earliest printed bible (printed prob. by Gutenberg before 1456), so called because the first known copy was in the library (*Bibliothèque Mazarine*) which Mazarin founded in Paris.
măzari'ne (-ēn) n. & adj. Deep rich blue.
Mă'zdaism n. Zoroastrianism. [Avestan *mazda* good principle in Persian theology (see AHURA-MAZDA)]
māze n. Confusing and baffling network of winding and intercommunicating paths with hedges

MAZE

on either side, designed as a puzzle for those who try to find their way in it; labyrinth; (fig.) confusion, bewilderment. ~ v.t. Confuse, bewilder. **mā'zȳ** adj. **mā'zĭlȳ** adv. **mā'zĭnĕss** n.
mă'zer n. (hist.) Hardwood drinking bowl, usu. silvermounted.

MAZER
Maple wood with silver rim and base

mazŭr'ka n. Lively Polish dance; music for this, in triple time. [Polish, = 'woman of province of Mazovia']
Măzzi'ni (-tsē-), Giuseppe (c 1805-72). Italian patriot and republican; agitated for the liberation of Italy, and spent many years in exile.
M.B. abbrev. *Medicinae baccalaureus* (L, = Bachelor of Medicine).

M.B.E. *abbrev.* Member (of the Order) of the British Empire.

m/c, Mc *abbrev.* Megacycle.

M.C. *abbrev.* Master of Ceremonies; Member of Congress (*or* Council); Military Cross.

M.C.C. *abbrev.* Marylebone Cricket Club.

M.Ch. *abbrev. Magister chirurgiae* (L, = Master of Surgery).

Md. *abbrev.* Maryland.

M.D. *abbrev. Medicinae doctor* (L, = Doctor of Medicine); mentally deficient.

mē[1] (*or* **mĭ**) *pron.* Objective (accus., dat.) case of I.

mē,[2] **mi** (mē) *n.* (mus.) 3rd note of hexachord and of major scale in movable-doh systems; note E in fixed-doh system. [see UT]

Me. *abbrev.* Maine; *Maître* (French advocate's title).

mead[1] *n.* Alcoholic liquor of fermented honey and water.

mead[2] *n.* (poet.) = MEADOW.

meadow (mĕ′dō) *n.* Piece of grassland, esp. one used for hay; low-lying ground, esp. near river; ~ *grass*, poa, esp. *Poa pratensis*; ~ *saffron*, autumn crocus; *mea′dowsweet*, rosaceous plant, esp. *Filipendula ulmaria*, common in meadows, growing to a height of about 2 feet, with dense heads of creamy-white and very fragrant flowers.

mea′gre (-ger) *adj.* Lean, scanty. **mea′grely** *adv.* **mea′greness** *n.*

meal[1] *n.* Edible part of any grain or pulse (usu. exc. wheat) rather coarsely ground; (Sc.) oatmeal; (U.S.) maize; *mea′lworm*, larva of beetle *Tenebrio molitor* which feeds on meal. **mea′ly** *adj.* Of, like, meal; (of boiled potatoes) dry and powdery; (also ~-*mouthed*), apt to mince matters, soft-spoken. **mea′liness** *n.*

meal[2] *n.* Customary, or any, occasion of taking food; food so taken; ~-*time*, usual time of eating.

mea′lie *n.* (usu. pl.) (S. Afr.) Maize; corn-cob.

mean[1] *n.* 1. Condition, quality, amount, equally removed from two opposite extremes. 2. (pl.) That by which a result is brought about; pecuniary resources; wealth; ~*s test*, official inquiry into financial resources of applicant for assistance from public funds. ~ *adj.* Equally far from two extremes; (math.) intermediate in value, position, etc., between two other quantities, points, etc.; average. **mea′ntime, mea′nwhile** *advs.* (also *in* or *for the meantime*) In the intervening time.

mean[2] *adj.* Inferior, poor; shabby; ignoble, small-minded; stingy. **mea′nly** *adv.* **mea′nness** (-n-n-) *n.*

mean[3] *v.* (past t. & past part. *meant* pr. měnt). Purpose; design, destine; intend to convey or indicate; signify, import. **mea′ning** *n.* What is meant. **mea′ningful**

adj. Significant. **mea′ningless** *adj.* **mea′ninglessness** *n.*

mea′ning *adj.* Expressive, significant. **mea′ningly** *adv.*

měă′nder *v.i.* Wind about; wander at random. ~ *n.* 1. (pl.) Sinuous windings, circuitous journey, winding paths, etc. 2. (geog.) Twisting course of river in its flood plain. 3. Fret pattern (see FRET and ill.). [f. MAEANDER]

mea′sles (-zlz) *n.* 1. Acute infectious disease of man (*Rubeola*), caused by a virus, and characterized by fever, skin rash, and inflammation of the conjunctival membranes and air passages; German ~: see GERMAN[2]. 2. Disease in swine, caused by tapeworm. **mea′sly** *adj.* Of, affected with, measles; (slang) contemptible, worthless.

measure (mĕ′zher) *n.* 1. Size or quantity found by measuring; vessel of standard capacity for measuring liquids; rod, tape, etc., for measuring; system of measuring; degree, extent, amount; stratum or bed of mineral; (math.) quantity contained in another an exact number of times; *greatest common* ~, largest quantity exactly dividing each of two or more given quantities. 2. Prescribed extent or quantity. 3. Metre; time of piece of music; (archaic) dance. 4. Suitable action; legislative enactment. ~ *v.* Ascertain extent or quantity of by comparison with fixed standard or thing of known size; mark off; be of specified length etc.; deal *out*; bring into competition *with*; ~ *up to*, meet the requirements of; *measuring worm*, larva of geometrid moth. **mea′surable** *adj.* **mea′surably** *adv.* **mea′surement** *n.* **mea′sured** (-erd) *adj.* Rhythmical, regular in movement; carefully weighed.

meat *n.* Animal flesh as food, usu. excluding fish and poultry; (archaic) food; meal; ~-*fly*, bluebottle. **mea′ty** *adj.* Full of meat; (fig.) full of substance; of or like meat.

Meath (-dh). North-eastern maritime county of Leinster, Ireland.

meā′tus *n.* (pl. -*us*, -*uses*). (anat.) External opening of channel, duct, passage, in the body, as *auditory* ~, channel of the ear (ill. EAR[1]).

Mĕ′cca. City now in Saudi Arabia, the birthplace of Muhammad and the chief place of Muslim pilgrimage.

měchă′nic(-k-) *n.* Skilled workman, esp. one who makes or uses machinery. **měchă′nics** *n.* Branch of applied mathematics treating of motion; mechanism, functioning; science of machinery.

měchă′nical (-k-) *adj.* Of machines or mechanism; like machines, automatic; working, produced, by machines; belonging to the science of mechanics; ~ *advantage*, ratio of load to effort; *the* ~ *powers*, the lever, wheel and axle, pulley, inclined plane, wedge, and screw. **měchă′nically** *adv.* **měchă′nicalness** *n.*

mě′chanism (-k-) *n.* 1. Way a machine works; structure, parts, of a machine; (fig.) framework, structure, technique; (physiol.) system of mutually adapted parts working together. 2. (philos.) Theory that the origin of life can be ascribed to chemical and physical forces (opp. VITALISM). **mě′chanist** *n.* 1. Expert in mechanics. 2. (philos.) Adherent of mechanism. **měchani′stic** *adj.*

mě′chanize (-k-) *v.t.* Make mechanical; replace manual labour with machinery; (mil.) equip with tanks etc. **měchaniza′tion** *n.*

Mě′chlin (-k-) *n.* (also ~ *lace*) Fine bobbin lace orig. made at Malines, a town in Belgium. [Flemish *Mechelen* Malines]

Med. *abbrev.* (slang) Mediterranean (Sea).

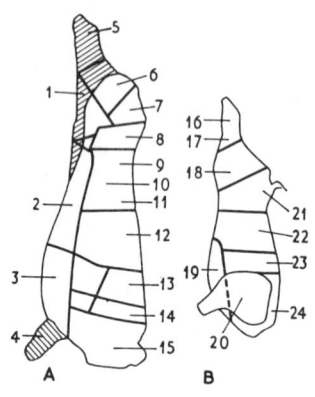

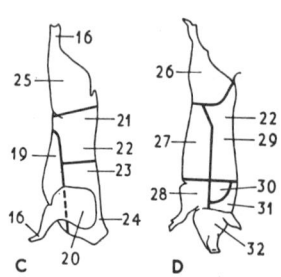

CUTS OF MEAT

A. BEEF (LONDON CUTTING). B. VEAL. C. MUTTON. D. PORK

A. 1. Thick flank or top rump. 2. Thin flank. 3. Brisket. 4. Shin. 5. Leg. 6. Topside and silverside. 7. Aitchbone. 8. Rump steak. 9. Sirloin. 10. Undercut or fillet. 11. Wing-rib. 12. Fore-rib. 13. Middle rib. 14. Chuck. 15. Clod and sticking. B. 16. Shank. 17. Knuckle. 18. Fillet. 19. Breast. 20. Shoulder. 21. Chumpchops. 22. Loin. 23. Best end of neck. 24. Middle neck. C. 25. Leg. D. 26. Leg or gammon. 27. Belly. 28. Hand or forehock. 29. Tenderloin. 30. Bladebone. 31. Spare-rib or chine. 32. Head

MEDAL

mĕ′dal n. Piece of metal, usu. in form of coin, struck or cast with inscription and device to commemorate event etc., or awarded as distinction to soldier, scholar, etc., for services rendered; ~ **play**, (golf) scored by strokes, not holes as in a match.

mĕ′dicable adj. Admitting of remedial treatment.

mĕ′dical adj. Of medicine; requiring, supplying, medical not surgical treatment. ~ n. (colloq.) Student of medicine; (colloq.) medical examination for fitness.

mĕdi′cament (or mĕ′-) n.

MEDUSA

round it, or the peoples of this region; M~ **Sea**, inland sea lying between S. Europe and N. Africa, communicating with the Atlantic by the Strait of Gibraltar and with the Persian Gulf by the Suez Canal. **Mĕditerrā′nĕan** n. Mediterranean Sea.

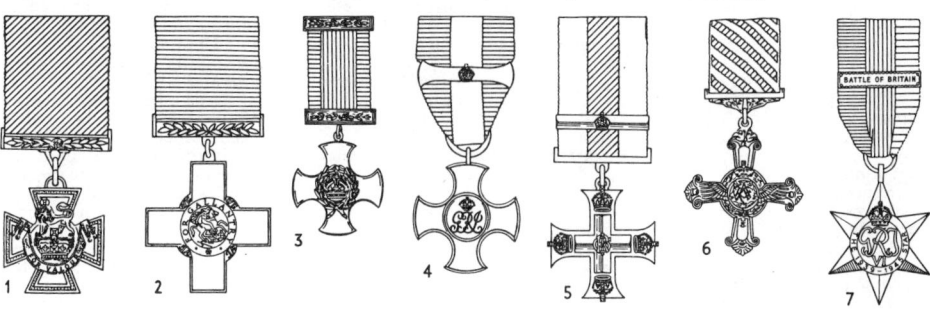

MEDALS AND DECORATIONS
1. Victoria Cross. 2. George Cross. 3. Distinguished Service Order. 4. Distinguished Service Cross. 5. Military Cross and Bar. 6. Distinguished Flying Cross. 7. 1939–45 Star, with clasp for Battle of Britain

mĕdă′llion (-yon) n. Large medal; medal-shaped picture, panel, etc.

mĕ′dallist n. 1. Winner of prize-medal. 2. Engraver, designer, of medals.

mĕ′ddle v.i. Busy oneself unduly *with*; interfere *in*. **mĕ′ddlesome** adj. Given to meddling. **mĕ′ddlesomenėss** n.

Mēde n. One of the earliest Iranian inhabitants of Persia; *the law of the ~s and Persians*, an immutable law (see Dan. 6: 8).

Mē′dian, Mē′dish adjs.

Mēdē′a. (Gk legend) Sorceress, daughter of Aeetes king of Colchis; helped JASON to obtain the Golden Fleece; married him but was deserted by him in Corinth and avenged herself by killing their two children.

mē′dia n. (pl. *-ae*). 1. (phonet.) Voiced stop consonant (*b, d, g*), as dist. f. TENUIS. 2. (anat.) Middle membrane of blood or lymph vessel.

mediaeval: see MEDIEVAL.

mē′dial adj. Situated in the middle; of average size. **mē′dially** adv.

Median¹ see MEDE.

mē′dian² adj. Situated in the middle. ~ n. 1. (anat.) Median artery, vein, nerve, etc. 2. (math.) Each of three lines drawn from the angles of a triangle to the middle points of the opposite sides and meeting in a point within it (ill. TRIANGLE).

mē′diant n. (mus.) 3rd note of any scale (ill. SCALE³).

mē′diate adj. Involving an intermediary. **mē′diately** adv. **mē′diāte** v. Form connecting link; intervene (between two persons etc.) for purpose of reconciling them; be the medium for bringing about (result). **mēdiā′tion, mē′diātor** ns. **mē′diator′ial, mē′diatory** adjs.

Substance used in curative or palliative treatment.

mĕ′dicāte v.t. Treat medically; impregnate with medicinal substance. **mĕdicā′tion** n.

Mĕ′dici (-chi). Name of the ruling family of Florence from 1434; orig. merchants and bankers; grand dukes of Tuscany 1569–1737; patrons of art and letters, esp. Cosimo dei (or de') ~ (1389–1464), his son Piero (1416–69), Piero's son Lorenzo 'the Magnificent' (1449–92), and Lorenzo's son Giovanni (1475–1521), who became Pope Leo X; Giulio (1478–1534) became Pope Clement VII; Catarina (CATHERINE DE MÉDICIS) married Henri II; Maria (MARIE DE MÉDICIS) married Henri IV. **Mĕdicē′an** adj.

mĕdi′cinal adj. Of medicine; curative.

mĕ′dicine (-dsn or -dĭsn) n. Art of restoring and preserving health, esp. by means other than surgery; substance taken internally for this purpose; ~ **man**, tribal magician of primitive peoples, esp. N. Amer. Indians.

mĕ′dicō n. (slang) Doctor.

mĕdiē′val, mĕdiae′val adj. Of the Middle Ages. **mĕdiē′valist, mĕdiē′valism** ns.

Mĕdi′na (-ē-). City now in Saudi Arabia, to which Muhammad fled from Mecca and where he died and was buried.

mĕdiō′cre (-ker) adj. Of middling quality, indifferent. **mĕdiŏ′crity** n. Mediocre quality; mediocre person.

mĕ′ditāte v. Plan mentally; exercise the mind in contemplation *on*. **mĕditā′tion** n. **mĕ′ditātive** adj. **mĕ′ditātively** adv.

mĕditerrā′nĕan adj. (of land) Remote from coast; (of water surfaces) land-locked; M~, of the Mediterranean Sea, the region

mē′dium n. (pl. *-s, -ia*). 1. Middle quality, degree, etc. 2. Means, agency. 3. (art) Method by which work of art is produced, branch of art (e.g. painting, sculpture); (also) liquid substance in which pigments are ground in preparation of paint, substance which makes pigment adhere to ground (e.g. oil, gum). 4. (spiritualism) Person claiming to be the vehicle for spirits' communication with human beings (*mental* ~) or to have the power of moving objects at a distance (*physical* ~). ~ adj. Intermediate between two degrees etc.; average, moderate; ~ **wave**, electromagnetic wave having a length between 100 and 800 metres (in broadcasting, between 200 and 550 metres).

mē′diumism n. Profession or occupation of a spiritualistic medium. **mēdiumi′stic** adj.

mĕ′dlar n. (Tree, *Mespilus germanica*, with) fruit like small brown apple, eaten when decayed.

mĕ′dley n. Heterogeneous mixture.

Mĕdoc (mā′dŏk) n. Wine produced in Médoc, a district in the Bordeaux region.

mĕdū′lla n. 1. Marrow of bones; spinal marrow. 2. Central parts of some organs, esp. kidney (ill. KIDNEY). 3. Cellular inner part of animal hair. 4. Soft internal tissue of plants (ill. STEM¹). 5. (also ~ *oblongata*) Brain-stem, prolonged hindmost segment of brain (ill. BRAIN). **mĕdŭ′llary** adj.

Mĕdū′sa¹. (Gk myth.) One of the Gorgons, the only mortal one; slain by Perseus, who cut off her head.

mĕdū′sa² n. (pl. *-sae*). (zool.) Sexually reproductive form of hydrozoan or scyphozoan coelenterates, with jelly-like body and stinging tentacles (pop. *jellyfish*).

[555]

meed n. (poet.) Reward; merited portion (*of* praise etc.).
meek adj. Piously humble and submissive; tamely submissive. **mee′klў** adv. **mee′knėss** n.
meer′kāt n. Suricate.
meer′schaum (-sham) n. Hydrated magnesium silicate, occurring in soft white masses, used for tobacco-pipe bowls; pipe with bowl made of this. [Ger., = 'seafoam']
meet[1] adj. (archaic) Suitable, fit. **mee′tlў** adv. **mee′tnėss** n.
meet[2] v. (past t. & past part. *mėt*). Come into contact or company (with); assemble; become perceptible to; satisfy (demand); experience. ∼ n. Assembly for hunting etc.
mee′ting n. (esp.) Assembly of people for entertainment, worship, etc.; duel; race-meeting; ∼-*house*, Quakers' place of worship.
M.E.F. abbrev. Middle East Forces.
mėga-, mėg- prefix. Great; (phys., prefixed to names of units of measurement, force, etc.) one million times (abbrev. M), as in *megacycle, megawatt*, etc. **mėgacėphă′lĭc** adj. Largeheaded.
mě′gacýcle n. 1,000,000 cycles, as unit in measuring frequency of electromagnetic waves (abbrev. m/c, Mc).
Mėgaer′a (-gēra). (Gk myth.) One of the Furies (see FURY).
mě′galĭth n. (archaeol.) Large stone used in construction or as a monument. **mėgali′thĭc** adj.
mėgalomā′nia n. 1. (psychiatry) Form of insanity marked by delusions of grandeur. 2. Passion for doing things on an extravagant scale. **mėgalomā′niăc** n.
mėgalosau′rus n. Huge carnivorous reptile of extinct genus *M*∼.
mě′gaphōne n. Large speaking-trumpet, used for making the voice travel to a distance.
mě′gapŏd, -pōde n. Member of family of birds, almost all in Australasian region, whose eggs are left to hatch without incubation.
Mě′gara. City of ancient Greece, on the Isthmus of Corinth. **Mėgār′ian** adj. & n. (Native, inhabitant) of Megara; (adherent) of the school of philosophy established at Megara by Eucleides, a pupil of Socrates, noted for its study of dialectics and its invention of logical fallacies or puzzles. **Mėgār′ĭc** adj. & n.
mě′garon n. (Gk antiq.) Rectangular living apartment.
mě′gascōpe n. Kind of camera obscura or magic lantern for throwing a magnified image on to a screen. **mėgascō′pĭc** adj. 1. Pertaining to a megascope. 2. MACROSCOPIC.
mě′gāss n. Fibrous residue after expression of sugar from cane.
mėgathēr′ium n. Large herbivorous sloth-like mammal of genus *M*∼.
mě′gaton (-tŭn) n. Explosive force equal to 1,000,000 tons of TNT.
mě′gawatt (-ŏt) n. 1,000,000 watts (abbrev. mW, MW).
mėgi′lp (-g-) n. Any of various preparations of varnish, oil, etc., which artists mix with paint to facilitate handling or hasten drying.
mě′grim n. Migraine; whim; (pl.) low spirits; staggers in horses and cattle. [Fr. *migraine* (f. Gk *hemi-* half, *kranion* skull)]
meiō′sis (mī-) n. (pl. -ōsēs). 1. Understatement, freq. ironical or jocular. 2. (biol.) Splitting of cell or nucleus without increase in number of chromosomes, so that each of the resulting two cells or nuclei has only half the chromosomes of the original one (cf. MITOSIS). 3. Var. of MIOSIS. **meiō′tĭc** adj.
Meissen (mī′sn). German town (near Dresden, Saxony) where the earliest European porcelain factory was founded, 1710, and still exists; ∼ *china*, porcelain made there (freq. called *Dresden china*).
Meissonier (mėsŏnyā), Jean Louis Ernest (1811–91). French painter of military and historical subjects.
mei′stersinger (mī-, -z-) n.pl. German lyric poets and musicians of 14th–17th centuries, organized in guilds and using elaborate technique; (sing.) member of such guild. [Ger., = 'mastersingers']
Mě′khitarĭst (-χ-) n. Member of a community of Armenian monks founded at Constantinople in 1701 by Peter Manong Mekhitar (1676–1749), Armenian religious reformer, and transferred in 1717 to the island of San Lazzaro, S. of Venice.
mėlanchō′lia (-k-) n. Mental illness characterized by depression (obsolesc. as psychol. term). [Gk *melas* black, *khole* bile]
mėlanchō′lĭc (-k-) adj. (of person) Melancholy; liable to melancholy.
mě′lancholў (-k-) n. 1. (Habitual tendency to) sadness and depression; pensive sadness. 2. (hist.) One of the four humours. ∼ adj. Sad, saddening.
Mėlă′nchthŏn (-k-). Graecized name of Philip Schwartzerd (1497–1560), German humanist, who was professor of Greek at Wittenberg and a supporter of Luther and the Reformation. [Gk *melas* black, *hkthon* earth]
Mėlanē′sia (-z-). General term for islands of W. Pacific including New Hebrides, New Caledonia, Fiji, etc. **Mėlanē′sian** adj. & n. [Gk *melas* black (from the colour of the predominant native race, the Papuans), *nēsos* island]
mélange (mālah′nzh) n. Mixture, medley.
mě′lanin n. Dark-brown or black pigment found in hair, skin, or tissues.
mě′lanĭsm n. Darkness of colour resulting from abnormal development of black pigment in epidermis, hair, etc.
mėlanŏ′chroī (-k-) n.pl. Caucasians with dark hair and pale complexion. **mėlanŏ′chroid** adj.
mėlanŏ′ma n. (path.) Dark-coloured tumour.
mėlanŏ′sĭs n. Morbid deposit, abnormal development, of black pigment in tissue. **mėlanŏ′tĭc** adj.
Mě′lba, Dame Nellie. Helen Porter Mitchell (1859–1931), Australian soprano singer, born near Melbourne, from which she took her professional name.
Mě′lbourne[1]. City of Australia, capital of Victoria.
Mě′lbourne[2], William Lamb, Viscount Melbourne (1779–1848). English statesman; prime minister 1834 and 1835–41.
Mě′lchiŏr (-k-). Traditional name of one of the Magi, a king of Nubia.
Mělchi′zėdėk (-lk-). King of Salem and the priest of the most high God, to whom Abraham paid tithes (Gen. 14: 18); he is sometimes quoted as the type of self-originating power, with reference to Heb. 7: 3–4.
mėld v. (cards) Declare (card(s)) for score; make meld. ∼ n. Melding; card(s) melded.
Mėlēā′ger[1] (-g-). (Gk myth.) Hero at whose birth the Fates declared that he would die when a brand then on the fire was consumed; his mother Althaea seized the brand and kept it; when Meleager grew up he slew a boar which was ravaging the country, but his fellow huntsmen, Althaea's brothers, quarrelled with him for giving away its head to the huntress Atalanta, and he killed them; whereupon Althaea threw the brand into the fire.
Mėlēā′ger[2] (-g-) (*c* 140–*c* 70 B.C.). Greek poet; lived at Tyre and Cos, author of short poems on love and death, and of many epigrams in the Greek Anthology.
mêlée (mě′lā) n. Mixed fight, skirmish.
mě′line adj. (zool.) Of the subfamily Melinae, the badgers and skunks.
mě′liorāte v. Improve. **mėliorā′tion** n.
mě′liorĭsm n. Doctrine that the world may be made better by human effort (opp. PESSIMISM). **mě′liorĭst** n.
mėlli′ferous adj. Yielding, producing, honey.
mėlli′fluous (-loo-) adj. (of voice, words, music) Sweet-sounding. **mėlli′fluence** n. **mėlli′fluent** adj.
mě′llow (-ō) adj. Soft and rich in flavour, colour, or sound; softened by age or experience; genial, jovial; partly intoxicated. **mě′llowlў** adv. **mě′llownėss** n.

mě'llow v. Make or become mellow; ripen.
mělō'dĕon, -dĭon, -dĭum n. Wind-instrument with keyboard and bellows worked by pedals; kind of accordion.
mělō'dĭc adj. Of melody; ~ *minor*, (mus.) minor scale with major 6th and 7th when ascending and minor 6th and 7th when descending (so called as more suitable for melody than HARMONIC minor; ill. SCALE[3]).
mělō'dĭous adj. Of, producing, melody; sweet-sounding. **mělō'dĭously** adv. **mělō'dĭousnĕss** n.
mě'lodĭst n. Singer; composer of melodies.
mě'lodrama (-rah-) n. Sensational dramatic piece with violent appeals to emotions and happy ending; language, behaviour, suggestive of this; (formerly) play, or passage in play, using spoken voice against musical background. **mělodramă'tĭc** adj. **mělodramă'tĭcally** adv. **mělodrā'matĭst** n. **mělodrā'matīze** v.t.
mě'lodў n. Sweet music; arrangement of single notes in musically expressive succession; principal part in harmonized music.
mě'lon n. (Any of several gourds bearing) sweet fruit, esp. the *musk*~, *Cucumis melo*, and *water*~, *Citrullus vulgaris*; *honeydew* ~, smooth-skinned melon with very sweet greenish flesh.
Mē'lŏs. Ancient name of Milos.
Mělpŏ'měnē. (Gk & Rom. myth.) Muse of tragedy.
mělt[1] v. (past part. *mě'ltĕd, mō'lten*). (Cause to) become liquefied by heat; soften, be softened; dissolve; pass imperceptibly *into*; ~ *away*, dissolve, disappear; ~ *down*, reduce (metal articles etc.) to molten metal for use as raw material; ~*water* (n.) water formed by melting of snow and ice, esp. from glacier. ~ n. Molten metal.
mělt[2] n. Var. of MILT.
mě'lton n. Kind of cloth with very close-cut nap, used for overcoats etc. [*Melton Mowbray*, town in Leicestershire]
Mě'lville, Herman (1819-91). American sailor, author of 'Moby Dick' and other adventure stories.
mem. abbrev. Memento (L, = remember).
mě'mber n. 1. Limb or other bodily organ, constituent portion of complex structure. 2. Person belonging to a society etc.; *M ~ of Parliament*, (abbrev. M.P.) person formally elected to the House of Commons. **mě'mbership** n.
mě'mbrāne n. Fine layer of connective tissue enveloping an organ, lining a cavity, or separating adjacent parts in a living organism; (palaeog.) parchment skin. **mě'mbrā'nèous, mě'mbranous** adjs.
mĕmě'ntō n. Object serving as reminder or warning, or kept as memorial; ~ *mō'rī* (L, = remember you must die), warning or reminder of death, e.g. skull.

Mě'mnŏn. (Gk legend) Ethiopian prince slain at Troy; a colossal statue at Thebes (in reality that of Amenhotep III), which gave forth a musical note when struck by the rays of the rising sun, was supposed to represent him.
mě'mō. abbrev. Memorandum.
mě'moir (-wār) n. Record, history, written from personal knowledge or special sources of information; (auto-)biography; essay on learned subject by expert.
mĕmorabĭ'lĭa n.pl. Memorable things. [L]
mě'morable adj. Likely or worthy to be remembered. **mĕmorabĭ'lĭtў** n. **mě'morablў** adv.
mĕmorā'ndum n. (pl. *-da*). Note to help the memory, record for future use; informal letter without signature etc.
mĕmōr'ial adj. Commemorative, of memory. ~ n. Memorial object, monument, custom, etc.; (usu. pl.) chronicle; statement of facts as basis of petition etc.; *M~ Day*, (U.S.) day commemorating members of armed forces who died on active service (30 May in most States, also 26 April, 10 May, or 3 June in South). **mĕmōr'ialīze** v.t. Commemorate; address memorial to.
mě'morīze v.t. Put on record; commit to memory.
mě'morў n. 1. Faculty by which things are recalled to or kept in the mind; recollection; posthumous repute; length of time over which memory extends. 2. Part of computer in which information is stored during its operation.
Mě'mphis. Early capital of ancient Egypt, on W. bank of Nile S. of Cairo.
memsahib: see SAHIB.
mě'nace n. Threat. ~ v.t. Threaten. **mě'nacinglў** adv.
ménage (měnah'zh *or* mā-) n. Household.
mĕnā'gerie (*or* -nah-) n. Collection of wild animals kept in captivity for exhibition etc.
Mě'nai Strait (-nī). Channel separating Anglesey from NW. Wales.
Mĕnă'nder (342-291 B.C.). Greek poet and writer of comedies.
mĕnd v. Restore to sound condition, repair; improve; rectify; regain health. ~ n. Repaired place; *on the* ~, improving.
mĕndā'cious (-shus) adj. Lying. **mĕndā'ciouslў** adv. **mĕndā'cĭtў** n.
Mě'ndel, Gregor Johann (1822-84). Abbot of Brünn, Moravia; his experiments in the cross-fertilization of garden peas led to the formulation of ~'s *laws* of heredity, showing that certain characteristics, as height, colour, etc., depend on the presence of hereditary determining factors (later called *genes*) which may be either dominant or recessive. **Mĕndē'lian** adj. **Mě'ndelism** n.
Mĕndeleev (-lā'ĕf), Dmitri Ivanovich (1834-1907). Russian chemist; discovered the PERIODIC law.
mĕndelē'vĭum n. (chem.) Transuranic element, symbol Md, at. no. 101. [f. MENDELEEV]
Mě'ndelssohn (-sn), Jacob Ludwig Felix (1809-47). German-Jewish musical composer of oratorios, concert-overtures, etc.
mě'ndĭcant adj. Begging; living on alms. ~ n. Beggar; mendicant friar. **mě'ndĭcancў, měndĭ'cĭtў** ns.
Mĕnělā'us. (Gk legend) King of Sparta; brother of Agamemnon, and husband of Helen, who was stolen from him by Paris and restored after the fall of Troy.
mě'nfŏlk (-ōk) n. Men collectively, esp. of family or community.
mĕnhā'den n. Kind of large herring (*Brevoortia gunteri* and *B. patronus*) found on E. coast of N. America, used for manure and yielding a valuable oil. [Amer. Ind.]
mě'nhir (-ēr) n. (archaeol.) Tall upright monumental stone. [Breton, = 'long stone']
mē'nial adj. Servile, degrading. ~ n. Household servant; servile person. **mē'niallў** adv.
meninges: see MENINX.
měningī'tis (-j-) n. Inflammation of the meninges.
mĕni'ngocēle (-ngg-) n. (path.) Tumour on the meninges.
mē'ninx n. (pl. *měni'ngēs* pr. -z). Any of three membranes (*dura mater*, *arachnoid*, *pia mater*) enveloping brain and spinal cord (ill. SPINE). **mĕni'ngēal** (-j-) adj.
mĕni'scus n. (pl. *-cī*). Lens convex on one side and concave on the other (ill. LENS); convex or concave upper surface of a column of liquid; (math.) figure of crescent form.
Mě'nnonīte n. Member of a Christian sect which arose in Friesland in the 16th c., maintaining principles similar to those of the Anabaptists; they baptize only after confession of faith and will not take oaths or undertake military or State service; German Mennonites settled in Russia under Catherine the Great, but when rendered liable to conscription in the 19th c. many emigrated to U.S. and Brazil; most are farmers. [f. *Menno* Simons (1492-1559), their early leader]
mĕnō'logў n. Calendar, esp. that of Greek Church, with biographies of saints and martyrs.
mě'nopause (-z) n. Period of life, generally between 40 and 50, in women, at which menstruation ceases. **mě'nopausal** adj.
menōr'ah (-ā-) n. Candelabrum used in Jewish worship.
mĕnorrhā'gia (-erā-) n. Excessive menstruation.
mě'nsēs (-z) n.pl. Discharge of blood and tissue debris from uterus of primates, normally at monthly intervals. [L, = 'months']

MENSHEVIK

Mĕ'nshėvĭk n. Member of the moderate Socialist party in Russia, which was in the minority at the Socialist conference in 1903 and was overthrown by Lenin and the Bolsheviks at the Revolution of 1917, after being in power for a brief period. [Russ. *menshe* smaller]
mĕ'nstrual (-ōō-) adj. 1. (astrol.) Monthly. 2. (physiol.) Of the menses.
mĕ'nstruāte v.i. Discharge the menses. **mĕnstruā'tion** n.
mĕ'nstruŭm (-rōō-) n. (pl. -a). (pharm.) Solvent.
mĕ'nsūrable adj. Measurable; (mus.) having fixed time or rhythm.
mĕ'nsūral adj. Of measure; (mus.) measurable.
mĕnsūrā'tion n. Measuring; (math.) branch of mathematics concerned with measurement of lengths, areas, and volumes.
mĕ'ntal adj. Of, relating to, the mind; (slang) feeble-minded; ~ *age*, age at which normal children reach a certain stage of mental development, used as standard for assessing the feeble-minded or precocious (e.g. a subnormal boy of 17 who has the mental development of a normal 10-year-old has a mental age of 10); ~ *arithmetic*, calculations performed without the use of written figures; ~ *deficiency*, congenital feeble-mindedness, condition of person who is unequal to the conduct of ordinary affairs; ~ *home, hospital*, institutions for care of persons suffering from mental disorder or defect; ~ *patient*, one under care for disordered mind. **mĕ'ntallў** adv.
mĕntă'litў n. Mental quality; mode of thinking; (degree of) intellectual power; (loosely) mind, disposition, character.
mĕ'nthŏl n. Crystalline camphor-like substance obtained from mint-oils.
mĕ'ntion v.t. Refer to; state incidentally; cite formally for meritorious achievement; *not to ~*, in addition to. **~** n. Mentioning.
Mĕ'ntŏr[1]. (Gk legend) Friend of Odysseus and guide and adviser of the young Telemachus.
mĕ'ntŏr[2] n. Experienced and trusted counsellor. [f. MENTOR[1]]
mĕ'nū n. Bill of fare. [Fr., = 'detailed list', f. adj. = 'small']
Mĕphĭstŏ'phelēs (-z). In the legend of FAUST, the demon to whom Faust sold his soul. **Mĕphistŏphē'lĕan, -lĭan** adj.
mĕphi'tĭs n. Noxious emanation, esp. from the earth; noisome stench. **mĕphi'tĭc** adj.
mĕr'cantile adj. Trading; of merchants or trade; mercenary, fond of bargaining; ~ *marine*, shipping employed in commerce; ~ *system*, that based on the old economic theory that money is the only form of wealth and that the object of trade is to export goods at the highest prices. **mĕr'cantilism, mĕr'cantilist** ns.

Mĕrcā'tor, Gerardus. Latinized name of *Gerhard Kremer* (1512–94), Flemish geographer; inventor of a system of projecting maps (~'s *projection*) in which the globe is projected on to a cylinder and the meridians of longitude are at right angles to the parallels of latitude (ill. PROJECTION).
mĕr'cĕnarў adj. Working merely for money or other reward; having love of money as motive; hired (now only of soldiers serving in a foreign army). ~ n. Hired soldier. **mĕr'cĕnarinĕss** n.
mĕr'cer n. Dealer in textile fabrics, esp. silks etc. **mĕr'cerў** n. [L *merx* merchandise]
mĕr'cerīze v.t. Prepare (cotton) for dyeing by treating with solution of caustic potash etc. which produces a silky lustre. [John *Mercer* (1791–1866), inventor]
mĕr'chandīse (-z) n. Mercantile commodities; goods for sale.
mĕr'chant n. Wholesale trader, esp. one trading with foreign countries; (slang, esp. in compounds) person, individual (chiefly in disparagement, as *speed-~*); (U.S.) retail trader; *mer'chantman*, merchant ship; ~ *navy, service, shipping*, commercial shipping; ~ *ship*, ship of merchant navy. **mĕr'chantable** adj. Saleable, marketable.
Mĕr'cia (-sha). Anglian kingdom founded in the 6th c. by the *Mercians* (= men of the border) between Wessex, Northumbria, and Wales; an earldom under Canute and his successors until the Norman Conquest; name revived in *West ~ Authority*, area of police administration covering the counties of Hereford and Worcester, and Salop.
mĕr'cĭful adj. Disposed to mercy; compassionate. **mĕr'cĭfullў** adv. **mĕr'cĭfulnĕss** n.
mĕr'cĭlĕss adj. Showing no mercy; pitiless, unrelenting. **mĕr'cĭlĕsslў** adv. **mĕr'cĭlĕssnĕss** n.
mercūr'ial adj. Born under the planet Mercury; of or like mercury or quicksilver; sprightly, ready-witted, and volatile (from supposed influence of the planet). **mercūr'iallў** adv. **mercūriā'litў** n.
mercūr'ialism n. Mercurial poisoning.
mercūr'ialīze v.t. Affect with mercury.
mercūr'ĭc adj. (chem.) Of compounds in which mercury has a valency of two; ~ *chloride*, corrosive sublimate ($HgCl_2$), formerly used in dilute aqueous solution as an antiseptic for wounds and for sterilizing non-metallic surgical instruments.
mercūr'ous adj. (chem.) Of compounds in which mercury has a valency of one; ~ *chloride*, calomel.
Mĕr'cūrў[1]. 1. (Rom. myth.) God of eloquence, skill, trading, and thieving, and messenger of the gods, early identified with HERMES.

MERINGUE

2. (astron.) Planet nearest to the sun, the smallest planet of the solar system (ill. PLANET). [L *Mercurius*, f. *merx* merchandise]
mĕr'cūrў[2] n. Silvery-white metallic element of high density, symbol Hg, at. no. 80, at. wt 200·59, pop. called *quicksilver*; its high density, its property of not wetting glass, and the wide range of temperature at which it is liquid make it valuable for scientific instruments esp. thermometers and barometers; it dissolves many metals, forming amalgams, and its compounds are used in medicine as purgatives and stimulants.
mĕr'cў n. Forbearance and compassion towards an offender, enemy, or person in one's power; disposition to forgive; act of mercy, gift of God, blessing; *at the ~ of*, wholly in the power of or subject to; *~-killing*, killing with the intention of preventing needless suffering; *~-seat*, golden covering of Ark of Covenant; hence, throne of God.
mēre[1] n. Lake.
mēre[2] adj. Pure, unmixed; barely or only what it is said to be, nothing more than. **mēr'elў** adv.
Mĕ'rĕdĭth, George (1828–1900). English novelist and poet; author of 'Diana of the Crossways', 'The Ordeal of Richard Feverel', 'The Egoist', etc.
mĕrĕtrĭ'cious (-shus) adj. Showily attractive, flashy. **mĕrĕtrĭ'ciouslў** adv. **mĕrĕtrĭ'ciousnĕss** n. [L *meretrix* prostitute]
mĕrgă'nser n. Any of various fish-eating ducks of great diving powers, with long narrow serrated bill hooked at the tip, inhabiting northern parts of Old World and N. America. [L *mergus* diver, *anser* goose]
mĕrge v. Lose, cause (thing) to lose, character or identity in something else; join or blend gradually (*into, with*). **mĕr'ger** n. Absorption of estate etc. in another; consolidation of one trading company or firm with another.
mĕri'dĭan n. Great circle passing through celestial poles and zenith of any place on earth's surface (ill. CELESTIAL) or passing through the poles and any place on the earth (ill. EARTH); point at which star or sun attains its highest altitude; prime, full splendour. ~ adj. Of noon; (fig.) of the period of greatest splendour, vigour, etc.
mĕri'dĭonal adj. Of the south (of France, or of Europe); southern. ~ n. Inhabitant of a southern country, esp. of France or S. Europe.
Mĕrimée (mārēmā), Prosper (1803–70). French novelist and playwright.
meri'ngue (-răng) n. Confection made of sugar and beaten white of egg, baked till crisp; shell of meringue filled with whipped cream.

meri′nō (-rē-) *n.* Variety of sheep with fine silky wool, orig. bred in Spain; fine yarn or soft fabric of this wool; fine woollen yarn.

Mĕriŏ′nèthshire. Former county of N. Wales, since April 1974 part of Gwynedd.

mĕ′ristĕm *n.* (bot.) Cell or region where growth is initiated.

mĕ′rit *n.* Quality of deserving well or being entitled to reward or gratitude; goodness; (pl.) good works, deserts; intrinsic rights and wrongs (of case etc., esp. law); *Order of* M~, (abbrev. O.M.) British order, limited in membership, for high and distinguished civil or military service, founded in 1902. ~ *v.t.* Deserve (reward, punishment).

mĕritŏ′cracў *n.* (Élite of) system in which position is determined by academic ability.

mĕritŏr′ious *adj.* Deserving praise, reward, etc. (often as term of limited praise, = well-meant, well-meaning). **mĕritŏr′iouslў** *adv.* **mĕritŏr′iousnèss** *n.*

mêrle *n.* (archaic) Blackbird.

mêr′lin[1] *n.* Small European falcon, *Falco columbarius aesalon*; N. Amer. pigeon hawk, *F. columbarius columbarius*.

Mêr′lin[2]. In Arthurian legend, a magician and bard who aided and supported King Arthur and made the Round Table.

mêr′lon *n.* Solid part of embattled parapet between two embrasures (ill. CASTLE).

mêr′maid *n.* (masc. *mêr′măn*) Fabled being inhabiting the sea, with human head and trunk and tail of a fish. [f. MERE[1]]

MERMAID
(From a wall-painting at Beauvois, *c* 1303)

Mêr′maid Tă′vern. Tavern in Bread Street, near Cheapside, London (with an entrance in Friday Street); meeting-place of the Friday Street Club, founded by Sir Walter Ralegh and frequented by Shakespeare, Ben Jonson, and other wits and men of letters; it was destroyed in the Great Fire in 1666.

mĕ′roblăst *n.* (physiol.) Ovum of two parts, one of which is germinal and the other nutritive.

mĕrohē′dral *adj.* (of crystal) Having less than the full number of faces of the type of symmetry to which it belongs.

Mĕrŏvi′ngian (-j-) *adj. & n.* (Member) of the line of Frankish kings founded by Clovis (481–511) and reigning in Gaul and Germany until 752.

mĕ′rrў *adj.* Mirthful, hilarious; full of animated enjoyment; slightly tipsy; *make* ~, be festive; ~-*andrew*, mountebank's assistant; clown, buffoon, (also fig.); ~-*go-round*, revolving machine carrying wooden horses, cars, etc., for riding on or in; roundabout; ~-*making*, festivity; ~ *monarch*, Charles II of England; ~-*thought*, wishbone. **mĕ′rrilў** *adv.* **mĕ′rrinèss** *n.*

Mêr′sey (-zĭ). English river rising in the Peak district and flowing into the Irish Sea near Liverpool.

Mêr′seysīde (-zĭ-). Metropolitan county of NW. England (since April 1974), comprising Liverpool and surrounding districts.

me′sa (mā-) *n.* High rocky tableland with precipitous sides.

mésalliance (mĕză′liahṅs) *n.* Marriage with a social inferior.

mĕ′scăl *n.* 1. Strong spirit distilled from fermented sap of wild agave. 2. PEYOTE.

mĕ′scalin, -ine *n.* Active principle in peyote.

mĕsĕmbrĭă′nthèmum, -brў̄- *n.* S. African plant of genus M~ with bright pink or white flowers which open around midday; figmarigold. [Gk *mesēmbria* noon, *anthemon* flower]

mĕ′senterў *n.* Fold of peritoneum attaching intestinal canal to posterior wall of abdomen. **mĕsentĕ′ric** *adj.* **mĕsĕnteri′tis** *n.* Inflammation of the mesentery.

mĕsh *n.* One of the spaces between the threads of a net; (pl.) net. ~ *v.* Catch in a net; (of gearwheels etc.) engage, interlock.

Mĕ′shach (-k). One of three Jewish youths who came unharmed from a furnace into which they were thrown by Nebuchadnezzar (Dan. 3).

me′sial (mēz- *or* mĕs-) *adj.* Of, in, directed towards, middle line of a body. **me′siallў** *adv.*

mĕ′smerism (-z-) *n.* (archaic) Hypnotism. **mĕsmĕ′ric** *adj.* **mĕ′smerist** *n.* **mĕ′smerīze** *v.t.* Hypnotize; fascinate, compel by fascination. [f. F.A. *Mesmer* (1734–1815), Austrian physician]

mesne (mēn) *adj.* (law) Intermediate; ~ *lord*, one who is himself a tenant of a superior lord but has tenants holding from him; ~ *profits*, those received from an estate by an occupier in unlawful possession, as e.g. after the expiry of a lease.

mĕ′socārp (*or* -z-) *n.* (bot.) Middle layer of pericarp (ill. FRUIT).

mĕ′sodêrm (*or* -z-) *n.* (physiol.) Middle of three layers of cells formed by embryo at early stage, layer from which skeletal muscles, heart muscle, and blood are developed.

mĕsogă′ster (*or* -z-) *n.* Membrane attaching stomach to dorsal walls of abdomen. **mĕsogă′stric** *adj.*

mĕsoli′thic (*or* -z-) *adj.* (archaeol.) Of the Stone Age between palaeolithic and neolithic.

mĕ′sŏn (*or* mĕz-) *n.* Elementary particle intermediate in mass between proton and electron; *mu-*~: see MUON.

mĕ′sopause(-z; *or* -z-)*n.* Top of the mesosphere (ill. ATMOSPHERE).

mĕ′sophўll (*or* -z-) *n.* (bot.) Inner tissue of leaf (ill. LEAF).

mĕ′sophўte (*or* -z-) *n.* Plant needing a moderate amount of moisture (opp. HYDROPHYTE, XEROPHYTE).

Mĕsopotă′mia. Region of SW. Asia, the larger part of modern Iraq, between the rivers Tigris and Euphrates; centre of the ancient civilizations of SUMER, ASSYRIA, and BABYLON; scene (1915–16) of a disastrous British campaign against the Turks. **Mĕsopotă′mian** *adj.* [Gk, = '(country) between the rivers' (*mesos* middle, *potamos* river)]

mĕ′sosphēre (*or* mĕz-) *n.* Part of atmosphere above stratosphere, in which temperature generally falls with increasing height (ill. ATMOSPHERE).

mĕ′sotrŏn (*or* mĕz-)*n.* = MESON.

Mĕsozō′ic (*or* -z-) *adj. & n.* (geol.) (Of) the era or group of systems between Cainozoic and Palaeozoic, characterized by the appearance of flowering plants and the emergence and extinction of dinosaurs (ill. GEOLOGY).

Mĕ′spŏt. (slang) Mesopotamia.

mĕ′squīte, -quit (-kēt) *n.* N. Amer. shrub of mimosa family, the seed-pods of which are used as cattle-fodder. [Mexican *misquitl*]

mĕss *n.* 1. (archaic) Portion of food; concoction, medley. 2. Dirty or untidy state; difficult situation, trouble; *make a* ~ *of*, bungle. 3. Spilt liquid etc. 4. Company of persons who take meals together, esp. in armed forces; taking of such a meal, place where it is eaten; ~-*tin*, soldier's metal utensil, used as plate or cup or for cooking. ~ *v.* 1. Make dirty or untidy; potter

[559]

about. 2. Take meals, esp. as member of a mess. **mĕ′ssў** adj. Untidy, dirty. **mĕ′ssilў** adv. **mĕ′ssinĕss** n.
mĕ′ssage n. Communication sent from one person to another; inspired utterance of a prophet or sage; teaching or moral of book, play, etc.; mission, errand. ~ v.t. Send as message; transmit (plan etc.) by signalling.
Mĕssali′na (-lē-) (d. 48 A.D.). 3rd wife of Emperor CLAUDIUS, proverbial for her profligacy.
mĕ′ssenger (-j-) n. Bearer of message.
Mĕssi′ah (-a) n. In O.T. prophetic writings, the promised deliverer of the Jews; in Christian doctrine, Jesus Christ, regarded as this deliverer; name of an oratorio by Handel, based on O.T. prophecies. **Mĕssiă′nic** adj. Of or relating to the or a Messiah. [Heb. *māšīaḥ* anointed]
messieurs: see MONSIEUR.
Mĕssi′na (-sē-). City and harbour of NE. Sicily; *Strait of* ~, that separating Sicily from Italy.
Messrs. (mĕ′serz) abbrev. Messieurs, pl. of Mr., prefixed as title to name of firm etc. or introducing list of men.
mĕ′ssuage (-wĭj) n. Dwelling-house with its outbuildings and land.
mĕ′stizō (-tē-) n. Spanish or Portuguese half-caste, esp. child of Spaniard and American Indian. [Span., f. L *miscere* mix]
met: see MEET².
met. abbrev. Meteorology etc.
mĕtabŏ′lic adj. Of metabolism; *basal* ~ *rate*, (abbrev. B.M.R.) measure of the energy used up by the body while maintaining itself in a condition of complete rest.
mĕtă′bolism n. Process in a cell or organism by which nutritive material is built up into living matter (*constructive* ~, *anabolism*) or by which protoplasm is broken down to perform special functions (*destructive* ~, *catabolism*). **mĕtă′-bolīze** v.t.
mĕtă′bolīte n. Substance undergoing change during metabolism.
mĕtacar′pus n. (anat.) Set of bones (five in man) connecting carpus to phalanges (ill. HAND); part of hand in which these are situated. **mĕtacar′pal** adj. & n. (Bone) of the metacarpus.
mĕ′tage n. Official measuring of coal etc.; duty paid for this.
mĕtagĕnĕ′sis n. (biol.) Reproduction of new generations by processes alternately sexual and asexual. **mĕtagĕnĕ′tic** adj.
mĕ′tal n. 1. One of a class of elements of which gold, silver, copper, iron, lead, and tin are examples; alloy of these. 2. Material for making glass, in molten state. 3. Broken stone (*road-*~) for macadam roads or railway ballast. 4. (pl.) Rails of a railway line. ~ v.t. Furnish or supply with metal; mend (road) with metal.

mĕtă′llic adj. Of or like metal; yielding metal.
mĕtalli′ferous adj. Bearing, producing metals.
mĕ′tallīze v.t. Render metallic; vulcanize (rubber). **mĕtallīzā′-tion** n.
mĕtallŏ′graphў n. Study, description, of metals and alloys, their structure and properties.
mĕ′talloid adj. Having form or appearance of metal. ~ n. Element having physical properties of a metal and chemical properties of a non-metal, e.g. tellurium.
mĕtă′llurgў (or mĕ′ta-) n. Science of the extraction, working, and properties of metals and their alloys. **mĕtallūr′gic, -ical** adjs. **mĕtă′llurgist** n.
mĕ′tamēre n. (zool.) One of a series of more or less similar segments of an animal body, as of a worm. **mĕtamĕ′ric** adj. (zool.) Of metameres; (chem.) having same percentage composition and molecular weight, but different chemical properties. **mĕtă′merism** n.
mĕtamor′phic adj. (geol., of rocks) Altered after formation by heat or pressure or both. **mĕtamor′phism** n. Metamorphic process.
mĕtamor′phosis n. (pl. *-osēs*). Change of form, esp. magic transformation as of person into beast or plant etc.; changed form; change of character, circumstance, etc.; (zool.) change, usually rapid, between immature form and adult. **mĕtamor′phōse** (-z) v.t. Change in form, change nature of.
mĕ′taphor n. Figure of speech in which name or descriptive term is transferred to an object to which it is not properly applicable (e.g. *a glaring error*); instance of this; *mixed* ~, combination of inconsistent metaphors. **mĕtaphŏ′ric, -ical** adjs. **mĕtaphŏ′rically** adv.
mĕ′taphrāse (-z) n. Translation, esp. word-for-word rendering, as dist. from *paraphrase*. ~ v.t. Translate thus. **mĕtaphrā′stic** adj.
mĕtaphў′sics (-z-) n. Branch of philosophy dealing with first principles of things, including such concepts as being, substance, space, time, identity, etc. **mĕtaphў′sical** adj. Of metaphysics; ~ *poets*, term used to designate certain 17th-c. English poets, including Donne, Cowley, Herbert, and Vaughan, addicted to 'witty conceits' and far-fetched imagery. **mĕtaphў′sically** adv. **mĕtaphў̆si′cian** (-shan) n. [Gk *ta meta ta phusika* the works (of Aristotle) placed after the 'Physics']
mĕ′taplăsm n. (biol.) Non-living constituent part of protoplasm.
mĕtapŏ′litics n. Abstract political science (often contempt.).
mĕtapoli′tical adj. **mĕtapoli′ti′cian** (-shan) n.
Metastasio (mātastah′zĭō).

Pietro Bonaventure Trapassi (1698–1782), Italian poet and librettist for Gluck, Handel, Haydn, Mozart, etc.
mĕtă′stasis n. (pl. *-es*). (path.) Transference of disease from a primary focus to one in another part of the body by way of natural passages or of blood or lymph vessels. **mĕtastă′tic** adj.
mĕtatar′sus n. Set of bones (five in man) connecting tarsus to phalanges (ill. FOOT); part of foot or hind limb in which these are situated. **mĕtatar′sal** adj. & n. (Bone) of the metatarsus.
mĕtă′thĕsis n. (pl. *-esēs*). 1. (gram.) Transposition of letters or sounds. 2. (chem.) Substitution of one radical or atom for another in a molecule. **mĕtathĕ′tical** adj.
mĕtazō′an adj. & n. (zool.) (Member) of the order Metazoa, comprising multicellular animals with differentiated tissues, a nervous system, and co-ordination between the various cells.
mēte v.t. (literary) Measure; portion *out*, allot (punishment, reward).
mĕtĕmpsўchō′sis (-k-) n. (pl. *-osēs* pr. -z). Supposed migration of soul at death into another body.
mĕ′teor n. One of the small solid bodies in the solar system which become luminous when passing into earth's atmosphere; (fig.) any bright, dazzling, but transient object. **mĕtĕŏ′ric** adj. Of the atmosphere; dependent on atmospheric conditions; of meteors; (fig.) dazzling, rapid.
mĕ′teorīte n. Fallen meteor, fragment of rock or nickel iron which has fallen from space on to earth's surface.
mĕ′teoroid n. Body moving through space, of same nature as those which by passing into earth's atmosphere become visible as meteors. **mĕtĕoroi′dal** adj.
mĕtĕorŏ′logў n. Study of, science treating of, atmospheric phenomena, esp. for forecasting weather. **mĕtĕorolŏ′gical** adj. **mĕtĕorolŏ′gically** adv. **mĕtĕorŏ′logist** n.
mē′ter n. Apparatus for measuring, esp. automatically, and recording quantity of gas, water, electricity, etc., passing through, or time elapsed, etc. ~ v.t. Measure with meter.
mĕ′thāne n. (chem.) Colourless inflammable gas (CH₄) formed by decay of vegetable matter in marshy places and coal-seams.
mĕthi′nks v.*impers.* (archaic) It seems to me.
mĕ′thod n. Procedure; way of doing anything, esp. according to a regular plan; systematic or orderly arrangement; orderliness and regularity. **mĕthŏ′dic, -ical** adjs. **mĕthŏ′dically** adv.
Mĕ′thodism n. Religious movement, founded by John WESLEY, his brother Charles, and George WHITEFIELD, in reaction against

[560]

apathy in the Church of England, and developed by missionary tours in Georgia, U.S., and in Gt Britain; the meetings, often in the open air, were characterized (as now) by lay preaching and hymn-singing; the movement later gave rise to various sects, but the principal groups (United Methodist Church, Primitive Methodists, and Wesleyan Methodists) united in 1932. **Mĕ'thodĭst** adj. & n. [*Methodists*, applied to associates of the Wesleys at Oxford forming a religious society (nicknamed the 'Holy Club'), prob. as following a specified 'method' of devotional study]
mĕths n. (colloq.) Methylated spirits.
Mĕthū'selah (-*zela*). Patriarch, grandfather of Noah, said (Gen. 5: 27) to have lived 969 years, hence regarded as type of longevity.
mĕ'thȳl (*or* mē'thĭl) n. (chem.) Univalent organic radical (CH₃); ~ *alcohol*, colourless volatile liquid distilled from wood and also made synthetically; wood-spirit. **mĕ'thȳlāte** v.t. Mix (alcohol) with wood-spirit, usu. to render it unfit for drinking and therefore exempt from duty, as *methylated spirit*.
mĕtĭ'cūlous adj. Extremely attentive to minute details. **mĕtĭ'cūlouslȳ** adv.
métier (mā'tyā) n. Trade or profession; line.
Mĕtŏ'nĭc cȳ'cle. Period of 19 solar years, after the lapse of which the new and full moons return to the same day of the year; it was the basis of the Greek calendar and is still used for calculating movable feast days, such as Easter. [f. *Meton*, Athenian astronomer (5th c. B.C.)]
mĕtŏ'nȳmȳ n. Substitution of name of an attribute or adjunct for that of the thing meant (e.g. the *turf* for *horse-racing*). **mĕtonȳ'mĭcallȳ** adv.
mĕ'tōpe n. (archit.) Square space between triglyphs in Doric frieze (ill. ORDER);˙ carving etc. on this.
mē'tre¹ (-*er*) n. Any form of poetic rhythm, determined by character and number of feet; group of metrical feet.
mē'tre² (-*er*) n. (abbrev. m) Basic unit of length in the metric system (approx. 39.37 in.), orig. representing one ten-millionth of a quadrant of the meridian passing through Paris, since 1960 defined as 1,650,763.73 wavelengths in a vacuum of the radiation corresponding to the transition between the quantum states ²p_{10}-⁵d_5 of the krypton-86 atom; ~-*kilogramme-second*, (abbrev. M.K.S.) applied to a system of units of measurement based on the metre, kilogramme, and second as units of length, mass, and time.
mĕt'rĭc adj. Of˛the metre or metric system; using the metric system; ~ *system*, decimal measuring system based on the metre, orig. devised in 1791 by the French Academy of Sciences, with the metre, litre, and kilogramme (orig. the gramme) as units of length, capacity, and mass; ~ *ton*, 1,000 kilogrammes. **mĕtrĭcā'tion** n. Conversion to the metric system.
mĕ'trĭcāte v.
mĕ'trĭcal adj. Of, composed in, metre; of, involving, measurement, as ~ *geometry*. **mĕ'trĭcallȳ** adv.
Mĕ'trŏ, Métro (mātrō) n. (colloq.) Metropolitan (underground) Railway of Paris.
mĕtrŏ'logȳ n. Science, system, of weights and measures. **mĕtrolŏ'gĭcal** adj.
mĕ'tronōme n. (mus.) Instrument marking time by means of a graduated inverted pendulum with a sliding weight. **mĕtronŏ'mĭc** adj.
mĕtrŏ'polis n. Chief city, capital; see of metropolitan bishop. [Gk *mētropolis* parent State (*mētēr* mother, *polis* city)]
mĕtropŏ'lĭtan adj. Of a metropolis; of, forming (part of) State as dist. from its colonies or dependencies; ~ *bishop, archbishop*, one who has authority over the bishops of a province. ~ n. Metropolitan bishop or archbishop; inhabitant of a metropolis. **mĕtropŏ'lĭtanate** n. Office, jurisdiction, of a metropolitan bishop.
Mĕ'tternich (-*x*). Prince Clemens Wenzel Lothar Metternich-Winneburg (1773–1859), Austrian statesman; led the Congress of Vienna in devising the settlement of Europe after the Napoleonic Wars.
mĕ'ttle n. Quality of disposition; natural vigour and ardour, spirit, esp. of a horse. **mĕ'ttlesome** adj. High-spirited.
Mĕtz. Fortified town of E. France, on the R. Moselle.
Meuse (mɜrz). (Du. *Maas*) River of NE. France, Belgium, and Netherlands.
mew¹ n. Gull, esp. the common gull, *Larus canus*; sea-mew.
mew² v. (of hawk) Moult; shut up (hawk) in mew; shut *up*, confine. ~ n. Cage for hawks.
mew³ v.i. Cry like cat. ~ n. Cat's cry.
mewl, mūle v.i. Cry feebly, whimper; mew like a cat.
mews (-z) n. Series of private stables built round a yard or on both sides of a lane (now freq. converted into dwellings etc.); area containing these. [f. MEW², orig. of royal stables ón site of hawks' mews]
Mĕ'xĭcŏ. Federal republic of southern N. America and Central America; orig. inhabited by various Amer. Indian peoples, esp. Maya, Aztecs; was a Spanish colony ('New Spain'), c 1519–1821; since then it has been a republic except for the years 1864–7 when MAXI-MILIAN² was emperor; the presidency of Diaz (1877–80 and 1884–1911) was followed by a period of revolution; the question of the possession of Texas led to war between the United States and Mexico in 1846–8, Texas having applied for admission to the American Union as early as 1836; *Gulf of ~*, area of Atlantic Ocean, almost surrounded by the southern coast of N. America the coast of Mexico, and Cuba. **Mĕ'xĭcan** adj. & n.
Meyer (mī'er), Conrad Ferdinand (1825–96). Swiss poet and historical novelist.
Meyerbeer (mī'erbār), Giacomo (Jakob) (1791–1864). German-Jewish composer of operas.
mēzēr'ēon n. Deciduous shrub (*Daphne mezereum*) with fragrant purple flowers.
mĕ'zzanine (-ēn; *or* -ts-) adj. & n. (Low storey) between two higher storeys, esp. between ground and 1st floors.
mĕ'zzō (-dzō *or* -tsō) adv. (mus.) Moderately; ~ *forte*, moderately loud; ~ *piano*, moderately soft. **mĕ'zzō-soprā'nō** (-dzō *or* -tsō; -ah-) n. (Person with, part for) voice between contralto and soprano.
mĕ'zzotint (-dz- *or* -ts-) n. Method of engraving on copper or steel in which the plate is roughened uniformly, lights and half-lights being produced by scraping away the roughness, deep shadows by leaving it; print produced in this way. ~ v.t. Engrave in mezzotint.
mf abbrev. Mezzo-forte.
M.F. abbrev. = Medium FREQUENCY.
M.F.H. abbrev. Master of Foxhounds.
mg abbrev. Milligramme(s).
Mgr abbrev. Monseigneur; Monsignor (pl. Mgri).
mho (mō) n. Unit of electrical conductance, the reciprocal of the ohm; thus, a conductor having a resistance of 4 ohms has a conductance of 0·25 mho.
mi (mē) n. (mus.) = ME².
M.I. abbrev. 1. Military Intelligence (numeral indicates department). 2. Mounted Infantry.
miaow (miow') n. & v.i. (Make) cat's cry, mew.
miā'sma (-z-) n. Noxious exhalation from marshes, putrid matter, etc. **miā'smĭc** adj.
Mic. abbrev. Micah (O.T.).
mī'ca n. One of a group of minerals composed of aluminium silicate combined with other silicates, occurring as small glittering scales in granite etc., or as larger crystals separable into thin transparent plates, used as a dielectric and insulator in electrical equipment etc. **mĭcā'ceous** (-sh*u*s) adj. [L, = 'crumb']
Mī'cah (-*a*). Hebrew minor prophet, a contemporary of Isaiah; book of O.T. containing his prophecies.
Mĭcaw'ber, Mr. In Dickens's

[561]

'David Copperfield', a sanguine idler trusting that something good will turn up. **Micaw′berism** n. **Micaw′berish** adj.
M.I.C.E. abbrev. Member of the Institution of Civil Engineers.
micĕ′lle n. (chem.) Minute particle formed by an aggregate of molecules, found in certain colloidal solutions.
Mich. abbrev. Michaelmas; Michigan.
Mī′chael (-kel), St. One of the archangels, usu. represented slaying a dragon (see Rev. 12: 7); commemorated 29 Sept.; *Order of St. ~ and St. George*, British order of knighthood (instituted 1818), awarded esp. for distinguished services abroad.
Mī′chaelmas (-kel-). Feast of St. Michael, 29 Sept., a quarter-day; *~ daisy*, herbaceous perennial of genus *Aster*, native in N. America, flowering at Michaelmas; *~ goose*, goose traditionally eaten at Michaelmas; *~ Term*, in universities etc., the autumn term beginning in late Sept. or early Oct.
Michelă′ngĕlō Buŏnarrō′ti (-kelănj-, bwō-) (1475–1564). Italian sculptor, painter, and poet; one of the greatest artists of the Renaissance; famous esp. for his frescoes in the Sistine Chapel at Rome.
Michelet (mēshelă), Jules (1798–1874). French historian.
Michĕlō′zzō (-kĭlŏtsō), Michelozzi (1396–1472). Italian architect; designed the Riccardi Palace in Florence.
Mī′chelson (-k-), Albert Abraham (1852–1931). Amer. physicist; devised with E. W. Morley the *~-Morley experiment*, which attempted to discover the effect of the velocity of the earth on the velocity of light, as a means of measuring the velocity of the earth through the ether; the failure to discover any such effect was the starting-point for the theory of RELATIVITY.
Mī′chigan (-sh-). State in north-central U.S., with its northern boundary formed by Lakes Huron and Superior; admitted to the Union in 1837; capital, Lansing; *Lake ~*, one of the chain of great lakes in N. America.
mi′ckey n. *take the ~ (out of)*, (slang) tease.
Mī′ckey Mouse. (R.A.F. slang) Electrical distributor which releases bombs from aircraft. [f. name of mouse-like character in Walt Disney's cartoons]
micro- prefix. Small, minute (contrasted with *macro-*); also used in names of units, = one millionth of (symbol μ), as in *micro-ampere, microfarad*.
mī′crōbe n. (pop.) Microorganism, esp. one of the bacteria causing diseases and fermentation. **micrō′bial, micrō′bic** adjs.
mīcrobiō′logў n. Study of micro-organisms. **mīcrobiŏ′logĭst** n.
mīcrocĕphă′lĭc adj. Small-headed.
micrococcus: see COCCUS.
mi′crocŏsm n. Little world, world in miniature; miniature representation *of*; man, society, as an epitome of the world or universe. **microcŏ′smic** adj.
mi′cro-dŏt n. Photograph reduced to the size of a dot.
mi′crofilm n. Very small film; photographic reproduction on this, projected on screen for reading etc. *~ v.t.* Photograph on microfilm. [trade-name]
mi′crolith n. (archaeol.) Minute worked flint, usu. for mounting as part of a composite tool, found esp. in mesolithic cultures.
micrŏ′mĕter n. Precision instrument, variously designed, for measuring minute distances.

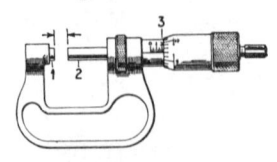

MICROMETER
1. Anvil. 2. Spindle. 3. Scale

mi′cron n. One millionth of a metre (symbol μm).
Micronē′sia (-z-; *or* -zha). Division of Oceania comprising the small NW. Pacific islands including the Mariana, Caroline, Marshall, and Gilbert Islands. **Micronē′sian** adj. & n.
micrō-ŏr′ganism n. Any of the organisms not visible to the unaided eye, as bacteria, protozoa, unicellular algae and fungi, and viruses.
mi′crophōne n. Instrument producing electrical impulses corresponding to the vibrations of sound waves falling on it and thus performing an essential part in telephonic and radio transmission. **microphŏ′nic** adj.
mi′croscōpe n. Lens or combination of lenses magnifying near objects so that details invisible to the naked eye are revealed. **microscŏ′pĭc** adj. Of a microscope; with the functions of a microscope; so minute as only to be seen clearly with a microscope. **microscŏ′pical** adj. Pertaining to a microscope. **microscŏ′pically** adv. **micrŏ′scopў, micrŏ′scopist** ns.
mi′crosōme n. (biol.) Small particle in a cell, not visible with an ordinary microscope.
mi′crostructure n. (metallurgy) Arrangement of crystals observable under a microscope. **microstrŭ′ctural** (-cher-) adj.
mi′crotōme n. Instrument for cutting very thin sections of organic tissue for examination under the microscope. **micrŏ′tomў** n.

mi′crotōne n. (mus.) Interval smaller than a semitone.
mi′crōwāve n. Electromagnetic wave having a wavelength between about 1 mm and 30 cm.
mi′crurgў n. Art or science of dissection and injection under a microscope. **micrūr′gical** adj.
mictūri′tion n. Urination.
mi′ctūrāte v.i. Urinate.
mid adj. Middle of; intermediate; (phon.) pronounced with the tongue or part of it in a middle position between high and low; *mi′dbrain*: see BRAIN; *~-off, -on, -wicket*, (position of) cricketers on off, on, sides, in front of batsman and near bowler (ill. CRICKET); *mi′drib*, main vein of a leaf etc. (ill. LEAF, ALGA).
Mī′das. (Gk legend) King of Phrygia; was given by Dionysus the power of turning everything he touched into gold; unable to eat or drink, he prayed to be relieved of the gift, and was instructed to wash in the river Pactolus, whose sands turned to gold at his touch; another time, when Midas declared Pan a better flute-player than Apollo, Apollo turned his ears into an ass's, and Midas tried to hide them, but his barber whispered the secret to some reeds, which repeated it whenever the wind rustled them.
mi′dday′ (-d-d-) n. Noon (often attrib.).
mi′dden n. Dung-hill, refuse-heap.
mi′ddle adj. Equidistant from extremities; intermediate in rank, quality, etc.; (gram.) of a voice of the verb, as in ancient Greek, expressing reflexive action of the verb on the subject or intransitive action; (of languages) in a stage of development between the old and modern forms, as *M~*

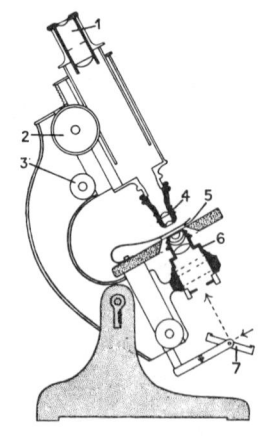

MICROSCOPE
1. Eyepiece. 2. Coarse adjustment head. 3. Fine adjustment head. 4. Objective. 5. Slide. 6. Condenser. 7. Mirror for directing light into condenser

[562]

MIDDLESEX

ENGLISH; ~ age, period between youth and old age; ~-aged (adj.); M~ Ages, period of history intermediate between ancient and modern times, variously calculated, but commonly applied to period from the fall of the Roman Empire in the West (5th c.) to the beginning of the Renaissance (middle of 15th c.); M~ Atlantic States, New York, New Jersey, and Pennsylvania; ~ class, class of society between upper and lower, including professional and business classes (often attrib.); ~ distance, that part of a picture which lies between the foreground and the background; M~ East, States lying between the Near and Far East, including those countries between Egypt and Iran; M~ Kingdom: see KINGDOM; mi'ddleman, trader intermediate between producer and consumer; ~ rib, cut of beef between fore- and wing-rib (ill. MEAT); ~ term, (logic) term in a syllogism common to both premisses; ~ watch, (naut.) watch between midnight and 4 a.m.; ~-weight, boxer of weight between welter-weight and heavyweight (see BOXING); M~ West, that part of U.S. occupying the N. half of the Mississippi River basin, including the States of Ohio, Indiana, Illinois, Michigan, Wisconsin, Iowa, and Minnesota; M~ Western(er). ~ n. Middle part or point in position or time; middle part of the body, waist; (gram.) middle voice or form of verb. ~ v.t. (naut.) Fold, double, in the middle.

Mi'ddlesĕx (-dls-). Former English county on the Thames, since 1965 mainly part of Greater London, with small part in Surrey.

Mi'ddleton (-dlt-) Thomas (1570-1627). English writer of satirical comedies of contemporary manners and of romantic comedies.

mi'ddling adj. & adv. (commerc.) Of goods of middle size or quality; moderately good; secondrate; (colloq.) fairly well (in health).

mi'ddlings (-z) n.pl. Grades of commodities, such as flour, of second quality or fineness.

Middx. abbrev. Middlesex.

mi'ddy n. (colloq.) Midshipman.

Mi'dgărd. (Scand. myth.) Region, surrounded by the sea, in which men live; ~ Serpent, monstrous serpent, the offspring of Loki, thrown by Odin into the sea, where, with its tail in its mouth, it encircled the earth.

midge n. Gnat, small insect; (zool.) member of dipterous family Chironomidae.

mi'dgĕt n. Extremely small person; dwarf; also attrib.

Mid Glamŏr'gan. County of S. Wales (since April 1974), comprising the central part of the former county of Glamorgan and parts of the former counties of Breconshire and Monmouthshire.

Mi'diănīte adj. & n. (Member) of a nomadic people of N. Arabia often mentioned in the O.T., traditionally descended from Midian son of Abraham (Gen. 25: 1), proverbial for leading Israel astray.

midinĕ'tte n. Parisian shopgirl or seamstress.

mi'dland n. Part of a country remote from the sea or borders; the Midlands, the counties of England S. of the Humber and Mersey and N. of the Thames, except Norfolk, Suffolk, Essex, Hertfordshire, Gloucestershire, and the counties bordering on Wales; WEST MIDLANDS: see entry. ~ adj. Of, in, the midland or (M~) Midlands.

Midlō'thian (-dh-). Former Scottish county on S. coast of Firth of Forth, since May 1975 part of the region of Lothian.

mi'dnight (-nīt) n. Middle of the night, 12 o'clock at night (often attrib.).

Mi'drăsh n. (pl. -im, pr. -ă'shĕm). Ancient Jewish commentary on part of the Hebrew scriptures.

mi'driff n. Diaphragm in mammals.

mi'dship n. Middle part of ship or boat; mi'dshipman, (hist., in British Navy) junior officer ranking between cadet and sub-lieutenant.

mi'dships adv. Amidships.

midst n. Middle. ~ adv. Amidst.

mi'dsŭmmer n. Period of summer solstice, about 21 June; M~ Day, 24 June, an English quarterday; ~ madness, extreme folly, supposed to be due to midsummer moon and heat.

mi'dwīfe n. (pl. -ves). Woman who assists others in childbirth.

mi'dwīferў (-frī) n.

mien n. (literary) Bearing or look.

might[1] (mīt): see MAY[1]; ~-have-been, past possibility.

might[2] (mīt) n. Great (bodily or mental) strength; power to enforce one's will.

mighty (mī'tĭ) adj. Powerful, strong in body or mind. ~ adv. (colloq.) Very, extremely. **mi'ghtĭlў** adv. **mi'ghtĭness** n.

mignonĕ'tte (mĭnyo-) n. 1. Plant with fragrant greyish-green blossoms (Reseda odorata). 2. (hist.) Fine, open-work French pillow-lace.

mi'graine (or mē-) n. Recurrent paroxysmal headache, often accompanied by nausea, visual disturbances, and other severe symptoms. [Fr., f. Gk hemi half, kranion skull]

mi'grant adj. That migrates. ~ n. Migrant bird etc.

mīgrā'te v.i. Move from one place of abode, or esp. one country, to another; (of birds, fishes, and animals) go from one habitat to another, esp. come and go regularly with the seasons. **mīgrā'tion** n. **mī'grătorў** adj.

Mĭk'adō (-kah-) n. Popular title, as used by foreigners, of the Em-

MILITANT

peror of Japan. [Jap. mi august, kado door]

mīke n. (slang) Microphone.

mil n. $\frac{1}{1000}$ of an inch, 0·0254 mm; $\frac{1}{1000}$ of a Cyprus pound.

Mĭlă'n. (It. Milano) Chief city of Lombardy, N. Italy.

Mĭlănē'se (-z) adj. Of Milan; ~ silk, finely woven material of silk or artificial silk. ~ n. Native, inhabitant, of Milan; Milanese silk.

mĭlch adj. Giving, kept for, milk; ~-cow, cow kept for milk; (fig.) source of regular (and easy) profit.

mīld adj. Gentle; not severe or harsh or drastic; not bitter; ~ steel, malleable and tough steel, having a low percentage of carbon. **mī'ldlў** adv. **mī'ldness** n.

mīld n. Mild beer.

mī'ldew n. Growth of minute fungi on plants or on leather etc. exposed to damp. **mī'ldewў** adj.

mī'ldew v. Taint, be tainted, with mildew.

mīle n. British unit of linear measure of 1,760 yards (also statute ~); race extending over one mile; geographical ~, one minute of longitude (1/60°) measured on the equator, 6,087·2 ft; nautical, sea, ~, length of one minute of latitude, standardized at 6,080 ft but actually varying with latitude (6,046-6,108 ft); mi'lestone, stone set up on road to indicate the miles to and from a given place; (fig.) stage, event, in life, progress, etc. [L mille thousand (the Roman mile being 1,000 paces)]

mī'leage (-lĭj), **mī'lage** n. Distance in miles; travelling allowance at fixed rate per mile; number of miles in which a vehicle uses a given amount of fuel.

mī'ler n. (colloq.) Man, horse, trained specially to run a mile; also in comb. as two-~.

Mĭlē'siăn[1] (-z-) adj. & n. (Inhabitant) of Miletus, ancient Greek city of Asia Minor.

Mĭlē'siăn[2] (-shan) adj. & n. Irish(man). [f. Milesius, a legendary Spanish king whose sons are said to have conquered Ireland c 1300 B.C.]

mī'lfoil n. Common yarrow (Achillea millefolium), which has many finely divided leaves.

mī'liarў adj. (path.) Marked by eruption of small red pustules resembling millet-seeds, as ~ fever; ~ tuberculosis, form of tuberculosis, usu. acute, in which small tubercular nodules are distributed throughout the body.

milieu (mē'lyêr) n. (pl. -x, -s, pr. -z). Environment, state of life, social surroundings.

mi'litant adj. Engaged in warfare; warlike, combative; Church ~, Christian Church considered as at war on earth with the powers of evil, contrasted with the heavenly Church triumphant. **mi'litancў** n. **mi'litantlў** adv.

mi'litant n. Militant person.

[563]

mi'litarism n. Spirit, tendencies, of the professional soldier; undue reliance on, and exaltation of, military force and methods; **mi'litarist** n.

mi'litarīze v.t. Make military or warlike; instil principles of militarism into. **militariza'tion** n.

mi'litary̆ adj. Of, done by, befitting, soldiers, or the army (opp. *civil*); ~ *age*, age of eligibility for admission to the armed forces; ~ *band*, combination of wood-wind, brass, and percussion instruments; M~ *Cross*, (abbrev. M.C.) decoration awarded to army captains, lieutenants, and warrant officers for bravery in battle, instituted 1914 (ill. MEDAL); M~ *Medal*, (abbrev. M.M.) similar decoration awarded to warrant and non-commissioned officers and men; ~ *police*, body of soldiers doing police duty in the army. **mi'litarily̆** adv. **mi'litary̆** n. Soldiery.

mi'litāte v.i. (of facts, evidence, etc.) Have force, tell (*against* conclusion or result).

mili'tia (-sha) n. Military force, esp. citizen army; (U.S.) all men liable to military service; **mili'tiaman**, member of the militia.

milk n. Opaque white fluid secreted by female mammals for nourishment of their young; cow's milk as article of food; milk-like fluid of certain plants, as the juice of the coconut, the latex of the caoutchouc, etc.; preparation of drugs, herbs, etc., resembling milk in appearance, as ~ *of almonds*, ~*-and-water*, feeble, insipid; ~ *bar*, bar selling non-alcoholic drinks, esp. made with milk, and refreshments; ~ *fever*, fever to which women are liable after childbirth during lactation; ~*-leg*, inflammatory condition of leg, in women after childbirth, accompanied by white swellings; **mi'lkmaid**, woman who milks or is employed in dairy; **mi'lkman**, man who sells or delivers milk; ~ *pudding*, baked pudding made of rice, sago, tapioca, etc., and sweetened milk; ~*-punch*, drink made of spirits and milk; ~ *shake*, (orig. U.S.) glass of milk or milk and egg flavoured and shaken up; **mi'lksop**, effeminate or spiritless fellow; ~*-sugar*, lactose; ~ *tooth*, one of the first, temporary set of teeth in young mammals (ill. TOOTH); **mi'lkwort**, any plant of genus *Polygala*, growing in meadows, formerly supposed to increase milk in cows eating it. ~ v.t. Draw milk from (cow, ewe, goat, etc.); get money out of, exploit (person); extract juice, virus, etc., from (snake etc.).

mi'lky̆ adj. Of, like, mixed with, milk; (of liquid) cloudy, not clear; effeminate, weakly amiable; M~ *Way*, galaxy as seen from the earth, forming a faintly luminous band of innumerable stars indistinguishable to the naked eye.

mill¹ n. Building or apparatus for grinding corn; machine for grinding any solid substance to powder; any machine, or building fitted with machinery, for manufacturing processes etc., as *saw-*, *cotton-*~; *put through, go through the* ~, subject to, undergo, training or experience; be severely disciplined; **mi'llboard**, stout pasteboard for bookbinding; ~*-dam*, dam across a stream to make water available for mill; ~*-pond*, pond formed by a mill-dam; *like a* ~*-pond*, said of very calm sea; ~*-race*, current of water that drives mill-wheel (ill. WATER); **mi'llstone**, one of pair of circular stones used in grinding corn; (fig.) heavy burden, crushing weight; *Millstone Grit*, hard siliceous rock of carboniferous system, found immediately below Coal Measures; ~*-wheel*, one that turns the machinery of a water-mill; **mi'llwright**, one who constructs mills. ~ v. Grind or treat in mill; produce grooves etc. in (metal) by rotary cutter; produce regular markings on edge of (coin, esp. in past part.: ill. COIN); thicken (cloth) by fulling; beat (chocolate) to a froth; beat, strike, fight (person); (of cattle etc.) move round and round in a mass; **milling machine**, rotary cutter for metal.

mill² n. (U.S.) one-thousandth part of a dollar, as a money of account.

Mill³, John Stuart (1806–73). English political economist; author of 'On Liberty' (1859) and 'Utilitarianism' (1861).

Mi'llais (-ā), Sir John Everett (1829–96). English painter; founder, with W. Holman Hunt and D. G. Rossetti, of the PRE-RAPHAELITE Brotherhood.

millenā'rian adj. Of, expecting, the millennium. ~ n. Believer in the millennium.

mi'llenary̆ adj. Consisting of a thousand (esp. years).

mille'nnium n. Period of a thousand years; period of one thousand years foretold in Rev. 20: 1–5 in which Christ will reign on earth; period of happiness and prosperity. **mille'nnial** adj.

mi'llepēde, milli- n. Myriapod with numerous legs placed on each of the segments in double pairs (ill. MYRIAPOD).

mi'ller¹ n. One who works or owns a flour or corn mill; (entom.) popular name for some varieties of white or white-powdered insects; cockchafer; ~*'s-thumb*, pop. name of a small freshwater fish, *Cottus gobio*, also called the bull-head.

Mi'ller², Joe (1684–1738). English actor; *Joe* ~*'s Jests, or Wits' Vade Mecum*, a collection of coarse witticisms, many of them old, published after his death; hence, *a Joe* ~, a stale joke.

mille'simal adj. Thousandth.

mi'llet n. Any of several cereal plants, esp. *Panicum miliaceum*, native of India, growing 3 or 4 ft high and bearing a large crop of minute nutritious seeds; seed of this; ~ *grass*, tall N. Amer. woodland grass, *Milium effusum*.

milli- prefix. One thousandth of (abbrev. m).

mi'lliard (-yerd) n. One thousand millions.

mi'llibăr n. (meteor.) One thousandth of a BAR² (abbrev. mbar).

mi'llième (-yĕm) n. One thousandth of a pound in Egypt and the Sudan.

mi'lligrămme n. One thousandth of a gramme (abbrev. mg).

mi'llilitre (-lēter) n. One thousandth of a litre.

mi'llime (or -ēm) n. One thousandth of a Tunisian dinar.

mi'llimētre (-ter) n. One thousandth of a metre. (abbrev. mm).

mi'lliner n. Maker or seller of women's hats. **mi'llinery̆** n. [f. MILAN; orig. = vendor of Milan goods]

mi'llion (-yon) n. Cardinal number equal to one thousand thousand, 1,000,000 (abbrev. m.); also as ordinal when followed by other numbers; one million pounds, dollars, etc.; enormous number; *the* ~, the bulk of the population; the masses. ~ adj. Amounting to one million.

millionair'e (-yon-) n. Person who possesses a million pounds, dollars, etc.; person of great wealth.

millipede: see MILLEPEDE.

mi'llisĕcond n. One thousandth of a second (abbrev. msec.).

Mills bomb (-z, -m). Oval hand grenade. [invented by Sir William *Mills* (1856–1932)]

Mi'lō (6th c. B.C.). Greek athlete of Crotona, Italy, famous for his strength; a pupil of Pythagoras, whose life he is said to have saved by holding up the roof of the school when a pillar gave way.

Mi'lŏs (or mē-). (also *Milō*) Greek island in the Cyclades; *Venus de Milo*, Hellenistic marble statue of Aphrodite (now in the Louvre) found here in 1820.

mi'lreis (-rā-) n. 1. Portuguese gold coin superseded in 1911 by the escudo. 2. Brazilian money of account, 1,000 reis, replaced in 1942 by the cruzeiro.

milt n. Spleen of mammals; roe of male fish. **mi'lter** n. Male fish in the breeding season.

Milti'adēs (-z) (d. *c* 488 B.C.). Athenian statesman and general, victor at MARATHON.

Mi'lton, John (1608–74). English Puritan poet; author of the epics 'Paradise Lost' and 'Paradise Regained' and many other poems. **Miltō'nian, Miltŏ'nic** adjs.

mīme n. 1. (Gk & Rom. antiq.) Kind of simple farcical drama, characterized by mimicry and dialogue for this. 2. Similar modern performance, play with mimic gestures and action usu.

[564]

M.I.M.E. without words. 3. Actor in a mime; buffoon, jester. ~ v. Act in mime.
M.I.M.E., M.I.Mech.E. *abbrevs.* Member of the Institution of Mining, Mechanical, Engineers.
mi′meograph(*or* -ahf)*n.* Apparatus in which stencils are placed for making copies of written pages. ~ *v.t.* Reproduce by mimeograph.
mime′sis *n.* (zool.) Protective similarity of one species of animal to another, the second being distasteful or poisonous to predators.
mime′tic *adj.* Of, addicted to, imitation, mimicry, or mimesis.
mi′mic *adj.* Feigned, esp. to amuse; sham; imitative. ~ *n.* Person who mimics. ~ *v.t.* Copy speech or gestures of, esp. to amuse others, imitate closely. **mi′micry** *n.* Mimicking; thing that mimics another; (zool.) mimesis.

mi′ndful *adj.* Taking thought or care (of). **mi′ndfully** *adv.* **mi′ndfulness** *n.*
mine[1] *poss. pron.* Abs. and pred. form of MY; (archaic & poet., used before initial vowel or silent 'h', or following a noun) = MY.
mine[2] *n.* 1. Excavation from which minerals are extracted; (fig.) abundant source (*of* information etc.). 2. (mil.) Subterranean gallery in which explosive is placed to destroy enemy's fortifications etc. 3. (mil., nav.) Case containing charge of high explosive, detonated acoustically, electrically, or on contact; *mi′nefield*, sea or land area sown with mines; ~-*layer*, vessel for laying sea-mines; ~-*sweeper*, vessel for sweeping and destroying sea-mines. ~ *v.* Dig for minerals; burrow or make subterranean passage in; lay, sow, mines under or in.

mini- *prefix.* Miniature, (very) small, as *mi′nibus*; ~-*skirt*, very short skirt.
mi′niate *v.t.* Paint with vermilion; illuminate (manuscript). [L *minium* red lead]
mi′niature (-nya- *or* -nicher) *n.* 1. Picture in illuminated manuscript. 2. Painted portrait on small scale and with minute finish; reduced image or representation. ~ *adj.* Represented, designed, on a small scale; ~ *camera*, camera producing negatives less than 6 sq. in. in area, (esp.) one using 35-mm film. **mi′niaturist** (*or* -cher-) *n.* Painter of miniatures. [L, as prec.]
Mi′nicoy I′slands (ilandz): see LACCADIVE ISLANDS.
mi′nikin *n.* (print.) Size of type (approx. 3–3½ point) smaller than brilliant.

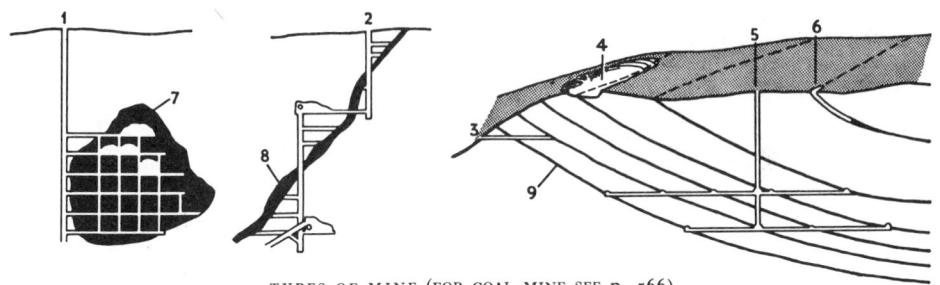

MINISTER

TYPES OF MINE (FOR COAL-MINE SEE p. 566)
1, 2. Deep level. 3. Adit. 4. Opencast. 5. Horizontal. 6. Drift. 7. Body of ore. 8. Lode or vein. 9. Seam

mimō′sa (-z-) *n.* Leguminous plant of genus *M*~, including the sensitive plant.
mi′na, my′na, mi′nor[2] *ns.* Bird of starling family, of SE. Asia, esp. common starling of India (*Gracula religiosa*); grackle. **minā′ceous**(-shus)*adj.* Threatening. **minā′ceously** *adv.*
mi′naret *n.* Tall slender tower or turret of mosque, with projecting balcony, from which muezzin proclaims the hour of prayer. [Arab. *manāra*]
mi′natory *adj.* Threatening.
mince *v.* Cut (meat etc.) very small; walk, speak, with affected delicacy; *not* ~ *matters*, be outspoken esp. in condemnation. ~ *n.* Minced meat; *mi′nceмeat*, mixture of raisins, currants, apples, suet, spices, etc.; *make mincemeat of*, (fig.) destroy, demolish utterly; ~-*pie*, small patty filled with mincemeat.
mind *n.* Seat of consciousness, thought, volition, and emotion; intellectual powers; memory; opinion; *have a good* ~ *to*, feel tempted or inclined to (*do* something). ~ *v.* Bear in mind; heed; take charge of; be vexed; have an objection (to).
mī′ndèd *adj.* Disposed, inclined; (colloq.) alive to importance of, keenly interested in, as *air*-, *politically* ~.

mi′nenwerfer (mē-, -vār-) *n.* Mine-thrower. [Ger.]
mi′ner *n.* Worker in mine.
mi′neral *n.* 1. Substance (e.g. metal, coal, salt) got by mining. 2. (chem.) Element or compound occurring naturally as a product of inorganic processes. 3. (pop.) Substance which is neither animal nor vegetable. 4. (usu. pl.) Mineral water (see below). ~ *adj.* Of, belonging to, minerals; belonging to any of the species into which inorganic substances are divided; ~ *water*, water naturally impregnated with mineral(s), esp. those of a medicinal character; (also *mineral*) bottled aerated soft drink.
minerā′logy *n.* Scientific study of minerals. **mineralō′gical** *adj.* **mineralō′gically** *adv.* **minerā′logist** *n.*
Miner′va. (Rom. myth.) Goddess of wisdom, identified with Greek Athene (which led to her being regarded also as the goddess of war).
minestrō′ne *n.* Soup containing vegetables and pasta. [It.]
minever: see MINIVER.
Ming. Name of dynasty which ruled in China 1368–1644; hence, porcelain etc. of this period.
mi′ngle (-nggl) *v.* (Cause to) mix; blend; unite *with*.
mi′ngy(-ji)*adj.* (colloq.) Stingy, mean.

mi′nim *n.* 1. (mus.) Note (○ or ♩) half as long as semibreve. 2. Smallest fluid measure, $\frac{1}{60}$ drachm. 3. Object of smallest size or importance.
mi′nimal *adj.* Very minute, the least possible.
mi′nimalist *n.* Person willing to accept minimum of his demands as compromise (opp. MAXIMALIST).
mi′nimize *v.t.* Reduce to, estimate at, smallest possible amount or degree. **minimizā′tion** *n.*
mi′nimum *n.* (pl. -*ma*). Least amount attainable, usual, etc. (opp. MAXIMUM); ~ *thermometer*, one registering lowest temperature within a period; ~ *wage*, lowest wage that may be legally offered.
mi′nimus *adj.* (in schools) Youngest of the name, as *Jones* ~; (hort.) very small variety.
mi′nion (-yon) *n.* Spoilt darling, favourite; (contempt.) servile agent; (print.) size of type (7 point), between nonpareil and brevier.
mi′nister *n.* 1. Executive agent; person in charge of a government department; ~ *of the Crown*, minister who is a member of the Cabinet; ~ *of State*, departmental senior minister intermediate between head of department and junior minister. 2. Diplomatic representative ranking below ambassador. 3. Clergyman (esp. Nonconformist). ~ *v.i.* Be

[565]

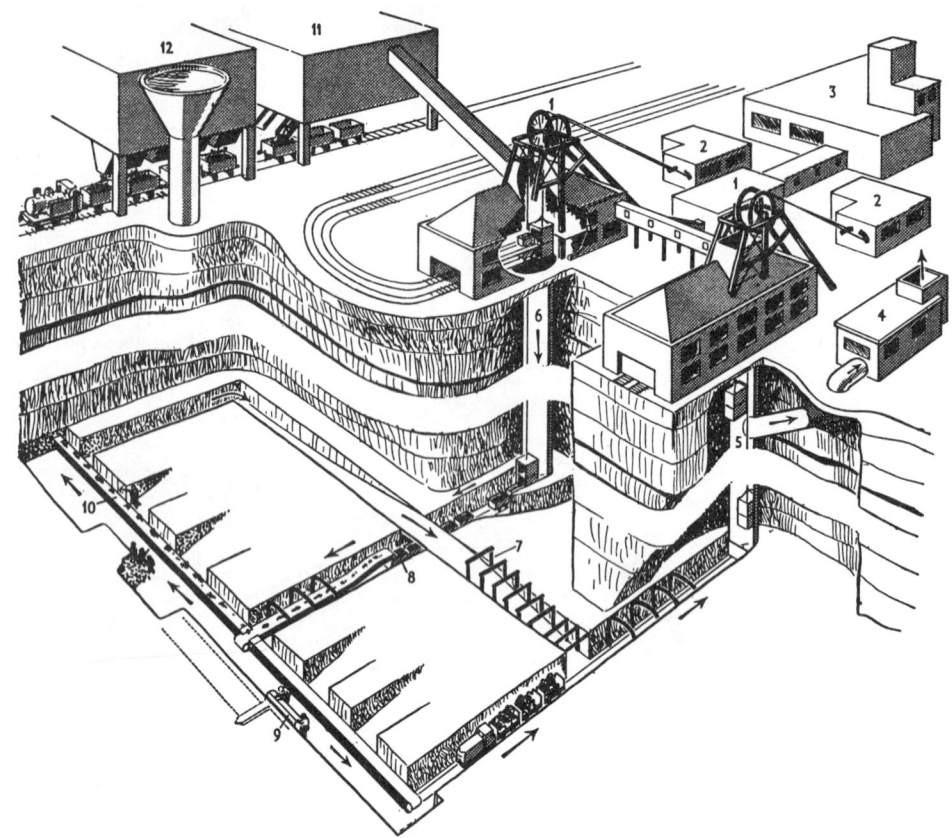

DIAGRAM OF A COAL-MINE

1. Head-gear. 2. Winding engine house. 3. Pit-head baths and canteen. 4. Fan house. 5. Upcast air-shaft. 6. Downcast air-shaft. 7. Pit props. 8. Mine-cars ready to be loaded into cage. 9. Cutting machine at coal face. 10. Conveyor. 11. Screens. 12. Washery

serviceable or contributory; officiate as minister of religion.
minister′ial *adj.* Of a minister or his office; of the government.
minister′ialist *n.* Supporter of the government.
ministra′tion *n.* Ministering, esp. in religious matters. **mi′nistrant** *adj. & n.*
mi′nistry *n.* 1. Priestly office; ministers of a church. 2. Office of minister of State; ministerial department of government, the building belonging to it; ministers forming a government.
mi′niver, mi′never *n.* Plain white fur used in ceremonial costume, esp. that of peers; ~ *pure*, (Fr. *puré*) powdered, i.e. spotted, miniver. [Fr. *menu vair* (*menu* small, *vair* kind of fur)]
mink *n.* Small semi-aquatic stoat-like animal of the family Mustelidae, esp. *Mustela vison* of N. America, valued for its thick brown fur; this fur.
Minn. *abbrev.* Minnesota.
mi′nnesinger *n.* German lyric poet and song-writer of the 12th to 14th centuries. [OHG *minna* love]
Minnesō′ta. State in north-central U.S. on Canadian border; admitted to the Union in 1858; capital, St. Paul.
mi′nnow (-ō) *n.* Small freshwater fish, in Gt Britain *Phoxinus phoxinus*, common in streams, ponds, etc.
Minō′an *adj. & n.* (Person) of the Bronze Age civilization (lasting from *c* 3000 to 1100 B.C.) revealed by excavations made in the Palace of Minos at Knossos in Crete.
mi′nor¹ *adj.* 1. Lesser (not followed by *than*); comparatively unimportant, as ~ *poet, prophet*; (in schools) younger of the name, as *Jones* ~ ; ~ *canon*, clergyman attached to a cathedral but not a member of the chapter; ~ *suit*, (bridge) diamonds or clubs; ~ *term*, (logic) subject of conclusion of categorical syllogism, contained in the ~ *premiss*. 2. (mus.) Of intervals less by a semitone than the corresponding major intervals (ill. INTERVAL); ~ *key, mode*, one having a scale containing a minor 3rd (and a minor 6th and 7th; ill. SCALE³); *in a* ~ *key*, (fig.) doleful. ~ *n.* 1. (law) Person below full age (in Engl. law below 18, formerly 21, years). 2. Minor interval, key, chord, etc. 3. Minor term or premiss. 4. MINORITE.
minor² : see MINA.
Minor′ca. Second largest of the Balearic Islands, in W. Mediterranean; hence, (also ~ *fowl*) black domestic fowl introduced from Spain.
Mi′norīte *n.* Franciscan friar, so called because the Franciscans regarded themselves as of humbler rank than members of the other orders.
minŏ′rĭty *n.* 1. (law) State, period, of being under legal age (see MINOR¹). 2. Smaller number or part, esp. smaller party voting against majority; number of votes cast for this.

[566]

MINOS

Mī′nŏs. Legendary king of Crete; in Attic tradition a cruel tyrant who every year exacted a tribute of Athenian youths and maidens, to be devoured by the Minotaur; *Palace of* ~, name given to the remains of the Bronze Age palace at Knossos.

Mī′notaur. (Gk myth.) Monster half-man, half-bull, offspring of Pasiphaë and a bull, confined in Crete in a labyrinth made by Daedalus; eventually slain by Theseus.

M.Inst.C.E. *abbrev.* Member of the Institution of Civil Engineers.

mi′nster *n.* Church of a monastery; any large church.

mi′nstrel *n.* Medieval singer or musician; poet; one of a band of entertainers with blackened faces, singing Negro songs etc.

mi′nstrelsy *n.* Minstrels' art, poetry; body of minstrels.

mint[1] *n.* Aromatic culinary herb of genus *Mentha*, esp. *M. viridis*, garden mint or spearmint; peppermint; ~ *sauce*, sauce made of finely chopped mint, vinegar, and sugar, used esp. with roast lamb.

mint[2] *n.* Place, usu. under State control, where money is coined; (fig.) source of invention; vast sum *of money*; *in* ~ *condition*, (as if) newly issued from a mint, perfect. ~ *v.t.* Coin (money); invent.

mi′ntage *n.* Coinage, money, esp. that issued from a particular mint at a specified time.

minuë′t *n.* Slow stately dance; music for this, in triple time; piece of music in this rhythm and style, often as movement of suite or sonata.

mi′nus *prep.* With the deduction of (symbol —); (colloq.) deprived of. ~ *adj.* (indicating subtraction) Less; negative; (after number etc.) less than. ~ *n.* Minus sign or quantity.

mi′nuscūle (*or* -ŭ′s-) *adj.* Small; (palaeog.) written in minuscule. ~ *n.* (palaeog.) (Letter in) small cursive script developed in the early Middle Ages, dist. from MAJUSCULE or uncial (ill. SCRIPT); (mod. typ.) lower-case letter.

mi′nute[1] (-ĭt) *n.* 1. Sixtieth part of an hour or of a degree (symbol ′); short time. 2. Memorandum, brief summary, (pl.) official record of proceedings at a meeting. 3. ~-*gun*, gun fired at intervals of a minute as a signal of distress by a ship at sea; ~-*hand*, hand indicating minutes on watch or clock. ~ *v.t.* Draft; make a minute of.

minū′te[2] *adj.* Very small; precise, going into details. **minū′telў** *adv.* **minū′teness** *n.*

minū′tia (-shĭa) *n.* (usu. in pl. -*tiae*) Trivial point; small detail.

minx *n.* Pert girl.

Mī′ocēne *adj.* & *n.* (geol.) (Of) the third epoch or system of the Tertiary period, after the Oligocene and before the Pliocene (ill. GEOLOGY).

mīō′sĭs *n.* (less usu. *meiosis*, *my-*) Constriction of the pupil of the eye.

Mirabeau (mērabō), Honoré Gabriel de Riqueti, Comte de (1749–91). French statesman and author; an important figure in the first National Assembly.

mi′racle *n.* Event due to supernatural agency; remarkable event or object; ~ *play*, mystery play. **mirăˊcūlous** *adj.* **mirăˊcūlouslў** *adv.* **mirăˊcūlousness** *n.*

miraˊge (-ahzh) *n.* Optical illusion, common in sandy deserts, caused by refraction of nearly horizontal light-rays by the hotter, and therefore less dense, layers of air near the surface, by which a distant object, directly invisible, appears to be near at hand, as though reflected in a sheet of water (also fig.).

Mirandola: see PICO DELLA MIRANDOLA.

mīre *n.* Swampy ground, boggy place; mud. ~ *v.* Sink in, bespatter with, mud. **mīr′ў** *adj.*

mi′rror *n.* Polished or very smooth surface which reflects images; looking-glass; (fig.) pattern, example; ~ *image*, image etc. with similar parts reversed as if reflected in a mirror. ~ *v.t.* Reflect as in a mirror (lit. & fig.).

mĭr̄th *n.* Rejoicing, merriment. **mĭr̄′thful** *adj.* **mĭr̄′thfully** *adv.* **mĭr̄′thfulness** *n.* **mĭr̄′thless** *adj.*

mis- *prefix.* Amiss, bad(ly), wrong(ly), unfavourably, or intensifying unfavourable meaning contained in verb, as *misdoubt*.

misadvĕ′nture *n.* Ill luck, bad fortune; (law) accidental homicide committed in doing a lawful act.

misalli′ance *n.* Unsuitable marriage.

mi′santhrōpe (*or* -z-) *n.* Hater of mankind; one who avoids human society. **misănthrŏ′pic, -ical** *adjs.* **misănˊthropist** *n.* **misă′nthropў** *ns.*

misapplў′ *v.t.* Apply wrongly. **misăpplicāˊtion** *n.*

misăpprehĕ′nd *v.t.* Misunderstand. **misăpprehĕ′nsion** *n.*

misapprōˊpriate *v.t.* Apply dishonestly to one's own use. **misapprōpriāˊtion** *n.*

misbecōˊme (-ŭm) *v.t.* Suit ill.

misbegŏ′tten *adj.* Illegitimate (often as vague term of opprobrium).

misbehāˊve *v.refl.* & *i.* Behave improperly. **misbehāˊviour** (-yer) *n.*

misc. *abbrev.* Miscellaneous; miscellany.

miscăˊlcūlāte *v.* Calculate wrongly. **miscălcūlāˊtion** *n.*

mi′scaˊll (-awl) *v.t.* Call by wrong name.

miscăˊrriage (-rĭj) *n.* Spontaneous abortion; failure of letter etc. to reach destination; ~ *of justice*, failure of court to do justice. **miscăˊrry** *v.i.* 1. Fail of success; go astray. 2. Suffer a miscarriage.

MISERERE

miscėgėnāˊtion *n.* Interbreeding between races, esp. sexual union of whites with Negroes.

miscellāˊnea *n.pl.* Miscellany; odds and ends.

miscellāˊneous *adj.* Of mixed character, of various kinds.

miscė′llanў (*or* miˊsĭ-) *n.* Medley; miscellaneous writings etc. collected together.

mischăˊnce (-ah-) *n.* (Piece of) ill luck, ill success.

mĭˊschief (-chĭf) *n.* Harm, evil, wrought by person or particular cause; worker of mischief; vexatious or annoying conduct, esp. of children; playful malice. **mĭˊschievous** (-ĭv-) *adj.* **mĭˊschievouslў** *adv.* **mĭˊschievousness** *n.*

mĭˊscĭble *adj.* Capable of being mixed, esp. (of liquids) to form a homogeneous substance. **miscĭbĭˊlitў** *n.*

misconceiˊve *v.* Have wrong idea of, misunderstand. **misconcĕ′ption** *n.*

miscŏˊndŭct *n.* Bad management; improper conduct, esp. adultery. **miscondŭˊct** *v.t.* & *refl.*

miˊsconstrūˊe (-ōō; *or* -kŏˊ-) *v.t.* Put wrong construction on (word, action). **misconstrŭˊction** *n.*

miscouˊnt *v.t.* Count wrongly. **miˊscount** *n.* Wrong count, esp. of votes.

miˊscrėant *n.* Vile wretch, villain.

mĭˊs-cūˊe *v.i.* (billiards) Fail to strike the ball properly. ~ *n.* Such a stroke.

misdāˊte *v.t.* Put wrong date on.

misdeaˊl *v.* Make mistake in dealing (cards). ~ *n.* Wrong deal.

miˊsdeeˊd *n.* Evil deed.

misdėmeaˊnant *n.* Person convicted of misdemeanour.

misdėmeaˊnour (-er) *n.* Misdeed; (law) any indictable offence (before 1967 regarded as less than felony).

miˊsdirĕˊct *v.t.* Direct wrongly; put wrong name, address, etc., on letter etc.; give wrong instructions to, specif. (of a judge) give wrong instructions to a jury; aim badly or without precision. **misdirĕˊction** *n.*

miˊsdōˊing (-ōō-) *n.* Misdeed.

misdouˊbt(-dowt)*v.t.*Have misgivings or suspicions about; doubt.

mise en scène (mēz ahn sān). Scenery and properties of an acted play; (fig.) setting of an event or action. [Fr.]

miˊser (-z-) *n.* One who lives miserably in order to hoard wealth. **miˊserlў** *adj.* **miˊserlĭness** *n.*

miˊserable(-z-) *adj.* Wretchedly unhappy, uncomfortable, or poor; causing wretchedness; pitiable, mean. **miˊserablў** *adv.*

misère (mēzār′) *n.* Call in solo whist (see SOLO).

Misererˊė[1] (-zerāˊrĭ). One of the Penitential Psalms (Ps. 51), beginning *Miserere mei Deus* (L, = 'Have mercy upon me O God'); cry for mercy.

[567]

miserer'e² (-zerārī) n. (erron.) = MISERICORD, sense 2.
misĕ'ricŏrd (-z-) n. 1. Room set apart in a monastery, where monks might take special food as an indulgence. 2. Projection on under-side of hinged seat in choir stall, serving when seat is turned up to support person standing (ill. STALL¹). 3. (hist.) Thin pointed dagger used in medieval warfare for giving *coup de grâce* to a fallen knight.
mi'serў (-z-) n. 1. Wretched state of mind or circumstances. 2. = MISÈRE.
misfea'sance (-fēz-) n. Wrongful exercise of lawful authority, as dist. from MALFEASANCE.
misfīr'e v.i. (of gun) Fail to go off; (of internal combustion engine) fail to ignite (also transf.) ~ n. Failure to explode or ignite.
mi'sfit n. Garment etc. that does not fit; (fig.) person badly adjusted to his work or surroundings.
misfŏr'tūne n. Calamity, bad luck.
misgi̇̆'ve (-g-) v.t. (past t. -*gāve*, past part. -*given*) (of heart, mind, etc.) Suggest misgivings to. **misgi̇̆'ving** n. Apprehension, uneasy doubt.
mishă'ndle (-s-h-) v.t. Handle (person, thing) roughly, rudely, or improperly.
mi'shăp (-s-h-) n. Unlucky accident.
mishear' (-s-h-) v.t. (past t. & past part. -*heard* pr. -hĕ́rd). Hear amiss or imperfectly.
mi'shi̇̆'t (-s-h-) v.t. Hit wrongly or inaccurately, esp. at games. ~ n. Faulty hit.
Mi'shnah (-a). Codification of Jewish oral law, made by Rabbi Judah ha-Nasi in 2nd c. A.D. [post-bibl. Heb. *mishnāh* teaching by repetition, traditional law]
mislay' v.t. (past t. & past part. -*laid*). Put (thing) by accident where it cannot readily be found; hence, (euphemism for) lose.
mislea'd v.t. (past t. & past part. -*lĕd*). Lead astray, give wrong impression to.
mismă'nage v.t. Manage badly or wrongly. **mismă'nagement** n.
mi'snā'me v.t. Call by wrong name.
mi'snō'mer n. Wrongly applied name.
misŏ'gamў n. Hatred of marriage. **misŏ'gamist** n.
misŏ'gynў (or -g-) n. Hatred of women. **misŏ'gynist** n.
misplā'ce v.t. Put in wrong place; bestow (affection etc.) on ill-chosen object. **misplā'cement** n.
mi'spri̇̆'nt n. Error in printing. **mispri̇̆'nt** v.t.
mispri̇̆'sion n. (law) Wrong action or omission, esp. on part of public official; ~ *of treason*, concealment of knowledge of a felony or of treason, by person not actively involved.
mispronou'nce v.t. Pronounce wrongly. **mispronŭnciā'tion** n.
mi'squō'te v.t. Quote wrongly. **misquotā'tion** n.
mi'srea'd v.t. Read or interpret wrongly.
misrĕprĕsĕ'nt (-zĕ-) v.t. Represent wrongly, give false account of. **misrĕprĕsĕntā'tion** n.
mi'sru'le (-ōōl) v.t. Rule badly. ~ n. Bad government; *Lord* (also *Abbot*, *Master*, etc.) *of M*~, in the late 15th and early 16th centuries, person appointed at court, in nobleman's house, or in a college or Inn of Court, to superintend Christmas revels.
miss¹ v. Fail to hit, reach, meet, find, catch, or perceive; pass over; regret absence of; fail. ~ n. Failure; (colloq.) *give* (a thing) *a* ~, pass by, leave alone.
miss² n. Title of (*M*~) or form of address to girl or unmarried woman with no superior title; girl (usu. contempt.); *misses*, applied to a range of garment sizes for women; so *junior miss*, (attrib.) for adolescent girls. [abbrev. of MISTRESS]
Miss. abbrev. Mississippi.
mi'ssal n. (R.C. Ch.) Book containing the service of the Mass for whole year; (loosely) book of hours, prayers, etc., esp. one that is illuminated.
mi'ssel n. (also ~-*thrush*) Large thrush (*Turdus viscivorus*) which feeds partly on mistletoe-berries. [OE *mistel* basil, mistletoe]
mis-shā'pen adj. Deformed.
mi'ssile n. Object or weapon capable of being thrown or shot.
mi'ssing adj. Not present, not found; ~ *link*, pop. name of hypothetical intermediate type of animal between anthropoid apes and man.
mi'ssion n. 1. Body of persons sent to foreign country to conduct negotiations etc. 2. Body sent by religious community to convert heathen; field of missionary activity; missionary post; organization in a district for conversion of the people; course of religious services etc. for this purpose. 3. Errand of political or other mission. 4. Operational sortie. 5. Person's vocation or divinely appointed work in life.
mi'ssionarў adj. Of religious missions. ~ n. Person doing missionary work.
mi'ssioner n. Missionary; person in charge of parochial mission.
mi'ssis, **mi'ssus** (-ĭz) n. (vulg.) Mistress; form of address to woman, without any name following; (joc.) wife. [oral equivalent of MRS.]
Mississi'ppi. 1. Greatest river of N. America, rising in Minnesota and flowing south to the Gulf of Mexico. 2. Southern State of U.S. lying E. of the lower Mississippi River, admitted to the Union 1817; capital, Jackson. 3. ~ *Scheme*: see LAW⁴.

mi'ssive n. Written message, letter.
Missour'i (-oorī). 1. One of the main tributaries of the Mississippi, flowing into it from the W. above St. Louis, and rising in the Rocky Mountains. 2. State in central U.S. lying W. of the Mississippi River; admitted to the Union in 1821; capital, Jefferson City.
mi'ssў n. Affectionate, playful, or contemptuous form of address to girl or young woman, = MISS² (not followed by name).
mist n. 1. Water-vapour precipitated in droplets smaller and more densely aggregated than those of rain; (meteor.) state of atmospheric obscurity (less dense than fog) produced by this, in which visibility exceeds 1 km. 2. Dimness or blurred effect caused by tears in the eyes etc. **mi'stў** adj. **mi'stilў** adv. **mi'stinĕss** n. **mist** v. Cover, be covered, (as) with a mist.
mistā'ke v. (past t. -*tōō'k*, past part. -*tā'ken*). Misunderstand, take in wrong sense; be in error; take (one thing) erroneously *for* another; err in choice of. ~ n. Misunderstanding; something incorrectly done through ignorance or inadvertence. **mistā'kenlў** adv. **mistā'kennĕss** (-n-n-) n. **mistā'kable** adj.
mi'ster n. Title prefixed to surname of man with no superior title (always written *Mr.*); (vulg.) form of address to man, without any name following; man without title of nobility.
mi'stī'me v.t. Time wrongly, do or perform at wrong time.
mi'stletoe (-sltō) n. Parasitic plant (*Viscum album*) with whitish sticky berries, growing on apple-trees etc., associated in England with Christmas, and anciently venerated by Druids when found growing on the oak.
mi'stral (or -ah'l) n. Violent cold northerly or north-westerly wind in Mediterranean provinces of France etc., blowing esp. down Rhône valley. [L *magistralis* masterful]
mi'strĕss n. 1. Woman in authority over servants; female head of household. 2. Woman who has power to control or dispose *of*, as *you are* ~ *of the situation*, *you are your own* ~ (also fig.). 3. Woman who has thorough knowledge (*of* subject). 4. Woman who has a continuing sexual relationship with a man other than her husband; (formerly) woman loved and courted by a man. 5. Female teacher in school or of special subject, as *music* ~. 6. *M*~ *of the Robes*, lady charged with care of Queen's wardrobe; *wardrobe* ~: see WARDROBE.
mi'strŭ'st v.t. Not trust; have uneasy doubts or suspicions about. ~ n. **mistrŭ'stful** adj. **mistrŭ'stfullў** adv. **mistrŭ'stfulnĕss** n.
misŭnderstă'nd v. (past t. &

past part. -st**ōō**d). Not understand rightly, misinterpret. **misŭnderstă′nding** n.
mi′sū′se (-z) v.t. Use wrongly, ill-use. ~ (-s) n.
Mĭtă′nnian adj. & n. (Native, language) of a Hurrian State (*Mitanni*) established c 1500 B.C. in N. Mesopotamia.
mīte[1] n. (orig.) Flemish copper coin of small value; hence (pop.) coin of very small value, esp. (also *widow's* ~) small money contribution (see Mark 12: 42); small object, esp. a child.
mīte[2] n. Any of several small arachnids of the order Acari, found as parasites.

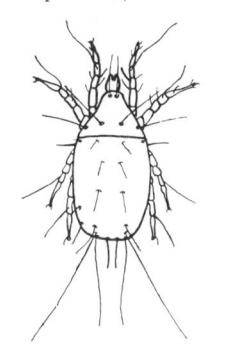

CHEESE-MITE (approx. × 100)

Mĭ′thras. (Pers. myth.) God of light, often identified with the sun. **Mĭthrā′ic** adj. **Mĭ′thrāism** n. Religion involving worship of Mithras, introduced among the Romans under the Empire and spread over most of N. and W. Europe during the first three centuries A.D., becoming the principal rival at that time of Christianity.
Mĭthrĭdă′tēs (-z). Name of 3 kings of Parthia and of several kings of Pontus; *Mithridates VI Eupator* (131–63 B.C.), of Pontus, called 'the Great', tried to drive the Romans out of Asia Minor, but was defeated by Sulla, and finally in 66 B.C. by Pompey; he was said to have rendered himself proof against poisons by taking them constantly in small quantities. **Mĭthrĭdă′tic** adj.
mĭ′tĭgāte v.t. Appease; alleviate, reduce severity of. **mĭtĭgā′tion** n. **mĭ′tĭgātorў** adj.
mĭtochŏ′ndrion (-k-) n. (pl. -*ia*). Thread-like or granular organelle with outer and inner membrane, concerned in release of metabolic energy (ill. CELL).
mĭtō′sis n. (pl. -*osēs* pr. -z). (biol.) Splitting of cell or nucleus accompanied by doubling of number of chromosomes, so that each of the resulting two cells or nuclei has the same number as the original one (cf. MEIOSIS). **mĭtŏ′tic** adj.
mitrailleu′se (-trahyēr̄z) n.

Many-barrelled breech-loading machine-gun designed to fire bullets in rapid succession or simultaneously.
mi′tral adj. (anat.) Of the mitral valve; ~ *valve*, two-cusped valve (so called from fancied resemblance to bishop's mitre) between left atrium and ventricle of human heart, preventing reflux of blood into atrium when ventricle contracts (ill. HEART).
mi′tre[1] (-ter) n. Bishop's tall pointed head-dress, deeply cleft at the top (ill. VESTMENT); episcopal office or dignity. **mi′tred** (-terd) adj. Wearing a mitre.
mi′tre[2] (-ter) n. (carpentry) Joint in which line of junction bisects the angle (usu. a right angle) between the two pieces, as in picture-frame; (also ~ *square*) device with blade set at angle of 45° for striking lines on something to be mitred (ill. SQUARE). ~ v. Join in mitre; shape to a mitre.
mitt n. Mitten; (slang, pl.) boxing-gloves.
mi′tten n. Glove leaving fingers and thumb-tip bare; glove having no separate partitions for fingers, but only for thumb.
Mi′ttў, Walter. Hero of story by James Thurber, given to extravagant day-dreams.
mix v. Mingle, blend, into one mass; compound; have intercourse *with*; ~ *in, it*, (colloq.) join in fighting; ~ *up*, confuse; ~-*up* (n.) confused fight, mêlée. ~ n. Mixture of materials (e.g. concrete, plastics) ready for a process.
mixed (-kst) adj. Of diverse qualities or elements; (of company) not select, containing persons of doubtful status; comprising both sexes; for persons of both sexes, as ~ *bathing*; ~ *farming*, farming involving both crops and livestock; ~-*up*, muddled; (of persons) confused, esp. emotionally.
mi′xer n. (esp.) 1. In sound films etc., apparatus that controls contributions of various microphones. 2. Apparatus, usu. electrical, for mixing or pulping food in cookery. 3. *good, bad,* ~, (colloq.) person who gets on well, badly, with others.
Mixolў′dian adj. ~ *mode,* ancient Greek MODE; also, 7th of the ecclesiastical modes with G as final and D as dominant (ill. MODE).
mi′xture n. Mixing; what is mixed, esp. medicinal preparation; mechanical mixing of two or more substances, involving no change in their character, opp. to *chemical combination*; (in internal combustion engine) gas or vaporized fuel mixed with air to form the explosive charges.
mi′zzen, mi′zen n. (naut.) Fore-and-aft sail on after side of ~-*mast*, the aftermost mast of a three-masted ship (ill. SHIP).
mi′zzle[1] v.impers. Drizzle.
mi′zzle[2] v.i. (slang) Run away, decamp.

mk abbrev. Mark (coin).
M.K.S. abbrev. Metre-kilogramme-second (system of measurement).
ml abbrev. Millilitre(s).
M.L.A. abbrev. Member of the Legislative Assembly; Modern Language Association.
Mlle abbrev. Mademoiselle (pl. *Mlles*).
mm abbrev. Millimetre(s).
MM. abbrev. Messieurs.
M.M. abbrev. Military Medal.
Mme abbrev. Madame (pl. *Mmes*).
m.m.f. abbrev. Magnetomotive force.
M.Mus. abbrev. Master of Music.
M.N. abbrev. Merchant Navy.
mnėmŏ′nic (n-) adj. Of, intended to aid, the memory. ~ n. Mnemonic rhyme etc.; (pl.) mnemonic art or system.
Mnēmŏ′sўnē (nēmŏz-). Mother of the Muses. [Gk, = 'memory'].
Mo. abbrev. Missouri.
M.O. abbrev. Medical Officer; money order.
mō′a n. Any of various large extinct flightless birds of New Zealand, resembling ostrich (many species in family Dinornithidae). [Maori]
Mō′ăb. Ancient country of the Dead Sea.
Mō′abīte n. (fem. *Moabitėss*) Member of a Semitic people traditionally descended from Lot (Gen. 19: 37), living in Moab. ~ adj. Of Moab or the Moabites; ~ *Stone,* a monument erected by Mesha, king of Moab, c 850 B.C., which describes the campaign between Moab and Israel of 2 Kings 3 and furnishes the earliest known inscription in the Phoenician alphabet; now in the Louvre, Paris.
moan n. Low inarticulate sound expressing pain or grief. ~ v. Utter moan; lament.
moat n. Deep, wide, usu. water-filled, ditch round castle, town, etc. (ill. CASTLE). **moa′tėd** adj. Surrounded by a moat.
mŏb n. Riotous or tumultuous crowd; rabble; promiscuous gathering. **mŏ′bbish** adj. **mŏb** v.t. Attack in a mob; crowd round and molest.
mŏ′b-că′p n. Woman's round usu. frilled indoor cap covering whole head, worn in 18th and early 19th centuries.
mō′bīle adj. Movable; characterized by freedom of movement; (of troops etc.) that may be easily moved from place to place; of changing expression, volatile. **mōbī′lĭtў** n. **mō′bīle** n. Piece of sculpture with parts free to move in currents of air; similar object of cardboard etc.
mō′bĭlīze v. Render movable, bring into circulation; call up, assemble, prepare, for war etc. **mō′bilīzable** adj. **mōbilīzā′tion** n.
mŏ′ccasin n. 1. Amer. Indian

[569]

MOCHA — MODIFY

soft shoe of deerskin etc. 2. Amer. viper of genus *Agkistrodon*.

mŏ'cha (-ka) *n.* Coffee of fine quality orig. coming from Mocha, seaport of S. Yemen; flavouring of (chocolate and) coffee.

mŏck *v.* Hold up to ridicule, ridicule by imitation, counterfeit; set at nought; jeer, scoff; befool, tantalize; *mo'cking-bird*, Amer. passerine song-bird, *Mimus polyglottos*, that imitates other birds' notes. ~ *n.* Mockery; object of derision. ~ *adj.* Sham, counterfeit, pretended; *~-heroic*, burlesque imitation of, burlesquely imitating, the heroic style; ~ *moon* = PARASELENE; ~ *orange*, shrub of genus *Philadelphus*, esp. *P. coronarius*, with creamy-white very fragrant flowers; sometimes called syringa; *~-sun* = PARHELION; *~-turtle soup*, soup made of calf's head to imitate real turtle soup; *~-up*, scale model.

mŏ'ckerў *n.* Derision; laughing-stock; impudent simulation; ludicrously or insultingly futile action.

mŏd *n.* Gaelic congress for music and poetry, initiated 1891 in Scotland as equivalent of Welsh eisteddfod.

mō'dal *adj.* Of mode or form as opp. to substance; (mus.) of mode; (logic) involving affirmation of possibility, necessity, or contingency; (gram.) of the mood of a verb, (of particle) denoting manner. **modă'litў** *n.* **mō'dallў** *adv.*

mōde *n.* 1. Way, manner, in which thing is done; prevailing fashion or conventional usage. 2. (mus.) Ancient Greek scale system (as AEOLIAN, DORIAN, IONIAN, LYDIAN, MIXOLYDIAN, PHRYGIAN); any of the scale-systems similarly named in medieval ecclesiastical music (see also AUTHENTIC, PLAGAL); in more modern music the two (MAJOR and MINOR) chief scale-systems. 3. (statistics) That value of a character or graded quality at which the instances are most numerous.

mŏ'del *n.* Representation in three dimensions of projected or existing structure or material object; design, pattern; object of imitation; (copy of) garment etc. by recognized designer; person employed to pose for artist etc. or to display clothes by wearing them; lay figure for shop windows etc. ~ *adj.* That is a model; exemplary, excellent of its kind. ~ *v.* 1. Mould, fashion; produce in clay, wax, etc. 2. Wear for display; act as artist's model. **mŏ'delling** *n.* Making models, manipulating clay etc.; representation of form in sculpture or of material relief and solidity in painting.

mŏ'derate *adj.* Avoiding extremes, temperate; tolerable, mediocre; not excessive. **mŏ'derately** *adv.* **mŏ'derateness** *n.* **mŏ'derate** *n.* Person, esp. politician, of moderate views. **mŏ'derāte** *v.* Make or become less violent or excessive; act as moderator.

mŏderā'tion *n.* 1. Moderating, moderateness. 2. *Moderations*, 1st public examination at Oxford University for degree of B.A. in certain faculties.

mŏ'derātor *n.* 1. Mediator; Presbyterian minister presiding over presbytery, synod, or general assembly. 2. (nuclear phys.) Material used to dilute fissile material so as to control nuclear reaction. **mŏ'derātorship** *n.*

mŏ'dern *adj.* Of the present and recent times; new-fashioned, not antiquated; of school subjects, not concerned with the classics; ~ *face*, style of printing type (ill. TYPE). **modĕ̄r'nitў**, **mŏ'dernèss** *ns.*

mŏ'dernĭsm *n.* Modern usage, expression, etc.; modern fashion in art; mode of theological inquiry in which the traditions and doctrines of Christianity are examined in the light of modern thought. **mŏ'dernĭst** *n.* Person favouring modernism. **mŏdernĭ'stĭc** *adj.* (esp., of style) Following new fashions and innovations, advanced.

mŏ'dernīze *v.t.* Make modern. **mŏdernīzā'tion** *n.*

mŏ'dest *adj.* Not overestimating one's own merits; not excessive; unpretentious; retiring, bashful; decorous, avoiding indecency. **mŏ'destlў** *adv.* **mŏ'destў** *n.*

mŏ'dĭcŭm *n.* Small quantity or portion.

mŏ'difў *v.t.* Tone down; alter without radical transformation; (gram.) qualify sense of (word etc.); change vowel by mutation. **mŏdĭfī'able** *adj.* **mŏdĭfĭcā'tion** *n.* Act of modifying, state of being modified; change made in vowel by mutation, graphic representation of this (¨).

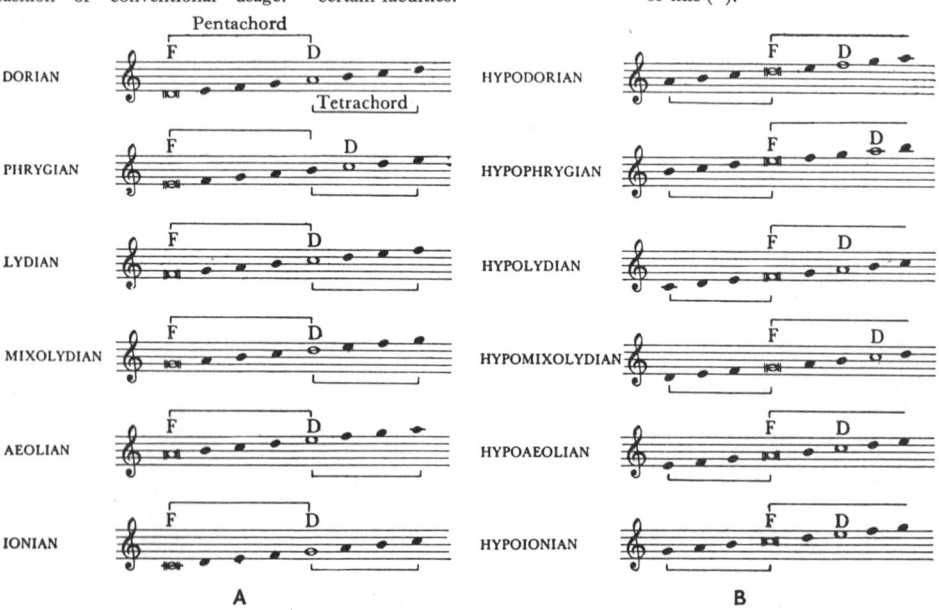

A. INTERVALS OF AUTHENTIC MODES. B. INTERVALS OF PLAGAL MODES
F = Final. D = Dominant

[570]

mŏdi′llion (-yon) *n.* (archit.) Projecting bracket under corona of cornice in Corinthian and other orders (ill. ORDER).
mō′dish *adj.* Fashionable, **mō′dishly** *adv.* **mō′dishness** *n.*
mōdi′ste (-ēst) *n.* Milliner, dressmaker.
mŏ′dom *n.* Minced form of *madam*, esp. in affected pronunciation of shop assistants to customers.
Mŏ′drĕd, Mōr′drĕd. In Arthurian legend, Arthur's nephew, who treacherously seized the kingdom during Arthur's absence and was killed by him in the last battle in Cornwall.
Mŏds (-z) *n.pl.* (colloq.) Moderations (Oxf. Univ.)
mŏ′dūlar *adj.* ~ *design*, (archit.) design based on a module or unit which is repeated throughout the building.
mŏ′dūlāte *v.* 1. Adjust, tone down; attune to a certain pitch or key, vary in tone. 2. (mus.) Pass from one key to another. 3. (radio) Vary the frequency, amplitude, etc., of (a wave) by the effect of another. **mŏdūlā′tion** *n.* Modulating, effect produced by this; *amplitude* ~, (abbrev. A.M.) transmission of signals by modulating the amplitude of the transmitted radio wave but keeping its frequency constant; *frequency* ~, (abbrev. F.M.) transmission of signals by modulating the frequency of the radio wave but keeping its amplitude constant.
mŏ′dūlātor *n.* 1. (mus.) Chart used in tonic sol-fa system for exercise in sight-singing. 2. (radio) Apparatus used for modulating a carrier wave.
mŏ′dūle *n.* Unit of standard of measurement, as for flow of water; (archit.) unit of measurement for determining the proportions of a building, in classical architecture usu. half the diameter of a column at the base (ill. ORDER); independent unit forming section of spacecraft.
mŏ′dūlus *n.* (math.) 1. Constant multiplier or coefficient, esp. for converting Napierian into common logarithms. 2. Number by which two others are divided (see CONGRUENCY).
mō′dus *n.* Method, manner, mode; ~ *operandi*, method, system, of working; plan of operations; ~ *vivendi*, mode of living, esp. arrangement between disputants pending settlement.
Mŏgŭ′l (or mō′-) *n.* 1. Mongolian, esp. one of the Muslim followers of Babur, who established an empire in India in 1526 which reached its zenith under Akbar and Aurangzeb, but declined after this, the last emperor being deposed by the British in 1857; *Great* ~, Mogul emperor. 2. *m*~, important or influential person. [Pers. *mugal*, *-ul*, pr. of *Mongol*]

M.O.H. *abbrev.* Medical Officer of Health.
mō′hair *n.* (Yarn or fabric made from) hair of Angora goat; imitation of this made of a mixture of wool and cotton. [Arab. *muḳayyar* cloth of goat's hair (lit. 'select, choice', f. *ḳayyara* choose)]
Mohă′mmĕd. Var. of MUHAMMAD. **Mohă′mmĕdan** *adj.* & *n.* Muslim.
Mō′hawk *n.* 1. (Member of) a tribe of N. Amer. Indians belonging to the Iroquois; language of this tribe. 2. (skating) Step from an edge on one foot to the same edge on the other foot in an opposite direction.
Mōhi′can (-hēk-) *n.* (Member of) a warlike tribe of N. Amer. Indians, of Algonkin stock, formerly occupying W. parts of Connecticut and Massachusetts.
mō′hō *n.* Discontinuity between earth's crust and mantle. **mō′-hōle** *n.* Hole drilled through seabed to mantle. [f. A. *Mohorovičić* (1857–1936), Yugoslav seismologist]
Mō′hŏck *n.* (hist.) One of a class of aristocratic ruffians who infested the London streets at night in the early years of the 18th c. [f. MOHAWK]
Mohs (mōs), Friedrich (1773–1839), German mineralogist, inventor of *Mohs' scale*: see HARDNESS, 2.
moi′dore *n.* Former Portuguese gold coin current in England in early 18th c. [Port. *moeda d'ouro* money of gold]
moi′ety *n.* Half, esp. in legal use; (loosely) either of two parts into which thing is divided.
moil *v.i.* Drudge.
moire (mwär) *n.* Watered silk fabric. [Fr., perh. f. Engl. *mohair*]
moiré (mwär′ā) *adj.* (of silk) Watered; (of metals) having clouded appearance like watered silk. ~ *n.* (Fabric with) appearance like that of watered silk. [Fr., f. *moirer* water (silk)]
Moissan (mwăsah̀n), Henri (1852–1907). French chemist; first isolated fluorine; Nobel Prize for chemistry 1906.
moist *adj.* Slightly wet, damp; rainy. **moi′stness** *n.*
moi′sten (-sn) *v.* Make or become moist.
moi′sture *n.* Liquid diffused through air or solid, or condensed on a surface. **moi′sturīze** *v.* Make moist; add moisture to.
moi′ther (-dh-) *v.* Worry, perplex; be incoherent or wandering.
mōke *n.* (slang) Donkey.
mol *abbrev.* MOLE⁴(s).
mō′lar¹ *adj.* & *n.* Grinding (tooth), back tooth of mammals (ill. TOOTH). [L *mola* millstone]
mō′lar² *adj.* (phys.) Of, acting on or by, masses (freq. opp. MOLECULAR); ~ *solution*, (chem.) solution containing one gramme molecule of a specified substance per litre.

molă′ssēs (-z) *n.* Thick viscid syrup, drained from raw sugar during manufacture; (U.S.) treacle. [Port *melaço*, f. LL *mellaceus* like honey]
Mŏldā′via. 1. (hist.) Danubian principality, from which, together with Wallachia, the kingdom of Rumania was formed in 1859. 2. Constituent republic of the U.S.S.R., formed from territory ceded by Rumania in 1940; capital, Kishinev.
mōle¹ *n.* Abnormal pigmented prominence on skin.
mōle² *n.* Small animal of genus *Talpa* with velvety, usu. blackish-grey fur, very small eyes, and very short strong fore-limbs for burrowing; ~-*hill*, mound of earth thrown up by mole; *mo'leskin*, mole's fur; strong, soft, fine-piled cotton fustian with surface shaved before dyeing, used for trousers etc.
mōle³ *n.* Massive structure, esp. stone, serving as pier or breakwater.
mōle⁴ *n.* Amount of a particular substance containing as many elementary entities (atoms, molecules, etc.) as there are atoms in 0·012 kg of carbon-12 (abbrev. mol).
mŏ′lĕcūle *n.* 1. (chem., phys.) One of the minute groups of atoms of which material substances consist; smallest particle to which a compound can be reduced by subdivision without losing its chemical identity. 2. (loosely) Small particle. **molĕ′cūlar** *adj.* Of molecules; ~ *weight*, weight of a molecule of a substance relative to weight of hydrogen atom.
molĕ′st *v.t.* Meddle with injuriously or with hostile intent. **mŏlĕstā′tion** *n.*
Molière (mŏliar̄). Stage-name of Jean Baptiste Poquelin (1622–73), French author of comedies satirizing contemporary manners.
Mō′linism *n.* 1. Religious doctrine taught by the Spanish Jesuit Luis Molina (1535–1600), that the efficacy of grace depends simply on the will that freely accepts it. 2. Doctrine of religious quietism taught by the Spanish mystic Miguel de Molinos (1640–96). **Mō′linist** *n.*
mō′ll *n.* (U.S. slang) Gangster's female companion.
mŏ′llify *v.t.* Soften, appease. **mŏllificā′tion** *n.*
mō′llusc *n.* Any animal of the phylum Mollusca which comprises soft-bodied unsegmented invertebrates (usu. having a hard protective shell) and includes limpets, snails, cuttlefish, oysters, etc. (ill. MUSSEL). **mŏllŭ′scan, mollŭ′scoid, mollŭ′scous** *adjs.*
mŏ′lly-cŏ′ddle *n.* Milksop. ~ *v.t.* Coddle.
Mō′lŏch¹ (-k). Canaanite god to whose image children were sacrificed as burnt-offerings: see Lev. 18: 21, 2 Kings 23: 10;

[571]

MOLOCH

hence, power or influence to which everything is sacrificed.

mŏ′lŏch² (-k) *n.* Australian thorn-lizard or thorn-devil, *Molochus horridus*.

Mŏ′lotŏv (-f), Vyacheslav Mikhailovich (1890–). Russian statesman, minister for foreign affairs in U.S.S.R., 1939-49, 1953-6; ~ *cocktail*, crude incendiary hand-grenade, consisting of a bottle of inflammable liquid and a wick, orig. used as anti-tank missile in 1939-45 war.

mŏ′lten *adj.*: see MELT¹; (esp.) liquefied by heat.

Mŏ′ltke (-e), Helmuth von, Count (1800-91). Prussian field marshal; reorganized the Prussian army before the Franco-German War of 1870-1.

mŏ′ltō *adv.* (mus.) Very (preceding mus. direction, as ~ *allegro*).

Molŭ′ccas (-z). Islands of Indonesia, SE. of Philippines.

mō′lў *n.* (Gk myth.) Fabulous plant with white flower and black root, given by Hermes to Odysseus as a charm against the sorceries of Circe.

molў′bdenīte *n.* Molybdenum disulphide (MoS$_2$), a soft flaky black mineral resembling graphite.

molў′bdenum *n.* (chem.) Greyish-white metallic element resembling tungsten and having a very high melting-point, a constituent of special steel alloys; symbol Mo, at. no. 42, at. wt 95·94. [Gk *molubdos* lead]

mō′ment *n.* Point of time, instant; importance, weight; (mech.) measure of power of a force to cause rotation round an axis.

mō′mentary *adj.* Lasting but for a moment. **mō′mentarilў** *adv.* **mō′mentarinĕss** *n.*

mō′mentlў *adv.* Every moment.

momĕ′ntous *adj.* Important; weighty. **momĕ′ntouslў** *adv.* **momĕ′ntousnĕss** *n.*

momĕ′ntŭm *n.* (mech.) Quantity of motion of a moving body, product of mass multiplied by velocity; (pop.) impetus gained by movement.

Mŏ′mmsen, Theodor (1817-1903). German historian and archaeologist; author of a 'History of Rome'.

Mŏ′mus. (Gk myth.) God of mockery; expelled from heaven for his criticisms and ridicule of the gods; hence, a fault-finder.

Mon. *abbrev.* Monday; Monmouthshire.

Mŏ′na. Island anciently inhabited by Druids, lying between England and Ireland; supposed to be the Isle of Man or Anglesey.

mŏ′nachal (-k-) *adj.* Monastic. **mŏ′nachism** *n.*

Mŏna′cō (-ah-). Independent principality, under French protection since 1861, on French Riviera, including Monte Carlo within its borders; capital, Monaco.

mŏ′nad *n.* 1. (hist.) Number one, unit. 2. (philos.) Ultimate unit of being (e.g. a soul, an atom, a person, God), esp. in philosophy of LEIBNIZ. 3. (biol.) Primary individual organism assumed as first term in a genealogy. **monă′dic** *adj.* **mŏ′nadism** *n.* Theory of monadic nature of matter or of substance generally, applied esp. to philosophy of Leibniz.

mŏnadĕ′lphous *adj.* (bot.) (of stamens) Having filaments united into one bundle.

Mŏ′naghan (-*a*-han). Inland county of Ulster in the Republic of Ireland.

Mŏ′na Li′sa (lēza). Portrait, now in the Louvre, of a lady traditionally identified as the wife of Francesco del Gioconda, painted by Leonardo da Vinci and famous for its strange smile.

mŏ′narch (-k) *n.* 1. Sovereign with title of king, queen, emperor, or equivalent; supreme ruler (often fig.). 2. Large orange-and-black butterfly (*Danaus plexippus*). **monarchal**, **monăr′chic**, **-ical** *adjs.*

mŏ′narchism (-k-) *n.* Principles of, attachment to, monarchy. **mŏ′narchist** *n.*

mŏ′narchy (-kī) *n.* (State under) monarchical government.

mŏ′nasterў *n.* Residence of community of monks.

monă′stic *adj.* Of monks or monasteries; secluded, austere. **monă′sticallў** *adv.* **monă′sticism** *n.*

mŏ′nazīte *n.* Phosphate mineral, containing thorium and rare-earth elements, found in alluvial sands in India and Brazil.

Monck: see MONK².

Mo′nday (mŭ-; *or* -dī) *n.* 2nd day of the week; *Black* ~, (school slang) first day of term. [OE *Monan dæg* (= moon's day), rendering of LL *lunae dies*]

monde (mawňd) *n.* Fashionable world, society; set in which one moves.

Mŏnet (-nā), Claude (1840-1926). French Impressionist painter.

mo′netarў (mŭ-) *adj.* Of coinage or money.

mo′netīze (mŭ-) *v.t.* Put in circulation as money; give standard value to (metal) in coinage of a country. **monetīzā′tion** *n.*

mo′ney (mŭ-) *n.* (pl. -s). 1. Current coin; coin and promissory documents representing it, esp. (*paper* ~) government and bank-notes; (econ.) anything generally accepted in settlement of debts. 2. (with pl.) Particular coin. 3. (pl., archaic or legal) Sums of money. 4. ~ *of account*, monetary denomination used in reckoning, esp. one not currently issued as coin or note, as Engl. *guinea*, U.S. *mill*; ~ *bill*, a bill, originating in the House of Commons, involving expenditure or raising of money for public purposes; ~*-changer*, one whose business it is to change money at a fixed rate; ~*-grubber*, one bent on accumulating money; avaricious person; ~*-lender*, one who lends

MONEY

MONASTERY

1. Gatehouse. 2. Church. 3. Abbot's lodging. 4. Store-rooms. 5. Cloister. 6. Garth. 7. Chapter house. 8. Kitchen. 9. Refectory or frater. 10. Dorter or dormitory. 11. Infirmary. 12. Bakehouse. 13. Mill

money at interest; ~*-market*, sphere of operations of dealers in loans, stocks and shares; ~ *order*, order for payment of money, issued by a post-office; ~*-spinner*, pop. name of a small red garden spider supposed to bring good luck in money matters; *mo′neywort*, creeping herb (*Lysimachia nummularia*) with round leaves and single yellow flower; creeping-jenny. **mo′neyed** (-nĭd) *adj.* Wealthy.

[572]

mo'nger (mŭngg-) *n.* Dealer, trader (chiefly in combination, as *fishmonger, ironmonger,* and fig. *scandalmonger*).

mongo (mŭ'nggō) *n.* $\frac{1}{100}$ of a tugric.

Mŏ'ngol (-ngg-) *adj. & n.* 1. (Member, language) of a pastoral people of Mongolia. 2. (Person) with Mongoloid characteristics. 3. *m~*, person afflicted with mongolism.

Mŏngō'lia (-ngg-). Region in Asia including *Inner* and *Outer ~*: see MONGOLIAN.

Mŏngō'lian (-ngg-) *adj.* Of the Mongols or their language; Mongoloid; *Inner ~ Autonomous Region*, autonomous region of China (formerly Inner Mongolia); capital, Huhehot; *~ People's Republic*, republic N. of China (formerly Outer Mongolia); capital, Ulan Bator. *~ n.* Mongolian person.

mŏ'ngolism (-ngg-) *n.* Type of mental deficiency characterized by a Mongoloid appearance.

• **Mŏ'ngoloid** (-ngg-) *adj. & n.* 1. (Person) resembling the Mongolians, esp. (member) of the yellow-skinned division of mankind with high cheekbones, small nose, and broad face, found esp. in Mongolia and adjacent countries and including most of the Asian peoples. 2. = MONGOL, sense 3.

mŏ'ngōōse (-ngg-) *n.* (pl. *-gooses*). 1. Small carnivorous mammal of Old World tropics esp. of genus *Herpestes,* esp. the Indian mongoose (*H. griseus*). 2. Species of lemur found in Madagascar (*Lemur mongoz*).

mo'ngrel (mŭngg-) *adj. & n.* (Animal, esp. dog) of no definable breed or type, resulting from various crossings; hybrid. **mo'ngrelism** *n.* **mo'ngrelīze** *v.t.*

Mŏ'nica, St. (332–87). Mother of St. AUGUSTINE[1].

mŏ'nism *n.* (philos.) Any theory denying the duality of matter and mind, as dist. from DUALISM and PLURALISM. **mŏ'nist** *n.* **mŏni'stic** *adj.*

moni'tion *n.* Warning; official or legal (esp. ecclesiastical) notice (admonishing a person to refrain from a specified offence).

mŏ'nitor *n.* 1. One who admonishes (archaic). 2. (fem. *mo'nitrĕss*) Senior pupil in school with disciplinary functions. 3. One who is appointed to listen to and report on foreign broadcasts, telephone conversations, etc. 4. Receiving apparatus used in monitoring; detector for induced radioactivity, esp. in atomic plant workers. 5. Kind of Old World tropical lizard of genus *Varanus,* supposed to give warning of the vicinity of crocodiles (ill. LIZARD). 6. (hist.) Ironclad with low freeboard and revolving gun-turrets, for coast defence, so called from name of first vessel of this type, designed by Capt. Ericsson, in the Amer. Civil War, 1862. *~ v.t.*

Act as monitor of (broadcast etc.). **mŏnitŏ̄r'ial** *adj.* Admonishing; connected with, pertaining to, school monitors.

monk[1] (mŭ-) *n.* Member of community of men living apart from the world under religious vows and according to a rule; *monkshood,* aconite. **mo'nkdom** *n.* **mo'nkish** *adj.*

Monk[2], **Monck** (mŭ-), George (1608–70). English general and admiral; supporter and trusted adviser of Cromwell; instrumental in restoring the monarchy (1660); created first Duke of Albemarle.

mo'nkey (mŭ-) *n.* 1. One of a group of mammals allied to and resembling man and ranging from anthropoid apes to marmosets; any animal of order Primates except

MONKEYS
1. Marmoset. 2. Macaque

man, the tarsiers, and the lemurs, usu. restricted to the small, long-tailed members, as dist. from the large, short-tailed apes. 2. Mischievous, playful young person. 3. Machine hammer for pile-driving. 4. (slang) £500. 5. *his ~ is up,* he is angry or enraged; *~ bread,* fruit of the baobab tree; *~ engine,* engine which lifts the head of a pile-driver; *~-jacket,* sailor's short close-fitting jacket; *~-nut,* peanut; *~ puzzle,* S. Amer. coniferous tree, *Araucaria imbricata,* with broad prickly spines growing at intervals down the branches; *~-wrench,* wrench or spanner with adjustable jaw. *~ v.i.* Fool *about,* play mischievous tricks (*with*).

Monmouth (mŭ'nmŭth), James Scott, Duke of (1649–85). Illegitimate son of Charles II and Lucy Walters; collected an army in the W. of England and led it against James II; was defeated at Sedgemoor, captured, and beheaded.

Mo'nmouthshire (mŭnm*u*-).

Former English county on Welsh border N. of Severn estuary, since April 1974 the main part of Gwent, with smaller parts in Mid Glamorgan and South Glamorgan.

mŏno-, mon- *prefix.* Alone, sole, single.

mŏnobā'sic *adj.* (chem., of an acid) Having only one acidic hydrogen atom in its molecule.

mŏnocăr'pic, mŏnocăr'pous *adjs.* (bot.) Bearing fruit once and then dying.

mŏnochlamy̆'dĕous (-k-) *adj.* (bot.) Having only one floral envelope; having a single perianth.

mŏ'nochŏrd (-k-) *n.* Musical instrument with single string, used for mathematical determination of musical intervals.

mŏ'nochrōme (-k-) *n. & adj.* (Picture etc.) having only one colour, or executed in different shades of one colour. **mŏnochromă'tic** *adj.*

mŏ'nocle *n.* Single eye-glass.

mŏnocli'nic *adj.* (of a crystal) Having one of the axial intersections oblique (ill. CRYSTAL).

mŏnocŏty̆lē'don *n.* Plant having a single cotyledon or seed-leaf (ill. SEEDLING). **mŏnocŏty̆lē'donous** *adj.*

monō'cūlar *adj.* Of, adapted for, one eye, as *~ microscope.*

mŏ'nocȳte *n.* One of the several forms of leucocytes or white blood-cells (ill. BLOOD).

mŏ'nodrama (-rah-) *n.* Dramatic piece for performance by a single person.

mŏ'nody̆ *n.* 1. (Gk antiq.) Lyric ode sung by a single voice. 2. Dirge, elegy. **monŏ'dĭc** *adj.* **mŏ'nodist** *n.*

monoe'cious (-nē'shus) *adj.* (bot.) Having reproductive organs of both sexes on same plant (but, if a flowering plant, in different flowers; ill. FLOWER).

monŏ'gamy̆ *n.* Condition, rule, or custom of being married to only one person at a time, as dist. from *polygamy.* **monŏ'gamist** *n.* **monŏ'gamous** *adj.*

mŏ'nogrăm *n.* Character composed of two or more interwoven letters. **monogrammă'tic** *adj.*

mŏ'nogrăph (*or* -ahf) *n.* Treatise on single object or class of objects. **monŏ'grapher, monŏ'graphist** *ns.* **mŏnogră'phic** *adj.* **mŏnogră'phically** *adv.*

mŏ'nolith *n.* 1. Single block of stone as pillar or monument. 2. (building) Mass of concrete, masonry, etc., forming a solid element in a structure. 3. Political or social structure presenting an indivisible or unbroken unity. **mŏnoli'thic** *adj.* Of, like, a monolith; unified and homogeneous; not exhibiting deviation or minority interests.

mŏ'nolŏgue (-g) *n.* Soliloquy; dramatic composition for a single performer. **mŏnolŏ'gical** *adj.* **monŏ'logist** *n.* **monŏ'logīze** *v.i.*

[573]

mŏnomā'nĭa n. Form of insanity, obsession of the mind by a single idea or interest. **mŏnomā'nĭăc** n.

mŏ'nomărk n. One of a system of registered marks (letters and figures) identifying articles, goods, addresses, etc.

mŏ'nomêr n. (chem.) 1. One of the units forming a polymer molecule (see POLYMER). 2. Compound which can undergo polymerization.

mŏnomĕ'tallism n. Use of standard currency based on one metal.

monŏ'mĭal adj. & n. (alg.) (Expression) consisting of a single term.

mŏnophŏ'nĭc adj. (of recording) Sounding as from a single source (opp. STEREOPHONIC).

mŏ'nophthŏng n. Single vowel sound, as dist. from *diphthong*.

mŏ'nophthŏngīze (-ngg-) v.t. Reduce (diphthong) to a monophthong.

Monŏ'physite n. One who holds, contrary to the CHALCEDONIAN definition, that there is only one nature, part divine and part human, in the person of Christ, the human element being totally subordinate to the divine.

mŏ'noplāne n. Aeroplane with one plane, as distinct from *biplane*.

monŏ'polist n. Holder or supporter of monopoly.

monŏ'polīze v.t. Secure monopoly of. **monŏpolĭzā'tion** n.

monŏ'poly n. Exclusive possession or control; exclusive trading privilege.

mŏ'norail n. Railway in which the track consists of a single rail.

mŏnosȳ'llable n. Word of one syllable. **mŏnosÿllă'bĭc** adj.

mŏ'nothēism n. Doctrine that there is only one God. **mŏ'nothēist** n. **mŏnothēi'stic** adj.

mŏ'notōne n. Sound continuing or repeated on one note, or without change of tone. **monotŏ'nic** adj. 1. (mus.) In monotone. 2. (math., of a sequence) Such that all members of it either do not increase or do not decrease.

monŏ'tonous adj. Having no variation in tone or cadence; lacking in variety, always the same. **monŏ'tonously** adv. **monŏ'tonousnĕss, monŏ'tony** ns.

mŏ'notrēme n. (zool.) Mammal of sub-class Monotremata, primitive egg-laying forms of Australasia including duck-billed platypus and spiny ant-eaters.

mŏ'notȳpe n. 1. Print taken from a freshly painted card, plate, or block. 2. M~, trade-name of printing apparatus which casts and sets up type in single letters by means of a perforated roll which has been previously produced on another part of the apparatus.

mŏnovā'lent adj. (chem.) Having a VALENCY of 1. **mŏnovă'lence, mŏnovā'lency** ns.

mŏnŏ'xīde n. (chem.) Oxide with one oxygen atom in the molecule.

Monroe (munrō'), James (1758–1831). 5th president of U.S., 1817–25; formulator (1823) of the ~ *Doctrine* that interference by any European State in the Spanish-American republics would be regarded as an act unfriendly to the U.S., and that the American continents were no longer open to European colonial settlement.

Mŏns (-z). Town in Hainaut, Belgium, near the French frontier, where the British Expeditionary Force fought its first battle (1914) in the war of 1914–18.

Mŏnseigneur (-sānyêr) n. Title or form of address to French dignitaries, esp. princes, cardinals, and bishops (abbrev. Mgr). [Fr.]

Monsieur (mosyêr) n. (pl. *Messieurs*, pr. māsyêr). Title of (corresp. to *Mr.*) or form of address to (*Sir*) Frenchman; (hist.) second son or younger brother of king of France.

Mŏnsi'gnor (-sēnyôr) n. (pl. -s or -i). (R.C. Ch.) Ecclesiastical title attached to office or distinction usu. bestowed by pope; in some countries (e.g. France) = MONSEIGNEUR. [It.]

mŏnsōō'n n. Seasonal wind prevailing in southern Asia, from south-west (*wet* ~) in summer and north-east (*dry* ~) in winter; rainy season accompanying SW. monsoon. [prob. f. Arab. *mausim*, lit. season]

mŏ'nster n. 1. Imaginary animal compounded of elements from various creatures. 2. Person or thing of portentous appearance or size. 3. Inhumanly cruel or wicked person. 4. (path.) Grossly malformed product of human conception.

mŏ'nstrance n. (R.C. Ch.) Receptacle in which the consecrated Host is exposed for veneration, consisting usu. of a glass or crystal case set in a gold or silver frame (ill. CIBORIUM).

mŏnstrŏ'sity n. Monstrousness; misshapen or outrageous thing.

mŏ'nstrous adj. Like a monster; huge; outrageous. **mŏ'nstrously** adv. **mŏ'nstrousnĕss** n.

Mont. abbrev. Montana; Montgomeryshire.

mŏ'ntage (-ahzh) n. 1. (cinemat.) Selection, cutting, and arrangement of shots; presentation of a series of shots as a connected sequence. 2. (Picture etc. produced by) juxtaposition of (parts of) photographs etc.

Mŏnta'gna (-ahnya), Bartolomeo (d. 1523). Italian painter.

Mŏ'ntagū, Lady Mary Wortley (1689–1762). English letter-writer and traveller.

Mŏntaigne (-ān), Michel Eyquem de (1533–92). French writer; author of 'Essais' which reveal a sagacious and tolerant philosophy of life, stressing the fallibility of the human reason and the relativity of human science.

Mŏntă'na. State of U.S., on the Canadian border E. of the Rocky Mountains; admitted to the Union in 1889; capital, Helena.

mŏ'ntāne adj. Of, inhabiting, mountainous country.

Mŏntā'nus (2nd c.). Founder, in Phrygia, of Montanism. **Mŏ'ntanism** n. Heretical Christian movement which reacted against the growing secularism of the Church, desired a stricter adhesion to the principles of primitive Christianity, and prepared for the earthly kingdom of Christ. **Mŏ'ntanist** n.

Mont Blanc (mawṅ blahṅ). Mountain in France on Italian border; highest in Europe (4810 m, 15,782 ft).

montbretia (monbrē'sha) n. English name of a commonly cultivated and extensively naturalized hybrid plant of two species of the genus *Crocosmia*. [A. F. E. Coquebert de *Montbret* (1780–1801), French botanist]

Montcalm (mŏnkahm), Louis-Joseph de Montcalm-Gozon, Marquis de (1712–59). French soldier; defended Quebec against Wolfe and was mortally wounded in the battle which followed the scaling of the Heights of Abraham.

mŏ'ntè n. Spanish-American game of chance, played with 45 cards.

Mŏ'ntè Cărʹlō. One of the three communes of Monaco; famous as a gambling resort.

Mŏ'ntè Cassi'nō (-sē-). Hill midway between Rome and Naples, site of the principal monastery of the Benedictine Order, founded by St. Benedict c 529. The monastery, previously demolished and rebuilt several times, was almost totally destroyed in a battle between German and Allied forces in 1944, but has since been restored.

Mŏntĕnĕ'grō. Former monarchy of SE. Europe, on the Adriatic; since 1919 a part of Yugoslavia. **Mŏntĕnĕ'grĭn** adj. & n.

Mŏntespan (-ăṅ), Françoise-Athénaïs de Pardaillan, Marquise de (1641–1707). Mistress of Louis XIV, to whom she bore seven children.

Montesquieu (mawṅteskyêr), Charles Louis de Secondat de (1689–1755). French political philosopher; author of 'L'Esprit des Lois' (1748), in which he analysed the types of political constitution and denounced the abuses of the French monarchy.

Mŏntĕssŏr'ĭ, Maria (1870–1952). Italian educationalist; originator of a system of training small children by the use of apparatus teaching manual dexterity, the matching of colours or shapes, etc., under less rigid discipline than was formerly common.

Mŏntèver'dĭ (-vār-), Claudio (1567–1643). Italian composer of instrumental music, madrigals, and operas.

Mŏntĕzū′ma II (1466–1520). Aztec emperor of Mexico at the time of the Spanish conquest; was seized and held as a hostage by Cortez, and mortally wounded when his people attempted to rescue him.

Mŏ′ntfort, Simon de (1208?–65). Norman-English earl of Leicester; married Eleanor, sister of Henry III of England; led the barons in a revolt against the king, 1263, and captured him at Lewes, 1264; summoned, 1265, a parliament which included, besides the barons, knights, and ecclesiastics, two citizens from every borough in England.

Montgolfier (mawṅgŏlfyā), Joseph Michel (1740–1810), and Jacques Etienne (1745–99), brothers. French inventors of a balloon raised by heated air.

Montgo′mery (-gŭ-), Bernard Law, Viscount Montgomery of Alamein (1887–1976). British field marshal; commander of 8th Army from 1943 during the N. African campaign; C.-in-C. of British group of armies in France and Germany, 1944–6.

Montgo′meryshire (-gŭ-). Former Welsh inland county on the English border, since April 1974 the N. part of Powys.

month (mŭ-) n. Period in which moon makes a complete revolution (*lunar* ~); one of 12 portions into which conventional year is divided (*calendar* ~); (loosely) period of 4 weeks.

mo′nthly (mŭ-) adj. Done, recurring, payable, etc., once a month; ~ *rose*, semi-single pink China rose, which flowers for several months. ~ adv. Once a month; every month. ~ n. Magazine etc. published each month; (pl.) menses.

Montmartre (mawṅ-, -tr) District in the N. of Paris; during the 19th c. the artistic quarter and the site of many famous cafés and cabarets.

Montrachet (mawṅrăshā) n. White wine produced in Montrachet in the Côte d'Or district of France.

Mŏntrèa′l (-awl). Canadian city and port on the St. Lawrence River.

Montrō′se (-z), James Graham, Marquis of (1612–50). Scottish soldier; played a large part in Scottish history in the reign of Charles I; he was first a Covenanter but fought for Charles in Scotland during the Civil War.

Mont St. Michel (mawṅ săṅ mĕshĕl). Islet off the coast of Normandy, a rocky peak crowned by a medieval Benedictine abbey-fortress.

mŏ′nŭment n. Anything that by its survival commemorates person, action, or event, esp. erection intended to do this; work of enduring value; *the M*~, a Doric column 202 ft high in the City of London, designed by Robert Hooke and Sir Christopher Wren (1671–7) to commemorate the Great Fire of 1666, which broke out in Pudding Lane near by.

mŏnūmĕ′ntal adj. Like, of, serving as, a monument; colossal, stupendous; ~ *mason*, tombstone-maker. **mŏnūmĕ′ntallў** adv. **mŏnūmĕntă′litў** n.

mŏnūmĕ′ntalize v.t. Record, commemorate, as by monument.

moo v.i. & n. (Make) lowing sound.

mooch v.i. (slang) Loaf *about*; slouch *along*.

mood[1] n. Frame of mind or state of feelings. **moo′dў** adj. Subject to changes of mood; depressed, sullen. **moo′dilў** adv. **moo′dinėss** n.

mood[2] n. 1. (gram.) Group of forms in conjugation of verb serving to indicate function in which it is used, as INDICATIVE, IMPERATIVE, SUBJUNCTIVE ~. 2. (logic) Any of the classes into which each of the figures of a valid categorical syllogism is divided.

Moo′dў and Să′nkey. Dwight Lyman Moody (1837–99) and Ira David Sankey (1840–1908), American religious revivalists and hymn-writers.

moon n. 1. Earth's satellite, a secondary planet reflecting light from sun to earth during night, and revolving round the earth in one lunar month; first manned landing on moon was made on 21 July 1969 by U.S. astronauts Edwin Aldrin (1930–) and Neil Armstrong (1930–). 2. Aspect of moon at any one time as *full* ~, *new* ~, etc. 3. Any planetary satellite. 4. (poet.) Month. 5. *moo′ncalf*, born fool; ~*-daisy*, *moo′n-flower*, ox-eye daisy; *moo′nlight*, light of moon (often attrib.); *moonlight flitting*, removal of household goods by night to avoid paying rent; *moo′nlighting*, (U.S.) working at a second job after one's regular working hours; *moo′nlit*, lit up by moon; *moo′nshine*, moonlight; (fig.) visionary talk or ideas; illicitly distilled or smuggled spirits, esp. whisky; hence, *moo′nshiner*, (U.S.) illicit distiller, smuggler of spirits; *moo′nstone*, variety of felspar having a pearly lustre, used as a gem; *moo′nstruck* (adj.) lunatic, distracted or dazed, a condition formerly supposed to be due to the moon's influence. **moo′nў** adj. Of, like, the moon; listless, stupidly dreamy. **moon** v.i. Go *about* dreamily or listlessly.

moor[1] n. Tract of unenclosed, often heather-covered, waste land, or of similar land preserved for shooting (also *moor′land*); ~*-cock*, male red grouse; *moor′hen*, waterhen. **moor′ish**, **moor′ў** adjs.

moor[2] v.t. Attach (boat etc.) by rope to shore or something fixed. **moor′age** n. Place, charge, for mooring. **moor′ings** (-z) n.pl. Place where vessel can be moored.

Moor[3] n. One of a Muslim people of mixed Berber and Arab race, inhabiting NW. Africa, who in the 8th c. conquered Spain (see also MOROCCO[1]). **Moor′ish** adj.

Moore[1], Francis (1656–1715). Astrologer and quack physician; advertised his pills by publishing an almanac forecasting weather etc., 1699; *Old* ~*'s Almanac*, any of various imitations of this.

Moore[2], George (1852–1933). Irish novelist; author of 'Esther Waters', 'The Brook Kerith', 'Héloïse and Abelard', etc.

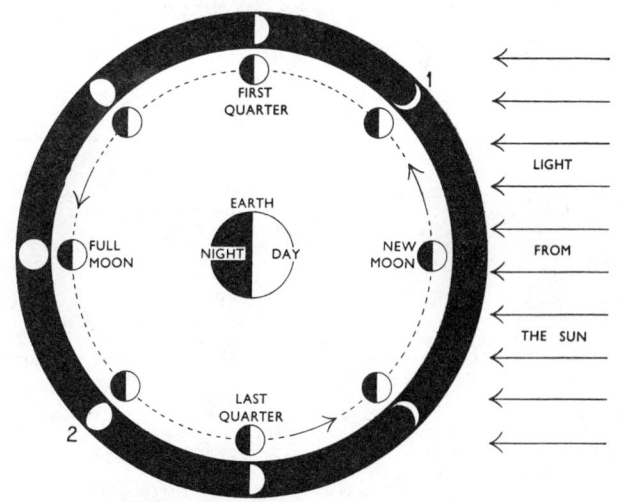

PHASES OF THE MOON
The diagram shows how the light from the sun falls on the moon, giving the appearance as in the black ring. 1. Crescent. 2. Gibbous

Moore³, Henry (1898–). English sculptor.
Moore⁴, Sir John (1761–1809). English soldier; C.-in-C. in the Peninsular War, 1808; was mortally wounded at Coruña during the retreat, and buried there in 1809.
moose n. (pl. *moose*). See ELK, 1.
moot n. (hist.) (Legislative or judicial) meeting. ~ *adj*. That can be argued, debatable. ~ *v.t*. Raise (question etc.) for discussion.
mop n. Bundle of yarn etc. fixed to stick for use in cleaning, polishing, etc.; *Mrs. M~*, joc. name for charwoman. ~ *v.t*. Clean or wipe with or as with mop; wipe tears, sweat, etc., from (brow etc.); ~ *up*, wipe up (as) with mop; (slang) absorb (profits etc.), dispatch, finish off, make an end of; (mil.) complete occupation of (place) by capturing or killing remaining enemy troops.
mope v.i. Be dull, dejected, and spiritless. ~ *n*. Person who mopes; (chiefly pl.) gloomy state of mind.
mo'pish adj. **mo'pishness** n.
mo'ped n. Motorized bicycle.
moquě'tte (-k-) n. Fabric with velvety pile, made of wool on basis of cotton or jute, used in upholstery etc.
mor n. Humus formed under acid conditions (opp. MULL⁴).
morai'ne n. Debris of sand, clay, and boulders deposited by melting glacier (ill. MOUNTAIN).
mo'ral adj. Concerned with character or disposition, or with the distinction between right and wrong; morally good, virtuous, righteous; ~ *certainty*, probability so great as to admit of no reasonable doubt; ~ *courage*, courage to encounter odium, contempt, etc., rather than abandon right course; ~ *philosophy*, ethics; *M~ Re-Armament*, (abbrev. M.R.A.) name of the ideological campaign launched by Dr Buchman in 1938 as an extension of the OXFORD Group; ~ *support*, psychological support, encouragement; ~ *victory*, defeat, indecisive result, that eventually produces the moral effects of victory. **mo'rally** adv.
mo'ral n. Moral teaching (of fable, story, etc.); (pl.) habits or conduct from point of view of morality.
mora'le (-ahl) n. Mental state or condition, esp. (of troops) as regards discipline and confidence.
mo'ralism n. Natural system of morality; principles of conduct based on distinction between right and wrong; not on religion.
mo'ralist n. One who practises or teaches morality; adherent of moralism. **morali'stic** adj.
morā'lity n. 1. Moral principles or rules; moral conduct. 2. Kind of drama (popular in 16th c.) inculcating moral or spiritual lesson.
mo'ralīze v. Indulge in moral reflection; interpret morally or symbolically. **moralīzā'tion** n.

morā'ss n. Wet swampy tract, bog.
morator'ium n. Legal authorization to debtor to postpone payment.
Morā'via. Province of Czechoslovakia. **Morāv'ian** adj. & n. 1. (Native, inhabitant) of Moravia. 2. (One) of a Hussite Protestant sect, the 'Unity of Moravian brethren' founded in Saxony in the early 18th c. by emigrants from Moravia, who obtained many adherents in England and the American colonies.
Morayshire (mǔ'rĭ-). Former county of NE. Scotland S. of Moray Firth, since May 1975 part of the region of Grampian.
mor'bid adj. (of mind, ideas, etc.) Unwholesome, sickly; (med.) of the nature, or indicative, of disease. **mor'bidly** adv. **mor'-bidness** n. **morbi'dity** n. Morbidness; prevalence of disease (in a district).
morbi'fic adj. Causing disease, pathogenic.
mor'dant adj. (of sarcasm etc.) Caustic, biting; pungent, smarting; (of acids) corrosive. ~ *n*. Substance used for fixing textile dyes; acid used in etching. **mor-dācious** (-shus) adj. **mor-dă'city**, **mor'dancỹ** ns.
mor'dent n. (mus.) Grace consisting of two timeless notes rapidly inserted before principal note, in *upper* ~, consisting of principal note, note above, and back to principal note, in *lower* ~, of principal note, note below, and back to principal note.
more¹ adj. & n. Greater number, quantity, or degree (of). ~ *adv*. To a greater extent, in a greater degree, additionally.
More², Henry (1614–87). English Platonist and poet.
More³, Sir Thomas (1478–1535). English statesman, author of 'Utopia' (1516), a description, in Latin, of an imaginary perfect State; he succeeded Wolsey as Lord Chancellor, 1529, but resigned in 1532, refusing to take any oath that would impugn the pope's authority or assume the justice of Henry VIII's divorce from Catherine of Aragon; he was therefore indicted of high treason, found guilty, and beheaded; canonized (as St. Thomas ~), 1935.
Morē'a. Peloponnese.
moree'n n. Woollen or woollen and cotton fabric with a rib or twill in it, used esp. for curtains.
more'llo n. Dark-coloured bitter cherry.
moreo'ver (mōrō-) adv. In addition.
More'sque (-k) adj. Moorish in style or design.
Mor'gan, John Pierpont (1837–1913). American banker who amassed a large fortune.
morganā'tic adj. (of a marriage) Between man of exalted rank and woman of lower rank in which it is provided that the wife and her children shall not share the rank or inherit the possessions of the husband. ·[OHG *morgangeba* gift from husband to wife the morning after consummation of marriage]
Mor'gan le Fay. 'Morgan the Fairy', a magician, sister of King Arthur; see also FATA MORGANA.
morgue (-g) n. Building (esp. one formerly in Paris) in which bodies of persons found dead are exposed for identification; (journalism) repository of material for obituary notices.
mo'ribund adj. In a dying state.
Mori'scō n. Descendant of the Moors in Spain.
Mor'land, George (1763–1804). English painter of animals, genre, and landscape.
Mor'ley, John, first viscount Morley of Blackburn (1838–1923). English liberal politician and author, famous esp. for his 'Life of Gladstone' (1903).
Mor'mon n. Member of the 'Church of Jesus Christ of Latter-day Saints', founded in New York State 1830, by Joseph Smith of Vermont; he claimed that a parallel volume to the Bible, the 'Book of Mormon', had been revealed to him, and that its author, the prophet Mormon, had been one of a race which had colonized America from Palestine in ancient times; the sect grew rapidly but met with hostility esp. for advocating polygamy (which they did until 1890); eventually, led by Brigham YOUNG, they migrated to Utah and there founded Salt Lake City in 1847. **Mor'monism** n.
morn n. (poet.) Morning; dawn.
mor'ning n. Early part of daytime, ending at noon or at time of midday meal; *good* ~, form of greeting; ~ *coat*, man's tail-coat with front sloped away; ~ *dress*, men's formal daytime wear; ~-*glory*, Amer. plant of genus *Ipomoea*, with showy flowers; *M~ Prayer*, morning service in Church of England; ~-*room*, sitting-room, other than dining- or drawing-room; ~ *sickness*, nausea commonly experienced in morning in early months of pregnancy; ~ *star*, Venus (or other planet or bright star) seen to the east before sunrise; ~-*watch*, (naut.) watch at sea from 4 a.m. to 8 a.m.
Moro'ccō¹. Country of NW. Africa, bounded on N. and W. by the Mediterranean Sea and Atlantic Ocean and on S. and E. by Algeria; inhabited by people descended from Berbers, Arabs, and Moors; formerly a French Protectorate, with a Spanish sphere of influence; since 1956 an independent kingdom; capital, Rabat; summer capital, Tangier. **Moro'ccan** adj. & n.
moro'ccō² n. Fine flexible leather made orig. in Morocco, now also elsewhere, from goatskins tanned with sumac; imitation

[576]

of this made from calf- or sheepskins, grained to resemble true morocco; *Levant* ~, high-grade, large-grained morocco, used for book-binding.

moroccoë'tte *n.* Textile material for bookbinding, imitating morocco.

mŏr'on *n.* Adult whose mental development corresponds to that of a normal average child between the ages of 8 and 12; (colloq.) very stupid person. **mŏrŏ'nic** *adj.*

morōse' *adj.* Sour-tempered, sullen, and unsocial. **morō'sely** *adv.* **morō'seness** *n.*

mŏr'phême *n.* (philol.) Morphological element considered in respect of its functional relations to a linguistic system.

Mŏr'pheus (-fūs). (Rom. myth.) Son of Somnus, god of sleep, and himself the god of dreams.

mŏr'phia *n.* Morphine.

mŏr'phine (-ēn) *n.* Alkaloid narcotic principle of opium, used to alleviate pain. **mŏr'phinism** *n.* Effect of morphine; excessive use of morphine.

mŏrphogĕ'nĕsis *n.* (biol.) Development of form in organisms.

mŏrphŏ'logy *n.* 1. Study of the form of animals and plants. 2. Study of the form of words, branch of philology dealing with inflexion and word-formation. 3. *social* ~, study of the structure of society, i.e. of social groups and institutions. **mŏrpholŏ'gical** *adj.* **mŏrpholŏ'gically** *adv.* **mŏrphŏ'logist** *n.*

Mŏ'rris, William (1834–96). English designer, printer, poet, and prose writer; advocated the revival of medieval hand-craftsmanship and inspired the Arts and Crafts Movement; founded, with Burne-Jones and other Pre-Raphaelites, a firm of decorators (1861), also the Kelmscott Press (1890); was active as a socialist.

mŏ'rris dance (dah-). English traditional dance in fancy costume, usu. representing characters from Robin Hood legend. [*morys*, var. of MOORISH]

mŏ'rrow (-rō) *n.* (literary) Next day.

mŏrse¹ *n.* = WALRUS.

mŏrse² *n.* Fastening or clasp (often jewelled) of a cope (ill. VESTMENT).

Mŏrse³, Samuel Finley Breese (1791–1872). American inventor of recording telegraph, deviser of the ~ *code*, a telegraphic alphabet in which letters are represented by combinations of short and long electrical contacts, sounds, flashes, etc. ('dots and dashes').

mŏr'sel *n.* Mouthful; small piece, fragment.

mŏrt *n.* Note sounded on horn announcing killing of deer.

mŏr'tal *adj.* Subject to or causing death, fatal; (of enemy) implacable; (of sin) deadly, entailing spiritual death (opp. VENIAL); accompanying death, as ~ *agony*; (slang) long and tedious. **mŏr'tally** *adv.* **mŏr'tal** *n.* One who is subject to death; (facet.) person.

mŏrtă'lĭty *n.* Mortal nature; loss of life on large scale; death-rate.

mŏr'tar *n.* 1. Hard vessel in which ingredients are pounded with a pestle. 2. Short gun with large bore for throwing shells at high angles. 3. Mixture of lime, sand, and water used to make joints between stones and bricks in building; ~*-board*, board for holding builders' mortar; cap with stiff flat square top, resembling this, worn as part of academic dress. ~ *v.t.* Bind, join (bricks or stones) together with mortar; fire upon with mortars.

mŏr'tgage (mŏrg-) *n.* Conveyance of property as security for money-debt, with provision for reconveyance on repayment of the sum secured; deed effecting this. ~ *v.t.* Make over by mortgage; pledge in advance. **mŏrgagee'** (-jē) *n.* Holder of mortgage. **mortgagor'** (-jŏr) *n.* Person who pledges property etc. in mortgage. [OF *mort gage* dead pledge]

mortice: see MORTISE.

mŏrti'cian (-shan) *n.* (U.S.) Undertaker.

mŏr'tify *v.* 1. Chasten (the body, passions, etc.) by self-denial. 2. Cause (person) to feel humiliated, wound (feelings). 3. (of flesh) Become gangrenous. **mŏrtifĭcā'tion** *n.*

mŏr'tise, mŏr'tice *n.* Hole or cavity into which end of some other part of framework or structure is fitted (ill. JOINT¹); ~ *lock*, lock housed within a mortise (ill. LOCK²). ~ *v.t.* Cut mortise in, fasten with mortise.

mŏr'tmain *n.* Condition of lands etc. held inalienably by corporation; *in* ~, (fig.) inalienable. [OF f. med. L *mortua manus* dead hand]

Mŏr'ton, John (1420?–1500). English prelate and statesman; lord chancellor 1487; ~'s *fork*, argument he used in demanding gifts for the royal treasury: that if a man lived handsomely he was obviously rich, and if simply, that economy must have made him so.

mŏr'tūary *adj.* Of or for burial or death. ~ *n.* Place for temporary reception of corpses.

mosā'ic¹ (-z-) *n.* (Production of) picture or pattern of small cubes of coloured stone, glass, etc., cemented together (also fig. of any diversified whole); (also ~ *disease*) plant virus disease causing mottled patches on leaves. ~ *adj.* Of or like such work. ~ *v.t.* Decorate with mosaics; combine (as) into mosaic. **mosā'icist** *n.* [med. L *mosaicus*, f. Gk *mousaikos* of the Muses]

Mosā'ic² (-z-) *adj.* Of MOSES; ~ *law*, ancient Hebrew law contained in the Pentateuch.

mŏschatĕ'l (-sk-) *n.* Small plant (*Adoxa moschatellina*), having pale-green flowers with a musky smell.

Mŏ'scovite *adj. & n.* = MUSCOVITE.

Mŏ'scow (-kō). (Russ. *Moskva*) Capital city of U.S.S.R. and R.S.F.S.R.; capital of Russia from 1240 to 1703 (when the capital was transferred to St. Petersburg) and from 1918.

Mŏ'seley (-zlĭ), Henry Gwyn-Jeffreys (1887–1915). English physical chemist; first produced experimental evidence (from X-ray spectra) for the allocation of atomic numbers to elements; ~ *number*, (formerly) atomic number.

Mosĕ'lle (-z-) *n.* Dry white wine produced in valley of river Moselle, which rises in Vosges Mountains and flows into Rhine at Coblenz.

Mō'ses (-ziz). Hebrew patriarch, the great law-giver of the Jews; led them from Egypt after the captivity there; was inspired by God on Mount Sinai to write down the Ten Commandments on tablets of stone (Exod. 20); died before the Promised Land was reached (Joshua 1: 34).

Mŏ'slem (*or* -z-) *adj. & n.* Var. of MUSLIM.

mŏsque (-sk) *n.* Muslim place of worship. [Fr. *mosquée*, f. Arab. *masjid*]

mŏsquī'tō (-kē-) *n.* Two-winged fly of the family Culicidae, gnat; (esp.) species of *Culex* and *Anopheles*, females of which have a long blood-sucking proboscis (*illustration, p. 578*); ~*-curtain,-net*, fine-meshed net for keeping mosquitoes from room, bed, etc.; ~ *craft*, collective name for small naval vessels, as motor torpedo-boats etc.

mŏss *n.* Peat-bog; small herbaceous cryptogamous plant growing in bogs, or in crowded masses

A ·—
B —···
C —·—·
D —··
E ·
F ··—·
G ——·
H ····
I ··
J ·———
K —·—
L ·—··
M ——
N —·
O ———
P ·——·
Q ——·—
R ·—·
S ···
T —
U ··—
V ···—
W ·——
X —··—
Y —·——
Z ——··
1 ·————
2 ··———
3 ···——
4 ····—
5 ·····
6 —····
7 ——···
8 ———··
9 ————·
0 —————

MORSE CODE

MOST

on ground, wood, stone, etc.; ~ *rose*, cabbage-rose (*Rosa centifolia*), with moss-like growth on calyx and stalk; ~-*trooper*, 17th-c. freebooter on Scottish border. **mŏ′ssў** *adj.* Of or like moss; overgrown with moss. **mŏ′ssĭnĕss** *n.*

MOSS

A. *POLYTRICHUM* FEMALE (LEFT) AND MALE. B. SPHAGNUM
1. Capsule or theca

mōst *adj. & n.* Greatest number, quantity, or degree (of). ~ *adv.* In a great or the greatest degree. **mō′stly** *adv.* For the most part.
Mōsu′l (-ōōl). Vilayet of Mesopotamia (Iraq), roughly corresponding to ancient Assyria; town on right bank of Tigris, opposite site of Nineveh.
mot (mō) *n.* (pl. *mots* pr. mōz). Witty saying; ~ *juste* (pr. zhōōst), expression that conveys a desired shade of meaning with more precision than any other. [Fr.]
mōte[1] *n.* Particle of dust, esp. speck seen floating in sunbeam.
mote[2]: see MOTTE.
mōtĕ′l (*or* mō′-) *n.* Roadside hotel or group of separate small buildings for accommodation of motorists. [blend of *motor*+*hotel*]
mōtĕ′t *n.* (mus.) Anthem in R.C. or Lutheran Church, generally unaccompanied; non-ecclesiastical work on similar lines. [Fr., dim. of *mot* word]
mŏth *n.* Popular name for the majority of insects belonging to the order Lepidoptera, those not *butterflies*, distinguished from them

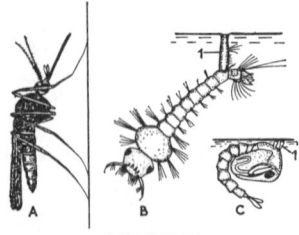

MOSQUITO
A. ADULT FEMALE. B. LARVA. C. PUPA
1. Spiracles at surface of water

by not having clubbed antennae and by being mostly nocturnal in habit; clothes-moth or any other insect whose larvae feed on fabrics;

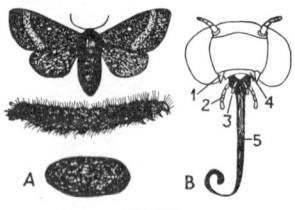

MOTH
A. ADULT, CATERPILLAR, AND COCOON. B. HEAD
1. Mandible. 2. Labial palp. 3. Maxillary palp. 4. Labrum. 5. Proboscis

(fig.) person hovering round temptation, as a moth flutters about light; ~-*ball*, small ball of naphthalene etc. used to keep moths away from fabrics etc.; (also) airtight plastic cover sprayed on and enclosing working parts of gun-mountings, machinery, etc. of ship; ~-*eaten*, injured by moths; (fig.) antiquated, time-worn. **mŏ′thy** *adj.* Infested by moths.
mo′ther (mŭdh-) *n.* Female parent (also transf.); head of female religious community (often ~ *superior*); title of or form of address to elderly woman (vulg.); incubator, artificial apparatus for rearing chickens; ~ *country*, country in relation to its colonies; native land; *mo′thercraft*, skill in rearing children; ~ *earth*, earth as mother of its inhabitants (facet.) the ground; ~ *goddess*, (esp.) goddess representing the fertility of nature; *M*~ *Hubbard*, person in nursery rhyme; full loose dress, esp. that imposed by missionaries on native women in the Pacific; ~-*in-law*, wife's or husband's mother; ~-*of-all*, part of spinning-wheel supporting the maidens (ill. SPINNING); ~-*of-pearl*, pearly iridescent lining of certain shells, as of oysters, mussels, etc., used in making buttons etc.; ~ *of vinegar*, mucilaginous substance produced in vinegar during fermentation by bacteria (usually of the Acetobacter family); *Mother's Day*, (orig. U.S.) day for honouring one's mother (in England = Mothering Sunday (see below); in U.S. a Sunday in May); ~ *ship*, ship acting as base for submarines, aircraft, etc.; ~ *tongue*, one's native language; ~ *wit*, native wit, common sense. **mo′therhood** *n.* **mo′therlĕss** *adj.* **mo′ther** *v.* Take care of as a mother; *mo′thering*, (esp.) custom of visiting parents and giving or receiving presents on mid-Lent Sunday (*Mothering Sunday*).
mo′therly (mŭdh-) *adj.* Befitting or resembling a mother. **mo′therlĭness** *n.*

MOUJIK, MUZHIK

mōti′f (-ēf) *n.* Distinctive feature or dominant idea of a design or composition; (mus.) FIGURE.
mō′tile *adj.* (zool., bot.). Capable of motion.
mō′tion *n.* 1. Moving, movement; gait; gesture. 2. Proposition formally made in deliberative assembly; (law) application to judge or court for some rule or order of court. 3. Evacuation of bowels. 4. ~ *picture*, (esp. U.S.) moving picture (see MOVE). **mō′tionlĕss** *adj.* **mō′tion** *v.* Make motion to direct or guide (person).
mō′tĭvāte *v.t.* Supply a motive to, be the motive of. **mōtĭvā′tion** *n.*
mō′tĭve *adj.* Tending to initiate motion; ~ *power*, esp. form of mechanical energy used to drive machinery. ~ *n.* 1. That which induces a person to act, e.g. desire, fear, circumstance. 2. = MOTIF. ~ *v.t.* Motivate.
mō′tley[1] *adj.* Parti-coloured; heterogeneous. ~ *n.* Jester's motley garb.
Mŏ′tley,[2] John Lothrop (1814–77). Amer. historian of the Netherlands.
mō′tor *n.* Motive agent or force; motor muscle or nerve; apparatus or engine supplying motive power for vehicle or machinery, esp. internal combustion engine; motor-car. ~ *adj.* 1. Giving, imparting, or producing motion; ~ *area*, that part of frontal lobe of mammal's brain from which muscular activity of opposite side of body is most easily evoked; ~ *nerve*, any nerve consisting of fibres which carry impulses from spinal cord or brain to induce contractions of muscle. 2. Driven by motor, as ~-*bike* (colloq.), -*boat*, -*cycle*; ~-*car*, motor-driven, usu. four-wheeled passenger road vehicle (*illustration, p. 552*). 3. Of, for, involving, motor vehicles; *mo′torcade*, (U.S.) procession of motor-cars; *mo′torway*, arterial road for fast-moving motor-traffic. ~ *v.* Go, convey, by motor-car. **mō′torist** *n.* Driver of motor-car.
mō′torize *v.t.* Supply or equip with motor transport; furnish with motor engine. **mōtorĭzā′tion** *n.*
mŏtte, mōte *n.* Mound, hillock, as site of castle, camp, etc. (ill. CASTLE).
mŏ′ttle *v.t.* Mark or cover with spots or blotches.
mŏ′ttō *n.* Inscription (esp. heraldic) or saying expressing appropriate sentiment or aspiration; maxim adopted as rule of conduct; short quotation prefixed to book or chapter, suggestive of the contents; riddle or joke etc. on slip of paper inside cracker.
mou′fflon (mōō-) *n.* Wild sheep of S. Europe, esp. *Ovis musimon*, native of Corsica.
moujik, muzhik (mōō′zhĭk) *n.* Russian peasant.

[578]

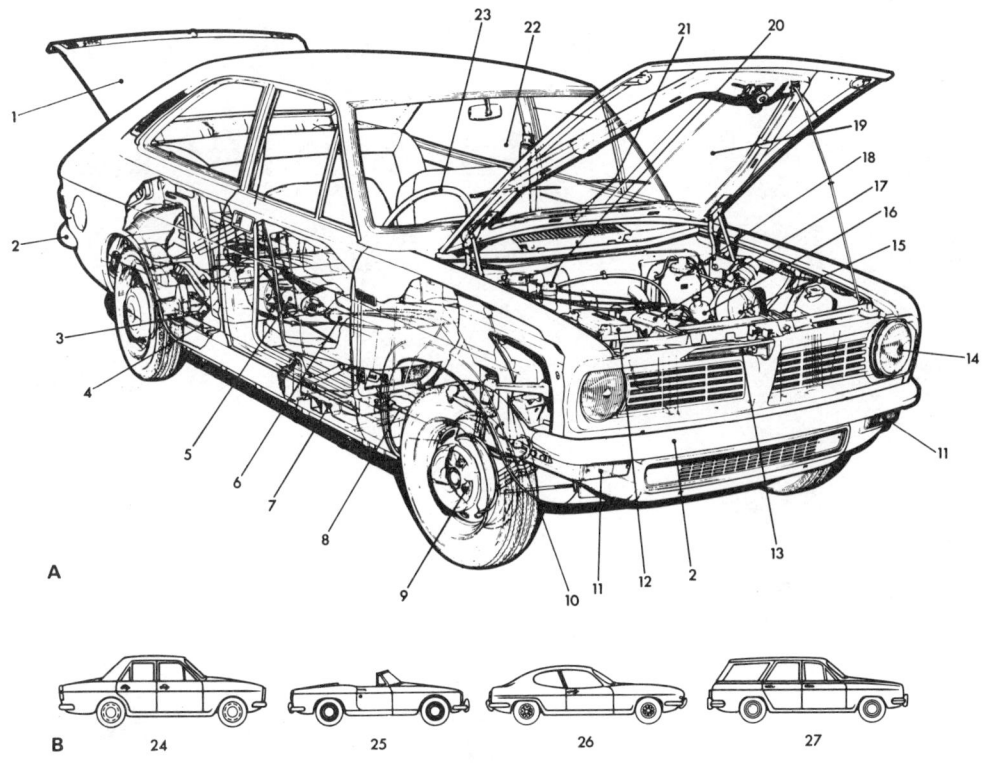

A. 1. Boot lid. 2. Bumper. 3. Rear shock-absorber. 4. Rear spring. 5. Differential. 6. Propeller shaft. 7. Chassis. 8. Torsion bar. 9. Wheel nut. 10. Brake hose. 11. Side-light/flashing indicator. 12. Battery. 13. Radiator. 14. Headlight. 15. Air cleaner. 16. Carburettor. 17. Cylinder head (rocker box). 18. Windscreen washer. 19. Bonnet. 20. Clutch and brake fluid reservoir. 21. Windscreen wipers. 22. Windscreen. 23. Steering wheel. B. 24. Saloon. 25. Convertible. 26. Coupé. 27. Estate car

mould[1] (mōld) *n.* Loose or broken earth, surface soil; the earth of the grave; soil rich in organic matter; ~-*board*, curved iron plate at back of plough-share that turns over furrow-slice (ill. PLOUGH).
mould[2] (mōld) *n.* Woolly or furry fungous growth forming on surfaces in moist warm air.
mould[3] (mōld) *n.* Matrix, vessel, in which fluid or plastic material is cast or shaped; pudding etc. shaped in mould; form, shape, distinctive nature. ~ *v.t.* Shape in or as in a mould; shape (bread) into loaves; model. **mou′lder**[1] *n.* (esp.) Person employed in making moulds for casting.
mou′lder[2] (mōl-) *v.i.* Turn to dust by natural decay, crumble away.
mou′lding (mōl-) *n.* Moulded object; ornamental contour given to stone-, wood- or metal-work; material, esp. long string of wood, prepared for this (*illustration, p. 580*).
mou′ldy[1] (mōl-) *adj.* Covered with MOULD[2]; mouldering; (slang) dull, wretched. **mou′ldiness** *n.*

mou′ldy[2] *n.* (naval slang) Torpedo.
Moulin Rouge (mōōlǎṅ rōōzh). Cabaret or *café chantant* in Montmartre, Paris, frequented in the late 19th and early 20th centuries by painters, poets, and other artists.
moult (mōlt) *v.* (of birds or animals) Shed feathers, fur, skin, etc., which are later replaced by new growth; shed (feathers etc.) thus. ~ *n.* Moulting.
mound[1] *n.* Embankment; heap, bank, hillock, of earth etc.
mound[2] *n.* Ball of gold etc. representing earth, surmounting crown etc.; (her.) figure of this as a bearing.
mount[1] *n.* Mountain, hill (abbrev. Mt, preceding name, as *Mt Everest*); (palmistry) fleshy prominence on palm of hand.
mount[2] *v.* Ascend; climb on to; increase in amount; amount *to*; set on horseback, furnish (person) with saddle-horse; put in position for use or exhibition; put (picture) in a MOUNT[3]; fit (gems etc.) in gold etc.; fix (object) on microscope slide; display specimen (e.g. butterfly); put (play) on stage; (mil.) organize (an offensive).
mount[3] *n.* Margin surrounding picture, card on which drawing is mounted; ornamental metal parts of thing; horse for person to ride.
mou′ntain (-tĭn) *n.* Natural elevation of earth's surface of impressive height, esp. over 1,000 ft (*illustration, p. 580*), large heap or pile; *the M~*, extreme party led by Danton and Robespierre in French Revolution, so called from occupying highest position in chamber of assembly; ~ *ash*, ROWAN tree; ~ *dew*, whisky, esp. illegally distilled; ~ *sickness*, difficult breathing, muscular weakness, mental lethargy, etc., caused by rarefied air at high altitudes.
mountaineer′ (-tĭn-) *n.* Mountain-climber. ~ *v.i.* Climb mountains.
mou′ntainous (-tĭn-) *adj.* Abounding in mountains; huge.
Mountbă′tten, Louis, 1st Earl Mountbatten of Burma (1900–). British naval and military leader; last viceroy (1947) and first

[579]

MOUNTEBANK   MOUSTERIAN

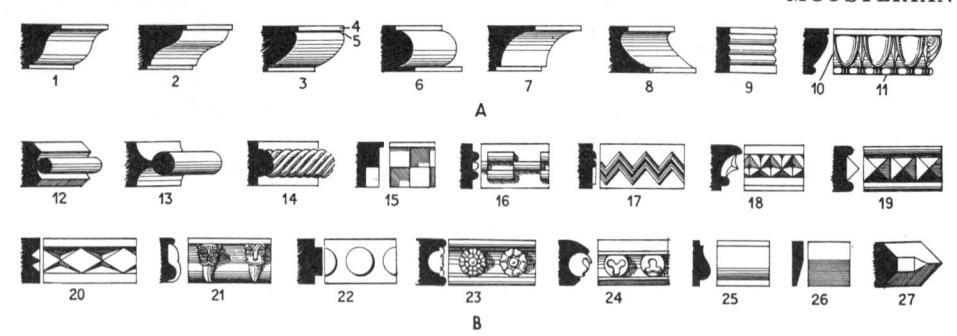

MOULDINGS WITH PROFILES: A. CLASSIC. B. MEDIEVAL

1. Cyma recta. 2. Ogee or cyma reversa. 3. Ovolo. 4. Fillet. 5. Quirk. 6. Torus. 7. Cavetto. 8. Scotia. 9. Reed. 10. Egg-and-tongue. 11. Bead-and-reel. 12. Bowtel. 13. Roll. 14. Cable. 15. Square billet. 16. Roll billet. 17. Zig-zag or chevron. 18. Nail-head. 19. Dog-tooth. 20. Lozenge. 21. Beakhead. 22. Pellet. 23. Rosette. 24. Ball-flower. 25. Bolection. 26. Bevel. 27. Chamfer with stopped end

MOUNTAIN AND GLACIER

1. Pass. 2. Peak. 3. Cirque. 4. Saddle. 5. Shoulder. 6. Col. 7. Arête. 8. Couloir. 9. Chimney. 10. Névé. 11. Lateral moraine. 12. Medial moraine. 13. Crevasses. 14. Séracs. 15. Terminal moraine

governor-general of India (1947–8).

mou′ntĕbănk *n.* Itinerant quack (archaic); impudent charlatan. [It. *montambanco* = *monta in banco* mount on bench]

Mou′ntie, -tў *n.* (colloq.) Member of the Royal Canadian Mounted Police.

mourn (môrn) *v.* Sorrow, grieve, lament, esp. lament death of; put on mourning. **mour′ner** *n.* One who mourns; person attending funeral.

mour′nful (môr-) *adj.* Exhibiting, expressing, or feeling, mourning or deep sorrow. **mour′nfullў** *adv.* **mour′nfulnĕss** *n.*

mour′ning (môr-) *n.* (esp.) Feeling or expression of sorrow; (wearing of) black clothes as sign of bereavement; ∼-*band*, band of black crape or other material worn round sleeve as sign of mourning; ∼-*card*, black-edged card giving name and date of death of deceased person; ∼-*paper*, black-edged notepaper.

mouse *n.* (pl. *mīce*). Small rodent esp. of genus *Mus*; timid or shy person; ∼-*ear*, hawkweed; *mousetrap*, trap for catching mice. **mou′sў** *adj.* **mouse** (*or* -z) *v.i.* Hunt for or catch mice; search *about* for something. **mou′ser** *n.* Animal that catches mice, esp. cat.

mousse (-ōōs) *n.* Dish of whipped cream, or cream and beaten eggs etc., flavoured with fruit etc. or containing meat or fish. [Fr., = 'froth']

mousta′che (mustahsh) *n.* Hair growing on upper lip, esp. of a man; similar hair round mouths of some animals, as cats etc.; ∼-*cup*, drinking-cup with partial cover to prevent the moustache from becoming wet.

Mouster′ian (mōō-) *adj.* Of a middle palaeolithic culture, characterized by flints worked usu. on one side only, and associated with Neanderthal Man, found in many localities in W. Asia, Europe, and

[580]

N. Africa. [Le *Moustier*, a rock-shelter in Dordogne, France]

mouth *n.* (pl. pr. -dhz). External orifice in head, with cavity behind it containing apparatus for mastication and organs of vocal utterance; person viewed as consumer of food; opening or entrance of anything; outfall of river; ~-*organ*, thin rectangular box containing series of metal reeds, tuned to a particular key and fitted in separate compartments so as to be capable of separate sounding by either blowing or sucking; **mou'thpiece**, part of some portable wind-instruments placed before or between lips; similar part of tobacco-pipe; part of telephone spoken into; one who speaks on behalf of others; ~-*to*-~, applied to a method of resuscitation in which a person places his mouth on the patient's and breathes expired air into his lungs. ~ (-dh) *v.* Utter or speak pompously, declaim; take (food) in, touch with, mouth; train (horse) to answer to bit and reins; grimace. **mou'thful** *n.*

mou'thỹ (-dhĭ) *adj.* Ranting, bombastic; prolix.

mo'vable (moō-) *adj.* That can be moved; (of property) that can be removed, personal as opp. to *real*; ~-*doh*: see SOLMIZATION. **movabi'litỹ, mo'vablenèss** *ns.*

move (moōv) *v.* Change position (of); change abode; stir, rouse; cause (bowels) to act; affect with emotion; propose as resolution; *moving picture*, continuous picture showing objects in motion, produced by projecting on to a series of photographs of the scene with successive positions slightly changed; *moving staircase*, escalator. ~ *n.* Moving of piece at chess etc.; way in which piece is allowed to move; act of moving from rest; change of abode or premises; device, trick, action to some end.

mo'vement (moōvm-) *n.* Moving; moving mechanism of watch etc.; principal division of (usu. instrumental) musical work; combined action or endeavour of body of persons for some special end.

mo'ver (moō-) *n.* (esp.) One who moves a proposal; *prime* ~, initial source (natural or mechanical) of motive power; author of fruitful idea.

mo'vie (moō-) *n.* (colloq.) Moving picture.

mow[1] (mō) *n.* Stack of hay, corn, etc.

mow[2] (mō) *v.* (past part. *mown*). Cut down grass, corn, etc., with scythe or machine; (fig.) cut, sweep down, like grass; *mowing-machine*, machine for cutting grass etc. **mow'er** *n.* Person who mows grass etc.; mowing-machine, lawn-mower.

mow[3] *n.* & *v.i.* (Make) a grimace.

mō'xa *n.* Down from dried leaves of *Artemisia moxa* or similar soft combustible material, used to cauterize the skin. [Jap. *mokusa* (*moe kusa* burning herb)]

Mōzambi'que (-bēk). Former Portuguese colony in E. Africa; gained independence in 1975; capital, Maputo.

Mōză'rabic *adj.* Of those Christians in Moorish Spain who were allowed the exercise of their own religion on condition of owing allegiance to the Moorish king and conforming to certain Moorish customs.

Mō'zărt (-ts-), Wolfgang Amadeus (1756–91). Austrian composer of symphonies, chamber-music, and operas, as 'Figaro', 'Don Giovanni', 'The Magic Flute'.

mp. *abbrev.* Mezzo piano.

m.p. *abbrev.* Melting-point.

M.P. *abbrev.* Member of Parliament; military police.

m.p.g., m.p.h. *abbrevs.* Miles per gallon, per hour.

M.P.S. *abbrev.* Member of the Pharmaceutical (*or* Philological *or* Physical) Society.

Mr. (mǐ'ster) *n.* Written form of MISTER.

M.R. *abbrev.* Master of the Rolls.

M.R.A. *abbrev.* MORAL Re-Armament.

M.R.B.M. *abbrev.* Medium range ballistic missile.

M.R.C.P.(E., I.) *abbrevs.* Member of the Royal College of Physicians (of Edinburgh, of Ireland).

M.R.C.S.(E., I.) *abbrevs.* Member of the Royal College of Surgeons (of Edinburgh, of Ireland).

M.R.C.V.S. *abbrev.* Member of the Royal College of Veterinary Surgeons.

M.R.G.S. *abbrev.* Member of the Royal Geographical Society.

Mrs. (mǐ'sĭz) *n.* Title prefixed to name of married woman with no superior title. [abbrev. of MISTRESS]

MS. *abbrev.* (pl. MSS.). Manuscript.

M.Sc. *abbrev.* Master of Science.

M.S.E. *abbrev.* Member of the Society of Engineers.

msec *abbrev.* Millisecond(s).

M.S.L. *abbrev.* Mean sea-level.

M.S.M. *abbrev.* Meritorious Service Medal.

M.T. *abbrev.* Motor Transport.

Mt *abbrev.* Mount.

M.T.B. *abbrev.* Motor torpedo-boat.

mū *n.* 13th (later 12th) letter of Greek alphabet (*M*, μ), corresponding to *m*; μ, (phys. etc.) symbol for one millionth; μ, *mu*, (radio) symbol for amplification factor of a valve; ~-*meson*: see MUON.

much *adj.* & *n.* Great number, quantity, or degree (of). ~ *adv.* In a great degree; pretty nearly; for a large part of one's time. **mŭ'chnèss** *n. much of a* ~, very much alike.

mu'cilage *n.* Viscous substance obtained from plants by maceration; adhesive substance. **mūcilă'ginous** *adj.*

mŭck *n.* Farmyard manure; (colloq.) dirt, filth. ~ *v.* Manure; ~ *about*, (slang) loaf; go about aimlessly; ~ *out*, clean out (stable etc.); ~ *up*, (slang) bungle. **mŭ'ckỹ** *adj.*

mŭ'cker *n.* (slang) Heavy fall; *come a* ~, come to grief.

mū'cŏr *n.* Fungus of genus *M*~ including many common moulds, such as those forming on bread, jam, etc.

mū'cous *adj.* Secreting or covered by mucus; ~ *membrane*, inner surface-lining of hollow organs of the body. **mūcŏ'sitỹ** *n.*

mū'crō *n.* (bot., zool.) Pointed part of an organ. **mū'cronate** *adj.*

mū'cus *n.* Sticky secretion of mucous glands usu. forming a protective covering for mucous membrane.

mŭd *n.* Wet soft soil or earthy matter, mire; ~ *bath*, bath in mud impregnated with salts, as a remedy for rheumatism etc.; ~-*flat(s)*: see FLAT[2] *n.*; **mu'dguard**, guard over wheel of cycle or other vehicle as protection against mud; **mu'dlark**, person searching for saleable articles in mud at low tide; street arab; ~-*pie*, mud formed by children in the shape of a pie; ~-*slinging*, (fig.) personal abuse, invective.

mŭ'ddle *v.* Bewilder, confuse; bungle; act in confused, unmethodical and ineffective manner; ~ *through*, finish successfully despite lack of method. ~ *n.* Muddled condition.

mŭ'ddỹ *adj.* Like mud; covered with, abounding in, mud; thick, turbid; not clear, mentally confused. **mŭ'ddĭlỹ** *adv.* **mŭ'ddĭnèss** *n.* **mŭ'ddỹ** *v.* Make or become muddy.

mudéjar (moōdhā'hăr) *n.* 1. Christianized Moor in medieval Spain. 2. Muslim of northern Spain. ~ *adj.* Of a style of architecture and decorative art in Spain and Portugal esp. in 12th–15th centuries.

mū'dra *n.* Symbolic conventional gesture of the hands in Indian and Asian art or dancing.

muĕ'zzin (moō-) *n.* Official of Muslim mosque who proclaims hour of prayer from minaret. [Arab. *mu'addin* ('*addana* proclaim)]

mŭff[1] *n.* Tubular covering esp. of fur into which hands are thrust to keep them warm (ill. COAT); similar contrivance for the feet (*foot-*~); *radiator* ~, protection for car radiator.

mŭff[2] *n.* (colloq.) Duffer, bungler; failure. ~ *v.t.* Bungle, make muddle of; miss (catch at cricket).

mŭ'ffin *n.* Light flat circular spongy cake eaten toasted and buttered. **mŭffineer'** *n.* Covered dish for keeping toasted muffins hot.

muffle *n.* Chamber or covering in furnace or kiln which protects contents from direct contact with fire. ~ *v.t.* Wrap, cover *up* for warmth; wrap up (oars, bell, drum, etc.) to deaden sound; wrap up (head of person) to prevent his speaking; repress, deaden, sound of (curse etc., usu. in past part.).

muffler *n.* Wrap or scarf worn round neck for warmth; silencer in engine; felt pad between hammer and strings of a piano.

mufti *n.* 1. Muslim priest or expounder of law. 2. Plain clothes worn by anyone who has the right to wear a uniform. [Arab. *al-muftī* official expounder of Islamic law]

mug *n.* Drinking-vessel, usu. cylindrical and with handle; (slang) face, mouth; (slang) stupid person, dupe. ~ *v.* 1. (slang) Study hard (*at* subject); ~ *up*, (slang) get up (subject). 2. (slang) Rob (person in street), esp. with violence.

mugger *n.* Broad-snouted Indian crocodile (*Crocodylus palustris*) venerated by many Hindus.

muggins (-z) *n.* Simpleton (slang); children's game of cards; game of dominoes in which the object is to make the sum of the two ends of the line a multiple of five.

Muggletonian *adj. & n.* (Member) of an English religious sect founded by Lodowick Muggleton (1609–98) and his cousin John Reeve (d. 1658), who claimed to be the two 'witnesses' of Rev. 11: 3–6.

muggy *adj.* (of weather etc.) Damp, warm, and oppressive. **mugginess** *n.*

mugwump *n.* (U.S.) Great man, chief; political independent, (esp.) Republican who refused to support party's nominee in presidential election of 1884. [N. Amer. Ind.]

Muhammad (*c* 570–632). Prophet of Islam, whose utterances are preserved in the KORAN; born at Mecca and buried at Medina; declared himself the Prophet, *c* 611, and sought to turn his fellow-Arabs from the local gods whom they then worshipped to the ancient religion of Abraham and other O.T. patriarchs and prophets; meeting opposition in Mecca, he fled to Medina in 622; this flight (the HEGIRA) is regarded as beginning the Muslim era. **Muhammadan** *adj. & n.* Muslim.

Muhammad Ali (ah-) (1769–1849). Viceroy of Egypt; founder of royal house of Egypt.

mulatto *n.* (pl. ~*s*). Offspring of one white and one Negro parent. ~ *adj.* Of brownish-yellow colour, as mulattos. [Span. *mulato* young mule]

mulberry *n.* 1. Tree of genus *Morus*, with dark-purple or white edible berries, and leaves which are used for feeding silkworms; fruit of this; dark-purple colour. 2. (Cover-name for) prefabricated harbour(s) towed across the English Channel and erected off the Normandy beaches during the invasion of Europe, June 1944.

mulch *n.* Half-rotten straw, grass mowings, leaves, etc., spread on the ground to protect roots of plants or trees or conserve moisture etc. ~ *v.t.* Cover or spread with mulch.

mulct *v.t.* Punish (person) by a fine; deprive (person *of*). ~ *n.* Fine imposed for offence.

mule[1] *n.* 1. Offspring of he-ass and mare; hence, stupid or obstinate person. 2. Kind of spinning jenny invented by S. Crompton.

mule[2] *n.* Kind of usu. backless slipper (ill. SHOE).

muleteer *n.* Mule-driver.

mulish *adj.* Obstinate as a mule, intractable. **mulishly** *adv.* **mulishness** *n.*

mull[1] *n.* Thin soft kind of plain muslin. [shortened f. *mulmull*, f. Hind. *malmal*]

mull[2] *v.t.* Make a mess or muddle of; ruminate, ponder *over*. ~ *n.* Mess, muddle.

mull[3] *v.t.* Make (wine, beer) into hot drink with sugar, spices, yolk of egg, etc.

mull[4] *n.* Humus formed under non-acid conditions (opp. MOR).

mullah *n.* Muslim learned in theology and sacred law; expounder of the Koran. [Hind. *mulla*, ult. adapted f. Arab. *mawlā*]

mullein (-lin) *n.* Herbaceous plant of genus *Verbascum*, with woolly leaves and erect woolly spike of yellow flowers.

muller *n.* Stone or piece of thick glass used for powdering drugs, pigments, etc., on a slab; apparatus for grinding ores.

mullet *n.* 1. Edible sea-fish; grey ~, greenish-grey fish of the Mediterranean (genus *Mugil*) or Gt Britain (*Crenimugil*); red ~, member of family Mullidae, esp. *Mullus*, some species of which are bright red. 2. (her.) Figure like rowel of spur or five-pointed star (ill. HERALDRY).

mulligatawny *n.* Highly flavoured E. Indian soup, made with curry-powder and hot seasonings; ~ *paste*, curry paste used for this. [Tamil *milagutannir* pepper-water]

mullion (-yon) *n.* Vertical shaft, usu. of stone, dividing lights in a window (ill. WINDOW). **mullioned** (-nd) *adj.* Furnished with mullions.

multi- *prefix.* Much, many.

multifarious *adj.* Having great variety. **multifariously** *adv.* **multifariousness** *n.*

multiform *adj.* Having many forms; manifold. **multiformity** *n.* Variety, diversity (opp. *uniformity*).

multilateral *adj.* Having many sides; (of agreement, treaty, etc.) in which more than two sides or States participate; ~ *trade*, trade carried on between several countries without the necessity of balancing trade or payments between them.

multimillionaire (-lyon-) *n.* Person with a fortune of several millions (of pounds, dollars, etc.).

multinomial *adj. & n.* (alg.) (Expression) of more than two terms connected by + or −.

multipara *n.* (med.) Pregnant woman who has borne one child or more.

multiparous *adj.* Producing more than one at birth.

multipartite *adj.* Divided into many parts.

multiple *adj.* Of many parts, elements or individual components; (math.) repeated, occurring more than once; (elect.) of a circuit with a number of parallel conductors; ~ *store*, retail business with branches in many places. ~ *n.* (math.) Number or quantity containing another an exact number of times; *lowest* (*least*) *common* ~, (abbrev. L.C.M.) least quantity that contains two or more given quantities exactly, as 12 is the L.C.M. of 3 and 4.

multiplex *adj.* Manifold, of many elements.

multipliable, multiplicable *adjs.* Capable of being multiplied.

multiplicand *n.* (math.) Number which is to be multiplied by another.

multiplication *n.* Multiplying; (math.) finding the quantity produced by taking a given quantity (MULTIPLICAND) as many times as there are units in another given quantity (MULTIPLIER); ~ *table*, set of numbers, usu. 1 to 12, with the products of multiplication by the same numbers successively. **multiplicative** *adj.*

multiplicity *n.* Manifold variety; great number *of*.

multiplier *n.* That which multiplies; (math.) number by which another number is multiplied; (elect.) device for multiplying intensity of force, current, etc., to bring it to a desired strength; (econ.) proportion of an increment of a consumer's income to the consequent increment of saving.

multiply *v.* Produce large number of (instances etc.); breed (animals), propagate (plants); (math.) perform process of multiplication (symbol ×).

multitude *n.* Great number; throng; *the* ~, the many, the common people. **multitudinous** *adj.* **multitudinously** *adv.* **multitudinousness** *n.*

mum[1] *int.* Hush! silence! ~ *adj.* Strictly silent or secret. ~ *v.i.* Act in dumb show.

mum[2] *n.* (colloq.) Mother.

mumble *v.* Speak or utter indistinctly or with lips partly closed. ~ *n.*

mumbo-jumbo *n.* Meaningless ritual; mystifying or obscure language etc., intended to confuse.

[582]

MUMMER

[f. name of grotesque idol said to have been worshipped by certain Negro tribes]

mŭ'mmer *n.* Actor in traditional popular performance in dumb show. **mŭ'mmerў** *n.* Mummer's performance; 'play-acting', buffoonery.

mŭ'mmifў *v.t.* Make into a mummy. **mŭmmĭfĭcā'tion** *n.*

mŭ'mmў[1] *n.* Dead body preserved from decay by embalming, esp. one so preserved by the ancient Egyptians; dried-up body; rich brown pigment obtained from bitumen; ~-*case*, case of wood, modelled to shape of human body, in which Egyptian mummies were placed for burial. [Arab. *mūmiyā*', med. L. *mumia* (Pers. *mūm* wax)]

mŭ'mmў[2] *n.* (Child's word for) mother.

mŭmps *n.* Virus infection which causes acute inflammation of parotid gland and consequent swelling of neck and face; (colloq.) fit of the sulks.

mŭnch *v.* Eat with noticeable action of the jaws.

Mŭnchausen (-ow'zn), Baron. Hero of a book of fantastic traveller's tales (1785) written in English by a German, Rudolph Erich Raspe; the original Freiherr von Münchhausen is said to have served in the Russian army against the Turks and to have related extravagant tales of his prowess.

mŭ'ndāne *adj.* Worldly. **mŭndā'nelў** *adv.* **mŭndā'neness.** (-n-n-) *n.*

mŭ'ngo[1] (-nggō) *n.* Cloth made from rags of heavily felted woollen cloth, like SHODDY but inferior.

Mungo[2]: see KENTIGERN.

Mū'nich (-k). (Ger. *München*) Capital of Bavaria; ~ *pact*, agreement between England, France, Germany, and Italy, signed at Munich on 29 Sept. 1938, under which part of Czechoslovakia was ceded to Germany.

mŭnĭ'cĭpal *adj.* Of the local self-government or corporate government of city or town. **mŭnĭ'cĭpallў** *adv.* **mŭnĭ'cĭpalĭsm, mŭnĭ'-cĭpalĭst** *ns.*

mŭnĭcĭpă'lĭtў *n.* Town, district, having local self-government; governing body of this.

mŭnĭ'cĭpalĭze *v.t.* Take over (private industries) and administer under municipal government. **mŭnĭcĭpalĭzā'tion** *n.*

mŭnĭ'fĭcent *adj.* Splendidly generous. **mŭnĭ'fĭcentlў** *adv.* **mŭnĭ'fĭcence** *n.*

mū'nĭments *n.pl.* Title-deeds etc. preserved as evidence of rights or privileges.

mŭnĭ'tion *n.* (pl. exc. in comb.). Military weapons, ammunition, equipment, and stores. ~ *v.* Provide, furnish with munitions.

Mŭ'nster. Province and ancient kingdom of SW. Ireland, including the counties of Cork, Waterford, Tipperary, Limerick, Clare, and Kerry.

mŭ'ntjăc *n.* Small horned deer (*Muntiacus*) of E. Indies and SE. Asia.

Mŭntz mĕ'tal. Alloy of copper and zinc used esp. for sheathing the bottoms of ships. [G. F. Muntz (1794–1857) of Birmingham, inventor]

mū'on *n.* (phys.) Mu-meson, meson having a mass of 206·7 times that of the electron.

mūr'al *adj.* Of, on, a wall; ~ *crown*, (Rom. antiq.) garland given to soldiers who first scaled walls of a besieged town. ~ *n.* Mural painting.

Murat (mūră), Joachim (1767–1815). French marshal; brother-in-law of Napoleon, by whom he was made king of Naples, 1808.

mūr'der *n.* Unlawful killing of person with malice aforethought, dist. from (*accidental* or *justifiable*) *homicide* and *manslaughter.* ~ *v.t.* Kill unlawfully and with malice aforethought; massacre, butcher; (fig.) spoil by bad execution, representation, etc. **mūr'-derer, -ėss** *ns.* **mūr'derous** *adj.* **mūr'derouslў** *adv.*

mūre *v.t.* (archaic or literary) Confine as in prison; shut *up*.

mūr'ĕx *n.* (pl. -*icēs*, -*exes*). Mollusc of genus *M*~ allied to whelks, yielding purple dye.

Mūri'llō, Bartolomé Esteban (1617–82). Spanish painter of genre and religious pictures.

mŭrk *n.* Darkness, gloom. ~ *adj.* (archaic, poet.) Dark, gloomy. **mŭr'kў** *adj.* Dark, gloomy; (of darkness) thick. **mŭr'kĭlў** *adv.* **mŭr'kĭness** *n.*

mŭr'mur *n.* Subdued continuous sound; (med.) sound of this kind heard in auscultation; muttered grumbling or repining; subdued or nearly inarticulate speech. **mŭr'murous** *adj.* **mŭr'murous-lў** *adv.* **mŭr'mur** *v.* Produce murmur; speak or say in murmur.

mūr'phў *n.* (slang) Potato. [Irish surname]

mŭ'rrain (-ĭn) *n.* Infectious disease in cattle.

Murray[1] (mŭ'rĭ), Sir James Augustus Henry (1837–1915). Scottish philologist, editor of the 'Oxford English Dictionary'.

Murray[2] (mŭ'rĭ), John (1745–93). Founder of the famous publishing house, whose son John (1778–1843) started the 'Quarterly Review' and was Byron's publisher.

mŭ'rrey *adj. & n.* Purplish-red (colour).

murrhine (mūr'ĭn) *adj.* ~ *glass*, Modern delicate glassware from the East, with small particles of coloured metal embedded in it. [L *murra* substance of which precious vases were made]

Mus.B., Bac. *abbrev. Musicae baccalaureus* (L, = Bachelor of Music).

mŭ'scadine *n.* = MUSCAT.

mŭ'scarine *n.* Poisonous alkaloid obtained from fungus *Amanita muscaria.* **mŭscari'nic** *adj.*

MUSHROOM

mŭ'scat *n.* Kind of grape with flavour or odour of musk. **mŭscatĕ'l, -dĕ'l** *n.* Muscat; strong sweet white wine prepared from muscats; muscat raisin.

mŭ'scle (-sl) *n.* Contractile fibrous band or bundle producing motion in animal body (*illustration*, *p. 557*); muscular strength; ~-*bound*, having the muscles stiff and enlarged owing to excessive exercise. ~ *v.i.* (slang) Force one's way *in*. [L *musculus* little mouse, f. fancied resemblance to a mouse]

Mŭ'scovў. (hist.) Principality of Moscow; Russia in the period (16th and 17th centuries) when that principality was dominant; ~ *duck*, tropical Amer. duck, *Cairina moschata*, with slightly musky smell. **Mŭ'scovite** *adj. & n.* (Native, inhabitant) of Muscovy or of Moscow. [*Muscovia*, latinized form of Russ. *Moskva* Moscow]

mŭ'scūlar *adj.* Of, in, the muscles; having well-developed muscles; ~ *Christianity*, Christian life of cheerful, physical activity, as described in the writings of Charles Kingsley. **mŭscūlă'rĭtў** *n.*

mŭ'scūlature *n.* System, arrangement, of muscles.

mŭscūlo- *prefix.* Of muscle.

Mus.D., Doc. *abbrev. Musicae doctor* (L, = Doctor of Music).

mūse[1] (-z) *v.i.* Ponder, reflect (*on*); gaze meditatively (*on* scene etc.).

Mūse[2] (-z) *n.* (Gk & Rom. myth.) One of the nine goddesses who presided over the arts and sciences (Calliope, epic poetry; Clio, history; Erato, erotic poetry; Euterpe, lyric poetry; Melpomene, tragedy; Polyhymnia, sacred song; Terpsichore, dancing; Thalia, comedy; Urania, astronomy); they were daughters of Zeus and Mnemosyne, born at the foot of Mt Olympus; Mt Helicon was sacred to them, and Mt Parnassus was one of their chief seats; hence, *m*~, poet's inspiring goddess, poet's genius.

mūsĕ'tte (-z-) *n.* Small soft-toned French bagpipe; dance for this, pastoral; reed stop on organ.

mūsē'um (-z-) *n.* Building or room for storing and exhibiting objects illustrative of antiquities, natural history, the arts, etc.; ~-*piece*, object fit for a museum; person or thing regarded merely as a survival or curiosity. [Gk *mouseion* seat of the Muses]

mŭsh *n.* Soft pulp; (U.S.) porridge made from maize flour. **mŭ'shў** *adj.* Soft, pulpy; (fig.) weakly sentimental, rubbishy. **mŭ'shĭness** *n.*

mŭ'shrŏŏm *n.* Popular name of any edible fungus, esp. *Agaricus campestris*, the common field-mushroom, proverbial for its rapid growth (ill. FUNGUS); (fig.) upstart; (attrib.) growing suddenly,

[583]

MUSIC　　　　　　　　　　　　　　　　　　　　　　　　　　　　　　　　MUSK

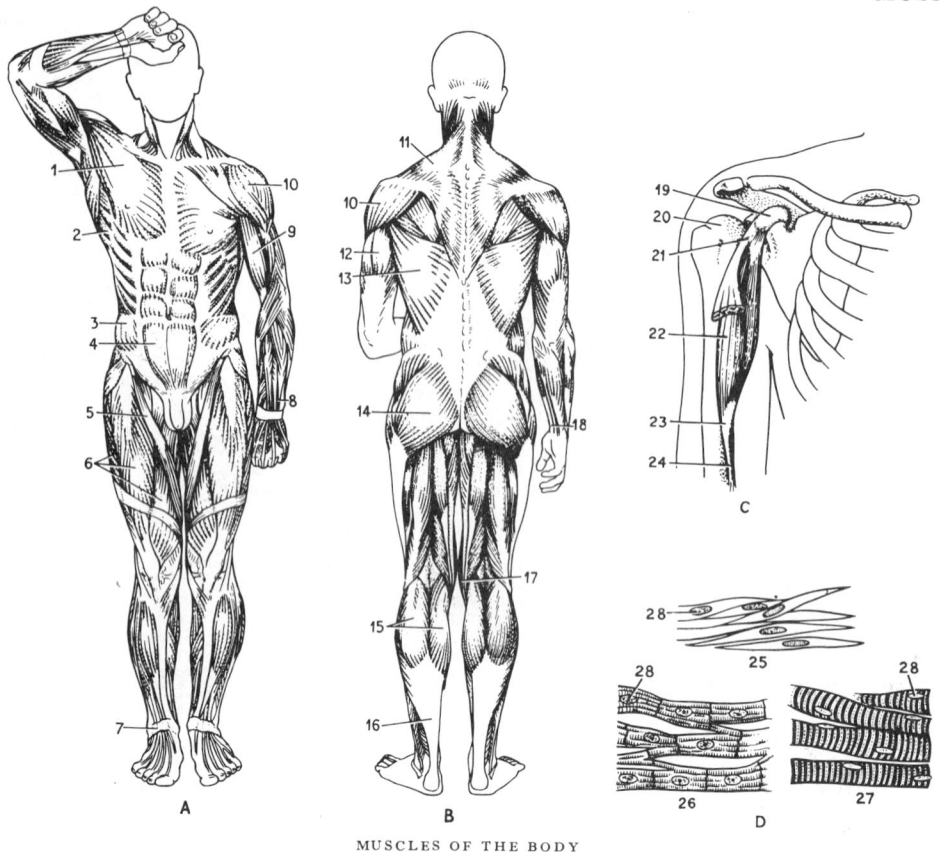

MUSCLES OF THE BODY
A. FRONT. B. BACK. C. PARTS OF A MUSCLE. D. MUSCLE-CELLS

A. 1. Pectoral muscle. 2. Serratus anterior. 3. External oblique muscle. 4. Rectus abdominis. 5. Sartorius. 6. Quadriceps. 7. Fascia. 8. Extensor tendons of hand and fingers. 9. Biceps. 10. Deltoid. B. 11. Trapezius. 12. Triceps. 13. Latissimus dorsi. 14. Gluteal muscles. 15. Gastrocnemius. 16. Achilles tendon. 17. Hamstrings. 18. Flexor tendons of hand and fingers. C. 19. Coracoid process of scapula. 20. Head of humerus. 21. Origin of muscle. 22. Body of muscle. 23. Tendon. 24. Insertion of muscle. D. 25. Plain (visceral) muscle. 26. Cardiac muscle. 27. Striated (somatic) muscle. 28. Nucleus

as ~ *growth*, *suburb*, etc.; ~ *cloud*, mushroom-shaped cloud, esp. resulting from nuclear explosion. ~ *v.i.* Have or assume the shape of a mushroom; spring up rapidly. **mŭ'shrōōming** *n.* Gathering mushrooms.

mŭ'sĭc(-z-) *n.* Art of combining sounds for reproduction by the voice or various kinds of musical instruments in rhythmic, melodic, and harmonic form so as to express thought or feeling and affect the emotions; sounds so produced; pleasant sound, e.g. song of a bird, murmur of a stream, etc.; written or printed score of musical composition; *face the* ~, face the consequences of actions etc. without shirking; ~ *drama*, Wagnerian form of opera in which music and the other elements are combined on equal terms and made subservient to dramatic expression; ~-*hall*, theatre for variety entertainments; ~-*stool*, stool with adjustable height of seat for piano-player.[Gk *mousikē* (*tekhnē*) (art) of the Muses (*Mousa* Muse)]

mŭ'sĭcal (-z-) *adj.* Of, resembling, fond of or skilled in, music; melodious, harmonious; set to, accompanied by, music; ~-*box*, mechanical musical instrument containing a revolving cylinder furnished with small pegs which strike on strips of metal, graduated to produce different notes; ~ *chairs*, drawing-room game in which a number of players move round a row of chairs, less by one in number than the players, until music ceases, when the one who finds no seat is eliminated, and a chair is removed before the next round; ~ *comedy*, light dramatic entertainment of songs, dialogue, and dancing connected by a slender plot; ~ *glasses*, set of glasses, graduated in tone, struck by small sticks; similar instrument with glass bowls or tubes; ~ *instrument*, any of a variety of instruments with which music is produced, usu. classified as *stringed*, *wind*, and *percussion*. **mŭ'sĭcallў** *adv.* **mŭ'sĭcalnĕss** *n.*
mŭ'sĭcal *n.* Film or theatrical piece (not opera or operetta) of which music is essential element.
mūsĭ'cian (-zĭshan) *n.* Person skilled in art or practice of music. **mūsĭ'cianship** *n.* Skill, insight, in interpreting and performing music.
mūsĭcŏ'lŏgў (-z-) *n.* All study of music except that directed to proficiency in performance or composition. **mūsĭcŏ'lŏgĭst** *n.* **mūsĭcŏlŏ'gĭcal** *adj.*
musique concrète (mūzěk kawṅkrět). CONCRETE music. [Fr.]

mŭsk *n.* Odoriferous reddish-brown substance secreted in a gland or sac by male musk-deer, used as a basis of perfumes; any of various plants with musky smell (but the plant commonly called 'musk', *Mimulus moschatus*, has now no scent); ~-*deer*, small

[584]

hornless deer (*Moschus*) of Central Asia; ~-*duck*, Muscovy duck; also, an Australian duck, *Biziura lobata*, so called from the musky smell of the male; ~ *melon*, common melon; ~-*ox*, ruminant (*Ovibos moschatus*) allied to sheep and bovines, with curved horns and shaggy pelt, now found only in Arctic America; ~-*rat*, large aquatic rodent (*Ondatra zibethica*) common throughout N. America, also called musquash; ~-*rose*, variety of climbing rose with fragrant white flowers; ~-*tree*, -*wood*, any of a variety of trees having a musky smell. **mŭ′skỹ** *adj*.

mŭ′skĕg *n*. Level swampy or boggy area in some regions of Canada.

mŭ′skĕt *n*. (hist.) Hand-gun, esp. unrifled, carried by infantry soldier. [It. *moschetto* sparrow-hawk]

[illustrations of muskets and firing mechanisms]

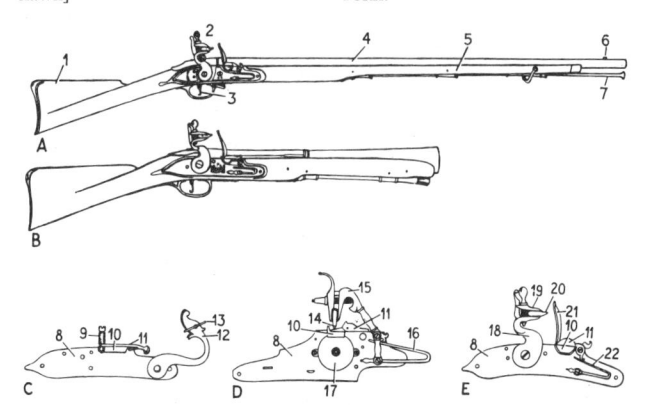

A. FLINTLOCK MUSKET, *c* 1800. B. BLUNDERBUSS, *c* 1750. C. MATCHLOCK, *c* 1650. D. WHEEL-LOCK, *c* 1650. E. FLINTLOCK, *c* 1740

A. 1. Butt. 2. Flintlock. 3. Trigger. 4. Barrel. 5. Stock. 6. Bayonet stud. 7. Ramrod. C. 8. Lockplate. 9. Pan cover screw and flash-guard support. 10. Pan. 11. Pan cover. 12. Serpent. 13. Screw for tightening serpent jaws on match. D. 14. Iron pyrites. 15. Dog. 16. Dog spring. 17. Wheel enclosed in wheel case. E. 18. Cock. 19. Upper jaw. 20. Flint. 21. Steel. 22. Pan cover spring

mŭskĕteer′ *n*. (hist.) Soldier armed with musket.

mŭ′skĕtrỹ *n*. (mil.) Instruction, practice, in rifle-shooting.

Mŭ′slĭm (*or* mōō-; *or* -z-) *n*. One who professes Islam. ~ *adj*. Of Muslims.

mŭ′slĭn (-z-) *n*. Fine delicately woven cotton fabric. [*Mosul*, town in Iraq where muslin was orig. made]

Mus.M. *abbrev. Musicae magister* (L, = Master of Music).

mŭ′squash (-ŏsh) *n*. MUSK-rat or (esp.) its fur. [Algonquian *muskwessu*]

mŭ′ssel *n*. Any of several genera of marine or freshwater bivalve molluscs, esp. *Mytilus*, the common edible sea-mussel, and *Unio*, the freshwater pearl-forming mussel.

Musset (mūsā), Alfred de (1810–57). French romantic poet.

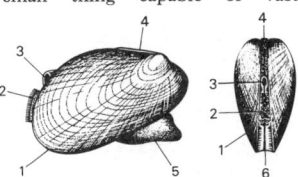

Mussoli′ni (mōōsolē-), Benito (1883–1945). Italian FASCIST politician; dictator 1922–43.

Mussōr′gskỹ (mōō-), Modest Petrovich (1839–81). Russian musician; composer of the opera 'Boris Godunov' (1874).

Mŭ′ssulman *adj*. & *n*. (pl. *-s*). Muslim.

mŭst[1] *n*. New wine; unfermented or incompletely fermented grape-juice.

mŭst[2] *adj*. & *n*. (Male elephant or camel) in state of dangerous frenzy. [Pers. *mast* intoxicated]

mŭst[3] *v*. (followed by inf. without *to*) Be obliged to; be certain to. ~ *n*. (colloq.) Something that should not be missed.

mŭ′stăng *n*. 1. Wild or half-wild horse of Mexico, California, etc. 2. Small red Texas grape.

Mustapha Kemal: see ATATÜRK.

mŭ′stard *n*. Plant of genus *Sinapis*, with yellow flowers and black or white seeds contained in pods; hot pungent powder made from the crushed seeds of this plant, mixed to a paste with water (*English* ~) or with vinegar, spices, etc. (*French* ~) and used as a condiment with meat; *grain of* ~ *seed*, small thing capable of vast development (Matt. 13: 31); ~ *and cress*, salad made of cress and young shoots or leaves of white mustard plant; ~ *gas*, dichlorodiethyl sulphide, a colourless oily liquid with faint garlic odour, the vapour of which is one of the vesicant gases used in chemical warfare; ~ *plaster*, plaster containing mustard, applied to the skin; ~-*pot*, vessel for holding mustard at table.

mŭ′ster *n*. Assembling of men for inspection, instruction, etc.; *pass* ~, undergo muster without censure; bear examination or inspection; come up to standard; ~-*roll*, official list of officers and men in army or ship's company (also fig.). ~ *v*. Collect or assemble for inspection etc.; collect, bring or come together; summon (courage, strength, etc., *up*).

mŭ′stỹ *adj*. Spoiled with damp; moist and fetid; mouldy; (fig.) stale, antiquated. **mŭ′stĭnĕss** *n*.

mŭ′table *adj*. Liable to change, fickle. **mŭtabĭ′lĭtỹ** *n*.

mŭ′tant *adj*. & *n*. (biol.) (Individual) differing from its parents as a result of mutation.

mŭtā′tion *n*. 1. Change, alteration. 2. (biol.) Occurrence of a new form differing from its parents as a result of change in the gene structure of a reproductive cell; mutant. 3. (gram.) Change in vowel sound through influence of another vowel in following syllable.

mutatis mutandis (mōōtah′tēs mōōtă′ndēs). With the necessary alterations or changes. [L]

mŭtch *n*. (Sc.) Woman's or child's close-fitting linen cap.

mŭte[1] *adj*. 1. Silent; not capable of speech, dumb; (of hounds) not giving tongue. 2. Not expressed in speech, as ~ *appeal*; (law, of prisoner) refusing to plead. 3. (of consonants) Stopped; produced with a closing at some point in throat or mouth, as *b*, *p*, *t*, etc.; (of letters) not pronounced, although written, as *e* in *mute*. **mŭ′telỹ** *adv*. **mŭ′tenĕss** *n*.

mŭte *n*. 1. Dumb person; actor without speaking part in a play; hired mourner at funeral. 2. (mus.) Clip for deadening resonance of strings of violin etc.; pad for deadening sound of wind instrument. 3. Mute consonant. ~ *v.t.* Deaden, soften, sound of a musical instrument with a mute; tone down.

mŭte[2] *v*. (birds) Excrete faeces, discharge thus.

mŭ′tĭlāte *v.t.* Injure, make imperfect, by depriving of part. **mŭtĭlā′tion** *n*.

mŭtĭneer′ *n*. One who mutinies.

mŭ′tĭnous *adj*. Guilty of mutiny, rebellion. **mŭ′tĭnouslỹ** *adv*.

mŭ′tĭnỹ *n*. Open revolt against constituted authority, esp. refusal of five or more members of armed forces to obey orders of a superior officer. ~ *v.i.* Take part in mutiny.

[585]

mū'tism *n.* Muteness, silence; dumbness.

mū'tter *v.* Speak, utter, in low and barely audible tones, with mouth nearly closed. ~ *n.* Muttering.

mū'tton (-tn) *n.* Flesh of sheep as food; *dead as* ~, quite dead; ~-*chop*, piece of rib or loin of mutton, usu. served fried or grilled; ~-*chop whiskers*, short bushy whiskers shaped like a mutton-chop.

mū'tūal *adj.* (of feelings, actions, etc.) Felt, done, by each to(wards) the other, as ~ *affection, benefit*; performed by joint action, done in common; (improp.) common to two or more persons, as *our* ~ *friend*; (insurance) of a system by which insured persons are shareholders of a company and share in its profits; ~ *fund*, (U.S.) UNIT trust. **mū'tūally** *adv.* **mūtūā'litў** *n.* Reciprocity, interdependence.

mū'tūalism *n.* (ethics) Doctrine that mutual dependence is necessary to social well-being. **mū'tūalist** *n.*

mū'tūle *n.* (archit.) Block projecting under Doric cornice (ill. ORDER).

mū'zzle *n.* 1. Projecting part of animal's head including nose and mouth (ill. DOG); snout. 2. Arrangement of straps or wires over animal's mouth to prevent its biting, eating, etc. 3. End of firearm from which the projectile is discharged (ill. CANNON); ~-*loader*, firearm loaded at muzzle, dist. f. *breech-loader*; ~ *velocity*, velocity of projectile at its discharge from muzzle of a gun. ~ *v.t.* Put muzzle on (animal, and fig. a person); impose silence on, restrict freedom of speech of.

mū'zzў *adj.* Mentally hazy; stupid with drink. **mū'zzilў** *adv.* **mū'zziness** *n.*

M.V. *abbrev.* Motor vessel; (also (m.v.) muzzle velocity.

M.V.D. Secret police of U.S.S.R., 1946-60. [initials of Russ. *Ministérstvo Vnútrennikh Del*, ministry of internal affairs]

M.V.O. *abbrev.* Member of the (Royal) Victorian Order.

mW, MW *abbrev.* Megawatt(s).

Mx *abbrev.* Maxwell(s).

mў *poss. pron.* Possessive case of *I* used as attrib. adj., belonging to, affecting, me; prefixed to some terms of address, as ~ *lord*. ~ *int.* Exclamation of surprise etc. (*oh* ~!).

M.Y. *abbrev.* Motor Yacht.

mўă'lgia (-ja) *n.* Pain in muscle or muscles.

mў'alism *n.* Kind of sorcery practised esp. in W. Indies.

mў'all (-awl) *n.* Australian acacia with hard sweet-scented wood used for pipes. [native *maial*]

mўcē'lium *n.* (bot.) Vegetative part of a fungus, consisting of microscopic hyphae or threads (ill. FUNGUS).

Mўcē'nae. City of ancient Greece in the plain of Argos; first inhabited *c* 3000 B.C. by peoples akin to the Minoans of Crete; in the Bronze Age (*c* 2100-1150 B.C.) occupied by a people whose language was probably an early form of Greek, who built the Lion Gate and beehive tombs which still survive. **Mўcēnae'an** *adj. & n.*

mўcŏ'logў *n.* Study of fungi. **mўcŏ'logist** *n.*

mўcorrhī'za (-rī-) *n.* (bot.) Association of a fungus with the roots of certain plants, in which the fungus forms a layer around or within the outer tissue of the roots.

mўcŏ'trophў *n.* State of a plant living in symbiosis with a fungus.

mўelī'tis *n.* Inflammation of the spinal cord.

myna : see MINA.

mўocār'dium *n.* Muscular substance of the heart. **mўocār'dial** *adj.*

mўogĕ'nic *adj.* Produced by, arising in, the muscles.

mўŏ'logў *n.* Study of muscles. **mўolŏ'gical** *adj.* **mўŏ'logist** *n.*

mўŏ'pathў *n.* Any affection of the muscles.

mў'ōpe *n.* Short-sighted person.

mўŏ'pia *n.* Short-sightedness, a condition of the eye in which the rays from distant objects are brought to a focus before they reach the retina and so form a blurred image.

mўŏ'pic *adj.* Short-sighted.

myosis : see MIOSIS.

mўosō'tis *n.* (bot.) Small plant of genus *M*~, of which the forget-me-not is a species, with pink, blue, or white flowers.

mў'otōme *n.* One of the serially repeated muscle blocks in a developing metamerically segmented animal (ill. LANCELET).

mў'riad *adj. & n.* Ten thousand; (of) indefinitely great number.

mў'riapŏd *adj. & n.* (zool.) (Animal) with many legs, of the

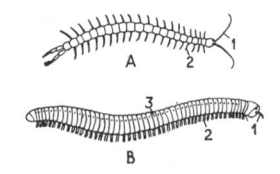

MYRIAPODS
A. CENTIPEDE. B. MILLEPEDE

1. Antenna. 2. Legs. 3. Pores for the escape of products of stink glands

class of arthropods which includes the centipedes and millepedes.

mўriora'ma (-rah-) *n.* Entertainment consisting of a large number of pictures and views.

Myr'midon[1] (mêr-) *n.* (Gk legend) One of a warlike people on the S. borders of Thessaly who followed Achilles to the siege of Troy.

myr'midon[2] (mêr-) *n.* Faithful follower; unscrupulously faithful attendant.

mўrŏ'balan *n.* Dried astringent plum-like fruit of certain E. Indian trees, containing tannin and used in dyeing, tanning, etc.

myrrh (mêr) *n.* Gum-resin, obtained from certain plants of genus *Commiphora*, used in perfumes and incense, and in medicine as astringent and antiseptic mouth-wash.

myr'tle (mêr-) *n.* (bot.) Shrub of genus *Myrtus*, esp. *M. communis*, the European myrtle with dark glossy evergreen leaves and white fragrant flowers.

mўsĕ'lf *pron.* Emphatic and reflexive form corresponding to *I*, ME.

Mў'sia (-sh-). Ancient region of NW. Asia Minor. **Mў'sian** *adj. & n.*

Mўsōr'e. State of S. India; capital, Bangalore.

mў'stagŏgue (-g) *n.* Teacher of mystical doctrines. **mўstagŏ'-gic, -ical** *adjs.*

mўstēr'ious *adj.* Full of, wrapt in, mystery; (of persons) delighting in, affecting, mystery. **mўstēr'iouslў** *adv.* **mўstēr'iousness** *n.*

mў'sterў *n.* 1. Hidden or inexplicable matter; secrecy, obscurity; ~ *trip*, pleasure excursion to an unannounced destination. 2. Religious truth known only by divine revelation; religious rite, esp. (pl.) Eucharist; (pl.) secret religious rites of Greeks, Romans, etc. 3. (also ~ *play*) Medieval drama based on Bible story or legend of saint.

mў'stic *adj.* Spiritually symbolic; occult, esoteric; enigmatical. ~ *n.* One who seeks by contemplation and self-surrender to attain union with the Deity, or who believes in the spiritual apprehension of truths beyond the understanding. **mў'stical** *adj.* Of mystics or mysticism; spiritually significant, connected with God in some way transcending understanding. **mў'sticallў** *adv.* **mў's-ticism** *n.*

mў'stifў *v.t.* Bewilder; hoax, humbug. **mўstificā'tion** *n.*

mўsti'que (-ēk) *n.* Atmosphere of mystery and veneration investing some doctrines, arts, professions, etc., or personages; any professional skill or technique which mystifies and impresses the layman.

mўth *n.* Fictitious (primitive) tale, usu. involving supernatural persons, embodying some popular idea concerning natural or historical phenomena; fictitious person or thing; fictitious idea or belief etc., esp. one that has been accepted uncritically. **mў'thic, -ical** *adjs.* **mў'thicallў** *adv.*

mў'thicize *v.t.* Treat (story etc.) as myth, interpret mythically. **mў'thicism** *n.*

mȳthŏ′graphȳ *n.* Representation of myths in painting or sculpture.
mȳthŏ′logȳ *n.* Body of myths, esp. as relating to particular person or subject or current in a particular country; study of myths; picture etc. illustrating a myth.
mȳthŏ′loger, mȳthŏ′logist *ns.* Student of myths. **mȳtholŏ′gical** *adj.* **mȳthŏlŏ′gically** *adv.* **mȳthŏl′ogīze** *v.t.* Treat of myths and mythology; invent myths.
mȳxoedē′ma (-*ed*-) *n.* Disorder due to deficient secretion of the thyroid gland.
mȳxomatō′sis *n.* Contagious, usu. fatal disease of rabbits, caused by a virus.
mȳxomȳ′cēte *n.* (bot.) Slime fungus, member of a group of organisms which pass part of their life-cycle in an amoeboid state and later reproduce by spores.

N

N, n (ĕn). 1. 14th letter of modern English and 13th of ancient Roman alphabet, representing historically Gk *nu* and Semitic *nun*; earlier Greek forms were И and И, corresponding to Phoenician И; usu. denoting a voiced nasal consonant with front closure (point of tongue touching teeth or teeth-ridge), but sometimes also sonant or vowel, and before *g*, *k*, a nasal. with back tongue-closure. 2. (print.) = EN. 3. (math.) Indefinite number; *to the nth(power)*, to any required power; (fig.) to any extent, to the utmost.
n. *abbrev.* Nano-; neuter; nominative; noon; noun.
N. *abbrev.* Nationalist; Navigator; New; newton(s); North.
N.A.A.F.I. *abbrev.* Navy, Army, and Air Force Institutes; *Naa′fi* (nă-), (colloq.) canteen organized by this.
Nā′aman. Syrian captain cured of leprosy by Elisha, who told him to bathe in Jordan (2 Kings 5).
năb *v.t.* (slang) Apprehend, arrest; catch in wrong-doing.
Năbatae′an *adj. & n.* (Member, Aramaic language) of an Arab people who established a kingdom centred on Petra (now in Jordan) which became the Roman province of Arabia in A.D. 105.
nā′bŏb *n.* 1. = NAWAB. 2. (hist.) Retired servant of East India Company, esp. between battle of Plassey, 1757, and appointment of Warren Hastings, 1772, returning to England with large fortune and orientalized ways. 3. Any ostentatiously wealthy person.
Nā′bŏth. Israelite who was stoned to death because he would not give up his vineyard to Ahab (1 Kings 21); ~*'s vineyard*, possession that one will stick at nothing to secure.
Năbūchodŏ′nosor (-*kod*-). = NEBUCHADNEZZAR.
nacě′lle *n.* 1. Outer casing of aircraft's engine (ill. AEROPLANE). 2. Car of airship. 3. Projecting housing on dashboard of motor vehicle for instrument dials.
nā′cre (-*ker*) *n.* (Shell-fish yielding) mother-of-pearl. **nā′crēous, nā′crous** *adjs.*
nā′dir (-ēr) *n.* Point of heavens diametrically opposite zenith or directly under observer (ill. CELESTIAL); (transf.) lowest point, place or time of great depression. [Arab. *nazir (as-samt)* opposite to (zenith)]
Nae′vius, Gnaeus (d. 201 B.C.). Early Roman poet and dramatist.
nae′vus *n.* (path.) Congenital lesion of skin, birth-mark, a network of hypertrophied blood-vessels causing sharply defined red patch level with skin surface; (also) pigmented mole.
năg¹ *n.* Small riding-horse or pony; (colloq.) horse.
năg² *v.* Find fault or scold persistently (*at* person); annoy thus. **nă′gging** *adj.* (esp. of pain) Gnawing, persistent.
Na′ga (nah-) *n.* 1. (Hindu myth.) One of a race of semi-human serpents, genii of rain, rivers, etc. 2. Member of one of a group of tribes inhabiting parts of Assam and Burma.
Na′galănd (nah-). State of NE. India; capital, Kohima.
naga′na (-*gah*-) *n.* Disease carried by certain species of tsetse fly affecting domestic animals and some wild ones. [Zulu *nakane*]
Nagar Haveli: see DADRA AND NAGAR HAVELI.
Nah. *abbrev.* Nahum.
Nahua′tl (-*wah*-) *adj. & n.* (Member, language) of a group of peoples of S. Mexico and Central America.
Nā′hum. Hebrew minor prophet; book of O.T. containing his prophecy against Nineveh (beginning of 7th c. B.C.).
nai′ad (nī-) *n.* Water-nymph (esp. in Gk myth.).
nail *n.* 1. Horny oval-shaped protective covering of modified epidermis on upper surface of tip of finger or toe; claw, talon. 2. Hard excrescence on upper mandible of some soft-billed birds. 3. Small metal spike, usu. with point and broadened head, driven in with hammer to hold things together or as peg or ornament; *hit the ~ on the head*, give true explanation, propose or do right thing, hit the mark; *on the ~*, (chiefly of payment) without delay. 4. ~-*brush*, small brush for cleaning finger-nails; ~-*head*, architectural ornament shaped like head of nail (ill. MOULDING); ~-*file*, ~-*scissors*, instruments for paring finger-nails. ~ *v.t.* Fasten with nail(s); fix or keep fixed (person, attention, etc.); secure, catch, engage, succeed in getting hold of; ~ *to the counter*, expose as false or spurious (in allusion to shopkeepers' practice of dealing thus with bad coins).
nai′ler *n.* Nail-maker.
nai′nsōōk *n.* Fine soft cotton fabric with high gloss on one side. [Hind. f. *nain* eye, *sukh* pleasure]
naira (nī′ra) *n.* Principal monetary unit of Nigeria, = 100 kobos.
Nair′nshire. Former county of NE. Scotland, S. of Moray Firth, since May 1975 part of the region of Highland.
Nairō′bi(nīr-). Capital of Kenya.
naïve, naive (nah-ē′v) *adj.* Artless, innocent, unsophisticated; amusingly simple. **naï′velȳ** *adv.* **naï′vetē** (-vtā), **naï′vetȳ** *ns.*
nā′kĕd *adj.* 1. Unclothed; not covered by clothing; defenceless. 2. Unsheathed; plain, undisguised, exposed for examination. 3. Devoid *of*; treeless, leafless, barren; without ornament; (of rock) exposed; (of light, flame, etc.) not placed within case or receptacle; (bot., zool.) without pericarp, leaves, hairs, scales, etc. 4. Without addition, comment, support, etc. 5. ~ *boys*, *ladies*, autumn crocus; ~ *eye*, eye unassisted by telescope, microscope, etc.; ~ *truth*, strict truth, without concealment or addition. **nā′kĕdlȳ** *adv.* **nā′kĕdnĕss** *n.*

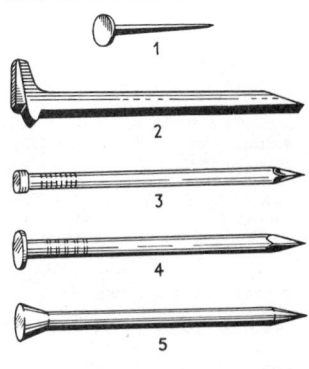

NAILS

1. Cut tack. 2. Steel rail dog. 3. Lost head oval wire brad. 4. Round wire nail. 5. Masonry fixing pin

N.A.L.G.O., Nă'lgō *abbrev.* National and Local Government Officers' Association.

nă'mbў-pă'mbў *adj.* & *n.* Sentimental, pretty, trifling (work of art); (person) lacking in vigour. [formed on name of *Ambrose Philips* (d. 1749), pastoral poet]

năme *n.* Word by which individual person, animal, place, or thing is spoken of or to; person as known, famed, or spoken of; family, clan; reputation; merely nominal existence, practically non-existent thing; *by the ~ of*, named; *call ~s*, describe by uncomplimentary names; *in the ~ of*, invoking; acting as deputy for or in the interest of; *keep one's ~ on, take one's ~ off, the books*, remain, cease to be, member of college, club, etc.; *put one's ~ down for*, apply as candidate etc.; *~-day*, day of saint after whom person is named; *~-part*, that after which play is named, title-role; *na'mesake*, person or thing with same name as another. *~ v.t.* Give name to, call by right name, appoint (to office etc.); specify; (of Speaker) mention (M.P.) as disobedient to Chair.

nā'melèss (-ml-) *adj.* Obscure, left unnamed; unknown; bearing no name or inscription; indefinable; too bad to be named.

nā'melў (-mlĭ) *adv.* That is to say.

Nămĭ'bĭa: see SOUTH WEST AFRICA.

Na'na Sah'ĭb (nah-). Name by which Dandu Panth (b. *c* 1821), a Mahratta, became known as leader of INDIAN Mutiny.

nă'ncў *n.* Effeminate man or boy; homosexual (also used attrib.). [pet form of the fem. name *Ann*]

nănkee'n *n.* Chinese cloth of natural buff-yellow cotton; cloth of dyed cotton resembling this; pale buff-yellow colour; (pl.) trousers of nankeen. [f. NANKING]

Nănkĭ'ng. City of China, on Yangtze, capital of China during two first reigns of Ming dynasty, and capital of Nationalist government from 1929 until the Japanese invasion of China in 1937. [Chin., = 'southern capital']

nă'nnў *n.* Child's nurse (also *nannie*); *~-goat*, she-goat. [pet form of female name *Ann*]

năno- *prefix.* (abbrev. n) One thousand millionth of, as *nanosecond*.

Nă'nsen, Fridtjof (1861–1930). Norwegian Arctic explorer, scientist, and statesman; League of Nations high commissioner for refugees after war of 1914–18; *~ passport*, (hist.) League of Nations passport for stateless refugees.

Nantes (nahṅt). City of W. France, on River Loire; *Edict of ~*, edict of Henry IV of France (1598) granting toleration to Protestants, revoked by Louis XIV (1685).

Nanteuil (nahṅtēryĕ), Robert (1623–78). French engraver of portraits, famous for his portraits of Louis XIV, Mazarin, Colbert, etc.

Năntŭ'ckėt. Island in Atlantic S. of Cape Cod, Massachusetts, U.S.

Nā'omĭ. Mother-in-law of RUTH (Ruth 1).

nā'ŏs *n.* (Gk antiq.) = CELLA (ill. TEMPLE[1]).

năp[1] *v.i.* Sleep lightly or briefly; *catch napping*, find asleep; take unawares or off guard. *~ n.* Short sleep, doze, esp. by day.

năp[2] *n.* Surface given to cloth by raising the fibres; soft or downy surface. *~ v.t.* Raise nap on (cloth). **nă'plèss** *adj.*

năp[3] *n.* 1. Card-game in which each player is given five cards and calls the number of tricks he expects to win; *go ~*, call five tricks; stake all one can; *~ hand*, hand suitable for going nap. 2. Tip that horse etc. is certain to win. *~ v.t.* Tip (horse etc.) as certain winner. [abbrev. of *Napoleon*]

napa: see NAPPA.

nă'palm (-ahm) *n.* Mixture of aluminium salts of naphthenic acid from crude petroleum with palmitic and stearic acids obtained from coconut oil, for jellying petrol for incendiary use in war (whence *~ bomb*). [*na*(phthenic)+*palm*(itic)]

năpe *n.* Back of neck.

nā'perў *n.* Household, esp. table, linen.

Nă'phtalī. Son of Jacob and Bilhah (Gen. 30 : 7–8); tribe of Israel, traditionally descended from him.

nă'phtha *n.* Orig., inflammable volatile liquid (a constituent of asphalt and bitumen) issuing from earth in some places; now, kinds of inflammable oil got by dry distillation of organic substances, esp. coal, shale, and petroleum.

nă'phthacēne *n.* Orange-yellow crystalline aromatic hydrocarbon.

nă'phthalēne *n.* White crystalline aromatic hydrocarbon, $C_{10}H_8$, with peculiar smell and pungent taste, obtained from coal-tar etc. and used in the manufacture of dyes and chemicals and for soil fumigation.

nă'phthēne *n.* One of a series of hydrocarbons occurring in petroleum, shale-tar, etc.

nă'phthŏl *n.* Either of two white crystalline hydroxyl derivatives of naphthalene, distinguished as *α-naphthol* and *β-naphthol*, used as disinfectants, in manufacture of dyes, etc.

Nā'pier, **Ne'per** (nā-), John (1550–1617). Scottish mathematician; inventor of logarithms and of the modern notation of decimal numbers; *~'s bones, rods*, graduated slips of bone, wood, etc., for performing multiplications and divisions. **Nāpier'ian** (-ēr-) *adj.*

nă'pkin. Square of material used for wiping lips or fingers at meals, or in serving certain dishes (*table-~*); piece of towelling or tissue worn by baby to absorb excreta; *~-ring*, ring for holding rolled-up table-napkin.

Nā'ples (-lz). (It. *Napoli*) City and seaport of SW. Italy. [L *Neapolis* f. Gk *nea polis* new city]

Napō'lèon[1]. Name of several French rulers: *Napoleon I*, Napoléon Bonaparte (1769–1821), French soldier of Corsican family; became First Consul of France, 1799, and Emperor of the French, 1804; conquered large parts of Europe; after various defeats, abdicated and withdrew to Elba 1814; returned to Paris, 1815; was defeated at Waterloo 3 months later and again abdicated; was exiled to St. Helena, where he died; *Napoleon II*, Napoléon François Joseph Charles, Duke of Reichstadt (1811–32), son of Napoleon I and Marie Louise; king of Rome; known as Napoleon II (although he never ruled France) because Napoleon I abdicated in his favour in 1814; *Napoleon III*, Charles Louis Napoléon Bonaparte (1808–73), nephew of Napoleon I; elected president of the French Republic 1848; proclaimed emperor 1852; captured by the Germans at SEDAN 1870, and deposed.

napō'lèon[2] *n.* 1. French gold coin of value 20 francs, issued by Napoleon I. 2. Kind of long boot. 3. = NAP[3] *n.*

Napŏlèō'nic *adj.* Of Napoleon I; *~ Wars*, series of campaigns (1799–1815), of French armies under Napoleon against Austria, Russia, Gt Britain, Portugal, Prussia, and other powers.

nă'ppa, **nă'pa** *n.* Leather prepared from sheep- or goat-skin by special tawing process. [f. *Napa*, county and town in California]

năppe *n.* 1. Sheet of water falling over weir etc. 2. (geol.) Recumbent fold or anticline (ill. ROCK[1]).

nă'ppў *n.* (colloq.) Baby's napkin.

napu (nah'poo) *n.* Any of various species of chevrotain. [Malay]

nar'cèine *n.* Bitter crystalline narcotic alkaloid present in opium.

narcĭ'ssĭsm *n.* (psychol.) Excessive or erotic interest in one's own body or personality. **narcĭssĭ'stĭc** *adj.* [f. NARCISSUS[2]]

narcĭ'ssus[1] *n.* Bulbous plant of genus N~ including the daffodil, esp. *N. poeticus*, bearing in spring heavily-scented single white flower with undivided corona with a red crisped edge.

Narcĭ'ssus[2]. (Gk myth.) Beautiful youth who, falling in love with his reflection in a spring, pined away, and was changed into the flower that bears his name.

nar'colĕpsў *n.* Disease characterized by irresistible attacks of true sleep, usually of brief duration. **narcolĕ'ptĭc** *adj.*

narcō'sĭs *n.* Operation or effects of narcotics; state of insensibility.

narcō'tĭc *adj.* Inducing drowsiness, sleep, stupor or insensibility

[588]

NARD

(also fig.). ~ n. Narcotic drug or influence.
nārd n. (Plant, prob. *Nardostachys jatamansi*, yielding) aromatic balsam of ancients, usu. called *spikenard*.
nār'ghilė (-gī-) n. Hookah. [Pers. *nārgīl* coconut]
nārk n. (slang) Police spy; informer. ~ v. Act as nark. [Romany *nak* nose]
Nărragă'nsett n. Member, Algonquian language, of an Amer. Indian tribe, formerly inhabiting parts of Rhode Island.
narrā'te v.t. Relate, recount, give continuous account of. **narrā'tion, narrā'tor** ns.
nă'rrative n. Tale, story, recital of facts; kind of composition or talk that confines itself to these. ~ adj. In the form of, concerned with, narration.
nă'rrow (-ō) adj. Of small width in proportion to length, confining; restricted; with little margin; illiberal, prejudiced, exclusive, whence ~*-minded(ly)*, ~*-mindedness*; searching, precise; (phonet.) tense; ~ *boat*, canal barge with narrow beam (ill. BARGE); ~ *gauge*, (on railway) gauge of less than 4 ft 8½ in. (but formerly ~ *gauge* meant 4 ft 8½ in., the British standard gauge); ~ *goods*, braids, ribbons, etc.; ~ *seas*, English Channel and Irish Sea. **nă'rrowly** adv. **nă'rrowness** n. **nă'rrow** n. (usu. pl.) Narrow part of sound, strait, river, pass, etc. ~ v. Make or become narrower, diminish, lessen, contract.
nār'thěx n. Porch or vestibule in early Christian church, extending across width of nave at opposite end from main altar, and used by those not in full communion (ill. BASILICA).
nār'whal (-wəl) n. Arctic delphinoid cetacean (*Monodon monoceros*), the male having a very long spirally twisted straight tusk developed from one, or sometimes both, of its two teeth (ill. WHALE¹).
nār'ӯ adj. (U.S. dial.) Not a, no. [var. of *ne'er a*]
nā'sal (-z-) adj. Of the nose; (of sounds) produced with nose passages open (as *n, m, ng*); (of voice etc.) characterized by unusual or disagreeable number of sounds produced by means of nose. **nā'sally** adv. **nasă'lĭtӯ** n. **nā'salīze** v. **nāsalīzā'tion** n. **nā'sal** n. Nasal letter or sound.
nă'scent adj. In the act of being born; just beginning to be, not yet mature; ~ *state*, (chem.) highly active condition of certain elements, esp. hydrogen, at the moment of liberation from a compound. **nă'scencӯ** n.
Nā'sebӯ (-zbĭ). Village of Northamptonshire, scene of battle (1645) in which Puritan army under Fairfax and Cromwell won decisive victory over Royalists under Charles I and Prince Rupert.

Năsh¹, John (1752–1835). English architect; designer of the terraces near Regent's Park, London; also of Regent St (buildings since replaced) and other parts of London.
Năsh², Richard (1674–1762). 'Beau Nash', English man of fashion, master of ceremonies at Bath.
Năsh³, -e, Thomas (1567–1601). English poet, dramatist, and pamphleteer.
Nā'smȳth¹, Alexander (1758–1840). Scottish landscape and portrait painter.
Nā'smȳth², James (1808–90). Scottish engineer, inventor of the steam-hammer.
nāso- (-z-) *prefix*. Of the nose, as in ~*-frontal*, of nose and forehead.
Nă'ssau¹ (-ow). Territory of central Germany on E. bank of the Rhine; formerly an independent grand duchy; incorporated 1866 with kingdom of Prussia.
Nă'ssau² (-aw). Capital city of Bahama Islands, on N. shore of New Providence.
Nā'sser, Gamel Abdel (1918–70). Egyptian army officer and politician; premier of Egypt 1954–6, president 1956–8; president of United Arab Republic 1958–70.
nastūr'tium (-shəm) n. 1. (bot.) Cruciferous pungent-tasting plant of genus *N*~ including watercress. 2. (pop.) One of an unrelated group of garden plants of genus *Tropaeolum*, mostly climbers, having spurred flowers in shades of red and yellow.
nā'stӯ (nah-) adj. Unpleasant to taste or smell; disgusting; obscene; spiteful; extremely disagreeable. **nā'stĭlӯ** adv. **nā'stĭness** n.
Nat. *abbrev.* Nathaniel; National(ist).
nă'tal¹ adj. Of, from, birth.
Nată'l². Eastern coastal province of Republic of South Africa; first settled by a few British traders in 1823, then by Boers in 1838, becoming a Boer Republic; annexed by British, 1845; representative government, 1856; responsible government, 1893; province of the Union of South Africa, 1910; capital, Pietermaritzburg. [named *Terra Natalis* by Vasco da Gama because he sighted the entrance to what is now Durban harbour on Christmas Day, 1497]
natā'tion n. Swimming.
nātatōr'ial, nā'tatorӯ adjs. Swimming, of swimming.
Nă'tchez n. Member of former Amer. Indian tribe, of lower Mississippi River, conquered and scattered by French in 1730.
nā'tēs (-z) *n.pl.* (anat.) 1. Buttocks. 2. Anterior pair of optic lobes of brain.
Nā'than. Hebrew prophet of time of David and Solomon (2 Sam. 7, 12, etc.).
Nathă'năĕl. Disciple of Christ (John 1: 45 ff., 21: 2), freq. identified with St. BARTHOLOMEW.

NATIONAL

nā'tion n. 1. Society united under one government in a State; considerable group of people having common descent or history. 2. (in medieval and some Sc. universities) Body of students from particular country or district.
nă'tional adj. Of a (or the) nation; common to the whole nation, concerned with its interests as dist. from those of a faction or region; ~ *anthem*, song adopted by a nation as an expression of patriotism, and played or sung on formal and ceremonial occasions; in Britain, poem and air 'God save the King' (or Queen) of unknown origin, first printed 1744; *N*~ *Assembly*, (esp., hist.) first revolutionary assembly of France 1789–91; ~ *bank*, (U.S.) any of numerous commercial banks chartered under the federal government in accordance with the banking Acts of 1863–4, empowered to receive, lend, and transmit money, and to issue currency notes; *N*~ *Coal Board*, public corporation, constituted 1946, controlling the nationalized coal industry of the United Kingdom; *N*~ *Convention*, (hist.) elected assembly which governed France 1792–5, abolished royalty, and established republic; (U.S. politics) convention of major political party which nominates candidate for presidency etc.; *N*~ *Debt*: see DEBT; *N*~ *Gallery*, gallery for permanent exhibition of pictures belonging to a nation, esp. that in Trafalgar Square, London; *N*~ *Government*, coalition government in Britain 1931–5, formed by Ramsay Macdonald; *N*~ *Grid*, grid used on British Ordnance Survey maps, based on the Transverse Mercator projection; *N*~ *Health Service*, British system, which came into force in 1948, providing a medical service financed chiefly by taxation; *N*~ *Insurance*, system of compulsory contributions from all persons and employers for providing State assistance in sickness, unemployment, retirement, etc.; *N*~ *Library of Scotland*, Advocates' Library (see ADVOCATE); ~ *park*, (orig. U.S.) extensive area set aside by government action for the preservation of historic or prehistoric sites and of flora and fauna, and for the benefit of the public; *N*~ *Portrait Gallery*, public collection in London, initiated 1856, of portraits of 'eminent persons in British history'; *N*~ *Savings*, savings deposited with the Government through the National Savings Bank, National Savings Certificates, and Premium Bonds; *N*~ *Socialist German Workers' Party*, party with ultra-nationalistic, anti-Semitic, and totalitarian programme which acquired dictatorial power in Germany under HITLER in 1933; hence *N*~ *Socialism*, *N*~ *Socialist*; *N*~ *Trust*, privately

[589]

NATIONALISM

subscribed trust (incorporated 1907) for preservation of places of historic interest or natural beauty in England, Wales, and N. Ireland; N~ Trust for Scotland, trust in Scotland (founded 1931) with similar aims. na'tionally adv.
na'tional n. 1. Person legally considered a member of a specified State. 2. the N~, (colloq.) the GRAND National.
na'tionalism n. Patriotic feeling, principle, or efforts; policy of national independence. na'tionalist n. nationali'stic adj.
nationa'lity n. National quality; nation, existence as a nation; ethnic group; fact of belonging to a particular nation or ethnic group; cohesion due to common history etc.; person's status as member of a nation, alterable by legal process.
na'tionalize v.t. Make national; make into a nation; naturalize (foreigner); transfer (land, mines, railways, etc.) from private ownership and control to that of the State. nationaliza'tion n.
na'tive n. 1. One born, or whose parents are domiciled, in a particular place or country; original or usual inhabitant of country as dist. from strangers or foreigners, esp. one of non-European race; (Austral.) white born in Australia. 2. Indigenous animal or plant. 3. Oyster reared wholly or partly in British waters, esp. in artificial beds. ~ adj. 1. Belonging to a person or thing by nature, innate, natural to; of one's birth; where one was born; belonging to one by right of birth. 2. (of metals etc.) Occurring naturally in pure state; occurring in nature, not produced artificially. 3. Born in a place (esp. of non-Europeans), indigenous, not exotic; of the natives of a place.
na'tivism n. 1. (philos.) Doctrine of innate ideas. 2. (U.S.) Prejudice in favour of natives against strangers, esp. immigrants. na'tivist n.
nati'vity n. Birth, esp. of Christ; picture of Christ's nativity; festival of birth of Christ (Christmas) or of Virgin (8 Sept.) or St. John Baptist (24 June); (astrol.) horoscope.
N.A.T.O., Nā'tō abbrev. North Atlantic Treaty Organization.
na'tter v.i. (colloq.) Chat cosily, gossip; chatter, esp. trivially or fretfully.
na'tterjack n. Species of small toad (Bufo calamita) found in Britain and NW. Europe, with yellow stripe down back and running, not hopping, gait.
Nattier (nätyā), Jean-Marc (1685–1766). French portrait painter; ~ blue, soft shade of blue much used by him.
na'tty adj. Spruce, trim. na'ttily adv. na'ttiness n.
na'tural (-cher-) adj. 1. Based on the innate moral sense, instinctive, as ~ law, ~ justice. 2. Constituted by nature, ~ day: see DAY;

~ selection: see DARWIN[1]. 3. Normal, conformable to the ordinary course of nature, not exceptional or miraculous; ~ death, by age or disease, not by violence. 4. Not enlightened, unregenerate, as ~ man; not communicated by revelation, as ~ religion, ~ theology. 5. Physically existing, not spiritual or intellectual or fictitious, as the ~ world; ~ life, duration of person's life on earth. 6. Existing in or by nature, not artificial; innate, inherent; self-sown, uncultivated; ~ gas, inflammable gas occurring underground, consisting chiefly of methane and other simple paraffins and often found associated with petroleum. 7. Lifelike; unaffected, easy-mannered; not disfigured or disguised. 8. Not surprising; to be expected. 9. Consonant or easy to (person etc.). 10. Destined to be such by nature, as ~ enemies. 11. So related by nature only, illegitimate, as ~ child, son. 12. Dealing with nature as a study; ~ classification, classification of species into natural orders, esp. Jussieu's arrangement of plant species acc. to likeness as opp. to Linnaeus's sexual system; ~ history, formerly, systematic study of all natural objects, animal, vegetable, and mineral; now usu., study of animal life, freq. implying popular rather than scientific treatment; aggregate of facts about the natural objects or characteristics of a place or class; so ~ historian; ~ order, (esp.) order resulting from natural classification; ~ philosophy, (hist.) natural science; physics; so ~ philosopher; ~ science: see SCIENCE. 13. (mus.) Not sharp or flat; (of scale or key) having no sharps or flats; ~ scale, scale of C major. na'turalness n. na'tural n. 1. Person half-witted from birth. 2. (mus.) Note in natural scale; white key on piano; sign ♮ used to cancel preceding sharp or flat. 3. (cards, in vingt-et-un) Hand making 21 as first deal. 4. (colloq., orig. U.S.) Person etc. naturally endowed (for); easy or obvious choice (for).
na'turalism (-cher-) n. 1. Moral or religious system on purely natural basis; philosophy excluding supernatural or spiritual. 2. Faithful representation of nature or reality in literature, art, etc.
na'turalist n. 1. One who believes in or studies naturalism. 2. Student of animals or plants. naturali'stic adj. Of, according to, naturalism in philosophy, literature, etc.; of natural history.
naturali'stically adv.
na'turalize (-cher-) v. Admit (alien) to citizenship; adopt (foreign word, custom, etc.); introduce (animal, plant) into new environment. naturaliza'tion n.
na'turally (-cher-) adv. (esp.) As might be expected, of course.

NAVAL

na'ture n. 1. Thing's essential qualities, person's innate character; general characteristics and feelings of mankind; specified element of human character; person of specified character; kind, sort, class; by ~, innately. 2. Inherent impulses determining character or action; vital force, functions, or needs; resin or sap in wood; against ~, unnatural, immoral. 3. Creative and regulative physical power conceived of as immediate cause of phenomena of material world; these phenomena as a whole; these personified; naturalness in art etc.; in the course of ~, in the ordinary course; in ~, in real fact; state of ~, unregenerate condition (opp. state of grace); condition of man before society is organized; uncultivated or undomesticated state of plants or animals; bodily nakedness.
naught (nawt) n. Nothing, nought; (arith.) cipher, nought.
naughty (naw'tĭ) adj. (now used almost exclusively of, to, or by children) Wayward, disobedient, badly behaved; (archaic) wicked, blameworthy, indecent. nau'ghtily adv. nau'ghtiness n.
nau'plius n. Larval form of certain crustaceans.
Naŭ'ru (-ōorōō). Pacific island near the equator, formerly under Australian administration; independent republic since 1968 with limited form of membership of the Commonwealth. Naŭ'ruan adj. & n.
nau'sea n. Feeling of sickness; sea-sickness; loathing. nau'seate v.t. Affect with nausea.
nau'seous adj. Causing nausea; offensive to taste or smell, nasty; disgusting, loathsome. nau'seously adv. nau'seousness n.
Nausi'cäa. (Gk legend) Daughter of Alcinous; she found the shipwrecked Odysseus on the shore and took him to her father's palace.
nautch n. Indian exhibition of professional dancing-girls; ~-girl, one of these.
nau'tical adj. Of sailors or navigation, naval, maritime; ~ mile: see MILE. nau'tically adv.
nau'tilus n. 1. (also paper ~) Small two-gilled cephalopod mollusc of warm seas (genus Argonauta), related to octopus, the female of which secretes in two of its arms a translucent single-chambered false shell. 2. (also pearly ~) Four-gilled cephalopod of Indian and Pacific Oceans (genus N~), having, in both sexes, a many-chambered true shell.
Na'vahō, Na'vajō (-ahō) n. (Member of) an Amer. Indian people of N. Arizona and New Mexico; ~ blanket, bright-coloured woollen blanket with geometrical pattern, made by Navaho women.
na'val adj. Of ships, esp. ships of war; of the (or a) navy; ~ officer, officer in navy; (U.S., also) customs

[590]

official; ~ *stores*, supplies for warships. **nā'vally** *adv*.

Năvari'nō (-rē-). Seaport and bay of S. Greece; scene of naval battle (1827) in which allied Russians, French, and British defeated Turks and Egyptians.

Navār're. (Span. *Navarra*) Province of N. Spain; (hist.) medieval kingdom which included also parts of SW. France.

nāve[1] *n*. Hub of wheel (ill. WHEEL).

nāve[2] *n*. Body of church from inner door to chancel or choir, usu. separated by pillars from aisles (ill. CHURCH).

nā'vel *n*. Depression in front of belly left by severance of umbilical cord; central point of anything; ~ *orange*, large orange with navel-like formation at top; ~*-string*, umbilical cord; *na'velwort*, wall penny-wort.

nă'vĭcĕrt *n*. Consular certificate granted to a neutral ship testifying that her cargo is correctly described according to the manifest and does not contravene contraband regulations, first put into operation 16 March 1916. ~ *v.t*. Authorize with a navicert. [L *navis* ship + *cert*(ificate)]

navi'cūlar *adj*. Boat-shaped; ~ *bone*, tarsal bone (ill. FOOT); ~ *disease*, disease in feet of horses. ~ *n*. Navicular bone or disease.

nă'vĭgable *adj*. Affording passage for ships; seaworthy; (of balloon) dirigible. **năvĭgabi'litў** *n*.

nă'vĭgāte *v*. Voyage, sail ship; sail over, up, down (sea, river); manage, direct course of (ship, aircraft, etc.) with the aid of instruments.

năvĭgā'tion *n*. Navigating; methods of determining position and course of ship, aeroplane, etc., by geometry and nautical astronomy; voyage; *inland* ~, communication by canals and rivers.

năvĭ'gator *n*. 1. One charged with or skilled in navigation; sea explorer. 2. (orig. name for) Navvy.

nă'vvў *n*. 1. Labourer employed in excavating etc. for canals, railways, roads, etc. 2. Mechanical excavator. [abbrev. of *navigator*]

nā'vў *n*. 1. Branch of armed forces using ships (in U.K., *Royal* N~); ~(-)*blue*, (of) the dark blue used in British naval uniform; ~*-cut*, cake tobacco finely sliced; N~ *Department*, U.S. department of State controlling the navy; ~ *list*, official publication containing list of officers of navy etc.; ~*-yard*, (now U.S.) government dockyard. 2. Navy blue.

nawa'b (-wawb) *n*. 1. Distinguished Muslim in Pakistan. 2. (hist.) Muslim noble in the Mogul Empire. [Arab. *nā'ib* deputy]

Nă'xŏs. Greek island, largest of the Cyclades; in ancient times a centre of the worship of Dionysus.

nay *adv*. No (archaic); or rather, and even, and more than that. ~ *n*. The word *nay*; *say* ~, utter denial or (usu.) refusal, refuse; *yea and* ~, shilly-shally.

Năzarē'ne *n*. 1. Native, inhabitant, of Nazareth; *the* ~, Jesus Christ. 2. (obs., in Muslim and Jewish use) Christian. 3. Member of an obscure early Jewish-Christian sect allied to Ebionites. 4. Member of a group of German romantic painters in early 19th c. with aims resembling those of Pre-Raphaelites. ~ *adj*. Of Nazareth or Nazarenes.

Nă'zarĕth. Town of Lower Galilee, now in Israel; home of Joseph and Mary, parents of Jesus, who spent his youth there.

Nă'zarīte[1] *n*. (rare) = NAZARENE 1.

Nă'zarīte[2] *n*. One of a Hebrew sect who abstained from all products of the vine, from cutting the hair, etc. (Num. 6). [Heb. *nāzîr* one consecrated, devoted]

nāze *n*. Promontory, headland, ness.

Nazi (nah'tsĭ) *n*. & *adj*. (Member, adherent) of the NATIONAL Socialist German Workers' party. **Na'zĭdom**, **Na'z(i)ism** *ns*. **na'zifў** *v.t*. **nazifĭcā'tion** *n*. [repr. pron. of *Nati-* in Ger. *Nationalsozialist* National Socialist]

n.b. *abbrev*. No ball.

N.B. *abbrev*. New Brunswick; North Britain; *nota bene* (L, = note well).

N.B.G., n.b.g. *abbrev*. (colloq.) No bloody good.

N.C. *abbrev*. North Carolina.

N.C.B. *abbrev*. National Coal Board.

N.C.O. *abbrev*. Non-commissioned officer.

N.C.U. *abbrev*. National Cyclists' Union.

n.d. *abbrev*. No date; not dated.

N. Dak. *abbrev*. North Dakota.

NE. *abbrev*. North-east(ern).

Neagh (nā), Lough. Lake of NE. Ireland, largest in the British Isles.

Neă'nderthal (-tahl). Valley in Rhineland, Germany; ~ *man*, type of man (ill. PRIMATE) widely distributed in palaeolithic Europe in the early stages of the last glaciation, with long low wide skull, retreating forehead, and massive brow-ridges (so called because parts of skeleton were discovered in a cave in this valley, 1857).

neap *adj*. Of those tides occurring soon after moon's 1st and 3rd quarters in which high-water level is at lowest. ~ *n*. Neap tide. ~ *v*. (of tides) Tend towards neap; reach highest point of neap-tide; (pass., of ship) be prevented from getting off by neaping of tides.

Něapŏ'lĭtan (nēa-) *adj*. Of Naples; ~ *ice*, ice-cream in layers of various colours and flavours; ~ *violet*, sweet-scented double variety of cultivated violet. ~ *n*.

Native, inhabitant, of Naples. [see NAPLES]

near *adv*. To, at, a short distance, in(to) proximity in space or time; nearly; (with *not*) anything like; closely; parsimoniously; ~ *at hand*, within easy reach; not far in the future; ~ *by*, not far off; hence, *nearby* (*adj*.); *go, come* ~ (*to do, doing*), nearly do. ~ *prep*. Near in space, time, condition, or resemblance, to. ~ *adj*. 1. Closely related, intimate. 2. (of horse, part of vehicle etc.) Left (i.e. on the side where one mounts; opp. OFF; so ~*-side*). 3. Close at hand, close to, in place or time; (of road or way) direct. 4. (of guess, translation, escape, etc.) Close, narrow. 5. (of persons) Niggardly. 6. ~ *distance*, part of scene between background and foreground; N~ *East*, SE. parts of Europe; Balkan States together with Asia Minor; ~ *miss*, (of shell, bomb, etc.) not a hit, but falling close enough to damage the target; something that narrowly misses its objective; ~*-sighted*, short-sighted. ~ *v*. Draw near (to), approach.

near'lў *adv*. Closely, almost; *not* ~, nothing like.

neat[1] *n*. Any animal of ox kind; (collect.) cattle; ~*-herd*, cowherd; ~*'s foot, tongue*, foot, tongue, of ox as food; ~*'s leather*, ox-hide.

neat[2] *adj*. 1. (of liquor, esp. alcoholic) Undiluted. 2. Nicely made or proportioned; pleasantly simple or compact; deft, dextrous, cleverly done; tidy, methodical; (of language, style, etc.) brief, clear, and pointed, cleverly phrased, epigrammatic. **nea'tlў** *adv*. **nea't-nĕss** *n*.

neath *prep*. (poet.) Beneath.

nĕb *n*. 1. (Sc.) Beak; nose; snout; tip, spout, point. 2. Handle of scythe.

Neb. *abbrev*. Nebraska.

Nĕbrā'ska. State in central U.S., admitted to the Union in 1867; capital, Lincoln.

Nĕbūchadnĕ'zzar, -rĕ'zzar (-k-). King of Babylon 605-562 B.C.; built the great walls of the city; after the rebellion of Jehoiakim of Judah he besieged and took Jerusalem 597; when ZEDEKIAH revolted, he took it again and destroyed it, 588.

nĕ'būla *n*. (pl. *-ae*). 1. Clouded speck on cornea causing defective sight. 2. (astron.) Cloud of dust or gas within the galactic system illuminated by neighbouring stars. 3. (astron.) Luminous mass believed to consist of an enormous number of stars, usu. not separately discernible, situated outside the galactic system. **nĕ'būlar** *adj*. Of nebula(e); ~ *hypothesis*, theory that solar and stellar systems developed from nebulae.

nĕ'būlous *adj*. 1. Of, like, nebula(e). 2. Cloud-like; hazy, vague, indistinct, formless; clouded, turbid. **nĕbŭlō'sĭtў** *n*.

[591]

nĕ'bŭlў, -lé (-lā) *adj.* (her.) Wavy, serpentine (ill. HERALDRY).
nĕcĕssār'ian *n.* & *adj.* = NECESSITARIAN.
nĕ'cĕssarĭlў (*or* -sĕ'r-) *adv.* As a necessary result, inevitably.
nĕ'cĕssarў *adj.* Indispensable, requisite; requiring to, that must, be done; determined by predestination or natural laws, not by free will; happening or existing by necessity; (of concept etc.) inevitably resulting from nature of things or the mind, inevitably produced by previous state of things; (of agent) having no independent volition. ~ *n.* Thing without which life cannot be maintained; (loosely) desirable thing not generally regarded as a luxury; *the* ~, (slang) money or action needed for a purpose.
nĕcĕssĭtār'ian *n.* & *adj.* (Person) denying free will and maintaining that all action is determined by antecedent causes. **nĕcĕssĭtār'ianism** *n.*
nĕcĕ'ssĭtāte *v.t.* Force, compel, to do (now rare); render necessary; involve as condition, accompaniment, or result.
nĕcĕ'ssĭtous *adj.* Poor, needy.
nĕcĕ'ssĭtў *n.* 1. Constraint or compulsion regarded as a law prevailing through the material universe and governing all human action; constraining power of circumstances, state of things compelling to certain course; *of* ~, unavoidably. 2. Imperative need (*for*); indispensability; indispensable thing, necessary. 3. Want, poverty, hardship, pressing need.
nĕck *n.* 1. Part of body that connects head with shoulders; flesh of animal's neck as food, this as cut of meat (ill. MEAT); part of garment covering or lying next to neck; *break one's* ~, dislocate cervical vertebrae, be killed so; *get it in the* ~, (slang) suffer fatal or severe blow; *save one's* ~, escape being hanged (also transf.); *stick one's* ~ *out*, (colloq.) expose oneself to danger; ~ *and crop*, headlong, bodily; ~ *and* ~, running even in race; ~ *or nothing*, desperate(ly), staking all on success. 2. Narrow part *of* vessel, esp. of bottle near mouth, or *of* passage, pass, or channel; pass, narrow channel, isthmus; narrow connecting part between two parts of thing; (archit.) lower part of capital. 3. (geol.) Conical hill consisting of igneous rock which has accumulated in throat of volcano and been exposed later when the mountain itself weathered away. 4. ~-*band*, part of garment round neck; *ne'ckcloth*, cravat; *ne'ckerchief* (-chĭf), kerchief worn round neck; *ne'cklace*, ornament of precious stones, beads, etc., worn round neck; *ne'cktie*, (esp.) narrow band of woven or knitted material placed round neck and tied in front; ~-*verse*, (hist.) Latin verse printed in black-letter (usu. beginning of

51st psalm) by reading which person claiming benefit of clergy might save his neck. ~ *v.i.* (slang, orig. U.S.) Hug, exchange kisses and caresses.
Nĕ'ckar. River of S. Germany, flowing into the Rhine from E.
Nĕcker (-ār), Jacques (1732–1804). French financier and statesman; finance minister to Louis XVI.
nĕ'cking *n.* (archit.) Part of column between shaft and capital (ill. ORDER).
nĕ'cklĕt *n.* Ornament, small fur, etc., worn round neck.
nĕ'cromăncў *n.* Act of predicting by means of communication with the dead; magic, enchantment. **nĕ'cromăncer** *n.* **nĕcromă'ntĭc** *adj.*
nĕcrŏ'phagŏus *adj.* Feeding on carrion.
nĕcrŏ'phĭlў *n.* Morbid preoccupation with corpses, death, etc.
nĕcrŏ'polis *n.* Cemetery.
nĕ'crŏpsў, nĕcrŏ'scopў *ns.* Post-mortem examination, autopsy.
nĕcrŏ'sis *n.* (path.) Death of circumscribed piece of tissue, esp. mortification of bones. **nĕcrŏ'tĭc** *adj.* **nĕ'crotīze** *v.i.*
nĕ'ctar *n.* 1. (Gk myth.) Drink of the gods; any delicious drink. 2. Sweet fluid or honey produced by plants. **nĕctār'ean, nĕctār'eŏus, nĕctari'ferous** *adjs.*
nĕ'ctarīne (*or* -ēn) *n.* Kind of peach with thin downless skin and firm flesh.
nĕ'ctarў *n.* (bot.) Glandular organ or tissue secreting nectar, occurring mainly in flowers, occasionally in leaves and stems (ill. FLOWER).
N.E.D. *abbrev.* New English Dictionary (= O.E.D.).
N.E.D.C. *abbrev.* National Economic Development Council.
nĕ'ddў[1] *n.* Donkey. [dim. of *Edward*]
Nĕ'ddў[2]. (colloq.) = N.E.D.C.
née (nā) *adj.* (before married woman's maiden name) Born, as *Mrs. Smith, née Jones.*
need *n.* 1. Necessity arising from circumstances of case; imperative demand for presence or possession *of*; *have* ~ *of*, require, want. 2. Emergency, crisis, time of difficulty; destitution, lack of necessaries, poverty. 3. Thing wanted, respect in which want is felt, requirement. ~ *v.* Be necessary (archaic); stand in need of, require; be needy; be under necessity or obligation to or *to* do. **nee'dful** *adj.* Requisite, necessary, indispensable; *the* ~, what is necessary, esp. (slang) the money required. **nee'dfulnĕss** *n.*
nee'dle *n.* 1. Instrument used in sewing, usu. small slender piece of polished steel with fine point at one end and hole or eye for thread at other; knitting-needle; one of parallel wires forming part of stocking-frame or Jacquard loom. 2. Piece of magnetized steel used as

indicator compass or in magnetic or electrical apparatus (also *magnetic* ~); strip of gold or silver of standard fineness used with touchstone in testing purity of these metals. 3. Pointed etching or engraving instrument; long slender pointed instrument used in surgery; pointed end of hypodermic or other syringe; steel pin exploding cartridge of breechloader; (in gramophones etc.) small pointed instrument transmitting vibrations from record to soundbox; stylus used in recording. 4. Obelisk; sharp rock, peak; beam of wood, esp. used as temporary support in underpinning; sharp slender leaf of fir or pine; (chem. etc.) needle-shaped crystal. 5. ~-*bath*, showerbath with fine strong spray; ~-*fish*, any of various fishes with very fine teeth, esp. garfish; *nee'dleful*, length of thread etc. put into needle; ~ *game, match*, one closely contested and arousing personal feeling or animosity; ~-*gun*, (hist.) early type of breech-loader using percussion cap; ~-*point*, fine sharp point; *nee'dlepoint* (*lace*), lace made with needle (see LACE); *nee'dlewoman*, woman who sews, seamstress; *nee'dlework*, sewing, embroidery, etc. ~ *v.* Sew, pierce, operate on, with needle; goad, irritate (colloq.); thread (one's way) between or through things; underpin with needle beams; form needle-shaped crystals.
nee'dlĕss *adj.* Unnecessary, uncalled for. **nee'dlĕsslў** *adv.* **nee'dlĕssnĕss** *n.*
needs (-z) *adv.* Of necessity (now only after or before *must*).
nee'dў *adj.* Poor, indigent, necessitous. **nee'dĭlў** *adv.* **nee'dĭnĕss** *n.*
ne'er (nār) *adv.* (poet.) Never; ~-*do-well, -weel*, good-for-nothing (person.)
nĕfār'ious *adj.* Wicked, iniquitous. **nĕfār'iouslў** *adv.* **nĕfār'iousnĕss** *n.*
Nĕfertī'tī (-tē-) (14th c. B.C.) Wife of AKHNATEN.
nĕgā'te *v.t.* Nullify; deny existence of, imply or involve non-existence of; be the negation of.
nĕgā'tion *n.* 1. Denying; negative statement or doctrine; refusal, contradiction, denial *of*. 2. (logic) Affirmation of difference or exclusion. 3. Absence or opposite of something actual or positive; negative or unreal thing, nonentity.
nĕ'gatorў *adj.*
nĕ'gatīve *adj.* 1. Expressing or implying denial, prohibition, or refusal; wanting, consisting in the want of, positive attributes; of opposite nature to thing regarded as possible. 2. (math., phys., etc.) Denoting quantities to be subtracted from others; less than zero; in the opposite direction to that which (arbitrarily or by convention) is regarded as positive; (elect.) having a negative charge; ~ *charge*,

NEGATIVISM

one of the two kinds of electric charge, the charge of an electron (cf. POSITIVE, 6); ~ **pole**, region of excess of electrons, cathode; also (magnetism) applied to the south-seeking pole of a magnet and the corresponding (north) pole of the earth; ~ **sign**, minus sign. 3. (phot.) Applied to image in which lights appear dark and shadows light (see *n.* 3 below). **nĕ′gatively** *adv.* **nĕ′gativeness, nĕgativ′ity** *ns.* **nĕ′gative** *n.* 1. Negative statement, reply, or word; right of veto; in the ~, negative(ly), no. 2. Negative quality, want of something; (math.) negative or minus quantity. 3. (phot.) Print in which lights and shadows of nature are reversed, made by direct action of light on an emulsion deposited on glass or other transparent substance, and used for producing a positive print. ~ *v.t.* Veto, reject, refuse to accept or countenance; disprove (inference, hypothesis); contradict (statement); neutralize (effect). **nĕ′gativism** *n.* Doctrine characterized by denial of accepted beliefs etc. **nĕ′gativist** *n.*

Nĕ′gĕv. Semi-desert region of Israel between Beersheba and the Gulf of Aqaba.

nĕglĕ′ct *v.t.* Disregard, slight; leave uncared-for; omit to do. ~ *n.* Neglecting, being neglected; negligence. **nĕglĕ′ctful** *adj.* **nĕglĕ′ctfully** *adv.* **nĕglĕ′ctfulness** *n.*

nĕgligĕ(nĕ′glĕzhā) *n.* Free-and-easy or unceremonious attire, esp. woman's loose garment worn on informal occasions.

nĕ′gligence *n.* Want of proper care or attention, (piece of) carelessness; *contributory* ~, negligence on a person's part that has helped to bring about the injury that he has suffered. **nĕ′gligent** *adj.* **nĕ′gligently** *adv.*

nĕ′gligible *adj.* That need not be regarded, that may be neglected.

nĕgō′tiāte (-shi-) *v.* 1. Confer (*with* another) with view to compromise or agreement; arrange (affair), bring about (desired object) by negotiating. 2. Transfer (bill) to another for a consideration; convert into cash or notes, get or give value for (bill, cheque) in money. 3. Clear, get over, dispose of (fence, obstacle, difficulty). **nĕgō′tiable** *adj.* **nĕgō′tiant, nĕgōtiā′tion, nĕgō′tiātor** *ns.*

Nĕ′grĕss *n.* Female Negro.

Nĕgrī′llō *n.* Small Negro; one of dwarf Negroid people of Central and S. Africa.

Negrī′ Sĕmbi′lan (-ē, -ēl-). State of Malaysia; capital, Seremban.

Nĕgri′to (-rē-) *n.* One of a small Negroid people in Malayo-Polynesian region.

Nĕ′grō *n.* (pl. -*es*). Member, esp. male, of black-skinned woolly-haired flat-nosed thick-lipped people esp. of Africa. ~ *adj.* Of Negroes.

Nĕ′groid *adj.* & *n.* (Member) of the division of mankind with Negro characteristics.

nĕ′gus[1] *n.* Mixture of sweetened and flavoured wine (esp. port or sherry) and hot water. [Col. F. *Negus*, d. 1732, inventor]

Nĕ′gus[2] *n.* Supreme ruler of Ethiopia.

Neh. *abbrev.* Nehemiah.

Nĕhĕmī′ah (-*a*) (4th c. B.C.) Jewish governor of Judaea under Artaxerxes; rebuilder of walls of Jerusalem; *Book of* ~, historical book of O.T. (in Vulgate, 2 Esdras), giving account of rebuilding of walls of Jerusalem and of various reforms (see CHRONICLER).

Nehru (nār′ōō), Pandit Jawaharlal (1889–1964). Indian Congress leader; 1st prime minister of India 1947–64.

neigh (nā) *v.i.* & *n.* (Utter) cry (as) of horse.

neighbour (nā′ber) *n.* Dweller next door, near, in same street, village, or district, or in adjacent country, esp. regarded as one who should be friendly or as having claim on others' friendliness; person or thing next or near another; (*attrib.*) neighbouring. ~ *v.* Adjoin, border upon, border *on.* **nei′ghbourless** *adj.* **nei′ghbourship** *n.* **neighbourhood** (nā′ber-) *n.* Neighbourly feeling or conduct; nearness, vicinity *of*; neighbours, people of a district, district (in U.S., freq. *attrib.*, as in ~ *school* etc.); (town planning) part of large city planned as a unit with own shopping centre etc. **neighbourly** (nā′ber-) *adj.* Like a good neighbour, friendly, helpful. **nei′ghbourliness** *n.*

nei′ther (nīdh-; *or* nē-) *adv.* (introducing mention of alternatives or different things, about each of which a negative statement is made) Not either; not, nor yet; (strengthening preceding negative) either. ~ *adj.* & *pron.* Not the one or the other.

Nĕjd. Region of Arabia on Persian Gulf, forming with Hejaz and Asir the kingdom of Saudi Arabia.

nĕk *n.* (S. Afr.) = COL.

nĕ′llÿ *n.* Large sea-bird *Macronectes giganteus*), the giant petrel. [prob. the feminine name]

Nĕ′lson[1] *n.* (wrestling) Class of holds (*double, full, half, quarter* ~) in which arm is passed under opponent's from behind and the hand applied to his neck.

Nĕ′lson[2], Horatio, Viscount Nelson, Duke of Bronté (1758–1805). British admiral and naval hero, killed in the battle of TRAFALGAR.

nĕ′matocÿst *n.* Cell in jelly-fish, sea-anemones, etc., containing coiled thread that can be projected as sting (ill. JELLY).

nĕ′matoid, nĕ′matōde *adjs.* & *ns.* (Worm) of slender unsegmented cylindrical shape, of the phylum Nematoda.

nem. con., nem. dis., diss.

NEOPLATONISM

abbrevs. Nemine contradicente, dissentiente (L, = with no dissentients).

nĕmē′sia (-zha) *n.* S. Afr. flowering plant of genus *N*~, many of which are cultivated as hardy annuals, with variously coloured irregular, slightly spurred flowers. [Gk *nemesis* snapdragon]

Nĕ′mĕsis. (Gk myth.) Daughter of Night and goddess of vengeance; regarded as personification of the gods' resentment at, and punishment of, insolence towards them; hence *n*~, retributive justice.

nĕmŏ′phila *n.* Ornamental herbaceous annual, often cultivated, of N. Amer. genus *N*~.

Nĕ′nnius (active 796). Welsh historian; compiler or reviser of 'Historia Britonum', giving oldest legends of King ARTHUR[1].

neo- *prefix.* New; modern, later or lately found or invented etc.

nĕodÿ′mium *n.* (chem.) Metallic element of rare-earth group; symbol Nd, at. no. 60, at. wt 144·24. [NEO + DIDYMIUM]

Nĕ′ogēne *adj.* & *n.* (geol.) (Of) the later period of the Tertiary era including the Miocene and Pliocene epochs.

nĕoli′thic *adj.* Of the later Stone Age (as contrasted with PALAEOLITHIC), characterized by ground or polished stone implements and by great advances in food production and simple skills.

nĕolō′gian *adj.* Of, inclined to, marked by, neologism in theology. ~ *n.* Neologist in theology.

nĕŏ′logism, nĕŏ′logÿ *ns.* 1. Coining or using of new words, new-coined word. 2. Tendency to, adoption of, novel or rationalistic religious views. **nĕŏ′logist** *n.*

nĕ′ŏn *n.* 1. (chem.) Colourless, odourless, inert, gaseous element present in minute quantities in the atmosphere; symbol Ne, at. no. 10, at. wt 20·179; ~ *light*, bright orange-red light obtained by passing an electrical discharge through a tube or bulb containing neon at low pressure, extensively used for illuminated signs in advertising, etc.; also light of blue, green, etc. obtained by mixing other inert gases with neon.

nĕ′ophrŏn *n.* Egyptian vulture (*N*~ *percnopterus*) of India and Africa; bird of same genus. [name of man turned into vulture in *Metamorphoses* of Antoninus Liberalis]

nĕ′ophÿte *n.* New convert, esp. among primitive Christians or Roman Catholics; newly ordained R.C. priest, novice of religious order; beginner, novice, tyro.

nĕ′oplăsm *n.* (path.) Autonomous new growth in some part of the body, tumour.

Nĕoplā′tonism *n.* Philosophical and religious system, chiefly consisting of a mixture of Platonic ideas with Oriental mysticism,

[593]

which originated at Alexandria in the 3rd c. and is represented in the works of Plotinus, Porphyry, and Proclus. **Nĕoplătŏ′nĭc** adj. **Nĕoplā′tonist** n.

Nĕoptŏ′lĕmus. (Gk legend) Son of ACHILLES; in the Trojan War he killed PRIAM, and ANDROMACHE fell to his lot when the TROJAN captives were distributed.

nĕotē′rĭc adj. Recent, new-fangled, modern.

Nĕpa′l (-awl). Independent kingdom NE. of India, on frontier of Tibet; capital, Katmandu. **Nĕpălē′se** (-z) adj. & n.

nĕpĕ′nthĕs (-z) n. 1. (also *nepenthe*) Egyptian drug mentioned in the 'Odyssey' as banishing grief; (poet.) any drug having this power. 2. Pitcher-plant of genus N~.

nĕ′phew (or -vū) n. Brother's or sister's son.

nĕphŏ′logў n. Study of clouds.

nĕ′phrīte n. = JADE, sense 1. [Gk *nephros* kidney, from its supposed value in kidney-disease]

nĕphrī′tĭc adj. Of or in the kidneys, renal.

nĕphrī′tĭs n. Inflammation of the kidneys.

ne plus u′ltra (nā ploŏs ōō-). Farthest or highest point attained or attainable. [L, = 'not more beyond' (supposed inscription on Pillars of Hercules)]

Nē′pŏs, Cornelius (c 99–c 24 B.C.). Roman historian, friend of Cicero, Atticus, and Catullus.

nĕ′potism n. Favouritism shown to relatives esp. in conferring offices; (hist.) practice on the part of some medieval and renaissance popes of showing special favour to their natural children, who were known euphemistically as their 'nephews'. **nĕ′potist** n.

Nĕ′ptūne. 1. (Rom. myth.) God of the sea, identified with POSEIDON. 2. (astron.) Third largest of the planets (ill. PLANET), with two known satellites, discovered 1846 as a result of mathematical computations of J. C. Adams in England and Leverrier in France; symbol Ψ. **Nĕptū′nian** adj. & n.

Nĕ′ptūnist n. (geol.) Adherent (esp. in 18th c.) of the view that the action of water played a principal part in the formation of rocks (opp. VULCANIST). **Nĕ′ptunism, Nĕptū′nianism** ns.

nĕptū′nium n. (chem.) Transuranic element, not found in nature, occurring as a temporary stage in the formation of plutonium from uranium 238; symbol Np, at. no. 93, at. wt 237·0482.

Nēr′ēid n. 1. (Gk myth.) One of the sea-nymphs, daughters of Nereus. 2. n~, (zool.) Marine polychaete worm.

Nēr′eus (-rūs). (Gk myth.) Sea-deity having the power, like Proteus, of assuming various forms.

Nēr′ī, St. Philip (1515–95). Italian churchman; founder of the Congregation of the Oratory, an order of secular priests.

nerī′nĕ (or -rē-) n. S. Afr. autumn-flowering bulbous plant of genus N~, with red or pink lily-like flowers.

Nēr′ō. Nero Claudius Caesar Augustus Germanicus (A.D. 37–68), Roman emperor 54–68; proverbial for tyranny and brutality.

nēr′olī n. Essential oil from flowers of bitter orange, used in perfumery. [f. name of Italian princess supposed to have invented it]

Nēr′va, Marcus Cocceius (c A.D. 35–98). Roman emperor 96–98.

nēr′vāte adj. (bot.) (of leaves) Having ribs. **nērvā′tion** n.

nērve n. 1. Sinew, tendon (now only poet. exc. in *strain every* ~, make all possible effort); vigour, energy, well-strung state. 2. (bot.) Rib, esp. midrib, of leaf. 3. (anat.) Fibre or bundle of fibres connecting and conveying impulses of

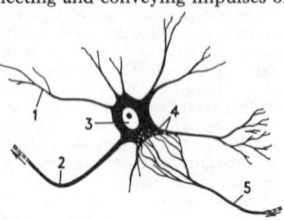

NERVE-CELL OR NEURON

1. Dendrite. 2. Beginning of axon. 3. Nucleus. 4. Synapse. 5. End of axon of another cell

sensation and motion between brain or spinal cord or ganglionic organ and some part of body; nervous fibre; (pl.) bodily state in regard to physical sensitiveness and interaction between brain and other parts, disordered state in these respects, exaggerated sensitiveness, nervousness; *get on one's* ~*s*, affect one with irritation, impatience, fear, etc.; ~*-centre*, ganglion, group of closely connected nerve-cells associated in performing some function; ~ *gas*, poison gas that attacks the nervous system, esp. affecting respiration. 4. Coolness in danger; boldness; assurance; (slang) audacity, impertinence; *lose one's* ~, become timid or irresolute. ~ *v.t.* Give strength, vigour, or courage. to; ~ *oneself*, brace oneself (to face something unpleasant).

nēr′velĕss (-vl-) adj. Inert, wanting in vigour or spirit, listless; (of style) diffuse; (bot., entom.) without nervures; (anat., zool.) without nerves. **nēr′velĕsslў** adv. **nēr′velĕssnĕss** n.

NEREID

nēr′vous adj. 1. Of the nerves; ~ *breakdown*, (colloq.) loss of emotional and mental stability; ~ *system*, system of specialized conducting tissue which enables an organism to co-ordinate its activity in relation to its environment. 2. Sinewy, muscular; (of style) vigorous, terse. 3. Having disordered or delicate nerves; excitable, highly strung, easily agitated, timid. **nēr′vouslў** adv. **nēr′vousnĕss** n.

nēr′vure (-yer) n. 1. One of the tubes strengthening an insect's wing (ill. INSECT). 2. Principal vein of leaf (ill. LEAF).

nēr′vў adj. 1. Nervous; trying to the nerves; irritable, apprehensive. 2. (U.S. colloq.) Insolent, courageous.

nĕ′science (or -shĭ-) n. Not knowing, absence of knowledge *of*. **nĕ′sciĕnt** adj. & n. Ignorant (*of*); agnostic.

nĕss[1] n. Promontory, headland, cape.

Nĕss[2], Loch. Lake in Invernessshire, Scotland, forming part of Caledonian Canal.

-nĕss suffix. Having a specified state or condition.

Nĕ′ssus. (Gk myth.) Centaur shot by Heracles for trying to carry off his wife Deianira; Nessus' blood-stained tunic, given to Deianira as a charm to reclaim an unfaithful husband, eventually caused Heracles' death.

nĕst n. Structure or place made or chosen by bird for laying eggs and sheltering young; animal's or insect's abode or spawning or breeding place; snug or secluded retreat, lodging, shelter, bed, receptacle; haunt *of* robbers etc.; fostering-place of vice etc.; brood, swarm; collection, series of similar objects; set *of boxes, tables,* etc., fitting one inside another; ~*-egg*, real or imitation egg left in nest to induce hen to go on laying there; sum of money kept as reserve or nucleus. ~ *v*. Make or have nest in specified place; take to nest-building; take birds' nests.

nĕ′stle (-sl) *v.* Make nest (now rare); settle oneself, be settled, comfortably *down, in, among,* etc., leaves, wraps, chair, etc.; press oneself affectionately (*close*) *to* person; lie half-hidden or embedded; push (head, shoulder, etc.) affectionately or snugly *in*; hold embraced (usu. in past. part.).

nĕ′stling (-sl-) n. Bird too young to leave nest.

Nĕ′stŏr[1]. (Gk legend) King of Pylos; in old age led his subjects to the Trojan War, where his wisdom, justice, and eloquence were proverbial; hence, wise old man.

Nĕ′stŏr[2] (c 1056–c 1114). Russian monk; reputed author of earliest Russian chronicle.

Nĕstŏr′ius (d. c 451). Syrian ecclesiastic; disciple of St. Chrysostom and patriarch of Constantinople (428–31); held that Christ had distinct human and divine persons and hence that the Virgin Mary should not be called 'Mother of God'; was condemned by the Councils of Ephesus (431) and Chalcedon (451). **Něstōr′ian** *adj.* & *n.* **Něstōr′ianism** *n.*

nět[1] *n.* Meshed fabric of twine, cord, hair, etc.; piece of this used for catching fish etc. or for covering, confining, protecting, carrying, etc.; moral or mental snare; reticulation, network; net stroke; **ne′tball**, game between teams of seven players, the object being to throw a large ball like a football

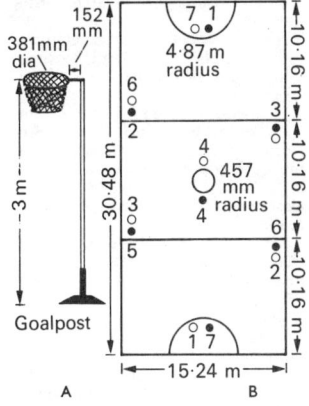

A. NET. B. NETBALL PITCH WITH POSITIONS OF PLAYERS

1. Goal shooter. 2. Goal attack. 3. Wing attack. 4. Centre. 5. Wing defence. 6. Goal defence. 7. Goal-keeper

so that it falls through a net suspended from a ring on the top of a post; ~-*cord*, cord supporting top of a tennis net; ~ *stroke*, stroke in which ball hits this; **ne′twork**, arrangement with intersecting lines and interstices resembling those of net; complex system *of* railways, rivers, canals, etc., ramification; broadcasting system of several stations linked together. ~ *v.* Cover, confine, catch, with net(s); fish (river etc.) with nets, set nets in (river); make netting; make (purse, hammock, etc.) by netting.

nět[2], **nětt** *adj.* Free from deduction, remaining after necessary deductions; ~ *price*, real price off which discount is not allowed; ~ *profit*, true profit, actual gain after working expenses have been paid; ~ *weight*, weight excluding wrappings. ~ *v.t.* Gain or yield (sum) as net profit.

ně′ther (-dh-) *adj.* (archaic or joc.) Lower. **ně′thermōst** *adj.*

Ně′therlands (-dh-, -z). (Du. *Nederland*) 1. Small kingdom in N. Europe, in English freq. called Holland; capital, Amsterdam, seat of govt., The Hague, principal language Dutch. 2. (hist.) Low Countries, the whole area of the Rhine, Meuse, and Scheldt deltas, that now occupied by Holland, Belgium, Luxembourg, and small parts of France and Germany. During the Middle Ages it was divided among numerous countships and dukedoms; by the mid-16th c. these were united under the Habsburg emperor Charles V, but in the wars of religion the N. (Dutch) part revolted (1555–88) and became an independent Protestant Republic (*United Provinces of the* ~, or States General); meanwhile the S. part passed to the Spanish Habsburgs (*Spanish* ~) and later, in 1713, to the Austrian Habsburgs (*Austrian* ~). In 1815 both N. and S. were united under a monarchy (*Kingdom of the* ~), but the S. revolted in 1830 and became an independent kingdom, BELGIUM. **Ně′therlander** *n.* **Ně′therlandish** *adj.*

ně′tsuke (-sōōkǎ) *n.* Carved or otherwise ornamented piece of ivory etc. once worn by Japanese as bob or button on cord by which articles were suspended from girdle.

nett: see NET[2].

ně′tting *n.* (esp.) Netted string, wire, or thread; piece of this.

ně′ttle *n.* Plant of genus *Urtica*, with two common species (*U. dioica* and *U. urens*) growing profusely on waste land and noted for stinging properties of leaf-hairs (ill. FLOWER); plant resembling this, esp. dead-nettle; ~-*rash*, skin eruption in patches like those produced by nettle-stings, urticaria. ~ *v.t.* 1. Beat or sting with nettles; get *oneself* stung with nettles. 2. Irritate, provoke.

neum, **neume** (nū-) *n.* (mus.) Sign in plainsong indicating note

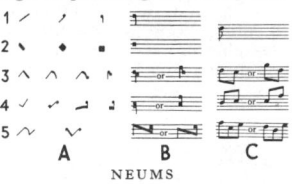

A B C

NEUMS

A. EARLY NEUMS. B. NEUMS USED NOW. C. MODERN EQUIVALENT

Accents: 1. Acute. 2. Grave. 3. Circumflex. 4. Grave+acute. 5. Acute+grave+acute

or group of notes to be sung to a single syllable.

neur′al (nūr-) *adj.* Of the nerves; of the nervous system.

neurǎ′lġia (nūr-) *n.* Affection of nerves (usu. of head or face) causing intense intermittent pain. **neurǎ′lġic** *adj.*

neurasthē′nia (nūr-) *n.* Functional nervous weakness, nervous debility. **neurasthě′nic** *adj.*

neurǎ′tion (nūr-) *n.* Distribution of nervures.

neuri′tis (nūr-) *n.* Inflammation of nerve(s). **neuri′tic** *adj.*

neuro- (nūr-) *prefix.* Of nerves. **neuroġli′a** (nūr-) *n.* Non-nervous tissue present in nervous system.

neurŏ′loġy (nūr-) *n.* Scientific study of the anatomy, functions, and diseases of the nervous system. **neurolŏ′ġical** *adj.* **neurŏ′loġist** *n.*

neurō′ma (nūr-) *n.* Tumour on a nerve or in nerve-tissue.

neur′ŏn, -ōne (nūr-) *n.* Nerve-cell with its appendages, the basic structural unit of the nervous system (ill. NERVE).

neur′opǎth (nūr-) *n.* Person of abnormal nervous sensibility; person affected by nervous disease. **neuropǎ′thic** *adj.* **neurŏ′pathў** *n.*

neurŏ′pterous (nūr-) *adj.* Of the Neuroptera, an order of insects having four naked membranous transparent wings with reticulate neuration.

neurō′sis (nūr-) *n.* (pl. -*ōsēs*). (path., psychol.) Derangement of normal function due to disorders of nervous system, esp. such as are unaccompanied by demonstrable organic change. **neurŏ′tic** *adj.* & *n.* (Person) affected with neurosis. **neurŏ′tically** *adv.* **neurŏ′ticism** *n.*

neu′ter *adj.* 1. (gram.) Neither masculine nor feminine; (of verb) intransitive. 2. Neither male nor female; (bot.) having neither pistils nor stamens; (entom.) sexually undeveloped, sterile. ~ *n.* 1. Neuter noun, adjective, verb, or gender. 2. Sexually undeveloped female insect, esp. bee or ant; castrated animal, person with characteristics of neither sex. ~ *v.t.* Castrate.

neu′tral *adj.* 1. Not assisting either of two belligerent States, belonging to a State remaining inactive during hostilities, exempted or excluded from warlike operations; taking neither side in dispute or difference of opinion, indifferent, impartial. 2. Not distinctly marked or coloured, indefinite, vague, indeterminate; (of colour) greyish or brownish; (of sound) indistinct, obscure. 3. (chem.) Neither acid nor alkaline; (elect.) neither positive nor negative. 4. Neuter, asexual. **neu′trally** *adv.* **neutrǎ′litў** *n.* **neu′tral** *n.* 1. Neutral State or person; subject of neutral State. 2. (mech.) Position of gear mechanism in which the propelling mechanism may revolve freely without transmitting power to the parts to be driven.

neu′tralize *v.t.* Counterbalance, render ineffective by opposite force or effect; exempt or exclude (place) from sphere of hostilities. **neutralizā′tion** *n.*

neutri′nō (-rē-) *n.* Neutral elementary particle of negligible mass.

neu′tron *n.* Electrically neutral particle of almost the same mass

[595]

Nev. *abbrev.* Nevada.

Nĕ'va. River of N. Russia, draining Lakes Ladoga, Onega, and Ilmen into Gulf of Finland, and running through Leningrad.

Nèva'da (-vah-). State of western U.S., admitted to the Union in 1864; capital, Carson City. **Nèva'dan** *adj.* (esp., geol.) Of an episode of mountain formation during the Mesozoic era (ill. GEOLOGY).

névé (nĕ'vā) *n.* Expanse of granular snow not yet compressed into ice at head of glacier (ill. MOUNTAIN).

nĕ'ver *adv.* At no time, on no occasion, not ever; not at all; (colloq., expressing surprise or incredulity) surely not; ~ *a*, not a, no — at all; ~ *a one*, none; ~ *mind*, do not be troubled (about); *nevermo're*, at no future time; *the ~-never*, (colloq.) hire-purchase; *~-never land*, imaginary place; ~ *so*, (in conditional clauses) to unlimited extent, ever so; ~ *the*, (with comparative) none the; *nevertheless*, notwithstanding, but for all that.

Nĕ'vis. Island in the West Indies, part of the State of St. Kitts.

new *adj.* Not existing before, now first made, brought into existence, invented, introduced, known or heard of, experienced, or discovered; unfamiliar *to*; renewed, fresh, further, additional; later, modern, newfangled; of recent growth, origin, arrival, or manufacture, now first used, not worn or exhausted; not yet accustomed *to*, fresh *from*; (of family or person) lately risen in position; *new'comer*, person lately arrived; *N~ Deal*: see DEAL³; *newfangled*, different from the good old fashion, having no merit but novelty; *N~ Forest*, wooded district in Hampshire, formerly a royal hunting-ground; *~-laid*, (of eggs) recently laid; *~ learning*, study of the Bible and the Greek classics in their original language at the time of the Reformation and Renaissance in England; ~ *moon*, moon when first visible as a crescent after conjunction with sun, time of such appearance; *N~ Model Army*, army organized by English Parliament, 1645, with Sir Thomas Fairfax as general; *N~ Order*, (f. Ger., *die neue Ordnung*) (esp.) Hitler's plan for the reconstruction of the States of Europe on the basis of a National-Socialist regime; ~ *poor*, *rich*, classes recently impoverished, enriched; *new'-speak*, (joc. in derogatory sense) reformed version of a language [f. George Orwell's novel *1984*]; *N~ Style*; see STYLE; *N~ Testament*: see TESTAMENT; *N~ Town*, (esp.) town built under the New Towns Acts, 1946-66, financed from government funds and managed by a development corporation; *N~ World*, the Americas, discovered at a comparatively late period; *N~ Year*, coming or lately begun year, first few days of year; *N~ Year's Day*, (U.S. freq. *N~ Year's*), 1 Jan.; *N~ Year honours*, titles of honour conferred annually by the British Sovereign and announced on New Year's Day. **new'ish** *adv.* **new'ness** *n.* **new** *adv.* Newly, recently, just; anew.

New Bri'tain (-*an*). Island of Bismarck Archipelago.

New Brŭ'nswick (-z-). SE. maritime province of Canada; capital, Fredericton.

New'castle upŏ'n Tyne (-kahsl *or* -kă'sl). City and port of the metropolitan county of Tyne and Wear, with important coal-shipping and ship-building industries; university, 1963.

new'el *n.* (archit.) Centre pillar or (*open* or *hollow ~*) well of winding stair; post supporting stair-handrail at top or bottom (ill. STAIR).

New E'ngland (ingg-). Part of U.S. comprising NE. States of Maine, New Hampshire, Vermont, Massachusetts, Rhode Island, and Connecticut. **New E'nglander** *n.* Native, inhabitant, of New England.

New'foundlănd (-fu-; *or* -fow'ndland). Large island, with famous fisheries, at mouth of St. Lawrence River; discovered and claimed for England 1497 by John Cabot; formerly a Dominion of the British Empire; joined with Canada as one of its provinces, 1949; capital, St. John's; ~ *dog*, large dog of a breed native to N. America, with thick coarse coat, noted for sagacity, good temper, strength, and swimming powers (ill. DOG). **New'foundländer** *n.*

New'gate. Former London prison, orig. the W. gatehouse of City of London, used for this purpose from 12th c.; burnt down 1780 by Gordon rioters and rebuilt; demolished 1902 and replaced by present Central Criminal Court; ~ *Calendar*, (hist.) publication, first issued 1773, giving accounts of the prisoners and their crimes.

New Gui'nea (gĭ-). Pacific island N. of Australia, divided into (1) the Indonesian province of West Irian, and (2) PAPUA New Guinea.

New Hă'mpshire. NE. State of U.S., one of the original thirteen States of the Union (1788); capital, Concord.

New Hĕ'brĭdës (-z). Group of islands in W. Pacific, under joint French and British administration; capital, Vila.

New Hŏ'lland. Former name of Australia.

New Ir'eland (īrl-). Island of Bismarck archipelago.

New Jĕr'sey (-zĭ). Middle Atlantic State of U.S., one of the original thirteen States of the Union (1787); capital, Trenton.

New'lands (-z), John Alexander Reina (1837-98). English chemist who formulated the Law of Octaves (see OCTAVE).

new'ly *adv.* Recently, just; in new manner; *newlywed(s)* (*adj.* & *n.pl.*) recently married (couple).

New'man, John Henry (1801-90). English theologian and author; as an Anglican clergyman, was one of the founders of the Oxford or TRACTARIAN movement; was received into R.C. Church 1845; published his 'Apologia pro Vita sua' 1864; was created cardinal 1879.

New'märkĕt. 1. Market-town in Suffolk, England, near which is a heath used for horse-racing since early 17th c. 2. (19th c.) Close-fitting coat (~ *coat*) for men or women, orig. worn for riding. 3. Card-game, in which the object is to play the same cards as certain duplicates which are exhibited and on which stakes are laid.

New Mĕ'xĭcō. State of south-west U.S.; admitted to the Union in 1912; capital, Santa Fe.

New Prŏ'vidence. Island of BAHAMAS.

news (-z) *n.* Tidings, new information, fresh event reported; wireless or television report of this; *new'sagent*, dealer in newspapers etc.; *new'scast*, radio or television broadcast of news; *new'scaster*, broadcaster of news on radio or television; *~-letter*, (orig.) letter sent out periodically with the news to country towns etc.; now, periodical sent by post to subscribers; *new'smonger*, gossip; *new'spaper(-s-)*, printed, now usu. daily or weekly, publication containing news, advertisements and literary matter; *new'sprint*, paper for printing newspapers on; *new's-reel*, cinema film giving items of recent news; *~-stand*, stall for sale of newspapers; *new'svendor*, newspaper-seller.

New South Wāles (-lz). State of SE. Australia; capital, Sydney.

new'sў (-zĭ) *adj.* (colloq.) Full of (sensational) news.

newt *n.* Small tailed amphibian of the order Urodela.

New'ton¹ (-tn), Sir Isaac (1642-1727). English natural philosopher; formulator of laws of motion and law of gravitation. **Newtō'nian** *adj.* & *n.* (Follower) of Newton or his theory of the universe.

new'ton² (-tn) *n.* (abbrev. N) Unit of force in M.K.S. system, equal to the force producing an acceleration of 1 metre per second per second on a mass of 1 kilogramme.

New Yŏrk. 1. Middle Atlantic State of U.S., one of the original thirteen States of the Union (1788); capital, Albany. 2. Largest city of U.S., in New York State at mouth of Hudson River. **New**

Yŏr'ker n. Native, inhabitant, of New York City.

New Zea'land. Member State of the Commonwealth, occupying two large and many smaller islands in S. Pacific c 1,000 miles SE. of Australia; the islands were discovered by Tasman 1642 and visited by Cook 1769; became an English colony; acquired self-government 1852 and dominion status 1907; capital, Wellington.

New Zea'lander n. Native, inhabitant, of New Zealand. [f. ZEELAND]

nĕxt adj. Lying, living, being, nearest or nearest to; nearest in relationship or kinship; soonest come to, first ensuing, immediately following, coming nearest in order etc., to, immediately before; ~ door, (door of the) nearest or adjoining house (also fig.); ~-door to, almost; ~ friend, (law) person acting on behalf of a minor or person of unsound mind; ~ world: see WORLD. ~ prep. In or into the next place, on the next occasion, in the next degree, to. ~ n. Next person or thing; ~ of kin, person nearest of kin (to).

nĕ'xus n. Bond, connection.

Ney (nā), Michel (1769–1815). French soldier, marshal of France; one of Napoleon's marshals; supported the Bourbons when Napoleon abdicated, but joined forces with him when he returned from Elba; commanded the Old Guard at Waterloo; was shot for treason.

N.F. abbrev. Newfoundland; Norman French.

N.F.S. abbrev. National Fire Service.

N.F.U. abbrev. National Farmers' Union.

ngwee (engwā') n. $\frac{1}{100}$ of a kwacha.

N.H. abbrev. New Hampshire.

n.h.p. abbrev. Nominal horsepower.

N.H.S. abbrev. National Health Service.

N.I. abbrev. National Insurance.

Niă'gara. N. Amer. river flowing from Lake Erie into Lake Ontario and forming part of boundary between Canada and U.S.A.; famous for its waterfalls over 45 m (150 ft) high.

nĭb n. Pen-point; point of tool etc.; (pl.) fragments of crushed cocoa-beans.

nĭ'bble v. Take small bites at; bite gently or cautiously or playfully. ~ n. Act of nibbling, esp. of fish· at bait.

Nĭ'bėlungs, -lungen (nēbĭlōongz, -ōongen) n.pl. (Germanic legend) Race of dwarfs in Norway.

Nĭ'belungenlied. 13th-c. German poem (embodying a story found in the EDDA) telling of the life and death of SIEGFRIED and of KRIEMHILD's revenge.

nĭ'blick n. Golf-club (no. 8 iron) with heavy lofted head, used esp. for playing out of bunkers.

nĭbs (-z) n. (slang) his ~, burlesque title (after his Grace etc.).

Nĭcae'a. (Turk. Iznik) Ancient city of Bithynia, scene of two oecumenical councils, the first (325) dealing with the Arian controversy and the second (787) the question of images.

Nĭcarā'gūa. Central American republic, between Honduras and Costa Rica; independent since 1821; capital, Managua.

nīce adj. 1. Fastidious; punctilious; requiring precision or discrimination; minute, subtle. 2. (colloq.) Agreeable, delightful; satisfactory; kind, friendly, considerate; generally commendable.

nī'cely adv. nī'cenĕss n.

Nĭcē'ne (or nī'-) adj. Of Nicaea; ~ Creed, formal statement of Christian belief based on decisions of first Council of Nicaea, official creed of Orthodox, Roman Catholic, and some Protestant Churches.

nī'cĕty n. Punctiliousness; precision, accuracy; minute distinction, subtle or unimportant detail, (pl.) minutiae; to a ~, as closely or precisely as possible.

niche n. Shallow recess in wall to contain statue, vase, etc.;

NICHE OR TABERNACLE

(fig.) place or position adapted to the character, or suited to the merits, or a person or thing. ~ v.t. Place (as if) in a niche.

Nĭ'cholas¹ (-k-). (Russ. Nikolai) Name of two emperors of Russia: Nicholas I (1796–1855), emperor 1825–55; his accession, after the death of his brother Alexander I and the abdication of his brother Constantine, was marked by the DECEMBRIST revolution, which he subdued and punished mercilessly; Nicholas II (1868–1918), emperor of Russia 1894–1917; forced to abdicate, March 1917; killed with his family, 1918.

Nĭ'cholas² (-k-), St. (d. 326). Bishop of Myra in Asia Minor; patron of sailors and of children (cf. SANTA CLAUS), and patron saint of Russia; commemorated 6 Dec.

Nĭ'ciăs (d. 413 B.C.). Athenian statesman and general in Peloponnesian War; negotiated a peace (421 B.C.) which was only temporary.

nick¹ n. Notch, groove, serving as catch, guide, mark, etc.; in the ~ of time, just at the right moment, only just in time. ~ v. Make nick(s) in, indent; make incision at root of (horse's tail) to make him carry it higher; (slang) catch, arrest; filch; (in hunting, racing, etc.) cut in.

Nick². Old ~, the Devil.

nĭ'ckel n. 1. (chem.) Hard silvery-white lustrous malleable ductile metallic element much used esp. in alloys; symbol Ni, at. no. 28, at. wt 58·71. 2. (U.S.) Five-cent piece (of copper and nickel alloy). 3. ~ silver, alloy of nickel, zinc, and copper, formerly used for cutlery; ~ steel, alloy of iron with nickel. ~ v.t. Coat with nickel. [abbrev. of Ger. kupfernickel copper-coloured ore from which nickel was first got (kupfer copper, nickel demon, w. ref. to disappointing nature of ore, which yielded no copper); cf. COBALT]

nĭ'ck-năck n. = KNICK-KNACK.

nĭ'cknāme n. Name added to or substituted for proper name of person, place, or thing. ~ v.t. Call (person etc. by a nickname), give nickname to.

Nĭcobăr' I'slands (īlandz). Group of islands in Bay of Bengal, administered (with Andaman Islands) by the Republic of India.

Nĭcodē'mus. Member of the Sanhedrin who helped Joseph of Arimathea to bury Jesus Christ (John 3, 7, 19).

nĭcōtiā'na (-shĭ-) n. Tobacco plant; any of several plants of genus N~, esp. N. alata, a garden variety with greenish-white flowers, grown for its sweet scent. [f. Jacques Nicot, who introduced tobacco into France in 1560]

nĭ'cotine (-ēn) n. Poisonous alkaloid contained in tobacco, from which it is obtained as a pungent oily liquid soluble in water. nicotĭ'nic adj. ~ acid, crystalline acid (C₆H₅NO₂), produced by oxidation of nicotine, a member of the vitamin B group.

nĭ'cotinism (-ēn-) n. Morbid state produced by excessive use of tobacco.

nĭ'ctāte, nĭ'ctĭtāte vbs.i. Close and open the eyes, wink; chiefly in nict(it)ating membrane, third or inner eyelid of many animals, vestigial in man (ill. EYE). nictā'tion, nictĭtā'tion ns.

nīdamĕ'ntal adj. (zool.) Secreting shell-covering material.

nīde n. Brood of pheasants.

nĭ'dĭfĭcāte, nĭ'dĭfy vbs.i. Build nest(s). nīdĭfĭcā'tion n.

nĭ'dus n. Place in which insects etc. deposit eggs; place in which spores or seeds develop; place of origin or development of disease etc.; place in which something is deposited or lodged.

Niebuhr (nē'boor), Barthold Georg (1776–1831). German historian of ancient Rome.

niece *n.* Brother's or sister's daughter.

niĕ′llō *n.* Black metallic amalgam of sulphur added to copper, silver, lead, etc., for filling engraved lines in silver or other metal, as decoration; (specimen of) such ornamental work; ~ *print*, print taken from engraved plate which is to be filled with niello.

Nier′steiner (-tīn-) *n.* White Rhine wine. [*Nierstein*, German village in Hesse, on left bank of Rhine]

Nietzsche (nē′che), Friedrich Wilhelm (1844–1900). German philosopher; originator of idea of 'superman' and of doctrine of perfectibility of man through forcible self-assertion and superiority to ordinary morality. **Nie′tzschēan** *adj.*

ni′ftў *adj.* (slang) Neat, smart, clever.

Ni′ger (-g-). 1. River of W. Africa, flowing in a curve from NE. frontier of Sierra Leone to Gulf of Guinea. 2. Republic in W. central Africa; capital, Niamey. [L, = 'black']

Nīgēr′ia. Republic in W. Africa, member State of the Commonwealth, occupying basin of lower Niger, with coastline on Gulf of Guinea; formerly a British protectorate; independent 1960; capital, Lagos.

ni′ggard *n.* Stingy person, grudging giver *of.* ~ *adj.* (rhet. & poet.) Niggardly.

ni′ggardlў *adj.* Parsimonious, stingy, sparing, scanty; giving or given grudgingly or in small amounts. **ni′ggardlinĕss** *n.*

ni′gger *n.* (Offensive term for) Negro or other dark-skinned person; dark shade of brown; *work like a* ~, work very hard.

ni′ggle *v.i.* Spend time, be overelaborate, on petty details. **ni′ggling** *adj.* Trifling, petty; lacking in breadth, largeness, or boldness of effect; (of handwriting) cramped.

nigh (nī) *adv., prep., & adj.* (archaic, poet., or dial.) Near.

night (nīt) *n.* Dark period between twilight and dawn, time from sunset to sunrise, darkness then prevailing, the dark; end of daylight; weather, experiences, or occupation of a night; *make a* ~ *of it*, spend night in festivity; ~ *out*, festive evening; evening on which servant is allowed out; ~-*bird*, (esp.) owl or nightingale; person who goes about by night; ~-*blindness*: see NYCTALOPIA; ~-*cap*, covering for the head, worn in bed; drink taken before going to bed; ~-*clothes*, clothes worn in bed; ~-*club*, club open at night for dancing, supper, etc.; *ni′ghtdress*, *ni′ghtgown*, loose garment worn by women or children in bed; *ni′ghtfall*, end of daylight; ~-*glass*, short refracting telescope for use at night; *ni′ghtjar*, nocturnal bird of family Caprimulgidae, with harsh cry; ~-*life*, entertainments open at night; ~-*light*, short thick candle or other dimly burning light for use at night, esp. in sick-rooms; ~-*line*, line left with baited hooks to catch fish by night; *ni′ghtmare*, female monster sitting upon and seeming to suffocate sleeper, incubus; oppressive, terrifying, or fantastically horrible dream; haunting fear, thing vaguely dreaded; ~ *office*, Matins and Lauds; ~-*piece*, (painting of) night scene or landscape; ~-*school*, school, class, held in evening for those at work during day; ~-*soil*, (archaic) contents of cesspools etc., removed at night; ~-*stick*, (U.S.) stick carried by policemen at night; ~-*watch*, (person or party keeping) watch by night; Hebrew or Roman division (one of three or four) of the night.

ni′ghtingāle¹ (nītĭngg-) *n.* Small reddish-brown migratory bird of genus *Luscinia*, in Gt Britain *L. megarhyncos*, celebrated for the melodious song of the male, often heard at night during the breeding season.

Ni′ghtingāle² (nītĭngg-), Florence (1820–1910). English reformer; founder of modern nursing profession; organized hospital unit for Crimean War and established new type of war hospital in Crimea.

ni′ghtlў (nīt-) *adj.* Happening, done, existing, etc., in the night; happening every night. ~ *adv.* Every night.

ni′ghtshāde (nīt-) *n.* Any of various plants of genus *Solanum*, esp. *black* ~ (*S. nigrum*), with white flowers and black poisonous berries, *woody* ~ (*S. dulcamara*), with purple flowers and bright-red berries; *deadly* ~, belladonna; *enchanter's* ~, plant of genus *Circaea* with white flowers.

ni′ghtў (nītī) *n.* (colloq.) Nightdress.

nigrĕ′scent *adj.* Blackish. **nigrĕ′scence** *n.* Becoming black; blackness.

ni′gritūde *n.* Blackness.

ni′hilĭsm (or nī′ĭ-) *n.* 1. Negative doctrines, total rejection of current beliefs, in religion or morals; (philos.) scepticism that denies all existence. 2. Doctrines of extreme revolutionary party in 19th-and 20th-c. Russia (orig. used of a small group in the 1860s who repudiated the established order and its standards). **ni′hilist** *n.* **nīhilĭ′stic** *adj.* [L *nihil* nothing]

Nī′kė. (Gk myth.) Goddess of victory, freq. identified with Athene; ~ *of Samothrace*: see WINGED Victory.

Ni′kon (nē-). Nikita Minin (1605–81), Russian churchman; patriarch of Moscow 1652–66; reformed Church discipline and ritual.

nil *n.* Nothing (esp. in scoring at games etc.); ~ *admirari*, (L, = 'to wonder at nothing') nonchalance, attitude of being surprised at, or admiring, nothing.

Nīle. Longest river of Africa, flowing from E. Central Africa 4,000 miles northwards to Mediterranean; *Blue* ~, tributary joining the Nile at Khartoum; *White* ~, part of Nile above Khartoum; *Battle of the* ~, naval battle (1798) fought in Aboukir Bay, near Alexandria, where Nelson's overwhelming victory over the French fleet restored British prestige in the Mediterranean and enabled England to recapture Malta and Minorca; ~ *green* = EAU de Nil.

nī′lgai (-gī) *n.* Large shorthorned Indian antelope (*Boselaphus tragocamelus*), male of which is bluish or iron-grey; Indian Blue Bull. [Pers. *nīl* blue, *gāw* ox]

Nīlŏ′tic *adj.* Of the river Nile, the Nile region, or its inhabitants.

nĭ′mble *adj.* Quick in movement, agile, swift; (of mind etc.) versatile, clever, quick to apprehend. **nĭ′mblenĕss** *n.* **nĭ′mblў** *adv.*

nimbostrā′tus *n.* (meteor.) Type of low cloud, dark grey and sometimes trailing (ill. CLOUD).

nĭ′mbus *n.* Bright cloud or halo investing deity, person, or thing; bright disc, aureole, round or over head of saint etc. in picture.

nimī′etў *n.* Excess.

ni′minў-pi′minў *adj.* Mincing, prim.

Ni′mrŏd. Great-grandson of Noah, traditional founder of the Babylonian dynasty, noted as a great hunter (Gen. 10: 8–10).

ni′ncompōōp *n.* Simpleton.

nīne *adj.* Amounting to nine; *the N*~, the Muses; ~ *days' wonder*, novelty that attracts much attention but is soon forgotten; *ni′nepin*, pin used in *ninepins*, game of knocking down nine wooden pins by throwing a ball or bowl at them. ~ *n.* One more than eight; symbol for this (9, ix, or IX); card with 9 pips; 9 o'clock; size etc. indicated by 9; set of 9 things or persons; (U.S.) baseball team; *to the* ~*s*, to perfection (esp. in *dressed up to the* ~*s*). **nī′nefōld** *adj. & adv.*

nī′netee′n (-nt-) *adj. & n.* One more than eighteen (19, xix, or XIX). **nī′netee′nth** *adj.* ~ *hole*, (colloq.) bar-room in golf club-house.

nī′netў (-ntī) *adj.* Amounting to ninety. ~ *n.* Cardinal number, nine times ten (90, xc, or XC); set of 90 things or persons; *nineties*, (pl.) numbers etc. from 90 to 99; these years of century or life.

Ni′nĕveh (-vī). Ancient capital of Assyrian Empire, on right bank of Tigris.

Ni′ngsia (-sh-). Autonomous region of China; capital, Yinchuan.

Ni′nian, St. (d. *c* 432). Briton trained in Rome and sent to convert pagans in N. Britain; he was consecrated bishop and his see was established in Galloway.

ni′nnў *n.* Simpleton.
ninon (nē′nawn) *n.* Light silk dress-fabric.
ninth *adj.* Next after eighth. ~ *n.* Ninth part (see PART¹, 1); ninth thing etc.; (mus.) interval of octave and second. **ni′nthlў** *adv.* In the ninth place.
Ni′obĕ. (Gk legend) Daughter of Tantalus; Apollo and Artemis, enraged because she boasted herself superior to their mother Latona, slew her six sons and five of her six daughters; Niobe herself was turned into a rock, and her tears into streams that trickled from it. **Nī′obids** (-z) *n.pl.* Children of Niobe.
niō′bium *n.* (chem.) Rare metallic element very similar to tantalum and usu. found associated with it; symbol Nb, at. no. 41, at. wt 92·9064. [named after NIOBE]
nip¹ *v.* Pinch, squeeze sharply, bite; pinch *off*; check growth of; (of cold) affect injuriously, pain; (slang) move rapidly or nimbly. ~ *n.* Pinch, sharp squeeze, bite; (check to vegetation caused by) coldness of air; ~ *and tuck*, (U.S.) neck and neck.
nip² *n.* Small quantity of spirits etc. ~ *v.* Take nips (of).
Nĭp³ *adj. & n.* (slang) Japanese. [abbrev. NIPPONESE]
ni′pa (*or* nē-) *n.* Kind of E. Indian palm (*N~ fruticans*), with creeping trunk, large feathery leaves, and large round bunches of fruit; alcoholic drink made from the sap of this tree.
ni′pper *n.* (esp.) 1. (slang) Young boy. 2. (pl.) Implement with jaws for gripping or cutting; forceps, pincers, pliers; (usu. pl.) crustacean's great claw.
ni′pple *n.* 1. Small projection in which mammary ducts terminate in mammal of either sex; teat, esp. on woman's breast; teat of nursing-bottle. 2. Nipple-like protuberance on skin, glass, metal, etc.; small rounded elevation on mountain; (hist.) perforated projection of musket-lock on which percussion-cap is placed.
Nipponē′se (-z) *adj. & n.* Japanese. [f. *Nippon*, Jap. name for Japan, f. *ni-pun* sunrise (*ni* sun, *pon* origin)]
ni′ppў *adj.* (colloq.) Cold; nimble.
N.I.R.C. *abbrev.* National Industrial Relations Court.
nīrva′na (-vah-) *n.* In Buddhist theology, extinction of individual existence and absorption into supreme spirit, or extinction of all passions and desires and attainment of perfect beatitude. [Sansk. *nirvāna* blowing out, extinction]
ni′si *conj.* (legal) Unless; *decree, order,* etc., ~, decree etc. valid unless cause is shown for rescinding it before appointed time at which it is made absolute; ~ *pri′us,* hearing of civil causes by judges of assize, court-business of this kind (from Latin words of writ, 'unless before', directing sheriff to provide jury on certain day unless the judges come sooner). [L]
Ni′ssen hŭt. Tunnel-shaped hut made of corrugated iron with a cement floor. [Lt.-Col. P. N. *Nissen,* inventor (1871–1930)]
nit *n.* Egg of louse or other parasitic insect (ill. LOUSE).
ni′trāte *n.* Salt of nitric acid; potassium or sodium nitrate used as fertilizer. **nitrā′te** *v.t.* Treat, impregnate, or cause to interact, with nitric acid. **nitrā′tion** *n.*
ni′tre (-ter) *n.* Saltpetre, potassium nitrate (KNO₃).
ni′tric *adj.* Of nitre; ~ *acid,* clear, colourless, pungent, highly corrosive liquid (HNO₃); ~ *oxide,* colourless gas (NO), obtained by the action of nitric acid on copper turnings or by the combination of nitrogen and oxygen at high temperatures.
ni′trifў *v.* Turn into nitre, make or become nitrous. **nītrificā′tion** *n.*
nītrobĕ′nzēne *n.* Poisonous yellow liquid (C₆H₅NO₂) used in the preparation of aniline etc.
nitrocĕ′llulōse *n.* = CELLULOSE nitrate.
ni′tro-chalk (-awk) *n.* Fertilizer consisting of a mixture of calcium carbonate and ammonium nitrate.
ni′tro-cŏ′mpound *n.* Organic substance containing the group —NO₂.
ni′trogen *n.* Colourless tasteless odourless gaseous element forming about four-fifths of the atmosphere and occurring also in nature as nitrates, and as proteins in animal and vegetable tissues, used commercially in the large-scale synthesis of ammonia; symbol N, at. no. 7, at. wt 14·0067; ~ *cycle,* continuous series of processes by which nitrogen and nitrogenous compounds are converted into substances that can be utilized by plants, thence transferred to animals, and finally re-converted by decay of plant and animal tissue; ~ *fixation,* process by which atmospheric nitrogen is combined with other elements (1) in the manufacture of commercially important nitrogen compounds, as nitric acid, fertilizers, etc., (2) in nature by soil bacteria, and thereby made available to plants as food. **nitrŏ′genous** *adj.* Of, belonging to, containing, nitrogen. **nitrŏ′genīze** *v.t.* Combine with nitrogen or nitrogenous compounds.
ni′tro-glў′cerine *n.* Glyceryl trinitrate, a yellowish oily violently explosive liquid formed by action of a mixture of nitric and sulphuric acid on glycerine; a constituent of dynamite, gelignite, and cordite.
ni′trous *adj.* Of, like, impregnated with, nitre; (chem.) of, containing, nitrogen, esp. of compounds in which nitrogen has a lower valency than nitric compounds; ~ *acid,* acid (HNO₂) containing less oxygen than nitric acid; ~ *oxide,* colourless sweet-smelling gas (N₂O), used as a mild anaesthetic, laughing-gas.
ni′twit *n.* (slang) Person of little intelligence.
nix¹ *n.* (slang) Nothing.
nix² *n.* (fem. *ni′xie*) Water-elf.
Ni′xon, Richard Milhous (1913–). 37th president of U.S., 1969–74 (resigned).
Nizā′m (-ahm) *n.* Title of former ruler of Hyderabad.
Nĭzh′ni Nŏv′gorod. Former name of GORKY².
N.J. *abbrev.* New Jersey.
N.K.V.D. Secret police of U.S.S.R., 1939–45. [initials of *Naródnўi Komissariát Vnu-trennikh Del,* people's commissariat of internal affairs]
N.L. *abbrev.* National Liberal.
N.L.C., N.L.F. *abbrevs.* National Liberal Club, Federation.
N.Mex. *abbrev.* New Mexico.
NNE. *abbrev.* North-north-east.
NNW. *abbrev.* North-north-west.
nō¹ *adj.* Not any; not a, quite other than a; hardly any; ~ *ball,* (umpire's announcement of) unlawfully delivered ball in cricket; *no-ball* (*v.*) pronounce (bowler) to have bowled no ball; *no′body,* no person; person of no importance; ~ *man,* no person; ~ *man's land,* piece of waste, unowned or debatable ground, esp. (mil.) the space between opposed lines; ~ *one,* no person; (as *adj.*) no single; ~ *side,* (Rugby footb.) (announcement of) end of game; ~ *trumps,* (cards), (bid calling for) hand played without trump suit; *no′ways* (archaic), *no′wise,* in no manner, not at all; ~ *whit,* (archaic or joc.) not at all. ~ *adv.* 1. (as alternative after *or*) Not. 2. (with comparatives) By no amount, not at all; ~ *more,* nothing further; not any more; no longer, never again, to no greater extent; just as little, neither. 3. Particle expressing negative reply to request, question, etc. ~ *n.* Word, answer, 'no'; (pl., *noes*) voters against a motion.
Nō², Noh (nō) *n.* Traditional Japanese drama evolved from the rites of Shinto worship and practically unchanged since 15th c.
Nᵒ, No. *abbrevs.* (pl. Nᵒˢ, Nos.) *Numero* (L, = in number); number.
n.o. *abbrev.* Not out.
N.O. *abbrev.* Natural order.
Nōā′chian (-k-) *adj.* Of Noah or his times.
Nō′ah (-*a*) Patriarch, represented as 10th in descent from Adam; at God's command he made the ARK which saved his family and specimens of every animal from the flood sent by God to destroy the world; his sons Shem, Ham, and Japheth were regarded as ancestors of all the races of mankind (Gen. 5–10); ~*'s ark,* child's toy model

[599]

of the ark with figures of Noah, his family, and the animals.
nŏb¹ *n.* (slang) Head; (cribbage) knave of same suit as turn-up card, counting one to holder.
nŏb² *n.* (slang) Member of upper classes. **nŏ'bbў** *adj.* (slang) Suitable for a nob, smart, elegant.
nŏ'bble *v.t.* (slang) Tamper with (race-horse) to prevent its winning; secure partiality of by underhand means; get hold of (money etc.) dishonestly; catch (criminal).
Nōbě'l, Alfred Bernhard (1833-96). Swedish chemist and engineer; inventor of dynamite and other high explosives; founder, by his will, of the five ~ *Prizes*, which are awarded annually to the persons adjudged by Swedish learned societies to have done the most significant work during the year in physics, chemistry, medicine, and literature, and to the person who is adjudged by the Norwegian parliament to have rendered the greatest service to the cause of peace; a ~ *Prize* for economic sciences was added in 1969.
nōbē'lium *n.* (chem.) Transuranic element, symbol No, at. no. 102.
nobi'liarў (-lya-) *adj.* Of (the) nobility; ~ *particle*, preposition (as French *de*, German *von*) prefixed to title.
nobi'litў *n.* 1. Noble character, mind, birth, or rank. 2. Persons of noble rank as a class; (in England) the peerage.
nō'ble *adj.* 1. Illustrious by rank, title, or birth, belonging to the nobility. 2. Of lofty character or ideals; showing greatness of character, magnanimous; splendid, magnificent, stately; impressive in appearance; excellent, admirable; (of metals such as gold, silver, sometimes platinum) resisting chemical action; *no'bleman, no'blewoman,* person of noble rank, peer(ess); **nō'blenèss** *n.* **nō'blў** *adv.* **nō'ble** *n.* 1. Nobleman. 2. (hist.) English gold coin, orig. minted by Edward III.
noblĕsse *n.* Class of nobles (esp. of foreign country); ~ *oblige* (-ēzh), privilege entails responsibility. [Fr.]
nŏck *n.* Notch at ends of bow for holding string; notch at butt end of arrow for receiving bowstring. ~ *v.t.* Set (arrow) on string.
nō'ctūle *n.* Great bat (*Nyctalus noctula*), European species of brown bat, the largest found in Britain.
nŏctŭr'nal *adj.* Of, in, done by, active in, the night.
nŏ'ctŭrne *n.* Soft, dreamy musical composition; (paint.) night-piece.
nŏd *v.* Incline head slightly and quickly in salutation, assent, or command; let head fall forward in drowsiness, be drowsy, make mistake from inattention; *nodding acquaintance*, slight acquaintance; ~ *n.* Nodding of the head; this as sign of absolute power; *land of N~*, (with pun on Gen. 4: 16), sleep.

N.O.D. *abbrev.* Naval Ordnance Department.
nŏ'dal *adj.* Of a node.
nŏ'ddle *n.* (colloq.) Head.
nŏ'ddў *n.* 1. Simpleton. 2. Soot-coloured tropical sea-bird (*Anous stolidus*), resembling tern but with shorter wings and tail not so forked.
nōde *n.* 1. (bot.) Point at which leaves spring (ill. LEAF). 2. (path.) Hard tumour esp. on gouty or rheumatic joint. 3. (astron.) Intersecting point of planet's orbit and ecliptic or of two great circles of celestial sphere (ill. CELESTIAL). 4. (phys.) Point or line of rest in vibrating body. 5. Central point in system. 6. (math.) Point at which curve crosses itself.
nŏ'dūle *n.* Small rounded lump of anything, small node in plant; small knotty tumour, ganglion. **nŏ'dūlar, nŏ'dūlātĕd, nŏ'dūlōse, nŏ'dūlous** *adjs.* **nŏdūlā'tion** *n.*
nŏ'dus *n.* Knotty point, difficulty, complication in plot of story etc.
Nōě'l *int.* Exclamation of joy, used in Christmas carols. [OF, f. L *natalis* natal]
nōě'tic *adj.* Of the intellect, purely intellectual or abstract; given to intellectual speculation. **nōě'tics** *n.* Science of the intellect.
nŏg¹ *n.* Pin, peg, small block, of wood; wood block built into wall in place of a brick so that interior woodwork may be nailed to it; snag or stump on tree. ~ *v.t.* Secure with nogs; build in form of nogging. **nŏ'gging** *n.* Brickwork between wooden quarters of framing (ill. HALF-timber).
nŏg² *n.* Kind of strong beer brewed in E. Anglia; EGG-nog.
nŏ'ggin *n.* Small mug; small measure, usu. ¼ pint, of liquor.
Noh: see No².
noil *n.* Short fibre combed from yarn during preparation.
noise (-z) *n.* Sound, esp. loud or harsh one; din, clamour; ~*s off*, in a play, sounds, usu. loud or confused, produced off the stage. **noi'selĕss** *adj.* **noi'selĕsslў** *adv.* **noi'selĕssnĕss** *n.* **noise** *v.t.* Make public, spread *abroad*.
noi'some *adj.* Harmful, noxious; ill-smelling; objectionable, offensive. **noi'somenĕss** *n.*
noi'sў (-zĭ) *adj.* Clamorous, turbulent; full of, making much, noise; loud. **noi'sĭlў** *adv.* **noi'sinĕss** *n.*
nō'lĕns vō'lĕns (-z, -z) *adv.* Willy-nilly. [L, = 'unwilling, willing']
nō'lī me tă'ngerĕ (mā, -ngg-). 1. Warning against interference etc.; person, thing, that must not be touched or interfered with. 2. (Old name for) lupus. 3. Painting representing appearance of Jesus Christ to Mary Magdalen at the sepulchre (John 20: 17). [L, = 'touch me not' (Vulgate, John 20: 17)]

nō'llĕ prō'sĕquī. (Entry on court record of) abandonment of part or all of suit by plaintiff or prosecutor. [L, = 'refuse to pursue']
nom. *abbrev.* Nominal; nominative.
nō'măd *n.* & *adj.* (Member of tribe) roaming from place to place for pasture; wanderer, wandering. **nomă'dic** *adj.* **nō'madism** *n.*
nō'mbril *n.* (her.) Point on an escutcheon midway between the true centre (fesse point) and the base point (ill. HERALDRY).
nŏm de guerre (gār). Pseudonym, sobriquet, assumed name under which person fights, plays, writes, etc. [Fr., = 'war name']
nŏm de plume (-ōom). Writer's pseudonym, pen-name. [Eng. formation on Fr. words *nom* name, *de* of, *plume* pen]
nō'měnclātor (-n-k-) *n.* 1. (hist.) Slave or client in ancient Rome charged with supplying his master, when canvassing for office, with names of persons met; usher assigning places at banquet. 2. Giver of names, esp. in classification.
nomě'nclature (*or* nō'-) *n.* System of names for things; terminology of a science etc.; systematic naming. **nomě'nclative** *adj.*
nō'minal *adj.* Of, as, like, a noun; of, in, names; existing in name only, (of price etc.) very small, trifling; not real or substantial; consisting of, giving, the names. **nō'minallў** *adv.*
nō'minalism *n.* (philos.) Doctrine of the scholastics that universal or abstract concepts are mere names, without any corresponding reality (opp. REALISM). **nō'minalist** *n.* **nŏminali'stic** *adj.*
nō'mināte *v.t.* Name or appoint (date, place); appoint, propose for election, to office. **nŏminā'tion** *n.* (esp.) Right of nominating for appointment. **nō'minātor, nŏminee'** *ns.*
nō'minative *adj.* 1. (gram.) Of the case of the subject of a verb. 2. Of, appointed by, nomination. ~ *n.* (Word in) nominative case; ~ *absolute*, construction like Latin ablative absolute, as *this being so, I did nothing.* **nŏminati'val** *adj.* Of the nominative case.
nŏn- *prefix.* Not (now freely prefixed to nouns, adjectives, etc.)
nŏn-ă'ccĕss (-ăks-) *n.* (law) Impossibility of access for sexual intercourse.
nō'nage *n.* Being under age, minority; immaturity, early stage.
nŏnagēnār'ian *adj.* & *n.* (Person) aged 90 years or more but less than 100.
nō'nagon *n.* Plane figure with 9 angles and 9 sides. **nonă'gonal** *adj.*
nŏn-appear'ance *n.* Failure to appear, esp. in court of law.
nō'narў *adj.* (arith., of scale of notation) Having nine as basis.
nŏn-belli'gerent *adj.* & *n.*

[600]

(State) not taking active or open part in war. **nŏn-belli′gerencў** *n.*
nŏnce *n.* Time being, present occasion (only in *for the* ∼); ∼-*word*, word coined for a special occasion and used only for a short time.
nŏ′nchalant (-sh-) *adj.* Unexcited, unmoved, cool, indifferent. **nŏ′nchalantlў** *adv.* **nŏ′nchalance** *n.*
nŏn-collē′giate *adj.* Of the students (in certain universities) not attached to any particular college or hall; not having a collegiate system.
nŏn-cŏm *n.* (colloq.) Noncommissioned officer.
nŏn-cŏ′mbatant *adj.* Not fighting. ∼ *n.* Civilian in time of war; member of army etc. whose duties do not include fighting.
nŏn-commi′ssioned (-shond) *adj.* Not holding commission (esp. of army officers such as *sergeant*, *corporal*).
nŏn-commi′ttal *adj.* Refusing to commit oneself to particular view or course of action.
nŏn-commū′nicant *adj. & n.* (Person) who does not attend communion service, esp. (one) who is not member of the Church of England.
nŏn cŏ′mpŏs mĕ′ntis. Not in one's right mind. [L]
nŏn-condū′cting *adj.* That does not conduct heat or electricity. **nŏn-condū′ctor** *n.*
nŏnconfōr′mĭst (-n-k-) *n.* One who does not conform to doctrine or discipline of an established Church, esp. member of Church dissenting from Anglican Church (usu. not including Roman Catholics); Protestant dissenter. **nŏnconfōr′mitў** *n.* Principles, practice, the body, of nonconformists, Protestant dissent; failure to conform (*to*); want of correspondence between things.
nŏn-cō-ŏperā′tion *n.* Refusal or failure to co-operate with authority, esp. as policy of GANDHI and his followers in India from *c* 1919.
nŏ′ndĕscript *adj. & n.* (Person, thing) not easily classified, neither one thing nor another, hybrid.
none[1] (nŭn) *pron.* Not any *of*; no person, no one (now rare); no persons. ∼ *adj.* (usu. ellipt.) No, not any; not to be counted in specified class. ∼ *adv.* By no amount, not at all; ∼ *the less*, nevertheless.
nōne[2] *n.* = NONES, 2.
nonĕ′ntitў *n.* Non-existence, non-existent thing, figment; person or thing of no importance, cipher.
nōnes (-nz) *n.pl.* 1. (Rom. antiq.) 9th day (by inclusive reckoning) before IDES; 7th of March, May, July, Oct., and 5th of other months. 2. N∼, (R.C. Ch.) canonical HOUR, (orig. said at) 9th hour of day (3 p.m.).
nŏn-ĕssĕ′ntial (-shal) *adj. & n.* (Thing) that is not essential.

nonesuch: see NONSUCH.
nōnĕ′t *n.* (mus.) Composition for nine instruments or voices.
nŏn-ĕxi′stent (ĭgz-) *adj.* Not existing. **nŏn-ĕxi′stence** *n.*
nŏn-fi′ction *adj. & n.* (Of) prose writings that are not fiction, poetry, or drama.
nŏn-flăm *adj.* (of cinema-film etc.) Not inflammable.
nŏn-flă′mmable *adj.* Non-inflammable.
noni′llion (-lyon) *n.* 9th power of million, 1 with 54 ciphers; (U.S.) 10th power of a thousand, 1 with 30 ciphers.
nŏn-inflă′mmable *adj.* That cannot be set on fire.
nŏn-intervĕ′ntion *n.* Absence of intervention; esp., in international politics, systematic refusal to interfere in affairs of another nation.
Nō′nius[1]. Latinized name of Pedro Nuñez (1492–1577), Portuguese mathematician.
nō′nius[2] *n.* Contrivance invented by Nuñez for graduating mathematical instruments, of which the VERNIER is an improved form. [f. NONIUS[1]]
nŏn-jur′or (joor-) *n.* (hist.) Beneficed clergyman who refused to take oath of allegiance to William and Mary in 1689. **nŏn-jur′ing** *adj.*
nŏnparei′l (-rĕl) *adj.* Unequalled, peerless. ∼ *n.* 1. Person or thing without equal, something unique. 2. (print.) Size of type (6 point) intermediate between emerald and ruby. 3. Kind of finch. 4. Kind of moth.
nŏn-pār′tў *adj.* That may be dealt with irrespective of political partisanship.
nŏnplŭ′s *n.* State of perplexity, standstill. ∼ *v.t.* (past t. -*ssed*) Reduce to hopeless perplexity. [L *non plus* not more]
nŏn pŏ′ssūmus. Statement of inability, refusal to act or move. [L, = 'we cannot']
nŏn-rĕ′sĭdent(-z-)*adj.* Sojourning in place only for short time or residing elsewhere; not residing at one's place of work; (of post) not requiring holder to reside. ∼ *n.* Non-resident person.
nŏn-rĕsi′stance (-zĭs-) *n.* (Principle of) not resisting authority even when it is unjustly exercised.
nŏ′nsense *n.* Absurd or meaningless words or ideas, foolish or extravagant conduct, worthless things, rubbish (freq. as exclamation of contempt); *no* ∼, no foolish or extravagant conduct, no foolery or humbug; ∼ *verse*(*s*), verse(s) having no sense or an absurd one. **nŏnsĕ′nsical** *adj.* **nŏnsĕ′nsicallў** *adv.*
nŏn sĕ′qultur. Illogical inference, paradoxical result. [L, = 'it does not follow']
nŏn-skid *adj.* (of tyres or road surface) Designed to prevent or limit skidding.
nŏn-smō′ker *n.* Person who does not smoke; railway-compart-

ment etc. in which smoking is not permitted.
nŏn-stār′ter *n.* (esp., colloq.) Idea, plan, etc., not worth consideration.
nŏn-stŏp *adj. & adv.* Travelling, performing, etc. without stopping at intermediate points. ∼ *n.* Non-stop train etc.
no′nsŭch, no′nesŭch (nŭns-) *n.* 1. Person or thing that is unrivalled, paragon. 2. Kind of lucerne.
nō′nsuit (-ūt) *n.* (law) Stoppage of suit by judge when plaintiff fails to make out legal case or bring sufficient evidence. ∼ *v.t.* Subject to nonsuit.
nŏn trŏ′ppō. (mus.) Not too much. [It.]
nŏn-U *adj.* (colloq.) Not characteristic of the upper classes.
nŏn-ū′nion *adj.* Not belonging to a trade-union; not made by union labour.
nŏn-ū′ser (-z-) *n.* (law) Neglect to use a right, by which it may become void.
nōō′dle[1] *n.* Simpleton.
nōō′dle[2] *n.* Strip or ball of pasta, used esp. in soup. [Ger. *Nudel*]
nook *n.* Secluded corner or place; recess.
noon *n.* 12 o'clock in the day; *noo′nday, noo′ntide,* (poet.) noon. [L *nona* (*hora*) ninth hour; orig., 3 p.m.]
noose *n.* Loop with running knot, tightening as string is pulled, of halter; (fig.) the marriage tie; snare or bond. ∼ *v.t.* Capture with noose, ensnare; make noose on (cord); arrange (cord) in noose *round* neck etc.
nō′pal *n.* Amer. cactus, *Nopalea cochinellifera,* cultivated for support of cochineal-insect.
nor *conj.* Neither (archaic); and not, and no more, neither, and not either.
nor′ *abbrev.* North.
Nōr′dic *adj. & n.* (Person) of the physical type of the Germanic peoples of N. Europe, esp. the Scandinavians, with tall stature, long narrow head, bony frame, and light colouring of hair, eyes, and skin.
Nōre. Sandbank at mouth of Thames off Sheerness; *Mutiny of the* ∼, mutiny which broke out, 1797, in fleet stationed there, occasioned by bad food and inadequate pay.
Nōr′folk (-*ok*). Eastern maritime county of England, since April 1974 including E. parts of the former county of Suffolk; ∼ *jacket*, man's loose-fitting single-breasted belted jacket with box-pleats back and front (ill. COAT).
norm *n.* Standard quantity to be produced, or amount of work to be done.
nōr′mal *adj.* 1. Rectangular (rare); standing at right angles, perpendicular. 2. Conforming to standard, regular, usual, typical;

NORMALIZE

of average intelligence; mentally or emotionally sound. **nōr'mally** adv. **nōrmä'litў**, **nōr'malcў** ns. **nōr'mal** n. (geom.) Normal line (ill. EVOLUTE[1]); usual state, level, temperature, etc.
nōr'malize v.t. Make normal. **nōrmalīzā'tion** n.
Nōr'man n. Native or inhabitant of NORMANDY belonging to or descended from mixed Scandinavian and Frankish people inhabiting that part of France; orig. one of the Northmen or Scandinavians who conquered Normandy in 10th c. ~ adj. Of the Normans or Normandy; (archit.) of the style of round-arched Romanesque architecture developed by Normans and employed in England after Norman Conquest, with characteristic geometrical ornament; ~ *Conquest*, conquest of England by Normans under William of Normandy, 1066; ~ *French*, form of medieval French spoken by Normans; later form of this in English legal use, law French.
Nōr'mandy. 1. Region and former province of NW. France with coastline on English Channel; given by Charles the Simple to Rollo, first Duke of Normandy, 912; united to England intermittently from Norman Conquest until 1204. 2. Name of English royal house, including William I and II, Henry I, and Stephen.
nōr'mative adj. Of, establishing, a norm.
Nōrn n. (Scand. myth.) Personification of fate or destiny, usu. in form of a virgin goddess, Skuld, Urd, Urdar, Verdandi.
Nŏ'rroy and U'lster (ŭ-). The 3rd King of Arms of England, whose jurisdiction is N. of river Trent. [AF *nor* north +*rey, roy* king]
Nōrse adj. Of ancient Scandinavia, esp. Norway; of the language of its inhabitants. ~ n. *Old* ~, Germanic language of medieval Scandinavia.
nōrth[1] adv. Towards, in, the north. ~ n. 1. Point of horizon to the left of an observer who faces the rising sun at the equinox; this direction. 2. Cardinal point of the compass 90° to the left of east and 90° to the right of west. 3. (usu. *the N*~) That part of a country, district, etc., which lies to the north; in England, region north of the Humber estuary; in U.S., States lying north of the Mason and Dixon line. 4. *N*~, bridge-player sitting opposite South and to the right of East. ~ adj. Lying towards, in, the north; (of wind) blowing from the north; *N*~ *Atlantic Treaty Organization*, international organization with headquarters in Brussels, set up to carry out provisions of treaty (signed in 1949) for mutual defence; ~ *country* (from, characteristic of) north of

England or Gt Britain; so ~-*countryman*; *N*~ *Island*, principal northern island of New Zealand; *Nor'thman*, native or inhabitant of Scandinavia, esp. Norway; *N*~ *Riding*: see RIDING[2]; *N*~ *Sea*, part of Atlantic between mainland of Europe and E. coast of Gt Britain; ~ *star*, pole-star. **nōr'thward** adv., adj., & n. **nōr'thwardlў** adv. & adj. **nōr'thwards** (-z) adv.
North[2], Christopher. Pseudonym of John WILSON[2].
North[3], Frederick, Earl of Guilford (1732–92; better known as Lord North). English statesman; supporter of George III.
North Amĕ'rica. Northern part of the continent of America, including Central America, Mexico, U.S., and Canada.
Northä'mptonshire. East midland county of England.
Northants. abbrev. Northamptonshire.
North Căroli'na. South Atlantic State of U.S.; one of the original thirteen States of the Union (1789); capital, Raleigh.
Nōr'thcliffe, Alfred Charles William Harmsworth, Viscount (1865–1922). British newspaper owner, founder of the 'Daily Mail' and chief proprietor of 'The Times' from 1908 until his death.
North Dakō'ta. State in northwestern U.S.; admitted to the Union in 1889; capital, Bismarck.
nōrth-east adv. & n. (Direction or compass-point) between north and east. ~ adj. Of, in, to, from, the north-east; ~ *passage*, passage for ships along northern coasts of Europe and Asia, formerly thought of as possible route to Far East. **nōrth-ea'ster** n. North-east wind. **nōrth-ea'sterlў** adv., adj., & n. **nōrth-ea'stern** adj. **nōrth-ea'stward** adv., adj. & n. **nōrth-ea'stwardlў** adv. & adj. **nōrth-ea'stwards** (-z) adv.
nōr'ther (-th-) n. (U.S.) Strong cold north wind blowing in autumn and winter over Texas, Florida, and Gulf of Mexico.
nōr'therlў (-dh-) adj. In the north; (of wind) blowing from the north. ~ adv. Towards the north. ~ n. North wind.
nōr'thern (-dh-) adj. Of the north; lying or directed towards the north; (poet.) coming from the north; *N*~ *hemisphere*: see HEMISPHERE; ~ *lights*, aurora borealis. **nōr'therner** n. (also *N*~) Native, inhabitant, of the north. **nōr'thernmōst** adj.
Nōr'thern Ir'eland (-dh-, īrl-). Autonomous unit of United Kingdom, constituted in 1920 (see IRELAND), comprising six counties, Armagh, Down, Londonderry, Antrim, Tyrone, and Fermanagh; capital, Belfast.
Nōr'thern Tĕ'rritorў (-dh-). Territory in N. Australia; the administration was taken over from South Australia by the

NOSE

Commonwealth of Australia in 1911.
nōr'thing (-th-) n. Northward progress or deviation esp. in sailing; distance due north.
Northumb. abbrev. Northumberland.
Northŭ'mberland. Extreme NE. county of England (some former areas of which became part of the metropolitan county of Tyne and Wear in April 1974).
Northŭ'mbria. Ancient Anglo-Saxon kingdom, extending from Humber to Forth; name revived in ~ *Authority*, area of police administration covering Northumberland and the metropolitan county of Tyne and Wear. **Northŭ'mbrian** adj. & n. (esp.) (Of) the Anglo-Saxon dialect spoken in Northumbria.
nōrth-wĕst adv. & n. (Direction or compass-point) between north and west. ~ adj. Of, in, to, from, the north-west; ~ *passage*, presumed route along N. coast of America from Atlantic to Pacific; *Northwest Territories*, part of Canada lying N. of 60th parallel; *Northwest Territory*, region of U.S. north of the Ohio river. **nōrth-wĕ'ster** n. 1. North-west wind. 2. = SOUTH-WESTER, 2. **nōrth-wĕ'sterlў** adv., adj., & n. **nōrth-wĕ'stern** adj. **nōrth-wĕ'stward** adv., adj., & n. **nōrth-wĕ'stwardlў** adv. & adj. **nōrth-wĕ'stwards** (-z) adv.
North Yōr'kshire. County of NE. England (since April 1974), comprising most of the former North Riding of Yorkshire and parts of the East and West Ridings.
Norvic. abbrev. (Bishop) of Norwich (replacing surname in his signature).
Nōr'way. Kingdom of N. Europe occupying W. part of Scandinavian peninsula, founded 872; united with Denmark 1397–1814, and thereafter with Sweden under a personal union of the crowns which was dissolved in 1905; capital, Oslo.
Nōrwē'gian (-jan) adj. Of Norway or its people or language. ~ n. 1. Norwegian person. 2. Language of Norway, in its literary form almost identical with Danish.
nōr-wĕ'ster n. 1. = NORTH-WESTER 1, 2. 2. Glass of strong liquor.
Nŏ'rwich (-rĭdzh or -rĭch). City and county town of Norfolk; ~ *School*, school of landscape painting here, c 1803–34.
nose (nōz) n. 1. Member of face or head above mouth, containing nostrils and serving as organ of smell (ill. HEAD); sense of smell; *as plain as the ~ on your face*, easily seen; *lead by the ~*, make (person) submissively do one's bidding; *pay through the ~*, be charged exorbitant price; *poke, thrust, one's ~*, pry or intrude *into*; *put person's ~ out of joint*, supplant,

[602]

disconcert, or frustrate him; *speak through the* ~, speak with nasal twang; *turn up one's* ~ *at*, show disdain for; *under person's* ~, right in front of him. 2. Open end or nozzle of pipe, tube, bellows, etc.; prow; projecting part. 3. ~*-ape*, proboscis monkey; ~*-bag*, bag of fodder hung to horse's head; ~*-band*, lower band of bridle passing over nose and attached to cheek-straps (ill. SADDLER); ~*-dive*, aircraft's downward plunge, with nose first; (*v.i.*) perform nose-dive; ~*-flute*, musical instrument blown with nose, among Siamese, Fijians, etc.; *no'segay*, bunch of (esp. sweet-scented) flowers; ~*-monkey*, proboscis monkey; ~*-rag*, (slang) pocket-handkerchief; ~*-ring*, ring fixed in nose of bull etc. for leading, or worn in nose as ornament. ~ *v.* Perceive smell of, discover by smell; detect, smell *out* (fig.); rub with the nose, thrust nose against or into; sniff (*at* etc.), pry or search (*after, for*); push one's way, push (one's *way*), with the nose (esp. of ship); ~ *over*, (of aircraft) fall nose forward.

nō'ser (-z-) *n.* Strong head wind.

nō'sey (-zĭ) *adj.* (esp., slang) Inquisitive, curious; *N*~ *Parker*, (slang) inquisitive person.

nō'sing (-z-) *n.* Rounded edge of step, moulding, etc., or metal or rubber shield for it.

nŏsŏ'logy̆ *n.* (Branch of medical science dealing with) classification of diseases.

nŏstă'lgia *n.* 1. Severe homesickness. 2. Sorrowful longing *for* conditions of a past age; regretful or wistful memory of earlier time. nŏstă'lgic *adj.*

nō'stoc *n.* Unicellular alga of genus *N*~ with cells arranged in intertwining rows which form gelatinous mass. [name invented by Paracelsus]

Nŏstradā'mus. Latinized name of Michel de Notredame (1503–66), Provençal astrologer of Jewish origin; favourite of Catherine de Médicis and physician to Charles IX of France.

nō'stril *n.* Either opening in nose admitting air to lungs and smells to olfactory nerves.

nō'strum *n.* Medicine prepared by person recommending it, quack remedy, patent medicine; pet scheme for political or social reform etc. [L, neut. of *noster* our]

nō'sy̆ (-zĭ) *adj.* = NOSEY.

nŏt *adv.* Expressing negation; now archaic following verbs other than auxiliaries and the verb *be* (freq. as *n't* joined to verb); ~*-being*, non-existence.

nō'ta bē'ne (-nā). (abbrev. N.B.) Mark well, observe particularly. [L]

nŏtabi'lity̆ *n.* Prominent person; being notable.

nō'table *adj.* Worthy of note, remarkable, striking, eminent. ~ *n.* Eminent person; (pl., French hist.) assembly of members of the privileged classes summoned by the king in an emergency.

nō'tary̆ *n.* Person publicly authorized to draw up or attest contracts etc., protest bills of exchange etc., and perform other formal duties (chiefly used about foreign countries, exc. in ~ *public*). notār'ial *adj.* notār'ially̆ *adv.*

notā'tion *n.* Representing of numbers, quantities, etc., by symbols; any set of symbols used for this, esp. in arithmetic, algebra, and music.

nŏtch *n.* V-shaped indentation or incision on edge or across surface; nick on stick etc., by way of keeping count; (U.S.) deep narrow pass. ~ *v.t.* Make notches in; score, mark, record, by notches; make (number of runs) at cricket; fix or insert by means of notches.

nōte *n.* 1. Written sign representing pitch and duration of a musical sound; key of pianoforte etc.; single tone of definite pitch made by musical instrument, voice, etc.; (single tone in) bird's song or call. 2. Sign, token, characteristic, distinguishing feature; stigma, mark of censure; mark *of exclamation* or *interrogation*; (theol.) sign or proof of genuine origin, authority, and practice. 3. Brief record of facts etc. to assist memory or serve as basis for fuller statement or as help in speaking (usu. pl.); annotation appended to passage in book etc. 4. Short or informal letter; formal diplomatic communication; (usu. ~ *of hand*) written promise to pay sum by certain time; BANK²-note. 5. Distinction, eminence; notice, attention. 6. *no'tebook*, book for taking notes or containing notes and memoranda; ~*-paper*, paper of size or quality used for correspondence. ~ *v.t.* Observe, notice, give attention to; set down, set *down*, as thing to be remembered or observed; annotate; *noted*, celebrated, well known *for*. nō'te-worthy (-twēr̆dhĭ) *adj.* Worthy of note or attention, remarkable.

no'thing (nŭ-) *n.* No thing; not anything, nought; trifle, very inferior thing; (arith.) no amount, nought; non-existence, what does not exist; (with pl.) trifling thing, event, remark, person; *come to* ~, turn out useless, fail, not amount to anything; *make* ~ *of doing*, do without hesitation or as ordinary matter. ~ *adv.* Not at all, in no way.

no'thingness (nŭ-) *n.* Non-existence, the non-existent; worthlessness, triviality, unimportance.

nō'tice *n.* 1. Intimation, warning; placard etc. conveying information or directions; formal intimation of something or instructions to do something, announcement by party to agreement that it is to terminate at specified time (esp. between landlord and tenant or employer and employee). 2. Heed, attention, cognizance, observation; *take* ~, give heed. 3. Short comment, review, etc., in newspaper or journal etc. ~ *v.t.* Remark upon, speak of; perceive, take notice of; treat with attention, favour, or politeness. nō'ticeable (-sa-) *adj.* nō'ticeably̆ *adv.*

nō'tifiable *adj.* (of diseases) That must be notified to public health authorities.

nō'tify̆ *v.t.* Make known, announce, report; inform, give notice to. nōtificā'tion *n.*

nō'tion *n.* General concept under which particular thing may be classed; idea, conception; view, opinion, theory; inclination, disposition, desire; (U.S., pl.) haberdashery, small wares, esp. cheap useful articles of some ingenuity; (pl.) traditional special vocabulary of Winchester College.

nō'tional *adj.* (of knowledge etc.) Speculative, not based on experiment or demonstration; (of things etc.) existing only in thought, imaginary; (of persons) fanciful. nō'tionally̆ *adv.*

nō'tochord (-k-) *n.* In CHORDATE animals, rudimentary spinal cord, rod of tissue lying along back below nerve cord (ill. LANCELET); in vertebrates, elongated cord of embryonic tissue from which vertebral column develops.

notōr'ious *adj.* Well or commonly known; undisguised, talked of, generally known to deserve the name; unfavourably known (*for*). notōr'iously̆ *adv.* nōtorī'ety̆ *n.*

Notre-Dame (nŏtre-dahm). Church dedicated to the Virgin Mary, esp. cathedral church of Paris. [Fr., = 'Our Lady']

Nŏ'ttingham (-ng-am). County town of Nottinghamshire; university, 1948.

Nŏ'ttinghamshire (-ng-am-). Midland county of England (some former areas of which became part of the metropolitan county of S. Yorkshire in April 1974).

Notts. *abbrev.* Nottinghamshire.

nō'tum *n.* (pl. *-ta*). (zool.) Dorsal part of thorax in insects.

nŏtwithstă'nding *prep.* In spite of, not the less for. ~ *adv.* Nevertheless, all the same. ~ *conj.* (archaic) Although, in spite of the fact *that*.

nougat (noō'gah) *n.* Sweet of sugar, honey, almonds or other nuts, and egg-white.

nought (nawt) *n.* Nothing (literary, exc. in arith.); figure o, cipher; *come, bring, to* ~, be ruined, fail; ruin, baffle; *set at* ~, disregard, ridicule; ~*s and crosses*, game in which each of 2 players tries to mark 3 noughts or crosses in line on a grid of 9 spaces.

nou'menŏn *n.* (pl. *-mena*) (philos.) Object of purely intellectual intuition, devoid of all phenomenal attributes. nou'menal *adj.* nou'menally̆ *adv.*

[603]

[Gk, = '(thing) apprehended' (*noeō* apprehend); taken by Kant as antithesis to *phenomenon*]
noun *n.* (gram.) Word used as name of person, place, thing, state, or quality.
nou′rĭsh (nŭ-) *v.t.* Sustain with food; foster, cherish, nurse, (feeling, hope, etc.) in one's heart. **nou′rĭshĭng** *adj.* **nou′rĭshment** *n.* Sustenance, food; nourishing.
nous *n.* (Gk philos.) Mind, intellect; (colloq.) common sense, gumption.
nouveau riche (nōōvō rēsh). (pl. *-x, -s*). Newly enriched person, parvenu. [Fr.]
Nov. *abbrev.* November.
nō′va *n.* (pl. *-vae*). Star showing sudden great increase in light and energy and then subsiding, formerly mistaken for new star.
Nŏva′lĭs (-vah-). Pseudonym of F. L. von HARDENBERG.
Nō′va Scō′tia (-sha). Province of SE. Canada, comprising peninsula projecting into Atlantic, and the adjoining Cape Breton Island; capital, Halifax. **Nō′va Scō′tian** *adj. & n.*
Nō′vaya Zĕmlya′ (-ah). Arctic territory comprising two large islands off NE. coast of European U.S.S.R. [Russ., = 'new land']
nŏ′vel[1] *n.* 1. Fictitious prose narrative of sufficient length to fill one or more volumes; *the ~*, this type of literature. 2. (Rom. law) New decree supplementary to Codex, esp. one of those made by Justinian.
nŏ′vel[2] *adj.* Of new kind or nature, strange, hitherto unknown.
nŏvelĕ′tte *n.* 1. Short novel, story of moderate length, romantic novel without literary merit. 2. (mus.) Composition of free form with several themes.
nŏ′velist *n.* Novel-writer. **nŏvelĭ′stĭc** *adj.*
nŏ′velize *v.t.* Convert into a novel. **nŏvelĭzā′tion** *n.*
novĕ′lla *n.* (pl. *-s* or *-le*, pr. -lā). Short novel. [It.]
nŏ′veltў *n.* New or unusual thing or occurrence; novel character *of* something.
Nŏvĕ′mber. 11th month of Gregorian (9th of Julian) calendar, with 30 days. [L *novem* nine]
novĕ′na *n.* (R.C. Ch.) Special prayers or services on 9 successive days.
nŏ′vĭce *n.* Person received in religious house on probation before taking the vows; new convert; inexperienced person, beginner, tyro.
novĭ′cĭate, novĭ′tĭate (-shĭat) *n.* Novice's probationary period, initiation, or apprenticeship; novice; quarters assigned to novices.
nŏ′vocaine (-kān) *n.* Synthetic drug used as a local anaesthetic. [trade-name]
now *adv.* 1. At the present time; by this time; immediately; in the immediate past; then, next, by that time; (*every*) ~ *and then*, ~ *and again*, from time to time, inter-

mittently. 2. In sentences expressing command, request, reproof, etc., with purely temporal sense weakened or effaced. ~ *conj.* Consequently upon or simultaneously with the fact that. ~ *n.* This time, the present (chiefly after prepositions). **now′adays** (-z) *adv. & n.* (At) the present day.
Nowĕ′l (nō-) *int.* = NOEL.
nō′where (-ār) *adv.* In, at, to, no place.
nŏ′xious (-kshus) *adj.* Harmful, unwholesome; **nŏ′xiouslў** *adv.* **nŏ′xiousnĕss** *n.*
noyade (nwahyahd) *n.* Execution by drowning, esp. as practised at Nantes during the Reign of Terror, 1794. [Fr.]
noyau (nwahyō′) *n.* Liqueur of brandy flavoured with fruit-kernels.
nŏ′zzle *n.* Projecting vent; small spout of hose-pipe etc.
n.p. *abbrev.* Net personalty; new paragraph.
N.P. *abbrev.* Notary Public.
nr *abbrev.* Near.
N.R. *abbrev.* North Riding.
N.R.A. *abbrev.* National Rifle Association; (U.S.) National Recovery Administration.
n.s. *abbrev.* Not sufficient (funds to meet cheque).
N.S. *abbrev.* New style; Nova Scotia.
N.S.B. *abbrev.* National Savings Bank.
N.S.P.C.C. *abbrev.* National Society for the Prevention of Cruelty to Children.
N.S.W. *abbrev.* New South Wales.
N.T. *abbrev.* New Testament; Northern Territory (Australia).
N.T.P. *abbrev.* Normal temperature and pressure.
nū *n.* 14th (later 13th) letter of Greek alphabet (N, *v*), corresponding to n.
nū′ance (*or* -ah′ns) *n.* Delicate difference in or shade of meaning, feeling, opinion, colour, etc.
nŭb *n.* 1. Small knob or lump, esp. of coal. 2. Point or gist (*of* matter or story). **nū′bble** *n.* = NUB, 1. **nū′bblў** *adv.*
Nū′bia. Region of NE. Africa in Nile valley between Aswan and Khartoum. **Nū′bian** *adj. & n.* (Native, inhabitant, monosyllabic language) of Nubia.
nū′bĭle *adj.* Marriageable (esp. of women). **nū′bĭlĭtў** *n.*
nū′chal (-kl) *adj.* Of the nape of the neck.
nū′cĭfōrm *adj.* Nut-shaped.
nū′cleăr *adj.* 1. Of or constituting a nucleus. 2. Of, using, concerned with, nuclear energy or weapons; ~ *bomb*, ATOMIC bomb; ~ *energy*, ATOMIC energy; ~ *fission*, splitting of a heavy nucleus into (usu. two) parts with resulting release of large amounts of energy; ~ *fuel* any substance from which atomic energy can be readily obtained.
nū′cleāse *n.* (chem.) Enzyme

which induces hydrolysis of nucleic acid.
nū′clĕāte *v.* Form (into) a nucleus. **nūclĕā′tion** *n.* **nū′clĕāte** *adj.*
nū′clĕĭc *adj.* ~ *acid*, one of a group of acids found in all living cells, combining with proteins to form nucleoproteins.
nūclĕō′lus *n.* (pl. *-lī*). Spherical body observable in nucleus of living resting cells but disappearing during mitosis (ill. CELL).
nū′clĕŏn *n.* (phys.) Proton or neutron of an atomic nucleus.
nūclĕŏ′nĭc *adj.* **nūclĕŏ′nĭcs** *n.* Branch of physics which treats of atomic nuclei esp. in practical applications, as in engineering.
nūclĕoprō′tein *n.* One of a group of compounds found in plant and animal cells, consisting of a protein combined with a nucleic acid.
nū′clĕŭs *n.* (pl. *-lĭī*). Central part or thing round which others are collected; kernel of aggregate or mass; central part of ovule or seed; body, present in nearly all living cells, containing chromosomes (ill. CELL); group of nerve-cells in the central nervous system concerned with a particular function; (phys., chem.) internal core of an atom, surrounded by electrons and containing the positive charge of the electrically neutral atom; (astron.) bright dense part forming head of comet.
nūde *adj.* Naked, unclothed, undraped; ~ *contract*, (law) one lacking a consideration and therefore void unless under seal. ~ *n.* Nude figure, in painting, etc.; *the* ~, the undraped human figure; the condition of being naked. **nū′dĭtў** *n.*
nŭdge *v.t.* Push slightly with elbow to draw attention privately; draw attention of. ~ *n.* Such a push.
nū′dĭst *n.* One who advocates or practises going unclothed. ~ *adj.* Of nudists. **nū′dĭsm** *n.*
nū′gatorў *adj.* Trifling, worthless, futile; inoperative, not valid.
nŭ′ggĕt *n.* Rough lump of native gold or platinum.
nui′sance (nūs-) *n.* Anything injurious or obnoxious to the community or a member of it for which legal remedy may be had; obnoxious person, offensive object, annoying action; anything disagreeable.
N.U.J. *abbrev.* National Union of Journalists.
nŭll *adj.* Not binding, invalid; without character or expression; (rare) non-existent, amounting to nothing.
nū′llah (*-a*) *n.* (Ind.) Stream, watercourse, ravine. [Hind. *nālā* brook]
nū′llĭfў *v.t.* Cancel, neutralize. **nŭllĭfĭcā′tion** *n.*
nū′llĭpōre *n.* Form of marine vegetation having power of secreting lime like coral polyp.

[604]

nŭ'llĭtў n. Being null, invalidity; act, document, etc., that is null; nothingness; a mere nothing.

Num. abbrev. Numbers (O.T.).

N.U.M. abbrev. National Union of Mineworkers.

Nŭ'ma Pŏmpĭ'lĭus. Legendary 2nd king of Rome, successor to Romulus; revered by ancient Romans as founder of nearly all their religious institutions.

nŭmb (-m) adj. Deprived of feeling or power of motion. **nŭ'mblў** (-mlĭ) adv. **nŭ'mbnèss** n. **nŭmb** v.t. Make numb; stupefy, paralyse.

nŭ'mber n. Count, sum, company, or aggregate, of persons, things, or abstract units; symbol or figure representing such aggregate; person or thing (esp. single issue of periodical) whose place in series is indicated by such figure; numerical reckoning; (sing. or pl.) large (or *large, small*, etc.) collection or company (*of*), (pl.) numerical preponderance; (gram.) property in words of denoting that one, two, or more persons or things are spoken of, form of word expressing this; item (as song, dance) esp. on a programme; (pl.) groups of musical notes, metrical feet, verses; *Numbers*, 4th book of O.T., earlier part of which contains census of Israelites; *his ~ is up*, he is doomed, his hour is come; (*times*) *out of ~, without ~*, innumerable (times); *~ one*, oneself, esp. as object of selfish care; (nav. slang) first lieutenant; *~-plate*, plate bearing a number, esp. that on registered vehicle; *N~ 10*, (used for) 10 Downing Street, Prime Minister's official residence. **nŭ'mberlèss** adj. **nŭ'mber** v.t. Count, ascertain number of; include, regard as, *among*, *in*, or *with* some class; assign a number to, distinguish with a number; have lived, live (so many years); have, comprise (so many); equal, amount to; (pass.) be restricted or few in number.

nŭ'merable adj. That can be numbered.

nŭ'meral adj. & n. (Word, figure, group of figures) denoting a number; of number.

nŭ'merate adj. & n. (Person) familiar with the basic principles of mathematics and science. **nŭ'meracў** n. State or condition of being numerate.

nūmerā'tion n. Method or process of numbering or computing; calculation; assigning of numbers; (arith.) expression in words of number written in figures.

nŭ'merātor n. Number above line in vulgar fraction, showing how many of the parts indicated by the denominator are taken; person who numbers.

nūmĕ'rĭcal adj. Of, in, denoting, etc., number. **nūmĕ'rĭcallў** adv.

nūmerŏ'logў n. Study of (esp. occult) significance of numbers. **nūmerolŏ'gĭcal** adj. **nūmerŏ'logĭst** n.

nū'merous adj. Comprising many units; coming from many individuals. **nū'merouslў** adv.

Nūmĭ'dĭa. Ancient kingdom and Roman province of N. Africa, comprising approximately modern Algeria.

nū'mĭnous adj. Divine; suggesting or revealing the presence or influence of a god. [L *numen* divine will, divinity]

nūmĭsmă'tĭc (-z-) adj. Of coins or coinage. **nūmĭsmă'tĭcallў** adv. **nūmĭsmă'tĭcs, nūmĭ's-matĭst, nūmĭsmatŏ'logў** ns.

nŭ'mmarў, nŭ'mmŭlarў adjs. Of, in, coin.

nŭ'mmŭlīte n. Disc-shaped fossil protozoan of order Foraminifera (many species, some very large).

nŭ'mskŭll n. Blockhead.

nŭn n. Woman living in convent under religious vow; *~'s veiling*, thin woollen material.

nŭ'nlīke, nŭ'nnĭsh adjs.

nŭ'n-buoy (-boi) n. (naut.) Buoy consisting of two cones placed base to base.

Nŭnc dĭ'mĭttĭs. Canticle beginning thus (L, = 'Lord, now lettest thou thy servant depart'; first words of Song of Simeon, Luke 2: 29); hence, farewell.

nŭ'ncĭō (-sh-) n. Diplomatic representative of the pope at foreign court. **nŭ'ncĭature** (-sha-) n. (Tenure of) office of nuncio.

nŭ'ncūpāte v.t. Declare (will etc.) orally, not in writing. **nŭncūpā'tion** n. **nŭ'ncŭpatĭve** adj.

Nuñez, Pedro: see NONIUS[1].

nŭnnā'tion n. Addition of final *n* in declension of (orig. Arabic) nouns.

nŭ'nnerў n. House, community, of nuns.

nŭ'ptĭal (-shal) adj. Of marriage or wedding. *~* n. (usu. pl.) Wedding.

N.U.R. abbrev. National Union of Railwaymen.

Nūr'embĕrg. (Ger. *Nürnberg*) City of Bavaria; *~ laws*, series of laws, enacted under the Nazi regime, depriving Jews in Germany of certain civil rights and prohibiting intermarriage between Germans and Jews; *~ trials*, trials of war criminals conducted at Nuremberg after war of 1939–45.

nūrse[1] n. 1. Woman employed to look after young child (so *nur'semaid*, maid-servant employed thus); wet-nurse. 2. (fig.) Something which nourishes or fosters some quality etc. 3. Person, usu. woman, charged with or trained for care of the sick or infirm. 4. (entom.) Sexually imperfect bee, ant, etc., caring for the young brood, worker; (zool.) individual in asexual stage or metagenesis. *~* v. 1. Suckle (child), give suck, act as wet-nurse; act as nursemaid to, have charge of; foster, tend, promote development of; manage (plants, estate) with solicitude; cherish (grievance etc.); (pass.) be brought up. 2. Wait upon (sick person); try to cure (sickness); be sick-nurse; *nursing home*, house (freq. under private management) receiving surgical cases, invalids, etc. 3. Clasp or hold carefully or caressingly; sit close over (fire); keep in touch with (constituency) in order to obtain votes; (billiards) keep balls together for series of cannons.

nūrse[2] n. Any of various dogfish or sharks; *~ hound*, kind of small shark, *Scyliorhinus stellaris*.

nŭr'selĭng (-sl-), **-slĭng** n. Infant, esp. in relation to its nurse.

nŭr'serў n. 1. Room assigned to children and their nurses; *day ~*, institution taking charge of young children during day. 2. Practice, institution, sphere, place, by or in which qualities or classes of people are fostered or bred. 3. Plot of ground in which young plants are reared for transplantation, esp. one in which trees or plants are reared for sale; fish-rearing pond; place where animal life is developed. 4. *~-garden*, see sense 3; *~ governess*, person combining duties of nurse and governess; *nur'seryman*, owner of nursery-garden; *~ rhyme*, simple short traditional verse for young children; *~ school*, school for young children, esp. those under 5 years of age.

nursĭng: see NURSELING.

nŭr'ture n. Bringing up, training, fostering care; nourishment. *~* v.t. Nourish, rear, foster, train, educate.

N.U.S. abbrev. National Union of Students.

nŭt n. 1. Fruit consisting of hard or leathery indehiscent shell enclosing edible kernel (ill. FRUIT); kernel of this; (slang) head; (*dead*) *~s on*, (slang) devoted to, fond of; *off one's ~*, out of one's mind. 2. Small toothed projection on spindle engaging with cog-wheel, small spur-wheel; small block of metal etc. pierced with female screw for adjusting or tightening bolt (ill. SCREW[1]); holder for tightening or relaxing horsehair of fiddle-bow. 3. Very small lump of coal etc. 4. (slang) Eccentric or insane person. 5. *~-brown*, coloured like ripe hazel-nut; *~-butter*, substance resembling butter, made from nut-oil; *nu't-cracker*, (usu. pl.) instrument for cracking nuts; prominent chin and nose with points near each other; brown corvine bird (*Nucifraga caryocatactes*) rare in Britain; *~-gall*, gall found on dyer's oak; *nu'thatch*, small creeping bird (*Sitta europaea*) feeding on nuts; *~-oil*, oil from nut-kernels; *nu't-shell*, hard exterior covering of nut; something extremely small; *in a nutshell*, briefest possible way of expressing something; *~-tree*, tree bearing nuts, esp. hazel.

nŭ'ttĭng n. Gathering nuts.

[605]

N.U.T. *abbrev.* National Union of Teachers.
nū'tant *adj.* (bot.) Drooping.
nūtā'tion *n.* Nodding; (astron.) oscillation of earth's axis making motion of pole of equator round pole of ecliptic wavy; oscillation of spinning top in its precession around an axis.
nŭ'mĕg *n.* Hard aromatic spheroidal seed from fruit of evergreen E. Ind. tree (*Myristica fragrans*), used as spice; ~-*apple*, fruit of nutmeg-tree, containing mace and nutmeg.
nŭ'tria *n.* Fur of the coypu.
nŭ'trient *adj. & n.* (Substance etc.) serving as or providing nourishment.
nŭ'triment *n.* Nourishing food.
nūtrī'tion *n.* (Supplying or receiving of) nourishment, food.
nūtrī'tional *adj.* Of, relating to, nutrition.
nūtrī'tious (-shus) *adj.* Nourishing, efficient as food. **nūtrī'tiouslў** *adv.* **nūtrī'tiousnèss** *n.*
nū'tritive *adj.* Serving as food; concerned in nutrition.
nŭts *adj.* (slang) Crazy.
nŭ'ttў *adj.* Abounding in nuts; tasting like nuts, of rich mellow flavour.
nŭx vŏ'mĭca. Seed of pulpy fruit of E. Ind. tree (*Strychnos nux-vomica*), yielding strychnine.
nŭ'zzle *v.* Nose; burrow, press, rub, sniff, with the nose; press nose or press (nose) *into*, *against*; nestle, lie snug.
NW. *abbrev.* North-west(ern).
N.W.T. *abbrev.* North-west Territories (Canada).
N.Y. *abbrev.* New York.
nya'la (-ah-) *n.* Large S. Afr. antelope (*Tragelaphus angasi*), one of the bush-bucks.
nyă'nza *n.* In Central Africa, large lake (esp. in place-names).
nўctalōp'ia *n.* 1. Night-blindness, inability to see in a dim light. 2. (rare) Inability to see clearly except at night.
N.Y.C. *abbrev.* New York City.
nў'lŏn *n.* Any of a group of long-chain synthetic polymeric amines of which the structural units or molecules can be oriented in one direction, and which are thus capable of being formed into filaments of great tensile strength; textile fibre of this structure and character; (pl.) garments, esp. women's stockings, made of this.
nŷmph *n.* 1. (myth.) One of class of semi-divine maidens inhabiting sea, rivers, fountains, woods, or trees; (poet.) young and beautiful woman. 2. (zool.) Immature insect which from time of hatching has a general resemblance to the adult (ill. DRAGON-fly). 3. Edible frog.
nŷ'mpha *n.* (pl. -*ae*). (anat.) One of the labia minora.
nymphae'a *n.* Aquatic plant of genus *N*~ which includes the common white water-lily.
nў'mpholĕpsў *n.* Ecstasy or frenzy caused by desire of the unattainable. **nў'mpholĕpt** *n.* Person inspired by violent enthusiasm, esp. for an ideal. **nўmpholĕ'ptic** *adj.*
nўmphomā'nia *n.* (path.) Morbid and uncontrollable sexual desire in women. **nўmphomā'niăc** *n.*
nўstă'gmus *n.* Rapid involuntary oscillation of eyeball; *miner's* ~, form of this affecting persons who work in cramped quarters and poor light. **nўstă'gmĭc** *adj.*
N.Z. *abbrev.* New Zealand.

O

O¹, o (ō). 1. 15th letter of modern English and 14th of ancient Roman alphabet, representing a variety of mid-back-round vowels, and corresponding in form to ancient Greek *O*, derived from Phoenician and ancient Semitic ○, ◊, ▽ (Heb. **y**), which represent not a vowel but a glottal stop. 2. *O*, O-shaped mark, circle; cipher or nought.
O², **oh** (ō) *int.* Exclamation expressing various emotions or prefixed to vocative name.
o' *prep.* Short for *of*, *on*, in some phrases as (= *of*) *o'clock*, *will-o'-the-wisp*, *man-o'-war*, (= *on*) *cannot sleep o' nights*.
O. *abbrev.* Observer; Ohio.
oaf *n.* (pl. -*s*, *oaves*). Awkward lout. **oa'fĭsh** *adj.* [ON. *dlfr* elf]
oak *n.* 1. (also ~-*tree*) Forest tree of genus *Quercus* with hard timber, bearing acorn as fruit; any of various trees or plants resembling this; (Austral.) tree of genus *Casuarina*; *durmast* ~: see DURMAST; *poison* ~: see POISON. 2. Wood of the oak; this as material for ships; (univ.) outer door of set of rooms. 3. Leaves of oak. 4. *the Oaks*, (f. name of estate near Epsom) race for 3-year-old fillies, founded 1779 and run at Epsom on Friday after the Derby. 5. ~-*apple*, globular oak-gall; *Oak-apple Day*, anniversary of restoration of Charles II (29 May), when oak-apples or oak-leaves are worn in memory of his hiding in an oak-tree at Boscobel on 6 Sept. 1651; ~-*fern*, smooth 3-branched polypody, *Thelypteris dryopteris*; ~-*gall*, excrescence on various species of oak produced by punctures of gall-flies (ill. GALL³). **oa'ken** *adj.* (chiefly poet.) Made of oak.
oa'kum *n.* Loose fibre got by untwisting and picking old hemp ropes and used esp. in caulking; *pick* ~, make this, esp. as formerly common task of convicts and paupers.
O.A.P. *abbrev.* Old age pension(er).
oar (ōr) *n.* Long stout wooden shaft widened and flattened at one end into a blade, used to propel (row) a boat by leverage against a rowlock which serves as a fulcrum (ill. BOAT), esp. pulled by one rower with both hands, as dist. from a scull (one hand) and a sweep (two rowers); oarsman; *put in one's* ~, interfere; *rest on one's* ~*s*, lean on handles of oars, raising blades out of water; (fig.) suspend one's efforts, take things easy; *oar'lock*, rowlock; *oar'sman*, rower; *oar's-manship*; *oar'weed*, large littoral alga, esp. *Laminaria*. ~ *v.* Row.
O.A.S. *abbrev.* On active service; Organisation of American States.
oā'sĭs *n.* (pl. *ōāsēs* pr. -z). Depression in desert where cultivation is possible owing to presence of water (also fig.).
oast *n.* Hop-drying kiln; ~-*house*, building containing this.
oat *n.* (pl.) (Grain yielded by) hardy cereal, *Avena sativa*, grown in cool climates as food for man and horses; (sing., rare exc. in comb.) oat-plant, variety of oats; (sing., poet.) oat-stem used as musical pipe by shepherds etc., pastoral or bucolic poetry; *wild* ~*s*: see WILD; *oa'tcake*, thin unleavened cake of oat-meal; *oa'tmeal*, meal made from oats; oatmeal porridge; greyish fawn (colour). **oa'ten** *adj.* (chiefly poet.) Made of oats.
Oates (ōts), Titus (1649–1705). Fabricator of the POPISH Plot, 1678; was condemned and imprisoned for perjury, but subsequently released and granted a pension.
oath *n.* (pl. pr. ōdhz). 1. Solemn appeal to God (or to something sacred), in witness of truth of statement or binding character of promise. 2. Name of God, or of something sacred, used as expletive to give emphasis or express anger etc.; piece of profanity in speech.
O.A.U. *abbrev.* Organisation of African Unity.
Ob (ŏb), **O'bĭ³** (ō-). River of Asiatic U.S.S.R., flowing

northwards into *Gulf of Ob*, an arm of the Arctic Ocean.
ob. *abbrev.* Obiit.
Obad. *abbrev.* Obadiah.
Obadi'ah (ō-, -a). Hebrew minor prophet; shortest book of O.T., bearing his name.
ŏbblĭga'tō (-ah-) *adj. & n.* (pl. -os). (mus.) (Part, accompaniment) forming integral part of composition; often wrongly used for *ad libitum*, of which it is the opposite. [It.]
ŏ'bdūrate *adj.* Hardened, impenitent, stubborn. **ŏ'bdūrately** *adv.* **ŏ'bdūracy** *n.*
O.B.E. *abbrev.* Officer of the (Order of the) British Empire.
ō'bĕah, ō'bī² *n.* Sorcery or witch-doctoring associated with the snake-god Obi whose worship was introduced by W. African Negro slaves into W. Indies and U.S.
obē'dience *n.* 1. Obeying as act, practice, or quality; submission to another's rule; compliance with law or command. 2. (eccles., esp. R.C.) (Sphere of) authority; district or body of persons subject to some rule.
obē'dient *adj.* Submissive to, complying with, superior's will; dutiful. **obē'diently** *adv.*
obēdiē'ntiary (-sha-) *n.* Holder of any office under superior in monastery or convent.
obei'sance (-bā-) *n.* Gesture, esp. bow or curtsy, expressing submission, respect, or salutation.
ŏ'bĕlisk *n.* 1. Tapering shaft of stone, square or rectangular in section with pyramidal apex; mountain, tree, etc., of similar shape. 2. (also *obelus*) Mark (—, ÷), used in ancient MSS. to indicate that word or passage is spurious etc.; mark (†) of reference to note in margin etc.; *double* ~, ‡.
ŏ'bĕlize *v.t.* Mark with obelisk as spurious etc.
Oberä'mmergau (ō-, -gow). Village in Upper Bavaria where the inhabitants vowed in 1633 that they would perform a Passion Play as an act of thanksgiving for deliverance from the plague; since 1680 the play has been performed every 10 years exc. for 1810, 1920, and 1940.
O'beron (ō-). In W. European folklore, king of the fairies.
obē'se *adj.* Corpulent. **obē'sity** *n.*
obey' (-ā) *v.* Perform bidding of, be obedient (to); execute (command).
ŏ'bfuscāte *v.t.* Darken, obscure; stupefy, bewilder. **ŏbfuscā'tion** *n.*
ō'bī¹ *n.* Japanese woman's bright-coloured sash.
obi²: see OBEAH.
Obi³: see OB.
ŏ'bĭit. Died (with date of death). [L]
ŏ'bit *n.* Obituary; date of person's death.
ō'biter *adv.* By the way, in passing; ~ *di'ctum, di'cta*, judge's expression(s) of opinion on matters of law, given in course of argument or judgment but not essential to decision and therefore without binding authority; incidental remark(s). [L]
obi'tūary *n.* Notice of death, esp. in newspaper, brief biography of deceased person. ~ *adj.* Recording a death; concerning deceased person. **obi'tūarist** *n.*
ŏ'bjĕct¹ *n.* 1. Thing placed before eyes or presented to sense; material thing; thing observed with optical instrument or represented in picture. 2. Person or thing of pitiable or ridiculous aspect. 3. Person or thing to which action or feeling is directed, subject *of* or *for*; thing aimed at, end, purpose; *no* ~, not to be taken into account; forming no obstacle. 4. (philos.) Thing thought of or apprehended as correlative to the thinking mind or subject; external thing; non-ego. 5. (gram.) Substantive word, phrase, or clause governed by active transitive verb or by preposition; *direct, indirect,* ~, that primarily, secondarily, affected by action. 6. ~*-ball*, that at which player aims his ball in billiards etc.; ~*-glass, -lens*, lens in telescope etc. nearest the object; ~ *lesson*, instruction about material object that is present for inspection; (fig.) striking practical application of some principle.
objĕ'ct² *v.* Bring forward or state in opposition, urge as objection; state objection; express or feel disapproval. **objĕ'ctor** *n.*
objĕ'ctify *v.t.* Present as object of sense; make objective; express in concrete form, embody.
objĕ'ction *n.* Objecting, thing objected; adverse reason or statement; expression or feeling of disapproval or dislike. **objĕ'ctionable** *adj.* Open to objection; undesirable, unpleasant, offensive. **objĕ'ctionably** *adv.*
objĕ'ctive *adj.* 1. Belonging to what is presented to consciousness; that is the object of perception or thought, as dist. from perceiving or thinking subject; external to the mind, real. 2. Dealing with outward things and not with thoughts or feelings, exhibiting actual facts uncoloured by exhibitor's feelings or opinions. 3. (gram.) Constructed as, appropriate to, the object. 4. ~ *point*, point aimed at; (orig. mil.) point towards which advance of troops is directed. **objĕ'ctively** *adv.* **objĕ'ctiveness, ŏbjĕcti'vity** *ns.* **objĕ'ctive** *n.* 1. Objectglass (ill. MICROSCOPE). 2. (gram.) Objective case. 3. Object or purpose aimed at in an action; (mil.) position to the attainment or capture of which an operation is directed, objective point.
objĕ'ctivism *n.* Tendency to lay stress on the objective; doctrine that knowledge of non-ego is prior in sequence and importance to that of ego. **objĕ'ctivist** *n.*

objet d'art (ŏbzhā där). Object (esp. small) of artistic interest, curio. [Fr.]
ŏ'bjurgāte *v.t.* Chide, scold. **ŏbjurgā'tion** *n.* **ŏ'bjurgātory** *adj.*
ŏ'blāte¹ *n.* Person dedicated to monastic or religious life or work.
ŏ'blāte² (*or* oblā't) *adj.* (geom., of spheroid) Flattened at the poles (ill. CONE).
oblā'tion *n.* (Presenting bread and wine to God in) Eucharist; thing offered to God, sacrifice, victim; donation for pious uses. **oblā'tional, ŏ'blatory** *adjs.*
ŏ'bligāte *v.t.* Bind (person, esp. legally) *to* do; (U.S.) oblige.
obligā'tion *n.* 1. Binding agreement, esp. one enforceable under legal penalty, written contract, or bond; constraining power of a law, precept, duty, contract, etc.; one's bounden duty, a duty, burdensome task; *of* ~, obligatory. 2. (Indebtedness for) service or benefit.
obli'gatory (*or* ŏ'b-) *adj.* Legally or morally binding; imperative, not merely permissive; constituting an obligation.
oblī'ge *v.t.* 1. Bind by oath, promise, contract, etc., *to* (archaic, legal); be binding on. 2. Make indebted by conferring favour, gratify *by, with*; (colloq.) make contribution to entertainment (*with*); (pass.) be bound (*to*) by gratitude. 3. Constrain, compel, *to* do.
obligee' *n.* (law) Person to whom another is bound by contract or to whom bond is given.
oblī'ging *adj.* Courteous, accommodating, ready to do kindness, complaisant. **oblī'gingly** *adv.* **oblī'gingness** *n.*
ŏ'bligor *n.* (law) One who binds himself to another or gives bond.
oblī'que (-ēk) *adj.* 1. Slanting; declining from vertical or horizontal; diverging from straight line or course; (geom.) (of line etc.) inclined at other than right angle, (of angle) acute or obtuse, (of cone etc.) with axis not perpendicular to plane of base; (anat.) neither parallel nor perpendicular to body's or limb's long axis; (bot., of leaf) with unequal sides. 2. Not going straight to the point, roundabout, indirect. 3. (gram.) ~ *case*, any case other than nominative or vocative (occas. also the accusative); ~ *narration, oration, speech*, indirect speech. **obli'quely** (-ēklī) *adv.* **obli'quity** *n.*
obli'terāte *v.t.* Blot out, efface, erase, destroy. **obliterā'tion** *n.*
obli'vion *n.* Having or being forgotten; disregard, unregarded state.
obli'vious *adj.* Forgetful, unmindful, (*of*); (poet.) of, inducing, oblivion. **obli'viously** *adv.* **obli'viousness** *n.*
ŏ'blŏng *adj.* Elongated in one direction (usu. as deviation from exact square or circular form);

OBLOQUY

(geom.) rectangular with adjacent sides unequal. ~ *n.* Oblong figure or object.

ŏ'bloquy (-kwĭ) *n.* Abuse, detraction; being generally ill spoken of.

obnŏ'xious (-kshus) *adj.* 1. (now rare) Exposed, liable, *to* harm or evil. 2. Offensive, objectionable, disliked. **obnŏ'xiously** *adv.* **obnŏ'xiousness** *n.*

ŏ'bōe *n.* Musical instrument of wood-wind family (ill. WOOD[1]), played vertically, with a double reed, having a range of nearly three octaves upwards from the B flat below middle C, and a plaintive incisive tone; organ reed-stop imitating this. **ō'bōist** *n.*

ŏ'bol *n.* Coin and weight of ancient Greece, ⅙ of a drachma.

obscē'ne *adj.* 1. (archaic) Repulsive. 2. Indecent, esp. grossly or repulsively so; lewd; (law, of publications) tending to deprave and corrupt. **obscē'nely** *adv.* **obscē'nity** *n.*

obscūr'ant *n.* Opponent of inquiry, enlightenment, and reform. **obscūr'antism** *n.* **obscūr'antist** *n.* & *adj.*

obscūr'e *adj.* 1. Dark, dim; (of colour) dingy, dull, indefinite. 2. Indistinct, not clear; (of vowel) not clearly enunciated. 3. Hidden, remote from observation; unnoticed; unknown to fame, humble. 4. Unexplained, doubtful; not perspicuous or clearly expressed. **obscūr'ely** *adv.* **obscūr'ity** *n.* **obscūr'e** *v.t.* Make obscure, dark, indistinct, or unintelligible; dim glory of, outshine; conceal from sight. **ŏbscūrā'tion** *n.*

ŏbsecrā'tion *n.* Earnest entreaty.

ŏ'bsequent *adj.* (of stream or valley) Following a course opposite to the original slope of the land (opp. CONSEQUENT).

ŏ'bsequies (-kwĭz) *n.pl.* Funeral rites, funeral. **obsē'quial** *adj.*

obsē'quious *adj.* Servile, fawning. **obsē'quiously** *adv.* **obsē'quiousness** *n.*

obsēr'vance (-z-) *n.* Keeping or performance of law, duty, ritual, etc.; act of religious or ceremonial character, customary rite; rule of a religious order. **obsēr'vancy** *n.*

obsēr'vant (-z-) *adj.* 1. Attentive in observance. 2. Acute or diligent in taking notice. ~ *n.* Member of branch of Franciscan order observing the strict rule. **obsēr'vantly** *adv.*

ŏbservā'tion (-z-) *n.* 1. Noticing or being noticed; perception, faculty of taking notice; (mil.) watching of fortress or hostile position or movements. 2. Observing scientifically, accurate watching and noting of phenomena as they occur in nature; taking of altitude of sun or other heavenly body to find latitude or longitude; reading or value of any observed quantity, esp. when noted down. 3. Remark, statement, esp. one of the nature of comment. **ŏbservā'tional** *adj.* **ŏbservā'tionally** *adv.*

obsēr'vatory (-z-) *n.* Building etc. whence natural, esp. astronomical, phenomena may be observed.

obsēr've (-z-) *v.* 1. Keep, follow, adhere to, perform duly. 2. Perceive, watch, mark, take notice of, become conscious of; examine and note (phenomena) without aid of experiment. 3. Say, esp. by way of comment; make remark(s) *on.* **obsēr'ver** *n.* (esp.) Interested spectator; person carried in aircraft to note enemy's position etc.; person trained to watch and identify aircraft.

obsē'ss *v.t.* Dominate or preoccupy the thoughts of (a person). **obsē'ssion** *n.* **obsē'ssive, obsē'ssional** *adjs.*

obsi'dian *n.* Dark vitreous volcanic rock with appearance like bottle-glass, used by primitive societies for knives etc. [f. personal name *Obsius*]

ŏbsolē'scent *adj.* Becoming obsolete; gradually disappearing. **ŏbsolē'scence** *n.*

ŏ'bsolēte *adj.* Disused, discarded, antiquated. **ŏ'bsolēteness** *n.*

ŏ'bstacle *n.* Hindrance, impediment; ~ *race,* one in which artificial or natural obstacles have to be passed.

obstě'tric, -ical *adjs.* Of midwifery; of, relating to, obstetrics. **obstě'trics** *n.* Branch of medicine and surgery concerned with the care of women before, during, and immediately after, childbirth. **ŏbstětri'cian** (-shan) *n.*

ŏ'bstinate *adj.* Firmly adhering to one's own course, not yielding to argument or persuasion; inflexible, self-willed; (of disease etc.) not yielding readily to treatment. **ŏ'bstinately** *adv.* **ŏ'bstinacy** *n.*

obstrě'perous *adj.* Noisy, vociferous; turbulent, unruly, noisily resisting control. **obstrě'perously** *adv.* **obstrě'perousness** *n.*

obstrŭ'ct *v.* Block up, fill with impediments, make impassable or difficult of passage; prevent or retard progress of, impede; practise (esp. Parliamentary) obstruction. **obstrŭ'ction** *n.* Blocking or being blocked, making or becoming more or less impassable, hindering, esp. of Parliamentary business by talking against time; obstacle. **obstrŭ'ctionism, obstrŭ'ctionist** *ns.*

obstrŭ'ctive *adj.* Causing, intended to produce, obstruction. **obstrŭ'ctively** *adv.* **obstrŭ'ctiveness** *n.*

obtai'n *v.* 1. Acquire, have granted one, get. 2. Be prevalent, established, or in vogue. **obtai'nable** *adj.*

obtě'cted *adj.* (entom.) (of pupa) Having limbs etc. indistinctly discernible through outer covering.

OCCIDENT

obtě'st *v.* (archaic) Adjure, supplicate, call to witness; protest. **ŏbtěstā'tion** *n.*

obtrŭ'de (-ōōd) *v.t.* Thrust forward (*on, upon*) importunately. **obtru'sion** *n.* **obtru'sive** *adj.* **obtru'sively** *adv.* **obtru'siveness** *n.*

obtŭ'nd *v.t.* (med.) Blunt, deaden (sense, faculty).

ŏ'btūrāte *v.t.* Stop up, close, seal. **ŏbtūrā'tion** *n.*

obtū'se (-s) *adj.* 1. Of blunt form, not sharp or pointed; (geom., of plane angle) greater than right angle (ill. ANGLE[1]). 2. Dull, not acute; stupid, slow of perception. **obtū'sely** *adv.* **obtū'seness** *n.*

ŏ'bvērse *adj.* 1. Narrower at base or point of attachment than at apex. 2. Answering as counterpart to something else. **ŏ'bvērsely** *adv.* **ŏ'bvērse** *n.* Side of coin or medal bearing head or principal design (opp. REVERSE; ill. COIN); face of anything meant to be presented, front; counterpart of a fact or truth.

obvēr't *v.t.* (logic) Infer another proposition with contradictory predicate by changing quality of (proposition). **obvēr'sion** *n.*

ŏ'bviāte *v.t.* Clear away, get rid of, get round, neutralize (danger, inconvenience, etc.).

ŏ'bvious *adj.* Open to eye or mind, clearly perceptible, palpable, indubitable. **ŏ'bviously** *adv.* **ŏ'bviousness** *n.*

O.C. *abbrev.* Officer Commanding.

ŏcari'na (-ē-) *n.* Small egg-shaped metal or porcelain musical wind instrument with whistle-like mouthpiece and finger-holes. [It. *oca* goose]

O'Cā'sey, Sean (1884–1964). Irish playwright, author of 'Juno and the Paycock', 'The Plough and the Stars', etc.

O'ccam (ŏ-), William of (*c* 1300–*c* 1349). English scholastic philosopher; founded a speculative sect reviving the doctrines of Nominalism; ~*'s razor,* principle that assumptions introduced to explain something must not be unnecessarily multiplied.

occā'sion *n.* Juncture suitable for doing something, opportunity; reason, ground, justification, need; subsidiary, incidental, or immediate cause; (particular time marked by) special occurrence; (pl.) affairs, business. ~ *v.t.* Be the occasion or cause of; bring about, esp. incidentally; cause.

occā'sional *adj.* Arising out of, made or meant for, acting on, special occasion(s), as ~ *verse;* happening irregularly as occasion presents itself; coming now and then, not regular or frequent; ~ *table,* small table for use as required. **occā'sionally** *adv.*

O'ccident (ŏks-) *n.* (chiefly poet.) The West; western Europe; Europe; Europe and America; America; European as opp. to

[608]

Oriental civilization. **ŏccĭdĕ'ntal** *adj.* **ŏccĭdĕ'ntallў** *adv.* **ŏccĭdĕ'ntalism, ŏccĭdĕ'ntalist** *ns.*
ŏ'ccĭput (ŏks-) *n.* Back of head. **occĭ'pĭtal** *adj.* Of the occiput (~ *bone,* ill. HEAD; ~ *lobe,* ill. BRAIN).
occlu'de (-ōōd) *v.t.* Stop up, close, obstruct; (chem.) absorb and retain (gases); *occluded front,* (meteor.) warm front forced upwards by cold front when the cold air overtakes the warm and flows in underneath it.
occlu'sion (-ōō-) *n.* Act or process of occluding; overlapping position of upper and lower teeth when jaws are brought together, bite; (phonet.) momentary closure of vocal passage as in formation of stop consonants; (chem.) absorption of gases by certain substances.
occlu'sive (-ōōs-) *adj.* Tending to occlude; (phonet., of a consonant) produced with occlusion.
occŭ'lt[1] *adj.* Kept secret, esoteric; recondite, mysterious, beyond the range of ordinary knowledge; involving the supernatural, mystical, magical; *the ~,* the supernatural. **occŭ'ltlў** *adv.* **occŭ'ltnĕss** *n.*
occŭ'lt[2] *v.* Conceal, cut off from view by passing in front (usu. astron.); *occulting light,* in lighthouse etc., light that is cut off at regular intervals.
ŏccultā'tion *n.* (astron.) Eclipse of one heavenly body by another, usu. larger, passing between it and the earth.
occŭ'ltism *n.* Theory of, belief in, occult forces and powers.
ŏ'ccŭpant *n.* Person holding property, esp. land, in actual possession; one who occupies, resides in, or is in, a place; one who establishes title to ownerless thing by taking possession. **ŏ'ccŭpancў** *n.*
ŏccŭpā'tion *n.* 1. Occupying or being occupied; taking or holding possession, esp. of country or district by military force; tenure, occupancy; ~ *bridge, road,* private bridge, road, for occupier of land. 2. What occupies one, means of filling one's time; temporary or regular employment, business, calling, pursuit. **ŏccŭpā'tional** *adj.* (esp. of disease etc.) Incidental to, caused by, one's occupation; ~ *therapy,* treatment of disease by means of purposeful occupation, as handicrafts, cultural activities, etc.
ŏ'ccŭpў *v.t.* Take possession of (country etc.) by military force or settlement; hold (office); reside in, tenant; take up or fill (space, time); be in (place, position); keep engaged. **ŏ'ccŭpīer** *n.* Person in (esp. temporary or subordinate) possession, esp. of land or house; holder, occupant.
occŭr' *v.i.* Be met with, be found, exist, in some place or conditions; come into one's mind; come into being at a point or period of time.

occŭ'rrence *n.* Happening; incident, event.
ocean (ō'shan) *n.* Great body of water surrounding the land of the globe; one of the main areas into which this is geographically divided (usu. reckoned as five, the *Atlantic, Pacific, Indian, Arctic, and Antarctic* (*Southern*) *Oceans*); *the* sea; immense expanse or quantity of anything.
Ŏcĕā'nĭa (ōs- *or* ōsh-). Islands of the Pacific Ocean and adjacent seas, sometimes including Australasia and Malaysia. **Ŏcĕā'nĭan** *adj. & n.*
ŏcĕă'nic (*or* ōsh-) *adj.* Of the ocean; *O~,* of Oceania.
Ŏcĕ'anid (ō-) *n.* (Gk myth.) One of the ocean nymphs, daughters of Oceanus and Tethys.
oceanŏ'graphў (ōsha-) *n.* Branch of science concerned with the study of the ocean, the composition and characteristics of the water, plant, and animal life, and the ocean floor. **oceanŏ'grapher** *n.*
Ŏcĕ'anus (ō-). (Gk myth.) Son of Uranus and Ge, and father of the Oceanids and river gods; personification of the river encircling the whole world.
ocĕ'llus *n.* (pl. *-lī*). 1. One of the simple as dist. from the compound eyes of insects and some other arthropods etc. (ill. INSECT). 2. One facet of a compound eye. 3. Eye-like spot on insects, fishes, etc.
ŏ'cĕllate, -ātĕd *adjs.*
ŏ'cĕlot *n.* One of the larger cats (*Felis pardalis*) of Central and S. America, with grey body marked with elongated fawn spots edged with black, and white or whitish underparts marked with black. [Fr., abbrev. by Buffon f. Mex. *tlal*(*ocelotl* jaguar) *of the field,* and applied to a different animal]
och (ŏχ) *int.* (Ir. & Sc.) Oh, ah.
ŏchlŏ'cracў (-kl-) *n.* Mob rule.
ŏ'chlocrăt *n.* **ŏchlocră'tic** *adj.*
ochre (ō'ker) *n.* Mineral or class of minerals consisting of hydrated ferric oxide mixed with varying proportions of clay, used as pigment, ranging in colour from light yellow to deep orange or brown. **ŏ'chrĕous, ŏ'chrous** *adjs.*
o'clŏ'ck *adv.* (of time) By the clock.
O'Cŏ'nnell, Daniel(1775–1847). 'The Liberator', Irish Catholic political leader; advocated Catholic emancipation and repeal of the union of Gt Britain and Ireland.
oct. *abbrev.* Octavo.
Oct. *abbrev.* October.
ŏcta-, ŏct- *prefix.* Eight.
ŏ'ctachŏrd (-kôrd) *n.* (mus.) Series of 8 notes, e.g. the diatonic scale; any 8-stringed musical instrument.
ŏ'ctad *n.* Group of 8.
ŏ'ctagon *n.* Plane figure of 8 angles and sides; object or building of such section. ~ *adj.* Octagonal. **octā'gonal** *adj.* **octă'gonallў** *adv.*
ŏctahĕ'dron *n.* Solid figure of 8 faces, usu. 8 triangles; body, esp. crystal, of regular octahedral form; *regular ~,* figure contained by 8 equal and equilateral triangles (ill. SOLID). **ŏctahĕ'dral** *adj.*
ŏ'ctāne *n.* (chem.) Hydrocarbon of the paraffin series (C_8H_{18}); ~ *number,* measure of the anti-knock properties of a petrol; *high ~,* (of petrol) having good anti-knock properties.
ŏ'ctant *n.* Eighth part of circle; either arc of $\frac{1}{8}$ of circumference or $\frac{1}{8}$ of area contained between two radii at angle of 45°; one of 8 parts into which solid figure or body is divided by three planes intersecting (usu. at right angles) at central point; (astron.) point in planet's apparent course 45° from another planet, esp. point at which moon is 45° from conjunction or opposition with sun; alternative name for QUADRANT.
ŏ'ctastўle *adj. & n.* (Portico or building) with 8 columns at end or in front (ill. TEMPLE[1]).
ŏ'ctave *n.* 1. (eccles.) Eighth day after a festival (both days being counted); period of 8 days beginning with a festival. 2. Group or stanza of 8 lines, octet. 3. (mus.) Note 8 diatonic degrees above or below given note (both notes being counted), and produced by vibrations of twice or half the rate (ill. INTERVAL); interval between any note and its octave; series of notes etc. extending through this interval; two notes an octave apart played or sung together; organ-stop sounding an octave higher than ordinary pitch; ~ *coupler,* device connecting organ-keys an octave apart. 4. Eighth position in fencing, that of parrying or attacking in low outside line with sword-hand in supination (ill. FENCE). 5. *law of ~s,* that formulated (1863–6) by J. A. R. Newlands, who noted that the chemical elements, when arranged in order of their atomic weights, exhibited a recurring regularity of properties after each series of 8 elements, an anticipation of the PERIODIC law.
Octā'via (ŏ-) (d. 11 B.C.). Sister of Augustus and wife of Mark Antony.
Octā'vian (ŏ-): see AUGUSTUS.
ŏctā'vō *n.* (abbrev. 8vo, oct.). Book or page given by folding sheets three times or into 8 leaves; size of this, varying according to size of sheet (crown, demy, etc.).
octĕ'nnial *adj.* Lasting, recurring every, 8 years.
octĕ't, -ĕtte *n.* (Composition for) 8 voices or instruments in combination; set of 8; group of 8 lines, esp. the first 8 of a sonnet.
ŏcti'llion (-lyon) *n.* One million raised to the 8th power (1 followed by 48 ciphers); (U.S.) one thousand raised to the 9th power (1 followed by 27 ciphers).
ŏcto-, ŏct- *prefix.* Eight.
Octō'ber (ŏ-). 10th month of Gregorian (8th of Julian) calendar,

with 31 days; ~ *revolution*, see Russian REVOLUTION. [L *octo* eight]
Octō'brist (ŏ-) *n*. Member of Russian moderate liberal political party, whose principles of constitutional government were proclaimed in the imperial Manifesto of Oct. 1905.
octodĕ'cĭmō *n*. (abbrev. 18mo) (Size of) book or page given by folding sheets into 18 leaves.
octogĕnār'ian *adj*. & *n*. (Person) aged 80 years or more but less than 90.
ō'ctonary *adj*. Of 8; consisting of 8; proceeding by eights. ~ *n*. Group of 8; 8-line stanza.
ō'ctopŏd *n*. Cephalopod of the order Octopoda with 8 arms.
ō'ctopus *n*. Cephalopod mollusc with 8 arms, provided with suckers, surrounding mouth.
octorōō'n *n*. Offspring of quadroon and white, person of one-eighth Negro blood.
ŏctosyllă'bic *adj*. & *n*. Eight-syllable (verse). **ŏctosy̆'llable** *adj*. & *n*. (Verse, word) of 8 syllables.
ō'ctroi (-rwah) *n*. Duty levied in some continental countries on goods entering town; place where, officials by whom, it is levied.
O.C.T.U., O'ctū (ŏ-). *abbrev*. Officer Cadets Training Unit.
ō'ctŭple *adj*. Eightfold. ~ *n*. Product (*of*) after multiplication by 8. ~ *v.t*. Multiply by 8.
ō'cūlar *adj*. Of, for, by, with, etc., the eye(s) or sight, visual. ~ *n*. Eyepiece of optical instrument.
ō'cūlarist *n*. Maker of artificial eyes.
ō'cūlist *n*. Medical practitioner who specializes in diseases of the eye.
ŏd *n*. Hypothetical power once held to pervade nature and account for magnetism, crystallization, chemical action, mesmerism, etc. [arbitrary formation of Baron von Reichenbach (1788–1869)]
ō'dalĭsque (-k) *n*. (hist.) Eastern female slave or concubine, esp. in Turkish sultan's seraglio. [Fr., f. Turk. *odalik*]
ŏdd *adj*. 1. Remaining over after division or distribution into pairs; (of number) not divisible by 2; numbered or known by such a number; (appended to number, sum, weight, etc.) with something over of lower denomination etc.; by which round number, given sum, etc., is exceeded; ~ *trick*, (whist) single trick by which one side wins when the score is 7–6. 2. Additional, casual, beside the reckoning, unconnected, unoccupied, incalculable; forming part of incomplete pair or set. 3. Extraordinary, strange, queer, remarkable, eccentric. 4. *O'ddfellow*, member of friendly society of Oddfellows (founded prob. in early part of 18th c.) with rites imitative of freemasonry; ~ *job*, casual disconnected piece of work. **ō'ddly** *adv*. **ō'ddness** *n*. **ŏdd** *n*.

(golf) Handicap given by deduction of one stroke from the score at each hole; stroke by which one player is above his opponent at a particular hole.
ō'dditȳ *n*. Strangeness; peculiar trait; queer person; fantastic object, strange event.
ō'ddments *n.pl*. Odds and ends.
ŏdds (-z) *n.pl*. (freq. treated as sing.). Inequalities; difference; variance, strife; balance of advantage; equalizing allowance to weaken competitor; ratio between amounts staked by parties to bet, advantage conceded by one of the parties in proportion to assumed chances in his favour; chances or balance of probability in favour of some result; ~ *and ends*, remnants, stray articles; ~-*on*, (of chance or probability) in favour of some result etc.
ōde *n*. 1. (orig.) Poem meant to be sung; *choral* ~, song of chorus in Greek play etc. 2. Rhymed (or, rarely, unrhymed) lyric, often in form of address, usu. of exalted style and enthusiastic tone, often in varied or irregular metre, and usu. between 50 and 200 lines in length.
O'der (ō-). European river rising in Carpathians and flowing NW. to Baltic.
Odĕ'ssa. Ukrainian city and seaport on NW. coast of Black Sea.
O'din (ō-). (Scand. myth.) Supreme god and creator, god of victory and the dead; represented as an old one-eyed man of great wisdom.
ō'dious *adj*. Hateful, repulsive. **ō'diously** *adv*. **ō'diousness** *n*.
ō'dium *n*. General or widespread dislike or reprobation incurred by person or attaching to action; ~ *theologicum*, bitterness proverbially characterizing theological discussions.
Odoā'cer (ō-) (*c* 434–93). First barbarian ruler of Italy, proclaimed king by the German soldiers; defeated several times and finally assassinated by Theodoric the Ostrogoth.
odō'mĕter *n*. Instrument for measuring distance travelled.
odŏntoglŏ'ssum *n*. Orchid of genus *O*~ with large beautifully coloured flowers.
odontō'lŏgȳ *n*. Scientific study of the teeth. **odontolō'gĭcal** *adj*. **odontō'logist** *n*.
odorĭ'ferous *adj*. Diffusing (usu. agreeable) scent, fragrant. **odorĭ'ferously** *adv*.
ō'dorous *adj*. (chiefly poet.) Odoriferous. **ō'dorously** *adv*.
ō'dour (-er) *n*. Pleasant or unpleasant smell; fragrance; (fig.) savour, trace; ~ *of sanctity*, sweet or balsamic odour supposed to be exhaled by dying or exhumed saint; reputation for holiness.
ō'dourless *adj*.
Ody̆'sseus (-sūs). (Gk legend) King of Ithaca, called Ulysses by the Romans; renowned for cun-

ning; he survived the Trojan War, but Poseidon kept him from home 10 years while his wife PENELOPE waited in Ithaca. **O'dy̆ssey**[1] (ō-). Greek epic poem attributed to Homer, in 24 books, describing the wanderings and return of Odysseus.
ō'dy̆ssey[2] *n*. Long adventurous journey.
O.E.C.D. *abbrev*. Organization for Economic Co-operation and Development.
oecology: see ECOLOGY.
oecūmĕ'nical (ēk-), **ēc-** *adj*. (eccles.) Of or representing the whole Christian world or universal church, general, universal, catholic; world-wide.
O.E.D. *abbrev*. Oxford English Dictionary.
oedĕ'ma (ĭd-) *n*. (path.) Abnormal accumulation of fluid in tissue, dropsy. **oedēmă'tic**, **oedĕ'matous** *adjs*.
Oe'dipus (ēd-). (Gk legend) Son of Laius king of Thebes, and Jocasta; he unwittingly killed his father and married his own mother, and when the facts were discovered, went mad and put out his own eyes, while Jocasta hanged herself; ~ *complex*, (psychol.) manifestation of infantile sexuality in relations of (esp. male) child to parents, with attraction towards parent of opposite sex and jealousy of other parent.
Oenō'nē (ēn-). (Gk legend) Nymph of Mount Ida and lover of Paris, who deserted her for Helen.
o'er (ōr) *adv*. & *prep*. (poet.) = OVER.
oer'stĕd (ēr-) *n*. Unit of magnetic intensity in c.g.s. electromagnetic system. [Hans Christian *Oersted* (1777–1851), Danish physicist]
oesŏ'phagus (ēs-) *n*. Canal leading from mouth to stomach, gullet (ill. ALIMENTARY).
oe'strogen (ēs-) *n*. Female hormone inducing oestrus and causing development of secondary sexual characteristics.
oe'strus (ēs-) *n*. Period of sexual activity in female mammals. **oe's-trous** *adj*.
of (ŏv *or* ov) *prep*. From; concerning; out of; among; relating to.
ŏff *adv*. Away, at or to a distance; (so as to be) out of position, not on or touching or dependent or attached; loose, separate, gone; so as to break continuity or continuance, discontinued, stopped, not obtainable, abstaining from, averse to; to the end, entirely, so as to be clear; (of food) deteriorated, unfit for consumption; *well, badly, comfortably*, etc., ~, so circumstanced or supplied with money; ~ *and on*, intermittently, waveringly, now and again. ~ *prep*. From; away, down or up from; disengaged or distant from; (so as to be) no longer on; *o'ffhand*, extempore, without premeditation, curt, casual,

[610]

unceremonious; *offha'nded(ly)* (adv.); *offha'ndedness* (n.); ~-*peak*, outside peak hours; ~ *shore*, a short way out to sea; ~-*shore wind*, one blowing seawards; *offsi'de*, (footb., hockey) of a player in a position on the field where he may not kick, handle, or hit the ball. ~ *adj.* 1. Farther, far; (of horse or vehicle) right (opp. NEAR; so ~-*side*); (cricket) towards, in, coming from, that side of the field which the batsman faces when playing. 2. Subordinate, divergent; disengaged. 3. ~-*chance*, slight or remote chance; ~-*licence*, licence to sell beer etc. for consumption off the premises; ~-*season*, season when business is less active than usual. ~ *n*. (cricket) The off side.

O'ffa (ŏ-) (d. 796). King of Mercia 757-96; ~'s *Dyke*, series of earthworks running from near mouth of Wye to near mouth of Dee, built or repaired by Offa as a boundary between Mercia and Wales.

o'ffal *n*. Refuse, waste stuff, scraps, garbage; parts cut off in dressing carcass of animal killed for food, orig. entrails, now a trade term for edible organs such as liver, kidneys, etc.; carrion, putrid flesh; low-priced fish; bran or other by-product of grain (freq. pl.).

O'ffalў (ŏ-). County of Leinster; formerly called King's County.

O'ffenbach (ŏ-, -ahχ), Jacques (1819-80). French composer of burlesque opera (*opera bouffe*), of German-Jewish origin.

offĕ'nce *n*. 1. Attacking, aggressive action. 2. Wounding of the feelings; wounded feeling, annoyance, umbrage. 3. Transgression, misdemeanour, illegal act. offĕ'ncelĕss *adj.*

offĕ'nd *v.* 1. Commit an offence (*against*). 2. Wound feelings of, anger, cause resentment or disgust in, outrage. offĕ'ndedlў *adv.* offĕ'nder *n*.

offĕ'nsive *adj.* 1. Aggressive, intended for or used in attack. 2. Meant to give offence, insulting. 3. Disgusting, repulsive. offĕ'nsivelў *adv.* offĕ'nsiveness *n*.

offĕ'nsive *n*. Attitude of assailant, aggressive action; attack, offensive campaign or stroke.

o'ffer *v.* 1. Present to deity, revered person, etc., by way of sacrifice; give in worship or devotion. 2. Hold out in hand, or tender in words or otherwise, for acceptance or refusal; make proposal of marriage; show for sale; give opportunity to enemy for (battle); express readiness *to* do; essay, try to show (violence etc.); show an intention *to* do. 3. Present to sight or notice; present itself, occur. ~ *n*. Expression of readiness to give or do if desired, or to sell on terms; proposal, esp. of marriage; bid. o'ffering *n*. Thing offered.

o'ffertorў *n*. Part of Mass or Communion service at which offerings are made, offering of these, gifts offered; collection of money at religious service.

o'ffice *n*. 1. Piece of kindness, attention, service, (*ill* ~) disservice. 2. Duty attaching to one's position, task, function. 3. Position with duties attached to it; place of authority, trust, or service, esp. of public kind; tenure of official position, esp. that of minister of State. 4. Ceremonial duty; (eccles.) authorized form of worship; (introit at beginning of) Mass or Communion service, any occasional service. 5. Place for transacting business; room etc. in which clerks of an establishment work, counting-house; (with qualification, as *booking-*~, *inquiry* ~) room etc. set apart for business of particular department of large concern, local branch of dispersed organization, or company for specified purpose; (U.S.) consulting-room of doctor etc. 6. (with capital) Quarters, staff or collective authority of a Government department, as *Home O*~; *Scottish O*~, that under Secretary of State for Scotland. 7. (pl.) Parts of house devoted to household work, storage, etc. 8. (slang) Hint, private intimation, signal (esp. in *give the* ~). 9. *Holy O*~: see HOLY.

o'fficer *n*. 1. Holder of public, civil, or ecclesiastical office; king's servant or minister, appointed or elected functionary; president, treasurer, secretary, etc., of society; bailiff, catchpole, constable. 2. Person holding authority in armed forces or mercantile marine, esp. one with a commission in the armed forces. ~ *v.t.* Provide with officers; act as commander of.

offi'cial (-shǎl) *adj.* Of an office, the discharge of duties, or the tenure of an office; holding office, employed in public capacity; derived from or vouched for by person(s) in office, properly authorized; usual with persons in office; (med., of drug etc.) conforming to a description in a pharmacopoeia. offi'ciallў *adv.* offi'cialdom, offi'cialism *ns.* offi'cialize *v.t.*

offi'cial *n*. 1. Person holding public office or engaged in official duties. 2. Presiding officer or judge of archbishop's, bishop's, or esp. archdeacon's court.

offi'ciāte (-sh-) *v.i.* Discharge priestly office, perform divine service; act in some official capacity, esp. on particular occasion. offi'ciant *n*.

offi'cinal *adj.* (of herb or drug) Used in medicine or the arts. offi'cinallў *adv.*

offi'cious (-shŭs) *adj.* 1. (Given to) offering service that is not wanted, doing or undertaking more than is required, intrusive, meddlesome. 2. (diplomacy, opp. *official*) Informal, unofficially friendly or candid, not binding. offi'cious1ў *adv.* offi'ciousness *n*.

o'ffing *n*. Part of visible sea distant from shore or beyond anchoring ground; position at distance from shore; *in the* ~, (fig.) near by; ready or likely to appear.

o'ffish *adj.* (colloq.) Inclined to aloofness. o'ffishness *n*.

o'ffprint *n*. Separate copy of article etc. that was originally part of larger publication.

o'ffscourings (-z) *n.pl.* Refuse, dregs.

o'ffsĕt *n*. 1. Short side-shoot from stem or root serving for propagation; offshoot, scion, mountain spur. 2. Compensation, set-off, consideration or amount diminishing or neutralizing effect of contrary one. 3. (surv.) Short distance measured perpendicularly from main line of measurement. 4. (archit.) Sloping ledge in wall etc. where thickness of part above is diminished (ill. BUTTRESS). 5. Bend made in pipe to carry it past obstacle. 6. (printing, engraving) Transfer of ink from a newly printed surface to another surface so that the final impression is in the same sense as the plate or type (~ *proof*, engraver's trial proof made thus as aid to working); ~ *lithography*, method of printing in which ink is transferred from a lithographic stone or plate to a rubber roller and thence, while still wet, to paper. ~ *v.t.* Counterbalance, compensate for; print by offset.

o'ffshōōt *n*. Side-shoot or branch; derivative.

o'ffspring *n*. Descendant.

O'flăg (ŏ-) *n*. German prison camp for officers. [Ger., abbrev. of *Offizier* officer, *Lager* camp]

O.F.M. *abbrev.* Order of Friars Minor.

O.F.S. *abbrev.* Orange Free State.

ŏft *adv.* Often (archaic exc. in comb.); ~-*times*, (archaic) often.

often (ŏ'fn) *adv.* Many times, at short intervals; in many instances; ~-*times*, (archaic) often.

ogam: see OGHAM.

ō'gēē *n*. S-shaped curve; (archit.) cyma reversa (ill. MOULDING); ~ *arch*, arch with two ogee curves meeting at apex (ill. ARCH¹).

ogham (ŏ'gam), ŏ'gam *n*. Ancient British and Irish alphabet of characters formed by parallel strokes arranged along either side of, or crossing, continuous medial line, e.g. edge of stone; inscription in this; one of the characters.

⊢B	⊢H	⊢M	⊢A
⊨L	⊨D	⊨G	⊨O
⊫V or F	⊫T	⊫NG	⊫U
⊨S	⊨C	⊨ST or Z	⊨E
≣N	≣Q	≣R	≣I

X as vowel, E; as consonant, C.

OGHAM

ō'gīve *n*. Diagonal groin or rib of vault; pointed or Gothic arch. ogī'val *adj.*

ō'gle *v.* Cast amorous glances,

eye amorously. ~ n. Amorous glance.
O.G.P.U., Ogpu (ŏ'gpōō): see G.P.U.
ō'gre (-er) n. (fem. **ō'gréss**) (in legend etc.) Man-eating giant; hence, terrifying person. **ō'greish, ō'grish** adjs.
O'gȳgēs (ŏ-,-z). (Gk myth.) First king of Thebes, in whose reign a destructive flood occurred. **Ogȳ'gian** adj. Of Ogyges; of obscure antiquity, of great age.
oh; see O².
Ohi'ō. State in NE. central U.S., part of Middle West admitted to the Union in 1803; capital, Columbus; ~ *River*, chief eastern tributary of Mississippi.
Ohm[1] (ōm), Georg Simon (1787-1854). German physicist who determined mathematically the law of the flow of electricity.
ohm[2] (ōm) n. Unit of electrical resistance, resistance of a circuit in which potential difference of one volt produces current of one ampere. **oh'mic** adj. [f. OHM[1]]
O.H.M.S. abbrev. On His (or Her) Majesty's Service.
ohō' int. Exclamation of surprise or exultation.
oil n. 1. One of a large group of liquid viscid substances with characteristic smooth and sticky feel, lighter than water and insoluble in it, inflammable, and chemically neutral, used as lubricants, in perfumery etc. (*essential* or *volatile* ~), and as fuel etc. (*mineral* ~); *drying* ~, any of those oils which by exposure to air harden into varnishes; *non-drying* ~, one which decomposes by exposure, used as lubricant, in making soap, etc. 2. Oil-colour (freq. pl.). 3. (pl.) Oilskins. 4. ~-*bomb*, incendiary bomb containing oil; ~-*cake*, mass of compressed linseed etc. left when oil has been expressed, used as cattle-food or manure; ~-*can*, can for holding oil, esp. with long nozzle for oiling machinery; *oi'lcloth*, fabric waterproofed with oil, oilskin; canvas coated with preparation containing drying oil, used to cover tables etc.; ~-*colour*, paint made by grinding pigment in a drying oil; ~-*engine*, one driven by explosion of vaporized oil mixed with air; ~-*field*, tract of oil-bearing strata; *oi'lman*, maker or seller of oils; ~-*meal*, ground oil-cake; ~-*paint*, oil-colour; ~-*painting*, art of painting, picture painted, in oil-colours; ~-*paper*, paper made transparent or waterproof by soaking in oil; ~-*shale*, rock from which petroleum can be produced by distillation; ~-*silk*, oiled silk; *oi'lskin*, cloth water-proofed with a drying oil; garment or (pl.) coat and trousers of this; *oi'lstone*, fine-grained stone used with oil as whetstone; ~-*well*, well yielding mineral oil. ~ v. 1. Apply oil to, lubricate. 2. Turn into oily liquid. 3. Impregnate or treat with oil. **oiled** (-ld) adj.

(esp.) 1. ~ *silk*, silk waterproofed with a drying oil. 2. (slang) Slightly drunk.
oi'ler n. Oil-can for oiling machinery; ship built for carrying oil.
oi'lȳ adj. 1. Of, like, covered or soaked with, containing much, oil. 2. (of manner etc.) Fawning, too smooth. **oi'lilȳ** adv. **oi'liness** n.
oi'ntment n. Emollient preparation applied to skin to heal or beautify, unguent.
Oireachtas (ēr'axthăs). Legislature of the Republic of Ireland, consisting of the President and two houses, **Dáil Eireann** and **Seanad Eireann** [Ir., = 'assembly']
Oisin: see OSSIAN.
Oji'bwā, -way n. Member of a large group of N. Amer. Indians of Algonquian linguistic stock, belonging to region of Great Lakes.
O.K. (ō kā) adj. (orig. U.S. slang) All right. ~ n. & v.t. (Mark with) the letters 'O.K.', esp. as denoting approval of contents of document etc.; sanction. [initials of *Old Kinderhook* (Kinderhook, near Albany, New York, birthplace of Democratic candidate, Martin van Buren) used c 1840 as a slogan and passing into a term of approval, being interpreted as abbrev. of *oll korrekt*, mis-spelling of *all correct*]
oka'pi (-ah-) n. Rare ungulate mammal, *Okapia johnstoni*, related to giraffes, found in dense forests of W. Africa.
ōkay' adj. & v.t. = O.K.
Okhŏ'tsk (oχ-), Sea of. Arm of NW. Pacific Ocean, lying between Kamchatka peninsula and mainland of Siberia.
Okla. abbrev. Oklahoma.
Oklahō'ma (ō-). State in south-central U.S., admitted to the Union in 1907; capital, Oklahoma City.
ŏ'kra, ŏ'krō n. Tall malvaceous African plant (*Hibiscus esculentus*, called also *gumbo*) cultivated in W. Indies, southern U.S., etc., the young fruits of which are used as a vegetable and for thickening soups, and the stem-fibres for ropes.
Ol. abbrev. Olympiad.
O'lăf (ō-). Name of two kings of Norway: *Olaf I Tryggvason* (c 969-1000), king 995-1000; raided coast of France and British Isles until he became a Christian; began conversion of Norway to Christianity; *Olaf II* (995-1030), 'St. Olaf', 'Olaf the Fat'; patron saint of Norway; king of Norway 1015-28; active in diffusion of Christianity in his kingdom until his expulsion by CANUTE.
Olā'us Mă'gnus (1490-1558). Swedish ecclesiastic; archbishop of Uppsala; author of a history of the northern peoples (1555).
O'lbers (ŏ-,-z), Heinrich Wilhelm Matthias (1758-1840). German astronomer; discoverer of several comets and some minor planets.
ōld adj. 1. Advanced in age, far

on in natural period of existence, not young or near its beginning; having characteristics, experience, feebleness, etc., of age; worn, dilapidated, shabby. 2. (appended to period of time) Of age (as *10 years* ~); (ellipt.) person or animal, esp. race-horse, of specified age (as *three-year*-~). 3. Practised or inveterate *in* action or quality, or as agent etc. 4. Dating from far back; made long ago; long established, known, familiar, or dear; ancient, not new or recent, primeval; (of language) belonging to the earliest known period or stage; *of* ~ *standing*, long established. 5. Belonging only or chiefly to the past; obsolete, obsolescent, out of date, antiquated, antique; concerned with antiquity; not modern, bygone, former. 6. ~-*age pension(er)*, (person receiving) retirement pension; *O*~ *Bailey*, English Central Criminal Court, on site of NEWGATE prison, situated in ancient bailey of London city wall between Lud Gate and New Gate; *O*~ *Believers*, Russian sect originating in 17th c. in protest against liturgical reforms of patriarch NIKON; *O*~ *Bulgarian*, Old SLAVONIC; *O*~ *Catholics*, group of small national Churches which have separated at various times from Rome, now in full communion with C. of E.; ~-*clothes-man*, dealer in discarded clothes; *O*~ *Colony*, part of Massachusetts within original limits of Plymouth colony; *O*~ *Contemptibles*: see CONTEMPTIBLE; ~ *countries*, countries long inhabited or civilized; *the* ~ *country*, *home*, etc., (used by colonials etc. of) mother country; *O*~ *Dominion*, Virginia; ~ *English sheep-dog*, medium-sized breed of dog with very long, shaggy, whitish coat and short or no tail; ~ *face*, style of printing type as dist. from modern face (ill. TYPE); *O*~ *Faithful*, geyser in Yellowstone National Park, Wyoming, erupting regularly at intervals of a little over an hour; ~-*fashioned*, belonging to a fashion that has gone or is going out; *O*~ *Glory*, (U.S.) the Stars and Stripes; ~ *gold*, colour of tarnished gold; *O*~ *Guard*, French Imperial Guard created by Napoleon I in 1804; (transf.) established influential conservative group; ~ *hand*, practised workman; person of experience in (*at*) something; *O*~ *Harry*, *O*~ *Nick*, the Devil; *O*~ *Hickory*, (U.S.) nickname of Andrew JACKSON[1], from his toughness of character; *O*~ *Hundred(th)*, tune (first published 1551) set to 100th psalm in old version of metrical psalms, and usually sung to doxology; *O*~ *Lady of Threadneedle Street*, familiar name for Bank of England; ~ *maid*, elderly spinster; person who is overprecise; (cards) round game in which object is to avoid holding of unpaired card; ~-*maidish* (adj.); ~ *man*, southernwood; (naut. slang)

[612]

ship's captain; (colloq.) husband; the ~ man, one's unregenerate self; ~ man of the sea, (from character in 'Arabian Nights' tale of Sindbad the Sailor) person who cannot be shaken off; ~ man's beard, kind of moss; traveller's joy and other species of *Clematis*; ~ master, (painting by) great painter of former times, esp. 13th–17th centuries in Europe; O~ Moore: see MOORE[1]; O~ Pretender: see PRETENDER; ~ school tie, necktie of characteristic pattern as worn by former members of a particular (public) school; used symbolically to denote extreme loyalty to a traditional mode of thought or behaviour; O~ Stone Age, PALAEOLITHIC age; ~ style: see STYLE; O~ Testament: see TESTAMENT; ~ time, of former times; ~-timer, (U.S.) one whose experience goes back to old times; one of long standing; old-fashioned person or thing; O~ Vic, theatre in Waterloo Road, London, opened 1818 as Coburg Theatre and renamed Victoria 1833, which was reopened 1880 by Emma Cons as a 'temperance music-hall' and under the management of Lilian Baylis (1912-37) became the headquarters of a company performing Shakespeare's plays and other classics; ~ wives' tale: see WIFE; ~ woman, (colloq.) wife; fussy or timid man; O~ World, eastern hemisphere; ~-world, of the old world, not American; (also) belonging to old times; ~ year, year just ended or about to end. ŏ'ldĭsh adj. ŏld n. Old time (only in *of old* (adj. & adv.) as *men of old, of old there were giants*).

Oldcastle (ō'ldkahsl), Sir John (d. 1417). English soldier; a leader of the Lollards; was arrested, but escaped and lived as an outlaw; was recaptured and executed as a heretic; Shakespeare used his name in 'Henry IV' but changed it, after a protest, to Falstaff.

ŏ'lden *adj*. (archaic & literary) Old-time, of a former age.

Oldenbar'nĕvĕldt (ō-, -fĕlt), Johan van (1547–1619). Dutch statesman; supporter of William the Silent in struggle for independence of the Netherlands; his execution under Maurice of Nassau is regarded as a judicial murder.

ŏ'ldster *n*. Old person.

ōlĕā'ceous (-shus) *adj*. Of the Oleaceae or olive family of plants, including jasmine etc.

ōlĕā'ginous *adj*. Having properties of or producing oil; oily, fatty, greasy.

ōlĕā'nder *n*. Evergreen poisonous Levantine shrub (*Nerium oleander*) with leathery lanceolate leaves and handsome red or white flowers.

ō'lĕfīne *n*. (chem.) Any member of the ethylene series of hydrocarbons.

ō'lĕogrăph (*or* -ahf) *n*. Picture printed in oil-colours.

ō'lĕo-margari'ne (-ēn; *or* j-) *n*. Fatty substance extracted from clarified beef-fat and made into margarine with addition of butyrin, milk, etc.

ō'lĕo-rĕ'sĭn (-z-) *n*. Natural product containing a volatile oil and a resin, e.g. exudation from coniferous tree.

ō'lĕum *n*. (chem.) Fuming (or Nordhausen) sulphuric acid ($H_2SO_4 xSO_3$), a solution of sulphur trioxide in sulphuric acid.

ōlfă'ction *n*. Smelling, sense of smell. ōlfă'ctĭve *adj*. ōlfă'ctory *adj*. Concerned with smelling.

oli'banum *n*. Aromatic gum resin obtained from trees of genus *Boswellia*, used as incense.

ŏ'lĭd *adj*. Rank-smelling, fetid.

ŏ'lĭgarch (-k) *n*. Member of oligarchy.

ŏ'lĭgarchy̆ (-kĭ) *n*. Government, State governed, by a few persons; members of such a government. ŏlĭgar'chĭc, -ĭcal *adjs*. ŏlĭgar'chĭcally̆ *adv*.

ŏlĭgŏcar'pous *adj*. (bot.) Having few fruits.

O'lĭgocēne (ō-) *adj*. & *n*. (geol.) (Of) the 3rd epoch or system of the Tertiary period (ill. GEOLOGY).

ō'lĭō *n*. Mixed dish, hotchpotch, stew of various meats and vegetables; medley, miscellany.

ōlĭvā'ceous (-shus) *adj*. Olive-green, of dusky yellowish green.

ŏ'lĭvary̆ *adj*. (anat.) Olive-shaped, oval.

ŏ'lĭve *n*. 1. Evergreen tree (*Olea europaea*), esp. the cultivated variety, with narrow leaves green above and hoary below and axillary clusters of small whitish flowers, bearing small oval drupes, blackish when ripe, with bitter pulp abounding in oil, and hard stone, cultivated in Mediterranean countries etc. for its fruit and oil; fruit of this tree; any tree of the genus *Olea*, tree or shrub resembling this. 2. Leaf, branch, or wreath of olive as emblem of peace. 3. Olive-shaped gasteropod mollusc (*Oliva*). 4. (pl.) Slices of beef or veal rolled up with onions and herbs and stewed in brown sauce. 5. Olive-colour. 6. ~*-branch*, branch of olive-tree, esp. as emblem of peace (freq. fig.); ~*-crown*, garland of olive as sign of victory; ~*-oil*, clear, pale-yellow, non-drying oil obtained from pulp of olives, used in cookery, salads, as a medicine, as a lubricant, and in the manufacture of toilet soap, etc.; *Mount of Olives*, ridge facing Temple mount at Jerusalem on the east, with Garden of Gethsemane on western slope. ~ *adj*. Coloured like unripe olive, dull yellowish green; (of complexion etc.) brownish yellow; of colour of olive foliage, dull ashy green with silvery sheen.

ŏ'lĭver[1] *n*. Tilt-hammer attached to axle and worked by treadle, for shaping nails etc.

O'lĭver[2] (ŏ-). In the Charlemagne cycle of legends, one of Charlemagne's paladins and the close friend of ROLAND.

ŏ'lĭvīne *n*. Yellowish-green mineral, a magnesium silicate, found in basalt and gabbro.

ŏ'lla podrī'da (-rē-). = OLIO. [Span., lit. 'rotten pot']

Oly̆'mpia. Plain on N. bank of river Alpheus about 20 miles from W. coast of Peloponnese; in ancient Greece a great religious centre second only to Delphi, and site of the OLYMPIC Games.

Oly̆'mpĭăd *n*. 1. Period of 4 years between celebrations of OLYMPIC Games, used by ancient Greeks in dating events, 776 B.C. being 1st year of 1st Olympiad. 2. Meeting of modern Olympic Games.

Oly̆'mpĭan *adj*. Of Olympus, celestial; (of manners) magnificent, condescending, superior; aloof. ~ *n*. Dweller in Olympus, one of the greater ancient Greek gods; person of superhuman calmness and detachment.

Oly̆'mpĭc *adj*. Of Olympia in Greece; of the Olympic Games; ~ *Games*, (1) athletic contests held by the ancient Greeks every 4th year at Olympia and including foot-races, boxing, wrestling, and chariot- and horse-races; (2) international amateur athletic contests begun in 1896 as revival of ancient Greek games and held every 4th year, organized by an international committee which decides where each festival is to be held and including athletics, gymnastics, combative sports, swimming, equestrian sports, the pentathlon, and art. Oly̆'mpĭcs *n.pl.* Olympic Games.

Oly̆'mpus. Lofty mountain in Greece at E. end of range dividing Thessaly from Macedonia; in Greek mythology the court of Zeus and home of the gods.

O.M. *abbrev*. Order of Merit.

Om (ŏm) *n*. In Hinduism etc., mystic and holy word regarded as summing up all truth.

O'man (ō-) *n*. Sultanate in SE. Arabia; capital, Muscat.

O'mar (ō-) (*c* 581–644). 2nd Muslim caliph, 634–44; reputed builder of *Mosque of* ~, on platform of Temple at Jerusalem, a much-altered Byzantine church, containing rock on which, acc. to Jewish legend, Abraham prepared to sacrifice Isaac, and from which, acc. to Muslims, Muhammad ascended to heaven.

O'mar Khayyám (ō-,kī-yah'm). 'Umar Khayyām (*c* 1100), Persian astronomer, mathematician, and epigrammatist, many of whose quatrains were translated into English by Edward FitzGerald.

omā'sum *n*. Ruminant's third stomach (ill. RUMINANT).

ŏ'mbre (-ber) *n*. Card-game for three, very popular in 17th–18th centuries, played with 40 cards (the eights, nines, and tens of ordinary pack being thrown out).

[613]

ŏ'mbudsman (-bŏŏdz-) n. Official who investigates complaints of maladministration, esp. by Government departments, in U.K. (O~), Parliamentary Commissioner for Administration. [Swed., = 'commissioner']

O'mdurmăn (ŏ-). Town of Sudan on left bank of Nile opposite Khartoum; chosen by the MAHDI as his capital, 1884; scene of a battle, 1898, in which an Anglo-Egyptian army under KITCHENER defeated the dervishes.

ŏ'mĕga n. Last letter of Greek alphabet (Ω, ω), corresponding to o (pr. ŏ). [Gk, = 'great o']

ŏ'melĕt, -ĕtte (ŏml-) n. Dish of eggs lightly beaten and cooked usu. in butter in a frying-pan, often with savoury or sweet filling.

ŏ'mĕn n. Event or object portending good or evil, prognostic, presage; prophetic signification.

omĕ'ntum n. (anat.) Fold of peritoneum connecting stomach with other viscera, caul (ill. ABDOMEN). **omĕ'ntal** adj.

omi'cron n. 16th (later 15th) letter of Greek alphabet (O, o) corresponding to o (pr. ŏ). [Gk, = 'small o']

ŏ'minous adj. Of evil omen, inauspicious, threatening. **ŏ'minously** adv.

omi'ssion n. Omitting, non-inclusion; non-performance, neglect, duty not done.

omi't v.t. Leave out, not insert or include; leave undone, neglect doing, fail to do.

ŏ'mnibus n. (pl. -es). 1. (in formal use) = BUS. 2. Volume containing a number of stories, plays, etc. ~ adj. Serving several objects at once; comprising several items. [L, = 'for all', i.e. everyone]

ŏmnicŏ'mpĕtent adj. Having jurisdiction in all cases.

ŏmnifār'ious adj. Of all sorts.

ŏmni'potence n. Infinite power; God; great influence. **ŏmni'potent** adj. **ŏmni'potently** adv.

ŏmniprĕ'sence (-z-) n. Ubiquity; being widespread or constantly met with. **ŏmniprĕ'sent** adj.

ŏmni'science (or -shens) n. Infinite knowledge; God; wide information or the affectation of it. **ŏmni'sciĕnt** adj. **ŏmni'sciĕntly** adv.

ŏ'mnium gă'therum (-dh-). Miscellaneous assemblage of persons or things, queer mixture. [mock L]

ŏmni'vorous adj. (of animals) Feeding on both plants and flesh; (fig.) taking in everything, esp. in choice of reading. **ŏmni'vorously** adv. **ŏmni'vorousnĕss** n. **ŏ'mnivŏre** n.

O'mphalè (ŏ-). (Gk legend) Queen of Lydia whom Hercules served for 3 years as a slave, doing female tasks while she wore his lion's skin.

ŏ'mphalŏs n. 1. (Gk antiq.) Boss on shield; conical stone at Delphi supposed to be central point of earth. 2. Centre, hub.

ŏn prep. 1. (So as to be) supported by, attached to, covering, or enclosing; ~ one, about one's person. 2. With axis, pivot, basis, motive, standard, confirmation, or guarantee, consisting in. 3. (So as to be) close to, in the direction of, touching, arrived at, against, just at. 4. (of time) During, exactly at, contemporaneously with, immediately after, as a result of; ~ the instant, immediately; ~ time, punctual(ly). 5. In manner specified by adj., or state or action specified by noun; concerning, about, while engaged with, so as to affect; taking (a drug) regularly. 6. Added to. 7. (U.S.) Against (a person); (colloq., esp. of treat of any kind) to be paid for by; have something ~, have advantage over. ~ adv. 1. (So as to be) supported by, attached to, covering, enclosing, or touching, something. 2. In some direction, towards something; farther forward, towards point of contact, in advanced position or state; with continued movement or action, in operation or activity; broadside, end, head, etc., ~, with that part forward; send ~, send in front of oneself, in advance; gas, water, etc., is ~, gas, water, etc., is turned on, running, or procurable by turning tap; get, be, ~, make, have made, bet. 3. ~ to (compound prep. corresponding to on as into to in, but usu. written as two words), to a position on. ~ adj. (cricket) Towards, from, or in that part of the field behind the batsman as he stands to play; ~ licence, licence for selling beer etc. to be drunk on the premises. ~ n. (cricket) The on side.

ŏn- prefix. On, as in o'ncoming, approach(ing).

ŏ'nager n. Wild ass, esp. the species Equus onager of Central Asia, with broad brown stripe along the back.

ŏ'nanism n. Interrupted coition; masturbation. [f. Onan (see Gen. 38: 9)]

O.N.C. abbrev. Ordinary National Certificate.

once (wŭns) adv. 1. For one time or on one occasion only; multiplied by one, by one degree; ~ and again, ~ or twice, a few times; ~ (and) for all, in final manner, definitively; ~ in a way, while, very rarely. 2. (in negative or conditional etc. clause) Ever, at all, even for one or the first time. 3. On a certain but unspecified past occasion; at some period in the past, former(ly). 4. at ~, immediately, without delay; at the same time; for (this, that) ~, on one occasion by way of exception; ~-over, (colloq.) single and rapid survey or examination. ~ conj. As soon as; if once; when once. ~ n. One time, performance, etc.

one (wŭn) adj. 1. Being, amounting to, the lowest cardinal number, number of a single thing without any more; a; ~ or two, a few. 2. Only, without others; forming a unity, united; identical, the same, unchanging; a particular but undefined, to be contrasted with another; become ~, coalesce; made ~, married. ~ n. The lowest cardinal number; its symbol (1, i, or I); one o'clock; size etc. indicated by 1; die-face or domino with one pip; single thing, person, or example; also, freq. used as substitute for repetition of noun previously expressed or implied; a ~, (slang) remarkable person, (esp.) joker; at ~, reconciled in agreement; go ~ better, bid, offer, risk, more by one point; ten etc. to ~, long odds, high probability; ~ and all, all jointly and severally; ~ another, formula of reciprocity with one orig. subjective and another objective or possessive; ~-off, (colloq.) single example; ~ too many for, too hard etc. for ... to deal with; ~ up (on), having gained an advantage (over); ~-upmanship, art or practice of demonstrating superiority. ~ pron. A particular but unspecified person (archaic); person of specified kind; any person, esp. the speaker, spoken of as representing people in general.

one- (wŭn) in comb.: ~-eyed, having only, blind of, one eye; ~-horse, drawn or worked by single horse; (fig.) petty, poorly equipped; ~-man, requiring, consisting of, done or managed by, one man; ~-sided, having, occurring on, one side only; larger etc. on one side; partial, unfair, prejudiced; ~-sidedly (adv.), ~-sidedness (n.); ~-step, ballroom dance in quick time with steps resembling walk; ~-time, former; ~-track, (of mind) that is fixed on one line of thought or action; ~-way, (of thoroughfares) along which traffic is permitted in one direction only.

Onĕ'ga. Second largest European lake, in U.S.S.R., near Finnish border.

Onei'da (ŏ-) n. Member of a N. Amer. Indian tribe of Iroquoian stock, formerly living round Oneida Lake in New York State; ~ Community, Christian communist society founded 1848 at Oneida Creek, New York State, by J. H. Noyes (1811–86), whose members held that true sinlessness could be realized through communion with Christ; dissolved and formed (1881) into a joint-stock company.

O'Nei'll, Eugene Gladstone (1888–1953). American playwright, author of 'The Emperor Jones,' 'Mourning Becomes Electra', 'The Iceman Cometh', etc.

ŏneirŏ'logy (-nī-) n. Study, psychological interpretation, of dreams. **oneirolŏ'gical** adj.

ONENESS

ŏneirŏ'logist n. **oneir'omăncў** n. Divination by dreams.
o'nenĕss (wŭn-n-) n. Being one, singleness; singularity, uniqueness; wholeness, unity, union, agreement; identity, changelessness.
o'ner (wŭ-) n. (slang) Remarkable or pre-eminent person or thing.
ŏ'nerous adj. Burdensome, causing or requiring trouble. **ŏ'nerouslў** adv. **ŏ'nerousnĕss** n.
onesĕ'lf (wŭn-) pron. Emphatic and reflexive form corresp. to ONE.
onion (ŭ'nyon) n. (Plant, *Allium cepa*, with) edible rounded bulb of close concentric leaves, with pungent smell and flavour, used as culinary vegetable; ~ *dome*, bulbous dome with pointed top found esp. on towers of Russian Orthodox churches; ~-*fly*, small fly (*Delia antiqua*) harmful to onion bulbs; ~ *shell*, molluscan shell of rounded form; ~-*skin*, outermost or any outer coat of onion; very thin smooth translucent kind of paper. **o'nionў** adj.
ŏ'nlŏoker n. One who looks on.
ō'nlў adj. That is (or are) the one (or all the) specimen(s) of the class, sole. ~ adv. Solely, merely, exclusively; and no one or nothing more, besides, or else; and that is all. ~ conj. Only thing to be added being; with this restriction, drawback, or exception only; but then.
ŏnomă'stic adj. Relating to name(s).
ŏnomatopoe'ia (-pēa) n. Formation of names or words from sounds resembling those associated with the object or action to be named, or seemingly naturally suggestive of its qualities (e.g. *cuckoo*, *rustle*); word so formed. **ŏnomatopoe'ic**, **ŏnomatopŏĕ'tic** adjs. **ŏnomatopoe'icallў**, **ŏnomatopŏĕ'ticallў** advs.
Onŏnda'ga (ŏ-, -dah-) n. Member of a N. Amer. Indian tribe of Iroquoian stock, living in New York State, one of the Six Nations, and guardians of the council-fire of the Iroquois.
ŏ'nrŭsh n. Onset.
ŏ'nsĕt n. Attack, assault, impetuous beginning.
ŏ'nslaught (-awt) n. Onset, fierce attack.
Ont. abbrev. Ontario.
Ontār'iŏ (ŏ-). Province of SE. Canada; capital, Toronto; *Lake* ~, smallest and most easterly of the Great Lakes, lying between the province and New York State.
ŏ'nto (-ōō) prep.: see ON.
ŏntogĕ'nĕsis n. = ONTOGENY.
ŏntogĕnĕ'tic adj. **ŏntogĕnĕ'ticallў** adv.
ŏntŏ'gĕnў n. (biol.) History of the development of an individual organism (opp. PHYLOGENY).
ŏntŏ'logў n. Department of metaphysics concerned with the essence of things or being in the abstract. **ŏntolŏ'gical** adj. **ŏntolŏ'gicallў** adv.
ō'nus n. Burden, duty, responsibility.
ŏ'nward adv. & adj. (Directed) farther on, towards the front; with advancing motion. **ŏ'nwards** (-z) adv.
ŏ'nўx n. 1. Type of chalcedony with different colours in layers, a form of silica, regarded as semi-precious stone. 2. (path.) Opacity of lower part of cornea, resembling finger-nail, caused by infiltration of pus behind it or between its layers.
ōō'dles (-lz) n.pl.(colloq.) Super-abundance (*of money* etc.).
ōōf n. (slang) Money. [for Yiddish *oof-tish* = Ger. *auf dem tische* on the table]
ōogĕ'nĕsis n. (biol.) Process leading to production of ripe ovum from germ-cell.
ō'olite n. Rock, freq. a limestone, composed of minute spheres of carbonate, resembling fish-roe in appearance, found esp. in the Jurassic strata. **ōoli'tic** adj.
ōō'logў n. Study, collecting, of birds' eggs. **ōō'logist** n.
ōō'lŏng n. Dark-coloured kind of tea grown in China and Taiwan: see TEA. [Chin. *wu* black, *lung* dragon]
ōōm n. (S. Afr.) Uncle; *Oom Paul*, President KRUGER.
oomiak n. Var. of UMIAK.
ōoze n. 1. Wet mud, slime, esp. in river-bed or estuary or on ocean bottom. 2. Tanning liquor, infusion of oak-bark etc. 3. Exudation; sluggish flow; something that oozes. **ōō'zў** adj. **ōō'zilў** adv. **ōō'zinĕss** n. **ōoze** v. (of moisture) Pass slowly through the pores of a body, exude, percolate; exude moisture; emit (moisture, information, etc.); (fig.) leak *out* or *away*.
op. abbrev. Operation; operator; opus.
o.p. abbrev. Out of print; over proof.
O.P. abbrev. Observation post; opposite prompt (side); *Ordinis Praedicatorum* (L, = of the Order of Preachers, i.e. Dominicans).
opā'citў n. Being opaque.
ō'pal n. Amorphous quartz-like form of hydrated silica, some kinds of which are valued as gems and show changing colours (common ~, milk-white or bluish with green, yellow, and red reflections); (commerc.) semi-translucent white glass.
ōpalĕ'scence n. Changing of colour as in an opal. **ōpalĕ'scent** adj. Showing opalescence, iridescent.
ō'paline (or -ēn) adj. Opal-like; opalescent. ~ n. Opal glass.
opā'que (-k) adj. Not transmitting light, not transparent; obscure, not lucid; dull-witted. **opā'quelў** adv. **opā'quenĕss** n.
ŏp ärt. Style of abstract art using contrasting colours, often black and white, to create optical illusions, esp. of movement. (*Illustration, p. 616.*)
op. cit. abbrev. *Opere citato* (L, = in the work quoted).
ōpe v. (poet.) Open.

OPEN

ō'pen adj. 1. Not closed or blocked up; allowing of entrance, passage, or access; having gate, door, lid, or part of boundary withdrawn; unenclosed, unconfined, uncovered, bare, exposed, undisguised; public, manifest; not exclusive or limited; (of cheque) not crossed. 2. (of vowel) Produced with wider opening of oral cavity than close vowel; (mus., of organ pipe) not closed at top; (mus., of string) not stopped by finger; (of note) produced by such pipe or string, or without aid of slide, key, or piston. 3. Expanded, unfolded, outspread; spread out, not close, without intervals; porous; communicative, frank. 4. ~ *air*, outdoors; ~-*and-shut*, (colloq.) immediately obvious; *with* ~ *arms*, heartily; ~-*armed* (adj.); ~ *boat*, undecked boat; *o'pencast*, (of mine or mining) with overlying soil and rocks removed and underlying deposits worked by surface quarrying (ill. MINE[2]); (of coal etc.) obtained thus; ~ *country*, country unenclosed or affording wide views; *the* ~ *door*, principle of free commerce for all comers; *with* ~ *eyes*, not unconsciously or under misapprehension; in eager attention or surprise; so ~-*eyed* (adj.); ~ *hand*, freedom in giving, generosity; ~-*handed* (adj.), ~-*handedly* (adv.), ~-*handedness* (n.); ~-*heart surgery*, surgery performed on the exposed heart with the bloodstream diverted through a machine; *keep* ~ *house*, entertain all comers; ~ *letter*, letter addressing an individual but published in newspaper etc.; ~ *mind*, accessibility to new ideas; unprejudiced or undecided state; ~-*minded* (adj.), ~-*mindedly* (adv.), ~-*mindedness* (n.); ~ *mouth*, mouth opened in voracity etc., and esp. in gaping stupidity or surprise; ~-*mouthed* (adj.), ~ *order*, formation with wide spaces between men or ships; ~ *prison*, prison with minimal security restrictions; ~ *question*, matter on which differences of opinion are legitimate; ~ *syllable*, syllable ending with a vowel; O~ *University*, university (established 1969) with no formal requirements for entry to its first degree courses, and providing instruction by a combination of television, radio, and correspondence courses and by audio-visual centres; ~ *verdict*, (at an inquest) verdict expressing no positive conclusion; *o'penwork*, pattern with interstices in material. **ō'pennĕss** (-n-n-) n.
ō'pen n. *the* ~, open space or country or air, public view. ~ v. 1. Make or become open or more open; start, establish, set going (business, campaign, etc.); ~ *case*, (of counsel in law court) make preliminary statement before calling witnesses; ~ *debate*, be first speaker; ~ *the door to*, give opportunity for; ~ *one's eyes*, show surprise; ~ *the eyes of*, undeceive,

[615]

OPENING

enlighten. 2. Commence speaking; make a start; begin to be sold; (of hounds) begin to give tongue. 3. (naut.) Get view of by change of position; come into full view. 4. ~ *out*, unfold, develop, expand; become communicative; open throttle of a motor engine, accelerate; ~ *up*, make accessible; bring to notice, reveal; begin firing *on*. ō'**pener** *n.* (esp.) Device for opening bottles, tins, etc.

ō'**pening** (-pn-) *adj.* (esp.) Initial, first. ~ *n.* (esp.) Gap, passage, aperture; commencement, initial part; counsel's preliminary statement of case; opportunity, favourable conjuncture *for*; (chess) recognized sequence of moves for beginning game.

ō'**penly** *adv.* Without concealment, publicly, frankly.

ŏ'**pera** *n.* Dramatic performance or composition of which music is an essential part; branch of art concerned with this; *comic* ~, opera of humorous character; *grand* ~, opera, usu. on serious theme, without spoken dialogue; *light* ~, = OPERETTA, 2; *opéra bouffe*, *opera buffa*, French, Italian, types of comic opera (Ital. *buffa* comic); *opéra comique*, opera with spoken dialogue, not necessarily humorous; ~*-glass(es)* small binoculars for use at opera or theatre; ~*-hat*: see HAT; ~ *house*, theatre for performance of opera.

ŏ'**perable** *adj.* (med.) That admits of being operated upon.

ŏ'**perāte** *v.* 1. Be in action, produce an effect, exercise influence; play *on*, try to act *on*; have desired effect. 2. Perform surgical or other operation; carry on war-

OPERATION

like operations; deal or speculate in stocks and shares. 3. Bring about, accomplish; (chiefly U.S.) manage, work, conduct. 4. Conduct, be in charge of (machine, apparatus). ŏ'**perāting** *n.* (esp.) ~ *table*, table for use in surgery; ~ *theatre*, room reserved in hospital etc. for the performance of surgical operations. ŏ'**perātor** *n.*

ŏperă'**tic** *adj.* Of, like, opera. ŏperă'**tically** *adv.*

ŏperā'**tion** *n.* 1. Working, action, way thing works; efficacy, validity, scope. 2. Active process, activity, performance; discharge of function; financial transaction. 3. Act or series of acts performed with hand or instrument on some part of body to remedy deformity, injury, disease, pain, etc.; (esp.) piece of surgery. 4. Strategic movement of troops, ships, etc. 5. (math.)

CURTAIN IN THE BREEZE

AN EXAMPLE OF OP ART

[616]

OPERATIVE

Subjection of number or quantity to process affecting its value or form, e.g. multiplication. **ŏperā'tional** *adj.* (esp.) Engaged on, used for, warlike operations.

ŏ'perative *adj.* 1. Having effect, in operation, efficacious; practical, not theoretical or contemplative. 2. Of surgical operations. **ŏ'peratively** *adv.* **ŏ'perative** *n.* Worker, esp. in factory.

opĕr'cūlum *n.* Gill-cover of fish (ill. FISH¹); lid or valve closing aperture of shell of mollusc when tenant is retracted; similar lid-like structure in plants etc. **opĕr'cūlar, opĕr'cūlate, -ātĕd** *adjs.*

ŏperĕ'tta *n.* 1. Short opera. 2. Opera in simple popular style.

ŏ'perōse *adj.* Requiring, showing, or taking, great pains, laborious. **ŏ'perōsely** *adv.* **ŏ'perōseness** *n.*

Ophē'lia. In Shakespeare's 'Hamlet', daughter of Polonius, who went mad and drowned herself because of HAMLET's treatment of her and his killing of her father.

ŏ'phicleide (-īd) *n.* Obsolete wind-instrument of powerful tone, development of the serpent, consisting of conical brass tube bent double, with (usu.) eleven keys, serving as bass or alto to key-bugle.

ophī'dian *adj.* & *n.* (Member) of the Ophidia, a suborder of reptiles comprising snakes.

O'phir (ō-). (O.T.) Unidentified region (perhaps in SE. Arabia) famous for its fine gold and precious stones.

ŏphthă'lmia *n.* Inflammation of the eye, esp. affecting the conjunctiva.

ŏphthă'lmic *adj.* Of, relating to, or situated near, the eye.

ŏphthălmŏ'logў *n.* Study of the eye and its diseases. **ŏphthălmŏ'logist** *n.*

ŏphthă'lmoscōpe *n.* Instrument for inspecting the interior of the eye, esp. the retina.

ŏ'piate *adj.* (archaic) Containing opium, narcotic, soporific. ~ *n.* Drug prepared from opium; sleep-inducing drug, narcotic.

O'pie (ō-), John (1761-1807). English painter of portraits and historical pieces.

opī'ne *v.t.* Express or hold the opinion (*that*).

opī'nion (-yon) *n.* Judgement or belief based on grounds short of proof; views or sentiment, esp. on moral questions, prevalent among people in general; formal statement by expert consulted; professional advice; *have no* ~ *of*, think unfavourably of.

opī'nionātĕd, opī'nionative (-nyo-) *adjs.* Obstinate in opinion, dogmatic; self-willed. **opī'nionātĕdnĕss** *n.*

ō'pium *n.* Dried latex from unripe capsules of a poppy (*Papaver somniferum*), of reddish-brown colour, with heavy smell and bitter taste, smoked or eaten as stimulant, intoxicant, or narcotic, and used in medicine as sedative; ~ *den*, haunt of opium-smokers.

opŏ'panăx *n.* Fetid gum-resin obtained from root of a yellow-flowered parsnip-like umbelliferous plant, *O*~ *chironium*, formerly used in medicine; gum-resin obtained from *Commiphora kataf*, used in perfumery.

opŏ'ssum *n.* Member of the Didelphidae, an Amer. family of small marsupials, mostly arboreal,

AMERICAN OPOSSUM

some aquatic, of nocturnal habits, with usu. prehensile tail; (Austral.) phalanger.

opp. *abbrev.* Opposite.

ŏ'ppilāte *v.t.* (med.) Block up, obstruct. **ŏppilā'tion** *n.*

oppō'nent *n.* Person opposed or on the opposing side in a contest etc.

ŏ'pportūne *adj.* (of time) Suitable, well-selected, favourable; (of action or event) well-timed, done or occurring at favourable juncture. **ŏ'pportūnely** *adv.* **ŏ'pportūnenĕss** (-n-n-) *n.*

ŏ'pportūnism *n.* Policy of doing what is opportune or at the time expedient, in politics, as opp. to rigid adherence to principles; method or course of action adapted to the circumstances of the moment. **ŏ'pportūnist** *n.*

ŏpportū'nitў *n.* Favourable juncture, good chance, opening.

oppō'se (-z) *v.t.* 1. Place, produce, or cite as obstacle, antagonist, counterpoise, or contrast *to*; represent as antithetical. 2. Set oneself against, withstand, resist, obstruct; propose the rejection of; act as opponent or check. **oppō'sed** (-zd) *adj.* (esp.) Contrary, opposite, contrasted; hostile, adverse. **oppō'sable** *adj.* (of digit, esp. thumb) Capable of being applied so as to meet another.

ŏ'pposite (-z-) *adj.* 1. Facing, front to front or back to back (with); ~ *number*, person or thing similarly placed in another set etc. to the given one. 2. Of contrary kind, diametrically different *to* or *from*;

OPTICAL

the other of a contrasted pair. **ŏ'ppositely** *adv.* **ŏ'ppositenĕss** *n.* **ŏ'pposite** *n.* Opposite thing or term. ~ *adv.* In opposite place or direction; on opposite sides. ~ *prep.* In an opposite place or direction to; *play* ~, have (specified actor or actress) as one's leading man or lady; ~ *prompt*, (theatr.) of side of stage to actors' right (abbrev. O.P.)

ŏpposi'tion (-z-) *n.* 1. Placing opposite; diametrically opposite position (esp. astron., of two heavenly bodies when their longitude differs by 180°; opp. CONJUNCTION). 2. Contrast, antithesis; (logic) relation between two propositions with same subject and predicate but differing in quantity or quality or both. 3. Antagonism, resistance, being hostile; any party opposed to some proposal; *O*~, chief Parliamentary party opposed to that in office. **ŏpposi'tional** *adj.* (psychol.) Apt to take an opposing point of view.

opprĕ'ss *v.t.* Overwhelm with superior weight or numbers, or irresistible power; lie heavy on, weigh down (spirits etc.); govern tyrannically, keep under by coercion, subject to continual cruelty or injustice. **opprĕ'ssion, opprĕ'ssor** *ns.* **opprĕ'ssive** *adj.* **opprĕ'ssively** *adv.* **opprĕ'ssivenĕss** *n.*

opprō'brious *adj.* Conveying reproach, abusive, vituperative. **opprō'briously** *adv.*

opprō'brium *n.* Disgrace attaching to some act or conduct, infamy, crying of shame.

oppu'gn (-ūn) *v.t.* Controvert, call in question; (rare) attack, resist, be in conflict with.

ŏpsō'nic *adj.* Of, produced by, arising from, opsonins; ~ *index*, index of proportion of opsonins present in blood.

ŏ'psonin *n.* Heat-sensitive substance, present in serum, which promotes destruction of bacteria by white blood-corpuscles.

ŏpt *v.i.* Exercise an option, make a choice; ~ *out* (*of*), choose not to take part (in).

ŏptā'tive *adj.* (gram.) Expressing wish; ~ *mood*, set of verbal forms of this kind. **ŏptā'tively** *adv.* **ŏptā'tive** *n.* Optative mood, verbal form belonging to it.

ŏ'ptic *adj.* Of the eye or sense of sight; ~ *disc*, BLIND spot (ill. EYE); ~ *nerve*, 2nd cranial nerve, from eyeball to fore-brain, conducting the impulses responsible for visual sensations (ill. EYE). ~ *n.* Eye (now usu. joc.). **ŏ'ptics** *n.* Science of sight, branch of physics dealing with properties etc. of light.

ŏ'ptical *adj.* Visual, ocular; of sight or light in relation to each other; belonging to optics; constructed to assist sight or on the principles of optics; ~ *activity*, (chem.) property possessed by

[617]

certain transparent solids and liquids of rotating the plane of polarization of polarized light passing through them. ŏ'pticallў adv.

optĭ'cian (-shan) n. Maker or seller of optical instruments.

ŏ'ptimė n. One placed in second (senior ~) or third (junior ~) division in mathematical tripos at Cambridge (see also WRANGLER). [L, = 'best', 'very well']

ŏ'ptimism n. Doctrine, esp. as set forth by Leibniz, that the actual world is the best of all possible worlds; view that good must ultimately prevail over evil in the universe; sanguine disposition, inclination to take bright views. ŏ'ptimist n. & adj. optimĭ'stic adj. ŏptimĭ'sticallў adv.

ŏ'ptimum n. (biol.) That degree or amount of heat, light, food, moisture, etc. most favourable for growth or other vital processes; (also attrib.) best. [L, = 'best']

ŏ'ption n. Choice, choosing, thing that is or may be chosen; liberty of choosing, freedom of choice; purchased right to call for or make delivery within specified time of specified stocks etc. at specified rate; local ~: see LOCAL.

ŏ'ptional adj. Not obligatory.

ŏptŏ'mėter n. Instrument for testing refracting power and visual range of the eye. ŏptŏ'mėtrȳ n. ŏptŏ'mėtrist n.

ŏ'pŭlent adj. Rich; abounding, abundant, well stored. ŏ'pŭlentlȳ adv. ŏ'pŭlence n.

ŏ'pus n. (pl. opuses, opera). Musical composition or set of compositions as numbered among works of composer in order of publication etc. (abbrev. op.); magnum ~, great literary undertaking, writer's or other artist's chief production. [L, = 'work'] opū'scule, opū'sculum (pl. -la) ns. Minor musical or literary composition.

ŏr[1] n. (her.) Gold or yellow (ill. HERALDRY).

ŏr[2] prep. & conj. (archaic) Before.

or[3] (ŏr, er) conj. Introducing alternatives.

Or. abbrev. Oregon.

O.R. abbrev. Other ranks.

ŏ'rache (-ich) n. Herb or small shrub, often mealy, of various species of genus Atriplex, commonest by the seashore.

ŏ'racle n. Place at which ancient Greeks etc. were accustomed to consult the gods for advice or prophecy; response, freq. ambiguous or obscure, given at such place; holy of holies or mercy-seat in Jewish temple; (vehicle of) divine inspiration or revelation; infallible guide, test, or indicator; authoritative, profoundly wise, or mysterious judge, judgement, prophet, etc.; work the ~, secure desired answer from oracle by tampering with priests etc.; (fig.) bring secret influence to bear in one's favour.

orăcūlar adj. Of an oracle;

obscure like an oracle. orā'cūlarlў adv.

ŏr'al adj. Spoken, verbal, by word of mouth; of the mouth; done or taken by the mouth. ŏr'allў adv. ŏr'al n. Oral examination.

ŏ'range[1] (-inj) n. 1. Evergreen tree, Citrus aurantium and allied species, native of the East, widely cultivated in S. Europe and other warm, temperate, or subtropical regions, with fragrant white flowers and large globose many-celled berries with sub-acid juicy pulp and tough outer rind of bright reddish-yellow; fruit of this; bitter ~, SEVILLE orange; mock ~: see MOCK; ~s and lemons, nursery game in which song beginning with these words is sung and players take sides acc. to which fruit they name in answer to question; ~-blossom, flowers of orange or mock orange, freq. worn or carried by brides at wedding; ~-flower water, fragrant aqueous solution of orange flowers; ~(-wood) stick, small stick of orange-wood used for manicuring nails. 2. Colour of orange-rind, reddish-yellow. ~ adj. Orange-coloured. [Arab. nāranj]

Orange[2]. (pr. orahṅzh) Small town (orig. a Roman colony) and principality on River Rhône, which passed in 16th c. to the house of Nassau, subsequently rulers of the Netherlands; hence, (pr. ŏ'rinj) House of ~, Dutch royal house; William of O~: see WILLIAM[2]. [L Arausio name of the town]

Orange[3] (ŏ'rinj). Epithet applied to the ultra-Protestant party in Ireland, in ref. to the secret political Association of Orangemen, formed 1795 for defence of Protestantism and maintenance of Protestant ascendancy in Ireland, and prob. named from wearing of orange badges etc. as symbol of adherence to William III, prince of ORANGE[2], and the Protestant succession in Ulster. O'rangĭsm n.

ŏrangea'de (-jăd) n. Drink of sweetened orange-juice and water; synthetic substitute for this.

Orange Free Stāte (ŏ'rinj). Inland province of the Republic of S. Africa; first settled by Boers trekking from Cape Colony (1836-8); annexed by Britain 1848, but restored in 1854 to Boers who established the Orange Free State Republic; annexed by Britain as Orange River Colony in 1900; responsible government, 1907; province of the Union of South Africa (1910) as Orange Free State; capital, Bloemfontein. [f. House of ORANGE[2]]

Orange Ri'ver (ŏ'rinj). Longest river of S. Africa, running westward into Atlantic across almost whole breadth of the continent.

ŏ'rangerȳ (ŏrĭnj-) n. Building, hothouse, for protection of orange-trees; esp., in 17th-c. mansions, (part of) building having solid N.

wall and large freq. arched windows on S. side.

ŏr'ang-u'tăn, -ou'tăng (-ōō-) n. Large long-armed mainly arboreal anthropoid ape, Pongo pygmaeus, of Borneo, Sumatra, and formerly Java (ill. APE). [Malay orang-uton man of the woods]

orā'te v.i.(joc.) Make an oration.

orā'tion n. Formal address, harangue, or discourse, esp. of ceremonial kind; (gram.) direct ~, oblique ~: see these words.

ŏ'rator n. Maker of a speech; eloquent public speaker; Public O~, official at Oxford and Cambridge speaking for university on ceremonial occasions.

ŏratōr'iō n. Semi-dramatic musical composition usu. on sacred theme performed by soloists, chorus, and orchestra, without action, scenery, or costume. [It., orig. of musical services at Oratory of St. Philip Neri, Rome]

ŏ'ratorȳ[1] n. (Art of making) speeches, rhetoric; highly coloured presentment of facts, eloquent or exaggerating language. ŏratŏ'rĭcal adj. ŏratŏ'rĭcallȳ adv.

ŏ'ratorȳ[2] n. 1. Small chapel, place for private worship. 2. O~, R.C. society of simple priests without vows, founded at Rome in 1564, for plain preaching and popular services; any branch or house of this.

ŏrb n. Circle, disc, ring (now rare); sphere, globe; heavenly body; eyeball, eye (poet.); globe surmounted by cross as part of regalia (ill. REGALIA), symbolizing domination of the world by Christ. ~ v. Enclose in, gather into, orb.

ŏrbĭ'cūlar adj. Circular, discoid, ring-shaped; spherical, globular, rounded; (fig.) forming complete whole. ŏrbĭ'cūlarlȳ adv.

ŏr'bit n. 1. Eye-socket; border round eye of bird or insect. 2. Curved course esp. of planet, comet, satellite, spacecraft, or binary star; complete circuit of this; (fig.) range, sphere, of action; in ~, travelling in an orbit. ~ v. (Cause to) travel in an orbit (round).

ŏr'bital adj. Of an orbit. ~ n. (phys.) That part of the region surrounding an atomic nucleus in which an associated electron is most likely to be found; mathematical equation describing this.

ŏrc, ŏr'ca n. Cetacean, esp. the killer whale (Orcinus orca).

Orcā'dian (ŏr-) adj. & n. (Native or inhabitant) of Orkney. [L Orcades the Orkney Islands]

Orcagna (ŏrkah'nya). Andrea di Cione (d. 1377), Florentine painter, sculptor, and architect.

ŏr'chard n. Enclosure with fruit-trees.

ŏrchĕ'stic (-k-) adj. Of dancing.

ŏr'chĕstra (-k-) n. 1. Semicircular space in front of stage in ancient Greek theatre, where chorus danced and sang. 2. Part of modern theatre or concert room

ORCHESTRATE

assigned to band or chorus; body of instrumental performers, or combination of stringed, woodwind, brass, and percussion instruments, in theatre or concert room; ~ pit, pit for orchestra in front of stage (ill. THEATRE). **orchĕ′stral** *adj.*

ŏr′chĕstrāte *v.* Arrange, or score, for orchestral performance. **ŏrchĕstrā′tion** *n.*

ŏrchĕstri′na(-kĭstrē-), **ŏrchĕ′strion** (-k-) *ns.* Any of various mechanical instruments imitating orchestral effects.

ŏr′chĭd (-k-) *n.* Plant of the Orchidaceae, a large and widely distributed order of monocotyledons with three sepals and three petals, of which one (the lip or labellum) is usu. much larger than the others and of special colour or shape (ill. FLOWER); esp. one of the exotic cultivated species, freq. brilliantly coloured or grotesquely shaped. **ŏrchĭdā′ceous** (-shus) *adj.*

ŏr′chĭl *n.* Red or violet dye from certain lichens, esp. *Roccella tinctoria.*

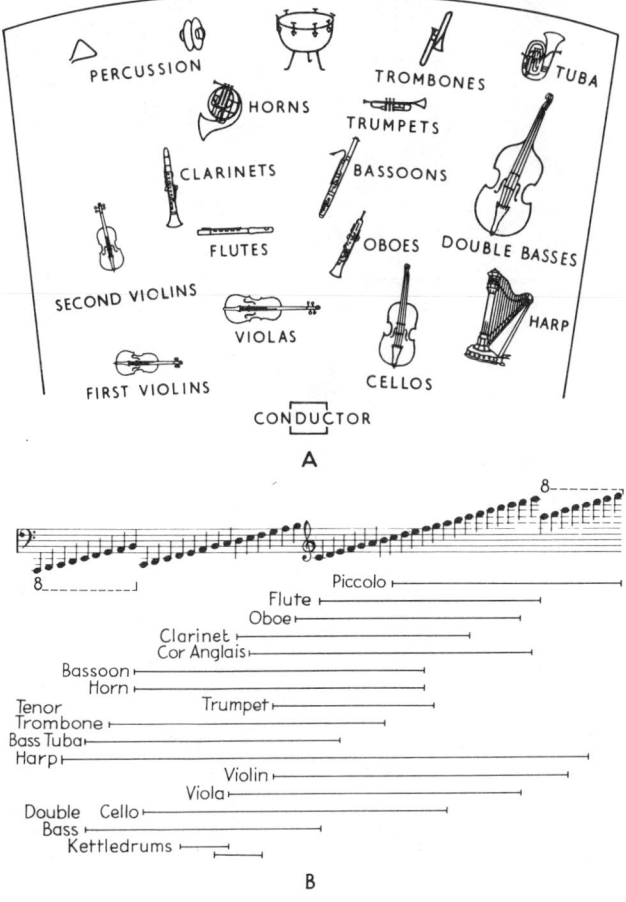

ŏr′chĭs (-k-) *n.* = ORCHID, esp. wild one.

ord. *abbrev.* Ordained; order; ordinary.

ŏrdai′n *v.t.* 1. Appoint ceremonially to Christian ministry; confer holy orders (esp. those of deacon or priest) on. 2. Destine, appoint; appoint authoritatively, decree, enact.

ordĕ′al (*or* ŏr′dĕl) *n.* Experience that tests character or endurance, severe trial; (hist.) primitive (esp. ancient Teutonic) mode of deciding suspected person's guilt or innocence by subjecting him to physical test such as plunging of hand in boiling water, safe endurance of which was taken as divine acquittal.

ORDER

ŏr′der *n.* 1. Rank of community, social division, grade or stratum; definite rank in State; separate and homogeneous set of persons. 2. Kind, sort. 3. ~s *of angels*: see ANGEL. 4. Grade of Christian ministry; (pl.) status of clergyman; *holy* ~s, orders of bishops, priests, and deacons; *minor* ~s, in R.C. Church (until 1973) orders of acolyte, exorcist, reader, and doorkeeper; *in* ~s, ordained; *take* ~s, be ordained. 5. Fraternity of monks or friars, or formerly of knights, bound by common rule of life; one of the companies (*Orders of Chivalry*), usu. instituted by sovereign, to which distinguished persons are admitted by way of honour or reward, insignia worn by member of such a company. 6. (archit.) Mode of treatment with established proportions between parts, esp. one of the *five* (*classical*) ~s of column and entablature (Doric, Ionic, Corinthian, Tuscan, and Composite, the first three of Greek origin, the others Roman) (*illustration, p.620*). 7. (archit.) Row of voussoirs (ill. ARCH[1]). 8. (math.) Degree of complexity. 9. (biol.) Classificatory group below *class* and above *family*; *natural* ~, (bot.) order of plants allied in general structure, not merely agreeing in single characteristic as in Linnaean system. 10. Sequence, succession, manner of following; regular array, condition in which every part or unit is in its right place; tidiness; normal, healthy, or efficient state; (mil.) equipment, uniform, etc., for some purpose; *in* (*good*) ~, fit for use; *out of* ~, not systematically arranged; not working rightly. 11. Constitution of the world, way things normally happen, collective manifestations of natural forces or laws. 12. Stated form of divine service; principles of decorum and rules of procedure accepted by legislative assembly or public meeting, or enforced by its president; ~, ~!, protest against infringement of this; *rise to* (*a point of*) ~, interrupt debate etc. with inquiry whether something being said or done is in or out of order; ~ *of the day*, programme, business set down for treatment; prevailing state of things. 13. Prevalence of constituted authority, law-abiding state. 14. Act or instance of ordering; authoritative direction or instruction (freq. pl.); (banking etc.) instruction to pay money or deliver property signed by owner or responsible agent; direction to manufacturer, tradesman, etc., to supply something; pass admitting bearer gratis, cheap, or as privilege, to theatre, museum, etc.; *in* ~, suitable, fitting, appropriate; *in short* ~, (U.S.) without delay, immediately; *large* or *tall* ~, (colloq.) difficult undertaking; *made to* ~, made according to special directions, to suit individual measurements etc.

A. POSITION OF PLAYERS IN A MODERN ORCHESTRA.
B. RANGE OF ORCHESTRAL INSTRUMENTS

[619]

ORDERLY   ORDINATION

ORDERS OF ARCHITECTURE

A. GREEK DORIC.   B. GREEK IONIC.   C. GREEK CORINTHIAN.   D. ROMAN CORINTHIAN.   E. COMPOSITE.
F. TUSCAN

A. 1. Acroterion. 2. Taenia. 3. Guttae. 4. Mutule. 5. Triglyph. 6. Metope. 7. Abacus. 8. Echinus. 9. Annulet. 10. Hypotrachelium. 11. Flute. 12. Arris. 13. Module. B. 14. Volute. 15. Stria. 16. Apophyge. 17. Plinth. C. 18. Acanthus. D. 19. Corona. 20. Modillion. 21. Dentil. 22. Fascia. F. 23. Necking. 24. Astragal.

(opp. *ready-made*); *money, postal* ~, kinds of Post Office cheque for remitting money; *on* ~, ordered but not yet supplied; *O*~ *in Council*, sovereign order on some administrative matter given by advice of Privy Council; ~ *to view*, requisition from estate agent to occupier to allow client to inspect premises. 15. *in* ~ *to do*, with a view to, for the purpose of, doing; *in* ~ *that*, with the intention or to the end that. ~ *v.t.* 1. (archaic) Put in order, array, regulate. 2. State with authority that (action must be performed, person must perform action); prescribe; command or direct to go *to*, *away*, etc.; direct tradesman etc. to supply (article).

ōr′derlў *adj.* Methodically arranged or inclined, regular, obedient to discipline, not unruly, well-behaved; (mil.) on duty, concerned with carrying out orders; ~ *book*, book kept in orderly room for entering orders etc.; ~ *officer*, officer on duty for the day; ~ *room*, one set apart in barracks etc. for administrative business. **ōr′derliness** *n.* **ōr′derlў** *n.* Soldier in attendance on officer to execute orders etc.; attendant in (esp. military) hospital.

ōr′dinal *adj.* Of or defining a thing's position in a series (~ *numbers* = first, second, etc.). ~ *n.* 1. Ordinal number. 2. Prescribed form of ceremony to be observed at consecration of bishops and ordination of priests and deacons; book containing words and directions for this ceremony.

ōr′dinance *n.* Authoritative direction, decree; religious rite; (U.S.) by-law.

ōr′dinarў *adj.* 1. Regular, normal, customary, usual; not exceptional, not above the usual, commonplace; ~ *seaman*, (abbrev. O.S.) lower rating than *able seaman*. 2. Having immediate or *ex officio* and not deputed jurisdiction. ~ *n.* 1. Ordinary authority; *the O*~, archbishop in province, bishop in diocese; (*Lord*) *O*~, in Scotland, one of five judges of Court of Session constituting Outer House. 2. Rule or book laying down order of divine service. 3. Public meal provided at fixed time and price in tavern etc. 4. (her.) Charge of earliest, simplest, and commonest kind, esp. chief, pale, bend, fess, bar, chevron, cross, or saltire (ill. HERALDRY). 5. Ordinary condition, course, etc.; what is ordinary; *in* ~, (of officials etc.) by permanent appointment, not temporary or extraordinary; (of ships) laid up, not in commission. **ōr′dinarilў** *adv.* **ōr′dinariness** *n.*

ōr′dinate *n.* (geom.) Any of series of parallel chords of conic section in relation to bisecting diameter (esp. used of half the chord, from curve to diameter); straight line from any point drawn parallel to one co-ordinate axis and meeting the other (correlative to ABSCISSA; ill. GRAPH).

ōrdinā′tion *n.* 1. Arrangement in ranks, classification. 2. Conferring of holy orders, admission to church ministry. 3. Decreeing, ordainment.

[620]

ōrdinee' *n.* Newly ordained deacon.

ōr'dnance *n.* Mounted guns, artillery; branch of public service dealing esp. with military stores and materials; ~ *survey*, official survey of Gt Britain (and formerly Ireland), orig. carried out under Master-General of the Ordnance, now by a civil department partially staffed by the R.E.; ~ *datum*, sea-level as defined for ordnance survey, mean sea-level at Newlyn, Cornwall, derived from the mean of hourly readings between 1915 and 1921.

Ordovi'cian (ōr-, -sh-) *adj. & n.* (geol.) (Of) the second period or system of the Palaeozoic era, between Cambrian and Silurian (ill. GEOLOGY). [*Ordovices*, ancient tribe in N. Wales]

ōr'dūre (*or* -dyer) *n.* Excrement, dung.

ōre[1] *n.* Solid naturally-occurring mineral aggregate from which one or more valuable constituents may be recovered by treatment; (poet.) metal, esp. precious metal.

öre (ēr'e) *n.* $\frac{1}{100}$ of a krone; $\frac{1}{100}$ of a krona.

ōr'ĕăd *n.* (Gk myth.) Mountain nymph.

ore'ctic *adj.* Of desire or appetite.

Oreg. *abbrev.* Oregon.

O'rĕgon (ŏ-). Pacific State of U.S.; admitted to the Union in 1859; capital, Salem; ~ *pine*, name for Douglas fir, esp. in timber trade; ~ *Trail*, (U.S. hist.) route from Missouri across Oregon, used by emigrants esp. 1842–7.

Orĕ'stēs (-z). (Gk legend) Son of AGAMEMNON and Clytemnestra; killed his mother and her lover Aegisthus in revenge because they had murdered his father; was pursued by the Furies until he was pardoned by Artemis, having rescued her statue (and his sister Iphigenia) from the island of Tauris; became king of Argos, Sparta, and Mycenae, and married Hermione, daughter of Menelaus.

ōrfe *n.* Fish, golden-yellow variety of the ide.

orfray: see ORPHREY.

ōr'gan *n.* 1. Part of animal or vegetable body adapted for special vital function, as ~s *of digestion*, *speech*, etc. 2. Person's voice with ref. to its power or quality. 3. Medium of communication, esp. newspaper or journal representing a party, cause, etc. 4. Musical instrument consisting essentially of pipes arranged in ranks (*stops*) which are supplied with wind by a bellows or electric fan and sounded by means of keys arranged in rows (*manuals*) and pedals, each key or pedal controlling the mechanism (usu. a valve) which admits air to a particular pipe (*illustration*, *p. 622*). 5. Any of various keyboard instruments producing more or less similar effects by different means, as AMERICAN ~, ELECTRONIC ~. 6. *barrel-*~: see BARREL; *choir* ~: see

CHOIR ORGAN; *great* ~, principal manual of an organ, linked with the louder stops; *mouth-*~: see MOUTH; *pedal* ~: see PEDAL[1]; ~-*blower*, person or mechanism working organ bellows; ~-*builder*, maker of organs; ~- *grinder*, player on barrel-organ; ~-*loft*, loft or gallery in which organ is placed, freq. above organ screen; ~-*pipe coral*, coral of genus *Tubipora*, forming vertical tubules; ~-*screen*, ornamental screen between nave and choir in church; ~-*stop*, set of pipes of similar tone-quality in organ; handle or knob of mechanism that brings such a set into action; *swell* ~: see SWELL *n.* 3.

ōr'gandie (*or* -ă'-) *n.* Thin stiff translucent muslin.

ōrganĕ'lle *n.* (biol.) Part of a cell, having a particular function.

ōrgă'nic *adj.* 1. Of the bodily organs, vital; (path., of disease) affecting structure of an organ (opp. *functional*). 2. Having organs or organized physical structure; of animals or plants; (chem., of compound substances) occurring naturally as constituent of organized bodies, formed from such compounds (all of which contain or are derived from hydrocarbon radicals); ~ *chemistry*: see CHEMISTRY. 3. Constitutional, inherent, fundamental, structural; organized, systematic, co-ordinated.

ōrgă'nically *adv.*

ōr'ganism *n.* Living animal or plant; anything capable of maintaining the processes characteristic of life, esp. reproduction; (material structure of) individual animal or plant; whole with interdependent parts compared to living being.

ōrgani'smic *adj.*

ōr'ganist *n.* Player of organ.

ōrganizā'tion *n.* (esp.) Organized body, system, or society.

ōr'ganize *v.* 1. Furnish with organs, make organic, make into living being or tissue (usu. in past part.); become organic. 2. Form into an organic whole; give orderly structure to, frame and put into working order; make arrangements for, get up (undertaking involving co-operation). **ōr'ganizer** *n.*

ōr'ganŏn, ōr'ganum *n.* Instrument of thought, system of or treatise on logic. [Gk *organon* tool, work; *Organon* was the title of Aristotle's logical writings, and *Novum* (new) *Organum* that of Bacon's]

ōrganothĕ'rapy *n.* Treatment of disease with animal organs or extracts of these.

ōrgă'nza *n.* Thin stiff transparent fabric of silk or synthetic fibre.

ōr'ganzine (-ēn) *n.* Strongest kind of silk thread, in which main twist is in contrary direction to that of strands.

ōr'găsm *n.* Paroxysm of excitement or rage; climax of venereal excitement in a sexual act. **ōrgă'stic** *adj.*

ōrgiă'stic *adj.* Of the nature of an orgy.

ōr'gy̆ *n.* 1. (Gk & Rom. antiq., usu. pl.) Secret rites in worship of various gods, esp. festival in honour of Dionysus (Bacchus), celebrated with extravagant dancing, singing, drinking, etc. 2. Drunken or licentious revel; (pl.) revelry, debauchery.

ōr'iel *n.* Large windowed polygonal recess projecting usu. from upper storey and supported from ground or on corbels; (also ~ *window*) window of oriel, projecting window of upper storey (ill. WINDOW).

Or'ĭent[1] (ōr-) *n.* 1. The East or countries E. of Mediterranean and S. Europe; (poet.) eastward part of sky or earth. 2. (*o*~) Orient pearl.

ōr'ĭent *adj.* 1. (of precious stones, esp. pearls, of finest kinds, as coming anciently from the East) Lustrous, sparkling, precious. 2. (archaic, of sun etc.) Rising, nascent.

ōr'ĭĕnt[2] *v.t.* 1. Place (building etc.) so as to face east; build (church) with chancel end due E.; bury with feet eastward. 2. Place or exactly determine position of with regard to points of compass, settle or find bearings of; (fig.) bring into clearly understood relations; ~ *oneself*, determine how one stands.

ōrĭĕ'ntal *adj.* Of the Orient, esp. Asiatic; occurring in, coming from, the East, haracteristic of its civilization etc.; (of pearls) orient. **ōrĭĕ'ntally** *adv.* **Orĭĕ'ntal** *n.* Native, inhabitant, of the Orient. **Orĭĕ'ntalism** *n.* **ōrĭĕ'ntalize** *v.* Make, become, Oriental.

ōr'ĭentāte *v.t.* = ORIENT[2]. **ōrĭentā'tion** *n.*

ōrienteer'ing *n.* Cross-country racing on foot, using map and compass.

ŏ'rifice *n.* Aperture, mouth of cavity, perforation, vent.

ŏ'riflămme *n.* Sacred banner of St. Denis, a banderole of two or three points of (orange-)red silk attached to a lance, received by early French kings from abbot of St. Denis on starting for war; anything, material or ideal, serving as rallying-point in struggle; bright conspicuous object, blaze of colour, etc. [Fr., f. L *aurum* gold, *flamma* flame]

ŏrigă'mi (-ah-) *n.* Japanese art of folding paper into decorative forms; example of this.

Or'igen (ōr- *or* ŏ'-) (*c* 185–253). Christian theologian and scholar of Alexandria.

ŏ'rigin *n.* Derivation, beginning or rising from something; extraction; source, starting-point.

ori'ginal *adj.* 1. Existent from the first; primitive, innate, initial, earliest; ~ *sin*, (Christian theol.) innate depravity common to all human beings in consequence of the Fall of man. 2. That has served as pattern, of which copy or

[621]

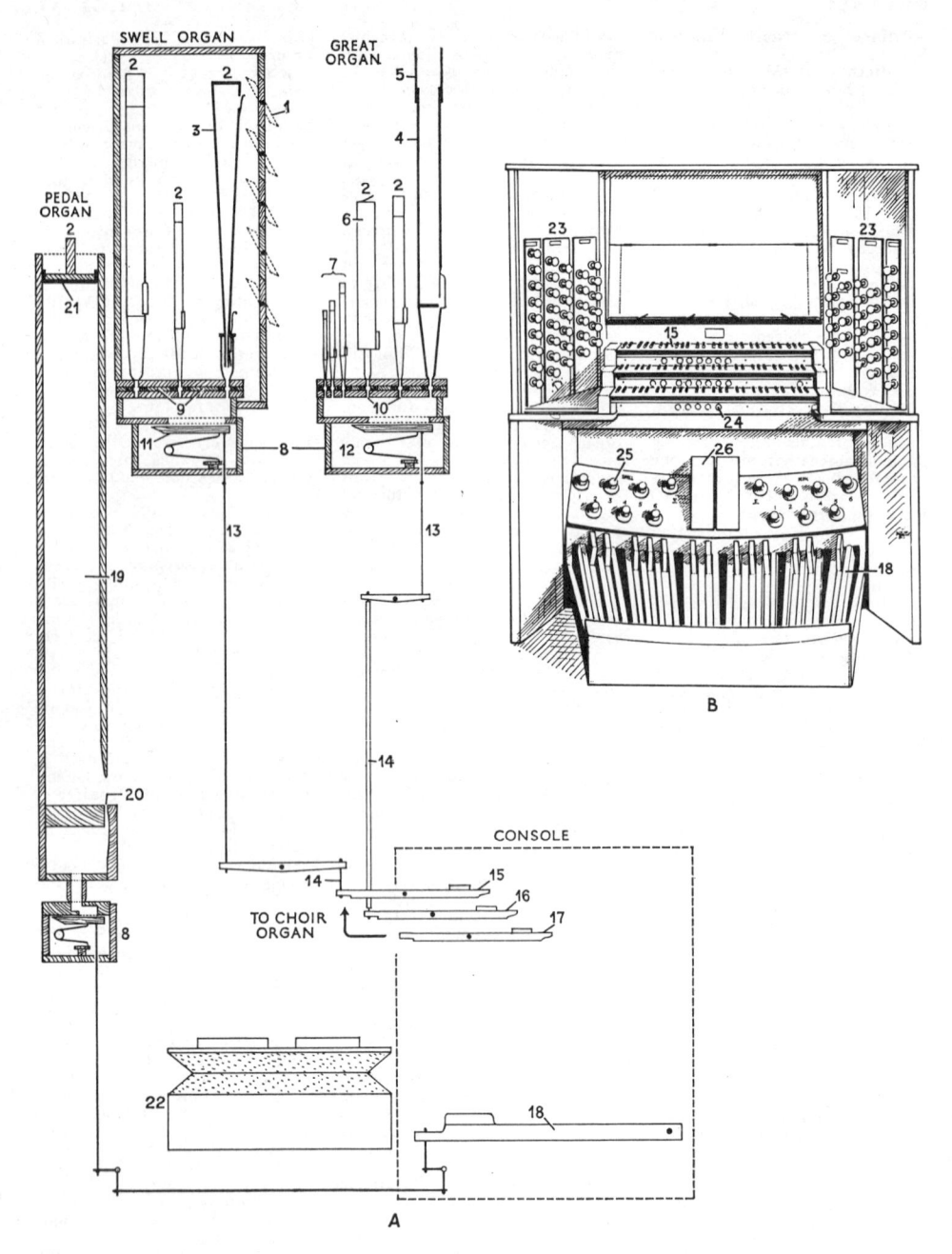

ORGAN WITH TRACKER ACTION: A. DIAGRAMMATIC SECTION. B. CONSOLE

1. Swell. 2. Rank of pipes or stop. 3. Reed-pipe (section). 4. Diapason: open metal flue-pipe (section). 5. Tuning slide to vary length of pipe when tuning. 6. Wooden open flue-pipe. 7. Mixture stop: 3 ranks of pipes on one slide, each note of keyboard thus playing 3 pipes of this stop simultaneously. 8. Wind-chest. 9. Stop slide. 10. Wind groove. 11. Pallet admitting wind into wind groove and thence to pipes. 12. Lower part of wind-chest supplied with wind from wind reservoir. 13. Tracker. 14. Sticker. 15. Swell organ manual. 16. Great organ manual. 17. Choir organ manual (mechanism, wind-chest, and pipes omitted). 18. Pedal organ keyboard or pedal-board. 19. Bourdon stopped wood pipe (section). 20. Flue of pipe. 21. Tampion or pipe stopper. 22. Bellows. 23. Stop knobs. 24. Thumb-pistons controlling manual stops. 25. Toe-pistons controlling pedal stops. 26. Swell pedals

[622]

translation has been made; not derivative or dependent, first-hand, not imitative; novel in character or style, inventive, creative; thinking or acting for oneself. **ori′ginally** *adv.* **originā′lity** *n.* **ori′ginal** *n.* Pattern, archetype; thing from which another is copied or imitated; eccentric person.

ori′gināte *v.* Give origin to, initiate, cause to begin; have origin, take rise. **originā′tion**, **ori′ginātor** *ns.*

Orinō′cō (ŏ-). River of northern S. America, flowing N. and E. through Venezuela to Atlantic Ocean.

ōr′iōle *n.* 1. Bird of genus *Oriolus*, esp. *O. oriolus* (golden ~), a summer visitor to Europe, the male of which has rich yellow and black plumage. 2. Unrelated Amer. bird of family Icteridae, mostly with yellow or orange and black coloration.

Ori′on. 1. (Gk legend) Giant and hunter of Boeotia, changed at his death into a constellation. 2. (astron.) Conspicuous constellation containing many bright stars; ~'s belt, three bright stars in short line across Orion. **Ori′onid** *n.* Any of a shower of meteors with radiant point in Orion.

o′rison (-zn) *n.* (archaic) Prayer.

Ori′ssa. State of E. India; capital, Bhubaneswar.

Or′kney (ōr-). Islands area of Scotland (since May 1975), former county of ~ *Islands*, a group of islands off N. coast.

Orlă′ndō (ōr-). Italian form of ROLAND.

ōrle *n.* (her.) Narrow band following outline of shield but not extending to edge of it (ill. HERALDRY).

Orlē′anist (ōr-). (Fr. hist.) Adherent of those princes of the house of Orleans who were descended from Louis XIV's younger brother Philippe and whose descendant Louis Philippe reigned as king of France 1830–48.

Orleans (ōrlē′anz). (Fr. *Orléans*) French city on River Loire; besieged by the English, 1428, and relieved by Joan of Arc.

ōr′lop *n.* Lowest deck of a ship which has three or more decks. [Du. *overloop* covering]

Or′mazd, Or′muzd (ōr-). In the Zoroastrian system, the supreme deity, principle of goodness and light, in perpetual conflict with Ahriman.

ōr′mer *n.* Haliotis.

ōr′molu (-lōō) *n.* Gilded bronze used for the mounts of furniture and other decorative metalwork, esp. in 18th-c. France; imitation of this, esp. gold-coloured alloy of copper, zinc, and tin; articles made of or decorated with this. [Fr. *or moulu* ground gold (for use in gilding)]

Ormuz, Hormuz (ōr′mōōz, hŏr-). Ancient city on island at mouth of Persian Gulf; an important centre of commerce in Middle Ages.

ōr′nament *n.* 1. (eccles., usu. pl.) Accessories of church or worship (e.g. altar, chalice, service-books, vestments, organ, bells, etc.). 2. Thing used or serving to adorn; quality or person whose existence or presence confers grace or honour. 3. Adorning, being adorned, embellishment; features or work added for decorative purposes. 4. (pl., mus.) Grace notes. **ōrnamĕ′ntal** *adj.* **ōrnamĕ′ntally** *adv.* **ōr′namĕnt** *v.t.* Adorn, beautify. **ōrnamĕntā′tion** *n.*

ōrnā′te *adj.* Elaborately adorned; embellished. **ōrnā′telȳ** *adv.* **ōrnā′teness** *n.*

ōrnithŏ′logȳ *n.* Branch of zoology dealing with birds. **ōrnithŏ′logist** *n.* **ōrnitholŏ′gical** *adj.*

ōrnithorhȳ′ncus (-rĭnk-) *n.* Platypus.

ōrogĕ′nĕsis, ōrŏ′genȳ *ns.* (geol.) Process of mountain formation, esp. by folding of earth's crust. **ōrogĕ′nic** *adj.*

ōrŏ′graphȳ *n.* Branch of physical geography dealing with mountains. **ōrogrā′phic** *adj.*

Orō′sius, Paulus (5th c.). Spanish priest, historian, and theologian.

ōr′otŭnd *adj.* Magniloquent, pompous. [L *ore rotundo* with round mouth]

ōr′phan *n.* & *adj.* (Child) bereaved of parent(s). ~ *v.t.* Bereave of parent(s). **ōr′phanage** *n.* (hist.) Institution for care of orphans.

Orpheus (ōr′fūs). (Gk legend) Legendary Thracian pre-Homeric poet; son of Calliope or another Muse; played so marvellously on the lyre (given to him by Apollo) that wild beasts were spellbound by his music; visited Hades and charmed Pluto into releasing his wife Eurydice from the dead, but lost her because he failed to obey the condition that he must not look back at her until they had reached the world of the living.

Or′phic (ōr-) *adj.* Of Orpheus or Orphism. **Or′phism, Or′phicism** (ōr-) *ns.* Mystic religion of ancient Greece, originating in 7th or 6th c. B.C. and based in poems (now lost) attributed to Orpheus, emphasizing the mixture of good (or divine) and evil in human nature and the necessity that the individual should rid himself of the evil part by ritual and moral purification throughout a series of reincarnations.

ōr′phrey, ōr′fray *n.* One of the bands or panels, freq. embroidered, with which an ecclesiastical vestment is decorated (ill. VESTMENT); similar band or panel hung over altar frontal; cross-shaped piece on the back of a chasuble.

ōr′piment *n.* Bright-yellow mineral, arsenious trisulphide (As_2S_3), used as a pigment.

ōr′pine, -pin *n.* Succulent herbaceous plant (*Sedum telephium*) with smooth fleshy leaves and corymbs of purple flowers.

Or′pington (ōr-) *n.* (One of) a breed of large hardy dual-purpose poultry, usu. buff, with white legs. [town in Kent]

ŏ′rrery *n.* Clockwork model of the planetary system. [named after Charles Boyle, 4th Earl of Orrery, c 1700]

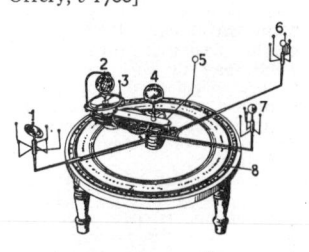

ORRERY, c 1800
1. Saturn and its satellites. 2. Earth. 3. Moon. 4. Sun. 5. Mars. 6. Uranus and its satellites. 7. Jupiter and its satellites. 8. Zodiac calendar scale

ŏ′rris[1] *n.* (also ~*-root*) Powdered violet-scented root of three species of iris used in perfumery etc.

ŏ′rris[2] *n.* Lace or braid of gold and silver thread, used esp. in 18th c.

Orsini (ōrsē′nĭ), Felice (1819–58). Italian patriot and revolutionary; executed for an attempt in 1858 on the life of Napoleon III.

ōrt *n.* (dial. & archaic; usu. pl.) Refuse scrap(s), leavings.

Ortē′lius (ōr-), Abraham (1527–98). Flemish geographer and mapmaker of Antwerp.

ōrthochromă′tic (-kr-) *adj.* (phot.) Reproducing colours in their correct relative intensities.

ōr′thoclāse *n.* Common felspar, occurring in crystals or masses with two cleavages at right angles.

ōrthodŏ′ntics *n.* Branch of dental surgery concerned with the correction of malformations of the teeth. **ōrthodŏ′ntic** *adj.* **ōrthodŏ′ntist** *n.*

ōr′thodŏx *adj.* Holding correct or currently accepted opinions esp. on religious doctrine; not heretical, original, or independent in mind; generally accepted as right or true, esp. in theology; in harmony with what is authoritatively established; approved, conventional; *O~ Church*, (also *Eastern* or *Greek Church*) part of Christian Church separated from Catholic Church in 9th c., recognizing patriarch of Constantinople as head; any of the national Churches of Russia, Bulgaria, Rumania, etc., in communion with this. **ōr′thodŏxȳ** *n.* Being orthodox.

ōr′thoëpȳ *n.* Study of correct pronunciation. **ōrthoë′pic** *adj.* **ōrthoë′pist** *n.*

ōrthogĕ′nĕsis *n.* View of evolution according to which variations

[623]

follow a defined direction and are not merely sporadic and fortuitous.
ŏrthŏ'graphў *n.* 1. Correct or conventional spelling; spelling with reference to its correctness. 2. Orthographic projection. ŏrthogră'phĭc *adj.* (of perspective projection in maps, elevations, etc.) In which point of sight is supposed to be at infinite distance, so that rays are parallel (ill. DRAWING). ŏrthogră'phical *adj.* Of orthography. ŏrthogră'phicallў *adv.*
ŏrthopae'dic *adj.* Of, relating to, orthopaedics. ŏrthopae'dics *n.* Branch of surgery dealing with abnormalities and injuries of the locomotor system. ŏrthopae'dist *n.*
ŏrthŏ'pterous *adj.* Of the order Orthoptera of insects, including grasshoppers, crickets, etc., with straight narrow fore wings, broad longitudinally folded hind wings, and incomplete metamorphosis.
ŏrthŏ'ptic *adj.* Of, concerning, the right or normal use of the eyes. ŏrthŏ'ptics *n.* Correction of defective vision by means of exercises of the eye-muscles. ŏrthŏ'ptist *n.*
ŏrthorhŏ'mbic (-rŏm-) *adj.* (cryst.) Having the three axes mutually at right angles and unequal (ill. CRYSTAL).
ŏrthoscŏ'pĭc *adj.* Having, producing, correct vision; free from, constructed to correct, optical distortion.
ŏr'tolan *n.* One of the buntings (*Emberiza hortulana*), a small bird of Europe, N. Africa, and W. Asia, esteemed as table delicacy.
Or'wĕll (ôr-), George: see BLAIR[1].
ŏ'rўx *n.* Large antelope (genus *O~*) of Africa and Arabia, with long straight pointed horns.
O.S. *abbrev.* Old style; ordinary seaman; Ordnance Survey; outsize.
O.S.A. *abbrev.* Order of St. Augustine.
O'sāge (ō-) *n.* Member of N. Amer. Indian tribe of Siouan linguistic stock, formerly occupying territory in Missouri and Arkansas; ~ *orange*, N. Amer. thorny tree of mulberry family with large yellow fruit and hard flexible yellow wood.
O.S.B. *abbrev.* Order of St. Benedict.
O'sborne (ŏz-). Former English royal residence in Isle of Wight; purchased by Queen Victoria, 1845; presented to the nation by Edward VII, 1902; used as a Naval College, 1903–21.
O'scan (ŏ-) *adj.* & *n.* (Of) the ancient Italic language spoken in Campania and farther S., and surviving only in inscriptions in an alphabet derived from Etruscan.
O'scar (ŏ-) *n.* Gold-plated statuette awarded annually by the Academy of Motion Picture Arts and Sciences, of Hollywood, California, for highest achievement in film production; (loosely)

similar award. [arbitrary use of Christian name]
ŏ'scillāte *v.* 1. Swing like pendulum, move to and fro; vacillate. 2. (of radio receiver) Radiate electromagnetic waves owing to faulty operation or construction. ŏscillā'tion *n.* ŏ'scillatorў *adj.*
ŏsci'lloscōpe *n.* Device in which variations in an electrical quantity produce a temporary trace on the fluorescent screen of a cathode-ray tube.
O'sco-U'mbrian (ō-, ŭ-) *adj.* & *n.* (Of) the group of Italic languages comprising Oscan, Umbrian, and Volscian.
ŏ'scŭlar *adj.* Of the mouth; of kissing; (math.) that osculates.
ŏ'scŭlāte *v.* 1. Kiss (usu. joc.). 2. (biol., of species etc.) Have contact through intermediate species etc.; have common characters *with.* 3. (math., of curve or surface) Have contact of higher order with, coincide in three or more points. ŏ'scŭlant, ŏ'scŭlatorў *adjs.* ŏscŭlā'tion *n.*
ŏ'scŭlum *n.* (pl. *-la*). Mouth-like aperture; mouth of sponge (ill. SPONGE).
O.S.F. *abbrev.* Order of St. Francis.
osier (ō'zher) *n.* (Shoot of) species of willow, esp. *Salix viminalis*, with tough pliant branches used in basket-work; attrib., of osiers.
Osī'rĭs. (Egyptian myth.) God of the underworld and husband of Isis; sometimes identified with the sun.
O'slō (ŏz-). Capital city of Norway, on SE. coast; formerly (1624–1925) called Christiania in honour of King Christian IV, who refounded it.
O'sman (ŏz-), O'thman[2] (ŏ-) (1259–1326). Turkish sultan and conqueror; founder of Ottoman or Osmanli dynasty; declared himself sultan on collapse of Seljuk Empire. Osmā'nli (ŏz-) *adj.* & *n.* Ottoman. [f. OSMAN]
ŏ'smium (ŏz-) *n.* (chem.) Metallic element of the platinum group, hard, brittle, bluish-white, and of high density; symbol Os, at. no. 76, at. wt 190·2. [Gk *osmē* smell]
ŏsmō'sĭs (ŏz-) *n.* Tendency of a solvent, when separated from a solution by a suitable membrane (often animal or vegetable), to pass through the membrane so as to dilute the solution. ŏsmŏ'tic *adj.* ~ *pressure*, pressure produced by the solvent in osmosis.
ŏ'sprey (or -ā) *n.* 1. Large diurnal bird of prey, *Pandion haliaetus*, found on inland waters and preying on fish; fish-hawk. 2. Egret plume worn as ornament on hat etc.
O'ssa (ŏ-). Lofty mountain in Thessaly, Greece, S. of Olympus; see also PELION.
ŏ'ssēous *adj.* Consisting of bone, ossified; having bony skeleton; abounding in fossil bones.

O'ssĭan (ō-), Oisin (ō'shēn). Legendary Gaelic 3rd-c. warrior and bard. Ossiă'nĭc *adj.* Of Ossian; of the style or character of the rhythmic prose of MACPHERSON's supposed translation of the poems of Ossian; hence, bombastic, grandiloquent.
ŏ'ssicle *n.* (anat.) Small bone, esp. one of three in the middle ear (ill. EAR[1]); small piece of bony, chitinous, or calcareous substance in animal framework.
ŏ'ssifў *v.* Turn into bone; harden; make or become rigid, callous, or unprogressive. ŏssificā'tion *n.*
ŏ'ssŭarў *n.* Place or receptacle for bones of the dead.
Ostade (ŏstah'de). Name of two Dutch painters: *Adriaen van* ~ (1610–84), genre painter and etcher; *Isack van* ~ (1621–49), his brother and pupil, genre and landscape painter.
ŏstĕ'nsible *adj.* Professed, for show, put forward to conceal the real. ŏstĕ'nsiblў *adv.*
ŏstĕ'nsorў *n.* Receptacle for displaying the Host to congregation, monstrance.
ŏstentā'tion *n.* Pretentious display, esp. of wealth or luxury; showing off; attempt or intention to attact notice. ŏstentā'tious (-shus) *adj.* ŏstentā'tiouslў *adv.*
ŏstĕo- *prefix.* Bone.
ŏstĕŏ'logў *n.* Branch of anatomy concerned with the study of the skeleton and the structure of bones.
ŏstĕŏ'pathў *n.* Theory of disease and method of cure based on assumption that deformation of part of skeleton, notably the spine, and consequent interference with nerves and blood-vessels, are the cause of most diseases. ŏstĕopă'thĭc *adj.* ŏ'stĕopăth *n.* Practitioner of osteopathy.
O'stia (ŏ-). Ancient city and harbour of Latium, Italy; said to be the first colony founded by Rome; it was buried, and its ruins were preserved, by the gradual silting up of the River Tiber.
ŏ'stler (ŏsl-) *n.* (hist.) Stableman at inn.
ŏ'stracize *v.t.* 1. (at ancient Athens) Banish (dangerously powerful or unpopular citizen) for 10 or 5 years by voting with potsherds or tiles (*ostraka*) on which name of person to be banished was written. 2. Exclude from society, refuse to associate with. ŏ'stracism *n.*
ŏ'strich *n.* Very large swift-running bird (*Struthio camelus*) of sandy plains of Africa and formerly Arabia, with small wings useless for flight, and habit of swallowing hard substances to assist working of gizzard; proverbial for self-delusion owing to the (unfounded) belief that when pursued it buries its head in the sand imagining that it cannot then be seen; ~ *plume*, wing or tail feather of ostrich as ornament.

[624]

O'strogŏth (ō-) *n.* Member of eastern branch of GOTHS, who towards end of 5th c. conquered Italy, and under their leader THEODORIC established a kingdom in Italy, Sicily, and Dalmatia which lasted until 555. **Ostrogŏ'thic** *adj.*

O'swald[1] (ŏz-), St. (*c* 605–42). King of Northumbria; defeated and slew British king Ceadwalla, 634; classed by Bede as one of the seven greatest Anglo-Saxon kings; commemorated 5 Aug.

O'swald[2] (ŏz-), St. (d. 992). English churchman, archbishop of York; commemorated 28 Feb.

O.T. *abbrev.* Old Testament.

Otaheite (ōtahē'tĭ). = TAHITI.

ō'tarў *n.* Member of the Otariidae, a mainly Antarctic family of seals with small external ear, including fur seals and sea-lions; eared seal.

O.T.C. *abbrev.* Officers' Training Corps.

o'ther (ŭdh-) *adj.* Not the same as one or more or some already mentioned or implied; separate in identity, distinct in kind; alternative, further, or additional; *every* ~, every alternate; *the* ~, the one remaining; *the* ~ *day*, a few days ago; *on the* ~ *hand*, in contrast (with fact or argument just mentioned); ~ *than*, different from; ~ *things being equal*, with conditions alike in everything but the point in question; *the* ~ *world*, life after death; ~*-world*, concerned with or thinking of this only; ~*-worldly* (*adj.*). ~ *n.* or *pron.* (orig. elliptic use of adj.) Other person, thing, specimen, etc.; *someone or* ~, a person unknown. ~ *adv.* Otherwise.

o'therwīse (ŭdh-, -z) *adv.* In a different way; if circumstances are or were different, else, or; in other respects; in a different state.

O'thman[1] (ō-) (*c* 574–656). 3rd Muslim caliph, son-in-law of Muhammad.

Othman[2]: see OSMAN.

Otho, Othonian: see OTTO[2].

ō'tic *adj.* Of the ear.

ō'tiōse (or -shĭ-) *adj.* Not required, serving no practical purpose. **ō'tiōselў** *adv.* **ō'tiōsenĕss** *n.*

otī'tis *n.* Inflammation of the ear.

ō'tō-rhī'nō-lărўngō'logў (-rĭ-) *n.* Branch of medicine dealing with diseases of ear, nose, and throat.

otta'va rī'ma (-tah-, rē-). Italian stanza of eight 11-syllabled lines (10-syllabled in English), the first six lines rhyming alternately, the last two forming a couplet.

Ottawa (ŏ'tawa). City of Ontario and capital of Canada, situated on the ~ *River*, a tributary of the St. Lawrence.

ō'tter *n.* 1. Aquatic fur-bearing carnivorous mammal of genus *Lutra* and related genera, feeding chiefly on fish, with webbed feet and pointed tail somewhat flattened horizontally; fur of this; ~*-hound*, dog of breed used for hunting otter. 2. Fishing-tackle of float with line and several hooks; kind of fishing gear used in trawling. 3. (mine-sweeping) Steel frame shaped like a box-kite for holding sweep-wires at required depth.

ŏ'ttō[1] *n.* ~ *of roses* = ATTAR.

O'ttō[2] (ō-), **O'thō** (ō-). Name of several Holy Roman emperors and German kings: *Otto I* (912–73), 'the Great', German king 936–73; crowned emperor by pope, 962; *Otto II* (955–83), son of Otto I, crowned 967, sole emperor 973–83; *Otto III* (980–1002), son of Otto II crowned 996, emperor 983–1002; *Otto IV* (*c* 1182–1218), crowned 1209, emperor 1198–1212 (deposed). **Ottō'nian, Othō'nian** *adjs.* Of the dynasty of these emperors; of this age.

ŏ'ttoman[1] *n.* Cushioned seat like sofa or chair without back or arms (freq. a box with cushioned top).

O'ttoman[2] (ō-) *adj.* Of the Ottoman Empire; ~ *Empire*, Turkish Empire founded *c* 1300 by OSMAN and lasting until 1919. ~ *n.* Turk.

O'tway (ŏ-), Thomas (1652–85). English Restoration playwright, author of 'Venice Preserved' etc.

O.U. *abbrev.* Oxford University (esp. in names of clubs, as *O.U.B.C.*, Boat Club, *O.U.D.S.*, Dramatic Society); *O.U.P.*, Oxford University Press.

oublië'tte (ōō-) *n.* Secret dungeon with entrance only by trap-door above.

ouch *int.* Exclamation of pain or annoyance.

Ou'denarde (ōō-). (Flem. *Oudenaarde*, Fr. *Audenarde*) Town of E. Flanders, Belgium; scene (1708) of victory of Marlborough and Prince Eugene over French forces under Vendôme.

ought[1] (awt) *n.* (vulg.) Figure denoting nothing, nought.

ought[2] (awt) *v. aux.* Expressing duty, rightness, shortcoming, advisability, or strong probability.

ougiya (ōōgēya) *n.* Principal monetary unit of Mauritania.

Ouida (wē'da). Pen-name of Marie Louise de la Ramée (1839–1908), English novelist.

Ouija (wē'jah) *n.* Board with letters, signs, etc., used with planchette for obtaining messages in spiritualist séances. [trade-name; Fr. *oui* yes; Ger. *ja* yes]

ounce[1] *n.* (abbrev. oz.). Unit of weight, $\frac{1}{16}$ lb. in avoirdupois, $\frac{1}{12}$ lb. in troy weight; *fluid* ~, 8 (fluid) drachms, $\frac{1}{20}$ of imperial pint; (U.S.) $\frac{1}{16}$ of pint; (fig.) very small quantity. [L *uncia* twelfth (of pound or foot)]

ounce[2] *n.* 1. (poet.) Lynx or other vaguely identified feline beast. 2. (zool.) Snow leopard (*Uncia uncia*) of highlands of central Asia, smaller and lighter in colour than leopard but with similar markings.

our (owr) *poss. pron.* Possessive case of WE used as attrib. adj., with abs. and pred. form **ours** (pr. -z), belonging to us.

oursĕ'lf (owr-) *pron.* (pl. *-selves*). Emphatic and reflexive form corresp. to WE, US (usu. pl. exc. in formal use).

Ouse (ōōz). Name of several English rivers: 1. River of North Yorkshire formed by junction of Swale and Ure, and forming, with Trent, the Humber estuary. 2. *Great* ~, river of Midlands, flowing into the Wash. 3. River of East Sussex running into English Channel at Newhaven.

ousel: see OUZEL.

oust *v.t.* Put out of possession, eject, expel *from*, drive out; force oneself or be put into the place of.

out *adv.* 1. Away from or not in or at a place, the right or normal state, the fashion, etc.; not at home; (of calculation) inaccurate; (of player or side) having finished innings; (boxing) unable to put up a defence, e.g. ~ *for the count* (i.e. the counting of seconds from one to ten); not at work, on strike; (of fire etc.) not burning. 2. In(to) the open, publicity, hearing, sight, notice, etc.; ~ *for*, ~ *to do*, (colloq.) engaged in seeking; ~ *and about*, able to leave bed or house. 3. To or at an end, completely; (in oral communication by radio etc., as indication) transmission ends; ~ *and away*, by far; ~ *and* ~, thorough(ly), surpassing(ly). 4. ~ *of*, from within; not within; from among; beyond range of; (so as to be) without; from, owing to, by use of (material); at specified distance from; beyond; transgressing rules of; (of animals) having as dam; ~ *of doors*, in, into, the open air; ~ *of it*, not included, forlorn, at a loss; ~*-of-the-way*, remote; uncommon, remarkable; ~ *of this world*, (esp.) superlatively good. ~ *prep.* Out of (now only in *from* ~). ~ *adj.* External, living etc. outside. ~ *n.* (pl.) *ins and* ~*s*: see IN.

out- *prefix.* External; detached; out of; to excess; so as to surpass.

ou'tbăck *adj. & n.* (Austral.) (Of) the more remote settlements.

outbi'd *v.t.* Outdo in bidding, offer more than.

ou'tboard (-ôrd) *adj.* On, towards, nearer to, outside of ship or aircraft; (of motor-boat) with engine and driving apparatus attached outside boat at stern. ~ *adv.* To, towards, outside of ship or aircraft.

outbrā've *v.t.* Defy, stand against bravely; outdo in bravery, finery, splendour, etc.

ou'tbreak (-brāk) *n.* Breaking out of emotion (esp. anger), hostilities, disease, fire, volcanic energy, etc.; outcrop; insurrection.

ou'tbuilding (-bĭ-) *n.* Outhouse.

ou'tbŭrst *n.* Explosion of feeling, esp. expressed by vehement words; volcanic eruption.

ou'tcast (-kahst) *adj. & n.* (Person) cast out from home and

[625]

OUTCASTE

friends; homeless and friendless (vagabond).

ou′tcaste (-kahst) *n. & adj.* (Person) who has lost or been expelled from his caste, or who does not belong to a caste.

outcla′ss (-ahs) *v.t.* Belong to higher class than, completely beat or surpass.

ou′tcome (-kŭm) *n.* Issue, result.

ou′tcrŏp *n.* Emergence of stratum, vein, or rock, at surface (ill. ROCK¹).

ou′tcrȳ *n.* Clamour, uproar.

outdi′stance *v.t.* Get far ahead of.

outdo′ (-ōō) *v.t.* Surpass, excel.

ou′tdoor (-dôr) *adj.* Done, existing, or used outdoors; ~ *relief*, (hist.) relief given to persons not resident in workhouse or institution. **outdoor′s** (-z) *adv.* Out of doors.

ou′ter *adj.* Farther from centre or inside, relatively far out; external, of the outside; objective, physical, not subjective or psychical; ~ *man*, personal appearance, dress; ~ *world*, people outside one's own circle. ~ *n.* (Hit on) outermost of three circles round bull's-eye on target (opp. *inner*). **ou′termōst** *adj.*

outfā′ce *v.t.* Look out of countenance, stare down; confront fearlessly or impudently, brave, defy.

ou′tfield *n.* Outlying land of farm; outlying region of thought etc.; (cricket) part of field remote from wickets.

ou′tfit *n.* Complete equipment; (U.S.) party travelling or in charge of herds of cattle etc.; (slang) organized group of persons. ~ *v.t.* Provide with outfit; supply *with*. **ou′tfitter** *n.* Supplier of equipment; retailer of men's ready-made clothes.

outflă′nk *v.t.* Get beyond flank of (opposing army), outmanœuvre by flanking movement.

ou′tflow (-ō) *n.* What flows out, amount flowing out.

outgĕ′neral *v.t.* Defeat by superior generalship.

ou′tgō *n.*, **outgō′ings** (-z) *n.pl.* Expenditure, outlay. **outgō′** *v.t.* Go faster than; surpass.

outgrow′ (-ō) *v.t.* Grow faster, get taller, than; get too big for (clothes); get rid of (childish habit, ailment, taste) with advancing age.

ou′tgrowth (-ōth) *n.* Offshoot; excrescence.

out-hĕ′rod *v.t.* ~ *Herod*, be more violent or hectoring than Herod (represented in old mystery plays as a blustering tyrant); outdo, surpass.

ou′thouse (-t-h-) *n.* House, building, shed, belonging to and near or built against main house.

out′ing *n.* Pleasure-trip, holiday away from home.

out-jŏ′ckey *v.t.* Out-manœuvre.

ou′tlander *n.* 1. (esp. poet.) Alien. 2. = UITLANDER.

outlă′ndish *adj.* Foreign looking or sounding; unfamiliar, bizarre, uncouth. **outlă′ndishly** *adv.* **outlă′ndishness** *n.*

outla′st (-ahst) *v.t.* Last longer than.

ou′tlaw *n.* Person deprived of protection of the law, banished or exiled person. ~ *v.t.* Proscribe, declare outlaw. **ou′tlawrȳ** *n.* Condition of, condemnation as, outlaw.

ou′tlay *n.* What one spends, expenses.

ou′tlĕt *n.* Means of exit or escape, vent, way out.

ou′tlier *n.* Outlying or detached part of something; (geol.) part of stratum or formation at some distance from main body to which it belongs, the intervening part having been removed by denudation.

ou′tline *n.* Line(s) enclosing the apparently plane figure presented by any object to sight, contour, external boundary; sketch containing only contour lines and no shading; rough draft, verbal description of essential parts only, summary; (pl.) main features, general principles. ~ *v.t.* Draw or describe in outline; mark outline of.

outli′ve *v.t.* Live beyond; come safely through, get over effect of; live longer than.

ou′tlŏŏk *n.* What one sees on looking out, view, prospect; person's general view of life; what seems likely to happen.

ou′tlying *adj.* Situated far from a centre, remote.

outmanœu′vre (-ōōver) *v.t.* Get the better of by superior strategy.

outmă′tch *v.t.* Be more than a match for.

outmō′dĕd *adj.* Out of date, old-fashioned.

ou′tmŏst *adj.* Outermost.

outnŭ′mber *v.t.* Exceed in number.

ou′tpātient (-shent) *n.* One receiving treatment at hospital etc. without being lodged in it.

outpoi′nt *v.t.* (yachting) Sail closer to the wind than.

ou′tpōst *n.* Detachment on guard at some distance from army to prevent surprise.

ou′tpouring (-pôr-) *n.* Effusion; verbal or literary expression of emotion.

ou′tput (-ŏŏt) *n.* Amount produced by manufacture, mining, labour, etc.; product; current etc. produced by electrical device; goods or services supplied to customers and for which V.A.T. must be charged.

ou′trāge *n.* Forcible violation of others' rights, sentiments, etc.; deed of violence, gross or wanton offence or indignity. ~ *v.t.* Do violence to, subject to outrage, injure, insult, violate; infringe (law, morality, etc.) flagrantly. **outrā′geous** (-jus) *adj.* Immoderate, extravagant, extraordinary; violent, furious; grossly cruel, immoral, offensive, or abusive. **outrā′geously** *adv.* **outrā′geousness** *n.*

OUTSPAN

Ou′tram (ōō-), Sir James (1803–63). English general and hero of the Indian Mutiny, one of the relievers of Lucknow.

outrā′nge *v.t.* (of guns etc.) Have longer range than.

outré (ōōtrā) *adj.* Outside the bounds of propriety, eccentric. [Fr.]

ou′t-relie′f *n.* OUTDOOR relief.

ou′trider *n.* Mounted attendant riding before, behind, or with carriage.

ou′trigged (-gd) *adj.* (of boat) Having outriggers.

ou′trigger *n.* 1. Beam, spar, framework, rigged out and projecting from or over ship's side for various purposes; bracket supporting rowlock beyond boat's side to enable a long oar to be conveniently used in a narrow boat; boat with such outriggers; ~ *canoe*, canoe having a long float parallel to its side, attached by beams (ill. CANOE). 2. Projecting beam etc. in building. 3. Extension of splinter-bar enabling extra horse to be harnessed outside shafts; horse harnessed thus.

outri′ght (-rīt) *adv.* Altogether, entirely, once for all, not by degrees or instalments or half-and-half; without reservation, openly. **ou′tright** *adj.* Downright, direct, thorough. **ou′trightness** *n.*

outri′val *v.t.* Outdo as a rival.

outru′n *v.t.* Outstrip in running; pass the limit of.

ou′tsĕt *n.* Start, commencement.

outshi′ne *v.t.* Surpass in brightness, splendour, or excellence.

ou′tsi′de *n.* 1. Outer side or surface; (of path) side away from wall or next to road. 2. Outer part, exterior; outward aspect. 3. Highest computation. ~ *adj.* Situated on, derived from, the outside; not belonging to some circle or institution; greatest existent or possible; ~ *broker*, one not member of Stock Exchange; ~ *edge*, skating movement on outer edge of skate; ~ *left*, *right*, (footb. etc.) player positioned nearest edge of field (ill. ASSOCIATION); ~ *porter*, one conveying luggage from station. **outsi′de** *adv.* On or to the outside, the open air, open sea, etc.; not within. ~ *prep.* External to; beyond the limits of; at or to the outside of.

outsi′der *n.* Non-member of some circle, party, profession, etc., uninitiated person, layman; person without special knowledge, breeding, etc., or not fit to mix with good society; horse or person not thought to have a chance in race or competition.

ou′tsize *n.* Person or thing larger than the normal, esp. ready-made article of dress larger than the standard size (also attrib.).

ou′tskirts *n.pl.* Outer border, fringe, of city, district, etc.

outsmā′rt *v.t.* Outwit, be smarter than.

ou′tspăn *v.* (S. Afr.) Unyoke,

OUTSPOKEN

unharness. ~ n. Act, time, or place of outspanning.

outspō'ken adj. Frank, unreserved. **outspō'kenly** adv. **outspō'kenness** (-n-n-) n.

ou'tsprea'd (-ĕd) adj. Spread out.

outstă'nding adj. Prominent; still unsettled. **outstă'ndingly** adv.

outstay' v.t. Stay beyond limits of, exhaust by staying; stay longer than.

outstri'p v.t. Pass in running etc.; surpass in competition or relative progress or ability.

ou't-thrŭst (-t-th-) n. Outward thrust or thrusting pressure in any structure.

outvie' v.t. Excel in competition, rivalry, or emulation.

outvō'te v.t. Outnumber in voting.

ou'tward adj. Outer (archaic); directed towards the outside; bodily, external, material, visible, apparent, superficial; ~ form, appearance. ~ adv. In an outward direction; ~-bound, (of ship or passenger) going away from home. **ou'twardly** adv. **ou'twardness** n. **ou'twards** (-z) adv.

outwei'gh (-wā) v.t. Exceed in weight, value, importance, or influence.

outwi't v.t. Prove too clever for, overreach, take in.

ou'twork (-wĕrk) n. Part of fortifications lying outside parapet; detached or advanced part of fortification.

outwŏr'n adj. Worn out; exhausted, spent.

ouzel, ousel (ōō'zl) n. 1. Any of several black European thrushes, esp. ring ~. 2. WATER ouzel. 3. (obs.) Blackbird.

ō'val adj. Egg-shaped, ellipsoidal; having the outline of an egg, elliptical. ~ n. Closed curve with one axis longer than the other, like ellipse or outline of egg; thing with oval outline; the O~, the Surrey County cricket ground, Kennington Oval, in London.

ō'vary n. Organ of female reproductive system, that in which ova or eggs are produced (ill. PELVIS); in plants, lowest part of pistil, ultimately becoming fruit or seed-vessel (ill. FLOWER). **ovār'ian** adj.

ō'văte adj. (biol.) Egg-shaped, oval.

ovā'tion n. 1. (Rom. antiq.) Lesser triumph. 2. Enthusiastic reception, spontaneous applause.

oven (ŭ'vn) n. Enclosed chamber or compartment for baking, heating, drying, etc.; Dutch ~: see DUTCH; o'venware, dishes that can be used for cooking food in an oven.

ō'ver adv. 1. Outward and downward from brink (as push ~ the edge) or from erect position (lean ~). 2. So as to cover or touch whole surface (paint it ~). 3. With motion above something so as to pass across something (climb ~).

4. So as to produce fold or reverse position (bend it ~; turn ~, turn other side of leaf up). 5. Across street or other space or distance; (cricket, as umpire's direction) change ends for bowling etc.; ~ against, in opposite situation to, in contrast with. 6. With transference or change from one hand, party, etc., to another; (in radio communication etc., as indication) changing from transmission to reception. 7. Too, in excess; in addition, besides; more; apart; ~ and above, moreover, into the bargain. 8. From beginning to end, with repetition, with detailed consideration (read ~, talk (matter) ~). 9. At an end, done with (the war is ~). ~ n. Number of balls (usu. 6 or 8) bowled from either end of wicket before change is made to other end; play during this time. ~ prep. 1. Above, on, at all or various points upon; to and fro upon, all through, round about; concerning, engaged with; ~ all, from end to end. 2. With or so as to get or give superiority to; beyond, more than; ~ and above, besides, not to mention. 3. Out and down from, down from edge of; so as to clear; across, on or to the other side of; throughout, through duration of, till end of; stumble ~, be tripped up by.

ōver- prefix. Over; upper, outer; superior; excessive.

over-ă'ct v. Act (part, emotion, etc.), act part, with exaggeration.

ō'verall (-awl) n. Garment worn over others as protection against wet, dirt, etc.; (pl.) outer trousers, leggings, or combination suit for dirty work; (mil., pl.) officer's full-dress tight trousers (ill. CAVALRY). ~ adj. Taking into account all features or aspects; inclusive.

ō'ver-ărm adv. & adj. = OVERHAND.

ōverawe' v.t. Restrain, control, or repress by awe.

ōverbă'lance v. (Cause to) lose balance and fall; outweigh.

ōverbear' (-bār) v.t. (past t. -bōre, past part. -bōrne). Bear down or upset by weight or force; put down, repress, by power or authority; surpass in importance etc., outweigh. **ōverbear'ing** adj. Domineering, masterful. **ōverbear'ingly** adv. **ōverbear'ingness** n.

ōverblow'n (-ōn) adj. (of flower) Too fully open, past its prime.

ō'verboard (-ŏrd) adv. From within ship into water; throw ~, (fig.) abandon, discard.

overbŭr'den v.t. Burden too much, overload, overcharge.

O'verbury (ō-), Sir Thomas (1581-1613). English poet and writer of 'Characters'; slowly poisoned in the Tower by agents of the divorced Countess of Essex, for his opposition to her marriage with his friend Robert Carr, later Earl of Somerset.

OVERFLOW

ōvercă'll (-awl) v.t. (bridge) Bid more on (hand) than it is worth; bid higher than (opponent, previous bid, one's partner when opponent has not done so). **ō'vercall** n. Bid made over partner's bid.

ōvercă'pitalīze v.t. Fix or estimate capital of (company etc.) too high.

ōvercă'st (-ahst) v.t. 1. Cover (sky etc.) with clouds or darkness (usu. in past part. overcast). 2. Sew over raw edges of (material, esp. with blanket or buttonhole stitch) to prevent unravelling.

ōverchăr'ge v.t. 1. Charge too highly with explosive, electricity, etc. 2. Put exaggerated details or too much detail into (description etc.). 3. Charge too high a price for (thing) or to (person); charge (specified sum) beyond right price. **ō'verchăr'ge** n. Excessive charge.

ō'vercoat n. Large coat worn over ordinary clothing, esp. in cold weather.

ōvercome' (-kŭm) v. (past t. -cāme, past part. -come). Prevail over, master, get the better of; be victorious. ~ adj. (esp.) Exhausted, made helpless, deprived of self-possession.

ōvercrow'd v. Crowd to excess; esp., crowd more people into a space than there is proper accommodation for.

ōverdo' (-ōō) v.t. (past t. -did, past part. -done pr. -dŭn). Carry to excess, go too far in; cook too long (esp. in past part.); overtax strength of (esp. in past part.).

ō'verdōse n. Excessive dose.

ō'verdraft (-ahft) n. Overdrawing of bank account; amount by which draft exceeds balance.

ōverdraw' v. (past t. -drew, past part. -drawn). 1. Draw cheque in excess of (one's account) or in excess of one's account. 2. Exaggerate in describing.

ōverdrĕ'ss v. Dress with too much display and ornament.

ōverdri've v.t. Drive too hard, drive or work to exhaustion. **ō'verdrive** n. (mech.) System by which a speed higher than that maintained by the engine is passed to the propeller shaft.

ōverdū'e adj. More than due; late, in arrear.

ōverea't v. (past t. -ate pr. -ĕt, past part. -eaten). Eat to excess; ~ oneself, overeat.

ōverĕ'stimăte v.t. Estimate too highly. ~ n. Too high an estimate.

ō'verfall (-awl) n. Turbulent stretch of sea etc. caused by set of tide or current over submarine ledge or meeting of currents.

ō'verflow (-ō) n. What overflows or is superfluous; outlet for excess liquid; ~ meeting, meeting elsewhere of those who have not found room at demonstration etc. **ōverflow'** v. Flow over (brim etc.), flood (surface); extend beyond limits of; (of receptacle) be so full that contents overflow; (of

[627]

OVERFLY

kindness, harvest, etc.) be very abundant. **overflow'ing** n. & adj. **overflow'ingly** adv.

overfly' v.t. (past t. -*flew*, past part. -*flown* pr. -flōn). (of aircraft) Fly over (territory); fly beyond.

ō'verglāze n. Second glaze applied to pottery over first glaze. ~ adj. (of painting etc.) Done on glazed surface.

overgrow' (-ō) v. (past t. -*grew*, past part. -*grown* pr. -grōn). Grow over, cover with growth; grow too large; grow too big etc. for.

ō'verhănd adv. & adj. With hand above object held; with hand above shoulder in bowling etc.; with hand or arm out of water in swimming.

overhă'ng v. (past t. & past part. -*hŭng*). Jut out over, jut; (fig.) impend (over.) **ō'verhăng** n. Thing that overhangs; fact or amount of overhanging.

overhau'l v.t. Pull to pieces for purpose of examining, examine condition of; (esp. naut.) catch up, come up with.

overhea'd (-hĕd) adv. On high; in the sky; in the storey above. **ō'verhead** adj. Placed overhead; ~ *charges* etc., those due to office expenses, management, interest on capital, and other general needs of a business. **ō'verheads** (-z) n.pl. Overhead charges.

overhear' v.t. (past t. & past part. -*heard* pr. -hĕrd). Hear as eavesdropper or unperceived or unintended listener.

overjoy'ed (-joid) adj. Transported with joy (*at*).

ō'verkill n. Greater (capacity for) destruction than is necessary (also fig.).

overlā'den adj. Overloaded, overburdened.

overlă'nd adv. By land and not sea. **ō'verland** adj. Entirely or partly by land.

overlā'p v. Partly cover; cover and extend beyond; partly coincide. **ō'verlăp** n. Thing that overlaps; fact or amount of overlapping.

overlay' v.t. (past. t. & past part. -*laid*). Cover surface of *with* coating etc. **ō'verlay** n. Thing laid over something, coverlet, small tablecloth, etc.

overlea'f adv. On other side of leaf (of book etc.).

overlea'p v.t. (past t. & past part. -*leapt* pr. -lĕpt). Leap over, surmount; omit, ignore.

overli'e v.t. (past t. -*lay*, past part. -*lain*). Lie on top of, smother (child) thus.

overloa'd v.t. Load to excess. **ō'verload** n. Excessive load or charge, as of electric current.

overloo'k v.t. 1. Have prospect of or over from above; be higher than. 2. Fail to observe, take no notice of, condone. 3. Superintend, oversee. 4. Bewitch with evil eye.

ō'verlōrd n. Supreme lord, suzerain. **ō'verlōrdship** n.

ō'verly adv. (dial. & U.S.) Over, excessively.

ō'vermăntel n. Ornamental carving, mirror, etc., over mantelpiece (ill. FIRE).

overma'ster (-mah-) v.t. Master completely, get victory over, overcome.

overmŭ'ch adj., n., & adv. Too much.

over-nī'ce adj. Too fastidious. **over-nī'ceness, over-nī'cety** ns.

overni'ght (-nīt) adv. On the preceding evening (in relation to following day); through the night (till the following morning). **ō'vernight** adj. Done etc. overnight.

ō'verpass (-ahs) n. Roadbridge over another road, esp. a motorway.

overpersuā'de (-sw-) v.t. Persuade in spite of reluctance.

overpi'tch v.t. Bowl (cricketball) so that it pitches too near wicket.

ō'verplŭs n. Surplus, superabundance.

overpow'er v.t. Reduce to submission, subdue, master; be too intense or violent for, overwhelm. **overpow'ering** adj. **overpow'eringly** adv.

overpri'nt v.t. Print (photographic print) darker than intended; print (additional matter or another colour) on already printed surface, esp. of postage-stamp.

overprodū'ce v.t. Produce in excess of demand or of defined amount. **overprodū'ction** n.

ō'verprōōf adj. Containing more alcohol than proof spirit.

overrā'te v.t. Have too high an opinion of; assess too high for rating purposes.

overrea'ch v. 1. (refl.) Strain *oneself* by reaching too far; (of horse) injure fore foot by striking it with hind hoof. 2. Circumvent, outwit, get the better of by cunning or artifice.

overri'de v.t. (past t. -*rōde*, past part. -*ridden*). 1. Exhaust (horse) by riding. 2. Ride over (enemy's country) with armed force; trample (person) under one's horse's hoofs; (fig.) trample under foot, set aside, refuse to comply with, have or claim superior authority to. 3. Slip or lie over, be superimposed on; (surg., of fractured bone) overlap.

ō'verrider n. Protective device on bumper of motor vehicle.

overru'le (-rōōl) v.t. Set aside (decision, argument, etc.) by superior authority; annul decision or reject proposal of (person).

overrŭ'n v.t. (past t. -*răn*, past part. -*run*). Flood, harry and spoil (enemy's country); swarm or spread over; exceed (limit).

oversea', -sea's (-z) advs. Across or beyond sea. **ō'versea, -seas** adjs.

oversee' v.t. Superintend, look after (workmen, execution of work, etc.). **ō'verseer** n.

ō'versew (-sō) v.t. (past part. -*sewn* pr. -sōn, -*sewed* pr. -sōd). Sew together (two pieces of stuff) so that every stitch passes in the same direction through both and the thread between the stitches lies over the edges (ill. STITCH).

overshā'dow (-ō) v.t. Cast a shadow over; (fig.) be more conspicuous than, outshine.

ō'vershoe (-ōō) n. Shoe of rubber, felt, etc., worn outside another.

overshōō't v.t. (past t. & past part. -*shŏt*). Send missile, go, beyond (mark etc.); ~ *the mark*, go too far, exaggerate, overdo something.

ō'vershŏt adj. (of wheel) Turned by water flowing above it (ill. WATER).

ō'versight (-sīt) n. 1. Supervision. 2. Omission to notice, mistake of inadvertence.

ō'verslaugh (-aw) n. (mil.) Passing over of turn of duty in consideration of another duty that takes precedence of it.

oversleep' v.refl. & i. (past t. & past part. -*slĕpt*). Miss intended hour of rising by sleeping too long.

ō'verspill n. (esp.) Surplus population of town etc., accommodated elsewhere.

overstā'te v.t. State too strongly, exaggerate. **ō'verstā'tement** n.

oversteer' v.i. (of vehicle) Have tendency to steer towards the inner side on a curve. **ō'versteer** n. Oversteering.

overstĕ'p v.t. Pass over (boundary).

overstrai'n v.t. Damage by exertion; make too much of (argument etc.). **ō'verstrain** n.

ō'verstrŭ'ng adj. 1. (of piano) With strings arranged in sets crossing each other obliquely. 2. (of person, nerves, etc.) Intensely strained.

oversŭbscri'be v.t. (usu. in past part.) Subscribe more than amount of (loan etc.).

ōvēr't adj. Openly done, unconcealed, patent. **ōvēr'tly** adv.

overtā'ke v.t. (past t. -*tōōk*, past part. -*tāken*). Come up with, catch up; (of storm, misfortune, etc.) come suddenly upon; (of vehicle) pass (vehicle) travelling in same direction.

overtă'x v.t. Make excessive demand on (person's strength etc.); burden with excessive taxes.

overthrow' (-ō) v.t. (past t. -*threw*, past p. -*thrown* pr. thrōn). Upset, knock down; cast out from power; vanquish, subvert; put an end to. **ō'verthrow** n. 1. Defeat, subversion. 2. (cricket) Fielder's return not stopped near wicket and so allowing further run(s).

ō'vertime adv. Beyond regular hours of work. ~ n. Time during which workman etc. works beyond regular hours; payment for this.

ō'vertōne n. (mus.) Harmonic; (subtle or elusive) secondary quality, colour, etc.; implication.

ō'verture n. 1. Opening of negotiations with another (usu.

[628]

pl.); formal proposal or offer. 2. (mus.) Orchestral piece beginning opera, oratorio, etc.; *concert* ~, one-movement composition in same style.

ōvertūr'n *v.* Upset; (cause to) fall down or over; overthrow, subvert; abolish. **ō'vertūrn** *n.*

ōverwee'ning *adj.* Arrogant, presumptuous.

ō'verwei'ght (-wāt) *n.* Preponderance; excessive weight. ~ *adj.* Beyond weight allowed or desirable. **ōverwei'ght** *v.t.* Impose too great weight or burden on.

ōverwhě'lm *v.t.* Bury beneath superincumbent mass, submerge utterly; crush, bring to sudden ruin; overpower with emotion etc.; deluge *with*. **ōverwhě'lming** *adj.* Irresistible by numbers, amount, etc. **ōverwhě'lmingly** *adv.*

ōverwī'nd *v.t.* (past t. & past part.: *-wound*). Wind too far.

ōverwor'k (-wêrk) *v.* (Cause to) work too hard; weary or exhaust with work. **ō'verwor'k** *n.* Excessive work.

ōverwrou'ght (-rawt) *adj.* 1. Over-excited; suffering reaction from excitement. 2. Too elaborate.

ōvibō'vine *adj.* & *n.* (Animal) having character intermediate between sheep and ox; musk-ox.

O'vid (ŏ-). Publius Ovidius Naso (43 B.C.–*c.* A.D. 18), Roman poet; author of 'Ars Amatoria', 'Metamorphoses', 'Fasti', etc. **Ovi'dian** *adj.*

ō'vidŭct *n.* (anat., zool.) One of pair of ducts carrying eggs from ovary.

ō'vifôrm *adj.* Egg-shaped.

ō'vīne *adj.* Of, like, sheep.

ōvī'parous *adj.* (zool.) Producing young by means of eggs expelled from body before being hatched.

ōvipō'sitor (-z-) *n.* (zool.) Organ with which female animal, insect, etc., deposits eggs.

ō'void *adj.* Solidly or superficially egg-shaped, oval with one end more pointed. ~ *n.* Ovoid body.

ō'volo *n.* Convex moulding of quarter-circle or quarter-ellipse section, receding downwards (ill. MOULDING). [It. *uovolo* little egg]

ōvo-tě'stis *n.* (zool.) Organ in certain animals which produces both ova and spermatozoa; hermaphrodite gland.

ōvovīvī'parous *adj.* (zool.) Producing young by means of eggs which hatch before reaching exterior (cf. OVIPAROUS).

ōvūlā'tion *n.* Development of ova; discharge of ova from ovary in mammals. **ō'vūlāte** *v.i.*

ō'vūle *n.* (bot.) Female germ-cell of seed-plant (ill. FLOWER).

ō'vūlar *adj.*

ō'vum *n.* (pl. *-a*) (biol.) Female germ-cell capable of developing into new individual when fertilized by male sperm; egg esp. of mammals, fish, or insects. [L, = 'egg']

owe (ō) *v.* Be under obligation to pay, repay, or render; be in debt (*for*); be indebted for *to*.

O'wen (ō-), Robert (1771–1858). English philanthropist and socialist; had great influence on the co-operative movement.

ow'ing (ō-) *pred. adj.* Yet to be paid, owed, due; ~ *to* (also used adverbially), attributed to, caused by.

owl *n.* 1. Bird of prey, esp. nocturnal, of the order Strigiformes, with large head, raptorial beak, large eyes directed forwards, and soft plumage enabling it to fly noiselessly, feeding on mice, small birds, etc. 2. Solemn person. **ow'lish** *adj.* **ow'lishly** *adv.* **ow'lishness** *n.*

ow'lět *n.* Owl, young owl.

own[1] (ōn) *adj.* 1. (appended to poss. adj. or case) In full ownership, proper, peculiar, individual, and not another's; (abs.) private property, kindred, etc: *of one's* ~, belonging to one; *hold one's* ~, maintain position, not be defeated; *on one's* ~, (colloq.) independently, on one's own account, responsibility or resources; *get one's* ~ *back*, be revenged (*on*). 2. (without possessive): ~ *brother, sister*, etc., with both parents the same; ~ *cousin*, first cousin.

own[2] (ōn) *v.* 1. Have as property, possess. 2. Acknowledge authorship, paternity, or possession, of; admit as existent, valid, true, etc.; submit to (person's sway etc.) without protest; ~ *up*, (colloq.) make frank confession. **ow'ner, ow'nership** *ns.* **ow'nerless** *adj.*

ŏx *n.* (pl. *oxen*). Large domestic bovine animal, esp. male castrated and used as draught animal or reared for food; any bovine animal; ~*-eye daisy*, common meadow plant, *Chrysanthemum leucanthemum*, with flowers having a yellow disc and long white rays; *o'xherd*, cowherd; *o'xlip*, kind of primula; (pop.) hybrid of primrose and cowslip; *o'xtail*, tail of ox, much used for soup-making.

ŏxă'lic *adj.* ~ *acid*, highly poisonous and intensely sour acid (COOH)₂ found in wood-sorrel etc., used in bleaching etc. [Gk *oxalis* wood-sorrel]

O'xbridge (ŏ-). Oxford and Cambridge Universities considered jointly.

Oxf. *abbrev.* Oxford.

O'xfăm (ŏ-) *abbrev.* Oxford Committee for Famine Relief.

O'xford (ŏ-). City on River Thames in Oxfordshire, seat of university organized as a *studium generale* soon after 1167, the first of its colleges, University College, being founded in 1249; ~ *accent*, style of pronouncing English pop. supposed to be characteristic of members of Oxford University; ~ *blue*, dark blue; ~ *frame*, picture-frame the sides of which cross each other and project at the corners; ~ *Group*, international religious movement founded by Dr. Frank N. D. Buchman in Oxford in 1921 (see MORAL Re-Armament); ~ *movement*: see TRACTARIANISM; ~ *shoe*, kind of low walking-shoe laced over instep (ill. SHOE). **ŏ'xfords** (-z) *n.pl.* Oxford shoes. [*ox(en)+ford*]

Oxfôr'diăn (ŏ-) *adj.* & *n.* (esp.) Pertaining to, adherent of, the view that the works attributed to Shakespeare were written by Edward de Vere, 17th Earl of Oxford.

O'xfordshire (ŏ-). South-east midland county of England, since April 1974 including N. parts of the former county of Berkshire.

ŏ'xidāse *n.* (physiol., bact.) One of a group of enzymes concerned with the uptake of oxygen by living cells (respiration).

ŏ'xīde *n.* Compound of oxygen with another element or with a radical.

ŏ'xidīze *v.* Cause to combine with oxygen; cover (metal) with coating of oxide, make rusty; take up or enter into combination with oxygen, rust; *oxidized silver*, silver with dark coating of silver sulphide. **ŏxidā'tion** *n.*

Oxon. *abbrev.* Oxoniensis (L, = of Oxford); (Bishop) of Oxford (replacing surname in his signature); Oxfordshire; Oxford University.

Oxō'nian (ŏ-) *adj.* & *n.* (Member) of Oxford University; (native or inhabitant) of Oxford. [*Oxonia* latinized name of Oxford]

ŏ'xter *n.* (Sc. & dial.) Armpit.

O'xus (ŏ-). Former name of the Amu Darya, great river of Central Asia, rising in Pamirs and flowing into Sea of Aral.

ŏxy̆-acě'ty̆lēne *adj.* Using mixture of oxygen and acetylene (esp. of flame produced in this way for cutting and welding metals).

ŏ'xy̆gen *n.* (chem.) Colourless, tasteless, odourless, gaseous element, essential to life and to combustion, comprising about one-fifth of the air, and present in combination in water and most minerals and organic substances; symbol O, at. no. 8, at. wt 15·9994; ~ *tent*: see TENT.

ŏ'xy̆genāte (*or* ŏksĭ'-) *v.t.* Supply, treat, or mix with oxygen, oxidize; charge (blood) with oxygen by respiration. **ŏxy̆genā'tion** *n.*

ŏ'xy̆genīze *v.t.* Oxygenate.

ŏxy̆hy̆'drogen *adj.* Of a mixture of oxygen and hydrogen.

ŏ'xy̆měl *n.* Syrup of honey and vinegar.

ŏxy̆môr'on *n.* (rhet.) Figure of speech with pointed conjunction of seeming contradictories (e.g. *faith unfaithful kept him falsely true*).

ŏxy̆ō'pia *n.* Abnormal keenness of vision.

ŏxy̆tō'cin *n.* Hormone produced by pituitary gland, stimulating muscle of uterus; synthetic form of this. **ŏxy̆tō'cic** *adj.*

ŏ'xy̆tōne *adj.* & *n.* (Gk. gram.) (Word) with acute accent on last syllable.

[629]

oy′er *n.* Criminal trial under writ of ~ *and terminer,* commission to judges on circuit to hold courts.
ōyĕ′z, ōyĕ′s *int.* Uttered, usu. thrice, by public crier or court officer to bespeak silence and attention. [OF *oyez,* imper. pl. of *oir* hear]
oy′ster *n.* Edible bivalve mollusc of family Ostreidae, usu. eaten alive, esp. the common European *Ostrea edulis* and the Amer. *O. virginica* and *O. lurida* (Californian ~); oyster-shaped morsel of meat in fowl's back; ~-*bank, -bed,* part of sea-bottom where oysters breed or are bred; ~-*bar,* counter where oysters are served; ~-*catcher,* maritime wading-bird (*Haematopus*) with black-and-white or black plumage and brilliant red feet and beak; ~-*farm,* sea-bottom used for breeding oysters; ~-*knife,* knife of shape adapted for opening oysters.
oz. *abbrev.* Ounce(s).
O′zark Mou′ntains (ō-, -tĭnz). (also *Ozarks*) Group of highlands between Arkansas and Missouri rivers, in States of Missouri, Arkansas, Oklahoma, Kansas, and Illinois, U.S.

ozŏ′cerīte, -k- *n.* Wax-like brownish-yellow aromatic fossil resin occurring in bituminous shales etc. and used for candles, insulators, etc.
ō′zōne *n.* 1. Allotropic form of oxygen with three atoms to the molecule (O_3), a pale-blue gas with a peculiarly pungent smell, formed by action of electric discharge or ultra-violet light, used for sterilizing water and purifying air. 2. (pop.) Invigorating, bracing air, esp. that of the seaside. **ozŏ′nĭc** *adj.*

P

P, p (pē). 16th letter of modern English and 15th of ancient Roman alphabet, corresponding to Gk *pi* (Π, π) and Semitic ꜓, ꜓, and representing a voiceless labial stop; *mind one's P's and Q's,* be careful not to do or say the wrong thing.
P. *abbrev.* Parking (place); pawn.
p. *abbrev.* Page; participle; past; pence, penny; pico-.
p. *abbrev.* Piano.
pa[1] (pah) *n.* (colloq.) Papa.
pa[2] (pah) *n.* Native fort in New Zealand. [Maori]
P.A. *abbrev.* Press Association.
p.a. *abbrev.* Per annum.
Pa. *abbrev.* Pennsylvania.
pa′ă′nga (-ngga) *n.* Tonga dollar, = 100 seniti.
pă′bulum *n.* Food, sustenance.
pă′ca *n.* Spotted cavy (*Cuniculus paca*), a nocturnal rodent of Central and S. America.
pāce[1] *n.* 1. Single step in walking or running; space traversed in this, as vague measure of distance (about 30 in.); space between successive stationary positions of same foot in walking (about 5 ft). 2. Mode of walking or running, gait; any of various gaits of (esp. trained) horse, etc.; amble; *put (person) through his* ~*s,* test his qualities in action, etc. 3. Speed in walking or running; rate of progression; *go the* ~, go at great speed; (fig.) indulge in dissipation; *keep* ~, advance at equal rate *with*; *pa′cemaker,* rider, runner, etc., who sets pace for another in race etc.; electrical device for stimulating the heart muscle. ~ *v.* Walk with slow or regular pace; traverse thus; measure (distance) by pacing; (of horse) amble; set pace for (rider, runner, etc.). **pā′cer** *n.* (esp.) Horse that paces.
pā′cĕ[2] *prep.* By leave of, with all deference to. [L, abl. of *pax* peace].
pacha: see PASHA.

pă′chӯdĕrm (-k-) *n.* Large thick-skinned mammal esp. elephant or rhinoceros. **păchӯdĕr′matous** *adj.*
paci′fĭc[1] *adj.* Tending to peace, of peaceful disposition. **paci′fĭcally** *adv.*
Paci′fĭc[2] *adj.* Of, adjoining, the Pacific Ocean; ~ *Ocean,* largest body of water on earth's surface, bounded by N. and S. America and Asia and Australia. ~ *n.* Pacific Ocean. [so named by Magellan, its first European navigator, because he experienced calm weather there]
păcĭfĭcā′tion *n.* Pacifying; being pacified. **paci′fĭcatorӯ** (or pă-, -kăt-) *adj.*
pă′cifism *n.* (Support of) policy of avoiding or abolishing war by use of arbitration in settling international disputes. **pă′cĭfist** *n.*
pă′cify *v.t.* Make calm or quiet; reduce (country etc.) to state of peace.
păck *n.* 1. Bundle of things wrapped up or tied together for carrying esp. on shoulders or back; (commerc.) method of packing for the market. 2. Set, lot (usu. derog., as ~ *of fools, lies,* etc.); group of Cub Scouts or Brownies; large quantity. 3. Number of animals or birds kept together or naturally congregating; group. 4. (Rugby footb.) Forwards of team. 5. Set of playing-cards. 6. Large area of large pieces of floating ice (~-*ice*) driven or packed together into nearly continuous mass. 7. Quantity of fish, fruit, etc., packed in a season etc. 8. (med.) Swathing of body or part of it in wet sheet, blanket, etc.; sheet etc. so used; wad of gauze etc. for packing an orifice; *ice* ~, compress of crushed ice. 9. Substance (esp. paste) applied to skin or hair as cosmetic treatment; treatment using this. 10. ~ *drill,* military punishment of marching up and down in full marching order; ~-*horse,* horse for carrying packs; *pa′ckman,* pedlar; ~-*saddle,* one adapted for supporting packs; *pa′ckthread,* stout thread for sewing or tying up packs. ~ *v.* 1. Put (things) together into bundle, box, bag, etc., for transport or storing (freq. ~ *up,* esp. abs.); (of things) admit of being packed *well, easily,* etc. 2. Prepare and put up (meat, fruit, etc.) in tins etc. for preservation. 3. Put closely together; crowd together; form into pack. 4. Cover (thing) with something pressed or wedged tightly round; (med.) wrap (body etc.) tightly in wet cloth. 5. Fill (bag, box, etc.) with clothes etc.; cram (space etc. *with*); load (beast) with pack. 6. Take oneself off with one's belongings; *send* (person) *packing,* dismiss him summarily; ~ (person) *off,* send him away; ~ *up,* (slang) retire from fight, contest, etc.; cease to function. 7. [prob. different wd] Select (jury etc.) so as to secure partial decision. 8. *packing-case,* case or framework for packing goods; *packing-needle,* large needle for sewing up packages in stout cloth.
pă′ckaġe *n.* Bundle of things packed, parcel; box etc. in which goods are packed; ~ *deal,* (colloq.) inclusive bargain or transaction; ~ *tour,* planned tour at a fixed inclusive price. ~ *v.t.* (commerc.) Make up into, enclose in, a package.
pă′cker *n.* (esp.) One who packs meat, fruit, etc., for market; machine for packing.
pă′ckĕt *n.* 1. Small package; (colloq.) considerable sum of money (esp. lost or won); *catch, get, stop a* ~, (colloq.) be (mortally) hit by bullet etc. 2. (also ~-*boat*) Mail-boat.
păct *n.* Agreement, covenant.
păd[1] *n.* 1. (slang) Road. 2. Easy-paced horse. ~ *v.* Tramp along (road etc.) on foot; travel on

[630]

foot; walk with dull-sounding steps. **păd²** *n.* Soft stuffed saddle without tree; part of double harness to which girths are attached; piece of soft stuff used to raise surface, diminish jarring, absorb fluid, etc.; guard for parts of body in cricket etc.; number of sheets of blotting-, writing-, or drawing-paper fastened together at edge; fleshy cushion forming sole of foot in some quadrupeds; paw of fox, hare, etc.; water-lily leaf; socket of brace, tool-handle; flat surface for helicopter take-off, rocket launching, etc.; (slang) bed, lodging. ~ *v.t.* Furnish with a pad, stuff; fill out (sentence etc.) with superfluous words; *padded cell*, room with padded walls in mental hospital. **pă'dding** *n.* Substance of pad, e.g. felt, hair, kapok, etc.; superfluous words in sentence etc.
păd³ *n.* Open pannier used as measure of fruit etc.
pă'ddle *n.* 1. Small spade-like implement with a long handle. 2. Short oar with blade at one or both ends used without rowlock; one of the boards fitted round circumference of paddle-wheel; paddle-shaped instrument; action or spell of paddling; (zool.) fin or flipper; ~-*wheel*, wheel for propelling ship, with boards round and at right angles to the circumference so as to press backward against the water. ~ *v.* Move on water, propel canoe, by means of paddles; row gently; walk with bare feet in shallow water; dabble.
pă'ddock¹ *n.* Small field, esp. as part of stud farm; enclosure near race-course, where horses are assembled before race; similar enclosure at motor-racing track; (Austral. & N.Z.) field (of any size).
pă'ddock² *n.* (archaic, dial.) Frog or toad.
pă'ddy¹ *n.* Rice in the straw or in the husk; rice-field. [Malay *padi*]
pă'ddy², **pă'ddywhăck** *ns.* (colloq.) Rage, fit of temper. [f. PADDY³]
Pă'ddy³. (Nickname for) Irishman. [pet-form of *Padraig* Patrick]
Pădere'wski (-rĕf-), Ignacy Jan (1860–1941). Polish pianist and statesman; prime minister of Poland 1919–21 and 1940–1.
pă'dlŏck *n.* Detachable lock hanging by hinged or pivoted hoop on object fastened. ~ *v.t.* Secure with padlock.
pa'dre (pah'drā) *n.* (nav., mil., & air force slang). Chaplain. [Port. etc. = 'father', 'priest']
padrō'nè *n.* Master of Mediterranean trading-vessel; Italian employer of street musicians, begging-children, etc.; proprietor of Italian inn.
Pă'dŭa. (It. *Padova*) City of NE. Italy. **Pă'dŭan** *adj.* & *n.*

pă'dŭasoy *n.* Strong corded silk fabric much worn in 18th c.
pae'an *n.* Song of praise or thanksgiving; shout or song of triumph, joy, or exultation. [Gk *paian* hymn to Apollo under name of Paian]
pae'derasty, **pĕd-** *n.* SODOMY.
paediă'tric *adj.* Of diseases of children. **paediă'trics** *n.* Study of children's diseases. **paediatrī'cian** (-shan) *n.* Specialist in paediatrics.
paĕ'lla (pah-) *n.* Spanish dish of rice with chicken, vegetables, etc., seasoned with saffron.
pae'on *n.* Metrical foot of three short syllables and one long, the latter occurring in any position in the group. **paeŏ'nic** *adj.*
pā'gan *n.* & *adj.* Heathen, esp. in antiquity. **pā'ganism** *n.* **pā'ganize** *v.*
Păgani'ni (-nē-), Niccolo (1782–1840). Italian violin virtuoso.
pāge¹ *n.* Boy, usu. in livery, employed (esp. in hotels) to attend to door, go on errands, etc. (also ~-*boy*); boy employed as personal attendant of person of rank; small boy attending bride at wedding; (hist.) boy in training for knighthood and attached to knight's service; ~ *of honour*, *of the presence*, etc., officers of royal household. ~ *v.t.* (orig. U.S.) Communicate with by means of page; call name of (person sought) in public rooms of hotel etc.
pāge² *n.* One side of leaf of book etc. ~ *v.t.* Put consecutive numbers on pages of (book etc.).
pă'geant (-jent) *n.* Brilliant spectacle, esp. procession, arranged for effect; spectacular representation of past history of place etc.; (hist.) tableau, allegorical device, etc., on fixed stage or moving car; (fig.) empty or specious show. **pă'geantry** *n.* Splendid display; empty show.
pă'ginal *adj.* Of pages; page for page. **pă'ginary** *adj.*
pă'gināte *v.t.* Page (book etc.). **păginā'tion** *n.*
pagō'da *n.* Temple or sacred building in India, China, etc., esp. tower, usu. of pyramidal form, built over relics of Buddha or a saint; ornamental imitation of this; (hist.) gold coin of S. India. ~-*tree*, one of several kinds of Chinese, Japanese, and Indian trees, growing in pagoda form.
pagūr'ian *adj.* Of hermit-crabs. ~ *n.* Hermit-crab.
pah *int.* Exclamation of disgust.
Pahang (pahŭ'ng). State of Malaysia through which flows the river Pahang; capital, Kuantan.
Pah'lavī, **Peh'levī** (pāl-). *n.* Iranian language, the ancestor of modern Persian, used in Persia from *c* 3rd c. onwards, distinguished from other dialects of Middle Persian chiefly by its script, which has some Aramaic characters. [Pers. *Pahlav* Parthia]
paid *adj.*: see PAY¹; (esp.)

put ~ *to*, (colloq.) settle the affairs of, finish off; ~-*up capital*, that part of the subscribed capital of an undertaking which has actually been paid.
pail *n.* 1. Bucket. 2. (U.S.; also *dinner-*~) Vessel in which workman's midday meal etc. is carried.
paillasse (pălyă's *or* pă'-) *n.* = PALLIASSE.
paillette (pălyĕ't) *n.* Piece of bright metal used in enamel painting; spangle.
pain *n.* 1. Sensation experienced when the body is injured, or afflicted by certain diseases; suffering, distress, of body or mind; (pl.) labour pains of childbirth. 2. (pl.) Trouble taken; *pai'nstaking*, careful, industrious. 3. Punishment (now only in ~s *and penalties*, *on* or *under* ~ *of*). ~ *v.t.* Inflict pain upon. **pai'nful** *adj.* **pai'nfully** *adv.* **pai'nfulness** *n.* **pai'nlĕss** *adj.* **pai'nlĕssly** *adv.* **pai'nlĕssness** *n.*
Paine, Thomas (1737–1809). English political theorist; advocated independence of Amer. colonies in his 'Common Sense' (1776) and other works; wrote 'The Rights of Man' (1791–2); associated himself with the French Revolutionists and was made a member of the National Convention.
paint *n.* Solid colouring-matter, suspended in a liquid vehicle used to impart colour to a surface; something, esp. medicament, put

CHINESE PAGODA

[631]

on like paint with brush; cosmetic colouring-matter applied to face etc. ~ *v.t.* 1. Portray, represent, in colours; adorn (wall etc.) with painting; (fig.) represent in words vividly as by painting. 2. Cover surface of with paint, apply paint of specified colour to; ~ *the town red*, cause commotion by riotous spree etc. 3. Apply liquid or cosmetic to (skin, face, etc.). 4. *painted lady*, orange-red butterfly (*Vanessa cardui*) with black and white spots. **pai′nting** *n.*

pai′nter[1] *n.* 1. One who paints pictures. 2. Workman who coats woodwork etc. with paint; ~*'s colic*, form of colic to which painters who work with lead paints are liable. **pai′nterly** *adj.* (transl. of Ger. *malerisch*) (of work of art) Executed with attention to light and shade, mass, tone, etc., rather than line (opp. LINEAR).

pai′nter[2] *n.* Rope attached to bow of boat for making it fast to ship, stake, etc. (ill. BOAT).

pair *n.* 1. Set of two, couple (esp. of things that usu. exist or are used in couples); article consisting of two corresponding parts not used separately; second member of a pair; ~ *royal*, set of 3 cards of same denomination or of 3 dice turning up same number. 2. Engaged or married couple; mated couple of animals; two horses harnessed together. 3. (parl.) Two voters on opposite sides absenting themselves from division by mutual agreement; person willing to act thus. 4. Flight (*of stairs, steps*). ~ *v.* Arrange, be arranged, in couples; unite in love or marriage; mate; unite (*with* one of opposite sex); ~ *off*, put two by two; go off in pairs; (parl.) make a pair; (colloq.) marry (*with*).

pai′sa (pī-) *n.* (pl. *paise* pr. -sā). $\frac{1}{100}$ of a rupee in India, Pakistan, and Bangladesh.

Pai′sley (-zlĭ). Town of Strathclyde near Glasgow; ~ *shawl*, shawl in soft bright colours, orig. made at Paisley; ~ *pattern*, characteristic pattern of such shawl.

pajamas: see PYJAMAS.

Pakista′n (pah-, -ahn). Muslim State in SE. Asia, formed in 1947 from regions where Muslims predominated; since 1956 an independent republic, member State of the Commonwealth until 1972; capital, Islamabad. **Pakista′nī** *adj. & n.* [earlier *Pakstan*, f. initials of *P*unjab, *A*fghan Frontier, *K*ashmir, *S*ind, and last three letters of *Baluchistan*]

păl *n.* (slang) Comrade, mate. ~ *v.i.* (usu. ~ *up*) Associate, make friends (*with*). [Engl. Gipsy *pal* brother, mate]

pă′lace *n.* Official residence of sovereign, archbishop, or bishop; stately mansion; spacious building for entertainment, refreshment, etc. [L *Palatium* PALATINE HILL, Augustus's house built on it]

pă′ladin *n.* Any of the Twelve Peers of Charlemagne's court, of whom the Count Palatine was the chief; knight errant.

Pă′laeocēne *adj. & n.* (geol.) (Of) the earliest epoch of the Tertiary period (ill. GEOLOGY).

Pă′laeogēne *adj. & n.* (geol.) (Of) the earlier part or system of the Cainozoic era, including the Palaeocene, Eocene, and Oligocene epochs.

pălaeo′graphy *n.* Study of ancient writing and inscriptions. **pălaeo′grapher** *n.* **păleogră′phic** *adj.*

pălaeoli′thic *adj.* Of the earlier Stone Age (as contrasted with NEOLITHIC), characterized by chipped stone implements and weapons.

pălaeŏntŏ′logў *n.* Study of extinct animals and plants. **pălaeŏntŏ′logist** *n.*

Pălaeozō′ic *adj. & n.* (geol.) (Of) the era or group or systems containing ancient forms of life, including the periods from Cambrian to Permian (ill. GEOLOGY).

palae′stra, palĕ′stra *n.* (Gk antiq.) Wrestling-school, gymnasium.

palamino: see PALOMINO.

pălankee′n, pălanqui′n (-nkēn) *n.* Covered litter for one, in India etc., carried usu. by four or six men. [Malay *palangki*]

pă′latable *adj.* Pleasant to the taste; (fig.) agreeable to the mind. **pă′latably** *adv.*

pă′latal *adj.* Of the palate; (of sound) produced by placing tongue against or near the palate, usu. hard palate. ~ *n.* Palatal sound. **pă′latalize** *v.t.* Make palatal, modify into palatal sound.

pă′late *n.* 1. Roof of the mouth in vertebrates, partly bony and partly fleshy structure separating cavity of mouth from that of nose (ill. HEAD); *bony* or *hard* ~, front part of this; *soft* ~, back part of this, pendulous fold of musculomembranous tissue separating mouth-cavity from pharynx. 2. Sense of taste; mental taste, liking.

pală′tial (-shal) *adj.* Like a palace; splendid.

pală′tinate *n.* Territory under a palatine; (*Rhine*) *P*~ (hist., Ger. *Pfalz*), State under rule of Count Palatine of the Rhine, constituting (with *Upper P*~) an electorate of the Holy Roman Empire, orig. including district immediately dependent on Aachen, later comprising two districts higher up Rhine, now part of *Rhineland-P*~, a State of the Federal Republic of Germany.

pă′latine[1] *adj.* 1. Of a palace; palatial. 2. Possessing royal privileges, having jurisdiction (within the territory) such as elsewhere belongs to the sovereign alone. 3. Of or belonging to a count or earl palatine; *count* ~, orig. in the later Roman Empire a count (*comes*) attached to the imperial palace and having supreme judicial authority in certain causes; under the German emperors, a count (Ger. *Pfalzgraf*) having supreme jurisdiction in his fief; in Engl. hist., an *earl* ~, the proprietor of a county palatine, now applied to the earldom of Chester and duchy of Lancaster, dignities which are attached to the Crown; *county* ~, in England, county of which the earl had orig. royal privileges, with exclusive jurisdiction (now Cheshire and Lancashire, formerly also Durham, Pembroke, Ely, etc.); *earl* ~: see above. ~ *n.* Office of imperial palace; lord having sovereign power over province or dependency of empire or realm; (Engl. hist.) earl palatine; *P*~, PALATINE HILL.

pă′latine[2] *adj.* Of the palate. ~ *n.* Either of two bones forming hard palate.

Pă′latine Hill. One of the seven hills of Rome, that on which the first Roman settlement was made; later, site of imperial palaces.

pala′ver (-lah-) *n.* Conference, discussion, esp. in tribal custom; profuse or idle talk. ~ *v.i.* Engage in palaver.

pāle[1] *n.* 1. Pointed piece of wood for fence etc., stake. 2. Boundary; enclosed place; *the P*~, (hist.) part of Ireland under English jurisdiction. 3. (her.) Vertical stripe (usu. ⅓ of breadth) in middle of shield (ill. HERALDRY); (*party*) *per* ~, (of shield) divided by vertical line through the middle.

pāle[2] *adj.* (of person or complexion) Of whitish or ashen appearance; (of colours) faint; faintly coloured; of faint lustre, dim; *pa′leface*, supposed N. Amer. Ind. name for white man. **pā′lelў** *adv.* **pā′lenĕss** *n.* **pāle** *v.* Grow or make pale; (fig.) become pale in comparison (usu. *before* or *beside*).

pā′lĕa *n.* (pl. *-eae*). 1. (bot.) Chaff-like bract or scale, esp. one of the inner bracts enclosing the stamens and pistil in the flower of grasses (ill. GRASS). 2. (ornith.) Wattle, dewlap.

Pă′lĕstine. Former name of country of Asia at E. end of Mediterranean, now divided between ISRAEL and JORDAN; ancient home of the Jews and the Holy Land of Christendom; it was conquered by the Romans, 65 B.C., and by Arabs, A.D. 634; thenceforward, except when ruled by Crusaders (1098–1187), it remained under Muslim dominion until the defeat of Turkish and German forces by the British at Megiddo, 1917; under British mandate, 1923–48. **Pălĕsti′nian** *adj. & n.*

palestra: see PALAESTRA.

Pălĕstri′na (-rē-), Giovanni

pă′letot (-etō) *n.* (19th c.) Loose outer garment for man or woman (ill. COAT).

pă′lĕtte *n.* Artist's thin usu. oval or rectangular board or plate, with hole for thumb, for arranging and mixing colours on; range of colours used by particular artist or on particular occasion; ∼-*knife*, flexible steel blade with handle for mixing colours, also used for applying them to canvas; similar knife used in cooking.

Pā′ley, William (1743–1805). English archdeacon and theologian; author of 'Evidences of Christianity' (1794) and 'Natural Theology' (1802), in which he finds proof of the existence of God in the design apparent in natural phenomena and particularly in the human body.

pa′lfrey (pawl-) *n.* (archaic, poet.) Saddle-horse for ordinary riding, esp. for ladies.

Pā′li (pah-) *n.* Indo-Aryan language spoken in N. India in the 5th–2nd centuries B.C.: as the language of a large part of the Buddhist scriptures it was brought to Sri Lanka and Burma, and, though not spoken there, became the vehicle of a large literature of commentaries and chronicles. [for Sansk. *pāli-bhāsā* (*pāli* canon, *bhāsā* language)]

pă′likar *n.* Member of the band of a Greek or Albanian military chief, esp. during war of Independence (1821–8).

pă′limpsĕst *n.* Parchment or other material used for a second time after the original writing has been erased.

pă′lindrŏme *n. & adj.* (Word, verse, etc.) that reads the same backwards as forwards (e.g. *madam*). **pălindrŏ′mic** *adj.*

pā′ling *n.* (Fence of) pales.

pălingĕ′nĕsis (-nj-) *n.* Regeneration; revival.

pă′linōde *n.* Poem in which author retracts things said in former poem; recantation.

pălisā′de *n.* 1. Fence of pales or of iron railings; (mil.) strong pointed wooden stake, of which a number are fixed deeply in ground in close row as defence. 2. (bot.) Internal tissue of a leaf in which the cells are elongated and arranged in rows resembling a stockade (ill. LEAF). ∼ *v.t.* Furnish, enclose, with palisade.

pā′lish *adj.* Slightly pale.

pall[1] (pawl) *n.* 1. Cloth, usu. of black, purple, or white velvet, spread over coffin, hearse, or tomb; ∼-*bearer,* person holding up corner of pall at funeral. 2. Woollen vestment (now a narrow band passing over shoulders, with short lappets) worn by pope and some metropolitans or archbishops; (fig.) mantle, cloak.

pall[2] (pawl) *v.* Become insipid (now only fig.); satiate, clog.

Pallā′dian *adj.* 1. Of Pallas ATHENE. 2. Of PALLADIO or his style (∼ *window*, ill. WINDOW).

Pallā′dianism *n.* Style, opinions, of the followers of Palladio.

Palladiō (-lah′-). Andrea di Pietro (1508–80), Italian architect of Vicenza, who revived classical Roman styles and had great influence through his 'Four Books of Architecture' (1570), esp. in England on Inigo Jones and others. [It., = 'man of Pallas (Athene)']

pallā′dium[1] *n.* Image of the goddess Pallas in the citadel of Troy, on which the safety of the city was held to depend, reputed to have been brought thence to Rome; safeguard.

pallā′dium[2] *n.* (chem.) Hard silvery-white metallic element of the platinum group; symbol Pd, at. no. 46, at. wt 106·4. [f. the asteroid *Pallas*]

Pă′llas. 1. (Gk myth.) One of the names (of unknown meaning) of ATHENE. 2. (astron.) Second largest of the asteroids.

pă′llĕt[1] *n.* Straw bed; mattress.

pă′llĕt[2] *n.* 1. Flat wooden blade with handle, used by potters etc. 2. Projection on part of a machine, engaging with teeth of wheel and converting reciprocating into rotatory movement, or vice versa (ill. CLOCK[1]). 3. Valve in upper part of wind-chest in organ, admitting wind to groove beneath set of pipes when corresponding key of keyboard is depressed (ill. ORGAN). 4. Portable platform for transporting and storing loads.

pă′llĕt[3] *n.* (her.) Ordinary like PALE[1] but half as long.

pă′lliăsse (*or* -ă′s) *n.* Straw mattress.

pă′lliāte *v.t.* Alleviate (disease) without curing; extenuate, excuse.

pălliā′tion *n.*

pă′lliative *adj. & n.* (Thing) serving to palliate.

pă′llid *adj.* Pale, sickly-looking. **pă′llidly** *adv.* **pă′llidnĕss** *n.*

pă′llium *n.* 1. Man's large rectangular cloak, esp. among Greeks. 2. Archbishop's or Pope's PALL[1]. 3. Integumental fold or mantle of mollusc.

pă′ll-mă′ll (*or* pĕl mĕl) *n.* 16th- and 17th-c. game in which a boxwood ball was driven with a mallet through an iron ring suspended at the end of a long alley. [It. *palla* ball, *maglio* mallet]

Păll Măll (*or* pĕl mĕl). Street in London on site of pall-mall alley, noted for its clubs.

pă′llor *n.* Paleness.

palm[1] (pahm) *n.* 1. Tree or shrub of an order of monocotyledons widely distributed in warm climates, with stem usu. upright and unbranched, head or crown of very large pinnate or fan-shaped leaves, and fruit of various forms; leaf of palm-tree as symbol of excellence; supreme excellence, prize for this. 2. Branch of various trees substituted for palm in northern countries, esp. in celebrating Palm Sunday. 3. ∼-*oil*, oil obtained from various palms; (with pun on PALM[2]) bribe-money; *P∼ Sunday*, Sunday before Easter, on which Christ's entry into Jerusalem is celebrated, freq. with processions in which branches of palm are carried. **palmā′ceous** (-shŭs) *adj.*

palm[2] (pahm) *n.* Part of hand between wrist and fingers, esp. its inner surface; part of glove that covers this; *grease person's* ∼, bribe him. ∼ *v.t.* Impose fraudulently, pass *off* (thing *on* person); conceal (cards, dice, etc.) in hand in sleight-of-hand etc.; bribe.

pă′lmar *adj.* Of, in, the palm of the hand.

pă′lmary *adj.* Bearing the palm, pre-eminent.

pă′lmate, -ātĕd *adjs.* Shaped like open palm or hand.

Palm Beach (pahm). Winter resort in Florida, U.S.; ∼ *suit,* trade-name for man's suit of lightweight fabric of cotton and wool or mohair.

pa′lmer (pahm-) *n.* 1. Pilgrim who had returned from Holy Land with palm branch or leaf; itinerant monk under vow of poverty. 2. (also ∼-*worm*) One of various kinds of destructive hairy-caterpillars of migratory or wandering habits; hairy artificial fly.

Pa′lmerston (pahm-), Henry John Temple, 3rd Viscount (1784–1865). British statesman; foreign minister for many years; prime minister 1855–8, 1859–65.

pălmĕ′tte *n.* Ornament somewhat like palm-leaf.

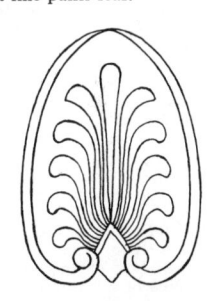

PALMETTE

pălmĕ′ttō *n.* Any of various small species of palms, esp. dwarf fan-palm (*Chamaerops humilis*) of S. Europe and N. Africa, and cabbage palmetto (*Sabal palmetto*) of south-eastern U.S.

pă′lmipĕd, -pēde *n. & adj.* Web-footed (bird).

pa′lmistry (pahm-) *n.* Art or practice of telling character or fortunes from the lines etc. in palm of hand. **pa′lmist** *n.*

palmy (pah′mĭ) *adj.* Of, like,

[633]

abounding in, palms; triumphant, flourishing (esp. in ~ *days*).
pălmy̆r'a¹ *n*. Species of palm (*Borassus flabellifer*) grown in India and Sri Lanka with fan-shaped leaves used for matting etc.
Pălmy̆r'a². (Aram. *Tadmor*) Ancient city at an oasis in the Syrian Desert on the caravan route from Damascus to the Euphrates; prosperous under the Roman Empire but destroyed in 3rd c. A.D. **Pălmy̆r'ēne** *adj. & n*.
pălomi'nō, păla- (-mē-) *n*. Golden-sand-coloured horse with white mane and tail.
pălp *n*. (also *pa'lpus*, pl. *-pī*) Jointed sense-organ in insects etc., feeler (ill. INSECT). **pă'lpal** *adj*.
pă'lpable *adj*. That can be touched or felt; readily perceived by senses or mind. **pălpabĭ'lĭty̆** *n*.
pă'lpably̆ *adv*.
pă'lpāte *v.t*. Examine by touch, handle, esp. in medical examination. **pălpā'tion** *n*.
pă'lpēbral *adj*. Of the eyelids.
pă'lpĭtāte *v.i*. Pulsate, throb; tremble. **pălpĭtā'tion** *n*. Throbbing; increased activity of heart due to exertion, agitation, or disease.
pa'lsgräve (pawlz-) *n*. German count PALATINE¹.
pa'lstave (pawl- *or* pŏl-) *n*. (archaeol.) Metal celt shaped to fit into split handle (instead of having socket into which handle fits; ill. CELT²).
palsy (paw'lzĭ *or* pŏl-) *n*. Paralysis (also fig.); *cerebral ~*, condition of weakness, imperfect control of movement, and spasticity, following damage to brain at birth. *~ v.t.* Paralyse.
pa'lter (pawl- *or* pŏl-) *v.i*. Shuffle, equivocate; haggle; trifle.
pa'ltry̆ (pawl- *or* pŏl-) *adj*. Worthless, petty, contemptible. **pa'ltrĭnèss** *n*.
palū'dal (*or* pă'-) *adj*. Of a marsh; malarial.
palū'stral, palū'strīne *adjs*. Of, inhabiting, marshes.
pā'ly̆ *adj*. (her.) Divided by vertical stripes (ill. HERALDRY).
păm *n*. Knave of clubs, esp. in five-card loo.
Pamir', Pamir's (-ēr, -ērz). Mountain system of central Asia.
pă'mpas *n.pl*. Vast treeless grassy plains of S. America south of the Amazon, esp. great plain of Argentina stretching from Atlantic coast to Andes, and from Rio Colorado to Gran Chaco; *~ grass*, gigantic grass (*Cortaderia selloana*) with silvery-coloured silky panicles on stalks sometimes 12 or 14 ft high, introduced into European gardens from S. America. [Quechua *pampa* plain]
pă'mper *v.t*. Over-indulge.
pă'mphlĕt *n*. Small unbound treatise, esp. on subject of current interest. **pămphlĕteer'** *n*. Writer of pamphlets. *~ v.i*. write pamphlets. [prob. f. *Pamphilet, Panflet*,

familiar name of 12th-c. Latin amatory poem or comedy 'Pamphilus, seu de Amore']
Pămphy̆'lia. Ancient region of S. Asia Minor. **Pămphy̆'lian** *adj. & n*.
păn¹ *n*. 1. Metal or earthenware vessel, usu. shallow and freq. open, for domestic purposes; pan-like vessel in which substances are heated etc.; contents of pan, panful. 2. Pan-shaped depression or concavity of any vessel or structure; part of lock that held priming in obsolete types of gun (ill. MUSKET). 3. Hollow in ground, esp. salt-pan. 4. Hard substratum of soil, more or less impervious to moisture. *~ v. ~ off, out*, wash (gold-bearing gravel) in pan; *~ out*, yield gold, (fig.) succeed, work (*well* etc.).
pan² (pahn) *n*. Betel-leaf; combination of this with areca-nut etc. for chewing. [Hind. *pān*]
păn³ *v*. (cinemat.) Pivot (camera) to obtain panoramic effect or follow moving object; (of camera) be pivoted thus.
Păn⁴. (Gk myth.) God of flocks and shepherds; orig. and chiefly an Arcadian deity, represented with the horns, ears, and legs of a goat; he invented the musical pipe (PAN-PIPE) and was reputed to cause sudden groundless fear such as that felt by travellers in remote and desolate places.
păn- *prefix*. All.
pănacē'a *n*. Universal remedy.
panā'che (-sh *or* -ahsh) *n*. Tuft, plume, of feathers, esp. as headdress or on helmet; (fig.) display, swagger.
pana'da (-nah-) *n*. 1. Dish of bread boiled to pulp and flavoured with cinnamon, sugar, etc. 2. Thick mixture of flour cooked with butter and milk, used esp. for binding together other ingredients.
păn-A'frican (ă-) *adj*. Of, for, all Africans.
Pănama¹ (-mah'). Republic of Central and S. America, lying between Costa Rica and Colombia; its capital city, at Pacific end of Panama Canal; *~ Canal*, canal connecting Atlantic and Pacific Oceans through narrow isthmus of Panama, built between 1882 and 1914, and under the control of the U.S.
pănama² (-mah') *n*. (also *~ hat*) Fine soft plaited hat made from undeveloped leaves of stemless screw-pine (*Carludovica palmata*) of tropical S. America, or an imitation of this.
păn-Amĕ'rican *adj*. Of all States of N. and S. America; of all Americans.
pă'ncāke (-nk-) *n*. Thin flat cake of batter fried in pan; *flat as a ~*, quite flat; *P~ Day*, Shrove Tuesday, from practice of eating pancakes on that day; *~ landing*, (slang) landing of aircraft without use of undercarriage; *~ make-up*, make-up in cake form.

~ v.i. (slang) Make a pancake landing.
Pă'nchĕn La'ma (lah-). = TASHI LAMA.
pănchromă'tĭc (-k-) *adj*. (phot.) Equally sensitive to all colours of spectrum, representing all colours in proper intensities.
păncră'tĭc *adj*. 1. Of the pancratium. 2. (of eyepiece) Capable of adjustment to many degrees of power. **păncrā'tĭum** *n*. (Gk antiq.) Athletic contest combining wrestling and boxing.
pă'ncrĕăs *n*. Gland near stomach discharging a digestive secretion (*pancreatic juice*) through ducts into duodenum, and also producing INSULIN which it passes directly into the blood-stream (ill. ABDOMEN). **păncrĕă'tĭc** *adj*.
pă'nda *n*. Raccoon-like animal (*Ailurus fulgens*) of SE. Himalayas, with reddish-brown fur and long bushy ring-marked tail; *giant ~*, large rare bear-like black-and-white mammal (*Ailuropoda melanoleuca*) of E. Tibet and Szechuan; *~ car*, police patrol car with broad stripe on sides and roof.
Pă'ndarus. (Gk legend) One of the Trojan leaders; in the medieval legend of Troilus and Cressida, Cressida's uncle, who acted as go-between for the lovers.
Pănde'an *adj*. Of PAN⁴.
pă'ndĕct *n*. (usu. pl.) Compendium in fifty books of Roman civil law made by order of Justinian in 6th c.; complete body of laws.
păndĕ'mĭc *adj. & n*. (Disease, usu. infectious) of world-wide distribution.
păndĕmō'nium *n*. Abode of all demons; place of lawless violence or uproar; utter confusion. [wd formed by Milton]
pă'nder *n*. Go-between in amorous intrigues, procurer; one who ministers to evil designs. *~ v.* Minister (*to* base passions, evil designs) (also fig.); act as pander to. [f. PANDARUS]
P. & O. *abbrev*. Peninsular & Oriental (Steamship Co.).
păndŏr'a¹, păndŏr'e *n*. Wire-stringed musical instrument of cither type.
Păndŏr'a². (Gk myth.) First woman, made by Hephaestus at the order of Zeus to punish the human race because PROMETHEUS had stolen fire from heaven for their use; she became wife of Epimetheus, brother of Prometheus, and from a box (*~'s box*) given her by Zeus she let loose all the evils that afflict mankind, hope alone remaining in the bottom of the box.
pă'ndour (-oor), **pă'ndoor** *n*. (pl.) Force of rapacious and brutal soldiers raised by Austria against the Turks in 18th c.
pāne¹ *n*. Single sheet of glass in compartment of window (ill. WINDOW); rectangular division of

chequered pattern etc. **pā'nelĕss** *adj.*

pāne² *n.* Pointed, edged, or ball-shaped end of hammer opposite face (ill. HAMMER).

pănĕgy̆'rĭc *n.* & *adj.* Laudatory (discourse). **pănĕgy̆'rĭcal** *adj.*

pă'nĕgy̆rīze *v.t.* Speak, write, in praise of, eulogize. **pănĕgy̆'rĭst** *n.*

pă'nel *n.* 1. Stuffed lining of saddle; kind of saddle, usu. a pad without framework. 2. Slip of parchment, esp. that on which sheriff entered names of jurors; list of jurymen, jury; (Sc. law) person(s) indicted, accused; *on the* ~, on his trial. 3. (hist.) List of doctors registered in a district as accepting patients under National Health Insurance Act (1913); *on the* ~, (of doctor) so registered; (of patient) under the care of such doctor. 4. Group of people gathered esp. as experts, to hold discussion, make judgement, etc. 5. Distinct section, esp. of surface, as of wainscot, door, etc., often sunk below or raised above general level (ill. WAINSCOT); strip of material in dress etc. ~ *v.t.* Saddle (beast) with panel; fit (wall, door, etc.) with panels; ornament (dress etc.) with panels. **pă'nelling** *n.*

păng *n.* Shooting pain; sudden sharp mental pain.

păngō'lĭn (-ngg-) *n.* Scaly ant-eater, large mammal of genus *Manis* (order Pholidota), of tropical Asia and Africa (ill. ANT-eater). [Malay *penggoling* roller]

pă'nhăndle *n.* Handle of pan; (U.S.) narrow prolongation of State or territory extending between two others. ~ *v.* (U.S. slang) Beg. **pă'nhăndler** *n.* (U.S. slang) Beggar.

păn-Hĕ'llēnĭsm *n.* Political union of all Greeks. **păn-Hellĕ'nĭc** *adj.*

pă'nĭc¹ *n.* (also ~ *grass*) Grass of genus *Panicum* including Italian millet, freq. cultivated as cereal grain.

pă'nĭc² *adj.* (of terror) Unreasoning, excessive. ~ *n.* Infectious fright; sudden general alarm leading to hasty measures. ~ *v.* Affect, be affected, with panic. **pă'nĭcky̆** *adj.* [Gk *panikos* of PAN⁴, reputed to cause panic]

pă'nĭcle *n.* (bot.) Compound inflorescence in which some pedicels branch again or repeatedly, forming loose irregular cluster, as in oats (ill. INFLORESCENCE).

Panjabi: see PUNJABI.

pănjă'ndrum *n.* Mock title of exalted personage; pompous official or pretender. [app. invented by S. Foote, 1720–77, in a piece of nonsense verse]

Pă'nkhŭrst, Mrs Emmeline (1858–1928). English leader of militant suffragism.

pă'nnage *n.* (Right of, payment for) pasturage of swine; acorns, beech-mast, etc., as food for swine.

pănne *n.* Soft long-napped dress-material resembling velvet.

pă'nnier *n.* 1. Basket, esp. one of those carried, usu. in pairs, by beast of burden or on the shoulders. 2. Frame distending woman's skirt at the hips, part of skirt looped up round hips.

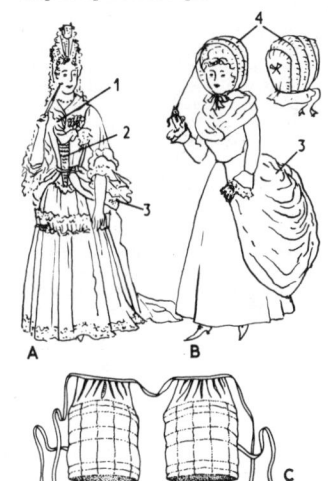

PANNIERS
A. *c* 1693. B. *c* 1780.
C. LINEN PANNIERS STIFFENED WITH CANE *c* 1730–50
1. Steenkirk. 2. Stomacher. 3. Pannier. 4. Calash

pă'nnĭkĭn *n.* Small metal drinking-vessel; its contents.

păn'oply̆ *n.* Complete suit of armour (now usu. fig.). **pă'noplied** (-lĭd) *adj.*

pănŏ'ptĭcon *n.* Bentham's proposed circular prison with cells built round a central well, whence the warders could at all times see the prisoners; (U.S.) circular prison of this type.

pănora'ma (-rah-) *n.* Picture of landscape etc. arranged on inside of cylindrical surface or successively rolled out before spectator; continuous passing scene; unbroken view of surrounding region. **pănorā'mĭc** *adj.* **pănorā'mĭcally̆** *adv.*

pă'n-pīpe(s) *n.* Musical instrument of graduated series of reeds forming scale, with open ends level. [f. PAN⁴]

pă'nsy̆ (-zĭ) *n.* 1. Wild or cultivated plant, *Viola tricolor*, with variously coloured flowers; heartsease. 2. (colloq.) Effeminate man; male homosexual.

pănt *v.* Gasp for breath; yearn (*for, after, to*); throb violently; utter gaspingly. ~ *n.* Gasp, throb.

Păntă'gruĕl (-rōō-). One of the characters of RABELAIS, giant son of Gargantua, represented as a great eater and drinker and an extravagant and satirical humorist. **Pāntagruĕ'lĭan** *adj.*

păntalĕ'ttes (-ts) *n.pl.* Long loose frilled drawers worn by girls *c* 1825–53.

Pāntaloō'n. Venetian character in Italian comedy represented as foolish old man wearing spectacles, pantaloons, and slippers; clown's butt and abettor in harlequinade or pantomime. [It. *Pantalone*, perh. f. San Pantaleone, favourite Venetian saint]

păntaloō'ns (-z) *n.pl.* Garment of breeches and stockings in one piece; tight-fitting trousers fastened with ribbons or buttons below calf, or strap passing under boots (ill. COAT); (chiefly U.S., archaic) trousers.

păntĕ'chnĭcon (-k-) *n.* Furniture warehouse (orig. name of a bazaar in London where all kinds of artistic work were sold); furniture-removing van.

pă'nthĕĭsm *n.* Doctrine that God is everything and everything is God; worship of all the gods. **pă'nthĕĭst** *n.* **pănthĕĭ'stĭc, -ĭcal** *adjs.*

pă'nthĕon(or-ē'on)*n.* 1. Temple dedicated to all the gods, esp. the circular one still standing in Rome, erected in early 2nd c. A.D. prob. on site of an earlier one built by Agrippa. 2. Building (esp. former church of St. Geneviève in Paris) in which illustrious dead are buried or have memorials. 3. Deities of a people collectively.

pă'nther *n.* 1. = LEOPARD, esp. male (now chiefly *black* ~, black form of leopard common in S. India). 2. (U.S.) Puma.

pă'ntĭes (-ĭz) *n.pl.* (colloq.) Short-legged knickers.

pă'ntĭ-hōse (-z) *n.* = TIGHTS, 1.

pă'ntĭle *n.* Roof tile transversely curved to ogee shape, one curve being much larger than the other (ill. ROOF).

păntĭsŏ'cracy̆ *n.* (Southey's and Coleridge's name for) a community in which all are equal and all rule.

Păntŏ'crator *n.* (Representation of) Christ as ruler of universe.

pă'ntogrăph (*or* -ahf) *n.* 1. Instrument of four rods jointed together in parallelogram form, with tracing-points on one free end and one terminal joint, for copying plans etc. on any scale. 2. (elect.)

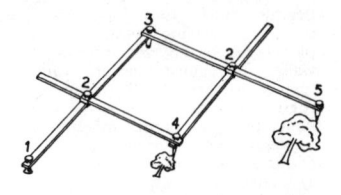

PANTOGRAPH
1. Fixed pivot. 2. Adjustable pivots. 3. Sliding pivot with ball foot. 4. Ivory point. 5. Pencil point

pantomime Device on top of electrically-operated vehicle that conveys current from overhead wires (ill. LOCOMOTIVE). **păntogră'phĭc** adj. **pă'ntomīme** n. 1. (hist.) Roman actor performing in dumb show. 2. Dramatic entertainment now usu. produced at Christmas time and based on a traditional fairy-tale, with singing, dancing, acrobatics, clowning, topical jokes, a transformation scene, and certain stock roles, esp. PRINCIPAL boy and DAME. 3. Dumb show. **păntomĭ'mĭc** adj.

pă'ntrȳ n. Room in which bread and other provisions, or (butler's, housemaid's, ~) plate, table-linen, etc., are kept; pa'ntryman, butler or his assistant.

pănts n.pl. 1. Men's drawers; (colloq.) knickers. 2. (U.S.) Trousers.

pă'nzer (-tser) n. Armour; freq. attrib., as ~ division. [Ger.]

Paolo Veronese: see VERONESE.

păp¹ n. 1. (archaic) Nipple of woman's breast; corresponding part of man. 2. Paps, local name for conical hilltops side by side.

păp² n. Soft or semi-liquid food for infants or invalids; mash, pulp.

papa' (-ah; U.S. pah'-) n. (Child's name for) father.

pā'pacȳ n. Pope's (tenure of) office; papal system.

pā'pal adj. Of the pope or his office; ~ cross, cross with three transoms (ill. CROSS); P~ States, district of central Italy until 1870 subject to the Apostolic See. **pā'pallȳ** adv. **pā'palism, pā'palist** ns.

papāverā'ceous (-shus) adj. Of the poppy family. **papā'verous** adj. Of, like, allied to, the poppy.

papaw' n. 1. Palm-like tree (Carica papaya) of S. America; fruit of this, usu. oblong, of dull orange colour, with thick fleshy rind and numerous black seeds embedded in pulp, used as food. 2. (U.S., also paw'paw) Small N. Amer. tree (Asimina triloba) with purple flowers; oblong edible fruit of this, with bean-like seeds embedded in sweet pulp.

pā'per n. 1. Substance composed of fibres interlaced into a compact web, made from linen and cotton rags, straw, wood, certain grasses, etc., which are macerated into a pulp, dried and pressed into a thin flexible sheet, used for writing, printing, drawing, wrapping up parcels, covering the interior of walls, etc.; substance of similar texture, as that made by wasps for their nests; substance made from paper-pulp, as papier mâché etc. 2. Negotiable documents, e.g. bills of exchange; bank-notes etc. used as currency (opp. coin). 3. (slang) (Persons admitted by) free passes to theatre etc. 4. (pl.) Documents proving person's or ship's identity, standing, etc.; send in one's ~s, resign. 5. Set of questions in examination; essay, dissertation, esp. one read to learned society. 6. Newspaper. 7. Paper used as wrapper or receptacle; small paper parcel; sheet of paper with pins or needles stuck in it. 8. on ~, hypothetically, to judge from statistics, etc.; pa'perback, (book) bound in paper, freq. as cheap reprint; ~-boy, boy who sells or delivers newspapers; ~-chase, cross-country run in which trail of torn-up paper is laid by one or more runners to set a course for the rest; ~-hanger, one who hangs wallpaper; ~-knife, blunt knife for cutting open leaves of book etc.; ~-mill, mill in which paper is made; pa'perweight, small heavy object laid on loose papers to prevent their being scattered; ~-work, clerical work involving keeping of records etc. **pā'perȳ** adj. **pā'per** v.t. Enclose in paper; decorate (wall etc.) with wall-paper; furnish with paper; (slang) fill (theatre etc.) by means of free passes.

Pā'phŏs. Ancient city on W. coast of Cyprus, sanctuary of a goddess identified by Greeks with Aphrodite. **Pā'phian** adj. Of Paphos; of illicit sexual love.

papier mâché (pă'pyä mah'shā). Moulded paper pulp used for boxes, trays, etc. [Fr., = 'chewed paper']

papīlionā'ceous (-yonāshus) adj. (bot.) With corolla like a butterfly (i.e. having a large upper petal, two lateral petals, and two narrow lower petals between these).

papĭ'lla n. Small nipple-like protuberance in a part or organ of the body; (bot.) small fleshy projection on plant. **pă'pillarȳ, pă'pillate, pă'pillōse** adjs.

papĭ'llon (-lyon) n. (Breed of) toy dog with ears suggesting form of butterfly.

pā'pĭst n. Advocate of papal supremacy; Roman Catholic (usu. in hostile sense). **papĭ'stĭc, -ical** adjs. **papĭ'stĭcallȳ** adv. **pā'pĭstrȳ** n.

papōō'se n. N. Amer. Indian young child.

pă'ppus n. (bot.) Downy appendage on seeds of thistles, dandelions, etc. (ill. FRUIT). **păppō'se** adj.

pă'prĭka (or -rē'-) n. Ripe fruit of sweet pepper; red condiment made from this. [Hungarian]

Pă'pūa. Territory of Australia 1905–49, consisting of SE. New Guinea and adjacent islands; merged in administrative union with New Guinea as ~ New Guinea in 1949, under Australian trusteeship; independent 1975; capital, Port Moresby. **Pă'pūan** adj. & n. (Native, inhabitant, language) of New Guinea and other islands of Melanesia; (member) of long-headed dark-skinned race with woolly hair and broad nose.

parachronism

pă'pūla, pă'pūle ns. Pimple; small fleshy projection on plant. **pă'pūlar, pă'pūlōse, pă'pūlous** adjs.

păpȳrā'ceous (-shus) adj. (bot.) Of the nature of, thin as, paper.

papȳr'us n. (pl. -ri). Aquatic plant of sedge family (Cyperus papyrus), with creeping rootstock sending up long stems which bear spikelets of flowers in large clusters; writing material prepared by ancient Egyptians etc. by soaking, pressing, and drying strips of papyrus stem, laying them side by side, and placing similar layers over these at right angles; MS. written on this. **păpȳrŏ'logȳ, păpȳrŏ'logĭst** ns.

pār¹ n. Equality, equal footing; average or normal amount, degree, or condition; (golf) number of strokes which scratch player should require for hole or course, allowing two putts for each green; ~ of exchange, recognized value of one country's currency in terms of another's; above ~, at a premium; at ~, (of stocks etc.) at face value; below ~, at a discount; below the average degree, quality, etc.; not in one's usual health. [L, = 'equal(ity)']

pār² n. (colloq.) Paragraph.

par³: see PARR¹.

Pār'a¹. State in N. Brazil; its capital city (officially Belem), on S. estuary of Amazon; ~ rubber, native rubber obtained from Hevea brasiliensis (and other species), tree growing on banks of Amazon.

pār'a² n. 1/100 of a Yugoslav dinar.

pă'ra³ n. (colloq.) Paragraph.

para- prefix. Beside; beyond; wrong; irregular.

pară'basis n. Part sung by chorus in Greek comedy, addressed to audience in the poet's name.

părabĭō'sĭs n. (zool.) Phenomenon in which individuals are conjoined by common tissues, as in Siamese twins. **părabĭō'tĭc** adj.

pă'rable n. Fictitious narrative used to point a moral or illustrate some spiritual relation or condition; short allegory.

pară'bola n. Plane curve formed by intersection of cone with plane parallel to its side (ill. CONE).

părabŏ'lĭc, -ical adjs. 1. Of, expressed in, a parable. 2. Of, like, a parabola. **părabŏ'licallȳ** adv.

pară'boloid n. Solid some of whose plane sections are parabolas, esp. that generated by revolution of parabola about its axis (~ of revolution, ill. CONE).

Păracĕ'lsus, Philippus Aureolus. Name taken by Theophrastus Bombastus von Hohenheim (1493–1541), German-Swiss physician, alchemist, and astrologer.

pară'chronism (-k-) n. Error in chronology.

[636]

PARACHUTE

pă′rachute (-shoot) *n.* Umbrella-shaped apparatus of silk or other material attached by ropes to person or heavy object falling or being dropped from a height, esp.

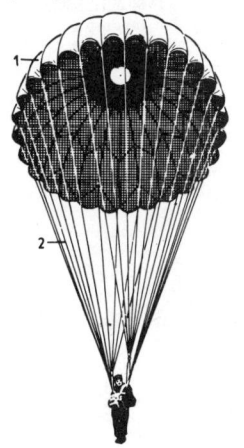

PARACHUTE
1. Canopy. 2. Rigging lines

from aircraft, and designed to be expanded by the air it is falling through (or other means) and by its resulting drag to reduce the speed of falling to some desired limit, usu. one consistent with safety; ~ *troops*, invading troops landing from aircraft by parachute. ~ *v.* Convey, descend, by parachute. **pă′rachutist** *n.*
pă′raclēte *n.* Holy Ghost as advocate or counsellor (John 14: 16, 26, etc.); (occas.) Jesus Christ as advocate (1 John 2: 1).
parā′de *n.* 1. Display, ostentation; serial display or recital of events etc. (e.g. *programme* ~ of the B.B.C.). 2. Muster of troops etc. for inspection, esp. one held regularly at set hours; ground used for this. 3. Public square or promenade. ~ *v.* 1. Assemble (troops etc.) for review or other purpose; march through (streets etc.) with display; march in procession with display. 2. Display ostentatiously.
pă′radigm (-ĭm) *n.* Example, pattern, esp. of inflexion of noun, verb, etc.; **păradigmă′tic** (-ĭg-) *adj.*
pă′radīse *n.* Garden of Eden (also *earthly* ~); heaven; region, state, of supreme bliss; *bird of* ~ : see BIRD. **păradīsā′ical, parādī′sal, părādī′sīac, -īacal** *adjs.* [O. Pers. *pairidaeza* park].
pă′rados *n.* Elevation of earth behind fortified place to secure it from rear attack or fire, esp. mound along back of trench.
pă′radox *n.* Statement contrary to received opinion; seemingly absurd though perhaps really well-founded statement; self-contradictory, essentially absurd or

false, statement; person, thing, conflicting with preconceived notions of what is reasonable or possible. **păradŏ′xĭcal** *adj.* **păradŏ′xĭcally** *adv.* **păradŏxĭcă′lĭty** *n.*
pă′raffin *n.* 1. (usu. ~ *wax*) White tasteless odourless waxy substance, chemically a mixture of higher hydrocarbons, solid at ordinary temperatures and obtained by distillation of petroleum etc., used for making candles, rendering paper waterproof (*waxed paper*), etc.; *liquid* ~, liquid form of petroleum jelly, used as mild laxative. 2. (chem.) Any of a series of saturated hydrocarbons of which methane is the simplest member; paraffin oil; ~ *oil*, mixture of hydrocarbons obtained by distillation of petroleum, used as fuel, illuminant, solvent, etc.; kerosene. [L *parum* little, *affinis* having affinity, referring to the relative unreactivity of the paraffins]
păragŏ′gė *n.* (gram.) Addition of letter or syllable to a word. **păragŏ′gĭc** *adj.*
pă′ragon *n.* 1. Model of excellence, supremely excellent person or thing, model (*of* virtue etc.). 2. Perfect diamond, 100 carats or more. 3. (print.) Large size of type, between great primer and double pica (two-line long primer, 20 point).
pă′ragrăph (*or* -ahf) *n.* Distinct passage or section in book etc., usu. marked by indentation of first line; symbol (usu. ¶) formerly used to mark new paragraph, now as reference mark; detached short item of news etc. in newspaper. ~ *v.t.* Write paragraph about; arrange (article etc.) in paragraphs. **pă′ragrapher, pă′ragraphist** *ns.* **păragră′phic** *adj.*
Pă′raguay (-gwā *or* -gwī). Inland republic of S. America; capital, Asuncion. **Păraguay′an** *adj.* & *n.*
pă′rakeet, pă′rr- *n.* Any of

PARALLELOGRAM

several small esp. long-tailed kinds of parrot. [OF, f. It. *parrochetto* dim. of *parroco* parson, or *parrucchetto* dim. of *parrucca* peruke]
parā′ldėhȳde *n.* Polymer of aldehyde ($C_8H_{12}O_3$), used as a sedative.
părali′psis, -lei′psis (-lĭ-) *n.* Trick of securing emphasis by professing to omit all mention of subject, e.g. *I say nothing of his antecedents, how from youth upwards etc.*
pă′rallăx *n.* Apparent displacement of object, caused by actual change of point of observation; angular amount of this displacement. **părallă′ctic** *adj.*

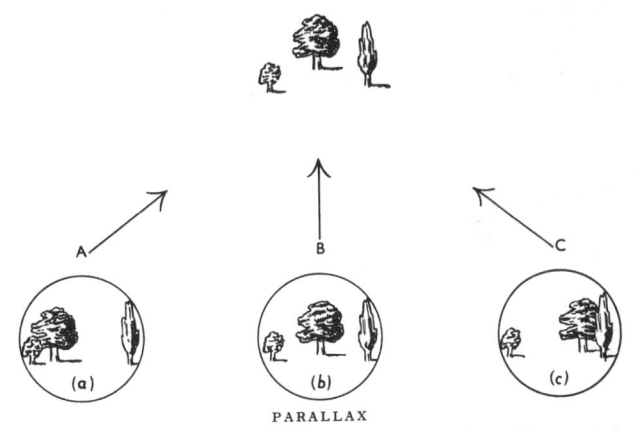

PARALLAX
a, b, c show the appearance of the trees to spectators at *A, B,* and *C* respectively

pă′rallĕl *adj.* (of lines) Continuously equidistant (*to*); precisely similar, analogous, or corresponding; ~ *bars*, pair of horizontal parallel bars supported on posts for gymnastic exercises; ~ *circuit*, (elect.) circuit connecting the same two points as are connected by another circuit (ill. CIRCUIT); ~ *ruler*, two rulers connected by pivoted cross-pieces or single ruler fitted with rollers, for drawing parallel lines. ~ *n.* 1. (also ~ *of latitude*) Each of the parallel circles marking degrees of latitude on earth's surface on globe; line on map corresponding to one of these. 2. Person, thing, precisely analogous to another; comparison. 3. Parallel position. 4. Two parallel lines (||) as reference mark. ~ *v.t.* Represent as similar, compare (*with, to*); find, mention, something parallel or corresponding to; be parallel, correspond, to.
părallĕlĕ′pipĕd (*or* -epī′p-) *n.* Solid contained by parallelograms (ill. PRISM).
pă′rallĕlism *n.* Being parallel; comparison or correspondence of successive passages, esp. in Hebrew poetry.
părallĕ′logrăm *n.* Four-sided rectilineal figure whose opposite

[637]

sides are parallel (ill. QUADRI-LATERAL); ~ *of forces*, (parallelogram illustrating) theorem that if two forces acting at a point be represented in magnitude and direction by two sides of a parallelogram, their resultant is represented by a diagonal drawn from that point.

para'logism *n*. Illogical reasoning, esp. of which reasoner is unconscious; fallacy.

pă'ralyse (-z) *v.t.* Affect with paralysis; render powerless, cripple.

para'lysis *n*. Affection marked by impairment or loss of motor or sensory function of nerves; (fig.) state of utter powerlessness.

păraly'tic *adj. & n*. (Person) affected with paralysis. **paraly'tically** *adv*.

păramăgnĕ'tic *adj.* (of substance, as tungsten, aluminium, manganese, and chromium) Tending to become magnetized in the presence of a magnetic field and lie with its long axis parallel to the field (cf. DIAMAGNETIC). **parama'gnetism** *n*.

paramă'tta *n*. Light dress fabric of merino wool and silk or cotton. [*Paramatta*, town in New South Wales]

para'meter *n*. (math.) Quantity constant in case considered, but varying in different cases.

părami'litary *adj.* Ancillary to or as substitute for armed forces.

pă'ramō *n*. High treeless plateau in tropical S. America.

păramoe'cium (-mē-) *n*. Ciliated freshwater protozoan of genus *P~* (ill. PROTOZOA).

pă'ramount *adj.* Supreme; pre-eminent; superior (*to*). **pă'ramountly** *adv*. **pă'ramountcy** *n*.

pă'ramour (-oor) *n*. Illicit lover of married person.

pa'răng (pah-) *n*. Large heavy Malay sheath-knife.

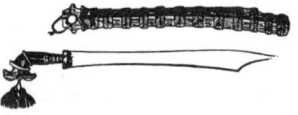

PARANG WITH SCABBARD

păranoi'a *n*. Form of mental illness characterized by systematic delusions. **păranoi'ăc** *adj. & n*.

pă'ranoid *adj.* Resembling, characterized by, paranoia.

pă'rapet *n*. Low wall at edge of balcony, roof, etc., or along sides of bridge etc.; (mil.) defence of earth, stone, etc., to conceal and protect troops, esp. mound along front of trench. **pă'rapĕttĕd** *adj*. Having a parapet.

pă'răph *n*. Flourish after a signature, orig. as precaution against forgery.

păraphernă'lia *n.pl.* Personal belongings; accessories, odds and ends of equipment; (formerly) articles of personal property that law allowed married woman to keep and treat as her own.

pă'raphrāse (-z) *n*. Free rendering or amplification of a passage, expression of its sense in other words; any of a collection of metrical paraphrases of passages of Scripture (esp. psalms) used in Church of Scotland etc. ~ *v.t.* Express meaning of (passage) in other words. **păraphră'stic** *adj.* **păraphră'stically** *adv*.

păraphrē'nia *n*. Variety of schizophrenic mental illness (esp. paranoid form), occurring in later life.

păraplē'gia *n*. Paralysis confined to the lower limbs. **păraplē'gic** *adj. & n*. (Person) affected with paraplegia.

părapsychŏ'logy (-*as*ĭk-) *n*. Study of mental phenomena lying outside the sphere of ordinary psychology; study of psychical phenomena. **părapsychŏlŏ'gical** *adj*.

pă'rasăng *n*. Ancient Persian measure of length (about 3¼ miles).

părasēlē'nē *n*. Bright spot on lunar halo, mock-moon.

pă'rasīte *n*. 1. Interested hanger-on, toady. 2. Animal, plant, living in or upon another and deriving nutriment from it to the detriment of the host; (loosely) plant that climbs about another plant, walls, etc. **părasĭ'tic, -ical** *adjs.* **pă'rasĭtism** *n*. **pă'rasītīze** *v.t.* Infest as a parasite.

părasō'l (or pă'-) *n*. Light umbrella used to give protection from the sun; ~ *pine*: see UMBRELLA pine.

părasympathĕ'tic *adj.* Of that part of the nervous system which consists of fibres connecting with nerve cells grouped within or near the viscera, so called because its peripheral nerves often run alongside those of the sympathetic system.

părasy̆'nthĕsis *n*. (philol.). Derivation from a compound. **părasy̆nthĕ'tic** *adj*.

părată'xis *n*. (gram.) Placing of clauses etc. one after another, without words to indicate co-ordination or subordination. **părătă'ctic** *adj.* **pără tă'ctically** *adv*.

părathȳr'oid *adj.* ~ *gland*, one of four small bodies adjacent to thyroid gland, producing a secretion which maintains the balance between the calcium in the blood and that in the bones. ~ *n*. Parathyroid gland.

pă'ratroōps *n.pl.* Parachute troops. **pă'ratroōper** *n*.

păraty̆'phoid *n*. Form of enteric fever milder than true typhoid and bacteriologically distinguishable from it.

pă'ravāne *n*. Apparatus towed from bows of a ship at a depth regulated by its vanes, with saw-edged jaws for cutting the moorings of submerged mines.

părazō'an *adj. & n*. (Member) of the Parazoa, a division of the animal kingdom comprising aquatic animals (sponges), with 2 layers of cells but little co-ordination between the cells and no nervous system.

păr'boil *v.t.* Boil partially; (fig.) overheat.

păr'bŭckle *n*. Method of using a rope to raise or lower casks and cylindrical objects, the middle being secured at the upper level

PARBUCKLING

and both ends passed under and round the object and then hauled or let slowly out. ~ *v.t.*

păr'cel *n*. 1. (archaic) Part (esp. in *part and* ~); piece of land, esp. as part of estate. 2. Goods etc. wrapped up in single package; ~ *post*, branch of postal service concerned with parcels. 3. (commerc.) Quantity dealt with in one transaction. ~ *adv.* (archaic) Partly; ~ *gilt*, partly gilded, esp. (of cup etc.) with inner surface gilt. ~ *v.t.* 1. Divide (usu. *out*) into portions; make (*up*) into parcel(s). 2. (naut.) Cover (caulked seam) with canvas strips and pitch; wrap (rope) with canvas strips. **păr'celling** *n*. (esp., naut.) Strip of canvas, usu. tarred, for binding round rope.

păr'cenary *n*. Joint heirship. **păr'cener** *n*. Coheir.

părch *v*. Roast slightly; make or become hot and dry.

păr'chment *n*. Skin (strictly, inner part of split skin of sheep) dressed and prepared for writing, painting, etc.; parchment-like skin, esp. husk of coffee-bean; ~ *paper*, thick, strong, specially toughened paper. [LL *pergamena* of PERGAMUM]

părd[1] *n*. (archaic) Leopard.

părd[2], păr'dner *ns*. (U.S. slang) Partner.

păr'don *n*. Forgiveness; (law) remission of legal consequences of crime; courteous forbearance (esp. in *I beg your* ~, formula of apology); (eccles.) indulgence, esp. (*P*~, in Brittany) festival at which this is granted, festival of patron saint.

PARDONER

~ *v.t.* Forgive; make allowance for, excuse. **par'donable** *adj.* **par'donably** *adv.*
par'doner *n.* (hist.) Person licensed to sell pardons or indulgences.
pare *v.t.* Trim (thing) by cutting away irregular parts etc.; cut away skin, rind, etc., of (fruit etc.); shave, cut *off, away* (edges etc.); (fig.) diminish little by little. **par'er, par'ing** *ns.*
parego'ric *n.* Camphorated tincture of opium flavoured with aniseed and benzoic acid; anodyne. ~ *adj.* Soothing.
pare'nchyma (-ngk-) *n.* 1. (anat.) Proper tissue of gland, organ, etc., as dist. from flesh and connective tissue. 2. (bot.) Tissue of cells of about equal length and breadth placed side by side, usu. soft and succulent, found esp. in softer parts of leaves, pulp of fruits, etc. (ill. LEAF). **pare'nchymal, parenchy'matous** *adjs.*
par'ent *n.* Father or mother; forefather; animal, plant, from which others are derived; (fig.) source, origin. **pare'ntal** *adj.* **pare'ntally** *adv.*
par'entage *n.* Descent from parents, lineage.
pare'nthesis *n.* (pl. -*theses*). Word, clause, sentence, inserted into a passage to which it is not grammatically essential, and usu. marked off by brackets, dashes, or commas; (sing. or pl.) round brackets () used for this. **pare'nthesize** *v.t.* Insert as parenthesis; put between marks of parenthesis; **parenthe'tic** *adj.* Of, inserted as a, parenthesis; (fig.) interposed. **parenthe'tically** *adv.*
parer'gon *n.* Ornamental accessory or addition; subordinate or secondary work or business. **parer'gic** *adj.*
pa'resis *n.* Partial paralysis or weakening of muscular power. **pare'tic** *adj.*
par excellence (-lahns). By virtue of special excellence, above all others that may be so called. [Fr.]
par'get *n.* Plaster spread upon wall, ceiling, etc., roughcast; (also *pargeting*) ornamental relief work in plaster. ~ *v.t.* Cover with parget or plaster; adorn with pargeting.
parhe'lion (-lyon) *n.* Spot on solar halo at which light is intensified, mock sun. **parheli'acal, parhe'lic** *adjs.*
pa'riah (-*a*; *or* pari'*a*) *n.* Member of very extensive low caste in S. India; member of low or no caste; (fig.) social outcast; ~-*dog*, yellow vagabond dog of low breed in India etc. [Tamil *paṛaiyar* (hereditary) drummers]
Par'ian *adj.* Of Paros; ~ *marble*, fine-textured white marble obtained from Paros, famous since 6th c. B.C. and much used by sculptors. ~ *n.* Native, inhabitant, of Paros.

pari'etal *adj.* 1. Of the wall of the body or of any of its cavities; ~ *bones*, pair forming part of sides and top of skull (ill. HEAD). 2. (bot.) Of or on the walls of a hollow structure etc.
pa'ri-mutue'l (-rē-) *n.* System of betting, carried on by a mechanical apparatus, in which the winners divide the losers' stakes less a percentage for managerial expenses (see TOTALIZATOR).
pa'ri pa'ssu (pah-, -sōō). With equal pace; simultaneously and equally. [L]
Pa'ris[1]. Capital city of France, on river Seine; *plaster of* ~: see PLASTER; ~ *green*, vivid light-green pigment prepared from arsenic trioxide and copper acetate. [*Parisii*, L name of Gallic tribe which settled there]
Pa'ris[2]. (Gk legend) Son of Priam and Hecuba; as a baby he was left to die because of a prophecy that he would bring destruction upon Troy, but shepherds found him and brought him up; awarded APPLE of discord to Aphrodite, who had offered him the fairest woman in the world; she enabled him to abduct HELEN, thus bringing about the Trojan War in which he was killed and Troy sacked.
Pa'ris[3], Matthew (d. 1259). English chronicler and illuminator of manuscripts; a monk of St. Albans.
pa'rish *n.* 1. Subdivision of diocese, having its own church and clergyman; inhabitants of this. 2. District (freq. identical with original parish) constituted for purposes of civil government, esp. (hist.) for poor-law administration. 3. ~ *clerk*, official performing various church duties, and formerly leading the congregation in responses; ~ *council*, administrative body in civil parish; ~ *register*, book recording christenings, marriages, and burials, at parish church. **pari'shioner** (-sho-) *n.* Inhabitant of parish.
Pari'sian (-z-) *adj. & n.* (Native, inhabitant) of PARIS[1].
parisylla'bic *adj.* (of Greek and Latin nouns) Having same number of syllables in nominative as in oblique cases of singular.
pa'rity *n.* Equality; parallelism, analogy; equivalence in another currency, being at par.
park[1] *n.* 1. Large enclosed piece of ground, usu. with woodland and pasture, attached to country house etc.; enclosure in town ornamentally laid out for public recreation; large tract of land kept in natural state for public benefit; *the P~*, (now) HYDE PARK; (formerly) St. James's Park. 2. (Space occupied by) artillery, stores, etc., in encampment; area where vehicles may be left temporarily. 3. Enclosed area for oyster-breeding, overflowed by sea at high tide. ~ *v.* Enclose (ground) in or as park; arrange (artillery etc.) com-

PARLOUR

pactly in a park; place or leave (vehicle) in park etc. temporarily; (transf.) leave in suitable place until required; *parking meter*, coin-operated meter which registers time allowed for a vehicle to be parked.
Park[2], Mungo (1771–1806). Scottish surgeon; explored river Niger, 1795–7; published his 'Travels in the Interior of Africa', 1799; returned to the Niger, 1805, and perished there.
par'ka *n.* Long fur jacket with attached hood worn in Arctic regions; garment resembling this.
Par'khurst. Convict prison in Isle of Wight, built 1830, orig. for boys.
par'kin *n.* (north.) Gingerbread made with oatmeal and treacle.
Par'kinson's disea'se (-z, zēz). Chronic progressive disease of the nervous system (*Paralysis agitans*, 'shaking palsy') characterized by tremor, muscular rigidity, defective gait, and emaciation. [James *Parkinson*, British physician (1755–1824)]
Par'kinson's law (-z). Theory that work expands to fill the time available for doing it. '[C. N. *Parkinson*, 1909–]
par'ky *adj.* (slang) Chilly.
par'lance *n.* Way of speaking.
par'ley *n.* Conference for debating of points in dispute, esp. (mil.) discussion of terms. ~ *v.* Discuss terms (*with*); speak (esp. foreign languages).
par'liament(-lam-) *n.* 1. Council forming with the sovereign the supreme legislature of United Kingdom, consisting of the House of Lords (see LORD) and the House of Commons (see COMMON) (*illustration, p. 640*); corresponding legislative assembly in other countries; *Long, Rump, Short P~*: see these words. 2. (obs.; also ~ *cake*) Thin crisp cake of gingerbread.
parliamentar'ian (-lam-) *n.* Skilled debater in parliament; adherent of Parliament in Civil War of 17th c. ~ *adj.* Parliamentary.
parliame'ntary (-lam-) *adj.* Of a parliament; enacted, established, by parliament; (of language) admissible in Parliament, (colloq.) civil; *P~ Commissioner (for Administration)*, title of ombudsman in U.K.; ~ *train*, (hist.) train carrying passengers at rate not above 1*d.* a mile, which every railway company was obliged by Act of Parliament (7 & 8 Vict., c. 85) to run daily each way over its system.
par'lour (-ler) *n.* 1. Apartment in convent for conversation with outsiders etc. 2. In mansion, town hall, etc., smaller room apart from great hall, for private conversation etc. 3. (now rarely used) Ordinary sitting-room of family in private house; ~ *game*, game (esp. word-game or quiz) played

[639]

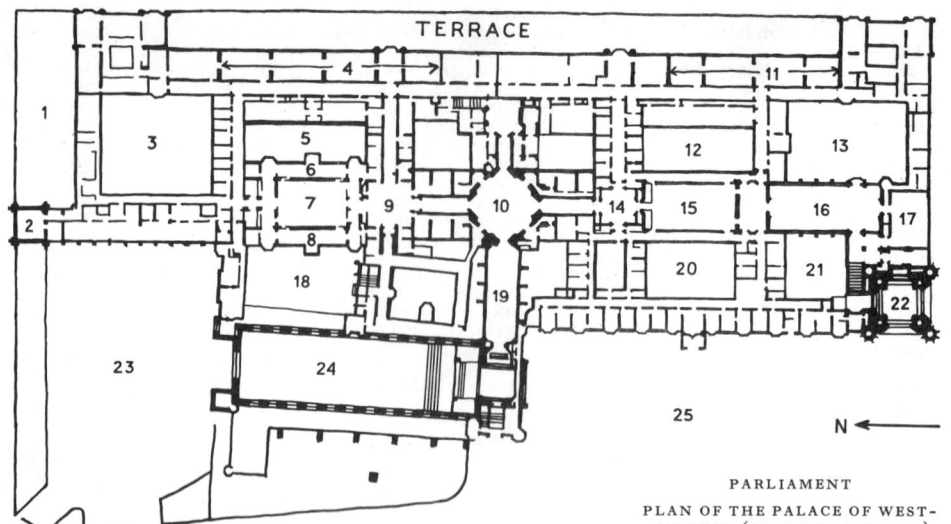

PARLIAMENT

PLAN OF THE PALACE OF WESTMINSTER (PRINCIPAL FLOOR)

1. Speaker's Green. 2. Big Ben. 3. Speaker's Court. 4. Commons Library. 5. Commons Court. 6. 'No' Division Lobby. 7. House of Commons. 8. 'Aye' Division Lobby. 9. Commons Lobby. 10. Central Lobby. 11. Peers' Library. 12. Peers' Court. 13. Royal Court. 14. Peers' Lobby. 15. House of Lords. 16. Royal Gallery. 17. Queen's Robing Room. 18. Star Chamber Court. 19. St. Stephen's Hall. 20. State Officers' Court. 21. Chancellor's Court. 22. Victoria Tower. 23. New Palace Yard. 24. Westminster Hall. 25. Old Palace Yard

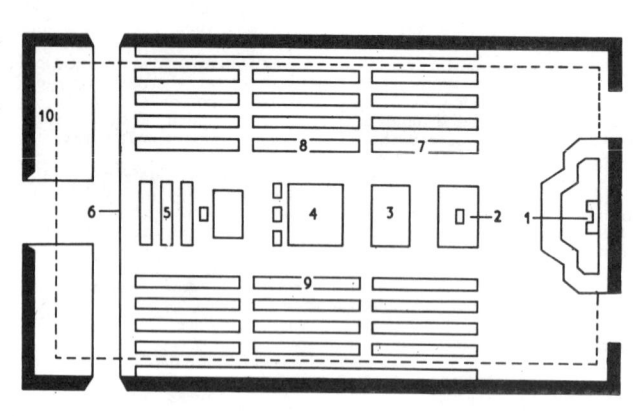

HOUSE OF LORDS

1. Throne. 2. Woolsack on which the Lord Chancellor sits. 3. Woolsack on which judges sit at the opening of Parliament. 4. Table of the House. 5. Cross-benches where independent peers sit. 6. Bar of the House. 7. Bishops' seats. 8. Government peers' seats. 9. Opposition peers' seats. 10. Public Gallery above

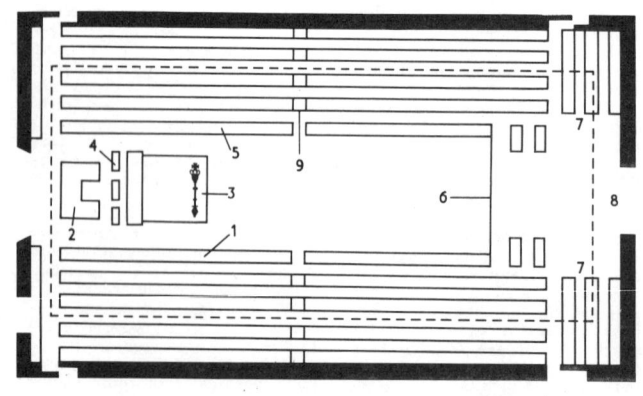

HOUSE OF COMMONS

1. Government Front Bench. 2. Speaker's chair. 3. Table of the House. 4. Clerks' chairs. 5. Opposition Front Bench. 6. Bar of the House. 7. Cross-benches. 8. Public Gallery above. 9. Gangway

PARLOUS

indoors. 4. Room in inn more private than tap-room. 5. (U.S.) Luxuriously fitted railway carriage. 6. Place of business, as *beauty* ~. 7. ~-*maid*, maid who waits at table.

par'lous *adj.* (archaic, joc.) Perilous; hard to deal with.

Par'ma. City and province (formerly a duchy) of N. Italy; ~ *violet*, sweet-scented cultivated violet.

Parmĕ'nidēs (-z). (6th c. B.C.) Greek philosopher of Elea (Italy); founder of the ELEATIC school.

Parmĕsä'n (-z-; *or* pär'-) *adj.* Of Parma; *esp.* applied to hard easily grated kind of cheese made there and in other parts of N. Italy.

Parnă'ssian *adj.* Of Parnassus; ~ *School*, founded by Leconte de Lisle, group of 19th-c. French poets, who insisted on importance of form and the *mot juste* and distrusted romantic sensibility and emotion as subjects of poetry. [f. title, 'Le Parnasse Contemporain', of three series of collections of their poetry, published 1866–76]

Parnă'ssus. Lofty mountain of Greece, N. of Delphi; associated in classical Greece with worship of Apollo and the Muses.

Parnĕ'll, Charles Stewart (1846–91). Irish nationalist political leader, who succeeded in converting Gladstone to his home-rule scheme.

paro'chial (-k-) *adj.* Of a parish; (fig.) confined to narrow area; narrow, provincial. **parō'-chially** *adv.* **parō'chialism** *n.*

pă'rody *n.* Composition in which an author's characteristics are ridiculed by imitation; feeble imitation, travesty. ~ *v.t.* Imitate (composition etc.) humorously. **pă'rodist** *n.*

parō'le *n.* Word of honour, esp. prisoner's promise that he will not attempt escape, or will return to custody if liberated, or will refrain from taking up arms against captors for stated period; (mil.) password used only by officers or inspectors of guard (as dist. f. COUNTERSIGN); *on* ~, (liberated) on parole. ~ *v.t.* Put (prisoner) on parole.

păronomā'sia (-z-) *n.* Pun.

pă'roquĕt (-k-) *n.* Var. of PARAKEET.

Par'ŏs. Greek island in Aegean Sea, famous for its marble (see PARIAN).

pă ́rō'tid *adj.* Situated near the ear, esp. ~ *gland*, (in man, largest of three salivary glands) situated in front of ear (ill. GLAND[1]). ~ *n.* Parotid gland. **păroti'tis** *n.* (path.) Inflammation of parotid gland, mumps.

pă'roxysm *n.* Fit of disease; fit (*of* rage, laughter, etc.). **păroxy'smal** *adj.* [Gk *oxuno* goad, render acute]

parŏ'xytone *adj. & n.* (Gk gram.) (Word) with acute accent on last syllable but one.

păr'pen *n.* Binder, 3. (ill. MASONRY).

păr'quet (-kī *or* -kā) *n.* Wooden flooring of pieces of wood, freq. of different kinds, arranged in pattern. ~ *v.t.* Floor (room) thus. **păr'quĕtry.**

părr[1]**, păr**[3] *n.* Young salmon; ~ *marks*, dark cross-bands on this.

Părr[2]**,** Catherine (1512–48). 6th wife of Henry VIII, whom she outlived.

pă'rricīde *n.* 1. One who murders his father. 2. Murder of father, parent, near relative, or one whose person is considered sacred. **părrici'dal** *adj.*

pă'rrot *n.* Bird of large mainly tropical group (order Psittaciformes) with short hooked bill, and freq. brilliant plumage, many species of which can be taught to repeat words and sentences; person who repeats another's words or imitates his actions unintelligently; ~ *disease*, PSITTACOSIS; ~-*fish*, any of various fishes with brilliant colouring or strong hard mouth like parrot's bill. ~ *v.t.* Repeat (words etc.) mechanically.

pă'rry[1] *v.t.* Ward off, avert (weapon, blow, etc.). ~ *n.* Warding off. [L *parare* prepare]

Pă'rry[2]**,** Sir Charles Hubert Hastings (1848–1918). English musical composer.

Pă'rry[3]**,** Sir William Edward (1790–1855). English rear-admiral and Arctic explorer; author of four narratives of voyages to the Polar Sea.

parse (-z) *v.t.* Describe (word) grammatically, stating inflexion, relation to sentence, etc.; resolve (sentence) into component parts of speech and describe them grammatically.

păr'sĕc *n.* (astron.) Unit in measuring stellar distances, distance at which a star would have an annual PARALLAX of one second of an arc, equivalent to 206,265 astronomical units (3·258 lightyears). [*par*(*allax*)+*sec*(*ond*)]

Pärsee' *adj. & n.* 1. (One) of the followers of ZOROASTER, descendants of those Persians who fled to India in 7th and 8th centuries to escape Muslim persecution. 2. (Of) the Iranian dialect of the Parsee religious literature.

Pär'sifal. Hero of Wagner's music-drama of the same name, character based on that of Sir PERCEVAL in the Arthurian cycle.

pär'simony *n.* Extreme or excessive carefulness in employment of money, etc.; reluctance to give or spend. **pärsimō'nious** *adj.* **pärsimō'niously** *adv.* **pärsimō'niousness** *n.*

pär'sley *n.* Biennial umbelliferous plant (*Petroselinum crispum*) with white flowers and aromatic leaves, finely divided and curled in commonly cultivated variety, used for seasoning and garnishing dishes; *cow, fool's, hedge,* ~, umbelliferous plants with finely divided leaves.

pär'snip *n.* Biennial umbelliferous plant (*Pastinaca sativa*) with pinnate leaves, yellow flowers, and (in cultivated variety) large, pale yellow, sweet, fleshy, and nutritious root used as culinary vegetable; root of this.

pär'son *n.* Rector; vicar or any beneficed clergyman; (colloq.) any clergyman; ~*'s nose*, rump of cooked table bird. **pärsō'nic, -ical** *adjs.*

pär'sonage *n.* Rector's or other incumbent's house.

pärt[1] *n.* 1. Some but not all of a thing or number of things; division or section; section of book etc., esp. as much as is issued at one time; each of several equal portions of a whole (as *third, fourth* etc. ~, one of 3, 4, etc., equal parts); individual component of machine etc.; ~ *of*, a part of, some of. 2. Portion allotted, share; interest, concern; person's share in action, his function, business, duty. 3. Character assigned to actor on stage; words spoken by actor on stage; copy of these; (fig.) character sustained by anyone. 4. Melody assigned to particular voice or instrument in concerted music. 5. (archaic, pl.) Abilities, capacities. 6. (pl.) Region. 7. Side in dispute. 8. *for my* ~, as far as I am concerned; *in* ~, partly; *take in good* ~, not be offended at; *the most* ~, the greatest part, most; *for the most* ~, in most cases, mostly; *on the* ~ *of*, proceeding from; done etc. by; *take* ~, assist (*in*); *take the* ~ *of*, support, back up; ~ *and parcel* (emphatic) constituent, element; essential portion; ~ *of speech*, each of the grammatical categories of words (noun, adjective, pronoun, verb, adverb, preposition, conjunction, interjection); ~-*song*, song for three or more voiceparts, usu. without accompaniment and in simple harmony. ~ *adv.* In part, partly; ~-*owner* etc., owner etc. in common with another or others; ~-*payment*, payment in part; ~-*time* (*adj.*) employed for, taking up, only part of the working-day; ~-*timer* (*n.*).

pärt[2] *v.* Divide into parts, suffer division; separate (hair), as with comb, on each side of dividing line or *parting*; (naut.) break, suffer breaking of (rope), (of rope) break; separate (combatants, friends, etc.); quit one another's company; (colloq.) part with one's money, pay; (archaic) distribute (thing) in shares; ~ *company*, dissolve companionship (*with*); ~ *from, with*, say good-bye to; ~ *with*, give up, surrender (property etc.).

pär'ting *n.* (esp.) Leave-taking; dividing line of combed hair; ~ *of the ways*, point at which road divides into two or more; (fig.)

[641]

PARTAKE

moment for decision in choice between alternative courses.
partā'ke v. (past t. -tōok, past part. -tā'ken). Take a share in; take a share (in, of, with); take, esp. eat or drink some or (colloq.) all of; have some (of quality etc.).
parterre (-tār') n. 1. Level space in garden occupied by flower-beds. 2. Part of ground-floor of auditorium of theatre, behind orchestra (ill. THEATRE).
parthenogĕ'nĕsis n. (biol.) Reproduction from gametes without fertilization, esp. among invertebrates and lower plants.
Pār'thenon. Temple of Athene Parthenos ('the maiden') on the Acropolis at Athens, erected 447–438 B.C. under Pericles' administration and decorated with sculptures by Phidias or his school.
Pār'thian adj. Of Parthia, an ancient country of Asia, SE. of Caspian Sea; ~ shot, (fig.) parting shot (so called from the trick used by Parthians of shooting arrows while in real or pretended flight). ~ n. Native, inhabitant, of Parthia.
parti' (-ē) n. Person regarded as eligible etc. in the marriage market.
par'tial (-shal) adj. 1. Biased, unfair; ~ to, having a liking for. 2. Forming only a part; not complete or total. **par'tially** adv.
partiā'lity (-shi-) n. Bias, favouritism; fondness (for).
par'tible adj. That can or must be divided (among; esp. of heritable property).
parti'cipate v. Have share in; have share (in); have something of.
par'ticipant adj. & n. **participā'tion** n.
par'ticiple n. Verbal adjective qualifying noun but retaining some properties of verb, e.g. tense and government of object. **particī'pial** adj.
par'ticle n. Minute portion of matter; smallest possible amount; minor part of speech, esp. short indeclinable one; prefix or suffix having distinct meaning.
par'ticoloured (-ŭlerd) adj. Partly of one colour, partly of another.
parti'cular adj. 1. Relating to one as distinguished from others, special; one considered apart from others, individual; P~ *Baptists*, body of Baptists holding Calvinistic doctrines of ~ *election* and ~ *redemption*, i.e. divine election and redemption of only some of the human race. 2. Worth notice, special. 3. Detailed, minute; scrupulously exact; fastidious (about).
particulā'rity n. **parti'cularly** adv. **parti'cular** n. Detail, item; (pl.) detailed account; in ~, especially.
parti'cularism n. Doctrine of PARTICULAR election or redemption; exclusive devotion to a party, sect, etc.; principle of leaving political independence to each

State in an empire etc. **parti'cularist** n.
parti'cularīze v.t. Name specially or one by one, specify. **particularīzā'tion** n.
pārti'culate adj. Of the nature of a particle; composed of particles.
parti' pris (-tē, prē). Preconceived view, bias.
partisă'n[1] (-z-; or pār'-) n. Adherent of party, cause, etc., esp. unreasoning one; (hist.) member of light irregular troops employed in special enterprises; (in war of 1939–45) guerrilla (applied orig. to Russians resisting in parts of their country occupied by the enemy). ~ *adj.* **partisă'nship** n.
pār'tisan[2] (-zan), -zan n. (hist.) Long-handled spear like halberd (ill. SPEAR).
pār'tīte adj. (bot., entom.) Divided (nearly) to the base.
parti'tion n. 1. Division into parts; such part; structure separating two such parts, esp. slight wall. 2. (law) Division of real property between joint tenants etc. by which co-tenancy is abolished and individual interests are separated. ~ v.t. Divide into parts; ~ off, separate (part of room etc.) by a partition.
par'titive adj. Dividing into parts; (gram.) denoting part of a collective whole; ~ *genitive*, that used to indicate that only a part of a collective whole is considered or spoken of, expressed in English by *of*, e.g. *one of many*, *pick of the bunch*. **par'titively** adv. **par'titive** n. Partitive word.
Pār'tlet. (archaic) Used as proper name for a hen, esp. *Dame* ~. [OF *Pertelote*, female proper name]
par'tly adv. With respect to a part; in some degree.
par'tner n. 1. Sharer; person associated with others in business of which he shares risks and profits; wife, husband; companion in dance; player associated with another in whist, tennis, etc. 2. (naut., pl.) Timber framework round hole in deck through which mast, pump, etc., passes. ~ v.t. Associate as partners; be partner of. **par'tnership** n.
par'tridge n. Any of various game-birds, esp. British and Central European *common* or *grey* ~ (*Perdix perdix*); (U.S.) any of various birds of grouse or pheasant family; ~-*wood*, W. Indian hard red wood with darker parallel stripes, used for cabinet work.
partūr'ient adj. About to bring forth young. **parturī'tion** n. Act of bringing forth young.
pār'ty[1] n. 1. Those on one side in a contest etc., esp. considered collectively; persons united in maintaining cause, policy, etc., in opposition to others; system of taking sides on public questions, system of parties. 2. Body of persons travelling or engaged to-

PASS

gether. 3. Social gathering, esp. of invited guests at private house. 4. Each of the two or more persons making the two sides in legal action, contract, marriage, etc.; *third* ~, person or persons other than these, esp. in insurance matters. 5. Participator, accessory (*to* action). 6. (now vulg. or joc.) Person. 7. ~ *line*, telephone line shared by number of subscribers; (also) set policy of political party; ~ *wall*, wall shared by each of the occupiers of the two buildings etc. that it separates.
pār'ty[2] adj. (her.) Divided into parts of different tinctures (ill. HERALDRY).
pār'venu n. Person of obscure origin who has gained wealth or position, upstart.
pār'vis n. Enclosed area in front of cathedral, church, etc. [OF *pare(v)is*, f. LL *paradisus* PARADISE, court in front of St. Peter's, Rome]
pas (pah) n. 1. Precedence. 2. Step in dancing. [Fr.]
P.A.S. abbrev. Para-aminosalicylic acid, a drug used in treatment of pulmonary tuberculosis.
Păscal (-kahl), Blaise (1623–62). French mathematician, physicist, and religious philosopher; author of 'Lettres à un Provincial' and 'Pensées'.
pă'schal (-k-) adj. Of the Jewish Passover; of Easter.
pasha, pacha (pah'sha) n. Title, placed after name, formerly used by senior officers in Turkish dominions. **pa'shalic** n. Jurisdiction of pasha.
Pashtu (pŭ'shtōō), **Pŭ'shtu** adj. & n. (Of) the language of the Afghans, belonging to the Eastern Iranian group of the Indo-European family.
Pasi'phaë (-aē). (Gk legend) Wife of Minos and mother of the Minotaur.
pă'sque-flower (-sk-) n. Anemone (*Anemone pulsatilla*) with bell-shaped purple flowers. [Fr. *passefleur* surpassing flower, with assim. to *Pasque* Easter]
păsquină'de (-kw-) n. Lampoon, satire, orig. one affixed to public place. [*Pasquino*, statue at Rome on which Latin verses were annually posted]
pass[1] (pahs) v. (past part. *passed* or as adj. *past*). 1. Move onward, proceed; circulate, be current; be transported from place to place; change; die; go by; come to an end; ~ *for*, be accepted as; ~ *by the name of*, be currently known by the name of. 2. Get through, effect a passage; go uncensured, be accepted as adequate; (of bill in parliament, proposal, etc.) be sanctioned; (of candidate) satisfy examiner. 3. (law) Adjudicate (*on, upon*); (of judgement) 'be given (*for* plaintiff etc.). 4. (cards etc.) Decline, declare inability, to play, bid, make trump, etc.; throw up

[642]

PASS

one's hand. 5. Leave on one side or behind as one goes; go across (sea, frontier, mountain range). 6. (of bill) Be examined and approved by (House of Commons etc.); reach standard required by (examiner, examination); ~ *muster*: see MUSTER. 7. Outstrip, surpass; be beyond compass or range of, transcend (any faculty or expression). 8. Transport (usu. with prep. or adv.) move, cause to go; emit from the body as excrement; cause to go by; hand round, transfer; give currency to; pledge (word etc.); (footb. etc.) transfer (ball) to another player on the same side. 9. Cause, allow, (bill in parliament, candidate for examination, etc.) to proceed after scrutiny. 10. Spend (*time* etc.); utter (criticism, judicial sentence, *upon*). 11. ~ *away*, die, come to an end; ~ *by*, omit, disregard; walk etc. past; ~ *off*, (of sensations etc.) fade away; (of proceedings) be carried through; palm off (thing *for* or *as* what it is not); distract attention from (awkward situation etc.); ~ *out*, (colloq.) die; become unconscious (from drinking etc.); ~ *over*, omit; make no remark upon; ~ *the time of day*: see TIME; ~ *through*, experience; ~ *water*, urinate. ~ *n*. 1. Passing, esp. of examination; (university) attainment of standard that satisfies examiners but does not entitle to honours. 2. Critical position, juncture, predicament. 3. Written permission to pass into or out of a place, be absent from quarters etc.; ticket authorizing holder to travel free on railway etc. 4. Thrust in fencing; juggling trick; passing of hands over anything, esp. in mesmerism; (footb. etc.) transference of ball to another player on same side; *make a* ~ *at*, (colloq.) try to attract sexually. 5. ~-*book*, book supplied by bank to person having current or deposit account, showing all sums deposited and drawn; ~-*key*, private key to gate etc. for special purposes; master-key; *pa'ssman*, one who takes pass degree at university; *pa'ssword*, selected word or phrase distinguishing friend from enemy.

pass² (pahs) *n*. Narrow passage through mountains (ill. MOUNTAIN); (mil.) such passage viewed as key to a country; navigable channel, esp. at river's mouth; passage for fish over weir; *sell the* ~, (fig.) betray a cause.

pa'ssable (pah-) *adj*. (esp.) That can pass muster, fairly good. **pa'ssably** *adv*.

pàssaca'glia (-ahya) *n*. (mus.) Instrumental composition in 3/4 time, based on an unvarying ground; (orig.) Spanish or Italian dance-tune. [It., perh. f. Sp. *pasar* pass, *calle* street, because freq. played in street]

pă'ssage¹ *n*. 1. Passing, transit; transition from one state to another; liberty, right, to pass through; voyage, crossing from port to port; right of conveyance as passenger by sea; *bird of* ~, see BIRD. 2. Passing of a measure into law. 3. Way by which person or thing passes; corridor etc. giving communication between different rooms in house. 4. (pl.) What passes between two persons mutually, interchange of confidences, etc. 5. (also ~ *of* or *at arms*) Fight (freq. fig.). 6. Part of speech or literary work taken for quotation etc.

pă'ssage² *v*. (of horse or rider) Move sideways, by pressure of rein on horse's neck and of rider's leg on opposite side; make (horse) do this.

pă'ssant *adj*. (her.) (of beast) Walking and looking to dexter side, with three paws on ground and dexter fore-paw raised (ill. HERALDRY).

Passchendaele (pă'shendāl). Ridge and village in Flanders E. of Ypres, captured by Canadians 6 Nov. 1917 at end of 3rd battle of Ypres.

passé (pă'sā) *adj*. (fem. *passée*) Past the prime; behind the times. **passementerie** (pahsmahntrē) *n*. Trimming of gold or silver lace, braid, beads, etc. [Fr.]

pă'ssènger (-j-) *n*. Traveller in (public) conveyance by land, air, or water; traveller in motor-car who is not driving; ineffective member of team, crew, etc.; *foot-*~, traveller on foot; ~ *pigeon*, N. Amer. wild pigeon (*Ectopistes migratorius*) capable of long sustained flight (now extinct).

păsse-păr̄tou't (-tōō) *n*. 1. Master-key. 2. Adhesive tape fastening edges of glass to mount of photograph or small picture as substitute for frame. [Fr., = 'pass everywhere']

pa'sser (-ah-) *n*. One who passes; ~-*by*, one who passes, esp. casually.

pă'sserine *adj*. & *n*. (Bird) of the order Passeriformes (perchers).

pă'ssible *adj*. (theol.) Capable of feeling or suffering. **păssibi'lity** *n*.

pă'ssim *adv*. (of allusions, phrases, etc., to be found in specified author or book) Here and there, throughout, in all parts.

pa'ssing (pah-) *n*. ~-*bell*, bell rung at moment of person's death; ~-*note*, (mus.) note not belonging to harmony, interposed for purpose of passing smoothly from one to the other of two notes essential to it. ~ *adj*. (esp.) Transient, fleeting, cursory, incidental. ~ *adv*. (archaic) Very.

pă'ssion *n*. 1. Strong emotion; outburst of anger; sexual love; strong enthusiasm (*for*). 2. P~, sufferings of Christ during his last days and (esp.) on the cross; (musical setting of) narrative of

[643]

PAST

this from Gospels; ~ *flower*, flower of genus *Passiflora* of (chiefly climbing) plants with parts supposed to suggest instruments of Christ's Passion, the corona representing the crown of thorns, etc.; ~-*fruit*, granadilla; *P*~ *Play*, mystery play representing Christ's Passion; *P*~ *Sunday*, 2nd Sunday before Easter; *Pa'ssiontide*, fortnight before Easter; *P*~ *Week*, week following Passion Sunday (but in Anglican usage freq. = week before Easter, Holy Week). ~ *v.i.* (poet.) Feel or express passion. **pă'ssionlèss** *adj*. **pă'ssionlèssnèss** *n*.

pă'ssional *adj*. Of, marked by, passion. ~ *n*. Book of the sufferings of saints and martyrs.

pă'ssionate *adj*. Easily moved to anger; dominated by, easily moved to, strong feeling; due to, showing, passion. **pă'ssionately** *adv*. **pă'ssionatenèss** *n*.

Pă'ssionist *n*. Member of order (Congregation of the Discalced Clerks of the most Holy Cross and Passion of our Lord Jesus Christ), founded in Italy, 1720, pledged to do their utmost to keep alive the memory of Christ's Passion.

pă'ssive *adj*. 1. Suffering action, acted upon; (gram.) applied to a voice of the verb comprising those forms in which action of verb is treated as attribute of thing towards which action is directed (loosely, of verb) in which the subject is acted on by something or suffers the action. 2. Offering no opposition, submissive; ~ *resistance*: see RESISTANCE. 3. Not active, inert; ~ *debt*, one on which no interest is paid. **pă'ssively** *adv*. **pă'ssiveness, passi'vity** *ns*. **pă'ssive** *n*. Passive voice or form of verb.

Pa'ssŏver (pah-) Jewish spring feast, held on evening of the 14th Nisan and the seven following days (Nisan approx. = April), commemorating the 'passing over' (i.e. sparing) of the houses of the Israelites whose doorposts were marked with the blood of the lamb, when the Egyptians were smitten with the death of their first-born (see Exod. 12); ~ *bread*, *cake*, kind of thin dry unleavened biscuit-like bread eaten during Passover.

pa'ssport *n*. Document issued by competent authority serving as identification of person and his nationality, esp. when travelling abroad; (fig.) thing that ensures admission.

past¹ (pah-) *adj*.: see PASS¹; (esp.) Gone by in time; just gone by; (gram.) expressing past action or state; ~ *master*, one who has been master in guild, freemasons' lodge, etc.; thorough master (*in, of*, subject). ~ *n*. Past time; what has happened in past time; person's past life or career, esp. one that will not bear inquiry.

past² (pah-) *prep*. Beyond in

time or place; beyond the range or compass of. ~ *adv.* So as to pass by, as *hastens* ~.

pă'sta *n.* Dried flour-paste used in Italian cooking, in various shapes such as macaroni, spaghetti, vermicelli, etc.

pāste *n.* Flour moistened and kneaded, with lard, butter, suet, etc., as cooking material; any of various sweet doughy confections; relish of pounded fish, meat, etc.; adhesive; any soft plastic mixture; mixture of clay, water, etc., used in making pottery; hard vitreous composition used in making imitation gems; *pa'steboard*, stiff substance made by pasting together sheets of paper; (attrib., fig.) unsubstantial, flimsy. ~ *v.t.* Fasten with paste; stick *up* on wall etc. with paste; cover (as) by pasting on or over; (slang) beat, thrash; bomb heavily; ~-*down*, (in book) that part of the end-paper which is pasted to the inside of the cover.

pă'stel *n.* Drawing instrument consisting of a stick of powdered pigment bound with gum, usu. covered with paper; drawing made with pastels (usu. in several colours); (attrib., of light colour) soft, subdued. **pă'stellist** *n.*

pă'stern *n.* Part of horse's foot between fetlock and hoof (ill. HORSE); corresponding part in other animals.

Pă'sternăk, Boris Leonidovich (1890–1960). Russian novelist and poet.

Pāsteur (-tēr̄), Louis (1822–95). French chemist and biologist; founder of bacteriology and inventor of method of inoculation for hydrophobia.

pă'steurīze (-ter-) *v.t.* Partially sterilize by Pasteur's method, prevent or arrest fermentation in (milk etc.) by keeping for some time at a temperature (55°–60 °C.) which does not greatly affect chemical composition. **păsteurīzā'tion** *n.*

păsti'ccio (-ēchīō) *n.* = PASTICHE, 1.

păsti'che (-ēsh) *n.* 1. Medley, esp. musical composition, picture, made up from various sources. 2. Literary or other work of art composed in the style of a known author.

pă'stil, păsti'lle (-tēl) *n.* 1. Small roll of aromatic paste burnt as fumigator etc. 2. Small sweet, freq. medicated; lozenge.

pa'stime (pah-) *n.* Recreation; game, sports.

Pă'ston lĕ'tters (-z). Collection of private correspondence (1440–86) of a well-to-do Norfolk family named Paston; of great historical value and interest.

pa'stor (pah-) *n.* Minister in charge of (esp. continental Protestant) church or congregation; person exercising spiritual guidance. [Anglo-Fr., f. L. *pastor* shepherd]

pa'storal (pah-) *adj.* 1. Of shepherds; (of land) used for pasture; (of poems etc.) portraying country life. 2. Of a pastor; *P*~ *Epistles*, those of Paul to Timothy and Titus, dealing with pastor's work. **pa'storally** *adv.* **pa'storal** *n.* 1. Pastoral play, poem, etc. or picture. 2. (mus.) = PASTORALE. 3. Letter from pastor, esp. bishop, to clergy or people. **pa'storalism** *n.* Convention of pastoral poetry etc.

pastorale (pahstorah'-) *n.* (pl. -*ali* pr. -lē, or -*ales*). 1. Simple opera etc. with rural subject. 2. Slow quiet instrumental composition with notes flowing in groups of three and usu. with drone notes in bass suggesting bagpipe.

pa'storate (pah-) *n.* Pastor's (tenure of) office; body of pastors.

pă'strỹ *n.* Paste of flour, fat, water, etc., rolled and baked; articles of food (pies, tarts, etc.) made wholly or partly of this; ~-*cook*, one who makes pastry, esp. for public sale.

pa'sturage (pahscher-) *n.* Pasturing; herbage for cattle etc.; pasture-land.

pa'sture (pah-) *n.* Herbage for cattle; (piece of) land covered with this. ~ *v.* Lead, put, (cattle) to pasture; (of sheep etc.) eat down (grassland); put sheep etc. on (land) to graze; graze. **pa'sturable** *adj.*

pă'stỹ[1] *n.* Pie of meat etc. seasoned and enclosed in crust of pastry and baked without dish.

pā'stỹ[2] *adj.* Of, like, paste; of pale complexion.

păt[1] *n.* Stroke, tap, esp. with hand as caress etc.; small mass (esp. of butter) formed (as) by patting; sound made by striking lightly with something flat. ~ *v.* Strike (thing) gently with flat surface; flatten thus; strike gently with inner surface of fingers, esp. to mark sympathy, approbation, etc.; beat lightly *on*; ~ *on the back*, express approbation of; ~-*ball*, (contempt.) poor or feeble lawn tennis.

păt[2] *adv.* & *adj.* Apposite(ly), opportune(ly); ready for any occasion.

Păt[3]. (colloq.) Nickname for Irishman.

pata'ca (-tah-) *n.* Monetary unit of Macau, = 100 avos.

Pătagō'nia. Southern region of S. America, in Argentina between Andes and Atlantic. **Pătagō'nian** *adj.* & *n.* [f. obs. *Patagon*, one of the S. Amer. Indians, of great stature, inhabiting this region]

pătch *n.* 1. Piece of cloth, metal, etc., put on to mend hole or rent or strengthen weak place; piece of court-plaster etc. put over wound; pad worn to protect injured eye; *not a* ~ *on*, not comparable to, nothing to. 2. Small piece of black silk or court-plaster worn esp. in 17th and 18th centuries to show off complexion. 3. Large or irregular spot on surface; piece of ground; number of plants growing on this; ~ *pocket*, pocket sewn on like patch; *strike a bad* ~, have a run of bad luck. ~ *v.t.* Put patch(es) on; serve as patch to; piece (things) together; appear as patches on (surface); ~ *up*, repair with patches; put together hastily; (fig.) repair; set to right (matter, quarrel, etc.); *pa'tchwork*, work made up of fragments of different colours sewn together (freq. fig.). **pă'tchỹ** *adj.* **pă'tchilỹ** *adv.* **pă'tchiněss** *n.*

pătě'tchouli (-ōōli) *n.* Odoriferous plant (*Pogostemon cablin*) of Silhat, Penang, and Malaysia; penetrating and lasting perfume prepared from this.

pāte *n.* (colloq.) Head, often as seat of intellect.

pâté (pah'tā *or* pă-) *n.* Paste of meat etc.; patty; ~ *de foie gras* (fwah grah), paste of liver of fatted geese. [Fr.]

patée: see PATY.

pătě'lla *n.* Knee-cap (ill. SKELETON). **patě'llar, patě'llate** *adjs.*

pă'ten *n.* Shallow dish used for bread at Eucharist (ill. CHALICE); thin circular plate of metal.

păt'ent (in England pā- in *letters* ~, ~ *office*, pā- usu. in all other senses; in U.S. pā- in sense 2, pă- usu. in all other senses), *adj.* 1. (of rights etc.) Conferred, protected, by *letters* ~, open document under seal, esp. royal, granting right, title, etc., esp. sole right for a term to make, use, or sell some invention; (fig.) to which one has proprietary claim; (colloq.) such as might be patented, ingenious, well-contrived. 2. (of door etc.) Open; (fig.) plain, obvious. 3. ~ *leather*: see LEATHER; ~ *log*: see LOG[1]; ~ *medicine*, proprietary medicine, esp. one of which formula is not disclosed on container (but in U.K. disclosure is now obligatory). **pā'tentlỹ** *adv.* **pā'tencỹ** *n.* **pă'tent** *n.* Letters patent; government grant of exclusive privilege of making or selling new invention; invention, process, so protected; (fig.) sign that one is entitled to something, possesses a quality, etc.; *P*~ *Office*, office from which patents are issued; ~-*roll*, roll of patents issued in Great Britain in a year. ~ *v.t.* Obtain patent for (invention).

pătentee' *n.* Taker-out or holder of a patent, person for the time being entitled to the benefit of a patent.

pā'ter[1] *n.* (slang) Father.

Pā'ter[2], Walter Horatio (1839–94). English essayist, critic, and humanist; author of 'Studies in the History of the Renaissance' (1873) and 'Marius the Epicurean' (1885).

pă'terfami'liăs *n.* (Rom. law & joc.) Head of family.

patēr'nal *adj.* Of a father;

[644]

fatherly; related through the father, on the father's side. patēr'nally adv.

patēr'nitў n. Fatherhood; one's paternal origin; (fig.) authorship, source.

pă'ternŏster n. 1. Lord's Prayer, esp. in Latin; bead in rosary indicating that paternoster is to be said. 2. (also ~ line) Weighted fishing-line with hooks and sinkers at intervals. [L pater noster our father].

path (pah-) n. Footway, esp. one merely beaten by feet, not specially constructed; track laid for foot or cycle racing; line along which person or thing moves; **pa'thfinder**, (esp.) aircraft (or its pilot) sent ahead of main force to locate and mark out bombing targets. **pa'thlĕss** adj.

Pathan (-tah'n) adj. & n. (Member) of a Pashtu-speaking people inhabiting E. Afghanistan, NW. Pakistan, and other parts of the India peninsula.

pathĕ'tĭc adj. Exciting pity or sadness; of the emotions; ~ fallacy, ascription of human emotion to inanimate nature. **pathĕ'tĭcallў** adv.

păthogĕ'nĕsĭs n. Mode of development of a disease.

păthogĕ'nĭc adj. Capable of producing disease.

pathŏ'logў n. Systematic study of bodily diseases, their causes, symptoms, and treatment. **pathŏ'logĭst** n. **păthŏlŏ'gĭcal** adj.

pā'thŏs n. Quality in speech, events, etc., that excites pity or sadness. [Gk, = 'suffering']

pā'tience (-shens) n. 1. Calm endurance of pain or any provocation; forbearance; quiet and self-possessed waiting for something; perseverance; have no ~ with, (colloq.) be unable to bear patiently; out of ~, provoked so as no longer to have patience. 2. (cards) Game, usu. for one person, in which object is to arrange cards in some systematic order.

pā'tient (-shent) adj. Having, showing, patience. **pā'tientlў** adv. **pā'tient** n. Person under medical treatment, esp. with reference to his doctor.

pă'tina n. Incrustation, usu. green, on surface of old bronze, esteemed as ornament; (by extension) gloss on woodwork etc., produced by long use. **pă'tĭnātĕd** adj. **pătĭnā'tion** n.

pă'tĭō n. Inner court open to sky; paved usu. roofless area adjoining a house. [Span.]

Pă'tmŏre, Coventry Kersey Dighton (1823–96). English poet.

Pă'tmŏs. Greek island of Sporades group in Aegean Sea, where, acc. to legend, St. John lived in exile and saw the visions of the Apocalypse.

Pă'tna. Capital city of Bihar; ~ rice, long-grained rice, orig. that of Patna, now also grown elsewhere, esp. in U.S.

pă'tois (-wah) n. Regional dialect of common people; jargon.

pā'trĭārch (-k) n. 1. Father and ruler of family or tribe; one of the forefathers of Abraham, as ancestors of the human race; Abraham, Isaac, Jacob, or any of Jacob's twelve sons, as progenitors of the Hebrew peoples. 2. (in early and Orthodox Churches) Bishop, esp. of Antioch, Alexandria, Constantinople, Jerusalem, or Rome; (in R.C. Church) bishop ranking next above primates and metropolitans and immediately below the pope. 3. Founder of an order, science, etc.; venerable old man; oldest living representative (of). **pātrĭār'chal** adj.

pā'trĭārchate (-k-) n. Office, see, residence, of ecclesiastical patriarch; rank of tribal patriarch.

pā'trĭārchў (-ki) n. Government by father or eldest male of tribe or family; community so organized.

patrĭ'cian (-shan) n. 1. Ancient Roman noble (contrasted with PLEBEIAN), one belonging to one of the original citizen families from whom, in first ages of Republic, senators, consuls and pontifices were exclusively chosen; member of noble order in later Roman Empire; officer representing Roman emperor in provinces of Italy and Africa. 2. Nobleman, esp. (hist.) in some medieval Italian republics. ~ adj. Noble, aristocratic; of the ancient Roman nobility.

patrĭ'ciate (-shyat) n. Patrician order, aristocracy; rank of patrician.

pā'trĭcĭde n. Parricide. **pātrĭcī'dal** adj.

Pă'trĭck, St. (c 389–c 461). Patron saint of Ireland; prob. of mixed Roman and British parentage; missionary to Ireland, from which, according to legend, he drove all snakes; commemorated 17 Mar.; Order of St. ~, order of chivalry, instituted 1783; St. ~'s cross, red saltire on white ground, the national cross of Ireland (ill. FLAG⁴).

pă'trĭmonў n. Property inherited from one's father or ancestors, heritage; endowment of church etc. **pătrĭmō'nĭal** adj.

pā'trĭot n. One who defends or is zealous for his country's freedom or rights. **pătrĭŏ'tĭc** adj. **pătrĭŏ'tĭcallў** adv. **pă'trĭŏtĭsm** n.

patrĭ'stĭc adj. Of (the study of the writings of) the Fathers of the Church.

Patrŏ'clus. (Gk legend) Grecian warrior at siege of Troy, friend of Achilles; slain by Hector.

patrō'l n. Going the rounds of garrison, camp, etc.; perambulation of town etc. by police; detachment of guard, police constable(s), told off for this; ships, aircraft, guarding sea-route, etc.; routine operational flight of aircraft; detachment of troops sent out to reconnoitre; unit of Scouts or Guides (six under ~-leader);

patrō'lman, (U.S.) constable attached to particular beat or district; ~ wagon, (U.S.) police van for prisoners. ~ v. Act as patrol; go round (camp, town, etc.) as patrol. [Fr. *patrouiller*, orig. = 'paddle in mud']

pā'tron n. 1. One who countenances, protects, or gives influential support to; customer, esp. regular one, of shop, restaurant, etc.; (usu. ~ saint) tutelary saint of person, place, craft, etc. 2. (Rom. antiq.) Former owner of manumitted slave; protector of CLIENT in return for certain services. 3. One who has right of presenting clergyman to benefice.

pă'tronage n. 1. Support, encouragement, given by patron; customer's support. 2. Right of presentation to benefice or office. 3. Patronizing airs.

patrō'nal (or pă'tro-) adj. Of a patron saint.

pă'tronīze v.t. 1. Act as patron towards, support, encourage. 2. Treat (person, thing) as if with consciousness of one's superiority.

pătronў'mĭc adj. & n. (Name) derived from that of a father or ancestor.

patrōō'n n. (U.S. hist.) Possessor of landed estate with manorial privileges (abolished c 1850) granted under old Dutch governments of New York and New Jersey to members of the (Dutch) West India Company.

pă'tten n. (hist.) Wooden sole with leather loop passing over instep, mounted on oval iron ring, for raising wearer's shoe out of mud etc. (ill. SHOE).

pă'tter¹ n. Jargon of any profession or class; oratory, speechifying, of cheapjack, mountebank, conjurer, etc.; rapid speech introduced into (comic) song. ~ v. Repeat (prayers etc.) in rapid mechanical way; talk glibly. [f. PATERNOSTER]

pă'tter² v. Make rapid succession of taps, as rain on windowpane; run with short quick steps; cause (water etc.) to patter. ~ n. Succession of taps.

pă'ttern n. 1. Excellent example; (attrib.) perfect, ideal, model. 2. Model from which thing is to be made; (founding) figure from which mould is made for casting. 3. Sample (of tailor's cloth etc.). 4. Decorative design as executed on carpet, wallpaper, cloth, etc.; distribution of shots, bombs, etc., on target; ~-welding, welding of alternate strips of twisted or plaited iron and steel, producing a pattern. 5. (fig.) Arrangement of things or actions, as ~ of behaviour, life, etc. ~ v.t. Model (thing after, upon design, etc.); decorate with pattern.

Pă'ttĭ, Adelina (1843–1919). Italian operatic soprano, born in Madrid. Naturalized British in 1898.

pă'ttў n. Little pie or pasty;

[645]

PATY, PATÉE

pa′ttypan, small tin pan or shape for baking patties.

paty, patée (pah′tī) adj. (her.) Of cross, having nearly triangular arms, very narrow where they meet and widening towards extremities (ill. HERALDRY). [Fr. (croix) pattée (cross) in which extremities are widened like an open paw (patte paw)]

pau′city n. Smallness of number or quantity.

Paul[1], St. (d. c A.D. 67). Jew, also called Saul, of Tarsus, with the status of a Roman citizen; was converted to Christianity soon after martyrdom of Stephen; became 'Apostle of the Gentiles' and the first great Christian missionary and theologian; his missionary journeys are described in the Acts of the Apostles, and his letters (Epistles) to the Churches form part of the N.T.; martyred at Rome; commemorated with St. Peter, 29 June.

Paul[2]. Name of six popes: Paul III (Alessandro Farnese, 1468-1549), pope 1534-49, patron of art, established the constitution of the Jesuits (1540); Paul VI (Giovanni Battista Montini, 1897-1978), pope 1963-78.

Paul[3] (1754-1801). Emperor of Russia 1796-1801; son of Peter III and Catherine the Great; was murdered when he refused to abdicate.

pau′ldron n. (hist.) Piece of armour covering shoulder (ill. ARMOUR).

Pau′line adj. Of St. Paul, his writings or his doctrines; ~ epistles, those in New Testament attributed to St. Paul. ~ n. 1. Pupil of St. Paul's School, London. 2. Member of one of many orders dedicated to St. Paul.

Paul Jōnes (-nz). Ballroom dance during which dancers change partners at intervals indicated by change of music.

paulō-pōst-fū′ture n. (Gk gram.) Tense expressing state resulting from future act, future perfect. [mod. L, = 'future a little after']

Paul Prȳ. Inquisitive person. [character in comedy by J. Poole, 1825]

paunch n. Belly, abdomen; protruding belly; rumen (ill. RUMINANT). ~ v.t. Disembowel.

pau′per n. Person without means of livelihood, beggar; (hist.) recipient of poor-law relief; (law) person allowed to sue or defend in forma pauperis. pau′perism, pauperīzā′tion ns. pau′perīze v.t.

Pausā′nïas[1] (5th c. B.C.). Spartan general; commanded Greek forces which defeated Persians in battle of Plataea, 479 B.C.

Pausā′nïas[2] (2nd c. A.D.). Greek traveller and geographer.

pause (-z) n. Interval of inaction or silence, esp. from hesitation; break made in speaking or reading;

(mus.) mark (⌢ or ⌣) placed over or under note or rest as sign that it is to be lengthened; give ~ to, cause to pause or hesitate. ~ v.i. Make a pause, wait; linger upon (word etc.).

pā′vage n. Paving; tax, toll, towards paving of streets.

pā′van, pava′ne (-ahn) n. Stately dance of 16th and 17th centuries in which dancers were elaborately dressed; music for this, in slow duple time.

pāve v.t. Cover (street, floor, etc.) with or as with pavement; (fig.) prepare (the way for).

pā′viour n.

pā′vé (-ā) n. Pavement; setting of jewels placed close together.

pā′vement (-vm-) n. Covering of street, floor, etc., made of stones, tiles, wooden blocks, asphalt, etc., esp. paved footway at side of road; (zool.) pavement-like formation of close-set teeth etc.; ~ artist, one who draws in chalks on pavement to get money from passers-by.

Pavī′a (-vēa). Town of Lombardy, Italy, old capital of Lombard kingdom, where François I of France was defeated and captured in 1525 by the army of the Emperor Charles V.

pavi′lion (-yon) n. 1. Tent, esp. large peaked one; light ornamental building, esp. one attached to cricket or other ground for spectators and players; projecting (usu. highly decorated) subdivision of building. 2. Part of brilliant-cut gemstone below girdle (ill. GEM). ~ v.t. Enclose (as) in, furnish with, pavilion. [L papilionem, butterfly, in LL, tent]

Pă′vlŏv (-f), Ivan Petrovich (1849-1916). Russian physiologist; Nobel Prize for medicine, 1904; noted for research on conditioned reflexes.

Pă′vlōva (or -lŏ′-), Anna Matveevna (1885-1931). Russian ballerina.

pă′vonīne adj. Of, like, a peacock.

paw n. Foot of beast having claws or nails; fur from lower part of animal's leg; (colloq.) hand. ~ v. Strike with paw (of horse) strike (ground), strike ground, with hoofs; (colloq.) handle awkwardly or rudely.

paw′kȳ adj. (Sc., dial.) Sly, cunning; shrewd; dryly humorous. paw′kīly adv. paw′kīness n.

pawl n. Short pivoted catch engaging with toothed wheel to prevent recoil (ill. WINDLASS); (naut.) short bar used to prevent capstan, windlass, etc., from recoiling. ~ v.t. Secure (capstan etc.) with pawl.

pawn[1] n. One of the pieces of smallest size and value in chess (ill. CHESS); (fig.) unimportant person used by another as a mere tool. [AF poun, f. med. L pedonem footsoldier]

pawn[2] n. Thing, person, left in

PAY

another's keeping as security, pledge; state of being pledged; paw′nbroker, one who lends money upon interest on security of personal property pawned; paw′nbroking, his occupation; paw′nshop, pawnbroker's place of business. ~ v.t. Deposit (thing) as security for payment of money or performance of action; (fig.) pledge.

pawnee′[1] n. Person with whom pawn is deposited.

Paw′nee[2] n. Indian of a N. Amer. confederacy, formerly living in Nebraska, now in Oklahoma.

paw-paw: see PAPAW.

păx n. 1. Tablet with representation of Crucifixion etc., kissed at Mass by priests and congregation; kiss of peace as liturgical form at High Mass. 2. ~ vobis, (as salutation) peace to you. 3. (school slang, as int.) Peace, truce. 4. ~ Britannica, peace imposed by British rule; ~ Romana, peace between nationalities within Roman Empire. [L, = 'peace']

pay[1] v. (past t. & past part. paid). 1. Give (person) what is due in discharge of debt or for services done or goods received; recompense (work); hand over (money owed); hand over amount of (debt, wages, etc.); (fig.) reward, recompense; ~ for, hand over the price of, bear the cost of; (fig.) be punished for; ~ in, pay to banking account; ~ off, pay in full and discharge or be quit of (ship's crew, creditor, etc.); (colloq.) bring success; ~ (person) out, punish or have revenge on him; ~ up, pay full amount of (arrears; or abs.); ~ one's way, not get into debt. 2. Render, bestow (attention, court, compliment, etc., to). 3. (of business etc.) Yield adequate return to (person); yield adequate return. 4. (naut.) ~ off, (of ship) fall off to leeward when helm is put up; ~ out, away, let out (rope) by slackening it. 5. ~-as-you-earn, (abbrev. P.A.Y.E.) method of collecting income tax by current deduction from earnings; ~-off, (orig. U.S.) time of reckoning; dénouement. 6. paying guest, resident in boarding-house etc. ~ n. Amount paid; wages, hire, salary; (attrib., mining) containing precious metal or other mineral in sufficient quantity tc be profitably worked; in the ~ of, employed by; ~-bed, hospital bed for the use of which payment is made; ~-day, day on which payment (esp. of wages) is (to be) made; (Stock Exch.) day on which transfer of stock has to be paid for; pay′load, weight of goods, passengers, etc., carried by aircraft etc.; paymaster, officer, official, who pays troops, workmen, etc.; Paymaster-General, head of Treasury department through which payments are made; ~ packet, packet

[646]

containing employee's wages; ~-roll, list of employees receiving regular pay.
pay² *v.t.* (naut.) Smear with tar, pitch, etc., to render waterproof.
pay'able *adj.* That must be paid, due; that may be paid; (of mine etc.) profitable.
P.A.Y.E. *abbrev.* Pay-as-you-earn.
payee' *n.* Person to whom payment is made.
Paym. *abbrev.* Paymaster.
pay'ment *n.* Paying; amount paid; (fig.) recompense.
pay'nim *n.* (archaic) Pagan, esp. Muslim.
P.B.I. *abbrev.* (colloq.) Poor bloody infantry.
p.c. *abbrev.* Per cent; postcard.
P.C. *abbrev.* Police constable; Privy Council(lor).
p.c.u. *abbrev.* Passenger car unit (in measuring capacity of road).
pd *abbrev.* Paid.
p.d.q. *abbrev.* (slang) Pretty damn quick.
pdr *abbrev.* Pounder (of fish, gun, etc.).
P.D.S.A. *abbrev.* People's Dispensary for Sick Animals.
p.e. *abbrev.* Personal estate.
P.E. *abbrev.* Physical education.
pea *n.* Hardy climbing leguminous plant (*Pisum sativum*), with large papilionaceous flowers and long pods each containing a row of round seeds; any of various related leguminous plants; seed of this as food; *green* ~*s*, peas gathered for food while still green, soft, and unripe; *everlasting* ~, plant (*Lathyrus latifolius*) cultivated for its variously-coloured flowers; *sweet* ~: see SWEET; *pea'nut*, (fruit of) *Arachis hypogaea* of W. Africa and W. Indies, with pod ripening underground, containing two seeds like peas, valued as food and for their oil; *peanut butter*, paste of ground peanuts; ~-*shooter*, toy weapon, tube from which dried peas are shot by blowing; ~ *soup*, soup made from (esp. dried) peas; (attrib., esp. of fog) suggestive of this in its dull-yellow colour or thick consistency; ~-*souper*, (colloq.) thick yellow fog.
peace *n.* 1. Freedom from, cessation of, war; ratification or treaty of peace between powers previously at war. 2. Freedom from civil disorder; *the (king's, queen's)* ~, general peace of the realm as secured by law; so *breach, commission, justice, officer, of the* ~. 3. Quiet, tranquillity; mental calm. 4. *at* ~, in state of friendliness, not at strife (*with*); *hold one's* ~, keep silence; *keep the* ~, prevent, refrain from, strife; *make one's* ~ (*with*), become reconciled (*with*); *make* ~, bring hostilities to an end. 5. *pea'cemaker*, one who brings about peace; ~-*offering*, propitiatory gift; (bibl.) offering presented as thanksgiving to God; ~-*pipe*, calumet.
pea'ceable (-sa-) *adj.* Disposed,

tending, to peace; free from disturbance, peaceful. **pea'ceableness** *n.* **pea'ceably** *adv.*
pea'ceful (-sf-) *adj.* Characterized by, belonging to a state of, peace; not violating or infringing peace. **pea'cefully** *adv.* **pea'cefulness** *n.*
peach¹ *n.* Large roundish fruit with downy white or yellow skin flushed with red, highly flavoured sweet pulp, and rough furrowed stone; tree (*Prunus persica*) bearing this, a native of Asia very early introduced into Europe; peach-colour; (slang) person or thing of superlative merit, attractive young woman; ~-*blow*, (glaze on some Oriental porcelain of) delicate purplish or pink; ~-*brandy*, spiritous liquor made from peach juice; ~-*colour(ed)*, (of) colour of ripe peach, a soft yellowish-pink. **pea'chy** *adj.* Like a peach, esp. in colour and softness. [L *persicum* (*malum*) Persian (apple)]
peach² *v.i.* (slang) Turn informer; inform (*against, on*).
pea'cock¹ *n.* 1. Male bird of any species of *Pavo*, esp. of *P. cristatus*, native of India, with striking plumage and upper tail coverts marked with iridescent ocelli, able to expand its tail erect like fan (freq. as type of ostentatious display). 2. European butterfly (*Nymphalis io*) with ocellated wings. 3. ~ *blue*, lustrous blue of peacock's neck-feathers; ~-*coal*, iridescent coal; ~-*throne*, former throne of kings of Delhi, adorned with representation of fully expanded tail coverts of peacock composed of precious stones. ~ *v.i.* Make display; strut about ostentatiously. **pea'cockery** *n.* **pea'cockish** *adj.*
Pea'cock², Thomas Love (1785–1866). English satirical novelist.
pea'fowl *n.* Peacock or peahen.
pea'hen *n.* Female of the peacock.
pea'-jacket *n.* Sailor's short double-breasted overcoat of coarse woollen cloth.
peak¹ *n.* 1. Projecting part of brim of cap; (naut.) narrow part of ship's hold, esp. (*forepeak*) at bow; upper outer corner of sail extended by gaff (ill. SAIL¹). 2. Pointed top, esp. of mountain (ill. MOUNTAIN); point, e.g. of beard; highest point in curve or record of fluctuations (whence ~-*load*, greatest frequency or maximum of electric power, traffic, etc.; ~-*hour*, time of day when this occurs). **pea'ky**¹ *adj.*
peak² *v.i.* Waste away; *peaked*, sharp-featured, pinched. **pea'ky**² *adj.* Sickly, puny.
peak³ *v.* (naut.) Tilt (yard) vertically; raise (oar blades) almost vertically.
Peak⁴. Hilly district in NW. Derbyshire.
peal *n.* Loud ringing of bell(s), esp. series of changes on set of

bells; set of bells; loud volley of sound, esp. of thunder or laughter. ~ *v.* Sound forth in a peal; ring (bells) in peals; utter sonorously.
pear (pār) *n.* (Fleshy fruit, tapering towards stalk, of) the tree *Pyrus communis*, or other species with similar fruit; *alligator, avocado, prickly*, ~: see these words.
pearl (pěrl) *n.* 1. Concretion, usu. white or bluish-grey, formed round foreign body within shell of certain bivalve molluscs, having beautiful lustre and highly prized as gem; precious thing, finest example (*of* its kind); pearl-like thing, e.g. dewdrop, tear, tooth; *mother-of-*~: see MOTHER¹. 2. (print.) Size of type (approx. 5 point) between ruby and diamond. 3. Small fragment of various substances. 4. ~-*ash*, commercial potassium carbonate; ~-*barley*, barley reduced by attrition to small rounded grains; ~ *button*, button made of mother-of-pearl or imitation of it; ~-*diver*, one who dives for pearl-oysters; ~-*fisher*, one who fishes for pearls; ~ *oyster*, oyster of family Pteriidae which often produce pearls; ~-*shell*, mother-of-pearl as naturally found. ~ *v.* Sprinkle with pearly drops; make pearly in colour etc.; reduce (barley, etc.) to small pearls; form pearl-like drops; fish for pearls.
pear'ly *adj.* ~ *king*, costermonger wearing clothes decorated with many pearl buttons (so ~ *queen*); **pearl** *adj.* Of the colour of pearl.
Pearl Har'bor (pěrl, -ber). Harbour on island of Oahu, near Honolulu, Hawaii, site of U.S. naval base, bombed in surprise attack by Japan, 7 Dec. 1941.
pear'lite (pěr-) *n.* Microstructural constituent of iron, a conglomerate of cementite and ferrite.
pear'main (pār-; *or* permā'n) *n.* Kind of apple. [prob. f. L *parmanus* of Parma]
Pear'y (pēr-), Robert Edwin (1856–1920). American Arctic explorer; reached N. Pole on 6 April 1909.
pea'sant (pěz-) *n.* Countryman, rustic, esp. one working on land as small farmer or labourer. **pea'santry** *n.* (Body of) peasants.
pease (-z) *n.* Peas, esp. in ~ *pudding*; (archaic) *pea'secod*, peapod.
peat *n.* Accumulation of partially decayed vegetable matter found in damp or marshy regions; cut piece of this, used as fuel; ~-*bog*, broken ground whence peats have been cut; ~-*reek*, smoke of, whisky distilled over, peat-fire. **pea'ty** *adj.*
peau-de-soie (pō-de-swah) *n.* Rich thick silk material with dull satin surface on both sides. [Fr. = 'silk skin']
pě'bble *n.* 1. Small stone worn and rounded by natural action; ~-*dash*, mortar with small pebbles in it as coating for wall. 2. Colourless transparent rock-crystal used

[647]

pěcā'n *n.* Species of hickory (*Carya illinoensis*) common in Ohio and Mississippi valleys; olive-shaped finely flavoured nut of this.

pě'ccable *adj.* Liable to sin. **pěccabi'lity** *n.*

pěccadi'llō *n.* Trifling offence.

pě'ccant *adj.* Sinning; (med.) morbid, inducing disease. **pě'ccancy** *n.*

pě'ccarỹ *n.* Small gregarious pig (of genus *Tayassu*) of S. and Central America.

pěcca'vi (-ah-) *n.* Confession of guilt. [L, = 'I have sinned']

pêche mě'lba (pǎsh). Confection of ice-cream and peaches. [Fr., after name of Dame Nellie MELBA, Australian prima donna]

pěck[1] *n.* Measure of capacity for dry goods, 2 gallons, ¼ bushel; vessel used as peck measure.

pěck[2] *v.* 1. Strike (thing) with beak; pluck *out* thus; make (hole) thus; aim *at* with beak; (colloq.) eat in nibbling fashion. 2. Strike with pick or other pointed tool. 3. *pecking order*, hierarchy apparently recognized among domestic birds (also transf.). ~ *n.* Stroke with beak; mark made with this; (joc.) kiss like bird's peck; (slang) victuals; ~ *order*, pecking order.

pě'cker *n.* Bird that pecks; kind of hoe; (slang) courage, resolution (in *keep one's* ~ *up*, perh. orig. = beak):

pě'ckish *adj.* (colloq.) Somewhat hungry.

Pě'cksniff, Mr. Unctuously hypocritical character in Dickens's novel 'Martin Chuzzlewit'; hence, a canting hypocrite. **Pěcksni'ffian** *adj.*

pě'ctěn *n.* (pl. *-ens* or *-ines* pr. -ǐnēz). (zool.) 1. Comb-like structure of various kinds (in animals), e.g. stiff hairs on legs of bees. 2. Bivalve mollusc of genus *P*~, with radiating ribs suggesting comb on rounded shell, scallop. **pě'ctinate, -ātěd** *adjs.*

pě'ctin *n.* (chem.) White gelatinous substance soluble in water, closely related to the carbohydrates, formed in the ripening of fruits, and constituting the gelatinizing agent in vegetable juices. **pě'ctic** *adj.*

pě'ctoral *adj.* Of the breast or chest (~ *muscle*, ill. MUSCLE); remedying diseases of the chest; worn on the breast; ~ *cross*, cross of precious metal worn on the breast by bishops, cardinals, and abbots. ~ *n.* Ornamental breastplate, esp. that of Jewish high priest.

pě'ctōse *n.* (chem.) Insoluble substance related to cellulose and occurring with it in vegetable tissues, esp. in unripe fruits and fleshy roots, converted by the action of acids into PECTIN.

pě'culāte *v.* Embezzle. **pěcūlā'tion, pě'cūlātor** *ns.*

pěcū'liar *adj.* Belonging exclusively *to*; belonging to the individual; particular, special; singular, strange, odd; *P*~ *People*, the Jews as God's chosen people; (also) sect founded in London, 1838, without creed or church organization, relying on prayer and anointing for the cure of disease. ~ *n.* 1. Peculiar property, privilege, etc. 2. (hist.) Parish, church, exempt from jurisdiction of diocese in which it lies. 3. *P*~, member of the Peculiar People.

pěcūliǎ'ritỹ *n.* Being peculiar; characteristic; oddity.

pěcū'liarlỹ *adv.* As regards oneself alone, individually; especially, more than usually; oddly.

pěcū'niarỹ *adj.* (Consisting) of money; (of offence) having pecuniary penalty. **pěcū'niarilỹ** *adv.*

pě'dagogue (-ǒg) *n.* Schoolmaster, teacher (usu. contempt.). **pědagǒ'gic, -ical** *adjs.* **pědagǒ'gically** *adv.*

pě'dagǒgỹ, pědagǒ'gics *ns.* Science of teaching.

pě'dal[1] *n.* 1. Lever worked by the foot to transmit power in machine, e.g. bicycle. 2. Footlever in various musical instruments; in harp, for altering pitch of strings; in organ, each of (wooden) keys played upon by feet (ill. ORGAN), (also) foot-lever for drawing out several stops at once, opening swell-box, etc.; in piano, foot-lever for raising dampers from strings, thus sustaining tone and making it fuller (*loud* ~), or for softening tone (*soft* ~) by shifting hammers so as to strike only one or two strings instead of three, by diminishing length of blow, or by interposing strip of cloth between hammers and strings. 3. (mus.) Note sustained or reiterated in one part (usu. bass) through a series of harmonies. 4. ~*-board*, row of pedals in an organ or pedal piano; ~ *note*, note sounded by the pedals of an organ; (also) in brass instruments, one of the fundamental notes which are below their normal compass; ~ *organ*, that part of an organ controlled by the pedals; ~ *piano*, piano constructed with a pedal board. ~ *v.* Work pedals of bicycle etc.; work (bicycle etc.) thus; play on organ pedals.

pě'dal[2] *adj.* (zool.) Of the feet or foot, esp. of mollusc.

pě'dal[3] *adj.* ~ *straw*, lower and thicker part of Italian straw grown for plaiting.

pě'dant *n.* One who overrates or parades book-learning or technical knowledge, or insists on strict adherence to formal rules. **pědǎ'ntic** *adj.* **pědǎ'ntically** *adv.* **pě'dantrỹ** *n.*

pě'date *adj.* (zool.) Footed.

pě'ddle *v.* Follow occupation of pedlar; trade or deal in as pedlar.

pě'děstal *n.* Base supporting column in construction; base of statue etc.; each of two supports of knee-hole writing-table; foundation; ~*-table*, one with massive central support. ~ *v.t.* Set, support, on pedestal.

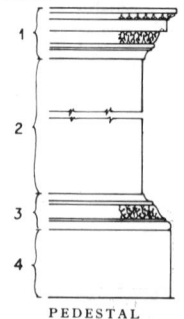

PEDESTAL
1. Cornice. 2. Dado. 3. Base. 4. Socle

pědě'strian *adj.* Going, performed, on foot; of walking; for those who walk; prosaic, dull, uninspired; ~ *crossing*, crossing-place for pedestrians over highway. ~ *n.* One who walks or goes on foot. **pědě'strianism** *n.*

pě'dicel, pě'dicle *ns.* (bot., zool.) Small, esp. subordinate, stalk-like structure in plant or animal (ill. INFLORESCENCE). **pědi'cūlate** *adj.*

pědi'cūlar, pědi'cūlous *adjs.* Lousy. **pědiculō'sis** *n.* Infestation with lice.

pě'dicūre *n.* 1. Chiropody. 2. Chiropodist. ~ *v.t.* Cure or treat (feet) by removing corns etc.

pě'digree *n.* Genealogical table; ancestral line (of man or animal); derivation (of word); ancient descent; (attrib.) having known line of descent. **pě'digreed** *adj.* [OF *pie de grue* crane's foot, mark ⅄ denoting succession in pedigrees]

pě'diment *n.* Triangular low-pitched gable crowning front of building in Greek style, esp. over portico (ill. TEMPLE[1]); similarly placed member of same or other form in Roman and Renaissance styles; *broken* ~, one without an apex. **pědimě'ntal, pě'dimentěd** *adjs.* (*Illustration, p. 649.*)

pě'dlar *n.* Travelling vendor of small wares, usu. carried in pack; (fig.) retailer (of gossip etc.).

pědǒ'lǒgỹ *n.* Science of soils.

pědǒ'mēter *n.* Instrument for estimating distance travelled on foot by recording number of steps taken.

pědŭ'ncle *n.* (bot.) Stalk of flower, fruit, or cluster, esp. main stalk bearing solitary flower or subordinate stalks (ill. INFLORESCENCE); (zool.) stalk-like process in animal body. **pědŭ'ncular, pědŭ'nculāte** *adjs.*

Pee'blesshire (-blz-). Former inland county of S. Scotland, since May 1975 part of the Borders region.

[648]

PEEK

peek v.i. Peep, peer; ∼-a-boo, (now U.S.) peep-bo. ∼ n. Peep, glance (take a ∼ at).

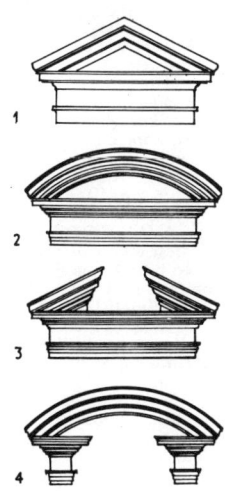

PEDIMENTS
1. Triangular. 2. Segmental. 3. Broken. 4. Open

peel[1] n. (hist.) Small square tower built in 16th c. in border counties of England and Scotland.

peel[2] n. Shovel, esp. baker's shovel, pole with broad flat disc at end for thrusting loaves etc. into oven.

peel[3] v. Strip peel, rind, bark, etc., from (fruit, vegetable, tree, etc.); take *off* (skin, peel, etc.); become bare of bark, skin, etc., (of bark, surface, etc.) come off or *off* like peel; (slang, of person) strip for exercise etc.; (colloq.) *keep one's eyes peeled*, keep a sharp look-out. ∼ n. Rind, outer coating, of fruit; *candied* ∼, candied rind of various species of citrus fruit, used in cookery and confectionery. **pee'ler**[1] n. **pee'lings** (-z) n.pl. What is peeled off.

Peel[4], John (1776–1854). Huntsman of Cumberland, England; hero of hunting-song 'D'ye ken John Peel?'.

Peel[5], Sir Robert (1788–1850). English statesman; prime minister 1834–5; formed ministry (1841–6) which repealed corn laws; founded Conservative Party and police force.

pee'ler[2] n. (archaic, colloq.) Policeman; (hist.) member of Irish constabulary, founded under secretaryship of Sir Robert PEEL[5].

peep[1] v.i. & n. (Make) feeble shrill sound of young birds, mice, etc.; chirp, squeak.

peep[2] v.i. Look through narrow aperture; look furtively; come cautiously or partly into view, emerge; (fig.) show itself unconsciously; *peeping Tom*, voyeur (f. name of tailor in story of Lady GODIVA). ∼ n. Furtive or peering glance; first appearance, esp. *of dawn*, *of day*; ∼-*of*-*day boys*, Protestant organization in Ireland (1784–93), searching opponents' houses at daybreak for arms; ∼-*hole*, small hole to peep through; *peepshow*, small exhibition of pictures etc. viewed through lens in small orifice; ∼-*toe*(*d*) *sandal*, shoe, one which allows tip of big toe to be seen.

pee'p-bō n. Game of hiding and suddenly appearing to child.

pee'per n. One who peeps; (slang) eye.

pee'pul, pi'pal (pē-) n. Indian species of fig-tree (*Ficus religiosa*) regarded as sacred.

peer[1] n. (fem. *peer'ess*) 1. Equal in civil standing or rank; equal in any respect. 2. Member of one of the degrees (duke, marquis, earl, viscount, baron) of nobility in United Kingdom; noble (of any country); *life* ∼, (since 1958) one whose title is not hereditary; ∼ *of the realm*, one of the peers of the United Kingdom, all of whom when of age may sit in the House of Lords. ∼ v. Rank with, equal; rank as equal *with*; make (man) a peer.

peer[2] v.i. Look narrowly; appear, peep out; come in sight.

peer'age n. Peers; nobility, aristocracy; rank of peer; book containing list of peers with genealogy etc.

peer'less adj. Having no equal, unrivalled. **peer'lessly** adv. **peer'lessness** n. [f. PEER[1]]

peeved (-vd) adj. (slang) Irritated.

pee'vish adj. Querulous, irritable. **pee'vishly** adv. **pee'vishness** n.

pee'wit, pēw- n. Lapwing; its cry; (U.S.) any of various N. Amer. flycatchers (*Sayornis*). [imit.]

pĕg n. 1. Pin, bolt, of wood, metal, etc., usu. round and slightly tapering, for holding together parts of framework etc., stopping up vent of cask, hanging hats etc. on, holding ropes of tent, tightening or loosening strings of violin etc. (ill. STRINGED), marking cribbage-score etc.; clothes-peg; (fig.) occasion, pretext, theme (*to hang discourse etc. on*); *off the* ∼, (of garment) bought ready-made; *take* (person) *down a* ∼ *or two*, humble him; ∼ *leg*, wooden leg; ∼-*top*, pear-shaped spinning-top with metal peg; ∼-*top trousers*, trousers wide at hips, narrow at ankles. 2. Drink, esp. of brandy and soda-water. ∼ v. Fix with peg; (Stock Exch.) prevent price of (stock etc.) from falling or rising by freely buying or selling at given price; mark score with pegs on cribbage-board; mark *out* boundaries of (mining-claim etc.); strike, pierce, aim *at*, with peg; (slang) throw (stone), throw stones etc. (*at*); drive pegs into (cricket-bat); work (*away*) persistently (*at*); ∼ *down*, restrict (*to*· rules etc.); ∼ *out*, (croquet) hit peg with ball as final stroke in game; (slang) die, be ruined.

Pĕ'gasus. 1. (Gk myth.) Winged horse, favourite of the Muses, sprung from blood of MEDUSA[1]; a blow of its hoof gave rise to the fountain Hippocrene on Mt Helicon. 2. (astron.) Northern constellation, figured as a winged horse, containing three stars of the 2nd magnitude forming with one star of Andromeda a large square (*square of* ∼).

Pehlevi: see PAHLAVI.

peignoir (pā'nwär) n. Woman's loose dressing-gown.

peine forte et dure (pān fôrt ā dūr). (hist.) Pressing to death, form of punishment inflicted on persons arraigned for felony who refused to plead. [Fr., = 'severe and hard punishment']

Peisistratus: see PISISTRATUS.

pē'jorative (*or* pijŏ'-) adj. & n. Depreciatory (word).

pēke n. Pekingese dog.

pēkinē'se (-z) n. = PEKINGESE, 2.

Pĕki'ng. Capital city of China; ∼ *man*, hominid, *Pithecanthropus pekinensis*, represented by at least a dozen skulls and other remains found near Peking from 1929 onwards. [Chin., = 'northern capital']

Pĕkingē'se (-z) adj. Of Peking. ∼ n. 1. Native, inhabitant, of Peking. 2. (Breed of) small dog of the pug type, with long silky coat, flat face, and prominent eyes, orig. brought to Europe from Summer Palace at Peking in 1860.

pĕ'kōe n. Superior kind of black tea. [Chin. *pek-ho* white down (leaves being picked young with down on them)]

pĕlă'gian[1], **pĕlā'gic** adjs. Of, inhabiting, the open sea. **pĕlā'-gian** n. Pelagic animal.

Pĕlā'gius (d. c 420). Latinized name of a British (or Irish) lay monk and theologian who denied the Catholic doctrine of original sin and maintained that the human will is capable of good without the help of divine grace; his doctrines were condemned by Pope Zosimus in 418. **Pĕlā'gian** adj. & n. **Pelā'gianism** n.

pĕlärgō'nium n. Plant of genus *P*∼ with showy flowers and fragrant leaves (pop. called *geranium*). [Gk *pelargos* stork]

Pĕlă'sgian (-zj- *or* -zg-) n. One of the pre-Greek inhabitants of Greece and the islands and coasts of the E. Mediterranean. **Pĕlă's-gic** adj. Of Pelasgians.

pĕ'lerine (*or* -ēn) n. (hist.) Woman's long narrow cape or tippet (ill. CLOAK).

Pē'leus (-lūs). (Gk legend) King of Thessaly and father, by Thetis, of Achilles.

pĕlf n. Money, wealth (usu. contempt.).

Pē'liăs. (Gk legend): see JASON.

[649]

PELICAN

pĕ'lican *n.* Large gregarious fish-eating bird of genus *Pelecanus* with large membranous pouch between lower mandibles of long hooked bill, used for storing fish

PELICAN

(the fable, of Egyptian origin, that the pelican feeds or revives its young with its own blood app. referred originally to another bird); ~ *crossing*, pedestrian crossing controlled by traffic lights operated by pedestrians.
Pē'lion. Wooded mountain near coast of SE. Thessaly, Greece; in Gk myth., home of centaurs; the giants were said to have piled Olympus on Mt. Ossa and Ossa on Pelion in their attempt to reach heaven and destroy the gods.
pėli'sse (-ēs) *n.* (hist.) Woman's mantle with armholes or sleeves,

PELISSE
A. AS CLOAK, *c* 1786. B. AS COAT, *c* 1806
1. Boa. 2. Reticule

reaching to ankles; child's outdoor garment worn over other clothes; cape or cloak worn as part of military uniforms (ill. CAVALRY).
pĕllă'gra *n.* Deficiency disease, endemic in countries whose populations live chiefly on cereals with low protein content (as maize), characterized by disorders of the skin, digestion, and nervous system. [It., perh. orig. *pelle agra* rough skin]

pĕ'llĕt *n.* Small ball of paper, bread, etc.; pill; small shot; circular boss in coins etc.; (her.) a roundel sable (ill. HERALDRY).
pĕ'llĕtėd *adj.* Formed into a pellet.
pĕ'llĭcle *n.* Thin skin; membrane; film. **pėlli'cūlar** *adj.*
pĕ'llĭtory *n.* 1. (also ~ *of Spain*) Composite plant (*Anacyclus pyrethrum*), native of Barbary, with pungent root used as local irritant etc. 2. (also ~ *of the wall*) Low bushy plant (*Parietaria officinalis*) with small ovate leaves and greenish flowers, growing on or at foot of walls.
pĕ'll-mĕ'll *adv.* In disorder, promiscuously; headlong, recklessly. ~ *adj.* Confused; tumultuous. ~ *n.* Confusion, medley, mêlée.
pėllū'cĭd *adj.* Transparent, clear; clear in style or expression; mentally clear. **pėllū'cĭdlȳ** *adv.* **pėllūci'dĭtȳ** *n.*
pĕ'lmĕt *n.* Valance or narrow pendent border concealing curtain-rods above window or door (ill. WINDOW). [prob. f. Fr. *palmette*, conventional palm-leaf design on cornice]
Pĕ'loponnēse, Pĕloponnē'sus. That part of Greece S. of Isthmus of Corinth. **Pĕloponnē'sian** (-shan) *adj.* ~ *War*, war (431–404 B.C.) waged by Sparta and her allies upon Athens and Athenian Empire resulting in the surrender of Athens and transfer, for a brief period, of leadership of Greece to Sparta.

PEMBROKESHIRE

Pĕ'lŏps. (Gk myth.) Son of TANTALUS[1], brother of NIOBE, and father of ATREUS.
pėlō'ta *n.* Basque ball-game resembling tennis or rackets, played in large walled court with curved wickerwork racket attached to leather glove. [Span., = 'ball' (f. L *pila*)]
pĕlt[1] *n.* Skin of sheep or goat with short wool on; skin of fur-bearing animal, esp. undressed; raw skin of sheep etc. stripped of wool or fur. **pĕ'ltrȳ** *n.* Pelts collectively.
pĕlt[2] *v.* Assail with missiles; (of rain etc.) beat with violence; strike *at* repeatedly with missiles; go on throwing (missiles). ~ *n.* Pelting.
pĕ'lta *n.* Small light shield of ancient Greeks, Romans, etc. (ill. SHIELD); (bot.) shield-like structure. **pĕ'ltate** *adj.*
pĕ'lvis *n.* 1. Basin-shaped cavity at lower end of trunk in most vertebrates, formed in man by innominate bones with sacrum and coccyx. 2. Funnel-shaped origin of ureter, having a wide end which lies within the kidney (ill. KIDNEY). **pĕ'lvic** *adj.*
Pĕ'mbroke. *n.* 1. Variety of Welsh corgi with short tail (ill. DOG). 2. ~ *table*, table on 4 fixed legs with hinged flaps that can be spread out and supported on brackets (ill. TABLE). [town in S. Wales]
Pĕ'mbrokeshire. Former county of SW. Wales, since April 1974 part of Dyfed.

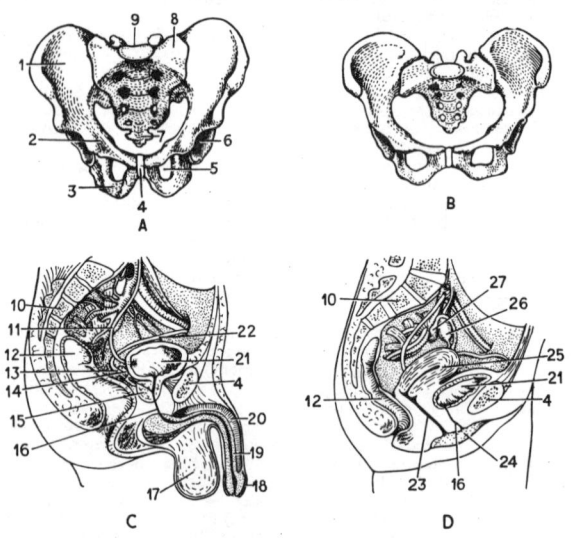

HUMAN PELVIS AND PERINEUM
A., C. MALE. B., D. FEMALE

A. 1. Ilium. 2. Pubis. 3. Ischium. 4. Pubic symphysis. 5. Obturator foramen. 6. Articular surface of head of femur. 7. Coccyx. 8. Sacrum. 9. Articular surface of 5th lumbar vertebra. C. 10. Spine. 11. Ureter. 12. Rectum. 13. Vas deferens. 14. Seminal vesicle. 15. Prostate gland. 16. Urethra. 17. Scrotum enclosing testicles. 18. Foreskin or prepuce. 19. Penis. 20. Erectile tissue. 21. Bladder. 22. Spermatic duct. D. 23. Vagina. 24. Labium. 25. Uterus or womb. 26. Ovary. 27. Fallopian tube

Pembs. *abbrev.* Pembrokeshire.
pĕ′mmican *n.* N. Amer. Indian food of lean meat dried, pounded, mixed into paste with melted fat and pressed into cakes; beef similarly treated and freq. flavoured with currants etc. for Arctic and other travellers.
pĕn[1] *n.* Small enclosure for cows, sheep, poultry, etc.; enclosure resembling this, as *submarine*-~; (W. Ind.) farm, plantation. ~ *v.t.* Enclose, shut *up*, shut *in*; shut up (cattle etc.) in pen.
pĕn[2] *n.* Quill feather with quill pointed and split into two sections, for writing with ink; small instrument of gold, steel, etc., similarly pointed and pointed into rod of wood etc. (~-*holder*), pen and pen-holder together; any contrivance for writing with fluid ink; writing, style of this; BALL[1]-*point* ~, FOUNTAIN-~: see these words; ~-*and-ink*, (attrib., of drawing etc.) done, made, with pen and ink; ~-*and-wash*, (attrib.) using both pen and brush; ~-*feather*, quill-feather of bird's wing; ~-*friend*, friend with whom one corresponds without meeting; *pe′nknife*, small knife usu. carried in pocket, orig. for making or mending quill pens; *pe′nman*, one who writes a (*good*, *bad*, etc.) hand; author; *pe′nmanship*, skill in writing, style of handwriting; action or style of literary composition; ~-*name*, literary pseudonym; ~-*pushing*, (colloq.) clerical work; so ~-*pusher*; ~ *wiper*, appliance usu. of small pieces of cloth for wiping pen after use. ~ *v.t.* Write, compose and write (letter etc.).
pĕn[3] *n.* Female swan.
pĕn[4] *n.* (U.S. slang) Prison. [abbrev. of *penitentiary*]
pen. *abbrev.* Peninsula.
P.E.N. *abbrev.* (International Association of) Poets, Playwrights, Editors, Essayists, and Novelists.
pĕ′nal *adj.* Of punishment, concerned with inflicting this; (of offence) punishable, esp. by law; inflicted as punishment; used as place of punishment; ~ *servitude*, imprisonment for three years or longer with compulsory labour (abolished in Britain in 1948).
pē′nally *adv.*
pē′nalize *v.t.* Make, declare, penal; (sport.) subject competitor to penalty or comparative disadvantage (also freq. fig.).
pĕ′nalty *n.* Punishment, esp. (exaction of) sum of money, for breach of law, rule, or contract; money thus paid; (sport, etc.) disadvantage imposed on competitor for breaking rule or winning previous contest; (bridge) points added to opponents' score when declarer fails to make his contract; ~ *area*, (Assoc. footb.) area in front of goal within which breach of certain rules involves award of penalty kick (ill. ASSOCIATION); ~ *kick*, (Assoc. & Rugby footb.) free kick allowed for certain infringements of rules.

pĕ′nance *n.* (R.C. & Orthodox Churches) Sacrament including contrition, confession, satisfaction, and absolution for sin; act of self-mortification as expression of penitence, esp. one imposed by priest; *do* ~, perform such act.
Pěnă′ng. State of Malaysia; capital, George Town.
pĕna′tes (-ahtēz) *n.pl.* (Rom. myth.) Gods of the store-room, worshipped, together with the lares (see LAR[2]), by households.
pence: see PENNY.
penchant (pah′nshahn) *n.* Inclination, liking, (*for*).
pĕ′ncil (-sl) *n.* 1. Artist's paintbrush (archaic); (fig.) painter's art or style. 2. Instrument for drawing or writing, esp. (*lead* ~) of graphite enclosed in wooden cylinder or in metal case with tapering end; pencil-shaped object; ~-*case*, case for holding pencils etc. 3. (optics) Set of rays meeting at a point. 4. (geom.) Figure formed by set of straight lines meeting at a point. ~ *v.t.* Tint or mark (as) with lead pencil; jot down with pencil; (esp. in past part.) mark delicately with thin concentric lines of colour or shading.
Pĕ′nda (577–*c* 655). King of Mercia; champion of heathenism against Christianity.
pĕ′ndant *n.* 1. Hanging ornament, esp. one attached to necklace, bracelet, etc. 2. (naut., pr. pĕ′nant, also spelt *pennant*) Short rope hanging from head of mast etc. with eye at lower end for receiving hooks of tackles; tapering flag, esp. that flown at mast-head of vessel in commission (ill. FLAG[4]); *broad* ~, short swallow-tailed pendant distinguishing commodore's ship in squadron. 3. Shank and ring of watch by which it is suspended. 4. Match, parallel, companion, complement (*to*).
pĕ′ndent *adj.* Hanging; overhanging; undecided, pending; (gram.) of which the construction is incomplete. **pĕ′ndency** *n.*
pĕndĕ′ntė lī′tė. (law) Pending the suit.
pĕndĕ′ntive *n.* (archit.) Each of the spherical triangles formed by the intersection of a dome by two pairs of opposite arches springing from the four supporting columns (ill. DOME).
pĕ′nding *adj.* Undecided, a-waiting decision or settlement. ~ *prep.* During; until.
pĕndră′gon *n.* Ancient British or Welsh prince; *Uther P*~: see UTHER PENDRAGON. [Welsh, = 'chief leader', f. *pen* head, *dragon* dragon standard, f. L *draco* dragon, standard of cohort]
pĕ′ndūlāte *v.i.* Swing like a pendulum.
pĕ′ndūline *adj.* (of nest) Suspended; (of bird) building such nest.
pĕ′ndūlous *adj.* Suspended, hanging down; oscillating. **pĕ′ndūlously** *adv.*
pĕ′ndūlum *n.* Body suspended so as to be free to swing, esp. rod with weighted end regulating movement of clock's works (ill. CLOCK[1]); person, thing, that oscillates; *swing of the* ~, (fig.) tendency to alternation of power etc.; (billiards) ~ *cannon*, ~ *stroke*, succession of cannons off two balls jammed in pocket-mouth.
Pĕnĕ′lopė. (Gk legend) Wife of Odysseus; when her husband did not return after fall of Troy, she told her importunate suitors that she would marry one of them when she had finished the piece of weaving on which she was engaged, but every night she undid the work that she had done during the day.
pĕ′neplain *n.* (geol.) Area of land reduced almost to a plain by erosion.
pĕnĕtrā′lia *n.pl.* Innermost shrine or recesses.
pĕ′nĕtrāte *v.* Find access into or through, pass through; make a way (*with*, *through*, *to*); (of sight) pierce through; permeate; imbue (*with*); (fig.) see into, find out, discern (design, the truth, etc.).
pĕ′nĕtrāting *adj.* (esp.) Gifted with or suggestive of insight; (of voice etc.) easily heard through or above other sounds. **pĕnĕtrabi′lity**, **pĕnĕtrā′tion** *ns.* **pĕ′nĕtrable**, **pĕ′nĕtrative** *adjs.*
pĕ′nguin (-nggw-) *n.* Any bird of the family Spheniscidae, including several genera of sea-birds of the southern hemisphere, with wings reduced to scaly flippers with which they swim under water.
pĕ′nial *adj.* Of the penis.
pĕ′nicillate *adj.* (biol.) Furnished with, forming, small tuft(s); marked with streaks as of pencil or brush.
pĕnici′llin *n.* Substance obtained from the mould *Penicillium notatum*, effective against many micro-organisms of disease (the first ANTIBIOTIC to be used therapeutically, during war of 1939–45). [L *penicillus* painter's brush, f. brush-like sporangia of the mould]
pĕni′nsūla *n.* Piece of land almost surrounded by water, or projecting far into the sea.
pĕni′nsular *adj.* Of (the nature of) a peninsula; *P*~ *War*, that carried on in Spain and Portugal (1808–14) between French under Napoleon and English, Spanish, and Portuguese under Wellington. ~ *n.* Inhabitant of a peninsula.
pĕni′nsūlāte *v.t.* Make (land) into a peninsula.
pē′nis *n.* Organ of urination and copulation in male animals (ill. PELVIS).
pĕ′nitent *adj.* That repents, contrite. ~ *n.* Repentant sinner; person doing penance under direction of confessor; (pl.) any of various R.C. congregations or orders associated for mutual discipline, giving religious aid to criminals etc. **pĕ′nitently** *adv.* **pĕ′nitence** *n.*

pĕnĭtĕ'ntial (-shal) adj. Of penitence or penance; ~ psalms, those expressing penitence (Pss. 6, 32, 38, 51, 102, 130, 143). pĕnĭtĕ'ntially adv.

pĕnĭtĕ'ntiary (-sha-) n. 1. Office in papal court deciding questions of penance, dispensations, etc.; Grand P~, cardinal presiding over this. 2. Reformatory prison; (U.S.) State prison. ~ adj. Of penance; of reformatory treatment of criminals.

Pĕnn, William (1644–1718). English Quaker, founder of Pennsylvania, 1681.

Penn., Penna abbrevs. Pennsylvania.

pĕ'nnant n. = PENDANT, sense 2; PENNON; (U.S.) flag awarded as distinction.

pĕ'nni n. (pl. -ia). 1/100 of a markka.

pĕ'nnifŏrm adj. (biol.) Having the form or appearance of a feather.

pĕ'nnilĕss adj. Having no money; poor, destitute.

Pĕ'nnine Chain. (also Pennines) System of hills in N. England, running northwards from the PEAK¹ to the Lake District.

pĕ'nnon n. Long narrow flag, triangular or swallow-tailed (ill. FLAG¹), esp. as military ensign of lancer regiments; long pointed streamer of ship; flag.

Pĕnnsylvā'nia. Middle Atlantic State of U.S.; one of the original thirteen States of the Union (1787); capital, Harrisburg. [named 1681 in honour of Admiral Sir William Penn, father of William PENN, founder of the colony]

pĕ'nny n. (pl. pence of amounts, pennies of individual coins as such). 1/100 of a British POUND¹; until 1971, 1/12 of a shilling; (bibl.) denarius; a pretty ~, a good sum of money; turn an honest ~, earn money by an odd job; ~-a-line, (of writing) cheap, superficial; ~-a-liner, hack writer; ~-farthing, early kind of bicycle with large front wheel and small rear one; ~-in-the-slot, (of mechanical devices esp. for the automatic supply of commodities) actuated by the fall of a penny inserted through a slot; ~-pinching (adj.) niggardly; (n.) niggardliness; ~ post, post for conveyance of letters at ordinary charge of one penny, esp. that established in the United Kingdom on 10 Jan. 1840 on the initiative of Rowland Hill; pe'nnyweight, (abbrev. dwt) measure of weight, 24 grains, 1/20 of an ounce troy; ~ wise, (over-)careful in small expenditures; pe'nnywort, name of two plants: (1) wall ~ (navelwort), perennial herb (Umbilicus rupestris) with rounded concave leaves, growing in crevices of rocks and walls; (2) marsh ~ (white-rot), small creeping or floating plant (Hydrocotyle vulgaris),

with rounded leaves, growing in marshy places; pe'nnyworth, pe'nnorth (-nerth), as much as can be bought for a penny.

pĕnnyroy'al n. Kind of mint (Mentha pulegium) with small leaves and prostrate habit, formerly cultivated for its supposed medicinal virtues.

pēnŏ'logў n. Study of punishment and of prison management. pēnolŏ'gical adj. pēnŏ'logĭst n.

pĕ'nsile adj. Hanging down, pendulous; (of bird etc.) that constructs pensile nest.

pĕ'nsion n. 1. Periodical payment made esp. by government or employer in consideration of past service, old age, widowhood, etc. 2. Consultative assembly of members of Gray's Inn. 3. Boarding-house where a fixed rate for board and lodging is charged (also pr. pahńsyawń); this charge; accommodation provided thus. ~ v.t. Grant pension to; buy over with pension; ~ off, dismiss with pension. pĕ'nsionable adj. Entitled, entitling person, to pension.

pĕ'nsionary n. Recipient of a pension; creature, hireling; (hist.) chief municipal magistrate of Dutch city; Grand P~, first minister of Holland and Zealand (1619–1794). ~ adj. Of a pension.

pĕ'nsioner n. Recipient of pension; hireling, creature; (Camb. Univ.) undergraduate who is not a scholar on the foundation of a college, or a sizar, but pays for his own commons etc.

pĕ'nsive adj. Plunged in thought; melancholy. pĕ'nsivelў adv. pĕ'nsiveness n.

pĕ'nstŏck n. Sluice, flood-gate (ill. HYDRO-ELECTRIC).

pĕnt adj. Closely confined, shut in or up.

pĕnta-, pĕnt- prefix. Five.

pĕ'ntachŏrd (-k-) n. Musical instrument with 5 strings; system or series of 5 notes (ill. MODE).

pĕ'ntacle n. Figure used as symbol, esp. in magic; prop. = pentagram.

pĕ'ntăd n. Set, group, of 5.

pĕ'ntagon n. Plane figure of 5 angles and sides; P~, U.S. Department of Defense at Washington [from the shape of its building]. pĕntă'gonal adj.

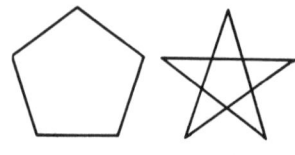

A. PENTAGON.   B. PENTAGRAM

pĕ'ntagrăm n. Five-pointed star formed by producing sides of pentagon both ways till they intersect, formerly used as mystic symbol.

pĕntahĕ'dron n. Solid figure of 5 faces. pĕntahĕ'dral adj.

pĕntă'merous adj. (bot.) Having parts of flower-whorl 5 in number; (zool.) consisting of 5 joints.

pĕntă'meter n. 1. (Gk & L pros.) Verse composed of two equal parts each having 2½ dactylic feet, thus:

−∪∪ | −∪∪ | − || −∪∪ | −∪∪ | ⌣

(spondees may be substituted for dactyls in the first half), used alternately with hexameter to form elegiac couplet. 2. (Engl. pros.) Line of verse of 5 feet, e.g. heroic or iambic verse of 10 syllables, thus:

∪/ | ∪/ | ∪/ | ∪/ | ∪/ |

pĕ'ntāne n. Any of a group of paraffin hydrocarbons containing 5 carbon atoms, including several colourless volatile liquids occurring in petroleum.

pĕ'ntaprĭsm (-zm) n. Prism having 5 faces, with 4 angles of 112·5° and one of 90° on each face, enabling light rays to be reflected at 90° without inverting the image (ill. CAMERA).

Pĕ'ntateuch (-tūk) n. First 5 books of O.T. (Genesis, Exodus, Leviticus, Numbers, Deuteronomy) traditionally ascribed to Moses. Pĕ'ntateuchal adj.

pĕntă'thlŏn n. 1. In ancient Greece, athletic contest of 5 events in each of which the same competitors took part (foot race, long jump, javelin-throwing, discus-throwing, wrestling). 2. Similar contest in modern times, comprising 5 different events.

pĕntatŏ'mic adj. (chem.) Containing 5 atoms in the molecule.

pĕntatŏ'nic adj. (mus.) Consisting of 5 notes or sounds; ~ scale, scale without semitones (ill. SCALE³).

pĕntă'valent adj. (chem.) Having a valency of 5; quinquivalent.

Pĕ'ntĕcŏst. 1. Jewish harvest festival observed on 50th day after the 2nd day of Passover (Lev. 23: 15, 16). 2. WHIT Sunday. pĕntĕcŏ'stal adj. [Gk pentēkostē (hēmera) fiftieth (day)]

Pĕntĕ'licus. Mountain NE. of Athenian plain, famous for its marble, milky-white but weathering to golden-brown, used for many of chief buildings and sculptures of ancient Athens.

Pĕnthĕsilĕ'a. (Gk legend) Queen of Amazons; came to help of Troy after death of Hector and was slain by Achilles.

pĕ'nthouse (-t-h-) n. Sloping roof, esp. as subsidiary structure attached to wall of main building; awning, canopy, or the like; structure with sloping top round three sides of tennis court (ill. TENNIS); (orig. U.S.) separate flat, house, or other structure on roof of block of flats or other building.

Pĕ'ntland Fĭrth. Channel separating Orkney Islands from mainland of Scotland.

[652]

Pĕ′ntland Hills (-z). (also *Pentlands*) Range of rounded hills in Lothian, Borders, and Strathclyde regions of Scotland.

pĕ′ntōde *n.* Electronic amplifying valve with 5 main electrodes.

Pĕ′ntonville. Prison in Islington, London.

pĕ′ntōse *n.* (chem.) Sugar with 5 carbon atoms in the molecule.

pĕntstĕ′mon (*or* pĕ′-) *n.* N. Amer. herbaceous plant of genus *P~*, allied to foxglove with showy flowers, usu. tubular and two-lipped.

pĕnŭ′lt, pĕnŭ′ltĭmate *adjs.* Last but one. *~ ns.* Last syllable but one.

pĕnŭ′mbra *n.* Partly shaded region around shadow of opaque body, esp. round total shadow of moon or earth in eclipse (ill. ECLIPSE); lighter outer part of sunspot; partial shadow. **pĕnŭ′mbral** *adj.*

pĕnūr′ious *adj.* Poor, scanty; stingy, grudging. **pĕnūr′iouslў** *adv.* **pĕnūr′iousnĕss** *n.*

pĕ′nūrў *n.* Destitution, poverty; lack, scarcity, (*of*).

pĕ′on *n.* 1. (also pr. pūn) In India, office-messenger, attendant, orderly. 2. In Span. Amer., daylabourer; in Mexico etc., debtor held in servitude by creditor until debts are worked off. **pĕ′onaġe** *n.* Employment, service, of peons.

pĕ′onў *n.* Plant of genus *Paeonia* with large, handsome, crimson, pink, or white, globular, flowers, in cultivation freq. double.

people (pē′pl) *n.* Persons composing community, tribe, race, or nation; persons belonging to a place or forming a company or class etc.; subjects of king etc.; congregation of parish priest etc.; parents or other relatives; commonalty; body of enfranchised or qualified citizens; persons in general; *People's Charter*: see CHARTER. *~ v.t.* Fill with people, populate, fill (place *with*); inhabit, occupy, fill (esp. in past part.).

pĕp *n.* (orig. U.S. slang) Vigour, go, spirit; *~-pill*, pill containing stimulant drug; *~-talk*, talk meant to inspire hearers to exceptional effort etc. *~ v.t.* Fill *up* or inspire with energy and vigour. [abbrev. of *pepper*]

P.E.P. *abbrev.* Political and Economic Planning.

Pĕ′pin, Pi′ppin². Name of several members of the Carolingian family: *Pepin I* (of Landen) (d. 639), Frankish mayor of the palace; *Pepin II* (of Héristal) (d. 714), Frankish ruler, father of Charles Martel; *Pepin III* 'the Short' (714–68), Frankish king, younger son of Charles Martel and father of Charlemagne.

pĕ′plum *n.* Short flounce from waist of garment.

pĕ′pper *n.* 1. Pungent aromatic condiment got from dried berries of plants of genus *Piper*, used whole (*peppercorns*) or ground into powder; climbing shrub of East Indies, cultivated also in W. Indies, from which this is chiefly got; *black ~*, shrub (*P. nigrum*); most usual form of the condiment, prepared from slightly unripe berries; *white ~*, milder form prepared from ripe berries, or from black by removing outer husk. 2. Capsicum; *red ~*, (large red or yellow edible fruit of) plant *Capsicum annuum*; cayenne pepper. 3. *~-and-salt*, (cloth) of dark and light threads woven together, showing small dots of dark and light intermingled; *~-box*, small usu. round box with perforated lid for sprinkling pepper (also *~-castor, -pot*); irregular buttress in Eton fives-court; *pe′ppercorn*, dried berry of black pepper, esp. as nominal rent; *~-pot*, pepper-castor. *~ v.t.* Sprinkle, treat, with pepper; besprinkle as with pepper; pelt with missiles.

pĕ′ppermint *n.* Kind of mint, *Mentha piperita*, cultivated for its essential oil; this oil, with characteristic pungent aromatic flavour leaving after-sensation of coolness; sweet flavoured with this.

pĕ′pperў *adj.* Of, like, abounding in, pepper; (fig.) pungent, stinging, hot-tempered.

pĕ′psin *n.* Enzyme contained in gastric juice, converting proteins into peptones in presence of dilute acid.

pĕ′ptic *adj.* Digestive; *~ gland*, gland secreting gastric juice; *~ ulcer*, any ulcer of the digestive system.

pĕ′ptōne *n.* Any of a class of easily soluble albuminoid substances into which proteins are converted by action of pepsin etc.

pĕ′ptonīze *v.t.* (esp.) Subject (food) to artificial process of partial digestion, as aid to weak digestion.

Pepys (pēps), Samuel (1633–1703). English diarist; secretary of Admiralty 1673–9, 1684–8.

pĕr *prep.* 1. Through, by means of (esp. in L phrases, for which see entries); *~ post*, by post; *as ~ usual*, (joc.) as usual. 2. For each; *~ cent*, (symbol %) in every hundred; *~ head*, for each person; *~ hour*, in each hour (of speed); *~ second per second*, (abbrev. per sec./sec.) per second every second (of rate of acceleration).

per- *prefix.* Completely, very; to destruction, to the bad; (in chem. compounds) denoting maximum of some element in combination.

pĕradvĕ′nture *adv.* (archaic) Perhaps. *~ n.* Uncertainty, chance, conjecture; *beyond, without*, (*all*) *~*, without doubt.

perai: see PIRANHA.

Perak (pār′a *or* pēr′a). State of Malaysia; capital, Ipoh.

peră′mbūlāte *v.t.* Walk through, over, or about; travel through and inspect (territory); formally establish boundaries of (parish etc.) by walking round them. **perămbūlā′tion** *n.* **peră′mbūlătorў** *adj.* **peră′mbūlātor** *n.* Carriage for one or two children, usu. with four wheels, pushed by hand.

pĕr ă′nnum. (So much) by the year. [L]

percā′le *n.* Plain-woven cotton fabric resembling calico, but finer and wider.

perceī′ve *v.t.* Apprehend with the mind, observe, understand; apprehend through one of the senses, esp. sight.

percĕ′ntaġe *n.* Rate, proportion, per cent; (loosely) proportion.

pĕr′cept *n.* (philos.) Object of perception; mental product, as opp. to action, of perceiving. **percĕ′ptūal** *adj.*

percĕ′ptĭble *adj.* That can be perceived by senses or intellect. **percĕptĭbi′litў** *n.* **percĕ′ptĭblў** *adv.*

percĕ′ption *n.* 1. Act, faculty, of perceiving; intuitive recognition (*of*); (philos.) action by which the mind refers its sensations to external object as cause. 2. (law) Collection (of rents etc.). **percĕ′ptional** *adj.* **percĕ′ptive** *adj.* **percĕ′ptivelў** *adv.* **percĕ′ptiveness, percĕpti′vitў** *ns.*

Pĕr′cevāl, Sir. Hero of a group of folk-tales later associated with the Arthurian cycle; in later versions, one of the knights successful in the quest for the holy GRAIL².

pĕrch¹ *n.* Common European spiny-finned freshwater fish (*Perca fluviatilis*) used as food; related N. Amer. species, *P. flavescens* (*yellow ~*).

pĕrch² *n.* 1. Horizontal bar for bird to rest upon; anything serving for this; (fig.) elevated or secure position. 2. Centre pole of some four-wheeled vehicles; horizontal bar used in softening leather. 3. (also *pole, rod*) Measure of length, esp. for land, 5½ yds; measure of area (also *square ~*), 30¼ sq. yds. *~ v.* Alight, rest, as bird (*on* bough etc.); settle, alight (*on*); place (as) on perch. **pĕr′cher** *n.* Passerine bird with feet adapted for perching.

perchă′nce (-ah-) *adv.* By chance (archaic); possibly, maybe.

pĕr′cherŏn (-she-; *or* pār′sherawn) *n.* Strong swift horse of breed originating in le Perche, district in department of Orne, N. France.

perci′pient *adj.* Perceiving, conscious. *~ n.* One who perceives, esp. (telepathy etc.) something outside range of senses. **perci′pience** *n.*

pĕr′colāte *v.* Filter, ooze, through (freq. fig.); permeate; strain (liquid etc.) through pores etc. **pĕrcolā′tion** *n.*

pĕr′colātor *n.* (esp.) Apparatus for making coffee by allowing water to filter repeatedly through ground coffee.

pĕr cŏ′ntra. (On) the opposite side (of an account etc.). [L]

percŭ′ss *v.t.* (med.) Tap gently with finger or instrument for purposes of diagnosis etc.

percu'ssion n. Forcible striking of one (usu. solid) body against another; (med.) percussing; ~ *instrument*, (mus.) instrument played by percussion, esp. struck with a stick or the hand (drum, triangle, tambourine) or struck together in pairs (cymbals); ~ *cap*, small copper cap or cylinder in firearm, containing fulminating powder and exploded by percussion of a hammer. **percu'ssive** adj.

Per'cy[1], Sir Henry (1366-1403), called Hotspur. Eldest son of 1st Earl of Northumberland; helped to place Henry IV on throne; revolted, 1403, and was killed at battle of Shrewsbury.

Per'cy[2], Thomas (1768-1808). English antiquary; editor of 'Reliques of Ancient English Poetry', a collection of ballads, metrical romances, and historical songs.

per di'em (dē-). (So much) by the day. [L]

perdi'tion n. Eternal death, damnation.

perdu', **-du'e** adj. Hidden; (mil.) placed as an outpost in hiding (esp. in *lie* ~).

perdur'able adj. Permanent; eternal; durable. **perdurabi'lity** n. **perdur'ably** adv.

pe'regrināte v.i. (joc.) Travel, journey. **peregrinā'tion** n.

pe'regrine (or -ēn) n. (also ~ *falcon*) Species of falcon (*Falco peregrinus*) esteemed for hawking (so called because the young were not taken from the nests but caught on their passages from their breeding-places).

Père Lachaise: see LA CHAISE.

pere'mptory (or pě'-) adj. 1. Decisive, final; esp. (law) ~ *mandamus*, in which the command is absolute; ~ *writ*, enforcing defendant's appearance without option. 2. (of statement or command) Admitting no denial or refusal; absolutely fixed, essential; (of person etc.) dogmatic, imperious, dictatorial. **pere'mptorily** adv. **pere'mptoriness** n.

pere'nnial adj. Lasting through the year; (of stream) flowing through all seasons of the year; lasting long or for ever; (of plant) living several years (cf. ANNUAL). **pere'nnially** adv. **pere'nnial** n. Perennial plant.

per'fèct adj. 1. Complete, not deficient; faultless; (of lesson) thoroughly learned; thoroughly trained or skilled (*in*); exact, precise; entire, unqualified. 2. (gram., of tense) Denoting completed event or action viewed in relation to the present; *future* ~, expressing action completed at the time indicated. 3. (bot.) Having all four whorls of the flower; (mus., of interval) not augmented or diminished, in normal form (ill. INTERVAL); ~ *cadence*, one consisting of direct chord of tonic preceded by dominant or subdominant chord. **per'fèctly** adv. **per'fèctness** n.

per'fèct n. Perfect tense. **perfe'ct** v.t. Complete, carry through; make perfect; improve. **perfècti-bi'lity** n.

perfè'ction n. Completion; making perfect; full development; faultlessness; perfect person or thing; highest pitch, extreme, perfect specimen or manifestation (*of*); (with pl.) accomplishment.

perfè'ctionist n. One who holds that perfection may be attained in religion, morals, politics, etc.; one who insists upon perfection; *P*~, member of the ONEIDA Community. **perfè'ctionism** n.

perfè'cto n. (U.S.) Large thick cigar tapering to point at both ends.

perfer'vid adj. Very fervid.

per'fidy n. Breach of faith, treachery. **perfi'dious** adj. **perfi'diously** adv. **perfi'diousness** n.

perfō'liate adj. (bot.) Having the stalk apparently passing through the leaf (ill. LEAF).

per'forāte v. Make hole(s) through, pierce; esp. make rows of holes in (sheet) to separate stamps, coupons, etc.; make an opening into; pass, extend, through; penetrate (*into*, *through*, etc.). **perforā'tion** n.

perfor'ce adv. Of necessity.

perfor'm v. Carry into effect (command, promise, task, etc.); be agent of; go through, execute (public function, play, piece of music, etc.); act in play, sing, etc.; (of trained animals) execute feats or tricks, esp. at public show. **perfor'mer** n. **perform'ing** adj.

perfor'mance n. Execution (*of* command etc.); carrying out, doing; notable feat; performing of play, public exhibition.

per'fūme n. Odorous fumes of burning substance; sweet smell; smell; fluid containing essence of flowers etc., scent. **per'fūmelèss** adj. **perfū'me** (or pér'-) v.t. Impart sweet scent to, impregnate with sweet smell (esp. in past part.).

perfū'mer n. Maker, seller, of perfumes. **perfū'mery** n.

perfū'nctory adj. Done merely for sake of getting through a duty, acting thus, superficial, mechanical. **perfū'nctorily** adv. **perfū'nctoriness** n.

perfū'se (-z) v.t. Besprinkle (*with*); cover, suffuse; pour (water etc.) through or over. **perfū'sion** n. **perfū'sive** adj.

Pér'gamēne adj. & n. (Native, inhabitant) of Pergamum.

Pér'gamum. (Turk. *Bergama*) Ancient city of NW. Asia Minor, the capital of the Attalid kings (3rd–2nd c. B.C.), under whom it became a centre of art and learning, and manufactured parchment for the books of its famous library.

per'gola n. Arbour, covered walk, formed of growing plants trained over trellis-work.

Pergole'se (-āzĭ), Giovanni Battista (1710-36). Italian composer of cantatas, operas, and much sacred music, of which his 'Stabat Mater' is best known.

perhă'ps (or *colloq.* prăps) adv. It may be, possibly.

pēr'ī n. (Pers. myth.) Fairy, good (orig. evil) genius, beautiful being.

pěri- *prefix*. Round, about.

pě'riănth n. Outer part or envelope of flower, enclosing stamens and pistils (ill. FLOWER); corolla and calyx, or either of these.

pě'riăpt n. Thing worn about the person as charm, amulet.

pěricăr'dium n. Membranous sac enclosing heart. **pěricăr'diăc**, **pěricăr'dial** adjs.

pě'ricărp n. Wall of ripened ovary of plant (ill. SEED).

pěrichŏ'ndrium (-k-) n. Membrane enveloping cartilages (except at joints).

pě'riclāse n. Mineral consisting of magnesia with small admixture of iron protoxide, found in greenish crystals or grains in ejected masses of crystalline limestone at Vesuvius etc.

Pě'riclēs (-z) (*c* 495-429 B.C.). Athenian statesman and military commander, under whose administration (460-429 B.C.) Athens reached the summit of her power. **Pěriclē'an** adj.

pěricli'nal adj. (geol.) Dome-like.

peri'copē n. Short passage, paragraph; portion of Scripture read in public worship.

pěricrā'nium n. Membrane enveloping skull; (joc.) skull, brain; intellect.

peri'dium n. (bot.) Outer envelope, enclosing spores, of some fungi.

pě'ridŏt n. (Jeweller's name for) olivine.

pě'rigee n. That point in planet's (esp. moon's) orbit at which it is nearest to earth (opp. *apogee*). **pěrigē'an** adj.

Pěrigord (pěrigōr). District (ancient province) in SW. France; ~ *pie*, meat pie flavoured with truffles.

peri'gynous adj. (of stamens) Situated around pistil or ovary; (of flower) having such stamens (ill. FLOWER).

pěrihē'lion (-yon) n. That point in planet's orbit at which it is nearest to sun (opp. *aphelion*).

pě'ril n. Danger, risk. **pě'rilous** adj. **pě'rilously** adv. **pě'rilousness** n.

peri'mĕter n. 1. Circumference, outline, of closed figure; length of this; ~ *track*, concrete runway round an airfield. 2. Instrument for measuring the field of vision. **peri'mĕtry** n. Measurement of field of vision. **pěrimě'tric** adj.

pěrinē'um n. (anat.) Lower end of trunk with its contents, extending from coccyx or tail-bone to pubic symphysis (ill. PELVIS). **pěrinē'al** adj.

[654]

PERIOD

pēr'iod *n.* 1. Round of time marked by recurrence of astronomical coincidences; time of planet's revolution; time during which disease runs its course; menses. 2. Indefinite portion of history, life, etc.; any portion of time; (attrib., esp. of furniture, architecture, etc.) of, characteristic of, a particular (past) period. 3. Complete sentence, esp. one of several clauses; (pl.) rhetorical language; full pause at end of sentence, full stop (.) marking this; set of figures marked (by comma etc.) in large number, as in numeration, recurring decimals, etc.; *put a ~ to*, bring to an end.

pēriŏ'dĭc *adj.* 1. Of revolution of heavenly body (*~ motion*); recurring at (regular) intervals. 2. Expressed in (rhetorical) periods. 3. (chem.) *~ law*, statement of fact that properties of chemical elements are periodic functions of their atomic weights, i.e. that when they are arranged in order of those weights, elements having similar chemical and physical properties occur at regular intervals; *~ table*, table of chemical elements illustrating this law. **pēriodǐ'cǐtў** *n.*

pēriŏ'dĭcal *adj.* = PERIODIC, 1; (of magazine, miscellany, etc.) published at regular intervals, e.g. monthly. **pēriŏ'dĭcally** *adv.* **pēriŏ'dĭcal** *n.* Periodical magazine etc.

pēriŏ'stěum *n.* Dense fibrovascular membrane enveloping bones (except where they are covered by cartilage), from inner layer of which bone-substance is produced (ill. BONE). **pēriŏ'stěal** *adj.*

pěripatě'tĭc *adj.* 1. *P~*, of the school of Aristotle, Aristotelian (from Aristotle's custom of teaching while walking in the Lyceum at Athens). 2. Walking from place to place on one's business, itinerant. **pěripatě'tĭcally** *adv.* **pěripatě'tĭc** *n.*

pěripětei'a (*or* -īa), **-tī'a** *n.* Sudden change of fortune in drama or life.

peri'phery *n.* Bounding line esp. of closed curvilinear figure; external boundary or surface. **peri'pheral** *adj.* (esp.) Applied to equipment used in conjunction with a computer without being an integral part of it, and to operations involving such equipment. **peri'pherally** *adv.* **peri'pheral** *n.* Peripheral device.

peri'phrasis *n.* (pl. *-es* pr. -ēz). Roundabout way of speaking, circumlocution; roundabout phrase. **pěriphrǎ'stĭc** *adj.* **pěriphrǎ'stĭcally** *adv.*

peri'pteral *adj.* (of temple) Surrounded by a single row of columns (ill. TEMPLE¹).

peri'que (-ēk) *n.* Kind of dark strong-flavoured Louisiana tobacco.

pě'rĭscōpe *n.* Apparatus of tube and mirrors giving view of things above surface to observer in submarine or trench, or enabling

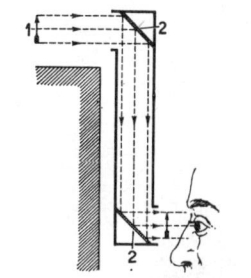

DIAGRAM OF A PERISCOPE
1. Object. 2. Mirrors reflecting at 90° rays of light from object

person to see over the heads of others in a crowd. **pěriscŏ'pĭc** *adj.* Enabling one to see distinctly for some distance round axis of vision.

pě'rĭsh *v.* Suffer destruction, lose life, come to untimely end; (of cold or exposure) reduce to distress or inefficiency (usu. in pass.). **pě'rĭshĭng** *adj.* (of cold etc.). **pě'rĭshĭngly** *adv.*

pě'rĭshable *adj.* Liable to perish; subject to speedy decay. **pě'rĭshables** (-lz) *n.pl.* Things, esp. foodstuffs in transit, of this nature.

pě'rĭspěrm *n.* (bot.) Nutritive tissue outside embryo-sac in some seeds.

pě'rĭspōme, pěrĭspō'měnon (pl. *-ena*) *adjs. & ns.* (Gk gram.) (Word) with circumflex accent on last syllable.

peri'stalĭth *n.* (archaeol.) Ring of standing stones round burial-mound etc.

pěrĭstǎ'lsĭs *n.* (physiol.) Automatic muscular movement consisting of successive waves of contraction and relaxation, by which contents of alimentary canal etc. are propelled along it. **pěrĭstǎ'ltĭc** *adj.* **pěrĭstǎ'ltĭcally** *adv.*

pěrĭsterŏ'nĭc *adj.* Of pigeons.

pě'rĭstōme *n.* 1. (bot.) Fringe of small teeth round mouth of capsule in mosses. 2. (zool.) Part round mouth in various invertebrates (ill. PROTOZOON).

pě'rĭstўle *n.* Row of columns surrounding temple, court, cloister, etc. (ill. TEMPLE¹); space so surrounded.

pěrĭthē'cĭum *n.* (pl. *-cia*). (bot.) Cup-shaped or flask-shaped receptacle enclosing fructification in certain fungi.

pěrĭtonē'um *n.* (anat.) Double serous membrane lining cavity of abdomen, of complex form, with numerous folds investing and supporting abdominal viscera (ill. ABDOMEN). **pěrĭtonē'al** *adj.* **pěrĭtonī'tĭs** *n.* Inflammation of (part of) peritoneum.

PERMIAN

pě'rĭwĭg *n.* Wig (ill. WIG). [Fr. *perruque* peruke]

pě'rĭwĭnkle¹ *n.* Plant of genus *Vinca*, esp. the European *lesser* and *greater ~* (*V. minor, V. major*), evergreen trailing shrubs with light-blue starry flowers; (also *~ blue*) colour of these flowers.

pě'rĭwĭnkle² *n.* Gasteropod mollusc (*Littorina*), esp. common European coast species (*L. littorea*), with dark-coloured turbinate shell, much used for food.

pēr'jure *v.refl.* Forswear *oneself*; *perjured*, guilty of perjury; involving perjury. **pēr'jurer** *n.*

pēr'jury *n.* Swearing to statement known to be false; wilful utterance of false evidence while on oath; breach of oath.

pěrk¹ *n.* (slang) Perquisite.

pěrk² *v.* Lift (*up*) one's head, carry oneself smartly or briskly; smarten *up*; hold *up* (head, tail) self-assertively. **pěr'kў** *adj.* Self-assertive, saucy, pert. **pěr'kĭlў** *adv.* **pěr'kĭněss** *n.*

Pěr'kin, Sir William Henry (1838–1907). English chemist, discoverer of aniline dyes.

Pěr'lĭs. State of Malaysia; capital, Kangar.

pěr'līte *n.* Obsidian or other vitreous rock with concentric structure, expansible by heating.

pěrm¹ *n.* (colloq.) PERMANENT wave.

pěrm² *n.* (colloq.) Permutation. *~ v.t.* Permutate.

pěr'mafrŏst *n.* Permanently frozen subsoil etc. in Arctic regions. [f. *perma*(*nent*) *frost*]

pěr'malloy *n.* Nickel steel alloy, containing about 78% nickel, characterized by a very high permeability in low magnetic fields, extensively used in submarine cables where this quality is valuable. [f. *perm*(*eable*) *alloy*]

pěr'manent *adj.* Lasting, intended to last, indefinitely; *~ magnet*, one whose property continues after the magnetizing agent has been removed; *~ wave*, artificial wave in hair which lasts until hair grows out; *~ way*, finished road-bed of railway. **pěr'manently** *adv.* **pěr'manence** *n.* Being permanent. **pěr'manency** *n.* Being permanent; permanent thing or arrangement.

permǎ'ngānate (-ngg-) *n.* (chem.) Salt of permanganic acid; (also *potassium ~, ~ of potash*) crystalline substance (KMnO₄), dark purple when dissolved, used as a disinfectant, stain, etc. **permangǎ'nĭc** *adj. ~ acid*, acid (HMnO₄) known only in solution and from its salts.

pěr'měāte *v.* Penetrate, pervade, saturate; diffuse itself *through, among*, etc. **pěr'měable** *adj.* **pěrměabĭ'lĭtў** *n.*

pēr mē'nsěm. (So much) by the month. [L]

Pěr'mian *adj. & n.* (geol.) (Of) the latest period or system of the

[655]

PERMISSIBLE

Palaeozoic (ill. GEOLOGY). [f. *Perm*, former province of E. Russia]
permi′ssible *adj.* Allowable.
permissibi′lity *n.*
permi′ssion *n.* Consent or liberty (*to* do).
permi′ssive *adj.* Giving permission; tolerant of behaviour that some might condemn; ~ *legislation*, legislation giving powers, but not enjoining their use. **permi′ssively** *adv.* **permi′ssiveness** *n.*
permi′t *v.* Give consent or opportunity; admit *of*. **pĕr′mĭt** *n.* Written order giving permission esp. for landing or removal of dutiable goods, entry into a place, etc.
pĕrmūtā′tion *n.* (math.) Variation of order of a set of things lineally arranged; each of different arrangment of which such a set is capable; (in football pools etc.) set of combinations of certain items. **pĕr′mūtāte** *v.t.* Arrange in different order or combination.
permū′te *v.t.* Put in different order, change sequence of (things etc.).
pĕrn *n.* Honey-buzzard.
perni′cious (-shus) *adj.* Destructive, ruinous, fatal; ~ *anaemia*, progressive and, unless checked, fatal form of anaemia. **perni′ciously** *adv.* **perni′ciousness** *n.*
perni′ckety *adj.* (colloq.) Fastidious; ticklish, requiring careful handling.
pĕrnoctā′tion *n.* Passing the night; (eccles.) all-night vigil.
Perón (pārŏ′n), Juan Domingo (1895–1974). Argentinian general; seized government and became dictator 1943; elected president 1946, 1951; exiled, after a revolution, 1955; returned to Argentina in 1972; elected president 1973. **Peroni′sta** *n.* Supporter of Peron.
pĕ′rorāte *v.i.* Sum up and conclude speech; speak at length. **pĕrorā′tion** *n.*
perŏ′xide *n.* (chem.) Compound of oxygen with another element containing greatest possible proportion of oxygen; (also ~ *of hydrogen*) colourless liquid (H₂O₂) used in aqueous solution as oxidizing and bleaching agent and antiseptic, in pure state a concentrated source of oxygen. ~ *v.t.* Bleach (esp. hair) with peroxide.
perpĕ′nd *v.t.* (archaic) Ponder, consider.
pĕrpendi′cūlar *adj.* 1. At right angles to plane of horizon; (loosely) very steep; erect, upright; (joc.) in standing position. 2. (geom.) At right angles (*to* given line, plane, or surface). 3. *P*~, (archit.) of the style of English Gothic architecture prevailing from the middle of the 14th c. to the middle of the 16th c., characterized by the vertical lines of its tracery (ill. WINDOW). **pĕrpendi′cūlarly** *adv.*
pĕrpendiculā′rity *n.* **pĕrpendi′cular** *n.* Plumb-rule or other instrument for showing perpendicular line; perpendicular line; *the* ~, perpendicular line or direction.
pĕr′pĕtrāte *v.t.* Perform, commit (crime, blunder, etc.). **pĕrpĕtrā′tion, pĕr′pĕtrātor** *ns.*
perpĕ′tūal *adj.* Eternal; permanent during life; applicable, valid, for ever or for indefinite time; continuous; (colloq.) frequent, repeated; ~ *curate*: see CURATE; ~ *motion*, motion of hypothetical machine that once set going should continue for ever unless stopped by external force or worn out. **perpĕ′tūally** *adv.*
perpĕ′tūāte *v.t.* Make perpetual; preserve from oblivion. **perpĕtūā′tion** *n.*
pĕrpĕtū′ity *n.* Quality of being perpetual; perpetual possession or position; perpetual annuity; *in, to, for,* ~, for ever.
perplĕ′x *v.t.* Bewilder, puzzle; complicate, confuse (matter); entangle, intertwine. **perplĕ′xedly, perplĕ′xingly** *advs.*
perplĕ′xity *n.* Bewilderment; cause of this; entangled state.
pĕr prōcūrātiōn′em (-shǐ-). (abbrev. *per pro*(*c*)., *p.p.*) By proxy, by the action of (person signing document). [L]
pĕr′quisite (-z-) *n.* Casual profit, esp. (law) that coming to lord of manor beyond regular revenue; thing that has served its primary use and to which subordinate or servant has then a customary right; customary gratuity.
Perrault (pĕrō), Charles (1628–1703). French poet, critic, and author of fairy-tales.
pĕ′rry *n.* Cider-like drink from expressed fermented juice of pears.
pĕr sē. By or in itself, intrinsically. [L]
pĕr′sĕcūte *v.t.* Pursue with enmity and injury (esp. holder of opinion held to be heretical); harass, worry; importune (*with* questions etc.). **pĕrsĕcū′tion** *n.* ~ *mania*, insane delusion that one is persecuted. **pĕr′sĕcūtor** *n.*

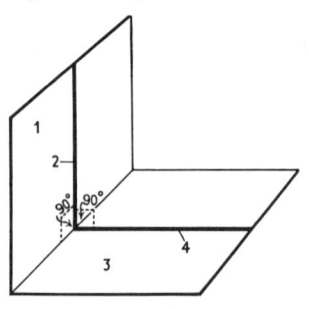

PERSIMMON

Pĕr′sĕid *n.* (astron.) One of a group of shooting stars appearing yearly near beginning of August and having their radiant near the constellation Perseus.
Persĕ′phonĕ. (Gk myth.) Daughter of Zeus and DEMETER; called by the Romans Proserpina; goddess of spring; while gathering flowers she was carried off by Pluto and made queen of Hell; Demeter persuaded Zeus to let her return to earth for 6 (or 8) months of each year.
Persĕ′polis. Ancient capital of Persian Empire, now in S. Iran.
Pĕr′seus (-sūs). 1. (Gk myth.) Hero, son of Zeus and DANAE; cut off the head of the gorgon MEDUSA[1], and gave it to Athene; saved ANDROMEDA from a sea-monster, married her, and founded the city of Mycenae. 2. (astron.) Northern constellation between Cassiopeia and Taurus.
pĕrsĕvēr′ance *n.* Steadfast pursuit of an aim, constant persistence; (theol.) continuance in state of grace.
pĕrsĕvēr′e *v.i.* Continue steadfastly, persist (*in, with*). **pĕrsĕvēr′ingly** *adv.*
Pĕr′sia (-sha). Ancient and (now) alternative name of IRAN.
Pĕr′sian (-shan) *adj.* Of Persia or its language or people; ~ *blinds*, PERSIENNES; ~ *cat*, cat of domesticated breed, with long silky hair, bushy tail, and round head; ~ *carpet, rug*, carpet or rug made in Persia, usu. oblong, of very fine skilful weave, of silk or wool pile and traditional, freq. geometrical, patterns; ~ *Empire*, empire formed (6th c. B.C.) by conquests of Media, Lydia, and Babylonia under Cyrus, including at its greatest all western Asia, Egypt, and parts of eastern Europe, and overthrown by Alexander the Great, 331 B.C.; ~ *Gulf*, landlocked sea extending in south-easterly direction from confluence of Euphrates and Tigris and communicating with Arabian Sea through Strait of Hormuz and Gulf of Oman; ~ *knot*, kind of knot used in carpet making (ill. WEAVE); ~ *lamb*, caracul; ~ *Wars*, wars in which Darius and Xerxes vainly attempted to conquer Greece (499–449 B.C.), but the defeat of Xerxes at SALAMIS, 479, decided the issue). ~ *n.* 1. Native, inhabitant, of Persia. 2. Indo-European Iranian language; *Middle* ~, Pahlavi; *Old* ~, ancient W. Iranian language, known from cuneiform inscriptions. 3. Persian cat.
pĕrsiĕ′nnes (-nz) *n.pl.* Outside window-blinds of light horizontal laths.
pĕr′sĭflage (-flahzh) *n.* Light raillery, banter.
persi′mmon *n.* Yellowish-orange plum-like astringent fruit, becoming sweet when softened by frost, of the Amer. tree *Diospyros*

[656]

persist *virginiana*; large red fruit of Chinese and Japanese species, *D. Kaki*.

persi'st *v.i.* Continue firmly or obstinately (*in* opinion, course, etc.) esp. against remonstrance etc. **persi'stence, persi'stency** *ns.* **persi'stent** *adj.* (esp., of horns, hair, leaves, etc.) Remaining after such parts normally wither or fall off. **persi'stently** *adv.*

Pĕr'sius. Aulus Persius Flaccus (A.D. 34–62), Roman poet and satirist.

pĕr'son *n.* 1. Individual human being; living body of human being; *young* ~, young man or (usu.) woman (and esp. when speaker does not wish to specify her social position); *in* ~, personally, oneself. 2. (law) Human being (*natural* ~) or body corporate (*artificial* ~) with recognized rights and duties. 3. Character in play or story. 4. (theol.) Each of three distinctions or modes of divine being in the Godhead, God the Father, Son, Holy Ghost. 5. (gram.) Each of three classes of personal pronouns, and corresponding distinctions in verbs, indicating the person(s) speaking (*first* ~), spoken to (*second* ~), and spoken of (*third* ~).

persō'na *n.* (pl. *-nae*). (Jungian psychol.) Outer aspect of personality as revealed to other persons.

pĕr'sonable *adj.* Handsome, comely.

pĕr'sonage *n.* Person of rank or importance; person; character in play etc.

persō'na gra'ta (-ah-). Acceptable person. [L]

pĕr'sonal *adj.* 1. One's own, individual, private; done, made, etc., in person; of the body; ~ *equation*: see EQUATION. 2. Directed, referring (esp. hostilely) to an individual; making, given to making, personal remarks. 3. ~ *property, estate*, etc., (law) chattels or chattel interests in land, all property except land and those interests in land that pass to one's heir. 4. (gram.) Of, denoting, one of the three persons (esp. in ~ *pronoun*). **pĕr'sonally** *adv.* In person, in one's own person; for one's own part.

pĕrsonă'lity *n.* 1. Being a person; personal existence or identity; distinctive personal character; person; *multiple* ~, (psych.) apparent existence of two or more distinct and alternating personalities in a single individual. 2. (of remarks) Fact of being personal; (usu. pl.) personal remarks.

pĕr'sonalize *v.t.* Personify; mark with one's name etc. **pĕrsonaliză'tion** *n.*

pĕr'sonalty *n.* Personal estate.

pĕr'sonate[1] *adj.* (bot.: of two-lipped corolla) Having the opening of the lips closed by upward projection of the lower (as in snap-dragon).

pĕr'sonate[2] *v.t.* Play the part of; pretend to be (person), esp. for fraudulent purpose. **personā'tion, pĕr'sonātor** *ns.*

pĕrsŏnifică'tion *n.* Personifying; person, thing, viewed as striking example or embodiment *of*.

pĕrsŏ'nify *v.t.* Attribute personal nature to (abstraction); symbolize (quality) by figure in human form; embody (quality) in one's own person, exemplify typically (esp. in past part.).

pĕrsonnĕ'l *n.* Body of persons employed in an organization, as distinct from the equipment.

perspĕ'ctive *n.* Art of delineating solid objects on a plane surface so as to give the same impression of relative positions, magnitudes, etc., as the actual objects do when viewed from a particular point (ill. DRAWING); picture so drawn; apparent relation between visible objects as to position, distance, etc.; (fig.) relation in which parts of subject are viewed by the mind; view, prospect (lit. and fig.); *in* ~, drawn according to rules of perspective; foreshortened. ~ *adj.* Of, in, perspective. **perspĕ'ctively** *adv.*

pĕr'spĕx *n.* Plastic material, much lighter than glass, used esp. for windscreens and transparent parts of aircraft. [trade-name, irreg. f. L *perspicere* look through]

pĕrspĭcā'cious (-sh*u*s) *adj.* Having mental penetration or discernment. **pĕrspĭcā'ciously** *adv.* **pĕrspĭcă'city** *n.*

perspi'cuous *adj.* Easily understood, clearly expressed; (of person) clear in expression. **perspi'cuously** *adv.* **pĕrspĭcū'ity, perspi'cuousness** *ns.*

perspīr'able *adj.* Allowing the passage of perspiration; that can be thrown off in perspiration.

pĕrspīrā'tion *n.* Sweating; sweat. **perspīr'atory** *adj.*

perspīr'e *v.* Sweat.

persuā'de (-sw-) *v.t.* Cause (person, oneself) to have belief (*of, that*); induce (*to* do, *into* action); persuaded, convinced (*of, that*). **persuā'dable, persuā's-ĭble** *adjs.* **persuāsĭbĭ'lity** *n.*

persuā'sion (-swā-) *n.* Persuading; persuasiveness; conviction; religious belief, sect holding this.

persuā'sive (-swā-) *adj.* Able to persuade, winning. **persuā's-ively** *adv.* **persuā'siveness** *n.*

pĕrt *adj.* Forward, saucy, in speech or conduct; (U.S. and dial.) lively, sprightly, cheerful. **pĕr'tly** *adv.* **pĕr'tness** *n.*

pertai'n *v.i.* Belong as part, appendage, or accessory, *to*; be appropriate *to*; have reference, relate, *to*.

Pĕr'thshire. Former inland county of central Scotland, since May 1975 part of Central and Tayside regions.

pĕrtĭnā'cious (-sh*u*s) *adj.* Stubborn, persistent, obstinate. **pĕr-tĭnā'ciously** *adv.* **pĕrtĭnā'ciousness, pĕrtĭnă'city** *ns.*

pĕr'tinent *adj.* Pertaining, relevant, apposite, (*to* matter in hand etc.); to the point. **pĕr'tinently** *adv.* **pĕr'tinence, pĕr'tinency** *ns.*

pertŭr'b *v.t.* Upset, disquiet, throw into agitation. **pĕrturbā'tion** *n.*

Peru (perōō'). Republic of Pacific coast of S. America; inhabited during the Middle Ages by the Incas (see INCA); won independence of Spain 1821; capital, Lima.

Pĕrugi'nō (-ōōjĕ-). Pietro Vannucci (*c* 1450–1523), Italian painter of Umbrian school, one of the masters of Raphael. [*Perugia*, Italian city]

peru'ke (-ōōk) *n.* Wig (ill. WIG).

peru'se (-ōōz) *v.t.* Read thoroughly or carefully; read; examine carefully. **peru'sal** *n.*

Peru'vian (-rōō-) *adj.* Of Peru or its people; ~ *bark*, cinchona bark. ~ *n.* Native, inhabitant, of Peru. [*Peruvia*, latinized name of PERU]

pervā'de *v.t.* Spread through, permeate, saturate. **pervā'sion** *n.* **pervā'sive** *adj.* **pervā'sively** *adv.* **pervā'siveness** *n.*

pervĕr'se *adj.* Persistent in error; different from what is reasonable or required; wayward; peevish; perverted, wicked; (of verdict) against weight of evidence or judge's direction. **pervĕr'sely** *adv.* **pervĕr'seness, pervĕr'sity** *ns.*

pervĕr't *v.t.* Turn aside (thing) from its proper use; misconstrue, misapply (words etc.); lead astray (person, mind) from right opinion or conduct, or esp. religious belief. **pervĕr'sion** *n.* **pervĕr'sive** *adj.* **pĕr'vĕrt** *n.* Perverted person; apostate; homosexual.

pĕr'vious *adj.* Affording passage (*to*); permeable; (fig.) accessible (*to* reason etc.). **pĕr'viousness** *n.*

pĕse'ta (-sā-) *n.* Principal monetary unit of Spain, = 100 centimos

pĕ'sewa (-swa) *n.* $\frac{1}{100}$ of a cedi.

Peshi'tta (-shē-) *n.* Principal Syriac version of the Bible.

peshwa (pā'shwah) *n.* (hist.) Hereditary sovereign (earlier, chief minister) of the former Mahratta State in India. [Pers. *pēšvā* chief, leader]

pĕ'sky *adj.* (U.S. slang) Troublesome, confounded, annoying, plaguy.

pe'sō (pā-) *n.* (pl. *-s*). Principal monetary unit in Argentina, Bolivia, Colombia, Cuba, Dominican Republic, Mexico, Philippines, and Uruguay.

pĕ'ssary *n.* Instrument, medicated plug, inserted into or worn in vagina to prevent uterine displacements or as contraceptive.

pĕ'ssimism *n.* Tendency to look at the worst aspect of things; doctrine that this world is the worst possible, or that all things

[657]

tend to evil. **pĕ′ssimist** n. **pĕssĭmi′stic** adj. **pĕssĭmi′stically** adv.
pĕ′ssimum n. Worst or most unfavourable condition, amount, or degree.
pĕst n. Troublesome or destructive person, animal, or thing; (obs.) pestilence.
Pĕstalŏ′zzi (-tsĭ), Jean Henri (1746-1827). Swiss reformer of elementary education; believed the faculties should be developed in natural order, beginning with sense perception; made much use of object-lessons.
pĕ′ster v.t. Trouble, plague.
pĕ′sticide n. Substance for destroying pests, esp. insects.
pĕsti′ferous adj. Noxious, pestilential; (fig.) having moral contagion, pernicious.
pĕ′stilence n. Any fatal epidemic disease, esp. bubonic plague. **pĕ′stilent** adj. Destructive to life, deadly; (fig.) injurious to morals etc.; (colloq.) troublesome, plaguy. **pĕ′stilentlў** adv. **pĕstilĕ′ntial** (-shəl) adj.
pĕ′stle (-sl) n. Club-shaped instrument for pounding substances in a mortar; various mechanical appliances for pounding, stamping, etc. ~ v. Pound (as) with pestle; use pestle.
pĕstŏ′logў n. Study of pests (esp. harmful insects) and the methods of dealing with them.
pĕt[1] n. Animal tamed and kept as favourite or treated with fondness; darling, favourite (often attrib.); ~ aversion, what one specially dislikes; ~ name, one expressing fondness or familiarity. ~ v. Treat as a pet, fondle, caress; (orig. U.S.) indulge in hugging, kissing, and fondling.
pĕt[2] n. Offence at being slighted, ill-humour.
Pet. abbrev. Peter (N.T.).
Pétain (pātăn), Henri Philippe Benoni Omer Joseph (1856-1951). Marshal of France; defender of Verdun, 1916; head of State in VICHY France 1940-4.
pĕ′tal n. Each of the divisions of the corolla of a flower, usu. when separate (ill. FLOWER). **pĕ′taloid** adj.
pĕ′talon n. Gold plate worn on linen mitre of Jewish high priest.
pĕtăr′d n. Small engine of war, orig. of metal, later wooden box charged with powder, formerly used to blow in door etc.; kind of firework, cracker; hoist with one's own ~: see HOIST[2].
pĕ′tasus n. (Gk antiq.) Low-crowned broad-brimmed hat, esp. as worn by Hermes; winged hat of Hermes.
pĕt′-cŏ′ck n. Small stop-cock for draining, letting out steam, etc.
pĕ′ter[1] v.i. (orig. U.S. mining colloq.) ~ out, give out, come to an end.
Pē′ter[2], St. (d. c 67). Apostle, orig. called Simon; most prominent of the disciples during the ministry of Jesus and in the early Church; martyred, probably in Rome; in R.C. tradition, founder and first bishop of Church of Rome, and in popular belief keeper of the door of heaven; commemorated with St. Paul, 29 June; (*Epistle of St.*) ~, either of the two epistles of N.T. ascribed to him; ~'s *pence*, in England, annual tribute of a penny from every householder having land of a certain value, paid to the papal see at Rome from Anglo-Saxon times until discontinued by statute in 1534; also, voluntary contributions of Roman Catholics to papal treasury since 1860; *rob* ~ *to pay Paul*, take away from one person, cause, etc., to pay, give, etc., to another. [Gk *petros* rock]
Pē′ter[3], **pē′ter** n. 1. = BLUE peter. 2. (whist) Signal or call for trumps.
Pē′ter[4]. Name of three tsars of Russia: *Peter I* (1672-1725), 'the Great', reigned 1682-1725; founded St. Petersburg (Leningrad); created the Russian navy; introduced many elements of Western civilization into Russia; *Peter II* (1715-30), grandson of Peter I, reigned 1727-30; *Peter III* (1728-62), maternal grandson of Peter I, reigned 1761-2; murdered prob. by orders of his wife, CATHERINE[1] the Great.
Pē′ter Lŏ′mbard (c 1100-60). Bishop of Paris; author of 'Sententiae', a collection of opinions of the Fathers, dealing with God, incarnation, redemption, and the nature of the sacraments; called 'magister sententiarum'.
Pē′terlōō′. Name for event of 1819, the 'Marches to Massacre', when a large and peaceable meeting in St. Peter's Field, Manchester, assembled to petition for repeal of the Corn Laws, was violently dispersed by yeomanry and hussars, with over 600 casualties.
Pē′ter Păn. Hero of J. M. Barrie's play (1904) of the same name, a boy who never grew up.
pē′tersham n. Thick ribbed stiffened cotton ribbon used for waist-bands of skirts; corded ribbon with silk or rayon warp used for hat-bands. [Viscount *Petersham*, c 1812]
Pē′ter the Hĕr′mĭt (c 1050-1115). French priest; preacher of First CRUSADE.
pĕ′thĭdine (-ēn) n. Synthetic soluble analgesic, related to morphine.
pĕ′tĭōle n. (bot.) Leaf-stalk (ill. LEAF). **pĕ′tĭolar, pĕ′tĭolate** adjs.
peti′te (-ēt) adj. (of woman) Of small dainty build.
petit four (-tē fōōr). Very small fancy cake. [Fr.]
pĕti′tion n. Asking, supplication, request; formal written supplication, request; formal written supplication from one or more persons to sovereign etc.; (law) kinds of formal written application to a court; *P*~ *and Advice*, (hist.) remonstrance presented to Cromwell by Parliament, 1657; *P*~ *of Right*, (hist.) parliamentary declaration of rights and liberties of the people assented to by Charles I in 1628. ~ v. Make petition to (sovereign etc. *for, to*); ask humbly (*for, to*). **pĕtĭ′tionarў** adj. **pĕtĭ′tioner** n. (esp.) Plaintiff in divorce suit.
pĕtĭ′tio prĭnci′pĭī (-shĭō). Begging the question. [L]
petit măl (-tē) n. Mild form of epilepsy (opp. *grand mal*). [Fr.]
petit point (-tē pwań). Tent-stitch (ill. STITCH).
Pē′tra. Ancient Nabataean and Edomite capital in SW. Jordan.
Pĕ′trărch (-k). Francesco Petrarca (1304-74), Italian poet and humanist; famous for his odes and sonnets to 'Laura'. **Pĕtrăr′chan** adj. ~ *sonnet*: see SONNET.
pĕ′trel n. Any of various seabirds of the order Procellariiformes (which includes also the shearwaters and albatrosses); *storm* ~, *stormy* ~, small bird (*Hydrobates pelagicus*) with black-and-white plumage.

STORM PETREL

Length 152 mm

Pē′triburg abbrev. (Bishop) of Peterborough (replacing surname in his signature).
pē′trī dĭsh. Shallow covered dish used for culture of microorganisms etc. [J. R. *Petri* (d. 1921), German bacteriologist]
pĕtrĭfăc′tion n. Petrifying; petrified substance or mass.
pĕ′trifў v. Convert into stone or stony substance, be so converted (esp. of dead organism becoming fossilized); (fig.) paralyse, stupefy, with astonishment, terror, etc.; deprive (mind etc.) of vitality, stiffen.
Pĕ′trine adj. Of St. PETER[2].
petro- *prefix*. Rock.
pĕtrochĕ′mical (-kĕ-) n. Substance obtained from petroleum or natural gas. ~ adj. Of petrochemicals or petrochemistry.
pĕtrochĕ′mistrў (-kĕ-) n. Chemistry of rocks or of petroleum.
pĕ′troglўph n. Rock-carving (usu. prehistoric). **pĕtroglў′phic** adj.
Pĕ′trogrăd. Name of St. Petersburg from 1917 to 1924, when it was renamed LENINGRAD.
pĕtrŏ′graphў n. Scientific description of formation and composition of rocks. **pĕtrŏ′grapher** n. **pĕtrogră′phic, -ical** adjs.

pe′trol n. Low-boiling fraction of crude petroleum consisting almost entirely of a mixture of various hydrocarbons and used as a fuel in internal combustion engines (in U.S. called *gasoline*).

petro′leum n. Crude oil; inflammable mineral oil, varying from light yellow to dark brown or black, found in many places in the upper strata of the earth, containing large numbers of different hydrocarbons and used esp. as source of oils for illumination and mechanical power; ~ *jelly*, translucent gelatinous hydrocarbon mixture derived from petroleum and used as an unguent, lubricant, etc. [L & Gk *petra* rock, L *oleum* oil]

petro′lic adj. Of petrol or petroleum.

petro′logy n. Study of origin, structure, etc., of rocks. **petrolo′gic, -ical** adjs. **petrolo′gically** adv. **petro′logist** n.

pe′tronel n. (hist.) Large pistol or carbine used esp. by horse-soldiers in 16th–17th centuries (ill. PISTOL). [Fr. *poitrine* chest (because butt-end rested against chest in firing)]

Petro′nius Ar′biter (āi-), Gaius (d. A.D. 66). Roman satirist; arbiter of taste (*elegentiae arbiter*) at Nero's court; committed suicide to avoid being killed by Nero.

pe′trous adj. Of, like, rock; esp. (anat.) applied to dense hard part of temporal bone forming protective case for internal ear.

pe′tticoat n. Woman's undergarment hanging from waist or shoulders; (elect.) skirt-shaped portion of insulator; ~ *government*, predominance of woman in the home or in politics.

pe′ttifog v.i. Practise legal chicanery; quibble, wrangle, about petty points. **pe′ttifogger** n. Inferior legal practitioner; rascally lawyer; petty practitioner in any department. **pe′ttifoggery** n. **pe′ttifogging** adj.

pe′ttish adj. Peevish, petulant, easily put out. **pe′ttishly** adv. **pe′ttishness** n.

pe′ttitoes (-ōz) n.pl. Pig's trotters.

pe′tty adj. Unimportant, trivial; little-minded; minor, inferior, on a small scale; ~ *cash*, small cash items of receipt or expenditure; ~ *officer*, officer in navy corresponding in rank to N.C.O.; ~ *sessions*: see SESSION. **pe′ttily** adv. **pe′ttiness** n.

pe′tulant adj. Peevishly impatient or irritable. **pe′tulantly** adv. **pe′tulance** n.

petu′nia n. Herbaceous plant of S. Amer. genus P~, with variously coloured flowers of funnel shape; dark violet or purple colour.

petu′ntse (-ōon-) n. White earth, made by pulverizing a partially decomposed granite, used in China with kaolin for making porcelain. [Chin. *pai* white, *tun* stone, with suffix, *-tze*]

pew n. Place (often enclosed and raised) in church appropriated to a family (*family* ~) or others; fixed bench with back in church. ~ *v.t.* Furnish with pews, enclose in pew.

pewit: see PEEWIT.

pew′ter n. Grey alloy of tin and lead or other metal, resembling lead in appearance when dull, but capable of receiving a high polish; utensils of this; pewter pot.

peyō′te (pā-) n. Mexican cactus, *Lophophora Williamsii*; hallucinogenic drug produced from tops of this.

P.F. *abbrev.* Procurator Fiscal.

p.f.c. *abbrev.* (U.S.) Private first class.

pfe′nnig n. 1/100 of a Deutsche mark or East German mark.

P.G. *abbrev.* Paying guest.

P.G.A. *abbrev.* Professional Golfers' Association.

pH (chem.) Symbol for common logarithm, with sign reversed, of hydrogen ion concentration, expressed in gramme equivalents per litre; ~ *scale*, scale on which the acidity or alkalinity of a solution is measured, pH 7·0 representing neutrality, lower values acidity, and higher ones alkalinity.

Phae′dra. (Gk legend) Daughter of Minos and wife of Theseus; became enamoured of Hippolytus, son of Theseus and the Amazon Hippolyta, and caused his death when he rejected her advances.

Phae′drus (1st c. A.D.). Macedonian slave; author of fables about animals, based on those of Aesop and others, in Latin verse.

Phā′ethon. (Gk myth.) Son of the sun-god Helios; drove his father's chariot too near the earth and was killed by Zeus with a thunderbolt to save the earth from destruction.

phā′eton (or fāt-) n. Light four-wheeled open carriage usu. drawn by pair of horses. [f. PHAETHON]

HIGH PERCH PHAETON

phage (fahzh) n. (bacteriology) Destroyer of bacteria.

phăgedae′na n. Spreading ulcer. **phăgedae′nic** adj.

phă′gocyte n. Blood-cell, esp. leucocyte, capable of ingesting and destroying dead or foreign material.

phā′lange (-j) n. = PHALANX 3.

phală′ngeal (-j-) adj. (anat.) Of a phalanx.

phală′nger (-j-) n. Any of the Australian opossums, small marsupials (of several genera) of arboreal habits, with thick woolly fur and freq. prehensile tail; *flying* ~, one of those which have a flying membrane, flying opossum, [mod. L, invented by Buffon f. Gk *phalanggion* spider's web, from webbed toes of hind feet]

phă′lanstery n. (Buildings of) socialistic PHALANX.

phă′lanx n. 1. (Gk antiq.) Line of battle, esp. body of Macedonian infantry drawn up in close order. 2. Set of persons banded together for common purpose (cf. FALANGE); community of about 1800 persons, as proposed by Fourier, living together as one family, and holding property in common. 3. (pl. *phalanges*, pr. -jēz; anat.) Any of the bones of the fingers or toes (ill. HAND, FOOT).

phă′larōpe n. Any of several related species of small wading and swimming bird allied to snipe.

phă′llus n. Image of penis, venerated in some religious systems as symbolizing generative power in nature. **phă′llic** adj. **phă′llism, -icism** ns.

phă′nerogăm n. (bot.) Plant that has stamens and pistils, flowering plant. **phănerogă′mic, phănero′gamous** adjs.

phă′ntăsm n. Illusion, phantom; illusive likeness (*of*); supposed vision of absent (living or dead) person. **phăntă′smal, phăntă′smic** adjs.

phăntăsmagōr′ia n. Exhibition of optical illusions produced chiefly by means of magic lantern first given in London in 1802; shifting scene of real or imagined figures. **phăntăsmagō′ric** adj.

phantasy: see FANTASY.

phă′ntom n. Apparition, spectre; image (*of*); vain show, form without substance or reality; mental illusion; (attrib.) apparent, illusive, imaginary.

Phār′aoh (-rō). Title of ruler of ancient Egypt; ~*'s serpent*, chemical toy made of mercury thiocyanate in shape of a small cone which on being ignited forms a long serpent-like coil. [Hebraized version of Egyptian title meaning 'great house']

Phă′rīsee n. Member of Jewish sect of 1st c. B.C. to 1st c. A.D. distinguished by their strict observance of the traditional and written law, represented in N.T. as having pretensions to superior sanctity; hence, self-righteous person: formalist; hypocrite. **Phărisā′ic, -ical** adjs. **Phă′risāism, Phă′risēeism** ns. [Heb. *parush* separated]

phărmaceu′tical adj. Of, engaged in, pharmacy; of the use or sale of medicinal drugs. **phărmaceu′tically** adv. **phărmaceu′tics** n.

phăr′macist n. Pharmaceutical chemist; qualified person engaged in pharmacy.

phărmaco′logy n. Science

[659]

concerned with the nature and action of drugs. **pharmacŏ'logĭst** n.
pharmacopoe'ia (-pēa) n. Book (esp. one officially published) containing list of drugs with directions for use; stock of drugs. **pharmacopoe'ial** adj.
phar'macy n. Preparation and (esp. medicinal) dispensing of drugs; pharmacist's shop.
Pharŏs[1]. Island off Alexandria on which stood a tower lighthouse built by Ptolemy Philadelphus; the lighthouse itself.
phar'ŏs[2] n. Lighthouse or beacon to guide mariners. [f. PHAROS[1]]
Pharsā'lia. Territory of the town of Pharsalus in Thessaly, where Pompey was decisively defeated by Julius Caesar 48 B.C.
pharў'ngal (-ngg-), **pharў'ngĕal** (-j-) adjs. Of the pharynx.
pharyngī'tis n. Inflammation of the membranes of the pharynx.
pharyngo- (-ngg-) prefix. Pharyngal.
pharў'ngŏcēle (-ngg-) n. Abnormal enlargement at base of pharynx.
pharў'ngŏscōpe (-ngg-) n. Instrument for inspecting pharynx.
phă'rynx n. Cavity, with enclosing muscles and mucous membrane, connecting mouth and nasal passages with oesophagus (ill. HEAD); corresponding part in invertebrates (ill. FLATworm).
phāse (-z) n. 1. Stage of change or development. 2. (astron.) Aspect of moon or planet acc. to amount of illumination (esp. applied to new moon, first quarter, full moon, last quarter). 3. (phys.) Particular stage or point in a recurring sequence of movements or changes, e.g. a vibration or undulation; time (measured from an arbitrary zero) at which a vibration attains a particular state; three-~ (of alternating currents), supplied in three parts differing in phase by one-third of a period or 120°; also of electric apparatus, producing or using such currents. 4. (physical chem.) Each of three different physical states, usu. solid, liquid, and gas, in which a substance can exist. **phā'sĭc** adj.
phāse v.t. Schedule, order; ~ in, out, bring into or out of use gradually.
Ph.B., Ph.D. abbrevs. Philosophiae baccalaureus, doctor (L, = Bachelor, Doctor, of Philosophy).
phea'sant (fĕz-) n. Long-tailed bright-plumaged gallinaceous game-bird, esp. Phasianus colchicus, long naturalized in Europe; any of various unrelated birds resembling this; ~-eyed, (of flowers) with rings of colour like pheasant's eye; ~'s eye, any of various flowers with dark centre, esp. Adonis annua and common narcissus. [Gk Phasianos (bird) of the river Phasis]
Pheidias: see PHIDIAS.
Pheidi'ppidēs (fī-, -z).(Gk hist.) Athenian runner dispatched to solicit help from Sparta upon the news of the Persian landing at MARATHON, 490 B.C.
phĕnă'cĕtin n. White crystalline substance (ethyl ether of acetanilide), used in medicine as antipyretic.
pheno-, phen- prefix. (chem.) Denoting certain substances derived from coal-tar (orig. in manufacture of illuminating gas).
phēnobar'bitōne n. Hypnotic and sedative drug ($C_{12}H_{12}O_3N_2$).
phē'nŏl n. 1. Hydroxy-benzene (C_6H_5OH), commonly called carbolic acid, obtained from coal-tar and used esp. as an antiseptic. 2. Any of the hydroxy compounds of benzene and its homologues with the hydroxyl groups attached to the nucleus, e.g. cresol, thymol, pyrogallol.
phĕnŏ'mĕnal adj. Of the nature of a phenomenon; cognizable by, evidenced only by, the senses; concerned with phenomena; remarkable, prodigious. **phĕnŏ'mĕnally** adv.
phĕnŏ'mĕnalism. Doctrine that phenomena are the only objects of knowledge. **phĕnŏ'mĕnalist** n. **phĕnŏmĕnali'stĭc** adj.
phĕnŏ'mĕnon n. (pl. -ena). Thing that appears or is perceived, esp. thing the cause of which is in question; (philos.) that of which a sense or the mind directly takes note, immediate object of perception; remarkable person, thing, occurrence, etc.
phē'notÿpe n. (biol.) Organism as it appears, as dist. from its genetic constitution (genotype).
phēnotÿ'pĭc adj. Appearing in an organism as a result of its genetic potentialities in a given environment.
phē'nÿl n. Monovalent organic radical C_6H_5.
phē'romōne n. Substance secreted and released by animal for detection and response by other of same species. **pheromō'nal** adj.
phew int. Exclamation of impatience, disgust, exhaustion, relief, etc.
phī n. Letter of Greek alphabet ($Φ, φ$), = ph.
phī'al n. Small glass bottle, esp. for medicine.
Phī Bē'ta Kă'ppa. Honour society in some U.S. universities and colleges; election for membership is based on high academic qualifications in one of three groups: undergraduates studying the liberal arts, graduates, and distinguished alumni and faculty members; founded in 1776 at College of William and Mary, Williamsburg, Virginia, [f. the initial letters $Φ, B, K$, of Gk philosophia biou kubernētēs philosophy the guide to life]
Phī'diăs, Pheid'iăs (fī-) (5th c. B.C.). Greek sculptor; famous in antiquity for colossal statues of gold and ivory which have not survived; the sculptures of the Parthenon were prob. made under his supervision.
Phil. abbrev. Philippians (N.T.).
Philadĕ'lphia. Chief city of PENNSYLVANIA, founded by William Penn and other Quakers. [Gk, = 'brotherly love']
Philadĕ'lphian adj. & n. 1. (Member) of short-lived mystical religious sect established in England in 2nd half of 17th c. 2. (Native, inhabitant) of Philadelphia.
philă'nder v.i. Make love esp. in trifling manner. **philă'nderer** n.
phi'lanthrōpe n. Philanthropist.
philanthrŏ'pĭc adj. Loving one's fellow men, benevolent, humane. **philanthrŏ'pically** adv.
philă'nthropĭst n. Lover of mankind; one who exerts himself for the well-being of his fellow men. **philă'nthropĭsm** n.
philă'nthropĭze v. Practise philanthropy; make (persons) objects of this; make philanthropic.
philă'nthropÿ n. Love, practical benevolence, towards mankind.
philă'tĕlÿ n. Stamp-collecting. **philatĕ'lĭc** adj. **philă'tĕlĭst** n. [Gk philos lover of, ateleia exemption from payment]
Philē'mon. Epistle to ~, book of N.T., epistle of St. Paul to a well-to-do Christian living prob. at Colossae.
philharmŏ'nĭc adj. & n. (Person) fond of music (freq. used in names of musical societies, orchestras, etc.).
phi'lhellēne (-lel-) adj. & n. (Person) loving or friendly to the Greeks or (hist.) supporting the cause of Greek independence. **philhellē'nĭc** adj. **philhĕ'llĕnism, philhĕ'llĕnist** ns.
Phi'lip[1], St. Name of two persons in N.T.: (1) Apostle, commemorated with St. James the Less, 1 May; (2) 'the Evangelist', one of seven deacons appointed to superintend the secular business of the Church at Jerusalem (Acts 6: 6).
Phi'lip[2]. Name of several kings of France: Philip I (1052–1108), reigned 1060–1108; Philip II (1165–1223), 'Philip Augustus', reigned 1180–1223; reconquered Normandy from English; Philip III (1245–85), 'the Bold', reigned 1270–85; Philip IV (1268–1314), 'le Bel', reigned 1285–1314; in his reign the papacy was established at Avignon; Philip V (c 1294–1322), reigned 1316–22; Philip VI (1293–1350), reigned 1328–50; his reign saw beginning of Hundred Years War.
Phi'lip[3]. Name of several kings of Spain: Philip II (1527–98), reigned 1556–98; married Mary I of England; Philip III (1578–1621), reigned 1598–1621; Philip IV

(1605–65), reigned 1621–65; *Philip V* (1683–1746), reigned 1700–46; founder of Bourbon dynasty in Spain.

Phi′lip⁴ (382–336 B.C.). King of Macedonia 359–336; reorganized Macedonian army and conquered Greece; father of Alexander the Great.

Phi′lippi (*or* -lī′-). Ancient city of Macedonia, fortified by Philip of Macedon and named after him; scene of battle (42 B.C.) in which Octavian and Mark Antony defeated Brutus and Cassius.

Phili′ppian *adj.* Of Philippi. ~ *n.* Native, inhabitant, of Philippi; (*Epistle to the*) ~s, book of · N.T., epistle of St. Paul to the Church at Philippi.

Phili′ppic *n.* Any of the three speeches of Demosthenes against Philip of Macedon; (also) Cicero's speeches against Antony; hence (*p*~) bitter invective.

Phi′lippine (-ēn) *adj.* Of the ~ *Islands* (or *Philippines*), an archipelago in E. Pacific lying between SE. coast of China and Borneo, formerly a colony of U.S., since 1946 an independent republic; capital, Manila. [f. PHILIP³ II of Spain]

Phi′listine *n.* 1. One of the warlike inhabitants of ancient Philistia, a district comprising the fertile Mediterranean coastal plain from Jaffa to Egypt, who in early times constantly harassed the Israelites. 2. Illiberal person, one whose interests are material and commonplace. **phi′listine** *adj.* Uncultured, commonplace, materialistic. **phi′listinism** *n.* [Vulgate *Philistīnī*; sense 2 taken f. Ger. *philister*, used by univ. students of townsmen, allegedly since 1693 when a student was killed at Jena in a 'town-and-gown' brawl and the sermon at his funeral was based on the text 'The Philistines be upon thee!']

phillŭ′mĕnist (*or* -loō-) *n.* Student or collector of matchbox labels.

philŏ′logў *n.* Science of language. **philŏ′logĭst** *n.* **philŏlŏ′gĭcal** *adj.* **philolŏ′gĭcallў** *adv.* **philŏ′logīze** *v.i.*

Phi′lomĕl, Philomē′la. (Gk myth.) Daughter of Pandion, a legendary king of Athens; was turned into a swallow and her sister Procne into a nightingale (or, in Latin versions, into a nightingale, and Procne into a swallow).

philoprogĕ′nitĭve *adj.* Prolific; (phrenology) loving one's offspring. **philoprogĕ′nitĭvenĕss** *n.*

philŏ′sopher *n.* Lover of wisdom; student of philosophy; one who regulates his life by the light of philosophy; one who shows philosophic calmness in trying circumstances; ~'s *stone*, supreme object of alchemy, substance supposed to change other metals into gold or silver.

philosŏ′phĭc, -ical *adjs.* Of, consonant with, philosophy; skilled in, devoted to, philosophy (freq. in titles of societies); wise; calm; temperate; *Philosophical Society*: see ROYAL Society. **philosŏ′phĭcallў** *adv.*

philŏ′sophism *n.* Philosophizing system (usu. contempt., esp. of the French Encylopaedists).

philŏ′sophīze *v.* Play the philosopher; speculate, theorize; moralize; render philosophic.

philŏ′sophў *n.* 1. Love, study, or pursuit, of wisdom or knowledge, esp. that which deals with ultimate reality, or with the most general causes and principles of things; philosophical system; system for conduct of life; MORAL ~, NATURAL ~: see these words. 2. Serenity, resignation.

phi′ltre (-ter), **phi′lter** *n.* Love-potion.

phĭz¹ *n.* (colloq.) (Expression of) face. [abbrev. of PHYSIOGNOMY]

Phĭz². Pseudonym of Hablot Knight Browne (1815–82), illustrator of 'The Pickwick Papers' and other novels by Dickens.

phlĕbī′tis *n.* Inflammation of walls of a vein. **phlĕbī′tic** *adj.*

phlĕbŏ′tomў *n.* Cutting into a vein, blood-letting, an early and now obsolete form of medical treatment.

Phlĕ′gĕthon. (Gk & Rom. myth.) River of fire, one of the five rivers of Hades.

phlegm (-ĕm) *n.* 1. Thick slimy substance secreted by mucous membrane of respiratory passages; (hist.) one of the four humours. 2. Coolness, sluggishness, apathy (supposed to result from predominance of phlegm in constitution). **phlĕgmă′tic** (-gm-) *adj.* **phlĕgma′tĭcallў** *adv.*

phlŏ′ĕm *n.* (bot.) Softer portion of the fibro-vascular tissue, as dist. from the xylem or woody portion; soft bast (ill. STEM¹).

phlogī′stic (*or* -g-) *adj.* Of phlogiston; (med.) inflammatory.

phlogī′ston (*or* -g-) *n.* Hypothetical substance formerly supposed to exist in combustible bodies.

phlŏx *n.* Plant of N. Amer. genus *P*~ of chiefly herbaceous plants with clusters of usu. showy salver-shaped flowers. [Gk, = 'flame']

phō′bia *n.* Fear, horror, or aversion, esp. morbid.

Phoe′bĕ, Phoe′bus (fē-). (Gk myth.) Artemis and Apollo as goddess of moon and god of sun; moon and sun personified. [Gk, = 'bright', 'radiant']

Phoenī′cia (finish- *or* -ēsh-). Ancient country of E. Mediterranean, a narrow strip along the coast of the modern Lebanon, including Tyre and Sidon. **Phoenī′cian** (-shan) *adj. & n.* (Member) of the Semitic people who inhabited this area from at least 2000 B.C., famous as pioneers of navigation and trade (Carthage was their colony) and as craftsmen, regarded by the Greeks as inventors of letters, since the Greek alphabet was based on the Phoenician.

phoe′nĭx (fē-) *n.* Mythical bird, the only one of its kind, that after living five or six centuries in the Arabian desert burnt itself on a funeral pile and rose from the ashes with renewed youth to live through another cycle; paragon.

Phoe′nĭx Pȧrk (fē-). Park in Dublin; ~ *Murders*, assassination (6 May 1882), by the Irish Invincibles, of Lord Frederick Cavendish, Secretary for Ireland, and Thomas Burke, the Undersecretary.

phŏn *n.* (phys.) Unit used in measuring sound.

phōne¹ *n.* Elementary sound of spoken language.

phōne² *n. & v.* (colloq.) Telephone.

phō′nēme *n.* (phonet.) Group of variants regarded as essentially the same vocal sound.

phonĕ′tic *adj.* Representing vocal sounds, esp. (of systems of spelling) using always same symbol for same sound; of the sounds of spoken language. **phonĕ′tĭcallў** *adv.* **phŏnĕti′cian** (-shan) *n.*

phonĕ′tics *n.* Study of phonetic phenomena; (as pl.) phonetic phenomena.

phō′nĕtist *n.* One versed in phonetics, advocate of phonetic spelling.

phō′ney, phō′nў *adj.* (slang) Sham, false, counterfeit.

phŏ′nic *adj.* Of sound, acoustic; of vocal sounds.

phō′nogrăm *n.* 1. Symbol representing sound, syllable, or word, e.g. figure of a house (*pr* in Egyptian) standing for the sound 'pr' (ill. HIEROGLYPH). 2. Sound-record made by phonograph.

phō′nogrăph (*or* -ahf) *n.* Early form of gramophone, using cylinders, not discs; (U.S.) gramophone. ~ *v.t.* Record, reproduce, by phonograph. **phonogră′phic** *adj.* **phonogră′phĭcallў** *adv.* **phonŏ′graphў** *n.*

phonō′logў *n.* Science of vocal sounds; system of sounds in a language. **phŏnolŏ′gic, -ĭcal** *adjs.* **phŏnolŏ′gĭcallў** *adv.* **phonŏ′logĭst** *n.*

phō′sgēne (-z-) *n.* Carbonyl chloride (COCL₂), a poisonous colourless gas with a characteristic suffocating smell.

phŏ′sphate *n.* (chem.) Salt or ester of phosphoric acid; substance containing this, used as a fertilizer. **phŏsphă′tic** *adj.*

phŏ′sphide *n.* (chem.) Compound of phosphorus with other element or radical.

phŏ′sphite *n.* Salt of phosphorous acid.

phŏ′sphor *n.* 1. Phosphorus; esp. in ~-*bronze*, -*copper*, etc.,

[661]

alloys of phosphorus with metals named. 2. Fluorescent material, esp. that used to form screen of cathode-ray tube.
phŏsphorĕ'scence n. Radiation similar to fluorescence but detectable after excitation ceases; emission of light without combustion or perceptible heat. **phŏsphorĕ'sce** v.i. Emit phosphorescence. **phŏsphorĕ'scent** adj.
phŏsphŏ'ric adj. Containing phosphorus in its higher valency.
phŏ'sphorite n. Form of apatite; variety of calcium phosphate.
phŏ'sphorous adj. Containing phosphorus in its lower (trivalent) valency.
phŏ'sphorus n. (chem.) Nonmetallic element found in all animal and vegetable organisms and in some minerals (symbol P, at. no. 15, at. wt 30·97376) and occurring in several allotropic forms: yellow ~, white or cream-coloured wax-like highly inflammable solid, not found in free state, oxidizing rapidly in air, appearing luminous, and transformed esp. in sunlight into red ~, a stable dark-red micro-crystalline powder, non-poisonous and less readily inflammable, used in safety matches; ~ necrosis, gangrene of jawbone due to white phosphorus, formerly prevalent in match industry. [L phosphorus morning star (Gk phōs light, phorus bringing)]
phōt n. (phys.) Unit of illumination equal to one LUMEN per sq. cm.
phō'tō n. Photograph (colloq.); ~-finish, close finish of race in which winner is identified by photography.
phōtochĕ'mistry (-k-) n. Branch of chemistry dealing with the chemical action of light. **phōtochĕ'mical** adj.
phō'tocŏpy n. & v.t. (Make) photographic copy (of).
phōtō-ĕlĕ'ctric adj. Marked by or utilizing emission of electrons from solid, liquid, or gaseous bodies, when exposed to light of suitable wave-lengths; ~ cell, cell or vacuum-tube that uses the photo-electric effect to produce an electric current. **phōtō-ĕlĕctri'cĭty** n.
phōtogĕ'nic adj. 1. Producing or emitting light. 2. Suitable for photography; photographing well (of person as good subject for photography).
phōtogrǎ'mmĕtry n. Process of making surveys or geodetic measurements by photography.
phō'tograph (or -ahf) n. Picture, likeness, taken by means of chemical action of light on sensitive film. ~ v. Take photograph of; ~ well, badly, be a good, bad, subject for photography. **phōtō'grapher, phōtō'graphy** ns. **phōtogrǎ'phic** adj. **phōtogrǎ'phically** adv.

phōtogravūr'e n. Printing process in which the subject-matter is photographically etched into a polished copper cylinder; this process. ~ v.t. Reproduce by photogravure.
phōtolĭthŏ'graphy n. Lithographic process in which printing plates are made photographically.
phōtō-mĕchǎ'nical (-k-) adj. Pertaining to the production of pictures by mechanical printing from a photographic plate.
phōtō'mĕter n. Instrument for measuring intensity of light. **phōtomĕ'tric** adj. **phōtō'mĕtry** n.
phō'tŏn n. Quantum unit of light or other radiant energy equal to the product of Planck's constant h and the frequency v.
phōtō'pic adj. ~ vision, vision of normal persons in bright daylight, with perception of detail and accurate recognition of colour (cf. SCOTOPIC).
phō'tosphēre n. Luminous envelope of sun or star from which its light and heat radiate (ill. SUN).
phō'tostǎt n. Apparatus for making photographic copies of documents etc.; copy made by this. **phōtostǎ'tic** adj. [tradename]
phōtosy̆'nthĕsis n. (bot.) Process by which carbon dioxide is converted into carbohydrates by chlorophyll under influence of light. **phōtosy̆nthĕ'tic** adj. **phōtosy̆nthĕ'tically** adv.
phōtothĕ'rapy n. Treatment of skin affections etc. by action of light.
phōtotrŏ'pic adj. (of plant leaves etc.) Bending or turning towards or away from a source of light. **phōtotrŏ'pism** n.
phrāse (-z) n. 1. Mode of expression, diction; idiomatic expression; small group of words, usu. without predicate, esp. preposition with the word(s) it governs, equivalent to adjective, adverb, or noun; short pithy expression; (pl.) mere words; ~-monger, person addicted to finesounding phrases. 2. (mus.) Short and more or less independent passage forming part of longer passage or of whole piece. **phrā'sal** (-z-) adj. ~ verb, (gram.) idiomatic phrase consisting of verb and adverb, often followed by a preposition, as put up with. **phrāse** v.t. Express in words; divide (music) into phrases; group (notes) in phrase.·
phrā'seōgrǎm (-z-) n. Written symbol representing a phrase, esp. in shorthand. **phrā'seōgrǎph** (or -ahf) n. Word for which there is a phraseogram.
phrāseō'logy (-z-) n. Choice or arrangement of words; mode of expression. **phrāseōlŏ'gical** adj. **phrāseōlŏ'gically** adv.
phrā'try n. (Gk hist.) Politico-religious division of people, arising orig. from kinship; in Athens,
each of three subdivisions of the phyle or tribe; (transf.) tribal division among primitive peoples.
phrĕǎ'tic adj. (geol., of water) Situated underground, but reachable by wells.
phrenĕ'tic adj. Frantic; fanatic.
phrĕ'nic adj. (anat.) Of the diaphragm.
phrĕnŏ'logy n. Study of external contours of cranium as index to development and position of organs supposedly belonging to the different mental faculties. **phrĕnolŏ'gical** adj. **phrĕnolŏ'gically** adv. **phrĕnŏ'logist** n.
Phry̆'gia. Ancient region of central and N. Asia Minor. **Phry̆'gian** adj. Of Phrygia or its people or language; ~ bonnet, cap, conical cap with top bent over in front, cap of liberty; ~ mode, ancient Greek MODE, reputedly warlike in character; 3rd of ecclesiastical modes, with E as final and C as dominant (ill. MODE). ~ n. Native, inhabitant, language, of Phrygia.
phthǎ'lic adj. ~ acid, any of three isomeric acids, $C_6H_4(COOH)_2$.
phthǐ'sis (fth- or th-) n. Pulmonary tuberculosis; (formerly) any progressive wasting disease. **phthi'sical** adj. Of, having, phthisis.
phŭt adv. go ~, (colloq.) come to grief, collapse. [Hind. phatnā burst]
phylǎ'ctery n. 1. Small leather box containing Hebrew texts (Deut. 6: 4-9, 11: 13-21; Exod. 13: 1-10, 11-16) on vellum, worn by Jews during morning prayer as reminder of obligation to keep the law; (usu. ostentatious) religious observance. 2. Amulet, charm.
phy̆'lē n. Ancient Greek clan or tribe; in Attica, political, administrative, and military unit, based on geographical division.
phy̆lĕ'tic adj. (biol.) Of a phylum or line of descent.
phy̆'llite n. Slate which glitters owing to presence of minute scales of mica.
phy̆'llōde n. (bot.) Flattened petiole resembling a leaf (ill. LEAF).
phy̆'llotǎxy, -tǎxis ns. Arrangement of leaves on a stem.
phylloxēr'a (or -ŏ'kse-) n. Any of several plant-lice of genus P~, esp. species very destructive to grape-vine.
phy̆logĕ'nesis n. = PHYLOGENY.
phy̆lŏ'geny n. (biol.) History of the evolution of a kind or type of organism (opp. ONTOGENY).
phy̆'lum n. (pl. -la). (biol.) Major division of animals or plants, above CLASS, comprising those of the same general form.
phy̆'sic (-z-) n. Art of healing; medical profession; (colloq.) medicine. ~ v.t. Dose with physic.
phy̆'sical (-z-) adj. 1. Of matter, material; of the body; of, according to the laws of, natural philo-

[662]

PHYSICIAN

sophy; ~ *chemistry*: see CHEMISTRY; ~ *geography*, that dealing with natural features. 2. Of the science of physics. **phy̆'sĭcally** *adv*.

phy̆sĭ'cian (-zĭshan) *n*. Medical practitioner, esp. one specializing in medical (opp. *surgical*) diagnosis and treatment; (fig.) healer.

phy̆'sĭcky̆ (-z-) *adj*. Suggestive of physic.

phy̆'sĭcs *n*. Science of the properties and nature of matter in general (excluding chemistry), the various forms of energy, and the mutual interaction of energy and matter. **phy̆'sĭcist** *n*.

phy̆sĭŏ'cracy̆ (-z-) *n*. Government according to natural order, esp. that advocated by political economists (followers of Francis Quesnay) in 18th-c. France, who held that the soil is the sole source of wealth and only proper object of taxation and that security of property and freedom of industry and exchange are essential. **phy̆'sĭocrăt** (-z-) *n*. **phy̆sĭocră'tĭc** *adj*.

phy̆sĭŏ'gnomy̆ (-zĭŏn-) *n*. Art of judging character from features of face or form of body; cast of features, type of face; (vulg.) face; external features of country etc.; characteristic (moral or other) aspect. **phy̆sĭognŏ'mĭc, -ĭcal** *adjs*. **phy̆sĭognŏ'mĭcally̆** *adv*. **phy̆sĭŏ'gnomist** *n*.

phy̆sĭŏ'graphy̆ (-z-) *n*. Description of nature, of natural phenomena, or of a class of objects; physical geography. **phy̆sĭŏ'grapher** *n*. **phy̆sĭogră'phĭcal** *adj*.

phy̆sĭŏ'logy̆ (-z-) *n*. Science dealing with the functions of living organisms or their parts; these functions. **phy̆sĭolŏ'gĭcal** *adj*. **phy̆sĭolŏ'gĭcally̆** *adv*.

phy̆sĭothĕ'rapy̆ (-z-) *n*. Treatment of disease by exercise, massage, heat, light, electricity, or other physical agencies, not by drugs. **phy̆sĭothĕ'rapist** *n*.

phy̆sĭ'que (-zēk) *n*. Bodily structure, organization, and development.

phy̆to- *prefix*. Plant.

pī[1] *n*. 17th (later 16th) letter of Greek alphabet (Π, π) corresponding to *p*; esp. (math.) as symbol of ratio of circumference of circle to diameter (3·14159).

pī[2] *adj*. (school slang) Pious; ~-*jaw*, sermonizing, moral lecture.

pĭă'cular *adj*. Expiatory.

pĭă'ffe *v.i.* (of horse etc.) Move as in trot, but slower. **pĭă'ffer, pĭă'ffe** *ns*. Action of piaffing.

pī'a mā'ter. (anat.) Delicate fibrous innermost meninx, consisting of a network of bloodvessels, covering the brain and spinal cord (ill. SPINE). [med. L transl. of Arab. anatomical term = 'tender mother']

pīanĭ'ssĭmō *adv.*, *n*. (pl. *-os*), & *adj*. (mus.) (Passage performed) very soft(ly).

pī'anist (pē-) *n*. Player on piano.

pīanĭ'stĭc *adj*. Of, adapted for playing on a piano.

pīa'nō[1] (pyah-) *adv.*, *n.* (pl. *-os*), & *adj.* (mus.) (Passage performed) soft(ly). [It.]

pĭă'nō[2], **pĭănofŏ'rtè** *ns*. Large musical instrument played by means of keys which cause hammers to strike on metal strings (the

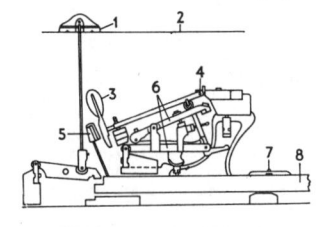

GRAND PIANO ACTION

1. Damper or sordine. 2. String. 3. Hammer. 4. Pivot of hammer. 5. Check. 6. Levers lifting hammer. 7. Pivot of key. 8. Key

vibrations being stopped by dampers); *cottage* ~, small upright piano; *grand* ~, large wing-shaped piano of full tone with strings arranged horizontally; *player* ~, mechanical piano, pianola; *upright* ~, piano with strings in vertical position; ~ *organ*, mechanical piano constructed like barrel-organ. [It., earlier *piano e forte* soft and strong, i.e. loud]

pĭănō'la *n.* (orig.) Device, attachable to piano, by means of which music can be reproduced mechanically; (now usu.) piano incorporating such a mechanism: hammers are made to strike the strings by means of air pressure and the passage of air to particular hammers is regulated by perforations in a revolving roll (~ *roll*). [trade-name]

pĭă'stre (-ter), **-ter** *n*. $\frac{1}{100}$ of a pound in Egypt, Lebanon, Sudan, and Syria.

pĭă'zza (-tsa) *n*. Public square or market-place, esp. in Italian town; (U.S.) verandah of house. [It., ult. f. Gk *plateia* (*hodos*) broad (street)]

pibroch (pē'brŏx) *n*. Series of variations for bagpipe, chiefly martial. [Gael. *piobaireachd*, f. *piobair* piper]

pī'ca *n*. (print.) Size of type (12 point), of about 6 lines to the inch; *small* ~, size (11 point), between long primer and pica; *double* ~ (prop. *double small* ~), size equal to 2 lines of small pica.

pĭcadŏr' *n.* Mounted man with lance in bullfight.

Pī'cardy̆. (Fr. *Picardie*) Former province of N. France between Normandy and Flanders, comprising the modern department of Somme and parts of Pas-de-Calais, Aisne, and Oise.

pĭcarĕ'sque (-k) *adj*. (of a style of fiction) Dealing with adventures of rogues.

PICK

pĭcarōō'n *n*. Rogue; thief; pirate; pirate ship.

Pĭcă'ssō, Pablo (1881–1973). Spanish painter, one of the original exponents of CUBISM.

pĭcayu'ne (-yōōn) *n*. (U.S.) 5-cent piece or other small coin; (colloq.) small, mean, or insignificant person or thing. ~ *adj*. (colloq.) Mean, contemptible, paltry.

Pĭccadĭ'lly̆. Street in West End of London. [f. *Pickadilly Hall*, a tailor's house so nicknamed f. *pickadill* scallop at edge of doublet]

pĭ'ccalĭllĭ *n*. Pickle of chopped vegetables, mustard, and hot spices.

pĭ'ccaninny̆ *n*. Negro child.

pĭ'ccolō *n*. Small flute, an octave higher than the ordinary flute. [It., = 'small']

pĭchĭcĭă'gō *n*. Small pink burrowing armadillo (genus *Chlamyphorus*) of Argentina. [perh. f. native *pichey* little armadillo, Span. *ciego* blind]

pick[1] *n*. Tool consisting of an iron bar, usu. curved with a point at one end and a point or chisel-edge at the other, with a wooden

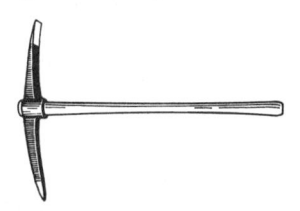

PICK

handle passing through the middle perpendicularly, used for breaking up hard ground etc.; instrument for picking, tooth-pick.

pick[2] *v*. 1. Break surface of (ground etc.) with or as with pick; make (hole etc.) thus. 2. Probe (teeth etc.) with pointed instrument to remove extraneous matter; clear (bone, carcass) of adherent flesh. 3. Detach (flowers, fruit, etc.) from place of growth. 4. (of birds) Take up (grains etc.) in bill; (of persons) eat in small bits; (colloq.) eat. 5. Select carefully; ~ *and choose*, select fastidiously. 6. Pull asunder (esp. ~ *oakum*); ~ *to pieces*, pull asunder; (fig.) criticize hostilely. 7. ~ *a lock*, open a lock (esp. with intent to rob) with pointed instrument etc.; ~ *a pocket*, steal its contents; ~ *a quarrel*, contrive to quarrel *with*; ~ *and steal*, pilfer; ~ *off*, pluck off; shoot deliberately one by one; ~ *on*, select; single out for criticism etc.; ~ *out*, take or choose from a number of others, distinguish from surrounding objects; relieve (ground colour *with* another); make out (meaning of passages etc.), play (tune) by ear; ~ *up*, break up (ground etc.)

[663]

with pick; lay hold of and take up; raise from a fall etc.; gain, acquire (livelihood, profit, tricks, information); take (person, or thing) along with one; regain; recover health; make acquaintance with casually (or *with*); succeed in receiving by wireless, seeing with searchlight, etc.; (games) select (sides) by alternate choosing; (of motor etc.) recover speed, accelerate. 8. **pi′cklock**, person who picks locks; instrument used for this; ~-*me-up*, stimulating drink; **pi′ckpocket**, one who steals from pockets; ~-*up*, picking up (of ball in cricket, etc.); game between sides chosen by picking up; (colloq.) casual esp. unintroduced acquaintance; power (of motor, etc.) to accelerate; mechanism (replacing sound-box of gramophone) which converts impulses imparted to needle by record into electrical impulses which can then be amplified; small motor truck with open body. **pi′cker** *n*. **pick** *n*. 1. Picking; selection; best part *of*. 2. (weaving) Thread, group of threads, of weft.

pi′ck-a-băck *adv*. On shoulders or back like a bundle.

pi′ckăxe *n*. = PICK¹. ~ *v*. Break (ground etc.) with pickaxe; work with pickaxe.

pi′ckerel *n*. Young pike.

pi′ckėt *n*. 1. Pointed stake or peg driven into ground to form palisade, tether horse, etc.; (hist.) (stake with pointed top on which person stood as) form of military punishment. 2. (mil.) Small body of troops sent out to watch for enemy or held ready in quarters; party of sentinels, outpost; (now, chiefly) camp-guard doing police duty in garrison town etc. 3. (usu. pl.) Man or body of men stationed by trade-union to dissuade men from work during strike etc. ~ *v*. Secure (place) with stakes; tether; post (men) as picket; beset with pickets during strike etc.; act as picket.

pi′cking *n*. (esp., pl.) Gleanings, remaining scraps; pilferings.

pi′ckle *n*. Brine, vinegar, or similar liquor in which flesh, vegetables, etc., are preserved; food, esp. (usu. pl.) vegetables preserved in pickle and eaten as relish; acid solution for cleaning purposes etc.; (fig.) plight, predicament; mischievous child. ~ *v.t.* Preserve in pickle; treat (wood etc.) with acid solution. **pi′ckled** (-ld) *adj*. (slang) Drunk.

Pi′ckwick, Mr. Samuel. Hero of Dickens's novel 'The Pickwick Papers'. **Pickwi′ckian** *adj*. Of Mr. Pickwick or the Pickwick Club; applied to uncomplimentary language which should not be interpreted literally ('Pickwick Papers', ch. i).

pi′cnic *n*. Pleasure party including meal out of doors. ~ *v.i.* Take part in picnic. **pi′cnicker** *n*.

pico- *prefix*. (abbrev. p) One billionth of (10^{-12}).

Pi′cō dĕlla Mĭră′ndola (pē-), Giovanni (1463-94). Italian humanist and neo-Platonic philosopher; pioneer in the study of Hebrew philosophy and the Cabbala.

picot (pē′kō) *n*. Small loop of twisted thread, one of series forming edging to lace, ribbon, etc. (ill. LACE).

picotee′ *n*. Carnation, tulip, etc., of which flowers have light ground with darker edging to petals.

picquĕ′t (-kėt) *n*. Var. of PIQUET.

pi′cric *adj*. ~ *acid*, trinitrophenol, intensely bitter yellow crystalline substance used, in aqueous solution, as a treatment for burns etc., and formerly as a high explosive (lyddite).

Pict *n*. One of an ancient, prob. pre-Celtic, people formerly inhabiting parts of N. Britain and Ireland, later (9th c.) united with Scots. **Pi′ctĭsh** *adj*.

pi′ctŏgrăph (*or* -ahf) *n*. Pictorial symbol which stands for the thing depicted, e.g. representation of an eye standing for 'eye' (ill. HIEROGLYPH); primitive writing or record consisting of these. **pictŏgră′phĭc** *adj*. **pictŏ′graphy** *n*.

pictŏr′ĭal *adj*. Of, expressed in, pictures; illustrated; picturesque. **pictŏr′ĭally** *adv*. **pictŏr′ĭal** *n*. Journal of which pictures are main feature.

pi′cture *n*. 1. Painting, drawing, of objects esp. as work of art; portrait; beautiful object; (fig.) symbol, type, figure. 2. Scene, total visual impression produced; mental image; *be*, *put*, *in the* ~, have, give, all the relevant information; *out of the* ~, irrelevant; *clinical* ~, total idea of diseased condition formed by physician. 3. Visible reproduction of film; image on television screen; (pl.) exhibition of cinematographic film(s), place where these are exhibited. 4. ~-*card*, court-card; ~-*gallery*, (hall etc. containing) collection of pictures; ~ *hat*, woman's wide-brimmed hat resembling those in pictures by Reynolds and Gainsborough; ~ *palace*, cinema; ~ *postcard*, postcard with picture on back; ~-*writing*, mode of recording events etc. by pictures, as in hieroglyphs etc.; ~ *window*, large window facing attractive view. ~ *v.t.* Represent in picture; describe graphically; imagine.

picture′sque (-cherĕsk) *adj*. Like, fit to be the subject of, a striking picture; (of language etc.) strikingly graphic, vivid. **pictŭrĕ′squely** *adv*. **pictŭrĕ′squeness** *n*.

pi′ddle *v.i.* (archaic) Work, act, in trifling way; (colloq. or childish) urinate. **pi′ddling** *adj*. (colloq.) Trivial.

pi′dgĭn *n*. 1. (also *pigeon*) Person's concern or responsibility. 2. Jargon chiefly of English words used esp. between Chinese and European (also ~ *English*); mixed simplified form of English used elsewhere. [Chin. corrupt. of *business*]

pie¹ *n*. Magpie.

pie² *n*. Dish of meat, fruit, etc., encased in or covered with or surrounded by paste and baked; any of various other baked dishes of meat, fish, etc.; *have a finger in the* ~, be (esp. officiously) concerned in the matter; *pie′crust*, baked paste of pie; *pie′man*, vendor of pies; ~ *in the sky*, (slang) heavenly or paradisiacal state.

pie³ *n*. (print.) Confused mass of type such as results from breaking down of a forme; (fig.) chaos. ~ *v.t.* Make (type) into pie.

pie′bald (pībawld) *adj*. Of two colours irregularly arranged, esp. black and white; (of horse) with black and white patches on body and legs; (fig.) motley, mongrel. [f. PIE¹ (magpie)]

piece *n*. 1. One of the distinct portions of which thing is composed; *in* ~*s*, broken; *break to* ~*s*, break into fragments; *pull or tear to* ~*s*, (fig.) criticize severely. 2. Enclosed portion *of* (land); detached portion (*of* a substance); definite quantity in which thing is made up; cask (*of* wine etc.) varying in capacity; *a* ~ *of one's mind*, one's candid opinion, rebuke. 3. Example, specimen; ~ *of work*, product of work; task. 4. Cannon, gun, pistol; man at chess, draughts, etc.; coin; ~ *of eight*, (hist.) Spanish dollar (which was marked with figure 8), of value of eight reals. 5. Picture; literary or musical composition, usu. short; drama. 6. *by the* ~, (payment etc.) according to amount done (not time taken); *of a* ~, uniform, consistent, in keeping (*with*); ~-*goods*, textile fabrics (esp. Lancashire cotton goods) woven in recognized lengths; ~-*work*, work paid for by the piece. ~ *v.t.* Put together, form into a whole; join thread in spinning; fit *on* (thing *to* another); eke *out*; make *out* (story, theory, etc.) by combination of parts; join *together*; patch *up*.

pièce de résistance (pyĕs de răzĕstahṅs). Most substantial dish at meal (also fig.). [Fr.]

pie′cemeal (-sm-) *adv*. Piece by piece, part at a time. ~ *adj*. Done etc. piecemeal.

pied (pīd) *adj*. Particoloured. **Pie′dmŏnt** (*or* pyä-). (It. *Piemonte*) District of NW. Italy, united with Italy 1859. **Piedmŏntē′se** (-z) *adj*. & *n*.

pier *n*. Solid structure of stone etc., extending into sea or tidal river, to protect or enclose a harbour; structure of iron or wood, open below, running out into sea, lake, etc. and used as promenade and landing-stage; support of spans of bridge; pillar (ill. ARCADE); solid masonry between windows etc.; ~-*glass*, large tall mirror, orig. used to fill up this; ~-*table*, table for standing against pier between windows. (*Illustration*, *p. 665*.)

[664]

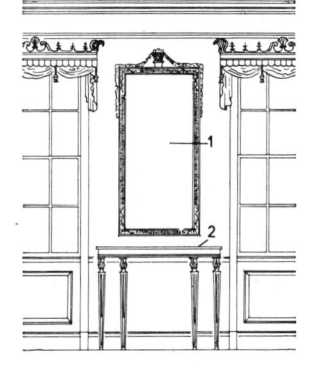

PIER, LATE 18TH C.
1. Pier-glass. 2. Pier-table

pierce[1] *v.* Penetrate; prick (*with* pin etc.); make hole in; force one's way through or into; penetrate *through, into*, etc. **pier'-cingly** *adv.*
Pierce[2], Franklin (1804–69), 14th president of U.S. 1853–7.
Piēr'ia. District on N. slopes of Mt OLYMPUS, whence the cult of the Muses was prob. carried to Helicon. **Pier'ian** *adj.* Of Pieria; of the Muses.
pierrot (pēr'ō) *n.* (fem. *pierrette*) French pantomime character with whitened face and loose white dress; itinerant entertainer (esp. member of troupe) similarly dressed. [Fr., dim. of *Pierre* Peter]
pietà (pyātah') *n.* Picture, sculpture, of Virgin Mary holding dead body of Christ on her lap. [L *pietas* piety]
pi'etism *n.* Movement for revival of piety in the Lutheran Church begun by P. J. Spener about 1670; pious sentiment, exaggeration or affectation of this. **pi'etist** *n.* **piēti'stic, -ical** *adjs.* **pi'ety** *n.* Quality of being pious.
piēzōĕlĕctri'city (*or* pēz-) *n.* Electricity or electric polarity produced by pressure on a non-conducting crystal. **piēzōĕlĕ'ctric** *adj.*
piēzō'mĕter *n.* Any of various instruments for measuring (something connected with) pressure.
pi'ffle *v.i.* Talk or act feebly, trifle. ~ *n.* Twaddle. **pi'ffling** *adj.* Trivial, worthless.
pig *n.* 1. Swine; flesh of (usu. young or sucking) pig as meat; (colloq.) greedy, dirty, sulky, obstinate, or annoying person; *buy a* ~ *in a poke*, buy something without seeing it or knowing its value. 2. Oblong mass of metal (usu. cast-iron) cooled in a mould into which it is run from smelting-furnace. 3. ~-*headed*, obstinate, stupid; ~-*iron*: see 2 above, and IRON; ~ *jump*, (of horse) jump sportively from all four legs not brought together as in buck- jumping; *pi'gnut*, earth-nut, esp. tuber of *Conopodium denudatum*; *pi'gskin*, (leather made of) pig's skin; (slang) saddle; *pi'gsticking*, hunting of wild boar with spear; *pi'gsty*, = STY[1]; ~'*s wash, pi'gwash*, swill of brewery or kitchen given to pigs; *pi'gtail*, tobacco twisted into thin rope or roll; plait of hair hanging from back of head, esp. as worn by Chinese under the Manchus, by young girls, and formerly by soldiers and sailors. ~ *v.* Bring forth (pigs), bring forth pigs; herd together like pigs, live in disorderly or untidy fashion.
pi'geon[1] (-jĭn *or* -jon) *n.* 1. Bird of the family Columbidae, dove, esp. (*rock-*~) the rock-dove, *Columba livia*, which haunts rocks and large buildings and is also domesticated in many varieties produced by fancy breeding; *carrier* ~, homing pigeon for carrying message attached to its neck or leg; *clay* ~: see CLAY; *homing* ~, pigeon trained to fly home over long distances; *wood-*~, ring-dove, *Columba palumbus*, a wild bird eaten as game; ~ *breast*, deformed human breast laterally constricted; ~-*hole*, small recess for pigeon to nest in; one of a set of compartments in cabinet etc. for papers, etc. (ill. DESK); (*v.t.*) deposit (document) in this, put aside (matter) for future consideration; assign (thing) to definite place in memory; ~ *pair*, boy and girl twins, or boy and girl as sole children; ~'*s milk*, partly-digested food with which pigeons feed their young; imaginary article for which children are sent on fool's errand; ~-*toed*, (of persons or horses) turning toes or feet inwards. 2. (colloq.) Person who is rooked or plucked.
pigeon[2]: see PIDGIN.
pi'ggery *n.* Pig-breeding establishment; pigsty; dirty place; piggishness.
pi'ggish *adj.* Like a pig, esp. greedy or dirty. **pi'ggishly** *adv.* **pi'ggishness** *n.*
pi'ggy *n.* 1. (nursery, colloq.) Little pig; ~-*bank*, money-box esp. of china, made in the shape of a pig. 2. Game of tip-cat. ~ *adj.* Piggish.
pi'glĕt, pi'gling *ns.* Young pig.
pi'gment *n.* Colouring-matter in a paint, or dye; (biol.) natural colouring-matter of a tissue. **pigmĕ'ntal, pi'gmentary, pi'g- mĕnted** (*or* -mĕ'-) *adjs.* **pigmĕntā'tion** *n.* Colouring (esp. of tissue) by pigment.
pigmy: see PYGMY.
pīke[1] *n.* 1. Long wooden shaft with steel or iron head, infantry weapon superseded by bayonet (ill. SPEAR); (dial.) pickaxe, spike. 2. Peaked top of hill. 3. Large voracious freshwater fish (*Esox lucius*) of northern temperate zone, with long slender snout (prob. abbrev. of *pike fish*, from its pointed snout). ~ *v.t.* Thrust through, kill with pike.
pīke[2] *n.* Toll-bar; toll; turnpike road.
pīke[3] *v.i.* (dial. & U.S.) Depart, go off.
pī'kelĕt (-kl-) *n.* Crumpet or (in some districts) muffin. [Welsh (*bara*) *pyglyd* pitchy (bread)]
pī'ker *n.* (U.S.) Cautious gambler; mean-spirited person.
pī'kestaff (-kstahf) *n.* Wooden shaft of pike; *plain as a* ~ (orig. *packstaff*, smooth staff used by pedlar), quite plain.
pĭlă'f, -ăff, pĭlau' (-ow), pĭlaw' *n.* Oriental dish of rice with meat, spices, etc.
pĭlă'ster *n.* Column of rectangular section projecting from a wall (ill. DOOR).
Pī'late, Pontius. Roman governor of Judaea A.D. 26–36; presided at trial of Jesus Christ.
pilch *n.* Infant's garment worn over napkin.
pĭ'lchard *n.* Small sea-fish (*Sardina pilchardus*) allied to herring but smaller and rounder, found esp. off the coasts of Cornwall, Devon, and W. France; related fish found elsewhere.
pĭ'lcŏrn *n.* Variety of cultivated oat in which husk does not adhere to grain.
pīle[1] *n.* 1. Pointed stake or post; heavy beam or column of wood, concrete, steel, etc., driven or bored into the ground as support for heavy structure; ~-*driver*, machine for driving piles into the ground. 2. (her.) Charge in form of wedge, usu. point downwards (ill. HERALDRY). ~ *v.t.* Furnish with piles; drive piles into.
pīle[2] *n.* 1. Heap of things laid more or less regularly upon one another; lofty mass of buildings. 2. Series of plates of dissimilar metals, such as copper and zinc, laid one upon another alternately, with cloth or paper moistened with an acid solution placed between each pair, for producing electric current; any similar arrangement for producing electric current. 3. (also *atomie* ~) Nuclear REACTOR. 4. (colloq.) Heap of money, fortune. 5. (also *funeral* ~) Heap of combustibles on which corpse is burnt. ~ *v.t.* Heap up (freq. with *up, on*); load (table, etc., *with*); ~ *arms*, place (usu. four) rifles with butts on ground and muzzles interlocked; ~ *up*, (naut.) run (ship) on rocks or aground; ~-*up*, (colloq.) collision involving several vehicles.
pīle[3] *n.* 1. Soft hair, down, wool of sheep. 2. Soft surface of some woven fabrics, produced by weaving in extra yarns and cutting them short (as in ~ *velvet*) or by knotting them on to warp threads (as in ~ *carpet*) (ill. WEAVE).
pīle[4] *n.* (Popular name for) haemorrhoid (usu. pl.); *pī'lewort*, lesser celandine (from reputed efficacy against piles).

[665]

pī′leus n. (pl. *-leī*). (bot.) Cap-like part of mushroom or other fungus (ill. FUNGUS).
pī′lfer v. Steal, esp. in small quantities. **pī′lferer** n.
pī′lgrim n. One who journeys to sacred place as act of religious devotion; person regarded as journeying to a future life; traveller; *P~ Fathers*, earliest English Puritan settlers of colony of Plymouth, Massachusetts, and esp. those who left Delft Haven and Plymouth, England, in the *Mayflower* in 1620; *P~ Trust*, trust founded in 1930 by Stephen Harkness, Amer. millionaire, for the benefit of Gt Britain, and used for preservation of historic buildings etc., for art and learning, and for social welfare. ~ v.i. Wander like a pilgrim.
pī′lgrimage n. Pilgrim's journey; (fig.) mortal life viewed as a journey; *P~ of Grace*, rising in Yorkshire in 1536 to protest against dissolution of the monasteries. ~ v.i. Go on a pilgrimage.
pīli′ferous adj. (chiefly bot.) Having hair.
pī′liform adj. (chiefly bot.) Hair-shaped.
Pīlipi′no (-pē-) n. Language of Filipinos, based on Tagalog.
pill n. 1. Small ball or disc of medicine to be swallowed whole; *the~*, (colloq.) oral contraceptive. 2. (fig.) Something unpleasant that has to be accepted. 3. (slang or joc.) Ball; (pl.) billiards. 4. *~-box*, shallow cylindrical box for holding pills; cap shaped like this; (mil.) small round concrete emplacement; *pi′llwort*, plant of genus *Pilularia*, with small globular involucres.
pi′llage n. Plunder, esp. as practised in war. ~ v.t. Sack, plunder. **pi′llager** n.
pi′llar n. Vertical structure of stone, wood, metal, etc., slender in proportion to height, used as support or ornament; post, pedestal; upright mass of air, water, etc.; (mining) solid mass of coal etc. left to support roof of the working; (fig.) person who is a main supporter (*of*); *from ~ to post*, to and fro, from one resource to another; *~-box*, hollow pillar about 5 ft high in which letters may be posted; *Pillars of Hercules*, two promontories, Calpe (Gibraltar) in Europe and Abyla (Ceuta) in Africa, at E. end of Strait of Gibraltar, anciently supposed to have been parted by the arm of Hercules and regarded as the western limits of the inhabited world. ~ v.t. Support (as) with pillars.
pi′llion (-yon) n. 1. (hist.) Woman's light saddle; cushion attached to hinder part of saddle for second rider, usu. woman. 2. Seat for passenger behind saddle of motor-cycle or scooter. 3. *ride ~*, travel on pillion.
pi′lliwinks n. (hist.) Instrument of torture for squeezing fingers.
pi′llory n. Wooden framework with holes for head and hands of offender exposed to public ridicule etc. ~ v.t. Put in the pillory; (fig.) expose to ridicule.

PILLORY

pi′llow (-ō) n. Cushion as support for head, esp. in bed; (techn.) pillow-shaped block or support; *~-case*, *-slip*, washable cover for pillow; *~-fight*, mock fight with pillows in bedroom; *~ lace*, lace plaited with bobbins on a pillow (ill. LACE). ~ v. Rest, prop up, (as) on pillow.
pillule: see PILULE.
pīlocar′pine n. Alkaloid obtained from jaborandi, used in pharmacy.
pī′lōse, pī′lous adjs. Covered with hair. **pīlō′sity** n.
pī′lot n. 1. Person qualified to take charge of ships entering or leaving a harbour, or wherever navigation requires local knowledge; steersman (archaic). 2. One who operates flying controls of an aircraft, one duly qualified to do so; automatic device for maintaining an aeroplane in flight. 3. (fig.) Guide, esp. in hunting-field; (attrib.) small-scale, experimental. 4. *~-cloth*, thick blue woollen cloth for greatcoats, etc.; *~-engine*, locomotive engine going on ahead of a train to make sure that the way is clear; *~-fish*, small silvery-blue dark-barred fish of warm seas (*Naucrates ductor*), said to act for shark as pilot or guide to food; *~ lamp*, electric indicator light or control light; *~ light*, small gas burner kept alight to kindle large burner as required; *~ officer*, lowest commissioned rank in R.A.F. ~ v.t. Conduct as pilot; act as pilot on. **pī′lotage** n. **pī′lotless** adj. (of aircraft) Without human pilot aboard, guided by remote control.
pilous: see PILOSE.
Pī′lsen. German name of Plzen, town of Czechoslovakia, famous for lager beer (*Pilsener*).
Pilsu′dski (-soot-), Joseph (1867–1935). Polish soldier and statesman; first marshal of Poland; chief of state 1918–23; prime minister and virtual dictator 1926–8, 1930–5.
Pī′ltdown. Down near Lewes, East Sussex, where prehistoric remains of a human skull and ape-like lower jaw and of worked flints and bone implements were discovered (1912); they were claimed as belonging to the early Pleistocene period but proved by scientific tests (1953) to have been assembled as a hoax.
pī′lūle, pī′llūle n. Small pill. **pī′lūlar** adj.
pīmē′ntō n. 1. (Dried aromatic berry of) West Indian evergreen tree, *Pimenta officinalis*; allspice. 2. Any of various peppers.
Pī′mlicō. District of SW. London, on left bank of Thames.
pimp n. Man who solicits clients for a prostitute or brothel. ~ v.i. Act as pimp.
pi′mpernĕl n. Small annual (*Anagallis arvensis*) found in cornfields and waste ground, with scarlet (also blue or white) flowers closing in cloudy or rainy weather.
pi′mping adj. Small, mean; sickly.
pi′mple n. Small solid round tumour of the skin, usu. inflammatory. **pi′mpled** (-ld), **pi′mplў** adjs.
pin n. Thin piece of metal with sharp point and round flattened head for fastening together parts of dress, papers, etc.; peg of wood or metal for various purposes; peg on musical instrument, (ill. STRINGED); skittle; (pl. colloq.), legs; DRAWING-~, HAIRpin, SAFETY-~ : see these words; *split ~*, metal cotter to be passed through hole and held there by the gaping of its split end; *~s and needles*, tingling sensation in limb recovering from numbness; *pi′ncushion*, small cushion for sticking pins in to keep them ready for use; *~-feather*, ungrown feather; *~-head*, (fig.) minute thing; *~-hole*, hole made by pin or into which peg fits; *~-money*, (orig.) allowance to woman for dress expenses etc.; hence, very small sum; *~-point*, point of a pin; (attrib. of targets) small and requiring very accurate and precise bombing and shelling; (v.t.) locate or bomb (such target) with the accuracy and precision required (also fig.); *pi′nprick* (fig.) trifling irritation; *~-spot*, small round spot or part of pattern on fabric; *~-stripe*, very narrow stripe in textile fabric; *pi′ntail*, duck or grouse with pointed tail; *~-tuck*, narrow ornamental tuck; *~-wheel*, small catherine-wheel; *~-worm*, threadworm (*Enterobius vermicularis*) parasitic in human rectum. ~ v.t. Fasten (*to, together, up*) with pin(s); transfix with pin, lance, etc.; seize and hold fast; bind (person *down*) *to* (promise, arrangement); ~ *up*, (archit.) underpin; fasten (on wall etc.) by means of a pin; *~-up* (n.).

[666]

(picture pinned up on wall etc. portraying) glamorous young woman or celebrity.

pi′nafore *n.* Washable sleeveless covering worn over dress etc. to protect from dirt; ~ *dress*, dress without sleeves or collar, for wearing over blouse or jumper.

pince-nez (păn′snā) *n.* Pair of eyeglasses with spring to clip on to nose. [Fr., = 'pinch-nose']

pi′ncers (-z) *n.pl.* (also *pair of* ~) Gripping tool made of two limbs pivoted together forming pair of jaws with manipulating handles;

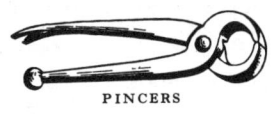

PINCERS

similar organ in crustaceans, etc.; ~ (also *pincer*) *movement*, (mil.) operation involving the convergence of two forces on enemy position like the jaws of a pair of pincers.

pinch *n.* Nip, squeeze; as much as can be taken up with tips of finger and thumb; (fig.) stress (of poverty etc.); *at a* ~, in a strait or exigency. ~ *v.* Nip with finger and thumb, cause pain or injure by squeezing; (of cold, hunger, etc.) nip, shrivel; stint; be niggardly; sail (vessel) close-hauled; (slang) steal; arrest.

pi′nchbeck *n.* Gold-like alloy of copper and zinc used in cheap jewellery etc. ~ *adj.* Made of pinchbeck; counterfeit, sham. [Christopher *Pinchbeck*, London watch- and toy-maker (*c* 1730)]

Pi′ndar (518–438 B.C.). Greek lyric poet. **Pinda′ric** *adj.* Of Pindar; resembling the style, diction, etc., of Pindar; ~ *ode*, (Engl. pros.) ode with irregular number of feet in lines and arbitrary disposition of rhymes.

pine¹ *n.* Tree of genus *Pinus* with evergreen needle-shaped leaves growing in sheathed clusters of two or more, many species of which afford timber, tar, and turpentine; ~-*cone*, characteristic organ of the pine, containing its seeds; ~-*kernel*, edible seed of some pine-trees.

pine² *v.i.* Languish, waste away, from grief, disease, etc.; long eagerly (*for, after, to*).

pi′neal *adj.* (anat.) Shaped like a pine-cone; ~ *body*, small conical body of unknown function behind third ventricle of brain (ill. BRAIN).

pi′neapple (-nă-) *n.* Juicy edible collective fruit of *Ananas*, surmounted by crown of small leaves (so called from resemblance to pine-cone); (slang) hand-grenade, bomb.

Pi′ner′**o** (or -nārō), Sir Arthur Wing (1855–1934). English playwright.

pi′nery *n.* Place in which pineapples are grown; plantation of pines.

pi′nfold *n.* Pound for stray cattle etc. ~ *v.t.* Confine in this.

ping *n.* Abrupt ringing sound as of rifle bullet flying through air. ~ *v.i.* Produce abrupt ringing sound; fly with this. [imit.]

pi′ng-pŏng *n.* Table tennis.

pi′nguid (-nggw-) *adj.* (usu. joc.) Fat, oily, greasy.

pi′nion¹ (-nyon) *n.* Terminal segment of bird's wing; any flight-feather of wing; (in carving) part of wing corresponding to forearm; (poet.) wing. ~ *v.t.* Cut off pinion of (wing, bird) to prevent flight; bind the arms of (person), bind (arms); bind (person etc.) fast *to*.

pi′nion² (-nyon) *n.* Small cogwheel engaging with larger one; cogged spindle engaging with wheel (ill. GEAR).

pĭnk¹ *n.* 1. Garden plant, species of *Dianthus*, esp. *D. plumarius*, native of E. Europe, with white, crimson, pink, or variegated sweet-smelling flowers; allied or similar plant. 2. Finest example of excellence, flower; *in the* ~, (slang) quite well. 3. Pale red slightly inclining to purple. 4. Fox-hunter's red coat; cloth of this; fox-hunter. ~ *adj.* Of pale red colour of various kinds, as *rose, salmon,* ~; (joc.) mildly communist; ~ *disease,* disease of children, characterized by extreme weakness and wasting and pink rash on skin; ~-*eye,* contagious fever of horses; contagious ophthalmia in man, marked by redness of the eyeball.

pĭnk² *n.* (hist.) Sailing-vessel esp. with narrow stern (orig. small and flat-bottomed).

pĭnk³ *n.* Young salmon; (dial.) minnow.

pĭnk⁴ *v.t.* Pierce with sword etc.; ornament (leather etc.) with perforations; cut scalloped or zigzag edge on; adorn, deck (freq. ~ *out*); *pinking shears,* dressmaker's serrated shears for cutting zigzag edge.

pĭnk⁵ *v.i.* (of internal combustion engine) Knock, emit dull metallic sound from detonation of (part of) charge, due to poor quality of fuel. [app. imit.]

Pi′nkerton, Allan (1819–84). Amer. detective of Scottish origin; founded (1850) a detective agency; forestalled an attempt on life of Abraham Lincoln, 1861; wrote his reminiscences.

pi′nna *n.* (pl. -ae) 1. Broad upper part of external ear (ill. EAR¹). 2. Primary division of pinnate leaf (ill. LEAF). 3. Fin, fin-like structure.

pi′nnace *n.* Man-of-war's double-banked (usu. eight-oared) boat; also applied to other ships' boats, now usu. driven by motor; (hist.) small, usu. two-masted, vessel.

pi′nnacle *n.* Small ornamental turret usu. ending in pyramid or cone, crowning a buttress, roof, etc.; natural peak; (fig.) culmination, climax. ~ *v.t.* Set (as) on pinnacle; form the pinnacle of; furnish with pinnacles.

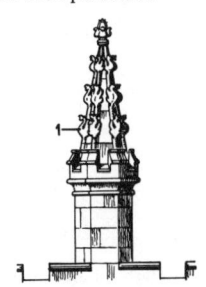

MEDIEVAL PINNACLE
1. Crocket

pi′nnate *adj.* 1. (bot., of compound leaf) With series of leaflets on each side of common stalk (ill. LEAF). 2. (zool.) With branches, tentacles, etc., on each side of an axis. **pi′nnately** *adv.*

pi′nner *n.* (esp.) Coif with two long side-flaps pinned on.

pi′nnothere *n.* Small crab of genus *Pinnotheres,* inhabiting shells of oysters, mussels, etc., and sharing their food.

pi′nnūle *n.* 1. (bot.) Secondary division of pinnate leaf (ill. FERN). 2. (zool.) Part, organ, like small wing or fin. 3. Sight at end of index of astrolabe etc. **pi′nnūlar** *adj.*

pi′nny *n.* (nursery colloq.) Pinafore.

pinochle, -cle (pē′nokl) *n.* (U.S.) Card-game like bezique; occurrence of queen of spades and knave of diamonds together at this game.

piño′lè *n.* Flour made from parched cornflour mixed with sweet flour of mesquite-beans, sugar, spice, etc. [Aztec *pinolli*]

pint *n.* Measure of capacity, ⅛ gallon, 20 fluid ounces in U.K., 16 in U.S.

pi′nta *n.* (colloq.) Pint of milk.

pi′ntle *n.* Bolt or pin, esp. one on which some other part turns (ill. BOAT).

pi′nto *adj.* & *n.* (south-western U.S.) Piebald (horse). [Span., = 'painted']

pinx. *abbrev.* Pinxit.

pi′nxit, pinxēr′unt. (So-and-so) painted it (in signature to picture, inscription on engraving etc.). [L]

pi′ny *adj.* Of, like, abounding in, pines.

pi′on *n.* (phys.) Pi-meson, meson having a mass of approx. 270 times that of the electron.

pioneer′ *n.* 1. Member of military unit equipped to prepare road for troops. 2. Beginner of enterprise; original explorer. ~ *v.* Act as pioneer (to); conduct; open up (road etc.) as pioneer.

pi′ous *adj.* Devout, religious; (archaic) dutiful; ~ *fraud:* see FRAUD. **pi′ously** *adv.*

[667]

pip[1] *n.* Disease of poultry, hawks, etc., marked by thick mucus in throat and often by white scale on tip of tongue; *the* ~, (slang) a feeling of disgust, depression, or bad temper.

pip[2] *n.* Each spot on playing-cards, dice, or dominoes, or star on army officer's shoulder; single blossom of clustered inflorescence; rhomboidal segment of surface of pineapple; image that an object produces on a radar screen.

pip[3] *n.* Seed of apple, pear, orange, etc.

pip[4] *n.* Signaller's name for letter P.

pip[5] *n.* High-pitched momentary sound, usu. produced mechanically, as in a radio time-signal. [imit.]

pip[6] *v.* (colloq.) Blackball; defeat; fail (in) examination; hit with shot; do for.

pipal: see PEEPUL.

pipe *n.* 1. Tube of wood, metal, etc., esp. for conveying water, gas, etc. 2. Musical wind-instrument consisting of single tube blown by mouth; each of tubes by which sounds are produced in organ (ill. ORGAN); boatswain's whistle, sounding of this; (pl.) bagpipes. 3. Voice, esp. in singing; song, note, or bird. 4. Tubular organ, vessel, etc., in animal body; cylindrical vein of ore; channel of decoy for wild fowl. 5. Narrow tube of clay, wood, etc., with bowl at one end, for drawing in smoke of tobacco; quantity of tobacco held by this; *King's, Queen's,* ~, furnace at London Docks used formerly for burning contraband tobacco; ~ *of peace*, calumet; *put that in your* ~ *and smoke it*, digest that fact etc. if you can. 6. Cask for wine, esp. as measure usu. = 105 gal. 7. ~-*clay*, fine white clay used for tobacco-pipes and (esp. by soldiers) for cleaning white breeches, belts, etc.; (*v.t.*) whiten with pipe-clay; ~-*dream*, (orig. U.S.) kind of extravagant fancy induced by smoking opium; hence, notion unlikely to be realized; ~-*line*, line of pipes for conveying petroleum, gas, or water across country; channel of supply, communication, etc.; ~ *major*, N.C.O. commanding regimental pipers; ~-*rack*, rack for tobacco-pipes; ~-*stone*, hard red clay used by Amer. Indians for tobacco-pipes. ~ *v.* 1. Play (tune etc.) on pipe; lead, bring, (person etc.), by sound of pipe; summon (crew) by sounding whistle; utter in shrill voice; ~ *down*, (naut.) dismiss from duty; (slang) be less noisy or cocksure; ~ *one's eye*, (colloq.) weep. 2. Propagate (pinks etc.) by cuttings taken off at joint of stem. 3. Trim (garment), ornament (cake etc.) with piping (see below). 4. Furnish with pipes.

pi'per *n.* One who plays on pipe, esp. strolling musician; bag-pipe-player; *pay the* ~, defray cost, bear expense or loss, of proceeding etc.

pipe'tte *n.* Slender tube filled usu. by suction, used in laboratories for measuring and transferring small quantities of liquid.

pi'ping *n.* (esp.) Ornamental pipe-like fold of cloth, often enclosing cord, for trimming edge of seam of garment, upholstery, etc.; ornamental cord-like line of icing on cake etc. ~ *adj.* (esp.) *the* ~ *times of peace*, those characterized by pastoral piping as opp. to more martial music; (*quasi-adv.*) ~ *hot*, so hot as to make piping or hissing sound.

pipistre'lle *n.* Small bat of genus *Pipistrellus*.

pi'pit *n.* Bird of a group superficially resembling larks but allied to the wagtails, of *Anthus* and related genera, including meadow ~, *A. pratensis.* [prob. imit.]

pi'pkin *n.* Small earthenware pot or pan.

pi'ppin[1] *n.* Any of several kinds of apple raised from seed.

Pippin[2]: see PEPIN.

pi'p-squeak *n.* (slang) Insignificant person, petty object.

piquant (pē'kant) *adj.* Agreeably pungent, sharp, appetizing; (fig.) pleasantly stimulating or disturbing to the mind. **pi'quantly** *adv.* **pi'quancy** *n.*

pique[1] (pēk) *v.t.* Irritate, wound the pride of; arouse (interest, curiosity); plume (oneself). ~ *n.* Ill-feeling, resentment.

pique[2] (pēk) *n.* Winning of 30 points at piquet before opponent begins to count. ~ *v.* Score a pique (against).

piqué (pē'kā) *n.* Stiff fabric, usu. cotton, with lengthwise ribs.

pique't (-kĕt) *n.* Card-game for two players with pack of 32 cards, points being scored on various groups or combinations of cards.

pīr'acy (or pĭr-) *n.* Action of a pirate; *air* ~, hijacking of aircraft.

Pīrae'us. Chief port of Athens.

pirā'gua (-gwa) *n.* 1. Long narrow canoe made from a single tree-trunk. 2. Two-masted sailing-barge. [Carib, = 'dug-out']

Pirandĕ'llo, Luigi (1867–1936). Italian playwright and novelist.

pira'nha (-ahnya), **pira'ya** (-ahya), **perai'** (-rī) *ns.* Tropical Amer. voracious freshwater fish (*Serrasalmo piraya*) with serrated belly and strong lancet-shaped teeth.

pīr'ate *n.* (Ship used by) sea-robber; marauder; one who infringes another's copyright; bus etc., that encroaches on recognized routes. ~ *v.* Plunder; reproduce (book etc.) without leave for one's own profit; play the pirate. **pīrā'tical** *adj.* **pīrā'tically** *adv.*

piro'gue (-ōg) *n.* = PIRAGUA.

pirouette (-ōŏet) *n.* & *v.i.* (ballet) Spin round on one foot or on point of toe. [Fr. = 'top']

Pisa (pē'za). City of Tuscany, N. Italy; *Leaning Tower of* ~, campanile of cathedral, built 1174–1350, about 180 ft high and leaning some 16 ft from the perpendicular.

pis aller (pēz ălā). Course etc. taken for want of a better. [Fr. *pis* worse, *aller* go]

pi'scary *n. common of* ~, right of fishing in another's water in common with owner (and others).

pi'scatory *adj.* Of fishermen or fishing; addicted to fishing. **piscatōr'ial** *adj.*

Pi'scēs (-z; *or* -skēz). The Fishes, a constellation; 12th sign (⟩⟨) of the zodiac, which sun enters about Feb. **Pi'scēan** *adj.* & *n.*

pi'sciculture *n.* Artificial rearing of fish. **piscicu'ltural** (-cher-) *adj.*

pisci'na (-sē-) *n.* 1. Fish-pond; ancient Roman bathing-pond. 2. (eccles.) Perforated stone basin for carrying away water used in rinsing chalice etc. (ill. FENESTELLA).

pi'scine[1] (*or* -ēn) *n.* Bathing-pool.

pi'scine[2] *adj.* Of fish.

pisci'vorous *adj.* Fish-eating.

pisé (pēzā) *n.* Stiff clay or earth (and gravel) rammed between boards (removed as it hardens) as building-material. [Fr., = 'pounded']

Pi'sgah (-zga). Mountain of Transjordan, NE. of Dead Sea, from which Moses viewed the Promised Land (Deut. 3: 27) before his death.

pish *int.* Exclamation of contempt, impatience, or disgust. ~ *v.i.* Say 'pish!'

pisho'gue (-ōg) *n.* (Ir.) Sorcery; charm, spell.

Pīsi'dia. Ancient region of S. Asia Minor. **Pīsi'dian** *adj.* & *n.*

pi'sifōrm (*or* pĭz-) *adj.* Pea-shaped; ~ *bone*, small bone of upper row of carpus (ill. HAND).

Pīsi'stratus, Peis- (pī-) (*c* 605–527 B.C.). Athenian statesman and soldier; became tyrant of Athens in 560 B.C.; was twice expelled, but returned to power.

pi'smīre *n.* Ant. [f. *piss* (from smell of ant-hill), and obs. *mire* ant, f. Du *mier*.]

piss *v.* (vulg.) Urinate; discharge with the urine; wet with urine. ~ *n.* Urine.

pistă'chiō (-sh-; *or* -tah-) *n.* Tree, *Pistacia vera*, of W. Asia, cultivated in S. Europe; nut of this, with greenish edible kernel; colour of the kernel.

piste (pē-) *n.* Ski-run.

pi'stil *n.* Organ of flower bearing ovules, comprising ovary, style, and stigma (ill. FLOWER). **pi'stillate** *adj.*

pi'stol (-tl) *n.* Small firearm, usu. with curved butt, held and fired by one hand; ~ *grip, handle,* handle shaped like butt of pistol (ill. RIFLE). (*Illustration, p. 669.*)

[668]

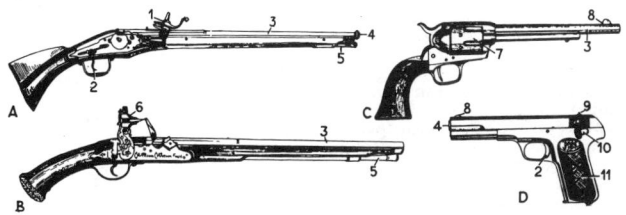

PISTOLS: A. GERMAN WHEEL-LOCK PETRONEL, c 1600. B. ENGLISH FLINTLOCK PISTOL, c 1650. C. COLT 45 SINGLE-ACTION 6-CHAMBERED REVOLVER, 1873. D. BROWNING 9 MM. SHORT AUTOMATIC PISTOL

1. Wheel-lock. 2. Trigger. 3. Barrel. 4. Muzzle. 5. Ramrod. 6. Flintlock. 7. Chambers. 8. Foresight. 9. Backsight. 10. Safety-catch. 11. Magazine holding eight rounds

pĭstō′le n. (hist.) Foreign gold coin, esp. Spanish.

pĭ′ston n. Disc or short cylinder fitting closely within cylindrical vessel in which it moves to and fro, used in steam-engine, pump, etc., to impart or receive motion by means of ~-*rod* (ill. COMBUSTION); sliding valve in cornet etc. (ill. BRASS); ~-*ring*, metallic expansible packing-ring fitted on piston.

pĭt n. 1. Natural hole in ground; hole made in digging for mineral etc. or for industrial purposes; (shaft of) coal-mine; depression in floor of workshop enabling persons to reach underside of motor vehicles for inspection or repair; covered hole as trap. 2. *the ~, hell*. 3. (hist.) Enclosure for cock-fights etc. 4. Hollow in animal or plant body or on any surface; depressed scar, as after smallpox; (bot.) hollow between plant cells on either side of lamella (~ *membrane*); ~ *of the stomach*, depression between cartilages of false ribs. 5. That part of auditorium of theatre etc. which is on floor of house; now usu. the part of this behind stalls (ill. THEATRE); people occupying this. 6. (U.S.) Part of floor of exchange appropriated for special branch of business. 7. (usu. pl.) Place at side of motor-racing track for refuelling etc. 8. *pi′tfall*, covered pit as trap; (fig.) unsuspected snare or danger; ~-*head*, top of shaft of coal-mine, or ground immediately around it; *pi′tman*, collier; (U.S.) connecting rod. ~ v. Put into a pit (esp. vegetables etc. for storage); set (cock etc.) to fight in pit (*against* another), (fig.) match (*against*); make pits, esp. scars, in (esp. in past part.); (path., of flesh etc.) retain impression of finger etc. when touched.

pĭt-a-păt adv. & n. (With) sound as of light quick steps.

Pĭ′tcairn I′sland (īl-). Small island in S. Pacific (British since 1839), inhabited by descendants of mutineers of the *Bounty*.

pĭtch[1] n. Black or dark-brown tenacious resinous substance, the residue from distillation of tar or turpentine, hard when cold but becoming viscid and semi-liquid when heated, used for caulking seams of ships, protecting wood from moisture, road-making, etc.; ~ *black*, with no light at all; so ~ *dark*(ness); *pi′tchblende*, mineral containing uranium oxide, one of the chief sources of radium and uranium; ~-*pine*, specially resinous kinds of pine; ~-*stone*, obsidian or other vitreous rock looking like pitch. **pĭ′tchy** adj. Of, like, dark as, pitch. **pitch** v.t. Smear, cover, coat, with pitch.

pĭtch[2] v. 1. Fix and erect (tent, camp); encamp; fix, plant, (thing) in definite position; pave (road) with set stones; (cricket) ~ *wickets*, fix stumps in ground and place bails; *pitched battle*, battle of set kind, not casual. 2. (mus.) Set at particular pitch; (fig.) express in particular style. 3. Throw, fling; (in games) throw (flat object) towards a mark; throw (ball) to batter in baseball etc.; (of ball etc.) land, fall in specified manner or position); fall heavily. 4. (slang) Tell (tale, yarn). 5. (of ship) Plunge in longitudinal direction. 6. Incline, dip (of stratum, roof, etc.). 7. ~ *in*, (colloq.) set to work vigorously; ~ *into*, (colloq.) assail forcibly with blows, words, etc.; make vigorous attack on; ~ *on*, happen to select. 8. ~-*and-toss*, game of skill and chance in which coins are pitched at a mark, and afterwards tossed up by players in turn, each keeping those that turn up 'heads'. ~ n. 1. Pitching; mode of delivering ball in cricket, baseball, etc. 2. Place at which street performer, bookmaker, etc. is stationed; (cricket) place between and about wickets; area for playing football etc. on. 3. Height to which falcon etc. soars before swooping on prey; height, degree, intensity (*of* quality etc.); (mus.) quality of musical sound depending on comparative rapidity of vibrations producing it, degree of acuteness (international standard pitch is set by fixing the A above middle C at 440 vibrations per second); ~-*pipe*, small pipe blown by mouth to set pitch for singing or tuning. 4. Degree of slope; steepness of roof's slope. 5. (mech.) Distance between successive points or lines, e.g. between successive teeth of cog-wheel; ~-*wheel*, toothed wheel engaging with another.

pĭ′tcher[1] n. (esp.) Player who delivers ball, esp. in baseball (ill. BASEBALL); stone used for paving.

pĭ′tcher[2] n. Vessel, usu. of earthenware, with handle or two ears and usu. a lip, for holding liquids; (bot.) modified leaf in pitcher-form; ~-*plant*, any of various plants with such leaves, freq. containing liquid secretion by which insects are caught and digested. **pĭ′tcherful** n.

pĭ′tchfŏrk n. Long-handled fork with two sharp prongs for pitching hay etc.; tuning-fork. ~ v.t. Cast (as) with pitchfork; (fig.) thrust (person) forcibly (*into* office, position, etc.).

pĭ′tèous adj. Such as to cause pity, deplorable. **pĭ′tèouslў** adv. **pĭ′tèousnĕss** n.

pĭth n. 1. Spongy cellular tissue in stem and branches of dicotyledonous plants (ill. STEM[1]); similar tissue lining rind of orange etc.; spinal cord; (fig.) essential part, quintessence. 2. Physical strength, vigour; force, energy. **pĭ′thlĕss** adj. **pith** v.t. Slaughter (animal) by severing spinal cord.

pĭthē′cănthrōpe n. Large fossil hominid, esp. *Pithecanthropus* (or *Homo*) *erectus* (JAVA man; ill. PRIMATE).

pĭthē′coid adj. & n. Ape-like (animal).

pĭ′thŏs n. (pl. *-oi*). (archaeol.) Store-jar.

pĭ′thў adj. Of, like, full of, pith; condensed and forcible, terse. **pĭ′thĭlў** adv. **pĭ′thĭnĕss** n.

pĭ′tiable adj. Deserving of pity or contempt. **pĭ′tiablenĕss** n. **pĭ′tiablў** adv.

pĭ′tiful adj. Arousing pity; contemptible. **pĭ′tifullў** adv. **pĭ′tifulnĕss** n.

pĭ′tilĕss adj. Showing no pity. **pĭ′tilĕsslў** adv. **pĭ′tilĕssnĕss** n.

Pĭ′tman, Sir Isaac (1813–97). English inventor of a system of shorthand based on sounds instead of letters.

pĭ′ton (pē-) n. Metal spike or peg used in mountaineering as support or belaying pin.

Pitot (pētō), Henri (1695–1771). French physicist; ~ *tube*, right-angled tube open at both ends, used in anemometers and for determining velocity of fluids (ill. ANEMOMETER); similar device used for measuring velocity of aircraft (ill. AEROPLANE).

pĭ′tpăn n. Central American dug-out boat.

Pitt, William, 1st Earl of Chatham (1708–78). English Whig statesman; prime minister 1766–8; his second son William (1759–1806), was prime minister 1783–1801, 1804–6.

pi′ttance n. 1. (hist.) Pious bequest to religious house for extra food etc. 2. Allowance, remuneration, esp. scanty one; small number or amount.

pĭtū′ĭtary adj. Of or secreting phlegm, mucous; ~ **gland**, small bilobed ductless gland at base of brain producing hormones which regulate many important bodily functions and co-ordinate the working of other endocrine organs (ill. BRAIN). ~ n. Pituitary gland. **pĭtū′ĭtous** adj. **pĭtū′ĭtrĭn** n. Hormone produced by pituitary gland; solution of this used medicinally.

pĭ′tў n. 1. Feeling of tenderness aroused by distress or suffering; take ~ on, feel or act compassionately towards. 2. Regrettable fact, ground for regret; more's the ~, so much the worse. ~ v.t. Feel pity for. **pĭ′tўĭnglў** adv.

Pī′us. Name of twelve popes: Pius II (Enea Silvio de Piccolomini, 1405–64); pope 1458–64; author and patron of letters; Pius IV (Giovanni Angelo Medici, 1499–1565); pope 1559–65, reconvened Council of TRENT in 1562; Pius IX (Giovanni Maria Mastai-Jenetti, 1792–1878); pope 1846–78; during this pontificate the temporal power of the papacy was lost and the doctrine of papal infallibility proclaimed; Pius XI (Achille Ratti, 1857–1939); pope 1922–39; the breach between Church and State was healed in this pontificate and the Vatican City State founded; Pius XII (Eugenio Pacelli, 1876–1958); pope 1939–58.

pĭ′vot n. Short shaft or pin on which something turns or oscillates; (mil.) man on whom body of troops wheels; (fig.) cardinal or central point. **pĭ′votal** adj. **pĭ′vot** v.i. Turn as on pivot, hinge (on).

pĭ′xў, pĭ′xĭe n. Supernatural being akin to fairy. **pĭ′xĭlātĕd** adj. (orig. U.S.) Enchanted, slightly crazy.

Pizăŕŕ′o, Francisco (c 1471–1541). Spanish discoverer and conqueror of Peru.

pizz. abbrev. Pizzicato.

pizza (pī′tsa) n. Italian dish of flat open crust containing cheese etc.

pizzĭca′to (pĭtsĭkah′tō) adv., n. (pl. -os), & adj. (mus.) (Passage, note, played) by plucking string of violin etc. with finger instead of using bow. [It.]

pĭ′zzle n. (vulg.) Penis of animal, esp. that of bull, formerly used as flogging instrument.

pl. abbrev. Place; plate; plural.

P.L.A. abbrev. Port of London Authority.

plā′cable adj. Easily appeased, mild, forgiving. **plăcabĭ′lĭtў** n. **plā′cablў** adv.

plā′card n. Document printed on one side of single sheet for posting up, poster. ~ v.t. Set up placards on (wall etc.); advertise (wares etc.) by placards; display (poster etc.) as placard.

placā′te (U.S. plā′-) v.t. Pacify, conciliate. **placā′tion** n. **placāt′ory** adj.

plāce n. 1. Particular part of space; part of space occupied by person or thing. 2. City, town, village, etc.; group of houses in town etc., usu. one not forming a street; residence, dwelling; country-house with surroundings; building, spot, devoted to specified purpose; another ~, (in House of Commons use) House of Lords. 3. Particular spot on surface etc.; particular point or passage in book etc. 4. Rank, station; position of figure in series as indicating its value in decimal or similar notation; step in progression of argument, statement, etc.; (racing) position among placed competitors. 5. Proper or natural position; space, seat, accommodation, for person etc. at table, in conveyance, etc.; in ~ of, instead of; take the ~ of, be substituted for. 6. Office, employment, esp. government appointment; duties of office etc. 7. give ~ to, make room for; be succeeded by; in, out of, ~, (un)suitable, (in)appropriate; take ~, happen. 8. ~ brick, brick imperfectly burnt from being on windward side of kiln; ~-kick, (footb.) kick made when ball is previously placed by another player for that purpose on ground. ~ v.t. 1. Put in particular place; arrange in their proper places. 2. Appoint (person) to post; find situation etc. for. 3. Invest (money); dispose of (goods) to customer; put (order for goods etc.) into hands of firm etc. 4. Repose (confidence etc., in, on). 5. Assign rank to; locate; state position of (usu. any of first three horses or runners) in race; identify fully, determine who (or what) a particular person (or thing) is, assign to a class; be placed, be among first three. 6. Get (goal) by place-kick.

placē′bō n. (pl. -s, -es). 1. Medicine given to humour patient (also used in experiments to test the effect of drugs, the drug being given to one group and the placebo to those who act as 'controls'). 2. (eccles.) Opening antiphon of the vespers for the dead. [L, = 'I shall be acceptable', first wd of Ps. 114: 9 in Vulgate]

placĕ′nta n. (pl. -ae). 1. Spongy vascular structure (in some mammals and some other vertebrates) formed by the interlocking of foetal and maternal tissue, through which the foetus is supplied with nutriment and rid of waste products (ill. EMBRYO). 2. (bot.) Part of carpel to which ovules are attached. **placĕ′ntal** adj.

plā′cer n. Deposit of sand, gravel, etc., in bed of stream etc., containing valuable minerals in particles.

plă′cĕt (-k-) n. (formerly, esp. in universities) Expression of assent given by saying 'placet' (L, = 'it pleases'). [L]

plă′cĭd adj. Mild; peaceful; serene. **plă′cĭdlў** adv. **placĭ′dĭtў** n.

plă′ckĕt n. Pocket, esp. in woman's skirt; opening or slit at top of skirt for convenience in putting on or off.

plă′coid adj. (of scales) Plate-shaped; (of fish) with placoid scales.

plā′gal adj. (mus., of ecclesiastical modes) Having their sounds comprised between the dominant and its octave, with final near middle of the compass (ill. MODE; cf. AUTHENTIC); ~ cadence, one in which chord of subdominant immediately precedes that of tonic.

plā′giarize v.t. Take and use another person's (thoughts, writings, inventions) as one's own. **plā′giarism, plā′giarist, plā′giarў** ns.

plăgiocĕphă′lĭc adj. Having anterior part of skull more developed on one side, posterior on the other.

plă′gioclāse n. (Mineral of the soda-lime felspar group (so called because they cleave obliquely). **plăgioclă′stĭc** adj. Having oblique cleavage.

plā′giostōme n. Fish with mouth placed transversely beneath snout, as shark, ray.

plāgue (-g) n. 1. Affliction, esp. as divine punishment; (colloq.) nuisance, trouble. 2. Pestilence, esp. oriental or bubonic plague; Great P~, bubonic plague that visited London in 1665; ~-spot, spot on skin characteristic of plague; locality infected with plague; (fig.) source or symptom of moral corruption. ~ v.t. Afflict with plague; (colloq.) annoy, bother.

plā′guy (-gĭ) adj. & adv. (archaic) Annoying(ly); exceeding(ly).

plaice n. European marine flatfish, Pleuronectes platessa, much used as food; allied American species.

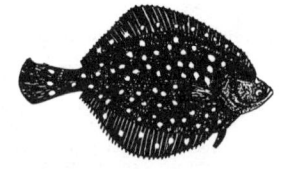

PLAICE

plaid (plăd, Sc. plād) n. Long piece of twilled woollen cloth, usu. with chequered or tartan pattern, outer article of Highland costume; cloth used for this, other fabric with tartan pattern. (Illus., p. 671.)

plain[1] adj. 1. Clear, evident; simple, readily understood; not elaborate or intricate. 2. Unembellished, (of drawings etc.) not

[670]

PLAIN

PLAID
1. Glengarry. 2. Sporran. 3. Plaid. 4. Kilt. 5. Trews. 6. Balmoral. 7. Tam-o'-shanter

coloured; (of food) not rich or highly seasoned; not luxurious; so ~ *cook*, person able to do ~ *cooking*, simple cooking. 3. Outspoken, straightforward. 4. Unsophisticated, ordinary, simple; of homely manners, dress, or appearance; not beautiful, ill-favoured. 5. ~*-chant*, plain-song; ~ *clothes*, ordinary civil or citizen dress, not uniform or fancy dress; ~ *dealing*, candour, straightforwardness; ~ *knitting*, stitch in which second needle is inserted through loop on first from left to right, and yarn is looped over first needle from the back (ill. KNITTING); ~ *sailing*, sailing in a plain course, with no difficulty or obstruction; (fig.) simple course of action; *plai'nsong*, traditional church music sung in unison in medieval modes and in free rhythm depending on accentuation of the words; ~*-spoken*, outspoken. ~ *adv.* Clearly; plainly.
plai'nly *adv.* **plai'nness** (-n-n-) *n.* **plain** *n.* 1. Level tract of country; *plai'nsman*, inhabitant of a plain. 2. Plain knitting.
plain² *v.i.* (archaic, poet.) Mourn; complain; emit plaintive sound.
plaint *n.* 1. (law) Accusation, charge. 2. (poet.) Lamentation, complaint.
plai'ntiff *n.* Party who brings suit into court of law, prosecutor.
plai'ntive *adj.* Expressive of sorrow; mournful. **plai'ntively** *adv.* **plai'ntiveness** *n.*
plait (-ăt) *n.* 1. Interlacing of three or more strands of hair, ribbon, straw, etc. 2. Fold, crease (now usu. PLEAT). ~ *v.t.* Form (hair, straw, etc.) into plait.
plăn *n.* Drawing, diagram, made by projection on flat surface, esp. one showing relative position of parts of (one floor of) a building; large-scale detailed map of town or district; table indicating times, places, etc., of intended proceedings, etc.; scheme of arrangement;

project, design; way of proceeding; (perspective) any of the imaginary planes, perpendicular to line of vision, passing through objects shown in picture. **plă'nless** *adj.* **plăn** *v.t.* Make a plan of (ground, existing building); design (building to be constructed etc.); scheme, arrange beforehand.
plănch (-sh) *n.* Slab of metal, stone, etc.; esp. of baked fire-clay used in an enamelling oven.
plă'nchet (-sh-) *n.* Plain disc of metal of which coin is made.
plănche'tte (-sh-) *n.* Small usu. heart-shaped board supported by two castors and a pencil, which when one or more persons rest their fingers lightly on the board is supposed to write without conscious direction.
Planck (-ŭnk), Max (1858–1947). German physicist; Nobel Prize for physics, 1918; originator of the QUANTUM theory; ~'s *constant*, (phys.) constant in the expression for the quantum of energy, symbol h, numerical value 6.61×10^{-27}.
plāne¹ *n.* Tall spreading tree of genus *Platanus*, with broad angular palmately-lobed leaves, and bark which scales off in irregular patches.
plāne² *n.* Tool for smoothing surface of woodwork by paring shavings from it, consisting of wooden or metal stock from smooth bottom of which projects a steel blade; similar tool for smoothing metal; *moulding* ~, one for making mouldings; *smoothing* ~, one used to finish surface. ~ *v.t.* Smooth (wood, metal) with plane; pare *away* or *down* (irregularities) with plane.
plāne³ *n.* 1. Surface such that the straight line joining any two points in it lies wholly in it; imaginary surface of this kind in which points or lines in material bodies lie; level surface. 2. Flat thin object, esp. one used in aerostatical experiments; (one of) the principal supporting surface(s) in an aeroplane; aeroplane; each

PLANETARIUM

of natural faces of a crystal. 3. Main road in mine. 4. (fig.) Level (*of* thought, knowledge, etc.). 5. ~ *sailing*, art of determining ship's place on the theory that she is moving on a plane; (fig., now usu. *plain sailing*) simple course. ~ *v.i.* Travel, glide (*down* etc.) in aeroplane; (of speedboat etc.) skim over water. ~ *adj.* Perfectly level, forming a plane; (of angle, figure, etc.) lying in a plane; ~ *chart*, one on which meridians and parallels of latitude are represented by equidistant straight lines, used in plane sailing; ~*-table*, surveying instrument used for measuring angles in mapping, consisting of a circular drawing-table mounted on a tripod and a ruler for pointing at the object observed; (*v.t.*) survey (area) with this.
plă'nėt¹ *n.* 1. (hist.) Heavenly body distinguished from fixed stars by having apparent motion of its own, esp. (astrol.) with reference to its supposed influence on persons and events. 2. Each of the heavenly bodies revolving in approximately circular orbits round sun (*primary* ~s), or of those revolving round these (*secondary* ~s or *satellites*); *major* ~s, (in order of distance from sun) Mercury, Venus, Earth, Mars, Jupiter, Saturn, Uranus, Neptune, Pluto (*illustration*, p. 672); *minor* ~s, asteroids (with orbits between those of Mars and Jupiter);

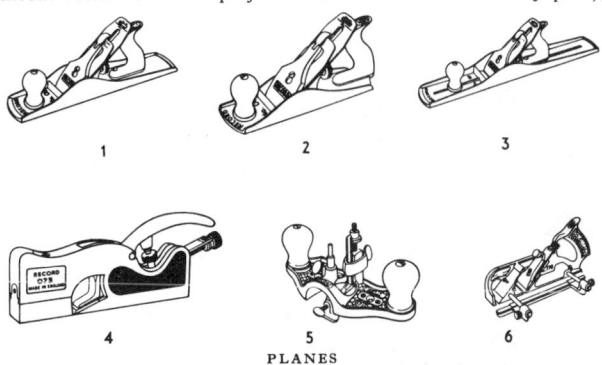

PLANES
1. Jack-plane. 2. Smoothing plane. 3. Trying-plane. 4. Rabbet plane. 5. Router plane. 6. Fillister plane

~*-gear(ing)*, gearing in which planet-wheels are used (ill. GEAR); ~*-wheel*, one of two or more gear-wheels in mesh with a central sun-wheel and an outer annulus which may be free to revolve (giving direct drive) or prevented from revolving (when drive from sun-wheel to planet-wheels effects a reduction in speed).
plă'nėt² *n.* Chasuble.
plănėtār'ium *n.* Model or structure representing planetary system, orrery; apparatus which projects representation of the heavens on inner surface of dome; building housing this.

[671]

PLANETARY

```
┌─────────────────────────┐
│         SUN             │
└─────────────────────────┘
  o  MERCURY
  O  VENUS
  O  EARTH
  o  MARS
 ∴∴∴∴∴  ASTEROIDS
         JUPITER
         SATURN
         URANUS
         NEPTUNE
  O  PLUTO
```

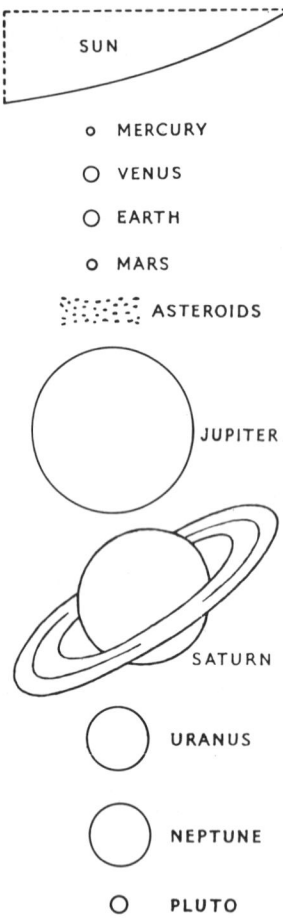

SIZES AND POSITIONS OF THE PLANETS IN RELATION TO THE SUN

plă'nėtarў *adj.* Of planets; terrestrial, mundane; wandering, erratic.

plă'ngent (-j-) *adj.* (of sound) Thrilling, vibrating, moaning, insistent. **plă'ngencў** *n.*

plani'mėter *n.* Instrument for mechanically measuring area of irregular plane figure. **plani'mėtrў** *n.* Measurement of plane surfaces.

plă'nish *v.t.* Flatten (sheet metal etc.) with smooth-faced hammer; flatten out (coining-metal) between rollers.

plă'nisphēre *n.* Device for showing the part of the heavens visible at a given time and place. **plănisphĕ'rĭc** *adj.*

plănk *n.* Long flat piece of smoothed timber, 50–150 mm thick, 225 or more mm wide; (fig.) item of political or other platform or programme; *walk the ~*, walk blindfold into sea along plank laid over side of ship, esp. as pirates' method of disposing of victims; *~-bed*, bed of boards, without mattress. *~ v.t.* Furnish, cover, floor, with planks; (U.S.) cook (fish) by splitting open and fixing to board; (slang) put *down* (esp. money on the spot).

plă'nkton *n.* (biol.) Collective name for all the forms of drifting or floating organic life found at various depths in the ocean or in fresh water.

plāno- *prefix.* Flatly, in a flattened manner; comb. of plane with another surface.

plāno-cŏ'ncāve, -cŏ'nvĕx *adjs.* With one surface plane and the other concave, convex (ill. LENS).

plănogră'phĭc *adj.* (of printing) Done from a flat surface (ill. PRINT).

plant (-ah-) *n.* 1. Living organism generally capable of living wholly on inorganic substances and having neither power of locomotion nor special organs of sensation or digestion, member of the vegetable kingdom (freq. restricted to the smaller plants, excluding trees and shrubs); *~-louse*, any of various insects infesting plants, esp. aphis. 2. Mode of planting oneself, pose. 3. Fixtures, implements, machinery, etc., used in industrial process. 4. (slang) Planned swindle or burglary; hoax. *~ v.t.* 1. Place (tree, shoot, seed, etc.) in ground that it may take root and grow; naturalize (animals, fish, etc.); cause (idea etc.) to take root *in* (mind); *~ out*, transfer (plant) from pot or frame to open ground; set out (seedlings) at intervals. 2. Fix firmly (*in, on,* ground, etc.); station (person), esp. as spy; *~ oneself*, take up a position. 3. Establish, found (community, city, church); settle (person) in place as colonist etc. 4. Furnish land *with* plants, district *with* settlers, etc.). 5. Deliver (blow, thrust) with definite aim. 6. (slang) Conceal (stolen goods etc. on innocent person's premises to incriminate him); bury, place (gold-dust, ore) in mining claim to encourage prospective buyer; devise (fraudulent scheme).

Plăntă'gėnėt. Orig., nickname of Geoffrey, Count of Anjou, father of Henry II of England; adopted as surname (*c* 1460) by Richard, Duke of York; applied to the whole royal house which occupied English throne 1154–1399 (Henry II to Richard II). [L *planta* sprig, *genista* broom, w. ref. to Geoffrey's habit of wearing on his helmet a sprig of the common broom of Anjou]

plă'ntain¹ (-tĭn) *n.* Plant of genus *Plantago*, esp. *greater ~* (*P. major*), low herb with broad flat leaves spread out close to ground and dense cylindrical spikes of seeds much used for cage-birds.

plă'ntain² (-tĭn) *n.* Tree-like

PLASTER

tropical herbaceous plant (*Musa paradisiaca*) allied to banana, with immense undivided oblong leaves, cultivated for its fruit borne in long densely clustered spikes; long pod-shaped somewhat fleshy fruit of this.

plă'ntar *adj.* (anat.) Of the sole of the foot.

plăntā'tion *n.* 1. Assemblage of planted growing plants, esp. trees. 2. Estate on which cotton, tobacco, etc., are cultivated (formerly by servile labour). 3. (hist.) Colonization; colony.

plā'nter (-ah-) *n.* 1. Cultivator of soil; (in Ireland) English settler on forfeited lands in 17th c., (19th c.) person settled in evicted tenant's holding. 2. Occupier of plantation, esp. in (sub-)tropical countries. 3. Machine for planting.

plă'ntigrāde *adj.* (zool.) That walks on its soles (cf. DIGITI-GRADE, on toes); (of human being) placing whole sole on ground at once in walking, flat-footed. *~ n.* Plantigrade animal.

plă'nxtў *n.* (Ir. mus.) Animated harp-tune, slower than jig, moving in triplets.

plaque (-ahk) *n.* Ornamental tablet of metal, porcelain, etc., plain or decorated; small tablet as badge of rank in honorary order.

plăsh¹ *n.* Marshy pool; puddle. **plă'shў¹** *adj.*

plăsh² *v.* Strike surface of (water) so as to break it up; splash. *~ n.* Splash, plunge. **plă'shў²** *adj.*

plăsh³ *v.t.* Bend down (branches, twigs) and interweave them to form hedge; make, renew (hedge) thus.

plăsm *n.* = PLASMA, 2.

plă'sma (-z-) *n.* 1. Green variety of quartz. 2. (physiol.) Coagulable solution of salts and protein in which corpuscles are suspended. 3. (phys.) Ionized gas in which numbers of electrons and positive ions are approximately equal. **plăsmă'tĭc, plă'smĭc** *adjs.*

plăsmō'dĭum (-z-) *n.* 1. (biol.) Mass of naked protoplasm formed by fusion or aggregation of amoeboid bodies (ill. PROTOZOON). 2. Protozoan of genus *P~*, causing malaria in man.

plăsmŏ'lўsĭs (-zm-) *n.* Contraction of protoplasm of vegetable cell due to loss of water to solution with which it is in contact.

Plă'ssey. Village of Bengal, scene of victory (1757) of CLIVE over forces of Nawab Suraj ud Daula, through which Bengal passed into British hands.

pla'ster (-ah-) *n.* 1. Curative application consisting of some substance spread upon muslin etc. and capable of adhering at temperature of the body. 2. Soft plastic mixture, esp. of lime, sand, and hair, spread on walls etc. to form smooth surface;

[672]

plasterboard, board containing plaster core, used for walling, ceilings, etc. 3. Sulphate of lime, gypsum; ~ *of Paris*, fine white plaster of calcined gypsum used to make moulds or casts, as cement etc. (orig. prepared from gypsums of Montmartre, Paris). **pla′stery** *adj.* **pla′ster** *v.t.* Cover with or like plaster; apply, stick, etc., like plaster to; coat, bedaub; (slang) bomb or shell heavily; *pla′stered*, (slang) drunk. **pla′sterer** *n.*
plă′stic (*or* -ah-) *adj.* 1. Moulding, giving form to clay, wax etc.; produced by moulding; capable of being (easily) moulded; (fig.) pliant, supple; ~ *arts*, those concerned with modelling, e.g. sculpture, ceramics; ~ *bomb*, bomb of soft pliable explosive substance; ~ *clay*, (geol.) middle group of Eocene beds; ~ *surgery*, repair or replacement of lost, damaged, or deformed tissue etc. 2. Causing growth of natural forms, formative; (biol.) capable of forming living tissue, accompanied by this process. **plă′stically** *adv.* **plă′stic** *n.* Any of a group of substances, natural or synthetic, chiefly polymers of high molecular weight, that can be moulded into any form by heat or pressure or both. **plăsti′city** *n.*
plă′sticine (-ēn; *or* -ah-) *n.* Composition of specially treated clay, used as a substitute for modelling clay. [trade-name] **plă′sticize** (*or* -ah-) *v.* Make, become, plastic. **plă′sticizer** *n.*
plă′stid *n.* (bot.) One of the small bodies in plant cells, containing pigments or food reserves.
plă′stron *n.* 1. Fencer's leather-covered breastplate; ornamental front to woman's bodice; breast-covering of cloth worn by lancers (ill. CAVALRY); (hist.) steel breastplate (ill. ARMOUR). 2. Ventral part of shell of tortoise or turtle (ill. TORTOISE); analogous part in other animals.
plăt *n.* Patch, plot, of ground.
Pla′ta (-ah-), Rio de la. River Plate, long funnel-shaped estuary on E. side of S. America, between Argentina and Uruguay: scene (1939) of naval battle between German 'pocket battleship' *Admiral Graf Spee*, subsequently scuttled, and 3 British cruisers, *Ajax*, *Achilles*, and *Exeter*. [Span., = 'river of silver', with ref. to export of silver from the region]
plāte[1] *n.* 1. Flat thin usu. rigid sheet of metal etc. of even surface and more or less uniform thickness; this as part of mechanism etc., esp. one of the sheets of which a ship's armour and steam-boilers are composed; (anat., zool., & bot.) thin flat organic structure or formation. 2. The portion of a denture which fits to the mouth and holds the teeth. 3. Smooth piece of metal etc. for engraving; impression from this, esp. as illustration of book; full-page illustration of book; book-plate. 4. Piece of metal with name or inscription for affixing to something; (baseball) (flat piece of metal or stone, marking) home base. 5. Stereotype or electrotype cast of page of composed movable types, from which sheets are printed. 6. Thin sheet of metal, glass, etc., coated with sensitive emulsion, for taking photographs; *whole* ~, (photograph the size of) one of these measuring 16·5 × 21·6 cm (6½ × 8½ in.); *half*-~, 12 × 16·5 cm (4¾ × 6½ in.); *quarter*-~, 9 × 11·5 cm (3¼ × 4¼ in.). 7. Horizontal timber laid along top of wall to support ends of joists or rafters, or at top or bottom of a framing (ill. ROOF). 8. (collect. sing.) Table and domestic utensils of silver, gold, or other metals; silver or gold cup as prize for (orig. horse-) race, such race; *selling*-~: see SELL. 9. Shallow usu. circular vessel, now usu. of earthenware or china, from which food is eaten; contents of this; similar vessel used for collection in churches etc. 10. ~-*basket*, basket for spoons, forks, etc.; ~ *clutch*: see CLUTCH[1]; ~ *glass*, flat glass of fine quality cast, ground, and polished in a continuous ribbon; ~-*layer*, man employed in laying and repairing railway lines; ~-*mark*, = HALLMARK; (also) impression left on margin of engraving by edge of plate; imitation of this on mount of photograph; whence ~-*marked* (*adj.*); ~-*powder*, powder for cleaning silver etc.; ~-*rack*, rack in which domestic plates are kept or placed to drain after washing; ~-*rail*, early form of railroad, flat strip of iron etc. with projecting flange, on which colliery trams are run; ~ *tracery*: see TRACERY. **plā′teful** *n.* **plāte** *v.t.* Cover (esp. ship) with plates of metal for protection, ornament, etc.; cover (other metal) with thin coat of silver, gold, tin, etc.; make a plate of (type) for printing.
Plāte[2], River: see PLATA.
plă′teau (-tō; *or* -tō′) *n.* Elevated tract of comparatively flat or level land, table-land.
plă′telèt (-tl-) *n.* (also *blood* ~) Ovoid or circular body suspended in the plasma, important in blood-clotting (ill. BLOOD).
plă′ten *n.* Iron plate in printing-press by which paper is pressed against inked type; corresponding part in typewriter etc.
plā′ter *n.* One who plates with silver etc.; one who makes or applies plates in ship-building; inferior racehorse, competing chiefly for plates.
plă′tform *n.* 1. Raised level surface, natural or artificial terrace; raised surface along side of line at railway station, from which passengers enter the carriages, and upon which they alight on leaving the train. 2. Raised flooring in hall or open air from which speaker addresses audience; (fig.) political basis of party etc. programme, esp. (U.S.) declaration issued by representatives of party assembled to nominate candidates for election.
plā′ting *n.* (esp.) Coating of gold, silver, etc.; plate-racing.
plă′tinize *v.t.* Coat with platinum.
plă′tinoid *n.* Alloy of nickel, zinc, copper, etc.; any of the metals found associated with platinum.
plă′tinotype *n.* (Print produced by) a process of photographic printing depending on the use of platinum salts.
plă′tinum *n.* (chem.) Somewhat rare metallic element, white, of high density, ductile and malleable, unaffected by simple acids and fusible only at very high temperatures; symbol Pt, at. no. 78, at. wt 195·09; ~ *black*, platinum in form of finely divided black powder; ~ *blonde*, woman with flaxen or nearly white hair; ~ *metal*, any of the elements found with and resembling platinum, as iridium, osmium, palladium, etc.
plă′titūde *n.* Commonplaceness; commonplace remark, esp. one solemnly delivered. **plătitū′dinous** *adj.* **plătitū′dinously** *adv.*
Plā′tō (*c* 429-347 B.C.). Greek philosopher, pupil of SOCRATES and author of Dialogues (based on his teaching and on the doctrines of Pythagoras), including 'Protagoras', 'Gorgias', 'Phaedo', 'Symposium', 'Republic', 'Phaedrus', 'Parmenides', 'Theaetetus', 'Sophist', 'Philebus', 'Timaeus', 'Laws', and the 'Apology'.
Platō′nic *adj.* Of Plato or his doctrines; esp. applied to love or affection for one of the opposite sex entirely free from sensual desire (orig. used without reference to women).
Plā′tonism *n.* Philosophical system of Plato, of which central conception is existence of a world of ideas, divine types, or forms of material objects, which ideas are alone real and permanent, while individual material things are but their ephemeral and imperfect imitations. **Plā′tonist** *n.* Follower of Plato; *Cambridge* ~*s*, group of 17th-c. philosophers (Ralph Cudworth, Henry More, John Smith, Nathanael Culverwel, and others) with headquarters in University of Cambridge.
platoō′n *n.* (hist.) Small infantry detachment, esp. a unit for volley-firing etc.; volley fired by it; (now, in British Army) sub-division of a company, a tactical unit commanded by a lieutenant and divided into three sections.
plă′tter *n.* (chiefly archaic) Flat dish or plate, freq. of wood.
plătyhĕ′lminth *n.* One of the phylum Platyhelminthes, including tapeworms and flukes; flatworm.

[673]

plă′tўpus n. (also *duck-billed ~*) Primitive aquatic and burrowing mammal (*Ornithorhynchus anatinus*) of Tasmania and SE.

DUCK-BILLED PLATYPUS

Australia, which has a bony duck-like beak and flattened tail, and lays shelled eggs. [Gk *platas* broad, *pous* foot]

plă′tўrrhine (-rin) adj. 1. (anthrop.) Having a broad nose with flat bridge. 2. (zool.) Of the Platyrrhini, a group of New World monkeys with broad flat nose. ~ n. Platyrrhine monkey.

plau′dĭt n. (usu. pl.) Round of applause; emphatic expression of approval. [shortened f. L *plaudite* applaud, imper. of *plaudere*, customary appeal for applause by Roman actors at end of play]

plau′sĭble (-z-) adj. (of arguments etc.) Seeming reasonable or probable; (of persons) fair-spoken (usu. implying deceit). **plausibĭ′lity** n. **plau′sĭbly** adv.

Plau′tus, Titus Maccius (d. c 184 B.C.). Roman comic dramatist.

play v. 1. Move about in lively or capricious manner, frisk, flit, flutter, pass gently; strike lightly; alternate rapidly; (of part of mechanism etc.) have free movement. 2. Allow (fish) to exhaust itself by pulling against line; direct (light *on, over*, etc.); (of light) pass (*over, along*, etc.). 3. Perform, execute (trick, prank, etc.). 4. Amuse oneself, sport, frolic; employ oneself in the game of; pretend for fun; (of ground etc.) be in good etc. condition for play; contend against (person) in game; employ (person) to play in game, include in team; (dial., esp. of workmen on strike) abstain from work; ~ *at*, engage in (game); (fig.) engage in (work etc.) in trivial or half-hearted way; ~ *ball*, (U.S.) co-operate (with); ~ *fair, foul,* play or (fig.) act (un)fairly; ~ *false*, deceive, betray; ~ *the game*, observe the rules of the game, play fair (freq. fig.); ~ *into the hands of*, act so as to give advantage to (opponent or partner); ~ *the market*, speculate in the stock market; ~ *up*, put all one's energy into the game etc.; be mischievous or unruly, exasperate by such behaviour; ~ *upon words*, pun; ~ *with*, amuse oneself with, trifle with, treat lightly; *played out*, exhausted of energy, vitality, or usefulness; 5. Move (piece in chess etc.); take (playing-card) from one's hand and lay it face upwards on table in one's turn; strike (ball) in specified, esp. defensive, manner; ~ *one's cards well*, (fig.) good make use of opportunities;

~ *on*, (cricket) play the ball on to one's own wicket and so put oneself out; ~ *off*, oppose (person against another) esp. for one's own advantage; cause (person) to exhibit himself disadvantageously; pass off as something else. 6. Perform on (musical instrument), perform (*on* instrument); perform (music *on* instrument); ~ *back*, reproduce (newly recorded music etc.); ~ (congregation etc.) *in, out*, play on organ etc., as they come in, go out; ~ *on*, make use of (person's fears, credulity, etc.). 7. Perform (drama) on stage; act (*in* drama); act (part) in drama; (fig.) act in real life the part of (*the deuce, the man, truant*, etc.); ~ *up to*, act in drama so as to support (another actor); (fig.) back up; flatter, toady. ~ n. 1. Brisk, light, or fitful movement; activity, operation; freedom of movement, space for this, scope for activity; *make* ~, act effectively, esp. (racing, hunting) exercise pursuers or followers. 2. Amusement; playing of game; manner, style, of this; cessation of work (of workmen on strike etc.); *at* ~, engaged in playing; *in* ~, not seriously; (of ball) being used in ordinary course of play; *out of* ~, (of ball) temporarily removed from play according to rules; ~ *on words*, pun. 3. Dramatic piece, drama. 4. Gaming, gambling. 5. *~-acting*, playing a part, posing; *~-actor*, actor (usu. contempt.); *~-bill*, bill, placard, announcing theatrical play; *play′boy*, man fond of pleasure and gaiety; *~-day*, school holiday, weekday on which miners etc. do not work; *play′fellow*, companion in (usu. children's) play; *play′goer*, frequenter of theatre; *play′ground*, piece of ground used for play, esp. at school; ~ *group*, group of children below school age, organized for playing etc. under supervision; *play′house*, theatre (obs. exc. in title); *play′mate*, playfellow; ~ *pen*, portable wooden enclosure for keeping young child out of harm's way; *play′thing*, toy; (fig.) person, etc., treated as mere toy; *play′wright*, dramatist.

play′er n. (esp.) Person engaged at the time, person skilful, in a game; professional player at cricket etc.; actor, performer on musical instrument; *~-piano*: see PIANO².

play′ful adj. Frolicsome, sportive; humorous, jocular. **play′fully** adv. **play′fulness** n.

play′ing n. (esp.) ~-*card*: see CARD², 2.

plea n. Pleading, argument, excuse; (law) formal statement by or on behalf of defendant; (hist.) action at law; *Court of Common P~s*: see COMMON; *special ~*, defendant's plea alleging new fact.

pleach v.t. Entwine, interlace; esp. = PLASH³ v.

plead v. 1. Address court as advocate on behalf of either party; maintain (cause) in court; allege formally as plea; (fig.) allege as excuse etc.; ~ *guilty*, admit liability or guilt, ~ *not guilty*, deny it. 2. Ask earnestly *for* help etc.; ~ *with*, make earnest appeal to (person). **plea′dĭngly** adv. **plea′der** n.

plea′ding n. (esp.) Formal (now usu. written) statement of cause of action or defence; *special ~*, see SPECIAL.

plea′sance (plĕz-) n. (archaic) Pleasure, enjoyment; pleasure-ground, esp. one attached to mansion.

plea′sant (plĕz-) adj. Agreeable to mind, feelings, or senses. **plea′santly** adv. **plea′santness** n.

plea′santry (plĕz-) n. Jocularity; humorous speech, jest.

please (-z) v. 1. Be agreeable (to); ~ *oneself*, do as one likes, take one's own way; *be pleased with*, derive pleasure from. 2. Be pleased, like; have the will or desire, think proper; (also *if you* ~) if you like (as courteous qualification to request etc.). **pleased** (-zd), **plea′sing** adjs. **plea′sĭngly** adv.

plea′surable (plĕzh-) adj. Affording pleasure. **plea′surableness** n. **plea′surably** adv.

plea′sure (plĕzh-) n. 1. Feeling of satisfaction; sensuous gratification as object of life. 2. Will, desire.

pleat n. Fold, crease; esp., flattened fold in cloth; *accordion ~s*, narrow pleats resembling accordion bellows, *box ~*, double pleat; *inverted ~*, reverse form of box pleat, *knife ~s*, narrow overlapping pleats. ~ v.t. Fold (cloth etc.) in pleats.

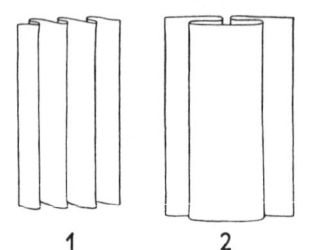

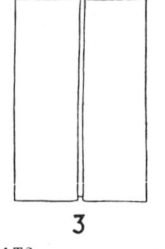

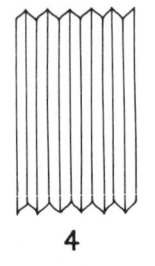

PLEATS

1. Knife. 2. Box. 3. Inverted. 4. Accordion

plebei'an (-bēan) *n.* Commoner in ancient Rome; commoner. ~ *adj.* Of low birth; of the common people; coarse, base, ignoble. **plebei'anness** (-n-n-) *n.*

plĕ'biscīte *n.* 1. (Rom. hist.) Law enacted by the commons (plebeians) voting by tribes. 2. Direct vote of all electors of State on important public question; public expression of community's opinion, with or without binding force.

plĕ'ctrum *n.* (pl. -*ra*). Small spike of ivory, quill, metal, etc., sometimes attached to a ring fitting on the finger, for plucking strings of guitar, zither, etc.; part of keyboard instrument with same function (ill. HARPSICHORD).

plĕdge *n.* 1. Thing handed over to person as security for fulfilment of contract, payment of debt, etc., and liable to forfeiture in case of failure; thing put in pawn. 2. Thing given as token of favour etc. or of something to come; drinking of a health, toast. 3. Vow, promise; *the* ~, solemn engagement to abstain from intoxicants. 4. State of being pledged. ~ *v.t.* 1. Deposit as security, pawn. 2. Promise solemnly; bind (oneself) by pledge. 3. Drink to the health of.

Plei'ad (plī-). 1. One of the Pleiades. 2. Name given by critics of Alexandria to the seven most eminent Greek tragic poets of reign of Ptolemy II. 2. (*la Pléiade*) Group of French poets, including Ronsard and du Bellay, of latter part of 16th c., animated by a common veneration for writers of antiquity and a desire to improve the quality of French verse.

Pleiades (plī'adēz). 1. (Gk myth.) Seven daughters of Atlas, turned on their deaths into a constellation. 2. (astron.) Conspicuous constellation or cluster of stars in Taurus.

plein air (plĕn ār) *attrib.* Of the Impressionist style of painting (originated in France *c* 1870) concerned with representing effects of atmosphere and light that cannot be observed in studio. **plein-air'ism(e), -air'ist(e)** *ns.* [f. Fr. *en plein air* in the open air]

Plei'stocēne (plī-) *adj.* & *n.* (geol.) (Of) the earlier part or system of the Quaternary period, characterized by the formation of glaciers and in which man first appeared (ill. GEOLOGY). [Gk *pleistos* most, *kainos* new]

plĕ'nary *adj.* Entire, absolute unqualified; (of assembly) attended by all members; ~ *inspiration*: see INSPIRATION. **plĕ'narily** *adv.*

plĕnipotĕ'ntiary (-sha-) *adj.* Invested with full power, esp. as ambassador deputed to act at discretion; (of power) absolute. ~ *n.* Person invested with full power.

plĕ'nitūde *n.* Fullness, completeness; abundance.

plĕ'ntēous *adj.* (chiefly poet.) Plentiful. **plĕ'ntēously** *adv.* **plĕ'ntēousness** *n.*

plĕ'ntiful *adj.* Abundant, copious. **plĕ'ntifully** *adv.* **plĕ'ntifulness** *n.*

plĕ'nty *n.* Abundance, as much as one could desire. ~ *adv.* (colloq.; with adj. followed by *enough*) Quite.

plĕ'num *n.* Space filled with matter; full assembly.

plĕ'onăsm *n.* (gram.) Redundancy of expression. **pleonă'stic** *adj.* **pleonă'stically** *adv.*

plēsiosaur'us *n.* (pl. -*ri*, -*ruses*). Member of a genus (*P*~) of extinct marine reptiles with long neck, small head, short tail, and four large paddles. [Gk *plesios* near, *sauros* lizard]

plĕ'thora *n.* (path., obs.) Morbid condition marked by excess of red corpuscles in blood; (fig.) over-supply, glut. **plĕthŏ'ric** *adj.* **plĕthŏ'rically** *adv.*

pleura (-oora) *n.* Either of two serous membranes lining thorax and enveloping lungs in mammals (ill. LUNG).

pleur'al (-oor-) *adj.* Of the pleura; of a pleuron.

pleur'isy (-oor-) *n.* Inflammation of the pleura, marked by pain in chest or side, fever, etc. **pleuri'tic** *adj.*

pleurodȳ'nia (-oor-) *n.* Pain caused by inflammation of intercostal muscles.

pleur'on (-oor-) *n.* (pl. -*ra*). Either of the two side plates of the exoskeleton in arthropods.

pleuro-pneumō'nia (-ooronū-) *n.* Pneumonia complicated with pleurisy, esp. as contagious disease of horned cattle.

plĕxi'mĕter *n.* (med.) Thin plate of ivory etc. placed on body and struck with plexor in medical percussion.

plĕ'xor *n.* (med.) Small hammer used with pleximeter.

plĕ'xus *n.* Network of nerve fibres or minute blood-vessels in animal body; network, complication.

pli'able, pli'ant *adjs.* Bending, supple; (fig.) yielding, compliant. **pliabi'lity, pli'ancȳ** *ns.* **pli'ablȳ, pli'antly** *advs.*

pli'ca *n.* (pl. -*ae*). Fold, as of skin or membrane; (path., also ~ *polo'nica*), matted condition of hair due to filth and neglect. [L]

pli'cāte *adj.* (bot., zool., geol.) Folded. **plicā'ted** *adj.* **plicā'tion** *n.* Folding; fold; folded condition.

pli'ers (-z) *n.pl.* (also *pair of* ~) Pincers having long jaws, usu. with parallel surfaces, sometimes toothed, for bending wire, holding small objects, etc.

PLIERS

plight[1] (-īt) *v.t.* (archaic) Pledge (troth, faith, etc., esp. in past part.); engage *oneself* (*to* person).

plight[2] (-īt) *n.* Condition, state (usu. unhappy).

pli'msoll *n.* Rubber-soled canvas shoe worn for sports etc.

Pli'msoll mărk. Load line(s) on merchant ship's side indicating

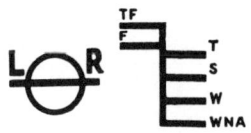

PLIMSOLL MARK AND LOAD LINES

L R, Lloyd's Register. Horizontal lines on right show variations of loading depths allowed in water of differing densities. TF, tropical fresh water. F, fresh water. Sea water: T, tropics. S, summer. W, winter. WNA, winter North Atlantic

limit to which it may be legally loaded. [Samuel *Plimsoll* (1824-98), Engl. radical M.P., largely instrumental in passing Merchant Shipping Act, 1876]

plinth *n.* Lower square member of base of column (ill. ORDER); projecting part of wall (or piece of furniture) immediately above ground.

pli'nthīte *n.* (min.) Kind of brick-red clay found among trap rocks of Antrim and the Hebrides.

Pli'nȳ. ~ *the Elder* (Gaius Plinius Secundus, *c* A.D. 23-79), Roman author of a 'Natural History', who perished in the eruption of Vesuvius; ~ *the Younger*, his nephew (Gaius Plinius Caecilius Secundus, *c* A.D. 61-*c* 112), famous for his published 'Letters'.

Pli'ocēne *adj.* & *n.* (geol.) (Of) the latest epoch or system of the Tertiary period (ill. GEOLOGY). [Gk *pleion* more, *kainos* new]

plŏd *v.* Walk laboriously, trudge; drudge, slave (*at*); make (one's way) laboriously. ~ *n.* Laborious walk or work. **plŏ'dder** *n.* **plŏ'dding** *adj.* Slow and painstaking. **plŏ'ddingly** *adv.*

plŏnk *n.* (orig. Austral. slang) Cheap or inferior wine.

plŏ'sive *adj.* & *n.* (phonet.) Explosive (consonant).

plŏt *n.* 1. Piece of ground, usu. small. 2. Plan, story, of play, poem, novel, etc. 3. Conspiracy; sly plan. ~ *v.t.* Make plan or map of (existing object, place or thing to be laid out, constructed, etc.); mark the position of values of a variable on a graph or the like; plan, contrive (evil object, or abs.). **plŏ'tter** *n.*

Plōti'nus (*c* A.D. 205-69). Egyptian-born founder of NEOPLATONISM.

plough (-ow) *n.* Implement for cutting furrows in soil and turning it up, consisting essentially of a vertical coulter which cuts the

[675]

PLOVER   PLUME

furrow from the unploughed ground, a *plou′ghshare* which cuts the furrow horizontally underneath, and a mould-board which turns it over, drawn by horses etc. with plough, esp. before sowing; rout *out*, cast *up*, thrust *down* (roots, weeds) with plough; furrow, scratch (surface) as with plough; produce (furrow, line) thus; ~ *back*, plough (grass, clover, etc.) into soil to enrich it; (fig.) reinvest (profits) in business etc. 2. Advance laboriously (*through* snow, book, etc.); (of ship etc.) cleave (surface of water, its way, etc.). 3. (slang) Reject (candidate) in examination; (of candidate) fail. **plou′ghable** *adj.*

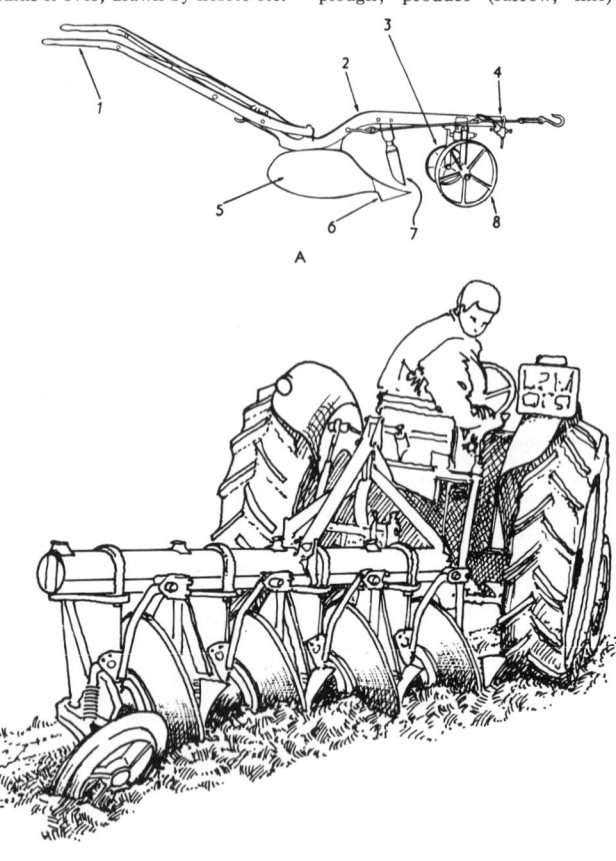

plo′ver (plŭ-) *n.* Gregarious bird of family Charadriidae, found in open country and nesting on the ground; *green* ~, lapwing.

ploy *n.* 1. (north.) Expedition, undertaking, occupation, job. 2. Stratagem, manœuvre.

plŭck *n.* 1. Plucking, twitch. 2. Rejection, failure, in examination. 3. Heart, liver, and lungs, of beast as food. 4. Courage, spirit. ~ *v.* 1. Pull off, pick (flower, feather, hair); pull at, twitch; tug, snatch, *at*; strip (bird) of feathers; (archaic) pull, drag, snatch (*away, off*, etc.). 2. Plunder, swindle. 3. Reject (candidate) in examination. 4. ~ *up heart, spirits, courage*, take courage. **plŭ′ckў** *adj.* Brave, spirited. **plŭ′ckilў** *adv.* **plŭ′ckiness** *n.*

plŭg *n.* 1. Piece of wood etc. fitting tightly into hole, used to fill gap or act as wedge etc.; freq. in technical use, e.g. pin etc. for making electrical contacts, sparking plug (see SPARK); natural or morbid concretion acting thus; kinds of stopper for vessel or pipe; fire-plug. 2. Tobacco pressed into cake or stick; piece of this cut off for chewing. ~ *v.* Stop (*up*) with plug; (slang) shoot; (slang) strike with fist; (colloq.) plod (*away at* work etc.); (slang) popularize (song etc.) by frequent repetition.

plŭm *n.* 1. Roundish fleshy fruit of *Prunus domestica*, drupe with sweet pulp and flattish pointed stone; tree bearing this. 2. Dried grape or raisin as used for puddings, cakes, etc.; sugar-plum; *French* ~, fine kind of prune. 3. (fig.) Good thing; best of a collection; prize in life. 4. ~ *cake*, cake containing raisins, currants, etc.; ~ *duff*, plain flour and suet pudding with raisins or currants; ~ *pudding*, boiled or steamed pudding of flour, suet, bread-crumbs, raisins, currants, eggs, spices, etc., eaten esp. at Christmas.

plu′mage (-ōō-) *n.* Bird's feathers.

plŭmb (-m) *n.* Ball of lead, esp. that attached to plumb-line; ~-*line*, string with weight attached for testing perpendicularity of wall, etc.; sounding-lead, plummet; *out of* ~, not vertical; ~-*rule*, mason's plumb-line attached to board. ~ *adj.* Vertical; (cricket, of wicket) level, true; (fig.) downright, sheer. ~ *adv.* Vertically; (fig.) exactly; (U.S., slang) quite, utterly. ~ *v.* 1. Sound (sea), measure (depth), with plummet; make vertical. 2. Work as plumber.

plŭmbā′gō *n.* 1. Graphite. 2. Herbaceous plant of genus *P*~, with spikes of tubular white, blue, or purplish flowers, leadwort.

plŭ′mbĕous *adj.* Of, like, lead; lead-glazed.

plŭ′mber (-mer) *n.* Artisan who fits and repairs pipes, cisterns, tanks, etc.

plŭ′mbing (-mi-) *n.* System of water and drainage pipes in a building etc.

plŭ′mbĭsm *n.* Poisoning caused by absorption of lead into the system.

plume (-ōōm) *n.* Feather, esp. large one used for ornament; feathery ornament in hat, hair, etc.; (zool.) feather-like part or formation. ~ *v.t.* Furnish with

PLOUGHS

A. HORSE-DRAWN SINGLE-FURROW PLOUGH. B. TRACTOR-MOUNTED 4-FURROW DISC PLOUGH

1. Handle. 2. Beam. 3. Land wheel. 4. Head. 5. Mould-board. 6. Share. 7. Coulter. 8. Furrow wheel

(or now, by tractor), and guided by *plou′ghman*; ploughed land; instrument resembling plough, for cutting up blocks of ice, clearing away snow, etc.; *the P*~: see URSA; ~-*beam*, central beam of plough; ~-*boy*, boy who leads plough-horses etc.; ~-*land*, (hist.) as much land as could be ploughed by one team of 8 oxen in a year, unit of assessment in northern and eastern counties of England after Norman Conquest; arable land; *ploughman*: see above; *P*~ *Monday*, first after Epiphany on which beginning of ploughing season was celebrated; *ploughshare*: see above; ~-*tail*, rear of plough. ~ *v.* 1. Turn up (earth, or abs.)

[676]

plume(s); pride *oneself* (*on* esp. something trivial or to which one has no claim); (of bird) preen (feathers).

plŭ′mmèt *n.* (Weight attached to) plumb-line; sounding-lead; weight attached to fishing-line to keep float upright. ~ *v.i.* Plunge.

plŭ′mmy̆ *adj.* Of, abounding in, plums; (colloq., of voice) speaking as if with a plum in the mouth; (colloq.) rich, good, desirable.

plumō′se (-ōō-) *adj.* Feathered; featherlike.

plŭmp[1] *adj.* (esp. of persons or parts of body) Full, rounded, fleshy, filled out. ~ *v.* Make or become plump, fatten *up*, swell *out*. **plŭ′mply̆** *adv.* **plŭ′mpnèss** *n.*

plŭmp[2] *v.* Drop or plunge with abrupt descent; vote *for* (one candidate alone, when one might vote for two); ~ *for*, vote for, choose (something). ~ *n.* Abrupt plunge, heavy fall. ~ *adv.* With sudden or heavy fall; flatly, bluntly. ~ *adj.* Direct, unqualified.

plŭ′mper *n.* Ball, disc, formerly carried in mouth to fill out hollow cheeks.

plu′mūle (-ōō-) *n.* Rudimentary stem of embryo plant (ill. SEED); little feather of down.

plu′mūlar, plumūlā′ceous (-shus) *adjs.*

plu′my̆ (-ōō-) *adj.* Plume-like; feathery; adorned with plumes.

plŭ′nder *v.t.* Rob (place, person) forcibly of goods, esp. as in war; rob systematically; steal, embezzle. ~ *n.* Violent or dishonest acquisition of property; property so acquired; (slang) profit, gain. **plŭ′nderer** *n.*

plŭ′nderage *n.* Plundering, esp. embezzling of goods on shipboard; spoil thus obtained.

plŭnge (-j) *v.* Thrust violently (*into* liquid, cavity, etc.); throw oneself, dive, (*into*); enter impetuously; descend abruptly and steeply; (of horse) throw itself violently forward; (of ship) pitch; (slang) gamble deeply, run into debt. ~ *n.* Plunging, dive; place for plunging; (fig.) critical step; ~-*bath*, one large enough to dive into.

plŭ′nger (-j-) *n.* (esp.) 1. Part of mechanism that works with plunging motion. 2. (slang) Gambler, speculator.

plu′pĕr′fèct (-ōō-) *adj.* & *n.* (gram.) (Tense) expressing action completed prior to some past point of time specified or implied (as *I had seen*). [L *plus quam perfectum* more than perfect]

plur′al (-oor-) *adj.* (gram.) Denoting more than one (or, in languages with dual form, more than two); more than one in number; ~ *vote*, vote of one person in more than one constituency. **plur′ally̆** *adv.* **plur′al** *n.* Plural form.

plur′alism (-oor-) *n.* 1. Holding of more than one office, esp. benefice, at a time. 2. (philos.) System that recognizes more than one ultimate principle. **plur′alist** *n.* **plurali′stic** *adj.*

plurā′lity̆ (-oor-) *n.* State of being plural; large number, multitude; holding of two or more benefices or offices; benefice, office, held with another; majority (*of* votes etc.).

plur′alize (-oor-) *v.* Make plural, express in the plural; hold more than one benefice.

pluripre̅′sence (-oor-, -z-) *n.* Presence in more than one place at same time.

plŭs *prep.* With the addition of (symbol +); (colloq.) with, and also. ~ *adj.* Extra (indicating addition); positive; (after number etc.) more than; ~-*fours*, long wide knicker-bockers, suit with these, freq. associated with golf, so named because, to produce the overhang, the length was orig. increased by 4 in. (ill. COAT). ~ *n.* Plus sign or quantity. [L, = 'more']

plŭsh *n.* Cloth of silk, cotton, etc., resembling velvet but with longer and softer pile; (pl.) footman's plush breeches. **plŭ′shy̆** *adj.*

Plu′tărch (-ōō-, -k) (*c* A.D. 46–120). Greek biographer and moral philosopher, author of 'Parallel Lives' of eminent Greeks and Romans.

plu′tărchy̆ (-ōō-, -kĭ) *n.* Plutocracy.

Plu′tō[1] (-ōō-). 1. (Gk & Rom. myth.) God of the infernal regions, brother of ZEUS and Poseidon. 2. (astron.) Planet, remoter than Neptune, discovered in 1930 (ill. PLANET).

Plu′tō[2] (-ōō-). Pipe-line laid for conveying fuel stores under English Channel in invasion of France, 1944. [f. initials of *Pipeline under the ocean*]

plutŏ′cracy̆ (-ōō-) *n.* Rule of the wealthy; ruling class of wealthy persons. **plu′tocrăt** *n.* **plutocră′tic** *adj.*

plu′ton (-ōō-) *n.* (geol.) Any body of rock that has crystallized deep in the earth's crust and has been exposed later by erosion.

plutŏ′nic *adj.* [f. PLUTO[1]]

Plutō′nian (-ōō-) *adj.* Of Pluto or his kingdom; infernal.

Plu′tonist (-ōō-) *n.* Adherent (esp. in 18th c.) of the theory that most geological phenomena are due to the action of internal heat (opp. NEPTUNIST). **Plu′tonism** *n.*

plutō′nium (-ōō-) *n.* (chem.) Transuranic element, not found in nature, formed from uranium in a nuclear reactor, used as a nuclear explosive; symbol Pu, at. no. 94, principal isotope at. wt 239. [named after planet PLUTO[1]]

plu′vial (-ōō-) *adj.* Of rain, rainy; (geol.) caused by rain. ~ *n.* (eccles. hist.) Long cloak as ceremonial vestment.

pluviŏ′mĕter (-ōō-) *n.* Rain-gauge. **pluviomĕ′trical** *adj.*

ply̆[1] *n.* Fold, thickness, layer, of cloth, etc.; strand of rope, etc.; *two*-, *three*-, etc. ~, having two etc. thicknesses or strands; *ply′wood*, strong thin board made by gluing or cementing layers of wood together with grains crosswise.

ply̆[2] *v.* 1. Use, wield vigorously (tool, weapon); work at (business, task); supply (person etc.) persistently *with* (food etc.); assail vigorously (*with* questions, arguments). 2. Work to windward (naut.); (of vessel, its master, coach, etc.) go to and fro *between* (places); (of porter, cabman, etc.) attend regularly for custom (*at* place).

Ply̆′mouth[1] (-muth). City of Devon, seaport and naval base; ~ *Brethren*, Calvinistic religious sect founded at Plymouth *c* 1830, with no formal creed or official order of ministers.

Ply̆′mouth[2] (-muth). Town of Massachusetts, landing-place of PILGRIM Fathers; ~ *Rock*, (1) granite boulder at Plymouth on which Pilgrim Fathers are supposed to have stepped from *Mayflower*; (2) Amer. domestic fowl of medium size and usu. with grey plumage barred with blackish stripes and yellow beak, legs, and feet.

p.m. *abbrev. Post meridiem*; *post mortem.*

P.M. *abbrev.* Prime Minister; Provost Marshal.

P.M.G. *abbrev.* Paymaster-General.

p.m.h. *abbrev.* Production per man-hour.

P.M.O. *abbrev.* Principal Medical Officer.

P.M.R.A.F.N.S. *abbrev.* Princess Mary's Royal Air Force Nursing Service.

P.N.E.U. *abbrev.* Parents' National Educational Union.

pneumă′tic (nū-) *adj.* Of, acting by means of, wind or (compressed) air; containing, connected with, air-cavities, esp. in bones of birds; ~ *dispatch*, conveyance of parcels etc. along tubes by compression or exhaustion of air; ~ *trough*, trough for collecting gases in jars over surface of water or mercury; ~ *tyre*, one inflated with air. **pneumă′tically̆** *adv.*

pneumă′tic *n.* Pneumatic tyre.

pneumă′tics *n.* Science of mechanical properties of air or other gases.

pneu′matocy̆st (nū-) *n.* Air-sac (in body of bird etc.).

pneumocŏ′ccus (nū-) *n.* (pl. -*cī*). Infective micro-organism (*Diplococcus pneumoniae*) in pneumonia.

pneumocŏniŏ′sis (nū-) *n.* (pl. -*sēs*). Any of a group of chronic lung diseases (e.g. silicosis) caused by inhaling abrasive dust.

pneumogă′stric (nū-) *adj.* Of lungs and stomach; ~ *nerve*, vagus nerve.

pneumonĕ′ctomy̆ (nū-) *n.* Surgical removal of a lung.

pneumo′nia (nū-) *n.* Acute inflammation of the lungs, converting their normally spongy tissue into a solid mass, caused esp. by infection with pneumococcus. **pneumo′nic** *adj.*
pneumothŏr′ax (nū-) *n.* Presence of air or gas in the pleural cavity, whether accidental or effected deliberately, e.g. to collapse a lung in treatment of pulmonary tuberculosis.
pnxt *abbrev.* Pinxit.
P.O. *abbrev.* Petty Officer; Pilot Officer; postal order; Post Office.
pō′a *n.* Grass of genus *P~*, widely distributed in temperate and cold regions.
poach[1] *v.t.* Cook (egg) without its shell by boiling in water or steaming; cook (fish, fruit, etc.) by simmering.
poach[2] *v.* 1. Trample, cut *up* (turf etc.) with hoofs; (of land) become sodden by being trampled. 2. Encroach, trespass (*on* person's *preserves* (freq. fig.), lands, etc.), esp. in order to steal fish or game; trespass on (land etc).; capture (game, fish) by illicit or unsportsmanlike methods; (in various games) enter on partner's portion of field or court, depriving him of some of his share in the game. **poa′cher** *n.*
Pōcahō′ntas (1595–1617). Daughter of Powhattan, an Amer. Indian chief in Virginia; according to the story of an English colonist, Capt. John Smith, she rescued him from death at the hands of her father, who had imprisoned him; she was seized as a hostage, 1612, and married a colonist, John Rolfe; was taken to England, 1616, and died there.
pō′chard *n.* Diving-duck, esp. *Aythya ferina*, of Europe, N. Asia, and N. America, male of which has bright reddish-brown head and neck.
pŏchĕ′tte (-sh-) *n.* Woman's envelope-shaped handbag.
pŏck *n.* Eruptive spot esp. in smallpox.
pŏ′ckĕt *n.* 1. Bag, sack, esp. as measure of hops (168 lb.) or wool (= half sack). 2. Small bag inserted in garment for carrying small articles, as money, etc.; (fig.) pecuniary resources; *put one's pride in one's ~*, humble oneself; *in ~*, having money available; having (so much) as profit; *out of ~*, losing money (by some transaction); *out-of-~ expenses*, actual outlay incurred. 3. Pouch at each corner and on each side of billiard table into which balls are driven (ill. BILLIARDS); pouch-like compartment in bag, suitcase, etc.; cavity in earth filled with gold or other ore; cavity in rock esp. (geol.) filled with foreign matter; AIR pocket; isolated area occupied by the enemy, forces occupying this. 4. (attrib.) Of suitable size or shape for carrying in pocket; small, diminutive; *~ battleship*,

(esp. German) ship armoured and equipped like, but smaller than, a battleship; *~-book*, notebook, book-like case for papers, currency notes, etc., carried in pocket; (U.S.) handbag; *~ borough*: see BOROUGH; *~ handkerchief*, one carried in pocket; *~ money*, money for occasional expenses, esp. that allowed to children. **pŏ′ckĕtful** *n.* **pŏ′ckĕt** *v.t.* Put into one's pocket; confine as in pocket; hem in (competitor) in race; appropriate, usu. dishonestly; submit to (affront, injury); conceal, suppress (feelings); (billiards) drive (ball) into pocket. **pŏ′ckĕtĕd** *adj.* Fitted with, enclosed in, pocket(s).
pōcocūră′ntė *adj. & n.* Indifferent, uncaring (person). [It., = 'caring little']
pŏd[1] *n.* Socket of brace and bit (ill. DRILL).
pŏd[2] *n.* Long seed-vessel, esp. of leguminous plants (ill. FRUIT); cocoon of silkworm; case of locust's eggs; narrow-necked eel-net. *~ v.* Form pods; shell (peas etc.).
pŏd[3] *n.* Small herd of seals or whales. *~ v.t.* Drive (seals etc.) into pod or bunch for purpose of clubbing them.
podă′gra (*or* pŏ′da-) *n.* (med.) Gout, esp. in feet. **podă′gral, podă′gric, podă′grous** *adjs.*
pŏdĕsta′ (-ah) *n.* (hist.) Governor appointed by Frederick Barbarossa over one or more Lombard cities; chief magistrate in medieval Italian towns and republics. [It.]
pŏ′dgў *adj.* Short, thick, and fat.
pō′dium *n.* Continuous projecting base or pedestal; raised platform round arena of amphitheatre (ill. AMPHITHEATRE); continuous bench round room.
pŏdophў′llin *n.* (chem.) Yellow bitter resin of cathartic properties from root of *Podophyllum peltatum*, plant of eastern N. America, with long thick creeping rhizomes, large long-stalked palmate leaves, and solitary white flower.
pŏ′dzŏl *n.* Stratified soil in which various materials have been leached from the upper layers and redeposited in a well-defined lower stratum. **pŏ′dzolize** *v.* Make into, become, podzol. **pŏdzolizā′tion** *n.*
Pōe, Edgar Allan (1809–49). American poet and critic; author of 'Tales of Mystery and Imagination'.
pō′ĕm *n.* Metrical composition, esp. of elevated character; elevated composition in prose or verse; (fig.) something (other than a composition of words) akin to or compared to a poem.
pō′ĕsў (-zĭ) *n.* (archaic) Art, composition, of poetry; poems collectively.
pō′ĕt *n.* (fem. *poetĕss*) Writer of poems; writer in verse, esp. one possessing high powers of imagi-

nation, expression, etc.; *~ laureate*: see LAUREATE; *Poets' Corner*, part of south transept of Westminster Abbey containing graves or monuments of several great poets. **pōĕtă′ster** *n.* Inferior poet.
pōĕ′tic *adj.* Of, proper to, poets or poetry; having the good qualities of poetry; *~ justice, licence*: see JUSTICE, LICENCE. **pōĕ′tical,** *adj.* Of, proper to, poets or poetry; written in verse. **pōĕ′ticallў** *adv.*
pōĕ′tics *n.* Part of literary criticism dealing with poetry; treatise on poetry, esp. (*P~*) that of Aristotle.
pōĕ′ticīze *v.t.* Make (theme) poetic.
pō′ĕtīze *v.* Play the poet, compose poetry; treat poetically; celebrate in poetry.
pō′ĕtrў *n.* Art, work, of the poet; expression of beautiful or elevated thought, imagination, or feeling in appropriate language and usu. in metrical form; poems; quality (in anything) that calls for poetical expression; *prose ~*, prose having all the qualities of poetry except metre.
pō′gō stick. Toy consisting of a stick with handles and a pair of pedals attached to a spring, used for jumping about.
pŏ′grom *n.* Organized massacre, orig. that of Jews in Russia (1905–6). [Russ., = 'destruction' (*grom* thunder)]
poi′gnant (poinyant *or* poin-) *adj.* Sharp, pungent, in taste or smell; painfully sharp; pleasantly piquant. **poi′gnantlў** *adv.* **poi′gnancў** *n.*
Poincaré (pwăṅkără), Raymond (1860–1934). French statesman, president during war of 1914–18.
poinsĕ′ttĭa *n.* Plant of Mexican species of *Euphorbia, E. pulcherrima*, with large scarlet bracts surrounding small yellowish flowers. [f. J. R. *Poinsett*, Amer. minister to Mexico, who discovered it]
point *n.* 1. Small dot on a surface. 2. Stop or punctuation-mark; dot, small stroke, used in Semitic script to indicate vowels or distinguish consonants; dot separating integral from fractional parts in decimals, as *two ~ five* (2·5). 3. Single item, detail, particular; thing under discussion; *beside the ~*, irrelevant(ly); *make a ~*, establish proposition, prove contention; *make a ~ of*, treat as essential, insist on; *to the ~*, relevant(ly). 4. Distinctive trait, characteristic, as *good, bad, ~*; *strong ~*, thing one is good at. 5. Salient feature of story, joke, etc.; pungency, effectiveness. 6. Unit in appraising qualities of exhibit in show or achievements of competitor in contest; unit (of varying value) in quoting price of stocks etc.; unit of value in rationing; *give ~s to*, allow (opponent) to count so many points at starting,

POINT-BLANK

(fig.) be superior to; *win on ~s*, (boxing) win by securing more points in a number of rounds, not by knock-out. 7. (print.) Unit of measurement for type bodies, in Britain and U.S. 0·0138 in. ($\frac{1}{72}$ in., $\frac{1}{12}$ of a pica). 8. (geom.) That which has position but not magnitude, as the intersection of two lines. 9. Precise place or spot, as *~ of contact*. 10. (hunting) Spot to which straight run is made, such run; *~-to-~ race*, race over course defined only by certain landmarks. 11. (her.) Any of 9 particular spots on shield used for determining position (ill. HERALDRY). 12. Stage, degree, in progress or increase, esp. of temperature, as *boiling-~*, *freezing-~*. 13. Precise moment for action etc.; exact moment (of death etc.). 14. (mus.) Important phrase or subject, esp. in contrapuntal music; (archaic) snatch of melody, esp. *~ of war*, short phrase sounded on instrument as signal. 15. Sharp end of tool, weapon, pin, pen, etc.; sharp-pointed tool, e.g. etching needle; (elect.) contact, terminal; socket; (also *~ lace*) lace made wholly with needle. 16. Tip; promontory, esp. in names, as *Start P~*; (pl.) extremities of a horse or dog; (pl., of Siamese cat) coloured ears, feet, tail, and face; (ballet, usu. pl.) tips of toes; *the ~*, (boxing) point of the jaw, tip of chin as spot for knock-out blow. 17. Tine of deer's horn. 18. Tapering movable rail by which train is directed from one line to another (ill. RAIL¹). 19. Tapered division on backgammon board (ill. BACKGAMMON). 20. (hist.) Tagged lace for lacing bodice, attaching hose to doublet, etc. (ill. DOUBLET). 21. (naut.) Short piece of cord at lower edge of sail for tying up a reef. 22. Horizontal direction on compass (ill. COMPASS); corresponding point of horizon, direction. 23. (cricket) (Position of) fieldsman placed more or less in line with popping-crease a short distance on off side of batsman (ill. CRICKET). 24. (of dog) Act of pointing. 25. *at all ~s*, in every part; *in ~*, apposite; *in ~ of fact*, as a matter of fact; *on the ~ of*, on the very verge of (action, *doing*); *~ of honour*, matter regarded as vitally affecting one's honour. 26. *~-duty*, that of constable stationed at particular point to regulate traffic etc.; *poi′ntsman*, man in charge of railway points; constable on point-duty. *~ v.* 1. Sharpen (pencil etc.); furnish with point; give point to (words, actions). 2. Insert points in Semitic script; mark (Psalms etc.) for chanting, by means of points. 3. Fill in joints of (masonry etc.) with mortar etc.; prick *in* (manure), turn *over* (soil), with point of spade. 4. Direct attention *to*, *at*, by or as by extending finger; (of dog) indicate presence of (game) by standing rigidly, looking towards it; direct (finger, weapon, etc., *at*); direct attention of (person *to*); aim *at*, tend *towards*; *~ out*, indicate, show.

poi′nt-blā′nk *adj. & adv.* With aim or weapon level; at short range; (fig.) direct(ly). [prob. f. *blank* white spot in centre of target]

point d'appui (pwǎṅ dǎpwē). (mil.) Point of support, rallying-place. [Fr.]

point-dėvi′ce *adj.* (archaic) Perfectly correct, extremely neat or precise. *~ adv.* In point-device manner. [app. f. Fr. *à point devis* to the point arranged, or arranged to the proper point]

poi′ntėd *adj.* Having, sharpened to, a point; (of remark, etc.) having point, penetrating, cutting; emphasized, made evident; (of Semitic script) having the vowels marked. **poi′ntėdlỹ** *adv.* **poi′ntėdnėss** *n.*

poi′nter *n.* (esp.) 1. Index hand of clock, balance, etc. 2. Rod used for pointing to words etc. on blackboard, map, etc. 3. Dog that on scenting game stands rigidly, with muzzle stretched towards it and usu. one foot raised. 4. (pl.) Two stars in Great Bear, straight line through which points nearly to pole-star. 5. (colloq.) Hint.

pointillé (pwǎ′ṅtĭlā) *adj.* 1. (of bookbinding) Decorated with gilt dots. 2. (of picture) Painted with numerous small spots of two or more pure colours which at a distance produce the effect of a mixed colour, whence **poi′ntillism** *n.* **poi′ntillist** *n.* Painter using technique of pointillism.

poi′nting *n.* (esp.) 1. (Insertion of) points in Semitic script, Psalms, etc. 2. (Insertion of) facing in joints of masonry etc. (ill. MASONRY).

poi′ntlėss *adj.* Without a point, blunt; without point, meaningless; not having scored a point. **poi′ntlėsslỹ** *adv.* **poi′ntlėssnėss** *n.*

poise (-z) *v.* Balance; hold suspended or supported; carry (one's head etc.) in specified way; be balanced; hover in air etc. *~ n.* Balance, equilibrium; state of indecision, suspense; carriage (of head etc.); (orig. U.S.) ease of manner, grace, assurance.

poi′son (-zn) *n.* Substance that when introduced into or absorbed by a living organism destroys life or injures health, esp. (pop.) one that destroys life by rapid action and when taken in small quantity; (fig.) baneful principle, doctrine, etc.; *~ gas*: see GAS; *~ ivy*, N. Amer. trailing or climbing sumac, *Rhus toxicodendron*, with trifoliate leaves, producing poisonous effects when touched; *~ oak*, low-growing variety of poison-ivy, allied plant (*R. diversiloba*) of Pacific N. America; *~ pen*, anonymous writer of libellous or scurrilous

POLAR

letters; *~-tree*, *poi′sonwood*, any of various trees with poisonous properties, esp. species of *Rhus*. **poi′sonous** *adj.* **poi′sonouslỹ** *adv.* **poi′son** *v.t.* Administer poison to; kill, injure, thus; produce morbid effects in (blood etc.); infect (air, water, etc.), smear (weapon) with poison; corrupt, pervert (person, mind); destroy, spoil (pleasure etc.); render (land etc.) foul and unfit for its purpose by noxious applications, etc. **poi′soner**, **poi′soning** *ns.*

Poitiers (pwătyā). Town of W. France, where armies of England under Edward the BLACK Prince defeated those of France under King John (1356).

pōke¹ *n.* Bag, sack (now dial. exc. in *buy a pig in a ~*: see PIG).

pōke² *v.* Thrust, push (thing *in*, *up*, *down*, etc.) with hand, arm, point of stick, etc.; stir (fire) with poker; produce (hole etc. *in*) by poking; make thrusts with stick, etc. (*at* etc.); thrust forward, esp. obtrusively; pry (*into*); *~ about*, look here and there; busy oneself in a desultory way; *~ fun at*, ridicule; *~ one's head*, carry head thrust forward, stoop. *~ n.* 1. Poking; thrust, nudge. 2. Device fastened on cattle etc., to prevent their breaking through fences. 3. Projecting brim or front of woman's bonnet; *~ bonnet*, bonnet with this.

pō′ker¹ *n.* Stiff metal rod with handle, for poking fire; kinds of instrument used in poker-work; *red-hot ~*: see RED; *~-work*, (design produced by) burning on wood with heated implement.

pō′ker² *n.* Card-game for two or more players, each of whom receives five cards, who bet on the value of their hands, the winner being the one who holds the strongest hand or who succeeds in bluffing the others into throwing in their hands; *~-face*, (person with) face that does not reveal thoughts or feelings.

pō′kỹ *adj.* (of place, room, etc.) Confined, mean, shabby.

pola′cre (-ahker), **polă′cca** *n.* Three-masted Mediterranean merchant vessel. [Fr. *polacre*, *polaque* Polish, Pole]

Pō′land. Country of NE. Europe, formerly a kingdom, which was divided by three partitions of 1772, 1793, and 1795 between Prussia, Russia and Austria; reconstituted by Napoleon under the title of the Duchy of Warsaw, but re-partitioned at the Congress of Vienna (1815); recognized as an independent republic by treaties of Versailles (1919) and Riga (1921); invaded and overrun by German and later by Russian armies, 1939, and again recognized as an independent republic in 1945; capital, Warsaw.

pō′lar *adj.* 1. Of, near, either pole of the earth or of the celestial sphere; *~ bear*, white bear,

[679]

Thalarctos maritimus; ~ *circle*, Arctic or Antarctic Circle, at distance of 23° 28′ from the poles (ill. EARTH); ~ *distance*, angular distance of point on sphere from nearer pole. 2. Having polarity, having associated positive and negative poles (either electrical or magnetic); (of forces) acting in two opposite directions; (of molecules) symmetrically arranged in definite directions. 3. (geom.) Relating to a pole. 4. (zool.) Of poles of nerve-cell, ovum, etc. 5. (fig.) Analogous to pole of the earth or to pole-star; directly opposite in character. ~ *n*. (geom.) Curve related in particular way to given curve and fixed point called pole; in conic sections, straight line joining points at which tangents from fixed point touch curve.
pōlarī'mĕter *n*. Instrument for measuring polarized light or degree of polarization. **pōlarī'mĕtrў** *n*. Measurement of polarization.
polā'rĭscŏpe *n*. Instrument for showing polarization of light or viewing objects in polarized light. **polărĭscŏ'pĭc** *adj*.
polā'rĭtў *n*. Tendency of magnetized bar etc. to point with its extremities to magnetic poles of earth; tendency of a body to place its mathematical axis in particular direction; possession of two poles having contrary qualities; electrical condition of body as positive or negative; (fig.) direction (of thought, feeling, etc.) towards a single point.
pō'larīze *v*. 1. Restrict vibrations of (transverse waves, esp. light) so that they have different amplitudes in different directions. 2. Give polarity to. **pōlarīzā'tion, pō'larīzer** *n*.
pō'lder *n*. Piece of low-lying land reclaimed from sea or river in Netherlands.
pōle[1] *n*. 1. Long slender rounded piece of wood or metal, esp. as support for tent, telegraph wires, etc.; wooden shaft fitted to carriage of vehicle and attached to yokes or collars of horses etc.; *under bare* ~*s*, (naut.) with no sail set; *up the* ~, (slang) in a fix; crazed or tipsy; ~-*jump*, -*jumping*, -*vault*, jump etc. with help of pole held in hands. 2. (as measure) Rod, perch, 5½ yds; (also *square* ~) 30¼ square yds. ~ *v.t.* Furnish with poles;,push, move, with pole.
pōle[2] *n*. 1. Either of the two points (*north* and *south* ~) in celestial sphere about which the stars appear to revolve; N. and S. extremities of earth's axis (ill. EARTH); ~-*star*, star of Ursa Minor, now about 1¼° distant from north pole of the heavens. 2. (geom.) Each of two points of a circle of the sphere in which axis of that circle cuts surface of sphere; fixed point to which others are referred. 3. Each of two opposite points on surface of magnet at which magnetic forces are manifested; each of two terminal points (POSITIVE and NEGATIVE) of electric cell, battery, etc. 4. (biol.) Extremity of main axis of any spherical or oval organ. 5. (fig.) Each of two opposed principles etc., hence ~*s apart*.
Pōle[3] *n*. Native or inhabitant of Poland.
pō'le-ăxe *n*. Battle-axe; axe formerly used in naval warfare as weapon and for cutting ropes etc. (ill. BATTLE-axe); halbert; butcher's axe with hammer at back. ~ *v.t.* Slaughter (beast etc.) with pole-axe.
pō'lecăt (-lk-) *n*. Small dark-brown fetid carnivorous European mammal of weasel family, esp. *Mustela putorius*.
pō'lĕmărch (-k) *n*. (Gk hist.) Military commander-in-chief, with varying civil functions; in Athens, 3rd archon, who orig. had military functions.
polĕ'mĭc *adj*. Controversial, disputatious. ~ *n*. Controversial discussion; (pl.) practice of this, esp. in theology; (sing.) controversialist. **polĕ'mĭcal** *adj*. **polĕ'mĭcally** *adv*.
polĕ'nta *n*. Italian dish of milk thickened with maize, barley, chestnut meal, etc.
polī'ce (-ēs) *n*. Civil administration, public order; department of government concerned with this; civil force responsible for maintaining public order; (collect.) members of this; any body officially employed to keep order, enforce regulations, etc.; ~ *authority*, committee responsible for local police force; ~-*dog*, employed by police to track criminals, etc.; *polī'ceman, polī'cewoman*, member of police force; ~-*officer*, policeman, policewoman; ~ *state*, State regulated by means of a national police having secret supervision and control of the citizens' activities; ~ *station*, office of local police force. ~ *v.t.* Control (country etc.) by means of police; furnish with police; (fig.) administer, control.
pō'lĭcў[1] *n*. 1. Political sagacity; statecraft; prudent conduct, sagacity; craftiness; course of action adopted by government, party, etc. 2. (Sc., usu. pl.) Park round country seat etc.
pō'lĭcў[2] *n*. (also ~ *of assurance, insurance* ~) Document containing contract of assurance or insurance.
pō'lĭō *n*. (colloq.) Poliomyelitis. **pō'lĭomўĕlī'tĭs** *n*. (in full *acute anterior* ~) Infectious disease of the central nervous system, with temporary or permanent paralysis. [Gk *polios* grey, *muelos* marrow]
pō'lĭsh[1] *v*. Make, become, smooth and glossy by friction; (fig.) make elegant or cultured, refine; smarten *up*; ~ *off*, finish off quickly. **pō'lĭsher** *n*. **pō'lĭsh** *n*. Smoothness, glossiness, produced by friction; such friction; substance used to produce polished surface; (fig.) refinement.
Pō'lĭsh[2] *adj*. Of Poland or the Poles; ~ *Corridor*: see CORRIDOR. ~ *n*. Language of Poland, belonging to Western branch of Slavonic languages.
polī'te *adj*. Of refined manners, courteous; cultivated, cultured; well-bred; (of literature etc.) refined, elegant. **polī'telў** *adv*. **polī'tenĕss** *n*.
pŏ'lĭtĭc *adj*. 1. (of person) Sagacious, prudent; (of action etc.) judicious, expedient; scheming, crafty. 2. *body* ~: see BODY. **pŏ'lĭtĭclў** *adv*. **pŏ'lĭtĭcs** *n*. Science and art of government; political affairs or life; (as pl.) political principles.
polī'tĭcal *adj*. 1. Of the State or its government; of public affairs; of politics; (of person) engaged in civil administration. 2. Having an organized polity. 3. Belonging to, taking, a side in politics. 4. ~ *economy*: see ECONOMY; ~ *geography*, that dealing with boundaries, divisions, and possessions of States; ~ *prisoner*, one imprisoned for a political offence. **polī'tĭcally** *adv*.
pŏlĭtĭ'cian (-shən) *n*. One skilled in politics, statesman; one interested or engaged in politics, esp. as profession; (U.S.) one who makes a trade of politics.
polī'tĭcō *n*. Political agent, officer, or resident.
pō'lĭtў *n*. Condition of civil order; form, process, of civil government; organized society, State.
Pŏlk, James Knox (1795–1849). 11th president of U.S., 1845–9.
pŏ'lka *n*. Lively dance of Czech origin, with music in duple time; music for this; ~-*dot*, one of a pattern of dots of uniform size and arrangement.
pŏll[1] *n*. 1. Human head (now dial. or joc.); part of head on which hair grows; ~-*tax*, tax levied on every person. 2. Counting of voters esp. at parliamentary or other election; voting at election; number of votes recorded. 3. Questioning of a sample of the population in order to estimate trend of public opinion. **pŏ'llster** *n*. (colloq.) One who takes public-opinion polls. **pŏll** *v*. 1. Crop the hair of (archaic); cut off top of (tree, plant), esp. make a pollard of; cut off horns of (cattle, esp. in past part.). 2. Take the votes of; (of candidate) receive (so many votes); give (vote); give one's vote. ~ *adj*. (of legal writing or deed) Polled or cut even at edge, executed by single party and therefore not indented.
Pŏll[2]. (also *poll parrot*) Conventional name of parrot.
pŏ'llack, pŏ'llock *n*. Sea-fish (*Pollachius pollachius*) allied to cod but with lower jaw protruding, used as food.
pŏ'llan *n*. Freshwater fish

POLLARD

(*Coregonus albula*) allied to trout of Irish inland loughs.

pŏ′llard *n*. 1. Animal that has cast or lost its horns; ox, sheep, goat, of hornless variety. 2. Tree polled so as to produce close rounded head of young branches. 3. Bran sifted from flour; fine bran containing some flour. ~ *v.t.* Make a pollard of (tree).

pŏ′llĕn *n*. Fine powdery substance discharged from anther of flower, male element that fertilizes ovules; ~ *count*, index of amount of pollen in air, published as warning to sufferers from respiratory ailments. **polli′nic, pŏllini′ferous** *adjs*. **pŏ′llen** *v.t*. Pollinate.

pŏ′llĕx *n*. Innermost digit of fore-limb; in man, thumb.

pollĭcĭtā′tion *n*. (civil law) Promise not yet formally accepted, and therefore revocable.

pŏ′llināte *v.t*. Sprinkle with pollen, shed pollen upon. **pollinā′tion** *n*.

pŏllĭ′nium *n*. Pollen grains united into a mass.

pollock: see POLLACK.

pollū′te (*or* -ōōt) *v.t*. Destroy the purity or sanctity of; make (water etc.) foul or filthy. **pollū′tion** *n*. (esp.) Contamination or defilement of man's environment.

Pŏ′llux. 1. (Gk myth.) Twin brother of CASTOR. 2. (astron.) Bright star in the constellation Gemini.

pō′lō[1] *n*. Game of Eastern origin resembling hockey, played on horseback by teams of usu. four players, with long-handled mallets (~*sticks*) and wooden ball; *water* ~, handball game played by swimmers with ball like football; ~ *neck*, high round turnover collar.

Pō′lō[2], Marco (1254–1324). Venetian traveller; reached the court of Kublai Khan in China; spent 17 years in China and wrote an account of his experiences.

pŏlonai′se (-z) *n*. 1. (hist.) Woman's dress consisting of bodice with skirt open from waist downwards. 2. (Music for) slow dance in triple rhythm of Polish origin, with intricate march or procession of dancers in couples. [Fr., fem. of *polonais* Polish]

polō′nium *n*. (chem.) Radioactive metallic element discovered by P and M. Curie in pitchblende; symbol Po, at. no. 84, principal isotope at. wt 210. [med. L *Polonia* Poland]

polō′nÿ *n*. Sausage, usu. with bright-red skin, of partly cooked pork. [app. f. *Bologna*]

pŏ′ltergeist (-gīst) *n*. Noisy spirit manifesting its presence by mischievous behaviour, such as the overturning of furniture, breaking of crockery, etc. [Ger.]

pŏltrōō′n *n*. Spiritless coward. **pŏltrōō′nerÿ** *n*.

poly- *prefix*. Many.

pŏlÿă′ndrous *adj*. 1. (Of, practising, polandry. 2. (bot.) With numerous stamens. **pŏlÿă′ndrÿ** *n*. Plurality of husbands.

pŏlÿă′nthus *n*. Cultivated primula with flowers of various colours.

Polÿ′bius (*c* 200–*c* 118 B.C.). Greek historian.

Pŏ′lÿcărp, St. (*c* 69–*c* 155). Bishop of Smyrna, martyr, and Father of the Church; commemorated 26 Jan.

pŏ′lÿchaete (-k-) *adj. & n*. (Animal) of the Polychaeta, a class of the Annelida comprising worms, mostly marine, with many bristles on the foot-stumps.

pŏlÿchromă′tic (-k-) *adj*. Many-coloured.

pŏ′lÿchrōme (-k-) *adj*. Painted, printed, decorated, in many colours. ~ *n*. Work of art in several colours, esp. coloured statue. **pŏlÿchrō′mic, pŏ′lÿchrōmous** *adjs*. **pŏ′lÿchrōmÿ** *n*. Art of painting in several colours, esp. as applied to ancient pottery or sculpture.

pŏlÿclĭ′nic *n*. Clinic devoted to various diseases.

Pŏlÿclī′tus, Pŏlÿcleī′tos (-lī-) (5th c. B.C.). Greek sculptor; his statue of the Doryphoros or Spearbearer was known as 'The Canon' or rule, as being an ideal representation of human proportions.

polÿ′gamous *adj*. 1. Having more than one wife or (less usu.) husband at once. 2. (zool.) Having more than one mate at one time. 3. (bot.) Bearing some flowers with stamens only, some with pistils only, some with both, on same or different plants. **pŏlÿgă′mic** *adj*. **polÿ′gamist, polÿ′gamÿ** *ns*.

pŏ′lÿglŏt *adj*. Of many languages; speaking or writing several languages; (of book, esp. Bible) written in several languages. ~ *n*. Polyglot person or book. **pŏlÿglŏ′ttal, pŏlÿglŏ′ttic** *adjs*.

pŏ′lÿgon *n*. Figure (usu. plane rectilinear) with many (usu. more than four) angles or sides; ~ *of forces*, polygon illustrating theorem relating to number of forces acting at a point, each represented in magnitude and direction by one side of the figure. **polÿ′gonal** *adj*. **polÿ′gonallÿ** *adv*.

pŏlÿ′gonum *n*. Plant of large and widely distributed genus *P*~ (including knot-grass, bistort, etc.) with swollen stem-joints sheathed by stipules, and small flowers.

polÿ′gÿnous (-g-) *adj*. 1. Of, practising, polygyny. 2. (bot.) With many pistils, styles, or stigmas. **polÿ′gÿnÿ** *n*. Plurality of wives.

pŏlÿhē′dron *n*. Many- (usu. more than 6-) sided solid. **pŏlÿhē′dral, pŏlÿhē′dric** *adjs*.

Pŏlÿhÿ′mnia. (Gk & Rom. myth.) Muse of the mimic art.

pŏ′lÿmăth *n*. Scholar of varied learning. **polÿ′mathÿ** *n*.

pŏ′lÿmer *n*. (chem.) Compound formed by the combination of a (usu. very large) number of identical molecules of a simpler substance. **pŏlÿmĕ′ric** *adj*. (of compounds) Composed of the same elements in the same proportions but differing in molecular weight.

polÿ′merize *v*. (chem., of a number of identical molecules) Combine together to form a polymer. **pŏlÿmerĭză′tion** *n*.

polÿ′merous *adj*. (biol.) Composed of many parts, members, or segments.

pŏ′lÿmorph *n*. Leucocyte of a class in which the nuclei occur in various forms.

pŏlÿmor′phic, -mor′phous *adjs*. Multiform; esp. (biol.) of a species) of which more than one form exists in a population.

pŏlÿmor′phism *n*. Diversity occurring within biological populations, determined genetically or by environment.

Pŏlÿnē′sia (-z-; *or* -zha). General name for all islands in central and W. Pacific or (more usu.) for the easternmost of the three great groups of these islands, including New Zealand, Hawaii, the Marquesas, and Samoa. **Pŏlÿnē′sian** *adj. & n*. (Member) of a black-haired brown-skinned people inhabiting Polynesia.

pŏlÿneurī′tis *n*. (path.) Multiple neuritis, condition in which many peripheral nerves are inflamed simultaneously.

pŏ′lÿp *n*. 1. (zool.) Single individual of a coelenterate or other colony (ill. CORAL); similar individual of a non-colonial form, e.g. sea-anemone (ill. HYDRA). 2. (path.) Small tumour with a stalk, formed by overgrowth of tissue. **pŏ′lÿpoid, pŏ′lÿpous** *adjs*.

pŏlÿpĕ′ptīde *n*. Substance formed by union of three or more amino-acids.

Pŏlÿphē′mus. (Gk legend) CYCLOPS from whom Odysseus and some of his companions escaped by putting out his one eye while he slept.

pŏ′lÿphōne *n*. Written character having more than one phonetic value.

POLONAISE *c* 1778
1. Petticoat

[681]

POLYPHONIC

pŏlўphŏ'nĭc adj. 1. (mus.) Of polyphony, contrapuntal. 2. (of written character) Having more than one phonetic value. 3. Producing many sounds.

polў'phonў n. (mus.) Simultaneous combination of number of parts each forming an individual melody; style of composition in which parts are so combined; counterpoint.

pŏ'lўploid adj. & n. (biol.) (Organism) having a chromosome number which is a multiple greater than 2 of the basic group number.

pŏ'lўpŏd adj. & n. (Animal) with many feet.

pŏ'lўpŏdў n. Fern of large and widely distributed genus *Polypodium*, esp. *P. vulgare*, growing on moist rocks, old walls, and trees.

pŏ'lўpŏre n. Fungus of the family Polyporaceae whose members have large fruiting bodies in which the spores are produced in tubes.

pŏ'lўpus n. (pl. *-pi*). (path.) Polyp.

polўstў'rēne n. Transparent thermoplastic material, a polymer of styrene.

pŏlўsyllă'bĭc adj. (of word) Having many syllables; marked by polysyllables. **pŏlўsyllă'bĭcallў** adv. **pŏlўsy'llable** n. Polysyllabic word.

pŏlўsynthĕ'tĭc adj. (of language) Combining several words of a sentence into one.

pŏlўtĕ'chnĭc (-k-) adj. Dealing with, devoted to, various arts. **Pŏlўtĕ'chnĭc** n. College of higher education providing courses in various subjects.

pŏ'lўthēĭsm n. Belief in, worship of, many gods or more than one god. **pŏ'lўthēĭst** n. **pŏlўthēĭ'stĭc** adj.

pŏ'lўthēne n. Thermoplastic material used for packaging etc.

polўvi'nўl adj. ~ chloride, (abbrev. P.V.C.) vinyl plastic used for insulation, as fabric for clothing and furnishings, etc.

pŏlўzō'an adj. & n. = BRYOZOAN.

pŏm n. (colloq.) Pomeranian dog.

pomace (pŭ'mĭs) n. Mass of crushed apples in cider-making before or after juice is pressed out; any pulp; refuse of fish, etc., after oil has been extracted, used as fertilizer.

poma'de (-ahd) n. Scented ointment (perh. orig. from apples) for hair and skin of head. ~ v.t. Anoint with pomade.

pomă'nder n. Ball of mixed aromatic substances placed in wardrobes etc. or (hist.) carried as guard against infection; spherical case for this. [OF. *pomme d'ambre* apple of amber]

pomā'tum n. & v.t. Pomade.

pōme n. (bot.) Succulent inferior fruit with firm fleshy body enclosing carpels forming core, e.g. apple, pear, quince (ill. FRUIT; poet.) apple. **pomi'ferous** adj. Bearing pomes.

pŏ'megrănate (-mg-) n. Large roundish many-celled berry about size of orange with tough golden or orange rind and acid reddish pulp enveloping the many seeds; tree (*Punica granatum*) bearing this, native to N. Africa and W. Asia.

pŏ'mĕlō n. Shaddock, grape-fruit.

Pŏmerā'nia. (Ger. *Pommern*) Province of Poland with sea-coast on Baltic, formerly part of Prussia. **Pŏmerā'nian** adj. & n. (Native, inhabitant) of Pomerania; (also ~ *dog*) dog of small breed with long thick silky hair, usu. black or white, pointed muzzle, pricked ears, and prominent eyes.

pŏ'mfrĕt-cāke (*or* pŭ-) n. Pontefract-cake. [f. *Pomfret* earlier sp. of Pontefract]

pŏ'mĭcŭlture n. Fruit-growing.

Pŏmmar'd (-ār) n. Dry red wine produced near Pommard in Burgundy.

po'mmel (pŭ-) n. 1. Rounded knob esp. at end of sword-hilt (ill. SWORD). 2. Upward projecting front part of saddle (ill. SADDLERY). ~ v.t. Strike or beat (as) with pommel of sword; beat with fists.

pŏ'mmy n. (Austral. & N.Z. slang) Immigrant from Britain.

pomŏ'logў n. Science of fruit-growing. **pŏmolŏ'gĭcal** adj. **pomŏ'logĭst** n.

Pomō'na. (Rom. myth.) Goddess of fruit-trees.

pŏmp n. Splendid display, splendour.

Pŏmpadour[1] (-oor), Marquise de (1721-64). Jeanne Antoinette Poisson le Normant d'Étoiles, mistress of Louis XV of France.

pŏ'mpadour[2] (-oor) n. Style of women's hairdressing with hair turned back from forehead in high roll. [f. POMPADOUR[1]]

Pŏmpei'i (-āē). Ancient town of Campania, Italy, buried by eruption of Mt Vesuvius in A.D. 79 and since 1755 gradually laid bare by excavation.

Pŏ'mpey[1]. Gnaeus Pompeius Magnus (106-48 B.C.), Roman general and consul; member, with Julius Caesar and Crassus, of the 1st triumvirate; later he opposed Caesar and was defeated by him at Pharsalia, 48 B.C.

Pŏ'mpey[2]. (naval slang) Portsmouth.

pŏ'm-pŏm[1] n. Automatic quick-firing gun. [imit.]

pŏ'mpŏm[2], **pŏ'mpŏn** ns. Ornamental tuft or bunch of silk threads, ribbon, etc., on hat, shoe, dress, etc.; variety of chrysanthemum or dahlia with small globular flowers.

pŏ'mpous n. Magnificent, splendid; self-important, consequential; (of language) inflated. **pŏ'mpouslў** adv. **pŏ'mpousnĕss**, **pŏmpŏ'sitў** ns.

PONTIFICAL

pŏnce n. & v.i. Pimp.

Pŏ'nce de Leŏ'n (-thā, lā-) Juan (c 1460-1521). Spanish conqueror of Puerto Rico and discoverer of Florida.

pŏ'nchō n. (pl. *-s*). S. Amer. cloak, oblong piece of cloth with slit in middle for head.

pŏnd n. Small body of still water artificially formed by hollowing or embanking; natural pool or small lake; (joc.) sea, esp. Atlantic Ocean; ~*-lily*, water-lily; ~*-skater*, bug of family Gerridae etc. which moves rapidly on surface of fresh water; *po'nd-weed*, aquatic herb (esp. *Potamogeton*) growing in still waters. ~ v. Hold back, dam up (stream); form a pool or pond.

pŏ'ndage n. Capacity of pond; storage of water.

pŏ'nder v. Weigh mentally, think over; think *on*, muse *over*. **pŏ'nderinglў** adv.

pŏ'nderable adj. Having appreciable weight. **pŏnderabi'litў** n.

pŏnderā'tion n. Weighing, balancing.

pŏ'nderous adj. Heavy; unwieldy; laborious; laboured. **pŏ'nderouslў** adv. **pŏ'nderousness**, **pŏnderŏ'sitў** ns.

Pŏ'ndĭchĕrrў. Union territory in SE. India; its capital.

pŏ'nē[1] n. In some card-games, player who leads, or his partner.

pōne[2] n. Orig., N. Amer. Ind. bread, thin cakes of maize flour cooked in hot ashes; now, in southern U.S., any maize bread; also, very fine light bread made with eggs, milk, etc., and baked in flat cakes.

pŏngee' (-j-; *or* pŭ-) n. Soft, freq. unbleached fabric of Chinese or Japanese silk, made from cocoons of a wild silkworm feeding on oak-leaves; imitation of this in cotton etc. [perh. f. Chin. *pun-chi* own loom]

pŏ'niard (-y-) n. Dagger (ill. DAGGER). ~ v.t. Stab with poniard.

pŏns (-z) n. (anat.) Band of nerve fibres in brain connecting two hemispheres of cerebellum, and medulla with cerebrum [ill. BRAIN], also called ~ *Varolii* ('bridge of Varoli', after an Italian 16th-c. anatomist). [L, = 'bridge']

pŏns ăsĭnōr'um (-z). Geometrical proposition (5th in 1st book of Euclid) that if a triangle has two of its sides equal, the angles opposite those sides are equal (so called because beginners find it difficult). [L, = 'bridge of asses']

Pŏ'ntĕfrăct-cāke n. Small round flat cake of liquorice, made at Pontefract, West Yorkshire.

pŏ'ntĭfĕx (pl. *-i'ficĕs*, pr. -z). (Rom. antiq.) Member of principal college of priests in Rome; ~ *maximus*, head of this; pope.

pŏ'ntĭff n. Pope; bishop; chief priest.

pŏntĭ'fĭcal adj. Of, befitting, a pontiff; solemnly dogmatic; ~

[682]

Mass, Mass celebrated by bishop while wearing full vestments. **pŏnti'fically** *adv.* **pŏnti'fical** *n.* Office-book of Western Church containing forms for rites to be performed by bishops; (pl.) vestments and insignia of bishop.
pŏnti'ficate *n.* Office of pontifex, bishop, or pope; period of this. **pŏnti'ficāte** *v.i.* Officiate as bishop, esp. at Mass; assume airs of pontiff, act pompously or dogmatically.
pŏ'ntil *n.* Iron rod for handling and rapidly twirling soft glass, esp. crown glass, in process of manufacture.
pŏ'ntine *adj.* Of the PONS.
pŏntōō'n¹ *n.* Flat-bottomed boat used as ferry-boat etc.; one of several boats, hollow metal cylinders, etc., used to support temporary bridge (ill. BRIDGE¹); caisson.
pŏntōō'n² *n.* Corruption (orig. soldiers') of the name of the card-game VINGT-ET-UN.
pŏ'ntý *n.* = PONTIL.
pŏ'nȳ *n.* 1. Horse of any small breed, esp. not more than 13 or (pop.) 14 hands high. 2. (slang) £25. 3. (U.S. slang) School crib. 4. *po'nytail*, hair worn drawn back, gathered at crown of head, and hanging loose behind.
pōō'dle *n.* Dog of breed with long curling hair, usu. black or white, often elaborately clipped and shaved (ill. DOG). [Ger. *pudel(hund)*, f. *pudeln* splash]
pooh (pōō or pŏōh) *int.* Exclamation of impatience or contempt. **pooh-pooh'** *v.t.* Express contempt for, make light of.
Pooh-Bah' (pōō-) *n.* Holder of many offices at once. [name of character in Gilbert and Sullivan's 'The Mikado']
pōōl¹ *n.* Small body of still water, usu. of natural formation; puddle of any liquid; deep still place in river; *the P~ (of London)*, part of Thames immediately below London Bridge. ~ *v.t.* Make (hole) for insertion of wedge in quarrying; undermine (coal).
pōōl² *n.* 1. (in some card-games) Collective amount of players' stakes and fines; receptacle for these. 2. Game on billiard-table in which each player has ball of different colour with which he tries to pocket the others in fixed order, winner taking the whole stakes; similar game in U.S. with balls numbered from 1 to 15, number of ball pocketed being added to player's score. 3. Collective stakes in betting etc.; arrangement between competing parties by which prices are fixed and business divided to do away with competition; common fund, e.g. of profit of separate firms; common supply of commodities, persons, etc. 4. *football ~*, (colloq. *the ~s*) system of betting on results of football matches. ~ *v.t.* Place in common fund; merge

(supplies from several sources); (of competing companies etc.) share (traffic, profits).
pōōp *n.* Stern of ship; aftermost and highest deck (ill. SHIP). ~ *v.t.* (of wave) Break over stern of (ship); (of ship) receive (wave) over stern.
poor *adj.* 1. Lacking means to procure comforts or necessaries of life; ill supplied, deficient (*in* possession or quality); (of soil) unproductive; *the ~*, poor people as a class. 2. Scanty, inadequate, less than is expected; paltry, sorry; spiritless, despicable; humble, insignificant. 3. (expr. pity or sympathy) Unfortunate, hapless. 4. *~-box*, money-box esp. in church for relief of the poor; *~-house*, (hist.) institution where paupers were maintained; *P~ Law*, (hist.) law relating to support of paupers; *~-spirited*, timid, cowardly; *~ white*, (U.S.) contemptuous name given by Negroes to white people of no substance.
poor'ly *adv.* Scantily, defectively; with no great success. ~ *pred. adj.* Unwell.
poor'ness *n.* Defectiveness; lack of some good quality or constituent.
pŏp¹ *v.* 1. Make small quick explosive sound as of cork when drawn; let off (firearm etc.); fire gun (*at*); *~-gun*, child's toy gun shooting pellets by compression of air with piston. 2. Put (*in, out, down*, etc.) quickly or suddenly; move, come, go (*in* etc.) thus; put (question) abruptly; *~ the question*, (colloq.) propose marriage. 3. (slang) Pawn; *~-shop*, pawnbroker's shop. 4. (U.S.) Parch (maize) till it bursts open; *po'pcorn*, maize so parched. ~ *n.* Abrupt, not very loud, explosive sound; (colloq.) effervescing drink; (slang) pawning; *in ~*, in pawn. ~ *adv.* With (the action or sound of) a pop. [imit.]
pŏp² *n.* = POPPA.
pŏp³ *adj.* (of music, art, etc.) Popular. ~ *n.* (Record of) popular music.
Pŏp⁴. Social and debating club at Eton. [L *popina* cookshop (orig. meeting-place)]
pop. *abbrev.* Population.
pōpe¹ *n.* 1. Bishop of Rome as head of the Roman Catholic Church; *P~ Joan*, fabulous female pope placed by some chroniclers *c* 855, under name of John; card-game played with pack from which eight of diamonds is removed, and a tray with eight compartments holding stakes to be won by players playing certain cards; *~'s eye*, lymphatic gland surrounded with fat in middle of leg of mutton; *~'s nose*, PARSON's nose. 2. (fig.) Person assuming or credited with infallibility. **pō'pedom** *n.*
pōpe² *n.* Parish priest of Greek Church in U.S.S.R. etc. [Russ. *pop*]

Pōpe³, Alexander (1688–1744). English poet, satirist, and translator of Homer.
pō'pery *n.* (in hostile use) Papal system, Roman Catholicism.
pŏ'pinjay *n.* 1. (archaic) Parrot; (hist.) figure of parrot on pole as mark to shoot at. 2. Fop, coxcomb.
pō'pish *adj.* Of popery, papistical; *P~ Plot*, supposed plot to murder Charles II and suppress Protestantism, deposed to by Titus OATES and largely fabricated by him (1678). **pō'pishly** *adv.*
pŏ'plar *n.* Large tree of rapid growth (genus *Populus*), freq. with tremulous leaves; soft light loose-textured wood of this.
pŏ'plin *n.* Closely woven fabric with corded surface, orig. of silk warp and worsted weft, now freq. of cotton. [It. *papalina* papal (because made in the papal town Avignon)]
popli'tēal *adj.* Of the hollow at back of knee.
Pŏ'pocătĕpĕ'tl. Volcanic mountain, dormant since 1802, in Mexico.
pŏ'ppa *n.* (U.S.) Papa.
pŏ'ppet *n.* 1. (dial. or colloq.) Small person, esp. as term of endearment. 2. (also *~-head*) Lathe-head. 3. (mining) Frame at top of shaft supporting pulleys for ropes used in hoisting. 4. (naut.) Short piece of wood for various purposes, e.g. forming rowlocks of boat, supporting ship in launching (ill. LAUNCH¹). 5. *~-valve*, mushroom-shaped valve operated by cams etc., used in engines to ensure quick action (ill. COMBUSTION).
pŏ'pple *n.* (esp., cricket) *~-crease*: see CREASE.
pŏ'pple *v.i.* & *n.* Ripple.
pŏ'ppy *n.* Plant or flower of genus *Papaver* of temperate and subtropical regions, having milky juice with narcotic properties, showy flowers of scarlet or other colour, and roundish capsules containing numerous small seeds; artificial poppy (also *Flanders ~*) worn on Poppy Day; *Californian ~*, ESCHSCHOLTZIA; *horn(ed) ~*, any plant of genus *Glaucium*, distinguished by its long horn-like capsules; *Iceland ~*: see ICELAND; *opium ~*: see OPIUM; *prickly ~*, any plant of genus *Argemone*, esp. *A. mexicana*, with yellow or white flowers and prickly leaves and capsules; *Shirley ~*: see SHIRLEY POPPY; *P~ Day*, (formerly) Armistice Day, (now) REMEMBRANCE Sunday, on which artificial poppies are worn (now because poppies were very conspicuous on the Flanders battlefields); *~-head*, capsule of poppy; (archit.) carved finial crowning end of seat in church (ill. STALL¹).
pŏ'ppycŏck *n.* (orig. U.S. slang) Nonsense, rubbish.
pō'pulace *n.* The common people.
pŏ'pular *adj.* 1. Of, carried on by, the people; adapted to the

[683]

POPULARIZE

understanding, taste, or means of the people; prevalent among the people; ~ **front**, political group representing leftist elements. 2. Liked, admired, by the people or by people generally or a specified class. **pŏ'pularly** adv. **pŏpŭlă'rity** n.

pŏ'pularize v.t. Make popular, cause to be generally known or liked; extend to the common people; present in popular form. **pŏpularīzā'tion** n.

pŏ'pulāte v.t. Inhabit, form the population of, (country, town, etc.); supply with inhabitants. **pŏpulā'tion** n. Degree in which place is populated; total number of inhabitants; people of a country etc.

Pŏ'pulist n. 1. Adherent of a Russian political movement (c 1870–80) advocating collectivism. 2. Adherent of a U.S. political party (1892–1904) aiming at public control of railways, graduated income tax, etc.

pŏ'pulous adj. Thickly inhabited. **pŏ'pulousness** n.

pŏr'beagle n. Shark of genus *Lamna*, esp. *L. nasus*, up to 3·12 m long and with pointed snout.

pŏr'celain (-slĭn), n. Finest and hardest kind of earthenware, consisting largely of kaolin or felspathic clay, baked at a high temperature and usu. covered with a coloured or transparent glaze; article or vessel of this; (attrib.) of porcelain, (fig.) delicate, fragile; ~-*shell*, cowrie. **pŏrcĕllā'nèous, pŏrcĕllā'nic, pŏrcĕ'llanous** adjs. [It. *porcellana* (*porcella* dim. of *porca* sow, f. resemblance of the shell to hog's back)]

pŏr'celainīze (-slĭn-) v.t. Convert (clay, shale, etc.) into porcelain or similar substance.

pŏrch n. 1. Covered approach to entrance of building. 2. (U.S.) Verandah. 3. *the P*~, public ambulatory in market-place of ancient Athens to which Zeno and his disciples resorted; Stoic school or philosophy.

pŏr'cine adj. Of or like swine.

pŏr'cūpīne n. 1. Rodent esp. of genus *Hystrix*, with body and tail covered with long erectile spines; similar arboreal rodent

PORCUPINE

(*Erethizon dorsatum*) of North America. 2. Any of several machines with many spikes or teeth, e.g. for heckling flax etc.

pōre¹ n. Minute opening in skin of animal body (ill. SKIN) or membrane of plant, for transpiration, absorption, etc.; external opening of duct exuding sweat; *taste* ~, external opening of taste-bud.

pōre² v. ~ *over*, be absorbed in studying (book etc.); (fig.) meditate, think intently upon (subject).

pŏr'gy (-gi) n. (U.S.) Sea-fish of family Sparidae related to the bass, of wide distribution.

pŏr'ism (*or* pō'r-) n. (math.) Proposition affirming possibility of finding condition that will make a given problem capable of innumerable solutions. **pŏrismă'tic, pŏri'stic** adjs.

pŏrk n. Flesh of swine as food; ~-*barrel*, (U.S. fig.) Federal treasury viewed as source of grants for local purposes; ~-*butcher*, one who slaughters pigs for sale; ~-*pie*, cylindrical pie of chopped pork; (attrib., of hat) with flat crown and no brim, or brim turned up all round.

pŏr'ker n. Pig raised for food; young fattened hog.

pŏrn n. (colloq.) Pornography.

pŏrnŏ'cracy n. Dominant influence of prostitutes, esp. in government of Rome in 10th c.

pŏrnŏ'graphy n. Explicit description or exhibition of sexual activity in literature, films, etc., intended to stimulate erotic feelings; literature etc. of this kind. **pŏrnŏ'grapher** n. **pŏrnogră'phic** adj.

pŏroplă'stic adj. Both porous and plastic, esp. of material used in surgical splints etc.

pŏr'ous adj. Full of pores; not watertight. **pŏr'ousness, pŏrŏ'sity** ns.

pŏr'phyrīte n. Rock resembling porphyry but with slightly different composition of crystals.

pŏr'phyry¹ n. Volcanic purplish-red rock composed of large crystals set in a fine-grained ground mass, anciently quarried in Egypt as material for statues etc.

Pŏr'phyry². Porphyrius (A.D. 233–c 305), scholar and philosopher; orig. called Malchus; by birth prob. a Syrian; became a disciple of Plotinus at Rome; author of numerous works in Greek.

pŏr'poise (-pus) n. Small whale of genus *Phocaena*, esp. *P. phocaena* which is about 1·8 m long, blackish above and paler beneath, and has a blunt rounded snout.

PORPOISE

pŏrrā'ceous (-shus) adj. Leek-green.

porrĕ'ct v.t. 1. (biol.) Stretch out, extend (part of body). 2. (eccles. law) Tender, submit (document).

[684]

PORTAL

pŏ'rridge n. Soft food made by stirring oatmeal or other meal or cereal in boiling water or milk.

pŏ'rringer (-j-) n. Small basin from which soup etc. is eaten.

PORRINGER

Pŏr'sèna, Pŏrsĕ'nna, Lars. (Rom. hist.) King of Clusium in Etruria, who vainly laid siege to Rome (508 B.C.) in an attempt to restore the exiled Tarquinius Superbus (see TARQUIN) or (acc. to another tradition) conquered and ruled Rome.

pŏrt¹ n. Harbour; town, place, possessing harbour, esp. one where customs officers are stationed.

pŏrt² n. 1. (chiefly Sc.) Gate, gateway, esp. of walled town. 2. Opening in side of ship for entrance, loading, etc.; aperture in cylinder for passage of steam, water, etc.; curved mouthpiece of some bridle-bits; (also ~-*hole*) aperture in ship's or aircraft's side for admission of light and air (ill. SHIP); aperture in wall etc. for firing through.

pŏrt³ n. External deportment, carriage, bearing. ~ v.t. (mil.) Carry (rifle, sword) diagonally across and close to the body, with barrel or blade opposite middle of left shoulder.

pŏrt⁴ n. Left-hand side of ship looking forward (formerly called larboard) (ill. BEARING); corresponding side of aircraft). ~ v. Turn (helm) to left side of ship; (of ship or aircraft) turn to port side.

pŏrt⁵ n. Heavy sweet fortified wine, dark red or (less freq.) white, made in the Douro valley of Portugal; wine of similar type made in other countries (but by various Anglo-Portuguese treaties only Douro wines may be sold in U.K. under the name of 'port'). [*Oporto*, seaport where the wine is shipped]

pŏr'table adj. Movable, convenient for carrying. **pŏrtabi'lity** n.

pŏr'tage n. Carrying, carriage; cost of this; carrying of boats or goods across land between two navigable waters, place at which this is necessary. ~ v.t. Convey (boat, goods) over a portage.

pŏr'tal¹ n. Door(way), gate-(way), esp. elaborate one.

pŏr'tal² adj. Of the *porta* or

transverse fissure of the liver; ~ *vein*, great vein (*vena portae*) formed by union of veins from stomach, intestine, and spleen, conveying blood to the liver (ill. BLOOD).

portamĕ'ntō *n.* (pl. *-os*). (mus.) Gliding continuously from one pitch to another, in singing or in playing a bowed instrument or trombone; in piano-playing, half-staccato. [It., = 'carrying']

Port Ar'thur (ār-). Harbour in S. Manchuria, leased to Russia 1898; besieged and taken by Japanese, 1904, in Russo-Japanese war; restored to U.S.S.R. in 1945.

por'tative *adj.* (chiefly hist.) Portable, esp. applied to kind of small organ.

portcu'llis *n.* Strong heavy grating blocking gateway of fortress, made to slide up and down in vertical grooves (ill. CASTLE).

portcu'llised (-st) *adj.*

Porte. (hist.) Ottoman court at Constantinople, Turkish Government until 1923 (also *Sublime* or *Ottoman* ~). [Fr. *la Sublime Porte*, transl. of Ottoman Turkish *bāb-i-'alī* high gate, title of central office of Turkish Government]

porte-cochère (pōrt-koshār') *n.* Gateway and passage for vehicles through house into courtyard. [Fr.]

portĕ'nd *v.t.* Foretell, foreshadow, as an omen; give warning of.

por'tĕnt *n.* Omen, significant sign; prodigy, marvellous thing.

portĕ'ntous *adj.* **portĕ'ntously** *adv.*

por'ter[1] *n.* (fem. *por'tress*) Gate-keeper, door-keeper, esp. of large building, public institution, etc.

por'ter[2] *n.* Person employed to carry burdens, esp. employee of railway company who handles luggage; (U.S.) attendant in Pullman coaches etc.; ~*'s knot*, pad resting on shoulders and secured to forehead used by porters in carrying loads. **por'terage** *n.* Work of porters; charge for this.

por'ter[3] *n.* Dark-brown bitter beer, like stout but weaker, brewed from charred or browned malt (now chiefly in Ireland); *por'terhouse*, (U.S.) house at which porter, etc., was retailed; place where steaks, chops, etc., were served, chop-house; *porterhouse steak*, choice cut of beef between sirloin and tenderloin. [short for *porter's ale* etc., app. because orig. brewed for porters and other labourers]

portfō'liō *n.* Case, usu. like large book-cover, for keeping loose sheets of paper, drawings, etc.; such receptacle containing official documents of State department, (fig.) office of minister of State; *minister without* ~, one not in charge of any department of State.

por'ticō *n.* Colonnade, roof supported by columns at regular intervals, usu. attached as porch to a building (ill. TEMPLE[1]).

portière (pōrtyār') *n.* Curtain hung over door(way).

por'tion *n.* Part, share; dowry; one's destiny, one's lot; amount of a dish served to a person in a restaurant etc.; some (*of*) anything. ~ *v.t.* Divide (thing) into shares, distribute *out*; assign (*to* person) as share; give inheritance or dowry to.

Port'land, Isle of. Peninsula on coast of Dorset, England, site of a convict prison converted (1921) into a Borstal institution; ~ *cement*, kind of cement hardening in water and resembling Portland stone when set; ~ *stone*, yellowish-white limestone from Isle of Portland, extensively used for building.

Port'land Club. London card-playing club, the recognized authority on the games of whist and bridge.

Port'land Vase (vahz). Roman vase (*c* 1st c. A.D.) of dark-blue transparent glass with engraved figure decoration in white opaque glass; acquired in 18th c. by Duchess of Portland from Barberini Palace, Rome; now in British Museum, where it was damaged by a madman in 1845.

por'tly *adj.* Bulky, corpulent; of stately appearance. **port'liness** *n.*

portma'nteau (-tō) *n.* (pl. -*s*, -*x*, pr. -z). Oblong case for carrying clothing etc., opening like book with hinges in middle of back; ~ *word*, word like those invented by Lewis Carroll, blending the sounds and combining the meanings of two others (e.g. *slithy* = lithe and slimy).

portola'nō (-lah-) *n.* (hist.) Book of sailing directions with description of harbours etc., illustrated with charts. [It.]

Porto Rico: see PUERTO RICO.

por'trait (-rit) *n.* Likeness of person or animal made by drawing, painting, photography, etc.; verbal picture, graphic description; (fig.) type, similitude. **por'traitist** *n.* Maker of portraits.

por'traiture (-richer) *n.* Portraying; portrait; graphic description.

portray' *v.t.* Make likeness of: describe graphically. **portray'al** *n.*

por'treeve *n.* (hist.) Chief officer of town or borough; officer inferior to mayor in some towns.

Port-Royal (pōr rwäyäl'). Cistercian convent near Versailles which from 1636 onwards became the home of the community of JANSENIST influence in France; the institution was persecuted by the Jesuits and dispersed in 1709.

Port Said (sīd). Seaport of Egypt, at N. end of Suez Canal.

Por'tsmouth (-*muth*). City and port of Hampshire; chief naval station of Gt Britain.

Por'tugal. Republic (kingdom until 1910) occupying W. part of Iberian peninsula; capital, Lisbon.

Portuguē'se (-gēz) *adj.* Of Portugal or its people or language; ~ *man-of-war*, marine hydrozoan of genus *Physalia*. ~ *n.* Portuguese person; Romance language of Portugal, spoken also in Brazil.

pōse[1] (-z) *n.* Attitude of body or mind, esp. one assumed for effect; (dominoes) posing, right to pose. ~ *v.* Lay down (assertion, claim, etc.); propound (question); place (artist's model etc.) in certain attitude; assume an attitude, esp. for artistic purposes; set up, give oneself out, *as*; (dominoes) place first domino on table.

pōse[2] (-z) *v.t.* Puzzle (person) with question or problem. **pō'ser** *n.* (esp.) Puzzling question or problem.

Posei'don (-sī-). (Gk myth.) God of the sea, brother of ZEUS and Pluto; identified by the Romans with Neptune.

pōseur' (-zēr) *n.* Affected person.

pŏsh *adj.* (slang) Smart, stylish; first-rate, high-class.

Pŏsidō'nius (*c* 135-51 B.C.). Syrian-Greek Stoic philosopher.

pŏ'sit (-z-) *v.t.* Assume as fact, postulate; put in position, place.

posi'tion (-z-) *n.* 1. (chiefly logic and philos.) Proposition; laying down of this. 2. Bodily posture, attitude. 3. Mental attitude, way of looking at question. 4. Place occupied by a thing, site, situation; *in* (*out of*) ~, in (out of) its proper place; (mil.) place where troops are posted esp. for strategical reasons. 5. Situation in regard to other persons or things; condition. 6. Rank, social status; official employment. 7. Situation of vowels in syllable, esp. (Gk & L pros.) of short vowel before two consonants, making syllable metrically long. ~ *v.t.* Place in position; determine position of. **posi'tional** *adj.*

pŏ'sitive (-z-) *adj.* 1. Explicitly laid down; definite; unquestionable. 2. Absolute, not relative; (gram., of degree of adjective or adverb) expressing simple quality, without qualification or comparison; (colloq.) downright, out-and-out. 3. (of person) Confident, assured; opinionated; (also) given to constructive action. 4. (philos.) Dealing only with matters of fact, practical. 5. Marked by presence, not absence, of qualities; tending in the direction regarded as that of increase or progress. 6. (math., phys., etc.) Greater than zero; in the direction which for purposes of calculation is to be regarded as upwards from zero; (elect.) having a positive charge; ~ *charge*, one of the two kinds of electric charge, that of the atomic nucleus as dist. from the negative charge of the electrons (the terms *positive* and *negative* were applied to electricity before the discovery of electrons and their meaning is now purely conventional); ~ **pole**, region of deficiency of electrons, anode; also (magnetism) applied to the north-seeking pole of a magnet and the corresponding (south) pole of the earth; ~ **sign**, the sign +, plus sign. 7. (photog.) Showing the lights and shades as seen in nature. 8. ~ **organ**, small (orig. portable) organ occas. used to supplement large one in church. **pŏ'sĭtĭvely** *adv.* **pŏ'sĭtĭveness, pŏsĭtĭ'vĭtў** *ns.* **pŏ'sĭtĭve** *n.* Positive degree, adjective, quantity, photograph, etc.

pŏ'sĭtĭvism (-z-) *n.* Philosophical system of Auguste Comte, recognizing only positive facts and observable phenomena and abandoning all inquiry into causes or ultimate origins; religious system founded upon this. **pŏ'sĭtĭvist** *n.* **pŏsĭtĭvĭ'stĭc** *adj.*

pŏ'sĭtrŏn (-z-) *n.* (phys.) Positive particle with mass equal to that of the electron and electrically its counterpart. [*posit(ive elect)ron*]

pŏ'ssĕ *n.* 1. Body of police or (~ *cōmĭtā'tus*) of men summoned to aid sheriff. 2. *in* ~, in possibility, in potentiality (opp. *in esse*). [L, = 'to be able'; in med. L, 'power']

possĕ'ss (-zĕs-) *v.t.* Hold as property, own; have (faculty, quality, etc.); maintain (*in* patience etc.); (of demon or spirit) occupy, dominate (person etc.); ~ *oneself of*, take, get for one's own; *be possessed of*, own, have. **possĕ'ssor** *n.* **possĕ'ssorў** *adj.*

possĕ'ssion (-zĕ-) *n.* 1. Possessing; actual holding or occupancy; (law) visible power of exercising such control as attaches to (but may exist apart from) lawful ownership; *in* ~, (of thing) possessed; (of person) possessing; *man in* ~, one placed in charge of chattels on which there is a warrant for distress; *in* ~ *of*, having in one's possession; *in the* ~ *of*, possessed or held by; ~ *is nine points* (or *tenths*) *of the law*, possession or occupancy gives every advantage short of actual lawful ownership. 2. Thing possessed; subject territory, esp. foreign dominion(s); (pl.) property, wealth.

possĕ'ssĭve (-zĕs-) *adj.* Of possession; indicating possession; desirous of keeping as one's own. **possĕ'ssĭvely** *adv.* **possĕ'ssĭveness** *n.* **possĕ'ssĭve** *n.* (Word in) possessive case.

pŏ'ssĕt *n.* (archaic) Drink made of hot milk curdled with ale, wine etc., and freq. flavoured with spices, formerly much used as remedy for colds etc.

pŏssĭbĭ'lĭty *n.* State, fact, of being possible; thing that may exist or happen; capability of being used, improved, etc.

pŏ'ssĭble *adj.* That can exist, be done, or happen; that may be or become; tolerable to deal with, reasonable, intelligible. **pŏ'ssĭbly** *adv.* In accordance with possibility; perhaps, maybe, for all one knows to the contrary. **pŏ'ssĭble** *n.* Highest possible score, esp. in rifle practice; possible candidate, member of team, etc.

pŏ'ssum *n.* (colloq.) Opossum; *play* ~, feign illness, death, etc.

pŏst[1] *n.* 1. Stout piece of timber usu. cylindrical or square and of considerable length placed vertically as support in building; stake, stout pole, for various purposes; post marking point in a race; winning-post. 2. Vertical mass of coal left as support in mine; thick compact stratum of sandstone etc. ~ *v.t.* Stick (paper etc., usu. *up*) to post or in prominent place; advertise (fact, thing, person) by placard; enter the name of in a public list; publish name of (ship) as overdue or missing; placard (wall etc.) with bills.

pŏst[2] *n.* 1. (hist.) One of series of men stationed with horses along roads at intervals, the duty of each being to ride forward with letters to next stage; (hist.) courier, letter-carrier; mail-cart. 2. Single dispatch of letters, letters so dispatched; letters taken from post office or pillar-box on one occasion; letters delivered at one house on one occasion. 3. Official conveyance of letters, parcels, etc.; post office or postal letter box; *by return of* ~, (hist.) by same courier who brought the dispatch; (now) by next mail in opposite direction. 4. ~-*bag*, mail-bag; ~-*boy*, letter-carrier; postilion of stage-coach etc.; *po'stcard*, card of regulation size for conveyance by post; ~-*chaise* (-sh-), (hist.) travelling carriage hired from stage to stage or drawn by horses so hired; ~-*free*, carried free of charge by post or with postage prepaid; ~-*haste*, with great expedition; ~-*horn*, horn of kind formerly used by postman or guard of mail-coach to announce arrival; ~-*horse*, one of those formerly kept at inns etc. for use of posts or travellers; *po'stman*, one who delivers or collects letters; *po'stmark*, official mark stamped on letters etc., esp. one giving place, date, and hour of dispatch or arrival, and serving to deface stamp; *po'stmark* (*v.t.*); *po'st-*

POSSET POT

master[1], (fem. *po'stmistress*) official in charge of a post office; ~ *office*, room or building in which postal business is carried on; ~-*office box*, numbered box in post office, for receiving letters addressed to particular firm or person; *P*~ *Office*, public corporation responsible for posts etc. in Britain; ~-*paid*, on which postage has been paid. ~ *adv.* (archaic) With post-horses; express, with haste. ~ *v.* 1. (hist.) Travel with relays of horses; travel with haste, hurry. 2. Put (letter etc.) into post office or letter-box for transmission. 3. (book-keeping) Carry (entry) from auxiliary book to more formal one, esp. from day-book or journal to ledger; (also ~ *up*) complete (ledger etc.) thus; (fig.) supply (person) with full information.

pŏst[3] *n.* 1. Place where soldier is stationed, (fig.) place of duty; position taken by body of soldiers, force occupying this; fort; (also *trading-*~) place occupied for purposes of trade esp. in uncivilized country. 2. Situation, employment; (naval, hist.) commission as officer in command of vessel of 20 guns or more; ~ *captain*, holder of such commission. 3. (mil.) *first, last*, ~, bugle-call giving notice of hour of retiring for night (*last* ~ is also blown at military funerals etc.). ~ *v.t.* Direct (soldiers etc.) to go to a specified station etc.; (mil., naval) commission (person) as captain.

pŏst- *prefix.* After, behind.

pŏ'stage *n.* Amount charged for carriage of letters etc. by post, now usu. prepaid by ~ *stamp*, adhesive label to be affixed (or stamp embossed or impressed) on envelope etc., having specified value, or by franking.

pŏ'stal *adj.* Of the POST[2] *n.*; ~ *order*: see ORDER, 14; (*Universal*) *P*~ *Union*, union of governments of various countries for regulation of international postage.

pŏst-clă'ssĭcal *adj.* Occurring later than the classical period of (esp. Greek and Latin) language, literature, or art.

pŏstdā'te *v.t.* Affix, assign, to (document, event, etc.) a date later than the actual one.

pŏstdĭlū'vĭan (*or* -ōō-) *adj.* & *n.* (Person) existing, occurring after the Flood.

pŏst-ĕ'ntrў *n.* Late or subsequent entry (for race, in book-keeping, etc.).

pŏ'ster *n.* 1. (also *bill-*~) One who posts bills. 2. Placard displayed in public place.

pŏste rĕ'stante (-ahnt) *n.* Department in post office in which letters are kept till applied for.

pŏstēr'ĭor *adj.* 1. Later, coming after in series, order, or time 2. Hinder; as viewed from behind. ~ *n.* (sing. or pl.) Buttocks. **pŏstērĭŏ'rĭtў** *n.* **pŏstēr'ĭorlў** *adv.*

pŏstĕ'rĭtў *n.* Descendants; all succeeding generations.

[686]

pŏ'stern n. Back door; side way or entrance.
pōst-ĕxi'lian, -ĕxi'lic (or ĕgz-) adjs. Subsequent to the Babylonian exile of the Jews.
pōst-fi'x v.t. Append (letters) at end of word. **pō'stfĭx** n. Suffix.
pōst-ģlā'cial (or -āshal) adj. (geol.) Occurring or formed after a glacial period. ~ n. Post-glacial period.
pōstgră'dūate adj. (of course of study) Carried on after graduation. ~ n. Student taking post-graduate course.
pŏst hŏc ẽr'gō prŏ'pter hŏc. 'After this, therefore on account of this', used to ridicule the tendency to confuse sequence with consequence. [L]
pō'sthūmous (-tū-) adj. Occurring after death; (of child) born after death of its father; (of book etc.) published after author's death.
pŏ'stil n. (hist.) Marginal note, comment, esp. on text of Scripture; commentary.
pŏsti'lion, -llion (-yon) n. One who rides the near horse of the leaders when four or more are used in a carriage, or near horse when one pair only is used and there is no driver on box.
Pōst-Imprĕ'ssionism n. Comprehensive term for various developments in painting (Neo-Impressionism, Expressionism, Cubism, etc.) which followed IMPRESSIONISM in late 19th and early 20th centuries. **Pōst-Imprĕ'ssionist** n. One of the painters responsible for Post-Impressionism (as Cézanne, Gauguin, Van Gogh, Picasso). **pōst-imprĕssioni'stic** adj.
pŏstli'minȳ n. (Rom. law) Right of banished person to resume civic privileges on return; (international law) restoration to their former state of persons and things taken in war, when they come again into the power of the nation they belonged to.
pō'stlūde n. (mus.) Concluding piece or movement played at end of oratorio.
pō'stmaster[1] (-mah-) n. See POST[2] n.
pō'stmaster[2] (-mah-) n. Scholar of Merton College, Oxford. **pō'stmastership** n.
pŏst merī'dĭem. (abbrev. p.m.) Between noon and midnight. **pōst-meri'dian** adj. [L]
pōst-mŏr'tem adj. After death. ~ n. Examination made after death to determine its cause; analysis of event after its occurrence, esp. of game of bridge.
pōstnā'tal adj. Occurring after birth or childbirth.
pōst-nŭ'ptial (-shal) adj. Subsequent to marriage.
pōst-ŏ'bit adj. Taking effect after death. ~ n. Bond securing to lender a sum to be paid on death of a specified person from whom borrower has expectations.

pōst-ŏr'al adj. Situated behind the mouth.
pōstpō'ne (or pōsp- or posp-) v. Cause to take place at later time than the present or the one arranged. **postpō'nement** n.
pōst'posi'tion (-zi-) n. Particle, etc. (as Engl. -wards) which is placed after the word whose sense it modifies. **pōstpō'sitive** adj.
pōst-prā'ndial adj. (chiefly joc.). Done etc. after dinner.
pō'stscript n. (abbrev. P.S.) Additional paragraph esp. at end of letter after signature.
pō'stūlant n. Candidate esp. for admission into religious order.
pō'stūlate n. Thing claimed or assumed as basis of reasoning, fundamental condition; prerequisite; (geom.) claim to take for granted possibility of simple operation, e.g. of drawing straight line between any two points; simple problem of a self-evident nature (dist. from AXIOM). **pō'stūlāte** v. Demand, require, claim, take for granted; stipulate for; (eccles. law) nominate or elect to ecclesiastical dignity, subject to sanction of superior authority. **pōstūlā'tion** n.
pō'sture n. Carriage, attitude of body or mind; condition, state (of affairs, etc.). ~ v. Dispose the limbs of (person) in particular way; assume posture.
pōst-war' (-wŏr) adj. Of the period after a war, esp. the world war of 1914–18 or that of 1939–45; Post-War Credits, credits arising out of the temporary reduction of certain income tax allowances during 1941–2 and 1945–6.
pō'sy (-zi) n. Bunch of flowers; (archaic) short motto, line of verse, etc., inscribed within ring.
pŏt[1] n. 1. Rounded vessel of earthenware, metal, glass etc., for holding liquids or solids; chamber-pot; ink-pot, flower-pot, tea-pot, coffee-pot, etc.; such vessel for cooking; drinking vessel of pewter etc.; contents of pot; vessel, usu. of silver, as prize in athletic sports, (slang) any prize in these; make the ~ boil, keep the ~ boiling, make a living; go to ~, (colloq.) be ruined or destroyed. 2. Fish-pot, lobster-pot; chimney-pot. 3. Large sum; (racing slang) large sum staked or betted; (also big ~) important person. 4. ~-belly, (person with) protuberant belly; ~-boiler, work of literature etc. done merely to make a living; writer or artist who produces this; ~-bound, (of plant) with roots filling flower-pot and wanting room to expand; ~-boy, po'tman, publican's assistant; ~-cheese, (U.S.) cheese of coagulated milk from which water is separated by heating in a pot; po'therb (-t-h-), herb grown in kitchen garden; ~-hook, hook over fireplace for hanging pot etc. on, or for lifting hot pot (ill. FIRE); curved stroke in handwriting, esp. as made in learning to write; ~-house, ale-house;

~-hunter, sportsman who shoots anything he comes across; person who takes part in contest merely for sake of prize; ~ lead, black-lead esp. as used for hull of racing yacht; ~ luck, whatever is to be had for a meal; ~-metal, stained glass coloured in melting-pot so that the colour pervades the whole; ~ roast, meat cooked slowly in covered dish; ~-shot, shot taken at game merely to provide a meal; shot aimed at animal etc. within easy reach (also fig.); ~-still, kind of still in which heat is applied directly and not by steam-jacket; ~-valiant, valiant because drunk; ~-wall(op)er, householder voter (before 1832).
pŏ'tful n. **pŏt** v. Place (butter, fish, minced meat, etc., usu. salted or seasoned) in pot or other vessel to preserve it; plant (plant) in pot; (billiards) pocket; bag (game), kill (animal) by pot-shot; shoot (at); seize, secure.
pŏt[2] n. (chiefly dial.) Pot-hole.
pŏt[3] n. (slang) Marijuana.
pō'table adj. Drinkable. **pō'tables** (-lz) n.pl. (usu. joc.) Drinkables.
potă'mic adj. Of rivers.
pō'tăsh n. Alkaline substance, crude potassium carbonate; (also caustic ~) potassium hydroxide (KOH), white brittle substance, soluble in water and deliquescent in air, with powerful caustic and alkaline properties. [Du. pot-asschen, because orig. got by lixiviating vegetable ashes and evaporating the solution]
potă'ssium n. (chem.) Light metallic element, one of the alkali metals, which is soft at ordinary temperatures, oxidizes immediately on exposure to air, and instantly decomposes water on contact with it, liberating and igniting hydrogen which burns with a characteristic violet flame; symbol K (f. kalium), at. no. 19, at. wt 39·102. [latinized form of POTASH]
potā'tion n. Drinking; (usu. pl.) tippling; draught. **pōt'atory** adj.
potā'tō n. (pl. -es). 1. Batata or sweet potato. 2. Plant (Solanum tuberosum), native of Pacific slopes of S. America, introduced into Europe late in 16th c., with roundish or oval starch-containing tubers used for food; tuber of this; ~ beetle, COLORADO beetle; ~-ring, (usu. silver) ring used as stand for a bowl in which potatoes were brought to table in Ireland. [Haitian batata]
pōtee'n, -thee'n n. Irish whiskey from illicit still.
Pote'mkin (-tyŏm-), Grigori Aleksandrovich, Prince (1739–91). Russian soldier and statesman, favourite of Catherine the Great.
pō'tent[1] adj. Powerful, mighty (chiefly poet. or rhet.); having sexual power; (of reasons etc.) cogent; (of drugs etc.) strong. **pō'tentlȳ** adv. **pō'tencȳ** n.

[687]

**pō'tent² **adj. (her., of line parting a field) Resembling a series of crutch-heads (ill. HERALDRY); (of cross) having limbs terminating in crutch-heads.

**pō'tentāte **n. Monarch, ruler.

**potē'ntial **(-shal) adj. Capable of coming into being or action, latent; (gram.) expressing potentiality or possibility; ~ *energy*, (phys.) energy existing in potential form, not as motion; ~ *function*, mathematical function by differentiation of which the force at any point in space arising from any system of bodies etc. can be expressed. **potē'ntially **adv. **potē'ntial **n. 1. Potential mood. 2. (Amount of energy or quantity of work denoted by) potential function; possibility, potentiality; resources that can be employed for an undertaking. **potěntiā'litỹ **(-shiăl-) n. Inherent, latent, capacity to exert power; possibility, promise, of development.

**potē'ntialīze **(-sha-) v.t. Make potential; convert (energy) into potential condition.

**potē'ntiāte **(-shī-) v.t. Endow with power; make possible.

**potěntiō'mĕter **(-shī-) n. Instrument for measuring differences of electrical potential.

**potheen **: see POTEEN.

**pŏ'ther **(-dh-) n. Choking smoke or cloud of dust; noise, din; verbal commotion or fuss.

**pŏ't-hōle **n. (geol.) Deep hole of more or less cylindrical shape; esp. one formed by wearing away of rock by rotation of a stone, or gravel, in an eddy of running water, or in glacier bed; depression or hollow in road-surface caused by traffic etc. **pŏ't-hōler, pŏ't-hōling **ns. Explorer, exploring of pot-holes.

**pō'tion **n. Dose, draught, of liquid medicine or of poison.

**Pō'tiphar. **Egyptian officer whose wife tried to seduce Joseph and then falsely accused him of an attempt on her virtue (Gen. 39).

**Potō'măc. **River of U.S. flowing into Chesapeake Bay and forming part of N. boundary of Virginia.

**potpourri **(pō'pōorĭ or -ē') n. Mixture of dried petals and spices kept in jar for its perfume; musical or literary medley. [Fr., lit. rotten pot]

**pŏ'tshĕrd **n. (archaeol.) Broken piece of earthenware.

**pŏtt **n. Size of writing- or printing-paper, usu. 394 × 318 mm (15 × 12½ in.), so called from original watermark of a pot.

**pŏ'ttage **n. (archaic) Soup, stew (esp. with ref. to Gen. 25: 34).

**pŏ'tter¹ **n. Maker of earthenware vessels; ~'s *lathe*, machine rotating the ~'s *wheel*, on which, as it spins rapidly round, the potter moulds the clay. **pŏ'ttery **n. Earthenware (sometimes distinguished from PORCELAIN); potter's work or workshop; *the Potteries*, district in N. Staffordshire, chief centre of English pottery industry.

**pŏ'tter² **v. Work in feeble or desultory manner (*at, in*); dawdle, loiter (*about* etc.); trifle *away* (time, etc.).

**pŏ'ttle **n. (archaic) Measure for liquids, half gallon; pot etc. containing this; small wicker or chip basket for strawberries etc.

**pŏ'ttō **n. Reddish-grey loris (*Perodicticus potto*) a slow-moving arboreal mammal of Africa.

**Pŏtt's frā'cture. **Fracture of lower end of fibula, usu. accompanied by dislocation of ankle (ill. BONE).

**pŏ'ttỹ **adj. (slang). 1. Insignificant, trivial. 2. Foolish, crazy.

**pouch **n. Small bag or detachable outside pocket for carrying e.g. tobacco; soldier's leather ammunition bag; mail-bag; bag-like receptacle in which marsupials carry their undeveloped young; cheek-pouch or other bag-like natural receptacle; (bot.) bag-like cavity in plant, esp. purse-like seed-vessel. ~ *v*. Put into pouch; take possession of, pocket; make (part of dress) hang like pouch, hang thus.

**pouffe **(pōof) n. 1. Low stuffed seat or cushion. 2. Woman's high roll or pad of hair. 3. Part of dress gathered up in bunch.

**poult **(pōlt) n. Young of domestic fowl, turkey, pheasant, etc.

**poult-de-soie **(pōodeswah') n. Fine corded silk. [Fr.]

**pou'lterer **(pōl-) n. Dealer in poultry.

**pou'ltice **(pōl-) n. Paste of bread, linseed, etc., usu. made with boiling water and spread on muslin etc., applied to sore or inflamed part. ~ *v.t.* Apply poultice to.

**pou'ltrỹ **(pōl-) n. Domestic fowls, ducks, geese, turkeys, etc., reared for food.

**pounce¹ **n. Claw, talon, of bird of prey; pouncing, sudden swoop. ~ *v*. Swoop down upon and seize; make sudden attack *on*, seize eagerly *on*.

**pounce² **n. Fine powder, formerly used to prevent ink from spreading on unsized paper etc.; powdered charcoal etc. dusted over perforated pattern to transfer design to object beneath. ~ *v.t.* Smooth (paper etc.) with pumice or pounce; transfer (design) by use of pounce, dust (pattern with pounce).

**pou'ncĕt-bŏx **n. (archaic) Small box with perforated lid for perfumes.

**pound¹ **n. 1. (abbrev. lb.) Measure of weight, 16 oz. avoirdupois, 12 oz. troy. 2. (also ~ *sterling*; written £ before figure) Principal monetary unit of the United Kingdom, = 100 pence. 3. Principal monetary unit of various Commonwealth countries and of Egypt (£E), Israel, Lebanon, Sudan (£S), and Syria. 4. ~-*cake*, rich cake containing 1 lb. (or equal weight) of each of chief ingredients; ~ *note*, bank- or treasury-note for £1. ~ *v.i.* (coining) Test weight of coins by weighing the number that ought to weigh 1 lb.

**pound² **n. Enclosure for detention of stray cattle or of distrained cattle or goods till redeemed; enclosure for animals; (fig.) place of confinement; (hunting) difficult position; ~ *lock*, lock with two gates. ~ *v.t.* Shut (cattle etc.) in pound. **pou'ndĕd **adj. (of rider in hunt) In enclosed place from which he cannot get out to follow the chase.

**pound³ **v. Crush, bruise, as with pestle; thump, pummel, with fists etc.; knock, beat (*to pieces, into a jelly*, etc.); deliver heavy blows, fire heavy shot (*at* etc.); walk, run, ride, make one's way, heavily.

**Pound⁴, **Ezra Loomis (1885–1972). Amer. poet; one of the founders of IMAGISM.

**pou'ndage **n. Commission, fee, of so much per pound sterling; percentage of total earnings of a business, paid as wages; payment of so much per pound weight; charge on postal order etc.

**pou'ndal **n. (phys.) Unit of force which acting on a mass of 1 lb. will impart to it an acceleration of 1 ft per sec. per sec., corresponding to the DYNE except that pound and foot replace gramme and centimetre.

**pou'nder¹ **n. Thing that, gun firing shot that, weighs a pound or specified number of pounds; thing worth, person possessing, specified number of pounds sterling.

**pou'nder² **n. (esp.) Instrument for pounding with or in, pestle, mortar.

**pour **(pōr) v. Cause (liquid, granular substance, light, etc.) to flow, discharge copiously; discharge (missiles etc.) copiously or in rapid succession; send *forth, out* (words, music, etc.); flow (*forth, out, down*) in stream (also fig. of crowd etc.); (of rain) descend heavily; (fig.) come (*in, out*) abundantly. ~ *n*. Heavy fall of rain, downpour; (founding) amount of molten metal etc. poured at a time. **pour'ing **adj.

**pourparler **(poorpărlā) n. (usu. in pl.) Informal discussion preliminary to negotiation. [Fr.]

**pour'point **(poor-), **pŭr'point **n. (hist.) Padded and quilted doublet.

**poussĕ'tte **(pōo-) n. Country-dance figure in which two couples, each with hands joined, dance round one another.

**Poussin **(pōosăṅ), Nicolas (1594–1665). French painter in the classical tradition.

**pout¹ **n. = BIB³.

**pout² **v. Protrude (lips), protrude lips, (of lips) protrude, esp. as sign of displeasure. ~ *n*. Protrusion of the lips.

[688]

pou'ter n. Person, animal, that pouts; (esp.) domestic variety of rock-pigeon with great power of inflating crop.
pŏ'vertў n. Indigence, want; deficiency (*in*, *of*); inferiority, poorness; ~-*stricken*, poor.
P.O.W. *abbrev*. Prisoner of war.
pow'der n. Mass of dry particles or granules, dust; medicine in the form of powder; cosmetic powder applied to face, skin, or hair; gunpowder; ~-*blue*, powdered smalt, esp. for use in laundry; (of) pale blue colour; ~-*flask*, case for carrying gunpowder; ~-*horn*, powder-flask orig. and esp. of horn; ~-*magazine*, place where gunpowder is stored; ~ *metallurgy*, moulding of finely ground (esp. metal) powders into intricate shapes to which solidity is restored afterwards by special treatment; ~-*monkey*, boy formerly employed on board ship to carry powder to guns; ~-*puff*, soft pad for applying powder to skin. ~ *v.t.* Sprinkle powder upon, cover (with powder etc.); apply powder to (hair, face, etc.); decorate (surface) with spots or small figures; reduce to powder. **pow'derў** *adj*.
pow'er n. 1. Ability to do or act; vigour, energy; particular faculty of body or mind. 2. Active property, as *heating* ~. 3. Government, influence, authority (*over*); personal ascendancy (*over*); political ascendancy. 4. Authorization, delegated authority; ~ *of attorney*: see ATTORNEY. 5. Influential person, body, or thing; State having international influence; *the* ~*s that be*, (w. ref. to Rom. 13: 1) constituted authorities. 6. Deity; (pl.) order of angels (see ANGEL). 7. Mechanical energy as opp. to hand-labour (freq. attrib., as ~-*lathe*, ~-*loom*); capacity for exerting mechanical force, esp. horsepower; electrical power distributed to consumer; ~ *factor*, ratio between actual power delivered and apparent power suggested by voltage and current. 8. (math., of a number or algebraic quantity) Product of a specified number of factors, each of which is the number or quantity itself, the specified number of factors being the *index*. 9. Magnifying power of lens. 10. (slang) Large number or amount. 11. ~ *dive*, (of aircraft), dive made without shutting off the motor power; ~ *egg*, engine with its auxiliaries compacted into one removable unit; ~ *politics*, diplomacy backed by (threat of) force; ~ *station*, station in which electric power is generated for distribution. ~ *v.t.* Supply with mechanical power.
pow'erful *adj*. Having great power or influence. **pow'erfullў** *adv*.
pow'erlėss *adj*. Without power; wholly unable (*to* help etc.). **pow'-**

erlėsslў *adv*. **pow'erlėssnėss** *n*.
pow'wow *n*. 1. N. Amer. Indian medicine-man or sorcerer. 2. Magic ceremonial, conference, of N. Amer. Indians. 3. (colloq.) Conference or meeting. ~ *v.i.* Hold powwow; (colloq.) confer.
Pow'ўs (pō-). Inland county of Wales (since April 1974), comprising the former counties of Montgomeryshire and Radnorshire and most of the former county of Breconshire.
pŏx *n*. Syphilis.
pŏzzola'na (-tsolah-) *n*. Volcanic ash found at Pozzuoli, near Naples, much used for hydraulic cement.
pp. *abbrev*. Pages.
pp. *abbrev*. Pianissimo.
p.p. *abbrev*. Past participle; *per procurationem*.
P.P. *abbrev*. Parcel post; Parish Priest.
P.P.C. *abbrev*. (written on cards etc.) *Pour prendre congé* (Fr., = to take leave).
P.P.E. *abbrev*. Philosophy, Politics, and Economics.
ppm *abbrev*. Parts per million.
P.P.S. *abbrev*. Parliamentary Private Secretary; *post postscriptum* (L, = further postscript).
pr *abbrev*. Pair; -pounder.
P.R. *abbrev*. Proportional representation.
P.R.A. *abbrev*. President of the Royal Academy.
praam: see PRAM[1].
prăc'ticable *adj*. That can be done, feasible; that can be used, (of road etc.) that can be traversed; (theatr., of door, window, etc.) real, that can be used as such. **prăcticabi'litў**, **prăc'ticablenėss** *ns*. **prăc'ticablў** *adv*.
prăc'tical *adj*. 1. Of, concerned with, shown in, practice; available, useful, in practice; engaged in practice, practising; ~ *joke*: see JOKE. 2. Inclined to action rather than speculation. 3. That is such in effect though not nominally, virtual. **prăc'ticalnėss, prăcticā'litў** *ns*. **prăc'ticallў** *adv*. In a practical manner; virtually, almost.
prăc'tice *n*. 1. Habitual action or carrying on; method of legal procedure; habit, custom; repeated exercise in an art, handicraft, etc.; spell of this. 2. Professional work, business, or connection, of lawyer or doctor. 3. (archaic) Scheming, (usu. underhand) contrivance, artifice (esp. pl.); *sharp* ~: see SHARP. 4. (arith.) Mode of finding value of given number of articles or quantity of commodity at given price, when quantity or price or both are in several denominations. 5. *in* ~, in the realm of action; actually; lately practised in skill or ability; *put in(to)* ~, carry out.
prăcti'cian (-shan) *n*. Worker, practitioner.
prăc'tīse *v*. Perform habitually, carry out in action; exercise, pur-

sue (profession); exercise oneself in or on (art, instrument, or abs.); exercise (*in* action or subject); (archaic) scheme, contrive; ~ *on*, impose upon, take advantage of. **prăc'tīsed** (-st) *adj*. Experienced, expert.
prăctĭ'tioner *n*. Professional or practical worker, esp. in medicine; *general* ~: see GENERAL.
Pra'dō (prah-). Spanish national museum of painting and sculpture, at Madrid, containing part of the royal collections. [Span., = 'meadow', f. the adjoining park]
praelĕ'ctor *n*. Var. of PRELECTOR.
praemūnīr'ė *n*. (law) Writ charging sheriff to summon person accused (orig.) of prosecuting in a foreign court a suit which is cognizable in England, or (later) of asserting or maintaining papal jurisdiction in England; *Statute of P*~, statute of 16 Richard II, on which writ is based. [L; so called because the words *praemunire facias* warn (so-and-so to appear) occur in the writ]
praepŏ'stor *n*. (public school) Prefect, monitor.
prae'tor *n*. (Rom. hist.; orig.) Consul as leader of army; (later) annually elected magistrate performing some duties of consul. **praetôr'ial** *adj*.
praetôr'ian, prĕtōrian *adj*. Of a praetor; ~ *guard*, bodyguard of a Roman general or emperor. ~ *n*. Man of praetorian rank, soldier of praetorian guard.
prăgmă'tic, -ical *adjs*. 1. Meddlesome; dogmatic. 2. Of philosophical pragmatism. 3. (-*ic*) Treating facts of history with reference to their practical lessons. 4. (-*ic*, hist.) Of the affairs of a State; ~ *sanction*, imperial or royal ordinance issued as fundamental law, esp. that of the Emperor Charles VI in 1724 settling Austrian succession. **prăgmă'ticallў** *adv*. **prăg'matism** *n*. 1. Officiousness; pedantry. 2. Matter-of-fact treatment of things. 3. Philosophical doctrine that estimates any assertion solely by its practical bearing upon human interests. **prăg'matist** *n*.
prăg'matīze *v.t.* Represent as real; rationalize (a myth).
Prague (-ahg). (Czech *Praha*) Capital city of Czechoslovakia.
prair'ie *n*. Large treeless tract of level or undulating grassland, esp. in N. America; ~ *chicken, hen*, N. Amer. grouse of genus *Tympanuchus*; ~-*dog*, N. Amer. burrowing rodent (*Cynomis*) of squirrel family; ~ *oyster*, raw egg seasoned and swallowed in spirits; ~ *schooner*, large covered wagon of kind used by emigrants in crossing N. Amer. plains.
praise (-z) *v.t.* Express warm approbation of, commend the merits of; glorify, extol the attributes of. ~ *n*. Praising, commendation.

[689]

prai′seworthy (-zwērdhĭ) *adj.* Worthy of praise, commendable. **prai′seworthily** *adv.* **prai′seworthiness** *n.*

Pra′krĭt (prah-) *n.* Any of the vernacular Indo-European dialects of India, as dist. from Sanskrit; all these collectively.

pra′line (-ahlēn) *n.* Sweet made by browning nuts in boiling sugar.

pram[1], **praam** (prahm) *n.* Flat-bottomed boat used in Baltic etc. for shipping cargo etc.; flat-bottomed boat mounted with guns; Scandinavian ship's boat corresp. to dinghy.

prăm[2] *n.* (colloq.) Perambulator; milkman's hand cart.

prance (-ah-) *v.* (of horse) Rise by springing from hind legs; cause (horse) to do this; (fig.) walk, behave, in elated or arrogant manner. ~ *n.* Prancing (movement).

prā′ndial *adj.* (joc.) Of dinner.

prăng *v.t.* 1. (R.A.F. slang) Bomb (target) hard from air; crash (aircraft). 2. (slang) Dent, damage by impact. ~ *n.*

prănk[1] *n.* Mad frolic, practical joke. **prā′nkful, prā′nkish** *adjs.*

prănk[2] *v.* Dress, deck (*out*); adorn, spangle (*with*); show oneself off.

prāseōdў′mium (-z-) *n.* (chem.) Metallic element of rare-earth group forming leek-green salts; symbol Pr, at. no. 59, at. wt 140·9077. [Gk *prasios* leek-green, (DI)DYMIUM].

prāte *v.* Chatter; discourse foolishly; talk solemn nonsense. **prā′ter** *n.*

prā′tique (-k; *or* pratē′k) *n.* Licence to hold intercourse with a port, granted to a ship after quarantine or on showing clean bill of health.

prā′ttle *v.* Talk or say in childish or artless fashion. **prā′ttler** *n.* **prā′ttle** *n.* Childish chatter, small talk.

prawn *n.* Small lobster-like marine decapod crustacean of genus *Palaemon, Penaeus*, etc., larger than shrimp. ~ *v.i.* Fish for prawns.

prā′xis *n.* Accepted practice, custom; (gram.) set of examples for practice.

Prăxi′tĕlēs (-z) (4th c. B.C.). Greek sculptor, creator of 'Apollo Slaying a Lizard' and 'Hermes with the Infant Dionysus'.

pray *v.* Make devout supplication to (God, object of worship); beseech earnestly (*for, to, that*); ask earnestly for; engage in prayer, make entreaty; ~ (contr. of *I pray you*), used parenthetically for emphasis, e.g. *what, ~, is the use of that?*

prayer (prār) *n.* Solemn request to God or object of worship; formula used in praying; form of divine service consisting largely of prayers; action, practice, of praying; entreaty to a person; thing prayed for; ~-*book*, book of forms of prayer, esp. *Book of Common P~*: see COMMON; ~-*meeting*, religious meeting at which several persons offer prayer; ~-*wheel*, revolving cylindrical box inscribed with or containing prayers, used esp. by Buddhists of Tibet. **prayer′ful** *adj.* **prayer′fully** *adv.* **prayer′fulness** *n.*

P.R.B. *abbrev.* Pre-Raphaelite Brotherhood.

pre- *prefix.* Before.

preach *v.* Deliver sermon or religious address, deliver (sermon); give moral advice in obtrusive way; proclaim, expound (the Gospel, Christ, etc.) in public discourses; advocate, inculcate (quality, conduct, etc.) thus. **prea′cher** *n.* **prea′chment** *n.* (usu. contempt.)

prea′chify *v.i.* Preach, moralize, hold forth, tediously.

prea′chy *adj.* (colloq.) Fond of preaching or holding forth.

Prē-ă′damīte *adj.* & *n.* (One of supposed race) existing before time of Adam. **pre-adā′mic** *adj.*

prēă′mble *n.* Preliminary statement in speech or writing; introductory part of statute, deed, etc. ~ *v.i.* Make preamble.

prē-arrā′nge (-j) *v.t.* Arrange beforehand. **prē-arrā′ngement** *n.*

Preb. *abbrev.* Prebendary.

prĕ′bend *n.* (chiefly hist.) Cathedral benefice, usu. revenue from one manor of the cathedral estates. **prĕ′bendal** (*or* pribĕ′-) *adj.*

prĕ′bendary *n.* Holder of prebend (chiefly hist.); (in Church of England) member of a chapter of certain cathedrals (since 19th c. usu. *canon*).

Prē-Că′mbrian *adj.* & *n.* (geol.) (Of) the earliest period or system, occurring before the Cambrian (ill. GEOLOGY).

prĕcār′ious *adj.* Held during the pleasure of another; question-begging; doubtful, uncertain; dependent on chance; perilous. **prĕcār′iously** *adv.* **prĕcār′iousness** *n.*

prē-ca′st (-ah-) *adj.* (of concrete) Cast in blocks before use in construction.

prĕ′catory *adj.* Of, expressing, entreaty; ~ *words*, (in will) words requesting that a thing be done; ~ *trust*, precatory words that are held to be binding.

prĕcau′tion *n.* Prudent foresight; measure taken beforehand to ward off evil or ensure good result. **prĕcau′tionary** *adj.*

prĕcē′de *v.* Go before in rank or importance; come before in order; walk or proceed in advance of; come before in time; cause to be preceded *by*.

prĕ′cēdence (*or* prĭsē′-) *n.* Priority in time or succession; superiority, higher position; (usu. prĭsē′-) right of preceding others in ceremonies and social formalities.

prĕ′cēdent *n.* Previous case taken as example for subsequent cases or as justification; (law) decision, procedure, etc., serving as rule or pattern. **prĕ′cēdĕnted** *adj.* Having a precedent; supported by precedent.

prĕcē′ntor *n.* (in some Presbyterian churches etc.) One who leads singing of congregation (fem. *prĕcē′ntrix*); (in English cathedrals) member of clergy in general control of musical arrangements, in old foundations ranking next to dean and having succentor as his deputy, and in new foundations being a minor canon. **prĕcē′ntorship** *n.*

prĕ′cĕpt *n.* Command, maxim; moral instruction; writ, warrant. **prĕcĕp′tive** *adj.*

prĕcĕp′tor *n.* (fem. *prĕcĕp′trĕss*) Teacher, instructor. **prĕcĕp-tōr′ial** *adj.*

prĕcĕp′tory *n.* (hist.) Subordinate community of Knights Templars; estate, buildings, of this.

prĕcĕ′ss *v.i.* (of rapidly revolving globe, spinning top, etc.) Sway in such a way that its axis describes a circle.

prĕcĕ′ssion *n.* ~ *of the equinoxes*, earlier occurrence of the equinoxes in each successive sidereal year through a slow change in the direction of the earth's axis, which moves (like the axis of a spinning top) so that the pole of the equator describes an approximate circle round the pole of the ecliptic once in about 25,800 years.

prē-Chrĭ′stian (-kr-) *adj.* Before Christ, before Christianity.

prē′cinct *n.* 1. Space enclosed by walls or other boundaries of a place or building, esp. of place of worship; boundary; (pl.) environs. 2. (town planning) Area from which main-road (or all) traffic is excluded. 3. Subdivision of county or city or ward for election and police purposes.

prĕciō′sity (-ĕsh-) *n.* Affectation of refinement or distinction.

prĕ′cious (-shus) *adj.* 1. Of great price, costly; of great non-material worth; ~ *metals*, gold, silver, (sometimes) platinum; ~ *stone*, stone of great value, used in jewellery. 2. Affectedly refined in language, workmanship, etc. 3. (colloq., as intensive) Out-and-out (*made a ~ mess of it*). 4. Beloved; (abs. as *n.*) beloved person. ~ *adv.* (colloq.) Extremely, very. **prĕ′ciously** *adv.* **prĕ′ciousness** *n.*

prĕ′cipice *n.* Vertical or steep face of rock, cliff, mountain, etc.

prĕcĭ′pĭtāte[1] *v.t.* 1. Throw down headlong, hurl, fling; hurry, urge on; hasten the occurrence of. 2. (chem.) Cause (a solid substance) to be deposited from a solution by the addition of another solution; condense (vapour) into drops and so deposit. **prĕcĭpĭtā′tion** *n.* (esp., meteor.) Fall of rain, sleet, snow, or hail.

[690]

prĕcī'pĭtāte (*or* -at) *n.* (chem.) Substance precipitated from solution; moisture condensed from vapour by cooling and deposited.
prĕcī'pĭtate[2] *adj.* Headlong, violently hurried; hasty, rash, inconsiderate. **prĕcī'pĭtatelў** *adv.* **prĕcī'pĭtatenĕss, prĕcī'pĭtance, prĕcī'pĭtancў** *ns.*
prĕcī'pĭtous *adj.* Of, like, a precipice; steep. **prĕcī'pĭtouslў** *adv.* **prĕcī'pĭtousnĕss** *n.*
prĕcīs (-ā'sē) *n.* Summary, abstract.
prĕcī'se *adj.* Accurately expressed, definite, exact; punctilious, scrupulous in observance of rules etc. **prĕcī'selў** *adv.* In precise manner; (in emphatic or formal assent) quite so. **prĕcī'senĕss** *n.*
prĕcī'sian (-zhan) *n.* One who is rigidly precise or punctilious, esp. in religious observance. **prĕcī'sianism** *n.*
prĕcī'sion *n.* Accuracy; (attrib., of apparatus) designed for exact or precise work.
prē-clă'ssical *adj.* Before the classical age (usu. of Greek and Roman literature or civilization).
prēclu'de (-ōōd) *v.t.* Exclude, prevent, make impracticable. **prēclu'sĭve** (-lōō-) *adj.*
prēcō'cious (-shus) *adj.* (of plant) Flowering or fruiting early; (of person) prematurely developed in some faculty; (of actions etc.) indicating such development. **prēcō'ciouslў** *adv.* **prēcō'ciousnĕss, prēcō'cĭtў** *ns.*
prēcŏgnī'tion *n.* 1. Antecedent knowledge. 2. (Sc. law) Preliminary examination of witnesses etc., esp. in order to know whether there is ground for trial. **prēcŏ'gnĭtĭve** *adj.*
prē-Cŏlŭ'mbian *adj.* Before the discovery of America by Columbus.
prēconcei've *v.t.* Conceive beforehand, anticipate in thought. **prēconcĕ'ption** *n.* (esp.) Prejudice.
prē-condī'tion *n.* Prior condition, one that must be fulfilled beforehand.
prē'conize *v.t.* Proclaim publicly; summon by name; (of pope) approve publicly the appointment of (bishop). **prēconiză'tion** *n.*
prē-Cŏ'nquĕst *adj.* Before the Norman Conquest.
prē-cŏ'nscious (-shus) *adj.* Antecedent to consciousness; (psychol.) of the foreconscious. ~ *n.* Foreconscious.
prēcŭ'rsor *n.* Forerunner, harbinger; one who precedes in office etc. **prēcŭ'rsorў** *adj.* Preliminary, introductory, serving as harbinger (*of*). **prēcŭ'rsĭve** *adj.*
prēdā'cious (-shus) *adj.* (of animals) Predatory. **prēdă'cĭtў** *n.*
prē'dator *n.* Animal that preys upon others.
prē'datorў *adj.* Of, addicted to, plunder or robbery; (of animals) preying upon others.

prēdĕcea'se *v.t.* Die before (another). ~ *n.* Death before another's.
prē'dĕcĕssor *n.* Former holder of any office or position; thing to which another thing has succeeded; forefather.
prĕdĕ'lla *n.* (Painting on vertical face of) altar-step; (painting, sculpture, on) raised shelf at back of altar (ill. ALTAR); small painting(s) done as pendant to altarpiece. [It., = 'stool']
prēdĕstinār'ian *adj. & n.* (Holder of the doctrine) of predestination.
prēdĕ'stĭnāte *v.t.* (of God) Foreordain (person) to salvation or *to* (any fate), *to* (do); determine beforehand. **prēdĕ'stĭnate** *adj.*
prēdĕstĭnā'tion *n.* God's appointment from eternity of some of mankind to salvation and eternal life; God's foreordaining of all that comes to pass; fate, destiny.
prēdĕ'stine *v.t.* Determine beforehand; appoint as if by fate; (theol.) predestinate.
prēdĕtĕr'mine *v.t.* Decree beforehand; predestine; (of motive, etc.) impel (person) beforehand. **prēdĕtĕr'minate** *adj.* **prēdĕtĕrminā'tion** *n.*
prē'dial *adj.* Of land or farms; rural, agrarian; attached to, tenanting, farms or the land.
prĕ'dicable *adj.* That may be predicated or affirmed. **prĕdicabĭ'lĭtў** *n.* **prĕ'dicable** *n.* Predicable thing, esp. (pl.) Aristotle's classes of predicates viewed relatively to their subjects (viz. genus, definition, property, accident).
prĕdĭ'cament *n.* 1. Thing predicated, esp. (pl.) ten categories of predications formed by Aristotle. 2. Unpleasant, trying, or dangerous situation.
prĕ'dĭcant *adj.* (of religious order, esp. Dominicans) Engaged in preaching.
prĕ'dĭcate *n.* (logic) What is predicated; what is affirmed or denied of the subject by means of the copula (e.g. *a fool* in *he is a fool*); (gram.) what is said of the subject, including the copula (e.g. *is a fool* in preceding example); quality, attribute. **prĕ'dĭcate** *v.t.* Assert, affirm, as true or existent; (logic) assert (thing) about subject. **prĕdĭcā'tion** *n.*
prĕdĭ'cative *adj.* Making a predication; (gram., of adj. or n., opp. *attributive*) forming part or the whole of the predicate. **prĕdĭ'catively** *adv.*
prĕdĭ'ct *v.t.* Forecast, prophesy. **prĕdĭ'ctable, prĕdĭ'ctive** *adjs.* **prĕdĭ'ction** *n.* **prĕdĭ'ctor** *n.* (esp.) Instrument for determining range etc. of aircraft to be engaged in anti-aircraft fire.
prē-dĭgĕ'st *v.t.* Render (food) easily digestible before introduction into stomach. **prē-dĭgĕ'stion** (-schon) *n.*
prĕdĭka'nt (-ahnt) *n.* Minister of Dutch Protestant Church, esp. in S. Africa.
prēdĭlĕ'ction *n.* Special liking, partiality, (*for*).
prēdispō'se (-z) *v.t.* Render liable, subject, or inclined (*to*). **prēdisposĭ'tion** (-z-) *n.* State of mind or body favourable *to.*
prēdŏ'mĭnāte *v.i.* Have or exert control (*over*); be superior; be the stronger or main element, preponderate. **prēdŏ'minance** *n.* **prēdŏ'minant** *adj.* **prēdŏ'mĭnantlў** *adv.*
prēdȳnă'stic *adj.* Of the period before the first dynasty, esp. in Egypt.
prē-ē'minent *adj.* Excelling others; distinguished beyond others in some quality. **prē-ē'minentlў** *adv.* **prē-ē'minence** *n.*
prē-ē'mpt *v.t.* Obtain by preemption; (U.S.) occupy (public land) so as to have right of preemption; (fig.) appropriate beforehand.
prē-ē'mption *n.* Purchase by one person etc. before opportunity is offered to others; right of actual occupant to purchase public land thus at nominal price, on condition of his improving it. **prē-ē'mptive** *adj.* (esp., in bridge, of bid) Higher than necessary, so as to prevent opponents from exchanging information by bidding.
preen *v.t.* (of bird) Trim (feathers) with beak and oil secreted by gland; trim *oneself*, smooth and adorn *oneself* (also fig., show satisfaction).
pref. *abbrev.* Preference; preferred; prefix.
Pref. *abbrev.* Preface.
prē'făb (*or* -ă'b) *n.* (colloq.) Prefabricated building.
prēfă'bricāte *v.t.* Make (building etc.) in sections for assembly on a site. **prēfăbricā'tion** *n.*
prē'face *n.* Introduction to book stating subject, scope, etc.; preliminary part of a speech; introduction to central part of Eucharistic service. ~ *v.* Furnish (book etc.) with preface, introduce (*with*); lead up to (event etc.); make preliminary remarks. **prēfator'ial, prē'fatorў** *adv.*
prē'fĕct *n.* 1. (Rom. hist.) Any of various civil and military officers e.g. civil governor of province, colony, etc. 2. Chief administrative officer of French department; ~ *of Police*, head of police administration of Paris and the department of the Seine. 3. (in some schools) Senior pupil authorized to maintain discipline. **prēfĕ'ctoral, prēfĕctōr'ial** *adjs.*
prē'fĕcture *n.* (Period of) office, official residence, district under government, of a prefect. **prēfĕ'ctural** (-cher-) *adj.*
prēfĕr' *v.t.* 1. Promote (person *to* office). 2. Bring forward, submit (statement, information, etc., *to* person in authority etc. *against* offender etc.). 3. Choose rather,

like better; *preferred stock*, PRE-FERENCE stock. **prē'ferable** *adj*. **prē'ferably** *adv*.

prē'ference *n*. Liking of one thing better than another; thing one prefers; prior right esp. to payment of debts; favouring of one person or country before others in business relations, esp. favouring of country by admitting its products at lower import duty; ~ *stock, share*, one on which dividend is paid before any is paid on ordinary stock.

preferē'ntial (-shal) *adj*. Of, giving, favouring, preference; (of duties etc.) favouring particular countries. **preferē'ntially** *adv*.

prefēr'ment *n*. Advancement, promotion; appointment, esp. ecclesiastical, giving social or pecuniary advancement.

prefi'gure (-ger) *v.t.* Represent beforehand by figure or type; picture to oneself beforehand. **prefigurā'tion, prefi'gurement** *ns.* **prefi'gurative** *adj*.

prē'fix *n*. Verbal element placed at beginning of word to qualify meaning or (in some languages) as inflexional formative; combining form; word (esp. preposition or adverb) used in combination; title placed before name. **prēfi'x** (*or* prē'-) *v.t.* Add (*to* book etc.) as introduction; join as prefix (*to* word).

prēfōr'm *v.t.* Form beforehand. **prēfōrmā'tion** *n*. Previous formation.

prēfōr'mative *adj*. Forming beforehand; prefixed as formative element, esp. in Semitic languages. ~ *n*. Preformative letter or syllable.

prē'gnable *adj*. Capable of being captured.

prē'gnant *adj*. 1. (of woman or female animal) With child(ren) or young in the womb. 2. Teeming with ideas, imaginative, inventive; fruitful in results; (of words or acts) having a hidden meaning, significant, suggestive; ~ *construction*, (gram.) one in which more is implied than the words express. **prē'gnantly** *adv*. **prē'gnancy** *n*.

prēhē'nsile *adj*. (zool., of tail or limb) Capable of grasping.

prēhē'nsion *n*. Grasping, seizing; mental apprehension.

prēhistō'ric *adj*. Of the period antecedent to history. **prēhistō'rically** *adv*.

prēhi'story *n*. Prehistoric matters or times. **prēhistōr'ian** *n*.

prē-igni'tion *n*. Too-early ignition in internal combustion engine.

prējū'dge *v.t.* Pass judgement on before trial or proper inquiry; form premature judgement upon. **prējū'dgement, prējudicā'tion** (-jōō-) *ns*.

prē'judice (-jōō-) *n*. Preconceived opinion, bias; injury that results or may result from some action or judgement; *without* ~, without detriment to existing right or claim. ~ *v.t.* Impair the validity of (right, claim, etc.); cause (person) to have a prejudice (*against, in favour of*).

prējudi'cial (-jōōdi'shal) *adj*. Causing prejudice, detrimental (*to*). **prējudi'cially** *adv*.

prē'lacy *n*. Office, rank, see, of a prelate; prelates collectively; church, government by prelates.

prē'late *n*. High ecclesiastical dignitary, e.g. (arch)bishop, metropolitan, patriarch; (hist.) abbot or prior. **prēlā'tic, -ical** *adjs*. **prēlā'tically** *adv*.

prē'lature *n*. Prelacy.

prēlē'ct *v.i.* Discourse, lecture (esp. in university). **prēlē'ction, prēlē'ctor** *ns*.

prēli'minary *adj*. Introductory, preparatory. ~ *n*. Preliminary arrangement.

prē'lūde *n*. Performance, action, event, condition, serving as introduction (*to* another); (mus.) introductory movement or piece of music, esp. one preceding fugue or forming first part of suite; short piece of music of similar type and on one theme. ~ *v*. Serve as prelude to, introduce, foreshadow; introduce with a prelude; be, give, a prelude *to*; (mus.) play a prelude. **prēlū'sion** *n*. **prēlū'sive** *adj*.

prēmatūr'e (*or* prē'-) *adj*. Occurring, done, before the usual or proper time, too early, hasty; ~ *baby*, baby born before expected date or weighing under 2,500 g (5½ lb.). **prēmatūr'ely** *adv*. **prēmatūr'eness, prēmatūr'ity** *ns*.

prēmaxi'lla *n*. Bone forming front of upper jaw in vertebrates, bearing the incisors. **prēmaxi'llary** *adj*.

prēmēdicā'tion *n*. Administration of sedative or hypnotic drug to patient before giving general anaesthetic.

prēmē'ditāte *v.t.* Think out, design, beforehand. **prēmē'ditātedly** *adv*. **prēmēditā'tion** *n*.

prē'mier (*or, esp.* U.S., prē-) *adj.* (now chiefly slang and journalese) First in position, importance, order, or time. ~ *n*. Prime minister. **prē'miership** *n*.

première (prē'myār) *n*. First performance of play etc.

prē'mise, prē'miss *n*. 1. (logic, freq. *premiss*) Previous statement from which another is inferred; *major* and *minor* ~, two propositions from which the conclusion is derived in a SYLLOGISM. 2. (pl.) Aforesaid, foregoing, esp. (law) aforesaid houses, lands, or tenements. 3. (pl.) House, building, with grounds and appurtenances. **prēmi'se** (-z) *v.t.* Say, write, by way of introduction.

prē'mium *n*. 1. Reward, prize (now chiefly in *put a* ~ *on*, provide or act as incentive to). 2. Amount to be paid in consideration of contract of insurance. 3. Sum additional to interest, wages, etc., a bonus; fee for instruction in profession etc.; charge for changing one currency into another of greater value; *at a* ~, at more than nominal value; (fig.) in high esteem. 4. *P*~ (*Savings*) *Bond*, government bond not bearing interest, but with periodical chance of cash prize.

prēmō'lar *adj. & n*. (Tooth) developed between canines and molars, (in man) bicuspid (ill. TOOTH).

prēmoni'tion *n*. Forewarning; presentiment. **prēmō'nitor** *n*. **prēmō'nitorý** *adj*.

Prēmōnstrātē'nsian (-shan) *adj. & n*. (Member) of R.C. order of regular canons founded (12th c.) by St. Norbert at Prémontré, France.

prē-nā'tal *adj*. Existing, occurring, before birth or childbirth.

prē'ntice *n. & v.t.* Apprentice (archaic; now chiefly in ~ *hand*, inexpert hand).

prēoccupā'tion *n*. Prepossession, prejudice; occupation of a place beforehand; occupation, business, that takes precedence of all others; mental absorption.

preò'ccupý *v.t.* Engage beforehand, engross (mind etc.); appropriate beforehand. **preò'ccupied** (-id) *adj*. Distrait, with thoughts elsewhere.

prē-ōrdai'n *v.t.* Appoint beforehand; foreordain.

prēp *adj*. Preparatory (as ~ *school*). ~ *n*. (colloq.) (Period of) school preparation, homework.

prep. *abbrev*. Preposition.

prē-pă'ck, -pă'ckage *vbs. t*. Pack (goods) ready for sale before distributing them.

prēparā'tion *n*. 1. Preparing; (usu. pl.) thing(s) done to make ready (*for*); (abbrev. *prep*) preparation of lessons by pupils as part of school routine; (mus.) preparing of a discord. 2. Substance, e.g. food or medicine, specially prepared.

prēpă'rative *adj. & n*. Preparatory (act.). **prēpă'ratively** *adv*.

prēpă'ratorý *adj*. Serving to prepare, introductory (*to*); ~ *school*, school where pupils are prepared for higher, esp. public, school. **prēpă'ratorily** *adv*.

prēpār'e *v*. Make ready (*for*); make (food, meal) ready for eating; make mentally ready or fit (*for* news, *to* hear, etc.); get (lesson, speech, etc.) ready by previous study, get (person) ready by teaching (*for* college, examination, etc.); make preparations (*for, to* do, etc.); make (chemical product etc.) by regular process; (mus.) lead up to (discord) by sounding the dissonant note in it as consonant note in preceding chord; *be prepared*, be ready or willing (*to* do).

prēpaý' *v.t.* (past t. & past part. *-paid*) Pay (charge) beforehand; pay (postage), pay postage of (parcel etc.) beforehand, e.g. by affixing stamp. **prēpaý'ment** *n*.

[692]

prepĕ′nse adj. Deliberate, intentional (chiefly in malice ~, intention to injure).

prepŏ′nderāte v.i. Weigh more, be heavier; be of greater moral or intellectual weight; be the chief element, predominate; ~ over, exceed in number, quantity, etc. **prĕpŏ′nderance** n. **prĕpŏ′nderant** adj. **prĕpŏ′nderantlў** adv.

prĕposi′tion (-z-) n. Indeclinable word serving to mark relation between the noun or pronoun it governs and another word (e.g. the italic words in: found him at home, wait in the hall, what did you do it for?, the bed that he slept in, won by waiting, came through the roof, that is what I was thinking of). **prĕposi′tional** adj. **prĕposi′tionallў** adv.

prĕpossĕ′ss (-zĕs) v.t. Imbue, inspire (with); (of idea etc.) take possession of (person); prejudice, usu. favourably. **prĕpossĕ′ssing** adj. (esp.) Making a favourable impression. **prĕpossĕ′ssinglў** adv. **prĕpossĕ′ssingnĕss, prĕposse′ssion** ns.

prĕpŏ′sterous adj. Contrary to nature, reason, or common sense; perverse, foolish; absurd. **prĕpŏ′sterouslў** adv. **prĕpŏ′sterousnĕss** n.

prĕpō′tent adj. Very powerful; more powerful than others. **prĕpō′tence, prĕpō′tencў** ns.

prē′pūce n. Loose integument covering end of penis (ill. PELVIS). **prĕpū′tial** (-shal) adj.

Prē-Rǎ′phaelite (or -fel-) adj. & n. (Member, follower) of the ~ Brotherhood, a group of young English artists and men of letters including Holman Hunt, Millais, D. G. and W. M. Rossetti, formed c 1848 to resist existing conventions in art and literature by a return to standards which they supposed to have existed in European art before the time of Raphael. **Prē-Rǎ′phaelism, -itism** ns.

prē-rēlea′se adj. & n. (Film) exhibited before date fixed for release.

prĕrĕ′quisite (-z-) adj. & n. (Thing) required as previous condition.

prĕrŏ′gative n. 1. royal ~, right of the sovereign, theoretically subject to no restriction. 2. Peculiar right or privilege; natural, or divinely given advantage, privilege, faculty. 3. ~ court (hist.) archbishop's court for probate of wills etc. ~ adj. Privileged, enjoyed by privilege; (Rom. hist.) having the right to vote first.

Pres. abbrev. President.

prē′sage n. Omen, portent; presentiment, foreboding. **prĕsā′geful** (-jf-) adj. **prē′sage** (or prīsā′j) v.t. Portend, foreshadow; give warning of (event etc.) by natural means; (of person) predict; have presentiment of.

prĕsbўō′pia (or -z-) n. Form of long-sightedness incident to old age, caused by loss of power of accommodation. **prĕsbўō′pic** adj.

prē′sbўter (-z-) n. (in early Christian Church) One of several officers managing affairs of local church; (in Episcopal Church) minister of second order, priest; (in Presbyterian Church) elder. **prĕsbў′teral, prĕsbўtēr′ial** adjs. **prĕsbў′terate, prē′sbўtership** ns.

Prĕsbўtēr′ian (-z-) adj. Of the ~ Church, Church recognizing no higher office than that of presbyter or elder and holding doctrines that are Protestant with a strong element of Calvinism; the national Church of Scotland; ~ Church in England: see UNITED Reformed Church. ~ n. Member of the Presbyterian Church. **Prĕsbўtēr′ianism** n.

prē′sbўterў (-z-) n. 1. Eastern part of chancel beyond choir, sanctuary (ill. CHURCH). 2. Body of presbyters, esp. court above kirk session; district represented by this. 3. (R.C. Ch.). Priest's house.

prē′scient (-shĭ-) adj. Having foreknowledge or foresight. **prē′scientlў** adv. **prē′science** n.

prĕsci′nd v. Cut off (part from whole), esp. prematurely or abruptly; ~ from, leave out of consideration.

Prē′scott, William Hickling (1796-1859). American historian, author of 'The History and Conquest of Mexico' and 'The History and Conquest of Peru'.

prĕscrī′be v. 1. Lay down or impose authoritatively; (med.) advise use of (medicine etc.). 2. Assert prescriptive right or claim (to, for).

prē′script n. Ordinance, law, command.

prĕscri′ption n. 1. Prescribing; physician's (usu. written) direction for composition and use of medicine. 2. (law, also positive ~) Uninterrupted use or possession from time immemorial, or for period fixed by law as giving title or right; such title or right; negative ~, limitation of the time within which action or claim can be raised; (fig.) ancient custom viewed as authoritative, claim founded on long use.

prĕscri′ptive adj. Prescribing; based on prescription, as ~ right (see PRESCRIPTION, 2); prescribed by custom. **prĕscri′ptivelў** adv.

prē′sence (-z-) n. 1. Being present; place where person is; the ~, ceremonial attendance on person of high esp. royal rank; ~-chamber, one in which great personage receives guests etc. 2. Carriage, bearing. 3. ~ of mind, calmness and self-command in sudden emergencies.

prē′sent[1] (-z-) adj. 1. Being in the place in question (chiefly pred.); being dealt with, discussed, etc. 2. (archaic) Ready at hand; ready with assistance. 3. Existing, occurring, being such, now; (gram., of tense) denoting action etc. now going on. ~ n. Present time; present tense; at ~, now; for the ~, just now, as far as the present is concerned; by these ~s, by this document (now legal or joc.).

prē′sent[2] (-z-) n. Gift.

prĕsĕ′nt[3] (-z-) v. 1. Introduce (to); introduce (person) to sovereign at court; (of theatr. manager) cause (actor) to take part in play, produce (play); recommend (clergyman) to bishop for institution (to benefice); ~ oneself, appear esp. as candidate for examination etc. 2. Exhibit (to); show (quality etc.); (of idea etc.) offer, suggest itself; (physiol., of part of unborn child) be foremost at outlet of womb; (law) bring formally under notice, submit (complaint, offence, to authority); (mil. etc.) aim (weapon at), hold out (weapon) in position for aiming; hold (firearm) in position for taking aim; (also ~ arms) hold firearm etc. in deferential position in saluting. 3. Offer, give, as present; offer (compliments, regards, to); deliver (bill, etc.) for acceptance etc.; ~ (person) with (thing), present it to him. ~ n. Act of aiming weapon, esp. firearm; position of weapon when aimed; position of 'present arms' in salute.

prĕsĕ′ntable (-z-) adj. Of decent appearance, fit to be introduced or go into company; suitable for presentation as a gift etc. **prĕsĕntabi′litў** n. **prĕsĕ′ntablў** adv.

prĕsĕntā′tion (-z-) n. 1. Presenting, esp. formal; gift, present; exhibition, theatrical representation, etc.; formal introduction, esp. at court. 2. (metaphys.) All the modification of consciousness directly involved in the knowing or being aware of an object in a single moment of thought. **prĕsĕntā′tional** adj.

prĕsĕntā′tionism (-z-) n. (metaphys.) Doctrine that in perception the mind has immediate cognition of the object.

prĕsĕ′ntative (-z-) adj. (of benefice) To which patron has right of presentation; serving to present an idea to the mind; (metaphys.) of (the nature of) presentation.

prĕsĕntee′ (-z-) n. Clergyman presented to benefice; person recommended for office; person presented at court; recipient of present.

prĕsĕ′ntient (-shĭ-) adj. Having a presentiment (of).

prĕsĕ′ntiment (-z-) n. Vague expectation, foreboding.

prĕsĕ′ntive (-z-) adj. (of word) Presenting an object or conception directly to the mind (opp. SYMBOLIC).

prē′sentlў (-z-) adv. Soon; (U.S.) at present.

prĕsĕ'ntment (-z-) *n.* 1. Theatrical representation. 2. Delineation, portrait. 3. Statement, description (*of*); act, mode, of presenting to the mind. 4. (law) Statement on oath by jury of fact within their knowledge. 5. (eccles.) Formal complaint of offence made by parish authorities to bishop or archdeacon at his visitation.

prĕservā'tion (-z-) *n.* Preserving, being preserved, or keeping from injury or destruction; state of being well or ill preserved.

prĕsĕr'vative (-z-) *adj.* & *n.* (Drug, measure, etc.) tending to preserve; (substance, esp. chemical) for preserving perishable foodstuffs etc.

prĕsĕr've (-z-) *v.t.* Keep safe (*from* harm etc.); keep alive; maintain (state of things); retain (quality, condition); prepare (fruit, meat, etc.) by boiling with sugar, pickling, etc., to prevent decomposition or fermentation; keep from decomposition, by chemical treatment etc.; keep (game, river, etc.) undisturbed for private use; *well-preserved*, (of elderly person) showing little sign of age. ~ *n.* 1. (also pl.) Preserved fruit; jam. 2. Ground set apart for protection of game (freq. fig.); piece of water for fish. **prĕsĕr'ver** *n.*

prĕsī'de (-z-) *v.i.* Occupy chair of authority at meeting of society or company; sit at head of table; exercise control, sit or reign supreme; *presiding officer*, person in charge of polling-station at election.

prĕ'sidency (-z-) *n.* Office of president; period of this; district administered by president.

prĕ'sident (-z-) *n.* Head of temporary or permanent body of persons, presiding over their meetings and proceedings; head of some colleges; person presiding over meetings of academy, literary or scientific society, etc.; (U.S.) person presiding over proceedings of bank or company; head of advisory council, board, etc.; elected head of government in U.S. and other modern republics; (hist.) governor of province, colony, etc.; *Lord P~ of the Council*, English crown officer presiding at meetings of Privy Council. **prĕsidĕ'ntial** (-shal) *adj.* **prĕsidĕ'ntially** *adv.*

prĕsi'diary *adj.* Of, having, serving as, a garrison.

prĕsi'dium (or -z-) *n.* Presiding body or standing committee (esp. in communist organization).

prĕss¹ *v.* 1. Exert steady force against (thing in contact); move by pressing; exert pressure, bear with weight or force; squeeze (juice etc. *from* etc.); compress, squeeze, (thing) to flatten or shape or smooth it, or to extract juice etc.; iron (clothes etc.). 2. Bear heavily on in attack etc.; weigh down, oppress; produce strong mental or moral impression, esp. weigh heavily *on* (mind, person); *be pressed for*, have barely enough (time etc.); ~ *the button*, set electric machinery in motion (freq. fig.); ~-*stud*, fastener of which the two parts engage by pressure. 3. Be urgent, demand immediate action; urge, entreat; urge (course etc. *upon* person). 4. Insist on strict interpretation of (words etc.). 5. Force (offer, gift, etc. *upon*). 6. (golf) Attempt to hit harder than can be done with accuracy. 7. Crowd, throng; hasten, urge one's way, *on*, *forward*, etc. ~ *n.* 1. Crowding; crowd (*of* people etc.); throng, crush, in battle. 2. Pressure, hurry, of affairs; pressing; (naut.) ~ *of sail*, *canvas*, as much sail as wind etc. will allow. 3. Kinds of instrument for compressing, flattening, or shaping, or for extracting juice, etc. 4. Machine for printing; printing-house or establishment; art, practice, of printing; newspapers generally; *in the ~*, being printed; *freedom of the ~*, right to print and publish anything without censorship; ~-*agent*, person employed by theatre, actor, etc., to attend to advertising and other publicity; ~-*box*, reporter's enclosure, esp. at sports events; ~ *conference*, prearranged interview given to journalists by celebrity, official, etc.; ~ *cutting*: see CUTTING; ~-*gallery*, gallery for reporters esp. in House of Commons; *pre'ssman*, journalist; operator of printing-press. 5. Large usu. shelved cupboard for clothes, books, etc., esp. standing in recess in wall; ~-*mark*, = SHELF-mark.

prĕss² *v.t.* Force to serve in army or navy (hist.); ~ *into service*, take for use in an emergency; ~ *n.* (hist.) Compulsory enlistment in navy or (less usu.) army; ~-*gang*, (hist.) body of men employed to press men.

prĕ'ssing¹ *adj.* (esp.) Urgent; importunate; persistent. **prĕ'ssingly** *adv.*

prĕ'ssing² *n.* Gramophone record; series of records made at one time from one mould.

prĕ'ssure (-sher) *n.* 1. Exertion of continuous force, force so exerted upon or against a body by another body, or by a liquid or gas, in contact with it; amount of this, expressed by the force upon a unit area; *blood-~*: see BLOOD; *high*, *low*, (*atmospheric*) ~: see ATMOSPHERIC; *high-~*, (of compound engines or turbines) used esp. of those in which steam is used at different pressures in different parts of the machine; ~-*casting*, metal casting obtained by injecting fluid metal under pressure into a rigid mould; ~-*cooker*, strong sealed metal vessel for cooking in steam at high pressure; ~-*flaking*: see FLAKE² *v.*; ~ *mine*, mine detonated by pressure. 2. Affliction, oppression; trouble, embarrassment; constraining influence; ~ *group*, body of people exerting pressure upon legislature etc. by concerted agitation. ~ *v.t.* (fig.) Pressurize.

prĕ'ssurize (-sher-) *v.t.* Maintain normal air pressure artificially, esp. in aircraft at high altitudes; (fig.) exert pressure on, force by pressure.

Prĕ'ster John (jŏn). Fabulous Christian priest and king believed in the Middle Ages to rule over an empire in Asia; in 15th c. identified with the king of Abyssinia.

prĕstidi'gitātor *n.* Conjurer. **prĕstidigitā'tion** *n.*

prĕsti'ge (-ēzh) *n.* Influence, reputation, derived from past achievements, associations, etc. **prĕsti'gious** (-jus) *adj.*

prĕsti'ssimō *adv.*, *n.* (pl. -*os*), & *adj.* (mus.) (Passage performed) very quick(ly). [It.]

prĕ'stō¹ *adv.*, *n.* (pl. -*os*), & *adj.* (mus.) (Passage performed) quick(ly). [It.]

prĕ'stō² *adv.* (in conjurer's formula, *esp. hey ~!*) Quickly. ~ *adj.* Rapid, juggling.

Prĕ'stonpăns (-z). Village of East Lothian, near which the Young PRETENDER gained victory (1745) over English royal forces under Sir John Cope.

prē-strĕ'ssed (-st) *adj.* (of concrete) Strengthened by compression with steel rods under tension, to counteract stress.

prĕsū'me (-z-) *v.* Take the liberty, venture (*to* do); assume, take for granted; be presumptuous, take liberties; ~ *upon*, take advantage of, make unscrupulous use of. **prĕsū'mable** *adj.* **prĕsū'mably**, **prĕsū'mingly** *advs.*

prĕsū'mption (-z-) *n.* Arrogance, assurance; taking for granted, thing taken for granted; ground for presuming; (law) ~ *of fact*, inference of fact from known facts; ~ *of law*, assumption of truth of thing until contrary is proved; inference established by law as universally applicable to certain circumstances.

prĕsū'mptive (-z-) *adj.* Giving ground for presumption; *heir ~*, one whose right of inheritance is liable to be defeated by birth of nearer heir.

prĕsū'mptuous (-z-) *adj.* Unduly confident, arrogant, forward. **prĕsū'mptuously** *adv.* **prĕsū'mptuousnèss** *n.*

prĕsuppō'se (-z-) *v.t.* Assume beforehand; involve, imply. **prĕsuppositi'on** *n.* Presupposing; thing assumed beforehand as basis of argument etc.

prĕtĕ'nce *n.* 1. Claim (*to* merit etc.); *in ~*, (her.) borne on an inescutcheon to indicate pretension or claim (ill. HERALDRY). 2. Ostentation, display; false profession of purpose, pretext; pretending, make-believe.

prĕtĕ'nd v. 1. Feign, give oneself out (*to* be or do); make-believe in play; profess falsely to have; allege falsely. 2. Venture, aspire, presume (*to* do); lay claim *to* (right, title, etc.); ~ *to*, try to win (person, person's hand) in marriage; profess to have (quality etc.).
prĕtĕ'nder n. One who makes baseless pretensions (*to* title etc.); Old P~, James Francis Edward Stuart (1688–1766), James II's son, called by Jacobites James III; took part in the unsuccessful Scottish rising of 1715; Young P~, Charles Edward Stuart (1720–88), son of the Old Pretender; led the rebellion of 1745.
prĕtĕ'nsion n. Assertion of a claim; justifiable claim; pretentiousness.
prĕtĕ'ntious (-shus) adj. Making claim to great merit or importance, esp. when unwarranted; ostentatious. **prĕtĕ'ntiously** adv. **prĕtĕ'ntiousness** n.
prēter- prefix. Past, beyond.
prēterhū'man adj. Beyond what is human, superhuman.
prē'terite adj. (gram.) Expressing past action or state; ~-*present*, (of tense) orig. preterite but now used as present (e.g. *can, dare, may*). ~ n. Preterite tense or verb.
prēteri'tion n. Omission, disregard (*of*); (theol.) passing over of the non-elect.
prētermi't v.t. Omit to mention, do, or perform; neglect; leave off (custom, continuous action) for a time; (improp.) leave off. **prētermi'ssion** n.
prēternā'tural (-cher-) adj. Outside the ordinary course of nature; supernatural. **prēternă'turally** adv.
prē'tĕxt n. Ostensible reason, excuse.
prĕtŏ'nic adj. Coming immediately before stressed syllable.
Prētōr'ia. Capital city of Transvaal and administrative capital of Republic of South Africa. [Andries Wilhelmus Jacobus *Pretorius* (1799–1853), S. African Boer leader, one of founders of Transvaal]
prē'ttify v.t. Make pretty; represent with finicking prettiness.
prē'tty adj. 1. Beautiful in diminutive or trivial way; attractive to eye, ear, or aesthetic sense. 2. Good, fine (also iron.); *a ~ penny*, a good deal of money. 3. (abs. as n.) Pretty one, pretty thing. 4. ~-~, overdoing the pretty, aiming too much at prettiness; ~-*pretties*, pretty things. **prē'ttyish** adj. **prē'ttily** adv. **prē'ttiness** n. **prē'tty** adv. Fairly, moderately, as *~ good, ~ well*.
prē'tzel n. Crisp salted biscuit, freq. baked in form of a knot.
preux chevalier (prer shěvălyā). Gallant knight. [Fr.]
prēvai'l v.i. Gain the mastery, be victorious (*against, over*); be the more usual or prominent, predominate; exist, occur, in general use or experience, be current; ~ *upon*, persuade. **prēvai'ling**, **prē'valent** adjs. **prē'valently** adv. **prē'valence** n.
prēvă'ricāte v.i. Speak, act, evasively; quibble, equivocate. **prēvărică'tion**, **prēvă'ricātor** ns.
prēvē'nient adj. Preceding, previous; having in view the prevention (*of*); ~ *grace*, (theol.) grace preceding repentance and predisposing the heart to seek God.
prēvē'nt v.t. 1. Hinder, stop. 2. (archaic) Meet, deal with (wish, question, etc.) before it is expressed; (theol., of God) go before, guide. **prēvē'ntable**, **prēvē'ntible** adjs. **prēvē'ntion** n.
prēvē'ntative adj. & n. Preventive.
prēvē'nter n. (esp., naut.) Rope, chain, bolt, etc., used to supplement another.
prēvē'ntive adj. Serving to prevent, esp. (med.) to keep off disease; of the department of Customs concerned with prevention of smuggling; ~ *detention*, (law) imprisonment of habitual criminal for period of corrective training etc. **prēvē'ntively** adv.
prēvē'ntive n. Preventive agent, measure, drug, etc.
prē'view (-vū) n. View of a picture, film, etc., arranged before it is open to public view.
prē'vious adj. Coming before in time or order; prior *to*; (slang) done or acting hastily; ~ *question*, (parl.) question whether vote shall be taken on main question (put to avoid putting of main question). **prē'viously** adv. **prē'viousness** n. **prē'vious** adv. Previously (usu. ~ *to*, before, prior to).
prēvi'se (-z) v.t. Foresee, forecast. **prēvi'sion** n. **prēvi'sional** adj. **prēvi'sionally** adv.
Prévost d'Exiles (prāvō dĕgzĕl), Antoine François (1697–1763). 'L'Abbé Prévost', French novelist and miscellaneous writer; author of 'Manon Lescaut'.
prē-war' (-wŏr) adj. Before the war (esp. of 1914–18 or of 1939–45).
prey (prā) n. Animal hunted or killed by carnivorous animal for food; person, thing, that falls a victim (*to* sickness, fear, etc.); *bird, beast, of ~*, one that kills and devours animals. ~ v.i. ~ *on, seek, take*, as prey, plunder; exert baneful or wasteful influence upon.
Prī'ăm. (Gk legend) Last king of Troy, father of 50 sons and many daughters; slain by Neoptolemus after the fall of Troy.
prī'apism n. Licentiousness; (path.) persistent erection of penis. [f. PRIAPUS]
Prīā'pus. (Gk myth.) God of fertility whose cult spread from Asia Minor to Greece and Italy; he became the god of gardens and herds and is represented as small, grotesque, and misshapen.
price n. Money for which thing is bought or sold; (betting) odds; (fig.) what must be given, done, sacrificed, etc., to obtain a thing; *above, beyond, without, ~*, so valuable that no price can be stated; *at any ~*, whatever it may cost; (with neg.) on any terms, for any consideration; *at a ~*, at a relatively high cost; *what ~ . . .?*, (slang) taunting allusion to worthlessness or failure of something; *~ on person's head*, reward offered for his death or capture; *~-ring*, association of traders formed to maintain price of product or commodity. ~ v.t. Fix, inquire, the price of (thing for sale); estimate the value of.
priced (-st) adj. To which a price is assigned.
pri'celess (-sl-) adj. Invaluable; (slang) incredibly or extremely amusing, absurd, etc. **pri'celessness** n.
pri'cey adj. (colloq.) Expensive.
prick n. Pricking, puncture; mark made by pricking; (archaic) goad for oxen, esp. in *kick against the ~s*, (fig.) hurt oneself by useless resistance (see Acts 9: 5); *~-ears*, erect pointed ears of some dogs etc.; conspicuous ears of person, esp. Roundhead. ~ v. Pierce slightly, make minute hole in; cause sharp pain to; feel pricking sensation; make a thrust (*at, into*, etc.); disable (bird) by shooting; mark off (name etc. in list) with a prick; mark (pattern *off, out*) with dots; (archaic) spur, urge on (horse); advance on horseback; *~ in, out, off*, plant (seedlings etc.) in small holes pricked in earth; *~ up*, (of animal) erect (ears) when on the alert; (of animal's ears) rise or stand erect; ~ *up one's ears*, (fig.) become suddenly attentive.
pri'cker n. (esp.) Pricking instrument, e.g. awl.
pri'ckĕt n. 1. Male of fallow deer in second year, with straight unbranched horns. 2. Spike to stick candle on.
pri'ckle n. Thorn-like process developed from epidermis of plant and capable of being peeled off with it; (pop.) small thorn; hard-pointed spine of hedgehog etc. ~ v. Affect, be affected, with sensation as of prick.
pri'ckly adj. Armed with prickles; tingling; ~ *heat*, inflammatory disease of the skin (*miliaria*) accompanying profuse sweating, caused by blocking of the sweat glands; ~ *pear*, species of cactus of genus *Opuntia*, with pear-shaped fleshy edible fruit; this fruit. **pri'ckliness** n.
pride n. 1. Unduly high opinion of one's own qualities, merits, etc., considered the first of the 'seven deadly sins'; arrogant bearing or conduct; ~ *of place*, exalted position, consciousness of this, arrogance. 2. (also *proper ~*) Sense

[695]

of what befits one's position, preventing one from doing unworthy thing; *false* ~, mistaken feeling of this kind. 3. Feeling of elation and pleasure; object of this feeling, esp. in names of plants, as *London* ~; *best condition*; *take* ~ *in*, be proud of; ~ *of the morning*, mist or shower at sunrise. 4. *peacock in his* ~, (her.) peacock with tail expanded and wings drooping. 5. Company (of lions). ~ *v.refl.* ~ *oneself on*, be proud of. **pri'deful** *adj.* (chiefly Sc.). **pri'defully** *adv.* **pri'deless** *adj.*
Pride's Purge (-z) Exclusion (1648) of about 130 Presbyterians and Royalists, supporters of Charles I, from the Long Parliament, carried out by Col. Thomas Pride and a body of troops who arrested members at the door of the House of Commons.
prie-dieu (-dyēr) *n.* Kneeling-desk; chair with tall sloping back for use in praying.
priest *n.* 1. Clergyman, esp. one above deacon and below bishop with authority to administer sacraments and pronounce absolution (now usu. *clergyman*, exc. in official and R.C. use); minister of the altar, esp. officiant at Eucharist; official minister of non-Christian religion (fem. *prie'stèss*); *high* ~: see HIGH; *prie'stcraft*, ambitious or worldly policy of priests; ~'*s hole*, secret chamber in house where R.C. priests hid during times of persecution; ~-*ridden*, held in subjection by priest(s); ~-*vicar*, minor canon in some cathedrals. 2. Mallet used to kill fish when spent (chiefly in Ireland); kind of artificial fly. ~ *v.t.* Make (person) a priest. **prie'sthōod** (-t-h-), **prie'stling** *ns.* **prie'stlèss**, **prie'stlīke** *adjs.*
Prie'stley, Joseph (1733-1804). English chemist, man of science, and theologian; 'discoverer' of oxygen and inventor of the 'pneumatic trough'.
prie'stly *adj.* Of, like, befitting, a priest; *P*~ *Code*, (O.T. criticism) one of the constituent elements of the Hexateuch, constituting framework of whole in its existing form.
prig *n.* Precision in speech or manners; conceited or didactic person. **pri'ggery, pri'ggism** *ns.* **pri'ggish** *adj.* **pri'ggishly** *adv.* **pri'ggishness** *n.*
prim *adj.* Consciously or affectedly precise; formal, demure. ~ *v.* Assume prim air; form (face, lips, etc.) into prim expression. **pri'mly** *adv.* **pri'mness** *n.*
pri'macy *n.* Office of a primate; pre-eminence.
pri'ma dō'nna (prē-). Principal female singer in opera. [It., = 'first lady']
pri'ma fā'cĭe (-sh-) *adv. & adj.* (Arising) at first sight, (based) on the first impression. [L]
pri'mage¹ *n.* Percentage addition to freight, paid to owners or freighters of vessels.
pri'mage² *n.* Amount of water carried off suspended in steam from boiler.
pri'mal *adj.* Primitive, primeval; chief, fundamental.
pri'marȳ *adj.* Earliest, original; of the first rank in a series, not derived; of the first importance, chief; (geol., *P*~) of the lowest series of strata, Palaeozoic; (biol.) belonging to first stage of development; ~ *amputation*, one performed before inflammation supervenes; ~ *assembly*, *meeting*, meeting for selection of candidates for election; ~ *colour*: see COLOUR; ~ *education*, that which begins with the rudiments of knowledge, esp. that provided for children under 11 years; ~ *feather*, one of large flight feathers of bird's wing, growing directly from manus (ill. BIRD); ~ *planets*, those revolving directly round sun as centre; ~ *school*, school for primary education. ~ *n.* Primary planet, meeting, feather, etc.; *P*~, (geol.) Primary period. **prī'marily** *adv.*
prī'mate (or -āt) *n.* 1. Archbishop; *P*~ *of all England*, archbishop of Canterbury; *P*~ *of England*, archbishop of York. 2. (pl. pr. -āts *or* -ātēz) (zool.)

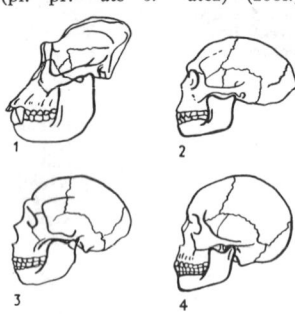

SKULLS OF PRIMATES
1. Gorilla. 2. Pithecanthrope. 3. Neanderthal man. 4. Man (*Homo sapiens*)

Member of order of mammals including man, apes, monkeys, tarsiers, and lemurs.
prīme¹ *n.* 1. State of highest perfection; best part (*of* thing). 2. Beginning, first age, of anything; *P*~, (R.C. Ch.) canonical HOUR, (orig. said at) first hour of day. 3. Prime number. 4. (mus.) Fundamental note or tone; lower of any two notes forming an interval. 5. Position in fencing, first of the eight parries or guards in sword-play, used to protect the head (ill. FENCE); thrust in such position. ~ *adj.* 1. Chief, most important; ~ *minister*, principal minister of any sovereign or State (now official title of first minister of State in Gt Britain). 2. First-rate (esp. of cattle and provisions), excellent. 3. Primary, fundamental; (arith., of number) having no integral factors except itself and unity (e.g. 2, 3, 5, 7, 11). 4. ~ *cost*: see COST; ~ *mover*: see MOVER; ~ *vertical* (*circle*), great circle of the heavens passing through E. and W. points of horizon and through zenith, where it cuts meridian at right angles.
prīme² *v.* Supply (firearm, or abs.) with gunpowder for firing charge (hist.); wet (pump) to make it start working; equip (person *with* information etc.); inject petrol into (carburettor or cylinder of internal combustion engine); fill (person *with* liquor); cover (wood, canvas, etc.) with glue, gesso, oil, etc. to prevent paint from being absorbed; (of engine-boiler) let water pass with steam into cylinder in form of spray.
prī'mer¹ *n.* (esp.) Cap, cylinder, etc., used to ignite powder of cartridge etc. (ill. CARTRIDGE).
prī'mer² *n.* 1. Elementary school-book for teaching children to read; small introductory book; (hist.) prayer-book for use of laity esp. before Reformation. 2. *great* ~, (print.) size of type between paragon and English (about 18 point); *long* ~, size between small pica and bourgeois (about 10 point); *two-line long* ~, PARAGON.
primēr'ō *n.* Gambling card-game fashionable *c.* 1530-1640, in which four cards were dealt to each player and each card had three times its ordinary value.
primē'val, **primae'val** *adj.* Of the first age of the world; ancient, primitive. **primē'vally** *adv.*
prī'ming¹ *n.* (esp.) 1. Gunpowder placed in pan of firearm. 2. Train of powder connecting fuse with charge in blasting etc. 3. Mixture used by painters for preparatory coat. 4. Preparation of sugar added to beer. 5. Hasty imparting of knowledge, cramming.
prī'ming² *n.* Acceleration of the tide taking place from neap to spring tides (opp. LAG¹).
primi'parous *adj.* Bearing child for the first time. **primĭpă'ra** *n.* Primiparous woman.
pri'mitive *adj.* Ancient; of early, simple, or old-fashioned kind; (gram., of words) radical, not derivative; (math., of line, figure, etc.) from which another is derived, from which some construction begins, etc.; (geol.) (of peoples) at an early stage of cultural development; (geol.) Palaeozoic; (biol.) appearing in early stage of evolution; only slightly evolved from ancestral types; *P*~ *Methodism*, *Methodist*, principles, member, of *P*~ *Methodist Connexion*, society of Methodists founded 1810 by Hugh Bourne by secession from main body. **pri'mitively** *adv.* **pri'mitiveness** *ns.* **pri'mitive** *n.* (Picture by) painter of period before Renaissance; (picture by) untutored painter who ignores rules of perspective etc. (chiefly

[696]

U.S.); primitive word, line, etc.; (P~) Primitive Methodist.

Pri′mō de River′a (prē-, -vār′a), Miguel, Marques de Estella (1870–1930). Spanish general, premier and dictator (1923–30).

primogĕ′nitor n. Earliest ancestor; (loosely) ancestor.

primogĕ′niture n. Fact of being the first-born of the children of the same parents; (also *right of* ~) right of succession belonging to first-born, esp. feudal rule by which the whole real estate of an intestate passes to the eldest son.

primōr′dial adj. Existing at or from the beginning, primeval. **primōr′dially** adv. **primōrdiă′lity** n.

pri′mrōse (-z) n. Plant (*Primula vulgaris*) bearing pale-yellowish flowers in early spring, growing wild in woods and hedges and on banks, and with many cultivated varieties (ill. FLOWER); colour of flower of this; *evening* ~, plant of genus *Oenothera*, with large pale-yellow flowers opening in evening; *P~ Day*, anniversary of death of DISRAELI (who died 19 April 1881); *P~ League*, political association formed 1883 in memory of Disraeli and in support of his principles of conservatism; ~ *path*, pursuit of pleasure (w. ref. to 'Hamlet', 1. iii. 50).

pri′mūla n. Herbaceous perennial of genus *P~*, of low growing habit with yellow, white, pink, or purple flowers mostly borne in umbels. **prīmūlā′ceous** (-shus) adj.

prī′mum mō′bĭlĕ. Outermost sphere added in Middle Ages to Ptolemaic system of astronomy, supposed to revolve round earth from E. to W. in 24 hours, carrying with it the (8 or 9) contained spheres; (fig.) prime source of motion or action. [med. L, lit. 'first moving thing']

pri′mus[1] adj. (in schools) Eldest (or of longest standing) of the name, as *Jones* ~. ~ n. Presiding bishop in Scottish Episcopal Church. [L, = 'first']

Pri′mus[2] n. (also ~ *stove*) Portable stove burning vaporized paraffin oil. [trade-name]

prince n. 1. Sovereign ruler (now rhet.); ruler of small State, actually or nominally feudatory to king or emperor; *P~ of Peace*, Christ; ~ *of darkness*, Satan. 2. (Title of) male member of royal family, esp. (in Gt Britain) son or grandson of king or queen; *P~ of Wales*, title (since 1301) conferred upon eldest son and heir apparent of English sovereign; ~ *of Wales's feathers*, triple ostrich plume, first adopted as crest by the Black Prince. 3. (as Engl. rendering of foreign titles) Noble usu. ranking next below duke; (as courtesy title in some connections) duke, marquis, earl; (fig.) chief, greatest (*of*); ~ *of the* (*Holy Roman*) *Church*,

title of cardinal. 4. ~ *bishop*, bishop who is also a prince; *P~ Consort*, husband of reigning female sovereign being himself a prince; esp., Albert, Prince of Saxe-Coburg, as husband of Queen Victoria; *P~ Imperial*, Napoléon Eugène Louis Jean Joseph (1856–79), son of Napoleon III, killed with British forces in Zulu war of 1879; *Princes in the Tower*, Edward V and his brother Richard, Duke of York, sons of Edward IV, alleged to have been lodged in the Tower of London and there murdered in 1483; *P~ Regent*, prince who acts as regent; esp., George Prince of Wales (afterwards George IV) during mental incapacity of George III (1811–20); ~'s (or *P~ Rupert's*) *metal*, gold-coloured alloy of about three parts of copper and one of zinc. **pri′ncedom, pri′nceling** ns.

Prince E′dward I′sland (ĕ-, il-). Smallest province of Canada, a large island in the Gulf of St. Lawrence; capital, Charlottetown.

pri′ncely (-sli) adj. (Worthy) of a prince; sumptuous, splendid. **pri′nceliness** n.

pri′ncĕss (or -ĕ′s *exc. when followed by name*) n. 1. (Title of) queen (archaic); wife of prince, daughter or grand-daughter of sovereign; ~ *royal*, (title conferrable on) sovereign's eldest daughter. 2. *attrib.* (of dress etc.) Made in panels with flared skirt and without a seam at the waist.

Pri′nceton (-st-). Borough in New Jersey; university for men, orig. a college (1746), at Princeton, N.J.

pri′ncipal adj. First in rank or importance, chief; main, leading; (of money) constituting the original sum invested or lent; ~ *boy*, hero of pantomime, traditionally acted by a woman; ~ *clause, sentence*, (gram.) one to which another is subordinate; ~ *parts*, parts of verb from which the others can be derived. ~ n. 1. Head, ruler, superior; head of some colleges. 2. Person for whom another acts as agent etc.; person directly responsible for crime, either as actual perpetrator (~ *in the first degree*) or as aiding (~ *in the second degree*); person for whom another is surety; combatant in duel. 3. Any of the main rafters on which rest the purlins that

support the common rafters (ill. ROOF). 4. Capital sum as distinguished from interest, sum lent or invested on which interest is paid. 5. Organ-stop of same quality as open diapason, but an octave higher in pitch. **pri′ncipalship** n.

principă′lity n. Government of a prince; State ruled by a prince; (pl.) order of angels (see ANGEL); *the P~*, Wales.

pri′ncipally adv. For the most part, chiefly.

pri′ncipate n. 1. (Rom. hist.) Rule of early emperors while some republican forms were retained. 2. State ruled by a prince.

pri′nciple n. 1. Fundamental source, primary element; fundamental truth as basis of reasoning etc.; law of nature seen in working of machine etc.; (phys. etc.) general or inclusive law exemplified in numerous cases; general law as guide to action. 2. (pl. and collect. sing.) Personal code of right conduct; *on* ~, from settled moral motive. 3. (chem.) Constituent of a naturally occurring substance, esp. one giving rise to some quality etc.

prink v. Smarten, dress up; titivate, esp. in front of a mirror.

print n. 1. Indentation in surface preserving the form left by pressure of some body; mark, spot, stain. 2. Language embodied in printed form, printed lettering; handwritten letters imitating this. 3. State of being printed; *book is in* ~, (i) in printed form, (ii) on sale, not *out of* ~ (sold out). 4. (chiefly U.S.) Printed publication, esp. newspaper. 5. Printed cotton fabric. 6. Picture, design, printed from block or plate; (photog.) picture produced from negative. ~ *v.t.* 1. Impress, stamp, (surface *with* seal, die, etc.; mark or figure *on, in*, surface); (fig.) impress (*on* mind, memory). 2. Produce (book, picture, etc., or abs.) by applying inked types, blocks, or plates to paper, vellum, etc. (*illustration, p. 698*); cause (book, MS.) to be so printed; express, publish, in print; write (words etc.) in imitation of typography; ~-*out*, computer output in printed form. 3. Mark (textile fabric) with decorative design in colours; transfer (coloured design) from paper etc. to unglazed surface of pottery; (photog.) produce (picture) by transmission of light through negative. 4. *printed circuit*, (elect.) circuit of conductive strips on a non-conducting material. **pri′ntable** adj.

pri′nter n. (esp.) One who prints books; owner of printing business; printing instrument; *Printers' Bible*, Bible which contains the misreading *Printers* for *Princes* in Ps. 119: 161; ~'s *devil, pie*: see DEVIL, PIE[3].

pri′or[1] n. (fem. *prioress*) Superior officer of religious house or order; (in abbey) officer next

PRINCE OF WALES'S FEATHERS

[697]

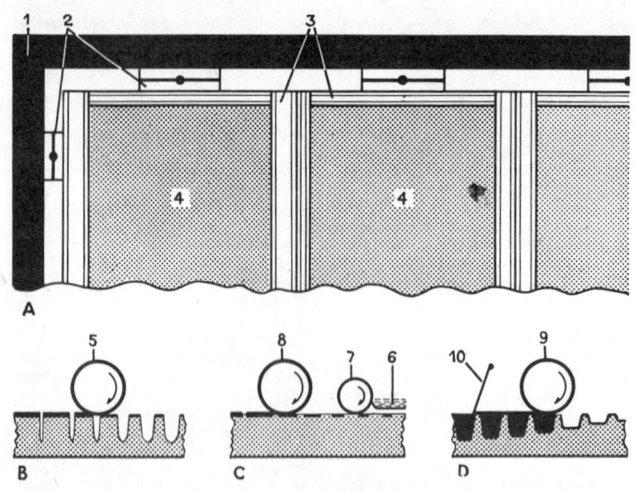

A. PART OF A FORME READY FOR PRINTING. B, C, D. METHODS OF PRINTING: B. LETTERPRESS (SURFACE). C. LITHOGRAPHY (PLANOGRAPHIC). D. PHOTOGRAVURE OR GRAVURE (INTAGLIO)

1. Chase. 2. Quoins which, when expanded, lock forme up tight, i.e. make it rigid. 3. Metal spacing material. 4. Pages of imposed type. 5. Ink roller inking surface. 6. Water. 7. Water roller wetting non-greasy section of surface to repel ink. 8. Ink roller inking greasy section of surface. 9. Ink roller filling depressions. 10. Doctor blade cleaning ink off surface

under abbot; (hist.) chief magistrate in some Italian republics. **pri′orship** n.
pri′or² adj. Earlier; antecedent in time, order, or importance. ~ adv. ~ to, before. **priŏ′rity** n. Condition or quality of being earlier in time, or of preceding something else; precedence in order, rank, or dignity; interest having prior claim to consideration, often with qualification, as first, top ~.
Pri′or³, Matthew (1664-1721). English poet and diplomatist.
pri′ory n. Monastery, nunnery, governed by prior or prioress.
Pri′scian (-sh-), (6th c. A.D.), Latin grammarian of Constantinople; break ~'s head, violate the rules of grammar.
prise: see PRIZE³.
prism n. Solid figure whose two ends are similar, equal, and parallel rectilineal figures and whose sides are parallelograms; transparent body of this form, usu. of triangular section, which splits light into a rainbow-like spectrum. **pri′smal** (-z-) adj.
prismă′tic (-z-) adj. Of, like, a prism; (of colours) distributed by transparent prism, (also) brilliant; ~ astrolabe: see ASTROLABE; ~ binoculars, glasses, type of field-glasses each telescope of which contains two right-angled prisms so placed as to secure a better stereoscopic effect with a shorter tube than an ordinary binocular (ill. BINOCULAR); ~ colour, one of the seven colours (violet, indigo, blue, green, yellow, orange, and red) into which a ray of white light is separated by a prism; ~ compass, hand compass furnished with a prism enabling the compass to be read while taking a bearing or sight. **prismă′tically** adv.
pri′smoid (-z-) n. Body, figure, resembling a prism, with similar but unequal parallel polygonal ends. **prismoi′dal** adj.
pri′son (-zn) n. Place in which person is kept in captivity, esp. building to which person is legally committed while awaiting trial or for punishment; custody, confinement. ~ v.t. (poet., rhet.) Imprison.
pri′soner (-zn-) n. Person kept in prison; (also ~ of war), member of the enemy's armed forces captured in war; ~ of State, State ~, one confined for political reasons; take (person) ~, seize and hold as prisoner; ~s' bars, base, game played by two parties of boys etc.,

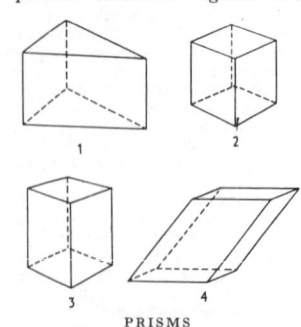

1. Wedge. 2. Cube. 3. Box. 4. Parallelepiped

each occupying distinct base or home, aim of each side being to make prisoner by touching any player who leaves his base.
pri′ssy adj. Prim, over-decorous.
pri′stine (or -ĕn) adj. Ancient, primitive, unspoilt.
pri′thee (-dhī) int. (archaic) Pray, please. [= (I) pray thee]
pri′vacy n. Being withdrawn from society or public interest; avoidance of publicity.
privat-docent (prĕvah′t dōtsĕ′nt) n. (in German universities) Private teacher or lecturer recognized by university but not on salaried staff.
pri′vate adj. 1. Not holding public office or official position; ~ member (of House of Commons), one not member of Ministry; ~ soldier, ordinary soldier not holding commissioned or non-commissioned rank. 2. Kept, removed, from public knowledge; not open to the public; ~ house, dwelling-house of private person (opp. to shop or office, public house or public building); ~ means, income not derived from employment; ~ parts, genitals; ~ school, school owned and managed by private individual, not vested in a public body. 3. One's own; individual, personal, not affecting the community; confidential. 4. (of place) Retired, secluded; (of person, archaic) given to retirement. **pri′vately** adv. **pri′vate** n. 1. Private soldier. 2. in ~, privately; in private life. 3. (pl.) Private parts.
privateer′ n. (hist.) Armed vessel owned and officered by private persons holding commission from government (letters of marque) and authorized to use it against hostile nation, esp. in capture of merchant shipping; commander, (pl.) crew, of this.
privā′tion n. Loss, absence (of quality), as cold is the ~ of heat; want of the comforts or necessaries of life.
pri′vative adj. Consisting in, marked by, the loss, removal, or absence of some quality or attribute, as cold is merely ~ (cf. prec.); denoting privation or absence of quality etc.; (gram.) expressing privation. **pri′vatively** adv.
pri′vet n. Bushy evergreen shrub (Ligustrum vulgare) with smooth dark-green leaves, clusters of small white flowers, and small shining black berries, much used for hedges; other species of Ligustrum or similar (usu. evergreen) shrub.
pri′vilėge n. Right, advantage, immunity, belonging to person, class, or office; special advantage or benefit; monopoly, patent, granted to individual, corporation, etc.; bill of ~, petition of peer demanding to be tried by his peers; parliamentary ~, any or all

of numerous privileges which belong to the Houses of Parliament or to their individual members in virtue of their office (freq. used of M.P.'s immunity in discussing matters which if discussed by others might become subject of legal action); *writ of* ~, writ to deliver privileged person from custody when arrested in civil suit. ~ *v.t.* Invest with privilege; allow (*to* do) as privilege; exempt (*from* burden etc.). **pri'vilėged** (-jd) *adj.*

pri'vity *n.* 1. Being privy (*to*). 2. (law) Any relation between two parties that is recognized by law, e.g. that of blood, lease, service.

pri'vy *adj.* Hidden, secluded, secret; ~ *to*, in the secret of (person's designs, etc.); *P*~ *Council*, sovereign's private counsellors; (in Gt Britain) body of advisers chosen by sovereign (now chiefly as personal dignity), together with princes of the blood, archbishops, etc.; ~ *parts*, (archaic) private parts; ~ *purse*, allowance from public revenue for monarch's private expenses; keeper of this; ~ *seal*, (hist.) seal affixed to documents that are afterwards to pass, or that do not require, the Great Seal. **pri'vily** *adv.* **pri'vy** *n.* 1. Lavatory. 2. (law) Person having a part or interest in any action, matter, or thing.

prize[1] *n.* Reward given as symbol of victory or superiority, to student in school or college who excels in attainments, to competitor in athletic contest, to exhibitor of best specimen of manufactured products, works of art, etc., in exhibition; (fig.) anything striven for or worth striving for; money or money's worth offered for competition by chance, in lottery, etc.; ~-*fight*, boxing-match for money; ~-*fighter*; *pri'zeman*, winner of prize; ~-*ring*, enclosed area (now usu. square), for prize-fighting. ~ *v.t.* Value highly.

prize[2] *n.* Ship, property, captured at sea in virtue of rights of war; (fig.) find or windfall; ~-*court*, department of admiralty court concerned with prizes; ~-*money*, money realized by sale of prize. ~ *v.t.* Make prize of.

prize[3], **prise** (-z) *v.t.* Force (lid etc. *up*, *out*, box etc. *open*) by leverage. ~ *n.* Leverage, purchase.

prō[1] *n.* (colloq.) Professional.

prō[2] *adv.* & *n.* (Argument) in favour of a proposition etc. (usu. pl., in ~*s and cons*, CON[4]). [L]

pro- *prefix.* 1. In front of, for, on behalf of, on account of. 2. Favouring or siding with.

P.R.O. *abbrev.* Public Record Office; Public Relations Officer.

prō'a *n.* Malay boat, esp. fast sailing-boat of type used in Malay archipelago, with large triangular sail and sharp stem and stern and one side flat and straight (instead of curved) to reduce leeway, having a small canoe or the like rigged parallel to it like an outrigger.

prŏbabi'liorism *n.* (R.C. casuistry) Doctrine that the side on which evidence preponderates ought to be followed. **prŏbabi'liorist** *n.*

prŏ'babilism *n.* Doctrine that where authorities differ any course may be followed for which a recognized doctor of the Church can be cited; theory that there is no certain knowledge, but may be grounds of belief sufficient for practical life. **prŏ'babilist** *n.*

prŏbabi'lity *n.* Quality of being probable; (most) probable event; (math.) likelihood of an event, measured by the ratio of the favourable cases to the whole number of cases possible; *in all* ~, most likely.

prŏ'bable *adj.* That may be expected to happen or prove true, likely. **prŏ'bably** *adv.* **prŏ'bable** *n.* Probable candidate, competitor, member of team, etc.

prō'bate (*or* -āt) *n.* Official proving of will; verified copy of will with certificate as handed to executors.

probā'tion *n.* Testing of conduct or character of person, esp. of candidate for membership in religious body; moral trial or discipline; (law) method of dealing with offenders by placing them under supervision; ~ *officer*, person appointed to befriend and supervise such offenders. **probā'tionary** *adj.* Of, serving for, done in the way of, probation; undergoing probation.

probā'tioner *n.* Person on probation, esp. novice in religious house, nurse in training, offender under probation.

prō'bative *adj.* Affording proof, evidential.

prōbe *n.* Blunt-ended surgical instrument for exploring wound etc.; act of probing; device used for exploring outer space and transmitting back data. ~ *v.t.* Explore (wound, part of body) with probe; penetrate (thing) with sharp instrument; (fig.) examine closely, sound.

prŏ'bity *n.* Uprightness, honesty.

prŏ'blem *n.* Doubtful or difficult question; thing hard to understand; (geom.) proposition in which something has to be done; (logic) question (usu. only implied) involved in a syllogism; (phys., math.) inquiry starting from given conditions to investigate a fact, result, or law; (chess, bridge, etc.) arrangement of pieces on board, or of cards dealt, etc., in which player is challenged to accomplish specified result, often under prescribed conditions; (attrib.; of child) difficult to train; (of literature etc.) treating subject of social or other problem.

prŏblĕmā'tic, **-ical** *adjs.* Doubtful, questionable; (logic) enunciating or supporting what is possible but not necessarily true. **prŏblĕmā'tically** *adv.*

prŏ'blemist, **-atist** *n.* One who studies or composes (esp. chess) problems.

probŏsci'dėan, **-ian** *adj.* Of, like, having, a proboscis; of the order Proboscidea, containing elephants and extinct allied animals with long flexible proboscis and incisors developed into long tusks. ~ *n.* Proboscidean animal.

probŏ'scis *n.* Elephant's trunk; long flexible snout of tapir etc.; elongated part of mouth in some insects (ill. MOTH); sucking organ in some worms; (joc.) human nose; ~-*monkey*, large, long-tailed, Bornean ape (*Nasalis larvatus*) the male of which has nose projecting far beyond mouth.

prō-cathē'dral *adj.* & *n.* (Church) used as substitute for a cathedral.

procē'dure (-dyer) *n.* Proceeding; mode of conducting business (esp. in parliament) or legal action. **procē'dural** *adj.*

procee'd *v.i.* Go on, make one's way, (*to*); go on (*with*, *in*, action etc., *to* do, *to* another course etc.); adopt course of action; go on to say; come forth, issue, originate; take legal proceedings *against*; (of action) be carried on, take place. **procee'ding** *n.* (esp.) Action, piece of conduct; (pl.) record of account of doings of a society; *legal* ~*s*, (steps taken in) legal action.

prō'ceeds (-z) *n.pl.* Produce, outcome, profit.

prō'cĕss[1] *n.* 1. Progress, course; *in* ~ *of time*, as time goes on; natural or involuntary operation, series of changes; course of action, proceeding, esp. method of operation in manufacture, printing, photography, etc. 2. (Print from block produced by) method (e.g. chemical or photographic) other than simple engraving by hand; ~-*block*, block for printing from, produced by such method. 3. Action at law; formal commencement of this; summons or writ; ~-*server*, sheriff's officer who serves processes or summonses. 4. (anat., zool., bot.) Outgrowth, protuberance. ~ *v.t.* 1. Institute legal process against (person.) 2. Treat (material), preserve (food), reproduce (drawing etc.) by a process.

procĕ'ss[2] *v.i.* (colloq.) Walk in procession.

procĕ'ssion *n.* 1. Proceeding of body of persons (or of boats etc.) in orderly succession, esp. as religious ceremony or on festive occasion; body of persons doing this; (fig.) ill-contested race. 2. (theol.) Emanation of the Holy Ghost. ~ *v.* Go in procession; walk along (street) in procession.

procĕ'ssional *adj.* Of processions; used, carried, sung, in processions. ~ *n.* Processional

[699]

processionary hymn, (eccles.) office-book of processional hymns etc.

proce'ssionary adj. Going in procession (esp. of caterpillars of the moth *Cnethocampa processionea*).

procès-verbal (prŏsĕ-vārbahl) n. Written report of proceedings, minutes; (Fr. law) written statement of facts in support of charge. [Fr.]

prō'chronism (-k-) n. Referring of event etc. to an earlier than the true date, as *races held in June and called by a ~ the Mays*.

proclai'm v.t. Announce publicly and officially; declare (war, peace); announce officially the accession of (sovereign); declare (person, thing) officially to be (traitor etc.); declare publicly or openly (thing, *that*); place (district etc.) under legal restrictions, prohibit (meeting etc.), by declaration. **prŏclamā'tion** n. **proclă'matory** adj.

procli'tic adj. & n. (Gk gram.) (Monosyllable) closely attached in pronunciation to following word and having itself no accent.

procli'vity n. Tendency (*to, towards*, action or habit, esp. bad one).

Prō'clus (c A.D. 410-85). Neoplatonic philosopher.

Prō'cnè, Prō'gnè. (Gk myth.) Sister of PHILOMEL.

prōcō'nsul n. 1. (Rom. hist.) Governor of Roman province, in later republic usu. an ex-consul; (under empire) governor of senatorial province. 2. (rhet.) Governor of modern colony etc.; (*pro-consul*) deputy consul. **prōcō'nsūlar** adj. **prōcō'nsūlate, prōcō'nsulship** ns.

procrā'stināte v.i. Defer action, be dilatory. **procrăstinā'tion** n. **procrā'stinative, procră'stinatory** adjs.

prō'crēate v.t. Generate (offspring). **prōcrēā'tion** n. **prō'crēative** adj.

Procrŭ'stēs (-z). (Gk legend) Robber who laid travellers on a bed and made them fit by cutting off their limbs or stretching them; he was killed by Theseus. **Procrŭ'stean** adj. Compelling conformity by violent means.

prō'ctor n. 1. Each of two officers (*senior, junior, ~*) in some universities, appointed annually and charged with various functions, esp. discipline of undergraduates. 2. (law) Person managing causes in court (now chiefly eccles.) that administers civil or canon law; *King's, Queen's, P~*, official who may intervene in probate, divorce, and nullity cases when collusion or suppression of facts is alleged. **prōctōr'ial** adj.

prō'ctorize v.t. Exercise proctor's authority on (undergraduate etc.). **prōctorīzā'tion** n.

procŭ'mbent adj. Lying on the face, prostrate; (bot.) growing along the ground.

prōcūrā'tion n. 1. Procuring, obtaining; bringing about; (fee for) negotiation of loan. 2. Function, authorized action, of attorney or agent. 3. (eccles.) Provision of entertainment for bishop or other visitor by incumbent etc., now commuted to money payment. 4. Procurer's trade or offence.

prō'cūrator n. 1. (Rom. hist.) Treasury officer in imperial province. 2. Agent, proxy, esp. one who has power of attorney. 3. Magistrate in some Italian cities. 4. *~ fiscal*, officer of sheriff's court in Scotland acting as public prosecutor of a district and with other duties similar to those of coroner. **prōcūrator'ial** adj. **prō'cūrātorship** n.

prō'cūratory n. Authorization to act for another.

prō'cūrātrix n. Inmate of nunnery managing its temporal concerns.

procūr'e v. Obtain by care or effort, acquire; act as procurer or procuress; (archaic) bring about. **procūr'able** adj. **procūr'ance, procūr'ement** ns.

procūr'er n. (fem. *procūr'ess*) Pimp.

prŏd v.t. Poke with pointed instrument, end of stick, etc.; goad, irritate. *~* n. Poke, thrust; pointed instrument.

prŏ'dĭgal adj. Recklessly wasteful; lavish *of*; *P~ Son*, repentant wastrel in parable (Luke 15: 11-32). **prŏ'dĭgally** adv. **prŏdĭgă'lity** n. **prŏ'dĭgal** n. Prodigal person.

prŏ'dĭgalīze v.t. Spend lavishly.

prodī'gious (-jus) adj. Marvellous, amazing; enormous; abnormal. **prodī'giously** adv. **prodī'giousness** n.

prŏ'dĭgy n. Marvellous thing, esp. one out of the course of nature; wonderful example *of* (some quality); person endowed with surprising qualities, esp. precocious child.

prŏ'drome n. Preliminary book or treatise (*to* another); (med.), premonitory symptom. **prŏ'drōmal, prodrŏ'mic** adjs.

prodū'ce v.t. 1. Bring forward for inspection or consideration; bring (play, performer, book, etc.) before the public. 2. (geom.) Extend, continue (line *to* a point). 3. Manufacture (goods) from raw materials etc. 4. Bring about, cause (sensation etc.). 5. Yield (produce); bear, yield (offspring, fruit). **prodū'cible** adj. **prō'dūce** n. Amount produced, yield, esp. in assay of ore; agricultural and natural products collectively; result (*of* labour, efforts, etc.).

prodū'cer n. 1. (pol. econ.) One who produces articles of consumption (opp. *consumer*); person who produces a play etc.; person financing a film and controlling its production (cf. DIRECTOR). 2. (also *gas ~*) Special form of furnace for making *~ gas*, an inflammable gas containing carbon monoxide together with nitrogen, made by passing air through red-hot coke and used for gas-engines etc.

prō'duct n. Thing produced by natural process or manufacture; result; (math.) quantity obtained by multiplying quantities together; (chem.) compound formed during chemical reaction.

prodŭ'ction n. Producing; thing(s) produced; literary or artistic work.

prodŭ'ctive adj. Producing, tending to produce; producing abundantly; (econ.) producing commodities of exchangeable value. **prodŭ'ctively** adv. **prodŭ'ctiveness** n. **prŏducti'vity** n. (esp.) Efficiency in industrial production.

prō'em n. Preface, preamble; beginning, prelude. **proē'mial** adj.

Prof. abbrev. Professor.

profā'ne[1] adj. Not belonging to what is sacred or biblical; not initiated into religious rites or any esoteric knowledge; (of rites etc.) heathen; irreverent, blasphemous. **profā'nely** adv. **profā'neness** (-n-n-) n. **profă'nity** n. (esp.) Profane words or acts.

profāne[2] v.t. Treat (sacred thing) with irreverence or disregard; violate, pollute (what is entitled to respect). **prŏfanā'tion** n.

profĕ'ss v. 1. Lay claim to (quality, feeling); pretend (*to* be or do); openly declare; take vows of religious order; receive into religious order. 2. Make (law, medicine, etc.) one's profession or business. 3. Teach (subject) as professor; perform duties of a professor.

profĕ'ssed (-st) adj. Self-acknowledged; alleged, ostensible; claiming to be duly qualified; that has taken the vows of a religious order. **profĕ'ssedly** adv.

profĕ'ssion n. 1. Declaration, avowal; declaration of belief in a religion; vow made on entering, fact of being in, a religious order. 2. Vocation, calling, esp. one that involves some branch of learning or science; body of persons engaged in this, esp. (theatr. slang) actors.

profĕ'ssional adj. Of, belonging to, connected with, a profession; following occupation (esp. one usu. engaged in as pastime or by amateurs) as means of livelihood; making a trade of something usu. or properly pursued from higher motives; maintaining a proper standard, businesslike, not amateurish. *~* n. Professional man, esp. (abbrev. *pro*) sportsman playing for money (opp. *amateur*). **profĕ'ssionally**.

profĕ'ssionalism n. Qualities, stamp, of a profession; practice of employing professionals in sport etc. **profĕ'ssionalize** v.t.

profĕ'ssor n. 1. One who

[700]

makes profession (*of* a religion). 2. Public teacher of high rank, esp. holder of a chair in university (prefixed as title, abbrev. Prof.). **profe′ssorate, profe′ssorship** *ns.* Position, period of activity, of university professor. **profe̊ssŏr′ial** *adj.* **profe̊ssŏr′ially** *adv.* **prŏ′ffer** *v.t. & n.* (literary) Offer.
profi′cient (-shent) *adj. & n.* Adept, expert (*in, at*). **profi′ciently** *adv.* **profi′ciency** *n.*
prō′file *n.* Drawing, silhouette, or other representation, of side view esp. of human face; side outline esp. of human face; flat outline piece of scenery on stage; (fort.) transverse vertical section of fort; comparative thickness of earthwork etc.; (journalism) biographical sketch of a subject, usu. accompanied by a portrait. ∼ *v.t.* Represent in profile; give a profile to.
prŏ′fit *n.* Advantage, benefit; pecuniary gain, excess of returns over outlay (usu. pl.); ∼ *and loss account*, (book-keeping) account in which gains are credited and losses debited so as to show net profit or loss at any time; ∼*-sharing*, sharing of profits esp. between employer and employed. **prŏ′fitless** *adj.* **prŏ′fitlessly** *adv.* **prŏ′fitlessness** *n.* **prŏ′fit** *v.* Be of advantage to; be of advantage; be benefited or assisted.
prŏ′fitable *adj.* Beneficial, useful; yielding profit, lucrative. **prŏ′fitableness** *n.* **prŏ′fitably** *adv.*
prŏfiteer′ *v.i.* Make inordinate profits on sale of necessary supplies or goods, esp. in time of war. ∼ *n.* Profiteering person.
prŏ′fligate *adj. & n.* Licentious, dissolute, or recklessly extravagant (person). **prŏ′fligately** *adv.* **prŏ′fligacy** *n.*
prō forʹma. Done for form's sake, as a matter of form; ∼ *invoice*, invoice sent to purchaser in advance of goods to show him how much will be payable. [L]
profou′nd *adj.* 1. Having, showing, great knowledge or insight; demanding deep study or thought. 2. (of state or quality) Deep, intense, unqualified. 3. Having, coming from, extending to, a great depth. **profou′ndly** *adv.* **profou′ndness, profŭ′ndity** *ns.* **profou′nd** *n.* (poet.) Vast depth.
profū′se *adj.* Lavish, extravagant (*in, of*); exuberantly plentiful. **profū′sely** *adv.* **profū′seness, profū′sion** *ns.*
prŏg *n.* (slang) Proctor at Oxford or Cambridge University. ∼ *v.t.* Proctorize.
proge̊′nitive *adj.* Capable of, connected with, the production of offspring.
proge̊′nitor *n.* (fem. *proge′nitress*) Ancestor; (fig.) political or intellectual predecessor, original of a copy. **progenitor′ial** *adj.*

proge̊′niture *n.* (Begetting of) offspring.
prŏ′geny̆ *n.* Offspring; descendants; (fig.) issue, outcome.
proge̊′sterōne *n.* Hormone produced by the ovaries (or prepared synthetically) that prepares the uterus for pregnancy.
proglŏ′ttid *n.* = PROGLOTTIS.
proglŏ′ttis *n.* (pl. *-ides̆*). Propagative segment of tapeworm.
prōgnā′thous *adj.* With projecting jaws; (of jaws) projecting. **prŏgnā′thic** *adj.* **prŏ′gnathism** *n.*
prŏgnō′sis *n.* (pl. *-oses̆*). Prognostication, esp. (med.) forecast of course of disease.
prŏgnō′stic *n.* Pre-indication, omen (*of*); prediction, forecast. ∼ *adj.* Foretelling, predictive (*of*).
prŏgnō′sticāte *v.t.* Foretell, presage. **prŏgnŏstica′tion** *n.* **prŏgnŏ′sticative, prŏgnŏ′sticatory** *adjs.*
prō′grăm *n.* 1. (U.S.) = PROGRAMME. 2. Series of coded instructions for a computer. ∼ *v.t.* Express (problem) as a program; instruct (computer) by means of a program.
prō′grămme *n.* 1. Descriptive notice of series of events, e.g. of course of study, concert, etc.; definite plan of intended proceedings. 2. Entertainment etc., esp. consisting of several items; a broadcast production. 3. = PROGRAM, 2. 4. ∼*-music*, music intended to suggest series of scenes or events.
prō′gress *n.* 1. Forward or onward movement in space; advance, development. 2. (hist.) State journey, official tour. **progre̊′ss** *v.i.* Move forward or onward; be carried on: advance, develop.
progre̊′ssion *n.* 1. Progress. 2. (mus.) Passing from one note or chord to another. 3. (math.) Succession of series of quantities, between every two successive terms of which there is some constant relation; *arithmetical* ∼, series in which each number increases or decreases by the same quantity, as 2, 4, 6, etc.; *geometrical* ∼, series in which the increase or decrease is by a common ratio, as 3, 9, 27. 4. (astron.) Movement of planet in order of signs of zodiac, i.e. from west to east. **progre̊′ssional** *adj.*
progre̊′ssionist *n.* Advocate of or believer in progress, e.g. in political or social matters.
progre̊′ssive *adj.* 1. Moving forward; proceeding step by step, successive; ∼ *whist* etc., whist etc. played by several sets of players at different tables, certain players passing after each round to next table. 2. Advancing in social conditions, character, efficiency, etc.; favouring progress or reform; (of disease) continuously increasing. **progre̊′ssively** *adv.* **progre̊′s-**

sivene̊ss *n.* **progre̊′ssive** *n.* Advocate of progressive policy.
prohi′bit *v.t.* Forbid, debar.
prōhibi′tion *n.* 1. Forbidding; edict, order, that forbids. 2. Forbidding by law of sale of intoxicants for common consumption. 3. (law) Writ from High Court of Justice forbidding inferior court to proceed in suit deemed beyond its cognizance. **prōhibi′tionist** *n.* Advocate of prohibition (esp. of sale etc. of intoxicants).
prohi′bitive *adj.* Prohibiting; (of tax etc.) serving to prevent the use or abuse of something; (of price) so high that it precludes purchase. **prohi′bitively** *adv.* **prohi′bitiveness** *n.* **prohi′bitory** *adj.*
proje̊′ct *v.* 1. Plan, contrive; form a project of. 2. Cast, throw, impel; cause (light, shadow) to fall on surface; (fig.) cause (idea etc.) to take shape. 3. Jut out, protrude. 4. (geom.) Draw straight lines from a centre through every point of (given figure) to produce corresponding figure on a surface by intersecting it; draw (such lines), produce (such corresponding figure); make projection of (earth, sky, etc.). **prŏ′je̊ct** *n.* Plan, scheme; (in schools) scheme of study lasting for a limited period (e.g. one term) during which the pupils make their own inquiries and record their findings.
proje̊′ctile *adj.* 1. Impelling, as ∼ *force*. 2. Capable of being projected by force, esp. from gun. ∼ *n.* Projectile missile, shell, bullet.
proje̊′ction *n.* 1. Throwing, casting. 2. Protruding; protruding thing; thrusting forward. 3. Planning; mental image viewed as objective reality. 4. (geom.) Projecting of a figure (see PROJECT *v.* 4); ∼ *of a point*, point in derived figure corresponding to point in original figure. 5. (geog.) Any orderly system of representing the meridians and parallels of the earth (or celestial sphere) by lines on a plane surface, e.g. by first projecting the meridians on to a cone (*conical* ∼) or a cylinder (*cylindrical* ∼) (*illustration, p. 702*). 6. Display of film in cinema by throwing image on screen (and producing corresponding sound). 7. (alchemy) Transmutation of metals by casting *powder of* ∼ (powder of philosophers' stone) into crucible containing them.
proje̊′ctionist *n.* Person who projects slides or cinema film.
proje̊′ctive *adj.* Mentally projecting or projected; (geom.) of, derived by, projection; ∼ *property* (of a figure), property unchanged after projection. **proje̊′ctively** *adv.*
proje̊′ctor *n.* 1. One who forms a project; promoter of bubble companies. 2. Apparatus for projecting rays of light, as from a lighthouse lantern; apparatus for

[701]

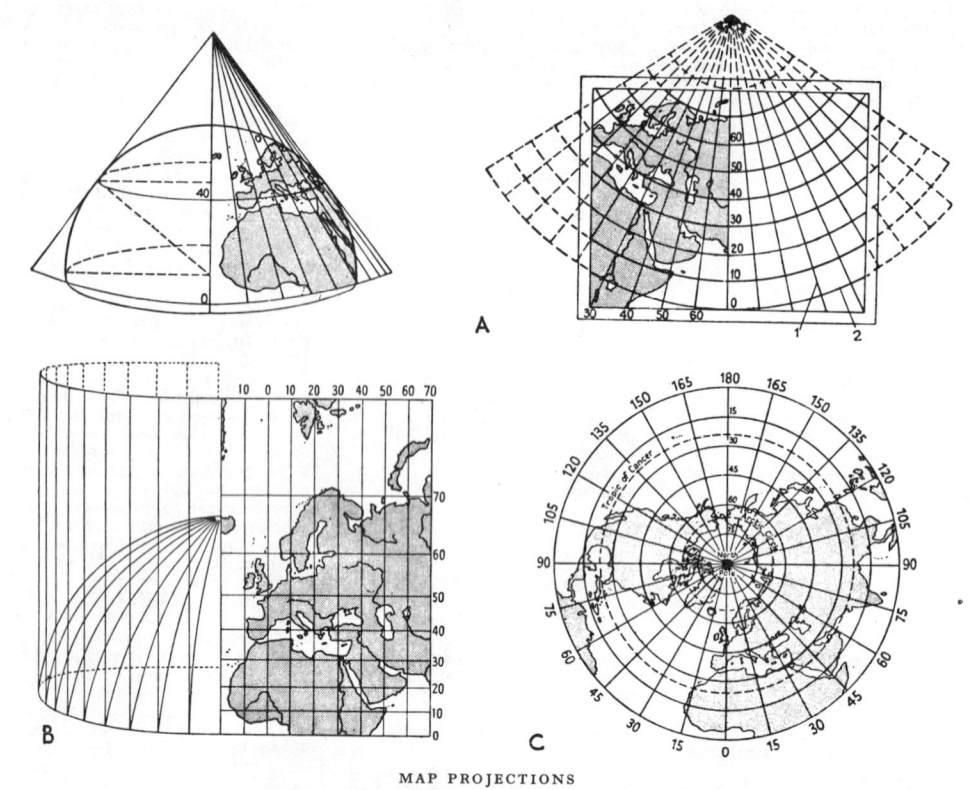

PROKOFIEV PROMENADE

MAP PROJECTIONS
A. CONICAL.   B. CYLINDRICAL OR MERCATOR.   C. ZENITHAL

1. Line of longitude. 2. Line of latitude. In A the meridians are projected on to a cone which touches the earth along a parallel, in this case 40° N. In B the meridians are projected on to a cylinder touching the earth, in this case at the equator. In C the surface of projection is a plane tangential to a point on the earth's surface, in this case the North Pole

throwing a picture on to a screen, as a cinematograph (*sound* ~, one for sound film, producing corresponding sound at same time).
Prokŏ'fiĕv (-f), Sergey Sergeevich (1891–1953). Russian composer and pianist.
Prol. *abbrev.* Prologue.
prolă'pse *v.i.* (path.) Slip forward or down out of place. **prō'-lăpse, prolă'psus** *ns.* (path.) Slipping forward or down of part or organ, esp. of uterus or rectum.
prō'lāte (*or* -ā't) *adj.* Growing, extending, in width; (fig.) widely spread; (gram.) prolative; (geom., of spheroid) lengthened in direction of polar diameter (ill. CONE).
prō'lātelÿ *adv.*
prolā'tive *adj.* (gram.) Serving to extend or complete predication (in 'you can go' *go* is the prolative infinitive).
prōle *n.* (colloq.) Proletarian.
prōlĕgŏ'mĕnon *n.* (usu. in pl. *-ena*). Preliminary discourse or matter prefixed to book etc.
prōlĕgŏ'mĕnarÿ, prōlĕgŏ'mĕnous *adjs.*
prōlĕ'psis *n.* (pl. *-psēs*). Anticipation; (gram.) anticipatory use of adjectives, as in *So those two brothers and their* murdered *man Rode past fair Florence*. **prolĕ'ptic** *adj.* **prolĕ'pticallÿ** *adv.*
prōlĕtār'ian *adj.* & *n.* (Member) of the proletariat. **prōlĕtār'ianism** *n.*
prōlĕtār'iat *n.* 1. (Rom. hist.) Lowest class of community in ancient Rome, regarded as contributing nothing to the State but offspring. 2. (freq. contempt.) Lowest class of community; (econ.) class which is dependent on daily labour for subsistence, and has no reserve of capital; sometimes, all wage-earners; *dictatorship of the* ~, Communist ideal of domination by the proletariat after the suppression of capitalism and the bourgeoisie.
prolĭ'ferāte *v.* Reproduce itself, grow, by multiplication of elementary parts; produce (cells etc.) thus; (of human beings etc.) multiply. **prolĭferā'tion** *n.* **prolĭ'ferative** *adj.*
prolĭ'ferous *adj.* (bot.) Producing leaf or flower buds from leaf or flower; producing new individuals from buds; (zool.) multiplying by budding etc.; (path.) spreading by proliferation.
prolĭ'fic *adj.* Producing (much) offspring; abundantly productive (*of*), abounding *in*. **prolĭ'fically** *adv.* **prolĭ'ficacÿ, prolĭfĭ'cĭtÿ, prolĭ'ficnĕss** *ns.*
prō'lix (*or* -olĭ'ks) *adj.* Lengthy, wordy, tedious. **prō'lixlÿ** *adv.* **prolĭ'xitÿ** *n.*
prōlŏ'cūtor *n.* Chairman esp. of lower house of convocation of either province of Church of England.
prō'logīze (-j-), **prō'loguīze** (-gīz) *vbs. i.* Write, speak, a prologue.
prō'lŏgue (-g) *n.* Preliminary discourse, poem, etc., esp. introducing play; act, event, serving as introduction (*to*). ~ *v.t.* Introduce, furnish, with a prologue.
prolŏ'ng *v.t.* Extend in duration; extend in spatial length; lengthen pronunciation of. **prōlŏngā'tion** (-ngg-) *n.*
prŏm *n.* (colloq.) Promenade concert.
prŏmĕna'de (-ahd) *n.* Walk, ride, drive, taken for exercise, amusement, or display, or as

[702]

social ceremony; place, esp. paved public walk for this; (U.S.) school or college ball or dance; ~ *concert*, one at which (part of) audience is not provided with seats and can move about; ~ *deck*, upper deck on a passenger vessel, where passengers may walk about. ~ *v.* Make a promenade through (place); lead (person) about a place esp. for display.

Promē'thean (-thūs). (Gk myth.) Son of the Titan Iapetus; he made mankind out of clay, taught them many arts, and stole fire for them from heaven; to punish him, Zeus chained him to a rock in the Caucasus, where a vulture fed each day on his liver, which was restored in the night. **Promē'thean** *adj*. Of, like, Prometheus in his skill or punishment.

promē'thium *n.* (chem.) Radioactive element of the rare-earth group, formed by the fission of uranium; symbol Pm, at. no. 61, principal isotope 147.

prŏ'minent *adj.* Jutting out, projecting; conspicuous; distinguished. **prŏ'minently** *adv.* **prŏ'minence** *n.* Being prominent; thing that projects; *solar* ~, cloud of incandescent hydrogen projecting from sun (ill. SUN).

promi'scūous *adj.* Of mixed and disorderly composition; indiscriminate; (esp.) having sexual intercourse with many persons. **promi'scūously** *adv.* **promi'scūousnĕss, prŏmiscū'ity** *ns.*

prŏ'mīse *n.* Assurance given to a person that one will do or not do something or will give or procure him something; thing promised; (fig.) ground of expectation of future achievements or good results. ~ *v.* Make (person) a promise to give or procure him (thing); make (person) a promise (*to, that*); make promise; (fig.) afford expectation of, seem likely (*to*); hold out good etc. prospect; ~ *oneself*, look forward to; *Promised Land*, Canaan, as promised to Abraham and his posterity (Gen. 12: 7, 13: 15, etc.); heaven, any place of expected felicity.

prŏmisee' *n.* (law) Person to whom promise is made.

prŏ'mising *adj.* Likely to turn out well, hopeful, full of promise. **prŏ'misingly** *adv.*

prŏ'missory *adj.* Conveying or implying a promise; ~ *note*, signed document containing written promise to pay stated sum to specified person or to bearer at specified date or on demand.

prŏ'montory *n.* Point of high land jutting out into sea etc., headland; (anat.) any of various protuberances in body.

promō'te *v.t.* 1. Advance, prefer (person *to* position, higher office); (chess) raise (pawn) to rank of queen etc. 2. Help forward, encourage (process, result); support actively the passing of (law), take necessary steps for passing of (local or private act of parliament). 3. (eccles. law) Set in motion (office of ordinary or judge) in criminal suit in ecclesiastical court, institute (such suit). **promō'ter** *n.* (esp., *company* ~) One who promotes formation of joint-stock company (freq. with implication of fraud or sharp practice). **promō'tion** *n.* Promoting; *sales* ~, (commerc.) information or instruction given to dealer by manufacturer or agent to enable him to sell a product. **promō'tive** *adj.*

Promō'tor Fide'ī (-dāī). (R.C. Ch.) Officer of Sacred Congregation of Rites at Rome who advances all possible arguments against candidate for beatification or canonization. [L, = 'promoter of the faith']

prŏmpt[1] *adj.* Ready in action, acting with alacrity; made, done, etc., readily or at once; (commerc., of goods) for immediate delivery and payment. **prŏ'mptitūde, prŏ'mptnĕss** *ns.* **prŏmpt** *n.* Time-limit for payment of account, stated on ~-*note*.

prŏmpt[2] *v.t.* 1. Incite, move (person etc. *to*); inspire, give rise to (feeling, thought, action). 2. Supply (actor, reciter) with the words that come next; assist (hesitating speaker) with suggestion. ~ *n.* Thing said to help memory, esp. of actor; ~-*book*, copy of play for prompter's use; ~-*box*, prompter's box on stage; ~-*side*, side of stage to actor's left. **prŏ'mpter** *n.* One who prompts, esp.(theatr.) person stationed out of sight of audience to prompt actors.

prŏ'mulgāte *v.t.* Make known to the public, disseminate, proclaim. **prŏmulgā'tion, prŏ'mulgātor** *ns.*

pronā'ŏs *n.* (Gk antiq.) Space in front of body of temple, enclosed by portico and projecting side walls (ill. TEMPLE[1]).

prō'nāte *v.t.* (physiol.) Put (hand, fore-limb) into prone position. **pronā'tion** *n.* **pronā'tor** *n.* (anat.) Muscle that effects or helps pronation.

prōne *adj.* 1. Having the front or ventral part downwards, lying face downwards; (loosely) lying flat, prostrate. 2. (of ground) Having downward aspect or direction; (loosely) steep, headlong. 3. Disposed, liable (*to*). **prō'nenĕss** (-n-n-) *n.*

prŏng *n.* Forked instrument, e.g. hay-fork; each pointed member of fork; ~-*buck*, ~-*horn*(*ed antelope*), N. Amer. deer-like ruminant (*Antilocapra americana*), male of which has deciduous horns with short prong in front. ~ *v.t.* Pierce, stab, turn up (soil etc.) with prong.

pronŏ'minal *adj.* Of (the nature of) a pronoun. **pronŏ'minally** *adv.*

prŏ'noun *n.* Word used instead of (proper or other) noun to designate person or thing already mentioned, known from context, or forming subject of inquiry; *demonstrative* ~*s*, this, that, these, those; *distributive* ~*s*, each, either; *indefinite* ~*s*, any, some, etc.; *interrogative* ~*s*, who? what? which?; *personal* ~*s*, I, we, thou, you, he, she, it, they; *possessive* ~*s*, adjectives representing possessive case of personal pronouns (my, our, etc.) with absolute forms (mine, ours, etc.); *reflexive* ~*s*, myself, ourselves, etc.; *relative* ~*s*, who, which, that, what.

pronou'nce *v.* 1. Utter, deliver (judgement, curse, etc.) formally or solemnly; state, declare, as one's opinion; pass judgement, give one's opinion. 2. Utter, articulate, esp. with reference to different modes of pronunciation; *pronouncing dictionary*, one in which pronunciation is indicated. **pronou'nceable** *adj.* **pronou'nced** (-st) *adj.* (esp.) Strongly marked, decided. **pronŭnciamĕ'ntō** *n.* Proclamation, manifesto, esp. (in Spanish-speaking countries) one issued by insurrectionists.

pronŭnciā'tion *n.* Mode in which a word is pronounced; a person's way of pronouncing words.

prōōf *n.* 1. Evidence sufficing or helping to establish a fact; spoken or written legal evidence; proving, demonstration; (Sc. law) evidence given before judge, upon record or issue in pleading, trial before judge instead of by jury. 2. Test, trial; (place for) testing of firearms or explosives; ~ *stress*, (eng.) load slightly greater than that which a mechanism etc. will normally have to bear. 3. Standard of strength of distilled alcoholic liquors; ~ *spirit*, standard mixture of pure alcohol and water (containing 57.3% alcohol by volume) in terms of which the alcoholic strengths of liquors are computed for excise purposes (e.g. if 100 volumes of a liquor contain enough alcohol to make 70 volumes of proof spirit the liquor is defined as '70% proof' or '30% under proof'). 4. Trial impression taken from type, in which corrections etc. may be made; each of limited number of careful impressions made from engraved plate before printing of ordinary issue and usu. (also ~ *before letters*) before inscription is added; *artist's, engraver's,* ~, one taken for examination or alteration by him; *signed* ~, early proof signed by artist; ~-*reader*, person employed in reading and correcting printers' proofs; so ~-*read* (*v.*). 5. Rough uncut edges of shorter or narrower leaves of book, left to show it has not been cut down in binding. ~ *adj.* (of armour) Of tried strength; impenetrable esp. as second element of compound, as *bo'mbproof, wi'ndproof*). ~ *v.t.* Make (thing) proof; make (fabric etc.) waterproof; submit (mechanism etc.) to proof stress.

prŏp[1] *n.* Rigid support, esp. one not forming structural part of thing supported; (fig.) person etc. who upholds institution etc. ~ *v.t.* Support (as) by prop, hold *up* thus.

prŏp[2] *n.* (colloq.) Stage property; (pl.) property-man etc.

prŏp[3] *n.* (colloq.) Aircraft propeller.

prop. *abbrev.* Proposition.

prŏpagă'nda *n.* 1. (*Congregation, College, of*) *the P*~, committee of cardinals of R.C. Ch. in charge of foreign missions. 2. Association, organized scheme, for propagation of a doctrine or practice; doctrines, information, etc., thus propagated (freq. with implication of bias or falsity, esp. in politics); efforts, schemes, principles, of propagation. **prŏpagă'ndist** *adj.* & *n.* **prŏpagă'ndīze** *v.*

prŏ'pagāte *v.* 1. Multiply specimens of (plant, animal, disease, etc.) by natural process from parent stock; (of plant etc.) reproduce (*itself*). 2. Hand down (quality etc.) from one generation to another. 3. Disseminate (statement, belief, practice). 4. Extend the action or operation of, transmit, convey in some direction or through some medium. **prŏpagā'tion, prŏ'pagātor** *ns.* **prŏ'pagātive** *adj.*

prŏ'pāne *n.* (chem.) Colourless inflammable hydrocarbon gas (C_3H_8), one of the paraffin series, occurring in natural gases.

prŏparŏ'xytone *adj.* & *n.* (Gk gram.) (Word) with acute accent on last syllable but two.

prope'l *v.t.* Drive forward, give onward motion to. **pope'llent** *adj.* Propelling.

prope'llant *n.* Propelling agent; explosive that propels projectile from firearm; fuel or oxidizer for propelling a rocket.

prope'ller *n.* (esp.) Revolving shaft with blades usu. set at an angle and twisted like thread of screw, for propelling ship; similar device on an aircraft producing the thrust which drives it forward.

prope'nsity *n.* Inclination, tendency (*to, for*).

prŏ'per *adj.* 1. (archaic) Own; (astron.) ~ *motion*, that part of apparent motion of fixed star etc. supposed to be due to its actual movement in space. 2. Belonging, relating, exclusively or distinctively (*to*); (her.) represented in natural colouring; ~ *name, noun*, name used to designate an individual person, animal, town, ship, etc. 3. Accurate, correct; (usu. following its noun) strictly so called, real, genuine; thorough, complete (colloq.); handsome (archaic); ~ *fraction*, one whose value is less than unity. 4. Suitable, right; in conformity with demands of society, decent, respectable. **prŏ'perly** *adv.* Fittingly, suitably; rightly, duly; with good manners; (colloq.) thoroughly.

prŏpĕrispŏ'mĕnon *adj.* & *n.* (Gk gram.) (Word) with circumflex accent on last syllable but one.

Propĕr'tius (-shus), Sextus (*c* 51 –*c* 15 B.C.). Roman elegiac poet.

prŏ'perty *n.* 1. Owning, being owned; thing owned; landed estate; ~ *qualification*, one based on possession of property; ~ *tax*, one levied directly on property. 2. (theatr.) Portable thing, as article of costume, furniture, etc., used on stage; ~-*man*, -*master*, (fem. -*mistress*), person in charge of stage properties. 3. Attribute, quality; (logic) quality common to a whole class but not necessary to distinguish it from others.

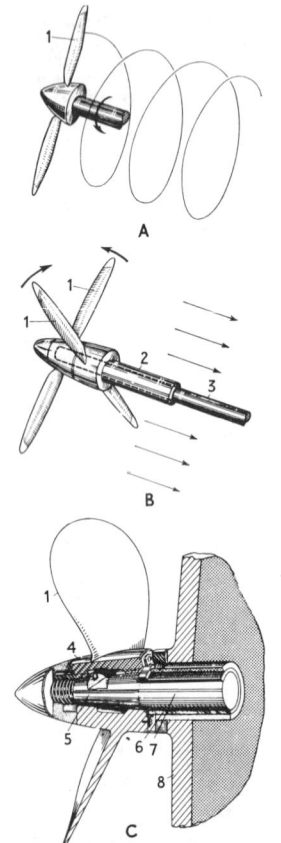

PROPELLERS. A. SINGLE ROTATION AIRCRAFT PROPELLER. B. CONTRAPROP. C. MARINE PROPELLER OR SCREW

1. Blade. 2. Back shaft. 3. Front shaft. 4. Boss. 5. Tail-end shaft. 6. Stern tube. 7. Shaft. 8. Hull. The arrows behind the propellers in *A* and *B* show the direction of the slipstreams

prŏ'phĕcў *n.* Faculty of a prophet; prophetic utterance; foretelling of future events.

prŏ'phĕsy̆ *v.* Speak as a prophet, foretell (future events); (archaic) expound the Scriptures.

prŏ'phĕt *n.* (fem. *pro'phĕtĕss*) Inspired teacher, revealer or interpreter of God's will; spokesman, advocate (*of*); one who foretells events; (pl.) prophetical writers of the O.T., the first four (Isaiah, Jeremiah, Ezekiel, Daniel) being called the *major* ~s since more of their writings have survived, and the last twelve (from Hosea to Malachi), the *minor* ~s whose extant writings are relatively short; *the P*~, Muhammad; (also) Joseph Smith, founder of Mormonism.

prophĕ'tic *adj.* Of a prophet; predicting, containing a prediction *of*. **prophĕ'tical** *adj.* **prophĕ'tically** *adv.*

prŏphy̆lă'ctic *adj.* & *n.* (Medicine, measure) tending to prevent disease. **prŏphy̆lă'ctically** *adv.* **prŏphy̆lă'xis** *n.* Preventive treatment of disease.

propi'nquity *n.* Nearness in place; close kinship; similarity.

prōpiŏ'nic *adj.* ~ *acid*, colourless liquid with odour resembling that of acetic acid, present in products of the distillation of wood.

propi'tiāte (-shi-) *v.t.* Appease (offended person etc.); make propitious. **propi'tiā'tion** *n.* Appeasement; atonement; (archaic) gift etc. meant to propitiate.

propi'tiatory (-sha-) *adj.* Serving, meant, to propitiate.

propi'tious (-shus) *adj.* Well-disposed, favourable; suitable *for*, favourable *to*. **propi'tiously** *adv.*

propor'tion *n.* Comparative part, share; comparative relation, ratio; due relation of one thing to another or between parts of a thing; (pl.) dimensions; (math.) equality of ratios between two pairs of quantities, set of such quantities; (arith.) method by which, three quantities being given, a fourth may be found which is in same ratio to third as second is to first. ~ *v.t.* Make proportionate *to*.

propor'tional *adj.* In due proportion, corresponding in degree or amount; ~ *representation*, method of parliamentary representation designed to allow the various political parties to be represented in proportion to their voters and characterized by the use of the transferable vote, i.e. the filling up of seats, where a quota is not secured by first choices, by the transference of votes from second choices, and so on. **propŏrtionă'lity** *n.* **propŏr'tionally** *adv.* **propŏr'tionate** *adj.* **propŏr'tionately** *adv.*

propō'sal (-z-) *n.* Act of proposing something; offer of marriage; scheme of action etc. proposed.

[704]

propō′se (-z) *v.* Put forward for consideration, propound; set up as an aim; nominate (person) as member of society etc.; offer (person, person's health, etc.) as toast; make offer of marriage (*to*); put forward as a plan; intend, purpose.

prŏposi′tion (-z-) *n.* 1. Statement, assertion, esp. (logic) form of words consisting of predicate and subject connected by copula; (math., abbrev. *prop.*) formal statement of theorem or problem, freq. including the demonstration. 2. Proposal; (U.S.) task, project, problem for solution. **prŏposi′tional** *adj.* **prŏposi′tion** *v.t.* (U.S.) Make a proposition to.

propou′nd *v.t.* Offer for consideration, propose (question, problem, scheme, etc.); produce (will) before proper authority in order to establish its legality.

prōprae′tor *n.* (Rom. hist.) Ex-praetor with authority of praetor in province not under military control.

proprī′etary *adj.* Of a proprietor; holding property; held in private ownership (esp. of medicines etc. of which manufacture or sale is restricted by patent or otherwise to particular person(s)). ~ *n.* Proprietorship; body of proprietors.

propri′etor *n.* (fem. *propri′étress*) Owner. **proprietōri′al** *adj.* **proprietōr′ially** *adv.* **propri′etorship** *n.*

propri′ety *n.* Fitness, rightness, correctness of behaviour or morals; (pl.) details of correct conduct.

prō-prō′ctor *n.* Assistant or deputy proctor in university.

propu′lsion *n.* Driving or pushing forward; means of this; (fig.) impelling influence. **propu′lsive** *adj.*

prō′pyl *n.* (chem.) Hydrocarbon radical C_3H_7; ~ *alcohol*, colourless liquid (C_3H_7OH), occurring in fusel-oil and separated by distillation, used as a solvent. **prō′pylēne** *n.* Colourless hydrocarbon gas (C_3H_6), occurring esp. in the gases from the cracking of petroleum.

prŏpylae′um *n.* (pl. *-aea*). Entrance to temple; *Propylaea*, entrance to the · Acropolis at Athens.

prō rā′ta. Proportional(ly).

prorō′gue (-g) *v.* Discontinue meeting of (British Parliament etc.) without dissolving it; be prorogued. **prōrogā′tion** *n.*

prōsā′ic (-z-; *or* pro-) *adj.* Like prose, lacking poetic beauty; unromantic, commonplace, dull. **prōsā′ically** *adv.*

proscē′nium *n.* 1. (Gk & Rom. antiq.) Stage. 2. (in theatre) Space between curtain or drop-scene and orchestra, esp. with the enclosing arch (ill. THEATRE).

proscri′be *v.t.* Put (person) out of protection of law; banish, exile; reject, denounce (practice etc.) as dangerous etc. **proscri′ption** *n.* **proscri′ptive** *adj.*

prōse (-z) *n.* Ordinary non-metrical form of written or spoken language; (eccles.) piece of rhythmical prose or rhymed accentual verse sung or said between epistle and gospel at certain Masses; *prosy discourse.* ~ *v.* Talk prosily; turn (poem etc.) into prose.

prŏ′sėcūte *v.t.* 1. Follow up, pursue (inquiry, studies); carry on (trade, pursuit). 2. Institute legal proceedings against or with reference to.

prŏsėcū′tion *n.* Prosecuting; carrying on of legal proceedings against person; prosecuting party; (law) exhibition of criminal charge before court.

prŏ′sėcūtor *n.* (fem. *prŏsėcū′trix*) One who prosecutes, esp. in criminal court; *public* ~, law officer conducting criminal proceedings in public interest.

prŏ′sėlyte *n.* Convert from one opinion, creed, or party, to another; Gentile convert to Jewish faith. ~ *v.t.* Make proselyte of. **prŏ′sėlytism, prŏ′sėlytizer** *ns.* **prŏ′sėlytize** *v.t.*

prosė′nchyma (-ngk-) *n.* (bot.) Tissue of elongated cells placed with their ends interpenetrating, esp. fibro-vascular tissue. **prosė′nchymal, prŏsėnchy′matous** *adjs.*

Prosėr′pina. Latin name of PERSEPHONE.

prō′sify (-z-) *v.* Turn into prose, make prosaic; write prose.

prō′sody *n.* Science of versification. **prosō′dic** *adj.* **prō′sodist** *n.*

prŏsōpopoe′ia (-pēia) *n.* (rhet.) Introduction of pretended speaker; personification of abstract thing.

prŏ′spect *n.* 1. Extensive view of landscape etc.; mental scene. 2. Expectation; what one expects. 3. (colloq.) Possible or likely purchaser, subscriber, etc. 4. (mining) Spot giving prospects of mineral deposit; sample of ore for testing, resulting yield. **prospe′ct** *v.* Explore region (*for* gold etc.); explore (region) for gold etc., work (mine) experimentally; (of mine) promise (well, ill; specified yield). **prospe′ctor** *n.*

prospe′ctive *adj.* Concerned with, applying to, the future; expected, future, some day to be. **prospe′ctively** *adv.*

prospe′ctus *n.* Circular describing chief features of school, commercial enterprise, forthcoming book, etc.

prŏ′sper *v.* Succeed, thrive; make successful. **prospe′rity** *n.*

prŏ′sperous *adj.* Flourishing, successful, thriving; auspicious. **prŏ′sperously** *adv.*

prŏ′stāte *n.* (also ~ *gland*) Large gland, accessory to male generative organs and surrounding neck of bladder and commencement of urethra (ill. PELVIS). **prŏstă′tic** *adj.*

prŏ′sthėsis *n.* 1. (surg.) Making up of deficiencies (with artificial teeth, limb, etc.); this as branch of surgery. 2. (gram.) Addition of letter or syllable at beginning of word. **prŏsthė′tic** *adj.* Of prosthesis; (biochem.) of a group or radical of a different kind added or substituted in a compound.

prŏ′stitūte *n.* Woman who offers her body to indiscriminate sexual intercourse for payment. ~ *v.t.* Make a prostitute of; (fig.) sell for base gain, put (abilities etc.) to ignoble use. **prŏstitū′tion** *n.*

prŏ′strāte (*or* -at) *adj.* Lying with face to ground, esp. as token of submission or humility; lying in horizontal position; overcome, overthrown; physically exhausted; (bot.) lying flat on ground. **prostrā′te** (*or* prŏ′-) *v.t.* Lay flat on ground; cast *oneself* down prostrate; (fig.) overcome, make submissive; (of fatigue etc.) reduce to extreme physical weakness. **prŏstrā′tion** *n.*

prŏ′style *adj.* & *n.* (That has) portico with not more than four columns (ill. TEMPLE[1]).

prō′sȳ (-zĭ) *adj.* Commonplace, tedious, dull. **prō′sily** *adv.* **prō′sinėss** *n.*

prōtăctī′nium *n.* (chem.) Radioactive element of the actinium series, which by disintegration yields actinium; symbol Pa, at. no. 91, at. wt 231·0359.

prŏtă′gonist *n.* Chief person in drama or plot of story; leading person in contest, champion of cause, etc.

Prŏtă′gorăs (5th c. B.C.). Greek sophist philosopher of Abdera; portrayed in Plato's dialogue of that name.

prō′tamine *n.* (chem.) One of the simple basic proteins, present only in sperm, containing a higher percentage of nitrogen than most proteins.

prŏtă′ndrous *adj.* Having stamens ripening before the stigmas.

prō tă′ntō. So far, to such an extent. [L]

prŏ′tasis *n.* (pl. *-asēs*). (gram., rhet.) Introductory clause, esp. clause expressing condition, opp. APODOSIS. **prŏtă′tic** *adj.*

prō′tėan *adj.* Variable, versatile; or of like Proteus.

protė′ct *v.t.* Keep safe, defend, guard (*from*, *against*); provide (machinery etc.) with appliances to prevent injury from it; (econ.) guard (home industry) against competition, by imposing tariffs on foreign goods; (commerc.) provide funds to meet (bill, draft).

protė′ction *n.* Protecting, defence; patronage; protecting person or thing; safe-conduct; system or policy of protecting home industries by tariffs etc.; security from threatened violence, obtained

[705]

PROTECTIVE

by payment to racketeers; such payment. **prote̅'ctionism, prote̅'ctionist** ns.

prote̅'ctive adj. Serving to protect; ~ *custody*, detention of person by State supposedly for his own protection. **prote̅'ctively** adv. **prote̅'ctiveness** n.

prote̅'ctor n. Person who protects; thing, device, that protects; regent in charge of kingdom during minority, absence, etc., of sovereign; *Lord P~ of the Commonwealth*, title of Oliver Cromwell 1653-8 and Richard Cromwell 1658-9. **prote̅'ctoral** adj.

prote̅'ctorate n. 1. Office of protector of kingdom or State; period of this, esp. of the protectorate of Oliver and Richard Cromwell. 2. Authority assumed by a strong State over a weak or underdeveloped one which it protects and partially controls; period of such authority; State so protected.

prote̅'ctory n. (R.C. Ch.) Institution for care of destitute or delinquent children.

protégé (prŏ'tăzhā) n. (fem. *-ée*). Person under protection or patronage of another.

prō'teiform adj. Multiform, extremely changeable.

prō'tein n. Any of a class of organic compounds (of carbon, hydrogen, oxygen, nitrogen, and often sulphur) forming an important part of all living organisms and the essential nitrogenous constituents of the food of animals.

prō te̅'mpōre (abbrev. *pro tem*.) For the time, temporary, temporarily. [L]

prō'test n. Formal statement of dissent or disapproval, remonstrance; written statement of dissent from motion carried in House of Lords signed by any peer of minority; written declaration, usu. by notary public, that bill has been duly presented and payment or acceptance refused; solemn declaration. **prote̅'st** v. Affirm solemnly; write a protest in regard to (bill); make (freq. written) protest *against* (action, proposal). **prote̅'ster, prote̅'stor** ns. **prote̅'stingly** adv.

prō'testant n. 1. *P~*, member, adherent of, any of the Christian Churches or bodies that repudiated papal authority and were separated from Roman communion in the Reformation (16th c.), or of any Church or body descended from them; (hist., usu. pl.) those German princes and free cities who dissented from the decision of the Diet of Spires (1529), which reaffirmed the edict of the Diet of Worms against the Reformation; German adherents of Reformed doctrines and worship. 2. (*also* prote̅'-) One who protests. **Prō'testantism** n. **Prō'testant** adj. Of Protestants or Protestantism; ~ *Episcopal Church*, official style of Church in U.S. descended from and in communion with Church of England.

prŏtēstā'tion n. Solemn affirmation; protest.

Prō'teus[1]. (Gk myth.) Seagod, son of Oceanus and Tethys, with power of assuming different shapes.

prō'teus[2] n. (zool.) Blind white urodele (*Proteus anguinus*) living in caves in Yugoslavia.

prōthala̅'mion n. Song or poem celebrating a marriage.

prō'thesis n. 1. (eccles.) Placing of the elements etc. in readiness for use in the Eucharistic office; credence-table, part of the church where this stands. 2. (gram.) = PROSTHESIS. **prothe̅'tic** adj.

prō'tium n. Common isotope of hydrogen, as dist. from the heavy isotopes deuterium and tritium.

proto- prefix. 1. First, primary, primitive. 2. (chem.) Indicating a substance held to be the parent of the substance to the name of which it is prefixed, as *protoactinium* (= PROTACTINIUM).

prō'tocol n. Original draft of diplomatic document, esp. of terms of treaty agreed to in conference and signed by the parties; formal statement of transaction; rigid prescription or observance of precedence and deference to rank as in diplomatic and military services; official formula at beginning and end of charter, papal bull, etc. ~ v. Draw up protocols; record in protocol. [Gk *protokollon* flyleaf glued to case of book (*kolla* glue)]

prōtogȳ'nous (-g-) adj. Having stigmas ripening before the stamens.

prōtoma̅r'tyr (-er) n. First person martyred for a cause (esp. applied to first Christian martyr, St. Stephen).

prō'ton n. (phys. chem.) Fundamental atomic particle forming part (or in hydrogen the whole) of the nucleus, having a single positive electric charge equal and opposite to that of the electron.

prōtonō'tary n. Chief clerk in some law courts, esp. (hist.) Chancery, Common Pleas, and King's Bench, (orig. in Byzantine court); *P~ Apostolic(al)*, (R.C. Ch.) member of the chief college of prelates in the Curia.

prō'tophyte n. Unicellular plant.

prō'toplasm n. Viscous translucent substance, the essential matter of living organisms, the substance of which cells principally consist, capable of being irritated, of moving spontaneously, contracting itself, assimilating other matter, and reproducing itself, differentiated (in most organisms) into the *nucleus*, or reproductive part, and the *cytoplasm*, a viscous fluid forming the general body of the cell. **prōtopla̅'smic** adj.

PROUD

prō'toplast n. Mass of cytoplasm which is visibly distinct from the rest. **prōtopla̅'stic** adj.

prō'totype n. Original thing or person in relation to any copy, imitation, representation, later specimen, improved form, etc. **prō'totypal, prōtotȳ'pical** adjs.

prōtozō'ic adj. (geol., of strata) Containing earliest traces of living beings.

prōtozō'on n. (pl. *-zoa*). Member of the Protozoa, a division of the

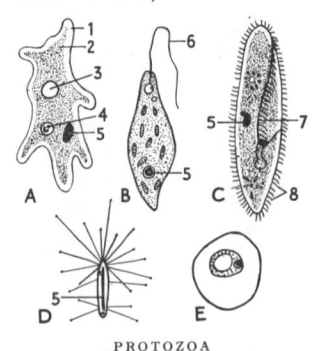

PROTOZOA

A. AMOEBA.
B. FLAGELLATE (*EUGLENA*).
C. CILIATA (*PARAMOECIUM*).
D. SUCTORIA (*PODOPHRYA*).
E. PLASMODIUM IN RED CORPUSCLES (ANNULAR STAGE)

1. Ectoplasm. 2. Endoplasm. 3. Contractile vacuole. 4. Gastric vacuole. 5. Nucleus. 6. Flagellum. 7. Peristome. 8. Cilia

animal kingdom comprising animals of the simplest type each essentially consisting of a simple cell, usu. of microscopic size.

protra̅'ct v.t. 1. Prolong, lengthen out; extend. 2. Draw (plan of ground etc.) to scale.

protra̅'ctile adj. (zool.) (of organ etc.) That can be extended.

protra̅'ction n. 1. Protracting; action of protractor muscle. 2. Drawing to scale.

protra̅'ctor n. 1. Instrument for setting off and measuring angles, usu. in form of graduated semicircle. 2. (physiol.) Muscle serving to extend limb etc.

protru̅'de (-ōōd) v. Thrust forth, cause to project; stick out, project; obtrude. **protru̅'sion** n. **protru̅'sible, -ive** adjs.

protū'berant adj. Bulging out, prominent. **protū'berance** n.

proud adj. 1. Valuing oneself highly or too highly, esp. on the ground *of* (qualities, rank, etc.); haughty, arrogant; feeling oneself greatly honoured; feeling or showing a proper pride; (of actions etc.) showing pride; of which one is or may be justly proud. 2. (of things) Imposing, splendid; slightly projecting; (of flesh) overgrown, round healing wound; (of waters) swollen, in flood. ~ adv. *do someone ~*,

[706]

PROUDHON

treat someone generously or lavishly. **prou'dly** adv.
Proudhon (-ōōdawṅ), Pierre Joseph (1809–65). French socialist and writer on politics and economics.
Proust (-ōōst), Marcel (1871–1922). French novelist; author of the series of volumes grouped under the title 'A la Recherche du Temps perdu', remarkable for their conception of the unreality and reversibility of time and for their minute psychological analysis.
Prov. abbrev. Proverbs (O.T.).
prove (-ōōv) v. 1. Test qualities of, try (archaic exc. in technical uses); subject (manufactured article etc.) to testing process; (arith.) test correctness of (calculation); take proof impression of (composed type, stereotype plate, etc.). 2. Establish as true, demonstrate truth of by evidence or argument; establish genuineness and validity of, obtain probate of (will). 3. Show itself, turn out, to be (or to be or do) ~ *oneself*, prove one's ability, character, etc. **pro'ven** adj. *not* ~, (Sc. law) not proved (verdict used when evidence is legally insufficient to justify conviction).
prŏ'vĕnance n. (Place of) origin.
Prŏvençal (-vahṅsah'l) adj. & n. (pl. -caux). Native, inhabitant of Provence; (of) the Romance language spoken in S. France, esp. in the old province of Provence.
Prove'nce (-vahṅs). District, former province, of SE. France east of the lower Rhône; orig. a Roman province, the first to be established outside Italy. [L *provincia (romana)* (the Roman) province]
prŏ'vĕnder n. Food, provisions, esp. for horses.
prŏ'vĕrb n. Short pithy saying in general use, adage, saw; byword, thing that is proverbial or matter of common talk; (*Book of*) *Proverbs*, didactic poetical book of O.T. consisting of maxims ascribed to Solomon and others.
prověr'bial adj. Of, expressed in, proverbs; that has become a proverb or byword, notorious, **prověr'bially** adv. **prověrbiă'lĭtў** n.
provĭ'de v. 1. Make due preparation (*for, against*); stipulate (*that*); (freq. ~ *with*) give or lend (what is needed); make provision, esp. secure maintenance (*for*). 2. (hist.) Appoint (incumbent *to* benefice); (of pope) appoint (successor *to* benefice not yet vacant).
provĭ'dĕd, provĭ'ding conjs. On the condition or understanding (*that*).
prŏ'vidence n. 1. Foresight, timely care; thrift. 2. Beneficent care of God or nature; *special* ~, particular instance of this. 3. P~, God.

prŏ'vĭdent adj. Having or showing foresight, thrifty. **prŏ'vĭdentlў** adv.
prŏvĭdĕ'ntial (-shal) adj. Of, by, divine foresight or interposition; opportune, lucky. **prŏvĭdĕ'ntiallў** adv.
prŏ'vince n. 1. (Rom. hist.) Territory outside Italy under Roman governor. 2. Administrative (esp. principal) division of country or State, esp. one that has been historically, linguistically, etc., distinct; (eccles.) district under archbishop or metropolitan; *the* ~s, all parts of country outside the capital. 3. Sphere of action, business; branch of learning etc.
provĭ'ncial (-shal) adj. Of a province; of the provinces; having the manners, speech, narrow views or interests, etc., associated with or attributed to inhabitants of provinces. **provĭ'nciallў** adv. **provĭ'nciă'lĭtў** (-nsh-) n. **provĭ'ncialize** (-sha-) v.t. **provĭ'ncial** n. 1. Inhabitant of a province or the provinces; countrified person. 2. (eccles.) Head of, chief of religious order in, a province.
provĭ'ncialism (-sha-) n. Provincial manner, mode of thought, etc.; word, phrase, peculiar to province(s); attachment to one's province rather than country.
provĭ'sion n. 1. Providing (*for, against*); provided amount *of* something; (pl.) supply of food, eatables and drinkables. 2. Legal or formal statement providing for something; clause of this; (Engl. hist., pl.) certain early statutes or ordinances; *Provisions of Oxford*, ordinances for checking king's misrule etc. drawn up (1258, in Henry III's reign) by barons under Simon de Montfort. 3. (hist.) Appointment to benefice not yet vacant. ~ v.t. Supply with provisions. **provĭ'sionment** n.
provĭ'sional adj. For the time being, temporary, subject to revision. **provĭ'sionallў** adv. **provisionă'lĭtў, provĭ'sionalness** ns.
provī'so (-z-) n. Stipulation; clause of stipulation or limitation in document.
provīs'or (-z-) n. (hist.) Holder of provision or grant (esp. from pope) of right of next presentation to benefice not yet vacant; *Statute of Provisors*, act of 25 Edw. III (1350–1) to prevent pope from granting such provisions.
provī'sorў (-z-) adj. Conditional; making provision.
prŏvocā'tion n. Incitement, instigation, irritation.
provō'cative adj. Tending to provocation (*of* curiosity etc.); intentionally irritating.
provō'ke v.t. Rouse, incite (*to*); irritate; instigate, tempt, allure; call forth (anger, inquiry, etc.); cause. **provō'king** adj. **provō'kinglў** adv.

PRUNT

prŏ'vost n. 1. Head of some university colleges and of Eton College; (U.S.) administrative officer in some universities; (hist.) head of chapter or religious community; Protestant clergyman in charge of principal church of town etc. in Germany etc. 2. Head of Scottish municipal corporation or burgh, corresponding to *mayor* in England. 3. (mil., usu. **provō'**) Officer of military police in garrison, camp, etc.; ~-*marshal*, head of military police in camp or on active service; master-at-arms of ship on which court martial is to be held; chief police official in some colonies; ~-*sergeant*, sergeant of military police.
prŏ'vostship n.
prow n. Fore-part immediately about stem of boat or ship.
prow'ĕss n. Valour, gallantry.
prowl v. Go about in search of plunder or prey; traverse (streets, place) thus. **prow'ler** n. **prowl** n. Prowling.
prox. abbrev. Proximo.
prox. acc. abbrev. *Proxime accessit*.
prŏ'xĭmal adj. (anat.) Situated towards centre of body or point of attachment. **prŏ'xĭmallў** adv.
prŏ'xĭmate adj. Nearest, next before or after; approximate. **prŏ'xĭmatelў** adv.
prŏ'xĭmĕ accĕ'ssĭt (aks-). (pl. *accesserunt*, pr. -ār'ŏont). (Position of) person who is nearly equal (to actual winner of prize, scholarship, etc.). [L, = 'he came very near']
prŏxĭ'mĭtў n. Nearness in space, time, etc.; ~ *of blood*, kinship.
prŏ'xĭmō adj. (abbrev. prox.) Of next month. [L]
prŏ'xў n. Agency of substitute or deputy; person authorized to act for another; writing authorizing person to vote on behalf of another, vote so given; (attrib.) done, given, made, by proxy.
prude (-ōōd) n. Person of extreme (esp. affected) propriety in conduct or speech. **pru'derў** n. **pru'dish** adj. **pru'dishlў** adv. **pru'dishness** n.
pru'dent (-ōō-) adj. Sagacious, discreet, wordly-wise. **pru'dentlў** adv. **pru'dence** n.
prudĕ'ntial (-ōō-,-shal) adj. Of, involving, marked by, prudence. **prudĕ'ntiallў** adv.
prune[1] (-ōō-) n. Dried plum; colour of its juice, dark reddish purple; ~*s and prisms*, prim and mincing manner of speaking etc.
prune[2] (-ōō-) v.t. Trim (tree etc.) by cutting away superfluous branches etc.; lop *off, away* (branches etc.); (fig.) remove (superfluities), clear *of* what is superfluous; *pruning-hook*, curved knife used for pruning.
prunĕ'lla (-ōō-) n. Strong silk or worsted stuff used formerly for barristers' gowns etc. and later for uppers of women's shoes.
prŭnt n. Piece of ornamental

[707]

glass laid on to vase etc.; tool for applying this.
prur'ient (-oor-) *adj.* Given to the indulgence of lewd ideas. **prur'iently** *adv.* **prur'ience, prur'iencȳ** *ns.*
pruri'gō (-oor-) *n.* Disease of skin marked by violent itching.
pruri'tus (-oor-) *n.* (med.) Itching of skin.
Prŭ'ssia (-sha). (Ger. *Preussen*) Former State of N. Europe; a kingdom 1701-1871; the dominant federal State of Germany 1871-1918; a republic 1918-46.
Prŭ'ssian (-shan) *adj.* Of Prussia, its people or language; ~ *blue* [so-called from its discovery in Berlin, 1704], deep greenish-blue pigment of great covering power, formerly regarded as ferric ferrocyanide. ~ *n.* Prussian person or language; *Old* ~, language which became extinct in 17th c., belonging to the Baltic group of languages.
prŭ'ssic *adj.* Of, got from, Prussian blue; ~ *acid*, solution in water of hydrocyanic acid.
prȳ[1] *v.i.* Look, peer, inquisitively; inquire impertinently *into*. **prȳ'ing** *adj.* **prȳ'inglȳ** *adv.*
prȳ[2] *v.t.* (U.S.) Variant of PRIZE[2].
prȳtanē'um *n.* (Gk antiq.) Public hall, esp. one in Athens for entertainment of ambassadors, presidents of senate, and specially honoured citizens.
Ps(s). *abbrev.* Psalm(s) (O.T.).
P.S. *abbrev.* Police sergeant; postscript; (also p.s.) prompt side.
psalm (sahm) *n.* Sacred song, hymn; (*Book of*) *Psalms*, book of O.T. consisting of psalms (pop. *Psalms of David*). **psa'lmist** *n.* Author of a psalm; *the P*~, David.
Psălmană'zar (să-), George (c 1679-1763). Assumed name of a Frenchman who represented himself as a pagan from Formosa and invented a language ('Formosan') and a religious system; he later repented the imposture, which is described in his Memoirs, and became a serious scholar; he was a friend of Dr Johnson.
psa'lmodȳ (săl- *or* sahm-) *n.* Practice, art, of singing psalms, hymns, anthems, etc., esp. in public worship; arrangement of psalms for singing, psalms so arranged. **psalmō'dic** *adj.* **psa'lmodist** *n.*
psa'lter (sawl- *or* sŏl-) *n.* 1. *P*~, Book of Psalms; version of this. 2. Copy of the Psalms esp. for liturgical use.
psaltē'rium (sawl- *or* sŏl-) *n.* Omasum.
psa'lterȳ (sawl- *or* sŏl-) *n.* Ancient and medieval triangular stringed instrument, like dulcimer, but played by plucking with fingers or plectrum.
psēphŏ'logȳ (sē-) *n.* Statistical analysis of votes cast in elections. **psephŏ'logist** *n.*
pseudo-, pseud- (*or* s-) *prefix.* False(ly), seeming(ly), professed-(ly) but not real(ly).
pseu'dō-ărchā'ic (sū-, -k-) *adj.* Artificially archaic in style etc.
Pseudo Dionysius: see DIONYSIUS.
pseu'dogrăph (sū-; *or* -ahf) *n.* Literary work purporting to be by a person other than the real author.
pseu'domŏrph (sū-) *n.* False form, esp. (min.) crystal etc. consisting of one compound but having the form proper to another. **pseudomŏr'phic, -mŏr'phous** *adjs.*
pseu'donȳm (sū-) *n.* Fictitious name, esp. one assumed by author. **pseudŏ'nȳmous** *adj.* Writing, written, under a false name. **pseudonȳ'mitȳ** *n.*
pseu'dopŏd, -pō'dium (sū-) *ns.* (pl. -*s*, -*ia*). Temporary protrusion of protoplasm in a protozoon, for movement or feeding.
pshaw (psh- *or* sh-) *int.* & *n.* Exclamation of contempt or impatience. ~ *v.* Say 'pshaw!' (*at*).
psi *n.* Letter of Greek alphabet (Ψ, ψ), '= ps; ~ *phenomena*, psychical phenomena supposedly independent of bodily processes, e.g. telepathy, clairvoyance.
p.s.i. *abbrev.* Pounds per square inch.
psi'ttacīne (sĭ-) *adj.* Of parrots, parrot-like.
psi'ttacoid (sĭ-) *adj.* Like, akin, to the Psittacidae or parrots.
psittacō'sis (sĭ-) *n.* Contagious disease of birds, esp. parrots, characterized by diarrhoea and wasting, and causing bronchial pneumonia when communicated to human beings.
psōrī'asis (s-) *n.* Non-contagious skin disease marked by red scaly patches.
Psyche[1] (psī'kĭ *or* s-). (Gk myth.) Soul personified as beloved of Eros and represented in art with butterfly wings, or as butterfly.
psyche[2] (sī'kĭ) *n.* Soul, spirit, mind.
psychěděl'ic (sĭk-) *adj.* (of drug) Hallucinatory, giving illusion of freedom from limitations of reality; suggesting experience or effect of such drugs.
psychī'atrȳ (sĭk- *or* sīk-) *n.* Study and treatment of mental disease. **psȳchiă'tric, -ical** *adjs.* **psȳchī'atrist** *n.*
psȳ'chic (sĭk-) *adj.* Psychical; susceptible to psychic or occult influences. ~ *n.* Psychic person.
psȳ'chical (sĭk-) *adj.* 1. Of the soul or mind. 2. Of phenomena and conditions apparently outside domain of physical law and therefore attributed by some to spiritual or hyperphysical agency. **psȳ'chicallȳ** *adv.*
psychōană'lȳsis (sĭk-) *n.* Therapeutic method, devised by FREUD, of dealing with certain mental disorders by bringing to light complexes or repressed affects persisting in the unconscious mind; branch of psychology dealing with unconscious mind. **psȳchōă'nalȳse** (-z) *v.t.* **psȳchōanalȳ'tic, -ical** *adjs.* **psȳchōă'nalȳst** *n.*
psychokinē'sis (sīk-) *n.* Supposed interference with physical causation by mental influence.
psycholŏ'gical (sĭk-) *adj.* Of psychology; of, relating to, the mind; ~ *moment*, [f. Fr. mistranslation of Ger. *moment* (neut.) potent element, momentum, as *moment* (masc.) moment of time], psychologically appropriate moment; (esp. joc.) nick of time; ~ *warfare*, achieving aims by acting on enemy's minds. **psȳcholŏ'gicallȳ** *adv.*
psychŏ'logȳ (sĭk-) *n.* Science of the nature, functions, and phenomena of human mind and conduct; treatise on, system of, this; mental characteristics; *analytical* ~, introspective analysis of mental processes; (also) method of psychological inquiry akin to psychoanalysis, system elaborated by C. G. JUNG. **psȳchŏ'logist** *n.*
psychŏ'metrȳ (sĭk-) *n.* 1. Alleged faculty of divining from physical contact or proximity the qualities of an object or of persons etc. that have been in contact with it. 2. Measurement of mental abilities etc. **psȳchomě'tric** *adj.*
psychōmō'tor (sĭk-) *adj.* Of motion resulting from mental activity.
psychōneurō'sis (sĭk-) *n.* (pl. -ōsēs). Functional disorder of the nervous system characterized by anxiety, depression, or obsessional states, without any ascertainable organic disease. **psȳchōneurō'tic** *adj.* & *n.*
psy'chōpăth (sĭk-) *n.* Mentally deranged person; emotionally unstable person. **psȳchōpă'thic** *adj.*
psychōpathŏ'logȳ (sĭk-) *n.* Pathology of the mind.
psychŏ'pathȳ (sĭk-) *n.* Mental disease or disorder, esp. one affecting character or moral sense.
psychō'sis (sĭk-) *n.* (pl. -ōsēs). Severe form of mental illness involving the entire personality. **psychŏ'tic** *adj.*
psychōsōmă'tic (sĭk-) *adj.* (of illness) Involving both mind and body; (esp.) exhibiting physical symptoms but instigated by mental processes.
psychōthě'rapȳ (sĭk-) *n.* Treatment of disease by action on the mind only, by hypnotism, suggestion etc. **psȳchōthěrapeu'tic** *adj.* **psȳchōthě'rapist** *n.*
psychrŏ'meter (sĭk-) *n.* Wet-and-dry-bulb thermometer, used for measuring the relative humidity of the atmosphere.
pt *abbrev.* Part; pint; point; port.
P.T. *abbrev.* Physical training.
ptăr'migan (t-) *n.* Grouse of genus *Lagopus* with black or grey plumage in summer and white in winter, inhabiting high altitudes in Scotland and northern Europe, the Alps and Pyrenees, and

western N. America. [Gaelic *tarmachan*]
Pte *abbrev.* Private (soldier).
ptĕrodă'ctўl (t-) *n.* Extinct winged reptile, one of the pterosaurs.

RECONSTRUCTION OF A PTERODACTYL

ptĕ'ropŏd (t-) *n.* Mollusc of the group Pteropoda with middle part of foot expanded into winglike lobes for swimming.
ptĕ'ropus (t-) *n.* Member of genus *P~* of large tropical and subtropical bats, flying-fox.
ptĕ'rosaur (t-) *n.* One of the Pterosauria, an extinct order of mesozoic flying reptiles, with one digit of each forefoot prolonged to great length and supporting flying-membrane.
P.T.O. *abbrev.* Please turn over.
Ptŏlĕmā'ic (t-) *adj.* 1. Of the PTOLEMIES. 2. Of the astronomer PTOLEMY; *~ system,* astronomical system elaborated by Ptolemy, in which the relative motions of the sun, moon, and planets are explained as taking place round a stationary earth.
Ptŏ'lĕmies (t-, -z). Dynasty of kings named Ptolemy, of Macedonian origin, that ruled over Egypt from death of Alexander the Great until Roman conquest in the reign of Cleopatra.
Ptŏ'lĕmў (t-). Claudius Ptolemaeus (2nd c. A.D.), Greek astronomer, mathematician, and geographer of Alexandria.
ptŏ'maine (t-; *or* tomā'n) *n.* One of a group of organic amine compounds, some of which cause toxic symptoms when injected or taken by mouth; *~ poisoning,* (formerly, erron.) food poisoning. [Gk *ptoma* corpse]
ptō'sis (tō-) *n.* (pl. *-sēs*.) (path.) Drooping of one or both upper eyelids; downward displacement of any organ.
pŭb *n.* (colloq.) Public house; *~ crawl,* calling at several pubs and drinking at each.
pū'bertў *n.* Being functionally capable of procreation; *age of ~,* age at which puberty begins (in Engl. law, 14 in boys, 12 in girls).
pū'bēs (-z) *n.* Hypogastric region, covered with hair in the adult.
pūbĕ'scence *n.* 1. Arrival at puberty. 2. (bot.) Soft down on leaves and stems of plants; downiness; (zool.) soft down on parts of animals, esp. insects. **pūbĕ'scent** *adj.*
pū'bĭc *adj.* Of pubes or pubis.
pū'bĭs *n.* Part of innominate bone forming anterior wall of pelvis (ill. PELVIS).

pŭ'blĭc *adj.* 1. Of, concerning, the people as a whole. 2. Done by or for, representing, the people. 3. Open to, shared by, the people; provided by, managed or controlled by, the community as a whole. 4. (universities) Of, for, acting for, the whole university (as dist. from colleges etc.). 5. *~ health,* protection of the public from disease and epidemics by provision of adequate sanitation and standards of hygiene etc.; *~ house,* establishment providing alcoholic liquors to be consumed on the premises; *P~ Orator:* see ORATOR; *~ relations officer,* (abbrev. P.R.O.) person who gives out information to the public in connection with some department etc.; *~ school,* (in Britain) endowed grammar- (usu. boarding-) school administered by a board of governors, and of which the headmaster is a member of the Headmasters' Conference; (also, in Scotland and U.S. etc.) school provided at public expense and managed by public authority as part of system of public (and usu. free) education; *~ utilities,* services or supplies commonly available in large towns, as buses, drainage, water, gas, electricity, etc. 6. Open to general observation, done or existing in public; of, engaged in, the affairs or service of the people; *~-spirited,* animated or prompted by zeal for the common good. **pŭ'blĭclў** *adv.* **pŭ'blĭc** *n.* 1. (Members of) the community in general; section of the community; *in ~,* publicly, openly. 2. (colloq.) Public house.
pŭ'blĭcan *n.* 1. (Rom. hist.) One who farmed public taxes; tax-gatherer. 2. Keeper of public house.
pŭblĭcā'tion *n.* Making publicly known; issuing of book, engraving, music, etc., to the public; book etc. so issued.
pŭ'blĭcist *n.* 1. Writer on, person skilled in, international law. 2. Writer on current public topics, esp. journalist. 3. Publicity agent.
pŭblĭ'cĭtў *n.* Being or making public; esp. (business of) advertising or making things or persons publicly known; *~ agent,* person employed for this purpose.
pŭ'blĭcīze *v.t.* Bring to public notice, advertise.
pŭ'blĭsh *v.t.* Make generally known, noise abroad; announce formally, promulgate (edict etc.); ask, read (banns of marriage); issue copies of (book etc.) for sale to the public. **pŭ'blĭsher** *n.* (esp.) One whose business is producing copies of books etc., and distributing them to booksellers etc. or to the public.
Puccī'nī (pōōchē-), Giacomo (1858–1924). Italian operatic composer, famous for his 'La Bohème', 'Tosca', and 'Madame Butterfly'.

pūce *adj.* & *n.* Purplish-brown.
pŭck[1] *n.* Rubber disc used in ice hockey.
Pŭck[2]. Merry mischievous sprite or goblin believed, esp. in 16th and 17th centuries, to haunt the English countryside; also called Robin Goodfellow or Hobgoblin; in earlier superstition, an evil demon.
pŭ'cker *v.* Contract, gather (*up*), into wrinkles, folds, or bulges, intentionally or as fault e.g. in sewing. *~ n.* Such wrinkle etc.
pu'dding (pŏŏ-) *n.* Soft or stiffish mixture of animal or vegetable ingredients, esp. mixed or enclosed in flour or other farinaceous food, cooked by boiling, steaming, or baking; intestine of pig etc. stuffed with minced meat, suet, oatmeal, etc.; sweet course of meal; (naut.) pad, tow binding, to prevent chafing, etc.; *~-cloth,* cloth in which some puddings are tied up for boiling; *~ face,* large fat face; *~-stone,* conglomerate rock of rounded dark pebbles set in a brown matrix, resembling plum pudding in appearance.
pŭ'ddle *n.* 1. Small dirty pool, esp. of rain on road etc. 2. Clay (and sand) mixed with water as watertight covering for embankments etc. *~ v.* 1. Dabble, wallow (*about*) in mud or shallow water; busy oneself in untidy way; make (water) muddy. 2. Knead (clay and sand) into, make, line (canal etc.) with, puddle. 3. Stir about (a mixture of molten cast iron and iron ore) in a reverberatory furnace so as to expel the carbon and convert it into malleable iron. **pŭ'ddler** *n.* **pŭ'ddlў** *adj.*
pŭ'dencў *n.* Modesty.
pŭdĕ'ndum *n.* (usu. in pl. *-da*). External genital organs. **pŭdĕ'ndal** *adj.* [L *pudere* be ashamed]
pŭdge *n.* (colloq.) Short thick or fat person, animal, or thing. **pŭ'dgў** *adj.*
puĕ'blŏ (pwĕ-) *n.* (pl. *-s*). 1. Spanish (-American) town or village, esp. communal village or settlement of Indians in Arizona, New Mexico, and adjacent parts of Mexico and Texas. 2. *P~,* member of a group of Indian peoples of several linguistic stocks, dwelling in pueblos in semi-desert areas in SW. of N. America.
pū'erīle *adj.* Boyish, childish; trivial. **pū'erīlelў** *adv.* **pūerī'lĭtў** *n.*
puĕr'peral *adj.* Of, due to, childbirth.
Puĕr'tŏ Rī'cō (pwĕr-, rē-). Easternmost island of Greater Antilles, taken by U.S. in Spanish-American war (1898); capital, San Juan.
pŭff *n.* 1. Short quick blast of breath or wind; sound (as) of this; small quantity of vapour, smoke, etc., emitted at one puff. 2. Round soft protuberant mass of material in dress, of hair of head, etc.;

POWDER-puff. 3. Piece, cake, etc., of light pastry, esp. of ~ *paste*, *pastry*, light flaky pastry. 4. Unduly or extravagantly laudatory review of book, advertisement of tradesman's goods, etc., esp. in newspaper. 5. ~ *adder*, large very venomous African viper (esp. *Bitis arietans*) which inflates upper part of body when excited; ~-*ball*, fungus (*Lycoperdon*) with ball-shaped spore-case, emitting spores in cloud of fine powder when broken; ~ *sleeve*, puffed sleeve. ~ *v.* 1. Emit puff of air or breath; come *out*, *up*, in puffs; breathe hard, pant; put out of breath; utter pantingly; emit puffs, move with puffs; blow (dust, smoke, light object, *away*, *out*, etc.) with puff; smoke (pipe) in puffs. 2. Blow *out*, *up*, inflate; become inflated, swell *up*, *out*; ~ *up*, elate, make proud (esp. in past part.); *puffed sleeve*, short very full sleeve gathered at shoulder and lower edge. 3. Advertise (goods etc.) with exaggerated or false praise.

pŭ′ffin *n.* Sea-bird of *Fratercula* and related genera, esp. *F. arctica* of N. Atlantic with very large furrowed particoloured bill.

pŭ′ffy *adj.* Gusty; short-winded; puffed out; corpulent. **pŭ′ffiness** *n.*

pŭg[1] *n.* Dwarf squat-faced breed of dog like miniature bulldog; ~-*nose(d)*, (having) short squat or snub nose.

pŭg[2] *n.* Loam or clay mixed and prepared for brickmaking etc. ~ *v.t.* Prepare (clay) for brickmaking by kneading and working it into soft and plastic condition; pack (space, esp. that under floor, to deaden sound) with pug, cement, etc.

pŭg[3] *n.* (Ind.) Footprint of a beast. ~ *v.t.* Track by pugs. [Hindi *pag* footprint]

pŭg[4] *n.* (slang) Pugilist.

pŭ′ggaree (-rī) *n.* Indian's light turban; thin scarf of muslin etc. worn round hat and sometimes hanging down behind to keep off sun.

pŭ′gilist *n.* Boxer, fighter. **pŭ′gilism** *n.* **pŭgili′stic** *adj.* **pŭgili′stically** *adv.*

Pŭ′gin, Augustus Welby Northmore (1812–52). English architect; one of the leaders of the Gothic revival; designer of the decorative detail of the Houses of Parliament.

pŭgnā′cious (-shŭs) *adj.* Disposed to fight, quarrelsome. **pŭgnā′ciously** *adv.* **pŭgnă′city** *n.*

puisne (pū′nĭ) *adj.* (law) Later, of subsequent date; ~ *judge*, inferior or junior judge in superior courts of common law. ~ *n.* Puisne judge.

pū′issant (or pwĭs-) *adj.* (archaic) Having great power or influence, mighty. **pū′issantly** *adv.* **pū′issance** *n.*

pūke *v.* Vomit.

pŭ′kka *adj.* (Ind.) Real, genuine, true; permanent, solidly built; ~ *sahib*, (freq. derisive) real gentleman. [Hindi *pakkā* cooked, ripe; thorough, permanent]

pul (pool) *n.* 1/100 of an afghani.

pŭ′lchritūde (-k-) *n.* Beauty.

pūle *v.i.* Cry querulously or weakly, whine. **pū′lingly** *adv.*

Pu′litzer (pōō-), Joseph (1847–1911). American newspaper-owner and editor, of Hungarian origin, one of the founders of American sensational journalism; ~ *Prize*, one of a group of money prizes established under his will and offered annually to American citizens for work in music, journalism, American history and biography, poetry, drama, and fiction.

pull (pool) *v.* 1. Exert upon (thing) force tending to draw it to oneself; draw (thing etc.) towards oneself or in direction so regarded; exert pulling force; pluck (plant, freq. *up*) by root; proceed with effort (*up* hill etc.); (of horse) strain against bit; (U.S.) draw or fire (gun etc.); ~ *person's leg*: see LEG. 2. Draw, suck, *at* (pipe, tankard, etc.); tear, pluck, *at*. 3. Print upon (sheet), print (copy, proof), orig. in old hand-press by pulling bar towards one. 4. Move (boat), move boat, by pulling oar; (of boat) be rowed, be rowed by (so many oars); ~ *one's weight*, row with effect in proportion to one's weight; perform one's due share of work etc. 5. (slang) Arrest; make raid on (gambling-house etc.). 6. Check (horse), esp. so as to make him lose race. 7. (cricket) Strike (ball, or abs.), strike ball bowled by (bowler), from off to leg; (golf) hit (ball, or abs.) widely to the left, or (of left-handed player) to the right. 8. ~ *a face*, distort features into grimace; ~ *about*, pull from side to side; treat roughly; ~ *down*, demolish (building etc.); lower in health, spirits, price, etc.; ~ *in*, (of train) arrive at station; (of vehicle) move in (nearer) to roadside; (colloq.) arrest (person); ~-*in* (*n.*) place (esp. with refreshment room etc.) where vehicles may pull in; ~ *off*, win (prize, contest); ~ *out*, row out; draw out of (a position); (colloq.) abandon project etc.; (of train) move out of station; (of vehicle) move out from roadside or line of traffic; ~-*out* (*n.*) page or plate in book that folds out from front edge of leaves to facilitate reference; *pu′llover*, garment for upper part of body, pulled on over head; ~ *through*, get (person), get oneself, safely through (danger, illness, etc.); ~-*through* (*n.*) cord with which cleaning-rag is drawn through rifle; ~ *together*, work in harmony; ~ *oneself together*, rally, recover oneself; ~ *up*, cause (person, horse, vehicle) to stop; reprimand; check oneself; advance one's relative position in race etc. ~ *n.* 1. Act of pulling, wrench,

tug; force thus exerted; (fig.) means of exerting influence, interest with the powerful; *have the* ~ *on*, *of*, *over*, etc., have (esp. unfair) advantage over. 2. (print.) Rough proof. 3. Spell of rowing; pulling at bridle to check horse; (cricket, golf) pulled stroke; deep draught of liquor; draw at pipe. 4. Handle etc. by which pull is applied.

pu′llet (pōō-) *n.* Young fowl, esp. hen from time she begins to lay till first moult.

pu′lley (pōō-) *n.* One of the simple mechanical powers, consisting of grooved wheel(s) for cord etc. to pass over, mounted in block and used for lifting a weight or changing direction of power;

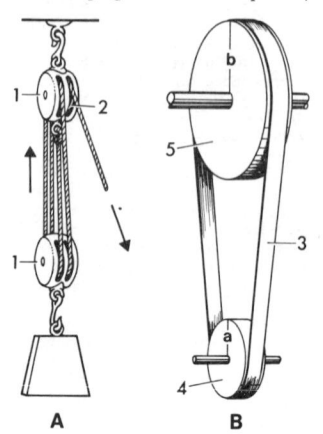

A. PULLEY, HOIST, OR TACKLE.
B. BELT DRIVE

A. 1. Block. 2. Pulley or sheave. The theoretical mechanical advantage is 4:1. B. 3. Belt. 4. Driving pulley. 5. Driven pulley. The theoretical mechanical advantage is in the ratio of *b* to *a*

wheel, drum, fixed on shaft and turned by belt, used esp. to increase speed or power. ~ *v.t.* Hoist, furnish, work, with pulley.

Pu′llman (pōō-) *n.* (also ~ *coach*) Type of comfortable railway carriage with fitted tables on which refreshments can be placed; sleeping-car. [George M. *Pullman* (1831–97), Amer. designer]

pŭ′llūlāte *v.i.* (of shoot, bud) Sprout out, bud; (of seed) sprout; (fig.) develop, spring up. **pŭ′llūlant** *adj.* **pullūlā′tion** *n.*

pŭ′lmonary (or pōō-) *adj.* Of, in, connected with, the lungs; having lungs or lung-like organs; affected with, subject to, lung-disease. **pŭ′lmonate**, **pŭlmŏ′nic** *adjs.*

pŭlp *n.* Fleshy part of fruit; any fleshy or soft part of animal body, e.g. nervous substance in interior cavity of tooth; soft formless mass, esp. that of linen, wood, etc., from which paper is made; ore pulverized and mixed with water; ~ *magazine*, trashy

[710]

PULPIT

magazine. ~ v. Reduce to pulp; remove pulp from (coffee-beans); become pulpy. **pŭ′lpў** adj.
pu′lpit (poŏ-) n. Raised enclosed platform from which preacher in church or chapel

PULPIT
1. Sounding board

delivers sermon; profession of preaching, preachers; (in small sailing vessel) guard-rail, usu. waist-high, fixed at bow or stern.
pulque (poo'lkē) n. Mexican fermented drink from sap of agave etc.
pŭ′lsar n. Cosmic source of rapidly pulsating radio signal.
pŭlsā′te (or pŭ′-) v. Expand and contract rhythmically, beat, throb; vibrate, quiver, thrill; agitate (diamonds) with pulsator. **pŭlsā′tion** n. **pŭ′lsatorў** adj. **pŭlsā′tor** n. Machine operating with throbbing movement.
pŭ′lsatile adj. Of, having the property of, pulsation; (of musical instrument) played by percussion.
pŭlsati′lla n. Pasque-flower, kind of anemone; its extract used in pharmacy.
pŭlse[1] n. Rhythmical throbbing of arteries as blood is pumped into them from the heart, used, as felt in wrists, temples, etc., to measure the heart rate; each successive beat of arteries or heart; (fig.) throb, thrill, of life or emotion; rhythmical recurrence of strokes, e.g. of oars; single beat or vibration of light, sound, etc.; (mus.) beat. **pŭ′lsèlèss** adj. **pŭ′lsèlèssnèss** n. **pŭlse** v. Pulsate; send out, in, etc., by rhythmic beats.
pŭlse[2] n. Edible seeds of leguminous plants, e.g. peas, beans, lentils; (with pl.) any kind of these.
pŭ′lverīze v. Reduce to powder or dust, crumble into dust; divide (liquid) into spray; (fig.) demolish, crush, smash. **pŭlverīzā′tion** n.
pŭlvĕ′rŭlent adj. Powdery, of dust; covered with powder; (of rock etc.) of slight cohesion, apt to crumble.
pū′ma n. Large Amer. feline quadruped, Felis concolor.
pŭ′mĭce n. (also ~-stone) Very light porous stone formed by the solidified froth on the surface of glassy lava, used, freq. powdered, for polishing and abrading; piece

of this for removing stains etc. from the skin.
pŭ′mmel v.t. Strike repeatedly, esp. with fist.
pŭmp[1] n. Machine for moving fluid from one place to another, e.g. raising water, or for compressing or rarefying gas, or for similar purpose, e.g. inflating tyres, formerly always with rod and

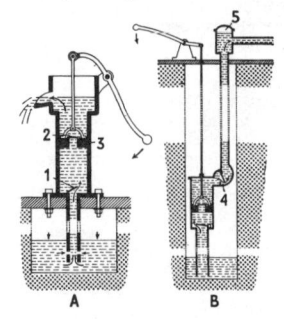

A. SUCTION-PUMP. B. FORCE-PUMP

1. Flap valve or clack. 2. Piston valve. 3. Piston. 4. Delivery valve. 5. Air bottle to give even flow

piston, now freq. rotary in action; action of working a pump; stroke of pump; (fig.) attempt at extracting information from person; ~-handle (v.) (colloq.) shake (person's hand) effusively; ~-room, room where pump is worked, esp. at spa where medicinal water is dispensed. ~ v. 1. Work a pump; remove, raise, (water etc.) thus; make dry by pumping; inflate (pneumatic tyre), inflate tyres of (bicycle etc.). 2. Bring out, pour forth (on) as by pumping; elicit information from (person) by artful or persistent questions. 3. (of exertion) Put completely out of breath. 4. (of mercury in barometer) Rise and fall instantaneously.
pŭmp[2] n. Light shoe, usu. without fastening, for dancing etc.
pu′mpernickel (poŏ-) n. German wholemeal rye bread, dark brown and freq. sweetened and spiced.
pŭ′mpkin n. Trailing plant, Cucurbita pepo, with heart-shaped five-lobed leaves; large egg-shaped or globular fruit of this, with edible layer next to rind, used in cookery and for cattle.
pŭn[1] n. Humorous use of word to suggest different meanings, or of words of same sound with different meanings, play on words. ~ v.i. Make puns (on).
pŭn[2] v.t. Consolidate (earth, rubble) by pounding or ramming; work up to proper consistency with punner.
pu′na (poō-) n. High bleak plateau in Peruvian Andes; mountain sickness.
pŭnch[1] n. Instrument or

PUNCHINELLO

machine for cutting holes in leather, metal, paper, etc., or for driving a bolt etc. out of a hole (starting ~) or forcing a nail beneath a surface (driving ~); tool or machine for impressing design or stamping die on material; bell-~, conductor's ticket-punch with bell to announce punching of ticket.
pŭnch[2] v. 1. Strike, esp. with closed fist; prod with stick etc., esp. (U.S.) drive (cattle) thus; punch(ing)-ball, inflated ball held by elastic bands etc., and punched as form of exercise; ~-up (n., slang) fight with fists, brawl. 2. Pierce (metal, leather, railway ticket, etc.) as or with punch; pierce (hole) thus; drive (nail etc. in, out) with punch. ~ n. Blow with fist; (slang) vigour, momentum, effective force; pull one's punches, refrain from using one's full force; ~-drunk (adj.) stupefied through being severely punched; ~-drunkenness (n.) morbid condition in pugilists, marked by muscular failure and mental confusion, and resulting from repeated head concussions caused by punches; ~-line, line giving point of joke etc.
pŭnch[3] n. Drink usu. of wine or spirits mixed with hot water or milk, sugar, lemons, spice, etc.; similar mixture taken cold; bowl

PUNCH-BOWL AND LADLE

of punch; ~-bowl, bowl in which punch is mixed; round deep hollow in hill(s).
pŭnch[4] n. (also Suffolk ~) Short-legged thickset draught horse.
Pŭnch[5]. Hook-nosed humpbacked buffoon, English variant of a stock character derived from Italian popular comedy who appeared in Italy as Pulcinella, in France as Polichinelle, in England as Punchinello or Punch; now preserved chiefly as title of an English humorous weekly periodical (founded 1841) and in ~ and Judy, open-air puppet-show performed at fairs etc. [Neapolitan dial. policenella, dim. of policena turkey-cock, prob. with ref. to its hooked beak]
pŭ′ncheon[1] (-chon) n. Short post, esp. one supporting roof in coal-mine.
pŭ′ncheon[2] (-chon) n. (hist.) Large cask for liquid etc. holding from 72 to 120 gals. (ill. CASK).
Pŭnchĭnĕ′llō. = PUNCH[5].

[711]

pŭ′nctāte *adj.* (biol., path.) Marked or studded with points, dots, or holes. **pŭnctā′tion** *n.*

pŭnctī′liō *n.* (pl. *-s*). Precise or subtle point of ceremony or honour; petty formality. [It. *puntiglio* little point]

pŭnctī′lious (-lyus) *adj.* Attentive to punctilios; very careful about detail. **pŭnctī′liouslў** *adv.* **pŭnctī′liousnèss** *n.*

pŭ′nctūal *adj.* Observant of appointed time; in good time, not late. **pŭ′nctūallў** *adv.* **pŭnctū-ă′litў** *n.*

pŭ′nctūāte *v.t.* Insert stops, commas, etc., in (writing), mark or divide with stops, commas, etc.; (fig.) interrupt (speech etc.) *with* exclamations etc. **pŭnctūā′tion** *n.* Practice, art, of punctuating; insertion of vowel and other points in Semitic languages.

pŭ′nctum (pl. *-a*), **pŭ′nctūle** *ns.* (biol., path.) Speck, dot, spot of colour or elevation or depression on surface. **pŭ′nctūlate** *adj.* **pŭnctūlā′tion** *n.*

pŭ′ncture *n.* Pricking, prick, esp. accidental pricking of pneumatic tyre; hole thus made. ~ *v.* Prick, pierce; experience a puncture.

pŭ′ndit *n.* Hindu learned in Sanskrit and in philosophy, religion, and jurisprudence of India; (joc.) learned expert or teacher.

pŭ′ngent (-j-) *adj.* 1. Sharp-pointed (bot.); (of reproof, etc.) biting, caustic; mentally stimulating, piquant. 2. Affecting organs of smell or taste, or skin etc., with pricking sensation. **pŭ′ngentlў** *adv.* **pŭ′ngencў** *n.*

Pū′nic *adj.* Of Carthage, Carthaginian; of the character attributed by the Romans to the Carthaginians, treacherous, perfidious; ~ *Wars*, three wars between Romans and Carthaginians (264-241, 218-201, 149-146 B.C.); in the 1st, Rome captured Sicily, her first province, from the Carthaginians under HAMILCAR; in the 2nd, the Carthaginians under HANNIBAL invaded Italy and the Romans after long resistance drove them out and destroyed the position of Carthage as a great Mediterranean power; in the 3rd, Carthage itself was besieged and destroyed.

pŭ′nish *v.t.* Cause (offender) to suffer for offence, chastise, inflict penalty on (offender); inflict penalty for (offence); (colloq.) inflict severe blows on (opponent in boxing), tax severely the powers of (competitor in race etc.), take full advantage of (weak bowling, stroke at tennis, etc.), make heavy inroad on (food etc.). **pŭ′nishable, pŭ′nishing** *adjs.* **pŭ′nishment** *n.*

pŭ′nitive *adj.* Inflicting punishment, retributive. **pŭ′nitorў** *adj.*

Pŭ′njab (-ahb). State of India (formerly NW. province of British India); capital, Chandigarh. **Pŭn-ja′bī, Pănja′bī** *n.* Native, inhabitant, Indo-Aryan language, of Punjab.

pŭnk *n.* (chiefly U.S.) Rotten wood, fungus growing on wood, used as tinder; anything worthless.

pŭ′nka, -kah (-ka) *n.* (E. Ind.) Portable fan usu. of leaf of palmyra; large swinging cloth fan on frame worked by cord.

pŭ′nner *n.* Tool for ramming earth about post etc.

pŭ′nnèt *n.* Small chip basket for fruit or vegetables.

pŭ′nster *n.* Maker of puns.

pŭnt[1] *n.* Flat-bottomed shallow boat, broad and square at both ends, propelled by long pole thrust against bottom of river etc. ~ *v.* Propel (punt, boat, or abs.) thus; convey in a punt. **pŭ′nter**[1] *n.*

pŭnt[2] *v.t.* (Rugby footb.) Kick (ball) after it has dropped from the hands and before it reaches ground. ~*n.* Punting kick; ~*-about*, kicking about of football for practice, ball so used.

pŭnt[3] *v.i.* (at faro and other card-games) Lay stake against bank; (colloq.) bet on horse etc. **pŭ′nter**[2] *n.* **pŭnt** *n.* Player who punts; point in faro.

pŭ′ntў *n.* = PONTIL.

pū′nў *adj.* Undersized; weak, feeble; petty. **pū′ninèss** *n.*

pŭp *n.* Puppy; *in* ~: see IN; *sell person a* ~, swindle him esp. by selling thing on prospective value. ~ *tent*, small tent of simple design. ~ *v.* Bring forth (pups, or abs.).

pū′pa *n.* (pl. *-ae*). Insect in its inactive pre-adult form, after larva but before imago (ill. MOSQUITO); chrysalis of butterfly or moth. **pū′pal** *adj.* **pū′pāte** *v.i.* Become a pupa. **pūpā′tion** *n.*

pū′pil *n.* 1. One who is taught by another, scholar; (law) person below age of puberty and under care of guardian; ~*-teacher*, (hist.) boy, girl, teaching in elementary school under head teacher and concurrently receiving general education from him or elsewhere. 2. Opening (circular, in man) in centre of iris of eye regulating passage of light to the retina (ill. EYE). **pū′pillage** *n.* Nonage, minority; being a pupil. **pū′pillar, pū′pillarў** *adjs.* **pūpillă′ritў** *n.*

pū′ppèt *n.* Figure, usu. small, representing human being etc., esp. one with jointed limbs moved by strings etc., or (*glove* ~) one made to fit over the operator's hand so that its head and arms may be manipulated by his fingers; person whose acts are controlled by another; ~*-play*, *-show*, one with puppets as characters; ~ *state, country*, one professing to be independent but actually under the control of some greater power. **pŭ′ppétrў** *n.* [Fr. *poupette* doll]

pŭ′ppў *n.* Young dog; conceited young man; ~ *fat*, temporary fat of adolescents. **pŭ′p-pўdom, pŭ′ppўhŏŏd, pŭ′ppўism** *ns.* **pŭpp′ўish** *adj.*

Pura′na (poorah-) *n.* Any of a class of Sanskrit sacred poems, containing mythology of Hindus. **Pura′nic** *adj.* [Sansk. *purāṇa* ancient legend]

Pūr′bèck, Isle of. Peninsula on coast of Dorset; ~ *marble*, name for the finer qualities of a hard limestone quarried there for building and paving.

pūr′blind *adj.* Partly blind, dim-sighted; (fig.) obtuse, dull. ~ *v.t.* Make purblind.

Pūr′cĕll, Henry (*c* 1658-95). English musical composer, best known for his opera 'Dido and Aeneas'.

pūr′chase *n.* 1. Buying; (law) acquisition of property by one's personal action, not by inheritance; thing bought; annual return from land; (hist.) practice of buying commissions in army; ~*-money*, price (to be) paid; ~ *tax*, tax levied on goods sold by retailer. 2. Mechanical advantage, leverage, fulcrum; appliance for gaining this, esp. (naut.) rope, windlass, pulley. ~ *v.t.* Buy; acquire (*with* toil, blood, etc.); (naut.) haul up (anchor etc.) by means of pulley, lever, etc. **pūr′chaser** *n.*

pūr′dah (*-a*) *n.* (in India, Pakistan, etc.) Curtain, esp. one serving to screen women from sight of strangers; striped material for curtains; (fig.) Indian system of secluding women of rank.

pūre *adj.* Not mixed or adulterated; (of sounds) not discordant, esp. (mus.) perfectly in tune; of unmixed descent, pure-blooded; mere, simple, nothing but, sheer; not corrupt; morally undefiled, guiltless, sincere; sexually chaste; (Gk gram. etc.), (of vowel) preceded by another vowel, (of stem) ending in vowel, (of consonant) not accompanied by another; ~ *mathematics*, theoretical mathematics, not including practical applications. **pūr′elў** *adv.* **pūr′enèss** *n.*

purée (pūr′ā) *n.* Pulp of cooked vegetables or fruit passed through sieve.

pūr′fle *n.* (archaic) Border, esp. embroidered edge of garment. ~ *v.t.* Adorn (robe) with purfle: ornament (edge of building *with* crockets etc.); beautify. **pūr′fling** *n.* (esp.) Inlaid bordering on back and belly of fiddles.

pūrgā′tion *n.* Purification, purging; purging of bowels; spiritual cleansing, esp. (R.C. Ch.) of soul in purgatory; (hist.) clearing of oneself from accusation or suspicion by oath or ordeal.

pūr′gative *adj.* Aperient; serving to purify. ~ *n.* Purgative medicine.

pūr′gatorў *n.* Condition, place of spiritual purging, esp. (R.C. Ch.) of souls departing this life in grace of God but requiring to be cleansed from venial sins etc.; place of temporary suffering or

[712]

expiation. ~ *adj.* Purifying.
purgatōr′ial *adj.*
purge *v.t.* Make physically or spiritually clean; rid (political party, army, etc.) of objectionable, alien, or extraneous elements or members; remove by cleansing process; (of medicine) clear (bowels) by evacuation; clear (of charge, suspicion); (law) atone for, wipe out, (offence, sentence) by expiation and submission. ~ *n.* 1. Aperient medicine. 2. Purging; ridding of objectionable or hostile elements; PRIDE'S ~: see entry.
pūrificā′tion *n.* Purifying; ritual cleansing, esp. that of woman after childbirth enjoined by Jewish law; P~ (*of the Blessed Virgin Mary*), festival (in Western Church, 2 Feb.) of presentation of Christ in the Temple on completion of days of Virgin Mary's purification (Luke 2: 22). **pūr′ificātory** *adj.*
pūr′ificātor *n.* (eccles.) Cloth used at communion for wiping chalice and paten, and fingers and lips of celebrant.
pūr′ify *v.t.* Make pure, cleanse (*of*, *from*, impurities, sin, etc.); make ceremonially clean; clear of foreign elements.
Pūr′im. Jewish festival on 14 and 15 of month Adar (Feb.-March), commemorating defeat of Haman's plot against the Jews (Esther 9).
pūr′ist *n.* Stickler for, affecter of, scrupulous purity esp. in language. **pūr′ism** *n.* **pūrĭ′stĭc**, **-ical** *adjs.*
Pūr′itan *n.* 1. (hist.) Member of that party of English Protestants who regarded the Reformation under Elizabeth as incomplete and demanded further purification of the Church from forms and ceremonies still retained; any of those who later separated from the Established Church on points of ritual, polity, or doctrine, held by them to be at variance with pure New Testament principles. 2. One who is, or is thought or affects to be, extremely strict, precise, or scrupulous in religion or morals. **pūrită′nic**, **-ical**, **P-** *adjs.* **Pūr′-itanism** *n.*
pūr′ĭty *n.* Pureness, cleanness, freedom from physical or moral pollution.
purl[1] *n.* 1. Cord of twisted gold or silver wire for bordering; chain of minute loops, each loop of this, ornamenting edges of lace, ribbon, etc. 2. (knitting) Stitch in which second needle is inserted through loop on first from right to left, and yarn is looped over second needle from the front (ill. KNITTING). ~ *v.* Border with purl; make purl stitches in knitting.
purl[2] *v.i.* (of brook etc.) Flow with whirling motion and babbling sound. ~ *n.* Purling motion or sound.
purl[3] *n.* (hist.) Ale or beer with wormwood infused; hot beer mixed with gin.

pur′ler *n.* (colloq.) Headlong fall.
pur′lieu (-lū) *n.* Tract on border of forest, (orig.) one earlier included in it and still partly subject to forest laws; place one habitually frequents; (pl.) outskirts, outlying region. [prob. f. AF *puralé* perambulation to settle boundaries]
pur′lin *n.* Horizontal beam running along length of roof, resting on principals and supporting common rafters or boards (ill. ROOF).
purloi′n *v.t.* Steal, pilfer.
pur′ple *n.* 1. Colour mixed of red and blue in varying proportions. 2. (also *Tyrian* ~) Colour got from the molluscs *Purpura*, *Thais*, and *Murex*, and associated with the dress and rank or office of emperors, consuls, kings, etc.; crimson; *the* ~, imperial, royal, or consular rank, power, or office; scarlet official dress of cardinal's rank or office. ~ *adj.* Of the colour purple; ~ *passage*, literary passage marked by exaggerated style. **pur′plish**, **pur′ply** *adjs.* **pur′ple** *v.* Make, become, purple.
purpoint: see POURPOINT.
pur′port *n.* Meaning, sense, tenor, of document or speech. **purpōr′t** *v.t.* (of document or speech) Have as its meaning, convey, state; profess, be intended to seem (*to do*).
pur′pose *n.* Object, thing intended; fact, faculty, of resolving on something; *on* ~, in order (*to*, *that*); designedly, not by accident; *to the* ~, relevant, useful for one's purpose; *to good*, *little*, *no*, etc., ~, with good, little, etc., effect or result. ~ *v.t.* Design, intend. **pur′posely** *adv.* **pur′poseful** *adj.* **pur′posefully** *adv.* **pur′posefulness** *n.* **pur′poseless** *adj.* **pur′poselessly** *adv.* **pur′poselessness** *n.*
pur′posive *adj.* Having, serving, done with, a purpose; having purpose and resolution.
pur′pura *n.* Disease, due to morbid state of the blood or bloodvessels, characterized by purple or livid spots on skin. **purpūr′ic** *adj.*
pur′pure *n.* (her.) Purple. (ill. HERALDRY).
pur′purin *n.* Red dye orig. got from madder.
purr *v.* (of cat or other feline animal, fig. of person) Make low continuous vibratory sound expressing pleasure; utter, express (words, contentment) thus. ~ *n.* Purring sound. [imit.]
purse *n.* Small pouch of leather etc. for carrying money on the person, orig. closed by drawing strings together; (fig.) money, funds; sum collected, subscribed, or given, as present or as prize for contest; bag-like natural or other receptacle, pouch, cyst, etc.; *public* ~, national treasury; ~-*bearer*, one who has charge of another's or a company's money;

official carrying Great Seal before Lord Chancellor in purse; ~-*net*, bag-shaped net for catching rabbits etc., mouth of which can be drawn close with cords; ~-*proud*, puffed up by wealth; ~-*strings*, strings for closing mouth of purse; *hold the* ~-*strings*, have control of expenditure. ~ *v.* Contract (lips etc., freq. *up*) in wrinkles; become wrinkled.
pur′ser *n.* Officer on ship who keeps accounts and usu. has charge of provisions; in passenger ship, head of stewards' department, superintending comfort and requirements of passengers.
pur′slane (-in) *n.* Low succulent herb, *Portulaca oleracea* var. *sativa*, formerly used in salads and pickled.
pursū′ance *n.* Carrying out, pursuing, esp. in *in* ~ *of* (plan etc.).
pursū′ant *adj.* Pursuing. ~ *adv.* Conformably *to*.
pursū′e *v.* Follow with intent to capture or kill; (fig.) persistently attend, stick to; seek after, aim at; proceed in compliance with (plan etc.); proceed along, continue, follow (road, inquiry, studies, etc.); go in pursuit. **pursū′er** *n.* (esp. civil & Sc. law). Prosecutor.
pursui′t (-sūt) *n.* Pursuing; profession, employment, recreation, that one follows.
pur′suivant (-swi-) *n.* Officer of College of Arms below herald; (poet.) follower, attendant.
pur′sy̆ *adj.* Short-winded, puffy; corpulent.
pur′ulent (-rōō-) *adj.* Of, full of, discharging, pus. **pur′ulently** *adv.* **pur′ulence** *n.*
purvey′ (-vā) *v.* Provide, supply (articles of food) as one's business; make provision, act as purveyor.
purvey′ance (-vāans) *n.* Purveying; (hist.) right of crown to provisions etc. at price fixed by *purveyor*, and to use of horses etc.
purvey′or (-vā-) *n.* One whose business it is to supply (esp.) articles of food, dinners etc., on large scale; (hist.) officer making purveyance for sovereign.
pur′view (-vū) *n.* Enacting clauses of statute; scope, intention, range (*of* act, document, etc.); range of physical or mental vision.
pus *n.* (path.) Yellowish viscid fluid formed by the liquefaction of dead tissues, usu. containing leucocytes, cell debris, and bacteria.
Pū′sey (-zī), Edward Bouverie (1800–82), English churchman, one of the leaders of the Oxford or TRACTARIAN movement. **Pū′seyism**, **Pū′seyite** *ns.*
push (pŏō-) *v.* 1. Exert upon (body) force tending to move it away; move thus; exert such pressure; (billiards) make push-stroke; (cause to) project, thrust out, forward, etc.; make one's way forcibly or persistently, force (*one's way*) thus; ~ *off*, (of person in boat) push against bank etc. with oar

[713]

to get boat out into stream etc.; (slang) leave, go away. 2. Exert onself, esp. to surpass others or succeed in one's business etc.; urge, impel; follow up (claim etc.); carry (action, matter, etc.) to further point, or to farthest limit; press the adoption, use, sale, etc., of (goods, etc.) esp. by advertisement; press (person) hard, esp. in passive. **pu′sher** *n.* (esp., slang) Illegal seller of drugs. **pu′shing** *adj.* **pu′shingly** *adv.* **push** *n.* 1. Act of pushing, shove, thrust; (billiards) stroke in which ball is pushed, not struck; thrust of weapon, beast's horn, etc.; *give, get, the* ~, (slang) dismiss, be dismissed. 2. Vigorous effort, (mil.) attack in force; exertion of influence; pressure of affairs, crisis, pinch. 3. Enterprise, determination to get on, self-assertion. 4. Contrivance etc. pushed or pressed to operate mechanism. 5. ~-*ball*, game in which very large ball is pushed, not kicked, towards opponents' goal; ~-*bicycle*, (slang) -*bike*, bicycle worked by pedalling; ~-*button* (*adj.*) operated by pressing a button (also transf.); ~-*chair*, light chair on wheels for pushing; ~-*stroke*, push (in billiards etc.). **pu′shful** *adj.*
Pu′shkin (pōō-), Alexander Sergeevich (1799–1837). Russian poet and prose-writer, the first national poet of Russia.
Pushtu : see PASHTU.
pūsillă′nimous (or -z-) *adj.* Faint-hearted, mean-spirited. **pūsillă′nimously** *adv.* **pūsillani′mity** *n.*
puss (pŏŏs) *n.* Cat (esp. as conventional proper name); (quasi-proper name for) hare; (colloq.) girl; ~ *in the corner*, children's game in which player standing in centre tries to capture one of the bases as the others change places; ~ *moth*, large downy-looking European moth (*Cerura vinula*), with whitish or light-grey forewings marked with darker colour. **pu′ssy** (pŏŏ-) *n.* Cat (esp. in nursery use); ~ *willow*, goat willow (*Salix caprea*) and allied species, with silky catkins; (U.S.) glaucous willow (*S. discolor*). **pu′ssyfoot** (pŏŏ-) *v.i.* (U.S. colloq.) Tread softly or lightly; proceed warily; avoid committing oneself. [nickname of Amer. prohibition lecturer, W. E. Johnson (1862–1945), given on account of his stealthy methods when a magistrate]
pu′stūlāte *v.* Form into pustules.
pu′stūle *n.* Pimple; *malignant* ~, anthrax. **pu′stūlar, pu′stūlous** *adjs.*
put[1] (pŏŏt) *v.* (past t. & past part. *put*). 1. Propel, hurl (*the weight, stone*) from hand placed close to shoulder, as athletic exercise; (naut.) proceed, take one's course (*back, in, off, out,* etc.). 2. Move (thing etc.) so as to place it in some situation; convey (person) across river etc.; harness (horse etc.) *to* vehicle. 3. Bring into some relation, state, or condition; translate *into* another language, turn (*into* speech or writing, words); apply *to* use or purpose; submit *to* vote etc.; subject *to* (suffering); ~ *an end, stop, to,* bring to an end, stop; ~ *upon,* oppress, victimize; ~ (horse) *at,* urge him towards (obstacle etc.). 4. ~ *about*: see ABOUT; ~ *away,* divorce (archaic); lay by (money etc.) for future use; (slang) consume (food, drink); ~ *back,* check the advance of, retard; move back the hands of (clock); restore to former place; ~ *by,* lay aside esp. for future use; ~ *down,* suppress by force or authority; take down, snub, put to silence; put (animal) to death; cease to maintain (expensive thing); account, reckon; write on paper; ~ *forth,* exert (strength, effort, etc.); (of plant) send out (buds, leaves, etc.); ~ *forward,* thrust into prominence; advance, set forth (theory etc.); ~ *in,* install in office etc.; present formally (evidence, plea, etc.) as in law-court; interpose; throw in (additional thing); (colloq.) pass, spend (time); make (an appearance); ~ *off,* postpone; postpone engagement with (person); evade (person, demand, freq. *with* excuse, etc.); hinder, dissuade *from*; foist (thing *upon* person); remove, take off (clothes); (of boat etc.) leave shore; ~ *on,* clothe oneself or another with; assume, take on (character, appearance); develop additional (flesh, weight); add (*to*); stake (*on* horse etc.); advance the hands of (clock); bring into action, exert (force, speed, steam, etc.); appoint, arrange for, (person) to bowl etc., (train) to run etc.; ~ *out,* dislocate (joint); (cricket) cause (batsman) to be out; extinguish; disconcert, confuse; annoy, irritate; put to inconvenience; exert (strength etc.); lend (money) at interest, invest; give (work) to be done off the premises; ~ *through,* carry out (task); place (person) in telephonic connection with another through exchange(s); ~ *together,* form (whole) by combination of parts; ~ *up,* employ as jockey; cause (game bird) to rise from cover; raise (price); offer (prayer), present (petition); propose for election; publish banns; offer for sale by auction or for competition; pack in parcel, place in receptacle for safe keeping; sheathe (sword); lodge and entertain; construct, build; ~ *person's back up,* enrage him; ~ (*person*) *up to,* inform him of, instruct him in, instigate him; ~ *up with,* submit to, tolerate; ~-*up* (*adj.*) fraudulently concocted. ~ *n.* Throw, cast, of the weight or stone.
put[2] *v.* (rare) Var. of PUTT.
pū′tative *adj.* Reputed, supposed. **pū′tatively** *adv.*

pŭ′tlŏg *n.* One of the short horizontal timbers on which scaffold-boards rest (ill. SCAFFOLDING).
pū′trefy *v.i.* Become putrid, rot, go bad; fester, suppurate. **pūtrefă′ction** *n.* **pū′trefăctive** *adj.*
pūtre′scent *adj.* In process of rotting, of, accompanying, this process. **pūtre′scence** *n.*
pū′trid *adj.* Decomposed, rotten; foul, noxious; (fig.) corrupt; (slang) of poor or bad quality, unpleasant. **pū′tridly** *adv.* **pū′tridnĕss, pūtri′dity** *ns.*
putsch (pōōch) *n.* Attempt at revolution, *coup d'état*. [Swiss Ger., = 'thrust', 'blow']
pŭtt *v.* Strike golf-ball, strike (golf-ball) gently and carefully with the putter so as to make it roll along the putting-green with the object of getting it into the hole; *pu′tting-green*, smooth piece of turf round each hole on golf-course on which the ball is putted; similar piece of ground usu. with 9 or 18 holes for putting. ~ *n.* Putting stroke.
pŭ′ttee *n.* Long strip of cloth wound spirally round leg from ankle to knee for protection and support. [Hind. *patti* bandage]
pŭ′tter *n.* Straight-faced club used in putting.
pŭ′tty *n.* 1. (*jewellers'* ~) Powder of calcined tin (and lead) for polishing glass or metal. 2. (*plasterers'* ~) Fine mortar of lime and water without sand. 3. (*glaziers'* ~) Cement of whiting, raw linseed oil, etc., for fixing panes of glass, filling up holes in woodwork, etc. ~ *v.t.* Cover, fix, join, fill *up,* with putty.
pŭ′zzle *n.* Bewilderment, perplexity; perplexing question, enigma; problem, toy, contrived to exercise ingenuity and patience. ~ *v.* Perplex; be perplexed; make *out* by exercising ingenuity and patience. **pŭ′zzlement** *n.* **pŭ′zzlingly** *adv.*
P.V.C. *abbrev.* Polyvinyl chloride.
p.w. *abbrev.* Policewoman.
pxt *abbrev. Pinxit*.
pya (pē′a) *n.* $\frac{1}{100}$ of a kyat.
pȳae′mia *n.* Severe infection of the blood by virulent bacteria accompanied by acute fever and formation of abscesses in liver, lungs, kidneys, etc.
pȳelŏ′graphy *n.* X-ray examination of kidneys and ureters.
pȳ′elogrăm *n.* X-ray produced by pyelography.
Pȳgmā′lion (-yon). (Gk legend) King of Cyprus who made a statue of a woman and fell in love with it; he prayed Aphrodite for a wife like it, and she endowed the statue with life.
pȳ′gmȳ, pi- *n.* 1. One of a diminutive race of men stated in ancient history and tradition to have inhabited parts of Ethiopia or India. 2. Member of a Negrillo people of very small stature.

[714]

pyjamas

3. Very small person or thing. ~ *adj.* Of pygmies; dwarf; stunted. [Gk *pugmē* length from elbow to knuckle]

pyjamas (-ah′maz), **paj-** (U.S.) *n.pl.* Loose silk or cotton trousers tied round waist, worn by both sexes in the East and adopted esp. for night wear by Europeans; sleeping suit of loose trousers and jacket. [Hind. *pāē jāma*, *pā jāma* loose drawers]

py′lon *n.* 1. Gateway, esp. of Egyptian temple, with two truncated pyramidal towers connected by lower architectural member containing the gate. 2. Structure used to mark out aeroplane course; tall (metal) structure for supporting power cables.

pȳlōr′us *n.* (anat.) Opening from stomach into duodenum; part of stomach where this is (ill. ALIMENTARY canal). **pȳlŏ′ric** *adj.* [Gk *pulōros* gate-keeping]

Pym, John (1584–1643). English statesman and Parliamentary leader; one of the five members whom Charles I attempted to seize before the outbreak of the Civil War.

pyorrhoea (pīorē′a) *n.* Disease of the tooth-sockets, accompanied by a discharge of pus and slight local haemorrhage.

pȳr′acănth, pȳracă′nthus *ns.* Evergreen thorny shrub of genus *Pyracantha* with white flowers and scarlet berries.

pў′ramid *n.* Monumental structure of stone etc. with polygonal or (usu.) square base and sloping sides meeting at apex, constructed by ancient Egyptians over a royal burial chamber and by Aztecs and Mayas as stepped platform for a temple; solid of this shape with base of three or more sides; pyramid-shaped thing or pile of things; fruit-tree trained in pyramid shape (ill. FRUIT); (pl., billiards) game played (usu.) with fifteen coloured balls arranged in triangle and one cue-ball. **pўră′midal** *adj.* ~ *tract*, great tract of motor nerve fibres running down spine, concerned in voluntary movement. **pўră′midallў** *adv.*

Pў′ramus *n.* (Rom. legend) Youth of Babylon, lover of Thisbe; forbidden to marry by their parents, who were neighbours, they conversed through a chink in the wall and agreed to meet at a tomb outside the city; here Thisbe was frightened away by a lioness, and Pyramus, finding her bloodstained cloak and supposing her dead, stabbed himself; Thisbe, finding his body, threw herself upon his sword.

pȳre *n.* Heap of combustible material, esp. funeral pile for burning corpse.

pȳr′ēne *n.* (chem.) Solid aromatic hydrocarbon obtained from dry distillation of coal etc.

Pȳrenēē′s (-z). Range of mountains in SW. Europe separating Spain from France. **Pȳrēnē′an** *adj.*

pȳrē′thrum *n.* Any of several chrysanthemums, esp. *Chrysanthemum coccineum* and *C. cinerariifolium*; (also ~ *powder*) insecticide made from powdered heads of this.

pȳrĕ′xia *n.* (med.) Fever.

pȳr′idine (*or* pī-) *n.* (chem.) Colourless volatile liquid base with offensive odour, present in bone-oil and coal-tar, whence it is obtained by distillation.

pȳrī′tēs (-z; *or* pī-) *n.* (*iron* ~) Iron sulphide (FeS_2) occurring as a mineral; (*copper* ~) double sulphide of copper and iron ($Cu_2S.Fe_2S_3$). **pȳrī′tic** *adj.*

pȳr′ō *n.* (colloq.) Pyrogallol.

pȳro-ĕlĕ′ctric *adj.* Becoming electrically polar when heated.

pȳrogă′llol *n.* (also *pyrogallic acid*). White crystalline substance, tri-hydroxy-benzene, very soluble in water, used as a developer in photography etc.

pȳrogĕ′nic *adj.* Fever-producing.

pȳrŏ′latry *n.* Fire-worship.

pȳr′omăncў *n.* Divination by fire.

pȳromā′nia *n.* Incendiary mania. **pȳromā′niăc** *n.*

pȳrŏ′meter *n.* Instrument for measuring high temperatures.

pȳrotĕ′chnic, -ical (-tĕk-) *adjs.* Of (the nature of) fireworks; (fig., of wit etc.) brilliant, sensational. **pȳrotĕ′chnicallў** *adv.* **pȳrotĕ′chnics** *n.* Art of making, display of, fireworks. **pȳrotĕ′chnist, pȳr′otĕchnў** *ns.*

pȳrŏ′xēne *n.* Black crystalline mineral common in igneous rocks.

pȳrŏ′xylin *n.* Any of a class of highly inflammable compounds (nitrates of cellulose), less highly nitrated than gun-cotton, produced by treating vegetable fibres with a mixture of nitric and sulphuric acids. **pȳroxў′lic** *adj.*

Pў′rrhic[1] (-rĭk) *adj. & n.* (Of) a war-dance of the ancient Greeks, performed in armour, with mimicry of actual warfare.

pў′rrhic[2] (-rĭk) *adj. & n.* (Metrical) foot of two short or unstressed syllables, ⏑ ⏑.

Pў′rrhic[3] (-rĭk) *adj.* Of PYRRHUS; ~ *victory*, victory achieved at too great a cost (from saying attributed to Pyrrhus after battle of Asculum, where he routed the Romans but lost the flower of his army: 'One more such victory and we are lost').

Pў′rrhō (-rō) (*c* 360–270 B.C.). Greek Sceptic philosopher of Elis. **Pyrrhō′nian** *adj.* ~ *school*, school of philosophy founded by Pyrrho, holding that nothing can be certainly known and that suspension of judgement is true wisdom and the source of happiness.

Pў′rrhus (-rus) (319–272 B.C.). King of Epirus, military adventurer who fought a series of campaigns against Rome in Italy and Sicily (280–275); see also PYRRHIC[3].

Pȳthă′gorăs (6th c. B.C.). Greek philosopher and mathematician of Samos; his philosophical teaching included the doctrine of the immortality and transmigration of the soul, and he evolved the idea that the explanation of the universe is to be sought in numbers and their relations; *theorem of* ~, geometrical proposition, of which Pythagoras is credited with discovering the proof, that the square on the hypotenuse of a right-angled triangle is equal to the sum of the squares on the other two sides. **Pȳthăgorē′an** *adj. & n.*

Pў′thia. (Gk hist.) Priestess of Apollo at Delphi, who delivered the oracles.

Pў′thian *adj.* Of Delphi; ~ *Apollo*, Apollo as giver of oracles at Delphi; ~ *games*, one of four national festivals of ancient Greece, held near Delphi and said to have been founded by Apollo when he slew the Python. ~ *n.* 1. Native, inhabitant, of Delphi. 2. PYTHIA.

pȳ′thon *n.* 1. (*P*~, Gk myth.) Huge serpent or monster slain near Delphi by Apollo. 2. Member of genus *P*~ of large non-venomous snakes inhabiting the tropical regions of the Old World, or of related genera, which kill their prey by constriction; other related snakes. **pȳthŏ′nic** *adj.*

Pў′thonĕss *n.* = PYTHIA.

pўx *n.* 1. (eccles.) Vessel, often of precious metal, in which host

PYX

is reserved. 2. Box at Royal Mint in which specimen gold and silver coins are deposited to be tested at annual *trial of the* ~ by jury of Goldsmiths' Company.

pўxi′dium *n.* (bot.) Seed-capsule of which the top comes off like lid of box (ill. FRUIT).

Q

Q, q (kū). 17th letter of modern English and 16th of ancient Roman alphabet, derived from Phoenician ϙ, ϟ, $ (representing guttural *k* sound). The letter, followed by *v*, was used in Latin to represent kw-, and *qu-* is used in English to represent this sound in many native English words as well as in those derived from Latin, even when these have now the pronunciation *k-* (as in words derived through French).
q. *abbrev.* Query.
Q. *abbrev.* Queen.
Qaraite: see KARAITE.
Q.A.R.A.N.C. *abbrev.* Queen Alexandra's Royal Army Nursing Corps.
Q.A.R.N.N.S. *abbrev.* Queen Alexandra's Royal Naval Nursing Service.
Qa′tar (kah-). Sheikdom on peninsula on W. coast of Persian Gulf; capital, Doha.
Q.B., Q.C. *abbrev.* Queen's Bench, Counsel.
Q.E.D. *abbrev. Quod erat demonstrandum.*
Q.F. *abbrev.* Quick-firing (gun).
Q fĕ′ver. Disease allied to typhus but milder, caused by a different variety of rickettsia. [f. Queensland, Australia, where first observed]
Q.H.C., Q.H.P., Q.H.S. *abbrevs.* Honorary Chaplain, Physician, Surgeon, to the Queen.
qintār′ (k-) *n.* $\frac{1}{100}$ of a lek.
q.l. *abbrev. Quantum libet* (L, = as much as is desired).
Q.M., Q.M.G., Q.M.S. *abbrevs.* Quartermaster (General, Sergeant).
q.p. *abbrev. Quantum placet* (L, = as much as is desired).
qr *abbrev.* Quarter.
q.s. *abbrev. Quantum sufficit.*
qt *abbrev.* Quart(s).
q.t. *abbrev.* (slang) Quiet (*on the* ~).
qu. *abbrev.* Quasi; query.
quā *adv.* As, in the capacity of.
quăck[1] *v.i.* & *n.* (Utter) harsh cry characteristic of duck.
quăck[2] *n.* Ignorant pretender to skill esp. in medicine and surgery; charlatan. **quă′ckerў** *n.* **quăck** *adj.* Fraudulent, (esp.) alleged to cure disease.
quad (-ŏd) *n.* Quadrangle; quadrat; (colloq.) quadruplet.
Quadragĕ′sima (-ŏd-). First Sunday in Lent. **quadragĕ′simal** *adj.* Lasting 40 days (of fast, esp. Lent); Lenten. [L, = 'fortieth (day)']
quadrangle (kwŏ′drănggl) *n.* Four-sided figure, esp. square or rectangle; four-sided court (partly) enclosed by parts of large building, such court with buildings round

it. **quadră′ngŭlar** *adj.* **quadră′ngŭlarlў** *adv.*
qua′drant (-ŏd-) *n.* 1. Quarter of circumference of circle; plane figure enclosed by two radii of circle at right angles and arc cut off by them (ill. CIRCLE); quarter of sphere. 2. Object, esp. graduated strip or plate of metal, shaped like quarter circle. 3. Instrument, usu.

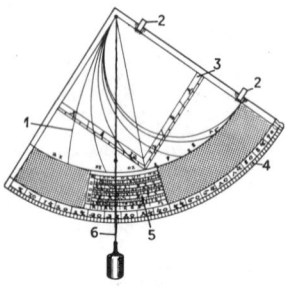

MEDIEVAL QUADRANT FOR TIME TELLING AND SURVEYING

1. Unequal (planetary) hour line. 2. Sight. 3. Shadow square. 4. Scale of 90°. 5. Cursor (half missing) to enable instrument to be used in any latitude. 6. Plumb-line and bob

with calibrated arc of 90°, used for measuring angles and formerly (now superseded by SEXTANT) altitudes.
qua′drat (-ŏd-) *n.* Small metal block used by printers in spacing (*em* ~, larger size, thus □ : *en* ~, smaller size, ▯).
qua′drate (-ŏd-) *adj.* Square, rectangular (rare exc. anat. in names of squarish parts of body); ~ *bone*, bone in heads of birds, amphibia, reptiles, and fish, by which lower jaw is articulated to skull. ~ *n.* Quadrate bone, muscle, etc.
quadră′tic (-ŏd-) *adj.* (math.) Involving the second and no higher power of an unknown quantity or variable (esp. ~ *equation*). ~ *n.* Quadratic equation. **quadră′tics** *n.* Branch of algebra dealing with quadratic equations.
qua′drature (-ŏd-) *n.* (math.) Expression of area bounded by curve, esp. circle, by means of equivalent square; (astron.) either of two points in space or time at which moon is 90° distant from sun; position of heavenly body in relation to another 90° away.
quadrĕ′nnial (-ŏd-) *adj.* Occurring every, lasting, 4 years.
quadri- (-ŏd-) *prefix.* Four.
qua′dric (-ŏd-) *adj.* (math.) Of the 2nd degree. ~ *n.* Quadric function; surface whose equation is in the 2nd degree.

qua′drĭcĕps (-ŏd-) *n.* Large muscle at front of thigh with 4 heads or attachments (ill. MUSCLE).
quadri′ga *n.* (pl. *-ae*). Ancient chariot with 4 horses abreast.
quadrilă′teral (-ŏd-) *adj.* & *n.* (Figure) bounded by 4 straight lines; (space, area) having 4 sides.

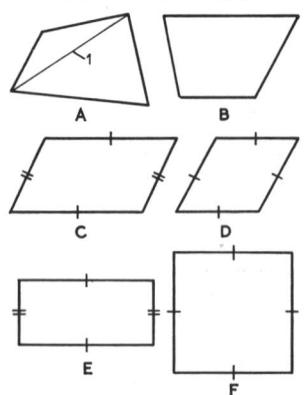

QUADRILATERALS

A. TRAPEZOID. B. TRAPEZIUM. C. PARALLELOGRAM OR RHOMBOID. D. RHOMB OR RHOMBUS. E. RECTANGLE. F. SQUARE

1. Diagonal

quadri′lle[1] *n.* Card-game fashionable in 18th c., played by 4 persons with 40 cards (i.e. an ordinary pack without the 8s, 9s, and 10s).
quadri′lle[2] *n.* Square dance for 4 couples, containing 5 figures; music for this. [Fr. f. Span. *cuadrilla* squadron (*cuadra* square)]
quadri′llion(-yon) *n.* 4th power of a million (1 followed by 24 ciphers); (U.S.) 5th power of a thousand (1 followed by 15 ciphers).
quadrĭnō′mial (-ŏd-) *adj.* Consisting of 4 algebraic terms.
quadripăr′tite (-ŏd-) *adj.* Consisting of 4 parts; shared by or involving 4 parties.
qua′drirēme (-ŏd-) *n.* Ancient galley with 4 banks of oars.
quadrĭsўllă′bic (-ŏd-) *adj.* Four-syllabled. **quadrĭsў′llable** *n.* Word of 4 syllables.
quadrĭvā′lent (-ŏd-) *adj.* (chem.) = TETRAVALENT.
quadri′vium *n.* In Middle Ages, the higher division of the 7 liberal arts, comprising arithmetic, geometry, astronomy, and music.
quadrōō′n *n.* Offspring of white and mulatto, person of quarter-Negro blood. [Span. *cuarteron* (*cüartō* 4th)]

[716]

qua'druped (-ŏdrōō-) *n.* Four-footed animal, esp. four-footed mammal. ~ *adj.* Four-footed.
quadru'pedal (-rōō-) *adj.*
qua'druple (-ŏdrōō-) *adj.* Fourfold, consisting of 4 parts or involving 4 parties; amounting to 4 times the number or amount *of*, equivalent to fourfold the amount of, superior by 4 times in amount or number *to*; ~ *rhythm* or *time*, (mus.) with 4 beats to a measure. **qua'druply** *adv.* **qua'druple** *n.* Number or amount 4 times greater than another. ~ *v.* Multiply by 4.
qua'druplet (-ŏdrōō-) *n.* One of 4 children born at a birth.
quadru'plicate (-ŏdrōō-) *adj.* Fourfold, 4 times repeated or copied. ~ *n. in* ~, in 4 exactly similar examples or copies; (pl.) 4 such copies. **quadru'plicāte** *v.t.* Multiply by 4; make in quadruplicate. **quadruplicā'tion** *n.*
quadrupli'cĭty̆ (-ŏdrōō-) *n.* Fourfold nature, being fourfold.
quae're *v.imper.* (introducing a question) Ask, inquire. ~ *n.* Question, query.
quae'stor *n.* (Rom. hist.) Magistrate in charge of public funds, as treasury officer etc. **quaestōr'ial** *adj.* **quae'storship** *n.*
quaff (-ahf *or* -ŏf) *v.* Drink, drain (cup etc.), in long or copious draughts.
quağ *n.* Quagmire. **quă'gğy̆** *adj.*
quă'gga *n.* Species of zebra (*Equus quagga*) of S. Africa, now extinct; (also, erron.) Burchell's zebra (*Equus burchelli*).
quă'gmīre *n.* Quaking bog, fen, marsh, slough.
Quai d'Orsay (kā, ōr-). Quay on left bank of Seine at Paris, on which stands French Ministry of Foreign Affairs; hence, French foreign policy.
quail[1] *n.* Migratory bird of Old World and Australia allied to partridge, esp. European species (*Coturnix coturnix*) esteemed as food; any of various Amer. birds resembling this; ~-*call*, -*pipe*, whistle with note like quail's used for luring the birds into net.
quail[2] *v.* Flinch, be cowed, give way *before* or *to*; (rare) cow, daunt.
quaint *adj.* Attractive or piquant in virtue of unfamiliar, esp. old-fashioned, appearance, ornamentation, manners, etc.; daintily odd. **quai'ntly̆** *adv.* **quai'ntness** *n.*
quāke *v.i.* Shake, tremble, rock to and fro; *qua'king grass*, grass of genus *Briza* with slender footstalks trembling in wind. **quā'kĭnglȳ** *adv.* **quā'kȳ** *adj.* **quāke** *n.* Act of quaking; earthquake.
Quā'ker *n.* Member of the religious society (Society of Friends) founded by George Fox in 1648–50, distinguished by peaceful principles and plainness of dress and manners; ~*s' meeting*, religious meeting of the Friends, silent except when some member feels stirred to speak; hence, silent meeting, company in which conversation flags. **Quā'kerism** *n.*
Quā'kerish *adj.* [nick-name of early members of the society, who were said to 'tremble at the Word of the Lord']
qualificā'tion (-ŏl-) *n.* 1. Modification, restriction, limitation; restricting or limiting circumstance. 2. Quality, accomplishment, etc., fitting person or thing (*for* post etc.). 3. Condition that must be fulfilled before right can be acquired or office held; document attesting such fulfilment. 4. Attribution of quality. **qua'lificātorȳ** *adj.*
qua'lifȳ (-ŏl-) *v.* 1. Attribute quality to, describe *as*; (gram., of adj.) express some quality of noun. 2. Invest or provide with the necessary qualities, make competent, fit, or legally entitled (*for*, *to*); make oneself competent (*for*) or capable of holding some office, exercising some function, etc. 3. Modify (statement etc.), make less absolute or sweeping, subject to reservation or limitation; moderate, mitigate, esp. make less violent, severe, or unpleasant.
qua'litative (-ŏl-) *adj.* Concerned with, depending on, quality.
qua'litȳ (-ŏl-) *n.* 1. Degree of excellence, relative nature or kind or character (opp. QUANTITY); class or grade of thing as determined by this; general excellence. 2. Faculty, skill, accomplishment, characteristic trait, mental or moral attribute. 3. (archaic) High rank or social standing. 4. (logic, of proposition) Being affirmative or negative. 5. (of sound, voice, etc.) Distinctive character apart from pitch or loudness, timbre.
qualm (-ahm *or* -awm) *n.* Momentary faint or sick feeling, queasiness: misgiving, sinking of heart; scruple of conscience.
qua'ndarȳ (-ŏn-) *n.* State of perplexity, difficult situation, practical dilemma.
quant (-ŏn-) *n.* Punting-pole used by E.-coast bargemen etc., with prong to prevent its sinking in mud. ~ *v.* Propel (boat), propel boat, with quant.
qua'ntic (-ŏn-) *n.*(math.) Rational integral homogeneous function of two or more variables.
qua'ntifȳ (-ŏn-) *v.t.* 1. (logic) Determine application of (term, proposition) by use of *all*, *some*, etc. 2. Determine quantity of, measure, express as quantity. **qua'ntifīable** *adj.* **quantificā'tion** *n.*
qua'ntitative (-ŏn-) *adj.* Measured or measurable by, concerned with, quantity; of, based on, the quantity of vowels. **qua'ntitatīvelȳ** *adv.*
qua'ntitȳ (-ŏn-) *n.* 1. Property of things that is regarded as determinable by measurement of some kind; amount, sum; (pros. etc.) length or shortness of sounds or syllables; (mus.) length or duration of notes; (logic) degree of extension given by proposition to term forming its subject. 2. Specified or considerable portion, number, or amount of something; amount of something present; (pl.) large amounts or numbers, abundance. 3. (math.) Thing having quantity, figure or symbol representing this; *negligible* ~, (transf.) person etc. that need not be reckoned with; *unknown* ~, (transf.) person or thing whose action cannot be foreseen; ~ *surveyor*, one who measures up and prices builders' work.
quant. suff. *abbrev. Quantum sufficit.*
qua'ntum (-ŏn-) *n.* (pl. *-ta*). Sum, amount; share, portion; (phys.) discrete unit quantity of energy, proportional to frequency of radiation, emitted from or absorbed by atom; ~ *dynamics, mechanics,* etc., dynamics, etc., taking account of quanta; ~ *number,* one of a set of integers or half-integers describing the energy level of a particle or system of particles; ~ *theory*, theory originated by M. Planck (1910) and extended by N. Bohr, which accounts for certain atomic phenomena by assuming that radiant energy (heat, light, etc.) is emitted from atoms only in discrete amounts or quanta and not continuously.
qua̅'ntum sŭ'ffĭcĭt. (abbrev. *quant. suff.* or *q.s.*) As much as suffices (in prescriptions); sufficient quantity; to sufficient extent. [L]
qua'rantīne (-ŏr-, -ēn) *n.* (Period, orig. 40 days, of) isolation imposed on infected ship, or on persons (esp. travellers) who might spread contagious or infectious diseases; (period of) isolation for animals (esp. dogs and cats) after landing from abroad. ~ *v.t.* Impose such isolation on, put in quarantine. [prob. f. It. *quarantina* 40 days]
quār'ē ĭ'mpĕdĭt. (law) Writ issued against objector in cases of disputed presentation to benefice. [L, = 'why does he hinder?']
qua'renden, -der (kwŏ-) *n.* Early deep-red apple common in Somerset and Devon.
quark (*or* -ōrk) *n.* (One of three kinds of) hypothetical component of sub-atomic particles.
qua'rrel[1] (kwŏ-) *n.* Short heavy arrow or bolt used in crossbow or arbalest (ill. BOW[1]).
qua'rrel[2] (kwŏ-) *n.* Occasion of complaint against person or his actions; violent contention or altercation *between* persons, rupture of friendly relations. ~ *v.i.* Take exception, find fault *with*; contend violently (*with* person), fall out, have dispute, break off friendly relations. **qua'rrelsome** *adj.* **qua'rrelsomelȳ** *adv.* **qua'rrelsomeness** *n.*
qua'rrȳ[1] (kwŏ-) *n.* Object of

QUARRY

pursuit by bird of prey, hounds, hunters, etc.; intended victim or prey. [OF *curée* (*cuir* skin); orig. sense, parts of deer placed on hide and given to hounds]

qua'rry[2] (kwŏ-) *n.* 1. Excavation made by taking stone for building etc. from its bed; place whence stone, or (fig.) information etc., may be extracted. ~ *v.* Extract (stone) from quarry; form quarry in (hill, etc.); cut or dig (as) in quarry; (fig.) extract (information etc.), search documents, etc., laboriously.

qua'rry[3] (kwŏ-) *n.* Diamond-shaped pane of glass (ill. WINDOW); square floor-tile. [earlier *quarrel*, f. It. *quadrello*, dim. of *quadro* square]

quart[1] (-ôr-) *n.* Measure of capacity, quarter of gallon, 2 pints; pot or bottle containing this amount.

quart[2] (kârt) *n.* 1. (also carte) Fourth of the 8 positions in fencing (ill. FENCE). 2. Sequence of 4 cards in piquet etc. ~ *v.* (fencing) Use the position quart; draw back (head etc.) in this.

quar'tan *adj.* & *n.* (archaic) (Fever) with paroxysm every 3rd (by inclusive reckoning 4th) day.

quarte *n.* Var. of QUART[2].

quar'ter (-ôr-) *n.* 1. Fourth part; one of 4 equal or corresponding parts; fourth part of; *bad~of an hour*, short unpleasant experience. 2. Quarter of dollar, 25 cents, as amount or coin (U.S. & Canada). 3. One of 4 parts, each including a limb, into which beast's or bird's carcass is divided; (pl.) similar parts of traitor quartered after execution; (freq. pl.) haunch(es) of living animal or man. 4. Either side of ship abaft the beam (ill. BEARING). 5. Side of boot or shoe from centre back to vamp (ill. SHOE). 6. (her.) One of 4 divisions of quartered shield, charge occupying quarter placed in chief. 7. Dry measure of 8 bushels. 8. Fourth part of cwt., 28 lb. (in U.S. 25 lb.). 9. Fourth part of fathom. 10. Quarter-mile race or running-distance. 11. Fourth part of year for which payments become due on quarter-day. 12. Fourth part of lunar period, moon's position between 1st and 2nd or 3rd and 4th of these (ill. MOON). 13. Point of time 15 minutes before or after any hour o'clock. 14. (Region lying about) point of compass; direction; district, locality; portion or member of community, some thing or things, without reference to actual locality. 15. Division of town, esp. one appropriated to or occupied by special class. 16. (pl.) Lodgings, abode, esp. place where troops are quartered or stationed; assigned or appropriate places, station; *beat for ~s*, (naut.) summon crew to action stations; *winter ~s*, place occupied, esp. by troops, for winter. 17. Exemption from death offered or granted to enemy in battle who will surrender. 18. ~ *binding*, (of book) with narrow strip of leather at back and none elsewhere (ill. BOOK); ~*-butt*, (billiards) cue of short length; ~*-day*, day on which quarterly payments are due, tenancies begin and end, etc. (in England and Ireland, Lady Day 25 Mar., Midsummer Day 24 June, Michaelmas 29 Sept., Christmas 25 Dec.; in Scotland, Candlemas 2 Feb., Whitsunday 15 May, Lammas 1 Aug., Martinmas 11 Nov.); ~*-deck*, part of upper deck between stern and after-mast; officers of ship or navy; ~*-ill*, disease in cattle and sheep causing putrefaction in one or more of the quarters; *quar'termaster*, (naut.) petty officer in charge of steering, signals, hold-stowing, etc.; (mil., abbrev. Q.M.) regimental officer with duties of assigning quarters, laying out camp, and looking after rations, clothing, equipment, etc.; *quartermaster general*, (abbrev. Q.M.G.) staff officer at head of department controlling quartering, equipment, etc.; *quartermaster sergeant*, non-commissioned officer assisting quartermaster and ranking as staff-sergeant; ~*-note*, (U.S.) crotchet; ~*-plate*, photographic plate or film $9 \times 11 \cdot 5$ cm ($3\frac{1}{4} \times 4\frac{1}{4}$ in.), photograph produced from it; ~*-section*, (U.S. & Canada) quarter of square mile of land, 160 acres; ~ *sessions*, court of limited civil and criminal jurisdiction and of appeal held quarterly until 1971 by justices of peace in counties and by recorder in boroughs; *quar'terstaff*, stout iron-tipped pole 6–8 ft long formerly used by English peasantry as weapon; ~*-tone*, (mus.) half a semitone. ~ *v.t.* 1. Divide into 4 equal parts; (hist.) divide (traitor's body) into quarters. 2. (her.) Place, bear (charges, coats of arms) quarterly on shield; add (another's coat) to one's hereditary arms; place in alternate quarters *with*; divide (shield) into quarters or into divisions formed by vertical and horizontal lines. 3. Put (esp. soldiers) into quarters; station or lodge in specified place. 4. (of dogs) Range or traverse (ground) in every direction.

quar'terage (-ôr-) *n.* Quarterly payment; a quarter's wages, allowance, pension, etc.

quar'tering (-ôr-) *n.* (esp., her., pl.) Coats marshalled on shield to denote alliances of family with heiresses of others (ill. HERALDRY).

quar'terly (-ôr-) *adj.* 1. Occurring every quarter of a year. 2. (her.) Divided quarterly or by lines at right angles (ill. HERALDRY). ~ *n.* Quarterly review or magazine. ~ *adv.* 1. Once every quarter of a year. 2. (her.) In the four, or in two diagonally opposite, quarters of a shield.

quar'tern (-ôr-) *n.* Quarter of a pint; (also ~*-loaf*) 4-pound loaf.

QUATRAIN

quartĕ't, -ĕ'tte (-ôr-) *n.* 1. (mus.) (Composition for) 4 voices or instruments in combination; players or singers rendering this; *piano ~*, three stringed instruments with piano; *string ~*, two violins, viola, and cello. 2. Set of 4 persons or things.

quar'tō (-ôr-) *n.* (also 4to, 4°). Size given by folding sheet of paper twice; book consisting of sheets so folded; ~ *paper*, paper folded so as to form 4 leaves out of original sheet; paper of size or shape of quarter-sheet.

quartz (-ôr-) *n.* Any of several varieties of silica, massive or crystallizing in hexagonal prisms; *fused ~*, type of glass made by melting quartz, capable of withstanding very high temperature and used for scientific apparatus, ultra-violet lamps, etc.

quar'tzīte (-ôr-) *n.* Hard sandstone containing quartz grains.

quā'sār (or -z-) *n.* Very small star-like cosmic source of light and radio waves.

quash (-ŏ-) *v.t.* Annul, make void, reject as not valid, put an end to (esp. by legal procedure or authority).

quā'sī (or -z-) *adv.* That is to say, as if it were.

quāsi- (or -z-) *prefix.* Seeming(ly), not real(ly); practical(ly); half-, almost.

Quă'simō'dō Sŭ'nday. First Sunday after Easter. [f. first two words of introit of Mass of the day]

quassia (-ŏ'sha) *n.* S. Amer. tree (*Quassia amara*), found esp. in Surinam; wood, bark, or root of this and other trees (now esp. *Picraena excelsa*, bitter wood tree, of W. Indies etc., yielding bitter medicinal tonic and also much used horticulturally for destroying aphids. [S. Amer. tree named by Linnaeus after *Graman Quassi*, Surinam Negro, who discovered its medicinal properties in 1730]

quătercĕntĕ'nary (or -ŏt-) *n.* 400th anniversary.

quatĕr'nary *adj.* 1. Having 4 parts; (chem.) compounded of 4 elements or radicals. 2. *Q~*, (geol.) of the period or system subsequent to the Tertiary, of recent and present-day formations, yielding fossils of shells, bones, and plants, all of which represent species still living. ~ *n.* 1. Set of 4 things; number 4. 2. *Q~*, (geol.) Quaternary period or system (ill. GEOLOGY).

quatĕr'nion *n.* Set of 4; quire of 4 sheets folded in two; (math.) quotient of two vectors or operator that changes one vector into another (so named as depending on 4 geometrical elements); (pl.) form of calculus of vectors in which this operator is used.

quatorzain (kă'terzān) *n.* 14-line poem, irregular sonnet.

quatrain (kwŏ'trĭn) *n.* Stanza of 4 lines, usu. with alternate rhymes.

quatre (kătr or kā'ter) n. Four in dice.

Quatrebras (kătrebrah). Small village near Brussels, Belgium, scene of battle (1815) between French under Marshal Ney and English, two days before WATERLOO.

qua'trefoil (kă-) n. 4-cusped figure, esp. as opening in architectural tracery, resembling symmetrical 4-lobed leaf or flower (ill. WINDOW).

quattrocĕ'ntō (-ahtrŏch-) n. 15th century as period of Italian art and literature. [It., = 'four hundred', short for *mil quattrocento* 1400].

quā'ver v. Vibrate, shake, tremble (esp. of voice or musical sound); use trills in singing; sing with trills; say in trembling tones. ~ n. 1. Trill in singing; tremulousness in speech. 2. (mus.) Note (♪) half as long as crotchet. **quā'veringlȳ** adv. **quā'verȳ** adj.

quay (kē) n. Solid stationary artificial landing-place usu. of stone or iron, lying alongside or projecting into water, for (un)loading ships. **quay'age** n. Quay-room; due levied on ships using quay or goods (un)loaded there.

Que. abbrev. Quebec.

quean n. (archaic) Impudent or ill-behaved girl, hussy.

quea'sȳ (-zī) adj. (of person, stomach) Easily upset, inclined to sickness or nausea; (of conscience etc.) tender, scrupulous. **quea'siness** n.

Quĕbĕ'c. Province of E. Canada; its capital, on the St. Lawrence River, orig. settled by the French, and captured from them by a British force under Wolfe, 1759.

Quechua (kĕ'chwa) n. Member of a group of Inca tribes; language of these tribes, still spoken among Peruvian Indians. **Que'chuan** adj. & n.

queen n. 1. King's wife (also ~ *consort* for distinction from next sense; ~ *dowager*, wife of late king; ~ *mother*, queen dowager who is mother of sovereign); also prefixed to personal name as title. 2. Female sovereign ruler, usu. hereditary; Q~ *Empress*, title assumed by Queen Victoria as Queen of England and Empress of India. 3. Adored female (Q~ *of grace*, Q~ *of heaven*, the Virgin Mary); ancient goddess (Q~ *of heaven*, Juno, *of love*, Venus, *of night*, Diana, etc.); person's sweetheart or wife or mistress; majestic woman; belle, mock sovereign, on some occasion (as Q~ *of the May* at May festival); personified best example of anything regarded as feminine. 4. Person, country, etc. regarded as holding sway over some sphere (~ *of the Adriatic*, Venice). 5. Perfect female of bee (ill. BEE), wasp, ant, or termite. 6. Female cat used for breeding. 7. (chess) Piece with greatest freedom of movement, placed next to king at beginning of game (ill. CHESS). 8. One of court-cards in each suit, bearing figure of a queen. 9. ~-*bee*, fully developed female bee; ~-*cake*, small soft rich currant-cake, freq. heart-shaped; ~-*post*, one of two upright timbers between tie-beam and principal rafters of roof-truss (ill. ROOF); Q~'s BENCH, COUNSEL, ENGLISH, EVIDENCE, PROCTOR, SHILLING: see these words. **quee'n-like** adj. **queen** v. 1. Make (woman) queen; ~ *it*, play the queen. 2. (chess) Advance (pawn) to opponent's end of board, where it is replaced by a queen or other piece; (of pawn) reach this position.

quee'ning n. Kind of apple.

quee'nlȳ adj. Fit for, appropriate to, a queen; majestic, queenlike. **quee'nliness** n.

Quee'nsberrȳ Rules (-z-, roolz). Set of rules for boxing in Gt Britain, based on those drawn up 1867 under supervision of 8th Marquess of Queensberry.

Queen's Cou'ntȳ (-z-). Former name of LEIX.

Quee'nsland (-z-). State of NE. Australia; capital, Brisbane. **Quee'nslānder** n.

queer adj. Strange, odd, eccentric; of questionable character, shady, suspect; out of sorts, giddy, faint; *in Q~ Street*, (slang) in a difficulty, in debt, trouble, or disrepute. **queer'lȳ** adv. **queer'ness** n. **queer** n. (slang) Homosexual. ~ v.t. (slang) Spoil, put out of order; esp. ~ *the pitch*, spoil chances of success *for* another, esp. by unfair means.

quĕll v.t. (poet. & rhet.) Suppress, forcibly put an end to, crush, overcome, reduce to submission.

quĕnch v.t. Extinguish (chiefly poet. or rhet.); cool, esp. with water (heat, heated thing); stifle, suppress (desire, speed, etc.); slake (thirst). **quĕ'nchlĕss** adj. That cannot be quenched.

quenĕ'lle (ke-) n. (cookery) Seasoned ball of fish or meat pounded to paste.

quēr'ist n. One who asks questions.

quĕrn n. Hand-mill for grinding corn; small hand-mill for pepper etc.

quĕ'rulous (-rōō-) adj. Complaining, peevish. **quĕ'rulouslȳ** adv. **quĕ'rulousnĕss** n.

quēr'ȳ n. Question; mark of interrogation (?), or word *query* or *qu.*, used to indicate doubt of correctness of statement in writing. ~ v. Ask, inquire; put a question; call in question, question accuracy of.

Quesnay (kěnā), François (1694–1774). French economist, founder of physiocratic school.

quĕst n. Official inquiry, jury, etc., making it (now only in vulg. *crowner's* ~, coroner's inquest); seeking by inquiry or search; thing sought, esp. object of medieval knight's pursuit; *in* ~ *of*, seeking. ~ v. Go *about* in search of something; (of dogs etc.) search (*about*) for game; (poet.) search for, seek *out*.

quĕ'stion (-chon) n. 1. Interrogative statement of some point to be investigated or discussed; problem; subject for discussion in meeting etc., esp. in Parliament; subject of discussion, debate, or strife; *the* ~, the precise matter receiving or requiring discussion or deliberation; *beg the* ~: see BEG; *in* ~, under consideration; *it is a* ~ *of*, what is required or involved is; *out of*, *past*, *without*, etc., ~, certainly, undoubtedly; *out of the* ~, foreign to the subject; not to be considered or thought of. 2. Sentence in interrogative form, meant to elicit information, interrogation, inquiry; ~-*mark*, mark of interrogation (?). 3. Action of questioning; (hist.) application of torture as part of judicial examination. **quĕ'stionlĕss** adj. **quĕ'stion** v.t. Ask questions of, interrogate, subject (person) to examination; seek information from study of (phenomena, facts); call in question, throw doubt upon, raise objections to. **quĕ'stioninglȳ** adv.

quĕ'stionable (-chon-) adj. (esp.) Doubtfully true; not clearly consistent with honesty, honour, or wisdom. **quĕ'stionablȳ** adv.

quĕstionnair'e (or -sch-; or kē-) n. Series of questions usu. for obtaining information on special points esp. in statistical investigations.

quĕ'tzal (kĕ-) n. 1. Extremely beautiful Central Amer. bird (*Pharomachrus mocino*), cock of which has very long golden-green tail-coverts. 2. Principal monetary unit of Guatemala, = 100 centavos. [Aztec *quetzalli* tail-feather of this bird]

Quĕtzalcōa'tl (kĕ-, -ahtl). (Aztec myth.) God worshipped as bestower of arts of civilization on mankind, having as symbol a plumed serpent (snake with quetzal feathers instead of scales); also, a hero whose connection with the god is obscure.

queue (kū) n. 1. Pigtail of hair or wig (ill. WIG). 2. Line of persons, vehicles, etc., awaiting their turn to be attended to or proceed. ~ v.i. Form *up* in, take one's place in, queue.

qui'bble n. Play on words, pun; equivocation, evasion; unsubstantial or purely verbal argument etc., esp. one depending on ambiguity of word. ~ v.i. Use quibbles. **qui'bbler** n. **qui'bbling** adj.

quiche (kēsh) n. Open pastry case containing sweet or savoury filling.

quick adj. 1. (archaic or dial.) Living, alive; (of hedge etc.) composed of living plants, esp. hawthorn. 2. Vigorous, lively, active; prompt to act, perceive, be

[719]

affected, etc.; (of fire) burning strongly, (of oven) hot. 3. Moving rapidly, rapid, swift; done in short time or with little interval. 4. ~-**change**, (of actor etc.) quickly changing costume or appearance to play another part; **qui'cklime**, = LIME¹, 2; ~ **march**, (mil.) march in quick time (esp. as word of command); ~ *one*, quick drink; **qui'cksand**, (bed of) loose wet sand readily swallowing up any heavy object resting on it; **qui'ckset**, (of hedge) formed of living plants; (*n*.) live slips of plants, esp. hawthorn, set in ground to grow; quickset hedge; **qui'cksilver**, mercury; (*v.t*.) coat back of (mirror-glass) with amalgam of tin; ~ *step*, step used in quick time; (mus.) march in military quick time; fast foxtrot; ~ *time*, rate of marching now (in British army) reckoned as 128 paces of 33 in. to the minute, or four miles an hour; ~ *trick*, (bridge) card that should take trick in first or second round of suit, ace or king. **qui'ckly** *adv*. **quick** *n*. Tender or sensitive flesh below skin or esp. nails; tender part of wound or sore where healthy tissue begins; seat of feeling or emotion. ~ *adv*. Quickly, at rapid rate, in comparatively short time; (imper.) make haste; ~-*firer*, -*firing gun*, gun in which the propellant is contained in a metal cartridge case (opp. BREECH-loading).

qui'cken *v*. 1. Give or restore natural or spiritual life or vigour to; animate, stimulate, rouse, inspire, kindle; receive, come to, life; (of human female) reach stage of pregnancy at which foetus makes clearly perceptible movements. 2. Accelerate; make or become quicker.

qui'ckie *n*. (colloq.) Thing hastily done or made; film so produced.

qui'ckness *n*. Readiness or acuteness of perception or apprehension; speed, rapidity, suddenness; hastiness (*of temper*).

quid¹ *n*. (slang; pl. same) Sum of £1; one-pound bank-note.

quid² *n*. Lump of tobacco etc. for chewing.

qui'ddity *n*. 1. Essence of a thing, what makes a thing what it is. 2. Quibble, captious subtlety.

qui'dnunc *n*. Newsmonger, person given to gossip. [L *quid what, nunc* now]

quid pro quo. Compensation, return made, consideration. [L, = 'something for something']

quie'scent *adj*. Motionless, inert, silent, dormant. **quie'scently** *adv*. **quie'scence** *n*.

qui'et *n*. Peaceful condition of affairs in social or political life; silence, stillness; freedom from disturbance, agitation, etc., rest, repose, peace of mind; unruffled deportment, calm. ~ *adj*. 1. Making no stir, commotion, or noise; not active; free from excess, not going to extremes; avoiding or escaping notice, secret, private; *on the* ~, secretly, covertly. 2. Free from disturbance, interference, or annoyance; calm, unruffled, silent, still. **qui'etly** *adv*. **qui'etness**, **qui'etude** *ns*. **qui'et** *v*. Reduce to quietness, soothe, calm; become quiet. **qui'eten** *v*. Quiet.

qui'etism *n*. 1. Form of religious mysticism (originated *c* 1675 by a Spanish priest, Molinos) consisting in passive devotional contemplation with extinction of will and withdrawal from all things of the senses. 2. State of calmness and passivity. **qui'etist** *n*. **quieti'stic** *adj*.

quie'tus *n*. Acquittance, receipt, given on payment of account etc. (now rare); release from life, extinction, final riddance. [med. L *quietus* (*est*) (he is) quit, used as receipt form]

quiff *n*. Curl plastered down on forehead, formerly affected by men; also, lock of (man's) hair brushed upwards in front.

quill *n*. Hollow stem of feather (ill. FEATHER); whole large feather of wing or tail; pen, plectrum, fishing-float, or toothpick, made of this; spine of porcupine; bobbin of hollow reed, any bobbin; musical pipe made of hollow stem (archaic); curled-up piece of cinnamon or cinchona bark; ~-*coverts*, feathers covering base of quill-feathers; ~-*driver*, (colloq.) clerk, journalist, author; ~-*feather*, stiff, comparatively large, feather of edge of bird's wing, similar feather of tail.

quilt *n*. Coverlet, esp. made of padding enclosed between two layers of fabric and kept in place by lines of stitching. ~ *v.t*. Cover, line, etc., with padded material; make or join together after the manner of a quilt. **qui'lting** *n*.

quin *n*. (colloq.) Quintuplet.

qui'nary *adj*. Of the number 5; consisting of 5 things.

quince *n*. Hard acid yellowish pear-shaped fruit used as preserve or as flavouring; small tree (*Cydonia oblonga*) bearing this; *Japanese* ~, fruit of garden japonica (*Chaenomeles lagenaria*). [ult. f. L *Cydonium* of Cydonia in Crete]

quincente'nary *n*. 500th anniversary.

Quincey, Thomas De: see DE QUINCEY.

qui'ncunx *n*. (Arrangement of) 5 objects set so that 4 are at corners of square or rectangle and the other at its centre, esp. as basis of arrangement in planting trees.

qui'nine (-ēn) *n*. Alkaloid found in cinchona bark and used in treatment of malaria and as febrifuge and tonic; (pop.) quinine sulphate, usual form in which it is taken. [Peruv. *kina* bark]

qui'none (or -ō'n) *n*. 1. Crystalline compound ($C_6H_4O_2$) obtained by oxidizing aniline. 2. General name for a benzene derivative in which 2 oxygen atoms replace 2 hydrogen.

quinquagēnā'rian *adj*. & *n*. (Person) aged 50 or more but less than 60.

Quinquagĕ'sima. Sunday before Lent. [med. L *quinquagesima* (*dies*) 50th day, so called as the 50th day before Easter by inclusive reckoning or loosely as the Sunday before Quadragesima Sunday]

quinque-, **quinqu-** *prefix*. Five.

quinquĕ'nnium *n*. 5-year period. **quinquĕ'nnial** *adj*. 5-year-long, 5-yearly.

quinquepar'tite *adj*. Divided into, consisting of, 5 parts.

qui'nquereme *n*. Ancient galley with 5 banks of oars.

quinquivā'lent *adj*. (chem.) Having a valency of 5.

qui'nsy (-zǐ) *n*. Abscess forming round the tonsil usu. as a complication of tonsillitis. [Gk *kunagkhē* (*kuōn kun-* dog, *aghkōm* throttle)]

quint *n*. 1. Musical interval of a 5th; organ-stop giving tone a 5th higher than normal. 2. (also pr. kǐ-) Sequence of 5 of same suit in piquet.

qui'ntain (-tǐn) *n*. (hist.) (Medieval military exercise of tilting at) post set up as mark and often provided with sandbag to swing round and strike unskilful tilter.

qui'ntal *n*. Weight of 100 lb.; hundredweight, 112 lb.; 100 kilograms. [Arab. *kintār*]

qui'ntan *adj*. & *n*. (archaic) (Fever) with paroxysm every 4th (by inclusive reckoning 5th) day.

quinte (kǎnt) *n*. Fifth thrust or parry of the 8 positions in fencing (ill. FENCE).

quintĕ'ssence *n*. 1. (ancient and medieval philos.) 5th substance, apart from the four elements, composing the heavenly bodies entirely and latent in all things, extraction of which was one of the aims of alchemy. 2. Most essential part of any substance, refined extract; purest and most perfect form, manifestation, or embodiment, *of* some quality or class. **quintĕssĕ'ntial** (-shal) *adj*. [*quinta essentia* 5th essence]

quintĕ't, -**ĕ'tte** *n*. 1. (mus.) (Composition for) 5 voices or instruments in combination; players or singers rendering this; *clarinet, piano*, etc., ~, 4 stringed instruments plus instrument named. 2. Set of 5 persons or things.

Quinti'lian (-yan). Marcus Fabius Quintilianus (b. *c* A.D. 30–5), Roman rhetorician, author of 'De Institutione Oratoria', the 10th book of which contains judgements on Greek and Roman writers.

quinti'llion (-yon) *n*. 5th power of a million (1 with 30 ciphers); (U.S.) cube of a million (1 with 18 ciphers).

qui'ntuple *adj*. Fivefold; consisting of 5 things or parts. ~ *v*. Multiply, increase, fivefold.

qui'ntuplet *n*. 1. Set of 5

[720]

things; (mus.) group of 5 notes played in the time of 4. 2. One of 5 children born at a birth.
quintu'plicate *adj.* Quintuple.
quip *n.* Sarcastic remark, clever hit, smart saying, verbal conceit; quibble.
qui'pu (-oō; *or* kē'-) *n.* Ancient-Peruvian device for sending messages, keeping accounts, etc., by variously knotting threads of various colours. [Peruv., = 'knot']
quire[1] *n.* 4 sheets of paper etc. folded to form 8 leaves as in medieval MSS.; any collection of leaves one within another in MS. or book; 24 sheets of writing paper; *in ~s*, (of book) in folded sheets, unbound.
quire[2] *n. & v.* (archaic) Choir.
Qui'rinal. One of the hills on which ancient Rome was built; site of Italian royal residence 1870–1947, now of official residence of president of the republic.
quirk *n.* 1. Quibble, quip; trick of action or behaviour; twist or flourish in drawing or writing. 2. (archit.) Acute hollow between convex part of moulding and soffit or fillet (ill. MOULDING).
quirt *n.* (U.S.) Short-handled riding whip with braided leather lash used in western U.S. and Span. America. *~ v.t.* Lash with quirt.
qui'sling (-z-) *n.* Person co-operating with an enemy who has occupied his country. **qui'slingite** *adj. & n.* [Major Vidkun *Quisling*, a Norwegian who collaborated with the Germans when they invaded Norway 1940]
quit[1] *pred. adj.* Free, clear, absolved (archaic); rid *of*; *qui't-claim*, renunciation of right; (*v.t.*) renounce claim to, give up (thing) *to*; *~-rent*, (usu. small) rent paid by freeholder or copyholder in lieu of service.
quit[2] *v.t.* 1. (archaic) Rid oneself *of*; behave, acquit, conduct (oneself) *well*, etc. 2. Give up, let go, abandon; depart from, leave; (abs., of tenant) leave occupied premises. **qui'tter** *n.* (U.S.) Shirker, one who abandons project etc.
quitch *n.* (also *~-grass*) COUCH[2]-grass.

quite *adv.* 1. Completely, wholly, entirely, altogether, to the utmost extent, in the fullest sense, positively, absolutely. 2. Rather, to some extent, as *~ a long time*; *~ a few*, a fair number.
quits *pred. adj.* On even terms by retaliation or repayment.
qui'ttance *n.* (archaic, poet.) Release *from*; acknowledgement of payment, receipt.
qui'ver[1] *n.* Case for holding arrows; *~ full (of children)*, large family (see Ps. 127: 5).
qui'ver[2] *v.* Tremble or vibrate with slight rapid motion: (of bird) make (wings) quiver. *~ n.* Quivering motion or sound.
qui vive (kē vēv). *on the ~*, on the alert. [Fr., = '(long) live who?', i.e. 'on whose side are you?', as sentinel's challenge]
Qui'xote, Don. Hero of romance (1605–15) by CERVANTES, written to ridicule the books of chivalry; hence, enthusiastic visionary, pursuer of lofty but impracticable ideals. **quixo'tic** *adj.* **qui'xotry** *n.*
quiz *n.* Odd or eccentric person, in character or appearance (now rare); one who quizzes; hoax, banter, ridicule (now rare); (orig. U.S.) informal oral examination of class or pupil, now, general knowledge test, esp. one organized as an entertainment or competition. *~ v.t.* Regard with mocking air; look curiously at, observe the ways or oddities of, survey through an eyeglass; (orig. U.S.) put series of questions to (person). **qui'zzical** *adj.* **qui'zzically** *adv.*
quod *n.* (slang) Prison. *~ v.t.* (slang) Imprison.
quŏd ĕ'rat dĕmŏnstra'ndum. (abbrev. Q.E.D.) Which was to be proved (formula concluding geometrical demonstration etc.) [L]
quŏd vi'dē. (abbrev. q.v.) Which see (in cross-references etc.). [L]
quoif (koif) *n.* Var. of COIF.
quoin (koin) *n.* 1. External angle of building; stone or brick forming angle, corner-stone (ill. MASONRY); internal corner of room. 2. Wedge for locking type in forme (ill. PRINT), raising level of gun, keeping barrel

from rolling, etc. *~ v.t.* Raise or secure with quoins.
quoit (*or* koit) *n.* Heavy, flattish ring of wood, rope, etc., thrown to encircle iron peg or to stick in ground near it; (pl.) game in which quoits are thrown thus.
quo'ndam *adj.* Sometime, former. [L, = 'formerly']
Quorn. Celebrated pack of fox-hounds, hunting in Leicestershire, named after Quorndon Hall where the kennels now are.
quor'um *n.* Fixed number of members that must be present to make proceedings of assembly, society, board, etc., valid. [L, = 'of whom']
quot. *abbrev.* Quotation etc.
quo'ta *n.* Part or share which is, or ought to be, contributed by one to a total sum or amount; part or share of a total which belongs, is given, or is due, to one. [L *quota (pars)* how great (a part), f. *quot* how many]
quota'tion *n.* 1. (print.) Large quadrat used for filling up blanks (orig. between marginal references). 2. Quoting, passage quoted; amount stated as current price of stocks or commodities; *~-marks*, inverted commas (see COMMA).
quote *v.t.* Cite or appeal to (author, book, etc.) in comfirmation of some view, repeat or copy out passage(s) from; repeat or copy out (borrowed passage) usu. with indication that it is borrowed; (abs.) make quotations (*from*); adduce or cite *as*; state price of (usu. *at* figure). *~ n.* (colloq.) Passage quoted; (usu. pl.) quotation-mark(s).
quŏth *v.t.*, 1st & 3rd pers. past indic. (archaic) Said.
quoti'dian *adj.* Daily, of every day; commonplace, trivial; *~ fever, ague*, fever with paroxysms recurring every day. *~ n.* Quotidian fever or ague.
quo'tient (-shent) *n.* Result given by dividing one quantity by another.
Qur'an (kurah'n). Var. of KORAN.
qursh (koŏ-) *n.* 1/20 of a riyal.
q.v. *abbrev. Quantum vis* (L, = as much as you wish); *quod vide*.
qy *abbrev.* Query.

R

R, r (är). 18th letter of modern English and 17th of ancient Roman alphabet, derived through early Gk Ρ, Ρ from Phoenician ٩; in modern standard English representing, before a vowel, an open voiced consonant, with almost no trill, in formation of which the point of the tongue approaches

the palate a little way behind the teeth; in other positions, an obscure vowel sound, disappearing altogether after some vowels.
R, ℞ *abbrevs.* Rupee.
R. *abbrev.* Réaumur; *Regina*; *retarder* (on timepiece regulator, Fr., = to retard); *Rex*; River.
r. *abbrev.* Right; röntgen(s); run(s).

℞ *abbrev.* (in medical prescriptions) *Recipe* (L, = take).
⓫ Symbol for 'Registered' (of trade-mark).
Ra (rah). (Egyptian myth.) Sun-god, freq. represented with head of falcon.
R.A. *abbrev.* Royal Academy (*or* Academician); Royal Artillery.

R.A.A.F. *abbrev.* Royal Australian Air Force; Royal Auxiliary Air Force.

rā'bbĕt *n.* 1. Step-shaped reduction cut along edge, face, or projecting angle of wood, etc., usu. to receive edge or tongue of another piece (ill. JOINT¹); ~ *plane*, tool for making groove along an edge (ill. PLANE²). 2. Elastic beam fixed so as to give rebound to large fixed hammer. ~ *v.t.* Join, fix, with rabbet; make rabbet in.

rā'bbī *n.* 1. Title of Jewish scholar or teacher of civil and religious law from New Testament times on. 2. Spiritual leader of a Jewish community and senior officer in synagogue; *Chief R~*, ecclesiastical head of United Synagogue in Gt Britain. **rā'bbīn** *n.* (archaic) Rabbi. **rā'bbīnate, rā'bbīnism, rā'bbīnist** *ns.* **rabbī'nĭcal** *adj.* **rabbī'nĭcallў** *adv.*

rā'bbĭt *n.* Burrowing herbivorous gregarious mammal (*Oryctolagus cuniculus*), native to W. Europe, allied to the hare but with shorter legs and smaller ears, brownish-grey in natural state, also black, white, or pied in domestication; (slang) poor performer at any game, esp. cricket, golf, or lawn tennis; ~*-punch*, (boxing) punch on back of neck. ~ *v.i.* Hunt rabbits.

rā'bble¹ *n.* Disorderly crowd, mob; contemptible or inferior set of people; lowest classes of the populace.

rā'bble² *n.* Iron bar with bent end for stirring molten metal in puddling.

Rabelais (-lā), François (*c* 1495–1553). French physician, humanist, and satirical writer; author of 'Pantagruel' and 'Gargantua'. **Răbelai'sian** (-z-), *adj.* Of or like Rabelais; having the exuberance and coarse humour characteristic of Rabelais.

rā'bĭd *adj.* Furious, violent, raging, unreasoning; (esp. of dog) affected with rabies; of rabies. **rā'bĭdlў** *adv.* **rā'bĭdnĕss, rabī'dĭtў** *ns.*

rā'bies (-z) *n.* Canine madness, a contagious disease principally of the dog but occas. affecting other domestic animals and also man in which case it is usu. known as *hydrophobia*).

R.A.C. *abbrev.* Royal Armoured Corps; Royal Automobile Club.

raccoon: see RACOON.

rāce¹ *n.* 1. Onward sweep or movement, esp. strong current in sea or river; course of sun or moon, course of life. 2. Channel of stream; track or channel in which something moves or slides, as that of a shuttle crossing the web or the balls in a ball-bearing (ill. BEARING). 3. Contest of speed between runners, ships, horses, etc., or persons doing anything; (pl.) series of these for horses at fixed time on regular course; ~-*card*, programme of races; *ra'cecourse*, ground for horse-racing; *ra'cehorse*, horse bred or kept for racing; ~-*meeting*, horse-racing fixture. ~ *v.* Compete in speed *with*; have race with, try to surpass in speed; cause (horse etc.) to race; indulge in horse-racing; make (person, thing) move at full speed; go at full speed; (of machinery) move, revolve with uncontrolled speed, when resistance is diminished, as when the propeller of a ship is raised out of the water.

rāce² *n.* Group of persons, animals, or plants connected by common descent; posterity *of* (person); house, family, tribe, or nation regarded as of common stock; distinct ethnical stock; any great division of living creatures; descent, kindred; class of persons etc. with some common feature; (biol.) subdivision of a species; variety.

racē'me *n.* (bot.) Inflorescence opening successively from base to apex, with flowers on short lateral stalks springing from a central stem, as in hyacinth, lily of the valley, etc. (ill. INFLORESCENCE).

racē'mĭc *adj.* (chem.) Derived from grapes or grape-juice; ~ *acid*, colourless crystalline acid, an optically inactive variety of tartaric acid, found in the juice of grapes.

rā'cĕmōse *adj.* (bot.) Arranged in, having form of, a raceme; (anat.) arranged in, having form of, a cluster, as e.g. the pancreas.

rā'cer *n.* (esp.) Horse, yacht, motor-car, etc., used for racing.

rachĕ'l¹ (-sh-) *adj.* & *n.* (Of) pale fawn shade used in cosmetics.

Rā'chel². Second wife of Jacob and mother of Joseph and Benjamin (Gen. 29–35).

rā'chĭs (-k-) *n.* (pl. -*ides* pr. -ĭdēz). 1. (bot.) Axis of inflorescence with flower-stalks at short intervals, as in grasses; axis of pinnately compound leaf or frond (ill. LEAF). 2. (anat.) Vertebral column or cord from which it develops. 3. (ornith.) Feather-shaft, esp. part bearing barbs (ill. FEATHER).

rachī'tĭs (-k-) *n.* Rickets. **rachī'tĭc** *adj.*

Rachmă'nĭnŏv (raχ-, -f), Sergey Vasilyevich (1873–1943). Russian composer and pianist.

rā'cial (-shal) *adj.* Of, belonging to, characteristic of, race. **rā'cially** *adv.*

rā'cialism (-sha-) *n.* (Encouragement of) racial antagonism; belief in the superiority of a particular race; social or political system based on this. **rā'cialist** *n.*

Răcine (-ēn), Jean (1639–99). French tragic poet and dramatist; author of 'Phèdre', 'Andromaque', 'Athalie', etc.

rā'cĭsm *n.* 1. Theory that distinctive characteristics, abilities, etc., are determined by race. 2. = RACIALISM. **rā'cĭst** *n.*

răck¹ *n.* 1. Driving clouds. 2. Destruction (only in ~ *and ruin*). ~ *v.i.* (of clouds) Drive before wind.

răck² *n.* 1. Fixed or movable frame of wooden or metal bars for holding fodder; framework with rails, bars, pegs, or shelves, for keeping articles on or in. 2. Cogged or indented bar or rail gearing with wheel, pinion, or worm, or serving with pegs etc. to adjust position of something (ill. GEAR); ~-*railway*, railway with cogged rail between bearing-rails; ~-*wheel*, cog-wheel. ~ *v.* Fill *up* stable-rack with hay or straw for the night; fasten (horse) *up* to rack; place in or on rack.

răck³ *v.t.* 1. Stretch joints of (person) by pulling esp. with instruments of torture made for the purpose; (of disease etc.) inflict tortures on; shake violently, injure by straining, task severely. 2. Exact utmost possible amount of (rent); oppress (tenants) with excessive rent; exhaust (land) with excessive use; ~-*rent* (*n.*) extortionate rent equal or nearly equal to full annual value of land; (*v.t.*) extort this from (tenant) or for (land); ~-*renter*, tenant paying, landlord exacting, rack-rent. ~ *n.* Instrument of torture, frame with roller at each end to which victim's wrists and ankles were tied so that his joints were stretched when rollers were turned; *on the* ~, (fig.) in state of acute mental or physical suffering, in keen anxiety or suspense.

răck⁴ *n.* (archaic) Arrack.

răck⁵ *n.* Horse's gait between trot and canter, both legs of one side being lifted almost at once, and all four feet being off ground together at moments. ~ *v.i.* Progress thus.

răck⁶ *v.t.* Draw off (wine etc.) from the lees.

rā'ckĕt¹, rā'cquet (-kĭt) *n.* Bat used in tennis, rackets, etc., network of cord, catgut, nylon, etc., stretched across elliptical frame with handle attached (ill. LAWN²); (pl.) ball-game for two or four persons played with rackets in a closed four-walled court, each player striking the ball in turn and trying to keep it rebounding from the end wall of the court; ~-*ball*, small hard kid-covered ball of cork and string; ~-*press*, press for keeping racket taut and in shape.

rā'ckĕt² *n.* 1. Disturbance, uproar; social excitement, gaiety, dissipation; trying experience (esp. in *stand the* ~, come successfully through test, face consequences of action). 2. (slang) Dodge, game, line of business; scheme, procedure, for obtaining money etc. by dubious or illegal means, esp. as form of organized crime. ~ *v.i.* Live gay life; move about noisily. **rā'ckĕtў** *adj.* Noisy; dissipated.

RACKETEER

racketeer' *n.* Member of (orig. U.S.) criminal gang practising extortion, intimidation, violence, etc., esp. on large scale.
racketeer'ing *n.* Systematic extortion of money by threats, violence, or other illegal methods.
racŏnteur' (-tēr) *n.* (fem. *-euse* pr. -ērz) Teller of anecdotes.
racoo'n, racc- *n.* N. Amer. nocturnal carnivore, *Procyon lotor*, with bushy tail and pointed snout.
racquet: see RACKET[1].
ra'cy *adj.* Of distinctive quality or vigour, not smoothed into sameness or commonness; lively, spirited, piquant. **ra'cily** *adv.* **ra'ciness** *n.*
rad[1] *n.* (phys.) Unit of absorbed dose of ionizing radiation, corresponding to 100 ergs per gramme of absorbing material.
rad[2] *abbrev.* Radian(s).
R.A.D.A. *abbrev.* Royal Academy of Dramatic Art.
ra'dar *n.* System for ascertaining direction and range of aircraft, ships, coasts, and other objects by sending out electromagnetic radiations of short wavelength and interpreting the reflections of these produced by certain types of surface; apparatus used for this. [f. *radio detection and ranging*]
R.A.D.C., R.A.E.C. *abbrevs.* Royal Army Dental, Educational, Corps.
Ra'dcliffe, Mrs Ann (1764–1823). English author of romances of mystery and terror.
ra'ddle *n.* Red ochre. ~ *v.t.* Paint with raddle; colour (skin) crudely.
ra'dial *adj.* 1. Arranged like rays or radii, having position or direction of a radius; having spokes or radiating lines; acting or moving along lines that diverge from a centre; ~ *axle*, axle (of railway-carriage etc.) assuming position of radius to curve of track; ~ *engine*, internal combustion engine with cylinders arranged like spokes of wheel; ~ *velocity*: see VELOCITY. 2. Of the radius of the forearm.
ra'dially *adv.* **ra'dial** *n.* Radial nerve or artery.
ra'dian *n.* (abbrev. rad) Angle at centre of circle (approx. 57·296°) subtending arc whose length is equal to the radius.

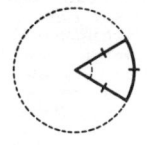

RADIAN

ra'diant *adj.* Emitting rays of light; beaming with joy, hope, etc.; issuing in rays, bright, shining, splendid; extending or operating radially; (her.) having wavy points; ~ *heat*, electromag-

netic radiation emitted by hot bodies, having a wavelength greater than that of visible light and capable of crossing a vacuum; ~ *heat therapy*, treatment, esp. of injured muscles and joints, by such radiation; ~ *point*, point from which rays or radii proceed; (astron.) apparent focal point of meteoric shower. **ra'diantly** *adv.* **ra'diance** *n.* **ra'diant** *n.* Point or object from which light or heat radiates; (astron.) radiant point.
ra'diate[1] *adj.* Having divergent rays or parts radially arranged. **ra'diately** *adv.*
ra'diate[2] *v.* Emit rays of light, heat, etc.; issue in rays; diverge or spread from central point; emit (light, heat, etc.) from centre; transmit by radio.
radia'tion *n.* Manner in which the energy of a vibrating body is transmitted in all directions by a surrounding medium; emission and diffusion of heat-rays; emission of Röntgen or X-rays, or the rays and particles characteristic of radioactive substances; ~ *sickness*, sickness caused by exposure to ionizing radiation.
ra'diator *n.* (esp.) Metal case containing arrangement of pipes heated with hot air, steam, etc., and radiating warmth into room; that part of the engine-cooling system of most motor vehicles and certain types of aeroplane engine in which the circulating fluid is air-cooled.
ra'dical *adj.* 1. Of the root(s); naturally inherent, essential, fundamental; forming the basis, primary. 2. Affecting the foundation, going to the root; (pol.) desiring or advocating fundamental or drastic reforms; (hist.) of, belonging to, extreme section of Liberal party or opinion. 3. (philol.) Of the roots of words. 4. (mus.) Of the root of a chord. 5. (bot.) Of, springing direct from, the root, or the main stem close to it. 6. (math.) Of the root of a number or quantity; ~ *sign*, sign $\sqrt{}$ ($\sqrt[3]{}$, $\sqrt[4]{}$, etc.) used to indicate that the square (cube, fourth, etc.) root of the number to which it is prefixed is to be extracted. **ra'dically** *adv.* **ra'dical** *n.* 1. Fundamental thing or principle. 2. (pol.) Person holding radical opinions. 3. (philol.) Root. 4. (math.) Quantity forming or expressed as root of another; radical sign. 5. (chem.) Element or atom, or group of these, forming base of compound and remaining unchanged during ordinary chemical reactions to which this is liable.
ra'dicle *n.* 1. Part of plant embryo that develops into primary root (ill. SEED); small root (ill. SEEDLING). 2. (anat.) Root-like subdivision of nerve or vein. 3. (chem.) Radical. **radi'cular** *adj.*
ra'dio *n.* 1. Transmission and reception of messages etc. by

RADIOLARIAN

means of electromagnetic waves of frequency between 10^4 Hz and 3×10^{11} Hz approx. (see FREQUENCY), either as acoustic signals (RADIOTELEPHONY) or as morse code signals (RADIOTELEGRAPHY); wireless, broadcasting. 2. Radio receiver. 3. (attrib.) Of radio-telephony or radiotelegraphy; concerned with phenomena occurring at radio frequency. 4. ~-*astronomy*, branch of astronomy dealing with investigation of celestial bodies by radar, and with electromagnetic radiations from outside earth's atmosphere; ~ *receiver*, apparatus which detects signals transmitted by radio-frequency waves and reproduces them as audible sounds; ~ *star*, source of radiation in space; ~ *telescope*: see TELESCOPE; ~ *transmitter*, apparatus which gives out signals by producing power at radio frequencies, delivering it to an aerial and radiating it.
radioa'ctive *adj.* Of, exhibiting, radioactivity. **radioacti'vity** *n.* (phys.) Property possessed by certain elements of high atomic weight (radium, thorium, uranium, etc.) of spontaneously emitting alpha, beta, or gamma rays (which are capable of penetrating opaque bodies and affecting a photographic plate even when separated by thin sheets of metal), by the disintegration of the nuclei of the atoms, or induced in certain non-radioactive elements by exposure to the action of bombarding particles.
radiocar'bon *n.* Radioactive isotope of carbon existing in organic matter and having its origin in the radioactive carbon dioxide produced by the interaction of cosmic ray neutrons and atmospheric nitrogen at high altitudes; ~ *dating*, method of dating organic materials from ancient deposits, esp. archaeological remains of the period 30,000 B.C. to A.D. 1000, made possible by the discovery that after the death of plants and animals the radiocarbon content decays at a regular rate (by half in every period of *c* 5600 years); also called *carbon-14 dating*.
radiogonio'meter *n.* Apparatus for discovering direction from which electromagnetic impulses are coming.
ra'diogram *n.* 1. Image produced on photographic plate by X-rays. 2. Message sent by radiotelegraphy. 3. Radio receiver combined with gramophone.
ra'diograph (*or* -ahf) *n.* 1. Instrument for measuring and recording the duration and intensity of sunshine. 2. = RADIOGRAM, 1.
radiogra'phic *adj.*
radio'graphy *n.* Photography by means of X-rays. **radio'grapher** *n.*
radiolar'ian *n.* Protozoon of the order Radiolaria, with siliceous skeleton and radiating pseudopodia.

[723]

rădĭolocā'tion n. Determination of the position or course of ships, aircraft, etc., by means of RADAR.
rădĭŏ'logy̆ n. Scientific study of X-rays, radioactivity, and other radiations, and (esp.) the use of these in medicine. rădĭolŏ'gical adj. rădĭŏ'logĭst n.
rădĭŏ'mĕter n. Instrument showing conversion of radiant energy into mechanical force.
ră'dĭŏphāre n. Radio transmitting station sending out signals to enable ships, aircraft, etc., to determine their position.
rădĭŏ'scopy̆ n. Examination of the internal structure etc. of opaque bodies by means of X- or other rays.
ră'dĭosŏnde n. Miniature radio transmitter, carried aloft in a balloon and descending by parachute, broadcasting to observers on the ground information about atmospheric conditions at various levels.
rădĭŏtĕlĕ'graphy̆ n. Transmission and reception of morse code signals by electromagnetic waves of radio frequency. rădĭŏtĕ'lĕgrăm n. Message transmitted by radiotelegraphy.
rădĭŏtĕlĕ'phony̆ n. Transmission and reception of acoustic signals by electromagnetic waves of radio frequency. rădĭŏtĕ'lĕphŏne n. Apparatus used in radiotelephony.
rădĭŏthĕrapeu'tics, rădĭŏthĕ'rapy̆ ns. Treatment of disease by X-rays, radium, or other forms of radiation.
ră'dĭsh n. Cruciferous plant, *Raphanus sativus*; fleshy slightly pungent root of this, often eaten raw as relish or in salads.
ră'dĭum n. (chem.) Rare radioactive metallic element isolated from pitchblende in 1898 by P. and M. Curie; symbol Ra, at. no. 88, at. wt 226·0254; (pop.) any of various salts of this element, used in radiotherapy etc.; ~ emanation, RADON; ~ needle, needle with hollow tip enclosing radioactive material, used in radiotherapy for treating underlying tissue.
ră'dĭus n. (pl. -iī). 1. Thicker and shorter bone of forearm in man (ill. SKELETON); corresponding bone in beast's foreleg or bird's wing. 2. (math.) Straight line from centre to circumference of circle or sphere (ill. CIRCLE); radial line from focus to any point of curve; ~ *vector*, variable line drawn to curve from fixed point, esp. (astron.) from sun or planet to path of satellite. 3. Any of set of lines diverging from a point like radii of circle, object of this kind (e.g. spoke). 4. Circular area as measured by its radius; *four-mile* ~, that of which Charing Cross, London, is the centre. 5. (bot.) Outer rim of composite flower-head (e.g. daisy); radiating branch of umbel.

ră'dĭx n. (pl. -*ices* pr. -īsēz). Number or symbol used as basis of numeration scale; source or origin *of*. [L, = 'root']
Ră'dnorshire. Former inland county of S. Wales, since April 1974 part of Powys.
ră'dŏn n. (chem.) Chemically inert heavy gaseous radioactive element, the first disintegration product of radium; symbol Rn, at. no. 86, principal isotope at. wt 222. [f. *radium* and the termination of *argon*, *neon*, etc.]
ră'dūla n. File-like structure in molluscs used to scrape off particles of food and draw them into the mouth.
Rae'burn (rāb-), Sir Henry (1756–1823). Scottish portrait-painter.
R.A.F. *abbrev*. Royal Air Force.
răff n. Riff-raff.
Raffaello Sanzio: see RAPHAEL².
ră'ffia n. Palm of genus *Raphia*; soft fibre from leaves of *R. ruffia* and *R. taedigera*, used for tying up plants and making hats, baskets, mats, etc.
ră'ffish *adj*. Disreputable, dissipated, esp. in appearance. ră'ffishly̆ *adv*. ră'ffishnĕss n.
ră'ffle¹ n. Lottery in which article is assigned by lot to one person of a number who have each paid a certain part of its value. ~ *v*. Take part in raffle *for* (thing); sell (thing) by raffle.
ră'ffle² n. Rubbish.
raft (rah-) n. Collection of logs, casks, etc., fastened together in the water for transportation; flat floating structure of timber, etc., for conveying persons or things, esp. as substitute for boat in emergencies; floating accumulation of trees, ice, etc. ~ *v*. Transport (as) on raft; form into a raft; cross (water) on raft(s); work raft.
ra'fter¹ (rah-) n. Man who rafts timber.
ra'fter² (rah-) n. One of the sloping beams forming framework on which slates etc. of roof are upheld (ill. ROOF). ~ *v.t*. Furnish with rafters; plough (land) so that earth from furrow is turned over on same breadth of unploughed ground next it.
R.A.F.V.R. *abbrev*. Royal Air Force Volunteer Reserve.
răg¹ n. Torn or frayed piece of woven material; one of the irregular scraps to which cloth etc. is reduced by wear and tear; (usu. with neg.) smallest scrap of cloth or sail; remnant, odd scrap, irregular piece; (contempt.) flag, handkerchief, newspaper, etc.; (pl.) tattered clothes; (collect.) rags used as material for paper, stuffing, etc.; ~-*bag*, bag in which scraps of linen etc. are kept for use; ~-*bolt*, bolt with barbs to keep it tight when driven in; (*v.t*.) join together with these; ~-*book*, children's book with pages of untearable cloth; ~ *doll*, stuffed doll made of cloth; ~ *fair*, old-clothes

sale held in Houndsditch; ~ *paper*, good-quality paper made from rags; ~ *tag* (*and bobtail*), riff-raff; ra'gtime, popular music of U.S. Negro origin, with much syncopation; ~ *trade*, (colloq.) business of making and selling women's clothes; ~-*wheel*, wheel with projections catching in links of chain that passes over it, sprocket-wheel; ra'gwort, common yellow-flowered ragged-leaved plant (*Senecio Jacobaea*) and other species of *Senecio*.
răg² n. Large coarse roofing-slate; hard coarse stone breaking up in thick slabs.
răg³ n. Act of ragging, noisy disorderly conduct; (in some universities) annual parade of students in fancy dress to collect money for charity. ~ *v*. Annoy, tease, torment; esp., (univ. slang) play rough jokes upon, throw into wild disorder (person's room etc.) by way of practical joke; act in this way.
ră'gamŭffin n. Person in ragged dirty clothes.
R.A.G.C. *abbrev*. Royal and Ancient Golf Club, St. Andrews.
rāge n. (Fit of) violent anger; violent operation of some natural force or some sentiment; poetic, prophetic, or martial ardour; vehement desire or passion *for*; object of widespread temporary enthusiasm or fashion. ~ *v.i*. Rave, storm, speak madly or furiously, be full of anger; (of wind, sea, passion, battle, etc.) be violent, be at the height, operate unchecked, prevail. rā'gingly̆ *adv*.
ră'ggĕd (-g-) *adj*. Rough, shaggy, hanging in tufts; of broken jagged outline or surface, full of rough or sharp projections; faulty, wanting finish, smoothness, or uniformity; rent, torn, frayed, in ragged clothes; ~ *robin*, common English crimson-flowered wild plant (*Lychnis floscuculi*); ~ *school*, (hist.) free school for poor children. ră'ggĕdly̆ *adv*. ră'ggĕdnĕss n.
ră'glan n. Overcoat without shoulder-seams, top of sleeve being carried up to neck; ~ *sleeve*, sleeve of this kind (ill. SLEEVE). [f. Lord *Raglan*, British commander in Crimean War]
Ră'gnarŏk (-ĕrk) n. (Scand. myth.) Great battle between gods and powers of evil (Scand. equivalent of *Götterdämmerung*) ending in the destruction of both and the disappearance of the old order, replaced by a new and happier scheme of things and the return of Balder from the nether world.
ră'gout (-ōō) n. Meat in small pieces stewed with vegetables and highly seasoned. ~ *v.t*. Make into a ragout.
ră'guly̆ *adj*. (her.) Like a row of sawn-off branches (ill. HERALDRY).
raid n. Sudden incursion of military force into or upon a

[724]

RAIKES

country for the purposes of plunder or attack; (international law) hostile invasion by military forces of territory of a State at peace unauthorized by the government of the country from which the raiding forces come; AIR-raid; sudden descent of police etc. upon suspected premises or illicit goods. ~ v. Make raid *into* etc.; make raid on. **rai′der** n.

Raikes (-ks), Robert (1735–1811). English promoter of Sunday schools.

rail[1] n. 1. Horizontal or inclined bar or continuous series of bars of wood or metal used to hang things on, as top of banisters, as part of fence, as protection against contact or falling over, or for similar purpose; any horizontal piece in frame of wooden panelling (ill. WAINSCOT). 2. Iron bar or continuous line of bars laid on ground as one side or half of railway track; railway (esp. *by* ~); ~-*chair*, metal clamp, attached to sleeper, in which railway line rests and is secured; *rai′lhead*, farthest point reached by railway under construction; (mil.) point on railway at which road transport begins; *rai′lman*, railwayman; *rai′lroad*, (esp. in U.S.) railway; (*v.*) transport, travel, by rail; accomplish (action) with great speed, rush *into*, *through*, etc.; *rai′lway*,

track or set of tracks of iron or steel rails for passage of trains of cars drawn by locomotive engine and conveying passengers and goods; tracks of this kind worked by a single company, whole of the organization and persons required for their working; (hist.) road laid with rails for heavy horse-carts; *rai′lwayman*, person employed on railway. ~ *v.* Furnish or enclose with rail (often ~ *in*, *off*); provide with rail; lay (railway route) with rails; convey (goods), travel, by rail.

rail[2] n. Any of various small birds of the family Rallidae, of which the LANDrail and the *water* ~ (*Rallus aquaticus*) are members.

rail[3] *v.i.* Use abusive language (*at*, *against*).

rai′lage n. Charges for freight etc. made by railway.

rai′ling *n.* (esp.) Fence or barrier of rails etc.

rai′llery n. (piece of) good-humoured ridicule, rallying.

rai′ment n. (poet., rhet.) Clothing, dress.

rain n. Condensed moisture of atmosphere falling visibly in separate drops; fall of such drops; (rain-like descent of) falling liquid or solid particles or bodies; (pl.) showers of rain; *the* ~*s*, rainy season in tropical countries; *rai′ncoat*, (waterproof) coat worn as protection against rain; ~ *day*, day

RAISE

when recorded rainfall is 0·2 mm or more; *rai′ndrop*, single drop of rain; *rai′nfall*, shower; quantity of rain falling within given area in given time; ~ *forest*, forest characteristic of rainy tropical regions; ~-*gauge*, instrument measuring rainfall; *rai′nproof*, impervious to rain; (*n.*) rainproof coat; (*v.t.*) make rainproof; ~-*spell*, period of 15 or more rain days (see above); ~-*shadow*, region shielded from rainfall by surrounding region; *rai′nwater*, water which has fallen from clouds as rain (not got from wells). **rai′nless** *adj.* **rain** *v.* 1. *it* ~*s*, *it is raining*, rain falls; there is a shower of (something falling etc.); *it* ~*s cats and dogs*, it rains violently; *it* ~*s in*, rain penetrates house etc. 2. Send down rain; fall or send down in showers or like rain.

rai′nbow (-ō) n. Arch showing PRISMATIC colours in their order formed in sky (or across cataract etc.) opposite sun by reflection, double refraction, and dispersion, of sun's rays in falling drops of rain, spray, etc.; (attrib.) many-coloured; *lunar* ~, (rarely seen) rainbow formed by moon's rays; ~ *fish*, any of various bright-coloured Amer. and New Zealand fishes; ~ *trout*, Californian species of trout (*Salmo irideus*).

rai′ny *adj.* In or on which rain is falling or much rain usu. falls; (of clouds, wind, etc.) laden with, bringing, rain; ~ *day*, (fig.) time of esp. pecuniary need.

Rais, Rĕtz, Gilles de (1404–40). Marshal of France; supporter of Joan of Arc; tried and hanged for murder (the number of his victims was said to be 140); his name is associated with legend of BLUEBEARD.

raise (-z) *v.t.* 1. Set upright, make stand up, restore to or towards vertical position; rouse; ~ *from the dead*, restore to life; ~ *the country*, etc., rouse inhabitants in some emergency; *raised pie*, *pastry*, etc., pie etc. standing without support of dish at sides. 2. Build up, construct; propagate; (chiefly U.S.) rear, bring up (person); utter, make audible; start; give occasion for, elicit; set up, advance; ~ *a laugh*, cause others to laugh; ~ *one's voice*, speak; speak more loudly; 3. Elevate, put or take into higher position; extract from earth; direct upwards; promote to higher rank; make higher or nobler; cause to ascend; make (voice) louder or shriller; increase amount of, heighten level of; (naut.) come in sight of (land, ship); ~ *bread* etc., cause it to rise with yeast etc.; ~ *Cain*, *hell*, etc., (colloq.) make a disturbance; become violently angry; ~ *one's eyebrows*, look supercilious or shocked; ~ *one's hat*, take hat off in greeting. 4. Levy, collect, bring together, procure, manage to get. 5. Relinquish, cause enemy

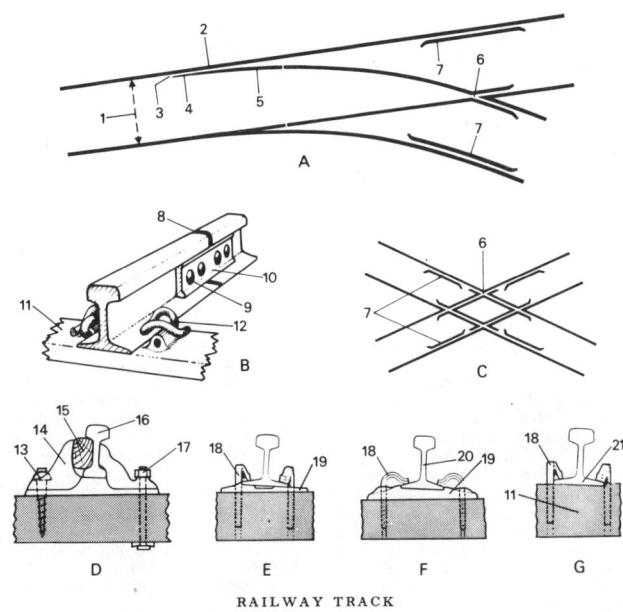

RAILWAY TRACK

A. POINTS. B. METHOD OF JOINING AND FIXING RAIL. C. DIAMOND CROSSING. D. BULL-HEADED RAIL IN CHAIR. E. FLAT-BOTTOMED RAIL ON SINGLE SHOULDER BASE-PLATE. F. DITTO ON DOUBLE SHOULDER BASE-PLATE. G. DITTO WITHOUT BASE-PLATE

1. Gauge. 2. Stock rail. 3. Throw of point. 4. Point. 5. Tongue. 6. Frog. 7. Guard-rail. 8. Gap. 9. Fish bolt. 10. Fish-plate. 11. Sleeper. 12. Spring clip. 13. Screw. 14. Chair. 15. Key. 16. Head. 17. Bolt. 18. Spike. 19. Base-plate. 20. Web. 21. Base

[725]

to relinquish (siege, blockade). ~ n. Increase in amount, esp. of stakes at poker, bid at bridge, etc., (U.S.) rise (in salary etc.).
rai′sin (-zn) n. Partially dried grape.
raison d'être (rāzawǹ dātr). What accounts for or justifies or has caused a thing's existence. [Fr.]
raj (rahj) n. (Ind.) Sovereignty, rule.
rajah, raja (rah′ja) n. (hist.) Indian king or prince (also as title of petty dignitary or noble in India, or of Malay or Javanese chief).
ra′jahship n. [Hind. *rājā*]
Ra′jasthan (rah-, -tahn). State in NW. India; capital, Jaipur.
Rajput (rah′jpoot). Member of Hindu land-owning warrior caste of NW. India.
rāke[1] n. Implement consisting of pole with cross-bar toothed like comb at end for drawing together hay etc., or smoothing loose soil or gravel; wheeled implement drawn by horse or tractor for same purpose; implement resembling rake used for other purposes, e.g. by croupier drawing in money at gaming-table. ~ v. Collect, draw *together*, gather *up*, pull *out*, clear *off*, (as) with rake; clean or smooth with rake; search (as) with rake, ransack; make *level*, *clean*, etc., with rake; use rake, search as with rake; sweep with shot, enfilade, send shot along (ship) from stem to stern; sweep with the eyes; (of window etc.) have commanding view of; ~-*off*, (slang, orig. U.S.) profit or commission made, often illegitimately, by one or more persons concerned in a transaction.
rāke[2] n. Dissipated or immoral man of fashion. [f. earlier *rakehell* (RAKE[1] v.)]
rāke[3] v. (of ship, its bow or stern) Project at upper part of bow or stern beyond keel; (of masts or funnels) incline from perpendicular towards stern; give backward inclination to. ~ n. Amount to which thing rakes; raking position or build.
rā′kish[1] adj. (As) of, like, a RAKE[2].
rā′kish[2] adj. (of ship) Smart and fast-looking, seeming built for speed (freq. with implication of suspicious or piratical character). [perh. same wd as prec., with extra association of raking masts]
râle (rahl) n. (path.) Sound additional to that of respiration heard in auscultation of unhealthy lungs.
Raleigh, Ralegh (raw′li *or* rah- *or* ră-), Sir Walter (*c* 1552-1618). English military and naval commander, explorer, and poet; explored the eastern seaboard of America; and wrote accounts of his adventures; fell out of favour with Elizabeth I; was convicted of conspiring against James I, 1603, reprieved, but eventually executed.

rall. abbrev. *Rallentando*.
rāllentă′ndō adv., n. (pl. *-os*), & adj. (mus.) (Passage performed) gradually slower. [It.]
ră′lline adj. Belonging to the Rallidae (see RAIL[2]).
ră′llÿ[1] v. Reassemble, get together again, after rout or dispersion, (cause to) renew conflict; bring, come, together as support or for concentrated action; revive (faculty etc.) by effort of will, pull oneself together, assume or rouse to fresh energy. ~ n. 1. Act of rallying, reunion for fresh effort; recovery of energy; mass-meeting; competitive event over public roads for motorists or motorcyclists. 2. (lawn tennis etc.) Series of strokes made between service and failure to return the ball.
rā′llÿ[2] v.t. Banter.
răm[1] n. 1. Uncastrated male sheep. 2. the *R*~: see ARIES. 3. (hist.) Swinging beam for breaching walls, battering-ram; (warship with) projecting beak at bow for charging side of other ships. 4. Falling weight of piledriving machine; rammer; hydraulic water-raising or lifting machine; piston of hydrostatic press; plunger of force-pump; *ra′mjet* jet engine for aircraft in which the motion through the air provides compression. ~ v.t. 1. Beat down (soil etc.) into solidity with wooden block etc.; make (post, plant, etc.) firm by ramming soil round it; drive (pile etc.) *down*, *in*, etc., by heavy blows; force (charge) home, pack (gun) tight, with ramrod; squeeze or force into place by pressure; (abs.) use rammer; *ra′mrod*, (hist.) rod for ramming home charge of muzzle-loader (ill. PISTOL). 2. (of ship) Strike with ram; dash or violently impel *against*, *at*, etc. **ră′mmer** n.
răm[2] n. (naut.) Boat's length over all.
R.A.M. abbrev. Royal Academy of Music.
Rămada′n (-ahn). 9th month of Muslim year, rigidly observed as 30 days' fast during hours of daylight.
Rā′man, Sir Chandrasekhara Venkata (1888-1970). Indian physicist; Nobel Prize for physics, 1930; ~ *effect*, appearance of additional lines (~ *lines*) in the spectrum of light when scattered by the molecules of a substance; ~ *spectrum*, spectrum so obtained.
Rama′yana (-mah-). Ancient Sanskrit epic poem (500-300 B.C.).
ră′mble v.i. Walk for pleasure and without definite route; wander in discourse, talk or write disconnectedly. ~ n. Rambling walk.
ră′mbler n. (esp.) Any of several kinds of freely climbing rose, esp. the *crimson* ~.
ră′mbling adj. Peripatetic, wandering; disconnected, desultory, incoherent; (of plants) strag-

gling, climbing; (of house, street, etc.) irregularly planned. **ră′mblinglỹ** adv.
Rambouillet (rahǹbwēyā), Cathérine de Vivonne-Pisani, Marquise de (1588-1655). Founder of first French salon, in which most distinguished persons of her day met and conversed.
R.A.M.C. abbrev. Royal Army Medical Corps.
Rameau (rahmō), Jean Philippe (1683-1764). French composer of operas and harpsichord music.
Ramée[1], Marie Louise de la: see OUIDA.
Ramée[2], Pierre de la: see RAMUS.
ră′mėkin, ră′mėquin (-kin) n. Small quantity of cheese baked with bread-crumbs, eggs, etc.; (also ~ *case*, *dish*) small mould in which this is baked.
ramē′ntum n. (chiefly in pl. *-ta*). (bot.) Thin membranous scale formed on surface of leaves and stalks.
Ră′mėsės, Ră′msės (-z). Name of several Egyptian kings of 19th and 20th dynasties; *Rameses II* (? 1292-1225 B.C.) is sometimes supposed to have been the Pharaoh who oppressed the Jews.
rāmifică′tion n. Ramifying, (arrangement of) tree's branches; subdivision of complex structure comparable to tree's branches.
rā′mifỹ v. Form branches, subdivisions, or offshoots; branch out; (usu. pass.) cause to branch out, arrange in branching manner.
Ră′millies (-liz). Belgian village near Louvain, scene (1706) of Marlborough's victory over French; ~ *wig*, wig with long plait behind tied with bow at top and bottom (ill. WIG).
ră′mmish adj. Rank-smelling.
rāmō′se adj. Branched, branching.
rămp[1] n. Slope, inclined plane joining two levels of ground, esp. in fortification, or of wall-coping; difference in level between opposite abutments of rampant arch; upward bend in stair-rail. ~ v. 1. (chiefly of lion) Stand on hind-legs with fore-paws in air, assume or be in threatening posture; (now usu. joc.) storm, rage, rush about. 2. Furnish or build with ramp; (of wall) ascend or descend to different level.
rămp[2] n. (slang) Swindle; levying of exorbitant prices.
rămpā′ge v.i. Behave violently, storm, rage, rush about. ~ n. Violent behaviour. **rămpā′geous** (-jus) adj. **rămpā′geouslỹ** adv. **rămpā′geousnėss** n.
ră′mpant adj. Ramping (chiefly of lion, esp. in her.; ill. HERALDRY); violent or extravagant in action or opinion, arrant, aggressive, unchecked, prevailing; rank, luxuriant; (of arch etc.) having one abutment higher than the other, climbing. **ră′mpantlỹ** adv. **ră′mpancỹ** n.
ră′mpärt n. Broad-topped and

usu. stone-parapeted defensive mound of earth; (fig.) defence, protection. ~ v.t. Fortify or protect (as) with rampart.

răˊmpion n. Flower (*Campanula rapunculus*), with white tuberous roots.

Răˊmsay[1] (-zĭ), Allan (1686–1758). Scottish poet; also, his son (1713–84), portrait-painter.

Răˊmsay[2] (-zĭ), Sir William (1852–1916). British chemist; discoverer of helium, argon (with Rayleigh), and neon in the atmosphere; Nobel Prize for chemistry, 1904.

Răˊmsden (-z-), Jesse (1735–1800). English optician and instrument maker.

Ramses: see RAMESES.

răˊmshăckle adj. Tumbledown, rickety.

răˊmson n. Broad-leaved garlic, *Allium ursinum*; bulbous root of this, eaten as relish.

Răˊmus. Latinized name of Pierre de la Ramée (1515–72), French philosopher; a victim of the massacre of St. Bartholomew.

ran: see RUN[1].

R.A.N. abbrev. Royal Australian Navy.

ranch (rah-) n. Cattle-breeding establishment in U.S., Canada, etc. ~ v.i. Conduct ranch. [Span. *rancho* mess, persons feeding together]

răˊncid adj. Smelling or tasting like rank stale fat. **răˊncidnèss** n.

rănciˊditў n.

răˊncour (-ker) n. Inveterate bitterness, malignant hate, spitefulness. **răˊncorous** adj. **răˊncorouslў** adv.

rănd[1] n. 1. Strip of leather placed under quarters of shoe to level it before heel-lifts are attached. 2. (S. Afr.) Highlands on either side of river valley; *the R*~, gold-mining district near Johannesburg in the Transvaal.

rănd[2] n. Principal monetary unit of the Republic of South Africa, = 100 cents.

R. and A. abbrev. Royal and Ancient Golf Club, St. Andrews.

răndăˊn[1] n. Style of rowing in which middle one of three rowers pulls a pair of sculls, stroke and bow an oar each; boat for this.

răndăˊn[2] n. Spree. [var. of *random*]

răˊndom n. *at* ~, at haphazard; without aim, purpose, or principle; heedlessly. ~ adj. Made, done, etc., at random. [OF *random* great speed (*randir* gallop)]

răˊndў adj. Loud-tongued, boisterous, lusty (Sc.); (of cattle etc., dial.) wild, restive; lustful, in lustful mood. **răˊndinèss** n.

ranee: see RANI.

Răˊnelagh (-la). Former place of public amusement in Chelsea, London, opened 1742, closed 1803; now part of grounds of Royal Hospital, Chelsea, and scene of the Royal Horticultural Society's show (Chelsea Flower Show). [named after Earl of *Ranelagh*, an earlier owner]

range (-j) n. 1. Row, line, tier, or series, of things, esp. of buildings or mountains; horizontal direction, lie; (U.S.) series of townships lying between two successive meridian lines six miles apart. 2. Liberty to range; area over which ranging takes place or is possible, (U.S.) stretch of grazing or hunting ground; piece of ground with targets for shooting; area over which plant etc. is distributed, area included in or concerned with something, scope, compass, register; limits of variation, limited scale or series; distance attainable by gun or projectile, distance between gun, camera, etc., and objective; *raˊngefinder*, instrument for estimating this distance. 3. Cooking fireplace, usu. with oven(s), boiler(s), and iron top plate with openings for saucepans, etc. ~ v. 1. Place or arrange in a row or ranks or in specified situation, order, or company; run in a line, reach, lie spread out, extend; be found or occur over specified district; vary between limits; be level (*with*), rank or find right place *with* or *among*. 2. Rove, wander; go all about (place), sail along or about (coast, sea). 3. (of gun) Throw projectile over, (of projectile) traverse, (distance).

raˊnger (-j-) n. (esp.) 1. Keeper of royal or other park 2. (pl.) Body of mounted troops. 3. (U.S.) Member of commando unit. 4. *R*~, member of senior branch of Girl Guides Association.

Rangoōˊn (-ngg-). Capital city and seaport of Burma, on Rangoon river, one of the mouths of the Irrawaddy.

raˊngў (-j-) adj. (chiefly U.S.) Adapted for ranging, of long slender form.

raˊni, -nee (rah-) n. (hist.) Hindu queen or princess. [Hind. *rānī, rāni* fem. of RAJAH]

rănk[1] n. 1. Row, line (now chiefly of taxis standing); (mil.) number of soldiers drawn up in single line abreast; *the* ~*s*, ~ *and file*, common soldiers; (transf.) ordinary people, as dist. from their leaders. 2. Distinct social class, grade of dignity, station; high station; *all* ~*s*, persons of every grade or rank in army etc.; *persons of* ~, members of nobility; ~ *and fashion*, high society. 3. Place in a scale. ~ v. Arrange (esp. soldiers) in rank; classify, give certain grade to; have rank or place. **răˊnker** n. (Commissioned officer who has been) a soldier in the ranks.

rănk[2] adj. Too luxuriant, coarse, choked with or apt to produce weeds; foul-smelling, offensive, loathsome, corrupt; flagrant, virulent. **răˊnklў** adv. **răˊnknèss** n.

Ranke (rah'ngke), Leopold von (1795–1886). German historian; author of 'The Popes of Rome' etc.

răˊnkle v.i. (of wound etc.) Fester (archaic); (of unpleasant experience, insult, etc.) remain as painful memory, cause continued bitterness or resentment. [OF (*d*)*rancle* festering sore, f. LL *dracunculus*, dim. of *draco* serpent]

răˊnsăck v.t. Thoroughly search; pillage, plunder.

răˊnsom n. (Liberation of prisoner of war or other captive in consideration of) sum of money or value paid for release; *king's* ~, large sum. ~ v.t. Redeem, buy freedom or restoration of; set free on payment of ransom, demand ransom from or for.

rănt v. Use bombastic language; declaim, tirade; preach noisily. ~ n. Piece of ranting, tirade; empty turgid talk. **răˊnter** n. (esp., 19th c. colloq.) Primitive Methodist preacher.

ranŭˊnculus n. (pl. *-lī*). Plant of genus *R*~ including buttercups, crowfoot, esp. the cultivated *R. asiaticus*. **ranŭnculăˊceous** (-shus) adj.

R.A.O.C., R.A.P.C. abbrevs. Royal Army Ordnance, Pay, Corps.

răp[1] n. Smart slight blow; sound made by knocker on door etc.; sound as of striking wooden surface supposed to be produced by spirit at seance; (colloq.) blame, punishment (esp. in *take the* ~). ~ v. Strike (esp. person's knuckles smartly; make the sound called a rap; ~ *out*, utter abruptly; (of supposed spirit) express (message etc.) by raps.

răp[2] n. Counterfeit coin passing current for halfpenny in Ireland in 18th c.; the least bit (esp. in *not care a* ~).

răp[3] n. Skein of 120 yds of yarn.

rapāˊcious (-shus) adj. Grasping, extortionate, predatory. **rapāˊciouslў** adv. **rapāˊcitў** n.

rāpe[1] v.t. Take by force (poet.); violate chastity of, force sexual intercourse on. ~ n. Carrying off by force (poet.); ravishing or violation of a woman; (law) unlawful sexual intercourse with a woman without her consent.

rāpe[2] n. (hist.) One of the former administrative districts of Sussex.

rāpe[3] n. Plant (*Brassica napus*) grown as food for sheep etc. and for its seed, *rapeseed*, which yields oil; coleseed; ~-*cake*, rapeseed pressed into flat cake after extraction of oil and used as food for livestock; ~ *oil* (also known as *colza oil*), oil made from rapeseed and used as lubricant etc.; *raˊpeseed*: see above.

rāpe[4] n. Refuse of grapes after wine-making, used in making vinegar.

Răˊphael[1]. One of the archangels; commemorated 24 Oct.

Răˊphael[2]. Raffaello Sanzio *or* Santi (1483–1520), great painter

of Italian Renaissance. **Răphaelĕ′sque** (-k) *adj.* In the style of Raphael.
ră′pid *adj.* Characterized by, moving or acting with, great speed; (of slope) descending steeply.
ră′pidlў *adv.* **rapi′ditў** *n.*
ră′pid *n.* (usu. pl.) Steep descent in river-bed, with swift current.
ră′pier *n.* Light slender sword for thrusting only (ill. SWORD).
ră′pīne *n.* (rhet.) Plundering, robbery.
răpparee′ *n.* (hist.) 17th-c. Irish irregular soldier or freebooter.
răppee′ *n.* Coarse kind of snuff made from dark rank leaves. [Fr. (*tabac*) *râpé* rasped (tobacco)]
răppōr′t (*or* -ōr) *n.* Communication, relationship, connection, esp. (in spiritualism) communication through a medium with alleged spirits.
răpprōchement (-shmahṅ) *n.* Re-establishment or recommencement of harmonious relations, esp. between States. [Fr.]
răpscă′llion (-yon) *n.* Rogue.
răpt *adj.* (orig. past part. of RAPE[1]) Snatched away bodily or carried away in spirit from earth, consciousness, or ordinary thoughts and perceptions; absorbed, enraptured, intent.
răptōr′ial *adj.* Predatory, (as) of predatory birds or animals; (zool.) of the Raptores, an order of birds of prey, including eagles, hawks, buzzards, etc. ~ *n.* Raptorial bird.
ră′pture *n.* (Expression of) ecstatic delight. **ră′pturous** (-tyer-) *adj.* **ră′pturouslў** *adv.*
rār′a ā′vĭs (*or* rah-). Rarity, kind of person or thing rarely encountered. [L, = 'rare bird']
rāre[1] *adj.* 1. (of air or gases) Not dense; with constituent particles not closely packed together. 2. Uncommon, unusual, seldom found or occurring; of uncommon excellence, remarkably good; very amusing. 3. ~ *earth*, basic oxide of a ~-*earth element*, any of the elements from lanthanum to lutetium inclusive in the PERIODIC system, together with those of scandium and yttrium; ~ *gas*, one of the group of INERT gases, of which all but radon occur in small amounts in the atmosphere. **rār′elў** *adv.* **rār′enėss** *n.*
rāre[2] *adj.* (of meat) Underdone.
rār′ebĭt (rārb-): see WELSH[1] rabbit.
rār′ee-show (-ō) *n.* Show carried about in a box, peep-show; any show or spectacle.
rār′efў *v.* Lessen density or solidity of (esp. air); purify, refine; make subtle; become less dense. **rārėfă′ction** *n.* **rār′efăctive** *adj.*
rār′itў *n.* Rareness; uncommon thing, thing valued as being rare.
R.A.S.C. *abbrev.* Royal Army Service Corps.
ra′scal (rah-) *n.* Rogue (freq. used playfully to child etc.). **rască′litў** *n.* **ra′scallў** *adj.*

rase: see RAZE.
răsh[1] *n.* Eruption of the skin in spots or patches.
răsh[2] *adj.* Hasty, impetuous, overbold, reckless; acting or done without due consideration. **ră′shlў** *adv.* **ră′shnėss** *n.*
ră′sher *n.* Thin slice of bacon or ham.
Ra′smussen (rahsmoo-), Knud Johan Victor (1879–1933). Danish Arctic explorer and ethnologist.
rasp (rah-) *n.* Coarse kind of file with separate teeth raised by means of pointed punch (ill. FILE). ~ *v.* Scrape with rasp; scrape roughly; grate upon, irritate; make grating sound.
ra′spatorў (rah-) *n.* Rasp used in surgery.
ra′spberrў (rahzb-) *n.* (Plant, *Rubus idaeus*, bearing) white, yellow, or usu. red subacid fruit of many small juicy drupelets arranged on conical receptacle; (slang) sound or gesture expressing derision or dislike; ~-*cane*, raspberry plant.
Răspu′tin (-poo-), Grigori Efimovich (1871–1916). Russian monk, an illiterate peasant who acquired great influence over the household of Nicholas II; he was assassinated as result of a conspiracy among a small group of nobles.
răt *n.* 1. Rodent of genus *Rattus*, esp. the *black* or *house*-~ (*R. rattus*), found esp. on shipboard,

A. BROWN RAT. B. BLACK RAT

and the larger *brown* or *grey* ~ (*R. norvegicus*) which is now the commoner, both regarded as pests, infesting sewers, warehouses, docks, etc., and acting as carriers of several diseases; rodent resembling this. 2. (pol.) Person who deserts his party when in difficulties as rats are said to leave doomed house or ship. 3. Workman who refuses to join strike or takes striker's place or accepts less than trade-union wages. 4. *musk-*~, *water-*~: see MUSK, WATER; *smell a* ~, have suspicions; ~*s!* (slang) nonsense!; ~-*catcher*, person whose business is to catch rats; (slang) unconventional hunting dress; *ra′tsbane*, rat-poison (now only literary); ~'*s-tail*, thing shaped like rat's tail, e.g. kind of file; ~-*tail*, hairless tail of horse; (also) = GRENADIER, 3; ~-*tailed*, (of spoon) with tail-like prolongation of handle along back of bowl (ill. SPOON); ~-*trap*, trap for rats; (cycle pedal) having two parallel steel plates with teeth

on edges to prevent the foot slipping. ~ *v.i.* Hunt or kill rats; play the rat in politics etc.; betray one's friends. **ră′tter** *n.*
rătafī′a (-ēa) *n.* Liqueur flavoured with almonds or kernels of peach, apricot, or cherry; kind of biscuit similarly flavoured.
ratan: see RATTAN.
rătăplă′n *n.* Drumming sound. ~ *v.* Play (as) on drum; make rataplan. [Fr., imit.]
rătch, **ră′tchėt** *ns.* Set of angular or saw-like teeth on edge of bar or wheel, into which a cog, click, or pawl may catch, usu. for the purpose of preventing reversed motion (ill. WINDLASS); (also ~-*wheel*) wheel with rim so toothed. ~ *vbs.t.* Provide with ratchet, give ratchet form to.
rāte[1] *n.* 1. Estimated value or worth; price, sum paid or asked for single thing. 2. Amount or number of one thing corresponding or having some relation to certain amount or number of another thing; value as applicable to each piece or equal quantity of something; basis of exchange; amount (*of* charge or payment), esp. in relation to some other amount or basis of calculation; assessment on property levied by local authorities for local purposes, hence, *ra′tepayer*; degree of speed, relative speed; relative amount of variation, increase, etc. 3. Standard in respect of quality or condition; class, kind, sort; class of (esp. war-) vessels; degree of action, feeling, etc. 4. *at any* ~, at all events, at least; *at this* (*that*) ~, things being so, under these circumstances. ~ *v.* Estimate worth or value of; assign fixed value to in relation to monetary standard; consider, regard as; (naut.) class under certain rating; rank or be rated *as*; (usu. pass.) subject to payment of local rate, value for purpose of assessing rates on.
rāte[2] *v.* Scold angrily.
rā′teable (-ta-) *adj.* Liable to payment of local rates. **rā′teablў** *adv.* **rāteabĭ′litў** *n.*
ra′tel (rah-) *n.* S. Afr. and Indian carnivorous mammal (*Mellivora capensis*) allied to weasel, honey badger.
rā′ter *n.* Vessel etc. of specified rate.
rāthe (-dh) *adj.* (poet.) Coming, blooming, etc., early in the year or day.
Rathenau (rah′tenow), Walther (1867–1922). German industrialist and statesman, of Jewish origin; assassinated 1922.
ra′ther (rahdh-) *adv.* 1. More truly or correctly, more properly speaking; more readily, all the more. 2. More (so) than not; to some extent, somewhat, slightly. 3. By preference, for choice, sooner (*than*); more properly. 4. (colloq., freq. pr. rahdhĕr′, in answer to question) Most emphatically, yes without doubt.

[728]

ra'tify *v.t.* Confirm or make valid (esp. what has been done or arranged for by another) by giving consent, approval, or formal sanction. **ratifica'tion** *n.*

răti'ne (-ēn) *n.* Dress-fabric of rough open texture resembling sponge-cloth.

ra'ting *n.* (esp.) 1. Amount fixed as local rate. 2. (naut.) Person's position or class in warship's crew; member of ship's company who is not a commissioned officer. 3. Any of the classes into which racing yachts are distributed by tonnage.

ra'tio (-sh-) *n.* Quantitative relation between two similar magnitudes determined by number of times one contains the other integrally or fractionally (*27 and 18 are in the* ~ *of three to two* or *3:2*; *the* ~*s 1:5 and 20:100 are the same*).

ratio'cinate *v.i.* Reason, carry on process of reasoning. **ratiocina'tion** *n.* **ratio'cinative** *adj.*

ra'tion *n.* Fixed allowance or individual share of provisions, esp. daily allowance for person or animal in armed forces; (pl.) provisions. ~ *v.t.* Put on fixed allowance of provisions etc.; share (food etc.) in fixed quantities.

ra'tional *adj.* Endowed with reason, reasoning; sensible, sane; based on, derived from, reason or reasoning; not foolish, absurd, or extravagant; (math., of ratio or quantity) expressible without radical signs. **ra'tionally** *adv.* **rationă'lity** *n.*

rationa'le (-ah-) *n.* Reasoned exposition of principles; logical or rational basis *of*.

ra'tionalism *n.* Practice of explaining the supernatural in religion in a way consonant with reason, or of treating reason as the ultimate authority in religion as elsewhere; theory that reason is foundation of certainty in knowledge. **ra'tionalist** *n.* & *adj.* **ratională'stic** *adj.* **rationali'stically** *adv.*

ra'tionalize *v.* 1. Explain, explain *away*, by rationalism; bring into conformity with reason; be or act as a rationalist. 2. (math.) Clear from irrational quantities. 3. Reorganize (industry etc.) on scientific lines, with elimination of waste of labour, time, and materials, and reduction of other costs. **rationaliza'tion** *n.*

Ra'tisbŏn. (Ger. *Regensburg*) Town of Bavaria; scene of victory of Napoleon over the Austrians, 1809.

ra'tīte *adj.* & *n.* (Bird) having a flat unkeeled breast-bone.

ra'tline, ra'tling *ns.* (usu. pl.) (One of) small lines fastened across ship's shrouds like ladder-rungs (ill. SAIL¹).

ratoō'n *n.* New shoot springing from root of plant, esp. sugar-cane, after cropping. ~ *v.* Send up ratoons; cut down (plant) to induce ratooning.

rattă'n, rată'n *n.* Climbing palm of genus *Calamus* with long thin pliable jointed stems, growing chiefly in E. Indies; piece of rattan stem used as cane or for other purposes; rattans used as material in building etc.

rǎt-tă't, rătată't, ră't-tăt-tă't *ns.* Rapping sound, esp. of knocker. [imit.]

ra'ttle *v.* 1. Give out rapid succession of short sharp hard sounds, cause such sounds by shaking something; move or fall with rattling noise; drive, run, ride, briskly; make rattle. 2. Say or recite rapidly; talk in lively thoughtless way. 3. (slang) Shake nerves of, fluster, frighten. ~ *n.* 1. Instrument or plaything made to rattle, esp. in order to give alarm or to amuse babies; end of rattlesnake's tail (see below); any of several plants with seeds that rattle in their cases when ripe, esp. *yellow* ~, *cock's-comb.* 2. Rattling sound; uproar, noisy gaiety, stir; rattling sound in throat caused by partial obstruction; noisy flow of words; empty or trivial talk; lively incessant talker. 3. ~*-brain, -head, -pate,* (person with) empty head; *ra'ttlesnake*, venomous Amer. snake of genus *Crotalus* with horny rings at end of tail making rattling noise when vibrated; ~*-trap*, rickety, shaky (vehicle etc.).

ra'ttler *n.* (esp.) Rattlesnake.

ra'ttling *adj.* (slang) Remarkably good, fast, etc. ~ *adv.* Remarkably, extremely.

ra'tty *adj.* Rat-like, esp. (slang) snappish, irritable.

rau'cous *adj.* Hoarse, harsh-sounding. **rau'cously** *adv.*

ra'vage *v.* Devastate, plunder; make havoc. ~ *n.* Devastation, damage, (esp., pl.) destructive effects *of*.

R.A.V.C. *abbrev.* Royal Army Veterinary Corps.

rāve¹ *n.* Rail of cart; (pl.) permanent or removable framework added to sides of cart to increase capacity.

rāve² *v.* Talk wildly or furiously (as) in delirium; (of sea, wind, etc.) howl, roar; utter with ravings; speak or write with rapturous admiration *about* or *of*, go into raptures. ~ *n.* Act, instance, of raving. ~ *adj.* (of review of play, book, etc.) Extravagantly enthusiastic.

ra'vel¹ *v.* 1. Entangle or become entangled, confuse, complicate. 2. Disentangle, unravel. ~ *n.* Entanglement, knot, complication; frayed or loose end.

Răvěl², Maurice (1875–1937). French musical composer.

ra'velin (-vl-) *n.* (fort.) Outwork of two faces forming salient angle outside main ditch before the curtain.

ră'ven¹ *n.* Large black hoarse-voiced bird (*Corvus corax*), feeding chiefly on carrion or other flesh; related species. ~ *adj.* Of glossy black.

rā'ven² *v.* Plunder, go plundering *about*, seek *after* prey or booty; prowl for prey; eat voraciously; have ravenous appetite for.

Ravě'nna. City of Emilia in NE. Italy, founded before Roman era; became the western capital of the Empire after the fall of Rome, and was the seat of THEODORIC's court; was added to the papal States, 1509; passed to Italy, 1860.

ră'venous *adj.* Voracious; very hungry. **ră'venously** *adv.*

ravi'ne (-ēn) *n.* Deep narrow gorge, mountain cleft.

raviŏ'li *n.* (Italian dish of) small pasta cases containing meat etc., served in savoury sauce. [It.]

ră'vish *v.t.* 1. Carry off (person, thing) by force (now rare); rape. 2. Enrapture. **ră'vishing** *adj.* Entrancing. **ră'vishingly** *adv.* **ră'vishment** *n.*

raw *adj.* 1. Uncooked; in natural or unwrought state, not yet dressed or manufactured; ~ *edge*, (of cloth) edge without hem or selvage; ~ *grain*, unmalted grain; ~ *hide*, untanned leather; rope or whip of this; ~ *material*, that out of which any process of manufacture makes the articles it produces; ~ *silk*, silk as reeled from cocoons; ~ *spirit*, undiluted spirit. 2. Crude, not brought to perfect composition or finish; uncultivated, uncivilized, brutal; ~ *deal*, (colloq.) harsh or unfair treatment. 3. (of persons, esp. soldiers) Inexperienced, untrained, unskilled. 4. Stripped of skin, excoriated; sensitive to touch from being so exposed; ~*-boned*, with projecting bones hardly covered with flesh, gaunt. 5. (of weather etc.) Damp and chilly, bleak. ~ *n.* Raw place on esp. horse's skin; *touch on the* ~, wound feelings etc. of person on points on which he is sensitive. **raw'něss** *n.*

ray¹ *n.* 1. Single line or narrow beam of light; straight line in which radiant energy capable of producing sensation of light is propagated to or from given point; analogous propagation-line of heat or other non-luminous physical energy; (fig.) remnant or beginning of enlightening or cheering influence; BECQUEREL, RÖNTGEN, ~*s*, X-RAY: see these words. 2. Any of the lines forming a pencil or set of straight lines passing through one point; any of a set of radiating lines, parts, or things; (bot.) marginal part of composite flower, as daisy; (zool.) radial division of starfish or other echinoderm. ~ *v.* Issue, come *forth, off, out,* in rays; radiate (poet.) **rayed** (rād), **ray'-lěss** *adjs.*

ray² *n.* Fish of genus *Raia*, closely allied to skate. (*Illustration, p.730*).

ray³, re (rā) *ns.* (mus.) Second note of hexachord and of major scale in movable-doh systems; note D in 'fixed-doh' system. [see UT]

Ray[4], John (1628–1705). English naturalist.

RAY

Ray'leigh (-lĭ), John William Strutt, 3rd Baron (1842–1919). English mathematician and physicist; discoverer (with Ramsay) of argon.

ray'ŏn n. Textile fibre made from cellulose; any of various textiles made from such fibre.

ray'onȳ, rayonné (-nā) adj. (her., of a division between parts of the field) Having flame-like indentations (ill. HERALDRY).

răze, răse (-z) v.t. Completely destroy, level with the ground.

razee' n. Ship reduced in rating by removal of upper deck(s). ~ v.t. Reduce rating of (ship) by removal of upper deck(s).

răz'or n. Sharp-edged instrument used in shaving hair from skin; ~-*back*, back sharp as razor's edge; kind of whale, rorqual; *ra'zorbill*, any of various birds with a bill shaped like a razor, esp. *Alca torda*, a species of auk; ~-*edge*, keen edge; sharp mountain ridge; critical situation; sharp line of division; ~-*fish*, bivalve mollusc of family Solenidae with long narrow shell like razor-blade; ~-*shell*, (shell of) razor-fish. [f. OF *rasor*, f. *raser*]

ră'zzle n. Spree (usu. in *go on the* ~).

R.B. abbrev. Rifle Brigade.

R.B.A., R.B.S. abbrevs. Royal Society of British Artists, of British Sculptors.

R.C. abbrev. Red Cross; right centre (of stage); Roman Catholic.

R.C.A.F. abbrev. Royal Canadian Air Force.

R.C.M. abbrev. Royal College of Music.

R.C.M.P. abbrev. Royal Canadian Mounted Police.

R.C.N. abbrev. Royal Canadian Navy; Royal College of Nursing.

R.C.O., R.C.P. abbrevs. Royal College of Organists, of Physicians.

R.C.S. abbrev. Royal College of Surgeons; Royal Corps of Signals.

Rd abbrev. Road.

R.D. abbrev. Refer to drawer (in banking); Royal (Naval Reserve) Decoration.

R.D.C. abbrev. Rural District Council.

re[1]: see RAY[3].

rē[2] *prep.* In the matter of (chiefly in legal and business use as first word of headline stating matter to be dealt with). [L, ablative of *res* thing]

re- *prefix.* 1. Once more; afresh; repeated. 2. Back, with return to previous state.

R.E. abbrev. Royal Engineers.

reach v. Stretch out, extend; stretch out the hand etc., make reaching motion or effort (lit. & fig.); succeed in touching or grasping with hand or anything held in it, etc., extend to; come to, arrive at; hand, pass or take with outstretched hand; (naut.) sail with the wind abeam (ill. SAIL[2]); ~-*me-down*, (slang) ready-made (garment). ~ n. 1. Act of reaching out; extent to which hand, etc., can be reached out; scope, range, compass. 2. Continuous extent, esp. part of river etc. lying between two bends, or of canal between two locks. 3. (naut.) Tack.

rĕă'ct v.i. Act in return (*upon* agent or influence); act, display energy, in response to stimulus; act in opposition to some force; move or tend in reverse direction; undergo change (esp. chemical change) under some influence.

rĕă'ctance n. (elect.) That part of the impedance of an alternating-current circuit which is due to capacitance or induction or both.

rĕă'ction n. 1. Responsive or reciprocal action; return of previous condition after interval of opposite (e.g. depression after excitement); (loosely) opinion, impression; (physiol.) response of organ etc. to external stimulus; (chem.) interaction of two or more substances resulting in chemical change. 2. Retrograde tendency esp. in politics. **rĕă'ctionarȳ** adj. & n. (Person) inclined or favourable to reaction.

rĕă'ctive adj. Tending to react.

rĕă'ctor n. 1. (nuclear phys.) Atomic pile, large-scale assembly in which nuclear reactions in fissile material are controlled by the introduction of absorbing non-fissile materials. 2. (med.) Animal, patient, reacting positively to a foreign substance.

read v. (past t. & past part. *read* pr. rĕd). 1. Discover or expound significance of (dream, riddle, etc.); foresee, foretell (esp. *the future, one's fortune*). 2. (Be able to) convert into the intended words or meaning (written, printed, or other symbols, or things, expressed by their means); reproduce mentally or vocally, while following their symbols with eyes or fingers, the words of (author, book, letter, etc.); study by reading; study (subject) at university; find (thing) stated, find statement, in print, etc.; convey when read, run; (of recording instrument) present (figure, etc.) to one reading it; ~ *proofs*, read printer's proofs and mark for correction. 3. Interpret (statement, action) in certain sense; assume as intended in or deducible from writer's words, find implications; (of manuscript, editor, etc.) give as the word(s)

probably used or intended by author; ~ *well, ill,* etc., (of written matter) sound or affect reader thus. 4. Bring into specified state by reading; ~ *oneself in,* (of incumbent) enter upon office by public reading of 39 Articles etc. ~ (rĕd) adj. (esp., in active sense) *well* ~, versed *in* subject by reading; with good knowledge of literature. ~ (rĕd) n. Time spent in reading.

rea'dable adj. Interestingly written; legible. **rea'dablenĕss, readabi'litȳ** ns. **rea'dablȳ** adv.

rĕaddrĕ'ss v.t. Change address of (letter).

Reade, Charles (1814–84). English novelist, author of 'The Cloister and the Hearth' etc.

rea'der n. (esp.) 1. Person employed by publisher to read and report on proffered MSS.; printer's proof-corrector. 2. Person appointed to read aloud, esp. (*lay-*~) parts of service in church; member of university staff ranking next to professor. 3. Book containing passages for exercise in reading, instruction in foreign language, etc. **rea'dership** n. Office of university reader.

rea'dilȳ (rĕd-) adv. Without showing reluctance, willingly; without difficulty.

rea'dinĕss (rĕd-) n. Prompt compliance, willingness; facility, prompt resourcefulness, quickness in argument or action; ready or prepared state.

rea'ding[1] n. (esp.) 1. Literary knowledge, scholarship. 2. One of successive occasions on which Bill must have been presented to each House of Parliament before it is ready for royal assent; *first* ~, that permitting introduction of Bill; *second* ~, that accepting general principles; *third* ~, that accepting details as amended in committee. 3. Entertainment at which something is read to audience. 4. Word(s) read or given by an editor etc. or found in MS. in text of a passage; interpretation, view taken, rendering. 5. Figure etc. shown by graduated instrument. 6. (Specified quality of) matter to be read. 7. ~-*desk*, desk for supporting book, etc., lectern; ~-*room*, room in club, library, etc., for persons wishing to read.

Rea'ding[2] (rĕd-). County town of Berkshire; university, 1926.

rea'dȳ (rĕdi) adj. With preparations complete; in fit state; with resolution nerved, willing; apt, inclined; about *to*; prompt, quick, facile; provided beforehand; within reach, easily secured; unreluctant; easy; fit for immediate use; *make* ~, prepare; ~ *money*, cash, actual coin; payment on the spot; ~ *reckoner*, (collection of) table(s) showing results of arithmetical calculations commonly required in business etc. ~ adv. Beforehand, so as not to require doing when the time comes; ~-*made*, (of clothes) made in standard

[730]

shapes and sizes, not to customer's individual measure. ~ *n.* Position in which rifle is held before the present; (slang) ready money. ~ *v.t.* Prepare.

reā′gent *n.* Chemical substance used to produce a chemical reaction.

re′al¹ (rāel) *n.* Former silver coin and money of account used in Spain and some Spanish-speaking countries. [Span., f. L *regalis* regal]

rē′al² (or rī-) *adj.* 1. Actually existing as a thing or occurring in fact, objective; genuine, rightly so called; natural, not artificial or depicted; actually present or involved, not merely apparent; ~ *answer*: see TONAL answer; *the ~ presence*, the actual presence of Christ's body and blood in the Eucharist; *the ~ thing*, the thing itself, not an imitation or inferior article. 2. (law, of actions, etc.) Relating to things, esp. real property; (of estate, property) consisting of immovable property, as land and houses; (philos. etc.) relating to, concerned with, things. ~ *adv.* (usu. with adjs.) Really; (chiefly Sc. & U.S.) very, extremely. ~ *n.* Real thing; what actually exists, esp. opp. the ideal.

reā′lgar *n.* Arsenic disulphide (As₂S₂), red orpiment, red arsenic, used as pigment and in fireworks. [Arab. *rahj al-ğār* dust of the cave]

rē′alism (or rī-) *n.* 1. Scholastic doctrine that universal or general ideas have objective existence; belief that matter as object of perception has real existence. 2. Practice of regarding things in their true nature and dealing with them as they are; fidelity of representation, rendering precise details of real thing or scene. **rē′alist** *n.* **reāli′stic** *adj.* **reāli′sticallў** *adv.*

reā′litў *n.* Property of being real; resemblance to original; real existence, what is real, what underlies appearances; existent thing; real nature *of.*

rē′alize (or rī-) *v.t.* 1. Convert (hope, plan, etc.) into fact; give apparent reality to, make realistic, present as reality. 2. Conceive as real; apprehend clearly or in detail. 3. Convert (securities, property) into money (freq. abs.); amass (fortune, specified profit), fetch as price. **reālizā′tion** *n.*

rē′ally (or rī-) *adv.* In fact, in reality; positively, indeed; (interrog.) is that so?

realm (rělm) *n.* Kingdom; sphere, province, domain.

re′alpŏlĭti′k (rāah-, -ēk) *n.* Politics based on realities and material needs, not on ideology or ethics. [Ger., = 'real politics']

rē′ăltor (or rī-) *n.* (U.S.) Real-estate agent or broker (prop. one who is a member or affiliated member of the National Association of Real Estate Boards).

rē′altў (or rī-) *n.* Real estate.

ream¹ *n.* Twenty quires or 480 sheets of paper (often 500, to allow for waste); (freq. pl.) large quantity of paper; *printers' ~*, 516 sheets. [Arab. *rizmah* bundle]

ream² *v.t.* Widen (hole in metal) with reamer; turn over edge of (cartridge-case etc.); (naut.) open (seam) for caulking. **rea′mer** *n.* Borer (ill. DRILL¹).

reap *v.* Cut (grain or similar crop), cut grain, etc., with sickle etc. in harvest; gather in thus, or fig. as harvest; harvest crop of (field etc.); *reaping-hook*, sickle.

rea′per *n.* 1. One who reaps; (fig.) death. 2. (also ~ *and binder*) Mechanical device for reaping crops (and binding sheaves) without manual labour.

rear¹ *n.* 1. Hindermost part of army or fleet; back of, space behind, position at back, of, army or camp or person; back part of anything; *bring up the ~*, come last. 2. *(attrib.)* Hinder, back-; *~-admiral*, flag-officer in navy, next below vice-admiral; (U.S.) highest rank in navy (except in special circumstances); *~-arch*, inner arch of window or. door opening when of different size or form from outer (ill. WINDOW); *rear′guard*, body of troops detached to protect rear, esp. in retreats; *rear′guard action*, engagement between rearguard and enemy; *~-lamp*, *-light*, red light at back of vehicle; *~-vault*, vaulted space connecting arched window or door head with arch in inner face of wall (ill. WINDOW). **rear′mōst** *adj.* Furthest back.

rear′ward *adj., adv. & n.* **rear′-wards** (-z) *adv.*

rear² *v.* 1. Raise, set upright, build. 2. Bring up; breed; cultivate. 3. (of horse etc.) Rise on hind feet.

reā′rm *v.* Arm again, esp. with more modern weapons or after disarming. **reārm′ament** *n.*

rea′son (-zn) *n.* 1. (Fact adduced or serving as) argument, motive, cause, or justification; (logic) one of premisses of syllogism, esp. minor premiss when given after conclusion; *~ of state*, political justification, esp. for immoral proceeding. 2. Intellectual faculty characteristic esp. of human beings by which conclusions are drawn from premisses; intellect personified; (tr. Kant's *Vernunft*) faculty transcending the understanding and providing *a priori* principles, intuition. 3. Sanity; sense; sensible conduct; what is right, practical, or practicable; moderation; *hear, listen to, ~*, allow oneself to be persuaded; *it stands to ~*, it cannot reasonably be denied. **rea′sonlĕss** *adj.* **rea′son** *v.* 1. Use argument *with* person by way of persuasion; persuade by argument *out of, into.* 2. Form or try to reach conclusions by connected thought; discuss *what, whether*, etc.; conclude, assume as step in argument, say by way of argument, *(that)*; express in logical or argumentative form; think *out*; *reasoned amendment*, one in which reasons are embodied with a view to directing course of debate. **rea′soning** *adj. & n.*

rea′sonable (-zn-) *adj.* 1. Endowed with reason, reasoning (rare). 2. Of sound judgement, sensible, moderate, not expecting too much, ready to listen to reason. 3. Agreeable to reason, not absurd, within the limits of reason; not greatly less or more than might be expected; inexpensive, not extortionate; tolerable, fair. **rea′sonablenĕss** *n.* **rea′sonablў** *adv.*

reassur′e (-shoor) *v.* Restore (person etc.) to confidence; confirm again in opinion or impression; reinsure. **reassur′ance** *n.*

Réaumūr (rāō-), René Antoine Ferchault de (1687-1757). French scientist; *~ scale*, scale in which the freezing-point of water is 0° and the boiling-point 80°.

reave, reive *v.* (past t. & past part. *rĕft*). (archaic, poet.) Commit ravages (usu. *reive*); forcibly deprive *of* (usu. in past part.); take by force, carry off. **rei′ver** *n.* Marauder, raider.

rēbā′bative *adj.* Repulsive.

rē′bāte¹ *n.* Deduction from sum to be paid, discount, drawback. **rēbā′te** *v.t.* (archaic) Diminish, reduce force or effect of; blunt, dull.

rēbā′te² *n. & v.t.* = RABBET.

rē′bĕc, -ĕck *n.* Medieval three-stringed instrument, early form of fiddle. [Arab. *rabāb*]

Rēbĕ′cca. Wife of Isaac and mother of Jacob and Esau (Gen. 25: 20 ff.).

rē′bel *n.* Person who rises in arms against, resists, or refuses allegiance to, the established government; person or thing that resists authority or control; *(attrib.)* rebellious, of rebels, in rebellion. **rĕbĕ′l** *v.i.* Act as rebel *(against)*, feel or manifest repugnance to some custom etc. *(against).*

rĕbĕ′llion (-yon) *n.* Organized armed resistance to established government, esp. (Sc. hist.) either of the Jacobite risings of 1715 and 1745; open resistance to any authority; *the Great R~*, (Engl. hist.) Royalist name for the Civil War of 1642-51.

rĕbĕ′llious (-lyus) *adj.* In rebellion; disposed to rebel, insubordinate, defying lawful authority; (of diseases, things) difficult to treat, unmanageable, refractory. **rĕbĕ′lliouslў** *adv.* **rĕbĕ′lliousnĕss** *r.*

rē′boant *adj.* (poet.) Re-echoing loudly.

rēbou′nd *v.i.* Spring back after impact; have reactive effect, recoil upon agent. ~ (or rē′-) *n.* Act of rebounding, recoil; reaction after emotion.

rēbŭ′ff *n.* Check given to one who makes advances, proffers help or sympathy, shows interest or

[731]

curiosity, makes request, etc.; snub. ~ v.t. Give rebuff to.

rěbū'ke v.t. Convey stern disapproval or censure to (person) *for* fault etc. ~ n. Rebuking, being rebuked; reproof.

rē'bus n. Enigmatic representation of name, word, etc., by pictures etc. suggesting its syllables.

rěbǔ't v.t. Force or turn back, give check to; refute, disprove (evidence, charge). rěbǔ'ttal, rěbǔ'tment ns.

rěbǔ'tter n. (esp., law) Defendant's answer to plaintiff's surrejoinder.

rěcǎ'lcĭtrant adj. & n. Obstinately disobedient or refractory (person). rěcǎ'lcĭtrance n.

rěcǎ'll (-awl) v.t. Summon back from or to a place, from different occupation, inattention, digression, etc.; bring back *to* memory, cause to remember; recollect, remember; revive, resuscitate; revoke, annul (decision etc.), take back (gift). ~ n. Summons to return to or from a place; signal to return; possibility of recalling, revoking, or annulling; recollection, remembrance.

rěcǎ'nt v. Withdraw and renounce (opinion, statement, etc.) as erroneous or heretical; disavow former opinion, esp. with public confession of error. rěcăntā'tion n.

rē'cǎp v. (colloq.) Recapitulate. ~ n. Recapitulation.

rěcǎpǐ'tūlāte v.t. Give heads or substance of (what has already been said); summarize, restate briefly. rěcǎpǐtūlā'tion n.

rěcǎ'st (-ah-) v.t. (esp.) Refashion, remodel, reconstruct; give new form or character to.

rē'ccē (rě'ki), rē'ccō n. (services' slang) Reconnaissance.

recd *abbrev.* Received.

rěcē'de v.i. Go back or farther off; become more distant; slope backwards; withdraw(*from* opinion etc.); decline in character or value.

rěcei'pt (-ēt) n. 1. (archaic) Recipe. 2. Amount of money received; fact or action of receiving or being received into person's hands or possession; written acknowledgement of such receipt, esp. of payment of sum due. 3. (archaic) Place where money is officially received; esp. ~ *of custom*, custom-house. ~ v.t. Write or print receipt on (bill).

rěcei've v.t. 1. Take into one's hands or possession; accept (something proffered); accept or buy (stolen goods) from thief; take (bread and wine of Eucharist); admit, consent or prove able to hold, provide accommodation for; submit to, endure; admit (impression etc.) by yielding or adaptation of surface. 2. Entertain as guest; greet, welcome; give specified reception to; admit to membership of society etc.; give credit to, accept as true; (abs.) receive company, hold reception. 3. Acquire, get, come by; be given or provided with; have sent to or conferred or inflicted on one. 4. (radio etc.) Transform incoming electromagnetic waves into the original signal, as sound or as light on screen.

rěcei'ver n. (esp.) 1. Person appointed by receiving-order of court to administer property of bankrupt or property under litigation. 2. Person who receives stolen goods. 3. Receptacle etc. for receiving something in machine or instrument, esp. earpiece of telephone; radio or television receiving set.

rěcē'nsĭon n. Revision of, revised, text.

rē'cent adj. Not long past, that happened or existed lately, late; not long established, lately begun, modern; *R~*, (geol.) of the latter part of the Quaternary period or system, including the present time (ill. GEOLOGY). rē'cently adv. rē'centness, rē'cency ns. Rē'cent n. (geol.) Recent epoch.

rěcě'ptacle n. 1. Containing vessel, place, or space. 2. (bot.) Common base of floral organs, axis of cluster (ill. FLOWER).

rěcě'ptĭon n. 1. Receiving, being received; receiving esp. of person, being received, into a place or company; formal or ceremonious welcome; occasion of receiving guests, assembly held for this purpose; ~ *room*, room available or suitable for receiving guests (esp. opp. *bedroom*). 2. Receiving of ideas or impressions into the mind. 3. Welcome or greeting of specified kind; demonstration of feeling towards person or project; *warm ~*, vigorous resistance or enthusiastic welcome. 4. (radio etc.) Receiving signals, efficiency with which they are received.

rěcě'ptĭonist n. Person employed to receive clients, patients, etc.

rěcě'ptĭve adj. Able or quick to receive impressions or ideas.

rěcě'ptĭvely adv. rěcě'ptĭveness, rěcěptĭ'vĭty (or rī-) ns.

rěcě'ptor n. 1. Receiving apparatus, receiver. 2. (physiol.) Minute organ at peripheral end of sensory nerve, capable of specially sensitive response to a particular form of energy, as light or heat; (also) specialized region of cell.

rěcě'ss n. 1. Temporary cessation from work, vacation, esp. of Parliament. 2. Retired or secret place; receding part of mountain chain etc., niche or alcove of wall; (anat.) fold or indentation in organ. ~ v.t. Place in a recess; set back; provide with recess(es).

rěcě'ssĭon n. 1. Receding, withdrawal, from a place or point; receding part of object etc.; illusion of distance in picture. 2. (orig. U.S.) Temporary decline or set-back in industrial or economic activity or prosperity.

rěcě'ssĭonal adj. Of the parliamentary recess; ~ *hymn*, hymn sung while clergy and choir withdraw after service. ~ n. Recessional hymn.

rěcě'ssĭve adj. 1. Tending to recede. 2. (biol., of an inherited character) Not manifest in the organism which inherits it, though liable to be manifest in the next generation; having its effect obscured by a DOMINANT character.

Rē'chabĭte (-k-) n. 1. One of a Jewish family, descended from Jonadab son of Rechab, who refused to drink wine or live in houses (Jer. 35: 2-19). 2. One who abstains from intoxicating liquors, esp. member of the Independent Order of Rechabites, a benefit society founded 1835.

réchauffé (rāshōfā) n. Warmed-up dish; rehash. [Fr.]

recherché (-shār'shā) adj. Devised or got with care or difficulty; choice, far-fetched, thought out.

rěcī'dĭvĭst n. One who relapses into crime. rěcī'dĭvĭsm n.

rē'cĭpe n. 1. Statement of ingredients and procedure for preparing dish etc. 2. (archaic) Medical prescription or remedy prepared from it. 3. Expedient, device, etc., for effecting something. [2nd pers. sing. of L *recipere* receive (i.e. take) as used in prescriptions]

rěcĭ'pĭent adj. Receptive. rěcĭ'pĭency n. rěcĭ'pĭent n. Person who receives something.

rěcĭ'procal adj. Given, felt, shown, etc., in return; felt or shared by both parties, mutual; inversely correspondent, complementary, esp. (math.) based on inverse relationship; (gram.) reflexive, expressing mutual action or relationship ('*each other*' is a reciprocal pronoun); rěcĭ'procally adv. rěcĭ'procal n. Equivalent, counterpart, complement; (math.) function or expression so related to another that their product is unity ($\frac{1}{3}$ is the reciprocal of 5).

rěcĭ'procāte v. 1. (mech.) Go with alternate backward and forward motion; give such motion to. 2. Give and receive mutually, interchange; return, requite (affection etc.); make a return (*with*). rěcĭprocā'tĭon n.

rěcĭprŏ'cĭty n. Reciprocal condition, mutual action; principle or practice of give-and-take, esp. interchange of privileges between States as basis of commercial relations.

rěcī'tal n. 1. Detailed account *of* a number of connected things or facts, relation *of* the facts of an incident etc., a narrative; part of document stating facts. 2. Act of reciting; musical entertainment given by one person.

rěcĭtā'tĭon n. (esp.) Reciting as entertainment, poem or passage recited; (U.S.) repetition of prepared lesson or exercise, examination

recitati′ve (-ēv) n. Musical declamation, between song and ordinary speech, of kind usual in narrative and dialogue parts of opera and oratorio; words, part, given in recitative.

recī′te v. 1. Repeat aloud or declaim (poem, passage) from memory, esp. before audience; give recitation. 2. Rehearse (facts) in document; mention in order, enumerate.

recī′ter n. Person who recites; book of passages for recitation.

reck v. (rhet., poet.; in neg. & interrog. sentences only). Care, be troubled, concern oneself; ~ of, pay heed to, take account of, care about.

re′ckless adj. Devoid of caution, regardless of consequences, rash; heedless of danger etc. **re′cklessly** adv. **re′cklessness** n.

re′ckon v. 1. Ascertain (number, amount), ascertain number or amount of, by counting or usu. by calculation, compute; start from, go on to, in counting; count up, sum up character of; arrive at as total; include in computation; make calculations, cast up account or sum; settle accounts with. 2. Count in, place in class among, with, in; take for, regard as, consider (to be); conclude after calculation, be of the confident opinion (that); rely, base plans, on.

re′ckoner n. (esp.) Aid to reckoning; ready ~: see READY.

re′ckoning n. (esp.) Statement of amount due, bill; day of ~, time when something must be atoned for or avenged; out in one's ~, mistaken in a calculation or expectation; dead ~: see DEAD.

reclai′m v. Win back, recall, from wrong course, error, etc.; reform, tame, civilize; bring back (land) into cultivation from a waste state or from the sea. ~ n. Reclaiming, reclamation.

reclamā′tion n. Reclaiming, being reclaimed.

réclame (rāklahm) n. Art or practice by which publicity is secured. [Fr.]

re′clinate adj. (biol.) Bending downwards.

reclī′ne v. Lay (esp. one's head, body, limbs) in more or less horizontal or leaning position; assume or be in recumbent position, lie, lean, sit with back or side supported at considerable inclination.

reclu′se (-ōōs) adj. & n. (Person) given to or living in seclusion, retirement, or isolation, esp. as religious discipline.

recogni′tion n. Recognizing, being recognized.

recŏ′gnizance (or -kŏn-) n. Bond by which person engages before court or magistrate to observe some condition, e.g. to keep the peace, pay a debt, or appear when summoned; sum pledged as surety for such observance.

recŏ′gnizant (or -kŏn-) adj. Showing recognition (of favour etc.).

re′cognīze v.t. 1. Acknowledge validity, genuineness, character, claims, or existence of; accord notice or consideration to; discover or realize nature of; treat as, acknowledge for; realize or admit that. 2. Know again, identify as known before. **re′cognizable** adj. **recognizabi′lity** n. **re′cognizably** adv.

recoi′l v.i. Retreat before enemy etc.; start or spring back, shrink mentally, in fear, horror, or disgust; rebound after impact; spring back to original position or starting-point; (of firearms) be driven backwards by discharge, kick. ~ n. Act, fact, sensation, of recoiling. **recoi′lless** (-l-l-) adj. (chiefly of guns).

recollě′ct v.t. Succeed in remembering, recall to mind, remember. **recollě′ction** n. Act, power, of recollecting; thing recollected, reminiscence; person's memory, time over which it extends. **recollě′ctive** adj.

recommě′nd v.t. 1. Give (oneself or another, one's spirit, etc.) in charge to God, a person, his care, etc. 2. Speak or write of, suggest, as fit for employment or favour or trial; make acceptable, serve as recommendation of. 3. Counsel, advise. **recommě′ndable**, **recommě′ndatory** adjs. **recommendā′tion** n.

re′compense v.t. Requite, reward or punish; make amends to (person) or for (another's loss, injury, etc.). ~ n. Reward, requital; atonement or satisfaction for injury; retribution.

re′concile v.t. 1. Make friendly after estrangement. 2. (eccles.) Purify (church etc.) by special service after profanation. 3. Bring into state of acquiescence or submission (to). 4. Adjust, settle (quarrel etc.); make (facts, statements, etc.) consistent or accordant; make compatible or consistent, regard or show as consistent (with). **re′concilable** adj. **re′concilement, reconciliā′tion** ns.

re′condīte (or rikŏ′-) adj. Abstruse, out of the way, little known; dealing in recondite knowledge or allusion, obscure. **re′conditely** adv. **re′conditeness** n.

recondi′tion v.t. Restore to proper, habitable, or usable condition, overhaul, repair.

recŏ′nnaissance (-nīsans) n. Reconnoitring survey or party.

reconnoi′tre (-ter) v. Approach and try to learn position and condition or strategic features of (enemy, district), make reconnaissance.

recŏr′d v.t. Register, set down for remembrance or reference, put in writing or other legible shape; represent in some permanent form, esp. on gramophone record or otherwise for reproduction; recording angel, angel supposed to register men's good and bad actions. **rě′cŏrd** n. 1. State of being recorded or preserved in writing, esp. as authentic legal evidence; official report of proceedings and judgement in cause before court of record, copy of pleading etc. constituting case to be decided by court; piece of recorded evidence or information, account of fact preserved in permanent form, document or monument preserving it; object serving as memorial of something; court of ~, court whose proceedings are recorded and valid as evidence of fact; matter of ~, something recorded and thereby established as fact; off the ~, (orig. U.S.) unofficial(ly); on ~, legally or otherwise recorded; (Public) R~ Office, building in which State papers and other public documents are kept. 2. Trace made by marker in groove of revolving disc or cylinder, from which sounds can afterwards be reproduced by means of a gramophone or other device; similar trace made on tape or wire by mechanical, magnetic, photographic, or other means; grooved disc, cylinder, etc., bearing such trace; ~ player, apparatus for reproducing sound of record as oscillating electrical current (which is amplified electronically). 3. Facts known about person's past. 4. Best performance or most remarkable event of its kind on record; (attrib.) best hitherto recorded; break, beat, the ~, outdo all predecessors.

recŏr′der n. (esp.) 1. Part-time judge presiding over certain Crown Courts; County Court judge of Belfast and of Londonderry; R~ of the Corporation of London, circuit judge sitting at Central Criminal Court. 2. Recording-apparatus in instruments. 3. Wood-wind instrument resembling flageolet, played vertically, and varying in range.

recŏr′ding n. (esp.) Process of registering wave-form by mechanical, photographic, electrical, or magnetic means for subsequent reproduction on gramophone, cinematograph, radio, television, etc.; disc, film, or tape on which the wave-form has been registered; programme so reproduced.

recou′nt[1] v.t. Narrate, tell in detail.

re-cou′nt[2] v.t. Count afresh. **rē′-count** n.

recou′p (-ōōp) v. Compensate for (loss), compensate (for); (law) deduct, keep back (part of sum due), make such deduction; (refl.) recover what one has expended or lost. **recou′pment** n.

recou′rse (-ōrs) n. Resorting or betaking of oneself to possible

reco′ver (-kŭ-) v. 1. Regain possession, use, or control of; acquire or find (out) again; reclaim; (refl.) regain consciousness, calmness, or control of limbs or senses. 2. Secure restitution or compensation, secure (damages) by legal process. 3. Bring or come back to life, consciousness, health, or normal state or position; ~ *sword*, bring it back after thrust etc.; (mil.) hold it upright with hilt opposite mouth. 4. Retrieve, make up for; get over, cease to feel effects of. ~ *n.* Position to which sword etc. is brought back in fencing or drill; act of coming to this.

reco′very (-kŭ-) n. Act or process of recovering or being recovered; (law) obtaining of a thing, right, damages, etc., by verdict or judgement of a court of law; *common* ~, (hist.) process, based on a legal fiction, by which entailed estate was commonly transferred from one party to another.

rĕ′crĕant adj. & n. Craven, coward(ly), apostate. **rĕ′crĕantly** adv. **rĕ′crĕancy** n.

rĕ′crĕāte[1] v. (of pastime, holiday, employment, etc.) Refresh, entertain, agreeably occupy; amuse oneself, indulge in recreation. **rĕcrĕā′tion** n. (esp.) Means of recreating oneself, pleasurable exercise or employment; ~ *ground*, public playground. **rĕ′crĕative** adj.

rē-crĕā′te[2] v.t. Create anew.

rĕ′crĕment n. (physiol.) Secretion that is re-absorbed by the body, as saliva, bile.

rĕcri′mĭnāte v.i. Retort accusation, indulge in mutual or counter charges. **rĕcrĭmĭnā′tion** n. **rĕcri′minative**, **rĕcri′minātory** adjs.

rĕcrūdĕ′sce (-ōōd-) v.i. (of sore, disease, etc., or fig.) Break out again. **rĕcrūdĕ′scence** n. **rĕcrūdĕ′scent** adj.

rĕcruī′t (-ōōt) n. Newly enlisted and not yet trained member of armed forces; person who joins society etc.; tyro. ~ v. 1. Enlist recruits for (armed forces, society, etc.); enlist (person) as recruit; get or seek recruits. 2. Replenish, fill up deficiencies or compensate wear and tear in, refresh; (seek to) recover health etc. **rĕcruī′tment** n.

rĕ′ctal adj. Of or by the rectum.

rĕ′ctangle (-nggl) n. Plane rectilinear 4-sided figure with 4 right angles, esp. one with adjacent sides unequal (ill. QUADRILATERAL).

rĕctă′ngūlar (-ngg-) adj. Shaped, having base or sides or section shaped, like rectangle; placed, having parts or lines placed, at right angles. **rĕctă′ngūlarly** adv.

rē′ctĭfȳ v.t. 1. Put right, correct, amend, reform, adjust (method, calculation, statement, etc.); abolish, get rid of, exchange for what is right (error, abuse, omission, etc.). 2. (chem.) Purify or refine esp. by renewed distillation. 3. (geom.) Find straight line equal in length to (curve). 4. (elect.) Change (current) from alternating to direct. **rĕctĭfĭcā′tion**, **rĕ′ctĭfĭer** ns.

rĕctĭlĭ′nĕar, -ĕal adjs. In or forming a straight line; bounded or characterized by straight lines. **rĕctĭlĭ′nĕarly** adv. **rĕctĭlĭnĕā′rĭtȳ** n.

rĕ′ctĭtūde n. Moral uprightness, righteousness.

rĕ′ctō n. Right-hand page of open book; front of leaf of book or manuscript (opp. VERSO).

rĕ′ctor n. 1. (in C. of E.) Parish incumbent, (hist.) one entitled to receive all tithes of parish; (in Protestant and Sc. Episcopal Ch.) minister in charge of parish; (R.C. Ch.) head parish priest. 2. Head of university, college, school, or religious institution, esp. Jesuit college or seminary (esp. abroad); in England only of heads of Lincoln and Exeter Colleges, Oxford; in Scotland of headmaster of secondary schools etc.); Lord R~, president of a Scottish university elected by the students. **rĕ′ctorate**, **rĕ′ctorship** ns. **rĕctŏr′ial** adj.

rĕ′ctory n. Rector's benefice; rector's house.

rĕ′ctrix n. (pl. -ices pr. -isēz). One of the strong feathers of bird's tail, directing flight (ill. BIRD).

rĕ′ctum n. Final section of the large intestine terminating at the anus (ill. ALIMENTARY). [L *rectum* (*intestinum*) straight (intestine)]

rĕ′ctus n. (pl. -ī). Straight muscle (~ *abdominis muscle*, ill. MUSCLE).

rĕcŭ′mbent adj. Lying down, reclining (~ *fold*, ill. ROCK[1]). **rĕcŭ′mbently** adv. **rĕcŭ′mbency** n.

rĕcū′perāte v. Restore, be restored or recover, from exhaustion, illness, loss, etc. **rĕcūperā′tion** n. **rĕcū′perative** adj.

rĕcūr′ v.i. Go back in thought or speech *to*; (of idea etc.) come back to one's mind etc., return to mind; (of problem etc.) come up again; occur again, be repeated; *recurring curve*, one that returns upon itself, e.g. circle; *recurring decimal*, decimal fraction in which a digit or series of digits is repeated indefinitely (indicated by dots above figures, as 0·142857). **rĕcū′rrence** n.

rĕcū′rrent adj. Occurring again, often, or periodically; (of nerve, vein, etc.) turning back so as to reverse direction. **rĕcū′rrently** adv. **rĕcū′rrent** n. Recurrent artery or nerve, esp. one of the two recurrent laryngeal nerves.

rĕcūr′ve v. Bend backwards. **rĕcūr′vate** adj. **rĕcūr′vature** n.

rē′cūsant (-z-; *or* rĭkū′-) n. & adj. (Person) who refused to attend Church of England services (hist.); (person) refusing submission to authority or compliance with regulation. **rĕ′cūsance, rĕ′cūsancȳ** ns.

rĕcū′se (-z) v.t. (rare) Reject (person, his authority); object to (judge) as prejudiced.

rĕd adj. 1. Of or approaching the colour seen at lower or least refracted end of visible spectrum, of shades varying from crimson to bright brown and orange, esp. those seen in blood, sunset clouds, rubies, glowing coals, human lips, and fox's hair; stained or covered with blood; (of eyes) bloodshot, or with lids sore from weeping; (of persons or animals) having red or tawny hair; (of certain peoples, esp. N. Amer. Indians) having reddish skin; (of places etc.) coloured red on maps to indicate British possession or control. 2. Marked or characterized by blood, fire, or violence; anarchistic or communistic. 3. Soviet-Russian. 4. ~ *admiral*: see ADMIRAL; *R~ Army*, Soviet-Russian army; ~ *arsenic*, REALGAR; ~ *bark*, superior kind of cinchona; ~ *biddy*, intoxicating drink of cheap red wine and methylated spirits; *re′dbird*, any of various small red-plumaged Amer. birds; ~-*blooded*, full of vigour and zest; *R~ Book of the Exchequer*, volume of charters, statutes, surveys, etc., compiled in 13th c.; *R~ Book of Hergest*, Welsh 14–15th-c. MS. containing Mabinogion, etc.; *re′dbreast*, (formerly) robin; *re′dbrick*, applied attrib. to modern English universities, as built of red brick, in distinction from Oxford and Cambridge; *re′dcap*, (colloq.) military policeman; ~ *carpet*, (fig.) elaborate form of reception for dignitaries etc.; ~ *cent*, (U.S.) smallest coin, orig. of copper (in *don't care a* ~ *cent* etc.); *re′dcoat*, (hist.) British soldier, so called from the scarlet uniform formerly worn by most regiments of the army; *R~ Crescent*, organization in Muslim countries, analogous to the Red Cross; ~ *cross*, St. George's cross; *R~ Cross*, emblem of red cross on white ground (Swiss flag with colours reversed) adopted at the Geneva Convention of 1864 for the international societies organized for the treatment of sick and wounded in war and borne by ambulances, hospitals, etc., attached to such service; ~ *currant*, (fruit of) currant-bearing shrub *Ribes rubrum*; ~ *deer*, reddish-brown species of deer (*Cervus elaphus*) of Europe, W. Asia, and N. Africa; common deer of N. Amer., Virginia deer (*Odocoileus virginianus*); ~-*eye*,

[734]

rudd; any of various Amer. fishes; ~ *fish*, male salmon in spawning season; red gurnard; any of various Amer. fishes; ~ *flag*, symbol of revolution or socialism; (also) danger signal; R~ *Flag*, revolutionary song; ~ *giant*, (astron.) star in intermediate stage of evolution, with reddish hue; ~ *gold*, gold alloyed with copper; (also, archaic and poet.) real gold, money; ~ *gum*, (eucalyptus tree yielding) reddish resin; ~*-handed*, in the act of crime; ~ *hat*: see HAT; ~ *heat*, being red-hot; temperature of red-hot thing; ~ *herring*, herring reddened by being cured in smoke; irrelevant question introduced to turn attention from the real one (as *draw a* ~ *herring across the track*, with ref. to use of herring in exercising hounds); ~*-hot*, heated to redness; highly excited, enthusiastic, furious; ~*-hot poker*, flame-flower (*Tritoma*), with tall spike of red flowers; ~ *lamp*, (formerly) night-sign of doctor or chemist; ~ *lane*, (colloq.) throat; ~ *lead*, red oxide of lead, much used as pigment; ~*-letter*, (of day) marked with red letter(s) in calendar as saint's day or festival; memorable as date of joyful occurrence; ~ *light*, red lamp as danger signal; ~*-light district*, district containing many brothels; R~ *Lion and Sun*, organization in Iran analogous to Red Cross; ~ *man*, N. Amer. Indian; ~ *meat*, beef, mutton, etc., as dist. from veal, pork, or chicken; re′dpoll, red-coated passerine bird, esp. *Carduelis flammea*; ~ *poll*, one of a breed of red-haired polled cattle; ~ *rag*, thing that excites person's rage as red object is supposed to enrage bull; ~ *sanders*, red sandalwood; R~ *Sea*, long narrow strip of water between Asia and Africa, connected with Mediterranean by Suez Canal and with Arabian Sea by Gulf of Aden; re′dshank, red-legged wading bird (*Tringa totanus*); ~ *shift*: see SHIFT, 1; ~*-short*, (of iron) brittle while red-hot; re′dskin, N. Amer. Indian; ~ *spider*, small red spider-like mite, of family Tetranychidae, infesting plants; re′dstart, red-tailed European song-bird (*Phoenicurus phoenicurus*); ~*-streak*, red-streaked apple formerly esteemed for cider making; ~ *tape*, pink tape used for tying legal documents etc.; excessive use of or adherence to formalities esp. in public business; re′dwing, red-winged thrush (*Turdus iliacus*); N. Amer. red-winged blackbird (*Agelaius phoeniceus*); S. Afr. red-winged francolin; re′dwood, red wood obtained from many tropical trees, used in dyeing etc.; tall Californian timber-tree (*Sequoia sempervirens*); ~ *worm*, kind of earth-worm used as fishing bait. rĕ′dden (-dn) *v*. rĕ′ddish *adj*. rĕ′dlў *adv*. rĕ′d-

nĕss *n*. rĕd *n*. Red colour; shade of red; red colour in roulette and rouge-et-noir; red ball at billiards; red cloth or clothes; one of former three squadrons or divisions (the ~, *white*, *blue*) of British fleet; radical, republican, anarchist, or (esp.) communist; *in the* ~, (bookkeeping) showing a debit; *see* ~, become so angry as to lose self-control.

rĕdă′ct *v.t*. Put into literary form, edit. rĕdă′ction, rĕdă′ctor *ns*.

rĕdă′n *n*. (mil.) Fieldwork with two faces forming salient angle.

rĕdd *v.t*. (Sc.) Clear up, arrange, tidy, put right, settle.

rĕ′ddle *n*. = RUDDLE.

rēde *n*. (archaic) Counsel, advice; narrative. ~ *v.t*. (archaic) Advise; read (riddle, dream).

rēdee′m *v.t*. 1. Buy back, recover by expenditure of effort or by stipulated payment. 2. Compound for, buy off, (charge or obligation) by payment; perform (promise); purchase the freedom of, save (one's life), by ransom; save, rescue, reclaim; (of God or Christ) deliver from sin and damnation. 3. Make amends for, counterbalance (fault, defect); save *from* a defect. rēdee′mable *adj*. rēdee′mer *n*. (esp. of Christ).

rēdē′mption *n*. Redeeming or being redeemed, esp. the deliverance from sin and damnation wrought by Christ's atonement; thing that redeems; purchase. rēdē′mptive *adj*.

rēdeploy′ment *n*. Improved organization and arrangement of factories as a means of increasing output.

rĕ′dingōte (-ngg-) *n*. Woman's long double-breasted outer coat with skirt sometimes cut away in front(ill. COAT). [Fr., f. Engl. *riding-coat*]

rēdi′ntĕgrāte *v.t*. Restore to wholeness or unity; renew or re-establish in united or perfect state. rēdĭntĕgrā′tion *n*.

Rĕ′dmond, John Edward (1856–1916). Irish political leader; leader of Parnellites after Parnell's death.

rĕ′dolent *adj*. Fragrant (now rare); having a strong smell; strongly suggestive or reminiscent *of*. rĕ′dolence *n*.

rēdou′ble[1] (-dŭ-) *v*. Intensify, increase; make or grow greater or more intense or numerous.

rēdou′ble[2] (-dŭ-) *v.t*. (bridge) Double again (bid already doubled by opponent). ~ *n*. Instance of redoubling.

rēdou′bt (-owt) *n*. (fort.) Outwork or fieldwork, usu. square or polygonal and without flanking defences.

rēdou′btable (-owt-) *adj*. Formidable.

rēdou′nd *v.i*. Result in, have effect of, contributing or turning *to* some advantage or disadvantage; turn *to* credit etc.; (of advan-

tage, honour, disgrace, etc.) result, attach, *to* (person), recoil or come back *upon*.

rēdrĕ′ss *v.t*. Readjust, set straight again; set right, remedy, make up for, rectify (distress, wrong, damage, etc.). ~ *n*. Reparation for wrong, redressing of grievances, etc.

rēdū′ce *v*. 1. Bring *to* certain order or arrangement, *to* a certain form or character; convert (*in*)*to* different physical state or form, esp. crush *to* powder etc. 2. Bring by force or necessity *to* some state or action, subdue, bring back to obedience. 3. Bring down, lower; weaken, impoverish; diminish, contract; ~ *to the ranks*, degrade (non-commissioned officer) to rank of private; *reduced circumstances*, poverty after prosperity. 4. (surg.) Restore (dislocated, fractured, or ruptured part) to proper position. 5. (chem.) Remove from (a compound) oxygen or other electronegative atom or group; add to (compound) hydrogen or other electro-positive atom or group. 6. (arith.) Change (number, quantity) (*in*)*to* another denomination or different form. 7. (logic) Bring syllogism into different form. 8. (intrans.) Lessen one's weight. rēdū′cer *n*. (esp., photog.) Agent for reducing the density of negatives etc. rēdū′cible *adj*.

rēdū′ction *n*. Reducing or being reduced; reduced copy of picture, map, etc.

rēduī′t (-dwēt) *n*. (fort.) Keep for garrison to retire to and hold when outworks are taken.

rēdū′ndant *adj*. Superfluous, pleonastic; copious, luxuriant, full; (of employee or his post) liable to be dispensed with because no longer necessary. rēdū′ndantlў *adv*. rēdū′ndance, rēdū′ndancў *ns*.

rēdū′plicāte *v.t*. Make double, repeat; (gram.) repeat (letter, syllable), form (tense) by reduplication.

rēdūplicā′tion *n*. Doubling, repetition; counterpart; (gram.) repetition of syllable or letter in word-formation, part so repeated.

rē-ĕ′chō (-kō) *v*. Echo; echo again and again, resound.

reed *n*. 1. (Tall straight stalk of) firm-stemmed water or marsh plant of genus *Phragmites*; (collect.) reeds, growth or bed of reeds; reeds or wheat-straw for thatching, used as lath for plastering etc.; *broken* ~, (fig.) unreliable person or thing. 2. Musical pipe of reed or straw, (fig.) pastoral poetry; one of two vibrating concave wedge-shaped pieces of reed or cane fixed face to face on metal tube as part of mouthpiece of oboe or bassoon (ill. WOOD); small metal tube with opening closed by vibrating metal tongue in lower end of organ-pipe; metal tongue, slip of cane, producing sound by vibration, in organ-pipe,

[735]

clarinet, etc.; (pl.) reed instrument(s). 3. Weaver's instrument of metal wires (formerly thin strips of reed or cane) fixed into parallel bars of wood, for separating threads of warp and beating up weft (ill. LOOM¹). 4. (archit.) One of a set of small semi-cylindrical mouldings (ill. MOULDING). 5. ~-babbler, -bird, -warbler, -wren, bird (esp. the common British *Acrocephalus scirpaceus*) frequenting reed-beds; ~-bunting, -sparrow, common British bird (*Emberiza schoeniclus*) frequenting reedy places; ~-mace, large persistent fruiting head of the water-plant *Typha*; the plant itself; ~ pen, reed sharpened for use in (esp. large) writing; ~-pipe, musical pipe made of reed; reeded organ-pipe (ill. ORGAN); ~-stop, organ-stop consisting of reed-pipes. ~ v.t. Thatch with reed; make (straw) into reed; fit (musical instrument, organ-pipe) with reed.

ree′dling n. Bearded titmouse (*Panurus biarmicus*).

ree′dy adj. 1. Abounding with reeds; made of reed (chiefly poet.); like a reed in weakness, slenderness, etc. 2. (of voice) Like reed-instrument in tone, scratchy, not round and clear. **ree′diness** n.

reef¹ n. One of three or four strips across top of square or bottom of fore-and-aft sail that can be taken in or rolled up to reduce sail's surface; ~ knot, knot consisting of two bights each enclosing the other's parallel-laid shanks, ordinary double-knot made symmetrically (ill. KNOT); ~-point, one of a set of short ropes to secure the sail when reefed (ill. SAIL¹). ~ v. Take in reef(s) of sail; shorten (topmast, bowsprit, etc.).

reef² n. Ridge of rock, shingle, or sand, at or just above or below surface of water; (gold-mining) lode of auriferous quartz, bed-rock.

ree′fer¹ n. 1. One who reefs; (slang) midshipman. 2. Reef-knot. 3. Close double-breasted stout jacket.

ree′fer² n. Marijuana cigarette.

reek n. 1. (Sc. & literary) Smoke; vapour, visible exhalation. 2. Foul or stale odour; fetid atmosphere. ~ v.i. Emit smoke (chiefly of houses after conflagration or object burnt in open air); emit vapour, steam; smell unpleasantly (usu. of). **ree′ky** adj. (chiefly Sc. & literary); *Auld Reekie*, Edinburgh.

reel¹ n. Rotatory apparatus on which thread, silk, yarn, paper, wire, etc., is wound at some stage of manufacture; apparatus capable of easy revolution for winding and unwinding cord, line, etc.; small cylinder with rim at each end, on which sewing-cotton, etc. is wound for convenience; cylinder on which length of cinematographic film is wound; quantity of such a film wound on a reel (the standard length of one reel is 1,000 ft); revolving part in machine; (*straight*) *off the* ~, without stopping, uninterruptedly. ~ v. Wind on reel; take (cocoon silk etc.) *off*, draw (fish, log-line, etc.) *in* or *up*, by use of reel; rattle (story, list, etc.) *off* without pause or apparent effort.

reel² v.i. Be in a whirl, be dizzy, swim; sway, stagger; stand, walk, or run unsteadily; rock from side to side, swing violently, be shaken physically or mentally; seem to shake. ~ n. Reeling motion.

reel³ n. Lively, esp. Scottish, dance, usu. of 2 (foursome ~) or 4 (eightsome ~) couples in line, forming a chain figure.

re-ĕ′ntrant adj. & n. (Angle) that points inward (opp. SALIENT).

re-ĕ′ntry n. (esp.) 1. (law) Act of re-entering upon possession of lands, tenements, etc., previously granted or let to another. 2. *card of* ~, (bridge, whist) high card that can be relied on to give holder the lead again by winning a trick. 3. Return of rocket etc. into earth's atmosphere from outer space.

reeve¹ n. (hist.) Chief magistrate of town or district; (Canada) president of village or town council.

reeve² n. Female RUFF².

reeve³ v.t. (naut.) Thread (rope etc.) *through* ring or other aperture; thread (aperture, block, etc.) with rope; fasten (rope, block, etc.) *in*, *on*, *to*, something by reeving.

refe′ction n. Refreshment by food or drink; slight meal, repast.

refe′ctory (*or in monastic use* rĕ′fi-) n. Room used for meal in monasteries etc. (ill. MONASTERY); ~ *table*, long narrow table (ill. TABLE).

refer′ v. 1. Trace or ascribe *to* person or thing as cause or source; assign *to* certain date, place, or class. 2. Commit, hand over, *to* person etc.; send on or direct (person), make appeal or have recourse, *to* some authority or source of information; cite authority or passage; ~ *back*, postpone consideration of (proposal etc.) by reference *to* specified authority. 3. (of statement etc.) Have relation, be directed, (of hearer) interpret as directed, *to*; make allusion, direct attention, *to*. 4. *referred pain*, pain felt at a point in a sensory system remote from the part actually affected. **rĕ′ferable** adj.

referee′ n. Arbitrator, person to whom dispute is to be or is referred for decision; umpire, esp. in football. ~ v. Act as referee (for), esp. in football.

rĕ′ference n. 1. Referring of matter for decision, settlement, or consideration, to some authority; scope given to such authority. 2. Relation, respect, correspondence, *to*; *in*, *with*, ~ *to*, regarding, as regards, about; *without* ~ *to*, irrespective of. 3. Allusion *to*. 4. Direction *to* book, passage etc. where information may be found; mark used to refer reader of text to note etc.; act of looking up passage etc. or of referring another or applying to person, for information; *book of* ~, ~ *book*, book designed for consultation rather than for continuous reading; ~ *library*, library where books may be consulted without being taken away. 5. Person named by one applying for post or offering goods etc. as willing to vouch for him or them; (loosely) testimonial. ~ v.t. Provide (book) with references to authorities etc. **referĕ′ntial** (-shal) adj.

referĕ′ndum n. Referring of question at issue to electorate for direct decision by a general vote.

rĕfi′ll v.t. Fill again. **rē′fill** n. Supply of material to refill container when contents are used up.

refi′ne v. 1. Free from dross, impurities, or defects; purify, clarify; become pure. 2. Polish, improve, make or become more elegant or cultured; use or affect subtlety of thought or language; improve *upon* by introducing refinements.

refi′nement (-nm-) n. Refining or being refined; fineness of feeling or taste, polished manners, etc.; subtle or ingenious manifestation *of* (luxury etc.), piece of elaborate arrangement; piece of subtle reasoning, fine distinction.

refi′ner n. (esp.) Person whose business is to refine metal, sugar, etc. **refi′nery** n. Place where raw material (e.g. sugar, petroleum) is refined.

refi′t v. Restore (ship) to serviceable condition; (of ship) undergo renewals and repairs. **rē′fit**, **refi′tment** ns.

reflā′tion n. Inflation of currency after deflation to restore system to its previous condition.

reflĕ′ct v. 1. (of surface or body) Throw (heat, light, sound, etc.) back, cause to rebound; (of mirror etc.) show image of, reproduce to eye or mind, exactly correspond in appearance or effect to; (of action etc.) bring back or cause to rebound (credit, discredit, etc.), bring discredit, *on* person etc. 2. Go back in thought, meditate, or consult with oneself (*on*). 3. Make disparaging remarks *on*.

reflĕ′ction, -ĕ′xion (-kshon) n. 1. Reflecting or being reflected; reflected light, heat, colour, or image; *angle of* ~, that made by reflected ray with perpendicular to the surface (ill. INCIDENCE). 2. (Piece of) censure, animadversion; thing bringing discredit *on*. 3. Reconsideration, meditation; mental faculty dealing with products of sensation and perception; idea arising in the mind; thought expressed in words.

reflĕ′ctive adj. 1. Giving back reflection or image. 2. Concerned in reflection or thought; thoughtful,

[736]

given to meditation. **reflĕ′ctively** adv. **reflĕ′ctiveness** n.
reflĕ′ctor n. Body or surface reflecting rays, esp. piece of glass, metal, etc., usu. concave, for reflecting in required direction; apparatus for reflecting images; (telescope etc. provided with) concave mirror for bringing parallel light to a focus.
rē′flĕx n. 1. Reflected light, colour, or glory; (painting etc.) light reflected from a surface in light to one in shade; reflection, image. 2. Reflex action; *conditioned* ~: see CONDITION v.t. ~ adj. Recurved; reflected; (of thought etc.) turned back upon the mind itself or its operations; coming by way of return or reflection; ~ *action*, involuntary action of muscle, nerve, etc., excited as automatic response to stimulus of sensory nerve (e.g. sneezing); ~ *angle*: see ANGLE¹; ~ *camera*, hand camera in which, by means of a pivoted mirror, the reflected image can be seen and focused up to the point of exposure (ill. CAMERA). ~ v.t. Bend back, recurve (only in past part.; chiefly bot. and her.).
reflĕ′xive adj. & n. (gram.) (Word, form) implying agent's action upon himself; (verb) of which subject and object are the same person or thing; (personal pronoun or possessive adjective) referring to subject. **reflĕ′xivelȳ** adv.
rē′fluent (-lōō-) adj. Flowing back. **rē′fluence**, n.
rē′flŭx n. Flowing back.
refōr′m v. Make or become better by removal or abandonment of imperfections, faults, or errors; abolish, cure (abuse, malpractice); *reformed churches*, Protestant Churches which have accepted the principles of the Reformation; esp. (*Reformed*) applied to Calvinist bodies, esp. contrasted with Lutherans. ~ n. Removal of abuse(s) esp. in politics; improvement made or suggested; *R~ Bill*, (in U.K.) any of several Bills to reform the representation of the people in Parliament; 1st, that of William Pitt, 1785, defeated; 2nd, that of Lord John Russell, 1831, defeated in House of Lords; 3rd (1st *R~ Act*), that of Earl Grey, passed 1832; *R~ Club*, London Club founded 1832 as rival to Carlton Club. **refōr′mative** adj.
reformā′tion n. Reforming or being reformed, esp. radical change for the better in political, religious, or social affairs; *R~*, 16th-c. religious movement directed to reform of doctrines and practices of Church of Rome and ending in establishment of reformed or Protestant Churches of central and NW. Europe.
refōr′matorȳ adj. Tending or intended to produce reform. ~ n. Institution to which juvenile offenders are sent for reform purposes.
refōr′mer n. One who reforms; leader in the 16th-c. REFORMATION; advocate or supporter of parliamentary reform, esp. of the reform movement of 1831–2.
refōr′mĭsm n. Policy of reforming existing institutions rather than abolishing or revolutionizing them.
refră′ct v.t. 1. Deflect (ray of light, energy, etc.) at certain angle at point of passage from one medium into another of different density; *refracting telescope*: see TELESCOPE. 2. (ophthalm.) Determine refractive condition of (eye). **refră′ction** n. 1. Instance of refracting. 2. (ophthalm.) Process of testing eye to determine refractive condition, esp. in order to correct error. **refră′ctive** adj.
refră′ctor n. Refracting medium, lens, or telescope.
refră′ctorȳ adj. Stubborn, unmanageable, rebellious; (of wounds etc.) not yielding *to* treatment; (of substances) hard to fuse or work. **refră′ctorilȳ** adv. **refră′ctorinĕss** n. **refră′ctorȳ** n. Substance, as fireclay, graphite, silica, specially resistant to the action of heat and suitable for lining furnaces etc. where high temperatures must be withstood.
refrai′n¹ n. Recurring phrase or line, esp. at end of stanzas.
refrai′n² v. 1. (archaic) Curb. 2. Abstain (*from*).
refră′ngĭble (-j-) adj. That can be refracted. **refrăngĭbi′litȳ** n.
refrĕ′sh v. Impart fresh vigour to, by food, rest, etc., reanimate, reinvigorate; freshen up (memory); restore (fire etc.) with fresh supply; refresh oneself, take refreshment.
refrĕ′sher n. (esp.) Extra fee paid to counsel in prolonged or frequently adjourned cases; (attrib., of course of instruction etc.) serving to refresh memory or make up to date.
refrĕ′shment n. Refreshing or being refreshed in mind or body; thing, esp. (usu. in pl.) food or drink, that refreshes.
refri′gerāte v. Make, become, cool or cold; expose (food) to low temperature in order to preserve it. **refri′gerant** adj. & n. (Medium etc.) that refrigerates. **refrĭgerā′tion** n.
refri′gerātor n. (esp.) Cupboard or room in which ice can be made and food etc. kept cold by the mechanical production of low temperature.
refri′geratorȳ n. Cold-water vessel through which worm of still passes, for condensing alcoholic and other vapours. ~ adj. That refrigerates.
reft: see REAVE.
refū′el v. Replenish with, take on, fresh supply of fuel.
rē′fūge n. (Place of) shelter from pursuit, danger, or trouble; person, thing, course, that gives shelter or is resorted to in difficulties; (also *street* ~) raised part of roadway on busy crossings etc. for pedestrians.
refūgēē′ n. Person escaped, esp. to foreign country, from religious or political persecution, war, etc.
refū′lgent adj. Shining, gloriously bright. **refū′lgentlȳ** adv. **refū′lgence** n.
refŭ′nd v. Pay back (money received or taken, expenses incurred by another); reimburse; make repayment. **rē′fŭnd** n. Repayment.
refū′sal (-z-) n. 1. Act or instance of refusing. 2. Right or privilege of deciding to take or leave a thing before it is offered to others.
refū′se¹ (-z) v. Say or convey by action that one will not accept, submit to, give, grant, gratify, consent; deny (*to* person etc.), refuse request of; make refusal; (of horse) stop short at (fence etc.), fail to take jump.
rĕ′fūse² n. & adj. (What is) rejected as worthless or left over after use.
refū′te v.t. Prove falsity or error of (statement, argument, etc.), rebut or repel by argument. **refū′tal**, **rĕfūtā′tion** ns.
rēgai′n v.t. Recover possession of; reach (place) again; recover (*feet*, *footing*, etc.).
rē′gal adj. Of or by kings; fit for a king, magnificent. **rē′gallȳ** adv.
rēgā′le v. Entertain choicely with food, *with* food, etc. (freq. iron.); give delight to; feast (*on*). **rēgā′lement** n.
rēgā′lia¹ n.pl. Insignia of royalty used at coronations; decorations or insignia of an order.

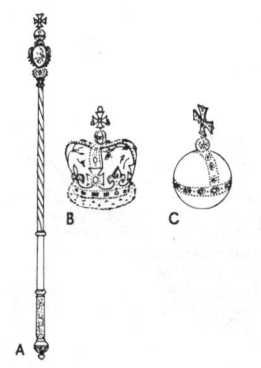

ROYAL REGALIA
A. SCEPTRE. B. CROWN. C. ORB

rēgā′lia² n. Large cigar of special quality.
rē′galĭsm n. Doctrine of sovereign's ecclesiastical supremacy.
rēgă′litȳ n. Attribute of kingly power, being king; royal privilege.

regār'd v. 1. Gaze upon; bestow attention or notice on, show interest in. 2. Give heed to; take into account in regulating actions or conduct; show consideration for; pay attention, give heed. 3. Look on *as* being something; look on *with* some feeling; consider. 4. Concern, have relation to; *as* ~*s*, so far as relates to. regār'ding *prep*. In or with regard to. regār'd *n*. 1. Look, gaze; observant attention or heed; consideration; care or concern *for*. 2. Thing or circumstance looked to or taken into account, respect; *in* ~ *to*, *of*, *with* ~ *to*, in respect of, with respect or reference to. 3. Esteem, kindly feeling or respectful opinion (*for*); (pl.) as expression of friendliness in letter etc. regār'dful *adj*. regār'dfully *adv*. regār'dless *adj*. (freq. slang as ellipt. adv., = 'regardless of cost'). regār'dlessly *adv*. regār'dlessness *n*. regār'dant *adj*. (her.) Looking backward (ill. HERALDRY).

regā'tta *n*. Meeting for boat or yacht races.

regēlā'te *v.i.* Freeze again; esp., of pieces of ice with moist surfaces, fuse at temperature above freezing-point. regēlā'tion *n*.

rē'gency *n*. (Period of) office of regent or regency-commission; *R*~, (Engl. hist.) period (1810-20) in which George, Prince of Wales, acted as regent; (attrib.) of the style of architecture, dress, etc., of this period.

regē'nerāte *v*. 1. Invest with new and higher spiritual nature; improve moral condition of; breathe new, more vigorous, and higher life into. 2. Generate again; bring or come into renewed existence. regē'nerāte, regē'nerative *adjs*. regēnerā'tion *n*.

Re'gensburg (rāg-): see RATISBON.

rē'gent *n*. 1. Person appointed to administer kingdom during minority, absence, or incapacity of monarch. 2. (U.S.) Member of governing board of some universities. ~ *adj*. (placed after n.) Acting as, having position of, regent; *Prince R*~, (Engl. hist.), George, Prince of Wales (later George IV), who was regent 1810-20 during incapacity of George III; *Regent's Park*, London, park laid out 1814 by John Nash and later containing Zoological Gardens.

rē'gicīde *n*. 1. Killer or participator in killing of a king; (Engl. hist.) one of those concerned in trying and executing Charles I. 2. Killing of a king. rē'gicīdal *adj*.

regime, ré- (rāzhē'm) *n*. Method of government; prevailing system of things; *ancien* ~: see ANCIEN RÉGIME.

rē'gimen *n*. 1. (med.) Prescribed course of exercise, way of life, and esp. diet. 2. (gram.) Relation of syntactic dependence between words, government.

rē'giment *n*. 1. (rare) Rule, government. 2. Army recruiting and training unit with permanent depot and often local name, consisting of a varying number of battalions, grouped for operational purposes into brigades; (freq. pl.) large array or number, legion. ~ *v.t.* Form (men) into regiment or regiments; organize (workers, labour) in groups or according to a system.

regimē'ntal *adj*. Of a regiment; military, maintaining or demanding strict discipline. regimē'ntals (-z) *n.pl*. Dress worn by regiment; military uniform.

regimēntā'tion *n*. Regimenting, organizing.

Rēgī'na *n*. (abbrev. R.) Reigning queen (esp. in signatures to proclamations, as *Elizabeth R*., Elizabeth Regina, and in titles of crown lawsuits, as ~ *v. Jones*, the Queen versus Jones). [L]

rē'gion (-jon) *n*. Tract of country, place, space, of more or less definitely marked boundaries or characteristics; separate part of world or universe; sphere or realm *of*; part of the body round or near some organ etc. rē'gional *adj*.

rē'gister *n*. 1. Book in which entries are made of details to be recorded for reference; official or authoritative list kept e.g. of births, marriages, and burials or deaths, shipping, medical practitioners, qualified voters in constituency, etc.; ~ *office*, registry. 2. (Set of pipes controlled by) slides in an organ; compass of voice or instrument (*upper*, *lower*, etc., ~, part of this). 3. Adjustable plate for widening or narrowing an opening and regulating draught, esp. in fire-grate. 4. Recording indicator of speed, force, etc. 5. (print.) Exact correspondence of printed matter on two sides of leaf or of impressions of colour-blocks in colour-print; (photog.) correspondence of focusing screen with plate or film. 6. ~ *ton*, cubic measure, 100 cubic feet. ~ *v*. 1. Set down (name etc.) formally, record in writing; enter or cause to be entered in particular register; (U.S.) enter name in register of hotel or lodging-house; (fig.) make mental note of; send (letter, parcel, etc.) by registered post; *registered envelope*, envelope sold by post office for enclosing letter etc. to be sent by *registered post*, the acceptance of which is registered at the post office and a receipt given to the sender. 2. (of instrument) Record automatically, indicate; (of person) express or show (emotion etc.) in face, or in any manner. 3. (print. etc.) Correspond, make correspond, exactly.

regīstrā'tion *n*.

regīstrār' *n*. 1. Official recorder, person charged with keeping register; judicial and administrative officer of the High Court and County Court; *R~ General*, administrative head of either the Office of Population Censuses and Surveys or of the General Register Office (Scotland). 2. Doctor on hospital staff ranking between consultant and senior house officer. regīstrār'ship *n*.

rē'gistrary *n*. Registrar of Cambridge University.

rē'gistry *n*. 1. Registration. 2. Place, office, where registers are kept; ~ *office*, (esp.) place where registers of births, marriages, etc., are kept, and where marriages may be performed without religious ceremony.

rē'gius *adj*. (of certain professorships at Oxford, Cambridge, and Scottish universities) Founded by a monarch (esp., by Henry VIII at Oxford and Cambridge), or to which appointment is made by the Crown; ~ *professor*, one holding such a chair. [L, = 'royal']

rē'gnal *adj*. Of a reign; ~ *day*, anniversary of sovereign's accession; ~ *year*, year of sovereign's reign, dated from moment of accession.

rē'gnant *adj*. Reigning (*Queen R*~, queen who rules in her own right and not as consort); predominant, prevalent.

regōr'ge *v*. Disgorge; gush or flow back again.

rē'gress *n*. Going back; declension, backward tendency. rēgrē'ss *v.i.* Move backwards.

regrē'ssion *n*. Backward movement, retreat; return of curve; relapse, reversion. regrē'ssive *adj*. regrē'ssively *adv*. regrē'ssiveness *n*.

regrē't *v*. Remember (something lost) with distress or longing, feel sorrow for loss of; grieve at, feel mental distress on account of; feel regret. ~ *n*. Sorrow for loss; repentance or sorrow for something done or left undone; (intimation of) sorrow or disappointment at inability to do something, esp. accept invitation. regrē'tful *adj*. regrē'tfully *adv*. regrē'ttable *adj*. regrē'ttably *adv*.

Regt *abbrev*. Regiment.

rē'gular *adj*. 1. (eccles.) Bound by religious rule; belonging to religious or monastic order. 2. Following or exhibiting a principle; harmonious, consistent, systematic; symmetrical; *the five* ~ *solids*, tetrahedron or triangular pyramid bounded by 4 triangles, hexahedron or cube by 6 squares, octahedron by 8 triangles, dodecahedron by 12 pentagons, and icosahedron by 20 triangles. 3. Acting, done, recurring, uniformly or calculably in time or manner; habitual, constant, not capricious or casual; orderly; *keep* ~ *hours*, do same thing at same time daily. 4. Conforming to a standard, in order; properly constituted or

[738]

qualified, not defective or amateur, devoted exclusively or primarily to its nominal function. 5. (gram., of verbs, nouns, etc.) Following a normal type of inflexion. 6. (colloq.) Complete, thorough, indubitable. 7. ~ *army*, army of ~ *soldiers*, professional soldiers as opp. to volunteers, militia, or temporary levies. **rĕ′gŭlarlў** *adv.* **rĕ′gŭlar** *n.* One of the regular clergy; regular soldier; (colloq.) regular customer, contributor, etc. **rĕgŭlă′rĭtў** *n.* **rĕ′gŭlarize** *v.t.* **rĕgŭlarĭzā′tion** *n.*
rĕ′gŭlāte *v.t.* Control by rule, subject to restrictions; moderate, adapt to requirements; adjust (machine, clock) so that it may work accurately. **rĕ′gŭlative** *adj.* **rĕgŭlā′tion** *n.* 1. Regulating, being regulated. 2. Prescribed rule, authoritative direction; (attrib.) fulfilling what is laid down by regulations, ordinary, usual, formal.
rĕ′gŭlātor *n.* (esp.) Device for regulating passage of steam, air, etc.; device for regulating speed of watch etc. by adjusting balance.
rĕ′gŭlus[1] *n.* 1. (chem.) Metallic content of mineral, liberated by reduction and sinking to bottom in crucible; impure metallic product of smelting various ores. 2. Golden-crested wren, *R*~ *regulus*. [L, dim. of *rex* king]
Rĕ′gŭlus[2], Marcus Atilius. Roman consul in 267 and 256 B.C.; captured in the Punic War, he was sent to Rome to negotiate peace, but refused to do so, returned to Carthage and was put to death with torture.
rĕgŭr′gĭtāte *v.* Gush back; (of stomach or receptacle) pour or cast out again. **rĕgŭrgĭtā′tion** *n.*
rĕhabĭ′lĭtāte *v.t.* Restore to rights, privileges, reputation, etc., reinstate; restore to previous condition; enable (disabled person) to earn his living or attain some degree of independence. **rĕhabĭlĭtā′tion** *n.*
rĕhă′sh *v.t.* Put (material) into new form without real change or improvement. **rĕ′hăsh** *n.* Presentation of same material in new form.
rĕhear′sal (-hĕr-) *n.* Rehearsing; practising of play etc. before performing it in public; *in* ~, in process of being rehearsed.
rĕhear′se (-hĕrs) *v.t.* Recite, say over, repeat from beginning to end; give list of, recount, enumerate; have rehearsal of (play, part, etc.); practise for later public performance.
Rĕhobō′am[1]. Son of Solomon; succeeded him as king of Israel; the northern tribes broke away from his rule and set up a new kingdom under Jeroboam, after which he continued as first king of JUDAH.
rĕhobō′am[2] *n.* Wine-bottle of largest size, holding equivalent of 8 standard bottles. [f. REHOBOAM[1]]

Reich (rīχ) *n.* German State or commonwealth; *First* ~, the Holy Roman Empire, A.D. 962–1806; *Second* ~, 1871–1918; *Third* ~, Nazi regime, 1933–45.
Reichstadt (rī′χshtăt), Duke of. Title of NAPOLEON[1] II.
Reichstag (rī′χstahχ or -g). Supreme legislature of the former German Empire and of the Republic; building in Berlin in which this met, burnt down on Nazi accession to power (1933).
Reichswehr (rī′χsvār). German armed forces, 1919–45.
reign (rān) *n.* Sovereignty, rule, sway; period during which sovereign reigns; ~ *of terror*, time in which community lives in dread of death or outrage, esp. that (1793–4) during the French Revolution. ~ *v.i.* Hold royal office, be king or queen; exercise authority, hold sway, rule; be acknowledged as supreme.
rēimbūr′se *v.t.* Repay (person who has expended money, out-of-pocket expenses). **rēimbūr′sement** *n.*
Reims: see RHEIMS.
rein (rān) *n.* Long narrow strap with each end attached to bit, used to guide or check horse etc. in riding or driving (freq. pl. in same sense) (ill. HARNESS); (fig.) means of control; *draw* ~, stop one's horse, pull up; *give* ~ *to*, let have free scope. ~ *v.t.* Check or manage with reins; pull *up* or *back*, hold *in* with reins; (fig.) govern, restrain, control.
rēincăr′nāte *v.t.* Incarnate again. **rēincăr′nate** *adj.* **rēincărnā′tion** *n.* Incarnation of the soul, after death of body, in another human or animal body.
rei′ndeer (rān-) *n.* Caribou sub-arctic deer (*Rangifer tarandus*) with large branching or palmated antlers in both sexes, used for drawing sledges and kept in herds for its milk, flesh, and hide.
rēinfor′ce *v.t.* Strengthen or support by additional men or material or by increase of numbers, quantity, size, thickness, etc.; *reinforced concrete*, concrete with steel bars or wire netting embedded in it to increase its tensile strength. ~ *n.* Thicker part of gun next breech (ill. CANNON); strengthening part, band, etc., added to object.
rēinfor′cement (-sm-) *n.* Reinforcing, being reinforced; anything that reinforces; (freq. pl.) additional men, ships, aircraft, etc., for military, naval, or air force.
reins (rānz) *n.pl.* (archaic) Kidneys; loins.
rēinstā′te *v.t.* Restore to, replace *in*, lost position, privileges, etc.; restore to health or proper order. **rēinstā′tement** *n.*
rēinsur′e (-shoor) *v.t.* Insure again, esp. (of insurer or underwriter) against risk one has undertaken.

rēi′terāte *v.t.* Repeat, do over again or several times.
reive, reiver: see REAVE.
rĕjĕ′ct *v.t.* 1. Put aside as not to be accepted, practised, believed, chosen, used, etc. 2. Cast up again, vomit, evacuate. **rĕjĕ′ction** *n.* **rĕ′jĕct** *n.* Thing rejected.
rĕjoi′ce *v.* Cause joy to, make glad; feel great joy; be glad (*to*, *that*, *in*, *at*); make merry, celebrate some event. **rĕjoi′cings** (-z) *n.pl.*
rĕjoi′n *v*, 1. Reply to charge or pleading, esp. to plaintiff's reply to defendant's plea (law); say in answer, retort. 2. Join again.
rĕjoi′nder *n.* What is rejoined or said in reply, retort.
rĕju′venāte (-jōō-) *v.* Make or become young again. **rĕjuvenā′tion** *n.*
rĕlā′pse *v.i.* Fall back, sink again, into wrong-doing, error, heresy, weakness, or illness, etc. ~ *n.* Act or fact of relapsing, esp. deterioration in patient's condition after partial recovery.
rĕlā′te *v.* 1. Narrate, recount. 2. Bring into relation, establish relation between; have reference *to*, stand in some relation *to*.
rĕlā′tĕd *adj.* (esp.) Connected, allied, akin by blood or marriage.
rĕlā′tion *n.* 1. Narration; a narrative; (law) laying of information before Attorney-General for him to take action upon. 2. Way in which one thing is thought of in connection with another; any connection, correspondence, or association between things or persons. 3. Kinsman, kinswoman, relative. **rĕlā′tionship** *n.* Being related; kinship.
rĕ′lative *adj.* 1. (gram.) Referring, and attaching a subordinate clause, to an expressed or implied antecedent; (of clause) attached to antecedent by relative word. 2. Comparative; in relation to something else; proportioned to something else; involving or implying comparison or relation; having application or reference *to*, with reference *to*; ~ *humidity*: see HUMIDITY. **rĕ′lativelў** *adv.* **rĕ′lative** *n.* 1. (gram.) Relative word, esp. pronoun, as *who*, *which*, *that*, *what*. 2. (philos.) Relative thing or term. 3. Kinsman, kinswoman; one related by blood or marriage.
rĕ′lativism *n.* Doctrine that knowledge is of relations only.
rĕlati′vitў *n.* 1. Relativeness, 2. Branch of physics concerned with correlation of descriptions of phenomena by observers using frames of reference in relative motion with respect to each other; (*special*) *theory of* ~, theory, mainly due to Einstein, based on principle of constant velocity of light and showing that all motion is relative, treating space and time as four related dimensions and invalidating previous conceptions of geometry; (*general*) *theory of* ~,

[739]

that developed by Einstein in 1915 extending the special theory to include cases of acceleration and the phenomena of gravity.

rĕlă′x v. Cause or allow to become loose, slack, or limp; enfeeble, enervate, mitigate, abate; grow less tense, rigid, stern, etc. **rĕlăxā′tion** n. Partial remission of penalty, duty, etc.; cessation from work; recreation, amusement; diminution of tension, severity, precision, etc.

rē′lay n. 1. (or rīlā′). Set of fresh horses substituted for tired ones; gang of men, supply of materials, etc., similarly used. 2. (rē′lā′) Switch or other device by which one electric current is made to control another; instrument used in long-distance telegraphy to reinforce weak current with local battery. 3. ~ race, one between teams of which each person does part of the distance, the 2nd etc. members starting when the 1st etc. end. ~ v. Arrange in, provide with, replace by, get, relays; pass on or rebroadcast (radio signal, programme, etc., originating at, and received from, another station).

rĕlea′se v.t. 1. (law) Remit (debt), surrender (right), make over (property) to another. 2. Set free, liberate, deliver, unfasten (from). 3. (cinemat.) Exhibit (film etc.) for first time, or generally. 4. Make (information) public. ~ n. 1. Deliverance, liberation, from trouble, life, duty, confinement, etc. 2. Written discharge, receipt; legal conveyance of right or estate to another, document effecting this. 3. Handle, catch, etc., that releases part of machine etc. 4. Public exhibition of cinema film etc. for first time or generally; film etc. so shown. 5. Statement etc. containing information, issued for publication.

rĕ′lēgāte v.t. Banish to some place of exile; consign or dismiss to some usu. inferior position, sphere, etc.; transfer (matter) for decision or execution, refer (person) for information etc. to; transfer (sports team) to lower section of league etc. **rĕlĕgā′tion** n.

rĕlĕ′nt v.i. Relax severity, become less stern; abandon harsh intention, yield to compassion. **rĕlĕ′ntlĕss** adj. **rĕlĕ′ntlĕsslў** adv. **rĕlĕ′ntlĕssnĕss** n.

rĕ′lĕvant adj. Bearing upon, pertinent to, the matter in hand. **rĕ′lĕvantlў** adv. **rĕ′lĕvance**, **rĕ′lĕvancў** ns.

rĕlī′able adj. That may be relied upon; of sound and consistent character or quality. **rĕlīabĭ′litў**, **rĕlī′ablenĕss** ns. **rĕlī′ablў** adv. **rĕlī′ance** n. Trust, confidence; thing depended upon. **rĕlī′ant** adj.

rĕ′lic n. 1. Part of holy person's body or belongings kept after his death as object of reverence;

memento, souvenir; (pl.) dead body, remains, of person. 2. (pl.) What has survived destruction or wasting, remnant, residue, scraps; (sing.) surviving trace or memorial of custom, period, people, etc.; object interesting for its age or associations.

rĕ′lict n. Widow.

rĕlie′f[1] n. 1. Alleviation of or deliverance from pain, distress, anxiety, etc.; redress of hardship or grievance. 2. Feature etc. that diversifies monotony or relaxes tension. 3. Assistance given to the poor or needy, esp. (hist.) that given under the Poor Law; ~ work, organized effort to help victims of earthquake or other calamity; ~ works, building etc. operations started to give work to unemployed. 4. Reinforcement and esp. raising of siege of besieged town. 5. (Replacing of person or persons on duty by) person(s) appointed to take turn of duty.

rĕlie′f[2] n. Method of moulding, carving, or stamping in which design stands out from plane or curved surface with projections proportioned and more or less closely approximating to those of objects imitated (HIGH, LOW[2], ~ : see the adjs.); piece of sculpture etc. in relief; appearance of being done in relief given by arrangement of line or colour or shading; distinctness of outline, vividness; ~ map, map in which the conformation of an area of the earth's surface is shown by (exaggerated) elevations and depressions or by suitable colouring.

rĕlie′ve v.t. 1. Bring, give, be, relief to; ease, free, from pain, discomfort, etc.; make less burdensome, monotonous, etc.; release from watch or other duty by becoming or providing a substitute; raise siege of; relieving arch, one built into wall to relieve pressure or weight upon wall (ill. ARCH[1]); relieving officer, (hist.) official who took charge of the poor or insane whose relatives were unable to care for them. 2. Bring into relief, make stand out.

rĕlie′vō n. (pl. -s) = RELIEF[2].

rĕlī′gion (-jon) n. 1. Human recognition of superhuman controlling power and esp. of a personal God or gods entitled to obedience and worship, effect of such recognition on conduct or mental attitude; particular system of faith and worship, as Christian, Muslim, Buddhist, ~. 2. Monastic condition, being monk or nun (enter into, be in, ~, enter or be member of a monastic order). 3. make a ~ of, make a point of (esp. doing some habitual action). **rĕlī′giōse** adj. Morbidly or excessively religious. **rĕlīgiŏ′s-itў** n. Being religious or religiose.

rĕlī′giŏus (-jus) adj. 1. Imbued with religion, god-fearing, devout. 2. Of, concerned with, religion;

scrupulous, conscientious. 3. Of, belonging to, an order of monks or nuns. **rĕlī′giouslў** adv. **rĕlī′-giousnĕss** n. **rĕlī′gious** n. Member of a religious order.

rĕlī′nquish v.t. Give up, abandon, resign, surrender; let go (something held). **rĕlī′nquishment** n.

rĕ′liquarў n. Receptacle for relic(s).

rĕlī′quiae n.pl. Remains; (geol.) remains of early animals or plants.

rĕ′lish n. 1. Flavour, distinctive taste of; slight dash or tinge of; appetizing flavour, attractive quality; thing eaten with plainer food to add flavour. 2. Enjoyment of food or other things; zest; liking for. ~ v. Serve as relish to, make piquant etc.; get pleasure out of, like, be pleased with; taste, savour, smack, suggest presence of; effect taste well, badly, etc.

rĕlŭ′ctant adj. Struggling, offering resistance, hard to work, get, or manage (esp. poet.); unwilling, disinclined (to). **rĕlŭ′ctantlў** adv. **rĕlŭ′ctance** n.

rĕlŭ′me (or -ōom) v.t. (poet.) Rekindle; make bright again; light up again.

rĕlў′ v.i. Put one's trust, depend with confidence, on.

rĕmai′n v.i. 1. Be left over after removal of some part or quantity, or after part has been done or dealt with in some way. 2. Be in same place or condition during further time; continue to exist, be extant; be left behind; continue to be (something specified). ~ n. (usu. pl.) What remains over, surviving members, parts, or amount; (usu. pl.) relic(s) of obsolete custom or of antiquity; (pl.) works, esp. those not before published, left by author; (pl.) dead body.

rĕmai′nder n. 1. (law) Residual interest in estate devised to another simultaneously with creation of estate; right of succession to title or position on holder's decease. 2. Residue, remaining persons or things; (arith.) number left after subtraction; copies of book etc. left unsold when demand has ceased and often offered at reduced price. ~ v.t. Treat or dispose of (edition) as remainder.

rĕma′nd (-ah-) v.t. Send back (prisoner) into custody to allow of further inquiry. ~ n. Recommittal to custody; ~ home: see COMMUNITY home.

rĕ′manĕt n. Remaining part, residue; postponed lawsuit or parliamentary Bill. [L, = 'it remains']

rĕmā′rk v. Take notice of, perceive, regard with attention, observe; say by way of comment; make comment on. ~ n. Noticing, observing, commenting; written or spoken comment, anything said. **rĕmā′rkable** adj. Worth notice, exceptional, striking, conspicuous. **rĕmārkabĭ′litў**, **rĕmā′rkablenĕss** ns. **rĕmā′rkablў** adv.

[740]

Rĕ′mbrandt (-ant). Rembrandt Harmensz van Rijn (pr. rīn) (1606-69), greatest painter of the Dutch school, and also a great etcher; has been called the 'King of Shadows', from his practice of painting pictures illuminated by a clear but limited light, emerging in the midst of masses of shadow. **R.E.M.E.** *abbrev.* Royal Electrical and Mechanical Engineers. **rĕ′mĕdў** *n.* Cure for disease, healing medicine or treatment; means of removing, counteracting, or relieving any evil; redress, legal or other reparation; the small margin within which coins are minted are allowed to vary from the standard fineness and weight (also called the *tolerance*). ~ *v.t.* Rectify, make good. **rĕmĕ′dĭable, rĕmĕ′dĭal** *adj.* **rĕmĕ′mber** *v.t.* 1. Retain in, recall to, the memory, recollect, not forget (freq. abs.). 2. Fee, reward, tip; mention in one's prayers; convey greetings from (person) to another. **rĕmĕ′mbrance** *n.* Remembering, being remembered, memory, recollection; keepsake, souvenir, memorial; (pl.) greetings conveyed through third person; *R~ Sunday*, Sunday nearest 11 Nov., as day of remembrance of those who lost their lives in the wars of 1914-18 and 1939-45. **rĕmĕ′mbrancer** *n.* One who reminds another; reminder, souvenir; *City R~*, officer representing Corporation of City of London before parliamentary committees etc.; *King's, Queen's, R~*, officer collecting debts due to sovereign. **rĕ′mĕx** *n.* (pl. *rĕmi′gēs*). One of principal feathers of bird's wing. [L, = 'rower'] **rĕmī′nd** *v.t.* Put (person) in mind *of, to* do, etc. **rĕmī′nder** *n.* Thing that reminds or is meant to remind. **rĕmī′ndful** *adj.* Acting as reminder, reviving the memory, *of*. **rĕmĭnī′sce** *v.i.* (colloq.) Indulge in reminiscence(s). **rĕmĭnī′scence** *n.* Remembering; act of recovering knowledge by mental effort; expression, fact, etc., recalling something else; remembered fact or incident; (pl.) collection in literary form of person's memories etc. **rĕmĭnī′scent** *adj.* Recalling past things; given to or concerned with retrospection, mindful or having memories *of*; reminding or suggestive *of*. **rĕmĭnī′scentlў** *adv.* **rĕmī′se¹** (-ēz) *n.* 1. (archaic) Coach-house; carriage hired from livery-stable. 2. (fencing) Second thrust made for recovery from first. ~ *v.i.* Make remise in fencing. **rĕmī′se²** (-īz) *v.t.* (law) Surrender, make over (right, property). **rĕmī′ss** *adj.* Careless of duty, lax, negligent; lacking force or energy. **rĕmī′sslў** *adv.* **rĕmī′ssnĕss** *n.* **rĕmī′ssible** *adj.* That may be remitted. **rĕmī′ssion** *n.* Forgiveness *of* sins etc., forgiveness of sins; remittance of debt, penalty, etc.; diminution of force, effect, degree, violence, etc. **rĕmī′ssive** *adj.* **rĕmī′t** *v.* 1. Pardon (sins etc.); refrain from exacting, inflicting, or executing (debt, punishment, sentence). 2. Abate, slacken, mitigate; partly or entirely cease from or cease. 3. Refer (matter for decision etc.) *to* some authority; send back (case) to lower court; send or put back (*in*)*to* previous state; postpone, defer, *to* or *till*. 4. Transmit, get conveyed by post etc. (money etc.). **rĕmī′ttance** *n.* Money sent to person; sending of money; ~ *man*, emigrant subsisting on remittances from home. **rĕmī′ttent** *adj. & n.* (Fever) that abates at intervals. **rĕmī′tter** *n.* (law) Substitution, in favour of holder of two titles to estate, of the more valid for the other by which he entered on possession; remitting of case to other court. **rĕ′mnant** *n.* Small remaining part, quantity, or number; small remaining quantity, part, or piece, esp. end of piece of cloth etc. left over after rest has been used or sold. **rĕmō′nĕtīze** (-mŭ-) *v.t.* Restore (metal etc.) to former position as legal tender. **rĕmŏnĕtĭzā′tion** *n.* **rĕmŏ′nstrance** *n.* 1. (hist.) Formal statement of public grievances; *Grand R~*, that presented by House of Commons to Crown in 1641; (eccles. hist.) document presented (1619) by Dutch Arminians to States of Holland, on differences between themselves and strict Calvinists. 2. Remonstrating, expostulation; protest. **rĕmŏ′nstrant** *adj. & n.* (esp.) Of, member of, Arminian party in Dutch Reformed Church. **rĕ′monstrate** (*or* rĭmŏ′-) *v.* Make protest, expostulate; urge in remonstrance. **rĕmŏ′nstrative** *adj.* **rĕ′mora** *n.* 1. Fish (of family Echenaedidae) which attaches itself to sharks, turtles, ships, etc., by means of adhesive organ on top of head, sucking-fish. 2. Obstruction, impediment (because the fish was formerly supposed to stay the course of the ship to which it adhered). **rĕmō′rse** *n.* Bitter repentance for wrong committed; compunction, compassionate reluctance to inflict pain or be cruel. **rĕmō′rseful(lў), rĕmō′rseless(lў)** *adjs. & advs.* **rĕmō′rselĕssnĕss** *n.* **rĕmō′te** *adj.* Far apart; far away or off in place or time; not closely related; distant, widely different, *from*; out-of-the-way,

secluded; (chiefly superl., of idea etc.) slight(est), faint(est); ~ *control*, control from a distance. **rĕmō′telў** *adv.* **rĕmō′tenĕss** *n.* **rĕmou′nt** *v.* 1. Mount (hill, horse, etc.) again; go up again, get on horseback again; provide (cavalry) with fresh horses. 2. Go back *to* specified date, period, source. **rĕ′mount** *n.* (mil.) Horse to replace another which is worn out or killed. **rĕmō′vable** (-ōō-) *adj.* (esp., of magistrate or official) Subject to removal from office, holding office during pleasure of Crown or other authority. **rĕmovabĭ′lĭtў** *n.* **rĕmō′val** (-ōō-) *n.* Removing; being removed. **rĕmō′ve** (-ōōv) *v.* 1. Take off or away from place occupied, convey to another place; change situation of; get rid of, dismiss; convey (furniture etc.) to another place for persons changing house. 2. Change one's residence; go away *from*. **rĕmō′ved** (-vd) *adj.* (esp.) Distant or remote *from*; (of cousins) *once, twice*, etc., ~, with difference of one, two, etc., generations. **rĕmō′ve** *n.* 1. (archaic) Dish that succeeds another at table. 2. Promotion to higher form at school; (at some schools) a certain form or division. 3. Act of removing, removal. 4. Distance (*rare*); stage in gradation, degree, esp. in consanguinity. **rĕmū′nĕrāte** *v.t.* Reward, pay for services rendered; serve as or provide recompense for (toil etc.) or to (person). **rĕmūnĕrā′tion** *n.* **rĕmū′nerative** *adj.* **rĕmū′nerativelў** *adv.* **rĕmū′nerativenĕss** *n.* **Rĕ′mus.** (Rom. legend) Twin brother of ROMULUS. **Rĕnai′ssance** (*or* -ahṅs) *n.* Great revival in 14th-16th centuries of art and letters, under influence of classical models, beginning in Italy; style of art or architecture characteristic of this period (freq. attrib.); *r~*, any similar revival. **rē′nal** *adj.* Of the kidneys. **Renan** (renahṅ), Ernest (1823-92). French scholar, philosopher, and historian; author of 'Origines du Christianisme', in which he applied the method of the historian to the biblical narrative. **rĕnă′scence** *n.* Rebirth, renewal; RENAISSANCE. **rĕnă′scent** *adj.* Springing up anew, being reborn. **rĕncŏ′ntre** (-t*er*; *or* rahṅkawṅtr) Encounter, battle, skirmish, duel; casual meeting. [Fr.] **rĕnd** *v.* (past t. & past part. *rĕnt*). Tear, wrench (*off, away, apart,* etc.); split or divide in two, in pieces, or (usu.) into factions. **rĕ′nder** *v.t.* 1. Give in return; give back, restore (archaic); hand over, deliver, give *up*, surrender (chiefly archaic); pay (tribute etc.), show (obedience etc.), do (service etc.); submit produce for

[741]

inspection or payment. 2. Reproduce, portray; give representation or performance of, execute; translate. 3. Make, cause to be, convert into. 4. Melt (fat) *down*, extract by melting; cover (stone, brick) with first coat of plaster; ~-*set*, plaster (wall etc.) with two coats; (plastering) of two coats. **rĕ′ndering** *n*. (esp.) Coat of plaster. **rĕ′nder** *n*. (law) Return in money, kind, or service, made by tenant to superior.

rendezvous (rah′ndāvōō) *n*. Place appointed for assembling of troops or ships or aircraft; place of common resort; meeting-place agreed on, meeting by agreement. ~ *v.i.* Meet at rendezvous.

rĕndi′tion *n*. 1. (now rare) Surrender of place or person. 2. (orig. U.S.) Rendering, performance, of dramatic role, musical piece, etc.; translation.

rĕ′negāde *n*. Apostate, esp. from Christianity to Islam; deserter of party or principles, turncoat. ~ *v.i.* Turn renegade.

rėnew′ *v*. 1. Restore to original state, make (as good as) new; regenerate; patch, fill up, reinforce, replace. 2. Get, begin, make, say, or give, anew; continue after intermission; grant or be granted continuation of *bill, lease*. **rėnew′al** *n*.

Rĕ′nfrewshire (-rōō-). Former county of SW. Scotland, S. of River Clyde, since May 1975 part of the region of Strathclyde.

rĕ′nifōrm *adj*. Kidney-shaped.

rĕ′nmĭ′nbĭ′ *n*. (or *yuan*) Principal monetary unit of China, = 10 jiao or 100 fen.

rĕ′nnėt[1] *n*. Curdled milk found in stomach of unweaned calf, used in curdling milk for making cheese, junket, etc.; preparation of inner membrane of calf's stomach, or of kinds of plant, used for this and other purposes.

rĕ′nnėt[2] *n*. Kind of smallish, firm-fleshed dessert apple, good for keeping.

Rĕ′nnie, John (1761–1821). Scottish civil engineer; designed London bridge, Southwark bridge, and (the original) Waterloo bridge.

Renoir (-nwår), Pierre Auguste (1841–1919). French Impressionist painter.

rėnou′nce *v*. Resign, surrender, esp. completely and formally; cast off, repudiate; discontinue, give up, esp. openly; (law) refuse or resign right or position, esp. as heir or trustee; (cards) follow with card of another suit for want of right one. **rėnou′ncement** *n*.

rĕ′novāte *v.t.* Make new again, repair, (house, garment, etc.); restore to good condition or vigour. **rĕnovā′tion, rĕ′novātor** *ns*.

rėnow′n *n*. Celebrity, fame, high distinction. **rėnow′ned** (-nd) *adj*. Famous, celebrated.

rĕnt[1] *n*. Tear in garment etc.; opening in clouds etc. resembling tear; cleft, fissure, gorge.

rĕnt[2] *n*. Tenant's periodical payment to owner or landlord for use of land, house, or room; payment for hire of machinery etc.; ~-*charge*, periodical charge on land etc. reserved to one who is not the owner; ~-*free*, exempt from rent; ~-*roll*, register of person's lands etc. with rents due from them; sum of person's income from rents; ~-*service*, (tenure by) personal service in lieu of or addition to rent. ~ *v*. Take, occupy, use, at a rent; let or hire for rent; be let *at* specified rent; impose rent on (tenant).

rėnt[3]: see REND.

rĕ′ntal *n*. Income from rents; amount paid or received as rent.

rĕ′nter *n*. One who holds land etc. by payment of rent; distributor of cinematographic films to exhibitors.

rentier (rahńtyā) *n*. One who derives his income from property, investments, etc. [Fr.]

rėnŭncia′tion (-sīā) *n*. Renouncing, document expressing this; self-denial, giving up of things. **rėnŭ′nciative** (-sha-), **rėnŭ′nciatorў** (-sha-) *adjs*.

rĕp[1], **rĕpp** *ns*. Textile fabric with corded surface, resembling poplin but heavier, used for curtains, upholstery, etc.

rĕp[2] *n*. (slang) Person of loose character. [perh. f. *reprobate* (*n*.)]

rĕp[3] *n*. (colloq.) Repertory (theatre).

rĕp[4] *n*. Representative, (esp.) commercial traveller.

rėpai′nt *v.t.* Paint again. **rĕ′-paint** *n*. Repainted golf-ball.

rėpair′[1] *v.i.* Resort, have recourse, go often or in numbers, *to*.

rėpair′[2] *v.t.* Restore to good condition, mend, by replacing or refixing parts or compensating loss or exhaustion; remedy, set right again, make amends for (loss, wrong, error). ~ *n*. Restoring to sound condition; *in good* ~, in good (working) condition.

rėpă′nd *adj*. (bot., zool.) Having an undulating margin, wavy.

rĕ′parable *adj*. (of loss etc.) That can be repaired.

rĕparā′tion *n*. Repairing or being repaired, repair; making of amends, compensation (esp., pl., that paid to victorious country by defeated one for damage done in war). **rėpă′rative** *adj*.

rėpărtee′ *n*. Witty retort; (making of) witty retorts.

rėpa′st (-ah-) *n*. (Food supplied for or eaten at) meal.

rėpă′triāte *v.t.* Restore or return to native land. ~ *n*. Person who has been repatriated. **rėpătriā′tion**.

rėpay′ *v*. (past t. & past part. *-paid*). Pay back (money); return, retaliate (blow, service, visit, etc.); give in recompense *for*; make repayment to (person); make return for, requite (action); make repayment. **rėpay′ment** *n*.

rėpea′l *v.t.* Revoke, rescind, annul (law etc.). ~ *n*. Abrogation, repealing; cancelling of Union between Great Britain and Ireland, esp. as demanded by O'CONNELL in 1830 and 1841–6.

rėpea′t *v*. Say or do over again; recite, report, reproduce; recur, appear again or repeatedly; (of watch etc.) strike last quarter etc. over again when required; (of firearm) fire several shots without recharging magazine; (refl.) recur in same form, say or do same thing over again. ~ *n*. Repeating, esp. of item in programme in response to encore; pattern repeated in cloth, paper, etc.; (mus.) passage intended to be repeated, mark indicating this; (commerc.) fresh consignment similar to previous one, order given for this. **rėpea′table** *adj*. **rėpea′tėdlў** *adv*.

rėpea′ter *n*. (esp.) Watch, firearm, etc. that repeats.

rėpĕ′l *v.t.* 1. Drive back, repulse, ward off; refuse admission, acceptance, or approach to. 2. Be repulsive or distasteful to. **rėpĕ′llent** *adj*. **rėpĕ′llentlў** *adv*.

rĕ′pėnt[1] *adj*. (chiefly bot.) Creeping, esp. growing along or just under surface of ground.

rėpĕ′nt[2] *v*. Feel contrition, compunction, sorrow, or regret for what one has done or left undone; think with contrition or regret *of*. **rėpĕ′ntance** *n*. **rėpĕ′ntant** *adj*. **rėpĕ′ntantlў** *adv*.

rėpercŭ′ssion *n*. Repulse or recoil after impact; return or reverberation of sound, echo; indirect effect or reaction *of* event or act. **rėpercŭ′ssive** *adj*.

rĕ′pertoire (-twår) *n*. Stock of dramatic or musical pieces etc. which company or player is accustomed or prepared to perform.

rĕ′pertorў *n*. 1. Storehouse, magazine, or repository, where something may be found. 2. Repertoire; ~ *company*, theatrical company which keeps a stock of plays ready for performance, or (now usu.) one which presents a different play each week etc. (whence ~ *system*).

rĕpėti′tion *n*. Repeating or being repeated; recitation of something learnt by heart, piece set to be learnt and recited; copy, replica; comparative ability of musical instrument to repeat same note in quick succession. **rėpėti′tious** (-shus), **rėpĕ′titive** *adjs*.

rėpī′ne *v.i.* Fret, be discontented (*at*).

rėpi′que (-ēk) *n*. (piquet) Winning of 30 points on cards alone before beginning to play (and before adversary begins to count), entitling player to begin his score at 90. ~ *v*. Score repique against; win repique.

rėplā′ce *v.t.* Put back in place; take place of, succeed, be substituted for; fill up place of (*with, by*), find or provide substitute for; (pass.) be succeeded, have one's or

REPLENISH

its place filled *by*, be succeeded. **rĕplā′ceable** *adj*. **rĕplā′cement** *n*.
rĕplĕ′nish *v.t.* Fill up again (*with*). **rĕplĕ′nishment** *n*.
rĕplē′te *adj*. Filled, stuffed, fully imbued, well stocked, *with*; gorged, sated (*with*). **rĕplē′tion** *n*.
rĕplĕ′vin *n*. Restoration or recovery of distrained goods on security given for submission to trial and judgement; writ granting, action arising out of, replevin. ~, **rĕplē′vy̆** *vbs.t.* Recover by replevin.
rĕ′plica *n*. Duplicate made by original artist of his picture etc.; facsimile, exact copy.
rĕply̆′ *v*. Make answer, respond, in word or action (*to*, *that*). ~ *n*. Act of replying; what is replied, response; (law) pleading by plaintiff after delivery of defence, final speech of counsel in trial; ~ *coupon*, coupon for prepaying reply to letter, exchangeable abroad for stamps; ~-*paid*, (of telegram) with cost of reply paid by sender.
rĕpōr′t *v*. Relate, give an account of; convey, repeat (something said or heard); take down (law-case, speech, etc.) in writing, esp. with view to publication in newspaper; give formal account or statement of; make report; relate or state as result of observation or investigation; name (person) to superior authority as having offended in some way; (refl. & intrans.) make known to some authority that one has arrived or is present; ~ *progress*, state what has been done so far; *move to* ~ *progress*, in House of Commons, propose that debate be discontinued, freq. for obstructive purposes. ~ *n*. 1. Common talk, rumour; way person or thing is spoken of, repute. 2. Account given or opinion formally expressed after investigation or consideration, (esp.) account by teacher of pupil's conduct and progress; description, epitome, or reproduction of scene, speech, law-case, etc., esp. for newpaper publication; ~ *stage*, that reached by Bill in House of Commons when chairman of committee announces conclusion of committee's dealings with it between second and third readings. 3. Sound of explosion; resounding noise.
rĕpōr′tage (or -ahzh) *n*. (Style of) reporting events for the press.
rĕpōr′ter *n*. (esp.) One employed to report events for newspaper.
rĕpō′se¹ (-z) *v.t.* Place (trust etc.) *in*.
rĕpō′se² (-z) *v*. Rest; lay (*one's head* etc.) to rest; give rest to, refresh with rest; lie, be lying or laid, esp. in sleep or death; be supported or based *on*. ~ *n*. Rest, cessation of activity or excitement, respite from toil; sleep; peaceful or quiescent state, stillness, tranquillity; restful effect; composure or ease of manner. **rĕpō′seful** *adj*. **rĕpō′sefully̆** *adv*.
rĕpō′sitory̆ (-z-) *n*. Receptacle; place where things are stored or may be found, museum, warehouse, shop, etc.; burial-place; recipient of confidences or secrets.
repou′ssé (-ōosā) *adj*. & *n*. (Ornamental metal work) hammered into relief from reverse side.
repp: see REP¹.
repr. *abbrev*. Represent etc.; reprinted.
rĕprĕhĕ′nd *v.t.* Rebuke, blame, find fault with. **rĕprĕhĕ′nsible** *adj*. **rĕprĕhĕ′nsibly̆** *adv*. **rĕprĕhĕ′nsion** *n*.
rĕpresĕ′nt (-z-) *v.t.* 1. Bring clearly before the mind, esp. by description or imagination; point out explicitly or seriously, freq. in expostulation etc.; describe as having specific character or quality. 2. Display to the eye, make visible; (esp.) exhibit by means of painting, sculpture, etc.; reproduce in action or show, play, perform, act the part of. 3. Symbolize, serve as embodiment of; serve as specimen or example of; stand for or in place of, denote *by* a substitute; take or fill the place of, be substitute for in some capacity; (esp.) be accredited deputy for (number of persons) in deliberative or legislative assembly. **rĕpresĕntā′tion** *n*. *proportional* ~: see PROPORTIONAL.
rĕpresĕ′ntative (-z-) *adj*. Serving to represent; esp. typical of a class; holding place of, acting for, larger body of persons (esp. the whole people) in government or legislation; of, based upon, system by which people is thus represented. **rĕpresĕ′ntatively̆** *adv*. **rĕpresĕ′ntativeness** *n*. **rĕpresĕ′ntative** *n*. 1. Sample, specimen; typical embodiment *of*. 2. Agent, delegate, substitute; person appointed to represent sovereign or nation in foreign court or country; one representing section of community as member of legislative body; *House of Representatives*, lower house of U.S. Congress or of a State legislature.
rĕprĕ′ss *v.t.* Check, restrain, put down, keep under; reduce to subjection, subdue, suppress, quell; (psychol.) actively exclude (distressing idea or memory) from the field of conscious awareness. **rĕprĕ′ssion** *n*. **rĕprĕ′ssive** *adj*. **rĕprĕ′ssively̆** *adv*.
rĕprie′ve *v.t.* Suspend or delay execution of (condemned person); give respite to. ~ *n*. Reprieving, being reprieved; (warrant for) remission or commutation of capital sentence; respite.
rĕ′primand (-ah-) *n*. Official rebuke. ~ *v.t.* Rebuke officially.
rĕ′print *v.t.* Print again, esp. in new edition. ~ *n*. Reproduction in print of matter previously printed; new impression.
rĕpri′sal (-z-) *n*. Act of retaliation (freq. pl.); (hist.) forcible seizure of foreign subjects' persons or property in retaliation.
rĕprī′se (-z) *n*. (law) Rent-charge or other payment to be made yearly out of estate.
rĕproa′ch *v.t.* Express, convey, disapproval to (person) for fault etc. (freq. *with*). ~ *n*. Reproaching; thing that brings disgrace or discredit (*to*); opprobrium, disgraced or discredited state. **rĕproa′chful** *adj*. **rĕproa′chfully̆** *adv*. **rĕproa′chfulness** *n*.
rĕ′probāte *v.t.* Express or feel disapproval of, censure; (of God) cast off, exclude from salvation. **rĕprobā′tion** *n*. **rĕ′probate** (or -āt) *adj*. & *n*. (Person) cast off by God, hardened in sin, of abandoned character, immoral.
rĕprodū′ce *v*. (esp.) Produce copy or representation of; multiply by generation. **rĕprodŭ′ction** *n*. **rĕprodŭc′tive** *adj*. **rĕprodŭ′ctively̆** *adv*. **rĕprodŭ′ctiveness** *n*.
rĕprōō′f¹ *n*. Blame; rebuke, expression of blame.
rĕ-prōō′f² *v.t.* Render (coat etc.) waterproof again.
rĕpro′ve (-ōov) *v.t.* Rebuke.
rĕ′ptant *adj*. (biol.) Creeping, crawling.
rĕ′ptile *n*. Crawling animal; (biol.) member of the Reptilia, a class of cold-blooded, lung-breathing vertebrates which includes snakes, lizards, crocodiles, turtles, and tortoises. ~ *adj*. Creeping. **rĕpti′lian** (-lyan) *adj*.
Rĕ′pton. English public school in Derbyshire, founded 1556.
rĕpŭ′blic *n*. A State in which supreme power rests in the people and their elected representatives and officers, as opp. to one governed by king etc.; any community or society with equality between members; *1st*, *2nd*, *3rd*, *4th*, *5th R*~: see FRANCE¹; ~ *of letters*, (all those engaged in) literature.
rĕpŭ′blican *adj*. 1. Of, constituted as, characterizing, republic(s); advocating or supporting republican government. 2. *R*~, *R*~ *party*, the political party which opposes the DEMOCRATIC party in U.S.; it was formed in 1854 and its first leader to achieve the presidency was Abraham LINCOLN²; (also, hist.) first party which supported Jefferson. ~ *n*. Person supporting or advocating republican government; *R*~, member, supporter, of U.S. Republican party. **rĕpŭ′blicanism** *n*.
rĕpū′diāte *v.t.* Divorce (wife); cast off, disown (person, thing); refuse to accept or entertain, or to have dealings with; refuse to recognize or obey (authority) or discharge (obligation, debt). **rĕpūdiā′tion** *n*.
rĕpŭ′gnance *n*. Contradiction, incompatibility, of ideas, statements, tempers, etc.; antipathy, aversion (*to*, *against*).
rĕpŭ′gnant *adj*. Contradictory

[743]

(to), incompatible (with); distasteful, objectionable, to.

repu'lse v.t. Drive back (attack, attacking enemy) by force of arms; rebuff (friendly advances etc.); refuse (request, offer, etc.). ~ n. Repulsing or being repulsed; rebuff.

repu'lsion n. 1. (phys.) Tendency of bodies to repel each other or increase their mutual distance; *capillary* ~: see CAPILLARY. 2. Aversion, disgust.

repu'lsive adj. 1. (phys.) Exercising repulsion. 2. Exciting aversion or loathing, disgusting. **repu'lsively** adv. **repu'lsiveness** n.

re'pūtable adj. Of good repute. **re'pūtably** adv.

repūtā'tion n. What is generally said or believed about the character of a person or thing; state of being well reported of, credit, respectability, good fame; *the* credit or distinction *of*.

repū'te v.t. (usu. pass.) Be generally considered, reckoned, spoken, or reported of. **repū'ted** adj. (esp.) Supposed, accounted; ~ *pint*, bottle of beer etc. sold as imperial pint. **repū'tedly** adv. **repū'te** n. Reputation.

reque'st n. 1. Act of asking for something, petition; thing asked for; *by* ~, in response to expressed wish. 2. State of being sought after, demand. ~ v.t. Seek permission *to* do; ask to be given, allowed, or favoured with; ask (person) *to* do *that*.

re'quiem n. Mass for repose of souls of the dead; musical setting for this; dirge. [L(accus.), = 'rest', first word of Introit in Mass for the Dead]

requiē'scat n. Wish for repose of the dead. [L *requiescat in pace* 'may he rest in peace']

requīr'e v.t. 1. Demand of (person) *to* do; demand or ask in words, esp. as of right; lay down as imperative. 2. Need, call for, depend for success, etc., on. **requīr'ement** n.

re'quisite (-z-) adj. Required by circumstances, necessary. ~ n. Requirement; what is required or necessary.

requisi'tion (-z-) n. Requiring, demand made, esp. formal and usu. written demand that some duty should be performed; order given to town etc. to furnish specified military supplies; being called or put into service. ~ v.t. Demand use or supply of for military purposes or public services; demand such supplies etc. from (town, individual, etc.); press into service, call in for some purpose.

requī'te v.t. Make return for, reward or revenge (*with*); make return to, repay with good or evil; give in return. **requī'tal** n.

rēre- *prefix*. (archit.) Var. of REAR[1].

rēr'edos (rērd-) n. Ornamental screen covering wall at back of altar (ill. ALTAR).

rescī'nd v.t. Abrogate, revoke, annul, cancel. **rescī'ssion** (-zhn) n.

rē'script n. 1. Roman emperor's written reply to appeal for guidance esp. from magistrate on legal point; pope's decretal epistle in reply to question, any papal decision; official edict or announcement of ruler or government. 2. Rewriting; thing rewritten.

rē'scūe v.t. Deliver from or *from* attack, custody, danger, or harm; (law) unlawfully liberate (person), forcibly recover (property). **rē'scūer** n. **rē'scūe** n. Rescuing, being rescued; succour; deliverance; illegal liberation, forcible recovery.

resear'ch (-sêr-) n. Careful search or inquiry *after*, *for*; (freq. pl.) endeavour to discover facts by scientific study of a subject, course of critical investigation. ~ v. Make researches (into).

resē'ct v.t. (surg.) Cut out or pare down (bone, cartilage, nerve, etc.). **resē'ction** n.

resē'da n. 1. Herbaceous plant of genus R~ which includes mignonette and dyer's weed. 2. (pr. re'si-) Pale greyish-green colour as of mignonette.

resē'mble (-z-) v.t. Be like, have similarity to or some feature or property in common with. **resē'mblance** n.

resē'nt (-z-) v.t. Show or feel indignation at, feel injured or insulted by. **resē'ntful** adj. **resē'ntfully** adv. **resē'ntment** n.

reservā'tion (-z-) n. (esp.) 1. (eccles.) Right reserved to pope of nomination to vacant benefice; power of absolution reserved to superior in certain cases; practice of retaining for some purpose a portion of the Eucharistic elements (esp. the bread) after celebration. 2. (law) Right or interest retained in estate being conveyed; clause reserving this. 3. (orig. U.S.) Tract of land reserved for special purpose, esp. for exclusive occupation by native tribe. 4. Express or tacit limitation or exception made about something; *mental* ~, qualification tacitly added in making statement, taking oath, etc. 5. (orig. U.S.) Engaging of seat, room, etc., in advance; seat etc. so engaged.

resēr've (-z-) v.t. 1. Keep for future use, enjoyment, or treatment, keep back for later occasion, hold over; keep *oneself* in reserve *for*. 2. Retain possession or control of, esp. by legal or formal stipulation; set apart, destine, *for* future use or fate; engage (seat, room, etc.) beforehand; (pass.) be left by fate *for*, fall *for* or only *to*. **resēr'ved** (-vd) adj. (esp.) Reticent, slow to reveal emotions or opinions, uncommunicative. **resēr'vedly** adv. **resēr've** n. 1. Something reserved for future use, extra stock or amount; *in* ~, unused but available. 2. (banking) That part of the assets held in the form of cash; (in central banks) that part of the assets held in the form of gold or foreign exchange. 3. (in joint-stock companies) That part of the profit which is not distributed to shareholders but added to capital; *hidden* ~, part of the profit concealed in the balance-sheet by the device of assessing the value of assets below its true level. 4. Troops withheld from action to reinforce or to cover retreat; forces not in regular service, liable to be called out in emergencies; (in games) extra player chosen in case substitute should be needed. 5. Tract of land reserved for some special purpose; = RESERVATION 3; *nature* ~, one where wild life is left undisturbed by man. 6. (at exhibitions etc.) Distinction conveying that exhibit will have prize if another is disqualified. 7. Limitation, exception, restriction, or qualification, attached to something; *without* ~, fully; (of auction sale) not subject to a fixed price's being reached; ~ *price*, stipulated price, less than which will not be accepted. 8. Self-restraint; avoidance of exaggerated or ill-proportioned effects in art etc.; reticence; want of cordiality or friendliness; intentional suppression of truth.

resēr'vist (-z-) n. Member of reserve forces.

rē'servoir (-zervwâr) n. Receptacle constructed of earthwork, masonry, etc., in which large quantity of water is stored; any natural or artificial receptacle esp. for or of fluid; place where fluid etc. collects; part of machine, organ of body, holding fluid; reserve supply or collection *of* knowledge, facts, etc. **rē'servoired** (-vwârd) adj. Stored in a reservoir.

resē't[1] v. (Sc.) Receive (stolen goods); receive stolen goods. **resē'tter** n. **resē't** n. Receiving of stolen goods.

resē't[2] v.t. Set again (gem, book or its type, etc.).

reshū'ffle v.t. Shuffle again; interchange (appointments, responsibilities, etc.) within a group. ~ n.

resī'de (-z-) v.i. Have one's home, dwell permanently; (of officials) be in residence; (of power, rights, etc.) rest or be vested *in* person etc.; (of qualities) be present or inherent *in*.

re'sidence (-z-) n. Residing; place where one resides, abode *of*; house esp. of considerable pretension, mansion; *in* ~, living or staying regularly at or in some place for the discharge of special duties, or to comply with some regulation.

rē'sidency (-z-) n. (hist.) Area in a protected State under authority of a resident governor; official residence of such a governor. **rĕ'sĭdent** (-z-) *adj.* Residing; (of birds etc.) staying all the year round, not migrating; staying at or in some place in fulfilment of duty or compliance with regulation. ~ *n.* 1. Permanent inhabitant (opp. *visitor*). 2. (hist.) Resident governor or political representative.

rĕsĭdĕ'ntial (-z-, -shal) *adj.* Suitable for or occupied by private houses; connected with residence; (of post) requiring holder to live at place of work.

rĕsĭdĕ'ntiarў (-z-, -sha-) *n.* Ecclesiastic bound to residence. ~ *adj.* Bound to, requiring, of or for, official residence.

rĕsĭ'dūal (-z-) *adj.* Remaining, left over, left as residuum; (of error etc.) left unexplained or uncorrected; (math.) resulting from subtraction. ~ *n.* Residual quantity; remainder; substance of the nature of a residuum.

rĕsĭ'dūarў (-z-) *adj.* Of the residue of an estate; of, being, a residuum, residual, still remaining.

rĕ'sĭdūe (-z-) *n.* Remainder, rest, what is left or remains over; what remains of estate after payment of charges, debts, and bequests; (chem. etc.) residuum.

rĕsĭ'dūum (-z-) *n.* What remains, esp. (chem. etc.) substance left after combustion or evaporation.

rĕsī'gn (-zīn) *v.* Relinquish, surrender, give up, hand over (office, right, property, charge, hope, etc.); reconcile *oneself*, one's *mind*, etc. (*to*); give up office, retire; (chess) discontinue play and admit defeat. **rĕsī'gned** (-zīnd) *adj.* Submissive, acquiescent, having resigned oneself to sorrow etc. **rĕsī'gnedlў** *adv.*

rĕsĭgnā'tion (-z-) *n.* (esp.) 1. Resigning of an office, document conveying this. 2. Being resigned, uncomplaining endurance of sorrow or other evil.

rĕsĭ'lience (-z-) *n.* Rebound, recoil; elasticity, power of resuming original shape or position after compression, bending, etc. **rĕsĭ'liencў** *n.* Resilience; buoyancy, power of recovery. **rĕsĭ'lient** *adj.* **rĕsĭ'lientlў** *adv.*

rĕ'sĭn (-z-) *n.* Adhesive, highly inflammable substance, hardening on exposure to air, formed by secretion in trees and plants and exuding naturally from many of them (as fir and pine) or obtained by incision, and used in making varnishes etc. and in pharmacy. ~, **rĕ'sĭnate** *vbs. t.* Rub or treat with resin. **rĕsĭnā'ceous** (-sh*u*s), **rĕsĭnĭ'ferous** *adjs.* Yielding, containing resin.

rĕ'sĭnous (-z-) *adj.* Of, containing, resin; produced by burning resin.

rĕsĭ'st (-z-) *v.* Stop course of, withstand action or effect of; strive against, oppose; offer resistance. **rĕsĭ'stant, rĕsĭ'stent, rĕsĭ'stĭble, rĕsĭ'stĭve** *adjs.* **rĕsĭstĭ'vĭtў** *n.* **rĕsĭ'st** *n.* Composition applied to surfaces for protection from some agent employed on them, esp. in textile printing to parts that are not to take dye.

rĕsĭ'stance (-z-) *n.* 1. Power of resisting; (also ~ *movement*), any (esp. underground) organization resisting authority, esp. that resisting German authority in occupied countries during the war of 1939–45; *passive* ~, resistance without resort to violence or active opposition; *non-co-operation*. 2. Hindrance, impeding or stopping effect, exercised by material thing upon another; (elect., magn., heat) non-conductivity; (elect.) measure of capacity in a conducting body to resist flow of a current (the resistance of a circuit is given by OHM's law as the ratio of the applied voltage (electromotive force) to the current which flows); part of apparatus used to offer definite resistance to current; *line of* ~, direction in which resistance acts; *line of least* ~, (fig.) easiest method or course.

rĕsĭ'stlĕss (-z-) *adj.* 1. That cannot be resisted. 2. Unresisting. **rĕsĭ'stlĕsslў** *adv.*

rĕsĭ'stor (-z-) *n.* Device used to introduce resistance into an electrical circuit.

rĕsŏ'lūble (-z-; or rĕ'-) *adj.* That can be resolved; analysable *into*.

rĕ'solūte (or -ōōt) *adj.* Determined, decided, bold, not vacillating, unshrinking, firm of purpose. **rĕ'solūtelў** *adv.*

rĕsolū'tion (-z-; or -lōō-) *n.* 1. Separation into components, decomposition, analysis; conversion *into* another form; (med.) disappearance of inflammation, return of diseased tissue to normal state; (pros.) substitution of two short syllables for one long; (mus.) process by which discord is made to pass into concord; (mech.) replacing of single force by two or more which are jointly equivalent; (optics) quality of optical instruments whereby definition of fine detail is obtained. 2. Solving of doubt, problem, question, etc. 3. Formal expression of opinion by legislative body or public meeting; form proposed for this. 4. Resolve, thing resolved on; determined temper or character, boldness and firmness of purpose.

rĕsŏ'lve (-z-) *v.* 1. Dissolve, disintegrate, analyse, break up into parts, dissipate, convert or be converted *into*; reduce by mental analysis *into*; (mus.) convert (discord), be converted, into concord. 2. Solve, explain, clear up, settle. 3. Decide upon, make up one's mind *upon* action or *to* do; form mentally or (of legislative body or public meeting) pass by vote the resolution *that*; (of circumstances etc.) bring (person) to resolution *to* do, *upon* action. **rĕsŏ'lved** (-vd) *adj.* (esp.) Resolute. **rĕsŏ'lve** *n.* Determination or resolution come to in the mind; (poet.) resolution, steadfastness.

rĕsŏ'lvent (-z-) *adj. & n.* (chiefly med. & chem.) (Drug, application, substance) effecting resolution of tumour etc. or division into component parts.

rĕ'sonant (-z-) *adj.* (of sound) Re-echoing, resounding; (of body) causing reinforcement or prolongation of sound, esp. by vibration; (of place) echoing, resounding, *with*. **rĕ'sonantlў** *adv.* **rĕ'sonance** *n.*

rĕ'sonāte (-z-) *v.i.* Produce or show resonance. **rĕ'sonātor** *n.* (esp.) Appliance for increasing sound by resonance.

rĕsōr'b *v.t.* Absorb again. **rĕsōr'bence** *n.* **rĕsōr'bent** *adj.*

rĕsōr'cĭnōl (-z-) *n.* Synthetic substance ($C_6H_4(OH)_2$), used in the production of various dyestuffs and drugs.

rĕsōr'ption *n.* Resorbing, being resorbed; (path.) disappearance of tissue by absorption into body fluids.

rĕsōr't (-z-) *v.i.* 1. Turn for aid *to*. 2. Go in numbers or often *to*. ~ *n.* 1. Thing to which recourse is had, what is turned to for aid, expedient; recourse; *in the last* ~, as a last expedient. 2. Frequenting, being frequented. 3. Place frequented, usu. for specified purpose or quality (as *health, holiday, seaside,* ~).

rĕsou'nd (-z-) *v.* 1. (of place) Ring or echo (*with*); (of voice, sound, etc.) produce echoes, go on sounding, fill place with sound; be much mentioned or repeated, be celebrated. 2. Repeat loudly (praises etc.); re-echo. **rĕsou'ndĭnglў** *adv.*

rĕsour'ce (-sōrs *or* -zōrs) *n.* 1. (usu. pl.) Means of supplying a want, stock that can be drawn on; (pl.) country's collective means for support and defence. 2. Expedient, device; means of relaxation or amusement; skill in devising expedients, ingenuity. **rĕsour'ceful** *adj.* **rĕsour'cefullў** *adv.* **rĕsour'cefulnĕss** *n.* **rĕsour'celĕss** *adj.* **rĕsour'celĕssnĕss** *n.*

rĕspĕ'ct *n.* 1. Reference, relation. 2. Heed or regard *to, of*, attention *to*; ~ *of persons*, partiality or favour shown esp. to the powerful. 3. Particular detail, point, aspect. 4. Deferential esteem felt or shown towards person or quality; state of being esteemed or honoured; (pl.) polite messages or attentions. ~ *v.t.* 1. Be directed, refer or relate, to. 2. Treat or regard with deference, esteem, or honour; treat with consideration, spare. 3. (her., of charges) Look at, face.

rĕspĕc'table *adj.* 1. Deserving

RESPECTFUL

respect. 2. Considerable in number, size, quantity, etc.; fairly good, tolerable. 3. Of good or fair social standing, worthy; befitting respectable persons. **rĕspĕctabĭ'lĭtў** n. **rĕspĕ'ctablў** adv.
rĕspĕ'ctful adj. Showing deferential esteem. **rĕspĕ'ctfullў** adv. **rĕspĕ'ctfulnĕss** n.
rĕspĕ'ctĭve adj. Pertaining to, connected with, each individual, group, etc., of those in question; separate, several, particular. **rĕspĕ'ctĭvelў** adv.
Rĕspĭ'ghĭ (-pēgĭ), Ottorino (1879–1936). Italian musical composer.
rĕ'spīrable adj. That can be breathed, fit for breathing.
rĕspīrā'tion n. Breathing; single inspiration and expiration; (biol.) process by which an organism utilizes oxygen from its environment and gives out carbon dioxide; *artificial* ~, any of various methods of restoring the natural function of breathing when this has been suspended; ~ *pump*, = RESPIRATOR, 2.
rĕ'spīrātor n. 1. Apparatus worn over mouth and nose to warm or filter inhaled air or prevent inhalation of poisonous gases etc., gas-mask. 2. Device for maintaining respiration artificially.
rĕspīr'e v. Inhale and exhale air; breathe; breathe again, take breath, recover hope or spirit, get rest or respite. **rĕ'spīrătorў** adj.
rĕ'spīte n. Delay permitted in the discharge of an obligation or suffering of a penalty; interval of rest or relief. ~ *v.t.* Grant respite to; postpone execution or exaction of (sentence, obligation).
rĕsplĕ'ndent adj. Brilliant, dazzlingly or gloriously bright. **rĕsplĕ'ndentlў** adv. **rĕsplĕ'ndence, rĕsplĕ'ndencў** ns.
rĕspŏ'nd v.i. Make answer; act in response (*to*). ~ *n.* 1. (eccles.) Responsory; response to versicle. 2. (archit.) Half-pillar or half-pier attached to wall to support arch, freq. as termination of arcade (ill. ARCADE).
rĕspŏ'ndent adj. Making answer; responsive *to*; in position of defendant. ~ *n.* One who answers, esp. one who defends thesis; defendant in divorce case.
rĕspŏ'nse n. Answer; (eccles.) responsory; any part of liturgy said or sung by congregation in answer to priest; (mus.) repetition by one part of a theme given by another part.
rĕspŏnsĭbĭ'lĭtў n. Being responsible; charge for which one is responsible.
rĕspŏ'nsĭble adj. Liable to be called to account, answerable; morally accountable for actions, capable of rational conduct; of good credit and repute, reliable, trustworthy; involving responsibility. **rĕspŏ'nsĭblў** adv.
rĕspŏ'nsĭons (-z) n.pl. (hist.) First examination (abolished 1960) (from which candidates were freq. exempted by other qualifications) for Oxford B.A. degree.
rĕspŏ'nsĭve adj. Answering; by way of answer; responding readily to or *to* some influence, impressionable, sympathetic; (of liturgy etc.) using responses. **rĕspŏ'nsĭvelў** adv. **rĕspŏ'nsĭvenĕss** n.
rĕspŏ'nsorў n. (eccles.) Anthem said or sung by soloist and choir after lesson.
rĕst¹ v. 1. Take repose by lying down, esp. in sleep; lie in death or the grave; cease, abstain or be relieved from exertion, action, movement, or employment; be at ease or in peace, stay, remain; give rest or repose to, lay to rest; allow to rest or remain inactive or quiescent; (theatr. slang) be temporarily unemployed. 2. Have place or position, place, set, lay, (*on*); (of eyes) be directed (*on*); lie or lean, lay, *on* for repose or support; rely, depend, be based, base, found, allow to depend *on*. 3. *resting-place*, place provided or used for resting; *last resting-place*, the grave. ~ *n.* 1. Repose or sleep, esp. in bed at night; intermission of, freedom from, labour, exertion, or activity; freedom from distress, trouble, etc.; quiet or tranquillity of mind; repose of the grave; *at* ~, tranquil, inert; settled; *set at* ~, satisfy, assure; settle; *day of* ~, sabbath; *lay to* ~, bury. 2. Place of resting or abiding; lodging-place or shelter provided for sailors, cabmen, or other class. 3. Prop, support; what something rests on. 4. (mus.) Interval of silence, pause, indicated by various signs according to duration, as *breve* ~ 𝄺, *semibreve* ~ 𝄻, *minim* ~ , or ~, *crotchet* ~ 𝄽 or 𝄾, *quaver* ~ 𝄾, *semiquaver* ~ 𝄿, etc.; pause in elocution, caesura in verse. 5. ~*-cure*, rest in bed as medical treatment; ~*-day*, day spent in rest; ~*-house*, dak-bungalow (in India); boarding-house or inn.
rĕst² v.i. Remain over (now rare); remain in specified state; ~ *with*, be left in the hands or charge of. ~ *n.* Remainder or remaining parts or individuals (*of*); (banking) reserve fund; (tennis etc.) rally, spell of sending ball etc. backwards and forwards without intermission; *for the* ~, as regards anything beyond what has been specially mentioned.
rĕst³ n. (hist.) Contrivance fixed to cuirass to receive butt-end of lance when couched for the charge.
rĕ'staurant (-orahṅ) n. Place where meals or refreshments may be had.
rĕstaurateur' (-orahtēr) n. Restaurant-keeper.
rĕ'stful adj. Favourable to repose, free from disturbing influences, soothing. **rĕ'stfullў** adv. **rĕ'stfulnĕss** n.

RESULTANT

rĕ'st-hărrow (-ō) n. Field-plant (*Ononis*) with tough roots.
rĕstĭtū'tion n. Restoring of or *of* thing to proper owner; reparation for injury; restoring of thing to its original state; resumption of original shape or position by elasticity; ~ *of conjugal rights*, resumption of cohabitation demanded in matrimonial suit.
rĕ'stĭve adj. (of horse) Refusing to go forward, obstinately moving backwards or sideways when being driven or ridden, intractable, resisting control; (of person) unmanageable, rejecting control, fidgety. **rĕ'stĭvelў** adv. **rĕ'stĭvenĕss** n.
rĕ'stlĕss adj. Finding or affording no rest; uneasy, agitated, unpausing, fidgeting. **rĕ'stlĕsslў** adv. **rĕ'stlĕssnĕss** n.
rĕstorā'tion n. (esp.) 1. *R*~, (period of) re-establishment of monarchy in England with return of Charles II in 1660. 2. Representation of original form of ruined building, extinct animal, etc.; action or process of restoring to original form or perfect condition.
rĕstŏ'rătĭve adj. Tending to restore health or strength. ~ *n.* Restorative food, medicine, or agency.
rĕstōr'e v.t. 1. Give back, make restitution of. 2. Repair, alter, (building, painting, etc.) so as to bring back as nearly as possible to original form, state, etc.; reproduce or represent in original form; reinstate, bring back to dignity or right; bring back *to* health, cure. 3. Re-establish, renew, bring back into use; replace or insert (words etc. in text, missing parts of thing etc.); replace, bring *to* former place or condition. **rĕstōr'er** n.
rĕstraī'n v.t. Check or hold in *from*, keep in check or under control or within bounds, repress, keep down; confine, imprison. **rĕstraī'nĕdlў** adv. With restraint.
rĕstraī'nt n. 1. Restraining, being restrained; check; controlling agency or influence; confinement; *without* ~, freely, copiously. 2. Constraint, reserve.
rĕstrĭ'ct v.t. Confine, bound, limit (*to, within*). **rĕstrĭ'ctĕdlў** adv. **rĕstrĭ'ction** n. **rĕstrĭ'ctĭve** adj. ~ *practices*, arrangements in industry and trade which restrict or control competition between firms; arrangements by groups of workers to control output or restrict the entry of new workers. **rĕstrĭ'ctĭvelў** adv.
rĕsŭ'lt (-z-) v.i. Arise as consequence, effect, or conclusion *from*; end *in* specified way. ~ *n.* Consequence, issue, outcome; quantity, formula, etc., obtained by calculation.
rĕsŭ'ltant (-z-) adj. Resulting. ~ *n.* Product, outcome; force which is equivalent of two or more

forces acting from different directions at one point; composite or final effect of any two or more forces. **rĕsū′me** (-z-) *v.* 1. Get or take again or back; recover; reoccupy. 2. Begin again; go on (with) after interruption; recommence. 3. Make résumé of.
résumé (rā′zūmā) *n.* Summary, epitome, abstract.
rĕsū′mption (-z-) *n.* Resuming.
rĕsū′mptive *adj.* **rĕsŭ′mptivelў** *adv.*
rĕsū′pinate *adj.* (bot., of leaf etc.) Inverted, upside-down.
rĕsūr′gent *adj.* That rises or tends to rise again. **rĕsūr′gence** *n.*
rĕsurrĕ′ct (-z-) *v.t.* (colloq.) Raise from the dead (rare); revive practice or memory of; take from grave, exhume.
rĕsurrĕ′ction (-z-) *n.* 1. R~, rising of Christ from the grave; rising again of men at the last day. 2. Revival from disuse, inactivity, or decay; restoration to vogue or memory. 3. ~-man, body-snatcher. **rĕsurrĕ′ctional** *adj.* **rĕsurrĕ′ctionist** *n.* (esp.) Body-snatcher.
rĕsū′scitāte *v.* Revive, return or restore to life, consciousness, vogue, vigour, etc. **rĕsŭscitā′tion, rĕsū′scitātor** *ns.* **rĕsū′scitative** *adj.*
Reszke (rĕ′skĕ), Jean de (1850–1925). Polish tenor singer.
rĕt *v.t.* Soften (flax, hemp) by soaking in water or exposing to moisture.
rĕtā′ble (*or* rĕ′tabl) *n.* Frame enclosing decorated panels on or above back of altar, altarpiece (ill. ALTAR); shelf above back of altar.
rē′tail *n.* Sale of goods in small quantities (freq. attrib. and in adverbial expressions; opp. WHOLESALE). **rētai′l** (*or* rē′-) *v.* 1. Sell (goods) by retail; (of goods) be retailed. 2. Recount, relate details of. **rētai′ler** (*or* rē′-) *n.*
rētai′n *v.t.* 1. Keep in place, hold fixed; *retaining wall*, one supporting and confining mass of earth or water. 2. Secure services of (esp. barrister) by engagement and preliminary payment; *retaining-fee*, = RETAINER, 1. 3. Keep possession of, continue to have; continue to practise or recognize, allow to remain or prevail, keep unchanged; bear in mind, remember.
rētai′ner *n.* 1. Retaining, being retained; fee paid to barrister to secure his services; sum paid to secure special services; (U.S.) authorization to lawyer to act in case. 2. One who retains. 3. (hist.) Dependant or follower of person of rank or position; (joc.) servant.
rētā′liāte *v.* Repay (esp. injury, insult, etc.) in kind; retort (accusation) *upon* person; make return or requital (esp. of injury). **rētāliā′tion** *n.* **rētā′liative, rētā′liatorў** *adjs.*

rĕtār′d *v.* Make slow or late, delay progress, arrival, accomplishment, or happening of; (esp. of physical phenomena, e.g. motion of tides, or celestial bodies) happen, arrive, behind normal or calculated time. **rĕtār′dĕd** *adj.* (esp., of child) With mental or physical development behind what is normal at his age. **rĕtārdā′tion** *n.* **rĕtār′dative, rĕtār′datorў** *adjs.* **rĕtār′d** *n.* Retardation; *in* ~, delayed; ~ *of tide* or *high water*, interval between full moon and following high water.
rĕtār′der *n.* Substance used to delay chemical action.
rĕtch *v.i.* Make motion of vomiting, esp. ineffectually and involuntarily. ~ *n.* Retching motion or sound.
rĕtĕ′ntion *n.* Retaining; esp. (med.) retaining in body of secretion (esp. urine) usually evacuated.
rĕtĕ′ntive *adj.* 1. (of memory) Tenacious, not forgetful. 2. Tending, inclined, apt, to retain. 3. (surg. etc.) Serving to keep dressing etc. in place. **rĕtĕ′ntivelў** *adv.* **rĕtĕ′ntiveness** *n.*
rĕtiā′rius *n.* (Rom. antiq.) Gladiator using net to entrap his opponent. [L.]
rē′ticence *n.* Reserve in speech, avoidance of saying too much or of speaking freely. **rē′ticent** *adj.* **rē′ticentlў** *adv.*
rē′ticle *n.* Network of fine threads or lines in object-glass of optical instrument to help accurate observation.
rētĭ′cūlar *adj.* Net-like.
rētĭ′cūlāte *v.* Divide, be divided or marked, into a network; arrange, be arranged, in small squares or with intersecting lines. **rētĭ′cūlāte** *adj.* **rētĭ′cūlātelў** *adv.* **rētĭcūlā′tion** *n.*
rē′ticūle *n.* 1. Reticle. 2. (archaic) Lady's bag of woven or other material carried or worn to serve purpose of pocket.
rētĭ′cūlum *n.* (pl. *-la*). 1. Second stomach of ruminant (ill. RUMINANT). 2. Net-like structure, reticulated membrane, etc.
rē′tiform *adj.* Net-like, reticulated.
rĕ′tĭna *n.* (pl. *-as, -ae*). Innermost layer or coating, sensitive to light, at back of eyeball, in which optic nerve terminates (ill. EYE).
rĕ′tĭnal *adj.*
rĕ′tĭnūe *n.* Suite or train of persons in attendance upon someone.
rētīr′e *v.* 1. Withdraw, go away, seek seclusion or shelter; withdraw to usual place or occupation, *to* bed, etc.; retreat, move back or away, recede; vanish *from* sight. 2. Cease *from* or give up office or profession or employment or business, esp. after having made a competence or earned a pension; compel (officer, employee) to retire; give up candidature; (cricket) voluntarily terminate one's innings. 3. (mil.) Lead back

(troops etc.), move back. 4. (finance) Withdraw (bill, note) from operation or currency. **rētīr′ed** (-īrd) *adj.* (esp.) 1. Withdrawn from society or observation; secluded. 2. ~ *list*, list of retired officers. **rētīr′ing** *adj.* (esp.) Shy; fond of seclusion. **rētīr′e** *n.* Signal to troops to retire.
rētīr′ement (-īrm-) *n.* (esp.) Seclusion; secluded place; condition of having retired from work.
rētōr′t[1] *v.* 1. Repay (esp. injury) in kind; cast back *on* offending party, use (argument etc.) *against* its author. 2. Make, say by way of, repartee, counter-charge, or counter-argument. ~ *n.* Incisive reply, repartee; turning of argument or charge against its author; piece of retaliation.
rētōr′t[2] *n.* Vessel usu. of glass with long downward-bent neck

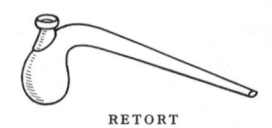

RETORT

used in distilling liquids; vessel for purifying mercury by distillation; clay or iron cylinder in which coal is heated to produce gas; furnace in which iron is heated with carbon to produce steel. ~ *v.t.* Purify (mercury) by distilling from retort.
rētōr′tĕd *adj.* Recurved, bent or twisted backwards.
rētōr′tion *n.* 1. Bending back. 2. Retaliation, esp. by one State on subject of another.
rētou′ch (-tŭch) *v.t.* Amend or improve by fresh touches, touch up (esp. photographic negative or print).
rētrā′ce *v.t.* Trace back to source or beginning; look over again; trace again in memory; go back over (one's steps, way, etc.).
rētră′ct *v.* 1. Draw (esp. part of one's body or of machine) back or in; (of such part etc.) shrink back or in, be capable of being retracted; (phonet.) pronounce with tongue retracted. 2. Withdraw, revoke, cancel; acknowledge falsity or error of; disavow; retract opinion or statement. **rētră′ctable, rētră′ctile** *adjs.* **rētrăctā′tion, rētră′ction** *ns.*
rētreā′d (-ĕd) *v.t.* Furnish (tyre) with fresh tread. **rē′tread** *n.* Tyre renovated thus.
rētreā′t *v.* Go back, retire, relinquish a position (esp. of army etc.); recede; (chiefly in chess) move (piece) back from forward or threatened position. ~ *n.* 1. Act of, (mil.) signal for, retreating; (mil.) bugle-call at sunset; *beat a* ~, retreat, abandon undertaking. 2. Withdrawing into privacy or security; (place of) seclusion; place of shelter; (eccles.) temporary retirement for religious exercises.

[747]

rětrē'nch v. 1. Reduce amount of (esp. expenses etc.); economize; cut off, remove, cut out. 2. (fort.) Furnish with inner line of defence, usu. consisting of trench and parapet. **rětrē'nchment** n.
rětri'al n. Retrying of a case in a court of law.
rětrĭbū'tion n. Recompense, usu. for evil, vengeance, requital. **rětri'būtive** adj. **rětri'būtivelỹ** adv.
rětrie've v. 1. (of dogs) Find and bring in (killed or wounded game). 2. Recover by investigation or effort of memory, restore to knowledge or recall to mind; regain possession of. 3. Rescue from bad state etc.; restore to flourishing state, revive (esp. fortunes etc.); repair, set right (loss, disaster, error). ~ n. Possibility of recovery.
rětrie'ver n. Dog of breed specially adapted for retrieving game (ill. DOG).
retro- prefix. Backwards, back.
rětroā'ct v.i. React; operate in backward direction; have retrospective effect. **rětroā'ction** n. **rětroā'ctive** adj. **rětroā'ctivelỹ** adv.
rē'trocēde[1] v.i. 1. Move back, recede. 2. (of gout) Strike inward. **rětrocē'dent** adj.
rē'trocēde[2] v.t. Cede (territory) back again.
rětrocē'ssion n. Act of retroceding (see RETROCEDE[1,2]). **rětrocē'ssive** adj.
rē'trochoir (-kwīr) n. Part of cathedral or large church behind high altar (ill. CHURCH).
rē'troflěx adj. Turned backwards.
rětrogradā'tion n. 1. (astron.) Apparent backward motion of planet in zodiac; motion of heavenly body from east to west; backward movement of lunar nodes on ecliptic. 2. Retrogression.
rē'trogrāde adj. 1. (astron.) In or showing retrogradation. 2. Directed backwards, retreating; reverting, esp. to inferior state, declining; inverse, reversed. **rē'trogrādelỹ** adv. **rē'trogrāde** v.i. Show retrogradation, move backwards, recede, retire, decline, revert.
rětrogrě'ss v.i. Go back, move backwards, deteriorate. **rětrogrě'ssive** adj. **rětrogrě'ssivelỹ** adv.
rětrogrě'ssion n. Backward or reversed movement; return to less advanced state, decline, deterioration; (astron.) retrogradation.
rē'tro-rŏckĕt n. Auxiliary rocket producing thrust in opposite direction or at oblique angle to course of spacecraft etc., used for decelerating etc.
rē'trospěct n. Regard or reference to precedent, authority, or previous conditions; view or survey of past time or events.

rětrospĕ'ction n. Action of looking back, esp. into the past, indulgence or engagement in retrospect. **rětrospĕ'ctive** adj. Of, in, proceeding by, retrospection; (of statutes etc.) operative with regard to past time, not restricted to the future, retroactive. **rětrospĕ'ctivelỹ** adv.
retroussé (-ōō'sā) adj. (of nose) Turned up at tip.
rē'trovĕrtĕd adj. Turned backwards (esp. path., of uterus).
rětūr'n v. 1. Come or go back; revert. 2. Bring, convey, give, send, put, or pay, back or in return or requital; (in games) respond to (play of one's partner or opponent, esp. partner's lead); give, render (thanks). 3. (archit.) Continue (moulding etc.) round angle of structure. 4. Say in reply, retort. 5. Report in answer to official demand for information, state by way of report or verdict; (of sheriff) report as having been appointed to serve on jury or sit in Parliament; (of constituency) elect as member of Parliament; returning officer, official responsible for conducting parliamentary election and announcing name of person elected. ~ n. 1. Coming back; coming round again; return ticket; (many) happy ~s (of the day), birthday or festival greeting; ~ ticket, ticket for journey to place and back again to point of departure. 2. Side or part receding, usu. at right angles, from front or direct line of any work or structure. 3. (Coming in of) proceeds or profit of undertaking. 4. Giving, sending, putting, or paying back; thing so given, sent, etc., esp. report of sheriff etc. in answer to writ or official demand for information; (returning officer's announcement of) candidate's election as member of Parliament; (also ~ match) match between same sides as before.
rětū'se adj. (of leaf, part of insect, etc.) Having a broad or rounded end ended with depression in centre.
Retz: see RAIS.
Reu'ben (rōō-). Hebrew patriarch, eldest son of Jacob and Leah (Gen. 29: 32); tribe of Israel traditionally descended from him.
rēū'nion (-yon) n. Reuniting, being reunited; social gathering, esp. of intimates or persons with common interests.
rēūnī'te v. Bring or come together again, join after separation.
Reu'ter (roi-), Paul Julius, Baron von (1816–99), German-born British founder of a telegraphic news agency (Reuters), now owned and directed by various newspaper associations of Gt Britain and the Commonwealth.
rěv n. (mech.) Revolution. ~ v. Cause (internal combustion engine) to run quickly, esp. before bringing it into use, speed up;

(of engine) revolve, be speeded up.
Rev. abbrev. Revelation (N.T.); Reverend.
rěvălorīzā'tion n. Action or process of establishing fresh value for something, esp. a currency. **rěvă'lorīze** v.t.
Revd. abbrev. Reverend.
rěvea'l[1] v.t. Disclose, make known, in supernatural manner (esp. of God); disclose, divulge, make known; display, show, let appear.
rěvea'l[2] n. Internal side surface of opening or recess, esp. of doorway or window-aperture (ill. WINDOW).
rěvei'llĕ (-vălĭ or -vĕlĭ) n. Military waking-signal sounded in morning on bugle or drums. [Fr. réveillez, imper. pl. of réveiller awaken, f. L vigilare keep watch]
rě'vel v.i. Make merry, be riotously festive, feast; take keen delight in. **rě'veller** n. **rě'vel** n. Revelling; (occasion of indulgence in) merry-making (freq. pl.). **rě'velrỹ** n.
rěvelā'tion n. 1. Disclosing of knowledge, knowledge disclosed, to man by divine or supernatural agency; R~ (of St. John the Divine), (pop. Revelations), last book of N.T., the Apocalypse. 2. Striking disclosure; revealing of some fact.
rěvelā'tionist n. 1. R~, author of the Apocalypse. 2. One who believes in divine revelation.
rě'venant (or revenahṅ) n. One who returns, esp. after long absence or from the dead; ghost.
rěvĕ'nge (-j) v. Avenge oneself (on a person); inflict punishment, exact retribution, for (injury, harm, etc.); avenge (person). ~ n. Revenging, act done in revenging; desire to revenge, vindictive feeling; (in games) opportunity given for reversing former result by return game. **rěvĕ'ngeful** adj. **rěvĕ'ngefullỹ** adv. **rěvĕ'ngefulněss** n.
rě'věnūe n. Income, esp. of large amount, from any source; (pl.) collective items or amounts constituting this; (sing.) annual income of Government or State, from which public expenses are met; department of civil service collecting this; inland ~: see INLAND; ~ cutter, officer, etc., one employed to prevent smuggling.
rěvěr'berāte v. Return, reflect, re-echo (sound, light, etc.); be reflected or re-echoed; (of flame, heat, etc.) be forced back into, over, upon (furnace, substance, etc.); subject to action of reverberatory furnace. **rěvěrberā'tion** n. **rěvěr'berant, rěvěr'berative** adjs.
rěvěr'berātor n. Reflector, reflecting lamp.
rěvěr'beratorỹ adj. Reverberating; ~ furnace, furnace with a shallow hearth and low arched roof from which the heat contained in the products of combustion is reverberated.

revēr′e¹ v.t. Regard as sacred or exalted, hold in deep and usu. affectionate or religious respect, venerate.

Revēr′e², Paul (1735–1818). American patriot, famous for his midnight ride from Charlestown to Lexington (1775) to give warning that British troops were advancing from Boston.

rĕ′verence n. Revering; capacity for this; gesture indicating respect, bow or curtsy (archaic); being respected or venerated; your, his, ~, (archaic, joc., or vulg., esp. in Ireland) titles used to, of, clergyman. reverĕ′ntial (-shal) adj. reverĕ′ntially adv. rĕ′verence v.t. Regard with reverence, venerate.

rĕ′verend adj. Deserving reverence by age, character, or associations; esp. as respectful epithet applied to members of the clergy, freq. (abbrev. Rev. or Revd.) prefixed to name and designation of clergyman; of, connected with, the clergy; Very R~, (in C. of E.) title of dean, Right R~ of bishop, Most R~ of archbishop; R~ Mother, title or form of address to mother superior of convent.

rĕ′verent adj. Feeling or showing reverence. rĕv′erently adv.

rĕ′verie n. (Fit of) musing daydream(ing); (mus.) instrumental composition suggesting dreamy or musing state.

revēr′s (-ēr) n. Turned back edge of coat etc. displaying under surface; material covering this edge.

revēr′se adj. Opposite or contrary (to) in character or order, back or backwards, upside-down; ~ gear, one permitting vehicle to be driven backwards. revēr′sely adv. revēr′se n. 1. Contrary (of); in ~, with the position reversed, the other way round; (of vehicle) in reverse gear, moving backwards. 2. (Device on) side of coin, medal, etc., which does not bear main device or inscription; verso (of leaf in book etc.); back. 3. Piece of misfortune, disaster, esp. defeat in battle. ~ v. Turn the other way round or up, or inside-out; invert; transpose; convert to opposite character or effect; cause (engine etc.) to work in contrary direction; revoke, annul (decree, act, etc.); drive (vehicle) backwards; (dancing, esp. in waltz) move or turn in opposite direction. revēr′sal n. revēr′sible adj.

revēr′sĭ (or -ē) n. 1. (obs.) Card-game in which object was to avoid winning tricks. 2. Game played on draught-board with counters coloured differently above and below.

revēr′sion n. 1. (Return to grantor or his heirs, right of ultimate succession to) estate granted till specified date or event, esp. death of original grantee; sum payable on person's death, esp. by way of life insurance; thing to which one has a right or expects to succeed when relinquished by another. 2. Return to a previous state, habit, etc., esp. (biol.) to ancestral type. revēr′sional adj. revēr′sionally adv. revēr′sionary adj.

revēr′sioner n. One who has the reversion of an estate, office, etc.

revēr′t v. 1. (of property, office, etc.) Fall in by reversion. 2. Return to former condition, primitive state, etc.; fall back into wild state. 3. Recur to subject in talk or thought. revēr′tible adj. (of property) Subject to reversion.

revē′t v.t. Face (rampart, wall, etc.) with masonry etc., esp. in fortification. revē′tment n. Retaining-wall or facing (ill. CASTLE).

review′ (-vū) n. 1. Revision, esp. legal. 2. Display and formal inspection of troops, fleet, etc.; pass in ~, (fig.) examine, be examined. 3. General survey or reconsideration of subject or thing. 4. Published account or criticism of literary work, play, cinema film, etc. (esp. a new or recent one). 5. Periodical publication with articles on current events, new books, art, etc. 6. Second view. ~ v. View again; subject to esp. legal revision; survey, glance over, look back on; hold review of (troops etc.); write review of (book etc.), write reviews. review′er n. (esp.) Writer of review(s).

revī′le v. Call by derogatory names, abuse; talk abusively. revī′ler n. revī′ling adj. revī′lingly adv.

revī′se (-z) v.t. Read carefully over, examine, go over again, in order to correct, improve, or amend (literary matter, printer's proofs, law, etc.); Revised Version, (abbrev. R.V.) revision (1870–84) of Authorized or 1611 Version of Bible. revī′sal, revī′sion ns. revī′sionism n. Departure from authoritative (esp. Marxist) doctrine. revī′sionist n. revī′sional, revī′sory adjs. revī′se n. (print.) Proof-sheet embodying corrections made in earlier proof.

revī′val n. 1. Bringing or coming back into vogue, use, etc.; restoring of old play etc. to stage etc.; ~ of learning, letters, the Renaissance in its literary aspect. 2. Reawakening of religious fervour; campaign with meetings etc. to promote this. 3. Restoration to bodily or mental vigour or to life of consciousness.

revī′valism n. State or kind of religion characterized by revivals. revī′valist n.

revī′ve v. Come or bring back to life, consciousness, existence, vigour, notice, activity, validity, or vogue; (chem.) convert or restore (metal, esp. mercury) to natural form. revī′ver n. (esp., slang) Stimulating drink.

revī′vify v.t. Restore to animation, activity, vigour, or life. revivifĭcā′tion n.

revī′vor n. (law) Proceeding for revival of suit after death of party etc.

revō′ke v. 1. Repeal, annul, withdraw, rescind, cancel (decree, consent, promise, permission). 2. (whist etc.) Make a revoke. ~ n. Card-player's failure to follow suit when he holds a card of that suit. rĕ′vocable, rĕ′vocătory adjs. rĕvocā′tion n.

revōlt′ v. 1. Cast off allegiance; make rising or rebellion; fall away from or rise against ruler; go over to rival power. 2. Feel revulsion or disgust at, rise in repugnance against, turn in loathing from; affect with strong disgust, nauseate. revō′lting adj. revō′ltingly adv. revōlt′ n. 1. Act of revolting, state of having revolted; rising, insurrection. 2. Sense of loathing; rebellious or protesting mood.

rĕ′volŭte (or -ōōt) adj. (bot.) Rolled backwards, downwards, or outwards.

revolū′tion (or -lōō-) n. 1. Revolving; motion in orbit or circular course, or round axis or centre; rotation; single completion of orbit or rotation, time it takes. 2. Complete change, turning upside-down, great reversal of conditions, fundamental reconstruction; esp. forcible substitution by subjects of new ruler or polity for the old; (Engl. hist.) expulsion (1688) of Stuart dynasty under James II and transfer of sovereignty to William and Mary; (Amer. hist.) overthrow of British supremacy by War of Independence, 1775–81; (Fr. hist.) = FRENCH Revolution; (Russ. hist.) series of revolutionary movements in Russia in 1917, beginning with a revolt of workers, peasants, and soldiers in March (February Old Style, hence February ~) and formation of a provisional government, and culminating in the Bolshevik ~ in November (October Old Style, hence October ~), which led to the establishment of the U.S.S.R. revolū′tionize v.t.

revolū′tionary (or -lōō-) adj. Of revolution; involving great and usu. violent changes. ~ n. One who instigates or favours political revolution; one who takes part in a revolution.

revolū′tionist (or -lōō-) n. Revolutionary.

revŏlve′ v. Turn round or round and round; rotate; go in circular orbit; roll along.

revŏl′ver n. (esp.) Pistol with mechanism by which set of cartridge-chambers is revolved and presented in succession before hammer, so that several shots may be fired without reloading (ill. PISTOL).

revū′e n. Theatrical entertainment purporting to give a review (often satirical) of current fashions, events, etc.; (freq.) entertainment consisting of numerous unrelated scenes or episodes.

[749]

rĕvŭ'lsion n. 1. Sudden violent change of feeling, sudden reaction in taste, fortune, etc. 2. (rare) Drawing or being drawn away. 3. (med.) Counter-irritation, treatment of one disordered organ etc. by acting upon another.
rĕvŭ'lsive adj. (chiefly med.) Of, producing, revulsion. ~ n. Counter-irritant application.
rėwar'd (-ôrd) n. Return or recompense for service or merit, requital for good or evil; sum offered for detection of criminal, restoration of lost property, etc. ~ v.t. Repay, requite, recompense.
Rĕx n. (abbrev. R.) Reigning king (cf. REGINA).
rĕ'xine (-ēn) n. Kind of artificial leather used in upholstery etc. [trade-name]
Rey'kjavík (rākya-). Capital city of Iceland.
Rey'nard (rĕn- or rān-). (Name for) fox, esp. as hero of cycle of medieval folk-stories.
Rey'nolds (rĕn-, -z), Sir Joshua, (1723–92). English portrait-painter; first president of Royal Academy, where he delivered his 'Discourses'.
r.f. abbrev. Radio FREQUENCY; rangefinder.
R.F. abbrev. Radio FREQUENCY; Royal Fusiliers.
R.F.C. abbrev. Reconstruction Finance Corporation (U.S.); Rugby Football Club.
R.G.S. abbrev. Royal Geographical Society.
Rh abbrev. Rhesus (factor).
R.H. abbrev. Royal Highlanders; Royal Highness.
R.H.A. abbrev. Royal Hibernian Academy; Royal Horse Artillery.
rhă'bdomăncў (ră-) n. Divination by means of a rod, as in water-divining.
Rhădamă'nthus (ră-). (Gk myth.) Son of Zeus and Europa, and one of the judges in the lower world; hence, stern and incorruptible judge.
Rhae'tia (rēsh-). (Rom. hist.) District and Roman province in the Alps. **Rhae'tian** adj. ~ Alps, chain in central part of Alpine mountain system, in E. Switzerland.
Rhae'tic (rē-) adj. (geol.) Of the topmost division of the Triassic in Europe. ~ n. Rhaeto-Romanic.
Rhaeto-Romă'nic (rē-) adj. & n. (Of) a group of Romance dialects spoken in some parts of the Alps, esp. SE. Switzerland and N. Italy; Ladin.
rhă'psōde (ră-) n. Ancient Greek reciter of epic, esp. Homeric, poems.
rhă'psodў (ră-) n. 1. (Gk antiq.) Epic poem or part of one suitable for recitation at one time. 2. Enthusiastic extravagant high-flown utterance or composition; emotional musical composition of indefinite form. **rhăpsŏ'dic, -ical** adjs. **rhăpsŏ'dically** adv. **rhă'p-sodīze** v. Recite as rhapsode; talk or write rhapsodies (about, on, etc.). **rhă'psodist** n.
rhea[1] (rē'a) n. S. Amer. three-toed ostrich-like bird of genus R~.
Rhea[2] (rē'a). (Gk myth.) One of the Titans, wife of Cronus and mother of Zeus, Demeter, Poseidon, and Hades.
Rheims (rēmz). (Fr. Reims) Ancient cathedral city of N. France, centre of champagne trade.
Rhē'mish (rē-) adj. Of Rheims; ~ Testament, New Testament of DOUAI-Rheims Bible.
Rhē'nish (rē- or rĕ-) adj. Of the Rhine or neighbouring regions.
rhē'nium (rē-) n. (chem.) Rare, very hard, very heavy metallic element resembling manganese in properties, found in ores of tantalum and platinum; symbol Re, at. no. 75, at. wt 186·2. [L Rhenus Rhine]
rhĕŏ'logў (rē-) n. Science dealing with the flow and deformation of matter.
rhĕ'ostăt (rē-) n. Device for varying the resistance to an electric current.
rhē'sus (rē-) n. Small catarrhine monkey (Macaca mulatta) common in N. India; ~ factor, (abbrev. Rh) inheritable antigen usu. present in human red blood cells (so called because first observed in rhesus monkeys), capable of causing a serious reaction (e.g. if Rh-positive blood cells enter the circulation of Rh-negative individuals from an Rh-positive foetus during pregnancy, antibodies may develop and subsequent Rh-positive offspring may suffer from a form of haemolytic anaemia; if they enter the circulation of Rh-negative individuals by transfusion, antibodies may develop with possibly serious consequences); ~-positive, -negative, having, without, rhesus factor. [arbitrary use of Gk Rhēsos, mythical king of Thrace]
rhē'tor (rē-) n. Ancient Greek or Roman teacher or professor of rhetoric.
rhē'toric (rĕ-) n. (Treatise on) the art of persuasive or impressive speaking or writing; language designed to persuade or impress (freq. with implication of insincerity, exaggeration, etc.).
rhĕtŏ'rical (rĭ-) adj. Expressed with a view to persuasive or impressive effect; artificial or extravagant in language; of the nature of rhetoric; of the art of rhetoric; given to rhetoric, oratorical; ~ question, question asked not for information but to produce effect. **rhĕtŏ'rically** adv.
rhĕtori'cian (rĕ-, -shan) n. Rhetor; rhetorical speaker or writer.
rheum (rōōm) n. (archaic) Watery secretion or discharge of mucous membrane etc.; catarrh; (pl.) rheumatic pains.

rheumă'tic (rōōm-) adj. Of, suffering from, rheumatism; subject to, producing, produced by, this; ~ fever, acute non-infectious febrile disease with inflammation and pain of joints. ~ n. Rheumatic patient; (pl., colloq.) rheumatism. **rheumă'tically** adv. **rheumă'tickў** adj.
rheu'matism (rōōm-) n. Pain in joints and soft tissues of the locomotor system, esp. in collagen; (pop.) rheumatoid arthritis.
rheu'matoid (rōōm-) adj. Having the character of rheumatism; ~ arthritis, chronic progressive general disease of uncertain origin, leading to inflammatory changes in the tissues, esp. joints.
rheu'mў (rōōmĭ) adj. (archaic) Consisting of, flowing with, rheum; (of air) damp, raw.
R.H.G. abbrev. Royal Horse Guards.
rhī'nal (rī-) adj. (anat. etc.) Of nostril or nose.
Rhine (rī-). (Ger. Rhein) Great European river, rising in Switzerland and flowing northwards through W. Germany and Holland to North Sea; ~ wine, wine produced in valley of Rhine, usu. white, light, and dry. **Rhī'nelănd**, Valley of the Rhine; ~-Palatinate, State of the Federal Republic of Germany; capital, Mainz.
rhī'nestone (rīns-) n. 1. Kind of rock-crystal. 2. Artificial gem of colourless paste cut like diamond. [f. RHINE]
rhī'nō[1] (rī-) n. (slang) Money.
rhī'nō[2] (rī-) n. (pl. -os). (slang) Rhinoceros.
rhinŏ'ceros (rī-) n. Large mammal of Africa and S. Asia, usu. with a horn on nose (or, in some species, two) and very thick freq. folded skin. **rhinŏcerŏ'tic** adj.
rhinŏ'logў (rī-) n. Branch of medicine dealing with diseases of the nose.
rhinoplă'stic (rī-) adj. Of plastic surgery of the nose.
rhī'noscōpe (rī-) n. Instrument for inspecting nasal cavity. **rhinŏ'-scopў** n. Examination of nasal cavity with rhinoscope.
rhī'zoid (rī-) adj. (bot.) Resembling a root. ~ n. Root-hair or filament (ill. LIVERWORT).
rhī'zōme (rī-) n. Prostrate or

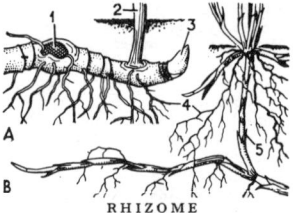

RHIZOME
A. SOLOMON'S SEAL.
B. COUCH-GRASS

1. Last year's scar. 2. Present year's shoot. 3. Next year's bud. 4. Adventitious roots. 5. Scale leaf

subterranean root-like stem emitting roots from the lower side and sending up leafy shoots from the upper surface.
rhō (rō) *n.* 20th (later 17th) letter of Greek alphabet (*P*, *ρ*), corresponding to *r*.
Rhōde I′sland (rōd īl-). Atlantic State of north-eastern U.S., one of the original thirteen States of the Union (1790); capital, Providence; ~ *Red*, (one of) an Amer. breed of domestic fowls with brownish-red plumage.
Rhodes[1] (rōdz). (Gk *Rhodos*) Most easterly island of Aegean Sea, largest of the Dodecanese, acquired by Italy 1912 and restored to Greece 1946; its principal city and harbour; *Knights of* ~, Knights HOSPITALLERS.
Rhodes[2] (rōdz), Cecil John (1853–1902). English imperialist, largely instrumental in extending British territory in S. Africa and in development of Rhodesia; ~ *scholarship*, one of the scholarships endowed at Oxford University under will of Cecil Rhodes, and awarded annually to students from countries of the Commonwealth, the U.S., South Africa, and West Germany; hence ~ *scholar*.
Rhōdē′sia (rō-, -zha *or* -zia *or* -sha). Territory of Central Africa, colonized chiefly by British settlers, lying S. of Zambesi River, bordered by Zambia, Botswana, the Transvaal, and Mozambique; declared independence from Gt Britain in 1965; republic established 1970; capital, Salisbury. **Rhōdē′sian** *adj.* & *n.* [named after Cecil RHODES[2]]
Rhō′dian (rō-) *adj.* & *n.* (Native, inhabitant) of Rhodes.
rhō′dium (rō-) *n.* (chem.) Hard white metallic element of the platinum group, used as a protective coating for silver articles, and in some special alloys for scientific purposes; symbol Rh, at. no. 45, at. wt 102·9055. [Gk *rhodon* rose, from the colour of some of its salts]
rhōdodē′ndron (rō-) *n.* Evergreen shrub or low tree with large flowers of genus *R*~ which includes azaleas. [Gk *rhodon* rose, *dendron* tree]
rhŏmb (rŏm) *n.* = RHOMBUS (ill. QUADRILATERAL); lozenge- or diamond-shaped object, marking, formation, etc.; (cryst.) rhombohedron. **rhŏ′mbic** *adj.*
rhŏmbohē′dron (rō-) *n.* (Crystal in shape of) solid bounded by six equal rhombs. **rhŏmbohē′dral** *adj.*
rhŏ′mboid (rō-) *adj.* Of or near the shape of a rhomb; ~ *muscle*, either of two muscles connecting spinous process of last cervical and first dorsal vertebrae with scapula. ~ *n.* 1. Quadrilateral figure having its opposite sides and angles equal (ill. QUADRILATERAL). 2. Rhomboid muscle. **rhŏmboi′dal** *adj.* Rhomboid; having

shape of a rhomboid. **rhŏmboi′dallў** *adv.*
rhŏ′mbus (rŏ-) *n.* 1. Plane equilateral figure with opposite angles equal, two being acute and two obtuse (ill. QUADRILATERAL). 2. Flatfish of genus *R*~ comprising turbot and brill.
Rhŏ′ndda (rŏ-). District in Mid Glamorgan on River Rhondda, esp. coal-mining area in lower part of valley.
Rhône (rōn). Great river rising in Switzerland and flowing eastward through Lake of Geneva into France and southward to Mediterranean.
R.H.S. *abbrev.* Royal Horticultural Society; Royal Humane Society.
rhu′bȧrb (rōō-) *n.* 1. (Purgative made from) root of Chinese and Tibetan species of the herb *Rheum*, orig. imported into Europe through Russia and the Levant, now usu. called *Turkey*, *East Indian*, *or Chinese* ~. 2. Plant of the genus *Rheum*, esp. (*garden* ~) any species having heart-shaped smooth deep-green leaves, growing on thick fleshy stalks which are cooked and eaten as fruit. [L *rhabarbarum* foreign rha or rhubarb (*rha* Gk perh. f. ancient name *Rha* of River Volga)]
rhŭmb (rŭm) *n.* Any one of the 32 points of the compass; angular distance (11° 15′) between two successive points of the compass; (also ~ *line*) line on the surface of a sphere which makes equal oblique angles with all meridians, indicating the course of an object moving always in the same compass direction.
rhȳme (rīm) *n.* Agreement in terminal sounds of two or more words or metrical lines, such that (in English prosody) the last stressed vowel and any sounds following it are the same, while the preceding sounds are different (examples: *which*, *rich*; *peace*, *increase*; *descended*, *extended*); verse marked by rhymes; poem with rhymes; employment of rhyme; word providing a rhyme (*to* another); *feminine*, *masculine* ~: see FEMININE, MASCULINE; ~ *royal*, stanzas of seven ten-syllable lines, rhyming *a b a b b c c*; *nursery* ~: see NURSERY; *neither* ~ *nor reason*, nothing reasonable. ~ *v.* Write rhymes, versify; put or make (story etc.) into rhyme; (of words or lines) terminate in sounds that form a rhyme, form a rhyme *to* or *with*; use (words) as rhymes; *rhyming dictionary*, book in which words are arranged in groups according to the sound of their last syllable or syllables; *rhyming slang*, vocabulary (esp. in Cockney use) dating from early 19th c., of rhyming substitutions for certain words, e.g. *apples and pears* = stairs.
rhȳ′olīte (rī-) *n.* Fine-grained volcanic rock.

rhȳthm (rĭdhm) *n.* Metrical movement determined by relation of long and short, or stressed and unstressed, syllables in foot or line, measured flow of words and phrases in verse or prose; (mus.) systematic grouping of notes, beats, measures, and phrases, giving an effect of forward movement; (art etc.) harmonious correlation of parts, movement with regulated succession of strong and weak elements or of opposite or different conditions; ~ *method*, method of contraception involving avoidance of sexual intercourse as time of ovulation recurs. **rhȳ′thmic**, **-ical** *adjs.* **rhȳ′thmicallў** *adv.*
R.I. *abbrev.* Rhode Island; Royal Institute (of Painters in Water-colours); Royal Institution.
R.I.A. *abbrev.* Royal Irish Academy.
ria (rē′a) *n.* River mouth formed by the submergence of a valley or valleys.
ri′al (rē-) *n.* Principal monetary unit of Iran, = 100 dinars; ~ *saidi*, principal monetary unit of Oman, = 100 baiza.
Riä′ltō. Single-span 16th-c. marble bridge over Grand Canal, Venice, in centre of the old mercantile quarter.
ria′ta (-ah-) *n.* = LARIAT.
rib *n.* 1. One of the curved bones articulated in pairs to spine and enclosing and protecting thoracic cavity and its organs (ill. SKELETON); one of these bones from animal carcass, with the meat adhering to it, as food (ill. MEAT); (joc., with ref. to Gen. 2: 21) wife, woman; *sternal*, *true*, ~, one of those attached to sternum or breastbone; *asternal*, *false*, *floating*, ~, one of those not so attached. 2. Denser, firmer, or stronger part extending along or through organ or structure (in aircraft, ill. AEROPLANE); spur of mountain, vein of ore, ridge between furrows, wave-mark on sand; central vein of leaf, shaft or quill of feather, nervure of insect's wing; one of ship's curved timbers to which planks are nailed, or corresponding ironwork; arch supporting vault, groin, raised moulding on groin or across ceiling etc. (ill. VAULT[1]); wooden or iron beam helping to carry bridge; hinged rod of umbrella frame; curved piece of wood forming side of violin etc.; combination of plain and purl stitches in knitting, producing a rib-like fabric with a certain elasticity (ill. KNITTING). ~ *v.* Provide with ribs, act as ribs of; mark with ridges; plough with ribs between furrows, rafter; knit in rib stitch.
R.I.B.A. *abbrev.* Royal Institute of British Architects.
ri′bald *adj.* Scurrilous, irreverent. ~ *n.* Ribald person. **rī′baldrў** *n.*

[751]

ri′band *n.* (archaic) Ribbon.
ri′bband *n.* Wale, strip, scantling, or light spar, of wood, used esp. in shipbuilding to hold ribs in position; in launching, square timber on outer side of bilge-ways to prevent cradle from slipping outwards.
ri′bbon *n.* (Piece or length of) silk, satin, or other fine material woven into narrow band, esp. for adorning costume; ribbon of special colour etc. worn to indicate membership of knightly order, possession of medal, order, or other distinction, membership of club, college, etc.; long narrow strip of anything, ribbon-like object or mark; (pl.) driving-reins; *blue* ~: see BLUE; ~ *building, development,* building of houses etc. in narrow strips along main roads; ~-*fish*, fish with very long slender flattened body, esp. *Regalecus glesne*; ~-*grass*, grass with long slender leaves, esp. variegated variety of *Phalaris*; *R*~ *Society*, Roman Catholic secret society, associated with agrarian disorders, in 19th c. in Ireland.
ribonūclē′ic *adj.* ~ *acid*: see RNA.
R.I.C. *abbrev.* Royal Institute of Chemistry; (hist.) Royal Irish Constabulary.
Ricār′do, David (1772–1823). English political economist of the free-trade school, author of 'Principles of Political Economy and Taxation', which deals with the causes determining the distribution of wealth. **Ricār′dian** *adj.*
Ri′ccio (-chō). Var. of RIZZIO.
rice *n.* Seeds (usu. pearl-white), used as staple food in many Eastern countries, and elsewhere in puddings, savoury dishes, etc., of an annual cereal grass (*Oryza sativa*) cultivated in marshy or easily flooded ground in warm climates; this plant; ~-*bird*, -*bunting*, (esp.) bobolink; ~-*paper*, thin paper made from rice-straw; Chinese painting-paper (so named in error) made from pith of tree *Tetrapanax papyriferum*; edible paper used in baking; ~ *pudding*, baked pudding of sweetened milk and rice.
rich *adj.* 1. Wealthy, having riches; abounding in or *in* natural resources or some valuable possession or production, fertile; abundant, ample. 2. Valuable; splendid, costly, elaborate. 3. (of food) Containing a large proportion of fat; (of cake etc.) containing a large proportion of fat, eggs, fruit, etc. 4. (of colours, sounds, etc.) Mellow, deep, full, not thin. 5. (of incidents) Highly amusing, full of entertainment. **ri′chnėss** *n.*
Ri′chard. Name of three kings of England: *Richard I* (1157–99), 'Cœur de Lion', reigned 1189–99, 3rd son of Henry II; a leader in the Third Crusade, on his return from which he was captured and held to ransom by Leopold of Austria; *Richard II* (1367–1400), reigned 1377–99, son of the Black Prince, deposed and imprisoned by Henry IV, *Richard III* (1452–85), reigned 1483–5, last king of House of York; younger brother of Edward IV; he was defeated and killed at BOSWORTH FIELD.
Ri′chardson, Samuel (1689–1761). English novelist; author of 'Pamela', 'Clarissa Harlowe', and 'Sir Charles Grandison'.
Richelieu (rēshelyēr), Armand Jean du Plessis, Duc de (1585–1642). French cardinal and statesman; prime minister of Louis XIII 1624–42; founder of French Academy.
ri′chės (-z) *n.* (usu. as pl.) Wealth; valuable possessions.
ri′chlÿ *adv.* In rich manner; amply, fully, thoroughly.
Ri′chter (-χ-), Johann Paul Friedrich (1763–1825). German romantic novelist, who wrote under name of 'Jean Paul'.
rick[1] *n.* Stack of hay, corn, etc., esp. one regularly built and thatched; ~-*cloth*, canvas cover for unfinished rick; ~-*yard*, enclosure for ricks. ~ *v.t.* Form into rick(s).
rick[2] *n.* & *v.t.* Wrench, sprain.
ri′ckėts *n.* Disease of children marked by softening of the bones and consequent distortion (bowlegs, curvature of spine, etc.), usu. associated with a deficiency of vitamin D resulting from malnutrition or lack of sunlight.
rickė′ttsia *n.* One of a group of micro-organisms of genus *R*~, apparently intermediate between bacteria and viruses. [H. T. *Ricketts*, Amer. pathologist]
ri′ckėtÿ *adj.* Of (the nature of), suffering from, rickets; shaky, insecure. **ri′ckėtinėss** *n.*
ri′ckshaw *n.* = JINRICKSHAW.
ri′cochėt (-sh-; *or* -ā) *n.* Rebounding of projectile or other object from an object which it strikes, hit made after this; (mus.) effect produced by letting fiddle-bow bounce on strings. ~ *v.t.* (of projectile) Glance or skip with rebound(s).
ri′ctus *n.* (anat., zool.) Gape of mouth or beak.
rid *v.t.* (past t. & past part. *rid*). Make free, disencumber, *of* (usu. in past part. with *be* or *get*, as *get* ~ *of him*); (archaic) abolish, clear away. **ri′ddance** *n.* (esp. in *good* ~! as exclamation of joy).
ri′ddel *n.* Curtain at side of altar (ill. ALTAR).
ridden: see RIDE.
ri′ddle[1] *n.* Question, statement, or description, designed or serving to test ingenuity of hearers in divining its answer, meaning, or reference; conundrum, enigma; puzzling or mysterious fact, thing, or person. ~ *v.* Speak in, propound, riddles; solve (riddle).
ri′ddle[2] *n.* Coarse sieve for corn, gravel, cinders, etc.; board or metal plate set with pins, for straightening wire. ~ *v.t.* 1. Pass (corn etc.) through riddle, sift; (fig.) test (evidence, truth). 2. Fill (ship, person, etc.) with holes esp. of gunshot; (fig.) subject to searching criticism, refute (person, theory) with facts.
ride *v.* (past t. *rōde*, past part. *ri′dden*). 1. Sit on and be carried by horse etc.; go on horseback etc. or on bicycle etc. or in train or other vehicle; sit, go, be on something as on horse, esp. astride; sit on and manage horse; (of boat etc.) lie at anchor; float buoyantly; (of sun etc.) seem to float; (of things normally level or even) project or overlap; ~ *for a fall*, ride, (fig.) act, recklessly; ~ *down*, overtake on horseback; allow one's mount to trample on (person); ~ *out the storm*, (of ship, and fig.) come safely through it; ~ *to hounds*, go hunting; ~ *up*, (of garment) work upwards when worn. 2. Traverse on horseback etc., ride over or through. 3. Ride on; sit heavily on; oppress, haunt, dominate, tyrannize over. 4. Give ride to, cause to ride. ~ *n.* Journey in vehicle; spell of riding on horse, bicycle, person's back, etc.; road esp. through woods for riding on; *take for a* ~, (U.S. slang) kidnap and murder; make a fool of.
ri′der *n.* (esp.) 1. (naut., pl.) Additional set of timbers or iron plates strengthening ship's frame; (sing.) overlying rope or rope-turn. 2. Additional clause amending or supplementing document, esp. parliamentary Bill at third reading; corollary, naturally arising supplement; expression of opinion, recommendation, etc., added to verdict. 3. Piece in machine etc. that surmounts or bridges or works over others.
ridge *n.* Line of junction in which two sloping surfaces meet; any narrow elevation across surface; long narrow hill-top, mountain range, watershed; (agriculture) one of a set of raised strips separated by furrows; (gardening) raised hotbed for melons etc.; (meteor.) elongated region of higher barometric pressure between two of lower; ~-*piece*, beam along ridge of roof (ill. ROOF); ~-*pole*, horizontal pole of long tent; ~ *rib*, rib following ridge of vault (ill. VAULT[1]); ~-*tile*, tile used for ridge of roof; *ri′dgeway*, road along ridge. ~ *v.* Break up (land) into ridges; mark with ridges; plant (cucumbers etc.) in ridges; gather (esp. of sea) into ridges.
ri′dicule *n.* Holding or being held up as object of contemptuous laughter. ~ *v.t.* Treat with ridicule.
ridi′culous *adj.* Deserving to be laughed at, absurd, unreasonable. **ridi′culouslÿ** *adv.* **ridi′culousnėss** *n.*

[752]

ri′ding[1] *n.* (esp.) Road for riders; green track through or beside wood; ~-*habit*: see HABIT; ~-*lamp*, *-light*, light shown by ship riding at anchor.

ri′ding[2] *n.* One of three administrative districts (*East*, *West*, and *North*) into which the former county of Yorkshire was divided (until April 1974); (hist.) similar division of other county in U.K. or its colonies. [for *thriding*, f. THIRD]

Ri′dley, Nicholas (*c* 1500–55). English bishop and Protestant martyr; burnt as heretic at Oxford with Latimer.

riel *n.* Principal monetary unit of the Khmer Republic, = 100 sen.

Rie′mănn, Georg Friedrich Bernhard (1826–66). German mathematician, originator of a non-Euclidean system of geometry; ~'*s surface*, (math.) surface imagined by Riemann for the uniform representation of a function defined by an algebraic equation, such that if the algebraic function has *n* branches, the corresponding Riemann's surface consists of *n* planes superimposed on one another and infinitely close together.

Riĕ′nzi (-ntsĭ), Nicholas (or Cola) di (*c* 1313–54). Tribune of the people at Rome; led rebellion against nobles and established a republic (1347), but was excommunicated and exiled; he returned to Rome 7 years later and was assassinated.

Rie′vaulx (-vō; *or* rī′verz). Village in North Yorkshire, with ruins of Cistercian abbey.

Rif. (also *Riff*) Mountain system of Mediterranean coast of Morocco.

rife *pred. adj.* Of common occurrence, met with in numbers or quantities, prevailing, current, numerous; well provided *with*.

Riff *n.* (also *Rif*) Member of a Berber people living in N. Morocco.

ri′ff-răff *n.* Rabble, disreputable persons.

ri′fle *v.* 1. Search and rob, esp. of all that can be found in various pockets or storing-places; carry off as booty. 2. Make spiral grooves in (gun or its barrel or bore) to produce rotatory motion in projectile; *rifled*, having such grooves or (of projectile) projecting studs or ribs to fit them. 3. Shoot with rifle. ~ *n.* 1. One of the grooves made in rifling a gun. 2. Portable firearm, esp. musket or carbine, with rifled bore; (pl.) troops armed with rifles; *ri′fleman*, soldier armed with rifle, esp. member of certain specially raised regiments or companies; ~-*range*, distance rifle carries; place for rifle-practice.

rift *n.* Cleft, fissure, chasm, in earth or rock (freq. fig.); rent, crack, split, in an object, opening in cloud, etc.; ~ *valley*, valley with steep parallel walls, formed by subsidence of earth's crust (ill. ROCK[1]).

rig[1] *v.* Provide (ship), (of ship) be provided, with necessary spars, ropes, etc.; prepare for sea in this respect; fit (*out*, *up*) with or *with* clothes or other equipment; set *up* (structure) hastily or as makeshift or by utilizing odd materials. ~ *n.* Way ship's masts, sails, etc., are arranged; (transf.) person's or thing's look as determined by clothes etc.; outfit, costume, also ~-*out*.

rig[2] *n.* Trick, dodge, way of swindling; (commerc.) corner. ~ *v.t.* Manage or conduct fraudulently; ~ *the market*, cause artificial rise or fall in prices.

rig[3] *n.* Imperfectly developed or partially castrated male animal.

Ri′ga (rē-). Seaport and capital city of Latvia; *Gulf of* ~, inlet of Baltic Sea between Latvia and Estonia.

rigadōō′n *n.* (hist.) Lively and complicated dance for two persons; music for this, in $\frac{4}{4}$ or $\frac{2}{4}$ time.

Ri′gel (-gl). (astron.) Very bright star of first magnitude in foot of constellation Orion.

ri′gger *n.* (esp.) One who attends to the rigging of an aircraft.

ri′gging *n.* (esp.) 1. Ropes etc. used to support masts (*standing* ~) and work or set yards, sails, etc. (*running* ~)(ill. SHIP). 2. Operation of adjusting and aligning the various surfaces of an aircraft.

right (rīt) *adj.* 1. Straight (archaic; now only in ~ *line*, ~-*lined*); ~ *angle*: see ANGLE[1]; involving right angles, not oblique; *at* ~ *angles*, turning or placed with right angle; ~ *ascension*, (astron.) celestial longitude; ~ *cone*, *cylinder*, *prism*, etc., cone, etc., with ends or base perpendicular to axis; ~ *sailing*, sailing due N., S., E., or W. 2. Just, morally good, required by equity or duty, proper; (freq. in comb., as ~-*minded*, ~-*principled*). 3. Correct, true; preferable or most suitable; less wrong or not wrong; in good or normal condition, sound, sane, satisfactory, well-advised, not mistaken; *get* ~, bring or come into right state; *put*, *set*, ~, restore to order, health, etc.; correct mistaken ideas of; justify *oneself* usu. *with* person; *in one's* ~ *mind*, sane, not mad; ~ *side*, side (of fabric etc.) meant for use or show; *on the* ~ *side of*, younger than (specified age); in good books or favour of (person). 4. (archaic) Rightful, real, veritable, properly so called; ~ *whale*: see WHALE[1]. 5. (of position) On or towards side of body opposite the left and of which the hand is normally more used; having corresponding relation to front of any object; (of bank of river etc.) on right hand of person looking downstream; ~ *about*, (turn) so far to right as to face opposite way; *send*, etc., *to the* ~ *about*, dismiss summarily; ~ *and left*, to or on both sides, on all hands; with, of, to both hands or sides; pugilist's two blows in quick succession with different hands; ~ *arm*, (fig.) most reliable helper; ~ *hand*, hand on right side; this as the better hand;

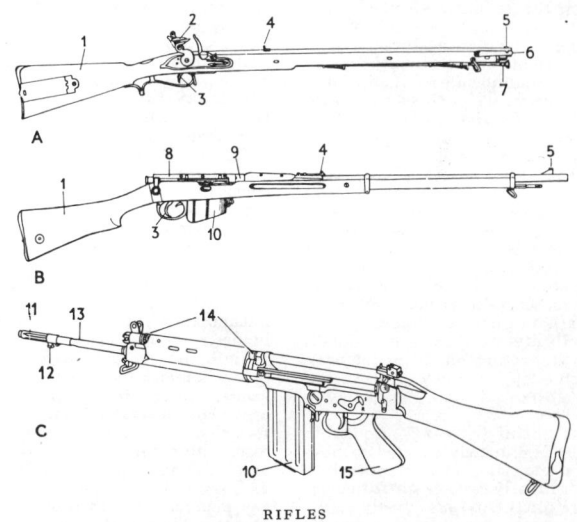

RIFLES

A. FLINTLOCK, MUZZLE-LOADING 'BAKER' RIFLE, *c* 1800. B. SHORT MAGAZINE 'LEE-ENFIELD' MK III (SMLE), BREECH-LOADING MAGAZINE RIFLE, *c* 1907. C. AUTOMATIC OR SELF-LOADING RIFLE (SLR) FN DESIGN *c* 1955

1. Butt. 2. Flintlock. 3. Trigger. 4. Backsight. 5. Foresight. 6. Muzzle. 7. Ramrod. 8. Bolt. 9. Breech. 10. Magazine. 11. Flash eliminator. 12. Bayonet lug. 13. Barrel. 14. Gas cylinder. 15. Pistol grip

region or direction on this side of person; chief or indispensable assistant; ~-*hand*, placed on the right hand; ~-*hand man*, chief or indispensable assistant; ~-*hand screw*, screw with thread turning to right; ~-*handed*, using right hand more than left; (of blow etc.) struck, made, with right hand; ~ *turn*, turn right into a position at right angles with original one; ~ *wing*, (esp.) extreme right in politics (see *n.*, sense 5). **ri'ghtnėss** *n.* **right** *v.* 1. Restore to proper, straight, or vertical position; (refl.) recover one's balance, (of ship) recover vertical position. 2. Make reparation for or to, avenge (wrong, wronged person); vindicate, justify, rehabilitate; correct (mistakes etc.), correct mistakes in, set in order. ~ *n.* 1. What is just; fair treatment; *the ~*, what is right, the cause of truth or justice; *by ~(s)*, if right were done; *in the ~*, with truth or justice on one's side. 2. Justification; fair claim; being entitled to privilege or immunity; thing one is entitled to; *assert, stand on, one's ~s*, refuse to relinquish them; *Declaration* or *Bill of R~s*, Bill declaring rights and liberties of England, and succession to the Crown, passed in 1689; *divine ~*: see DIVINE; ~ *of way*, right of using path etc. over another's ground; path etc. so used; right of one travelling vehicle to take precedence over another. 3. (pl.) Right condition, true state; *set* or *put to ~s*, arrange properly. 4. Right-hand part, region, or direction; (boxing) right-handed blow. 5. Conservative members of continental legislature, those who sit on right of chamber; hence, more traditional part of any political group. **ri'ghtlėss** *adj.* **right** *adv.* 1. Straight; all the way *to, round*, etc.; completely *off, out*, etc.; (U.S.) straight away, immediately. 2. Exactly, quite; very, to the full; ~-*down*, thorough(ly). 3. Justly, properly, correctly, aright, truly, satisfactorily; *it serves him ~*, it is no worse than he deserves. 4. To right hand. ~ *int.* Exclamation of agreement or consent (also, slang, ~ *oh!*, ~ *you are!*). **ri'ghtward** *adj. & adv.*
ri'ghteous (rīchus) *adj.* Morally good; acting in a moral way, virtuous; morally justifiable. **ri'ghteously** *adv.* **ri'ghteousnėss** *n.*
ri'ghtful (rīt-) *adj.* Equitable, fair; legitimately entitled to position etc.; that one is entitled to. **ri'ghtfully** *adv.* **ri'ghtfulnėss** *n.*
ri'ghtly (rīt-) *adv.* Justly, fairly; properly, correctly, accurately; justifiably.
ri'gid *adj.* Not flexible, stiff, unyielding; inflexible, harsh, strict, precise. **ri'gidly** *adv.* **rigi'dity** *n.*
ri'gmarōle *n.* Rambling or meaningless talk or tale. [app. f. obs. *ragman roll* list, catalogue]

ri'gor (*or* rī'ger) *n.* (path.) Sudden chill with shivering; (also ~ *mortis*) stiffening of body after death.
ri'gour (-ger) *n.* Severity, strictness, harshness; (pl.) harsh measures; (sing.) strict enforcement *of* rules etc.; extremity or excess *of* weather, hardship, famine, etc., great distress; austerity of life, Puritanic strictness of observance or doctrine; logical accuracy, exactitude. **ri'gorous** *adj.* **ri'gorously** *adv.*
Rigve'da (-vă-) *n.* Oldest and most important of the Vedas (see VEDA). [Sansk.]
Ri'ksdăg *n.* Parliament of Sweden.
rīle *v.t.* (slang, orig. U.S.) Raise anger in, irritate.
Ri'lke (-ke), Rainer Maria (1875–1926). Austrian lyric poet and writer of lyrical prose.
rill *n.* Small stream, runnel, rivulet. **ri'llėt** *n.*
rille *n.* (astron.) Long narrow trench or valley on moon's surface.
rim *n.* Outer ring of wheel (not including tyre), connected with nave or boss by spokes etc. (ill. WHEEL); outer frame of sieve etc.; edge, margin, border, esp. a raised one, etc., of more or less circular object. ~ *v.t.* Furnish with rim, serve as rim to, edge, border. **ri'mlėss** *adj.*
Rimbaud (răṅbō), Arthur (1854–91). French symbolist poet.
rīme[1] *n. & v.* = RHYME.
rīme[2] *n.* 1. (meteor.) Water-droplets from cloud or fog which freeze on hill-tops, high branches, etc., esp. in windy weather. 2. (chiefly poet.) Hoar-frost. ~ *v.t.* Cover with rime. **rī'mў** *adj.*
Ri'mmon *n.* Deity worshipped at Damascus (2 Kings 5: 18).
Ri'mskў-Kôr'sakŏv (-f), Nikolay Andreevich (1844–1908). Russian musical composer.
rind *n.* Bark of tree or plant; peel of fruit or vegetable; harder enclosing surface of cheese or other substance; skin of bacon etc.; external aspect, surface. ~ *v.t.* Strip bark from.
ri'nderpėst *n.* Virulent infectious disease of ruminant animals, with fever, dysentery, and inflammation of mucous membranes.
ring[1] *n.* 1. Circlet, usu. of precious metal and often set with gem(s), worn round finger as ornament or token (esp. of betrothal or marriage) or signet, or (usu. with defining word) hung to or encircling other part of body. 2. Circular object or appliance of any material and any (but esp. of no great) size. 3. Raised, sunk, or otherwise distinguishable line or band round cylindrical or circular object, rim; circular fold, coil, bend, structure, part, or mark; excision of bark round branch or trunk of tree; one of the expanding circular ripples caused by some-

thing falling or being thrown into water; (also *annual ~*) one of the concentric circular bands of wood constituting yearly growth of a tree (ill. STEM[1]). 4. Persons, trees, etc., disposed in a circle, such disposition; (chem.) number of atoms so united that they can be represented graphically in cyclic form. 5. Combination of traders etc. to monopolize and control a particular trade, market, or policy, or (*price-~*) to stabilize or keep up price of goods. 6. Circular enclosure for some sport, performance, or exhibition (esp. in circus); space marked off (usu. rectangular) for prize-fight or wrestling-match, enclosed space for bookmakers etc., or for displaying livestock etc.; *the ~*, pugilism; bookmakers. 7. Circular or spiral course; *make ~s round*, excel or surpass easily. 8. ~-*bark* (*v.t.*) cut ring in bark of (tree) to kill it or to check its growth and bring it into bearing; ~-*bolt*, bolt with ring attached for fastening rope to etc.; ~-*bone*, (horse-disease with) deposit of bony matter on pastern-bones; ~-*cartilage*, cricoid; ~-*dove*, wood-pigeon; ~-*fence*, one completely enclosing estate etc.; ~-*finger*, third finger esp. of left hand; *ri'ngleader*, leader of persons acting in defiance of law or rules etc.; ~-*master*, manager of circus performance; ~-*neck*, ring-necked bird; ~-*necked*, with band(s) of colour round neck; ~-*net*, kind of salmon-net; ~-*ouzel*, bird (*Turdus torquatus*) allied to blackbird, with white ring or bar on breast; ~ *road*, circular road passing round a town; *ri'ngside seat*, seat close to (boxing or circus etc.) ring; seat providing close view; ~-*snake*, common European grass-snake; ~-*stand*, stand (usu. branched) for keeping finger-rings on; ~-*straked*, (bibl.) marked with rings of colour round body; ~-*tail*, female of hen-harrier; golden eagle till its third year; ring-tailed opossum or phalanger; ~-*tailed*, with tail ringed in alternate colours; (of phalanger or lemur) with tail curled at end; ~-*velvet*, velvet fine enough to be drawn through a ring; *ri'ngworm*, any of several contagious diseases (*tinea*) of the skin, hair, or nails, caused by fungi and characterized by ring-shaped patches. **ri'nged** (-ngd), **ri'nglėss** *adjs.* **ring** *v.* 1. (of hawk etc.) Rise in spirals; (of hunted fox) take circular course. 2. Encompass (*round, about, in*); hem in (game, cattle) by riding or beating in circle round them. 3. Put ring upon; put ring in nose of (pig, bull). 4. Ring-bark. 5. Cut (onions etc.) into rings.
ring[2] *v.* (past t. *rang* or rarely *rŭng*; past part. *rŭng*). 1. Give out clear resonant sound (as) of

vibrating metal; (of bell) convey summons by ringing; (of place) resound, re-echo (*with*); (of utterance or other sound) linger *in* one's ears, memory, etc.; (of ears) be filled with sensation as of bell-ringing or *with* sound; ~ *true, false*, (of coin tested by throwing on counter, and fig. of sentiments, etc.). 2. Make (bell) ring; throw (coin) on counter to test it; ring bell as summons; sound (peal, knell, etc.) on bell(s); announce (hour etc.) by sound of bell(s); usher *in, out*, with bell-ringing; ~ *off*, terminate telephone call; ~ *up*, make telephone call to; ~ *the bell*, (colloq.) achieve complete success; strike a sympathetic or responsive note; ~ *the changes*, see CHANGE; ~ *the curtain up* or *down* in theatre, direct it by bell to be raised or lowered; ~ *the knell of*, announce or herald the end or abolition of. ~ *n.* Set *of* (church) bells; ringing sound; ringing tone in voice etc.; resonance of coin or vessel; act of ringing bell, sound so produced; a call on the telephone.

ri′nger (-g-) *n.* 1. Quoit that falls round pin. 2. Fox that runs in ring when hunted. 3. Bell-ringer; device for ringing bell.

ri′nghăls *n.* S. African hooded snake (*Haemachatus haemachatus*) with light band round neck. [Du., f. *hals* neck]

ri′nglet *n.* Curly lock of hair, curl; (rare) small ring, fairy ring on grass, ring-shaped mark, etc. **ri′nglĕtĕd, ri′nglĕtў** *adjs.*

rink *n.* Stretch of ice used for game of curling; sheet of natural or artificial ice for skating, building containing this; floor for roller-skating; (division of) bowling-green.

rinse *v.t.* Wash out or *out* (vessel, mouth) by filling with water etc. and shaking and emptying; pour liquid over or wash lightly; put (clothes etc.) through clean water to remove soap; clear (soap, impurities) *out* or *away* by rinsing; wash (food) *down* with liquor. ~ *n.* Rinsing or being rinsed; preparation used for rinsing the hair, esp. for tinting it.

Rīo de Janeir′ō (rē′ō). Seaport and former capital of Brazil.

Rio Grănde (rē′ō; *or* -dĭ). N. Amer. river rising in S. Colorado and flowing south and east through New Mexico and along N. boundary of Mexico to Gulf of Mexico.

rī′ot *n.* 1. Loud revelry, revel; unrestrained indulgence in or display or enjoyment of something. 2. (hunting) Following of any scent indiscriminately; *run* ~, (orig. of hounds, now usu. fig.) act without restraint or control, disregard all limitations. 3. Disorder, tumult, disturbance of the peace, outbreak of lawlessness, on part of a crowd; *R*~ *Act*, act (1715) providing that if twelve or more persons unlawfully or riotously assembled refuse to disperse within an hour after specified part has been read by a competent authority they shall be considered as felons; *read the R*~ *Act*, announce that some course of action or conduct must cease. **rī′otous** *adj.* **rī′otouslў** *adv.* **rī′otousnĕss** *n.* **rī′ot** *v.* Make or engage in riot; revel. **rī′oter** *n.*

rip¹ *n.* Worthless horse, screw; dissolute person, rake.

rip² *v.* 1. Cut or tear (thing) quickly or forcibly away from something; make long cut or tear in, cut or tear vigorously apart; split (wood, rock), saw (wood) with the grain; strip (roof) of tiles or slates and laths; make (fissure, passage) by ripping; open *up* (wound etc.) again; come violently asunder, split; ~*-cord*, cord for releasing parachute, opening balloon gas-bag, etc.; ~*-saw*, saw for ripping wood. 2. Rush along; *let her* ~, do not check speed or interfere. ~ *n.* Rent made by ripping, tear.

rip³ *n.* Stretch of broken water in sea or river, overfall.

R.I.P. *abbrev. Requiesca(n)t in pace* (L, = may he or she, they, rest in peace).

ripār′ian *adj.* Of, on, riverbank. ~ *n.* Riparian proprietor.

ripe *adj.* Ready to be reaped, gathered, eaten, drunk, used, or dealt with; fully developed, mellow, mature; prepared or able to undergo something, in fit state *for.* **rī′pelў** *adv.* **rī′penĕss** *n.* **rī′pen** *v.*

ripō′ste *n.* Quick return thrust in fencing; counter-stroke; retort. ~ *v.i.* Deliver riposte.

ri′pper *n.* One who rips; tool for ripping roof; rip-saw.

ri′pple¹ *n.* Toothed implement used to clear away seeds from flax. ~ *v.t.* Treat with ripple.

ri′pple² *n.* Ruffling of water's surface, small wave(s); wavy or crinkled appearance in hair, ribbons, etc.; gentle lively sound that rises and falls; method of firing torpedoes in succession. **ri′pplў** *adj.* **ri′pple** *v.* Form, flow in, show, agitate or mark with, sound like, ripples.

ri′p-roar′ing *adj.* (U.S.) Uproarious, boisterous, full of vigour, spirit, or excellence.

Ripūār′ian *adj.* Of the ancient Franks living on Rhine between Moselle and Meuse; ~ *law*, code observed by them.

Rĭp văn Wĭ′nkle. Hero of a story (1820) by Washington Irving; he fell asleep in the Catskill Mountains and awoke after 20 years to find the world completely changed.

rise (-z) *v.* (past t. *rose* pr. rōz, past part. *risen* pr. rī′zn). 1. Get up from lying, sitting, or kneeling position; get out of bed; (of meeting etc.) cease to sit for business; recover standing or upright position, become erect; leave ground; come to life again (freq. *from the dead*). 2. Cease to be quiet; abandon submission, make revolt; *gorge, stomach*, ~*s*, indignation or disgust is felt. 3. Come or go up; grow upwards; ascend, mount, soar; project or swell upwards; become higher, reach higher position, level, price, pitch, or amount; increase; incline upwards; come to surface; (of fish) come to surface of water to take fly, bait, etc.; become or be visible above or *above* surroundings; (of sun, moon, etc.) appear above horizon; develop greater energy or intensity; be progressive; (of dough etc.) swell with yeast or other agent; (of spirits) become more cheerful; ~ *in the world*, attain higher social position. 4. Develop powers equal *to* (an *occasion* etc.). 5. Have origin, begin to be, flow, *from, in, at*, etc. 6. Make or see (fish, bird, etc.) rise; (naut.) ~ *ship, land*, etc., see it appear above horizon. ~ *n.* 1. Ascent, upward slope; knoll, hill. 2. Social advancement; upward progress; increase in power, rank, value, price, amount, height, pitch, wages, etc. 3. Movement of fish to surface; *have, get, take, a* ~ *out of*, (fig.) draw (person) into display of temper or other foible. 4. Vertical height of step, arch, incline, etc.; riser of staircase. 5. Origin, start; *give* ~ *to*, induce.

rī′ser (-z-) *n.* (esp.) Vertical piece connecting two treads of stair (ill. STAIR).

rī′sible (-z-) *adj.* Inclined to laugh; of laughter; laughable, ludicrous. **risibi′lĭtў** *n.* **rī′siblў** *adv.*

rī′sing (-z-) *n.* (esp.) 1. Insurrection, revolt. 2. (naut.) Narrow strake of board fastened inside frame of boat to support thwarts (ill. BOAT). ~ *adj.* That rises; advancing towards maturity (*the* ~ *generation*) or towards a specified age (as ~ *5, 14*, etc.); (of ground) sloping upwards.

risk *n.* Hazard; chance of or *of* bad consequences, loss, etc.; exposure to mischance; *at* ~, exposed to risk; *run* ~*s, run a* or *the* ~, expose oneself, be exposed, to loss etc. ~ *v.t.* Expose to chance of injury or loss; venture on, take the chances of.

rī′skў *adj.* 1. Hazardous, full of risk. 2. [after Fr. *risqué*] Involving suggestion of indecency, offending against propriety. **rī′skĭlў** *adv.* **rī′skinĕss** *n.*

Risōrgĭme′ntō *n.* Movement of middle 19th c. for union and liberation of Italy, associated with names of Cavour, Mazzini, and Garibaldi. [It., = 'resurrection']

risŏ′ttō *n.* Italian dish of rice cooked in savoury stock.

risqué (rĭskā) *adj.* = RISKY, 2. [Fr.]

ri′ssōle *n.* Fried ball or cake of minced meat or fish coated with breadcrumbs etc.

ritardă′ndō *adv., n.* (pl. *-os*), & *adj.* (mus.) (Passage performed) more slowly. [It.]

rite *n.* Religious or solemn ceremony or observance; form of procedure, action required or usual, in this.

rītornĕ′llō *n.* (mus.) Instrumental refrain, interlude, or prelude in a vocal work. [It., *dim.* of *ritorno* return]

ri′tūal *adj.* Of, with, consisting in, involving, religious rites. **ri′tūallỹ** *adv.* **ri′tūal** *n.* Prescribed order of performing religious service; book containing this; performance of ritual acts. **ri′tūalism** *n.* (Excessive) practice of ritual. **ri′tūalīst** *n.* **ritūali′stic** *adj.* **ritūali′stically** *adv.*

rī′val *n.* Person's competitor for some prize (esp. woman's or man's love) or in some pursuit or quality (also of things). ~ *attrib. adj.* That is a rival or are rivals. ~ *v.t.* Vie with, be comparable to, seem or claim to be as good etc. as. **rī′valrỹ** *n.* [L *rivalis*, orig. = 'on same stream', f. *rivus* stream]

rīve *v.* (past t. *rīved*, past part. *rī′ven*). Tear apart, rend, lacerate, tear *off, away*, etc.; split (esp. wood, stone); rend (heart etc.), be rent, with painful thoughts or feelings; cleave, split, crack; admit of splitting. **rī′ven** *adj.*

rī′ver *n.* Copious stream of water flowing in channel to sea, lake, marsh, or another river; copious flow or stream *of*; (freq. attrib.; ~-*bottom*, (U.S.) low-lying alluvial land along banks of river; ~-*god*, tutelary deity supposed to dwell in and preside over river; ~-*horse*, hippopotamus. **rī′vered** (-*erd*), **rī′verlĕss** *adjs.* \rī′verain *adj.* Of river or its neighbourhood; situated, dwelling, by river. ~ *n.* Person dwelling by river.

rī′verīne *adj.* Of, on, river or its banks, riparian.

rī′vĕt *n.* Nail or bolt for holding together metal plates etc., its headless end being beaten out or pressed down after insertion. ~ *v.t.* Clinch (bolt); join or fasten with rivets; fix, make immovable; concentrate, direct intently (eyes etc. *upon*); engross (attention), engross attention of. **rī′vĕter** *n.*

Riviēr′a (-ārā). Strip of coast of N. Italy and S. France, between mountains and Mediterranean, famous for its beauty, fertility, and mild climate; hence, extended to other coasts (as *Cornish* ~) regarded as similar in some respects.

rī′vière (-vyār) *n.* Necklace of diamonds or other gems, esp. of more than one string.

ri′vūlĕt *n.* Small stream.

ri′x-dŏllar *n.* Silver coin and money of account current in various European countries from 16th to 19th centuries. [Du. *rijksdaler, (rijk* kingdom, *daler* dollar)]

riyal (rē′ahl) *n.* Principal monetary unit of Qatar (= 100 dirhams), Saudi Arabia (= 20 qursh), and Yemen Arab Republic (= 40 bugshas).

Ri′zziō (-ts-), David (*c* 1533–66). Italian secretary to MARY, QUEEN OF SCOTS, murdered by Darnley.

R.M. *abbrev.* Resident Magistrate; Royal Mail; Royal Marines.

R.M.A. *abbrev.* Royal Military Academy (Sandhurst).

R.M.S. *abbrev.* Royal Mail Steamer.

r.m.s. *abbrev.* Root-mean-square.

R.M.S.P. *abbrev.* Royal Mail Steam Packet (Company).

R.N. *abbrev.* Royal Navy.

RNA *abbrev.* Ribonucleic acid, any of the class of nucleic acids containing ribose, present in the nucleoli and cytoplasm of living cells and concerned in the synthesis of proteins.

R.N.C., R.N.D. *abbrevs.* Royal Naval College, Division.

R.N.L.I. *abbrev.* Royal National Lifeboat Institution.

R.N.R., R.N.V.R. *abbrevs.* Royal Naval (Volunteer) Reserve.

R.N.Z.A.F., R.N.Z.N. *abbrevs.* Royal New Zealand Air Force, Navy.

roach[1] *n.* Small freshwater fish (*Rutilus rutilus*) of the carp family of N. European rivers; (U.S.) small fish resembling this.

roach[2] *n.* (naut.) Upward curve in foot of square sail.

road[1] *n.* 1. (usu. pl.; also *roa′dstead*) Piece of water near shore in which ships can ride at anchor. 2. Line of communication between places for use of foot-passengers, riders, and vehicles; way of getting *to*; one's way or route; *the* ~, *the* highway; *on the* ~, travelling; *royal* ~, smooth or easy way (*to* success etc.); *rule of the* ~, custom regulating side to be taken by vehicles, riders, or ships, meeting or passing each other; *take the* ~, set out; *take to the* ~, (formerly) become a highwayman, (now) become a tramp. 3. Underground passage or way in mine; (U.S.) railroad, railway. 4. ~-*book*, book describing roads of country etc., itinerary; ~-*hog*, reckless, dangerous, or bad-mannered driver of motor vehicle etc.; ~-*house*, inn on main road in country district; **roa′dman**, man employed in repairing roads; ~-*metal*, broken stone for road-making; ~-*sense*, capacity for intelligent behaviour on roads, esp. in traffic; ~-*side*, border of road (esp. attrib.); *roadstead*: see sense 1; **roa′dway**, road; central part of road, esp. part used by vehicular traffic; **roa′dworthy**, (of vehicle) fit to be used on the road; hence **roa′dworthiness**. **roa′dlĕss** *adj.*

road[2] *v.t.* (of dog) Follow up (game-bird) by foot-scent.

roa′dster *n.* Ship at anchor in roadstead; horse, bicycle, etc., for use on the road; two- or three-seater motor-car with open body.

roam *v.* Ramble, wander; walk or travel unsystematically over, through, or about (country, seas, etc.). **roa′mer** *n.* **roam** *n.* Ramble, rambling walk.

roan[1] *adj.* (of animal) With coat in which the prevailing colour is thickly interspersed with another, esp. bay, sorrel, or chestnut mixed with white or grey. ~ *n.* Roan horse or cow.

roan[2] *n.* Soft sheepskin leather used in bookbinding as substitute for morocco. [perh. f. *Rouen*]

roar (rōr) *n.* Loud deep hoarse sound (as) of lion, person or company in pain or rage or loud laughter, the sea, cannon, thunder, furnace, etc. ~ *v.* Utter, send forth, roar; (of horse) make loud noise in breathing due to disease; (of place) be full of din, re-echo; say, sing, utter (words etc.) in loud tone; make *deaf, hoarse,* etc., put *down,* by roaring. **roar′er** *n.* (esp.) Roaring horse.

roar′ing (rōr-) *adj.* (esp.) Riotous, noisy, boisterous, brisk; stormy; ~ *forties*: see FORTY.

roast *v.* Cook (esp. meat) by exposure to open fire or (improperly for *bake*) in oven; heat or calcine (ore) in furnace; heat (coffee-beans) in preparation for grinding; expose to fire or great heat; ridicule, banter, chaff; undergo roasting; *roa′sting-jack*, appliance keeping meat in motion while roasting. ~ *n.* Roast meat or a dish of it; operation of roasting; *rule the* ~, (archaic) be master. **roa′sting** *adj.* (esp.) Very hot. **roa′ster** *n.* (esp.) Kind of oven for roasting; utensil for baking meat etc. in; ore-roasting furnace; coffee-roasting apparatus; fowl etc. fit for roasting or baking.

rŏb *v.t.* Despoil (person etc.) of or *of* property by violence; feloniously plunder; deprive *of* what is dear; (abs.) commit robbery. **rŏ′bber** *n.* **rŏ′bbery** *n.* Stealing (with threat) of force.

Rŏ′bbia, della. Name of Florentine family of sculptors in glazed terracotta: *Luca* ~ (1400–82); *Andrea* ~, his nephew (1435–1525); *Giovanni* ~, son of Andrea (1469–1529).

rōbe *n.* 1. Long loose outer garment, esp. one worn as indication of wearer's rank, office, profession, etc., gown, vestment; dressing-gown, bath-wrap; *the long* ~, (dress of) legal or clerical profession. 2. (U.S., Canada) Dressed skin of animal used as garment or rug. ~ *v.* Invest (person) in robe; dress; assume one's robes or vestments.

Rŏ′bert[1]. Name of two kings of France: *Robert I* (*c* 865–923), king of the Franks (922–3),

Robert grandfather of Hugh Capet; *Robert II* (*c* 970–1031), king of France 996–1031, son of Hugh Capet.

Rŏ'bert[2] (d. 1035), 'the Devil' or 'the Magnificent'. Duke of Normandy and father of William the Conqueror; figures in many legends in consequence of his violence and cruelty.

Rŏ'bert[3]. Name of three kings of Scotland: *Robert I*: see BRUCE; *Robert II*, 'the Steward' (1316–90), son-in-law of Robert I, reigned 1371–90; *Robert III* (*c* 1340–1406), illegitimate son of Robert II, reigned 1390–1406.

Robert Guiscard (rōbār gēskār), (*c* 1015–85). Norman adventurer, one of Norman conquerors of S. Italy and Sicily.

Rŏ'berts, Frederick Sleigh, 1st Earl Roberts of Kandahar (1832–1914). English field marshal; defeated Afghans near Kabul, and led famous march from Kabul to Kandahar; commander-in-chief in S. Africa 1899–1900.

Robespierre (rōbzpyār), Maximilien François Marie Isidore de (1758–94). French revolutionist; leader of extreme party and chief promoter of the Reign of Terror; overthrown and guillotined 1794.

rŏ'bin *n*. Small brown redbreasted European bird (*Erithacus rubecula*); (U.S.) red-breasted thrush (*Turdus migratorius*); any of various birds of Australia, New Zealand, India, etc., some having red breasts; ~'*s eye*, herb Robert. [OF. dim. of *Robert*]

Rŏ'bin Gōō'dfĕllow (-ō). = PUCK[2].

Rŏ'bin Hōōd. Legendary outlaw, hero of many ballads and plays, who robbed the rich and helped the poor; associated esp. with Sherwood Forest in Nottinghamshire; said to have lived in 12th–13th centuries.

robi'nia *n*. N. Amer. tree or shrub of genus *R*~ which includes the locust tree. [*Robin*, royal gardener in Paris, who introduced these trees to Europe (1635)]

Rŏ'binson Crū'sōe (krōō-). Hero of a novel (1719) by DEFOE, based on adventure of Alexander Selkirk, who lived alone on the uninhabited Pacific island of Juan Fernandez for 5 years (1704–9).

rŏ'borant *adj*. & *n*. (med.) Strengthening (drug).

rŏ'bŏt *n*. Apparently human automaton; machine-like person, soulless automaton; automatic traffic-signal; ~ *bomb*, flying bomb. [term in play 'R.U.R.' by Karel Čapek for mechanical apparatus doing work of a man; f. Czech *robota* compulsory labour, *robotnik* serf]

Rŏb Roy[1]. Robert Macgregor or Campbell (1671–1734), Scottish Highland freebooter and cattlelifter.

Rŏb Roy[2]. Pseudonym of John Macgregor (1825–92), Scottish traveller, inventor of ~ *canoe*, a decked-over canoe with doublebladed paddle.

Robt *abbrev*. Robert.

robŭ'st *adj*. Of strong health and physique; vigorous; (of exercise etc.) tending to or requiring strength, invigorating. **robŭ'stlỹ** *adv*. **robŭ'stnĕss** *n*.

robŭ'stious *adj*. Boisterous, self-assertive, noisy.

rŏc *n*. Gigantic bird of Eastern legend.

R.O.C. *abbrev*. Royal Observer Corps.

rŏ'cambōle *n*. N. European species of leek (*Allium scorodoprasum*).

rŏche moutonnée (-sh, mōōtō'nā). (geol.) Small mass of rock shaped by glacial action, with one side smooth and gently sloping and the other rough steep and irregular. [Fr.]

Rŏ'chĕster, John Wilmot, Earl of (1648–80). English poet, wit, and libertine; favourite of Charles II.

rŏ'chĕt *n*. Surplice-like vestment used chiefly by bishops and abbots (ill. VESTMENT).

rŏck[1] *n*. 1. Large rugged mass of stone forming cliff, crag, or prominence; large detached stone, boulder; (U.S.) stone of any size; (fig.) source of danger or destruction; sure foundation or support, shelter or protection; (U.S. slang, pl.) money; *on the* ~*s*, in financial straits; (of (esp. alcoholic) drink) served with ice cubes; *R*~ *of ages*, Christ. 2. Hard and massive stone; (geol.) any formation of

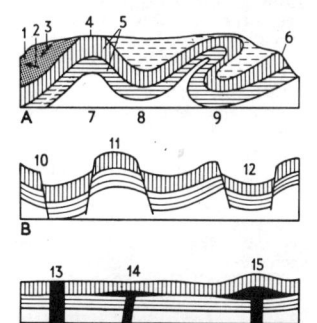

ROCK FORMATIONS
A. FOLDS. B. FAULTS.
C. INTRUSIONS

A. 1. Bedding plane (at right angle to 5). 2. Strike. 3. Dip. 4. Outcrop. 5. Strata. 6. Escarpment. 7. Anticline. 8. Syncline. 9. Recumbent fold or nappe. B. 10. Fault. 11. Horst. 12. Rift valley. C. 13. Dike. 14. Sill. 15. Laccolith

natural origin in the earth's crust, whether composed of a single mineral or an aggregate of many. 3. Hard confection of candied sugar, esp. flavoured with peppermint. 4. (usu. *blue* ~) Rock-pigeon. 5. ~ *barnacle*: see BARNACLE[2]; ~-*bed*, base of rock; ~-*bottom*, (slang, of prices etc.) very lowest; ~-*cake*, bun with rugged surface; ~ *cod*, any of various Amer. and Australian fishes; ~-*crystal*, crystallized quartz; ~-*dove*: see PIGEON; ~-*drill*, rock-boring tool or machine; ~-*fish*, fish frequenting rocks or rocky bottoms; ~-*garden*, rockery; ~-*oil*, native naphtha; ~-*pigeon*: see PIGEON; ~-*plant*, plant growing among rocks or suitable for rockeries; ~-*rose*, plant of genus *Cistus* with yellow, pink, or salmon flowers; ~-*salmon*, fishmongers' name for dogfish; ~-*salt*: see SALT *n*. 1; ~-*tar*, petroleum; ~-*work*, rough stonework resembling or imitating rocks; rockery.

rŏck[2] *v*. Move gently to and fro (as in cradle; set or keep (cradle etc.), be, in such motion; (goldmining) work (cradle), work cradle; shake in cradle, sway, cause to sway, from side to side; shake, oscillate, reel; ~-*shaft*, one that oscillates about axis without making complete revolutions; ~-*staff*, part of apparatus working smith's bellows. ~ *n*. Rocking motion, spell of rocking.

rŏck[3] *n*. (hist.) Distaff.

Rŏ'ckefĕller, John Davison (1839–1937). Amer. financier and philanthropist who made a large fortune from petroleum; established and endowed four charitable foundations, including ~ *Foundation*, fund established 1913 'to promote the well-being of mankind throughout the world'; ~ *Institute for Medical Research*, founded 1901 in New York.

rŏ'cker *n*. (esp.) One of the curved bars upon which cradle, chair, etc., rocks; rocking-chair; gold-miner's cradle; mezzotint engraver's cradle for roughening surface of plate (ill. ENGRAVING); skate with highly curved blade; *rocking turn*.

rŏ'ckerỹ *n*. Artificial heap of rough stones and rock for growing rock-plants.

rŏ'ckĕt[1] *n*. Cruciferous plant of genus *Hesperis*, esp. *H. matronalis*, sweet-scented after dark; *blue* ~, of any various kinds of wolf's-bane (*Aconitum*) or larkspur (*Delphinium*). [It. *ruchetta* f. L *eruca* because formerly applied to the salad-plant *Eruca sativa*]

rŏ'ckĕt[2] *n*. 1. Cylindrical case that can be projected to a height or distance by the reaction of the gases discharged from the rear when its (highly combustible) contents are ignited, used as firework, for signalling, to carry life-line, propel military warhead, put spacecraft into orbit, etc.; ~ *propulsion*, propulsion by means of the reaction of gases expelled backward from the rocket at high velocity. 2. Shell or bomb propelled by rocket. ~ *v.t.* Bound

upwards like rocket; (of game-bird) fly straight upwards, fly fast and high; (of prices) rise rapidly.
ro'cketry n. Science, practice, of rocket propulsion.
Ro'ckies (-īz) n.pl. Rocky Mountains.
ro'cking adj. That rocks; swaying, oscillating; ~-*chair*, chair mounted on rockers; ~-*horse*, child's wooden horse on rockers; ~-*stone*, large stone or boulder so poised that it rocks easily; ~-*turn*, turn in skating from any edge to same in opposite direction with body revolving away from convex of first curve.
ro'cky[1] adj. Of rock, full of or abounding in rocks; like rock in ruggedness, firmness, solidity, etc.; *R~ Mountains*, (also *Rockies*) great mountain range of western N. America, extending from the Mexican frontier to the Arctic regions.
ro'cky[2] adj. Unsteady, tottering.
rocŏ'cŏ adj. Of the style of decoration, originating in France and Italy in the late 17th c. and prevalent in Europe until c 1770, characterized esp. by scroll-work, shell motifs, asymmetrical effects, and lightness of colouring; (erron.) of the style of the 18th c. in general; (loosely) airily fantastic, frivolous, sophisticated, merely ornamental. ~ n. Rococo style. [Fr., f. *rocaille* rock-work (in ref. to encrusting grottoes with shells)]
rŏd n. Slender straight round stick growing as shoot on tree or cut from it or made from wood, switch, wand (freq. as symbol of office etc.), such stick, or bundle of twigs, for use in caning or flogging; fishing-rod; (as measure) = PERCH[2]; slender metal bar, connecting bar, shaft; rod-shaped structure; *a ~ in pickle*, a punishment in store.
ro'dent adj. Of the *Rodentia*, an order of mammals having only one pair of strong incisors in each jaw and no canine teeth (including rats, voles, beavers, mice, etc.); *~ ulcer*, (path.) slow-growing form of cancer causing extensive destruction of tissue. ~ n. Rodent mammal.
rŏde'o (-dāō) n. Round-up of cattle for branding etc.; exhibition of cowboys' skill.
Rŏdin (-dăn), Auguste (1840–1917). French sculptor.
Ro'dney, George Brydges, Baron (1718–92). English admiral; victor over Spanish fleet off Cape St. Vincent (1780) and over a French fleet off Dominica (1782).
rŏdomontā'de n. & adj. Boastful, bragging (saying or talk). ~ v.i. Brag. [It. *Rodomonte*, character in Ariosto's 'Orlando Furioso']
Rŏdri'guez (-rēgĕz). British island in Indian Ocean, dependency of Mauritius, which is nearly 400 miles to westward.
rŏe[1] n. (also *~ deer*) Small European and W. Asiatic species of deer (*Capreolus capreolus*); ~-*buck*, male roe.
rŏe[2] n. Mass of eggs (*hard ~*) in fish's ovarian membrane; *soft ~* male fish's milt; ~-*stone*, oolite.
Roentgen[1], **roentgen**[2] n. Varr. of RÖNTGEN[1], RÖNTGEN[2].
Roffen. abbrev. (Bishop) of Rochester (replacing surname in his signature).
rogā'tion n. 1. (usu. pl.) Solemn supplication consisting of litanies chanted on *R~ days*, Monday, Tuesday, and Wednesday preceding Ascension Day, prescribed days of prayer and fasting on which intercession is made esp. for the harvest; *R~ Sunday*, Sunday before Ascension Day. 2. (Rom. antiq.) Law proposed before the people by consul or tribune.
Rŏ'ger[1]. Masculine proper name: *Jolly ~*, pirates' black flag; (*Sir*) *~ de Coverley*, English country dance, with dancers facing each other in two rows; the music of this.
rŏ'ger[2] adv. Response used in oral communication by radio etc. to indicate that a message has been received and understood.
rōgue (-g) n. Idle vagrant (archaic); dishonest, unprincipled person (freq. playfully of mischievous child etc.); inferior plant among seedlings; wild beast, esp. elephant, driven or living apart from the herd and of savage temper; horse that shirks work on racecourse or in hunting-field.
ro'guery (-ge-) n. **ro'guish** (-gĭ-) adj. (esp.) = ARCH[2]. **ro'-guishly** adv. **ro'guishness** n.
roi'ster v.i. Revel noisily, be uproarious (esp. in part. *roistering* as adj.). **roi'sterer**, **roi'stering** ns.
Rŏ'land. Hero of medieval (esp. French and Italian) legend, one of the paladins of Charlemagne; became friend of Oliver, another paladin, after single-handed combat in which neither won; was killed in a rearguard action at Roncevaux in the Pyrenees; *a ~ for an Oliver*, an equal exchange.
rōle, **rôle** (rōl) n. Actor's part; one's task or function.
rōll[1] n. 1. Cylinder formed by turning flexible fabric over and over upon itself without folding; quantity of textile fabric rolled thus (esp. as definite measure of cloth); (U.S.) quantity of notes or bills rolled together, person's money; (archit.) volute of Ionic capital. 2. Document, esp. official record, in this form; *Master of the Rolls*, one of four *ex officio* judges of Court of Appeal, with charge of rolls, patents, and grants that pass the great seal, and of Chancery records; *the Rolls*, former building in Chancery Lane, London (now represented by Public Record Office), where these documents were kept. 3. List of names (freq. fig., as in *~ of fame*, *~ of saints*); official list of those qualified to act as solicitors; *strike off the ~s*, debar from practising as solicitor; *~-call*, calling over of list (as in school or army) so that each person present answers to his name and absentees are detected; *~ of honour*, (esp.) list of those who have died for their country in war. 4. More or less (semi-) cylindrical straight or curved mass of anything however formed; (*also bread ~*) small loaf for one person; (archit., also *~-moulding*) moulding of convex section, (ill. MOULDING); *ro'llmop*, salted spiced herring rolled up and skewered. 5. Cylinder, roller; in steel mill, grooved cylinder, usu. one of a set revolving simultaneously, beneath which or between which white-hot ingots are passed to shape them. 6. Bookbinder's revolving patterned tool for marking cover.
rōll[2] v. 1. Move, send, go, in some direction by turning over and over on axis; (cause to) go, convey, with smooth rolling or sweeping motion (freq. fig.); undulate; make revolve between two surfaces; wrap (*up in*) by rolling motion; (of eyes) change direction (*of*) with rotatory motion. 2. Wallow, turn about in fluid or loose medium; (of animal) lie on back and kick about; sway or rock, walk with swaying gait as of sailor, reel. 3. (of sound) Utter, be uttered, sound, with vibratory, undulating, or trilling effect. 4. Flatten by passing roller over or by passing between rollers; shape (metal) by passing between or beneath rolls. 5. Turn over and over upon itself into more or less cylindrical shape. 6. Form into cylindrical or spherical shape or accumulate into mass, by rolling. 7. *~-on* (n.) light corset made of elastic; (adj.) applying (liquid) by means of a rotating ball in the neck of a container; *~-top desk*, desk with flexible cover sliding in curved grooves. **rōlled** (-ld) adj. (esp.) *~ gold*, base metal with thin coating of gold applied by rolling. **rō'lling** adj. & n. (esp.) *~ mill*, mill which rolls steel into thin sheets or strips; *~-pin*, cylindrical roller for rolling out dough; *~-press*, press with rollers for various purposes; *~-stock*, railway company's wagons and trucks. **rōll** n. 1. Rolling motion; spell of rolling; rolling gait; turn of aircraft about its longitudinal axis through 360° (used on return to airfield as sign of victory; ill. AEROBATICS). 2. Quick continuous beating of drum; long peal of thunder or shout; rhythmic flow of words.
Rŏlland (-ahṅ), Romain (1866–1944). French novelist, essayist, and man of letters.
rō'ller n. (esp.) 1. Cylinder of wood, stone, metal, etc., used alone or as rotating part of machine for lessening friction, smoothing

[758]

ground, pressing, stamping, crushing, flattening, spreading printer's ink, rolling up cloth on, etc.; hollow cylinder of plastic, wire, etc., for rolling hair for setting; ~ **bandage**, long surgical bandage rolled up for convenience of applying. 2. Long swelling wave. 3. Breed of tumbler-pigeon. 4. Brilliant-plumaged crow-like bird (esp. *Coracias garrulus*); canary with trilling or rolling song. 5. ~-**skate**, skate-like contrivance with small wheels or rollers instead of blade, for skating on smooth flooring etc.; ~-*towel*, towel with ends joined, running on roller.

rŏ′llick *v.i.* Be jovial, indulge in high spirits, enjoy life boisterously, revel (chiefly in part, *rollicking* as adj.). ~ *n.* Exuberant gaiety; frolic, spree, escapade.

Rŏ′llŏ (d. *c* 932). Leader of Normans who settled at mouth of River Seine, and first Duke of Normandy.

rō′lў-pō′lў *n.* Pudding made of sheet of paste covered with jam etc., formed into roll, and boiled or baked. ~ *adj.* (usu. of children) Podgy, plump.

rom. *abbrev.* Roman (type).

Rom. *abbrev.* Romans (N.T.).

Romā′ic *adj.* & *n.* (Of) the vernacular language of modern Greece.

Rŏmains (-ăṅ), Jules. Pseudonym of Louis Farigoule (1885–1972), French novelist, poet, and playwright.

Rō′man *adj.* 1. Of ancient or modern Rome or the Roman republic or Empire. 2. Of the Roman Catholic Church. 3. (of nose) Having prominent upper part or bridge like those seen in portraits of ancient Romans. 4. *r*~, of the modern kind of lettering or type which most directly represents that used in ancient Roman inscriptions, of the kind now in ordinary use in W. Europe and the New World; upright, as dist. from *italic* (ill. TYPE). 5. (of numerals) Expressed in letters of the Roman alphabet, thus: I = 1, V = 5, X = 10, L = 50, C = 100, D = 500, M = 1000; the letters composing a number are ranged in order of value and the number meant is found by addition, e.g. MDCLXVI = 1666; if a letter or set of letters is placed before a letter of higher value, it is to be subtracted from it before the addition is done, e.g. IIC = 98, MCM = 1900. 6. ~ *candle*, tube discharging coloured balls in fireworks; ~ *Catholic*, (member) of that part of the Western or Latin Christian Church which owes its allegiance to the Bishop of Rome (the Pope); so ~ *Catholicism*; ~ *Empire*, that established by Augustus 27 B.C. and divided by Theodosius A.D. 395 into the Western Empire with Rome as its capital and the Eastern Empire with Byzantium as its capital (see BYZANTINE); *Holy* ~ *Empire*, confederation of Germanic States regarded as the revival of the Western Empire, formed in 962 when Otto I was crowned emperor (or sometimes regarded as originating with Charlemagne in 800); so *Holy* ~ *Emperor*; ~ *law*, system of law of ancient Rome, esp. as codified under the Emperor JUSTINIAN; code, modified or derived from the Justinian code, in force in many parts of Europe in modern times; ~ *road*, road surviving from the period of Roman rule. ~ *n.* 1. Native, inhabitant, of ancient or modern Rome, the Roman republic or Empire; (*Epistle to the*) ~*s*, book of N.T., epistle of St. Paul to the Church at Rome. 2. (disparagingly) Roman Catholic. 3. *r*~, roman lettering or type.

Romā′nce[1] *adj.* & *n.* (Of) the vernacular language of France, descended from Latin; (of) the whole group of languages descended from Latin, including French, Spanish, Portuguese, Italian, Rumanian, etc.; derived or descended from Latin; composed in a Romance language.

romā′nce[2] *n.* 1. Medieval tale, usu. in verse, of some hero of chivalry (orig. because written in Romance, i.e. not in Latin). 2. Prose or rarely verse tale (esp. of the class prevalent in 16th and 17th centuries) with scene and incidents remote from everyday life; class of literature consisting of such tales; set of facts, episode, love affair, etc., suggesting such tale by its strangeness or moving nature; romantic or imaginative character or quality; exaggeration, picturesque falsehood. 3. (mus.) Short composition of simple or informal character. ~ *v.i.* Invent romances; exaggerate fantastically. **romā′ncer** *n.*

Rŏmanĕ′sque (-sk) *adj.* Of the style of art and architecture prevalent in W. Europe between the end of the classical period and the rise of Gothic style, (esp.) of the style prevalent from mid-11th c. until end of 12th c., characterized by the use of massive stone vaulting and the round-headed arch, often with richly carved columns and capitals, and sculptured figures (in ref. to English buildings called 'Norman'); *First* ~, style of architecture originating in Italy in 9th c. ~ *n.* Romanesque style.

Romā′nia. Var. of RUMANIA.

Romā′nic *adj.* (of languages) = ROMANCE[1].

Rŏ′manīze *v.t.* Render Roman in character; bring under the influence or rule of Rome.

Romāno- *prefix.* Roman, Roman and —.

Roma′nov (-ahnof). Surname of the imperial dynasty ruling in Russia from the accession of Michael Romanov (elected tsar 1613) to 1917.

Romă′nsh *adj.* & *n.* (Of) the Rhaeto-Romantic dialect spoken in the Grisons, E. Switzerland.

romă′ntic *adj.* Characterized by, suggestive of, given to, romance; imaginative, remote from experience, visionary; (of projects etc.) fantastic, unpractical, quixotic, dreamy; (of music, literary or artistic method, etc., opp. CLASSIC) preferring grandeur, picturesqueness, passion, or irregular beauty to finish and proportion, subordinating whole to parts or form to matter; *R*~ *Movement*, *Revival*, movement of European literature and art of late 18th and early 19th centuries. **romă′nticallў** *adv.* **romă′nticĭsm, romă′nticĭst** *ns.* **romă′ntĭc** *n.* Romantic person; (pl.) romantic ideas or talk; *R*~, participant in the Romantic Movement.

Rŏ′manў *adj.* & *n.* (Of) a gipsy or the gipsies; (of) the language of the gipsies, an Indo-European language related to Hindi.

romau′nt *n.* (archaic) Romance or tale of chivalry etc.

Rōme. (It. *Roma*) 1. City on River Tiber, about 20 miles from sea near centre of W. coast of Italy, founded 753 B.C.; a republic from *c* 500 B.C. until the reign of Augustus (*c* 31 B.C.), and conqueror and chief city of most of the known world; in modern times, capital city of Italy (*King of* ~, title given to NAPOLEON[1] II at his birth). 2. Rome as see of the Pope and original capital of Western Christendom; hence, the Roman Catholic Church.

Rō′mĕŏ. Hero of Shakespeare's romantic tragedy 'Romeo and Juliet'; hence, romantic young lover.

Rŏ′mney[1]. Town and former port in Kent, one of the CINQUE PORTS.

Rŏ′mney[2](*or* rŭ-), George (1734–1802). English portrait painter.

rŏmp *v.i.* (of children etc.) Play about together, chase each other, wrestle, etc.; (racing slang) get *along*, *past*, etc., without effort, come *in* or *home* as easy winner. ~ *n.* Child or woman fond of romping, tomboy; spell of romping, boisterous play. **rŏ′mper** *n.* (sing. or pl.) Garment, usu. covering trunk only, for young child to play in.

Rŏ′mūlus. (Rom. legend) Founder of Rome, one of the twin sons of Mars by the vestal Rhea Silvia, exposed at birth with his brother Remus and found and suckled by a she-wolf.

Roncevaux, Roncesvalles (rawńsevō, -văl). Village in Navarre, N. Spain, in W. Pyrenees, site of legendary defeat of rearguard of Charlemagne's army and death of ROLAND.

rŏ′ndeau (-ō) *n.* Poem of 10 or 13 lines having only two rhymes throughout and with opening words used twice as refrain.

RONDEL

rŏ'ndel *n.* Poem of 13 or 14 lines, with two rhymes only, and with the first two lines recurring after the sixth, and the first two or the first only at the end.

rŏ'ndō *n.* Piece of music (freq. as last movement of sonata) in which principal theme recurs twice or oftener in same key, after introduction of contrasting themes.

rŏ'ndūre (*or* -dyer) *n.* (poet.) Round outline or object.

rŏ'nèo *v.t.* Reproduce by means of a *Roneo*, a type of duplicating machine.

Ronsard (rawṅsar̄), Pierre de (1524–85). French lyric poet, chief figure in the PLEIAD.

Rö'ntgen[1] (rŏntyen *or* rĕr̄-; *or* -jen), Wilhelm Konrad von (1845–1923). German physicist, discoverer of X-RAYS, hence freq. called *∼-rays*; *∼ therapy*, treatment of disease by X-rays.

rö'ntgen[2] (rŏntyen *or* rĕr̄-; *or* -jen) *n.* (abbrev. r) Quantity of X or gamma radiation used as unit of radioactivity. [f. RÖNTGEN[1]]

rōod *n.* 1. (esp. *holy ∼*) Cross of Christ (archaic); crucifix, esp. one raised on middle of *∼ screen*, wooden or stone carved screen separating nave and choir; *∼-arch*, arch between nave and choir; *∼-loft*, gallery above roodscreen. 2. Measure of land, properly 40 sq. poles or a quarter acre but varying locally; esp. as loose term for small piece of land.

rōof *n.* Upper covering of house or building, usu. supported by its walls; top of covered vehicle, esp. when used for outside passengers; *∼ of the mouth*, palate; *∼ of the world*, high mountain range; *∼-spotter*, observer on top of a building to spot hostile aircraft; *∼-tree*, ridge-pole of roof. **rōo'fage, rōo'fing** *ns.* **rōo'flèss** *adj.* **rōof** *v.t.* Cover with roof; be roof of.

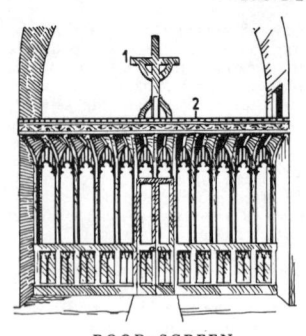

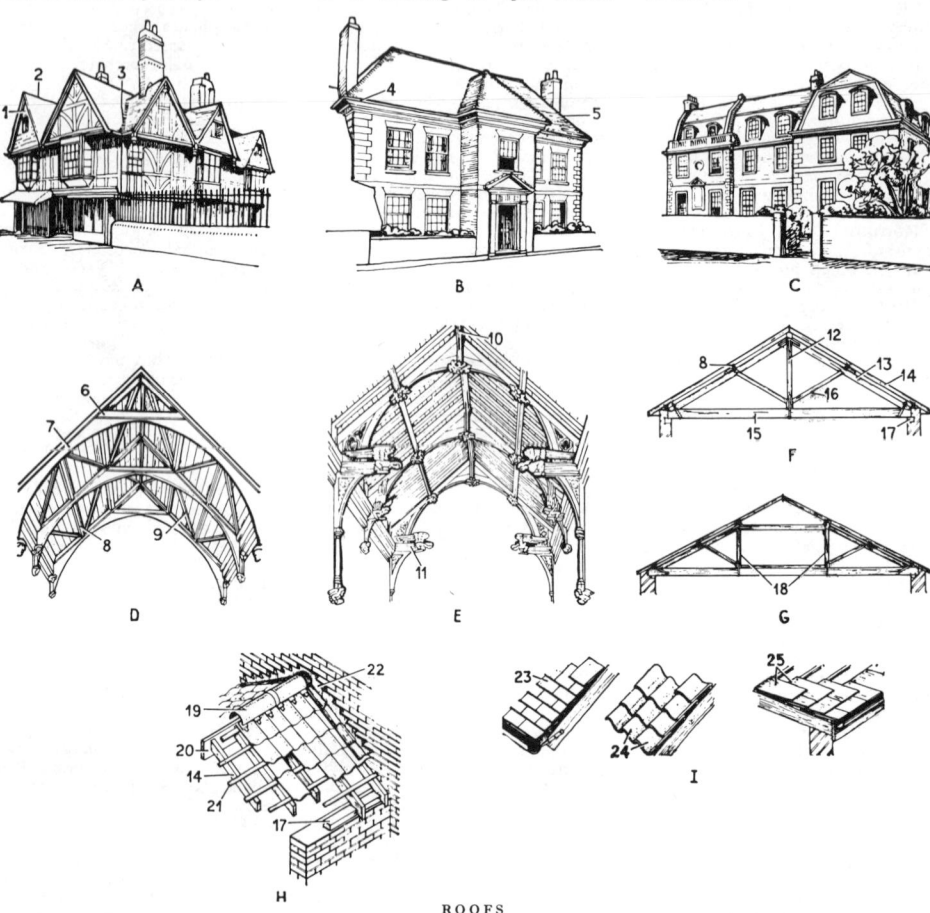

ROOF

ROOD-SCREEN
1. Rood. 2. Rood-loft

ROOFS
A. GABLED.   B. HIPPED.   C. MANSARD.   ROOF-TRUSSES: D. ARCH-BRACED COLLAR-BEAM.
E. HAMMER BEAM. F. KING-POST. G. QUEEN-POST. H. ROOF CONSTRUCTION. I. TILES AND SLATES

1. Gable. 2. Ridge. 3. Valley. 4. Eaves. 5. Hip. 6. Collar-beam. 7. Arched brace. 8. Purlin. 9. Wind brace. 10. Ridge-pole. 11. Hammer beam. 12. King-post. 13. Principal rafter. 14. Common rafter. 15. Tie-beam. 16. Strut. 17. Wall-plate. 18. Queen-posts. 19. Ridge-tile. 20. Ridge-piece. 21. Batten. 22. Flashing. 23. Tiles. 24. Pantiles. 25. Slates

[760]

roo'fer n. (colloq.) Letter of thanks for entertainment sent by departed visitor (f. stock phrase *under your hospitable roof*).

roo'inek (rō-) n. Englishman, esp. new-comer, in S. Africa. [S.-Afr. Du., = 'red-neck' (*rood red*)]

rook[1] n. Common black raucous-voiced European and Asiatic bird (*Corvus frugilegus*) of crow family, nesting in colonies; cheat, swindler, esp. at dice or cards; ~-*rifle*, rifle of small bore for rook-shooting. ~ v.t. Defraud by cheating at dice, cards, etc.; charge (customer) extortionately.

rook[2] n. (chess) One of 4 pieces which at beginning of game are set in corner squares, and have power of moving in a straight line forwards, backwards, or laterally over any number of unoccupied squares (ill. CHESS). [f. (ult.) Arab. *rukh*].

roo'kery n. (Clump of trees with) colony of rooks; colony of penguins etc. or seals; (archaic) crowded cluster of mean houses or tenements.

roo'kie, roo'ky n. (army slang) Recruit.

room n. 1. Space that is or might be occupied by something; capaciousness, ability to accommodate contents; *in the ~ of*, instead of, in succession to, as substitute for; *make ~*, vacate standing-ground etc., or post etc., *for* another, withdraw, retire; clear a space *for* by removal of others. 2. Opportunity, scope, *to do or for*. 3. Part of house or other building enclosed by walls or partitions; (pl.) set of these occupied by person or family, apartments or lodgings; (transf., sing.) company in a room; ~ *service*, (department of hotel responsible for) serving food and drinks to a guest in his room. **roo'mful** n. **room** v.i. (U.S.) Have room(s), lodge, board; *rooming house*, lodging house. **roo'mer** n. (U.S.) Lodger.

roo'my adj. Capacious, large, of ample dimensions.

Roosevelt[1] (rō'ze-), Franklin Delano (1882–1945). 32nd president of U.S., 1933–45.

Roosevelt[2] (rō'ze-), Theodore (1858–1919). 26th president of U.S., 1901–9.

roost[1] n. Tumultuous tidal race off various parts of Orkneys and Shetlands.

roost[2] n. Bird's perching- or resting-place, esp. hen-house or part of it in which fowls sleep; *come home to ~*, come back upon originator; *rule the ~*, be the leader or master. ~ v. (of birds etc.) Settle for sleep, be perched or lodged for night; provide with sleeping-place. **roo'ster** n. (esp. U.S.) Domestic cock.

root[1] n. 1. Part of plant normally below earth's surface and serving to attach it to earth and convey nourishment to it from soil; (pl.)

such part divided into branches or fibres; (sing.) corresponding organ of epiphyte, rootlet attaching ivy to its support; permanent underground stock of plant; (hort.) small plant with root for transplanting; (bibl.) scion, offshoot;

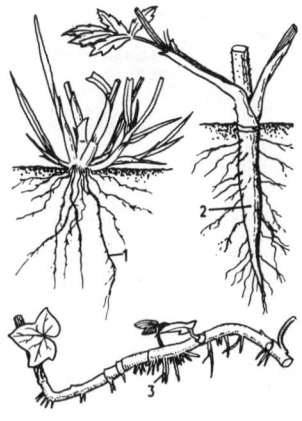

ROOTS
1. Fibrous root (grass). 2. Tap-root (wild carrot). 3. Adventitious root (ivy)

pull up by the ~s, uproot; *take, strike, ~*, begin to draw nourishment from soil; get established; *roo'tstock*, primary form whence offshoots have arisen. 2. (Plant, such as turnip, carrot, etc. with) root used for food or in medicine. 3. Imbedded part of some bodily organ or structure, as hair, tooth, nail; part of thing attaching it to greater or more fundamental whole. 4. Source or origin (*of*); basis, dependence, means of continuance, or growth; bottom, essential substance or nature. 5. (math.) Number, quantity or dimension which when multiplied by itself a requisite number of times produces a given expression (symbol √); value(s) of an unknown quantity. which will satisfy a given equation; ~ *mean square*, (abbrev. r.m.s.) square root of the arithmetic mean of the squares of a set of numbers. 6. (philol.) Ultimate unanalysable element of language, forming basis of vocabulary. 7. (mus.) Fundamental note of chord. **roo'tlet** n. **root** v. (Cause to) take root; fix firmly to the spot; establish.

root[2], **rout** vbs. 1. (of swine etc.) Turn up ground with snout, beak, etc., in search of food; turn *up* (ground) thus. 2. Search *out*, hunt *up*, rummage *among, in*, **roo'tle** v. Root.

rope n. 1. (Piece of) stout cord (technically, over 1 in. in circumference); *the ~*, halter for hanging person; *the ~s*, those enclosing boxing-ring or other arena; *give one* (*enough*) *~* (*to hang himself*),

plenty of ~, etc., not check him, trust to his bringing about his own discomfiture; *know the ~s*, be familiar with the conditions in some sphere of action; ~ *of pearls* etc., pearls etc. strung together. 2. Viscid or gelatinous stringy formation in beer or other liquid. 3. ~-*dancer, -dancing*, performer, performance, on tight-rope; ~-*ladder*, two long ropes connected by cross-ropes as ladder; ~'*s-end*, short piece of rope used for flogging person; ~-*walk*, long piece of ground used for twisting rope; ~-*yarn*, (piece of the) material (esp. when unpicked) of which rope-strands consist. **rō'py** adj. Rope-like; forming viscid glutinous or slimy threads; (slang) extremely poor or inferior. adj. **rō'piness, rō'ping** ns. **rōpe** v. 1. Fasten or secure with rope; catch with rope; (mountaineering) connect (party) with rope, attach (person) to rope, put on rope; use ropes in towing etc.; enclose, close *in*, shut *off*, (space) with rope; ~ *in*, draw into some enterprise. 2. Become ropy or viscid.

Roquefort (rŏ'kfor) n. Blue cheese of a type orig. made at Roquefort, a town in S. France, usu. of ewes' milk and ripened in limestone caves, with strong characteristic flavour.

rō'quelaure (-kelor) n. (hist.) Man's cloak (18th and early 19th centuries) reaching to knees. [Fr., f. Duke of *Roquelaure* (1656–1738)]

rō'quet (-ki) n. (croquet) Hitting another player's ball with one's own. ~ v. Cause one's ball to strike, (of ball) strike, another.

ror'qual n. Whale of genus *Balænoptera*, with dorsal fin; *Sibbald's ~*, blue whale (see WHALE[1]). [Norw. *raud* red, *hval* whale]

Rō'sa (-z-), Salvator (1615–73). Italian landscape painter and etcher.

rō'sace (-z-) n. Rose-window; rose-shaped ornament or design.

rosa'ceous (-zāshus) adj. Of the order Rosaceae, of which the rose is the type.

rosa'niline (-z-; or -ēn) n. Magenta dye.

rosar'ian (-z-) n. 1. Rose-fancier. 2. *R~*, (R.C. Ch.) member of a Confraternity of the Rosary.

rō'sary (-z-) n. 1. Rose-garden, rose-bed. 2. (R.C. Ch.) Form of prayer in which 15 decades of Aves are repeated, each decade preceded by Paternoster and followed by Gloria; book containing this; string of 165 beads for keeping count in this.

Roscius (rŏ'shus). Quintus Roscius Gallus (d. 62 B.C.), Roman comic actor.

Rŏscŏ'mmon. Inland county of province of Connacht.

rōse (-z) n. 1. (Prickly bush or shrub of genus *Rosa* bearing) a

[761]

beautiful and usu. fragrant flower usu. of red, yellow, or white colour; (with defining word) any of various other flowering plants; ~ *of Sharon*, unidentified Eastern plant; (also) species of St. John's wort; *bed of* ~*s*, perfect conditions, pleasant easy post or condition; *path strewn with* ~*s*, life of delight; *under the* ~, in secret. 2. Representation of the flower in heraldry or decoration, esp. as national emblem of England; rose-shaped design; rosette worn on shoe or clerical hat; protuberance round base of animal's horn or eye of some birds; sprinkling-nozzle of watering-pot or hose; rose diamond; rose-window; *golden* ~, ornament blessed by pope on 4th Sunday in Lent (*R*~ *Sunday*) and sent as compliment to R.C. sovereign, city, etc.; *Wars of the Roses*, series of civil wars in England during reigns of Henry VI, Edward IV, and Richard III (15th c.), between followers of house of York (with white rose as badge) and of house of Lancaster (red rose), ended (exc. for rebellion of Lambert Simnel) by the accession in 1485 of the Lancastrian Henry Tudor, Earl of Richmond (Henry VII), who united the two houses by marrying Elizabeth, daughter of Edward IV. 3. Light crimson colour, pink; (usu. pl.) rosy complexion. 4. ~-*apple*, (edible sweet-scented fruit of) small tropical tree (*Eugenia*) with beautiful foliage; ~-*bay*, oleander; willow-herb; *ro'sebud*, bud of rose; ~-*bush*, rose plant; ~-*chafer*, beetle of genus *Cetonia*, frequenting roses, very destructive in grub-state; ~-*colour*, rosy red, pink; (fig.) pleasant state of things or outlook; ~-*coloured*, rosy; (fig.) optimistic, cheerful; ~-*cut*, (of gem) hemispherical with upper surface cut into many triangular facets (ill. GEM); ~-*diamond*, rose-cut diamond; ~-*gall*, excrescence on dog-rose etc. made by insect (ill. GALL); ~-*leaf*, leaf, usu. petal, of rose; *crumpled* ~-*leaf*, (fig.) slight vexation alloying general felicity; ~-*nail*, nail with head shaped like rose diamond; ~-*noble*, (hist.) 15th–16th c. gold coin of varying value stamped with rose; ~-*pink*, rose-colour(ed); ~-*red*, red as (of) a rose; *R*~ *Sunday*, see sense 2; ~-*water*, perfume distilled from roses; ~ *window*, round window, usu. filled with tracery suggesting rose-shape or divided by spoke-like mullions (ill. WINDOW); *ro'sewood*, any of various kinds of valuable close-grained fragrant cabinet wood. ~ *adj.* Coloured like a pale-red rose, of warm pink.

rosé (rōzā) *n.* Short for *vin rosé* (văṅ), pink table-wine, the pale colour being produced by removing the grape-skins during fermentation. [Fr.]

rō'sēāte (-z-)*adj.* Rose-coloured. **rō'sēately** *adv.*

Rō'sebery (-zb-), Archibald Philip Primrose, 5th Earl of (1847–1929). British Liberal statesman, foreign secretary in Gladstone's governments of 1886 and 1892, and prime minister 1894–5.

rō'semary (-zm-) *n.* Evergreen fragrant shrub (*Rosmarinus officinalis*), native of S. Europe, with leaves used in perfumery etc., and taken as emblem of remembrance. [L *ros* dew, *marinus* marine]

rōsē'ola (-z-) *n.* (path.) Any reddish rash. **rōsē'olar, rōsē'olous** *adjs.*

Rosē'tta stōne (-z-). Stone found near Rosetta on the W. mouth of the Nile by Napoleon's soldiers in 1799; its inscription, in Egyptian hieroglyphics, demotic characters, and Greek, made it possible to decipher hieroglyphics.

rōsē'tte (-z-) *n.* Rose-shaped ornament for dress or harness made of ribbons, leather strips, etc.; rose diamond; rose-like object or arrangement of leaves, parts, etc.; (archit.) carved or moulded conventional rose on wall etc. (ill. MOULDING); rose window.

Rōsicru'cian (-zĭkrōōshan) *n.* Member of supposed society in 17th and 18th centuries (reputed to have been founded 1484 by a Christian Rosenkreuz, but first mentioned 1614), which was said to claim secret and magic knowledge of transmutation of metals, prolongation of life, power over elements and elemental spirits, etc.; member of one of several later organizations professing principles derived from or attributed to this society. **Rōsicru'cianism** *n.* [L *rosa crux* rose cross, as transl. of Ger. *Rosenkreuz*]

rŏ'sin (-z-) *n.* Resin (esp. of solid residue after distillation of oil of turpentine from crude turpentine). ~ *v.t.* Smear, seal up, rub (e.g. fiddle-bow or -string), with rosin.

Rŏsĭnă'ntĕ (-z-) *n.* Don Quixote's horse; hence, poor worn-out horse, hack.

rosō'liō (-z-) *n.* S. European cordial of spirits, raisins, sugar, etc. [It., f. L *ros* dew, *solis* of the sun, the cordial being orig. made from the plant sundew]

RoSPA *abbrev.* Royal Society for the Prevention of Accidents.

Rŏss¹, Rŏ'ss-shire. Former county of Scotland joined with Cromarty in 1890 to form Ross AND CROMARTY.

Rŏss², Sir James Clark (1800–62). English admiral and polar explorer; commander of the Antarctic expedition of *Erebus* and *Terror* (1839–43).

Rŏss³, Sir John (1777–1856). Arctic explorer, author of two narratives of voyages (1818 and 1829–33) in search of the Northwest passage.

Rŏss⁴, Sir Ronald (1857–1932). English physician and bacteriologist; demonstrated transmission of malaria by mosquito-bites.

Rŏss and Crŏ'marty. Former county of N. Scotland, extending from N. Sea to Atlantic, since May 1975 part of the region of Highland.

Rossē'tti (-z-). Name of English family of Italian origin: Dante Gabriel ~ (1828–82), poet and painter, and his brother William Michael ~ (1829–1919), critic, both members of the PRE-RAPHAELITE Brotherhood; Christina Georgina ~ (1830–94), their sister, poet.

Rŏssi'ni (-sē-), Gioacchino Antonio (1792–1868). Italian composer of 'The Barber of Seville', 'William Tell', and other operas.

Rŏstand (-tahṅ), Edmond (1868–1918). French poet and dramatist, author of 'Cyrano de Bergerac'.

rŏstĕ'llum *n.* (pl. *-la*). 1. (bot.) Short beak-shaped process on stigma of many violets and orchids. 2. (zool.) Protruding fore-part of head of tapeworm (ill. TAPE).

rŏ'ster *n.* List or plan showing turns of duty or leave for individuals or companies esp. of a military force. [Du. *rooster* list, orig. gridiron (*rooster* roast) w. ref. to parallel lines]

rŏ'stral *adj.* (of column etc.) Adorned with actual or sculptured etc. beaks of ancient war-galleys (zool. etc.) of, on, the rostrum. **rostrā'tĕd** *adj.* (of column etc.) Rostral; (zool. etc.) having, ending in, a rostrum.

rŏ'strum *n.* (pl. *-ra*, *-rums*). 1. Platform for public speaking (orig. that in Roman forum adorned with beaks of captured galleys); pulpit; office etc. that enables person to gain the public ear. 2. (Rom. antiq.) Beak of war-galley. 3. (zool., entom., bot.) Beak, stiff snout, beak-like part. **rŏ'strate, rŏ'striform** *adjs.* Beak-like.

rō'sy̌ (-zĭ) *adj.* Coloured like a red rose (esp. of complexion as indicating health, of blush, wine, sky, etc.); (fig.) rose-coloured, promising, hopeful; ~ *cross*, supposed emblem of Rosicrucians. **rō'sily** *adv.* **rō'siness** *n.*

rŏt *n.* 1. Decay, putrefaction, rottenness (esp. in timber); virulent liver-disease of sheep; (slang) sudden series of unaccountable failures. 2. (slang) freq. as int. of incredulity or ridicule) Nonsense; absurd statement, argument, or proposal; foolish course; undesirable state of things. ~ *v.* Undergo natural decomposition, decay, putrefy; cause to rot, make rotten; (fig.) gradually perish from want of vigour or use; (slang) spoil or disconcert; banter, tease; ~-*gut*, (liquor) injurious to stomach.

rō'ta *n.* 1. List of person acting, or duties to be done, in rotation; roster. 2. (R.C. Ch.) Supreme ecclesiastical and secular court. [L, = 'wheel']

ROTARIAN

Rōtār'ian *adj.* & *n.* (Member) of a ROTARY² Club.
rō'tarў¹ *adj.* Acting by rotation. ~ *n.* Rotary machine, esp. type of engine, as the turbine, in which the necessary rotary motion is obtained directly, instead of being converted, as in the *reciprocating engine.*
Rō'tarў² *adj.* ~ *Club*, Local organization of business men, first founded 1905 by Paul Harris in Chicago and imitated in Gt Britain 1911; it includes not more than one representative of each business, profession, or institution in the community and aims at furthering business service and social relations and promoting international understanding and goodwill; ~ *International*, international organization of Rotary Clubs. ~ *n.* Rotary movement or organization.
rō'tate¹ *adj.*(bot.) Wheel-shaped.
rotā'te² *v.* Move round axis or centre, revolve; arrange (esp. crops) or take in rotation. **rō'tatorў, rō'tative** *adjs.*
rotā'tion *n.* Rotating; recurrence, recurrent series or period, regular succession in office etc.; ~ *of crops*, growing of different crops in regular order to avoid exhausting soil. **rotā'tional** *adj.*
rotā'tor *n.* Revolving apparatus or part; (anat.) muscle that rotates a limb etc.
rōte *n.* Mere habituation, knowledge got by repetition, unintelligent memory (only in *by* ~).
Rō'thschild. Name of a Jewish family of financiers, founders at Frankfurt-on-Main, towards end of 18th c., of famous banking-house, with branches at Paris, Vienna, London, and Naples.
rō'tifer *n.* Member of the phylum Rotifera of minute (usu. microscopic) metazoan animals

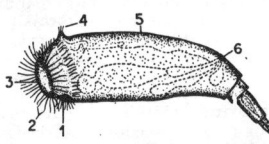

ROTIFER
1. Mouth. 2. Cilia. 3. Trochal disc. 4. Dorsal feeler. 5. Cuticle. 6. Anus

with (usu.) ring(s) of beating cilia giving the impression of revolving wheels; wheel-animalcule.
rōtogravūr'e (*or* -ā'vyer) *n.* Photogravure printed on rotary machine.
rō'tor' *n.* Rotary part of machine; rotating system of a helicopter (ill. HELICOPTER).
rō'ttĕn *adj.* 1. Affected with rot; perishing of decay; falling to pieces, friable, easily breakable or tearable, from age or use. 2. (of sheep) Affected with the rot. 3. Morally, socially or politically corrupt. 4. (slang) Disagreeable, regrettable, ill-advised. 5. ~

borough: see BOROUGH; ~-*stone*, decomposed siliceous limestone used as polishing powder. **rŏ'ttenlў** *adv.* **rŏ'ttenness** (-n-) *n.*
Rŏ'tten Row (rō). Wide track in Hyde Park, London, for horse-riders.
rŏ'tter *n.* (slang) Person objectionable on moral or other grounds.
Rŏ'tterdăm. City and principal port of the Netherlands, on river Meuse.
rotū'nd *adj.* Round, circular (rare); (of mouth) rounded in speaking etc.; (of speech etc.) as from rotund mouth, sonorous, sounding, grandiloquent; (of persons) plump, podgy. **rotū'ndlў** *adv.* **rotū'ndităў** *n.*
rotū'nda *n.* Building of circular ground-plan, esp. one with dome; circular hall or room.
rou'ble (roō-) *n.* Principal monetary unit of U.S.S.R., = 100 copecks.
roué (roō'ā) *n.* Debauchee, rake. [Fr., past part. of *rouer* break on wheel, = one deserving this]
Rouen (roōahn). City of N. France, on river Seine; ancient capital of Normandy.
rouge¹ (roōzh) *n.* Fine red powder made (originally) from safflower and used for colouring cheeks and lips; any cosmetic used thus; red plate powder of oxide of iron; red in ~ *et noir* (ā nwar), card-game played on table with two red and two black diamond-shaped marks upon which stakes are placed. ~ *adj.* Red (only in *R*~ *Croix*, ~ *Dragon*, two pursuivants of English College of Arms, so called from their badges). ~ *v.* Colour, adorn oneself, with rouge.
rouge² (roōj) *n.* In Eton football, scrummage, touch-down counting as point to opponents.
rough (rŭf) *adj.* 1. Of uneven or irregular surface; not smooth, level, or polished; diversified or broken by prominences; hairy, shaggy, coarse in texture, rugged. 2. Not mild, quiet, or gentle; unrestrained, violent, stormy, boisterous, disorderly, riotous; harsh, unfeeling; grating, strident. 3. Deficient in finish, elaboration, or delicacy; incomplete, rudimentary; entirely or partly unwrought; merely passable; inexact, approximate, preliminary. 4. ~ *and ready*, not elaborate, just good enough; not over-particular; roughly efficient or effective; ~-*and-tumble*, irregular, scrambling, disorderly, regardless of procedure rules; (*n.*) haphazard fight, scuffle; **rou'ghcast**, (coat, coated, with) plaster of lime and gravel for walls; (*v.*) coat (wall) with roughcast; ~ *coat*, first coat of plaster laid on; ~ *coating*, roughcast; ~ *diamond*: see DIAMOND; ~-*dry*, dry (clothes) without ironing; ~-*grind*, give preliminary grinding to (edged

ROUND

tool etc.); ~-*hew*, shape out roughly, give crude form to; ~-*house*, (orig. U.S.) disturbance, row; ~ (*luck*) *on*, bearing, what bears, hardly (on person); ~-*neck*, (U.S.) rowdy fellow; ~ *passage*, crossing over rough sea (also fig.); ~-*rider*, horsebreaker, man who can ride unbroken horses; irregular cavalryman; ~-*shod*, (of horse) having shoes with the nail-heads projecting; *ride* ~-*shod over*, treat arrogantly or inconsiderately. **rou'ghen** *v.* **rou'ghish** *adj.* **rou'ghlў** *adv.* **rou'ghness** *n.* **rough** *adv.* In rough manner. ~ *n.* 1. Rough ground; (golf) rough uncut ground bordering the fairway or between the tee and the green. 2. One of the spikes inserted in roughing horse. 3. Hard part of life, piece of hardship. 4. Rowdy, ruffian. 5. Unfinished or natural state. 6. Rough drawing etc. ~ *v.t.* 1. Turn *up* (feathers, hair, etc.) by rubbing against the grain. 2. Secure (horse, its shoes) against slipping by insertion of spikes or projecting nails in shoes. 3. Shape or plan *out*, sketch *in*, roughly; give first shaping to. 4. ~ *it*, do without ordinary conveniences of life.
rou'ghage (rŭf-) *n.* Less useful or refuse part of crops (U.S.); indigestible fibrous matter or cellulose in foodstuffs.
roulade (roōlah'd) *n.* Florid passage of runs, etc., in solo vocal music, usu. sung to one syllable.
rouleau (roōlō') *n.* Number of gold or other coins made up into cylindrical packet; coil or roll, esp. as trimming.
roulĕ'tte (roō-) *n.* 1. Gambling game played on table with revolving centre, on which ball is set in motion, and finally drops into one of set of numbered compartments. 2. (math.) Curve traced by point on curve rolling over another

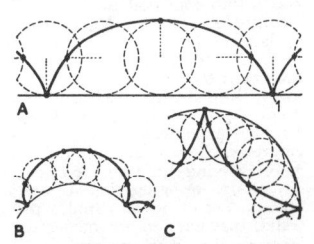

ROULETTES: A. CYCLOID (TROCHOID). B. EPICYCLOID. C. HYPOCYCLOID
1. Cusp

fixed curve. 3. Revolving toothed wheel for making dotted lines in engraving (ill. ENGRAVING); similar wheel for perforating postage stamps.
Roumā'nia (roō-). Var. of RUMANIA.
round¹ *adj.* 1. Spherical, circular, or cylindrical, or approaching

[763]

these forms; presenting convex outline or surface; done with or involving circular motion; (of cheeks) plump. 2. Entire, continuous, all together, not broken or defective or scanty, sound, smooth; complete (as ~ *dozen*); plain, genuine, candid, outspoken; (of voice etc.) full and mellow; *be* ~ *with*, (archaic) speak home truths to. 3. ~ *arch*, semicircular arch characteristic of Romanesque architecture; ~-*arm*, (of bowling) with arm swung horizontally; ~ *dance*, one in which dancers form a ring; ~ *figure*(*s*), round number; figure given as an approximate estimation; ~ *game*, one in which each player plays on his own account; ~ *hand*, writing with bold curves; *Rou'ndhead*, member of Parliamentary party in civil war of 17th c. (from custom of wearing hair close-cut); ~ *house*, (hist.) lock-up or place of detention; (naut.) cabin or set of cabins on after-part of quarterdeck, chiefly in old sailing-ships; ~ *number*, number (as tens, hundreds, etc.) stated without odd units; ~ *robin*, written petition with signatures radiating from centre of circle to conceal order in which they were written; ~ *shot*, spherical ball for smooth-bore cannon; ~ *shoulders*, shoulders so bent forward that back is convex; ~ *sum*, considerable sum of money; *R*~ *Table, Table R*~, that round which King Arthur and his knights are supposed to have sat, so that none might have precedence; ~-*table conference*, conference at which parties present are all on equal footing; ~-*top*, platform about masthead, formerly circular; ~ *towel*, roller towel; ~ *trip*, *voyage*, circular tour or trip, outward and return journey; *rou'ndworm*, nematode worm, often parasitic, e.g. species infesting human intestines. **rou'nden** *v.* **rou'ndish** *adj.* **rou'ndness** *n.*

round[2] *n.* 1. Round object; rung of ladder; large round piece *of* beef, cut from haunch; slice of toast etc.; *the* ~, form of sculpture in which figure stands clear of any ground, as dist. from *relief*; rounded or convex form. 2. Circumference, bounds, extent, *of*. 3. Revolving motion; circular, circuitous, or recurring course; circuit, cycle, series; (mil., pl.) watch that goes round inspecting sentries, circuit it makes; (golf) playing of all holes in course once; *daily* ~, ordinary occupations of the day; *make, go, one's* ~*s*, take customary walk, esp. of inspection; *rou'ndsman*, tradesman's employee going round for orders and with goods. 4. (mus.) Kind of canon for three or more voices singing the same melody, the first voice completing a phrase before the next enters, and so on. 5. Allowance of something distributed or measured out; one of set or series; one bout or spell; one stage in competition; single discharge of shot by firearm; ammunition for this; (archery) fixed number of arrows discharged at fixed distance.

round[3] *adv.* 1. With more or less circular motion, with return to starting-point after such motion, with rotation, with change to opposite position; by circuitous way; through, throughout; *bring, come,* ~, restore to, recover, consciousness; bring, come, incidentally or informally; (cause to) veer to a different opinion etc. 2. To, at, affecting, all or many points of a circumference or area or members of a company etc.; in every direction from a centre or within a radius; *an all-*~ *man*, one of varied talents; *show* ~, take (person) to all points of interest. 3. ~ *about*, in a ring (about), all round; on all sides (of); with change to opposite position; circuitously; about, approximately; piece of circumlocution; merry-go-round; place, as road junction, where all traffic must follow circular course; (*adj.*) circuitous; circumlocutory; plump or stout. ~ *prep.* So as to encircle or enclose; with successive visits to, at or to points on the circumference of; in various directions from or with regard to; having as axis of revolution or central point; so as to double or pass in curved course, having thus passed, in the position that would result from thus passing; ~ *the clock*, for 24 hours; unceasingly.

round[4] *v.* 1. Invest with, assume, round shape; round the lips in pronouncing (vowel); bring to complete, symmetrical, or well-ordered state (freq. ~ *off*). 2. Gather *up* (cattle) by riding round (freq. transf.), whence ~-*up* (*n.*) this action. 3. (naut.) Sail round, double (headland etc.). 4. Turn round (rare, chiefly naut.). 5. ~ *on*, make unexpected retort to, turn on; inform against.

rou'ndel *n.* 1. Small disc, esp. decorative medallion etc. 2. Rondeau; rondel.

rou'ndelay *n.* Short simple song with refrain.

rou'nders (-z) *n.pl.* Game with bat and ball between two sides of nine players, the unit of scoring being the round or complete run of player through all the bases arranged in a circle.

rou'ndly *adv.* 1. In thoroughgoing manner; bluntly, with plain speech; without qualification, severely. 2. In circular way.

roup[1] (rōōp) *n.* Highly infectious poultry-disease characterized by an acute fever generally ending in death. **rou'py** *adj.*

roup[2] (rowp) *v.t.* (Sc. & north.) Sell by auction. ~ *n.* Auction.

rouse[1] (-z) *n.* (archaic) Draught of liquor, bumper; toast; revel, drinking-bout.

rouse[2] (-z) *v.* 1. Startle (game) from lair or cover; bring out of a state of sleep, quiescence, etc.; provoke temper of, inflame with passion; evoke (feelings). 2. Stir (fire, liquid, esp. beer while brewing); (naut.) haul vigorously *in, out, up.* 3. Cease to sleep; become active. **rou'sing** *adj.* (esp.) Exciting, stirring; (of fire) blazing strongly; (of trade) brisk, lively.

Rousseau[1] (rōōsō), Henri (1844–1910). French painter; a customs officer, hence called 'le douanier'.

Rousseau[2] (rōōsō), Jean Jacques (1712–78). French philosopher, advocate of return to natural state, in which man is both good and happy; the 'Contrat Social' (1762), expounding the view that society is founded on a contract and that the head of a State is not the people's master but their mandatory, had profound influence on French thought and prepared the way for the Revolution.

Rousseau[3] (rōōsō), Pierre Étienne Théodore (1812–67), French landscape painter of BARBIZON school.

rout[1] *n.* 1. Assemblage or company esp. of revellers or rioters; (law) assemblage of three or more persons engaged in unlawful act; riot, tumult, disturbance, clamour, fuss. 2. (archaic) Large evening party or reception. 3. Disorderly retreat of defeated army or troops; *put to* ~, utterly defeat. ~ *v.t.* Put to rout.

rout[2] *v.* = ROOT[2]; (also) force or fetch *out* (of bed or from house etc.). **rou'ter** *n.* (esp., also ~ *plane*) Kind of plane used in moulding (ill. PLANE[2]).

route (rōōt, *mil.* rowt) *n.* Way taken in getting from starting-point to destination; (mil.) marching orders; *column of* ~, formation of troops on the march; ~-*march*, training march of soldiers etc. ~ *v.t.* Plan route of (goods etc., esp. by rail).

routine (rōōtē'n) *n.* Regular course of procedure, unvarying performance of certain acts; set form, fixed arrangement (e.g. of steps in dancer's performance); (attrib.) performed by rule or habitually. **routi'nism, routi'nist** *ns.*

roux (rōō) *n.* (cookery) Flour cooked in melted fat, used to thicken sauces etc. [Fr. = 'red', 'browned']

rōve[1] *v.* Wander without fixed destination, roam, ramble; (of eyes) look in various directions; wander over or through; (angling) troll with live bait; *roving commission*, authority granted by the Admiralty to the officer in command of a vessel to cruise wherever he may think fit; (transf.) authority given to pursue an inquiry or investigation in whatever quarters it may be considered necessary. ~ *n.* Act of roving. [orig. term used in archery, = 'shoot at casual mark with range not determined']

rōve² *n.* Sliver of cotton, wool, etc., drawn out and slightly twisted. ~ *v.t.* Form into roves.

rō'ver¹ *n.*

rōve³ *n.* Small metal plate or ring for rivet to pass through and be clinched over.

rō'ver² *n.* 1. (archery) Mark chosen at undetermined range; mark for long-distance shooting. 2. Wanderer; *R~*, former name for VENTURE Scout. 3. (croquet) (Player of) ball that has passed all hoops, but not pegged out.

rō'ver³ *n.* Sea-robber, pirate.

row¹ (rō) *n.* Number of persons or things in a more or less straight line; row of houses, street with this on one or each side (freq. in street names); line of seats in theatre etc.; row of plants in garden etc.; *the R~*, ROTTEN ROW; *a hard~ to hoe*, (U.S.) a difficult task.

row² (rō) *v.* Propel boat, propel (boat), convey (passenger) in boat, with oars or sweeps; row race with; be oarsman of specified number in boat; (of boat) be fitted with (so many *oars*); ~ *down*, overtake in rowing, esp. bumping, race; *~-boat*, (U.S.) rowing-boat; *rowed out*, (of crew) exhausted by rowing; *row'ing-boat*, boat propelled with oars. **row'er** *n.* **row** *n.* Spell of rowing, boat-excursion.

row³ *n.* (colloq.) Disturbance, commotion, noise, dispute; shindy, free fight; being reprimanded; *make*, *kick up*, *a ~*, raise noise; make protest. ~ *v.t.* Reprimand.

row'an (or rō-) *n.* (also ~ *tree*) Mountain ash, tree (*Sorbus aucuparia*) with pinnate leaves and scarlet berries.

row'dÿ *adj. & n.* Rough, disorderly, and noisy (person). **row'diness, row'dÿism** *ns.*

Rowe (rō), Nicholas (1674–1718). English playwright and poet; author of 'Tamerlane', 'The Fair Penitent', etc.

row'el *n.* Spiked revolving disc at end of spur (ill. SPUR); (now rare) circular piece of leather etc. with hole in centre, inserted between horse's skin and flesh to discharge exudate. ~ *v.t.* Urge with rowel.

Row'landson (rō-), Thomas (1756–1827). English caricaturist and illustrator.

row'lock (rŏl- *or* rŭl-) *n.* Pair of thole-pins or other contrivance on boat's gunwale serving as point of support for oar (ill. BOAT).

Row'ton, Montague William Lowry-Corry, Baron (1838–1903). English originator of scheme of ~ *Houses*, model lodging-houses for poor men at prices similar to those of common lodging-houses.

Rŏ'xburghshire (-brŏ-). Former inland border county of Scotland, since May 1975 part of the Borders region.

roy'al *adj.* 1. Of, from, suited to, worthy of, belonging to family of, in service or under patronage of, a king or queen; *R~ Academy of Arts*, institution, founded 1768 in London under patronage of George III, for annual exhibition of works of contemporary artists and establishment of school of art, housed in Burlington House, Piccadilly, since 1869; ~ *blue*, deep vivid blue; ~ *borough*, *burgh*, one holding charter from crown; ~ *evil*, KING's evil; *R~ Exchange*, building in Cornhill, London, for dealings between merchants, orig. founded by Sir T. Gresham in 1566, twice destroyed by fire, in its present form opened in 1844; *R~ Institution*, society founded 1799 in London for diffusion of scientific knowledge; ~ *jelly*, substance secreted by worker honey-bees, fed to all larvae in their first few days of life and afterwards only to those selected to develop into queens; ~ *oak*, oak in which Charles II hid after battle of Worcester (1651); sprig of oak worn to commemorate Restoration of Charles II (1660); ~ *oak day*, 29 May; *R~ Society*, scientific society founded 1660 in London from nucleus of Philosophical Society (founded 1645) to promote scientific discussion esp. in the physical sciences; ~ *standard*, banner with royal arms (ill. FLAG⁴). 2. Kingly, majestic, stately, splendid; first-rate; on great scale; of exceptional size etc.; *battle ~*, free fight; heated dispute; ~ *backstay*, *mast*, *sail*, that above topgallant (ill. SHIP); ~ *fern*, flowering fern *Osmunda regalis*; ~ *stag*, one with head of twelve or more points. **roy'ally** *adv.* **roy'al** *n.* 1. Royal stag. 2. Royal mast or sail. 3. Size of paper, 610 × 483 mm for writing and 635 × 508 mm for printing; ~ *octavo* etc., octavo etc. folded from this. 4. (colloq.) Member of royal family.

Roy'al George (jŏrj). English naval vessel which sank at Spithead 1782 while at anchor undergoing repairs, with Admiral Kempenfelt and about 800 visitors and crew.

roy'alist *n.* Monarchist, supporter of monarchy as institution or of the royal side in civil war etc. **roy'alism** *n.* **royali'stic** *adj.*

roy'altÿ *n.* 1. Office, dignity, or power of king or queen; sovereignty. 2. Royal persons; member of royal family. 3. Prerogative of privilege of sovereign (usu. pl.); royal licence to work minerals etc. 4. Sum paid to patentee for use of patent or to author, composer, etc., for each copy of his book, piece of music, etc., sold, or for each public performance of his work given.

R.P.S. *abbrev.* Royal Photographic Society.

R.Q.M.S. *abbrev.* Regimental Quartermaster-Sergeant.

R.R.C. *abbrev.* Royal Red Cross.

Rs, ₨ *abbrevs.* Rupees.

R.S. *abbrev.* Royal Scots; Royal Society.

R.S.A. *abbrev.* Royal Scóttish Academy; Royal Society of Arts.

R.S.D., R.S.E. *abbrevs.* Royal Society of Dublin, of Edinburgh.

R.S.F. *abbrev.* Royal Scots Fusiliers.

R.S.F.S.R. *abbrev.* Russian Soviet Federal Socialist Republic.

R.S.M. *abbrev.* Regimental Sergeant-Major.

R.S.O. *abbrev.* Railway sub-office.

R.S.P.C.A. *abbrev.* Royal Society for the Prevention of Cruelty to Animals.

R.S.V.P. *abbrev. Répondez s'il vous plaît* (Fr. = 'answer, if you please').

R.S.W. *abbrev.* Royal Scottish Society of Painters in Watercolours.

R.T., R/T *abbrevs.* Radiotelegraphy; radiotelephony.

Rt Hon. *abbrev.* Right Honourable.

R.T.O. *abbrev.* Railway Transport Officer.

R.T.R. *abbrev.* Royal Tank Regiment.

Rt Revd. *abbrev.* Right Reverend.

R.U. *abbrev.* Rugby Union.

rŭb *v.* 1. Subject to friction, slide one's hand or an object along over or up and down the surface of; polish, clean, abrade, chafe, make *bare*, *dry*, *sore*, etc., by rubbing; slide (hands, object) *against*, *on* or *over* something, (objects) *together*, with friction; bring *away*, *off*, or *out*, force *in*, *into*, *through*, reduce *to* powder, etc., bring size or level of *down*, spread *over*, groom *down*, freshen or brush *up*, mix *up* into paste, by rubbing (lit. & fig.); ~ *in*, (fig., colloq.) emphasize; ~ *noses*, rub nose against another's in greeting; ~ *one's hands* (*together*), rub each with the other, usu. in sign of keen satisfaction; ~ *shoulders*, come into contact *with* other people; ~ (*up*) *the wrong way*, stroke against the grain, irritate or repel as by stroking cat upwards. 2. Apply by rubbing. Make facsimile or design of (sepulchral brass or stone) by rubbing paper laid on it with coloured chalk etc. 3. Come into or be in sliding contact, exercise friction, *against* or *on*; (of bowl) be retarded or diverted by unevenness of ground; (fig., of person etc.) go *along*, *on*, *through*, with more or less restraint or difficulty; (of cloth, skin, etc.) get frayed, worn, sore, or bare with friction. ~ *n.* Spell of rubbing; (bowls) inequality of ground impeding or diverting bowl, being diverted etc. by this; (transf.) impediment or difficulty; (golf) ~ *of the green*, accidental interference with course or position of ball.

rŭ'b-a-dŭb *n. & v.i.* (Make) rolling sound of drum. [imit.]

[765]

ruba′tō (rōōbah′tō) *n.* (mus.) In full, *tempo* ~, time occasionally slackened or hastened for the purposes of expression. [It., = 'robbed']

rŭ′bber[1] *n.* 1. Person who rubs, as Turkish-bath attendant who rubs bathers. 2. Implement used for rubbing; part of machine operating by rubbing. 3. (from its use in erasing pencil-marks; also *indiarubber*) Elastic solid made from the milky juice (latex) of certain plants and trees (esp. *Hevia brasiliensis*) of S. America, Africa, the E. Indies, etc., and used for many purposes in industry, e.g. for making pneumatic tyres, waterproofing cloth; piece of this or other substance for erasing pencil-marks; (pl.) galoshes, rubber boots, rubber-soled shoes; *ru′bberneck*, (U.S. slang) sightseeing tourist, inquisitive person; (*v.*) act as rubberneck; ~ *stamp*, stamp for quickly endorsing papers with signature, date, etc., whence ~-*stamp* (*v.*) give (unconsidered) endorsement to others' decision. **rŭ′bberў** *adj.* **rŭ′bber** *v.* 1. Coat or cover with rubber. 2. (U.S. slang) Turn head to look at something.

rŭ′bber[2] *n.* Three successive games (or two games won by same side) between sides or persons at bridge, whist, cribbage, backgammon, etc.

rŭ′bbish *n.* Waste material, debris, refuse, litter; worthless material or articles, trash; absurd ideas or suggestions, nonsense (freq. as excl. of contempt). **rŭ′bbishў** *adj.*

rŭ′bble *n.* Waste fragments of stone, brick, etc., esp. from old or demolished buildings; pieces of undressed stone used, esp. as filling-in, for walls (ill. MASONRY); (geol.) loose angular stones etc. forming upper covering of some rocks; water-worn stones. **rŭ′bblў** *adj.*

Rŭ′bbra, Edmund (1901–). British composer of orchestral and choral music.

rubĕfā′cient (rōō-, -shent) *n.* & *adj.* (med.) (Counter-irritant etc.) producing redness or slight inflammation. **rubĕfā′ction** *n.*

ru′bĕllite (rōō-; *or* -bĕ′-) *n.* Red variety of tourmaline.

Ru′bĕns (rōōbinz), Sir Peter Paul (1577–1640). Flemish painter and diplomatist, active at Antwerp and in Italy, France, Spain, and England.

ru′bicĕlle (rōō-) *n.* Orange-red or yellow variety of spinel.

Ru′bicon (rōō-). Ancient name of a small stream flowing into Adriatic, forming part of boundary of Cisalpine Gaul; by taking his army across it, i.e. outside his own province, Julius Caesar committed himself to war against the Senate and Pompey; hence, *cross*, *pass*, *the* ~, take decisive step, esp. at outset of enterprise; ~ *bezique*, card-game, kind of bezique in which four packs are used, 9 cards being dealt by three to each player.

ru′bicŭnd (rōō-) *adj.* (esp. of complexion) Ruddy. **rŭbicŭ′ndităў** *n.*

rubi′dium (rōō-) *n.* (chem.) Rare soft silvery metallic element, one of the alkali metals; symbol Rb, at. no. 37, at. wt 85·4678. [L *rubidus* red, from two red lines in its spectrum]

rubi′ginous (rōō-) *adj.* Rusty, rust-coloured.

Ru′binstein (rōō-, -īn), Anton Grigorevich (1829–94). Russian-Jewish pianist and musical composer.

ru′bric (rōō-) *n.* Heading of chapter, section, etc., also special passage or sentence, written or printed in red or in special lettering; direction for conduct of divine service (prop. in red) inserted in liturgical book; (red-letter entry in) calendar of saints (now rare). **ru′brical** *adj.* **ru′bricallў** *adv.* **rubri′cian** (-shan), **ru′bricist** *ns.* **ru′bricāte** *v.t.* Mark with, print or write in, red; furnish with rubrics. **rubricā′tion, ru′bricātor** *ns.*

ru′bў (rōō-) *n.* 1. Rare and valuable precious stone (*true or Oriental* ~), a species of corundum, of colour varying from deep crimson to pale rose-red; less valuable stone (*spinel* ~), an aluminate of magnesium, or a rose-pink variety of this (*balas* ~); ~ *wedding*, 40th anniversary of wedding. 2. Colour of ruby, a rich glowing purple-tinged red; red wine. 3. (print.) Size of type (5½ point) intermediate between nonpareil and pearl. ~ *adj.* Of ruby colour.

ruche (rōōsh) *n.* Frill or gathering of lace etc. as trimming, esp. one with both edges sewn to garment; parallel rows of gathering. ~ *v.t.* Ornament, gather, thus.

rŭck[1] *n.* Main body of competitors left out of the running, undistinguished crowd or general run of persons or things.

rŭck[2], **rŭ′ckle** *ns.* & *vbs.* Crease, wrinkle.

rŭ′cksăck (*or* rōō-) *n.* Bag for carrying walker's necessaries, slung by straps from both shoulders and resting on back.

rŭ′ckus *n.* (U.S.) = RUCTION.

rŭ′ction *n.* (slang, usu. pl.) Disturbance, tumult.

rŭdbĕ′ckia *n.* Plant of genus *R* ~ of the aster family, native to N. America, much grown in gardens. [Olaus *Rudbeck* (1630–1702), Swedish botanist]

rŭdd *n.* Freshwater fish (*Scardinius erythrophthalmus*) of the carp family resembling roach, red-eye.

rŭ′dder *n.* Broad flat wooden or metal piece hinged to vessel's stern-post for steering with (ill. BOAT); similar device on an aircraft (ill. AEROPLANE); (fig.) guiding principle, etc.; (brewing) paddle for stirring malt in mash-tub. **rŭ′dderlĕss** *adj.*

rŭ′ddle *n.* Red ochre, esp. of kind used for marking sheep. ~ *v.t.* Mark or colour (as) with ruddle.

rŭ′ddock *n.* (dial.) Robin.

rŭ′ddў *adj.* 1. Freshly or healthily red; reddish. 2. (slang) = BLOODY, 3. **rŭ′ddilў** *adv.* **rŭ′ddinĕss** *n.*

rude (rōōd) *adj.* 1. Primitive, simple; in natural state; uncivilized, uneducated; roughly made, contrived, or executed. 2. Violent, not gentle; unrestrained, startling, abrupt. 3. Vigorous, hearty, (chiefly in ~ *health*). 4. Insolent, impertinent, offensive. **ru′delў** *adv.* **ru′denĕss, ru′derў** (slang) *ns.*

ru′diment (rōō-) *n.* 1. (pl.) Elements or first principles of or *of* knowledge or some subject. 2. (pl.) Imperfect beginning of something that will develop or might have developed. 3. Part or organ incompletely developed, as a vestigial one or one having no function. **rudimĕ′ntarў** *adj.*

rue[1] (rōō) *v.t.* (pres. part. *rueing*). Repent of, bitterly feel the consequences of, wish undone or unbefallen. ~ *n.* (archaic) Repentance, dejection at some occurrence. **rue′ful** *adj.* Doleful, dismal; *Knight of the* ~ *countenance*, Don QUIXOTE. **rue′fullў** *adv.* **rue′fulnĕss** *n.*

rue[2] (rōō) *n.* Evergreen shrub (*Ruta graveolens*) with bitter strong-scented leaves.

rŭff[1] *n.* Deep projecting starched frill of several separately goffered folds of linen or muslin worn round neck, esp. in 16th c. (ill. DOUBLET); projecting or conspicuously coloured ring of feathers or hair round bird's or beast's neck; kind of domestic pigeon resembling jacobin.

rŭff[2] *n.* Bird of sandpiper kind (*Philomachus pugnax*) of which male has ruff and ear-tufts in breeding-season; (esp.) male of this (the female is called *reeve*).

rŭff[3] *n.* Small olive-brown freshwater fish of perch family (*Acerina cernua*), with rough prickly scales and brown and black spots.

rŭff[4] *n.* & *v.* Trump(ing) at whist, bridge, etc.

rŭ′ffian *n.* Brutal violent lawless person. **rŭ′ffianism** *n.* **rŭ′fianlў** *adj.*

rŭ′ffle *v.* 1. Disturb smoothness or tranquillity of; (of bird) erect (feathers) in anger etc.; (fig.) irritate, perturb. 2. Suffer ruffling. 3. Gather (lace etc.) into a ruffle. ~ *n.* 1. Perturbation, bustle (rare); rippling effect on water. 2. Ornamental gathered or goffered frill of lace etc. worn at opening of garment, esp. about wrist, breast, or neck; ruff of bird etc.

ru′fous (roo-) *adj.* (chiefly biol.) Reddish brown.

rŭg *n.* 1. Large wrap or coverlet of thick woollen etc. stuff. 2. Floor-mat of shaggy material or thick pile, esp. (freq. *hearth-~*) laid down before fireplace.

Rŭgbei′an (-ēan) *adj. & n.* (Member) of Rugby School.

Rŭ′gbў. Town in Warwickshire, site of public school founded 1567; ~ *football*, one of the two main types of football (the other being ASSOCIATION football), played with 15 players a side (in Rugby Union) or 13 (in Rugby

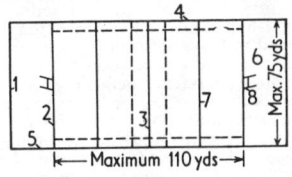

RUGBY UNION FOOTBALL GROUND

League), with an elliptical football punted, dropped, or passed from hand to hand, the object being to touch down behind the opponents' line and score a try, and to kick the ball over the crossbar of the H-shaped goal; ~ *League* (esp. in N. England), ~ *Union*, organizations of clubs playing Rugby football.

rŭ′ggėd (-g-) *adj.* Of rough uneven surface; unsoftened, unpolished; lacking gentleness or refinement; harsh in sound; austere, unbending; involving hardship. **rŭ′ggėdlў** *adv.* **rŭ′ggėdnėss** *n.*

rŭ′gger (-g-) *n.* (colloq.) Rugby football.

rugō′se (roo-) *adj.* (chiefly biol.) Wrinkled, corrugated. **rugō′selў** *adv.* **rugō′sitў** *n.*

Rüh′mkorff (room-), Heinrich Daniel (1805–77). German physicist, inventor of induction-coil named after him.

Ruhr (roor). River of W. Germany, flowing into Rhine on right bank at Ruhrort; coal-mining district, with iron and steel and other heavy industries, along this river.

ru′in (roo-) *n.* Downfall, fallen or wrecked state (lit. or fig.); (freq. pl.) what remains of building, town, structure, etc., that has suffered ruin; (sing.) what causes ruin, destroying agency, havoc. ~ *v.t.* Reduce (place) to ruins; bring to ruin. **ruinā′tion** *n.*

ru′inous (roo-) *adj.* In ruins, dilapidated; bringing ruin, disastrous. **ru′inouslў** *adv.* **ru′inousnėss** *n.*

rule (rool) *n.* 1. Principle to which action or procedure conforms or is bound or intended to conform; dominant custom, canon, test, standard, normal state of thing's; *as a* ~, usually, more often than not; *by* ~, in regulation manner, mechanically; *standing* ~, one made by corporation to govern its procedure; *work to* ~, adhere with excessive strictness to rules of work so as to slow production etc. as a form of industrial protest; ~ *of three*, method of finding fourth number from three given numbers, of which first is in same proportion to second as third is to unknown fourth; ~ *of thumb*, rough practical method based on experience or practice, not theory. 2. Sway, government, dominion; *bear* ~, hold sway. 3. (eccles.) Code of discipline observed by religious order; (law) order made by judge or court with reference to particular case only; (hist.) *the* ~, limited area outside Fleet and King's Bench prisons in which prisoners, esp. debtors, were allowed to live on certain terms. 4. Graduated, freq. jointed, strip of metal or wood used for measuring, esp. by carpenters etc.; (print.) thin slip of metal for separating headings, columns, etc., short (*en* ~) or long (*em* ~) dash in punctuation etc. ~ *v.* 1. Exercise sway or decisive influence over; keep under control, curb; (pass.) consent to follow advice, be guided *by*; *ruling passion*, motive that habitually directs one's actions. 2. Be the ruler(s), have the sovereign control of or *over*, bear rule. 3. (of prices etc.) Have specified general level, be for the most part. 4. Give judicial or authoritative decision; ~ *out*, exclude, pronounce irrelevant or ineligible. 5. Make parallel lines across (paper); make (straight line) with ruler or mechanical help.

ru′ler (roo-) *n.* 1. Person or thing bearing (esp. sovereign) rule. 2. Straight strip or cylinder (usu. of wood) used in ruling paper or lines. **ru′lership** *n.*

ru′ling (roo-) *n.* (esp.) Authoritative pronouncement, judicial decision.

rŭ′lley *n.* Flat four-wheeled dray, lorry.

rŭm[1] *n.* 1. Spirit distilled from products of sugar-cane chiefly in W. Indies and Guiana. 2. (U.S.) Any intoxicating liquor; ~*-runner*, (U.S.) smuggler of alcoholic liquor.

rŭm[2] *adj.* (slang) Odd, strange, queer; ~ *start*, surprising occurrence. **rŭ′mlў** *adv.* **rŭ′mnėss** *n.*

Rumā′nia (roo-). Country of SE. Europe, on the Black Sea, formed by union in 1861 of Moldavia and Wallachia; a monarchy from 1881 to 1947, when it was declared a republic; capital, Bucharest. **Rumā′nian** *adj. & n.* 1. (Native, inhabitant) of Rumania. 2. (Of) the language of Rumania, a Romance language much influenced by Slavonic.

rŭ′mba *n.* Cuban Negro dance; ballroom dance imitative of this.

rŭ′mble[1] *v.* Make sound (as) of thunder, earthquake, heavy cart, wind in the bowels, etc.; *go along*, *by*, etc., making or in vehicle making such sound; utter, say, give *out*, *forth*, with such sound. ~ *n.* 1. Rumbling sound. 2. Hind part of carriage or (U.S.) motorcar arranged as extra seat or for luggage; ~*-seat*, (U.S.) dickeyseat.

rŭ′mble[2] *v.t.* (slang) Detect, understand, see through.

rŭmbŭ′stious *adj.* (colloq.) Boisterous, uproarious.

ru′měn (roo-) *n.* Ruminant's first stomach (ill. RUMINANT).

ru′minant (roo-) *n.* Animal that chews the cud. ~ *adj.* 1. Belonging to the ruminants. 2. Given to, engaged in, rumination.

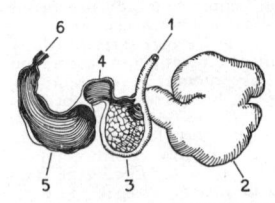

STOMACHS OF A RUMINANT

1. Gullet. 2. Paunch or rumen. 3. Reticulum or honeycomb. 4. Omasum. 5. Abomasum or maw. 6. Intestine

ru′mināte (roo-) *v.* 1. Chew the cud. 2. Meditate, ponder. **rumin ā′tion** *n.* **ru′minative** *adj.* **ru′minativelў** *adv.*

rŭ′mmage *v.* Ransack, make search in or *in*, make search; fish *out* or *up* from among other things; disarrange, throw *about*, in search. ~ *n.* Things got by rummaging, miscellaneous accumulation; rummaging search; ~*-sale*, clearance sale of unclaimed articles at docks etc.; jumble sale.

rŭ′mmer *n.* Large drinking-glass. [f. W.Fl. *rummer*, Ger. *römer*, f. *roemen* praise, boast]

rŭ′mmў[1] *adj.* (slang) = RUM[2].

rŭ′mmў[2] *n.* Card-game played by 3 or more players with 2 packs of cards, the object being to get rid of cards by forming sequences or sets and 'declaring' them.

ru′mour (roomer) *n.* General talk, report, or hearsay, of doubtful accuracy; current but unverified statement or assertion. ~ *v.t.* (chiefly pass.) Report by way of rumour.

rŭmp *n.* 1. Tail-end, posterior, buttocks, of beast or bird, or rarely of person; ~ *steak*, steak cut from ox's rump (ill. MEAT). 2. Small or contemptible remnant of a parliament or similar body, esp. (hist.) that of the Long Parliament, either from its Restoration (1659) to its final dissolution (1660), or from PRIDE'S PURGE (1648) to its first dissolution (1653).

rŭ′mple *v.t.* Crease, ruffle.

rŭ′mpus *n.* (slang) Disturbance, brawl, row, uproar; ~ *room*, (U.S.) room for games, parties, etc.

[767]

rŭ'm-tŭm n. Light racing-boat for one sculler, with outriggers and sliding seat, used on lower Thames.

rŭn v. (past t. răn, past part. rŭn). 1. (of persons) Move legs quickly (one foot being lifted before the other is set down) so as to go at faster pace than walking; (of animals) go at quick pace, amble, trot, gallop, etc.; (start to) cross cricket-pitch to score run; flee, abscond; go or travel hurriedly, precipitately, etc.; ~ down, over, up, etc., pay flying visit (to). 2. Compete in or in race; seek election etc.(for parliament, president, etc.). 3. Go straight and fast (of fish, ship, etc.); advance (as) by rolling or on wheels, spin round or along, revolve (as) on axle; go with sliding, smooth, continuous, or easy motion; be in action; work freely; be current or operative; (of play) be performed; (of train, bus, etc.) ply; (of fire, news, etc.) spread rapidly from point to point; ~ in the family, be found in all members of it; ~ in the head, (of tune etc.) seem to be heard over and over again. 4. (of colour in fabric, ink on paper, etc.) Spread from marked or dyed to other parts. 5. (of thought, eye, etc.) Pass in transitory or cursory way. 6. (of liquid, sand, etc., vessel etc.) Flow, be wet, drip, flow with; (of nose, eyes, etc.) drop mucus or tears; (of candle) gutter; (of sore) suppurate; person's blood ~s cold, he is horrified; feeling ~s high, excitement, partisanship, etc., is prevalent etc.; the sands are running out, time of grace etc. is nearly up; ~ dry, cease to flow, be exhausted; ~ low, short, become scanty. 7. Extend, be continuous; have a certain course or order, progress, proceed; have a tendency, common characteristic, or average price or level. 8. (with cognate object) Pursue, follow, traverse, cover; make way swiftly through or over; wander about in; perform; essay, be exposed or submit to; ~ the blockade: see BLOCKADE; ~ a chance, stand a chance; ~ errands, messages, perform errands, be a messenger; ~ the gauntlet: see GAUNTLET²; ~ rapids, shoot them; ~ risk, see RISK. 9. Sew loosely or hastily with RUNNING stitches; ~-and-fell seam, flat seam with one edge stitched down over the other (ill. SEAM). 10. Chase, hunt; have running race with; ~ hard or close, press severely in race, competition, or comparative merit; ~ to earth, chase to its lair; (fig.) discover after long search. 11. Make run or go; smuggle (contraband goods) by evading coastguard etc.; keep (coach, steamer, business, person, etc.) going, manage, conduct operations of; ~ the show, (slang) dominate in an undertaking etc.; ~ (thing) fine, leave very little margin of time or amount concerning it. 12. ru'n-about(adj.) roving; (n.) light motor-car, aeroplane, etc.; ru'naway, fugitive; bolting (horse); (of marriage) after elopement; ru'nway, track or gangway; specially prepared surface on airfield for taking off and landing; groove in which thing slides; place for fowls to run in. 13. (with preps.) ~ across, fall in with; ~ after, pursue with attentions; seek society of; give much time to; ~ against, fall in with; ~ at, assail by charging or rushing; ~ into, incur (debt); fall into (practice etc.); be continuous or coalesce with; have collision with; reach or attain; ~ on, (of person's thoughts) be engrossed by; ~ over, review, glance over, repeat, recapitulate; touch (notes of piano etc.) in quick succession; (of vehicle) pass over (animal etc.); ~ through, examine cursorily; peruse; deal successively with; consume (estate etc.) by reckless or quick spending; pervade; ~ to, reach (amount, number, etc.); have money or ability, (of money) be enough, for; fall into (ruin); (of plants) tend to develop chiefly (seed); indulge inclination towards. 14. (with advs.) ~ about, bustle, hurry from one person etc. to another; play or wander without restraint; ~ away, flee, abscond, elope; (of horse) bolt; get clear away from competitors in race; ~ away with, carry off; accept (notion) hastily; consume (money etc.); (of horse etc.) bolt with; ~ down, (of clock etc.) stop for want of winding; (of health etc.) become enfeebled from overwork, poor feeding, etc.; knock down or collide with; overtake in pursuit; discover after search; disparage; ~ in, (of combatant) rush to close quarters; (Rugby footb.) carry ball over opponents' goal-line and touch it down; bring (new machinery) to proper condition by careful working; (colloq.) arrest and take to prison; ~ off, flee; flow away; digress suddenly; write or recite fluently; produce on machine; drain (liquid) off; decide (race) after tie or trial heats; ~ on, be joined together (of written characters); continue in operation; elapse; speak volubly, talk incessantly; (print.) begin in same line as what precedes; ~ out, come to an end; exhaust one's stock of; escape from containing vessel; advance from block to hit ball in cricket; (of rope) pass or be paid out; jut out; come out of contest in specified position etc., complete required score etc.; complete (race); advance so as to project; put down wicket of (batsman, while he is running); exhaust oneself by running; ~ over, overflow; ~ through, pierce with sword etc.; draw line through (written words); ~ up, grow quickly; rise in price; amount to; be runner-up; accumulate (number, sum, debt) quickly; force (rival bidder) to bid higher; force up (price etc.); erect (wall etc.) to great height or in unsubstantial or hurried way; add up (column of figures); (of aircraft) approach (target) preparatory to dropping bombs. ~ n. 1. Act or spell of running; short excursion or visit; (cricket) traversing of pitch by both batsmen without either's being put out, point scored thus or otherwise; at a ~, running; on the ~, fleeing; bustling about; with a ~, rapidly; a ~ for one's money, some enjoyment etc. in return for expenditure or effort. 2. Rhythmical motion; way things tend to move; direction. 3. (mus.) Rapid scale-wise passage. 4. Continuous stretch, spell, or course; distance travelled by a ship in a specific time; long series or succession; general demand; in the long ~: see LONG¹; a ~ on the bank, sudden demand from many customers for immediate repayment. 5. Common, general, average, or ordinary type or class; class or line of goods; batch or drove of animals born or reared together; shoal of fish in motion. 6. Regular track of some animals; enclosure for fowls etc.; range of pasture; trough for water to run in. 7. (chiefly U.S.) Small stream or water-course. 8. Part of ship's bottom narrowing towards stern. 9. (chiefly U.S.) Ladder in stocking etc. 10. Licence to make free use of; the ~ of one's teeth, free board. 11. ~-back, additional space at either end of tennis court; ~-down, progressive reduction, esp. in the numbers of armed forces; ~-in, act of running in at football; final stretch of race; ~-of-the-mill (adj.) ordinary, not outstanding; ~-off, deciding race after dead heat; ~-up, race between greyhounds up to hare's first turn; (golf) low approach shot; (of aircraft) approach to target (also fig.).

rŭ'ncible adj. (Orig.) nonsense word used by Edward Lear; ~ spoon, (now) three-pronged pickle fork, curved like spoon, with one sharp edge.

rune (rōon) n. 1. Letter or character of earliest Teutonic

ᚠ ᚢ ᚦ ᚨ ᚱ ᚲ ᚷ ᚹ ᚺ ᚾ ᛁ ᛃ ᛇ ᛈ
F U Th O R C G W H N J I P
                                                  A H

ᛉ ᛋ ᛏ ᛒ ᛖ ᛜ ᚻ ᛚ ᛗ ᛟ ᛇ ᚫ ᛠ
[X]S T B E Ng D L M Œ A Æ Y Ea

RUNES WITH ROMAN
EQUIVALENTS

alphabet (most extensively used by Scandinavians and Anglo-Saxons), dating from at least 2nd or 3rd c.

A.D. and based on Roman or Greek letters modified to make them suitable for cutting on wood or stone; similar character of mysterious or magic significance; ~-staff, magic wand inscribed with runes; runic. 2. (Division of) Finnish poem, esp. one of the separate songs of the Kalevala.

rŭng n. Bar attached at each end as rail, spoke, or cross-bar in chair etc., or esp. in ladder.

ru'nic (roo-) adj. Of, in, marked with, runes; (of poetry etc.) such as might be written in runes, esp. ancient Scandinavian or Icelandic. ~ n. (print.) Display lettering with thick face and condensed form.

rŭ'nlĕt¹ n. (archaic) Cask of varying size for wine etc.

rŭ'nlĕt² n. Small stream.

rŭ'nnable adj. Proper for the chase.

rŭ'nnel n. Brook, rill; gutter.

rŭ'nner n. (esp.) 1. Messenger, scout, collector, or agent for bank etc.; tout; (hist., esp. *Bow-Street* ~) police officer. 2. Water-rail (RAIL²). 3. Revolving millstone. 4. (naut.) Rope rove through single block, with one end passed round tackle-block and other attached to hook. 5. Naked creeping stem thrown out from base of main stem of strawberry or

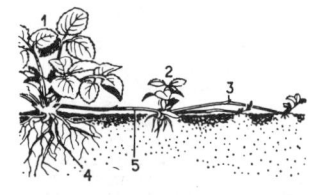

STRAWBERRY RUNNERS
1. Parent plant. 2. Young plant. 3. Scale leaf. 4. Roots. 5. Runner

other plant, and itself taking root; any of various kinds of cultivated bean (esp. SCARLET ~) which twine round stakes for support. 6. Ring etc. that slides on rod, strap, etc. 7. Long piece of wood or metal, curved at end(s), supporting body of sledge etc.; blade of skate, skate with blade curving up at toe. 8. Groove or rod for thing to slide along; roller for moving heavy article. 9. Long narrow strip of (embroidered) cloth etc., placed along or across table etc. as ornament; long narrow rug or strip of carpet. 10. ~-*up*, competitor or team taking second place.

rŭ'nning n. (esp.) Condition of ground to be run or raced on; row of running stitches (ill. STITCH); *in*, *out of*, *the* ~, with good, no, chance of winning; *make*, *take up*, *the* ~, set the pace, take the lead; ~-*board*, narrow gangway on either side of keel-boat (U.S.); footboard extending along either side of locomotive, motor-car, etc. ~ *adj*. That runs; (placed after

noun) in successsion, following each other without interval; ~ *fight*, fight kept up while one is retreating; ~ *fire*, successive shots from different points; ~ *hand*, writing in which pen etc. is not lifted after each letter; ~ *head-(line)*, title, heading of page, repeated or varying according to content; ~ *jump*, one in which jumper runs to the take-off; ~ *knot*, knot that slips along rope to enlarge or diminish loop; ~ *stitch*, one of a line of small straight stitches made by passing needle in and out through material.

rŭ'nny adj. Tending to run or flow; excessively fluid.

Rŭ'nnymēde. Meadow at Egham on S. bank of Thames near Windsor, famous for its association with Magna Carta, which was signed by King John on the meadow or on the island near by.

rŭnt n. 1. Ox or cow of small breed. 2. Smallest animal of a litter; dwarfed or undersized person. 3. Large breed of domestic pigeon.

rupee' (roo-) n. Monetary unit of India, Nepal, and Pakistan (= 100 paise) and of Sri Lanka and Mauritius (= 100 cents). [Hind. *rūpiyah*, f. Sansk. *rūpya* wrought silver]

Ru'pert (roo-), Prince, Count Palatine of the Rhine and Duke of Bavaria (1619–82). Son of Frederick V of Bohemia and Elizabeth, daughter of James I of England; general of the horse in army of Charles I in English Civil War; admiral in fleet of Charles II after Restoration; *Prince ~'s drops*, pear-shaped drops of glass with long tail, made by dropping melted glass into water, and remarkable for the property, due to internal strain, of disintegrating explosively into powder when the tail is broken off or the surface scratched; *Prince ~'s metal*, gold-coloured alloy of about three parts copper and one of zinc.

rupiah (roopē'a) n. Principal monetary unit of Indonesia, = 100 sen. [see RUPEE]

rŭ'pture n. 1. Breach of harmonious relations, disagreement and parting. 2. (path.) Abdominal HERNIA. 3. Breaking, breach. ~ *v.* Burst, break (cell, vessel, membrane); sever (connection etc.); affect with hernia; suffer rupture.

R.U.R. *abbrev*. Royal Ulster Rifles; 'Rossum's Universal Robots' (title of play by K. ČAPEK).

rur'al (roor-) *adj*. In, of, suggesting, the country; pastoral or agricultural. **rur'ally** *adv*. **rurā'lĭty, ralizā'tion** *ns*. **rur'alīze** *v*.

ruridĕcā'nal (roor-) *adj*. Of rural dean (see DEAN) or deanery.

Rur'ĭk (roor-), (d. 879). Reputed founder of Russian empire, Varangian chief who settled in

Novgorod in 862; founder of dynasty which ruled Russia until 1598.

Ruritā'nia (roor-). Imaginary kingdom in central Europe, scene of two novels by Sir Anthony Hope (Hawkins), 'The Prisoner of Zenda' and 'Rupert of Hentzau'; hence, scene of romantic adventure and court intrigue in modern European setting. **Ruritā'nian** *adj. & n.*

ruse (rooz) *n*. Stratagem, feint, trick.

rŭsh¹ *n*. Marsh or water-side plant of order Juncaceae, with naked slender tapering pith-filled stems (prop. leaves) formerly used for strewing floors and still for making chair bottoms and plaiting baskets etc.; stem of this; (collect.) rushes as a material; thing of no value; ~-*bearing*, annual northern-English festival on occasion of carrying rushes and garlands to strew floor and decorate walls of church; ~ *candle*, one made by dipping pith of a rush in tallow; *ru'shlight*, rush candle; feeble light or glimmer; ~ *ring*, ring made of rush(es) formerly used in (esp. mock) weddings.

rŭsh² *v*. 1. Impel, drag, force, carry along, violently and rapidly; (mil.) take by sudden vehement assault; pass (obstacle etc.) with a rapid dash; swarm upon and take possession of (goldfield, platform at meeting, etc.); charge (customer) exorbitant price (colloq.). 2. Run precipitately, violently, or with great speed; go or resort without proper consideration; flow, fall, spread, roll, impetuously or fast; ~ *at*, charge. ~ *n*. Act of rushing, violent or tumultuous advance, spurt, charge, onslaught; (football) combined dash of several players with the ball; sudden migration of large numbers, esp. to new goldfield; strong run *on* or *for* some commodity; (pl., cinema) preliminary showings of film before cutting; ~ *hour*, time at which traffic is busiest. ~ *adj*. (colloq.) Urgent; (to be) done in haste.

rŭsk *n*. Piece of bread pulled or cut from loaf and rebaked.

Rŭ'skin, John (1819–1900). English writer on art and social subjects.

Rŭ'ssell¹, Bertrand Arthur William, 3rd Earl Russell (1872–1970). English philosopher; author of many works on philosophy, logic, education, economics, and politics.

Rŭ'ssell², George William (1867–1935). Irish poet and painter, widely known under his pseudonym 'A.E.'.

Rŭ'ssell³, Lord John, 1st Earl Russell (1792–1878). British Whig statesman; introducer (1832) of Reform Bill into Parliament; prime minister 1846–52 and 1865–6.

Rŭ'ssell⁴, Sir William Howard (1821–1907). English war corre-

[769]

RUSSET

spondent, special correspondent of 'The Times' in Crimean War.

ru′sset *n.* 1. (hist.) Coarse home-spun reddish-brown or grey cloth worn by peasants. 2. Reddish-brown. 3. Rough-skinned russet-coloured apple. ~ *adj.* 1. Reddish-brown. 2. (archaic) Rustic, homely, simple.

Ru′ssia (-sha) *n.* Vast territory of E. Europe and N. Asia, until 1917 an empire under the autocratic rule of the tsars, since 1917 a federation of socialist republics (see UNION OF SOVIET SOCIALIST REPUBLICS); ~ *leather*, fine leather tanned with birch-, willow-, or oak-bark and rubbed with birch-oil (which imparts characteristic smell) as protection against insects.

Ru′ssian (-shan) *adj.* Of Russia or the U.S.S.R., its people or language; ~ *ballet*, form of ballet developed at the beginning of the 20th c. at the Imperial School of Ballet at St. Petersburg from older Italian ballet; ~ *wolfhound*, = BORZOI. ~ *n.* 1. Russian person. 2. Russian language, any of the three principal languages or dialects (*Great* ~, *Little* ~, *White* ~) forming the eastern group of Slavonic languages, esp. Great Russian.

Ru′ssian So′viet Fe′deral So′cialist Repu′blic. (abbrev. R.S.F.S.R.) Largest and most important of the constituent republics of the U.S.S.R.; it occupies more than three-quarters of the total area of the Union, contains more than half its population, and consists of twelve autonomous republics and numerous provinces; capital, Moscow.

Russo- *prefix.* Of Russia and —; ~-*Japanese War*, war between Russia and Japan, 1904–5, in which Russia was decisively defeated at sea and on land.

rust *n.* 1. Yellowish-brown coating formed on iron or steel by oxidation, esp. as effect of moisture, and gradually corroding the metal; similar coating on other metals; colour of this; (fig.) impaired state due to disuse or inactivity, inaction as deteriorating influence. 2. (Plant-disease with rust-coloured spots caused by) any of various fungi; blight, brand. **ru′stless** *adj.* **rust** *v.* Contract rust, undergo oxidation or blight; (of bracken etc.) become rust-coloured; lose quality or efficiency by disuse or inactivity; affect with rust, corrode.

ru′stic *adj.* Rural; having the appearance or manners of country-people, characteristic of peasants, unsophisticated, unpolished, uncouth, clownish; of rude or country workmanship; of untrimmed branches or rough timber; (of lettering) irregularly formed (ill. SCRIPT); (archit.) with rough-hewn or roughened surface or with chamfered joints. **ru′stically** *adv.* **rusti′city** *n.* **ru′stic** *n.* Countryman, peasant.

ru′sticate *v.* 1. Retire to, sojourn in, the country, lead a rural life; countrify. 2. Send down temporarily from university as punishment. 3. Mark (masonry) with sunk joints or roughened surface (ill. MASONRY). **rustica′tion** *n.*

ru′stle (-sl) *v.* 1. Make sound (as) of dry leaves blown, rain pattering, or silk garments in motion; go with rustle; cause to rustle. 2. (U.S.) Get, acquire, pick up, by one's own exertions (also ~ *up*); steal (cattle or horses). ~ *n.* Sound of rustling. **ru′stler** *n.* (esp., U.S.) Cattle or horse thief.

ru′sty[1] *adj.* Rusted, affected with rust; of antiquated appearance; (of voice) croaking, creaking; stiff with age or disuse; antiquated, behind the times; impaired by neglect, in need of furbishing; rust-coloured; (of black clothes) discoloured by age. **ru′stily** *adv.* **ru′stiness** *n.*

ru′sty[2] *adj.* Rancid (esp. of bacon). [obs. *resty*, f. OF *reste* left over, stale]

rut[1] *n.* Track sunk by passage of wheels; established mode of procedure, beaten track, groove. **ru′tty** *adj.* **rut** *v.t.* Mark with ruts (usu. in past part.).

rut[2] *n.* Periodic sexual excitement of male deer (also of goat, ram, etc.). **ru′ttish** *adj.* **rut** *v.i.* Be affected with rut.

ruth[1] (rooth) *n.* (archaic) Pity, compassion.

Ruth[2] (rooth). 1. Moabite woman; her widowed mother-in-law Naomi, a Jewess, returned to her own country, and Ruth being also a widow went with her; in Bethlehem Ruth gleaned corn in the fields of Boaz, who proved to be her husband's kinsman and married her. 2. Book of O.T. telling story of Ruth.

Ruthe′nia (roo-). Former province of Czechoslovakia, since 1945 incorporated in the Ukraine. **Ruthe′nian** *adj.* & *n.*

ruthe′nium (roo-) *n.* (chem.) Rare metallic element of the platinum group, a hard, greyish-white metal; symbol Ru, at. no. 44, at. wt 101·07. [med. L *Ruthenia* Russia (from its discovery in the Urals)]

Ru′therford, Ernest, 1st Baron Rutherford of Nelson (1871–1937). Physicist, born in New Zealand; professor at Montreal, Manchester, and, from 1919, Cavendish Professor of Physics at Cambridge; investigated the nature of radioactive transformations and the structure of the atom; Nobel Prize for chemistry 1908.

ru′thless (roo-) *adj.* Without pity. **ru′thlessly** *adv.* **ru′thlessness** *n.*

Ru′tland. Former midland county, the smallest county in England, since April 1974 part of Leicestershire.

Ruy Lo′pez (roo′ĭ). Conventional opening in game of chess. [f. name of Spanish author of book on chess (1561)]

Ruysdael (roi′sdahl), Jacob van (*c* 1628–82). Dutch landscape-painter and etcher.

R.V. *abbrev.* Revised Version (of Bible).

Rwa′nda (roo-). Republic in central Africa east of Zaire; independent 1962; capital, Kigali.

R.W.S. *abbrev.* Royal Society of Painters in Water-colours.

Rx, **℞** *abbrevs.* Tens of rupees.

Ry *abbrev.* Railway.

rye[1] *n.* (Grain of) a cereal, *Secale cereale*, widely grown in N. Europe as food-crop, in England chiefly as fodder; (U.S.) rye-whisky; ~-*grass*, fodder grass of genus *Lolium*, esp. *L. perenne*, common rye, and *L. italicum*, Italian rye; ~-*whisky*, whisky made from rye.

Rye[2]. Town and former harbour of East Sussex, England, one of the CINQUE PORTS.

Rye House Plot. Plot (1683) to assassinate Charles II and his brother James, Duke of York, for alleged complicity in which Lord William Russell and Algernon Sidney were executed. [f. name of a house in Hertfordshire]

ry′ot *n.* Indian peasant.

R.Y.S. *abbrev.* Royal Yacht Squadron.

S

S, s (ĕs). 1. 19th letter of modern English and 18th of ancient Roman alphabet, derived in form (through early Latin and Greek Ϛ, Ϛ, Ϛ), from Phoenician W (Hebrew ⱳ), representing *s* or *sh* in Semitic languages, in modern English representing chiefly a voiceless sibilant (*s*) initially or when doubled in combination with a voiceless consonant, and the corresponding voiced sound (*z*) finally and medially between vowels, but frequently representing also the phonetic combinations (sy), (zy), as in *sure*, *vision* (in this dictionary written sh, zh). 2. Thing shaped like S.

s. *abbrev.* Second; shilling; singular; solidus, -i; son.

S. *abbrev.* Saint; Signor; South(ern); Sudanese (£S).

S.A.

S.A. *abbrev.* Salvation Army; sex appeal; South Africa; *Sturm Abteilung* (Ger. = storm detachment; political militia of Nazi party).
Saar (zär *or* s-). River of France and W. Germany, right-bank tributary of 'Moselle; Saarland.
Saar'land. Mining and industrial district surrounding the Saar river, since 1957 a 'Land' of the Federal German Republic; capital, Saarbrücken.
Sä'ba. Ancient country (biblical *Sheba*) of S. Arabia including modern Yemen. **Sabae'an** (-bē-), **Sabē'an** *adj.* & *n.*
Sa'bah (sahba). State of Malaysia, formerly British North Borneo; capital, Kota Kinabalu.
Sā'baism *n.* Star-worship. [Heb. *ṣābā* host]
Sā'bāoth *n.pl.* Hosts, armies (*Lord of* ~, Rom. 9:29, James 5:4).
săbbatār'ian *n.* Sabbath-keeping Jew; Christian favouring strict observance of Sunday as holy day. ~ *adj.* Of sabbatarian tenets. **săbbatār'ianism** *n.*
să'bbath *n.* 1. (also ~ *day*) Seventh day of week (Saturday) as day of religious rest enjoined on Israelites; also, the Christian Sunday, esp. as day of obligatory abstinence from work and play. 2. Period of rest. 3. *Witches'* ~: see WITCH[1]. [Heb. *šabbāt*, f. *šābat* to rest]
sabbă'tical *adj.* Of, appropriate to, the sabbath; ~ *year*, 7th year in which Israelites were to cease tilling and release debtors and Israelite slaves; year of absence from duty for purposes of study and travel, granted to teachers in universities etc. at certain intervals.
sabbă'tically *adv.*
Sabě'llian[1] *adj.* & *n.* (Rom. hist.) (Member) of a group of tribes in ancient Italy including Sabines, Samnites, Campanians, etc.
Sabě'llian[2] *adj.* & *n.* (Holder) of doctrine of Sabellius (3rd c.), African heresiarch, that the Father, Son, and Holy Spirit are merely aspects of one Divine person.
Sā'bian *adj.* & *n.* 1. (Member) of a sect classed in Koran with Muslims, Jews, and Christians, as believers in the true God. 2. (erron.) (Adherent) of SABAISM. [Arab. *sābi*']
Să'bine *adj.* & *n.* (Member) of a tribe in ancient Italy, whose lands were in the neighbourhood of Rome, celebrated in legend as having taken up arms against the Romans to avenge the carrying off of their women by the Romans at a spectacle to which they had been invited.
sā'ble[1] *n.* Small dark-brown-furred arctic and subarctic carnivorous marten (*Martes zibellina*, European species; *M. americana*, American); its skin or fur.
sā'ble[2] *n.* 1. (her.) Black (ill. HERALDRY); (poet., rhet.) the colour black; (poet., rhet.; pl.)

mourning garments. 2. ~ *antelope*, large stout-horned antelope of S. and E. Africa (*Hippotragus niger*), male of which is dark glossy brown with white belly. ~ *adj.* (poet., rhet.) Black, dusky; gloomy, dread; *his* ~ *Majesty*, the Devil.
sā'bot (-ō) *n.* 1. Shoe hollowed out from one piece of wood, worn by French peasants etc.; wooden-soled shoe. 2. (mil.) Wooden disc riveted to spherical projectile to keep it in place in bore of piece; metal cup strapped to conical projectile to make it conform to rifling grooves of gun; (mech.) shoe or armature of pile, boring-rod, etc.
sā'botage (-ahzh) *n.* Deliberate destruction of machinery, damaging of equipment, manufacture of faulty product, etc., by dissatisfied or disaffected workmen, or by enemy agents esp. in wartime. ~ *v.t.* Commit sabotage on; (fig.) destroy, render useless. **săboteur'** (-êr) *n.* One who commits sabotage.
sā'bra *n.* Native-born Israeli.
sā'bre (-ber) *n.* Cavalry sword with curved blade (ill. SWORD); implement for removing scum from molten glass; ~-*toothed lion, tiger*, large extinct feline mammal with long sabre-shaped upper canines. ~ *v.t.* Cut down or wound with sabre.
sā'bretache (-ertäsh) *n.* Flat leather bag worn suspended by long straps from the sword-belt as part of the full uniform of cavalry and artillery officers (ill. CAVALRY).
săc[1] *n.* Bag-like membrane enclosing cavity in animal or vegetable organism; membranous envelope of hernia, cyst, tumour, etc.
săc[2]: see SACK[1] *n.* 2.
să'ccadic *adj.* Jerky, twitching; ~ *movement*, (psychol.) sudden movement of eyes from one point of fixation to another, as in reading.
să'ccate *adj.* Dilated into form of sac (bot.); encysted.
să'ccharāte (-k-) *n.* Salt of saccharic acid.
săcchă'ric (-k-) *adj.* ~ *acid*, dibasic acid (HOOC(CHOH)$_4$COOH) formed by oxidation of dextrose.
săcchari'ferous (-k-) *adj.* Sugar-bearing.
săcchari'mēter (-k-) *n.* Instrument for determining the amount of sugar in a solution by polarized light.
să'ccharin, -ine (-k-; *or* -ēn) *n.* White intensely sweet crystalline substance prepared from toluene and used as a substitute for sugar.
să'ccharine *adj.* Sugary (also fig.); of, containing, like, sugar.
să'ccharoid (-k-) *adj.* (geol.) Granular like sugar. ~ *n.* Sugar-like substance.
să'ccharōse (-k-) *n.* = SUCROSE.
să'cciform (-ks-) *adj.* Sac-shaped.

SACKBUT

să'ccūle *n.* Small sac or cyst.
să'ccūlar, să'ccūlate, -ātĕd *adjs.*
săccūlā'tion *n.*
săcerdō'tal *adj.* Of priest(s) or priesthood, priestly; (of doctrines etc.) ascribing sacrificial functions and supernatural power to ordained priests, claiming excessive authority for the priesthood. **săcerdō'tally** *adv.* **săcerdō't-alism, săcerdō'talist** *ns.*
să'chem *n.* 1. Supreme chief of some American Indian tribes. 2. (U.S.) One of 12 high officials in Tammany Society.
să'chet (-shā) *n.* Small perfumed bag; (packet of) dry perfume for laying among clothes etc.
Săchs (-ks), Hans (1494-1576). German shoemaker of Nuremberg, one of the MEISTERSINGER; author of several plays.
săck[1] *n.* 1. Large, usu. oblong, bag of coarse flax, hemp, etc., usu. open at one end, and used for storing and conveying goods; sack with contents; amount (of corn, coal, flour, wool, etc.) usu. put in sack as unit of measure or weight; *give, get, the* ~, dismiss, be dismissed, from service (perh. f. Fr. phrase referring to giving of passport). 2. Woman's short loose dress of sack-like appearance; (hist., also ~ *dress, săc, săcque*, pr. -k) woman's loose gown esp. of late 17th-18th c., or voluminous train hanging loosely from shoulders of gown. 3. *sa'ckcloth*, coarse fabric of flax or hemp, sacking; (fig.) mourning or penitential garb (esp. in *sackcloth and ashes*); ~-*race*, race between competitors with lower part of body in sacks. **să'ckful** *n.* **săck** *v.t.* Put into sack(s); (colloq.) give the sack to, dismiss from service. **să'cking** *n.* Closely woven material of hemp, jute, flax, etc., for sacks etc.
săck[2] *v.t.* Plunder (captured town etc.) ~ *n.* Act or instance of sacking.
săck[3] *n.* (hist.) Any of various white wines formerly imported from Spain and the Canaries. [Fr. *vin sec* dry wine]
să'ckbut *n.* (mus.) Old name for

[771]

sacque: see SACK¹ *n*. 2.

să'cral *adj*. (anat.) Of the sacrum.

să'crament *n*. Religious ceremony or act symbolizing or conferring grace (in the Eastern, pre-Reformation Western, and R.C. Churches one of the seven rites of baptism, confirmation, the Eucharist, penance, extreme unction, orders, and matrimony; by many Protestants restricted to baptism and the Eucharist); thing of mysterious and sacred significance, sacred influence, symbol, etc.; oath or solemn engagement taken; (also blessed or holy ~, ~ *of the altar*) Eucharist; consecrated elements, esp. the bread or Host.

săcramĕ'ntal *adj*. Of (the nature of) a or the sacrament; attaching great importance to the sacraments. ~ *n*. Observance analogous to but not reckoned among the sacraments, e.g. use of holy water or sign of the cross. **săcramĕ'ntally** *adv*. **săcramĕ'ntalism, săcramĕ'ntalist** *ns*.

săcramentār'ian *n*. 1. S~, (hist.) name given in 16th c. and afterwards to Zwinglians and Calvinists who repudiated the Lutheran doctrine of Consubstantiation and the doctrine of Transubstantiation and denied the Real Presence, holding that the bread and wine were only symbols of the body and blood of Christ. 2. One who holds definite views on the efficacy of the sacraments. ~ *adj*. Pertaining to a sacrament or the sacraments; pertaining to sacramentarians. **săcramentār'ianism** *n*.

sacrār'ium *n*. 1. (Rom. antiq.) Shrine; adytum of temple; place in house where Penates were kept. 2. Sanctuary, part of church within altar-rails. 3. (R.C. Ch.) Piscina.

să'crĕd *adj*. Consecrated, esteemed dear, *to* a deity; dedicated, reserved, appropriated, *to* some person or purpose; made holy by religious association, hallowed; safeguarded or required by religion, reverence, or tradition; indefeasible, inviolable, sacrosanct; S~ *College*: see COLLEGE; ~ *concert*, concert of sacred music; ~ *cow*, (contempt.) idea, institution, etc., held to be immune from criticism; S~ *Heart*, (R.C. Ch.) heart of Jesus Christ or Mary, as object of devotion; ~ *music, poetry,* music, poetry, on religious themes. **să'crĕdly** *adv*. **să'crĕdness** *n*.

să'crifice *n*. 1. Slaughter of animal or person, surrender of possession, as offering to a deity, (fig.) act of prayer, thanksgiving, or penitence as propitiation; what is thus slaughtered, surrendered, or done, victim, offering; (eccles.) the Crucifixion, the Eucharist as either a propitiatory offering of the body and blood of Christ or an act of thanksgiving. 2. Giving up of thing for the sake of another that is higher or more urgent; thing thus given up, loss thus entailed; *make the supreme* ~, die for one's country. ~ *v*. Offer (as) sacrifice (*to*); give up, treat as secondary or of inferior importance, devote *to*; resign oneself to parting with. **săcrifi'cial** (-shal) *adj*. **săcrifi'cially** *adv*.

să'crilege *n*. Robbery or profanation of sacred building, outrage on consecrated person or thing, violation of what is sacred. **săcrilĕ'gious** (-jus) *adj*. **săcrilĕ'giously** *adv*. [L *sacrilegus* one who steals sacred things (*sacer* holy *legere* gather)]

să'cring *n*. (archaic) Consecration of elements in the Mass; ordination and consecration of bishop, sovereign, etc.; ~-*bell*, bell rung at elevation of Host.

să'crist *n*. Official keeping sacred vessels etc. of religious house or church.

să'cristan *n*. Sexton of parish church; SACRIST.

să'cristy *n*. Repository for vestments, vessels, etc., of a church.

să'crosănct *adj*. Secured by religious sanction against outrage, inviolable. **săcrosă'nctity** *n*.

să'crum *n*. Composite triangular bone of ankylosed vertebrae forming back of pelvis (ill. PELVIS). **sā'cral** *adj*. [L *os sacrum* sacred bone (from sacrificial use)]

săd *adj*. 1. Sorrowful, mournful; showing or causing sorrow. 2. (contempt., usu. joc.) Shocking; deplorably bad; incorrigible. 3. (of pastry, bread, etc.) Heavy, doughy; (of colour) dull, neutral-tinted. **să'dden** *v*. **să'ddish** *adj*. **să'dly** *adv*. **să'dness** *n*.

să'ddle *n*. 1. Rider's seat placed on back of horse etc. (usu. concave, of leather, with side-flaps and girths and stirrups (ill. SADDLERY), or forming part of bicycle etc., or of some agricultural machines; part of shaft-horse's harness that bears shafts (ill. HARNESS); *in the* ~, mounted; (fig.) in office or control. 2. Saddle-shaped thing, e.g. ridge between two summits, support for cable or wire on top of suspension-bridge pier or telegraph-pole; part of back of various animals, as dog (ill. DOG); joint of mutton or venison consisting of the two loins. 3. *sa'ddleback*, (archit.) tower-roof with two opposite gables; saddle-backed hill; various birds and fishes (esp. grey or hooded crow); (*adj*.) saddle-backed; *sa'ddlebacked*, with upper outline concave, (archit.) having saddleback; ~-*bag*, one of pair of bags laid across horse, etc., behind saddle; kind of carpeting (in imitation of Eastern saddle-bags of camels) used in upholstering chairs etc.; ~-*bow*, arched front of saddle; ~-*cloth*, cloth laid on horse's back under saddle; ~-*horse*, horse for riding; ~-*tree*, frame of saddle; tulip-tree. ~ *v.t.* Put saddle on (horse etc.); burden (person) *with* task, responsibility, etc.; put (burden) *on* person.

să'ddler *n*. Maker of or dealer in saddles and other equipment for horses; (mil.) man in charge of saddlery of cavalry regiment. **să'ddlery** *n*. (*Illustration, p. 773.*)

Să'ddūcee *n*. Member of a Jewish sect of 1st c. B.C.–1st c. A.D., opposed to the Pharisees, who repudiated oral tradition and accepted the written Law only, rejecting belief in the resurrection of the body and the existence of angels and spirits. [Heb. *ṣĕdūkiy* prob. = descendant of Zadok]

Sade (sahd), Donatien Alphonse, Count (generally known as Marquis) de (1740–1814). French author, whose accounts of sexual perversions have given his name to SADISM.

sadhu (sah'doo) *n*. Hindu holy man, sage, or ascetic. [Sansk. *sādhu* good]

să'dism (*or* sah-) *n*. Deriving of pleasure from the infliction of cruelty upon others, esp. as method of sexual gratification **să'dist** *n*. **sadi'stic** *adj*. [f. Count D. A. de SADE]

Sadō'wa (-va). Village in Bohemia, scene of a battle (also called Königgrätz) in which the Austrians were defeated by the Prussians in 1866.

s.a.e. *abbrev*. Stamped addressed envelope.

safār'i *n*. Journey or expedition in E. Africa esp. for hunting. [Swahili, f. Arab. *safar* journey]

sāfe¹ *n*. Ventilated cupboard for provisions (also *meat*-~); strong locked repository for valuables; ~-*deposit*, building containing a number of separate safes or strong-rooms, which can be hired for the deposit of valuables etc.

sāfe² *adj*. 1. Uninjured (pred. after *bring, come, keep*, etc.); secure, out of or not exposed to danger. 2. Affording security or not involving danger; *on the* ~ *side*, with margin of security against risks. 3. Debarred from escaping or doing harm. 4. Cautious and unenterprising; consistently moderate; that can be reckoned on, unfailing, certain *to* do or be; sure to become. 5. ~ *cŏ'nduct*, (document conveying) privilege granted by sovereign, commander, etc., of being protected from arrest or harm on particular occasion or in district; ~ *keeping*, custody. **sā'fely** *adv*. **sā'feness** *n*.

sā'feguard (-gård) *n*. Safe conduct; (usu.) proviso, stipulation, quality, or circumstance that tends to prevent some evil or protect. ~ *v.t.* Guard, protect (esp. rights, etc.) by precaution or stipulation.

sā'fety *n*. Being safe, freedom from danger or risks; safeness, being sure or likely to bring no danger; (gun with) safety-bolt

SADDLERY

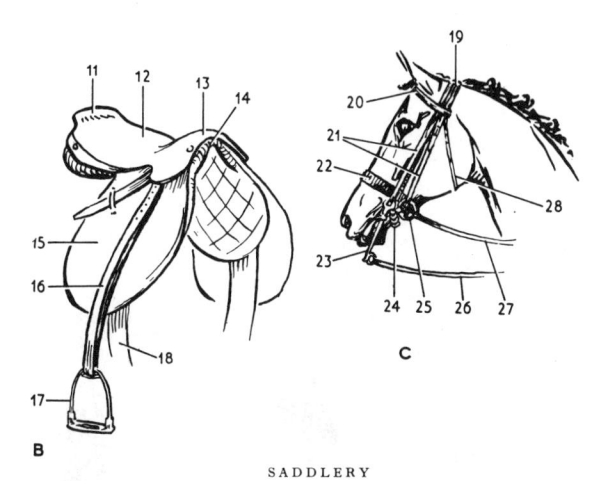

A. HORSE SADDLED AND BRIDLED. B. HUNTING SADDLE (FACING RIGHT). C. DOUBLE BRIDLE

1. Racing bridle. 2. Big ring snaffle. 3. Running martingale. 4. Breastplate. 5. Rein. 6. Boot. 7. Stirrup. 8. Weight cloth (for racing). 9. Racing saddle. 10. Saddle-cloth. 11. Cantle. 12. Seat. 13. Pommel. 14. Saddle-tree. 15. Flap. 16. Stirrup-leather. 17. Stirrup-iron. 18. Girth. 19. Head-piece. 20. Brow band. 21. Cheek-straps. 22. Nose band. 23. Curb. 24. Curb chain. 25. Snaffle. 26. Curb rein. 27. Snaffle rein. 28. Throat lash

or -catch; *play for* ~, avoid risks in game etc.; ~ *belt*, strap securing occupant to seat in aircraft, motor vehicle, etc.; ~*-bolt*, *-catch*, device for locking guntrigger (ill. PISTOL); ~ *curtain*, fireproof curtain in theatre that can be lowered to cut off auditorium from stage; ~*-fuse*, fuse that can be ignited at a safe distance from the charge; ~*-glass*, glass so made as to prevent splintering; ~*-lamp*, miner's lamp so constructed as to prevent the flame from coming into direct contact with fire-damp and causing an explosion; ~*-match*, one igniting only on specially prepared surface; ~*-pin*, pin bent back on itself so as to form a spring, with guard or sheath to cover point; ~ *razor*, razor with guard to prevent blade from cutting deeply; ~*-valve*, valve in steam-boiler opening automatically to relieve excessive pressure; (fig.) means of giving harmless vent to excitement etc.

să'fflower *n.* Thistle-like plant (*Carthamus tinctorius*) yielding red dye; dried petals of this; dye made from them.

să'ffron *n.* Kind of crocus (*Crocus sativus*) cultivated for its flowers, the stigmas of which yield an orange-yellow substance used for colouring and flavouring food; this substance; colour of this; *bastard* ~, the plant safflower; ~*-cake*, cake flavoured with saffron; tablet of pressed saffron. ~ *adj.* Of saffron colour. ~ *v.t.* Colour with or like saffron.

să'franin *n.* (chem.) Yellow colouring-matter of saffron; synthetic orange-red dye-stuff.

săg *v.* Sink or subside under weight or pressure; hang sideways, be lopsided; have downward bulge or curve in middle, cause to curve thus; (commerc.) decline in price; (of ship) drift to leeward. ~ *n.* Sagging; amount that rope etc. sags.

sa'ga (sah-) *n.* Medieval Icelandic or Norwegian prose narrative, esp. one embodying history of Icelandic family or Norwegian king; story of heroic achievement or adventure, long family chronicle. [ON, = 'narrative'.]

sagā'cious (-shus) *adj.* Mentally penetrating, gifted with discernment, practically wise, acuteminded, shrewd; (of speech etc.) showing sagacity; (of animals) exceptionally intelligent, seeming to reason or deliberate. sagā'ciouslў *adv.* sagā'citў *n.*

să'gamōre *n.* = SACHEM, 1.

sāge[1] *n.* Aromatic herb (*Salvia officinalis*) with dull greyish-green leaves; its leaves used in cookery; any plant of the genus *Salvia*; *sa'gebrush*, any of various N. Amer. hoary-leaved shrubs of genus *Artemisia*, freq. covering large flat tracts in Western States; ~ *cheese*, cheese flavoured and mottled by addition of sage-infusion to the curd; ~*-green*, greyish-green colour of sage leaves.

sāge[2] *adj.* Wise, discreet, judicious, having the wisdom of experience, or of indicating profound wisdom (freq. iron.); wise-looking, solemn-faced. sā'gelў *adv.* sā'geness *n.* sāge *n.* Profoundly wise man (freq. iron.), esp. any of the ancients traditionally reputed wisest of their time; *the seven* ~*s*: see SEVEN.

să'ggar *n.* 1. Case of baked fireproof clay enclosing pottery while it is baked. 2. Case in which cast iron can be decarbonized and made malleable.

Sagi'tta. The Arrow, a northern constellation.

să'gittal *adj.* (anat.) In the same plane as the sagittal suture (suture between parietal bones of skull; ill. HEAD), i.e. longitudinal and from front to back. sagi'ttallў *adv.*

Săgittār'ius. The Archer, a southern constellation; 9th sign (♐) of the zodiac, which the sun enters about 22 Nov. Săgittār'ian *adj.* & *n.*

să'gittāte *adj.* (bot., zool.) Shaped like arrow-head.

sā'gō *n.* Palm or cycad esp. of

SAHARA

genus *Metroxylon*; kind of starch used in cookery for puddings etc., obtained from pith of these plants.
Sahar´a. Great desert of N. Africa; hence, any great arid tract (also fig.). **Sahar´an, Sahar´ic** *adjs.*
sah´ib *n.* 1. (fem. *mĕ´msahib*) Former title or form of address used by Indians to European; also as honorific affix (*Jones* ~). 2. (colloq.) Gentleman.
said (sĕd) *adj.*: see SAY; (esp.) aforesaid.
sai´ga (*or* sī-) *n.* Kind of antelope (*S~ tartarica*) of Russian steppes.
sail[1] *n.* 1. Piece of canvas or other textile material extended on rigging to catch wind and propel vessel; (collect.) some or all of ship's sails; *full ~*, with all sail spread (lit. & fig.); *take in ~*, (fig.) moderate one's ambitions; *under ~*, with sails set. 2. (collect.) Ships; ship (esp. in *S~ ho!*, cry announcing that ship is in sight). 3. Wind-catching apparatus, now usu. set of boards, attached to arm of windmill (ill. WINDMILL); sail-fish's dorsal fin, tentacle of nautilus, float of Portuguese man-of-war; (also *wind-~*) funnel-shaped bag on ship's deck giving ventilation; *~-arm*, arm of windmill; *sai´lcloth*, canvas for sails; kind of coarse linen; *~-fish*, fish with large dorsal fin, esp. basking shark. **sai´llèss** (-l-l-) *adj.*
sail[2] *v.* 1. (of vessel or person on board) Travel on water by use of sails or engine-power; start on voyage. 2. Walk in stately manner; travel over or along, navigate, glide through (sea, sky, etc.); (of bird etc.) glide in air. 3. Control navigation of (ship), set (toy boat) afloat. 4. *~ close to* or *near the wind*, sail nearly against it; (fig.) come near transgressing a law or moral principle; *~ into*, (slang) inveigh against, rate, attack. *~ n.* Voyage or excursion in sailing-vessel; voyage of specified duration; *sai´lplane*, high-performance glider.
sai´ler *n.* Ship of specified sailing-power.
sai´ling *n.* (esp.) *plain ~*: see PLAIN[1]; *~-master*, officer navigating yacht; *~ orders*, instructions to captain of ship for departure, destination, etc.; *~-ship*, *vessel*, vessel propelled by sails, not engines.

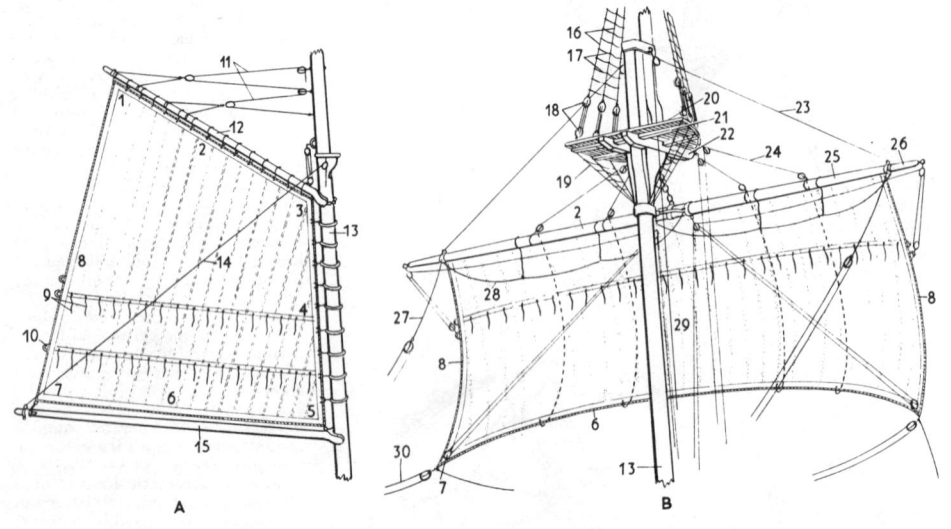

SAILING

PARTS OF SAILS, SPARS, AND RIGGING
A. FORE-AND-AFT. B. SQUARE

1. Peak. 2. Head. 3. Throat. 4. Luff. 5. Tack. 6. Foot. 7. Clew. 8. Leech. 9. Reef-points. 10. Cringle. 11. Halyards. 12. Gaff. 13. Mast. 14. Topping lift. 15. Boom. 16. Topmast shrouds. 17. Ratlines. 18. Dead-eyes. 19. Futtock shrouds. 20. Top. 21. Cross-trees. 22. Trestle-trees. 23. Lift. 24. Bunt-line. 25. Yard. 26. Yard-arm. 27. Brace. 28. Foot-rope. 29. Bunt. 30. Sheet.

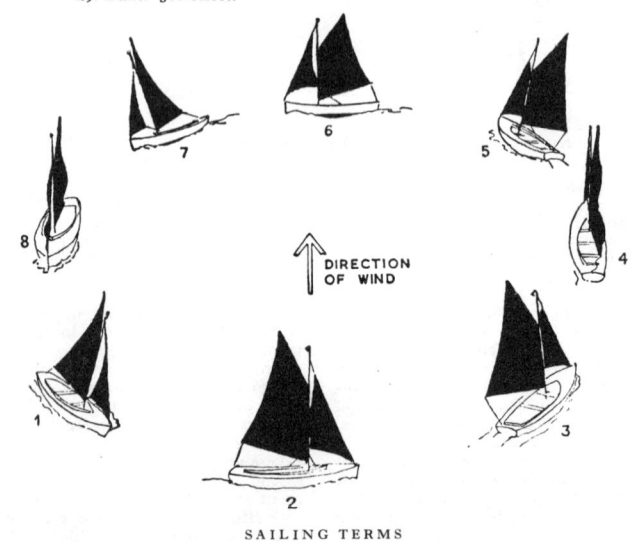

SAILING TERMS

1. Close-hauled on the starboard tack. 2. Reaching on the starboard tack. 3. Running on the starboard gybe. 4. Gybing for wearing. 5. Running on the port gybe. 6. Reaching on the port tack. 7. Close-hauled on the port tack. 8. Coming about

[774]

SAILOR

sai′lor *n.* One who is employed in navigating a ship; member of ship's company below rank of officer; *good, bad, ~,* person not, very, liable to sea-sickness; *~ hat,* straw hat with narrow brim and flat top; *~-man,* (vulg. and joc. for) sailor; *~s' home,* institution for lodging sailors cheaply ashore; *~'s knot,* any of various knots used by sailors; kind of knot used in tying neck-tie, so that both ends hang down. **sai′lorlў** *adj.*
sai′nfoin *n.* Low-growing perennial herb (*Onobrychis viciifolia*) with pinnate leaves and pink flowers, cultivated as fodder. [Fr. *sain* wholesome, *foin* hay]
saint (when unstressed snt *or* sent) *adj.* Holy; canonized or officially recognized by the Church as having won by exceptional holiness a high place in heaven and veneration on earth (usu., esp. abbrev. St. or S., pl. Sts., SS., as prefix to name(s) of person or archangel(s) as *St. Paul, St. Michael;* hence in names of churches and of towns called after their churches, and in Christian and family names, as *St. John* (sĭ′njon), taken from patron saint etc.). *~ n.* One of the blessed dead or other member of the company of heaven; canonized person; (bibl., archaic, and in some modern sects) one of God's chosen people, member of Christian Church or of some (esp. puritanical) branch of it; Mormon; person of great, real, or affected holiness; *patron ~,* saint selected as heavenly protector of person or place, esp. church, often named after him; *~'s day,* Church festival in memory of a saint, freq. observed as holiday. **sai′ntlīke, sai′ntlў** *adjs.* **sai′ntliness, sai′nthōŏd** (-t-h-) *ns.*
saint *v.t.* Canonize, admit to the calendar of saints; call or regard as a saint; *sainted,* worthy to be or be regarded, of saintly life; hallowed, sacred.
St. A′ndrews (ă-, -ōŏz). Town in Fife, on E. coast of Scotland; seat of the Royal and Ancient Golf Club, the governing body of the game of golf; university, 1410.
St. Asaph. *abbrev.* (Bishop) of St. Asaph (replacing surname in his signature).
Saint-Cyr (săn sēr). College for French army cadets, established 1806 near Versailles in the buildings of a former convent school founded by Louis XIV for young ladies of the nobility; transferred, after the buildings were destroyed in the war of 1939–45, to Coétquidan in Brittany.
St. Dŭ′nstan's (-z). Organization for the care of British soldiers, sailors, and airmen blinded in war, founded 1915 by Sir Arthur Pearson.
˳Sainte-Beuve (sănt bĕrv), Charles Augustin (1804–69). French literary critic.

St. Edm. & Ipswich. *abbrev.* (Bishop) of St. Edmundsbury and Ipswich (replacing surname in his signature).
St. Helĕ′na. Island in the S. Atlantic, in British possession, the place of Napoleon's exile (1815–21).
St. Jā′mes's (-mzĭz). Old Tudor palace of the kings of England in London, built by Henry VIII; *Court of ~,* official title of the British court, to which ambassadors from foreign countries are accredited.
Saint-Just (săn zhŭst), Louis Antoine Léon (1767–94). French revolutionary.
St. Kĭ′lda. Island of the Outer Hebrides.
St. Kitts. Island in the West Indies, formerly in British possession; independent (with Nevis) 1967; capital, Basseterre.
St. Law′rence (lŏr-). River of N. America, flowing from Lake Ontario to the Atlantic.
St. Lĕ′ger. Annual horse-race for 3-year-old colts and fillies, held in September at Doncaster; instituted by Lt-Gen. St. Leger in 1776.
St. Lu′cia (lōōsha). Island in the West Indies, formerly in British possession; independent (as an Associated State) 1967; capital, Castries.
St. Paul's (-z). Cathedral church of the bishop of London, in the City; designed by Sir Christopher Wren and built 1675–1710 on the site of a medieval church (*Old ~*) destroyed in the Great Fire.
St. Pē′ter's (-z). Basilica of St. Peter adjoining the Vatican palace in Rome, built during the years 1506–1626 from plans drawn by Bramante and adapted by Michelangelo.
St. Pē′tersbŭrġ (-z-). Former name of LENINGRAD.
Saint-Pierre (săn pyār), Jacques Henri Bernardin de (1737–1814). French author of the romantic novel 'Paul et Virginie'.
Saint-Saëns (săn sahń), Charles Camille (1835–1921). French musical composer, famous for his symphonic poems and the opera 'Samson and Delilah'.
Saint-Simon[1] (săn sēmawń), Claude Henri, Comte de (1760–1825). French socialist; advocated the State control of property and division of profits among the workers according to the value of their work. **Saint-Si′monĭsm** *n.*
Saint-Simon[2] (săn sēmawń), Louis, Duc de (1675–1755). French writer of memoirs of the reign of Louis XIV.
St. Sophī′a. Principal church of Constantinople; built by Emperor Justinian (532–7); converted into a mosque after the capture of Constantinople by the Turks (1453); a museum since 1935.
St. Stē′phens (-venz). The House of Commons, so called from

SALAMANDER

the ancient chapel of St. Stephen, Westminster, in which the House used to sit (1537–1834).
St. Vĭ′ncent. Island in the West Indies, formerly in British possession; independent (as an Associated State) 1969; capital, Kingstown.
Sā′is. Ancient capital of Lower Egypt, in the Nile delta. **Sāĭ′tĭc** *adj.* Of Sais; *~ dynasties,* 26th–30th of the Egyptian kings.
saithe (-dh) *n.* = COAL-fish.
sāke *n. for the ~ of,* (for someone's or something's) *~,* out of consideration for, in the interest of (someone or something); *for goodness', heaven's, ~,* form of entreaty or exclamation; *for old sake's, time's, ~,* in memory of old days.
sake (sah′kĭ) *n.* Japanese fermented liquor made from rice.
sā′ker *n.* 1. Large falcon (*Falco sacer*) used in hawking, esp. the female, which is larger than the male. 2. (hist.) Old form of cannon.
Sakyamū′nĭ (sah-): see BUDDHA.
sal (sahl) *n.* Indian timber-tree (*Shorea robusta*), yielding resin.
salaa′m (-ahm) *n.* Oriental salutation 'Peace'; Indian obeisance accompanying this, low bow of head and body with right palm on forehead. *~ v.* Make salaam (to). [Arab. *salām*]
salable. Var. of SALEABLE.
salā′cious (-shus) *adj.* Lustful; (of literature) dealing with or suggestive of lewdness. **salā′ciouslў** *adv.* **salā′ciousnĕss, salā′cĭtў** *ns.*
să′lad *n.* Cold dish of usu. uncooked vegetables; cold dish of meat, fish, etc., with salad (e.g. *chicken ~*); vegetable (e.g. lettuce, endive) suitable for eating raw in salads; *~ days,* one's inexperienced youth; *~-dressing,* mixture of oil, vinegar, etc., used for seasoning salad; *~-oil,* olive or other vegetable oil used for dressing salads.
Să′ladin (1137–93). Sultan of Egypt, who invaded Palestine and captured Jerusalem.
Sălamă′nca. Province of W. Spain; capital of this province, scene of a battle (1812) in which the French were defeated by Wellington.
să′lamănder *n.* 1. Lizard-like animal supposed to live in fire; figure of this used as emblem; person who can endure great heat; spirit supposed to live in fire. 2. (zool.) Tailed urodele amphibian,

SALAMANDER

related to newts, of family Salamandridae. 3. (hist.) Red-hot iron or poker used for firing gunpowder etc. 4. Iron plate used hot for browning top of pudding etc. **sălamă′ndrian, sălamă′ndrine**

[775]

adjs. **sălămă′ndroid** *adj. & n.*
sala′mè, -ĭ (-lah-) *n.* Italian highly seasoned sausage, freq. flavoured with garlic.
Să′lamis. Island off SW. coast of Attica, near the Piraeus, scene of a naval battle in 480 B.C. in which the Persian fleet under Xerxes was defeated by the Greeks.
săl ammŏ′niăc : see AMMONIAC.
salār′iat *n.* Salaried class.
sa′larў *n.* Fixed periodical payment made to person doing other than manual or mechanical work, which is remunerated by *wages*.
să′laried (-ĭd) *adj.* Receiving a salary. [L *salarium*, orig. soldier's salt-money, f. *sal* salt]
săle *n.* Exchange of a commodity for money or other valuable consideration, selling; amount sold; public auction; rapid disposal at reduced prices of (part of) shop's stock at end of season etc.; charity bazaar; *for, on,* ~, offered for purchase; *white* ~, sale of household linen etc.; ~*-ring*, ring of buyers at auction; *sa′lesman, sa′leswoman*, person engaged in selling goods in shop, etc., or as middleman between producer and retailer; *sa′lesmanship*, skill in selling; *sales resistance*, (orig. U.S.) opposition or apathy of the prospective customer regarded as requiring to be overcome by salesmanship; *sales talk*, persuasive reasoning to prospective customer.
sā′leable (-labl) *adj.* Fit for sale; finding purchasers. **sāleabĭ′litў** *n.*
Sā′lĕm. Place mentioned in Gen. 14: 18 as the seat of the kingdom of Melchizedek, doubtfully identified with Jerusalem; hence, a Nonconformist chapel.
să′lĕp *n.* Nutritive meal, starch, or jelly, from dried tubers of orchidaceous plants, esp. of genus *Orchis.* [Arab. *ta′lab*]
Sales (sahl) *or* sahl), St. Francis of (1567–1622). French R.C. bishop of Geneva. **Sălē′sian** (-zhan) *adj. & n.* (Member) of an order named after St. Francis of Sales.
Sa′lford (saw-). Town in Greater Manchester; university, 1967.
Sā′lian¹ *adj.* (Rom. religion) Of the Salii or priests of Mars.
Sā′lian² *adj. & n.* (Member) of Frankish tribe on the lower Rhine from which the Merovingians were descended.
Sā′lĭc, Săli′que(-ēk) *adj.* Of the Salian Franks; *Salic Law*, code of law of the Salian Franks which maintains that a woman can have no portion of the inheritance of the 'Salian land'; alleged fundamental law of the French monarchy excluding females from dynastic succession.
să′lĭcĕt *n.* Organ-stop one octave higher than SALICIONAL.
să′lĭcĭn *n.* Bitter crystalline substance got from willow-bark etc. and used medicinally.
salĭ′cional (-shon-) *n.* Organ-stop of soft reedy tone like willow-pipe.
să′lĭcўl *n.* (chem.) Radical of salicylic acid. **sălĭcў′lĭc** *adj.* ~ *acid,* (C₆H₄(OH)COOH) orig. obtained from salicin but now made synthetically, used as antiseptic and in treatment of rheumatism etc., esp. in the form of its acetyl ester, aspirin. **salĭ′cўlate** *n.* Salt of salicylic acid.
sā′lient *adj.* 1. Leaping or dancing (pedantic, joc.); (of water etc., poet.) jetting forth. 2. (of angle, esp. in fortification) Pointing outwards. 3. Jutting out; prominent, conspicuous, most noticeable. **sā′liently** *adv.* **sā′lience, sā′liencў** *ns.* **sā′lient** *n.* Salient angle or part in fortification; projecting section of line of offence or defence.
sālĭĕ′ntian (-shĭan) *adj. & n.* (Member) of the Salientia, a superorder of amphibians comprising frogs and toads, the adult forms of which have no tails or gills but have strong hind legs for leaping or swimming.
Sălier′ĭ (-yārĭ), Antonio (1750–1825). Italian musical composer.
salĭ′ferous *adj.* (geol.) (of stratum) Containing much salt.
sā′līne *adj.* (of natural waters, springs, etc.) Impregnated with salt or salts; (of taste) salt; of chemical salts, of the nature of a salt; (of medicines) containing salt(s) of alkaline metals or magnesium. ~ *n.* Salt lake, spring, marsh, etc.; salt-pan, salt-works; saline substance; saline purge; *physiological* ~, solution of sodium chloride approx. equivalent to salt concentration of body fluids in mammals. **salĭ′nitў** *n.*
Salique: see SALIC.
Sa′lisburў¹ (sawlz-). Capital city of Rhodesia.
Sa′lisburў² (sawlz-), Robert Arthur Talbot Gascoyne Cecil, 3rd Marquis of (1830–1903). British Conservative statesman; prime minister 1885–6, 1886–92, 1895–1902.
salĭ′va *n.* Colourless, normally alkaline, liquid, the mixed secretion of salivary glands and mucous glands of the mouth, which mixes with food in mastication; spittle. **să′livarў** (*or* salĭ′-) *adj.* Secreting or conveying, of, existing in, saliva (~ *gland,* ill. GLAND).
să′livāte *v.* Produce unusual secretion of saliva in (person), usu. with mercury; secrete or discharge saliva, esp. in excess. **săliva′tion** *n.*
să′llenders (-z) *n.pl.* Dry eruption inside hock of horse's leg (cf MALLENDERS, of knee).
să′llĕt *n.* (hist., in armour) Light globular head-piece without crest and with lower part curving outwards behind (ill. ARMOUR).
să′llow¹ (-ō) *n.* Willow-tree, esp. of low-growing or shrubby kinds; shoot or wood of this. **să′llowў** *adj.*
să′llow² (-ō) *adj.* (of skin or complexion) Sickly yellow or yellowish-brown in colour; having skin of this colour. ~ *v.* Make, grow, sallow. **să′llowish** *adj.* **să′llowness** *n.*
Să′llust. Gaius Sallustius Crispus (86–35 B.C.), Roman historian; accompanied Caesar in his African war and became governor of Numidia.
să′llў¹ *n.* 1. Rush (*out*) from besieged place upon enemy, sortie; excursion; ~-*port*, opening in fortified place for making sallies from. 2. Sudden start into activity, outburst; outburst, flash (esp. *of wit*); witticism, piece of banter, lively remark. 3. Projection, prominence (archit., carpentry, etc.). ~ *v.i.* Make sally (usu. *out*); go *forth* or *out* on journey, for a walk, etc.
să′llў² *n.* First movement of bell when set for ringing, bell's position when set; part of bell-rope prepared with inwoven wool for holding.
Să′llў³. Familiar for *Sarah: Aunt* ~: see AUNT; ~ *Lunn*, kind of sweet light tea-cake served hot (perhaps f. name of a girl hawking them at Bath *c* 1800).
sălmagŭ′ndi *n.* Dish of chopped meat, eggs, anchovies, onions, etc., with oil and condiments; general mixture, miscellaneous collection. [Fr. *salmigondis*]
să′lmi *n.* Ragout, esp. of game-birds, partly roasted and then stewed with wine or sauce. [Fr., prob. short for prec.]
să′lmon (săm-) *n.* Large silver-scaled pink-fleshed fish of genus *Salmo,* esp. *S. salar* which ascends rivers to spawn, much prized for food and sport; any of various other fishes (esp. *Oncorhynchus*) of same family, or resembling salmon; ~-*ladder,* -*leap,* -*pass,* -*stair,* series of steps or other arrangement for allowing salmon to pass dam and ascend stream; ~-*pink,* (of) the orange-pink colour of salmon-flesh; ~ *trout,* sea-trout (*Salmo trutta* of northern European rivers). ~ *adj.* Salmon-pink.
sălmonĕ′lla *n.* Micro-organism of the genus *S*~, members of which are responsible for many forms of enteritis, typhoid fever, etc. [D. E. *Salmon* (1850–1914), Amer. pathologist]
să′lmonid *adj. & n.* (zool.) (Fish) of the family Salmonidae (salmon, trout, etc.).
Salō′mè. Stepdaughter of Herod Antipas; she danced before him, and at the bidding of her mother, Herodias, asked for the head of John the Baptist in a charger (i.e. a dish) as a reward (see Matt. 14).
Sălomŏ′nĭc, Sălomŏ′nian *adjs.* Of, as of, Solomon.
să′lon (-awṅ) *n.* Reception-room in continental, esp. French, great house; (assembly of notabilities in) reception-room of

SALONICA

(esp. Parisian) lady of fashion; (exhibition in) gallery etc. for showing works of art, photographs, etc., esp. (*the S~*) annual exhibition of living artists' pictures in Paris; room or establishment where hairdresser, dressmaker, etc., receives clients; ~ *music*, light music for drawing-room.

Salŏ'nica (*in Gk hist.* sălŏnī'ka). (Gk *Thessaloniki*, the ancient THESSALONICA) Seaport in NE. Greece, capital of Macedonia; scene of campaign in war of 1914-18, by French and British in support of Serbia, during which they occupied Salonica (Oct. 1915).

salōō'n *n.* 1. Hall or large room, esp. in hotel or place of public resort, fit for assemblies, exhibitions, etc. 2. Large cabin for first-class or for all passengers on ship etc., esp. serving as lounge; (also *~-car, ~-carriage*) luxurious railway carriage without compartments serving as lounge. 3. Public room(s) or gallery for specified purpose (*billiard-, dancing-, shooting-~*, etc.). 4. (U.S.) Drinking-bar. 5. Saloon (motor-) car (see below). 6. ~ *bar*, first-class bar in English public-house; *~-car, -carriage*, see sense 2; ~ *car*, motor-car with closed body and no partition behind driver (ill. MOTOR); ~ *deck*, deck reserved for saloon passengers; *~-keeper*, keeper of saloon bar; ~ *pistol, rifle*, one adapted for short-range practice in shooting-saloon.

salōō'p *n.* = SALEP; hot drink of salep or sassafras formerly sold as substitute for coffee at London street-stalls.

Să'lop. West midland county of England (until April 1974 called Shropshire). **Salŏ'pian** *adj.* & *n.* 1. (Native) of Salop. 2. (Member) of Shrewsbury School. [AF *Sloppesberie* Shrewsbury]

sălpĭglŏ'ssĭs *n.* Showy-flowered herbaceous garden-plant allied to petunia, orig. from Chile. [Gk *salpigx* trumpet, *glōssa* tongue]

să'lsĭfy̆ *n.* European biennial composite plant (*Tragopogon porrifolius*) with long cylindrical fleshy roots eaten as vegetable, purple goat's-beard.

salt (sawlt *or* sŏlt) *n.* 1. (also *common ~*) Sodium chloride, a substance with characteristic taste, very abundant in nature (in the sea, and in crystalline form), used as a condiment, as a preservative of food, and in many industrial processes; *rock-~*, impure brownish salt found in salt-mines; *white ~*, this refined for household use; *table ~*, finely powdered salt for table use; *eat person's ~*, be his guest or dependant; *take ~ with*, be guest or; *take with a grain of ~*, accept (statement etc.) with reserve; *worth one's ~*, efficient, useful; *the ~ of the earth*, people for whose existence the world is better, moral élite (see Matt. 5: 13). 2. Vessel for table salt, salt-

CEREMONIAL SALT

cellar (now chiefly in trade use; and hist. in *above the ~*, seated with family and their equals, and *below the ~*, among servants and dependants). 3. Sting, piquancy, pungency, wit. 4. (chem.) Substance formed from an acid when all or part of its hydrogen is replaced by a metal or metallic radical. 5. (old chem.) Solid soluble non-inflammable substance (obs. exc. in some compound names as *~s of lemon, Glauber's ~*, etc.). 6. (also *~ bottom, ~-marsh*) Marsh overflowed by sea, freq. used as pasture or for collecting water for salt-making. 7. (pl.) Exceptional rush of sea-water up river. 8. Experienced sailor (esp. *old ~*). 9. *sa'ltbush*, plant of genus *Atriplex*; *~-cat*, mass of salt mixed with gravel, cummin-seed, urine, etc., to attract pigeons and keep them at home; *~-cellar*, vessel holding salt for table use; (colloq.) one of hollows at base of neck; *~-glaze*, glaze made by throwing salt on to stoneware while in furnace; *~-grass*, (U.S.) grass growing in salt meadows; pasture-grass of arid plains of western States; *~-lick*, place where animals collect to lick earth impregnated with salt; *~-marsh*, see 6 above; *~ meadow*, (chiefly U.S.) meadow liable to be flooded with salt water; *~-mine*, mine yielding rock-salt; *~-pan*, depression near sea, vessel, used for getting salt by evaporation; *~-spoon*, spoon usu. with short handle and roundish deep bowl for helping salt; *sa'ltwort*, any of various maritime and salt-marsh plants (esp. *Salsola Kali*, prickly saltwort, and other species of *Salsola*). ~ *adj.* Impregnated with, containing, tasting of, cured or preserved or seasoned with, salt; (of plants) growing in sea or salt-marshes; (of tears, grief, etc.)

SALVAGE

bitter, afflicting; (of wit etc.) piquant (rare); ~ *horse*, (naut. slang) salt beef; ~ *water*, sea-water; *tears*; *~-water*, of, living in, the sea. **sa'lty̆** *adj.* **sa'ltinĕss, sa'ltnĕss** *ns.* **salt** *v.t.* 1. Preserve, season, or treat with salt; *~ away, down*, put by, store away (money etc.). 2. Render piquant, enliven. 3. Make (mine etc.) appear to be paying one by fraudulently introducing rich ore etc.

săltā'tion *n.* Leaping, dancing, a jump; sudden transition or movement.

sa'lter (sawl- *or* sŏl-) *n.* Manufacturer of, dealer in, salt; DRY-salter; workman at salt-works; person who salts fish etc.

sa'ltern (sawl- *or* sŏl-) *n.* Salt-works; set of pools for natural evaporation of sea-water.

să'ltigrăde *adj.* (zool.) Moving by jumping.

sa'lting (sawl- *or* sŏl-) *n.* = SALT *n.* 6.

să'ltīre *n.* (her.) Ordinary in form of St. Andrew's cross (X), dividing shield etc. into four compartments (ill. HERALDRY).

saltpē'tre (sawltpēt*er or* sŏl-) *n.* Nitre, potassium nitrate (KNO₃), white crystalline salty substance used as constituent of gunpowder, in preserving meat etc.; *Chili or cubic ~*, sodium nitrate (NaNO₃). [prob. f. L *sal petrae* salt of stone, because it occurs as an incrustation on stones]

salū'brious (-ōō- *or* -ū-) *adj.* Healthy (chiefly of air, climate, etc.). **salu'briously̆** *adv.* **salu'brĭty̆** *n.*

salu'kĭ (-ōō-) *n.* Tall swift slender silky-coated dog, Arabian gazelle-hound.

să'lūtary̆ *adj.* Producing good effect, beneficial.

sălūtā'tion *n.* (Use of) words spoken or written to convey interest in another's health etc., pleasure at sight of or communication with him, or courteous recognition of his arrival or departure; greeting.

salū'te (*or* -ōōt) *v.* Make salute or salutation (to); (archaic) kiss. ~ *n.* Gesture expressing respect, homage, or courteous recognition; (mil., nav., etc.) prescribed movement (esp., of hand to forehead) or position of body or weapons, use of flag(s), discharge of gun(s), in sign of respect; (fencing) formal performance of certain guards, etc., by fencers before engaging; kiss, as greeting.

Să'lvadōr (*or* -dōr'), El. Republic of Central America, on the Pacific coast; capital, San Salvador.

să'lvage *n.* (Payment made or due for) saving of a ship or its cargo from loss by wreck or capture; rescue of property from fire etc.; saving and utilization of waste material of all kinds; property salvaged. ~ *v.t.* Make salvage of, save from wreck, fire, etc.

[777]

sălvā′tion n. 1. Saving of the soul; deliverance from sin and its consequences, and admission to heaven, brought about by the merits of Christ's death. 2. Preservation from loss, calamity, etc.; thing that preserves from these.

Sălvā′tion Ar′mў (ār-). Religious missionary body founded by the Rev. William (afterwards known as 'General') Booth in 1878 and organized on a quasi-military basis and engaging in evangelical and charitable work among the destitute throughout the world. **Sălvā′tionist** n. Member of the Salvation Army.

sălve[1] (or sahv) n. Healing ointment for sores or wounds; mixture of tar and grease for smearing sheep; something that soothes wounded feelings or uneasy conscience. ~ v.t. Anoint (wound etc.); smear (sheep); soothe (pride, self-love, conscience, etc.).

sălve[2] v.t. Save (ship, cargo) from loss at sea or (property) from fire etc.

Să′lvĕ[3] n. (also ~ *regina*; L, = 'hail, queen') R.C. antiphon beginning thus, recited after Divine Office from Trinity Sunday to Advent; music for this.

să′lver n. Metal tray for handing refreshments or presenting letters, visiting-cards, etc. [f. Fr. *salve* tray for presenting certain things to king, f. Span. *salva* assaying of food (*salvo* safe)]

să′lvia n. Plant of genus S~, comprising the sages; flower of this cultivated for its bright-blue or scarlet colour.

să′lvo[1] n. (pl. -s). (archaic) Saving clause; quibbling evasion; expedient for saving reputation or soothing feelings.

să′lvo[2] n. (pl. -*es*, -s). Simultaneous discharge of artillery, rockets, etc.; burst of applause.

săl volă′tile. Alcoholic solution of ammonium carbonate flavoured with the oils of lemon and nutmeg and used as a restorative in faintness etc. [mod. L, = 'volatile salt']

să′lvor n. Person, ship, making or assisting in salvage.

Să′lzbūrg (-lts-). Town in Austria where a summer festival of music and drama has been held annually, except in war-time, since 1920.

Sam. *abbrev.* Samuel (O.T.).

samār′a n. Winged one-seeded indehiscent fruit, single (as in ash) or double (as in sycamore) (ill. FRUIT).

Samār′ia. Ancient capital of Israel, the northern kingdom of the Hebrews (see ISRAEL[2], 3); region surrounding this, west of the Jordan, bounded by Galilee and Judaea.

Samă′ritan n. 1. Native, inhabitant, language, of Samaria; member of Jewish sect accepting only the Pentateuch. 2. *good* ~, person always ready to help the unfortunate (with ref. to Luke 10: 33 etc.). 3. Member of 'The Samaritans Incorporated', an organization founded in 1953 to enable help, compassion, and friendship to be given (esp. through telephone service) to the suicidal and despairing. ~ *adj.* Of Samaria or Samaritans. **Samă′ritanism** n. Charitableness, charity.

samār′ium n. (chem.) Element of rare-earth group, symbol Sm, at. no. 62, at. wt 150·4.

Sămarkă′nd. City of Uzbekistan; TAMBURLAINE's capital.

să′mba n. Brazilian dance of African origin; ballroom dance imitative of this.

să′mbăr, -būr n. Indian elk (*Rusa unicolor*), distributed over SE. Asia.

să′mbō[1] n. (also *zambo*) Half-breed, esp. between Negro and Indian.

Să′mbō[2]. Nickname for Negro.

Săm Browne. Leather belt with a supporting strap passing over the right shoulder, worn by officers in the British Army. [f. name of Gen. Sir *Samuel* J. *Browne*, 1824–1901]

sāme *adj.* 1. Not different; (freq. as emphatic substitute for) the, that, those, the very. 2. (pred.) Not changed; not varying; equally acceptable. 3. Aforesaid. 4. (*abs.* and as *pron.*) *the* ~, the same person; the same thing; (archaic, legal, commercial) the aforesaid thing or person. 5. *the* ~ (*adv.*) in the same manner; *all the* ~, nevertheless; *just the* ~, in spite of changed conditions. **sā′menĕss** n.

să′mel *adj.* (of brick, tile) Imperfectly baked.

Sā′mian *adj.* Of Samos; ~ *ware*, orig., pottery made of Samian earth; extended to a fine kind of pottery found extensively on Roman sites. ~ n. Native, inhabitant, of Samos.

să′mīte n. (hist.) Rich medieval dress-fabric of silk sometimes interwoven with gold. [late Gk *hexamitum* (*hex* six, *mitos* thread), perh. = fabric in which weft-threads are caught only at every 6th warp-thread]

să′mlĕt n. Young salmon.

Săm′nīte *adj. & n.* (Member) of an ancient tribe of S. Central Italy, inhabiting the district of Samnium.

Samō′a. Group of Polynesian islands, of which the eastern part (*American* ~) is a U.S. territory; *Western* ~, republic, independent since 1962; member State of the Commonwealth; capital, Apia. **Samō′an** *adj. & n.*

Sā′mŏs. Greek island in the Aegean.

Sā′mothrāce. Greek island in the Aegean; *Winged Victory of* ~: see WINGED.

să′movăr n. Russian tea-urn. [Russ., = 'self-boiler']

Să′moyĕd (-mo-) n. 1. Member, language, of a Mongolian people of Siberia. 2. Dog of white Arctic breed, used for pulling sledges. **Sămoyĕ′dĭc** *adj. & n.*

să′mpăn n. Small boat used in river and coastal traffic of China, Japan, and neighbouring islands, rowed with a scull from the stern and usu. having a sail of matting and an awning. [Chin. *san-pan* boat (*san* three, *pan* board)]

să′mphīre n. Cliff-plant (*Crithmum maritimum*) with aromatic saline fleshy leaves used in pickles. [Fr. (*herbe de*) *St. Pierre* St. Peter's (herb)]

sa′mple (sah-) n. Small separated part of something illustrating qualities of the mass etc. it is taken from, specimen, pattern. ~ v.t. Take or give samples, try the qualities, get representative experience, of. **sa′mpler**[1] n.

sa′mpler[2] (sah-) n. 1. Piece of embroidery worked as specimen of proficiency, usu. containing alphabet and various decorative motifs. 2. (forestry) Young tree left standing when others are cut down.

Să′mson. Israelite judge famous for his strength (Judges 13–16); he confided to a woman, Delilah, that his strength lay in his hair, and she betrayed him to the Philistines, who cut off his hair while he slept and captured and blinded him; but when his hair grew again his strength returned and he pulled down the pillars of the house of Gaza, destroying himself and a large concourse of Philistines; hence, man of phenomenal strength; ~ ('s) *post*, (naut.) strong supporting pillar or post in a ship usu. resting on the keelson and supporting a deck beam; post in a whaler to which harpoon-rope is attached.

Să′mŭel. Hebrew prophet who rallied the Israelites after their defeat by the Philistines and became their ruler; (*1st* and *2nd Book of*) ~, two books of O.T. covering the history of Israel from Samuel's birth to the end of the reign of David.

să′murai (-ōōrī) n. (pl. same). In

SAMOVAR

1. Lid of water container. 2. Lid of charcoal container. 3. Tap

[778]

SANATIVE, SANATORY

Japanese feudal system, military retainer of the daimios; any member of military caste; (now) Japanese army officer.

sā′native, sā′natory *adjs.* Healing, of or tending to physical or moral health, curative.

sănatōr′ium *n.* (pl. *-ia*). Establishment for treatment of chronic diseases (as tuberculosis) or for convalescents; room or building in school or college for the sick.

sănbĕni′tō (-nē-) *n.* Penitential scapular-shaped yellow garment with red St. Andrew's cross before and behind worn by confessed and penitent heretic under Spanish Inquisition; similar black garment painted with flames and devils worn by impenitent heretic at auto-da-fé. [Span. *sambenito* f. *San Benito* St. Benedict, because shaped like scapular introduced by him]

Să′ncho Pă′nza (-kō). The squire of Don Quixote, who accompanies him on his adventures; he is an ignorant and credulous peasant, but has a store of proverbial wisdom and is thus a foil to his master.

sā′nctify *v.t.* Consecrate, make holy; purify from sin; give authority to, justify. **sănctifĭcā′tion** *n.*

sănctimō′nious *adj.* Making a show of sanctity or piety. **sănctimō′niouslў** *adv.* **sănctimō′niousnĕss** *n.*

sā′nction *n.* 1. (hist.) Law or (esp. eccles.) decree; *pragmatic ~*: see PRAGMATIC. 2. Penalty or reward for (dis)obedience attached to a law, clause containing this, (now esp.) penalty imposed for non-compliance with international agreement; consideration operating to enforce obedience to any rule of conduct. 3. Confirmation or ratification of law etc. by supreme authority; express authoritative permission; countenance or encouragement given to action etc. by custom etc. *~ v.t.* Authorize; countenance; permit.

sā′nctitūde *n.* (now rare) Saintliness.

sā′nctitў *n.* Saintliness; sacredness; inviolability; (pl.) sacred obligations, feelings, etc.

sā′nctuarў *n.* 1. Place recognized as holy part of church within altar-rails (ill. CHURCH). 2. Sacred place for retiring to which fugitive from law, or debtor, was secured by medieval Church law against arrest or violence; place in which similar immunity was established by custom or law; place of refuge; (right of affording) such immunity. 3. (hunting etc.) Close time or place for bird, beast, or fish.

sā′nctum *n.* Holy place in Jewish etc. tabernacle or temple; person's private room, study, den; *~ sanctorum*, holy of holies.

Să′nctus *n.* Hymn (from Isa. 6: 3) beginning '*Sanctus, sanctus, sanctus*' or 'Holy, holy, holy',

forming conclusion of Eucharistic preface; music for this; ~ *bell*, bell in turret at junction of nave and chancel, or handbell, rung at the Sanctus.

sănd[1] *n.* Minute fragments resulting from wearing down of esp. siliceous rocks and found covering parts of the sea-shore, river-beds, deserts, etc.; (also pl.) shoal or submarine bank of sand; (usu. in pl.) grain of sand; (pl.) expanse or tracts of sand; *sa′ndbag*, bag filled with sand, used for making trenches, for protecting buildings etc. against blast and splinters, as ballast, as weapon leaving no mark on victim, as draught-excluder, etc.; (*v.t.*) protect with sandbags; fell with blow from sandbag; *~-bank*, shoal in sea or river; *~-bar*, sandbank at mouth of harbour or river; *~-bath*, vessel of heated sand as equable heater in chemical processes; *sa′ndblast*, jet of sand impelled by compressed air or steam for giving rough surface to glass etc.; (*v.t.*) clean with a sandblast; *~-box*, (hist.) castor for sprinkling sand over wet ink; mould of sand used in founding; box of sand on locomotive for sprinkling slippery rails; (golf) receptacle for sand used in teeing; *~-casting*, metal casting obtained from sand mould; process of making such castings; *~-devil*, (S. Afr.) small whirlwind; *~-fly*, small fly or midge (*Simulium*); kind of fishing-fly; *sa′ndglass*, device for measuring intervals of time,

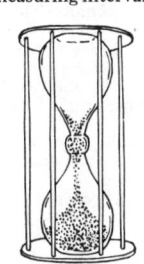

SANDGLASS OR HOURGLASS

consisting of wasp-waisted reversible glass with two bulbs containing sand which takes a definite time in passing from upper to lower bulb, now practically obsolete except for measuring the time required to boil an egg; *~-hill*, dune; *~-hopper*, small jumping crustacean of family Talitridae, most species of which burrow in sand of sea-shore; *S~-man*, (nursery name for) personification of sleep or sleepiness; *~-martin*: see MARTIN; *sa′ndpaper*, paper with layer of sand or other abrasive stuck on for smoothing or polishing wood etc.; (*v.t.*) polish with sandpaper; *~-piper*, bird of family Scolopacidae, esp. *Actitis hypoleucos* or the N. Amer. *A. macularia*, haunting open wet sandy places; *~-shoes*, shoes for

SANDWICH

use on sands, usu. of canvas with rubber or hemp soles; *sa′ndstone*, sedimentary rock composed of small grains usu. of quartz cemented together; *New Red Sandstone*, (geol.) Permian and Triassic series (esp. in NW. England); *Old Red Sandstone*, (geol.) continental Devonian series; *~-storm*, desert storm of wind with clouds of sand. *~ v.t.* Sprinkle, cover, mix, or polish with sand.

Sănd[2] (sahn), George. Pen-name of Armandine Lucile Amore Dupin-Dudevant (1804-76), French novelist, friend of Alfred de Musset and Chopin, author of 'Indiana', 'Lélia', 'Consuelo', etc.

sā′ndal[1] *n.* Sole without upper, attached to foot by thongs passing over instep and round ankle; modification of this, worn by ancient Greeks and Romans, by some orientals, as modern revival, etc. *~ v.t.* Put sandals on (foot, person; esp. in past part.).

sā′ndal[2], **sā′ndalwŏŏd** *ns.* Any of various scented woods, true sandalwood being obtained from species of Asian tree of genus *Santalum*; *red ~*, inodorous dye-wood (*Pterocarpus santalinus*).

sā′ndărăc, -ch -(k) *n.* 1. REAL-GAR. 2. (also *gum ~*) Resin exuding from NW. African tree *Tetraclinis articulata*, used in making spirit varnish.

sā′nd-blind *adj.* (archaic & dial.) Dim-sighted, purblind. [prob. for *samblind*, f. OE *sam*-half-]

sā′nderling *n.* Common small wading bird of sea-shores (*Calidris alba*).

sa′nders (sah-, -z) *n.* Sandalwood.

Să′ndhŭrst. Training college, now at Camberley, Surrey, for officers of the British Regular Army, officially known as 'The Royal Military Academy, Sandhurst', being an amalgamation of the Royal Military College at Sandhurst in Berkshire (founded 1799) and the Royal Military Academy at Woolwich, London (founded 1741).

S. & M. *abbrev.* (Bishop) of Sodor and Man (replacing surname in his signature).

Să′ndown. Race-course near Esher, Surrey.

Săn′dringham (-ng-am). Country seat of the sovereign of England, in Norfolk, near the Wash, on an estate purchased by Edward VII, when Prince of Wales.

sā′ndwich *n.* Two or more slices of bread etc. with meat or other relish between; slice of bread spread with filling and rolled; cake of two or more layers with jam etc. between; *open ~*, one with top layer of bread etc. omitted; *Victoria ~*, sandwich cake; *~-board*, board carried by sandwich-man (see below); *~-boat*, (in bumping race) boat rowing last in higher and first in lower division on same day; *~ course*,

[779]

training, course of study, training, in which periods of theoretical and practical work alternate; ~-*man*, man walking street with two advertisement-boards hung one before and one behind. ~ *v.t.* Insert (thing, statement etc.) between two of another character. [perh. f. name of 4th Earl of *Sandwich* (1718-92), said to have eaten slices of cold beef between slices of toast, while gaming for 24 hours]
sǎ'ndў[1] *adj.* Covered with sand; sand-coloured, (of hair) yellowish-red; having such hair. sǎ'ndǐnĕss *n.*
Sǎ'ndў[2]. Familiar for *Alexander*: (nickname for) Scotsman.
sāne *adj.* Of sound mind, not mad; sensible, rational. sā'nelў *adv.* sā'nenĕss (-n-n-) *n.*
Sǎn Franci'scō. City and seaport of California, U.S.
sǎngaree' (-ngg-) *n.* Cold drink of wine diluted and spiced. [Span. *sangria* 'bleeding', a drink of red wine and lemon-water]
sang-de-bœuf (sahṅ -d*e*- bẽrf) *n.* & *adj.* (Of) deep-red colour of some old Chinese porcelain. [Fr., = 'ox's blood']
sang-froid (sahṅ-frwah') *n.* Composure, coolness, in danger or under agitating circumstances. [Fr., = 'cold blood']
sangrail, sangreal: see GRAIL[2].
sǎ'nguinarў (-nggw-) *adj.* Attended by, delighting in, bloodshed or slaughter, bloody, bloodthirsty; (of laws) prescribing death for slight offences. sǎ'nguinarilў *adv.* sǎ'nguinarinĕss *n.*
sǎ'nguine (-nggw-) *adj.* 1. Blood-red. 2. (hist.) Belonging to that one of the four HUMOURS supposed to be characterized by predominance of blood over other humours, and indicated by ruddy face and courageous, hopeful, and amorous disposition; (mod., of complexion) ruddy, florid. 3. Habitually hopeful, confident; expecting things to go well. sǎ'nguinelў *adv.* sǎ'nguinenĕss *n.*
sǎ'nguine *n.* Crayon coloured brownish-red esp. with iron oxide; drawing made with this.
sǎngui'nēous (-nggwǐ-) *adj.* Of blood; blood-coloured; full-blooded, plethoric.
sǎ'nhĕdrin, -im (-nǐ-) *n.* (Jewish hist.) Highest court of justice and supreme council, of 71 members, in ancient Jerusalem, esp. between 5th c. B.C. and A.D. 70. [late Heb., f. Gk *sunedrion* (*sun* together, *hedra* seat)]
sǎ'nicle *n.* Umbelliferous plant (*Sanicula europaea*).
sǎnitār'ium *n.* (pl. *-ia*). (U.S.) = SANATORIUM.
sǎ'nitarў *adj.* Of the conditions that affect health, esp. with regard to dirt and infection; free from or designed to obviate influences deleterious to health; ~ *towel*, pad used in menstruation. sǎ'nǐtarilў *adv.* sǎ'nitarinĕss *n.*
sǎnitā'tion *n.* Measures conducing to the preservation of public health, esp. efficient drainage and disposal of sewage, ventilation, pure water supply; (specif.) drainage and disposal of sewage in houses and towns generally.
sǎ'nitў *n.* Being sane, mental health; tendency to avoid extreme views.
Sankey: see MOODY AND SANKEY.
Sǎn Mari'no (-ēnō). Small republic near Rimini, Italy, on the Adriatic; its capital.
sǎns[1] (-z) *prep.* (archaic) Without.
sǎns[2] (-z) *n.* = SANSERIF.
sans cérémonie (sahṅ sěrěmonē). Without the usual ceremony or polite forms. [Fr.]
sǎnscūlŏ'tte (-z-; *or* sahṅk-) *n.* Republican of Parisian lower classes in French Revolution; any extreme republican or revolutionary. [Fr., lit. 'breechless']
sans doute (sahṅ dōōt). Doubtless. [Fr.]
sǎnsĕ'rif *n.* & *adj.* (Form of type) without serifs (ill. TYPE).
sans façon (sahṅ fǎsawṅ). Outspokenly, unceremoniously. [Fr.]
sans-gêne (sahṅ-zhěn) *n.* Disregard of ordinary forms of civility and politeness. [Fr.]
Sǎ'nskrit *adj.* & *n.* (Of) the ancient, classical, and sacred language of the Hindus in India, in which the Vedic hymns were composed, the oldest known member of the Indo-European family of languages. Sǎnskri'tic *adj.*
sans peur et sans reproche (sahṅ pẽr ā sahṅ r*e*prŏsh). Of chivalrous character. [Fr., = 'without fear and without reproach', said orig. of Seigneur de BAYARD]
sans-souci (sahṅ-sōōsē) *n.* Carelessness, unconcern; *Sans-Souci*, palace at Potsdam built 1745-7 for Frederick the Great. [Fr.]
Sǎ'nta Claus (-z). Father CHRISTMAS. [U.S., f. Du. *Sint Klaus*, St. NICHOLAS]
Sǎntǎnder' (-ār̃). Province of N. Spain; its capital.
Sanu'si (-ōō-). Var. of SENOUSI.
sǎp[1] *n.* Juice in plants; (also ~-*wood*) soft layers of wood growing between the bark of trees and the heart-wood, alburnum (ill. STEM[1]); ~-*green*, pigment made from buckthorn berries, (of) colour of this. sǎ'plĕss, sǎ'ppў *adjs.* sǎp *v.t.* Drain or dry (wood) of sap; remove sap-wood from (log); (fig.) exhaust vigour of.
sǎp[2] *n.* Making of trenches or tunnels to cover assailant's approach to besieged place or enemy's trenches; covered siege-trench; (fig.) insidious or slow undermining of belief, resolution, etc.; ~-*head*, front end of sap. ~ *v.* Dig sap, approach by sap; undermine, make insecure by removing foundations; (fig.) destroy insidiously.
sǎp[3] *n.* (slang) Simpleton, fool.
sǎ'pajou (-jōō) *n.* CAPUCHIN monkey.
sǎ'pǎnwōōd, sǎ'pp- *n.* Tree (*Caesalpinia sappan*) of tropical Asia and the Indian Archipelago yielding red dye-wood; its wood.
sapē'lĕ *n.* African tree of genus *Entandrophragma* yielding hardwood used for making furniture; its wood.
sǎ'pǐd *adj.* Having (esp. agreeable) flavour, savoury, palatable, not insipid. sapi'ditў *n.*
sā'pient *adj.* Wise (now rare); would-be wise, of fancied sagacity, aping wisdom. sā'pientlў *adv.* sā'pience *n.*
săpiĕ'ntial (-sh*a*l) *adj.* Of wisdom; ~ *books*, (in O.T. and Apocrypha) Proverbs, Ecclesiastes, Song of Solomon, Wisdom, Ecclesiasticus.
sǎp'ling *n.* Young tree; (fig.) a youth; greyhound in first year.
sǎpodi'lla *n.* Large evergreen tropical Amer. tree (*Achras zapota*), with durable wood and edible fruit; fruit of this.
sǎponā'ceous (-shus) *adj.* Of, like, containing, soap; soapy.
sapŏ'nifў *v.* (chem.) Convert (fat or oil) into soap by boiling with alkali; convert (an ester) into its constituent acid and alcohol; be converted thus. sapŏnificā'-tion *n.* ~ *value*, in the analysis of oils and fats, the number of milligrams of potassium hydroxide neutralized in the saponification of one gramme of the substance.
sā'pŏr *n.* Quality perceptible by taste; distinctive taste; sensation of taste.
sappanwood: see SAPANWOOD.
sǎ'pper *n.* (esp.) Private of Royal Engineers.
Sǎ'pphic (sǎf-) *adj.* Of SAPPHO; ~ *verse*, metre used by Sappho and imitated in Latin by Horace, consisting of $-\cup-\bar{\cup}-\cup\cup-\cup-\bar{\cup}$ thrice repeated and followed by $-\cup\cup-\bar{\cup}.$ ~ *n.* Sapphic metre; *sapphics*, Sapphic verse.
sǎ'pphīre (sǎf-) *n.* Transparent blue precious stone, variety of alumina akin to ruby; (min.) any precious transparent native crystalline alumina, including sapphire and ruby; bright blue of sapphire, azure. ~ *adj.* Of sapphire blue.
Sappho (sǎ'fō). Greek lyric poetess of Lesbos (flourished 610 B.C.); according to legend, she threw herself into the sea in despair at her unrequited love for Phaon.
sǎprogĕ'nic *adj.* Causing or produced by putrefaction.
sǎ'prophile *adj.* & *n.* (Bacterium) inhabiting putrid matter.
sǎ'prophуte *n.* Vegetable organism living on decayed organic matter. sǎprophу'tic *adj.*
sǎ'rabǎnd *n.* Stately Spanish dance in triple time; music for this or in rhythm of it (often with long note on second beat of bar).

Să'racen *n.* (hist.) Member of the nomadic peoples of the Syro-Arabian desert; hence, Arab; by extension, Muslim, esp. with reference to the crusades; ~ *corn*, *buckwheat*; ~'*s head*, head of a Saracen, Arab, or Turk, used as a charge in heraldry, as an inn-sign, etc. **Săracĕ'nĭc** *adj.* Of, connected with, the Saracens; of Islamic architecture.

să'rafăn *n.* Long sleeveless cloak or veil as part of Russian peasant woman's dress.

Sār'ah (-*a*). Wife of Abraham and mother of Isaac (Gen. 17: 15 ff.).

Săraje'vō (-jā-). City of Yugoslavia, formerly capital of Bosnia, where the Archduke Francis Ferdinand of Austria was assassinated on 28 June 1914.

Sărasa'tĕ (-ahti), Pablo de (1844–1908). Spanish violinist and composer.

Sărato'ga. Scene, near the Hudson River, U.S., of the decisive victory of the American army under Gates over the British under Burgoyne in 1777, in the American War of Independence, and of the surrender of Burgoyne and his army; ~ *trunk*, (19th c.; f. *Saratoga Springs*, fashionable watering-place in New York State) lady's travelling trunk.

Să'rawăk (*or* sarah'-). State of Malaysia; capital, Kuching.

sār'căsm *n.* Bitter or wounding irony or ironical remark. **sār-că'stic** *adj.* **sărcă'sticăllў** *adv.*

sār'cĕllў *adj.* (her., of cross) Having the points split and curled back (ill. CROSS).

sarcenet: see SARSENET.

sārcō'ma *n.* (path.) Malignant tumour of connective tissue.

sārcŏ'phagŭs *n.* (pl. -*gi* pr. -gī). Stone coffin, esp. one adorned with sculpture or bearing inscription etc. [L, f. Gk *sarkophagos*, orig. = flesh-consuming (stone) (*sar* flesh, -*phagos* eating)]

sār'coplăsm *n.* Component of muscular tissue, substance filling the spaces in between the fibres.

sārd *n.* Yellow or orange cornelian. [f. *Sardis* in Lydia]

Sārdană'palus (*or* -năpah'-) (d. 626 B.C.). Last king of Assyria, notorious for his luxury and effeminacy.

sār'dīne[1] *n.* Precious stone mentioned in Rev. 4: 3, prob. = SARD.

sārdi'nē[2] (-ēn) *n.* Young pilchard, freq. cured and tinned tightly packed in oil; *like ~s*, packed tight, very crowded.

Sārdi'nĭa. Large island W. of the Italian mainland, formerly a kingdom (including Savoy and Piedmont), which became by expansion part of the kingdom of Italy in 1861. **Sārdi'nian** *adj.* & *n.*

sār'dĭus *n.* = SARD.

sārdŏ'nic *adj.* (of laughter etc.) Bitter, scornful, mocking, sneering, cynical. **sārdŏ'nĭcăllў** *adv.* [Gk *sardonios* Sardinian, substituted for Homeric *sardanios* (epithet of bitter or scornful laughter) because of belief that convulsive laughter ending in death resulted from eating a Sardinian plant]

sār'donўx *n.* Variety of onyx with white layers alternating with sard.

sārgă'ssō *n.* Seaweed of genus *Sargassum* with berry-like air-vessels, found floating in island-like masses in Gulf Stream.

Sārgă'ssō Sea. Region in N. Atlantic, S. of the 35th parallel. [f. prevalence in it of SARGASSO]

Sār'gent, John Singer (1856–1925). American portrait and genre painter, chiefly active in England.

sa'ri (sah-) *n.* Length of material wrapped round the body, worn as main garment by Hindu women.

sārk[1] *n.* (Sc. & north.) Shirt or chemise.

Sārk[2]. One of the Channel Islands.

Sārmā'tia (-sh*a*). Ancient name of a region N. of the Black Sea inhabited by ancestors of the Slavs, used occasionally by English poets to signify Poland. **Sārmā'tian** *adj.* & *n.*

sărŏ'ng *n.* Malay and Javanese garment, long piece of cloth worn as skirt, tucked round waist or under armpits.

sārsaparĭ'lla *n.* Any of various kinds of tropical Amer. smilax (esp. *Smilax ornata*, Jamaica smilax); dried roots of these, or extract of them, used as tonic etc.

sār'sen *n.* One of the large boulders of sandstone found scattered on chalk downs, esp. in Wiltshire. [prob. f. SARACEN]

sār'senĕt, sār'cenet (-sn-) *n.* Fine soft silk material used esp. for linings. [f. Anglo-Norman *sarzinett*]

Sarto: see ANDREA DEL SARTO.

sārtōr'ĭal *adj.* Of tailors or tailoring; of men's clothes.

sārtōr'ius *n.* Long narrow muscle crossing thigh obliquely in front (ill. MUSCLE). [mod. L, so called as being concerned in producing tailor's cross-legged working position]

Sār'um[1]. Ecclesiastical name of Salisbury, Wiltshire, and its diocese; *Old ~*, hill 2 miles from Salisbury on which Norman castle and town were built, now deserted; ~ *use*, form of liturgy used in the diocese of Salisbury from the 11th c. to the Reformation. [med. L., supposed to be due to a mis-reading of an abbreviated form of L *Sarisburia* Salisbury]

Sarum[2]. *abbrev.* (Bishop) of Salisbury (replacing surname in his signature).

săsh[1] *n.* Ornamental scarf worn over one shoulder or round waist by man, usu. as part of uniform or insignia (ill. CAVALRY), or by woman or child round waist. [Arab. *shāsh* muslin, band twisted round head as turban]

săsh[2] *n.* Frame, usu. of wood, fitted with pane(s) of glass forming (part of) window, esp. sliding frame or one of pair of frames made to slide up and down; glazed sliding light of glass-house or garden-frame; (now U.S.) casement; ~-*cord*, -*line*, strong cord used for attaching sash-weights to sash; ~ *cramp*: see CRAMP[2]; ~-*pocket*, space on each side of window-frame in which sash-weights run; ~-*pulley*, pulley over which sash-cord runs; ~-*weight*, weight attached to sash-cord at each side of sash to counterbalance it; ~ *window*, window with frames that slide up and down (ill. WINDOW). [corrupt. of CHASSIS]

Sask. *abbrev.* Saskatchewan.

Săskă'tchĕwan. 1. River of Canada, flowing from the Rocky Mountains to Lake Winnipeg. 2. Province of central Canada; capital, Regina.

săss *n.*, **să'ssў** *adj.* (dial., now chiefly U.S.) Varr. of SAUCE, SAUCY.

sassā'bў *n.* Large antelope (*Damaliscus lunatus*) of central and S. Africa, resembling hartebeest but with more regularly curved horns.

să'ssafrăs *n.* Tree of genus *S*~ of laurel family, esp. N. Amer. *S. albidum*, with green apetalous flowers and dimorphous leaves; dried bark of root of this used medicinally and for flavouring.

Sāssā'nian, Sā'ssanid *ns.* Member of the Sassanian dynasty. ~ *adjs.* Of the family of Sassan, rulers of the Persian Empire A.D. 211–651; of this period in Persia.

Sā'ssenach (-ahχ) *n.* (Sc. & Ir. for) Englishman. [Gael. & Ir. form of *Saxon*]

Sat. *abbrev.* Saturday.

Sā'tan. The Devil, Lucifer. **sată'nic** *adj.* (also *S~*) Of, like, or befitting Satan, diabolical; *S~ school*, Southey's designation for Byron, Shelley, and their imitators. **sată'nicăllў** *adv.* [Heb. *šāṭān* enemy]

Sā'tanĭsm *n.* Worship of the Devil with a travesty of Christian ceremonial and with celebration of the Black Mass; diabolical wickedness. **Sā'tanist** *n.*

Sătanŏ'logў *n.* (History or collection of) beliefs concerning the Devil.

satār'a *n.* Heavy ribbed and lustred woollen cloth. [f. *Satara* in India]

să'tchel *n.* Small bag, esp. for carrying school-books, freq. with straps to hang over shoulders.

sāte *v.t.* Gratify (desire, appetite, etc.) to the full; surfeit.

satee'n *n.* Cotton fabric, glossy on one side, woven like satin.

[781]

să'tellĭte *n.* 1. Follower, henchman, hanger-on; member of great man's retinue, underling. 2. Small or secondary planet revolving round larger one; (also) artificial body launched from the earth and encircling it or other celestial body. 3. (also ~ *state*) State nominally independent but dominated by powerful neighbour. 4. ~ *town*, small town built near larger one to house excess population.

sā'tiate (-shyat) *adj.* Sated, satiated. **sā'tiāte** *v.t.* Sate. **sātiā'tion** (sāsh-) *n.*

satī'ety *n.* State of being glutted or satiated; feeling of disgust or surfeit caused by excess.

să'tin *n.* Fabric of silk or similar yarn with glossy surface on one side produced by twill weave in which weft-threads are almost concealed by warp, or vice versa (ill. WEAVE); ~-*flower*, honesty; greater stitchwort; Australian umbelliferous plant (*Actinotus helianthi*); any of various other plants; ~ *gypsum*, fibrous kind of gypsum with pearly lustre; ~-*stitch*, in embroidery, long straight stitches laid close together, producing smooth surface (ill. STITCH); *sa'tinwood*, (hard light-coloured wood with satiny surface, of) Indian tree (*Chloroxylon swietenia*) and various W. Indian, Australian, etc., trees. **să'tĭn, să'tĭnў** *adjs.* Resembling satin; very smooth.

sătĭnĕ't, -ĕ'tte *n.* Satin-like fabric partly or wholly of cotton or synthetic fibre.

să'tīre *n.* Poem or prose composition ridiculing vice or folly; lampoon; branch of literature containing such compositions; use of ridicule, sarcasm, or irony to expose folly. **satī'ric, satī'rical** *adjs.* **satī'rically** *adv.* **să'tĭrist** *n.* Writer of satires; satirical person. **să'tĭrīze** *v.t.* Write satires on; describe satirically.

sătĭsfă'ction *n.* 1. Payment of debt, fulfilment of obligation, atonement *for*; thing accepted by way of satisfaction; (eccles.) performance of penance; (theol.) atonement made by Christ for sins of men. 2. Opportunity of satisfying one's honour by duel, acceptance of challenge to duel. 3. Satisfying, being satisfied, in regard to desire or want or doubt; thing that satisfies desire or gratifies feeling.

sătĭsfă'ctory *adj.* 1. (theol.) Serving as atonement for sin. 2. Sufficient, adequate, (of argument) convincing; such as one may be content or pleased with. **sătĭsfă'ctorĭlў** *adv.* **sătĭsfă'ctorĭness** *n.*

să'tĭsfў *v.* 1. Pay (debt), fulfil (obligation), (now rare except in *law*); pay (creditor); make atonement or reparation. 2. Meet expectations or desires of, come up to (notion etc.), be accepted by (person etc.) as adequate, content; give satisfaction, leave nothing to be desired; fully supply needs of, put an end to (appetite etc.) by fully supplying it; furnish with adequate proof, convince; adequately meet (objection, doubt, etc.); (math.) be a solution e.g. of an equation; (pass.) be content or pleased (*with*), demand no more than, consider it enough *to* do; ~ *examiners*, (at English universities) pass examination without attaining honours. **să'tĭsfўĭng** *adj.* **să'tĭsfўĭnglў** *adv.*

să'trăp *n.* 1. Holder of provincial governorship in ancient Persian Empire. 2. Subordinate ruler, colonial governor, etc. (freq. with implication of luxury or tyranny). **să'trapў** *n.* Office, province, of satrap. [Pers. *khsatrapava* province guardian]

Să'tsūma (*or* -ū'-) *n.* 1. (also ~ *ware*) Kind of Japanese glazed pottery with a yellow ground. 2. *s~*, kind of small orange. [Former province of Japan]

să'turāte (-cher-) *v.t.* 1. Soak thoroughly, imbue *with*. 2. (phys. etc.) Cause to absorb or hold the maximum quantity of moisture, electrical charge, etc., that can be held under given conditions of temperature etc.; (chem.) cause (a substance) to combine with or dissolve the maximum quantity possible of another substance. 3. Bomb (target) from the air so thoroughly that anti-aircraft defences are powerless. **să'turātĕd** *adj.* (esp., of a solution) Containing the maximum quantity possible of the dissolved substance at a given temperature (cf. *unsaturated*, able to dissolve more than it contains); (also, of chemical compounds, esp. hydrocarbons) containing no double bonds and hence unable to undergo addition reactions (*unsaturated*, containing one or more double bonds and capable of such reactions). **săturā'tion** *n.*

Să'turday (*or* -dĭ) *n.* 7th day of the week; *Holy ~*: see HOLY. [OE, f. L, *Saturni dies* day of Saturn]

Să'tŭrn. 1. (Rom. myth.) Ancient Italian god of agriculture, ruler of the world in a golden age of innocence and plenty, later identified with the Greek CRONUS. 2. (astron.) Major planet, next in size to Jupiter, distinguished by its 10 satellites or moons and its engirdling system of rings (ill. PLANET); (astrol.) leaden planet supposed to produce a cold sluggish gloomy temperament in those born under its influence. 3. (alchemy) The metal lead.

Sătŭrnā'lia *n.* (also as pl.). (Rom. antiq.) Yearly festival of Saturn, held in December, observed as a time of unrestrained merrymaking with temporary release of slaves, predecessor of the modern Christmastide; hence, *s~*, scene or time of wild revelry or tumult. **Sătŭrnā'lian** *adj.*

Satŭr'nian *adj.* Of the god or the planet Saturn; ~ *age*, the supposed golden age when Saturn reigned; ~ *metre*, *verse*, metre used in early Latin poetry before the introduction of Greek metres, generally taken to have consisted of a line of three iambic feet and an extra syllable followed by one of three trochees. ~ *n.* 1. Supposed inhabitant of Saturn. 2. *s~*, Saturnian metre; (pl.) Saturnian verse.

să'turnĭne *adj.* 1. Born under, influenced by, the planet Saturn (astrol.); sluggish, cold and gloomy in temperament, (of looks etc.) suggesting such temperament. 2. Of lead; of, affected by, lead-poisoning.

sătyagra'ha (-grah-). Passive resistance to government, non-violent disobedience, as policy of GANDHI and his followers in India, initiated *c* 1919. [Hind., = 'soul force']

să'tўr (*-er*) *n.* (Gk myth.) One of a class of woodland spirits, in pre-Roman period freq. confused with sileni but from 4th c. B.C. usu. represented as being young with ears, tail, and legs of goat, and budding horns; (fig.) type of lustfulness.

sătўrī'asis *n.* Excessive sexual excitement in males.

satў'ric *adj.* Of satyrs; ~ *drama*, form of ancient Greek drama burlesquing the legends of the gods and having a chorus dressed as satyrs.

sauce *n.* 1. Preparation, usu. liquid or soft, taken as relish with some article of food; (fig.) something that adds piquancy; (U.S.) vegetables or fruits as part of meal or as relish; (techn.) solution of salt and other ingredients used

SATYR

SAUCEPAN   SAWYER

in some manufacturing processes; *hard* ~, sauce which is not liquid; *tar'tare* ~, sharp-flavoured sauce consisting of mayonnaise with chopped gherkins, capers, herbs, etc., served with fish. 2. (colloq.) Impudence. 3. ~-*alone*, hedge-weed (*Alliaria petiolata*) formerly used to flavour salads and sauces; ~-*boat*, vessel in which sauce is served; ~-*box*, impudent person. ~ *v.t.* 1. Season with sauces or condiments (rare); (fig.) make piquant, add relish to. 2. (slang) Be impudent to, cheek.

sau'cepan (-sp-) *n.* Kitchen utensil of metal with a cover and long handle projecting from side, in which food is boiled.

sau'cer *n.* Shallow vessel for standing esp. tea- or coffee-cup on, to catch liquid that may be spilled from it; any small shallow vessel resembling this; round shallow depression in the ground; *flying* ~: see FLYING.

sau'cỹ *adj.* Impudent; (slang) smart-looking. **sau'cilỹ** *adv.* **sau'cinèss** *n.* [orig. = savoury, flavoured with sauce]

Sau'dī Arā'bia (sow-). Kingdom in Arabia formed in 1932 by the union of Nejd and the Hejaz; capital, Riyadh. **Sau'dī Arā'bian** *adj. & n.*

sauerkraut (sow'erkrowt) *n.* German dish of cabbage cut fine and pickled in brine. [Ger.]

Saul. 1. First king of Israel (11th c. B.C.) 2. (also ~ *of Tarsus*) Original name of St. PAUL[1].

sau'na (*or* sow-) *n.* Steam bath or bath-house, of Finnish origin.

sau'nter *v.i.* Walk in leisurely way, stroll. ~ *n.* Leisurely ramble or gait. **sau'nteringlỹ** *adv.*

saur'ian *adj. & n.* (Of or like) a lizard.

sau'sage (sŏs-) *n.* Meat minced, seasoned, and stuffed into long cylindrical case made from intestine, bladder, or other animal tissue, or synthetic material; short length of this made by twisting or tying the containing case; (colloq.) sausage-shaped object, esp. observation balloon, wind-sleeve; ~-*meat*, meat minced and seasoned to be used in sausages or as stuffing etc.; ~ *roll*, sausage or sausage-meat enclosed in roll of pastry and baked.

sauté (sō'tā) *adj. & n.* (cookery) (Dish of meat, vegetables, etc.) quickly and lightly fried by being tossed in fat over heat. ~ *v.t.* Fry lightly.

Sauterne (sōtār'n) *n.* Light sweet white wine from the Bordeaux region. [*Sauternes*, name of a district of Gironde, France]

să'vage *adj.* 1. Uncultivated, wild (archaic); uncivilized, in primitive state; fierce, cruel, furious; (colloq.) angry, out of temper. 2. (her., of human figure) Naked. **să'vagelỹ** *adv.* **să'vage-nèss, să'vagerỹ** *ns.* **să'vage** *n.* Member of savage tribe, esp. one living by hunting or fishing; brutally cruel or barbarous person. ~ *v.t.* (of animal, esp. horse) Attack and bite (person etc.).

savă'nnah (-*a*) *n.* Wide tree-less plain, great tract of meadow-like land, esp. in tropical America.

să'vant (-ahṅ) *n.* Man of learning, scholar.

sava'te (-aht) *n.* Kind of French boxing in which blows are given with feet as well as hands. [Fr.]

săve[1] *v.* 1. Rescue, preserve, deliver from danger, misfortune, harm, or discredit; bring about spiritual salvation of, preserve from damnation; prevent loss of (game etc.), (footb. etc.) prevent opponent from scoring; ~ *the situation*, find or provide way out of difficulty. 2. Keep for future use, husband, reserve, put by; lay by money; live economically; ~-*as-you-earn*, (abbrev. S.A.Y.E.) method of collecting savings by current deduction from earnings; ~ *up*, try to accumulate money by economy. 3. Relieve from need of expending (money, trouble, etc.) or from exposure to (annoyance etc.). ~ *n.* Act of preventing other side from scoring in football etc.; (bridge) action taken to avoid heavy loss.

săve[2] *prep.* Except, but. ~ *conj.* (archaic) Unless, but.

să'velọy *n.* Highly seasoned dried sausage. [corrupt. of Fr. *cervela* (It. (*cervello* brain), named as orig. made f. pig's brain)]

să'vin, -ine *n.* European and W. Asiatic small bushy evergreen shrub (*Juniperus sabina*) with dark-green leaves and small bluish-purple berries; dried tops of this, used as drug; any of various similar shrubs, esp. (U.S.) red cedar (*J. virginiana* and *J. horizontalis*). [L (*herba*) *Sabina* Sabine herb]

să'ving *n.* (esp., usu. pl.) Sum of money saved and put by; ~*s bank*, bank receiving small deposits at interest and devoting profits to the benefit of depositors. ~ *adj.* (esp.) Making a reservation, furnishing a proviso. ~ *prep. & conj.* = SAVE[2] *prep. & conj.*

să'viour (-vyer) *n.* Deliverer, redeemer; *the, our, S*~, Christ.

săvoir faire (-vwār). Quickness to see and do the right thing, tact, address. [Fr.]

Săvonarō'la, Girolamo (1452–98). Dominican monk, whose sermons at Florence gave expression to the religious reaction against the artistic licence and social corruption of the Renaissance; he became the leader of the democratic party in Florence after the expulsion of the Medici, but aroused the hostility of Pope Alexander VI and was burnt at the stake as a heretic.

să'vorỹ *n.* Herb of genus *Satureia* of mint family, used in cooking; esp. *S. hortensis* (summer ~), and *S. montana* (winter ~).

să'vour (-ver) *n.* Characteristic taste, flavour; power of affecting sense of taste; essential virtue or property; tinge, hint, smack, *of*. **să'vourlèss** *adj.* **să'vour** *v.* Appreciate flavour of, enjoy; smack or suggest presence *of*.

să'vourỹ (-eri) *adj.* With appetizing taste or smell; free from bad smells, fragrant (now only with negative); (of dishes etc.) of stimulating or piquant flavour and not sweet. ~ *n.* Savoury dish, esp. one served at end of dinner.

Savoy'[1]. Former duchy in NW. Italy forming part of the kingdom of Sardinia; ceded to France in 1860.

Savoy'[2], The. Precinct between the Strand, London, and the Thames, so called from having been given by Henry III in 1246 to Peter of Savoy, who built a palace here.

savoy'[3] *n.* Rough-leaved hardy cabbage grown for winter use. [f. SAVOY[1]]

Savoy'ard (-oi-) *n.* 1. Native of SAVOY[1]. 2. Member of the D'Oyly Carte Company which originally performed the Savoy Operas.

Savoy' O'peras (ŏperaz): see GILBERT[3].

să'vvỹ *v.* (slang) Know. ~ *n.* (slang) Knowingness, wits. [orig. Negro- and pidgin English, after Span. *sabe usted* you know]

saw[1] *n.* Tool, worked by hand or mechanically, for cutting wood, metal, stone, bone, etc., consisting essentially of plate, band, or tube of steel, one edge of which (except in some stone-cutting saws) is formed into continuous series of teeth (*illustration, p.* 785); (zool.) part or organ with saw-like teeth; *hand-*~, saw managed by one hand; ~-*buck*, saw-horse; *saw'dust*, tiny fragments of wood produced in sawing, used for stuffing, packing, etc.; ~-*edged*, with serrated edge; *saw'fish*, sea-fish (*Pristis*) with snout ending in long flat projection with teeth on each edge; *saw'fly*, insect of family Tenthredinidae, usu. very destructive to vegetation, with saw-like ovipositor; ~-*horse*, frame or trestle for supporting wood being sawn; *saw'mill*, mill in which wood is sawn into planks or logs by machinery; ~-*pit*, excavation with framework over mouth holding timber to be sawn with long two-handled saw by two men, one in pit and other on raised platform. ~ *v.* Cut (wood etc.) with, make (boards etc.) with, use, saw; move backward and forward, divide (the air etc.) with motion as of saw or person sawing; admit of being sawn *easily*, *badly*, etc.; (bookbinding) make incisions to receive binding-bands in (gathered sheets); *saw'bones*, (slang) surgeon.

saw[2] *n.* Proverbial saying, old maxim.

saw'der *n. soft* ~, flattery, cajoling talk. [app. = SOLDER]

saw'yer *n.* 1. Man employed in sawing timber. 2. (U.S.)

[783]

Uprooted tree held fast by one end in stream etc. with free end bobbing up and down with current.

săx[1] *n.* Chopping-tool for trimming slates.

săx[2] *n.* (colloq.) Saxophone.

sā′xatile *adj.* Living or growing among rocks.

săxe *n.* (also ~ *blue*) Shade of bright slightly greenish blue. [Fr. *Saxe* Saxony]

Săxe-Cō′burg-Gō′tha (-ta). Name of the English royal house from the accession of Edward VII in 1901 (changed to *Windsor* in 1917).

să′xhŏrn *n.* Brass instrument of trumpet kind made in seven sizes, of which the three with lowest range are called tubas (ill. BRASS). [invented 1845 by Adolphe *Sax*, Belgian instrument-maker]

să′xifrage *n.* Alpine or rockplant of genus *Saxifraga*, with tufted foliage and panicles of white, yellow, or red flowers. [L *saxifraga* spleenwort, f. *saxum* rock, *frangere* break (prob. because growing in rock-clefts)]

Să′xō Grammă′ticus (d. *c* 1210). Danish chronicler.

Să′xon *n.* Member, language, of a Germanic people which in the early centuries of the Christian era dwelt in a region near the mouth of the Elbe, and of which one portion, distinguished as the Anglo-Saxons, conquered and occupied part of Britain in the 5th and 6th centuries, while the other, the Old Saxons, remained in Germany; native of modern Saxony; Englishman as opp. to Irish and Welsh, Scottish Lowlander as opp. to Highlander; Germanic elements in the English language; *plain* ~, homely direct speech. ~ *adj.* Connected with, pertaining to, the Saxons, their language or country; (of English words) of Germanic origin.

Săxō′nian *adj.* & *n.* (geol.) (Of) a division of the European Permian.

Să′xonism *n.* Word, idiom, surviving in English, derived from Anglo-Saxon (opp. LATINISM).

Să′xonỹ[1]. Former province of E. central Germany on the upper reaches of the Elbe, earlier part of the larger kingdom of Saxony; *Lower* ~, province of Germany; capital Hanover.

să′xonỹ[2] *n.* Fine kind of wool; any of various kinds of cloth (~ *coating*, ~ *flannel*, ~ *cord*) made from it. [f. SAXONY[1]]

să′xophōne *n.* Keyed wind instrument with conical tube, made of brass but regarded as belonging to wood wind group (ill. WOOD[1]), its mouthpiece being equipped with a reed like a clarinet's. [invented *c* 1840 by Adolphe *Sax*, Belgian instrument-maker; cf. SAXHORN]

say (past t. & past part. **said**, pr. sĕd) *v.* Utter, recite, rehearse, in ordinary speaking voice; put into words, express; adduce or allege in argument or excuse; form and give opinion or decision; select as example, assume, take as near enough. **say′ing** *n.* (esp.) Sententious remark, maxim. **say** *n.* (Opportunity of saying) what one has to say; share in decision; ~*-so*, (U.S. colloq.) assertion; authority.

S.A.Y.E. *abbrev.* SAVE[1]-as-you-earn.

sc. *abbrev. Scilicet; sculpsit.*

S.C. *abbrev.* South Carolina; Special Constable.

scăb *n.* 1. Dry rough inscrustation formed over sore in healing, cicatrice. 2. Cutaneous disease in animals, resembling scabies. 3. Parasitic disease of plants causing scab-like roughness. 4. (slang) Mean low fellow; (orig. U.S.) blackleg. **scă′bbỹ** *adj.* **scăb** *v.* Form scab, heal over.

scă′bbard *n.* Sheath of sword, bayonet, etc. (ill. SWORD); ~ *fish*, long, silver-coloured, eel-like sea fish (*Lepidopus caudatus*).

scā′bies (-z) *n.* Contagious skin-disease due to a parasite, the mite *Sarcoptes scabiei.*

scā′bious *n.* Herbaceous plant of genus *Scabiosa*, with blue, pink, or white pincushion-shaped aggregate flowers. [med. L. *scabiosa* (*herba*), named as specific against itch, f. SCABIES]

scā′brous *adj.* 1. (zool., bot.) (etc.) With rough surface, scurfy. 2. Salacious; indecent.

scăd *n.* Fish of family Carangidae including the horse mackerel, with enlarged plates on side of body.

scă′ffold *n.* 1. Temporary raised platform for execution of criminals; *the* ~, death at executioner's hands. 2. SCAFFOLDING, 1. ~ *v.t.* Attach scaffolding to.

scă′ffolding *n.* 1. Temporary structure of wooden poles (or metal tubes) and planks providing platform(s) for workmen to stand on while erecting or repairing building (*illustration, p.785*). 2. Materials for making such structure. 3. Temporary framework for other purposes (also fig.).

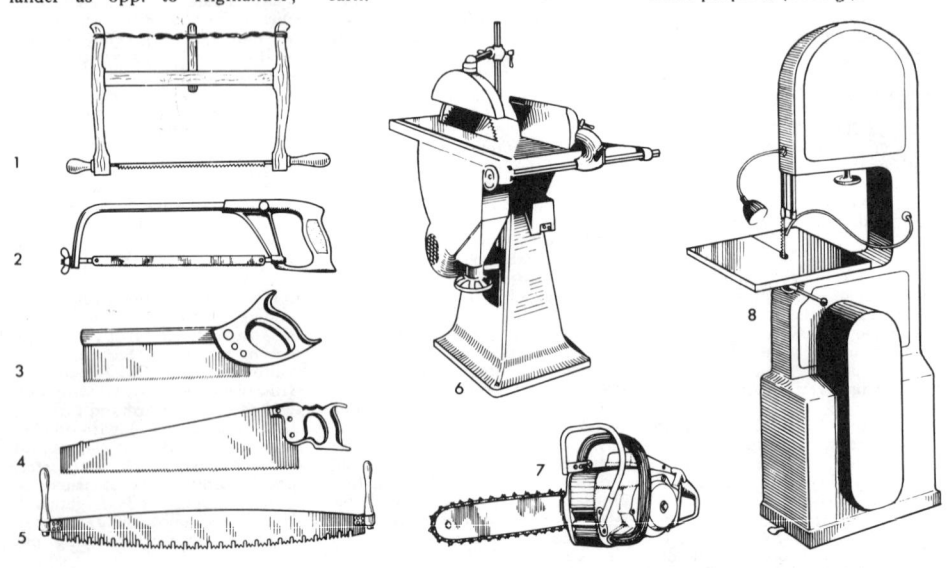

SAWS

1. Bow-saw. 2. Hack-saw. 3. Tenon saw. 4. Hand-saw. 5. Cross-cut saw. 6. Circular saw in machine. 7. Chain saw. 8. Band-saw in machine

SCAGLIOLA

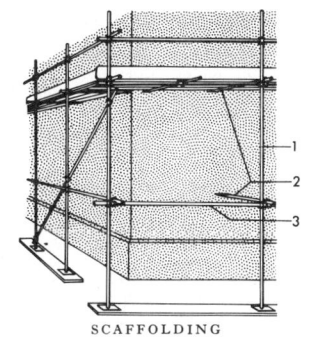

SCAFFOLDING
1. Standard. 2. Putlog fixed in wall. 3. Ledger

scăgliō'la (-ălyō-) *n.* Kind of plaster-work (of gypsum and glue with surface of marble dust etc.) imitating stone. [It. *scagliuola*, dim. of *scaglia* chip of marble]

scā'lar *adj. & n.* (math.) (Of) a quantity that has only magnitude.

scă'lawăg, -ll- *n.* Varr. of SCALLYWAG.

scald[1] (-aw-) *v.t.* Injure or pain with hot liquid or vapour; affect like boiling water; cleanse with boiling water; pour hot liquid over; heat (liquid, esp. milk) nearly to boiling-point. ~ *n.* Injury to skin by scalding.

scald[2], **skald** (-aw-) *n.* Ancient Scandinavian composer and reciter of poems in honour of heroes and their deeds.

scāle[1] *n.* 1. One of the small thin membranous horny or bony outgrowths or modifications of skin in many fishes, reptiles, etc., freq. overlapping, and forming covering for (part of) the body (ill. FISH). 2. Flattened membranous plate of cellular tissue (usu. rudimentary or degenerate leaf) as covering of leaf-buds of deciduous trees etc. (ill. BULB). 3. Protective covering of many female insects (~-*bug*, -*insect*) of family Coccidae infesting and injuring various plants (ill. BUG). 4. Thin plate, lamina, or film of any kind; (fig., after Acts 9: 18) what causes physical or moral blindness; (usu. collect.) film of oxide forming on iron or other metal when heated and hammered or rolled; hard deposit of 'fur' in boilers etc.; incrustation of lime or dirt on bottom of salt-pan; tartar on teeth. 5. ~-*armour*, armour of small overlapping plates of metal, horn, etc.; ~-*board*, very thin board for hat-boxes, veneer, etc.; ~-*insect*: see sense 3; ~ *leaf*, modified leaf resembling scale (ill. RHIZOME). **scā'lў** *adj.* Covered with, having, scales. **scāle** *v.* Take away scale(s) from; form, come off in, drop, scales; (of scales) come *off*.

scāle[2] *n.* 1. Pan of balance; weighing instrument, esp. (also *pair of* ~s) one consisting of beam pivoted at middle and with dish, pan, board, etc., suspended at either end (ill. BALANCE); *hold the* ~s *even*, judge impartially; *turn the* ~, exceed weight in other pan etc. of balance, outweigh other considerations, motives, etc. 2. *the Scales*: see LIBRA. ~ *v.t.* Weigh (specified amount).

scāle[3] *n.* 1. (mus.) Definite series of sounds ascending or descending by fixed intervals; any

DIATONIC

1 2 3 4 5 6 7 8
Major

Harmonic

Melodic   Minor

CHROMATIC

WHOLE TONE

PENTATONIC

SCALES
1. Tonic. 2. Supertonic. 3. Mediant. 4. Subdominant. 5. Dominant. 6. Submediant. 7. Leading note. 8. Tonic (octave above 1). 1–2, 2–3, 4–5, 5–6, 6–7 are tones; 3–4, 7–8 are semitones

of graduated series of sounds into which octave may be divided; any of these series as subject of instruction or practice. 2. Series of degrees, graduated arrangement, system, or classification; standard of measurement, calculation, etc.; (arith.) system of numeration or numerical notation, in which the value of a figure depends on its place in the order (the usual or *denary* ~ is that in which successive places from right to left represent units, tens, hundreds, etc.); relative dimensions, proportion which representation of an object bears to the object itself. 3. Set of marks at measured distances on line for use in measuring or making proportional reductions or enlargements; rule determining intervals between these; piece of metal, wood, etc., apparatus, on which they are marked. ~ *v.* 1. Climb with ladder or by clambering; *scaling-ladder*, one used in escalades. 2. Represent in dimensions proportional to actual ones; reduce to common scale; ~ *up*, *down*, make larger, smaller, in due proportion. 3. (of quantities etc.) Have common scale, be commensurable.

SCAMPI

scā'lēne (*or* -ē'n) *adj.* ~ *cone*, *cylinder*, one of which axis is not perpendicular to base; ~ *muscle*, scalenus; ~ *triangle*, triangle with no two sides equal (ill. TRIANGLE).

scālē'nus *n.* (pl. -*nī*). (anat.) One of set of triangular muscles (three on each side of neck) extending from cervical vertebrae to first or second rib (ill. HEAD).

Scăl'iger, Joseph Justus (1540–1609). Renaissance scholar of Italian origin, known as 'the founder of historical criticism'; revolutionized the study of ancient chronology; his father, *Julius Caesar* ~ (1484–1558), Italian physician, scholar, and philologist.

scallawag: see SCALAWAG.

scā'llion (-yon) *n.* Shallot; Welsh onion (kind of *Allium* intermediate in appearance between onion and leek); onion which fails to bulb but forms long neck and strong blade. [OF *eschaloigne*, see SHALLOT]

sca'llop (-ŏl-) *n.* 1. Bivalve mollusc of genus *Pecten*, with shell having ridges radiating from middle of hinge and edged with small rounded lobes; one valve of this as utensil in which various dishes (of fish, minced meat, etc., with bread-crumbs or sauce) are cooked and served; (hist.) pilgrim's cockle-shell worn as sign that he had visited shrine of St. James at Compostella. 2. One of series of rounded projections at edge of garment etc. 3. = ESCALLOP, 3. ~ *v.t.* 1. Bake in scallop-shell or similar shallow pan or dish. 2. Ornament (edge, material) with scallops. **sca'lloping** *n.* (esp.) Edging ornamented with scallops.

scā'llywăg *n.* (colloq., orig. U.S.) Rogue, rascal, disreputable person; (U.S. hist.) native white of southern State accepting Republican principles after Civil War.

scălp *n.* Top of head (now dial.); skin of upper part of head, with hair covering it, this cut or torn from man's head as battle trophy by Amer. Indians (freq. fig.). ~ *v.t.* Take scalp of (freq. fig.).

scā'lpel *n.* Small straight knife used in surgery and dissection.

scă'lper, scau'per, scōr'per *ns.* Engraver's tool for hollowing out bottom of sunken designs (ill. ENGRAVING).

scă'mmonў *n.* Kind of convolvulus (*Convolvulus scammonia*) of Syria and Asia Minor, with fleshy root; gum-resin obtained from this, used as a purgative.

scămp[1] *n.* Rascal, knave (freq. joc.).

scămp[2] *v.t.* Do (work etc.) in perfunctory or inadequate way.

scă'mper *v.i.* Run or caper about nimbly, rush hastily. ~ *n.* Scampering run.

scă'mpi *n.pl.* Large prawns; dish of these. [It.]

[785]

scăn *v.* 1. Analyse, test metre of (verse) by examining number and quantity of feet and syllables; (of verse) be metrically correct. 2. Look intently at all parts successively of. 3. Resolve (a picture) into elements of light and shade in a pre-arranged number and pattern of lines as a stage in televising. 4. (radar) Traverse (region) with controlled beam.

scă'ndal *n.* (Thing that occasions) general feeling of outrage or indignation, esp. as expressed in common talk; malicious gossip; (law) public affront, irrelevant abusive statement in court. **scă'ndalous** *adj.* **scă'ndalously** *adv.* **scă'ndalmonger** (-ŭngg-) *n.* One who invents or spreads scandals.

scă'ndalīze[1] *v.t.* Offend moral feelings, sense of propriety, etc.; shock.

scă'ndalīze[2] *v.t.* (naut.) Reduce area of (sail) by lowering peak and tricing up tack. [alteration of obs. *scantelize*, f. SCANTLE]

Scăndinā'via. Geographical term for Sweden, Norway, and Denmark, together with the adjacent islands and Iceland. **Scăndinā'vian** *adj. & n.* (Native, inhabitant, family of languages) of Scandinavia.

scă'ndĭum *n.* (chem.) Rare metallic element (discovered 1879 in Scandinavian mineral euxenite) usu. included in rare-earth group; symbol Sc, at. no. 21, at. wt 44·9559. [L *Scandia* Scandinavia]

scă'nner *n.* (esp.) 1. Instrument which scans television pictures. 2. (radar) Apparatus that directs beam in scanning (SCAN, 4).

scă'nsion (-shon) *n.* Metrical scanning; way verse scans.

scănsōr'ial *adj.* (of feet of birds and animals) Adapted for climbing; that is given to climbing.

scănt *adj.* Barely sufficient, deficient, with scanty supply *of*.

scă'ntling *n.* 1. Small beam or piece of wood; block or slice of stone of fixed size. 2. Size to which stone or timber is to be cut; set of standard dimensions for parts of structure, esp. in ship-building. 3. Trestle for cask.

scă'ntў *adj.* Of small extent or amount; barely sufficient. **scă'ntilў** *adv.* **scă'ntiness** *n.*

Sca'pa Flow (-ah-, flō). British naval base in the Orkney Islands.

scāpe[1] *v.t.* (archaic) Escape.

scāpe[2] *n.* 1. (archit.) Shaft of column. 2. (bot.) Long flower-stalk rising directly from root or rhizome of plant having only radical leaves. 3. (entom.) First segment of antenna (ill. INSECT). 4. (ornith.) Shaft of feather.

scā'pegoat (-pg-) *n.* (in Mosaic ritual of Day of Atonement) Goat allowed to escape into wilderness, the sins of the people having been symbolically laid upon it (see Lev. 16); hence, person blamed or punished for sins of others.

scā'pegrăce (-pg-) *n.* Reckless or careless person, esp. young man or boy constantly in scrapes. [= 'one who escapes the grace of God']

scā'phoid *adj.* (anat.) Shaped like a boat; ~ *bone*, first proximal carpal bone in mammals (ill. HAND). ~ *n.* Scaphoid bone.

s. caps *abbrev.* Small capital letters.

scă'pŭla *n.* (pl. *-lae*). Shoulderblade (ill. SKELETON).

scă'pŭlar *adj.* Of the scapula; ~ *arch*, shoulder girdle; ~ *feather*, feather growing from scapular region (ill. BIRD). ~ *n.* 1. (eccles.) Monk's short cloak covering shoulders; badge of affiliation to religious order consisting of two strips of cloth hanging down breast and back and joined across shoulders, worn under clothing. 2. Bandage for shoulder-blade. 3. Scapular feather. **scă'pularў** *n.* = SCAPULAR *n.* 1, 3.

scār[1] *n.* Trace of healed wound, sore, or burn, cicatrice (freq. fig.); mark on plant left by fall of leaf etc., hilum (*leaf-*~, ill. STEM[1]). ~ *v.* Mark with scar or scars; heal over, form scar.

scār[2] *n.* Precipitous craggy part of mountain-side.

scā'rab *n.* Dung-beetle (*Scarabaeus sacer*) revered by ancient Egyptians as symbol of resurrection and immortality; gem or stone in form of beetle, with intaglio design on flat under-side, worn in ring or as pendant round neck, esp. by ancient Egyptians, Etruscans, etc.

scărabae'id *adj. & n.* (Beetle) of lamellicorn family Scarabaeidae, including cockchafers, dung-beetles, etc.

scărabae'us *n.* (pl. *-ae'ī*). Scarab.

scă'ramouch *n.* (archaic) Boastful poltroon, braggart. [Fr., f. It. *Scaramuccia*, stock character in Italian farce]

scārce *adj.* Insufficient, not plentiful, scanty; seldom met with, rare; *make oneself* ~, go away, keep away. ~ *adv.* (archaic, poet., rhet.) Scarcely. **scār'celў** *adv.* Hardly, barely, only just. **scār'ceness** *n.* **scār'citў** *n.* (esp.) Dearth of food.

scār'cement (-sm-) *n.* Setback in wall etc.; ledge resulting from this.

scāre *v.t.* Strike with sudden terror, frighten; frighten away, drive off; *scar'ecrow*, device for frightening birds away from crops, usu. figure of man in ragged clothes; bogy; badly dressed or grotesque person. ~ *n.* Sudden fright or alarm; esp. general public alarm caused by baseless or exaggerated rumours. **scār'emonger** (-mŭngg-) *n.* Alarmist.

scārf[1] *n.* Long narrow strip of material worn for ornament or warmth round neck, over shoulders, from one shoulder to opposite hip, or round waist, with ends hanging; square of material worn at neck; ~*-pin*, usu. ornamental pin for fastening scarf; ~*-ring*, ring through which ends of neck-tie are thrust; ~*-skin*, outer layer of skin, epidermis.

scārf[2] *v.t.* Join ends of (pieces of timber, metal, or leather) by bevelling or notching so that they overlap without increase of thickness and then bolting, brazing or sewing them together. ~ *n.* Joint made by scarfing (ill. JOINT[1]); notch, groove.

scār'ĭfier (*or* skă-) *n.* Agricultural machine with prongs for loosening soil.

scār'ĭfў (*or* skă-) *v.t.* Make superficial incisions in (surg.); make sore, wound (now fig.); break up ground with scarifier. **scărĭfĭcā'tion** *n.*

scār'ious *adj.* (bot.) Thin, dry, and membranous (of bracts etc.).

scārlati'na (-tē-) *n.* Scarlet fever (pop. applied to what is supposed to be a milder form of the disease).

Scārlă'tti. Name of two Italian composers: *Alessandro* ~ (1658-1725), founder of the Neapolitan school of opera; *Domenico* ~ (1685-1757), his son; composer of many sonatas.

scār'lĕt *adj.* Of brilliant red colour inclining to orange; ~ *fever*, contagious fever, due to streptococcal infection, with scarlet eruptions of skin and mucous membrane of mouth and pharynx; ~ *hat*, cardinal's hat, esp. as symbol of the rank of cardinal; ~ *pimpernel*, red-flowered common pimpernel (*Anagallis arvensis*); ~ *runner*, red-flowered climbing bean (*Phaseolus multiflorus*); ~ *woman*, prostitute; (also) abusive epithet applied to the Church of Rome (in allusion to Rev. 17: 1-5). ~ *n.* Scarlet colour; scarlet cloth or clothes. [perh. f. Pers. *sagalat* scarlet cloth]

scā'roid *adj. & n.* (Fish) of family Scaridae of fishes inhabiting warm seas and including scarus etc.

scārp *n.* Inner wall or slope of ditch in fortification (ill. CASTLE); any steep slope. ~ *v.t.* Give steep face to, slope steeply.

scār'per *v.i.* (slang) Go, make off.

scār'us *n.* Mediterranean parrot-fish esteemed by Romans as food; bright-coloured fish of genus *S*~ allied to wrasse family, with coalescent teeth giving beak-like appearance to jaws.

scāthe (-dh) *v.t.* Injure, esp. by fire, lightning, etc. (poet.); wither with fierce invective or satire. **scā'thing** *adj.*

scătŏ'logў *n.* 1. Study of coprolites. 2. Preoccupation with excrement. 3. Preoccupation with obscenity in literature. **scătolŏ'gical** *adj.*

scătŏ'phagous *adj.* Feeding on, eating, dung.

[786]

scă′tter v. 1. Throw here and there, strew, sprinkle; (of gun, cartridge) distribute (shot); (phys.) diffuse by reflection from particles. 2. Separate and disperse in flight etc. 3. ~-*brain*, heedless person; ~-*brained*, heedless, desultory. **scă′ttered** (-erd) adj. (esp.) Not situated together, wide apart; sporadic. **scă′tter** n. Act of scattering; extent of distribution, esp. of shot. **scă′tty** adj. (slang) Scatter-brained, crazy.

scaup n. (also ~ *duck*) Diving duck of genus *Aythya*, esp. *A. marila*, of N. European, Asiatic, and American coasts, the head of the male being black glossed with green.

scauper: see SCALPER.

scă′vénger (-j-) n. Person employed to keep streets etc. clean by carrying away refuse; animal feeding on carrion, garbage, or any decaying organic matter. **scă′vėnge** v. Be, act as, scavenger.

scă′zon n. (Gk & L. pros.) Iambic trimeter ending with spondee or trochee instead of iambus, ◡–|◡–|◡–|◡–|◡–|–◡|; choliamb. [Gk *skazōn* f. *skazō* limp]

S.C.C. abbrev. Sea Cadet Corps.

scena (shā′nah) n. (Words and music of) scene in Italian opera; long vocal solo with recitatives and arias, and with orchestral accompaniment. [It.]

scenario n. (pl. -s). 1. (shānär′iō) Skeleton libretto of play or opera. 2. (sinär′iō) Complete plot of film play, with all necessary directions for actors, details of scenes, etc. **scė′narist** n. Composer of scenario, sense 2. [It., f. *scena* scene]

scėne n. 1. (hist.) Stage, esp. of Greek or Roman theatre. 2. Place where action of (part of) play, novel, etc., is supposed to take place; locality of event. 3. Portion of a play during which action is continuous, or (esp. of French plays) in which no intermediate entries or exits occur; subdivision (rarely, the whole) of an act; episode, situation, as subject of narrative or description; action, episode, situation, in real life. 4. Stormy encounter or interview; agitated colloquy, esp. with display of temper. 5. Any of the pieces of painted canvas, woodwork, etc., used to represent scene of action on stage; picture presented by these to audience; (transf.) landscape or view spread before spectator like scene in theatre; *behind the* ~s, amidst actors and stage-machinery; (fig.) acting upon information not accessible to the public. 6. *change of* ~, variety of surroundings esp. secured by travel; ~-*dock*, space near stage where scenes are stored (ill. THEATRE); ~-*painter*, painter of theatrical scenery; ~-*shifter*, person helping to change scenes in theatre.

scė′nery n. 1. Accessories used in theatre to make stage resemble supposed scene of action. 2. General appearance of natural features etc. of place or district; picturesque features of landscape. **scė′nic** adj. Of, on, on the stage; of the nature of a show, picturesque in grouping; having fine natural scenery, giving landscape views; ~ *railway*, miniature railway running through artificial scenery. **scė′nically** adv.

scėnt v. 1. Discern by smell; perceive as if by smell, detect. 2. Impregnate with odour, perfume. ~ n. 1. Distinctive odour, esp. of agreeable kind; odour of man or animal as means of pursuit by hound, trail; (in paper-chase) paper strewn by 'hares' as trail for 'hounds'. 2. (of animals, esp. dogs) Power of detecting or distinguishing smells; (fig.) flair. 3. Liquid perfume made by distillation from flowers etc.

scė′psis (sk-) n. Philosophic doubt, sceptical philosophy.

scė′ptic (sk-) n. One who doubts the possibility of real knowledge of any kind; one who doubts the truth of the Christian or of all religious doctrines; person of sceptical temper, or unconvinced of the truth of a particular fact or theory. **scė′ptical** adj. Inclined to suspense of judgement, given to questioning truth of facts and soundness of inferences; incredulous, hard to convince. **scė′ptically** adv. **scė′pticism** n.

scė′ptre (-ter) n. Staff borne in hand as symbol of regal or imperial authority (ill. REGALIA); (fig.) royal or imperial dignity, sovereignty. **scė′ptred** (-terd) adj.

Sch. abbrev. Scholar; school.

schadenfreude (shah′denfroide) n. Malicious enjoyment of others' misfortunes. [Ger., f. *schaden* damage, *Freude* joy]

schäppe (sh-), **shăp** n. Fabric or yarn made from waste silk.

schė′dūle (sh-; U.S. sk-) n. Tabulated statement of details, inventory, list, etc., esp. as appendix or annexe to principal document; (chiefly U.S.) timetable; *on* ~, at time provided for in timetable. ~ v.t. Make schedule of; enter in schedule; *scheduled territories*, until 1972, group of countries, mostly in the Commonwealth, with currencies linked to sterling and between which payments were freely made in sterling (*sterling area*); since 23 June 1972 (when the pound was floated) consisting only of the United Kingdom and the Republic of Ireland.

Scheldt (skĕlt). River flowing from the Aisne department, France, through Belgium and Holland to the North Sea.

Schė′lling (sh-), Friedrich Wilhelm Joseph von (1775–1854). German philosopher; regarded nature as a single living organism working towards self-consciousness, a faculty dormant in inanimate objects and fully awake only in man, whose being consists in 'intellectual intuition' of the world he creates.

schė′ma (sk-) n. Diagram, outline; (Kantian philos.) form (a product of the imagination) through which what is perceived is subsumed under a 'category'. **schėmă′tic** adj. **schėmă′tically** adv.

schėme (sk-) n. 1. Systematic arrangement; table of classification or of appointed times; plan for doing something. 2. Artful or underhand design. ~ v.i. Make plans, plan esp. in secret or underhand way. **schė′mer** n. **schė′ming** adj.

scherză′ndō (skärts-) adv., n. (pl. -os), & adj. (mus.) (Passage performed) playful(ly) or sportive(ly). [It.]

schėrzo (skār′tsō) n. (mus.) Vigorous (properly light and playful) composition, independent or as movement in work of sonata type. [It., f. Teut. (Ger. *Scherz* merriment, prank, jest)]

Schiedă′m (sk-) n. Kind of gin made at Schiedam, a town in NW. Netherlands.

Schi′ller (sh-), Johann Christoph Friedrich von (1759–1805). German dramatist, lyric poet, and historian; author of the dramas 'Die Räuber', 'Don Carlos', 'Wallenstein', 'Maria Stuart', 'Die Jungfrau von Orleans', 'Die Braut von Messina', 'Wilhelm Tell', etc.

schi′lling (sh-), n. Principal monetary unit of Austria, = 100 groschen.

schi′pperkė (sk- *or* sh-) n. Kind of small black dog, tailless, smooth-haired and with prick ears, orig. bred in the Netherlands and Belgium and used as a watch-dog on barges. [Du. dim. of *schipper* boatman]

schism (sĭ-) n. Breach of unity of a Church, separation into two Churches or secession of part of Church owing to difference of opinion on doctrine or discipline; offence of promoting schism. **schismă′tic** (sĭz-) adj. & n. (Person) tending to, guilty of, schism; (member) of seceded branch of a Church.

schist (sh-) n. Fine-grained metamorphic rock with component minerals arranged in more or less parallel layers, splitting in thin irregular plates. **schi′stōse, schi′stous** adjs.

schiză′nthus (sk-) n. Flowering annual of genus S~, native of Chile, with finely divided leaves and showy variegated flowers, usu. white, violet, or crimson.

schi′zoid (skĭtz-; *or* -dz-) adj. Of, resembling, afflicted with, schizophrenia. ~ n. Schizophrenic person.

schizomy′cete (sk-) *n.* Member of class Schizomycetae of minute, freq. single-celled, lowly organisms between algae and fungi, including bacilli, bacteria, etc. **schizomyce′tous** *adj.*

schizophre′nia (skĭts-; *or* -dz-) *n.* Mental disease characterized by dissociation, delusions, and inability to distinguish reality from imagination. **schizophre′nic** *adj.* & *n.*

Schle′gel (schlägl). Name of two German Romantic critics: *August Wilhelm von* ~ (1767-1845), chiefly known in England for his translation into German, with the collaboration of others, of the plays of Shakespeare; *Friedrich von* ~ (1772-1829), his younger brother, Romantic critic and novelist.

Schleswig (shlĕ′svĭk). Former duchy of the Danish Crown, acquired by conquest by Prussia in 1864 and incorporated into the province of Schleswig-Holstein; the N. part of this territory was returned to Denmark in 1920 after a plebiscite held in accordance with the Treaty of Versailles; ~-*Holstein*, province of the Federal Republic of Germany; capital, Kiel.

Schlie′mann (shl-), Heinrich (1822-90). German archaeologist, who excavated Troy, Tiryns, and Mycenae.

schmaltz (shmawlts; *or* -ă-) *n.* Sickly sentimentality. [Ger.]

schmelz (shmĕlts) *n.* Kinds of coloured glass, esp. red kind used to flash white glass.

schnäpps (shn-) *n.* Strong hollands gin. [Ger. *Schnaps* mouthful, dram of liquor]

schnauzer (shnow′tser) *n.* Wire-coated black, black-and-brown, or pepper-and-salt terrier of German breed.

schni′tzel (shn-) *n.* Veal cutlet, esp. (*Wiener* ~) one fried in breadcrumbs in the Viennese style and garnished with lemon, anchovies, etc.

schnor′kel (shn-), **snor′kel** *n.* 1. Funnel providing German submarine with air, snort. 2. Breathing-tube for swimmer with head under water. [Ger. *schnorchel*]

scho′lar (sk-) *n.* 1. (archaic) Pupil. 2. Holder of scholarship. 3. Learned person, person versed in literature. **scho′larly** *adj.*

scho′larship (sk-) *n.* 1. Attainments of a scholar; learning, erudition. 2. (Right to) emoluments paid, during a fixed period, from funds of school, college, university, etc., or State, for defraying cost of education or studies, usu. granted after competitive examination.

schola′stic (sk-) *adj.* 1. Of schools or other educational establishments; educational, academic; pedantic, formal. 2. (As) of the SCHOOL¹men; dealing in logical subtleties. **schola′stically** *adv.*

schola′sticism *n.* **schola′stic** *n.* 1. Schoolman; modern theologian of scholastic tendencies. 2. Jesuit between novitiate and priesthood.

scho′liast (sk-) *n.* Writer of scholia (see foll.).

scho′lium (sk-) *n.* (pl. *-ia*). Marginal note, explanatory comment, esp. one by an ancient grammarian on a passage in a classical author.

Schö′nberg (shêr-), Arnold (1874-1951). Austrian composer who became a U.S. citizen; his works include chamber music, operas, etc.

school¹ (sk-) *n.* 1. Institution for educating children or giving instruction, usu. of more elementary or more technical kind than that given at universities; buildings, pupils, of this; time given to teaching; being educated in a school; (fig.) circumstances or occupation serving to discipline or instruct. 2. Organized body of teachers and scholars in any of higher branches of study in Middle Ages, esp. as constituent part of medieval university; any of the branches of study with separate examinations at university; (or pl.) hall in which university examinations are held; (pl.) such examinations. 3. Disciples, imitators, followers, of philosopher, artist, etc.; band or succession of persons devoted to some cause, principle, etc. 4. ~ *board*, (hist.) from 1870 to 1902, body of persons elected by ratepayers of a district to provide and maintain public elementary schools (hence called *board* ~*s*); **schoo′lboy**, boy at school; ~-*days*, time of being at school; **schoo′lgirl**, girl at school; ~-*ma'am*, -*marm*, (colloq.) schoolmistress; **schoo′lman**, teacher in medieval university; writer (9th-14th centuries) treating of logic, metaphysics, and theology as taught in medieval 'schools' or universities of Europe; **schoo′lmaster**, **schoo′lmistress**, teacher in school; **schoo′lroom**, room used for lessons in school or private house; ~-*teacher*, teacher esp. in infant or primary school. ~ *v.* Send to school, provide for education of (rare); discipline, bring under control, train or accustom *to.* **schoo′ling** *n.*

school² (sk-) *n.* Shoal (of fish, whales, etc.).

schoo′ner¹ (sk-) *n.* Small sea-going fore-and-aft rigged sailing vessel, orig. with only two masts, later with three or four, and usu. carrying one or more topsails.

schoo′ner² (sk-) *n.* (U.S.) Large tall beer-glass.

Schö′penhauer (sh-, -how-), Arthur (1788-1860). German pessimistic philosopher, who taught that the absolute reality is a blind and restless will, that all existence is essentially evil, and that release can be attained only by overcoming the will to live.

schörl (sh-) *n.* Black variety of tourmaline.

schottische (shŏtē′sh) *n.* Kind of dance like polka but slower; music for this. [Ger., = 'Scottish']

Schu′bert (shōō-), Franz Peter (1797-1828). Austrian musical composer, esp. famous for his songs.

Schu′mann (shōō-), Robert Alexander (1810-56). German Romantic musical composer, author of many songs and much piano and chamber music etc.

scia′tic (sī-) *adj.* Of the hip; of, affecting, the sciatic nerve; suffering from, liable to, sciatica; ~ *nerve*, each of two divisions of the sacral plexus, esp. the *great* ~ *nerve*, largest nerve in human body, emerging from pelvis and passing down back of thigh to foot.

scia′tica (sī-) *n.* Neuritis or neuralgia of sciatic nerve, with paroxysms of pain along course of nerve and its branches.

sci′ence (sī-) *n.* 1. Systematic and formulated knowledge; pursuit of this, principles regulating such pursuit. 2. Branch of knowledge, organized body of the knowledge that has been accumulated on a subject; *abstract* ~, theoretical, not applied, science; *applied* ~, one studied for practical purposes (opp. *pure* ~); *exact* ~, one admitting of quantitative treatment; *natural* ~, science(s) concerned with the physical world (as chemistry, biology), opp. abstract science(s); *pure* ~, science studied without its applications to practical use (opp. *applied* ~); ~ *fiction*, form of fiction which assumes an imaginary technological advance or change in environment etc. 3. Natural sciences collectively, the systematic study of the phenomena of the material universe and their laws. 4. (in sport, esp. boxing) Expert's skill as opp. to strength or natural ability.

scie′ntial (sī-, -shal) *adj.* Of knowledge. **scie′ntially** *adv.*

scienti′fic (sī-) *adj.* Of science, esp. the natural sciences; devised according to the rules of science for testing soundness of conclusions etc.; systematic, accurate; assisted by expert knowledge. **scienti′fically** *adv.*

sci′entist (sī-) *n.* One who studies or professes the natural sciences.

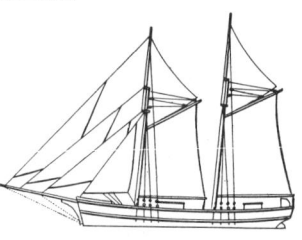

SCHOONER

Sciento′logy (sī-) *n*. Religious system based on study of knowledge and claiming to develop the highest potentialities of mankind. **Sciento′logist** *n*.
scī′licĕt (sī-) *adv*. (abbrev. *sc.*, *scil.*) That is to say, namely. [L, = *scire licet* it is permitted to know]
sci′lla (sĭ-) *n*. Liliaceous bulbous plant of genus *S*~, esp. the frequently cultivated blue-flowered *S. sibirica*.
Sci′lly, (sĭ-) Isles of. (also *Scillies*) Group of small islands off W. extremity of Cornwall.
sci′mitar (sĭ-) *n*. Oriental short curved single-edged sword, usu. broadening towards point.
scinti′lla (sĭ-) *n*. Spark, atom.
sci′ntillāte (sĭ-) *v.i*. Sparkle, twinkle (freq. fig.); emit sparks. **sci′ntillant** *adj*. **scintillā′tion** *n*.
scī′olist (sĭ-) *n*. Superficial pretender to knowledge, smatterer. **scī′olism** *n*. **scioli′stic** *adj*.
sci′on (sī-) *n*. Shoot of plant, esp. one cut for grafting or planting (ill. GRAFT[1]); descendant, young member of (esp. noble) family.
sci′rrhus (sĭrus; *or* sk-) *n*. (path.) Hard carcinoma; organ which has hardened. **sci′rrhoid**, **sci′rrhous** *adjs*. **scīrrhŏ′sitў** *n*.
sci′ssion (sĭ-) *n*. Cutting, being cut; division, split.
sci′ssors (sĭzerz) *n.pl*. 1. (also *pair of* ~) Cutting instrument consisting of pair of handled blades so pivoted that the instrument can be opened to X-shape and then closed with the object to be cut between the edges of the blades. 2. (wrestling) Hold in which opponent's head or body is clasped betweenlegs. **sci′ssor** *v.t*. Cut with scissors.
sclēr′a *n*. = SCLEROTIC *n*.
sclerĕ′nchўma (-k-) *n*. Hard tissue of coral; tissue of higher plants composed of cells with thickened and lignified walls, forming e.g. nutshell or seedcoat.
sclĕr′ogĕn *n*. Hard lignified matter deposited on inner surface of plant-cells.
sclĕrŏ′sis *n*. (pl. *-es* pr. *-ēz*). 1. (path.) Replacement of normal tissue, esp. of nervous system or arteries, by overgrowth of fibrous or supporting tissue, resulting in hardening and loss of function. 2. (bot.) Hardening of cell wall by lignification.
sclĕrŏ′tic *adj*. Of, affected with, sclerosis; of the sclerotic. ~ *n*. Hard opaque white outer coat covering eyeball except over cornea and forming white of eye (ill. EYE).
S.C.M. *abbrev*. State Certified Midwife; Student Christian Movement.
scŏff *v.i*. Speak derisively, esp. of something deserving respect, mock, jeer (*at*). **scŏ′ffer** *n*. **scŏff** *n*. Derisive jest; object of derision or scoffing.

scŏld *v*. Castigate (person) verbally *for* fault etc. **scŏ′lding** *n*. **scŏld** *n*. (archaic) Railing or nagging woman.
scŏ′lĕx *n*. (pl. *-icēs*). Anterior head-like part of tapeworm.
scŏnce[1] *n*. Flat candlestick with handle; bracket candlestick to hang on wall (ill. CANDLE).
scŏnce[2] *n*. (obs., joc.) Head, crown of head.
scŏnce[3] *n*. Small fort or earthwork, usu. covering a ford, pass, etc.
scŏnce[4] *v.t*. (Oxf. Univ.) Inflict forfeit of beer upon, for offence against table etiquette. ~ *n*. Forfeit imposed by sconcing.
scōne[1] *n*. Soft flat cake of flour, freq. with currants etc., usu. round or quadrant-shaped, orig. baked on a griddle.
Scone[2] (-ōōn). Village in Perthshire, ancient capital of the Scots where their kings were crowned; *stone of* ~: see CORONATION stone.
scōōp *n*. 1. Short-handled deep shovel for dipping up and carrying such materials as flour, grain, coal; long-handled ladle; instrument with spoon- or gouge-shaped blade for cutting out piece

MARROW SCOOP

from soft material or removing embedded substance, core, etc.; coal-scuttle. 2. Motion as of, act of, scooping; slurring of interval by singer or fiddler. 3. (orig. U.S. slang) Obtaining of news etc. by newspaper before, or to exclusion of, competitors, news so obtained; lucky stroke of business etc., large profit. ~ *v.t*. 1. Lift (*up*), hollow (*out*), (as) with scoop; slur (notes) in music. 2. (slang) Secure (large profit etc.) by sudden action or stroke of luck; get advantage over (rival) by obtaining newspaper scoop.
scōōt *v.i*. Run, dart, make off. **scōō′ter** *n*. 1. Child's toy vehicle, consisting of a narrow foot-board mounted on two tandem wheels, the front one attached to a long steering-handle, propelled by pushes of one foot on the ground, the other foot resting on the foot-board; (also *motor* ~) similar heavier vehicle for adults, with seat and motor. 2. (U.S.) Sail-boat with runners for use on either ice or water.
scō′pa *n*. (entom.) Small brush-like tuft of hairs esp. on bee's leg, by which pollen is gathered from hairs on body.
scōpe *n*. End aimed at, purpose (now rare); outlook, purview, sweep or reach of observation or action, range; opportunity, outlet; (naut.) length of cable out when ship rides at anchor.
scopŏ′lamine (*or* -ēn) *n*. = HYOSCINE.
scorbū′tic *adj*. & *n*. Of, like, (person) affected with, scurvy.

scorch *v*. 1. Burn surface of with flame or heat so as to discolour, injure, or pain; affect with sensation of burning; become discoloured, slightly burnt, etc., with heat; *scorched earth*, policy of destroying all means of sustenance and supply in a country that might be of use to an invading enemy. 2. (slang, of motorist etc.) Go at very high or excessive speed.
score *n*. 1. Notch cut, line cut, scratched, or drawn. 2. Running account kept by scores against customer's name, esp. for drink in old inns; reckoning, esp. for entertainment; *pay off old* ~*s*, (fig.) pay person out for past offence. 3. Number of points made by player or side in some games; register of items of this. 4. (mus.) Copy of composition on set of staves braced and barred together; *full* ~, with each part on separate staff. 5. (pl. same exc. in ~*s* = large numbers) Twenty, set of 20; weight of 20 (or 21) lb., used in weighing pigs or oxen. 6. Category, head. 7. (slang) Remark or act scoring off person; piece of good luck. ~ *v*. 1. Mark with notches, incisions, or lines, slash, furrow; make (line, notch, incision). 2. Mark *up* in inn-score; enter; (fig.) mentally record (offence *against* offender). 3. Record (score in cricket and other games), keep score; win and be credited with, make points in game, secure an advantage, have good luck; ~ *off*, (slang) worst in argument or repartee, inflict humiliation on. 4. (mus.) Orchestrate; arrange *for* an instrument; write out in score.
scōr′ia *n*. (pl. *-iae*, *-ias*). Cellular lava, fragments of this; slag. **scōriā′ceous** (-shus) *adj*.
scōr′ifў *v.t*. Reduce to scoria or slag, esp. in assaying. **scōrifica′tion**.
scorn *v.t*. Hold in contempt, despise; abstain from, refuse *to* do, as unworthy. ~ *n*. Contempt, derision; object of this. **scor′nful** *adj*. **scor′nfullў** *adv*. **scor′nfulness** *n*.
scorper: see SCALPER.
Scor′piō. The Scorpion, a constellation; 8th sign (♏), of the zodiac, which the sun enters about 23 Oct.
scor′pion *n*. 1. Arachnid with lobster-like claws and segmented tail that can be bent over to inflict poisoned sting on prey held in claws. 2. (O.T.) Kind of whip, prob. armed with metal points. 3. *the S*~: see SCORPIO. 4. ~*-shell*, kind of marine snail with long spine fringing outer lip of aperture.
scorzonēr′a *n*. Narrow-leaved yellow-flowered herb of genus *S*~, esp. *S. hispanica*, black salsify, with parsnip-like root used as vegetable.
Scŏt[1] *n*. 1. Native of Scotland. 2. (hist.) One of an ancient Gaelic-speaking people who migrated from Ireland to Scotland in 6th c.

[789]

scŏt² *n.* (hist.) Payment corresponding to modern tax, rate, or other assessed contribution; ~-*free*, unharmed, unpunished, safe, esp. in *get off, go, ~-free*.

Scŏtch¹ *adj.* Of Scotland or its inhabitants (the modern inhabitants of Scotland usu. prefer the form *Scottish* except in expressions like *Scotch tweeds, whisky*; in the dialect(s) of English spoken in the Lowlands of Scotland; ~ *barley*, pot barley with the husk ground off; ~ *broth*, mutton broth thickened with pearl barley and vegetables; ~ *cap*, GLENGARRY; ~ *collops*, collops of beef cut small and stewed; ~ *fir*, common N. European pine, *Pinus sylvestris*; *Sco'tchman, Sco'tchwoman* (Sc. *Scots-*), native of Scotland; ~ *mist*, thick wet mist; ~ *pebble*, variety of crystalline quartz, as agate, chalcedony, cairngorm, etc., cut and polished and used as an ornamental stone in brooches, etc.; ~ *terrier*, short-legged terrier with a rough, wiry, greyish coat and short erect tail (ill. DOG); ~ *whisky*, whisky, often having a smoky flavour of peat, as distilled in Scotland; ~ *woodcock*, scrambled eggs served on toast with anchovy paste. ~ *n.* 1. Scottish form of English. 2. (colloq.) Scotch whisky.

scŏtch² *v.t.* Make incisions in, score; wound without killing; crush, stamp out. ~ *n.* Slash; mark on ground for HOPSCOTCH.

scō'ter *n.* Large sea-duck (genus *Melanitta*) of northern coasts.

scō'tia (-sha) *n.* Concave moulding esp. in base of column (ill. MOULDING).

Scō'tism *n.* Scholastic philosophy of DUNS SCOTUS and his followers. **Scō'tist** *n.*

Scō'tland. Northern part of Great Britain, formerly a separate kingdom; capital, Edinburgh; the crowns of England and Scotland were united by the accession of James VI of Scotland (James I of England) to the English throne in 1603; the two parliaments were united by the Act of Union in 1707, when Scotland became a part of the United Kingdom.

Scō'tland Yȧrd. Headquarters of London metropolitan police, formerly in Great Scotland Yard, a short street off Whitehall; in 1890 moved to New Scotland Yard on Thames Embankment and in 1967 to Broadway, Westminster; allusively, the Criminal Investigation Department (C.I.D.) of the Metropolitan Police Force.

Scōto- *prefix.* Scottish.

scotō'pic *adj.* ~ *vision*, vision of normal persons in twilight, with some perception of form but poor recognition of colour (cf. PHOTOPIC).

Scŏts *adj.* Scottish; *Sco'tsman, Sco'tswoman*, native of Scotland. ~ *n.* Scottish (esp. Lowlands) form of English.

Scŏtt¹. Name of an English family of architects: *Sir George Gilbert* ~ (1811–78), restorer of Gothic churches and designer of the Albert Memorial, London; *George Gilbert* ~ (1839–97), his son, and *Sir Giles Gilbert* ~ (1880–1960), his grandson.

Scŏtt², Robert (1811–87): see LIDDELL.

Scŏtt³, Robert Falcon (1868–1912), captain R.N. Explorer, leader of two Antarctic expeditions, in the second of which the S. Pole was reached on 18 Jan. 1912, but Scott and the rest of the Pole party perished storm-bound in a blizzard on the return journey.

Scŏtt⁴, Sir Walter (1771–1832). Scottish writer of historical novels and verse romances, author of 'Waverley', 'Guy Mannering', 'Rob Roy', 'Heart of Midlothian', 'Kenilworth', 'Ivanhoe', etc.

Scō'ttĭcè *adv.* In the Scots language.

Scō'tticism *n.* Scots phrase, idiom, word, pronunciation, etc.

Scō'tticīze *v.* Imitate the Scots in idiom or habits; imbue with, model on, Scottish ways.

Scō'ttie *n.* (colloq.) Scotch terrier.

Scō'ttish *adj.* Connected with, pertaining to, Scotland, its people, language, etc.

Scotus, John Duns: see DUNS SCOTUS.

scou'ndrel *n.* Unscrupulous person, villain, rogue. **scou'ndrelly** *adj.*

scour¹ *v.t.* Cleanse or brighten by friction; clean out by flushing with water, or (of water) by flowing through or over; purge drastically; purge (worms) by placing in damp moss etc. to fit them for bait; clear (rust, stain) away, off, by rubbing etc. ~ *n.* Act, action, of scouring; artificial current or flow for clearing channel etc.; kind of diarrhoea in cattle.

scour² *v.* Rove, range, go along hastily; hasten over or along, search rapidly.

scourge (-ĕrj) *n.* Whip for chastising persons; person or thing regarded as instrument of divine or other vengeance or punishment. ~ *v.t.* Use scourge on; chastise, afflict, oppress. [LL *excoriare* strip off the hide]

scout¹ *n.* 1. Man sent out to reconnoitre position and movements of enemy (mil.); official of motorists' organization employed to assist motorists on road; ship, aircraft used for reconnoitring, esp. small fast single-seat aeroplane. 2. Male college servant at Oxford (formerly also at Yale and Harvard). 3. Act of seeking (esp. military) information. 4. *S~*, member of the *S~ Association* (formerly *Boy Scouts*), an organization founded (1908) by Lord Baden-Powell, for helping boys to develop character by training them in open-air activities. 5. *scou'tmaster*, officer in charge of scouts (sense 1); *Scou'tmaster*, man in charge of a group of Scouts (sense 4). ~ *v.i.* Act as scout.

scou'ter *n.* (esp., *S~*) Adult leader in Scout Association.

scout² *v.t.* Reject with scorn or ridicule.

scow *n.* (esp. U.S.) Kind of large flat-bottomed square-ended boat used esp. as lighter.

scowl *v.i.* Wear sullen look, frown ill-temperedly. ~ *n.* Scowling aspect, angry frown.

S.C.R. *abbrev.* Senior common-room.

scrȧ'bble *v.i.* Scratch or grope (*about*) to find or collect something.

scrȧg *n.* Lean skinny person, animal, etc.; bony part of animal's carcass, esp. of neck of mutton, as food; (slang) person's neck. **scrȧ'ggy** *adj.* **scrȧ'ggily** *adv.* **scrȧ'gginess** *n.* **scrȧg** *v.t.* Hang (on gallows), wring neck of, garotte.

scrȧm *v.i.* (slang) Go away quickly, get out (usu. as imper.).

scrȧ'mble *v.* 1. Make way over steep or rough ground by clambering, crawling, etc.; struggle to secure as much as possible of something from competitors; deal with in a hasty manner. 2. Cook (eggs) by stirring slightly in pan with butter, milk, etc., and heating; mix together indiscriminately or confusedly; alter frequency of the voice in telephoning or radiotelephony by means of automatic mechanical or electrical devices fitted to the transmitter so as to make the message unintelligible except to a person using a receiver fitted with a similar device. 3. (of military aircraft or their pilots) (Hasten to aircraft and) take off in response to alert. ~ *n.* 1. Eager struggle or competition (*for*). 2. Climb or walk over rough ground; motor-cycle race over rough ground.

scrȧ'mbler *n.* (esp.) Telephone or wireless transmitter fitted with a device for scrambling speech.

scrȧ'nnel *adj.* (archaic; of sound) Weak, reedy; unmelodious.

scrȧp¹ *n.* Small detached piece; shred or fragment; short piece of writing etc.; (pl.) odds and ends; (collect.) waste material, clippings, etc., of metal collected for reworking; metal wasted in production; residuum of melted fat; ~-*book*, book for collection of newspaper cuttings etc.; ~-*heap*, collection of waste material (freq. fig.); ~-*iron*, -*metal*, scrap. **scrȧ'ppy** *adj.* Fragmented, disconnected. **scrȧp** *v.t.* Consign to scrap-heap; condemn as past use; discard.

scrȧp² *n.* Fight, scrimmage, quarrel. ~ *v.i.* Engage in a scrap.

scrāpe *v.* 1. Clean, clear of projections, abrade, smooth, polish, etc., by drawing sharp or angular

SCRATCH

edge breadthwise over, or by causing to pass over such edge; take (projection, stain, etc.) *off*, *out*, *away*, by scraping. 2. Draw along with scraping sound, produce such sound from, emit such sound. 3. Pass along something so as to graze or be grazed by it or just avoid doing so; ~ *through*, get through with a squeeze or narrow shave (freq. fig.). 4. Amass by scraping, with difficulty, by parsimony, etc.; contrive to gain; practise economy. ~ *n*. 1. Act or sound of scraping; scraping of foot in bowing. 2. Awkward predicament, difficult position, esp. as result of escapade etc.

scrā′per *n*. (esp.) Scraping instrument in various technical operations; appliance fixed outside door of house, with horizontal blade for scraping mud etc. from shoes; (archaeol.) primitive wedge-shaped flint implement.

scrătch[1] *v*. 1. Score surface of, make long narrow superficial wounds in, with nail, claw, or something pointed; get (part of body) scratched; form, excavate, by scratching; scrape without marking, esp. with finger-nails to relieve itching; scratch oneself; make scratch; scrape *together* or *up*. 2. Score (something written) *out*, strike *off* with pencil etc.; erase name of, withdraw, from list of competitors etc. ~ *n*. 1. Mark or sound made by scratching; sound made by friction of needle in sound-recording apparatus and heard in playing of record etc.; spell of scratching oneself; slight wound. 2. Line from which competitors in race, or those receiving no start in handicap, start; zero, par, in games or contests in which handicaps are allowed; *come up to* ~, be ready to start race, match, etc., at the proper time; (fig.) be ready to embark on an enterprise, to fulfil one's obligations; *start from* ~, have no handicap (also fig.). ~ *adj*. Collected by haphazard, scratched together, heterogeneous.

Scrătch[2]. *Old* ~, the Devil.

scră′tchy̆ *adj*. (of drawing etc.) Done in scratches, careless, unskilful; (of pen) making scratching sound or given to catching in paper; (of action etc.) uneven, ragged. **scră′tchily̆** *adv*. **scră′tchiness** *n*.

scrawl *v*. Write, draw, in hurried, sprawling, untidy way; cover with scrawls. ~ *n*. Something scrawled; hasty or illegible writing.

scraw′ny̆ *adj*. (U.S.) Scraggy.

scream *v*. Utter piercing cry, normally expressive of terror, pain, sudden or uncontrollable mirth, etc.; make noise like this; utter in screaming tone. **screa′ming** *adj*. **screa′mingly̆** *adv*. (freq. in ~ *funny* etc.). **scream** *n*. Screaming cry or sound; (slang) irresistibly comical affair or person.

screa′mer *n*. (esp.) Large S. Amer. bird of family Anhimidae, with harsh cry; (slang) something that raises screams of laughter; (slang) exclamation mark.

scree *n*. (freq. pl.) (Mountain slope covered with) loose stones that slide when trodden on.

screech *n*. Loud shrill harsh cry; ~-*owl*, barn-owl, from its discordant cry, supposed to be of ill omen; small Amer. owl of genus *Otus* with harsh cry. ~ *v*. Make, utter with, screech.

screed *n*. 1. Long and tedious harangue, letter, etc. 2. (plastering etc.) Strip of accurately levelled plaster on wall, ceiling, etc., as guide in running cornice, laying coat of plaster, etc.; board, strip of wood, used for levelling concrete etc.

screen *n*. 1. Partition partly shutting off part of church or room, esp. that between nave and choir of church; ornamental wall masking front of building. 2. Movable piece of furniture designed to shelter from excess of heat, light, draught, etc., or from observation; any object utilized as shelter esp. from observation, measure adopted for concealment, protection afforded by these; SMOKE-screen; wind-screen; (cricket) movable erection of white canvas, wood, etc., placed so that batsman can see ball and bowler's arm more clearly. 3. Upright surface on which images are projected or received, objects displayed, etc.; (also *silver* ~) moving pictures, films; scree′n-*play*, (script of) film; 4. Body, part of optical, electrical, or other instrument, serving to intercept light, heat, electricity, etc.; (photog.) transparent plate ruled with fine cross-lines, through which picture etc. is photographed for half-tone reproduction; ~-*grid valve*, radio valve (tetrode, pentode, etc.) in which electrostatic capacity between anode and grid is much reduced. 5. Large sieve or riddle to separate coarser from finer parts of sand, grain, coal, etc. 6. ~ *printing*, serigraphy, stencil printing process in which ink is rolled through a screen of silk or similar material; similar process for reproducing pattern on fabrics; so ~-*printed*, ~ *v.t.* 1. Afford shelter to; hide partly or completely; (mil.) employ a body of men to cover (an army's movement); furnish (radio valve) with screen; prevent from causing electrical interference; ~ *off*, shut off by means of, conceal behind, screen. 2. Show (esp. cinematograph film) on screen. 3. Clean, sift, grade (coal, gravel, etc.) by passing through a screen; scrutinize, subject (person) to tests to establish reliability etc.

scree′nings (-z) *n.pl.* Material which has been screened; refuse separated by screening.

SCREW

scree′ver *n*. (slang) Pavement artist. **screeve** *v.i.*

screw[1] (-ōō) *n*. 1. Cylinder with spiral ridge (*thread*) running round it outside (*male* ~) or inside (*female* ~); metal male screw with

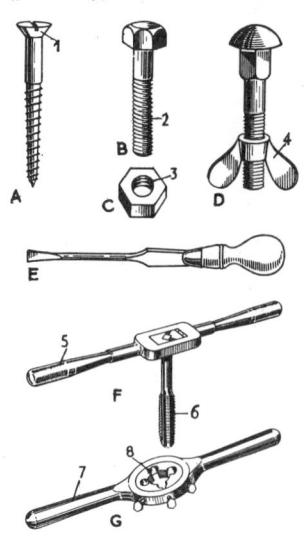

A. WOOD SCREW. B. BOLT. C. NUT. D. COACH BOLT. E. SCREW-DRIVER. F. TAP-WRENCH FOR CUTTING FEMALE SCREW THREADS. G. STOCK AND DIE FOR CUTTING MALE SCREW THREADS

1. Countersunk head. 2. Male thread. 3. Female thread. 4. Wing or butterfly nut. 5. Wrench. 6. Tap. 7. Stock. 8. Adjustable die

slotted head and sharp point for fastening pieces of wood etc. together, or with blunt end to receive nut and bolt things together; wooden or metal etc. screw as part of appliance for exerting pressure; *have a* ~ *loose*, be slightly mad; *put the* ~ *on*, *apply the* ~ *to*, (fig.) put moral pressure on, coerce. 2. Propeller (ill. PROPELLER). 3. One turn of a screw; oblique curling motion or tendency as of billiard-ball struck sideways and below centre. 4. Small twisted-up paper of tobacco etc. 5. Miser; stingy or extortionate person. 6. (slang) Salary, wages. 7. *screw′-driver*, tool with thin wedge-shaped end or blade for turning screws by slot in head; ~-*palm*, -*pine*, plant of tropical genus *Pandanus*, with slender palm-like stems and branches, with terminal crown of sword-like leaves; ~-*press*, press worked by screw; ~-*propeller* = sense 2 above; ~-*top*, (attrib., of jar, bottle, etc.) having lid that screws on. ~ *v.* 1. Fasten, tighten, etc., by use of screw or screws; turn (screw), twist round like screw; make tauter or more

[791]

SCREW

efficient; revolve like screw; take curling course, swerve. 2. Press hard on, oppress. 3. Be miserly; squeeze, extort *out* of. 4. Contort, distort, contract.
screw² (-ōō) *n.* Vicious, unsound, or worn-out horse.
screw'ball (-ōōbawl) *n. & adj.* (U.S. slang) Mad, crazy (person).
screw'y (-ōōi) *adj.* (U.S. slang) Mad, crazy, suspicious.
Scri'abin (-rēa-), Alexander Nikolaevich (1872-1915), Russian composer of piano and orchestral works.
scri'bble¹ *v.* Write hurriedly or carelessly. **scri'bbler¹** *n.*
scri'bble *n.* Careless writing, thing carelessly written, scrawl.
scri'bble² *v.t.* Card (wool, cotton) coarsely, pass through machine which does this. **scri'bbler²** *n.* Scribbling-machine.
scribe *n.* 1. Copyist, transcriber of manuscripts, calligrapher; (obs.) clerk, secretary. 2. Ancient Jewish maker and keeper of records etc.; member of class of professional interpreters of the Law after return from Captivity. 3. Tool for marking or scoring (wood, bricks, etc.) to indicate shape to be cut etc. ~ *v.t.* Mark with scribe.
scrim *n.* Open-weave fabric used in bookbinding, upholstery, plastering, etc.
scri'mmage *n.* Tussle, confused struggle, brawl; (Amer. footb.) play when holder of ball places it flat on ground with long axis at right angles to goal-line, and puts it in play; *lines of* ~, imaginary lines parallel to goal-line passing through points of ball resting on ground before being put in play. ~ *v.i.* Engage in scrimmage.
scrimp *v.* Skimp.
scri'mshank *v.i.* (mil. slang) Shirk duty. **scri'mshanker** *n.*
scrip¹ *n.* (archaic) Beggar's, traveller's, or pilgrim's wallet, satchel.
scrip² *n.* Provisional document of allotment issued to holder of stocks or shares entitling him to formal certificate when the necessary payments have been completed, and to dividends etc.; (collect.) such documents. [abbrev. of (*sub*)*scrip*(*tion receipt*)]
script *n.* 1. (law) Original document. 2. Handwriting, written characters; printed cursive characters, imitation of handwriting in type (*illustration, p. 793*); style of handwriting in which characters resemble those of print and are not joined together. 3. Manuscript, typescript, of play, film, etc.; text of broadcaster's announcement or talk; examinee's written answers. ~ *v.i.* (colloq.) Compose script of play etc.
scriptōr'ium *n.* (pl. -ia), Room set apart for writing, esp. in monastery.
scri'pture *n.* Sacred book or writings; Bible; (attrib.) taken from or relating to the Bible.
scri'ptural (-cher-) *adj.*
scri'vener *n.* (hist.) Writer, drafter of documents, notary, broker, moneylender.
scrō'fula *n.* Name formerly given to a prob. tubercular condition affecting the lymphatic glands and bones, also called KING's evil.
scrō'fulous *adj.*
scrōll *n.* 1. Roll of parchment or paper, esp. written on; book or volume of ancient roll form. 2. Ornamental design, esp. in architecture, made to imitate scroll of parchment more or less exactly; volute of Ionic capital or of chair etc., head of violin etc. (ill. STRINGED); flourish in writing; ribbon bearing heraldic motto etc.; any tracery of spiral or flowing lines. 3. ~ *gear, wheel,* (gear with) cog-wheel in shape of disc with cogs in spiral line on one face; ~ *saw*, fretsaw, saw stretched in frame, for carving curved lines; *scro'llwork*, ornament of spiral or curving lines, esp. as cut by scroll saw. ~ *v.* Curl or roll up like paper; adorn with scrolls.
Scrōōge, Ebenezer. Miserly curmudgeon in Charles Dickens's 'Christmas Carol'; hence, miser.
scrōōp *n.* Harsh grating noise; crisp rustle of silk. ~ *v.* Make scroop; treat (silk) with dilute mineral acids so that it will rustle crisply.
scrō'tum *n.* (anat.) Pouch or bag enclosing testicles (ill. PELVIS).
scrō'tal *adj.*
scrounge (-nj) *v.* (colloq.) Appropriate without leave; cadge; search about. **scrou'nger** *n.*
scrŭb¹ *n.* (Ground covered with) plant community dominated by shrubs; stunted or insignificant person, animal, etc.; ~-*oak, pine,* stunted oak, pine, of several Amer. species; ~ *typhus*, acute febrile disease, caused by bites of certain larval mites, esp. prevalent in Japan; Japanese river fever.
scrŭ'bby *adj.*
scrŭb² *v.* 1. Rub hard to clean or brighten, esp. with soap and water applied with hard-bristled brush (*scrubbing-brush*); use such brush; ~ *up*, (esp., of surgeons etc.) scrub hands and arms thoroughly before performing surgical operation. 2. Pass (coal-gas) through a scrubber to extract certain components. ~ *n.* Scrubbing, being scrubbed.
scrŭ'bber *n.* (esp.) Any of various apparatuses for removing impurities etc. from coal-gas etc. as (1) a tower in which gas ascends through coke or other material down which water or a watery solution trickles; (2) a vessel in which gas is forced through a liquid, or a tank in which the gas is forced over blades or brushes that rotate in a liquid.
scrŭff *n.* (also ~ *of the neck*) Back outer part of neck.
scrŭ'ffy *adj.* Unkempt.

SCULPT

scrŭm *n.* 1. (Rugby footb.) Formation in which two sets of forwards pack themselves together with heads down and try to obtain ball placed on the ground between them by pushing their opponents away from it; ~-*half*, half-back who puts ball into scrum. 2. (colloq.) Dense crowd.
scrŭ'mmage *n.* = SCRUM, 1.
scrŭ'mptious(-shus)*adj.*(slang) Delicious, delightful.
scrŭnch *n. &* v. CRUNCH.
scrŭ'ple (-ōō-) *n.* 1. In apothecaries' weight, unit equivalent to 20 grains or ⅓ drachm; symbol ℈. 2. Doubt, uncertainty, or hesitation in regard to right and wrong, duty, etc. ~ *v.i.* Hesitate owing to scruples *to do.*
scru'pulous (-ōōp-) *adj.* Conscientious even in small matters, not neglectful of details, punctilious; over-attentive to details, esp. to small points of conscience.
scru'pulously *adv.* **scru'pulousness, scrupulō'sity** *ns.*
scrutā'tor (-ōō-) *n.* One who examines, scrutineer.
scrutineer' (-ōō-) *n.* Person examining ballot-papers for irregularities.
scru'tinīze (-ōō-) *v.t.* Look closely at, examine in detail.
scru'tiny(-ōō-) *n.* Critical gaze; close investigation, examination into details; official examination of votes at election to eliminate irregularities or confirm numbers stated in return.
scrȳ *v.i.* Practise crystal-gazing. **scrȳ'er** *n.*
scŭd *v.i.* Run, fly, straight and fast, esp. with smooth or easy motion; (naut.) run before the wind. ~ *n.* Driving shower of rain, gust of wind.
Scudéry (-dārē), Madeleine de (1607-1701). French author of heroic romances.
scŭff *v.* Walk with dragging feet, shuffle; shuffle, drag along (feet); wear, rub, esp. with feet.
scŭ'ffle *v.i. & n.* (Engage in) confused struggle or scrambling fight.
sculduddery: see SKULDUGGERY.
scŭll *n.* Each of pair of short light oars used by single rower; oar used to propel boat by working it from side to side over stern, reversing blade at each turn. ~ *v.* Propel (boat), propel boat, with scull(s). **scŭ'ller** *n.* User of sculls; boat intended for sculling.
scŭ'llery *n.* Back kitchen, small room attached to kitchen for washing dishes etc.
scŭ'llion (-yon) *n.* (archaic & rhet.) Menial servant, washer of dishes and pots.
sculp *v.* (colloq.) Sculpture.
scŭ'lpin *n.* Small Amer. seafish of family Cottidae, with barbels on head.
scŭ'lpsĭt. (So-and-so) carved or sculptured or engraved (this).
sculpt *v.* (colloq.) Sculpture.

SCULPTOR   SCURRILOUS

SCRIPT

1. Rustic capitals, 4th–5th c. 2. Uncial, mid-5th c. 3. Half-uncial, 6th c. 4. Insular (Anglo-Saxon) majuscule, early 8th c. 5. Carolingian minuscule, early 9th c. 6. Gothic, *c* 1250. 7. Humanist script, late 15th c. 8. Italic, late 15th c. 9. Secretary hand, 1593. 10. Court hand, 1611. 11. Copperplate, 1673.

scŭ′lptor *n.* One who practises sculpture.

scŭ′lpture *n.* 1. Art of forming representations of objects etc. or abstract designs in the round or in relief by chiselling stone, carving wood, modelling clay, casting metal, or similar processes; work of sculpture. 2. (zool., bot.) Raised or sunk markings on shell etc. **scŭ′lptural** (-cher-) *adj.* **scŭ′lpturally** *adv.* **scŭ′lpture** *v.* Form by, represent in, sculpture; adorn with sculpture; be sculptor, practise sculpture. **scŭ′lptured** (-*erd*) *adj.* (esp., biol.) With markings etc. like those produced by sculpture.

scŭm *n.* Impurities that rise to surface of liquid; (fig.) worst part, refuse, offscourings. **scŭ′mmў** *adj.* **scŭm** *v.* Take scum from, skim; be, form, scum on; (of liquid) develop scum.

scŭ′mble *v.t.* Soften, make less brilliant, blend (colours, hard outlines in painting etc.) by applying coat of opaque or semi-opaque colour with nearly dry brush, by rubbing pencil- or charcoal-marks lightly, etc. ~ *n.* Softened effect produced by scumbling.

scŭ′pper[1] *n.* Opening in ship's side level with deck to drain off water.

scŭ′pper[2] *v.t.* (slang) Sink (ship, crew), disable, throw into disorder.

scŭrf *n.* Flakes on surface of skin cast off as fresh skin develops below, esp. those of head; any scaly matter on a surface. **scŭr′fў** *adj.* **scŭr′finĕss** *n.*

scŭ′rrilous *adj.* Grossly or

[793]

obscenely abusive; given to, expressed with, low buffoonery. **scŭ′rrilouslў** *adv*. **scŭrri′litў** *n*.
scŭ′rrў *v.i.* Run hurriedly, scamper. ~ *n*. Act of scurrying, rush, bustle; flurry, fluttering assemblage (e.g. of snowflakes) moving or driven rapidly through the air.
scŭr′vў[1] *adj*. (archaic) Contemptible, low, mean. **scŭr′vilў** *adv*.
scŭr′vў[2] *n*. Disease resulting from deficiency of vitamin C, characterized by swollen gums, haemorrhage esp. into skin and mucous membrane, and great debility, formerly common among sailors and others who lived for long periods without fresh vegetables; ~-*grass*, any of several cresses used against scurvy, esp. *Cochlearia officinalis*, found in Arctic regions.
scŭt *n*. Short tail, esp. of hare, rabbit, or deer.
scŭ′tage *n*. (hist.) Money paid to the Crown by feudal landowner in lieu of personal service.
scŭtch *v.t.* Dress (fibrous material, esp. retted flax) by beating. **scŭ′tcher** *n*. Hand tool for scutching flax; machine for scutching; part of threshing-machine for striking off the grain. **scŭtch** *n*. 1. Scutcher. 2. Bricklayer's tool for cutting bricks etc. 3. Refuse of scutched flax.
scŭ′tcheon (-chǒn) *n*. ESCUTCHEON; pivoted cover of keyhole (ill. DOOR); plate for name or inscription.
scŭtĕ′llum *n*. Small shield, plate, or scale, in plants; shield-like part of insect; one of the horny scales on bird's foot. **scŭ′tĕllate**, **scŭtĕ′llar** *adjs*. **scŭtĕllā′tion** *n*.
scŭ′tter *v.i.* Scurry.
scŭ′ttle[1] *n*. 1. Shallow open basket for carrying corn, earth, etc. 2. Metal or other receptacle for carrying and holding small supply of coal (*coal-*~) for a fire in a room. 3. Part of motor-car connecting bonnet with body.
scŭ′ttle[2] *n*. Lidded opening smaller than hatchway in ship's deck; similar opening in ship's side for ventilation, lighting, etc.; (U.S.) lidded opening in floor or roof of house. ~ *v.t.* Cut hole(s) in (ship, boat, etc.), sink thus.
scŭ′ttle[3] *v.i.* Scurry, run away, make off. ~ *n*. Hurried gait, precipitate flight or departure.
scŭ′tum *n*. (pl. *-ta*). (zool.) Bony, horny, etc., plate, esp. second of three parts forming upper surface of notum in insects; shield-like dermal plate in crocodile, turtle, etc. **scŭ′tal** *adj*.
Scў′lla (sĭ-). (Gk myth.) Female sea-monster who devoured sailors when they tried to navigate the narrow channel between her cave and the whirlpool CHARYBDIS; later legend substituted a dangerous rock for the monster and located it on the Italian side of the Strait of Messina; hence, ~ *and Charybdis*, two dangers such that to avoid the one is to court the other.
scўphozō′an (sĭ-) *adj*. & *n*. (Member) of the Scyphozoa, a class of coelenterates comprising the true marine jellyfishes.
Scўth (sĭ-) *n*. Member of a nomadic people, natives of Scythia, who overran W. Asia in 7th c. B.C.
scўthe (sīdh) *n*. Agricultural implement for mowing and reaping, with long thin slightly curved blade fastened at an angle with handle and wielded with long sweeping stroke. ~ *v.t.* Cut with scythe.

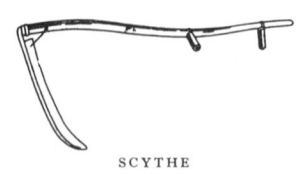

SCYTHE

Scў′thia (sĭ-; *or* -dh-). Ancient region of S. European and Asiatic Russia, between the Carpathians and the Don. **Scў′thian** *adj*. & *n*. 1. Scyth. 2. (Language) of Scythia.
s.d. *abbrev*. *Sine die*.
S. Dak. *abbrev*. South Dakota.
SE., SE *abbrevs*. South-east(ern).
sea *n*. 1. Continuous body of salt water covering most of earth's surface; part of this having certain land-limits or washing a particular coast and having a proper name; *at* ~, away from land, aboard ship; (fig.) perplexed, bewildered, at a loss; *the four* ~*s*, those bounding Gt Britain; *the high* ~*s*: see HIGH; *the seven s*~, the Arctic, Antarctic, N. and S. Pacific, N. and S. Atlantic, and Indian Oceans. 2. Local motion or state of the sea; swell, rough water. 3. Large quantity or level expanse *of*. 4. ~*-anchor*, floating, expanding anchor, usu. of canvas, used to keep a boat's head into the wind in rough weather; drag-anchor; ~*-anemone*, any of numerous usu. large and solitary polyps with bright colours and many petal-like tentacles surrounding mouth; ~*-bird*, bird frequenting sea; ~*-board*, coast bordering the sea; ~*-borne*, conveyed by sea; ~*-breeze*, cool breeze blowing landward from sea, usu. in daytime; ~*-calf*, common seal; ~ *chest*, sailor's chest; ~ *coal*, (archaic) coal (because formerly brought by sea from Newcastle to London etc.); coal mined from sea-coast veins; ~*-coast*, land adjacent to the sea; ~*-cock*, valve by which sea-water can be let into ship's interior; ~*-colander*, brownish seaweed with fronds perforated like a colander; ~*-cow*, manatee or other sirenian; ~*-cucumber*, one of the holothurians, esp. the bêche-de-mer; ~*-dog*, old sailor, privateer or pirate, esp. of Elizabethan days; = DOG, 7; ~*-eagle*, any of the various eagles feeding largely on fish, esp. the white-tailed eagle; ~*-ear*, haliotis; ~*-elephant*, elephant seal, large seal of S. hemisphere with proboscis; ~*-fan*, coral with fan-like skeleton; *sea′farer*, traveller by sea, sailor; *seafaring* (*adj*. & *n*.); ~ *food*, sea-fish, esp. shell-fish, as food; ~*-front*, part of town etc. facing sea; *sea′going*, (of ship) designed for open sea, not rivers, etc.; seafaring; ~*-green* (*adj*. & *n*.) (of) bluish green as of sea; *S*~-*green Incorruptible*, Carlyle's term for Robespierre; *sea′gull*, gull; ~*-hog*, porpoise; ~*-horse*, hippocampus, small fish covered with rough bony plates, with prehensile tail and forepart of body resembling horse's head and neck; walrus; (Gk & Rom. myth.) fabulous marine animal with forepart of horse and tail of fish, drawing sea-god's chariot; ~*-island cotton*, fine variety of long-stapled cotton, grown orig. and esp. on islands off coast of Georgia and S. Carolina; *sea′kale*, W. European cruciferous plant grown as culinary vegetable; *seakale beet*, CHARD; ~ *lane*, course prescribed for ocean steamers; ~*-lavender*, any maritime herb of genus *Limonium*, of plumbago family; ~*-lawyer*, argumentative or captious sailor; (also) TIGER-SHARK; ~ *legs*, ability to walk on deck of rolling ship; ~ *level*, mean level of sea, mean level between high and low tides, used as a standard for measurements of heights and depths; ~ *lily*, crinoid; ~*-lion*, any of several large eared seals; *sea′man* sailor; sailor below rank of officer; navigator; *sea′manship*, skill of

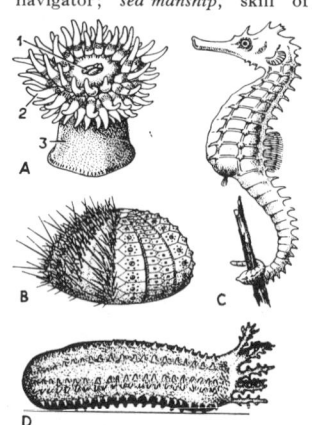

A. SEA-ANEMONE. B. SEA-URCHIN (HALF THE SPINES REMOVED). C. SEA-HORSE. D. SEA-CUCUMBER (HOLOTHURIAN)

1. Mouth. 2. Tentacles. 3. Column

[794]

good seaman; ~-*mark*, conspicuous object serving to guide or warn sailors in navigation; **sea'-mew**, common gull; ~-*mile*, nautical mile, one minute ($\frac{1}{60}°$) measured along a meridian; ~-*mouse*, pop. name of a marine annelid worm, covered with minute iridescent setae, of the genus *Aphrodite*; ~ *onion*, squill; ~-*pie*, dish of meat, vegetables, etc., baked or boiled together in crust of paste or in layers between crusts; ~-*pig*, porpoise; ~ *pink*, see THRIFT, 2; **sea'plane**, aeroplane fitted with floats to enable it to alight or take off from water (ill. AEROPLANE); **sea'port**, (town with) harbour or port on sea-coast; ~-*power*, naval strength, State having this; ~-*room*, unobstructed space at sea for ship to manœuvre in; ~-*rover*, pirate; ~-*salt*, salt obtained by evaporation from sea-water; **sea'-scape**, picture of a scene at sea; ~ *serpent*, sea-monster of great length and more or less resembling a serpent freq. reported to have been seen at sea; ~-*shanty*, = SHANTY[2]; ~-*shell*, shell of any salt-water mollusc; ~-*shore*, land close to sea, ground between high- and low-water marks; **sea'sick**, suffering from nausea and vomiting induced by motion of ship at sea; **sea'-sickness** (n.); **sea'side**, edge of sea, sea-coast as health or pleasure resort; ~-*slug*, marine gasteropod mollusc of which the shell is absent or internal; ~-*squirt*, sessile marine animal of sub-phylum Urochordata, which squirts water when touched (ill. ASCIDIAN); ~-*swallow*, tern; ~-*trout*, salmon trout; any of various sea-fishes; ~-*urchin*, marine animal of order Echinoidea, esp. one of nearly globular form covered with (freq. very sharp) movable spines; ~-*wall*, wall or embankment made to check encroachment of sea or act as breakwater; **sea'weed**, plant growing in sea, esp. marine alga (ill. ALGA); **sea'worthy**, (of ship) in fit state to put to sea; **sea'worthiness** (n.).

seal[1] *n.* Marine amphibious fish-eating mammal, of family Phocidae, with limbs developed into flippers and adapted for swimming, elongated body covered with thick fur or bristles, and short tail, hunted for its hides and oil; (also **sea'lskin**) skin or prepared fur of seals; coat, cape, etc., made of this. ~ *v.i.* Hunt seals, **sea'ler** *n.* (esp.) Ship or man engaged in seal-hunting.

seal[2] *n.* 1. (Impressed device on) piece of wax or other plastic material attached to document as evidence of authenticity of signature etc., or on folded letter, envelope-flap, door, lid of box, etc., so that it cannot be opened without breaking seal; impression stamped on a wafer etc. stuck to document as symbol equivalent to wax seal; decorative adhesive stamp other than postage-stamp; (fig.) mark of ownership; obligation to silence or secrecy. 2. Engraved stamp of metal or other hard material used to make impression on wax etc., used as seal; this as mark of office, esp. (pl.) as symbol of position of Lord Chancellor or Secretary of State; *Great S*~, seal used for authentication of important documents issued in name of highest executive authority; ~-*ring*, finger-ring with seal. 3. Substance used to close aperture etc., esp. water standing in drain-pipe to prevent ascent of foul air. ~ *v.t.* Place seal on (document), fasten (letter etc.), esp. with seal or sealing-wax; close tightly or hermetically; stop or shut *up*; (fig.) prove authenticity of (devotion etc.) *with* one's life etc.; set significant mark on; set apart, destine, devote; decide irrevocably; ~ *off*, cut off (an area) so as to prevent entry or exit. **sealed** (-ld) *adj.* (esp.) *S*~ *Book*, one of the presumed perfect copies of Book of Common Prayer certified by Great Seal in 1662 under Charles II; (fig.) something obscure *to* a person, beyond his capacity to understand; ~ *orders*, written instructions for a commander of a ship, esp. in time of war, in a sealed envelope, only to be opened at a stated time or place; ~ *pattern*, regulation pattern of weapon, uniform etc., officially accepted for armed services. **sea'ling** *n.* (esp.) ~-*wax*, coloured mixture of shellac, rosin, and turpentine, which becomes soft when heated and hardens as it cools, thus easily receiving and preserving the impression of a seal, used for sealing letters, documents, etc.

sea'lant *n.* Sealing substance.

Sea'lyham (-lĭam) *n.* Wiry-haired, long-bodied, short-legged terrier, usu. white with brown or grey markings on head, noted for spirit and gameness. [f. name of estate in Dyfed, Wales]

seam *n.* Line of junction between two edges, esp. those of two pieces of cloth etc. sewn together,

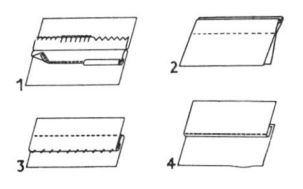

SEAMS

1. Flat seam, showing five different ways of finishing edges. 2. French seam. 3. Run-and-fell seam. 4. Lapped seam

or of boards fitted edge to edge; line, groove, furrow, formed by two abutting edges, mark resembling this; scar; line of purl stitches in knitting resembling sewn seam; thin layer or stratum, esp. of coal, between two wider strata (ill. MINE[2]); ~-*stitch*, (knitting) purl-stitch. ~ *v.* Join *together*, *up*, etc., with seam(s); (knitting) make seam-stitch; score or mark with seams, furrow, ridge.

sea'mstress (sĕm-), **sĕ'mpstress** *ns.* Sewing-woman.

sea'my *adj.* Showing seams; ~ *side*, wrong side of garment etc. where rough edges of seams are visible; (usu. fig.) of worst, roughest, or least presentable aspect, esp. of life.

Seanad Éireann (shă'nadh ār'an). Upper Chamber (Senate) of the Republic of Ireland, with 60 members. [Ir., = 'Irish senate']

séance (sā'ahns; *or* -ans) *n.* Sitting of society or deliberative body; meeting for exhibition or investigation of spiritualistic phenomena.

sear *v.t.* Wither up, blast (rare); scorch, esp. with hot iron, cauterize, brand; (fig.) render (conscience etc.) incapable of feeling. ~ *adj.* SERE.

search (sĕr-) *v.* Examine thoroughly (place, person, etc.) for what may be found or to find something of which presence is known or suspected; make search or investigation (*for*); ~ *me!* (slang, orig. U.S.) exclamation implying that the speaker has no knowledge of some fact or no idea what course to take. **sear'ching** *adj.* (of examination etc.) Thoroughgoing, leaving no loopholes. **sear'chingly** *adv.* **search** *n.* Act of searching, investigation, quest; *right of* ~, belligerent's right to stop neutral vessel and search it for contraband; **sear'ch-light**, lamp designed to throw strong beam of light in any desired direction, used in warfare for discovering hostile aircraft, observing movements of troops, passing ships, etc.; light from this; ~-*party*, party of persons going out to look for lost or concealed person or thing; ~-*warrant*, legally issued warrant to enter premises to search for suspected persons, stolen property, or other things kept or concealed in violation of law.

sea'son (-zn) *n.* 1. Each of the periods into which year is divided by earth's changing position in regard to sun, with particular conditions of weather etc., esp. one of the four equal periods (spring, summer, autumn, winter) marked by passage of sun from equinox to solstice and from solstice to equinox; or each of two periods, rainy and dry, into which year is divided in tropical climates; time of year when a plant flourishes, blooms, etc., or when an animal pairs, breeds, is hunted, etc., or which is regularly devoted to a particular occupation etc., or

[795]

when a particular place is most frequented (esp., in London, the time from May to July when fashionable society is assembled there). 2. Proper time, favourable opportunity; period of indefinite or various length; ~-ticket, ticket issued at reduced rates permitting any number of journeys to be taken, performances attended, etc., within year, month, or other specified length of time. ~ v. 1. Bring into efficient or sound condition by habituation, exposure, special preparation, use, or lapse of time; inure, mature; become fit for use by being seasoned. 2. Make palatable or piquant by introduction of salt, condiments, wit, jests, etc.; give zest to, flavour; temper, moderate.

sea'sonable (-z-) adj. Suitable to, of the kind usual at, the season; opportune, meeting the needs of the occasion. sea'sonably adv. sea'sonableness n.

sea'sonal (-z-) adj. Occurring at a particular season; (of trades, workers, etc.) dependent on the seasons, employed only during a particular season. sea'sonally adv.

sea'soning (-z-) n, (esp.) Substance for seasoning food (see SEASON v. 2).

seat n. 1. Manner of sitting, esp. on horse. 2. Place on which person sits; (right to) use of seat: right to sit as member esp. of Parliament etc.; authority or dignity symbolized by sitting on particular seat or throne; something made for sitting upon; part of chair etc. on which occupant sits; sitting part of body, buttocks; part of garment covering this; ~ belt, = SAFETY belt. 3. Site, location, temporary or permanent scene; country mansion, esp. with park or large grounds. ~ v.t. 1. Cause to sit, place oneself in sitting posture. 2. Fit or provide with seats; (of room etc.) have seats for (specified number). 3. Mend seat of (chair, trousers, etc.). 4. Establish in position; fix in particular place.

-seater n. (in comb.) single-~, two-~, etc., motor-car, aeroplane, etc., with seat(s) for one, two, etc.

sea'ting n. (esp.) Seats; arrangement, provision, of seats.

S.E.A.T.O., SEATO abbrev. South East Asia Treaty Organization.

sĕbā'ceous (-shus) adj. Of tallow or fat, fatty; ~ duct, gland, etc., organ secreting or conveying fatty matter which lubricates hair and skin (ill. SKIN).

Sĕbā'stian (-tyan) St. (3rd c.). Roman soldier and Christian martyr, usu. represented as youth pierced by many arrows.

Sĕbā'stopol. (Russ. Seva'stopol'). Seaport of the Crimea, besieged and destroyed by the English and French during the Crimean War, 1854–5.

sĕborrhoe'a (-rēa) n. Excessive discharge from the sebaceous glands. sĕborrhoe'ic adj.

sĕc¹ n. (colloq.) SECOND¹ n.
sĕc² adj. (of wine) Dry.
sĕc³ abbrev. = SECANT n. 1.
Sec. abbrev. Secretary.

sē'cant adj. (math.) Cutting, intersecting. ~ n. 1. (trig., function of angle in right-angled triangle) Ratio of side adjacent given acute angle to the hypotenuse (reciprocal of COSINE; ill. TRIGONOMETRY). 2. (geom.) Line cutting another, esp. straight line cutting curve at two or more points.

sē'cateurs (-êrz) n.pl. (also pair of ~) Short-bladed pruning shears operated with one hand.

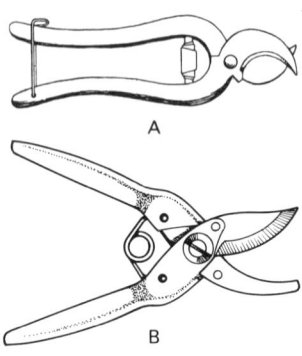

A. SECATEURS. B. PRUNER

sĕ'ccotine (-ēn) n. Liquid composition serving as a strong adhesive. [trade-name]

sĕcē'de v.i. Withdraw formally from membership esp. of Church or federation of States.

sĕcē'ssion n. Act of seceding, body of seceders; War of ~, AMERICAN Civil War (1861–5), which arose from an attempt by eleven of the Southern States to secede from the U.S. sĕcĕ'ssional adj. sĕcĕ'ssionism, sĕcĕ'ssionist ns.

sĕclu'de (-ōōd) v.t. Keep retired or away from company or resort.

sĕclu'sion (-ōō-) n. Secluding, being secluded; retirement, privacy, avoidance of intercourse; secluded place.

sĕ'cond¹ adj. Next after first in order of time, position, quality, etc.; next in rank, quality, degree, etc., to; other, another; (mus., of part) next below highest in concerted music; that performs such a part; S~ Advent: see ADVENT; ~ ballot, electoral method by which, if the winner on the first ballot has not polled more than half of the votes cast, a second is taken in which only he and the next candidate are eligible; ~ best, (what is) next in quality, inferior, to the first; come off ~ best, be worsted; ~ chamber, upper house in a legislature which consists of two chambers or houses; ~ class, class next to first; (U.S., of postal matter) consisting of periodicals sent from publishing office; ~-class (adj.) inferior in quality, second-rate; (adv.) by the second class; S~ Coming, Second Advent; ~ cousin: see COUSIN; ~ distance, portion of a picture between the foreground and background, middle distance; S~ Empire, (Ger. hist.) see GERMANY; (Fr. hist.) that of Napoleon III (1852–70); ~-hand, not new, not original, previously worn, used, etc., by another; ~ lieutenant, army officer of lowest commissioned rank; ~ nature, acquired tendency or habit that has become instinctive; ~-rate, of inferior quality, value, etc.; (of ship) rated in second class; ~-ra'ter; S~ Republic, French Republic of 1848–52; ~ sight, faculty, claimed by, or attributed to, some persons, of seeing, as in a vision, future events; ~ thoughts, reconsideration, decision or opinion after reconsidering matter. ~ n. 1. Second thing etc.; second person in race etc.; (person who takes) second class in examination. 2. (mus.) Next to highest part; interval of which the span involves only two alphabetical names of notes (ill. INTERVAL); harmonic combination of the two notes thus separated. 3. (pl.) Goods of quality inferior to best. 4. Supporter, helper, esp. person representing and supporting principal in duel. 5. Sixtieth part of minute of time or angular measurement; vaguely, a short time; ~ hand, hand or pointer in some watches and clocks recording seconds. 6. (in motor vehicle) Second gear. ~ adv. Second-class. ~ v.t. Supplement, support, back ŭp, esp. support (motion, mover) in debate, etc. as necessary preliminary to further discussion or adoption of motion. sĕ'conder n.

sĕcŏ'nd² v.t. 1. (mil.) Remove (officer) temporarily from regiment etc., with a view to staff or other extra-regimental appointment. 2. Transfer (official) temporarily to another department. sĕcŏ'ndment n.

sĕ'condary adj. Not in the first class in dignity, importance, etc., of minor importance, subordinate; subsidiary, auxiliary; not original or primary, derivative, belonging to a second stage or period; S~, (geol.) Mesozoic; ~ colour: see COLOUR; ~ education, education between primary or elementary and higher or university education; ~ feather, feather growing from second joint of bird's wing (ill. BIRD); ~ planet, planet's satellite; ~ school, school giving secondary education. sĕ'condarily adv. sĕ'condary n. Secondary feather, planet; S~, (geol.) Secondary period.

seco'nde (-kawnd) n. Second of

the eight parries in fencing (ill. FENCE).
sĕ'condlў *adv.* In the second place.
sē'crĕcў *n.* Being secret.
sē'crĕt *adj.* Hidden, concealed, not (to be) made known; known only to the initiated; not given to revealing secrets; ~ *agent*, spy; ~ *police*, political police of a totalitarian state; ~ *service*, services rendered to government, nature of which is not revealed, and which are paid for from special fund; *S~ Service*, (pop.) espionage department. **sē'crĕtlў** *adv.* **sē'crĕt** *n.* Thing (to be) kept secret; thing known only to initiated or to a limited number; mystery; *in ~*, secretly.
sĕcrĕtair'e *n.* Piece of furniture for keeping private papers etc., with shelf for writing on (ill. DESK).
sĕcrĕtār'iat, -ate *n.* Body or department of secretaries; place where secretary does business, keeps records, etc.; (premises of) department headed by Secretary-General.
sĕ'crĕtarў (-trĭ) *n.* 1. Person employed by another to assist him in correspondence, literary work, and other confidential matters; official appointed by society, company, etc., to keep its records, conduct correspondence, etc. 2. Principal assistant of government minister or ambassador etc.; *S~-General*, principal administrative officer of organization; *S~ of State*, minister of the Crown in charge of one of the major government departments. 3. ~ *bird*, long-legged long-tailed raptorial African bird (*Sagittarius serpentarius*), with crest of long feathers (thought to resemble pens stuck behind the ear). ~ *adj.* Applied to style of handwriting used chiefly in legal documents of 16th and 17th centuries (ill. SCRIPT). **sĕcrĕtār'ial** *adj.* **sĕ'crĕtarўship** *n.*
sĕcrē'te *v.t.* 1. Put into place of concealment. 2. Produce by secretion. **sĕcrē'torў** *adj.*
sĕcrē'tion *n.* 1. Concealing, concealment. 2. Action of gland etc. in extracting and elaborating certain substances from blood, sap, etc., to fulfil function within body or be excreted; any substance (as saliva, urine, resin) produced by such process.
sĕcrē'tive (*or* sē'krĭ-) *adj.* Given to making secrets, uncommunicative, needlessly reserved. **sĕcrē'-tivelў** *adv.* **sĕcrē'tivenĕss** *n.*
sĕct *n.* Body of persons agreed upon religious doctrines usu. different from those of an established or orthodox Church; party or faction in a religious body; religious denomination; school of opinion in philosophy, politics, etc. **sĕctār'ian** *adj.* & *n.* **sĕctār'ianism** *n.*
sect. *abbrev.* Section.
sĕ'ctarў *n.* Member of a sect, esp. (hist.) of English Protestant Dissenters in 17th–18th centuries.
sĕ'ctile *adj.* That can be cut (esp. of soft minerals).
sĕ'ction *n.* 1. Cutting (rare exc. in ref. to surgery etc.). 2. Part cut off from something; one of the parts into which something is divided; one of the minor subdivisions of a book etc. (usu. indicated by ~-*mark*, §, as § 15); (mil.) subdivision of platoon; part of community having separate interests or characteristics; thin slice of something cut off for microscopic examination; (U.S.) area of one square mile into which public lands are divided; (U.S.) part of sleeping-car containing two berths. 3. Cutting of solid by plane, (area of) figure resulting from this; representation of internal structure of something supposed to be cut thus (ill. DRAWING); *conic ~s*, (math.) study of curves of intersection produced by allowing plane to cut cone at various angles (ill. CONE). 4. Section-mark (see sense 2) used as mark of reference or to indicate beginning of section. **sĕ'ctional** *adj.* **sĕ'ctionallў** *adv.* **sĕ'ction** *v.t.* Arrange in, divide into, sections.
sĕ'ctor *n.* 1. Plane figure contained by two radii and the arc of a circle, ellipse, etc. (ill. CIRCLE); anything having this shape; ~ *of a sphere*, solid generated by revolution of plane sector about one of its radii. 2. Mathematical instrument, now consisting of two flat rules inscribed with various scales and stiffly hinged together, for mechanical solution of various problems; astronomical instrument, telescope turning about centre of graduated arc, for measuring angles. 3. (mil.) Subdivision of defensive position or system under one commander; territory for which one group, e.g. of airraid wardens, is responsible. **sĕctōr'ial** *adj.* 1. Of, like, sector of a circle. 2. (of tooth, esp. one of the pre-molars) Adapted for cutting. ~ *n.* Sectorial tooth.
sĕ'cular *adj.* 1. Occurring once in, lasting for, an age or a century; lasting or going on for ages or an indefinitely long time. 2. Concerned with the affairs of this world, worldly; not sacred; not monastic or ecclesiastical, temporal, profane, lay; sceptical of religious truth or opposed to religious education; ~ *arm*, (hist.) civil jurisdiction to which criminal was transferred by the Church for severer punishment; ~ *clergy*, *priests*, those not belonging to monastic orders (opp. *regular*). **sĕ'cularlў** *adv.* **sĕ'cularism** *n.* **sĕ'cularist** *n.* & *adj.* **sĕ'cularīze** *v.t.* **sĕcularīzā'tion**, **sĕcŭlă'ritў** *ns.* **sĕ'cular** *n.* Secular priest.
sĕcūr'e *adj.* 1. Untroubled by danger or apprehension; safe against attack, impregnable. 2. Reliable, certain not to fail or give way; (usu. pred.) in safe keeping, firmly fastened. 3. Having sure prospect *of*; safe *against*, *from*. **sĕcūr'elў** *adv.* **sĕcūr'e** *v.t.* 1. Fortify. 2. Confine, enclose, fasten, close, securely. 3. Guarantee, make safe against loss. 4. Succeed in getting, obtain.
sĕcūr'itў *n.* (esp.) 1. Thing deposited or hypothecated as pledge for fulfilment of undertaking or payment of loan; document as evidence of loan; certificate of stock, bond, exchequer bill, etc. 2. Precautions against theft, espionage, etc. 3. *S~ Council*, Council of the General Assembly of the United Nations, consisting of 15 members of which 5 (China, France, U.K., U.S.A., U.S.S.R.) are permanent and the remainder elected, charged with the duty of dealing with disputes between nations which threaten the peace of the world.
Sĕdă'n¹. Town of N. France, near Belgian border, scene (1870) of defeat of army of Napoleon III by Germans and of the French emperor's surrender.
sĕdă'n² *n.* 1. (also ~ *chair*) 17th–18th-c. portable covered-in chair

SEDAN CHAIR

for one person, usu. carried on poles by two men. 2. (U.S.) Motor-car with enclosed body for 4 to 7 persons including driver.
sĕdā'te *adj.* Tranquil, equable, composed, settled; not impulsive or lively. **sĕdā'telў** *adv.* **sĕdā'tenĕss** *n.*
sĕdā'tion *n.* (med.) Treatment by sedatives.
sĕ'dative *adj.* & *n.* (Drug etc.) tending to soothe.
sĕ'dentarў *adj.* Sitting; (of occupation etc.) requiring continuance in sitting posture; (of persons) accustomed or addicted to sitting still, engaged in sedentary occupation; (zool.) permanently attached; (of spiders) lying in wait until prey is in web. **sĕ'dentarilў** *adv.* **sĕ'dentarinĕss** *n.*
sĕdge *n.* Grass-like plant of genus *Carex*, growing in marshes or by waterside; bed of such plants; ~-*warbler*, small brown migratory bird of Europe and Asia (*Acrocephalus schoenobaenus*),

[797]

with sweet loud song, breeding among sedges. **sĕ′dgȳ** *adj.*
Sĕ′dgemoor (-jm-). Plain in Somerset, scene of battle (1685) in which Monmouth, who had landed at Lyme Regis as champion of the Protestant party, was defeated by troops of James II.
sĕdĭ′lĭa *n.pl.* Series of usu. three freq. canopied seats set in the S. wall of the chancel of a church.

SEDILIA

sĕ′dĭment *n.* Matter that settles to bottom of liquid, lees, dregs; (geol.) material carried by water or wind which settles and consolidates to make rocks. **sĕdĭmĕ′ntarȳ** *adj.* **sĕdĭmĕntā′tion** *n.*
sĕdĭ′tion *n.* Conduct or language directed unlawfully against State authority; public commotion, riot, not amounting to insurrection or rebellion and therefore not treason. **sĕdĭ′tious** (-shus) *adj.* **sĕdĭ′tiouslȳ** *adv.* **sĕdĭ′tiousnĕss** *n.*
sĕdū′ce *v.t.* Lead astray, tempt into sin or crime; persuade (esp. virgin) to have sexual intercourse with one. **sĕdū′cer** *n.*
sĕdŭ′ction *n.* Seducing, being seduced; thing that seduces.
sĕdŭ′ctive *adj.* (esp.) Alluring, enticing, winning. **sĕdŭ′ctivelȳ** *adv.* **sĕdŭ′ctivenĕss** *n.*
sĕ′dūlous *adj.* Diligent, persevering, assiduous, painstaking. **sĕ′dūlouslȳ** *adv.* **sĕ′dūlousnĕss, sĕdūlĭtȳ** *ns.*
sĕ′dum *n.* Fleshy-leaved plant of genus S~, cultivated for its foliage and pink, white, or yellow flowers.
see[1] *v.* (past t. *saw*, past part. *seen*). Have the faculty of discerning objects with the eyes, exercise this faculty; perceive objects by sight; perceive mentally; learn by reading; look at, visit; admit as visitor; ascertain by inspection, experiment, consideration, etc.; supervise; escort *home*, *to the door*, etc.; consider, judge; know by observation, experience; imagine; ~ *about*, attend to; take into consideration; ~ *over*, go over and inspect; ~ *through*, (esp., fig.) penetrate, see real character of through disguise or false appearance; continue to watch or take care of until the end, or until difficulties are overcome; ~ *to*, attend to; take special care about.
see[2] *n.* Office, position, jurisdiction, of a bishop; *Apostolic, Holy, Papal*, or *Roman S~*, office, jurisdiction, authority, of pope.
seed *n.* 1. (One of) grains or ovules of plants, esp. as used for sowing; seed-like fruit, any other part of plant (as bulb) used for propagating new crop; *go, run, to ~,* cease flowering as seed develops; (fig.) become shabby, worn-out, etc. 2. (bot.) Fertilized and ripened ovule of flowering

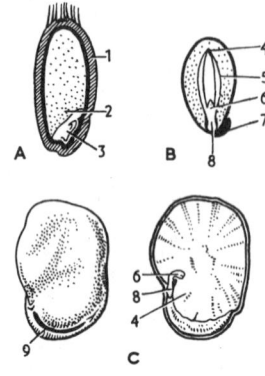

SEEDS
A. LONGITUDINAL SECTION OF WHEAT GRAIN (MONOCOTYLEDON). B. LONGITUDINAL SECTION OF CASTOR OIL SEED. C. EXTERIOR AND LONGITUDINAL SECTIONS OF BROAD BEAN (*B* AND *C* ARE DICOTYLEDONS)

1. Pericarp. 2. Albumen. 3. Embryo or germ. 4. Cotyledon. 5. Endosperm. 6. Plumule. 7. Aril. 8. Radicle. 9. Hilum

plant, containing embryo capable of developing by germination. 3. Sperm, semen, milt; germ or latent beginning *of* (idea etc.). 4. (bibl.) Progeny, descendants. 5. Seeded player. 6. ~*-cake*, cake flavoured with caraway seeds; ~*-corn*, grain preserved to sow for new crop; ~*-pearl*, very small pearl; *see′dsman*, dealer in seeds; ~*-time*, sowing-season; ~*-vessel*, pericarp; ~*-wool*, raw cotton before being cleaned of its seeds. **see′dlĕss** *adj.* Having no seeds.
seed *v.* Go to seed, produce or let fall seed; sprinkle (as) with seed; remove seeds from; disperse chemical material in (cloud) to make artificial rain; (sport, esp. lawn tennis) sort (competitors in competition or tournament) so that certain players do not meet in the early rounds; hence *seeded player*, one so selected.
see′dling *n.* Young plant raised from seed.

see′dȳ *adj.* 1. Full of seed. 2. Shabby, ill-looking; unwell, out of sorts. **see′dilȳ** *adv.* **see′dinĕss** *n.*
see′ing *conj.* Considering the fact *that*; since, because.
seek *v.* (past t. & past part. *sought* pr. sawt). Go in search of, look for; try to obtain or bring about, *to do*; ask for, request; make search; *be yet to ~,* be lacking. **see′ker** *n.* (esp.) *S~,* one of a small sect of English 17th-c. Independents who professed to be seeking further light on the true Church.
seem *v.i.* Have the appearance of, be apparently; appear *to be* or *do*; appear to exist; appear to be true or the fact. **see′ming** *adj.* Apparent; apparent only. **see′mingly** *adv.*
see′mlȳ *adj.* Decent, decorous, becoming. **see′mlinĕss** *n.*
seen: see SEE[1].
seep *v.i.* Ooze, percolate. **see′page** *n.*
seer *n.* Visionary, prophet, one gifted with second sight.
seer′sŭcker *n.* Thin linen, cotton, or other fabric with puckered surface, freq. striped, orig. of Indian manufacture. [Pers. *shīr o shakkar* milk and sugar]
see′-saw *adj. & adv.* With backward-and-forward or up-and-down motion. ~ *n.* Game in which two persons sit one at each end of a long board balanced on a central solid support and move each other up and down alternately; board thus used (freq. fig.). ~ *v.i.* Play at see-saw; move up and down as in game of see-saw; vacillate.
seethe (-dh) *v.* Cook by boiling (archaic); (fig.) boil, bubble, be agitated.
sĕ′gment *n.* 1. (geom.) Plane figure contained by chord and arc of circle (ill. CIRCLE); finite part

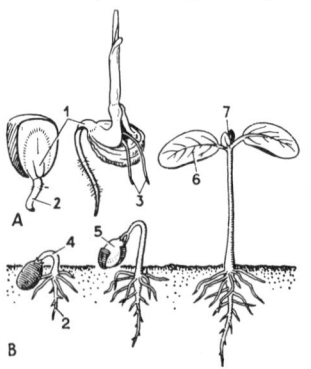

SEEDLINGS
STAGES IN GROWTH OF (A) MAIZE (MONOCOTYLEDON), (B) CASTOR OIL (DICOTYLEDON)

1. Root sheath. 2. Radicle. 3. Adventitious roots. 4. Hypocotyl. 5. Endosperm. 6. Cotyledon. 7. Epicotyl

segregate of line between two points; ~ *of a sphere*, part cut off by plane; (phys.) each of parts into which length of vibrating string etc. is divided by nodes. 2. Division, section, of something, esp. each of longitudinal divisions of body of some animals, somite, metamere. 3. Segmental arch. ~ *v.* Divide into segments; (of cell) undergo cleavage or divide into many cells. **segme′ntal** *adj.* (esp. of arch, pediment, etc.) Having form of segment of circle (ill. ARCH[1], PEDIMENT). **se′gmentary** *adj.* **segmenta′tion** *n.*
se′gregate *v.* Set apart, isolate; subject (people) to racial segregation; enforce racial segregation in (community, institution, etc.); separate from general mass and collect together, as in crystallization or solidification; (biol., of Mendelian hybrids) separate into dominants, recessives, and hybrids, in conformity with numerical law. **segrega′tion** *n.* (esp.) Enforced separation of different racial groups in a country, community, or institution. **segrega′tionist** *n.* **se′gregate** *adj.* Isolated, set apart (rare); (zool., bot., etc.) separated from the parent or from one another, not aggregated. ~ *n.* (zool., bot.) Species separated from aggregate species; (biol.) segregated individual.
seiche (sāsh) *n.* Oscillation of lake waters due to variation of barometric pressure.
Sei′dlitz pow′der (sĕdlĭts). Aperient medicine of two powders, one of tartaric acid, the other of potassium tartrate and sodium bicarbonate, mixed separately with water and then poured together to produce effervescence. [name of village in Czechoslovakia with spring impregnated with magnesium sulphate and carbon dioxide]
seigneur (sānyēr′) *n.* Feudal lord, lord of manor (formerly in France and Canada and still in Channel Islands). **seigneur′ial** *adj.*
seigneury (sā′nyerĭ) *n.* Territory governed by seigneur; in Canada, landed estate held (until 1854) by feudal tenure.
seignior (sā′nyer) *n.* (hist.) Feudal superior, lord of a manor; seigneur. **seigniōr′ial** *adj.*
sei′gniorage (sānyer-) *n.* Something claimed by sovereign or feudal superior as prerogative, esp. Crown's right to percentage on bullion brought to mint for coining; profit made on coins issued at a rate above their intrinsic value.
seigniory (sā′nyerĭ) *n.* Lordship, sovereign authority; domain of seignior.
seine[1] (*or* sān) *n.* (also ~ *net*) Fishing net hanging vertically in water, ends being drawn together to enclose fish. ~ *v.* Catch, catch fish, with seine; use seine in.

Seine[2] (sān). River of France on which Paris stands, flowing into the English Channel.
sei′sin (-z-), **sei′zin** *n.* (law) Possession of land by freehold; act of taking such possession; what is so held.
sei′smic (sīz-) *adj.* Of earthquakes; ~ *focus*, place below earth's surface where an earthquake originates.
sei′smograph (sīz-) *n.* Instrument for recording tremors of earthquakes. **seismo′graphy** *n.* **seismo′logy** *n.* Scientific study of earthquakes. **seismolo′gical** *adj.* **seismo′logist** *n.*
seize *v.* 1. (law) Put in possession *of*; take possession of, confiscate, by warrant or legal right, impound, attach. 2. Lay hold of forcibly or suddenly, snatch; grasp with hand or mind, comprehend quickly or clearly; lay hold eagerly *upon*. 3. (naut.) Lash, fasten with several turns of cord. 4. (of bearings or other moving part of machinery) Become stuck, jam, from undue heat or friction.
seizin: see SEISIN.
sei′zure (-zher) *n.* (esp.) Sudden attack of illness or paralysis.
sē′jant *adj.* (her.) Sitting with forelegs upright (ill. HERALDRY).
sejm (sām) *n.* Polish parliament.
Sĕ′khĕt (-kĕt). (Egyptian myth.) Goddess, wife of Ptah, who destroys the souls of the wicked in the underworld.
sĕ′lah. Hebrew word of unknown meaning occurring freq. in psalms and supposed to be a musical direction.
Selā′ngor. State of Malaysia; capital, Kuala Lumpur.
sĕ′ldom *adv.* Rarely, not often.
sĕlĕ′ct *adj.* Chosen for excellence, choice, picked; (of society etc.) exclusive, cautious in admitting members; *sele′ctman*,(U.S.) one of a board of annually elected officers managing various local concerns in New England towns. **sĕlĕ′ctness** *n.* **sĕlĕ′ct** *v.t.* Pick out as best or most suitable. **sĕlĕ′ction** *n.* Selecting, choice; what is selected; (biol.) sorting out in various ways of the types of animal or plant better fitted to survive, regarded as a factor in evolution. **sĕlĕ′ctive** *adj.* (esp., of radio receiver) Able to receive a desired frequency to the exclusion of others. **sĕlĕ′ctively** *adv.* **sĕlĕcti′vity** *n.*
sē′lenate *n.* Salt of selenic acid.

SEINE NET

Sĕlē′nĕ. (Gk myth.) Goddess of the moon, in later myths identified with Artemis.
sĕlē′nic *adj.* ~ *acid*, acid (H_2SeO_4), crystalline when pure, resembling sulphuric acid in many of its characteristics.
sĕlē′nious *adj.* ~ *acid*, colourless crystalline acid (H_2SeO_3).
sē′lenite *n.* 1. (min.) Calcium sulphate ($CaSO_4 2H_2O$), gypsum, in crystalline or foliated form; slip of this used to polarize light. 2. (chem.) Salt of selenious acid. **sĕlēni′tic** *adj.*
sĕlē′nium *n.* (chem.) Non-metallic element, chemically resembling sulphur and tellurium, having the property that its conductivity of electricity increases with intensity of light falling on it and hence used in various photo-electric devices; symbol Se, at. no. 34, at. wt 78·96; ~ *cell*, piece of selenium to which electrical connections are made, used as a photo-electric device etc. [Gk *selēnē* moon; named f. its association in nature with *tellurium*]
sĕlē′nodont *n.* & *adj.* (Mammal) with crescent-shaped ridges on crowns of teeth.
sĕlēno′graphy *n.* Science dealing with the physical geography of the moon, mapping the moon's surface.
Sĕleu′cid *adj.* & *n.* (Member) of the dynasty founded by Seleucus Nicator, one of the generals of Alexander the Great, ruling over Syria and a great part of W. Asia, 312–65 B.C.
sĕlf *n.* (pl. -*ves*). Person's or thing's own individuality or essence, person or thing as object of introspection or reflexive action; one's own interests or pleasure, concentration on these; (commerc., vulg., joc.) = myself, yourself, himself, etc. ~ *adj.* (of colour) Uniform, the same throughout; (of material) the same; (of flower) self-coloured.
sĕlf- *prefix.* Combining form of SELF; ~-*abuse*, masturbation; ~-*acting*, acting automatically; ~-*assertion*, insistence on one's own rights, claims, individuality, etc.; self-confidence; ~-*binder*, reaping-machine with apparatus for binding sheaves automatically; ~-*centred*, centred in oneself, itself; engrossed in self, preoccupied with one's own personality or affairs; ~-*colour(ed)*, (of) one uniform colour; ~-*command*, self-control; ~-*complacency*, complacency; ~-*complacent (adj.)*; ~-*confidence*, confidence in oneself; arrogant reliance on oneself; ~-*confident (adj.)*; ~-*conscious*, having consciousness of one's identity, actions, sensations, etc.; unduly or morbidly preoccupied with oneself; ~-*consciously (adv.)*, ~-*consciousness (n.)*; ~-*contained*, complete in itself; (of person) uncommunicative; ~-*control*, control of oneself, one's desires,

[799]

SELFISH

emotions, etc.; ~-*defence*, (esp.) in phr. *in* ~-*defence*, not by way of aggression; (*noble*) *art of* ~-*defence*, boxing; ~-*denial* (*n.*), ~-*denying* (*adj.*) sacrificing one's personal desires; ~-*denying ordinance*, (Engl. hist.) ordinance of Long Parliament (1645), forbidding members to accept any civil or military office; ~-*determination*, (esp.) people's decision of its political status, as form of government, independence, etc.; ~-*employed*, running own business etc.; ~-*esteem*, favourable opinion of oneself; ~-*evident*, not needing demonstration, axiomatic; ~-*forgetful*, with no thought of or concern for oneself; ~-*forgetfully* (*adv.*); ~-*forgetfulness* (*n.*); ~-*governing*, (esp., of colony, territory, etc.) governing itself; ~-*government* (*n.*); ~-*heal*, any of various plants credited with healing properties, esp. *Prunella vulgaris*, a blue-flowered mint of Europe and Asia; ~-*help*, providing for oneself without assistance from others; ~-*important*, having an exaggerated idea of one's own importance; ~-*importantly* (*adv.*); ~-*importance* (*n.*); ~-*indulgence*, indulgence of one's own desires for ease, pleasure, etc.; ~-*indulgent* (*adj.*), ~-*indulgently* (*adv.*); ~-*interest*, what one conceives to be for one's own interests; ~-*interested* (*adj.*), ~-*love*, selfishness, self-centredness; regard for one's own well-being or happiness; ~-*made*, made by one's own action or efforts; ~-*made man*, one who has risen from obscurity or poverty by his own exertions; ~-*opinionated*, obstinately adhering to one's own opinion; ~-*portrait*, artist's portrait of himself; ~-*possessed*, cool, composed, in command of one's faculties or feelings; ~-*possession* (*n.*); ~-*preservation* (*n.*), (esp.) natural instinct impelling living creatures to go on living and avoid injury; ~-*raising* (*adj.*), (of flour) not needing addition of baking-powder etc.; ~-*reliance*, reliance on one's own powers etc.; ~-*reliant* (*adj.*); ~-*respect* (*n.*) proper regard for one's dignity, standard of conduct etc.; ~-*righteous*, righteous in one's own esteem; ~-*sacrifice*, postponing private interest and desires to those of others; *se'lfsame* (*adj.*) (the) very same; ~-*satisfaction*, conceit; ~-*sealing*, having a device for filling up a hole in a structure caused by shot etc.; ~-*seeking* (*adj.* & *n.*) seeking one's own advantage only; ~-*service*, arrangement of shop, restaurant, etc., whereby customers help themselves and pay cashier afterwards (also *attrib*. of shop etc.); ~-*sown*, grown from chance-dropped seed; ~-*starter*, device for starting internal combustion engine without use of crank or auxiliary starting engine; ~-*styled*, having taken name or description on one's own initiative; ~-*sufficient*, requiring nothing from outside, independent; sufficient in one's own opinion, presumptuous; ~-*sufficiency* (*n.*) **sĕ'lflĕss** *adj.* Oblivious of self, incapable of selfishness. **sĕ'lflĕssnĕss** *n.*

Sĕ'lfish *adj.* Deficient in consideration for others, regarding chiefly personal profit or pleasure; actuated by, appealing to, self-interest. **sĕ'lfishlў** *adv.* **sĕ'lfishnĕss** *n.*

Sĕ'ljuk (-ōōk) *adj.* & *n.* (Member) of certain Turkish dynasties ruling over large parts of Asia from 11th c. to 13th c., or of branch of Turkish people to which these belonged. [f. name of reputed ancestor]

Sĕ'lkĭrk, Alexander (1676–1721). Scottish sailor; at his own request he was put ashore on the uninhabited island of Juan Fernandez, where he remained 1704–9; the original of 'Robinson Crusoe'.

Sĕ'lkirkshire. Former county of S. Scotland, since May 1975 part of the Borders region.

sĕll *v.* (past t. & past part. *sōld*). 1. Make over, dispose of, in exchange for money; keep stock of for sale, deal in; betray for money or other reward; promote sales (of); gain acceptance of, advertise or publish merits of; (of goods) be sold at a specific price; find purchaser(s); ~ *off*, sell remainder of (goods), clear out stock, at reduced prices; ~ *out*, (hist.) leave army by selling commission; sell (one's shares in company, whole stock-in-trade, etc.); ~ *up*, sell goods of (debtor) by distress or legal process. 2. (slang) Trick, take in. **sĕ'ller** *n.* One who sells; ~'*s market*, market in which supplies are short and prices high. **sĕ'lling** *n.* (esp.) ~-*plate*, *race*, etc., race in which winning horse is put up for

SEMEIOLOGY, SEMEIOTICS

auction. **sĕll** *n.* (slang) Hoax, take-in, swindle; disappointment; ~-*out*, betrayal; selling of all copies, seats, etc., commercial success.

sĕ'llable *adj.* (of goods) Finding purchasers easily.

sĕllotāpe *n.* & *v.t.* (Seal with) adhesive usu. transparent cellulose tape. [trade-name]

Sĕ'ltzer *n.* (also ~ *water*) Effervescent mineral water from Nieder-Selters, near Wiesbaden, Germany; similar artificial mineral water.

sĕ'lvage, **sĕ'lvĕdge** *ns.* Edge of piece of material so woven that weft will not unravel (ill. WEAVE); edge-plate of lock with opening for bolt.

sĕlvagee' *n.* Coil of rope-yarn bound together, used as sling etc.

sĕmă'ntēme *n.* Element of a language that expresses or denotes an image or idea.

sĕmă'ntĭc *adj.* Of meaning. **sĕmă'ntĭcs** *n.* Branch of philology concerned with meanings. **sĕmă'ntĭcĭst** *n.*

sĕ'maphŏre *n.* Signalling apparatus of post with one or more movable arms; signal(ling) by person holding flag in each hand. **sĕmaphŏ'rĭc** *adj.* **sĕmaphŏ'rĭcallў** *adv.* **sĕ'maphŏre** *v.* Signal, send by semaphore.

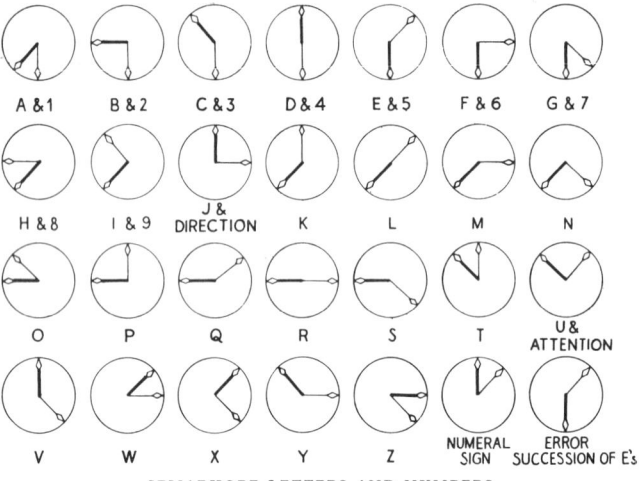

A & 1 B & 2 C & 3 D & 4 E & 5 F & 6 G & 7
H & 8 I & 9 J & DIRECTION K L M N
O P Q R S T U & ATTENTION
V W X Y Z NUMERAL SIGN ERROR SUCCESSION OF E's

SEMAPHORE LETTERS AND NUMBERS
The thick lines represent the right arm and thin lines the left arm

sĕmāsiŏ'logў *n.* Semantics.

sĕmă'tĭc *adj.* (biol., of colour, markings in animals) Serving to warn off enemies or attract attention.

sĕ'mblance *n.* Outward appearance; likeness, image, *of*; resemblance.

semé (sĕ'mā) *adj.* (her.) Sprinkled, strewn, covered, with small bearings of indefinite number (e.g. stars, fleurs-de-lis) arranged over field.

sĕmeiŏ'logў, **sĕmeiŏ'tĭcs**

[800]

SEMELE

(-mī-), **sēmi-** *ns.* Study of signs or sign language; (med.) study of symptoms of disease. **sēmeiŏ'tic, sĕmi-** *adj.*

Sĕ'mĕlė. (Gk myth.) Daughter of Cadmus and Harmonia and mother, by Zeus, of Dionysus; she entreated Zeus to come to her in his full majesty and was destroyed by his lightning.

sē'mĕn *n.* Seed, esp. of flowering plants; viscous whitish fluid secreted by male animal, containing spermatozoa.

sĕmė'ster *n.* Half-year course or term in German and other universities.

sĕmi- *prefix.* Half-, partly-, to some extent; partial(ly), imperfect(ly).

sĕ'mi-ă'nnūal *adj.* Half-yearly; lasting half a year (only). ~ *n.* Semi-annual plant.

sĕ'mibrēve *n.* (mus.) Longest note in general use (○), half as long as BREVE; in U.S. called 'whole note'.

sĕ'micīrcle *n.* Half of circle divided by its diameter, or half its circumference (ill. CIRCLE); anything in this shape. **sĕmicīr'cūlar** *adj.* ~ *canal,* any of the three curving fluid-filled channels, each in a different plane, opening into the cavity of the inner ear, jointly serving to inform the brain of changes in speed and direction during movements of the head (ill. EAR[1]).

sĕ'mi-cō'ke *n.* Fuel obtained by carbonizing coal etc. at low temperature.

sĕmicō'lon *n.* Punctuation-mark (;), indicating a more marked separation than the comma, and less than a full stop or colon.

sĕmi-condŭ'ctor *n.* Electrical conductor with resistance less than that of insulator but greater than that of metal etc.

sĕmi-cy̆'linder *n.* Half of cylinder cut longitudinally. **sĕmicy̆li'ndrical** *adj.*

sĕ'mi-dĕtă'ched (-cht) *adj.* (of house) Joined to another by party wall on one side only.

sĕmifi'nal *adj. & n.* (Match, round) preceding final.

sĕmiflu'id (-ōō-) *adj. & n.* (Substance) of consistency half-way between fluid and solid.

sĕmilū'nar (*or* -lōō-) *adj.* Half-moon-shaped, crescent.

sĕ'minal *adj.* Of seed, semen, or reproduction; germinal, reproductive, propagative; providing a source of future development; ~ *fluid,* semen. **sĕ'minally̆** *adv.*

sĕ'minar *n.* (Meeting of) group of advanced students pursuing special study; meeting for discussion.

sĕ'minary̆ *n.* Place of education (now rare exc. fig. or of R.C. and esp. Jesuit schools for training priests). **sĕ'minarist** *n.* Student in seminary; (hist.) R.C. priest educated in foreign seminary in 16th and 17th centuries, esp. at Douai for English mission.

Sĕ'minōle *adj. & n.* (Member) of tribe of N. Amer. Indians, allied to Creeks, formerly and still partly resident in Florida.

sĕ'mi-offi'cial (-sh*a*l) *adj.* Having some degree of official authority. **sĕ'mi-offi'cially̆** *adv.*

semiology, -otic: see SEMEIO-LOGY.

sĕ'mi-pŏr'celain (-slĭn) *n.* Kind of porcelain of inferior finish, resembling earthenware; kind of earthenware resembling porcelain.

sĕ'mi-prĕ'cious (-sh*u*s) *adj.* (of gems) Of less value than those called 'precious' (as amethyst, jade, garnet, etc.).

sĕ'miquāver *n.* (mus.) Note (♬) half as long as QUAVER.

Sĕmi'ramis. Mythical queen of Assyria of great beauty and wisdom, wife and successor of Ninus, reputed founder of Nineveh; she built many cities, including Babylon; ~ *of the North,* a term applied to (1) Margaret (1353-1412), daughter of Valdemar IV of Denmark and wife of Haakon VI of Norway, who became in 1381 regent of Norway and Denmark, and in 1388 ruler of Sweden; (2) Catherine II of Russia (1729-96), empress of Russia from 1762.

sĕ'mi-sŏ'lid *adj. & n.* Extremely viscous, partially solid (substance).

Sĕ'mite *n.* Member of any of the peoples supposed to be descended from SHEM (Gen. 10), including Jews, Arabs, Assyrians, Phoenicians, and other peoples of SW. Asia.

Sĕmi'tic *adj.* 1. Of the group of languages now spoken chiefly in N. Africa and SW. Asia, including Hebrew, Aramaic, Arabic, ancient Assyrian, and Ethiopic. 2. Of the Semites. ~ *n.* 1. Semitic family of languages. 2. Semite.

Sĕ'mitism *n.* 1. Semitic characteristics; (esp.) Jewish ideas, influence, etc. 2. Semitic word or idiom.

sĕ'mitōne *n.* (mus.) Interval of (approximately) half a tone (ill. SCALE[3]).

sĕ'mivowel *adj. & n.* (Vocal sound) partaking of nature of vowel and consonant, letter (e.g. *w, y*) representing this.

sĕmoli'na (-lē-) *n.* Hard portions of wheat which resist action of millstones and are collected in form of rounded grains and used in milk puddings, for making macaroni, etc.

sĕmpitĕr'nal *adj.* (rhet.) Everlasting, eternal.

sĕ'mplice (-plēchā) *adv.* (mus.) Simply. [It.]

sĕ'mpre (-ā). *adv*: (mus.) Throughout, as in ~ *forte,* loudly throughout. [It.]

sempstress: see SEAMSTRESS.

sĕn *n.* (pl. same). 1/100 of a Brunei dollar; 1/100 of a riel; 1/100 of a rupiah.

SENIOR

S.E.N. *abbrev.* State Enrolled Nurse.

Sen. *abbrev.* Senate; Senator; Senior.

sĕnār'ius *n.* Latin verse of 6 feet, esp. iambic trimeter.

sĕ'nary̆ *adj.* Of the number 6; (of system of numeration) of which radix is 6.

sĕ'nate *n.* 1. (Rom. hist.) Roman legislative and administrative body, orig. of representatives elected by patricians, later of appointed members and actual and former holders of various high offices. 2. Upper and less numerous branch of the legislature in various countries (in U.S. consisting of 2 members from each State of the Union). 3. Governing body of some British and Amer. universities; council in some Amer. colleges composed of members of faculty and elected students, and having control of discipline etc. 4. ~-*house,* place for meetings of senate.

sĕ'nator *n.* Member of senate. **sĕnatōr'ial** *adj.* **sĕ'natorship** *n.*

sĕnd *v.* (past t. & past part. *sĕnt*). Cause to go, dispatch, secure conveyance of, to some destination, *to, into, away,* etc.; drive, cause to go, *into* some condition, *to sleep,* etc.; send message or letter; (of deity) grant, bestow, inflict, bring about, cause to be; ~ *down,* rusticate, expel, from university; ~ *for,* summon; esp., of head of State, summon politician in order to offer him premiership; ~ *off,* send away; witness departure of (person) as sign of respect, etc.; ~-*off* (*n.*); ~ *up,* (esp., colloq.) satirize; ridicule by mimicry; (U.S.) send to prison; ~-*up* (*n.*). **sĕ'nder** *n.*

sĕ'ndal *n.* (hist.) (Garment of) thin rich silk material.

Sĕ'nĕca[1], Lucius Annaeus (*c* 4 B.C.–A.D. 65). Roman Stoic philosopher and author of tragedies; tutor and adviser to Nero; ordered to take his own life on charge of complicity in Piso's conspiracy.

Sĕ'nĕca[2] *n.* One of a numerous and warlike tribe of Iroquoian Indians, formerly occupying W. part of New York State.

Sĕnėga'l (-awl). River of W. Africa; republic of the French Community, lying to the S. of Senegal River; capital, Dakar.

sĕnė'scent *adj.* Growing old. **sĕnė'scence** *n.*

sĕ'nėschal (-sh*a*l) *n.* (hist.) Steward or major-domo in medieval great house.

sĕ'nīle *adj.* Belonging, incident, peculiar, to old age; having weakness of old age; ~ *dementia,* severe mental deterioration in old age. **sĕni'lity̆** *n.*

sĕ'nior *adj.* More advanced in age, older in standing; superior in age or standing *to*; of higher or highest degree; senior to another of the same name; (U.S.) belonging to final year in university,

[801]

school, etc.; ~ *partner*, head of firm; S~ *Service*, Royal Navy; ~ *wrangler*: see WRANGLER.

sēniŏ'rĭtў *n.* **sē'nior** *n.* One superior or worthy of deference etc. by reason of age; person of comparatively long service, standing, etc.; one's elder or superior in length of service, membership, etc.; senior wrangler, student, etc.

sĕni'tĭ (-nē-) *n.* 1/100 of a pa'anga.

sĕ'nna *n.* (Dried pods or leaflets, used as purgative, of) species of *Cassia*.

Sĕnnă'cherĭb (-k-). King of Assyria 705-681 B.C.; invaded Judah in reign of Hezekiah and was forced to retire on account of pestilence among his troops (2 Chron. 32).

sĕ'nnĕt *n.* (hist.) Signal call on trumpet (in stage-directions of Elizabethan plays).

sĕ'nnight (-ĭt) *n.* (archaic) Week. [for *seven-night*]

sĕñōr' (-ny-), **sĕñōr'a, sĕñōrī'ta** (-rē-) *ns.* (Title of or form of address to) Spanish man, woman, young or unmarried woman.

Sĕnou'si, -ssi, Sĕnu'ssi (-ōō-) *n.* Member of N. African Muslim religious sect, noted for fanatical and belligerent attitude, founded *c* 1835 by Sidi Muhammad Ben Ali es-Senousi.

sĕnsā'tion *n.* 1. Consciousness of perceiving or seeming to perceive some state or affection of one's body, its parts or senses, or of one's mind or its emotions; contents of such consciousness. 2. Excited or violent feeling, strong impression, as of horror, surprise, esp. among community; event, person, etc., arousing this. **sĕnsā'tional** *adj.* **sĕnsā'tionallў** *adv.*

sĕnsā'tionalism *n.* 1. (philos.) Theory that sensation is sole source of knowledge. 2. Pursuit of the sensational in literature, journalism, etc.

sĕnse *n.* 1. Any of those faculties, each dependent upon specialized groups of receptors connected with the brain, by which man and other animals are aware of their environment or recognize changes in their own bodily condition such as pain, movement of muscles and joints, or cold and warmth; *the five ~s*, those providing knowledge of the external world (sight, hearing, smell, taste, touch); *~-datum*, element of experience due to stimulation of a sense-organ; *~-organ*, part of body concerned in producing sensation. 2. (pl.) The senses considered as channels for gratifying the desire for pleasure. 3. (pl.) Person's sanity regarded as attested by possession of the senses. 4. Ability to perceive or feel; consciousness *of*; quick or accurate appreciation *of*; instinct regarding, insight into, specified matter. 5. Practical wisdom, judgement, common sense, conformity to these. 6. Meaning, way in which word etc.

is to be understood; intelligibility, coherence, possession of a meaning; *in a ~*, in a way, under limitations. 7. Prevailing sentiment among a number of people. ~ *v.t.* Perceive by sense; (esp.) be vaguely aware of.

sĕ'nselĕss (-sl-) *adj.* 1. Deprived of sensation; unconscious; unfeeling. 2. Extremely foolish. 3. Meaningless, purposeless. **sĕ'nselĕsslў** *adv.* **sĕ'nselĕssnĕss** *n.*

sĕnsĭbi'lĭtў *n.* 1. Capacity to feel. 2. Susceptibility, sensitiveness (*to*); delicacy of feeling; over-sensitiveness.

sĕ'nsĭble *adj.* 1. Perceptible by the senses; great enough to be perceived, appreciable. 2. Aware, not unmindful, *of*. 3. Of good sense, reasonable, judicious; moderate; practical. **sĕ'nsĭblenĕss** *n.* **sĕ'nsĭblў** *adv.*

sĕ'nsĭtĭve *adj.* Having sensibility *to*; very open *to* or acutely affected by external impressions, esp. those made by the moods or opinions of others in relation to oneself; (of instrument etc.) readily responding to or recording slight changes of condition; (chem.) readily affected by or responsive *to* appropriate agent; (photog., of paper, etc.) susceptible to influence of light; ~ *plant*, tropical Amer. plant (*Mimosa pudica*) with leaflets that fold together at slightest touch; plant with similar quality. **sĕ'nsĭtĭvelў** *adv.* **sĕ'nsĭtĭvenĕss, sĕnsĭtĭ'vĭtў** *ns.*

sĕ'nsĭtize *v.t.* Make sensitive; render (photographic paper etc.) sensitive to light; render (organism, tissue) sensitive to substance normally inert, or highly reactive to drug etc.

sĕnsōr'ĭal *adj.* Of the sensorium, sensation or sensory impressions.

sĕnsōr'ĭum *n.* Brain as seat of sensation; whole sensory apparatus.

sĕ'nsorў *adj.* Of sensation or the senses; ~ *nerve*, nerve consisting of fibres conducting impulses from the peripheral sense-organs to the central nervous system.

sĕ'nsūal (*or* -shōō-) *adj.* Of or dependent on the senses only, voluptuous; given to the pursuit of sensual pleasures or gratification of the appetites; licentious. **sĕ'nsūallў** *adv.* **sĕ'nsūalĭsm, sĕ'nsūalĭst, sĕnsūā'lĭtў** *ns.* **sĕnsūalĭ'stic** *adj.*

sĕ'nsŭm *n.* (philos.) SENSE-datum.

sĕ'nsŭous *adj.* Of, derived from, affecting, the senses. **sĕ'nsŭouslў** *adv.* **sĕ'nsŭousnĕss** *n.*

sent: see SEND.

sĕ'ntence *n.* 1. Judgement or decision of court (now rare exc. of decisions of ecclesiastical and admiralty courts); (judicial declaration of) punishment allotted to person condemned in criminal trial (also transf.). 2. (archaic) Pithy or pointed saying, maxim.

3. Series of words in connected speech or writing, forming grammatically complete expression of single thought, and usu. containing subject and predicate, and conveying statement, question, command, or request; loosely, part of writing or speech between two full stops; (mus.) group of two or more phrases forming a unit. ~ *v.t.* Pronounce judicial sentence on, condemn *to* a punishment.

sĕntĕ'ntĭous (-shŭs) *adj.* Aphoristic; full of, given to, pointed maxims; pompously moralizing. **sĕntĕ'ntĭouslў** *adv.* **sĕntĕ'ntĭousnĕss** *n.*

sĕ'ntĭent (-shĭ-) *adj.* Having the power of sense-perception, that feels or is capable of feeling. **sĕ'ntĭence** *n.* **sĕ'ntĭentlў** *adv.*

sĕ'ntĭment *n.* 1. Mental attitude; opinion, view. 2. Mental feeling, emotion, thought or reflection coloured by or proceeding from emotion; emotional thought expressed in literature, art, etc.; feeling or meaning (intended to be) conveyed by passage etc. 3. Refined and tender feeling; emotional weakness, mawkish tenderness, nursing of the emotions. **sĕntĭmĕ'ntal** *adj.* Swayed by or dictated by shallow emotion; designed to excite or gratify the softer emotions. **sĕntĭmĕ'ntallў** *adv.* **sĕntĭmĕ'ntalĭsm, sĕntĭmĕ'ntalĭst, sĕntĭmĕntă'lĭtў** *ns.* **sĕntĭmĕ'ntalĭze** *v.*

sĕ'ntĭnel *n.* Sentry; ~ *crab*, crab of Indian Ocean (*Podophthalmus vigil*) with very long eye-stalks.

sĕ'ntrў *n.* Soldier etc. posted to keep guard; ~*-box*, hut for sentry to stand in; ~*-go*, duty of pacing up and down as sentry.

sĕ'pal *n.* (bot.) One of leaves or divisions of calyx (ill. FLOWER).

sĕ'parate *adj.* Divided or withdrawn from others, detached, shut off; forming a unit that is or may be regarded as apart or by itself, distinct, individual, of individuals. **sĕ'paratelў** *adv.* **sĕ'paratenĕss** *n.* **sĕ'parates** (-ts) *n.pl.* Separate articles of dress suitable for wearing together in various combinations. **sĕ'parāte** *v.* Make separate, sever, disunite; keep from union or contact; part, secede *from*, go different ways; remove (substance) *from* another with which it is combined or mixed, as cream from milk, esp. by some technical process. **sĕ'parable** *adj.*

sĕparā'tion *n.* (esp.) Cessation of conjugal cohabitation without dissolution of marriage tie, either by mutual consent or (*judicial ~*) imposed by judicial decree; ~ *allowance*, allowance made by soldier to his dependants, augmented by Government.

sĕ'paratĭst *n.* One who favours separation; (esp., hist.) one of the 17th-c. Independents separated from the Church of England; one favouring Home Rule for Ireland or secession of southern States from U.S. **sē'paratism** *n.*

sē'parātor *n.* (esp.) Machine or appliance for separating, esp. cream from milk by centrifugal force.

Sĕphār'dim *n.pl.* Jews of Spanish or Portuguese descent. **Sĕphār'dic** *adj.* [mod. Heb., f. *sᵉp̱āraḏ*, a country mentioned once in O.T. and held in late-Jewish tradition to be Spain]

sē'pia *n.* (Rich brown colour of) pigment made from inky secretion of cuttle-fish; a sepia drawing. ~ *adj.* Of colour of sepia; drawn in sepia.

sē'poy *n.* (hist.) Native Indian soldier under European, esp. British, discipline; *S~ Mutiny*, Indian Mutiny. [Hind., f. Pers. *sipāhī* soldier (*sipāh* army)]

sē'psis *n.* (pl. *-es*). State of poisoning of the tissues or bloodstream, caused by bacteria.

sĕpt *n.* Clan, esp. in Ireland.

sĕpt-, sĕpti-, *prefix.* Seven.

Sept. *abbrev.* September.

sē'ptal *adj.* Of a septum or septa. **sē'ptate** *adj.* Having a septum or septa. **sĕptā'tion** *n.*

Sĕptĕ'mber. 9th month of Gregorian (7th of Julian) calendar, with 30 days. [L *septem* seven]

Sĕptĕ'mbrist. (Fr. hist.) Supporter of or participant in massacre of political prisoners in Paris, 2–6 Sept. 1792.

sĕptē'nary *adj.* Of or involving the number 7, on basis of 7, by 7s, septennial. ~ *n.* Set of 7.

sĕptĕ'nnial *adj.* Of, for, (recurring) every, 7 years.. **sĕptĕ'nnially** *adv.*

sĕptĕ't, -ĕtte *n.* 1. (mus.) (Composition for) 7 voices or instruments in combination. 2. Set of 7 persons or things.

sē'ptic *adj.* Putrefying; caused by or in a state of sepsis; ~ *tank*, tank in which organic matter in sewage is rapidly decomposed through agency of anaerobic bacteria. **sē'ptically** *adv.*

sĕpticae'mia *n.* Disease caused by pathogenic bacteria in the blood, blood-poisoning.

sĕptilā'teral *adj.* Seven-sided.

sĕpti'llion (-yon) *n.* 7th power of a million (1 followed by 42 ciphers); (U.S.) 8th power of a thousand (1 followed by 24 ciphers).

sē'ptime *n.* Seventh of the 8 parries in fencing (ill. FENCE).

sĕptūagēnār'ian *adj.* & *n.* (Person) aged 70 or more but less than 80.

Sĕptūagĕ'sima. Third Sunday before Lent. [L, = '70th']

Sĕ'ptūagint *n.* (symbol LXX) Greek version of Old Testament, traditionally said to have been the work of 72 Jewish translators in 3rd c. B.C.; copy of this. [L *Septuaginta* 70]

sē'ptum *n.* (pl. *-ta*). (anat., bot., zool.) Partition, dividing wall,

membrane, layer, etc., e.g. that between the nostrils.

sĕ'ptūple *adj.* & *n.* Sevenfold (amount). ~ Multiply by 7, increase sevenfold.

sĕpŭ'lchral (-k-) *adj.* Of sepulchre(s) or sepulture; suggestive of the tomb, funereal, gloomy, dismal.

sĕ'pulchre (-*ker*) *n.* Tomb, esp. cut in rock or built of stone or brick, burial vault or cave; *Holy S~*, cave in which Jesus Christ was buried outside walls of Jerusalem; *whited ~*, hypocrite (see Matt. 23: 27).

sĕ'pulture *n.* Burying, burial.

seq. *abbrev. Sequens, sequentes, -ia.* [L, = 'the following']

sĕquā'cious (-shus) *adj.* Following, attendant; coherent; lacking independence or originality, servile. **sĕquā'ciously** *adv.* **sĕquăcitȳ** *n.*

sē'quel *n.* What follows after, continuation or resumption of a story, process, etc., after pause or provisional ending; after-effects, upshot.

sĕquē'la *n.* (pl. *-ae*). (path.) Morbid condition or symptom following upon some disease.

sē'quence *n.* 1. (Order of) succession. 2. Set of things belonging next each other on some principle of order, series without gaps. 3. (mus.) Phrase or melody repeated at higher or lower pitch. 4. (eccles.) Composition in metrical prose or accentual metre said or sung after Alleluia and before Gospel. 5. (cinema) Incident in film story recorded consecutively, corresponding to scene of play. 6. (gram.) ~ *of tenses*, rule or practice according to which tense of verb in subordinate clause depends on that of verb in main clause (e.g. *I think you* are, *thought you* were, *wrong*). **sē'quent** *adj.* Following; successive; consecutive. **sĕquĕ'ntial** (-shal) *adj.* **sĕquĕ'ntiallȳ** *adv.*

sĕquĕ'ster *v.t.* 1. Seclude, isolate, set apart. 2. Confiscate, appropriate; seize temporary possession of (debtor's effects).

sĕquĕ'strāte (*or* sē'kwĭs-) *v.t.* = SEQUESTER (sense 2), divert (income of estate or benefice) temporarily from owner into other hands. **sĕquĕstrā'tion** *n.*

sĕquĕ'strum *n.* (path.) Portion of dead tissue, esp. bone, detached from surrounding parts. **sĕquĕ'stral** *adj.*

sē'quin *n.* 1. (hist.) Venetian gold coin. 2. Small circular spangle.

sĕquoi'a (-*a*) *n.* Very tall Californian coniferous tree of genus *S~*. [f. name (*Seqouiah*) of the Cherokee Indian who invented a syllabary for his language]

sérac (sĕră'k) *n.* One of the castellated masses into which a glacier is divided at steep points by the crossing of crevasses (ill. MOUNTAIN). [Swiss Fr., orig. name of a cheese]

sera'glio (-ahlyō) *n.* Walled palace, esp. (hist.) that of sultan at Constantinople; harem.

serai (-ī) *n.* = CARAVANSERAI. [Pers., = 'palace']

sē'raph *n.* (pl. *-im*). 1. (pl. also *-s*). One of the *seraphim*, in bibl. use the living creatures with three pairs of wings, seen in Isaiah's vision as hovering above the throne of God. 2. (pl.) Order of angels (see ANGEL). **sĕră'phic** *adj.* Of, resembling, the seraphim; angelic; *S~ Doctor*, St. BONAVENTURA. **sĕră'phicallȳ** *adv.*

Sĕrā'pis. (Egyptian myth.) God invented and introduced into Egypt by Ptolemy I to unite Greeks and Egyptians in common worship, combining the Egyptian Osiris with attributes of Zeus, Hades, and Aesculapius.

Sĕrb *n.* 1. Member, language, of a Slav tribe settled at the invitation of the emperor Heraclius in the Roman province of Moesia, S. of the Danube and N. of Thrace; Serbian. 2. Serbian language.

Sĕr'bia. Former Balkan kingdom, since 1919 part of Yugoslavia. **Sĕr'bian** *adj.* & *n.* (Native, inhabitant, language) of Serbia. **Sĕrbō-Crōā'tian** (-shian) *adj.* & *n.* Yugoslav.

Sĕrbō'nĭs. Boggy lake in the delta of the Nile, in which whole armies were said to have been swallowed up. **Sĕrbō'nian** *adj.* ~ *bog*, Serbonis; (fig.) difficult position from which escape is impossible.

sēre, sear *adjs.* (now poet. or rhet.) Dry, withered.

sĕrēnā'de *n.* Performance of music at night in open, esp. by lover under lady's window; piece of music suitable for such performance; instrumental composition in several movements. ~ *v.* Entertain with, perform, a serenade.

sĕrēnā'ta (-nah-) *n.* (mus.) Cantata, freq. pastoral, suitable for performance in open air; kind of suite usu. opening with march and including minuet.

Sĕrendi'b (-ēb). One of the ancient names of Sri Lanka.

sĕrendi'pitȳ *n.* Faculty of making happy discoveries by accident. [coined by Horace Walpole f. title of a fairy-tale, 'The Three Princes of Serendip']

sĕrē'ne *adj.* Clear and calm; unruffled; placid, tranquil, unperturbed. **sĕrē'nelȳ** *adv.* **sĕrē'nitȳ** *n.*

sĕrf *n.* Villein, person whose service is attached to the soil and transferred with it (hist.); oppressed person, drudge. **sĕr'fage, sĕr'fdom, sĕr'fhōod** *ns.*

sĕrge *n.* Kind of durable twilled worsted cloth. [L *serica* silk f. *Seres* the Chinese]

sergeant (sār'jant) *n.* Non-commissioned officer above corporal; police officer ranking

[803]

between inspector and constable; ~-at-arms: see SERJEANT, sense 2. ~-major, non-commissioned officer of highest grade.

Sergt abbrev. Sergeant.

sēr'ial adj. Of, in, forming, a series; (of story etc.) issued in instalments. **sēr'iallў** adv. **sēr'ial** n. Serial story. **sēr'ialize** v.t.

sĕriā'tim (or sēr-) adv. One after another, one by one in succession.

Sēr'ic adj. (rhet. etc.) Chinese.

sĕr'iculture n. Silkworm-breeding, production of raw silk.

sēr'ies (-z; or -iz) n. (pl. same). Succession, sequence, or set of similar or similarly related things etc.; set of successive issues of periodical, of literary compositions, of books issued by one publisher in common form and with some similarity of subject or purpose etc.; (geol.) set of strata with common characteristic; (chem.) group of elements with common properties or of compounds related in composition and structure; (math.) set of terms constituting progression or having common relation between successive terms; (elect.) set of circuits so arranged (in ~) that same current traverses all circuits (ill. CIRCUIT); (zool.) number of connected genera, families, etc.

sĕ'rif n. Cross-line finishing off a stroke of a letter (ill TYPE).

sĕ'rigraph (or -ahf) n. Print made by serigraphy. **sĕrī'graphў** n. SCREEN printing. **sĕrī'grapher** n.

sĕ'rin n. Small greenish finch (of genus Serinus) of Mediterranean countries, esp. S. canarius, wild canary.

sĕrinĕ'tte n. Instrument for teaching cage-birds to sing.

sĕriō-cō'mic adj. Partly serious and partly comic.

sēr'ious adj. Grave in appearance, manner, intention, purpose, etc., solemn, earnest, not frivolous, trifling, or playful; requiring earnest thought or application; important, not slight; earnest about things of religion, religious-minded. **sēr'iouslў** adv. **sēr'-iousnĕss** n.

serjeant (sār'jant) n. 1. (hist., also ~-at-law) Member of superior order of barristers (abolished 1880) from which Common Law judges were chosen; Common S~, circuit judge sitting at Central Criminal Court, appointed by Corporation of London as assistant to Recorder. 2. ~-at-arms, title of certain court, parliamentary, and city officials with ceremonial duties, esp., officer of each House of Parliament with duty of enforcing commands of the house, arresting offenders, etc.; officer with corresponding duties under other legislative assemblies; Serjeants' Inn, collegiate building of the now extinct order of serjeants-at-law, esp. that in Chancery Lane, London.

sĕr'mon n. Discourse delivered from pulpit and usu. based on text of Scripture, by way of religious exhortation or instruction; similar discourse on religious or moral subject delivered elsewhere or published; moral reflection(s), homily. S~ on the Mount, discourse of Christ recorded in Matt. 5-7. **sĕr'monize** v.

sēr'ous adj. Of, like, serum; whey-like; ~ gland, gland elaborating a watery, as opposed to a mucous, secretion; ~ membrane, delicate membrane lining closed cavities of the body.

sĕr'pent n. 1. Snake, esp. large snake; treacherous person. 2. Kind of firework with serpentine motion in air or on ground; Pharaoh's ~: see PHARAOH. 3. (mus.) Obsolete bass wind instrument of long wooden tube with several U-shaped bends, with finger-holes and mouthpiece like that of trumpet. 4. Curved or coiling object or part (esp., part of matchlock, ill. MUSKET).

sĕr'pentine adj. Of or like a serpent; writhing, coiling, tortuous, sinuous; cunning, subtle, treacherous; ~ verse, line beginning and ending with same word. ~ n. 1. (hist.) Kind of cannon. 2. Dull-green (or occas. red or brown) soft rock or mineral, chiefly hydrated magnesium silicate, with markings resembling those of snake's skin. 3. Waving or sinuous thing or line; the S~, ornamental water in Hyde Park, London.

sĕrpī'ginous adj. (of skin disease etc.) Creeping from one part to another. **sĕrpī'gō** n. Any creeping or spreading skin disease.

sĕ'rrate, sĕrrā'tĕd adjs. Having, forming, row of small projections like teeth of saw; notched like saw. **sĕrrā'tion** n.

sĕrrā'tus adj. (of muscle) Having serrated processes (~ anterior muscle, ill. MUSCLE).

sĕ'rried (-rĭd) adj. (of ranks etc.) Pressed close together, in close order, crowded.

sēr'um n. 1. Amber-coloured liquid which separates from clot when blood coagulates. 2. Blood serum as antitoxin or therapeutic agent; ~ eruption, sickness, manifestations following serum injection, e.g. skin eruption, fever, swelling of joints. 3. Watery animal fluid.

sĕr'val n. Long-legged African cat-like animal, Felis serval, with tawny black-spotted coat and large ears.

sĕr'vant n. One who has undertaken, usu. in return for salary or wages, to carry out orders of individual or corporate employer, esp. one who waits on master or mistress or performs domestic duties in household; devoted follower, person willing to serve another; C~ Servant: see CIVIL; public ~, State official; your obedient ~,

epistolary form preceding signature (now only in letters of official type).

sĕrve v. 1. Be servant (to), render service, be useful (to); be employed (in army, navy, etc.); be soldier, sailor, etc. (in war, against enemy, etc.); ~ at table, act as waiter. 2. Meet needs (of), avail, suffice, satisfy; perform function, be suitable, do what is required for; ~ one's apprenticeship, go through training; ~ sentence, undergo it; ~ (one's) time, undergo imprisonment, serve a sentence; serve apprenticeship. 3. Dish up, set (food) on table; set out ready; distribute; supply (person with); make legal delivery of (writ etc.), deliver writ etc. to (person); set ball, set (ball) in play; (tennis etc.) start play by striking ball towards opponent, into opposite court, etc.; (of male animal) cover (the female). **sĕr'ver** n. One who serves; (esp.) celebrant's assistant who arranges altar and makes responses. **sĕrve** n. (tennis etc.) = SERVICE[1], 5.

Sēr'via. Former name (until 1914) of SERBIA. **Sēr'vian**[1] adj. & n.

Sēr'vian[2] adj. Of, pertaining to, SERVIUS TULLIUS; ~ Wall, wall built around Rome by Servius Tullius.

sĕr'vice[1] n. 1. Being servant, serving a master; work or duty of a servant; duty which feudal tenant was bound to render to lord; person's disposal or behalf; use, assistance. 2. Department of royal or public employ or of work done to meet some general need; persons engaged, employment, in this, esp. army, navy, or air force; (attrib.) belonging, issued, etc., to armed force. 3. Liturgical form or office appointed for use on some occasion; single meeting of congregation for worship; musical setting of (parts of) liturgical service. 4. Legal serving of or of writ etc. 5. Act of serving ball in tennis etc., way of doing this, ball served. 6. Set of dishes, plates, etc., required for serving meal. 7. Set of trains, steamers, buses, etc., plying at stated times; supply or laying-on of gas, water, etc., through pipes to private houses etc.; provision of what is necessary for the due maintenance of a thing, esp. maintenance and repair work carried out by vendor after sale. 8. ~ area, (esp.) area surrounding broadcasting station within which reception is assured; ~ dress, ordinary uniform (opp. to full dress); ~ flat, one in which domestic service is provided by the management; ~ hatch, opening in wall through which dishes are passed from kitchen to dining-room; ~ industry, one providing services (as electricity, gas, etc.), not goods; ~-line, line marking limit short of which service must fall (ill. LAWN[2]); ~ module, module containing main

[804]

engine and power supplies of spacecraft; ~ *pipe*, one conveying water or gas from the main to a building; ~ *road*, road constructed and situated for convenient service of houses etc. lying off the main road. ~ *v.t.* Provide service for, do routine maintenance work on.

sẽr'vice² *n.* (also ~-*tree*) European tree (*Sorbus domestica*), like mountain ash, with small round or pear-shaped fruit edible when overripe; (also ~-*berry*) Amer. small tree or shrub (*Amelanchier canadensis*), with berry-like fruits, shad-bush.

sẽr'viceable (-sa-) *adj.* Profitable, useful, capable of rendering service; durable, hard-wearing, for rough or ordinary use rather than ornament. sẽr'viceableness *n.* sẽr'viceably *adv.*

sẽrviĕ'tte *n.* Table-napkin.

sẽr'vile *adj.* Of, being, suitable to, a slave or slaves; slavish, cringing, fawning, mean-spirited. sẽr'vilely (-l-li) *adv.* sẽrvĭ'litў *n.*

sẽr'vitor *n.* (archaic) Attendant, henchman, servant.

sẽr'vitūde *n.* Slavery, subjection, bondage.

Sẽr'vius Tŭ'llius. Semi-legendary 6th king of Rome (6th c. B.C.).

sẽr'vō-mē'chanĭsm (-k-) *n.* Power-assisted device usu. for controlling movement (e.g. a brake), freq. deriving its power from the source of energy over which it exercises control. sẽr'vōcontrō'l *n.* sẽr'vō-assĭ'stĕd *adj.*

sĕ'samĕ *n.* (Seeds of) E. Indian herbaceous plant (*Sesamum indicum*) yielding oil and used as food; *open* ~, password or charm at which doors or barriers fly open (see ALI BABA).

sĕ'samoid *adj.* Shaped like a sesame-seed, nodular (esp. of small independent bones developed in tendons passing over angular structure, as the kneecap or the navicular bone). ~ *n.* Sesamoid bone.

sēsqui- *prefix.* One and a half, the ratio 3:2, etc.

sēsquicĕntĕ'nnial *adj.* & *n.* (Of) 150th anniversary.

sēsquipĕdā'lian *adj.* (of word) One and a half feet long; cumbrous, pedantic.

sĕ'ssile *adj.* (bot., zool.) Immediately attached; without footstalk, peduncle, etc. (ill. INFLORESCENCE).

sĕ'ssion *n.* Sitting, continuous series of sittings, term of such sittings, of court, legislative or administrative body, etc., for conference or transaction of business; period between opening and prorogation of English parliament; (Sc., U.S., and in some English universities, etc.) part of year during which instruction is given; *Court of S*~, supreme civil court in Scotland; *petty* ~*s*, MAGISTRATES' courts. sĕ'ssional *adj.*

sĕ'stẽrce *n.* Ancient Roman coin, ¼ of denarius. sĕstẽr'tium (-sh*u*m) *n.* One thousand sesterces.

sĕstĕ't *n.* Sextet; last six lines of sonnet.

sĕt¹ *v.* (past t. & past part. *sĕt*).
1. Put, lay, stand; apply (thing) *to*; station, place ready; place, turn, in right or specified position or direction; dispose suitably for use, action, or display; plant (seed etc.) in ground; give sharp edge to (razor), bend teeth of (saw) alternately; ~ *sail*, hoist sail; begin voyage; ~ *table*, lay table for meal; ~ (*up*) *type*, arrange it for printing. 2. Join, attach, fasten; fix; determine, decide, appoint, settle, establish; put parts of (broken bone etc.) into right relative position after fracture or dislocation; insert (precious stone etc.) in gold etc. as frame or foil; 3. Bring by placing, arranging, etc., into specified state; make sit down *to* task, cause *to work*, apply oneself *to work*; exhibit or arrange as pattern or as material to be dealt with; draw up (questions, paper) to be answered by examinees; make insertions in (surface) *with*; ~ *to music*, provide (song, words) with music usu. composed for the purpose. 4. Put or come into a settled or rigid position or state; curdle, solidify, harden; take shape, develop into definiteness; fix (hair) when damped so that it dries in desired style. 5. (of sun, moon, etc.) Appear to descend towards and below horizon. 6. (of tide, current, etc.) Have motion, gather force, sweep along; show or feel tendency. 7. (of sporting dog) Take rigid attitude indicating presence of game; (of dancers) take position facing partners; (of garment) adapt itself to figure, sit *well, badly*, etc. 8. ~ *about*, begin, take steps towards; (colloq.) set on, attack; ~ *back*, impede or reverse progress of; (U.S. slang) cost (person) specified amount; ~-*back* (*n.*) reversal or arrest of progress; ~ *down*, put in writing; attribute *to*, explain or describe oneself *as*; allow (passenger) to alight; ~ *in*, arise, get vogue, become established; fit (part of garment) into the rest; ~ *off*, act as adornment or foil to, enhance, make more striking; start (person) laughing, talking, etc.; begin journey; ~-*off* (*n.*) thing set off against another, thing of which the amount or effect may be deducted from another by opposite tendency; counterpoise, counterclaim; embellishment, adornment *to* something; (archit.) sloping or horizontal member connecting lower and thicker part of wall etc. with upper receding part; ~ *on*, urge (dog etc.) to attack (person etc.); attack; ~ *out*, demonstrate; exhibit; declare; begin journey; ~ *to*, begin doing something, esp. fighting or arguing, vigorously; ~-*to* (*n.*) combat, esp. with fists; ~ *up*, start; occasion, cause; establish (person, oneself) in some capacity; place in view; raise, begin to utter (cry, protest, etc.); propound (theory); prepare (machine) for operation; ~-*up* (*n.*) manner or position in which a thing is set up; (orig. U.S.) structure or arrangement of an organization, or the like; ~ *up for*, make pretension to the character of.

sĕt² *adj.* (esp.) Unmoving; fixed; (of persons) determined or resolved *on*; (of speech) composed beforehand; (of phrases) customary; ~ *fair*, (of weather) fine without sign of breaking; ~ *piece*, fireworks arranged on scaffolding etc.; formal or elaborate arrangement, esp. in art or literature; *of* ~ *purpose*, intentionally, deliberately; ~ *scene*, stage-scene built up of more or less solid material; ~ *square*, draughtsman's appliance for drawing lines at certain angles, consisting of a plate of wood, metal, etc., in shape of right-angled triangle, with other angles of 60° and 30°, or 45° (ill. SQUARE).

sĕt³ *n.* 1. Number of things or persons belonging together as essentially similar or complementary; group, clique, collection; (tennis etc.) group of games counting as unit to side winning more than half of them; radio or television receiving apparatus. 2. Slip or shoot for planting; young fruit just set. 3. (poet.) Setting *of* sun or day. 4. Way current, wind, opinion, etc., sets; drift or tendency *of*; configuration, conformation, habitual posture; warp, bend, displacement, caused by continued pressure or position; (amount of) alternate deflexion of saw-teeth; fixing of damped hair. 5. Last coat of plaster on wall; timber frame supporting gallery etc. in coal-mine; width of body of type in printing (ill. TYPE); clutch of eggs; badger's burrow; granite paving-block; setter's pointing in presence of game; *dead* ~, pointed attack, determined onslaught *at* or *against*. 6. Theatrical or cinema setting, stage furniture, etc.

Sĕt⁴. (Egyptian myth.) God of evil, brother (or son) of Osiris and his constant enemy; represented with head of beast with long pointed snout.

sĕ'ta *n.* (pl. -*ae*). (bot., zool.) Stiff hair, bristle (ill. EARTHWORM). sĕtā'ceous (-sh*u*s) *adj.* Having bristles, bristle-like.

Sĕth. Third son of Adam (Gen. 4:25).

sĕ'ton *n.* (veterinary surg.) Thread or skein of thread drawn through fold of skin to promote drainage etc.

sĕtt *n.* Var. of SET³, in various technical uses; (esp.) paving-block.

sĕttee' *n.* Long seat with back and usu. arms, for more than one person (ill. SOFA).

sĕ'tter *n.* 1. (also ~-*up*) Worker who prepares a machine for an

[805]

operation, as dist. from the *machinist* who operates it. 2. One of several varieties of sporting dogs, with long silky coat, trained to stand rigid on scenting game, as *English* ~, white with brownish and black markings, *Gordon* ~, black with tan markings, *Irish* ~, dark red or chestnut colour. **sĕ'tting** *n.* (esp.) 1. Music to which words are set. 2. Frame in which jewel is set; surroundings or environment of anything; mounting of play, film, etc., scenery, stage furniture, etc. **sĕ'ttle**¹ *n.* Bench with high back and arms, and freq. with box or chest under seat (ill. SOFA). **sĕ'ttle**² *v.* 1. Establish, become established, in more or less permanent abode, place, or way of life; (cause to) sit down (or *down*) to stay for some time; cease from wandering, motion, change, disturbance, or turbidity; bring to, attain, fixity, composure, certainty, decision, etc., determine, decide, appoint. 2. Colonize, establish colonists in, settle as colonists in (country). 3. Subside, sink to bottom of liquid or into lower position. 4. Deal effectually with, dispose or get rid of, do for; pay (bill), pay bill; ~ *up* (*accounts*), draw up accounts and liquidate balance; *settling-day*, (esp.) fortnightly account day at Stock Exchange. 5. Bestow legally for life *on*. **sĕ'ttlement** (-lm-) *n.* (esp.) 1. (law) Conveyance of, creation of estate(s) in, property, esp. on marriage. 2. Company of social workers established in poor or crowded district to give educational, medical, recreational, etc., services. 3. Newly settled tract of country, colony. 4. *Act of S*~, Act (1701) by which succession to British Crown was settled upon the Electress Sophia of Hanover and her descendants. **sĕ'ttler** *n.* (esp.) One who settles in new colony or newly developed country, early colonist. **sĕ'ttlor** *n.* (law) One who makes a settlement of property. **sĕ'ven** *adj.* Amounting to seven, ~ *deadly sins*, pride, lechery, envy, anger, covetousness, gluttony, sloth; *S*~ *Dials*, district of London, formerly of narrow and squalid streets, with open space from which seven streets radiated, having a hexagonal (not seven-sided) column in centre with sundials at top; ~-*league boots*, (in fairy story of Hop-o'-my-Thumb) boots enabling wearer to go 7 leagues at each stride; ~ *sages of Greece*, Thales of Miletus, Solon of Athens, Bias of Priene, Chilo of Sparta, Cleobulus of Rhodes, Periander of Corinth, and Pittacus of Mytilene, to each of whom some wise maxim is attributed by ancient writers; ~ *seas*: see SEA; *S*~ *Sisters*, the PLEIADES; *S*~ *Sleepers*, in early Christian legend,

7 noble Christian youths of Ephesus who fell asleep in a cave while fleeing from the Decian persecution and woke 187 years later; *S*~ *Weeks' War*, that of 1866 between Austria and Prussia, as result of which Prussia became the predominant German power; *S*~ *Wonders of the World*, structures regarded as the most remarkable monuments of antiquity: the Pyramids, the Mausoleum at Halicarnassus, the Hanging Gardens of Babylon, the temple of Artemis at Ephesus, Pheidias's statue of Zeus at Olympia, the Colossus of Rhodes, and the Pharos at Alexandria; *S*~ *Years' War*, that waged 1756–63 by France, Austria, and Russia against Frederick the Great of Prussia and Gt Britain, in which France lost to Britain her possessions in America and India. ~ *n.* One more than six; symbol for this (7, vii, or VII); card with 7 pips; 7 o'clock; size etc. indicated by 7; set of 7 things or persons. **sĕ'venteen** *adj. & n.* One more than sixteen (17, xvii, or XVII). **sĕ'venteenth** *adj. & n.* **sĕ'venth** *adj.* Next after sixth; ~ *day*, Saturday (in Quaker speech and among sects keeping Saturday as sabbath); *S*~-*day Adventists*, millenarian and sabbatarian sect; ~ *heaven*, abode of supreme bliss, highest of 7 heavens in Muslim and some Jewish systems. **sĕ'venthly** *adv.* In the seventh place. **sĕ'venth** *n.* Seventh part (see PART¹, 1); seventh thing etc.; (mus.) interval of which the span involves 7 alphabetical names of notes (ill. INTERVAL); harmonic combination of notes thus separated. **sĕ'ventỳ** *adj.* Amounting to seventy; ~-*five* (*n.*) 75-mm gun; ~-*four*, (hist.) warship with 74 guns. ~ *n.* Cardinal number, seven times ten (70, lxx, or LXX); set of 70 things or persons; *seventies*, (pl.) numbers etc. from 70 to 79; these years of century or life. **sĕ'ventieth** *adj. & n.* **sĕ'ver** *v.* Separate, divide, part, disunite; cut or break off, take away, (part) from whole. **sĕ'verance** *n.* **sĕ'veral** *adj.* 1. Separate, distinct, individual, respective. 2. A few, more than two or three but not many. ~ *pron.* A moderate number of persons or things. **sĕ'verally** *adv.* **sĕ'veraltỳ** *n.* Individual or unshared tenure of estate etc. **sĕvēr'e** *adj.* Austere, strict, harsh; violent, vehement, extreme; trying, making great demands on endurance, energy, skill, etc.; unadorned, without redundance, restrained. **sĕvēr'elỳ** *adv.* **sĕvē'ritỳ** *n.* **Sévigné** (sāvēnyā), Marie de Rabutin-Chantal, Marquise de (1626–96). French letter-writer, whose letters to her daughter give a vivid picture of age of Louis XIV.

Sĕvi'lle (*or* sĕ'-). (Span. *Sevilla*) City and province of Andalusia, Spain; ~ *orange*, bitter orange, *Citrus aurantium*. **Sèvres** (sĕvr). Town near Paris, site of the French national porcelain factory, which was orig. a private undertaking at Vincennes, and was moved to Sèvres, under Louis XV's patronage, in 1756; porcelain from this factory. **sew** (sō) *v.* (past t. *sewed* pr. sōd, past part. *sewn* pr. sōn, *sewed*). Fasten, join (pieces of material, leather, etc.) by passing thread through series of punctures made by needle carrying the thread or with an awl; make by sewing; fasten together sheets of (book) by passing thread or wire through back fold of each sheet; use needle and thread or sewing-machine; *sewing-machine*, machine for sewing or stitching. **sew'age** (sū-) *n.* The spent water supply of a community, including wastes from domestic and trade premises etc. and ground water; ~ (*disposal*) *works*, plant for purifying sewage by artificial methods, rendering it fit for discharge into a river, lake, or tidal waters; ~ *farm*, agricultural land used for the treatment of sewage, portions being used in rotation for sewage disposal, cultivation, and crops. ~ *v.t.* Irrigate, fertilize, with sewage. **sew'er**¹ (sū-) *n.* Pipe or conduit for conveying sewage; ~-*gas*, foul air of sewers. ~ *v.t.* Provide, drain, with sewers. **sew'erage** *n.* **sew'er**² (sū-) *n.* (hist.) Attendant at meal who arranged table, seated guests, and superintended serving and tasting of dishes. **sĕx** *n.* Sum of the physiological differences in structure and function which distinguish the male from the female in animals and plants; males or females collectively; (loosely) sexual instincts, desires, etc., or their manifestation; sexual intercourse; (attrib.) arising from sex; ~ *appeal*, qualities attracting members of the opposite sex; ~ *chromosome*, one affecting the determination of sex of an organism; ~-*limited*, (of Mendelian character) expressed only in one sex although the controlling gene is not on a sex chromosome; ~-*linked*, (of Mendelian character) controlled by a gene which is carried on a sex chromosome. **sĕ'xlĕss** *adj.* **sĕx-**, **sĕxi-** *prefix.* Six. **sĕxagēnār'ian** *adj. & n.* (Person) aged 60 years or more but less than 70. **sĕxagē'narỳ** *adj.* Of 60; composed of, proceeding by, sixties. **Sĕxagē'sima.** Second Sunday before Lent. [L, = '60th'] **sĕxagē'simal** *adj.* Proceeding by sixties; of, based on, involving, division into 60 equal parts; ~ *fraction*, one whose denominator is 60 or a power of 60. **sĕxagē'simallỳ** *adv.*

sĕxcĕntē'narў adj. & n. (Of) 600 (esp. years); (of) 600th anniversary.

sĕxĕ'nnĭal adj. Lasting, (occurring) once in, 6 years.

sĕxĭ'llion (-yon) n. 6th power of a million (1 followed by 36 ciphers); (U.S.) 7th power of a thousand (1 followed by 21 ciphers).

Sĕxt n. (R.C. Ch.) Canonical HOUR, (orig. said at) sixth hour of day (noon).

sĕ'xtan adj. (archaic, of fever) With paroxysm every 5th (by inclusive reckoning 6th) day.

sĕ'xtant n. Instrument with mirrors and graduated arc of 6th part of circle, used by navigators

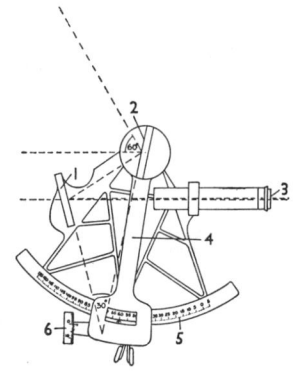

NAVIGATION SEXTANT

1. Horizon mirror. 2. Index mirror. 3. Eyepiece of telescope. 4. Index arm. 5. Graduated arc. 6. Decimal micrometer. The dotted lines indicate the direction of light from sun or star and horizon

for finding position by measuring altitudes of heavenly bodies or horizontal angles between terrestrial objects.

sĕxtĕ't, -ĕ'tte n. 1. (mus.) (Composition for) 6 voices or instruments in combination. 2. Set of 6 persons or things.

sĕxtĭ'llion (-yon) n. = SEXILLION.

sĕxtŏdĕ'cĭmō n. (abbrev. 16mo) Sheet of paper folded in 16 leaves; this way of folding; book of such sheets.

sĕ'xton n. Church officer having care of fabric and contents of church, and freq. with duties of bell-ringer and grave-digger.

sĕ'xtŭple adj. & n. Sixfold (amount). ~ v. Multiply by 6.

sĕ'xŭal (or -kshoō-) adj. 1. Of sex; of, occurring between, the two sexes; ~ intercourse, copulation, esp. of man and woman. 2. (biol.) Having sex or sexual organs; reproducing by union of male and female gametes (opp. asexual). 3. (bot., of classification) Based on distinction of sexes in plants. sĕ'xŭally adv. sĕ'xŭalist, sĕxŭā'lĭtў ns.

sĕ'xŭalĭze (or -kshoō-) v.t. Make sexual, attribute sex to. sĕxŭalĭzā'tion n.

sĕ'xў adj. (colloq.) Sexually attractive or provocative; engrossed with sex.

Seychelles (sāshĕ'lz). Group of islands in the Indian Ocean, since 1810 in British possession.

Sey'mour (sēmôr), Jane (c 1509-37). 3rd queen of Henry VIII of England and mother of Edward VI.

sf. abbrev. Sforzando.
s.f. abbrev. Sub finem.
S.F. abbrev. Science fiction.
S.F.A. abbrev. Scottish Football Association.

sfŏrzā'ndō (-ts-) adj., n. (pl. -os), & adv. (Passage performed) with sudden emphasis. [It.]

sfuma'tō (-oōmah-) adj. (painting) Having indistinct, blurred, outlines. [It., = 'smoked']

s.g. abbrev. Specific gravity.

s.g.d.g. abbrev. Sans guarantie du gouvernement (Fr., = without government guarantee).

Sgt abbrev. Sergeant.

sh int. = HUSH.

shă'bbў adj. Contemptible, paltry, dishonourable; dingy and faded from wear or exposure; worn, dilapidated; shabbily dressed; ~-genteel, attempting to look genteel or keep up appearances in spite of shabbiness. shă'bbĭlў adv. shă'bbĭnĕss n.

shăck n. (orig. U.S. & Canada) Roughly built hut or shanty. ~ v.i. ~ up (with), (slang) live (with) as husband and wife without marriage.

shă'ckle n. Metal loop or staple, bow of padlock, link closed

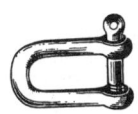

SHACKLE

by bolt for connecting chains etc., coupling link; (pl.) fetters, impediments, restraints; ~-bolt, bolt for closing shackle; bolt with shackle on end. ~ v.t. Fetter, impede, trammel.

Shă'ckleton (-lt-), Sir Ernest Henry (1874-1922). Irish-born explorer, whose ship, the Endurance, was crushed in the ice when he tried to cross the Antarctic, 1914-16.

shăd n. Any of various deep-bodied herring-like fishes of genus Alosa, much used as food; ~-berry, ~-bush, service-berry.

shă'ddock n. (Tree, Citrus grandis, bearing) largest citrus fruit, esp. large coarse pear-shaped varieties of this (the smaller and rounder being called grapefruit). [Capt. Shaddock, who introduced the plants into Barbados (1696)]

shāde n. 1. Comparative or partial darkness, esp. caused by more or less opaque object intercepting rays of sun or other source of light; comparative obscurity;

darker part of picture; (freq. pl.) place sheltered from sun, cool or sequestered retreat; (pl.) darkness of night or evening; the ~s, the abode of the dead, Hades. 2. Colour, esp. with regard to its depth or as distinguished from one nearly like it; gradation of colour; (painting) colour darkened by admixture of black; darker tone of a colour as dist. from tint. 3. Slight difference, small amount; unsubstantial or unreal thing. 4. Soul after death, ghost, disembodied spirit. 5. Screen excluding or moderating light, heat, etc.; eye-shield; glass cover for object. shā'delĕss (-dl-) adj. shāde v. Screen from excessive light; cover, keep off, or moderate power of (luminous object, light) with or as intervening object; make dark or gloomy; darken (parts of drawing etc.), esp. with parallel pencil lines, to give effects of light and shade or gradations of colour; (of colour, opinion, etc.) pass off by degrees into another colour or variety, make pass thus into another. shā'dĕd adj. shā'dĭng n.

shădoō'f, shădu'f (-oōf) n. Primitive device for raising water with bucket and pulley, used esp. in irrigation in Egypt etc.

shā'dow (-ō) n. 1. Shade; dark part of picture, room, etc.; patch of shade, dark figure projected by body intercepting rays of light, this regarded as appendage of person or thing; (fig.) inseparable attendant or companion. 2. Reflected image; delusive semblance or image; type, foreshadowing, adumbration; slightest trace; phantom, ghost. 3. Protection, shelter. 4. ~-boxing, boxing against imaginary opponent as form of training; ~ cabinet, a cabinet of the prospective members of which are at present in the Opposition; ~ factory, factory erected (sometimes duplicating an existing one) as a provision for future production (esp. of war materials); ~ square, device for giving tangents and cotangents, used by astronomer to deduce altitude of sun (i.e. angle subtended at observer between sun and horizon) from length of shadow cast by vertical gnomon on horizontal plane (ill. QUADRANT). shā'dowlĕss, shā'dowў adjs. shā'dow v.t. 1. Cast shadow over. 2. Indicate obscurely, set forth dimly or in slight outline, prefigure. 3. Follow closely; follow and watch secretly.

Shā'drăch (-k). One of three Jewish youths who came unharmed from a furnace into which they were thrown by Nebuchadnezzar (Dan. 3).

shaduf: see SHADOOF.

shā'dў adj. 1. Affording shade; shaded; on the ~ side of, older than (specified age). 2. Not able to bear the light, disreputable, of doubtful honesty. shā'dĭlў adv. shā'dĭnĕss n.

[807]

Shā′fīite (or shah-) adj. & n. (Member) of one of four sects of Sunnites. [f. Muhammad ibn Idrīs al-Shāfi'ī (767–819) their founder]
shaft (-ah-) n. 1. Long slender rod forming body of spear, lance, or arrow; spear (archaic); arrow; ray of light, streak of lightning. 2. Stem; part of column between base and capital (ill. ORDER); upright part of cross; part of chimney above roof; rib of feather (ill. FEATHER); more or less long, narrow, and straight part supporting or connecting part(s) of greater thickness etc.; part of golf-club between handle and head; handle, haft, of tool, etc. 3. (mech.) Long cylindrical rotating rod upon which are fixed parts for transmission of motive power in machine. 4. One of long bars between pair of which horse is harnessed to vehicle (ill. CART). 5. Vertical or inclined well-like excavation giving access to mine, tunnel, etc. (ill. MINE²); any similar well-like excavation or passage, as that in which lift runs etc.; ~ grave, (archaeol.) grave consisting of deep rectangular pit.
Sha′ftesburȳ(-ahfts-). Anthony Ashley Cooper, 3rd Earl of ~ (1671–1713), English moral philosopher; Anthony Ashley Cooper, 7th Earl of ~ (1801–85), philanthropist, active in many movements for the protection of the working classes and the benefit of the poor.
shǎg n. 1. Rough growth or mass of hair etc. 2. (archaic) Long-napped rough cloth. 3. Strong coarse kind of cut tobacco. 4. Cormorant, esp. *Phalacrocorax aristotelis*.
shǎ′ggȳ adj. Hairy, rough-haired; hirsute, villous; covered with rough tangled vegetation; (of hair) rough, coarse, tangled; ~ *dog story*, type of anecdote (orig. about a talking animal) with much detail and peculiar twist of humour at end. **shǎ′ggilȳ** adv. **shǎ′gginěss** n.
shagree′n n. Kind of untanned leather with rough granular surface made from skin of horse, ass, shark, seal, etc., and freq. dyed green; imitation of this; hard rough skin of some sharks, rays, etc., covered with calcified papillae, used for polishing.
shah n. Title of the sovereign ruler of Iran. [Pers., = 'king']
shaikh (-āk) n. Var. of SHEIKH.
shāke v. (past t. *shŏŏk*, past part. *shā′ken*). Move violently or quickly up and down or to and fro; (cause to) tremble, rock, or vibrate; jolt, jar; brandish; weaken, make less firm or stable; agitate, shock, disturb; ~ *down*, fell, remove, fetch or send down by shaking; *sha′kedown*, improvised bed; ~ *hand*(s), clasp right hands at meeting or parting, over concluded bargain, in congratulation, etc.; ~ *head*, move it from side to side in refusal, negation, disapproval, concern, etc.; ~ *off*,

get rid of by shaking; ~ *out*, empty of contents or dust, empty (contents or dust) from vessel, etc., by shaking; spread or open (sail, flag, etc.); ~ *up*, mix, loosen, by shaking; rouse with or as with shaking. ~ n. Shaking, being shaken; jolt, jerk, shock; crack in growing timber; (mus.) trill, rapid alternation of note with the note above; = MILK-shake; *no great* ~s, (colloq.) not very good.
shā′ker n. (esp.) 1. Vessel in which ingredients of cocktails are shaken. 2. *S*~, member of Amer. religious celibate sect living in mixed communities, orig. founded (1747) in Manchester, England, by secession from the Quakers, and named from dancing movements which formed part of their worship.
Shā′kespeare (-kspēr), William (1564–1616). England's greatest dramatist and poet. **Shākespear′ian** adj. ~ *sonnet*: see SONNET.
shǎ′kō n. Military cap, more or less cylindrical, with peak and upright plume or tuft (ill. CAVALRY). [Magyar *csákó*]
shā′kȳ adj. Unsteady, trembling, unsound, infirm; unreliable. **shā′kilȳ** adv. **shā′kinĕss** n.
shāle n. Very fine-grained laminated sedimentary rock consisting of consolidated mud or clay; ~-*oil*, oil obtained from bituminous shale. **shā′lȳ** adj.
shǎll (*unstressed* shăl *or* shl) v.aux. (past & conditional *should* pr. shŏŏd). Forming compound tenses or moods expressing: (1) (in 1st pers.) simple future action; (2) (in other persons) command; (3) (in all persons) obligation, intention, necessity, etc.
shallŏŏ′n n. Light twilled woollen fabric used chiefly for linings. [f. *Châlons*-sur-Marne, France]
shǎ′llop n. Light open boat for shallow water.
shallŏ′t n. Onion-like plant, *Allium ascalonicum*, native to Syria, with small clustered bulbs, resembling but milder than those of garlic, used for flavouring. [Fr. *eschalotte*, dim. of *eschaloigne* f. L *ascalonia*, f. *Ascalon* in Palestine]
shā′llow (-ō) adj. Of little depth (lit. & fig.), superficial, trivial. **shā′llowlȳ** adv. **shā′llownĕss** n. **shā′llow** n. Shallow place, shoal. ~ v. Become shallower; make shallow.
sha′lwār (-ŭlv-) n. Loose trousers worn by both sexes in some countries of S. Asia.
shǎm n. Imposture, pretence, humbug; person, thing, pretending or pretended to be something that he or it is not. ~ *adj*. Pretended, counterfeit, imitation. ~ v. Feign, simulate; pretend to be.
shǎ′man n. Priest or witch-doctor in shamanism. **shǎ′manism** n. Primitive religion of Ural-Altaic peoples of N. Asia in which

gods, spirits, and demons influencing all human life are believed to be responsive to shamans; any similar religion, esp. among N. Amer. Indians.
shā′mble v.i. Walk, run, in shuffling, awkward, or decrepit way. ~ n. Shambling gait.
shā′mbles (-blz) n.pl. (freq. with sing. construction). Butchers' slaughter-house; scene of carnage or chaotic confusion.
shāme n. Feeling of humiliation excited by consciousness of guilt or shortcoming, of appearing ridiculous, or of having offended against propriety etc.; fear of this as restraint on behaviour; state of disgrace, ignominy, or discredit; person or thing that brings disgrace; (colloq.) regrettable or unlucky thing. **shā′meful**, **shā′meless** adjs. **shā′mefully**, **shā′melĕsslȳ** advs. **shā′mefulnĕss**, **shā′melĕssnĕss** ns. **shāme** v.t. Bring shame on, be a shame to, make ashamed; put to shame by superior excellence; drive *into*, *out of*, through shame or fear of shame.
shā′mefaced (-mfāst) adj. Ashamed; embarrassed. **shā′mefācědlȳ** adv. **shā′mefācednĕss** n.
shǎ′mmȳ n. = CHAMOIS (leather).
shămpŏŏ′ v.t. 1. (rare) Massage, esp. as part of Turkish bath. 2. Wash (hair) with cleansing preparation; use cleansing preparation on surface of (carpet, upholstery, etc.). ~ n. Shampooing (preparation); *dry* ~, (n. & v.t.) (use) such preparation made for use without water. [prob. f. Hind. *cāṅpo*, imper. of *cāṅpnā* press, knead (dough or limbs)]
shǎ′mrŏck n. Trifoliate plant, used, according to tradition, by St. Patrick to illustrate doctrine of Trinity, and hence adopted as national emblem of Ireland; (now usu.) lesser yellow trefoil, *Trifolium minus*. [Ir. *seamróg*, dim. of *seamar* clover]
Shan (-ahn) n. Member, language, of a Thai people of Burma; ~ *State*, State of E. Burma.
shǎ′ndrȳdǎn n. Chaise with hood; rickety old-fashioned vehicle.
shǎ′ndȳ, **shǎ′ndȳgǎff** ns. Drink made of mixture of beer and ginger beer or lemonade.
Shǎnghai¹ (-hī′). Seaport of China.
shǎnghai² (-hī′) v.t. Drug or otherwise render insensible and ship as sailor while unconscious. [f. SHANGHAI¹]
Shǎngri-La′ (-ngg-, -ah) n. Imaginary hidden paradise on earth. [f. place in James Hilton's novel 'Lost Horizon' (1933)]
shǎnk n. 1. Leg, lower part of leg from knee to ankle; shin-bone, tibia; (part of) leg of bird (pop.); lower part of foreleg of horse; cut of meat (ill. MEAT). 2. Stem; straight part of nail, pin, fish-hook, etc.;

stem of key, spoon, anchor, etc. (ill. ANCHOR); shaft of tool between head etc. and handle; narrow part of boot or shoe beneath instep; body of type (ill. TYPE).
Shă′nnon. River of Ireland flowing from Cavan county to the Atlantic.
Shā′nsi′ (-sē). Province of N. China.
Shă′ntŭ′nġ[1] (or -tōō-). Maritime province of NE. China.
shăntŭ′nġ[2] n. Soft undressed Chinese silk, usu. undyed and sometimes mixed with cotton. [f. SHANTUNG[1]]
shăn′ty[1] n. Hut, cabin; mean roughly constructed dwelling. [Canadian-Fr. *chantier* log hut, f. Fr. = 'workshop'].
shă′nty[2] n. Sailors' song, sung while heaving, pulling, etc., with solo by *sha′ntyman* alternating with chorus.
shāpe n. 1. External form, contour, configuration; visible appearance characteristic of person, thing, etc.; guise; concrete presentment, embodiment; phantom (now rare); dimly seen figure. 2. Kind, description, sort. 3. Definite or regular form, orderly arrangement. 4. Mould for jelly, blancmange, etc.; jelly, etc., moulded in this; body or frame of hat before trimming; portion of material etc. cut or moulded to have particular shape. **shā′pelèss** adj. **shā′pelèssly** adv. **shā′pelèssnèss** n. **shāpe** v. Create, form, construct; model, mould, bring into desired or definite figure or form; frame mentally, imagine; assume form, develop into shape, give signs of future shape.
shā′pelў (-pli) adj. Well-formed or proportioned, of pleasing shape. **shā′peliness** n.
shār̆d, shĕrd ns. 1. = POTSHERD. 2. Hard wing-case of beetle, elytron (ill. BEETLE[2]).
shāre[1] n. Portion detached for individual from common amount; part one is entitled to have or expected to contribute, equitable portion; part one gets or contributes; part-proprietorship of property held by joint owners, esp. one of the equal parts into which company's capital is divided; ~-*cropper*, (U.S.) tenant farmer paying rent with part of his crop; *shar′eholder*, owner of shares in joint-stock company; ~-*pusher*, one who peddles shares by circular or advertisement instead of selling them on the market. ~ v. Apportion, give share of; give away part of; get or have share of; possess, use, endure, jointly with others; have share(s), be sharer(s); (in the language of some religious groups) communicate to others one's spiritual experiences; ~ *out*, distribute; ~-*out* (n.).
shāre[2] n. PLOUGHshare. (ill. PLOUGH); blade of seeding-machine or cultivator.

shār̆k n. Any of various long-bodied cartilaginous fish, esp.

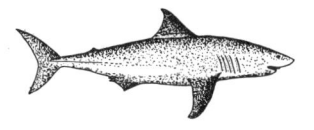

SHARK

large voracious kinds; rapacious person, swindler; ~(′s)-*fin*, fin of shark, used as table delicacy by Chinese; *shar′kskin*, skin of shark used as shagreen etc.; worsted twill-woven fabric; smooth fabric of rayon etc.
shār̆p adj. 1. Having keen edge or point, not blunt; peaked, pointed, edged; well-defined; abrupt, angular. 2. Keen, pungent, acid, tart; shrill, piercing; biting, harsh, severe, intense, painful. 3. Acute, sensitive, keen-witted, vigilant, clever; quick to take advantage, artful, unscrupulous, dishonest; ~ *practice*, relentless pursuit of advantage; trickery. 4. Vigorous, speedy, impetuous. 5. (mus.) Above true pitch, too high; (following name of note, as *C sharp* etc.) a semitone higher than the note named; (of key) having sharps in the signature. **shār̆′plў** adv. **shār̆′pnèss** n. **shār̆p** n. 1. Sewing-needle with sharp point. 2. (mus.) Note raised by a semitone above natural pitch; symbol (♯) indicating this raising. 3. (pl.) Finer parts of husk and coarser particles of flour of wheat and other cereals. ~ adv. Sharply; abruptly; punctually; (mus.) above true pitch; ~-*set*, hungry; *shar′p-shooter*, skilled shot, esp. one of division engaged in skirmishing and outpost work; shot attaining definite degree of skill in marksmanship. ~ v.i. Cheat, swindle, esp. at cards. **shār̆′per** n. Cheat, swindler, esp. at cards. **shār̆′pen** v. Make, become, sharp.
shă′tter v. Break suddenly and violently in pieces; utterly destroy, wreck.
shāve v. (past part. *shāved* or *shāven*). 1. Remove (hair), free (chin etc.) of hair, with razor; shave oneself; *shaving-brush*, brush for applying lather before shaving. 2. Cut or pare away surface of (wood etc.) with spokeshave, plane, or other sharp tool. 3. Pass close to without touching; miss narrowly, nearly graze. ~ n. 1. Shaving, being shaved. 2. Close approach without contact; narrow miss, escape, or failure. 3. Knife-blade with handle at each end for shaving wood etc.
shā′ven adj. Shaved, tonsured; closely clipped.
shā′ver n. (esp.) 1. (colloq.) Lad, youngster. 2. Electrical appliance for shaving hair from face.

Shā′vian adj. (In the manner) of G. B. SHAW[2].
shā′ving n. (esp.) Thin slice taken from surface with sharp tool; thin slice of wood cut off with plane.
shaw[1] n. (archaic & poet.) Thicket, wood.
Shaw[2], George Bernard (1856–1950). Irish playwright, critic, and writer on social and political subjects; author of the plays 'Man and Superman', 'Back to Methuselah', 'Candida', 'Pygmalion', 'Saint Joan', etc.
shawl n. Oblong or square piece of fabric, freq. folded into triangle, worn over shoulders or head, round neck, etc., or wrapped round baby. **shawled** (-ld) adj. Wearing shawl. [Pers. *shāl*]
shawm n. Obsolete musical instrument of oboe class, with double reed in globular mouth-piece.
shē pron. 3rd person nom. sing. fem. pronoun, denoting the female person or animal referred to; object, device, country, etc., personified as feminine. ~ n. Female animal.
sheaf n. (pl. -*ves*). Large bundle of cereal plants bound together after reaping; cluster or bundle of things laid lengthwise together; bundle or quiverful of 24 arrows. ~ v.t. Bind into sheaf or sheaves.
shear v. (past t. *sheared*, past part. *shōrn, sheared*). 1. Cut with sharp instrument (poet. & archaic); clip, cut with scissors or shears; clip wool from (sheep); (fig.) fleece, strip bare. 2. Distort or break, be distorted or broken by, the strain called a shear. ~ n. 1. (pl.) Cutting-instrument with two meeting blades pivoted as in scissors or connected by spring and passing close over each other edge to edge. 2. (mech.) Kind of strain produced by pressure in structure of a substance, its successive layers being shifted laterally over each other (ill. STRESS). 3. (pl., also ~-*legs*) see SHEER[4].
shear′ling n. Sheep once shorn.
shear′water (-waw-) n. Sea-bird of genus *Puffinus*, with long wings, skimming close to water in flight.
shea′t-fish n. Largest European freshwater fish, a large catfish (*Silurus glanis*), common in Danube and other central European rivers.
sheath n. (pl. pr. -*dhz*). Close-fitting cover, esp. for blade of weapon or implement; (bot., anat., etc.) sheath-like covering, investing membrane, tissue, skin, horny case, etc.
sheathe (-dh) v.t. Put into sheath; encase, protect with sheathing. **shea′thing** n. Protective layer of boards, metal plates, etc., on outside of bottom of wooden ship, on piece of machinery, roof, wall, etc.
sheave[1] n. Grooved wheel or

[809]

sheave pulley of pulley-block etc. (ill. PULLEY).

sheave² v.t. Gather (corn etc.) into sheaves.

Shē'ba. Biblical name of SABA; Queen of ~, Balkis, who visited Solomon (1 Kings 10).

shěbǎ'ng n. (U.S. slang) House, store, saloon, business.

shēbee'n n. (chiefly in Ireland) Pot-house; unlicensed house selling drink.

shěd¹ n. Slight structure for shelter, storage, etc., freq. built as lean-to, and sometimes with open front or sides; similar but large and strongly built structure on railway, wharf, aerodrome, etc.

shěd² v.t. (past t. & past part. shěd). Part with, let fall (off), drop; cause (blood) to flow; disperse, diffuse, spread abroad; ~ light on; illuminate, esp. fig.

sheen n. Splendour, radiance, lustre. **shee'nȳ¹** adj.

shee'nȳ² n. (slang, derog.) Jew.

sheep n. (pl. same). Wild or domesticated timid, gregarious, woolly, often horned, ruminant mammal of genus *Ovis*, closely allied to goat, bred for flesh and wool; (usu. pl.) member(s) of minister's flock, parishioners, etc.; person as stupid, poor-spirited, unoriginal, or timid as a sheep; ~-dip, preparation for cleansing sheep of vermin or preserving their wool; place for such cleansing; ~-dog, collie; Old English ~-dog, shaggy-coated bob-tailed dog used for guarding and herding sheep (ill. DOG); ~'s eyes, amorous glances; shee'pfold, enclosure for penning sheep; shee'pshank, knot for temporarily shortening rope, made by doubling rope in three parts and taking hitch over bight at each end (ill. KNOT); ~'s-head, (dish of) head of sheep; large foodfish of Atlantic coasts of U.S., with head supposed to resemble sheep's; shee'pskin, garment or rug of sheep's skin with wool on; leather of sheep's skin used in bookbinding, etc.; parchment of sheep's skin, deed or diploma engrossed on this; ~-walk, tract of land on which sheep are pastured; ~-wash, sheep-dip.

shee'pish adj. Embarrassed, shamefaced.

sheer¹ adj. Mere, unqualified, undiluted, absolute; (of textile fabric) thin, diaphanous; (of rock, fall, ascent, etc.) perpendicular, very steep and without a break. ~ adv. Plumb, perpendicularly, outright.

sheer² v.i. (naut.) Deviate from course; ~ off, swerve away; make off, esp. from person one dislikes.

sheer³ n. Upward slope of ship's lines towards bow and stern; deviation of ship from course.

sheer⁴ n. (pl.; also ~-legs or shear-legs) Hoisting apparatus of two or more poles attached at or near top and separated at bottom for masting ships or putting in engines etc., used in dockyards or on ~-hulk, dismasted ship used for the purpose. [var. of SHEAR; named from resemblance to pair of shears]

sheet n. 1. Rectangular piece of linen, cotton, etc., used as one of a pair of inner bedclothes. 2. Broad more or less flat piece of some thin material, as paper; complete piece of paper of the size in which it was made; newspaper. 3. Wide expanse of water, snow, ice, flame, colour, etc. 4. Rope or chain at lower corner of sail, used to extend it or alter its direction (ill. SAIL¹). 5. (pl.) Spaces of open boat forward of (*foresheets*) and abaft (*stern ~s*) thwarts (ill. BOAT). 6. in ~s, (of book) printed but not bound; *three ~s in the wind*, rather or very drunk. 7. ~-bend, kind of knot made between two ropes (ill. KNOT); ~ glass, kind made first as hollow cylinder which is cut open and flattened in furnace; ~ *iron, metal*, etc., spread by rolling, hammering, etc., into thin sheets; ~ *music*, music published in sheets, not in book form. ~ v.t. Furnish with sheets; cover with sheet; secure (sail) with sheet.

sheet-ā'nchor (-k-) n. Large, formerly always largest, anchor carried outside the waist of a ship, ready to be 'shot' or cast in an emergency; (fig.) one's best, surest, or only hope, refuge, or expedient.

Shē'ffield. City in South Yorkshire, famous for manufacture of cutlery and steel; university, 1905; ~ *plate*, copperware coated with silver by now disused process.

sheikh (-k; or -āk) n. Chief, head, of Arab tribe, family, or village; title of eminent Muslim.

shei'khdom n. Office, territory, of sheikh.

shei'la n. (Austral. & N.Z. colloq.) Girl.

shě'kel n. Ancient Babylonian, Phoenician, Hebrew, etc., weight; coin of this weight, esp. chief Jewish silver coin; (pl., colloq.) money, riches.

shě'ldrāke n. (fem. & pl. freq. shě'ldŭck or shěld dŭck). Brightplumaged wild duck of genus *Tadorna*, frequenting sandy coasts in Europe, N. Africa, and Asia.

shělf n. (pl. -ves). Projecting slab of stone or board let into or hung on wall to support things; one of boards in cabinet, bookcase, etc., on which contents stand; ledge, horizontal step-like projection in cliff-face etc.; reef or sandbank under water; *on the ~*, (fig.) put aside, done with; ~-mark, mark, number, on book indicating its place on library shelf.

shěll n. 1. Hard outer case enclosing kernel of nut, some kinds of seed or fruit, egg, some molluscs or crustaceans, etc. 2. Walls of unfinished or gutted building, ship, etc.; light narrow racing-boat; rough wooden coffin, inner coffin of lead, etc. 3. Explosive artillery projectile. 4. Apsidal end of schoolroom at Westminster School, form (intermediate between 5th and 6th) which orig. used this; in other English schools, an intermediate form. 5. ~-back, (joc.) old sailor; ~-bark (hickory), N. Amer. tree, *Carya ovata*, with rough shaggy bark of long narrow loosely adhering plates; *she'llfish*, any aquatic animal with shell, esp. crustacean or mollusc; ~-jacket, undress tight-fitting military jacket reaching only to waist behind, worn esp. as a mess-jacket by officers; ~-pink, delicate shade of pale pink; ~-shock, form of nervous breakdown provoked by exposure to battle conditions.

shělled (-ld), **shě'll-lèss**, **shě'llȳ** adjs. **shěll** v. 1. Take out of shell, remove shell or pod from; come away or off in thin pieces, scale off; ~ out, (slang) pay up, hand over (money); ~-out, (billiards) game of pyramids played by 3 or more persons; (slang) distribution of gains. 2. Bombard, fire at, with shells.

shěllǎ'c (or shě'-) n. Purified lac, esp. in thin plates, used in varnishes, insulating materials, gramophone records, on account of its high gloss, adhesiveness, and toughness. ~ v.t. Varnish, coat, with shellac.

Shě'lley, Percy Bysshe (1792–1822). English Romantic poet, author of 'Ode to the West Wind', 'To a Skylark', 'The Cloud', etc., and of the dramas 'The Cenci', 'Prometheus Unbound', etc.; *Mary Wollstonecraft ~* (1797–1851), his second wife, author of 'Frankenstein'.

shě'lter n. Thing serving as shield or barrier against attack, danger, heat, wind, etc.; screen or cabin to keep off wind, rain, etc.; place of safety or immunity; sheltered or protected state (usu. *seek, take ~*). ~ v. Act or serve as shelter to; protect, conceal, harbour, defend *from* blame, screen, shield; take shelter; *sheltered industries*, those not exposed to foreign competition, e.g. building and inland transport.

shě'ltie n. Small pony, esp. Shetland.

shělve¹ v.t. Put on shelf; provide with shelves, esp. bookshelves; put aside (question etc.) from consideration; remove (person) from office, employment, etc.

shě'lving n. (esp.) Shelves, material for shelves.

shělve² v.i. Slope gently.

Shěm. Eldest son of Noah (Gen. 10: 21).

shěmǒ'zzle n. (orig. East End slang) Rough-and-tumble, uproar.

Shē'nsi' (-ē). Province of N. China.

Shē'ol. Hebrew underworld, abode of the dead, represented as

[810]

shepherd (-perd) *n.* (fem. **she′pherdèss**) Person who guards, tends, and herds flock of sheep; pastor; *S~ Kings*, HYKSOS; *~'s pie*, pie of chopped or minced meat with crust of mashed potatoes; *~'s plaid*, (woollen cloth with) small black-and-white check pattern; *~'s purse*, common cruciferous white-flowered weed, *Capsella bursa-pastoris*, with pouch-like pods. ~ *v.t.* Tend as shepherd; marshal, conduct, guide, like sheep.

Shĕ′raton, Thomas (1751–1806). English furniture designer, author of 'The Cabinet Maker's and Upholsterer's Drawing Book' (1791–4) and similar works illustrating the style then in vogue; hence, style of furniture designed by Sheraton.

shĕr′bet *n.* Oriental cooling drink of sweetened and diluted fruit juice; effervescing drink or powder of flavoured sodium bicarbonate, tartaric acid, sugar, etc.; water-ice. [f. Turk. Pers. *šerbet* f. Arab. *šarba* drink]

shĕrd *n.* = POTSHERD.

Shĕ′ridan, Richard Brinsley (1751–1816). Irish playwright and member of Parliament; author of the comedies 'The Rivals', 'The School for Scandal', etc.

sheri′f (-ēf), **sheree′f** *n.* Descendant of Muhammad through his daughter Fatima; title of certain Arab princes, esp. sovereign of Morocco; chief magistrate or local governor of Mecca. [Arab. *šarif* noble, glorious]

shĕ′riff *n.* Chief executive officer of shire or county, charged with keeping of the peace, administration of justice under direction of the courts, execution of writs by deputy, presiding over elections, etc.; (in Scotland) sheriff-depute; (U.S.) elective officer responsible for keeping the peace in his county; *~-depute*, (in Scotland) judicial officer of a county or stewartry having jurisdiction in minor civil and criminal cases.

Shĕr′pa *n.* (fem. **Sherpa′ni** pr. -ahni). Member of a people of Mongolian origin living on slopes of Himalayas and speaking a language allied to Tibetan.

shĕ′rry *n.* Still wine made near Jerez de la Frontera in Andalusia, Spain, varying in colour from pale gold to dark brown and usu. fortified; similar wine made elsewhere, notably in S. Africa, Australia, California, and Cyprus. [Span. (*vino de*) *Xeres* (wine of) Jerez]

Shĕ′tland. Islands area of Scotland (since May 1975), former county of *~ Islands* (also *Shetlands*) group of islands NNE. of Scottish mainland; ~ *pony*, pony of small hardy rough-coated breed orig. from Shetland Islands; ~ *wool*, fine thin loosely twisted wool from Shetland sheep. ~ *n.* Shetland pony. **Shĕ′tlander** *n.*

shew (shō). Var. of SHOW *v.*; *shew′bread*, twelve loaves displayed in Jewish temple and renewed each sabbath.

Shiah (shē′a). Muslim sect (chiefly represented by Persians) holding that Muhammad's cousin and son-in-law Ali was the prophet's true successor and that the three first Sunnite caliphs were usurpers. [Arab. *al-ši'a* party, sect sc. of Ali]

shi′bbolĕth *n.* Test word, principle, opinion, etc., the use of or inability to use which reveals one's party, nationality, etc. (see Judges 12: 6); catchword, (esp. outworn or empty) formula, etc., distinguishing a party or sect. [Heb. *šibbōleṯ*]

shield *n.* Article of defensive armour carried in hand or on arm

A B C
SHIELDS
A. GREEK PELTA, 5TH C. B.C. B. MEDIEVAL SHIELD. C. 16TH-C. FIST BUCKLER
1. Umbo or boss

as protection from weapons of enemy; protective plate or screen in machinery etc.; person or thing serving as protection or defence; shield-like part in animal or plant; (her.) escutcheon (ill. HERALDRY); (U.S.) policeman's shield-shaped badge; *shie′ldbug*, flat broad insect (*Dolyoris baccarum*) with conspicuous shield behind head (ill. BUG). ~ *v.t.* Protect, screen, esp. from censure or punishment.

shie′ling *n.* (Sc.) Small hut used by shepherds, fishermen, etc., during the summer.

shift *n.* 1. Change of place or character; substitution of one thing for another; vicissitude; rotation; *red ~*, (astron.) apparent shift in spectra of light from distant galaxies towards the long-wave or red end of the spectrum, indicating that the galaxies are receding; *~-key*, key for adjusting typewriter when capitals etc. are to be used. 2. Expedient, device, stratagem, resource; dodge, trick, piece of evasion or equivocation. 3. Chemise. 4. Relay or change of workmen; length of time during which such relay works. ~ *v.* 1. Change or move from one position to another, change form or character. 2. Use expedients, contrive; manage, get along; ~ *for oneself*, depend on one's own efforts.

shi′ftlĕss *adj.* Lacking in resource; lazy, inefficient. **shi′ftlĕssly** *adv.* **shi′ftlĕssnĕss** *n.* ·

shi′ftў *adj.* Not straightforward, evasive, deceitful. **shi′ftilў** *adv.* **shi′ftinĕss** *n.*

Shi′īte (shē-) *n.* Member of the SHIAH sect.

shikār′ *n.* (Ind.) Hunting. **shikār′ee, shikār′i** *n.* Hunter, esp. professional guide or hunter in India.

shillelagh (-lā′la; *or* -lī) *n.* Irish cudgel of blackthorn or oak. [name of village in County Wicklow]

shi′lling *n.* (abbrev. *s.*) Monetary unit of Kenya, Somali Republic, Tanzania, and Uganda, = 100 cents; former monetary unit of U.K., = $\frac{1}{20}$ of a pound; *cut person off with a ~*, disinherit him; *take the King's (Queen's) ~*, enlist in the army, from the now obs. custom of giving a recruit a shilling.

shi′llў-shă′llў *n.* Vacillation, irresolution, indecision. ~ *v.i.* Vacillate, be irresolute or undecided. [orig. *shill I, shall I*]

shi′mmer *v.i.* & *n.* (Shine with) tremulous or faint diffused light.

shi′mmў *n.* (colloq. & nursery) CHEMISE.

shin *n.* Front of human leg below knee; lower part of leg of beef (ill. MEAT); *~-bone*, tibia; *~-guard*, guard worn at football or hockey to protect the shins. ~ *v.i.* Climb *up* by using arms and legs, without help of ladder, irons, etc.

shi′ndў *n.* (colloq.) Brawl, disturbance, row, noise.

shine *v.* (past t. & past part. *shōne*). Emit or reflect light, be bright, glow; be brilliant, excel, in some respect or sphere; (colloq.) make bright, polish (boots etc.). ~ *n.* Light, brightness; sunshine; lustre, sheen.

shi′ner *n.* (esp.) 1. Diamond; (pl., slang) money, coin. 2. (slang) Black eye. 3. (chiefly U.S.) Any of various small silvery freshwater fishes.

shi′ngle[1] (-nggl) *n.* 1. Thin rectangular piece of wood thicker at one end, used like roof-tile. 2. Shingled hair. ~ *v.t.* 1. Cover, roof, with shingles. 2. Cut (woman's hair) short so that it tapers from back of head to nape of neck.

shi′ngle[2] (-nggl) *n.* Small rounded pebbles on seashore; gravel. **shi′nglў** *adj.*

shi′ngles (-ngglz) *n.* (pop.) = HERPES *zoster*. [L *cingulum* girdle, because eruptions freq. appear round trunk]

Shi′ntō *n.* Ancient, more or less pantheistic, religion of Japan, based on worship of ancestors and of nature, gradually absorbed and superseded by Buddhism from 6th c. onwards, but re-established as the State religion after 1868, when the cult of the emperor as a descendant of the sun became its principal feature. **Shi′ntōism** *n.* **Shi′ntōist** *n.* [Chin. *shin* god, *tao* doctrine]

SHINTY

shi′ntȳ *n.* Game similar to hockey, played chiefly in N. Britain and N. America.
shi′nȳ *adj.* Glistening, shining, polished, rubbed bright. **shi′niness** *n.*
ship *n.* Any large sea-going vessel, propelled by sails, steam, or other mechanical means; ship; take ship, embark; take service on ship; deliver (goods) to forwarding agent for conveyance by land or water. 2. Fix (mast, rudder, etc.) in its place; remove (oars) from rowlocks and lay them inside boat; (of vessel) take in (water) over the side; ~ *a sea*, be flooded by wave.

SHOCK

buttoning down to waist in front.
shir′ting *n.* Material for shirts.
shir′tȳ *adj.* (slang) In a rage, annoyed.
shit *v.i.* (vulg.) Evacuate bowels. ~ *n.* (vulg.) 1. Faeces. 2. Applied contemptuously to a person.
Shiva: see SIVA.
shi′ver[1] *n.* Quivering or trem-

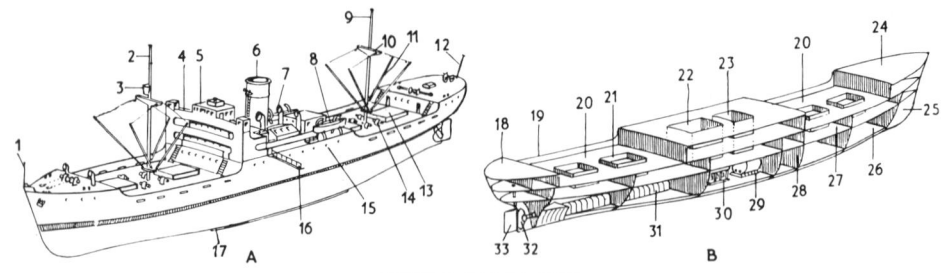

GENERAL CARGO SHIP
A. EXTERIOR (PORT SIDE). B. DIAGRAM TO SHOW CONSTRUCTION (STARBOARD SIDE)
A. 1. Jackstaff. 2. Foremast. 3. Crow's-nest. 4. Navigating bridge. 5. Wheel-house. 6. Funnel. 7. Cowl ventilators. 8. Lifeboat and davits. 9. Mainmast. 10. Cross-tree. 11. Derrick. 12. Ensign staff. 13. Cargo hatch. 14. Winch. 15. Porthole. 16. Accommodation ladder. 17. Bilge keel. B. 18. Poop. 19. Bulwark. 20. Well-deck. 21. Hatch coaming. 22. Engine casing to skylight. 23. Boiler casing to funnel. 24. Forecastle. 25. Forepeak. 26. Cargo hold. 27. 'Tween-decks. 28. Watertight bulkhead. 29. Boiler-room or stokehold. 30. Engine-room. 31. Shaft tunnel. 32. Propeller or screw. 33. Rudder

(specif.) sailing-vessel with bowsprit and three square-rigged masts, each divided into lower, top, and topgallant mast (*illustration, p 813*); (esp. U.S. Air Force) aircraft; ~('s) *biscuit*, hard coarse kind of biscuit made for keeping, formerly much used on board ship; *on shi′pboard*, (adv. phrase) on board ship; ~-*broker*, agent of a shipping company, transacting business for their ships when in port; agent for marine insurance business; *shi′pbuilder*, one whose business it is to build ships; *shi′pbuilding*; ~ *burial*, (archaeol.) burial in ship under mound; ~-*canal*, canal large enough for sea-going vessels; ~('s) *chandler*, dealer supplying ships with stores; *shi′pload*, quantity of something forming whole cargo; *shi′pmate*, fellow sailor; ~-*money*, (hist.) ancient tax levied on ports and maritime towns and counties of England in time of war to provide ships (revived by Charles I and abolished by statute in 1640); ~'*s articles*, terms on which seamen take service on her; ~'*s company*, crew of a ship, not including the officers; *shi′pshape*, in good order, trim and neat; ~'*s papers*, documents carried on board ship establishing ownership, nationality, nature of cargo, etc.; ~-*way*, inclined track on which a ship is built and down which she is launched; *shi′pworm*, worm-shaped mollusc that bores into ship's timbers; *shi′pwreck*, (cause, suffer) destruction of ship by storm, foundering, striking rock, etc.; (fig.) ruin; *shi′pwright*, shipbuilder, ship's carpenter; *shi′pyard*, shipbuilding establishment. ~ *v.* 1. Put, take, send away, on board -**ship** *suffix.* Having specified character, office, skill, etc.
shi′pment *n.* Putting of goods etc. on ship; amount shipped, consignment.
shi′pper *n.* Merchant etc. who sends or receives goods by ship.
shi′pping *n.* (esp.) Ships, esp. the ships of a country, port, etc.; ~-*agent*, person acting for (line of) ships at a port etc.; ~-*articles*, ship's articles; ~-*master*, official in whose presence ship's articles are signed, paying-off is done, etc.; ~-*office*, office of shipping-agent or -master.
shire *n.* County; *the* ~*s*, (loosely) the foxhunting counties of Leicestershire, Rutland (formerly), and Northamptonshire; ~ *horse*, draught-horse of heavy powerful breed, chiefly bred in midland counties of England.
-**shire** (-er) *suffix.* County.
shirk *v.t.* Avoid meanly, evade, shrink selfishly from (duty, responsibility, etc.). **shir′ker** *n.*
Shir′ley pŏ′ppȳ. Cultivated variety of common corn poppy with single or double flowers of various delicate colours. [f. Shirley Rectory, Croydon, England, where first produced]
shirr *v.t.* (orig. U.S.) Gather (material) with several parallel threads. ~ *n.* Shirring, shirred trimming.
shirt *n.* Man's loose sleeved garment for upper part of body; *in* ~-*sleeves*, without coat, or coat and waistcoat; ~-*blouse*, woman's blouse resembling a man's shirt; ~-*front*, breast of shirt, freq. stiffened or starched; dicky; ~-*tail*, back part of shirt below waist; *shir′twaister*, woman's dress bling, esp. of body under influence of cold, fear, etc. ~ *v.i.* Tremble, shake, quiver, esp. with cold or fear. **shi′veringlȳ** *adv.*
shi′ver[2] *n.* One of many small pieces into which thing is shattered by blow or fall. ~ *v.* Break into shivers.
shoal[1] *adj.* (of water) Shallow. ~ *n.* Shallow place in water, sand-bank or bar. ~ *v.i.* Grow shallow(er).
shoal[2] *n.* Multitude, crowd, great number, esp. of fish swimming in company. ~ *v.i.* Form shoals.
shŏck[1] *n.* Violent collision, concussion, or impact; one of the violent shakes or tremors of part of earth's surface constituting an earthquake; sudden and disturbing mental or physical impression; stimulation of nerve(s) with muscular contraction and feeling of concussion by passage of electric current through body; (path.) acute state of prostration accompanied by lowering of blood-volume and -pressure and weakening of pulse and respiration, commonly following accidents, wounds, or burns; ~-*absorber*, device for absorbing vibration in mechanically propelled vehicles (ill. MOTOR); device on aircraft to lessen shock of landing; ~ *tactics*, sudden and violent action; ~ *troops*, picked troops for offensive action; ~ *wave*, disturbance produced when body travels through medium at speed greater than that at which medium transmits sound, or by explosion. ~ *v.t.* Affect with intense aversion, disgust, or strong disapproval, scandalize; outrage sentiments, prejudices, etc., of;

[812]

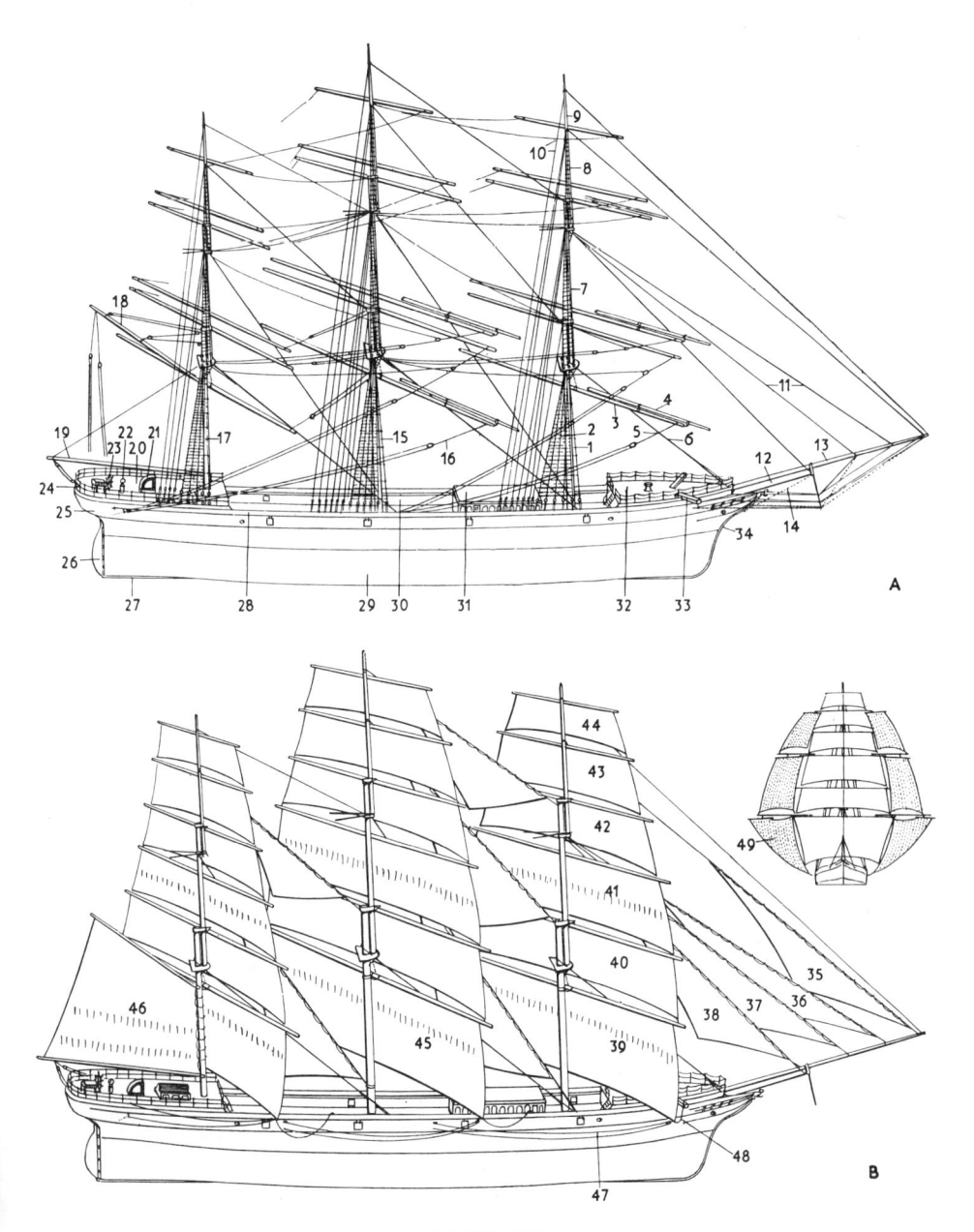

SAILING-SHIP
A. RIGGING. B. SAILS (SQUARE-RIGGED)

A. Masts, spars, and rigging: 1. Foremast. 2. Fore shrouds. 3. Fore-lower yard. 4. Stunsail boom. 5. Fore brace. 6. Forestay. 7. Fore topmast. 8. Fore-topgallant mast. 9. Fore-royal mast. 10. Fore-royal backstay. 11. Jib-stays. 12. Bowsprit. 13. Jib-boom. 14. Bobstay. 15. Main-mast. 16. Main-brace. 17. Mizzen-mast. 18. Gaff. 19. Boom. Decks and hull: 20. Poop. 21. Companion-way. 22. Binnacle (holding compass). 23. Wheel or helm. 24. Taffrail. 25. Counter. 26. Rudder. 27. Keel. 28. Bulwarks. 29. Bilge. 30. Waist or amidships. 31. Deckhouse (with galley). 32. Forecastle. 33. Cathead. 34. Stem. B. Sails: 35. Flying jib. 36. Outer jib. 37. Inner jib. 38. Fore-topmast staysail. 39. Foresail or fore-course. 40. Fore-lower topsail. 41. Fore-upper topsail. 42. Fore-lower topgallant sail. 43. Fore-upper topgallant sail. 44. Fore-royal. 45. Mainsail. 46. Spanker. 47. Fore-tack. 48. Foresheet. 49. Fore-lower stunsail.

(The names of the upper masts, sails, yards, stays, and braces attached to the main- and mizzen-masts follow those given for the foremast.)

[813]

SHOCK

cause to suffer shock; administer electric shock to. **shŏ'cking** *adj.* **shŏ'ckingly** *adv.* **shŏ'ckingness** *n.*
shŏck² *n.* Group of sheaves of corn etc. propped upright against each other in field to dry and ripen. ~ *v.t.* Arrange in shocks.
shŏck³ *n.* Unkempt or shaggy mass of hair; ~ *head(ed)*, (having) rough head of hair.
shŏ'cker *n.* (esp., colloq.) 1. Very bad specimen of anything. 2. Sensational novel.
shŏd *adj.*: see SHOE *v.t.*; (esp.) wearing shoes; tipped, edged, or sheathed with metal.
shŏ'ddy *n.* (Cloth of) woollen yarn made from shreds of knitted or loosely woven woollen fabrics (cf. MUNGO¹); inferior cloth, anything of worse quality than it claims or seems to have. ~ *adj.* Of poor material or quality.
shoe (-ōō) *n.* Outer covering for foot, of leather or other material,

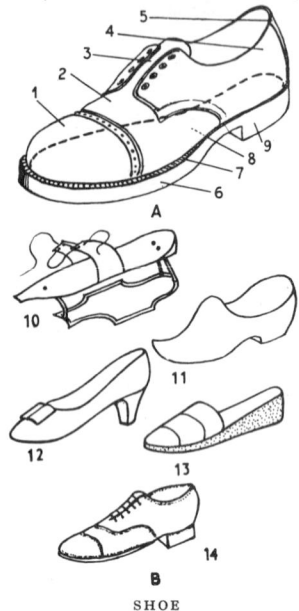

SHOE

A. PARTS OF A SHOE. B. KINDS OF SHOES

A. 1-5. Upper (1. Toecap. 2. Vamp. 3. Tongue. 4. Quarter. 5. Back strip). 6. Sole. 7. Welt. 8. Insole. 9. Heel. B. 10. Patten. 11. Clog. 12. Court shoe. 13. Mule. 14. Oxford shoe

with more or less stiff sole and lighter upper part, esp. not reaching above ankle; plate of metal, usu. iron, nailed to underside of horse's hoof; thing like shoe in shape or use, e.g. ferrule or metal sheath for pole etc., wheel-drag, socket; part of brake which presses lining against wheel to slow it down (ill. BRAKE⁴); (elect.) cast-iron block sliding over live rail to collect current therefrom; *shoe'black*, boy or man who, for a small charge, cleans boots and shoes of passersby; *shoe'horn*, curved piece of horn, metal, etc., for easing the heel into the back of a shoe; *shoe'lace*, lace for tying up shoe; *shoe'maker*, one who makes shoes; *shoe'string*, shoelace; *on a shoestring*, (fig.) with minimal expenditure. ~ *v.t.* (past t. & past part. *shŏd*, pres. part. *shoe'ing*). Fit with shoe(s).
shŏ'gun (-ōōn) *n.* (hist.) Japanese hereditary commander-in-chief and virtual ruler for some centuries until the office was abolished in 1868. [Jap., short for *sei-i-tai shōgun* barbarian-subduing great general]
shōō *int.* Exclamation used to frighten birds etc. away. ~ *v.* Utter shoo; drive *away* etc. thus.
shōōt *v.* (past t. & past part. *shŏt*). 1. Come or go vigorously or swiftly; pass quickly under (bridge), over (rapids), in boat; ~ *up*, (esp.) grow rapidly; *shooting star*, meteor. 2. Discharge or propel quickly; discharge (bullet etc.) from gun etc., cause (bow, gun, etc.) to discharge missile, discharge gun etc.; kill or wound with missile from gun etc.; hunt game etc. with gun, shoot the game *over* estate etc., shoot game *on* (estate etc.); (of gun etc.) go off, send missile; throw (dice); (footb. etc.) take shot at goal; ~ *down*, bring down (aircraft) by gunfire. 3. Photograph or (esp.) film. 4. (joinery) Plane edge of board accurately. **shōō'ter** *n.*
shōō'ting *n.* (esp.) Right of shooting over particular land; ~*-box*, sportsman's lodge for use in shooting season; ~*-brake*, vehicle used on shooting expeditions; ~*-gallery*, indoor place where shooting at targets with rifles is practised; ~*-range*, ground with butts for rifle practice; ~*-stick*, walking-stick which may be adapted to form a seat. **shōōt** *n.* 1. Young branch or sucker. 2. Shooting-party, expedition, practice, or land.
shŏp *n.* Building, room, etc., for retail sale of some commodity; workshop of a joiner; engineering works or yard; (slang) institution, trade, or business (esp. in *talk* ~); ~ *assistant*, salesman or saleswoman in retail shop; *sho'pkeeper*, owner and manager of shop; ~*-lifter*, pretended customer who steals goods in shop; *sho'pman*, assistant in shop; ~*-soiled*, soiled or faded by being shown in shop; ~ *steward*, person elected by fellow-workers in shop or department of factory etc. and acting as their spokesman in dealings with employer; *sho'pwalker*, attendant in large shop who directs customers to the department they may require; ~*-worn*, shop-soiled. ~ *v.* 1. Go to shop(s) to make purchases.

SHORT

2. (slang) Inform against. **shŏ'pper** *n.* 1. Person who shops. 2. Shopping-bag. **shŏ'pping** *n.* (esp.) Goods purchased in shop(s).
shōre¹ *n.* Land that skirts sea or large body of water; (law) land between ordinary high- and low-water marks; *in* ~, on water near(er) to shore; ~*-based*, operating from a base on shore. **shōr'eless** *adj.* **shōr'eward** *adj.* & *adv.*
shōre² *n.* Prop, beam, set obliquely against ship, wall, tree, etc., as support. ~ *v.t.* Support, prop *up*, with shores.
shorn: see SHEAR.
short *adj.* 1. Measuring little from end to end in space or time, soon traversed or finished; of small stature, not tall; not far-reaching, acting near at hand. 2. Deficient, scanty, in want *of*, below the degree *of*; (of weight, change, etc.) less than it should be; concise, brief, curt; (phonet., pros., of vowel or syllable) having the lesser of two recognized durations; (of stocks, broker, crops, etc.) sold, selling, etc., when amount is not in hand, in reliance on getting the deficit in time for delivery. 3. (of pastry, clay, etc.) Friable, crumbling. 4. ~*-arm*, with arm not fully extended; *shor'tbread*, *shor'tcake*, crisp dry cake made with flour and butter and sugar without liquid; ~ *circuit*, electric circuit through much smaller resistance than in the normal circuit, thus allowing a large current to flow through and causing overheating, fusing, etc.; ~*-circuit* (*v.t.*) cause short circuit in; shorten (process) by eliminating intermediate stages; *shortco'ming*, failure to come up to a standard, deficiency, defect; *shor'tfall*, output less than expected; shortage; *shor'thand*, stenography, system of graphic notation in which speech is recorded at great speed by using contractions, symbols, etc.; ~*-handed*, undermanned, understaffed; ~*-headed*, (ethnol.) having a head which is broad in proportion to its length, brachycephalic; *shor'thorn*, one of a short-horned breed of cattle orig. from NE. counties of England; ~ *line*, line across width of squash court (ill. SQUASH²); ~ *list*, list of selected candidates for a post from which it is intended to make the final selection; ~*-list* (*v.t.*) put on a short list; ~*-lived*, having a short life; brief, ephemeral; ~ *metre*, hymn stanza of four lines, of which the third has eight syllables and the others six; ~ *odds*, (in betting) nearly even chances; *S*~ *Parliament*, that which sat from 13 April to 5 May 1640; ~ *sight*, ability to see clearly what is comparatively near but not what is at a distance, myopia; ~*-sighted*, having short sight; (fig.) lacking imagination, deficient in foresight; ~*-sightedly*, ~*-sightedness*; ~ *story*, story with

[814]

a fully worked-out motif but of smaller compass than a novel; ~-*tempered*, having a temper easily roused; ~ *time*, condition of working fewer than the regular number of hours per day or days per week; ~-*wave*, radio wavelength of from approx. 10 to 100 metres; ~-*winded*, short of breath, becoming out of breath after slight exertion; ~-*windedly*, ~-*windedness*. **shōr'tnĕss** *n*. **shōrt** *adv*. Abruptly; before the natural or expected time; in short manner. ~ *n*. Short syllable or vowel, mark indicating that a vowel is short; (colloq.) short circuit; short cinema film; small drink of neat spirits; (pl.) short trousers reaching to any point between crutch and knee. ~ *v.t.* (colloq.) Short-circuit.
shōr'tage *n*. (Amount of) deficiency.
shōr'ten *v*. Become, make, actually or apparently short(er), curtail; reduce amount of (*sail*) spread.
shōr'tly *adv*. Before long; a short time *before*, *after*; in few words, briefly; curtly.
Shŏstakō'vich, Dmitri (1906–75). Russian composer of symphonies, operas, piano music, etc.
shŏt[1] *n*. 1. Single missile for cannon or gun, non-explosive projectile; (pl. same) small lead pellets of which a quantity is used for single charge or cartridge, esp. in sporting guns; injection; (slang) dram of spirits. 2. Discharge of cannon or gun; attempt to hit with projectile or missile; (fig.) attempt to guess or do something; aim or stroke, esp. in a game, as tennis, golf, billiards; (footb. etc.) attempt to drive a ball into the goal. 3. Possessor of specified skill with rifle, gun, pistol, etc. 4. Range, reach, distance to or at which thing will carry or act, as *ear-*, *rifle-*~. 5. Photograph; (portion of) film scene photographed as a unit. 6. ~-*gun*, smooth-bore gun for firing small-shot; ~-*gun wedding*, (orig. U.S.) forced wedding, esp. one necessitated by pregnancy; ~-*tower*, tower in which shot is made from molten lead poured through sieves at the top and falling into water at the bottom. ~ *v.t.* Load, weight, etc., with shot.
shŏt[2] *n*. Reckoning, (one's share of) tavern-bill.
shŏt[3] *adj.*: see SHOOT; (esp., of textile) woven with warp-threads of one colour and weft-threads of another, so that the fabric changes in tint when viewed from different points; ~ *edge*, (joinery) accurately planed edge.
should: see SHALL.
shou'lder (-ōl-) *n*. Part of body at which arm, foreleg, or wing is attached; either lateral projection below or behind neck; combination of end of upper arm with ends of collar-bone and shoulder-blade; joint of meat consisting of upper foreleg and adjoining parts (ill. MEAT); part of mountain, bottle, tool, etc., projecting like human shoulder; (pl.) upper part of back; body regarded as bearing burdens; *hard* ~, verge of motorway; ~-*belt*, band passing over one shoulder and under other arm; ~-*blade*, either of the pair of large flat bones of upper back, scapula; ~-*knot*, knot of ribbon or metal lace worn on shoulder of uniform or livery; ~-*strap*, band over shoulder connecting front and back of (esp. woman's) garment; band at shoulder of uniform keeping shoulder-belt in place and bearing name or number of regiment etc. ~ *v*. Push with shoulder, jostle, make one's *way* thus; take (burden) on one's shoulders (also fig.); ~ *arms*, (mil.) hold rifle vertically in front of shoulder with butt resting in palm of hand, the arm being fully extended downwards.
shout *n*. Loud cry expressing joy, grief, pain, defiance, etc., or to attract attention at a distance. ~ *v*. Utter shout; speak loudly; say loudly, call out.
shove (-ŭv) *n*. (Strong) push. ~ *v*. Push, esp. vigorously or roughly; jostle; (colloq.) put; ~ *off*, start from shore in boat. ~-*halfpenny*, SHOVELBOARD.
sho'vel (-ŭv-) *n*. Spade-like implement, freq. with slightly concave blade, for shifting coal, earth, grain, etc.; cue used in shovelboard; ~ *hat*, stiff broad-brimmed hat turned up at sides worn by some Church dignitaries. ~ *v.t.* Shift with shovel or spade.
sho'velboard (-ŭvelbōrd), **shŭ'ffleboard** (-flbōrd) *ns*. Game in which coin or other disc is driven along highly polished board or table by blow with hand into a series of divisions; shipboard game in which wooden or iron discs are pushed along decks with shovel into divisions marked by chalk etc.
sho'veler, -**ll**- (-ŭv-) *n*. Brightly coloured river duck (*Anas clypeata*) with large very broad bill.
show (-ō) *v*. (past t. *showed* pr. shōd; past part. *shown* pr. shōn; also occas. spelt *shew*, *shewed*, *shewn*). 1. Allow or cause to be seen, expose to view, exhibit, reveal, point out; be visible or noticeable, come into sight; appear in public; have some appearance. 2. Demonstrate, prove, expound; point out. 3. ~ *off*, display to advantage; act or talk for show, make ostentatious display of abilities etc.; ~ *up*, make, be, conspicuous or clearly visible; expose (fraud, impostor). 4. ~-*down*, (fig. from game of poker) final test, disclosure of achievements or possibilities. ~ *n*. 1. Showing; display; spectacle, exhibition, entertainment; exhibit; ~-*business*, profession of (esp. theatrical) entertainment (abbrev. *show'biz*); ~-*boat*, passenger-boat, esp. on Mississippi, used as theatre; ~-*case*, glazed case for exhibiting goods, curiosities, etc.; ~-*jumping*, competitive jumping on horse-back; ~ *of hands*, voting by raising of hands; *show'man*, exhibitor or proprietor of show; *show'manship*, (esp.) capacity for exhibiting one's wares, capabilities, etc., to the best advantage; *show'room*, room in which goods are exhibited for sale. 2. Outward appearance, semblance; parade, ostentation, pomp, display. 3. (slang) Concern, undertaking, organization; action, deed; opportunity of acting etc.
show'er *n*. 1. Brief fall of rain, *of* rain, hail, arrows, dust, etc.; (also ~-*bath*) bath in which water is sprayed from above. 2. (U.S.) Party for giving presents esp. to a prospective bride. **show'erў** *adj*. **show'eriness** *n*. **show'er** *v*. 1. Discharge, descend, come, in a shower; bestow (gifts etc.) lavishly (*upon*). 2. Take shower-bath.
show'ў (-ōi) *adj*. Striking, making good display; brilliant, gaudy. **show'ĭlў** *adv*. **show'ĭnĕss** *n*.
s.h.p. *abbrev*. Shaft horsepower.
shră'pnel *n*. Hollow projectile containing bullets scattered in shower by small bursting charge; fragments of any shell, bomb, etc., scattered by explosion. [Gen. H. *Shrapnel* (1761–1842), inventor of the shell during Peninsular War]
shred *n*. Scrap, fragment; small torn, broken, or cut piece; small remains; least amount. ~ *v.t.* Tear or cut into shreds.
shrew (-ōō) *n*. 1. Small mouse-like insectivore of *Sorex* and other genera, with long pointed snout.

A. SHREW. B. VOLE

2. Scolding woman. **shrew'ish** *adj*. Ill-tempered. **shrew'ishlў** *adv*. **shrew'ishnĕss** *n*.
shrewd (-ōōd) *adj*. 1. (archaic, of blow etc.) Severe. 2. Sagacious, sensible, discriminating, astute. **shrew'dlў** *adv*. **shrew'dnĕss** *n*.
Shrew'sbury (-rŏz- *or* -rōōz-). County town of Salop; English public school, founded 1552.
shriek *n. & v*. (Utter) loud shrill cry or sound of terror, pain, mirth, etc.; (make) high-pitched piercing sound.
shrie'valtў *n*. (Tenure of) sheriff's office or jurisdiction.

shrift n. (archaic) Confession (and absolution); now only in *short* ~, little time between condemnation and execution or punishment; scant attention.

shrike n. Bird of genus *Lanius* or related genera, with strong hooked beak, preying usu. on insects, but also on mice and small birds; butcher-bird.

shrill adj. (of sound) Piercing and high-pitched; producing such sounds. ~ v. (poet. and rhet.) Sound, utter, shrilly. **shri′lly** adv. **shri′llness** n.

shrimp n. Any of the small marine decapod crustaceans of *Crangon* and allied genera, esp. the common shrimp, *C. vulgaris*, inhabiting sandy coasts, a common article of food; diminutive or puny person. ~ v.i. Go catching shrimps.

shrine n. Casket, esp. one holding sacred relics; tomb, usu. sculptured or highly ornamented, of saint etc.; place where worship is offered or devotions paid to saint or deity; place hallowed by memory or associations.

Shri′ner n. Member of Ancient Arabic Order of Nobles of the Mystic Shrine, established in U.S. in 1872, and open only to Knights Templar and Freemasons of 32nd degree.

shrink v. (past t. *shrănk*, past part. *shrŭnk* and rarely in vbl, commonly in adj., use *shrŭ′nken*). Become, make, smaller; (of textile fabric) contract when wetted, cause to do this; cower, huddle *together*, recoil, flinch *from*; be averse *from*. **shri′nkage** n.

shrive v.t. (archaic; past t. *shrōve*, past part. *shri′ven*). Hear confession of, assign penance to, and absolve; ~ *oneself*, make one's confession.

shri′vel v. Contract or wither into wrinkled, folded, contorted or dried-up state.

Shrŏ′pshire. Former name of SALOP.

shroud n. 1. Winding-sheet, garment for the dead; (fig.) concealing agency. 2. (pl.) Set of ropes forming part of standing rigging and supporting mast or topmast (ill. SHIP). 3. (elect.) Enlargement of conductor to reduce strain on insulating material. ~ v.t. Clothe (corpse) for burial; cover or disguise.

Shrŏ′vetide (-vt-) n. Three days before Ash Wednesday, period for confession before Lent; so *Shrove Tuesday*. [f. SHRIVE]

shrŭb[1] n. Woody plant of less size than tree and usu. divided into separate stems from near the ground. **shrŭ′bby** adj.

shrŭb[2] n. Cordial of juice of acid fruit, sugar, and spirit (usu. rum). [Arab. *sharāb*]

shrŭ′bbery n. (Plantation of) shrubs.

shrŭg n. Raising and contraction of shoulders to express dislike, disdain, indifference, etc. ~ v. Raise (shoulders), raise shoulders, in shrug.

shrunk, shrunken: see SHRINK.

shŭck n. (chiefly U.S.) Husk, pod. **shŭcks** int. Exclamation of contempt or indifference. **shŭck** v.t. Remove shucks of, shell.

shŭ′dder v.i. & n. (Experience) sudden shivering due to fear, repugnance, or cold.

shŭ′ffle n. 1. Shuffling movement; shuffling of cards; general change of relative positions. 2. Piece of equivocation or sharp practice. 3. Quick scraping movement of feet in dancing. ~ v. Move with scraping, sliding, dragging, or difficult motion; manipulate (cards in pack) so that their relative positions are changed; intermingle, confuse, push about or together in disorderly fashion; put *in, off, on*, etc., clumsily or fumblingly; put (responsibility etc.) *off, on to*, another etc., get *out of* shiftily or evasively; keep shifting position, fidget, vacillate; prevaricate, be evasive.

shuffleboard: see SHOVEL-BOARD.

shŭn v.t. Avoid, keep clear of. **'shŭn!** abbrev. (as command) Attention!

shŭnt v. Divert (train, part of an electric current, etc.), diverge, on to a side track. **shŭ′nter** n. Railwayman shunting trains. **shŭnt** n. Turning, being turned, on to side track; conductor joining two points in an electric circuit so as to form a parallel circuit; such a circuit.

shŭt v. (past t. & past part. *shŭt*). Close (door, aperture, window, etc.), close door etc. of (room, box, etc.); become, admit of being, closed; keep *in, out*, etc., by shutting door etc.; ~ *down*, close, cease working; ~ *one's eyes to*, (fig.) ignore; ~ *in*, encircle, prevent free prospect or egress from or access to; ~ *off*, stop flow of (water, gas, etc.) by shutting valve; separate *from*; ~ *up*, close doors and windows of (house), close securely, decisively, or permanently, put away in box etc.; imprison; reduce to silence, shut one's mouth, stop talking; ~ *up shop*, cease business.

shŭ′tter n. (esp.) Movable wooden or iron screen placed outside or inside window to shut off light or ensure privacy or safety (ill. WINDOW); device for opening and closing aperture of photographic lens (ill. CAMERA); (pl.) louver-boards of organ's swell-box, regulating volume of sound from swell-organs. ~ v.t. Provide with shutters, put up shutters of.

shŭ′ttle n. Weft-carrier in a loom, a boat-shaped wooden implement with hollowed centre to hold the weft-thread, thrown or 'shot' from hand to hand by the weaver, or moved by mechanical means backwards and forwards across and through the warp; thread-holder in sewing-machine carrying lower thread through the loop of the upper one; (attrib.) denoting an out-and-back course, as in ~ *service, train*; *shu′ttlecock*, small piece of weighted cork or other light material with feathers projecting in a ring from one side, struck to and fro with a battledore in the old game of battledore and shuttlecock, and by a racket in badminton.

shȳ[1] adj. Easily startled, timid, avoiding observation, uneasy in company, bashful; avoiding company *of*, chary of *doing*; elusive; (as second element of compounds) frightened (of), averse (to), as *gun-, work-*~. **shȳ′ly** adv. **shȳ′ness** n. **shȳ** v.i. Start suddenly aside in alarm (*at* object or noise, esp. of horse). ~ n. Act of shying.

shȳ[2] v. (colloq.) Fling, throw. ~ n. Act of shying.

Shȳ′lŏck. Jewish usurer in Shakespeare's 'Merchant of Venice'; hence, hard-hearted and grasping money-lender.

shȳ′ster n. (orig. U.S. slang) Tricky, unscrupulous lawyer (or other professional man).

si (sē) n. (mus.) 7th note of major scale (same as TE) in movable-doh systems; note B in fixed-doh system.

S.I. abbrev. (Order of the) Star of India; Système International.

si′al n. (geol.) Lighter outer crust of earth's surface, composed mainly of solid or molten rocks rich in silica and alumina. [f. *si*lica and *al*umina]

Siă′m. Name until 1939 of THAILAND.

si′amăng (sēa-) n. Largest of the gibbons (*Symphalangus syndactylus*), found in Sumatra and the Malay peninsula.

Siamē′se (-z) adj. Of Siam or its people or language; ~ *cat*, cat of domesticated breed of a cream colour with chocolate markings; ~ *twins*, two male natives of Siam, Chang and Eng (1814–74), who were congenitally united by a thick fleshy ligament in the region of the waist; any pair of conjoined twins. ~ n. Siamese person; Siamese language, one of the Thai group; Siamese cat.

sib adj. (archaic & Sc.) Related, akin, (*to*). ~ n. (genetics) Brother or sister (disregarding sex). **si′bling** n. One of two or more children having one or both parents in common. **si′bship** n. (genetics) Group of children (disregarding sex) from the same two parents.

Sibelius (-bā′-), Johan Julius (Jean), (1865–1957). Finnish musical composer of tone-poems, symphonies, etc.

Sibēr′ia. Territory of U.S.S.R. in N. Asia, stretching from the Ural Sea to Yakutsk and forming the larger part of the Russian Soviet Federal Socialist Republic; used

as a place of exile for offenders.
Sīber'ian adj. Of Siberia; ~ crab: see CRAB²; ~ dog, dog of breed resembling the Eskimo dog, used for drawing sledges; ~ wallflower: see WALLflower.
si'bilant adj. Hissing, sounding like a hiss (of the consonants s, z, sh). **si'bilance, si'bilancy** ns. **si'bilant** n. (phon.) Sibilant speech-sound.
si'bȳl n. Any of the women who in ancient times acted in various places as mouthpiece of a god, uttering prophecies and oracles, the most famous of whom was the Cumaean sibyl at Cumae in S. Italy, who guided Aeneas through the underworld; prophetess, fortune-teller, witch.
sibȳ'lline (or sĭ'-) adj. Of a sibyl, oracular, mysteriously prophetic; S~ Books, collection of oracles kept in ancient Rome in temple of Jupiter Capitolinus and freq. consulted by magistrates for guidance; acc. to legend, 9 of these books were offered to Tarquin by a sibyl, who burnt 3 of them and then 3 more when they were refused because of their high price, and finally sold the last 3 at the same price as she had asked for them all.
sĭc adv. (freq. parenth.) So, thus, (used, spelt, etc.) with implication that this use is incorrect or absurd.
si'ccative adj. & n. (Substance etc.) of drying properties.
Si'cel, Sicul'ian ns. Native of ancient Sicily (opp. SICELIOT). ~ adjs. Of the Sicels or Siculians.
Sicĕ'liot n. Ancient Greek settler in Sicily (opp. native SICEL). ~ adj. Of the Siceliots.
Sicil'ian adj. Of Sicily; ~ Vespers, riot which broke out at a church near Palermo while the vesper-bell was ringing on Easter Monday 1282 and developed into a general massacre of the French in Sicily and the expulsion of the Angevins. ~ n. Native, inhabitant, of Sicily.
siciliē'nne, sicilia'na (-ah-) ns. (mus.) Slowish dance (in 6/8 or 12/8 time), freq. in minor key, much used by 18th-c. composers as movement in suite or sonata etc. [Fr. & It. fem. adj., 'Sicilian']
Si'cilȳ. Large island in Mediterranean, separated from 'toe' of Italy by Strait of Messina; in Italian possession since 1860; in ancient times colonized by the Greeks; capital, Palermo.
sick adj. 1. Ill, unwell (now chiefly U.S. and literary); disposed to vomit, vomiting. 2. Disordered, perturbed; suffering effects of; disgusted; pining for; surfeited and tired of; (of humour) morbid; suggesting callousness. 3. Of or for sick persons (~ benefit, leave). 4. ~-bay: see BAY³; ~-bed, invalid's bed; state of being invalid; ~ headache, headache caused by biliousness; ~-list, list of sick esp. in regiment, ship,
etc.; S~ Man of Europe, Turkey during latter part of 19th c.
si'cken v. Begin to be ill, show symptoms of illness; feel nausea or disgust (at etc.); affect with inclination to vomit, loathing, disgust, weariness, or despair. **si'ckening** adj. **si'ckeninglȳ** adv.
si'ckle n. Reaping-hook, short-handled semicircular-bladed implement used for lopping, trimming, etc. (ill. HOOK); anything sickle-shaped, esp. crescent moon; ~-feather, one of the long curved middle feathers of cock's tail.
si'cklȳ adj. Apt to be ill, chronically ailing; suggesting sickness, as of sick person, languid, pale; causing ill health or nausea; mawkish, weakly sentimental. **si'cklinĕss** n. **si'cklȳ** v.t. Cover over, o'er, with sickly hue (with ref. to 'Hamlet', III. i. 85).
si'cknĕss n. Being ill, disease; a disease; vomiting, inclination to vomit.
Siculian: see SICEL.
side n. 1. One of the more or less flat surfaces bounding an object, esp. more or less vertical outer or inner surface; such surface as distinguished from top and bottom, front and back, or ends; either surface of thing regarded as having only two; (math.) bounding line of superficial figure. 2. Either of two lateral surfaces or parts of trunk in persons or animals, esp. extending from armpit to hip or from foreleg to hindleg; part of object in same direction as observer's right or left and not directly towards or away from him, or turned in specified direction; part or region near margin and remote from centre or axis of thing; subordinate, less essential, or more or less detached, part; (attrib.) subordinate; ~ by ~, standing close together, esp. for mutual support. 3. Region external but contiguous to, specified direction with relation to, person or thing; partial aspect of thing; (cause represented by, position in company with) one of two sets of opponents in war, politics, games, etc.; team. 4. Position nearer or farther than, right or left of, dividing line. 5. Line of descent through father or mother. 6. (billiards) Spinning motion given to ball by striking it on side. 7. (slang) Assumption of superiority, swagger. 8. ~-arms, weapons worn at side, as swords, bayonets; **si'deboard**, piece of dining-room furniture, freq. with drawers and cupboards, for holding dishes, wine, plate, etc.; (pl., slang) side-whiskers (also si'deburns); ~-car, jaunting-car; car for passenger(s) attached to side of motor-cycle; kind of cocktail; ~-dish, extra dish, freq. of elaborate kind, at dinner, etc.; ~ drum: see DRUM¹; ~ effect, secondary, esp. undesirable, effect (as of drug) produced in addition to that intended;

si'delight, light at side of vehicle etc.; port or starboard light on ship under way; light coming from the side, (fig.) incidental light on subject etc.; ~-line, (esp.) boundary along side of field of play (ill. LAWN²); subsidiary, secondary, or additional business, pursuit, etc.; on the ~-lines (transf.) looking on but not participating; ~ road, minor or subsidiary road; road joining or diverging from main road; ~-saddle, saddle for rider, usu. woman, with both feet on one (usu. left) side of horse; ~-show, minor show attached to principal one (freq. fig.); ~-slip, skid; (of aircraft) move, motion, sideways; **si'desman**, assistant churchwarden; ~-step, step taken sideways; (v.t.) avoid, evade, (as) by stepping sideways; ~-street, street lying aside from main streets or roads; ~-stroke, swimming-stroke made lying on the side; ~-track, siding; (v.t.) turn into siding, shunt, postpone or evade treatment or consideration of; ~-view, view obtained sideways; profile; ~-walk, (chiefly U.S.) path at side of road for foot-passengers; ~-whiskers, hair left unshaven on cheeks. ~ v.i. Take part, be on same side, with.
si'delŏng (-dl-) adv. & adj. Inclining to one side, oblique(ly).
sidēr'eal adj. Of the stars; (of time) measured by the stars; ~ clock, astronomical clock regulated to sidereal time; ~ day, year: see DAY, YEAR.
si'derostăt n. (astron.) Instrument for keeping heavenly body in same part of telescope field.
si'deways (-dwāz) adv. & adj. Laterally, to or from a side.
si'ding n. Short track by side of railway line and connected with it by switches, for shunting etc.
si'dle v.i. Walk obliquely, esp. in furtive or unobtrusive manner.
Si'dney, Sir Philip (1554-86). English soldier, statesman, and poet; author of the prose romance 'Arcadia' and of a series of sonnets known as 'Astrophel and Stella'.
Si'don. (mod. Saida, Lebanon) Ancient seaport of the Phoenicians; see TYRE².
siege n. Surrounding or hemming in of a fortified place by a military force to compel its surrender or to take it by direct attack, period during which this lasts; besieging, being besieged.
Sie'gfried. Hero of first part of NIBELUNGENLIED, who forged the Nothung sword, slew Fafner, the dragon guarding the stolen Rhine gold, and helped Gunther to win Brunhild; at the instigation of Brunhild he was treacherously slain by Hagen, a Burgundian retainer.
Sie'gfried line. German line of fortifications along the W. border of Germany from Cleves to Basle,

SIENA   SILAGE

constructed prior to the war of 1939-45.

Siē′na. City of Tuscany, Italy.

Sienē′se (-z) *adj. & n.*

siĕ′nna *n.* Ferruginous earth used as pigment, brownish-yellow (*raw* ~) or reddish-brown (*burnt* ~). [It. (*terra*) *di Siena* (earth of) SIENA]

siĕ′rra *n.* In Spain and Spanish America, range of mountains with serrated outline. [Span., f. L *serra* saw]

Siĕ′rra Leō′ne. State on W. coast of Africa, between Liberia and Guinea; member State of the Commonwealth; independent 1961; capital, Freetown.

siĕ′sta *n.* Midday or afternoon rest in hot countries. [Span., f. L *sexta* (*hora*) 6th (hour)]

sieve (sĭv) *n.* Utensil consisting of usu. circular frame with meshed or perforated bottom, for separating finer from coarser parts of loose material, or for straining liquids or pulping solids; coarsely-plaited basket for market produce, this as a measure. ~ *v.t.* Put through, sift with, sieve.

si′ffleur (-êr) *n.* (fem. *si′ffleuse* pr. -êrz) Whistling artiste.

sift *v.* Put through sieve; separate, get *out*, by use of sieve; use sieve; fall as from sieve; sprinkle (sugar etc.) with perforated spoon, castor, etc.; closely examine details of, analyse character of. **si′fter** *n.*

sigh (sī) *n.* Prolonged deep audible respiration expressive of dejection, weariness, longing, relief, etc. ~ *v.* Give sigh or (of wind etc.) sound resembling sigh; utter or express with sighs; yearn, long, *for*.

sight (sīt) *n.* 1. Faculty of seeing (see SEE¹). 2. Seeing, being seen; way of looking at or considering thing; view, point or position commanding view, *of* something; range or field of vision; *at*, *on*, ~, as soon as person or thing has been seen; ~*-reading*, *-singing*, reading music, singing, at sight. 3. Thing seen, visible, or worth seeing; display, show, spectacle; ridiculous, shocking, or repulsive sight; (colloq.) great quantity (*of*); *si′ghtseeing*, act of going to see places or objects of special interest, beauty, etc.; *si′ghtseer* (*n.*). 4. Device for assisting precise aim with gun, bomb, etc., or observation with optical instrument (ill. GUN). ~ *v.t.* Get sight of, esp. by coming near; take observation of (star etc.) with instrument; provide (gun etc.) with sights, adjust sights of; aim (gun etc.) with sights. **si′ghting** *n.* Instance of seeing something, esp. aircraft etc.

si′ghtlĕss (sīt-) *adj.* Blind.

si′ghtlў (sīt-) *adj.* Pleasing to the sight, not unsightly.

si′gma *n.* Letter of Greek alphabet (Σ, σ or *s*; uncial C) corresponding to *s*.

si′gmoid *adj.* Crescent-shaped, like the uncial sigma C; having double curve like letter s; of the ~ *flexure*, curving portion of intestine between colon and rectum.

sign (sīn) *n.* 1. Significant gesture; mark or device with special meaning or used to distinguish thing on which it is put; written mark conventionally used for word, phrase, etc., symbol; token, indication, trace (*of* something); omen, portent; miracle as demonstration of divine power or authority; (path.) objective evidence or indication of disease etc. (cf. SYMPTOM). 2. Characteristic device, freq. painted on board, displayed by inn etc., board bearing name or inscription in front of shop etc. 3. Any of twelve equal divisions of zodiac named from constellations formerly situated in them. 4. *si′gnboard*, = sense 2; ~ *manual*, signature; ~*-painter*, painter of signboards, shop-front inscriptions, etc.; *si′gnpost*, post at cross-roads etc., with arm(s) indicating direction of place(s); (*v.t.*) provide with signpost(s), indicate, direct. ~ *v.* 1. Mark *with* sign of the Cross; mark with sign; make sign, intimate with sign. 2. Attest or confirm by adding one's signature; write (name) as signature; affix one's signature; make *over*, give *away*, etc., by signing; ~ *off*, *on*, end, begin, occupation, broadcast, etc., esp. by writing or announcing one's name; ~ *off*, (bridge) indicate by a conventional bid that one is ending bidding.

si′gnal¹ *n.* Pre-arranged or obvious sign conveying information or direction, esp. to person(s) at a distance; message made up of such signs; electrical impulse or radio wave transmitted or received; ~*-book*, book containing code of signals, and esp. in army, air force, and navy; ~*-box*, hut on railway from which signals are given or worked; *si′gnalman*, signaller. ~ *v.* Make signal(s); make signal(s) to; transmit, announce, by signal, direct (person) *to* do by signal. **si′gnaller** *n.*

si′gnal² *adj.* Remarkable, conspicuous, striking. **si′gnallў** *adv.*

si′gnalīze *v.t.* Distinguish, make conspicuous or remarkable.

si′gnatory *adj. & n.* (Party, esp. State) whose signature is attached to document, esp. treaty.

si′gnature *n.* 1. Name, initials, or mark written with person's own hand as authentication of document or other writing; distinguishing mark; stamp, impression. 2. Letter(s) or figure(s) placed by printer at foot of first page (and freq. other pages) of each sheet of book as guide in making up and binding; a sheet as distinguished by its signature; (mus.) sign(s) placed at beginning of piece of music, movement, etc., to indicate key and time (ill. STAVE); ~ *tune*, special tune used in broadcasting etc. to announce a particular programme or performer.

si′gnet *n.* Small seal, esp. one fixed in finger-ring; small seal orig. used by sovereigns of England and Scotland for private purposes and for certain official documents, in Scotland later serving as seal of Court of Session; *Writer to the S*~: see WRITER.

signi′ficance *n.* Being significant, expressiveness; meaning, import; consequence, importance.

signi′ficant *adj.* Having, conveying, a meaning; full of meaning, highly expressive or suggestive; important, notable. **signi′ficantlў** *adv.*

significā′tion *n.* (esp.) Exact meaning or sense.

signi′ficative *adj.* Signifying: having a meaning; serving as sign or indication *of*.

si′gnify *v.* Be sign or symbol of; represent, mean, denote; communicate, make known; be of importance, matter.

signor, signora, signorina (sē′nyōr, -ōr′a, -orē′na) *ns.* (Title of or form of address to) Italian man, woman, young or unmarried woman. [It.]

Sikh (sēk) *n.* Member of a monotheistic sect established in India (chiefly in Punjab) since 16th c.; esp., member of a martial community maintained by this sect; ~ *Wars*, wars between Sikhs and British, 1845 and 1848-9, culminating in the British annexation of the Punjab.

Si′kkim. Small independent State of E. Himalayas, an Indian protectorate; capital, Gangtok.

si′lage *n.* Preservation of green

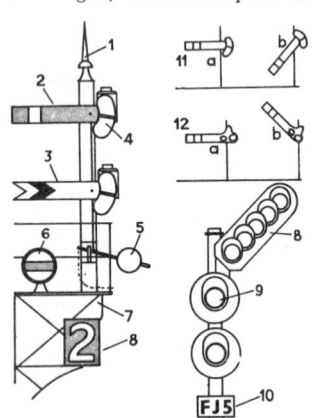

RAILWAY SIGNALS

1. Pinnacle. 2. Stop arm. 3. Distant arm. 4. Front spectacle. 5. Balance weight. 6. 'Banner' signal. 7. Gantry. 8. Route indicator. 9. Colour-light signal. 10. Identification plate. 11. Lower quadrant system. 12. Upper quadrant system (*a* stop, *b* proceed)

[818]

fodder in silo or pit without drying; fodder thus preserved.

Si′las. Member of early Church at Jerusalem (Acts 15: 22, 32, etc.), companion of St. Paul on his second missionary journey.

si′lence *n*. Abstinence from speech or noise, taciturnity, reticence; absence of sound, stillness, noiselessness; neglect or omission to mention, write, etc. ~ *v.t.* Make silent, reduce to silence; put down, repress (expression of opinion etc.); compel (gun, ship, etc.) to cease firing.

si′lencer *n*. (esp.) Device for rendering gun, internal combustion engine, etc., (comparatively) silent.

si′lent *adj*. Not speaking; not uttering, making, or accompanied by, any sound; (of letter) not pronounced; taciturn, speaking little; not mentioning or referring to, passing over, something. **si′lently** *adv*.

silē′nus[1] *n*. (pl. -*ī*). (Gk myth.) Kind of bearded woodland satyr sometimes with horse-tail and -legs.

Silē′nus[2]. (Gk myth.) Foster-father and teacher of Dionysus, freq. represented as a fat, jolly, drunken old man.

Silē′sia[1] (-sha). Ancient duchy and district of E. Europe, partitioned at various times between States of Prussia, Austria-Hungary, Poland, and Czechoslovakia.

silē′sia[2] (-sha) *n*. Thin, twilled cotton or linen cloth, used for dress-linings etc., orig. made in Silesia.

silhouĕ′tte(-lōō-; or sǐ′-) *n*. Portrait of person in profile showing outline only, this being filled in with black, cut out in paper, etc.; dark outline, shadow in profile, thrown up against lighter background. ~ *v.t.* Represent, exhibit, in silhouette. [named after Étienne de *Silhouette* (1709-67), French politician]

si′lica *n*. Silicon dioxide (SiO₂), a hard, white or colourless, widely distributed mineral present in many precious and other stones, esp. quartz, and sand, used in the manufacture of glass, bricks, etc.

si′licate *n*. Salt of silicic acid.

sili′ceous, sili′cious (-sh*u*s) *adj*. Containing or consisting of silica.

sili′cic *adj*. Of, formed from, silica.

sili′cify *v*. Convert, be converted, into silica.

si′licon *n*. (chem.) Non-metallic element occurring only in combination, manufactured commercially by reduction of sand and used in the manufacture of certain alloys; symbol Si, at. no. 14, at. wt 28·086; ~ **carbide**, very hard crystalline compound (SiC), used as an abrasive and as a refractory lining in furnaces etc.

si′licōne *n*. One of a group of synthetic resins containing silicon which resist effects of water and high temperatures, used in polishes, lubricants, insulators, etc.

silicō′sis *n*. (pl. -*sēs*). Chronic lung disease caused by inhalation of stone-dust and freq. affecting coal-miners, one of the group of diseases known as pneumoconioses.

si′liqua *n*. (bot.) Long pod-like seed-vessel (ill. FRUIT).

silk *n*. Strong soft lustrous fibre produced, to form their cocoons, webs, etc., by certain insect larvae, spiders, etc., esp. by 'silkworms' (see below); thread or textile fabric made from this; similar lustrous filament or fibre made by chemical processes from cellulose (*artificial* ~, now usu. *rayon*); silk gown of King's or Queen's Counsel (esp. in *take* ~, become K.C. or Q.C.); silky styles of female maize-flower; (attrib.) made of silk; ~ *cotton*, silky fibre, esp. kapok, covering seeds of tropical trees of family Bombacaceae, used for padding etc.; ~-*cotton tree*, tree yielding this, esp. *Ceiba pentandra*, kapok tree; ~ *hat*, tall stiff cylindrical hat covered with silk plush; ~-*screen printing*: see SCREEN printing; *si′lkworm*, mulberry-feeding caterpillar of moth (*Bombyx mori*), which spins cocoon of silk before changing into pupal state; caterpillar of other moths yielding silk cocoons of commercial value.

si′lken *adj*. Made of silk; clad in silk; soft or lustrous as silk.

si′lky *adj*. Like silk in smoothness, softness, fineness, or lustre. **si′lkiness** *n*.

sill *n*. 1. Horizontal piece or part at base of doorway or etc. window (ill. WINDOW). 2. Timber across the bottom of the entrance to a lock on a canal or river against which the gates close (ill. DOCK³). 3. Sheet of intrusive volcanic rock lying parallel to the bedding of other rocks (ill. ROCK¹).

si′llabŭb, sy̆ll- *n*. Dish of cream or milk mixed with wine etc. into soft curd and sometimes whipped or solidified with gelatine.

Si′llery *n*. Any of various kinds of sparkling and esp. still champagne made at or near Sillery, a village in Champagne.

si′lly *adj*. Innocent, simple, helpless (archaic); foolish, weak-minded, unwise, imbecile; ~ *season*, late summer as time when newspapers print trivial articles or discussions for lack of important news; ~ *mid-on*, *point*, etc., (cricket) fielder placed close up to batsman (ill. CRICKET). **si′llily** *adv*. **si′lliness** *n*.

si′lō *n*. Pit or airtight structure in which fodder is pressed to undergo fermentation for conversion into succulent winter feed. ~ *v.t.* Make silage of.

Silō′am. Spring and pool of water near Jerusalem, where the man born blind was bidden by Christ to wash (John 9: 7).

silt *n*. Sediment deposited by water in channel, harbour, etc. ~ *v.* Choke, be choked, (*up*) with silt.

Silūr′ēs (-z) *n.pl.* Members of a tribe in SE. Wales who resisted the Roman invasion (A.D. 43). **Silūr′ian** *adj. & n.* 1. (One) of the Silures. 2. (geol.) (Of) the period or system of the Palaeozoic between Ordovician and Devonian (ill. GEOLOGY).

silvan: see SYLVAN.

Silvā′nus. (Rom. myth.) Spirit of woods, fields, flocks, etc.

si′lver *n*. 1. (chem.) White lustrous ductile malleable metallic element, one of the precious metals, used chiefly with alloy of harder metal for coin, plate, etc., and in form of salts as the light-sensitive materials in photography; symbol Ag, at. no. 47, at. wt 107·868. 2. Silver coins; cupro-nickel coins now substituted for these in Britain; money in general (chiefly Sc.); silverware, silver plate; household cutlery. 3. (attrib.) *si′lversmith*, worker in silver, maker of silverware; *si′lverware*, articles made of silver. ~ *adj*. Wholly or chiefly of, coloured like, silver; having clear ringing sound; eloquent; (of lace etc.) containing silver threads; ~ *age*, (i) (Gk & Rom. myth.) second age of the world, inferior to golden age; (ii) second phase of classical Latin (see Silver LATIN); ~ *birch*, common white birch, *Betula alba*, from the colour of the bark; ~ *fir*, any of various firs with white or silvery colour on under-surface of leaves, esp. the central European and Asiatic *Abies alba*; ~-*fish*, various silvery fishes, esp. white variety of goldfish; small silvery wingless insect (*Lepisma saccharina*) found in damp places in

SILVER-FISH
(*Lepisma saccharina*)

houses; ~ *fox*, colour form of American red fox with highly prized black fur which appears silver-tipped because the long hairs are banded with white near tips; ~ *gilt*, silver gilded over; ~-*grey*, lustrous grey; S~ *Latin*: see LATIN; ~ *lining*, sign of hope in gloom; ~ *paper*, fine white tissue-paper; tinfoil; ~-*plate* (*v.t.*) plate with silver, electroplate; ~ *sand*, fine white pure quartz sand used in glass-making, for polishing, and in gardening for assisting plant-growth; *si′lverside*, upper and choicer side of a round of beef (ill. MEAT); *si′lverweed*, plant with silvery leaves, esp. a common wayside plant (*Potentilla argentea*) with leaves silvery-white underneath and yellow flowers. ~ *v.* Coat or plate with silver; give silvery appearance to; turn

[819]

SILVERY

(hair etc.), become, white or grey; provide (mirror-glass) with amalgam of tin and quicksilver.
si'lvery *adj.* Resembling silver in lustre, whiteness, ringing sound, etc.
si'ma *n.* (geol.) Part of earth's crust immediately below SIAL. [f. *si*licon and *ma*gnesium.]
Simenon (sēmenawn), Georges (1903–). Writer of crime fiction, born in Belgium; creator of MAIGRET.
Sī'mėon. Hebrew patriarch, son of Jacob and Leah (Gen. 29: 33); tribe of Israel traditionally descended from him.
Sī'mėon Stȳli'tės (-z), St. (*c* 390–459). First of the stylites; lived for 30 years on top of a pillar near Antioch in Syria.
si'mian *adj. & n.* (Of) one of the apes, esp. the anthropoid apes; ape(-like), monkey(-like).
si'milar *adj.* Like, alike, having mutual resemblance or resemblance *to*, of the same kind; (geom.) having same shape. **si'milarly** *adv.* **similă'rity** *n.*
si'milė *n.* Writer's or speaker's introduction of an object or scene or action with which the one in hand is compared for the purpose of illustration or ornament; passage effecting this.
simi'litūde *n.* Guise, outward appearance; (obs.) simile.
si'mmer *v.* Be, keep, on the point of boiling, cook slowly in liquid at temperature just below boiling-point (freq. fig.). ~ *n.* Simmering state.
Si'mnel, Lambert (*c* 1475–1525). English youth who impersonated the imprisoned Edward, Earl of Warwick (1475–99) immediately after the Wars of the Roses; he was crowned in Dublin as Edward VI, 1487, but defeated at Stoke, near Newark, by Henry VII, pardoned, and employed as a turnspit in the royal kitchen.
si'mnel cake. Rich decorated fruit cake made chiefly at midLent and Easter.
Si'mon. 1. St. PETER². 2. Apostle, member of the Zealot party (~ *Zelotes* or *the Canaanite*); commemorated with St. Jude, 28 Oct. 3. Kinsman of Jesus Christ (Matt. 13: 55, Mark 6: 3). 4. (also ~ *Magus*) Sorcerer of Samaria who was converted by Philip; he offered money to the Apostles if they would confer upon him the power to impart the Holy Ghost, and was rebuked by Peter (Acts 8: 9–19).
Simo'nidės (-z) (556–468 B.C.). Greek lyric poet.
si'mony *n.* Buying or selling of ecclesiastical preferment. [f. SIMON Magus]
simoō'm, simoō'n *n.* Hot dry suffocating dust-laden wind of Arabian, Syrian, etc., deserts.
si'mper *n.* Affected and self-conscious smile, smirk. ~ *v.* Smile in silly affected manner, smirk; utter with simper.
si'mple *adj.* 1. Not compound, complex, complicated, elaborate, involved, or composite; unmixed, consisting of one substance, ingredient, or element; presenting no difficulty; mere, pure, bare; ~ *equation*, one not involving second or any higher power of unknown quantity; ~ *interest*: see INTEREST; ~ *life*, life in more or less primitive conditions, without servants or luxuries; ~ *sentence*, one without subordinate clause. 2. Plain, unsophisticated, natural, artless; inexperienced; weak-minded; of low rank, ordinary; ~-hearted, -minded, ingenuous. **si'mply** *adv.* In simple manner; without exception, absolutely. **si'mpleness** *n.* **simpli'city** *n.* **si'mple** *n.* (archaic) Herb used medicinally; medicine made from this.
si'mpleton (-lt-) *n.* Foolish, gullible, or half-witted person.
si'mplify *v.t.* Make simple, make easy to do or understand. **simplifica'tion** *n.*
Simplon (sănplawn). Alpine pass in SW. Switzerland; ~ *tunnel*, railway tunnel, about 12 miles long, driven through Monte Leone, NE. of the pass.
Si'mpson, Sir James Young (1811–70). Scottish surgeon; introduced the use of chloroform as an anaesthetic.
simūlā'crum *n.* (pl. *-ra*). Image of something; shadowy likeness, deceptive substitute, mere pretence.
si'mūlāte *v.t.* Feign, counterfeit; pretend to be, wear guise of, mimic. **simūlā'tion** *n.* **si'mūlātor** *n.* (esp.) Machine simulating conditions experienced in flying aircraft, driving vehicle, etc., used esp. in training pilots etc.
simultā'nėous *adj.* Existing, occurring, operating, at the same time (*with*); ~ *equations*, equations involving the same values of the unknown quantity or quantities and solved in conjunction with each other. **simultā'nėously** *adv.* **simultā'nėousness** *n.*
sin¹ *n.* (A) transgression against divine law or principles of morality; offence *against* good taste, propriety, etc.; DEADLY, MORTAL, ORIGINAL ~: see these words; *seven deadly ~s*: see SEVEN. **si'nful, si'nless** *adjs.* **si'nfully, si'nlessly** *advs.* **si'nfulness, si'nlessness** *ns.* **sin** *v.i.* Commit sin; offend *against*. **si'nner** *n.*
sin² *abbrev.* Sine.
Sī'nāi (or -nīi). Peninsula at the N. end of the Red Sea; *Mount ~*, mountain in S. part of this peninsula, where (Exod. 19–34) the Ten Commandments and the Tables of the Law were given to Moses. **Sināi'tic** *adj.* Of Mount Sinai or the peninsula.
si'napism *n.* Mustard plaster.
since *adv.* From that time till now; within the period between then and now, subsequently, later;

SINGLE

ago, before now. ~ *prep.* From (specified time) till now; during the period between (specified past time) and now. ~ *conj.* 1. From the time that. 2. Seeing that, because, inasmuch as.
sincēr'e *adj.* Free from pretence or deceit, not assumed or put on, genuine, honest, frank. **sincēr'ely** *adv.* In a sincere manner; *yours ~*, polite formula used before signature in letter (e.g. to acquaintance) which is neither formal nor intimate. **sincĕ'rity** *n.*
si'ncipŭt *n.* Front part of head or skull.
Sĭnd. Region of W. Pakistan.
Sī'ndbād. (also *Sinbad* or ~ *the Sailor*) Hero of one of the tales in the 'Arabian Nights', who relates his fantastic adventures in a number of voyages.
sīne *n.* (trig., function of angle in right-angled triangle) Ratio of side opposite given acute angle to hypotenuse (abbrev. sin; ill. TRIGONOMETRY); ~ *curve*, graph in rectangular coordinates showing how this ratio varies with the angle.
si'nėcūre *n.* Office of profit or honour without duties attached, esp. benefice without cure of souls.
sī'nė dī'ē. (Adjourned) without any day for resumption of business etc. being specified; indefinitely. [L, = 'without day']
sī'nė quā nŏn. Indispensable condition or qualification. [L, = 'without which not']
si'new *n.* (Piece of) tough fibrous tissue uniting muscle to bone, tendon; (pl., loosely) muscles, bodily strength, wiriness (freq. fig., esp. in ~*s of war*, money). **si'newy** (-ūi) *adj.*
sing *v.* (past t. *săng*, past part. *sŭng*). Utter words or sounds, utter (words, sounds), in tuneful succession, esp. in accordance with a set tune; produce vocal melody, utter (song, tune); make inarticulate melodious, humming, buzzing, or whistling sounds, (of ears) have sensation of being filled with humming sound; compose poetry, celebrate in verse; ~ *out*, (slang) call out loudly. **si'nger** *n.*
Singapōr'e. Republic consisting of the island of Singapore and a number of smaller islands, S. of Malay peninsula; former British colony; member State of the Commonwealth, independent 1965.
singe (-j) *n.* Superficial burn. ~ *v.t.* Burn superficially or lightly, burn ends or edges of.
Singh (-ng) *n.* (Indian) Great warrior; title of warrior castes, as Rajputs and Sikhs.
Singhalese: see SINHALESE.
si'ngle (-nggl) *adj.* One only, not double or multiple, undivided, individual, separate; of, for, one person only; solitary, lonely, unaided; unmarried; (of flower) not double, having only one whorl or set of petals; (of game) with one person only on each side; (of

[820]

journey, ticket for this) not return; ~ **bed**, bed for use of one person only; ~**-breasted**, (of garments) having buttons on one edge, not double-breasted; ~ **combat**, combat between two persons; ~ **court**, court for single game (lawn tennis etc.); ~ **entry**, simple method of book-keeping in which transactions are entered in the ledger under one account only (opp. *double* ENTRY); ~ *file*, line of persons going one behind another, Indian file; ~**-handed**, (done etc.) without help from other persons; ~**-hearted**, sincere, honest; ~**-minded**, single-hearted; also, keeping one purpose in view; ~ **room**, room for use of one person only; ~**-stick**, (fighting or fencing with) basket-hilted stick. **sī′ṅgleness** *n.* **sī′ṅglȳ** *adv.*
sī′ṅgle *n.* Single ticket; (tennis etc.) single game (usu. pl.); hit for one in cricket; (pl.) twisted single threads of silk. ~ *v.t.* Choose *out* as example, to serve some purpose etc.
sī′ṅglet (-ngg-) *n.* Undershirt, vest; athlete's vest worn instead of shirt.
sī′ṅgleton (-ngglt-) *n.* (whist, bridge, etc.) Card which is the only one of its suit in the hand.
Sing Sing. New York State prison at Ossining, a suburb of New York City.
sī′ṅgsŏṅg *adj.* In, recited with, monotonous rhythm, rising and falling monotonously. ~ *n.* Monotonous rhythm or cadence; impromptu or informal vocal concert.
sī′ṅgūlar (-ngg-) *adj.* 1. (gram.) Denoting, expressing, one person or thing. 2. Unusual, uncommon, extraordinary, surprising; strange, odd, peculiar. **sī′ṅgūlarlȳ** *adv.* **siṅgūlā′ritȳ** *n.* (esp.) Eccentricity, oddness, strangeness. **si′ṅgūlar** *n.* Singular number; word in singular form.
Sīnhalē′se (-z), **Siṅgh-, Sī′nhala** *n.* 1.(Member of) the majority community in Sri Lanka. 2. Indo-European language spoken in Sri Lanka, closely related to Pali, with many Dravidian words. ~ *adj.*
sī′nister *adj.* 1. Of evil omen; unfavourable, harmful; wicked, corrupt, evil; ill-looking, malignant, villainous. 2. (her.) On left side of shield etc. (from bearer's point of view) (ill. HERALDRY).
sī′nistral *adj.* (of spiral shells) With whorls going to left; (of flat fishes) having left side of body turned uppermost.
sink[1] *n.* 1. Place in which foul liquid collects (now usu. fig.). 2. Large fixed basin for washing crockery etc., usu. rectangular, made of porcelain, stone, metal, etc., with pipe for escape of water to a drain, and usu. with supply of water connected with it. 3. *heat* ~, device for dissipating heat, (esp.) metal block, usu. covered with fins, which dissipates heat from transistor by radiation and convection (ill. TRANSISTOR).
sink[2] *v.* (past t. *sănk*, past part. *sŭnk* and rarely in vbl., commonly in adj., use *sŭ′nken*). 1. Become wholly or partly submerged in water, quicksand, snow, etc. (freq. fig.); fall slowly downwards, subside, descend, pass out of sight; pass, fall gently, lapse, degenerate, *into*; (of sun etc.) appear to move downwards towards or pass below horizon; penetrate, make way *in(to).* 2. Cause or allow to sink; send below surface of liquid or ground; lower level of; excavate, make by excavating; set aside, leave out of consideration; invest (money), lose by investment.
sī′nker *n.* (esp.) Weight used to sink fishing or sounding line.
Sī′nkiǎ′ṅg-Uighur (-wē′ger). Autonomous region of China; capital, Urumchi.
sī′ṅkiṅg *n.* (esp.) Internal bodily sensation caused by hunger or apprehension; ~-*fund*, fund of money periodically set aside from revenue, usu. to reduce principal of national, municipal, or company's debt.
Sinn Fein (shĭn fān). Irish society, founded 1905 by Arthur Griffith, aiming at political independence and revival of Irish culture and language; policy of this; extreme Irish nationalist party. [Ir., = 'we ourselves']
Sino- *prefix.* Of China and —, as ~-*Soviet.*
sinŏ′logȳ *n.* Study of Chinese language, history, customs, etc. **sī′nologūe** (-g), **sinŏ′logist** *ns.* Person versed in this.
sī′nophil, -phīle, sī′nophōbe *ns.* One who loves, hates, the Chinese.
Sīno-Tībě′tan *adj. & n.* (Of) the family of languages, mostly of the isolating type but orig. agglutinative, spoken over an area including N. India, Malay peninsula, China, and most of central and E. Asia (but not Japan).
sī′nter *n.* Siliceous deposit often found round hot springs. ~ *v.* Become or cause to become a solid mass.
sī′nūate *adj.* (esp. bot.) Wavy-edged. **sī′nūatelȳ** *adv.* **sinūā′tion** *n.*
sī′nūous *adj.* With many curves, tortuous, serpentine, undulating. **sī′nūouslȳ** *adv.* **sī′nūousness** *n.* **sinūō′sitȳ** *n.* Sinuousness; a curve or bend.
sī′nus *n.* 1. (anat., zool.) Cavity of bone or tissue, esp. one of the cavities in the bone of the skull which communicate with the nostrils (ill. HEAD). 2. (path.) Passage communicating with deep-seated abscess, fistula. 3. (bot.) Curve between lobes of leaf.
sinusī′tis *n.* Inflammation of sinus(es).
sio′miō (shō-) *n.* One of the inferior nobles of Japan who were vassals of the Shogun.
Sioux (sōō) *n.* (Member of) important group of N. Amer. Indian tribes, orig. of district W. and S. of Lake Superior, later of plains of Minnesota, N. and S. Dakota, and Nebraska. **Siou′an** *adj.*
sip *n.* Small mouthful of liquid; act of sipping. ~ *v.* Drink in sips, take sip of.
sī′phon *n.* Pipe or tube bent so that one leg is longer than the other and used for drawing off liquids by atmospheric pressure, which forces liquid up the shorter leg and over the bend in the pipe; aerated-water bottle from which liquid is forced out by pressure of gas through tube inserted in bottle; (zool.) tube-like organ, esp. in molluscs, serving as canal for passage of fluid etc. (ill. MUSSEL); siphuncle; ~ *barometer*, type of mercury barometer (ill. BAROMETER). **sī′phonal, siphŏ′nic** *adjs.* **sī′phon** *v.* Conduct, flow, (as) through siphon.
sī′phonet *n.* (zool.) Honey-tube of aphis.
sī′phuncle *n.* (zool.) Small canal or tube connecting shell-chambers in some cephalopods.
sī′ppet *n.* Small piece of (fried) bread or of toast served in soup, with meat, etc.
sīr *n.* 1. S~, title of honour placed before Christian name of knight or baronet. 2. Used (without name) in addressing master, superior in rank, age, etc., or an equal; sometimes with scornful, indignant, contemptuous, etc., force; (*Dear*) *S*~(*s*), opening of formal letter. ~ *v.t.* Address as *sir*.
sīr′car *n.* (Ind.) The Government of India; head of government or household; house-steward; Indian accountant. [Hind., f. Pers. *sarkar* (*sar* head, *kār* work)]
sīr′dar *n.* (Ind.) 1. Person in command, leader. 2. Sikh. [Urdu, f. Pers. *sar* head, *dār* possessor]
sīre *n.* 1. Father, forefather (poet.); male parent of beast, esp. stallion. 2. (archaic) = 'your majesty'. ~ *v.t.* Beget (esp. of stallions).
sīr′en *n.* 1. (Gk myth.) Any of several fabulous creatures, women or birds with women's heads, living on rocky isle to which they lured seafarers by their singing. 2. Sweet singer; dangerously fascinating woman, temptress; (attrib.) irresistibly tempting. 3. Apparatus producing loud sound by revolution of perforated disc over jet of compressed air or steam, used as ship's fog-signal, air-raid warning, etc.; ~ *suit*, one-piece suit of clothes, easily put on or off, for use during a night air-raid. 4. Eel-like tailed amphibian of family Sirenidae, with short forelegs and no hindlegs.
sīrē′nian *adj. & n.* (Member) of order Sirenia of large aquatic herbivorous mammals, including manatee and dugong.

Si′rius. (astron.) Dog-star, a brilliant white star in the constellation Canis Major, the brightest fixed star.

sir′loin n. Upper and choicer part of loin of beef (ill. MEAT).

sirŏ′ccō n. (pl. -s). Hot and blighting oppressive wind blowing from N. coast of Africa over Mediterranean and parts of S. Europe, esp. Italy, Malta, and Sicily. [It. s(c)irocco, f. Arab. šarūk east wind]

si′rrah n. (archaic) = SIR used in contempt, reproach, reprimand, etc.

sirree′ n. (U.S. colloq.) Sir.

si′rup n. (U.S.) = SYRUP.

si′sal n. (also ~-grass, -hemp) Strong durable white fibre of a W. Indian agave (Agave sisalina) and similar plants, used for cordage etc. [Sisal, former seaport of Yucatan]

Si′sera. Canaanite who led an army against the Israelites and was killed by JAEL (Judges 4, 5).

si′skin n. Small sharp-billed olive-green song-bird of Europe and Asia (Carduelis spinus), allied to goldfinch.

Si′sley, Alfred (1840–99). French Impressionist landscape-painter.

si′ssy: see CISSY.

si′ster n. 1. Daughter of same parents as another person; one considered as or filling the place of a sister. 2. Member of a religious sisterhood, nun; head nurse of hospital ward; S~, title of or form of address to either of these; S~ of Mercy, member of one of various religious organizations devoted to educational and charitable work, esp. that founded 1827 in Dublin. **si′sterly** adj.

si′sterhood n. 1. Being a sister, relation between sisters. 2. Society of women bound by monastic vows or devoting themselves to religious or charitable work.

Si′stine (or -ēn) adj. 1. Of, pertaining to, built by, one of the popes named Sixtus; ~ chapel, chapel in the Vatican, built by Sixtus IV, containing Michelangelo's painted ceiling and his fresco of the Last Judgement; ~ Vulgate, edition of the Vulgate issued under the papacy of Sixtus V. 2. ~ Madonna, painting by Raphael formerly in the Church of San Sisto, Piacenza, and later in Dresden.

si′strum n. (Egyptian antiq.) Jingling instrument of thin metal frame with transverse loose metal rods and handle by which it was shaken, used esp. in worship of Isis.

Si′syphus. (Gk myth.) Legendary king of Corinth, condemned for his misdeeds to Hades; his eternal task was to roll a large stone to the top of a hill from which it rolled back again to the plain. **Sisyphē′an** adj. (As) of Sisyphus, everlastingly laborious.

sit v. (past t. & past part. săt). 1. Take, be in, position in which weight of body rests on buttocks; occupy seat as judge, with administrative function, as member of council or legislative assembly, etc.; (of assembly) hold a session, transact business; pose (for portrait etc. to painter etc.); take examination. 2. (of birds and some animals) Rest with legs bent and body close to ground or perch; remain on nest to hatch eggs. 3. (chiefly of inanimate things) Be in more or less permanent position. 4. Seat oneself (usu. down); cause to sit (usu. down); sit on (horse); (of bird) sit on, hatch (eggs). 5. ~ down, seat oneself; (mil.) encamp before town etc. to besiege it; ~-down strike, one in which strikers refuse to leave the place where they are working; ~ down under, submit tamely to; ~-in, organized protest in which demonstrators occupy building etc.; ~ on, hold session concerning; (slang) repress, squash, snub; ~ out, remain to end of; outstay; take no part in (dance etc.), sit out dance; ~ up, rise from lying to sitting posture; sit erect; (of animal) sit on hind legs with forelegs straight or lifted in begging posture; remain out of bed. ~ n. (esp.) Set (of garment etc.).

si′tär n. Long-necked seven-stringed Indian musical instrument resembling a lute.

site n. Ground on which town, building, etc., stood, stands, or is to stand; ground set apart for some purpose. ~ v.t. Locate, place, provide with site.

si′trep n. (mil.) Situation report.

si′tter n. (esp.) 1. Person sitting for portrait etc.; (also ~-in) BABY-sitter. 2. Easy catch, stroke, shot, etc.; something that can hardly be bungled.

si′tting n. (esp.) 1. Time during which one sits or remains seated; meeting of legislature or other body; single occasion of sitting for artist etc. 2. Clutch of eggs. 3. ~-room, space for sitting; room used for sitting in (opp. bedroom, kitchen, etc.).

si′tuāte v.t. Place or put in position, situation, etc. **si′tuāted, si′tūate** adjs. In specified situation. **situā′tion** n. 1. Place, with its surroundings, occupied by something. 2. Set of circumstances, position in which one finds oneself; critical point or complication, position of affairs, in narrative, drama, etc. 3. Place or paid office, esp. of domestic servant.

sitz-bath (-bah-) n. Hip-bath. [Ger. Sitzbad, f. sitzen sit]

Si′va, Shi′va (sē- or shē-). (Hinduism) One of the supreme gods, third deity of the triad of which Brahma and Vishnu are the other members; he represents the principle of destruction and the regeneration which follows it; he has countless names and manifests himself in various shapes. **Si′vaism, Shi′vaism** ns. Worship of Siva or Shiva.

six adj. Amounting to six; ~-foot, measuring 6 feet; ~-foot way, (on railway) space between two parallel pairs of rails; S~ Counties, those of Northern Ireland (Antrim, Armagh, Down, Fermanagh, Londonderry, Tyrone); S~ Nations, (U.S. hist.) confederation of N. Amer. Indians consisting of the FIVE Nations and the Tuscaroras; si′xpence, sum of six pence; coin formerly worth this; ~-shooter, revolver capable of firing 6 shots without reloading. ~ n. One more than five; symbol for this (6, vi, or VI); card, die-face, or domino with 6 pips; 6 o'clock; size etc. indicated by 6; set of 6 things or persons. **si′xfōld** adj. & adv.

si′xer n. (colloq.) Hit for 6 runs in cricket.

sixte n. Sixth of the 8 positions in fencing (ill. FENCE).

si′xteen adj. One more than fifteen; sixteenmo, 16mo, sextodecimo. ~ n. The number sixteen (16, xvi, or XVI). **si′xtee′nth** adj. & n.

sixth adj. Next after fifth; ~ day, Friday (with the Society of Friends); ~ sense, supposed faculty by which a person perceives facts and regulates action without the direct use of any of the five senses. ~ n. Sixth part (see PART[1], 1); sixth thing etc.; sixth form in school; (mus.) interval of which the span involves 6 alphabetical names of notes (ill. INTERVAL); harmonic combination of notes thus separated. **si′xthly** adv. In the sixth place.

Si′xtine (or -ēn) adj. = SISTINE.

Si′xtus. Name of five popes, esp.: Sixtus IV, pope 1471–84, patron of art and letters, builder of the SISTINE Chapel, refounded the Vatican library; Sixtus V, pope 1585–90, reorganized the papal finances and initiated (1589) the Sistine Vulgate.

si′xty adj. Amounting to sixty. ~ n. Cardinal number, six times ten (60, lx, or LX); set of 60 things or persons; sixties, numbers etc. from 60 to 69; these years of century or life. **si′xtieth** adj. & n.

si′zar n. In University of Cambridge and at Trinity College, Dublin, student receiving allowance from the college and formerly charged with certain menial offices. **si′zarship** n. [f. SIZE[1], n. in obs. sense of 'portion']

size[1] n. Dimensions, magnitude; one of usu. numbered classes into which things, esp. garments, are divided in respect of size. ~ v.t. Group or sort in sizes or according to size; ~ up, estimate size of; (colloq.) form judgement of.

size[2] n. Glutinous substance, preparation of glue, shellac, etc.,

SIZEABLE

and water, used for glazing paper, stiffening textiles, mixing with colours, etc. ~ *v.t.* Treat with size.
sī′zeable (-za-) *adj.* Of fairly large size.
sī′zzle *v.i.* Make sputtering or hissing sound, esp. in frying, roasting, etc. ~ *n.* Sizzling noise.
S.J. *abbrev.* Society of Jesus.
S.J.A.(A., B.) *abbrev.* St. John Ambulance (Association, Brigade).
sjä′mbŏk (sh-) *n.* Rhinoceros-hide whip. ~ *v.t.* Flog with sjambok. [S. Afr. Du., f. Malay, *samboq*, f. Urdu *chābuk*]
S.J.C. *abbrev.* (U.S.) Supreme Judicial Court.
Skă′gerrăk. N. part of channel between S. Scandinavia and Denmark connecting North Sea with Baltic.
skald: see SCALD[2].
skăt *n.* Three-handed card game played with 32 cards.
skāte[1] *n.* Cartilaginous fish of family Rajidae, esp. *Raja batis*, large flat food-fish with very large pectoral fins giving fish a rhomboidal shape.
skāte[2] *n.* One of a pair of steel blades, each attached beneath boot-sole, enabling wearer to glide over ice; ROLLER-skate. ~ *v.i.* Move, glide, (as) on skates.
skean, skĕne *n.* Kind of knife or dagger formerly used in Ireland and Highlands of Scotland; ~-*dhu* (doō), dagger stuck in stocking as part of Highland costume.
skĕdă′ddle *v.* (colloq.) Run away, retreat hastily. ~ *n.* Precipitate retreat or flight, scurry.
skein (-ān) *n.* 1. Quantity of yarn or thread coiled and usu. loosely twisted. 2. Flight of wild geese or other wild fowl.
skĕ′lĕton *n.* Hard internal or external framework of bones, cartilage, shell, woody fibre, etc., supporting or containing animal or vegetable body; dried bones of human being or other animal fastened together in same relative positions as in life; very thin or emaciated person, etc.; mere outlines, supporting framework, main features or most necessary elements, *of* something; *attrib.* (of staff, company, regiment, etc.) of the minimum size, forming a nucleus or cadre that can be added to as occasion arises; ~ *key*, key fitting many locks by having large part of bit filed away; ~ *leaf*, leaf of which parenchyma has been removed or rotted away, so that only network of veins remains. **skĕ′lĕtal** *adj.*
skĕ′lĕtonīze *v.t.* Reduce to a skeleton.
Skĕ′lton, John (c 1460–1529). English poet, author of satires, ballads, and allegories.
skene: see SKEAN.
skĕp *n.* (see also SKIP[5]). Wooden or wicker basket or hamper of kinds varying locally; amount contained in skep, formerly as measure of capacity; straw or wicker beehive; (north.) coal-scuttle.
skĕtch *n.* Preliminary, rough, slight, merely outlined, or unfinished drawing or painting; brief account or narrative without detail, rough draft, general outline; short slight play, freq. of single scene; ~-*block*, -*book*, block or book of drawing-paper for making sketches on; ~-*map*, -*plan*, map, plan, with outlines but little detail. ~ *v.* Make or give sketch of; make sketches.
skĕ′tchy *adj.* Giving only a slight or rough outline; resembling a sketch; light, flimsy, hurried, rough. **skĕ′tchĭlў** *adv.* **skĕ′tchĭnĕss** *n.*

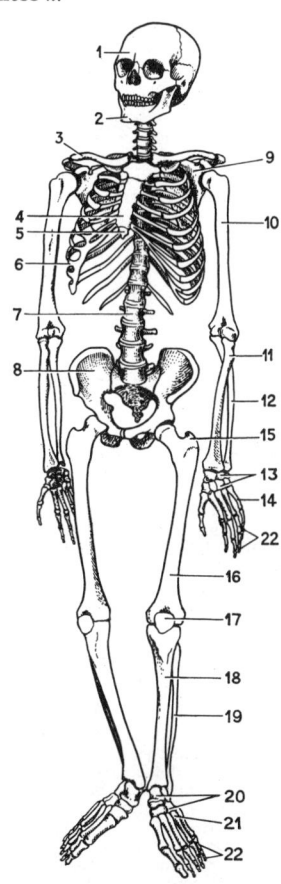

HUMAN SKELETON

1. Skull. 2. Mandible. 3. Clavicle or collar-bone. 4. Sternum or breastbone. 5. Xiphoid process. 6. Ribs. 7. Spine. 8. Pelvis. 9. Scapula or shoulder-blade. 10. Humerus. 11. Radius. 12. Ulna. 13. Carpal bones. 14. Metacarpal bones. 15. Trochanter. 16. Femur. 17. Patella or knee-cap. 18. Tibia. 19. Fibula. 20. Tarsal bones. 21. Metatarsal bones. 22. Phalanges

SKILFUL

skew *adj.* Oblique, slanting, squint, not symmetrical (now usu. archit., mech., etc.); ~ *arch*, arch springing from two points not level with each other. ~ *n.* Sloping top of buttress; coping of gable; stone built into bottom of gable to support coping.
skew′bald (-awld) *adj. & n.* (Horse) with brown and white patches all over body, and white, black, or brown (or mixed) mane and tail.
skew′er *n.* Pin for holding meat compactly together while cooking. ~ *v.t.* Fasten together, pierce, (as) with skewer.
ski (-ē *or* shē) *n.* (pl. -s). One of pair of long slender pieces of wood, usu. pointed and curved upward

SKIING TURNS
1. Stem turn. 2. Christiania. 3. Telemark

at front, fastened to boot and enabling wearer to glide over snow-covered surface; ~-*lift*, device for transporting skiers up mountain-side, usu. consisting of seats suspended from overhead cable; (also *water*-~) similar device for use on water. ~ *v.i.* Travel on skis.
skid *n.* 1. Piece of frame or timber serving as buffer, support, inclined plane, for logs, etc. 2. Braking device, esp. wooden or metal shoe, fixed under the wheel of a cart etc. and so preventing its turning when descending a steep hill; runner on aircraft to facilitate landing, protect tail or wings on landing, etc. (ill. AEROPLANE). 3. Act of skidding; ~-*pan*, surface artificially prepared to induce skidding, used for practice in controlling skidding vehicles. ~ *v.* 1. Support, move, protect, check, with skid(s). 2. (of wheel etc.) Slide without revolving, fail to grip ground, side-slip; (of vehicle etc.) slide sideways towards outside of curve when turning; slip, slide, esp. with (partial) loss of balance.
skiff *n.* Small light boat, esp. for rowing or sculling; long narrow outrigged racing-boat for one oarsman, covered in fore and aft with canvas.
ski′lful *adj.* Having or showing skill, practised, adept, expert, ingenious. **ski′lfullў** *adv.*

[823]

skill *n.* Expertness, practised ability, dexterity, facility in doing something.

skilled (-ld) *adj.* (esp., of workman etc.) Properly trained or experienced; (of work) requiring skill and experience.

ski′llet *n.* Metal cooking utensil usu. with three or four feet and long handle; (esp. U.S.) frying-pan.

ski′lly *n.* Thin watery porridge, gruel, or soup, usu. of oatmeal and water, formerly served in prison, workhouse, etc.

skim *v.* Take scum, cream, floating matter, from surface of (liquid), remove (cream etc.) from surface of milk etc.; pass over (surface), pass *over*, *along*, rapidly and lightly with close approach or very slight contact; read superficially, look over cursorily. ~ *adj.* ~ *milk*, milk with the cream removed.

ski′mmer *n.* (esp.) 1. Ladle, usu. perforated, or other utensil for skimming liquids. 2. Long-winged marine bird of genus *Rynchops*, obtaining food by skimming along surface of water with knife-like lower mandible immersed.

skimp *v.* Supply meagrely; be parsimonious. **ski′mpy** *adj.* Meagre, inadequate.

skin *n.* 1. Tough flexible continuous covering of human or other animal body, consisting of two layers, the *epidermis* or outer

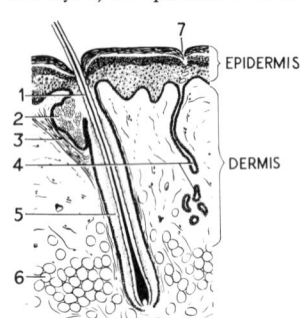

SECTION OF HUMAN SKIN
1. Hair in follicle. 2. Sebaceous gland. 3. *Erector pili* muscle. 4. Sweat glands. 5. Root sheath. 6. Fat and subcutaneous tissue. 7. Pore.

layer, and the *dermis* or inner layer, with (in mammals) its sebaceous glands, hair follicles, etc.; one of the separate layers of which skin is composed; hide of flayed animal, esp. of smaller animals, as sheep, goat, etc., with or without the hair or wool; vessel for wine or water made of animal's whole skin; *get under one's* ~, take a strong hold on, irritate. 2. Outer coating, peel, rind, of fruit, vegetable, etc.; thin film or pellicle; outer covering of ribs or frame of ship, boat, or aircraft (ill. AERO-

PLANE). 3. ~-*deep*, superficial, not deep or lasting; ~-*dive* (*v.i.* & *n.*) dive without diving-suit (usu. in ref. to deep diving with aqualung); so ~-*diver*; ~ *game*, (U.S. slang) swindle; ~-*tight*, (of garment) very close-fitting. **ski′nful** *n.* (slang) As much liquor as one can hold. **skin** *v.* 1. Cover (usu. *over*), as with skin; form, become covered (usu. *over*) with, new skin. 2. Strip skin from, flay; remove skin of. 3. (slang) Swindle, fleece; *ski′nflint*, niggard, miser.

skink *n.* Any lizard of the family Scincidae, e.g. *Scincus officinalis* of N. Africa and Arabia.

ski′nner *n.* (esp., now chiefly in name of a City company) Dealer in skins, furrier.

ski′nny *adj.* (esp.) 1. Lean, emaciated. 2. Mean, miserly.

skip[1] *v.* Jump about lightly, frisk, gambol, caper, move lightly from one foot to the other; spring or leap lightly and easily, esp. over rope revolved over head and under feet; shift quickly from one subject or occupation to another; omit, make omissions, in reading, dealing with a series, etc.; cause (bomb) to ricochet from a surface towards a target; hence, ~-*bombing*; *ski′pping-rope*, rope used for skipping. ~ *n.* Skipping movement, esp. quick shift from one foot to the other.

skip[2] *n.* Captain of side at bowls, curling, etc. [abbrev. of SKIPPER]

skip[3] *n.* College servant, scout, esp. at Dublin. [prob. f. obs. *skip-kennel* lackey]

skip[4] *n.* 1. Basket, cage, bucket, etc., in which men or materials are lowered and raised in mines and quarries. 2. Large container for rubbish etc.

skip[5], **skēp** *ns.* Wooden box for freshly caught fish; amount of fish contained in skip.

ski′pper *n.* Captain or master of ship, esp. small trading or fishing vessel; captain of aircraft; captain of side in cricket and other games. [MDu. or MLG *schipper*, f. *schip* ship]

skirl *n.* & *v.i.* (Make) shrill sound characteristic of bagpipes.

skir′mish *n.* Irregular engagement between two small bodies of troops, esp. detached or outlying parties of opposing armies; any contest or encounter. ~ *v.i.* Engage in skirmish.

ski′rret *n.* Kind of waterparsnip, the perennial umbelliferous plant *Sium sisarum*, formerly much used as table vegetable.

skirt *n.* Woman's outer garment hanging from waist, or this part of complete garment; underskirt, petticoat (archaic); flap of a saddle; border, rim, outskirts, boundary of anything; diaphragm or midriff of animal (esp. of beef) used for food; *divided skirt*, woman's garment, loose trousers resembling skirt; ~-*dancing*, dan-

cing accompanied by manipulation of long full flowing skirts or drapery. ~ *v.* Go along, round, or past the edge of; be situated along, go *along*, coast, wall, etc.; *skirting*(-*board*), narrow board round wall of room etc. close to floor (ill. WAINSCOT).

skit *n.* Light piece of satire, burlesque.

ski′tter *v.i.* Skip or skim along surface, esp., of wildfowl, along water in rising or settling; fish by drawing bait jerkily or skippingly over surface of water.

ski′ttish *adj.* Frivolous, excessively lively; spirited; (of horse etc.) nervous, excitable, fidgety. **ski′ttishly** *adv.* **ski′ttishness** *n.*

ski′ttle *n.* Pin used in ninepins or tenpins; (pl.) game of ninepins; ~ *alley*, place where skittles are set up. ~ *v.* Play skittles; knock down (skittles); (cricket) get (batsmen, side) *out* easily and rapidly.

skive *v.* 1. Split, pare (hide, leather). 2. (slang) Evade task etc. **ski′ver** *n.* (esp.) Thin soft kind of dressed leather split from grain-side of sheepskin and tanned in sumach; tool or machine for skiving leather.

ski′vvy *n.* (colloq.) Female domestic servant (usu. derogatory).

skū′a *n.* Large rapacious predatory bird of genus *Stercorarius* or related genera, esp. the great skua (*S. skua*), largest European species, of N. Atlantic coasts.

skŭldŭ′ggery, scŭldŭ′ddery *n.* (orig. U.S.) Rascally conduct, underhand plotting.

skŭlk *v.i.* Lurk, conceal oneself, avoid observation, esp. with sinister motive or in cowardice.

skŭll *n.* Bony case of the brain, cranium; whole bony framework of head (ill. HEAD); ~ *and crossbones*, representation of human skull with two thigh-bones crossed below it, as emblem of death; ~-*cap*, close-fitting brimless cap for top of head; (anat.) cranial portion of skull.

skŭnk *n.* Small N. Amer. mammal of weasel family (genus *Mephitis* and related genera), with black coat, usu. striped with white, and bushy tail, able to emit, when attacked, powerful and offensive odour from two anal glands; fur of this; low contemptible person. [Amer. Indian *segongw*]

Sku′pshtina (-ōōp-) *n.* Parliament of Yugoslavia.

skȳ *n.* Apparent arch or vault of heaven; climate, clime; colour of blue sky, sky-blue; ~-*blue*, colour of clear summer sky; ~-*high*, very high(ly); *sky′lark* common European lark, *Alauda arvensis*, which sings continuously while soaring; (*v.i.*) frolic, play tricks or practical jokes, indulge in horseplay; *sky′light*, window in roof or ceiling; ~-*line*, silhouette of anything against sky; visible horizon; ~-*marker*, parachute flare

[824]

dropped by raiding aircraft to mark the target area; ~ *pilot*, (slang) clergyman; *sky'rocket*, rocket exploding high in air; (*v.i.*) ascend like skyrocket, shoot up; ~-*sail*, light sail above royal in square-rigged ship; *sky'scraper*, very high building of many storeys; ~-*writing*, legible smoke-trails made by aircraft, esp. for advertising purposes. **skȳ'ey** *adj.* **skȳ'ward** *adj. & adv.* **skȳ'wards** (-z) *adv.* **skȳ** *v.t.* Hit, throw, (ball) very high; hang (picture) on top line or near ceiling in exhibition, hang picture of (artist) thus.

Skye. Largest island of Inner Hebrides; ~ *terrier*, small, long-bodied, short-legged, long-haired variety of Scotch terrier, of slate or fawn colour.

slăb¹ *n.* Flat, broad, comparatively thick piece of solid material, as stone, timber, etc.; large flat piece of cake, chocolate, etc.; (logging) rough outside piece cut from log or tree-trunk. ~ *v.t.* Cut slab(s) from (log, tree); cover, support, protect with slabs; roll steel ingots into slabs in *slabbing-mill*.

slăb² *adj.* (archaic, chiefly with ref. to 'Macbeth', IV. i. 32). Thick, viscous.

slă'bber *n. & v.* = SLOBBER.

slăck¹ *adj.* Sluggish, remiss, relaxed, languid, loose, inactive, negligent; (of heat etc.) gentle, moderate; ~ *water*, water with no apparent motion, esp. tidal water about turn of tide. **slă'cklў** *adv.* **slă'cknėss** *n.* **slăck** *n.* Slack part of rope; slack time in trade etc.; (pl.) trousers for informal or sports wear. ~ *v.* Slacken, make loose; take rest, be indolent, slow *up*; slake (lime); ~ *off*, abate vigour.

slăck² *n.* Very small or refuse coal, coal-dust.

slă'cken *v.* Make, become, loose or slack.

slă'cker *n.* Shirker, lazy person.

slăg *n.* Dross separated in fused vitreous state in smelting of ores; clinkers; volcanic scoria; ~ *wool*, mineral wool. ~ *v.i.* Form slag, cohere into slag-like mass.

slain: see SLAY.

slāke *v.t.* Quench, allay (thirst), cause (lime) to heat and crumble by action of water or moisture.

slā'lom (*or* -ah-) *n.* 1. Ski-race downhill on zig-zag course between artificial obstacles, usu. flags. 2. Canoe race in turbulent water through narrow passages ('gates') marked by poles.

slăm¹ *v.* Shut (door etc.) violently with loud bang; (of door etc.) shut thus; put *down* (object) with similar sound. ~ *n.* Sound (as) of slammed door.

slăm² *n.* Winning of all tricks (*grand* ~) or of all tricks but one (*little* ~) in whist, euchre, bridge, etc.

sla'nder (-ah-) *n.* False report maliciously uttered to person's injury; false oral defamation; defamation, calumny (cf. LIBEL). **sla'nderous** *adj.* **sla'nderously** *adv.* **sla'nderousnėss** *n.* **sla'nder** *v.t.* Utter slander about, defame falsely.

slăng *n.* Language in common colloquial use but considered to be outside standard educated speech and consisting either of new words or phrases or of current words used in new sense; cant, special language of some class or profession. ~ *adj.* Of, expressed in, slang. ~ *v.t.* Use abusive language to.

slă'ngy (-ngĭ) *adj.* Of the character of, given to the use of, slang. **slă'ngĭlў** *adv.* **slăngĭ'nėss** *n.*

slant (-ah-) *n.* Slope, oblique position; point of view, way of regarding something; bias. ~ *adj.* Sloping, inclined, oblique. ~ *v.* Slope, diverge from a line, have or take oblique direction or position; present (news etc.) in biased way.

slăp *n.* Smart blow esp. with palm of hand or something flat, smack. ~ *v.t.* Strike with such blow; ~-*bang*, violently, noisily; *sla'pdash*, hasty, careless, happy-go-lucky; (*adv.*) in slapdash manner; ~-*happy*, cheerfully casual; *sla'pstick*, (orig. U.S.) flexible lath used by harlequin in pantomime; (of) boisterous knockabout type of comedy; ~-*up*, (slang) first-rate, splendid, done regardless of expense. ~ *adv.* Suddenly, noisily, headlong.

slăsh *v.* Cut, cut at, with sweep of sharp weapon or instrument; make gashes (in); slit (garment) to show contrasting lining etc.; lash with whip, crack (whip); make drastic economies in (budget etc.). ~ *n.* (Wound or slit made by) slashing cut.

slăt *n.* Long narrow strip of wood or metal, lath, esp. one of a series forming a Venetian blind, one of the crosspieces of a bedstead on which the mattress rests. ~ *v.* Flap, strike, with noisy sound, esp. of sails, ropes, etc.

slāte¹ *n.* Very fine-grained grey metamorphic rock which cleaves perfectly in one direction, freq. at an angle to the bedding plane; thin usu. rectangular plate of this or other stone as roofing material ill. ROOF); tablet of slate, usu. framed in wood, for writing on; ~-*coloured*, ~-*grey*, dark, freq. bluish or greenish, grey of slate; ~-*pencil*, stick of soft slate used for writing on slate. **slā'tў** *adj.* **slāte** *v.t.* Cover, roof, with slates.

slāte² *v.t.* (colloq.) Criticize severely, scold, rate.

slă'ttern *n.* Sluttish woman. **slă'tternlў** *adj.*

slau'ghter (-awt-) *n.* Slaying, esp. of many persons or animals at once, carnage, massacre; ~-*house*, place for killing cattle or sheep, shambles. ~ *v.t.* Kill in ruthless manner or on great scale; butcher, kill for food.

slau'ghterous (-awt-) *adj.* Murderous.

Slav (-ahv) *n.* Member of any of the peoples belonging to the Slavonic linguistic group, inhabiting large parts of E. and central Europe, and including Russians, Poles, Czechs, Bulgarians, Serbo-Croats, Slovenes, etc. ~ *adj.* Of the Slavs or their languages.

slāve *n.* Person who is the legal property of another, servant completely divested of freedom and personal rights; human chattel; helpless victim *to*, *of*, some influence; submissive or devoted servant; drudge; ~ *bangle*, bracelet, wide bracelet freq. worn above elbow; ~-*driver*, superintendent of slaves at work; hard taskmaster; ~-*ship*, ship employed in slave-trade; ~ *States*, (U.S. hist.) those southern States of N. America in which slave-holding was legal; ~-*trade*, traffic in slaves, esp. former transportation of African Negroes to America. ~ *v.i.* Work like slave, drudge.

slā'ver¹ *n.* Ship or person engaged in slave-trade.

slā'ver² *n.* Saliva flowing or falling from mouth. **slā'verў¹** *adj.* **slă'ver** *v.* Let saliva run from mouth; wet with saliva, slobber.

slā'verў² *n.* Condition of a slave; slave-holding; drudgery.

slā'veў *n.* Hard-worked female domestic servant, maid of all work.

Slā'vĭc *adj. & n.* (chiefly U.S.) Slav.

slā'vĭsh *adj.* Of, like a slave, servile; showing no originality or independence. **slā'vĭshlў** *adv.*

Slavō'nia. District of N. Yugoslavia bordering on Hungary, between the Sava, Drava, and Danube rivers. **Slavō'nian** *adj. & n.* 1. (Native, inhabitant, language) of Slavonia. 2. (less freq.) Slavonic.

Slavŏ'nic *adj.* Of the Slavs; ~ *languages*, group of Indo-European languages spoken in E. and central Europe, including Russian, White Russian, Ukrainian, Polish, Czech, Bulgarian, Serbo-Croatian, and Slovene. ~ *n.* Slavonic languages; *Church* ~, *Old* ~, earliest written Slavonic language, a Bulgarian dialect fixed in writing towards end of 9th c., extinct as a vernacular but remaining the liturgical language of the Orthodox Church in Slav countries.

slaw *n.* (U.S.) Cole slaw.

slay *v.t.* (past t. *slew* pr. -ōō, past part. *slain*). (chiefly poet. and rhet.) Kill.

S/Ld *abbrev.* Squadron Leader. **slea'zў** *adj.* 1. Flimsy, loosely-woven. 2. Shoddy, shabby. 3. Squalid.

slĕd *n. & v.* (chiefly dial. & U.S.) = SLEDGE¹.

slĕdge¹ *n.* Vehicle mounted on

runners instead of wheels for conveying loads or passengers, esp. over snow or ice. ~ v. Travel, go, convey, in sledge.

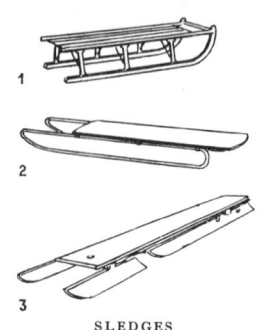

SLEDGES

1. Luge. 2. Steel skeleton toboggan. 3. Bob-sleigh

slĕdge[2] *n.* (also ~-*hammer*) Large heavy hammer usu. wielded with both hands, esp. that used by blacksmith (ill. HAMMER).
sleek *adj.* (of hair, fur, surface, etc.) Soft, smooth and glossy; sleek-haired or -skinned; of well-fed comfortable appearance. **slee′klў** *adv.* **slee′knĕss** *n.* **sleek** *v.t.* Make sleek.
sleep *n.* Bodily condition regularly and naturally assumed by man and other animals, in which the postural and other muscles are relaxed and consciousness is largely suppressed, though it may be re-established by a sensory disturbance; period or occasion of this; inert condition of some animals in hibernation; (fig.) death; rest, quiet, peace; ~-*walking*, somnambulism. ~ *v.* (past t. and past part. *slĕpt*). Be in state of sleep; fall, be, asleep; rest in death; spend in, affect by, sleeping; stay for the night *at, in,* etc.; provide sleeping-accommodation for; be inactive or dormant; (of top) spin so steadily as to seem motionless; *sleeping partner*, partner taking no share in actual working of business. **slee′ping** *n.* (esp.) ~-*bag*, bag, usu. lined or padded, for sleeping in, esp. out-of-doors; *S*~ *Beauty*, heroine of fairy-tale who slept for 100 years; ~-*car*, -*carriage*, railway carriage with berths or beds; ~-*draught*, drink inducing sleep, opiate; ~ *sickness*, (1) freq. fatal disease charaterized by extreme lethargy, prevalent in parts of W. and S. Africa and caused by a trypanosome (*Trypanosoma gambiense*) transmitted by the bite of the tsetse fly; (2) SLEEPY sickness; ~-*suit*, pyjamas; child's one-piece garment for night wear.
slee′per *n.* (esp.) Wooden beam etc. used as (usu. transverse) support for rails of railway etc. (ill. RAIL[1]); (colloq.) sleeping-car; rod or ring worn in place of earring in pierced ear lobe; ~ *wall*, wall supporting beams of floor.
slee′pў *adj.* Drowsy, ready for sleep; inactive, indolent, without stir or bustle; (of fruit, esp. pears) beginning to rot; ~ *sickness*, (pop.) ENCEPHALITIS lethargica. **slee′pilў** *adv.* **slee′pĭnĕss** *n.*
sleet *n.* Hail or snow falling in a half-melted state. **slee′tў** *adj.*
sleeve *n.* Part of garment covering arm; tube or hollow shaft

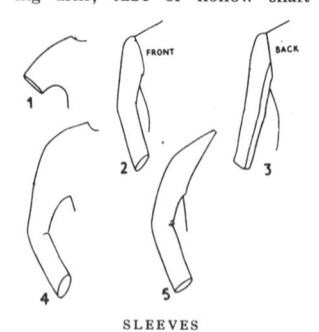

SLEEVES

1. Magyar. 2. Straight. 3. Tailored. 4. Dolman. 5. Raglan

fitting over rod, spindle, etc.; wind-sock, drogue; cover for gramophone record; ~-*board*, small ironing-board over which sleeves can be fitted for pressing; ~-*nut*, long nut with right- or left-hand screw-threads for connecting pipes or shafts conversely threaded; ~-*valve*, internal combustion engine's valve with sleeve(s) fitting interior of cylinder, sliding with piston, and so designed and controlled that inlet and exhaust ports are uncovered at proper stages in cycle. **sleeved** (-vd), **slee′velĕss** *adjs.*
sleigh (slā) *n.* Sledge, esp. as passenger-vehicle drawn by horse(s); ~-*bells*, small bells attached to sleigh or harness of sleigh-horse.
sleight (slīt) *n.* Dexterity, cunning, artifice (archaic exc. in) ~-*of-hand*, conjuring, trick(s) displaying great dexterity, esp. performed so quickly as to deceive the eye.
Sleĭ′pnir (slāp-). (Norse myth.) Odin's eight-footed horse.
slĕ′nder *adj.* Of small girth or breadth; scanty, slight, meagre. **slĕ′nderlў** *adv.* **slĕ′ndernĕss** *n.*
sleuth (slōō-) *n.* (also ~-*hound*) Blood-hound; detective. ~ *v.* Track, trail; play the detective.
slew, slue (-ōō) *v.* & *n.* Turn or swing round on axis.

slice *n.* Relatively thin flat broad piece or wedge cut from esp. meat, bread, or cake; share, portion; (golf) slicing stroke; kind of implement with thin broad blade used in cookery etc., esp. (*fish-*~) for lifting or serving fish. ~ *v.* Cut into slices, cut (piece) *off*; cut cleanly or easily; (golf) strike (ball) so that it flies or curves to right (or, in the case of a left-handed player, to the left).
slick *adj.* Sleek; smooth, plausible; adroit, deft, quick, cunning. **sli′cklў** *adv.* **sli′cknĕss** *n.* **slick** *n.* (also *oil* ~) Patch or film of oil on water. ~ *v.t.* Smooth, sleek.
sli′cker *n.* (U.S.) Long loose waterproof overcoat; (U.S. colloq.) well-dressed plausible rogue; (also *city-*~) well-dressed person from city.
slide *v.* (past t. & past part. *slĭd*). (Make) progress along smooth surface with continuous friction on same part of object progressing; glide over ice without skates in more or less erect posture; glide, go smoothly along, pass easily or gradually; *let* (something) take its own course; ~-*rule*, rule graduated along one edge according to the logarithms of the numbers from 1 to 100 and along the other according to the logarithms of the numbers from

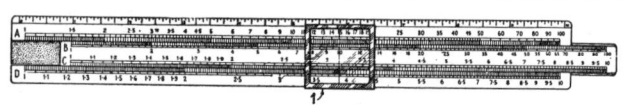

SLIDE-RULE
1. Cursor

1 to 10 (enabling squares and square roots to be read off directly), and having a similarly graduated sliding piece along its centre (enabling numbers to be multiplied or divided by adding or subtracting their logarithms); ~-*valve*, valve with sliding plate for opening and closing orifice, esp. in steam engine (ill. STEAM). ~ *n.* Act of sliding; track on ice made by sliding; slope prepared with snow or ice for tobogganing; inclined plane down which goods etc. slide to lower level; part(s) of machine on or between which sliding part works; part of machine or instrument that slides; *stop* ~, (organ) strip of wood perforated with holes under each rank of pipes, which stops off rank when moved sideways (ill. ORGAN); thing slid into place, esp. glass holding object for microscope (ill. MICROSCOPE); lantern-slide, photographic transparency; kind of clasp for keeping hair tidy.
sli′ding *adj.* That slides; ~ *door, lid, panel*, etc., door, lid, etc., drawn across aperture by sliding sideways instead of turning on hinges; ~ *rule*, slide-rule; ~ *scale*, scale (of payments, wages, etc.) rising or falling in proportion or

[826]

conversely to rise or fall of some other standard.

slight (-it) *adj.* Slender, slim, thin; not good or substantial, rather flimsy or weak; small in amount, degree, etc., unimportant, trifling. **sli′ghtly̆** *adv.* **sli′ghtnĕss** *n.* **slight** *n.* Instance of slighting or being slighted; contemptuous indifference or disregard. ~ *v.t.* Treat with indifference or disrespect, disregard, disdain, ignore.

Sli′go. Maritime county in Connacht.

slim *adj.* Slender, (gracefully) thin; small, slight, meagre. **sli′mly̆** *adv.* **sli′mnĕss** *n.* **slim** *v.* Make, become, slim, esp. by dieting, exercise, etc.

slime *n.* Fine oozy mud; any substance of similar consistency. ~ *v.t.* Cover with slime.

sli′my̆ *adj.* Of the consistency of slime; covered or smeared with slime; vile, disgusting; repulsively meek or flattering. **sli′mily̆** *adv.* **sli′minĕss** *n.*

sling[1] *n.* 1. Weapon, consisting of strap attached to two cords or to staff, for hurling stones etc.; ballista. 2. Belt, rope, etc., formed

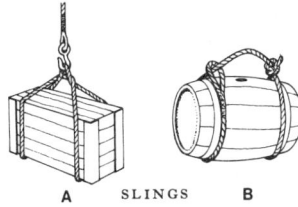

A. BALE SLING (STROP). B. BUTT SLING

into loop, with hooks and tackle, for securing bulky or heavy articles while being hoisted or lowered; strap, band, etc., supporting something suspended; bandage etc. formed into loop round neck to support injured arm. ~ *v.* (past t. & past part. *slŭng*). 1. Throw, cast, hurl; hurl (stone etc.) from sling, use sling. 2. Suspend with sling; hoist or transfer with sling; hang up, suspend, esp. between two points.

sling[2] *n.* (U.S.) Spirit, esp. gin, with water, sugar, etc., drunk hot or iced.

slink *v.i.* (past t. *slŭnk* or rarely *slănk*, past part. *slŭnk*). Move, go, in quiet, stealthy, or sneaking manner. **sli′nky̆** *adj.* (of woman's garment) Close-fitting.

slip[1] *n.* Finely ground clay, flint, etc., mixed with water to consistency of cream and used for making, cementing, decorating, etc., pottery, tiles, etc.; ~-*ware*, pottery coated with slip.

slip[2] *n.* 1. Act of slipping; blunder, accidental piece of misconduct; slip-stream; *give person the* ~, evade or escape from him.

2. Loose covering or garment, e.g. pillow-case, petticoat. 3. Leash for slipping dogs; device for suddenly loosing clip or attachment. 4. Inclined plane on which ships are built or repaired. 5. Long narrow strip of thin wood, paper, etc.; printer's proof on such paper. 6. Cutting taken from a plant for grafting or planting; scion; young, esp. slender, person. 7. (cricket) Fielder stationed for balls glancing off bat to off side behind batsman (ill. CRICKET[2]); (usu. pl.) this part of ground. ~ *v.* 1. Slide unintentionally for short distance; lose footing, balance, etc., by unintended sliding; go with sliding motion, move easily or unperceived, glide, steal; escape restraint or capture esp. by being slippery or hard to hold; make careless mistake (also, colloq., ~ *up*). 2. Let go (hounds etc.) from restraint of some kind; pull (garment etc.) hastily *on*, *off*; make pass or move stealthily, casually, or with gliding motion; escape from, give the slip to; (naut.) allow (anchor-cable) to run out when leaving anchorage hastily, drop (anchor) thus; (of animals) miscarry with, drop (young) prematurely.

slip- in comb.: ~-*case*, close-fitting case in which a book is issued and from or into which it can be readily slipped; ~-*carriage*, *coach*, etc., carriage that can be detached from railway train while running; ~-*knot*, knot that can be undone by a pull; knot that slips up and down rope etc. and tightens or loosens loop; ~-*road*, road giving access to or exit from motorway; ~-*stream*, current of air driven astern by propulsion unit of an aircraft producing the thrust which moves the aircraft forwards; *sli′pway*, inclined way leading into water in a dock or shipbuilders' yard (ill. LAUNCH[1]); runway for take-off of aircraft.

sli′pper *n.* Light loose comfortable indoor shoe; skid or shoe placed under wagon-wheel as drag; ~-*bath*, partly covered slipper-shaped bath.

sli′ppery̆ *adj.* With smooth, polished, oily, slimy, or greasy surface making foothold insecure, or making object etc. difficult to grasp or hold; (fig.) elusive, unreliable, shifty, unscrupulous; **sli′pperily** *adv.* **sli′pperinĕss** *n.*

sli′ppy̆ *adj.* Slippery; *be, look,* ~, (slang) look sharp, make haste.

sli′pshŏd *adj.* With shoes down at heel; slovenly, careless, unsystematic.

slit *n.* Long incision; long narrow opening comparable to cut. ~ *v.* Cut or tear lengthwise, make slit in, cut into strips; ~ *trench*, narrow trench made to accommodate a soldier or a weapon.

sli′ther (-dh-) *v.i.* Slide unsteadily, go with irregular slipping motion.

sli′ver *n.* Thin piece cut or split off; thin strip of wood torn from tree or timber, splinter; (fishing) side of small fish cut off as bait. ~ *v.* Break off as sliver, break up into slivers.

sli′vovitz (slē-) *n.* Alcoholic spirit distilled from plums esp. in Yugoslavia, plum brandy.

Sloane, Sir Hans (1660–1753). British physician and naturalist; bequeathed to the nation a library which formed the nucleus of the BRITISH Museum.

slŏ′bber *v.* & *n.* Slaver, drivel. **slŏ′bbery̆** *adj.*

slōe *n.* Blackthorn; its fruit; ~ *gin*, gin flavoured with sloes and sweetened.

slŏg *v.* Hit hard and freq. wildly, esp. in boxing and cricket; work hard and doggedly, plod. **slŏ′gger** *n.* **slŏg** *n.* Heavy random hit.

slŏ′gan *n.* Highland war-cry (Sc.); party-cry, watchword, motto; advertiser's phrase calculated to catch the eye. [Gael. *sluagh* host, *gairm* outcry]

sloop *n.* Small one-masted fore-and-aft-rigged vessel; (also ~ *of war*) small ship-of-war with guns on upper deck only.

slŏp[1] *n.* (pl.) Dirty water or liquid, waste contents of kitchen or bedroom vessels; (pl.) liquid or semi-liquid food of weak unappetizing kind; ~-*basin*, -*bowl*, basin for receiving rinsings of tea-cups; ~-*pail*, pail for removing bedroom slops. ~ *v.* Spill, (allow to) flow over edge of vessel; spill or splash liquid upon.

slŏp[2] *n.* (pl.) Ready-made, esp. cheap or badly made, clothes; (pl.) clothes and bedding supplied to sailors in navy; ~-*room*, room from which slops are issued on man-of-war; ~-*shop*, shop for cheap ready-made clothes.

slōpe *n.* Stretch of rising or falling ground; inclined surface or way; upward or downward inclination, deviation from horizontal or perpendicular. ~ *v.* Take, form, move in, be in, place or arrange in, a slope or inclined direction or position; (slang) make *off*, go away.

slŏ′ppy̆ *adj.* Wet, splashed, full of puddles; messy with liquid; watery and disagreeable; weak, slovenly, maudlin. **slŏ′ppily** *adv.* **slŏ′ppinĕss** *n.*

slŏsh *v.t.* (slang) Beat, thrash. **slŏshed** (-sht) *adj.* (slang) Drunk. **slŏsh** *n.* (slang) 1. Heavy blow. 2. = SLUSH.

slŏt[1] *n.* 1. Groove, channel, slit, long aperture, made in machine, fabric, etc., to admit some other part, esp. slit for coin that sets working ~-*machine*, automatic retailer of small wares. 2. (fig.) Place in series etc.; = OPENING, 3. ~ *v.t.* Provide with slot(s).

slŏt[2] *n.* Track of animal, esp. deer; trace, trail.

[827]

slōth *n.* 1. Laziness, indolence. 2. Long-haired slow-moving arboreal mammal of tropical Central and S. America, with two toes

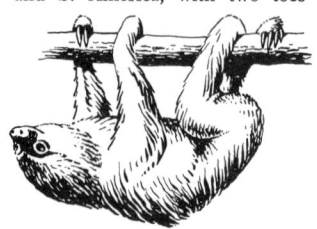

TWO-TOED SLOTH

with hook-like claws on each forefoot (genus *Chloloepus*) or three toes (*Bradypus tridactylus*); ~-**bear**, common shaggy black-haired bear (*Melursus ursinus*), feeding on fruit, insects, and honey, of India and Sri' Lanka. **slō′thful** *adj.* Lazy. **slō′thfully** *adv.* **slō′thfulness** *n.*
slouch *v.* Droop, hang down negligently; go, stand, etc., with loose ungainly stoop of head and shoulders; pull or bend down brim of hat, esp. over face. ~ *n.* Slouching gait or posture, stoop; downward bend of hat-brim; ~ *hat*, soft hat with wide flexible brim.
slough[1] (-ow) *n.* Quagmire, swamp, miry place; *S~ of Despond*, in Bunyan's 'Pilgrim's Progress', deep miry place between City of Destruction and wicket-gate at beginning of Christian's journey; state of hopeless depression.
slough[2] (-ŭf) *n.* Outer skin periodically cast by snake etc.; any part cast or moulted by an animal; dead tissue from surface of wound, ulcer, etc. ~ *v.* Drop off as slough; cast slough.
Slō′vǎk *adj. & n.* (Member) of a Slavonic people inhabiting chiefly Slovakia and S. Moravia; (of) their language. **Slova′kia** (-vah-). Territory forming the E. part of Czechoslovakia, formerly a part of Hungary.
slo′ven (-ŭv-) *n.* Person who is careless, untidy, or dirty in personal appearance or slipshod and negligent in work etc. **slo′venly** *adj.* **slo′venliness** *n.*
Slō′vēne *adj. & n.* (Member, language) of the Slavonic people inhabiting chiefly Slovenia and neighbouring parts of Yugoslavia. **Slōvē′nia**. Constituent republic of Yugoslavia, bordering on Austria and Italy; capital, Ljubljana. **Slōvē′nian** *adj. & n.* Slovene.
slow (-ō) *adj.* 1. Not quick, taking a long time to do a thing or traverse a distance; gradual; tardy, lingering; not hasty; (of clock etc.) behind correct time; (of surfaces) tending to cause slowness (*a ~ pitch, billiard-table*, etc.). 2. Dull-witted, stupid; deficient in liveliness or interest,

dull, tedious. 3. *slow′coach*, slow, idle, or indolent person; ~ *match*, slow-burning fuse or match for igniting explosives; ~ *motion*, action or speed of a film in which movements appear much slower than in nature, achieved either by exposing the film at high speed or by projecting it at reduced speed; ~ *poison*, poison of which repeated doses are injurious. **slow′ly** *adv.* **slow′ness** *n.* **slow** *adv.* Slowly. ~ *v.* Reduce one's speed, reduce speed of.
slow-worm (slō′-wẽrm) *n.* Small European legless lizard (*Anguis fragilis*), blindworm (ill. LIZARD).
slŭb *n.* Thick place or lump in yarn of thread; (attrib., of material etc.) with irregular effect produced by warp of uneven thickness.
slŭdge *n.* Thick greasy mud; sewage; muddy or slushy sediment or deposit; accumulation of dirty oil, esp. in sump of internal combustion engine; sea-ice newly formed in small pieces. **slŭ′dgy** *adj.*
slue *n. & v.* = SLEW.
slŭg[1] *n.* 1. Gasteropod mollusc with rudimentary or no shell, many kinds of which are very destructive to small plants. 2. Roughly or irregularly shaped bullet or other piece of metal; (printing) thick piece of metal used in spacing; line of type in linotype printing. 3. (eng., as measure in calculating acceleration) That mass to which a force of 1 lb. will impart an acceleration of 1 ft per second in every second.
slŭg[2] *n. & v.t.* (colloq., chiefly U.S.) (Strike with) hard heavy blow.
slŭ′g-abĕd *n.* (archaic) One who lies late in bed.
slŭ′ggard *n.* Lazy sluggish person.
slŭ′ggish *adj.* Inert, inactive, slow-moving, torpid. **slŭ′ggishly** *adv.* **slŭ′ggishness** *n.*
sluice (-ōos) *n.* (Gate in) dam or embankment with sliding gate or other contrivance for controlling volume or flow of water (ill. LOCK[2]); any device for regulating flow of water; artificial water-channel, esp. in gold-washing. ~ *v.* Provide with sluice(s); flood with water from sluice; rinse, pour or throw water freely upon; (of water etc.) rush (as) from sluice.
slŭm[1] *n.* Dirty squalid overcrowded street, district, etc. inhabited by the very poor. **slŭ′mmy** *adj.* **slŭm** *v.i.* Go about in slums for philanthropic or charitable purposes, or out of curiosity.
slŭm[2] *n.* Non-lubricating part of crude oil; gummy residue formed in lubricating oil during use.
slŭ′mber *n. & v.i.* Sleep (chiefly poet. and rhet.). **slŭ′mberous, -brous** *adj.* **slŭ′mberously, -brously** *adv.*

slŭmp *n.* Sudden decrease (esp. of commercial ventures, prices, etc.; opp. BOOM[3]); sudden or heavy fall in demand. ~ *v.i.* Undergo slump, fall in price; sit or flop down heavily and slackly.
slŭng: see SLING[1].
slur *v.* 1. Smudge, blur; pronounce indistinctly, with sounds running into one another; (mus.) sing, play, two or more notes smoothly and connectedly; mark with slur. 2. Pass lightly *over*, conceal, minimize. ~ *n.* 1. Slight, discredit, blame. 2. Slurred sound or utterance; (mus.) curved line (⌢, ⌣,) over or under two or more notes to be sung or played without a break or as smoothly as possible (ill. STAVE).
slŭ′rry *n.* Thin sloppy cement, mud, etc.
slŭsh *n.* Watery mud or water-saturated snow; soft greasy mixture of oil etc. or other materials, used to lubricate or protect machinery etc.; (fig.) silly sentiment. **slŭ′shy** *adj.*
slŭt *n.* Slovenly woman. **slŭ′ttish** *adj.* **slŭ′ttishly** *adv.* **slŭ′ttishness** *n.*
slȳ *adj.* 1. Cunning, wily, deceitful; practising concealment, working, moving, etc., in stealthy or underhand manner. 2. Knowing, arch, bantering, insinuating. **slȳ′ly** *adj.* **slȳ′ness** *n.*
slȳpe *n.* (archit.) Covered passage-way from transept or cloister of cathedral or monastic church to chapter house or deanery (ill. CHURCH).
S.M. *abbrev.* Sergeant-Major; short metre.
smăck[1] *n.* Flavour, taste; trace, tinge, suggestion, *of* something. ~ *v.i.* Have taste or savour *of*, suggest the presence *of*.
smăck[2] *n.* Sharp slight sound as of surface struck with palm of hand, lips parted suddenly, etc.; slap, sounding blow; loud kiss. ~ *v.* Strike with palm of hand or with something flat; part (lips) noisily, (of lips) be parted, in eager anticipation or enjoyment of food etc.; crack (whip). ~ *adv.* (colloq.) (As) with a smack, slap; outright, exactly.
smăck[3] *n.* Single-masted sailing-vessel, rigged like sloop or

CUTTER-RIGGED SMACK
1. Gaff sail

smacker n. (slang) Loud kiss; sounding blow; dollar, pound.

small (-awl) adj. Not large, of comparatively little size, strength, power, or number; consisting of minute units; (of agent) not acting on large scale; poor, mean, humble; ungenerous, not much of; unimportant, trifling; petty, paltry; ~ *arms*, portable firearms, esp. rifle, pistol, light machine-gun; ~ *beer*: see BEER; ~-*clothes*, (archaic) knee-breeches; ~-*holding*, agricultural holding smaller than farm; also, piece of land (1 to 50 acres) let or sold by a county council to a ~-*holder*; ~ *hours*: see HOUR; ~-*sword*, light tapering sword for thrusting only (ill. SWORD); ~ *talk*, ordinary social conversation, chat. ~ n. Small, slender, or narrow part of anything, esp. the back; (pl., colloq.) small articles of laundry, esp. underclothes; (pl., formerly, at Oxf. Univ.) responsions. ~ adv. Into small pieces, on small scale, etc.; *sing* ~, adopt humble tone or manner.

smallpox (-awl-) n. Acute contagious febrile disease (*variola*), often endemic in occurrence, characterized by pustular eruption, usu. leaving scars or pits on skin.

smalt (-awlt) n. Glass coloured deep blue with oxide of cobalt; this pulverized and used as pigment.

smarm, smalm (-ahm) v.t. (dial. & colloq.) Smooth, plaster *down*; flatter fulsomely. **smarmy** adj. Fulsomely flattering or ingratiating.

smart[1] n. Sharp pain, stinging sensation. ~ v.i. Feel, cause, smart.

smart[2] adj. 1. Severe, sharp; lively, vigorous, brisk. 2. Clever, quick, ingenious; quick at looking after one's own interests. 3. Alert, brisk; neat, trim; stylish, fashionable, elegant. **smarten** v. **smartly** adv. **smartness** n.

smash n. Breaking to pieces; violent fall, collision, or disaster; commercial failure, bankruptcy; violent and heavy blow; (lawn tennis) hard overhand stroke; ~-*up*, complete smash. ~ v. Break utterly to pieces, shatter, bash *in*; utterly rout and disorganize; break, come to grief, go bankrupt; (of vehicle etc.) crash; (lawn tennis) hit (ball) in smash; ~-*and-grab*, (colloq.) (of robbery) in which shop-window etc. is broken and goods snatched from behind it. ~ adv. With a smash. **smashing** adj. (slang) Very fine, wonderful.

smattering n. Slight superficial knowledge (*of*).

smear v. Daub with greasy or sticky substances or with something that stains, make greasy or sticky marks on; blot, obscure outlines of; (orig. U.S.) blacken character of, discredit publicly. **smeary** adj. **smear** n. Mark, blotch, made by smearing.

smell n. 1. Faculty of smelling, by which odours are perceived by means of the nose; act of smelling, sniff. 2. Property of things affecting sense of smell, odour; bad odour, stench. **smelly** adj. (colloq.) Smelling strongly, evil-smelling. **smell** v. (past t. & past part. *smelt*). 1. Perceive smell of, detect presence of by smell; use sense of smell, sniff *at*; hunt *out* by smell; (fig.) discover, find *out*, as if by smell; perceive smells, have sense of smell. 2. Emit smell; suggest or recall the smell *of*; stink, be rank. 3. *smelling-bottle*, small bottle of *smelling-salts*, preparation of ammonium carbonate and scent, to be sniffed as restorative in faintness etc.

smelt[1] n. Small edible fish esp. of genus *Osmerus*, allied to salmon, with greenish back, silvery sides and belly, and delicate tender rather oily flesh.

smelt[2] v.t. Fuse or melt (ore) to extract metal; obtain (metal) thus.

Smetana, Bedřich (1824–84). Czech musician, composer of 'The Bartered Bride', a humorous opera.

smew n. Small duck (*Mergus albellus*) of Europe and Asia, the smallest of the mergansers.

smilax n. 1. Liliaceous climbing plant, freq. with prickly stem, of genus S~, some tropical species of which yield sarsaparilla from tuberous root-stocks. 2. S. African climbing asparagus (*Asparagus asparagoides*) much used in decoration.

smile v. Express pleasure, amusement, affection, indulgent scorn, incredulity, etc., with slight more or less involuntary movement of features, upward curving of corners of mouth, parting of lips, etc.; look *on*, *at*, with such expression; express by smiling; drive *away*, bring *into* or *out of* (mood), by smiling; be, appear, propitious; look pleasant, have bright aspect; ~ *on*, show favour to, approve of. ~ n. Act of smiling; smiling expression or aspect.

smirch v.t. & n. Stain, soil, smear, spot (also fig.).

smirk v. & n. (Put on) affected or silly smile; simper.

smite v. (past t. *smote*, past part. *smitten*). Strike (*upon*), hit, chastise, defeat (chiefly poet. and rhet.); (chiefly in past part. *smitten*) strike, seize, infect, possess, *with* disease, love, etc.

smith[1] n. Worker in metal, esp. iron, blacksmith.

Smith[2], Adam (1723–90). Scottish political economist, author of 'The Wealth of Nations' (1776) which established political economy as a separate science.

Smith[3], Joseph (1805–44). Founder of the MORMON sect.

Smith[4], Sydney (1771–1845). English churchman, essayist, and wit; author of the 'Letters of Peter Plymley' (1807) in defence of Catholic emancipation.

smithereens (-dh-, -z) n.pl. (colloq.) Small fragments.

Smithfield. Orig., open space outside the NW. walls of City of London, a market for cattle and horses; later the central meat-market; in 16th c., scene of burning of heretics.

Smithsonian Institution (i-). Establishment for increase and diffusion of knowledge founded 1846 in Washington under will of an English mineralogist and chemist, James Smithson (1765–1829; earlier known as James Lewis Macie); it comprises a national museum, mainly of zoology and ethnology, and an astrophysical observatory.

smithy (-dhi) n. 1. Blacksmith's workshop, forge. 2. Blacksmith.

smock n. 1. Chemise (archaic). 2. Loose-fitting outer garment of shirt-like shape, freq. with gathered or smocked yoke. ~ v.t. Adorn with smocking. **smocking** n.

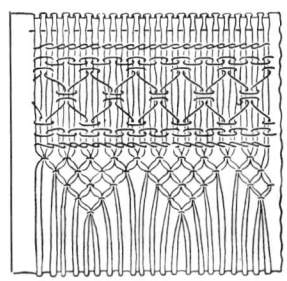

SMOCKING

Form of needlework with honeycomb ornamentation on basis of very close thick gathers.

smog n. Smoky fog.

smoke n. 1. Visible volatile product given off by burning or smouldering substances; cloud or column of this esp. used as signal etc. 2. Cigar or cigarette; spell of smoking tobacco etc. 3. ~-*bomb*, bomb emitting dense clouds of smoke on bursting, for forming smoke-screen; ~-*box*, chamber in steam boiler between flues and chimney-stack; ~-*screen*, dense volume of smoke diffused by funnel of vessel, smoke-bomb, etc., to conceal naval or military operations etc.; ~-*stack*, chimney, chimney-pipe. **smokeless** adj. Producing little or no smoke; free from smoke. **smoke** v. 1. Emit smoke or visible vapour, reek, steam; (of chimney, lamp, etc.) emit smoke, be smoky, as result of imperfect draught etc. 2. Colour, darken, obscure, with

[829]

SMOKER

smoke; preserve or cure by exposure to smoke; fumigate; suffocate, stupefy, drive *out*, rid of insects, etc., with smoke. 3. Inhale and exhale smoke of (tobacco, opium, etc.); smoke tobacco; bring *into* specified state by smoking; *smoking-car(riage)*, *compartment*, carriage, etc., for smokers on railway train; *smoking-concert*, concert at which smoking and drinking are allowed; *smoking-room*, room set apart for smoking in.

smō'ker n. (esp.) Person who habitually smokes tobacco; smoking-carriage on train.

smō'kў adj. Emitting, veiled or filled with, obscure (as) with, smoke; stained with, coloured like, smoke. **smō'kĭlў** adv. **smō'kĭnėss** n.

Smō'llėtt, Tobias George (1721-71). Scottish novelist, by profession a surgeon; author of 'Roderick Random', 'Peregrine Pickle', 'Humphrey Clinker', etc.

smōlt n. Young salmon at stage between parr and grilse, when it is covered with silvery scales and migrates to sea for first time.

smōōth (-dh) adj. With surface free from projections, wrinkles, lumps, or undulations; not rough, uneven, or hairy; (of ground etc.) not broken or obstructed, easily traversed; not harsh in sound, taste, etc.; pleasant, polite, unruffled; bland, insinuating, flattering; ~-*bore*, gun with unrifled barrel; ~-*faced*, hypocritically or plausibly bland, friendly, or polite; ~-*spoken*, -*tongued*, smooth, plausible, flattering, in speech; soft-spoken. **smōō'thlў** adv. **smōō'thnėss** n. **smōōth** v. Make or become smooth; free from impediments etc.; *smoothing-iron*, flat-iron; *smoothing plane*, one used for smoothing (ill. PLANE[2]). ~ n. Smoothing touch or stroke.

smōr'gasbord n. Buffet meal with a variety of hors-d'œuvres and other dishes. [Swed. *smörgåsbord*]

smo'ther (-ŭdh-) v. Suffocate, stifle, be suffocated or stifled, esp. with smoke; deaden or extinguish (fire) by excluding air with ashes etc.; suppress, conceal, cover (*up*); cover closely or thickly (*in*). ~ n. Dense or suffocating smoke, dust, fog, etc.

smou'lder (smōl-) v.i. Burn and smoke without flame (freq. fig.).

s.m.p. abbrev. *Sine mascula prole* (L, = without male issue).

smŭdge[1] n. Dirty mark, smear, blur, blot. ~ v. Soil, stain, smirch, smear.

smŭdge[2] n. (U.S.) Outdoor fire with dense smoke to drive away insects.

smŭg adj. Self-satisfied, consciously virtuous. **smŭ'glў** adv. **smŭ'gnėss** n.

smŭ'ggle v. Convey (goods), convey goods, clandestinely into or out of country to avoid payment of customs duties etc.; convey stealthily or secretly *in*, *out*, put *away* into concealment. **smŭ'ggler** n.

smŭt n. 1. Fungous disease of cereals and other plants, with (parts of) grain covered with blackish powdery spores; any fungus causing this. 2. (Black mark, smudge, made by) flake of soot. 3. Indecent or obscene talk or publications. **smŭ'ttў** adj. **smŭ'ttĭlў** adv. **smŭ'ttĭnėss** n. **smŭt** v.t. Mark with smut(s); infect (grain etc.) with smut.

Smŭts, Jan Christian (1870-1950). South African general, philosopher, and statesman; prime minister of the Union of S. Africa 1918-24, 1939-48.

Smyr'na (-ér-). Former name of Izmir.

snăck n. Slight, casual, or hurried meal; ~-*bar*, -*counter*, counter where sandwiches and other snacks may be obtained.

snă'ffle n. Simple kind of bridle-bit (ill. SADDLERY). ~ v.t. Put snaffle on (horse); (slang) appropriate, seize, purloin.

snăg n. Jagged projecting point, as stump or branch left on tree after pruning or cutting, trunk or large branch of tree embedded in bottom of river etc., with end pointed upwards; (fig.) impediment, obstacle, unexpected drawback. ~ v.t. Run upon or damage by a snag.

snail n. Any aquatic or terrestrial gasteropod mollusc with well-developed spiral or whorled shell capable of covering whole body;

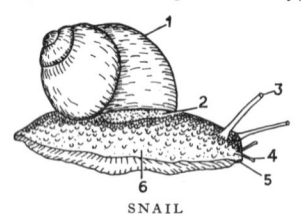

SNAIL

1. Shell. 2. Mantle. 3. Eye. 4. Tentacle. 5. Mouth. 6. Foot

slow-moving or indolent person; (also ~-*wheel*) spiral cam, esp. in striking mechanism of clock.

snake n. 1. Limbless reptile of sub-order Ophidia, serpent; (also, pop.) snake-like limbless lizard or amphibian; treacherous or ungrateful person; ~ *in the grass*, lurking danger, secret enemy; ~*s and ladders*, children's dice-game in which the hazards are marked by these depicted on a board. 2. *S~*, Amer. Indian of various Shoshonee groups of western U.S. 3. ~-*fence*, (U.S.) zigzag fence of split rails or poles; *sna'keroot*, (root of) any of various Amer. plants, esp. *Aristolochia serpentaria* and *Polygala senega*, reputed to be antidotes to snake-poison, and used in medicine; *sna'keshead*

SNARL

(*lily*), common fritillary, *Fritillaria meleagris*; *sna'keweed*, bistort; ~-*wood*, (wood, used as remedy for snake-poison, of) various E. Indian shrubs and trees of genus *Strychnos*; (hard heavy wood, with snake-like markings, of) S. Amer. timber-tree *Piratinera guianensis*. **snă'kў** adj. Infested with snakes; snake-like; (chiefly of hair of Furies) composed of snakes.

snake v.i. Make twisting course.

snăp n. 1. (Bite, cut, with) sudden quick closing of jaws or scissors; sudden break or fracture; sound of snapping, quick sharp sound. 2. Small crisp gingerbread cake or biscuit. 3. Spring-catch or one closing with snapping sound. 4. Card-game in which, when two cards of same value are turned up, the first player to call 'snap' has the right to take cards from other player(s). 5. Sudden, usu. brief, spell of frost or cold. 6. Alertness, vigour, energy; dash. 7. Snapshot. 8. (attrib., esp. of parliamentary and similar proceedings) Taken by surprise, brought on without notice, as ~ *debate* etc. 9. *sna'pdragon*, antirrhinum; Christmas game of plucking raisins from burning brandy; ~-*fastener*, press-stud; ~ *lock*, lock shutting automatically with spring when door etc. is closed; ~ *shot*, quick shot without deliberate aim; so ~-*shooter*; *sna'pshot*, instantaneous photograph, esp. with hand-camera; (v.) take such photograph (of). ~ v. 1. Make quick or sudden bite; speak irritably; say ill-tempered or spiteful things. 2. Pick *up* (esp. bargain) hastily. 3. Break sharply; produce sudden sharp sound from, emit sharp report or crack; close with snapping sound; ~ *fingers*, make audible fillip (*at*), esp. in contempt. 4. Take snapshot of. 5. *snapping turtle*, any of various large ferocious Amer. freshwater tortoises seizing prey with snap of jaws. **snă'pper** n. (esp.) Snap-fastener; snapping turtle; any of various carnivorous food-fishes (family Lutianidae) of warm seas.

snă'ppĭsh adj. Peevish, testy, malicious, ill-natured. **snă'ppĭshlў** adv. **snă'ppĭshnėss** n.

snă'ppў adj. 1. Snappish. 2. Quick, vigorous, lively, full of life or spring; *make it* ~, (colloq.) be quick about it.

snare n. Device for catching birds or animals, esp. with running noose of cord, wire, etc. (freq. fig. of temptation etc.); (surg.) wire loop or similar device for removing morbid growths; gut or rawhide string stretched across lower head of side-drum; ~-*drum*, side-drum. ~ v.t. Catch with snare.

snarl[1] n. (chiefly U.S.) Tangle, esp. of wool, hair, or the like; tangled condition. ~ v. Tangle (*up*), mix together confusedly.

snarl[2] v. (of dog etc.) Make

[830]

angry or quarrelsome sound with bared teeth; (of person) grumble viciously, use ill-tempered or surly language; express by snarling. ~ *n.* Act or sound of snarling.
snătch *v.* Make sudden snap or catch *at*, seize hurriedly or eagerly; rescue narrowly *from*; carry suddenly *away, from*. ~ *n.* Hasty catch or grasp, grab or snap *at*; brief period, short spell (*of*); small amount, fragment, short burst (*of* song, talk, etc.); brief view, glimpse. **snă'tchy̆** *adj.* In short spells, disconnected. **snă'tchily̆** *adv.*
sneak *n.* Mean-spirited or underhand person; telltale; (cricket) ball bowled along ground; ~-*thief*, one who steals what is in reach without breaking into buildings. ~ *v.* 1. Slink, go furtively. 2. (slang) Make off with, steal. 3. (school slang) Peach, tell tales. **snea'king** *adj.* (esp.) Furtive, not avowed.
snea'kers (-z) *n.pl.* (slang) Soft-soled shoes or slippers.
sneer *v.* Smile derisively (*at*); express or suggest derision or disparagement in speech or writing. ~ *n.* Sneering look or remark.
sneeze *v.i.* Make sudden involuntary convulsive expiration through the nose as a result of irritation of the mucous membrane, from catarrh, effect of dust, etc.; ~ *at*, despise, disregard, underrate. ~ *n.* Act of sneezing; sound thus produced.
snib *n.* (chiefly Sc.) Bolt, fastening, catch, of door, window, etc. ~ *v.t.* Bolt, fasten.
snick *n.* 1. Slight notch or cut. 2. (cricket) Batsman's light glancing blow deflecting ball slightly. ~ *v.t.* Make snick in; (cricket) slightly deflect (ball) with bat.
sni'cker *n.* & *v.i.* Whinny, neigh; snigger.
snickersnee' *n.* (joc.) Large knife. [f. earlier *snick-or-snee*, fight with knives, f. Du. *steken* thrust, *snijen*, cut]
snide *adj.* 1. (slang) Counterfeit, bogus. 2. (colloq.) Sneering. ~ *n.* Counterfeit jewellery or coin(s).
sniff *v.* Draw up air audibly through nose to stop it from running, in smelling *at* something, or as expression of contempt; draw (*up*) (air, liquid, scent), draw up scent of, into nose. ~ *n.* Act or sound of sniffing; amount sniffed up. [imit.]
sni'fter *n.* (slang) Small amount of spirits etc.
sni'fting-vălve *n.* Valve in steam-engine for blowing out air, steam, etc., or drawing in air (ill. LOCOMOTIVE].
sni'gger *v.i.* & *n.* (Utter) half-suppressed secretive laugh.
snip *v.* Cut with scissors etc., esp. in small quick strokes. ~ *n.* Act of snipping; piece snipped off; (sporting slang) something easily won or obtained, a certainty.

snīpe *n.* Wading bird of genus *Gallinago*, related to woodcocks, frequenting marshy places and having characteristic long straight

SNIPE
Length 266 mm

bill. ~ *v.* Shoot snipe; (mil.) shoot at (men) one at a time, usu. from cover and at long range; shoot, shoot *at*, thus. **sni'per** *n.*
sni'ppet *n.* Small piece cut off, snipping; (fig.) scrap, fragment, (pl.) odds and ends. **sni'ppety̆** *adj.*
sni'pping *n.* (esp.) Clipping, cutting.
snitch *v.* (slang) 1. Inform, peach. 2. Steal.
sni'vel *v.i.* Run at the nose; make sniffing or snuffling sound; be in tearful state, show maudlin emotion. ~ *n.* Running mucus; slight sniff; hypocritical emotion.
S.N.O. *abbrev.* Senior Naval Officer.
snŏb *n.* 1. (chiefly dial.) Cobbler; cobbler's apprentice. 2. Person who meanly or vulgarly admires, imitates, or seeks to associate with, those of superior social position or wealth, and looks down on those he considers inferior; also *transf.* of intellectual and artistic levels etc. **snŏ'bbish** *adj.* **snŏ'bbishly̆** *adv.* **snŏ'bbishnĕss, snŏ'bbery̆** *ns.*
snoek (-ōōk) *n.* (S. Afr.): see BARRACOUTA.
snōōd (*or* -ŏŏd) *n.* 1. Fillet or band for woman's hair; net etc. loosely confining hair at back. 2. (sea-fishing) Any of the short lines attaching baited hook to main line.
snōōk (*or* -ŏŏk) *n.* (slang) Contemptuous gesture with thumb to nose and fingers spread out; *cock a* ~, make this gesture.
snōō'ker *n.* (also ~ *pool*) Variety of pool played with 15 red balls, having a value of one each, and 6 balls of other colours, having values of 2 to 7, which the striker may only play at after having pocketed a red ball. **snōō'kered** (-erd) *adj.* With balls in such a position that direct play is impossible; (slang) defeated, baffled.
snōōp *v.i.* (slang, orig. U.S.) Pry inquisitively.
snōō'ty̆ *adj.* (slang, orig. U.S.) Contemptuous, supercilious.
snōōze *v.i.* & *n.* (Take) short sleep, esp. in day-time.
snōre *n.* & *v.* (Make) harsh or noisy respiration through mouth, or mouth and nose, during sleep.
snorkel : see SCHNORKEL.

Snŏ'rri Stur'lusŏn (stoor-) (1178–1244). Icelandic historian, author of the 'Heimskringla', a history of the kings of Norway, and of the 'Prose EDDA'.
snŏrt *n.* 1. Loud or harsh sound made by driving breath violently through nose, or noise resembling this. 2. Funnel providing submarine with air and enabling it to remain below surface for long periods. ~ *v.* Make sound of snort; express by snorting, utter with snorts.
snŏr'ter *n.* (esp.) Stiff gale; anything remarkable for size, violence, etc.
snŏt *n.* (vulg.) Mucus of the nose. **snŏ'tty̆** *adj.* (vulg.) Running or foul with snot. ~ *n.* (naval slang) Midshipman.
snout *n.* Projecting part of head of animal, including nose and mouth, (contempt.) person's nose; projecting part, structure, nozzle, etc., resembling snout.
snow (-ō) *n.* 1. Atmospheric vapour condensed and frozen into small, usu. hexagonal, crystals, and falling in soft white clusters of these known as flakes; fall of these, layer of them on ground; (usu. pl.) fall or accumulation of snow. 2. Something resembling snow, esp. in whiteness; white hair; (cookery) creamy or snowy-looking dish; white blossom etc. 3. (slang) Cocaine. 4. *snow'ball*, snow pressed into ball, esp. as missile; anything growing or increasing rapidly, like snowball rolled along ground; guelder rose; *snow'ball* (*v.*) pelt with, throw, snowballs; increase rapidly; *snow'-berry*, (fruit of) any of various plants or shrubs with white berries; ~-*bird*, any of various small white or partly white birds, esp. snow-bunting; ~-*blind*, with vision affected by glare of sun on snow; ~-*broth*, melted or melting snow; ~-*bunting*, small finch, *Plectrophenax nivalis*, breeding in Arctic regions, and common in Europe and N. America in winter, with brown-and-white or black-and-white plumage; ~-*drift*, snow piled up in heap by action of wind; *snow'drop*, (flower of) small early-flowering bulbous plant, *Galanthus nivalis*, with white pendent flower; *snow'flake*, one of flakes or small crystalline masses in which snow falls; any (white flower or) plant of bulbous genus *Leucojum*, esp. spring-flowering *L. vernum*, resembling snowdrop; ~ *goose*, white goose (*Anser coerulescens*) of N. America and N. Asia, breeding in Arctic regions; ~-*line*, level above which snow never completely disappears; *snow'man*, mass of snow formed into figure of man; ~-*plough*, device for clearing snow from railway track, road, etc.; ~-*shoe*, one of pair of racket-shaped frames of light wood strung with rawhide, enabling wearer to walk on surface

of snow; ~-*storm*, storm with heavy fall of snow; something resembling this, e.g. effect of electrical interference on a television screen; ~-*white*, white as snow, pure white. **snow′y** (-ŏĭ) *adj.* **snow** *v.* 1. *it snows*, *it is snowing*, snow falls. 2. Let fall as or like snow; strew, cover, (as) with snow; ~ *under*, bury in snow, (fig.) submerge, overwhelm; ~ *up*, block, imprison with fallen snow.

Snow′don (-ō-). Highest mountain (3,560 ft) of Wales.

snŭb[1] *v.t.* 1. Rebuff, reprove, humiliate, in sharp or cutting manner. 2. Check way of (ship) suddenly, esp. by rope wound round post. ~ *n.* Snubbing, rebuff.

snŭb[2] *adj.* (of nose) Short and turned up, whence *snub-nosed*.

snŭff[1] *n.* Charred part of candlewick, esp. as black excrescence obscuring light. ~ *v.* Trim snuff from (candle, wick) with fingers, scissors, etc.; ~ *out*, extinguish thus; (slang) die. **snŭ′ffers** (-z) *n.pl.* Scissors for snuffing candle, with box to catch snuff (ill. CANDLE).

snŭff[2] *n.* Powdered tobacco for sniffing up into nostrils; ~-*box*, small box for holding this; ~-*mill*, small mill for grinding snuff. **snŭ′ffў** *adj.* **snŭff** *v.* Sniff (*up*, *in*, *at*);

snŭ′ffle *v.* Sniff, esp. audibly or noisily; speak or say nasally, whiningly, or like one with a cold. ~ *n.* Sniff; snuffling sound or speech.

snŭg *adj.* Sheltered, comfortable, cosy; (of ship etc.) trim, neat, well protected from bad weather. **snŭ′glў** *adv.* **snŭ′gnėss** *n.* **snŭg** *n.* (dial. or slang) Bar-parlour of inn.

snŭ′ggerў *n.* Snug place, esp. private room or den; bar-parlour.

snŭ′ggle *v.* Move, lie, close *up to* for warmth; hug, cuddle.

sō[1] *adv.* To extent, in manner, with result, described or indicated; of the kind, in the condition, etc., already indicated, by that name or designation; on condition set forth or implied; indeed, as well; *just* ~, (pred.) in precise style etc.; *or* ~, or thereabouts; ~-*and*-~ (*n.*, *adj.*, & *adv.*) used as substitute for name or expression not exactly remembered or not needing to be specified, or (colloq., euphem.) for term of abuse etc.; ~-~, indifferently, only passably. ~ *conj.* In order that; with the result that; therefore.

sō[2] *n.* = SOL[2].

S.O. *abbrev.* Section Officer; Staff Officer; Stationery Office; sub-office.

soak *n.* Soaking; drinking-bout; hard drinker. ~ *v.* Place, lie, for some time in liquid, steep; make, be, saturated or wet through; take *up*, suck *in*, liquid; (of liquid) make way *in(to)*, *through*, by saturation; drink persistently, booze.

soap *n.* Cleansing agent, essentially sodium salts of fatty acids (palmitic, stearic) usu. forming lather when rubbed in water; *soft* ~, kind remaining semi-fluid, potassium salts of fatty acids; (fig.) flattery; ~-*box*, box or rough platform for open-air orators; (attrib.) of or like open-air oratory; ~-*bubble*, iridescent bubble made from thin film of soap and water; *soa′pflakes*, specially prepared flakes of soap for washing clothes etc.; ~ *opera*, (U.S. colloq.) sentimental radio or television serial; *soa′pstone*, steatite; *soa′psuds*, water impregnated with dissolved soap; *soa′pwort*, herbaceous plant of genus *Saponaria*, yielding detergent substances, esp. *S. officinalis*. ~ *v.t.* Rub, smear, lather, treat, with soap; (slang) flatter.

soa′pў *adj.* Like, smeared or impregnated with, suggestive of, soap; ingratiating, unctuous, flattering.

soar (sôr) *v.i.* Fly at, mount to, great height; hover or sail in air without flapping of wings or use of motor power.

sŏb *v.* Draw breath in convulsive gasps, usu. with weeping; utter with sobs; bring *oneself into* state, *to sleep*, with sobbing. ~ *n.* Convulsive catching of breath, esp. in weeping.

sō′ber *adj.* Not drunk; temperate in regard to drink; moderate, well-balanced, sedate, temperate; (of colour) quiet, inconspicuous. **sō′berlў** *adv.* **sō′ber** *v.* Make, become, sober.

Sobieski, John: see JOHN SOBIESKI.

Sōbra′nje, **-ye** (-ahnyĕ) *n.* Bulgarian elective national assembly.

sobri′etў *n.* Being sober.

sō′briquet (-kā) *n.* Nickname.

Soc. *abbrev.* Socialist; Society.

sō′cage *n.* (hist.) Feudal tenure of land by payment of rent or services other than military service.

sō′ccer (-k-) *n.* (colloq. ASSOCIATION football.

sō′ciable (-sha-) *adj.* Fitted or inclined for company of others, not averse to society, ready to converse; of, characterized by, friendly or pleasant companionship. **sō′ciablў** *adv.* **sōciabi′litў** *n.* **sō′ciable** *n.* 1. (hist.) Open four-wheeled carriage with seats facing each other, and box for driver; tricycle etc. with two seats side by side; Victorian S-shaped or circular couch. 2. (U.S.) Informal social gathering, esp. of church members.

sō′cial (-sha) *adj.* 1. Of, marked by, friendly intercourse; enjoyed, taken, in company with others; inclined to friendly intercourse, sociable. 2. Living in companies or more or less organized communities, gregarious. 3. Of, concerned with, interested in, society and its constitution, or the mutual relations of men or classes of men; ~ *contract*, contract assumed by Rousseau ('Contrat Social', 1762) and other writers by which true freedom was obtained by mutual agreement to substitute a state of law for a state of individualism; *S*~ *Credit*, economic doctrine propounded chiefly by C. H. Douglas (1879–1952), British social economist, according to which the potential abundance which modern industry can produce belongs to the whole community and ought to be made available to all by certain changes in the monetary policy, esp. the issue of National Dividends of Consumer Credit; *S*~ *Democrat*, member of socialistic political party, esp. (i) that founded in Germany 1863 by Ferdinand Lassalle, and united with Marxists 1875; (ii) Russian Marxist socialist party; (iii) moderate state-socialist party in Germany after 1919; ~ *history*, history of social behaviour; *S*~ *Revolutionary*, member of former Russian non-Marxist socialist party; ~ *science*, study of human society regarded as a science (freq. taken to include not only sociology but economics, political science, social anthropology, and social psychology); ~ *security*, (State provision of) financial and welfare benefits; ~ *services*, welfare services provided by the State; *S*~ *War*, (Gk hist.) war between Athenians and their allies, 357–355 B.C.; (Rom. hist.) war between Rome and her Italian allies, 90–89 B.C.; ~ *work*, practical sociology; so ~ *worker*. **sō′ciallў** *adv.* **sō′cial** *n.* Social gathering, esp. one organized by club, association, etc.

sō′cialism (-sha-) *n.* Political and economic principle that community as a whole should have ownership and control of all means of production and distribution (opp. CAPITALISM and INDIVIDUALISM); policy aiming at this; state of society in which this principle is accepted. **sō′cialist** *n.* **sōciali′stic** *adj.* **sōciali′sticallў** *adv.*

sō′cialize (-sha-) *v.t.* Make social or socialistic. **sōcializā′tion** *n.*

soci′etў *n.* 1. State of living in association with other individuals; customs and organization of ordered community; any social community. 2. Leisured, well-to-do, or fashionable persons regarded as distinct part of community. 3. Association with others, companionship, company. 4. Association of persons with common interest, aim, principle, etc.; *S*~ *of Friends*: see QUAKER; *S*~ *of Jesus*: see JESUIT; *Royal S*~: see ROYAL Society.

Soci′etў I′slands (īlandz). Group of islands in French Polynesia, including Tahiti; named by Capt. Cook in honour of Royal Society.

Soci'nian *adj.* & *n.* (Follower) of the doctrines of the Italian theologian *Socinus* (Lelio Sozzini, 1525–62) and his nephew Fausto Sozzini (1539–1604) who denied that Christ was divine. **Soci'nianism** *n.*

sŏciŏ'logў *n.* Study of human esp. civilized, society; study of social problems, esp. with a view to solving them. **sŏciŏlŏ'gical** *adj.* **sŏciŏlŏ'gically** *adv.* **sŏciŏ'logist** *n.*

sŏck[1] *n.* 1. Short stocking not reaching knee. 2. Light shoe worn by comic actors on ancient Greek and Roman stage; comedy. 3. = INSOLE, 2.

sŏck[2] *n.* (slang) Hard or violent blow. ~ *v.t.* Hit, strike hard; ~ (person) *one*, give him hard blow.

sŏ'ckėt *n.* Hollow, usu. cylindrical, part or piece for thing to fit into, revolve in, etc.; hollow or cavity in which eye, tooth, bone, etc., is contained; (elect.) device into which electric light bulb or plug fits to make an electrical connection.

sŏ'ckeye (-kī) *n.* Amer. fish, the blueback salmon, *Oncorhynchus nerka*. [Amer. Indian *sukai*]

sŏ'cle *n.* (archit.) Square block or plinth as support for pedestal, vase, statute, etc. (ill. PEDESTAL).

Socŏ'tra. Island E. of Gulf of Aden, in the People's Democratic Republic of Yemen; capital, Tamarida.

Sŏ'cratēs (-z) (469–399 B.C.). Greek philosopher, who was tried at Athens on a charge of corrupting the young by his teaching, and sentenced to death (by drinking hemlock); he left no writings, but his method and doctrines are preserved in the Dialogues of PLATO. **Socrā'tic** *adj.* Of, like, Socrates; ~ *irony*: see IRONY; ~ *method*, method of inquiry and instruction by series of questions. **Socrā'ticallў** *adv.*

sŏd[1] *n.* Turf, (piece of) upper layer of grass-land, with grass growing on it. ~ *v.t.* Cover (ground) with sods.

sŏd[2] *n.* (vulg.) Sodomite; also used as term of abuse.

sŏ'da *n.* 1. (also *washing* ~) Sodium carbonate (Na₂CO₃) an alkaline substance occurring naturally in mineral state or in solution, used in manufacture of glass, soap, etc., and obtained orig. from ashes of marine plants; *baking-*~, sodium bicarbonate. 2. Soda-water (see below). 3. ~-*biscuit*, ~ *bread*, ~ *cake*, ~-*scone*, biscuit, bread, etc., leavened with sodium bicarbonate; ~ *fountain*, apparatus for drawing soda-water kept under pressure; counter, shop, apparatus, for making and serving iced drinks, ice-cream, sundaes, etc.; ~-*water*, effervescent water charged under pressure with carbon dioxide and used alone or mixed with spirits, syrups, etc., as beverage. **sodă'litў** *n.* Confraternity, association, esp. Roman Catholic religious guild or brotherhood.

sŏ'dden *adj.* Saturated with liquid, soaked; heavy, doughy; stupid or dull with habitual drunkenness. [orig. past part. of SEETHE]

Sŏ'ddў, Frederick (1877–1956). English chemist, researcher in radioactivity; Nobel prize for chemistry 1921.

sŏ'dium *n.* (chem.) Soft silverwhite lustrous metallic element, oxidizing rapidly in air and reacting violently with water, closely resembling potassium in appearance and properties; symbol Na, at. no. 11, at. wt 22·9898; ~ *bicarbonate*, substance (NaHCO₃), used in baking (baking-soda) and medicinally as an antacid; ~ *carbonate*, common washing soda (Na₂CO₃); ~ *chloride*, common salt (NaCl); ~ *hydroxide*, caustic soda. [named by Sir H. Davy, 1807, f. *soda*]

Sŏ'dom. Ancient city near the Dead Sea, destroyed, along with Gomorrah, on account of its wickedness by fire from heaven (Gen. 18–19).

sŏ'domў *n.* Unnatural sexual intercourse by a man esp. with another male or with an animal. **sŏ'domite** *n.* Person practising sodomy. [f. SODOM]

Sŏ'dor. Medieval diocese comprising the Hebrides and the Isle of Man; now, as Sodor and Man, including only the Isle of Man.

S.O.E.D. *abbrev.* Shorter Oxford English Dictionary.

soĕ'ver *adv.* At all, of any kind, in any way (used with generalizing or emphatic force after words or phrases preceded by *how, what, who*, etc.).

-soĕver *suffix.* Soever.

sŏ'fa *n.* Long seat with raised back and end(s). [Arab. *ṣuffa*] (Illustration, *p. 834*.)

sŏ'ffit *n.* (archit.) Under-surface of architrave, lintel, arch, etc. (ill. ARCH[1]).

Sofi: see SUFI.

Sŏ'fia (*or* -ē'*a*). Capital city of Bulgaria.

sŏft *adj.* 1. Not hard; yielding to pressure, malleable, plastic, easily cut. 2. Of smooth surface or fine texture, not rough or coarse; (of weather etc.) mellow, mild; rainy, moist. 3. (of water) Not containing calcium or other mineral salts which prevent formation of lather with soap. 4. Not astringent, sour, or bitter; not crude or brilliant; not sharply defined; not strident or loud; (phonet.) voiced; (of Russian consonants) palatalized, (of vowels) causing palatalization; (of the letters *c, g*) pronounced as spirants, not stops. 5. Gentle, quiet, conciliatory; sympathetic, compassionate; maudlin, feeble, flabby, weak; silly; (of drink) non-alcoholic; (slang) easy. 6. ~ *coal*, bituminous coal; ~ *currency*, currency of which other countries have earned more than they can willingly spend in the country whose currency it is and for which other economical outlets are not easily found (cf. HARD); ~ *goods*, textiles; ~-*pedal*, restrain, tone down; ~-*shell*(*ed*), having a soft or flexible shell; having shell not yet hardened owing to recency of moult; ~ *soap*: see SOAP; ~ *sugar*, granulated or powdered sugar; *so'ftware*, (in computer) programmes etc. not forming part of machine; (audiovisual aids) recorded material, such as films, film strips, records, tapes, etc., as opp. to *hardware*, the permanent equipment, such as projectors, record players, etc., in which it is used; *so'ftwood*, (wood of) coniferous tree(s). **sŏ'ftlў** *adv.* **sŏftness** *n.* **sŏft** *adv.* Softly. ~ *int.* (archaic.) Wait a moment; hush!

sŏ'ften (-fn) *v.* Become, make soft or softer; reduce strength of a defended position by bombing or bombardment (often with *up*); *softening of the brain*, morbid, esp. senile, degeneration of brain.

S.O.G.A.T., SoGAT *abbrev.* Society of Graphical and Allied Trades.

sŏ'ggў *adj.* Sodden, saturated, heavy with moisture.

sōh (sō) *n.* = SOL[2].

Sŏ'hō (*or* -ō'). District of London S. of Oxford St and W. of Charing Cross Rd, with many foreign restaurants.

soigné (swah'nyā) *adj.* Carefully or elegantly arranged; well-groomed.

soil[1] *n.* The ground, upper layer of earth in which plants grow, consisting of disintegrated rock usu. with admixture of organic remains. **soi'lless** (-l-l-) *adj.*

soil[2] *v.* Make dirty, smear or stain with dirt; tarnish, defile; admit of being soiled. ~ *n.* Dirty mark, smear, defilement; ~-*pipe*, pipe conveying domestic sewage etc. to main sewer.

soil[3] *v.t.* Feed (cattle etc.) on fresh-cut green fodder.

soirée (swaˆr'ā) *n.* Evening party, social evening.

sŏ'journ (-*ern; or* sŭ-) *n.* & *v.i.* (Make) temporary stay in place.

sōke *n.* Right of local jurisdiction (hist.; now only in names of certain districts, as the *S*~ *of Peterborough*).

Sŏl[1] *n.* (Rom. myth.) The Sun personified.

sŏl[2] *n.* (mus.) 5th note of hexachord and of major scale in movable-doh system; note G in fixed-doh system (see SOLMIZATION). [see UT]

sŏl[3] *n.* (phys. chem.) Liquid solution or suspension of colloid. [for *solution*]

sŏl[4] *n.* Principal monetary unit of Peru, = 100 centavos.

sō'la *n.* Tall pithy-stemmed E. Indian swamp-plant; ~ *topee*, light sun-helmet of pith of this.

[833]

SOLACE   SOLEMNIZE

1. COUCH, EARLY 19TH C. 2. SETTLE, LATE 18TH C. 3. SETTEE, MID-18TH C. 4. DAY-BED, LATE 17TH C. 5. CHESTERFIELD, LATE 19TH C. 6. SOFA, MID-20TH C.

sŏ′lace *n*. Comfort, consolation. ~ *v.t.* Comfort, cheer, console.

sŏ′lan *n*. (also ~ *goose*) Gannet.

sŏlanā′ceous (-sh*u*s) *adj*. Belonging to the nightshade family of plants (Solanaceae).

solā′num *n*. Plant of large genus *S*~ of herbs, shrubs, and trees incl. nightshade, potato, etc.

sō′lar *adj*. Of, concerned with, determined by, emanating from, the sun; ~ *cell*, photoelectric device for converting solar radiation into electrical energy (ill. SPACECRAFT); ~ *day*: see DAY, 2; ~ *month*, exact twelfth of the year; ~ *plexus*, (anat.) complex of nerves situated in abdomen behind stomach; ~ *system*, sun with the 9 major planets and many minor planets, asteroids, comets, etc., held by its attraction and revolving round it; ~ *time*, time as shown on sundial ~ *n.* = SOLARIUM; (in medieval house) upper chamber, esp. for private use of family (ill. HOUSE).

solār′ium *n*. (pl. *-ia*). Room, balcony, etc., enclosed in glass or open to air, for sunbathing etc.

solā′tium (-shī-) *n*. Something given as compensation or consolation, esp. additional sum over and above actual damages.

sold : see SELL.

sŏ′lder (*or* sŏd-) *n*. Fusible metal or metallic alloy used for joining metal surfaces or parts. ~ *v.t.* Join with solder.

sŏ′ldier (-jer) *n*. Member of army, esp. private or non-commissioned officer; man of military skill and experience; (also ~ *ant*) fighting ant or termite, larger and with larger head and jaws than workers (ill. TERMITE); ~ *crab*, hermit-crab; ~ *of fortune*, one of adventurous character, willing to serve wherever his services are well paid. **sŏ′ldierlike, sŏ′ldierly** *adjs*. **sŏ′ldier** *v*. Serve as soldier; (naut. slang) shirk work; ~ *on*, (colloq.) keep going in spite of difficulties; plod on steadily. [OF *soude* pay f. L *solidus* gold coin]

sŏ′ldiery (-jerĭ) *n*. Soldiers of a State, in a district, etc.

sōle¹ *n*. Lower surface of foot, that part of it which rests or is placed on ground in standing or walking; part of boot or shoe on which wearer treads (freq. excluding heel; ill. SHOE); bottom, foundation, or under-surface, of plough, wagon, golf-club head, etc. ~ *v.t.* Provide (boot etc.) with sole.

sōle² *n*. Common European flatfish of genus *Solea*, highly esteemed as food; any of various other flatfishes, esp. edible ones.

sōle³ *adj*. One and only; exclusive; (law, of woman) unmarried. **sō′lely** (-l-lĭ) *adv*.

sŏ′lecĭsm *n*. Offence against grammar or idiom, blunder in speech or writing; violation of good manners or etiquette. **sŏ′lecĭst** *n*. **sŏlecĭ′stic** *adj*.

sŏ′lemn (-m) *adj*. Accompanied, performed, with religious rites or with ceremony; formal; ceremonious; impressive, awe-inspiring; serious, grave, earnest. **sŏ′lemnly** *adv*. **sŏ′lemness** *n*.

solĕ′mnĭty *n*. Rite, celebration, festival, ceremony; solemn character, appearance, behaviour, etc.

sŏ′lemnīze *v.t.* Celebrate, honour with ceremonies; duly

[834]

perform (marriage ceremony); make solemn. **sŏlemnīzā′tion** *n.*
sō′lĕn *n.* Razor-fish of genus *S~*.
sō′lĕnoid *n.* (elect.) Cylindrical coil of conducting wire which behaves as a bar magnet when a current is passed through it, and which can be used for producing magnets.
Sō′lent. W. part of channel between Isle of Wight and mainland of England.
sŏ′lfa′ (-ah) *n.* (mus.): see TONIC sol-fa.
Sōlferi′nō (-rē-). Village on Lake Garda, Italy, scene of defeat of Austrians by French and Sardinians, 1859.
Sol.-Gen. *abbrev.* Solicitor-General.
solĭ′cĭt *v.* Make appeals or requests to, importune; ask importunately or earnestly for; accost and importune for immoral purposes. **solĭcĭtā′tion** *n.*
solĭ′cĭtor *n.* 1. One who solicits or canvasses (chiefly U.S.). 2. (in English law) Member of legal profession qualified to advise clients and instruct barristers, but not to appear as an advocate except in certain lower courts; *S~-General*, law-officer of Crown ranking next to Attorney-General or (in Scotland) Lord Advocate; in U.S., similar officer appointed by president to assist Attorney-General; in some States, chief law officer.
solĭ′cĭtous *adj.* Anxious, troubled, concerned; anxious, eager (*to* do). **solĭ′cĭtously** *adv.*
solĭ′cĭtūde *n.* Being solicitous, anxiety, concern.
sŏ′lĭd *adj.* Of stable shape, not liquid or fluid, rigid, hard and compact; of three dimensions; of solid substance throughout, not hollow, without internal cavities or interstices, uninterrupted; homogeneous, alike all through; firm, substantial, well grounded, sober, real, genuine; concerned with solids; ~ *state*, (phys.) state of matter in which a body retains its own boundaries without the need of a container. **sŏ′lĭdly** *adv.* **sŏ′lĭdnĕss, solĭ′dĭty** *ns.* **solĭ′dĭfy** *v.* **sŏ′lĭd** *n.* (geom.) Body or magnitude of three dimensions; solid substance or body.
sŏlĭdă′rĭty *n.* Community of interests, sympathies, and action.
sŏlĭdŭ′ngūlar, -ate (-ngg-) *adjs.* = SOLIPED.
sŏ′lĭdus *n.* (pl. *-dī*). Gold coin of the Roman Empire, orig. worth *c* 25 denarii; shilling(s) (only in abbrev. *s.*); shilling line as in 7/6.
solĭ′loquy (-kwĭ) *n.* Talking to oneself or without addressing any person; instance of this, esp. on part of character in play. **solĭ′loquīze** *v.i.* Utter soliloquy.
sŏ′lĭpĕd *adj. & n.* Solid-hoofed (animal), as horse.
sŏ′lĭpsĭsm *n.* (metaphys.) View that the self is the only object of real knowledge or the only really existent thing. **sŏ′lĭpsĭst** *n.*
sŏlĭtair′e *n.* 1. Precious stone, usu. diamond, set by itself. 2. Card-game for one person, patience (now chiefly U.S.); game for one player, played on a board with marbles or pegs which are removed by jumping as in draughts, the object being to clear the board.
sŏ′lĭtary *adj.* Alone, living alone, not gregarious, without companions; single, separate; secluded, lonely. **sŏ′lĭtarĭly** *adv.* **sŏ′lĭtarĭnĕss** *n.* **sŏ′lĭtary** *n.* Recluse, hermit.
sŏ′lĭtūde *n.* Being solitary; lonely place.
sŏlmĭzā′tion *n.* Singing a passage at sight to the sol-fa syllables by any of the systems in use (fixed-, movable-, DOH).
sō′lō *n.* 1. Piece of vocal or instrumental music, dance, performed by one person or instrument, with or without subordinate accompaniment. 2. Any of various card-games in which one player plays or may play alone against the others. 3. Solo flight (see below). ~ *adj.* Alone, without companion or partners; ~ *flight*, aeroplane flight made without companion or instructor; ~ *whist*, form of whist in which person making highest bid (e.g. *solo*, five tricks; *misère*, no tricks; *abundance*, nine tricks) plays alone against the other three.
sō′lōĭst *n.* Musician etc. who performs alone or takes principal part.
Sŏ′lomon. King of Israel *c* 970–933 B.C.; son and successor of David; famed for his wisdom and magnificence; built the Temple at Jerusalem; *Judgement of ~*, his proposal to cut in two the baby that was claimed by two women at once (2 Kings 3: 16–28); *Song of ~*: see SONG; *~'s seal*, herbaceous plant (*Polygonatum multiflorum*) with broad sessile leaves and drooping greenish-white flowers on arching stems; also, magic symbol formed by two interlaced triangles forming a six-pointed star. **Sŏlomŏ′nĭc** *adj.*
Sŏ′lomon I′slands (īlandz). Group of islands in S. Pacific, E. of New Guinea; a protectorate of Britain except for the northernmost which belong to the Australian territory of Papua and New Guinea.
Sō′lon (*c* 638–558 B.C.). Early Athenian legislator and reformer of the constitution, renowned for his wisdom.
sŏ′lstice *n.* Time when sun is farthest from equator and appears to stand still, occurring twice yearly, on 21 or 22 June (*summer ~*) and 22 or 23 Dec. (*winter ~*), and corresponding with the longest and shortest days of the year; point in ecliptic reached by sun at solstice (ill. CELESTIAL). **sŏlsti′tial** (-shal) *adj.*
sŏ′lūble *adj.* That can be dissolved; that can be solved; ~ *glass*: = WATER-glass. **sŏlūbĭ′lĭty** *n.* **sŏ′lūbĭlīze** *v.*
solu′tion (-ōō- *or* -ū-) *n.* 1. Solving, being solved; instance or method of solving, explanation, answer. 2. Dissolving, being dissolved, conversion of solid or gas into liquid form by mixture with solvent; dissolved state; fluid substance produced by process of solution. 3. Breaking, breach (chiefly in ~ *of continuity*).
solu′tionist *n.* (esp.) Solver of newspaper puzzles.
Solū′trēan, Solū′trian (*or* -ōō-) *adj.* Of the later palaeolithic culture (immediately following the Aurignacian); named from remains found in a rock shelter at La Solutré, central France, with characteristic flint implements; worked by pressure-flaking.
sŏlve *v.t.* Explain, resolve, answer; (math.) find answer to (problem, etc.). **sŏ′lvable** *adj.* **sŏlvabĭ′lĭty** *n.*
sŏ′lvency *n.* Being financially solvent.
sŏ′lvent *adj.* 1. Able to pay all one's debts or liabilities. 2. That dissolves or can dissolve. ~ *n.* Substance (usu. liquid) capable of dissolving something; dissolving or disintegrating agent.
Sŏ′lway Fĭ̂rth. Arm of Irish Sea forming estuary of River Esk and W. part of boundary between England and Scotland.
Som. *abbrev.* Somerset.
Soma′lĭ (-mah-) *adj. & n.* (Member) of a dark-skinned Muslim Hamitic people inhabiting Somalia; (of) their language, belonging to the Ethiopian group of Hamitic languages.
Soma′lĭa (-mah-). Republic on E. coast of Africa, formed (1960) from the former protectorate British Somaliland and the former Italian colony of Somalia; capital, Mogadishu.

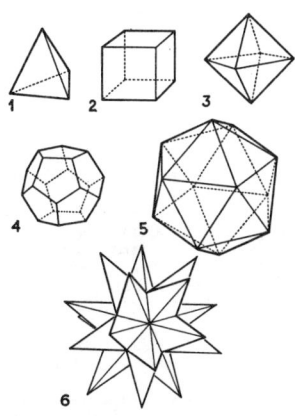

[835]

sŏmă′tĭc *adj.* Of the body, corporeal, physical; of the framework of the body as dist. from the internal organs; ~ *cell*, one of the cells forming tissues, organs, etc., of the body (dist. from GERM-*cell*).
sō′matōme *n.* One of the segments into which bodies of many animals are divided.
sŏ′mbre (*-er*) *adj.* Dark, gloomy, dismal. **sŏ′mbrelў** *adv.* **sŏ′mbrenėss** *n.*
sŏmbrer′o (-ārō) *n.* Broad-brimmed, usu. felt, hat, of kind common in Spain and Spanish America.
some (sŭm *or* sum) *adj.* Particular but unknown or unspecified; certain quantity or number of; appreciable or considerable quantity of; (colloq., emphat., orig. U.S.) such in the fullest sense, something like. ~ *pron.* Certain persons or things; a certain quantity or number. ~ *adv.* (slang) In some degree.
so′mebody (sŭmb-) *n.* & *pron.* Some person; person of some note or consequence.
so′mehow (sŭmh-) *adv.* In some indefinite or unspecified manner, by some means or other.
someone (sŭ′mwŭn) *n.* & *pron.* Somebody.
so′mersault (sŭ-) *n.* & *v.i.* (Make) acrobatic movement of the body turning head over heels or the reverse, either on the ground or in the air.
So′mersėt (sŭ-). County of SW. England.
So′mersėt House (sŭ-). 18th-c. building in the Strand, London, on site of palace built by a 16th-c. Duke of Somerset; contains offices of Revenue Department, principal Probate Registry, and Registrar-General of births, marriages, and deaths.
so′mething (sŭmth-) *n.* & *pron.* Some thing; some undetermined, unspecified, or unknown thing; important thing or person. ~ *adv.* (archaic, exc. in ~ *like*) In some degree.
so′metime (sŭmt-) *adv.* At some time; (archaic) formerly. ~ *adj.* Former. **so′metimes** (-z) *adv.* At some times.
so′mewhat (sŭmwŏt) *adv.* In some degree. ~ *pron.* (archaic) A certain amount, part, etc., *of* something.
so′mewhere (sŭmwār) *adv.* In, at, to, some place.
sō′mīte *n.* Segment of animal body, esp. of vertebrate or arthropod embryo, somatome (ill. LOBSTER). **somī′tĭc** *adj.*
Sŏmme. River of NE. France running into English Channel; scene of almost continuous heavy fighting from 1915 to 1917, esp. July–Nov. 1916.
sŏmnă′mbūlism *n.* Walking or performing other action during sleep; state characterized by this. **sŏmnă′mbūlĭst** *n.* **sŏmnăm-būlī′stĭc** *adj.*

sŏmnī′ferous *adj.* Inducing sleep, soporific.
sŏ′mnolent *adj.* Sleepy, drowsy; inducing drowsiness. **sŏ′mnolentlў** *adv.* **sŏ′mnolence, sŏ′mnolencў** *ns.*
son (sŭn) *n.* 1. Male child in relation to parent; male descendant; offspring, product, native, follower; ~*-in-law*, daughter's husband; ~ *of the soil*, native of district; worker on the land; dweller in the country. 2. *the S*~, second person of the Trinity; *S*~ *of God*, *S*~ *of Man*, Jesus Christ.
sō′nant *adj.* & *n.* Voiced (sound, letter).
sō′nar *n.* Device for detecting and locating submerged objects by reflection of sonic and ultrasonic waves.
sona′ta (-nah-) *n.* (orig.) Musical composition for instruments (usu. strings and keyboard) as opp. voice ('cantata'), in several movements, in *chamber* ~ usu. in dance rhythms, in *church* ~ of more abstract form and usu. including figure; later, composition for one or two instruments, in several (usu. four or three) movements contrasted in rhythm and speed but related in key; ~ *form*, composition in which two subjects are successively set forth, developed, and restated.
sŏnati′na (-tē-) *n.* Shorter or simpler form of sonata.
sŏnde *n.* = RADIOSONDE.
son et lumière (sŏn ā loomyār). Entertainment recounting history connected with a building etc. and using recorded sound together with lighting effects. [Fr., = 'sound and light']
sŏng *n.* Singing, vocal music; musical utterance of certain birds; short poem set to music or meant to be sung; short poem, esp. in rhymed stanzas; poetry, verse; *buy for a* ~, buy for very little; ~*-bird*, bird with musical song; *S*~ *of Solomon*, *S*~ *of Songs*, poetic book of O.T., traditionally ascribed to Solomon; *S*~ *of the Three Holy Children*, book of the Apocrypha telling of Daniel's three companions in the fiery furnace (Dan. 3: 23); ~ *sparrow*, common sparrow (*Melospiza melodia*) of eastern N. America, with sweet song; ~*-thrush*: see THRUSH[1].
sŏ′nglėss *adj.*
Song of Sol. *abbrev.* SONG OF Solomon.
sŏ′ngster *n.* (poet.) 1. (fem. so′ngstress) Singer. 2. Song-bird.
sō′nĭc *adj.* Of, using, sound waves, esp. (of apparatus) determining depth of water by reflection of sound waves; (of a mine) set off by sound vibrations; ~ *barrier*, sound barrier; ~ *boom*, explosive noise produced by aircraft flying faster than the speed of sound.
sŏ′nnėt *n.* Poem of 14 lines arranged according to any of various definite schemes, each line having normally 10 syllables in English verse (but in Italian verse 11, in French 12), of which the commonest forms in English are the *Petrarchan* or *Italian* ~, divided into an octave of 8 lines rhyming *a b b a a b b a* and a sestet of 6 lines with three rhymes more freely arranged, and the *Shakespearian* or *English* ~ which consists of three quatrains and a couplet.
so′nnў (sŭ-) *n.* Familiar form of address to boy.
sŏnorĕ′scent *adj.* Capable of converting light- or heat-radiations into sound. **sŏnorĕ′scence** *n.*
sonŏr′ous (*or* sŏ′-) *adj.* Resonant, (capable of) giving out esp. loud or rich sound; high-sounding. **sonŏr′ouslў** *adv.* **sonŏr′ousnėss, sonŏr′ĭtў** *ns.*
sōōn *adv.* Not long after present time or time in question, in a short time; early; willingly; *as or so* ~ *as*, the moment that, not later than, as early as; *sooner or later*, at some time or other.
sōōt *n.* Black carbonaceous substance or deposit in fine particles formed by combustion of coal, wood, oil, etc. ~ *v.t.* Smear, smudge, cover, choke (*up*), with soot; sprinkle or manure with soot. **sōō′tў** *adj.* **sōō′tĭlў** *adv.* **sōō′tĭnėss** *n.*
sōōth *n.* (archaic) Truth, fact.
sōōthe (-dh) *v.t.* Calm, tranquillize; reduce force or intensity of (passion, pain, etc.).
sōō′thsayer *n.* One who foretells future events, diviner.
sŏp *n.* Piece of bread etc. dipped or steeped in liquid before eating or cooking; (also ~ *to Cerberus*) something given to pacify or bribe. ~ *v.* Soak, steep (*in* liquid), take *up* (liquid) by absorption; *sopping* (*wet*), very wet, drenched. **sŏ′ppў** *adj.* Soaked, wet; (colloq.) mawkish, foolishly sentimental.
sŏ′phism *n.* Specious but fallacious argument, esp. one intended to deceive or mislead.
sŏ′phĭst *n.* 1. Paid teacher of rhetoric and philosophy in ancient Greece. 2. Captious or fallacious reasoner, quibbler. **sophĭ′stĭc, -ĭcal** *adjs.* **sophĭ′stĭcallў** *adv.* **sŏ′phĭstrў** *n.*
sŏ′phĭster *n.* Student in 2nd or 3rd year at Cambridge (i.e. Harvard, etc., in 3rd or 4th year at Trinity College, Dublin, and some Amer. universities.
sophĭ′stĭcāte *v.t.* 1. Render somewhat artificial by depriving of natural simplicity, as by education, worldly experience, etc. 2. Falsify by mis-statement or unauthorized alteration. **sophĭ′stĭcātėd** *adj.* (esp.) 1. (of person) Having fashionable tastes or style; (of things) satisfying such persons; (of peoples) of a fully developed culture or stage of civilization. 2. (of machinery etc.) Complex, intricate and versatile. **sophĭstĭcā′tion** *n.* **sophĭ′stĭcāte** *n.* Sophisticated person.

SOPHOCLES

Sŏ'phoclēs (-z) (495-406 B.C.). Athenian tragic poet; author of 'Oedipus the King', 'Oedipus at Colonus', 'Antigone', 'Electra', 'Trachiniae', 'Ajax', and 'Philoctetes'.

sŏ'phomōre n. (U.S.) 2nd-year student in Amer. universities and colleges. **sŏphomōr'ic** adj.

sŏpori'fic adj. & n. (Drug) tending to produce sleep.

sopra'no (-rah-) n. (pl. -os). Highest singing voice in women and boys (ill. VOICE); singer with such voice; musical part for this; ~ clef: see CLEF. **sopra'nist** n. Male adult singer retaining boy's soprano voice.

Sorā'bian adj. & n. = SORBIAN.

sōrb[1] n. (Fruit of) service-tree or rowan.

Sōrb[2] n. = WEND. **Sōr'bian** adj. & n.

Sōrbŏ'nne. Orig. a theological college founded in Paris by Robert de Sorbon, chaplain and confessor to Louis IX, c 1257; later, faculty of theology in University of Paris, suppressed 1792; now, seat of faculties of science and letters of University of Paris.

sōr'cerer n. (fem. sorceress) User of magic arts, wizard, magician. **sōr'cery** n.

sōr'did adj. Dirty, foul, squalid; ignoble, base; avaricious, mercenary. **sōr'didly** adv. **sōr'didness** n.

sōr'dine (-ēn) n. (mus.) Mute for bowed or wind instruments etc.; damper of a piano string (ill. PIANO[2]).

sōre n. Place where skin or flesh of animal body is diseased or injured so as to be painfully tender or raw. ~ adj. Painful, causing pain, distressing, irritating, grievous; suffering pain; irritable, sensitive; (colloq.) irritated, annoyed. **sōr'ely** adv. **sōr'eness** n. **sōre** adv. (archaic) Grievously, severely.

sōr'ghum (-gum) n. Plant of genus S~ of tropical grasses including the cereal Indian millet and the Chinese sugar-cane (sweet ~).

sori'tēs (-z) n. (logic) Series of propositions in which predicate of each is subject of next and conclusion is formed of first subject and last predicate. **sori'tic**, -ical adjs.

sorŏ'rity n. (U.S.) Women's college or university society.

sorŏ'sis n. (bot.) Fleshy or pulpy compound fruit, as pineapple, mulberry.

sŏ'rrel[1] n. Any of various small sour-tasting perennial plants of genera Rumex and Oxalis, freq. used in cookery.

sŏ'rrel[2] adj. & n. (Horse) of bright chestnut or reddish-brown colour; (having) this colour.

sŏ'rrow (-ō) n. Distress of mind caused by loss, suffering, disappointment, etc.; occasion or cause of this, misfortune, trouble. ~ v.i. Grieve, feel sorrow, mourn.

sŏ'rrowful adj. **sŏ'rrowfully** adv. **sŏ'rrowfulness** n.

sŏ'rry adj. 1. Feeling regret, regretful (freq. in expressions of sympathy or apology). 2. Wretched, paltry, shabby, mean. **sŏ'rrily** adv. **sŏ'rriness** n.

sŏrt n. Kind, species, variety (of); (print., usu. pl.) any particular letter or character in fount of type; of ~s, (colloq.) of a not very satisfactory kind; out of ~s, out of health, spirits, or temper; slightly unwell. ~ v. Separate into sorts; take out (certain sorts from others); (archaic) correspond, agree, with. **sŏr'ter** n. (esp.) Letter-sorter at a post-office.

sŏr'tēs (-z) n.pl. ~ Biblicae or Sacrae, Homericae, Virgilianae, divination by turning up at random a passage in the Bible, Homer, or Virgil. [L, pl. of sors lot, chance]

sŏr'tie n. Sally, esp. of beleaguered garrison; operational flight by an aircraft.

sōr'tilège n. Divination by lots; enchantment, magic.

sōr'us n. Cluster of sporecases or spores on under-surface of fern-leaves, in fungi, lichens, etc. (ill. FERN).

S O S (ĕs ō ĕs). International code-signal (three dots, three dashes, three dots) of extreme distress, used esp. by ships at sea; (colloq.) urgent appeal for help.

sŏstenu'tō (-nōō-) adv., n. (pl. -os), & adj. (Passage performed) in a sustained manner.

sŏt n. Person stupefied by habitual drunkenness. **sŏ'ttish** adj.
sŏ'ttishly adv. **sŏ'ttishness** n.

So'thĕby's (sŭdh-, -z). Auction-rooms in New Bond St, London, orig. founded 1744 at York St, Covent Garden, by Samuel Baker whose partner and nephew was John S. Sotheby (1740-1807); the first sale-room exclusively for books, manuscripts, and prints.

Sō'thic adj. Of the dog-star; ~ cycle, period of 1460 Sothic years or 1461 × 365 days; ~ year, ancient Egyptian year of 365 days 6 hours, computed from one heliacal rising of the dog-star to the next. [Gk Sóthis, f. the Egyptian name of the dog-star]

sŏ'ttō vō'ce (-chĕ). In an undertone, aside. [It.]

sou (sōō) n. Former coin of France, orig. worth $\frac{1}{20}$ livre; later, bronze coin worth 5 centimes, one worth 10 centimes; (colloq.) very small amount of money.

soubrĕ'tte (sōō-) n. Maid-servant or similar character (esp. with implication of pertness, coquetry, intrigue, etc.) in comedy, opera, etc.; actress playing such parts.

sou'chŏng (sōōsh-) n. Fine variety of China tea, in Lapsang ~ with smoky or tarry flavour. [Chin. siao-chung small sort]

Soudan: see MALI.

souffle (sōō'fl) n. (path.) Low

SOUND

murmuring sound heard in auscultation.

soufflé (sōō'flā) n. Light spongy savoury or sweet dish made by mixing a thick sauce or purée with the yolks and stiffly beaten whites of eggs and baking.

sough (sow) n. & v.i. (Make) rushing, sighing, or rustling sound, as of wind in trees.

sought (sawt) adj.: see SEEK; (csp.) ~-after, much in demand.

soul (sōl) n. 1. Spiritual or immaterial part of man; moral and emotional part of man; vital principle and mental powers of animals including man; animating or essential part, person viewed as this; personification or pattern of, embodiment of moral or intellectual qualities. 2. Departed spirit; disembodied spirit. 3. Person. **sou'llĕss** (-l-l-) adj. **sou'llĕssly** adv. **sou'llĕssness** n.

sou'lful (sōl-) adj. Having, expressing, appealing to, the (esp. higher) emotional or intellectual qualities; (colloq.) excessively emotional. **sou'lfully** adv. **sou'lfulness** n.

sound[1] adj. Healthy; not diseased, injured, or rotten; financially solid or safe; correct, logical, well-founded, valid; (of sleep) deep, unbroken; thorough, unqualified. **sou'ndly** adv. **sou'ndness** n. **sound** adv. Deeply, profoundly (asleep).

sound[2] n. Sensation produced in organs of hearing when surrounding air etc. vibrates so as to affect these; what is or may be heard; vibrations causing this sensation; utterance, speech, or one of the separate articulations composing this; impression produced by sound, statement, etc.; ~ barrier, extremely great resistance of air to object moving at speed near that of sound; ~-board, thin resonant board in musical instrument so placed as to reinforce tones; ~-bow, thickest part of bell, against which clapper strikes (ill. BELL[1]); ~-box, (in gramophone) box carrying reproducing or recording stylus or needle; ~ effects, sounds, other than speech or music, broadcast as part of programme; ~-film, film for recording sound; cinema film with sound-track; ~-hole, f-hole (ill. STRINGED); ~-post, small wooden peg beneath bridge of violin or similar instrument supporting belly and connecting it with back; ~-proof, preventing passage of sound; (v.t.) make sound-proof; ~-track, (area of film carrying) sound record on cinema film; ~-wave, one of a series of progressive longitudinal vibratory disturbances in air or other medium by which the auditory nerves are stimulated. **sou'ndlĕss** adj. **sound** v. Give forth sound (freq. fig., with reference to impression created); cause to sound; utter, pronounce; give

[837]

notice of by sound, cause to resound, declare, make known; examine (person etc.) by auscultation, examine medically.
sound[3] *n.* Surgeon's probe for sounding or exploring cavities of body. ~ *v.* Investigate, test depth or quality of bottom of (water), with line and lead or other apparatus; measure (depth) thus; (of whale) dive deeply; inquire, esp. in cautious or indirect manner, into sentiments or inclination of (person); (surg.) examine with a sound; *sounding-lead*, lead attached to line (*sounding-line*) used in sounding depth of water.
sound[4] *n.* 1. Narrow channel, esp. between island and mainland, or connecting two large bodies of water; arm of sea. 2. Swimming-bladder of cod, sturgeon, etc.
sou'nding[1] *adj.* Resonant, sonorous; high-sounding, imposing; *~-board*, board or screen over or behind pulpit etc. to reflect speaker's voice towards the audience (ill. PULPIT); sound-board.
sou'nding[2] *n.* (esp. pl.) Measurement of depth of water at specific places; places where such measurements can or have been taken.
soup (soop) *n.* 1. Liquid food made by stewing vegetables, meat, etc.; *in the ~*, (slang) in difficulties; *~-kitchen*, public institution where soup etc. is supplied free to the poor or in times of distress. 2. (U.S. slang) Nitro-glycerine, esp. when used to open safe. **sou'py** *adj.*
soupçon (soo'psawn) *n.* Trace or flavour (*of*); very small amount.
sour *adj.* With tart or acid taste, esp. as result of unripeness or of fermentation; rendered acid esp. by fermentation; affected or spoiled thus; (of smell) suggesting fermentation; (of soil) cold and wet, dank; (of person etc.) harsh, peevish, morose; *~-dough*, (U.S.) prospector, one who lives in the open, esp. in Alaska or Canada (from keeping piece of sour dough for making bread); *~-sop*, (large, succulent, slightly acid fruit of) tropical American tree, *Anona muricata*. ~ *n.* Acid solution used in bleaching, tanning, etc.; (U.S.) acid drink, usu. of whisky or other spirit with lemon- or lime-juice. **sour'ish** *adj.* **sour'ly** *adv.* **sour'ness** *n.* **sour** *v.* Make, become, sour.
source (sors) *n.* Spring, fountain-head, of stream or river; origin, chief or prime cause, *of*; document, work, etc., giving evidence, esp. original or primary, as to fact, event, etc.; literary work(s) from which later writers have derived inspiration, plots, etc.
sourdine (soordē'n) *n.* (mus.) = SORDINE; also, soft stop on harmonium.
Sousa (soo'za), John Philip (1854-1932). American bandmaster and composer of marches.
sou'saphone (sooz-) *n.* (mus.)

Bass wind-instrument of tuba kind. [f. J. P. SOUSA]
souse *n.* 1. Pickle made with salt; food in pickle, esp. head, feet, and ears of swine. 2. Sousing. ~ *v.* Put in pickle; plunge (*into* water etc.), soak (*in* liquid), drench. ~ *adv.* With sudden plunge.
soused (-st) *adj.* (slang) Drunk, 'pickled'.
soutache (soo'tahsh) *n.* Narrow flat ornamental braid.
soutane (sootah'n) *n.* Cassock of R.C. priest.
souteneur (sootener) *n.* Man living on earnings of prostitute. [Fr.,= 'protector']
sou'terrain (soo-) *n.* (chiefly archaeol.) Underground chamber or passage.
south *adv.* Towards, in, the south. ~ *n.* 1. Point of horizon directly opposite north; this direction. 2. Cardinal point of the compass opposite north. 3. (usu. *the S~*) That part of a country, district, etc., which lies to the south; (esp.) SOUTHERN States of U.S. 4. *S~*, bridge-player opposite North. ~ *adj.* Lying, towards, in, the south; (of wind) blowing from the south; *S~ Downs*, downs of East Sussex, West Sussex, and Hampshire; *sou'thdown*, small hornless sheep with short fine wool, yielding mutton of good quality, originating on South Downs; *S~ Island* central and largest island of New Zealand; *sou'thpaw*, left-handed (person), esp. in sport; *S~ Sea*, Pacific Ocean; *S~ Sea Company*, company formed in 1711 by Harley (later Earl of Oxford) to trade with Spanish America; in 1720 it assumed responsibility for the national debt in return for a guaranteed profit, a fever of speculation (*the ~ Sea Bubble*) set in, and shortly afterwards the company failed. **sou'thward** *adv.*, *adj.*, & *n.* **sou'thwards** (-z) *adv.* **south** *v.i.* Turn, veer, move, towards south; (astron.) cross meridian.
South A'frica (ă-). Republic in S. Africa; constituted in 1910 (as *Union of ~*) from the self-governing British colonies Cape of Good Hope, Transvaal, Natal, and Orange Free State; member State of the Commonwealth until 1961; administrative capital, Pretoria; seat of legislature, Cape Town. **South A'frican** *adj.* & *n.*
South Amĕ'rica. Southern part of the continent of America, joined to Central America by the isthmus of Panama. **South Amĕ'rican** *adj.* & *n.*
Southă'mpton. City and seaport in Hampshire; university, 1952.
South Austrā'lia (*or* ŏ-). State of S. Australia; capital, Adelaide.
South Căroli'na. Southeastern State of U.S. on Atlantic coast, one of the original States of the Union (1788); capital, Columbia.

Sou'thcott, Joanna (1750-1814). English religious fanatic; announced herself as the woman mentioned in Rev. 12; left a sealed box which was to be opened in a time of national crisis; it was opened in 1927, but contained nothing of interest.
South Dakō'ta. State in north central U.S.; admitted to the Union in 1889; capital, Pierre.
south-east *adv.* & *n.* (Direction or compass-point) between south and east. ~ *adj.* Of, in, to, from, the south-east. **south-ea'ster** *n.* South-east wind. **south-ea'sterly** *adv.*, *adj.* & *n.* **south-ea'stern** *adj.* **south-ea'stward** *adv.*, *adj.*, & *n.* **south-ea'stwardly** *adv.* & *adj.* **south-ea'stwards** (-z) *adv.*
sou'therly (sŭdh-) *adj.* In the south; (of wind) blowing from the south. ~ *adv.* Towards the south. ~ *n.* South wind.
sou'thern (sŭdh-) *adj.* Of the south; lying or directed towards the south; (poet.) coming from the south; *S~ Cross*: see CROSS; *S~ hemisphere*: see HEMISPHERE; *S~ States*, those in southern part of U.S., esp. those south of Mason and Dixon's line and east of New Mexico; *sou'thernwood*, hardy shrubby southern-European wormwood (*Artemisia abrotanum*) with fragrant aromatic leaves. **sou'therner** *n.* (also *S~*) Native, inhabitant, of the south. **sou'thernmōst** *adj.*
Sou'they (-dhī; *or* sŭ-), Robert (1774-1843). English poet, essayist, and historian; one of the Lake poets (see LAKE[1]).
South Glamŏr'gan. County of S. Wales (since April 1974), comprising the S. part of the former county of Glamorgan and part of the former county of Monmouthshire.
sou'thing (-th-) *n.* Southward progress or deviation, esp. in sailing; distance due south.
Southwark (sŭ'dherk). Inner London borough, famous in literary history on account of its ancient inns and theatres. [orig. the 'south work' or bridgehead at the south end of London Bridge]
south-wĕst *adv.* & *n.* (Direction or compass-point) between south and west. ~ *adj.* Of, in, to, from, the south-west. **south-wĕ'ster** *n.* 1. South-west wind. 2. (usu. *sou'-wester*) Waterproof hat with broad flap behind to protect the neck. **south-wĕ'sterly** *adv.*, *adj.*, & *n.* **south-wĕ'stern** *adj.* **south-wĕ'stward** *adv.*, *adj.*, & *n.* **south-wĕ'sterly** *adv.* & *adj.* **south-wĕ'stwards** (-z) *adv.*
South Wĕst A'frica (ă-). (also called *Namibia*) Territory in S. Africa between Cape Province and Angola; German protectorate 1880-1915; since 1919 a mandated territory of South Africa; capital, Windhoek.

[838]

South Yor'kshire. Metropolitan county of N. England (since April 1974), comprising Sheffield and the S. part of the former county of Yorkshire.

souvenir (soo'venēr or -ēr') n. Thing given, brought, kept, etc., for memento (*of* occasion, place, etc.). [Fr., = remember, f. L *subvenire* occur to the mind]

sou'wĕ'ster n. = SOUTH-WESTER.

sov., sovs abbrevs. Sovereign(s) (coin).

sŏ'vereign (-vrĭn) n. 1. Supreme ruler, esp. monarch. 2. Former British gold coin worth £1. ~ adj. Supreme; possessing sovereign power; (of remedies etc.) very good or efficacious. **sŏ'vereigntў** n.

sŏ'vĭet n. Council, esp. elected organ of government of district, republic, etc., or (*Supreme S*~) whole, of U.S.S.R.; the *S*~, the U.S.S.R. **sŏ'vĭetize** v.t. Change or convert to a form of government by soviets. [Russ. *sovet* council]

Sŏ'vĭet U'nĭon (ū-). Union of Soviet Socialist Republics (see entry).

sow[1] n. 1. Female of swine, adult female pig, esp. domestic one used for breeding. 2. Trough through which molten iron runs into side-channels to form pigs; large block of iron solidified in this. 3. ~-*bread*, wild cyclamen of central Europe, the fleshy tuberous root-stocks of which are eaten by swine; ~-*thistle*, plant of genus *Sonchus*, common European weed with sharply toothed thistle-like leaves and milky juice.

sow[2] (sō) v.t. Scatter (seed) on or in the earth; plant (ground *with* seed) by sowing; (fig.) cover thickly *with*. **sow'er** n.

soy n. (also ~ *sauce*, *soya* (-*bean*) *sauce*) Sauce for fish etc. made, chiefly in Japan, China, and India, from soya beans pickled in brine; **soya bean**. [Jap. colloq. f. *sho-yu* f. Chin. *shi-yu* (*shi* salted beans, *yu* oil)]

soy'a bean. (Seed of) a widely cultivated Asiatic bushy leguminous plant (*Soja hispida*), yielding valuable meal (*soya* (-*bean*) *flour*), oil, fertilizer, forage, etc. [f. SOY]

sŏ'zzled (-ld) adj. (slang) Very drunk.

s.p. abbrev. *Sine prole* (L, = without issue).

S.P. abbrev. Service Police; sparking plug; starting price.

spa (-ah) n. Watering-place, (place with) mineral spring. [f. *Spa*, watering-place in Belgium, fashionable in 18th c.]

spāce n. 1. Continuous extension viewed with or without reference to the existence of objects within it; the universe beyond the earth's atmosphere, the immeasurable expanse in which the solar and stellar systems, nebulae, etc., are situated; *spa'cecraft*, ~ *ship*, vehicle designed to travel outside the earth's atmosphere (*illustration, p. 813*); ~-*time*, (philos.) four-dimensional continuum resulting from a fusion of the concepts of space and time. 2. Interval between points or objects. 3. Interval of time. 4. (print.) Blank between words etc., piece of type-metal used to separate words etc. ~ *v.* Set at intervals, put spaces between; make space between words on typewriter etc.

spā'cious (-shus) adj. Enclosing a large space, having ample space, roomy. **spā'ciouslў** adv. **spā'ciousness** n.

spāde[1] n. Tool for digging or cutting ground, turf, etc., usu. with flattish rectangular blade socketed on wooden handle, with grip or cross-piece at upper end, grasped with both hands while blade is pressed into ground with foot; anything resembling this in form or use; ~-*guinea*, guinea coined 1789–99 with shield on reverse shaped like blade of pointed spade; *spa'dework*, (fig.) hard work, preliminary drudgery. ~ v.t. Dig up with spade.

spāde[2] n. (Playing-card with) black figure(s) resembling pointed spade; (pl.) suit of these cards. [Span. *espada* sword]

spā'dix n. (bot.); pl. -*ices* pr. -ī'sēz). Inflorescence consisting of thick fleshy spike, usu. enclosed in spathe (ill. INFLORESCENCE).

spaghĕ'tti (-gĕ-) n. Pasta formed into long rods, thinner than macaroni but thicker than vermicelli; ~ *junction*, (colloq.) complex intersection of roads. [It., = 'little strings']

spahi (spah'hē) n. 1. (hist.) Member of Turkish irregular cavalry disbanded c 1830. 2. (hist.) Member of native Algerian cavalry in service of French Government.

Spain. State occupying the larger portion of the Iberian peninsula, formed in the last quarter of the 15th c. by the union of Aragon and Castile and ruled over until 1931, when a republic was proclaimed, by sovereigns of the Aragon, Habsburg, and Bourbon dynasties; renamed a kingdom by Generalissimo Franco in 1947; capital, Madrid.

spall (-awl) n. Splinter, chip. ~ *v.* Splinter; (mining) prepare (ore) for sorting by breaking it up.

spăm n. Kind of tinned ham produced in U.S. [trade-name; f. *spiced ham*]

spăn[1] n. Distance from tip of thumb to tip of little finger, occas. of forefinger, of fully extended hand; this as measure (9 in.); short distance or time; whole extent of a period of time; full extent or stretch between abutments of arch, piers of bridge, wing-tips of aircraft, etc.; arch of bridge. ~ v.t. Stretch from side to side of, extend across; bridge (river etc.), form arch across; measure, cover, extent of (thing) with one's grasp etc.

spăn[2] n. (naut.) Rope with both ends made fast to afford purchase in loop, rope connecting stays or other uprights; (U.S., Canada, etc.) pair of horses, mules, etc., (S. Africa) team of oxen. ~ v.t. (now esp. S. Afr.) Inspan, harness or yoke (oxen, horses, etc.); (naut.) fasten, attach, draw tight. [Du. *spannen* fasten]

spă'ndrel n. Space between either shoulder of arch and surrounding rectangular moulding or framework, or between shoulders of adjoining arches and moulding above (ill. ARCADE).

spă'ngle (-nggl) n. Small round thin piece of glittering metal etc., esp. one of many sewn to dress etc. as ornament; any small sparkling object. **spă'nglў** adj. **spă'ngled** (-ld) adj. Covered (as) with spangles.

Spă'niard (-yard) n. Native of Spain.

spă'niel (-yel) n. Dog of various small or medium-sized breeds, usu. with long silky hair, large drooping ears, keen scent, and docile and affectionate disposition, used as sporting dogs esp. for starting and retrieving game, or kept as pets (ill. DOG). [OF. *espaignol* Spanish (dog)]

Spă'nish adj. Of Spain or its people or language; ~ *America*, those portions of America settled by Spaniards and now occupied by their descendants, including the greater part of S. America and some of the West Indian islands; ~ *American* (adj. & n.); ~ *Armada*: see ARMADA; ~ *black*, pigment obtained from charred cork; ~ *brown*, dark reddish-brown earth used as a pigment; ~ *chestnut*: see CHESTNUT; ~ *fly*, brilliant green beetle (*Lytta vesicatoria*) from which cantharides, used for raising blisters, is obtained; ~ *grass*, esparto grass; ~ *Main*, mainland of America adjacent to the Caribbean Sea, esp. that portion from the Isthmus of Panama to the mouth of the Orinoco; in later use, the sea contiguous to this; *War of* ~ *Succession*, that between France and Spain on the one side and England, Austria, and the United Provinces on the other, on the death of Charles II of Spain without issue (1701–14); ~ *windlass*, stick used as a lever for tightening cord or bandage. ~ *n.* Language of Spain, one of the Romance group.

spănk[1] v.t. & n. Slap or smack with open hand, esp. on buttocks.

spănk[2] v.i. Move or travel quickly or dashingly.

spă'nker n. (esp.) 1. Fast or spirited horse; (colloq.) person or thing of notable size or quality. 2. (naut.) Fore-and-aft sail set on aftermost mast of sailing vessel (ill. SHIP).

spă'nkĭng adj. (esp.) Very

[839]

SPANNER

large or fine, striking, notable, excellent; (of horse etc.) fast-moving, dashing, showy.

spă′nner *n.* Tool, usu. steel bar with jaw, socket, or opening at end(s), for turning nut of screw, bolt, coupling, etc. (*Illustration, p. 841*.)

spār¹ *n.* Stout pole, esp. such as is used for mast, yard, etc., of ship (ill. SHIP); either of main lateral members of wing of aircraft, carrying ribs (ill. AEROPLANE); ~ *deck*: see DECK¹. ~ *v.t.* Furnish with spars.

spār² *n.* Any of various more or less lustrous crystalline easily cleavable minerals as FLUORSPAR, ICELAND spar, etc.

spār³ *v.i.* Make motions of attack and defence with fists, use hands (as) in boxing; (fig.) dispute, bandy words; (of cocks) strike with feet or spurs, fight. ~ *n.* Sparring; boxing-match; cock-fight.

spă′rable *n.* Small wedge-shaped headless nail for soles and heels of boots. [orig. *sparrow-bill*]

spāre *adj.* 1. Scanty, frugal; lean, thin. 2. That can be spared, not required for ordinary use; re-

SPARE

served for future, emergency, or extraordinary use; ~ *part*, duplicate of part of machine, kept in readiness to replace loss, breakage, etc.; ~ *room*, room not ordinarily used, guest-room. **spār′ely** *adv.* **spār′eness** *n.* **spāre** *n.* Spare part. ~ *v.* 1. Be frugal or grudging of; be frugal. 2. Dispense with, do without. 3. Refrain from inflicting injury, affliction, or damage or punishment on, deal leniently or gently with; refrain from taking (life). **spār′ingly** *adv.* **spār′ingness** *n.*

SPACECRAFT

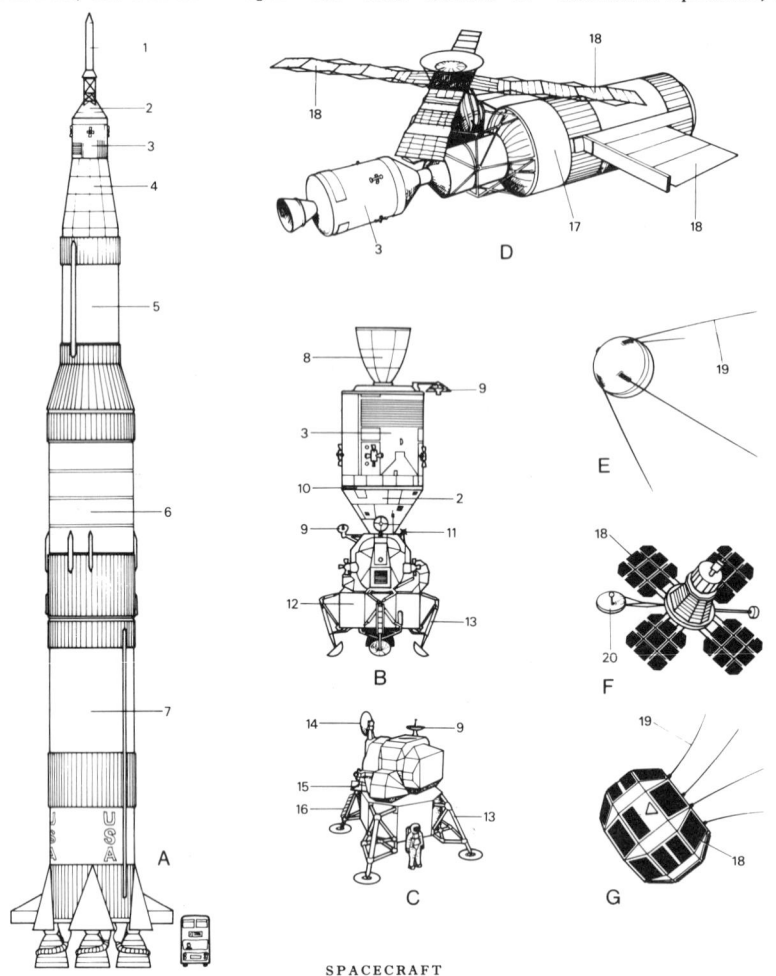

A. SATURN 5 LAUNCH VEHICLE WITH APOLLO SPACECRAFT IN PLACE. TOTAL HEIGHT 363 ft., c 1970. DOUBLE DECKER BUS IS SHOWN BESIDE FOR COMPARISON. B. COMMAND AND LUNAR MODULES IN DOCKED POSITION. C. LUNAR MODULE. D. SKY-LAB ORBITAL WORKSHOP 1973 (U.S.A.). E. FIRST ARTIFICIAL SATELLITE, SPUTNIK 1, 1957, 184 lb. (U.S.S.R.). F. LUNAR ORBITER 1966/7, 850 lb. (U.S.A.). G. PROSPERO 1971, 145 lb. (U.K.)

1. Launch escape system. 2. Command module. 3. Service module. 4. Lunar module housing. 5. Third stage of Saturn 5 launch vehicle. 6. Second stage. 7. First stage. 8. Service propulsion engine nozzle. 9. S-band antenna. 10. Heat shield. 11. V.H.F. antenna. 12. Lunar module. 13. Landing gear. 14. Rendezvous radar antenna. 15. Exit platform. 16. Ladder. 17. Workshop made from the third stage of a Saturn 5 launch vehicle. 18. Solar cell panels. 19. Radio antenna. 20. 36″ parabolic antenna

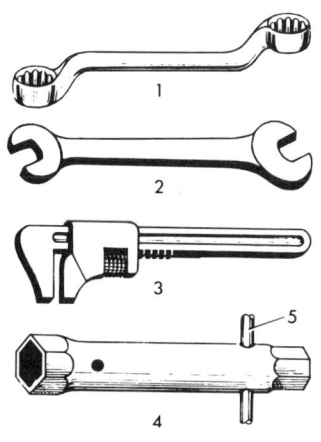

SPANNERS
1. Ring. 2. Open. 3. Adjustable spanner or wrench. 4. Box-spanner. 5. Tommy bar

spāre'-rib *n.* Part of closely-trimmed ribs of meat, esp. pork (ill. MEAT).

spărk[1] *n.* Fiery particle thrown off from burning substance, or still remaining in one almost extinguished, or produced by impact of one hard body on another; small bright object or point; (elect.) (brilliant flash of light accompanying) sudden disruptive discharge between two conductors separated by air etc.; electric spark for firing explosive mixture in internal combustion engine; (pl., colloq.) radio operator on ship; (fig.) flash (of wit etc.); scintilla, particle (of fire, some quality, etc.); ~-*plug*, (U.S.) sparking plug. ~ *v.* Emit spark(s) of fire or electricity; produce sparks at point where electric circuit is broken; ~ *off*, cause (esp. sudden or violent activity); *sparking plug*, electrical device fitting into the cylinder-head of an internal combustion engine, consisting of two electrodes across the space between which the current from the ignition system passes and so produces the spark which fires the explosive mixture in the cylinders (ill. COMBUSTION).

spărk[2] *n.* Gay fellow; gallant. **spăr'kish** *adj.* **spărk** *v.i.* Play the gallant.

spăr'kle *n.* Sparkling; gleam, spark. ~ *v.i.* Emit sparks; glitter, glisten, scintillate. **spăr'kler** *n.* (esp., colloq.) Diamond or other sparkling gem. **spăr'kling** *adj.* (of wines etc.) Effervescing with small glittering bubbles of carbon dioxide.

spă'roid (*or* spār-) *adj.* Of the Sparidae or sea-bream family of fishes.

spă'rrow (-ō) *n.* Small brownish-grey bird of genus *Passer*, either the *house-*~ (*P. domesticus*), a native of Europe introduced into N. America, common about buildings and in towns, or the *tree-*~ (*P. montanus*) of Europe, not associated with buildings; *hedge-*~, DUNNOCK; ~-*grass*, (colloq. corrupt. of) asparagus; ~-*hawk*, small hawk (*Accipiter nisus*) of N. Europe and Asia, preying on small birds; small N. Amer. falcon (*Falco sparverius*); any of various other small hawks and falcons.

spărse *adj.* Thinly dispersed or scattered, not crowded or dense, with wide distribution or intervals. **spăr'sely** *adv.* **spăr'senĕss** *n.*

Spăr'ta. Ancient capital (also called *Lacedaemon*) of LACONIA, the inhabitants of which were noted for the military organization of their State and for their rigorous discipline, simplicity, and courage.

Spăr'tacist *adj. & n.* (Member) of the extreme revolutionary Socialist party organized in Germany in 1918 under the leadership of Karl Liebknecht, who adopted the pen-name of 'Spartacus'.

Spăr'tacus. Thracian leader of an army of slaves who rebelled against Rome in 73–71 B.C.

Spăr'tan *adj.* Of Sparta (esp. with allusion to the characteristics of the Spartans); hence, austere, hardy; ~ *dog*, kind of bloodhound. ~ *n.* Native, inhabitant, of Sparta; hardy austere person.

spăsm *n.* Involuntary sudden and violent muscular contraction; sudden convulsive movement, convulsion.

spăsmŏ'dĭc (-zm-) *adj.* Of, caused by, subject to, spasm(s); occurring, done, jerkily or by fits and starts. **spăsmŏ'dĭcally** *adv.*

spă'stĭc *adj.* Of, characterized by, (esp. tonic) spasm(s). **spăstĭ'cĭty** *n.* **spă'stĭc** *n.* Person with cerebral PALSY.

spăt[1] *n.* Spawn of shellfish, esp. oyster. ~ *v.* (of oyster) Spawn.

spăt[2] *n.* (usu. pl.) Short gaiter covering instep and reaching little above ankle (ill. COAT). [abbrev. of SPATTERDASH]

spăt[3] *n.* (U.S.) Tiff, quarrel.

spăt[4] *n.* : see SPIT[2].

spă'tchcŏck *n.* Fowl hastily killed and dressed, split open and grilled. ~ *v.t.* Cook as, like, spatchcock; (colloq.) insert, interpolate (esp. incongruous matter).

spāte *n.* River-flood, esp. sudden; rush, outburst.

spāthe (-dh) *n.* (bot.) Large bract, freq. bright-coloured, enveloping inflorescence on same axis (spadix), as in arum etc. (ill. INFLORESCENCE).

spă'thic *adj.* Of or like SPAR[2], foliated, lamellar.

spă'tial (-shal) *adj.* Of, relating to, occupying, occurring in, space. **spă'tially** *adv.*

spă'tialize (-shal-) *v.t.* Make spatial; localize in space.

spă'tter *v.* Scatter (liquid, mud, etc.) here and there in small drops, splash (*with* mud, slander, etc.) thus, (of liquid) fall thus or with sound suggesting heavy drops. ~ *n.* Spattering, splash; pattering.

spă'tterdăsh *n.* (chiefly pl.) Long gaiter or legging to protect stockings etc. from mud etc. (ill. INFANTRY).

spă'tūla *n.* Flat broad-bladed knife-shaped implement used for spreading foods or ointments and for medical examination of certain organs etc. **spă'tūlar** *adj.*

spă'tūlate *adj.* With broadened rounded end like common form of spatula.

spă'vin *n.* Disease of hock in horses, marked by hard bony tumour or excrescence and caused by strain etc. **spă'vined** (-nd) *adj.*

spawn *n.* Minute eggs of frogs, fishes, etc., usu. extruded in large numbers and often forming coherent or gelatinous mass, fertilized by the MILT (ill. FROG[1]); (contempt.) brood, (numerous) offspring; mycelium of fungi. ~ *v.* Cast spawn; produce or generate as spawn or in large numbers.

spay *v.t.* Remove ovaries of (female animal).

S.P.C.K. *abbrev.* Society for Promoting Christian Knowledge.

S.P.E. *abbrev.* Society for Pure English.

speak *v.* (past t. *spōke*, archaic *spāke*; past part. *spō'ken*). Utter words or articulate sound in ordinary (not singing) voice; hold conversation; make oral address, deliver speech; utter (words); make known (opinion, *the truth*, etc.) thus; use (specified language) in speaking; state in words; be evidence of, indicate; ~ *for*, act as spokesman of or for; ~ *of*, mention; ~ *out, up*, speak freely; speak loud(er) or so as to be distinctly heard; ~-*easy*, (U.S. slang) illicit liquor shop.

spea'ker *n.* 1. One who speaks, esp. one who makes a speech. 2. *S*~, member of House of Commons chosen by the House to preside over debates, preserve order, etc.; similar officer of U.S. House of Representatives and other legislative bodies. 3. LOUD- speaker.

spea'king (-*ng*) *n.* Speechmaking; ~ *part*, part in play etc. containing words to be spoken; ~ *terms*, degree of acquaintanceship allowing exchange of conversation (*not on* ~ *terms*, (usu.) estranged); ~-*trumpet*, trumpet-shaped instrument for magnifying sound of voice; ~-*tube*, tube for conveying voice from one room or building to another, or from the inside to the outside of a closed carriage or motor-car, enabling the occupants to speak with the driver.

spear *n.* Thrusting or hurling weapon with long shaft and sharp-pointed head, usu. of iron or steel (*illustration, p. 842*); sharp-pointed and barbed instrument for catching fish etc.; ~-*grass*, grass with stiff pointed leaves; *spear'head*, (fig.) person(s) leading, anything in forefront of, attack; (*v.t.*) act as

[841]

spearhead for; *spear′mint*, common garden mint. ~ *v.t.* Pierce, strike, (as) with spear.

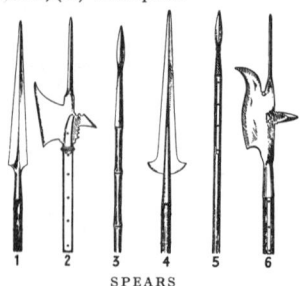

SPEARS

1. Long-bladed spear, *c* 1510. 2. Halberd, *c* 1500. 3. Cavalry lance, late 19th c. 4. Partisan, *c* 1510. 5. Pike, 16th–17th centuries. 6. English bill, *c* 1480

spĕc *n.* (colloq.) Speculation; *on* ~, experimentally, as a gamble.
spē′cial (-shal) *adj.* Of a particular kind, peculiar, not general; for a particular purpose; exceptional in amount, degree, kind, etc.; ~ *constable*: see CONSTABLE¹; ~ *correspondent*, correspondent appointed by newspaper to report on special facts; ~ *licence*, licence allowing marriage to take place without usual publication of banns or at time or place other than those legally appointed; ~ *pleader*, counsel employed to give an opinion on special points submitted to him; ~ *pleading*, (law) allegation of special or new matter as opp. to denial of allegations of other side; (pop.) specious but unfair argument, statement of case designed to support point of view rather than discover truth; ~ *train*, additional train for special purpose. spē′cially *adv.* In special manner, to special degree or extent; of special purpose, expressly. spē′cial *n.* Special constable, train, edition of newspaper, etc.
spē′cialist (-shal-) *n.* One who devotes himself to particular branch of profession, science, etc., esp. medicine.
spĕciă′lity (-shǐ-) *n.* Special feature or characteristic; special pursuit, product, operation, etc., thing to which person gives special attention.
spē′cialize (-shal-) *v.* 1. Make specific or individual; modify, limit (idea, statement). 2. (biol.) Adapt (organ etc.) for particular purpose, differentiate; be differentiated, become individual in character. 3. Be, become, a specialist. spĕcializā′tion *n.*
spē′cialty (-shal-) *n.* 1. (law) Special contract under seal. 2. Speciality.
spē′cie (-shē) *n.* Coin, coined money. [L *in specie* in kind]
spē′cies (-shēz *or* -shǐz) *n.* (pl. same) 1. (logic) Group subordinate to genus, containing individuals which have common attribute(s) and are called by a common name. 2. (biol.) Group of organisms which have certain characteristics not shared by other groups, usu. a group which is believed to be reproductively isolated, i.e. whose members will breed among themselves but not normally with members of other groups; sub-division of genus. 3. (loosely) Kind, sort.
spĕcǐ′fic *adj.* 1. Definite; distinctly formulated; precise, particular. 2. Of a species; possessing, concerned with, the properties characterizing a species. 3. (med., of remedies) Specially efficacious for a particular ailment etc.; (path.) characteristic. 4. ~ *gravity*: see GRAVITY; ~ *heat*: see HEAT. spĕcǐ′fically *adv.* spĕcǐ′ficness *n.* spĕcǐ′fic *n.* Specific remedy.
spĕcǐfǐcā′tion *n.* Specifying; specified detail, esp. detailed description of construction, workmanship, materials, etc., of work undertaken by engineer, architect, etc.; description by applicant for patent of nature, details, and use of invention.
spĕ′cǐfy *v.t.* Name expressly, mention definitely; include in specification.
spĕ′cimĕn *n.* Individual or part taken as example of class or whole, esp. serving as example of class or thing in question for purposes of investigation or scientific study; (med.) sample; (colloq.) person of a specified sort.
spē′cious (-shus) *adj.* Of good appearance; plausible; fair or right on the surface. spē′ciously *adv.* spē′ciousness, speciŏ′sǐty (-shǐ-) *ns.*
spĕck *n.* Small spot, dot, stain; particle (*of* dirt etc.); spot of rottenness in fruit. spĕ′ckless *adj.* spĕck *v.t.* Mark with specks.
spĕ′ckle *n.* Small speck, mark, or stain. ~ *v.t.* Mark with speckles.
spĕcs *n.pl.* (colloq.) Spectacles.
spĕ′ctacle *n.* 1. Public show, specially prepared or arranged display; object of public attention, curiosity, admiration, etc. 2. (*pair of*) ~*s*, pair of lenses to correct or assist defective sight set in frame supported on nose and usu. with side-pieces passing over ears. 3. Device on railway signal consisting of two frames containing red and green glass respectively (ill. SIGNAL). spĕ′ctacled (-ld) *adj.* Wearing spectacles; (of animals etc.) marked in way that suggests spectacles.
spĕctă′cular *adj.* Of, of the nature of, a spectacle or show; striking; imposing. spĕctă′cūlarly *adv.*
spĕctā′tor¹ *n.* One who looks on, esp. at show, game, etc. spĕctātōr′ial *adj.*
Spĕctā′tor², The. Daily periodical conducted by STEELE and ADDISON 1711–12 and revived by Addison in 1714, containing articles on manners, morals, and literature.
spĕ′ctral *adj.* 1. Ghostly, of ghosts. 2. Of spectra or the spectrum.
spĕ′ctre (-ter) *n.* Ghost, apparition.
spĕ′ctrogrăph (*or* -ahf) *n.* Instrument producing representation of a spectrum usu. on a screen or photographic plate. spĕctrogră′phic *adj.*
spĕ′ctroscōpe *n.* Optical instrument for producing and examining spectra. spĕctroscŏ′pic *adj.* spĕctroscŏ′pically *adv.*
spĕ′ctrum *n.* (pl. *-ra*). 1. Series of images formed when a beam of radiant energy is dispersed and then brought to focus, so that its component waves are arranged in order of wavelength; (esp.) coloured band into which beam of light is decomposed by prism etc.; after-image seen when eyes are turned away from bright-coloured object etc.; ~ *analysis*, analysis, esp. chemical analysis, by means of spectra. 2. Range, series, of interrelated ideas or objects.
spĕ′cūlar *adj.* Of (the nature of) a speculum or mirror; ~ *iron (ore)*, haematite.
spĕ′cūlāte *v.i.* 1. Engage in thought or reflection, esp. of conjectural or theoretical kind (*on*). 2. Buy or sell commodities etc. in expectation of rise or fall in their market value; engage in commercial operation, make investment, involving risk of loss. spĕ′cūlatīve *adj.* spĕ′cūlatīvely *adv.* spĕ′cūlativeness, spĕ′cūlator *ns.*
spĕcūlā′tion *n.* 1. Meditation on, inquiry into, theory about, a subject. 2. Speculative investment or enterprise, practice of speculating, in business.
spĕ′cūlum *n.* 1. (surg.) Instrument for dilating cavities of human body for inspection. 2. Mirror, usu. of polished metal, esp. in optical instruments; ~ *metal*, alloy of copper and tin taking high polish used as a reflector in telescopes. 3. Lustrous coloured patch on wing of some birds.
speech *n.* Act, faculty, or manner of speaking; thing said, remark; public address; language, dialect; *King's*, *Queen's* ~, ~ *from the throne*, statement of foreign and domestic affairs and of chief measures to be considered by Parliament, read at opening of parliamentary session; ~-*day*, annual day when prizes are presented and speeches made at a school; ~ *therapy*, remedial treatment of defective speech.
spee′chǐfy *v.i.* (contempt.) Make speeches, hold forth.
spee′chless *adj.* Dumb; temporarily deprived of speech by emotion etc. spee′chlessly *adv.* spee′chlessness *n.*

[842]

speed n. 1. Rate of time at which something moves, travels, proceeds, or operates; rapidity; (photog.) sensitivity of film etc. to light; length of exposure. 2. (archaic) Success, prosperity. 3. ~-*boat*, motor-boat etc. capable of very high speed; ~-*cop*, (orig. U.S.) policeman with duty of checking excessive speed of motorists; ~ *limit*, maximum speed permitted on road, to vehicle etc.; *spee'dway*, track for motor-racing, road intended only for fast motor vehicles. ~ v. 1. Go fast; travel at excessive or illegal speed; (archaic) send fast, send on the way. 2. (archaic) Be, make, prosperous; succeed; give success to. 3. Regulate speed of (engine etc.), cause to go at fixed speed; ~ *up*, increase speed of, increase rate of work, production; ~-*up* (n.).
speedŏ'mĕter n. Instrument for registering speed at which vehicle, esp. motor-car, is moving.
spee'dwĕll n. Plant, flower, of genus *Veronica* of small herbaceous plants with leafy stems and small blue (occas. pink or white) flowers.
spee'dў adj. Rapid, swift; prompt. **spee'dĭlў** adv. **spee'dĭnĕss** n.
spĕlĕŏ'logў n. Scientific study of caves. **spĕlĕŏ'logĭst** n.
spĕll[1] n. Words, formula, used as charm; incantation; attraction, fascination; *spe'llbinder*, (U.S.) political speaker who can hold audiences spellbound; *spe'llbound*, bound (as) by spell, fascinated, entranced.
spĕll[2] v. (past t. & past part. *spĕlt* or *spĕlled*, pr. -lt). Name or write in order letters of (word etc.); form words etc. thus; (of letters) make up, form (word); (fig.) signify, imply, involve; ~ *out*, make out (words etc.) laboriously letter by letter; state explicitly, explain in detail. **spĕ'llĭng** n. (esp.) ~-*bee*, competition in spelling.
spĕll[3] n. Turn of work, or *of* or *at* some occupation; short period. ~ v. (Allow to) rest for short period.
spellican: see SPILLIKIN.
spĕlt n. Variety of wheat (*Triticum spelta*) grown in parts of S. Europe.
spĕ'lter n. Zinc (now commerc.); zinc solder.
Spĕ'ncer[1], Herbert (1820–1903). English philosopher and sociologist; founder of evolutionist philosophy, the principle of which was laid down in his 'Programme of a System of Synthetic Philosqphy' (1860), to the elaboration of which he devoted the rest of his life.
spĕ'ncer[2] n. 1. Man's short double-breasted tailless coat worn at end of 18th and beginning of 19th centuries. 2. Woman's or child's close-fitting jacket or bodice (ill. COAT). [f. 2nd Earl *Spencer* (1758–1834)]
spĕnd (past t. & past part.

spĕnt). Pay out (money) for a purchase etc., pay out money; use, use up, consume, exhaust, wear out; be consumed; live or stay through (period of time); *spe'ndthrift*, extravagant person, prodigal (freq. attrib. or as adj.).
Spĕ'nser, Edmund (c 1552–99). English poet, author of 'The Faerie Queene' etc. **Spĕnsēr'ian** adj. Of Spenser; *s*~ *stanza*, stanza invented by Spenser, in which he wrote 'The Faerie Queene', consisting of eight 5-foot iambic lines, followed by an iambic line of 6 feet, rhyming *a b a b b c b c c*.
spĕnt adj.: see SPEND; (esp.) used up; exhausted.
spĕrm n. 1. Male generative fluid, semen; (biol.) spermatozoon. 2. ~ *oil*, spermaceti; ~ *whale*, large whale (*Physeter catodon*) found in warm oceans, with large head cavity containing spermaceti (ill. WHALE[1]).
spĕrmacē'tĭ n. White soft scaly solid, a mixture of fatty esters, separating from oil found in head of sperm whale and other cetaceans, and used for ointments, candles, etc. [med. L f. *sperma* seed, *cetus* whale (because it was thought to be whale-spawn)]
spĕr'mary n. Organ in which spermatozoa are produced, testis.
spĕrmă'tĭc adj. Of sperm or the spermary, seminal; ~ *cord*, structure connecting testicles with seminal vesicles.
spĕrmatogĕ'nesĭs n. Development of spermatozoa. **spĕrmatogĕnĕ'tĭc** adj.
spĕr'matophōre n. (zool.) Capsule formed by some animals containing compact mass of spermatozoa.
spĕrmatozō'on n. (pl. -*zōa*). Minute active fertilizing cell of male organism.

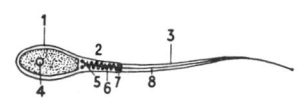

HUMAN SPERMATOZOON

1. Head. 2. Neck. 3. Tail. 4. Vacuole. 5. Centriole. 6. Mitochondria. 7. Annulus. 8. Axial filament

spew, spūe v. Vomit.
sp. gr. abbrev. Specific gravity.
sphă'gnum n. Moss of genus *S*~ growing in boggy and swampy places, used as packing, surgical dressings, etc. (ill. MOSS).
sphē'noid adj. Wedge-shaped; ~ *bone*, compound bone at base of skull (ill. HEAD). ~ n. 1. (anat.) Sphenoid bone. 2. (cryst.) Wedge-shaped crystal with 4 equal and similar triangular faces. **sphēnoi'dal** adj.
sphere n. 1. Body or space bounded by surface every point of which is equidistant from a point within called the centre (ill. CONE); ball, globe; heavenly body; globe

representing earth or apparent heavens. 2. Any of the (orig. 8, later 9 or 10) concentric transparent hollow globes formerly imagined as revolving with harmonious sound (*music of the* ~s)

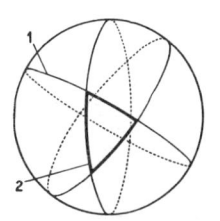

SPHERE

1. Great circle. 2. Spherical triangle

round earth and carrying with them moon, sun, planets, and fixed stars; sphere occupied by particular planet, star, etc.; field of action, influence, or existence, natural surroundings, place in society. ~ v.t. Enclose (as) in sphere; (poet.) exalt among the spheres, set aloft. **sphĕ'rĭc** adj. (poet.) Of the heavens, exalted.
sphĕ'rĭcs n. Spherical geometry and trigonometry.
sphĕ'rĭcal adj. 1. Sphere-shaped, globular. 2. Of, concerned with properties of, spheres; (of lines etc.) described in, on surface of, sphere. **sphĕ'rĭcallў** adv.
sphēr'oid n. Sphere-like but not perfectly spherical body, esp. one generated by revolution of ellipse about one of its axes (ill. CONE). **sphēroi'dal** adj.
sphĕ'rule (-ōōl) n. Small spherical body.
sphĭ'ncter n. Ring of muscle guarding or closing an orifice in the animal body, e.g. *anal*, *oral*, *pupillary*, ~; *cardiac* ~, sphincter guarding upper orifice of stomach.
sphĭ'ngĭd (-ngg-) adj. & n. (Member) of family Sphingidae or hawk-moths.
sphĭnx n. 1. (Gk myth.) Winged monster with woman's head and lion's body, which infested Thebes, killing all who could not answer the riddle it propounded, until the riddle was solved by OEDIPUS; (loosely) enigmatic or mysterious person. 2. Ancient Egyptian figure of a recumbent lion with the head of a man, ram, or hawk, esp. (*the S*~) the colossal 4th-Dynasty stone one near the Pyramids at Giza; any similar figure. (*Illustration*, *p. 844*). 3. (also ~-*moth*) = HAWK-moth.
sphў'gmogrăph (or -ahf) n. = SPHYGMOMETER.
sphўgmŏ'mĕter n. Instrument recording graphically the movements of the pulse and variations in arterial pressure.
spī'ca[1] n. (surg.) Form of spiral bandage with reversed turns, suggesting ear of wheat.
Spī'ca[2]. (astron:) Star of first magnitude in constellation Virgo.

[843]

SPHINX
A. EGYPTIAN. B. GREEK

spi′cate *adj.* (bot., zool.) Pointed, spiked, spike-shaped.

spice *n.* Any of various strong-flavoured or aromatic vegetable substances obtained from tropical plants, as ginger, cinnamon, nutmeg, allspice, used to season or preserve food etc.; spices collectively; slight touch, trace, dash, *of* some quality etc.; *spi′cebush*, N. Amer. aromatic shrub *Lindera benzoin* with small yellow flowers and scarlet berries. ~ *v.t.* Flavour or season with spice(s).

spick and span *adj. phr.* Smart and new; neat, trim. ~ *adv. phr.* [extended f. ME *span-new* (ON *spánn* chip)]

spi′cula *n.* (pl. *-ae*). Spicule; prickle.

spi′cule *n.* Small, slender, pointed or needle-like process or formation; esp. (zool.) small hard calcareous or siliceous body stiffening tissues of various invertebrates, as sponges etc. (ill. SPONGE). **spi′cular, spi′culate** *adjs.*

spi′cy *adj.* Of, flavoured or fragrant with, spice; (fig.) pungent, sensational, scandalous, somewhat improper. **spi′cily** *adv.* **spi′ciness** *n.*

spi′der *n.* 1. Eight-legged animal of order Araneida of arachnids, many species of which spin webs esp. for capture of insects as food; (loosely) spider-like arachnid. 2. (U.S.) Frying-pan, orig. one with legs or feet. 3. Kind of trap or phaeton with very large light wheels. 4. Part of machinery with radiating arms. 5. ~-*catcher*, any of various birds which catch or eat spiders, esp. E. Indian sunbirds; ~-*crab*, crab of group Oxyrhyncha with long slender legs; ~ *monkey*, tropical Amer. monkey of genus *Ateles* with long slender limbs and prehensile tail; *spi′derwort*, plant of Amer. genus *Tradescantia*, with ephemeral white, pink, or violet flowers and slender hairy stamens. **spi′dery** *adj.* Spider-like, esp. long and slender like spider's legs; like cobweb.

spie′geleisen (-gelīzn) *n.* Kind of pig-iron containing much manganese, used in making steel by the Bessemer process. [Ger., = 'mirror-iron']

spiel *n.* (U.S. slang) Talk, speech, story (esp. glib or persuasive one). ~ *v.i.* Talk volubly. [Ger., = 'game']

spi′got *n.* Small peg or plug esp. for insertion into vent-hole of cask; plain end of section of pipe fitting into socket of another.

spīke *n.* 1. Sharp point; pointed piece of metal, e.g. forming part of barrier, fixed in shoe-sole to prevent slipping, etc.; large stout nail. 2. (bot.) Inflorescence of sessile flowers on elongated simple axis (ill. INFLORESCENCE). 3. French lavender (obs.); *oil of* ~, ~-*oil*, essential oil distilled from lavender. **spī′ky** *adj.* **spīke** *v.t.* Furnish with spike(s); fix on, pierce, with spike(s); plug vent of (cannon) with spike.

spi′kelet (-kl-) *n.* (bot.) Small or secondary spike esp. as part of inflorescence of grasses etc. (ill. GRASS).

spi′kenard (-kn-) *n.* Ancient costly aromatic substance used in ointments etc. and obtained from the N. Indian plant *Nardostachys jatamansi*; this plant.

spīle *n.* Wooden peg or plug, spigot; (U.S.) small spout for conducting sap from sugar-maple etc. ~ *v.t.* Provide (cask, tree, etc.) with spile.

spill[1] *n.* Thin strip of wood, folded or twisted piece of paper etc., for lighting candle, pipe, etc.

spill[2] *v.* (past t. & past part. *spilt* or *spilled*). Allow (liquid etc.) to fall or run out from vessel, esp. accidentally or wastefully, run out thus; shed (blood); empty (sail) of wind (naut.); cause to fall from horse or vehicle; *spi′llway*, passage for overflow of surplus liquid (ill. DAM[1]). ~ *n.* Throw or fall, esp. from horse or vehicle; tumble.

spi′ller *n.* (dial. & U.S.) Long fishing-line with number of hooks; in mackerel-fishing, seine inserted into larger seine to take out fish, or used to hold part of catch.

spi′llikin, spĕ′llican *ns.* One of a heap of small rods or slips of wood, bone, etc., used in the game of *spillikins*, in which the object is to remove each rod with a hook without disturbing the rest.

spin *v.* (past t. *spăn* or *spŭn*, past part. *spŭn*). 1. Draw out and twist (wool, cotton, etc.) into threads, make (yarn) thus; be engaged in, follow, this occupation; (of insects) make (web, cocoon, etc.) by extrusion of fine viscous thread; ~ *out*, spend, consume (time etc.); prolong, extend; last out. 2. Revolve, turn (*round*), whirl; (aviation) make diving descent with continued rotation of aircraft; cause (minnow etc.) to revolve in water as bait for trout etc., fish thus. 3. ~ *drier*, machine which dries clothes etc. by rapid spinning in a rotating aerated drum. ~ *n.* Spinning motion, esp. in rifle bullet, in tennis ball, etc., struck aslant, or in aeroplane in diving descent (ill. AEROBATICS); brisk or short run, spell of driving, etc.

spi′nach (-ĭj) *n.* Plant (*Spinacia oleracea*) with succulent leaves used as vegetable; ~ *beet*, kind of beet (*Beta cicla*) with large succulent leaves used like those of spinach.

spi′nal *adj.* Of the spine; ~ *canal*, channel formed by arches of vertebrae, containing spinal cord; ~ *column*, spine; ~ *cord*, rope-like mass of nerve-cells and nerve-fibres enclosed within and protected by spinal column, co-ordinating activities of limbs and trunk and transmitting impulses between the brain and the tissues of the body (ill. SPINE).

spi′ndle *n.* 1. Slender rounded rod tapering at both ends, used to twist fibres of wool, flax, etc., into thread in spinning-frame (ill. SPINNING); steel rod by which thread is twisted and wound on bobbin; varying measure of length for yarn. 2. Pin, axis, that revolves or on which something revolves. 3. Anything spindle-shaped, esp. (biol.) spindle-shaped system of fibres formed during cell-division, to which the chromosomes become attached. 4. ~-*berry*, (bright-red fruit of) spindle-tree; ~-*shanks*, (person with) long thin legs; ~-*shaped*, with circular cross-section and tapering towards each end; ~-*tree*, ornamental European shrub of genus *Euonymus*, esp. *E. europaeus*, with hard fine-grained yellowish wood formerly much used for spindles. **spi′ndly** *adj.* Very thin.

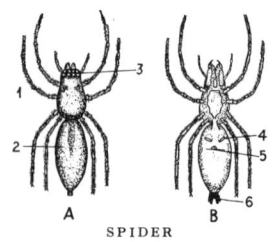

SPIDER
A. DORSAL VIEW. B. VENTRAL VIEW
1. Cephalothorax. 2. Abdomen. 3. Eyes. 4. Lung spiracle. 5. Genitals. 6. Spinnerets

[844]

spi′ndle v.i. Have, grow into, long slender form.
spi′ndrift n. Spray blown along surface of sea.
spine n. 1. In vertebrates, articulated series of vertebrae extending from skull to the hips (and

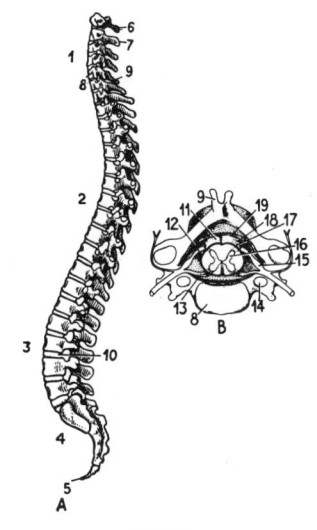

SPINE
A. VERTEBRAE. B. SECTION OF 5TH CERVICAL VERTEBRA

A. 1. Cervical vertebrae. 2. Thoracic vertebrae. 3. Lumbar vertebrae. 4. Sacrum. 5. Coccyx. 6. Atlas. 7. Axis. 8. Body of vertebra. 9. Spine of vertebra. 10. Intervertebral disc. B. 11. Spinal cord. 12. Posterior root of spinal nerve (sensory). 13. Anterior root (motor). 14. Foramen for vertebral artery. 15. Posterior root ganglion. 16. Grey matter. 17, 18, 19. Meninges (17. Pia mater, 18. Arachnoid. 19. Dura mater)

in some animals continued to form the tail) and forming the supporting axis of the body, backbone; ~-*chiller*, -*chilling*, (book, film, etc.) causing thrill of terror. 2. (bot.) Stiff sharp-pointed woody or hardened process, usu. a shoot; (anat.) sharp-pointed slender process of various bones; (zool.) thorn-like process or appendage in certain fishes, insects, etc., prickle of hedgehog, quill of porcupine, etc. 3. Ridge, sharp projection, of rock, ground, etc., resembling backbone. 4. Part of outer cover of book which protects and encloses the back (ill. BOOK).
spi′nel n. (min.) Hard crystalline (octohedral) mineral of various colours, essentially a compound of magnesium and alumina, esp. the deep-red variety (the gem ~ *ruby*).
spi′neless (-nl-) adj. Invertebrate; having no spines; (fig.) limp, weak.
spinē′t (*or* spī′-) n. Small keyboard instrument (17th–18th c.)

of harpsichord type but smaller, and with only one string to a note. [prob. f. name of Giovanni *Spinetti* of Venice (*c* 1550)]
spi′nnaker n. Large three-cornered sail carried on mainmast opposite mainsail of racing-yacht running before wind (ill. YACHT). [fanciful formation f. *Sphinx*, name of yacht first using it]
spi′nner n. (esp.) Spinning-machine; manufacturer engaged in (esp. cotton-)spinning; kind of (artificial) trout-fly, spinning bait.
spi′nneret n. 1. (zool.) Organ or process, esp. nipple-like process on spider's abdomen, tubule on lower lip of silkworm, for producing silk, gossamer, etc. (ill. SPIDER). 2. Contrivance of glass or metal with fine holes through which viscous solution is forced, to form filaments or threads, in making of filaments of synthetic fibre.
spi′nney n. Small wood, thicket.
spi′nning n. (esp.) ~ *jenny*, spinning-machine with several spindles; ~-*wheel*, simple spinning-apparatus in which spindle

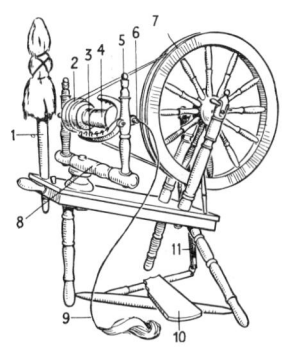

SPINNING-WHEEL
1. Distaff. 2. Flier or spindle whorl. 3. Hackle. 4. Bobbin. 5. Maiden. 6. Spindle. 7. Wheel. 8. Mother-of-all. 9. Yarn. 10. Treadle. 11. Footman

SPINET

is driven by wheel worked by hand or foot.
spi′nōse, spi′nous adjs. Armed or furnished with spines; slender and sharp-pointed like a spine.
Spinō′za, Benedict (Baurd) de (1632–77). Philosopher, a Dutch Jew of Portuguese origin; exponent of pantheism; rejected Cartesian dualism and held God to be the immanent cause of the universe with an infinite number of attributes, of which only two, thought and extension, are known to man, all individual things being modes of these. **Spinō′zism, Spinō′zist** ns.
spi′nster n. Unmarried woman, esp., in popular use, old maid. [orig. = 'woman who spins']
spinthă′riscōpe n. Instrument making radium emanations visible as tiny flashes or sparks on fluorescent screen.
spi′nūle n. (bot., zool.) Small spine. **spi′nūlōse, spi′nūlous** adjs.
spi′nў adj. Full of spines, prickly; (fig.) perplexing, troublesome, thorny.
spir′acle n. (zool.) Orifice or pore which (unlike a STIGMA) can be opened or closed for respiration in insects etc. (ill. INSECT); reduced first gill-slit in fishes, blow-hole of cetacean.
spirae′a(-ēa) n. Rosaceous plant or shrub of genus *S*~ with simple leaves and small pink or white flowers in panicles, racemes, or corymbs.
spīr′al adj. Coiled in cylindrical or conical manner; curving continuously round fixed point in same plane at a steadily increasing (or diminishing) distance from it. **spīr′allў** adv. **spīr′al** n. Anything of spiral form; (geom. etc.) continuous curve traced by point moving round fixed point in same

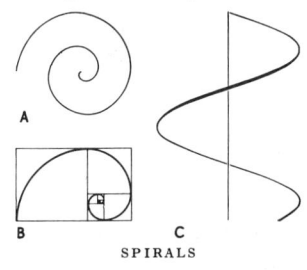

SPIRALS
A. ARCHIMEDEAN. B. VOLUTE. C. HELIX
The helix is three-dimensional

plane at steadily increasing or diminishing distance; curve traced by point simultaneously moving round and advancing along cylinder or cone; spiral nebula; flight in spiral path; progressive but gradual rise or fall, as of wages or prices; ~ v.i. Wind or move in spiral path, (of aircraft, pilot) descend (or ascend) in spiral path.

[845]

spīr'ant *adj. & n.* (Consonantal sound) formed by a constriction, but not a total closure, of the air-passage, so that the air-stream passes continuously and the sound is capable of being prolonged (opp. STOP *n.* 6).

spīre[1] *n.* Tapering structure in form of tall cone or pyramid rising above tower, esp. of church; tapering or pointed top of anything.

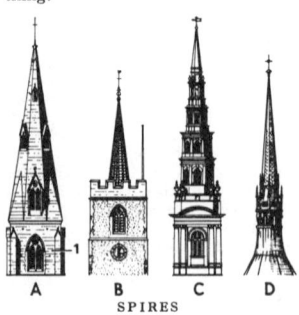

SPIRES

A. BROACH SPIRE. B. LEAD SPIRE ON PARAPETTED TOWER. C. STONE SPIRE OF MANY STORIES (17TH C.). D. FLÈCHE

1. Belfry

spīre[2] *n.* Spiral, coil; single fold or convolution of this.

spi'rit *n.* 1. Animating or vital principle, intelligent or immaterial part of man, soul; person viewed as possessing this, esp. with ref. to particular mental or moral qualities. 2. Rational or intelligent being not connected with material body; disembodied soul; incorporeal being, elf, fairy; ~-*rapping* professed communication with spirits by means of raps thought to be made by them. 3. Person's mental or moral nature or qualities; essential character or qualities, prevailing tone, general meaning, *of* something; mental or moral condition or attribute, mood; mettle, vigour, courage, energy, dash. 4. Strong alcoholic liquor got by distillation (usu. pl.); distilled extract, alcoholic solution *of* some substance; ~-*gum*, quick-drying gum used in fastening false hair, beard, etc., to actor's skin; ~ *lamp*, lamp, esp. for heating or boiling, fed by methylated or other spirits; ~ *level*, instrument for determining a true horizontal or vertical line or surface, usu. by centring an air-bubble in a hermetically sealed glass tube filled with spirit; ~(*s*) *of salts*, (commerc.) hydrochloric acid; ~(*s*) *of wine*, (archaic) ethyl alcohol. ~ *v.t.* Convey (*away*, *off*, etc.) rapidly and secretly (as) by agency of spirits.

spi'rited *adj.* 1. Full of spirit; animated, lively, brisk; courageous. 2. Having specified spirit(s). **spi'ritedly** *adv.* **spi'ritedness** *n.*

spi'ritism *n.* = SPIRITUALISM. **spi'ritist** *adj. & n.* **spiriti'stic** *adj.*

spi'ritless *adj.* Wanting in ardour, animation, or courage. **spi'ritlessly** *adv.* **spi'ritlessness** *n.*

spi'ritual *adj.* Of spirit as opp. to matter; of the soul esp. as acted upon by God; of, proceeding from, God, holy, divine, inspired; concerned with sacred or religious things; ecclesiastical; *Lords S~*, bishops and archbishops in the House of Lords. **spi'ritually** *adv.* **spi'ritualness** *n.* **spi'ritual** *n.* Characteristic religious song of Amer. Negroes.

spi'ritualism *n.* Belief that spirits of dead can communicate with the living, esp. through a medium; system of doctrines or practices founded on this. **spi'ritualist** *n.* **spirituali'stic** *adj.* **spirituali'stically** *adv.*

spirituā'lity *n.* 1. Spiritual quality. 2. (usu. pl.) What belongs or is due to the Church or to an ecclesiastic as such.

spi'ritualize *v.t.* Make spiritual. **spi'rituous** *adj.* Containing much alcohol; ~ *liquor*, one produced by distillation, not by fermentation alone.

spīr'ochaete (-kēt) *n.* Any of various slender flexible microorganisms with spiral bodies, many of which cause diseases in man.

spirt *v. & n.* = SPURT[2].

spit[1] *n.* 1. Slender pointed rod thrust into meat for roasting at fire (ill. FIRE). 2. Small low point of land running into water. ~ *v.t.* Pierce, transfix, (as) with spit.

spit[2] *v.* (past t. & past part. *spat*). Eject saliva; eject (saliva, food, etc., *out*) from mouth; (fig.) utter vehemently; (of cat etc.) make noise as of spitting as sign of anger or hostility; (of rain etc.) fall thinly; (of pen etc.) sputter; *spi'tfire*, fiery-tempered person. ~ *n.* Spittle; act, instance, of spitting; *the very ~ of*, exact counterpart of.

spit[3] *n.* Depth of earth pierced by full length of spade-blade.

spi'tchcock *n.* Eel split or cut up and boiled or fried. ~ *v.t.* Prepare (eel etc.) as spitchcock.

spite *n.* Ill-will, malice; *in ~ of*, notwithstanding. **spi'teful** *adj.* **spi'tefully** *adv.* **spi'tefulness** *n.* **spite** *v.t.* Thwart, mortify, annoy.

Spi'tsbergen (-g-). Archipelago in the Arctic Ocean, N. of Norway, under Norwegian sovereignty.

spi'ttle *n.* Saliva, spit.

spittoo'n *n.* Receptacle for spittle.

spiv *n.* Person, esp. flashily dressed, living on his wits as racing-tout, black-marketeer's agent, etc. **spi'vish** *adj.* **spi'vvery** *n.* Activity characteristic of a spiv. [prob. connected with Engl. colloq. and dial. *spiff*, flashily dressed person]

splăsh *v.* Bespatter (*with* water etc.); dash, spatter (liquid); (of liquid) fly about in drops or scattered portions; cause liquid to do this; step, fall, etc., *into* (water etc.) so as to cause it to splash; mark, mottle, with irregular patches of colour etc.; *spla'shdown*, landing of spacecraft in sea. **splă'shy** *adj.* **splăsh** *n.* Act, result, or sound of splashing; quantity of fluid splashed; dash of soda-water in spirits; large irregular patch of colour etc.; (colloq.) striking or ostentatious display or effect; ~-*board*, guard in front of vehicle to keep mud off occupants; ~ *headline*, in newspaper, conspicuous one designed to attract attention.

splăt *n.* Flat piece of wood forming central part of chair-back, whence ~-*back*(*ed*) (*adj.*) (ill. CHAIR).

splay *n.* (archit.) Slope or bevel; embrasure (ill. WINDOW). ~ *adj.* Wide and flat, spread or turned out; ~(-)*foot*, (having) broad, flat clumsy foot turned outwards. ~ *v.* Bevel; construct (aperture) with divergent sides, be so constructed.

spleen *n.* Dark-red abdominal organ (in mammals situated beneath diaphragm on left side) which is concerned in the formation of antibodies and the destruction of red blood-cells (ill. ABDOMEN); this as the supposed seat of the passions; moroseness, irritability, spite; *splee'nwort*, fern of genus *Asplenium*. **splee'nful** *adj.* **splee'nfully** *adv.* **splee'nfulness** *n.*

splĕ'ndent *adj.* Shining, bright, brilliant.

splĕ'ndid *adj.* Magnificent, grand, sumptuous, brilliant, gorgeous; excellent, very good or fine. **splĕ'ndidly** *adv.*

splĕndi'ferous *adj.* (colloq.) Magnificent, splendid.

splĕ'ndour *n.* Great brightness; magnificence, parade, pomp, brilliance.

splĕnĕ'tic *adj.* Ill-tempered, peevish; of the spleen. **splĕnĕ'tically** *adv.* **splĕnĕ'tic** *n.* Splenetic person.

splĕ'nic *adj.* Of, in, the spleen.

splice *n.* Joining of two ends of rope etc. by untwisting and

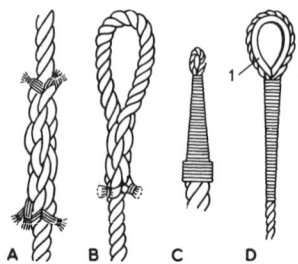

A. SHORT SPLICE. B. EYE SPLICE. C. BECKET. D. THIMBLE EYE

1. Thimble

[846]

interweaving strands at point of junction; overlapping join of two pieces of wood etc.; part of cricket-bat handle inserted in blade. ~ *v.t.* Join by splice; (colloq.) join in marriage; ~ *the main-brace*: see MAIN[1].
splint *n.* Appliance to keep in position or protect injured part, esp. strip of more or less rigid material for holding fractured bone in position; bony excrescence in cannon-bone of leg of horse or mule, usu. on inner side; ~-*bone*, either of two small metacarpal or metatarsal bones in leg of horse etc. (ill. HORSE); ~ *coal*, hard bituminous laminated coal giving great heat. ~ *v.t.* Put into splints, secure with splint(s).
spli′nter *n.* Rough, sharp-edged, or thin piece of wood, bone, stone, etc., broken or split off. ~-*bar*, cross-bar in horse-drawn vehicle supporting springs. **spli′ntery** *adj.* Like splinter(s); apt to splinter. **spli′nter** *v.* Split into splinters.
split *v.* (past t. & past part. *split*). Break forcibly, be broken, into parts, esp. with the grain or plane of cleavage; divide into parts, thicknesses, shares, etc.; divide into factions, groups, etc.; (slang) inform (*on*). ~ *adj.* (esp.) ~ *infinitive*, infinitive with adverb etc. inserted between *to* and verb, e.g. *seems to partly correspond*; ~ *personality*, alteration or dissociation of personality such as may occur in certain mental illnesses, esp. schizophrenia and hysteria; ~ *pin*, pin with one end split so that it may be spread open to keep it in position; ~ *ring*, ring consisting of two turns of spiral or helix pressed flat together, on which keys etc. may be strung; ~ *second*, very brief moment of time; ~-*stitch*, embroidery stitch in which the thread is divided (ill. STITCH). ~ *n.* Act, result, of splitting; cleft; rupture; anything formed by splitting, as single thickness of split hide; half-bottle of mineral water; split roll or bun; (pl.) in acrobatic dancing etc., movement in which body is lowered to floor between legs widely separated at right angles to trunk.
splŏdge *n.* = SPLOTCH.
splŏsh *n.* (colloq.) Quantity of water suddenly dropped or thrown.
splŏtch *n.* Large irregular spot or patch; blot, smear. **splŏ′tchy** *adj.* **splŏtch** *v.t.* Cover or splash with splotches.
splurge *n. & v.i.* (U.S.) (Make) noisy or ostentatious effort.
splu′tter *v.* Utter, talk, hastily and indistinctly or confusedly; scatter or fly in small splashes or pieces; make sputtering sound. ~ *n.* Spluttering (noise); fuss.
Spōde, Josiah (1754–1827). English china-manufacturer of Stoke-on-Trent, Staffs; hence, china made by him.

spoil *v.* (past t. & past part. *spoilt* or *spoiled*). 1. (archaic) Plunder, deprive (*of* thing) by force or stealth. 2. Destroy or impair good, valuable, or effective qualities of; prevent full exercise or enjoyment of; ~-*sport*, one who spoils sport or enjoyment of others. 3. Injure character of (person) by over-indulgence; cosset. 4. Deteriorate, decay, go bad. ~ *n.* (usu. pl. or collect. sing.) Plunder, booty, taken from enemy in war or acquired by violence; (chiefly U.S. and pl.) public offices etc. distributed among supporters of successful political party; ~*s system*, practice of such distribution.
spōke *n.* Each of set of bars or rods radiating from hub to rim of wheel (ill. WHEEL); each radial handle of steering-wheel; rung of ladder; *spo′keshave,* tool with blade or plane-bit between two

SPOKESHAVE

handles used for planing curved surface, shaping spokes, etc. ~ *v.t.* Furnish with spokes.
spoken: see SPEAK.
spō′kesman (-ks-) *n.* One who speaks for others, representative.
spōliā′tion *n.* 1. Despoiling, plundering, pillaging. 2. (eccles.) Appropriation of fruits of benefice by one incumbent to detriment of another. 3. (law) Destruction of, tampering with, document to destroy its value as evidence.
spŏndā′ic *adj.* Composed of spondees; (of hexameter) with spondee as 5th foot.
spŏ′ndee *n.* (pros.) Metrical foot of two long syllables, — —.
sponge (-ŭnj) *n.* 1. Any of various aquatic (chiefly marine) animals of the group Porifera, with

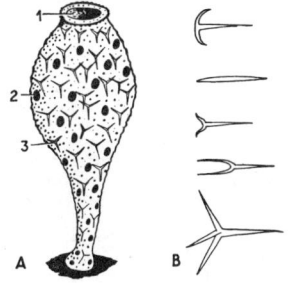

A. SPONGE. B. TYPES OF SPONGE SPICULES

1. Osculum. 2. Pore. 3. Spicule

tough elastic skeleton of interlacing fibres. 2. Soft, light, porous, easily compressible, highly absorbent framework remaining after living matter has been removed from various members of this group, used in bathing, cleansing

surfaces, etc.; porous rubber etc. used similarly. 3. Thing of sponge-like absorbency or consistence; sponge-cake; soft porous leavened dough in bread-making. 4. Immoderate drinker, soaker; person who contrives to live at others' expense. 5. Sponging; bath, swill, with sponge. 6. ~-*bag*, waterproof bag for toilet articles; (*adj.*, of trousers) of checked material; ~-*cake*, very light sweet cake of flour, beaten eggs, and sugar; ~-*cloth*, loose-textured cotton fabric with wrinkled surface. ~ *v.* 1. Wipe, cleanse, with sponge, wet *with* liquid applied with sponge; wipe out, efface, (as) with sponge; absorb, take *up* (liquid) with sponge. 2. Live on others as parasite, be meanly dependent *on* (esp. ~ *on* person *for* money etc.); *sponging-house,* (hist.) house kept by bailiff or sheriff's officer, used as place of preliminary confinement for debtors.
spo′nger (-ŭnj-) *n.* (esp.) One who sponges for money etc.
spo′ngiform (-ŭnj-) *adj.* (zool.) Formed like sponge.
spo′ngin (-ŭnj-) *n.* Horny or fibrous substance forming skeleton of many sponges.
spo′ngy (-ŭnjĭ) *adj.* Sponge-like; esp. porous, compressible, absorbent, or soft, as sponge.
spŏ′nsion *n.* Being surety for another; (international law) engagement on behalf of State by agent not specially authorized.
spŏ′nson *n.* Projection from ship's side, as gun-platform, triangular platform before or abaft paddle-box, etc.
spŏ′nsor *n.* Person making himself responsible for another; person who presents candidate for baptism and makes promises on behalf of infant being baptized, godparent; supporter; advertiser paying cost of broadcast programme into which advertisements of his wares are introduced; hence, person subscribing to charity in return for specified activity by another. **spŏnsŏr′ial** *adj.* **spŏ′nsorship** *n.* **spŏ′nsor** *v.t.* Act as sponsor for; support, advocate.
spŏntā′neous *adj.* Acting, done, occurring, without external cause; voluntary; (of movements etc.) involuntary, not due to conscious volition; ~ *combustion*, ignition of mass of material (e.g. straw) from heat generated within itself; ~ *generation*, abiogenesis, development of living organisms from non-living matter. **spŏntā′neously** *adv.* **spŏntā′neousness, spŏntanē′itў** *ns.*
spŏntoo′n *n.* (hist.) Kind of halberd used by some British infantry officers (ill. INFANTRY).
spoof *n. & v.t.* Swindle, hoax, humbug. [orig. game invented by Engl. comedian A. Roberts (1852–1933)]

spook *n.* (colloq.) Ghost. **spoo′kish, spoo′ky** *adjs.*
spool *n.* Reel for winding yarn, wire, photographic film, fishing-line, etc., on. ~ *v.t.* Wind on spool.
spoon *n.* Utensil consisting of round or usu. oval bowl and a handle, used for conveying soft or liquid food to mouth, in cooking, etc.; spoon-shaped thing, esp. wooden golf-club with slightly concave face; kind of artificial bait used in spinning for fish; *spoo′nbill*, any of various wading-birds (esp. of genus *Platalea*) related to ibises, with long bill expanded and flattened at tip; ~-*bread*, (U.S.) kind of bread, usu. of corn-meal, so soft that it must be served with spoon; ~-*fed*, fed with spoon like child; (fig.) pampered, coddled. ~ *v.* 1. Take, lift, etc., with spoon. 2. Behave amorously, make love, esp. in sentimental fashion.
spoo′nerism *n.* Accidental transposition of initial or other sounds of two or more words (e.g. *blushing crow*, for *crushing blow*). [Revd. W. A. *Spooner* (1844–1930), Warden of New Coll., Oxford]
spoo′ny *adj.* Soft, silly; sentimentally amorous. **spoo′nily** *adv.* **spoo′niness** *n.*
spoor *n.* Track, trail, of animal or person. ~ *v.t.* Trace by spoor.
spora′dic *adj.* Occurring in isolated instances or very small numbers; scattered, dispersed; occasional. **spora′dically** *adv.* **spora′dicalness** *n.*
spora′ngium (-j-) *n.* (pl. *-gia*). (bot.) Receptacle containing spores (ill. FERN).
spore *n.* Minute reproductive body produced by plants and some protozoa and capable of development into new individual independently (ill. FERN); ~-*case*, sporangium.
spo′rran *n.* Pouch, usu. of skin with hair left on, worn with the kilt, slung round the waist and hanging down in front (ill. PLAID). [Gael. *sporan*]
sport *n.* 1. Amusement, diversion, fun; plaything, toy; pastime(s), game(s), esp. of athletic or open-air character; pastime afforded by taking or killing wild animals, game, or fish; (pl.) (meeting for competition in) athletic pastimes. 2. Animal, plant, etc., exhibiting abnormal variation from parent stock or type. 3. (slang) Good fellow; sportsman. 4. ~*s car*, *model*, etc., car of open low-built fast type; ~*s coat*, *suit*, etc., coat etc. suitable for some outdoor sports or for informal wear; *spor′tsman*, *spor′tswoman*, person fond of sports, esp. hunting, shooting, etc.; good fellow; one displaying good qualities of sportsman, esp. desire for fair play, in ordinary life; *spor′tsmanlike*, befitting, worthy of, a sportsman. ~ *v.* 1. Divert oneself; take part in pastime. 2. (bot. etc.) Become, produce, a sport. 3. Wear, exhibit, produce, esp. ostentatiously.
spor′ting *adj.* Interested in sport; sportsmanlike; ~ *chance*, one involving risk but offering possibility of success. **spor′tingly** *adv.*
spor′tive *adj.* Playful. **spor′tively** *adv.* **spor′tiveness** *n.*
spor′ty *adj.* (slang) Sporting; characteristic of a sport, showy.
spo′rule *n.* (Small) spore. **spo′rular** *adj.*
spot *n.* 1. Speck, stain, small discolouring or disfiguring mark; eruptive mark on skin, pimple; dark mark on sun etc.; small, usu. roundish mark on surface; moral blemish, stain; (billiards) marked place on table, esp. that on which red ball is placed (ill. BILLIARDS); *in a* ~, in difficulties, in an awkward situation; *put on the* ~, (U.S. slang) determine assassination of. 2. Particular place, definite locality; *on the* ~, at once; at the very place; equal to situation, wide awake. 3. (colloq.) Small amount, particle, drop (*of*); a drink. 4. ~-*ball*, (billiards) ball marked with black spot; ~ *cash*, money paid, delivered, immediately on sale or other transaction; ~ *check*, check made at random; ~-*check* (*v.t.*); ~ *height*, (figure on map showing) elevation of a certain point; *spo′tlight*, (lamp or projector throwing) concentrated beam of light on one spot, esp. of stage (freq. fig.); (*v.t.*) illuminate (as) with spotlight, throw into relief, concentrate attention etc. on. **spo′tty, spo′tless** *adjs.* **spo′tlessly** *adv.* **spo′tlessness, spo′tlessness** *ns.* **spot** *v.* 1. Mark, stain, soil, with spots; (of textile etc.) be (liable to be) marked with spots. 2. (colloq.) Single out, detect, mark out, note; esp. single out (winner in race etc.) beforehand. 3. Act as spotter.
spo′tted *adj.* (esp.) Marked with spots (freq. in names of animals etc.); ~ *dog*, Dalmatian dog; PLUM-duff; ~ *fever*, pop. name for cerebro-spinal meningitis; (also) typhus.
spo′tter *n.* (esp.) Watcher on roof, observer in aircraft, etc., noting approach or position of enemy forces, effect of gun-fire or bombing, etc.
spouse (-z) *n.* Husband or wife.
spout *n.* Projecting tube, pipe, or lip, through which rainwater is carried off from roof, liquid is poured from teapot, kettle, etc., or issues from fountain, pump, etc.; jet, column, of liquid, etc.; whale's spiracle; sloping trough down which thing may be shot into receptacle; *up the* ~, (slang) pawned, pledged; ~-*hole*, spiracle of whale etc.; natural hole in rocks through which sea spouts. ~ *v.* Discharge, issue, forcibly in a jet; utter in declamatory manner, speechify.
S.P.Q.R. *abbrev. Senatus Populusque Romanus* (L, = the senate and people of Rome); small profits and quick returns.
S.P.R. *abbrev.* Society for Psychical Research.
sprain *v.t.* Wrench (joint of body, esp. ankle or wrist) violently so as to cause pain and swelling. ~ *n.* Act, result, of spraining.
sprat *n.* Small European herring, *Sprattus sprattus*, common on Atlantic coasts; any similar fish.
spra′tting *n.* Fishing for sprats.
sprawl *v.* Spread oneself, spread (limbs), out in careless or ungainly way; straggle. ~ *n.* Sprawling movement or attitude; straggling group or mass.
spray[1] *n.* Slender shoot or twig, graceful branch with flowers etc., esp. used for decoration or ornament.
spray[2] *n.* Water or other liquid dispersed in small mist-like drops by wind, waves, atomizer, etc.; preparation intended for spraying; instrument or apparatus for applying spray. ~ *v.* Scatter, diffuse, as spray; sprinkle (as) with spray.
spread (-ĕd) *v.* (past t. & past part. *spread*). Extend surface of, stretch out, cause to cover larger surface, by unrolling, unfolding, smearing, flattening out, etc.; cover surface of; show extended

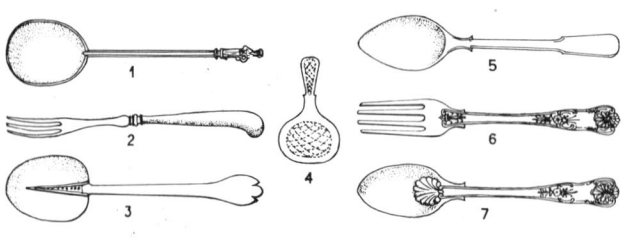

SPOONS AND FORKS
1. Apostle spoon. 2. Fork with pistol handle. 3. Rat-tailed spoon with trifid end to stem (back). 4. Caddy-spoon. 5. Fiddle pattern spoon. 6. King's pattern fork (back). 7. King's pattern spoon (back)

or extensive surface; diffuse, be diffused. ~ *adj.* (esp.) ~ *eagle*, representation of eagle with legs and wings extended; something resembling this; (attrib., U.S., in allusion to figure of spread eagle on U.S. flags etc.) bombastic, noisily patriotic, jingoistic; ~*-eagle* (*v.t.*) extend, fix, in form of spread eagle. ~ *n.* Spreading; being spread; extent or expanse, breadth, compass, span; feast, meal (colloq.); sweet or savoury paste for spreading on bread.
spree *n.* Lively frolic, bout of drinking, etc.
sprig *n.* 1. Small headless nail, usu. wedge-shaped; small projecting point. 2. Small branch, spray; ornament in form of sprig or spray. 3. (usu. contempt.) Youth, young man. ~ *v.t.* Ornament with sprigs.
spri′ghtly (-it-) *adj.* Vivacious, lively, gay. **spri′ghtliness** *n.*
spring *v.* (past t. *sprăng*, past part. *sprŭng*). 1. Leap, jump, move rapidly or suddenly, esp. from constrained position or by action of a spring; arise, take rise; originate; (of wood) warp, split, crack. 2. Rouse (game) from earth or cover; cause to spring, move suddenly, etc.; cause to work by a spring; produce, develop, suddenly or unexpectedly; explode (mine etc.); develop (leak); (slang) contrive the escape of (person from confinement etc.). ~ *n.* 1. Leap; power of springing, elasticity, springiness; place from which vault or arch springs or rises. 2. Elastic contrivance possessing property of returning to normal shape after being compressed, bent, coiled, etc., used for lessening or preventing concussion, as motivating power in clockwork etc. (ill. CLOCK); moving or actuating agency, motive; source, origin. 3. Place where water, oil, etc., wells up from underground rocks; flow of water etc. rising from earth. 4. Season between winter and summer, season in which vegetation begins, popularly reckoned in N. hemisphere as comprising March, April, and May, but astronomically as lasting from vernal equinox (20 or 21 March) to summer solstice (21 or 22 June). 5. (esp. pl.) Spring tide. 6. ~*-balance*, balance measuring weight by elasticity of steel spring (ill. BALANCE); ~*-bed*, (bed with) spring mattress; **spri′ngboard**, elastic board, esp. stout projecting board from end of which person jumps or dives; ~*-clean*, clean house etc. thoroughly, esp. in spring; ~ *gun*, gun discharged by spring when trespasser or animal stumbles on it; ~*-halt*, convulsive movement of horse's hind leg in walking; ~ *lock*, lock with bolt closing by means of spring; ~ *mattress*, one containing or consisting of springs; **spri′ngtail**, wingless insect of the order Collembola, leaping by means of long elastic caudal appendages; ~ *tide*, highest tide, occurring on days shortly after new and full moon; **spri′ngtide, spri′ngtime**, season of spring; ~*-water*, water from spring. **spri′ngless**, **spri′nglike, spri′ngy** (-nggĭ) *adjs.* **spri′nginess** *n.*
spri′ngbŏk *n.* S. African species of gazelle (*Antidorcas marsupialis*), springing lightly and suddenly in air when disturbed. [S. Afr. Du., f. *springen* spring, *bok* antelope]
springe (-j) *n.* Noose, snare, for catching small game.
spri′nger *n.* (esp.) 1. (archit.) Support from which arch springs (ill. ARCH[1]). 2. Medium-sized gundog of spaniel sort, freq. black-and-white, used for flushing game.
spri′nkle *v.* Scatter in small drops or particles; subject to sprinkling (*with* liquid etc.); (of liquid etc.) fall thus on. **spri′nkler** *n.* Contrivance for sprinkling (water on soil etc.). **spri′nkle** *n.* Slight shower (*of* rain etc.).
sprint *v.i.* Run etc. at top speed, esp. for short distance. ~ *n.* Short spell of sprinting; short race run at full speed over whole distance.
sprit[1] *n.* Small spar reaching diagonally from mast to upper outer corner of sail; **spri′tsail** (pr. -săl *or* -sl), sail extended by sprit (ill. BARGE).
sprit[2] *n. & v.* (chiefly dial.) Shoot, sprout.
sprite *n.* Elf, fairy, goblin.
sprŏ′cket *n.* Projection or tooth on rim of wheel engaging with links of chain; ~*-wheel*, wheel with sprockets (ill. TRACTOR).
sprout *v.* Begin to grow, shoot forth, put forth shoots; spring up, grow to a height; produce by sprouting. ~ *n.* Shoot, new growth, from plant; (pl.) young and tender side-shoots of plants of cabbage kind, Brussels sprouts.
spruce[1] (-ōōs) *n.* Kind of fir with dense foliage and soft light wood (also ~*-fir*); wood of this; ~ *beer*, fermented drink made from leaves and small branches of spruce. [AF. *Pruce* Prussia]
spruce[2] (-ōōs) *adj.* Trim, neat, smart in appearance. **spru′cely** *adv.* **spru′ceness** *n.* **spruce** *v.t.* Smarten (*up*), make spruce.
sprue[1] (-ōō) *n.* Tropical disease with chronic inflammation of bowel and ulceration of mouth. [Du. *spr(o)uw* THRUSH[2]]
sprue[2] (-ōō) *n.* Hole through which metal is poured into mould; metal filling sprue.
sprue[3] (-ōō) *n.* Asparagus of inferior quality.
sprŭng *adj.*: see SPRING; (esp.) 1. Furnished with springs. 2. (colloq.) Tipsy. 3. ~ *rhythm*, verse-rhythm invented by G. M. HOPKINS[1] in which each foot consists of a stressed first syllable followed by a varying number of unstressed syllables.

sprȳ *adj.* Active, nimble, lively. **sprȳ′ly** *adv.* **sprȳ′ness** *n.*
s.p.s. *abbrev. Sine prole superstite* (L, = without surviving issue).
spŭd *n.* 1. Small sharp narrow spade, occas. with prongs instead of blade, for digging up big-rooted weeds etc. 2. (colloq.) Potato. ~ *v.t.* Dig (*up, out*) with spud.
spue: see SPEW.
spūme *n. & v.i.* Froth, foam. **spū′mous, spū′mȳ** *adjs.* **spūmĕ′scence** *n.* Foaminess.
spŭn *adj.*: see SPIN; (esp.) that has undergone spinning; (of butter, sugar, etc.) drawn out into threads for ornamenting cakes etc.; ~ *glass*, glass drawn into thread while liquid; ~ *gold, silver*, thread wound round with gold or silver ribbon or wire; ~ *silk*, thread or fabric made from floss or waste silk, freq. mixed with cotton.
spŭnk *n.* Spirit, mettle, pluck. **spŭ′nkȳ** *adj.* [orig. 'spark']
spŭr *n.* 1. Small spike or spiked wheel attached to rider's heel for urging horse etc. forward; (fig.)

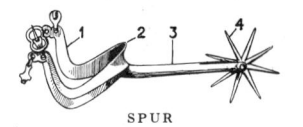

SPUR

1. Arm. 2. Crest. 3. Neck. 4. Rowel

incentive, stimulus; *on the* ~ *of the moment*, without premeditation; *win one's* ~*s*, gain knighthood (hist.); gain distinction, make a name. 2. Spur-shaped thing; hard process or projection on cock's leg, steel point fastened to this in cock-fight; range, ridge, mountain, etc., projecting from main system or mass; short branch or shoot, esp. one bearing fruit; (bot.) tubular protecting part, usu. nectary, of corolla or calyx (ill. FLOWER). 3. ~*-dog*, kind of small shark, *Squalus acanthias*. ~ *v.* Prick (horse) with spurs; incite, urge, prompt; provide with spur(s); ride hard, hasten.
spŭrge *n.* Plant of genus *Euphorbia*, with acrid milky juice with medicinal properties; ~ *flax, laurel*, shrubs of European and Asiatic genus *Daphne*.
Spŭr′geon (-jon), Charles Haddon (1834–92). English popular Baptist preacher.
spŭr′ious *adj.* Not genuine or authentic; not what it appears, claims, or pretends to be. **spŭr′iously** *adv.* **spŭr′iousness** *n.*
spŭrn *v.* Repel, thrust back, with foot; reject with disdain, treat with contempt.
spŭ′rry, -ey *n.* Plant of genus *Spergula*, with slender stems and narrow leaves, esp. the white-flowered *corn* ~ (*S. arvensis*), occas. used as fodder.
spŭrt[1] *v.i. & n.* (Make) short

sudden violent effort, esp. in racing.
spŭrt² *v.* (Cause to) gush out in a jet or stream. ~ *n.* Sudden gushing out, jet.
spu'tnik (spoo-) *n.* Russian earth SATELLITE (ill. SPACECRAFT). [Russ., = 'travelling companion']
spŭ'tter *v.* Emit with spitting sound; spit, splutter; speak, utter, rapidly or incoherently; speak in rapid or vehement fashion. ~ *n.* Sputtering; sputtering speech.
spū'tum *n.* (pl. *-ta*). Saliva, spittle; thick expectorated matter characteristic of some diseased states of lungs or throat.
spȳ *n.* Secret agent, one keeping secret watch on person, place, etc.; person employed by a government, esp. in time of war, to obtain information relating to defences, military and naval affairs, etc., of other countries. ~ *v.* 1. Act as spy (*on*, *upon*). 2. Discern, make out, esp. by careful observation; ~ *out*, explore secretly, discover thus; ~-*glass*, small hand telescope, field-glass.
sq. *abbrev.* Square; (also sqq.) *sequentes*, *sequentia* (L, = (and) the following lines etc., (and) what follows).
Sqn. Ldr. *abbrev.* Squadron Leader.
squab (-ŏb) *n.* Young, esp. unfledged, pigeon; short fat person; thickly stuffed loose cushion, esp. forming seat or back of seat of motor-car etc. ~ *adj.* Short and fat, squat.
squa'bble (-ŏbl) *v.i. & n.* (Engage in) petty or noisy quarrel.
squad (-ŏd) *n.* (mil.) Small number of men grouped or assembled for drill etc.; small party of persons; *flying* ~, detachment of police or other service organized for rapid movement in emergency.
squa'dron (-ŏd-) *n.* Division of cavalry regiment of between 100 and 200 men, 2 troops; division of fleet forming unit, esp. detachment employed on particular service; division of a military airforce, freq. of about 12 machines, with pilots, ground-staff, etc.; ~ *leader*, officer of R.A.F. next above flight lieutenant.
squa'lid (-ŏl-) *adj.* Dirty, foul, filthy, mean in appearance. **squa'lidly** *adv.* **squa'lidness** *n.*
squall (-awl) *n.* 1. Sudden violent gust (*of* wind, rain, etc.). 2. Discordant cry, scream. **squa'lly** *adv.* **squall** *v.* Scream loudly or discordantly; utter in harsh or screaming voice.
squă'loid *adj. & n.* (Fish) of or resembling genus *Squalus* of sharks.
squa'lor (-ŏl-) *n.* Squalid condition.
squä'ma *n.* (pl. *-ae*). (zool., anat., bot., etc.) Scale; scale-like portion of bone etc. **squä'mōse**, **squä'mous** *adjs.*

squa'nder (-ŏn-) *v.t.* Spend wastefully, dissipate.
squāre *n.* 1. Plane rectilinear rectangular figure with 4 equal sides (ill. QUADRILATERAL); object (approximately) of this shape; quadrilateral area, open space, esp. enclosed by buildings or dwellinghouses, buildings surrounding this; (U.S.) block (of buildings), area, surrounded by streets; body of troops drawn up in square formation; *on the* ~, honest, genuine; *be on the* ~, be a freemason. 2. Instrument for determining, measuring, or setting out

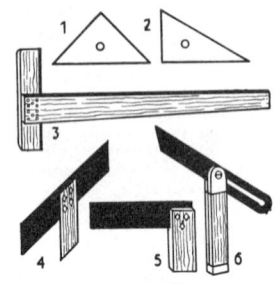

SQUARES

1, 2. Set squares (1. 45°, 2. 60°). 3. T square. 4. Mitre square. 5. Try-square. 6. Bevel

angles. 3. Product of number or quantity multiplied by itself. 4. (slang) Person of conservative or conventional tastes etc., one ignorant of or disliking current trends. ~ *adj.* 1. Of the (approximate) shape of a square; rectangular; angular, not round; approximating to square section or outline, solid, sturdy; of stated length on each of 4 sides forming square; ~ *foot*, *metre*, etc. (area equal to that of) square whose side is a foot, metre, etc.; ~ *measure*, measure expressed in such units; ~ *number*, square of an integer; ~ *root*, number or quantity which when multiplied by itself produces given number or quantity. 2. Properly arranged, in good order, on a proper footing; fair, honest; thorough, uncompromising; (of meal) solid, substantial. 3. (slang) Of conservative or conventional tastes etc. 4. ~ *dance*, one in which 4 couples face inwards from 4 sides; (loosely) country dance; *squar'ehead*, (U.S. colloq.) Scandinavian immigrant; German; ~ *peg* (*in a round hole*), person unsuited to his job; ~-*rigged*, having principal sails extended by horizontal yards slung to mast by middle (ill. SAIL¹); ~ *sail*, four-sided sail set from yards and slung at right angles to the mast (ill. SAIL¹). **squār'ely** *adv.* **squār'eness** *n.* **squār'ish** *adj.* **squāre** *adv.* Squarely. ~ *v.* 1. Make square or rectangular; mark (*out*) in squares; multiply (number, quantity) by itself; ~ *the circle*,

construct square equal in area to given circle (problem incapable of purely geometrical solution); freq. fig., attempt an impossibility. 2. Adjust, make or be consistent (*with*), reconcile; settle (accounts etc.), also (abs.) ~ *up*; conciliate or satisfy (person) esp. with bribe or compensation. 3. Assume boxing attitude, move *up to* (person) thus.
squă'rrōse *adj.* (Rough with scale-like processes) standing out widely.
squār'son *n.* (joc.) Clergyman who is squire of his parish. [f. *squire* and *parson*]
squash¹ (-ŏ-) *v.* Crush, squeeze flat or into pulp; be so crushed or squeezed; pack tight, crowd; (fig.) silence (person) with crushing retort. **squa'shy** *adj.* **squa'shiness** *n.* **squash** *n.* 1. Squashing; something squashed or crushed; crush, crowd; drink made of juice of crushed fruit, freq. in compounds as *lemon* ~. 2. (also ~ *rackets*) Game resembling rackets

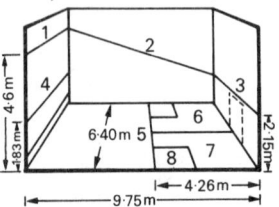

SQUASH RACKETS COURT

1. Front wall line. 2. Side wall line. 3. Back wall line. 4. Cut line. 5. Short line. 6. Forehand court. 7. Backhand court. 8. Service box

but played in a smaller court, by two persons, with a soft ball.
squash² (-ŏ-) *n.* (Gourd, used as vegetable etc., of) species of *Cucurbita*, genus of trailing herbaceous annual plants. [Amer. Ind. *askuta-squash*]
squat (-ŏt) *v.* 1. Sit with knees drawn up and heels close to or touching hams; crouch; put into this position; (colloq.) sit. 2. (orig. U.S.) Settle on or in uncultivated or unoccupied land, building, etc., without legal title or payment of rent; (Austral.) take up land as squatter. ~ *adj.* In squatting posture; short and thick, dumpy. ~ *n.* Squatting posture.
squa'tter (-ŏ-) *n.* Person who settles on common land or occupies a building, without right or permission; (Austral.) person acquiring title to pastoral land belonging to Government by settling on it; sheep-farmer, esp. on a large scale.
squaw *n.* N. American Indian woman or wife. [Amer. Ind.]
squawk *v.i. & n.* (Utter) harsh cry of pain or fear; (make) complaint.
squeak *v.* 1. Emit short, shrill, thin sound; utter in squeaking voice. 2. (slang) Turn informer. ~ *n.* Short thin high-pitched

[850]

sound; *narrow* ~, narrow escape, close shave.
squeal *v.* 1. Utter, emit, more or less prolonged loud shrill noise, esp. of pain or fright; utter with this sound. 2. (slang) Turn informer. ~ *n.* Sharp shrill sound.
squea'mish *adj.* Fastidious; of delicate stomach or conscience. **squeam'ishly** *adv.* **squeam'ishness** *n.*
squee'gee' *n.* Implement with rubber blade or roller for scraping, cleaning, squeezing away moisture, etc. ~ *v.t.* Treat with squeegee.
squeeze *v.* Press, compress hard, esp. so as to crush, drain liquid from, etc.; force by pressure, press out; force one's way; extort money etc. from, bring pressure to bear on, constrain; obtain (money etc.) *from, out of,* by extortion or pressure; take impression of (coin etc.), esp. with sheets of damp paper. ~ *n.* Application of pressure; crowd, crush; impression of coin etc.; *put the* ~ *on*, (colloq.) use forceful methods to secure payment.
squee'zer *n.* (esp.) Device for expressing juice from lemon and other fruits.
squelch *v.* Fall, stamp on (something soft), with crushing or squashing force; crush, squash; walk or tread heavily in water or wet ground, make sound (as) of this. ~ *n.* (Sound of) squelching. **sque'lchy** *adj.*
squib *n.* 1. Firework, straight tube filled with mixture burning with hissing sound and usu. with small explosion at end. 2. Short satirical composition, lampoon.
squid *n.* Any of various ten-armed cephalopod molluscs, esp. of genus *Loligo*, some of which are used for food and as fish bait.
squi'ffy *adj.* (slang) Drunk.
squi'ggle *n.* Curly mark.
squill *n.* Sea-onion, bulbous-rooted sea-shore plant, *Scilla maritima*, with bulbs used dried as diuretic and stimulant; other species of *Scilla*.
squinch *n.* (archit.) Straight or arched support across interior angle to carry dome or other superstructure (ill. DOME).
squint *n.* 1. Strabismus, abnormality of the eyes in which the visual axes do not coincide at the objective; stealthy or sidelong glance; (colloq.) glance, look. 2. (archit.) Oblique opening through wall of church etc., esp. affording view of altar from transept. ~ *adj.* Squinting, looking different ways. ~ *v.* Have the eyes turned in different directions, have strabismus; look obliquely at; give cast to (eye), cause to look asquint.
squire *n.* 1. Attendant on knight (hist.); follower; man escorting or attending on lady. 2. Country gentleman, esp. chief landed proprietor in district. ~ *v.t.* Attend upon, escort (woman).
squir'earchy (-ïrärkï) *n.*

Government by, influence of, landed proprietors, esp. in England before Reform Bill of 1832; class of landed proprietors. **squir'earch** *n.* **squir'earchal, squirear'chical** *adjs.*
squiree'n *n.* Small landowner, esp. in Ireland.
squirm *v.i.* Wriggle, writhe (freq. fig.). ~ *n.* Squirming movement.
squi'rrel *n.* Any of various rodents of the family Sciuridae, small and slender with long bushy tail, many being arboreal (*red* ~, *grey* ~, species found in Britain); *barking* ~, prairie-dog; ~(-*tail*) *grass*, grass of genus *Hordeum* with bushy spikelets; ~ *monkey*, small soft-haired long-tailed S. Amer. monkey of genus *Saimiri*.
squirt *v.* Eject (liquid etc.) in jet as from syringe; be so ejected, spurt. ~ *n.* 1. Syringe; small jet or spray. 2. (colloq.) Insignificant person, whippersnapper.
squitch *n.* COUCH²-grass.
Sr *abbrev.* Senior.
sr *abbrev.* Steradian(s).
S.R. *abbrev.* Scottish Rifles.
Sri Lä'nka (srē). Large island in Indian Ocean near S. point of India, until 1972 called Ceylon; independent republic, member State of the Commonwealth, since 1948; formerly a British colony; capital, Colombo. [Sanskrit name of the island]
S.R.N. *abbrev.* State Registered Nurse.
S.R.O. *abbrev.* Statutory Rules and Orders.
S.R.U. *abbrev.* Scottish Rugby Union.
SS. *abbrev.* Saints.
S.S. *abbrev.* Schutz Staffel (Ger., = protection patrol; Nazi police force); (also s.s.) steamship.
S.S.A.F.A. *abbrev.* Soldiers', Sailors', and Airmen's Families Association.
S.S.C. *abbrev.* Solicitor to the Supreme Court (Scotland).
S.S.E. *abbrev.* South-south-east.
S.S.J.E. *abbrev.* Society of St. John the Evangelist.
S.S.W. *abbrev.* South-south-west.
st. *abbrev.* Stem; stone (weight); stumped.
St. *abbrev.* Saint; Strait; Street.
stab *v.* Pierce, wound, with (usu. short) pointed weapon, needle, etc.; aim blow (*at*) with such weapon etc. ~ *n.* Act of stabbing, wound made thus; short stiff stroke with billiard-cue, bat, etc.; *have a* ~ *at*, (colloq.) make shot at, try; ~-*culture*, in bacteriology, culture in which inoculation is by means of needle thrust deep into medium.
sta'bilize *v.t.* Make stable, bring into a state of stability. **stabiliza'tion** *n.* (esp.) Maintenance of purchasing power of a country's currency by fixing its value in terms of gold.
sta'bilizer *n.* (esp.) 1. One of a

pair of retractable fins inserted into sides of ship's hull below waterline to prevent rolling. 2. (U.S.) Horizontal tail-plane of aircraft.
stā'ble¹ *n.* Building with stalls, loose-boxes, mangers, etc., for keeping horses; establishment for training racehorses, horses belonging to this (also transf.); *sta'bleboy*, ~ *lad*, *sta'bleman*, one who works in a stable. ~ *v.* Put, keep, (horse) in stable; be stabled. **stā'bling** *n.* (esp.) Accommodation for horses etc.
stā'ble² *adj.* Firmly fixed or established, not easily shaken, dislodged, decomposed, changed, destroyed, etc.; firm, resolute, steadfast. **stabi'lity, stā'bleness** *ns.* **stā'bly** *adv.*
stacca'tō (-aht-) *adv., n.* (pl. -*os*), & *adj.* (mus.) (Note etc. played) in detached disconnected manner, with breaks between successive notes.
stack *n.* 1. Circular or rectangular pile of hay, straw, sheaves of grain, etc., usu. with sloping thatched top; pile, esp. one arranged in orderly way; (colloq., pl.) large quantity, 'heaps'. 2. Group of chimneys etc. standing together (ill. CHIMNEY); chimney of house, factory, ship, locomotive, etc.; part of library where books are stored; aircraft circling airfield at various altitudes while awaiting their turn to land. ~ *v.t.* Pile, arrange, in stack(s).
stā'ddle *n.* 1. Young tree left standing when others are felled. 2. Platform of stone, wood, etc., supporting stack or rick; supporting framework.
stā'dium *n.* 1. Ancient Greek and Roman measure (about 600 ft.). 2. Enclosed athletic ground with tiers of seats for spectators.
Staël (stah-ĕl), Anne Louise Germaine, Madame de (1766-1817). French author, daughter of NECKER, wife of Swedish ambassador in Paris; hostess of a progressive and revolutionary salon.
staff (-ah-) *n.* (pl. -*s*, *stäves*). 1. stick used as aid in walking or climbing (now usu. literary); stick, rod, as sign of office or authority, as *pastoral* ~; shaft, pole, as support or handle, as *flagstaff*; rod used for measuring distances, heights, etc., in surveying etc. 2. (mus., pl. *staves*) = STAVE (now chiefly in ~ *notation*, musical notation on stave as dist. from sol-fa method). 3. Body of officers, not themselves in command, assisting a general or other commanding officer in the control of an army, brigade, etc., or in performing special duties; body of persons working under central direction, esp. in factory, educational institution, etc.; *general* ~, body of officers controlling an army from headquarters under the commander-in-chief; ~ *college*, (mil.) establishment for instruction and training of officers for staff

[851]

STAFFORDSHIRE

appointments; ~ *sergeant*, non-commissioned officer serving on regimental staff. ~ *v.t.* Provide with staff of officers, teachers, servants, etc.

Stă'ffordshire. County of central England.

Staffs. *abbrev.* Staffordshire.

stăg *n.* Male of (esp. red) deer; (Stock Exch.) person who applies for newly issued shares with a view to selling immediately on allotment at a profit; (attrib., orig. U.S.) for, of, males only, as ~-*party*; ~-*beetle*, large beetle of family Lucanidae of which males have long denticulated mandibles resembling stag's horns; ~-*hound*, hound of large breed used for hunting stags etc. ~ *v.i.* Act as a stag on the Stock Exchange.

stāge *n.* 1. Raised floor or platform, e.g. scaffold for workmen and their tools, platform used as gangway, landing-place, etc., surface on which object is placed for inspection through microscope, tier of shelves for plants, esp. in greenhouse. 2. Platform on which spectacles, plays, etc., are exhibited, esp. that in theatre, with scenery, etc. (ill. THEATRE); theatre, drama; actor's profession; (fig.) scene of action; *hold the* ~, *dominate conversation etc.* 3. Division of journey, process, development, etc.; point reached; regular stopping-place on stage-coach route where horses were changed; section of bus route for which a particular fare is charged; as much of journey as is performed without stopping for rest etc. 4. Propulsion section of rocket, which can be shed after firing (ill. SPACECRAFT). 5. ~-*coach*, (hist.) coach running regularly between two places for conveyance of passengers, parcels, etc. (ill. COACH); ~ *direction*, instruction in written or printed play for appropriate action etc.; ~ *door*, entrance from street for actors etc. to parts of theatre behind stage; ~ *fright*, nervousness at appearing before audience, esp. for first time; ~-*hand*, one of persons handling scenery, lights, etc., during performance on stage; ~-*manage (v.t.)* arrange, control, etc., as a stage-manager does; ~-*manager*, person in charge of stage-hands etc. and having general control of stage during performance, rehearsals, etc.; ~-*struck*, smitten with love for stage, esp. with desire to become actor; ~-*wait*, hitch, pronounced delay, in theatrical performance; ~ *whisper*, whisper loud enough to be heard by audience, one meant to be overheard. ~ *v.* Put (play) on stage, organize (exhibition, pageant, etc.); put (plants) on stage, esp. for exhibition at show; (of play) lend itself to stage production.

stā'ger *n. old* ~, experienced person, old hand.

stā'gger (-g-) *v.* 1. Walk or stand unsteadily or with swaying movement and irregular devious steps, totter, reel; cause to totter; (cause to) hesitate, waver in purpose, be unsettled or bewildered. 2. Arrange in zigzag, slanting, or overlapping order; arrange (crossing) so that side roads are not exactly opposite one another; arrange (hours of work, holidays, etc.) so that they do not coincide with those of others. ~ *n.* Act, effect, amount, of staggering; (pl.) diseased condition in animals resulting in unsteady gait, sudden falling, etc.

stā'ging *n.* (esp.) 1. Scaffolding, temporary platform or support. 2. Putting play on stage. 3. Travelling by stages; ~ *point*, *post*, place marking one stage of journey, esp. place for overnight stay for travellers.

825

Stă'gīrīte *n.* Native, inhabitant, of ancient Macedonian city of Stagira; *the* ~, Aristotle.

stă'gnant *adj.* Not flowing or running, without motion or current (freq. implying unwholesomeness); dull, sluggish, without activity or interest. **stă'gnantlÿ** *adv.* **stă'gnancÿ** *n.*

stăgnā'te (or stā'-) *v.i.* Be, become, stagnant. **stăgnā'tion** *n.*

stā'gÿ *adj.* Theatrical, dramatically artificial or exaggerated.

staid *adj.* Steady, sober, sedate. **stai'dlÿ** *adv.* **stai'dnèss** *n.*

stain *v.* 1. Discolour, soil; (fig.) sully, blemish. 2. Colour (textile fabrics, paper, wood, etc.) with pigment that penetrates instead of forming coating on surface; colour (tissues etc.) with pigment to render structure visible for examination with microscope etc.; colour (glass) with transparent colours. ~ *n.* Discoloration, spot or mark, esp. one caused by contact with foreign matter and not easily removable; dye etc. for staining; (fig.) blot, blemish.

stai'nlèss *adj.* (esp. of steel etc.) Alloyed with chromium so as not to be liable to rust or tarnish under ordinary conditions; made of such metal.

stair *n.* Each of succession of steps, esp. indoors; (pl.) set or flight of these; *below* ~*s*, in, to, basement, esp. as servants' part of house; **stair'case**, (part of building containing) flight, or series of flights, of stairs; ~-*rod*, rod for securing stair-carpet in angle between two steps; **stair'way**, staircase.

STAKE

stāke *n.* 1. Stick or post sharpened at one end for driving into ground, used to mark boundary, to support plant, as part of fence, etc.; post to which person was tied to be burnt alive; *the* ~, death by burning. 2. What is

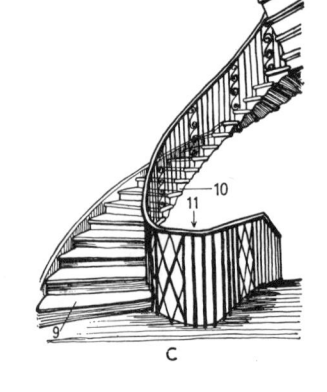

STAIRS

A. SPIRAL STAIRS. B. STAIRCASE WITH HALF-LANDINGS. C. CURVED STAIR WITH WINDERS

1. Newel. 2. Half-landing. 3. Tread. 4. Riser. 5. Newel post. 6. String-board. 7. Hand-rail. 8. Banister or baluster.
9. Winder. 10. Open string. 11. Well

[852]

staked or wagered on an event; (pl.) money etc. staked by entrants to be contended for, esp. in horse-race; (pl.) such race; (fig.) interest involved, something to be gained or lost; *at* ~, at issue, in question, risked. 3. ~-*boat*, moored or anchored boat as starting-point or mark for racing boats. ~ *v.t.* 1. Fasten, secure, support, with stake(s); mark *off*, *out*, with stakes. 2. Wager, risk (*on* event etc.); (fig.) hazard, risk loss of; (U.S.) furnish with money, supplies, etc., esp. in order to share gains.

Stakha′novīte (-χah-) *adj. & n.* (Member) of Soviet-Russian movement aiming at greater output in industry, initiated by Alexey Stakhanov, a Donetz miner, who in 1935 produced a phenomenal quantity of coal by a combination of new method and great energy.

stă′lactīte *n.* Icicle-like formation of crystalline calcium carbonate formed by dripping of water through overlying limestone and depending from roof or wall of cavern etc. **stălacti′tic** *adj.*

Stă′lăg *n.* German prison camp for non-commissioned officers and men. [abbrev. of Ger. *Stammlager* (*Stamm* main body, *Lager* camp)]

stă′lagmīte *n.* Deposit of calcium carbonate or other material on floor of cavern etc. resembling inverted stalactite and similarly formed. **stălagmi′tic** *adj.*

stāle *adj.* Not fresh; insipid, musty, or otherwise the worse for age; lacking novelty, trite; (of athlete) overtrained (similarly of other persons whose vigour is impaired by overwork); *sta′lemate*, (chess) position in which player can make no move without bringing his king into check, (fig.) deadlock, drawn contest; (*v.t.*) place (player, his king) in position of stalemate. **stā′lelў** (-l-li) *adv.* **stā′lenĕss** *n.* **stāle** *n.* Urine of horses and cattle. ~ *v.* 1. Make, become, stale or common. 2. (of horse etc.) Urinate.

Sta′lin (-ah-). Name adopted by Joseph Vissarionovich Dzhugashvili (1879–1953), Soviet statesman; by birth a Georgian; worked as an 'underground' revolutionary from 1904 until the Bolshevik revolution of 1917; by c 1929 he was established as undisputed successor to Lenin and leader of the Communist party and administration, retaining that position until his death; premier of U.S.S.R. 1941–53; later denounced by KHRUSCHEV. **Sta′linism** *n.* **Sta′linist** *adj. & n.* [Russ., = 'man of steel']

Sta′līngrăd (stahlin-g-). See VOLGOGRAD.

stalk[1] (-awk) *n.* Main stem of herbaceous plant, bearing flowers and leaves; attachment or support of leaf, flower, fruit, animal organ, etc.; stem, shaft, of object.

stalk[2] (-awk) *v.* 1. Pursue (game) stealthily; steal up to game under cover; *stalking-horse*, horse, screen, behind which hunter approaches game; (fig.) something used to conceal intentions or efforts; (pol.) candidate put forward to conceal another's candidacy or to draw votes from a rival. 2. Walk with stiff measured steps; stride in stately or imposing manner. ~ *n.* Act of stalking game; stealthy pursuit.

stall[1] (-awl) *n.* 1. (Division for one animal in) stable, cattle-shed, cow-house. 2. Fixed seat enclosed wholly or partly at back and sides, and freq. canopied, in choir

STALL, 15TH C.
1. Poppy-head. 2. Misericord on underside of upturned seat

or chancel of church or in chapter-house, for clergyman, dignitary of church, knight of one of higher orders of chivalry, etc.; (fig.) office or dignity of canon etc.; each of set of seats in part of theatre nearest stage, usu. between pit and orchestra (ill. THEATRE). 3. Booth, table, stand, in market etc., compartment in building, for exposure and sale of goods. 4. (coal-mining) Compartment in which coal is worked. 5. (Condition resulting from) stalling. ~ *v.* 1. Place, keep, (cattle etc.) in stall, esp. for fattening; furnish with stalls. 2. (Cause to) stick fast in mud, snow, etc.; stop (internal combustion engine) undesignedly, (of engine) be accidentally stopped; (cause to) lose flying-speed to point at which aircraft ceases to answer normally to controls; *stalling speed*, critical speed below which aircraft stalls.

stall[2] (-awl) *n.* Pickpocket's confederate distracting attention of victim during theft; (slang) act of stalling or stalling-off. ~ *v.* Act as stall for (pickpocket); (slang) stave *off* with trick, plausible tale etc., play for time thus, block, obstruct. [AF *estal* decoy-bird]

sta′llage (-awl-) *n.* Space or rent for, right to erect, stall(s) in market, etc.

stă′llion (-yon) *n.* Uncastrated male horse, esp. one kept for breeding.

sta′lwart (-awl-) *adj.* (chiefly literary) Stout, strong, sturdy; valiant, courageous, resolute. ~ *n.* Resolute uncompromising partisan, esp. of political party. **sta′lwartlў** *adv.* **sta′lwartnĕss** *n.*

Stămbou′l (-ōōl). (obs.) Istanbul.

stă′mĕn *n.* (bot.) Male fertilizing organ of flowering plants, with anther containing pollen supported on slender filament (ill. FLOWER).

stă′mina *n.* Staying-power, power of endurance.

stă′minal *adj.* Of stamina or stamens.

stă′mināte *adj.* Having stamens, esp. without pistils.

stă′minōde *n.* (bot.) Infertile, aborted or reduced stamen.

stă′mmer *v.* Falter or stumble in speech, esp. repeat involuntarily certain sounds in a word etc. several times in rapid succession through inability to complete the articulation; utter with stammer. ~ *n.* Stammering speech, tendency to stammer.

stămp *v.* 1. Bring down one's foot, bring down (foot), heavily on ground; ~ *out*, put an end to, crush, destroy; *stamping-ground*, (U.S.) animal's habitual place of resort. 2. Impress pattern, name, mark, upon with die or similar instrument; affix postage or other stamp to (document, envelope, etc.); assign a character to, characterize; impress *on* the memory. 3. Crush, pulverize (ore etc.). ~ *n.* 1. Act, sound, of stamping, esp. with foot. 2. Instrument for stamping pattern or mark, mark made by this; government's embossed or impressed mark, adhesive label with distinctive device, on deed or other document etc., to certify that duty, tax, etc., has been paid; postage stamp; mark impressed on, label etc. affixed to, commodity as evidence of quality etc.; (fig.) characteristic mark, impress (*of* some quality etc.); character, kind. 3. Heavy pestle operated by machinery for crushing ores; (pl.) stamp-mill. 4. *S~ Act*, Act for regulating stamp duties, esp. that of 1765 (repealed 1766) levying such duties on American colonies; ~-*collector*, one who collects postage stamps, philatelist; ~-*duty*, any duty collected by means of impressed or affixed stamps; ~-*mill*, apparatus for crushing ore, with series of stamps; ~-*paper*, paper with government revenue stamp; gummed marginal paper of sheet of postage stamps.

stămpē′de *n.* Sudden rush and flight of number of frightened horses, cattle, etc.; sudden unreasoning rush or action of persons

STANCE

in a body or mass. ~ *v.* (Cause to) take part in stampede.

stănce *n.* (golf etc.) Player's position for making stroke; pose, attitude.

stanch, staunch (-ah-, -aw-) *v.t.* Check flow of (esp. blood); check flow from (esp. wound).

stă'nchion (-shon) *n.* Upright bar, stay, or support (ill. GIRDER). ~ *v.t.* Provide, strengthen, support, with stanchion(s).

stănd *v.* (past t. & past part. *stood*). 1. Have, take, assume, erect attitude on one's feet; be set, remain, upright; be of specified height when standing; remain stationary, stop walking or moving on; be set, placed, or situated; remain firm, secure, valid, etc., or in specified condition; present a firm front; offer oneself as candidate, esp. for election to Parliament etc.; (naut.) sail, steer, in specified direction, to sea, etc. 2. Place, set, in upright or specified position. 3. Bear the brunt of, resist; endure, undergo (trial etc.); endure without succumbing or complaining. 4. Provide at one's expense. 5. *all standing*, (naut.) without dismantling or unrigging; (transf.) without time for preparation; ~ *by*, uphold, support, side with; adhere to, abide by; stand near, be a bystander, stand and look on; stand ready, be on the alert; ~*-by*, thing, person, that can be depended on; ~ *a chance*, have a chance or prospect (of success); ~ *down*, step down from witness-box; retire, withdraw; go off duty; ~ *for*, represent, signify, imply; (colloq.) tolerate, acquiesce in; ~ *in*, use (person) specified sum; (also) deputize; ~*-in*, favourable position; (cinema) person employed to take place of actor until lights, cameras, etc., are ready; deputy, substitute; ~ *off*, move away, keep one's distance; ~ *off half*, (Rugby footb.) half-back with position between scrum-half and three-quarters; ~*-o'ffish*, distant, reserved, not affable; ~*-o'ffishly (adv.)*, ~*-o'ffishness(n.)*; ~ *on*, insist on, observe scrupulously; ~ *out*, hold out, persist in opposition or endurance; be prominent or conspicuous; ~ *over*, be postponed; ~ *pat*, (in poker) play hand as dealt; oppose change, maintain one's position; ~*-pipe*, vertical pipe for conveying water, gas, etc., or with spout or nozzle for hose, for attachment to water-main; *sta'ndpoint*, point of view; *sta'ndstill*, halt, pause, cessation of movement or activity; ~ *to*, abide by, stick to, not desert; (mil.) take up position in preparation for an attack; ~ *to win, lose*, etc., be reasonably certain to win, lose, etc.; ~ *up*, rise to one's feet from sitting position etc.; maintain erect position; ~ *up for*, side with, maintain, support; ~*-up*, (of collar) high, not turned down or folded over; (of fight) fair and square, in which opponents stand up to one another without flinching or evasion; (of meal etc.) taken standing. ~ *n.* 1. Cessation from motion or progress, stoppage; stationary condition, esp. for resistance (*against*); position taken up. 2. Table, set of shelves, rack, etc., on or in which things may be placed; stall in market etc.; standing-place for vehicles etc.; raised structure for persons to sit or stand on; (U.S.) witness-box. 3. Standing growth or crop.

stă'ndard *n.* 1. Distinctive flag, as (*English*) *royal* ~, banner with royal arms (ill. FLAG⁴); flag of cavalry regiment (opp. to *colours* of infantry); (fig.) rallying principle; (bot.) vexillum, uppermost petal of sweet pea or other papilionaceous flower (ill. FLOWER). 2. Weight or measure to which others conform or by which the accuracy of others is judged (often attrib. as in ~ *pound, yard*, etc.); legal proportion of weight of fine metal and alloy in gold and silver coin (*monetary* ~) or in articles made of these metals; thing serving as basis of comparison. 3. Degree of excellence etc. required for a particular purpose; thing recognized as model for imitation etc.; (attrib. of book) recognized as possessing merit or authority; (in primary schools) each of several degrees of proficiency, class studying to reach this; ~ *of living*, degree of material comfort enjoyed by community, class, or person. 4. Average quality. 5. Measure of timber (varying in different countries). 6. Upright support (ill. SCAFFOLDING); upright water or gas pipe; upright holder for lamp in street or room; tree, shrub, trained on erect stem (not as espalier or dwarfed); tree left standing when others are felled. 7. ~*-bearer*, soldier etc. who bears standard; (fig.) prominent leader in cause; ~ *English*, the form of English used, with local variations, by the majority of cultured English-speaking people; ~ *lamp*, lamp set on tall holder standing on floor; ~ *time*, time established legally or by custom in country or region, usu. that of a specific time zone.

stă'ndardize *v.t.* Make to conform to standard, make uniform.

stăndardīzā'tion *n.*

stă'nding *n.* (esp.) Estimation in which person is held, repute; duration; ~*-room*, space to stand in. ~ *adj.* (esp.) Established, permanent, not made, formed, etc., for the occasion; ~ *orders*, series of instructions remaining in force until countermanded or repealed by a proper authority, esp. (mil.) orders not subject to change by an officer temporarily in command; (parliament) rules of procedure remaining in force through successive sessions (opp. *sessional orders*).

STAR

Stă'nford, Sir Charles Villiers (1852–1924). British organist, born in Dublin; composer of operas, symphonies, chamber music, songs, and church music.

Stă'nley, Sir Henry Morton (1841–1904). British explorer of Welsh birth; was sent in 1869 by Gordon Bennett, proprietor of the 'New York Herald', to find David Livingstone, who was believed to be lost in Central Africa.

stă'nnarў *n.* Tin-mine; *the Stannaries*, tin-mining districts of Cornwall and Devon.

stă'nnate *n.* (chem.) Salt of stannic acid.

stă'nnic *adj.* Of tin; (chem.) containing tin as quadrivalent element.

stă'nnous *adj.* Containing tin as bivalent element.

stă'nza *n.* Group of (usu. rhymed) lines of verses forming division of song or poem.

stă'pēs (-z) *n.* = STIRRUP bone (ill. EAR¹).

stăphўlocŏ'ccus *n.* (pl. *-ī*). Any of numerous micro-organisms, globular and tending to grow in clusters, causing various morbid conditions such as boils, carbuncles, and abscesses (ill. BACTERIUM). **stăphўlocŏ'ccal** *adj.* [Gk *staphulē* bunch of grapes, *kokkos* grain]

stă'ple¹ *n.* U-shaped bar or loop of metal with pointed ends to be driven into post, wall, etc., as hold for hook, bolt, etc. (ill. HASP); contrivance of similar shape or function, esp. bent wire used in bookbinding for wire-stitching. ~ *v.t.* Furnish, fasten, with staple; *sta'pling-machine*, bookbinder's wire-stitching machine. **stă'pler¹** *n.* (esp.) Device for stapling.

stă'ple² *n.* 1. Important or principal product or article of commerce; raw material; (fig.) chief element or material. 2. Fibre of wool, cotton, etc., considered with respect to its length and fineness. ~ *adj.* Forming a staple; having important or principal place among exports, industries, etc. ~ *v.t.* Sort, classify (wool etc.), according to fibre. **stă'pler²** *n.*

stăr *n.* 1. Celestial body appearing as luminous point esp. at night; (also *fixed* ~) such body so far from earth as to appear motionless except for diurnal revolution of the heavens; *binary* ~, two stars revolving round each other, or round a common centre; *double* ~, 2 fixed stars appearing to naked eye as one, esp. binary star; *multiple* ~, similar group of 3 to 6; *falling, shooting* ~, small meteor looking like rapidly moving star. 2. (astrol.) Heavenly body, esp. planet, considered as influencing human affairs or person's fortunes. 3. Thing suggesting star by its shape, esp. figure or object with radiating points; asterisk;

[854]

white spot on forehead of horse etc. 4. Actor, singer, etc., of great celebrity; brilliant or prominent person. 5. (pool) Additional life bought by player whose lives are lost. 6. S~ Chamber, (hist.) room in royal palace at Westminster (said to have had gilt stars on the ceiling) where the Privy Council tried civil and criminal cases, esp. those affecting Crown interests, until in 1640 the court (*Court of S~ Chamber*) was abolished as too arbitrary in its judgements; ~*-drift*, common proper motion of a number of fixed stars in same region; *star'fish*, echinoderm of the class Asteroidea with usu. five broad arms radiating from a central disc, esp. *Asterias*

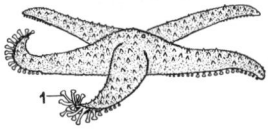

STARFISH
1. Tube-feet

rubens, form commonest on European coasts; ~*-gazer*, impractical idealist; ~*-gazing* (n.); *star'light*, light of the stars; (*adj*., also *star'-lit*); *S~ of Bethlehem*, plant of genus *Ornithogalum*, esp. *O. umbellatum*, with white stellate flowers; any of various other plants; ~ *sapphire*, cabochon sapphire, which shines like a cluster of stars; *S~-spangled Banner*, U.S. national anthem, with ref. to the Stars and Stripes (see below); ~*-stream*, either of two systematic drifts of stars (one of which comprises the nearer stars and moves towards Orion); *Stars and Stripes*, flag of the U.S.A. with 13 horizontal stripes, representing the 13 orig. States, and one star for each of the 50 States in the Union. **stär'dom** *n.* Status of star performer (see *n.*, sense 4); realm, sphere, of such stars. **stär'lĕt** *n.* Young star (sense 4). **stär'lĕss**, **stär'rў** *adjs.* **stär** *adj.* Brilliant, prominent, pre-eminent. ~ *v.* Set, adorn (as) with stars; mark with asterisk; present (actor etc.), appear, as a star (sense 4).
stär'board (-b*e*rd, naut. -bed) *n.* Right-hand side of boat or ship or aircraft looking forward (opp. PORT⁴) (ill. BEARING). ~ *v.t.* Turn, put, (helm) to starboard. [OE *steor* rudder]
stärch *n.* White odourless tasteless carbohydrate occurring widely in plants, esp. cereals, potatoes, etc., and forming an important constituent of human food; preparation of this for stiffening linen etc.; (fig.) stiffness of manner or conduct, formality; ~*-reduced*, containing less than normal proportion of starch. **stär'chў** *adj.* **stär'chilў** *adv.* **stär'chinĕss** *n.* **stärch** *v.t.* Stiffen with starch.

stāre *v.* Gaze fixedly with eyes wide open; open eyes in astonishment, be amazed; reduce (person) to specified condition by staring; be obtrusively conspicuous; ~ (person) *in the face*, (of thing) be glaringly obvious to. ~ *n.* Staring gaze.
stärk *adj.* Stiff, rigid; downright, sheer. ~ *adv.* Quite, completely (now chiefly in ~ *mad, naked*).
stär'ling¹ *n.* Bird (*Sturnus vulgaris*) with dark light-speckled plumage having metallic lustre, of gregarious habits and often nesting near human habitations; any bird of the passerine family Sturnidae or (loosely) the unrelated Amer. family Icteridae.
stär'ling² *n.* Outwork of piles protecting pier of bridge against force of stream, damage by floating objects, etc.
stärt *v.* 1. Make sudden movement from pain, surprise, etc., give start; move suddenly from one's place; rouse (game) from lair etc.; (of timbers etc.) spring from proper position, be displaced by pressure or shrinkage; cause, experience, starting of timbers etc. 2. Set out, begin journey, career, course of action, etc.; make a beginning (*on*); begin; originate, set going; cause to begin doing, cause or enable to commence course of action etc.; give signal to (persons) to start in race etc.; (also ~ *up*) cause (motor-engine) to begin to run; (of motor-engine) begin to operate. ~ *n.* 1. Sudden involuntary movement caused by surprise, fright, pain, etc.; (pl.) intermittent and sudden efforts or displays of energy. 2. Beginning of journey, action, race, career, etc.; starting-place of race; opportunity or assistance for starting career, course of action, etc.; advantage gained by starting first in race, journey; position in advance of competitors.
stär'ter *n.* (esp.) 1. Person giving signal to start in race. 2. Horse, competitor, starting in race etc. 3. Apparatus for starting motor-engine, esp. *self-*~. 4. Preliminary course of meal.
stär'ting *n.* (esp.) ~*-block*, shaped block for bracing the feet of runners at start of race; ~*-gate*, movable barrier for securing fair start in horse-race; ~*-post*, post from which competitors start in race; ~ *prices*, final odds on horse etc. at time of starting.
stär'tle *v.t.* Cause to start with surprise or fright; alarm; take by surprise.
stärve *v.* (Cause to) die of hunger; (cause to) suffer from lack of food; (colloq.) feel hungry; force *into* course of action, *out* etc., by starvation; (fig.) (cause to) suffer mental or spiritual want. **stärvā'tion** *n.*
stär'velĭng (-vl-) *n.* Starving or ill-fed person or animal.

stă'sĭs *n.* Stoppage of circulation of any body-fluids, esp. blood.
stāte¹ *n.* 1. Condition; manner or way of existence as determined by circumstances; (colloq.) excited or agitated condition of mind or feeling; (engraving etc.) stage of engraved or etched work, distinguishable variant of edition of book etc. 2. Rank, dignity; pomp; *in* ~, with all due ceremony; *lie in* ~, (of dead person) be ceremoniously exhibited in public place. 3. Organized political community under one government, commonwealth, nation; such community forming part of federation with sovereign government; civil government; *the States*, the UNITED STATES OF AMERICA; also, the legislative body in Jersey, Guernsey, and Alderney; *States General*, legislative assembly of clergy, nobles, and commons of whole realm in France before the Revolution, or in Netherlands from 15th c. to 1796. 4. (attrib.) ~ *capitalism*, system in which capital is owned or controlled by State; *S~ Department*, department of U.S. government dealing with foreign affairs; *S~-house*, (U.S.) building in which legislature of a State holds its sessions; *S~ rights*, (U.S.) rights and powers not delegated to the Federal government but reserved to individual States; ~*-room*, passenger's private cabin on ship; ~ *socialism*, system of State control of industries, railways, etc. **stā'telĕss** (-tl-) *adj.* Having no legal nationality, esp. because of change of government or alteration of boundaries of States. **stāte** *adj.* Of, for, concerned with, the State (sense 3); reserved for, employed on, occasions of state or ceremony.
stāte² *v.t.* Express, esp. fully or clearly, in speech or writing; specify (number etc.).
stā'telў (-tlĭ) *adj.* Dignified, imposing, grand. **stā'telinĕss** *n.*
stā'tement (-tm-) *n.* Stating, expression in words; presentation of musical theme or subject; thing stated; formal account of facts, as of liabilities and assets; account presented periodically by tradesman to customer.
stā'ter *n.* Any of various ancient Greek gold, silver, or electrum coins.
stā'tesman (-tsm-) *n.* Person skilled or taking leading parts in management of State affairs; *Elder S~*: see ELDER².
stă'tĭc *adj.* Of forces in equilibrium or bodies at rest (contrasted with *dynamic* or *kinetic*); acting by weight without motion; passive, not active or changing; (elect.) stationary, produced by friction; (radio) atmospheric; (of a store of water in a tank) having no pressure of its own and requiring to be pumped; ~ *line*, length of cord in top half of a parachute bag which on becoming taut releases

[855]

the parachute. ~ n. Atmospherics; static electricity. **stă′tical** adj. Of statics. **stă′tics** n. Branch of physical science concerned with bodies at rest and forces in equilibrium (contrasted with *dynamics*); (radio) atmospherics.

stă′tion n. 1. Place in which person or thing stands or is placed, esp. habitually or for definite purpose or duties; in India, (hist.) place in which English officials etc. resided; in Australia, sheep- or cattle-run with its buildings. 2. Position in life, (high) rank, status. 3. Stopping-place on railway with buildings for accommodation of passengers and goods, or goods only; these buildings; similar stopping-place for long-distance buses etc. 4. One of a series of holy places, esp. Roman churches, visited in turn for devotions; *Stations of the Cross*, series of 14 pictures or images of Christ's Passion (orig. crosses) in church or occas. in open air, before which devotions are performed. 5. ~*-house*, police station; ~*-master*, official in control of railway station; ~ *sergeant*, sergeant in charge of police station; ~ *wagon*, (U.S.) estate car. ~ v. Assign station or post to; post, place, in station.

stă′tionary adj. Remaining in one place, not moving; fixed, not movable; not changing in condition, quality, or quantity.

stă′tioner n. Tradesman selling writing-materials etc.; *Stationers' Company*, livery company of the City of London, founded 1556, comprising stationers, booksellers, printers, bookbinders, etc.; *Stationers' Hall*, hall of this company, at which register of copyrights is kept. **stă′tionery** n. Articles sold by stationer, as paper, pens, ink, etc.

stati′stics n. Branch of study concerned with collection and classification of (esp.) numerical facts; (also as pl.) facts so collected and classified. **stati′stical** adj. **stati′stically** adv. **stătisti′cian** (-shan) n.

Stā′tius (-shus), Publius Papinius (c A.D. 45-96). Roman poet, author of the THEBAID.

stă′tor n. Stationary part of machine or device (ill. DYNAMO).

stă′tuary n. Sculptor; (art of making) statues. ~ adj. Of statues; sculptured; suitable for statues.

stă′tūe n. Sculptural representation in the round of (esp.) deity, allegorical subject, or human being(s), usu. of life-size proportions.

stătŭě′sque (-k) adj. Resembling a statue, esp. in beauty or dignity.

stătŭě′tte n. Small statue.

stă′ture n. Height of (esp. human) body.

stā′tus n. 1. Social or legal position or condition, rank, standing. 2. (med.) ~ *lymphă′ticus*, bodily condition with excessive development of lymphatic tissue, in which sudden death may occur esp. in surgical anaesthesia. 3. ~ (*in*) *quo*, unchanged position, previous position, of affairs.

stă′tūte n. Written law of a legislative body; ordinance of corporation etc. intended to be permanent; *S~ of Wales, Westminster*: see WALES, WESTMINSTER. **stă′tūtable**, **stă′tūtory** adjs. Enacted, required, imposed, by statute.

staunch[1]: see STANCH.

staunch[2] adj. Trustworthy, loyal, firm; (of vessel etc.) watertight, airtight. **stau′nchly** adv. **stau′nchness** n.

stāve n. 1. Each of the narrow shaped pieces of wood etc. placed together vertically to form sides of cask etc. (ill. CASK). 2. Stanza, verse, of poem, song, etc. 3. (mus.) Set of (now 5) parallel horizontal lines on and between which notes

STAVE

1. Accolade. 2. Clef. 3. Key signature (A flat). 4. Time signature (Common or $\frac{4}{4}$). 5. Crotchet to be played *staccato*. 6. Quaver with value increased by half. 7. Semiquaver. 8. Bar line. 9. Leger line. 10. Tie. 11. Accidental (natural). 12. Slur. 13. Stave or staff. 14. Names of notes

are placed so as to indicate pitch; *great ~*, stave of 11 lines combining treble and bass clefs. ~ *v.t.* (past t. & past part. staved, also (chiefly naut.) *stōve*). 1. Break up (cask) into staves, break into, break hole *in* (boat, cask, etc.); crush, bash (*in*). 2. Furnish, fit (cask etc.) with staves. 3. ~ *off*, ward off, defer.

stay[1] n. Large rope supporting mast, leading from mast-head down to another mast or spar etc. (ill. SHIP); guy or rope supporting flagstaff etc.; tie-piece, cross-piece, holding parts together in aircraft etc. (ill. AEROPLANE); *stay′sail* (or -sl), triangular sail carried on stay. ~ *v.t.* Support, steady, with stay(s).

stay[2] v. 1. Check, stop (now chiefly literary); postpone (judgement etc.). 2. Support, prop (*up*), as with buttress etc. 3. Remain; dwell temporarily; pause in movement, action, speech; ~ *put*, (orig. U.S.) remain in one's, or its, place. 4. Hold out, show powers of endurance; hold out for (specified distance, *the course*). 5. ~*-at-home*, (person) remaining habitually at home; ~*-down strike*, one in which miners remain underground; ~*-in strike*, one in which workers do not leave place of employment; *staying-power*, endurance. ~ n. 1. Remaining, esp. dwelling temporarily, in a place; duration of this. 2. Suspension of judicial proceedings, esp. *of execution* of judgement delivered. 3. Prop, support; (pl.) corset; ~*-lace*, tape for lacing stays or bodice.

S.T.D. abbrev. Subscriber trunk dialling.

stead (-ĕd) n. *stand* (person) *in good ~*, be of advantage or service to; *in person's ~*, instead of him, as his substitute.

stea′dfast (-ĕd-) adj. Constant, firm, unwavering. **stea′dfastly** adv. **stea′dfastness** n.

stea′ding (-ĕd-) n. Farmstead, homestead.

stea′dy (-ĕdĭ) adj. Firm, not tottering, faltering, rocking, or shaking; stable; unwavering, resolute; settled, unvarying; regular, maintained at even rate of action, change, etc., not erratic. **stea′dily** adv. **stea′diness** n. **stea′dy** adv. Steadily (chiefly naut.); ~*-going*, staid, sober. ~ v. Make, become, steady.

steak (stāk) n. Thick slice or strip of meat (esp. beef) for grilling, frying, etc., esp. cut from hindquarters of animal (ill. MEAT); thick slice of fish cut through backbone.

steal v. (past t. *stōle*, past part. *stō′len*). 1. Take away dishonestly, and esp. secretly, what belongs to another; obtain surreptitiously or by surprise; win, get possession of, by insidious arts, attractions, etc.; ~ *the show*, unexpectedly outshine other performers. 2. Move secretly or unseen; ~ n. (chiefly U.S. colloq.) Stealing, theft; thing stolen.

stealth (-ĕl-) n. Secret, secret procedure; *by ~*, surreptitiously, clandestinely. **stea′lthy** adj. **stea′lthily** adv. **stea′lthiness** n.

steam n. Invisible vapour into which water is converted by heat; this used in specially contrived engines for generation of mechanical power; (pop.) steam mixed with air and with minute particles of water suspended in it, in form of white cloud or mist; (colloq.) energy, go; *stea′mboat*, boat, esp. large river- or coasting-boat, driven by steam; ~*-coal*, coal suitable for generating steam in boiler; ~*-engine*, engine in which motive power is steam (*illustration, p.857*); freq., steam-driven locomotive; ~*-gauge*, gauge showing pressure of steam in boiler; ~ *hammer*, hammer operated by steam; ~*-heating*, central heating in which steam is circulated through radiators; ~*-jacket*, casing round cylinder etc. that can be filled with steam; ~*-navvy*, steam-operated machine for digging or excavating; ~*-roller*, heavy locomotive engine with wide

[856]

STEAMER

wheels and roller for crushing road-metal, levelling roads, etc.; **stea′mship**, ship driven by steam;

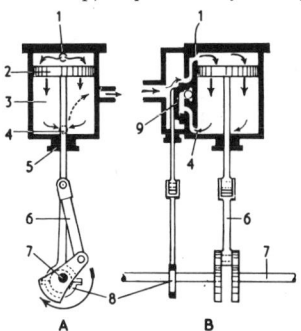

STEAM-ENGINE (DOWNWARD STROKE): A. END VIEW. B. SIDE VIEW
1. Inlet port. 2. Piston. 3. Cylinder. 4. Outlet port. 5. Gland. 6. Connecting rod. 7. Crankshaft. 8. Eccentric. 9. Slide-valve. On upward stroke 1 is outlet port and 4 is inlet port

~-*tug*, steamer for towing ships etc. **stea′my** *adj.* **steam** *v.* 1. Emit, give off, steam or vapour, exhale (steam, vapour), cover, bedew, (surface), (of surface) become covered, with condensed vapour; generate steam. 2. Travel, move, by agency of steam. 3. Treat with steam, expose to action of steam; cook by steam. **stea′mer** *n.* (esp.) 1. Vessel propelled by steam. 2. Vessel in which food is cooked by steam.
stē′arate *n.* Salt of stearic acid.
steă′ric *adj.* Derived from, containing, stearin; ~ *acid*, white crystalline fatty acid obtained from tallow etc.
stē′arin *n.* Any ester of glycerol and stearic acid, esp. white crystalline solid found in tallow and many other animal and vegetable fats; solid portion of any fixed oil or fat; (pop.) stearic acid used for making candles etc.
stē′atite *n.* (min.) Greyish-green or brown massive variety of talc with soapy feel, soapstone. **steati′tic** *adj.*
steed *n.* (poet., rhet., etc.) Horse, esp. war-horse.
steel *n.* Various hard, malleable, elastic alloys of purified iron with carbon (up to 1 %) and metals such as nickel, manganese, or chromium, used as material for tools, weapons, etc.; this in form of weapons or cutting tools (ill. MUSKET); rod of steel, usu. tapering and roughened, for sharpening knives; strip of steel for stiffening corset etc.; ~ *engraving*, engraving on, impression taken from, steel plate; ~ *wool*, very fine steel shavings used as abrasive. ~ *v.t.* Nerve, harden, fortify, (*against*).
Steele, Sir Richard (1672-1729). Irish essayist, playwright, and miscellaneous author; founder of

the 'Tatler' and (with Addison) 'Spectator'.
stee′ly *adj.* Of, hard as, steel; inflexible, obdurate.
stee′lyard *n.* Lever with unequal arms used as balance, the article to be weighed being suspended from shorter arm while counterpoise is slid along longer, graduated arm until equilibrium is produced (ill. BALANCE).
stee′nbŏck *n.* = STEINBOCK, 2.
stee′nkĭrk, steĭ′n- (-n-k-) *n.* (hist.) Man's or woman's neck-cloth with long lace ends hanging down or twisted and passed through ring (ill. COAT). [f. battle of *Steenkerke*, Belgium, 1692]
steep[1] *adj.* With precipitous face or slope, sloping sharply; (colloq., of price etc.) exorbitant, unreasonable; (of story etc.) exaggerated, incredible. **stee′ply** *adv.* **stee′pnèss** *n.* **stee′pen** *v.* **steep** *n.* Steep slope, precipice.
steep[2] *v.* Soak, be soaked, in liquid; (fig.) permeate, imbue, impregnate. ~ *n.* Process of steeping; liquid in which thing is steeped.
stee′ple *n.* Lofty structure, esp. tower with spire, rising above roof of church (ill. CHURCH); spire; *stee′-plechase*, horse-race across country (orig. perhaps with steeple as goal) or on made course with hedges, water-jumps, and other obstacles; foot-race of similar kind; *stee′plejack*, man who climbs steeples, tall chimneys, etc., to do repairs etc.
steer[1] *n.* Young, esp. castrated, male of ox kind; (U.S.) castrated male ox of any age.
steer[2] *v.* Guide (vessel), guide vessel, by rudder, helm, etc.; guide (motor-car, aircraft) by mecha-

STEM

nical means; (of vessel etc.) be guided; direct one's course; ~ *clear of*, avoid; *steering-wheel*, vertical wheel on ship, hand-wheel in motor-car etc. for steering (ill. MOTOR); *steer′sman*, one who steers ship, whence *steer′smanship*.
steer′able *adj.*
steer′age *n.* 1. Effect of helm on ship; ~ *way*, amount of way or motion sufficient for ship to answer helm. 2. Part of ship allotted to passengers travelling at cheapest rate.
stein (-īn) *n.* (chiefly U.S.) Large earthenware mug, esp. for beer. [Ger. = 'stone']
steĭ′nbŏck (-īn-) *n.* 1. Alpine ibex (*Capra ibex*). 2. Small S. and E. African antelope, *Raphicerus campestris*.
steinkirk: see STEENKIRK.
stē′lē *n.* (pl. *-ae*). 1. Upright slab with sculptured design or inscription, esp. as gravestone. 2. (bot.) Axial cylinder in stems and roots of vascular plants (ill. STEM[1]).
stē′llar *adj.* Of stars; star-shaped.
stē′llate, -ātèd *adjs.* Star-shaped, radiating from centre like rays of star (ill. SOLID).
stĕm[1] *n.* 1. Main body above ground, ascending axis, of tree, shrub, or other plant; stalk supporting leaf, flower, or fruit; ~ *stitch*, (needlework) kind of stitch used for stems and other slender lines in embroidery etc. (ill. STITCH). 2. Stem-shaped part or object, as slender upright support of cup, wineglass, etc., long slender part or tube of key, thermometer, tobacco-pipe, etc., pendant-shank of watch; ~-*winder*, watch wound by turning head on

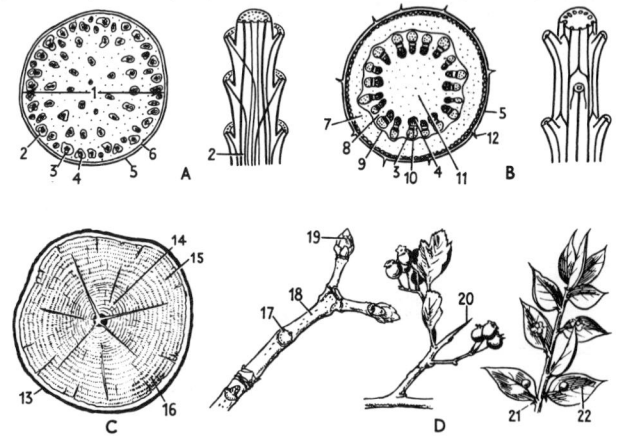

STEMS: TRANSVERSE AND LONGITUDINAL SECTIONS OF (A) MAIZE (MONOCOTYLEDON) AND (B) SUNFLOWER (DICOTYLEDON). C. TRANSVERSE SECTION OF TREE TRUNK. D. TWIGS OF HORSE-CHESTNUT, HAWTHORN, AND BUTCHER'S BROOM

A. 1. Stele. 2. Vascular bundle. 3. Phloem. 4. Xylem. 5. Epidermis. 6. Fibres. B. 7. Cortex. 8. Medulla. 9. Endodermis. 10. Cambium (forming fibre with phloem and xylem). 11. Pith. 12. Hair. C. 13. Bark. 14. Heart-wood. 15. Sap-wood. 16. Annual ring. 17. Leaf-scar. 18. Lenticel. 19. Bud. 20. Thorn. 21. True leaf. 22. Cladode

[857]

end of stem, not by key. 3. Part of word remaining essentially unchanged in inflexion, part to which flexional suffixes are added. 4. Line of ancestry; branch of family; stock, race. 5. (naut.) Curved upright timber or metal piece at fore end of vessel, to which ship's sides are joined (ill. BOAT); bows or forepart of vessel. ~ v. 1. Remove stem of. 2. Make headway against (tide, current, etc.). 3. ~ *from*, originate in.

stĕm² *v.t.* Check, stop, dam up (stream etc.); (skiing) check (oneself), check progress, by forcing heel of ski(s) outward from line of run; ~ *turn*, turn made by stemming one ski (ill. SKI).

stĕ′mma *n.* (pl. *-ata*). 1. Family tree; pedigree. 2. (zool.) Simple eye, facet of compound eye, in invertebrates (more usu. called *ocellus*). [L., f. Gk, = 'garland' (*stephō* crown)]

stĕnch *n.* Foul or offensive smell.

stĕ′ncil *n.* Thin sheet of metal, cardboard, etc. with holes cut in such a way that when a brush or roller charged with pigment is passed over it, desired design is produced on surface beneath (also ~*-plate*); decoration, lettering, so produced. ~ *v.t.* Produce (pattern) on surface, ornament (surface) with pattern, by means of stencil(s).

Stendhal (stahṅdahl). Pen-name of Henri Beyle (1783–1842), French novelist, author of 'Le Rouge et le Noir' and 'La Chartreuse de Parme'.

Stĕn gŭn. Small mass-produced sub-machine-gun usu. fired from the hip. [f. initials of *S*hepherd and *T*urpin, inventors, and *en*, as in BREN GUN]

stĕnŏ′graphў *n.* Art of writing in shorthand. **stĕ′nograph** (*or* -ahf) *n.* Writing, machine for writing, in shorthand. ~ *v.* Write in shorthand, act as stenographer. **stĕnŏ′grapher** *n.* **stĕnograˈphic** *adj.* **stĕnograˈphicallў** *adv.*

stĕ′nter *n.* Var. of TENTER².

Stĕ′ntor *n.* In the 'Iliad', a herald with voice as powerful as fifty voices of other men; hence (s~), person with very powerful voice. **stĕntor′ian** *adj.*

stĕp *v.* Lift and set down foot or alternate feet in walking etc.; go short distance, progress in some direction, by stepping; measure (distance) by stepping; (naut.) set up (mast) in step; ~ *down*, (elect.) lower voltage (of current) by means of a transformer; ~ *on the gas*: see GAS²; hence ~ *on it*, (slang) hurry; ~ *out*, walk vigorously, stride; behave, live, in lively, gay, extravagant, or dissipated manner; ~ *up*, (elect.) increase voltage of (current) by means of a transformer; increase (efficiency, production) in rate, volume, etc., speed up; *stepping-stone*, stone set in or projecting above water or muddy place as a help in crossing; (fig.) means of advancement or progress. ~ *n.* 1. Movement of stepping, distance gained by this; progress by stepping, course followed; manner of stepping; sound made by setting foot down; (fig.) action towards result, one of series of measures taken; *in* ~, stepping in time with other person(s) or music, stepping simultaneously and with corresponding legs with other person(s) or animal(s); *out of* ~, not in step. 2. Flat-topped structure, used singly or as one of series, to facilitate person's movement from one level to another; rung of ladder; foot-piece for entering, mounting, or alighting from vehicle; notch cut for foot in climbing; (pl.) step-ladder; (fig.) degree in an ascending scale, advance from one of these to another. 3. (naut.) Block or socket supporting mast etc. (ill. BOAT); (mech.) lower bearing on which vertical shaft revolves; step-like part or offset. 4. ~*-cut*, (of gem) cut in straight facets arranged round centre of stone (ill. GEM); ~*-dance*, dance for display of special steps (usu.) by individual performer; ~*-ladder*, kind of portable short ladder with flat steps and prop hinged to back for steadying.

stĕp- *prefix.* Having a specified relationship resulting from remarriage of a parent, as *ste′pbrother*, *ste′psister*, child of one's stepfather or stepmother; *ste′pchild* (*-daughter*, *-son*), child by previous marriage of one's wife or husband; *ste′pfather*, *ste′pmother*, husband, wife, of one's mother, father, by subsequent marriage.

stĕphanō′tis *n.* Tropical woody climbing plant of genus *S*~ with fragrant white waxy flowers. [Gk, = 'fit for a wreath' (*stephanos*)].

Stĕ′phen¹ (-ēv-), St. (d. *c* A.D. 35). First Christian martyr, stoned to death at Jerusalem (Acts 6, 7; commemorated 26 Dec.).

Stĕ′phen² (-ēv-), St. (*c* 977–1038). First king (997–1038) and patron saint of Hungary; commemorated 2 Sept.

Stĕ′phen³ **of Blois** (-ēv-, blwah) (*c* 1097–1154). Grandson, through his mother, of William the Conqueror; king of England 1135–54.

Stĕ′phenson (-ēv-), George (1781–1848). English engineer; built first railway (Stockton–Darlington, 1825) and greatly improved the locomotive engine.

stĕppe *n.* Vast plain, grassy and largely treeless, esp. in SE. Europe and Siberia. [f. Russ. *step′*]

sterā′dian *n.* (abbrev. sr) Solid angle at centre of sphere subtending a section on the surface whose area is equal to the square of the radius.

stĕrcorā′ceous (-sh*u*s), **stĕr′**-coral *adjs.* Of, produced by, dung or faeces.

stĕr′eŏ *n.* Stereotype; stereoscopic photograph or photography; stereophonic reproduction or equipment. ~ *adj.* Stereotyped; stereoscopic;. stereophonic.

stĕreo- *prefix.* Solid; three-dimensional; stereoscopic.

stĕ′reobāte *n.* (archit.) Solid mass of masonry as foundation for wall, columns, etc.

stĕreoche′mistry (-k-; *or* stĕ′r-) *n.* (Branch of chemistry dealing with) spatial arrangement of atoms etc. in molecule. **stĕreoche′mical** *adj.*

stĕrĕŏ′graphў (*or* stĕ′r-) *n.* Art of delineating forms of solid bodies on a plane. **stĕreogra′phic** *adj.*

stĕrĕŏ′metrў (*or* stĕ′r-) *n.* Art of measuring solids; solid geometry. **stĕreome′tric, -ical** *adjs.*

stĕrĕŏ′phonў (*or* stĕ′r-) *n.* System of separate microphones or loudspeakers designed to enhance the actuality of sounds. **stĕreopho′nic** *adj.* **stĕreopho′nicallў** *adv.*

stĕr′eoscōpe (*or* stĕ′r-) *n.* Instrument for obtaining single image giving impression of solidity or relief from two pictures (usu. photographs) of object from slightly different points of view. **stĕreosco′pic** *adj.* Of the stereoscope or stereoscopy. **stĕrĕŏ′-scopў** *n.* Vision of objects as solid or in three dimensions.

stĕr′eotype (*or* stĕ′r-) *n.* Printing-plate cast from mould of forme of type; method or process of printing from this. ~ *v.t.* Make stereotype(s) of, print from stereotype(s); (fig.) fix or perpetuate in unchanging form, formalize.

stĕ′rile *adj.* Barren; not producing, incapable of producing, fruit or offspring; free from living micro-organisms, as bacteria etc. **stĕ′rilelў** (-l-l-) *adv.* **steri′litў** *n.*

stĕ′rilize *v.t.* 1. Render (individual) incapable of producing offspring. 2. Render (object) free from contamination by micro-organisms by treating with heat, antiseptic, etc. **steriliza′tion** *n.*

stĕr′let *n.* Small species of sturgeon (*Acipenser ruthenus*) found in and near Caspian Sea, and used for making finest caviare.

stĕr′ling *n.* 1. British currency; ~ *area*, scheduled territories (see SCHEDULE *v.*). 2. (Articles made of) sterling silver. ~ *adj.* (of coins and precious metals) Genuine, of standard value or purity; (fig.) solidly excellent, genuine, not showy or specious; ~ *silver*, silver of a fineness formerly fixed by law for British silver coinage (92½% silver and 7½% copper). [orig. as n. = the English silver penny]

stĕrn¹ *n.* After or rear part of ship or boat, specif. that part of the hull abaft the sternpost (ill. BOAT); buttocks, rump; tail, esp. of fox-hound; ~*-chase*, pursuit of ship by another directly in its

[858]

wake; *ster'npost*, central upright timber or iron of stern, attached to keel and usu. bearing rudder; ~ *sheet(s)*, space in boat's stern, esp. aft of hindmost thwart (ill. BOAT); ~-*wheeler*, steamer with one large paddle-wheel at stern.

stērn² *adj.* Severe, strict, not lenient, rigorous in principle, punishment, or condemnation; hard, grim, harsh, gloomy. **stēr'nlỹ** *adv.* **stēr'nnĕss** (-n-n-) *n.*

stēr'nal *adj.* Of the sternum.

Stērne, Laurence (1713–68). English novelist, born in Ireland; author of 'Tristram Shandy' and 'A Sentimental Journey'.

Stēr'nhold, Thomas (d. 1549). Composer (with John Hopkins (d. 1570)) of English metrical version of the Psalms (complete edition, 1562).

stĕrno- *prefix.* Of the sternum and —, as ~-*mastoid muscle* (ill. HEAD).

stēr'num *n.* Bone or series of bones running along middle line of front of trunk, usu. articulated with some of ribs (ill. SKELETON); breast-bone of bird; ventral plate of body segment of arthropod.

stĕrnūtā'tion *n.* Sneezing, sneeze. **stĕrnū'tative, stĕrnū'tatorỹ** *adjs. & ns.* (Substance, e.g. snuff) causing sneezing.

stēr'nūtātor *n.* Poison gas that acts as a nose irritant.

stēr'oid *adj. & n.* (biochem.) (One) of a class of compounds with complex four-ring molecular structure, found in animal and plant cells or prepared synthetically and including the sterols, bile acids, and certain hormones.

stēr'ŏl *n.* (biochem.) One of a class of complex solid alcohols, as cholesterol, ergosterol, widely distributed in animals and plants.

stēr'torous *adj.* (of breathing etc.) Producing snoring or rasping sound. **stēr'torouslỹ** *adv.* **stēr'torousnĕss** *n.*

stĕt. Direction to printer, written in margin of MS. or proof, to cancel a correction made in the text, the letters thus restored being indicated by dots beneath them. [L, = 'let it stand']

stĕ'thoscōpe *n.* Instrument, consisting of ear tubes and a main tube to be applied to chest etc., for auscultation, esp. of heart or lungs. **stĕthoscŏ'pic** *adj.* **stĕthoscŏ'pically** *adv.* **stĕthŏ'scopỹ** *n.*

stĕ'tson *n.* Man's slouch hat with very wide brim. [maker's name]

stĕ'vedōre *n.* Man employed in loading and unloading ship's cargoes; (north.) charge-hand supervising dockers.

Stĕ'venson, Robert Louis (1850–94). Scottish essayist, novelist, and poet; author of 'Treasure Island', 'Dr Jekyll and Mr Hyde', 'Kidnapped', etc.

stew¹ *n.* (usu. pl., obs.) Brothel.

stew² *v.* Cook by long simmering in closed vessel with liquid; (of tea) make bitter or strong with too long soaking; (fig.) be oppressed by close or moist warm atmosphere; ~ *in one's own juice*, be left to suffer the consequences of one's own actions. ~ *n.* Dish of stewed meat, usu. with vegetables; (fig.) state of great alarm or excitement; ~-*pan*, -*pot*, pan, covered pot, for stewing.

stew³ *n.* Pond or tank for keeping live fish for table; artificial oyster-bed.

stew'ard *n.* 1. Person entrusted with management of another's property, esp. paid manager of great house or estate. 2. Purveyor of provisions etc. for college, club, ship, etc. 3. (fem. *stew'ardĕss*) Attendant waiting on passengers in ship or aircraft. 4. Official managing race-meeting, ball, show, etc. 5. *Lord High S~ of England*, official managing coronation or presiding at trial of peer; *Lord S~ of the* (*King's, Queen's*) *Household*, high court officer, with nominal duty of controlling sovereign's household above stairs. **stew'ardship** *n.*

stew'artrỹ *n.* Former territorial division of Scotland under jurisdiction of a steward.

St. Ex., St. Exch. *abbrevs.* Stock Exchange.

stg *abbrev.* Sterling.

stichomy'thia (-k-) *n.* Form of dramatic dialogue esp. in ancient Greek drama in which two characters speak one line of verse each alternately.

stĭck *v.* (past t. & past part. *stŭck*). 1. Thrust point of (pin, weapon, etc.) *in*(*to*), *through*; insert pointed thing(s) into, stab; (of mounted sportsman) spear (wild pig); fix on pointed thing, be fixed (as) by point *in*(*to*) or *on*; (colloq.) put in specified position. 2. ~ *out, up,* etc., protrude, (cause to) project; be, make, erect; ~ *up for*, maintain cause or character of, champion; ~ *up*, rob with violence, hold up; ~-*up* (*n.*). 3. Fix, become or remain fixed (as) by adhesion of surfaces; (cause to) adhere or cleave; (slang) endure, bear; ~ *at* or *to it*, persist, not cease trying. 4. Lose or deprive of power of motion through friction, jamming, suction, difficulty, etc.; ~-*in-the-mud*, slow, unprogressive (person); *sticking-plaster*, adhesive plaster for wounds etc.; ~-*jaw*, toffee etc. tending to stick jaws together and difficult to chew; ~-*pin*, (U.S.) (ornamental) pin, esp. tie-pin, that is merely stuck in, as dist. from safety-pin; ~-*up*, (*adj.*) that sticks up or projects. ~ *n.* 1. Short and relatively slender piece of wood; shoot or branch of tree cut to convenient length for use as walking-cane, bludgeon, staff, wand, support for climbing plant, etc.; fiddlestick, drumstick, composing-stick, etc.; implement used to propel ball in sports, as *hockey* ~; twigs or small pieces of wood as fuel; (fig.) person of no liveliness or intelligence, poor actor; ~ *of furniture*, (esp. in neg. or pl.) piece of furniture. 2. Slender more or less cylindrical piece *of* any material. 3. Number of aerial bombs released in close succession, or of parachute troops from an aircraft. 4. ~-*insect*, insect of family Phasmidae, usu. wingless, with long slender stick-like body resembling twigs of trees in which it lives; ~ *lac*, lac in natural state, encrusting the insects and small twigs.

stĭ'cker *n.* (esp.) 1. Adhesive label or other paper gummed on back. 2. Dogged or persistent person. 3. Rod in mechanism of organ or pianoforte working under compression (ill. ORGAN).

stĭ'cking *n.* Inferior meat at neck of beef (ill. MEAT).

stĭ'cklebăck (-lb-) *n.* Any of small spiny-finned fishes (family Gasterosteidae) of N. hemisphere.

stĭ'ckler *n.* ~ *for*, one who insists on or pertinaciously supports or advocates. [obs. *stickle* be umpire]

stĭ'ckỹ *adj.* Tending to stick or adhere, glutinous, viscous; (of racecourse, wicket) with yielding surface due to wet; (colloq.) unbending, awkward; (slang) highly unpleasant and painful, as in *he'll come to a ~ end*. **stĭ'ckilỹ** *adv.* **stĭ'ckinĕss** *n.*

stĭff *adj.* 1. Rigid, not flexible; unbending, unyielding, uncompromising, obstinate; lacking ease, grace, or freedom; formal, laboured, constrained, haughty; ~-*necked*, stubborn. 2. Not working freely, sticking, offering resistance; (of joints, limbs, etc.) not supple, unable to move without pain; ~ *neck*, affection in which head cannot be moved without pain. 3. Hard to cope with, trying, difficult. 4. (of moist or semi-liquid substance) Thick and viscous, not fluid. **stĭ'fflỹ** *adv.* **stĭ'ffnĕss** *n.* **stĭ'ffen** *v.* **stĭ'ffener, stĭ'ffening** *ns.* **stĭff** *n.* (slang) Corpse.

stĭ'fle¹ *v.* Smother; (cause to) feel oppressed or unable to breathe. **stĭ'fling** *adj.* **stĭ'flinglỹ** *adv.*

stĭ'fle² *n.* (also ~-*joint*) Joint between femur and tibia in horse and some other quadrupeds, corresponding to knee in man (ill. HORSE).

stĭ'gma *n.* (pl. -s, -ata). Mark branded on slave, criminal, etc. (archaic); (fig.) mark of disgrace or infamy, stain on one's good name; (path.) definite characteristic of some disease, morbid red spot on skin, esp. one bleeding spontaneously; (anat., zool.) spot, pore, natural mark, esp. spot on surface of ovary where rupture of Graafian follicle will occur; (bot.) receptive surface of the floral gynaecium to which pollen grains adhere (ill. FLOWER); (pl. -*ata*) marks resembling wounds on crucified body of Christ, said to

[859]

STIGMATIZE

have developed on bodies of some saints. **stigmă'tic** *adj.*

sti'gmatize *v.t.* Mark with stigmata, produce stigmata upon; (fig.) use opprobrious terms of, describe by disgraceful or reproachful name. **stigmatīzā'tion** *n.*

stīle[1] *n.* Arrangement of steps, rungs, etc., allowing passage to persons over or through fence or wall but excluding cattle etc.

stīle[2] *n.* Vertical bar of wainscot, sash, or other wooden framing (ill. WAINSCOT).

stĭlĕ'ttō *n.* (pl. *-s, -es*). Short dagger (ill. DAGGER); small pointed implement for making eyeletholes etc.

still[1] *adj.* Without or almost without motion or sound, silent, quiet, calm; (of wine etc.) not sparkling or effervescing; ~ *birth*, delivery of dead child; so ~*-born*; ~ *life*, representation in painting etc. of inanimate things, as fruit, flowers, etc. **stĭ'llness** *n.* **still** *n.* 1. Deep silence. 2. Photograph (other than moving picture), esp. single shot from cinema film. ~ *v.* Quiet, calm, appease, make still; (rare) grow still or calm. ~ *adv.* 1. Without motion or change. 2. Now as formerly; then as before; now, in contrast with future; even then, even now; nevertheless; even, yet; always, even.

still[2] *n.* Distilling apparatus, consisting essentially of a closed vessel for heating substance to be distilled, and spiral tube or worm for condensing the vapour so produced; ~*-room*, orig., room for distilling perfumes, cordials, etc.; later, housekeeper's store-room in large house.

sti'llage *n.* Stand or bench for keeping something, as a cask, from ground.

sti'lly *adj.* (poet.) Still, quiet.

stilt *n.* 1. Each of pair of poles, usu. held by hands or under arms, with foot-rest some way from lower end, for enabling person to walk over marshy ground, stream, etc., with feet raised above ground; one of set of piles or posts supporting building, etc. 2. Marsh bird of the widely distributed genus *Himantopus*, with very long slender legs and sharp slender bills.

sti'lted *adj.* (As) on stilts; (archit.) raised by a course of masonry, as ~ *arch* (ill. ARCH[1]); (of style, language, etc.) artificially lofty, formally pompous. **sti'ltedly** *adv.* **sti'ltedness** *n.*

Stĭ'lton *n.* (also ~ *cheese*) Rich blue-veined cheese, orig. made in Leicestershire and formerly sold to travellers at a coaching inn at Stilton, Huntingdonshire, on the Great North Road from London.

stĭ'mūlant *n.* Agent producing temporary increase of activity in part of organism; esp., alcoholic drink.

stĭ'mūlāte *v.t.* Apply stimulus to, act as stimulus on; animate, spur on, make more vigorous or active. **stĭmūlā'tion** *n.* **stĭ'mūlātive** *adj.*

stĭ'mūlus *n.* (pl. *-lī*). Something that rouses to activity or energy; rousing effect; thing that rouses organ or tissue to specific activity or function, effect of this. [L, = 'goad']

sting *n.* 1. Sharp-pointed organ in some insects and other animals, freq. connected with poison gland, and capable of giving painful or dangerous wound; poison-fang of snake; (bot.) stiff sharp-pointed hair emitting irritating fluid when touched. 2. Stinging, being stung; wound made, pain or irritation produced, by sting; rankling or acute pain of body or mind; keenness, vigour; stimulus. 3. ~*-ray*, ray esp. of family Dasyatidae, with long tapering tail armed with flattened sharp-pointed serrated spine(s) capable of inflicting severe wounds. ~ *v.* (past t. & past part. *stŭng*). 1. Wound with sting; (of some plants) produce kind of burning or itching rash or inflammation by contact with (skin); feel acute pain; be able to sting, have a sting; *stinging hair*, sting of plant; *stinging nettle*, common NETTLE. 2. (slang, chiefly *pass.*) Charge heavily, involve in expense, swindle.

stĭ'ngō (-nggō) *n.* (archaic) Strong beer.

stĭ'ngÿ (-jĭ) *adj.* Meanly parsimonious. **stĭ'ngilȳ** *adv.* **stĭ'ngĭness** *n.*

stĭnk *v.* (past t. *stănk* or *stŭnk*, past part. *stŭnk*). Have, emit, strong offensive smell; drive *out* with stench or suffocating fumes; cause to stink. ~ *n.* Strong offensive smell; (pl., slang) chemistry as subject of study; ~*-ball*, missile emitting suffocating vapour; ~*-bomb*, small bomb giving off offensive smell on bursting; ~*-horn*, any of various ill-smelling fungi, esp. *Ithyphallus impudicus*; *sti'nkwood*, any of various trees with unpleasant-smelling wood.

stĭ'nkard *n.* Stinking person or animal, esp. the teledu.

stĭ'nker *n.* Stinkard; (colloq.) anything particularly offensive or irritating.

stĭ'nking *adj.* That stinks (freq. in names of plants etc.); (slang) objectionable, obnoxious.

stint *n.* Limitation of supply or effort; fixed or allotted amount (of work etc.); (mining) area of coal-face to be worked in a shift. ~ *v.* Keep on short allowance, supply or give in niggardly amount or grudgingly.

stīpe *n.* (bot.) Footstalk, esp. stem supporting pileus of fungus, leaf-stalk of fern etc. (ill. FUNGUS); (zool.) stipes.

stī'pĕnd *n.* Salary, esp. of clergyman.

stīpĕ'ndiarȳ *adj. & n.* (Person) receiving stipend.

stī'pēs (-z) *n.* (zool.) Stalk-like

STITCH

part or organ, esp. second segment of maxilla of insect, eye-stalk, etc.; (bot.) stipe.

stī'pple *n.* Method of painting, engraving, etc., by use of dots or small spots to produce gradations of shade or colour; layer of paint applied roughly over layer of another colour which shows through in places; effect, work, so produced. ~ *v.* Engrave, paint, in stipple.

stĭ'pūlāte *v.* Require or insist upon as essential condition; make express demand *for* as condition of agreement. **stĭpūlā'tion** *n.*

stĭ'pūle *n.* One of pair of lateral appendages, freq. resembling small leaf or scale, at base of leaf in certain plants (ill. LEAF).

stĭr[1] *n.* Commotion, bustle, disturbance, excitement; slight movement; act of stirring. ~ *v.* Set, keep, (begin to) be, in (esp. slight) motion; agitate (soft or liquid or semi-liquid mass) with more or less circular motion, as with spoon, so as to mix ingredients, prevent burning in cooking, etc.; rouse (*up*), excite, animate, inspirit; *stir'about*, porridge made by stirring oatmeal or other meal into boiling water or milk. **stĭ'rring** *adj.* Exciting, stimulating. **stĭ'rringlȳ** *adv.*

stĭr[2] *n.* (slang) Prison.

Stĭr'ling. Town on river Forth, in Central region; university, 1967.

Stĭr'lingshire. Former county of S. Scotland, since May 1975 part of the Central region.

stĭ'rrup *n.* Support suspended by strap from side of saddle for rider's foot, now usu. iron loop with flattened base (ill. SADDLERY); something resembling this, esp. U-shaped clamp or support (of bow, ill. BOW[1]); (naut.) rope with eye at end supporting foot-rope; (also ~*-bone*) stirrup-shaped bone of middle ear, stapes (ill. EAR[1]); ~*-cup*, parting cup of wine etc. handed to rider on horseback; ~*-iron*, iron part of rider's stirrup; ~ *jar, vase*, (Gk antiq.) jar with solid neck joined to body by handle on each side; ~*-leather*, strap suspending stirrup from saddle; ~ *pump*, hand pump with stirrup-shaped foot-rest and short hose, used for extinguishing small fires.

stĭtch *n.* 1. Sudden sharp pain, esp. in the side of the body. 2. Each movement of threaded needle in and out of fabric in sewing, or of awl in shoe-making; loop of thread etc. left in fabric by this movement; single complete movement of needle, hook, etc., in knitting, crochet, embroidery, etc., part of work produced by this; (surg.) movement of needle in sewing up wound, loop of catgut etc. left in skin or flesh by this; method of making stitch, kind of work produced. 3. *sti'tchwort*, chickweed, esp. kind with erect

[860]

STITCHERY

stem and white starry flowers. ~ v. Sew, make stitches (in); fasten, make, ornament, with stitches.

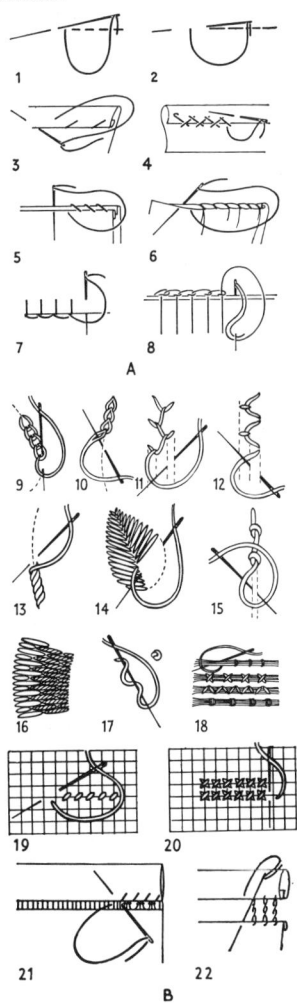

A. SEWING STITCHES.
B. EMBROIDERY STITCHES

A. 1. Running. 2. Backstitch. 3. Hemming. 4. Herring-bone. 5. Oversewing. 6. Whipping. 7. Blanket stitch. 8. Buttonhole stitch. B. 9. Chain-stitch. 10. Split-stitch. 11. Feather-stitch. 12. Fly-stitch. 13. Stem stitch. 14. Satin-stitch. 15. Coral stitch. 16. Long-and-short stitch. 17. French knot. 18. Couching. 19. Tent-stitch (*petit point*). 20. Cross-stitch (*gros point*). 21. Hem-stitching. 22. Faggotting

sti′tcherў *n.* Needlework.
sti′ver *n.* Most trifling coin or amount.
stŏ′a *n.* (pl. *-ae, -as*). 1. Portico in ancient Greek architecture (ill. TEMPLE¹). 2. S~, great hall at Athens, adorned with frescoes of battle of Marathon, in which Zeno of Citium lectured.
stoat *n.* European ERMINE, esp. in its brown summer form.
stŏck *n.* 1. Trunk or stem of tree; stump, butt; plant into which graft is inserted; (bot.) rhizome; (geol.) cylindrical intrusive body of igneous rock (freq. granite) of moderate size. 2. Body-piece serving as the base or holder for the working parts of an implement or machine, as whip, plough, gun, anchor, etc. (ill. ANCHOR). 3. (Source of) family or breed. 4. (hist., pl.) Instrument of punishment, wooden framework

STOCKS

set up in public place with holes for offender's feet or feet and hands. 5. (pl.) Timbers on which ship rests while building; *on the* ~*s*, in construction (also fig.). 6. Cruciferous plant of genus *Matthiola*, with fragrant flowers; *Virginian* ~, small cruciferous plant, *Malcolmia maritima*, with flowers of various colours resembling those of *Matthiola*. 7. Hard solid brick pressed in mould. 8. Close-fitting wide band for neck, worn esp. as part of riding-kit; piece of black or purple silk etc. worn below clerical collar. 9. Swarm or hive of bees. 10. Livestock. 11. Liquor made by stewing meat, bones, vegetables, etc., and used as foundation for soup etc. 12. Raw material of manufacture. 13. Fund, store ready for drawing on, equipment for trade or pursuit. 14. Subscribed capital of trading company, or public debt of nation, municipal corporation, etc., regarded as transferable property held by subscribers or creditors and subject to fluctuations in market value. 15. (obs.) Portion of tally given to payer (ill. TALLY). 16. *take* ~, make inventory of merchandise etc. in hand; (fig.) make careful estimate of one's position, prospects, resources, etc.; *take* ~ *of*, reckon up, evaluate, scrutinize; *take* ~ *in*, invest money in; (fig.) concern oneself in. 17. (*attrib.* or as *adj.*) Kept regularly in stock for sale or use; commonly used, constantly recurring in discussion etc.; ~ *actor, company,* (member of) company regularly performing together at particular theatre; *sto′ckbroker*, broker who buys and sells stocks for clients on com-

mission; ~ *car*, saloon car built (sometimes using part(s) of old car) for ~-*car racing*, racing on small oval circuit where cars may push or bump to gain places; ~-*dove*, woodland pigeon *Columba oenas*, nesting in hollow trees; ~ *exchange*, market, building, for buying and selling of stocks esp. (*S~ Exchange*) that in London; association of brokers and jobbers doing business in particular place or market; *sto′ckfish*, cod, hake, etc., split open and dried in the air without salt; ~-*gillyflower* = stock (sense 6); *sto′ckholder*, holder of stock in public funds etc., shareholder ~-*in-trade*, goods kept in stock, all requisites for a particular trade; ~-*jobber*, member of Stock Exchange dealing in stocks on his own account; *sto′ckman*, (chiefly Austral.) man employed to look after livestock; ~-*market*, traffic in stocks and shares; ~ *piece, play*, play forming part of repertory; *sto′ckpile*, (orig. U.S.) raw materials purchased and accumulated by country which cannot provide them in sufficient quantity from its own resources; *sto′ckpiling*, this practice; ~-*pot*, cooking-pot in which stock is made and kept; ~ *size*, size of ready-made garments regularly kept in stock; person able to wear these; ~-*still*, quite motionless; ~-*whip*, short-handled whip with very long lash for herding cattle; *sto′ckyard*, enclosure with pens etc. for sorting or temporary keeping of cattle. ~ *v.* 1. Fit (gun etc.) with stock. 2. Provide (shop, farm, etc.) with goods, livestock, or requisites. 3. Keep (goods) in stock.
stockā′de *n. & v.t.* (Fortify with) breastwork or enclosure of upright stakes.
Stŏ′ckholm (-hōm). Capital city and port of Sweden; ~ *tar*, kind of tar prepared from resinous pine-wood and used in shipbuilding and the manufacture of cordage, orig. exported from Stockholm.
stŏckinĕ′t (*or* stŏ′-) *n.* Fine elastic machine-knitted textile material used for undergarments etc.
stŏ′cking *n.* Close-fitting, usu. knitted, covering for foot and leg up to or above knee; surgical appliance resembling this; leg of bird or animal, when of different colour from body; ~-*frame*, -*loom*, -*machine*, knitting machine; ~ *stitch*, knitting-stitch resembling that commonly used in stockings, producing plain smooth surface (ill. KNITTING).
stŏ′ckist *n.* One who stocks specified goods for sale.
stŏ′ckў *adj.* Thickset, short and strongly built. stŏ′ckilў *adv.* stŏ′ckinĕss *n.*
stŏdge *n.* 1. Thick semi-solid mass, esp. of food. 2. Greedy eater. ~ *v.i.* Eat greedily.
stŏ′dġў *adj.* (of food) Heavy,

[861]

filling, thick or semi-solid; (of person, book, etc.) dull, heavy, solid, uninspired. **stŏ′dgily** *adv.* **stŏ′dginėss** *n.*

stoep (-oōp) *n.* (S. Afr.) Verandah at front (and occas. sides) of house.

stŏ′gie, stŏ′gy (-gi) *n.* (U.S.) Kind of long slender cigar or cheroot.

stŏ′ic *n.* 1. S~, philosopher of school founded *c* 315 B.C. by ZENO[1], who taught that virtue was the highest good, and inculcated repression of emotion, indifference to pleasure or pain, and patient endurance; later Stoic writers were Seneca, Epictetus, and Marcus Aurelius. 2. Person of great self-control, fortitude, or austerity. **stŏ′ical** *adj.* **stŏ′ically** *adv.* **stŏ′icism** *n.* [Gk *stoa* porch, hall in Athens where Zeno taught]

stōke *v.* Feed and tend (furnace), feed furnace of (engine etc.); act as stoker; ~ *up*, (fig., colloq.) feed, eat, esp. in hurried way; **sto′kehold**, apartment containing ship's boilers, where furnaces are tended; **sto′kehole**, space in front of furnace where stokers stand, opening through which furnace is tended, stokehold.

stō′ker *n.* One who feeds and tends furnace esp. of ship or steam-engine.

S.T.O.L. *abbrev.* Short take-off and landing (aircraft).

stōle *n.* 1. Long loose garment reaching to feet, esp. as outer dress of ancient Roman matron. 2. Ecclesiastical vestment, narrow strip of silk or linen worn over shoulders and reaching to or below knees (ill. VESTMENT); woman's wrap of similar shape.

stolen: see STEAL.

stŏ′lid *adj.* Not easily excited or moved, phlegmatic, dull and impassive. **stŏ′lidly** *adv.* **stoli′dity** *n.*

stō′lon *n.* 1. (bot.) Reclined or prostrate branch that strikes root and develops new plant (ill. GRASS). 2. (zool.) In hydrozoa etc., extension of body wall that develops buds, giving rise to new zooids.

stŏm′a *n.* (pl. -*s*, -*ata*). (anat., zool.) Small mouth-like opening, esp. in lower animals; (bot.) minute orifices in epidermis of plants, esp. of leaves, affording communication between outer air and intercellular spaces in interior tissue (ill. LEAF).

sto′mach (-ŭmak) *n.* Internal pouch or cavity in human or other animal body in which food is digested; in man, a dilatation of alimentary canal at upper left of abdomen (ill. ALIMENTARY); in some animals, esp. ruminants, one of several digestive cavities; (loosely) abdomen; (archaic) appetite *for* food; (fig.) relish, inclination, desire (*for* danger, conflict, an undertaking, etc.); ~-*ache*, pain in belly, esp. bowels; ~-*pump*, small pump or syringe for emptying stomach or introducing liquids into it. **sto′machal** *adj.* **sto′mach** *v.t.* Bear without resistance, endure (insult etc.).

sto′macher (-ŭmaker) *n.* (hist.) In women's dress of 15th–17th centuries, ornamental piece, freq. embroidered or set with gems, covering breast and pit of stomach (ill. PANNIER).

stomă′chic (-k-) *adj.* & *n.* Of the stomach; (drug etc.) promoting digestion or appetite.

stŏmati′tis *n.* Inflammation of the mouth.

stōne *n.* 1. Piece of rock, esp. of small or moderate size; hard compact material of which stones and rocks consist, particular kind of this; gem; piece of stone of definite form and size, for special purpose, as for building, paving, grinding, as a monument, etc. 2. Hard morbid concretion in body, esp. in kidney, urinary bladder, or gall-bladder, calculus; hard wood-like case of kernel in drupe; seed of grape etc.; testicle. 3. Unit of weight, usu. of 14 lb., but varying with different commodities from 8 to 24 lb. 4. *S~ Age*, stage of a culture marked by use of implements and weapons of stone, not metal; ~-*blind*, quite blind; **sto′nechat**, small European singing bird (*Saxicola torquata*), with plumage largely black and white; ~-*cold*, quite cold; **sto′necrop**, species of sedum, esp. *Sedum acre*, with bright yellow flowers and small cylindrical fleshy leaves, growing on rocks, old walls, etc.; ~-*dead*, quite dead; ~-*deaf*, completely deaf; **sto′nefish**, small tropical fish, *Synanceja verrucosa*, with erectile dorsal spines containing poison sacs; ~-*fly*, insect of order Plecoptera with larvae often found under stones in streams, used by anglers as bait; ~-*fruit*, drupe; ~ *of Destiny*, stone of Scone: see CORONATION stone; ~-*lily*, fossil crinoid; ~ *marten*, BEECH-marten; ~-*mason*, mason; ~-*pine*, species of pine (*Pinus pinea*) of S. Europe and Levant with wide-spreading branches and flat top; ~*'s throw*, short or moderate distance; **stonewa′ll**, (cricket) excessively cautious batting, (pol., esp. Austral.) parliamentary obstruction; **sto′neware**, hard dense kind of pottery made from very siliceous clay or mixture of clay with much flint or sand; **sto′nework**, masonry. ~ *v.t.* Pelt with stones, esp. put to death thus; take stones out of (fruit); face, pave, etc., with stone.

Stō′nehĕ′nge (-nhěnj) *n.* Prehistoric stone monument on Salisbury Plain, Wiltshire, consisting of concentric circles of dressed stones erected mainly in the Bronze Age; some of the larger stones carry lintels and among the smaller are blue stones which apparently come from SW. Wales.

stō′nў *adj.* Full of, covered with, having many, stones; hard, rigid, fixed, as stone, obdurate, unfeeling; (also ~-*broke*), (slang) utterly broke, without any money.

stood: see STAND.

stōōge *n.* (slang) Butt, foil, esp. for comedian; person deputed to do routine or spare work for another. ~ *v.i.* (slang) Act as stooge (*for*); move, travel *about*, *around*, in vehicle or aircraft.

stōōk *n.* & *v.t.* (Make into) shock of corn.

stōōl *n.* 1. Seat for one person, without arms or back, esp. wooden one on three or four legs; footstool. 2. (Place for) evacuation of bowels; faeces evacuated. 3. Stump of felled tree etc., esp. with new shoots. 4. (U.S.) Decoy-bird; (also ~-*pigeon*) decoy (freq. fig., esp. = police-spy). ~ *v.* Throw up young shoots or stems; (U.S.) decoy; act as stool-pigeon.

stōōp[1] *v.* 1. Bring one's head nearer ground by bending shoulders, trunk, etc., forward; carry head and shoulders bowed forward; incline (head, shoulders, back, etc.) forward and down; (fig.) descend from dignity, rank, etc., *to* action, *to* do. 2. (of hawk or other bird of prey) Swoop, descend steeply and swiftly, on quarry. ~ *n.* 1. Stooping carriage of back or shoulders; act of stooping. 2. Swoop of bird of prey on its quarry.

stōōp[2] *n.* (U.S. and Canada) Porch, platform, small verandah, before door of house.

stŏp *v.* 1. Close or almost close aperture or cavity by plugging, obstructing, etc., esp. block mouth(s) of (fox's earth), fill cavity in tooth with stopping, close (organ-pipe) at upper end with plug or cap; prevent or forbid passage through; make impervious or impassable. 2. Put an end to, arrest (motion etc.); check progress, motion or operation of; effectively hinder or prevent; suspend (payment etc.), give instructions to banker not to cash (cheque etc.). 3. (mus.) Press down (string of violin etc.) with finger to raise pitch of note, produce (note, sound) thus. 4. Cease, come to an end, cease from, discontinue; cease from motion, speaking, or action; make halt or pause; (colloq.) remain, stay, sojourn. 5. ~ *down*, reduce aperture of (lens); ~ *out*, (etching etc.) cover with varnish (parts of plate to be protected from action of acid); ~ *over*, (U.S.) halt (*at* place) and proceed by later conveyance.

stŏ′ppage *n.* **stŏp** *n.* 1. Stopping, being stopped; pause, check. 2. Punctuation-mark, esp. comma, semi-colon, colon, or period; *full ~*, period. 3. Batten, peg, block, etc., meant to stop motion of something at fixed point; something stopping aperture, plug. 4. (optics, photog.) Aperture.

stope 5. (mus.) ORGAN-stop; closing of hole in tube of wind instrument to alter pitch of note, hole so closed, metal key closing it; pressing with finger on string of violin etc. to raise pitch of note, part of string where this pressure is applied. 6. (phonet.) Consonant in formation of which passage of breath is completely obstructed, mute. **stop-** in comb: *sto′pcock*, tap or short pipe with externally operated valve to stop or regulate passage of liquid, gas, etc., key or handle for turning this; *sto′pgap*, makeshift, temporary substitute; ~*-knob*, handle or knob turning organ-stop on or off (ill. ORGAN); ~*-lamp, -light*, light, on rear of motor vehicle, that illuminates when brakes are applied; ~*-over*, (U.S.) act of stopping over; permission to passenger to break journey; ~*-press*, (news) inserted in paper after printing has begun; ~*-watch*, watch indicating fractions of a second by a hand that may be instantly stopped at will, used in timing races etc.

stōpe *n.* Working face of mine, area where ore is being extracted.

Stōpes (-ps), Marie Carmichael (1880–1958). English author; advocate of birth control.

stŏ′pper *n.* (esp.) Plug for closing bottle etc., usu. of glass or of same material as vessel. ~ *v.t.* Close or secure with stopper.

stŏr′age *n.* Storing of goods, method of doing this; space for storing; cost of warehousing; *cold* ~, storing of provisions under refrigeration; ~ *battery*, (elect.) apparatus for storing electrical energy in chemical form, accumulator; ~ *heater*, electric radiator storing in bricks etc. heat accumulated in off-peak hours.

stŏr′ăx *n.* 1. Fragrant gum-resin obtained from tree *Styrax officinalis*. 2. Fragrant honey-like balsam obtained from tree *Liquidambar orientalis*. 3. Tree yielding storax.

stōre *n.* 1. Abundance, provision, stock of something ready to be drawn upon; *in* ~, in reserve, for future use; *in* ~ *for*, awaiting (person). 2. (Gt Britain) Large shop selling goods of many different kinds; (U.S.) shop of any kind. 3. (pl.) Articles of particular kind or for special purpose accumulated for use; supply of things needed, stocks, reserves. 4. *attrib.* (of animals) Kept for breeding as part of farm stock or bought to be fattened; (U.S.) of store or shop; bought at shop; (of clothes) ready-made; *stor′ehouse*, place where things are stored; store, treasury; *stor′ekeeper*, person in charge of store(s); (U.S. etc.) shopkeeper; *stor′eroom*, room for storing goods or supplies, esp. of ship or household. ~ *v.t.* Furnish, stock (*with* something); lay *up* for future use, form stock of; deposit (goods, furniture, etc.) in warehouse for temporary keeping; have storage accommodation for.

stōr′ey, stŏr′y[2] *n.* (pl. *-eys, -ies*). Each stage or portion into which house or building is divided horizontally; anything compared to this.

stōriā′tion *n.* Decoration with designs representing historical, legendary, etc., subjects.

stōr′ied (-id) *adj.* 1. Adorned with representations of historical or legendary scenes. 2. Celebrated in history or story.

stŏrk *n.* Large wading bird of *Ciconia* and allied genera, with long legs and long stout bill, esp. the *common* or *white* ~ (*C. ciconia*), migratory European stork, often nesting on human habitations.

stŏrm *n.* Violent disturbance of atmosphere, with high winds and freq. thunder, heavy rain, hail, snow, etc.; wind of particular degree of violence, of force 10 or 11 on BEAUFORT scale; heavy discharge or shower (*of* blows etc.); violent disturbance of civil, political, domestic, etc., affairs; tumult, agitation, dispute, etc.; assault on fortified place, capture *of* place by such assault; *take by* ~, take by assault (freq. fig.); *S* ~ *and Stress* [tr. Ger. *Sturm und Drang*], movement in German literature, *c* 1770–82, characterized by extravagant representation of violent passion and rejection of classical rules of composition; ~ *in a teacup*, commotion about a trivial matter; ~*-centre*, central, comparatively calm, area of cyclonic storm; (fig.) centre round which storm of controversy, trouble, etc., rages; ~*-cloud*, heavy rain-cloud; ~*-cock*, missel-thrush; ~*-cone*, cone of tarred canvas hoisted as a storm-signal; ~ *lantern*, one with flame protected from wind and rain; ~ *petrel*: see PETREL; ~*-signal*, any device for signalling approach of a storm; ~ *troops*, shock-troops, esp. a Nazi semi-military organization; ~*-trooper*, member of this. ~ *v.* 1. Take by storm, rush violently, esp. to attack. 2. (of wind etc.) Rage, be violent; bluster, fume; scold.

stŏr′my *adj.* Characterized, marked, by storm(s); associated or connected with storms; ~ *petrel*: see PETREL. **stŏr′mily** *adv.* **stŏr′miness** *n.*

Stŏr′thing (-ti-), **-ting** *n.* Norwegian parliament. [Norw. *stor* great, *ting* assembly]

stŏr′y[1] *n.* Past course of life of person, institution, etc.; account given of incident or series of events; narrative meant to entertain hearer or reader, tale in prose or verse of actual or fictitious events; legend, myth, anecdote, novel, romance; (amusing) anecdote; plot (of novel, play, etc.); (orig. U.S.) account in newspaper, material for this; (colloq.) lie.

story[2]: see STOREY.

stŏtĭ′nka *n.* (pl. *-ki*). $\frac{1}{100}$ of a lev.

stoup (-ōōp) *n.* Vessel for holy water, usu. stone basin in wall of church or near church porch; (archaic) flagon, tankard, beaker.

stout *adj.* 1. Valiant, undaunted, resolute. 2. Of considerable thickness or strength. 3. Corpulent. **stou′tish** *adj.* **stou′tly** *adv.* **stou′tness** *n.* stout *n.* Heavy dark type of beer prepared with well-roasted barley or malt and sometimes caramelized sugar.

stōve[1] *n.* Portable or fixed closed apparatus to contain burning fuel or consume gas, electricity, etc., for use in warming rooms, cooking, etc.; ~*-pipe*, pipe to carry off smoke and gases from stove; (orig. U.S.) top hat, tall silk hat. ~ *v.t.* Dry, heat, in stove; fumigate, disinfect with sulphur or other fumes.

stove[2]: see STAVE *v.*

stow (-ō) *v.* Pack (*away*) in proper receptacles or convenient places, esp. (naut.) place (cargo) in proper order in hold etc.; fill (receptacle) with articles compactly arranged; (slang) desist, refrain from; ~ *away*, conceal oneself on board ship; *stow′away*, person hiding in ship, aircraft, etc. to avoid paying passage-money, to escape by stealth etc. **stow′age** *n.* (Cost of) stowing.

Stowe[1] (-ō). English public school founded 1923 at Stowe House in Buckinghamshire.

Stowe[2] (-ō), Mrs Harriet Elizabeth Beecher (1811–96). American author of 'Uncle Tom's Cabin', a novel describing the sufferings of Negro slaves.

S.T.P. *abbrev. Sanctae theologiae professor* (L, = Professor of Sacred Theology).

str. *abbrev.* Stroke (oar).

strabi′smus (-z-) *n.* Squinting, a squint. **strabi′smal, strabi′smic** *adjs.*

Strā′bō (*c* 64 B.C.–A.D. 19). Greek historian and geographer; native of Pontus in Asia Minor; wrote a 'Geography' of the Roman Empire.

Strā′chey (-chi), Giles Lytton (1880–1932). English literary critic and biographer.

Stråd *n.* STRADIVARIUS (instrument).

strā′ddle *v.* Spread legs wide apart in walking, standing, or sitting; (of legs) be wide apart; stand or sit across (thing) thus; part (legs) widely; drop shells beyond and short of a target in order to determine its range; drop bombs across (a target) beginning on one side and finishing on the opposite side. ~ *n.* 1. Action, position, of straddling. 2. (Stock Exch.) Contract giving holder right of either calling for or delivering stock at fixed price.

Strădĭvār′ius. Latinized name of Antonio Stradivari (*c* 1644–1737), most famous of a family of

Italian makers of stringed instruments; hence, violin or other stringed instrument made by member of this family.

strafe (-ahf; U.S. -āf) *v.t.* Bombard, worry with shells, bombs, sniping, etc.; reprimand sharply, abuse, thrash. ~ *n.* Strafing. [Ger., *Gott strafe England* God punish England, catchword in war of 1914–18]

Strā′fford, Sir Thomas Wentworth, 1st Earl of (1593–1641). English statesman, chief adviser to Charles I, whose authority he tried to restore; he was impeached in 1640, but when treason could not be proved the Commons (Long Parliament) brought in a Bill of Attainder and Strafford was executed.

strā′ggle *v.i.* Stray from the main body, be dispersed or scattered, grow irregularly or loosely. **strā′ggler** *n.* **strā′ggling** *adj.* **strā′gglingly** *adv.* **strā′ggly** *adj.* **strā′ggle** *n.* Body or group of scattered or straggling objects.

straight (-āt) *adj.* 1. Not crooked, not curved, bent, or angular; (geom., of line) lying evenly between any two of its points; (of hair) not curly or waving. 2. Direct, undeviating, going direct to the mark. 3. Upright, honest, candid; in proper order or place. 4. (orig. U.S.) Unmixed, undiluted, (of spirits) neat; (poker, or cards) in sequences, without gap; (of drama) without music. 5. *a ~ bat* (cricket) bat held upright, not inclining to either side (freq. fig.); *~-edge*, strip of wood, steel, etc., with a perfectly straight edge, for testing accuracy of plane surface, drawing straight lines, etc.; *a ~ fight*, (pol.) direct contest between two candidates. **strai′ghtness** *n.* **straight** *n.* Straight condition; straight part of something, esp. concluding stretch of race-course; sequence of cards in poker. ~ *adv.* In a straight line, direct, without deviation or circumlocution; in right direction, with good aim; ~ *away*, immediately, at once; *~-cut*, (of tobacco) cut lengthwise into long silky fibres; ~ *off*, without hesitation, deliberation, etc.; ~ *out*, frankly, outspokenly.

strai′ghten (-āt-) *v.* Make straight.

straightfor′ward (-āt-) *adj.* Honest, open, frank; (of task etc.) presenting no complications. **straightfor′wardly** *adv.*

strai′ghtway (-āt-) *adv.* (archaic) Straight away.

strain[1] *n.* Breed, stock; inherited tendency or quality, moral tendency forming part of a character.

strain[2] *n.* 1. Straining, being strained, pull, tension, exertion; injury or damage due to excessive exertion, tension, or force; deformation or distortion in any body due to stress, molecular displacement. 2. Melody, tune; passage, snatch, of music, poetry, etc.; tone, mode, etc., adopted in talking or writing; tenor, drift, general tendency or character. ~ *v.* 1. Stretch tightly, make taut; stretch beyond normal degree, force to extreme effort, exert to utmost; wrest, distort, from true intention or meaning; hug (person) *to* oneself, one's breast, etc. 2. Overtask; injure, try, imperil, by over-use, by making excessive demands on, etc. 3. Make intense effort; strive intensely *after*, try *at*. 4. Clear (liquid) of solid matter by passing through sieve etc.; filter (solids) *out* from liquid; (of liquid) percolate. **strained** (-nd) *adj.* (esp.) Artificial, forced, constrained; ~ *relations*, relations that are dangerously tense, nearly at breaking-point.

strai′ner *n.* (esp.) Utensil for straining or filtering.

strait *adj.* Narrow, limited; confined, confining; (archaic exc. in) ~ *jacket*, ~ *waistcoat*, strong garment for upper part of body, admitting of being tightly laced and usu. confining arms, used to restrain violent persons in mental hospital or prison; *~-jacket* (*v.t.*, fig.) restrict severely; *~-laced*, (now only fig.) severely virtuous, puritanical. ~ *n.* 1. Narrow passage of water connecting two seas or large bodies of water. 2. (usu. pl.) Difficult position; need, distress.

strai′ten *v.t.* (chiefly in past part.) Restrict in amount, scope, or range; reduce to straits; *straitened circumstances*, inadequate means of living, poverty.

strāke *n.* Section of iron rim of cart-wheel (ill. WHEEL); continuous line of planking or plates, of uniform breadth, from stem to stern of ship (ill. BOAT).

stramō′nium *n.* Thorn-apple; dried leaves of this, used in treatment of asthma etc.

strănd[1] *n.* Margin of sea, lake, or river, esp. part of shore between tide-marks; *the S~*, London street N. of Thames, orig. so called as occupying, with gardens of its houses, shore of Thames between cities of London and Westminster. ~ *v.* Run aground. **strā′ndėd** *adj.* (esp.) Left in a helpless position or without adequate resources.

strănd[2] *n.* Each of strings or wires twisted together to form rope, cord, cable, etc.; thread of woven material, string of beads, pearls, etc.; single hair; group of hairs.

strănge (-j) *adj.* Foreign, alien, not one's own, not familiar or well known (*to*); novel, queer, peculiar, surprising, unexpected; fresh or unaccustomed *to*, unacquainted, bewildered. **strā′ngely** *adv.* **strā′ngeness** *n.*

strā′nger (-j-) *n.* Foreigner; person in place, company, etc., to which he does not belong; person unknown to or *to* one; *I spy ~s*, formula in House of Commons demanding expulsion of all but members or officials before secret session.

strā′ngle (-nggl) *v.t.* Throttle, kill by external compression of throat; hinder growth of (plant) by overcrowding; (fig.) suppress; *stra′nglehold*, deadly grip (usu. fig.).

strā′ngles (-ngglz) *n.* Infectious febrile disease, caused by a streptococcus, in equine animals.

strā′ngulāte (-ngg-) *v.t.* Strangle (rare); (path., surg.) constrict (organ, duct, etc.) so as to prevent circulation or passage of fluid; *strangulated hernia*, hernia so constricted as to arrest circulation in protruding part. **străngulā′tion** *n.* Strangling, being strangled; strangulating.

strā′ngūry (-ngg-) *n.* (Disease characterized by) slow and painful emission of urine.

străp *n.* Leather band; flat strip of leather etc. of uniform breadth with buckle or other fastening for holding things together etc.; strip of metal used to secure or connect, leaf of hinge, etc.; *stra′phanger*, passenger in bus, train, etc., who must stand and hold on by strap for want of sitting space; *stra′pwork*, ornamental work of narrow band or fillet folded, crossed, interlaced, etc. **străp′less** *adj.* Without strap(s); (esp., of dress) without shoulder straps. **străp** *v.t.* Furnish, fasten, with strap; beat, flog, with strap; (surg.) close (wound), bind (part) up with adhesive plaster.

strappā′dō (*or* -ahdō) *n.* (pl. *-s*). (hist.) Form of punishment or torture in which victim was hoisted by rope, usu. by hands tied behind his back, and allowed to fall to length of rope. ~ *v.t.* Inflict strappado on.

strā′pping *adj.* (of persons). Strongly and stoutly built.

străss[1] *n.* Vitreous composition used for making artificial gems, paste. [Ger., said to be f. name of inventor, Josef *Strasser*]

străss[2] *n.* 1. Silk refuse. 2. Silky-looking waxed straw used as trimming etc.

strā′tagem *n.* Artifice, trick, trickery; device(s) for deceiving enemy.

stratē′gic *adj.* Of, dictated by, serving the ends of, strategy; ~ *bombing*, bombing designed to disrupt the enemy's internal economy, destroy morale, etc. (opp. TACTICAL *bombing*). **stratē′gical** *adj.* **stratē′gically** *adv.*

strā′tegy *n.* Generalship, art of war; art of planning and directing larger military movements and operations of campaign or war (opp. TACTICS); also transf. **strā′tegist** *n.*

Strā′tford-upŏ′n-A′von (ā-).

Town in Warwickshire, birthplace of Shakespeare.
Străthclȳ'de. Region of W. Scotland (since May 1975), comprising the city of Glasgow and the former counties of Argyllshire, Ayrshire, Buteshire, Dunbartonshire, Lanarkshire, and Renfrewshire.
străthspey' (-ā) *n.* 1. Type of country-dance tune; dance to this. 2. First part of a Scotch reel. [Sc. place-name]
stră'tifȳ *v.t.* Arrange in strata. **strătĭfĭcā'tion** *n.*
strati'graphȳ *n.* Study and description of stratified rocks; historical geology.
strătocū'mŭlus *n.* (meteor.) Type of low cloud, a layer of globular masses (ill. CLOUD).
stră'topause (-z) *n.* Top boundary of the stratosphere (ill. ATMOSPHERE).
stră'tosphēre *n.* Region of the atmosphere lying above the troposphere, in which the temperature does not decrease with increasing height (ill. ATMOSPHERE).
strā'tum (*or* -ah-) *n.* (pl. *-ta*). (geol.) Layer or bed of sedimentary rock (ill. ROCK¹); (biol.) layer of tissue; (archaeol.) layer of deposits in excavation etc. indicating distinct period or form of culture; (fig.) level or grade in social position, culture, etc.
strā'tus *n.* Continuous horizontal sheet of cloud (ill. CLOUD).
Strauss¹ (-ows), David Friedrich (1808–74). German theologian; author of a 'Life of Jesus', in which he attempted to prove that the biblical story of Jesus rested on a series of myths.
Strauss² (-ows). Name of a Viennese family of composers, famous esp. for dance music; *Johann* ~ (1825–99), composer of the 'Blue Danube' waltz and the opera 'Die Fledermaus'.
Strauss³ (-ows), Richard Georg (1864–1949). German composer of 'Der Rosenkavalier' and other operas and of orchestral music.
Stravi'nskȳ, Igor (1882–1971). Russian-born composer, famous esp. for ballet music.
straw¹ *n.* Dry cut stalks of various cereals used for bedding, thatching, litter for animals, plaited or woven as material for hats, beehives, etc.; stem of any cereal plant; single stalk or piece of straw; tube orig. of straw for sucking drink through; insignificant trifle; straw hat; *last* ~, last of a series of mishaps, irritations, etc., proving disastrous; *man of* ~, stuffed effigy; imaginary person set up as adversary etc.; person undertaking financial responsibility without means of discharging it; ~-*board*, coarse yellow cardboard made of straw pulp; ~-*colour*(*ed*), (of) the pale light-yellow colour of straw; ~ *vote*, (U.S.) unofficial vote, esp. as sample or indication of public opinion. **straw'ȳ** *adj.*
straw² *v.t.* (archaic) Strew.
straw'berry *n.* (Juicy edible pulpy, usu. red, fruit, dotted with small yellow seed-like achenes, and not properly a berry, of) plant of any species of genus *Fragaria*, stemless herbs with trifoliate leaves, white flowers, and slender trailing runners; colour of red strawberries; ~ *leaf*, leaf of strawberry, esp. as symbol of ducal rank (with ref. to strawberry leaves ornamenting duke's coronet); ~-*mark*, naevus birthmark, resembling strawberry; ~ *roan*, red roan; ~ *tree*, European evergreen tree, *Arbutus unedo*, with white flowers and strawberry-like fruit; (U.S.) spindle-tree.
stray *v.i.* Wander, go aimlessly; deviate from right way or (fig.) from virtue; lose one's way; get separated from flock, companions, home, or proper place. ~ *n.* Strayed domestic animal; homeless, friendly person, esp. child; (radio, usu. pl.) atmospherics. ~ *adj.* Strayed; scattered, sporadic, occasional, casually met with.
streak¹ *n.* Thin irregular line of different colour or substance from material or surface in which it occurs; flash (*of* lightning); vein of mineral; trait, strain, element, of character, etc. **strea'kȳ** *adj.* **strea'kilȳ** *adv.* **strea'kinėss** *n.*
streak *v.* Mark with streak(s).
streak² *v.i.* Move very fast.
stream *n.* Body of water flowing in bed, esp. rivulet or brook as dist. from river; current or flow of river, in sea, etc.; flow of any liquid, current of air, gas, etc.; continuous flow of persons etc. moving in one direction, or of words, events, influences, etc.; set of pupils in school grouped according to academic ability; ~-*line*, path of particle of fluid in motion, current of air, etc.; form of body (esp. motor-car or aircraft) calculated to offer minimum of resistance to air, water, etc.; *strea'mline* (*v.t.*) give this shape to; ~ *of consciousness*, (psychol.) thoughts and feelings considered as series of states constantly moving forward in time; (attrib.) applied to style of writing presenting individual's thoughts and feelings as continuous monologue. **strea'mȳ** *adj.* **stream** *v.* Flow or move as a stream; run with liquid; emit stream of; float or wave in wind, current of water, etc.; group (pupils) in stream.
strea'mer *n.* Pennon; ribbon etc. attached at one end and floating or waving at the other; (pl.) Aurora Borealis.
strea'mlėt *n.* Small stream.
street *n.* Road in town or village with houses on one side or both; this with its houses; *the S*~, (esp.) Fleet Street; (U.S.) Wall Street; *in the* ~, said of Stock Exchange business done after closing hours; *on the* ~*s*, living by prostitution; *up one's* ~, in keeping with one's tastes or abilities; *stree'tcar*,(U.S.)tramcar;~-*walker*, prostitute who solicits in street.
strĕngth *n.* Being strong; degree in which person or thing is strong; what makes strong; number of men in army, regiment, etc., of ships in fleet etc., men enrolled; *on the* ~, (mil.) entered on rolls of regiment etc.; *on the* ~ *of*, encouraged by, relying on, arguing from. **strĕ'ngthlėss** *adj.*
strĕ'ngthen *v.* Make, become, stronger.
strĕ'nūous *adj.* Vigorous, energetic, persistently and ardently laborious (esp. of action or effort). **strĕ'nūouslȳ** *adv.* **strĕ'nūousnėss** *n.*
Strĕ'phon. Shepherd whose lament for his lost Urania forms the opening of Sidney's 'Arcadia'; hence, fond lover.
strĕptocŏ'ccus *n.* (pl. *-cī*). Micro-organism of *genus S*~ of bacteria which form chains (ill. BACTERIUM), certain species of which produce infections in man (e.g. scarlet fever, puerperal fever, endocarditis) and are a freq. cause of septicaemia. **strĕptocŏ'ccal** *adj.*
strĕptomȳ'cin *n.* Antibiotic drug, produced from *Actinomyces griseus*, a mould-like micro-organism found in garden soil.
strĕss *n.* 1. Pressure *of* load, weight, some adverse force or influence etc.; condition of

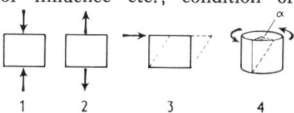

STRESSES AND STRAINS
1: Compressive stress. 2. Tensile stress. 3. Shear stress and strain. 4. Torsional stress and strain. α = angle of twist

things demanding or marked by strained effort; (mech.) force exerted between contiguous bodies or parts of a body. 2. Emphasis; greater relative force of utterance given to one syllable of word, one part of syllable, word in sentence, etc. ~ *v.t.* Lay the stress on, accent, emphasize; subject to mechanical stress; *stressed-skin construction*, (aircraft fuselage, wing, etc.) construction in which some or most of the stresses are borne by the skin (ill. AEROPLANE).
strĕtch *v.* 1. Make taut; tighten, straighten; place in tight-drawn or outspread state; lay (person) flat; (also ~ *oneself*) extend limbs to tighten muscles after sleeping etc.; ~ *one's legs*, take walking exercise; ~ *out*, extend (hand, foot, etc.) by straightening arm or leg; reach out hand. 2. Strain; exert to utmost or beyond legitimate extent; do violence to; exaggerate. 3. Have specified length or extension; be continuous between

[865]

points, to or from a point. 4. Draw, be drawn, admit of being drawn, out into greater length, extension, or size; (slang) hang (person). ~ *n.* Stretching, being stretched; continuous expanse, tract, or spell; (naut.) distance covered on one tack; (slang) term of imprisonment.

stre̓'tcher *n.* (esp.) 1. Brick or stone laid with length in direction of wall (ill. BRICK); bar or rod used as tie or brace, e.g. between legs of chair (ill. CHAIR); board in boat against which rower presses feet (ill. BOAT). 2. Frame on which artist's canvas is spread and drawn tight by wedges etc. 3. Oblong frame, with handles at each end, for carrying sick or wounded persons on; ~-*bearer*, one who helps to carry this.

strew (-ōō) *v.t.* (past part. *-ed* or *-n*). Scatter (sand, flowers, small objects) over a surface; cover (surface, object) *with* small objects scattered.

stri̓'a *n.* (pl. *-ae*). (anat., zool., geol., etc.). Linear mark on surface; slight ridge, furrow, or score; (archit.) fillet between flutes of classical column (ill. ORDER). **stri̓'ate** *adj.* **stri̓'ately** *adv.* **striā'te** *v.t.* **striā'tion** *n.*

stri̓'cken *adj.*: see STRIKE; (esp., of deer etc.) wounded; (of person, mind, etc.) afflicted with disease, frenzy, trouble, grief, etc.; ~ *field*, pitched battle or place where it was fought; ~ *in years*, (archaic) of advanced age.

stri̓'ckle *n.* Rod for striking off grain etc. level with rim of measure.

strict *adj.* 1. Exact, precise, accurately determined or defined. 2. Rigorous, allowing no evasion, stringent; (of discipline etc.) admitting no relaxation or indulgence. **stri̓'ctly** *adv.* **stri̓'ctness** *n.*

stri̓'cture *n.* 1. (usu. pl.) Adverse criticism, critical remark. 2. (path.) Morbid contraction of passage of the body, esp. urethra; contracted part.

stride *v.* (past t. & past part. *strōde*). Walk with long steps; pass over or *over* (obstacle etc.) with one step; bestride. ~ *n.* Striding; long step; distance covered by this; striding gait; *take in one's* ~, (of horse or rider) clear (obstacle) without changing gait; (fig.) deal with incidentally without interrupting course of action etc.

stri̓'dent *adj.* Loud and harsh, grating. **stri̓'dently** *adv.*

stri̓'dūlāte *v.i.* Make harsh grating shrill noise (esp., of grasshoppers etc.) by rubbing together hard parts of body. **strīdūlā'tion** *n.*

strife *n.* Condition of antagonism or discord; contention, struggle, dispute.

stri̓'gil (-j-) *n.* (Gk & Rom. antiq.) Instrument with curved blade for scraping away sweat and dirt from skin at bath etc.

strīke *v.* (past t. *strŭck*, past part. *strŭck* or in some phrases *stri̓'cken*). 1. Hit, hit upon or *on*, deliver blow(s) or stroke(s); afflict (with infirmity or death); (of disease etc.) attack suddenly; (of lightning) descend upon and blast. 2. Produce or record or bring into specified state by strokes or striking; impress, stamp, print (*with device etc.*); coin (money); touch (string or key of instrument), produce (note) thus; (of clock) sound (hour etc.) with stroke(s) on bell etc.; (of hour) be sounded thus; produce (fire, spark) by percussion of flint and steel, friction of match, etc. 3. Arrest attention of; occur to mind of; produce mental impression on, impress *as*. 4. Lower or take down (sail, flag, tent); signify surrender by striking flag, remove tents of (camp etc.); (theatr.) remove (scene etc.). 5. (of body of employees) Cease work by agreement among themselves or by order of trade union etc. in order to obtain remedy for grievance, better working conditions, etc. 6. (Cause to) penetrate; pierce, stab (as) with sharp weapon. 7. Turn in new direction, go *across*, *down*, *over*, etc.; take specified direction. 8. Level (grain etc.) with rim of measure by passing strickle over it. 9. Assume (attitude) suddenly and dramatically. 10. ~ *home*, get blow well in; ~ *in*, intervene in conversation etc.; ~ *off*, cancel, erase, (as) by stroke of pen; print; ~ *off the register*, *rolls*, remove (medical practitioner, solicitor) from official list for misconduct; ~ *out*, erase; open up (path, course) *for* oneself; lay about one with fists etc., begin to swim or skate; ~ *up*, begin to play or sing; start (acquaintance, conversation) esp. rapidly or casually. ~ *n.* 1. Concerted refusal to work by employees till some grievance is remedied; *on* ~, taking part in this; ~-*bound*, immobilized by a strike; ~-*breaker*, one who works for employer whose employees are on strike; ~ *pay*, trade union's allowance to workers on strike. 2. (U.S.) Sudden discovery of rich ore, oil, etc.; (fig.) sudden success or piece of good fortune. 3. (geol.) Horizontal course of stratum (ill. ROCK[1]). 4. (baseball) Unsuccessful attempt to hit pitched ball.

stri̓'ker *n.* (esp.) 1. Employee taking part in industrial strike. 2. Blacksmith's assistant who wields heavy sledge-hammer. 3. (in various games) Player who is to strike (in lawn tennis, opp. *server*); (footb. etc.) player whose function is to drive ball into goal.

stri̓'king *adj.* (esp.) Noticeable, arresting, impressive. **stri̓'kingly** *adv.* **stri̓'kingness** *n.*

string *n.* 1. Thin length of twisted fibre; piece of this or of leather, ribbon, or other material, used for tying up, lacing, drawing together, activating puppet, etc.; bowstring; (fig.) condition or limitation imposed; *first*, *second*, etc., ~, person or thing that chief, alternative, etc., reliance is placed on; *have two* ~*s to one's bow*, have two alternative resources; *pull* (*the*) ~*s*, control course of affairs; exert (esp. hidden) influence; *without* ~*s*, unconditionally. 2. Tendon, nerve, elongated muscle, etc., in animal body; tough piece connecting two halves of pod in beans etc.; thread of viscid substance. 3. Catgut, wire, etc., yielding musical tone(s) when stretched, in piano, harp, violin, and other instruments; (pl.) stringed instruments played with bow, players of these in orchestra etc. 4. Set of or *of* objects strung together; number of animals etc. in single file; set or stud of horses; number of things in row or line; continuous series or succession. 5. ~-*bean*, (U.S.) French or kidney bean; ~-*board*, board supporting ends of steps in staircase (ill. STAIR); ~-*course*, raised horizontal band or course running round or along building (ill. MASONRY); ~-*piece*, long piece of timber connecting and supporting parts of framework (ill. HALF-timber); ~ *quartet*, quartet of stringed instruments, esp. two violins, viola, and violoncello; music for this. ~ *v.* (past t. & past part. *strŭng*). Supply, fit, tie, with string(s); thread (beads etc.) on string; make (bow) ready for use by slipping loop of bow-string into its notch; remove strings of bean-pod; brace *up*, bring to specified condition of sensitiveness or tension; connect, put together in continuous series; arrange in row(s) or series; move in string or disconnected line (esp. ~ *out*).

stringed (-ngd) *adj.* (esp., of musical instruments) Having strings. (*Illustration, p. 840.*)

stri̓'ngent (-j-) *adj.* (of regulations, obligations, etc.) Rigorous, strict, binding, requiring exact performance. **stri̓'ngently** *adv.* **stri̓'ngency** *n.*

stri̓'nger *n.* Longitudinal stiffening member used in construction of ships (e.g. *deck* ~, *side* ~) and aircraft (ill. AEROPLANE).

stri̓'ngy (-ngi) *adj.* Fibrous, like string; (of liquid) ropy.

strip[1] *n.* Long narrow piece or tract (of textile material, land, paper, etc.); narrow flat bar of iron or steel, iron or steel in this form; strip CARTOON; ~ *lighting*, lighting with usu. tubular lamps arranged in line; ~-*mill*, place where steel slabs are rolled into strips for manufacture of tinplate.

strip[2] *v.* Denude, lay bare; deprive *of* covering, appurtenance, or property; undress; pull or tear off, *off* or *from* something; tear off (thread from screw, teeth from wheel); remove stalk and midrib from (tobacco-leaf); ~-*tease*,

[866]

STRIP

entertainment in which a young woman divests herself of her garments one by one before an audience. **stri′pper** *n.* (esp.) 1. Performer of strip-tease. 2. Device or solvent for removing paint, varnish, etc.

part. *stri′ven*). Endeavour, try hard, struggle; contend, vie.
strōbe *n.* (colloq.) Stroboscope; stroboscopic lamp.
strŏ′bīle *n.* (bot.) Cone of pine etc., inflorescence made up of imbricated scales (ill. CONIFER).

STRINGED INSTRUMENTS OF THE VIOLIN FAMILY WITH BOWS
A. VIOLIN. B. VIOLA. C. VIOLONCELLO OR CELLO. D. DOUBLE-BASS

1. Scroll. 2. Peg or pin. 3. Neck. 4. Finger-board. 5. Back. 6. Belly. 7. Bouts. 8. Bridge. 9. G string. 10. Tail-piece. 11. Chin-rest. 12. Sound hole or *f*-hole

strip³ *v.* Extract last milk from udder of (cow).
stripe¹ *n.* (archaic; chiefly pl.) Stroke or lash with whip etc.
stripe² *n.* Long narrow portion, usu. of uniform width, on surface, differing in colour or texture from adjacent parts; narrow strip of cloth, braid, etc., sewn on garment, esp. chevron indicating rank of non-commissioned officer.
stri′pў *adj.* **stripe** *v.t.* Mark, ornament, with stripe(s). **strīped** (-pt) *adj.*
strī′plīng *n.* Youth approaching manhood.
strīve *v.i.* (past t. *strōve*, past

strŏ′boscōpe *n.* 1. Instrument for determining speed of rotation or frequency of oscillation. 2. Kind of lamp used in instantaneous photography of rapidly moving objects. **strŏ′boscŏ′pic** *adj.*
strode: see STRIDE.
strōke¹ *n.* 1. Blow, shock given by blow; apoplectic or paralytic seizure; damaging or destructive discharge (of lightning). 2. Single effort put forth, one complete performance of recurrent action or movement; time or way in which such movements are performed; act or method of striking ball etc. in games; specially successful or

STRONG

skilful effort; ~ *of genius*, original or strikingly successful idea; ~ *of luck*, unforeseen opportune occurrence. 3. Mark made by movement in one direction of pen, pencil, paintbrush, etc.; detail in description etc. 4. Sound made by striking clock; *on the* ~ *of*, exactly at specified hour. 5. Oarsman rowing nearest stern and setting time of stroke. ~ *v.t.* Act as stroke to (boat, crew).
strōke² *v.t.* Pass hand etc. softly and usu. repeatedly in one direction over (hair, skin, etc.), as caress etc.; (needlework) arrange (gathers) neatly by drawing blunt point downwards from top of each; ~ *down*, soothe, mollify; ~ *the wrong away*, irritate, ruffle. ~ *n.* Act, spell, of stroking.
strōll *n.* Leisurely walk or ramble, saunter. ~ *v.i.* Walk in leisurely fashion; *strolling company, players*, etc., actors travelling about and giving performances in temporary buildings etc.
strō′ma *n.* 1. (anat.) Supporting framework of organ, usu. of connective tissue; spongy framework of red blood corpuscle etc. 2. (bot.) Fungous tissue in which perithecia or other organs of fructification are immersed. **stromă′tic** *adj.*
Strŏ′mbolī. One of the Lipari islands in the Mediterranean; an active volcano on this island.
strŏng *adj.* 1. Physically powerful, vigorous, or robust; performed with muscular strength; having great muscular, moral, or mental power or strength; powerful in arms, numbers, equipment, authority, etc. 2. Difficult to capture, break into, invade, or escape from, capable of resisting force or strain, resistant, tough. 3. Energetic, effective, vigorous, decided. 4. Convincing, striking; powerfully affecting the senses, passions, mind, etc. 5. (of drink) Having large proportion of flavouring element, solid ingredient, alcohol, etc. 6. (gram., of verbs) Forming inflexions by vowel-change in root syllable, rather than by addition of suffixes. 7. ~-*arm*, (colloq.) using force; ~-*box*, strongly made chest or safe for money, documents, etc.; ~ *drink*, alcoholic liquors; *stro′nghold*, fortified place; secure place of refuge or retreat; centre of support for cause etc.; ~ *man*, (esp.) one who performs feats of strength for entertainment; (colloq.) dictator; ~-*minded*, having strong, vigorous, or determined mind; ~ *point*, (esp.) something in which person excels; ~-*point*, (mil.) specially fortified position in a defence system; ~-*room*, fire- and burglar-proof room for valuables; ~ *waters*, (archaic) spirits.
strŏ′nglў *adv.* **strŏng** *adv. come it, go it* ~, act vigorously, boldly, recklessly, etc.; *be going* ~, be vigorous, thriving, or prosperous.

[867]

strŏ'ntia (-sha) *n.* Alkaline earth (SrO) the monoxide of strontium. **strŏ'ntian** *adj.* ~ *yellow*, (pigment of colour of) strontium chromate. **strŏ'ntianīte** *n.* Mineral, strontium carbonate. [f. *Strontian* in Highland]

strŏ'ntium (-shum) *n.* Soft easily fusible metallic element (silver-white when pure); symbol Sr, at. no. 38, at. wt 87·62; ~ *90*, radioactive isotope of strontium which is present in fall-out of nuclear fission and if ingested concentrates in bone-marrow.

strŏp *n.* 1. Strip of leather for sharpening razor, implement or machine serving same purpose. 2. Rope or sling for handling cargo. ~ *v.t.* Sharpen on or with strop.

strophă'nthĭn *n.* White crystalline bitter poisonous glucoside, used as a heart tonic, obtained from various species of *Strophanthus*, genus of plants of tropical Africa and Asia.

strŏ'phĕ *n.* (Lines recited during) movement made from right to left by chorus in ancient Greek choral dance; series of lines forming division of lyric poem. **strŏ'phic** *adj.*

strŭ'ctural (-kcher-) *adj.* Of structure; ~ *engineering*, design and construction of large structures, as dams, bridges, etc.; ~ *steel*, strong mild steel in shapes specially suitable for structural purposes. **strŭ'cturallў** *adv.*

strŭ'cture *n.* 1. Manner in which building or other complete whole is constructed; supporting framework or whole of essential parts of something; make, construction. 2. Thing constructed; complex whole; building. ~ *v.t.* Arrange, organize, give a structure to.

strŭ'ggle *v.i.* Throw one's limbs about in violent effort to escape grasp etc.; make violent or determined efforts under difficulties, strive hard; contend *with*, *against*, make one's way with difficulty *through*, *along*, etc. ~ *n.* Struggling; resolute contest, continued effort to resist force, free oneself from constraint etc.; determined effort or resistance; ~ *for existence*, *life*, competition between organic species, esp. as element in natural selection; continued effort to maintain life or obtain means of livelihood. **strŭ'ggling** *adj.* (esp.) Experiencing difficulty in making a living, getting recognition, etc. **strŭ'gglinglў** *adv.*

Strŭ'ldbrŭg *n.* In Swift's 'Gulliver's Travels', one of those endowed with immortality but not retaining or renewing youthful vigour.

strŭm *v.* Touch notes or twang strings of piano or other stringed instrument; play, esp. unskilfully, *on* (piano, guitar, etc.). ~ *n.* Sound made by strumming.

stru'ma (-oo-) *n.* 1. (med.) Goitre, or (formerly) scrofulous swelling. 2. (bot.) Cushion-like cellular dilatation of an organ. **stru'mōse, stru'mous** *adjs.*

strŭ'mpĕt *n.* (archaic) Prostitute.

strung: see STRING.

strŭt[1] *n. & v.i.* (Walk with) pompous or affected stiff gait.

strŭt[2] *n.* Bar, rod, etc., of wood, iron, etc., inserted in framework to resist pressure or thrust in direction of its length (ill. ROOF); brace. ~ *v.t.* Brace with strut(s).

'struth (-oo-) *int.* Exclamation (short for *God's truth*) used as oath.

strў'chnĭc (-k-) *adj.* Of strychnine; ~ *acid*, white crystalline substance obtained by heating strychnine with alkali.

strў'chnine (-knēn) *n.* Highly poisonous vegetable alkaloid obtained from plants of genus *Strychnos*, esp. the nux vomica, used in medicine as stimulant and tonic.

S.T.S. *abbrev.* Scottish Text Society.

Sts. *abbrev.* Saints.

Stū'art. Name of royal house of Scotland from the accession (1371) of Robert II, one of the hereditary stewards of Scotland, and of England from the accession of James VI of Scotland to the English throne as James I (1603) to the death of Queen Anne (1714).

stŭb *n.* Stump of tree, tooth, etc., left projecting; short remnant *of* pencil, cigar, etc.; pen with short blunt point; counterfoil of cheque, ticket, receipt, etc. ~ *v.t.* Grub up (stubs, roots), clear (land) of stubs; hurt (toe) by striking it against something; extinguish (cigarette) by crushing lighted end against something hard.

stŭ'bble *n.* Lower ends of grainstalks left in ground after harvest; short stubble-like growth of hair esp. on unshaven face.

stŭ'bborn *adj.* Unreasonably obstinate, obdurate, refractory, intractable. **stŭ'bbornlў** *adv.* **stŭ'bbornnĕss** (-n-n-) *n.*

Stŭbbs[1] (-z), George (1724–1806). English painter and engraver of horses.

Stŭbbs[2] (-z), William (1825–1901). English constitutional historian; bishop of Oxford 1889–1901.

stŭ'ccō *n.* Fine plaster used to cover walls, ceilings, etc., and for making cornices, mouldings, etc.; coarse plaster or cement for covering exterior surfaces of walls in imitation of stone. ~ *v.t.* Coat or ornament with stucco.

stŭck *adj.*: see STICK; (esp., of animal) that has been stabbed or had throat cut; ~-*up*, (colloq.) conceited, insolently exclusive.

stŭd[1] *n.* 1. Large-headed nail, boss, or knob, projecting from surface, esp. for ornament; rivet, cross-piece in each link of chain-cable; kind of two-headed button passed through one or more eyelets or buttonholes, esp. in shirt-front or to fasten collar to shirt. 2. Upright post in framing for lath-and-plaster partition walls (ill. HALF-timber); (chiefly U.S.) height of room as indicated by length of this. ~ *v.t.* Set with studs; be scattered over or about (surface). **stŭ'ddĕd** *adj.* (esp.) Thickly set or strewn *with*. **stŭ'ddĭng** *n.* (esp.) Woodwork of lath-and-plaster wall.

stŭd[2] *n.* Number of horses kept for breeding, hunting, racing, etc.; place where stud, esp. for breeding, is kept; ~-*book*, book giving pedigree of thoroughbred horses; ~-*farm*, place where horses are bred; ~-*horse*, stallion; ~-*poker*, (cards) kind of poker in which all but first round of cards are dealt face up.

stŭ'ddĭng-sail (*or* stŭ'nsl) *n.* = STUNSAIL.

stŭ'dent *n.* 1. Person engaged in or addicted to study; person undergoing instruction at university or other place of higher education or technical training. 2. (at some colleges) One who receives emoluments from foundation to enable him to pursue studies, scholar or fellow. **stŭ'dentship** *n.*

stŭ'dĭō *n.* (pl. -*s*). Work-room of sculptor, painter, photographer, etc.; room in which cinema-play is staged; room or premises used for transmission of broadcasts, or for making films or recordings; ~ *couch*, couch which opens out to form a bed.

stŭ'dĭous *adj.* Given to study, devoted to learning; careful to do, anxiously desirous *of*; studied, deliberate, zealous, anxious, painstaking. **stŭ'dĭouslў** *adv.* **stŭ'dĭousnĕss** *n.*

stu'dĭum gĕnera'lĕ (stoo-, -ah-). (hist.) University. [L, = 'general study']

stŭ'dў *n.* 1. Devotion of time and thought to acquisition of information esp. from books; (freq. pl.) pursuit of some branch of knowledge; careful examination or observation *of* (subject, question, object, etc.). 2. Thing to be secured by pains or attention; thing that is or deserves to be investigated. 3. Literary composition devoted to detailed consideration of a subject or problem or executed as exercise or experiment in style etc. 4. (painting etc.) Careful sketch made for practice in technique or as preliminary experiment for picture etc. or part of it; (mus.) composition designed to develop player's skill. 5. (theatr.) Learning of parts in play; *good*, *slow*, ~, person who learns part quickly, slowly. 6. Room used for literary occupation. ~ *v.* Make a study of, take pains to investigate or acquire knowledge of (subject) or to assure (desired result); examine carefully, read attentively, investigate (object); apply oneself to study; take pains *to* do. **stŭ′died** (-ĭd) *adj.* (esp.) Deliberate, intentional, affected.

stŭff *n.* 1. Material of which thing is made or which is or may be used for some purpose; articles of food or drink, produce of garden, farm, etc.; commodity dealt in or produced. 2. Textile material, esp. woollen fabric; ~ *gown*, gown of junior counsel. 3. Valueless matter; trash, nonsense; *do one's* ~, do what is required or what one is expected to do. ~ *v.* Pack, cram; stop *up*, fill; distend; fill out (skin of bird, beast, etc.) with material to restore original shape; fill (inside of bird, piece of meat, etc.) with forcemeat, seasoned breadcrumbs, herbs, etc., before cooking; cram food into, gorge (food); gorge oneself, eat greedily; ram or press into receptacle; gull, hoax, humbug. **stŭ′ffing** *n.* (esp.) Ingredients for stuffing fowl etc. in cookery; *knock the* ~ *out of* (person), reduce to state of flabbiness or weakness.

stŭ′ffy *adj.* Lacking fresh air or ventilation, close, fusty; without freshness, interest, smartness, etc.; easily offended or shocked, straitlaced. **stŭ′ffily** *adv.* **stŭ′ffiness** *n.*

stŭ′ltify *v.t.* Reduce to foolishness or absurdity; render worthless or useless; exhibit in ridiculous light.

stŭm *n.* Unfermented or partly fermented grape-juice, must. ~ *v.t.* Prevent from fermenting, secure (wine) against further fermentation in cask, by introduction of antiseptic.

stŭ′mble *v.* Lurch forward, have partial fall, from catching or striking foot or making false step; make blunder(s) in doing something; come accidentally *on* or *across*; *stumbling-block*, obstacle; circumstance that causes difficulty, hesitation, or scruples. **stŭ′mblingly** *adv.* **stŭ′mble** *n.* Act of stumbling.

stŭ′mer *n.* (slang) Worthless cheque, counterfeit coin or note.

stŭmp *n.* Projecting remnant of cut or fallen tree; part remaining of broken branch or tooth, brokenoff mast, amputated limb, etc.; fag-end, stub, of cigar, pencil, etc.; stalk of plant (esp. cabbage) with leaves removed; (pl., joc.) legs; stump of tree used by orator to address meeting from; cylinder of rolled paper etc. for softening pencil-marks and other uses in drawing; (cricket) one of three uprights of wicket (ill. CRICKET); ~ *speech*, open-air speech. ~ *v.* 1. Walk stiffly, clumsily, and noisily. 2. (cricket, of wicket-keeper) Put (batsman who is not in his ground) out by dislodging bail(s) while holding ball. 3. Nonplus, pose, cause to be at a loss. 4. Make stump speeches; traverse (district) doing this. 5. Use stump on (drawing etc.).

6. ~ *up*, pay over money required, produce (sum).

stŭ′mper *n.* (cricket) Wicket-keeper.

stŭ′mpy *adj.* Thickset, stocky; of small height or length in proportion to girth. **stŭ′mpily** *adv.* **stŭ′mpiness** *n.*

stŭn *v.t.* (of blow etc.) Knock senseless, reduce to insensibility or stupor; daze, bewilder, with strong emotion, din, etc. **stŭ′nner** *n.* (esp., slang) Stunning person or thing. **stŭ′nning** *adj.* (esp., slang) Splendid, delightful.

stung : see STING.

stunk : see STINK.

stŭ′nsail, stŭ′ns'l *n.* Sail set on small extra yard and boom beyond leech of square sail in light winds (ill. SHIP).

stŭnt[1] *n.* (colloq.) Special effort, feat; showy performance, skilful trick or manœuvre, esp. with aircraft; advertising device intended to attract public attention. ~ *v.i.* Perform stunt.

stŭnt[2] *v.t.* Retard growth or development of, dwarf, cramp.

stū′pa *n.* Monument, usu. dome-like, erected over relics of Buddha or at place associated with him.

stū′pefy *v.t.* Make stupid or torpid, deprive of sensibility; stun with amazement, fear, etc. **stūpefă′ction** *n.*

stūpĕ′ndous *adj.* Prodigious, astounding, esp. by size or degree. **stūpĕ′ndously** *adv.* **stūpĕ′ndousness** *n.*

stū′pid *adj.* In a state of stupor or lethargy; dull by nature, slow-witted, obtuse, crass, characteristic of persons of this nature; uninteresting, dull. **stū′pidly** *adv.* **stūpi′dity** *n.* **stū′pidness** *n.* Stupid person.

stū′por *n.* Dazed state, torpidity; helpless amazement.

stŭr′dy[1] *adj.* Robust, hardy, vigorous, strongly built. **stŭr′dily** *adv.* **stŭr′diness** *n.*

stŭr′dy[2] *n.* Vertigo in sheep and cattle caused by tapeworm in brain.

stŭr′geon (-jon) *n.* Any of various large fishes of rivers, lakes, and coastal waters of north temperate zone, with long almost cylindrical body and long tapering snout, esteemed as food and the source of caviare and isinglass, esp. *Acipenser sturio* of Atlantic coastal regions of Europe and N. America.

stŭ′tter *v.* Stammer; speak or say with continued involuntary repetition of parts of words, esp. initial consonants. ~ *n.* Act or habit of stuttering.

stȳ[1] *n.* (also *pigsty*) 1. Pen or enclosure for pigs. 2. Filthy room or dwelling. ~ *v.* Lodge in sty.

stȳ[2], **stye** *n.* Inflamed swelling on edge of eyelid.

Stȳ′gian *adj.* (As) of the Styx or of Hades; murky, gloomy, black as the Styx.

stȳle *n.* 1. Ancient writing-implement, small rod with pointed end for scratching letters on wax-covered tablets, and flat broad end for erasing and smoothing tablet; (poet.) pen, pencil; style-like thing, as graver, blunt-pointed probe, gnomon of sundial; (bot.) narrowed prolongation of ovary supporting stigma (ill. FLOWER); (zool.) small slender pointed process or part; pointed sponge-spicule. 2. Manner of writing, speaking, or doing, esp. as opp. to the matter expressed or thing done; manner of execution of work of art etc.; manner characteristic of person, school, period, etc.; (esp. correct or pleasing) way of doing something; kind, sort, pattern, type; mode of behaviour, manner of life; fashion, distinction, noticeably superior quality or manner, esp. with regard to appearance. 3. Descriptive formula, designation of person or thing; full title. 4. Mode of expressing dates; *New S*~, (abbrev. N.S.) according to the reformed or GREGORIAN calendar; *Old S*~, (abbrev. O.S.) according to the JULIAN calendar, used by all Christian nations until 1582. ~ *v.t.* Call by specified name or style; design, arrange, make, etc. in (esp. fashionable) style.

stȳ′lĕt *n.* Stiletto; graving-tool, pointed marking instrument; (surg.) slender probe, wire run through catheter for stiffening or cleaning; (zool.) piercing mouth-part of insects etc.

stȳ′lish *adj.* Noticeably conforming to fashionable standard of elegance; having good style. **stȳ′lishly** *adv.* **stȳ′lishness** *n.*

stȳ′list *n.* Person having or aiming at good style in writing or doing something. **stȳ′listic** *adj.* Of literary or artistic style. **stȳli′stically** *adv.*

stȳ′lite, stȳli′tēs (-z) *ns.* Medieval ascetic living on top of a pillar; SIMEON STYLITES: see entry.

stȳ′līze *v.t.* Conform (work of art etc., or part of it) to the rules of a conventional style. **stȳlīzā′tion** *n.*

stȳ′lō *n.* Stylograph.

stȳ′lobāte *n.* Continuous base supporting row(s) of columns (ill. ORDER).

stȳ′lŏgrăph (*or* -ahf) *n.* Fountain-pen with ink flowing from reservoir through fine perforated writing-point. **stȳlŏgră′phic** *adj.*

stȳlohy′oid *adj.* & *n.* (Muscle) connecting styloid process and hyoid bone.

stȳ′loid *adj.* Slender, pointed; ~ *process*, process projecting from base of temporal bone in man (ill. HEAD). ~ *n.* Styloid process.

stȳlomă′stoid *adj.* Common to the styloid and mastoid processes.

stȳlopō′dium *n.* (pl. *-dia*) Fleshy swelling at base of style in plants of carrot family.

stȳ′lus *n.* Style, ancient writing-

sty'mie n. (formerly, in golf) Position on the putting-green in which the opponent's ball lies in a direct line between the player's ball and the hole. ~ v.t. Put into position of having to negotiate stymie (freq. fig.).

sty'ptic adj. & n. (Substance) that contracts organic tissue and checks bleeding.

styr'ax n. Plant of genus S~ which comprises the storaxes.

styr'ene n. Liquid hydrocarbon ($C_6H_5CH:CH_2$), used as basis for many plastics.

Sty'ria. Province, formerly duchy, of S. Austria. **Sty'rian** adj. & n.

Styx. (Gk myth.) River of Hades over which Charon ferried the shades of the dead.

suā'sion (swā-) n. Persuasion, esp. in *moral* ~.

suave (swahv) adj. Bland, soothing, polite. **sua'vely** adv. **suā'vity** n.

sub n. Short for subaltern, submarine, subscription, substitute; money in advance on account of wages. ~ v. Pay or receive (part of wages in advance); sub-edit; substitute.

sub- prefix. (freq. with small letter changed by assimilation) 1. Under, below. 2. More or less, roughly; not quite; on the borders of. 3. Subordinate(ly); secondary; further.

subā'cid adj. Moderately acid or tart; somewhat biting.

subacū'te adj. (med.) Between acute and chronic.

sub-ā'gent n. Subordinate agent.

subahdār' (soo-) n. (hist., in India) 1. Provincial governor. 2. Chief native officer of company of sepoys. [Hind. (*sūba* province, *dār* master)]

subă'lpine adj. Of higher slopes of mountains (about 4,000-5,500 ft), between the Alp line and the timber line.

su'baltern adj. 1. Of inferior rank; subordinate. 2. (logic, of a proposition) Particular, not universal. ~ n. (mil.) Junior officer below rank of captain.

subā'queous adj. Existing, formed, performed or taking place, under water; adapted for use under water.

subar'ctic adj. Of regions somewhat south of Arctic Circle or resembling these in climate etc.

subato'mic adj. Occurring in, smaller than, an atom.

su'b-bā'sement (-sm-) n. Storey below basement.

subclā'vian adj. Lying or extending under clavicle; ~ *artery*, main trunk of arterial system of upper extremity (ill. BLOOD). ~ n. Subclavian artery, vein, or muscle.

subcli'nical adj. (of disease) Not yet presenting definite symptoms.

su'bcommittee n. Committee formed from main committee for special purpose.

subcō'nscious (-shus) adj. Of part of mind or mental field outside range of attention or imperfectly or partially conscious. ~ n. Subconscious part of mind.

subcō'ntinent n. Land-mass of great extent but smaller than those generally called continents.

subcō'ntract n. Contract for carrying out (part of) previous contract. **subcontra'ct** v. Make subcontract (for). **subcontra'ctor** n.

subcor'tical adj. Situated, formed, etc., below a cortex, esp. the cortex of the brain.

subcō'stal adj. Below a rib.

subcutā'neous adj. Lying, living, performed, etc., under the skin; hypodermic.

subdea'con n. (in some branches of the Church) Minister of order next below deacon; cleric or lay clerk assisting next below deacon at solemn celebration of Eucharist, epistoler.

subdiā'conate n. Office of subdeacon.

subdivī'de v. Divide again after first division. **subdivi'sion** n. Subdividing; subordinate division; (mil.) half of division.

subdŏ'minant n. (mus.) 4th note of ascending scale (ill. SCALE³).

subdū'e v.t. Conquer, subjugate, overcome, prevail over; reduce intensity, force, or vividness of (sound, colour, light).

sub-ĕ'dit v.t. Act as assistant editor of (paper etc.), prepare (copy) for supervision of editor. **sub-ĕ'ditor** n.

subēr'eous (or soo-), **su'berōse, su'berous** (or soo-) adjs. (bot.) Of, like, cork, corky.

subĕ'ric (or soo-) adj. Of cork; (chem.) ~ *acid*, white crystalline dibasic acid obtained by action of nitric acid on cork etc.

su'b-fă'mily n. (zool.) Taxonomic category below family and above tribe or genus.

sub fī'něm (or soob fē-). Towards the end (of chapter etc. referred to). [L]

subfū'sc adj. Dusky, dull, or sombre in colour. ~ n. Dark clothes worn on formal occasions in some universities.

su'b-head, -heading (-ĕd-) ns. Subordinate division of subject etc.; subordinate heading or title in chapter, article, etc.

sub-hū'man adj. Less than human; not quite human.

sub-i'ndex n. (math.) Inferior index written to right of symbol.

subjā'cent adj. Underlying, situated below.

su'bject n. 1. Person owing allegiance to government or ruling power esp. sovereign; any member of a State except the Sovereign, any member of a subject State. 2. (logic, gram.) That member of a proposition or sentence about which something is predicated; substantive word, phrase, or clause governing a verb. 3. (philos.) Thinking or feeling entity, the mind, the ego, the conscious self, as opp. to all that is external to the mind; the substance of anything as opp. to its attributes. 4. Theme of or *of* discussion or description or representation; matter (to be) treated of or dealt with; department of study. 5. (mus.) Principal phrase of a composition or movement; *first, second, ~,* first, second, to be introduced. 6. (chiefly med.) Person of specified usu. undesirable bodily or mental characteristics, as *hysterical, sensitive, ~.* 7. ~ *catalogue, index,* etc., catalogue, index, listing books, etc., according to subject; ~ *-heading,* heading in index collecting references to a subject; ~ *-matter,* matter treated of in book etc. ~ adj. Under government, not independent, owing obedience *to*; liable, exposed, or prone *to*; ~ *to,* conditional(ly) upon, on the assumption of. **subjě'ct** v.t. Subdue, make subject, (*to* one's sway etc.); expose, make liable, treat, *to.* **subjě'ction** n.

subjě'ctive adj. 1. Of, proceeding from, taking place within the thinking subject, having its source in the mind; personal, individual; introspective; imaginary, illusory. 2. (gram.) Of the subject; ~ *case,* nominative. **subjě'ctively** adv. **subjě'ctiveness, subjěcti'vity** ns.

subjě'ctivism n. Philosophical theory that all knowledge is merely subjective. **subjě'ctivist** n.

subjoi'n v.t. Add at the end, append.

sub ju'dĭce (joo-). (law, of case) Under judicial consideration, not yet decided. [L]

su'bjugāte (-joo-) v.t. Bring under the yoke or into subjection, subdue, vanquish. **subjugā'tion** n.

subjŭ'nctive adj. (gram.) Of a verbal mood used in classical language chiefly in subordinate or subjoined clauses; obsolescent in English exc. in certain uses, e.g. to express wish (*I wish it were over*), imprecation (*manners* be hanged!), and contingent or hypothetical events (*if he were here now*). **subjŭ'nctively** adv. **subjŭ'nctive** n. Subjunctive mood.

su'blease n. Lease granted to subtenant. **sublea'se** v.t. Let to subtenant.

sub-lě't v.t. (past t. & past part. *-let*). Let to subtenant.

sub-lieute'nant (-lĕft-, in navy *-let-*; U.S. -lōōt-) n. Officer ranking next below lieutenant.

su'blimate n. (chem.) Solid produced when a substance is sublimed. **su'blimāte** v.t. 1. (chem., obs.) = SUBLIME². 2. Transmute into something nobler, more sublime or refined; (psychol.)

divert energy of (primitive impulse) into activity socially more useful or regarded as higher in cultural or moral scale. **sŭblimā'tion** n. Action, process, of subliming or sublimating.
subli'me[1] *adj.* Of the most exalted kind, aloof from and raised far above the ordinary; inspiring awe, deep reverence, or lofty emotion by beauty, vastness, grandeur, etc.; *S~ Porte*: see PORTE. **subli'mely** *adv.* **subli'mity** n. **subli'me** n. What is sublime, sublimity.
subli'me[2] v. 1. (chem.) Subject (substance) to action of heat so as to convert it to vapour which on cooling is deposited in solid form; purify (substance) by this means; (of substance) undergo this process; pass from solid to gaseous state without liquefaction. 2. (fig.) Purify or elevate, become pure, as by sublimation; make sublime.
subli'minal *adj.* (psychol.) Below threshold of consciousness, too faint or rapid to be recognized; *~ advertising*, advertising done e.g. by rapid flashes on cinema or television screen which though not consciously seen by observers may affect their subsequent behaviour.
subli'ngual (-nggwal) *adj.* Under the tongue.
sublū'nary (*or* -lōō-) *adj.* Beneath the moon; between orbits of moon and earth; subject to moon's influence; of this world, earthly, terrestrial.
sŭb-machi'ne-gŭn (-shēn-) n. Light-weight machine-gun fired from waist or shoulder (ill. GUN).
sŭ'b-mănn *n.* (pl. *-men*). Markedly inferior, brutal or stupid, man.
sŭbmăr'ginal *adj.* Situated near margin.
sŭbmari'ne (-ēn; *or* sŭ'-) *adj.* Existing or lying under surface of sea; operating, operated, constructed, laid, intended for use, under surface of sea. *~ n.* Vessel,

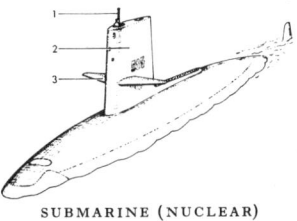

SUBMARINE (NUCLEAR)
1. Periscope. 2. Conning-tower.
3. Hydroplane

esp. warship, which can be submerged and navigated under water, used esp. for carrying and launching torpedoes and other missiles. **sŭbmă'riner** n. Member of crew of submarine.
sŭbmă'xillary (*or* -ĭ'l-) *adj.* Beneath lower jaw.
sŭbmē'diant n. (mus.) 6th note of ascending scale (ill. SCALE[3]).
sŭbmēr'ge v. (Cause to) sink or plunge under water. **submēr'gence, submēr'sion** ns.
submi'ssion n. Submissive, yielding, or deferential attitude, condition, conduct, etc.; submitting, being submitted.
submi'ssive *adj.* Inclined to submit, yielding to power or authority, humble, obedient. **submi'ssively** *adv.* **submi'ssiveness** n.
submi't v. 1. Surrender oneself, become subject, yield (*to* person, his authority, etc., or *to* judgement, criticism, or condition, etc.). 2. Bring under notice or consideration of person, refer *to* his decision or judgement; urge or represent deferentially (*that*).
sŭbnôr'mal *adj.* Less than normal, below normal.
sŭb-nū'clear *adj.* Occurring in, smaller than, an atomic nucleus.
sŭbôr'bital *adj.* Of less duration or distance than one orbit.
sŭ'bôrder n. (zool., bot.) Subdivision of order next below order in classification.
subôr'dinate *adj.* Of inferior importance of rank, secondary, subservient; (gram., of clause) dependent, being syntactically equivalent to noun, adjective, or adverb. *~ n.* Person under control or orders of superior. **subôr'dināte** *v.t.* Make subordinate, treat or regard as of minor importance, bring or put into subservient relation (*to*). **subôrdinā'tion** n. **subôr'dinative** *adj.*
subôr'n *v.t.* Bribe, induce, or procure (person) by underhand or unlawful means to commit perjury or other unlawful act. **subôrnā'tion** n.
sŭ'b-plŏt n. Secondary plot in play etc.
subpoe'na (-pēn-) n. Writ commanding person's attendance in court of justice. *~ v.t.* Serve subpoena on. [L *sub poena*, = 'under penalty', first words of writ]
sŭbpri'or n. Prior's assistant and deputy.
sŭbrogā'tion n. (law) Substitution of one party for another as creditor so that the same rights and duties apply.
sŭb rō'sa (-za). In confidence, in secret. [L = 'under the rose']
subscri'be v. 1. Write (one's name) at foot of document, sign one's name to (document etc.), signify assent or adhesion *to* by signing one's name; put one's signature *to* in token of assent, approval, etc.; express one's agreement etc. 2. Enter one's name in list of contributors: make or promise a contribution, contribute (specified sum) *to* or *to* common fund, society, etc., or *for* common object, raise or guarantee raising of by subscribing thus; *~ to*, undertake to buy (periodical) regularly. **subscri'ber** n. (esp.) One who rents telephone equipment for use via an exchange. **subscri'ption** n.

sŭ'bscript *adj.* Written below or underneath (math. etc., of index written below and to right of symbol, Gk gram., of *iota* written under ā, ē, or ō).
sŭ'bsĕction n. Subordinate division of section.
sŭ'bsĕquent *adj.* Following in order, time, or succession, esp. coming immediately after; (of stream or valley) tributary to CONSEQUENT stream or valley. **sŭ'bsĕquently** *adv.* **sŭ'bsĕquence** n.
subsēr've *v.t.* Be instrumental in furthering or promoting.
subsēr'vient *adj.* 1. Serving as means to further end or purpose. 2. Subordinate, subject (*to*); cringing, truckling, obsequious. **subsēr'viently** *adv.* **subsēr'vience** n.
subsi'de *v.i.* Sink down, sink to low(er) level (esp. of liquids or soil sinking to normal level); (of swelling etc.) go down; (of person, usu. joc.) sink *into*, *on to*, chair etc.; (of storm, strong feeling, clamour, etc.) abate, become less agitated, violent, or active; cease from activity or agitation. **sŭ'bsidence** (*or* -sī'-) *n.*
subsi'diary *adj.* Serving to assist or supplement, auxiliary, supplementary; subordinate, secondary; *~ company*, one of which another company (the 'holding company') holds more than half issued share capital. *~ n.* Subsidiary person or thing; subsidiary company.
sŭ'bsidīze *v.t.* Pay subsidy to.
sŭ'bsidy n. 1. Money grant from one State to another in return for military or naval aid etc. 2. Financial aid given by government towards expenses of an undertaking or institution held to be of public utility, or to producers of commodity etc. to enable goods or services to be provided at low(er) cost to consumer. 3. (Engl. hist.) Pecuniary aid granted to sovereign by Parliament for special needs.
sŭb sĭlĕ'ntĭō (*or* -shĭō). In silence, without remark; in hushed-up manner, privately. [L]
subsi'st v. 1. Exist as a reality; continue to exist, remain in being. 2. Maintain, support, keep, provide food or funds for, provision; maintain or support oneself.
subsi'stence n. Subsisting; means of supporting life, livelihood; *~ allowance*, allowance granted to employee for living expenses while travelling on employer's business; *~ diet*, minimum amount of food required to support life; *~ farming*, farming in which produce is consumed by farm household, with little or no surplus for selling.
sŭ'bsoil n. Soil lying immediately under surface soil; *~ plough*, plough with no mould-board, used to loosen soil at some depth below surface in ploughed furrows.
sŭbsŏ'nic *adj.* (of aircraft etc.)

[871]

Having speed less than that of sound (opp. SUPERSONIC).
sŭbspē′cies (-shēz *or* -shĭz) *n.* Subdivision of species.
sŭ′bstance *n.* 1. (philos.) What underlies phenomena, permanent substratum of things, that in which accidents or attributes inhere; essential nature; essence or most important part of anything, purport, real meaning. 2. Theme, subject-matter, material, esp. as opp. to form; reality, solidity, solid or real thing. 3. (archaic) Possessions, wealth. 4. Particular kind or species of matter.
sŭb-stă′ndard *adj.* Of less than required or normal quality or size.
substă′ntial (-shal) *adj.* 1. Having substance, actually existing, not illusory; of real importance or value, of considerable amount. 2. Of solid material or structure, not flimsy, stout; possessed of property, well-to-do, commercially sound. 3. That is such essentially, virtual, practical. **substă′ntially** *adv.* **substăntiă′lity** (-shĭ-).
substă′ntialism (-shal-) *n.* (philos.) Doctrine that there are substantial realities underlying phenomena.
substă′ntialize (-shal-) *v.* Invest with or acquire substance.
substă′ntiāte (-shĭ-) *v.t.* Give substantial form to; demonstrate or verify by proof or evidence. **substăntiā′tion** *n.*
substantī′val *adj.* Of, consisting of, substantive(s). **substantī′vally** *adv.*
sŭ′bstantive *adj.* 1. Having a separate and independent existence, not merely inferential or implicit or subservient. 2. (gram.) Expressing existence; denoting a substance; ~ *verb*, the verb *be*. 3. (law) Of, consisting of, rules of right administered by court as opp. to forms of procedure. 4. (mil.) Appointed to substantive rank; ~ *rank*, permanent rank in the holder's branch of the army, (as opp. to brevet, honorary, or temporary rank). 5. (of dye) Not requiring the use of a mordant. **sŭ′bstantively** *adv.* **sŭ′bstantive** *n.* (gram.) Noun.
sŭ′bstitūte *n.* Person or thing acting or serving in place of another. ~ *v.* Put in place of another; (cause to) act as substitute *for*. **sŭbstitū′tion** *n.* (esp., chem.) Replacement of one atom or radical in molecule by another. **sŭbstitū′tional, sŭ′bstitūtive** *adjs.*.
sŭbstră′tosphēre *n.* Layer of atmosphere immediately below stratosphere.
sŭbstrā′tum (*or* -ah-) *n.* (pl. -*ta*). What underlies or forms basis of anything.
subsū′me *v.t.* Bring (one idea, principle, etc.) *under* another, a rule, or a class. **subsū′mption** *n.*
sŭbtĕ′nant *n.* One who holds or leases from a tenant. **sŭbtĕ′nancy** *n.*
subtĕ′nd *v.t.* (geom.) (of chord, side of figure, angle) Be opposite to (angle, arc). **subtĕ′nse** *n.* Subtending line.
sŭ′bterfūge *n.* Evasion, shift; artifice or device adopted to escape or avoid force of argument, condemnation, or censure, or to justify conduct.
sŭbterrā′nean *adj.* Existing, lying, situated, formed, operating, taking place, performed, under surface of the earth; underground. **sŭbterrā′neous** *adj.* Subterranean. **sŭbterrā′neously** *adv.*
subtile (sŭ′tl) *adj.* (archaic) Subtle.
su′btilīze (sŭt-) *v.* Make subtle; elevate, sublime, refine; argue or reason, subtly (upon).
sŭ′b-tī′tle *n.* Subordinate or additional title of literary work etc.; caption of cinema film. ~ *v.t.* Add sub-title(s) to.
subtle (sŭ′tl) *adj.* Tenuous, rarefied (archaic); pervasive or elusive by reason of tenuity; fine or delicate, esp. to such an extent as to elude observation or analysis; making fine distinctions, having delicate perceptions, acute; ingenious, elaborate, clever; crafty, cunning. **su′btly** *adv.* **su′btlety** *n.*
sŭbtō′nic *n.* (mus.) Note next below tonic, 7th note of ascending scale.
sŭbtō′pia *n.* (iron.) Suburban paradise, spread of small houses over countryside. [f. *suburb* and UTOPIA]
subtră′ct *v.t.* Deduct (part, quantity, number) from or *from* whole or from quantity or number, esp. in arithmetic and algebra. **subtră′ction** *n.* **subtră′ctive** *adj.*
sŭ′btrahĕnd (-a-h-) *n.* (math.) Quantity or number to be subtracted.
sŭbtrŏ′pical *adj.* (Characteristic of regions) bordering on the tropics.
sŭ′būlate, sū′būliform *adjs.* (biol.) Awl-shaped, slender and tapering.
sŭ′bŭrb *n.* (One of) residential parts lying on or near outskirts of city. **subŭr′ban** *adj.*
subŭr′bia *n.* The suburbs (esp. of London) and their inhabitants.
subvĕ′ntion *n.* Grant from government etc., in support of enterprise of public importance, subsidy.
subvĕr′sion *n.* Overturning, ruin, overthrow from foundation.
subvĕr′sive *adj.* Tending to subvert or overthrow.
subvĕr′t *v.t.* Overthrow, overturn, upset, effect destruction or ruin of (religion, government).
sŭb vō′ce. (abbrev. *s.v.*) Under the (specified) word. [L]
sŭ′bway *n.* Underground passage for water-pipes, telegraph lines, etc., or for pedestrians to cross below road(s) etc.; (U.S.) underground railway.
sŭccĕdā′neum (-ks-) *n.* (pl. -*nea*). Substitute, esp. (med.) remedy, freq. inferior, substituted for another. **sŭccĕdā′neous** *adj.*
succee′d (-ks-) *v.* 1. Come next after and take the place of, follow in order, come next (to); be subsequent (to); come by inheritance or in due course to or *to* office, title, or property. 2. Have success, be successful; prosper; accomplish one's purpose; (of plan etc.) be brought to a successful issue.
succĕ′ntor (-ks-) *n.* Deputy to precentor in cathedral choir.
succès d'ĕstime (sōoksā, -ēm). Passably cordial reception given to performance or work out of the respect in which the performer or author is held rather than on account of the merits of the work itself. [Fr.]
succès fou (sōoksā fōō). Success marked by wild enthusiasm. [Fr.]
succĕ′ss (-ks-) *n.* Favourable issue; attainment of object, or of wealth, fame, or position; thing or person that succeeds or is successful; issue of undertaking (now rare exc. in *ill* ~). **succĕ′ssful** *adj.* **succĕ′ssfully** *adv.*
succĕ′ssion (-ks-) *n.* 1. Following in order, succeeding; series of things in succession; *in* ~, one after another in regular sequence. 2. (Right of) succeeding to the throne or any office or inheritance; set or order of persons having such right; *apostolic* ~, uninterrupted transmission of spiritual authority through bishops from the apostles downwards; ~ *duties*, taxes payable on succession to estate; *S*~ *States*, those resulting from dismemberment of Austria-Hungary after the war of 1914–18. **succĕ′ssional** *adj.*
succĕ′ssive (-ks-) *adj.* Coming one after another in uninterrupted sequence. **succĕ′ssively** *adv.*
succĕ′ssor (-ks-) *n.* Person or thing succeeding another.
succi′nct (-ks-) *adj.* Terse, brief, concise. **succi′nctly** *adv.* **succi′nctness** *n.*
sŭ′ccory *n.* = CHICORY, 2.
sŭ′ccotăsh *n.* (U.S.) Dish of beans and green maize cooked together (sometimes with salt pork). [Amer. Ind. *misquatash*]
sŭ′ccour (-ker) *v.t.* Come to assistance of, give aid to in need or difficulty. ~ *n.* Aid given in time of need.
sŭ′ccuba, sŭ′ccubus *ns.* (pl. -*bae*, -*bī*). Female demon supposed to have sexual intercourse with men in their sleep.
sŭ′cculent *adj.* Juicy; (bot.) having juicy or fleshy tissues, as the cactus. **sŭ′cculently** *adv.* **sŭ′cculence** *n.* **sŭ′cculent** *n.* Plant with fleshy foliage or stems or both.
succŭ′mb (-m) *v.i.* Sink under

pressure, give way to superior force, authority, etc.; (esp.) yield to effects of disease, wounds, etc., die.

sŭch *adj.* 1. Of the character, degree, or extent described, referred to, or implied; previously described or specified; ~ *as*, of the kind or degree that, the kind of (person or thing) that; for example, e.g. 2. So great, so eminent, etc. (freq. emphatic and exclamatory; (preceding attrib. adj., with adverbial force) so. 3. Particular, but not specified; ~-*and-such*, a particular but unspecified; *su'chlike*, (of) such a kind. ~ *pron.* That, the action, etc., referred to; such people *as*, those *who* (chiefly archaic or rhet.); (vulg. or commerc.) the aforesaid thing(s); *as* ~, as what has been specified.

sŭck *v.* 1. Draw (liquid, esp. milk from breast) into mouth by contracting muscles of lips, tongue, and cheeks so as to produce partial vacuum; (fig.) imbibe, absorb (knowledge etc.). 2. Apply lips, lips and tongue or analogous organs, to breast, food substance, etc., to absorb nourishment. 3. Perform action of sucking, use sucking action; (of pump etc.) make sucking or gurgling sound, draw in air instead of water. 4. ~ *at*, take pull at (pipe etc.); ~ *down, in,* (of whirlpool, quicksand, etc.) engulf; ~ *dry*, exhaust of contents by sucking; ~ *in, up,* (of absorbent substance) absorb; ~ *up to*, (school slang) toady to, curry favour with. ~ *n.* Action, act, spell, of sucking (*give* ~, *suckle*); drawing action of whirlpool etc.; small draught of *of* liquor.

sŭ'cker *n.* 1. Person or thing that sucks, esp. sucking-pig or young whale-calf; organ adapted for sucking; any of several csp. N. Amer. fish with mouths of form that suggests feeding by suction; piston of pump, syringe, etc. 2. Part, organ, or device adapted for adhering to object by suction; fish with suctorial disc by which it adheres to foreign objects. 3. Shoot thrown out by plant, esp. root under ground; axillary shoot in tobacco-plant. 4. (slang) Person easily victimized or gulled, greenhorn.

sŭ'cking *adj.* Not yet weaned; (fig.) budding, unpractised, immature; ~-*fish*, REMORA; ~-*pig*, young pig, esp. young milk-fed pig suitable for roasting whole.

sŭ'ckle *v.t.* Give suck to, feed at the breast. **sŭ'ckling** *n.* Unweaned child or animal.

su'crĕ (sōō-) *n.* Principal monetary unit of Ecuador, = 100 centavos.

sū'crōse *n.* Sugar ($C_{12}H_{22}O_{11}$) that comes from cane and from beet and is found widely in many plants.

sŭ'ction *n.* Action of sucking; production of complete or partial vacuum so that external atmospheric pressure forces fluid into vacant space or causes adhesion of surfaces; in internal combustion engine, = INDUCTION; ~ *pipe*, pipe leading from bottom of pump barrel to reservoir from which fluid is to be drawn; ~-*pump*, pump drawing liquid through pipe into chamber exhausted by piston (ill. PUMP[1]). **sŭ'ctional** *adj.*

sŭctōr'ial *adj.* (of organ) Adapted for sucking; (of animal) having suctorial organs; of the group Suctoria of protozoa, with tubular suctorial tentacles (ill. PROTOZOA).

Sudä'n (sōō-). 1. Region of Africa, S. of Sahara and Libyan deserts. 2. Republic in NE. Africa, south of Egypt; capital, Khartoum. **Sudanē'se** (-z) *adj.* & *n.*

sūdār'ium (*or* sōō-) *n.* (pl. *-ia*). Cloth for wiping face; esp. cloth with which St. Veronica wiped face of Christ on his way to Calvary, miraculously impressed with his features.

sūdatōr'ium (*or* sōō-) *n.* (pl. *-ia*). (Rom. antiq.) Room in which hot-air or steam-baths were taken to produce sweating.

sŭdd *n.* Impenetrable mass of floating vegetable matter impeding navigation on White Nile.

sŭ'dden *adj.* Happening, coming, performed, taking place, etc., without warning or unexpectedly, abrupt. ~ *adv.* (chiefly poet.) Suddenly. **sŭ'ddenly** *adv.* **sŭ'ddennĕss** (-n-n-) *n.* **sŭ'dden** *n.* (*all*) *of a* ~, suddenly.

Su'dermann (sōō-) Hermann (1857-1928). German playwright and novelist.

Sude'ten (-dā-). 1. (also *Sude'tēs* pr. -z) Mountain range in E. central Europe. 2. (also *Sude'tenland*) Mountainous region of N. Czechoslovakia, annexed by Germany in 1938 and returned in 1945. ~ *n.* Native, inhabitant, of Sudetenland.

sūdori'ferous (*or* sōō-) *adj.* Producing or secreting sweat. **sūdori'fic** *adj.* & *n.* (Drug) promoting or causing sweating.

Su'dra (sōō-) *n.* (Member of) the lowest of the 4 great Hindu castes, the artisans and labourers.

sŭds (-z) *n.pl.* Water impregnated with soap; frothy mass on top of soapy water, lather.

sūe[1] (*or* sōō) *v.* Institute legal proceedings, bring civil action, against; (usu. ~ *out*) apply before court for grant of (writ, legal process); bring suit; plead, appeal, supplicate (*for*).

Sue[2] (sü), Eugène (1804-57). French novelist, author of 'Les Mystères de Paris' etc.

suède (swäd) *n.* 1. Kid or other skin with flesh-side rubbed into nap, as material for gloves, shoes, etc. 2. (also ~-*cloth*) Woven fabric imitating this. [Fr. *Suède* Sweden]

sū'ĕt (*or* sōō-) *n.* Hard fat round the kidneys and loins of cattle and sheep, used in cooking or rendered down to form tallow; ~ *pudding*, pudding made with suet and usu. boiled in cloth or steamed. **sū'ĕtў** *adj.* Of or like suet; pale-complexioned.

Suetō'nius (swē-). Gaius Suetonius Tranquillus (*c* A.D. 70–*c* 160). Roman historian and antiquary.

Su'ĕz (sōō-). District of Lower Egypt at N. end of the Red Sea; seaport at S. end of the ~ *Canal*, a ship-canal across the Isthmus of Suez to Port Said, cut (1859-69) by Ferdinand de LESSEPS.

sŭ'ffer *v.* 1. Undergo, experience, be subjected to (pain, loss, grief, defeat, punishment, etc.); undergo pain, grief, or damage. 2. Permit *to do*; allow, put up with, tolerate. **sŭ'fferer, sŭ'ffering** *ns.*

sŭ'fferance *n.* 1. (archaic) Long-suffering, forbearance. 2. Sanction, or acquiescence, implied by absence of objection; tacit permission or toleration, esp. in *on* ~, under conditions of bare tolerance or tacit acquiescence.

suffi'ce *v.* Be enough, be adequate; satisfy, meet the needs of. **suffi'ciency** (-shen-) *n.* (esp.) Sufficient supply, adequate provision.

suffi'cient (-shent) *adj.* Sufficing; adequate, esp. in amount or number; enough; (archaic) competent, adequate in ability or resources. **suffi'ciently** *adv.* **suffi'cient** *n.* Enough, a sufficient quantity.

sŭ'ffix *n.* 1. (gram.) Verbal element attached to end of word as inflexional formative or to form new word. 2. (math.) Sub-index. ~ *v.t.* Add as suffix.

sŭ'ffocāte *v.* Kill, stifle, choke, by stopping respiration; produce choking sensation in, smother, overwhelm; feel suffocated. **sŭffocā'tion** *n.*

Sū'ffolk (-ŏk). East Anglian county of England.

sŭ'ffragan *adj.* ~ *bishop*, bishop appointed to assist diocesan bishop in particular part of his diocese; bishop in relation to his archbishop or metropolitan. ~ *n.* Suffragan bishop.

sŭ'ffrage *n.* 1. (eccles.) In Book of Common Prayer, intercessory petitions said by priest in litany, (pl.) set of versicles and responses; (archaic) intercessory prayer, esp. for souls of departed. 2. Vote; approval or consent expressed by voting; right of voting as member of body, State, etc., franchise.

sŭffragĕ'tte *n.* (hist.) Woman advocating political enfranchisement of women, esp. militantly or violently.

sŭ'ffragist *n.* Advocate of extension of political franchise, esp. to women.

suffū'se (-z) *v.t.* Overspread as

[873]

SUFI, SOFI

with a fluid, a colour, a gleam of light. **suffu′sion** n.

Su′fi (sōō-), **Sō′fi** n. Muslim ascetic mystic of sect which originated in 8th c. and later, esp. in Persia, embraced pantheistic views. **Su′fism, Sō′fism** n. [Arab. *ṣūfī* Muslim mystic, perh. f. *ṣūf* wool]

su′gar (-shŏŏ-) n. 1. Sweet crystalline substance ($C_{12}H_{22}O_{11}$), white when pure, obtained by evaporation from plant juices, esp. that of sugar-cane and sugar beet, and forming important article of human food, saccharose; (pl.) kinds of sugar. 2. Sweet words, flattery, anything serving purpose of sugar put round pill in reconciling person to what is unpalatable. 3. (chem.) Any of a group of carbohydrates, soluble in water and having a sweet taste, found esp. in plants and including glucose, lactose, saccharose, etc. 4. ~ *of milk*, lactose; ~*-almond*, sweet of almond with hard sugar coating; ~*-beet*, kind of white beet from which sugar is extracted; ~*-candy*: see CANDY¹, sense 1; ~*-cane*, perennial tropical and sub-tropical grass, *Saccharum officinarum*, with tall stout jointed stems, cultivated as a source of sugar; ~*-daddy*, (U.S. slang) elderly man who lavishes gifts on a young woman; ~*-loaf*, conical moulded mass of hard refined sugar; thing, esp. hill, in shape of a sugar-loaf; ~*-maple*, N. Amer. tree, *Acer saccharinum*, yielding maple sugar; ~*-plum*, small round or oval sweet of boiled sugar. **su′garlèss** adj. **su′gar** v.t. Sweeten, coat with sugar; make sweet or agreeable; form sugar, become crystalline or granulated like sugar; spread sugar mixed with gum etc. on (tree) to catch moths; ~ *off*, complete boiling down of maple syrup for sugar.

su′garў (shŏŏ-) adj. Like sugar; containing (much) sugar; (fig.) cloying, sentimental.

suggë′st (-j-) v.t. Cause (idea) to be present to mind, call up idea of; prompt execution or fulfilment of; put forward opinion or proposition (*that*), utter as a suggestion; give hint or inkling of, give impression of existence or presence of.

suggĕ′stible (-j-) adj. (esp.) Capable of being influenced by suggestion. **suggĕstibi′lity** n.

suggĕ′stĭō fă′lsī. Positive misrepresentation not involving direct lie but going beyond concealment of the truth (cf. SUPPRESSIO VERI).

suggĕ′stion (-jĕschon) n. Suggesting; idea, plan, or thought suggested, proposal; suggesting of prurient ideas; insinuation of belief or impulse into mind of subject by hypnosis or other means, such belief or impulse.

suggĕ′stĭve (-j-) adj. (esp.) Suggesting something indecent. **suggĕ′stĭvelў** adv. **suggĕ′stĭvenèss** n.

sū′icide (or sōō-) n. 1. Intentional self-slaughter; *commit* ~, kill oneself. 2. (fig.) Action destructive to one's own interests etc. 3. Person who has committed suicide. **sūĭcī′dal** adj. **sūĭcī′dally** adv.

sū′ī gĕ′neris (or sōō′ī) Of its own kind, peculiar, unique. [L]

suit (sūt or sōōt) n. 1. Suing in court of law, legal prosecution; process instituted in court of justice, law-suit. 2. Suing, supplication, petition; courting of a woman, courtship. 3. Set of outer garments, usu. coat (and sometimes waistcoat), and trousers or skirt; *sui′tcase*, case for carrying clothes, usu. box-shaped with flat hinged lid and one handle. 4. Any of the four sets (spades, clubs, hearts, diamonds) of playing-cards in pack, consisting of 13 cards (10 numbered consecutively and 3 court cards); *follow* ~, play card of suit led; (fig.) follow another's example. ~ v. 1. Accommodate, adapt, make fitting or appropriate, *to*. 2. Be agreeable or convenient to; be fitted or adapted to; be good for, favourable to health of; go well with appearance or character of, be becoming to; be fitting or convenient. **sui′ting** n. (esp.) Material for suits of clothing.

sui′table (sūt- or sōōt-) adj. Suited *to* or *for*; well fitted for the purpose; appropriate to the occasion. **sui′tablў** adv. **suitabi′litў, sui′tablenèss** ns.

suite (swēt) n. 1. Retinue, set of persons in attendance. 2. Set, series; number of rooms forming set used by particular person(s) or for particular purpose; set of furniture of same pattern. 3. (mus.) Old form of instrumental composition (c 1500–c 1750), later partly superseded by SONATA, and consisting of several (usu. four) movements based on dance tunes, in same or related keys; set of instrumental compositions related in theme etc. and freq. constituting music for ballet, incidental music for play, etc.

sui′tor (sūt- or sōōt-) n. 1. Party to law-suit; petitioner or plaintiff. 2. Wooer, one who seeks woman in marriage.

sū′lcate adj. (anat., bot.) Furrowed, grooved. **sulcā′tion** n.

sū′lcus n. Groove, furrow; esp. (anat.) fissure between two convolutions of brain (ill. BRAIN).

sŭlk v.i. Be sulky. ~ n. (usu. pl.) Sulky fit.

sŭ′lkў adj. Sullen, morose; silent, inactive, or unsociable from resentment or ill-temper. **sŭ′lkĭlў** adv. **sŭ′lkĭnèss** n. **sŭ′lkў** n. Light two-wheeled carriage for single person, esp. one used in trotting-races.

Sū′lla, Lucius Cornelius (138–78 B.C.). Roman dictator and general; instituted reforms of the constitution designed to increase the power

SULPHUREOUS

of the Senate and reduce that of the people and their tribunes.

sŭ′llage n. Filth, refuse, sewage.

sŭ′llen adj. Gloomy, ill-humoured. **sŭ′llenlў** adv. **sŭ′llennèss** (-n-n-) n.

Sŭ′llĭvan, Sir Arthur Seymour (1842–1900). English musical composer, in collaboration with W. S. GILBERT[3], of light satiric operas.

sŭ′llў v.t. (chiefly poet.) Soil, tarnish; be stain on, discredit.

sŭ′lpha adj. ~ *drug*, sulphonamide.

sŭ′lphamīde n. Amide of sulphuric acid, a colourless trigonal neutral compound ($SO_2(NH_2)_2$).

sŭlphani′lamīde n. Synthetic organic chemical compound ($H_2NC_6H_4SO_2NH_2$), from which most of the sulpha drugs are derived.

sŭ′lphāte n. Salt of sulphuric acid. ~ v. Treat, impregnate, with sulphuric acid or a sulphate; (elect.) form whitish scales of lead sulphate on plates of (storage battery); become sulphated. **sŭlphā′tion** n.

sŭ′lphīde n. Compound of sulphur with another element or a radical.

sŭ′lphīte n. Salt of sulphurous acid.

sŭlphŏ′namīde n. Any of a group of drugs derived from amides of sulphonic acids, capable of killing or preventing the multiplication of bacteria, e.g. streptococci, used in the treatment of many different infections.

sŭ′lphōne n. Any of a group of organic compounds containing the radical SO_2 united directly to two carbon atoms. **sulphŏ′nic** adj.

sŭ′lphur n. 1. (chem.) Greenish-yellow non-metallic inflammable element, burning with blue flame, widely distributed free and in combination, and used in manufacture of matches, gunpowder, and sulphuric acid, for vulcanizing rubber, as a disinfectant (as sulphur dioxide), and in medicine as a laxative, a sudorific, and an ingredient of ointments; symbol S, at. no. 16, at. wt 32·06; *flowers of* ~, pure sulphur in form of yellow powder; *liver of* ~, mixture of sulphur compounds used as a lotion in treatment of certain skin diseases. 2. In popular belief, material of which hell-fire and lightning were held to consist; (alchemy) one of the supposed ultimate elements, the principle of combustion. 3. Any of various yellow (or orange) butterflies of family Pieridae. 4. ~ *candle*, candle used for disinfection, giving off sulphur dioxide; ~*-yellow*, (of) the bright pale-yellow colour of sulphur.

sulphūr′ĕous adj. Of, like, suggesting, sulphur; with qualities associated with (burning) sulphur; full of sulphur of hell; sulphur-yellow.

[874]

sŭlphurĕ'ttĕd *adj.* Chemically combined with sulphur (now only in ~ *hydrogen*, hydrogen sulphide (H₂S), colourless gas with very offensive odour).

sŭlphūr'ic *adj.* Of, containing, sulphur; ~ *acid*, dense highly corrosive oily fluid, oil of vitriol (H₂SO₄); ~ *ether*, ether.

sŭ'lphurous *adj.* 1. Sulphureous. 2. (chem., of compounds) Containing sulphur of lower valency than sulphuric compounds; ~ *acid*, acid (H₂SO₃) present in solutions of sulphur dioxide in water.

sŭ'ltan *n.* 1. Sovereign of Muslim country, esp. (hist.) of Turkey. 2. Small white domestic fowl with heavily feathered legs and feet, orig. from Turkey. 3. (also *sweet* ~) Either of two sweet-scented annuals, *Centaurea moschata* (purple or white sweet ~), and *C. suaveolens* (yellow ~). **sŭ'ltanate** *n.* Rank, authority, of a sultan; jurisdiction, dominion, of a sultan. [Arab. *sulṭān* ruler, emperor]

sŭlta'na (-tah-) *n.* 1. Wife or concubine of sultan. 2. Bird of genus *Porphyrio*, chiefly of W. Indies, southern U.S., and Australia. 3. Small light-coloured seedless raisin grown esp. near Izmir; pale-yellow grape from which sultanas are produced.

sŭ'ltanĕss *n.* = SULTANA, 1.

sŭ'ltry *adj.* Oppressively hot, sweltering; (fig.) having strong sexual attraction. **sŭ'ltrily** *adv.* **sŭ'ltriness** *n.*

sŭm *n.* 1. Total amount resulting from addition of two or more numbers, quantities, magnitudes, etc.; total number or amount *of*; ~ *total*, total amount, aggregate (*of*). 2. Quantity or amount of or of money. 3. (Working out of) arithmetical problem. ~ *v.* 1. Find sum of; reckon, count, or total *up*; collect (*up*) into small compass. 2. ~ *up*, summarize, epitomize; form estimate or judgement of; (of judge in trial, or counsel concluding his client's case) recapitulate (evidence or arguments), with any necessary exposition of points of law, before jury considers its verdict; so *su'mming up* (*n.*).

sŭ'mac, -ch (-k; *or* shōō-) *n.* Shrub or small tree of genus *Rhus*; dried leaves etc., rich in tannin, of various plants of this genus, esp. the S. European *R. coriaria*, used in tanning, dyeing, and staining leather black, and as astringent. [Arab. *summāk*]

Suma'tra (-mah- *or* sŭ-). Large island of Indonesia, separated from the Malay Peninsula by the Strait of Malacca.

Sū'mer (*or* sōō-). Ancient district of Babylonia. **Sūmēr'ian** *adj.* & *n.* (Native, inhabitant) of Sumer; (of) the agglutinative language of the Sumerian inscriptions written in a cuneiform script.

sŭ'mmarīze *v.t.* Make or constitute a summary of, sum up.

sŭ'mmary *adj.* Compendious and (usu.) brief; dispensing with needless detail, performed with dispatch; (law, of proceedings) carried out rapidly by omission of certain formalities required by common law; *court of* ~ *jurisdiction*, court that can itself judge or convict. **sŭ'mmarily** *adv.* **sŭ'mmary** *n.* Summary account or statement, abridgement, epitome.

summā'tion *n.* Addition, summing (up); finding of total or sum.

summā'tional *adj.*

sŭ'mmer¹ *n.* 1. Warmest season of year, popularly reckoned in N. hemisphere as lasting from mid-May to middle or end of August, but astronomically as lasting from summer solstice (21 or 22 June) to autumnal equinox (22 or 23 Sept.); summer weather; (pl.) years of life or age (chiefly poet., as in *boy of ten* ~*s*); INDIAN, St. LUKE's, St. MARTIN²'s ~: see these words. 2. (*attrib.* or as *adj.*) ~ *ermine*, brown fur of ermine in summer; ~-*fallow*, (land) lying fallow during summer; ~-*house*, (usu. simple and light) building in park or garden providing cool shady place in summer; *S*~ *Palace*, ruined palace of Chinese emperors near Peking; ~ *pudding*, dish made by pressing stewed (esp. soft) fruit into a bowl lined and covered with bread or sponge-cake; ~ *school*, course of lectures etc. held during summer vacation, esp. at university; ~ *solstice*: see SOLSTICE; ~-*time*, season of summer; standard time, one hour in advance of ordinary time, adopted in some countries during summer to facilitate use of daylight (*double* ~-*time*, two hours in advance); ~-*weight*, (of clothes etc.) suitable in weight for use in summer. ~ *v.* Pass summer (*at* or *in* place); pasture (cattle) *at*, *in*.

sŭ'mmer² *n.* Horizontal beam, esp. main beam supporting girders or joists of floor.

sŭ'mmit *n.* Highest point, top, apex; highest degree; ~ *conference*, meeting of heads of States.

sŭ'mmon *v.t.* Call together by authority for action or deliberation, require presence or attendance of, bid approach; call upon *to* do; call *up* (courage, resolution, etc.) to one's aid; cite by authority to appear before court or judge to answer charge or give evidence.

sŭ'mmons (-nz) *n.* Authoritative call or urgent invitation to attend on some occasion or to do something; citation to appear before judge or magistrate. ~ *v.t.* Take out summons against.

sŭ'mmum bŏ'num. Chief or supreme good. [L]

sŭmp *n.* Pit or well for collecting water or other fluid, esp. in mine; oil-reservoir at bottom of crank-case of internal combustion engine (ill. COMBUSTION).

sŭ'mpter *n.* Pack-horse or its driver (archaic); ~-*horse*, -*mule*, etc., pack-animals.

sŭ'mption *n.* (logic) Major premiss.

sŭ'mptūary *adj.* Regulating expenditure; ~ *edict*, *law*, one which limits private expenditure in the interest of the State.

sŭ'mptūous *adj.* Costly, splendid, magnificent in workmanship, decoration, appearance, etc. **sŭ'mptūously** *adv.* **sŭ'mptūousness** *n.*

sŭn *n.* Star forming centre of system of worlds or planets, esp. the central body of the solar system, round which the earth and other planets revolve, and which

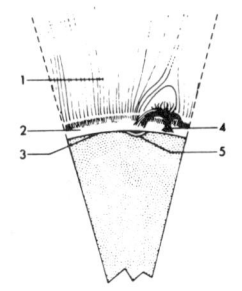

A SECTION OF THE SUN AND ITS ATMOSPHERE

1. Corona. 2. Chromosphere. 3. Photosphere. 4. Prominence. 5. Sun-spots or maculae

supplies them with light and warmth by its radiation; such light or warmth; (poet.) climate, clime; *a place in the* ~, position giving scope for development of individual or national life; *take the* ~, (naut.) make observation of meridian altitude of sun to determine latitude; ~-*and*-*planet gearing*, system of gearing in which axis of cogged wheel (*planet*-*wheel*) moves round that of central wheel (~-*wheel*) to which it communicates motion (ill. GEAR); ~-*bath*, exposure of skin to sun's rays; *su'nbathe*, take sun-bath; *su'nbeam*, beam of sunlight; ~-*blind*, awning over window; ~-*bonnet*, bonnet of cotton etc. shaped so as to shade eyes and neck from sun; *su'nburn*, tanning or superficial inflammation of skin caused by exposure to sun; brown colour produced thus; *su'nburnt* (*adj.*); ~-*burst*, burst of sunlight; piece of jewellery representing sun surrounded by rays; ~-*deck*, upper deck of ship; *su'ndew*, plant of genus *Drosera* of small herbs growing in bogs, with leaves covered with glandular hairs secreting viscid drops; *su'ndial*, contrivance for showing time by shadow cast by sun on surface marked with hours (*illustration*, *p.876*); ~ *disc*, (archaeol.) winged disc, symbol of sun god; ~-*dog*, parhelion, mock

[875]

sun; sǔ'ndown, sunset; sǔ'ndowner, (Austral.) tramp arriving at station at sunset so as to obtain food and night's lodging; sǔ'nfish, large fish (*Mola mola*) of warm seas, with round ungainly body and short fringe-like caudal fin; any of various small usu. brilliant-coloured Amer. freshwater fishes of family Centrachidae; sǔ'nflower, composite plant of genus *Helianthus*, chiefly native of N. America, with conspicuous yellow flower-heads whose disc and rays suggest figure of sun; ~-*glasses*, tinted spectacles for protecting eyes from sunlight or glare; ~ *god*, (myth.) god of the sun; ~-*hat*, broad-brimmed hat worn to protect head from sun; ~-*helmet*, hat with double crown for same purpose; ~ *lamp*, large lamp with parabolic mirror reflector used in motion-picture photography; lamp emitting ultra-violet rays; sǔ'nlight, light of sun; ~-*ray*, sunbeam; (*attrib.*) emitting, using, ultra-violet rays, esp. therapeutically; sǔ'nrise, (time of) sun's apparent ascent above eastern horizon; ~ *room*, room with walls largely of glass, designed to catch maximum amount of sunshine; sǔ'nset, (time of) sun's apparent descent below western horizon at end of day; glow of light or display of colour in sky at this time; (fig.) decline, close (esp. of life); sǔ'nshade, device providing protection from sun's rays, esp. parasol or awning over window; sǔ'nshine, unimpeded sunlight, fair weather; (fig.) cheerfulness, bright influence; ~-*spot*, one of the cavities in photosphere appearing as dark spots or patches on sun's surface, lasting from a few hours to several months, recurring in greatest numbers at intervals of a little over eleven years, and freq. accompanied by magnetic disturbances etc. on earth; sǔ'nstroke, prostration or collapse caused by exposure to excessive heat of sun; ~-*up*, (chiefly U.S.) sunrise; ~-*wheel*, central wheel of sun-and-planet gearing; sǔ'nwise, in direction of sun's apparent motion, clockwise. **sǔ'nlĕss** *adj*. **sǔ'nlĕssnĕss** *n*. **sǔn** *v*. Expose to the sun; ~ *oneself*, bask in sun.
Sun. *abbrev.* Sunday.
sǔ'ndae (-dā) *n*. (orig. U.S.) Confection of ice-cream with fruit, nuts, syrup, cream, etc.
Sǔ'nday (*or* -di) *n*. 1st day of the week, observed by Christians as day of rest and worship; *a month of* ~*s*, a very long time; ~ *best*, best clothes worn on Sunday; ~ *school*, school held on Sunday; now only for religious instruction, and usu. attached to parish or church congregation.
sǔ'nder *v*. (now poet. or rhet.) Separate, sever, keep apart.
sǔ'ndry *adj*. Divers, several; *all and* ~, one and all. ~ *n*. 1. (Austral.) An extra in cricket. 2. (pl.) Oddments, small items classed together without individual mention.
sung[1]: see SING.
Sung[2] (sŏo-). Name of dynasty which ruled in China 960-1279.
sǔnk, sǔ'nken *adjs.*: see SINK[2]; (esp., of eyes, cheeks, etc.) hollow, fallen in.
Sǔ'nna, -ah (-a) *n*. Traditional portion of Muslim law based on Muhammad's words or acts but not written by him, accepted as authoritative by the orthodox but rejected by the Shiites. **Sǔ'nni** (-nē), **Sǔ'nnīte** *adjs. & ns*. (Muslim) accepting the Sunna as well as the Koran.
sǔ'nny *adj*. Bright with or as sunlight; exposed to, warm with, the sun; cheery, bright in disposition. **sǔ'nnily** *adv*. **sǔ'nninĕss** *n*.
Sǔn Yăt-sĕn (1866-1925). Leader of Chinese revolutionary movement, 1911-12; 1st president of the Chinese Republic, 1921-2.
sǔp *v*. Take (liquid food) by sips or spoonfuls; take supper; provide supper for. ~ *n*. Mouthful of liquid, esp. soup; (*a*) *bite and* (*a*) ~, a little food and drink.
sup. *abbrev.* Superlative; *supra* (L, = above).
sǔ'per (*or* sōō-) *n*. (colloq. or slang for) Supernumerary actor; superintendent. ~ *adj*. (shop) Superfine; (slang) excellent, unusually good.
super- (*or* sōō-) *prefix*. On the top (of); over; beyond, besides, in addition; exceeding, going beyond, more than, transcending; of higher kind; to a degree beyond the usual.
superabou'nd (*or* sōō-) *v.i.* Be more abundant; abound excessively, be very or too abundant.
superabu'ndant *adj*. **superabu'ndance** *n*.
superă'nnūāte (*or* sōō-) *v.t.* Dismiss or discharge as too old; discharge with pension. **superănnūā'tion** *n*.
supĕr'b (*or* sōō-) *adj*. Grand, majestic, splendid, magnificent. **supĕr'bly** *adv*.
sǔ'percārgō (*or* sōō-) *n*. Merchant ship's officer superintending cargo and commercial transactions of voyage.
sǔ'perchārger (*or* sōō-) *n*. Device supplying internal combustion engine with air or explosive mixture at higher pressure than normal in order to increase its efficiency. **sǔ'perchārged** (-jd) *adj*.
supercǐ'liary (*or* sōō-) *adj*. Of the eyebrow, over the eye.
supercǐ'lious (*or* sōō-) *adj*. Haughtily contemptuous, disdainful, or superior. **supercǐ'liously** *adv*. **supercǐ'liousnĕss** *n*.
supercŏndŭctǐ'vity (*or* sōō-) *n*. Extremely high conductivity shown by certain substances at very low temperatures. **supercŏndǔ'ctive** *adj*.
sǔ'percōōl (*or* sōō-) *v.t.* Cool below freezing-point without solidification or crystallization.
superĕlĕvā'tion (*or* sōō-) *n*. Amount of elevation of outer above inner rail at curve on railway.
superĕrogā'tion (*or* sōō-) *n*. Performance of more than duty or circumstances require; esp. (R.C. theol.) performance of good works beyond what God requires, which constitute a store of merit which the Church may dispense to make up others' deficiencies.
sǔ'perfămily (*or* sōō-) *n*. (biol.) Set of related families within an order.
superfǐ'cial (-shal; *or* sōō-) *adj*. Of, on, the surface; not going deep, without depth; (of measures) involving two dimensions, of extent of surface, square. **superfǐ'cially** *adv*. **superficiā'lity** *n*. **superfǐ'cies** (-shēz; *or* sōō-) *n*. Surface.
sǔ'perfine (*or* sōō-) *adj*. Extremely fine in quality, of the very best kind.
superflu'ity (-lōō-; *or* sōō-) *n*. Superfluous amount.
supĕr'fluous (-lōō-; *or* sōō-) *adj*. More than enough, excessive, redundant; needless, uncalled-for. **supĕr'fluously** *adv*. **supĕr'fluousnĕss** *n*.
superhea't (*or* sōō-) *v.t.* Heat to very high temperature; esp. raise temperature of (steam) to increase its pressure. **superhea'ter** *n*.
sǔ'perhĕ't (*or* sōō-) *adj. & n*. Superheterodyne.
sǔ'perhĕ'terodyne (*or* sōō-) *adj. & n*. (Of) radio reception or receiver in which, by means of a local oscillator, a beat-note is set up with the incoming signal and amplified at the resulting intermediate frequency.
superhū'man (*or* sōō-) *adj*. Beyond (normal) human capacity, strength, etc.; higher than (that of) man.
superimpō'se (-z; *or* sōō-) *v.t.* Impose or place, cause to follow, succeed, etc., on or on something else. **superimposi'tion** *n*.
supericŭ'mbent (*or* sōō-) *adj*. Lying or resting on something else.
superindū'ce (*or* sōō-) *v.t.* Develop, bring in, introduce, induce, in addition.

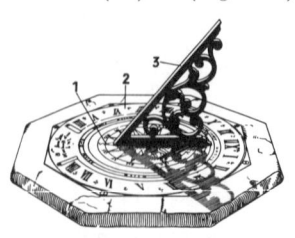

SUNDIAL (N. HEMISPHERE)
1. South point of compass. 2. Hour-scale. 3. Gnomon

[876]

sūperĭntĕ′nd (*or* soo-) *v.* Have or exercise charge or direction (of), oversee, supervise. **sūperĭntĕ′ndence** *n.* **sūperĭntĕ′ndent** *n.* Officer or official having control, oversight, or direction of business, institution, etc.; police officer above rank of inspector.

sūpēr′ior (*or* soo-) *adj.* 1. Upper, higher, situated above or farther up than something else; growing above another part or organ, that is higher than other(s) of the same kind; (of small letters, figures, etc.) printed or written above the line or near the top of other figures etc. 2. Higher in rank, dignity, degree, amount, quality, status, etc.; ~ *to*, above the influence or reach of, not affected or mastered by, higher in status or quality than. 3. Conscious, showing consciousness, of superior qualities; lofty, supercilious, dictatorial, etc. **sūpēr′iorlў** *adv.* **sūpērĭŏ′ritў** *n.* **sūpēr′ior** *n.* 1. Person of higher rank, dignity, or authority, superior officer or official; person or thing of higher quality or value than another. 2. Head of religious community (freq. *Father, Mother*, etc., *S~*).

sūpēr′lative (*or* soo-) *adj.* 1. Raised above or surpassing all others; of the highest degree. 2. (gram., of an inflexional form of an adjective or adverb, as *highest, fastest*) Expressing the highest or very high degree of the quality etc. denoted by the simple word. **sūpēr′lativelў** *adv.* **sūpēr′lative** *n.* (Word in) the superlative degree.

sū′permăn (*or* soo-) *n.* (pl. -*men*). Ideal superior man of the future, conceived by NIETZSCHE as evolved from normal human type; man of superhuman powers or achievement. [transl. Ger. *übermensch*]

sū′permārkĕt (*or* soo-) *n.* Self-service store selling food and household goods.

sūpēr′nal (*or* soo-) *adj.* (poet., rhet.) Heavenly, divine; of the sky; lofty.

sūpernă′tural (-ch*er*-; *or* soo-) *adj.* Due to, manifesting, some agency above the forces of nature; outside the ordinary operation of cause and effect. **sūpernă′turallў** *adv.* **sūpernă′turalnĕss** *n.*

sūpernă′turalism (-ch*er*-; *or* soo-) *n.* Belief in supernatural beings, powers, events, etc. **sūpernă′turalist** *n.* **sūpernăturali′stĭc** *adj.*

sū′per-nō′va (*or* soo-) *n.* Nova of immense brightness or intensity.

sūpernū′merarў (*or* soo-) *adj.* & *n.* (Person or thing) in excess of the normal number, esp. (extra person) not belonging to the regular body or staff but associated with it in some need or emergency; (actor) employed in addition to regular company, appearing on stage or in scene but not speaking.

sūperphŏ′sphāte (*or* soo-) *n.* Fertilizer made by treating phosphate-containing rock with sulphuric acid.

sūperpō′se (-z; *or* soo-) *v.t.* Place above or on something else; bring into same position so as to coincide. **sūperposĭ′tion** *n.*

sūpersă′tūrāte (*or* soo-) *v.t.* Add to (esp. solution) beyond saturation point. **sūpersătūrā′tion** *n.*

sūperscrībe (*or* soo-) *v.t.* Write upon, put inscription on or over; write (inscription) at top of or outside something. **sūperscrĭ′ption** *n.* **sū′perscrĭpt** *adj.*

sūpersē′de (*or* soo-) *v.* Set aside, cease to employ; adopt or appoint another person or thing in place of; take the place of, oust, supplant. **sūpersē′ssion** *n.*

sūpersŏ′nĭc (*or* soo-) *adj.* With a velocity greater than that of sound; (also, obs., of soundwaves) ULTRASONIC.

sūperstĭ′tion (*or* soo-) *n.* Irrational fear of unknown or mysterious, credulity regarding the supernatural; habit or belief based on such tendencies; irrational religious system, false or pagan religion. **sūperstĭ′tious** (-sh*u*s) *adj.* **sūperstĭ′tiouslў** *adv.* **sūperstĭ′tiousnĕss** *n.*

sū′perstrŭcture (*or* soo-) *n.* Building, upper part of building, any material or immaterial structure, resting upon something else or with some other part as a foundation; parts of warship or other vessel above main deck.

sū′pertăx (*or* soo-) *n.* Additional tax, esp. on incomes (in Gt Britain replaced in 1929–30 by the *surtax*).

sūpertŏ′nĭc (*or* soo-) *n.* (mus.) Note next above tonic, 2nd note of ascending scale (ill. SCALE[3]).

sūpervē′ne (*or* soo-) *v.i.* Occur as something additional or extraneous, follow closely upon some other occurrence or condition. **sūpervē′ntion** *n.*

sū′pervise (-z; *or* soo-) *v.t.* Oversee, superintend execution of performance of (thing), production, or work of (person); **sūpervĭ′sion**, **sū′pervisor** *ns.* **sūpervĭ′sorў** *adj.*

sū′pinate *v.t.* (physiol.) Turn (hand or fore-limb) so that back of it is downward or backward (opp. PRONATE). **sūpinā′tion** *n.*

sū′pine[1] (*or* soo-) *adj.* 1. Lying face upward; supinated. 2. Disinclined for exertion, indolent, lethargic, inert. **sū′pinelў** *adv.* **sū′pinenĕss** (-n-n-) *n.*

sū′pine[2] (*or* soo-) *n.* (gram.) Latin verbal noun with two cases, accus. sing. ending in -*tum*, -*sum*, used with verbs of motion to express purpose, and abl. sing. in -*tu*, -*su*, used with adjectives.

sū′pper *n.* Meal taken at end of day, esp. evening meal less formal and substantial than dinner; evening meal when dinner is taken at midday. **sū′pperlĕss** *adj.*

suppl. *abbrev.* Supplement.

supplă′nt (-ah-) *v.t.* Dispossess and take the place of, oust, esp. by dishonourable or treacherous means.

sū′pple *adj.* Easily bent, pliant, flexible; (fig.) compliant, accommodating, artfully or servilely complaisant or submissive. **sū′pplў**[2] *adv.* **sū′pplenĕss** *n.*

sū′pplĕment *n.* 1. Something added to supply a deficiency; part added to complete literary work etc., esp. special number or part of periodical dealing with particular item(s). 2. (math.) Amount by which arc is less than semicircle, or angle is less than 180°. ~ (*or* -ĕ′nt) *v.t.* Furnish supplement to. **sŭpplĕmĕ′ntal** *adj.* **sŭpplĕmĕ′ntarў** *adj.* (esp.) ~ *angle*, either of two angles which together make 180°.

sū′pplĭant *n.* Humble petitioner. ~ *adj.* Supplicating; expressing supplication. **sū′pplĭantlў** *adv.*

sū′pplĭcāte *v.* Make humble petition to or *to* person, for or *for* thing. **sŭpplĭcā′tion** *n.* **sū′pplĭcatorў** (*or* -āt-) *adj.*

supplĭ′er *n.* Person, firm, etc., that supplies.

supplў′[1] *v.t.* Furnish, provide (thing needed, or person, receptacle, etc. with or *with* thing needed); make up for (deficiency etc.). ~ *n.* 1. Provision of what is needed. 2. Stock, store, quantity, of or *of* something provided or available, esp. (econ.) marketed for purchase; (pl.) food and other stores necessary for armed force; (pl. or collect. sing.) sum of money granted by legislature for cost of government; *Committee of S~*, House of Commons sitting to discuss estimates for public service. 3. Person, esp. minister or schoolteacher, who supplies vacancy or acts as substitute for another.

supplў[2]: see SUPPLE.

suppōr′t *n.* Supporting, being supported; person or thing that supports. ~ *v.t.* 1. Carry (part of) weight of; hold up, keep from falling or sinking; keep from failing or giving way, give courage, confidence, or power of endurance to. 2. Endure, tolerate. 3. Supply with necessaries, provide for. 4. Lend assistance or countenance to; back up, second, further; bear out, substantiate; second, speak in favour of (resolution etc.). **suppōr′table** *adj.* **suppōr′tablў** *adv.* **suppōr′tive** *adj.*

suppōr′ter *n.* (esp., her.) One of pair of figures represented as holding up or standing one on each side of shield (ill. HERALDRY).

suppō′se (-z) *v.t.* 1. Assume as a hypothesis, as ~ *it were true*; in part. or imper. = if, as *supposing white were black you would be right*; also in imper. as formula of proposal, as ~ *we try again*.

SUPPOSITION

2. (of theory, result, etc.) Involve or require as condition, as *design in creation supposes a creator*. 3. Assume in default of knowledge, be inclined to think, accept as probable. 4. *be supposed*, have as a duty, as *he is supposed to clean the boots*; colloq., with neg., freq. = not be allowed, as *children are not supposed to go in*. **suppō′sed** (-zd) *adj*. (esp.) Believed to exist or have specified character. **suppō′sedly** *adv*. **suppō′sable** *adj*.
supposi′tion (-z-) *n*. What is supposed or assumed. **supposi′tional** *adj*.
supposi′tious (-zĭshus) *adj*. Hypothetical, assumed.
supposĭtĭ′tious (-zĭtĭ′shus) *adj*. Substituted for the real; spurious, false. **supposĭtĭ′tiously** *adv*. **supposĭtĭ′tiousness** *n*.
suppŏ′sĭtory (-z-) *n*. (med.) Cone or cylinder of medicated easily melted substance introduced into rectum, vagina, or urethra.
supprĕ′ss *v.t*. Put down, quell, put a stop to activity or existence of; withhold or withdraw from publication; keep secret or unexpressed, refrain from mentioning or showing. **supprĕ′ssion** *n*.
supprĕ′ssĭō ver′ī (vārī). Suppression of truth, misrepresentation by concealment of facts that ought to be made known. [L]
su′ppūrāte *v.i*. Form or secrete pus, fester. **suppūrā′tion** *n*. **su′ppūrative** *adj*.
sŭpra- (or sōō-) *prefix.* = SUPER-, esp. in scientific (esp. anat. and zool.) terms with senses above, higher than; on.
sŭpraclavĭ′cūlar (or sōō-) *adj*. Situated above the clavicle.
sŭpralăpsār′ian (or sōō-) *n*. (hist.) One of those Calvinists holding that predestination was antecedent to the creation and fall. ~ *adj*. Of the supralapsarians or their doctrine.
sŭpra-ōr′bĭtal (or sōō-) *adj*. & *n*. (Artery, vein, bone, nerve) above the orbit of the eye.
sŭprarē′nal (or sōō-) *adj*. & *n*. (Gland) situated above the kidney, adrenal.
sŭprĕ′macy (or sōō-) *n*. Being supreme, position of supreme authority or power; *Act of S~*, any Act of Parliament laying down position of sovereign as supreme head on earth of Church of England or supreme governor of England in spiritual and temporal matters, esp. that of 1534.
sŭprē′me (or sōō-) *adj*. Highest in authority or rank; greatest, of the highest quality, degree, or amount; *S~ Court*, (esp.) highest judicial body in U.S. Government, consisting of 9 members appointed for life by President with Senate's approval. **sŭprē′mely** *adv*.
Supt *abbrev*. Superintendent.
sūr′ah *n*. Soft twilled silk fabric used for scarves, linings, etc. [prob. f. *Surat*, town in Gujarat]

sūr′al *adj*. Of the calf of the leg.
surcea′se *n*. (archaic) Cessation, esp. temporary. ~ *v.i*. (archaic) Cease.
sūr′chārge *n*. Additional or excessive pecuniary charge, or load or burden; extra charge on understamped letter etc.; additional mark printed on face of stamp, esp. to change its value. **surchār′ge** *v.t*. Charge (person) additional or excessive price or payment; exact (sum) as surcharge; overload, fill or saturate to excess; print surcharge on (stamp).
sūr′cingle (-nggl) *n*. Band round horse's body, esp. to keep blanket, pack, etc., in place.
sūr′coat *n*. (hist.) Rich outer garment, esp. (13th–14th centuries)

SURCOAT
A. 13TH-C. MALE. B. 15TH-C. FEMALE
1. Coif. 2. Surcoat. 3. Gown. 4. Veil

loose garment worn over armour (ill. ARMOUR).
sūrd *adj*. & *n*. 1. (math.) Irrational (quantity, esp. root of integer). 2. Voiceless (speech sound).
sure (shoor) *adj*. 1. Certain, assured, confident, persuaded (*of*); having no doubt. 2. That may be relied on, trustworthy, unfailing, infallible; certainly true or truthful; safe; ~*-footed*, treading securely or firmly. 3. Certain *to* do or be; ~ *of*, certain to get, keep, have, etc.; *make ~*, act so as to be certain *of*. **sur′eness** *n*.
sure *adv*. Assuredly, undoubtedly, certainly; *as* certainly *as*.
sur′ely (shoorli) *adv*. 1. With certainty or safety (chiefly in *slowly but ~*). 2. Certainly, assuredly; (freq., expressing belief without absolute proof, or readiness to maintain a statement against possible denial) as may be confidently supposed, as must be the case.
sur′ety (shoorti) *n*. 1. Certainty (archaic; chiefly in *of a ~*, certainly). 2. Formal engagement, pledge, guarantee, bond, security, for fulfilment of undertaking; person undertaking to be liable for default of another, or for his appearance in court, payment of debt, etc.
sūrf *n*. Swell and white foamy

SURLY

water of sea breaking on rock or (esp. shallow) shore; ~*-board*, long narrow board for riding over heavy surf to shore; ~*-duck*, *-scoter*, N. Amer. sea-duck (*Melanitta perspicillata*) with black plumage and white-marked head and neck; ~*-riding*, sport of riding on surf-board. **sūr′fing** *n*. Surfriding.
sūr′face *n*. 1. Outermost boundary of any material body, upper boundary on top of soil, water, etc.; superficial area; (fig.) outward aspect or appearance of anything immaterial, what is presented to casual view or consideration. 2. (geom.) Continuous extent with two dimensions only (length and breadth, without thickness). 3. ~ *craft*, ship navigable on the surface of the sea (opp. SUBMARINE); ~ *mail*, mail carried by land or sea (opp. AIR *mail*); ~*-tension*, (phys.) tension of surface-film of liquid, due to attraction between its particles, which tends to bring it into form with smallest superficial area; ~*-water*, water that collects on and runs off from surface of ground etc. ~ *v*. Put special surface on (paper etc.); raise (submarine etc.), (of submarine etc.) rise, to surface.
sūr′feit (-fit) *n*. Excess, esp. in eating or drinking; oppression or satiety arising from excessive eating or drinking. ~ *v*. Overfeed; (cause to) take too much of something; cloy, satiate *with*.
surg. *abbrev*. Surgeon; surgery.
sûrge *v.i*. Rise and fall, toss, move to and fro (as) in waves or billows; (naut., of rope etc.) slip back or round with jerk. ~ *n*. Waves, a wave; surging motion; ~ *tank*, stand-pipe or storage reservoir to neutralize sudden changes of water pressure (ill. DAM).
sūr′geon (-jon) *n*. Person skilled in surgery; medical officer in army, navy, or military hospital; ~*-fish*, fish of genus *Acanthurus* with sharp movable spine (like lancet) on each side of tail.
sūr′gery *n*. 1. Manual or instrumental treatment of injuries or disorders of the body, esp. (also *operative ~*) involving incision of the skin. 2. Room where medical practitioner, dentist, or veterinary surgeon sees patients for consultation or treatment.
sūr′gical *adj*. Of surgeons or surgery. **sūr′gically** *adv*.
sūr′ĭcāte *n*. Burrowing four-toed mammal of S. Africa (*Suricata suricatta*), related to mongoose, and having grey black-striped fur; meerkat.
Surinā′m (soor-). Dutch colony in northern S. America, Netherlands Guiana; capital, Paramaribo; ~ *toad*, large aquatic toad (*Pipa pipa*) of Guiana and Brazil.
sūr′ly *adj*. Uncivil, churlishly ill-humoured, rude and cross. **sūr′lily** *adv*. **sūr′liness** *n*.

[878]

surmi′se (-z) *n.* Conjecture, idea formed without certainty and on slight evidence. ~ *v.* Infer doubtfully or conjecturally; conjecture, guess.

surmou′nt *v.t.* 1. Prevail over, overcome, get over (obstacle etc.). 2. Cap, be on the top of.

surmŭ′llĕt *n.* Red mullet.

sŭr′name *n.* Family name, name common to all members of family; (archaic) name or epithet added to person's name(s), esp. one derived from his birthplace or some quality or achievement. ~ *v.t.* Give surname to; give as surname.

surpa′ss (-ahs) *v.t.* Outdo, excel. **surpa′ssing** *adj.* That greatly exceeds or excels others, of very high degree. **surpa′ssĭnglў** *adv.*

sŭr′plĭce *n.* Loose full-sleeved white linen vestment worn, usu. over cassock, by clergy and choristers at divine service (ill. VESTMENT).

sŭr′plus *n.* What remains over, excess; (*attrib.*) that is in excess of what is taken, used, or needed; ~ *value*, (econ.) difference between value of wages paid and labour expended or commodity produced. **sŭr′plusage** *n.*

surprī′se (-z) *n.* 1. Catching or taking of person(s) unprepared. 2. Emotion excited by the unexpected, astonishment. 3. Thing, event, that excites surprise. ~ *v.t.* 1. Assail, capture, by surprise; come upon unexpectedly, take unawares. 2. Affect with surprise; be a surprise to; lead unawares, betray, *into* doing something not intended. **surprī′sing** *adj.* **surprī′singlў** *adv.*

sŭrrē′alism *n.* Movement in art and literature, which originated in France (1924), purporting to express the subconscious activities of the mind by representing the phenomena of dreams and similar experiences; art, literature, produced in accordance with this theory. **sŭrrē′alist** *n. & adj.* **sŭrrēalĭ′stic** *adj.* **sŭrrēalĭ′stically** *adv.*

sŭrrē′nder *v.* Yield up, give into another's power or control, relinquish possession of, esp. upon compulsion or demand; abandon claim under (insurance policy) in return for payment of consideration; abandon *oneself*, give *oneself* up *to* some influence, habit, emotion, etc.; (of army, fortress, etc.) yield to enemy or assailant; give oneself up, submit, cease from resistance; ~ *to one's bail*, appear in court at appointed time after being admitted to bail. ~ *n.* Surrendering, being surrendered; ~ *value*, amount to which insured is entitled if he surrenders insurance policy.

sŭrreptĭ′tious (-shus) *adj.* Underhand, secret, clandestine, done by stealth. **sŭrreptĭ′tiouslў** *adv.*

Sŭ′rrey[1] *n.* County of SE. England; university, at Guildford, 1966.

sŭ′rrey[2] *n.* (U.S.) Light four-wheeled carriage with two seats facing forwards. [f. county of SURREY[1]]

sŭ′rrogate *n.* Deputy, esp. of bishop or his chancellor; in New York and other States of U.S., judge with jurisdiction over probate of wills and settlement of estates.

surrou′nd *v.t.* Come, lie, be, all round or on all sides; invest, enclose, encompass, environ, encircle. ~ *n.* Border or edging, as of linoleum, boards, round carpet.

surrou′ndings (-z) *n.pl.* Things (collectively) surrounding person or thing, environs, environment.

Sŭr′sum cōr′da. Versicle beginning thus (L, = 'Lift up your hearts'), preceding preface in Latin Mass; corresponding versicle in Anglican rite.

sŭr′tăx *n.* Additional tax; graduated tax on incomes exceeding the amount to which the standard rate applies. ~ *v.t.* Impose surtax on.

Sŭr′tees (-z), Robert Smith (1805–64). English author of humorous sporting novels, in some of which the principal character is a grocer named Jorrocks.

surveĭ′llance (-văl-) *n.* Supervision; close guard or watch, esp. over suspected person.

survey′ (-vā) *v.t.* 1. Take general view of, scan. 2. Consider (situation, subject, etc.) as a whole, make or present survey of. 3. Examine condition of (building etc.) 4. Determine form, extent, etc., of (tract of ground etc.) by linear and angular measurements so as to settle boundaries or construct map, plan, or detailed description. **sŭr′vey** *n.* General or comprehensive view of something; inspection, examination in detail, esp. for specific purpose; account given of result of this; department or persons engaged in, operations constituting, act of, surveying of land etc., map or plan setting forth results of such survey.

survey′or (-vā-) *n.* Official inspector *of* (weights and measures, highways, etc.); person professionally engaged in surveying. **survey′orship** *n.*

survī′val *n.* Surviving; person or thing remaining as relic of earlier time.

survī′ve *v.* Outlive, continue to live or exist after death, cessation, or end of, or after the occurrence of (disaster, hardship, etc.); continue to live or exist, be still alive or existent. **survī′vor** *n.* **survī′vorship** *n.* (esp.) Right of person having some joint interest to take whole estate on death of other(s).

Susă′nna (sōōz-). Virtuous and beautiful wife of Joachim, accused of adultery by Jewish elders but proved innocent by Daniel; *Book of* ~, book of the Apocrypha telling of this.

suscĕ′ptible *adj.* 1. (predic.) Admitting *of*; open, liable, accessible, sensitive, *to*. 2. Impressionable; sensitive; readily touched with emotion; touchy. **suscĕptĭbĭ′lĭtў** *n.* **suscĕ′ptĭblў** *adv.*

suspĕ′ct *v.t.* 1. Imagine something evil, wrong, or undesirable in, have suspicions or doubts about; imagine something, esp. something wrong, about. 2. Imagine to be possible or likely, have faint notion or inkling of; surmise. **sŭ′spĕct** *adj.* Regarded with suspicion or distrust; of suspected character. ~ *n.* Suspected person.

suspĕ′nd *v.t.* 1. Debar from exercise of function or enjoyment of privilege; deprive (temporarily) of office; put a (temporary) stop to, put in abeyance, annul for a time, abrogate temporarily; defer; refrain from forming (judgement, opinion); ~ *payment*, fail to meet financial engagements; become insolvent. 2. (mus.) Prolong (one note of chord) to following chord. 3. Hang up; hold, cause to be held, in suspension. **suspĕ′ndĕd** *adj.* (esp.) ~ *animation*, temporary cessation of vital physical functions.

suspĕ′nder *n.* (esp.) Device attached to top of sock or stocking to hold it up; (pl., chiefly U.S.) braces.

suspĕ′nse *n.* State of usu. anxious uncertainty, expectation, or waiting for information; doubtfulness, uncertainty; ~ *account*, (book-keeping) account in which items are temporarily entered until proper place is determined.

suspĕ′nsion *n.* Suspending, being suspended; condition of being diffused in form of particles through fluid medium; (mus.) prolonging note of chord into following chord, discord so produced; ~ *bridge*, bridge in which roadway is suspended from ropes, chains, or wire cables extending between steel or masonry towers or other supports (ill. BRIDGE[1]).

suspĕ′nsorў *adj.* That suspends or holds suspended or supported (esp. some part or organ). ~ *n.* Suspensory bandage.

suspĭ′cion (-shon) *n.* Suspecting; feeling or state of mind of one who suspects; being suspected; slight belief or idea, faint notion, inkling; slight trace, very small amount *of*. ~ *v.t.* (chiefly U.S. and dial.) Suspect.

suspĭ′cious (-shus) *adj.* Prone to, feeling, indicating, open to, deserving of, exciting, suspicion. **suspĭ′ciouslў** *adv.* **suspĭ′ciousnĕss** *n.*

suspī′re *v.i.* (now poet.) Sigh. **sŭspīrā′tion** *n.*

Sŭ′ssĕx[1]. Former maritime

Sussex county of SE. England, since April 1974 divided into the counties of East Sussex and West Sussex; university, at Brighton, 1961.

Sŭ′ssex² *n.* Domestic fowl of English breed with speckled or red plumage.

sustai′n *v.t.* 1. Uphold or allow validity, rightfulness, truth, correctness, or justice of; be adequate as ground or basis for. 2. Keep from failing or giving way; keep in being, in a certain state or at the proper level or standard; keep up, keep going (sound, effort, etc.); keep up, represent (part, character) adequately. 3. Endure without failing or giving way; withstand; undergo, experience, suffer. 4. Hold up, bear weight of; be support of; bear, support (weight, pressure).

sŭ′stenance *n.* Livelihood; means of sustaining life, food.

sŭstentā′tion *n.* Support, upkeep, maintenance; support or maintenance of life; ~ *fund*, fund, esp. in Church of Scotland, to provide support for ministers.

sŭsŭrrā′tion *n.* Whispering, rustling.

Sŭ′therland (-dh-). Former county of N. Scotland, since May 1975 part of the region of Highland.

sŭ′tler *n.* Camp-follower selling provisions etc. to soldiers.

Su′tra (soo-) *n.* Aphorism, set of aphorisms, in Sanskrit literature. [Sansk. *sūtra* manual of aphoristic rules]

sŭttee′ *n.* (hist.) Hindu widow who immolated herself on husband's funeral pyre; such immolation. **sŭttee′ism** *n.* [Sansk. *satī* virtuous wife]

Sŭ′tton Hōō (-tn). Site near Woodbridge, Suffolk, of Saxon ship burial (*c* A.D. 650), probably of an East Anglian king.

su′ture (soo-) *n.* 1. (surg.) Joining of edges of wound etc. by stitch(es), stitch used for this. 2. (anat.) Seam-like line of junction of two bones, esp. of skull (ill. HEAD); (zool., bot.) line of junction of contiguous parts, as of valves in shell, plant's ovary, etc. **su′tural** *adj.* **su′ture** *v.t.* Stitch (wound).

sŭ′zerain (or soo-) *n.* Feudal overlord; sovereign or State having political control over another. **sŭ′zerainty** *n.*

s.v. *abbrev. Sub voce.*

svĕlte *adj.* Slim, willowy.

SW. *abbrev.* South-west(ern); static water.

swab (-ŏb) *n.* Mop or other absorbent mass used for cleansing or mopping up; pad of cotton-wool or other absorbent material for applying medicament, cleaning wound, etc.; specimen of morbid secretion etc. taken with swab. ~ *v.t.* Clean or wipe (as) with swab, mop *up* (as) with swab.

Swā′bia. Latinized form of *Schwaben*, former German duchy including Württemberg, Baden, and part of Bavaria. **Swā′bian** *adj. & n.*

swa′ddle (-ŏ-) *v.t.* Swathe in bandages, wrappings, etc.; *swaddling-clothes*, narrow bandages wrapped round new-born infant to prevent free movement (now chiefly fig.).

Swadeshi (swahdā′shǐ) *n.* (hist.) Movement in India, originating in Bengal, advocating the boycott of foreign, esp. British, goods. [Bengali, = 'native country']

swăg *n.* 1. Ornamental festoon of flowers, fruit, etc., fastened up at both ends and hanging down in

SWAG OR FESTOON

middle; carved or moulded representation of this. 2. (slang) Thief's booty; dishonest gains. 3. (Austral.) Bundle of personal belongings carried by tramp, miner, or bush-traveller; *swa′gman*, one travelling with a swag.

swāge *n.* Tool for bending cold metal, die or stamp for shaping metal by striking with hammer or

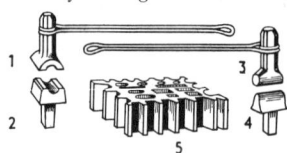

SWAGE AND FULLER

1. Top swage. 2. Bottom swage. 3. Top fuller. 4. Bottom fuller. 5. Swage-block

sledge; ~-*block*, smith's block of metal with perforations, grooves, etc., for this purpose. ~ *v.t.* Shape with swage.

swă′gger (-g-) *v.i.* Walk, carry oneself, as if among inferiors, with superior, insolent, or blustering manner; talk boastfully or braggingly. ~ *n.* 1. Swaggering gait or manner. 2. (also ~ *coat*) Woman's loose straight coat. 3. ~-*cane*, -*stick*, short light cane carried by army officers when walking out. ~ *adj.* (colloq.) Smart, fashionable.

Swahi′li (-hē-) *n.* (One of) Bantu people of Zanzibar and adjacent coast; (also *Kīswahi′li*) language of these, used as lingua franca in parts of E. Africa. [lit. 'of the coasts', f. Arab. *sawāhil* pl. of *sāhil* coast]

swain *n.* Countryman, young rustic, esp. shepherd (archaic); country gallant or lover; (joc.) suitor, lover.

swa′llow¹ (-ŏlō) *n.* Bird of genus *Hirundo* and related genera, esp. the migratory insect-eating *H. rustica* with long pointed wings and forked tail, swift curving flight and twittering cry, building mud-nests on buildings and associated (in N. Europe) with summer; (loosely) any of various other birds, esp. the unrelated swifts, resembling swallows in some respects; ~ *dive*, dive with head tilted backwards and arms spread sideways like swallow's wings; ~-*tail*, forked tail like swallow's; *swa′llowtail*, butterfly (of family Papilionidae, esp. *Papilio machaon*) in which border of each hind wing is prolonged into a tail-like process; cleft two-pointed end of flag or pennon, flag with this; swallow-tailed kite; (freq. pl.) swallow-tailed coat, man's ~-*tailed coat*, man's full-dress evening coat, with two long tapering tails; ~-*tailed kite*, white kite (*Elanoides forficatus*) of S. and Central America (rare in U.S.) with black wings and deeply forked tail; tropical African kite (*Chelictinia riocourii*).

swa′llow² (-ŏlō) *v.* Cause or allow (food etc.) to pass down one's throat; engulf, absorb, exhaust (usu. ~ *up*); accept (statement etc.) with ready credulity; put up with, stomach (affront); recant (words); keep down, repress (emotion). ~ *n.* 1. Gullet; act of swallowing; amount swallowed at once; capacity for swallowing. 2. (also ~-*hole*) Hole, esp. in limestone formations, through which stream disappears underground.

swa′mi (-wah-) *n.* Hindu religious teacher (esp. as form of address to Brahmin); (transf.) pundit. [Sansk. *svāmin* master, prince]

swamp (-ŏ-) *n.* Piece of wet spongy ground, marsh; (esp., N. America) tract of rich soil with trees etc., too moist for cultivation; (attrib., of many animals, birds, plants, etc.) growing, living, in swamps. **swa′mpў** *adj.* swamp *v.* Submerge, inundate, soak, with water (of boat) (cause to) fill with water and sink; overwhelm with numbers or quantity of anything.

swan¹ (-ŏn) *n.* Large web-footed swimming bird usu. of genus *Cygnus*, with long gracefully curved neck, esp. the domestic, mute, or tame swan, *C. olor*, with pure white plumage in adult, black legs and feet and red bill with black knob, occurring wild in NE. Europe and W. Central Asia, and semi-domesticated all over Europe and America, formerly

SWALLOW
Length 190 mm

[880]

supposed to sing melodiously just before its death; (fig.) singer, poet (see *S~ of* AVON); (*S~*, astron.) northern constellation Cygnus; ~ *dive*, (U.S.) swallow dive; ~-*goose*, largest goose (*Anṣer cygnoides*) of E. Asia; ~ *knight*, Lohengrin or other legendary hero brought by swan to succour country; ~ *maiden*, one of a class of legendary maidens capable of changing into swans; ~-*neck*, something of curved cylindrical form more or less like swan's neck; swa'nsdown, down or fine soft feathers of swan used for powder-puffs, trimmings, etc.; soft thick woollen cloth, thick cotton fabric with soft nap; swa'nskin, thick soft kind of flannel or other fabric; ~-*song*, legendary song of dying swan; last (esp. artistic) production of person etc.; ~-*upping*, annual expedition on Thames for marking swans on beak as property of Crown or some City corporation. swa'nlike *adj.*
swan[2] (-ŏn) *v.i.* (slang) Cruise, roam (esp. *around*).
swănk *n.* (slang) Ostentatious or pretentious behaviour, talk, etc., swagger, boastfulness, showing off. swă'nkў *adj.* swănk *v.i.* Show off, bounce, swagger.
swa'nnerў (-ŏ-) *n.* Place where swans are kept and reared.
swap (-ŏp), swŏp *ns.* & *vbs.* (slang) Exchange by way of barter.
Swara'j (-ahj) *n.* (hist.) Self-government of India, as the aim of Indian Nationalists. Swara'jĭst *n.* [Sansk., = 'self-ruling']
sward (-ôrd) *n.* (Stretch of) turf or greensward.
swarm[1] (-ôrm) *n.* Cluster of bees leaving hive or main body with queen bee to establish new hive; large or dense body, throng, multitude of persons, insects, etc., esp. moving about. ~ *v.i.* Move in a swarm; (of bees) gather in compact cluster round queen and leave hive in a body; congregate in number, be very numerous; (of places) be overrun or crowded.
swarm[2] (-ôrm) *v.* Climb *up* (rope, pole, tree) by clasping it with arms and legs alternately; climb up or *up* (any steep ascent) by clinging with hands and knees.
swart (-ôrt) *adj.* (archaic) Dark-hued, swarthy.
swar'thў (-ôrdhi) *adj.* Dark-complexioned, dark in colour. swar'thily *adv.* swar'thinėss *n.*
swash[1] (-ŏsh) *v.* (of water etc.) Wash about, make sound of washing or rising and falling; (archaic) strike violently; swa'shbuckler, swaggering bravo or ruffian, bully. ~ *n.* (Sound of) swashing.
swash[2] (-ŏ-) *adj.* (turning etc.) Inclined obliquely to axis of work; (print., of italic capitals) having flourished strokes at top and bottom, as *T*, *N*; ~-*plate*, rotating circular plate set at an oblique angle to its shaft, giving recipro-cating motion to rod resting on it and parallel to its shaft.
swa'stika (-ŏs-) *n.* Primitive and ancient symbol or talisman in form of cross with equal arms, each arm having a limb of same length projecting from its end at right angles, all in same direction (usu. direction of sun's course, i.e. clockwise) (ill. CROSS), found in various parts of the world, esp. Mexico, Peru, and Tibet, used in Germany and Austria from 1918 onwards as symbol of anti-Semitism or as emblem of Nazi Party. [Sansk. f. *svastika*, f. *svasti* well-being, good fortune, luck]
swat (-ŏt) *v.t.* Hit hard, crush (fly etc.) with blow.
swath (-aw-) *n.* (pl. pr. -dhz). Row or line of grass, corn, etc., as it falls when mown or reaped; space covered by mower's scythe, width of grass or corn so cut.
swāthe (-dh) *v.t.* Wrap up or round, envelop, like bandage or (as) with wrapping.
sway *v.* 1. Lean unsteadily to one side or in different directions by turns; have unsteady swinging motion; oscillate irregularly; waver, vacillate; give swaying motion to. 2. Govern the motion of; wield, control direction of; have influence over; govern, rule over. 3. *swayed*, *sway-back(ed)*, with back abnormally hollowed (esp. of horse). ~ *n.* 1. Swaying motion or position. 2. Rule, government.
Swa'zĭlănd (swah-). Kingdom in SE. Africa between Mozambique, Transvaal, and Natal; member State of the Commonwealth, formerly a British protectorate; independent 1968; capital, Mbabane.
swear (swār) *v.* (past t. swōre, past part. swōrn). 1. State something, state (thing) on oath, take oath; promise or undertake something by oath; promise to observe or perform (something); take (oath); confirm by oath; affirm emphatically or confidently; ~ *by*, (colloq.) profess or have great belief in; ~ *off*, forswear. 2. Utter profane oath, use profane language, to express anger or as expletive(s); ~-*word*, profane oath or word. 3. Cause to take oath, administer oath to; (also ~ *in*), admit to office or function by administering oath.
sweat (-ĕt) *n.* 1. Salty fluid secreted by glands beneath the skin and exuded through the pores, perspiration; something resembling sweat, drops of moisture on a surface; condition or fit of sweating; (colloq.) state of impatience or anxiety; ~-*band*, band of leather etc. as lining of hat or cap; ~ *gland*, minute coiled tubular gland beneath skin secreting sweat (ill. SKIN); ~-*shirt*, kind of sweater worn by athletes before or after exercise. 2. (chiefly colloq.) Drudgery, toil, laborious task; *old* ~, old soldier; ~-*shop*, workroom in which workers are sweated (see below). swea'tў *adj.* swea'tilў *adv.* swea'tinėss *n.* sweat *v.* 1. Exude sweat, perspire; emit or exude, ooze *out*, as or like sweat; cause (horse, athlete, etc.) to sweat by exercise etc.; exude or gather moisture in drops on surface; cause to exude moisture, force moisture out of; *sweating-pit*, (tanning) pit in which hides are sweated; *sweating-room*, room in Turkish bath etc. where persons are sweated; room in which cheeses are sweated or deprived of superfluous moisture; *sweating-sickness*, febrile disease, freq. rapidly fatal, with profuse sweating, epidemic in England in 15th and 16th centuries. 2. Work hard, toil, drudge; employ (workers) at starvation wages for long hours, exploit to the utmost; (of workers) work on such terms.
swea'ter (-ĕt-) *n.* (esp.) Pullover.
Swēde[1] *n.* Native of Sweden.
swēde[2] *n.* Large variety of turnip with yellow edible root, first introduced into Scotland from Sweden in 18th c.
Swē'den. Kingdom of E. Scandinavia; capital, Stockholm.
Swē'denbõrg, Emanuel (1688–1772). Swedish religious mystic and philosopher; held that God, as Divine Man, is infinite love and infinite wisdom, and the end of creation is the approximation of man to God; he taught that there is a symbolic sense to the Scriptures, of which he was the appointed interpreter. Swēdenbõr'gian (-j-) *adj.* & *n.* (Follower) of Swedenborg, (member) of the New Jerusalem Church. Swēdenbõr'gianĭsm *n.*
Swē'dĭsh *adj.* Of Sweden or its people or language; ~ *drill*, system of muscular exercises as a form of hygienic or curative treatment; ~ *nightingale*, nickname of Jenny LIND; ~ *turnip* = SWEDE[2]. ~ *n.* Indo-European language of Sweden, one of the Norse group.
sweep *v.* (past t. & past part. *swĕpt*). 1. Glide swiftly, speed along with impetuous unchecked motion, go majestically; extend in continuous curve, line, or slope. 2. Impart sweeping motion to; carry *along*, *down*, *away*, *off*, in impetuous course; clear *off*, *away*, *from*, etc. 3. Traverse or range swiftly, pass lightly across or along; pass eyes or hand quickly along or over; scan, scour, graze; (of artillery etc.) include in line of fire, cover, enfilade, rake. 4. Clear everything from; clear of dust, soot, litter, with broom; gather *up*, collect, (as) with broom; ~ *the board*, win all money on gaming-table; win all possible prizes etc. 5. ~-*net*, large fishing-net enclosing wide space; swee'pstake(s), (prize won in) race or contest in

[881]

which all competitors' stakes are taken by winner(s); form of gambling on horse-races etc. in which sum of participators' stakes goes to drawer(s) of winning or placed horse(s) etc. **swee'per** *n.* (esp.) 1. (footb. etc.) Player positioned in front of goalkeeper and behind other players. 2. = CARPET sweeper. **swee'ping** *adj.* (esp., of statement etc.) General, unqualified, regardless of limitations or exceptions. **sweep** *n.* 1. Sweeping, clearing up or away (now usu. *a clean ~*); moving in continuous curve (of an army, fleet, river, etc.); hostile reconnaissance by group of aircraft; sweeping motion or extension, curve in road, etc.; curved carriage drive leading to house. 2. Range or compass of something that has curving motion; extent, stretch, expanse, esp. such as can be taken in at one survey. 3. Long oar worked by rower(s) standing on barge etc.; long pole mounted as lever for raising bucket from well; gear for clearing submarine mines, usu. consisting of a long wire with a cutting device attached, streamed from a vessel (*mine-sweeper*) at the required depth. 4. Chimney sweep; (slang) low fellow, blackguard. 5. (colloq.) Sweepstake. **sweet** *adj.* 1. Tasting like sugar, honey, etc., corresponding to one of the primary sensations of taste; (of wine) tasting thus, containing unfermented natural sugar (opp. DRY). 2. Pleasing to the sense of smell, fragrant, perfumed. 3. Fresh and sound, not salt(ed) or sour or bitter or putrid. 4. Agreeable, attractive, gratifying; inspiring. affection, dear, amiable, gentle, easy; (colloq.) pretty, charming, delightful; *at one's own ~ will*, as one pleases, arbitrarily; *~ on*, (colloq.) very fond of, (inclined to be) in love with. 5. *~-and-sour*, cooked or prepared with seasoning of both sugar and vinegar or lemon; *~ bay*, = BAY¹, 1; (also) N. Amer. magnolia (*Magnolia virginiana*); *swee'tbread*, pancreas or thymus gland of animal, esp. calf, used for food; *~-brier*, eglantine (*Rosa rubiginosa*, and other species), with small hooked prickles, single flowers, and small aromatic leaves; *~ corn*, sweet-flavoured variety of maize or Indian corn; *swee'theart*, darling; either of pair of lovers; *~ herb*, fragrant culinary herb; *~ marjoram*, aromatic cultivated herb (*Origanum marjorana*); *swee'tmeat* = SWEET *n.* 1; *~ (spirits of) nitre*, spirit of nitrous ether, a pale yellow sweet-tasting aromatic liquid used as diuretic, diaphoretic, etc.; *~ oil*, any pleasant- or mild-tasting oil, esp. olive oil, rape oil; *~ pea*, climbing leguminous annual (*Lathyrus odoratus*) cultivated for its many-coloured, sweet-scented flowers; *~ potato*, (large sweet farinaceous tuberous root, eaten as vegetable, of) tropical climbing-plant (*Ipomoea batatas*) widely cultivated in warm regions; *~-scented*, having a sweet scent (freq. in names of plants, flowers, etc.); *swee'tsop*, (sweet pulpy fruit with thick green rind and black seeds of) tropical Amer. evergreen tree (*Annona squamosa*); *~ tooth*, taste for sweet things; *~-william*, cultivated species of pink (*Dianthus barbatus*), with closely clustered sweet-smelling freq. particoloured flowers. **swee'tly** *adv.* **swee'tness** *n.* **sweet** *n.* 1. Small shaped piece of something sweet, usu. made of boiled sugar or chocolate with fruit or other flavouring or filling. 2. (freq. pl.) Sweet dish(es) such as puddings, tarts, jellies, forming a course at table. 3. Sweet part (chiefly fig.); (usu. pl.) fragrance; (pl.) delights, pleasures, gratifications; (chiefly in voc.) darling. **swee'ten** *v.* **swee'tening** *n.* **swee'tie** *n.* (chiefly Sc.) = SWEET *n.* 1; (U.S.) sweetheart. **swee'ting** *n.* Kind of sweet apple. **swell** *v.* (past part. *swö'llen* or less usu. *swelled*). (Cause to) grow bigger or greater, dilate, expand; rise, raise, *up* from surrounding surface; bulge *out*; increase in volume, force, or intensity; (of emotion) arise and grow in mind with sense as of expansion; (of person, his heart, etc.) be affected with such emotion; (mus.) sing or play (note) with alternate *crescendo* and *diminuendo*. **swě'lled** (-ld) *adj.* (esp.) *~ head*, (colloq.) conceit. **swěll** *n.* 1. Being swollen; swollen part, protuberance, bulge. 2. Heaving of sea etc. with long rolling waves that do not break, as after storm; such waves collectively. 3. Gradual increase in loudness or force of sound; (mus.) *crescendo* followed by *diminuendo*, symbol denoting this (< >); mechanism in organ, harmonium, etc., for gradually varying force of tone, now usu. series of slats that can be opened or shut by means of pedal or lever worked by knee (ill. ORGAN); *~-box*, box, containing set of pipes or reeds, which is opened or closed by swell; *~ organ*, set of pipes enclosed in swell-box. 4. (colloq.) Fashionable or stylish person; person of good social standing; *~ mob(smen)*, (obs. slang) well-dressed pickpockets or swindlers. *~ adj.* (colloq.) Distinguished, first-rate; stylishly dressed or equipped; of good social position. **swě'lling** *n.* (esp.) Distension of injured or diseased part of body. **swě'lter** *v.i.* Be oppressed or oppressive with heat; sweat profusely, languish, be faint, with excessive heat. **swept**: see SWEEP. **swerve** *v.* Turn aside, (cause to) deviate from straight or direct course; (cricket etc.) cause (ball) to swerve in the air. *~ n.* Swerving motion; divergence from course.
S.W.G., s.w.g. *abbrev.* Standard wire gauge.
swift¹ *adj.* Fleet, rapid, quick; soon coming or passing, not long delayed; prompt, quick *to do*. *~ adv.* Swiftly (chiefly in combination, as *~-footed*). **swi'ftly** *adv.* **swi'ftness** *n.* **swift** *n.* Any of various swift-flying insectivorous birds of the numerous

SWIFT
Length 165 mm

and widely distributed family Apodidae superficially resembling swallows, esp. *Apus apus*, the common swift, a summer visitant in Europe.
Swift², Jonathan (1667–1745). Irish clergyman, Dean of St. Patrick's, Dublin; author of 'A Tale of a Tub', 'Gulliver's Travels', and other satires and political works.
swig *v.* (slang) Take draughts (of). *~ n.* (Act of taking) a draught of liquor.
swill *v.* Wash or rinse (*out*), pour water over or through, flush; drink greedily. *~ n.* 1. Liquid or partly liquid food, chiefly kitchen refuse, given to swine; pig-wash; inferior liquor. 2. Rinsing, swilling.
swim *v.* (past t. *swăm*, past part. *swŭm*). 1. Float on or at surface of liquid. 2. Progress at or below surface of water by working legs, arms, tail, webbed feet, fins, etc. (*illustration, p. 883*); traverse (distance etc.) thus; compete in (race) thus; cause (horse, dog, etc.) to progress thus; (fig.) go with gliding motion. 3. Appear to undulate, reel, or whirl, have dizzy effect or sensation; be flooded or overflow with or *with* or *in* moisture. 4. *~-bladder*, air-bladder of many fish (ill. FISH¹); *swimming-bath*, *-pool*, bath, pool, for swimming in; *swimming-bell*, bell-shaped swimming organ of jellyfish etc. *~ n.* Spell of swimming; (fig.) main current of affairs (*in, out of, the ~*); *~-suit*, bathing-costume.
swi'mmeret *n.* Abdominal appendage in some crustaceans (ill. LOBSTER).
swi'mmingly *adv.* (esp.) With easy and unobstructed progress.
Swi'nburne, Algernon Charles (1837–1909). English poet, author of 'Songs before Sunrise', 'Atalanta in Calydon', etc.
swi'ndle *v.* Cheat (person, money *out of* person, person *out of*

[882]

SWINE   SWOP

money). **swi′ndler** n. **swi′ndle** n. Piece of swindling, fraudulent scheme, imposition; something represented as what it is not, fraud.

melody, etc.) Vigorously rhythmical. 2. Gay, lively. **swi′ngingly** adv. **swi′ngle** (-nggl) n. Wooden sword-like instrument for beating flax and removing woody parts from it; striking or swinging part of flail; ~-*tree*, cross-bar pivoted in middle, to ends of which traces are fastened in cart, plough, etc. (ill. HARNESS). ~ v.t. Clean (flax) with swingle.

swink n. & v.i. (archaic) Toil.

swipe v. 1. Hit at or hit cricket-ball etc., hit (cricket-ball etc.) hard and recklessly, slog; (slang) steal by snatching. ~ n. 1. Reckless hard hit or attempt to hit. 2. (pl.) Washy or turbid or otherwise inferior beer.

swirl n. Eddy, whirlpool; eddying or whirling motion; twist, convolution, curl. ~ v. Eddy, carry (object), be carried, with eddying or whirling motion.

swish[1] n. Sound of switch or similar object moved rapidly through air, of scythe cutting grass, or object moving rapidly through water. ~ v. Make, move with, swish; flog with birch or cane.

swish[2] adj. (colloq.) Very smart.

Swiss[1] adj. Of Switzerland or its people; ~ *guards*, Swiss mercenary troops formerly by sovereigns of France etc. and still at Vatican; ~ *roll*, thin flat spongecake spread with jam etc. and rolled up. ~ n. Native (collect., people) of Switzerland.

swiss[2] n. (chiefly U.S.) Fine cotton fabric of plain weave freq. with dots or flecks formed by extra yarns (dotted ~).

switch n. 1. Slender tapering whip; thin flexible shoot cut from tree, something resembling this. 2. Device for making and breaking contact or altering connections in electric circuit; (on railway etc.) movable rail or pair of rails pivoted at one end at junction of tracks, used to deflect train etc. from one line to another. 3. Tress of dead or false hair, tied at one end, used in hairdressing. 4. ~-*back* (railway), form of railway used on steep slopes, with zigzag series of lines connected at ends by switches; railway used for amusement at fairs etc. with series of steep alternate ascents and descents, the momentum of each descent carrying the car or train (partly) up the following ascent; road with alternate ascents and descents; **swi′tchboard**, board or frame with set of switches for varying connection between a number of electric circuits, as of telephone, telegraph, etc.; **swi′tchman**, man who works switch(es), esp. on railway. ~ v. 1. Strike, whip, (as) with switch; flourish like a switch, whisk, lash, move with sudden jerk. 2. Turn (train etc.) on to another line by means of switch; turn (electric current, light, etc.) *on*, *off*, by means of switch, change (connection) *over* with switch; (fig.) turn off, divert; (cards) change suit in bidding or leading; ~-*over*, diversion of effort, activity, or production.

swi′ther (-dh-) v.i. (chiefly Sc.) Hesitate, be uncertain.

Swi′thin (-dh-), St. (d. 862). Bishop of Winchester, commemorated 15 July; acc. to legend, if it rains on this day there will be rain for the next 40 days.

Swi′tzerland. Federal republic of central Europe, consisting of 25 cantons inhabited by German-, French-, Italian-, and Romansh-speaking people; an independent State since it broke away from the Holy Roman Empire in 1499; capital, Berne.

swi′vel n. Simple joining or coupling device made so that object fastened can turn freely upon it, or so that each half of the swivel itself can turn independently; ring or staple turning on pin, or the like; ~ *bearing, chain, coupling, gun*, etc., one provided with or mounted on swivel; ~ *chair*, chair with seat turning horizontally on pivot; ~-*eye(d)*, (with) squinting eye. ~ v. Turn (as) on swivel.

swi′zzle n. 1. Compounded drink, esp. of rum or other spirit and bitters; ~-*stick*, stick used to stir drink into a froth or to make gas escape from champagne. 2. (school slang) Swindle; disappointment.

swollen: see SWELL.

swoon n. & v.i. (archaic) Faint.

swoop v. Come down or *down* with the rush of a bird of prey (often upon prey etc.); attack from a distance; (colloq.) snatch, seize, the whole of. ~ n. Act of swooping, esp. sudden pounce of bird of prey; *at one (fell)* ~, at a single blow or stroke.

swop: see SWAP.

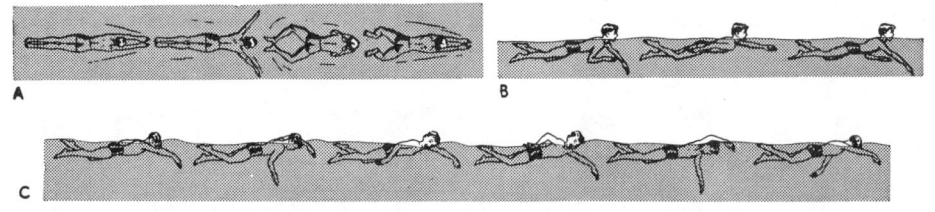

SWIMMING STROKES. A. BREAST-STROKE. B. DOG PADDLE. C. CRAWL

swine n. (pl. same). Animal of family Suidae of non-ruminant hoofed mammals, with stout body, thick skin, longish snout with terminal nostrils, and small tail; pig, esp. the common species *Sus scrofa*, domesticated for its flesh and regarded as type of greediness and uncleanness; person of greedy or bestial habits (used esp. as strong term of abuse); ~-*fever*, infectious disease of swine caused by virus and chiefly affecting intestines, hog cholera; **swi′neherd**, one who tends swine; ~-*plague*, infectious bacterial disease of swine resembling swine-fever but chiefly affecting lungs. **swi′nish** adj. **swi′nishly** adv. **swi′nishness** n.

swing v. (past t. & past part. **swung**). 1. Move with the to-and-fro or curving motion of object having fixed point(s) or side but otherwise free; sway or so hang as to be free to sway like pendulum, door, etc.; oscillate, revolve, rock, wheel; ~ *the lead*: see LEAD[1]. 2. Go with swinging gait. 3. Give (music) the character of swing music. 4. ~-*back*, hinged or pivoted back of photographic camera, allowing plate to be kept vertical when camera is tilted etc.; ~-*boat*, boat-shaped swing at fairs etc.; ~ *bridge*, kind of bridge that can be swung aside on pivot(s) to let ships etc. pass (ill. BRIDGE[1]); ~-*door*, -*gate*, door (esp. in two leaves hung separately and sprung), gate, that swings in either direction and closes of itself when released; ~ *glass*, looking-glass hung on pivots; ~-*wing*, (of aircraft) having wings that can be swung back. ~ n. 1. Act or process of swinging; swinging gait or rhythm; movement describing curve. 2. Seat slung by ropes or chains for swinging in; swing-boat; spell of swinging in either of these. 3. (also ~ *music*) Kind of jazz in which the time of the melody (usu. played by single instrument) is freely varied over simple harmonic accompaniment in strict time with strongly marked rhythm.

swi′ngeing (-jing) adj. Forcible; (colloq.) huge.

swi′nging adj. (esp. of gait,

[883]

SWORD

sword (sord) *n.* Offensive weapon for cutting or thrusting, consisting of long straight or curved blade with handle or hilt and cross-guard, sharp point, and usu. one or two sharp edges; *draw, sheathe, the* ~, begin, cease from, war; *fire and* ~, destruction spread (part of) word previously spelt out.
S.Y. *abbrev.* Steam yacht.
Sȳ′barīte *n.* Inhabitant of ancient Greek colony of Sybaris in S. Italy noted for luxury; hence (s~), luxury-loving person. **sȳbarĭ′tĭc** *adj.*

SYLLEPSIS

denoting a syllable; consisting of such symbols; (pros.) based on number of syllables. **sȳllă′bĭcallȳ** *adv.*
sȳllă′bĭcāte, sȳllă′bĭfȳ *vbs.t.* Divide into syllables. **sȳllăbĭcā′tion, sȳllăbĭfĭc′ātion** *ns.*
sȳ′llable *n.* Vocal sound(s)

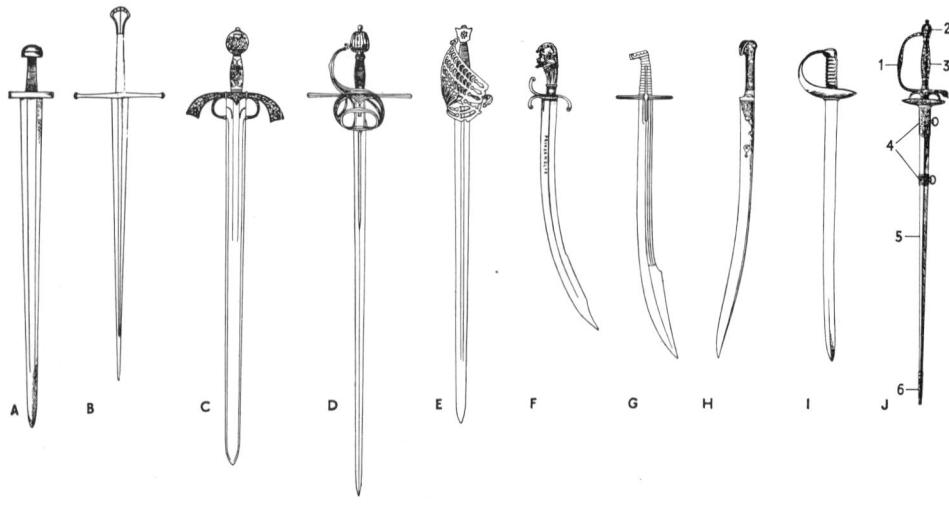

A. VIKING SWORD, 11TH C.   B. HAND-AND-A-HALF SWORD, EARLY 15TH C.   C. TWO-EDGED SWORD, *c* 1525.   D. RAPIER, *c* 1620.   E. VENETIAN BROADSWORD, *c* 1650.   F. FALCHION, *c* 1600–20. G. HUNGARIAN SABRE, *c* 1650.   H. TURKISH YATAGHAN, 19TH C.   I. NAVAL CUTLASS, *c* 1790. J. SMALL-SWORD, *c* 1790
1, 2, 3. Hilt (1. Knuckle-bow, 2. Pommel, 3. Grip).   4. Lockets.   5. Scabbard.   6. Chape

by invading army; *put to the* ~, kill, esp. after victory; ~*-arm*, right arm; ~*-bayonet*, bayonet that can be used as short sword; ~*-bearer*, person carrying sword for another, esp. municipal officer bearing sword before magistrate on ceremonial occasions; ~*-dance*, dance, esp. folk-dance, in which performers go through evolutions with swords, or one which is danced over naked swords laid on ground; ~*-fish*, large sea-fish used for food (*Xiphias gladius*), with upper jaw prolonged into sword-like point; ~*-grass*, grass with sharp-edged leaves; plant with sword-shaped leaves, as the gladiolus; ~*-lily*, gladiolus; ~*-play*, fencing; ~*-stick*, hollow walking-stick containing a sword-blade; *swor′dsman*, one skilled in use of sword; *swor′dsmanship*. **swor′dlīke** *adj.*
sworn *adj.*: see SWEAR; (esp.) bound by an oath; ~ *brother*, close friend; ~ *enemy, foe*, determined or irreconcilable enemy.
swŏt *n.* (school slang) Hard work or study; person who works hard, esp. at learning. ~ *v.* Work hard, esp. at books; study (subject) *up* hurriedly.
swum : see SWIM.
swŭng *adj.* : see SWING; (esp.) ~ *dash*, mark (~) used in place of

sȳ′camōre *n.* 1. Large Eurasian species of maple (*Acer pseudoplatanus*) grown as shady ornamental tree and for its wood. 2. (N. Amer.) Plane-tree (*Platanus*), esp. *P. occidentalis*. 3. (bibl., also *sycomore*) Species of fig (*Ficus sycomorus*) common in Egypt and Syria etc.
sȳce *n.* (archaic, in India) Groom. [Hind., f. Arab. *sā'is*]
sȳ′comōre *n.* = SYCAMORE, 3. [Gk *sukon* fig, *moron* mulberry]
sȳ′cophant *n.* Flatterer, parasitic person. **sȳ′cophancȳ** *n.* **sȳcophă′ntĭc** *adj.* [Gk *sukophantes* informer, f. *sukon* fig, *phainō* show (reason for name unknown)]
sȳcō′sis *n.* Skin-disease, esp. of bearded part of face, with inflammation of hair-follicles.
Sȳ′dney. Seaport and capital of New South Wales, Australia.
sȳ′ēnīte *n.* Crystalline rock allied to granite, mainly composed of felspar and hornblende. [L *Syenites* (*lapis*) (stone) of Syene, f. Gk *Suēnē* (mod. Aswan), town of Upper Egypt]
sȳ′llabarȳ *n.* Collection, system, or table of syllables, esp. of written characters each representing a syllable.
sȳllă′bĭc *adj.* Of, forming, syllable(s); (of written symbols)

forming a whole word or part of a word and uttered as an uninterrupted unit; character(s) representing this; least mention, hint, or trace (*of*). ~ *v.t.* Pronounce by syllables; articulate distinctly; (poet.) utter, speak.
syllabub : see SILLABUB.
sȳ′llabus *n.* (pl. *-buses*). 1. Concise statement of heads of discourse, contents of treatise, subjects of lectures, course of study, etc. 2. (R.C. Ch.) Summary statement of points decided, esp. catalogue of 80 heretical doctrines, practices, or institutions of rationalists, socialists, etc., appended to encyclical *Quanta cura* of Pope Pius IX (1864), or of 65 heretical propositions of Modernists issued by Pope Pius X (1907). [mod. L, based on misreading in Ciceronian MS. of *sittybas* f. Gk *sittuba* parchment label or title-slip on book]
sȳllĕ′psis *n.* (pl. *-sēs*). (gram.) Figure of speech by which word is made to apply to two or more other words in same sentence while properly applying to or agreeing with only one of them (e.g. *neither you nor he knows*), or applying to them in different senses (e.g. *in a flood of tears and a sedan-chair*). **sȳllĕ′ptĭc** *adj.* **sȳllĕ′ptĭcallȳ** *adv.*

[884]

sȳ'llogĭsm *n.* Form of reasoning in which conclusion is deduced from two premisses (major and minor) containing a common or middle term which is absent from the conclusion, e.g. (major premiss) *All men are mortal*; (minor premiss) *Socrates is a man: therefore* (conclusion) *Socrates is mortal*; deductive as opp. to inductive reasoning. **syllogĭ'stĭc** *adj.* **syllogĭ'stĭcallў** *adv.*
sȳ'llogīze *v.* Use syllogisms; throw (facts, arguments) into syllogistic form.
sȳlph *n.* In system of Paracelsus, mortal but soulless elemental spirit of the air; slender graceful woman; any of several S. Amer. humming-bird(s) with long, brightly coloured tail. **sȳ'lphlīke** *adj.* Slender and graceful.
sȳ'lvan, sĭ'lvan *adjs.* Of wood(s); consisting of, abounding in, furnished with, woods or trees.
Sȳ'lvĕster, St. (d. 335). Bishop of Rome 314–35, commemorated 31 Dec.
sym- *prefix.* With, together, alike.
symbĭō'sĭs *n.* (pl. -sēs). (biol.) Association of two different organisms living attached to one another or one as tenant of the other (used esp. of associations advantageous to both organisms, as dist. from PARASITISM; cf. ANTI-BIOSIS). **symbĭō'tĭc** *adj.* **symbĭō'tĭcallў** *adv.*
sȳ'mbol *n.* Thing standing for or representing something else, esp. material thing taken to represent immaterial or abstract thing, as an idea or quality; written character conventionally standing for some object, process, etc. **symbŏ'lĭc, -ĭcal** *adjs.* **symbŏ'lĭcallў** *adv.*
sȳ'mbolĭsm *n.* System, use, meaning, of symbols; doctrine of the Symbolists. **sȳ'mbolĭst** *n.* 1. One who uses symbols. 2. *S~*, member of a school of French poets (*c* 1880–*c* 1900) who aimed at arousing emotions etc. by sounds and rhythms rather than direct expression and attached symbolic meaning to particular objects, words, etc.
sȳ'mbolīze *v.t.* Be symbol of; represent by symbol; treat as symbolic or emblematic.
sȳ'mmĕtrȳ *n.* 1. (Beauty resulting from) right proportion between the parts of the body or any whole, balance, congruity, harmony. 2. Such structure as allows of an object's being divided by a point or line or plane or radiating lines or planes into two or more parts exactly similar in size and shape and in position relatively to the dividing point etc.; repetition of exactly similar parts in contrary or equally divergent directions; *axial ~,* symmetry about an axis; *bilateral ~,* about a plane; *radial ~,* about a point. 3. Approximation to such structure; possession by a whole of corresponding parts correspondingly placed. **symmĕ'trĭc, -ĭcal** *adjs.* **symmĕ'trĭcallў** *adv.*
sȳ'mmĕtrīze *v.t.*
sympathĕ'ctomȳ *n.* Surgical excision of sympathetic ganglion or part of sympathetic nerve.
sympathĕ'tĭc *adj.* 1. Of sympathy; full of, expressing, due to, effecting sympathy; (in literary criticism) capable of evoking sympathy, appealing *to* reader; *~ strike,* strike of workers not to remedy their own grievances but to support other strikers. 2. (of disorder, pain, etc.) Induced in organ or part of body by a similar or corresponding one in another; *~ string,* (mus.) string which vibrates with sympathetic resonance, enriching the tone. 3. (physiol.) Of that part of the nervous system consisting principally of a pair of ganglionated nerve trunks placed alongside the vertebral column and connected with nerve fibres which extend to the blood-vessels, viscera, sweat and salivary glands, and pupils. 4. *~ ink,* liquid composition, writing with which remains invisible until colour is developed by heat or chemical reagent. **sympathĕ'tĭcallў** *adv.*
sȳ'mpathīze *v.i.* Feel or express sympathy (*with*); suffer with or like another.
sȳ'mpathȳ *n.* Affinity or relation between things by virtue of which they are similarly or correspondingly affected by the same influence, or affect or influence each other; tendency to share, state of sharing, emotion, sensation, or condition of another person or thing; mental participation in another's trouble, compassion, commiseration; disposition to agree (*with*) or approve, favourable attitude of mind towards person, cause etc.
sympĕ'talous *adj.* (bot.) Having petals united.
sȳ'mphonȳ *n.* 1. Musical composition written in form of SONATA but for full orchestra and usu. comprising four movements; (archaic) any of various other kinds of instrumental music occurring in vocal composition as introduction, overture, or conclusion; *~ orchestra,* large orchestra including strings, wood wind, brass, and percussion instruments, playing chiefly symphonies or other works of serious artistic quality. 2. (archaic) Harmony of (esp. musical) sound, concord, consonance. **symphŏ'nĭc** *adj.* *~ poem,* orchestral work, usu. of descriptive or rhapsodic character, freq. resembling first movement of symphony or sonata. **symphŏ'nĭcallў** *adv.* **sȳ'mphonĭst** *n.*
sȳ'mphȳsĭs *n.* (pl. -sēs). (anat.) (Line of) union of two bones etc. originally separate, esp. union of two similar bones on opposite sides of body in median line, as of pubic bones (ill. PELVIS) or two halves of lower jaw-bone. **symphȳ'sĭal** *adj.*
sympō'dĭum *n.* (pl. *-dia*). (bot.) Apparent main axis or stem made up of successive secondary axes, as in vine. **sympō'dĭal** *adj.*
sympŏ'sĭum (-z-) *n.* (pl. *-sĭa*). 1. Ancient Greek drinking party,

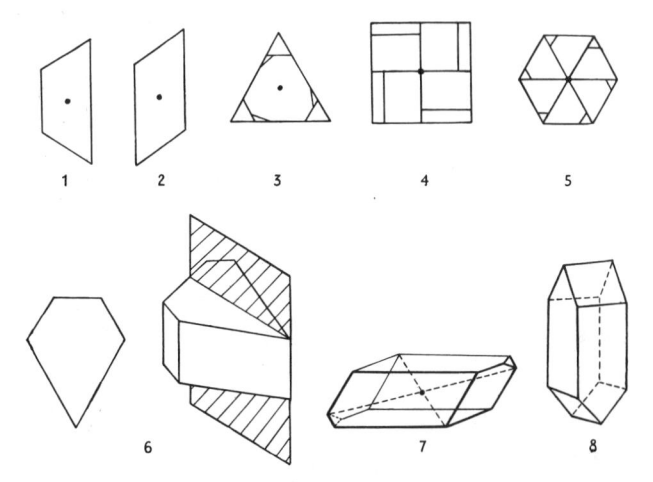

SYMMETRY IN CRYSTALS

1–5. Axes of symmetry. Each figure is brought into coincidence with itself by rotation round the axis perpendicular to the paper, through an angle of (1) 360°, (2) 180°, (3) 120°, (4) 90°, (5) 60°. 6. Plane of symmetry. This divides the figure into two parts which are mirror images of each other in that plane. 7. Centre of symmetry. A line drawn from the edge, corner, or plane through the centre, and produced an equal distance beyond it, reaches a corresponding part. 8. Inversion axis. The figure is brought into coincidence with itself on rotation through 90° round a vertical axis, accompanied by an inversion of every part through a centre of symmetry convivial meeting for drinking, conversation, and intellectual entertainment; the S~, title of one of Plato's dialogues recording such conversation. 2. Meeting or conference for discussion of some subject; collection of opinions delivered or articles contributed by number of persons on special topic. sympō'sial adj.

sy'mptom n. 1. Perceptible change in the body or its functions indicating presence of disease or injury, esp. (also subjective ~) one directly perceptible to the patient only; objective ~, one accompanied by signs (see SIGN n. 1). 2. Evidence or token of the existence of something. symptomă'tic adj. symptomă'tically adv.

sy'mptomatīze v.t. Be a symptom of.

syn- prefix. With, together, alike.

synaer'esis (-nēr-) n. (pl. -sēs). (gram.) Contraction, esp. of two vowels into diphthong or single vowel.

synaesthē'sia (-z-) n. Sensation in one part of body produced by stimulus in another part; production of mental sense-impression of one kind by stimulus of a different sense. synaesthē'tic adj.

sy'nagōgue (-g) n. Regular assembly of Jews for religious instruction or worship; building where this is held. synagōgal, synagō'gical adjs.

sy'năpse n. (anat.). Locus where a nervous impulse passes from the axon of one neuron to the dendrites of another (ill. NERVE).

syna'psis n. (pl. -sēs). 1. (biol.) Fusion of pairs of chromosomes, the first process in meiotic division of germ-cells. 2. (anat.) = SYNAPSE. syna'ptic adj.

synarthro'sis n. (anat.) Articulation in which bones are immovably fixed, as in sutures of skull and sockets of teeth.

sy'ncarp n. (bot.) Compound fruit, one arising from number of carpels in one flower (ill. FRUIT). syncar'pous adj.

synchondro'sis (-k-) n. (pl. -sēs). Nearly immovable articulation of two bones by layer of cartilage, as in spinal vertebrae.

sy'nchromesh (-k-) n. System of gearing, esp. in motor vehicles, in which the sliding gear-wheels are provided with small friction clutches which make contact with the non-sliding wheels before engagement, thus facilitating gear-changing by making both wheels revolve at the same speed. [abbrev. f. synchronized mesh]

sy'nchronīze (-k-) v. Occur at the same time, be contemporary or simultaneous (with); keep time (with); cause to go at same rate or function simultaneously; cause (clocks etc.) to indicate same time; add dialogue or other sound as synchronous accompaniment to (motion picture). synchronīzā'tion n.

sy'nchronous (-k-) adj. Existing or happening at same time, contemporary, simultaneous, (with); keeping time, proceeding at same pace (with), having coincident periods. sy'nchronously adv.

sy'nchrotron (-k-) n. An adaptation of the cyclotron designed for high acceleration of particles combined with a low-frequency magnetic field.

synclă'stic adj. (of curved surface) Having same kind of curvature in all directions.

sy'ncline n. (geol.) Rock-bed which forms a trough (opp. ANTICLINE; ill. ROCK¹). sy'nclinal (or -lī'-) adj.

sy'ncopāte v.t. 1. (gram.) Shorten (word) by omitting syllable(s) or letter(s) in the middle. 2. (mus.) Affect, modify, by syncopation. syncopā'tion n. (esp., mus.) Displacement of accent, or beat, by beginning note on normally unaccented part of bar (and freq. prolonging it into normally accented part), putting strong accent on normally weakly accented part of bar etc.

sy'ncopē n. 1. (path.) Fainting, sudden temporary loss of consciousness due to cerebral anaemia associated with a severe disturbance of the circulation. 2. (gram.) Shortening of word by dropping of syllable(s) or letters in the middle. sy'ncopal, syncō'pic adjs.

sy'ncrētism n. (Attempted) reconciliation of diverse or opposite tenets or practices, esp. in philosophy or religion. syncrē'tic, syncrēti'stic adjs. sy'ncrētīze v.

syndă'ctyl adj. & n. (Animal) having (some of) fingers or toes wholly or partly united, as kangaroos, web-footed birds, etc.

sy'ndesis n. (pl. -sēs). = SYNAPSIS.

sy'ndic n. Officer of government, with different powers in different countries, esp. each of four chief magistrates of Geneva; person representing and transacting affairs of a corporation; esp., in Cambridge University, member of special committee of senate.

sy'ndicalism n. Movement, orig. and esp. in France, for transfer of control and ownership of means of production and distribution to workers' unions. sy'ndicalist adj. & n. [Fr. syndicalisme, f. syndicat trade union]

sy'ndicate n. Body of syndics; combination of financiers etc. for promotion of financial or commercial undertaking; (journalism) combination of persons for syndicating articles etc. in newspapers.

sy'ndicāte v.t. Form into syndicate; publish simultaneously in a number of periodicals. syndicā'tion n.

sy'ndrōme (or -omī) n. Concurrence of several symptoms in a disease, set of concurrent symptoms characterizing it.

syne adv., prep., & conj. (Sc.) Since.

synĕ'cdochē (-kī) n. (gram., rhet.). Figure of speech in which, when a part is named, the whole it belongs to is understood (e.g. 50 sail for 50 ships).

sy'nergism, sy'nergy ns. (med.) Co-ordination in the action of muscles, organs, or drugs. synergĕ'tic, synĕr'gic adjs.

Synge (-ng), John Millington (1871–1909). Irish playwright, author of 'Riders to the Sea', 'The Playboy of the Western World', etc.

sy'nod n. 1. Assembly of clergy of church, diocese, nation, etc., for discussing and deciding ecclesiastical affairs; in Presbyterian churches, assembly of ministers and other elders constituting ecclesiastical court next above presbytery; General S~, supreme governing body (under Parliament) of the Church of England, constituted in 1969. 2. Any convention or council. sy'nodal, synŏ'dical adjs. synŏ'dically adv.

synoe'cious (-ēshus) adj. (bot.) Having male and female flowers in same flower-head, as many composites, or male and female organs in same receptacle, as some mosses (ill. FLOWER).

sy'nonym n. Word having same meaning as another in same language; another name (for). synŏ'nymous adj. synŏ'nymously adv.

synony'mic adj. Of or using synonyms.

synŏ'nymy n. Being synonymous; use of synonyms, esp. for amplification or emphasis; subject or study of, a collection of, synonyms.

synŏ'psis n. (pl. -sēs). Brief general survey; summary.

synŏ'ptic adj. Of, forming, furnishing, a synopsis; taking, affording, comprehensive mental view; (meteor.) of, affording, a comprehensive description of atmospheric conditions; S~, of the S~ Gospels, those of Matthew, Mark, and Luke, as giving an account of events under same general aspect or from same point of view. synŏ'ptical adj. synŏ'ptically adv. Synŏ'ptist n. Writer of a Synoptic gospel.

synostō'sis n. Bony ankylosis; joining of bones by osseous tissue.

synŏ'via n. (physiol.) Viscous fluid which is secreted by the inner lining membrane of the cavities of joints and the sheaths of tendons and lubricates them. synŏ'vial adj. Of, containing, secreting synovia; ~ fluid, synovia; ~ membrane, dense membrane of connective tissue secreting synovia (ill. BONE).

synovī'tis n. Inflammation of synovial membrane, freq. with swelling of joint.

[886]

sy̆ntăx n. (gram.) Arrangement of words in sentence showing their connection and relation; department of grammar dealing with usages of grammatical construction. **syntă'ctĭc** adj.
sy̆'nthĕsis n. (pl. -sēs). Putting together of parts or elements to make up a complex whole; (chem.) formation of a compound by combination of its elements or simpler compounds, esp. artificial production of organic compounds. **sy̆'nthĕsīze** v.t.
sy̆nthĕ'tĭc adj. Produced by synthesis, artificial. **sy̆nthĕ'tĭcally** adv. **sy̆nthĕ'tĭc** n. Artificially produced fibre etc.
sy̆'philis n. Venereal disease due to the micro-organism *Treponema pallidum*, usu. communicated by direct contact with an infected person, affecting first some local part (*primary* ~), secondly skin and mucous membrane (*secondary* ~), and thirdly bones, muscles, and brain (*tertiary* ~); *congenital* ~, condition in which the unborn child is infected through the maternal blood-stream. **sy̆phĭlĭ'tĭc** adj. & n. Of, (person) affected with, syphilis. [f. *Syphilus*, character in Latin poem on the subject (1530) by Girolano Fracastoro, Veronese physician]
sy̆philō'ma n. Syphilitic tumour.
Sy̆r'acūse (-z). City in Sicily, scene of a battle (413 B.C.) in the Peloponnesian War, in which the Athenians under Demosthenes and Nicias were defeated in their attempt to take the city and their fleet was destroyed. **Sy̆racū'san** (-z-) adj. & n.
Sy̆'ria. Republic in SW. Asia at E. end of Mediterranean; formed, with nearby regions, part of the Roman Empire from 64 B.C. to A.D. 36; chiefly under Arab domination until the Ottoman conquest in 1517; French mandated territory 1918-41; capital, Damascus. **Sy̆'rian** adj. & n.

Sy̆'riac adj. & n. (Of, in) the language of ancient Syria, a branch of Aramaic. **Sy̆'rĭacĭsm** n.
sy̆ri'nga (-ngga) n. Shrub of genus *S*~, esp. *S. vulgaris*, the common lilac; (pop.) mock orange. [Gk *surigx* pipe, w. ref. to use of stems cleared of pith as pipestems]
sy̆ri'nge (-j) n. Tube with nozzle and piston or bulb for drawing in quantity of liquid and

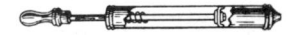

DIAGRAM OF GARDEN SYRINGE

ejecting it in stream or jet, for making injections, cleansing wounds, spraying plants, etc. ~ v.t. Sluice, spray, with syringe.
sy̆'rinx n. (pl. -es or -nges). 1. Pan-pipe. 2. (archaeol.) Narrow channel or tunnel cut in rock in ancient Egyptian tomb. 3. (anat.) Eustachian tube from throat to ear (ill. EAR[1]); (zool.) song-organ of birds, consisting of trachea and bronchi (ill. BIRD). **sy̆ri'ngēal** (-j-) adj.
Sy̆r'o- *prefix*. Syrian, as in ~-*Arabian*, -*Phoenician*.
sy̆'rup n. Water (nearly) saturated with sugar, this combined with flavouring as beverage or with drug(s) as medicine; condensed sugar-cane juice, part of this remaining uncrystallized at various stages of refining, molasses, treacle; *golden* ~, trade-name for pale kind; *maple* ~, syrup obtained by evaporating maple sap or dissolving maple sugar. **sy̆'rupy̆** adj.
sy̆stă'ltĭc adj. Contracting, esp. (physiol.) with alternate contraction (*systole*) and dilatation (*diastole*).
sy̆'stĕm n. 1. Complex whole, set of connected things or parts, organized body of material or immaterial things; (phys.) group of bodies moving about one another in space under some dynamic law, as that of gravitation, esp. (astron.) group of heavenly bodies moving in orbits about central body; (biol.) set of organs or parts in animal body of same or similar structure or subserving same function, animal body as an organized whole; ~s *design*, organization of data for electronic processing, or of data-processing equipment. 2. Department of knowledge or belief considered as organized whole; comprehensive body of doctrines, beliefs, theories, practices, etc., forming particular philosophy, religion, form of government, etc.; scheme or method of classification, notation, etc.; (cryst.) any of six general methods or types in which substances crystallize. 3. Orderly arrangement or method. **sy̆stĕmă'tĭc** adj. Methodical; arranged, conducted, according to system or organized plan; of system(s). **sy̆stĕmă'tĭcally** adv. **sy̆stĕmă'tĭcs** n. Scientific study of classification of the plant and animal kingdoms, taxonomy. **sy̆'stĕmatīze** v.t.
Système International (sĭstĕm ăntărnăshonahl). (also ~ *d'unités*) International System (of units): system based on the metre, kilogramme, second, ampere, kelvin, candela, and mole.
sy̆stĕ'mĭc adj. Of, affecting, a system; (esp., physiol.) of the system or body as a whole, or a particular system of bodily organs. **sy̆stĕ'mĭcally** adv.
sy̆'stŏlė n. Contraction of heart, alternating with DIASTOLE. **sy̆stŏ'lĭc** adj.
sy̆'zy̆gy̆ n. 1. (astron.) Point at which the heavenly bodies are in conjunction or opposition, esp. the moon with the sun. 2. (math.) Group of rational integral functions so related that if they are severally multiplied by other rational integral functions, the sum of the products vanishes identically.
Szechuan (sĕ'chwah'n). Province of China on the Yangtze Kiang.

T

T, t (tē). 1. 20th letter of modern English and 19th of ancient Roman alphabet, derived in form from Greek *T* (*tau*), from the Phoenician and ancient Semitic † Ӿ Ӽ X, and representing a voiceless dental (or in English, rather alveolar) stop, but in some combinations has the sound 'sh', in -*tual*, -*tue*, -*ture* freq. the sound represented in this dictionary by 'ch'; the combination -th- represents voiced and voiceless dental spirants, simple sounds for which the Roman alphabet has no single symbols; *to a T*, exactly, to a nicety. 2. Object etc. shaped like T; *T-bone steak*, beef-steak from thin end of loin, containing T-shaped bone; *T-junction*, junction, esp. of roads, in shape of T; *T-shirt*, short-sleeved usu. collarless (under-)shirt; *T square*, T-shaped instrument for obtaining or testing right angles and parallel lines (ill. SQUARE).
t. *abbrev*. Taken (betting); ton(s); tonne(s).
T. *abbrev*. Tenor; tera-; tesla(s); Turkish (in £T).
ta (tah) *int*. (nursery, colloq.) Thank you.

T.A. *abbrev*. Territorial Army.
Taal (tahl) n. Cape Dutch, Afrikaans. [Du., = 'language']
tăb n. Short broad strap, flat loop, strip, tag, attached by one end to object, or forming projecting tongue, by which thing can be taken hold of, hung up, fastened, identified, etc.; coloured tab, esp. red gorget patch worn by staff officer; (U.S. colloq.) account, check (esp. *keep a* ~ or ~*s on*).
T.A.B. *abbrev*. Typhoid-paratyphoid A and B vaccine.
tă'bard n. (hist.) Short surcoat

[887]

TABARET

open at sides and with short sleeves worn by knight over armour and emblazoned with armorial bearings (ill. ARMOUR); short-sleeved or sleeveless jerkin emblazoned with royal arms forming official dress of herald or pursuivant.

ta'baret n. Upholstery fabric with alternate satin and watered-silk stripes.

tabă'scō n. Pungent pepper made from fruit of *Capsicum annuum*; T~, trade-name of sauce made with this.

tă'bbў n. 1. (often attrib.) Plain weave (ill. WEAVE); plain-woven fabric, as watered taffeta. 2. (also ~ *cat*) Brownish, tawny, or grey cat with darker stripes; old maid, elderly gossiping woman. 3. Very hard concrete of mixture in equal proportions of lime and shells, gravel, or stones. ~ *v.t.* Water (fabric) by calendering; mark with dark stripes or streaks. [*'attābiy*, quarter of Baghdad where the fabric was woven]

tă'berdar n. Scholar of Queen's College, Oxford. **tă'berdarship** n. [*taberd* tabard, from the gown formerly worn]

tă'bernăcle n. 1. Temporary or slightly built dwelling, hut, booth, tent; *Feast of Tabernacles*, Jewish festival, held in October, commemorating Israelites' sojourn in tents in the wilderness. 2. (Jewish hist.) Curtained tent containing Ark of the Covenant, which served as portable sanctuary of Jews during their wandering in the wilderness. 3. Place of worship other than a church, esp. (hist.) one of the temporary structures used during rebuilding of churches after Fire of London; nonconformist, esp. Baptist or Methodist, place of worship. 4. (eccles.) Canopied niche or recess in wall or pillar (ill. NICHE); ornamental receptacle for pyx or eucharistic elements. 5. Socket, step, or hinged post for a mast that has to be lowered frequently, for passing under bridges, etc. 6. ~ *roof*, roof sloping at ends as well as sides to central ridge shorter than sidewalls; ~-*work*, ornamental carved work or tracery over niches, stalls, pulpits, etc. **tăbernă'cūlar** *adj*. **tă'bernăcle** v. Provide with shelter or tabernacle; dwell temporarily.

tă'bēs (-z) n. (path.) Slow progressive emaciation; ~ *dorsā'lis*, locomotor ataxia.

tabĕ'tic *adj.* Of, affected with, tabes, esp. locomotor ataxia. ~ *n.* Tabetic patient.

tă'bĭnĕt n. Watered poplin-like fabric of silk and wool made chiefly in Ireland.

tă'blature n. 1. (mus.) Old form of musical notation indicating string, fret, hole, etc., to be touched or stopped with fingers. 2. (fig., archaic) Mental picture.

tă'ble n. 1. Article of furniture consisting of flat top of wood or other solid material supported on legs or central pillar, esp. one on which meals are laid out, articles of

TABLE

use or ornament kept, work done, or games played; each half of folding backgammon board; provision or supply of food for meals, fare; company of persons at a table; *at* ~, at a meal or meals; *lay, lie, on the* ~, (in Parliament est.) postpone (measure, report), be postponed, indefinitely; *turn the* ~*s*, reverse relation between two persons or parties, cause a complete reversal of state of affairs; *T~ of the House*, central table in either of the Houses of Parliament (ill. PARLIAMENT). 2. Flat, usu. rectangular, horizontal or vertical surface in architecture etc.; flat part of machine tool on which work is put to be operated on; flat upper surface of faceted gem; large flat plate or sheet of crown-glass; crystal of flattened or short prismatic form; flat elevated tract of land, plateau, flat mountain-top. 3. Slab of wood, stone, etc.; matter written on this; ~*s of the law* (*covenant*), the Ten Commandments, the stones on which they were written; *the Twelve Tables*, laws drawn up by decemviri in Rome, 451 and 450 B.C., embodying most important rules of Roman law. 4. Tabulated statement or arrangement; arrangement of numbers, words, etc., esp. in columns and lines occupying single sheet, so as to exhibit set of facts or relations distinctly and comprehensively for study, reference, or calculation; *T~ of Kindred and Affinity* (also

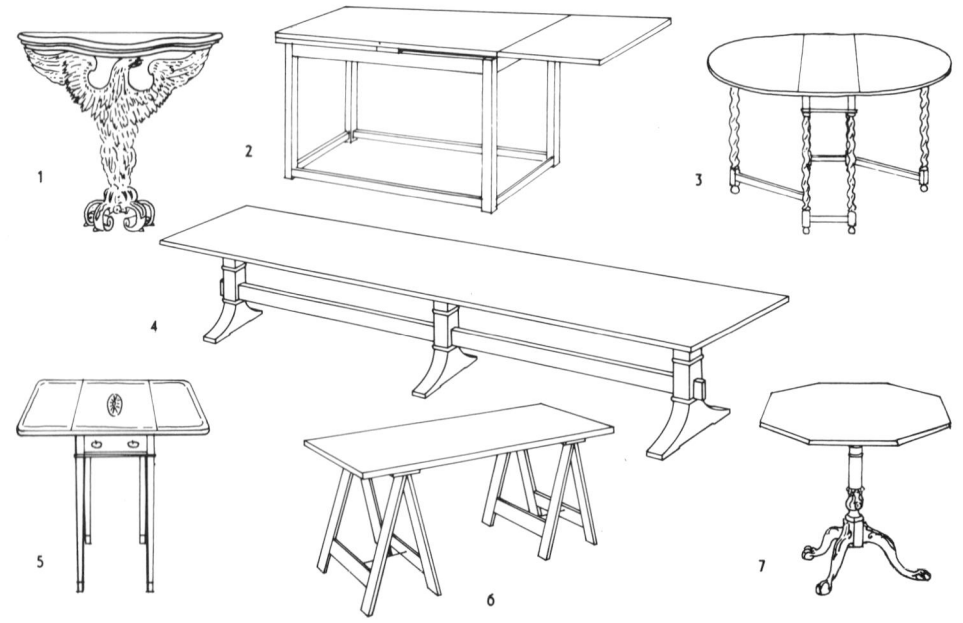

TABLES

1. Console-table.　2. Draw-table.　3. Gate-leg table.　4. Refectory table.　5. Pembroke table.　6. Trestle-table.　7. Tripod table.

T~ *of Affinity, of Prohibited or Forbidden Degrees*), list of the degrees or relationship by blood and by marriage within which marriage may not take place acc. to Church law. 5. ta′blecloth, cloth spread on table, esp. for meals; ~-*cut*, (of gem) cut with flat upper surface larger than culet and surrounded by small facets (ill. GEM); ~-*knife*, knife used at table, esp. of the size or shape used in cutting meat small; ~-*land*, extensive elevated region with level surface, plateau; ~-*linen*, tablecloths, napkins, etc.; T~ *Mountain*, flat-topped mountain with Cape Town at its foot; ~-*rapping, -turning*, production of raps or knocking sounds on table, moving or turning a table, without apparent or apparently adequate physical means, as spiritualistic phenomena; ta′blespoon, spoon, larger than dessert-spoon, used at table for serving vegetables, etc.; tablespoonful; ta′blespoonful, amount held by tablespoon; ~-*talk*, informal conversation at table; ~ *tennis*, game resembling lawn tennis, played with small round bats and celluloid ball on table with net stretched across it; ta′bleware, utensils and dishes etc. used at table. ~ *v.t.* Lay (measure, report, etc.) on table, esp. as way of postponing indefinitely; bring forward for discussion or consideration; join (timbers) together with projection in each fitting into groove in next; strengthen (sail) with wide hem.

tă′bleau (-lō) *n.* Presentation, esp. of group of persons etc., producing picturesque effect; striking or dramatic effect suddenly produced; ~ *curtains*, (theatr.) pair of curtains to draw across and meet in middle of stage; ~ *vivant* (vēvahṅ), representation of painting, statue, scene, etc., by silent and motionless person or group. [Fr., = 'picture']

table d′hôte (tahbl-dōt). 1. (obs.) Common table for guests at hotel etc. 2. (of meal) Served at fixed price for a stated series of courses (opp. *à la carte*). [Fr., = 'host's table']

tă′blĕt *n.* Small thin flat piece of ivory, wood, etc., for writing on, esp. each of set fastened together; pad of sheets of notepaper fastened together at top; small slab, esp. with or for inscription; small flat or compressed piece of solid confection, drug, etc., flattened lozenge; flat cake of soap.

tă′blier (-ā) *n.* (hist.) Apron-like part of woman's dress.

tă′bling *n.* (esp.) Broad hem at edge of sail to strengthen it.

tă′bloid *n.* 1. Anything in compressed or concentrated form. 2. Newspaper of small format, esp. one giving news in concentrated and simplified form.

tabōō′, tabu′ (-ōō) *adj.* Set apart as sacred or prohibited. ~ *n.* Ban, prohibition. ~ *v.t.* Put under taboo. [Polynesian wd]

tā′bor *n.* (hist.) Small drum used to accompany pipe or fife.

tă′borĕt, -ourĕt (-er-) *n.* Low seat or stool, without back or arms, for one person; embroidery frame. [Fr., = 'small tabor']

tabu: see TABOO.

tă′būla *n.* (anat.) Hard, flat surface of bone etc.; ~ *rasa*, erased tablet; (fig.) human mind at birth viewed as having no innate ideas; complete obliteration, a blank. [L, = 'table']

tă′būlar *adj.* 1. Of, arranged in, computed, etc., by means of, tables. 2. Broad, flat, and (usu.) comparatively thin, like a table; formed of, tending to split into, pieces of this form; (of crystal etc.) of short prismatic form with flat base and top. **tă′būlarlў** *adv.*

tă′būlāte *v.t.* Arrange, summarize, exhibit, in form of a table, scheme, or synopsis. **tăbūlā′tion** *n.* **tă′būlate** *adj.* Having flat surface, tabular.

tă′būlātor *n.* (esp.) Typewriter attachment for tabulating figures.

tă′c-au-tă′c (-ō-) *n.* (fencing) Parry followed immediately by riposte; rapid succession of attacks and parries.

tă′cĕt *v.imper.* (mus.) Let the voice or instrument remain silent. [L, = 'is silent']

tăch, tăche[1] (-sh) *n.* (bibl.) A clasp, link. [see TACK[1]]

tăche[2] (-sh) *n.* (sugar-boiling) Each of series of pans, esp. the last and smallest, in which sugar is evaporated.

tăchĕŏ′mĕter, tăchў′mĕter (-k-) *ns.* Surveying instrument for measuring distance by optical means. **tăchĕŏ′mĕtrў** *n.*

tă′chŏgrăph (-k-; *or* -ahf) *n.* Device on vehicle recording its speed and travel-time.

tăchŏ′mĕter (-k-) *n.* Any instrument for measuring the velocity of machines or the rate of flow of liquids. **tăchŏ′mĕtrў** *n.*

tăchўcăr′dia (-kĭ-) *n.* (path.) Abnormally rapid action of heart.

tăchў′grăphў (-k-) *n.* Stenography, (esp. ancient Greek or Roman) shorthand; form of Greek or Latin written in Middle Ages with many abbreviations and compendia. **tăchўgră′phic** *adj.*

tachymeter: see TACHEOMETER.

tă′cĭt *adj.* Implied, understood, inferred, but not openly expressed or stated; saying nothing, silent. **tă′cĭtlў** *adv.*

tă′cĭtŭrn *adj.* Reserved in speech, saying little, uncommunicative. **tăcĭtŭr′nĭtў** *n.*

Tă′cĭtus, Cornelius (*c* A.D. 56–117). Roman historian, son-in-law of Agricola; author of 'Agricola' (containing an account of Britain), 'Germania', 'Histories', and 'Annals'.

tăck[1] *n.* 1. Small sharp nail, usu. with large flat head, for fastening thin or light object to more solid one (ill. NAIL). 2. Fastening together, esp. in slight or temporary way; long slight stitch used in fastening together seams etc. before permanent sewing. 3. Rope used for securing lower corner of some sails; lower windward corner of sail, to which tack is attached (ill. SAIL[1]). 4. Tacking; ship's course in relation to direction of wind and position of sails; course obliquely opposed to direction of wind, one of consecutive series of such courses with wind alternately on port and starboard side; (fig.) course of action or policy. 5. (of varnish, printing-ink, etc.) Viscous condition. ~ *v.* 1. Attach with tacks, or in slight or temporary manner, esp. with long slight stitches; (fig.) annex, append (*to, on to*); (esp., Engl. hist.) append (clause relating to extraneous matter) *to* money-bill, to ensure its passing House of Lords. 2. Change ship's course by shifting tacks and sails; make run or course obliquely against wind, proceed to windward by series of such courses; (fig.) change one's course, conduct, policy, etc.

tăck[2] *n.* Foodstuff (chiefly in *hardtack*: see HARD, *soft* ~, bread, good fare).

tă′ckle *n.* 1. Apparatus, utensils, instruments, appliances, esp. for fishing or other sport. 2. (naut. pr. tā-) Rope(s) and pulley-block(s) or other mechanism for hoisting weights etc. (ill. PULLEY); windlass with its ropes and hooks; running rigging of ship. 3. (footb. etc.) Tackling; (Amer. footb.) each of two players (*right* ~, *left* ~), with positions next to the ends in the forward line. ~ *v.* Grapple with, grasp, lay hold of, with endeavour to hold, manage, or overcome; (football etc.) seize and stop, obstruct, intercept (opponent in possession of ball).

tă′ckў *adj.* (of gum, nearly dry varnish, etc.) Slightly sticky or adhesive. **tă′ckĭnĕss** *n.*

tăct *n.* Intuitive perception of what is fitting, esp. of the right thing to do or say; adroitness in dealing with persons or circumstances. **tă′ctful** *adj.* **tă′ctfullў** *adv.* **tă′ctfulnĕss** *n.* **tă′ctlĕss** *adj.* **tă′ctlĕsslў** *adv.* **tă′ctlĕssnĕss** *n.* **tă′ctic** *n.* (Piece of) tactics.

tă′ctical *adj.* Of tactics; adroitly planning or planned; ~ *bombing*, aerial bombing carried out in immediate support of military or naval operations. **tă′cticallў** *adv.* **tăctĭ′cian** (-shan) *n.* One versed or skilled in tactics.

tă′ctics *n.* (as sing. or pl.) Art or science of deploying and manœuvring air, military, or naval forces, esp. when in contact with the enemy (contrasted with *strategy*); (as pl.) procedure, device(s) for gaining some end.

tă′ctile *adj.* Of, perceived by, connected with, sense of touch;

TACTUAL

(painting etc.) appealing to sense of touch, producing effect of solidity. **tăcti′lĭtў** n.
tă′ctūal adj. Tactile. **tă′ctūallў** adv.
tă′dpōle n. Larva of frog or toad, from time it leaves egg until it loses gills and tail, esp. early stage of this when it seems to consist simply of round head with a tail (ill. FROG¹); larva of similar appearance in other animals.
Tădzhĭkista′n (tăj-, -ahn). Constituent republic of U.S.S.R., in central Asia; capital, Dushanbe.
tael (tāl) n. Chinese ounce (= 1⅓ oz. avoirdupois), esp. of silver as former monetary unit. [Malay *tahil* weight]
tae′nia, tē′nia ns. (pl. -iae). 1. (archit.) Band separating architrave from frieze in Doric order (ill. ORDER). 2. (anat.) Ribbon-like structure, esp. band of white nervous matter in brain and longitudinal muscles of colon. 3. (zool.) Tapeworm of genus *T*~ (ill. TAPE). **tae′nioid** adj.
tă′ffĕta n. Fine plain-woven usu. glossy fabric of silk or other material. [Pers. *tăftah* (*tăftan* twist)]
tă′ffrail (-ril) n. Rail round ship's stern (ill. SHIP). [Du. *tafereel* panel, dim. of *tafel* table]
Tăffў¹. (colloq.) Nickname for Welshman. [supposed Welsh pronunciation of *Davy*, David]
tă′ffў² n. (Sc., north., & U.S.) Toffee.
tă′fia n. Rum-like spirit distilled from molasses etc.
Tăft, William Howard (1857–1930). 27th President of U.S., 1909–13.
tăg¹ n. Metal etc. point at end of shoelace; small pendent piece or part, as loop at back of boot for pulling it on, ragged lock of wool on sheep, address-label for tying on, any loose or ragged end; brief and usu. familiar, trite or much-used quotation; refrain or catch of song etc., last words of speech in play etc.; *tagrag* (*and bobtail*): = RAG¹ *tag*. ~ v. Furnish with a tag; join (*to*, *on to*, *together*); find rhymes (*to verses*), string (rhymes) together; follow closely, trail or drag behind.
tăg² n. Children's game in which one pursues the others until he touches one, who in turn becomes pursuer.
Tăga′lŏg (-gah-) n. (Member, language) of principal Malayan people of Philippine Islands. [native name, f. *taga* native, *ilog* river]
Tăgŏr′e, Rabindranath (1861–1941). Indian poet and prose-writer; Nobel Prize for literature 1913.
Tā′gus. River of Spain and Portugal, flowing into Atlantic near Lisbon.
Tahī′tĭ (-hē-). One of the Society Islands in the S. Pacific, a French protectorate since 1843. **Tahī′tian** (-shan) adj. & n.

Tai : see THAI.
taĭga (tī′gah) n. Siberian pine-forest between tundra and steppe.
tail¹ n. 1. Hindmost part of animal, esp. when prolonged beyond rest of body; *turn* ~, run away. 2. Thing, part, appendage, resembling this, as luminous train of comet, twisted or braided tress of hair, stem of musical note, pendent posterior part of man's coat, esp. dress-coat; appendage of string and paper at lower end of kite; outer corner of eye; rear-end of column, procession, etc.; weaker members of sports team; hinder part of cart, plough, or harrow; rear part of aircraft; tail-race of mill etc.; reverse side of coin; (pl.) tail-coat. 3. ~ *bandage*, one divided into strips at end; *tai′lboard*, usu. hinged or removable board at back of cart, lorry, etc. (ill. CART); ~-*coat*, man's coat with long skirt divided at back and cut away in front (ill. COAT); ~-*end*, extreme end, concluding part; ~-*gate*, lower gate of canal-lock; ~-*lamp*, -*light*, light carried at back of train, cycle, car, etc.; ~-*piece*, piece forming tail; triangular piece of wood to which lower ends of strings are fastened in violin etc. (ill. STRINGED); small decoration at end of book, chapter, etc.; *tai′lplane*, horizontal stabilizing surface of tail of aircraft; ~-*race*, part of mill-race below wheel (ill. WATER); ~-*skid*, small skid or runner supporting tail of aircraft in contact with ground; ~-*spin*, (aviation) kind of spinning dive; ~-*stock*, one of two parts (~-*stock* and *headstock*) which hold the work in a lathe (ill. LATHE²); ~ *wind*, wind blowing in same direction as course of aircraft etc. ~ v. Furnish with tail; follow (person) inconspicuously to keep watch on him; cut or pull off what is regarded as tail, esp. of plant or fruit; ~ *away*, *off*, fall away in tail or straggling line; diminish and cease.
tail² n. (law) Limitation of freehold estate or fee to a person and (particular class of) the heirs of his body (freq. in phrase *in* ~). ~ adj. Limited to specified heirs; being in tail.
tai′lor n. (fem. *tai′lorĕss*) Maker of men's outer garments, or of such women's garments as have similar character, e.g. coats, suits, riding-clothes; ~-*bird,* various Asiatic passerine singing-birds (esp. of genus *Orthotomus*) which stitch together edges of leaves to form cavity for nest; ~-*made*, made by tailor, usu. with little ornament and with special attention to exact fit; ~'*s dummy*, lay figure for fitting or displaying clothes (freq. contempt., of persons). ~ v. Do tailor's work; make (garments etc.) by tailor's methods; (of fabric) admit of being tailored; furnish with clothes, dress. **tai′lored** (-erd)

TAKE

adj. (esp., of women's clothes) Made in plain fitted style.
tain n. Thin tinplate; tinfoil for backing mirror.
Taine (těn), Hippolyte Adolphe (1828–93). French literary critic and historian.
taint n. Spot, trace, of decay, corruption, or disease; corrupt condition, infection. ~ v. Introduce corruption or disease into, infect, be infected.
Taiwă′n (ti-). Island off SE. coast of China, ceded by China to Japan in 1895 and formally relinquished by Japan in 1952; headquarters of Chinese Nationalist Government since 1949; capital, Taipei. **Taiwanē′se** (-z) adj.
Tăjĭksta′n (-ahn). Var. of TADZHIKISTAN.
Taj Mahal (tahj mahah′l). Marble mausoleum of great splendour and beauty at Agra, India, built (1631–45) by the Mogul Emperor Shah-Jahan, in memory of his favourite wife. [corrupt. of Pers. *Mumtāz-i-Maḥall*, title of wife of Shah-Jahan, f. *mumtāz* distinguished, *maḥall* abode]
ta′ka (tah-) n. Monetary unit of Bangladesh, = 100 paise.
tāke v. (past t. *took*, past part. *tā′ken*). 1. Seize, grasp; capture; catch; (cards) win (trick); (of plant, seed, etc.) germinate, begin to grow; catch fancy or affection of; (of inoculation etc.) be successful or effective; *be taken ill*, fall ill. 2. Receive into body, as medicine, food, drink, etc.; bring or receive (person) into some relation to oneself; appropriate, enter into possession (of); secure, get, receive, by payment, esp. regularly, as a periodical; assume, charge oneself with, undertake; perform, discharge (function, service, etc.); range oneself on, ally oneself with, (side, in contest etc.); (gram.) have as proper construction; ~ *it*, (colloq.) endure punishment, affliction, etc., with fortitude. 3. Choose, adopt, take into use or employment; proceed or begin to deal with in some way; proceed to occupy; use (up), consume; need (specified size) *in* shoes, gloves, etc., 4. Obtain, derive, from some source or by some process; write (*down*) (notes, spoken words, etc.); obtain likeness, esp. by photography. 5. Receive, accept, enjoy (pleasure, money, wager, hint, etc.); exact (vengeance etc.); accept as true or correct, or in some specified way; face and attempt to get over, through, etc., negotiate; admit, absorb, contract, be affected by (moisture, infection, dye, a quality, etc.). 6. Grasp with mind, apprehend, understand; suppose, assume; regard, consider (*as*); feel, experience (emotion etc.). 7. Perform, do (action, movement, etc.); raise, make (objection, exception, etc.). 8. Carry, convey, cause to go with one; ~ *from*, *off*, carry away, remove, deprive or rid person or

[890]

thing of; subtract, deduct; be capable of being taken *off*, *out*, etc. 9. ~ *aim*, aim (*at*); ~ *charge*, make oneself responsible; ~ *fire*, become kindled or ignited, catch fire; ~ *care*, be careful; ~ *care of*, be careful of; be in charge of; (U.S.) deal with; ~ *hold* (*of*), grasp, seize, take under one's control; ~ *place*, (esp. of pre-arranged event) occur; ~ *possession*, enter into possession (*of*). 10. ~ *after*, resemble (person, esp. parent) in character, feature, etc.; ~ *away*, remove, subtract, detract *from*; ~ *back*, retract (words); ~ *down*, write down; humiliate, humble; pull down (building), lower, carry or cut down; ~ *in*, admit, receive (lodgers etc.); undertake (work) to be done in one's own house; conduct into house, room, etc.; include, comprise; reduce (garment etc.) to smaller compass, furl (sail); understand, comprehend; deceive, cheat; believe (false statement); subscribe to (newspaper etc.). ~-*in* (*n*.) fraud, deception; ~ *off*, remove; conduct away; deduct (part of price); drink off; mimic; jump, spring; (of aircraft or pilot) leave ground etc.at beginning of flight; ~-*off* (*n*.) caricature; spot from which jump etc. is made; aircraft's leaving of ground; ~ *on*, undertake (work, responsibility, etc.); play (person) *at* game; (colloq.) show violent emotion, be greatly agitated; ~ *out*, cause to come out; bring, convey, out; remove; accept payment or compensation in specified form; ~ *it out of*, exhaust, fatigue; exact satisfaction from; ~ *over*, succeed to possession or control of; ~-*over* (*n*.); ~ *to*, begin, begin to occupy oneself with; conceive a liking for; ~ *up*, lift up; shorten (garment); absorb; occupy, engage; adopt as protégé; interrupt, correct (speaker); enter upon; pursue (occupation, subject, inquiry, etc.); secure, fasten; accept (challenge); subscribe for, subscribe amount of (shares, loan, etc.); ~ *up with*, begin to consort with. ~ *n*. Amount (of fish, game, etc.) taken or caught; takings; (cinemat.) scene or part of scene photographed at one time without stopping camera, photographing of this.

tā'ker *n*. (esp.) One who takes a bet.

tā'king *n*. (esp.) State of agitation (archaic); (pl.) money received in business. ~ *adj*. Attractive, captivating, charming. **tā'kingly** *adv*.

tă'lapoin *n*. 1. Buddhist priest or monk. 2. Small W. Afr. monkey (*Cercopithecus talapoin*).

talār'ia *n.pl.* Winged sandals as attribute in classical art of Hermes, Iris, and others. [L]

ta'lbot (tawl- *or* tŏl-) *n*. Kind of large whitish hound (now extinct) with long hanging ears and heavy jaws, formerly used for tracking and hunting and supposed to be ancestral stock of bloodhound; representation of this in heraldry, as inn-sign, etc. [perh. f. family name *Talbot*]

ta'lbotype (tawl- *or* tŏl-) *n*. Photographic process invented by W. H. Fox Talbot in 1840, the basis of that now used.

tălc *n*. Soft, translucent, white, green, or grey mineral (a hydrated magnesium silicate) with greasy feel and shining lustre, freq. occurring in broad flat plates, used in making soap, toilet powder, paper, lubricants, etc.; (pop.) = MICA; ~ *powder*, talcum powder.

tă'lcum *n*. Talc; ~ *powder*, toilet powder of (usu. perfumed) powdered talc.

tāle *n*. 1. (archaic, rhet., poet.) Number, total. 2. Story, true or (usu.) fictitious narrative, esp. one imaginatively treated; idle or mischievous gossip, malicious report (esp. in *tell* ~*s*); ~-*bearer*, one who reports maliciously what is meant to be secret; ~-*teller*, one who tells tales.

tă'lent *n*. 1. Ancient weight and money of account, varying greatly with time, place, and people. 2. Special aptitude, faculty, gift [from the parable of the talents, Matt. 25: 14–30 etc.]; high mental ability; ~ *scout*, person engaged in searching for talented people, esp. theatrical etc. performers. **tă'lentĕd** *adj*.

tā'lēs (-z) *n*. (law) Writ for summoning jurors, list of persons who may be so summoned, to supply deficiency; *tā'lēsman* (or -lz-), person so summoned. [L *tales de circumstantibus* such of the bystanders, first words of the writ]

tă'lipēs (-z) *n*. Club-foot.
tă'lipĕd *adj*. & *n*. Club-footed (person).

tă'lipŏt, -pŭt *ns*. Fan-palm (*Corphyra umbraculifera*) of Ceylon and Malabar, of great height, and with enormous fan-shaped leaves used as sunshades, fans, and as writing-material.

tă'lisman (-z-) *n*. Charm, amulet, esp. stone, ring, etc., inscribed with astrological figures or characters and supposed to protect its wearer or bring him good fortune. **tălismă'nic** *adj*. [Arab. *tilsam*, f. Gk *telesma* (*telesmos* consecration, ceremony)]

talk (tawk) *v*. Convey or exchange ideas, information, etc., by speech, esp. familiar speech of ordinary intercourse; express, utter, discuss, in words; exercise faculty of speech; utter words; use (language); gossip; bring into specified condition etc. by talking; ~ *down*, silence (person) by louder or more effective talking; give instructions by radio to (pilot landing aircraft); ~ *down to*, address (person) in language suited to his supposed ignorance or stupidity; ~ *out*, get rid of (bill, motion, in Parliament) by prolong-

ing discussion till time of adjournment; ~ *to*, speak to, (colloq.) reprove. **ta'lker** *n*. **talk** *n*. Conversation; short address or lecture in conversational style, esp. one broadcast by radio; theme of gossip.

ta'lkative (tawk-) *adj*. Fond of talking. **ta'lkatively** *adv*. **ta'lkativeness** *n*.

ta'lkie, -y (tawkĭ) *n*. (slang) Cinema sound-film.

tall (tawl) *adj*. 1. (of persons) Of more than average height; (of things) high, lofty, higher than the average or than surrounding objects; of specified height; *ta'llboy*, tall chest of drawers, occas. in two sections, one standing above the other (ill. CHEST). 2. (of talk etc.) High-flown; exaggerated, highly coloured; ~ *order*, unreasonable or excessive demand. **ta'llish** *adj*. **ta'llness** *n*.

Tălleyrand-Pĕrigord (-rahn, pĕrĭgōr), Charles Maurice de, Prince de Benevent (1754–1838). French statesman.

tă'llow (-ō) *n*. Fat of animals, esp. of sheep and ox kinds, separated by melting and clarifying and used for making candles, soap, etc.; ~-*chandler*, (obs.) maker, seller, of tallow candles. **tă'llowy** *adj*.

tă'lly *n*. 1. (obs.) Piece of wood scored across with notches representing amount of debt or payment

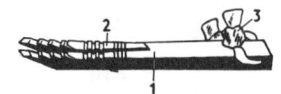

14TH-C. TALLY

1. Stock which is given to payer. 2. Foil which is kept by payee. 3. Seal. The notches represent the amount recorded, in this case £3. 13*s*. 4*d*. (3½£, 3*s*. 4*d*.)

and split lengthwise across notches, each party keeping half; account so kept. 2. Score, reckoning. 3. Distinguishing mark, ticket, label, attached to thing for identification etc. 4. Corresponding thing, counterpart, duplicate. 5. ~-*card*, (U.S.) score-card; *ta'llyman*, one who sells goods which are paid for by instalments; ~-*shop*, shop where such goods are sold. ~ *v*. Record, reckon, by tally; agree, correspond (*with*).

tă'lly-hō' *int*. Huntsman's cry to hounds, view-halloo. ~ *n*. 1. Cry of 'tally-ho'. 2. (hist.) Fast passenger-coach, orig. one running between London and Birmingham (1823–); (U.S.) large four-in-hand coach. ~ *v*. Utter cry of 'tally-ho!'; incite (hounds) with this cry.

tă'lma *n*. Woman's or man's long cape or cloak in first half of 19th c. [F. J. Talma (1763–1826), Fr. tragedian]

Tă'lmud *n*. Body of Jewish civil and ceremonial law, comprising the MISHNAH and the

[891]

GEMARA. **Tălmŭ′dĭc, -ĭcal** *adjs.* **Tă′lmudĭst** *n.*
tă′lon *n.* Claw, esp. of bird of prey; (cards) remainder of pack after cards have been dealt; shoulder of bolt against which key presses in turning it; handle end of sword-blade; (archit.) ogee moulding.
tă′lus[1] *n.* Slope, esp. (fort.) sloping side of wall or earthwork; (geol.) mass of rock debris gathering at the foot of a cliff.
tă′lus[2] *n.* (pl. *-lī*). (anat.) Anklebone (ill. FOOT); (path.) form of club-foot with toes drawn up and heel resting on ground.
tăm *n.* = TAM-O'-SHANTER.
tama′l, -a′lè (-ah-) *n.* Mexican dish of crushed maize with pieces of meat or chicken, red pepper, etc., wrapped in corn-husks and baked or steamed.
tamă′ndūa *n.* Arboreal anteater (*T~ tetradactyla*) of Central and S. America; lesser ant-eater.
tă′marack *n.* (Timber of) any of various Amer. larches, esp. *Larix laricina* of northern N. America.
tă′marind *n.* Large tropical tree (*Tamarindus indica*) with hard heavy timber, dark-green pinnate leaves, and racemes of fragrant red-streaked yellow flowers; fruit of this, brown pods with seeds embedded in brown or reddish-black acid pulp, used in medicine, as relish, etc. [Arab. *tamr-hindī* date of India]
tă′marisk *n.* Plant of genus *Tamarix*, esp. *T. gallica*, a graceful evergreen shrub or small tree with slender feathery branches and minute leaves, growing in sandy places.
tă′mbour (-oor) *n.* 1. Circular frame consisting of one hoop fitting closely within another, over which material is stretched for embroidering; embroidery worked on it; tambour-lace; ~-*lace*, kind in which pattern is embroidered or darned on machine-made net stretched in tambour. 2. (archit.) Cylindrical stone forming part of shaft of column; circular part of various structures; ceiled lobby with folding doors in church porch etc., to prevent draughts etc.; sloping buttress or projection in tennis court etc. (ill. TENNIS). 3. (fort.) Small defensive work of palisades, earth, etc., defending entrance or passage. ~ *v.* Decorate, embroider, on tambour.
tă′mbourĭn (-ber-) *n.* Long narrow drum used in Provence; (music for) dance accompanied by this.
tămbouri′ne (-berēn) *n.* Musical instrument consisting of a wooden hoop with a skin stretched over one side and pairs of small cymbals in slots round the circumference, played by shaking, striking with knuckles, or drawing finger(s) across parchment.
Tă′mburlaine, Tă′merlāne.

Timur Lenk or *Lang* 'lame Timur' (*c* 1335–1405), Tatar conqueror of much of Asia and E. Europe; ancestor of the Mogul dynasty in India.
tāme *adj.* 1. (of animals, birds, etc.) Made tractable, domesticated, not wild; (colloq., of land or plant) cultivated. 2. Submissive, spiritless, insipid. **tā′melў** *adv.* **tā′menèss** *n.* **tāme** *v.t.* Make gentle and tractable, break in, domesticate (wild beast, bird, etc.); subdue, curb, humble, reduce to submission. **tā′meable** (-ma-) *adj.*
Tă′mĭl *n.* Member of people of SE. India and part of Sri Lanka; Dravidian language of this people.
Tă′mĭl Nădu′ (-ōō). State in SE. India; capital, Madras.
Tă′mmanў. Fraternal and benevolent society of New York City, founded in 1789, developed out of one of the earlier patriotic societies; political organization of the Democratic party, identified with this society and notorious in 19th c. for corruption; ~ *Hall*, any of the successive buildings used as headquarters of Tammany; (transf.) members of Tammany. [f. name of Indian chief (late 17th c.) noted for wisdom and friendliness towards whites, and regarded (*c* 1770–90) as 'patron saint' of Pennsylvania and other northern colonies]
Tammuz: see THAMMUZ.
tă′mmў[1] *n.* Fine woollen or wool-and-cotton textile fabric, freq. with glazed finish.
tă′mmў[2] *n.* = TAM-O'-SHANTER.
tăm-o′-shă′nter *n.* Round woollen or cloth cap with flat baggy top much wider than head band (ill. PLAID). [f. hero of Burns's poem 'Tam o' Shanter']
tămp *v.t.* Plug (blast-hole etc.) with clay above firing-charge; ram down.
tă′mper *v.i.* ~ *with*, meddle with; alter, corrupt, pervert.
tă′mpion *n.* Plug for top of organ-pipe (ill. ORGAN); plug or cover for muzzle of gun.
tă′mpon *n.* Plug inserted in wound, body cavity, or orifice, to stop haemorrhage or absorb secretions. ~ *v.t.* Plug with tampon.
tă′mponage *n.*
tăn[1] *v.* 1. Convert (skin or hide) into leather by soaking in infusion of oak-bark or other substance rich in tannin, or by any other process. 2. Make, become, brown by exposure to sun or weather. 3. (slang) Beat, thrash. ~ *n.* 1. Crushed or bruised bark of oak or other trees, used for tanning (also ~-*bark*); spent bark from tan-pits used for covering riding-track, circus ring, etc.; track etc. covered with this. 2. Brown colour of tan; bronzed colour of skin that has been exposed to sun or weather. 3. ~-*bark*, see sense 1; ~-*pit*, -*vat*, pit, cistern, tank, etc., in which hides are tanned. ~ *adj.* Of the colour

of tan or tanned leather, yellowish or reddish brown.
tăn[2] *abbrev.* Tangent.
Ta′na (tah-). Lake in Ethiopia, source of the Blue Nile.
tă′nager (-j-) *n.* Amer. bird of sub-family Thraupidae, with numerous species, in which males are usu. bright-coloured.
Tă′nagra (*or* -ah′g-). Ancient town of Boeotia, NE. Greece, famous for terracotta figurines found in tombs mainly of 3rd and 4th centuries B.C.
Tă′ncrèd (*c* 1078–1112). Norman leader in 1st crusade.
T. & A.V.R. *abbrev.* Territorial and Army Volunteer Reserve.
tă′ndem *adv.* (of horses in harness) One behind the other; *drive* ~, drive horses so harnessed. ~ *n.* 1. Carriage driven tandem. 2. Bicycle with two or more seats one behind the other. [punning use of L *tandem* at length (of time)]
t. & o. *abbrev.* Taken and offered.
tăng[1] *n.* 1. Point, projection, esp. extension of knife, chisel, or other metal tool or instrument by which it is secured to its handle (ill. CHISEL). 2. Strong or penetrating taste or smell; characteristic quality; trace, touch, suggestion, *of* something. ~ *v.t.* Furnish with tang.
tăng[2] *n.* Any of various large coarse seaweeds, esp. species of *Fucus*.
T'ang, Tang (tă-). Name of dynasty which ruled in China A.D. 618–906, a period noted for territorial conquest and great wealth, and regarded as golden age of Chinese poetry and art; hence, porcelain etc. of this period.
Tănganyi′ka (-ngg-, -yē-). Mainland part of TANZANIA; *Lake* ~, large lake between Tanganyika and Congo. **Tănganyi′kan** *adj.* & *n.*
tă′ngent (-j-) *adj.* Of (the nature of) a tangent; (of line or surface) touching a line or surface, but not intersecting it. ~ *n.* 1. Straight line tangent to a curve (ill. CIRCLE); *fly, go*, etc., *off at a* ~, diverge suddenly from previous course or direction, or from matter in hand. 2. (trig., function of angle in right-angled triangle) Ratio of side opposite given acute angle to side opposite the other (abbrev. tan; ill. TRIGONOMETRY). 3. Upright piece that strikes string of clavichord (ill. CLAVICHORD). **tă′ngencў** *n.* **tăngĕ′ntial** (-shal) *adj.* **tăngĕ′ntiallў** *adv.*
tăngeri′ne (-jerēn) *n.* Small flattened deep-coloured sweet-scented variety of orange from Tangier; deep orange-yellow colour of this. ~ *adj.* Of colour of tangerine.
tă′ngible (-j-) *adj.* That may be touched, perceptible by touch; real, objective, definite. **tă′ngibleness, tăngibi′litў** *ns.* **tă′ngiblў** *adv.*

Tăṅġier' (-j-). (Arab. *Tanja*) Seaport and summer capital of Morocco, at SW. of Strait of Gibraltar.

tă'nġle[1] (-nggl) *v.* Intertwine, become twisted or involved, in confused mass; entangle; complicate. ~ *n.* Tangled condition or mass. **tă'nġlў** *adj.*

tă'nġle[2] (-nggl) *n.* Either of two seaweeds (*Laminaria digitata* and *L. saccharina*) with long leathery fronds, occas. used as food; any large seaweed.

tă'nġō (-nggō) *n.* Slow dance of Central African origin, brought by Negro slaves to Central America and thence to Argentina where it was influenced by European rhythms, fashionable in ballrooms since c 1910; music for this, in $\frac{2}{4}$ time.

tă'nġram (-ngg-) *n.* Chinese geometrical puzzle of square

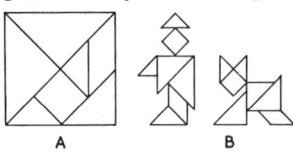

A. TANGRAM. B. TWO FIGURES WHICH CAN BE CONSTRUCTED WITH IT

divided into 7 pieces (5 triangles, a square, and a rhomboid), which can be fitted together to form many figures.

tănk *n.* 1. Large metal or wooden vessel for liquid, gas, etc.; part of locomotive tender containing water for boiler; ~-*car*, railway truck with large tank for carrying liquids; ~-*engine*, railway engine carrying its own fuel and water instead of drawing a tender (ill. LOCOMOTIVE). 2. In India, storage-pond or reservoir used for irrigation or as drinking-water. 3. (mil.) Armoured car carrying guns and mounted on caterpillar tracks, capable of traversing rough ground.

tă'nkaġe *n.* (Charge for) storage in tanks; cubic contents of (tanks).

tă'nkard *n.* Large one-handled drinking-vessel, esp. of pewter or silver, freq. with lid.

tă'nker *n.* Ship, aircraft, or vehicle for carrying mineral oil or other liquid in bulk.

tă'nnāte *n.* Salt of tannic acid.

Tă'nnenberġ. Village formerly in E. Prussia, now in Poland; scene of rout of Teutonic Knights by Poles and Lithuanians, 1410, and of heavy defeat of Russians by Germans, 1914.

tă'nner[1] *n.* One who tans hides.

tă'nner[2] *n.* (slang) Sixpence.

tă'nnerў *n.* Place where hides are tanned.

Tă'nnhäuser (-hoiz-). Legendary 13th-c. German minnesinger.

tă'nnic *adj.* ~ *acid*, complex glucoside found esp. in oak-galls, also in tea and many other plants.

tă'nnin *n.* Any of a group of substances extracted from oak-galls and various barks and having the property of converting hides into leather; also used in medicine, dyeing, etc.

tă'nsў (-zĭ) *n.* Species (*Tanacetum*) of erect herbaceous plants, esp. the strongly aromatic bitter-tasting *T. vulgare*, with deeply divided leaves and corymbs of yellow button-like flowers. [Gk *athanasia* immortality]

tă'ntalīte *n.* Rare heavy black mineral, the principal source of tantalum.

tă'ntalīze *v.t.* Torment, tease, by sight or promise of something desired that is kept out of reach or withheld. **tăntalīzā'tion** *n.* [f. TANTALUS[1]]

tă'ntalum *n.* (chem.) Rare metallic element of vanadium group, a very hard ductile greyish-white metal, used commercially in the manufacture of alloys where hardness and resistance to heat and to the action of acids are of importance, and formerly for electric-lamp filaments; symbol Ta, at. no. 73, at. wt 180·9479. **tăntă'lic** *adj.* [f. TANTALUS[1], with ref. to incapacity of tantalum to absorb acids]

Tă'ntalus[1]. (Gk myth.) King of Phrygia, son of Zeus and the nymph Pluto; he served the flesh of his son Pelops to the gods (or committed some other crime variously described) and after his death was condemned to stand in Tartarus, in water that receded when he tried to drink and under branches of fruit that always eluded his grasp.

tă'ntalus[2] *n.* Spirit-stand containing decanters which can be seen but not withdrawn until bar holding them is unlocked. [f. TANTALUS[1]]

tă'ntamount *adj.* Equivalent *to.*

tă'ntara (or -tär'*a*) *n.* Fanfare, flourish, of trumpets etc.

tănti'vў *int.* Exclamation expressing sound of galloping, esp. as hunting cry. ~ *n.* Swift movement, gallop, rush.

Ta'ntra (tŭ-) *n.* 1. One of a class of Hindu writings, in Sanskrit, of a mystical and magical nature. 2. One of a group of Buddhist writings of somewhat similar character. **Ta'ntric** *adj.* Of the Tantras; ~ *Buddhism*, form of Buddhism, with emphasis on magic, practised esp. in Tibet. **Ta'ntrism** *n.* Tantric Buddhism. [Sansk. *tantra* loom, doctrine, manual]

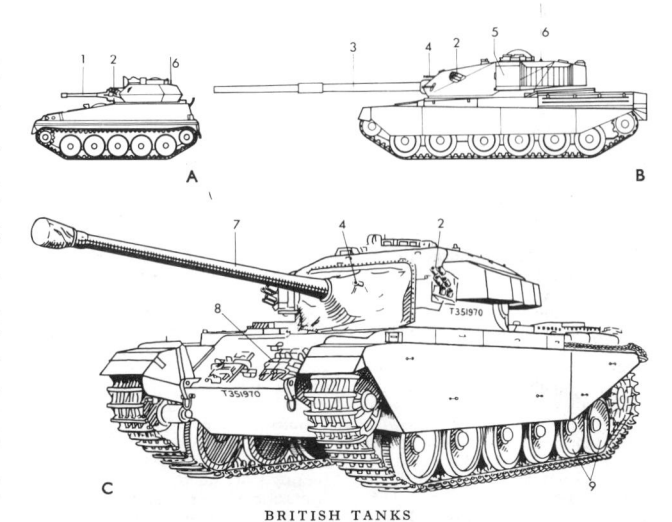

BRITISH TANKS

A. SIDE VIEW OF SCORPION LIGHT TANK, c 1972. B. SIDE VIEW OF CHIEFTAIN TANK, c 1972. C. CENTURION MARK III TANK, c 1950

1. 76 mm gun. 2. Smoke grenade dischargers. 3. 120 mm gun. 4. 7·62 mm machine gun. 5. Infra-red searchlight. 6. Radio aerial. 7. 83·4 mm gun. 8. Spare track links. 9. Road wheels

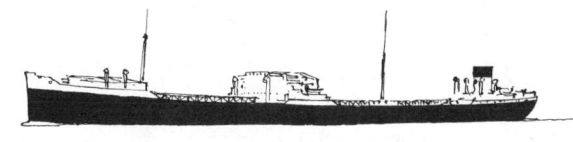

TANKER

tă′ntrum n. (colloq.) Outburst or display of bad temper or petulance.

Tănzani′a (-ēa; or -ā′nĭa). Republic in E. Central Africa, formed in 1964, consisting of Tanganyika and Zanzibar; member State of the Commonwealth; capital, Dar es Salaam. **Tănzani′an** adj. & n.

taoiseach (tē′shŏk) n. Prime minister of the republic of Ireland.

Ta′ōism (tah-; or tow′ĭ-) n. One of the three religions of China, orig. a system of conduct based on writings attributed to the philosopher LAO-TSE and later invested with magical beliefs and a large pantheon. **Ta′ōist** n. [f. Chin. *Tao tê king* 'Book of reason and virtue']

tăp[1] n. 1. Hollow or tubular plug with device for shutting off or controlling flow, through which liquid or gas may be drawn from pipe, cask, etc. (ill. COCK[1]); liquor from a particular tap, particular quality or kind of drink; (colloq.) tap-room; *on* ~, on draught, ready for immediate use or consumption. 2. Tool in shape of male screw of hard steel, for cutting female screw thread (ill. SCREW[1]). 3. ~*-room*, room in public-house etc. where liquors are kept on tap; ~*-root*, straight root growing vertically downwards, thick at top and tapering to a point (ill. ROOT[1]); ~*-water*, water from a tap, esp. that supplied through system of pipes and taps to house etc. ~ v.t. 1. Furnish (cask etc.) with tap; pierce (cask, tree, etc.) so as to draw off liquid, draw liquid from (any reservoir); draw off (liquid); (surg.) pierce body-wall of (person) to draw off accumulated liquid, drain (cavity) thus; (fig.) broach (subject). 2. Furnish (bolt, hole, etc.) with screw-thread. 3. Connect electric circuit to (another circuit), esp. as means of intercepting telegraph or telephone message, stealing current, etc.

tăp[2] v. 1. Strike lightly; cause (thing) to strike lightly (*against* etc.); strike gentle blow, rap; do tap-dancing. 2. Apply leather to (heel of shoe). ~ n. 1. Light blow, rap; sound of this; (pl., U.S. mil. and nav.) signal sounded on drum or bugle for lights out. 2. (U.S.) Piece of leather put on over worn sole in shoe-repairing. 3. ~*-dance*, kind of exhibition dance in which rhythm, esp. in elaborate syncopation, is tapped out with the feet; ~*-dancer, -dancing*; ~*-shoes*, shoes with metal plates.

tāpe n. 1. Narrow woven strip of cotton etc. used as string for tying garments etc.; piece of tape stretched across race-course between winning-posts. 2. Strip of tape, flexible metal, etc., used as measuring-line etc.; paper strip on which messages are printed in tape-machine (see below); strip of magnetic material on which sounds etc. are recorded. 3. ~*-machine*, receiving instrument of recording telegraph system; ~*-measure*, strip of tape or thin flexible metal marked for use as measure; ~*-recorder*, machine for recording and reproducing sounds on magnetic tape; *ta′peworm*, any of numerous cestode worms (*Taenia* and allied genera) parasitic in intestines of

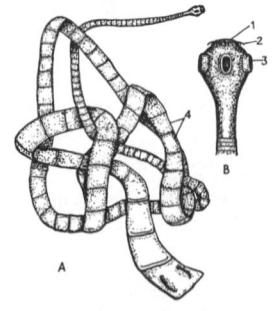

A. TAPEWORM. B. ENLARGEMENT OF SCOLEX

1. Rostellum. 2. Hooks. 3. Suckers. 4. Proglottides

man and other vertebrates, and having long flat body of numerous proglottides. ~ v.t. Furnish, measure, join, with tape(s); record on tape; *have* thing, person, *taped*, have summed up, understand completely.

tā′per n. 1. Slender wax candle; long wick coated with wax for lighting lamp etc. 2. Tapering. ~ *adj.* (chiefly poet. and rhet.) Tapering; ~ *bearing*, roller bearing tapered at one end (ill. BEARING). ~ v. (freq. ~ *off*) Make, become, gradually smaller towards one end; (cause to) grow gradually less.

tă′pĕstry̆ n. Thick hand-woven fabric, usu. of wool, with a pictorial or ornamental design formed by the weft-threads, these being carried back and forth across the parts where their respective colours are needed and not from selvage to selvage (ill. WEAVE); wall-hanging of this; embroidered, painted, or machine-woven fabric imitating or resembling tapestry; ~ *carpet*, kind of carpet in which design is printed on warp before weaving; ~*-needle*, short comparatively thick needle; ~*-stitch*, Gobelin stitch, embroidery stitch like cross-stitch but with all threads parallel with warp on right side of fabric.

tapē′tum n. (pl. *-ta*). 1. (zool.) Irregular sector in eyes of certain animals (e.g. cat) which shines owing to absence of black pigment. 2. (bot.) Layer of nutritive tissue esp. in reproductive organs.

tăpiō′ca n. Starchy granular foodstuff prepared from cassava and used in puddings etc. [Braz. tipioca juice of cassava (*tipi* dregs, *og, ók* squeeze out)]

tā′pir (*or* -ēr) n. Hoofed pig-like mammal of genus *Tapirus* of

TAPIR
Length c 2 m

tropical America and Malaya, with short flexible proboscis, related to rhinoceros.

tă′pis (-pē) n. *on the* ~, under discussion. [OF, = 'tapestry', perh. f. use of this for tablecloths]

tapŏ′tement (-tm-) n. (med.) Percussion as part of massage treatment.

tă′ppĕt n. Arm, collar, cam, etc., used in machinery to impart intermittent motion; ~ *loom*, loom in which hammers are worked by tappets; ~ *rod*, rod carrying tappet(s), used e.g. for opening and closing valves of internal combustion engine (ill. COMBUSTION).

tă′pster n. Person employed at bar to draw and serve liquor.

tăr[1] n. 1. Thick viscid inflammable black or dark-coloured liquid with heavy resinous or bituminous odour, obtained by distillation of wood, coal, or other organic substance, used for coating and preserving timber, cordage, etc., and as a preservative and antiseptic; source (by distillation) of a number of aromatic hydrocarbons and other substances which are starting materials for the manufacture of numerous chemicals and drugs; substances resembling this; ~*-brush*, brush used for applying tar; *a touch of the* ~*-brush*, a trace of Negro or Indian blood; *tar′heel*, (U.S., colloq.) nickname for inhabitant of pine-wood districts of N. Carolina; ~ *macadam*, (tradename) *tar′mac*, road-making material of crushed stone, slag, etc., mixed or covered with tar or other bituminous binder; ~*-water*, infusion of tar in cold water formerly used as medicine. ~ v.t. Cover, smear, with tar; ~ *and feather*, smear (person) with tar and cover him with feathers, as punishment or indignity.

tăr[2] n. (colloq., also *Jack* ~) Sailor. [perh. f. TARPAULIN]

tă′radĭddle, tă′rr- n. (colloq.) 1. Petty or trifling lie. 2. Pretentious nonsense.

tărantĕ′lla, tărantĕ′lle ns. Rapid whirling dance of S. Italian peasants, formerly supposed to be the remedy for, or the effect of, tarantism; music for this; instrumental composition in rhythm of tarantella, now always in § time, increasing in speed towards the end.

tă′rantism n. (obs.) Malady (prob. chorea) characterized by melancholy and overwhelming desire to dance, epidemic in S. Italy in 15th–17th centuries, and pop. supposed to be caused by bite of tarantula.

tară′ntūla n. Large black S. European spider of genus *Lycosa*, with slight poisonous bite formerly supposed to cause tarantism; any of various other large venomous spiders, esp. large hairy spiders of warm parts of America. **tară′ntūlar** adj. [f. *Taranto* in S. Italy]

tară′xacum n. Plant of genus *T*~ of weedy composite herbs, including dandelion, with bitter foliage and usu. yellow flowers; drug prepared from dried roots of dandelion (*T. officinale*) and used as tonic and laxative. [Pers. *talkh chakōk* bitter herb]

tărboo′sh n. Man's brimless (usu. red) felt etc. cap resembling a fez worn alone or as part of a turban by Muslims in certain countries of E. Mediterranean.

tăr′digrāde adj. Slow-moving, of the Tardigrada or water-bears, a phylum of minute aquatic animals which are primitive arthropods. ~ n. Tardigrade animal; water-bear, bear animalcule.

tăr′dō adj. & adv. (mus.) Slow(ly). [It.]

tăr′dȳ adj. Slow-moving, slow, sluggish; late, coming or done late. **tăr′dily** adv. **tăr′diness** n.

tāre¹ n. Any of various vetches; vetch-seed; (bibl.) darnel.

tāre² n. (Allowance made for) weight of wrapping, box, conveyance, etc., in which goods are packed; (chem.) weight of vessel in which substance is weighed. ~ v.t. Ascertain, allow for, tare of.

tărge n. (archaic & poet.) Shield, esp. light shield or buckler.

tăr′gĕt (-g-) n. Mark, esp. with concentric circles round central ring or spot, for shooting at; anything aimed at; (U.S.) disc-shaped railway signal indicating position of switch.

Tăr′gum (-ŏŏm) n. Any of various translations, interpretations, or paraphrases, in Aramaic, of parts of O.T., recorded in writing from *c* A.D. 100 onwards, but preserved from earlier times by oral transmission. **Tăr′gumist** n. [Heb. *targūm* translation, interpretation]

tă′riff n. 1. List of duties or customs to be paid on imports or exports; such duties collectively; law imposing these; duty on particular class of goods; ~ *reform*, esp. (U.S.) movement favouring general reduction of tariffs; (in England at beginning of 20th c.) extension of tariffs on imports, as opp. 'free trade'. 2. List or scale of charges at hotel, on railway, etc. [Arab. *ta'rīf* notification ('*arrafa* notify)]

tăr′latan n. Thin stiff muslin of very open weave, sometimes glazed.

tarmac, tarmacadam: see TAR¹.

tărn n. Small mountain lake.

tăr′nish v. Dull or dim lustre of, discolour by oxidation etc.; lose lustre; (fig.) sully, taint, stain. ~ n. Tarnishing, being tarnished; stain, blemish, tarnished coating.

tă′rō n. Either of two plants of the arum family, *Colocasia esculenta* and *C. antiquorum*, cultivated in Pacific islands and other tropical regions for the starchy edible root.

tă′rŏc, tă′rot (-ō) ns. One of a pack of 78 cards (*tarocchi*) first used in Italy in 14th c., and much used in fortune-telling, esp. any of the figured cards which constitute trumps; game played with these.

tărpau′lin n. Canvas made waterproof by coating or impregnating with tar and used as covering, esp. for ship's hatches, boats, etc.; other waterproof cloth used as covering; sailor's tarpaulin or oilskin hat.

Tărpei′an (-ēan) adj. Of a cliff (~ *Rock*) on the Capitoline Hill over which criminals were hurled in ancient Rome.

tăr′pon n. Large silvery marine game-fish (*Megalops atlanticus*) found in warmer waters of W. Atlantic.

Tăr′quin. Name of two semi-legendary, perhaps Etruscan, kings of ancient Rome, Tarquinius Priscus and Tarquinius Superbus (~ *the Proud*); when the latter was expelled (510 B.C.) the Republic was founded.

tă′rragon n. Plant of wormwood kind (*Artemisia dracunculus*), of S. Russia and E. Europe, with aromatic leaves used for flavouring salads etc.; ~ *vinegar*, vinegar flavoured with oil or leaves of tarragon. [Arab. *tarkhōn*, perh. f. Gk *drakōn* dragon]

tăr′rȳ¹ adj. Of, like, smeared or impregnated with, tar.

tă′rrȳ² v. (literary) Remain, stay; wait; delay, be late.

tăr′sal adj. Of the TARSUS¹.

tăr′sia n. = INTARSIA. [It.]

tăr′sier n. Small nocturnal tree-climbing animal of E. Indies with soft fur and large prominent eyes (esp. *Tarsius spectrum*), a primate related to the lemurs. [L *tarsus*, from formation of its foot]

tăr′sus¹ n. (pl. -*sī*). 1. (anat.) Ankle, collection of small bones (7 in man) between metatarsus and leg (ill. FOOT); third segment of bird's leg; (entom.) terminal segment of limb (ill. INSECT). 2. Tarsal plate, plate of condensed connective tissue stiffening eyelid.

Tăr′sus². City in SW. corner of Turkey, home of St. Paul.

tărt¹ n. 1. Pie containing fruit; piece of pastry spread on pie-plate etc. with jam, treacle, etc., on top. 2. (slang) Girl, woman, esp. of loose morals; prostitute.

tărt² adj. Sharp-tasting, sour, acid; cutting, biting. **tăr′tlȳ** adv. **tăr′tness** n.

tăr′tan n. Woollen cloth with stripes of various colours crossing at right angles, esp. in the distinctive pattern of a Highland clan; such pattern; other fabric with similar pattern. ~ adj. Made of, chequered like, tartan.

tăr′tar¹ n. 1. Acid potassium tartrate deposited in form of crust in wine-casks etc. during fermentation of grape-juice; *cream of* ~, purified tartar in form of white crystals, used in cookery; ~ *emetic*, poisonous white crystalline salt, potassium antimonyl tartrate, used in medicine, and in dyeing as mordant. 2. Hard deposit of calcium phosphate from saliva on teeth.

Tartar² : see TATAR.

tăr′tare sauce. Savoury sauce consisting of mayonnaise with capers, chopped gherkins and herbs, etc., served with fish etc.

tărtă′ric adj. Derived from tartar; ~ *acid*, organic acid present in numerous plants esp. unripe grapes, and used in calico printing and in manufacture of baking-powders and effervescent drinks.

Tăr′tarus. (Gk myth.) Infernal regions, or lowest part of them, where the Titans were confined; place of punishment in Hades.

Tărtăr′ean adj.

Tăr′tarȳ. Tatar regions of Asia and E. Europe, esp. high plateau of Asia and its NW. slopes.

tăr′tlĕt n. Small tart.

tăr′trāte n. Salt of tartaric acid.

Tăr′zăn n. Hero of African jungle stories by Amer. novelist Edgar Rice Burroughs (1875–1950); hence, man of very great strength and agility.

Tă′shī La′ma (lah-). Lama second in rank to Dalai Lama.

task (tah-) n. Piece of work imposed or undertaken as a duty etc.; any piece of work that has to be done; *take to* ~, find fault with, rebuke (*for*); ~ *force*, (U.S.) an armed force organized for operations under a unified command; *ta′skmaster*, (now usu. fig.) one who

TARSIER
Length 355 mm

sets a task, one who imposes heavy burden or labour. ~ v.t. Assign task to; occupy or engage fully, put strain upon.
Tă'sman (-z-), Abel Janszoon (c 1603–59). Dutch navigator and explorer, discoverer of TASMANIA, New Zealand, and Fiji Islands. ~('s) *Sea*, part of Pacific Ocean lying between New Zealand and SE. Australia.
Tăsmā'nia (-z-). State of Commonwealth of Australia, consisting of one large and several smaller islands SE. of the continent; discovered 1642 by TASMAN; formerly called Van Diemen's Land; capital, Hobart.
Tăsmā'nian (-z-) adj. Of Tasmania; ~ *devil*, nocturnal carnivorous marsupial (*Sarcophilus harrisii*) of savage appearance, about size of badger, with coarse black hair with white patches; ~ *wolf*, THYLACINE. ~ *n*. Native, inhabitant, of Tasmania.
Tăss. Telegraphic agency of U.S.S.R. [initials of Russ. *Telegráfnoe Agéntstvo Sovétskogo Soyúza*]
tă'ssel n. 1. Tuft of loosely hanging threads or cords as ornament for cushion, cap, etc.; tassel-like head of some plants, esp. staminate inflorescence at top of stalk of Indian corn; ribbon sewn into book to be used as bookmark. 2. = TORSEL. ~ *v.t.* Furnish with tassel; remove tassels of (Indian corn) to strengthen plant. [OF., perh. f. L *taxillus* small die]
tă'sset n. (hist., usu. pl.) One of the overlapping plates hanging from corslet and protecting thighs (ill. ARMOUR).
tă'ssie n. (Sc.) Small cup.
Tă'ssō, Torquato (1544–95). Italian poet, author of 'Jerusalem Delivered' etc.
tāste v. Learn flavour of (food etc.) by taking it into the mouth; eat small portion of; experience, have experience of; (of food etc.) have specified flavour, have flavour of. ~ *n.* 1. Sensation excited in taste buds by contact of some soluble things, flavour; ~ *bud*, one of a number of groups of narrow rod-shaped cells in epithelium of mouth, esp. of tongue. 2. Faculty of perceiving flavour of things by allowing them to touch the tongue. 3. Small portion (*of* food etc.) taken as sample. 4. Liking; predilection *for*. 5. Faculty of discerning and enjoying beauty or other excellence esp. in art and literature; sense of what is harmonious or fitting in art, language, or conduct (*in good* ~, manifesting this faculty; *in bad* ~, showing lack of it).
tā'steful (-tf-) adj. Having, showing, done in, good taste (TASTE *n.* 5). **tā'stefully** adv. **tā'stefulness** n.
tā'steless (-tl-) adj. 1. Flavourless, insipid. 2. Lacking physical sense of taste. 3. Lacking in good taste, or critical discernment and appreciation; not in good taste. **tā'stelessly** adv. **tā'stelessness** *n*.
tā'ster *n*. (esp.) 1. Person employed to judge quality of tea, wine, etc., by taste; (hist.) person employed to taste food before it was touched by his employer, esp. to guard against poison. 2. Shallow cup for tasting wines etc.; instrument for taking small portion from interior of cheese; skewer for testing condition of hams.
tā'sty adj. (colloq.) Savoury, appetizing. **tā'stily** adv. **tā'stiness** *n*.
tăt v. Do TATTING; make by tatting.
ta-ta' (-ah) int. (nursery or colloq.) Good-bye. **tă'ta** (-ah) *n*. A walk.
Ta'tar (tah-), **Tăr'tar** *n*. Member of any of numerous, mostly Muslim and Turkic, tribes inhabiting various parts of European and Asiatic Russia, esp. parts of Siberia, Crimea, N. Caucasus, districts along Volga, etc.; one of the mingled horde of Mongols, Turks, Tatars, etc., who overran E. Europe under Genghis Khan. ~ *adj.* Of the Tatars; ~ *Republic*, autonomous republic of R.S.F.S.R.; capital, Kazan. [Pers. *tātăr*; altered to *tartar* by association with TARTARUS]
Tāte, Nahum (1652–1715). English playwright and poet laureate (from 1692); author, with Nicholas Brady, of a metrical version of the Psalms (1696).
Tāte Gă'llery. National Gallery of British Art and of modern foreign painting and sculpture; built at Millbank, London, at the expense of Sir Henry Tate (1819–99), sugar manufacturer, to house a collection presented by him and other works accumulated by various bequests since 1841; opened in 1897.
Tă'tler, The. Periodical (consisting chiefly of short essays) published by Addison and Steele, 1709–11.
Ta'tra Mou'ntains(tah-, -tĭnz). (also *Tatras, High Tatra*) Highest group of central Carpathians, partly in N. Czechoslovakia, partly in Poland.
tă'tter *n*. Rag, irregularly torn piece, of cloth, paper, etc. **tă'ttered** (-erd) adj. Reduced to tatters.
tătterdemă'lion n. Ragged fellow, ragamuffin.
Tă'ttersall's (-z). Horse-dealing mart founded 1766 by Richard Tattersall in London, now at Newmarket; ~ *Committee*, unofficial organization concerned esp. with betting on horse-racing; ~ *Ring*, principal betting enclosure on any race-course.
tă'tting n. Kind of knotted lace made from sewing-thread with small flat shuttle-shaped instrument.
tă'ttle v.i. Gossip idly; repeat or discuss scandal. ~ *n*. Tattling; gossip. **tă'ttler** n.
tattōō'[1] *n*. 1. (mil.) Signal by drum or bugle in evening summoning soldiers to quarters; elaboration of this as military entertainment, usu. by torch or other artificial light, with music, troop exercises, etc. 2. Drumming, rapping; drum-beat; *devil's* ~: see DEVIL. ~ *v.* Rap quickly and repeatedly; beat devil's tattoo. [Du. *tap-toe*, lit. 'close the tap' (of the cask)]
tattōō'[2] v.t. Mark (skin) with permanent pattern or design by puncturing it and inserting pigment; make (design) thus. ~ *n*. Tattooing. [Tahitian *tatau*]
tă'tty[1] *n*. Cuscus-grass mat hung in doorway, window, etc., and kept wet to cool the air. [Hind. *ṭaṭṭi* wicker-frame]
tă'tty[2] adj. (colloq.) Tattered, shabby.
tau *n*. Letter of Greek alphabet (T, τ), corresponding to *t*; mark or cross (~ *cross*) in shape of this (ill. CROSS).
Tau'chnĭtz (towχ-). Name of family of German printers and publishers in 19th c., founders of a firm at Leipzig which issued cheap reprints of British and American copyright works for circulation in the continent of Europe (~ *editions*).
taunt v.t. Reproach, upbraid, (*with*) insultingly or contemptuously. ~ *n*. Insulting or provoking gibe; scornful reproach.
taur'ine adj. Of, like, a bull, bovine; of the zodiacal sign Taurus.
Taur'is. Name sometimes used for Crimea in ancient times, from *Tauri*, earliest known inhabitants of its S. coast.
taurŏ'machȳ (-kĭ) *n*. Bullfight(ing).
Taur'us. The Bull, a constellation; 2nd sign (♉) of the zodiac, which the sun enters about 21 April. **Taur'ēan** adj. & *n*.
taut adj. (of rope etc.) Tightly drawn, not slack; (of ship etc.) trim, neat. **tau'tly** adv. **tau'tness** *n*. **tau'ten** v.
tauto- *prefix*. Same.
tau'tochrōne (-k-) *n*. (math.) Curve upon which body sliding from state of rest under given force will reach lowest point in same time, from whatever point it starts. **tautŏ'chronism** *n*. **tautŏ'chronous** adj.
tautŏhē'dral adj. (cryst.) Having the same face or side in common.
tautŏ'logȳ *n*. Repetition of

TATTING

TAUTOMERISM

same word or phrase, or of same idea etc., in different words (e.g. *arrived one after the other in succession*). **tautŏ'logous, tautolŏ'gical** adjs. **tautolŏ'gicallў** adv.
tautŏ'merism n. (chem.) Property possessed by some organic compounds of behaving in different reactions as if they possessed two or more different constitutions. **tau'tomēr** n. Compound having property of tautomerism. **tautomĕ'ric** adj.
tautŏ'phonў n. Repetition of same (vocal) sound.
tă'vern n. (archaic) Inn or PUBLIC house.
taw[1] n. Large, freq. streaked or variegated, marble with which player shoots; game played with taws; line from which players shoot.
taw[2] v.t. Make (hides or skins) into leather by steeping in solution of alum and salt.
taw'drў adj. Showy or gaudy without real value. **taw'drilў** adv. **taw'drinèss** n. [f. *tawdry lace* sold at *St. Audry's* Fair, i.e. St. Etheldreda's, in Isle of Ely]
taw'nў adj. & n. (Of) brown colour with preponderance of yellow or orange; ~ *eagle*, brownish eagle (*Aquila rapax*) of Africa and Asia, with reddish backfeathers; ~ *owl*, common reddish-brown owl (*Strix aluco*) of Europe and N. Africa, with darker brown bars or markings. **taw'ninèss** n.
taws, -se (-z) n. (Sc.) Leather strap with end slit into narrow strips, for chastising children.
tăx n. Contribution levied on person, property, business, or articles of commerce, for the support of the State (in U.S. including rates levied by local bodies); oppressive or burdensome charge etc.; strain, heavy demand *on*; ~*-collector*, (archaic) ~*-gatherer*, collector of taxes; ~*-free*, exempt from taxes, esp. from income-tax; (of dividends or interest) having the income-tax paid by the company and not deducted from the distributed dividend or interest; *taxpayer*, one who pays taxes. ~ v. 1. Impose tax on, subject to taxation; make demands on, strain, burden. 2. (law) Assess (costs); examine and allow or disallow items of (costs of action etc.); *taxing-master*, official of law-court who taxes costs. 3. Accuse, charge (*with*); call to account, take to task. **tă'xable** adj. **tăxā'tion** n.
tă'xi n. Motor-car plying for hire, esp. one fitted with taximeter; (also *air* ~) aircraft plying for hire. ~ v. Go, convey, in taxi; (of aircraft) run along ground or over surface of water before taking off or after alighting.
tă'xidermў n. Art of preparing and mounting skins of animals in lifelike manner. **tăxidēr'mal, tăxidēr'mic** adjs. **tă'xidērmist** n.
tă'ximēter n. Automatic device fitted to taxi indicating fare due.
tă'xis n. 1. (biol.) Movement

of organism in a particular direction in response to external stimulus (e.g. towards or away from light or heat). 2. (surg.) Manipulative operation to restore displaced part or reduce hernia etc. 3. (Gk antiq.) Division of Greek army, varying in size in different States. 4. (gram.) Order, arrangement.
tăxŏ'nomў n. (biol.) (Laws and principles of) classification. **tăxŏ'nomer, tăxŏ'nomist** ns. **tăxonŏ'mic, -ical** adjs. **tăxonŏ'micallў** adv.
Tay. River of Scotland flowing into North Sea by *Firth of* ~, between Tayside and Fife; the first Tay Bridge, a railway bridge across the Firth of Tay (opened 1877), was blown down in 1879 while a passenger-train was crossing it.
Tay'lor[1], John (1580–1653). The 'Water-Poet', English pamphleteer and Thames waterman.
Tay'lor[2], Zachary (1784–1850). American soldier; 12th president of U.S., 1849–50.
Taysi'de. Region of Central Scotland (since May 1975), comprising the former counties of Angus, Kinross-shire, and N. Perthshire.
tazza (tah'tsa) n. Shallow ornamental bowl or cup mounted on a base.

ENGRAVED SILVER-GILT
TAZZA

T.B. abbrev. Torpedo-boat; tubercle bacillus; (colloq.) tuberculosis.
T.C.D. abbrev. Trinity College, Dublin.
Tchaikŏ'vskў (chĭköf'-), Peter Ilyich (1840–93). Russian composer.
Tchekov: see CHEKHOV.
T.D. abbrev. *Teachta Dála* (Ir., = Deputy of Dáil); Territorial (Officer's) Decoration.
tē n. (mus.) 7th note of major scale in movable-doh systems; note B in fixed-doh system.
tea n. 1. Dried and prepared leaves of the tea-plant, classed acc. to their method of manufacture as *green*, *black*, and *oolong* (the leaves of green tea are rolled and fired immediately, those of black tea are fermented or oxidized before firing, and those of oolong tea are only partially oxidized before firing); drink made by infusion from tea-leaves, with slight-

TEAK

ly bitter and aromatic flavour and moderately stimulant action, widely used as a beverage; meal at which this is served, esp. light meal in afternoon, or (*high* ~) evening meal. 2. (also ~*-plant*) Plant from which tea is obtained shrub (*Thea*) with fragrant white flowers and evergreen lanceolate leaves, cultivated from ancient times in China and Japan and grown also in India, Sri Lanka, etc. 3. Infusion made in same way as tea from leaves, blossoms, etc., of other plants, beef extract, fruit preserves, etc., and freq. used medicinally; (with defining word) plant used for tea, or the beverages prepared from this. 4. ~*-bag*, small permeable bag of tea-leaves for infusion; ~*-break*, interruption of work allowed for drinking tea etc.; *tea'cake*, light kind of flat sweet bun, freq. toasted, eaten at tea etc.; ~*-chest*, foil-lined cubical chest in which tea is exported; ~*-cloth*, tea-towel; (also) cloth for tea-table or tea-tray; *tea'cup*, cup from which tea is drunk; as measure, about 4 fluid ounces; ~*-garden*, garden in which tea etc. is served to public; ~*-gown*, woman's usu. flowing dress worn at tea etc.; ~*-leaf*, leaf of tea, esp. (pl.) leaves after infusion; ~*-plant*: see sense 2; ~*-planter*, proprietor or cultivator of tea plantation; *tea'pot*, vessel with spout in which tea is made; ~*-room*, room in which tea and other refreshments are served to public; ~*-rose*, delicate-scented half-hardy or tender varieties of cultivated rose derived from *Rosa odorata* of China; ~*-set*, set of cups and saucers, plates, etc., for tea; ~*-shop*, tea-room; *tea'spoon*, small spoon used for stirring tea etc.; teaspoonful; *tea'spoonful*, amount held by teaspoon, about ⅓ tablespoonful; ~*-taster*, one whose business is to test quality of tea by tasting samples; ~*-things*, tea-set as needed for meal; ~*-towel*, cloth for drying crockery etc. after washing. [Chin. (Amoy dial.) *t'e*, Mandarin *ch'a*]
teach v. Give (person) instruction or lessons in (a subject); show or make known to person (how to do something); give instruction to, educate, explain, state by way of instruction; be a teacher; ~*-in*, kind of oral symposium on subject of topical interest.
tea'chable adj. Apt to learn, docile; (of subject etc.) that can be taught. **teachabi'litў, tea'chablenèss** ns.
tea'cher n. (esp.) One who teaches in a school.
tea'ching n. (esp.) What is taught, doctrine.
teak n. (Yellowish-brown heavy durable oily wood of) large E. Indian tree (*Tectona grandis*) with large egg-shaped leaves and panicles of white flowers; (strong or

[897]

teal *n.* Small freshwater duck of *Anas* or other genera, widely distributed in Europe, Asia, and America, esp. *A. crecca*.

team *n.* 1. Two or more draught animals harnessed together; two or more beasts, or a single beast, with the vehicle they draw. 2. Set of players forming side in game or sport; set of persons working together; ~-*work*, combined effort, organized co-operation. ~ *v.* Harness in team; convey, transport, with team; (also ~ *up*) join, put together in a team (*with*).

tea'mster *n.* Driver of a team.

tear[1] *n.* 1. Drop of limpid saline fluid secreted by lachrymal gland appearing in or flowing from eye, as result of emotion, esp. grief, or of physical irritation, nervous stimulus, etc.; (pl.) weeping, sorrow, grief. 2. Something resembling a tear, esp. various gums exuding from plants in tear-shaped or globular beads, defect in glass caused by particle of vitrified clay, Prince Rupert's drop, etc. 3. ~-*duct*, lachrymal or nasal duct carrying off tears from eye to nose; lachrymal canal carrying tears to eyes; ~-*gas*, lachrymatory vapour used to disable opponents; ~-*gland*, lachrymal gland.

tear'ful *adj.* Shedding tears; mournful, sad. **tear'fully** *adv.* **tear'fulness** *n.* **tear'less** *adj.* **tear'lessly** *adv.* **tear'lessness** *n.*

tear[2] (tār) *v.* (past t. *tōre*, past part. *tōrn*). 1. Pull apart, away, or asunder, by force; rend, lacerate; make a tear or rent; (of thing) lend itself to tearing. 2. Move violently or impetuously, rush. ~ *n.* Damage caused by tearing; torn part or place in cloth etc.

tear'ing (tār-) *adj.* (esp.) Violent, overwhelming.

tease (-z) *v.t.* 1. Pull asunder fibres of, comb, card (wool, flax, etc.); comb surface of (cloth etc.) into nap with teasels etc. 2. Assail playfully or maliciously, vex, irritate, with jests, questions, or petty annoyances. ~ *n.* Person addicted to teasing.

tea'sel (-z-), **tea'zle** *n.* Plant of genus *Dipsacus*, herbs with prickly leaves and flower-heads, esp. *D. fullonum*, *fuller's* ~, heads of which have hooked prickles between flowers; dried prickly flower-head of fuller's teasel used for teasing cloth etc. so as to raise nap on surface; contrivance used as substitute for this. ~ *v.t.* Dress (cloth) with teasel(s).

tea'ser (-z-) *n.* (esp., colloq.) Difficult question, problem, or task, thing hard to deal with.

teat *n.* Nipple, small protuberance at tip of breast in female mammalia, upon which ducts of mammary gland open and from which milk is sucked by young; artificial structure resembling this, esp. contrivance of rubber etc. through which milk is sucked from bottle.

teazle: see TEASEL.

těc *n.* (slang) Detective.

těchne'tium (-knēshum) *n.* (chem.) Radioactive metallic element not found in nature, the first otherwise unknown element to be produced artificially (1937); symbol Tc, at. no. 43, at. wt 98·9062. [Gk *tekhnētos* artificial]

tě'chnic (-k-) *n.* Technical term or detail, technicality; (pl. rare) technique; (usu. pl.) technology.

tě'chnical (-k-) *adj.* 1. Of or (used) in a particular art, science, profession, handicraft, etc. 2. Of, for, in, the mechanical arts and applied science generally; ~ *hitch*, one caused by mechanical fault. 3. Regarded in specified way according to a strict interpretation of law or rule(s). **tě'chnically** *adv.* **těchnică'lity** *n.* Technical quality or character; technical point, detail, term, etc.

techni'cian (-knĭshan) *n.* Person skilled in the technique of an art or subject; person expert in the practical application of science.

Tě'chnicolor (-knĭkŭl-) *n.* (cinemat.) Process of colour photography in which the colours are separately but simultaneously recorded and then transferred to a single positive print. [tradename]

těchni'que (-knēk) *n.* Manner of execution or performance in painting, music, etc.; mechanical part of an art, craft, etc.; (loosely) method of achieving one's purpose.

těchnŏ'cracy (-kn-) *n.* Government or control of society by technical experts. **tě'chnocrăt** *n.* **těchnocră'tic** *adj.*

těchnŏ'logy (-k-) *n.* Scientific study of practical or industrial arts; practical arts collectively; terminology of particular art or subject. **těchnolŏ'gical** *adj.* **těchnŏ'logist** *n.*

techy: see TETCHY.

těctŏ'nic *adj.* Of building or construction; ~ *geology*, that part of geology which deals with structure in the rocks and in the earth's crust. **těctŏ'nics** *n.* Art of producing useful and beautiful buildings, furniture, vessels, etc.

těctōr'ial *adj.* Forming a covering; ~ *membrane*, the covering part of the inner ear.

tě'ctrix *n.* (pl. -*icēs*). (ornith.) = COVERT[1], 2.

těd *v.t.* Turn over and spread out (grass, hay) to dry. **tě'dder** *n.* Machine for drying hay.

Tě'ddy bear (băr). Child's toy bear. [named after Theodore Roosevelt]

Tě'ddy-boy *n.* (in 1950s) Youth affecting style of dress held to be characteristic of the reign of Edward VII.

Tě Dē'um. Ancient Latin hymn of praise beginning *Te Deum laudamus* 'We praise thee, O God', sung at matins in R.C. Ch. and Church of England, and as thanksgiving on special occasions; musical setting of this.

tē'dious *adj.* Tiresomely long, prolix, irksome. **tē'diously** *adv.* **tē'diousness** *n.*

tē'dium *n.* Weariness produced by tediousness, tedious circumstances.

tee[1] *n.* Letter T; T-shaped thing or part; ~-*shirt*, -*square*, = T-shirt, T-square (see T).

tee[2] *n.* (golf) Small mound of sand on which golfer places the ball for driving off at the start and after each hole; small piece of wood, rubber, etc., for the same purpose; place from which the ball is played at the beginning of play for each hole; mark aimed at in quoits, curling, etc. ~ *v.* Place (ball) on tee; ~ *off*, play ball from tee.

tee[3] *n.* Umbrella-shaped usu. gilded ornament crowning tope or pagoda. [f. Burmese *h'ti* umbrella]

teem[1] *v.i.* Be prolific, be stocked to overflowing *with*, be abundant.

teem[2] *v.t.* (dial., tech.) Empty, discharge, pour out (vessel, cart, coal, molten metal, etc.).

teen *n.* (archaic) Grief, misfortune.

tee'n-ā'ge *adj.* In the teens; of or for teenagers. **tee'nāger** *n.* Person in the teens.

teens (-z) *n.pl.* Years of person's age from 13 to 19.

tee'ny *adj.* (nursery) Tiny.

Tees (-z). English river flowing through Co. Durham and Cleveland into North Sea.

tee'ter *v.* Move like a see-saw; move unsteadily.

teethe (-dh) *v.i.* Grow or cut teeth. **tee'thing** *n.* (esp.) ~-*ring*, ring of bone, plastic, etc., for teething infant to bite on; ~ *troubles*, (fig.) difficulties etc. of early stages of anything.

teetō'tal *adj.* Of, advocating, total abstinence from intoxicants. **teetō'talism** *n.* **teetō'tally** *adv.* **teetō'taller** *n.* Total abstainer. [reduplicated form of *total*]

teetō'tum *n.* Child's four-sided top with sides lettered to determine the spinner's luck; any top spun with the fingers. [f. T (the letter on one side) and L *totum* the whole (stakes), for which it stood]

těg *n.* Sheep in its second year.

tě'gular *adj.* Of or like tiles.

tě'gŭment *n.* Natural covering of (part of) animal body. **tĕgŭmě'ntal**, **tĕgŭmě'ntary** *adjs.*

Teherā'n, Tehra'n (tărahn). Capital city of Iran.

teind (tēnd) *n.* (Sc.) Tithe.

Teirēsias: see TIRESIAS.

těknŏ'nymy *n.* Practice of naming the parent from the child.

tě'ktīte *n.* (geol.) Rounded glassy body of unknown origin, found in various parts of the world.

tělaesthē'sia (-zia) *n.* (psychol.) Perception of distant occurrences or objects otherwise than by means

[898]

of the recognized physical senses.
tĕlaesthĕ'tic *adj.* [Gk TELE- and *aisthēsis* perception]
tĕ'lamon *n.* (archit.) Male figure supporting an entablature (cf. CARYATID. [L, f. Gk *Telamōn* myth. person]
tĕle- *prefix.* Far; (esp.) in names of instruments, producing or recording results etc. at a distance; of, for, television.
tĕ'lĕcast (-ahst) *n.* Programme or item broadcast by television.
tĕlĕcommūnicā'tion *n.* Communication at a distance by telegraph, telephone, radio, etc.; (freq. pl.) science of this.
tĕ'lĕdu (-doo) *n.* Stinking badger of Java and Sumatra (*Mydaus javanensis*).
tĕlĕgĕ'nic *adj.* Suitable for being televised.
tĕlĕ'gonȳ *n.* (biol.) Theory of supposed transmission of characteristics from a previous sire to offspring of the same dam by a later sire. **tĕlĕgŏ'nic** *adj.*
tĕ'lĕgrăm *n.* Message sent by telegraph.
tĕ'lĕgrăph (or -ahf) *n.* Instantaneous conveyance of messages to any distance by means of two instruments so connected by electricity that the working of one excites movements in the other representing letters etc. acc. to some arranged code; apparatus needed for this; semaphore, signalling-apparatus; scoring-board with large figures or other means of making facts known to a distant observer; ~-*key*, device for making and breaking the electric circuit of a telegraph; ~-*line*, telegraphic connection; ~-*plant*, East Indian plant of the bean family whose leaves have spontaneous jerking motion; ~-*pole*, -*post*, pole, post, supporting telegraph wires; ~-*wire*, wire along which telegraphic messages may be transmitted. ~ *v.* Send (message *to* person, or abs.) by telegraph; make signals, convey by signals.
tĕlĕgraphē'se (-z) *n.* Elliptical style used in telegrams.
tĕlĕgrā'phic *adj.* Of, by, for, the telegraph; (of style) economically worded, with unessential words omitted; ~ *address*, abbreviated or other registered address used in telegrams. **tĕlĕgrā'phically** *adv.*
tĕlĕ'graphist *n.* Operator of a telegraph.
tĕlĕ'graphȳ *n.* Art of constructing, practice of communicating by, telegraph; *wireless* ~, transmission of signals through space by means of electromagnetic waves.
tĕlĕkinē'sis *n.* Movement at a distance from the motive cause or agent without material connection, esp. as a spiritualistic phenomenon.
Tĕlĕ'machus (-k-). In the 'Odyssey', son of Odysseus and Penelope.

tĕ'lĕmãrk *n.* Swing turn in skiing used to change direction or to stop short (ill. SKI). [f. *Telemark*, district in Norway]
tĕlĕmĕchă'nics (-k-) *n.* Art of remote control of machinery.
tĕ'lĕmēter *v.t.* Register (temperature, pressure, or other phenomena) at a distant meter, usu. by means of radio devices. ~ *n.*
tĕlĕŏ'logȳ *n.* Doctrine of final causes, view that developments are due to the purpose of design that is served by them. **tĕlĕolŏ'gic**, -**ical** *adjs.* **tĕlĕolŏ'gically** *adv.* **tĕlĕŏ'logism, tĕlĕŏ'logist** *ns.*
tĕlĕ'pathȳ *n.* Communication of impressions from one mind to another without the aid of the known senses. **tĕlĕpă'thic** *adj.* **tĕlĕpă'thically** *adv.* **tĕlĕ'pathīst** *n.* **tĕlĕ'pathīze** *v.*
tĕ'lĕphōne *n.* Instrument for converting the vibrations caused by sound, esp. that of the voice, into an electric current which passes along a wire and is reconverted into sound at the other end; system of communication by a network of telephones; ~ *exchange*: see EXCHANGE. **tĕlĕphŏ'nic** *adj.* **tĕlĕphŏ'nically** *adv.*
tĕ'lĕphōne *v.* Send (message), speak (*to* person), by telephone.
tĕlĕ'phonist *n.* Telephone operator.
tĕlĕ'phonȳ *n.* Art or science of constructing telephones; the working of a telephone or telephones.
tĕ'lĕphŏ'tō *adj.* Telephotographic; ~ *lens*, lens or combination of lenses for photographing distant objects.
tĕlĕphōtŏ'graphȳ *n.* Photography of objects at a distance by means of a telephoto lens. **tĕlĕphōtŏgră'phic** *adj.*
tĕ'lĕprint *n.* Message sent by teleprinter. ~ *v.* Send (message etc.), communicate, by teleprinter.
tĕ'lĕprinter *n.* Telegraphically operated kind of typewriter.
tĕ'lĕprŏmpter *n.* Electronic device for prompting television speaker by slowly unrolling his text in large letters outside the audience's sight. [trade-name]
tĕlĕrĕcō'rding *n.* Recording, on film, of television programme, esp. for re-transmission.
tĕ'lĕscōpe *n.* 1. Optical instrument for making distant objects appear nearer and larger, consisting of one or more tubes with an arrangement of lenses, or of one or more mirrors and lenses, by which the rays of light are collected and brought to a focus and the resulting image magnified; *reflecting* ~, one in which the image is produced by a mirror; *refracting* ~, one in which the image is reproduced by a lens (the object-glass). 2. *radio* ~, directional aerial system for collecting radio energy from different parts of the sky as an optical telescope

collects light from different stars, either steerable, as the 250-ft Jodrell Bank instrument in Cheshire, or fixed and directed by the earth's rotation to successive points in the sky. (*Illustration, p. 900.*) ~ *v.* Force or drive one into another like the sliding-tubes of a hand-telescope; close, slide together, in this manner; be forced one into the other (esp. of colliding railway trains).
tĕlĕscŏ'pic *adj.* Of, made with, a telescope; visible only through a telescope, as ~ *star*; consisting of sections that telescope. **tĕlĕscŏ'pically** *adv.*
tĕlĕ'scopist *n.* User of telescope.
tĕlĕ'scopȳ *n.* Use and making of telescopes.
tĕ'lĕview (-vū) *v.i.* Watch television. **tĕ'lĕviewer, tĕ'lĕviewing** *nn.*
tĕ'lĕvīse (-z) *v.t.* Transmit by television.
tĕ'lĕvision *n.* Simultaneous visual reproduction of scenes, objects, performances, etc., at a distance by means of a camera which converts the image into electrical impulses which are transmitted by radio to a receiver which converts them by means of a CATHODE-ray tube into a corresponding image on a screen; apparatus for reception of televised images (also ~ *set*); televised programme(s) or matter. **tĕ'lĕvisor** (-z-) *n.* Transmitting apparatus for television.
Tĕ'lĕx *n.* System of telegraphy in which printed messages are exchanged by teleprinters connected to the public telecommunication network.
Tĕ'lford, Thomas (1757–1834). Scottish civil engineer, designer of numerous roads and bridges (notably the Menai Bridge) and the Caledonian Canal; called by Southey the 'Colossus of Roads'.
tĕll[1] *v.* (past t. & past part. *tōld*). Relate or narrate; make known, divulge, state, express in words; inform or give information *of*, *about, how*, etc.; betray secret, inform against (person); ascertain, decide about, distinguish; produce marked effect on; count (votes, esp. in House of Commons); ~ *one's beads*, use rosary; ~ *person's fortune*, forecast his future by occult means; ~ *off*, number (party etc.), pick out (specified number of persons, person) *for* task or *to* do; (slang) tell (person) home truths; scold, reprimand; ~ *on*, inform against; ~ *tales*, reveal another's private affairs, misconduct, etc.
tĕll[2] *n.* Artificial mound found esp. in Near and Middle Eastern countries, consisting of accumulated remains of ancient settlements.
Tĕll[3], William. Legendary hero of the liberation in the 14th c. of Switzerland from Austrian oppression; the legend represents him as a skilled marksman who

TELLER

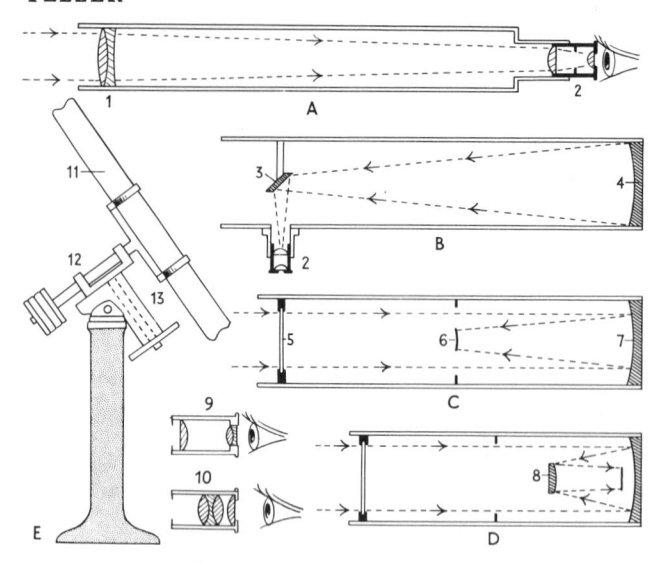

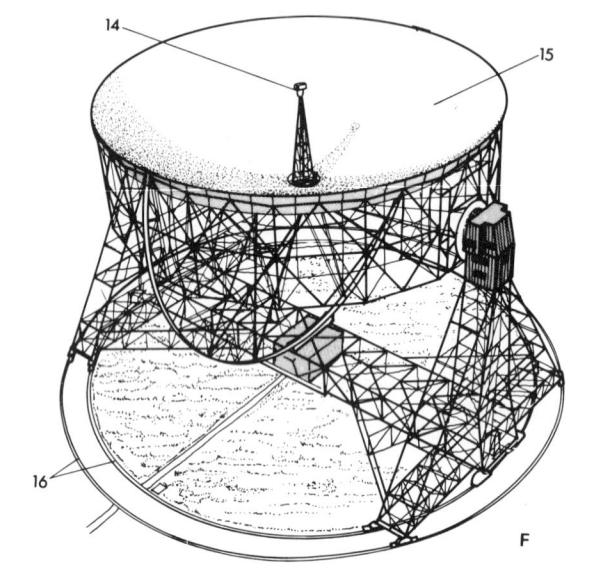

ASTRONOMICAL TELESCOPES
A. REFRACTING. B. NEWTONIAN REFLECTING. C. SCHMIDT PHOTOGRAPHIC. D. MODIFIED SCHMIDT GIVING FLAT FOCAL SURFACE. E. EQUATORIAL MOUNTING. F. RADIO TELESCOPE (JODRELL BANK)

1. Object glass. 2. Huyghenian eyepiece. 3. Flat mirror. 4. Parabolic concave mirror. 5. Glass correcting plate. 6. Curved focal surface. 7. Spherical mirror. 8. Convex mirror. 9. Achromatized Ramsden eyepiece. 10. Orthoscopic eyepiece. 11. Telescope tube. 12. Declination axis. 13. Polar axis. 14. 62 ft. aerial mast. 15. 250 ft. reflector (sheet steel bowl). 16. Railway tracks

refused to do honour to the hat of Gessler, the Austrian bailiff, placed on a pole, and was in consequence required to shoot with an arrow an apple placed on the head of his son; this he successfully did and with a second arrow shot Gessler.

tĕ'ller n. (esp.) Any of four persons appointed (two for each side) to count votes in House of Commons; person appointed to receive or pay out money in bank etc.

tĕ'lling adj. (esp.) Producing marked effect. **tĕ'llingly** adv.

TEMPERA

tĕ'lltāle n. 1. Person who tells about another's private affairs; (fig.) thing, circumstance, that reveals person's thoughts, conduct, etc., esp. attrib., as ~ *blush*, *stain*. 2. Kind of automatic registering device; (naut.) index near wheel to show position of the tiller.

tĕ'llūrāte n. Salt of telluric acid.

tĕllūr'ian adj. & n. (Inhabitant) of the earth.

tĕllūr'ic[1] adj. Of the earth; obtained from earth or soil.

tĕllūr'ic[2] adj. Of, derived from, TELLURIUM; ~ *acid*, acid (H_2TeO_4), analogous to sulphuric acid, obtained by oxidizing tellurium.

tĕllūr'ium n. (chem.) Rare, brittle, lustrous, silver-coloured element, formerly classed among the metals, but chemically belonging to the same family as sulphur and selenium; symbol Te, at. no. 52, at. wt 127·60.

tĕllūrous adj. Of, containing, tellurium, esp. of compounds containing a greater proportion of tellurium than those called *telluric*.

Tĕ'llus. (Rom. myth.) Goddess of the earth; earth personified, the planet Earth.

tĕ'llȳ n. (colloq.) Television (set).

tĕ'lpher n. Travelling unit in telpherage; (attrib.) employing or worked by telpherage. **tĕ'lpherage** n. Automatic electric transport of goods etc.

tĕ'lson n. Posterior abdominal region of some crustaceans and other arthropods (ill. LOBSTER).

Tĕ'luġu (-ōōgōō) adj. & n. (Language, member) of Dravidian people in Coromandel coast region of India, N. of Madras.

tĕmerār'ious adj. (literary) Rash, reckless. **tĕmerār'iouslȳ** adv.

tĕmĕ'ritȳ n. Rashness, audacity.

tĕmp. abbrev. *Tempore* (L, = 'in the time of', as *temp. Henry I*).

Tĕ'mpē. Ancient name of a beautiful valley in Thessaly, watered by R. Peneus, between Mts Olympus and Ossa.

tĕ'mper v. Bring (clay etc.) to the desired consistency by moistening and kneading; toughen and harden (metal, esp. steel, glass) by heating, sudden cooling, and reheating; (of metal etc.) come to proper hardness and elasticity by this means; modify, mitigate (*justice* etc.) by blending *with* (*mercy* etc.). ~ n. 1. Consistency of clay etc. obtained by tempering; degree of hardness and elasticity in steel etc. produced by tempering. 2. Habitual or temporary disposition of mind; fit of anger; composure under provocation.

tĕ'mpera n. Painting with colours which have been mixed with a natural emulsion (e.g. eggyolk) or an artificial emulsion (e.g. oil and gum), esp. the method used for movable pictures before the development of oil-painting.

[900]

TEMPERAMENT

tĕ′mperament *n.* 1. Characteristic combination of physical, mental, and moral qualities which together constitute the character of an individual and affect his manner of acting, feeling, and thinking; (also *artistic, musical* ~) emotional character of artist or musician. 2. (mus.) Adjustment of the tones of the scale (in the tuning of instruments of fixed tone, e.g. piano) so as to adapt the scale for use in all keys; *equal* ~, that in which the 12 semitones are at equal intervals.
tĕmperamĕ′ntal *adj.* Of, relating to, the temperament; liable to, marked by, variable or unaccountable moods. **tĕmperamĕ′ntallў** *adv.*
tĕ′mperance *n.* Moderation, self-restraint, in speech, conduct, etc., esp. in eating and drinking; moderation in use of, total abstinence from, alcoholic liquors as beverages; (attrib.) non-alcoholic, aimed at the restriction or prohibition of alcoholic drinks, as in ~ *drinks, league, legislation*; ~ *hotel*, hotel not supplying alcoholic drinks.
tĕ′mperate *adj.* Moderate, self-restrained; abstemious; (of climate) not exhibiting extremes of heat or cold, equable; ~ *zone*, zone between either tropic and the corresponding polar circle. **tĕ′mperatelў** *adv.* **tĕ′mperateness** *n.*

tĕ′mperature *n.* Degree or intensity of sensible heat of a body or of the atmosphere, esp. as shown by the thermometer; (med.) internal heat of the body in man, normally 37 °C (98·4 °F); (colloq.) body temperature above normal, fever; *take person's* ~, ascertain his internal heat with a clinical thermometer to detect any variation from the normal state of health; ~ *chart*, one showing a temperature curve; ~ *curve*, curve showing variations of temperature, esp. in clinical use.
tĕ′mpĕst *n.* Violent storm; (fig.) violent tumult or agitation.
tĕmpĕ′stŭous *adj.* (of weather, time, etc., and fig. of person or mood) Stormy, violent. **tĕmpĕ′stŭouslў** *adv.* **tĕmpĕ′stŭousnĕss** *n.*
Tĕ′mplar *n.* 1. Member of a powerful and wealthy religious and military order of knights (*Knights* ~s), chaplains, and men-at-arms; it was founded *c.* 1118 for the protection of the Holy Sepulchre and of Christian pilgrims to the Holy Land, and for some time occupied a building on or near the site of Solomon's Temple at Jerusalem; suppressed by Council of VIENNE, 1312. 2. Lawyer, student, with chambers in the Temple in London. 3. Member of an order of Freemasons (*Knights* ~s) or of a temperance society (*Good* ~s).

TEMPORAL

tĕ′mplate *n.* Pattern, gauge, usu. thin board or metal plate, used as a guide in cutting or drilling metal, stone, wood, etc.; timber or plate used to distribute weight in a wall or under a beam etc.; wedge for building-block under ship's keel.
tĕ′mple[1] *n.* Edifice dedicated to service of (esp. ancient Greek, Roman, Egyptian) god; any of the three successive religious edifices of the Jews in Jerusalem; place of Christian public worship, esp. Protestant church in France; (fig.) place in which God resides; *the T*~, the Inns of Court, Inner and Middle Temple, in London, the site of which formerly belonged to the Knights Templars; *T*~ *Bar*, gateway (removed 1879) that marked the westward limit of the City Corporation's jurisdiction, at junction of Fleet St. and the Strand in London.
tĕ′mple[2] *n.* Flat part of either side of the head between the forehead and the ear.
tĕ′mple[3] *n.* Device for keeping cloth taut on a loom.
tĕ′mplĕt *n.* Var. of TEMPLATE.
tĕ′mpō *n.* (pl. *-os*). (mus.) Speed at which a passage is (to be) played; (transf.) rate of movement, activity, or progress.
tĕ′mporal *adj.* 1. Of, in, denoting, time; (gram.) pertaining to time or tense. 2. Of this life

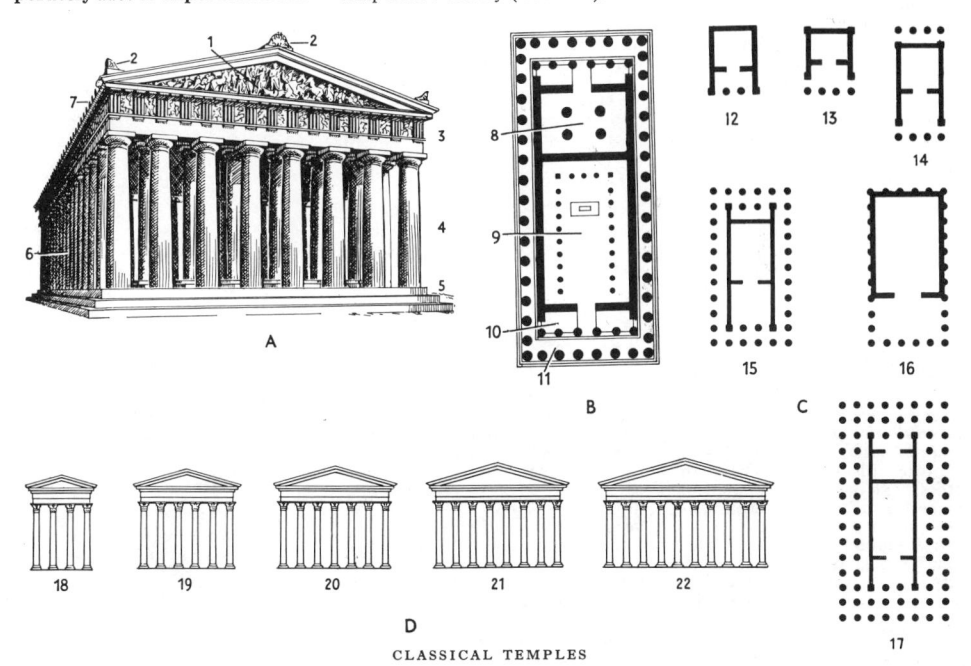

CLASSICAL TEMPLES
A, B. RECONSTRUCTION AND PLAN OF THE PARTHENON.
C, D. PLANS AND ELEVATIONS OF TEMPLES

A. 1. Pediment. 2. Acroterion. 3. Entablature. 4. Column. 5. Stylobate. 6. Peristyle. 7. Antefix. B. 8. Inner cella. 9. Cella or naos. 10. Pronaos. 11. Portico or stoa. C. 12. Distyle in antis. 13. Prostyle. 14. Amphiprostyle. 15. Peripteral. 16. Pseudo-peripteral. 17. Dipteral. D. 18. Tetrastyle. 19. Hexastyle. 20. Heptastyle. 21. Octastyle. 22. Decastyle

[901]

only, secular, lay (opp. *spiritual*); Lords T~, members of the House of Lords other than the bishops; ~ *power*, power of an ecclesiastic, esp. the pope, in temporal matters. 3. (anat.) Of the temples: ~ *bone*, compound bone of the side of the human skull (ill. HEAD). **tĕ'mporally** *adv.* **tĕ'mporalness** *n.* **tĕ'mporalty** *n.* Laity. **tĕ'mporal** *n.* Temporal bone.

těmporă'lĭty *n.* Secular possessions, esp. properties and revenues of a religious body or an ecclesiastic (usu. pl.); (law) temporariness.

tĕ'mporary *adj.* Lasting only for a time, transient; held, occupied, during a limited time only, not permanent. **tĕ'mporarily** *adv.* **tĕ'mporariness** *n.*

tĕ'mporize *v.i.* Pursue indecisive or time-serving policy; avoid committing oneself, act so as to gain time; comply temporarily with requirements of an occasion. **tĕmporīzā'tion, tĕ'mporīzer** *ns.*

tĕmporo- *prefix.* Of temples of head, as ~*-facial*, of temporal and facial regions.

tĕmpt *v.t.* Entice, incite; attract; (archaic) test or try the resolution of.

tĕmptā'tion *n.* Tempting or being tempted; thing that attracts, attractive course.

tĕ'mpter *n.* (fem. *te'mptress*) One who tempts (chiefly in bad sense); *the T~*, the Devil.

tĕ'mpting *adj.* Attractive, inviting. **tĕ'mptingly** *adv.*

tĕn *adj.* Amounting to ten; *te'npin*, pin used in *te'npins*, a game similar to ninepins, played with 10 pins; ~*-pounder*, (hist.) person having a vote in parliamentary election by occupation of property of rental value of £10. ~ *n.* One more than nine; symbol for this (10, x, or X); card with 10 pips; 10 o'clock; size etc. indicated by 10; set of 10 things or persons; *upper* ~ (for *ten thousand*), the aristocracy. **tĕ'nfōld** *adj.* & *adv.*

tĕ'nable *adj.* Capable of being maintained or defended against attack or objection; (of office etc.) that can be held *for* a specified time, *by* person, etc. **tĕnabĭ'lĭty, tĕ'nableness** *ns.*

tĕ'nace (-is) *n.* (whist) (Holding of) two cards, one next above, the other next below, the opponents' highest of the suit. [Span. *tenaza*, lit. 'pincers']

tĕnā'cious (-shus) *adj.* Holding fast; keeping firm hold (*of* property, rights, principles, etc.); (of memory)retentive;adhesive,sticky; strongly cohesive. **tĕnā'ciously** *adv.* **tĕnā'ciousness, tĕnā'cĭty** *ns.*

tĕnā'cŭlum *n.* (pl. *-la*). Surgeon's sharp hook used for taking up arteries.

tĕnā'il, -ai'lle *n.* (fort.) Outwork in main ditch between two bastions.

tĕ'nancy *n.* Act of holding property as a tenant; period of such holding; property, land, etc., held by a tenant.

tĕ'nant *n.* (law) Person holding real property by private ownership; person who occupies land or tenement under a landlord; inhabitant, dweller. ~ *v.t.* Occupy as tenant (esp. in past part.).

tĕ'nantable *adj.* Fit to be occupied by a tenant.

tĕ'nantry *n.* Tenants.

tĕnch *n.* European freshwater fish (*Tinca tinca*) of the carp family.

tĕnd[1] *v.i.* Move, be directed, in a certain direction; be apt or inclined, serve, conduce (*to* action, quality, etc., *to* do).

tĕnd[2] *v.* Take care of, look after (flocks, invalid, machine, etc.); wait *upon*; (naut.) watch (ship at anchor) so as to keep turns out of her cable. **tĕ'ndance** *n.* (archaic).

tĕ'ndency *n.* Bent, leaning, inclination (*towards, to,* thing, *to* do).

tĕndĕ'ntious (-shus) *adj.* (of writing etc.) Having an underlying purpose, calculated to advance a cause.

tĕ'nder[1] *n.* (esp.) 1. Small ship in attendance upon a larger one to supply her with stores, convey orders, etc. 2. Truck attached to a locomotive and carrying fuel, water, etc. (ill. LOCOMOTIVE). [f. TEND[2]]

tĕ'nder[2] *v.* Offer, present, give in (*one's services, resignation*, etc.); offer (money etc.) as payment; make a tender (*for* supply of thing or execution of work). ~ *n.* Offer, esp. offer in writing to execute work or supply goods at a fixed price; *legal* ~, currency recognized by law as acceptable in payment of a debt.

tĕ'nder[3] *adj.* Soft, not tough or hard; easily touched or wounded, susceptible to pain or grief; delicate, fragile, (lit. and fig., of reputation etc.); loving, affectionate, fond; solicitous, considerate; requiring careful handling, ticklish; *te'nderfoot,* (orig. U.S.) newcomer in camp, settlement, etc., novice, greenhorn; new recruit in Scout Association; ~*-hearted,* susceptible to, easily moved by, pity; kindly, compassionate; *te'nderloin,* middle part of loin of pork; (U.S.) undercut of sirloin. **tĕ'nderly** *adv.* **tĕ'nderness** *n.*

tĕ'nderīze *v.t.* Make (more) tender.

tĕ'ndĭnous *adj.* Of, connected with, resembling, a tendon.

tĕ'ndon *n.* Tough, fibrous tissue connecting a muscle to some other part (ill. MUSCLE); sinew; *Achilles* ~ : see ACHILLES.

tĕ'ndril *n.* Slender thread-like organ or appendage of a plant, often spiral in form, which stretches out and attaches itself to some other body so as to support the plant.

Tĕ'nĕbrae *n.pl.* (R.C. Ch.) Matins and Lauds for the last three days of Holy Week, at which the candles are successively extinguished. [L, = 'darkness']

tĕ'nĕment *n.* (law) Any kind of permanent property as lands, rents, held of a superior; dwellinghouse; portion of a house, tenanted as a separate dwelling; ~*-house*, house containing tenements. **tĕnĕmĕ'ntal** *adj.*

Tĕnerī'fe (-ēf). Largest of the Canary Islands.

tĕ'nĕt *n.* Principle, dogma, doctrine, of a person or school. [L, = 'he holds']

tenia : see TAENIA.

Tĕ'niers (-nyerz), David. Name of two Flemish painters, father (1582–1649) and son (1610–90), the younger being the more famous.

Tenn. *abbrev.* Tennessee.

tĕ'nner *n.* (colloq.) A ten-pound note, ten pounds.

Tĕnnĕssēē'. State in southeastern U.S., admitted to the Union in 1796; capital, Nashville.

Tĕ'nniel, Sir John (1820–1914). English painter and cartoonist; illustrator of the 'Alice' books of Lewis Carroll.

tĕ'nnĭs *n.* Game for two or four persons played by striking ball

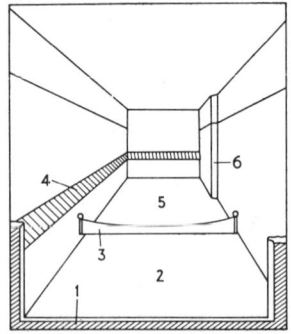

TENNIS COURT

1. Dedans. 2. Service side. 3. Net. 4. Penthouse. 5. Hazard side. 6. Tambour

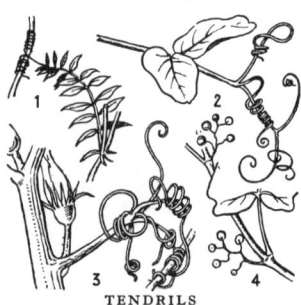

TENDRILS

1. Tendril formed from midrib of leaf (tare). 2. Tendril formed at end of leaf-bearing stem (pea). 3. Stem tendril (marrow). 4. Self-climbing tendril (Virginia creeper)

[902]

with racket (formerly with the palm of the hand) over a net stretched across a walled oblong court; LAWN² tennis; ~ *court*, court on which tennis or lawn tennis is played; ~ *elbow*, inflammatory condition of the elbow joint, caused by strain as in playing tennis. [app. f. OF *tenez* 'take', called by server to his opponent]

Tĕ'nnyson, Alfred, 1st Baron (1809–92). English poet; poet laureate from 1850; author of 'In Memoriam', 'Maud', 'Idylls of the King', 'Enoch Arden', etc. Tĕnnȳsō'nian *adj*.

tĕ'non *n*. Projection fashioned on the end or side of a piece of wood or other material, to fit into a corresponding cavity or mortice in another piece (ill. JOINT¹); ~ *saw*, fine saw for making tenons etc., having a thin blade, strong brass or steel back, and small teeth (ill. SAW¹). ~ *v.t.* Cut into a tenon; join by means of a tenon.

tĕ'nor *n*. 1. Settled or prevailing course or direction (esp. fig. *of one's life, way*, etc.); general purport, drift (*of* speech, writing, etc.); (law) true intent, exact copy. 2. (mus.) (Music for, singer with) high adult male voice, usually ranging from the octave below middle C to the A above it (ill. VOICE); viola; (usu. attrib.) applied to an instrument of any kind of which the range is approx. that of tenor voice; ~ *bell*, largest of a peal or set; ~ *clef*: see CLEF. [L *tenorem* holding on, (med. L) chief melody, formerly assigned to adult male voice]

tĕnŏ'tomy *n*. Surgical cutting of a tendon.

tĕnse¹ *n*. Any of the different forms or modifications in the conjugation of a verb which indicate the different times (*past*, *present*, or *future*) at which the action or state denoted by it is viewed as happening or existing, and also (by extension) the different nature of such action or state, as continuing (*imperfect*), completed (*perfect*), or indefinite (*aorist*).

tĕnse² *adj*. (of cord, membrane, fig. of nerve, mind, emotiŏn) Stretched tight, strained to stiffness, highly strung; (phon., of vowel) uttered with the tongue in a tense condition (opp. *slack*). tĕ'nsely *adv*. tĕ'nseness *n*. tĕnse *v*. Make, become, tense.

tĕ'nsible *adj*. Capable of being stretched out or extended. tĕnsibĭ'lity *n*.

tĕ'nsile *adj*. Of tension; capable of being drawn out or stretched. tĕnsĭ'lity *n*.

tĕ'nsion *n*. Stretching, being stretched; tenseness; mental strain or excitement, strained (political, social, etc.) state; (phys.) effect produced by forces pulling against each other; (elect.) stress along lines of force in a dielectric, formerly used as a synonym for potential, electromotive force, and mechanical force exerted by electricity, still so applied, in industrial and commercial use, in *high* and *low* ~. tĕ'nsional *adj*.

tĕ'nson, tĕ'nzon *n*. Contest of verse-making between troubadours, verse dialogue sung at such contests.

tĕ'nsor *n*. (anat.) Muscle that tightens or stretches a part.

tĕnt¹ *n*. Portable shelter of canvas, cloth, etc., supported by pole(s) and stretched by cords secured to pegs driven into the ground; *oxygen* ~, tent-like cover, enclosing head and shoulders or whole body, through which oxygen can be supplied to assist breathing; ~-*bed*, bed with a tent-like canopy; bed for use in a tent; ~-*fly*, piece of canvas pitched outside and over ridge of tent as extra protection from sun, rain, etc.; ~-*pegging*, cavalry exercise in which the rider tries at full gallop to carry off on point of his lance a tent-peg fixed in the ground; ~-*stitch*, series of parallel diagonal stitches (ill. STITCH). ~ *v.* Cover (as) with a tent; encamp in a tent.

tĕnt² *v.t.* Dilate (orifice of wound etc.) by inserting plug of lint etc. ~ *n*. Plug of lint, linen, etc., used for tenting.

tĕnt³ *n*. Sweet, dark-red Spanish wine, chiefly used as sacramental wine. [Span. *tinto* deep-coloured]

tĕ'ntacle *n*. Slender flexible process in animals, esp. invertebrates, serving as sensory or attachment organ (ill. JELLY); (bot.) sensitive hair or filament. tĕ'ntacled (-ld), tĕntă'cular, tĕntă'culate, -ātĕd *adjs*.

tĕ'ntative *adj*. Done by way of trial, experimental. tĕ'ntatively *adv*.

tĕ'nter¹ *n*. Person in charge of something, esp. of machinery in a factory.

tĕ'nter² *n*. Machine or frame for stretching cloth to set or dry; *te'nterhooks*, hooks to which cloth is fastened on a tenter; *on tenterhooks*, (fig.) in a state of suspense, distracted by uncertainty.

tĕnth *adj*. Next after the ninth. ~ *n*. Tenth part (see PART¹, I); tenth thing etc. tĕ'nthly *adv*. In the tenth place.

tĕ'nuis *n*. (pl. *tenŭēs*). (phonet.) Voiceless stop, as *p*, *t*, *k*.

tĕnŭ'ity *n*. Slenderness; (of air, fluid) rarity, thinness; (of style) simplicity, lack of grandeur.

tĕ'nŭous *adj*. Thin, slender; (of distinctions etc.) subtle, over-refined.

tĕ'nure (-yer) *n*. The holding *of* a piece of property or office; conditions or period of such holding.

tenu'tō (-ōō-) *adv., n*. (pl. -*os*), & *adj*. (mus.) (Sustained, note etc. sustained) to its full time value (contrasted with *staccato*). [It.]

tenzon: see TENSON.

tēocă'llĭ *n*. (archaeol.) Temple of Aztec or other Mexican aborigines, usu. built on a truncated pyramidal mound. [Nahuatl, f. *teotl* god, *calli* house]

tē'pee *n*. Conical tent, hut, or wigwam of the N. Amer. Indians.

tē'pefy *n*. Make, become, tepid. tĕpĕfă'ction *n*.

tĕ'phrite *n*. Ash-coloured volcanic rock.

tĕ'pid *adj*. Slightly warm, lukewarm (lit. and fig.). tĕpĭ'dĭty, tĕ'pidness *ns*. tĕ'pidly *adv*.

tĕpidā'rium *n*. (pl. -*ia*). (Rom. antiq.) Warm room in baths.

tēr *adv*. (mus., med.) Three times. [L]

tĕra- *prefix*. One billion times (abbrev. T).

tĕ'raph *n*. (pl. *teraphim*, also used as sing.). Small religious image venerated by Hebrews in pre-exilic times, also used in divination.

tĕratŏ'logy *n*. Tale or myth concerning prodigies, marvellous tale, collection of these; (biol.) study of monstrosities or abnormal formations, esp. in man. tĕratŏlŏ'gical *adj*.

tĕratō'ma *n*. Tumour made up of heterogeneous mixture of tissues.

tĕr'bium *n*. (chem.) Metallic element of rare-earth group found in combination in gadolinite and other minerals: symbol Tb, at. no. 65, at. wt 158·9254. [f. *Ytterby* in Sweden]

tĕrce *n*. Var. of TIERCE.

tĕr'cel *n*. Male hawk. [L *tertius* 3rd, from belief that the 3rd egg of a hawk produced a small male bird]

tĕrcentē'nary (*or* -sĕ'ntĭ-) *n*. 300th anniversary. ~ *adj*. Of 300 (esp. years). tĕrcentĕ'nnial *n*. & *adj*. Tercentenary.

tĕ'rĕbĕne *n*. Mixture of terpenes obtained by action of sulphuric acid on oil of turpentine and used as expectorant etc.

tĕ'rĕbinth *n*. Small S. European tree, *Pistacia terebinthus*, yielding Chian turpentine. tĕrĕbĭ'nthĭne *adj*. Of the terebinth; of turpentine.

terē'dō *n*. Shipworm of genus *T*~.

Tĕ'rence. Publius Terentius Afer (*c* 190–*c* 159 B.C.). Roman author of comedies, born at Carthage.

Tĕrē'sa (-za), St. (1515–82). Spanish mystic and religious reformer; born at Avila (as Teresa de Cepeda); became a Carmelite nun and founded the Discalced Carmelites, who follow a stricter rule; wrote 'The Way of Perfection' (1565) and other mystical works, and an autobiography.

tĕr'gal *adj*. Of the back, dorsal.

tĕr'giversāte *v.i.* Turn one's coat, desert one's party or principles, apostatize. tĕrgiversā'tion *n*.

tĕr'gum *n*. Dorsal surface of body segment of arthropod.

tĕrm *n*. 1. Boundary, limit, esp. of time; limited period;

[903]

completion of period of pregnancy, (normal) time of childbirth; (law) estate or interest in land, etc., for fixed period; (esp. Sc., also ~ *day*) quarter-day, each of days in year fixed for payment of rent, wages, etc. 2. Figure, post, stone, etc., marking boundary (= TERMINUS, 4). 3. Each period (usu. three or four in year) appointed for sitting of court of law, or for instruction and study in school, university, etc. 4. (math.) Each of two quantities composing a ratio or fraction; each of the quantities forming a series of progression; each of the quantities connected by signs of addition (+) or subtraction (−) in an algebraical expression or equation. 5. (logic) Word(s), notion, that may be subject or predicate of a proposition; hence, any word or group of words expressing a definite conception, esp. in particular branch of study etc.; (pl.) language employed, mode of expression; ~*s of reference*, terms defining scope of inquiry, action, etc. 6. (pl.) Conditions, esp. charge, price; ~*s of trade*, ratio between prices paid for imports and received for exports. 7. (pl.) Relation, footing. ~ *v.t.* Denominate, call.

tĕr'magant *n.* Brawling turbulent woman. [imaginary deity supposed in medieval times to be worshipped by Muslims]

tĕr'minable *adj.* That may be terminated (esp. after definite period).

tĕr'minal *adj.* Of, forming, a limit or terminus; situated at, forming, the end or extremity of something; of, forming, a term, termly; (med.) forming, suffering, the final stage of a fatal disease. tĕr'minally *adv.* tĕr'minal *n.* Terminating thing, extremity, esp. (structure or device forming) each of free ends of open electrical circuit, by connecting which circuit is closed (ill. BULB); (physiol.) end of nerve fibre or neuron; ornament at end of something; (U.S.) end of railway line, terminus.

tĕr'mĭnāte *v.* Bound, limit; bring, come, to an end, end (*at in*, *with*). tĕr'minative *adj.* tĕr'minatively *adv.* tĕr'minate *adj.* Determinate, finite, esp. (math.) not recurring or infinite, expressible in finite number of terms.

tĕrmĭnā'tion *n.* (esp.) Final syllable or letter(s) of word, (inflexional or derivative) ending, suffix.

tĕr'minātor *n.* (esp., astron.) Line of separation between dark and light parts of moon or planet.

tĕrmĭno'logy *n.* System of terms belonging to a science or subject; technical terms collectively. tĕrmĭnŏ'gical *adj.* tĕrmĭnŏlŏ'gically *adv.*

tĕr'mĭnus *n.* (pl. -*uses*, -*ī*). 1. Station at end of line of railway, bus-route, etc. 2. Point to which motion or action tends; ~ *ad quem*, ~ *a quo*, terminating-, starting-, point (of argument, policy, period, etc.). 3. (Rom. antiq., also *term*) Statue or bust of the god Terminus, who presided over landmarks and boundaries; figure of human bust supported on square pillar.

tĕr'mĭtary, tĕrmĭtār'ium *ns.* Termites' nest.

tĕr'mīte *n.* Pale-coloured soft-bodied social insect of order

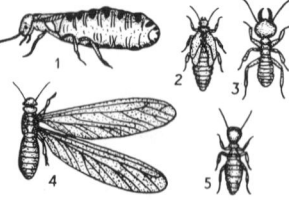

TERMITE
1. Queen.   2. Nymph.   3. Soldier.
4. Winged male.   5. Worker

Isoptera, chiefly tropical, and very destructive to timber; white ant.

tĕrn[1] *n.* Sea-bird esp. of genus *Sterna*, resembling gull but usu. smaller and more slender-bodied, with long, pointed wing and forked tail; sea-swallow.

tĕrn[2] *n.* Set of three, esp. three lottery-numbers drawn together and winning large prize; such prize.

tĕr'nary *adj.* Of, in, set(s) of three; composed of three parts or elements; (mus.) ~ *form*, form of movement with independent subject or tune followed by another in a related key and then by a repetition of the first.

tĕr'nate *adj.* Consisting of, arranged in, threes; (bot.) composed of three leaflets, (of leaves) in whorls of three. tĕr'nately *adv.*

tĕr'ne-plāte *n.* (also *terne*) Thin iron or steel coated with alloy of lead and tin, inferior tinplate. [Fr. *terne* dull, tarnished]

tĕrotĕchnŏ'logy (-k-) *n.* Maintenance engineering.

tĕr'pēne *n.* (chem.) Any of a large group of cyclic hydrocarbons which form the chief constituents of the volatile oils obtained by distilling plant material. [obs. *terpentin* TURPENTINE]

Tĕrpsi'chorė (-k-). (Gk & Rom. myth.) Muse of lyric poetry and dance. Tĕrpsichorē'an *adj.* Of Terpsichore; of dancing.

tĕ'rra ă'lba. Any of various white mineral substances; (esp.) pipe-clay. [L]

tĕ'rrace *n.* 1. Raised level place, natural or artificial, esp. raised in garden or level space in front of building on sloping ground; (geol.) horizontal shelf or bank bordering river, lake, or sea. 2. Row of houses on raised site or on face of rising ground; row of houses of uniform style built in one block. ~ *v.t.* Form into, furnish with, terrace(s).

tĕrracŏ'tta *n.* Hard unglazed pottery of fine quality used for decorative tiles, statuary, architectural decorations, etc.; statuette, figurine of this; brownish-red colour of this pottery. ~ *adj.* Of, made of, of the colour of, terracotta. [It., = 'baked earth']

tĕ'rra fĭr'ma. Dry land, firm ground. [L]

tĕrrai'n *n.* Tract of country considered with regard to its natural features etc., esp. (mil.) its tactical advantages, fitness for manœuvring, etc.

tĕ'rra ĭncŏ'gnĭta. Unknown or unexplored region. [L]

tĕrramār'ė *n.* (One of) a group of lake dwellings, esp. in the Po valley, Italy; ammoniacal earth found in these. [It., f. L *terra amara* bitter earth]

tĕrrā'ne *n.* (geol.) Connected series, group, or system of rocks or formations, area over which a group of formations is prevalent.

tĕ'rrapin *n.* Any of various N. Amer. edible tortoises of family Emydidae, found in fresh or brackish water, esp. the *diamond-backed* ~, (*Malaclemys*) of salt marshes of coasts of Atlantic and Gulf of Mexico, famous for its delicate flesh.

tĕrrā'quėous *adj.* Consisting of land and water; living in, extending over, land and water.

tĕrrē'ne *adj.* Of earth, earthy; terrestrial.

terreplein (tār'plān) *n.* (fort.) Surface of rampart behind parapet, esp. level space on which guns are mounted; level base of battery in field fortifications.

terrĕ'strial *adj.* Of the earth, of this world, worldly; of land as opp. to water; ~ *globe*, globe with map of earth on its surface. terrĕ'strially *adv.*

tĕ'rrėt *n.* Ring, esp. on swivel, to which chain, string, etc., is attached, esp. each of the loops or

ENAMELLED CELTIC TERRET
1ST CENTURY B.C.

strings on harness-pad for driving-reins to pass through.

terre-verte (tārvārt) *n.* Soft green earth used as pigment. [Fr., = 'green earth']

tĕ'rrible *adj.* Exciting, fitted to

[904]

excite, terror; awful, dreadful, formidable; (colloq.) very great, excessive. **tĕ′rrĭblў** *adv.*
tĕ′rrĭer[1] *n.* 1. Any of several kinds of usu. small active hardy dog orig. used to pursue quarry fox, badger, etc.) into burrow or earth (ill. DOG). 2. (colloq.) A Territorial.
tĕ′rrĭer[2] *n.* Register of landed property, with boundaries, acreage, etc.; rent-roll.
tĕrrĭ′fĭc *adj.* Causing terror; (colloq.) of great size, intensity, etc.; very good, admirable, etc. **tĕrrĭ′fĭcăllў** *adv.*
tĕ′rrĭfў *v.t.* Fill with terror, frighten.
tĕrrĭ′ne (-ēn) *n.* Earthenware vessel containing and sold with some table delicacy such as pâté de foie-gras.
tĕrrĭtōr′ĭal *adj.* Of territory; of a particular territory or locality, local; *T~ Army*, British Army of Home Defence instituted on territorial or local basis in 1908 and consisting of men living at home and doing only occasional periods of drill and other training, replaced in 1967 by *T~ and Army Volunteer Reserve*; similar force in other countries; ~ *waters*, that part of the seas adjacent to its shores over which a State claims jurisdiction, esp. within a minimum of 3 miles from low-water mark. **tĕrrĭtōr′ĭăllў** *adv.*
Tĕrrĭtōr′ĭal *n.* Member of Territorial Army etc.
tĕrrĭtōr′ĭalism *n.* System of Church government under which the civil rule has religious jurisdiction over the subjects of a State.
tĕ′rrĭtorў *n.* 1. Land under jurisdiction of sovereign, State, city, etc.; (large) tract of land, region; portion of country not yet admitted to full rights of a State or Province. 2. Area over which commercial traveller etc. operates; (zool.) area of habitat which a particular animal or group defends against others of the same species; (in games) half of field regarded as belonging to team whose goal etc. is in it. 3. (fig.) Sphere, province.
tĕ′rror *n.* Extreme fear; person or thing causing this; (colloq.) exasperating or tiresome person, troublesome child; *King of Terrors*, death personified.
tĕ′rrorĭst *n.* Person attempting to further his views or to rule by system of coercive intimidation. **tĕ′rrorĭsm** *n.* **tĕrrorĭ′stĭc** *adj.*
tĕ′rrorĭze *n.* Fill with terror; rule or maintain power by terrorism. **tĕrrorĭzā′tĭon** *n.*
tĕ′rrў[1] *n.* & *adj.* (Pile-fabric) with loops forming pile left uncut (ill. WEAVE).
Tĕ′rrў[2], Ellen Alicia (1848–1928). English actress.
Tĕrsă′nctus *n.* = SANCTUS; occas. = TRISAGION.
tĕrse *adj.* (of speech, style, writer) Free from cumbrousness and superfluity, smooth and concise; curt. **tĕr′selў** *adv.* **tĕr′sèness** *n.*

tĕr′tĭan (-shan) *adj.* 1. (archaic, of fever) With paroxysm recurring every other (by inclusive reckoning every 3rd) day. 2. *T~ Father*, Jesuit undergoing 3rd period of training or noviţiate after ordination. ~ *n.* 1. (archaic) Tertian fever. 2. Tertian Father. **tĕr′tĭanshĭp** *n.* Position of being a Tertian Father.
tĕr′tĭarў (-sha-) *adj.* 1. Of the third order, rank, class, stage, etc. 2. *T~*, (geol.) of the period subsequent to the Mesozoic, forming the earlier part of the Cainozoic, characterized by the appearance of mammals other than man. 3. (ornith., of wing-feathers) Borne on humerus. 4. ~ *colour*, (painting) one of the greyish hues obtained by mixing two secondary colours (e.g. purple with green). ~ *n.* 1. Tertiary colour; tertiary feather. 2. Member of 3rd order of monastic body. 3. *T~*, (geol.) Tertiary period or system (ill. GEOLOGY).
tĕr′tĭum quid (-shĭ-). Something (undefined) related in some way to two (definite or known) things but distinct from both. [L, = 'some third thing']
Tertŭ′llĭan (-lyan). Quintus Septimius Florens Tertullianus (*c* 160–*c* 220), Christian theological writer; a violent opponent of paganism and leader of the Montanist sect.
tĕrvă′lent *adj.* (chem.) = TRIVALENT.
terza rima (tār′tsa rē′ma). Form of verse in sets of three 10- or 11-syllabled lines rhyming *a b a, b c b*, etc., as in Dante's 'Divina Commedia'. [It., = 'third rhyme']
tĕ′sla *n.* (abbrev. T) Unit of magnetic induction in M.K.S. system. [f. N. *Tesla* (1856–1943), U.S. electrician]
tĕ′ssĕllāte *v.t.* Make into mosaic, form (esp. pavement) by combining variously coloured blocks into pattern. **tĕ′ssĕllātĕd** *adj.* Composed of, ornamented with, small coloured blocks arranged in pattern; (zool., bot.) marked, coloured, in regularly arranged squares or patches, reticulated. **tĕssĕllā′tĭon** *n.*
tĕ′ssera *n.* (pl. -ae). 1. (Gk & Rom. hist.) Small tablet of wood, bone, ivory, etc., used as token, tally, label, etc. 2. Each of small square pieces of marble, glass, tile, etc., of which mosaic pavement etc. is made up. 3. (math.) Curvilinear rectangle. **tĕ′sseral** *adj.* (esp., math.) Of the tesserae of a spherical surface.
tĕst[1] *n.* 1. (orig.) = CUPEL; now, cupel and iron frame containing it, forming movable hearth of reverberatory furnace. 2. Critical examination or trial of qualities of person or thing; means of so examining; standard for comparison or trial, circumstances suitable for this; (chem.) examination of substance under known conditions to determine its identity or that of one of its constituents, reagent used for this. 3. (colloq.) Test-match. 4. *T~ Act*, (esp.) act passed 1672 and repealed 1828, requiring holders of office under Crown to take oaths of supremacy and allegiance, receive Communion of Church of England, etc.; ~ *case*, (law) case in which decision is taken as settling a number of other cases involving same question of law; *~-match*, (esp., cricket) one of series of usu. five games played between sides representing England and Australia or other country, esp. of the Commonwealth, as test of superiority; *~-meal*, meal of specified quantity and composition given to enable gastric secretions etc. to be examined; ~ *paper*, (chem.) paper impregnated with substance which changes colour under certain conditions, used to test presence of these conditions; *~-piece*, composition performed by all entrants in musical or other competition; *~ pilot*, one who pilots aircraft on experimental flights; *~-tube*, (chem.) tube of thin glass closed at one end, used to hold substance under test etc. ~ *v.t.* Put to the test, make trial of; try severely, tax (endurance etc.); subject to chemical test.
tĕst[2] *n.* External covering or shell of tunicates.
tĕ′sta *n.* (bot.) Seed-coat.
tĕstā′ceous (-shus) *adj.* Having a shell, esp. a hard shell; of shells, shelly; (bot., zool.) of colour of tile or red brick, brownish-red.
tĕ′stacў *n.* Being testate.
tĕ′stament *n.* 1. (law) Will, esp. (formerly) disposition of personal as dist. from real property. 2. (colloq.) (Written) statement, affirmation, of (political) beliefs, principles, etc. 3. (bibl.) Covenant between God and man (archaic), hence, *Old*, *New*, *T~*, (abbrev. O.T., N.T.) main divisions of Bible consisting respectively of books of old or Mosaic, and new or Christian, dispensation; *T~*, copy of New Testament. **tĕstamĕ′ntarў** *adj.* Of (nature of), relating to, a will.
tĕ′stāte (*or -at*) *adj.* & *n.* (Person) that has left a valid will at death.
tĕstā′tor *n.* (fem. *testā′trĭx*) Person who makes or has died leaving a will.
tĕ′ster[1] *n.* Canopy esp. over four-poster bed (ill. BED).
tĕ′ster[2] *n.* Shilling of Henry VIII, esp. as debased and depreciated.
tĕ′stĭcle *n.* Testis, esp. in man and most other mammals (ill. PELVIS). **tĕstĭ′cūlar** *adj.*
tĕstĭ′cūlate *adj.* Having, shaped like, testicles; (bot., of some orchids) having two tubers of this shape.

tĕ'stifў v. Bear witness; (law) give evidence; affirm, declare, be evidence of, evince.

tĕstimō'nial n. Certificate of character, conduct, or qualifications; gift presented, esp. in public, as mark of esteem, in acknowledgement of services, etc.

tĕstimō'nialize v.t. Present with testimonial.

tĕstimonў n. Evidence, esp. (law) statement made under oath or affirmation.

tĕ'stis n. (pl. -tēs). Male organ in which sperms are produced; in man and most other mammals, each of two such organs enclosed in scrotum; testicle.

tĕstŏ'sterōne n. Male sex hormone secreted by testes; synthetic preparation of this.

tĕstū'dinate adj. Arched, vaulted, like tortoise-shell.

tĕstū'dō n. (pl. -dōs, -dinēs). (Rom. antiq.) Screen formed by body of troops in close array with overlapping shields; movable screen or roof under cover of which walls of besieged town could be attacked.

tĕ'stў adj. Irritable, touchy. tĕ'stilў adv. tĕ'stinĕss n.

tĕtă'nic adj. Of, like, producing, tetanus. ~ n. Remedy acting on spinal cord and tending to produce tetanic spasms.

tĕ'tanus n. 1. (med.) Painful and often fatal disease caused by micro-organism, usu. introduced through wound, and characterized by tonic spasm and rigidity of voluntary muscles. 2. (physiol.) Prolonged contraction of muscle produced by rapidly repeated stimuli.

tĕ'tanў n. (med.) Condition characterized by spasms of the extremities, caused by disturbance in activity of parathyroid glands and consequent deficiency of calcium.

tĕ'tchў, tĕ'chў adj. Peevish, irritable. tĕ'(t)chilў adv. tĕ(t)ch'inĕss n.

tête-à-tête (tā'tatā't) n. & adj. (Of) private conversation or interview between two persons. ~ adv. In private, without presence of third person.

tĕ'ther (-dh-) n. Rope, chain, halter, by which grazing animal is confined; end of one's ~, extreme limit of one's resources. ~ v.t. Make fast, confine, with tether (freq. fig.).

Tĕ'thўs. (Gk myth.) Sea deity, daughter of Uranus and Ge, and wife of Oceanus.

tetra- prefix. Four.

tĕ'trachōrd (-k-) n. Series of 4 notes with interval of perfect fourth between lowest and highest, as half of octave or unit of ancient Greek music (ill. MODE).

tĕ'trăd n. The number four; set or group of 4.

tetrada'ctўl adj. & n. (Animal) with 4 fingers or toes. tetrada'ctўlous adj.

tĕtra-ĕ'thўl (or -ē'thīl) adj. (chem.) Containing 4 ethyl groups; ~ lead, heavy colourless liquid used as anti-knock agent in internal combustion engine fuels.

tĕ'tragon n. Plane figure of 4 angles and sides. tĕtră'gonal adj. Having the form of a tetragon; (cryst.) having three axes at right angles and the two lateral axes equal (ill. CRYSTAL).

tĕ'tragrăm n. 1. Word of 4 letters. 2. Quadrilateral.

Tĕtragră'mmaton n. Hebrew word of 4 consonants (YHWH or JHVH) representing the incommunicable name of God.

tĕtrahĕ'dron n. Solid figure bounded by 4 plane triangles; triangular pyramid (ill. SOLID); crystal of this form. tĕtrahĕ'dral adj.

tĕtră'logў n. Series of 4 connected operas, plays, etc., esp. (Gk antiq.) series of 3 tragedies and a satyric drama produced at Athens at festival of Dionysus.

tĕtră'merous adj. Having 4 parts; (bot.) having parts arranged in series of 4.

tĕtră'mĕter n. 1. (Gk & L. pros.) Verse consisting of four dipodies in trochaic, iambic, or anapaestic metre. 2. (Engl. pros.) Line of verse of 4 feet.

tĕ'trapŏd adj. & n. (Vertebrate) having two pairs of limbs (zool.; now more usu. than quadruped on not necessarily implying walking on 4 feet).

tĕ'trarch (-k) n. One of 4 joint rulers; (Rom. hist.) governor of a fourth part of a country or province, any subordinate ruler. tĕ'trarchate, tĕ'trarchў ns. tĕtrar'chical adj.

tĕ'trastyle adj. & n. (Portico) of 4 columns (ill. TEMPLE[1]).

tĕtrasў'llable n. Word of 4 syllables. tĕtrasўllă'bic adj.

tĕtravā'lent adj. (chem.) Having a VALENCY of 4. tĕtravā'lence, tĕtravā'lencў ns.

tĕ'trōde n. Electronic amplifying valve with four main electrodes.

tĕ'tter n. (archaic, dial.) Any pustular skin-eruption, as eczema etc.

Teu'cer. (Gk legend) 1. Ancestor of the kings of Troy. 2. Son of Telamon and half-brother of Ajax, the greatest archer amongst the Greeks attacking Troy. Teu'crian adj. & n. Trojan.

Teu'ton n. 1. One of the ancient Teutones or Teutoni, a N. European people in ancient Roman times. 2. One of a N. European race of tall stature with long heads, blue eyes, and fair hair and skin, first appearing in Germany, Scandinavia, and the Netherlands. 3. German.

Teutō'nic adj. Of the Teutons or their languages (see GERMANIC); ~ Order, ~ Knights, religious and military order founded at Acre (1190) by German Crusaders; it was invited early in 13th c. to undertake conquest of heathen Prussians and colonization of lands eastward of Germany, where it became a powerful governing aristocracy and administered large territories; the battle of TANNENBERG (1410) began the disintegration of its power and it was eventually suppressed in 1809; resuscitated as a semi-religious knighthood esp. devoted to ambulance service in Austria in 1840; became mendicant order in 1929.

Tex. abbrev. Texas.

Tĕ'xas. State in south-central U.S., admitted to the Union in 1845; capital, Austin. Tĕ'xan adj. & n.

tĕxt n. 1. Wording of anything written or printed, esp. the very words and sentences as orig. written, as opp. to translation, commentary, notes, etc. 2. (print.) Type, as opp. to illustrations etc. 3. Passage of Scripture quoted as authority or esp. chosen as subject of sermon etc.; subject, theme. 4. te'xtbook, manual of instruction in any branch of science or study, work recognized as an authority; ~-hand, fine large kind of handwriting esp. used for manuscripts. tĕ'xtile adj. Of weaving; woven, suitable for weaving. ~ n. Textile fabric or material.

tĕ'xtūal adj. Of, in, the text. tĕ'xtūallў adv.

tĕ'xtūalist n. One who adheres strictly to the letter of the text; one well acquainted with text, esp. of Bible. tĕ'xtūalism n.

tĕ'xture n. Character of textile fabric, resulting from way in which it is woven; arrangement of constituent parts, structure, constitution; representation of surface of objects in work of art, (also) character of surface of paint in picture etc. tĕ'xtural (-cher-) adj. tĕ'xturallў adv.

T.F. abbrev. Territorial Force.

T.G.W.U. abbrev. Transport & General Workers' Union.

Thă'ckeray, William Makepeace (1811–63). English novelist, author of 'Vanity Fair', 'Henry Esmond', 'The Virginians', 'The Newcomes', etc.

Thai, Tai (tī) adj. Of Thailand or its people or languages. ~ n. 1. Native, inhabitant, of Thailand; (member of) a people of Mongolian stock who migrated southwards from S. China (c 10th c.) and now occupy parts of Thailand, Burma, North Vietnam, and Laos. 2. Language of Thailand. 3. Group of languages spoken over a wide area in SE. Asia. Thai'lănd. Kingdom in SE. Asia, until 1939 called Siam; capital, Bangkok. Thai'lănder n. [Siamese thai free]

Thă'is. Athenian courtesan who accompanied Alexander the Great on his Asiatic campaign and later became wife of Ptolemy Lagus, king of Egypt; hence, any cultured and intelligent courtesan.

thă′lamo-cŏr′tical adj. (physiol.) Involving the thalamus and cortex of the brain.

thă′lamus n. (pl. -mī). 1. (anat.) Interior region of brain where certain important sensory nerves, esp. the optic nerve, originate (hence sometimes called *optic* ~; ill. BRAIN). 2. (bot.) Receptacle of flower.

thalăs′sic adj. Of sea(s), esp. of smaller or inland seas as dist. from oceans.

tha′ler (tah-) n. Any of various former German silver coins.

Thā′lēs (-z) (end of 7th c. B.C.). Greek philosopher of Miletus, one of the 'seven sages', believed to have founded the geometry of lines, discovered several theorems, and advanced the study of astronomy; he regarded water as the principle of all material things.

Thali′a. (Gk & Rom. myth.) 1. Muse of comedy. 2. One of the Graces. **Thali′an** adj.

thali′domide n. Sedative drug, taking of which by pregnant women was followed c 1960 by birth of children with malformed limbs; so ~ *child*.

thă′llium n. (chem.) Soft bluish-white leaden-lustred metallic element; symbol Tl, at. no. 81, at. wt 204·37. **thăllic, thăll′ous** adjs. [Gk *thallos* green shoot, from brilliant green line in its spectrum]

thă′llophȳte n. Plant whose body is a thallus, e.g. seaweed, liverwort.

thă′llus n. (pl. -ī). Body of a primitive plant which is not divided into leaves, stem, and roots but consists of more or less uniform tissue (ill. ALGA). **thă′lloid** adj.

Thames (tĕmz). Chief river of England, on which London stands, rising in Gloucestershire and flowing into North Sea.

Thă′mmuz, Tam- (t-). 1. Syrian or Babylonian deity, god of agriculture and flocks, lover of Astarte, who brought him back from the lower world after his death. 2. 10th month of JEWISH calendar.

Thă′myris. (Gk legend) Thracian poet and musician, blinded by the muses for his arrogance.

than (dh-; emphat. -ăn) conj. Introducing second member of comparison.

thăne n. (Engl. hist.) One holding land of king or other superior by virtue of military service, with rank between ordinary freemen and hereditary nobles; (Sc. hist.) one, ranking with earl's son, holding land of the king, chief of a clan.

thănk v.t. Express gratitude to (person *for* thing); ~ *you*, I thank you (as polite formula of gratitude etc.). ~ n. (now only in pl.) (Expression of) gratitude; ~*s*, thank you; ~*s to*, owing to, as the result of; *tha′nksgiving*, expression of gratitude, esp. to God; form of words for this; *Thanksgiving* (*Day*), (U.S.) annual festival and legal holiday, on 4th Thursday of November, first held (1621) by the Plymouth colony in thankfulness for their first harvest; ~-*offering*, offering made as expression of gratitude esp. to God.

thă′nkful adj. Grateful, expressive of thanks. **thă′nkfully** adv. **thă′nkfulness** n.

thă′nkless adj. Not feeling or expressing gratitude; (of task etc.) not likely to win thanks, unprofitable. **thă′nklessly** adv. **thă′nklessness** n.

thăt (dh-) pron. 1. demonstr. (pl. *those* pr. -z) Person or thing referred to, observed, understood, in question, etc.; (coupled or contrasted with *this*) esp., the farther, less immediate or obvious, etc., of two; *and all* ~, and so forth; *at* ~, (orig. U.S.) at that standard, (even) in that capacity; too, besides; ~ *is* (*to say*), introducing explanation of preceding word, phrase, etc. 2. (unemphatic -at) rel. (introducing defining clause; often omitted) Who, whom, which. ~ adj. (pl. *those* pr. -z) Designating person or thing referred to etc.: the (used demonstratively not merely definitively); farther or less immediate of the two (opp. *this*); well-known (often implying censure or dislike, but sometimes admiration. ~ adv. (colloq.) To the extent or degree indicated (as ~ *far*, ~ *much*). ~ conj. Introducing dependent clause, esp. expressing result or consequence.

thătch n. Roof-covering of straw, reeds, etc. ~ v.t. Roof or cover with thatch; make (roof) of thatch.

thau′matrōpe n. Card or disc with two different figures drawn upon the two sides, which are apparently combined into one when the disc is rotated rapidly, used to demonstrate the persistence of visual impressions.

thau′matūrge n. Worker of miracles, wonder-worker. **thaumatūr′gic, -ical** adjs. **thau′maturgy** n.

thaw v. Reduce (frozen substance) to liquid state by raising its temperature above freezing-point; become liquid, flexible, or limp by rise of temperature after being frozen; (fig.) free, be freed, from coldness or stiffness, (cause to) unbend or become genial. ~ n. Thawing, melting of ice and snow after frost; warmth of weather that thaws.

the (before vowel dhĭ, before consonant dhe, emphatic dhē) adj. (the definite article) Denoting, or defining, or singling out person(s) or thing(s) already mentioned or under discussion, actually or potentially existent, unique, familiar, or otherwise sufficiently identified; applied to singular nouns as representing species, class, etc.; used with adjectives used abs.; emphatically, applied to person or thing best known or best entitled to the name. ~ adv. In that degree, by that amount, on that account; *the . . . the*, by how much . . . by so much; in what degree . . . in that degree.

thē′archy (-kĭ) n. Theocracy; system or order of gods.

Thē′atīne n. & adj. (R.C. Ch.) (Member) of an order of clerks regular founded 1524 in Italy to combat Lutheranism; (member) of the corresponding order of nuns, founded in early 17th c., now most numerous in U.S.

thē′atre (-ter) n. 1. Building or outdoor area for dramatic performances etc.; (Gk & Rom. antiq.) open-air structure in form of segment of circle rising gradually; room, hall, for lectures etc., with seats in tiers (illustration, p. 881). 2. Scene, field, of action. 3. = OPERATING theatre. 4. Natural formation of land resembling ancient Greek or Roman theatre. 5. Dramatic literature or art.

theă′trical adj. Of or suited to theatre; of acting or actors; calculated for effect, showy, artificial; **theă′trically** adv. **theă′tricalism, theătrică′lity** ns. **theă′tricals** (-z) n.pl. Theatrical performances, esp. by amateurs.

Thēbā′id. Latin epic poem (c A.D. 92) by Statius, concerned with expedition against Thebes to recover throne for Polynices from his brother Eteocles.

Thēbes (-bz). 1. Ancient capital (from time of 12th dynasty) of Upper Egypt, on site of modern Luxor. 2. (Gk *Thivai*) Ancient city of Boeotia, subject of many legends including those of Cadmus, Oedipus, and Antigone; from the late 6th c. B.C. the bitter enemy of Athens, and after the Peloponnesian War the rival of Sparta for the hegemony of Greece; it was razed to the ground in 335 B.C. but rebuilt, existed throughout Roman times, and was finally destroyed in 1311. **Thē′ban** adj. & n.

thē′ca n. 1. (bot.) Part of plant serving as receptacle, as pollen-sac of anther, spore-case, capsule of moss, etc. (ill. MOSS). 2. (zool., anat.) Case or sheath enclosing some organ or part.

thee (dh-) pron. Objective (accus., dat.) case of THOU; dial. and among Quakers occas. used for THOU.

thĕft n. Stealing; (law) act of dishonestly appropriating another's property with intent of permanently depriving him of it.

their (dhār) poss. pron. Possessive case of THEY used as attrib. adj. with abs. and pred. form *theirs* (pr. -z), belonging to, affecting, them.

thē′ism n. Belief in gods or

[907]

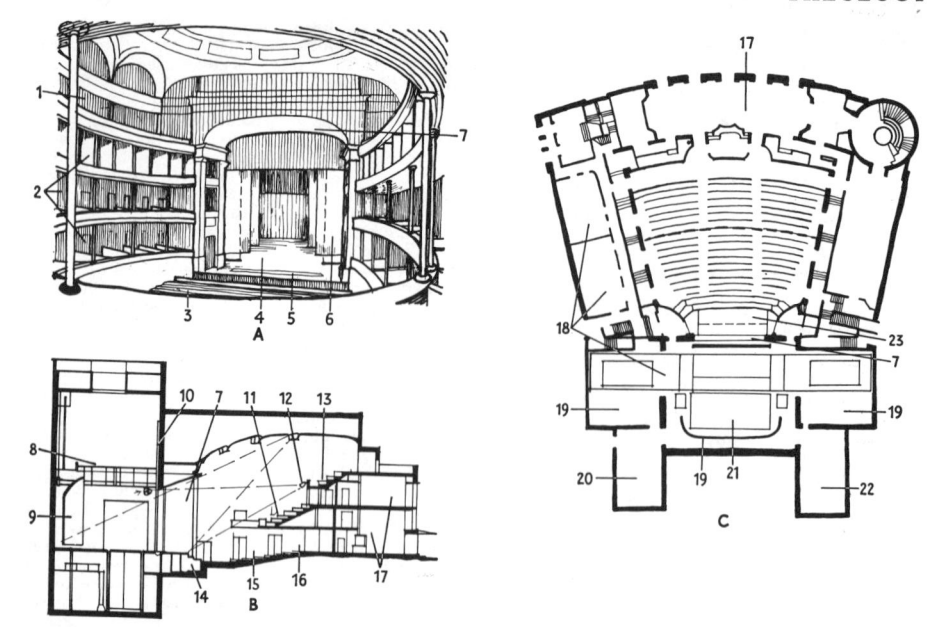

THEATRE: A. GENERAL VIEW OF AUDITORIUM AND STAGE. B. SECTION. C. PLAN

A. 1, 2, 3. Auditorium (1. Gallery, 2. Boxes, 3. Parterre). 4. Stage. 5. Footlights. 6. Wings or coulisses. 7. Proscenium opening. B. 8. Flies. 9. Back-cloth. 10. Safety curtain. 11. Dress circle. 12. Stage lights. 13. Balcony. 14. Orchestra pit. 15. Stalls. 16. Pit. 17. Foyers. C. 18. Green-room and dressing-rooms. 19. Scene-docks. 20. Stage carpenter's room. 21. Trap. 22. Property room. 23. Apron stage

(esp.) a god, as opp. to ATHEISM, PANTHEISM, POLYTHEISM, esp. belief in one God as creator and supreme ruler of universe. **thĕ′ĭst** n. **thĕĭ′stĭc, -ĭcal** adjs.
thĕm (dh-) pron. Objective (accus., dat.) case of THEY.
thĕmă′tĭc adj. Of, belonging to, constituting, a theme.
thēme n. 1. Subject of discourse, conversation, composition, etc., topic; school essay. 2. (mus.) Subject, tune, or passage developed in musical composition, and recurring as a principal part of its material; tune on which variations are constructed; ~ song, recurrent melody in a musical play or film. 3. (gram.) = STEM¹, 3.
Thĕ′mĭs. (Gk myth.) Goddess of law and justice.
Themĭ′stoclēs (-z) (c 524–459 B.C.). Athenian statesman and soldier, commander of the Athenian fleet at SALAMIS.
themsĕ′lves (dh-, -vz) pron. Emphatic and reflexive form corresponding to THEY, THEM.
thĕn (dh-) adv. At that time; next, afterwards, after that; now and ~, at one time and another, from time to time. ~ conj. In that case; therefore; it follows that; accordingly. ~ adj. Existing etc. at that time. ~ n. That time; every now and ~, from time to time.
thĕ′nar n. (anat.) Ball of muscle at base of thumb; palm of hand; sole of foot.
thĕnce dh-) adv. (archaic and literary) From that place, from there; from that source, for that reason. **thĕncefŏr′th, thĕncefŏr′ward** advs. & ns. From (from) that time forward.
theo- prefix. God.
thēobrō′mĭne n. Bitter white crystalline alkaloid, related to caffeine, obtained from seeds of cacao-tree.
thēocĕ′ntrĭc adj. Having God as its centre.
thēo′cracy̆ n. Government by God, directly or through a priestly class etc.; State so governed; the T~, the Jewish commonwealth from Moses to the monarchy.
thēo′crasy̆ n. Union of the soul with God through contemplation (among Neo-platonists, Buddhists, etc.).
thē′ocrăt n. Ruler in, subject under, a theocracy. **thēocră′tĭc** adj. **thēo′cratĭst** n. Believer in theocracy.
Thēŏ′crĭtus (3rd c. B.C.). Sicilian Greek poet; regarded as the originator of pastoral poetry.
thēŏ′dĭcy̆ n. Vindication of the divine providence in view of the existence of evil.
thēŏ′dolīte n. Surveying instrument for measuring horizontal and vertical angles, telescope rotating round a graduated circular plate and also free to swivel in vertical plane over a graduated arc. **thēŏdolĭ′tĭc** adj.
Thē′odore, Name of 3 tsars of Russia: Theodore I (1557–98),
succeeded his father Ivan the Terrible 1584; Theodore II (1589–1605), son of Boris Godunov, succeeded his father 1605 and was murdered in the same year; Theodore III (1661–82), succeeded his father Alexey 1679.
Thēŏ′dorĭc (c 454–526). King of the Ostrogoths, invader (488–93) and conqueror of Italy, which he ruled from Ravenna; attempted to revive the Western Roman Empire.
Thēodō′sius (-shĭ-). Name of 3 Emperors of the Eastern Roman Empire: Theodosius I (c 346–95), 'the Great', Roman general, born in Spain, became emperor of the East 379; Theodosius II (401–50) succeeded his father Arcadius as emperor 408; Theodosius III was proclaimed emperor 715 by the rebellious Byzantine army and deposed 717 by Leo III. **Thēodō′sian** adj. Of Theodosius; (esp.) ~ Code, code of all imperial legislation since time of Constantine, promulgated in 438 by Theodosius II.
thēŏ′gony̆ n. Genealogy of the gods; poem etc. dealing with this. **thēogŏ′nĭc** adj. **thēŏ′gonĭst** n.
thēolō′gian n. Person skilled in theology.
thēŏ′logy̆ n. Science of religion, study of God or gods, esp. of attributes and relations with man etc.; dogmatic ~, that based on the authoritative teaching of the Scriptures and the Church; natural

~, dealing with knowledge of God as gained from his works by the light of nature and reason; *positive*, *revealed*, ~, based on revelation; *speculative* ~, not confined to revelation but giving scope to human speculation; *systematic* ~, methodical arrangement of the truths of religion in their natural connection. theolō'gical *adj.* theolō'gically *adv.*
theŏ'machy (-ki), *n.* Strife among the gods.
theomōr'phic *adj.* Having the form or likeness of a god.
theŏ'phany *n.* Manifestation or appearance of God to man; Epiphany.
theōr'bō *n.* Large kind of lute with two necks and two sets of tuning-pegs, much used in 17th c.
thē'orĕm *n.* Universal or general proposition, not self-evident but demonstrable by chain of reasoning; algebraical or other rule, esp. expressed by symbols or formulae. theorĕmă'tic, -ical *adjs.*
theorē'tic, -ical *adjs.* Of, consisting in, relating to, conforming to, theory; existing only in theory, hypothetical; addicted to, constructing, dealing with, theories, speculative. theorĕ'tics *n.pl.* Theory, theoretical parts of science etc.
thē'ory *n.* Scheme or system of ideas or statements held to explain group of facts or phenomena, statement of general laws, principles, or causes of something known or observed; systematic conception or statement of principles of something, abstract knowledge, formulation of this; department of art or technical subject concerned with knowledge of its principles or methods, as opp. to *practice*; systematic statement of general principles of some branch of mathematics; mere hypothesis, conjecture, individual view or notion. thē'orist *n.* thē'orize *v.*
theŏ'sophy *n.* Philosophy professing to attain to knowledge of God by spiritual ecstasy, direct intuition, or special individual relations, esp. system of Jakob BOEHME; now usu., doctrines of the Theosophical Society. theosŏ'phic *adj.* theosŏ'phical *adj.* (esp.) *T~ Society*, society founded in 1875 in New York by Madame BLAVATSKY and others, advocating universal brotherhood, and following esp. Brahminic and Buddhistic teachings. theosŏ'phically *adv.* theŏ'sopher, theŏ'sophist *ns.* theŏ'sophize *v.i.*
thĕrapeu'tic, -ical *adjs.* Of the healing of disease, curative. thĕrapeu'tics *n.* Branch of medicine concerned with remedial treatment of disease.
thĕ'rapy *n.* Curative medical treatment.
Thĕrava'da (-vah-) *n.* One of the two great schools of Buddhism, surviving esp. in Sri Lanka, Burma, Thailand, and Khmer.
there (dhār, unemphatic dh*er*) *adv.* In or at that place; at that point in argument, situation, progress of affairs, etc.; to that place or point; used unemphatically to introduce sentence or clause in which verb comes before its subject (also, with the verb *to be*, without inversion); ther'e-*about*(s), near that place; near that number, quantity, etc.; there*a'fter*, (archaic) after that; there*a't*, (archaic) there; thereupon, at that; *thereby'* (or dhār'bī), (archaic) by or through that; *thereby hangs a tale*, in that connection there is something to be told; *therefor'*, (archaic) for that, for it; for that reason, on that account; *ther'efore*, in consequence of that; for that reason, accordingly, consequently; *therei'n*, (archaic) in that place; in that respect; *thereina'fter*, *therein-befor'e*, (archaic) later, earlier, in same document, etc.; *thereo'f*, (archaic) of that, of it; *thereo'n*, (archaic) on that, on it; *thereto'*, (archaic) to that, to it; in addition; *thereupo'n*, in consequence of that; soon, immediately, after that; (archaic) upon that; *therewi'th*, (archaic) with that; thereupon; *therewitha'l* (archaic) in addition, besides. ~ *n.* That place or point. ~ *int.* Exclamation expressing confirmation, triumph, dismay, etc.
ther'iăc *n.* Antidote to poison, esp. to bite of venomous serpent.
theriomōr'phic *adj.* Having form of a beast; of deity worshipped in form of a beast.
thĕrm *n.* Unit of heat, esp. 100,000 Btu as basis of charge for gas used as fuel.
ther'mae *n.pl.* (Gk & Rom. antiq.) Public baths.
ther'mal *adj.* Of heat; determined, measured, operated by heat; ~ *capacity*, (of a body) number of heat units required to raise its temperature by one degree; ~ *springs*, hot springs; ~ *unit*, unit of heat; *British T~ Unit*, (abbrev. Btu) amount of heat required to raise the temperature of one pound of water at its maximum density by one degree Fahrenheit. ~ *n.* Rising current of warm air.
thermă'ntidōte *n.* Apparatus used in hot countries for cooling the air.
Ther'midōr. 11th month of French Revolutionary calendar, covering parts of July and August. Thermidōr'ian *n.* (Fr. hist.) One of those taking part in overthrow of Robespierre on 9 Thermidor (27 July 1794).
ther'miŏn *n.* Electrically charged particle (electron or ion) emitted from a heated body. thermiŏ'nic *adj.* Of, emitting, thermions; ~ *valve*, vacuum tube, in which electrons emitted by a heated filament carry electric current in one direction, used as a rectifier of an alternating current and in radio receiving sets for the detection and amplification of radio waves.
thermi'stor *n.* Type of semiconductor in which the resistance decreases as the temperature rises.
ther'mīte *n.* Mixture of finely divided aluminium and oxide of iron or oxide of other metal, producing very high temperature (c 3000 °C) on combustion, used in smelting, welding, and as filling for incendiary bombs.
thermochĕ'mistry (-k-) *n.* Branch of chemistry dealing with the heat changes accompanying reactions. thermochĕ'mical *adj.* thermochĕ'mist *n.*
thermocou'ple (-kŭpl) *n.* Device consisting of two different metals joined at two places so that when a difference of temperature exists between the two joins an electromotive force is produced which can be used to measure that difference.
thermodynă'mics *n.* The science dealing with the relationship between thermal energy (heat) and all other forms of energy (mechanical, electrical, etc.); *1st law of* ~: during transformation of heat into another form of energy there is a constant relation between the amount of heat expended and energy gained; the same is true of the reverse process; *2nd law of* ~: heat cannot pass to its own accord from a colder to a hotter body. thermodynă'mic *adj.* thermodynă'mically *adv.*
thermoĕlĕctri'city *n.* Electricity developed by the action of heat at the junction of two different metals. thermoĕlĕ'ctric *adj.*
thermogĕ'nesis *n.* Generation of heat in an animal body.
thermolā'bīle *adj.* (biochem.) Sensitive to heat.
thermŏ'lȳsis *n.* (pl. -*sēs*). (chem.) Dissociation, decomposition, by action of heat.
thermŏ'meter *n.* Instrument for measuring temperature, freq. a graduated glass tube with bulb containing a substance (as mercury, alcohol) whose expansion and contraction under the influence of temperature can be accurately measured. thermomĕ'tric, -ical *adjs.* thermomĕ'trically *adv.* thermŏ'metry *n.* Science dealing

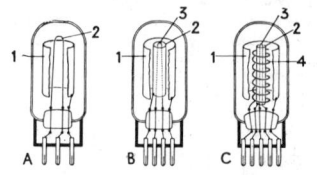

THERMIONIC VALVES

A, B. DIODES (A. DIRECT HEATING. B. INDIRECT HEATING). C. TRIODE

1. Anode. 2. Cathode. 3. Cathode heater. 4. Control grid

with the measurement of temperature.
thĕrmonū'clĕar *adj.* Of or concerned with reactions involving the fusion of atomic nuclei at very high temperatures, as in a hydrogen bomb.
thĕr'mophĭl, -phĭle *adj. & n.* (Organism, as certain bacteria) requiring high temperature for development.
thĕr'mopĭle *n.* Set of thermocouples arranged in series, used to detect radiant heat.
thĕrmoplă'stĭc *adj. & n.* (Substance) that becomes plastic when heated, hardens when cooled, and can do this repeatedly.
Thĕrmŏ'pўlae (-lē). Pass in Greece from Locris into Thessaly, orig. narrow but now much widened by recession of sea; scene of the heroic defence (480 B.C.) against the Persian army of Xerxes by 6,000 Greeks including 300 Spartans under LEONIDAS.
thĕr'mŏs *n.* (also ~ *bottle, flask, jug*) Kind of vacuum flask. [trade-name]
thĕr'mosĕtting *adj.* Becoming permanently hard and rigid when heated.
thĕr'mostăt *n.* Device which automatically maintains temperature at a constant value, or which gives notice of an undue change in temperature. **thĕrmostă'tĭc** *adj.* **thĕrmostă'tĭcallў** *adv.*
thĕrmotăx'ĭs *n.* (physiol.) Regulation of bodily heat.
thĕrmotrŏ'pĭc *adj.* (of plants etc.) Bending or turning towards or away from a source of heat. **thĕrmotrŏ'pĭsm** *n.*
thĕr'oid *adj.* Having beastlike propensities.
Thersī'tēs (-z). (Gk legend) Most ill-favoured of the Greeks in the Trojan War, a scurrilous reviler of the leaders.
thĕsaur'us *n.* (pl. *-rī*). Storehouse of information, esp. dictionary or encyclopaedia.
these: see THIS.
Thē'sĕus (or -sūs). (Gk legend) Hero, son of Aegeus, king of Athens (or of Poseidon); slayer of the Cretan Minotaur and hero of other famous exploits.
thē'sĭs *n.* (pl. *-ses* pr. -sēz). 1. Proposition laid down or stated, esp. as theme to be discussed and proved; dissertation to maintain and prove thesis, esp. submitted by candidate for university degree. 2. (pros., *also* thĕ-) Unstressed syllable in or part of metrical foot (opp. ARSIS).
Thē'spĭan *adj.* 1. Of Thespis; of tragedy or the dramatic art. 2. Of Thespiae, ancient city of Boeotia. ~ *n.* 1. Actor or actress. 2. Native, inhabitant, of Thespiae.
Thē'spĭs (6th c. B.C.). Greek dramatic poet, regarded as father of Greek tragedy.
Thess. *abbrev.* Thessalonians (N.T.).
Thĕssalō'nĭan *adj.* Of Thessalonica. ~ *n.* Native, inhabitant, of Thessalonica; (*Epistle to the*) ~s, either of two books of N.T., earliest extant letters of St. Paul, written from Corinth to the new Church at Thessalonica.
Thĕssalonī'ca. Ancient city in Macedonia, founded 316 B.C. by Cassander, a general of Alexander the Great; now SALONICA.
Thĕ'ssalў. District of N. Greece.
thē'ta *n.* 9th (later 8th) letter of Greek alphabet (Θ, θ), = *th*.
Thĕ'tĭs. (Gk myth.) Sea-nymph, mother of ACHILLES.
thĕ'ûrgў *n.* Operation of divine or supernatural agency in human affairs; system of magic among Neoplatonists, supposed to procure communication with beneficent spirits and produce miraculous effects by their aid. **thĕûr'gĭc, -ical** *adj.* **thĕ'ûrgĭst** *n.*
thews (-z) *n.pl.* Sinews, muscles; mental or moral vigour. **thew'-lĕss, thew'ў** *adjs.*
they (dhā) *pron.* 3rd person nom. pl. pronoun, plural of HE, SHE, IT.
thī'amīde *n.* Any of a class of compounds resembling amides but with sulphur in place of oxygen.
Thibet, Thibetan: see TIBET, TIBETAN.
thĭck *adj.* 1. Of great or specified depth between opposite surfaces; (of line etc.) broad, not fine. 2. Arranged closely, crowded together; numerous; abounding, packed, *with*; of great or considerable density, viscid, stiff; turbid, muddy, cloudy, not clear; (of soup) thickened. 3. Stupid, dull; (of voice) muffled, indistinct; (colloq.) intimate; *a bit* ~, (slang) excessive in some disagreeable quality, going beyond what is reasonable. 4. **thĭ'ckhead**, blockhead; ~-*headed*, stupid, slow-witted; **thĭ'ckset**, set or growing close together; heavily or solidly built; **thĭ'ckset** (*hedge*), close-grown hedge; ~-*skinned*, (fig.) not sensitive to criticism, reproach, insult, etc. **thĭ'ckĭsh** *adj.* **thĭ'cklў** *adv.*
thĭck *n.* Thick part of anything, esp. fight etc.; *through* ~ *and thin*, under all conditions, resolutely. ~ *adv.* Thickly.
thĭ'cken *v.* Make or become thick; make of stiffer consistence.
thĭ'ckĕt *n.* Dense growth of small trees, shrubs, underwood, etc.
thĭ'cknĕss *n.* Being thick; third dimension, dist. from *length* and *breadth*; what is thick; layer.
thief *n.* One who steals, esp. secretly and without violence.
thieve *v.* Be a thief, practise stealing; steal (thing). **thie'vĕrў** *n.* **thie'vĭsh** *adj.* **thie'vĭshlў** *adv.* **thie'vĭshnĕss** *n.*
Thiers (tēar), Louis Adolphe (1797–1877). French statesman and historian; negotiated peace with Germany 1870, suppressed the Commune, and became president of the republic 1871–3.
thigh (thī) *n.* Upper part of human leg, from hip to knee; corresponding part (or part pop. supposed to correspond) in other animals; ~-*bone*, bone of the thigh, femur.
thĭll *n.* Pole or shaft of wagon, cart, etc., esp. one of pair of shafts between which draught-animal is placed (ill. CART).
thĭ'mble *n.* Bell-shaped sheath of metal etc. worn on end of finger to push needle in sewing; (mech. etc.) ring, tube, sleeve, ferrule, etc.; (naut.) metal ring with concave outer surface round which rope is spliced (ill. SPLICE); **thĭ'mbleful**, small quantity (of spirits etc.) to drink; **thĭ'mblerĭg**, swindling game with three thimble-shaped cups and pea, bystanders betting which cup covers pea; **thĭ'mblerĭgger, thĭ'mblerĭggĭng** (*ns.*).
thĭn *adj.* Having opposite surfaces close together; of small diameter; slender; lean, spare, not plump; not dense; not full or closely packed; of slight density or consistence; wanting body, fullness, volume, or substance; (of lines) narrow, fine; (fig.) shallow, transparent, flimsy; *a* ~ *time*, a wretched or uncomfortable period; ~-*skinned*, (fig.) sensitive. **thĭ'nlў** *adv.* **thĭ'nnĕss** (-n-n-) *n.* **thĭ'nnĭsh** *adj.* **thĭn** *v.* Make or become thin; reduce in bulk or number; ~ *out*, reduce number of (esp. seedlings, by pulling up the less promising). ~ *adv.* Sparsely.
thine: see THY.
thĭng *n.* 1. What is or may be an object of perception, knowledge, or thought. 2. Entity, being, esp. inanimate object. 3. Piece of property, possession, (pl.) clothes, garments, esp. outdoor garments; (pl.) implements, utensils. 4. (pl.) Affairs, concerns, matters. 5. What is (to be) done, fact, deed, occurrence; what is said, expression, statement.
thĭ'ngamў, thĭ'ngumajĭg, thĭ'ngum(a)bŏb, thĭ'ngummў *ns.* (colloq.) Person, thing, indicated vaguely because speaker cannot remember or does not wish to use correct name or word; what's-his-name, what-d'you-call-it.
thĭnk *v.* (past t. & past part. *thought*, pr. -awt). Consider, be of opinion; form conception of; exercise mind in active way, form connected ideas; consider a matter, reflect; conceive notion of doing something, contemplate, intend; ~ *about*, consider; ~ *of*, consider; imagine; intend, contemplate; entertain idea *of*; hit upon; ~ *out*, consider carefully; devise (plan etc.); ~ *over*, reflect upon. **thĭ'nker** *n.* (esp.) Person of skilled or powerful mind.
thī'o-ă'cĭd *n.* Acid in which oxygen is partly or wholly replaced by sulphur.
thīocyă'nĭc *adj.* ~ *acid*, colourless unstable liquid acid (HCNS) with penetrating odour. **thīocў'anāte** *n.* Salt of this.

thīosū'lphāte n. Salt of thiosulphuric acid (H₂S₂O₃), extremely unstable acid; used in photography, formerly called *hyposulphite* (see HYPO).
thīrd adj. Next after second; ~-*class*, (esp.) poor, inferior; ~ *degree*, severe examination of prisoner to extort confession or information (orig. U.S.); (freemasonry) degree of master mason; *T~ Empire*: see GERMANY; ~ *man*, (cricket) fielder placed between point and short slip but farther out (ill. CRICKET); ~ *party*: see PARTY¹; ~ *rail*, (in some electric railways) rail through which current is conducted, lying alongside those on which train runs; ~-*rate*, inferior, decidedly poor, in quality; *T~ World*, underdeveloped countries of Asia, Africa, and Latin America, usu. not aligned with either the Communist or the Western nations. ~ n. Third part (see PART¹, 1); third thing, person, place, class, etc.; sixtieth of a second of time or angular measurement; (in motor vehicle) third gear; (pl.) goods of third degree of quality; (mus.) interval of which the span involves 3 alphabetical names of notes (ill. INTERVAL); harmonic combination of the two notes thus separated. **thīr'dly** adv. In the third place.
thīrst n. Uneasy or painful sensation caused by want of drink; desire for drink; (fig.) ardent desire, craving. **thīr'sty** adj. Feeling thirsty; dry, parched, arid; (colloq.) causing thirst; (fig.) eager, greedy. **thīr'stily** adv. **thīr'stiness** n. **thīrst** v.i. Feel thirst.
thīrtee'n adj. & n. One more than twelve (13, xiii, or XIII). **thīrtee'nth** adj. & n. **thīrtee'nthly** adv.
thīr'ty adj. Amounting to thirty; *Thirty-nine Articles*, articles of religion assented to by person taking orders in Church of England; ~-*two-mo* (-too'mō), 32mo, book with sheets folded into thirty-two leaves; *T~ Years' War*, war (1618-48) originating between Catholics and Protestants of Germany and later involving most of Western Europe. ~ n. Cardinal number, three times ten (30, xxx, or XXX); set of thirty things or persons; *thirties*, numbers etc. from 30 to 39; these years of century or life. **thīr'tieth** adj. & n. **thīr'tiethly** adv. **thīr'tyfold** adj. & n.
this (dh-) *demonstr. pron.* & *adj.* (pl. *thēse* pr. -z). The (person, thing, event, time) near, present, just mentioned (freq. opp. THAT). ~ adv. To the extent or degree indicated (as ~ *far*, ~ *much*).
Thi'sbē (-z-). (Rom. legend) Lover of PYRAMUS.
thi'stle (-sl) n. Prickly composite herbaceous, often woody, plant of *Carduus* and related genera, with stems, leaves, and involucres thickly armed with prickles, usu. globular flowerheads and most freq. purple flowers; (figure of this as) heraldic emblem of Scotland, and part of insignia of distinctively Scottish order of knighthood, *Order of the T~*, instituted 1687 by James II and revived 1703 by Queen Anne; *Knight of the T~*, member of this order; *thi'stledown*, pappus of thistle (freq. as type of lightness or flimsinesss). **thi'stly** adj.
thi'ther (dhĭdh-) adv. (archaic) To that place.
tho', **tho** (dhō) *conj.* & *adv.* = THOUGH.
thōle n. (also ~ *pin*) Pin in gunwale of boat as fulcrum for oar; each of two such pins between which oar plays (ill. BOAT).
Thŏ'mas¹ (tŏ-), St. Apostle who (John 20: 24-29) refused to believe that Christ had risen again unless he could see and touch his wounds; commemorated 21 Dec.; *doubting ~*, sceptic.
Thŏ'mas² (tŏ-), Dylan (1914-53). British poet, born in Wales; author of 'Under Milk Wood', a play for voices.
Thŏ'mas à Kĕ'mpĭs (tŏ-). Thomas Hämmerken (c 1380-1471), named from his birthplace, Kempen, near Düsseldorf; Augustinian monk, author of 'De Imitatione Christi'.
Thomas Aquinas, St.: see AQUINAS.
Thŏ'mism (tō-). System of theology and philosophy taught by St. Thomas AQUINAS. **Thŏ'mist** n. **Thŏmi'stic**, **-ical** adjs.
Thŏ'mpson¹ (tŏms-), Francis (1859-1907). English poet; author of 'Hound of Heaven', describing the poet's flight from God, the pursuit, and the overtaking.
Thŏ'mpson² (tŏms-), John Taliaferro (1860-1940). Amer. general; one of the inventors of the *Thompson sub-machine-gun*, a portable automatic weapon (ill. GUN).
Tho'mson¹ (tŏ-), James (1700-48). Scottish poet; author of 'The Seasons' etc.
Tho'mson² (tŏ-), James (1834-82). Scottish poet; author of 'The City of Dreadful Night' etc.
Thŏ'mson³, Sir Joseph John (1856-1940). English physicist; investigated cathode rays and the mass and charge of the particle now called the electron; Nobel Prize for physics 1906.
Thŏ'mson⁴ (tŏ-), William: see KELVIN².
thŏng n. Narrow strip of hide or leather etc. used as lace, strap, whip-lash, etc. ~ v.t. Furnish with thong; lash, strike with thong.
Thŏr. (Scand. myth.) God of thunder, war, and agriculture, represented as armed with hammer.
thŏr'ăx n. 1. (anat., zool.) Part of body of mammal between neck and abdomen, that enclosed by ribs, breast-bone, and vertebrae and containing chief organs of circulation and respiration. 2. (zool.) Middle section of body of insect etc. between head and abdomen (ill. INSECT). **thŏrā'cic** adj.
Thŏr'eau (-rō), Henry David (1817-62). American naturalist; author of 'Walden or Life in the Woods' (1854).
thŏr'ia n. Thorium oxide (ThO₂).
thŏr'ium n. (chem.) Radioactive metallic element which (like uranium) will undergo fission when bombarded with neutrons and is therefore a potential source of atomic energy; symbol Th, at. no. 90, at. wt 232·0381.
thŏrn n. 1. Stiff sharp-pointed process on stem or other part of plant; thorn-bearing bush or tree, esp. hawthorn, whitethorn, or other species of genus *Crataegus*. 2. Name of Old English and Icelandic runic letter þ (= th). 3. ~-*apple*, poisonous plant of genus *Datura*, esp. *D. stramonium*, jimson weed; *thor'nback*, common ray or skate (*Raja clavata*), with rows of short sharp spines along back and tail; ~-*bush*, any bush bearing thorns. **thŏr'nless** adj. **thŏr'ny** adj. (esp., fig.) Harassing, vexatious, difficult to handle, delicate, ticklish.
thorough (thŭ'ro) adj. Complete, unqualified, not superficial, out-and-out; ~ *bass*, figured bass, bass-part of piece of music written alone, with signs, esp. numerals, indicating chords or harmonies; *tho'roughbred*, (animal, esp. horse) of pure breed; (person) with characteristics associated with a thoroughbred animal; *tho'roughfare*, any public way open at both ends, esp. main road; ~-*going*, extreme, thorough, out-and-out; ~-*paced*, (of horse, archaic) thoroughly trained in all paces; (fig.) complete, unqualified. **tho'-roughly** adv. **tho'roughness** n. **tho'rough** adv. & prep. (archaic) Through.
thŏrp, **thŏrpe** n. (archaic & hist.) Village, hamlet.
Thos. *abbrev.* Thomas.
those: see THAT.
Thŏth (or tōt). (Egyptian myth.) God of wisdom and magic, the scribe of the gods, identified with the Greek Hermes and represented in human form with head of an ibis.
thou (dhow) *pron.* 2nd person nom. sing. pronoun (now archaic or poet.) denoting person addressed.
though (dhō) *conj.* In spite of the fact that; even if, granting that; *as ~*, as if. ~ adv. (colloq.) And yet, but yet, all the same, none the less.
thought¹ (-awt) n. Process, power, capacity, faculty, of thinking; what one thinks, what is or

[911]

THOUGHT

has been thought; idea, notion; consideration, heed; meditation; intention, purpose, design; ~-*reader*, *-reading*, (person capable of) direct perception of what is passing in another's mind; ~-*transference*, telepathy.
thought[2]: see THINK.
thou'ghtful (-awt-) *adj.* Engaged in, given to, meditation; showing thought or consideration; considerate (*of*), kindly. **thou'ghtfully** *adv.* **thou'ghtfulness** *n.*
thou'ghtless (-awt-) *adj.* Unthinking, heedless, imprudent, inconsiderate. **thou'ghtlessly** *adv.* **thou'ghtlessness** *n.*
thou'sand (-z-) *adj.* Amounting to one thousand; (loosely) very many; ~*-and-one*, of indefinitely great number; *T~ and One Nights*, the 'ARABIAN Nights'; *T~ Islands*, group of about 1,000 islands in St. Lawrence River. ~ *n.* Ten hundred; symbol for this (1,000, m, or M). **thou'sandfold** *adj. & adv.* **thou'sandth** *adj. & n.*
Thrāce. District of eastern Balkan peninsula, in ancient times including Bulgaria and eastern Macedonia. **Thrā'cian** (-shan) *adj. & n.* (Native, inhabitant) of Thrace; (of) its ancient Indo-European language, closely related to Illyrian, Phrygian, and Armenian.
thrall (-awl) *n.* Slave; bondage. **thra'ldom** *n.*
thrăsh *v.t.* Beat, esp. with stick or whip; conquer, surpass; thresh; ~ *out*, (fig.) discuss exhaustively, argue thoroughly.
thrā'sher *n.* (esp.) Kind of shark (*Alopias vulpinus*), with very long upper division of tail, with which it lashes an enemy.
thrasō'nical *adj.* Resembling *Thraso*, a braggart soldier in Terence's 'Eunuchus'; boastful, vainglorious. **thrasō'nically** *adv.*
thread (-ĕd) *n.* 1. Fine cord of spun-out fibres or filaments of flax, cotton, wool, glass, etc., esp. of two or more twisted together; thread-shaped or thread-like thing, e.g. fine line or streak of colour or light; spiral ridge of screw, each complete turn of this (ill. SCREW). 2. (fig.) Something represented as like thread, esp. course of human life; that which connects successive points in narrative, train of thought, etc., or on which things hang; continuous or persistent feature running through pattern of anything. 3. *threa'dbare*, with nap worn off and threads of warp and woof left bare; wearing such garments, shabby, seedy; (fig.) commonplace, trite, hackneyed; ~-*fish*, tropical fish of family Polycnemidae, with pectoral fin in long threads; *threa'dworm*, any of various threadlike worms, any nematode, esp. the pin-worm. **threa'dy** *adj.* **thread** *v.t.* Pass thread through eye of (needle); string (beads etc.) on thread,

make (chain etc.) thus; pick one's way through (street, crowded place, etc.), make one's *way* thus; form screw-thread on.
Threa'dneedle Street (-ĕd-). Street in City of London containing premises of Bank of England (the *Old Lady of* ~). [earlier *three-needle*, poss. f. a tavern with the arms of the Needlemakers]
threat (-ĕt) *n.* Declaration of intention to punish or hurt; (law) such menace of bodily hurt or injury to reputation or property as may restrain person's freedom of action; indication of coming evil.
threa'ten (-ĕtn) *v.* Use threats (against); try to influence by threats; announce one's intention (*to do*) as punishment or in revenge etc.; be source of danger to; presage, portend. **threa'teningly** *adv.*
three *adj.* Amounting to three; ~-*colour process*, printing-process in which coloured picture etc. is reproduced by superposition of the 3 primary colours or their complementaries; ~-*cornered*, having 3 angles or corners; (of contest etc.) between 3 persons; ~-*decker*, 3-decked ship, esp. (hist.) line-of-battle ship with guns on 3 decks; anything with 3 layers, tiers, etc.; ~-*dimensional*, (producing effect or illusion of) having depth in space as well as height and width; realistic; ~-*handed*, (of games) played by 3 persons; ~-*lane*, (of road) marked for 3 lines of traffic; *T~ Holy Children*, Shadrach, Meshach, and Abednego (Dan. 3: 12–30); ~-*legged*, (of race) run by pairs with a right and a left leg tied together; ~-*master*, vessel with 3 masts; ~-*mile limit*, limit of zone of territorial waters, extending 3 miles from coast; *three'pence* (thrĕp-, thrĭp-, thrŭp-), sum of 3 pence; *threepenny* (pr. as prec.) *adj.*), *threepenny bit*, former coin of Britain, worth threepence; ~-*ply*, having, woven with, three strands (of thread, yarn, etc.); (plywood) composed of 3 layers of wood; ~-*point landing*, landing of aircraft so that landing-wheels or floats and tail-skid or wheel touch ground etc. simultaneously; ~-*point turn*, forward–reverse–forward manœuvre to turn vehicle; ~-*quarter*, (of portraits) showing figure down to hips or knees; (Rugby footb. etc.) player with position between half-back and full-back; *the ~ R's*, reading, (w)riting, (a)rithmetic, regarded as fundamentals of education; basic knowledge in any field; *three'some*, (game etc., esp. golf) in which 3 persons take part. **three'fold** *adj. & adv.* ~ *n.* One more than two; symbol for this (3, iii, or III); card, die-face, or domino with 3 pips; 3 o'clock; size etc. indicated by 3; set of 3 things or persons; hit at cricket for 3 runs.
thrĕ'nōde, thrĕ'nody *ns.* Song

THROB

of lamentation, esp. for death, dirge. **thrĕnō'dial, thrĕnŏ'dic** *adjs.* **thrĕ'nodist** *n.*
thrĕsh *v.t.* Beat out or separate grain from (corn etc.) on *threshing floor* (prepared hard level for the purpose) or in *threshing machine*.
thrĕ'shōld (or -sh-h-) *n.* Piece of stone, timber, etc., lying below bottom of doorway; entrance; (fig.) point at which stimulus begins to produce its effect.
thrīce *adv.* (archaic or literary) Three times.
thrift *n.* 1. Frugality, economical management. 2. Plant of genus *Armeria*, esp. *A. maritima* (sea pink), sea-shore and alpine plant with pink, white, or purple flowers on naked stems rising from tuft of grass-like radical leaves. **thri'ftless** *adj.* **thri'ftlessly** *adv.* **thri'ftlessness** *n.* **thri'fty** *adj.* **thri'ftily** *adv.* **thri'ftiness** *n.*
thrill *n.* Nervous tremor caused by intense emotion or sensation, wave of feeling or excitement; sensational quality (of story etc.). ~ *v.* Penetrate with wave of emotion or sensation, be thus penetrated or agitated; (of emotion etc.) pass *through*, *over*, etc.; quiver, throb, (as) with emotion. **thri'ller** *n.* (esp.) Sensational play, story, etc. **thri'lling** *adj.* **thri'llingly** *adv.* **thri'llingness** *n.*
thrips *n.* Any minute insect, with four hair-fringed wings, of order Thysanoptera, many of which injure plants by feeding on their juices.

THRIPS

thrīve *v.i.* (past t. *thrōve* or *thrīved*, past part. *thri'ven* or *thrīved*). Grow or develop well and vigorously, flourish; prosper; grow rich.
thro', thrō (-ōō) *prep. & adv.* = THROUGH.
throat *n.* 1. Front of neck between chin and collar-bone, region containing gullet and wind-pipe; narrow passage, esp. in or near entrance of something, narrow part in a passage; *sore* ~, inflammation of lining membrane of gullet etc.; ~ *lash*, strap of bridle passing under horse's throat (ill. SADDLERY). 2. Forward upper corner of fore-and-aft sail (ill. SAIL[1]). ~ *v.t.* Groove, channel.
throa'ty *adj.* Guttural, uttered in the throat, hoarse. **throa'tily** *adv.* **throa'tiness** *n.*
thrŏb *v.i.* (of heart etc.) Beat strongly, palpitate, pulsate, vibrate. ~ *n.* Throbbing, violent beat or pulsation.

[912]

throe n. (usu. pl.) Violent pang(s); desperate or agonizing struggle, anguish.

thrŏmbō′sis n. (pl. -sēs). Localized clotting of blood within the heart or blood-vessels. **thrŏmbō′tic** adj.

thrŏ′mbus n. Blood-clot formed within vascular system which may impede circulation.

throne n. Chair of state for sovereign, bishop, etc., usu. decorated and raised on dais; sovereign power; seat for painter's model; (pl.) order of angels (see ANGEL). ~ v.t. Enthrone.

throng n. Crowd, multitude (of) esp. in small space. ~ v. Come, go, press, in multitudes; fill with crowd or as crowd does.

thrŏ′stle (-sl) n. 1. (literary or dial.) Thrush, esp. song-thrush. 2. Machine for spinning wool, cotton, etc., in which the processes of drawing, twisting, and winding are continuous.

thrŏ′ttle n. 1. Throat. 2. Valve controlling flow of steam in steam-engine or of fuel in internal combustion engine. ~ v.t. 1. Choke, strangle. 2. Control, obstruct, flow of (steam, fuel, etc.) in engine, esp. with throttle; (also ~ down) slow down (engine) thus.

through (-ōō) prep. From end to end or side to side of, between the sides, walls, parts, etc., of; from beginning to end of; by reason of, by agency, means, or fault of; (U.S.) up to and including. ~ adv. Through something; from end to end; to the end; ~ and ~, all the way through, completely, utterly; be, get, ~ (with), finish (with), come to end (of). ~ adj. Going, concerned with going, through; (of railway or other travelling) going all the way without change of train, line, etc.

throughou′t (-rōō-owt) prep. From end to end of; in every part of. ~ adv. In every part or respect.

throw (-ō) v. (past t. threw pr. -ōō, past part. thrown pr. -ōn). 1. Turn (wood etc.) in lathe, shape (pottery) on wheel; prepare and twist (silk etc.) into threads. 2. Project (thing) from hand or arm with jerking motion, esp. with sudden straightening of arm near shoulder-level, so that it passes through air or free space; (of gun etc.) shoot; cast, make specified cast, (with) dice; move (esp. part of the body) quickly or suddenly. 3. (of wrestler, horse, etc.) Bring (antagonist, rider) to the ground; (of snake) cast (skin); (of animals) bring forth (young). 4. Put carelessly or hastily on, off, etc. 5. (slang) Give (a party). 6. ~ away, (fig.) squander, waste; lose (chance etc.) by neglect; discard (card) when one cannot follow suit; ~-away (n.) printed paper, hand-bill, etc., not intended to be kept; ~ back, revert to ancestral type or character; ~-back (n.) such reversion, example of this; ~ in, add (thing) to bargain without extra charge; interpose (word, remark) in parenthesis or casually; ~ in one's hand, give up, withdraw from contest; ~ in one's lot with, decide to share fortunes of; ~-in (n.) (footb.) act of throwing in ball after it has gone out of play; ~ off, discard; get rid of; abandon (disguise); produce, deliver, in offhand manner; ~ oneself into, participate enthusiastically in; ~ oneself on, place one's reliance on; ~-on, (Rugby footb.) throwing ball forwards; ~ out, cast out; make (projecting or prominent addition to house etc.); suggest, insinuate; reject (bill in Parliament); eject; disturb, distract (person) from train of thought etc.; (cricket) put (batsman) out by throwing ball so as to hit his wicket; ~ over, desert, abandon; ~ up, vomit; resign (office); raise (hands, eyes, etc.) quickly or suddenly; ~ up the sponge, give in, confess oneself beaten. ~ n. 1. Throwing, cast; cast of dice; distance missile is or may be thrown; fall in wrestling; (geol., mining) (amount of vertical displacement caused by) fault in stratum. 2. (Extent of) action or motion of slide-valve, crank, cam, etc.; machine or instrument for imparting rotary motion.

throw′er (-ōer) n. One who throws; apparatus for throwing a depth charge.

throw′ster (-rō-) n. One who throws silk.

thrŭm¹ n. Fringe of warp-threads remaining on loom when web has been cut off, single thread of this; any loose thread or tuft.

thrŭm² v. Strum; sound monotonously, hum. ~ n. (Sound of) thrumming.

thrush¹ n. Small or medium-sized passerine bird of family Turdidae, esp. the European song-thrush, throstle, or mavis (Turdus philomelos) and the larger and less musical missel-thrush.

thrush² n. 1. Disease, esp. of infants, characterized by whitish vesicular specks on inside of mouth and throat etc. and caused by fungi of genus Candida. 2. Inflammatory suppurative disease of foot in animals, esp. of frog of horse.

thrust v. (past t. & past part. thrŭst). Push, drive, exert force of impact on or against; pierce through; make sudden push at with pointed weapon; force oneself through, past, etc., make way thus. ~ n. Thrusting, lunge, stab; (mech. etc.) thrusting force of one part of structure etc. on contiguous part, esp. horizontal or diagonal pressure of part of building against abutment or support, driving force exerted by paddle, propeller-shaft, or jet-stream in ship or aircraft, (effect of) compressive strain in earth's crust.

thrŭ′ster n. (esp.) One who pushes forward in hunting-field or rides too close to hounds; pusher.

Thūcy̆′dĭdēs (-z) (5th c. B.C.). Athenian historian of the Peloponnesian War.

thŭd n. & v.i. (Make, fall with) low dull sound as of blow on soft thing.

thŭġ n. Vicious ruffian; T~, (hist.) member of an association in India (suppressed 1830–40) of professional robbers and murderers, strangling their victims. **thŭ′ġġery** (-g-) n. **Thŭ′ġġee** (-gē) n. (hist.) Practice of Thugs.

thū′ja, thū′ya n. Tree or shrub of coniferous genus T~ (Arbor Vitae) including the N. Amer. (T. occidentalis) and Chinese (T. orientalis) varieties.

Thū′lē. Ancient Greek and Latin name of country 6 days' sail N. of Britain, supposed to be most northerly region in world; ū′ltĭma ~, highest or uttermost point or degree.

thū′lium n. (chem.) Rare metallic element found in combination in some rare earths; symbol Tm, at. no. 69, at. wt 168·9342. [f. THULE]

thŭmb (-m) n. Short thick inner digit, opposable to fingers, and with only two phalanges, of human hand; any inner digit opposable to and set apart from other digits; part of glove etc. covering thumb; ~s up! exhortation to cheerfulness or expression of satisfaction; rule of ~: see RULE; under one's ~, under influence or domination of; ~-index, reference-index consisting of grooves cut in, or tabs projecting from front edges of book, or margins so cut as to show initial letters or titles etc.; ~-mark, mark left on surface by (dirty) thumb; ~-nail, nail of thumb; ~-nail sketch, small or hasty portrait, brief word-picture; ~-print, impression of inner surface of top joint of thumb; thu′mbscrew, screw with flattened or winged head that may be turned with thumb and fingers; instrument of torture for compressing thumb(s); ~-tack, drawing-pin. **thŭ′mbless** adj. **thŭmb** v.t. Soil, wear, with thumb; handle with thumb or awkwardly or clumsily; make a request for (a ride in a vehicle) by sticking out a thumb in the direction one wishes to go.

Thŭ′mmĭm n.: see URIM. [Heb., = 'perfections']

thŭmp n. Heavy blow, bang; sound of this. ~ v. Beat heavily, esp. with fist; deliver heavy blows (at, on, etc.). **thŭ′mpĭnġ** adj. (esp., colloq.) Very large, striking, impressive. **thŭ′mper** n. (esp., colloq.) Large, striking, or impressive person or thing, esp. lie.

thŭ′nder n. Loud noise accompanying lightning (but appearing to follow it because of difference in speeds of light and sound) and due to sudden violent disturbance

[913]

of air by the electric discharge; any loud deep rumbling or resounding noise; terrifying, threatening, or impressive utterance(s); thu′nderbolt, imaginary bolt or dart formerly supposed to be the destructive agent when thing is struck by lightning, esp. as attribute of Thor, Jupiter, etc.; conventional representation of this; something very startling, terrible, or destructive; ~-clap, loud crash of thunder; ~-cloud, storm-cloud charged with electricity and producing thunder and lightning; ~-head, rounded cumulus cloud near horizon projecting above general body of cloud and portending thunder; ~-storm, storm with thunder and lightning; thu′nderstruck, (fig.) amazed, terrified, confounded. thŭ′nderlèss, thŭ′nderous, thŭ′nderў adjs. thŭ′nder v. 1. it ~s, it is thundering, there is thunder. 2. Sound with or like thunder; emit (threats etc.) in loud or impressive manner; fulminate. thŭ′nderer n. (esp., T~) Jupiter; (joc.) 'The Times' newspaper. thŭ′ndering adj. & adv. (esp., colloq.) Unusual(ly), decided(ly).
Thūr′ber, James (1894–1961). U.S. writer and illustrator.
thūr′ible n. Censer.
Thūri′ngia (-j-). (Ger. Thüringen) Region of central Germany. Thūri′ngian adj. & n. (Native, inhabitant) of Thuringia; (member) of an ancient tribe of central Germany conquered by Franks in 6th c.
Thurs. abbrev. Thursday.
Thūr′sday (-z-; or -dī) n. 5th day of the week; Holy ~: see HOLY. [OE thur(e)sdæg Thor's day, rendering LL dies Jovis day of Jupiter]
thŭs (dh-) adv. In this way, like this, as follows; accordingly, consequently, and so; to this extent, number, or degree. thŭ′snèss n. (colloq. & usu. joc.).
thuya: see THUJA.
thwăck n. & v.t. = WHACK.
thwart (-ôrt) n. Seat across boat, on which rower sits (ill. BOAT). ~ adv. & adj. (Lying) athwart. ~ prep. Athwart; ~-ship (adj.), -ships (adv.), (lying) across ship. ~ v.t. Frustrate, cross.
T.H.W.M. abbrev. Trinity high-water mark.
thy (dhī) poss. pron. Possessive case of THOU used as attrib. adj. with abs. and pred. form (also used before initial vowel and silent 'h') thine, belonging to, affecting, thee.
Thyĕ′stēs (-z). (Gk legend) Brother of ATREUS. Thyĕ′stēan adj.
thy̆′lacīne n. Tasmanian wolf, Thylacinus cynocephalus, a carnivorous marsupial resembling a dog in appearance, greyish-brown with conspicuous black markings on the hinder half of the back.

thyme (tīm) n. Shrubby herb of genus Thymus with fragrant aromatic leaves, chiefly of Mediterranean regions, esp. garden ~ (T. vulgaris), native of Spain and Italy, cultivated as pot-herb, and wild ~ (T. serpyllum), occurring on dry banks etc. throughout Europe.
thȳ′mic adj. Of the thymus.
thȳ′mol (or tī-) n. (chem.) White crystalline phenol obtained from oil of thyme, having pleasant aromatic smell and used as antiseptic.
thȳ′mus n. (pl. -mī). (anat.) Ductless glandular body (of uncertain function) situated near base of neck in vertebrates, in man disappearing or diminishing after childhood.
thȳ′roid adj. (anat.) Of the thyroid gland; ~ cartilage, large cartilage of the larynx consisting of two broad plates united in front at an angle, forming the 'Adam's apple'; ~ gland, large ductless gland lying near larynx and upper trachea in vertebrates and influencing growth and development, so called because of its proximity to the thyroid cartilage (ill. GLAND¹). ~ n. Thyroid gland; extract prepared from thyroid gland of some animals, used in treating goitre, cretinism, etc.
thȳrō′xin, -ine n. (chem.) White crystalline active principle of thyroid gland.
thyr′sus (-êr-) n. (pl. -sī). 1. (Gk antiq.) Staff tipped with ornament like pine-cone, attribute of Dionysus. 2. (bot.) Kind of inflorescence in which primary axis is racemose and secondary etc. cymose, as in lilac and horse-chestnut.
thysĕ′lf (dh-) pron. Emphatic and reflexive form corresponding to THOU, THEE.
ti (tē) n. Var. of TE.
tiar′a n. Ancient Persian form of head-dress; official head-dress of the pope, consisting of a high pointed cap encircled by three crowns, symbolic of the temporal, spiritual, and purgatorial sovereignty claimed by the papacy; papal office; jewelled coronet worn by women.
Tī′ber. River of central Italy flowing from Tuscan Appenines through Rome to Mediterranean Sea at Ostia.
Tibēr′iăs. Ancient town (built by Herod Antipas c A.D. 21 and named after Tiberius) on W. shore of Sea of Galilee.
Tibēr′ius. Tiberius Claudius Nero (42 B.C.–A.D. 37), Roman emperor A.D. 14–37.
Tibĕ′t, Th- (tī-). Mountainous country of central Asia, an autonomous region of China since 1965; capital, Lhasa. Tibĕ′tan, Th- adj. & n. (Native, inhabitant) of Tibet; (of) its language, allied to Burmese.
ti′bia n. (anat.) Inner and usu.

larger of two bones of lower leg, from knee to ankle, shin-bone (ill. SKELETON); tibiotarsus of birds; (entom.) fourth segment of insect's leg, between femur and tarsus. ti′bial adj.
tibiotâr′sus n. Tibia of birds, fused at lower end with some bones of tarsus.
Tibŭ′llus, Albius (c 50–19 B.C.). Latin elegiac poet.
tic n. Habitual local spasmodic contraction of muscles, esp. of face; (also ~ douloureux pr. dōōlerêr) trigeminal neuralgia, severe facial neuralgia with twitching of facial muscles.
Tī′chborne claī′mant. Arthur Orton (1834–98), a butcher, who came from Australia with claim to be Roger Charles Tichborne (1829–54), eldest son of 10th baronet, lost at sea; after a long trial (1871) Orton's ejectment action against the trustees of the Tichborne estates was lost, and he was found guilty of perjury.
tick¹ n. Any of several large blood-sucking mites of the order Acarina infesting hair or fur of various animals; similar parasitic dipterous insect (e.g. Melophagus) infesting birds, sheep, etc.
tick² n. Case of mattress, pillow, or bolster. ti′cking n. Strong hard linen or cotton material for making ticks.
tick³ n. 1. Quick light dry recurring sound, distinct but not loud, esp. of alternate check and release of train in escapement of clock or watch; (colloq.) time between two ticks of clock, moment, instant. 2. Small mark (√) set against items in list etc. in checking. ~ v. Mark (off item etc.) with tick; make ticking sound; wear away, out, etc., in ticking, (of tape-machine) throw off, out (message by ticking); what makes (person) ~, motivation; ~ off, (slang) reprimand; ~ over, (of internal combustion engines) run slowly with gears disconnected (also fig.).
tick⁴ n. (colloq.) Credit. [abbrev. of TICKET]
ti′cker n. (esp., colloq.) Watch; telegraphic tape-machine; (joc.) heart.
ti′ckèt n. Written notice for public information, esp. label, show-card; slip, usu. of paper or cardboard, bearing evidence of holder's title to some service or privilege, as railway journey, seat at entertainment, etc.; certificate of qualifications of pilot, ship's mate, or captain, etc.; pay-warrant, esp. discharge warrant of soldier etc.; ticket of leave; (U.S.) list of candidates of one party or group put forward for election; hence, (fig.) principles of a party; the ~, (slang) what is wanted, expected, etc.; ~-card, thick paper used for show-cards; ~-collector, railway official who takes or checks passengers' tickets; ~ of leave, licence giving convict his liberty, under

[914]

certain restrictions, before sentence has expired; ~-**punch**, tool for punching holes in tickets to show that they have been used. ~ *v.t.* Put ticket on (article for sale etc.).

ti′ckle *n.* Act, sensation, of tickling. ~ *v.* Touch or stroke (person, part of his body) lightly with finger-tips, feather, etc., so as to excite nerves and usu. produce laughter; cause or feel peculiar uneasy sensation as of being tickled; excite agreeably, amuse, divert; catch (trout etc.) by stroking lightly with hand.

ti′cklish *adj.* Easily tickled, sensitive to tickling; (of question etc.) difficult, critical, delicate, requiring careful handling. **ti′cklishly** *adv.* **ti′cklishness** *n.*

ti′ck-tă′ck *adv.* With repetitive sound as of ticking. ~ *n.* 1. Ticking sound. 2. System of signalling with arms etc. used by men employed by bookmakers at race-meetings.

ti′ck-tŏ′ck *adv. & n.* (With) repetitive sound as of a clock ticking.

t.i.d. *abbrev. Ter in die* (L, = 'three times a day', in medical prescriptions).

ti′dal *adj.* Of tides; (of motor traffic) running in opposite directions at different times of day; ~ *air*, (physiol.) volume of air breathed in and out of lungs during a normal respiration; ~ *river*, river affected by tides to some distance from mouth; ~ *stream*, horizontal water movement caused by tide-generating forces; ~ *wave*, wave caused by movement of tide; (pop.) exceptionally large ocean wave or very high water sometimes following earthquake or other local commotion; (fig.) widespread manifestation of feeling etc.

tidbit : see TITBIT.

ti′ddler *n.* Very small fish, esp. stickleback or minnow; (colloq.) very small thing.

ti′ddlywinks *n.* Game in which small counters are flipped across table into receptacle.

tīde *n.* 1. Time, season (archaic exc. in *Whitsuntide, Shrovetide*, etc.). 2. Flowing or swelling of sea, or its alternate rising (*flood-*~) and falling (*ebb* ~), twice in each lunar day, due to the attraction of moon (and sun); (fig.) something like a tide in ebbing and flowing, turning, etc.; flood-tide; *high, low* ~, completion of the flood, ebb, tide; NEAP, SPRING, ~: see these words; ~-*gate*, gate through which water passes into dock etc. at flood, and by which it is retained during ebb; ~-*lock*, double lock between tidal water and canal, basin, etc., beyond it; ~-*mark*, mark made by tide at high water; (colloq.) line between clean and dirty parts of body after partial wash; ~-*rip*, rough water caused by opposing tides; ~-*waiter*, (hist.) customs officer boarding ships to enforce customs regulations; *ti′dewater*, water affected by ebb and flow of tides; (U.S.) coastal land affected by tide; *ti′deway*, channel in which tidal current runs, tidal part of river. **ti′deless** *adj.* **tīde** *v.* 1. Drift with tide, esp. use tide to work in or out of harbour. 2. ~ *over*, (enable or assist to) get through difficult time, surmount difficulty, etc.

ti′dings (-z) *n.pl.* (now chiefly literary) (Piece of) news.

ti′dy *adj.* Neatly arranged, neat, orderly; (colloq.) pretty large, considerable. ~ *n.* Ornamental loose covering for chair-back etc.; receptacle for odds and ends. ~ *v.t.* Make neat, put in good order. **ti′dily** *adv.* **ti′diness** *n.*

tīe *v.* 1. Attach, fasten, with cord etc.; secure (shoe etc.) by tightening and knotting lace etc.; form into knot or bow; bind (rafters etc.) by cross-piece etc.; (mus.) unite (notes) by tie; restrict, bind (person etc.); ~ *up*, restrict, esp. annex conditions to (bequest etc.) to prevent its being sold or diverted from its purpose. 2. Make same score as (person) in game etc.; be equal in score *with.* ~ *n.* 1. Cord, chain, etc., used for fastening. 2. Neck-tie; fur necklet. 3. Rod, beam, etc., holding parts of structure together; (U.S.) railway sleeper. 4. (mus.) Curved line placed over or under two notes to indicate that sound is to be sustained, not repeated (ill. STAVE). 5. (elect.) Circuit or land-line coupling two electrical systems, power stations, etc. 6. (fig.) Thing that connects or unites in some way, link, bond. 7. Equality of score between competitors or sides in match or contest, drawn match; deciding match played after draw, match between victors in previous matches or heats; match between any pair of several competing players or teams. 8. ~-*bar*, metal rod holding parts of building together; ~-*beam*, horizontal beam connecting rafters (ill. ROOF); ~-*pin*, ornamental pin worn in neck-tie; ~-*up*, link; obstructed situation, standstill, esp. (U.S.) obstruction of traffic on railway etc. caused by strike, breakdown, etc.; ~-*wig*, wig with hair tied in knot behind.

Tieck, Ludwig (1773–1853). German Romantic poet and novelist.

tied (tīd) *adj.* (esp., of inn or public house) Of which the tenant is bound to take liquor from a particular brewing firm (opp. FREE house); (of dwelling house etc.) of which the tenant must work for the owner; (of foreign aid) that must be spent in the donor country.

Tie′polō (tyăp-), Giovanni Battista (1696–1770). Venetian painter.

tier *n.* Row, rank, esp. one of several placed one above another as in theatre. ~ *v.t.* Arrange or pile in tiers.

tierce *n.* T~, (R.C. Ch.) canonical HOUR, (orig. said at) third hour of day (9 a.m.). 2. Position in fencing, 3rd of eight parries, or corresponding thrust, in sword-play (ill. FENCE). 3. (mus.) Interval of two octaves and a major third (= major 17th) above fundamental note; organ-stop giving tones at this interval. 4. (hist.) Measure of capacity, one-third of pipe; cask or vessel holding this quantity.

Tiĕ′rra dĕl Fue′gō (fwā-). (Main island of) archipelago at S. point of S. America, discovered 1520 by Magellan; divided between Chile and Argentina.

tiers état (tyārz ātah). (Fr. hist.) Third ESTATE. [Fr.]

tiff *n.* (colloq.) Slight or petty quarrel. ~ *v.i.* Have a tiff.

ti′ffany *n.* (archaic) Kind of thin transparent silk or muslin. [OF *tifanie* theophany, i.e. Epiphany (because orig. worn on Twelfth Night)]

ti′ffin *n. & v.i.* (Ind.) (Take) light meal, lunch. [app. f. obs. *tiff* drink, sip]

tī′ger (-g-) *n.* 1. Large Asiatic carnivorous feline quadruped (*Panthera tigris*), maneless, of tawny-yellow colour with blackish transverse stripes and white belly, proverbial for ferocity and cunning. 2. Any of various other feline animals, esp. (in America) the jaguar and puma, and (in S. Africa) the leopard. 3. Fierce, cruel, or rapacious person or animal; formidable opponent in a game (opp. *rabbit*). 4. (obs., slang) Smartly liveried boy groom accompanying master in light vehicle. 5. (U.S. slang) Loud yell at end of burst of cheering. 6. ~-*beetle*, active carnivorous voracious beetle of family Cicindelidae; ~ *cat*, any of various moderate-sized feline beasts resembling tiger in markings etc.; (Austral.) carnivorous marsupial (*Dasyurus quoll*); ~('s)-*eye*, yellowish-brown quartz with brilliant lustre, used as gem; (U.S.) kind of crystalline pottery glaze resembling this; ~-*lily*, tall garden lily (*Lilium tigrinum*) of Asiatic origin with orange flowers spotted with black; ~-*moth*, moth of family Arctiidae, esp. *Arctia caja*, large scarlet-and-brown British species spotted and streaked with white; ~-*shark*, any of various large voracious spotted or streaked sharks, esp. *Galeocerdo cuvier*; ~-*wood*, wood from a tree native to Guiana, used in cabinet-making.

tī′gress *n.* Female tiger.

tī′gerish (-g-) *adj.* Like, cruel as, a tiger. **tī′gerishly** *adv.* **tī′gerishness** *n.*

tight (tīt) *adj.* 1. Close-textured, firmly constructed, so as to be impervious to fluid etc. 2. Closely held, drawn, fastened, fitting, etc.;

[915]

tense, taut, stretched so as to leave no slack; neat, trim, compact. 3. Produced by, requiring, great exertion or pressure; (colloq., of person) close-fisted, (of money) difficult to obtain. 4. (slang) Drunk. 5. ~-*fisted*, stingy, close-fisted; ~-*rope*, tightly stretched rope, wire, etc., on which acrobats and rope-dancers perform; ti′ghtwad, (U.S. slang) tight-fisted person. ~ *adv.* Tightly; ~-*laced*, having laces drawn tight, wearing tightly laced stays; (fig.) strait-laced. ti′ghten *v.* ti′ghtly *adv.* ti′ghtnĕss *n.* tights *n.pl.* 1. (also *pair of* ~) Closely fitting garment covering legs, feet, and lower part of body. 2. Leotard with legs and feet.

Ti′gris. River of E. Mesopotamia, joining Euphrates to form Shatt al Arab, which flows into the Persian Gulf.

T.I.H. *abbrev.* Their Imperial Highnesses.

ti′ki (tē-) *n.* (New Zealand) Maori large wooden or small ornamental greenstone image of creator of man or an ancestor.

ti′lburў *n.* Light open two-wheeled carriage fashionable in

TILBURY

first half of 19th c. [inventor's name]

Ti′lburў Dŏcks. Large passenger and goods docks on N. shore of Thames 26 miles below London Bridge.

ti′lde (-e) *n.* Diacritical mark (˜) placed in Spanish over *n* to indicate palatalized sound (ny) and in Portuguese over *a* and *o* to indicate nasal sound; swung dash.

tile *n.* 1. Thin slab of baked clay for covering roof (ill. ROOF), paving floor, lining wall, fireplace, etc., or making drains etc.; material of this, burnt clay; tiles collectively. 2. Decorated piece used in mah-jongg. 3. (slang) Hat, esp. silk hat. ~ *v.t.* Cover, line, with tiles; (freemasonry, usu. *tyle*) protect (lodge, meeting) from intrusion or interruption. ti′ler *n.* Tile-layer; (freemasonry, usu. *tyler*) door-keeper at lodge or meeting.

ti′le-fish *n.* Large deep-water yellow-spotted food-fish (*Lopholatilus chamaeleonticeps*), of coasts of New England etc.

till¹ *n.* Money-drawer, -box, etc., in bank, shop, etc.

till² *n.* Boulder-clay, stiff unstratified clay mixed with sand, gravel, and boulders.

till³ *v.t.* Labour upon (land) in order to produce crops. ti′llage, ti′ller¹ *ns.*

till⁴ *prep.* Up to, as late as. ~ *conj.* To the time that; up to (the point) when.

ti′ller² *n.* Shoot of plant springing from bottom of original stalk; sapling; sucker.

ti′ller³ *n.* Horizontal bar fixed to rudder head and acting as lever for steering (ill. BOAT).

ti′llite *n.* Rock composed of consolidated TILL².

tilt¹ *n.* Covering or awning of canvas etc. esp. for cart (ill. WAGON). ~ *v.t.* Furnish with tilt.

tilt² *v.* 1. (Cause to) incline abruptly from vertical or horizontal, (cause to) assume sloping or slanting position, heel over; (geol., pass., of strata) be inclined. 2. Engage in tilt; strike, thrust, run, *at*, with weapon. 3. Forge, work, with tilt-hammer. ~ *n.* 1. Tilting, sloping position. 2. Joust, combat between two armed men on horseback each trying to throw opponent from saddle with lance; *full* ~, at full speed, with full force or impetus; ~-*yard*, enclosed place for tilting, tilting-ground. 3. (also ~-*hammer*) Heavy forging hammer, fixed on pivot and alternately tilted up and dropped by action of cam-wheel or eccentric.

tilth *n.* Tillage, cultivation, husbandry; depth of soil dug or cultivated.

Tim. *abbrev.* Timothy (N.T.).

ti′mbal, tў′mbal *n.* (archaic or hist.) Kettledrum. [Fr. *timbale*, earlier *attabale*, f. Arab. *al ṭabl* the drum]

timbale (tăṅbahl) *n.* Dish of minced meat, fish, etc., cooked in drum-shaped mould of pastry etc. [Fr.]

ti′mber *n.* Wood prepared for building etc.; trees suitable for this; piece of wood, beam, esp. (naut.) any curved piece forming ribs of vessel (ill. BOAT); *standing* ~, trees, woods; ~-*wolf*, large grey wolf of northern N. America. ~ *v.t.* Support (roof of mine or working, sides and roof of tunnel, etc.) with timber. ti′mbered (-erd) *adj.* Made of timber or wood; wooded. ti′mbering *n.*

timbre (tăṅbr) *n.* Distinctive quality of musical or vocal sound depending on voice or instrument producing it, tone colour. [Fr., = 'clock-bell', 'drum', f. L *tympanum*]

ti′mbrel *n.* (chiefly bibl.) Tambourine or the like. [f. TIMBRE]

Tĭmbŭktu′ (-ōō). Town in central Mali near the Niger river; (pop. *Timbuctoo*) very remote place.

time *n.* 1. Indefinite continuous duration regarded as dimension in which sequence of events takes place (freq. personified, (*Father*) *T*~, esp. as old man with scythe and hourglass); finite duration as dist. from eternity; more or less definite portion of this associated with particular events or circumstances, historical or other period; (freq. pl.) conditions of life, prevailing circumstances, of a period; allotted or available portion of time, time at one's disposal; moment or definite portion of time destined or suitable for a purpose etc., esp. period of gestation, term of imprisonment, term of apprenticeship, length of round in boxing, part of football or other game, time to begin or end this; point of time; season; occasion; (payment for) amount of time worked; (amount of) time as reckoned by conventional standards; STANDARD ~, SUMMER-~: see these words; *a good* ~, period of enjoyment. 2. (mus.) Rhythm or measure of musical composition, marked by division into bars and denoted by ~ *signature*, usu. fraction showing number of aliquot parts of semibreve in each bar; tempo. 3. (pl.) Preceded by numeral and followed by number or expression of quantity etc., expressing multiplication, comparison, etc. 4. *all the* ~, during the whole time referred to; (U.S.) at all times; *at the same* ~, simultaneously; all the same; *at* ~*s*, now and then; *from* ~ *to* ~, occasionally; *in* ~, not late; early enough; eventually, sooner or later; following the time of music etc.; *in no* ~, rapidly, in a moment; ~ *of day*, hour by the clock; *pass the* ~ *of day*, engage in casual conversation. 5. ~ *and motion study*, systematic investigation of working methods in order to increase efficiency and establish standards; ~-*bomb*, bomb with time-fuse or other device so adjusted that it will explode after a predetermined interval, delayed-action bomb; ~-*card*, card with record of time worked; ~-*clock*, clock with device recording times, e.g. of arrival and departure of workmen etc.; ~-*constant*, mathematical expression giving indication of delay involved in heating, charging, moving, etc., when the process produces an opposing effect proportional to the temperature, charge, speed, etc.; ~-*exposure*, (photog.) exposure for regulated length of time, as dist. from instantaneous exposure; ~-*fuse*: see FUSE²; ~-*honoured*, respected on account of its antiquity; ~-*keeper*, watch, clock, esp. in ref. to accuracy; one who records time, esp. of workmen; ~-*lag*, interval of time between cause etc. and result or consequence; *ti′mepiece*, instrument for measuring time, chronometer; ~-*server*, opportunist; ~-*serving*, opportunism; ~-*sheet*, sheet of paper recording hours worked by employee(s) etc.; ~-*signal*, visible or audible signal, esp. radio signal, announcing the time of day; ~ *signature*, see sense 2; *ti′metable*, tabular list or

[916]

schedule of times of classes in school etc., arrival and departure of trains, boats, etc.; ~ *zone*, one of 24 regions, each bounded by two lines of longitude 15° apart, adopting as standard the mean solar time of the meridian in it distant from Greenwich a complete number of hours. ~ *v.* Choose the time for, do at chosen time; record time of event, duration of action, etc., keep time, harmonize (*with*).
ti′melĕss (-ml-) *adj.* Unending, eternal; not subject to time. ti′melĕsslў *adv.* ti′melĕssnĕss *n.*
ti′melў (-mlĭ) *adj.* Seasonable, opportune. ti′melinĕss *n.*
ti′meous (-m*u*s) *adj.* (chiefly Sc.) Timely.
ti′mid *adj.* Easily alarmed; shy. ti′mĭdlў *adv.* ti′mĭdnĕss, timĭ′dĭtў *ns.*
timŏ′cracў *n.* 1. In the Aristotelian sense: a polity with a property qualification for office. 2. In the Platonic sense: a polity (like that of Sparta) in which love of honour is said to be the dominant motive among the rulers. timocrăt′ic, -ical *adjs.*
timŏ′logў *n.* (philos.) Doctrine of values.
Tī′mon (5th c. B.C.). Athenian who became a misanthrope owing to the ingratitude of his friends.
Tī′mor (tē-). Island in southern Malay Archipelago; divided between Portugal and Indonesia. ~ *Sea*, part of Indian Ocean lying between Timor and NW. Australia.
ti′morous *adj.* Timid. ti′morouslў *adv.* ti′morousnĕss *n.*
Tĭ′mothў[1]. Convert and colleague of St. Paul; either of two Pauline epistles of N.T. addressed to him.
ti′mothў[2] *n.* (also ~ *grass*) Meadow grass (*Phleum pratense*), European grass with long cylindrical spikes, introduced into N. America from England for cultivation for hay in 18th c. [said to be f. *Timothy* Hanson, who introduced it into Carolina *c* 1720]
timpani : see TYMPANI.
Timur Lenk, Lang : see TAMBURLAINE.
tin *n.* 1. (chem.) Metallic element nearly approaching silver in whiteness, highly malleable, and taking a high polish, used in the manufacture of alloys as bronze, pewter, etc., and, on account of its resistance to oxidation, for making tinplate and lining culinary and other iron vessels; symbol Sn, at. no. 50, at. wt 118·69. 2. Vessel made of tin, or more usu. tinned iron, esp. a vessel in which meat, fish, fruit, etc., is hermetically sealed for preservation; tinplate, as the material of such vessels. 3. (slang) Money, cash. 4. (attrib. or as *adj.*) ti′nfoil, tin hammered or rolled into a thin sheet; sheet of this rubbed with mercury, formerly used for backing mirrors and precious stones; similar sheet of an alloy of tin and lead used for wrapping and packing; (*v.t.*) cover, coat, with tinfoil; ~ *god*, (fig.) base or unworthy object of veneration; ~ *hat*, (mil. slang) steel helmet; *T*~ *Lizzie*, nickname for a small cheap (orig. Ford) motor-car; ~-*opener*, instrument for opening hermetically sealed tins; *T*~ *Pan Alley*, world of composers, publishers, etc., of popular music; *tinplate*, sheet-iron or sheet-steel coated with tin; ~-*pot*, pot made of tin or tinplate; (attrib.) resembling or suggesting a tin-pot in quality or sound; hence contempt., of inferior quality; trivial; *ti′nsmith*, worker in tin, maker of tin utensils; ~ *soldier*, miniature toy soldier of metal, esp. lead; ~-*stone*, most commonly occurring form of tin ore, cassiterite (SnO$_2$); ~-*tack*, short iron nail coated with tin. ~ *adj.* Of tin; (colloq.) of steel or corrugated iron. ~ *v.t.* Cover, coat, with tin; pack (meat, fruit, etc.) in tins for preservation.
ti′namou (-ōō) *n.* S. American bird of the family Tinamidae, resembling grouse but related to rheas.
ti′ncal, ti′nkal *n.* Crude borax, found in lake-deposits in parts of Asia.
tinctōr′ial *adj.* Of, used in, dyeing; yielding, using, dye or colouring matter.
ti′ncture *n.* 1. (her.) Colour or metal used in coat of arms etc. (ill. HERALDRY). 2. Solution, usu. in alcohol or alcohol and ether, of medicinal substance or principle. 3. Slight flavour, spice, smack; smattering; tinge. ~ *v.t.* Colour slightly; tinge, flavour; affect slightly.
ti′nder *n.* Any dry inflammable substance readily taking fire from spark, esp. that formerly used in ~-*box* to catch spark from flint and steel for kindling fire etc. ti′ndery *adj.*
tine *n.* Prong, projecting sharp point of harrow, fork, etc. (ill. HARROW); pointed branch of deer's antler (ill. DEER).
ti′nĕa *n.* (path.) Ringworm.
ting *n.* & *v.i.* (Make) tinkling sound.
tinge (-j) *v.t.* Colour slightly, modify tint or colour of; (fig.) qualify, modify, slightly alter tone of. ~ *n.* Tint, slight colouring; flavour, touch.
ti′ngle (-nggl) *n.* & *v.* (Feel, cause) slight pricking or stinging sensation.
tinkal : see TINCAL.
ti′nker *n.* Mender (esp. itinerant) of kettles, pans, etc.; (Scotland and N. Ireland) gipsy; (U.S.) jack-of-all-trades; act of tinkering. ~ *v.* Repair, patch (*up*), roughly; work amateurishly or clumsily *at*, esp. in attempt to repair or improve.

ti′nkle *n.* & *v.* (Make, cause to make) succession of short light sharp ringing sounds, as of small bell.
ti′nner *n.* Tinsmith; one who tins meat, fruit, etc., canner.
tinni′tus *n.* (med.) Noises heard in the ear not due to external stimulation by sound-waves.
ti′nnў *adj.* Of or like tin; having a metallic taste; (of sound) thin and metallic.
ti′nsel *n.* Shining metallic gold- or silver-coloured material used in thin sheets, strips, or threads to give sparkling effect; fabric adorned with tinsel; (fig.) anything having or giving deceptively fine or glittering appearance, gaudy or showy but worthless thing. ti′nsĕllў *adj.* ti′nsel *adj.* Showy, gaudy, cheaply splendid. ~ *v.t.* Adorn with tinsel. [L *scintilla* spark]
tĭnt *n.* Colour, usu. slight or delicate, esp. one of several tones of the same colour; (in painting, esp.) lighter tone of a colour as dist. from *shade*, darker one; (engraving) effect produced by fine lines or dots set more or less closely together so as to produce an even tone. ~ *v.t.* Apply tint to, colour.
Tĭntă′gel. Village on coast of N. Cornwall, with ruins of castle; traditional birthplace of King Arthur.
Tĭ′ntern A′bbey (ă-). Ruins, on River Wye, Gwent, of a Cistercian abbey founded 1131 and dissolved by Henry VIII.
tĭntĭnnăbūlā′tion *n.* Ringing or tinkling of bell(s).
Tĭntorĕ′tto. Jacopo Robusti (1518–94). Venetian painter.
tī′nў *adj.* Very small.
tip[1] *n.* Extremity, end, esp. of small or tapering thing; small piece or part attached to thing to form serviceable end, ferrule, etc.; thin flat brush used for gilding; light horse-shoe for front part of hoof; (*on*) *ti′ptoe*, on the tips of the toes, standing or walking with heels raised from ground; *ti′ptoe* (*v.i.*) walk on tiptoe; ~-*top*, highest point of excellence; first-rate. ~ *v.t.* Furnish with tip.
tip[2] *v.* 1. (Cause to) lean or slant, tilt, topple, esp. with slight effort; overturn, cause to overbalance; discharge (contents of jug, wagon, etc., *out* etc.) thus. 2. Strike or touch lightly; (ninepins etc.) knock down (pin) otherwise than by direct impact of bowl; (slang) forecast as winner, esp. informally; ~ *off*, give private or secret information to; warn informally of danger etc.; ~ *the wink*: see WINK. 3. Give a tip to (see *n.*, sense 4). 4. ~-*and-run*, children's form of cricket in which batsman must run if he hits the ball; (attrib. of raid etc.) marked by hasty attack and immediate withdrawal from the scene; ~-*cat*, small piece of wood tapering at

[917]

both ends, which is struck with stick at one end so as to spring into air, and then knocked to a distance with same stick; game in which this is used; ~-*car*, -*cart*, etc., one pivoted so that its contents can readily be tipped out; ~-*up*, (of seat in theatre etc.) constructed so as to tip up to allow of passage between rows. ~ *n.* 1. Act of tipping or tilting; place where refuse etc. is tipped. 2. Light touch or blow. 3. Piece of useful private or special information given by expert, esp. about horseracing, money-market, etc.; useful hint or idea. 4. Small present of money, esp. for service rendered or expected.

Tipperār′ў. County of Munster, Ireland; song associated with the B.E.F. of 1914, the first words of which were *It's a long way to ~.*

ti′ppet *n.* 1. (hist.) Long narrow band of cloth attached to or forming part of dress, head-dress, or sleeve. 2. Woman's small cape or collar of fur, silk, etc., usu. with two ends hanging in front (hist.); similar garment worn as part of official costume by judges, clergy, etc. (ill. VESTMENT).

Ti′ppett, Sir Michael Kemp (1905–). English composer of orchestral and other works, including an oratorio 'A Child of Our Time' (1940).

ti′pple *v.* Drink strong drink habitually; take (drink) constantly in small quantities. **ti′ppler** *n.*
ti′pple *n.* Strong drink.
ti′pstaff (-ahf) *n.* (Metal-tipped staff as badge of) sheriff's officer.
ti′pster *n.* One who gives tips about races etc.
ti′psў *adj.* (Partly) intoxicated; unsteady, staggering, from effects of drink; ~-*cake*, cake soaked in wine or spirit and served with custard. **ti′psilў** *adv.* **ti′psiness** *n.*
tirā′de (*or* ti-) *n.* Long vehement speech esp. of denunciation or abuse; long declamatory passage. [It. *tirada* volley]
tīre[1] *v.* Make or grow weary.
tired (-īrd) *adj.* Weary (*of*); (slang) lazy. **tīr′edlў** *adv.* **tīr′edness** *n.* **tīr′eless** *adj.* **tīr′elesslў** *adv.* **tīr′elessness** *n.*
tire[2]: see TYRE[1].
tīre[3] *n.* (archaic) Head-dress, attire. ~ *v.t.* Adorn, attire.
Tīrē′sias. (Gk legend) Blind Theban prophet.
tir′esome (-īrs-) *adj.* Tending to tire, fatiguing, tedious; annoying. **tīr′esomelў** *adv.* **tīr′esomeness** *n.*
Tír na nÓg (tēr, nōg). Elysium in ancient Irish literature. [Irish, = 'land of the young']
tiro: see TYRO.
Tirol: see TYROL.
Tir′pitz (tēr-), Alfred von (1849–1930). German admiral.
Tī′rўns (-z). City of ancient Greece in the plain of Argos, near Mycenae, with Cyclopean walls of a Mycenaean palace and fortress.

'**tis** (-z). (archaic, poet., or dial.) Contraction of *it is*.
Tisī′phonė. (Gk myth.) One of the Furies (see FURY).
ti′ssūe (*or* -shōō) *n.* 1. Any (esp. rich or fine) woven stuff. 2. (biol.) Substance of animal or plant body, esp. of a particular part; organized mass of cells of similar kind, as *muscular ~, nervous ~*, etc. 3. (fig.) Interwoven series, set, collection (*of*). 4. (also ~ *paper*) Thin soft gauze-like unsized paper for wrapping delicate articles, toilet use, etc.; piece of tissue paper.
tit[1] *n.* (also *ti′tmouse*) Any of various small birds mostly of the common and widely distributed genus *Parus*, including the *blue ~* (*P. caeruleus*), *coal ~* (*P. ater*), and *great ~* (*P. major*).
tit[2] *n.* ~ *for tat*, equivalent given in return, blow for blow, retaliation.
Tit. *abbrev.* Titus (N.T.).
Tī′tan *n.* (Gk myth.) One of 12 gigantic children of Uranus and Ge (Oceanus, Coeus, Crius, Hyperion, Iapetus, Theia, Rhea, Themis, Mnemosyne, Phoebe, Tethys, Cronus), from two of whom (Cronus and Rhea) Zeus and the Olympians descended; hence, person of superhuman size, strength, etc.
titā′nic[1] *adj.* 1. *T~*, of the Titans. 2. Gigantic, colossal.
Titā′nic[2]. British passenger liner which sank after collision with an iceberg on her maiden voyage to New York in April 1912.
ti′tanite *n.* Monoclinic mineral (CaTiSiO$_5$), occas. used as a gem.
titā′nium *n.* (chem.) Grey metallic element widely distributed in combination in many minerals and clays, used esp. in the manufacture of alloy steels, symbol Ti, at. no. 22, at. wt 47·90.
titā′nic[3], **ti′tanous** *adjs.* [Gk *Titanes* Titans]
ti′tbit, ti′dbit *n.* Delicate bit, choice morsel.
tithe (-dh) *n.* 1. (hist.) Tenth of annual produce of agriculture etc. conceived as due to God and hence payable for support of priesthood, religious establishments, etc.; ~ *barn*, barn built to hold tithes paid in kind; ~ *rent charge*, money payment substituted for tithes, abolished in 1936. 2. (rhet.) Tenth part. ~ *v.t.* Subject to tithes. **tī′thing** *n.* (esp., hist.): see FRANK-PLEDGE.
Tithō′nus. (Gk myth.) Brother of Priam, loved by the dawn goddess, Eos, who asked Zeus to make him immortal but omitted to ask for eternal youth for him.
Tī′tian (-shan). Tiziano Vecellio (1477–1576), Venetian painter; ~ *red*, bright golden auburn, colour of the hair favoured by Titian in his pictures.
ti′tillāte *v.t.* Tickle, excite agreeably. **titillā′tion** *n.*
ti′tivāte *v.* (colloq.) Adorn,

smarten; adorn oneself; put finishing or improving touches to appearance (of).
ti′tlårk *n.* Meadow PIPIT.
ti′tle *n.* 1. Name (freq. descriptive) of book, poem, picture, piece of music, etc.; title-page. 2. Distinctive name or style; personal appellation denoting or relating to rank, function, office, attainment, etc. 3. (law) Legal right to possession of (esp. real) property, title-deeds as evidence of this; just or recognized right or claim (*to*). 4. (eccles.) Any of principal or parish churches in Rome, of which incumbents are cardinal priests. 5. Fineness of gold expressed in carats. 6. ~-*deed*, document constituting evidence of ownership; ~-*part*, -*role*, part in play etc. from which title is taken; ~-*page*, page at beginning of book bearing title.
ti′tled (-ld) *adj.* Having a title of nobility.
ti′tling *n.* (esp.) Impressing of name or title of book on cover.
ti′tmouse *n.* (pl. -*mice*). = TIT[1].
Ti′tō (tē-), Josip Broz, Marshal (1892–), prime minister of Yugoslavia 1945–53; president 1953– .
ti′trāte *v.t.* (chem.) Determine volumetrically quantity of constituent in (solution) by adding reagent of known strength until a point is reached at which reaction occurs or ceases. **titrā′tion** *n.*
tī′tre (-ter) *n.* (chem.) Strength of solution as determined by titration.
ti′tter *n.* & *v.i.* (Produce) laugh of suppressed or covert kind, giggle.
ti′ttle *n.* (archaic) Particle, whit. [late and med. L *titulus* stroke over letter, f. L *titulus* title]
ti′ttle-tă′ttle *n.* & *v.i.* (Indulge in) petty gossip, chatter.
ti′ttup *v.i.* Go, move, with up-and-down movement, mince, prance. **ti′ttupў** *adj.* [perh. imit. of sound of hoof-beat]
titūbā′tion *n.* Staggering, reeling, unsteadiness in gait or carriage (esp. path.).
ti′tūlar *adj.* Held by virtue of a title; such, existing, only in name; ~ *bishop*, (R.C. Ch.) bishop *in partibus infidelium*, one deriving his title from see lost to Roman pontificate; ~ *saint* etc., (R.C. Ch.) sacred person or thing giving name to church. **ti′tūlarlў** *adv.* **ti′tūlar** *n.* One who holds title to office, benefice, etc., esp. without performing functions thereof; (esp.) titular bishop.
Tī′tus[1]. Convert and helper of St. Paul; Pauline epistle of N.T. addressed to him.
Tī′tus[2]. Titus Flavius Sabinus Vespasianus (A.D. 40–81), Roman emperor 79–81; took Jerusalem (A.D. 70) after long siege.
tizz, ti′zzў *ns.* (slang) Dither.
tmē′sis *n.* (gram.) Separation of parts of compound word by intervening word(s), e.g. *to* us *ward*.

[918]

T.N.T. *abbrev.* Trinitrotoluene.
to (tōō *or* tŏŏ *or* to) *prep.* 1. In the direction of; as far as, not short of. 2. Used after words expressing comparison, ratio, proportion, relative position, agreement, or adaptation, correspondence, reference, etc. 3. Introducing indirect object, supplying place of dative; indicating person or thing for whose benefit, use, disposal, etc., thing is done, etc. 4. Used as sign of infinitive; expressing purpose, consequence, etc.; limiting meaning or application of adjective; used as sign of verbal noun etc.; used as substitute for infinitive. ~ *adv.* (tōō) To the normal or required position or condition, esp. to a standstill; ~ *and fro*, backwards and forwards, up and down, from place to place.
T.O. *abbrev.* Transport Officer; turn over.
toad *n.* Tailless leaping amphibian (*Bufo*), resembling a frog, but terrestrial in habits except at breeding season, more squat in shape, and having a warty skin; ~ *in a (the) hole*, sausage or other meat baked in batter; ~*-eater*, sycophant, obsequious parasite; ~*-fish*, any of various fishes with large heads or inflated bodies, of family Batrachoididae, of Amer. Atlantic coasts; ~*-flax*, common European and Asiatic herb (*Linaria vulgaris*) with showy spurred orange-spotted yellow flowers; various related plants; *toa′dstone*, any of various small stones formerly supposed to be found in head of toad and worn as jewel or amulet; *toa′dstool*, fungus with round disc-like top and slender stalk, esp. of inedible or poisonous kind.
toa′dy̆ *n.* Toad-eater, sycophant. **toa′dy̆ism** *n.* **toa′dy̆** *v.i.* Fawn upon, behave servilely (*to* person).
toast *n.* 1. (Slice of) bread browned at fire or other heat; ~*-rack*, rack for holding slices of dry toast. 2. Person or thing in whose honour a company is requested to drink (hist.), reigning belle of season etc.); call to drink, instance of drinking, thus; ~*-master*, one who proposes or announces toasts at public dinner etc. ~ *v.t.* 1. Brown, cook (bread, cheese, etc.) by exposure to heat of fire etc.; warm (one's feet etc.) before fire; *toasting-fork*, long-handled fork for toasting bread etc. 2. Drink to health or in honour of.
toa′ster *n.* Electrical device for toasting bread.
toba̱′ccō *n.* Tall annual plant of genus *Nicotiana*, esp. *N. tabacum*, native of tropical America, with white or pink tubular flowers and large ovate leaves used, dried and variously prepared, for smoking or chewing or in form of snuff; these dried leaves, or cigars, cigarettes, etc., manufactured from them; plant resembling tobacco or used for same purposes; ~ *heart*, affection of the heart due to excessive tobacco smoking.
toba̱′cconist *n.* Dealer in tobacco.
Tobago: see TRINIDAD AND TOBAGO.
Tobī′as. Son of Tobit in the Book of Tobit.
Tō′bit. *Book of* ~, book of the Apocrypha, a romance of the Jewish captivity telling the story of Tobit, a pious Jew.
tobŏ′ggan *n.* Long light narrow sledge curved up at the forward end used esp. in sport of coasting down prepared slopes of snow or ice (ill. SLEDGE[1]). ~ *v.i.* Ride on toboggan.
Tobru′k (-ōōk). Harbour and small town in Cyrenaica, Libya; occupied (Jan. 1941) by British and allied forces, besieged by Germans April–Nov. 1941, besieged again and taken June 1942; evacuated by Germans Nov. 1942.
tō′by̆ *n.* 1. (also *T~ jug*) Mug or small jug for ale etc. in form of stout old man wearing long full-skirted coat and three-cornered hat. 2. *T~*, name of trained dog in Punch and Judy show, usu. wearing frill round neck. [dim. of name *Tobias*]
tocca′ta (-kah-) *n.* (mus.) Composition for keyboard instrument, freq. as prelude to fugue etc., designed to exhibit touch and technique of performer. **toccatĕ′lla**, **toccati′na** (-tē-) *ns.* Short toccata.
Tŏc H (āch). Society with many branches, aiming at Christian fellowship and social service, founded 1915 by Rev. P. T. B. Clayton (1885–1972). [= *T.H.* (*toc* being signallers' name for T), initials of Talbot House, soldiers' club in Poperinghe in the Ypres Salient opened in memory of G. W. L. Talbot (killed 1915)]
Tochār′ian, Tokh- (-k-) *adj. & n.* (Member) of fairly highly cultured people living in first 1,000 years of Christian era in central Asia; (of) Indo-European language of these people, recovered (1904–8) from manuscripts and inscriptions found in ruined temples of northern Chinese Turkestan.
tō′csin *n.* (Bell rung as) alarm or signal. [Provençal *tocarsenh* (*tocar* touch, *senh* signal-bell, f. L *signum* sign)]
tŏd[1] *n.* (dial.) Fox.
tŏd[2] *n.* *on one's* ~, (slang) on one's own.
today′, to-day′ *adv. & n.* (On) this present day; (loosely) nowadays, (in) modern times.
tō′ddle *n.* Toddling walk. ~ *v.i.* (esp. of child) Walk with short unsteady steps; take casual walk.
tō′ddler *n.* (esp.) Child just learning to walk.
tō′ddy̆ *n.* 1. Fresh or fermented sap of various species of palm, used as beverage. 2. Sweetened drink of spirits and hot water. [Hind. *tārī*, f. *tār* palm-tree (Sansk. *tāla* palmyra)]
to-do′ (-dōō) *n.* Commotion.
tō′dy̆ *n.* Small insectivorous W. Indian bird of genus *Todus*, allied to the kingfisher.
toe (tō) *n.* One of five terminal members of foot, forepart of foot; part of stocking, shoe, etc., that covers toes; forepart of hoof; something suggesting a toe by its position, shape, etc., esp. outer end of striking-surface of golf-club; *on one's* ~*s*, (fig.) alert; *toe′cap*, piece of leather covering toe of boot or shoe; ~*-dance*, dance performed on extreme tips of toes; ~*-dancer*, *-dancing*; ~*-hold*, minimal foothold (also fig.); ~*-in*, *-out*, slight forward convergence, divergence, in setting of wheels of vehicle. ~ *v.t.* (pres. part. *toeing*). Furnish with toe, put new toe on (stocking etc.); touch or reach with toes; ~ *the line*, *mark*, etc., stand with tips of toes reaching line indicating starting-point in race etc.; (fig.) conform strictly to standard or requirement, esp. under pressure.
tŏff *n.* (slang) = SWELL *n.*, 4. ~ *v.t.* Dress *up* like a toff (esp. reflex. & pass.).
tŏ′ffee (-ĭ) *n.* Sweet of sugar or treacle, butter, and other ingredients boiled together and allowed to cool and harden; small piece of this; ~ *apple*, apple coated with toffee and stuck on stick for eating; ~*-nosed*, (slang) conceited, pretentious.
tŏg *n.* (pl., slang) Clothes. ~ *v.t.* Dress (*out*, *up*). **tŏ′ggery̆** *n.* Togs.
tō′ga *n.* Ancient Roman citizen's outer garment, flowing cloak

ROMAN COSTUME
1. Toga. 2. Tunic

or robe of single piece of stuff covering whole body except right arm, freq. with allusion to civil career or (~ *viri′lis*, pr. -ēl-, manly toga) to its assumption at age of manhood; (transf.) gown or other garb associated with some profession; (U.S.) office, esp. senatorship.
togĕ′ther (-gĕ′dh-) *adv.* In(to) company or conjunction, so as to unite, in union; simultaneously;

[919]

TOGGLE

uninterruptedly, in unbroken succession.
tŏ'ggle *n.* Short pin put through eye or loop of rope, link of chain etc. to keep it in place etc. (ill. HASP); any similar cross-piece on chain etc.; rod or screw with cross-piece or device enabling it to pass through hole in one position but not in other; movable pivoted cross-piece serving as barb in harpoon; (also ~-*joint*) two plates or rods hinged together endwise, so that force applied at the elbow to straighten the joint is transmitted to the outer end of each plate or rod; ~ *iron*, harpoon with toggle.
Tō'gō. Republic in W. Africa between Ghana and Dahomey; fully independent 1960; capital, Lomé.
toil[1] *v.i.* Work long or laboriously; move painfully or laboriously. **toi'ler** *n.* **toil** *n.* Labour, drudgery, hard and continuous work or exertion. **toi'lsome** *adj.* **toi'lsomenèss** *n.*
toil[2] *n.* (now only in pl.) Net, snare. [OF *toile* cloth, f. L *tela* web]
toi'lĕt *n.* Process of dressing, arranging hair, etc.; (style of) dress; dressing-room; lavatory; ~-*paper*, soft paper for use in lavatories; ~-*powder*, dusting-powder used after bath, shaving, etc.; ~-*roll*, roll of toilet-paper; ~-*set*, set of usu. matching articles used in dressing, as mirror, brush, comb, etc.; ~-*soap*, mild soap freq. perfumed and coloured; ~ *vinegar*, aromatic vinegar used in washing; ~ *water*, scented liquid used after washing. [Fr. *toilette*, orig. = cloth thrown over shoulders in dressing]
toi'lĕtrÿ *n.* (also *pl.*) (shop-word) Articles for use in making one's toilet.
toilette (twahlĕt') *n.* Dress, costume, esp. formal or fashionable dress. [Fr.]
Tokay' (*or* -kī) *n.* Rich sweet aromatic wine made near Tokay in Hungary; similar wine made in California etc.
tō'ken *n.* Sign, symbol (*of*); characteristic mark; thing serving to authenticate person, message, etc.; keepsake; small flat piece of stamped metal issued by tradesman, company, etc., and exchangeable for goods etc.; *book, record,* ~, voucher exchangeable for book(s), record(s); *gift* ~, voucher given as gift; *in* ~ *of*, in evidence of; ~ *payment*, proportionably small payment made by debtor, esp. State, as indication that debt or obligation is not repudiated; ~ *strike*, strike of workers lasting a few hours only; ~ *vote*, (parl.) vote of arbitrary (small) sum of money, proposed for purpose of enabling a public discussion to take place.
Tokharian : see TOCHARIAN.
Tō'kyō. Capital city of Japan,

at head of Tokyo Bay on SE. coast of main island; largest city in the world.
tō'lbōōth *n.* (Sc.) Town hall or guildhall; town prison. [f. TOLL[1] (*n.*), *booth*]
Tole'dō (-lā-) City of Spain, Spanish capital 1087–1560; long famous for manufacture of finely tempered sword-blades.
tŏ'lerable *adj.* Endurable; fairly good, not bad. **tŏ'lerablenèss** *n.* **tŏ'lerablÿ** *adv.*
tŏ'lerance *n.* Willingness to tolerate, forbearance; capacity to tolerate (esp. med.); (eng.) permitted variation in dimension.
tŏ'lerāte *v.t.* Endure, permit; allow to exist, be practised, etc., without interference or molestation; forbear to judge harshly; (med.) sustain use of (drug etc.) without harm. **tŏ'lerant** *adj.* **tŏ'lerantlÿ** *adv.*
tŏlerā'tion *n.* Tolerating; (esp.) recognition of liberty to uphold one's religious opinions and forms of worship or to enjoy all social privileges etc. without regard to religious differences; *Act of T*~, (in U.K.) that of 1688 conditionally freeing dissenters from some restrictions on their forms of worship.
tōll[1] *n.* Tax, duty, charge, paid for selling goods or setting up stall in market, for passage along public road or over bridge or ferry, for transport of goods by railway or canal etc.; *take* ~, (fig.) abstract a portion *of*; ~-*bar*, -*gate*, bar or gate across road to prevent passage without paying toll; ~-*bridge*, bridge at which toll is charged; ~-*house*, house occupied by collector of tolls at toll-gate or toll-bridge. ~ *v.i.* Take, pay, toll.
tōll[2] *v.* Cause (bell) to ring, ring bell, with slow uniform strokes, esp. for death or funeral; (of bell or clock) give out (stroke, knell, hour of day), give out measured sounds. ~ *n.* Tolling, stroke, of bell.
Tŏ'lpŭddle mâr'tyrs (-*erz*). Six farm labourers of village of Tolpuddle, Dorset, who attempted to form a union and were sentenced in 1834 to 7 years' transportation on a charge of administering unlawful oaths; their sentences were remitted, after public protest, in 1836.
Tŏlstoy' (*or* tŏ'-), Lev (Leo) Nikolaevich, Count (1828–1910). Russian novelist and social reformer, author of 'War and Peace', 'Anna Karenina', etc. **Tŏlstoy'an** *adj. & n.* (Follower) of doctrines of Tolstoy, who advocated simple living and practice of manual labour and held that all property is sinful.
Tŏ'ltĕc *n.* Member, language, of an Amer. Indian people, remarkable esp. as architects, who flourished in Mexico from the 9th c. onwards, having their capital

TOMAHAWK

at Tula, which they abandoned in 1168, when some of them moved to Yucatan and lived in association with the MAYA[2]. **Tŏ'ltĕcan** *adj. & n.*
tŏ'lū *n.* (also *balsam of* ~, ~ *balsam*) Fragrant brown balsam obtained by incision from tropical S. Amer. tree (*Myroxylon balsamum*) and used to flavour cough syrups and lozenges, as expectorant, and in perfumery. [f. (*Santiago de*) *Tolu* in Colombia]
tŏ'lūēne *n.* Colourless aromatic liquid hydrocarbon (*methyl benzene*) with smell like benzene and burning taste, orig. obtained from tolu balsam but now esp. from coal-tar, used in manufacture of explosives and other compounds. **tolū'ic** *adj.* ~ *acid*, any of four isomeric acids derived from toluene.
tŏ'lūŏl *n.* Commercial form of toluene.
Tŏm. Masculine proper name used in various collocations: (also *Great* ~) large bell at Christ Church, Oxford; *Great* ~ *of Lincoln*, large bell in central tower of Lincoln Cathedral; *Long* ~, large gun with long range; (naut.) long gun formerly carried amid-ships on swivel-carriage; *Old* ~, strong kind of gin; ~ *Collins*, drink of gin, sugar, lemon- or lime-juice and soda-water; ~, *Dick, and Harry* (usu. derog.), persons taken at random, ordinary people; ~ *Fool*, type of witlessness (also see TOM *n.*); ~ *o' Bedlam*, (hist.) madman discharged from BEDLAM and licensed to beg; ~ *Quad*: see Tom Tower; ~ *Thumb*, dwarf in nursery tale, no bigger than his father's thumb; any diminutive person; dwarf variety of various plants; ~ *Tiddler's ground*, game in which children run over territory of player called Tom Tiddler, crying 'We're on Tom Tiddler's ground, picking up gold and silver', while he chases them; place where money can be had for the picking up; ~ *Tower*, tower, built by Wren, over entrance to W. quadrangle (~ *Quad*) of Christ Church, Oxford, containing Great Tom. **tŏm** *n.* 1. Male animal, esp. cat (*to'mcat*). 2. *to'mboy*, wild romping girl, hoyden; *to'mcod*, any of various small Amer. fishes (*Microgadus*) resembling cod; *tomfoo'l*, witless fellow; (*adj.*) stupid, senseless; (*v.i.*) play the fool; *tomfoo'lery*, foolish trifling, foolish knick-knacks, etc.; *tomno'ddy*, blockhead, fool; (chiefly Sc.) puffin; *tomtit*, blue tit. [abbrev. of name *Thomas*]
tŏ'mahawk *n.* Light axe of

AMERICAN-INDIAN PIPE
TOMAHAWK

[920]

TOMALLEY

N. Amer. Indians, used as tool and as weapon of war; (Austral.) aboriginal stone hatchet, any hatchet. ~ v.t. Strike, kill, with tomahawk.
tŏ′malley n. Fat (often called 'liver') of N. Amer. lobster, green when cooked.
toma′tō (-mah-; U.S. -mā-) n. (pl. -oes). (Glossy red or yellow fleshy edible fruit of) S. Amer. plant (*Lycopersicon esculentum*) with weak trailing or climbing stem, irregularly pinnate leaves, and yellow flowers, widely cultivated, usu. as annual. [Mex. *tomatl*]
tomb (toōm) n. Excavation, chamber, vault, in earth or rock for reception of dead body; sepulchral monument; to′mbstone, memorial stone over grave.
tŏ′mbăc n. Alloy of copper and zinc used as material for cheap jewellery. [Malay]
tŏmbō′la (or tŏ′-) n. Kind of lottery resembling lotto.
tōme n. Volume, esp. large heavy one.
tomĕ′ntum n. 1. (bot.) Pubescence of matted woolly hairs. 2. (anat.) Flocculent inner surface of pia mater. **tō′mentōse, tomĕ′ntous** adjs.
tŏ′mmў n. 1. T~ (*Atkins*), private in British Army. 2. Short rod used as wrench or screwdriver. 3. (obs. slang) Bread, goods or provisions, esp. as given to workmen in lieu of wages; food carried by workmen. 4. ~ *gun*, Thompson sub-machine-gun (ill. GUN); similar automatic weapon; ~ *rot*, nonsense. [familiar form of *Tom*]
tomŏ′rrow (-ō) adv. & n. (On) the day after today.
tŏ′mtŏm n. Native E. Indian drum, usu. beaten with hands; any barbaric drum. [Hind. *tamtam*, imit.]
ton (tŭn) n. 1. (abbrev. t) Measure of weight; *long* ~, used for coal, 2,240 lb. avoirdupois; *metric* ~: see TONNE; *short* ~, used in U.S. and for metals, 2,000 lb. avoirdupois. 2. Measure of capacity (often varying) for timber (40 cu. ft), stone (16 cu. ft), salt (42 bushels), lime (40 bushels), coke (28 bushels), wheat (20 bushels), wine (see TUN), etc. 3. Unit of internal capacity of ship (for purposes of registered TONNAGE, 100 cu. ft; for purposes of freight, usu. 40 cu. ft). 4. (slang) 100 m.p.h., esp. on motorcycle (also ~-*up*). 5. (colloq., esp. pl.) Large number or amount. [var. of *tun*]
tŏ′nal adj. Of tone or tones; (of fugue) having *tonal* (opp. *real*) *answer*, in which intervals are modified instead of repeated exactly.
tōnă′litў n. 1. (mus.) That relation between notes in a composition which constitutes the key; strict observation of key scheme or mode of musical composition. 2. (painting) Colouring in respect of its lightness and darkness, tones of a picture in relation to one another.
tŏ′ndō n. Painting, carving in relief, within circular shape. [It., *rotondo* round]
tōne[1] n. 1. Sound, esp. with ref. to pitch, quality, and strength. 2. Particular quality, pitch, modulation, etc., of voice; intonation; pitch, inflexion, of spoken sound, expressing differences of meaning, esp. (in Chinese and similar languages) any of various inflexions or pitches distinguishing words which otherwise have the same sound. 3. (mus.) Sound of definite pitch and character produced by regular vibration of sounding body, musical note; each of the several tones(*fundamental* ~ and *overtones*) audible in sound of bell or similar instrument; (also) musical note without overtones. 4. (mus.) Interval of major second, e.g. C–D, E–F sharp (freq. *whole* ~, as opp. to *semitone*) (ill. SCALE[3]). 5. (mus.) *Gregorian* ~*s*: see GREGORIAN. 6. (med.) Degree of firmness or tension proper to strong and healthy organs or tissues of body. 7. Prevailing character of morals, sentiments, etc., in society or community; state of mind, mood. 8. Degree of lightness or darkness of colour(s); general effect of combination of light and shade, esp. in a picture or a scene in nature. 9. ~-*arm*, pick-up arm; ~-*colour*, (mus.) timbre; ~-*deaf(ness)*, insensitive(ness) to differences in pitch between musical tones; ~ *language*, language in which similar sounds are distinguished by tones (see 2 above); ~ *poem*, symphonic poem, orchestral composition of indeterminate form and illustrative character, based on poetic or literary rather than purely musical ideas. ~ v. Give tone or quality (of sound or colour) to; alter tone or colour of (photographic print) in finishing it; harmonize; ~ *down*, lower tone, quality, or character of; make, become, less emphatic; become lower or softer in tone or quality; ~ *up*, improve tone of, give higher or stronger tone to.
Tōne[2], Theobald Wolfe (1763–98). Irish revolutionary; one of the founders of the society of 'United Irishmen'.
tō′neless (-nl-) adj. (esp.) Without distinctive quality of sound or colour, dull, lifeless, unexpressive. **tō′nelesslў** adv. **tō′nelessness** n.
tŏng n. Chinese association, esp. secret society of Chinese in foreign country. [Chin. *t'ang* meeting-place]
tŏ′nga[1] (-ngga) n. Light two-wheeled carriage in India.
Tŏ′nga[2] (-ngga). (also *Tongan Islands* or *Friendly Islands*) Group of islands in S. Pacific E. of Fiji; kingdom, member State of the Commonwealth, independent since 1970; capital, Nukualofa. **Tŏ′ngan** adj. & n.

TONIC

tŏngs (-z) n.pl. (also *pair of* ~) Implement consisting of two limbs connected by hinge, pivot, or spring bringing together lower ends so that objects may be grasped which it is impossible or inconvenient to lift with hand.
tongue (tŭng) n. 1. Organ in floor of mouth, usu. protrusible and freely movable; in man and many other vertebrates tapering, blunt-tipped, muscular, soft and fleshy, used in taking in and swallowing food, as principal organ of taste, and in man of articulate speech; animal's tongue as article of food. 2. Action of speaking, faculty of speech, words, talk, language; speech or language of a people; *gift of* ~*s*, power of speaking in various languages, esp. as miraculously conferred on early Christians (Acts 2); *give* ~, (of hound) bark, esp. on finding scent; *hold one's* ~, be silent; (*speak*) *with one's* ~ *in one's cheek*, (speak) insincerely or mockingly. 3. Thing like tongue in shape or function, as pin of buckle, narrow strip of land between two bodies of water, clapper of bell, pole of wagon or other vehicle, strip of leather closing gap in front of boot or shoe (ill. SHOE), movable tapered piece of steel in railway-switch, projecting tenon along edge of board, to be inserted into groove or mortise of another board etc. (ill. JOINT[1]). 4. ~-*bit*, bit with plate to keep horse's tongue under mouthpiece; ~-*fish*, sole; ~-*grafting*, whip-grafting, in which wedge-shaped tongue of scion is inserted into cleft in stock; ~-*tie(d)*, (condition of) having fraenum of tongue too short, so that distinct speech is difficult or impossible; speechless, dumb, from embarrassment, shyness, etc.; ~-*twister*, sequence of words difficult to articulate quickly. ~ v. Utter, speak; furnish with tongue; interrupt stream of air with tongue in playing wind instrument.
tŏ′nic adj. 1. Producing tension, esp. of muscles; of, maintaining, restoring, tone or normal healthy condition of tissues or organs; strengthening, invigorating, bracing; (of spasm) with sustained muscular contraction; ~ *water*, carbonated water esp. for mixing with alcoholic drinks. 2. (mus.) Of, founded upon, tonic or keynote; ~ *major*, *minor*, major, minor scale or key, with same tonic as given major or minor; ~ *sol-fa*, system of sight-singing and notation in which tonic of all major keys is doh (and other notes correspondingly, as ray, me, fah, etc.) and tonic of all minor keys lah (and other notes correspondingly, as te, doh, etc.) with time-values shown by vertical lines, colons, etc. 3. Of tone or accent in speech. **tŏ′nicallў** adv. **tŏ′nic** n. 1. Tonic medicine or agent; invigorating influence. 2. Tonic

[921]

water. 3. (mus.) Keynote (ill. SCALE³).

toni′cĭtў *n.* Tonic quality or condition, tone.

toni′ght, to-ni′ght (-nīt) *adv. & n.* (On) the present night, (on) the night of today.

tŏ′nka bean. Black fragrant almond-shaped seed of large S. Amer. leguminous tree (*Dipteryx odorata* or *D. oppositifolia*), used for scenting tobacco, as ingredient in perfumes etc.; the tree itself.

to′nnage (tŭ-) *n.* 1. (Engl. hist., usu. ~ *and poundage*) Customs duties on wine imported in tuns or casks (and on every pound's-worth of goods imported or exported), usu. granted by parliament to sovereign, and illegally imposed on his own authority by Charles I in 1629. 2. Carrying capacity of ship expressed in tons of 100 cu. ft; ships collectively, shipping; charge per ton on cargo or freight; *displacement* ~, weight of water displaced by a ship when loaded up to her load-line, used in stating the tonnage of warships; *gross* ~, total cubic capacity of all spaces above and below the tonnage-deck; *net* or *register* ~, gross tonnage less space occupied by engines, crew's quarters, etc., tonnage for which vessels are registered and on which the assessment of dues and charges on shipping are based; *under-deck* ~, cubic capacity of space under tonnage-deck; ~-*deck*, second deck from below in ships with more than one deck.

tonne (tŭn) *n.* (abbrev. t) Unit of mass equal to 1000 kilogrammes, 2204·6 lb avoirdupois (formerly called *metric ton*).

tŏ′nneau (-ō) *n.* Rear part, containing back seats, of a motor-car (orig. with the door at the back).

tonŏ′mĕter *n.* Tuning-fork or other instrument for measuring the pitch of tones.

tŏ′nsil *n.* Either of a pair of small organs on either side of the root of the tongue, composed of lymphatic tissue and instrumental in protecting the throat from infection, but themselves liable to become septic (ill. HEAD). **tŏ′nsillar** *adj.* Of, affected by, the tonsils.

tŏnsillĕ′ctomў *n.* Surgical removal of the tonsils.

tŏnsilli′tis *n.* Inflammation of the tonsils.

tŏnsōr′ial *adj.* (usu. joc.) Of a barber or his work.

tŏ′nsure (-sher) *n.* Shaving of head (in Eastern Ch.) or part of it, esp. circular patch on crown (in R.C. Ch., until 1972), as religious practice, esp. as preparation to entering priesthood or monastic order; part of head thus shaved. ~ *v.t.* Shave head of, give tonsure to.

tŏ′ntine (-ēn; *or* -ē′n) *n.* Financial scheme by which subscribers to loan receive an annuity for life, increasing as their number is diminished by death, until last survivor enjoys whole income; any arrangement, as form of insurance, in which benefits shared among members are increased on death or default of any of them, or in which they are distributed among all remaining members at end of fixed period. [Lorenzo *Tonti*, Neapolitan banker, who instituted scheme in France *c* 1653]

tōō *adv.* 1. In addition, moreover, besides, also. 2. In excess; more than is right or fitting, more than enough; (colloq.) extremely, very.

tōōl *n.* Implement for working upon something, usu. one held in and operated by hand, but also including simple machines, as lathe; (cutting-part of) machine-tool; anything used in performing some operation or in any occupation or pursuit; person used as mere instrument by another; (bookbinding etc.) small stamp or roller for impressing design on leather; large kind of chisel; house-painter's brush; ~-*house*, -*shed*, shed, as in garden, where tools are kept; ~-*post*, (in lathe) upright piece in ~-*rest* holding or supporting tool (ill. LATHE²); ~ *v.* Work with tool; smooth surface of building-stone with large chisel; ornament (leather) with tool; (slang) drive, ride, (*along*) esp. in casual or leisurely manner.

tōō′ling *n.* (esp.) Dressing of stone with broad chisel; impressing of ornamental design with heated tools on leather, such design(s).

tōōt *n.* Note or short blast of horn, trumpet, or other wind instrument. ~ *v.* Sound (horn or other wind instrument); give out such sound.

tōōth *n.* (pl. *teeth*). 1. Each of the hard processes (in mammals usu. of dentine coated with cement round root and enamel in exposed part) attached, usu. in sockets, in a row to each jaw in most vertebrates except birds, with points, edges, or grinding surfaces, and used for biting, tearing, or chewing food, or as weapons of attack or defence; elephant's tusk; (fig.) sense of taste, taste, liking; *in the teeth of*, in spite of; in opposition to; in the face of (wind etc.); *put teeth in*(to), make (more) effective, make (law etc.) enforceable; *set one's teeth*, clench teeth firmly from indignation or fixed resolution (freq. fig.); *show one's teeth*, (usu. fig.) show hostility or malice, behave threateningly; ~ *and nail*, (usu. fig.) vigorously, fiercely. 2. Projecting part or point resembling tooth, as pointed process on margin of leaf; projecting point of rock; prong or tine of comb, saw, file, harrow, rake, fork, etc.; one of series of projections on edge of wheel, pinion, etc., engaging with corresponding ones on another, cog; (sing. only) rough surface on paper, canvas, etc., to which pencil-marks, colours, etc., adhere; roughness made on surfaces to be glued together. 3. *too′thache*, ache in tooth or teeth; ~-*brush*, small brush used for cleaning teeth; (*small*-)~-*comb*, comb with fine close-set teeth; ~-*paste*, -*powder*, paste, powder, for cleaning teeth; ~-*pick*, small pointed instrument of quill, wood, etc., used for removing matter lodged between teeth; (slang) very narrow pointed boat; (U.S. slang) bowie-knife (freq. *Arkansas* ~-*pick*); ~-*shell*, (long tubular tusk-shaped shell of) mollusc of *Dentalium* or allied genus. **tōō′thlĕss** *adj.* **tōō′thlĕsslў** *adv.* **tōō′thlĕssnĕss** *n.* **tōōth** *v.* Furnish with tooth or teeth; give rough surface to; (of cog-wheels etc.) interlock; *toothing-plane*, plane with serrated iron used to score and roughen surface.

tōō′thful *n.* Small mouthful, esp. of spirit.

tōō′thsome *adj.* Pleasant to eat. **tōō′thsomelў** *adv.* **tōō′thsomeness** *n.*

tōō′tle *v.i.* Toot gently or continuously, esp. on flute.

tōō′tsў *n.* (nursery or joc.) (also ~-*wōō′tsў*) Foot.

tŏp¹ *n.* 1. Summit, upper part, surface; highest place, rank, degree, etc.; end of anything conventionally regarded as the higher, e.g. end of billiard-table opposite baulk; (usu. pl.) part of plant growing above ground, esp. of vegetable grown for its root; *from* ~ *to toe*, from head to foot, in every part; *on* ~, (fig.) supreme, dominant. 2. Part or piece forming upper part or covering of something, e.g. platform near head of lower mast of ship (ill. SAIL¹), in warship, armoured platform on a short mast; topsail; upper part of leg of high boot, esp. broad band of material round this; gauntlet

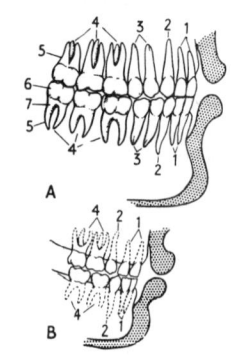

[922]

HUMAN TEETH
A. PERMANENT. B. MILK TEETH

1. Incisors. 2. Canine. 3. Premolars. 4. Molars. 5. Wisdom. 6. Crown. 7. Root

part of glove; turned-down part of leg of sock or stocking; stopper of bottle; hood of carriage, motor-car, etc. ~ adj. Highest in position or degree, that is at or on top; ~-boot, boot with high top, esp. with wide band of lighter colour or different material simulating turned-down top; ~-coat, overcoat; ~ drawer, uppermost drawer of series; (fig.) high social position or origin; ~-dress, apply material to surface of (land, road, etc.) without working it in; ~-dressing, material, esp. manure, so applied; topga'llant, mast, sail, yard, rigging, immediately above topmast and topsail (ill. SHIP); ~ hamper, upper masts, sails, and rigging; weight or encumbrance aloft (freq. fig.); ~ hat, tall silk hat (ill. COAT); ~-heavy, over-weighted at top, so as to be unstable; to'pknot, knot, bow of ribbon, tuft, crest, etc., worn or growing on top of head; to'pmast, smaller mast on top of lower mast, esp. second section of mast above deck; ~-notch, (colloq.) first-rate, excellent; ~ note, highest note of singer's compass; to'psail (or -sl), in square-rigged vessel, sail next above lower sail, sometimes divided into upper and lower topsails (double topsails); ~-sawyer, sawyer in upper position in saw-pit; (fig., archaic) person in superior position; ~ secret, extremely secret (esp. as security classification); ~ sergeant, (U.S. colloq.) chief or first sergeant of company, battery, etc.; to'pside, upper part of ship's side, above water-line or main deck; outer side of round of beef, cut from haunch between leg and aitchbone (ill. MEAT). ~ v. 1. Provide with top or cap; remove top of (plant) to improve growth etc.; reach top of (hill etc.); be at top of, have highest position in; exceed in height, overtop; hit (golf-ball) above centre, make (stroke) thus; ~ off, put end or finishing touch to. 2. (naut.) Tip up, slant, raise (yard); (of yard) rise, tip up; topping lift, line for raising boom (ill. SAIL¹). to'pping adj. (colloq.) Tip-top, excellent. to'pless adj.

tŏp² n. 1. Toy, usu. conical, spherical, or pear-shaped, rotating on point when set in motion by hand, spring, or string; humming-~, hollow, usu. metal top, with perforations, making humming noise in spinning; sleep like a ~, sleep soundly, (with ref. to apparent stillness of top spinning on vertical axis); ~-shell, marine snail of genus Trochus or family Trochidae, with short conical shell.

tō'păz n. 1. Silicate of aluminium usu. in yellow, white, pale-blue, or pale-green transparent lustrous prismatic crystals, classed as semi-precious stone; false ~, transparent pale-yellow variety of quartz; oriental ~, a precious stone, the yellow sapphire; pink ~, rose-coloured kind produced by exposing yellow Brazilian topaz to great heat. 2. (also ~ humming-bird) Either of two large brilliant-coloured S. Amer. humming-birds (Topaza pella, T. pyra).
tō'pazīne adj. Topaz-yellow.
tō'pazīte n. Rock consisting of quartz and topaz.
tōpe¹ n. Small European shark, Galeorhinus galeus; any of various related sharks.
tōpe² n. Buddhist monument, usu. a cylindrical tower surmounted by a cupola. [Sansk. stupa mound]
tōpe³ v.i. (now chiefly literary) Drink to excess, esp. habitually.
tō'per n.
tō'pee, tō'pĭ n. Light pith hat or helmet, esp. sola ~. [Hind. topi hat]
Tō'phĕt. Orig., place near Gehenna, S. of Jerusalem, where Jews made human sacrifices to strange gods (see Jer. 19: 4), later used for deposit of refuse; hence, place of eternal fire, hell.
tō'phus n. 1. Tufa. 2. (path.) Mineral concretion in the body, esp. on the joints or on a bone, in gout. 3. Dental tartar.
topi: see TOPEE.
tō'piarȳ adj. & n. (Of) the art of clipping and trimming shrubs etc. into ornamental or fantastic shapes. tōpiār'ian adj. tō'piarist n. [L topia landscape gardening or painting, f. Gk topos place]
tō'pic n. Subject of discourse, argument, etc., theme; (rhet., logic) class of considerations from which arguments can be drawn.
tō'pical adj. 1. Of topics; of topics of the day, containing local or temporary allusions. 2. (med.) Local. tō'picallȳ adv.
tō'pmŏst adj. Uppermost.
tŏpŏ'graphȳ n. Detailed delineation or description, physical features, of place; features of locality collectively; (study of) local distribution; (anat.) regional anatomy. tŏpŏ'grapher n. tŏpŏgră'phic, -ical adjs. tŏpŏgră'phicallȳ adv.
tŏpŏ'logȳ n. Branch of mathematics dealing with the properties of spaces (sets of points) in respect of their being one connected piece and of forming a boundary, independently of shape and size. tŏpŏlŏ'gical adj. tŏpŏlŏ'gicallȳ adv. tŏpŏ'logist n.
tŏpŏ'nȳmȳ n. Study of the place-names of a region.
tō'pper n. (esp., colloq.) Top hat.
tō'pple v. (Cause to) tumble or fall headlong, as if top-heavy.
tŏ'psȳ-tûr'vȳ adv. & adj. With the top where the bottom should be, upside down; in(to) utter confusion or disorder.
tōque (-k) n. 1. Small usu. brimless hat of folded or swathed material. 2. Monkey (Macaca sinica) of Ceylon, with tufted head.

tōr n. Craggy or rocky hill or peak, esp in Devon and Cornwall.
Tō'rah (-a) n. Pentateuch, the Mosaic Law; scroll of this used in synagogue. [Heb. tôrāh instruction, direction]
torc: see TORQUE.
tŏrch n. 1. Light for carrying in hand, consisting of piece of resinous wood or length of twisted hemp or flax soaked in resin, tallow, etc.; (fig.) source of conflagration, illumination, enlightenment, etc.; carry ~ for, (U.S. slang) have unrequited passion for; hand on the ~, pass on tradition. 2. (also electric ~) Small portable electric lamp. 3. (U.S.) Blow-lamp or other portable device for producing hot flame. 4. Any of various flowers suggesting flaming torch in shape or colour esp. (usu. pl.) mullein. 5. ~-bearer, (esp.) one who guards or hands on light of truth, civilization, etc.; ~-lily, RED-hot poker; ~-singer, (chiefly U.S.) singer of ~-songs, popular, esp. jazz, songs about unrequited love; ~-thistle, any columnar cactus of genus Cereus with stems sometimes used for torches.
tŏr'chŏn (-sh-; or -awṅ) n. (also ~ lace) Coarse strong linen bobbin-lace; similar machine-made linen or cotton lace; ~ paper, paper with rough surface used esp. for water-colours. [Fr., = 'duster' (torcher wipe)]
tōre n. = TORUS, senses 1 and 3.
tō'rėadōr n. Mounted bull-fighter (term still current in English but not in mod. Spanish). [Span. toro bull, f. L taurus]
torēr'o (-ārō) n. (pl. -s). Bull-fighter. [Span.]
toreu'tic (-roō-) adj. & n. (Of) the art of chasing, carving, and embossing, esp. metal.
tŏr'ment n. Severe bodily or mental suffering; cause of this.
tŏrmĕ'nt v.t. Subject to torment.
tŏrmĕ'ntor n.
tŏr'mentil n. Low-growing yellow-flowered herb (Potentilla tormentilla) of Europe and Asia, common on heaths and dry pastures, with strongly astringent roots.
tŏr'mina n.pl. (med.) Griping pains in bowels, colic. tŏr'minal adj.
torn: see TEAR².
tŏrnā'dō n. Violent storm, usu. with heavy rain, in which wind rotates or constantly changes direction, esp., in West Africa, Mississippi region of U.S., etc., destructive rotatory storm under funnel-shaped cloud like waterspout, advancing in narrow path for many miles; ~-cellar, -pit, underground shelter from tornadoes. [app. f. Span. tronada thunderstorm, assimilated to tornar turn]
tō'roid n. (geom.) Surface generated by the rotation of a plane closed curve about a line lying in its plane. ~ adj. Of,

[923]

TORONTO

resembling, a tore or toroid. **tŏroi′dal** adj.
Torŏ′ntō. Capital city of province of Ontario, Canada.
tŏrpē′dō n. 1. ELECTRIC ray, esp. *Torpedo nobiliana* found in Atlantic Ocean. 2. Self-propelled dirigible submarine missile, usu. cigar-shaped, carrying an explosive which is fired by impact with its objective, used for destroying or injuring ships at sea; similar missile discharged from aircraft (*aerial* ~); (U.S.) case containing explosive used for various military purposes, explosive cartridge for clearing obstructions etc. in oil-well, detonator placed on railway-line as fog-signal etc.; ~-*boat*, small fast lightly armoured vessel carrying torpedoes; ~-*boat destroyer* (now usu. *destroyer*), larger and more heavily armed torpedo-boat, orig. for attacking torpedo-boat (see also DESTROYER); ~-*net(ting)*, steel net round vessel or hung from a boom as a protection against torpedoes; ~-*tube*, steel tube through which torpedoes are discharged, usu. by compressed air. ~ *v.t.* Attack, damage, destroy, (as) with a torpedo. [L, name of the fish (*torpere* be numb)]
tŏr′pĕfў, tŏr′pifў v.t. Make torpid, benumb.
tŏr′pĭd adj. Benumbed; dormant; sluggish, inactive, dull. **tŏr′pĭdlў** adv. **tŏrpĭ′dĭtў, tŏr′pĭdnĕss** ns. **tŏr′pĭd** n. (Oxf. Univ.) Clinker-built eight-oared boat (orig. second boat of college) used for *Torpids*, college boat-races in early spring.
tŏr′por n. Torpidity.
tŏrque (-k), **tŏrc** n. 1. Necklace or collar, usu. of twisted metal,

CELTIC TORQUE

worn esp. by ancient Britons and Gauls. 2. (phys. etc.) Twisting or rotary force in piece of mechanism, moment of system of forces producing rotation.
Tŏrquĕma′da (-mah-), Tomas de (1420–98). Spanish Dominican monk; first inquisitor-general.
tŏ′rrĕfў v.t. Roast, scorch, or dry by heat; esp. dry (drugs etc.) on metallic plate by heat. **tŏrrĕfă′ction** n.
tŏ′rrent n. Swift violent rushing stream of water etc.; violent down-pour of rain; (fig.) violent flow (of words etc.). **tŏrrĕ′ntial** (-shal) adj. **tŏrrĕ′ntiallў** adv.
Tŏ′rrĕs Strait. Strait between Australia and New Guinea.
Tŏrricĕ′llĭ (-chĕ-), Evangelista (1608–47). Italian physicist and mathematician, deviser of experiment (1643) showing that height of mercury column in inverted closed tube corresponds to atmospheric pressure. **Tŏrricĕ′llĭan** (*or* -chĕ-) *adj.* ~ *tube*, early name for barometer; ~ *vacuum*, vacuum produced by filling closed tube with mercury and inverting it in cup of mercury.
tŏ′rrid adj. Scorched, parched, exposed to great heat; intensely hot, burning; ~ *zone*, region between the tropics of Cancer and Capricorn (ill. EARTH). **torri′ditў, tŏ′rridnĕss** ns.
tŏr′sel n. Block of stone, piece of iron or wood, in wall to support end of beam or joist (ill. FLOOR).
tŏr′sion n. Twisting, twist; *angle of* ~, (geom.) infinitesimal angle between two consecutive osculating planes of tortuous curve; ~ *balance*, apparatus for measuring minute horizontal forces by means of wire or filament which is twisted by the application of the force. **tŏr′sional** adj. **tŏr′sionallў** adv.
tŏr′sō n. (pl. -s). Statue lacking head and limbs; trunk of statue, or of human body; mutilated or unfinished work. [It., = 'stalk', 'stump', 'torso', f. L *thyrsus* (Gk *thursos* shaft, wand)]
tŏrt n. (law) Breach of a duty imposed by law (but not breach of contract), making offender liable to action for damages. [med. L *tortum* wrong f. L *torquere tort* twist]
tŏrtĭcŏ′llĭs n. (path.) Rheumatic or other affection of muscles causing twisting and stiffness of neck.
tŏrti′lla (-tēya) n. In Spanish America, thin flat cake of maize flour baked on flat plate of iron etc.
tŏr′tious (-shus) adj. Of, constituting, a tort.
tŏr′toise (-tus) n. Slow-moving four-footed reptile of land and

TORTOISE
1. Carapace. 2. Plastron

freshwater species of order Chelonia, with body enclosed in heavy shell, and head and legs retractile.
tŏr′toiseshĕll (-tesh-) n. 1. Carapace of turtle, esp. that of
TOSS

the hawksbill turtle (*Chelone imbricata*), semi-transparent, of rich yellowish-brown mottled colour, used for ornamental articles, in inlaying, etc. 2. (also ~ *butterfly*) Any of various butterflies with colouring resembling that of tortoiseshell, esp. the small ~ (*Aglais urticae*). 3. (also ~ *cat*) Cat of black, brown, and yellow mottled colouring.
tŏr′tūous adj. Full of twists or turns; (geom., of curve) of which no two successive portions are in same plane; (fig.) devious, circuitous, crooked, not straightforward. **tŏr′tūouslў** adv. **tŏr′tūousnĕss, tŏrtūŏ′sitў** ns.
tŏr′ture (-cher) n. Infliction of severe bodily pain, e.g. as punishment or to force confession or extort information; severe physical or mental pain. ~ *v.t.* Subject to torture; (fig.) strain, wrench, distort, pervert.
tŏ′rŭla n. (pl. -lae). Any of various non-spore-bearing yeasts which do not produce alcoholic fermentation.
tŏr′us n. (pl. -rī). 1. (archit.) Large convex moulding esp. at base of column (ill. MOULDING). 2. (bot.) Receptacle of flower, swollen summit of flower-stalk, supporting floral organs; (also) thickening of PIT membrane. 3. (Solid enclosed by) surface described by a conic section, esp. circle, rotating about a straight line in its own plane. [L, = 'protuberance', 'bed']
Tŏr′ў adj. & n. (now chiefly in colloq. & hostile use) Conservative; (hist.) (member) of the parliamentary and political party in England that opposed the exclusion of the Duke of York (James II) from the succession, inclined to the House of Stuart after 1689, accepted George III and the established order in Church and State, opposed the Reform Bill of 1832, and has been known officially (since *c* 1830) as 'Conservative'; cf. WHIG. **Tŏr′ўism** n. [Ir. *tóraidhe* pursuer, applied orig. to 17th-c. Irish outlaws who robbed and killed English settlers and soldiers]
tŏsh n. (slang) Rubbish, nonsense.
tŏss v. Throw (*up, away, to,* etc.), esp. lightly, carelessly, or easily; (of bull etc.) throw (person etc.) up with horns; throw (coin), throw coin (*up*), into air to decide choice etc. by way it falls; settle question or dispute with (person *for* thing) thus; throw back *head*, esp. in contempt or impatience; throw about from side to side, throw oneself about thus in bed etc.; roll about restlessly; roll or swing with fitful to-and-fro motion; throw (pancake) up so that it returns to pan when other side up; ~ *off*, drink off at a draught; dispatch (work etc.) rapidly or without apparent effort; ~ *up*,

[924]

toss coin. ~ *n.* Tossing; sudden jerk, esp. of head; tossing of coin; throw from horseback etc.; *full* ~, (cricket) ball which does not touch ground between wickets; ~-*up*, tossing of coin; doubtful question.

tŏt[1] *n.* Tiny child; small quantity (*of* drink, esp. spirits), dram.

tŏt[2] *v.* Add (*up*), mount *up* (*to*). [abbrev. of TOTAL or of L *totum* whole]

tō'tal *adj.* Complete, comprising or involving the whole; absolute, unqualified; ~ *war*, one in which all available resources are employed without reserve. tō'tally *adv.* tŏtă'lĭtў *n.* tō'tal *n.* Sum of all items, total amount. ~ *v.* Amount to, mount *up to*; reckon total of.

tŏtălĭtār'ian *adj.* Of, pertaining to, regime which permits no rival loyalties or parties and arrogates to itself all rights including those normally belonging to individuals. tŏtălĭtār'ianism *n.*

tō'talĭzātor *n.* Device for registering or finding total of something; esp. a machine for registering and indicating bets on each horse, dog, etc., in a race on the PARI-MUTUEL system.

tō'talĭze *v.* Collect into a total, find the total of.

tōte[1] *n.* (orig. Austral. colloq.) TOTALIZATOR.

tōte[2] *v.t.* (U.S.) Convey, transport, carry (supplies, timber, etc.).

tō'tem *n.* Natural, esp. animal, object assumed as emblem of family or clan; image of this; ~-*pole*, ~-*post*, post with carved and painted representation of totem, set up in front of N. Amer. Indian dwelling. tō'temism *n.*

t'o'ther, to'ther (tŭdh-) *pron.* & *adj.* The other.

tŏ'tter *v.i.* Walk with unsteady steps, go shakily or feebly; rock or shake on its base, as if about to overbalance or collapse. tŏ'ttering *adj.* tŏ'tteringlў *adv.* tŏ'tter *n.* Tottering gait. tŏ'tterў *adj.*

tou'can (tōō-) *n.* Tropical Amer. fruit-eating bird of *Rhamphastos* or allied genera, with huge light thin-walled beak and freq. brilliant colouring.

touch (tŭch) *v.* 1. Put hand or other part of body on or into contact with; bring (thing) into contact *with* another; be in, come into contact (with); (geom.) be tangent (to); (hist., of king) lay hand on (person) as cure for scrofula (also abs.). 2. Affect in some way by contact; strike (strings, keys) of musical instrument so as to make it sound; mark, draw (*in*), modify, alter, by touching drawing etc. with pencil or brush; add touches *to*; mark, modify, slightly *with* colour, expression, etc.; (of ship etc.) call at (port); reach, (fig.) approach in excellence etc. 3. Affect mentally or morally; affect with tender feeling, soften; rouse painful or angry feeling in; concern. 4. Treat of (subject) lightly or in passing. 5. Affect slightly, produce slightest effect on; have to do with in the slightest degree, esp. hurt or harm in the least degree; (usu. with neg.) eat or drink the smallest quantity of. 6. ~ *at*, call at (port); ~ *down*, alight on ground from the air; (Rugby footb.) make touch-down (see *n.* 3); ~ *for*, (slang) get (money) from (person); ~ *off*, make (sketch) hastily, make hasty sketch of; discharge (explosive etc.); ~ *on*, treat (subject) briefly; ~ *up*, give finishing, improving, or heightening touches to; jog (memory); strike (horse etc.) lightly with whip or spur. 7. ~-*and*-*go*, of uncertain result, risky; ~-*me*-*not*, plant of European genus *Impatiens*, esp. yellow balsam (*I. noli-me-tangere*) with seed-capsules which split open when touched; ~ *wood*, touch (wooden object) to avert ill luck; *tou'chwood*, children's game in which touching wood gives immunity from pursuit. ~ *n.* 1. Act or fact of touching, contact; faculty by which material things are perceived by their contact with some part of the body surface; sensation conveyed by touching, feel; light stroke with pencil, brush, etc., detail of any artistic work, slight act or effort in work of any kind; artistic skill, style of artistic work; manner of touching keys or strings of musical, esp. keyboard, instrument, manner or degree in which instrument responds to this. 2. (also ~ *mark*) Manufacturer's identifying mark on article of pewter. 3. Close relation of communication, agreement, sympathy, etc. (esp. *in*, *out of*, ~ *with*; *keep in*, *lose*, ~). 4. (footb.) Part of ground outside touch-line (ill. RUGBY); ~-*down*, (Rugby footb.) touching ball on ground behind opponents' goal-line; (Amer. footb.) scoring by being in possession of ball behind opponents' goal-line; ~-*judge*, umpire who marks where ball goes into touch; ~-*line*, boundary line on each side of field of play between goal-lines (ill. ASSOCIATION). 5. ~-*hole*, (hist.) small tubular hole in breech of cannon through which fire was applied to powder (ill. CANNON); ~-*needle*, slender rod of gold or silver of known fineness, used with touchstone to test fineness of gold or silver; ~-*paper*, paper impregnated with nitre so as to burn steadily without flame, formerly used for firing gunpowder etc.; *tou'chstone*, basa-nite, used to test fineness of gold and silver alloys by colour of streak produced by rubbing them on it; (fig.) standard, criterion; ~-*typewriting*, *typing*, typewriting by touch, i.e. without looking at keys; *tou'chwood*, wood or woody substance in such state as to catch fire readily, used as tinder; esp. soft white long-burning substance into which wood is converted by action of some fungi.

touché (tōō'shā) *int.* (fencing) Exclamation acknowledging a touch by opponent's foil; (transf.) acknowledgement of home thrust in argument. [Fr., = 'touched']

tou'ching (tŭ-) *prep.* (archaic or literary) Concerning, about. ~ *adj.* Affecting, pathetic. tou'chinglў *adv.* tou'chingnèss *n.*

tou'chў (tŭ-) *adj.* Easily taking offence, over-sensitive. tou'chilў *adv.* tou'chinèss *n.*

tough (tŭf) *adj.* Of close tenacious substance or texture; hard to break or cut, not brittle; (of food) difficult to masticate; (of clay etc.) stiff, tenacious; hardy, able to endure hardship; unyielding, stubborn; difficult; (colloq., of luck etc.) hard, severe, unpleasant; (slang, chiefly U.S.) ruffianly, hardened in crime. tou'ghlў *adv.* tou'ghnèss *n.* tou'ghen *v.* tough *n.* Street ruffian, tough person.

Toulon (toolawn) S. France. City, port, and naval base in S. France.

Toulouse-Lautrec (tōōlōōz lō-trĕk), Henri de (1864–1901). French painter and lithographer.

toupee, -pet (tōō'pā) *n.* 1. (hist.) Top-knot of hair esp. as crowning feature of wig; wig with this. 2. Patch, front, of false hair. [OF *toup* tuft]

tour (toor) *n.* 1. Journey through (part of) a country from place to place; rambling excursion, short journey, walk, esp. for sake of observing what is noteworthy; *grand* ~, (hist.) journey through France, Germany, Switzerland, and Italy, fashionable esp. in 18th c. as finishing course in education of young man of rank; *on* ~, touring. 2. (esp. mil.) Spell of duty in service, time to be spent at station; (occas., chiefly U.S.) shift. ~ *v.* Make tour (of); (of actor, theatrical company, etc.) travel from town to town fulfilling engagements, travel about (country) thus, take (entertainment) about thus; so *touring company*. tour'er *n.* Motor-car designed for touring, usu. with open body. tour'ing *n.* (esp.) ~-*car*, tourer.

touraco: see TURACO.

tour de force (toor, fôrs). Feat of strength or (esp.) skill. [Fr.]

tour'ism (toor-) *n.* Organized touring; accommodation and entertainment of tourists as industry.

tour'ist (toor-) *n.* Person who makes a tour; person who travels for pleasure; ~ *camp*, place offering simple accommodation to motorists etc.; ~ *class*, class of accommodation below first and second class in ships and aircraft. ~ *adv.* In tourist-class accommodation.

tour'maline (toor-; *or* -ēn) *n.* Brittle pyro-electric mineral, freq. occurring as crystals, a complex silicate of boron and aluminium with vitreous lustre, usu. black or blackish and opaque (*schorl*), also

TOURNAMENT

blue (*indicolite*), red (*rubellite*), and other colours, used in polariscopes and other optical instruments or as gem. [Sinhalese *tòramalli* (orig. found in Sri Lanka)]
tour′nament (toor- *or* tēr-) *n.* 1. (hist.) Medieval martial sport in which a number of mounted combatants in armour fought with blunted weapons for prize of valour; later, meeting for knightly sports and exercises. 2. Any contest in which a number of competitors play a series of games or take part in athletic events.
tournedos (toor′nedō) *n.* Small piece of fillet of beef grilled or sauté.
tour′ney (toor- *or* tēr-) *n. & v.i.* (hist.) (Take part in) tournament.
tourniquet (toor′nikă *or* tēr-) *n.* Bandage for arresting bleeding by compression, tightened by twisting a rigid bar put through it; surgical instrument usu. with pad and screw, for same purpose.
tou′sle (-zl) *v.t.* Pull about, handle roughly, make (esp. hair) untidy.
Toussaint Louverture (tōō-săṅ lōōvārtūr), François Dominique (1743–1803). Negro who led a rising in Haiti in 1791; later became a general in French army, and governor of the island 1796–1802, but was arrested, and died a prisoner in France.
tout *v.i.* Solicit custom, pester possible customers with applications (*for* orders); spy out movements and condition of racehorses in training. ~ *n.* One who touts.
tow¹ (tō) *n.* Coarse and broken fibres of flax or hemp, separated by heckling and ready for spinning; ~-head(ed), (having) head of very light-coloured straight hair. **tow′y** *adj.*
tow² (tō) *v.t.* Pull (boat, barge, etc.) along in water by rope or chain; pull (person, thing) along behind one; ~(*ing*)-*line*, -*rope*, line or rope by which something is towed; ~(*ing*)-*net*, fine-meshed drag-net towed near surface of water for collecting natural specimens; ~(*ing*)-*path*, path beside canal or navigable river for use in towing. **tow′age** *n.* **tow** *n.* Towing, being towed; *in* ~, being towed; *take in* ~, (fig.) take under one's guidance or patronage.
tō′ward¹ (-erd) *adj.* (archaic) Docile, apt. **tō′wardly** *adv.* **tō′wardness** *n.*
toward², **towards** (tōrd(z) *or* towōr′d(z)) *prep.* In the direction of; as regards, in relation to; near, approaching (in time); as contribution to. **toward** *adv.* (archaic) About to happen, at hand.
tow′el *n.* Absorbent cloth, paper, etc., for drying or wiping oneself or thing after washing; ~-*horse*, frame or stand on which towels are hung. ~ *v.t.* Wipe or dry with towel. **tow′elling** *n.* (esp.) Material for towels.
tow′er *n.* Tall, usu. square or circular structure, freq. forming part of church, castle, or other large building (ill. CHURCH); such structure (or whole fortress or stronghold of which it is part) used as stronghold or prison; (fig.) place of defence, protector (~ *of strength*, (of person) support); *the T*~ (*of London*), large assemblage of buildings on north bank of Thames eastwards of City of London, orig. fortress and palace and later a State prison, now used as repository of ancient armour and weapons and other objects of public interest; ~ *Hill*, rising ground by Tower of London, formerly a place of execution. ~ *v.i.* Reach high (*above* surroundings); (of eagle etc.) soar, be poised, aloft; (of wounded bird) shoot straight up. **tow′ering** *adj.* High, lofty; (fig., of rage, passion) violent.
town *n.* Inhabited place usu. larger and more regularly built than *village* and with more complete and independent local government or (in England) dist. from village by having periodical market or fair; (without *the*) business or shopping centre of a town or city; (without *the*) chief town of district or neighbourhood; (at Oxford, Cambridge, etc.) civic community as dist. from members of university (esp. in ~ *and gown*); *T*~, (West end of) London; *go to* ~, work enthusiastically, spend lavishly, etc. (*on*); *man about* ~, fashionable idler, esp. in London; *woman of the* ~, woman belonging to disreputable side of town life; ~ *clerk*, (until 1974) secretary to civic corporation, with charge of records, correspondence, legal business, conduct of municipal elections, etc.; ~ *hall*, building used for transaction of official business of town, often also used for public entertainments, court of justice, etc.; ~-*house*, town (as dist. from country) residence; (also) terraced house in town; ~-*meeting*, (U.S.) meeting of voters of town for transaction of public business, with certain powers of local government; ~-*planning*, construction of plans for regulation of growth and extension of town(s), provision and siting of amenities etc.; *tow′ns-people*, people of a town; ~ *talk*, common talk or gossip of people of town.
tow′nship *n.* (hist.) Community inhabiting manor, parish, etc.; manor or parish as territorial division (chiefly hist.); small town or village forming part of large parish, or being one of parishes into which larger parish has been divided; (U.S. and Canada) division of county with some corporate powers of local administration, district 6 miles square whether settled or not; (Austral.) site laid out for town.
tŏxae′mia *n.* Diseased condition due to presence of toxic substances in blood, usu. of bacterial origin; condition of pregnancy characterized by oedema and raised blood-pressure.
tŏxă′lbūmin *n.* (biochem.) Any toxic protein.
tŏ′xĭc *adj.* Of, affected or caused by, a poison or toxin; poisonous. **tŏ′xĭcally** *adv.* **tŏxī′-cĭty** *n.* [Gk *toxikon* poison for arrows (*toxa* arrows)]
tŏxĭcŏ′lŏgў *n.* Study of the nature and effects of poisons, their detection and treatment. **tŏxĭco-lŏ′gical** *adj.* **tŏxĭcolŏ′gĭcally** *adv.*
tŏxĭdēr′mĭc *adj.* Of skin disease produced by a toxin.
tŏ′xĭn *n.* Poisonous substance of animal or vegetable origin; esp. (path.) one of the poisons produced in a human or animal body by micro-organisms of disease, provoking the formation of antitoxins.
tŏxŏ′phĭlў *n.* Practice of, addiction to, archery. **tŏxŏ′phĭlite** *n. & adj.* (Student, lover) of archery. **tŏxŏphĭlī′tic** *adj.*
toy *n.* Plaything, esp. for child; knick-knack, small or trifling thing, thing meant rather for amusement than for serious use; (attrib., of dogs etc.) of diminutive breed or variety. ~ *v.t.* Trifle, amuse oneself (*with*); deal *with* in trifling, fondling, or careless manner.
Toy′nbee¹, Arnold (1852–83). English social reformer and economist; ~ *Hall*, the first social settlement, was erected in his honour in Whitechapel, London.
Toy′nbee², Arnold Joseph (1889–). English historian.
trāce¹ *v.* 1. Delineate, mark out, sketch, write esp. laboriously. 2. Copy (drawing etc.) by following and marking its lines, using a transparent sheet placed over it or similar device. 3. Follow the track or path of (person, animal, footsteps, etc.); follow course or line of, decipher; follow course or history of; observe or find vestiges or signs of. **trā′ceable** (-sa-) *adj.* **trāce** *n.* 1. Track left by person or animal walking or running, footprints or other visible signs of course pursued (usu. pl.); path of indicating spot in cathode-ray tube, shown as trace on a fluorescent screen. 2. Visible or other sign of what has existed or happened; minute quantity, esp. (chem.) too little to be measured; ~ *element*, substance which is essential, though only in minute amounts, to plant or animal life.
trāce² *n.* Each of pair of ropes, chains, or straps connecting collar of draught animal with swingletree etc. of vehicle (ill. HARNESS); *kick over the* ~*s*, (fig.) become insubordinate, act recklessly.
trā′cer *n.* (esp.) 1. (also ~ *bullet*, *shell*) Bullet etc. emitting smoke or flame which makes its course visible. 2. (also ~ *element*) Isotope which can be detected in minute

[926]

tra'cery n. Decorative stone open-work, esp. in head of Gothic window, in which patterns are formed by placing strips of stone inside a window opening (bar ~) or by perforating expanses of flat stone (plate ~) (ill. WINDOW); interlaced work of vault etc.; anything resembling or suggesting this.

tra'chea (-k-; or trakē'a) n. (pl. -eae). 1. Musculo-membranous tube from larynx to bronchial tubes, conveying air to lungs in air-breathing vertebrates (ill. LUNG). 2. Each of tubes forming respiratory organ in insects etc. 3. (bot.) Duct, vessel. **tra'cheal, tra'cheate** adjs.

tra'cheid (-k-; or trakē'id) n. Water-conducting element in the wood of vascular plants.

tra'cheocēle (-k-; or trakē'-) n. Tumour in or on trachea; goitre. **trachēŏ'tomy** (-k-) n. Incision of trachea; ~ tube, breathing-tube inserted into opening made by this.

trachō'ma (-k-) n. Contagious form of conjunctivitis with inflammatory granulation of inner surface of eyelids, freq. causing blindness. **trachŏ'matous** adj.

tra'chyte (-k-) n. Rough-surfaced, usu. light-coloured, volcanic rock consisting mainly of potash felspar. **trachy'tic** adj.

tra'cing n. (esp.) Copy made by tracing; record of self-registering instrument; ~-paper, tough semi-transparent paper for copying drawings etc.

track n. 1. Mark, series of marks, left by passage of anything, as wheel-rut, wake of ship, footprints; in one's ~s, on the spot, instantly; on the ~ of, in pursuit of, having a clue to; cover (up) ~s, conceal or screen actions etc. (of); keep ~ of, follow or grasp course, sequence, etc., of; make ~s (for), make off, make for. 2. Path, esp. one beaten by use, rough unmade road; line of travel or motion, course; train, sequence; prepared course for racing etc. (esp. cinder-~ for runners); continuous line of railway; (mech.) caterpillar track (ill. TRACTOR); ~ suit, loose garment worn by athlete before or between races, for warmth. 3. Transverse distance between wheels of vehicle. **tra'ckless** adj. **tra'cklessness** n. **track** v. Follow track or footsteps (of); pursue, follow up; (of wheels) run in same track, be in alignment; ~ down, pursue until caught or found.

tra'cker n. (esp., organ-building) Strip of wood or rod exerting pulling action between key and pallet (ill. ORGAN).

tract[1] n. Stretch, extent, region (of); region or area of natural structure, esp. bodily organ or system.

tract[2] n. Short treatise or discourse, esp. on religious subject. **tra'ctable** adj. (usu. of persons or animals) Easily handled, manageable, pliant, docile. **tractabi'lity, tra'ctableness** ns. **tra'ctably** adv.

Tractār'ian adj. & n. (Adherent, promoter) of Tractarianism. **Tractār'ianism** n. English high-church movement of 19th c. (later called the Oxford Movement) intended to restore high-church ideals of 17th c. and based on a series of 'Tracts for the Times' (1833–41) by Newman, Pusey, Keble, and others.

tra'ctāte n. Treatise.

tra'ction n. Drawing, pulling (esp. as dist. from pushing or pressure); drawing of vehicles or loads along road or track, esp. in ref. to form of power used for this; (med.) sustained pulling on limb etc., esp. by weights and pulleys, to correct dislocation, relieve pressure, etc.; ~-engine, steam or diesel engine used for drawing loads on ordinary road, across fields, etc.; ~-wheel, driving-wheel of locomotive etc. **tra'ctional, tra'ctive** adjs.

tra'ctor n. Traction-engine; motor-vehicle for drawing heavy loads etc., esp. one for farm-work.

TRACKED TRACTOR
1. Driving sprocket-wheel. 2. Caterpillar track

trad adj. & n. (slang) Traditional (jazz).

trade n. 1. Business, esp. mechanical or mercantile employment (opp. to PROFESSION), carried on as means of livelihood or profit; skilled handicraft. 2. Exchange of commodities for money or other commodities. 3. Persons engaged in a trade; the T~, (colloq.) licensed victuallers. 4. (usu. pl.) Trade-wind(s) (see below). 5. ~ cycle, recurring succession of trade conditions alternating between prosperity and depression; ~-mark, device, word(s) etc., used by manufacturer etc. to distinguish his goods, established by use and legally registered; ~-name, name of proprietary article; name by which a thing is called by the trade; name under which a person or firm conducts trade; ~ price, price at which an article is sold to retailers by manufacturers or wholesalers; **tra'desman**, person engaged in trade, esp. shopkeeper; (esp. in armed services) craftsman, man skilled in one of a number of specified crafts or trades; ~(s) union, organized association of employees in a trade or allied trades to protect and further their common interests; Trades Union Congress, (abbrev. T.U.C.) official representative body of trade unions in Gt Britain, founded 1868; ~ unionism, unionist; ~-wind, one of the winds blowing constantly towards the equatorial region of calms from about the 30th parallel north and south, being deflected westward by the earth's rotation so that they blow from the north-east in the N. hemisphere and from the south-east in the S. hemisphere (ill. WIND[1]). ~ v. Buy and sell, engage in trade; have commercial transaction (with); carry merchandise (to place); exchange in commerce, barter (goods); ~ in, barter, buy and sell (influence, offices, etc.), esp. corruptly; hand over (e.g. used car) in (part) payment or exchange (for thing); ~ on, take (esp. unscrupulous) advantage of (person's credulity or good nature, one's knowledge of secret etc.).

tra'ding n. (esp.) ~-post, station in sparsely populated area for exchanging local products for goods etc.; ~ stamp, stamp given by tradesman to customer, exchangeable for various articles.

tradi'tion n. Transmission of statements, beliefs, customs, etc., esp. by word of mouth or by practice without writing; what is thus handed down from generation to generation; long-established and generally accepted custom, practice, etc., an immemorial usage; (theol.) doctrine etc. held to have divine authority but not orig. committed to writing, esp., among Christians, body of teachings transmitted orally from generation to generation from earliest times and by Roman Catholics held to derive from Christ and the Apostles or to have authority of the Holy Spirit. **tradi'tional** adj. **tradi'tionally** adv. **tradi'tionalism, tradi'tionalist** ns. **traditionali'stic** adj.

tradū'ce v.t. Calumniate, misrepresent.

Trafă'lgar (archaic & poet. as in Span., trăfalgăr'). Cape on S. coast of Spain near which British fleet under NELSON (who was killed in the action) achieved great victory over combined fleets of France and Spain (21 Oct. 1805); ~ Square, square adjoining upper end of Whitehall, London, laid out 1829–41, and containing Nelson monument and other statues, freq. used for popular demonstrations.

tra'ffic n. 1. Trade (in commodity); now esp. dealing or

bargaining in something which should not be the subject of trade. 2. Transportation of goods, coming and going of persons, goods, or esp. vehicles or vessels, along road, railway, canal, etc.; amount of this; ~ *cop*, (U.S.) policeman regulating road traffic; ~ *lights*, *signal*, mechanical signal for controlling road traffic, esp. at junctions or crossings, by means of coloured lights etc.; ~ *warden*, person appointed to assist the police in road traffic duties, esp. in controlling the parking of vehicles. ~ *v*. Trade (*in*), carry on commerce; barter (esp. in sense of *n*. 1).
trăf'fĭcātor *n*. Direction indicator on vehicle.
tră'gacănth *n*. Gum exuded from various species of *Astragalus*, usu. obtained in dried whitish flakes, and used as vehicle for drugs, in the arts, etc. [Gk *tragakantha* goat's-thorn (*tragos* he-goat, *akantha* thorn)]
tragē'dian *n*. Writer of tragedies; actor in tragedies. **tragēdiē'nne** *n*. Actress in tragedies.
tră'gedy *n*. Literary composition, esp. play, of serious and usu. elevated character, with fatal or disastrous conclusion; branch of dramatic art dealing with sorrowful or terrible events in serious and dignified style; sad event, calamity, disaster. [Gk *tragōidia* app. goatsong (*tragos* goat, *ōidē* song)]
tră'gĭc *adj*. Of, in the style of, tragedy; ~ *irony*, used in ancient Greek tragedy of words having an inner esp. prophetic meaning for audience unsuspected by speaker. 2. Sad, calamitous, distressing. **tră'gĭcal** *adj*. (rare) Tragic. **tră'gĭcally** *adv*.
tră'gĭcŏ'mĕdy *n*. Drama of mixed tragic and comic elements. **trăgĭcŏ'mĭc, -ical** *adjs*. **trăgĭcŏ'mĭcally** *adv*.
tră'gopăn *n*. Asiatic pheasant of genus *T*~, with erectile fleshy horns on head of male, horned pheasant. [L f. Gk, reputed bird in Ethiopia (*tragos* goat+PAN³)]
Trahĕr'ne (-a-h-), Thomas (*c* 1637-74). English metaphysical poet and writer of religious works.
trail *n*. Part drawn behind or in the wake of a thing, long (real or apparent) appendage; hinder end of stock of gun-carriage, resting on ground when piece is unlimbered (ill. GUN); track left by thing that has moved or been drawn over surface; track, scent; beaten path, esp. through wild region; *at the* ~, (mil.) being trailed. ~ *v*. Draw along behind one, one on ground, drag (one's limbs, oneself) along, walk wearily, lag, straggle; hang loosely; (of plant) grow decumbently and stragglingly to some length, esp. so as to touch or rest on the ground; (mil.) carry (rifle etc.) in horizontal or oblique position with arm extended downwards; track, follow the track or wake of, shadow.

trai'ler *n*. (esp.) 1. Trailing plant. 2. Vehicle drawn along behind another, esp. caravan, luggage-carrier, small fire-pump, etc., designed to be drawn along behind a motor-car. 3. Excerpt(s) of cinema film exhibited in advance as an advertisement.
trai'ling *adj*. That trails; (esp.) ~ *edge*, rear edge of aircraft's wing, tail, or fin (ill. AEROPLANE); ~ *shoe*, rear shoe of brake (ill. BRAKE⁴).
train *v*. Bring (person, child, animal) to desired state or standard of efficiency, obedience, etc., by instruction and practice; subject, be subjected to, course of instruction and discipline (*for* profession, art, etc.); teach and accustom (*to do, to* action); bring, bring oneself, to physical efficiency by exercise and diet, esp. in preparation for sport or contest; cause (plant) to grow in required shape; point, aim, (firearm, camera, *on* object etc.). ~ *n*. 1. Trailing thing, esp. elongated part of skirt or robe trailing behind on ground, or sometimes carried on ceremonial occasions by page or attendant; long or conspicuous tail of bird; ~-*bearer*, person holding up train of another's robe. 2. Body of followers, retinue, suite; succession or series of persons or things; line of gunpowder or other combustible material to convey fire to explosive charge etc.; set of parts in mechanism actuating one another in series, esp. set of wheels and pinions actuating strikingpart or turning hands of clock or watch. 3. Number of railwaycarriages, vans, or trucks coupled together (usu. including locomotive drawing them); ~-*ferry*, ferry conveying railway-trains across water; ~-*sickness*, sickness or nausea caused by railway-travelling. **trai'nless** *adj*.
train-band *n*. (hist.) Company of citizen soldiers, organized in London and elsewhere in 16th, 17th, and 18th centuries. [abbrev. of *trained band*]
trainee' *n*. One who is being trained (for an occupation).
trai'ner *n*. (esp.) One who trains persons or animals for athletic performance, as race, boxing-match, etc.
trai'ning *n*. (esp.) *in* ~, undergoing physical training, physically fit as a result of this; *out of* ~, in poor condition from lack or cessation of training; (*teacher*) ~ *college*, former name for COLLEGE of Education; ~-*ship*, ship on which boys are trained for naval service or merchant navy.
train-oil *n*. Whale-blubber oil. [MDu. *traen*, app. = 'tear', 'drop']
traipse, trāpes (-ps) *v*. Walk in trailing or untidy way, walk about aimlessly or needlessly, trudge wearily; walk over (thus). ~ *n*.
trait (*or* trā) *n*. Feature (of face or esp. of mind or character), distinguishing quality.
trai'tor *n*. One who is false to his allegiance or acts disloyally (*to* his sovereign or country, his principles, religion, etc.). **trai'torous** *adj*. **trai'torously** *adv*. **trai'torousness** *n*.
Trā'jan. Marcus Ulpius Nerva Trajanus (*c* A.D. 52-117), Roman emperor 90-117, whose victories are commemorated on Trajan's Column in Rome.
tră'jĕctory (*or* trajĕ'-) *n*. Path of any body moving under action of given forces, esp. that of projectile in its flight through air; (geom.) curve or surface cutting all curves or surfaces of a given system at constant angle.
trăm¹ *n*. (also ~ *silk*) Silk thread of 2 or 3 loosely twisted strands used for weft of some velvets and silks. [L *trama* weft]
trăm² *n*. 1. Small iron truck running on rails; undercarriage of this. 2. (also *tra'mcar*) Passenger car running on rails on public road; *tra'mline*, track with rails flush with road surface on which tramcars are run; (pl., colloq.) either pair of long parallel lines bounding a lawn tennis court; *tra'mway*, rails along which tram runs. ~ *v*. Convey in tram, perform (journey) in tram; travel by tram. [app. same wd as LG *traam* beam, barrow-shaft]
tră'mmel *n*. 1. (also ~ *net*) Fishing-net consisting of fine net hung loosely between vertical walls

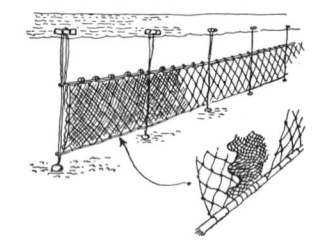

TRAMMEL NET WITH DETAIL TO SHOW INNER AND OUTER NETS

of coarser net, so that fish passing through carry some of the finer net through the coarser and are caught in the pocket thus formed. 2. Shackle, esp. one used in teaching horse to amble; (fig., usu. pl.) impediment to free movement or action. 3. Instrument for drawing ellipses, esp. cross with grooves in which move pins carrying beam and pencil; kind of gauge for adjusting and aligning machine parts; (now chiefly U.S.) kind of hook for holding kettle etc. at adjustable heights in fireplace. 4. ~-*wheel*, device for converting rotary into reciprocal motion, or vice versa, and consisting of wheel with crossing grooves in which slide blocks attached to connecting rod. ~ *v.t.* Confine, hamper, with trammels.

tramŏ'ntāne *adj.* (Situated, living) on other side of the Alps; (fig., from Italian point of view) foreign, barbarous; (of wind) blowing from beyond mountains, esp. Alps. ~ *n.* Tramontane person, wind.

trămp *v.* Walk with firm heavy tread; walk, go, traverse, on foot; be a tramp. ~ *n.* 1. Measured and continuous tread of body of persons or animals, sound of heavy footfalls. 2. Tramping, long or tiring walk or march; journey on foot, walking excursion. 3. Person who tramps roads in search of employment or as vagrant. 4. (also *ocean* ~, ~ *steamer*) Cargo-vessel not trading regularly between fixed ports, but taking cargoes wherever obtainable and for any port.

tră'mple *v.* Tread heavily and (esp.) injuriously (upon), crush or destroy thus (freq. fig.); put (fire) *out* by trampling. ~ *n.* Trampling.

tră'mpoline (*or* -ēn) *n.* Canvas sheet attached to horizontal framework by springs, providing resilient platform for acrobatics etc.

trance (-ah-) *n.* Sleep-like state, with more or less inertness to stimulus and subsequent amnesia; hypnotic or cataleptic condition, similar state of spiritualistic medium; mental abstraction from external things, absorption, ecstasy.

tră'nquil *adj.* Serene, free from agitation or disturbance. **tră'nquillў** *adv.* **trănqui'llitў** *n.* **tră'nquillize** *v.t.* **tră'nquillizer** *n.* (esp.) Sedative drug.

trans- *prefix.* Across, beyond, over, to or on farther side of.

trănsă'ct (*or* trah-; -z- *or* -s-) *v.t.* Perform, carry on, do (action, business, etc.). **trănsă'ction** *n.* Transacting, being transacted; what is transacted, piece of business; (pl.) proceedings, dealings; (usu. pl.) learned society's, esp. published, records of its proceedings.

trănsă'lpine (-z-; *or* trah-) *adj.* Situated, living, beyond the Alps (usu. from Italian point of view); passing across or through the Alps; *T~ Gaul*, Roman province including the present France, Switzerland, Belgium, and the Netherlands. ~ *n.* Person living beyond the Alps.

trănsatlă'ntic (-z-; *or* trah-) *adj. & n.* (Person living) across the Atlantic; esp., from European point of view, American; (of boat, aircraft, etc.) crossing the Atlantic.

Trănscaucă'sia (-nz-; -zĭa *or* -zha; *or* trah-). Region of U.S.S.R. lying beyond (i.e. S. of) the Caucasus, including the republics of Armenia, Azerbaijan, and Georgia. **Trănscaucă'sian** *adj. & n.*

trănscĕ'nd (*or* trah-) *v.t.* Go beyond, exceed, limits of; rise above, surpass, excel.

trănscĕ'ndent (*or* trah-) *adj.* That transcends ordinary limits, pre-eminent, supreme, extraordinary; (Kantian philos.) transcending, altogether outside, unrealizable in, experience. **trănscĕ'ndentlў** *adv.* **trănscĕ'ndencў** *n.* **trănscĕ'ndent** *n.* Transcendent thing.

trănscĕndĕ'ntal (*or* trah-) *adj.* 1. (Kantian philos.) Not derived from experience, *a priori*; (of any philosophy) based on recognition of *a priori* element in experience; (pop., vaguely) abstract, metaphysical, obscure, visionary. 2. (math.) Not capable of being produced by a finite number of ordinary algebraical operations of multiplication, addition, involution, or the inverse operations. **trănscĕndĕ'ntallў** *adv.*

trănscĕndĕ'ntalism (*or* trah-) *n.* Transcendental philosophy, esp. idealism of Schelling, Fichte, and Hegel (which does not recognize Kantian distinction between *transcendent* and *transcendental*), and religio-philosophical doctrine of Emerson and his followers; extravagant, vague, or visionary quality, philosophy, language, etc. **trănscĕndĕ'ntalist** *n. & adj.*

trănscŏntinĕ'ntal (-z-; *or* trah-) *adj.* Extending or passing across a continent.

trănscrī'be (*or* trah-) *v.t.* Copy out (esp. in writing), make copy of; write out (shorthand) in ordinary characters; (mus.) adapt (composition) for voice or instrument other than that for which it was orig. written. **tră'nscript** *n.* Written copy; (law) copy of legal record. **trănscrī'ption, trănscrī'ptive** *adj.*

trănsdū'cer (*or* trah-) *n.* Device that accepts power from one part of a system and emits power in a different form to another part, as between electrical, mechanical, or acoustic parts.

tră'nsĕpt (*or* trah-) *n.* (Either arm of) transverse part of cruciform church (ill. CHURCH). **trănsĕ'ptal** *adj.*

trănsfĕr' (*or* trah-) *v.* Convey, transmit, transport, hand over, from one person, place, etc., to another; (law) convey (title, property, etc.) by legal process; convey (design etc.) from one surface to another; change from one station, line, route, etc., to another to continue journey; transfer (esp. football-player, his services) to another club, group, etc. **tră'nsfer** *n.* 1. Transferring, being transferred, esp. (law) conveyance of property, as shares, etc., from one person to another; means or place of transfer, esp. (U.S.) conveyance of passenger and luggage from one station or line to another, place where trains etc. are transferred to ferry for water transport etc.; transfer ticket (see below). 2. Transferred thing; design etc. (to be) conveyed from one surface to another, (freq. coloured) design or picture on prepared paper from which it can be transferred to another surface, as with water or hot iron. 3. ~ *company*, (U.S.) company conveying passengers and luggage between stations or from station; ~*-fee, -money*, sum paid for transfer esp. of professional footballer to another club; ~ *ticket*, ticket allowing journey to be continued on another line or route.

trănsfĕr'able (*or* tră'- *or* trah-) *adj.* Capable of being transferred; ~ *vote*, electoral method for securing that elected candidate shall represent a majority, each voter signifying on his ballot-paper to which candidate his vote shall be transferred if no candidate has an absolute majority of first preferences.

tră'nsference (*or* trah-) *n.* (esp., psychol.) Transferring of emotions to new object.

trănsfigurā'tion (*or* trah-) *n.* Transfiguring, being transfigured; esp. change in appearance of Jesus on the mountain (Matt. 17: 2; Mark 9: 2, 3), Church festival (6 Aug.) commemorating this, picture representing it.

trănsfi'gure (-ger; *or* trah-) *v.t.* Alter form or appearance of, transform; esp. glorify, change so as to elevate or idealize.

trănsfi'x (*or* trah-) *v.t.* Pierce with, impale on, sharp-pointed instrument; pierce through, render motionless (with fear, grief, horror, etc.). **trănsfi'xion** (-kshon) *n.*

trănsfŏr'm (*or* trah-) *v.t.* Change shape or form of, esp. considerably; change in character, condition, function, nature, etc.; (phys.) change (one form of energy) into another; (elect.) change (current) in potential (as from high voltage to low) or type (as from alternating to continuous). **trănsformā'tion** (*or* trah-) *n.* Transforming, being transformed, metamorphosis, as of insects; (math.) change of form without alteration of value, as substitution of one geometrical figure for another of equal magnitude, or of one algebraical expression for another of same value; change of form of substance, as from solid to liquid, or of potential or type of electric current etc.; wig; ~ *scene*, (theatr.) elaborate spectacular scene in pantomime in which actors and scenery change their appearance in sight of audience.

trănsfŏr'mer (*or* trah-) *n.* (esp., elect.) Apparatus for changing potential or type of electric current, consisting usually of a few turns of comparatively thick wire and a coil of fine wire wound on a laminated iron core.

trănsfū'se (-z; *or* trah-) *v.t.* Cause (fluid, fig. quality etc.) to flow or pass from one vessel etc. to another; transfer (blood of one person or animal) into veins of another. **trănsfū'sion** *n.*

[929]

TRANSGRESS

trănsgrĕ′ss (*or* -z-; *or* trah-) *v.t.* Violate, infringe (law, command, esp. of God). **trănsgrĕ′ssion, trănsgrĕ′ssor** *ns.*
trănshi′p (*or* trah-) *v.* = TRANSSHIP. **trănshi′pment** *n.*
tră′nsient (-z-) *adj.* Not durable or permanent, brief, momentary, fleeting; ~ *chord, note,* (mus.) unessential one, serving only to connect. **tră′nsiently** *adv.* **tră′nsience, tră′nsiency** *ns.*
trănsi′stor *n.* Electronic device using the flow of electrons in a solid to perform most of the functions of a thermionic valve; radio

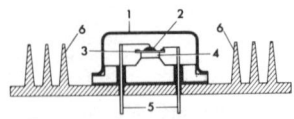

CROSS-SECTION OF A TYPICAL POWER TRANSISTOR MOUNTED ON A FINNED HEAT SINK

1. Metal shell. 2. Emitter. 3. Base. 4. Collector. 5. Terminals. 6. Finned heat sink

set using such device; also attrib., as ~ *radio.* **trănsi′storīzed** (-zd) *adj.* Fitted with transistors instead of valves.
tră′nsit (*or* -z-; *or* trah-) *n.* 1. Passing, passage, journey, conveyance, from one place to another. 2. (astrol.) Passage of planet across some region or point of zodiac; (astron.) passage of inferior planet across sun's disc, or of satellite or its shadow across planet's disc; passage of celestial body across meridian. 3. (colloq.) Transit-circle, -compass, or -instrument. 4. ~*-circle*, astronomical instrument, consisting of transit-instrument combined with meridian circle for determining right ascension and declination of star by observation of its transit; ~*-compass*, kind of theodolite for measurement of horizontal angles; ~*-duty*, duty on goods passing through a country; ~*-instrument*, astronomical telescope mounted at right angles to fixed east-and-west axis, for determining time of transit of celestial body; ~*-theodolite*, transit-compass; ~ *visa*, visa allowing passage through but not stay in a country. ~ *v.* (of heavenly body) Make transit (across).
trănsi′tion (-z-; *or* trah-) *n.* Passage from one condition, action, style, subject, stage of development, etc., to another; period of this; (mus.) modulation, esp. passing or brief, or into remote key. **trănsi′tional** *adj.* **trănsi′tionally** *adv.* **trănsi′tionary** *adj.*
tră′nsitive (*or* trah-) *adj. & n.* (Verb) expressing action which passes over to an object, requiring direct object to complete the sense. **tră′nsitively** *adv.* **tră′nsitiveness** *n.*

trā′nsitory (*or* trah-) *adj.* Not lasting; fleeting, momentary, brief. **tră′nsitorily** *adv.* **tră′nsitoriness** *n.*
Trănsjŏr′dan (-z- *or* trah-). (hist.) District of Palestine E. of river Jordan (now the major part of the Hashemite Kingdom of the Jordan).
trănslā′te (*or* -z-; *or* trah-) *v.* 1. Turn (word, sentence, book, etc.) from one language *into* another, express sense of it in another form of words. 2. Infer or declare the significance of, interpret (signs, movement, conduct, etc.). 3. Convey, introduce (idea, principle, design) *from* one art etc. *into* another. 4. Remove (bishop) to another see. 5. (bibl.) Convey to heaven without death. 6. (teleg.) Retransmit (message). 7. (mech.) Cause (body) to move so that all its parts follow same direction, impart motion without rotation to. **trănslā′tion** *n.* **trănslā′tional** *adj.*
trănsli′terāte (-z-; *or* trah-) *v.t.* Replace (letters of one alphabet or language) by those of another. **trănsliterā′tion** *n.*
trănslocā′tion (-z-; *or* trah-) *n.* Change of location, esp. (bot.) movement of dissolved substances inside plants.
trănslū′cent (-zlū-; *or* -lōō-; *or* trah-) *adj.* Allowing passage of light but so diffusing it as to prevent bodies lying beyond from being clearly distinguished. **trănslu′cence, trănslu′cency** *ns.*
trănslū′nary (-z-; *or* trah-; *or* -lōō-) *adj.* Lying beyond the moon; (fig.) insubstantial, visionary.
trănsmari′ne (-z-, -ēn; *or* trah-) *adj.* That is beyond the sea; crossing the sea.
tră′nsmīgrā′te (-z-; *or* trah-) *v.i.* Migrate; (of soul) pass after death into another body, either human or animal. **trănsmī′grant** *n.* (esp.) Person passing as emigrant from one country through another in which he does not intend to settle. **trănsmīgrā′tion** *n.* **trănsmī′gratory** *adj.*
trănsmi′ssion (-z-; *or* trah-) *n.* (esp.) 1. Gear by which power is transmitted from engine to axle in motor-car etc. 2. Transmitting by radio or television; programme etc. so transmitted.
trănsmi′t (-z-; *or* trah-) *v.t.* Send, convey, cause to pass or go, to another person, place, or thing; suffer to pass through, be medium for, serve to communicate (heat, light, sound, electricity, emotion, news). **trănsmi′ssible, trănsmi′ssive, trănsmi′ttable** *adjs.*
trănsmi′tter (-z-; *or* trah-) *n.* (esp.) Part of telegraphic or telephonic apparatus by means of which message etc. is transmitted; (part of) radio set or station for transmitting radio waves.
trănsmŏ′grify (-z-; *or* trah-) *v.t.* (joc.) Transform (esp. utterly,

TRANSPORT

grotesquely, or strangely). **trănsmŏgrĭfĭcā′tion** *n.*
trănsmūtā′tion (-z-; *or* trah-) *n.* Transmuting, being transmuted; (biol.) transformation of one species into another, evolution (esp. in Lamarckian theory). **trănsmū′te** (-z-; *or* trah-) *v.t.* Change form, nature, or substance of; convert (one element, substance, species, etc.) into another; esp. (alchemy) change (baser metal) into gold or silver.
trănsōcĕă′nic (-z- *or* -zōsh-; *or* trah-) *adj.* Situated, existing, beyond the ocean; crossing the ocean.
tră′nsom *n.* Cross-beam, cross-piece, esp. one spanning an opening; horizontal bar across window (ill. WINDOW); cross-bar separating door from fan-light above it; (U.S.) window above transom, esp. of door.
trănspaci′fic (-z-; *or* trah-) *adj.* Situated, being, beyond the Pacific Ocean; crossing the Pacific.
trănspăr′ency (*or* trah-; *or* -z-; *or* -păr-) *n.* Being transparent; transparent object or medium; esp. photograph or picture on transparent substance, to be viewed by transmitted light.
trănspăr′ent (*or* trah-; *or* -z-; *or* -păr-) *adj.* Transmitting light so that bodies lying beyond are completely visible; pervious to specified form of radiant energy, as heat-rays, X-rays; easily seen through, manifest, obvious, clear; candid, frank, open. **trănspăr′ently** *adv.*
trănspier′ce (-z-; *or* trah-) *v.t.* Pierce through.
trănspīr′e (*or* trah-) *v.* Emit through excretory organs of skin or lungs, send off in vapour; be emitted thus; (bot., of plant or leaf) exhale watery vapour; (of gas or liquid) move through capillary tube under pressure; (of secret etc.) come to be known; (misused for) occur, happen. **trănspirā′tion** *n.*
trănsplă′nt (-lah-; *or* trah-) *v.* Remove (plant) from one place and plant it in another; remove and establish, esp. cause to live, in another place; (surg.) transfer (living tissue or organ) from one part of body, or one person or animal, to another; bear transplanting. **tră′nsplant, trănsplantā′tion** *ns.*
trănspŏ′ntine (*or* -z-) *adj.* Of, on, the other side of the bridges in London, S. of the Thames; hence (from melodramas popular in the theatres there in 19th c.), cheaply or violently melodramatic.
trănspŏr′t (*or* trah-) *v.t.* 1. Carry, convey, from one place to another. 2. (hist.) Deport, convey (convict) to penal colony. 3. (usu. pass.) Carry away by strong emotion. **tră′nspŏrt** *n.*

[930]

transportation 1. Conveyance, carrying, of goods or passengers, from one place to another; means of conveyance, esp. vessel used in transporting troops or military stores, wagons or other vehicles carrying supplies of army etc. 2. Vehement (usu. pleasurable) emotion; (freq. pl.) fit of joy or rage.

trănsportā'tion (*or* trah-) *n.* Transporting; deportation, transfer to penal settlement; (U.S.) means of transport or conveyance.

trănspō'se (-z; *or* trah-) *v.t.* Alter order of (series of things) or position of (thing in series), interchange; esp. alter order of (letters) in word or (words) in sentence; (algebra) transfer (quantity) from one side of equation to the other; (mus.) put into different key, alter key of. **trănsposi'tion** *n.*

trănsrhē'nāne (-zrē-; *or* trah-) *adj.* Beyond the Rhine; German as opp. to Roman or French.

trăns-shī'p (-z-; *or* trah-) *v.* Transfer, change, from one ship, railway-train, etc., to another. **trăns-shī'pment** *n.*

Tră'ns-Sībēr'ian Rai'lway (-nz-; *or* trah-). Railway in U.S.S.R., built 1891-1904, running from the Urals to Vladivostok.

trănsubstă'ntiāte (-shī-; *or* trah-) *v.t.* Change from one substance into another.

trănsubstāntiā'tion (-shī-; *or* trah-) *n.* (esp., theol.) Doctrine that in the Eucharist a change is wrought in the elements at consecration, whereby the whole substance of the bread and wine is transmuted into the very Body and Blood of Christ, only the appearances (and other 'accidents') of bread and wine remaining.

trănsū'de (*or* trah-) *v.i.* Exude through pores in body or anything permeable.

trănsūră'nīc (*or* trah-) *adj.* (chem.) Belonging to a group of radioactive elements having atomic numbers and weights greater than those of uranium, not found in nature but produced artificially, e.g. in atomic pile.

Trănsvaa'l (-ahl; *or* trah-; *or* -z-). Province of the Republic of South Africa, lying N. of Orange Free State and separated from it by River Vaal.

trănsvēr'sal (-nz-; *or* trah-) *adj.* (of line) Cutting a system of lines. ~ *n.* Transversal line.

trănsvēr'se (-nz-; *or* tră'-; *or* trah-) *adj.* Situated, lying, across or athwart; ~ *magnet*, bar magnetized at right angles to its length, so that poles are at the sides, not at the ends. **trănsvēr'sely** *adv.* **tră'nsvērse** *n.* Transverse muscle, piece, etc.

trănsvē'stīsm (*or* -nz-; *or* trah-) *n.* Practice of dressing in clothes of opposite sex. **trănsvē'stīte** *n.* One who practises transvestism. ~ *adj.*

Trănsȳlvā'nīa (*or* trah-). Province of Rumania; before the war of 1914-18, part of Austria-Hungary. **Trănsȳlvā'nīan** *adj.*

tră'nter *n.* (now dial.) Carrier; hawker.

trăp[1] *n.* 1. Device, as pitfall, snare, mechanical contrivance, for catching animals; device allowing pigeon to enter but not leave loft; police arrangement for timing motorists over measured distance to ensure that those exceeding speed-limit are caught; (fig.) something by which one is caught, led astray, etc. 2. Trap-door; movable covering of opening, falling when stepped upon; door flush with surface in floor, ceiling, etc. 3. Device for suddenly releasing bird etc. to be shot at; compartment from which greyhound is released at start of race; pivoted wooden instrument for throwing ball into air in trap-ball. 4. Light, esp. two-wheeled (horse-)carriage on springs. 5. Device, usu. U-shaped section of pipe with standing water, for preventing upward escape of noxious gases from pipe; contrivance for preventing passage of steam, water, silt, etc. 6. (slang) Mouth. 7. ~-*ball*, game in which ball is thrown into air from 'heel' of shoe-shaped wooden device when other end is struck with bat, with which ball is then hit away; ~-*door*, hinged or sliding door flush with surface of floor, roof, wall, etc.; ~-*door spider*, spider living in burrow closed by one or more lids like trap-door(s); ~-*drum*, bass drum with other percussion instruments attached; so ~-*drummer*; ~-*nest*, nest-box for hen, with hinged door by which she can enter but not leave; ~-*shooting*, sport of shooting pigeons, balls, etc., released from spring trap. ~ *v.* Catch (as) in trap, snare, ensnare; set traps for game etc.; furnish with trap(s).

trăp[2] *n.* Any of various dark-coloured fine-grained igneous rocks, freq. columnar in structure, or in sheet-like masses rising like stairs.

trăp[3] *v.t.* (chiefly in past part.) Adorn with trappings, caparison. [OF *drap* cloth, covering]

trăp-cŭt *n.* = STEP-cut.

trapes: see TRAIPSE.

trapē'ze *n.* Horizontal crossbar suspended by ropes as apparatus for acrobatics etc. **trapē'zist** *n.* Performer on trapeze.

trapēz'ium *n.* 1. Quadrilateral with two sides (thought of as base and opposite side) parallel (ill. QUADRILATERAL). 2. (U.S.) = TRAPEZOID, 1. 3. (anat.) Bone of carpus articulating with metacarpal bone of thumb (ill. HAND); band of nerve-fibres in *pons Variolii* of brain. 4. *T*~, (astron.) trapezium-shaped group of four stars in great nebula of Orion. [Gk *trapezion*, dim. of *trapeza* table]

trapē'zius *n.* (anat.) Each of pair of large flat triangular muscles of back, extending over back of neck etc. (ill. MUSCLE).

trăpėzohē'dron *n.* Solid figure whose faces are trapeziums.

tră'pėzoid *n.* 1. Quadrilateral with no sides parallel (ill. QUADRILATERAL). 2. (U.S.) = TRAPEZIUM, 1. 3. (anat.) Second bone of distal row of carpus (ill. HAND). ~ *adj.* Of, in the form of, a trapezoid. **trăpėzoi'dal** *adj.*

tră'ppėan *adj.* (geol.) Of (the nature of) TRAP[2].

tră'pper *n.* (esp.) One engaged in trapping wild animals for their furs.

tră'ppings (-z) *n.pl.* Ornamental housing for horse; ornaments, embellishments, ornamental accessories.

Tră'ppist *adj. & n.* (Monk) of reformed Cistercian order established 1664 at monastery of La Trappe in Normandy and observing extremely austere discipline and perpetual silence except with confessors and in choir. **Tră'ppistine** *adj. & n.* (Member) of order of nuns established 1796 and affiliated with Trappists.

trăps *n.pl.* (colloq.) Personal effects, portable belongings, baggage. [app. shortening of *trappings*]

trăsh *n.* Waste or worthless stuff, refuse, rubbish; stripped-off leaves and tops of sugar-canes (*field*-~) or refuse after juice has been extracted (*cane*-~); worthless or disreputable people; *white* ~, poor white population of southern States of U.S.; ~-*ice*, broken ice mixed with water. **tră'shy** *adj.* **tră'shily** *adv.* **tră'shiness** *n.*

Tră'simēne (-z-). (It. *Trasimeno*) Lake near Perugia, Italy, where Hannibal fought and defeated the Romans (217 B.C.).

trăss *n.* Light-coloured volcanic tufa found esp. along lower Rhine and used for hydraulic cement.

trau'ma *n.* (pl. -*ata*, -*as*). Injury, wound; condition resulting from this; (psychol.) unpleasant or disturbing experience in which neurosis etc. originates. **traumă'tic** *adj.* **traumă'tically** *adv.* **trau'matism** *n.*

tră'vail *n. & v.i.* (archaic) (Suffer) pangs of childbirth; (make) painful or laborious effort. [OF *travail*, app. f. LL *trepalium* instrument of torture (L *tres* three, *palus* stake)]

tră'vel *v.* 1. Make journey, esp. of some length or to foreign countries; act as COMMERCIAL traveller; pass from one point or place to another, proceed; (of piece of mechanism) move, be capable of moving, along fixed course; (colloq.) bear transportation. 2. Journey through, pass over, traverse, cover (specified distance); cause (herds etc.) to journey. ~ *n.* 1. Travelling, esp. in foreign countries. 2. Single movement of part of mechanism; range, rate, mode of motion, of this. 3. ~ *agency*, *agent*, one

[931]

making arrangements, supplying tickets, etc., for travellers.
tră'veller n. One who travels; (esp.) COMMERCIAL traveller; ~'s *cheque*, cheque purchased from bank etc., encashable at any of the bank's agencies; ~'s *joy*, shrub (*Clematis alba* and other climbing species of *Clematis*) trailing over wayside hedges; ~'s *tale*, incredible or mendacious story.
tră'velling n. (esp.) ~ *clock*, small clock in case; ~ *fellowship*, *scholarship*, etc., one enabling holder to travel for purposes of study. ~ *adj*. That travels; ~ *crane*, crane that travels along esp. overhead support.
tră'velŏgue (-g) n. Illustrated narrative of travel.
tră'verse n. 1. Movement or part of structure which crosses another; (each lap of) ascending zigzag road; (mountaineering) more or less horizontal motion across face of precipice from one practicable line of ascent or descent to another, place where this is necessary; (naut.) zigzag course taken owing to contrary winds or currents, each leg of this; (surv.) single line of survey across region, tract of country so surveyed; (geom.) TRANSVERSAL line; (mil.) earthwork in form of parapet protecting covered way etc., double or quadruple right angle in trench (⌐, ⌐⌐); horizontal or lateral movement of gun; (eng.) platform for shifting engine etc. from one line of rails to another; sideways movement of part or machine; (archit.) gallery from side to side of church etc.; (hist.) curtain, partition across room etc., compartment so cut off; ~ *circle*, circular or segmental track on which gun-carriage is turned in traversing gun; ~ *sailing*, sailing on zigzag course; ~ *table*, table for computing nautical traverses. 2. (law) Formal denial of matter of fact alleged by other side. ~ v. 1. Travel or lie across; make a traverse in climbing; determine position of points, survey (road, river, etc.) by measuring lengths and azimuths of connected series of straight lines; turn (gun) (of needle of compass etc.) turn (as) on pivot; (of horse) walk crosswise; plane (wood) across grain; (of pulley) run over rope etc. that supports it. 2. (fig.) Consider, discuss, whole extent of (subject). 3. Deny, esp. (law) in pleading; thwart, frustrate (plan or opinion).
tră'vertine (or -ēn) n. White or light-coloured crystalline concretionary limestone deposited from springs etc. and used for building. [L *tiburtinus*, f. *Tibur* Tivoli, near Rome]
tră'vestў v.t. Make ridiculous by gross parody or imitation; be ridiculous imitation of. ~ n. Ridiculing treatment; ridiculous imitation.
trawl n. Large bag-net (~ *net*)

with mouth held open by beam or otherwise, dragged along bottom of sea etc. by boat; (U.S.) long buoyed line, anchored at ends, and with numerous short baited lines attached, for seafishing. ~ v. Fish with trawl or in trawler; catch with trawl.
traw'ler n. One who trawls; vessel used in fishing with trawl net.

A. TRAWLER. B. TRAWL
1. Gallows through which warps are run. 2. Warps. 3. Otter boards or trawl boards, which keep mouth of net open. 4. Floats to raise top of net

tray n. Flat shallow vessel usu. with raised rim for placing or carrying small articles on, steeping specimens in laboratory, holding correspondence on desk, etc.; shallow lidless box forming compartment of trunk.
T.R.C. *abbrev*. Thames Rowing Club.
trea'cherous (-ĕch-) *adj*. Violating faith or betraying trust; perfidious; not to be relied on, deceptive. **trea'cherously** *adv*. **trea'cherousnĕss, trea'cherў** ns.
trea'cle n. Uncrystallized syrup produced in refining sugar; golden syrup. **trea'clў** *adj*.
tread (-ĕd) v. (past t. *trŏd*, past part. *trŏ'dden*). Set down one's foot, walk, (of foot) be set down; go through (dance) esp. in stately measure; press or crush with feet, trample (*on*); (of male bird) copulate with; ~ *the boards*, be an actor, appear on stage; ~ *down*, press down with feet; trample on, destroy, oppress, crush; ~ *in*, press in or into earth etc. with feet; ~ *out*, stamp out; press out (wine, grain) with feet; ~ *under foot*, (fig.) trample on, destroy, treat contemptuously; ~ *water*, (in swimming) keep body erect and head above water while moving feet as in walking upstairs. ~ n. 1. Manner, sound, of walking. 2. (also ~-*board*) Top surface of step or stair (ill. STAIR); each step of treadmill; rung of ladder. 3. Piece of metal, rubber, or other substance placed on step to lessen wear or sound. 4. Part of wheel that touches ground or rails; part of rails that wheels touch. 5. Part of stilt on which foot rests. 6. Part of sole of shoe etc. that rests on ground. 7. Distance between

pedals of bicycle. 8. (of male bird) Copulation. 9. Round white spot on egg-yolk (formerly supposed to appear only in fecundated eggs). 10. *trea'dmill*, appliance for producing motion by the stepping of man or horse etc. on steps fixed to revolving cylinder, esp. kind formerly used in prisons as punishment; (fig.) monotonous routine; ~-*wheel*, treadmill or similar appliance.
trea'dle (-ĕdl) n. Lever moved by foot and imparting motion to machine, e.g. lathe, sewing-machine, bicycle. ~ v. Work treadle.
Treas. *abbrev*. Treasurer.
trea'son (-zn) n. 1. (also *high* ~) Violation by subject of his allegiance to sovereign or chief authority of State (e.g. compassing or intending sovereign's death, levying war against him, or adhering to his enemies); ~ *felony*, attempt to depose sovereign or levy war in order to compel change of measures, intimidate parliament, or stir up foreign invasion. 2. Breach of faith, disloyalty (*to* cause, friend, etc.). **trea'sonous** *adj*.
trea'sonable (-zn-) *adj*. Involving, guilty of, treason. **trea'sonableness** n. **trea'sonablў** *adv*.
trea'sure (-ĕzher) n. Wealth or riches stored up, esp. in form of precious metals or gems; accumulated wealth; anything valued or preserved as precious; beloved person, esp. child; (colloq.) very efficient or satisfactory person, esp. servant; ~-*house*, place where treasure is kept, treasury; ~-*trōve*, gold or silver, money, etc., found hidden in ground or other place, owner of which is unknown. ~ v.t. Store (*up*) as valuable; cherish, prize; (fig.) store, lay up (e.g. in memory).
trea'surer (-ĕzher-) n. (orig.) One charged with receipt and disbursement of revenues of king, noble, State, Church, etc.; now, one responsible for funds of public body or any corporation, society, or club; (U.S.) officer of Treasury Department who receives and keeps the moneys; (*Lord High*) *T*~ (*of England*), (hist.) third great officer of the Crown, controlling sovereign's revenues, with duties since reign of George I discharged by Lords of the Treasury. **trea'surership** n.
trea'surў (-ĕzherĭ) n. 1. Room, building, in which precious or valuable objects are preserved (freq. fig.); (esp. in book-titles) collection of treasured writings. 2. Funds or revenue of State, corporation, etc.; *T*~, in Gt Britain, department of State advising the Chancellor of the Exchequer, administering expenditure of public revenue, and co-ordinating the economic activities of other branches of government; building where business of this department is transacted;

corresponding institution in other countries; T~ **bench**: see BENCH; ~ **bill**, security given by a government in exchange for a loan of short duration (freq. 91 days); ~ **note**, (U.S.) demand note issued by Treasury Department, and legal tender for all debts; (in Engl. usage) currency note for £1 or 10s., issued by the Treasury 1914-28, later replaced by notes issued by the Bank of England. 3. (theatr. slang) Weekly payment of company of actors.
treat v. 1. Deal, negotiate (*with*), in order to settle terms. 2. Deal with (subject), deal with subject, in speech or writing; deal with in way of art, represent artistically; deal with to obtain particular result, esp. deal with disease etc. in order to relieve or cure. 3. Behave or act towards in specified way. 4. Entertain, esp. with food and drink, regale, feast. ~ n. Entertainment, esp. one given gratuitously, pleasure party; treating, invitation to eat or esp. drink; a great pleasure, delight, or gratification.
trea′tise (*or* -z) n. Book or writing treating in formal or methodical manner of particular subject.
trea′tment n. (Mode of) dealing with or behaving towards person or thing; esp. (method of) treating patient or disease.
trea′ty n. (Document embodying) formal contract between States relating to peace, truce, alliance, commerce, etc.; *in* ~, negotiating, treating; ~*-port*, port (esp. certain ports in Far East) opened to foreign commerce by treaty.
Trĕ′bĭzŏnd. (Turk. *Trabzon*) City and port of Turkey on Black Sea, once capital of an empire (1204-1461) founded by Alexius Comnenus.
trĕ′ble adj. 1. Threefold, triple; ~ *chance*, type of football pool paying (orig. 3) dividends to persons with highest number of points; ~ *crochet*, crochet stitch with 3 loops on hook together (ill. CROCHET). 2. Soprano; high-pitched, shrill; of treble pitch; ~ *bob*: see BOB²; ~ *clef*: see CLEF. ~ n. 1. Treble quantity, stitch, etc. 2. Treble voice, singer, string, etc. ~ v. Multiply, be multiplied, by 3.
trĕ′bŭchĕt (-sh-), **trĕ′bŭckĕt** n. 1. (hist.) Medieval military engine, pivoted lever with sling at one end, used for throwing heavy missiles. 2. Small tilting balance or pair of scales.
trĕcĕ′ntō (trăch-) n. 14th century as period of Italian art and literature. [It., = 'three hundred', short for *mil trecento* 1300]
tree n. Perennial plant with self-supporting woody main stem (usu. developing woody branches at some distance from ground); erect bush or shrub with single stem; piece of wood shaped for some purpose (as BOOT-tree, SADDLE-tree); gallows (archaic); cross of Christ (archaic & poet.); genealogical chart like branching tree (*family* ~, ~ *of* JESSE); *at the top of the* ~, in the highest position; *up a* ~, cornered, in a difficulty; ~ *agate*, agate with tree-like markings; ~*-calf*, (bookbinding) calf leather stained with acids in tree-like markings; ~*-creeper*, any of various birds which creep on trunks and branches of trees, esp. *Certhia familiaris* and Amer. variety of this; ~*-fern*, fern with upright woody stem, growing to size of tree, found in tropics, Australia, and New Zealand; ~*-frog*, toad-like or frog-like arboreal amphibian esp. of genus *Hyla*; ~*-nail*, pin of hard wood for fastening ship's timbers together; ~ *of knowledge of good and evil*, tree in garden of Eden bearing the forbidden fruit which was tasted by Adam and Eve (Gen. 3); ~ *onion*, variety of onion which produces bulbs on stems instead of flowers; ~ *oyster*, oyster found on roots of mangrove, esp. *Ostrea glomerata*; ~*-toad*, treefrog. ~ v.t. Cause to take refuge in tree, drive up a tree; stretch on boot-tree.
trĕ′foil n. 1. Plant of genus *Trifolium* with leaves of three leaflets, clover. 2. Ornamental figure resembling clover-leaf; (archit.) opening divided by cusps suggesting three-lobed leaf (ill. ARCH¹).
Treitschke (trī′chke), Heinrich von (1834-96). German historian and political writer.
trĕk v.i. (orig. S. Afr.) Travel, migrate, esp. by ox-wagon; make arduous journey or expedition. ~ n. (Stage of) journey made by trekking; *Great T*~, migration northward (1835-7) of large numbers of Boers, discontented with British rule in the Cape, to the areas where they eventually founded the Transvaal Republic and the Orange Free State.
trĕ′llis n. Structure of light bars crossing each other with open square or diamond-shaped spaces between, used as screen, as support for climbing plants, etc.; ~*-work*, trellis. ~ v.t. Furnish, support, (as) with trellis. [L *trilix* three-ply (f. *licium* warp-thread)]
trĕ′matōde n. Member of the Trematoda, a class of unsegmented parasitic flatworms.
trĕ′mble v.i. Shake involuntarily as with fear or other emotion, cold, or weakness; quiver; (fig.) be affected with fear, agitation, suspense, etc. ~ n. Trembling, quiver, tremor.
trĕ′mbly adj. (colloq.)
trĕ′mbler n. (esp.) Spring which makes electrical contact when shaken.
trĕ′mbling adj. ~*-bog*, bogland formed over water or soft mud, shaking at every tread. **trĕ′mblĭnglў** adv.
trĕmĕ′ndous adj. Awe-inspiring, terrible; (colloq.) extraordinarily great, immense. **trĕmĕ′ndouslў** adv. **trĕmĕ′ndousnĕss** n.
trĕ′molō n. (pl. -*os*). Tremulous or vibrating effect in certain instruments or human voice; organ-stop producing this effect. [It., = 'trembling']
trĕ′mor n. Tremulous or vibratory movement or sound, vibration, shaking, quaking; (instance, fit, of) involuntary agitation of body or limbs from physical weakness, fear, etc.
trĕ′mūlous adj. Trembling, quivering; shaky; timid; tremblingly sensitive or responsive. **trĕ′mūlouslў** adv. **trĕ′mūlousnĕss** n.
trĕnch n. Long narrow usu. deep hollow cut out of ground, esp. with earth thrown up as parapet to protect soldiers under fire or from bombing; ~*-coat*, thick, usu. lined, waterproof overcoat, orig. for wearing in trenches; ~*-feet, -foot*, affection of feet resembling chilblains, sometimes with gangrene, due to exposure to extreme cold and wet and prevalent among soldiers serving in trenches; ~ *fever*, low, intermittent, infectious fever carried by lice and common among men serving in trenches; ~*-gun, -mortar*, small mortar for throwing bombs etc. into enemy trenches at short range; ~ *warfare*, hostilities carried on from more or less permanent trenches. ~ v. 1. Make trench(es) or ditch(es) in (ground); make series of trenches in digging or ploughing (ground) so as to bring lower soil to surface; dig trench(es); cut (groove), cut groove in (wood etc.). 2. Encroach *on*; verge or border closely *on*.
trĕ′nchant adj. (archaic & poet.) Keen, sharp; (zool., of tooth etc.) having cutting edge; (fig.) keen, penetrating; vigorous, energetic. **trĕn′chantlў** adv. **trĕ′nchancў** n.
trĕ′ncher n. Flat square or usu. circular piece of wood on which meat etc. was formerly cut; any flat round piece of wood; MORTAR-board; *tre′ncherman*, feeder, eater, usu. qualified as *good, stout*, etc.
trĕnd n. General direction, course, tendency. **trĕ′ndў** adj. (colloq.) Following latest trends of fashion etc. **trĕnd** v.i. Have specified direction, course, or general tendency.
Trĕnggā′nu (-ng-gahnoo). State of Malaysia; capital, Kuala Trengganu.
Trĕnt¹. River of English midlands, flowing into North Sea by Humber.
Trĕnt². (It. *Trento*) City of N. Italy; scene of oecumenical council of R.C. Church, meeting from time to time, 1545-63, which defined the doctrines of the Church

[933]

in opposition to those of the Reformation, reformed discipline, and strengthened the authority of the Papacy.

trĕ′ntal *n.* (R.C. Ch.) Set of 30 requiem masses said daily or all on one day.

Trĕnti′nō (-tē-). Part of S. Tyrol with many Italian inhabitants, ceded by Austria to Italy after war of 1914–18.

trĕpă′n *n.* 1. Surgeon's cylindrical saw (obs.; superseded by TREPHINE). 2. (mining etc.) Heavy boring instrument for sinking shafts. ~ *v.t.* Operate on with trepan.

trĕpă′ng *n.* Edible marine sea-cucumber, esp. of genera *Holothuria* and *Actinopyga*, esteemed as luxury by Chinese etc.; bêche-de-mer. [Malay *trĭpang*]

trĕphi′ne (*or* -ēn) *n.* Surgeon's cylindrical saw with guiding centre-pin, for removing part of bone of skull. ~ *v.t.* Operate on with trephine. **trĕphinā′tion** *n.*

trĕpidā′tion *n.* Confused hurry or alarm, flurry, perturbation.

trĕ′spass *n.* Transgression, breach of law or duty; (law) actionable wrong committed against person or property of another, esp. wrongful entry upon another's lands with damage (however inconsiderable) to his real property. ~ *v.i.* 1. (archaic) Transgress, sin. 2. (law) Commit trespass, esp. enter unlawfully on land of another or his property or right; (fig.) make unwarrantable claim or undesired intrusion *on*, encroach *on*, infringe. **trĕ′spasser** *n.*

trĕss *n.* Lock, braid of (esp. woman's long) hair; (pl.) woman's hair.

trĕ′ssure (-syer *or* -sher) *n.* (her.) Small orle, narrow band one-quarter of width of bordure (ill. HERALDRY).

trĕ′stle (-sl) *n.* Supporting structure for table etc. consisting of horizontal beam with diverging legs, usu. two at each end, or of two frames hinged together or fixed at an angle; open braced framework of wood or metal for supporting bridge etc.; (naut., pl.) trestle-trees; ~-*bridge*, bridge supported on trestles; ~-*table*, table of board(s) laid across trestles or other supports (ill. TABLE); ~-*tree*, either of a pair of fore-and-aft horizontal timbers on mast, supporting cross-trees, top-mast, etc. (ill. SAIL¹).

trĕt *n.* Allowance of extra weight formerly made to purchasers of some goods for waste in transportation etc.

trews (-ōōz) *n.pl.* Close-fitting trousers or breeches combined with stockings, formerly worn by Scottish highlanders and Irish; close-fitting usu. tartan trousers worn by some Scottish regiments (ill. PLAID).

trey (-ā) *n.* Three at dice or cards.

T.R.H. *abbrev.* Their Royal Highnesses.

tri- *prefix.* Three, thrice.

trī′ăd *n.* Group or set of 3; (Welsh literature) form of composition with subjects or statements arranged in groups of 3; (mus.) chord of 3 notes, esp. note with its third and fifth (e.g. common chord without octave) (ill. CHORD); (chem.) group of 3 chemical elements having similar properties, as iron, nickel, and cobalt. **triă′dĭc** *adj.*

triădĕ′lphous *adj.* (Having stamens) united by filaments into 3 bundles.

trī′al *n.* 1. Examination and determination of causes at law by judicial tribunal. 2. Testing or putting to proof of qualities of thing; test, probation; trial match etc.; experimental treatment, investigation by means of experience; examination of person, esp. for Presbyterian ministry; (in some English public schools) terminal examination; (motor cycling) test of ability to ride over rough ground. 3. Being tried by suffering or temptation; painful test of endurance, patience, etc.; affliction, hardship. 4. Attempt, endeavour. 5. Something serving as sample, proof, etc., trial-piece. 6. ~ *balance*, in double-entry book-keeping, addition of all entries on each side of ledger, when debits should balance credits; ~ *eight*, provisional crew of eight-oared boat, from among whom members of final eight may be chosen; (pl., also) race between such crews; ~ *match*, etc., one leading to selection of persons for an important team etc.; ~-*piece*, anything made or taken as specimen; ~ *trip*, trip to test speed and other qualities of new vessel etc.

trī′ăngle (-nggl) *n.* Geometrical figure, esp. plane rectilineal figure, with 3 angles and 3 sides; any system of 3 points not in a straight line, with the 3 real or imaginary lines joining them; any 3-cornered body, object, or space, esp. musical percussion instrument consisting of steel rod bent into a triangle open at one corner and struck with a small steel rod, (naut.) kind of large tripod of 3 spars for hoisting weights etc.; (hist., usu. pl.) frame of 3 halberds joined at top to which soldier was bound for flogging; *eternal* ~: see ETERNAL; ~ *of forces*, theorem that 3 forces in equilibrium acting at one point can be represented by a triangle with sides parallel to their directions and proportional in length to their magnitudes; triangle representing such forces.

triă′ngŭlar (-ngg-) *adj.* Of the shape of a triangle, 3-cornered; 3-sided, between 3 persons or parties; ~ *numbers*, (math.) series of numbers (1, 3, 6, 10, 15, etc.) obtained by continued summation of the natural numbers 1, 2, 3, 4, etc. **triă′ngŭlarly̆** *adv.* **triăngŭlă′rity̆** *n.*

triă′ngŭlate (-ngg-) *adj.* Consisting of, marked with, triangles. **triă′ngŭlately̆** *adv.* **triă′ngŭlāte** *v.t.* Divide or convert into triangles; (surveying etc.) measure, map out, by measurement of sides and angles of series of triangles on determined base-line(s). **triăngŭlā′tion** *n.*

Trianon (trēanawṅ). Either of two small palaces in great park at Versailles; the larger (*Grand* ~) was built by Louis XIV 1687; the smaller (*Petit* ~), built by Louis XV 1762–8, belonged first to Madame du Barry and afterwards to Marie Antoinette; *Treaty of* ~, that between the Allied Powers and Hungary, 1920.

Trī′ăs *n.* (geol.) = TRIASSIC. **Triă′ssic** *adj. & n.* (geol.) (Of) the earliest period or system of the Mesozoic (ill. GEOLOGY). [G. *trias*, Gk *trias* group of 3, f. threefold sub-division of these rocks in Germany]

triă′tic *adj.* ~ *stay*, rope, or two ropes joined by spar, attached at ends to foremast and mainmast and used for hoisting boats etc.; stay between mast-heads of steamship.

triato̅′mic *adj.* Having 3 atoms in the molecule; having 3 replaceable atoms or groups.

trī′bal *adj.* Of tribe(s). **trī′bally̆** *adv.*

trī′balism *n.* Tribal system or organization.

trībā′sic *adj.* (chem.) Having 3 replaceable hydrogen atoms; containing 3 atoms of a univalent metal or 3 basic hydroxyl groups.

tribe *n.* 1. Group of primitive or barbarous clans under recognized chiefs. 2. (Rom. hist.) Each

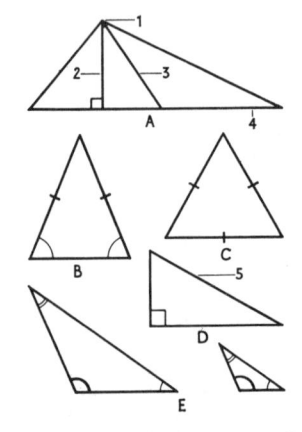

TRIANGLES: A. SCALENE. B. ISOSCELES. C. EQUILATERAL. D. RIGHT-ANGLED. E. TWO SIMILAR TRIANGLES

1. Vertex. 2. Altitude. 3. Median. 4. Base. 5. Hypotenuse

of the political divisions of the Romans (orig. 3, prob. representing clans, ultimately 35); (Gk hist.) = PHYLE. 3. Any similar division whether of natural or political origin; any of the 12 divisions of the people of Israel, each traditionally descended from one of the patriarchs; *Lost Tribes*, the 10 Israelite tribes (i.e. all but Judah and Benjamin) which revolted from the House of David and were deported by Shalmaneser, after which time their history is lost. 4. (biol.) Group ranking below sub-family and above genus (with name usu. ending in *-ini* for animals and *-eae* for plants). 5. Class, lot, set (usu. contempt.); (pl.) large numbers. tri'besman (-bz-) *n.* Man who is a member of a tribe.
tribŏ'logў *n.* Study of friction, wear, lubrication, and bearing design. tribolŏ'gical *adj.* tribŏ'logist *n.*
tri'brăch (-k) *n.* Metrical foot of 3 short syllables (⌣⌣⌣).
tribūlā'tion *n.* Great affliction, oppression, or misery. [L *tribulare* press, oppress, f. *tribulum* threshing-sledge]
tribū'nal *n.* 1. Judgement-seat; court of justice, judicial assembly; (fig.) place of judgement, judicial authority. 2. Board or committee appointed to adjudicate on claims of a particular kind, act as arbiters, etc.
tri'būne[1] *n.* 1. (Rom. hist.) Administrative officer, esp. one of 2 (later 5, then 10) orig. protecting interests and rights of plebs from patricians; one of 6 officers of legion, each in command for 2 months of year. 2. Protector of rights of people, popular leader, demagogue. tri'būnate, tri'būneship *ns.*
tri'būne[2] *n.* Raised floor for magistrate's chair in apse of Roman basilica (ill. BASILICA); bishop's throne, apse containing this, in basilica; platform, stage, pulpit; raised and seated area or gallery.
tri'būtarў *adj.* 1. Paying or subject to tribute; furnishing subsidiary supplies or aid, auxiliary, contributory; (of stream) flowing into a larger stream or a lake. ~ *n.* Tributary person or State; tributary stream.
tri'būte *n.* Money or equivalent paid by one sovereign or State to another in acknowledgement of submission or for protection or peace; obligation of paying this; (fig.) contribution, offering or gift as mark of respect, affection, etc.; (mining) proportion of ore, or its equivalent, paid to miner for labour.
trice[1] *n.* in *a* ~, in an instant.
trice[2] *v.t.* (naut.) Hoist *up* and secure with rope or lashing, lash *up*.
tricĕntē'narў, tricĕntē'nnial *adjs. & ns.* Tercentenary, tercentennial.

tri'cĕps *adj. & n.* (Muscle, esp. great extensor muscle of back of upper arm) with 3 heads or attachments (ill. MUSCLE).
tricĕ'ratŏps *n.* Gigantic dinosaur of genus *T*~ found in parts of U.S., with two large horns above eyes and one on nose.
trichī'na (-k-) *n.* (pl. *-ae*). Minute nematode worm (*Trichinella spiralis*) parasitic in muscles and intestines of man, pig, etc. trichinō'sis (-k-) *n.* Disease caused by introduction of trichinae from infected pork into alimentary canal. tri'chinous (-k-) *adj.* Of trichinae or trichinosis.
trichŏ'logў (-k-) *n.* Study of structure, functions, and diseases of hair. trichŏ'logist *n.*
tri'chōme (-k-) *n.* Any outgrowth of epidermis or superficial tissue of plant, as prickles, hairs, etc.
trichŏ'pter (-k-) *n.* Caddisfly. trichŏ'pterous *adj.*
trichŏ'tomў (-k-) *n.* Division into, classification or arrangement in, 3 (classes etc.); division of human nature into body, soul, and spirit. trichŏ'tomous *adj.*
trichrō'ic (-kr-) *adj.* Having or showing 3 colours; esp. of crystal, presenting 3 different colours when viewed in 3 different directions. tri'chrōism *n.*
trichromă'tic (-kr-) *adj.* Trichroic; esp. of or having 3 fundamental colour-sensations (red, green, violet) of normal vision; of (printing in) 3 colours. trichrō'matism *n.*
trick *n.* 1. Crafty or fraudulent device or stratagem, esp. of mean or base kind; hoax, joke; capricious, foolish, or stupid act; clever device or contrivance, stratagem, feat of skill or dexterity; knack (freq. in ~(*s*) *of the trade*); *do the* ~, achieve the desired result. 2. Peculiar or characteristic practice; habit, mannerism. 3. (cards) Cards played and won in one round; such round, point(s) gained by winning it. 4. (naut.) Time, usu. two hours, of duty at helm. ~ *v.* 1. Deceive by trick, cheat; cheat *out of*, beguile *into*, by trickery; practise trickery. 2. Dress, deck, decorate (usu. *out*, *up*). tri'ckerў *n.*
tri'ckle *v.* (Cause to) flow in drops or in scanty halting stream; (of ball) run slowly over surface of ground, cause to do this. ~ *n.* Trickling, small fitful stream; ~ *charger*, (elect.) device for slow continuous charging of an accumulator. tri'cklў *adj.*
tri'cksў *adj.* Full of tricks, playful.
tri'ckў *adj.* Crafty, given to tricks, deceitful; skilful in clever tricks or dodges, adroit, resourceful; (colloq.) requiring cautious or adroit action or handling, ticklish. tri'ckilў *adv.* tri'ckiness *n.*
tricli'nic *adj.* (cryst.) Having the 3 axes unequal and obliquely inclined (ill. CRYSTAL).

tri'colour (-ŭler) *n. & adj* (Flag, esp. that adopted as national flag of France at Revolution) having 3 colours.
tri'cōrn *adj. & n.* 3-cornered (cocked hat).
tri'cot (-ō; *or* trē-) *n.* Fabric knitted by hand or machine; ~*-stitch*, plain simple crochet stitch producing straight pattern.
tricŭ'spid *adj.* Having 3 cusps or points; ~ *valve*, (anat.) valve, consisting of 3 triangular segments, which guards the opening from the right atrium into the right ventricle of the heart (ill. HEART).
tri'cўcle *n.* 3-wheeled pedal- or motor-cycle. ~ *v.i.* Ride tricycle.
tri'dent *n.* 3-pronged instrument or weapon, esp. 3-pronged fish-spear or sceptre as attribute of Neptune or of Britannia; 3-pronged spear used by RETIARIUS.
Tridĕ'ntine *adj.* Of the Council of TRENT[2].
tri'dūum *n.* (R.C. Ch.) 3 days of prayer in preparation for feast or other solemn occasion.
triĕ'nnial *adj.* Existing, lasting, for 3 years; occurring, done, every 3 years. triĕ'nniallў *adv.* triĕ'nnial *n.* Triennial occasion, event, publication, etc.; esp. visitation of diocese by bishop every 3 years.
Triĕ'ste (trē-). Seaport in NE. Italy on the Adriatic; under Austrian control until end of 1914-18 war.
tri'fid *adj.* Split or divided into 3 by deep clefts or notches.
tri'fle *n.* 1. Thing, fact, circumstance, of slight value or importance; small amount, esp. of money; small article. 2. Sweet dish of sponge-cakes flavoured with wine, jam, etc., topped with custard or whipped cream. ~ *v.i.* Toy, play, dally, fidget, *with*; act or speak idly or frivolously. tri'fler *n.* tri'fling *adj.* Unimportant, paltry, insignificant; foolish, frivolous, idle. tri'flinglў *adv.*
trifō'liate *adj.* 3-leaved; consisting of 3 leaflets; having such leaves.
trifŏr'ium *n.* (pl. *-ia*). Gallery or arcade in wall over arches at sides of nave and choir (and occas. transepts) in some large churches (ill. CHURCH).
tri'fōrm *adj.* Having a triple form, existing or appearing in 3 forms.
trig[1] *adj.* (archaic) Trim, neat.
trig[2] *n.* (colloq.) Trigonometry.
tri'gamў *n.* Having 3 wives or husbands at same time. tri'gamist *n.* tri'gamous *adj.*
trigĕ'minal *adj.* Of the 5th and (in man) largest pair of cranial nerves, dividing into 3 main branches (ophthalmic, maxillary, and mandibular nerves).
tri'gger *n.* Movable catch or lever which is pulled or pressed to release a spring or otherwise set

mechanism in motion, esp. small steel catch for releasing hammer of lock in firearm (ill. GUN); ~ finger, forefinger of right hand; ~-fish, fish of *Balistes* and related genera, so called because pressure on second spine of anterior dorsal fin depresses first. ~ *v.t.* Initiate, set *off* a reaction etc.

tri′glyph *n.* (archit.) Ornament of frieze in Doric order, consisting of block or tablet with two vertical grooves and a half-groove on each side, alternating with metopes (ill. ORDER).

tri′gon *n.* 1. Triangle. 2. (astrol.) Set of 3 signs of zodiac distant 120° from each other; each of 4 such groups (*airy, earthy, fiery, watery*) into which the 12 signs are divided; triplicity, trine. 3. (zool.) Cutting region of crown of upper molar. **trigo′nic** *adj.*

tri′gonal *adj.* Triangular; having triangular cross-section (ill. CRYSTAL); of a trigon; (geom., cryst., of solid) having triangular faces, having 3 equal and equally inclined axes.

tri′gonoid *adj. & n.* (geom.) (Plane figure) contained by 3 arcs of equal radius meeting at angles.

trigonomĕ′mĕtrў *n.* Branch of mathematics dealing with measurement of sides and angles of triangles and with certain functions of their

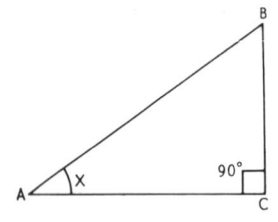

TRIGONOMETRICAL RATIOS
Sine $X = BC/AB$. Cosine $X = AC/AB$. Secant $X = AB/AC$. Cosecant $X = AB/BC$. Tangent $X = BC/AC$. Cotangent $X = AC/BC$

angles or angles in general. **trigonomĕ′tric, -ical** *adjs.* **trigonomĕ′trically** *adv.*

tri′grăm *n.* Inscription of 3 letters; figure of 3 lines or elements.

tri′grăph (*or* -ahf) *n.* Combination of 3 letters representing one sound.

trihĕ′dron *n.* Figure formed by 3 surfaces meeting in point. **trihĕ′dral** *adj. & n.*

tri′jugăte (-ōō- *or* -ōō′-) *adj.* (bot.) With 3 pairs of pinnate leaves.

trilă′teral *adj. & n.* (Figure) having 3 sides; triangle, triangular.

tri′lbў *n.* (also ~ *hat*) Soft felt hat with narrow brim and indented crown. [f. *Trilby* O'Ferrall, heroine of novel 'Trilby' (1894) by George Du Maurier]

trili′near *adj.* (math.) Of, contained by, having some relation to, 3 lines.

trili′ngual (-nggw-) *adj.* Speaking, using, expressed in, 3 languages.

trili′teral *adj.* Consisting of 3 letters, esp. (Semitic philol.) consisting of 3 consonants.

tri′lith, tri′lithon *ns.* Prehistoric structure of two upright stones with another resting on them as a lintel.

trill *n.* 1. (mus.) Rapid alternation of 2 notes a tone or semitone apart, shake. 2. (phon.) Pronunciation of consonant, consonant pronounced, with vibration of tongue or other part of speech-organs. 3. Tremulous high-pitched sound or note(s), esp. in singing of birds. ~ *v.* Utter, sing, produce, with trill(s); make trill(s).

tri′llion (-yon) *n.* 1. 3rd power of a million, unit followed by 18 zeros. 2. (U.S.) 4th power of a thousand, unit followed by 12 zeros.

trilō′bate (*or* tri′lo-) *adj.* Having, consisting of, 3 lobes.

tri′lobite *n.* Fossil arthropod with 3-lobed body found in Lower Palaeozoic rocks.

TRILOBITE

tri′logў *n.* (Gk antiq.) Series of 3 tragedies performed at Athens at festival of Dionysus; any series or group of 3 related dramatic or other literary works.

trim *adj.* In good order; well arranged or equipped; neat, spruce. **tri′mly** *adv.* **tri′mnĕss** *n.* trim *v.* 1. Set in good order, make neat or tidy; remove irregular or superfluous or unsightly parts from; remove (such parts) by clipping, planing, etc. 2. Ornament (with ribbon, lace, etc.); dress (windows). 3. Adjust balance of (vessel, aircraft) by distribution of cargo, passengers, etc.; arrange (sails etc.) to suit wind; (fig.) hold middle course in politics or opinion, adjust oneself to prevailing opinion etc., be a time-server. ~ *n.* 1. (naut.) State of being trimmed and rigged ready for sailing, battle (*fighting* ~), etc.; state of ship, cargo, etc., in reference to fitness for sailing, esp. proper balance in water on fore-and-aft line; difference between draught forward and draught aft; (aeron.) balance of aircraft in ref. to fore-and-aft in horizontal plane. 2. State, degree, of adjustment, readiness, or fitness; good order. 3. Trimming, being trimmed; interior furnishings of motor-car; (U.S.) visible woodwork round openings of house etc.; window-dressing. 4. Trimming or cutting off; anything cut off or out, trimmings.

tri′marăn *n.* Boat resembling catamaran but with 3 hulls side by side.

tri′mĕter *adj. & n.* (Verse) of 3 measures (usu. 3 feet, but 6 feet in classical trochaics, iambics, and anapaestics, which have 2 feet per measure).

tri′mmer (esp.) 1. One who trims between opposing parties in politics etc. or inclines to each of two opposite sides as interest dictates (orig. Lord Halifax or his followers, 1680–90). 2. One whose business is to stow coal or cargo in loading ship. 3. Short beam framed across an opening (as a stair-well or hearth) to carry the ends of those joists which cannot be extended across the opening (ill. FLOOR).

tri′mming *n.* (esp.) Ornamental addition to dress, hat, etc.; (pl.) accessories, usual accompaniments; (pl.) pieces cut off in trimming something.

trimor′phic, trimor′phous *adjs.* (of species etc.) Having 3 distinct forms; (bot.) having 3 distinct forms of organs on individuals of same species; (cryst., of substance) crystallizing in 3 fundamentally distinct forms. **tri′morph, trimor′phism** *ns.*

trine *adj. & n.* Threefold, triple (group); (thing) made up of 3 parts; (astrol.) (aspect) of 2 heavenly bodies distant from each other by a third part of the zodiac (120°). **tri′nal, tri′narў** *adjs.*

tri′ngle (-nggl) *n.* (archit.) Narrow straight, esp. square-sectioned, moulding.

Tri′nidăd and Tobā′gō. W. Indian islands off coast of Venezuela; member State of the Commonwealth, independent since 1962; capital, Port of Spain.

Trinĭtār′ian *adj. & n.* 1. (Member) of religious order of Holy Trinity, founded 1198 to redeem Christian captives from Muslims. 2. (Holder) of doctrine of Trinity of Godhead.

trinĭ′trate *n.* (chem.) Compound formed from 3 molecules of nitric acid by the replacement of 3 hydrogen atoms by a trivalent element or radical.

trinĭtrotŏ′luēne, -tŏ′luŏl *ns.* Derivative of toluene with 3 nitro (NO₂) groups, high explosive used as shell fillings and as ingredient of various explosives (abbrev. T.N.T.).

tri′nitў *n.* Being 3; group of 3; *the T~*, 3 persons or modes of being of the Godhead as conceived in orthodox Christian belief; Father, Son, and Spirit as constituting one God; *T~ sittings*, session of English High Court of Justice beinning on Tuesday following Trinity Sunday; *T~ Sunday*, Sunday after Whit Sunday, observed as festival in honour of the Trinity; *T~ term*, former 4th session (22 May–12 June) of English High Court of Justice;

university term beginning after Easter.

Tri'nity House, Corporation of. Guild or fraternity incorporated in 1514 and having official regulation of British shipping, including erection and maintenance of lighthouses, buoys, etc. and licensing of pilots.

tri'nkėt n. Small or trifling ornament or fancy article, esp. piece of jewellery.

trinō'mial adj. & n. (esp., math.) (Algebraical expression) consisting of 3 terms connected by plus or minus signs.

tri'o (-ēō) n. 1. (mus.) (Composition for) 3 voices or instruments in combination; composition in 3 parts; middle division of minuet or scherzo (orig. in 3-part harmony), or of march. 2. Set of 3 persons or things.

tri'ōde n. Electronic amplifying valve with 3 main electrodes (anode, cathode, and grid) (ill. THERMIONIC).

tri'olėt (or trē-) n. Verseform of 8 lines with 2 rhymes (a b a a a a b a b), and with 1st line recurring as 4th and 7th, and 2nd as 8th.

triŏ'xĭde n. (chem.) Compound of 3 atoms of oxygen with an element or radical.

trip v. 1. Walk, dance, skip, etc., with quick light tread, run lightly, move freely and quickly. 2. (freq. with *up*) Make false step, stumble; cause (person) to stumble by entangling or suddenly arresting his feet; make mistake, commit fault, inconsistency, or inaccuracy; detect in stumble, inconsistency, or inaccuracy. 3. Tilt, esp. (naut.) tilt or cant (yard or mast) in lowering it; (naut.) loose (anchor) from its bed and raise it clear of bottom; (mech.) release (catch, lever, etc.) by contact with projection, operate (mechanism) thus. ~ n. 1. Short voyage or journey, esp. each of series of such journeys over particular route; excursion for pleasure or health, esp. one at lower fare than usual; (colloq.) experience induced by hallucinatory or other drug. 2. Stumble; tripping or being tripped up. 3. Contrivance for tripping, projecting part of mechanism coming into contact with another part so as to cause or check movement; ~-*hammer*, massive machine hammer operated by trip; ~-*wire*, wire setting off explosive or warning device etc. when tripped over.

tripār'tite adj. Divided into, composed of, 3 parts or kinds; of, involving, such division; engaged in by, concluded between, 3 parties.

tripe n. First or second stomach of ruminant, esp. ox, prepared as food; (pl., vulg.) entrails; (slang) worthless or trashy product or thing.

triphi'bious adj. (of military operations) On land, sea, and in the air.

tri'phthŏng n. Combination of 3 vowel sounds in one syllable.

tri'plāne n. Aircraft with 3 superimposed main supporting surfaces.

tri'ple adj. Threefold, 3 times as much or as many, of 3 parts; *T~ Alliance*, (1) alliance of England, Sweden, and Netherlands against France, 1668; (2) that of France, Gt Britain, and Netherlands against Spain, 1717; (3) that of Germany, Austria, and Italy against Russia and France, 1882–3; ~ *crown*, papal tiara; *T~ Entente*: see ENTENTE; ~ *time*, (mus.) rhythm of 3 beats in the bar. **tri'plỹ** adv. **tri'ple** v. Increase threefold; be 3 times as great or as many as.

tri'plėt n. 1. Set of 3; esp. 3 successive lines of verse rhyming together; (mus.) group of 3 notes performed in the time of 2 of the same value; (microscope with) combination of 3 plano-convex lenses. 2. Each of 3 children born at a birth.

tri'plĕx adj. Triple, threefold; *T~ glass*, (trade-name) unsplinterable glass used in motor-cars, aircraft, etc., with a celluloid sheet cemented between two sheets of glass.

tri'plicate adj. Threefold, forming 3 exactly corresponding copies; ~ *ratio*, ratio of cubes of 3 quantities. ~ n. Each of set of 3 exactly corresponding copies or parts; *in* ~, in 3 exactly corresponding copies. **tri'plicāte** v.t. Triple, multiply by 3, make or provide in triplicate. **triplicā'tion** n.

tripli'city n. State of being triple; trio, triplet; trinity; (astrol.) TRIGON.

tri'pŏd n. 3-legged support, table (ill. TABLE), seat, etc., esp. frame or stand with 3 diverging legs, usu. hinged at top, for supporting camera, theodolite, etc.; (Gk antiq.) altar at Delphi on which priestess sat to utter oracles; imitation of this as prize in Pythian Games etc.

tripō'lar adj. (biol.) Having 3 poles.

Tri'poli[1]. Seaport and capital city of Libya. **Tripŏ'litan** adj.

tri'poli[2] n. Fine earth, freq. used as polishing powder, composed mainly of decomposed siliceous matter, esp. shells of diatoms. [f. TRIPOLI[1]]

trī'pŏs n. Honours examination for Bachelor of Arts (orig. only in mathematics) at Cambridge University. [app. altered f. L *tripus*, after Gk *tripous* TRIPOD; orig. applied to 3-legged stool on which B.A. sat to dispute humorously with candidates for degrees]

tri'pper n. (esp.) Excursionist, one who goes on a pleasure trip.

tri'ptych (-ĭk) n. Picture or carving, or set of 3, in 3 compartments side by side, with lateral panels usu. hinged so as to fold over central one, used esp. as altarpiece.

Tri'pura (-ōōra). Union territory in NE. India; capital, Agartala.

triquĕ'tra n. (pl. -ae). Triangular ornament of 3 interlaced arcs or lobes. **triquĕ'tral** adj.

TRIQUETRA

3-cornered; ~ *bone*, 3-cornered or cuneiform bone in wrist (ill. HAND).

triquĕ'trous adj. Triquetral, triangular, having 3 salient edges or angles; (bot., of stem) of triangular cross-section. **triquĕ'trously** adv.

trirī'ēme n. Ancient Greek or Roman warship with 3 banks of oars.

Trisā'giŏn (-g-) n. Liturgical chant used esp. in Eastern Churches, 'Holy God, Holy and mighty, Holy and immortal, have mercy upon us'; also occas. = SANCTUS.

trisĕ'ct v.t. Divide into 3, esp. (geom.) equal parts. **trisĕ'ction** n.

trī'smus (-z-) n. (path.) Lockjaw.

Tri'stan da Cu'nha (dah kōōnya). Small volcanic island in S. Atlantic about half-way between Cape of Good Hope and S. America, in British possession. **Tri'stram.** Knight, hero of a medieval legend; lover of ISEULT.

trisy'llable n. Word of 3 syllables. **trisyllă'bic** adj. **trisyllă'bically** adv.

trīte adj. Worn out by constant use or repetition, hackneyed, commonplace. **tri'tely** adv. **tri'tenėss** n.

tri'thēism n. Belief in 3 gods, esp. doctrine that 3 persons of Trinity are 3 distinct gods. **trī'thēist** n. **trithēi'stic, -ĭcal** adjs.

trī'tium n. (chem.) An isotope of hydrogen (at. wt 3, symbol H^3 or T).

Tri'ton[1]. (Gk myth.) Sea-god, son of Poseidon and Amphitrite, represented as a merman.

trī'ton[2] n. 1. (Gk myth.) One of a number of sea-gods in form of mermen, freq. represented with conch-shell trumpets (*illustration*, p. 938). 2. (zool.) Marine gasteropod of family Tritonidae with large spiral shell.

trī'tūrāte v.t. Grind, rub, pound, etc., to powder or fine particles, pulverize. **trĭtūrā'tion** n.

trī'umph n. 1. (Rom. antiq.)

[937]

TRIUMPHAL

Entrance of commander with army and spoils in solemn procession into Rome in celebration of victory. 2. Triumphing; victory, conquest, the glory of this; rejoicing in success, elation, exultation. ~ *v.i.* Celebrate a Roman triumph; be victorious, prevail; rejoice in victory, exult (*over*); rejoice, glory.
triŭ'mphal *adj.* Of, used in, celebrating, commemorating, a triumph or victory; ~ *arch*, arch erected, by Roman emperor or in modern times, in commemoration of victory etc.
triŭ'mphant *adj.* Victorious, successful; triumphing, exultant.
triŭ'mphantlў *adv.*
triŭ'mvir *n.* (pl. *-rs, -rī*). 1. (Rom. hist.) One of 3 public officers jointly charged with one department of administration; member of 1st or 2nd triumvirate (see below). 2. Member of any group of 3 jointly exercising power. **triŭ'mvirate** *n.* Office or function of triumvir; set of triumvirs; 1st ~, coalition of Pompey, Julius Caesar, and Crassus (60 B.C.); 2nd ~, administration of Mark Antony, Octavian (Augustus), and Lepidus (43 B.C.).
trī'ūne *adj.* 3 in one. **triū'nitў** *n.*
trivā'lent *adj.* (chem.) Having a valency of 3. **trivā'lence, trīvā'lencў** *ns.*
tri'vĕt *n.* Stand for pot, kettle, etc., placed over fire, orig. and properly on 3 feet, now freq. with projection(s) by which it may be secured on top bar of grate. *right as a ~*, thoroughly or perfectly right.
tri'vial *adj.* Of small value or importance, trifling, slight, inconsiderable. **tri'viallў** *adv.* **tri'vialness, tri'vialism, triviă'litў** *ns.* **tri'via** *n.pl.* [L *trivialis* commonplace f. *trivium* place where 3 ways meet (*via* way)]
tri'vium *n.* (hist.) Grammar, rhetoric, and logic, forming the lower division (the other being the QUADRIVIUM) of the seven liberal arts in medieval schools. [see TRIVIAL.]
trī-wee'klў *adj. & adv.* (Occurring, appearing, etc.) every 3 weeks or 3 times a week.
trīzō'mal *adj.* (math.) Related to sum of 3 square roots.
Trō'ăd. Ancient region of NW. Asia Minor of which ancient Troy was the chief city.

TRITON

troat *n. & v.i.* (Make) cry of rutting buck. [imit.]
trō'car *n.* Surgical stylet with (usu.) triangular point enclosed in metal tube or cannula, for withdrawing fluid from cavity etc.
trŏchā'ic (-k-) *adj.* Consisting of trochees, that is a trochee. ~ *n.* Trochee; (pl.) trochaic verse.
trō'chal (-k-) *adj.* Wheel-shaped; ~ *disc*, (zool.) flattened end of rotifer (ill. ROTIFER).
trochă'nter (-k-) *n.* (anat., zool.) Prominence or protuberance (usu., as in man, two in number) in upper part of thigh-bone, serving for attachment of certain muscles (ill. SKELETON); (entom.) second joint of insect's leg.
trŏche (-sh *or* -ch; *or* -ō'kĭ) *n.* Flat, usu. round, medicated tablet or lozenge.
trō'chee (-k-) *n.* (pros.) Metrical foot of two syllables, the 1st long or accented and the 2nd short or unaccented (— ⏑). [Gk *trokhaios* (*pous*) running (foot) (*trekhō*, run)]
trō'chilus (-k-) *n.* 1. Small Egyptian bird said by ancients to pick teeth of crocodile; small bird, esp. humming-bird. 2. (archit.) Concave moulding, scotia.
trō'chlea (-k-) *n.* (pl. *-ae*). (anat.) Pulley-like structure or arrangement of parts, as surface of inner condyle of humerus at elbow-joint, with which ulna articulates, fibrous ring through which superior oblique muscle of eye passes etc. **trō'chlear** (-k-) *adj.* Of, connected with, a trochlea; ~ *muscle*, superior oblique muscle of eye; ~ *nerve*, each of 4th pair of cranial nerves, motor nerves for trochlear muscles.
trō'choid (-k-) *n.* (geom.) Curve traced by a point on a circle rolling on a straight line, or by a curve rolling upon another curve (ill. ROULETTE); (anat.) pivot-joint. ~ *adj.* (anat., of joint) In which one bone turns upon another with rotary motion. **trochoi'dal** *adj.*
trochoi'dēs (-k-, -z) *n.* (anat.) Pivot-joint.
trŏ'dden *adj.*: see TREAD; (esp., of path) formed by treading, beaten.
trŏ'glodȳte *n.* Cave-dweller, caveman. **trŏglodȳ'tic** *adj.*
troi'ka *n.* (Russian vehicle drawn by) three horses abreast. [Russ.]
Troi'lus (*or* trō'ĭ-). (Gk legend) Son of Priam and Hecuba, killed by Achilles; in medieval legend, forsaken lover of CRESSIDA.
Trō'jan *adj.* Of TROY[1] or its inhabitants; ~ *horse*, see below; ~ (Gk legend) siege of Troy by Greeks under Agamemnon, undertaken in order to recover his brother's wife, HELEN; it lasted 10 years and ended in the destruction of Troy after the stratagem of the ~ *horse*, a huge wooden figure of a horse concealing soldiers within it which the Greeks caused the Trojans to bring inside the city. ~ *n.* 1. Native, inhabitant, of Troy. 2. Person of great energy, endurance, or bravery.
trŏll[1] *n.* Reel of fishing-rod; trolling-spoon. ~ *v.* 1. Sing out in carefree spirit. 2. Fish for, fish in (water), fish, with rod and line and dead bait or with spoon-bait (*trolling-spoon*) drawn along behind boat.
trŏll[2] *n.* (Scand. myth.) One of race of supernatural beings formerly conceived as giants, later, in Denmark and Sweden, as dwarfs, inhabiting caves and subterranean dwellings.
trŏ'lley *n.* 1. Kind of truck that can be tilted; costermonger's cart pushed by hand or drawn by donkey; low truck worked by hand-lever along the rails for conveying plate-layers etc. to work; (also ~*-table*) small table usu. on castors for use in serving food etc. 2. In tram etc., wheel running along overhead electric wire (~*-wire*), mounted usu. on a pole (~*-pole*) down which current is conveyed to vehicle; ~*-bus*, bus with motive power derived from trolley; ~*-car*, (U.S.) tram.
trŏ'llop *n.* Slatternly woman, slut.
Trŏ'llope, Anthony (1815–82). English novelist; author of novels set in imaginary cathedral city of Barchester, including 'The Warden', 'Barchester Towers', 'The Last Chronicle of Barset', etc.
trŏ'mba *n.* Organ-stop, variety of the loud tuba.
trombō'ne (*or* trō'-) *n.* Large brass wind-instrument, usu. of tenor or bass range, having a tube which is adjusted in length for different notes (ill. BRASS); organ reed-stop of similar tone. **trombō'nist** *n.*
trompe l'œil (trawṅp lĕryē). Painting in which objects represented have the illusion of reality; also attrib. [Fr. = 'deceives the eye']
trōōp *n.* 1. Body of soldiers, esp. cavalry unit under a captain, artillery unit, or unit of armoured vehicles; (pl.) armed forces; ~*-carrier*, aircraft for transporting troops; ~*-ship*, *-train*, vessel, train, for conveyance of troops. 2. Number of persons or things collected together as a group. 3. Company of patrols in the Scout Association. ~ *v.* Flock, assemble, move along in or as a troop; come or go in great numbers; ~ *the colour(s)*, (mil.) perform that part of ceremonial of mounting the guard in which the flag or colours are received.
trōō'per *n.* Cavalryman, horse-soldier; troop-ship; (Austral. & U.S.) mounted policeman.
trōpacocai'ne *n.* (pharm.) Local anaesthetic obtained from coca leaves grown in Java.
trŏpae'olum *n.* Plant of genus

TROPAEOLUM

[938]

T~ which comprises the nasturtiums. [Gk *tropaion* trophy, from resemblance of leaf to shield and of flower to helmet]
trōpe *n.* Figurative (e.g. metaphorical, ironical) use of a word; (eccles.) phrase or verse introduced as embellishment into some part of the Mass.
trŏ′phĭc *adj.* (biol.) Of nutrition; ~ *nerves*, nerves concerned with or regulating nutrition of tissues.
trŏ′phoblast (-ahst) *n.* Layer of cells enclosing embryo, serving to nourish it and (in mammals) to attach it to the wall of the uterus (ill. EMBRYO). **trŏphoblă′stĭc** *adj.*
trŏphoneurō′sĭs *n.* Functional disorder due to derangement of trophic action of nerves.
trŏ′phў *n.* (Gk & Rom. antiq.) Arms or other spoils taken from enemy set up as memorial of victory, painted or carved figure

TROPHY

of such memorial; (representation of) ornamental or symbolic group of objects; anything taken in war, hunting, etc., esp. if displayed as memorial; token or evidence of victory, power, skill, etc., prize, memento.
trŏ′pĭc *n.* Each of 2 circles of celestial sphere (northern ~ *of Cancer*, and southern ~ *of Capricorn*) parallel to equator and 23° 28′ north and south of it, where sun reaches its greatest declination north or south; each of 2 corresponding parallels of latitude on earth's surface; (pl.) torrid zone, region lying between these parallels. ~ *adj.* Tropical; ~ *bird*, sea-bird of the chiefly tropical genus *Phaethon*, resembling terns, with webbed feet, rapid flight, and usu. white·plumage marked with black.
trŏ′pĭcal[1] *adj.* Of, occurring in, inhabiting, peculiar to, suggestive of, the tropics; (fig.) very hot, ardent, or luxuriant; ~ *year*: see YEAR, sense 1. **trŏ′pĭcallў** *adv.*
trŏ′pĭcal[2] *adj.* Metaphorical, figurative. **trŏ′pĭcallў** *adv.*
trŏ′pĭsm *n.* (biol.) Turning of organism or part of one in particular direction in response to external stimulus or automatically.
tropŏ′logў *n.* Figurative speech or writing; figurative interpretation, esp. of Scriptures. **trŏpolŏ′gĭcal** *adj.* **trŏpolŏ′gĭcallў** *adv.*
trŏ′popause (-z) *n.* Boundary between the troposphere and the stratosphere (ill. ATMOSPHERE).
trŏ′posphēre *n.* Layer of atmospheric air extending from surface of earth to stratosphere, within which temperature falls with height (ill. ATMOSPHERE).
Trŏ′ssachs (-χs). Picturesque narrow wooded valley in Central region of Scotland.
trŏt *n.* Quadruped's gait between walk and gallop in which legs move in diagonal pairs almost together; similar gait between walking and running of man etc.; *on the* ~, on the go, continually moving. ~ *v.* (Make) go at a trot; cover (distance) by trotting; bring to specified condition by trotting; ~ *out*, lead out and show off paces of (horse); (fig.) produce, bring forward.
trŏth *n.* (archaic) Truth; faith, plighted word; *plight one's* ~: see PLIGHT[1].
Trŏ′tskў, Leon. Lev Davidovich Bronstein (1877–1940), Russian revolutionary leader; Soviet foreign commissar and minister of war and marine, 1918, organizer of Red Army, ordered to leave Russia 1929; advocate of world proletarian revolution and consistent opponent of Stalin; murdered in Mexico. **Trŏ′tskўĭsm** *n.* **Trŏ′tskўĭst** *n.*
trŏ′tter *n.* (esp.) Horse specially bred and trained for trotting; animal's foot, esp. used for food; (pl., joc.) human feet.
trŏ′tting *n.* (esp.) ~-*race*, race at trotting pace between horses each drawing a sulky on which the driver sits.
trou′badour (-ōōbadoor) *n.* One of a class of 11th–13th-c. lyric poets living in S. France, E. Spain, and N. Italy and singing in Provençal, chiefly of chivalry and gallantry. [Fr., f. Provençal *trobador*, f. *trobar* find, invent, compose in verse]
trou′ble (trŭb-) *n.* Affliction, grief, vexation, bother, inconvenience; pains, exertion; thing or person that gives trouble; *get into*, *be in*, ~, incur censure, punishment, etc.; (euphem., of unmarried woman) become, be, pregnant; ~-*maker*, one who stirs up trouble, agitator; ~-*shooter*, person employed to trace and remove cause of defective working, discontent, etc. ~ *v.* Disturb, agitate; distress, grieve; be disturbed or worried; subject, be subjected, to inconvenience or exertion.
trou′blesome (trŭbls-) *adj.* Causing trouble, vexatious; **trou′blesomelў** *adv.* **trou′blesomenèss** *n.*
trou′blous (trŭb-) *adj.* (archaic) Full of troubles, agitated.
trough (-ŏf) *n.* Long narrow open box-like wooden or other receptacle for holding water or food for animals, kneading dough, washing ore, etc.; wooden or other channel for conveying liquid; hollow or valley resembling trough. (meteor.) elongated region of lower barometric pressure between 2 of higher; ~ *of the sea*, hollow between 2 waves.
trounce *v.t.* Beat severely, castigate; defeat heavily; scold, abuse.
troupe (-ōōp) *n.* Company, troop, esp. of actors, acrobats, etc.
trou′per *n.* (esp.) Actor.
trou′ser (-z-) *n.* (pl., also *pair of* ~s) Loose-fitting two-legged outer garment extending (usu.) from waist to ankles; ~-*clips*, clips used by cyclists to confine trouser-legs at ankles; ~-*press*, contrivance for pressing legs of trousers so as to produce lengthwise crease. **trou′sering** *n.* Material suitable for trousers.
trousseau (trōō′sō) *n.* Bride's outfit of clothes etc.
trout *n.* Any of various small usu. speckled freshwater fish of genus *Salmo*, inhabiting rivers and lakes of temperate or colder parts of N. hemisphere, fished for sport and esteemed as food; *old* ~, (slang, derog.) oldish woman.
trouvere, trouveur (trōōvār, -ēr) *n.* One of a school of chiefly epic or narrative poets which originated in N. France in the 11th c. [Fr., f. OF *trover* find, invent (cf. TROUBADOUR)]
trove: see TREASURE-trove.
trŏ′ver *n.* (law) Finding and keeping of personal property; (also *action of* ~) common-law action to recover value of personal property illegally converted by another to his own use.
trow (*or* -ō) *v.t.* (archaic) Think, believe.
trow′el *n.* Flat-bladed tool with short handle used for spreading mortar etc.; gardener's short-handled tool with hollow scoop-like blade. ~ *v.t.* Spread, smooth, lay on, etc., (as) with trowel.

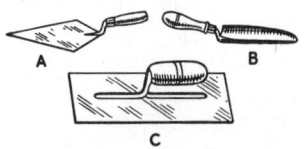

A. MASON'S TROWEL. B. GARDENER'S TROWEL. C. PLASTERER'S TROWEL OR FLOAT

Troy[1]. Ancient city in NW. Asia Minor, besieged by the Greeks in the TROJAN War; believed to be a figment of Greek legend until its remains were excavated between 1870 and 1890 by Heinrich Schliemann at Hissarlik.
troy[2] *n.* (also ~ *weight*) System of weights (1 lb. = 12 ounces = 240 pennyweights = 5760 grains)

[939]

used for precious metals etc. [prob. f. city of *Troyes* in France] **trs.** *abbrev.* Transpose.

tru′ant (-ōō-) *n.* One who absents himself from duty or business, esp. child who stays away from school without leave; *play ~*, act thus. *~ adj.* That plays truant or is a truant; shirking, idle, loitering, wandering. **tru′ancy** *n.*

truce (-ōōs) *n.* (Agreement for) temporary cessation of hostilities; respite or intermission from something disagreeable or painful; *~ of God*, (hist.) suspension of hostilities or private feuds ordered by Church during certain days and seasons in Middle Ages. **tru′celèss** *adj.*

trŭck[1] *n.* 1. Barter; (system of) payment of wages otherwise than in money; (fig.) dealings, intercourse. 2. Small miscellaneous articles, sundries; odds and ends, trash, rubbish; (U.S.) market-garden produce. *~ v.* Exchange, trade, barter; bargain, trade (*in*); pay or deal with on truck system.

trŭck[2] *n.* 1. Strong usu. 4- or 6-wheeled vehicle for heavy goods, lorry; open railway-wagon; barrow for moving luggage on railway-platform etc.; hand-cart; set of wheels in framework for supporting whole or part of railway-carriage etc. 2. (naut.) Wooden disc at top of mast with holes for halyards. *~ v.t.* Carry, convey, on truck. **trŭ′ckağe** *n.* (Cost of) conveyance by truck(s); supply of trucks.

trŭ′ckle *n.* (usu. *~-bed*) Low bed on wheels that may be pushed under another, esp. as formerly used by servants. *~ v.i.* Submit obsequiously, cringe (*to*). [n. f. L *trochlea* pulley f. Gk *trokhilia*; v. orig. in sense 'sleep in truckle-bed']

trŭ′cŭlent *adj.* Showing ferocity or cruelty; aggressive, savage, harsh. **trŭ′cŭlently** *adv.* **trŭ′cŭlence, trŭ′cŭlencў** *ns.*

trŭdġe *v.* Walk laboriously, wearily, or without spirit, but steadily; perform (distance) thus. *~ n.* Trudging; laborious or wearisome walk.

trŭ′dġen *n.* (also *~ stroke*) Hand-over-hand or double over-arm stroke in swimming with vigorous leg-kicks. [f. John *Trudgen* (19th c.), English swimmer]

true (-ōō) *adj.* 1. Consistent with fact or reality, not false or erroneous; *come ~*, be verified in experience, be fulfilled. 2. Agreeing with reason, correct principles, or recognized standard; real, genuine, correct, proper; not spurious, counterfeit, hybrid, or merely apparent; (of voice etc.) in good tune; conformable to the type; accurately placed, fitted, or shaped; (of ground etc.) level, smooth; *~ bill*, (hist.) bill of indictment found by Grand Jury sufficiently well-supported to justify hearing of case. 3. Steadfast in adherence (*to*), constant, loyal, faithful, sincere. 4. *~-blue*, (fig.) (person) of uncompromising loyalty or orthodoxy; *~-born*, of genuine birth, truly such by birth; *~-bred*, of true or pure breed, thoroughbred; *~-love knot*, *~ lover's knot*, (figure of) kind of knot symbolizing true love, usu. double-looped bow or knot formed of two loops intertwined. *~ adv.* Truly. *~ v.t.* Make (piece of mechanism etc.) true, adjust or shape accurately, make perfectly straight, smooth, level, etc.

trŭ′ffle *n.* Any of various edible central- and southern-European fungi of genus *Tuber*, esp. the French *T. melanospora*, usu. shaped like petals, with black warty exterior and rich flavour, esteemed as delicacy.

trŭġ *n.* Shallow garden-basket made of wood strips, with handle from side to side.

tru′ism (-ōō-) *n.* Self-evident truth, esp. of slight importance; hackneyed truth, platitude.

trŭll *n.* (archaic) Prostitute.

tru′lў (-ōō-) *adv.* Sincerely, genuinely; faithfully, loyally; accurately, truthfully.

Tru′man (trōō-), Harry S. (1884–1972). 33rd president of U.S., 1945–53.

trumeau (trōōmō′) *n.* (archit.; pl. *-x*). Piece of wall, pillar, between two openings, e.g. pillar dividing large doorway (ill. DOOR).

trŭmp[1] *n.* (archaic & poet.) (Sound of) trumpet.

trŭmp[2] *n.* Playing-card of suit ranking temporarily above other three; (colloq.) person of surpassing excellence, very helpful person; *turn up ~s*, (colloq.) turn out well or successfully; *~ card*, card turned up to determine which suit shall be trumps, any card of this suit; (fig.) valuable resource, important means of doing something, gaining one's point, etc. *~ v.* Put trump on, take (trick, card) with trump; play trump, take trick with trump; *~ up*, (colloq.) fabricate, invent.

trŭ′mperў *n.* Worthless stuff, trash, rubbish. *~ adj.* Showy but worthless, delusive, shallow. [Fr. *tromper* deceive]

trŭ′mpĕt *n.* Musical wind-instrument of bright ringing tone, consisting of narrow cylindrical, usu. metal, straight or curved tube with bell and cup-shaped mouth-piece and now usu. with valves (ill. BRASS); organ reed-stop with powerful trumpet-like tone; something shaped like trumpet, esp. ear-trumpet, speaking-trumpet, tubular corona of daffodil; sound (as) of trumpet, esp. elephant's loud cry; *~-creeper*, N. Amer. creeper (*Campsis radicans*) with large scarlet trumpet-shaped flowers; *~-flower*, any of various plants with trumpet-shaped flowers; *~-lily*, white arum lily; species of lily, esp. the Japanese *Lilium longiflorum*; *~-major*, chief trumpeter of band or regiment; *~-shell*, large marine univalve shell of *Triton* and allied genera; *~-vine*, trumpet-creeper. *~ v.* Proclaim (as) by sound of trumpet; celebrate, extol loudly; (of elephant) make loud sound as of trumpet.

trŭ′mpĕter *n.* 1. One who plays on or sounds trumpet, esp. cavalry-soldier giving signals with trumpet. 2. Any of various large S. Amer. birds of genus *Psophia*, allied to cranes, with loud trumpet-like note; *~ swan*, large N. Amer. wild swan, *Cygnus buccinator*, with loud sonorous note. 3. Fish making trumpeting noise when taken from water, esp. Austral. and N. Zealand marine food-fish of genus *Latris*.

trŭ′ncāte *adj.* Truncated. *~ v.t.* Cut short, cut off top or end of. **trŭncā′tĕd** *adj.* (esp.) (of cone or pyramid) With vertex cut off by plane section, esp. parallel to base; (of edge or solid angle) cut off by plane face, esp. one equally inclined to adjacent faces; (of crystal, solid figure, etc.) having such angles; (biol.) looking as if tip or end were cut off. **trŭncā′tion** *n.*

trŭ′ncheon (-chon) *n.* Short thick staff or club, esp. that carried by policeman. *~ v.t.* Strike or beat with truncheon.

trŭ′ndle *n.* 1. Small wheel; lantern-wheel, device of two discs connected by cylinder of parallel staves which engage with teeth of cog-wheel; roller with two arms for transmitting motion from stop-knob of organ. 2. Trundling. *~ v.* (Cause to) roll; draw, be drawn, along on wheel(s) or in wheeled vehicle.

trŭnk *n.* 1. Main stem of tree as dist. from roots and branches; shaft of column; human or animal body without head and limbs; main body or line of nerve, artery, etc., or of river, railway, telegraph, telephone, road, or canal system, as dist. from branches. 2. Box or chest with hinged lid for carrying clothes etc. while travelling; perforated floating box for keeping live fish; box-like passage, usu. of boards, used as shaft, conduit, shute, etc. 3. Elephant's long flexible nose. 4. (pl.) Short full breeches worn with hose or tights, trunk-hose; short close-fitting breeches worn by swimmers, boxers, etc. 5. *~-call*, telephone call to more or less distant exchange, involving use of trunk line; *~-fish*, fish of *Ostracion* and related genera, with body of angular cross-section and covered with bony hexagonal plates; *~-hose*, full, freq. padded, breeches reaching about half-way down thigh, worn in 16th and early 17th centuries (ill. DOUBLET); *~ line*, main line of railway, telephone

[940]

system, etc.; ~ **road**, important main road. **trŭ'nkful** n. **trŭ'nkless** adj.

trŭ'nnion (-nyon) n. Supporting cylindrical projection on each side of cannon or mortar (ill. CANNON); hollow gudgeon supporting cylinder in steam-engine and giving passage to steam.

Truron. abbrev. (Bishop) of Truro, Cornwall (replacing surname in his signature).

trŭss n. 1. Bundle of hay or straw (in England 60 lb. of new or 56 lb. of old hay, or 36 lb. of straw); compact cluster of flowers growing on one stalk. 2. Supporting structure or framework of bridge, roof, etc. (ill. ROOF); large corbel, projecting from face of wall and freq. supporting cornice etc.; (naut.) tackle for securing yard to mast, iron ring round mast with pivoted attachment to yard at centre. 3. Surgical appliance, now usu. pad with belt or spring, for support in cases of hernia etc. ~ v.t. 1. Tie (up), pack, in a bundle or parcel; tie, fasten (up) closely or securely; fasten limbs of (fowl etc. for cooking) to body with skewers etc.; (hist.) fasten (up) points or laces of (hose); tie up (points), tie up arms of (person). 2. Support or secure with truss(es).

trŭst n. 1. Confidence in, reliance on, some quality of person or thing, or truth of statement; confident expectation, hope; confidence in future payment for goods etc. supplied, credit; object of trust. 2. Condition of being trusted; obligation of one in whom confidence is placed or authority vested; (law) confidence reposed in person in whom legal ownership of property is vested to hold or use for benefit of another, property so committed, body of trustees; thing, person, duty, entrusted to one or committed to one's care; *in* ~, entrusted to person or body of persons, held as trust; *investment* ~, joint-stock company whose profits are drawn from investments distributed among a number of other companies and from the sale of these investments; ~ *company*, company formed or authorized to act as trustee or handle trusts; ~ *territory*, one under trusteeship of (State designated by) the United Nations. 3. Organized combination of producing or trading firms to reduce or defeat competition, control production and distribution, etc., esp. such a combination with central governing body holding majority or whole of stock of combining firms. ~ v. Have faith or confidence (in); place trust in, rely or depend on; hope; believe (statement), rely on truthfulness, etc., of (person); commit care or safety of (thing) *to* or *with* person; place or allow to be *in* place or condition or *to* do something, without fear of the consequences; entrust to care,

disposal, etc., of; give (person) credit *for* (goods).

trŭstee' n. Person to whom property is entrusted for benefit of another; one of number of persons appointed to manage affairs of an institution; (U.S.) one in whose hands debtor's property is attached in ~ *process*, judicial process by which goods, effects, and credits of debtor may be attached while in hands of third person; ~ *stock*, stock in which trust-funds are or may legally be invested.

trŭstee'ship n. Position of a trustee; status of area for whose government another State is instructed by the United Nations to be responsible.

trŭ'stful adj. Full of trust, confiding. **trŭ'stfullў** adv. **trŭ'stfulnėss** n.

trŭ'stworthy (-wêrdhĭ) adj. Worthy of trust, reliable. **trŭ'stworthinėss** n.

trŭ'stў adj. (chiefly archaic) Trustworthy. **trŭ'stĭlў** adv. **trŭ'stĭnėss** n. **trŭ'stў** n. (U.S.) Trustworthy convict granted special privileges.

truth (-ōōth) n. Quality, state, of being true; loyalty, honesty, accuracy, integrity, etc.; what is true, true statement or account, true belief or doctrine, reality, fact. **tru'thful**(-ōōth-) adj. Habitually speaking truth, not deceitful; true. **tru'thfullў** adv. **tru'thfulnėss** n.

try v. 1. Examine and determine (cause, question) judicially, determine guilt or innocence of (accused person) by consideration of evidence; test (quality), test qualities of (person, thing), by experiment; test effect or operation of, experiment with; attempt to ascertain by experiment or effort; subject to severe test or strain, strain endurance or patience of; ~ *on*, test fit or style of (garment) by putting it on; ~ *out*, put to the test, test thoroughly. 2. Attempt to do, perform, or accomplish; essay; make an effort, endeavour, attempt; ~ *for*, attempt to attain (object, position, etc.) or to reach (place); ~ *one's hand*, make attempt *at* for first time; ~ *it on*, begin some doubtful action etc. experimentally to see how much will be tolerated; attempt an imposition. 3. Dress (board etc.) to perfectly flat surface with trying-plane. 4. (also ~ *out*) Extract (oil) from blubber or fat by heat, extract oil from (fat etc.) thus, render. 5. ~-*on*, act or instance of trying it on (see 2 above); (colloq.) attempt to deceive; ~-*out*, experimental run, test of efficiency etc.; *try'sail* (or trī'sl), small strongly made fore-and-aft sail used as substitute for normal sail in stormy weather; ~-*square*, carpenter's instrument of two straight edges fixed at right angles, for laying off short perpendiculars (ill. SQUARE); ~-*works*, apparatus for rendering

blubber. ~ n. 1. Act of trying, attempt. 2. (Rugby footb.) Right of attempting to kick a goal, obtained by touching down ball on or behind opponents' goal-line, points (4) scored for this if goal is not successfully kicked; (Amer. footb., also ~ *for point*) attempt to score additional point after touch-down by scoring goal, crossing opponents' line again, or completing forward pass in opponents' end zone.

trȳ'ing n. (esp.) ~-*plane*, long heavy plane used for accurate squaring of timber (ill. PLANE²); ~-*square*, TRY-square. ~ adj. That tries; (esp.) exhausting; exasperating; difficult to bear.

trȳ'panosōme n. Parasite of *Trypanosoma* or allied genera of flagellate protozoa, infesting blood etc. of man and other animals and often causing disease. [Gk *trupanon* borer, *soma* body]

trȳ'psĭn n. Enzyme present in pancreatic juice, converting proteins into peptones.

trȳ'ptĭc adj. Of, produced by, trypsin.

trȳ'ptŏphān n. Crystalline amino-acid formed in tryptic digestion, the presence of which in the food of animals is necessary for proper growth.

trȳst n. (archaic) Appointed meeting, appointment. **trȳ'stĭngplāce** n. Appointed place for meeting.

tsär, czär (z-) n. (hist.) Emperor, title assumed c 1482 by Ivan Basilovich, Grand Duke of Muscovy, and used by emperors of Russia until 1917. [Russ. *tsar*, f. L CAESAR]

tsär'ėvich, cz- (z-) n. (hist.) (Title of) son of tsar (in Engl. usage, but erroneously, the eldest son and heir).

tsarė'vna, cz- (z-) n. (hist.) (Title of) daughter of tsar.

tsari'na, tsari'tsa, cz- (z-, -ēn-) ns. (hist.) (Title of) empress of Russia.

tsär'ĭsm, cz- (z-) n. (Devotion to, advocacy of) autocratic rule of tsars. **tsär'ĭst** adj. & n. **tsari'stĭc** adj.

tsĕ'tsė (or tĕt-) n. (also ~-*fly*) Fly of genus *Glossina*, abundant in parts of central and southern Africa and carrying disease to men and animals, esp. *G. palpalis*, carrier of the trypanosome causing sleeping sickness.

T.S.H. abbrev. Their Serene Highnesses.

tsuna'mi (tsōōnah-) n. Unusually large wave produced by submarine earthquake.

Tswa'na (tswah- or swah-) n. 1. (Member of) a Negroid people living between the Orange and Zambezi rivers in southern Africa. 2. Bantu language of this people.

T.T. abbrev. Teetotaller; Tourist Trophy; tuberculin-tested.

t.t.d. abbrev. Three times daily.

T.U. abbrev. Trade(s) Union.

[941]

tŭb *n.* Open cylindrical or slightly concave vessel, usu. of staves and hoops, with flat bottom; measure of capacity for butter or other commodities; slow clumsy ship; short broad boat, esp. stout roomy boat for rowing practice; (mining) box or bucket for conveying coal etc. to surface; (colloq.) bath; ~-*thumper*, ranting preacher or orator. ~ *v.* Bathe or wash in tub; plant, pack, in tub; (slang) coach, practise, in tub.

tū′ba *n.* (mus.) Brass wind-instrument, the bass of the horn family, usu. with wide conical bore and cup-shaped mouthpiece (ill. BRASS); esp. the euphonium (*tenor* ~), bombardon, and the lower-pitched saxhorns and sousaphone; player of this; sonorous high-pressure reed-stop in organ.

tŭ′bby *adj.* Tub-shaped; short and fat, round, corpulent.

tūbe *n.* 1. Long hollow cylinder esp. for conveying or holding liquids, pipe. 2. Main body of wind instrument. 3. Short cylinder of flexible metal with screw cap for holding semi-liquid substance, e.g. toothpaste, artists' paint. 4. Inner tube containing air in pneumatic tyre. 5. Hollow cylindrical organ in animal body, as *bronchial* ~; ~-*foot*, one of the tubular projections on body of echinoderm, used for locomotion and grasping (ill. STARFISH). 6. Cylindrical tunnel in which some London electric railways run; such railway. 7. (U.S.) Thermionic valve. **tū′bełèss** *adj.* (esp., of pneumatic tyre) Having no inner tube. **tūbe** *v.* Furnish with, enclose in, tube(s). **tūbed** (-bd) *adj.* (esp., of racehorse) Having tube inserted in air-passage.

tū′ber *n.* 1. Short, thick, more or less rounded, root or stem of

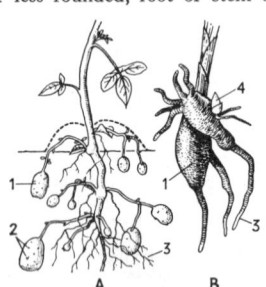

TUBERS
A. STEM TUBER (POTATO)
B. ROOT TUBER (ORCHID)

1. Tuber. 2. Eyes. 3. Roots. 4. Bud

plant, freq. bearing eyes or buds from which new plants may grow, as potato etc. 2. (anat.) Rounded swelling or protuberant part.

tū′bercle *n.* Small rounded projection or protuberance; esp. (path.) small rounded swelling on surface of body or in part or organ, esp. mass of granulation-cells characteristic of tuberculosis; (bot.) small tuber, or root-growth resembling this, small wart-like excrescence; ~ *bacillus*, bacillus *Myobacterium tuberculosis* causing tuberculosis. **tūber′cūlar** *adj.*

tūber′cūlin *n.* Sterile liquid prepared from cultures of tubercle bacillus and used for diagnosis and treatment of tuberculosis, esp. in children and cattle; ~ *test*, injection of tuberculin under skin, causing inflammation in tuberculous subjects; ~-*tested*, (esp., of milk) from cows shown by tuberculin test to be free of tuberculosis.

tūbērcūlō′sis *n.* Infectious disease in men and animals caused by tubercle bacillus and characterized by formation of tubercles in bodily tissues, esp. lungs (*pulmonary* ~). **tūber′cūlous** *adj.* (esp.) Affected with, of the nature of, tuberculosis.

tū′berōse *adj.* Tuberous. ~ (-z) *n.* Tropical liliaceous plant (*Polianthes tuberosa*) with creamy-white funnel-shaped fragrant flowers and tuberous roots. **tūberō′sitў** *n.* Tuberous formation or part; esp. (anat., zool.) large irregular projection of bone, usu. as attachment for muscle. [L *tuberosus* tuberous]

tū′berous *adj.* Of the form or nature of a tuber; covered or affected with, bearing, tubers; ~ *root*, (esp.) root thickened so as to resemble tuber but bearing no buds. **tū′berouslў** *adv.* **tū′berousnèss** *n.*

tūbi′colous *adj.* Living in a tube (of annelids and rotifers secreting tubular cases, spiders spinning tubular webs, etc.).

tūbili′nġual (-nggw-) *adj.* Having a tubular tongue, as honey-eaters.

tū′bing *n.* (esp.) Tubes collectively; length or piece of tube; material for tubes.

tū′bipoře *adj.* & *n.* (Member) of genus *Tubipora*, the organ-pipe corals.

tū′būlar *adj.* Tube-shaped; cylindrical, hollow, and open at one or both ends; constructed with, consisting of, tubes. **tū′būlous** *adj.*

tū′būle *n.* Small tube, minute tubular structure in animal or plant.

T.U.C. *abbrev.* Trades Union Congress.

tŭck[1] *n.* 1. Flattened fold in garment etc., secured by stitching, for ornament or to shorten the article. 2. (naut.) Part of vessel where ends of bottom planks meet under stern. 3. (slang) Eatables, esp. sweets and pastry; ~-*in*, -*out*, hearty meal; ~-*shop*, (school slang) shop where tuck is sold. 4. Tucking in of ends or edges, anything so tucked in; ~-*in*, part to be tucked in; (*adj.*) (esp., of woman's blouse etc.) designed to be tucked into top of skirt etc. 5. (also ~-*net*, -*seine*) Smaller net inside seine to gather and bring fish to surface. ~ *v.* 1. Put tuck(s) in, shorten or ornament with tuck(s); thrust or put (*away*) object into place where it is snugly held or concealed; thrust or turn (*in*) ends or edges of (anything pendent or loose, now esp. bedcoverings) so as to retain or confine them; be so disposed of; draw together into small compass. 2. ~ *in*, (slang) eat heartily.

tŭck[2] *n.* (archaic, chiefly Sc.) Blast, flourish (of trumpet); beat, tap (of drum).

tŭ′cker[1] *n.* (esp.) Piece of lace, linen, etc., worn by women inside or round top of bodice in 17th–18th c. (now chiefly in *best bib and* ~).

tŭ′cker[2] *v.t.* (U.S.) Tire (*out*), weary; *tuckered out*, exhausted, worn out.

tŭ′cker[3] *n.* (Austral. colloq.) Food.

tŭ′ckèt *n.* (archaic) Flourish on trumpet.

Tū′dor. 1. Name of English royal house from Henry VII to Elizabeth I, descended from Owen Tudor, who married Catherine, widowed queen of Henry V. 2. (attrib. or as *adj.*) Of the architectural style (latest development of Perpendicular) prevailing in England during reigns of Tudors; of, resembling, imitating, the domestic architecture of this period, with much half-timbering, brickwork freq. in patterns, elaborate chimneys, many gables, rich oriel windows, much interior panelling and moulded plasterwork, etc.; ~ *arch*, flattened four-centred arch characteristic of the period; ~ *rose*, conventional five-lobed decorative figure of rose,

TUDOR ROSE

esp. combination of red and white roses of York and Lancaster adopted as badge by Henry VII. **Tūdorĕ′sque** (-k) *adj.*

Tues. *abbrev.* Tuesday.

Tuesday (tū′zdā *or* -dĭ) *n.* 3rd day of the week. [OE *Tiwesdæg* (rendering L *dies Martis*) f. Tiw, Germanic deity identified with MARS]

tū′fa *n.* (geol.) Porous deposit of calcium carbonate laid down round mineral springs. **tūfā′ceous** (-shus) *adj.*

tŭff *n.* (geol.) Rock formed from volcanic ashes. [Fr. *tuffe* TUFA]

tŭft *n.* Bunch, collection, of threads, grass, feathers, etc., held or growing together at the base; gold tassel on cap, formerly worn by titled undergraduates at Oxford and Cambridge. **tŭ′ftў** *adj.* **tŭft** *v.t.* Furnish with tuft(s); (upholstery) secure padding of (mattress, cushion, etc.) with thread drawn through tightly at regular intervals, producing depressions in surface usu. ornamented with tuft or button. **tŭ′ftėd** *adj.* (esp., of birds) Having tuft of feathers on head, crested; (of plants etc.) growing in tuft(s), clustered, bearing flowers in tufts.

tŭg *v.* Pull with great effort or violently; make vigorous pull *at*; tow (vessel) by means of tug-boat. ~ *n.* 1. Tugging, violent pull; ~-*of-war*, decisive contest, struggle for supremacy; athletic contest between two teams hauling on rope, each team trying to pull other over line marked between them. 2. Trace, various other parts of harness; any chain, strap, or rope used for pulling. 3. (also

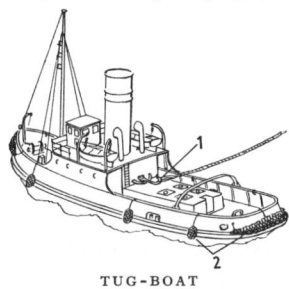

TUG-BOAT
1. Towing hook. 2. Rope fenders

~-*boat*) Small stoutly built steamer used to tow other vessels.
tŭ′gric (-ēk) *n.* Principal monetary unit of the Mongolian People's Republic, = 100 mongo.
Tuileries (twēlerē). Royal palace on N. bank of Seine in Paris, begun 1564 by Catherine de Médicis and later joined by wings to Louvre; destroyed by fire 1871.
tuï′tion *n.* Teaching, instruction. **tuï′tional, tuï′tionarў** *adjs.*
tŭ′lip *n.* (Flower of) bulbous spring-flowering plant of genus *Tulipa*, esp. any of the numerous cultivated varieties, with showy bell-shaped or cup-shaped flowers of various colours and markings; ~-*root*, disease of cereal and other plants caused by minute nematoid worm and marked by bulb-like swelling of lower stem; ~-*shell*, (large coloured shell of) marine gasteropod of family Fasciolariadae, esp. *Fasciolaria tulipa* of southern U.S.; ~-*tree*, large N. Amer. tree (*Liriodendron tulipifera*) with large greenish-yellow tulip-like flowers and soft white wood; any of various other trees with tulip-like flowers, as species of *Magnolia* etc.; ~-*wood*, light ornamental wood, used for cabinet-work etc., of tulip-tree; any of

various coloured and striped woods or trees producing these. [Turk. *tülbend-*(*lale*) turban (tulip)]
tülle *n.* Thin soft fine silk net, used for dresses, veils, etc. [Fr., name of town]
Tŭ′llў. Familiar name for Marcus Tullius CICERO.
tŭ′lwar *n.* Any of various Indian sabres.
tŭm *n.* (nursery or joc.) Stomach.
tŭ′mble *v.* 1. (Cause to) fall, esp. helplessly or violently; roll, toss, wallow; move in headlong or blundering fashion; overthrow, demolish; be overthrown, fall into ruin; handle roughly, disorder, rumple, disarrange by tossing; (fig.) stumble, blunder (*on*, *into*); ~ *to*, understand, grasp (esp. something hidden or not clearly expressed). 2. Perform leaps, somersaults, and other acrobatic feats; (of pigeon etc.) turn end over end in flight. 3. (also ~ *home*, of sides of ship) Slope inwards above greatest breadth. 4. ~-*bug*, (U.S.) dung beetle that rolls up balls of dung in which to lay its eggs; dor beetle; *tu′mbledown*, falling or fallen into ruin, dilapidated; ~-*home*, inward inclination of upper part of ship's sides; *tu′mbleweed*, (U.S.) any of various plants which in late summer are broken off and blown along by wind in light globular rolling mass. ~ *n.* Fall; tumbled condition, confused or tangled heap.
tŭ′mbler *n.* (esp.) 1. One who does somersaults, handsprings, etc., acrobat. 2. (also ~-*pigeon*) Variety of domestic pigeon turning over and over backwards in flight. 3. Kind of tapering cylindrical or barrel-shaped drinking-cup or (now usu.) glass without handle or foot, orig. with rounded or pointed bottom so that it would not stand upright, now with flat usu. heavy bottom. 4. Pivoted plate through which mainspring acts on hammer of gun-lock; pivoted piece in lock which must be moved into proper position by key etc. before lock can be opened (ill. LOCK²); any of various mechanisms or parts, as projecting piece on revolving shaft for operating another piece, movable part of tumbling gear, tumbling box, revolving barrel for washing hides, etc. 5. ~ *bearing*, bearing falling out of position or knocked aside to make way for gear travelling on shaft which it supports; ~ *gear*, tumbling gear; ~ *switch*, electric switch operated by pushing over small spring thumb-piece.
tŭ′mbling *n.* & *adj.* ~-*barrel*, tumbling box; ~-*bay*, outfall from river, canal, or reservoir, pool into which this falls; ~-*bob*, weighted lever or arm in machinery falling when moved to certain point; ~ *box*, rotating drum in which small articles are cleaned and polished by attrition or small castings have

cores broken out; ~ *gear*, gear with one or more idle wheels on swinging frame for producing reverse motion.
tŭ′mbrėl, -il *n.* 1. Tip-cart, esp. for dung (ill. CART). 2. Cart in which condemned persons were carried to the guillotine during the French Revolution. 3. Ammunition cart.
tŭ′mėfў *v.* (Cause to) swell; make, become, tumid, turgid, or bombastic. **tŭmėfă′ction** *n.*
tŭmė′scent *adj.* Swelling up, becoming tumid. **tŭmė′scence** *n.*
tŭ′mid *adj.* Swollen, swelling, morbidly affected with swelling; inflated, turgid, bombastic. **tŭ′midlў** *adv.* **tŭmi′ditў** *n.*
tŭ′mmў *n.* (esp. nursery) Stomach.
tŭ′mour (-mer) *n.* Abnormal or morbid swelling, overgrowth; BENIGN ~, MALIGNANT ~: see these words. **tŭ′morous** *adj.*
tŭ′mŭlt *n.* Commotion of a multitude, esp. with confused cries and uproar, public disturbance, riot, insurrection; commotion, agitation, disorderly or noisy movement, confused and violent emotion. **tŭmŭ′ltuous** *adj.* **tŭmŭ′ltuouslў** *adv.* **tŭmŭ′ltuousnėss** *n.*
tŭ′mŭlus *n.* (pl. -lī). Ancient sepulchral mound, barrow.
tŭn *n.* Large cask or barrel for wine, beer, etc.; measure of capacity, usu. 2 pipes or 4 hogsheads.
tū′na *n.* Tunny; *yellow-fin* ~, an albacore, *Thunnus albacares*.
tŭ′ndra *n.* Vast level treeless region of N. Europe, Asia, and N. America, with arctic climate and vegetation (chiefly mosses and lichens with dwarf shrubs etc.).
tūne *n.* Rhythmical succession of musical tones, air, melody (with or without harmony); being in proper pitch, correct intonation in singing or instrumental music; harmony or accordance in respect of vibrations other than those of sound; *in*, *out*, *of*, ~, in or out of the proper pitch or correct intonation; in or out of order or proper condition, (not) correctly adjusted; in or out of harmony (*with*); *to the* ~ *of*, to the (considerable or exorbitant) amount or sum of. ~ *v.* Adjust tones of (musical instrument) to standard of pitch, put in tune; attune, bring into accord or harmony; bring into proper or desirable condition; adjust (engine etc.) to run smoothly and efficiently, (radio receiver) to desired wavelength etc.; ~ *in*, adjust (radio receiver) to receive transmission; ~ *out*, cut off (radio signal) by tuning receiver; ~ *up*, raise one's voice; bring (instrument) up to proper pitch, adjust instruments for playing together; bring (engine etc.) into most efficient working order by esp. fine adjustments. **tū′nable** *adj.* (archaic) Harmonious, melodious.
tū′neful (-nf-) *adj.* Melodious,

[943]

musical. **tū′nefully** *adv.* **tū′nefulness** *n.*
tū′neless *adj.* Untuneful, unmusical; not in tune; songless, silent. **tū′nelessly** *adv.* **tū′nelessness** *n.*
tū′ner *n.* (esp.) One whose occupation is to tune pianos or organs.
tū′ngsten *n.* (chem.) Heavy steel-grey ductile metallic element, melting only at a very high temperature, occurring in combination in wolfram and other minerals, and used for electric-light filaments, electric contacts, sparking-plug points, hard steel alloys, etc.; symbol W (*wolfram*), at. no. 74, at. wt 183·85. **tū′ngstic** *adj.* [Swed. *tung* heavy, *sten* stone]
tū′nic *n.* 1. Ancient Greek and Roman short-sleeved body garment reaching to about knees (ill. TOGA). 2. Close-fitting short coat of police or military uniform. 3. Woman's loose garment for upper part of body; belted frock worn by women and children at games. 4. (anat., zool.) Membranous sheath or lining of organ or part; (bot.) integument of seed etc.
tū′nica *n.* (anat., zool.) Tunic.
tū′nicate *n.* Member of the sub-phylum Urochordata including the sea-squirts, having body enclosed in a hard TEST[2] and, at least in larval stage, a notochord; = ascidian. ~ *adj.* 1. (zool.) Enclosed in a sheath; of the tunicates. 2. (bot.) Consisting of a series of concentric layers, as a bulb.
tū′nicle *n.* (eccles.) Short vestment like dalmatic worn at Eucharist by subdeacon over alb or by bishop between alb and dalmatic.
tū′ning-fork *n.* Small 2-pronged steel instrument giving definite musical note of constant pitch when struck.
Tūni′sia (*or* -z-). Republic in N. Africa between Algeria and Libya; independent 1956, formerly a French protectorate; capital, Tunis. **Tūni′sian** *adj.* & *n.*
tū′nnel *n.* Subterranean passage under hill, river, roadway, etc., now esp. for railway; subterranean passage dug by burrowing animal; level or nearly level passage in mine etc.; tube, pipe, as that containing propeller-shaft in ship etc. ~ *v.* Make tunnel, make tunnel through.
tū′nny *n.* Large mackerel-like sea-fish of family Scombridae, esteemed as food and as game-fish; esp. *Thunnus thynnus*, fished from ancient times in Mediterranean and Atlantic.
tŭp *n.* 1. Male sheep, ram. 2. Device acting by impact, as striking-face of steam-hammer etc. ~ *v.t.* Copulate with (ewe).
tu′pelō (tōō-) *n.* Any of various large N. Amer. trees of genus *Nyssa*, growing in swamps or on river banks in southern U.S.; wood of this.
Tu′pí (tōō-) *n.* Member, language, of S.-Amer. Indian people living in parts of Brazil, esp. the Amazon valley.
tū quō′que (*or* tōō kwŏ-). The retort *So are you* (or *So did you* etc.). [L, = 'you too']
tur′acō, tour- (toor-) *n.* Long-tailed crested African bird of *Tauraco* and allied genera.
tŭr′ban *n.* Oriental men's head-dress of Muslim origin consisting of cap with long band or scarf of linen, cotton, or silk wound round it; woman's hat of scarf wound or twisted round (ill. SACK[1]); bright-coloured cotton cloth worn as head-dress by Negro women in southern U.S. and West Indies; ~ *lily*, Siberian lily with deep-red spotted flowers. [Turk. *tülbend*]
tŭr′barý *n.* Land where turf or peat may be dug for fuel; right to dig turf or peat on another's land.
tŭr′bid *adj.* Muddy, thick, not clear; (fig.) confused, disordered. **tŭr′bidly** *adv.* **turbi′dity̆, tŭr′bidness** *ns.*
tŭr′binal *adj.* Turbinate. ~ *n.* Turbinate bone.
tŭr′binate, -ātėd *adjs.* (of shell) Spiral with whorls decreasing rapidly in size; (bot.) inversely conical; *turbinate bone*, (anat.) one of scroll-like bones of the nose.
tŭr′bine *n.* Motor in which rotatory motion is produced by a fluid (water, steam, gas, etc.) impinging directly upon a series of vanes on the circumference of a revolving cylinder or disc, used to drive a ship, aircraft, generators for electric power, etc.
tŭrbo- *prefix.* Turbine, in compounds forming the name of machines driven by a turbine, or which are themselves turbines, as ~-*dynamo*, -*generator*; ~-*jet*, power unit of a jet-propelled aircraft; aircraft with turbo-jet engine; jet produced by a gas-turbine.
tŭr′bot *n.* Large European flat fish (*Scophthalmus maximus*) much esteemed as food; (loosely) any of various similar fish, as Californian diamond flounder.
tŭr′bulent *adj.* Disturbed, in commotion, disorderly, troubled, stormy; tumultuous, unruly, violent. **tŭr′bulently** *adv.* **tŭr′bulence** *n.*
Turcoman: see TURKOMAN.
tŭrd *n.* (vulg.) (Lump or piece of) excrement.
tŭr′dine *adj.* Of the sub-family Turdinae of true thrushes.
tūree′n *n.* Deep covered dish from which soup is served.
Tūrėnne, Henri de la Tour d'Auvergne, Vicomte de (1611–75). Marshal of France.
tŭrf *n.* (pl. -*fs* or -*ves*). Covering of grass etc. with matted roots, forming surface of grass-land; sod; slab or block of peat dug for fuel; *the T*~, grassy course used for horse-racing; institution, action, or practice of horse-racing; ~ *accountant*, book-maker. **tŭr′fy̆** *adv.* **tŭrf** *v.t.* Cover (ground) with turf; (slang) throw (person or thing) *out*.
Turgénev (toorgā′ny̆ef), Ivan Sergeevich (1818–83). Russian novelist; author of 'Fathers and Sons', 'Virgin Soil', etc.
tŭr′gid *adj.* Swollen, distended, puffed out; (fig., of language) pompous, bombastic. **tŭr′gidly̆** *adv.* **turgi′dity̆, tŭrgė′scence** *ns.* **tŭrgė′scent** *adj.*
tŭr′gor *n.* (bot.) Rigidity due to uptake of water into living cells or tissues.
Tūri′n. (Ital. *Torino*) Capital city of province of same name, Piedmont, Italy.
tūr′ion *n.* Scaly shoot produced from bud on underground stem.

TURION (ASPARAGUS)

Tŭrk *n.* 1. Native of Turkey; (hist.) native or inhabitant of the Ottoman Empire. 2. Member of a people speaking a Turkic language. 3. ~'*s cap*, kind of lily (*Lilium martagon*); ~'*s head*, long-handled broom with head of feathers, for dusting; knot resembling turban.
Tŭrkėsta′n, Tŭrki- (-ahn). Region of Central Asia, divided between U.S.S.R. and China.
Tŭr′key[1]. Country of Asia Minor and Europe, formerly part

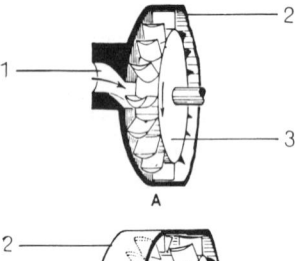

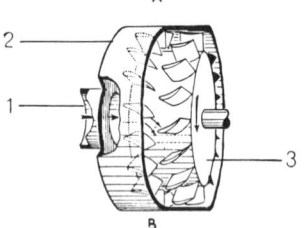

A. IMPULSE TURBINE.
B. REACTION TURBINE.
1. Steam intake. 2. Stator. 3. Rotor

[944]

TURKEY

of the Ottoman Empire, declared a republic in 1923; capital (since 1923), Ankara; ~ *carpet*, carpet made of wool, with a thick pile and bold design in red, blue, and green; ~ *red*, scarlet pigment made from madder or synthetically; cotton cloth dyed with this.

tūr′key² *n.* Large galinaceous bird of the Amer. genus *Meleagris*, with handsome plumage and naked wattled head, esp. *M. gallopavo*, found domesticated in Mexico in 16th c. and highly esteemed as table fowl (in England associated esp. with Christmas festivities, in U.S. with those of Thanksgiving); ~*-buzzard*, Amer. carrion vulture (*Cathartes aura*) with dark plumage and naked reddish head and neck; ~*-cock*, male of turkey; ~*-trot*, ragtime ballroom dance in vogue during war of 1914–18. [short for *turkey-cock, -hen,* orig. guinea-fowl, so-called f. being orig. imported through Turkey]

Tŭr′ki *adj. & n.* (Of, belonging to) a group of Ural-Altaic languages and peoples, including Turkish. **Tŭr′kĭc** *adj.*

Tŭr′kish *adj.* Of Turkey or the Turks; Turkic; ~ *bath*, hot-air or steam bath, inducing perspiration, after which body is washed, massaged, etc.; ~ *coffee*, strong usu. sweet black coffee made with very finely ground beans; ~ *delight*, sweet made of lumps of jelly flavoured with rosewater etc. and coated with icing-sugar; ~ *knot*, kind of knot used in carpet making (ill. WEAVE); ~ *tobacco*, aromatic tobacco grown esp. in Turkey and Greece; ~ *towel*, rough towel with a long nap usu. of uncut loops. ~ *n.* Language of Turkey.

Tŭr′kman *n.* Native of Turkmenistan. **Tŭrkmĕ′nĭan** *adj.*

Tŭr′kmĕn *n.* Turkoman language.

Tŭrkmĕnĭsta′n (-ahn), Constituent republic of U.S.S.R. lying between the Caspian Sea and Afghanistan; capital, Ashkhabad.

Tŭr′koman, Tŭrco- *n.* Member of a group of tribes of E. Turkic stock, living chiefly in Turkmenistan and parts of Iran and the Caucasus; Ural-Altaic language of these tribes; ~ *carpet*, *rug*, soft richly coloured carpet made by them. [Pers. *turkumān* Turk-like person]

Turku (tōōr′kōō). (Swed. *Ȧbo*) Port of SW. Finland.

tŭr′meric *n.* East Indian herb (*Curcuma longa*) of ginger family; pungent aromatic root-stock of this, used as condiment, esp. as chief ingredient in curry-powder and as yellow dye; ~*-paper*, unsized paper tinged with turmeric solution and used as test for alkalis, which turn it from yellow to brown.

tŭr′moil *n.* Agitation, commotion, trouble.

tūrn *v.* 1. Move on or as on axis; give rotary motion to, receive such motion; execute (somersault etc.) with rotary motion; change from one side to another, invert, reverse; (fig.) revolve mentally. 2. Give new direction to, take new direction; adapt, be adapted. 3. Move to other side of, go round, flank; pass round (*flank* etc. of army) so as to attack from flank or rear; cause to go, send, put. 4. Change in nature, form, condition, etc.; esp. change for the worse; (cause to) become; (of milk) (cause to) become sour. 5. Shape (object, material) in lathe; (of material) lend itself to treatment in lathe; give (esp. elegant) form to. 6. ~ *about*, turn so as to face in new direction; ~ *against*, become hostile to; ~ *down*, fold down; place upside down or face downwards; reduce flame of (gas, lamp, etc.) by turning tap etc.; (slang) reject (proposal, offer, etc.); ~ *in*, fold inwards; incline inwards; (colloq.) go to bed; ~ *off*, check flow of (water, electricity, etc.) by turning tap, switch, etc.; dismiss from employment; ~ *on* allow passage to (water, electricity, etc.) by turning tap etc.; depend upon; face hostilely, become hostile to; ~ *out*, expel; (cause to) point or incline outwards; produce; clear (receptacle, room, etc.) of its contents, put (contents) out of room, pocket, etc.; extinguish (light) by turning tap, switch, etc.; (cause to) assemble for duty etc.; get out of bed; be found, prove to be so; ~ *over*, reverse, invert; read (book) by turning over leaves; (cause to) fall over, upset; hand over, make over, transfer; do business to amount of; ~ *round*, face about; change to opposite opinion, state of mind, etc.; (of ship) discharge cargo and be ready for new voyage: ~ *to*, apply oneself to, set about; begin work; ~ *up*, turn (playing-card) face upwards; disinter; appear; happen; look up, refer to; nauseate, cause to vomit. 7. ~*-buckle*, coupling with internal screw-thread(s) for connecting metal rods, regulating their length, etc.; ~*-button*, small pivoted bar engaging with catch, edge of door, etc.; *tur′ncoat*, one who changes his principles or party, renegade; *tur′ncock*, person employed to turn on water from mains to supply-pipes etc.; ~*-down*, turned-down part of anything; (*adj.*) made to wear with upper part turned down; *tur′nkey*, one in charge of keys of prison; ~*-out*, (esp.) assemblage, muster; (style of) equipment, outfit, array; carriage with its horse(s) etc.; ~*-over*, (esp.) article in last column of newspaper page and continued overleaf; kind of pie or tart in which filling is laid on one half of rolled-out pastry and other half is turned over it; amount of money turned

TURNIP

over in business; *tur′npike*, (hist.) spiked barrier across road or passage, as defence against attack; (hist.) toll-gate; (hist. and U.S.) road with gates for collection of tolls; main road, highway; ~*-round*, (of ship) process of entering port, discharging, reloading, and leaving port (also of motor transport); *tur′nspit*, (hist., freq. contempt.) man or boy who turned spit upon which meat was cooked; dog of short-legged breed formerly used to turn a spit; *tur′nstile*, post with four radiating arms revolving horizontally as person passes through, in gateway, door, etc., similar device with mechanism for registering number passing through; *tur′ntable*, revolving platform, table, stand, etc., esp. one for reversing railway or other wheeled vehicles; ~*-up*, turned up part of anything, esp. of end of trouser-leg; turning up of card or die; (colloq.) commotion, tussle, fight. ~ *n.* 1. Turning; rotation, esp. single revolution of wheel etc.; (single) coil or twist. 2. (mus.) Ornament consisting of note above principal note, note itself, note below and note itself, performed instead of principal note or after it; *inverted* ~, similar figure begun on lower instead of higher note. 3. Change of direction or course, change of position by rotatory movement; curved or bent part of anything, bend, angle; turning back (esp. ~ *of the tide*). 4. Change, alteration; change of colour, condition, etc.; (colloq.) momentary shock caused by sudden alarm etc.; *on the* ~, (of food etc.) turning sour. 5. Act of good or ill will, (*good, bad,* ~, *service, disservice*); attack of illness, faintness, etc. 6. Opportunity, occasion, privilege, obligation, etc., coming successively to each of several persons, etc.; public appearance on stage before or after others, (performer of) item in variety entertainment; *in* ~, in succession; ~ (*and* ~) *about*, in turn; *serve one's, its* ~, answer purpose or requirement. 7. Character, tendency, disposition, formation.

tŭr′ner¹ *n.* (esp.) One who works with lathe. **tŭr′nerў** *n.* Use of lathe; objects fashioned on lathe; turner's workshop.

Tŭr′ner², Joseph Mallord William (1775–1851). English landscape-painter.

tŭr′ning *n.* (esp.) 1. Use of, art of using, lathe; (pl.) chips or shavings produced in process of turning. 2. Place where road, path, etc., turns or turns off from another; such road; ~*-point*, point at which decisive change takes place.

tŭr′nip *n.* Either of two biennial cruciferous plants (*Brassica rapa* and *B. napobrassica*) with fleshy globular or spheroidal root, toothed leaves, and yellow flowers; root of these, used as vegetable and for

[945]

tur′pentine *n.* Semifluid oleo-resin (*Chian* ~) exuded by tere-binth; (now usu.) yellowish viscous liquid oleo-resins, usu. solidifying on exposure (many varieties acc. to source, most having the same composition, $C_{10}H_{16}$), obtained from various coniferous trees; (also *oil of* ~, pop. *turps*) colourless or yellowish volatile inflammable oil, of pungent smell and taste, distilled from turpentines and used in mixing paints and varnishes etc.; ~-*tree*, terebinth; any tree yielding turpentine.

feeding cattle and sheep; (with defining word) any of various similar plants; (slang) large thick old-fashioned watch; ~-*tops*, young green shoots of turnips used as vegetable.

Tur′pin, Dick (1706–39). English highwayman.

tur′pitude *n.* Baseness, depravity, wickedness.

turps *n.* (colloq.) (Oil of) turpentine.

tur′quoise (-z; *or* -kwahz) *n.* Opaque or translucent sky-blue or blue-green hydrous aluminium phosphate found esp. in Persia and valued as gem; (also ~ *blue*) brilliant greenish-blue colour of turquoise. [OF (*pierre*) *turquoise* Turkish (stone)]

tu′rret *n.* Small or subordinate tower, esp. rounded addition to angle of building, freq. commencing at some height above ground; (mil., nav.) tower-like armoured usu. revolving structure in which guns are mounted in fort or tank or (usu.) warship; structure housing guns in aircraft; (mech.) rotating holder for various dies or cutting tools in lathe, drill, etc. ~ *v.t.* Furnish, equip, with turret(s) or turret-like structures; **tu′rreted** *adj.*

tur′tle[1] *n.* (now usu. ~-*dove*) Wild dove of genus *Streptopelia*, esp. the common European *S. turtur* with cinnamon-brown plumage and white-tipped tail-feathers, noted for its soft cooing and affection for its mate.

tur′tle[2] *n.* Reptile of any of the marine species (in U.S. also freshwater species) of the order Chelonia resembling tortoise but with limbs compressed into flippers or paddles; flesh of certain turtles as food, much used for soup; *turn* ~, turn over, capsize; ~-*back*, -*deck*, arched structure over part of deck of vessel to protect it from heavy sea; ~-*neck*, high close-fitting neck of knitted garment.

Tu′scan *adj.* Of Tuscany; (archit.) of the Tuscan order, simplest of the classical orders (ill. ORDER); ~ *straw*, fine yellow wheat-straw used for hats etc. ~ *n.* Native, inhabitant, language, of Tuscany.

Tu′scany. Region of W. central Italy.

Tuscaror′a *n.* Indian of tribe orig. of N. Carolina but since admission to Iroquois confederacy living mainly in New York.

tush[1] *int., n., & v.i.* (archaic) (Make) exclamation of impatient contempt.

tush[2] *n.* Long pointed tooth, esp. horse's canine tooth; small or stunted tusk in some Indian elephants.

tusk *n.* Long pointed tooth projecting beyond mouth in certain animals, as elephant, wild boar, etc.; tusk-like thing, as long protruding tooth, kind of tenon, etc. ~ *v.t.* Dig (*up*), tear, wound, with tusk; furnish with tusks.

tu′sker *n.* Elephant, wild boar, with developed tusks.

tu′ssah (-*a*), **tu′sser** *ns.* Varr. of TUSSORE.

Tussaud (tōōsō′), Marie (*née* Gresholtz) (1760–1850). Swiss founder of 'Madame Tussaud's', a permanent exhibition in London of wax models of eminent people (orig. victims of the French Revolution) from 1802 onwards.

tu′ssle *n. & v.i.* Struggle, scuffle.

tu′ssock *n.* Tuft, clump, small hillock, of grass, sedge, etc.; tuft of hair etc.; ~-*grass*, any of various grasses, esp. tall-growing stout grass (*Poa flabellata*) of Falkland Islands etc. introduced into Scotland as valuable fodder-grass; ~-*moth*, moth with larva covered with long tufts of hair. **tu′ssocky** *adj.*

tu′ssore *n.* (Strong coarse brownish silk produced by) any of various undomesticated Asiatic silkworms esp. *Antherae mylitta*. [Hindi *tasar* (Sansk. *tasara* shuttle)]

tut, tut-tut *int., n., & v.i.* (Make) exclamation of impatience, dissatisfaction, or rebuke.

Tutankha′men (tōō-, -ka̱h-) (14th c. B.C.). Egyptian king of XVIIIth dynasty who died at age of 18; successor and son-in-law of Akhnaton; his tomb at Karnak, containing remarkable treasures, was excavated in 1922.

tu′telage *n.* Guardianship, being under this; instruction, tuition.

tu′telary *adj.* Serving as protector, guardian, or patron, esp. of particular person, place, etc.; of a guardian, protective.

tu′tenag *n.* Zinc imported from China and E. Indies; white silver-like alloy of copper, nickel, and zinc, formerly used for domestic ware and fire-grates. [Marathi *tuttinag*]

tu′tor *n.* 1. Private teacher, esp. one having general charge of person's education; (in some British universities) graduate (usu. fellow of a college) directing studies of undergraduates assigned to him; (in some U.S. colleges) teacher ranking below instructor. 2. Instruction book in any subject. 3. (Rom. law) Guardian of a minor. **tu′torage, tu′torship** *ns.* **tutor′ial** *adj.* Of a tutor. ~ *n.* Period of individual instruction given to small group or single student. **tutor′ially** *adv.* **tu′tor** *v.* Act as tutor (to); exercise restraint over, subject to discipline.

tu′tti (tōō-) *adj. & n.* (Passage) to be rendered by all performers together. [It. = 'all']

tu′tti-fru′tti (tōō-, frōō-) *n. & adj.* (Confection, esp. ice-cream) made of or flavoured with various fruits. [It., = 'all fruits']

tu′tū (*or* tōō′tōō) *n.* Dancer's short skirt made of layers of stiffened frills.

tu-whi′t tu-whōō′ (tōō-, tōō-) *int., n., & v.i.* (Make) cry of owl. [imit. of cry of tawny owl]

tuxē′dō (*pl.* -*s*, -*es*) *n.* (U.S.) Dinner-jacket; man's evening dress including this. [name of fashionable country club at *Tuxedo* Park, N.Y.]

tuyère (twēyar′, tōōyar′, twēr′) *n.* Nozzle through which blast is forced into furnace etc.

T.V. *abbrev.* Television; terminal velocity.

T.V.A. *abbrev.* Tennessee Valley Authority.

twa′ddle (twŏ-) *n. & v.i.* (Indulge in) senseless, silly, or trifling talk or writing, (talk) nonsense.

twain[1] *adj. & n.* (archaic) Two. **Twain**[2], Mark. Pseudonym of Samuel Langhorne Clemens (1835–1910), Amer. humorist, author of 'Tom Sawyer' (1876), 'Huckleberry Finn' (1884), 'A Connecticut Yankee at the Court of King Arthur' (1889), etc. [call of leadsmen taking soundings on Mississippi where Clemens served as a pilot; = 2nd mark on cable, i.e. 2 fathoms]

twang *n.* Sharp ringing sound (as) of tense string of musical instrument or bow when plucked; nasal intonation; distinctive, esp. local, peculiarity of pronunciation. ~ *v.* (Cause to) make twanging sound; play on stringed instrument; utter, speak, with twang.

tweak *n.* Twist, sharp pull, pinch. ~ *v.t.* Seize and pull sharply with twisting movement, pull at with jerk, twitch.

Tweed[1]. River of S. Scotland, flowing into North Sea at Berwick.

tweed[2] *n.* Twilled woollen (or woollen mixture) cloth of usu. rough surface, dyed, freq. in several colours, before weaving. **twee′dy** *adj.* [formerly a tradename originating in a̱ misreading of *tweel*, Sc. form of TWILL, influenced by name of river TWEED]

Twee′ddale. Former name of Peeblesshire.

Tweedledu′m and Tweedledee′ (-ld-, -ld-). Two persons or things differing only or chiefly in name (orig. applied to the composers Handel and Bononcini in a satire by John Byrom containing the lines 'Strange all this Difference should be Twixt Tweedledum and Tweedle-dee!').

Tweedsmuir (-mūr): see BUCHAN[2].

'tween *prep.* Between; ~-*decks*,

(space) between decks (ill. SHIP).

twee′ny n. (colloq.) Between-maid.

tweet(-tweet) n. & v.i. (Utter) note of small bird.

twee′zers (-z) n.pl. (also pair of ~) Small pincer-like instrument for taking up small objects, plucking out hairs, etc. **twee′zer** v. Use, pull out with, tweezers.

twĕlfth adj. Next after eleventh; the T~, 12 August, on which grouse-shooting legally begins; T~-day, -night, 12th day after Christmas, 6 Jan., feast of Epiphany, formerly last day of Christmas festivities and observed as time of merry-making. ~ n. Twelfth part (see PART¹, 1); twelfth thing etc. **twĕ′lfthlў** adv.

twĕlve adj. Amounting to twelve; twe′lvemo, 12mo, duodecimo; twe′lvemonth, year. ~ n. One more than eleven (12, xii, or XII).

twĕn′tў adj. Amounting to twenty; ~-five, (esp., Rugby footb.) (space enclosed by) line drawn across ground 25 yards from each goal (ill. RUGBY). ~ n. Cardinal number, twice ten (20, xx, or XX); set of 20 things or persons; twenties, numbers etc. from 20 to 29; these years of century or life. **twĕ′ntiĕth** adj. & n. **twĕ′ntўfōld** adj. & adv.

twĕrp n. (slang) Silly or insignificant person.

twice adv. Two times; on two occasions; doubly, in double degree or quantity.

twi′ddle n. Slight twirl, quick twist; twirled mark or sign. ~ v. Trifle (with); twirl idly, play with idly or absently; ~ one's fingers, thumbs, keep turning them idly around each other (for lack of occupation); be idle. **twi′ddlў** adj.

twĭg¹ n. Small shoot or branch of tree or plant; divining-rod; (anat.) small branch of artery etc.; hop the ~, (colloq.) die.

twĭg² v. (slang) Understand, catch meaning (of); perceive, observe.

twi′light (-lit) n. Light diffused by reflection of sun's rays between daybreak and sunrise or (usu.) sunset and dark; period of this; faint light; (fig.) condition of imperfect knowledge, understanding, etc.; ~ of the gods, (transl. Ger. Götterdämmerung; Icel. ragna rökkr, orig. ragna rök judgement of the gods) in Scand. and Ger. myth., destruction of the gods and the world in conflict with the powers of evil; hence (fig.) complete downfall of a regime etc.; ~ sleep, (formerly) partial narcosis for dulling pains of childbirth.

twi′lit adj. Dimly illuminated (as) by twilight.

twill n. (Textile fabric with) surface of parallel diagonal ribs produced by passing weft-threads over one and under two or more (not one as in plain weaving) warp-threads (ill. WEAVE). ~ v.t. Weave with twill (esp. in past part.). [Sc. & north. variant of obs. twilly, OE twili, f. OHG zwilih, after L bilix (licium thread)]

twin adj. Forming, being one of, a closely related pair, esp. of children born together; (bot.) growing in pairs; consisting of 2 closely connected and similar parts; twi′nflower, (U.S.) either species of Linnaea (L. borealis of northern Europe and Asia and L. americana of northern N. America), prostrate plants with fragrant flowers growing in pairs; twi′nscrew, (esp. of steamer) having 2 screw propellers on separate shafts and revolving in opposite directions. ~ n. One of 2 children or young carried simultaneously in uterus and born at short interval (FRATERNAL, IDENTICAL, ~s: see these words); each of closely related pair; exact counterpart of person or thing; composite crystal consisting of 2 or more (usu. equal and similar) crystals in reversed position in respect to each other; the Twins: see GEMINI; ~-set, woman's matching jumper and cardigan. ~ v. Bear twins; join intimately together, couple, pair.

twine n. Strong thread or string of 2 or more strands of hemp, cotton, etc., twisted together, used for sewing coarse materials, tying packages, making nets, etc.; twining or trailing stem, spray, etc.; coil, twist. ~ v. Twist (strands) together to form twine, make (thread) thus; form (garland etc.) by interlacing; wreathe, clasp, twist; coil, wind; (of plant) grow in twisting or spiral manner.

twinge(-j) n. Sharp darting pain.

twi′nkle v. Shine with rapidly intermittent light, sparkle, glitter; emit (light etc.) thus; wink, blink, quiver; move to and fro, in and out, etc., rapidly, flit, flicker; in the twinkling of a eye, in a twinkling, in an instant. ~ n. Wink, blink, twitch, quiver; intermittent or transient gleam.

twĭrl v. Revolve rapidly, spin, whirl; turn (one's thumbs etc.) round and round idly, twiddle; twist, coil. ~ n. Whirling, twirling; anything that twirls, curved line, whorl of shell, etc.

twist v. Wind (strands etc.) one about another; form (rope etc.) thus; interweave; give spiral form to (rod, column, etc.) as by rotating ends in opposite directions; receive, grow in, spiral form; cause (ball, esp. in billiards) to rotate while following curved path; wrench out of natural shape, distort. **twi′stў** adj. twist n. 1. Thread, rope, etc., made by winding 2 or more strands etc. about one another; kinds of strong silk thread and of cotton yarn; roll of bread, tobacco, etc., in form of twist; paper packet with screwed-up ends. 2. Act of twisting, condition of being twisted; manner or degree in which thing is twisted; peculiar tendency of mind, character, etc.; twisting strain, torque; angle through which thing is twisted; dance involving rhythmic gyrations.

twi′ster n. (esp.) Liar, dishonest person, crook; twisting ball in cricket or billiards; girder.

twit¹ v.t. Reproach, upbraid, taunt.

twit² n. (slang) Foolish or insignificant person.

twitch¹ v. Pull with light jerk, pull at, jerk at, esp. to call attention; (of features, muscles, etc.) move or contract spasmodically. ~ n. 1. Sudden sharp pull or tug, jerk; sudden involuntary, usu. slight, contraction. 2. Noose tightened by stick, used to compress horse's lip or muzzle to keep him quiet during operation etc. **twi′tchў** adj.

twitch² n. (also ~-grass) COUCH²-grass.

twite n. Kind of linnet (Acanthis flavirostris) of N. Britain and Scandinavia; mountain linnet.

twi′tter v. (of bird) Utter succession of light tremulous notes, chirp continuously (freq. fig., of person); utter, express, thus. ~ n. Twittering; state of tremulous excitement.

'twixt prep. (poet.) Betwixt.

two (tōō) adj. Amounting to two; ~ or three, a few; ~-dimensional, having height and width; (of literary work) superficial, unconvincing; ~-edged, having 2 cutting edges; (fig.) cutting both ways, ambiguous; ~-faced, having 2 faces; deceitful, insincere; twofold, double, doubly; ~-handed, wielded with both hands; worked or wielded by hands of 2 persons; (of card-game etc.) for 2 persons; ~-line, (printing) having depth of 2 lines of size of type specified; twopence (tŭ′p-), sum of 2 pence twopenny (tŭ′p-), worth, costing, twopence; paltry, trumpery, trifling; Twopenny Tube, (hist.) Central London (underground) Railway, on which fare for any distance was orig. twopence; twopenny-halfpenny (tŭ′pnĭ-ha′pnĭ), (usu. fig.) petty, cheap, worthless; ~-piece (suit),coat and skirt or coat and dress meant to be worn together; ~-ply, of 2 strands, layers, or thicknesses; ~-step, ballroom dance with sliding steps in march or polka time; ~-stroke, (internal combustion engine) in which power stroke occurs on each revolution of crank-shaft (ill. COMBUSTION); T~ Thousand Guineas, annual horserace for 3-year-olds run at Newmarket; ~-time (v.t., U.S. slang) deceive; ~-way, (esp.) allowing passage of fluid in either of 2 directions; ~-way switch, device by which electric current can be switched on or off at either of 2 points. ~ n. One more than one; symbol for this (2, ii, or II); card, die-face, or domino with two pips; 2 o'clock; size etc. indicated by 2; set of 2 things or persons; hit at cricket for 2 runs; *in* ~ ~*s*, (colloq.) in a very short time; *put* ~ *and* ~ *together*, draw inference from facts.

Tȳ'burn. Place of public execution for Middlesex (until 1783) near what is now Marble Arch, London; ~ *tree*, the gallows. [orig. *Teobernan*, = 'boundary stream', name of former small tributary of Thames]

T.Y.C. abbrev. Thames Yacht Club.

Tȳchō'nĭan, Tȳchŏ'nĭc (-k-) *adjs.* Of (astronomical system of) Tycho BRAHE.

tȳcoō'n *n.* Business magnate. [Jap. *taikun* great lord, title applied by foreigners to shogun of Japan 1854-68 (Chin. *ta* great, *kuin* prince)]

tȳke *n.* Dog, cur; low fellow; (also *Yorkshire* ~) Yorkshireman.

tȳle, tȳ'ler[1] *ns.* Varr. of TILE, TILER.

Tȳ'ler[2], John (1790-1862). 10th president of U.S., 1841-5.

Tȳ'ler[3], Wat (d. 1381). English rebel, led Peasants' Revolt 1381.

tymbal: see TIMBAL.

tȳ'mpan *n.* 1. Appliance in printing-press interposed between platen etc. and sheet to be printed to equalize pressure, in handpresses usu. double frame covered with sheets of parchment or strong linen, with packing of blanket, rubber, etc., between. 2. (archit.) TYMPANUM.

tȳ'mpani, ti- *n.pl.* Kettledrums. **tȳ'mpanist** *n.*

tympă'nic *adj.* Of the or a tympanum; resonant when struck; ~ *bone*, bone supporting tympanic membrane; ~ *membrane*, thin membrane closing middle ear and serving to transmit vibrations from air to inner ear.

tympanī'tēs (-z) *n.* Distension of abdomen caused by gas or air in intestine or peritoneal cavity. **tympanī'tic** *adj.*

tȳ'mpanum *n.* 1. (anat.) Eardrum, middle ear, cavity in temporal bone filled with air, closed externally by tympanic membrane and containing chain of small bones by which sound vibrations are conveyed to inner ear (ill. EAR[1]); tympanic membrane; similar membrane in insects covering organ of hearing in leg etc.; (ornith.) bony labyrinth at base of trachea in some ducks with resonant membranes in walls. 2. (archit.) Vertical recessed face (usu. triangular) of pediment; space between lintel and arch of door etc., carving etc. on this (ill. DOOR).

Tȳ'ndale (-dl), William (d. 1536). English reformer and martyr, translator of the Bible.

Tȳne. River of NE. England, flowing into the North Sea near Newcastle.

Tȳne and Wear. Metropolitan county of NE. England (since April 1974), comprising Newcastle upon Tyne and areas formerly in SE. Northumberland and NE. Durham.

Tȳ'nwald (-wŏ-). Legislature of Isle of Man, consisting of assembly of governor, council acting as upper house, and House of Keys, to proclaim enacted laws to the people.

type *n.* 1. Person, thing, event, serving as illustration, symbol, or characteristic specimen, of another thing or of a class. 2. General form, character, etc., distinguishing particular class or group; kind, class, as distinguished by particular character. 3. (biol.) Species of genus regarded as most complete example of essential characteristics of genus, family, etc., and from which family etc. is named. 4. Biblical event regarded as symbolic or as foreshadowing a later one (its *antitype*). 5. Object, conception, work of art, serving as model for later artists. 6. Device on either side of medal or coin. 7. Small block, usu. of metal or wood, with raised letter, figure, etc., on its upper surface for use in printing; (collect.) set, supply, kind, of these. 8. ~-*cast*, cast (actor) in certain type of role because of predisposing characteristics; ~-*metal*, alloy of lead, antimony, and tin from which printing-types are cast; *ty'pescript*, (matter) written with typewriter; *ty'pesetter*, compositor; composing-machine; *ty'pewrite* (*v.*), write with typewriter; *ty'pewriter*, machine for writing in characters similar to those of print, the characters being produced by striking the paper through an inked ribbon by steel types arranged on separate rods or on a wheel and actuated by striking corresponding keys on a keyboard; (also, chiefly U.S.) typist. ~ *v.* 1. Be a type of, typify. 2. Determine type or group of, classify acc. to type. 3. Write with typewriter.

tȳ'phoid *n.* (also ~ *fever*) Infectious eruptive febrile disease

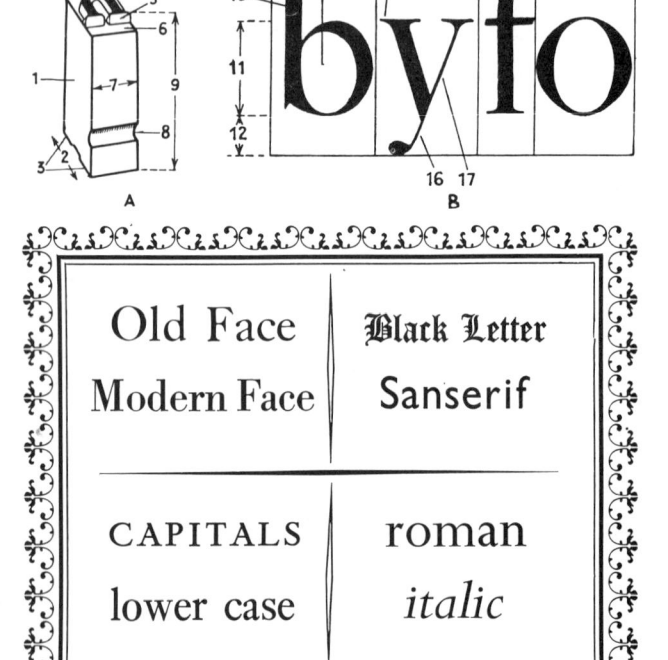

TYPE: A. PIECE OF TYPE. B. PARTS OF LETTERS. C. TYPE FACES, PRINTERS' FLOWERS, AND ORNAMENTAL RULES

A. 1. Stem or shank. 2. Body size. 3. Feet. 4. Face or printing surface. 5. Bevel. 6. Shoulder. 7. Set. 8. Nick. 9. Type-height. B. 10. Ascender. 11. x-height. 12. Beard. 13. Counter. 14. Serif. 15. Kern. 16. Descender. 17. Hair-line

TYPHOON

(formerly supposed to be variety of typhus) caused by ~ *bacillus* (*Bacillus typhosis*) and characterized by catarrhal inflammation of intestines. **tўphoi′dal** *adj.*
tўphoō′n *n.* Violent cyclonic storm, esp. one occurring in the China seas and adjacent regions.
tўphŏ′nic *adj.* [f. Chin. *tai fung*, dial. forms of *ta* big, *feng* wind]
tў′phus *n.* Acute contagious fever transmitted to man by body-lice or rat-fleas infected by *Rickettsia prowazekii*, and characterized by eruption of rose-coloured spots, extreme prostration, and usu. delirium. **tў′phous** *adj.*
tў′pical *adj.* Serving as type, symbol, or representative specimen, symbolical, emblematic; distinctive, characteristic. **tў′pically** *adv.*
tў′pify *v.t.* Represent by type or symbol, foreshadow; serve as type or example of.
tў′pist *n.* One who uses a typewriter.
tўpŏ′graphў *n.* Art, practice, of printing from types; style, appearance, of printed matter. **tўpŏ′grapher** *n.* **tўpogră′phic, -ical** *adjs.* **tўpogră′phicallў** *adv.*
tўpŏ′logў *n.* 1. Classification of archaeological remains etc. according to type. 2. Doctrine, interpretation, of biblical types and antitypes, study of these. **tўpolŏ′gical** *adj.* **tўpolŏ′gicallў** *adv.*
Tyr (tēr). (Scand. myth.) God of battle, equated with the Roman Mars.
tўră′nnical *adj.* Acting like, characteristic of, a tyrant; despotic, arbitrary, oppressive, cruel. **tўră′nnicallў** *adv.*
tўră′nnicīde *n.* Killer, killing, of tyrant. **tўrănnicī′dal** *adj.*
tў′rannize *v.* Play the tyrant; rule despotically or cruelly (*over*).
tўră′nnosaur *n.* Fossil dinosaur (*Tyrannosaurus rex*), largest known carnivore, which walked erect on hind feet, from late Cretaceous period of N. America.
tў′rannous *adj.* Ruling or acting tyrannically; oppressive, unjustly severe or cruel. **tў′rannouslў** *adv.*
tў′rannў *n.* 1. Government of, State ruled by, tyrant or absolute ruler. 2. Oppressive or despotic government; arbitrary or oppressive exercise of power; tyrannical act or behaviour.
tўr′ant *n.* 1. (Gk hist.) Absolute ruler who seized sovereign power without legal right; (despotic) usurper. 2. Oppressive, unjust, or cruel ruler, despot; person exercising power or authority arbitrarily or cruelly. 3. ~-*bird*,

UHLAND

-*flycatcher*, bird of American passerine family Tyrannidae.
tȳre[1], **tīre** *n.* 1. (usu. *tire*) Metal rim or hoop round wheel (ill. WAGON). 2. (usu. *tyre*; U.S. usu. *tire*) Endless rubber cushion, solid or tubular with air-inflated inner tube inside, fitted on rim of wheel of bicycle, motor-car; etc.
Tȳre[2]. (Arab. *Sur*) Ancient seaport of the Phoenicians on Lebanon coast; ~ *and Sidon*, towns referred to in N.T. as instances of sinfulness (Matt. 11: 21, 22; Luke 10: 13, 14).
Tȳ′rian *adj.* Of Tyre or its inhabitants; ~ *purple*, purple dye made from shellfish by the Tyrians and exported by them to ancient Greece and Rome. ~ *n.* Native, inhabitant, of Tyre.
tȳr′ō, tīr′ō *n.* Beginner or learner in anything, novice.
Tў′rol, Tī′rol (*or* -ŏ′l). Alpine province of W. Austria, the S. part of which was ceded to Italy after the war of 1914–18. **Tўrolē′se, Tirolē′se** (-z) *adj. & n.*
Tȳrō′ne. County of Northern Ireland.
Tў′rrhēne, Tўrrhē′nian *adjs. & ns.* ETRUSCAN.
tzär etc. (z-): Varr. of TSAR etc.
Tziġane (tsigah′n) *adj.* Of the Hungarian gipsies or their music. ~ *n.* Hungarian gipsy.

U

U, u (yōō). 1. 21st letter of modern English and 20th of ancient Roman alphabet, where it was identical in form and origin with *v*; now representing a vowel sound except after *g*, where it is freq. silent (*guard, plague*), in final -*que*, where it is always silent (*grotesque*), and after *q* in other positions, where it has the value of *w* (*quick, inquest*), as also in various words after *s* and *g* (*persuade, anguish*). 2. Object etc. shaped like U.
U (ōō) *n.* Burmese title of respect used before man's name.
U *abbrev.* Universal (i.e. for everyone, of cinema film); upper-class.
U.A.E. *abbrev.* United Arab Emirates.
ūbī′etў *n.* Being in definite place, local relation.
ūbī′quitў *n.* Omnipresence; being everywhere or in many places at the same time. **ūbī′quitous** *adj.* **ūbī′quitouslў** *adv.* **ūbī′quitousnėss** *n.*
U-boat *n.* German submarine. [Ger. *U-Boot*, abbrev. f. *Unterseeboot* submarine]
u.c. *abbrev.* Upper case (of print).
U.C.C.A. *abbrev.* Universities Central Council on Admissions.
ū′dal *n.* Kind of freehold right based on uninterrupted possession prevailing in N. Europe before the establishment of the feudal system and still existing in Orkney and Shetland.
ū′dder *n.* Pendulous baggy organ, provided with two or more teats, by which milk is secreted in cows and certain other female animals.
U.D.I. *abbrev.* Unilateral Declaration of Independence.
U.F.O., UFO (ū′fō) *abbrev.* Unidentified flying object.
Uġă′nda (ū-). Republic in central Africa, N. of Lake Victoria; member State of the Commonwealth, independent since 1962; capital, Kampala. **Uġă′ndan** *adj. & n.*
U′ġarit (ū-). Ancient city and trading centre at Ras Shamra, near Latakia in Syria, capital of Semitic kingdom powerful esp. in 15th–14th centuries B.C.
ugh (ŭ(h) *or* ōō(h)) *int.* Exclamation expressing disgust etc.
ŭ′ġlў *adj.* Unpleasing or repulsive to sight or hearing; morally repulsive, vile; disquieting, threatening; extremely awkward or unpromising (task, situation); ~ *customer*, unpleasantly formidable person; ~ *duckling*, dull or plain child who becomes brilliant adult (w. ref. to cygnet in a brood of ducklings in Hans Andersen's tale). **ŭ′ġlifў** *v.t.* **ŭ′ġlilў** *adv.* **ŭ′ġlinėss** *n.* **ŭ′ġlў** *n.* 1. Headdress of silk on wire frame, worn in mid-19th c. as protection to bonnet. 2. Mottled green citrus fruit produced by crossing grape-fruit with tangerine.
U′ġrian, U′ġric (ū-) *adjs. & ns.* (Language, member) of the E. branch of the Finno-Ugrian or Finnic peoples, specif. the Hungarians and Magyars. [*Ugra*, name of the country on both sides of the Ural mountains]
U.H.F. *abbrev.* Ultra-high FREQUENCY.
u′hlan (ōōl- *or* ūl-) *n.* Cavalryman armed with lance in some European armies, esp. former German army. [Fr., Ger., f. Polish (*h*)*ulan*, f. Turk. *oğlan* boy, servant]
U′hland (ōōl-), Johann Ludwig (1787–1862). German poet and ballad-writer.

UITLANDER

Ui′tlander (ätlŏn-) n. Outlander, esp. British resident in former S. African republics before Boer War (1899-1902). [(Cape) Du., f. *uit* out, *land* land]

U.K. abbrev. United Kingdom.

ukā′se n. 1. (hist.) Decree or edict, with force of law, of former Russian emperor or government. 2. Arbitrary order. [Russ. *ukaz* command]

Ukrai′ne (ū-; or -īn). Constituent republic of U.S.S.R., to the N. of the Black Sea; capital, Kiev. **Ukrai′nian** adj. & n.

ukule′le (-lāli) n. Small 4-stringed guitar of Portuguese origin which became popular in Hawaii and subsequently in U.S. and Europe. [Hawaiian, = 'jumping flea']

ŭ′lcer n. Open sore on external or internal surface of body, secreting pus; (fig.) corroding or corrupting influence, plague-spot. **ŭ′lcerous** adj. **ŭ′lcerously** adv.

ŭ′lcerāte v. Make, become, ulcerous. **ŭlcerā′tion** n.

u′lema (ōō-) n. (Member of) body of Muslim doctors of sacred law and theology esp. in the former Turkish Empire. [Arab. '*ulamā*' pl. of '*alim* learned]

U′lfilas (-). Var. of WULFILA.

ūli′ginōse, ūli′ginous adjs. Waterlogged, muddy, swampy; (bot.) growing in muddy places.

ŭ′llage n. Amount by which cask or bottle falls short of being quite full; remnant of liquor left in container that has lost part of its contents.

ŭ′lna n. (pl. *-ae*). Large inner bone of forearm, extending from elbow to wrist (ill. SKELETON); corresponding bone of foreleg in quadrupeds and of wing in birds. **ŭ′lnar** adj.

U′lster¹ (ŭ-). Former province of Ireland, comprising present Northern Ireland and the counties of Cavan, Donegal, and Monaghan; (loosely) Northern Ireland; university, at Coleraine, Co. Londonderry, 1970.

ŭ′lster² n. Long loose freq. belted overcoat, orig. of Ulster frieze. [f. ULSTER¹]

ult. abbrev. Ultimo.

ŭltēr′ior adj. Situated beyond; more remote; in the background, beyond what is seen or avowed. **ŭltēr′iorly** adv.

ŭ′ltimate adj. Last, final; beyond which there is no advance, progress, etc.; fundamental, elemental. **ŭ′ltimately** adv.

ultima Thule: see THULE.

ŭltimā′tum n. (pl. *-tums*, *-ta*). Final statement of terms, rejection of which by opposite party may lead to rupture, declaration of war, etc.

ŭ′ltimō adj. (abbrev. ult.) Of last month. [L]

ŭ′ltra adj. & n. (Person) holding extreme views, esp. in religion or politics. [orig. as abbrev. of Fr. *ultra-royaliste*]

ultra- prefix. Lying beyond or on the other side of; (with adjs.) going beyond, surpassing; having (the quality etc. expressed by the adj.) in extreme or excessive degree.

ultramari′ne (-ēn) adj. Situated beyond the sea; of the colour of ultramarine. ~ n. Brilliant deep-blue pigment got from lapis lazuli; imitation of this. [L *ultra* beyond, *mare* sea (w. ref. to foreign origin of lapis lazuli)]

ŭltramī′croscōpe n. Microscope using beam of light at right angles to its optical axis to detect particles beyond the range of an ordinary microscope. **ŭltramicrosco′pic** adj.

ŭltramō′ntāne adj. Situated S. of the Alps; Italian; favourable to the absolute authority of the pope in matters of faith and discipline. ~ n. One who resides S. of the Alps; person holding ultramontane views. **ŭltramō′ntānism, ŭltramō′ntānist** ns. [L *ultra* beyond, *mons* mountain]

ŭltramŭ′ndāne adj. Of or pertaining to things) lying outside the world or beyond the limits of the solar system.

ŭltra-shŏrt adj. (of radio wave) Having a wavelength below 10 metres.

ŭltrasŏ′nic adj. (of sound) So high-pitched as to be beyond the range of human hearing; (of sound frequency) above audio-frequency range.

ŭltra-vī′olėt adj. (phys.) Lying immediately beyond the violet end of the visible spectrum; of, producing, electromagnetic radiation with a wavelength shorter than that of visible light rays and having powerful actinic effect.

ŭ′ltra vīr′ēs (-z). Beyond one's powers; exceeding the powers granted by law. [L]

ŭ′lūlāte v.i. Howl, wail; (also) express joy. **ŭlūlā′tion** n.

Ulyanov (ōōlyah′nŏf), Vladimir Ilyich: see LENIN.

U′lÿssēs (ū-, -z; or ūlī′-). Roman name for ODYSSEUS.

ŭ′mbel n. (bot.) Inflorescence with pedicels of nearly equal length springing from common centre (ill. INFLORESCENCE). **ŭ′mbellate, ŭmbelli′ferous, ŭmbě′llifŏrm** adjs. **ŭmbě′llifer** n. [L *umbella* sunshade, dim. of *umbra* shadow]

ŭ′mber n. Brown earth (iron and manganese) used as pigment. ~ adj. Of the colour of umber. [Fr. (*terre d'*)*ombre* or It. (*terra di*) *ombra*, either = 'shadow' (L *umbra*) of f. fem. of L *Umber* Umbrian]

ŭmbi′lical (med. also -ī′k-) adj. Of, affecting, situated near, forming, umbilicus; ~ *cord*, flexible tube attaching foetus to placenta, navel-string (also transf.). **ŭmbī′licate, -ātėd** adjs. Resembling a navel.

ŭmbīli′cus n. Central depression in abdomen, marking point of attachment of umbilical cord,

UMPIRE

navel; small depression or hollow suggesting this; (geom.) point in surface through which all its lines of curvature pass.

ŭ′mbles (-lz) n.pl. (obs.) Edible offal of deer; *umble-pie*: see HUMBLE pie.

ŭ′mbō n. Boss of shield (ill. SHIELD); any round or conical projection, esp. most protuberant point of univalve shell or of each valve of bivalve shell. **ŭ′mbonal, ŭ′mbonate** adjs.

ŭ′mbra n. (pl. *-ae*). The earth's or moon's shadow in an eclipse, esp. the complete shadow as dist. from the *penumbra* (ill. ECLIPSE); dark central part of a sun-spot.

ŭ′mbral adj. [L, = 'shade']

ŭ′mbrage n. 1. Sense of slight or injury, offence. 2. (chiefly poet.) Shade. **umbrā′geous** (-jus) adj.

ŭmbrě′lla n. Light portable screen usu. circular and supported on central stick, used in hot countries as protection against sun, and in some Oriental and African countries as symbol of rank or state; portable protection against rain etc., made of silk or similar material fastened on slender ribs which are attached radially to stick and can be readily raised to form an arched circular canopy; structure resembling an umbrella, esp. (zool.) gelatinous disc or bell-shaped structure of jellyfish (ill. JELLY); (conch.) umbrella-shell, part of its shell like an open umbrella; screen of fighter aircraft or (in full ~ *barrage*) curtain of fire put up as protection against hostile aircraft; (fig.) general protection, aegis; ~-*bird*, S. or Central Amer. bird of genus *Cephalopterus*, esp. Brazilian *C. ornatus*, with black plumage and large crest curving forward from the back of the head; ~ *pine*, parasol pine (*Sciadopitys verticillata*), Japanese evergreen tree with symmetrical branches and needle-shaped leaves in umbrella-like whorls; ~-*shell*, limpet-like marine gasteropod of genus *Umbrella*.

U′mbria (ŭ-). District of ancient, province of modern, central Italy.

U′mbrian (ŭ-) adj. Of Umbria; ~ *school*, Renaissance school of painting to which Raphael and Perugino belonged. ~ n. Native, inhabitant, language, of Umbria.

umiak (ōō′myăk) n. Long open Eskimo boat of skins over wooden framework, paddled by women.

umlaut (ōō′mlowt) n. (in Germanic languages) Vowel change due to *i* or *u* (now usu. lost or altered) in following syllable, e.g. Ger. *mann männer, fuss füsse*, Engl. *man men, foot feet*; diacritical sign (¨) indicating this. [Ger. *um* about, *laut* sound]

ŭ′mpīre n. One who decides between disputants or contending parties and whose decision is usu. accepted as final; (law) third

[950]

UMPTEEN

person called upon to settle question submitted to arbitrators who cannot agree; person chosen to enforce rules of games or contest and settle disputes or doubtful points. ~ *v.* Act as umpire (in). [OF *nomper* peerless, in sense 'odd man' (*non* not, *per* PEER)]
u'mptee'n *adj. & n.* (slang) Indeterminate but large number (of). **u'mptee'nth** *adj.* [joc. formation, on analogy of *thirteen* etc.]
'un *pron.* (colloq. or dial.) One.
un-¹ *prefix.* Used with verbs and verbal derivatives and in forming new verbs from adjectives, nouns, etc., to signify contrary or reverse action to that of simple verb (or, rarely, intensification of negative force of verb, as in *unloose*), or deprivation or removal of some quality or property.
The number of words with this and the following prefix is almost limitless, and as the meaning usu. presents no difficulties, few such words are listed in this dictionary.
un-² *prefix.* Not (used freely and extensively with adjectives, esp. past participles, adverbs, and nouns).
U.N. *abbrev.* United Nations.
ŭnadŏ'ptĕd *adj.* (of road) Not taken over for maintenance by local authority.
ŭnalloy'ed (-oid) *adj.* Not mixed, pure.
ŭn-Amĕ'rican *adj.* Not American; (esp.) not of, not worthy or characteristic of, opposed to, against interests etc. of, the U.S.A.
ŭnă'nimous *adj.* All of one mind, agreeing in opinion; (of opinion, vote, etc.) formed, held, given, etc., with general agreement or consent. **ŭnă'nimouslў** *adv.* **ŭnani'mitў, ŭnă'nimousnĕss** *ns.*
ŭnassū'ming *adj.* Modest, not pretentious.
ŭnawār'es (-awārz) *adv.* Unexpectedly, unconsciously; by surprise.
ŭnbă'lanced (-st) *adj.* (esp.) Mentally unstable or deranged.
ŭnbeknow'nst (-bĭnōn-) *adj. & adv.* (colloq. or dial.) Without the knowledge (of).
ŭnbĕ'nd *v.* (past t. & past part. -*bĕnt*). Release, relax, from tension; straighten; become unconstrained or genial.
ŭnbo'som (-bōōz-) *v.* Disclose, reveal; ~ *oneself*, disclose one's secrets, thoughts, etc.
ŭnbri'dled (-ld) *adj.* Unrestrained, uncontrolled.
ŭnca'lled-fŏr (-n-kawld-) *adj.* Not required or requested; unprovoked, impertinent.
ŭncă'nnў (-n-k-) *adj.* Supernatural, mysterious, uncomfortably strange or unfamiliar. **ŭncă'nnilў** *adv.* **ŭncă'nninĕss** *n.*
u'ncial (*or* -shal) *adj.* Of, written in, a form of majuscule script resembling capitals but with some ascending and descending strokes, used in Greek and Latin MSS. of the 4th–8th centuries (ill. SCRIPT); *half-~*, intermediate between uncial and minuscule. ~ *n.* Uncial letter; uncial MS. [L *uncialis* in LL sense 'inch-high', 'large', f. *uncia* twelfth part of foot, inch]
u'ncĭfŏrm *adj. & n.* Hook-shaped (bone, process).
u'ncinate *adj.* -Hooked, furnished with hooks.
u'ncle *adj.* 1. Father's or mother's brother, aunt's husband; (children's colloq.) unrelated man who is a family friend; (U.S.) familiar form of address to elderly man, esp. (in southern U.S.) Negro; *U~ Sam*, Government (or people) of U.S. (perh. facetious expansion of initials *U.S.*). 2. (slang) Pawnbroker.
u'ncŏ *adj. & adv.* (Sc. & north. dial.) Extreme(ly), unusual(ly). ~ *n.* Stranger. [shortening of *uncouth*]
ŭncŏ'mmon (-n-k-) *adj.* Unusual, remarkable. ~ *adv.* (colloq.) Remarkably.
ŭncŏ'mpromising (-n-k-; -z-) *adj.* Refusing compromise; unyielding, stubborn.
ŭncŏ'nscionable(-n-k-; -shun-) *adj.* 1. Having no conscience, unscrupulous; (of actions) performed against dictates of conscience. 2. Not right or reasonable; excessive, shameless.
ŭncŏ'nscious (-n-k-; -shus) *adj.* Not conscious; ~ *mind*, (psychol.) those mental processes whose existence is inferred from their effects. ~ *n.* Unconscious mind; *collective* ~, (Jungian psychol.) alleged unconscious mental processes common to all mankind.
ŭncou'th (-n-kōōth) *adj.* Odd, uncomely, awkward, clumsy, in shape, sound, bearing, etc. **ŭncou'thlў** *adv.* **ŭncou'thnĕss** *n.* [OE *uncuth* = 'unknown', 'unfamiliar']
u'nction *n.* 1. Anointing with oil etc. as religious rite or symbol (esp. of investiture with kingship or other office); unguent; *extreme* ~; see EXTREME. 2. (Manner suggesting) deep spiritual or religious feeling; simulation of this, affected enthusiasm, gush.
u'nctŭous *adj.* 1. Of the nature or quality of an unguent, oily, greasy in feel, appearance, etc. 2. Full of (esp. simulated) unction, complacently agreeable or self-satisfied. **ŭ'nctŭouslў** *adv.* **ŭ'nctŭousnĕss** *n.*
u'nder *prep.* In or to position lower than, below, at the foot of; within, on the inside, of; inferior to, less than; supporting or sustaining; subjected to, undergoing, liable to, on condition of, subject to; governed, controlled, or bound by; in accordance with; in the form of; in the time of; (*speak* etc.) ~ *one's breath*, in a whisper; ~ *a cloud*: see CLOUD; ~ *the rose*, SUB ROSA; ~ *the sun*, anywhere on earth; ~ *way*: see WAY. ~ *adv.* In a lower place or subordinate condition. ~ *adj.* Lower. **ŭ'ndermōst** *adj.*
ŭnder- *prefix.* Below; beneath, lower than; insufficiently, incompletely; situated beneath, subordinate.
ŭnderă'ct *v.* Act (part) inadequately or with too much restraint.
ŭ'nderărm *adj. & adv.* (of bowling in cricket, service in lawn tennis) (Performed) with arm lower than the shoulder.
ŭnderbĭ'd *v.* (past t. & past part. -*bid*). Bid less than; bid too little (on); undercut.
ŭ'nderbrŭsh *n.* Undergrowth in forest.
ŭ'ndercărriage (-rĭj) *n.* Lower framework of a vehicle which supports the superstructure; landing-gear of an aeroplane.
ŭ'ndercliff *n.* Terrace or lower cliff formed by a landslip.
ŭ'nderclōthes (-ōdhz *or* -ōz), **ŭ'nderclōthing** (-dh-) *ns.* Clothing worn below outer garments, esp. next to the skin.
ŭ'ndercoat *n.* Under-layer of hair or down in certain long-haired animals; layer of paint used under finishing coat(s). **ŭ'ndercoating** *n.* (esp.) Paint for use as undercoat.
ŭ'ndercover (-ŭv-) *adj.* Acting, done, surreptitiously or secretly.
ŭ'ndercrŏft *n.* Crypt.
ŭ'ndercŭrrent *n.* Current flowing below surface or upper current; (fig.) suppressed or underlying activity, force, etc.
ŭndercŭ't *v.t.* Cut (away) below or beneath, esp. in carving; supplant by working for lower payment; undersell. **ŭ'ndercŭt** *n.* (esp.) Under-side of sirloin (ill. MEAT).
ŭ'nderdŏg *n.* Loser in fight etc.; one in state of subjection or inferiority.
ŭnderdo'ne (-ŭn) *adj.* Incompletely or insufficiently cooked.
ŭnderdraw' *v.t.* (past t. -*drew*, past part. -*drawn*). (esp.) Cover (inside of roof or under-side of floor) with boards or lath and plaster.
ŭnderĕ'stimāte *v.t.* Form or make too low an estimate (of).
ŭ'nderfĕlt *n.* Felt for laying under carpet.
ŭnderfoo't *adv.*: see FOOT.
ŭ'ndergărment *n.* Article of underwear.
ŭndergō' *v.t.* (past t. -*wĕnt*, past part. -*gone* pr. gŏn). Be subjected to, suffer, endure.
ŭndergră'dŭate *n.* Member of university who has not yet taken a degree.
ŭndergrou'nd *adv.* Below the surface of the ground; in(to) secrecy or concealment. **ŭ'nderground** *adj. & n.* (Railway) situated underground; (group, movement, etc.) conducted or existing in secret, esp. in resistance to established order etc.

ŭ'ndergrowth (-ōth) n. Growth of plants or shrubs under trees etc.
ŭnderhă'nd (or ŭ'-) adj. & adv. Clandestine(ly), secret(ly), not above-board; = UNDERARM.
ŭnderhŭ'ng adj. (of lower jaw) projecting beyond upper jaw; (of person, animal) having underhung jaw.
ŭnderlay' v.t. (past t. & past part. -laid). Raise or support or line etc. with something laid under. **ŭ'nderlay** n. Something laid under esp. carpet or mattress as protection or support.
ŭnderli'e v.t. (past t. -lay, past part. -lain). Lie, be situated, under; (fig.) be the basis or foundation of, lie under surface aspect of.
underli'ne v.t. Draw line(s) beneath (words etc.) for emphasis, emphasize. **ŭ'nderline** n. Caption below illustration.
ŭ'nderling n. (usu. contempt.) Subordinate.
ŭndermi'ne v.t. Make mine or excavation under; wear away base or foundation of; injure, wear out, etc., insidiously, secretly, or imperceptibly.
ŭndernea'th adv. & prep. At or to a lower place (than), below. **ŭ'nderneath** adj. & n. Lower (surface, part).
ŭ'nderpass (-ahs) n. (Crossing with) road etc. passing under another.
ŭnderpi'n v.t. Support or strengthen (building etc.) from beneath.
ŭ'nderplŏt n. = SUB-PLOT.
ŭnderpri'vilėged (-jd) adj. Not enjoying normal living standard or rights and privileges of society.
ŭnderrā'te v.t. Form too low an estimate of.
ŭndersĕ'll v. (past t. & past part. -sōld). 1. (of persons) Sell at a lower price than (another person); cut out by selling at a lower rate; (of thing) be sold thus. 2. Sell (thing) at too low a price.
ŭndershoō't v. (past t. & past part. -shŏt). (of aircraft) Land short of (the runway).
ŭ'ndershŏt adj. (of wheel) Turned by water flowing under it (ill. WATER).
ŭ'ndersigned (-īnd) adj. (Whose names are) signed below; the undersi'gned, undersigned person(s).
ŭndersi'zed (-zd) adj. Of less than normal size.
ŭndersta'nd v. (past t. & past part. -stoōd). Perceive the meaning of; know how to deal with; infer, esp. from information received; take for granted. **ŭndersta'nding** n. (esp.) Intelligence; agreement; convention, thing agreed upon. ~ adj. Intelligent, having understanding. **ŭndersta'ndingly** adv.
ŭndersta'tement (-tm-) n. Statement falling below or coming short of truth or fact. **ŭndersta'te** v.t.

ŭndersteer' v.i. (of vehicle) Have tendency to steer towards the outer side on a curve. **ŭ'ndersteer** n. Understeering.
ŭ'nderstŭdy n. Actor who studies part in order to play it at short notice in absence of usual performer. ~ v.t. Study (part) thus, act as understudy to.
ŭndertā'ke v. (past t. -toōk, past part. -tāken). Bind oneself to perform; engage in, enter upon (work, enterprise, etc.); promise (to do); guarantee; (colloq.) manage funerals. **ŭ'ndertāker** n. (esp.) One whose business is to carry out arrangements for funerals. **ŭndertā'king** n. (esp.) Work etc. undertaken, enterprise; business of funeral undertaker.
ŭ'ndertōne n. Low or subdued, underlying or subordinate, tone.
ŭ'ndertow (-tō) n. Current below sea-surface moving in contrary direction to surface current.
ŭ'ndertrick n. (bridge) Trick required to make bid or contract but not taken.
ŭ'nderwear (-wār) n. Underclothes.
ŭ'nderwood n. Small trees or shrubs, brushwood, growing beneath trees.
ŭ'nderworld (-wēr-) n. (esp.) Infernal regions; criminal section of society.
ŭnderwri'te (-der-rīt) v. (past t. -wrōte, past part. -wri'tten). (esp.) Subscribe (insurance policy), thereby accepting risk of insurance; undertake esp. marine insurance; agree to take up stock not bought by public in (new company or new issue). **ŭ'nderwriter** n.
ŭ'ndies (-dĭz) n.pl. (colloq.) Women's underclothes.
ŭndi'ne (-ēn) n. Female watersprite who by marrying a mortal and bearing a child might receive a soul. [invented by Paracelsus, f. L unda wave]
ŭndo' (-oō) v.t. (past t. -dĭd, past part. -done pr. -dŭn). Annul, cancel; open (parcel etc.); unfasten (laces, buttons, etc.); (poet.) ruin. **ŭndo'ing** n. (esp.) (Cause of) bringing to ruin. **ŭndo'ne** adj. (esp.) Unfastened; (poet.) ruined.
ŭndrĕ'ss v. Take off clothes (of). **ŭ'ndrĕss** n. (esp., mil. etc.) Uniform for ordinary occasions, as dist. from full or service dress (freq. attrib.).
ŭ'ndūlant adj. Undulating, rising and falling like waves; ~ fever, persistent remittent fever with profuse perspiration, swollen joints, and enlarged spleen, transmitted through milk esp. of cows with contagious abortion.
ŭ'ndūlate adj. With wave-like markings; having waved surface or outline, arranged in wave-like curves. **ŭ'ndūlately** adv. **ŭ'ndūlāte** v.i. Have wavy motion or look. **ŭ'ndūlāting** adj.
ŭndūlā'tion n. Wavy motion or form, gentle rise and fall, each wave of this; set of wavy lines.

ŭ'ndūlatŏry (or -ā'-) adj. Undulating, wavy; of, due to, undulation.
ŭndū'lў adv. Unrightfully, improperly; excessively.
ŭ'ndў, -dee adj. (her.) Wavy (ill. HERALDRY). [Fr. ondi, f. L unda wave]
ŭnear'ned (-ērnd) adj. (esp.) ~ income, revenue from interest payments etc., dist. from wages etc.
unear'th (-ērth) v.t. Dig up, disinter; force out of hole or burrow; (fig.) bring to light, disclose, find by searching.
ŭnear'thlў (-ērth-) adj. Celestial, not of this earth; supernatural, ghostly; (colloq.) not appropriate, absurdly early or inconvenient.
ŭnea'sў (-zĭ) adj. Restless, disturbed, uncomfortable in body or mind. **ŭnea'silў** adv.
ŭnėmploy'ed (-oid) adj. Not employed or occupied; not in use. **ŭnėmploy'ment** n.
UNESCO, Unĕ'scō (ū-) abbrev. United Nations Educational, Scientific, and Cultural Organization.
ŭnėxcė'ptionable adj. With which no fault can be found.
ŭnfai'thful adj. Failing in loyalty; not true to; adulterous. **ŭnfai'thfullў** adv.
ŭnfa'sten (-fahsn) v.t. Make loose; detach; open fastening(s) of.
ŭnfee'ling adj. Lacking sensibility, without feeling; harsh, cruel. **ŭnfee'linglў** adv.
ŭnfi't adj. Not fit, unsuitable; in poor health. ~ v.t. Make unsuitable (for).
ŭnfō'ld v. Open out; reveal; develop.
ŭnfŏr'tūnate adj. Unlucky; regrettable; ill-advised. **ŭnfŏr'tūnatelў** adv.
ŭnfrŏ'ck v.t. Deprive of priestly status.
ŭngai'nlў (-n-g-) adj. Awkward, clumsy, ungraceful. **ŭngai'nlinėss** n.
ŭngŏ'dlў (-n-g-) adj. Impious, wicked; (colloq.) outrageous.
ŭngo'vernable (-n-gŭv-) adj. Uncontrollable.
ŭ'ngual (-nggw-) adj. Of, like, bearing, a nail, claw, or hoof.
ŭ'nguent (-nggw-) n. Ointment, salve.
ŭngui'cūlate (-nggw-) adj. 1. (bot.) Having an unguis. 2. (zool.) Having nails or claws, as dist. from hooves.
ŭ'nguis (-nggw-) n. (pl. -gues, pr. -gwēz). 1. (bot.) Narrow base of certain petals. 2. (zool.) Nail, claw.
ŭ'ngula (-ngg-) n. (pl. -ae). 1. Hoof, claw, talon. 2. (math.) Cone, cylinder, with top cut off by plane oblique to base (ill. CONE).
ŭ'ngulate (-ngg-) adj. Hoof-shaped; (of mammals) having hoofs.
ŭnhă'llowed (-ōd) adj. Not consecrated; unholy, impious, wicked.

ŭnhă′nd v.t. (archaic) Take one's hands off (person or thing).
ŭnhea′lthў (-hĕl-) adj. Sickly; diseased; prejudicial or hurtful to health; unwholesome; (slang) dangerous.
ŭnhi′nge (-j) v.t. (chiefly in past part.). Derange, disorder (mind).
ūni- prefix. One; having, composed or consisting of, characterized by, etc., one (thing specified by second element).
U′niat, -ate (ū-) adj. & n. (Member) of any of those Christian Churches in E. Europe and the Near East) which accept the Catholic faith and acknowledge the pope's supremacy but retain their own organization and liturgy. [Russ. *uniyat* f. *uniya* union (L *unus* one)]
ūnică′meral adj. Having one (legislative) chamber.
UNICEF, U′nicĕf (ū-) abbrev. United Nations (International) Children's (Emergency) Fund.
ūnicĕ′llūlar adj. (esp. of organism) Having, composed of, a single cell.
ū′nicŏrn n. 1. Fabulous animal represented as having the body of a horse with a single horn projecting from its forehead; heraldic representation of this, usu. with legs of deer, lion's tail, and straight spirally twisted horn, esp. as supporter of royal arms of Gt Britain or Scotland. 2. (also ~-*shell*) Marine gasteropod with horn-like lip projecting from shell.
ū′nifŏrm adj. Being or remaining the same in different places, at different times, etc., unvarying, consistent; plain, unbroken, undiversified; conforming to one standard, rule, or pattern, alike, similar. **ū′nifŏrmlў** adv. **ū′nifŏrm** n. Distinctive dress of uniform cut, material, and colour worn by all members of particular military or other organization. ~ v. Make uniform; dress in uniform.
ūnifŏr′mĭtў n. Being uniform, sameness, consistency, conformity; *Act of U*~, (hist.) any of three Acts (passed in 1549, 1559, 1662), regulating public worship in Gt Britain and prescribing use of a particular Book of Common Prayer.
ū′nifў v.t. Reduce to unity or uniformity. **ūnificā′tion** n.
ūnilă′teral adj. One-sided; of, affecting, etc., one side (only); made by, binding on, affecting, one part only; *U*~ *Declaration of Independence*, declaration of independence from Gt Britain made by Rhodesia in 1965. **ūnilă′terallў** adv.
ūn′ion (-yon) n. 1. Uniting, joining, being united, coalition, junction; marriage; concord, agreement. 2. Body formed by combination of parts or members; TRADE union; (hist.) two or more parishes consolidated for administration of poor laws, workhouse erected by such union. 3. Kind of joint or coupling for pipes etc. 4. Union cloth; Union Jack; Union Society; *the U*~, (hist.) uniting of Scottish and English crowns (1603) or parliaments (1707); uniting of parliaments of Gt Britain and Ireland (1801); (formation of) the UNITED STATES OF AMERICA. 5. ~ *cloth*, fabric of different yarns woven together, esp. cotton and linen or cotton and wool; *U*~ *flag*, *Jack*, national flag of the United Kingdom, combining red cross of St. George and white saltire cross of St. Andrew surmounted by red saltire cross of St. Patrick, and retaining blue ground of banner of St. Andrew (ill. FLAG[4]); *U*~ *Society*, at Oxford, Cambridge, and some other universities, (premises of) general club and debating society open to all members, or all undergraduates, of university; ~ *suit*, (U.S.) undergarment combining vest and drawers, combinations.
ū′nionist (-nyo-) n. 1. Member of a trade union; advocate of trade unions. 2. One who desires or advocates union, esp. of particular legislative or political union, as (U.S.) supporter of Federal Union of U.S., esp. (in Civil War of 1861-5) as opp. Secessionist; (British politics) supporter of maintenance of parliamentary union between Gt Britain and Northern Ireland (freq. simply = Conservative). ~ *adj*. Of, supporting, belonging to, union, unionism, or unionists. **ū′nionism** n.
U′nion of Sŏ′viet Sō′cialist Repŭ′blics (ūnyon, -shal-). (abbrev. U.S.S.R.) Union now including fifteen constituent republics (Russian Soviet Federal Socialist Republic, Ukraine, Belorussia, Uzbekistan, Kazakhstan, Georgia, Azerbaijan, Lithuania, Moldavia, Latvia, Kirghizia, Tadzhikistan, Armenia, Turkmenistan, Estonia), orig. established after the Russian revolution of 1917; capital, Moscow.
ūni′que (-ēk) adj. Of which there is only one; unmatched, unequalled; having no like, equal, or parallel. **ūni′quelў** adv. **ūni′queness** n.
ū′nisĕx n. Adoption of similar fashions of dress and hair-style by members of both sexes.
ū′nison n. (mus.) Coincidence in pitch; sound or note of same pitch as another; combination of voices or instruments at same pitch; *in* ~, at same pitch; in concord, agreement, or harmony. **ūnisō′nal, ūnisō′nant** adjs. **ūni′sonance** n.
ū′nĭt n. 1. Single magnitude or number regarded as undivided whole, esp. the numeral 'one'; any determinate quantity, magnitude, etc., as basis or standard of measurement for other quantities of same kind. 2. One of the individuals or groups into which a complex whole may be analysed; that part of collective body or whole regarded as lowest or least to have separate existence; fractional interest in unit trust (see below). 3. Device with specified function forming element in complex mechanism etc.; piece of furniture for fitting with others like it or formed of complementary elements. 4. ~ *magnetic pole*, unit of magnetic pole strength equal to strength of pole that exerts a force of 1 dyne on an equal pole 1 cm distant; ~ *trust*, system of investment in which money subscribed by individual investors is pooled and invested by a management company, each subscriber acquiring a fractional interest in the aggregate of securities thus purchased and receiving a corresponding share of the total dividend. ~ *adj*. Of, being, forming, a unit, individual.
Unitār′ian (ū-) n. One who maintains that the Godhead is one person, not a Trinity; member of Christian body, which originated in England in 17th c., maintaining this belief; (also) one who advocates individual freedom of belief. ~ *adj*. Of Unitarians or their doctrine. **Unitār′ianĭsm** n.
ū′nĭtarў adj. Of, based on, proceeding from, etc., a unit or unity; individual, simple, that is a unit.
ūni′te v. Join together, make or become one, combine, consolidate, amalgamate; agree, combine, cooperate (*in*). **ūni′tĕd** adj. (esp.) *U*~ *Brethren*, Moravians; *U*~ *Irishman*, member of the Society of United Irishmen, a political association which was formed 1791 by Wolfe Tone, originally to promote union between Catholics and Protestants, and helped to organize the rebellion of 1798; *U*~ *Provinces*, (hist.) seven northern provinces of the Low Countries, allied from 1579 and later developed into the kingdom of Holland; *U*~ *Reformed Church*, formed in 1972 by union of Congregational Church in England and Wales and Presbyterian Church in England; *U*~ *States*, UNITED STATES OF AMERICA. **ūni′tĕdlў** adv.
Uni′tĕd A′rab E′mirātes (ū-, ă-, ĕ- -ts). (abbrev. U.A.E.) Union of seven emirates in or near the Persian Gulf forming an independent State, Abu Dhabi, Ajman, Dubai, Fujairah, Sharjah, and Umm al Qaiwain in 1971; Ras al Khaimah joined in 1972.
Uni′tĕd Ki′ngdom (ū-). (abbrev. U.K.) Kingdom consisting of Great Britain and Ireland (from 1801 to 1922); Great Britain and Northern Ireland (from 1922); capital, London.
Uni′tĕd Nā′tions (ū-, -z). (orig.) The nations at war with the Axis, 1939-45; hence, international

organization of these and other States established as successor to the League of Nations by the ~ *Charter* signed at San Francisco on 26 June 1945; its main object is the maintenance of peace and its six principal organs are the General Assembly, Security Council, Secretariat (at New York), International Court (at The Hague), Economic and Social Council, and Trusteeship Council; abbrev. U.N.
Uni′tĕd States of Amĕ′rica (ū-, -ts). (abbrev. U.S.A. or U.S.) Republic of N. America, bounded on N. by Canada and on S. by Mexico; federation of fifty States and the District of Columbia with federal capital at Washington D.C. Colonies were established in N. America in 17th c. by several European nations, esp. Spanish and French in S., Dutch in N., and British in E., who gained ascendancy over the rest; the colonies were ruled by Britain until 1775 when they revolted (War of American Independence, 1775-83); the thirteen original States agreed on a constitution (1787-8), and chose George Washington as first president (for U.S. presidents see Appendix VI and separate entries; see also AMERICA).
ū′nĭtў *n.* State of being one or single or individual; being formed of parts that constitute a whole; due interconnection and coherence of parts; thing showing such unity, thing forming complex whole; (math.) the numeral one as basis of number; harmony, concord, between persons etc.; any of the three Aristotelian principles of dramatic composition as adapted by French classical dramatists, by which a play should consist of one main action, represented as occurring at one time and in one place.
Univ. *abbrev.* University.
ūnĭvā′lent *adj.* (chem.) = MONOVALENT.
ū′nĭvălve *adj.* (zool., of shell) Composed of a single valve, (of mollusc) having such shell.
ūnĭvēr′sal *adj.* Of, belonging to, done, or used by, etc., all persons or things in the world or in the class concerned; applicable to all cases; ~ *donor*, person whose blood-group is such that his blood may be transfused into any other person irrespective of the latter's grouping; ~ *joint*, joint or coupling permitting of free movement in any direction of the parts joined, esp. one in which one connected part conveys rotary action to other; ~ *proposition*, (logic) proposition in which the predicate is affirmed or denied of the entire subject; ~ *suffrage*, suffrage extending to all persons over a specified age with the exception of certain minor categories. **ūnĭvēr′sallў** *adv.* **ūnĭvērsă′litў** *n.* **ūnĭvēr′-salīze** *v.t.* **ūnĭvēr′sal** *n.* (logic) Universal proposition; (philos.)

general notion or idea, thing that by its nature may be predicated of many.
ūnĭvēr′salism *n.* (theol.) Doctrine that all mankind will eventually be saved. **ūnĭvēr′salist** *n.* One who holds this doctrine, esp. (*U*~) member of an organized sect chiefly in U.S.
ū′nĭvēṙse *n.* All created or existing things, all creation; = COSMOS[1]; the world or earth; all mankind.
ūnĭvēr′sĭtў *n.* Whole body of teachers and scholars engaged at particular place in giving and receiving instruction in higher branches of learning; such persons as corporate body with definite organization and powers (esp. of conferring degrees), forming institution for promotion of higher education; colleges, buildings, etc., of such a body.
ŭnkĕ′mpt (-n-k-) *adj.* Uncombed, dishevelled; untidy, looking neglected.
ŭnki′nd (-n-k-) *adj.* Lacking kindness; unpleasant, harsh.
ŭnknow′n (ŭn-nōn) *adj.* Not known; not identified; *U*~ *Soldier, Warrior,* unnamed representative of a country's armed services killed in battle, buried in tomb serving as national memorial, esp. (*U*~ *Warrior*) representative of British casualties of 1914-18 war, buried in Westminster Abbey.
ŭnlea′sh *v.t.* Free from leash or restraint; set free in order to pursue, attack, etc.
ŭnlĕ′ss *conj.* If . . . not, except when.
ŭnlī′ke (or ŭ′-) *adj. & prep.* Not like, different (from).
ŭnlī′kelў (-klī) *adj.* Improbable; unpromising.
ŭnlī′stĕd *adj.* Not included in list, esp. of Stock Exchange prices or of telephone numbers.
ŭnloa′d *v.* Remove cargo or anything carried or conveyed (from); remove charge from (gun); relieve of burden; get rid of, sell (out).
ŭnlŏŏ′ked-fŏr (-kt-) *adj.* Not expected or foreseen.
ŭnlŏŏ′se *v.t.* Loose, untie.
ŭnlŭ′ckў *adj.* Unfortunate; unsuccessful; ill-contrived.
ŭnmă′n *v.t.* Deprive of courage, strength, firmness, etc.
ŭnmă′nnerlў *adj.* Rude, illbred.

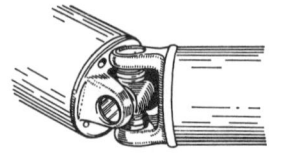

UNIVERSAL JOINT

ŭnmĕ′ntionable *adj.* Unspeakable.
ŭnmĭstā′kable *adj.* That cannot be mistaken or doubted.

ŭnmĭ′tĭgātĕd *adj.* Unqualified, absolute.
ŭnnă′tural (ŭn-năcher-) *adj.* Contrary or not conforming to nature; lacking natural feelings; artificial.
ŭnnĕ′cessarў (ŭn-n-) *adj.* Not necessary; more than necessary.
ŭnnēr′ve (ŭn-n-) *v.t.* Deprive of nerve, courage, self-control, etc.
ŭnnŭ′mbered (ŭn-n-, -erd) *adj.* Countless; not marked etc. with a number.
ŭnpă′rallĕled (-ld) *adj.* Having no parallel or equal.
ŭnpărliamĕ′ntarў (-la-) *adj.* Contrary to parliamentary usage, uncivil.
ŭnpĭ′ck *v.t.* Detach; undo stitches of (anything sewn or knitted).
ŭnplā′ced (-st) *adj.* Not placed, esp. in race or list.
ŭnplea′sant (-lĕz-) *adj.* Disagreeable. **ŭnplea′santlў** *adv.* **ŭnplea′santnĕss** *n.* (esp.) Disagreeable situation, action, etc.; hostility, quarrel.
ŭnpŏ′pŭlar *adj.* Not in popular favour; disliked.
ŭnprĕ′cĕdentĕd *adj.* For which there is no precedent, novel.
ŭnprĭ′ncipled (-ld) *adj.* Not having, not based on, etc., sound or honest principles of conduct.
ŭnprofĕ′ssional *adj.* Not professional; unworthy of a member of a profession.
ŭnqua′lified (-ŏlĭfīd) *adj.* Not qualified; not modified or limited.
ū′nquōte. Direction used in dictation to indicate the end of a quotation.
ŭnră′vel *v.* Take out of tangled or intertwined condition (freq. fig.); undo, pull out (woven or esp. knitted fabric); come undone, become unknit or disentangled.
ŭnrĕmĭ′tting *adj.* Incessant.
ŭnrĕ′st *n.* Disturbance, turmoil, trouble.
ŭnrī′vallĕd (-ld) *adj.* Having no rival or equal; supreme.
ŭnru′lў (-rōō-) *adj.* Not amenable to rule or discipline; turbulent. **ŭnru′linĕss** *n.*
ŭnsă′tūrātĕd *adj.* (chem.): see SATURATE, 2.
ŭnsā′vourў (-verĭ) *adj.* Not savoury; morally offensive.
ŭnscā′thed (-dhd) *adj.* Not injured or harmed.
ŭnscrĭ′ptĕd *adj.* Not made or read from a prepared script.
ŭnsea′t *v.t.* 1. (of horse) Throw (rider) from saddle. 2. Dislodge, deprive of seat, esp. in House of Commons.
ŭnsee′n *adj.* Not seen; without prior study. ~ *n.* Passage for translation without prior study.
ŭnshā′keable (-ka-) *adj.* Not to be shaken; firm, resolute.
ŭnsī′ghtlў (-sit-) *adj.* Unpleasing to the eye, ugly.
ŭnsolĭ′cītĕd *adj.* Not asked for; given or done voluntarily.
ŭnspea′kable *adj.* That may

not be spoken; indescribably repulsive or objectionable.
ŭnstrŭ′ng *adj.* 1. With strings relaxed or removed. 2. Not threaded on a string. 3. Weakened, unnerved.
ŭnstŭ′ck *adj.* Not stuck, loosened from being stuck; *come ~*, (fig., colloq.) fail, go wrong.
ŭnthi′nkable *adj.* Inconceivable.
ŭnti′dў *adj.* Not tidy, slovenly.
ŭnti′l *prep. & conj.* = TILL⁴.
ŭ′nto (-ōō) *prep.* (archaic) To.
ŭntō′ld *adj.* Not told; not counted; beyond count.
ŭntou′chable (-tŭ-) *n.* Non-caste Hindu (whom a caste man may not touch).
ŭntō′ward (or ŭntowôr′d) *adj.* Perverse, refractory (archaic); awkward; unlucky; unseemly. **ŭntō′wardlў** *adv.* **ŭntō′wardnĕss** *n.*
ŭntru′th (-rōō-) *n.* Being untrue; falsehood, lie.
ŭnū′sual (-zhōō-) *adj.* Not usual; remarkable. **ŭnū′suallў** *adv.*
ŭnū′tterable *adj.* That cannot be uttered; above or beyond description.
ŭnvâr′nished (-sht) *adj.* Not covered (as) with varnish; not embellished, plain.
ŭnwa′rrantable (-wŏ-) *adj.* Not justifiable.
ŭnwĕ′ll *adj.* Not in good health; indisposed.
ŭnwĕ′pt *adj.* Not wept for, not lamented.
ŭnwie′ldў *adj.* Slow or clumsy of movement, awkward to handle, wield, or manage, by reason of size, shape, or weight. **ŭnwie′ldinĕss** *n.*
ŭnwi′tting *adj.* Not knowing, not aware; not intentional. **ŭnwi′ttinglў** *adv.*
ŭnwri′tten (ŭnr-) *adj.* Not written (down); oral; traditional.
ŭp *adv.* To, in, a high or higher place, position, degree, amount, value, etc.; to or in a capital or university; to or in place farther north or otherwise conventionally regarded as higher; to or in the place in question or where the speaker etc. is; to or in erect or vertical position esp. as favourable to activity, out of bed, out of lying or sitting or kneeling posture, in(to) condition of efficiency or activity; (with verbs, usu.) expressing complete or effectual result etc.; *on the ~ and ~*, honest(ly); continually improving; *well ~*, in a high position; expert, well-informed, *in*; *~ against*, in(to) contact or collision with; (colloq.) faced or confronted by; *~ and down*, rising and falling; to and fro along; *~-and-downer*, (slang) row, quarrel; *~ in*, (colloq.) expert, well-informed, in subject etc.; *~ to*, as high or far as, up towards, so as to reach or arrive at; until; as much or as many as; fit or qualified for, capable of, able to deal with, ready for; on a level with; engaged in, occupying oneself with; (colloq.) obligatory or incumbent on; *~-to-the-minute*, (colloq.) with the latest information; in the latest style etc.; *~ with*, so as to overtake; on a level with. *~ prep.* To a higher point of, on or along in ascending direction; at or in a higher part of; *~ stream*, *u′pstream*, against the current, further from mouth, of river. *~ adj.* Moving, sloping, going, towards a higher point or to the capital; *~-and-coming*, alert and likely to succeed; *~-beat*, (mus.) unaccented beat, esp. last beat in bar; *~ grade*, (U.S.) upward slope; *on the ~-grade*, (fig.) improving; *~-gra′de* (v.t.) raise in status etc. *~ n. ~s and downs*, rises and falls; undulating ground; alternately good and bad fortune. *~ v.* 1. Drive up (swans) for marking. 2. Rise or raise abruptly. 3. (colloq.) Begin abruptly or boldly (to do something), *he ~s and says . . .*
u.p. *abbrev.* Under proof.
U.P. *abbrev.* United Presbyterian; United Press.
Upă′nishăd (ōō-; *or* -pŭn-) *n.* Any of various compositions forming the final part of the VEDIC literature, dealing with the nature of the soul and ultimate reality.
ŭ′pas *n.* (also *~ tree*) Fabulous Javanese tree poisoning all animal and vegetable life for miles around; (bot.) Javanese tree *Antiaris toxicaria*, yielding poisonous juice; poison obtained from this.
ŭpbrai′d *v.t.* Chide, reproach.
ŭ′pbringing *n.* Bringing up of young persons, early rearing and training.
ŭ′pcast (-ah-) *adj.* Turned upwards. *~ n.* (esp.) 1. (mining & geol.) (Fault caused by) upward dislocation of seam. 2. (mining) *~ (air-)shaft*, shaft through which air passes out of mine (ill. MINE²).
ŭ′p-cou′ntrў (-kŭn-) *n., adj., & adv.* (To, in, of) inland part of country.
ŭpdā′te *v.t.* Advance date of, bring up to date.
ŭp-ĕ′nd *v.* Set, rise up, on end.
ŭphea′ve (ŭp-h-) *v.* Lift up, raise; throw up with violence, esp. by volcanic action; rise up.
ŭphea′val *n.*
ŭ′phĭll (ŭp-h-) *adj.* Sloping upwards; (fig.) arduous, difficult, laborious. **ŭphi′ll** *adv.* With upward slope on hill, with slope in upward direction.
ŭphō′ld (ŭp-h-) *v.t.* (past t. & past part. *-held*). Hold up, keep erect, support; give support or countenance to; maintain, confirm (decision etc.).
ŭphō′lster (ŭp-h-) *v.t.* Furnish (room etc.) with hangings, carpets, etc.) provide (chair etc.) with textile covering, padding, etc., cover chair (*with, in*). **ŭphō′lsterer**, **ŭphō′lsterў** *ns.* [f. obs. *upholster, upholder* one who upholds, i.e. keeps in repair; *v.* back-formation]

ŭ′pkeep *n.* (Cost of) maintenance in good condition or repair.
ŭ′pland *n.* (freq. pl.) Piece of high ground, stretch of hilly or mountainous country. *~ adj.* Living, growing, situated, etc., on high ground.
ŭpli′ft *v.t.* Raise up, elevate (esp. fig.). **ŭ′plift** *n.* Raising, elevating; (colloq.) moral or intellectual edification.
upŏ′n *prep.* = ON.
ŭ′pper *adj.* Higher in place, situated above; superior in rank, authority, dignity, etc.; *~ case*: see CASE²; *~ crust*, (colloq.) aristocracy, highest social circles; *~-cut*, (boxing) short-arm upward blow; *~ deck*, highest continuous deck of ship; *~ hand*, mastery, control, or advantage (*of, over*); *~ house*, higher legislative assembly, esp. House of Lords. *~ n.* Upper part of boot or shoe (ill. SHOE); *on one′s ~s*, (colloq.) poor, having hard luck.
ŭ′ppermŏst *adj.* Highest in place or rank. *~ adv.* On or to the top.
U′pper Vŏ′lta (ŭ-). Inland republic of W. Africa, formerly part of the French Colony of the Ivory Coast; independent since 1960; capital, Ouagadougou.
ŭ′ppish *adj.* Self-assertive, pert, putting on airs. **ŭ′ppishlў** *adv.* **ŭ′ppishnĕss** *n.*
ŭprai′se (-z) *v.t.* Raise up, elevate, rear.
ŭ′pright (-rīt) *adj. & adv.* Erect, vertical; righteous, strictly honourable or honest. **ŭ′prightlў** *adv.* **ŭ′prightnĕss** *n.* **ŭ′pright** *n.* Upright PIANO²; post or rod fixed upright esp. as support to some structure.
ŭprī′sing (-z-) *n.* (esp.) Insurrection, popular rising against authority etc.
ŭ′proar (-ôr) *n.* Tumult, violent disturbance, clamour. **ŭproar′ious** *adj.* **ŭproar′iouslў** *adv.* **ŭproar′iousnĕss** *n.*
ŭprōō′t *v.t.* Tear up by the roots; eradicate, destroy.
ŭpsĕ′t¹ *v.* (past t. & past part. *upset*). Overturn, be overturned; disturb the peace, composure, temper, digestion, etc., of. *~ n.* Upsetting, being upset.
ŭ′psĕt² *adj. ~ price*, price fixed as lowest for which property offered at auction will be sold.
ŭ′pshŏt *n.* Final issue, conclusion.
ŭ′pside-dow′n *adv. & adj.* With the upper part under, inverted, in(to) total disorder. [altered from ME *up so down* up as if down]
ŭpsi′des (-dz) *adv.* (colloq., orig. Sc.) Even or quits *with*.
ŭpsī′lon *n.* Letter of Greek alphabet (Υ, υ), corresponding to u.
ŭpstā′ge *adv.* Away from front of stage; *~ of*, further upstage than. *~ adj.* (slang) Supercilious, haughty. *~ v.t.* Force (actor) to face away from audience by

getting or keeping upstage of him; (fig.) outshine; behave superciliously or haughtily towards.
ŭpstair's (-z) *adv.* Up the stairs. **ŭ'pstairs** *adj.* & *n.* (Of, in) upper floor of house etc.
ŭpstă'nding *adj.* Well set up, erect.
ŭ'pstărt *n.* One who has newly or suddenly risen in position or importance (freq. attrib.).
ŭ'pstrōke *n.* Upward line made in writing.
ŭ'pswĕ'pt *adj.* 1. (of hair) Brushed upwards towards top of head. 2. Curved or sloped upwards.
ŭ'ptāke *n.* (Sc. & colloq.) Understanding, apprehension.
ŭ'pthrŭst *n.* Upward thrust, esp. (geol.) one caused by volcanic or seismic action.
ŭ'ptĭght (-īt) *adj.* (colloq., orig. U.S.) 1. Tense, worried; annoyed. 2. Stiffly conventional.
ŭ'pward *adj.* & *adv.* (Directed) towards a higher place (lit. & fig.).
ŭ'pwards (-z) *adv.* (esp.) ~ *of*, more than.
Ur (ēr). Ancient city of Mesopotamia (at Tell Muqayyar in S. Iraq), a centre of Sumerian civilization, *c* 3000 B.C.; in O.T. called 'Ur of the Chaldees' (Gen. 11: 28, 31); laid waste by Babylonians *c* 1800 B.C.; partially rebuilt by Nebuchadnezzar of Babylon in 6th c. B.C.
ūrae'mĭa *n.* (path.) Presence in blood of urinary matter normally eliminated by kidneys; condition caused by failure of kidneys to function. **ūrae'mĭc** *adj.*
ūrae'us *n.* (Egyptian antiq.) Representation of (head and neck of) sacred asp or serpent, as emblem of supreme power, esp. in head-dress of ancient Egyptian divinities and sovereigns. [modern latinization of Gk *ouraios*, supposed to be ancient Egyptian for cobra]
Ur'al-Altā'ic (ūr-, ă-) *adj.* Of (the people of) the Urals and Altaic mountain ranges of central Asia; of a family of Finnic, Mongolian, Turkic, and other agglutinative languages of N. Europe and Asia.
Ur'al Mou'ntains (ūr-, -tĭnz). (also *Urals*) Mountain range in U.S.S.R. forming a natural boundary between Europe and Asia.
Ūrā'nĭa (ūr-). (Gk & Rom. myth.) 1. Muse of astronomy. 2. Title of Aphrodite, esp. in Oriental countries, and of various non-Greek goddesses.
ūrā'nĭum *n.* (chem.) Heavy greyish metallic radioactive element, found in pitchblende and minerals, capable of nuclear fission and hence used in the production of atomic energy and atomic bombs; symbol U, at. no. 92, at. wt 238·029. **ūrā'nĭc, ūrā'nous** *adjs.* [f. URANUS]
ūranŏ'graphў *n.* Descriptive astronomy.
ūranŏ'mĕtrў *n.* Measurement of stellar distances; map showing positions and magnitudes of stars.
Ur'anus (ūr-; *or* ūrā'-). 1. (Gk myth.) Personification of the sky, the most ancient of the Greek gods and the first ruler of the universe. 2. (astron.) 7th of the major planets, farthest from the sun except for Neptune and Pluto; discovered in 1781 by Sir W. Herschel (ill. PLANET).
ûr'ban[1] *adj.* Of, living or situated in, a city or town.
Ur'ban[2] (ēr-). Name of eight popes: *Urban II*, pope 1088–99, inaugurated the first crusade; *Urban VIII*, pope 1623–44, Florentine scholar and poet.
ûrbā'ne *adj.* Courteous, civil; bland, suave. **ûrbā'nelў** *adv.*
ûrbă'nĭtў *n.* [L *urbanus* of the city, refined, polished (*urbs* city)]
ûr'banize *v.t.* Render urban; remove rural character of (district or population). **ûrbanĭzā'tion** *n.*
ûr'chĭn *n.* 1. Hedgehog (archaic or dial.); *sea-~*: see SEA. 2. Roguish or mischievous boy; little fellow, boy. [ME *hurcheon* hedgehog, f. L *ericius*]
Urdu (oor'dōō). Literary form of Hindustani drawing vocabulary from Persian and using Persian–Arabic script; one of the national languages of Pakistan. [Hind., lit. = 'camp language']
ūr'ĕa (*or* ūrē'a) *n.* (chem.) Soluble nitrogenous crystalline compound (CO(NH₂)₂), present in urine of mammals, birds, and some reptiles, and also in blood, milk, etc.
ūrē'ter *n.* Either of two ducts conveying urine from kidney to bladder or cloaca (ill. KIDNEY).
ūrē'thra *n.* Duct through which urine is discharged from bladder (ill. PELVIS). **ūrē'thral** *adj.*
ûrge *v.t.* 1. Bring forward (fact etc.) earnestly to someone's attention; state as justification etc.; advocate pressingly. 2. Entreat pertinaciously, incite. 3. Drive forcibly, impel; hasten. ~ *n.* Impelling motive, force, pressure, etc.
ûr'gent *adj.* Pressing, calling for immediate action or attention; importunate, earnest and persistent in demand. **ûr'gentlў** *adv.* **ûr'gency** *n.*
Uriah (ūrī'a). Officer in David's army, husband of Bathsheba, whom David caused to be killed in battle (2 Sam. 11).
ūr'ĭc *adj.* Of urine; ~ *acid*, white crystalline acid found in urine of mammals, birds, etc.
Ur'ĭel (ūr-). One of the seven archangels enumerated in the 'Book of Enoch'.
Ur'ĭm (ūr-) *n.* ~ *and Thummim*, objects of unknown nature worn in or on the breastplate of the Jewish high priest in O.T. (Exod. 28: 30) by means of which the will of Jahweh was to be declared. [Heb., = 'lights']

ūrī'nal (*or* ūr'ĭ-) *n.* Vessel for receiving urine; building or structure for use of persons requiring to pass urine.
ūr'ĭnarў *adj.* Of urine.
ūr'ĭnāte *v.i.* Void urine. **ūrĭnā'tion** *n.*
ūr'ĭne *n.* Fluid secreted by kidneys in man and other mammals, stored in bladder and voided at intervals through urethra; similar fluid in other vertebrates. **ūr'ĭnous** *adj.*
ûrn *n.* 1. Vessel or vase with foot and usu. with rounded body, esp. as used for storing ashes of the dead, or as receptacle or measure; *ur'nfield*, cemetery (esp. of Bronze Age) of cinerary urns without permanent superstructure. 2. Large vessel with tap, in which water is kept hot or tea made.
ūr'odēle *n.* (zool.) Member of the amphibian order Urodela, comprising newts and salamanders.
ūrŏ'logў *n.* Study of diseases of urinary system. **ūrŏ'logist** *n.*
Ur'sa (ēr-). (astron.) ~ *Major*, the Great Bear, a northern constellation, also known as the Plough, (Charles's) Wain, Callisto; ~ *Minor*, the Little Bear, most northern constellation, containing the Pole Star. [L, = 'she-bear']
ûr'sine *adj.* Of, like, a bear.
Ur'sŭla (ēr-) *n.* British saint and martyr, who, acc. to legend, was put to death with 11,000 virgins, having been captured by Huns near Cologne when on a pilgrimage.
Ur'sŭline (ēr-) *adj.* & *n.* (Nun) of an order founded by St. Angela Merici at Brescia in 1537 for nursing the sick and teaching girls. [named after St. URSULA, patron saint of the foundress]
ûrtĭcār'ĭa *n.* (path.) NETTLE-rash.
Uruguay (oor'ōōgwī *or* ūī-). 1. River of S. America, flowing southwards from Brazil and joining the Plata river. 2. S. Amer. republic, lying to the E. of the Uruguay river, inaugurated in 1830; capital, Montevideo. **Uruguay'an** *adj.* & *n.*
ŭs (unstressed *us*) *pron.* Objective (accus., dat.) case of WE.
U.S. *abbrev.* United States (of America).
U.S.A. *abbrev.* United States of America; United States Army.
U.S.A.F. *abbrev.* United States Air Force.
ū'sage (ūz-) *n.* Manner of using or treating, treatment; habitual or customary practice, established use (esp. of word); quantity used; (law) habitual but not necessarily immemorial practice.
ū'sance (ūz-) *n.* Time allowed by commercial usage for payment of esp. foreign bill of exchange etc.
use (ūz) *v.* 1. Employ for a purpose or as instrument or material; exercise, put into operation, avail oneself of; ~ *up*, use the whole of, find a use for what remains of;

USEFUL

exhaust, wear out. 2. Treat in specified manner. 3. (now only in past t. **used** (ŭst)) Be accustomed, have as constant or frequent practice; (past part.) accustomed. **ū'sable** adj. **use** (ūs) n. 1. Using, employment, application to a purpose; right or power of using; availability, utility, purpose for which thing can be used, occasion for using. 2. Ritual and liturgy of a church, diocese, etc. 3. (law) Benefit or profit of lands etc. held by another solely for the beneficiary.

ū'seful (ūsf-) adj. Of use, serviceable; suitable for use, advantageous, profitable. **ū'sefullȳ** adv. **ū'sefulnèss** n.

ū'selèss (ūsl-) adj. Serving no useful purpose, unavailing; of inadequate or insufficient capacity, inefficient. **ū'selèsslȳ** adv. **ū'selèssnèss** n.

ū'ser (ūz-) n. (law) Continued use or exercise of right etc.; presumptive right arising from use.

ū'sher n. Official or servant who acts as doorkeeper or shows people to seats in church, lawcourt, etc.; official at court who walks before person of rank; under-teacher, assistant schoolmaster (now only as a traditional title, or contempt.). **ūshere͏̆'tte** n. Female usher esp. in cinema. **ŭ'sher** v.t. Act as usher to; precede (person) as usher, announce, show in, out (freq. fig.). [OF uissier f. L ostiarius doorkeeper (ostium door)]

U.S.N. abbrev. United States Navy.

U.S.P.G. abbrev. United Society for the Propagation of the Gospel.

ŭ'squėbaugh (-baw) n. Whisky. [Ir. & Sc. Gaelic uisge beatha water of life]

U.S.S. abbrev. United States Senate; United States Ship (or Steamer, Steamship).

U.S.S.R. abbrev. Union of Soviet Socialist Republics.

ū'sual (ūzho͞oal) adj. Commonly or ordinarily observed, practised, used, happening, to be found, etc.; current, ordinary, customary, wonted. **ū'suallȳ** adv. **ū'sualnèss** n.

ū'sŭfrŭct (ūz-) n. (law) Right of enjoying use and advantages of another's property, short of causing damage or prejudice to this; use, enjoyment (of something). **ūsŭfrŭ'ctūarȳ** adj. & n. Of usufruct, (person) enjoying usufruct.

ū'surer (ūzhu-) n. One who lends money at exorbitant or illegal rates of interest.

usūr'p (ūz-) v. Seize, assume, (power, right, etc.) wrongfully. **ūsurpā'tion** (ūzer-), **ūsūr'per** ns.

ū'surȳ (ūzh-) n. Practice of lending money at exorbitant interest, esp. at higher interest than is allowed by law; such interest. **ūsūr'ious** (ūz-) adj. **ūsūr'iouslȳ** adv. **ūsūr'iousnèss** n.

ŭt (or o͞ot) n. 1. (hist.) First note of the hexachord. 2. First note of octave in solmization, now usu. called DOH. [named, with the other five notes of the hexachord, after syllables from a Latin hymn: Ut queant laxis resonare fibris Mira gestorum famuli tuorum, Solve polluti labii reatum; because in this hymn the notes of the hexachord fell on these syllables]

Ut. abbrev. Utah.

U'tah (ū-; or, esp. U.S., -ta). State of western U.S., admitted to the Union in 1896; capital, Salt Lake City.

ūtė'nsil n. Instrument, implement, vessel, esp. in domestic use.

ū'terine adj. 1. Having the same mother but different fathers. 2. Of, situated in, connected with, the uterus.

ū'terus n. (pl. -ī). Womb, organ in which young are conceived, develop, and are protected till birth (ill. PELVIS).

U'ther Pĕndră'gon (ū-). In Arthurian legend, king of Britons and father of ARTHUR[1].

ūtilitār'ian adj. Of, consisting in, based on, utility, esp., regarding the greatest good of the greatest number as the chief consideration of morality; holding utilitarian views or principles. ~ n. One who holds or supports utilitarian views; one devoted to mere utility or material interests.

ūtilitār'ianism n. Utilitarian principles, doctrines, etc., esp. as expounded by BENTHAM and J. S. MILL[3].

ūti'litȳ n. 1. Usefulness, fitness for some desirable end or useful purpose, profitableness; power to satisfy human wants; useful thing; (public) utilities, (organizations supplying) gas, water, electricity, transport services, means of communication, etc., provided for some or all members of the community and regarded as so essential to the life of the community that they are subject to various forms of public control. 2. (attrib.)

V, v

Reared, kept, made, etc., for useful ends as opp. to display or show purposes; (hist., for some years from 1942) applied to clothes, furniture, etc., made in standardized form in accordance with the official allowance of material; ~ actor, man, actor of small parts.

ū'tilīze v.t. Make use of, turn to account, use. **ūtilīzā'tion** n.

ŭ'tmōst adj. Furthest, extreme; that is such in the highest degree. ~ n. Utmost point, degree, limit, extent, etc.; best of one's ability, power, etc.

Utō'pia (ū-). Name of the imaginary island governed on a perfect political and social system, which forms the title of a book by Sir Thomas More published in 1516; hence, any ideally perfect social and political system. **Utō'pian** adj. & n. (Inhabitant) of Utopia; (characteristic of) an ardent, but unpractical reformer. **ūtō'pianism** n.

Utrecht (ūtrĕ'χt). City and province of the Netherlands; Peace of ~, series of treaties, concluded here in 1713, which terminated the War of the Spanish Succession; ~ velvet, kind of mohair plush.

ū'tricle n. (bot., zool.) Small cell, sac, or bladder-like part or process, esp. one of two sacs in membranous labyrinth of the inner ear. **ūtri'cūlar** adj.

U'ttar Pradė'sh (o͞o-; or -āsh). State in N. India bordering on Tibet and Nepal; capital, Lucknow.

ŭ'tter[1] adj. Complete, total, unqualified. **ŭ'tterlȳ** adv. **ŭ'tternèss** n. **ŭ'ttermōst** adj.

ŭ'tter[2] v.t. 1. Emit audibly; express in spoken or written words. 2. Put (forged banknotes, base coin, etc.) into circulation. **ŭ'tterance** n. Uttering; power of speech; spoken words.

ū'vūla n. (pl. -ae). Conical fleshy prolongation hanging from middle of pendent margin of soft palate (ill. HEAD). **ū'vūlar** adj.

ŭxōr'ious adj. Excessively fond of one's wife; marked by such fondness. **ŭxōr'iouslȳ** adv. **ŭxōr'iousnèss** n.

U'zbĕk, U'zbĕg (o͞oz- or ŭz-) adj. & n. (Member, language) of a Turkic people of Turkestan and Uzbekistan.

Uzbĕkista'n (o͞oz- or ŭz; -ahn). Constituent republic of U.S.S.R., lying S. and SE. of the Aral Sea; capital, Tashkent.

V

V, v (vē). 1. 22nd letter of modern English and 20th of ancient Roman alphabet, adopted in form from early Greek vowel-symbol V, in English representing a labio-dental voiced spirant. 2. Roman numeral symbol for five. 3. V, symbol for allied victory in war of 1939–45; V day, 15 Aug 1945, day fixed for the official celebration of the end of the war; VE day, 8 May 1945, day fixed for

V. the official celebration of the end of hostilities in Europe; V**J** day, 15 Aug. 1945, celebrating end of hostilities in Japan; *V-sign*: see below. 4. *V-weapon*, flying bomb (*V1*) or rocket projectile (*V2*) of type devised by Germans and used towards end of war of 1939–45 [abbrev. f. Ger. *Vergeltung* retribution]. 5. Object etc. shaped like V; *V-formation*, formation of aircraft in flight in shape of V; *V-sign*, (orig. in war of 1939–45) first two fingers held up in shape of V, palm outward, as symbol of victory; similar sign, palm inward, as vulgar derisory gesture.
v. *abbrev.* Verb; verse; versus; *vide*.
V *abbrev.* Volt(s).
Va. *abbrev.* Virginia.
V.A. *abbrev.* Vicar Apostolic; Vice-Admiral; (Order of) Victoria and Albert.
Vaal (vahl). River of S. Africa, rising in Transvaal and flowing SW. into Orange River.
văc *n.* (colloq.) Vacation.
vā′cancў *n.* Being vacant; vacant space, breach, gap; lack of intelligence, inanity; unoccupied office, post, or dignity.
vā′cant *adj.* Empty, not filled or occupied; (of the mind) unoccupied with thought; without intelligence; (of person) with vacant mind; ~ *possession*, legal and auctioneer's term implying that immediate occupation and possession of a house etc. is offered. **vā′cantly** *adv.*
vacā′te (*or*, esp. U.S., vā′kāt) *v.t.* Leave (office, position) vacant; give up possession or occupancy of (house etc.); (law) make void, annul, cancel.
vacā′tion (*or*, esp. U.S., vā-) *n.* Vacating; time during which law-courts, schools, or universities are closed; (chiefly U.S.) holiday.
vă′ccināte (-ks-) *v.t.* Inoculate with a vaccine, esp. against smallpox. **vaccinā′tion** *n.*
vă′ccine (-ks-; *or* -ēn) *n.* Preparation of cowpox virus used for inoculation against smallpox; any preparation of micro-organisms used as an immunizing agent.
văcci′nia (-ks-) *n.* (path.) Cowpox.
vă′cillāte *v.i.* Swing or sway unsteadily; hover doubtfully; waver between different opinions, etc. **văcillā′tion** *n.*
vacū′itў *n.* Empty space; absolute emptiness; vacuousness, vacancy.
văcŭolā′tion *n.* (bot.) Formation of vacuoles during development of living cells.
vă′cŭole *n.* Space within protoplasm usu. filled with liquid (ill. CELL).
vă′cūous *adj.* Empty; void; unintelligent, vacant. **vă′cūouslў** *adv.* **vă′cūousnĕss** *n.*
vă′cūum *n.* Space entirely empty of matter; empty space; space, vessel, empty of air, esp. one from which air has been artificially withdrawn; ~ *bottle*, *flask*, *jar*, *jug*, vessel with double wall enclosing vacuum so that liquid in inner receptacle retains its temperature; ~ *brake*, brake operated by (partial) vacuum, used esp. on railway-trains; ~ *cleaner*, apparatus for removing dust etc. from carpets, upholstery, etc., by suction; ~ *pump*, pump for producing a vacuum; ~ *tube*, sealed glass or metal tube or bulb from which almost all the air has been removed, so that electrical current can flow between electrodes inside without disturbance by a gaseous atmosphere; such tube used in radio and electronics. ~ *v.t.* (colloq.) Clean with vacuum cleaner.
V.A.D. *abbrev.* (Member of) Voluntary Aid Detachment.
va′de-me′cum (vahdā mā-) *n.* Book or other thing carried constantly about the person, esp. handbook or manual. [L, = 'go with me']
vă′gabŏnd *adj.* Wandering, having no settled habitation or home; straying; (as) of a vagabond. ~ *n.* Vagabond person, esp. idle and worthless wanderer, vagrant; (colloq.) scamp, rascal. **vă′gabŏndage**, **vă′gabŏndism** *ns.* **vă′gabŏndĭsh** *adj.* **vă′gabŏndize** *v.i.*
vā′gal *adj.* Of the vagus.
vagār′ў *n.* Capricious or extravagant action, notion, etc.; freak, caprice.
vagī′na *n.* Sheath-like covering, organ, or part; membranous canal leading from vulva to uterus in female mammals (ill. PELVIS); analogous structure in some other animals. **vagī′nal** *adj.*
vā′grant *n.* One without settled home or regular work, wandering from place to place, tramp, wanderer; (law) idle and disorderly person liable to term of imprisonment. ~ *adj.* That is a vagrant; (as) of a vagrant; roving, itinerant. **vā′grantlў** *adv.* **vā′grancў** *n.*
vāgue (-g) *adj.* Indistinct, not clearly expressed or perceived, of uncertain or ill-defined meaning or character or appearance; forgetful, unbusinesslike. **vā′guelў** *adv.* **vā′guenĕss** *n.*
vā′gus *n.* Either of 10th pair of cranial nerves, with branches to thoracic and abdominal viscera etc.
vain *adj.* Unsubstantial, empty, of no effect, unavailing; having excessively high opinion (*of* one's own appearance, qualities, possessions, etc.); *in* ~, to no effect or purpose, vainly; *take in* ~, utter, use (name, esp. of God), needlessly, casually, or idly. **vai′nlў** *adv.*
vainglōr′ў (-n-g-) *n.* Boastfulness, extreme vanity. **vainglōr′ious** *adj.* **vainglōr′iouslў** *adv.* **vainglōr′iousnĕss** *n.*
vair *n.* Kind of grey-and-white squirrel-skin much used in 13th–14th centuries as lining or trimming (archaic); (her.) representation of this with small shield-shaped spaces of two tinctures, usu. azure and argent, arranged alternately (ill. HERALDRY).
Vaisya (vī′sya) *n.* (Member of) the 3rd of the four great Hindu castes, comprising merchants and agriculturalists. [Sansk. *vaiśya* peasant, labourer]
Vă′lais (-ā) Canton of Switzerland.
vă′lance *n.* Short curtain round frame or canopy of bedstead (ill. BED), above window or under shelf.
vāle¹ *n.* Valley (now chiefly poet. or in names).
vale² (vah′lā) *int.* & *n.* Farewell. [L, = 'be well!']
vălĕdĭ′ction *n.* (Words used in) bidding farewell.
vălĕdĭctōr′ian *n.* (U.S.) Senior scholar who delivers the valedictory oration on graduation etc.
vălĕdĭ′ctorў *adj.* & *n.* (Speech, oration) bidding farewell.
valence: see VALENCY.
Valĕ′ncia (*or* -sha). Town and province of E. Spain; hence, variety of almond, raisin, orange, and other fruits, produced there.
Valenciennes (vălahṅsyĕn). Town in NE. France, formerly Flemish; ~ *lace*, fine bobbin-lace made at Valenciennes in 17th and 18th centuries.
vā′lencў, **vā′lence** *ns.* (chem.) 1. Power which atoms possess of combining with one another to form molecules; ~ *bond*, linkage between two atoms in a molecule, formed either by the transfer of an electron from one atom to the other (*electrovalent bond*) or by the sharing of electrons, two to each link, between the atoms (*covalent bond*). 2. Number indicating the number of atoms of hydrogen with which a single atom of a given element can combine (an element with a valency of 1 is *univalent* or *monovalent*, of 2 *bivalent* or *divalent*, of 3 *tervalent* or *trivalent*, of 4 *quadrivalent* or *tetravalent*, etc.)
Vă′lentine¹, St. Name of several saints of whom most celebrated are two martyrs whose festivals fall on 14 Feb., both belonging to reign of the emperor Claudius.
Vă′lentine² *n.* 1. St. Valentine's day, 14 Feb., on which birds were believed to mate and sweethearts were chosen. 2. Sweetheart chosen on St. Valentine's day; gift given on this occasion (archaic); (also *v*~) letter or card, of sentimental or comic nature, sent, usu. anonymously, to person of opposite sex on St. Valentine's day.
Valera, Eamon de: see DE VALERA.
valēr′ian *n.* Any species of widely distributed herbaceous genus *Valeriana*, esp. *V. officinalis*

with small pink or white flowers and strong odour esteemed by cats; dried roots etc. of species of valerian used as carminative etc., or in scents etc.

vale′ric (*or* -ēr-), **valēriă′nic** *adjs.* Derived from valerian; ~ *acid*, any of four strong-smelling isomeric fatty acids.

Valerỹ (vălărī), Paul (1871–1945), French poet.

vă′lĕt (*or* -lā) *n.* (also ~ *de chambre*, pr. vălă de shahṅbr) Manservant attending on man's person and having charge of clothes etc.; one who cleans, presses, and mends clothes. ~ *v.t.* Wait on, act, as valet to.

vălĕtūdinăr′ian *adj. & n.* (Person) of infirm health, esp. unduly solicitous or anxiously concerned about health. **vălĕtūdinăr′ianism** *n.* **vălĕtū′dinarỹ** *adj.*

vă′lgus *n.* (path.) Deformity in which the legs are knock-kneed.

Vălhă′lla. (Scand. myth.) Hall assigned to heroes who have died in battle, in which they feast with Odin.

vă′liant (-ya-) *adj.* Brave, courageous. **vă′liantlỹ** *adv.* **vă′liance** *n.*

vă′lĭd *adj.* (of reason, argument, etc.) Sound, defensible, well-grounded; (law) sound and sufficient, executed with proper formalities. **vă′lĭdlỹ** *adv.* **vali′dĭtỹ** *n.*

vă′lĭdāte *v.t.* Make valid, ratify, confirm. **vălĭdā′tion** *n.*

vălī′se (-ēz) *n.* Kind of travelling-bag carried by hand (chiefly U.S.); large waterproof case for an officer's bedding and spare clothing, rolled up from one end and secured by straps.

Vă′lkỹrie (*or* -ēr′ī) *n.* (Scand. myth.) Each of twelve war-maidens supposed to hover over battlefields selecting those to be slain and conducting them to Valhalla.

Vallĕ′tta. Capital city and port of Malta.

vă′lley *n.* Long depression or hollow between hills, freq. with stream or river along bottom; stretch of country drained or watered by river-system; any depression or hollow resembling valley, esp. trough between waves; angle formed by intersection of two roofs or roof and wall (ill. ROOF); ~ *of the shadow of death*, experience of being near to death (Ps. 23: 4).

Vă′lley Fŏrge. Valley near Philadelphia where George Washington and Amer. Revolutionary army passed winter of 1777–8 in conditions of great hardship.

vă′llum *n.* (Rom. antiq.) Rampart surmounted by stockade, or wall, of earth, sods, or stone, as means of defence.

Vălois (-lwah). Medieval duchy of France; *House of* ~, French royal line 1328–1589.

vălō′nia, văll- *n.* Dried acorn cups of the ~ *oak* (*Quercus aegilops*), a Levantine evergreen oak, used in tanning, dyeing, etc.

vă′lorīze *v.t.* Fix or raise price of (commodity) by artificial means, esp. by centrally organized scheme. **vălorīzā′tion** *n.*

vă′lour (-ler) *n.* (now chiefly poet. and rhet.) Courage, esp. as shown in war or conflict. **vă′lorous** *adj.* **vă′lorouslỹ** *adv.*

Vălparai′sō (-īzō). Seaport and city of Aconcagua province, Chile.

valse (vahls *or* vawls) *n.* Waltz.

vă′lūable *adj.* Of great value, price, or worth. ~ *n.* (usu. pl.) Valuable thing or possession esp. small article.

vălūā′tion *n.* Estimation (esp. by professional valuer) of thing's worth; worth so estimated, price set on thing.

vă′lūe *n.* 1. Amount of commodity, money, etc., considered equivalent for something else; material or monetary worth of thing; worth, desirability, utility, qualities on which these depend; (econ.) amount of commodity, money, etc., for which something else is readily available; FACE, SURPLUS, SURRENDER, ~: see these words; ~ *judgement*, (philos.) subjective estimate of quality etc.; ~ *added tax*, (abbrev. V.A.T.) tax on amount by which the value of an article is increased by each stage in its production. 2. (math. etc.) Precise number or amount represented by figure, quantity, etc. 3. (mus.) Relative duration of tone signified by note. 4. (painting) Relation of part of picture to others in respect of light and shade, part characterized by particular tone. ~ *v.t.* Estimate value of, appraise, esp. professionally; have high or specified opinion of, prize, esteem, appreciate.

vă′lūelèss (-lū-) *adj.* Worthless. **vă′lūelèssnèss** *n.*

vă′lūer *n.* (esp.) One who estimates or assesses values professionally.

valū′ta *n.* Exchange value of one currency in terms of another; currency in respect of such value.

vă′lvate, vălved (-vd) *adjs.* Having valve(s).

vălve *n.* 1. Door controlling flow of water in sluice; device for controlling flow of any fluid, usu. acting by yielding to pressure in one direction only. 2. (anat.) Membranous fold or other device in organ or passage of body closing automatically to prevent reflux of blood or other fluid (ill. HEART). 3. (pop.) Thermionic valve (ill. THERMIONIC); vacuum tube used in radio etc. 4. (mus.) Device for varying length of tube in instruments of horn or trumpet kind (ill. BRASS). 5. (conch.) Each half of hinged shell, single shell of same form (ill. MUSSEL); (bot.) each half or section of dehiscent pod, capsule, etc.

vă′lvūlar *adj.* Of, like, acting as, furnished with, valve(s).

vă′mbrāce *n.* (hist.) Defensive armour for forearm (ill. ARMOUR).

vamōō′se *v.i.* (slang) Make off, decamp (from). [Span. *vamos let us go*]

vămp[1] *n.* 1. Upper front part of boot or shoe (ill. SHOE). 2. Something revamped up or patched; (mus.) improvised accompaniment, introductory bars of song etc. ~ *v.* 1. Put new vamp to (boot, shoe); repair, patch *up*. 2. Make *up*, produce (as) by patching; compose, put together (book etc.) out of old materials; serve up (something old) as new by addition or alteration; (mus.) improvise (accompaniment etc.), improvise accompaniments.

vămp[2] *n.* Adventuress, woman who exploits men. ~ *v.t.* Attract as vamp, allure. [abbrev. of *vampire*]

vă′mpīre *n.* 1. Reanimated corpse supposed in parts of central and E. Europe to leave grave at night and renew its life by sucking blood of sleeping persons; hence, person preying on others. 2. (also ~ *trap*) Stage trap-door allowing demon etc. to appear or disappear suddenly. 3. (also ~ *bat*) Any of various small bats of S. America which make an incision with their teeth and lap blood of animals (genera *Desmodus*, *Diaemus*, and *Diphylla*); any of various other bats, chiefly S. American, which do not lap blood, esp. the large *false* ~ (*Vampyrus spectrum*). **vămpī′ric, vă′mpīrish** *adjs.* **vă′mpīrism** *n.*

văn[1] *n.* (archaic) Winnowing-machine or shovel; (poet.) wing, esp. of bird.

văn[2] *n.* = VANGUARD.

văn[3] *n.* Covered vehicle for carrying goods; railway-truck for goods, luggage, mails, or for use of guard. [abbrev. of *caravan*]

văn[4] *n.* (lawn tennis) Advantage (esp. in ~ *in*, ~ *out*). [abbrev. of *vantage*]

vă′nadate *n.* Salt of vanadium.

vanā′dium *n.* (chem.) Extremely hard, steel-white metallic element found in small quantities in combination in many minerals; symbol V, at. no. 23, at. wt 50·941; ~ *steel*, steel alloyed with vanadium (and sometimes other elements). **vană′dĭc, vă′nadous** *adjs.* [ON *Vanadis*, a name of FREYA]

Văn A′llen (ă-), James Alfred (1914–). U.S. physicist; ~ (*radiation*) *belt*, either of two zones of intense radiation surrounding the earth.

Vă′nbrugh (-bru), Sir John (1664–1726). English playwright and architect.

Văn Bŭr′en, Martin (1782–1862). 8th president of U.S., 1836–40.

Văncou′ver (-kōō-). City and seaport of British Columbia,

VANDAL

Canada; ~ *Island*, large island off Pacific coast, opposite Vancouver. [George *Vancouver* (1758–98), Engl. navigator and explorer of W. coast of N. America]

Vă′ndal *n.* 1. One of an ancient Germanic people who invaded W. Europe, and settled in Gaul, Spain, etc., in 4th and 5th centuries and finally (428–9) migrated to N. Africa; in 455 they sacked Rome in a marauding expedition; their kingdom in N. Africa was overthrown by Belisarius in 533. 2. *v*~, wilful or ignorant destroyer of anything beautiful, venerable, or worthy of preservation. **vă′ndalĭsm** *n.* **văndalī′stic** *adj.*

Văn de Vĕ′lde (-de). Dutch family of artists; the best-known are Willem the younger (1633–1707), marine painter, and his brother Adriaen (1636–72), landscape-painter.

Văn Die′men's Lănd (-z). Old name of Tasmania. [named by Tasman after Anthony *Van Diemen* (1593–1645), Du. governor of Java, who sent him on his voyage]

Văn Dўck, Văndў′ke[1], Sir Anthony (1599–1641). Flemish portrait-painter who worked for some years, and died, in England; *Vandyke beard*, neat pointed beard of kind freq. found in his paintings; *Vandyke brown*, a deep-brown pigment; *Vandyke collar*, broad lace or linen collar with deeply indented edge, seen in portraits by Van Dyck.

văndў′ke[2] *n.* Each of deep points forming border of Vandyke collar. ~ *v.t.* Cut (cloth etc.) in vandykes.

vāne *n.* Weathercock; windmill-sail; blade, wing, or other projection attached to axis etc. so as to be acted on by current of air or liquid; barbs of a feather (ill. FEATHER); sight of surveying instrument.

vaně′ssa *n.* Butterfly of genus *V*~ that includes red admiral, painted lady, etc.

Văn Eyck (ik), Jan (d. ?1441). Flemish artist; pioneer, together with his brother Huibrecht or Hubert (d. 1426), in use of oils in painting.

Văn Gogh (gŏχ), Vincent (1853–90). Dutch Post-Impressionist painter, active chiefly in France.

vă′ngŭard (-gărd) *n.* Front part or foremost division of army, fleet, etc., moving forward or onward; (fig.) leaders of movement etc.

vanī′lla *n.* (Pod-like capsule of) tropical climbing orchid of genus *V*~, esp. *V. planifolia*; aromatic extract or synthetic preparation of this, used as flavouring or perfume.

vanī′llĭn *n.* (chem.) Fragrant principle of vanilla (C_6H_5CHO).

vă′nish *v.i.* Disappear from sight, esp. suddenly and mysteriously; pass, fade, away; cease to exist; (math.) become zero; *van-*

ishing cream, face cream which is quickly absorbed by skin; *vanishing point*, in perspective, point at which receding parallel lines appear to meet.

vă′nitў *n.* What is vain or worthless; futility, worthlessness, emptiness; empty pride, self-conceit and desire for admiration; ~ *bag*, *case*, woman's small handbag or case containing mirror, face powder, etc.; *V*~ *Fair*, (from Bunyan's 'Pilgrim's Progress') the world as scene of idle amusement and vain display; fashionable world of society.

vă′nquish *v.t.* (now chiefly rhet.) Conquer, overcome.

va′ntage (vah-) *n.* Advantage (esp. in lawn tennis); ~-*ground*, COIGN of vantage.

vă′pĭd *adj.* Insipid, flat. **vă′p-ĭdlў** *adv.* **vapĭ′dĭtў**, **vă′pĭdnĕss** *ns.*

vā′porīze *v.* Convert, be converted, into vapour. **vā′porīzer** *n.* (esp.) Apparatus for vaporizing liquid, fine spray. **vāporīzā′tion** *n.*

vā′pour (-er) *n.* Matter diffused or suspended in air, as mist, steam, etc., esp. form into which liquids are converted by action of heat; (phys.) gaseous form of normally liquid or solid substance; vaporized substance; (pl., archaic) depression, spleen. **vāporī′fic**, **vā′porous**, **vā′pourў** *adjs.* **vā′porouslў** *adv.* **vā′porousnĕss** *n.* **vā′pour** *v.i.* Emit vapour; talk fantastically or boastingly.

văquer′ō (-kārō) *n.* (in Spanish American and south-western U.S.) Herdsman, cowboy.

Vărana′sī (-ahzī). (formerly *Benares*) City on the Ganges in India, regarded as sacred by Hindu

Vără′ngian (-j-) *adj.* & *n.* (One) of the Scandinavian rovers who in 9th and 10th centuries traded, through Russia, with Constantinople, where they served as a bodyguard to the Byzantine emperors (~ *Guard*); and, under RURIK, established a dynasty at Novgorod.

vār′iable *adj.* Apt, liable, to vary or change, capable of variation; modifiable, alterable, changeable, shifting, inconstant; (of star) varying periodically in brightness or magnitude; (math. etc.) of quantity etc.) that may assume a succession of values, having different values under different conditions. **vāriabi′litў**, **vār′iablenĕss** *ns.* **vār′iablў** *adv.* **vār′iable** *n.* Variable quantity, star, or other thing; shifting wind, (pl.) parts of sea where steady wind is not expected.

vār′iance *n.* Disagreement, difference of opinion, lack of harmony (esp. in *at* ~); (law) discrepancy between two documents, statements, etc., that should agree.

vār′iant *adj.* Differing *from* something or from standard, type, etc. ~ *n.* Variant form, spelling, reading, etc.

VARNISH

vāriā′tion *n.* 1. Varying, undergoing or making modification or alteration, esp. from normal condition, action, or amount, or from standard or type; extent of this. 2. (astron.) Deviation of heavenly body from mean orbit or motion. 3. (of magnetic needle) Declination. 4. (math.) Change in function(s) of equation due to indefinitely small change of value of constants; *calculus of* ~*s*, branch of calculus dealing with variations of curves; ~ *of curve*, change of curve into neighbouring curve. 5. (mus.) One of series of repetitions of theme or tune with changes which do not disguise its identity.

vă′ricocēle *n.* Varicose swelling of spermatic veins.

vār′icoloured (-kŭlerd) *adj.* Of various colours, variegated in colour.

vă′ricōse *adj.* (of veins) Having permanent abnormal local dilatation; affected with, resembling, of, a varix or varices. **vāricō′sitў** *n.*

vār′iegāte (-rig-) *v.t.* Diversify in appearance, esp. in colour. **vār′iegātĕd** *adj.* **vāriegā′tion** *n.* Being variegated, esp. (bot.) presence of two or more colours in leaves, petals, etc.; defective or special development leading to such colouring; variegated marking.

varī′etў *n.* 1. Being varied, diversity, absence of monotony, sameness, or uniformity; collection of different things. 2. Different form *of* some thing, quality, or condition; kind, sort; (biol.) (plant, animal, belonging to) group distinguished by characteristics considered too trivial to allow of its classification as distinct species. 3. (also ~ *show*) Entertainment consisting of a number of different independent performances.

vār′ifōrm *adj.* Of various forms.

vār′iōle *n.* Something resembling smallpox mark, as small spherical body of variolite.

vār′iolite *n.* Rock with whitish small spherical bodies embedded in it. **vāriolī′tic** *adj.*

vāriōr′um *n.* & *adj.* (Edition, esp. of classical author or text) with notes of various editors or commentators. [L, gen. pl. of *varius* various]

vār′ious *adj.* Different, diverse; separate, several. **vār′iouslў** *adv.* **vār′iousnĕss** *n.*

vār′ix *n.* (pl. *-icēs*). 1. Permanent abnormal dilatation of vein or artery, usu. with tortuous development. 2. Prominent longitudinal ridge on surface of shell.

vār′lĕt *n.* (hist.) Knight's attendant or page; (archaic) menial, low fellow, scoundrel.

vār′mĭnt *n.* (U.S. & dial.) Vermin; mischievous or discreditable person or animal.

vār′nish *n.* Resinous matter dissolved in oil or spirit, used for spreading over surface to produce

[960]

a translucent and usu. glossy protective coating; preparation of certain other substances, e.g. wax, cellulose, for same purpose; surface so formed; gloss; superficial polish of manner; external appearance or display without underlying reality. ~ *v.t.* Coat with varnish; gloss (*over*), disguise; *varnishing day*, day before opening of exhibition of paintings on which exhibitors may retouch and varnish their work.

Vă'rrō, Marcus Terentius (116–27 B.C.). Roman antiquarian and prolific author of books of history, biography, grammar, geography, and of 'De Re Rustica', a treatise on agriculture.

vâr'sitў *n.* (colloq.) University (now chiefly in reference to sport, as ~ *boat*, *match*).

Vâr'una. (Hinduism) Supreme cosmic deity, creator, and ruler.

vârve *n.* (geol.) Pair of layers of alternately fine and coarse silt or clay, deposited annually in meltwater lakes etc. **vârved** (-vd) *adj.*

vâr'ў *v.* Change, make different, modify, diversify; suffer change; be or become different in degree or quality; be of different kinds; ~ (*inversely*) *as*, change in quantity or value in (inverse) proportion to.

Vasār'ī (*or* -z-), Giorgio (1511–74). Italian painter, architect, and author of 'Lives' of Italian painters, sculptors, and architects.

Vasco da Gama: see GAMA.

vă'sculār *adj.* (biol., anat.) Of tubular vessels; containing, supplied with, these; ~ *system*, system of tubes within an organism for conveying fluid, esp. blood, sap.

văs dĕ'ferĕns (-nz). (pl. *va'sa defere'ntia*). Spermatic duct (ill. PELVIS). [L *vas* vessel, *deferens* carrying down]

vase (vahz; U.S. vās *or* vāz) *n.* Vessel, usu. of greater height than width, used as ornament, for holding flowers, etc. or (archaeol.) as container.

vasĕ'ctomў *n.* Surgical removal of (part of) the vas deferens.

vă'sĕline (*or* -ēn) *n.* Kind of petroleum jelly. [trade-name, f. Ger. *wasser* water, Gk *elaion* oil]

Vă'shti. Queen of Ahasuerus, banished for refusing to appear before his guests (Esther 1: 9–19).

vā'sifōrm *adj.* Duct-shaped, tubular.

vāso-mō'tor (*or* -z-) *adj.* (of nerves) Acting on walls of blood-vessels so as to constrict or dilate these and thus regulate flow of blood.

vă'ssal *n.* 1. (hist., in feudal system) One holding lands on condition of homage and allegiance to superior. 2. Humble servant or subordinate, slave. **vă'ssalage** *n.* (hist.) Condition, obligations, service, of vassal; servitude, dependence; fief.

Vă'ssar Cŏ'llĕge. College, orig. for women, in State of New York, founded 1861 by Matthew Vassar, an Amer. brewer.

vast (vah-) *adj.* Of great extent or area; of great size or amount. **va'stlў** *adv.* **va'stnĕss** *n.*

văt *n.* 1. Large tub, cask, cistern, or other vessel for holding or storing liquids. 2. Dyeing liquor, esp. liquor containing dye in soluble non-dyeing form, which oxidizes and is deposited in fibres when textile steeped in the liquor is exposed to air; ~-*dye* (*n. & v.t.*) dye so used, dye thus. ~ *v.* Place, treat, mature, in vat.

V.A.T. *abbrev.* Value added tax.

Vă'tican. Pope's palace and official residence on Vatican Hill in Rome; 'the papal government;

GREEK VASE SHAPES
1. Amphora. 2. Crater. 3. Lecythus. 4. Hydria. 5. Cylix

~ *City*, independent papal state in Rome, including Vatican and St. Peter's, established 1929 by Lateran Council; ~ *Council*, (1) council of 1869–70, (2) similar council held 1962–65; ~ *Hill*, hill in Rome on W. bank of Tiber, opposite ancient Rome. **vatī'cināte** *v.* Prophesy, foretell. **vatĭcĭnā'tion** *n.*

Vauban (vōbahṅ), Sébastien le Prestre de (1633–1707). Marshal of France and constructor of fortifications.

vau'deville (*or* vōdv-) *n.* Variety entertainment. [Fr., prob. f. earlier (*chanson du*) *Vau de Vire* (song of) valley of the Vire, Normandy]

Vaughan (vawn), Henry (1622–95). Metaphysical poet and mystic, of Welsh birth and parentage.

Vaughan Wi'lliams (vawn, -yamz), Ralph (1872–1958). English composer of symphonies, choral works, etc.

vault[1] (*or* vŏlt) *n.* Arched structure of masonry usu. supported by walls or pillars and serving as roof or carrying other parts of building; any arched surface resembling this, esp. apparently concave surface of sky; room or other part of building covered by vault, esp. when subterranean and used as cellar for storing food, wine, etc.; room of this kind without arched roof, underground room, strongroom; (partly) underground burial chamber in cemetery or under church. ~ *v.t.* Construct with, cover (as) with vault; form vault over; make in form of vault.

vault[2] (*or* vŏlt) *n.* Leap, spring, performed by vaulting. ~ *v.* Leap, spring, esp. while resting on the hand(s) or with help of pole; spring over thus.

vaunt *n.* (archaic or rhet.) Boast. ~ *v.* Boast, brag, (of). **vau'ntinglў** *adv.*

Vauxhall (vŏ'ks-hawl *or* -awl). District of London on S. bank of Thames, site of a famous pleasure garden 1661–1859. [orig. *Falkes' Hall*, f. 13th-c. owner *Falkes* de Breauté]

V.C. *abbrev.* Vice-Chancellor; Victoria Cross.

v.d. *abbrev.* Various dates.

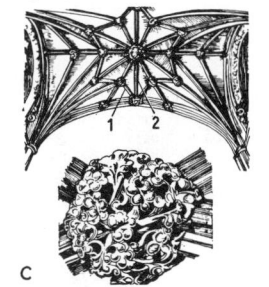

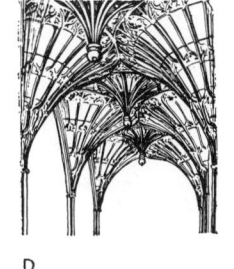

MEDIEVAL VAULTS: A. BARREL VAULT. B. GROINED CROSS-VAULT. C. RIBBED VAULT AND DETAIL OF BOSS. D. FAN VAULT
1. Lierne. 2. Ridge rib

V.D. *abbrev.* Venereal disease; Volunteer (Officer's) Decoration.

veal *n.* Calf's flesh as food.

vĕ′ctor *n.* 1. (math.) Quantity having both magnitude and direction. 2. (path.) Carrier of disease, esp. insect which conveys pathogenic organisms from one host to another. ~ *v.t.* (orig. U.S.) Direct (aircraft) on a course.

Ve′da (vā-) *n.* Ancient sacred literature of the Hindus; (esp.) the four collections of hymns known as the Rigveda, Yajurveda, Sāmaveda, and Atharvaveda. **Ve′dĭc** *adj.* [Sansk. *veda* (sacred) knowledge]

Vĕda′nta (-ahn-) *n.* 1. Final part of the Veda, the Upanishads. 2. Later system of monistic philosophy based on the Upanishads and taught principally by Śankara Ācārya. **Vĕda′ntĭc** *adj.* [Sansk. VEDA, *anta* end]

Vĕ′dda *n.* Aborigine of Sri Lanka.

Vee, vee *n.* Letter V, v.

veer *v.* Change direction, esp. (of wind) in clockwise direction; (of ship) turn with head away from wind, cause to turn thus; (fig.) change from one state, tendency, etc., to another, be variable.

vĕg (-j) *n.* (colloq.) Vegetable(s).

Vē′ga. (astron.) Brightest star in N. hemisphere, in constellation Lyra. [Arab. (*al nasr*) *al wāḳi'* 'the falling (vulture)', meaning the constellation Lyra]

Ve′ga Cär′pĭō (vā-), Lope Felix de (1562–1635). Spanish poet and playwright.

Vĕ′gan *n.* Vegetarian who eats no butter, eggs, cheese, or milk. ~ *adj.* Of Vegans or their diet.

vegă′nĭc *adj.* (esp., of manure) Containing vegetable organic matter only.

vĕ′gėtable *n.* Living organism belonging to plant kingdom, plant; (esp.) herbaceous plant cultivated for food. ~ *adj.* Of (the nature of) derived from, concerned with, comprising, plants; ~ *kingdom*, that division of organic nature to which plants belong; ~ *marrow*: see MARROW, 2.

vĕ′gėtal *adj.* Of (the nature of) plants; exhibiting, producing, phenomena of physical life and growth (usu. contrasted with *animal*).

vĕgėtār′ian *n.* One who eats no animal food, or none that is obtained by destruction of animal life. ~ *adj.* Of vegetarian(s); living on vegetables; consisting of vegetables. **vĕgėtār′ianism** *n.*

vĕ′gėtāte *v.i.* Grow as or like plant(s); (fig.) lead dull monotonous life without intellectual activity or social intercourse. **vĕ′gėtatĭvely** *adv.* **vĕ′gėtatĭveness** *n.*

vĕgėtā′tion *n.* 1. Vegetating; plants collectively, vegetable growths. 2. (path.) Morbid growth or excrescence on part of body.

ve′hement (vēi-) *adj.* Intense, violent, acting with great force; exhibiting, caused by, strong feeling or excitement. **ve′hementlỹ** *adv.* **ve′hemence** *n.*

ve′hicle (vēi-) *n.* 1. Carriage or conveyance for persons or goods, any means of transport, esp. by land. 2. Substance, usu. liquid, used as medium for application, administration, etc., of another substance, as drug; liquid in which pigment is suspended. 3. Thing, person, as means, channel, or instrument of expression, communication, etc. **vehi′cŭlar** (vĭhĭ-) *adj.*

Vehmgericht (fā′mgerĭχt) *n.* One of the secret tribunals having great power in Westphalia and elsewhere in Germany from end of 12th to middle of 16th c. [Ger., = 'secret court']

veil (vāl) *n.* 1. Piece of linen or other material as part of nun's head-dress, falling over head and shoulders; take the ~, become nun. 2. Piece of thin, usu. more or less transparent, material worn over head or face as part of head-dress or to conceal the face or protect it from sun, dust, etc.; curtain; (fig.) disguise, cloak, mask, anything which conceals or covers; *beyond the* ~, in(to) the next world; *draw a* ~ *over*, conceal, avoid discussing or dealing with. 3. Velum. ~ *v.t.* Cover (as) with veil; (fig.) conceal, disguise, mask. **vei′ling** *n.* (esp.) Material for veils, net.

vein (vān) *n.* 1. Each of the tubular vessels in which blood is conveyed from all parts of body back to heart (ill. BLOOD); (pop.) any blood-vessel. 2. (bot.) One of the slender bundles of tissue forming framework of leaf (ill. LEAF). 3. (entom.) Nervure of insect's wing (ill. INSECT). 4. Anything suggesting or resembling vein, esp. streak of different colour in wood, marble, etc., channel of water in ice etc.; (geol.) crack or fissure in rock, freq. filled with mineral matter; (min.) fissure containing metallic ore (ill. MINE²). 5. Distinctive character or tendency, cast of mind or disposition, mood. **vei′nlèss, vei′nỹ** *adjs.* **vein** *v.t.* Fill or cover (as) with vein(s). **vei′ning** *n.*

vėlā′men *n.* (pl. -*mĭna*). Enveloping membrane.

vĕ′lar *adj.* Of a velum, esp. velum of palate; (phon., of sound) formed with back of tongue near or touching soft palate. **vĕ′larīze** *v.t.* Pronounce with velar articulation.

Vėlă′zquez (-skwĭz *or* -skĭz) Diego Rodriguez de Silva y (1599–1660). Spanish artist, court painter to Philip IV.

veld (fĕlt) *n.* (S.Afr.) Fenced or unfenced grassland. [Afrikaans (formerly Du. *veldt*, = 'field')]

vĕllē′ĭtỹ *n.* Low degree of volition not prompting to action.

vĕ′llĭcāte *v.* Twitch, move convulsively. **vĕllĭcā′tion** *n.*

vĕ′llum *n.* Skin (strictly calfskin) dressed and prepared for writing, painting, etc.; imitations of this, esp. (commerc.) smooth-surfaced writing-paper.

vĕlŏ′cĭpĕde *n.* Any of various light vehicles propelled by riders, esp. early forms of bicycle and tricycle.

vĕlŏ′cĭtỹ *n.* Rapidity of motion, operation, or action; (mech.) time rate of change of position of body in a given direction; (loosely) (esp. high) speed; *actual* ~, speed at which a body moving on a curve actually moves as distinct from its *circular* ~ (speed at which it is moving round a point) and its *radial* ~ (speed at which it is moving away from or towards that point); *terminal* ~, maximum speed of falling object, when resistance of air equals pull of gravity.

vėlour, -ours (-oor′) *n.* Woven fabric with plush-like or velvety pile; felt with similar surface, used for hats; hat of this.

velskoen (fĕ′lskoon) *n.* Shoe of untanned hide, without nails, as used in S. Africa (Engl. *veldtshoe*). [Du. *vel* skin]

vē′lum *n.* (pl. -*la*). (anat., bot., zool.) Membrane or membranous partition; (esp.) soft PALATE (ill. HEAD and FUNGUS).

vĕ′lvėt *n.* Textile fabric having a dense smooth pile on one side formed by loops of additional weft-threads, the loops being usu. cut through during the weaving (ill. WEAVE); surface, substance, resembling this in softness or rich appearance, e.g. soft downy skin covering newly grown antlers of deer; *on* ~, in easy or advantageous position. ~ *adj.* Of, soft as, velvet; ~ *glove*, outward gentleness cloaking inflexibility. **vĕ′lvėtỹ** *adj.*

vĕ′lvėtee′n *n.* Cotton fabric resembling velvet; (pl.) velveteen trousers.

Ven. *abbrev.* Venerable.

vē′na căva (pl. -*ae -ae*). Each of two veins (*inferior* ~ and *superior* ~) conveying blood to right atrium of heart (ill. HEART).

vē′nal *adj.* (of person) That may be bribed, willing to lend support, exert influence, or sacrifice principles, from mercenary motive; (of action etc.) characteristic of venal person. **vē′nallỹ** *adv.* **vēnă′lĭtỹ** *n.*

vėnā′tion *n.* Arrangement of veins in a leaf or leaf-like organ.

vĕnd *v.* Sell (now rare exc. law); offer (esp. small articles) for sale, hawk; *vending machine*, (orig. U.S.) slot-machine. **vĕ′ndor** *n.*

vĕ′ndāce *n.* Small delicate freshwater fish (*Coregonus albula*), allied to trout, of some Scottish and English lakes.

Vendée (vahṅdā), La. Maritime department of W. France; *Wars of the* ~ (1793–6), insurrection of people of La Vendée against Republic. **Vĕndē′an** *adj. & n.*

Vendémiaire (vahṅdāmyār). 1st month of French revolutionary calendar, 22 Sept.–22 Oct. [L *vindemia* vintage]

vĕndĕ'tta *n.* Blood-feud, esp. one practised through generations, as in Corsica and parts of Italy.

vĕneer' *v.t.* Cover, overlay, (furniture etc.) with thin sheet of finer wood or other more beautiful or valuable material; (fig.) give merely specious or superficial appearance of some good quality to, gloss over. ~ *n.* Thin outer sheet used in veneering; (fig.) superficial appearance.

vĕ'nĕpŭncture, vĕ'nĭ- *n.* Puncture of vein, esp. by insertion of hollow needle for medical purposes or for extraction of blood specimen.

vĕ'nerable *adj.* Entitled to veneration on account of age, character, etc.; (in C. of E.) title of archdeacons; (in R.C. Ch.) title of one who has attained lowest of three degrees of sanctity but is not yet beatified or canonized; *V~ Bede*: see BEDE. **vĕnerabi'litў, vĕ'nerablenĕss** *ns.* **vĕ'nerablў** *adv.*

vĕ'nerāte *v.t.* Regard with feelings of respect and reverence; consider as exalted or sacred. **vĕnerā'tion** *n.*

vĕnēr'ĕal *adj.* Of, connected with, sexual desire or intercourse; (of disease) contracted by sexual intercourse with infected person; infected with venereal disease, as e.g. gonorrhoea or syphilis. [f. VENUS]

Vĕnē'tian (-shan) *adj.* Of Venice; ~ *blind,* window blind of horizontal slats that may be adjusted so as to admit or exclude light; ~ *glass,* decorative glassware made at Murano, near Venice, since 15th c., freq. very elaborate and sometimes fusing clear glass with opaque or with glass of various colours; ~ *lace,* one of several varieties of point lace; ~ *pearl,* imitation pearl made of solid glass; ~ *red,* reddish pigment consisting of ferric oxides; ~ *School,* school of painting centred in Venice in the 15th and 16th centuries, culminating in the work of Giorgione, Titian, Veronese, and Tintoretto; revival of this in 18th c.; ~ *window,* PALLADIAN window (ill. WINDOW). ~ *n.* Native, inhabitant, of Venice.

Vĕnĕzuē'la (-zwāla). S. Amer. republic on Caribbean Sea, formed 1830 after secession from the Republic of Colombia; capital, Caracas. **Vĕnĕzuē'lan** *adj.* & *n.* (Native, inhabitant) of Venezuela.

vĕ'ngeance (-jans) *n.* Avenging oneself on another, retributive or vindictive punishment, hurt or harm inflicted in revenge; *with a* ~, in an extreme degree, with great force or violence.

vĕ'ngeful (-jf-) *adj.* Seeking vengeance, disposed to revenge, vindictive. **vĕ'ngefullў** *adv.* **vĕ'ngefulnĕss** *n.*

vĕ'nial *adj.* (of sin or fault) Pardonable, excusable, not grave or heinous, (theol.) not MORTAL. **vĕ'niallў** *adv.* **vĕ'nialnĕss, vĕniā'litў** *ns.*

Vĕ'nice. (Ital. *Venezia*) Seaport of NE. Italy built on numerous islands in a lagoon of the Adriatic; formerly the chief European port for trade with the East, famous esp. for its beauty and (from 15th to 18th c.) as a centre of art; ~ *glass,* VENETIAN glass; ~ *treacle,* old antidote to poisonous bites compounded of many drugs mixed with honey, theriac; ~ *turpentine,* larch resin, used in painting.

venipuncture: see VENEPUNCTURE.

vĕ'nison (-nzn *or* -nĭzn) *n.* Deer's flesh as food.

Vĕnīzē'los (-zā-), Eleutherios (1864–1936). Greek statesman, born in Crete; several times prime minister of Greece between 1910 and 1933; supported Allied cause in the war of 1914–18 in opposition to king of Greece.

vĕ'nom *n.* Poisonous fluid secreted by certain snakes etc. and injected by biting or stinging; (fig.) bitter or virulent feeling, language, etc. **vĕ'nomous** *adj.* **vĕ'nomouslў** *adv.* **vĕ'nomousnĕss** *n.*

vĕ'nous *adj.* Of veins; veined; (of blood) having given up oxygen in capillaries and hence of dark-red colour, like blood contained in veins (opp. ARTERIAL). **vĕ'nōse** *adj.* (esp.) Having many or very marked veins. **vĕnō'sitў** *n.* (esp., med.) Condition in which arteries contain venous blood.

vĕnt[1] *n.* Opening or slit in garment, esp. slit in back of coat.

vĕnt[2] *n.* Hole or opening allowing passage out of or into confined space, as hole in top of barrel to admit air while liquid is drawn out, finger-hole in musical instrument etc.; anus, esp. of lower animals; (fig.) outlet, free passage, free play; ~*-hole,* vent. ~ *v.t.* Make vent in; give vent or free expression to.

vĕ'nter *n.* (anat.) Belly; protuberance or concave part of muscle or bone; (law) womb, mother.

vĕ'ntilāte *v.t.* Expose to fresh air, purify by air, oxygenate; cause air to circulate freely in (enclosed space); make public, discuss freely. **vĕntilā'tion** *n.*

vĕ'ntilātor *n.* (esp.) Contrivance, e.g. revolving fan, for ventilating building, ship, mine, etc.; opening in wall, freq. with grid, for same purpose.

Ventose (vahṅtōz). 6th month of French revolutionary calendar, 19 Feb.–20 Mar. [L *ventus* wind]

vĕ'ntral *adj.* Of the abdomen, abdominal; of the anterior or lower surface (opp. DORSAL). **vĕ'ntrallў** *adv.*

vĕ'ntricle *n.* (anat., zool.) Cavity of body, esp. cavity of heart from which blood is pumped into arteries (in mammals and birds, either of two such cavities; ill. HEART); one of series of communicating cavities in brain formed by enlargements of neural canal (ill. BRAIN). **vĕntrī'cūlar, vĕntrī'cŭlous** *adjs.*

vĕntrī'loquism, vĕntrī'loquў *ns.* Practice of speaking etc. without visible movement of the lips and in such a manner that the voice appears to come from some other person or object. **vĕntrīlō'quial, vĕntrī'loqui'stic, vĕntri'loquous** *adjs.* **vĕntrī'loquist** *n.* **vĕntrī'loquīze** *v.i.* [L *venter* belly, *loqui* speak]

vĕ'nture *n.* 1. Undertaking of a risk, risky undertaking; (archaic) property at stake, thing risked; *at a* ~, at random. 2. *V*~ *Scout,* member of senior branch of Scout Association. **vĕ'nturesome** *adj.* **vĕ'nturesomelў** *adv.* **vĕ'nturesomenĕss** *n.* **vĕ'nture** *v.* Dare; not be afraid, make bold *to* do, hazard (opinion etc.).

vĕ'nŭe *n.* (law) County, district, where jury is summoned to come for trial of case; (pop.) rendezvous.

vĕ'nŭle *n.* (anat.) Minute vein.

Vĕ'nus. 1. (Rom. myth.) Ancient Italian goddess, identified by the Romans with Aphrodite; ~ *de Milo*: see MILOS; *Mount of* ~, (palmistry) protuberance at base of the thumb; ~'s *comb,* annual of parsley family with comb-like fruit; marine snail (*Murex tenuisspina*) having rows of long spines on shell; ~'s *flytrap,* N. Amer. insectivorous plant (*Dionaea muscipula*); ~'s *hair,* delicate maidenhair fern; ~'s *slipper,* = LADY's slipper. 2. (astron.) 2nd planet in order of distance from sun, in orbit between Mercury and earth; the morning or evening star (ill. PLANET).

Vĕ'nusbĕ̄rg. Mountain, identified with Hörselberg in Thuringia, in the caverns of which, according to the Tannhäuser legend, Venus held her court.

verā'cious (-shus) *adj.* Speaking, disposed to speak, truth; true, accurate. **verā'ciouslў** *adv.* **verā'citў** *n.*

verā'nda, -dah (-da) *n.* Open roofed portico or gallery along side of house. [Hindi, f. Port. or Span. *varanda* railing]

vĕrb *n.* (gram.) Part of speech which expresses action, occurrence, or being.

vĕr'bal *adj.* 1. Of, concerned with, words; oral, not written; *verbatim;* ~ *note,* (diplomacy) unsigned note or memorandum as reminder of matter not of immediate importance. 2. Of (the nature of) a verb; ~ *noun,* noun derived from verb-stem and having some verbal constructions (as English nouns ending in *-ing*). **vĕr'ballў** *adv.*

vĕr'balism *n.* Verbal expression; predominance of merely verbal over real significance.

vĕr'balist *n.* One concerned with

[963]

words only, apart from reality or meaning.
vĕr′balize v.t. Make (noun etc.) into verb. **vĕrbalĭzā′tion** n.
verbā′tim adv. & adj. Word for word, in the exact words.
verbē′na n. Plant of genus V~ which comprises the vervains, esp. garden variety of this with blue, white, or crimson flowers.
vĕr′biage n. Needless abundance of words.
verbō′se adj. Using, expressed in, too many words. **verbō′sely** adv. **verbō′seness, verbŏ′sitў** ns.
verb. sap. Further explanation or statement is unnecessary. [abbrev. of L *verbum sat est sapienti* a word is sufficient for the wise]
Vercingĕ′torix. Gallic chief of the Arverni (occupants of the district now called Auvergne) in 52 B.C. in their war against Julius Caesar.
vĕr′dant adj. Green. **vĕr′dantly** adv. **vĕr′dancў** n.
vĕrd-ănti′que (-ēk) n. Ornamental green serpentine marble; green patina on bronzes, verdigris; (also *Oriental* ~) green porphyry. [OF, = 'antique green']
vĕr′derer n. (hist.) Judicial officer of royal forest, keeping forest assizes, etc.
Ver′di (vārdē), Giuseppe Fortunino Francesco (1813–1901). Italian composer of operas and church music.
vĕr′dict n. Decision of jury in civil or criminal cause on issue submitted to them; decision, judgement.
vĕr′digris (or -ēs) n. Green or greenish-blue deposit forming on copper or brass as a rust; copper acetate, obtained by action of dilute acetic acid on copper and used as pigment and mordant in dyeing. [OF *vert de Grece* green of Greece]
Verdŭn (vār-). Town and fortress on Meuse, NE. France, successfully held against the Germans in 1916.
vĕr′dure (-dyer) n. Fresh green colour of flourishing vegetation; green vegetation. **vĕr′durous** adj.
verge¹ n. 1. Extreme edge, brink, border; grass edging of path, flower-bed, etc. 2. (hist.) Area of 12 miles round king's court subject to jurisdiction of Lord High Steward (with ref. to his wand of office, see 3); (in 18th c.) precincts of Whitehall as place of sanctuary; (archit.) edge of tiles projecting over gable. 3. Wand, rod, carried before bishop, dean, etc., as emblem of office; shaft or spindle in various mechanisms, esp. of watch balance in old vertical escapement; (archit.) shaft of column. ~ v.i. Border *on*.
verge² v.i. Incline downwards or in specified direction.
vĕr′ger n. Official carrying rod or other symbol of office before dignitaries of cathedral, church, or university; one who takes care of interior of church and acts as attendant.
Vergil: see VIRGIL.
Verhaeren (-hār′en), Émile (1855–1916). Belgian poet.
vĕri′dical adj. Truthful, veracious. **vĕri′dicallў** adv.
vĕ′rifў v.t. Establish the truth or correctness of, examine for this purpose; (pass.) be proved true or correct by result, be borne out. **vĕ′rifiable** adj. **vĕrifĭabi′litў, vĕrifĭcā′tion** ns.
vĕ′rilў adv. (archaic) Really, in truth.
vĕrisimi′litūde n. Appearance of truth or reality; probability; apparent truth.
vĕ′ritable adj. Real, properly or correctly so called. **vĕ′ritablў** adv.
vĕ′ritў n. Truth; true statement; reality, fact.
vĕr′juice (-ōōs) n. Acid juice of crab-apples, unripe grapes, etc., used in cooking.
Verlaine (vārlĕn), Paul (1844–96). French lyric poet belonging to the Symbolist movement.
Vermeer′, Jan (1632–75). Dutch painter, of Delft.
vĕr′meil (-mĭl) n. Silver gilt; red varnish used to give lustre to gilding; orange-red garnet; (poet.) vermilion. ~ adj. (poet.) Vermilion.
vermĭcĕ′lli n. Pasta in long slender threads. [It., = 'little worms' (L *vermis* worm)]
vĕr′micide n. Substance used to kill (esp. intestinal) worms.
vermi′cūlar adj. Worm-like in form or movements; of worm-eaten appearance; marked with close wavy lines; (med.) of, caused by, intestinal worms.
vermi′cūlātĕd adj. Covered or ornamented with close wavy markings like those made by gnawing of worms or their sinuous movements (ill. MASONRY). **vermĭcūlā′tion** n.
vĕr′mifŏrm adj. Worm-shaped; ~ *appendix,* small worm-like blind tube extending from caecum in man and some other mammals (ill. ALIMENTARY).
vĕr′mifūge n. Substance that expels worms from intestines.
vermi′lion (-yon) n. Cinnabar; brilliant scarlet colour of this. ~ adj.. Of the colour of vermilion. ~ v.t. Colour (as) with vermilion.
vĕr′min n. (usu. collect.) Mammals and birds injurious to game crops, etc.; creeping or wingless insects etc. of noxious or offensive kind, esp. those infesting or parasitic on living beings or plants; noxious, vile, or offensive persons. **vĕr′minous** adj. (esp.) Infested with, full of, vermin; caused by vermin. **vĕr′minouslў** adv. **vĕr′minousnĕss** n.
Vermŏ′nt. New England State of U.S., admitted to Union in 1791; capital, Montpelier.
vĕr′mouth (-uth *or* -ōōth) n.

White wine flavoured with wormwood or other aromatic herbs, made esp. in France and Italy. [Fr., f. Ger. *wermuth* wormwood]
vernă′cūlar adj. (of language, idiom, word) Of one's own native country, native, indigenous, not of foreign origin or of learned formation. **vernă′cūlarlў** adv. **vernă′cūlarize** v.t. **vernă′cūlar** n. Vernacular language or dialect; homely speech.
vĕr′nal adj. Of, appropriate to, coming or happening in, spring; ~ *equinox*: see EQUINOX; ~ *grass,* kind of European grass (*Anthoxanthum odoratum*), sweet-smelling when dry and freq. grown for hay. **vĕr′nallў** adv.
vĕr′nalize v.t. Accelerate flowering by treatment of seed or seedlings. **vĕrnalĭzā′tion** n.
vernā′tion n. (bot.) Arrangement of leaves within leaf-bud.
Verne (vārn), Jules (1828–1905). French writer of science fiction, including 'Twenty Thousand Leagues under the Sea' etc.
vĕr′nicle n. Representation of Christ's face on sudarium of St. Veronica; any similar picture of Christ's face.
vĕr′nier n. Device consisting of graduated scale sliding along fixed scale, for measuring fractional parts of divisions of larger

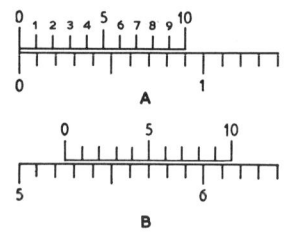

VERNIER SCALE

A. Main scale (lower) in units and tenths, with vernier (above) to read hundredths. B. Showing a reading of 5·25

scale. [after Pierre *Vernier* (1580–1637), French mathematician]
Verō′na. City of N. Italy.
Vĕ′ronal n. Hypnotic drug, diethylbarbituric acid ($C_8H_{12}N_2O_3$). [Ger. trade-name]
Vĕronē′se¹ (-z) adj. & n. (Native, inhabitant) of Verona.
Vĕronē′sĕ² (-nāzĭ). Paolo Cagliari (1528–88). Italian painter.
Verō′nĭca¹, St. Woman who, acc. to legend, wiped the sweat from the face of Christ on the way to Calvary (see SUDARIUM).
verō′nĭca² n. 1. Speedwell. 2. Vernicle. [f. VERONICA¹]
vĕrru′ca (-ōō-) n. Wart, wart-like formation or growth. **vĕ′rrucōse, vĕrru′cous** adjs.
Versailles (vārsī). Town SW. of Paris, which contains the royal palace built by Louis XIII and XIV; *Treaty of* ~, treaty which terminated the Amer. War of

[964]

VERSATILE

Independence in 1783; treaty signed on 28 June 1919 between Germany and the Allies which terminated the war of 1914-18.
vēr'satile *adj.* Turning easily or readily from one subject, occupation, etc., to another, showing facility in varied subjects, many-sided; (bot., zool.) turning, moving freely (as) on pivot or hinge. **vēr'satilely** (-l-li) *adv.* **versati'lity** *n.*
vērse *n.* 1. Words arranged according to rules of prosody and forming complete metrical line (now chiefly in ref. to Gk and Latin poetry). 2. Small number of metrical or rhythmical lines forming either a whole in themselves or a unit in a longer composition, stanza. 3. Metrical composition or structure; poetry esp. with ref. to metrical form as dist. from PROSE. 4. Each of the short sections into which the chapters of the Bible are divided. 5. Short sentence as part of liturgy; solo passage in anthem etc.
vērsed[1] (-st) *adj.* ~ *sine*, quantity obtained by subtracting cosine from unity.
vērsed[2] (-st) *adj.* Experienced, practised, skilled (*in* subject etc.).
vēr'sicle *n.* Each of a series of short sentences said or sung in liturgy, esp. sentence said by the minister or priest and followed by another (RESPONSE) from the people; (pl.) versicles and responses collectively.
vēr'sify *v.* Make verses; turn into, narrate in, verse. **versificā'tion** *n.*
vēr'sion *n.* 1. Rendering of work, passage, etc., into another language; particular form of statement, account, etc., given by one person or party. 2. (obstetrics) Turning of foetus in womb to facilitate delivery.
vers libre (vār lēbr). Free verse, verse with no regular metrical system and arranged in lines of irregular length, freq. unrhymed, but having certain rhythms. **versli'brist** (vārlē-) *n.*
vēr'sō *n.* Left-hand page of open book; back of leaf of book or manuscript (opp. RECTO); reverse of coin or medal.
vēr'sor *n.* (math.) In quaternions, factor expressing direction and amount of turning of vector.
vēr'sus *prep.* (abbrev. v.) Against.
vērt *n.* (her.) Green (ill. HERALDRY).
vēr'tebra *n.* (pl. *-ae*). Each of the bony segments composing the spinal column (ill. SPINE); (pl., loosely) backbone; *cervical vertebrae*, those of neck; *thoracic*, of ribs; *lumbar*, of loins; *sacral*, of hips; *caudal*, of tail. **vēr'tebral** *adj.* **vēr'tebrally** *adv.*
vēr'tebrāte *adj. & n.* (Animal) belonging to the Vertebrata, the division containing all animals having a cranium and a spinal column or a notochord and including mammals, birds, reptiles, amphibians, and fishes.
vērtebrā'tion *n.* Formation of, division into, vertebrae or similar segments.
vēr'tex *n.* (pl. usu. *-ices*). Top, highest part or point; top of the head; (math.) point opposite base of (plane or solid) figure, point where axis meets curve or surface, or where lines forming angle meet.
vēr'tical *adj.* Of, at, passing through, vertex or zenith, having position in heavens directly above given place or point; placed, moving, perpendicularly (ill. PERPENDICULAR); upright; of, at, affecting, vertex of the head; ~ *combine*, *trust*, one operating successive processes of manufacture or distribution of a product, as dist. from HORIZONTAL combine, trust; ~ *take-off*, (of aircraft) take-off directly upward (freq. attrib.). **vēr'tically** *adv.* **verticā'lity** *n.*, **vēr'tical** *n.* Vertical line, plane, or circle.
vēr'ticil *n.* (bot.) Number of similar organs or parts arranged in circle round axis. **vērti'cillate** *adj.* **vērti'cillately** *adv.*
vēr'tīgō (or -tī'-) *n.* Dizziness, condition with sensation of whirling and tendency to lose equilibrium. **verti'ginous** *adj.* Of vertigo; causing, tending to cause, giddiness. **verti'ginously** *adv.* **verti'ginousness** *n.*
vertu: see VIRTU.
Vertū'mnus. (Rom. myth.) Etruscan god.
Vē'rulam (-rōō-), **Verulā'mium.** Romano-British town whose modern name is St. Albans (Hertfordshire).
vēr'vain *n.* Common European herbaceous plant of genus *Verbena*, esp. *V. officinalis.*
vērve *n.* Vigour, enthusiasm, energy, esp. in literary work.
vēr'vet *n.* (also ~ *guenon*) Small greyish African monkey (*Cercopithecus aethiops pygerythrus*).
vē'ry *adj.* Real, true, genuine, properly so called or designated; *the* ~, used to emphasize identity, significance, extreme degree, etc. ~ *adv.* (used with adjs., advs., adjectival participles, but not other parts of verbs) In a high degree, to a great extent, extremely; ~ *well*, formula of consent or approval.
Vē'ry light (lit). Coloured flare fired from *Very pistol* esp. for night signalling or to provide temporary illumination in night-fighting. [invented by Lt S. W. *Very*, 1877]
vēsī'ca *n.* 1. (anat.) Bladder. 2. ~ *piscis*, pointed oval (O) used as an aureole in medieval art [L, = 'bladder of a fish']. **vē'sical** *adj.*
vē'sicāte *v.t.* Raise blisters on (skin etc.). **vē'sicant, vē'sicatory** *adjs. & ns.* (Substance) causing formation of blisters. **vesicā'tion** *n.*

VESTAL

vē'sicle *n.* Small bladder-like vessel, cavity, sac; (path.) small, usu. round, elevation of cuticle containing clear watery fluid. **vēsi'cūlar, vēsi'cūlate, -āted** *adjs.*
Vespā'sian (-zhan). Titus Flavius Vespasianus (A.D. 9–79), Roman emperor A.D. 70–79; began building the Colosseum.
Vē'sper. (poet.) = HESPERUS.
Vē'spers (-z) *n.pl.* (R.C. Ch.) Canonical HOUR; office said or sung towards evening, evensong; *vesper-bell*, bell that calls to Vespers; *Sicilian* ~: see SICILIAN.
vē'spertine *adj.* Of, taking place in, evening; (of animals etc.) appearing, active, (of flowers) blooming, in evening; (of star etc.) setting at or just after sunset.
Vēspu'cci (-ōōchē), Amerigo (1451–1512). Florentine merchant who settled in Spain; he claimed to have made a voyage in 1497 in which he discovered the mainland of S. America; in virtue of this claim, which has not been proved, his name was given to the continent of America.
vē'ssel *n.* 1. Hollow receptacle for liquid etc., esp. domestic utensil, freq. of circular section, used for preparing, storing, or serving food or drink; (bibl.) person regarded as containing or receiving some spiritual quality. 2. (anat., zool.) Membranous canal, duct, etc., in which body-fluids are contained or circulated, esp. artery or vein (*blood-~*); (bot.) woody duct carrying or containing sap etc., (rare) seed-vessel. 3. Any craft or ship, now usu. one larger than rowing-boat.
vēst[1] *n.* Waistcoat (now chiefly shop term and U.S.); knitted or woven undergarment for upper part of body; (also *vestee'*) part of front of woman's bodice etc., usu. piece of lace etc., filling opening at neck; ~-*pocket*, waistcoat pocket (chiefly attrib. of articles etc., as cameras) of small size.
vēst[2] *v.* 1. (chiefly pass.) Invest (person) *with* power, authority, etc.; put in full or legal possession of something, place or secure (something, freq. power or authority) in possession of person(s). 2. Become vested (*in* person), pass into possession of person(s). **vē'sted** *adj.* (esp. with *right*, *interest*) Established or secured in hands or under authority of certain person(s).
Vē'sta[1]. 1. (Rom. myth.) Goddess of hearth and household, daughter of Saturn, with temple in Rome whose sacred fire was tended by Vestal Virgins. 2. (astron.) One of minor planets or asteroids with orbit between Mars and Jupiter.
vēsta[2] *n.* Kind of short match, esp. with wax shaft. [f. VESTA[1]]
Vē'stal *adj.* 1. Of the goddess Vesta or the Vestal Virgins;

[965]

~ **Virgin**, (Rom. hist.) one of the (orig. 2, later 4, then 6) virgins consecrated to the service of Vesta and vowed to chastity. 2. *v*~, chaste, virgin. ~ *n.* Vestal Virgin; *v*~, chaste unmarried woman.

vĕ'stĭbūle *n.* 1. Antechamber, hall, lobby, between entrance door and interior of house or other building; porch of church etc. 2. (Gk & Rom. antiq.) Enclosed or partially enclosed space in front of main entrance of house. 3. (chiefly U.S.) Enclosed and covered-in entrance at end of railway coach giving access to carriage and usu. communicating with other coaches. 4. (anat.) Dilated entrance to a canal or cavity in the body; ~ *of inner ear*, cavity between middle ear and cochlea (ill. EAR¹); ~ *of mouth*, space between the lips and cheeks and the gums. **vĕstĭ'būlar** *adj.*

vĕ'stĭġe *n.* Trace, track, evidence (of something no longer existing or present); (biol.) organ or part which is small or degenerate in descendants but in ancestors was fully developed. **vĕstĭ'ġial** *adj.*

vĕ'stment *n.* Garment, esp. worn by king or official on ceremonial occasion; any of official garments of priests, choristers, etc., during divine service etc., esp. chasuble.

vĕ'strў *n.* Room or part of church used for keeping vestments, vessels, records, etc., for robing of clergy and choir, for parish meetings, etc.; (in English parishes) ratepayers of parish, representatives of these, assembled (freq. in vestry of parish church) for dispatch of parochial business; ~-*clerk*, clerk of such vestry; *ve'strўman*, member of parochial vestry.

Vĕsū'vĭus. Active volcano near Naples, Italy. **Vĕsū'vĭan** *adj.*

vĕt *n.* (colloq.) Veterinary surgeon. ~ *v.t.* Examine, treat (beast, person) medically; submit (scheme, work, etc.) to careful examination.

vĕtch *n.* Leguminous plant of *Vicia* (esp. *V. sativa*, common tare) or related genera, many of which are valuable for fodder; *kidney* ~, leguminous herb, *Anthyllis vulneraria*. **vĕ'tchlĭng** *n.* Any small plant of genus *Lathyrus*.

vĕ'teran *adj.* Grown old in service; experienced by long practice; (of army) composed of veteran troops; (of service) long-continued; ~ (*motor-*)*car*, early motor-car, (esp.) one built in or before 1904. ~ *n.* Veteran person, esp. soldier; (U.S.) ex-service man.

vĕ'terĭnarў *adj.* Of, for, concerned with (treatment of) diseases and injuries of cattle and other animals. **vĕ'terĭnarў, vĕterĭnār'ian** *ns.* Veterinary surgeon.

vē'tō *n.* Prohibition of proposed or intended act; (exercise of) constitutional right to prohibit passing or putting in force of an enactment or measure. ~ *v.t.* Exercise veto against. [L, = 'I forbid']

vĕx *v.t.* Anger by slight or petty annoyance, irritate; (archaic) grieve, afflict; (chiefly poet.) agitate, toss about, put into state of commotion.

vĕxā'tĭon *n.* Being vexed, irritation; vexing thing. **vĕxā'tĭous** (-shus) *adj.* **vĕxā'tĭouslў** *adv.* **vĕxā'tĭousnĕss** *n.*

vĕxed (-kst) *adj.* (esp.) ~ *question*, one much discussed or contested.

vĕxĭ'llum *n.* (pl. -*illa*). 1. (Rom. antiq.) Banner of Roman troops; body of troops under this 2. (eccles.) Small piece of linen or silk wound round upper part of crosier. 3. (bot.) Large upper petal of papilionaceous flower (ill. FLOWER). 4. (ornith.) Vane of feather. **vĕ'xĭllarў** *adj.*

v.f. *abbrev.* Very fair.
v.ġ. *abbrev.* Very good.
V.G. *abbrev.* Vicar-General.
V.H.F. *abbrev.* Very high FREQUENCY.

vī'a *prep.* By way of, through (specified place).

vī'able *adj.* Capable of maintaining separate existence (of child at birth etc.); able to live in particular environment; practicable; (bot., of seeds) having ability to germinate. **vĭabĭ'lĭtў** *n.* [Fr., f. *vie* life]

vī'adŭct *n.* Bridge-like structure carrying railway or road over valley, river, etc.

vī'al *n.* Small vessel for liquid medicines, now esp. small glass bottle.

vī'a mĕ'dĭa. Intermediate course between extremes. [L, = 'middle way']

vī'and *n.* (usu. pl.) Article(s) of food, provision(s), victual(s).

vĭā'tĭcum *n.* 1. Eucharist as administered to one (in danger of) dying. 2. (rare) Sum of money for travelling expenses, provisions for journey. [L, = 'travelling-money', f. *via* way]

vĭbrā'cŭlum *n.* (pl. -*la*). (zool.) Slender whip-like movable individual in some polyzoan colonies serving e.g. to prevent noxious material from settling.

vī'brant *adj.* Vibrating, thrilling, resonant. **vī'brantlў** *adv.* **vī'brancў** *n.*

vī'braphōne *n.* Percussion instrument with lids of resonators kept in constant motion by an electric current so as to produce a pulsating effect.

vībrā'te *v.* (Cause to) swing to and fro periodically, oscillate, quiver; set, be, in state of vibration; thrill; (of sound) strike ear with quivering or pulsating effect; (of pendulum) measure (seconds etc.) by vibration.

vī'bratĭle *adj.* Of vibration, vibratory; (of cilia etc.) capable of vibrating.

vībrā'tĭon *n.* (esp., phys.) Rapid reciprocating motion to and fro, up and down, etc., of particles of elastic body produced by

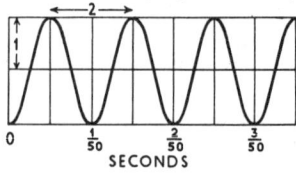

VIBRATION

1. Amplitude. 2. Wavelength or cycle. The frequency is 50 cycles per second. The wave traces a sine curve

CLERICAL VESTMENTS: A, B. BISHOP. C, D. PRIEST
1. Mitre. 2. Orphrey. 3. Morse. 4. Cope. 5. Crosier. 6. Chimere. 7. Rochet. 8. Surplice. 9. Tippet. 10. Cassock. 11. Hood. 12. Chasuble. 13. Alb. 14. Amice. 15. Maniple. 16. Stole

VEXILLUM

disturbance of its equilibrium. **vibrā'tional** *adj.*
vĭbra'tō (-ah-) *n.* (mus.) Effect akin to TREMOLO in singing and playing stringed instruments. [It.]
vībrā'tor *n.* Thing, person, that vibrates. **vī'bratorў** *adj.* Characterized by, causing, connected with, vibration; capable of vibrating.
vībrĭ'ssae *n.pl.* (anat., zool.) Stiff hairs about mouth of many animals (e.g. those in human nostrils, or whiskers of cat) freq. serving as organs of touch; bristle-like feathers about beak of some birds.
vībûr'num *n.* Shrub of widely distributed genus *V~* which includes guelder rose, laurustinus, wayfaring tree, etc.
vic *n.* V-shaped formation of aircraft in flight. [name of the letter V in the phonetic alphabet]
Vic. *abbrev.* Victoria.
vi'car *n.* 1. Earthly representative of God or Christ; (esp.) pope (*V~ of Christ*). 2. (in C. of E.) Parish incumbent formerly entitled to receive part (or none) of tithes of parish (cf. RECTOR); (loosely) perpetual curate; *~ choral*, clerical or lay assistant in some (esp. musical) parts of cathedral service; *~ general*, lay official assisting (arch)bishop in ecclesiastical causes etc.; (hist.) title given to Thomas Cromwell (1535) as king's representative in ecclesiastical affairs. 3. (in R.C. Ch.) One who represents another in ecclesiastical or religious matters, (esp.) bishop's deputy; *~ general*, bishop's representative in jurisdictional or administrative matters.
vi'carship *n.*
vi'carage *n.* Benefice, residence, of vicar.
vicār'ial *adj.* Of, serving as, a vicar.
vicār'ious *adj.* Deputed, delegated; acting, done, endured, for another; **vicār'iouslў** *adv.* **vicār'iousnèss** *n.*
vice[1] *n.* Evil, esp. grossly immoral, habit or conduct; depravity, serious fault; defect, blemish; fault, bad trick (of horse etc.).
vice[2] *n.* Tool with two jaws worked by screw for gripping

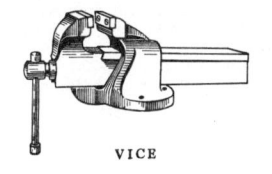

VICE

firmly and holding thing being worked upon by metal-worker, carpenter, etc.
vice[3] *n.* (colloq.) Vice-president, -chairman, -chancellor, etc., substitute, deputy.
vī'cè[4] *prep.* In the place of, in succession to.

vīce- *prefix.* Acting in place of, assistant, next in rank to.
vice-ă'dmiral *n.* Naval officer ranking next below admiral. **vice-ă'dmiraltў** *n.*
vice-cha'ncellor (-ah-) *n.* (esp., in universities) Acting representative of Chancellor, discharging most administrative duties. **vice-cha'ncellorship** *n.*
vicegĕ'rent (-sj-; *or* -jēr-) *n.* & *adj.* (Person) exercising delegated power, deputy. **vicegĕ'rencў** *n.*
vicĕnn'ial *adj.* Lasting, happening every, 20 years.
Vicĕ'ntè, Gil (*c* 1465-1536). Portuguese poet and playwright, sometimes called the Portuguese Shakespeare.
vice-rē'gent *n.* One acting in place of regent.
vī'cereine (-srän) *n.* Wife of viceroy.
vī'ceroy (-sr-) *n.* 1. Person acting as governor of country, province, etc., in name and by authority of supreme ruler; (hist.) representative of British Crown in India. 2. Handsome red-and-black Amer. butterfly, *Limenitis archippus.* **vicerē'gal, viceroy'al** *adjs.* **viceroy'altў** *n.*
vī'cè vēr'sa. The other way round, conversely.
Vichy (vēshi). Town in central France noted for mineral waters; *~ Government,* French Government, with headquarters at Vichy, which administered S. part of France (*~ France*) and collaborated with Germans after Franco-German armistice of 1940; *~ water,* effervescent mineral water from Vichy, freq. bottled.
vichyssoi'se (-shǐswahz) *n.* Cream soup of potatoes and leeks.
vī'cinage *n.* Neighbourhood, surrounding district; being or living near others, relation of neighbours.
vī'cinitў *n.* Surrounding district; nearness in place; close relationship; *in the ~ (of),* in the neighbourhood (of).
vī'cious (-shus) *adj.* 1. Of the nature of, addicted to, vice; evil; depraved. 2. (of language, reasoning, etc.) Incorrect, faulty, unsound, corrupt; intensifying its own causes; *~ circle:* see CIRCLE. 3. Having vices (esp. of horses); bad-tempered, spiteful. **vī'cious**l**ў** *adv.* **vī'ciousnèss** *n.*
vici'ssitūde *n.* Change of circumstances, esp. of condition or fortune.
Vĭ'cksbûrg. Town in Mississippi, on the Mississippi River, where, in 1863, the Federal forces under Grant besieged the Confederates, who surrendered on 4 July; this victory and Gettysburg marked the turning-point in the Amer. Civil War.
Vī'cō (vē-), Giovanni Battista (1668-1744). Italian philosopher, jurist, and historian.
vī'ctim *n.* Living creature sacrificed to a deity or in per-

formance of religious rite; person who is killed or made to suffer by cruel or oppressive treatment; (loosely) one who suffers injury, hardship, loss, etc.
vī'ctimīze *v.t.* Cause to suffer inconvenience, discomfort, annoyance, etc.; cheat, defraud; treat unjustly or with undue harshness, esp. by dismissal as result of strike. **victimīzā'tion** *n.*
vī'ctor *n.* (rhet.) Conqueror in battle or contest.
Vī'ctor Emmă'nūel (ĭ-). Name of three kings of Sardinia, two of whom became kings of Italy: *Victor Emmanuel I* (1759-1824), king of Sardinia 1802-21; *Victor Emmanuel II* (1820-78), first king of Italy 1861-78; *Victor Emmanuel III* (1869-1947), king of Italy 1900-46.
Victōr'ia[1] (1819-1901). Daughter of Edward, Duke of Kent, 4th son of George III; queen of Great Britain and Ireland 1837-1901; empress of India 1877-1901; married Prince Albert of Saxe-Coburg-Gotha, 1840; *Lake ~,* largest lake in Africa and chief reservoir of the Nile; *Order of ~ and Albert,* order of chivalry, instituted 1862; *~ and Albert Museum,* British national museum founded 1852 as a 'Museum of Ornamental Art', renamed by Queen Victoria after herself and her consort when she laid the foundation stone of its new building in South Kensington in 1899; *~ Cross,* (abbrev. V.C.) decoration awarded for conspicuous bravery to members of British and Commonwealth armed forces, first instituted by Queen Victoria in 1856 and struck from metal of guns captured at Sebastopol during the Crimean War; it consists of a cross paty of bronze with the Royal Crown surmounted by a lion in the centre, and, beneath, the inscription 'For Valour' (ill. MEDAL); *~ Falls,* waterfall on the Zambezi, discovered by David Livingstone in 1855.
Victōr'ia[2]. State of SE. Australia; capital, Melbourne.
Victōr'ia[3]. Capital of British Columbia, Canada, and principal city of Vancouver Island.
victōr'ia[4] *n.* 1. Light low four-wheeled carriage with collapsible hood, seats for (usu.) two

VICTORIA

passengers and raised driver's seat. 2. Gigantic water-lily of S. Amer. genus *V~*, with leaves sometimes 1·6 m in diameter. 3. Variety of large red luscious plum. [f. VICTORIA[1]]

[967]

Victō̄r′ian *adj.* Of, living in, characteristic of, the reign of Queen VICTORIA[1]; *Royal ~ Order*, order founded in 1896 by Queen Victoria and awarded for personal service to the sovereign. *~ n.* Person living in the reign of Queen Victoria.
vi′ctorine (-ēn) *n.* (hist.) Woman's fur tippet fastening in front with two loose ends hanging down.
victō̄r′ious *adj.* Triumphant, successful in contest or struggle; marked by, producing, victory. **victō̄r′iouslȳ** *adv.* **victō̄r′iousnèss** *n.*
vi′ctorȳ *n.* Supremacy achieved by battle or in war, defeat of enemy; triumph or ultimate success in any contest or enterprise.
victual (vĭ′tl) *n.* (usu. pl.) Food, provisions. *~ v.* Supply with victuals; lay in supply of victuals; eat.
victualler (vĭ′tler) *n.* Purveyor of victuals or provisions, esp. (*licensed ~*), keeper of public house, licensed to sell food and esp. drink for consumption on the premises; ship employed to carry stores for other ships.
vicuġna, -uña (-ōō′nya) *n.* S. Amer. mammal (*Vicugna vicugna*) of N. Andes, related to llama and alpaca, and with fine silky wool used for textiles; soft cloth made of this, imitation of it.
vĭ′dē (*or* vē′dā) *v.imp.* (as direction to reader) Refer to, consult. [L]
vĭde′lĭcĕt (-dā-) *adv.* (abbrev. *viz.*) That is to say, namely. [L]
vĭ′dēō *n.* (U.S.) Television; *~ recording*, *.tape*, recording, record on magnetic tape, of television programme.
vie *v.i.* (pres. part. *vȳ′ing*). Contend or compete for superiority in some respect (*with*), be rivals.
Vĭē′nna. (Ger. *Wien*) Capital of Austria; *Congress of ~*, conference (1814–15) of European statesmen which readjusted territories and governments throughout Europe after the Napoleonic Wars. **Vĭēnnē′se** (-z) *adj. & n.*
Vĭē′nne. Town in SE. France; scene of Oecumenical Council held 1311–12 when Pope Clement V suppressed the Knights TEMPLAR.
Vĭĕtnă′m. Country in SE. Asia, formed 1945 from the Tongking, Annam, and Cochin-China provinces of French Indo-China; since 1954 divided into *Democratic Republic of ~* (*= North ~*), capital Hanoi, and *Republic of ~* (*= South ~*), capital Saigon. **Vĭĕtnamē′se** (-z) *adj. & n.*
view (vū) *n.* Inspection by eye or mind; inspection by jury of place, property, etc., concerned in case; power of seeing, range of physical or mental vision; what is seen, scene, prospect; picture etc. representing this; mental survey, mental attitude; *in ~ of*, having regard to, considering; *on ~*, open to inspection; *point of ~*, position from which thing is viewed, way of looking at a matter; *private ~*, view of exhibition open only to invited guests, usu. on day before public opening; *with a ~ to*, for the purpose of, as a step towards; with an eye to, in the hope of getting; *view′finder*, attachment to camera showing view in range of camera lens; similar device used by painters; *~-halloo′*, shout of huntsman on seeing fox break cover; *view′point*, point of view. *~ v.t.* Survey with eyes or mind, form impression or judgement of.
view′er (vū′er) *n.* (esp.) One who watches television broadcast.
vĭ′ġil *n.* Keeping awake during usual time for sleep; eve of a festival, esp. eve that is a fast; watch kept on this; nocturnal service; (pl.) prayers at such service, esp. for the dead; *keep ~*, keep watch.
vĭġilance *n.* Watchfulness against danger or action of others, caution, circumspection; *~ committee*, (U.S.) self-appointed committee for maintenance of justice and order, esp. for summary punishment of crime when processes of law are considered inadequate. **vĭ′ġilant** *adj.* **vĭ′ġilantlȳ** *adv.*
vĭġilā′ntē *n.* (orig. U.S.) Member of vigilance committee.
vĭġnĕ′tte (vēny-) *n.* Decorative design, usu. small, on blank space in book, having edges shading off into surrounding paper; photograph with edges shading off into background; (fig.) character sketch or short description. *~ v.t.* Make vignette of esp. by shading off or softening away edges. [Fr., = 'little vine', ornamental design at end of chapter]
Vĭġny (vēnyē), Alfred de (1797–1863). French lyric poet, dramatist, and novelist, early leader of the Romantic movement.
vĭ′gour (-er) *n.* Active physical strength or energy; flourishing physical condition, vitality; mental or moral strength, force, or energy. **vĭ′gorous** *adj.* **vĭ′gorouslȳ** *adv.* **vĭ′gorousnèss** *n.*
Vī′king *adj. & n.* (One) of the Scandinavians during the period (8th–11th centuries) when they became active as traders esp. between Russia and W. Europe, and also took to piracy, plundering and temporarily occupying many of the coastal districts and river valleys of N. and W. Europe.
vila′yĕt (-lah-) *n.* Province or main administrative division of Turkey.
vīle *adj.* Despicable on moral grounds, base, depraved; worthless, of poor or bad quality; disgusting, filthy; shameful. **vī′lelȳ** (-l-lĭ) *adv.* **vī′lenèss** *n.*
vĭ′lifȳ *v.t.* Defame, traduce, speak evil of.

vĭ′lipĕnd *v.t.* (literary) Disparage, vilify.
vi′lla *n.* 1. (hist., esp. Roman) Country estate with house(s), farm(s), etc. 2. Italian country house. 3. Small house, detached or semi-detached, in suburban or residential district. **vi′lladom** *n.* Suburban villas or their residents; the comfortable or smug middle-class world. [L *villa* farmhouse]
vi′llaġe *n.* Assemblage of houses etc. in country district, larger than hamlet and smaller than town; (U.S.) small municipality with limited corporate powers. **vi′llaġer** *n.* Inhabitant of village (usu. implying rusticity).
vi′llain (-an) *n.* Person guilty or capable of great wickedness, scoundrel; character in play, novel, etc., whose evil motives or actions are important element of plot; (colloq., playful) rascal, scamp. **vi′llainȳ** *n.*
vi′llainous (-an-) *adj.* Worthy of a villain, wicked, vile; (colloq.) abominably bad. **vi′llainouslȳ** *adv.* **vi′llainousnèss** *n.*
villanĕ′lle *n.* Poem usu. of five three-line stanzas and final quatrain, with two rhymes throughout, the 1st and 3rd lines of the 1st stanza being repeated alternately as refrain in other stanzas and as final couplet in the quatrain.
vi′llein (-lĭn) *n.* (hist., in feudal system) Peasant cultivator entirely subject to a lord or attached to a manor. **vi′lleinaġe** *n.* Tenure of villein; being a villein, serfdom.
Villiers de l'Isle-Adam (vēlyā, lĕl-ahdahṅ), Philippe August Mathia, Comte de (1838–89). French Symbolist poet, dramatist, and novelist.
Villon (vēyawṅ), François (1431–*c* 1463). French lyric poet, writer of ballades and rondeaux.
vi′llōse, vi′llous *adjs.* Covered with (numerous close slender projections resembling) thickset hairs.
vi′llus *n.* (pl. *-lī*). (bot.) Long slender soft hair; (anat., zool.) slender hair-like projection, esp. of small intestine.
Vi′lnius. (also *Vĭ′lna*) Capital city of Lithuania.
vĭm *n.* (colloq., orig. U.S.) Vigour, energy.
vĭmi′nèous *adj.* Made of pliable twigs or wickerwork; (bot.) producing long flexible shoots or twigs.
vĭnaigrĕ′tte (-nĭg-) *n.* 1. Small ornamental bottle holding aromatic salts etc., smelling-bottle. 2. (also *~ sauce*) Sauce of oil, vinegar, etc., used esp. with salads.
Vi′ncent de Paul, St. (1576–1660). French Roman Catholic reformer, founder of 'Congregation of Priests of the Mission', a missionary society now usu. known as the Lazarists, and of a society of 'Sisters of Charity'. **Vĭncĕ′ntian** (-shan) *adj. & n.* (Member) of society founded by Vincent de Paul.

[968]

vi′nculum *n.* (math.) Straight line drawn over two or more terms denoting that these are subject to the same operations of multiplication, division, etc., by another term; (anat.) ligament, frenum. [L, = 'bond']

vi′ndicate *v.t.* Maintain the cause of (person, religion, etc.) successfully; establish the existence or merits or justice of (one's veracity, courage, conduct, character, assertion). vindica′tion *n.*

vi′ndicatory *adj.* Tending to vindicate; (of laws) punitive.

vindi′ctive *adj.* Revengeful, avenging, given to revenge; ~ *damages,* damages awarded not only to compensate plaintiff but also to punish defendant. vindi′ctively *adv.* vindi′ctiveness *n.*

vine *n.* Trailing or climbing woody-stemmed plant of genus *Vitis* (esp. *V. vinifera,* from the fruit of which wine is made) bearing grapes, grape-vine; any trailing or climbing plant.

vi′negar *n.* Sour liquid (dilute acetic acid) produced by acetous fermentation of wine, malt liquors, etc., and used as condiment, preservative, etc. vi′negary *adj.* Sour like vinegar, acid. vi′negar *v.t.* Season, treat, with vinegar. [OF *vin* wine, *aigre* sour]

vi′nery *n.* Glass-house for growing grapes.

vi′neyard (-ny-) *n.* Plantation of grape-vines, esp. for wine-making.

vingt-et-un (vănt ā ŭṅ) *n.* Card-game in which players' object is to obtain from dealer cards with values adding up to 21. [Fr., = 'twenty-one']

Vi′nland. Region of N. America, probably near Cape Cod, where a settlement was made in the 11th c. by Norsemen under Leif Ericsson. [f. legend that grape-vines were found there]

vi′no de pa′sto (vē-). Table wine, medium pale dry sherry. [Span., = 'wine for a meal']

vin ordinaire (văṅ, -āṙ). Cheap usu. red wine for ordinary use, usu. drunk when young.

vi′nous *adj.* Of, like, due to, addicted to, wine. vi′nously *adv.* vi′nousness *n.*

vi′ntage *n.* (Season of) grape-harvest; wine, esp. of good quality: wine made from grapes of particular district (freq. used with ref. to the age of a wine or the year when it was made; also used *attrib.* and *transf.*); ~ (*motor-*)*car,* motor-car built between 11 Nov. 1918 and 31 Dec. 1930. vi′ntager *n.* Grape-harvester.

vi′ntner *n.* Wine-merchant.

vi′nyl *n.* 1. (chem.) Univalent radical (CH$_2$CH) derived from ethylene, forming the basis of many plastics. 2. Synthetic material made from a vinyl compound.

vi′ol *n.* Late-medieval stringed musical instrument (now again in use), similar in shape to violin, but usu. with six strings and held downwards on or between the knees; ~ *da gamba, d'amore*: = VIOLA da gamba, d'amore.

vi′ola¹ *n.* Herbaceous plant of genus *V*~ which includes violets and pansies; hybrid garden-plant of this genus, more uniformly and delicately coloured than pansy. [L, = 'violet']

vio′la² *n.* 1. Member of violin family of musical instruments, slightly larger than violin, of lower pitch (its lowest note being C below middle C) and with less bright quality of tone (ill. STRINGED). 2. ~ *da gamba,* bass viol; ~ *d'amore,* tenor viol with sympathetic strings under finger-board, having very sweet affecting tone.

A. VIOLA D'AMORE. B. VIOLA DA GAMBA. C. BOW

violā′ceous (-shus) *adj.* (bot.) Of the violet family (Violaceae).

vi′olate *v.t.* Break (agreement, law, oath, etc.); treat profanely, break in upon (sanctuary, privacy, etc.); rape. violā′tion *n.*

vi′olence *n.* Violent treatment or conduct, outrage, injury; violent feeling or language, vehemence; intensity (*of*); (law) (intimidation by threat of) unlawful exercise of physical force.

vi′olent *adj.* Involving, caused by, acting with, great physical force or unlawful exercise of force; intense in force, effect, feelings, etc. vi′olently *adv.*

vi′olet *n.* 1. Plant of genus *Viola,* esp. (also *sweet* ~) the sweet-scented *V. odorata,* with purplish-blue, mauve, or white flowers; similar plant of various other genera. 2. Purplish-blue colour of the violet, colour at opposite end of spectrum from red. ~ *adj.* Of the colour violet.

violi′n *n.* Stringed musical instrument held under chin with left hand and played with bow or occas. by plucking (ill. STRINGED), having a resonant curvilinear sound-box of polished wood over which are stretched four strings tuned in fifths, the lowest note being G below middle C; part for violin in instrumental composition, player of this; *first* ~, violin player performing FIRST part; leader of such players; leader of string quartet; *second* ~, violin player performing SECOND part; ~ *family,* group of instruments including violin, viola, violoncello, and double bass. violi′nist *n.* Player of violin. [It. *violino* little VIOLA²]

vi′olist *n.* Player of viol.

violonce′llo (-chĕ-) *n.* (pl. *-os*). (usu. abbrev. *cello*) Large instrument of violin family played supported on floor between performer's knees, normally taking bass part in string ensembles but having very wide range (ill. STRINGED). violonce′llist *n.* (usu. abbrev. *cellist*) Player of violoncello. [It., dim. of *violone* double bass, f. VIOLA²]

V.I.P. *abbrev.* Very important person.

vi′per *n.* Venomous snake of family Viperidae, esp. adder; (fig.) malignant or treacherous person; ~*'s bugloss*: see BUGLOSS; ~*'s grass,* arrow-leaved yellow-flowered perennial herb (*Scorzonera hispanica*) with long thick edible root. vi′perine, vi′perish, vi′perous *adjs.*

virā′go (*or* -ah-) *n.* (pl. *-os*). Turbulent woman, termagant. [L, = 'female warrior', f. *vir* man]

vīr′al *adj.* (of disease) Caused by a VIRUS.

Virchow (fēṙ′kō), Rudolf (1821–1902). German pathologist and anthropologist; author of 'Cellular Pathology' (1858).

vi′relay *n.* (hist.) Short lyric poem of a kind which originated (14th c.) in France, consisting of short lines arranged in stanzas with only two rhymes, the end-rhyme of one stanza being the chief rhyme of the next.

vire′scence *n.* Greenness, esp. (bot.) in petals etc. normally of some other colour. vire′scent *adj.*

vīr′gate *n.* (hist.) English land-measure, usu. ¼ of a hide.

Vīr′gil. Publius Vergilius Maro (70–19 B.C.), Roman poet, whose chief works were the 'Aeneid', the epic poem of the Roman people, recounting the adventures of Aeneas and his Trojans; the 'Georgics', a didactic poem on agriculture and rearing of cattle and bees; the 'Eclogues' or 'Bucolics', pastoral poems. Virgi′lian *adj.* Of, in the style of, Virgil.

vīr′gin *n.* 1. Person, esp. woman, who has had no sexual intercourse; (eccles.) in early Christian times, unmarried or chaste woman distinguished for piety and steadfastness in religion. 2. (*Mary*) *the V*~, *the* (*Blessed*) *V*~ (*Mary*): see MARY¹; image or picture representing her. 3. *the V*~: see VIRGO. 4. ~ *birth,* (esp.) doctrine that Jesus Christ was born to the Virgin

Mary having no human father but conceived by the power of the Holy Spirit; ~'s bower, traveller's joy or other species of plant *Clematis*. ~ *adj*. That is a virgin; of, befitting, a virgin; spotless, not yet or not previously touched, handled, or employed; (of metal) made from ore by smelting; ~ *forest*, forest as yet untouched by man; *V*~ *Queen*, Elizabeth I of England; ~ *rock*, rock not yet cut into or quarried; ~ *soil*, soil not yet brought into cultivation etc. **vīrgi'nitў** *n*. Condition or quality of a virgin.
vīr'ginal *adj*. Being, befitting, belonging to, a virgin. **vīr'ginally** *adv*. **vīr'ginal** *n*. (freq. pl.) Keyboard instrument, earliest (16th

VIRGINAL
A form of spinet. Italian, about 1570. Length 5' 3"

and 17th centuries) and simplest form of harpsichord, with one string to a note, in box or case, usu. without legs.
Virgi'nia. South Atlantic State of U.S., one of the original thirteen States of the Union (1788), and site of first English settlement (1607) in America; capital, Richmond; ~ *creeper*, N. Amer. climbing plant *Parthenocissus quinquefolia*, cultivated for ornament; ~ *reel*, (U.S.) country-dance, called in England 'Sir Roger de Coverley'; ~ *tobacco*, variety of toacco grown in Virginia; any American tobacco. **Virgi'nian** *adj*. & *n*. [named in honour of Elizabeth I of England (VIRGIN Queen)]
Vīr'gin I'slands (īlandz) Group of about 100 small islands in W. Indies, mostly uninhabited; divided between Britain (with capital Road Town) and U.S. (with capital Charlotte Amalie).
Vīr'gō. The Virgin, a constellation; 6th sign (♍) of the zodiac, which the sun enters about 23 Aug. **Vīrgō'an** *adj*. & *n*.
viridě'scent *adj*. Greenish, somewhat green. **viridě'scence** *n*.
viri'dian *n*. 1. Yellowish-green colour. 2. Chromium oxide, an emerald-green pigment. ~ *adj*. Of the colour viridian.
viri'ditў *n*. Greenness, esp. of foliage or grass; mental or bodily freshness.
vi'rile *adj*. Of, characteristic of, a man; capable of procreation; having masculine vigour or strength. **viri'litў** *n*.
vīrō'logў *n*. Study of viruses. **vīrō'logist** *n*.
vīrtu', vĕrtu' (-ōō) *n*. (archaic) Love or knowledge of, taste for, the fine arts; *article, object, of* ~,

curio, antique, or other product of the fine arts.
vīr'tūal *adj*. That is so in essence or effect, although not formally or actually; ~ *focus*, (optics) apparent focus of reflected or refracted rays of light. **vīr'tūallў** *adv*. **vīrtūă'litў** *n*.
vīr'tūe *n.* Moral excellence, uprightness, goodness; a particular moral excellence, moral quality regarded as of special excellence or importance; chastity, esp. of women; good quality or influence, efficacy; *by, in,* ~ *of,* on the strength or ground of; (pl.) order of angels (see ANGEL). [L *virtus* worth, valour, f. *vir* man]
vīrtūō'sō (*or* -zō) *n*. (pl. *-si* pr. -sē). Person with special interest in or knowledge of works of art or virtu; person skilled in technique of an art, esp. of performance on musical instrument. **vīrtūō'sitў** *n*. [It. *virtuoso* learned, skilled, f. L *virtus* (see VIRTUE)]
vīr'tūous *adj*. Possessing, showing, moral rectitude; chaste. **vīr'tūouslў** *adv*. **vīr'tūousness** *n*.
vi'rŭlent (*or* -rōō-) *adj*. Poisonous; malignant, bitter; (of disease) extremely violent. **vi'rŭlentlў** *adv*. **vi'rŭlence** *n*.
vīr'us *n*. 1. Organic particle, much smaller than bacteria or other classifiable micro-organisms, existing only within cells of animal and plant bodies and capable of producing various diseases. 2. Poisonous substance, the product of disease, found in the tissues and body-fluids. 3. (fig.) Moral poison, malignity. [L, = 'poison']
vīs *n*. Force, strength; ~ *iněr'tiae* (-shiī), inertia, tendency to remain inactive. [L]
Vis. *abbrev.* Viscount.
visa (vē'za) *n*. Endorsement on passport permitting holder to enter or cross a particular country. ~ *v.t*. Mark with visa.
vi'sage (-z-) *n*. (now chiefly literary) Face.
vis-à-vis (vēz-ah-vē') *n*. Either of two persons or things facing or situated opposite each other. ~ *prep.* & *adv*. Over against, in comparison with; facing, face-to-face (with).
Visc. *abbrev.* Viscount.
viscacha : see VIZCACHA.
vi'scera *n.pl*. Internal organs of principal cavities of animal body, as intestines, heart, liver, etc. **vi'sceral** *adj*.
vi'scid *adj*. Glutinous, sticky. **vīsci'ditў** *n*.
vi'scōse *n*. Highly viscous solution of cellulose compound obtained by treating wood-pulp or cotton fibre with caustic soda and carbon disulphide, used in manufacture of rayon etc.
viscō'sitў *n*. Quality, degree, of being viscous; (phys.) body's property of resisting alteration in position of its parts relative to each other.
vi'scount (vīk-) *n*. Member

of 4th order of British peerage, between earl and baron; courtesy title of earl's eldest son. **vi'scountcў, vi'scountў** *ns*.
vi'scountess *n*. Wife or widow of viscount; peeress of 4th order of nobility.
vi'scous *adj*. Glutinous, gluey, sticky; having viscosity; intermediate between solid and fluid, adhesively soft. **vi'scouslў** *adv*. **vi'scousness** *n*.
vi'scus *n*. (anat.) Internal organ (sing. of VISCERA).
visé (vē'zā) *n*. & *v.t.* = VISA.
Vi'shnu (-ōō). (Hinduism) One of the principal deities, identified by his worshippers with the supreme deity and regarded as saviour of the world. **Vi'shnuism** *n*.
vi'sible (-z-) *adj*. Capable of being seen; that can be seen at particular time, under certain conditions, etc.; in sight; that can be perceived or observed, apparent, open, obvious. **vi'siblў** *adv*. **visibi'litў** *n*. (esp.) Conditions of light, atmosphere, etc., as regards distinguishing of objects by sight; possibility of seeing, range of vision, under such conditions.
Vi'sigŏth (-z-) *n*. West Goth, one of that branch of Goths which entered Roman territory towards end of 4th c. and subsequently established in Spain a kingdom overthrown by the Moors in 711–12. **Visigŏ'thic** *adj*.
vi'sion *n*. 1. Act or faculty of seeing, sight; perception of things by means of the light coming from them which enters the eye. 2. Power of discerning future conditions, sagacity in planning, foresight. 3. Thing, person, seen in dream or trance; supernatural apparition, phantom; thing, esp. of attractive or fantastic character, seen vividly in the imagination; person, sight, of unusual beauty. 4. Television picture (see PICTURE).
vi'sionarў *adj*. Given to seeing visions or indulging in fanciful theories; seen (only) in a vision, existing only in imagination; unreal, fantastic, unpractical. ~ *n*. Visionary person.
vi'sit (-z-) *v.t.* Go, come, to see (person, place, etc.) as act of friendship or social ceremony, on business, from curiosity, for official inspection, etc.; (of disease, calamity, etc.) come upon, attack; (bibl.) punish (person, sin), avenge (sins etc.) *upon* person, comfort, bless, (person *with* salvation etc.); *visiting-card*, small card of introduction giving person's name, address, etc., left in making call etc. ~ *n*. Call on a person or at a place; temporary residence with a person or at a place; occasion of going *to* doctor, dentist, etc., for examination or treatment, doctor's professional call on patient; formal or official call for purpose of inspection etc.

[970]

vi′sitant (-z-) *n.* 1. Migratory bird, as temporarily frequenting particular locality. 2. (poet., rhet.) Visitor. 3. V~ member of the VISITATION Order.

visitā′tion (-z-) *n.* 1. Official visit of inspection etc., esp. bishop's inspection of churches of his diocese. 2. (colloq.) Unduly protracted visit or social call. 3. Boarding of vessel belonging to another State to learn her character and purpose (*right of* ~, right to do this, not including right of search). 4. Divine dispensation of punishment or reward, notable experience, esp. affliction, compared to this. 5. V~ (*of Our Lady*), visit of Virgin Mary to her cousin Elizabeth (Luke 1: 39); day, 2 July, commemorating this; *V~ Order*, order of nuns founded in 1610, now concerned esp. with education. 6. (zool.) Unusual or large migration of animals.

vi′sitor (-z-) *n.* One who visits; esp., one with right or duty of supervision (usu. exercised periodically) over university, college, school, or the like; ~*s' book*, book in which visitors to a place enter their names.

vi′sor (-z-), **vi′zor** *n.* 1. (hist.) Movable front part of helmet, covering face, and with openings for seeing and breathing (ill. ARMOUR). 2. (hist.) Mask. 3. (U.S.) Peak of cap. 4. Movable shield fixed inside motor vehicle above windscreen to protect eyes from sunlight or glare; (usu. tinted) screen shading windscreen outside.

vi′sta *n.* View, prospect, esp. through avenue of trees or other long narrow opening; such an opening; (fig.) mental view of extensive period of time or series of events etc.

Vi′stula. River of Poland flowing from the Carpathians to the Baltic at Danzig.

vi′sual (-z- *or* -zh-) *adj.* Of, concerned with, seeing; used in seeing, received through sight; ~ *angle*, angle formed by two straight lines from extreme points of object to centre of eye; ~ *purple* purple-red pigment present in retinal rods of eyes, abundant in eyes of nocturnal animals. **vi′sually** *adv.*

vi′sualize(-z- *or* -zh-) *v.t.* Make mental vision or image of (something not present or not visible), make visible to imagination. **visualizā′tion** *n.*

vi′ta glass (-ahs). Special kind of glass for windows etc., which does not exclude ultra-violet or actinic rays of sunlight. [L *vita* life]

vi′tal *adj.* Of, concerned with, essential to, organic life; essential to existence or to the matter in hand; affecting life, fatal to life or to success, etc.; ~ *capacity*, (physiol.) volume of air that can be expelled from lungs after strongest possible inspiration; ~ *parts*, parts of body essential to life, as lungs, heart, brain, etc.; ~ *statistics*, those relating to births, deaths, health, disease, etc.; (colloq.) measurements of woman's bust, waist, and hips. **vi′tally** *adv.* **vi′tals** (-z) *n pl.* Vital parts of body.

vi′talism *n.* (philos.) Theory that life originates in a vital principle distinct from chemical and physical forces (opp. MECHANISM). **vi′talist** *n.* Adherent of vitalism. **vitali′stic** *adj.*

vitā′lity *n.* Vital power, ability to sustain life; (fig.) active force or power, activity, animation, liveliness.

vi′talize *v.t.* Put life or animation into, infuse with vitality or vigour. **vitalizā′tion** *n.*

vi′tamin *n.* Any of a number of substances essential for growth and nutrition, occurring in certain foodstuffs or produced synthetically; ~ *A*, present in liver-oils, butter-fat, green leaves, etc.; ~ *B*, any of a group present in yeast products, pulses etc., comprises a number of separate substances concerned esp. with the formation and functioning of important enzymes in the body; ~ *C*, ASCORBIC acid; ~ *D*, present in fish-liver oils and egg-yolk and apparently concerned in the deposition of calcium phosphate in bones; ~ *E*, present in germ-layer of wheat and green leaves, its absence causing sterility; ~ *K*, present in various foodstuffs, esp. green leaves, facilitating clotting of blood in post-operational jaundice and similar conditions. **vitami′nic**, **vitā′minous** *adjs.* **vi′taminize** *v.t.* Introduce vitamin(s) into (food). [orig. named *vitamine* f. L *vita* life and Engl. AMINE, in the belief that an amino-acid was present]

vitě′llin *n.* (biochem.) Chief protein of egg-yolk.

Vitě′llius, Aulus (A.D. 15–69). Roman emperor after the death of Otho (A.D. 69), defeated in the same year by Vespasian and murdered.

vitě′llus *n.* (embryol.) Yolk of an egg. **vitě′lline** *adj.* Of the vitellus; ~ *membrane*, membrane enclosing vitellus.

vi′tiate (-shi-) *v.t.* Impair the quality of, corrupt, debase; make invalid or ineffectual. **vitiā′tion** *n.*

vi′ticulture *n.* Cultivation of the vine.

Vitor′ia. Town in NE. Spain, where in 1813 Wellington defeated the French under Joseph Bonaparte and thus freed Spain from French domination.

vi′treous *adj.* Of (the nature of) glass; resembling glass in composition, brittleness, hardness, lustre, transparency, etc.; ~ *humour*: see HUMOUR, 3. **vi′treously** *adv.* **vitrěǒ′sity** *n.*

vi′trify *v.* Convert, be converted, into glass or glass-like substance; render, become, vi-treous. **vitrǐfǐā′ction, vǐtrǐfǐcā′tion** *ns.*

vi′triŏl *n.* 1. Any of various metallic sulphates used in the arts or medicinally, esp. iron sulphate; (also *oil of* ~) concentrated sulphuric acid. 2. (fig.) Causticity, acrimony, of feeling or utterance. **vitriǒ′lic** *adj.* (esp., fig.) Extremely caustic, scathing, bitter, or malignant.

Vītru′vius (-rōō-). Marcus Vitruvius Pollio (1st c. A.D.), Roman architect, whose book 'De architectura' had much influence on Renaissance building. **Vītru′-vian** *adj.* Of, in the style of, Vitruvius; ~ *scroll*, convoluted scroll-pattern as architectural ornament.

vi′tta *n.* (pl. *-ae*). 1. (Rom. antiq.) Fillet, garland. 2. Lappet of mitre. 3. (bot.) One of a number of oil-tubes in pericarp of fruit of most umbelliferous plants. **vi′ttāte** *adj.*

vǐtū′perāte *v.t.* Revile. **vǐtuperā′tion** *n.* **vǐtū′perative** *adj.* **vǐtū′peratively** *adv.*

Vī′tus, St. (*c* 300). Child martyr of the DIOCLETIAN persecution; *St. Vitus's dance*, (pop.) = CHOREA.

vī′va¹ (vē-) *n. & int.* (Salute, greeting, cry, of) 'long live . . .'. [It., 3rd pers. imperat. of *vivere* live]

vī′va² *n.* = VIVA VOCE.

vivace (vēvah′chä) *adv. & n.* (mus.) (Passage performed) in brisk and lively manner. [It.]

vīvā′cious (-shus) *adj.* Lively, animated. **vīvā′ciously** *adv.* **vivǎ′city** *n.*

vivandière (vēvahṅdyār′) *n.* Formerly, in French and other continental armies, woman following troops and selling provisions and liquor. [Fr.]

vivār′ium *n.* (pl. *-ia*). Place or enclosure for keeping living animals etc. as far as possible under natural conditions, for interest or scientific study.

vī′va vō′ce (-chi). Oral (examination); orally. [L, = 'with the living voice']

vive (vēv) *int.* Cry of 'long live', as in ~ *le roi* (rwah), long live the king. [Fr., 3rd pers. sing. imperat. of *vivre* live]

vǐvě′rrine *adj.* Of the Viverridae or CIVET family.

vī′vǐd *adj.* Strong, intense, glaring (esp. of colour, light, etc.); clearly or distinctly perceived or perceptible, intensely or strongly felt or expressed, (capable of) presenting subjects or ideas in clear and striking manner. **vī′vǐdly** *adv.* **vī′vǐdness** *n.*

vī′vify *v.t.* (chiefly fig.) Give life to, animate.

vīvǐ′parous *adj.* 1. (zool.) Bringing forth young in developed state, not hatching from egg (cf. OVIPAROUS). 2. (bot.) Germinating while still attached to the parent plant; having such seeds. **vīvǐ′parously** *adv.* **vīvǐ′parousness**, **vīvǐpǎ′rǐty** *ns.* **vīvǐ′pary** *n.* (bot. only).

vi'visect *v.t.* Perform vivisection upon. **vivisec'tion** *n.* Performance of surgical experiments on living animals in laboratory for the advancement of (esp. medical) knowledge. **vivisec'tionist** *n.* One who approves of or advocates this practice.

vi'xen *n.* 1. Female fox. 2. Ill-tempered quarrelsome woman. **vi'xenish** *adj.*

viz. *abbrev.* (usu. spoken as 'namely') = VIDELICET.

vi'zard *n.* (archaic) Mask; visor.

vizcă'cha (-s-), **vis-** *n.* Large burrowing S. Amer. rodent (*Lagostomus maximus*) with long soft fur, grey on back and yellowish-white beneath.

vizier' (*or* vī'zier) *n.* High administrative official in some Muslim countries, esp. (*grand ~*) chief minister of former Turkish Empire. [Arab. *wazīr* caliph's chief minister]

v.l. *abbrev.* *Varia lectio* (L, = variant reading).

Vlăch (-k) *n.* Member of a people speaking a Rumanian dialect living in parts of SE. Europe. [Slav., ult. f. Germanic *Walh* foreigner]

Vlă'dĭmir (-mēr), St. (*c* 956–1015). Grand duke of Kiev and prince of Russia; he was baptized in 988 and introduced the Orthodox Church into Russia.

Vlădĭvŏ'stŏk. Far Eastern seaport and naval base of U.S.S.R., terminus of Trans-Siberian railway.

V.O. *abbrev.* (Royal) Victorian Order.

voc. *abbrev.* Vocative.

vō'cable *n.* Word, esp. with ref. to form rather than meaning.

vocă'bŭlary *n.* List of words with their meanings, glossary; sum of words used in a language, or in a particular book or branch of science etc., or by a particular person, class, profession, etc.

vō'cal *adj.* Of, concerned with, uttered by, the voice; (poet.) endowed (as) with a voice; expressive, eloquent; (of music) composed for voice(s) with or without accompaniment; (phonet.) of a vowel, vocalic; *~ cords* or *folds*, voice-producing organs, two strap-like membranes stretched across the larynx, each having a medial edge which is free to vibrate in the airstream (ill. HEAD), determining pitch of voice by their length and frequency of vibration, women's being shorter than men's; *~ score*, musical score showing voice parts in full. **vō'cally** *adv.* **vō'cal** *n.* 1. Vowel. 2. (R.C. Ch.) Person entitled to vote in certain elections.

vocă'lic *adj.* Of, concerning, vowel(s); of the nature of a vowel; rich in vowels.

vō'calism *n.* Use of voice in speech or singing; system of vowels in a language. **vō'calist** *n.* Singer.

vō'calize *v.* Utter, make vocal; convert into, use as, vowel; furnish with vowels or vowel-points; sing, esp. on vowel-sound(s). **vōcalĭzā'tion** *n.*

vocā'tion *n.* Divine call to, sense of fitness for, a career or occupation; occupation, calling. **vocā'tional** *adj.* **vocā'tionally** *adv.*

vŏ'cative *adj.* (gram.) Of the case used in address or invocation. *~ n.* (Word in) vocative case.

vocĭ'ferāte *v.* Utter, cry out, noisily; shout, bawl. **vōcĭferā'tion** *n.*

vocĭ'ferous *adj.* Clamorous, noisy. **vocĭ'ferously** *adv.* **vocĭ'ferousnĕss** *n.*

vŏ'dka *n.* Alcoholic spirit made esp. in Russia by distillation of rye etc. [Russ., dim. of *voda* water]

Vŏ'gler (f-), Georg Joseph (1749–1814). German musical composer and organist, known as *Abt ~* (i.e. Abbé *~*).

vōgue (-g) *n.* Popularity, general acceptance or currency; prevailing fashion; *in ~*, in fashion, generally current; *~ word*, word currently popular.

voice *n.* 1. Sound uttered by the mouth, esp. human utterance in speaking, shouting, or singing; use of the voice esp. in spoken or (fig.) written words; opinion so expressed; right to express opinion; vote; (phonet.) sound uttered with vibration or resonance of vocal cords (dist. from *breath* or *whisper*);

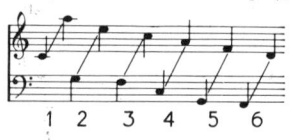

APPROXIMATE COMPASS OF SINGING VOICES

1. Soprano.   2. Contralto.   3. Alto.
4. Tenor.   5. Baritone.   6. Bass

(mus.) singing voice, quality of this. 2. (gram.) Set of forms of a verb showing relation of the subject to the action (ACTIVE, MIDDLE, PASSIVE, etc., *~*). 3. (mus.): see FUGUE. *~ v.t.* Give utterance to, express; (phonet.) utter with voice, change from voiceless to voiced; (mus.) regulate tone-quality of organ pipes. **voiced** (-st) *adj.* (esp., phonet.) Uttered with voice, sonant.

voi'celĕss (-sl-) *adj.* Speechless, dumb, mute; (phonet.) not voiced. **voi'celĕssly** *adv.* **voi'celĕssnĕss** *n.*

void *adj.* Empty, vacant; invalid, not binding; (poet., rhet.) ineffectual, useless; *~ of*, lacking, free from. *~ n.* Empty space. *~ v.t.* Render void or invalid; emit (excrement etc.).

voi'dance *n.* (esp., eccles.) Fact of benefice etc. being or becoming void or vacant.

voi'dĕd *adj.* (esp., of heraldic bearing) Having central area cut away, so as to show the field; (of velvet) having no pile in some parts, the pile-thread being buried in the foundation fabric.

voile *n.* Thin semi-transparent cotton, wool, or silk dress-material. [Fr., = 'veil']

vol. *abbrev.* Volume.

vō'lant *adj.* Flying, capable of flight; (her.) represented as flying; (poet.) nimble, rapid.

vō'lar *adj.* (anat.) Of palm of hand or sole of foot.

vŏ'latīle *adj.* Readily evaporating at ordinary temperatures; (fig.) changeable, flighty, lively, gay; evanescent, transient; *~ oil*, essential oil. **vŏlatĭ'lity** *n.*

volă'tilīze (*or* vŏ'la-) *v.* (Cause to) evaporate; make, become, volatile. **vŏlătilīzā'tion** *n.*

vŏl-au-vent (-ō-vahǹ) *n.* Pie, usu. for one person, of light puff pastry filled with sauce containing meat, fish, etc. [Fr., lit. 'flight in the wind']

vŏlcă'nic *adj.* Of, produced by, a volcano; characterized by volcanoes; *~ glass*, obsidian. **vŏlcă'nically** *adv.*

vŏlcā'nō *n.* (pl. *-oes*). Hill or mountain, more or less conical, composed partly or wholly of discharged matter, with crater(s) or other opening(s) in earth's crust

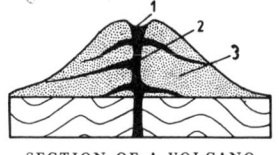

SECTION OF A VOLCANO

1. Crater.   2. Lava.   3. Tuff

through which steam, gases, ashes, rocks, and freq. streams of molten material are or have been periodically ejected; (fig.) violent, esp. suppressed, feeling, passion, etc. **vŏ'lcanism** *n.* Volcanic activity. [It., f. L. *Volcanus* VULCAN]

vōle *n.* Small rodent with short ears and tail, rounded snout, and herbivorous teeth; British species: *bank ~* (*Clethrionomys glareolus*), *field ~* (*Microtus agrestis*), and *water ~* (*Arvicola amphibius*).

Vŏ'lga. Longest river of Europe, rising in NW. of U.S.S.R. and flowing E., then S. to the Caspian Sea.

Vŏ'lgogrăd. City (formerly *Stalingrad*, 1925–61, previously *Tsaritsyn*) of U.S.S.R. on the lower Volga, where the German invasion of Russia was halted in Aug.–Nov. 1942.

volĭ'tion *n.* Act, power, of willing or resolving, exercise of the will. **volĭ'tional** *adj.* **volĭ'tionally** *adv.*

vŏ'lley *n.* Salvo, shower, of missiles (or fig. of oaths etc.); (tennis, lawn tennis, etc.) return

stroke at ball before it touches ground; (cricket) full pitch; ~-*ball*, game in which large inflated ball is struck with hands from alternate sides of high net without touching ground. ~ *v.* Discharge (missiles etc.), return, hit, bowl, (ball), in volley; fly in volley; make sound like volleys of artillery.
Vŏ'lscī *n.pl.* Ancient warlike people of E. Latium, subdued by Romans in 4th c. B.C. **Vŏ'lscĭan** *adj. & n.*
Vŏ'lsung (-ōong) *n.* (Scand. legend) Member of a family descending from Odin whose history is related in the 'Volsunga Saga'.
vŏlt[1] *n.* Unit of electromotive force, the electrical pressure that if steadily applied to a conductor whose resistance is 1 ohm will produce a current of 1 ampere (abbrev. V). [f. VOLTA]
vŏlt[2]: see VOLTE.
Vŏ'lta, Alessandro (1745–1827). Italian physicist, a pioneer of electrical science; first devised apparatus for chemically developing electric currents.
vŏ'ltaġe *n.* Electromotive force expressed in volts.
vŏltā'ic *adj.* Producing electricity, (of electricity) generated, by chemical action, after the method discovered by VOLTA; (consisting) of, caused by, connected with, such electricity.
Vŏltaire, François Marie Arouet de (1694–1778). French deist philosopher, historian, dramatist, and writer of historical and satirical poems and tales; famous for his anti-clericalism, his witty scepticism, and his influence on the leaders of the French Revolution.
vŏltā'mēter *n.* Instrument for measuring electricity by amount of electrolysis produced.
vŏlte, vŏlt *n.* (manège) Horse's sideways gait in circle; (fencing) quick movement to escape thrust. ~ *v.* Make a volte.
vŏlte-face (-fahs) *n.* Complete change of front in argument, politics, etc. [Fr.]
vŏ'ltmēter *n.* Any instrument for measuring voltage.
vŏ'lūble *adj.* Fluent, glib; speaking, spoken, with great readiness or fluency. **vŏlūbī'litӯ, vŏ'lūblenėss** *ns.* **vŏl'ūblӯ** *adv.*
vŏ'lūme *n.* 1. Collection of written or esp. printed sheets bound together to form a book; division of work (intended to be) separately bound. 2. Bulk, mass, quantity, esp. large quantity; space occupied by anything, esp. as measured in cubic units; size, dimensions, amount, *of.* 3. (usu. pl.) Wreath, coil, rounded mass, of smoke etc. 4. (mus. etc.) Quantity, power, fullness, of tone or sound.
vŏlūmĕ'tric *adj.* Of, pertaining to, measurement of volume. **vŏlūmĕ'trically** *adv.*
volū'minous *adj.* 1. Containing, consisting of, many coils or convolutions. 2. Consisting of many volumes; (of writer) producing many books etc. 3. Of great volume, bulky, ample. **volŭ'mĭnouslӯ** *adv.* **volū'minousnėss, volūminŏ'sitӯ** *ns.*
vŏ'luntarӯ *adj.* Done, acting, able to act, of one's own free will; purposed, intentional, not constrained; (of bodily action etc.) controlled by the will; brought about, produced, maintained, etc., by voluntary action; *V~ Aid Detachment*, group of men or women organized by the Order of St. John, the St. Andrew's Ambulance Association, or the British Red Cross Society, undertaking first aid and nursing duties; ~ *hospital*, one maintained by voluntary contributions. **vŏ'luntarilӯ** *adv.* **vŏ'luntarinėss** *n.* **vŏ'luntarӯ** *n.* (orig.) Extempore performance, esp. as prelude to other music; (now) organ solo played before, during, or after any church service; music composed for this.
volunteer' *n.* One who voluntarily offers his services or enrols himself for any enterprise, esp. for service in any of the armed forces; (hist.) member of British military company or force formed by voluntary enlistment and distinct from regular army. ~ *v.* Undertake, offer, voluntarily; make voluntary offer of one's services; be a volunteer.
volŭ'ptuarӯ *n. & adj.* Of, concerned with, (person) given up to, indulgence in luxury and gratification of the senses.
volŭ'ptuous *adj.* Of, derived from, marked by, addicted to, promising etc., gratification of the senses. **volŭ'ptuouslӯ** *adv.* **volŭ'ptuousnėss** *n.*
volŭ'te *n.* 1. (archit.) Spiral scroll forming chief ornament of Ionic capital and used also in Corinthian and Composite capitals (ill. ORDER). 2. Spiral conformation (ill. SPIRAL), convolution, esp. of spiral shell; marine gasteropod of genus *Voluta* and allied genera, chiefly tropical, and freq. with very handsome shell. ~ *adj.* Having the form of a volute, forming spiral curve(s).
volū'tion *n.* Convolution, spiral turn, whorl of spiral shell; rolling or revolving movement.
vŏ'lva *n.* (bot.) Membranous covering enclosing many fungi in early stages of growth (ill. FUNGUS).
vŏ'mit *v.* Eject contents of stomach through mouth; bring up, eject, (as) by vomiting, belch forth, spew out. ~ *n.* Matter ejected from stomach.
vōō'dōō *n.* System of religious or magical beliefs and practices among Negroes etc. of West Indies and America. ~ *v.t.* Bewitch, put voodoo spell on.
vorā'cious (-sh*u*s) *adj.* Greedy in eating; gluttonous. **vorā'ciouslӯ** *adv.* **vorā'ciousnėss, vorā'citӯ** *ns.*

vōr'tĕx *n.* (pl. *-icēs, -exes*). 1. Mass of fluid, esp. liquid, with rapid circular movement round axis and tendency to form vacuum or cavity in centre towards which bodies are attracted, whirlpool; anything likened to this, esp. by reason of rush or excitement, rapid change, or absorbing effect. 2. Whirling mass of air or vapour; (central part of) whirlwind. 3. In older theories of the universe, esp. that of Descartes, (cosmic matter carried round in) rapid rotatory movement round centre or axis, supposed to account for origin and phenomena of terrestrial and other systems. **vōr'tical** *adj.* **vōr'ticallӯ** *adv.*
vōr'ticism *n.* 1. Philosophical theory of vortices (see prec.). 2. Theory of a group of futurist painters etc., first expounded 1913 by Wyndham Lewis, that art should express the 'seething vortex of modern life'. **vōr'ticist** *n.*
Vōr'tigĕrn. Legendary British prince supposed to have invited the Jutes to Britain and to have married the daughter of Hengist.
Vosges (vōzh). Mountain system of E. France.
vō'tarӯ *n.* (fem. *vō'tarėss*) One bound by vow(s), esp. to religious life; devotee, devoted or zealous worshipper, ardent follower (*of*).
vōte *n.* Expression of one's acceptance or rejection signified by ballot, show of hands, voice, or otherwise; right to vote; opinion expressed, resolution or decision carried, by voting; votes collectively. ~ *v.* Give a vote, express choice or preference by ballot, show of hands, etc.; choose, elect, establish, ratify, grant, confer, by vote; pronounce, declare, by general consent; (colloq.) propose, suggest; *voting-paper*, slip of paper used in voting by ballot.
vō'tive *adj.* Dedicated, offered, consecrated, etc., in fulfilment of a vow.
vouch *v.* Confirm, uphold, (statement) by evidence or assertion; answer, be surety, *for.*
vou'cher *n.* Document, receipt, etc., to attest correctness of accounts or monetary transactions, authorize or establish payment, etc.; esp. document which can be exchanged for goods or services as token of payment made or promised.
vouchsā'fe *v.t.* Give, grant, bestow, in condescending or gracious manner; deign to give, condescend (*to do*).
voussoir (vōō'swär) *n.* Each of the wedge-shaped or tapered stones forming an arch (ill. ARCH[1]).
vow *v.t.* Promise, or undertake solemnly, esp. by a vow; make solemn resolve to exact (vengeance), harbour (hatred), etc. ~ *n.* Solemn promise or engagement, esp. to God or to any deity or saint.

vow′el *n*. Speech-sound produced by vibrations of vocal cords, modified or characterized by form of vocal cavities, but without audible friction (opp. to, but not sharply divided from, CONSONANT); letter or symbol representing such a sound, as a, e, i, o, u; ~-*point*, sign used to indicate vowel in certain alphabets, as Hebrew etc.

vŏx ăngĕ′lĭca (-j-). Organ-stop of soft pleasant tone, freq. with slight wave effect produced by two pipes not tuned exactly together. [L, = 'angelic voice']

vŏx hŭma′na (-mah-). Organ reed-stop, quality and tone of which resembles human voice. [L, = 'human voice']

vŏx pŏ′pŭlī. Voice of the people; public opinion, popular belief, general verdict. [L]

voy′age *n*. Journey, esp. to distant place or country, by sea or water. ~ *v*. Travel by water; traverse, travel over. **voy′ager** *n*.

voyeur (vwahyêr′) *n*. One who derives gratification from looking at sexual·organs or acts of others. **voyeur′ism** *n*.

V.R. *abbrev*. *Victoria Regina* (L, = Queen Victoria).

V.S. *abbrev*. Veterinary Surgeon.

Vt. *abbrev*. Vermont.

V.T.O.L. *abbrev*. Vertical takeoff and landing (aircraft).

Vŭ′lcan. (Rom. myth.) God of fire and patron of workers in metal, identified with Hephaestus.

Vŭ′lcanist *n*. = PLUTONIST.

vŭ′lcanīte *n*. Ebonite, black variety of rubber hardened by treatment with sulphur at high temperatures.

vŭ′lcanīze *v.t.* Harden and make (rubber etc.) more durable by chemical means, esp. by combining it with sulphur, either by subjection to great heat or at ordinary temperatures. **vŭlcanīzā′tion** *n*.

Vulg. *abbrev*. Vulgate.

vŭ′lgar *adj*. Of, characteristic of, the common people, plebeian, coarse, low; in common use, generally prevalent; ~ *fraction*: see FRACTION; ~ *tongue*, vernacular, popular or native language, esp. as opposed to Latin. **vŭ′lgarlў** *adv*. **vŭ′lgarism**, **vŭlgă′ritў** *ns*.

vŭlgār′ian *n*. Vulgar (esp. rich) person.

vŭ′lgarīze *v.t.* Make vulgar or commonplace; reduce to level of something usual or ordinary. **vŭlgarīzā′tion** *n*.

Vŭ′lgate. Latin version of Bible prepared (in the main) by St. Jerome, *c* 382–404; recension of this published 1592 by order of Pope Clement VIII, official text of R.C. Church. [L *vulgare* make public]

vŭ′lnerable *adj*. That may be wounded, open to attack, injury, or assault, not proof against weapon, criticism, etc.; (in contract bridge) that has won one game towards rubber, and therefore liable to double penalties. **vŭlnerabi′litў** *n*.

vŭ′lnerarў *adj. & n*. (Drug, preparation, etc.) useful in or used for healing wounds.

vŭ′lpīne *adj*. Of fox(es); characteristic of, like, fox; crafty, cunning.

vŭ′lture *n*. Any of various large raptorial birds feeding largely on carrion and often with head and neck almost naked; (fig.) rapacious person. **vŭ′lturine** (-cher-) *adj*.

vŭ′lva *n*. External female genital organ, esp. external opening of vagina.

vv. *abbrev*. Verses.

W

W, w (dŭ′belyōō). 23rd letter of modern English alphabet, originally a ligatured doubling of the Roman letter represented by *u* and *v* of modern alphabets, pronounced as a voiced bilabial spirant and, after vowels, as a *u*-glide, the second element of a diphthong.

w. *abbrev*. Wicket; wide; wife; with.

W. *abbrev*. Watt(s); Welsh; West.

W.A.A.C. *abbrev*. Women's Army Auxiliary Corps (in 1914–18 war). **Waac** (wăk) *n*. (colloq.) Member of W.A.A.C.

W.A.A.F. *abbrev*. Women's Auxiliary Air Force (1939–48). **Waaf** (wăf) *n*. (colloq.) Member of W.A.A.F.

wad (wŏd) *n*. Small bundle or mass of soft flexible material used as pad etc., esp. plug or disc of felt, cardboard, etc., keeping powder and shot compact in cartridge to prevent gas passing between shot and barrel when the cartridge is fired; (U.S.) tight roll, esp. of bank-notes, (colloq.) wealth, money. ~ *v.t.* Press, compress, roll into wad; line, pad, with wadding; furnish, plug, with wad.

wa′dding (wŏ-) *n*. (Soft pliable material for making) wads; loose, soft, fibrous material for padding, stuffing, etc.

wa′ddle (wŏ-) *v.i.* Walk with short steps and swaying motion natural to stout short-legged person or to bird with short legs set far apart, as duck. ~ *n*. Waddling gait.

wa′ddў (wŏ-) *n*. Wooden war-club of Australian aborigines.

wāde[1] *v*. Walk through water or any soft substance which impedes motion; walk through (stream etc.); (fig.) progress slowly or with difficulty (*through* book etc.); *wading bird:* = WADER, 1. ~ *n*. Act of wading.

Wāde[2], George (1673–1741). British field-marshal; served in Marlborough's army; was sent (1724) to the Highlands of Scotland, where he built numerous bridges and metalled roads.

wā′der *n*. (esp.) 1. Long-legged bird, as crane, heron, sandpiper, that wades in shallow water. 2. (pl.) High waterproof boots or long waterproof garments covering feet and legs and coming up above waist, worn by fishermen etc.

wa′dī, wa′dў (wah-) *n*. In N. Africa etc., rocky ravine or watercourse, dry except in rainy season.

w.a.f. *abbrev*. With all faults.

wā′fer *n*. Very thin light sweet crisp biscuit or cake now chiefly eaten with ices; thin disc of unleavened bread used at Eucharist; small disc of gelatine, flour and gum, etc., formerly used for sealing letters; disc of red paper stuck on legal document instead of seal. **wā′ferў** *adj*. **wā′fer** *v.t.* Attach or seal with wafer.

wa′ffle[1] (wŏ-) *n*. Small soft crisp batter-cake with honeycomb surface; ~-*iron*, utensil, usu. of two shallow metal pans hinged together, between which waffle is baked or fried.

wa′ffle[2] (wŏ-) *v.i. & n*. (slang) (Utter) wordy nonsense; twaddle.

waft (wah-) *n*. Act of waving, waving movement; whiff of odour, breath of wind; (naut., also *w(h)ĕft*), flag or some substitute, usu. knotted, hoisted as signal, etc. ~ *v*. Convey (as) through air or over water, sweep smoothly and lightly along.

wăg[1] *v*. Shake or move briskly to and fro, oscillate; *wa′gtail*, small bird of genus *Motacilla* with slender body and long tail which is freq. in wagging motion; any of various Amer. or Australian birds resembling this. ~ *n*. Single wagging motion.

wăg[2] *n*. Facetious person, habitual joker. **wă′ggerў** *n*. Action(s), humour, of a wag. **wă′ggish** *adj*. **wă′ggishlў** *adv*. **wă′ggishness** *n*.

wāge[1] *n*. Amount paid periodically, esp. by day or week or month, for work or service of employee (usu. pl.); requital, reward (usu. pl.); (pl., econ.) that part of total production of

WAGE

community which is the reward of all forms of labour (as dist. from remuneration received by capital); ~(s) council, board consisting of workers' and employers' representatives and with some independent members, set up in industries with insufficient arrangements for collective bargaining; ~ *slave*, person dependent on income obtained from (esp. unpleasant) labour.

wāge² *v.t.* Carry on (war etc.).

wā'ger *n.* Bet, stake; ~ *of battle*, (hist.) challenge by defendant to decide his guilt or innocence by single combat. ~ *v.t.* Bet, stake.

wă'ġġle *v.* Move (something held or fixed at one end), be moved, to and fro with short quick motions. ~ *n.* Act of waggling.

waġġon etc.: see WAGON etc.

Wa'ġner (vah-), Wilhelm Richard (1813–83). German composer of operas ('The Ring of the Nibelungen', 'Tristan and Isolde', 'The Mastersingers', 'Parsifal', etc.); revolutionized opera by his music-dramas for which he wrote both text and music, dispensing with set arias and choruses; spent his last years at BAYREUTH. **Waġnēr'ian** *adj. & n.* **Waġnerĕ'sque** (-k) *adj.*

wă'ġon, wă'ġġon *n.* Four-wheeled vehicle for drawing heavy loads often with removable semicylindrical tilt or cover, usu. drawn

WAGON

1. Tilt. 2. Dished wheel. 3. Tire. 4. Spring. 5. Axle-tree. 6. Shaft

by two or more horses; railway truck; vehicle for carrying water, whence *on the* ~, (slang) abstaining from alcohol; *tea* ~, trolley for conveying tea etc.; ~-*boiler*, -*ceiling*, -*roof*, -*vault*, one shaped like wagon-tilt.

wă'ġoner, wăġġ- *n.* Driver of wagon; *the W*~: see AURIGA.

wăġonĕ'tte, wăġġ- *n.* Four-wheeled horse-drawn vehicle, open or with removable cover, with facing side-seats and transverse seat(s) at front.

wagon-lit (vă'gawṅ-lē; *or* w-) *n.*

Sleeping-car on continental railway. [Fr. *wagon* wagon, *lit* bed]

Wă'ġram (v-). Place near Vienna where Napoleon defeated the Austrians in 1809.

wagtail: see WAG¹ *v.*

Waha'bi (wahah-) *n.* Member of Muslim sect, followers of Abd-el-Wahhab (*c* 1703–91) who acquired political power in Arabia in early 20th c.

waif *n.* (law) Any object or animal found ownerless; homeless and helpless person, esp. unowned or abandoned child; ~*s and strays*, odds and ends; homeless or neglected children.

wail *n.* Prolonged plaintive inarticulate cry of pain, grief, etc.; bitter lamentation; sound resembling cry of pain. ~ *v.i.* Utter wails or persistent and bitter lamentations or complaints; bewail, lament; *Wailing Wall*, high wall in Jerusalem, supposed to stand on the site of Temple of Herod the Great, to which Jews resort to pray and lament.

wain *n.* Wagon; (*Charles's*) *W*~ [Charles = Charlemagne; orig. called the Wain of Arcturus (a neighbouring star); Arcturus was confused with Arturus, King ARTHUR¹, who is associated with Charlemagne in legend]: see URSA.

wai'nscot *n.* Wooden panelling or boarding on room-wall; (hist.) imported oak of fine quality. ~ *v.t.* Line with wainscot.

wai'nscoting *n.* Wainscot or material for it.

waist *n.* Part of human body between ribs and hip-bones, normally slenderer than parts above and below it; middle narrower part of anything; part of garment covering waist, narrowed part of garment corresponding to waist (but sometimes worn higher or lower than position of this); (chiefly U.S.) bodice, blouse; (naut.) middle part of upper deck of ship, between quarter-deck and forecastle; *wai'stband*, band going round waist, esp. one forming upper part of lower garment; ~-*cloth*, loin-cloth; *wai'stcoat* (*or* -sk-), garment, usu. sleeveless and buttoned, covering upper part of body usu. down to waist, worn under outer garment; *wai'stline*, line of waist; measurement of this.

wait *v.* 1. Abstain from action or departure till some expected event occurs; pause, tarry; be expectant or on the watch. 2. Await, bide. 3. Act as attendant

WAGONETTE

WAIVE

on person; serve food and drink, shift plates at table; ~ (*up*)*on*, pay respectful visit to. 4. Defer (meal) till someone arrives. 5. ~-*a-bit*, [f. Afrikaans *wag-'n-bietje*] any of various plants and shrubs, esp. species of *Mimosa*, with hooked and clinging thorns. ~ *n.* 1. Act or time of waiting; *lie in* ~, lurk in ambush. 2. (pl.) Street singers of Christmas carols; (hist.) official bands of musicians maintained by a town or city.

wai'ter *n.* (esp., fem. *wai'tress*) Person employed at hotel, restaurant, etc., (or, U.S., in private house) to wait upon guests, take orders for meals, etc.; tray, salver (see DUMB waiter).

wai'ting *n.* (esp.) (Period of) official attendance at court; *in* ~, on duty, in attendance; ~ *game*, abstention from attempting to secure advantages in early part of game etc. in order to act more effectively at later stage; ~-*list*, list of persons waiting for appointment, next chance of obtaining something etc.; ~-*room*, room provided for persons to wait in, esp. at bus or railway station or for patients waiting to consult doctor etc.

waive *v.t.* Relinquish, refrain from insisting on, refuse to avail oneself of (advantage, privilege, claim, opportunity, etc.). **wai'ver** *n.* (law) Waiving.

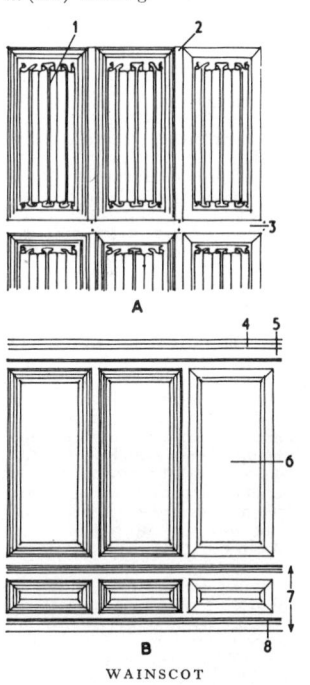

WAINSCOT

A. 16TH C. B. LATE 17TH C.

1. Linenfold. 2. Stile. 3. Rail. 4. Cornice. 5. Frieze. 6. Panel. 7. Dado. 8. Skirting

[975]

wāke¹ v. (past t. wōke, wāked; past part. wāked, wōken). Cease to sleep, rouse from sleep, (freq. ~ up); be awake (archaic except in pres. part.); cease, rouse, from sloth, torpidity, inactivity, etc.; rise, raise, from the dead; arouse, excite (feeling, activity, etc.), evoke (sound, echo, etc.); (chiefly Ir.) hold wake over; ~-robin, wild arum, *Arum maculatum*; (U.S.) liliaceous plant of genus *Trillium*; any of various arums.

wāke² n. 1. (hist.) (Vigil of) festival in commemoration of dedication of church. 2. (usu. pl.) Annual holiday in N. England. 3. (chiefly with ref. to Irish custom) Watch by corpse before burial; drinking, lamentation, feasting, etc., associated with this.

wāke³ n. Track left on water's surface by ship or other moving object; *in the ~ of*, following close behind; in imitation of; following as a result or consequence.

wā′keful (-kf-) adj. Keeping awake, esp. while others sleep; unable to sleep; marked by absence or want of sleep. wā′kefully adv. wā′kefulness n.

Wāke I′sland (il-). N. Pacific island under sovereignty of U.S.

wā′ken v. Cause to be, become, awake; wake up.

Walachia: see WALLACHIA.

Walbūr′ga (wŏ-), St. (c 710–79). English missionary to Germany, abbess of Heidenheim; commemorated 25 Feb. and 1 May (see WALPURGIS).

Wă′lcheren (vălk-). Island of the province of Zeeland in the Netherlands.

Waldĕ′nsēs (wŏ-, -z) n.pl. Puritanical religious sect which originated in S. France c 1170 through preaching of a rich Lyons merchant, Peter Waldo; was banned in 1184 and scattered by persecution into Germany and Bohemia; became a separately organized Church, which associated itself with the Protestant Reformation of the 16th c. and still exists, chiefly in N. Italy and in N. and S. America, though not officially tolerated until 1848. Waldĕ′nsian adj. & n.

Waldo, Peter: see WALDENSES.

wāle n. 1. Weal. 2. One of horizontal timbers connecting and bracing piles of trench, dam, etc.; (naut.) one of the broader thicker timbers extending along ship's sides at different heights. ~ v.t. Mark, furnish, with wales.

Wā′ler n. (Ind. colloq.) Horse, esp. cavalry-horse, imported from Australia, esp. New South Wales.

Wāles (-lz). Principality occupying extreme W. of central southern portion of Gt Britain; orig. independent; was conquered by Edward I and united with England by the *Statute of ~* (1284); university (1893), with colleges at Aberystwyth, Bangor, Cardiff, Lampeter, and Swansea;

capital, Cardiff; *Prince of ~*, title usu. conferred (since 1301) on eldest son of reigning sovereign of England.

Wălhă′lla (v-): = VALHALLA.

walk (wawk) v. 1. Travel, go, on foot; perambulate, tread floor or surface of, go over or along on foot; (of bipeds) progress by alternate movements of legs so that one foot is always on the ground, (of quadrupeds) go at gait in which there are always two, and during part of step three, feet on ground (opp. to *run*, *trot*, *gallop*, etc.); (of ghost etc.) appear. 2. Cause to walk with one; take charge of (hound-puppy at walk). 3. (archaic) Live with specified principle or in specified manner, conduct oneself. 4. ~ *away from*, (U.S.) outdistance easily; ~ *away with*, win (something) easily; ~ *off*, depart, esp. abruptly; ~ *off with*, carry away, steal; win; ~ *on*, play non-speaking part on stage; ~ *out*, (esp., colloq.) strike; hence ~-*out* (n.); ~ *out on*, abandon, esp. without warning; ~ *out with*, (colloq.) court; ~ *over*, (of horse) win race in which there is no other starter by going over (course) at walking pace; win a race or other contest with little or no effort; ~-*over* (n.) race in which winner walks over; ~ *the boards*, be actor; ~ *the hospitals*, be medical student; ~ *the plank*: see PLANK; ~ *the streets*, (esp.) be a prostitute; ~-*up*, (U.S. colloq.) block of flats in which there is no lift. 5. *walking delegate*, trade-union official who visits sick members, interviews employers, etc.; *walking-stick*, stick carried when walking and normally designed to give additional support to the body; *walking-stick (insect)*, STICK insect; *walking-stick palm*, Australian palm (*Bacularia monostachya*) with stems suitable for making walking-sticks; *walking-tour*, pleasure journey on foot. wa′lker n. walk n. 1. Walking gait, walking pace; manner of walking, spell of walking, esp. short journey on foot for exercise or pleasure. 2. Place for walking, tree-bordered avenue, broad path in garden or pleasure-ground, sidewalk, footpath; beat or round of forest official, hawker, etc.; course or circuit for walking; sheepwalk; place where hound-puppy is sent to accustom it to variety of surroundings (esp. in *at ~*, *put to ~*); place where game-cock is kept; *cock of the ~*, person whose supremacy in his own circle is undisputed. 3. Department of action, calling, profession, occupation (usu. ~ *of life*).

wa′lkie-ta′lkie (wawkĭ, tawkĭ) n. Radio transmitting and receiving set carried on the person.

Wă′ĭkўrie (v-; *or* -ēr′ĭ) n. = VALKYRIE.

wall (wawl) n. 1. Structure of stone, bricks, earth, etc., of some

height, serving as rampart, embankment, defensive enclosure of city, castle, etc., or to enclose or divide off house, room, field, garden, etc.; *drive*, *send*, *up the ~*, (slang) drive to distraction. 2. Something resembling wall in appearance or function; outermost part of hollow structure, as tyre etc. 3. (anat., zool., bot.) Outermost layer bounding organ, cell, etc. 4. *wa′llflower*, plant of genus *Cheiranthus*, esp. *C. cheiri*, with yellow or orange-brown fragrant flowers, growing wild on old walls, rocks, etc., and cultivated in gardens; (colloq.) woman sitting out dances for lack of partners; *Siberian wallflower*, small plant resembling wallflower, with bright orange flowers, called by horticulturists *Cheiranthus allionii*, but more probably an *Erysimum*; ~-*fruit*, fruit of trees grown against a wall; ~ *game*, kind of football peculiar to Eton, played against a wall; *wa′llpaper*, paper for covering interior walls of rooms; ~-*plate*, timber or other horizontal member laid on or in wall to support rafters, distribute pressure, etc. (ill. ROOF). ~ v.t. Provide or protect with wall; close (*up*, *in*), block, shut *up*, with wall(s).

wă′lla (wŏ-) n. Var. of WALLAH.

wa′llabў (wŏ-) n. Any of various smaller species of kangaroo.

Wa′llace¹ (wŏ-), Alfred Russel (1822–1913). English naturalist and traveller.

Wa′llace² (wŏ-), Sir William (1270?–1305). National hero of Scotland; resisted the English under Edward I, was captured by treachery and executed in London.

Wa′llace Collĕ′ction (wŏ-). Collection of art treasures made by the Seymour-Conway family and enlarged by Sir Richard Wallace (1818–90) and left to the nation in 1897, now housed in Manchester Sq., London.

Wallā′chia, Walā′chia (-k-; *or* wŏ-). Former principality of SE. Europe, united (1859) with Moldavia to form Rumania. Walla′chian adj. & n.

wallah (wŏ′la) n. (orig. Ind.) Person employed about or concerned with something; (colloq.) man, person. [Hind. -*wālā*, suffix equivalent in some uses to Engl. -*er*]

Wallenstein (vă′lenshtīn), Albrecht Eusebius von, Duke of Friedland (1583–1634). Bohemian general; led the Imperial troops in the Thirty Years War; was defeated by Gustavus Adolphus at Lutzen (1632) and assassinated by some of his own officers on account of suspected treason.

wa′llĕt (wŏ-) n. 1. (archaic) Bag, esp. pilgrim's or beggar's, for holding provisions etc. on journey. 2. Flat folding case for carrying in one's pocket, closed by flap or opening like book, for holding paper money, documents, etc.

wall-eye (waw′l-ī) *n.* Eye with iris whitish (or occas. streaked, particoloured, or different in colour from other eye) or with divergent squint. **wall-eyed** (-īd) *adj.* Having wall-eye; (U.S., of fishes) with large prominent eyes.

Walloo′n *adj.* & *n.* (Member, language) of people, of Gaulish origin and speaking a French dialect, forming chief part of population of SE. Belgium.

wa′llop (wŏ-) *n.* (colloq.) Heavy resounding blow, whack. ~ *v.t.* Thrash, beat.

wa′lloping *adj.* (esp., colloq.) Big, strapping, thumping.

wallow (wŏ′lō) *v.i.* Roll about in mud, sand, water, etc.; (of ship) roll helplessly; (fig.) take delight in gross pleasures etc. ~ *n.* Act of wallowing; place where buffalo, elephant, etc., goes to wallow; depression, mud-hole, dust-hole, formed by this.

Wa′llsĕnd (wawlz-). Town (at end of Hadrian's Wall) in Tyne and Wear; hence, fine grade of household coal.

Wall Street (wawl). Street in New York City, on or near which are concentrated chief financial institutions of U.S.; hence, the American money-market.

wa′lnut (waw-) *n.* Fruit, consisting of two-lobed seed enclosed in spheroidal shell covered with green fleshy husk, of various trees of genus *Juglans*, esp. *J. regia*; any tree of *Juglans* or some related genera; wood of walnut-tree, used in cabinet-making.

Wa′lpōle (waw- *or* wŏ-), Sir Robert, 1st Earl of Orford (1676–1745); British statesman, leader of WHIG party and first prime minister 1730–41; *Horace* ~, 4th Earl (1717–97), his son; author of a novel 'The Castle of Otranto', writings on art, and a series of letters.

Walpurgis Night (vălpoor′gĭs nit; *or* vahl-). Eve of 1 May, on which, acc. to German legend, a witches' Sabbath took place on the Brocken, a peak of the Harz mountains; named after St. WALBURGA, whose feast day on 1 May coincides with an old pagan feast with rites protecting from witchcraft.

wa′lrus (waw-) *n.* Large carnivorous amphibious mammal (*Odobenus rosmarus*) of Arctic seas, allied to seals and sea-lions, and chiefly distinguished by two long tusks; ~ *moustache*, man's long thick moustache hanging down over mouth.

Wa′lsingham (waw- *or* wŏ-), Sir Francis (*c* 1530–90). English statesman under Queen Elizabeth I.

Wa′lter (waw- *or* wŏ-), John (1738/9–1812). Founder of 'The Times' newspaper, London.

Walther vŏn der Vogelweide (vă′lter, fŏn, fō′gelvīde). Early 13th-c. German lyric poet, a minnesinger.

Wa′lton[1] (waw- *or* wŏ-), Izaak (1593–1683). English writer, remembered for his 'Compleat Angler' (1653) and 'Lives' of several contemporary writers.

Wa′lton[2] (waw- *or* wŏ-), Sir William Turner (1902–). English composer of orchestral music.

waltz (wawls *or* wŏls) *n.* Dance performed to music in triple time by couples who progress at the same time as they swing round and round with smooth sliding steps; music for this, or in its characteristic time and rhythm. ~ *v.* Dance waltz; move lightly, trippingly, etc.; move (person) as in waltz.

wa′mpum (wŏ-) *n.* Cylindrical white and mauve beads of polished ends of shells threaded to form broad belts and formerly greatly used by N. Amer. Indians of the E. coast as currency, as ornaments, or (as substitute for writing, through the figures and patterns used) for mnemonic or symbolic purposes, recording treaties, etc.

wan (wŏn) *adj.* Pale, pallid, colourless, sickly. **wa′nlў** *adv.* **wa′nnĕss** (-n-n-) *n.*

wand (wŏ-) *n.* Slender rod or staff carried as sign of office by verger, beadle, usher, etc.; staff used in enchantments by fairy or magician.

wa′nder (wŏ-) *v.* Roam, ramble, move idly or restlessly or casually about, stroll, saunter; go from country to country or place to place without settled route or destination; stray, diverge from right way, get lost; wind, meander; be unsettled or incoherent in mind, purpose, talk, etc., be inattentive or delirious, rave; traverse in wandering. **wa′nderer, wa′ndering** *ns.* **wa′ndering** *adj.* (esp.) *W~Jew*, person of medieval legend condemned to wander the earth without rest until Day of Judgement, as punishment for insulting Christ on way to crucifixion.

wa′nderlŭst (wŏ-; *or* vah′nderlŏost) *n.* Strong desire to wander or travel. [Ger.]

wanderoo′ (wŏ-) *n.* Langur of Sri Lanka (*Macaca senex*).

wāne *v.i.* Decrease in brilliance, size, or splendour, decline; lose power, vigour, importance, intensity, etc.; (of moon) undergo periodical decrease in extent of visible illuminated portion during second half of lunation. ~ *n.* (Period of) waning, decline; defect in timber which has bark or insufficient wood at corner or edge. **wā′ney** *adj.*

wă′nġle (-nggl) *v.t.* (slang) Accomplish, obtain, bring about, by scheming or contrivance; manipulate, fake, (account, report, etc.). ~ *n.* Act of wangling.

Wa′nsdўke (wŏnz-). Linear earthwork in two sections, in Somerset and N. Wessex, prob. built by Britons in the late Roman period.

want (wŏ-) *n.* Lack, absence, deficiency, *of*; lack of necessaries of life, penury, destitution; need, condition marked by lack of necessary or desirable thing; (chiefly pl.) something needed or desired. ~ *v.* Be without or have too little of, fall short (by specified amount) *of*; be in want; require; desire, wish for possession or presence of. **wa′ntĕd** *adj.* (esp.) Sought for by police. **wa′nting** *adj.* (esp.) Lacking *in*, unequal *to*; lacking, minus, without; (colloq.) mentally deficient.

wa′nton (wŏ-) *adj.* Sportive, capricious; luxuriant, wild (archaic & poet.); licentious, unchaste; unprovoked, reckless, arbitrary. **wa′ntonlў** *adv.* **wa′ntonnĕss** (-n-n-) *n.* **wa′nton** *n.* Unchaste woman. ~ *v.i.* (chiefly archaic and poet.) Gambol, frolic; luxuriate, revel, *in*; sport amorously or lewdly.

wă′pentāke (*or* wŏ-) *n.* (hist.) In some eastern and midland English shires (where Danish element in population was large), subdivision corresponding to HUNDRED of other counties.

wa′piti (wŏ-) *n.* N. Amer. ELK (*Cervus canadensis*).

war (wŏr) *n.* 1. Quarrel usu. between nations conducted by force, state of open hostility and suspension of ordinary international law prevalent during such quarrel, attack or series of attacks by armed forces; fighting as profession; (fig.) hostility between persons; *civil* ~, war between parts of one nation for supremacy; *cold* ~: see COLD; *holy* ~, war waged in support of some religious cause; *private* ~, feud between persons or families carried on in defiance of laws of murder etc.; (also) armed attack made by members of one State without government sanction upon another; ~ *of nerves*, attempt to wear down opponent by gradual destruction of morale. 2. Phrr.: *be at, make, wage*, ~, carry on hostilities; *declare* ~, announce that hostilities may be expected (also fig.); *go to* ~, begin hostilities. 3. ~-*cloud*, position in international affairs that threatens war; ~ *correspondent*, newspaper correspondent reporting on war; ~-*cry*, phrase or name shouted in charging or rallying to attack; party catchword; ~-*dance*, dance of primitive people before warlike excursion or after victory; ~-*god*, god worshipped as giving victory in war, esp. Ares or Mars; *war′head*, explosive head of torpedo, rocket, etc.; ~-*horse*, charger (now chiefly fig. in *old war-*~, person excited by memories of past combats or controversies); ~-*lord*, military commander (transl. of Ger. *Kriegsherr*, used esp. of William II of Germany and of Chinese civil-war generals); **war'-monger**, one seeking to bring about war; **war'mongering** (adj. & n.); **~-paint**, paint applied to face and body esp. by N. Amer. Indians before battle; (colloq.) one's best clothes and finery, ceremonial costume; **~-path**, (route taken by) warlike expedition of N. Amer. Indians; **on the ~-path**, (fig.) engaged in, preparing for, any conflict; **~-plane**, military aircraft; **war'ship**, ship armed and manned for war; **~-song**, song inciting to war or celebrating martial deeds; **war'time**, time of war; **~-whoop**, yell esp. of N. Amer. Indians in charging; **~-worn**, experienced or damaged in or exhausted by war. ~ v. (chiefly literary) Make war, be at war. **war'ring** adj. (esp.) Contending, discordant.

War. abbrev. Warwickshire.

War'bĕck (wŏr-), Perkin (1474–99). The 2nd of two pretenders to the English Crown in the reign of Henry VII (cf. SIMNEL); he claimed to be Richard, Duke of York, and led an insurrection in 1497, but was captured and hanged.

war'ble¹ (wŏr-) v. Sing softly and sweetly, sing with trills and quavers; (of small stream) make melody as it flows. ~ n. Warbling sound.

war'ble² (wŏr-) n. Small hard tumour produced by pressure of saddle on horse's back; swelling on back of cattle etc. produced by larva of warble fly; ~ fly, any of various dipterous insects whose larvae live under skin of cattle etc.

war'bler (wŏr-) n. (esp.) Any of various small Old World plain-coloured singing birds of family Parulidae; any of various small Amer. usu. bright-coloured birds; any of various small birds of Australia and New Zealand.

ward¹ (wŏrd) n. 1. Act of guarding or defending (now only in **keep watch and ~**); confinement, custody (archaic); guardianship of minor or other person legally incapable of conducting his affairs. 2. Minor under care of guardian or Court of Chancery. 3. Separate room or division of prison or hospital or (hist.) workhouse. 4. Administrative division of borough or city, or of Cumberland, Northumberland, and some Scottish counties. 5. Each ridge projecting from inside plate of lock, preventing passage of any key not having corresponding incisions; each incision in bit of key corresponding to ward of lock (ill. LOCK²). 6. BAILEY. 7. **~-maid**, woman employed to do domestic work in hospital ward; **war'dmote**, meeting of citizens of ward, esp. in City of London of liverymen of ward under presidency of alderman; **war'droom**, mess-room or living-space of naval commissioned officers below commanding officer. ~ v.t. Have in keeping, protect (chiefly now of God); parry (off blow), keep off (danger etc.).

Ward² (wŏrd), Mrs Augusta, better known as Mrs Humphry Ward (1851–1920). English novelist.

war'den¹ (wŏr-) n. 1. President, governor (of certain colleges, schools, hospitals, the CINQUE PORTS, etc.); governor of prison (esp. in old title **W~ of the Fleet**); 2. Churchwarden. 3. (also **air-raid ~**) Member of civil organization for assistance of civilian population in air-raids. 4. TRAFFIC warden. **war'denship** n.

war'den² (wŏr-) n. Variety of cooking-pear.

war'der (wŏr-) n. 1. (archaic) Sentinel, watchman on tower. 2. (fem. **war'dress**) Official in charge of prisoners in gaol.

Wardour Street (wŏr'der). Street in Soho, London, formerly occupied by dealers in antique and imitation-antique furniture (whence ~ **English**, pseudo-archaic diction in historical novels etc.) and now by the offices of film companies.

war'drobe (wŏr-) n. Place where clothes are kept, esp. large cupboard with hangers, movable trays, drawers, etc.; room where theatrical costumes and properties are kept; in royal or noble household, department charged with care of wearing apparel (chiefly in titles); person's stock of clothes; ~ **dealer**, dealer in second-hand clothes; ~ **mistress**, woman in charge of professional wardrobe of actor, actress, or theatrical company; ~ **trunk**, upright trunk in which dresses, coats, etc., are hung, and other clothes packed in separate drawers, etc.

wāre¹ n. Articles made for sale, goods; esp., vessels etc. of baked clay (usu. with defining word, as **Staffordshire ~, Wedgwood ~**); (pl.) things that person has for sale.

wāre² pred. adj. (poet.) Aware.

wāre³ (or wŏr) v.t. (usu. imper., esp. in hunting-field) Beware of, look out for.

war'ehouse (wăr̄h-) n. (Part of) building used for storage of merchandise, wholesaler's goods for sale, furniture or other property temporarily stored for owner; large retail shop; **bonded ~**: see BOND¹. ~ (-z) v.t. Store in warehouse.

war'fare (wŏr-) n. State of war, being engaged in war, conflict.

war'like (wŏr-) adj. Martial; skilled in, fond of, war; of, for use in, war; bellicose, threatening war.

war'lock (wŏr-) n. (archaic) Sorcerer.

warm (wŏrm) adj. 1. Of, at, rather high temperature, giving out considerable degree of heat (but less than that indicated by **hot**); (of persons etc.) glowing with exercise, excitement, eating and drinking, etc.; (of clothes etc.) serving to keep one warm. 2. (of feelings etc.) Sympathetic, affectionate, cordial; eager, emotionally excited, indignant; (of position etc.) difficult or dangerous to meet or maintain; (of conflict) vigorous, harassing; (of scent or trail) fresh, strong; (in children's games) near to the object sought, or to finding or guessing. 3. (of colour) Suggesting warmth; esp., of, containing, rich reds and yellows. 4. **~-blooded**, (of birds and mammals) having constant body-temperature normally higher than that of surrounding medium; (fig.) passionate, amorous, emotional; **~-hearted**, of, showing, proceeding from, generous and affectionate disposition. **wǎr'mlў** adv. **wǎr'mnĕss, wǎrmth** ns. **wǎrm** n. Warming, being warmed; warmth of atmosphere; **British ~**, short warm overcoat worn esp. by army officers. ~ v. Make warm; excite; become warm, animated, or sympathetic; ~ **up**, make, become, warm; re-heat (food etc.); (of radio, engine, etc.) come to efficient working temperature; **war'ming-pan**, long-handled covered metal (usu. brass) pan for holding live coals etc., formerly used for warming beds.

warn (wŏrn) v.t. Give timely notice to (person etc.) of impending danger or misfortune, put on guard, caution **against**; admonish; notify of something requiring attention, give previous notice to; ~ **off**, give notice to person to keep at distance, off private ground, etc.; ~ **off** (the course, the Turf), prohibit (offender against Jockey Club rules) from riding or running horses at its meetings.

war'ning (wŏr-) n. (esp.) Thing that serves to warn; notice of, or caution against, possible danger; notice of termination of business relation, esp. between landlord and tenant, employer and employee.

warp (wŏrp) v. 1. Make, become, crooked or perverted, bias, change from straight or right or natural state. 2. (naut.) Move (ship) by hauling on rope attached to fixed point; (of ship etc.) progress thus. 3. Choke, be choked, **up** with alluvial deposit; cover (land) with deposit of alluvial soil by natural or artificial flooding. ~ n. 1. Threads stretched lengthwise in loom to be crossed by weft (ill. WEAVE). 2. Rope used in towing or warping. 3. Crooked state produced in timber etc. by uneven shrinking or expansion; (fig.) perversion or perverse inclination of mind. 4. Sediment or alluvial deposit, esp. that left by turbid water kept standing on poor land.

wa'rrant (wŏ-) n. 1. Act, token, of authorization, sanction; justifying reason or ground for action, belief, etc.; proof, authoritative witness. 2. Document conveying authority or security; esp. written

[978]

WARRANTY

authorization to pay or receive money; executive authority's writ or order empowering officer to make arrest or search, execute judicial sentence, etc.; writing issued by sovereign, officer of State, etc., authorizing performance of some act; (mil., naval) official certificate of rank issued to officer lower than commissioned officer; ~ *officer*, officer holding office by warrant (in British armed forces now intermediate in rank between commissioned and non-commissioned officers). ~ *v.t.* Serve as warrant for, justify; guarantee. **wa′rranter**, (law) **wa′rrantor** *ns*.

wa′rranty (wŏ-) *n*. Authority, justification (*for*); (esp., law) express or implied undertaking by vendor that his title is secure or that thing sold fulfils specified conditions; in insurance contract, engagement by insured that certain statements are true or certain conditions shall be fulfilled.

wa′rren (wŏ-) *n*. Piece of land where rabbits breed or abound; (fig.) densely populated building or district; (hist.) piece of land enclosed and preserved for breeding game.

wa′rrior (wŏ-) *n*. Fighting man, valiant or experienced soldier (now poet. or rhet.); fighting man of tribe etc.

War′saw (wŏr-). (Pol. *Warszawa*) Capital city of Poland; ~ *Pact*, treaty of mutual defence and military aid, signed at Warsaw 14 May 1955, between U.S.S.R., Poland, Czechoslovakia, Hungary, Rumania, Bulgaria, Albania, and East Germany.

wart (wŏrt) *n*. Small round dry tough excrescence on skin caused by abnormal growth of papillae and thickening of epidermis over them; rounded excrescence or protuberance on skin of animal, surface of plant, etc.; ~-*hog*, African wild hog of genus (*Phacochoerus aethiopicus*), with large warty excrescences on face and large protruding tusks. **war′ty** *adj*.

Warwick[1] (wŏ′rĭk). County town of Warwickshire; university, at Coventry, 1965.

Warwick[2] (wŏ′rĭk), Richard Neville, Earl of (1428–71). Known as 'the Kingmaker'; instrumental in placing Edward IV on the throne in 1461 and in restoring Henry VI in 1470.

Warwickshire (wŏ′rĭk-). Midland county of England.

wār′y *adj*. (Habitually) on one's guard, circumspect, cautious, careful. **wār′ily** *adv*. **wār′iness** *n*.

wash (wŏ-) *v*. 1. Cleanse with liquid; take (stain, dirt, etc.) *out*, *off*, *away*, by washing; wash oneself or esp. one's hands (and face); wash clothes; (of textile material, dye, etc.) bear washing without deterioration; (fig.) purify; ~ *one's hands of*, decline responsibility for;

~ *up*, wash (table utensils etc.) after use. 2. Moisten; (of sea, river, etc.) flow past, beat upon (shore, walls, etc.), sweep *over*, surge *against*; make (channel etc.) thus; ~ *up*, sweep (object) on to shore etc. 3. Sift (ore), sift ore, sand, etc. (*for* gold etc.), by action of water; brush thin coating of watery colour over (wall, drawing, etc.); coat (inferior metal) thinly with gold etc. **washed** (-sht) *adj*. (esp.) ~ *out*, (of fabric) faded from being washed; (fig.) enfeebled, limp, exhausted; ~ *up*, (colloq.) having failed completely, finished. **wash′able** *adj*. **wash** *n*. 1. Washing, being washed; process of being laundered (esp. *in*, *at*, *the* ~); quantity of clothes etc. (to be) washed. 2. Lotion; liquid applied to hair esp. to cleanse it. 3. Thin even layer of transparent watercolour or diluted ink; coating of wall-colouring. 4. Solution applied to metal to give effect of gold or silver. 5. Visible or audible motion of agitated water, esp. waves caused by passage of vessel; disturbance in air caused by passage of aircraft. 6. Sandbank, tract of land, alternately covered and exposed by sea; low-lying often-flooded ground with shallow pools and marshes; shallow pool, backwater, etc.; (U.S.) dry bed of winter torrent; *the* W~, shallow-water bay of North Sea between Lincolnshire and Norfolk, forming estuary of several rivers. 7. Kitchen scraps or brewery refuse as food for pigs, liquid food for other animals. 8. Solid particles carried away or deposited by running water; soil from which gold or diamonds may be washed out. 9. Malt or other substance(s) steeped in water to ferment before distillation; washy or vapid liquor or (fig.) writing etc. **wash-** *prefix*. ~-*basin*, bowl for washing hands etc.; ~-*board*, corrugated board on which clothes etc. may be scrubbed; ~-*bottle*, (chem.) bottle containing liquid through which gases may be passed for purification; ~-*day*, day on which clothes are washed; ~-*drawing*, (drawing produced by) method of using washes of colour or ink; ~-*hand-stand*, piece of furniture for holding wash-basin, ewer, soap-dish, etc.; ~-*house*, outbuilding for washing clothes; ~-*leather*, soft esp. sheepskin leather dressed to resemble chamois, used for cleaning, etc.; ~-*out*, (esp.) (site of) removal by flood of part of hillside, road, track, railway, etc.; the washing out of a cavity of the body, result of this; (slang) disappointing failure, fiasco; ~-*room*, (U.S.) room with toilet facilities, lavatory; ~-*stand*, wash-hand-stand; ~-*tub*, tub for washing clothes etc.

Wash. *abbrev*. Washington.

wa′sher[1] (wŏ-) *n*. Person,

thing, that washes; *wa′sherman*, *wa′sherwoman*, person whose occupation is washing clothes.

wa′sher[2] (wŏ-) *n*. (esp.) Disc or flattened ring of metal, leather, rubber, fibre, etc., placed between two surfaces to relieve rotative friction or prevent lateral motion, under plunger of screw-down water-tap etc. to prevent leakage. under nut of bolt or tie-rod etc. (ill. COCK[1]).

wa′shery (wŏ-) *n*. Place where the washing of coal, ore, wool, etc., is carried on.

wa′shing (wŏ-) *n*. (esp.) Clothes, linen sent to the wash; ~-*day*, wash-day; ~-*machine*, machine for washing clothes etc.; ~-*soda*, form of sodium carbonate used in washing clothes etc.

Wa′shington[1] (wŏ-), George (1732–99). Commander-in-chief of the Continental Forces in the War of American Independence and first president of U.S., 1789–97.

Wa′shington[2] (wŏ-). Administrative capital of U.S., conterminous with the District of Columbia on the NE. bank of the Potomac River; founded during presidency of George Washington and named after him; ~ *Conference*, conference of world powers held in 1921 to discuss limitation of naval armaments and avoidance of conflict in the Far East.

Wa′shington[3] (wŏ-). Most northerly of the Pacific States of U.S., admitted to the Union in 1889; capital, Olympia.

wa′shy (wŏ-) *adj*. (of food etc.) Too much diluted, weak, sloppy, thin; (of colour) faded-looking, weak, pale; (of style, utterance, etc.) feeble, diffuse, wanting force or vigour. **wa′shily** *adv*. **wa′shiness** *n*.

wasp (wŏ-) *n*. Any of the superfamily Vespoidea of hymenopterous insects, often carnivorous, with slender body, abdomen attached to thorax by narrow stalk, usu. two pairs of fully-developed wings and often formidable sting; esp. the common wasp (*Vespa vulgaris* and *V. germanica*) and similar social species, with alternate rings of black and yellow on abdomen and marked taste for fruits and sweet things; ~ *waist*, -*waisted*, (having) very slender waist, esp. one produced by tight lacing.

wa′spish (wŏ-) *adj*. Irritable, petulantly spiteful, irascible; caustic. **wa′spishly** *adv*. **wa′spishness** *n*.

wa′spy (wŏ-) *adj*. Wasp-like; abounding in wasps.

wă′ssail (*or* -sl; *or* wŏ-) *n*. (archaic) Salutation in presenting cup of wine to guest; festive occasion, drinking-bout; liquor in which healths were drunk, esp. spiced ale drunk on Twelfth Night and Christmas Eve; ~-*bowl*, large bowl for this. ~ *v.i.*

Make merry; sit carousing and drinking healths. **wa′ssailer** n. [ON *ves heill* 'be in good health', form of salutation]
Wa′ssermann (vahs-),. August von (1866-1925). German pathologist; ~ *test*, blood test employed in diagnosis of syphilis.
wā′stage n. Loss or diminution by use, wear, decay, leakage, etc.; amount wasted.
wāste[1] n. 1. Desert, waste region; dreary scene or expanse. 2. Consumption, loss or diminution from use, wear and tear, etc.; wasting, useless or extravagant expenditure or consumption, squandering (*of*); run to ~, (of liquid) flow away so as to be wasted; (fig.) be expended uselessly. 3. Waste matter; useless remains (esp. of manufacturing process), scraps, shreds; esp. scraps, remnants, from manufacture of cotton, woollen, etc., yarn or textiles, used for cleaning machinery, absorbing oil, etc.; ~-*pipe*, pipe for carrying off used or superfluous water or steam. ~ *adj.* 1. (of land, region, etc.) Desert, uninhabited, desolate, barren; uncultivated; (fig.) monotonous, without features of interest; not built upon; *lay* ~, destroy, devastate, ruin; ~ *land*, land not utilized for cultivation or building. 2. Superfluous, refuse, left over; no longer serving a purpose; ~ *paper*, paper thrown away as spoiled, superfluous, useless, etc.; ~-*paper basket*, basket for this; ~ *product*, useless by-product of manufacture or physiological process.
wāste[2] v. 1. Lay waste; (law) bring (estate) into bad condition by damage or neglect. 2. Expend to no purpose or for inadequate result, use extravagantly, squander; run to waste. 3. Wear gradually away, be used up, lose substance or volume by gradual loss, decay, etc.; wither; reduce one's weight by training etc.
wā′steful (-tf-) *adj.* Given to, exhibiting, waste; extravagant. **wā′stefullў** adv. **wā′stefulnèss** n.
wā′ster n. (esp., colloq.) Dissolute or good-for-nothing person.
wā′strel n. Waster; waif; spendthrift.
watch (wŏ-) v. Remain awake for devotion or other purpose, keep vigil; be on the alert *for*, keep watch, be vigilant; exercise protecting care *over*; keep eyes fixed on, keep under observation, follow observantly. **wa′tcher**[1] n. **watch** n. 1. Watching, keeping awake and vigilant at night for guarding, attending, etc.; (hist.) each of (3, 4, or 5) periods into which night was anciently divided; (naut.) period of time (usu. 4 hours) for which each division of ship's company remains on duty, sailor's turn of duty; part, usu. one half, of officers and crew who together work ship during a watch; ~ *and* ~, arrangement by which 2 halves of ship's crew take duty alternately every 4 hours. 2. Watching, observing, with continuous attention, continued lookout, guard (*keep* ~); one who watches, look-out man; (hist.) man, body of men, charged with patrolling and guarding streets at night, proclaiming the hour, etc.; *W*~, early 18th-c. name of irregular Highland troops; *Black W*~, (from their dark-coloured tartan) some of these troops embodied (1739-40) as 42nd Regiment. 3. Small timepiece designed to be worn or carried in pocket etc. (ill. CLOCK). 4. ~-*chain*, chain attaching timepiece to one's person; *W*~ *Committee*, (hist., in a county borough) committee acting as local police authority; ~-*dog*, dog kept to guard house, property, etc.; ~-*fire*, fire burning at night as signal or for use of sentinel or other person(s) on watch; ~-*glass*, thin piece of glass, usu. concavo-convex, fitted over dial-plate of watch or used as receptacle for material under observation etc.; ~-*guard*, chain, cord, ribbon, etc., for securing watch on person; ~-*gun*, gun fired at changing of watch; ~-*key*, key for winding watch; **wa′tchman**, formerly, one who patrolled streets at night to safeguard life and property; now esp. man employed to guard building etc., esp. at night; ~-*night*, (religious service lasting till after midnight held on) New Year's Eve; ~-*pocket*, small pocket, usu. in waistcoat, for holding a watch; ~-*spring*, mainspring of watch; ~-*tower*, tower from which observation is kept of approach of danger; **wa′tchword**, (hist.) military password; (transf.) word or phrase expressing guiding principle or rule of action of party or individual.
wa′tchful (wŏ-) *adj.* Wakeful (archaic); accustomed to, engaged in, watching, vigilant; showing vigilance. **wa′tchfullў** *adv.* **wa′tchfulnèss** n.
wa′ter(waw-)n. 1. Transparent, colourless, tasteless, inodorous liquid (H_2O) composing seas, lakes, and rivers, falling as rain, issuing from springs, etc., and convertible into steam by heat and into ice by cold; this as supplied for domestic needs, esp. through pipes; sheet or body of water, (now chiefly Sc.) stream, river; liquid resembling (and usu. containing) water, as tears, saliva, urine, etc.; aqueous decoction, infusion, etc., used in medicine or as cosmetic or perfume; (freq. pl.) water of mineral spring(s) used medicinally for bathing or drinking; state of tide (in *high, low,* ~); *heavy* ~: see HEAVY; *strong* ~*s* (archaic), distilled alcoholic liquors; ~ *on the brain*, hydrocephalus; ~ *on the knee*, accumulation of inflammatory exudate in knee-joint. 2. Characteristic transparency and lustre of diamond or pearl; *of the first* ~, of the finest quality. 3. ~-*bath*, (esp., chem.) vessel containing water in or over which vessels containing chemical preparations etc. are placed for cooling, evaporating, etc.; ~-*bear*, = TARDIGRADE; ~ *bed*, (bed with) rubber mattress filled with water; ~-*biscuit*, unsweetened biscuit made with flour and water; ~ *boatman*, aquatic insect (*Notonecta*) with boat-shaped body and oar-like legs which swims upside-down over surface of water; ~-*bok, -buck*, S. African antelope of genus *Kobus*, frequenting riverbanks; ~-*borne*, (esp., of diseases) communicated by use of contaminated drinking-water etc.; (of seaplane) having landed on water; ~-*bottle*, bottle to hold drinking-water, esp. kind of flask carried by soldiers and travellers; ~-*buck*, water-bok; ~-*buffalo*, common domestic buffalo; ~-*butt*, barrel for catching rainwater; *W*~-*carrier*: see AQUARIUS; ~-*cart*, cart carrying water, esp. for sprinkling streets; ~-*clock*, water-operated machine for measuring time; ~-*closet*, (room etc. containing) lavatory flushed by water (abbrev. W.C.); ~-*colour*, artists' paint made of pigment mixed usu. with gum and diluted with water; esp., transparent variety of this, aquarelle; picture painted, art or method of painting, with such colours; ~-*cooled*, (of internal combustion engine) cooled by means of circulating water; ~-*cooler*, (esp.) small tank containing cooled drinking-water; **wa′ter-course**, (bed or channel of) stream of water, river, brook; **wa′tercress**, hardy perennial cress (*Nasturtium officinale*) growing in springs and clear running streams, and with pungent leaves used as a salad; ~-*cure*, = HYDROPATHY; ~-*diviner*, one who finds subterranean water with a dowsing-rod; **wa′terfall**, more or less perpendicular descent of water from a height, cascade; ~-*finder*, water-diviner; ~-*flag*, yellow iris; **wa′terfowl**, bird(s) frequenting water, esp. swimming game-bird(s); **wa′ter-front**, land or buildings abutting on river, lake, sea, etc.; ~-*gas*, gas (mixture of hydrogen and carbon monoxide), made by forcing steam over red-hot coke and used as fuel etc.; ~-*gilding*, gilding by application of liquid amalgam and subsequent evaporation of mercury; ~-*glass*, tube with glass bottom for observing objects under water; aqueous solution of sodium or potassium silicate, solidifying on exposure to air and used as cement, fire-proof paint, for preserving eggs, etc.; ~-*hammer*, concussion of water made when its flow through pipe is suddenly checked; ~ *hemisphere*: see HEMISPHERE; **wa′terhen**, any of various

ralline birds, esp. moorhen and Amer. coot; ~-*hole*, hole or hollow containing water, esp. in desert or dry bed of stream; ~-*ice*, frozen confection of flavoured water and sugar; ~-*jacket*, casing holding water, esp. casing through which water circulates in water-cooled engines, guns, etc.; ~-*jump*, place where horse must jump over water in steeplechase etc.; ~-*level*, (height of) surface of water; upward limit of saturation by water; ~-*lily*, aquatic plant of *Nymphaea* and related genera, and similar plants with broad floating leaves and showy fragrant flowers; ~-*line*, line on ship's side corresponding to surface of water when she is afloat, esp. proper line of floatation when ship is fully loaded; linear watermark in paper; wa'terlogged, filled or saturated with water so as to be unbuoyant, heavy and unmanageable; (of ground etc.) made useless by saturation with water; ~-*main*, chief pipe in system of watersupply; wa'terman, (esp.) boatman plying for hire on river etc.; wa'termark, distinguishing mark or design in paper visible when it is held up to light; ~-*meadow*, meadow periodically inundated by stream; ~-*melon*, large fruit (*Citrullus vulgaris*) with smooth hard rind, soft pink or red pulp, and abundant sweet watery juice; plant, native of tropical Africa and widely cultivated, bearing this; ~-*mill*, mill driven by water; ~-*mint*, aquatic plant of labiate genus *Mentha*; ~-*nymph*, nymph inhabiting or presiding over water, naiad; ~ *ouzel*: see DIPPER, 1; ~-*plantain*, plant of genus *Alisma*, with plantain-like leaves, growing in ditches etc.; W~ *Poet*, title adopted by the poet John TAYLOR[1]; ~ *polo*, game played in water by teams of swimmers with ball like football; ~-*power*, mechanical force derived from weight or motion of water; wa'terproof (adj.) impervious to water; (n.) waterproof garment or material; (v.t.) make waterproof; ~ *rail*: see RAIL[2]; ~-*rat*, aquatic rodent of genus *Arvicola*, water vole; (U.S.) muskrat; (Austral.) aquatic mouse of genus *Hydromys*; ~-*rate*, charge made for use of public watersupply; wa'tershed, summit or boundary line separating waters flowing into different rivers or river basins; whole catchment area of river system; ~-*ski* (v.i.) plane over water on water-skis, towed by boat; ~-*ski* (n.): see SKI; ~-*snake*, snake inhabiting or frequenting water, esp. nonpoisonous freshwater snake of *Natrix* and related genera; ~-*splash*, shallow stream or ford across road; (colloq.) water-jump; wa'terspout, (esp.) gyrating column of mist, spray, and water produced by action of whirlwind on part of sea and clouds above it; sudden

and violent fall of rain, cloudburst; ~-*table*, level at which porous rock etc. is saturated by underground water, height to which such water naturally rises in well etc. (ill. WELL[1]); (archit.) projecting horizontal course in wall to throw off rainfall; wa'tertight, so closely constructed or fitted that water cannot leak through; (of argument etc.) unassailable; *watertight compartment*, each of compartments with watertight partitions into which interior of ship is divided for safety; (fig.) division of anything regarded as kept entirely separate from rest; ~-*tower*, structure supporting elevated tank to secure necessary pressure for water-supply; fire-fighting apparatus for delivering water at considerable height; ~ *vole*: see VOLE; ~-*wagon*, wagon for carrying water; ~-*wagtail*, common pied wagtail; ~-*wave*, wave set when hair is damp; wa'terway, navigable channel; (naut.) channel round ship's deck to drain off water; ~-*weed*, aquatic plant without special use or beauty; ~-*wheel*, wheel rotated by action of water

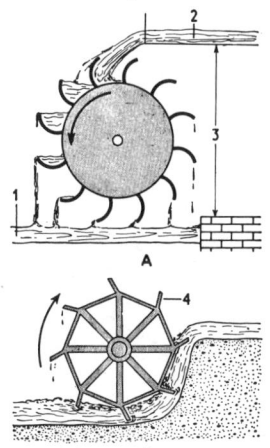

A

B

WATER-WHEEL
A. OVERSHOT. B. UNDERSHOT BREAST-WHEEL

1. Tail-race. 2. Mill-race. 3. Head of water. 4. Float

and driving machinery; wheel for raising water for irrigation etc. in boxes or buckets fitted on its circumference; ~-*wings*, inflated floats used as supports by persons learning to swim; wa'terworks, assemblage of machinery, buildings, engineering constructions, etc., for supplying town, ornamental fountain, etc., with water through pipes; (slang) tears. wa'terless adj. wa'ter v. 1. Give (animal) water to drink, (of animals) go to pool etc. to drink; furnish (ship etc.) with, take in, supply of water; supply water to

(plant, crop, etc.), esp. by pouring or sprinkling; add water to (drink etc.), dilute (freq. ~ *down*). 2. (of eyes) Fill and run with moisture, (of mouth) secrete abundant saliva in anticipation of appetizing food etc. 3. (commerc.) Increase nominal amount of (company's stock or capital) by issue of new shares without corresponding addition to assets. 4. (chiefly in past part.) Produce wavy lustrous finish on (silk or other textiles) by sprinkling with water and passing through calender. 5. *watering-can*, portable vessel for watering plants, with long tubular spout freq. ending with rose; *watering-cart*, water-cart; *watering-place*, pool, trough, etc., where animals obtain water; place where supply of water is obtained; spa; seaside holiday or health resort.
Wa'terford (waw-). Maritime county and city of Munster, Ireland; ~ *glass*, glassware produced at Waterford.
Waterloo' (waw-). Village S. of Brussels, Belgium, where on 18 June 1815 Napoleon was finally defeated by the British under the Duke of Wellington and the Prussians; hence, *meet one's* ~, suffer final defeat.
wa'tery (waw-) adj. Of, consisting of, water (esp. in ~ *grave*, place in which person lies drowned); full of, covered with, containing too much, water, suffused or running with, water; resembling water in colour, pale; washed out; (of liquids) too thin, diluted, having little or no taste; (fig.) vapid, insipid, feeble.
Wa'tling Street (wŏ-). Roman road running NW. across England from Richborough in Kent through London and St. Albans to Wroxeter in Salop.
Wat'son[1] (wŏ-), Dr. Stolid medical man in stories by Sir A. Conan Doyle; companion and assistant of Sherlock HOLMES; his qualities serve as a foil to his friend's brilliance.
Wa'tson[2] (wŏ-), Sir William (1858-1935). English poet.
Watt[1] (wŏt), James (1736-1819). Scottish inventor of the steam-engine.
watt[2] (wŏt) n. Unit of power in M.K.S. system, equivalent to 1 joule per second (abbrev. W); ~-*meter*, instrument for measuring electric power in terms of watts. [f. WATT[1]]
wa'ttage (wŏ-) n. Amount of electric power expressed in watts.
Watteau (wŏtō), Antoine (1684-1721). French genre-painter, whose pictures of shepherds and shepherdesses in the costumes of the 18th c. have caused his name to be given to various kinds of female dress, as ~ *bodice*, *dress*, *hat*, etc.
wa'ttle[1] (wŏ-) n. 1. Interlaced rods and twigs or branches used for fences and walls and roofs of

buildings; ~ *and daub*, this plastered with clay or mud as building material for huts etc. (ill. HALF-timber). 2. (from use of its long pliant branches for making wattle fences etc.) Any of various species of acacia with fragrant golden-yellow flowers (adopted as Austral. national emblem), and bark used in tanning. ~ *v.t.* Construct of wattle; interlace (twigs etc.) to form wattle; enclose, fill up, with wattle-work.

wa′ttle² (wŏ-) *n.* Fleshy, usu. bright-coloured, lobe pendent from head or neck of turkey, domestic fowl, and other birds; barb, fleshy appendage on mouth of some fishes.

Watts¹ (wŏ-), George Frederick (1817–1904). English painter of portraits and allegorical pictures.

Watts² (wŏ-), Isaac (1674–1748). English writer of hymns and poems for children.

wāve *n.* 1. Moving ridge or swell of water between two troughs; movement of sea etc. in which such waves are formed. 2. Undulating configuration or line in or on surface, as hair etc. 3. Something resembling or supposed to resemble a wave, esp. temporary heightening of emotion, influence, etc.; *heat, cold* ~, spell of hot or cold weather. 4. (phys.) Oscillatory condition which is propagated from place to place, such that the same type of vibration occurs all along the path with a difference of PHASE (i.e. slightly delayed in time; ill. VIBRATION); *heat, light, radio,* ~*s*, electromagnetic waves propagated through space; ~-*band*: see BAND, 4; ~-*form*, shape of wave, graphical or arithmetical specification of this; *wa′velength*, distance between successive points of equal phase in the direction of propagation of a wave, specific electromagnetic wave used by radio transmitting station; ~ *mechanics*, system of wave equations used to calculate the behaviour of atoms and subatomic particles when Newtonian mechanics no longer suffices. 5. Act or gesture of waving. ~ *v.* 1. Move in waves, undulate; move to and fro, shake, sway; impart waving movement to; wave hand in greeting or as signal; motion (person) *away, back, in,* etc., by movement of hand. 2. Give undulating surface, course, or appearance to, make wavy; (of hair, lines, etc.) have such appearance, be wavy.

wā′velĕt (-vl-) *n.* Small wave, ripple.

wā′ver *v.i.* Change, vary, fluctuate, shake, tremble; be irresolute, show doubt or indecision; falter, show signs of giving way. **wā′verer** *n.* **wā′veringlȳ** *adv.*

wā′vȳ *adj.* Undulating; forming undulating line or series of wavelike curves; *W*~ *Navy*, (colloq.)

Royal Naval Volunteer Reserve (from the wavy gold-lace stripes or rings formerly worn on sleeves). **wā′vilȳ** *adv.* **wā′vinĕss** *n.*

wăx¹ *n.* 1. Beeswax, sticky plastic yellowish substance of low melting-point secreted by bees from special abdominal glands, used as material of honeycomb; white brittle translucent odourless tasteless substance got from this by purifying and bleaching and used for candles, as plastic material for modelling, as basis of polishes, as air-excluding protective coating, etc. 2. Any of class of natural substances of plant or animal origin resembling beeswax in general properties and in being composed of fatty acids and alcohols; any of various hydrocarbons resembling beeswax. 3. Compound, chiefly of lac, used to receive impression of seal, sealing-wax. 4. Thick resinous composition used by shoemakers for rubbing thread, cobblers' wax. 5. Cerumen. 6. *wa′xberry*, (fruit of) wax myrtle; *wa′xbill*, any of numerous small birds of weaver-bird family with waxy-looking pink, red, or white beaks; ~ *candle*, candle of beeswax, paraffin wax, etc.; ~ *casting*, casting by making a wax model, laying a fireproof mould round it, melting out the wax, and pouring molten metal in its place; ~ *doll*, doll with head etc. of wax; person with pretty but unexpressive face; ~-*end*, thread coated with wax and usu. pointed with bristle, used by shoemakers; ~ *insect*, any of various wax-secreting insects, esp. a Chinese scale-insect (*Ericerus*); ~-*light*, taper or candle of wax; ~ *myrtle*, plant of genus *Myrica*, esp. either of two eastern N. Amer. species with aromatic foliage and small hard berries thickly coated with a white wax; ~ *paper*, paper coated with wax used as waterproof and airtight wrapping etc.; *wa′xwing*, any of various Amer. and Asiatic passerine birds of genus *Bombycilla*, esp. *B. garrulus*, with showy crest and red wax-like tips on wing-feathers; *wa′xwork*, modelling in wax; object modelled in wax, esp. life-size figure of person with wax head, hands, etc., coloured and clothed to look like life; (pl.) exhibition of such figures. ~ *v.t.* Smear, coat, polish, treat, with wax; *waxed paper*: see PARAFFIN.

wăx² *n.* (slang) Fit of anger.

wăx³ *v.i.* (of moon) Undergo periodical increase in extent of visible illuminated portion in first part of lunation, before full moon (opp. WANE); (archaic and poet.) grow, increase; change by growth or increase, become (*fat* etc.).

wă′xen *adj.* Made of, coated with, wax; resembling wax, esp. in smooth and lustrous surface, pallor, or softness and impressibility.

wă′xȳ¹ *adj.* Resembling wax, esp. easily moulded, or presenting smooth pale translucent surface; (of tissue) affected with amyloid degeneration. **wă′xinĕss** *n.*

wă′xȳ² *adj.* (slang) Angry; quick-tempered.

way *n.* 1. Road, track, path, street (esp. in phrases *across, over, the* ~, etc.); place of passage through door, crowd, etc.; (pl.) inclined structure, usu. of timber, on which ship is built and down which it is slid at launch (ill. LAUNCH); (pl.) parallel sills forming track for carriage or table of lathe or other machine; (pl.) inclined plane of parallel wooden rails or planks for sliding down heavy loads. 2. Route, line or course of travel for reaching place; opportunity for passage or advance, (fig.) freedom of action, scope, opportunity; travel or motion in particular direction, direction of motion, relative position, aspect; distance (to be) travelled, distance between places or to a place; (naut.) progress, rate of progress, through water, impetus gained by vessel in motion; *the other* ~ *about, round*, conversely, vice versa. 3. Path or course of life or conduct, (pl.) habits of life, esp. with regard to moral conduct; course of action, device, method, means; customary or usual, habitual or characteristic, manner of acting, behaving, speaking, etc., (pl.) habits; condition regarded as hopeful or the contrary; kind, sort (now only in *in the* ~ *of* and similar phrases), kind *of business*; ~*s and means*, methods, esp. of providing money. 4. *make* ~, open a passage (*for*), move to allow person to pass; leave place vacant *for* (successor etc.); *make one's* ~, proceed in certain direction or to certain place; make progress in career, advance in wealth, reputation, etc.; *pay one's* ~, pay expenses as they arise, without incurring debts; (of business etc.) be carried on at least without loss; *see one's* ~, (esp., fig.) feel justified in deciding *to do* something. 5. *by the* ~, by the road-side; while going along; (fig.) incidentally, in passing; *by* ~ *of*, via; in capacity or function of, as something equivalent to; in the habit of (*doing*), making a profession of, having a reputation for (*being, doing,* something); *under* ~, (of vessel) having begun to move through water (also freq. fig.). 6. ~-*bill*, list of passengers or goods on conveyance; *way′farer*, traveller, esp. on foot; *way′faring*, travelling, itinerant; *way′faring tree*, European and Asiatic shrub (*Viburnum lantana*), growing wild in hedges etc., with broad leaves downy beneath, dense cymes of white flowers, and green berries turning red and then black; also, the closely related Amer. shrub *V. alnifolium*; *waylay′*, lie in wait

[982]

for; wait for and accost or stop (person) to rob or interview him; **way′leave**, (rent or charge for) permission to convey minerals etc. across person's land, telephone wires over buildings, water-pipes or drains across private lands etc.; **way′side**, (land bordering) side of road or path; (*adj.*) situated on, growing at, lying near, etc., wayside; ~-*worn*, wearied by travel. ~ *adv.* (U.S. and dial.) Away; (esp.) at or to a great distance, far; ~ *back*, (colloq.) long ago; distant past; remote or rural. district; ~-*out*, (slang) exotic, esoteric.
Way′land (the) Smith. (Scand. myth.) Smith with supernatural powers; in English legend, supposed to have his forge in a dolmen near the White Horse on the Downs in SW. Oxfordshire.
way′ward *adj.* Childishly or capriciously self-willed or perverse, erratic, freakish, unaccountable. **way′wardly** *adv.* **way′wardness** *n.*
way′zgoose *n.* Annual festivity of printing-house.
Wb *abbrev.* Weber[3].
W.C. *abbrev.* Water-closet; West Central (London postal district).
W.C.A. *abbrev.* Women's Christian Association.
W/Cdr *abbrev.* Wing Commander.
we *pron.* 1st person nom. pl. pronoun denoting speaker and other person(s) associated with him as subject of sentence; used by sovereign or ruler, by newspaper writer or editor etc., instead of *I*.
W.E.A. *abbrev.* Workers' Educational Association.
weak *adj.* Wanting in strength, power or number; fragile, easily broken, bent, or defeated; wanting in vigour, feeble, sickly; wanting in resolution or power of resisting temptation, easily led; (of action etc.) not effective, showing weakness; (of argument etc.) unconvincing, logically deficient; (of liquid, esp. infusion) watery, thin; (of stress, a speech-sound, etc.) having relatively little force etc., (of word or syllable, esp. final syllable of verse) unstressed; (gram., of Germanic verbs) forming past tense by addition of suffix, (of Germanic nouns or adjs.) belonging to any declension in which Old Teut. stem ended in -*n*; ~ *ending*, (in verse) occurrence of unstressed monosyllable in normally stressed place at end of line; ~-*kneed*, (fig.) wanting in resolution or determination; ~-*minded*, lacking strength of purpose; mentally deficient. **wea′kly**[1] *adv.*
wea′ken *v.* Make, become, weak or weaker.
wea′kling *n.* Weak or feeble person or animal.
wea′kly[2] *adj.* Sickly, not robust, ailing.
wea′kness *n.* (esp.) Weak point,

failing, defect, foolish or self-indulgent liking *for*.
weal[1] *n.* Welfare, well-being, prosperity (now chiefly in ~ *and woe*), (archaic) *common* ~ = commonwealth.
weal[2] *n.* Ridge or mark raised on flesh by stroke of rod, lash, etc. ~ *v.t.* Raise weal(s) on.
weald *n.* Tract of country, formerly wooded, between N. and S. Downs of SE. England, including parts of Kent, Surrey, Hampshire, and East Sussex; ~ *clay*, upper stratum of the wealden, with abundant fossil remains.
wea′lden *n.* Series of lower Cretaceous freshwater strata above oolite and below chalk, best exemplified in the weald. ~ *adj.* Of the weald or wealden.
wealth (wĕl-) *n.* Abundant means, large possessions, being rich; abundance, profusion or lavish display *of*. **wea′lthy** *adj.* **wea′lthily** *adv.* **wea′lthiness** *n.*
wean *v.t.* Accustom (child or other young mammal) to food other than its mother's milk; (fig.) detach, alienate *from* accustomed object of pursuit or enjoyment, reconcile gradually to privation of something.
wea′nling *n.* Newly weaned child or other young mammal.
wea′pon (wĕp-) *n.* Instrument used in war or combat as means of attack or defence; any part of body (esp. of bird or beast) used for similar purpose, as claw, horn, etc.; any action or means used against another in conflict.
wear[1] (wār) *v.* (past t. *wōre*, past part. *wōrn*). 1. Be dressed in (habitually or on specific occasion); have on, be covered or decked with; dress (hair, beard, etc.), allow to grow, in specific fashion, or as opposed to shaving or wearing wig; (of ship etc.) fly (flag, colours); (transf. and fig.) bear, carry, exhibit, present (scar, appearance, title, etc.), carry in one's heart, mind, or memory. 2. Waste and impair, damage, deteriorate, gradually by use or attrition; suffer such waste, damage, or deterioration; come or bring into specified state by use, rub *away*, *down*, *off*, *out*, etc.; make (hole, groove, etc.) by attrition; exhaust, tire or tired *out*; put *down* by persistence; endure continued use *well*, *badly*, etc., remain specified time in working order or presentable state, last long; ~ *out*, use, be used, until usable no longer. 3. (of time) Go slowly and tediously *on*, pass (time), be passed, gradually *away*. 4. (slang) Accept, tolerate. **wear′able** *adj.* **wear′er** *n.* **wear** *n.* 1. Wearing or being worn on person, use as clothes; thing to wear, fashionable or suitable apparel. 2. Damage or deterioration due to ordinary use (freq. ~ *and tear*); capacity for resisting wear and tear.
wear[2] (wār) *v.* (past t. & past

part. *wōre*). (naut.) Put (ship) about, (of ship) come about, by turning head away from wind.
wear′isome *adj.* Causing weariness, monotonous, fatiguing. **wear′isomely** *adv.* **wear′isomeness** *n.*
wear′y *adj.* 1. Tired, worn out with exertion, endurance, wakefulness, etc., intensely fatigued; sick or impatient *of*; dispirited, depressed. 2. Tiring, toilsome, tedious, irksome. **wear′ily** *adv.* **wear′iness** *n.* **wear′y** *v.* Make, grow, weary.
wea′sand (-z-) *n.* (archaic) Windpipe; oesophagus and throat generally.
wea′sel (-zl) *n.* 1. Small slender-bodied reddish-brown carnivorous mammal (*Mustela nivalis*) closely allied to stoats and polecats and remarkable for ferocity and bloodthirstiness; ~-*faced*, having thin sharp features. 2. Tracked motor vehicle for use on snow and ice.
wea′ther (wĕdh-) *n.* Atmospheric conditions prevailing at a specified time or place with respect to heat or cold, quantity of sunshine, presence or absence of rain, snow, fog, etc., strength of wind; adverse, unpleasant, or hurtful condition of atmosphere, rain, frost, wind, etc., as destructive agents; (naut.) direction in which wind is blowing; *make heavy* ~ *of*, find trying or difficult; *under the* ~, (orig. U.S.) indisposed, not very well; in adversity; ~-*beaten*, worn, defaced, damaged, bronzed, hardened, etc., by exposure to weather; ~-*board*, one of series of overlapping horizontal boards covering outside of wall(s); sloping board over window or other opening to throw off rain; ~-*boarded*, -*boarding*; **wea′therbound**, detained by bad weather; ~-*chart*, diagram showing details of weather over wide area; **wea′thercoat**, (shopword) raincoat; **wea′thercock**, plate of metal, esp. in form of cock, fixed on vertical spindle and turning readily with head to wind, used as indication of direction of wind; (fig.) changeable or inconstant person; ~-*eye*, alertness to change in weather; *keep one's* ~-*eye open*, be watchful and alert; ~ *forecast*, forecast of weather to be expected in an ensuing period; ~-*gauge*, (naut.) position of a ship to windward of another; hence, position of advantage; ~-*glass*, barometer; ~-*house*, toy hygroscope in form of small house with figures of man and woman emerging from porches in wet and dry weather; ~-*map*, weather-chart; ~-*proof*, impervious to weather; ~-*ship*, ship acting as a meteorological station; ~-*station*, meteorological observation post; ~ *strip*, strip of material round window to exclude rain etc. ~ *adj.* (naut.) Windward. ~ *v.* 1. Expose to atmospheric changes; wear away, be worn

[983]

away, disintegrate, discolour, by exposure to weather. 2. (naut.) Pass, sail to windward of; withstand or come safely through (storm etc.); (fig.) come safely through (trouble, adversity, etc.).

weave v. (past t. wōve, past part. wō'ven and, chiefly in some trade phrases, wōve). Form fabric by carrying a continuous thread or threads (the *weft*) back and forth across a set of lengthwise threads (the *warp*) so that warp and weft are interlaced; operate loom; make (thread etc.) into fabric, (fabric out of thread etc., thus; (fig.) intermingle as if by weaving, form or introduce *into* connected whole thus; (cause to) move from side to side or in devious or intricate course; (R.A.F. slang) manœuvre aircraft thus, dodge, take evasive action. ~ n. Style, method, of weaving.

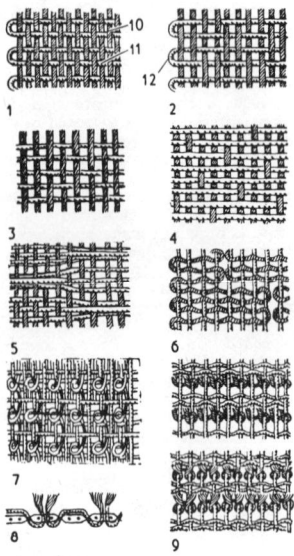

WEAVES
1. Plain (tabby). 2. Hopsack. 3. Twill. 4. Satin. 5. Huckaback. 6. Tapestry. 7. Terry. 8. Velvet (section). 9. Pile carpet weaves, Persian knots above and Turkish below. 10. Warp. 11. Weft. 12. Selvedge

wea'ver n. (esp.) 1. One who weaves fabrics. 2. (also ~-*bird*) Any of numerous Asiatic or African tropical birds of family Ploceidae, building elaborately interwoven nests.

wea'zened (-znd) adj. = WIZENED.

wĕb n. 1. Woven fabric, esp. whole piece in process of weaving or after coming from loom; (fig.) thing of complicated structure or workmanship, tissue. 2. Cobweb (freq. fig.); filmy texture spun by some caterpillars etc. 3. Tissue or membrane in animal body or plant; membrane or fold of skin connecting digits, esp. that between toes of aquatic bird or beast, forming palmate foot; vane of feather (ill. FEATHER); thin flat plate or part connecting more solid parts in machinery; centre part of girder between flanges (ill. GIRDER); (paper-making) (large roll of paper made on) endless wire-cloth on rollers carrying the pulp. 4. ~-*fingered*, having fingers united by fold of skin; ~-*foot*, ~-*footed*, (having) foot with webbed toes; ~-*offset*, (print.) offset process using continuous roll of paper; ~-*worm*, (U.S.) larva of various moths spinning large webs in which to feed or rest. ~ v.t. Cover with web or fine network; stretch threads of spider's web across (micrometer etc.); connect (fingers, toes) with web or membrane.

wĕ'bbing n. (esp.) Stout strong closely woven material in form of narrow bands, used in upholstery etc.

We'ber[1] (vä-), Carl Maria von (1786–1826). German composer of romantic operas, as 'Der Freischütz', 'Oberon', etc.

We'ber[2] (vä-), Wilhelm Eduard (1804–91). German physicist; devised the centimetre-gramme-second system of measurement of electrical quantities.

we'ber[3] (vä-) n. Unit of magnetic flux in M.K.S. system, equal to 10^8 maxwells (abbrev. Wb). [f. WEBER[2]]

Wĕ'bster[1], John (c 1580–c 1625). English writer of comedies and tragedies.

Wĕ'bster[2], Noah (1758–1843). Amer. lexicographer, advocate of reform of English spelling.

wĕd v. (past t. we'dded, past part. wĕ'dded or, rarely and not in adj. use, wĕd). Marry; unite, join, or couple intimately *with*; *be wedded to*, be obstinately attached to (pursuit etc.).

Wed. abbrev. Wednesday.

wĕ'dding n. Marriage ceremony with its attendant festivities; specified anniversary of this, as *silver* ~; ~-*breakfast*, entertainment usual between ceremony and departure for honeymoon; ~-*cake*, rich highly decorated cake eaten at wedding and sent in small portions to absent friends etc.; ~-*card*, card with names of pair sent to friends as announcement of wedding; ~-*day*, (anniversary of) day of wedding; ~-*march*, march (esp. Mendelssohn's) for performance at wedding; ~-*ring*, ring placed by bridegroom on bride's finger (usu. third finger of left hand) as part of wedding ceremony and usu. worn there constantly by married woman.

wĕdge n. 1. Piece of wood, metal, etc., thick at one end and tapering to thin edge at the other, used as tool operated by percussion or pressure on thick end for splitting wood, stone, etc., forcing things apart, widening opening, rendering separate parts immovable, etc. (ill. BEETLE[1]); (fig.) something that splits or separates; *thin end of the* ~, small beginning which it is hoped or feared may lead to something greater. 2. Anything shaped like a wedge. 3. American golf-club, a heavy lofted iron used for pitching. ~ v. Tighten, fasten tightly, by driving in wedge(s); split *off*, force *apart*, with wedge; drive, push, squeeze (object) into position where it is held fast; pack or crowd (*together*) in close formation or limited space.

Wĕ'dgwood, Josiah (1730–95). Founder of pottery works at Etruria, village (built for his workmen) near Stoke on Trent, England; hence, ware made at this factory, esp. fine porcelain with small cameo reliefs in white paste on a tinted matt ground; ~ *blue*, shade of blue characteristic of Wedgwood ware.

wĕ'dlock n. Married state; *born in, out of,* ~, having parents legally, not legally, married.

Wĕ'dnesday (wĕnz- or wĕdnz-; or -dĭ). 4th day of the week; *Ash* ~ : see ASH. [OE wódnes dæg day of WODEN; transl. of LL *Mercurii dies* day of Mercury]

wee adj. Tiny (chiefly Sc. and in nursery use); ~ *folk*, fairies; *W*~ *Free Kirk, W*~ *Frees,* nickname of minority of Free Church of Scotland that refused to enter union with United Presbyterian Church by which United Free Church was formed in 1900.

weed n. 1. Herbaceous plant not valued for use or beauty, growing wild or rank and regarded as cumbering ground or hindering growth of more valued plants. 2. (archaic) Tobacco; cigar. 3. (colloq.) Lanky and weakly horse or person. **wee'dless, wee'dy** adjs. ~ *weed* v. Clear ground of weeds; free (land, a crop, etc.) from weeds, remove (weeds); eradicate, remove, clear *out* (faults, inferior or superfluous individuals, etc.).

weeds (-z) n.pl. Deep mourning worn by widow (usu. *widow's* ~).

week n. 1. Cycle of 7 days usu. understood as beginning with Sunday; period of any 7 successive days; working days or hours of 7-day period, as *five-day* ~. 2. Seven days before or (esp.) after a specified day, as *Tuesday* ~. 3. *wee'kday*, any day other than Sunday; ~-*end*, holiday period at end of week, usu. from Saturday noon or Friday night to Monday; (v.i.) make week-end visit, etc.

wee'kly adj. Occurring, done, etc., once a week; of, for, lasting, a week. ~ *adv.* Once a week, every week. ~ *n.* Weekly newspaper or periodical.

ween v.t. (archaic & poet.) Think, consider, deem.

wee'ny adj. (colloq.) Tiny.

weep v. (past t. & past part. wĕpt). Shed tears; shed tears over, shed (tears), lament, utter, with tears; shed moisture in drops, exude drop of water, exude (water or other liquid); *Weeping Cross*, place-name occurring in several English counties, presumably indicating site of a cross, now destroyed (significance uncertain); *weeping willow*, large Asiatic species of willow (*Salix babylonica*), with long slender branches drooping towards ground, cultivated in Europe as ornamental tree and regarded as symbolical of mourning.

wee'per n. (esp.) 1. Capuchin monkey (*Cebus apella*) of S. America. 2. (pl.) Conventional sign of mourning, esp. hat-band or scarf of black crape worn at funeral. 3. (pl., slang) Long flowing side-whiskers. 4. Small mourning figure on tomb.

wee'ver n. Marine fish of genus *Trachinus* with many strong sharp venomous dorsal spines.

wee'vil n. Beetle of the large family Curculionidae, usu. of small size, with head elongated into kind of snout, freq. very destructive or having destructive larvae, boring into grain, fruit, nuts, bark of trees, etc.; any insect damaging stored grain. **wee'-viled, -ll-** (-ld), **wee'villy** adjs. Infested with weevils.

wĕft[1] n. Threads crossing from side to side of web and interwoven with warp (ill. WEAVE); yarn for weft-threads.

weft[2]: see WAFT.

Wei (wā). Name of several dynasties which ruled in China, esp. that of 386-535.

weigh (wā) v. 1. Heave up (ship's anchor) before sailing; ~ *anchor*, sail; ~ *up*, raise (sunk ship etc.) from bottom of water. 2. Find weight of with scales or other machine; balance in hands (as if) to guess weight of; take definite weight of, take specified weight from larger quantity (freq. ~ *out*); be equal to or balance (specified weight) in scales; (fig.) estimate relative value or importance of (*with*, *against*), consider, ponder, balance in the mind; have specified importance or value, be of account, have influence (*with*); ~ *one's words*, speak deliberately and in calculated terms. 3. ~ *down*, draw, bend, force, down by pressure of weight; depress, oppress, lie heavy on; ~ *in*, (of boxer or wrestler) be weighed before contest; (of jockey) be weighed after race; so ~-*in* (n.); ~ *in with*, (colloq.) introduce; present; ~ *on*, be burdensome, heavy, oppressive, on; ~ *out*, (of jockey) be weighed before race; so ~-*out* (n.); ~ *up*, (colloq.) appraise, form estimate of. 4. ~-*bridge*, platform scale, flush with road, for weighing vehicles etc.; ~-*house*, public building in which goods can be weighed officially; *wei'ghman*, man employed to weigh goods etc., esp., in colliery, one who weighs tubs of coal at pit-mouth; *weighing-machine*, contrivance for weighing, esp. one for heavy loads, of more complicated mechanism than simple balance. ~ n. Process or occasion of weighing; *under* ~, corruption (from association with phrase *weigh anchor*) of *under way* (see WAY, n.).

weight (wāt) n. 1. Force with which body is attracted to earth; product of mass of any body and the average force of terrestrial gravitation; mass or relative heaviness as property of material substances; amount that thing etc. weighs, expressed in units of some recognized scale; portion or quantity weighing definite amount; heavy mass, burden, load; (fig.) heavy burden of care, responsibility, etc.; importance, influence, authority; persuasive or convincing power (of argument etc.), preponderance (*of* evidence, authority) on one side of question. 2. Any of various systems, with series of units in fixed arithmetical relations, used for stating weight of anything; piece of metal etc. of known weight, used in scales for weighing articles; heavy piece of metal etc. used to pull or press down something, give impulse to machinery (e.g. in clock), act as counterpoise, etc.; heavy stone thrown from one hand close to shoulder in athletic sport of *putting the* ~; ~-*lifting*, athletic sport or exercise of lifting heavy weights; so ~-*lifter* (n.). **wei'ghtless** adj. **wei'ghtlessness** n. **weight** v.t. Attach a weight to, hold down with weight(s); impede or burden with load; add weight to (textiles or other commodities) by addition of adulterant etc.; (statistics) multiply components of (average) by compensating factors.

wei'ghty (wātǐ) adj. Heavy, weighing much; momentous, important; requiring or giving evidence of earnest thought, consideration, or application; influential, authoritative. **wei'ghtily** adv. **wei'ghtiness** n.

Weil (vīl), Adolf (1848-1916). German physician; ~'s *disease*, infectious febrile disease with severe jaundice, caused by a spirochaete.

Wei'mar (vī-). Town in Thuringia, Germany, famous as the residence of Goethe and Schiller and as the seat of the National Assembly of Germany (1919-33); ~ *Republic*, German republic (1919-33) the constitution of which was drawn up at Weimar.

weir (wēr) n. Dam or barrier across river etc. to retain water and regulate its flow; fence or enclosure of stakes etc. in river, harbour, etc., to catch or preserve fish.

weird[1] (wērd) n. (archaic or Sc.) Fate, destiny.

weird[2] (wērd) adj. Connected with fate; uncanny, supernatural; (colloq.) queer, fantastic. **weir'dly** adv. **weir'dness** n. [f. WEIRD[1], f. phrase ~ *sisters* the Fates, the witches, in Shakespeare's 'Macbeth']

Wei'smann (vīs-), August (1834-1914). German biologist. **Wei'smannism** n. Theory of heredity, which assumes the continuity of the germ-plasm and the non-transmission of acquired characteristics.

Wĕlch adj. Old spelling of WELSH retained in name of *Royal* ~ *Fusiliers*.

wĕ'lcome int. Exclamation of greeting, indicating pleasure at arrival of person(s) (often in phrases as ~ *home*, ~ *to Brighton*). ~ n. Saying 'welcome' to person; kind or glad reception or entertainment of person or acceptance of offer. ~ v.t. Say 'welcome' to, receive gladly. ~ adj. Gladly received; acceptable as visitor; ungrudgingly permitted *to* do something or given right *to* thing. [OE *wilcuma* (*wil*-) desire, pleasure, and *cuma* comer) one whose coming is pleasing, later changed to *wel*- (= WELL[2]) after OF *bien venu*]

wĕld[1] n. Plant *Reseda lutea*; yellow dye yielded by this.

wĕld[2] v. Unite (pieces of metal) into solid mass by hammering or pressure, or by fusion using an electric arc (*arc welding*), usu. when metal is soft but not melted; (of metal) admit of being welded; (fig.) unite intimately or inseparably. **wĕ'lder** n. **wĕld** n. Joint made by welding.

wĕ'lfāre n. Good fortune, happiness, or well-being (of person, community, etc.); *W*~ *State*, one having highly developed social services controlled or financed by the government; ~ *work*, organized effort for welfare of class or group; so ~ *worker*.

wĕ'lkin n. (literary, chiefly poet.) Sky, firmament.

wĕll[1] n. 1. (archaic & poet.) Spring, fountain; (fig.) source, origin. 2. Pit, esp. circular vertical excavation, usu. lined with masonry, sunk in ground to obtain supply of water (*illustration*, *p. 986*); shaft sunk in ground for obtaining oil, gas, brine, etc., for storage of ice, etc. 3. Enclosed space more or less resembling well-shaft, esp. central open space of winding or spiral staircase, lift-shaft, deep narrow space between surrounding walls of building(s) for light and ventilation, space on floor of law-court where solicitors sit, deep receptacle in piece of furniture, body of vehicle, etc.; (naut.) vertical shaft protecting pump in ship's hold; receptacle for liquid, esp. for ink in inkstand. 4. ~-*deck*, (naut.) space on main deck of ship enclosed by bulwarks and higher decks (ill. SHIP); ~-*head*,

[985]

WELL

(esp. fig.) chief source, fountain-head; ~-*room*, building where water from mineral spring is dispensed; ~-*spring*, head-spring of stream etc.; (fig.) fountain-head, source of perennial emanation or supply. ~ *v.i.* Spring (*up*, *out*, *forth*), from or as from fountain.

wĕll[2] *adj.* (chiefly predic.) In good health; in satisfactory state or position, satisfactory; advisable, right and proper. ~ *adv.* 1. In good manner or style, satisfactorily, rightly. 2. Thoroughly, carefully, completely, sufficiently; to a considerable distance, degree, or extent, quite. 3. Heartily, kindly, approvingly, laudatorily, on good terms. 4. Probably, easily, with reason, wisely, advisably. 5. *as* ~, with equal reason; preferably; in addition; *as* ~ *as*, (esp.) to the same extent, in the same degree, as much . . . as; in addition to, both . . . and, not only . . . but also. 6. In comb., esp. with past and present participles of vbs., and with adjs. ending in -*ed*, as ~-*advised*, (esp.) prudent, wary, wise; ~-*affected*, favourably disposed, inclined to be friendly (*towards*), loyal; ~-*appointed*, properly equipped or fitted out; ~-*balanced*, sensible, sane; equally matched; ~-*being*, happy, healthy, or prosperous condition; ~-*born*, of noble or distinguished family; ~-*bred*, having or displaying good breeding or manners, courteous, refined; of good breed or stock; ~-*conditioned*, of good disposition, morals, or behaviour; sound, healthy, in good physical condition; ~-*conducted*, properly directed or managed; well-behaved; ~-*connected*, (esp.) of good family and connections; ~-*disposed*, (esp.) disposed to be friendly or favourable (*towards*, *to*); ~-*doing*, virtuous conduct; ~ *done*, (*int.*) exclamation of approval; skilfully or rightly done; (of meat etc.) cooked thoroughly; ~-*favoured*, good-looking; ~-

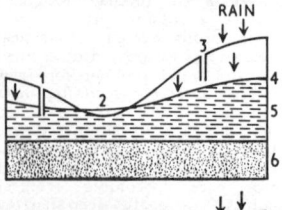

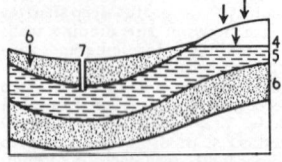

WELLS
1. Permanent well. 2. River. 3. Intermittent well. 4. Water-table. 5. Pervious rock. 6. Impervious rock. 7. Artesian well

found, fully furnished and equipped; ~-*founded*, (esp.) having foundation in fact, based on good grounds or reason; ~-*groomed*, (esp. of persons) with hair, skin, etc., carefully tended; ~-*grounded*, well-founded; well-trained in rudiments; ~-*heeled*, (colloq.) rich; ~-*informed*, having well-stored mind, fully furnished with general or special knowledge; ~-*intentioned*, having, showing, based on, good intentions; ~-*knit*, (esp., of person, his frame) strongly and compactly built, not loosely made; ~-*made*, (esp. of person or animal) of good build, well-proportioned; ~-*marked*, clearly defined, easy to distinguish or recognize; ~-*meaning*, well-intentioned (freq. with implication of inefficiency or unwisdom); *wellnigh*, very nearly, almost wholly; ~ *off*, fortunately situated; fairly or sufficiently rich; ~-*preserved*, kept in good condition; (of elderly person) of more youthful appearance than age merits; ~-*read*, well-informed by reading, learned (*in*), versed or skilled (*in*); ~-*rounded*, symmetrical, (of sentence etc.) full and well-turned; ~-*spoken*, (esp.) having good or ready speech, refined in speech; ~-*timed*, timely, opportune; ~-*to-do*, prosperous, well off; ~-*tried*, often tried or tested with good result; ~-*turned*, (esp., of speech) neatly finished, happily expressed; ~-*wisher*, one who wishes well to another, a cause, etc.; ~-*worn*, (esp.) trite, hackneyed. ~ *int.* Exclamation introducing remark or statement, expressing astonishment, relief, concession, etc., or resumption of talk or subject, qualified recognition of point, expectation, resignation, etc.

wĕ′lladay′, wĕllaway′ (-aw-) *ints.* (archaic) Exclamations of grief.

Wĕ′llington[1], Arthur Wellesley, 1st Duke of (1769–1852). British general and statesman; led the British forces in the Peninsular War, defeated Napoleon at Waterloo (1815); prime minister 1828–30; ~ *boot*, military boot reaching to the knee in front and cut away behind.

Wĕ′llington[2]. Capital of New Zealand, in North Island.

wĕ′llington[3] *n.* One of a pair of rubber etc. waterproof boots sometimes reaching to the knee; *W*~, Wellington boot. [f. WELLINGTON[1]]

Wĕllingtō′nia *n.* Sequoia. [named after the Duke of WELLINGTON[1]]

Wĕlls (-z), Herbert George (1866–1946). English writer of sociological novels, science fiction, and short stories. **Wĕ′llsian** *adj.*

Wĕlsh[1] *adj.* Of Wales or its people or language; ~ *corgi*: see CORGI; ~ *dresser*, open oak kind orig. made in Wales; ~ *flannel*, heavy variety with a bluish tinge

WEREWOLF

made from Welsh fleeces; ~ *harp*, large triple-strung harp orig. used in Wales; *We′lshman*, *We′lshwoman*, native of Wales; ~ *mutton*, mutton obtained from small breed of sheep pastured in Wales; ~ *rabbit*, dish consisting of seasoned melted or toasted cheese on buttered toast, sometimes incorrectly called ~ *rarebit*. ~ *n.* 1. (collect.) People of Wales. 2. Language of Wales, one of the Celtic group of languages.

wĕlsh[2] *v.i.* (of bookmaker etc.) Decamp without paying winner(s) of bet(s) (also ~ *on*).

wĕlt *n.* 1. Strip of leather sewn between edge of sole and turned-in edge of upper in soling boot or shoe (ill. SHOE); ribbed or reinforced border of knitted garment. 2. Ridge on flesh, esp. mark of heavy blow or healed wound, weal. ~ *v.t.* 1. Provide with welt. 2. Raise weals on, beat, flog.

wĕ′lter[1] *v.i.* Roll, wallow; be tossed or tumbled about; lie prostrate *in* (blood or gore); (fig.) be sunk or deeply involved *in*. ~ *n.* State of turmoil or upheaval; surging or confused mass.

wĕ′lter[2] *adj.* (of races etc.) For heavy-weight riders; *we′lterweight*, boxer of weight between lightweight and middleweight (see BOXING); (horse-racing) heavy-weight rider; extra weight (28 lb.) sometimes imposed in addition to weight for age.

wĕn *n.* More or less permanent benign tumour on skin, esp. of scalp; (fig.) abnormally large or congested city (*the great W*~, London).

Wĕ′ncĕslas[1], **-laus**[1], St., Duke of Bohemia (early 10th c.). National saint of Bohemia, commemorated 28 Sept.

Wĕ′ncĕslas[2], **-laus**[2] (1361–1419). King of Bohemia (as Wenceslas IV), king of Germany and Holy Roman Emperor (1378–1419).

wĕnch *n.* (now dial. or joc.) Girl or young woman. ~ *v.i.* (archaic) Associate with prostitutes.

wĕnd[1] *v.* Direct one's *way*; (archaic) go.

Wĕnd[2] *n.* Member of a Slavonic people of eastern Germany.

Wĕ′ndish *adj.* Of the Wends or their language. ~ *n.* Western-Slavonic language of the Wends.

Wĕ′nsleydāle (-z-). District of North Yorkshire, upper part of Ure valley; hence, sheep of long-woolled breed originating here; kind of cheese made in the valley.

went: see GO.

wĕ′ntletrăp (-lt-) *n.* Any marine gasteropod mollusc of genus *Scalaria*, with usu. white shell with many convolutions. [Du. *wenteltrap* winding stair, spiral shell]

wept: see WEEP.

werewolf (wer′woolf) *n.* In folklore, human being who changes into a wolf.

[986]

Wer'fel (vār-), Franz (1890–1945). Austrian expressionist poet, dramatist, and novelist.

Werther (vār´ter). Hero of Goethe's sentimental novel 'Die Leiden des jungen Werthers' (Sorrows of young Werther, 1774). **Werthēr'ian** *adj.* Morbidly sentimental. **Wer'therism** *n.*

We'ser (vāz-). One of the principal rivers of Germany, flowing into the North Sea.

Wĕ'sley (*or* -z-). *John* (1703–91), religious teacher and founder of METHODISM; *Charles* ~ (1707–88), his brother, author of many hymns; *Samuel Sebastian* ~ *n.* (1810–76), grandson of Charles, organist and composer of church music. **Wĕ'sleyan** *adj.* & *n.* (Follower) of John Wesley or his teaching. **Wĕ'sleyanism** *n.*

Wĕ'ssĕx. 1. Kingdom of WEST[1] Saxons. 2. Those counties of SW. England, principally Dorset, which are the scene of Thomas Hardy's novels.

wĕst[1] *adv.* Towards, in, the west; *go* ~, (esp.) go to America or the Western States; (fig.) die, perish, be destroyed. ~ *n.* 1. Point of horizon where sun sets at equinox; this direction. 2. Cardinal point of the compass lying opposite east. 3. (*usu.* the *W*~) That part of a country, district, etc., which lies to the west; Europe and America as dist. from Asia; (esp.) western Europe and America as dist. from Communist States of Asia and eastern Europe; States of U.S. west of Mississippi River; West End of London. 4. *W*~, bridge-player sitting opposite East and to the right of North. ~ *adj.* Lying towards, in, the west; coming from the west (~ *wind*); ~ *country*, (esp.) south-western counties (Somerset, Devon, etc.) of England; *W*~ *End*, (esp.) part of London lying west of Charing Cross and Regent St., and including fashionable shopping district, Mayfair, and the Parks; fashionable or aristocratic quarter of any town; *W*~ *Lothian*, former county in mid-Scotland, S. of the Firth of Forth, since May 1975 part of the region of Lothian; *W*~ *Point*, U.S. military reservation and academy on west bank of Hudson River, N.Y. State; *W*~ *Riding*: see RIDING[2]; *W*~ *Saxon*, (of) the Old English dialect spoken by divisions of Saxons in England occupying area S. of Thames and westward from Surrey and West Sussex; (member) of such peoples. **wĕ'stward** *adv., adj.,* & *n.* **wĕ'stwardly** *adv.* & *adj.* **wĕ'stwards** (-z) *adv.*

Wĕst[2], Benjamin (1738–1820). American painter, active chiefly in England.

wĕ'ster *adj.* (chiefly Sc.) Western. ~ *v.i.* Move, travel towards, draw near, the west (esp. of sun). **wĕ'sterly** *adj.* In the west; (of wind) blowing from the west. ~ *adv.* Towards the west. ~ *n.* West wind.

wĕ'stern *adj.* Of the west; occidental; lying or directed towards the west; (poet.) in, coming from, the west; *W*~, of the West as dist. from Communist countries; *W*~ *Church*, Latin or Roman Catholic Church (occas., including also Anglican Church or all churches of western Christendom) as dist. from Orthodox Church; *W*~ *Empire*: see ROMAN Empire; *W*~ *Islands*, islands area of Scotland (since May 1975), comprising the Outer Hebrides. ~ *n.* (esp.) Film or novel about adventures of cowboys, rustlers, etc., in western parts of N. America. **wĕ'sterner** *n.* (also *W*~) Native, inhabitant, of the west, esp. of western U.S. **wĕ'sternmōst** *adj.*

Wĕ'stern Austrā'lia (*or* ŏ-). State of W. Australia; capital, Perth.

wĕ'sternize *v.t.* Make Western, esp. make (Eastern country or people) more Western in institutions, ideas, etc.

Wĕst Glamŏr'gan. County of S. Wales (since April 1974), comprising the W. part of the former county of Glamorgan.

Wĕst I'ndies (ĭndĭz). Chain of islands extending from coast of Florida to Venezuela and enclosing Caribbean Sea, inhabited largely by black and coloured people whose ancestors were brought there from Africa by European settlers to work on the plantations. **Wĕst I'ndian** *adj.* & *n.*

wĕ'sting *n.* Westward progress or deviation, esp. in sailing; distance due west.

Wĕ'stinghouse, George (1846–1914). American inventor; ~ *brake*, kind worked by compressed air on railway trains.

Wĕstmea'th (-dh). County of Leinster, Ireland.

Wĕst Mi'dlands (-z). Metropolitan county of central England (since April 1974), comprising Birmingham, Wolverhampton, Coventry, and adjacent former county boroughs, and parts of the former counties of Warwickshire and Worcestershire.

Wĕ'stminster. City and inner London borough containing the Houses of Parliament (*Palace of* ~) and many government offices etc.; hence, British parliamentary life or politics; *Statute of* ~, statute of 1931 recognizing the equality of status of the Dominions as autonomous communities within the British Empire; ~ *Abbey*, collegiate church of St. Peter in the City of Westminster, several times reconstructed from a church orig. built by Edward the Confessor in the 11th c., scene of the coronation of English monarchs and burial-place of many kings, statesmen, soldiers, poets, etc.; ~ *Hall*, part of the old· Westminster Palace, built by William II and rebuilt, substantially in its present form, by Richard II; meeting-place of early parliaments and principal seat of justice from the time of Henry III until the 19th c.; ~ *School*, public school, founded 1560 by Queen Elizabeth. I, adjoining Westminster Abbey.

Wĕ'stmorland. Former county in NW. England, since April 1974 part of the county of Cumbria.

Wĕstphā'lia. (Ger. *Westfalen*) Former province of NW. Germany which from 1815 formed part of Prussia; now part of the province North Rhine–Westphalia (capital, Düsseldorf); *Peace of* ~, peace (1648) which ended the Thirty Years War. **Wĕstphā'lian** *adj.* & *n.* (esp.) ~ *ham*, kind made by smoking with juniper twigs and berries over a beechwood fire.

Wĕst Sŭ'ssĕx. County of SE. England (since April 1974), mainly comprising the W. part of the former county of Sussex.

Wĕst Virgi'nia. East central State of U.S., admitted to the Union in 1863; capital, Charleston.

Wĕst Yŏr'kshire. Metropolitan county of N. England (since April 1974), comprising Leeds, Bradford, and other former county boroughs, and parts of the former W. Riding of Yorkshire.

wĕt *adj.* 1. Soaked, covered, supplied with, etc., water or other liquid; rainy; employing, done by means of, water or other liquid; (naut., of vessel) liable to ship much water over bows or gunwale. 2. Addicted to, concerned with, supplying, alcoholic drinks; (U.S.) favouring sale of alcoholic liquors. 3. (U.S. slang) Mistaken. 4. (slang) Feeble. 5. ~ *blanket*: see BLANKET; ~ *bob*: see BOB[3]; ~-*bulb thermometer*, one having its bulb covered with wet muslin so that the difference between its reading and that of a dry-bulb thermometer indicates the amount of water vapour in the air; ~ *dock*, see DOCK[3]; ~-*fly*, (angling) artificial fly used under water; ~-*nurse*, woman employed to suckle another's child; ~-*nurse* (*v.t.*) act as wet-nurse to; foster, coddle; ~ *pack*, (med.) form of bath, in which patient is wrapped in wet sheets, esp. to reduce fever; ~ *plate*, (photog.) sensitized collodion plate exposed in camera while collodion is moist. **wĕ'tly** *adv.* **wĕ'tnĕss** *n.* **wĕ'ttish** *adj.* **wĕt** *v.t.* Make wet. ~ *n.* Moisture, liquid that wets something, rainy weather; (slang) a drink; (U.S.) one opposed to prohibition or in favour of allowing sale of alcoholic drinks.

wĕ'ther (-dh-) *n.* Castrated male sheep; *grey* ~*s*, hard sandstone boulders lying on surface of Devon and Wiltshire downs.

Wĕ'xford. Maritime county and city of Leinster, Ireland.

[987]

w.f. *abbrev.* (print.) Wrong fount.
W.F.T.U. *abbrev.* World Federation of Trade Unions.
whăck *n.* Heavy resounding blow, esp. with stick; (colloq.) portion, share, esp. large or full share. ~ *v.t.* Beat or strike vigorously.
whă′cker *n.* (slang) Unusually large thing or person.
whă′cking *adj.* (slang) Very large.
whāle[1] *n.* Any fish-like marine mammal of order Cetacea, with short fore-limbs like fins and tail with horizontal flukes, esp. one of the larger of these, hunted for oil, whalebone, etc.; (colloq., chiefly U.S.) something impressive in size or amount, or superlative in quality (~ *of a* . . .); *blue* ~, large bluish-grey whale, hunted for its oil; *Greenland* ~, whalebone whale, with very large head; *right* ~, whalebone whale, esp. of genus *Balaena*; ~*-back*, anything shaped like back of whale, esp. arched structure over deck of ship, kind of steam-boat, much used on the Amer. Great Lakes in early 20th c., with spoon bow and main decks covered in and rounded over; ~*-boat*, long narrow rowing-boat, sharp at both ends, used in whale-fishing or carried as lifeboat; *wha′lebone*, elastic horny substance growing in series of thin parallel plates in upper jaw of some whales and used in feeding, baleen; strip of this, used as stiffening in clothes etc.; *whalebone* ~, whale of sub-order Mysiceti having whalebone plates in upper jaw; ~*-oil*, oil obtained from blubber of whales. ~ *v.i.* Fish for whales. **whā′ler** *n.* Ship, man, engaged in whale-fishing.
whāle[2] *v.* (colloq., esp. U.S.) Beat, thrash; perform action vigorously or vehemently.
whăng *v.* (colloq.) Strike heavily and loudly; (of drum etc.) sound (as) under heavy blow. ~ *n.* Whanging sound or blow.
whăngee′ (-nggē) *n.* (Cane made from) any of various Chinese and Japanese bamboos of genus *Phyllostachys*. [Chin. *huang* kind of bamboo]
wharf (-ŏrf) *n.* Substantial structure of stone, timber, etc., at water's edge for loading or unloading of ships lying alongside. ~ *v.t.* Discharge (cargo), accommodate (ships), at wharf. **whar′fage** *n.* Provision of accommodation at wharf; charge made for this; wharfs collectively.
whar′finger (-ŏrfĭnj-) *n.* Owner or keeper of wharf.
Whar′ton (-ŏrtn), Edith (1862–1937). American novelist.
what *pron.* 1. (interrog.) What thing(s)?; what did you say?; *know* ~'*s what*, have good judgement; know the matter in hand, know what is fitting or profitable; ~ *not*, other things of the same kind, anything; ~*-not*, some indefinite or trivial thing; (19th c.) piece of furniture with shelves for knick-knacks; ~'*s-his* (or *-her*)-*name*, *d'you-call-it*, person, thing, whose correct name the speaker cannot recall. 2. (exclam.) What thing(s)!; how much! 3. (rel.) That or those which; the thing(s) that; anything that; a thing that. ~ *adj.* 1. (interrog.) Asking for selection from indefinite number or for specification of amount, number, kind, etc. 2. (exclam.) How great, how strange, how remarkable in some way; (before adjs.) how. 3. The . . . that, any . . . that, as much or many . . . as. ~ *adv.* 1. (interrog.) To what extent or degree?; how much? 2. ~ *with*, on account of, considering. ~ *int.* Exclamation of surprise.
whatĕ′ver (-ŏt-) *pron.* Anything that; any quantity etc. that; no matter what; something of the same kind; (colloq.) as emphatic extension of 'what' implying perplexity or surprise. ~ *adj.* All; any quantity etc. of; (with negatives) at all.
whatsōĕ′ver (-ŏt-) *pron. & adj.* (emphat.) Whatever.
whaup *n.* (Sc.) Curlew.
wheal *n. & v.* = WEAL[2].
wheat *n.* Cereal plant of genus *Triticum*, esp. *T. vulgare*, closely related to barley and rye; its grain, furnishing meal or flour, the chief bread-stuff in temperate countries; ~*-belt*, region in which wheat is chief agricultural product, e.g. prairie provinces of Canada; ~*-grass*, couch-grass; *whea′tmeal*, meal of wheat, esp. wholemeal.
whea′ten *adj.* Of wheat, of grain or flour of wheat.
whea′tear *n.* Small passerine bird of genus *Oenanthe* of N. parts of Europe, Asia, and America, esp. *O. oenanthe*, cock of which has bluish-grey back, blackish wings, and white rump and upper tail-feathers. [prob. *whit eeres* white arse]
Whea′tstone, Sir Charles (1802–75). English physicist and inventor; ~ *bridge*, device utilizing galvanometer for comparison of electrical resistances.
whee′dle *v.* Entice or persuade by soft words or flattery; obtain by such action; use soft words or flattery.
wheel *n.* 1. Circular frame or disc arranged to revolve on axis and used to facilitate motion of vehicle or for various mechanical purposes (*illustration, p. 989*); wheel-like structure or thing; instrument or appliance with wheel as essential part, e.g. bicycle; revolving firework in form of spiral; ancient instrument of torture. 2. Motion as of wheel, circular motion, motion of

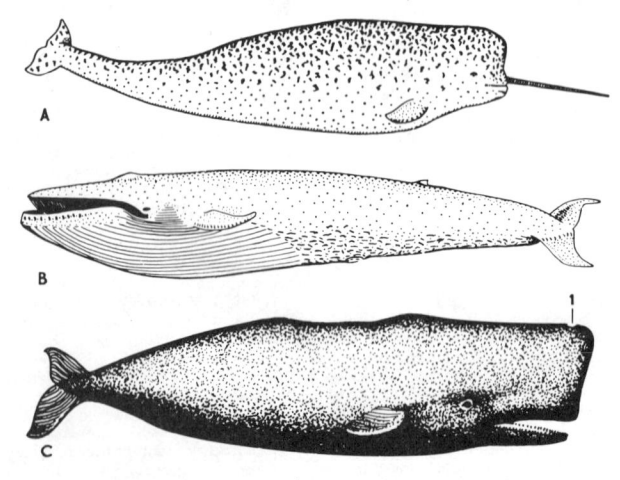

A. NARWHAL. B. SIBBALD'S RORQUAL. C. SPERM WHALE
1. Blowhole
Sibbald's rorqual (or blue whale) is the largest known living animal (30 m long)

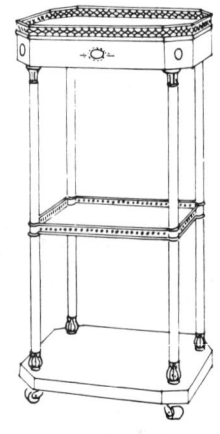

WHAT-NOT

[988]

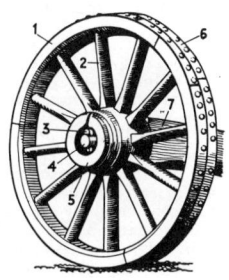

WHEEL

1. Felloe. 2. Spoke. 3. Linchpin. 4. Axle or arbor. 5. Hub or nave. 6. Strake. 7. Axle-tree

line as on pivoted end esp. as military evolution; *left, right, ~,* words of command to troops in line to swing round on left, right, flank as pivot. 3. *on ~s,* (fig.) with rapid easy motion; *~s within ~s,* intricate machinery, indirect or secret agencies. 4. *~-animal(cule),* rotifer; *~-back,* (chair with) wheellike back characteristic of those made by Hepplewhite c 1775; (also) traditional Windsor chair with wheel design in centre-piece of back (ill. CHAIR); *whee'lbarrow,* shallow open box with shafts and one wheel for carrying small loads on; *~-base,* distance between points of contact with ground or rail of front and back wheels of vehicle; *~-chair,* invalid's chair on wheels; *~-horse:* WHEELER; *~-house,* structure enclosing large wheel, esp. (naut.) superstructure containing steering-wheel; (archaeol.) stone-built circular house of the Iron Age in Scotland, with radial piers or stone slabs to support the roof; *~-load,* part of load of vehicle borne by single wheel; *~-lock* (gun with) lock in which powder was fired by friction of small wheel against flint (ill. MUSKET); *~-race,* part of millrace where mill-wheel is fixed; *~-spin,* rotation of wheels of (esp. motor) vehicle without traction, as on mud or ice; *~-tread,* part of tyre or rim that touches ground; *whee'lwright,* one who makes or mends wooden wheels of farm vehicles. *~ v.* 1. Turn on axis or pivot, (cause to) move in circle or spiral; change direction, face another way, turn *round* or *about.* 2. Push or pull (wheel-chair, bicycle, etc.). **wheeled** (-ld) *adj.* (esp). Having wheels.

whee′ler *n,* (esp.) Pole- or shaft-horse in four-in-hand, tandem, etc.; wheelwright; (in comb.) vehicle etc. having specif. no. of wheels, e.g. *three-~.*

wheeze *v.* Breathe hard with audible whistling or piping sound from dryness or obstruction in throat; utter with wheezing. *~ n.* 1. Sound of wheezing. 2. (orig., theatr. slang) Gag, esp. one frequently repeated; (slang) catch-phrase, trick or dodge. **whee′zy** *adj.* **whee′zily** *adv.* **whee′ziness** *n.*

wheft : see WAFT.

whĕlk[1] *n.* Marine gasteropod mollusc of *Buccinum* and allied genera, with spiral shell, esp. *B. undatum,* common in Europe and N. America and much used for food.

whĕlk[2] *n.* Pimple.

whĕlm *v.t.* (poet.) Overwhelm.

whĕlp *n.* Young dog, puppy; (archaic) young of lion, tiger, bear, and wolf; (derog.) youth. *~ v.* Bring forth (whelp(s)).

whĕn *adv.* (interrog.) At what time, on what occasion, in what case or circumstances?; say ~, (in pouring drink etc.) tell me when to stop. *~ conj.* At the time that, on the occasion etc., that; at which time etc., and (just) then; seeing that, considering that, since; whereas. *~ n.* Time, date, occasion.

whĕnce *adv.* & *conj.* (archaic) From where, from what or which place, source, circumstance, etc.; (with *place* etc.) from which. *~ n.* Source.

whĕnĕ′ver *adv.* & *conj.* At whatever time, on whatever occasion; every time that; (Sc. & Ir.) as soon as.

whĕnsŏĕ′ver *adv.* & *conj.* (emphat.) Whenever.

where (-âr) *adv.* (interrog.) At or in what place, position, or circumstances?; in what respect, in what, from what source, etc.?; to what place?; in comb. with preps., with the general meaning of the prep. followed by *what* or *which* (chiefly archaic or formal), as *wherea'fter, wherea't, whereby', wherefor', wherei'n, whereo'f, whereo'n, whereto', whereupo'n, wherewi'th. ~ conj.* In, at, to, etc., place in or at which; and there.

whereabou′ts (-āra-) *adv.* About where, in or near what place or position? **wher′eabouts** *n.* (Approximate) position or situation (of), place in or near which person or thing is.

wherĕa′s (-ârăz) *conj.* In view or consideration of the fact that, inasmuch as (chiefly in preamble of legal or other formal document); while on the contrary, but on the other hand.

wher′efore(-ârf-)*adv.* For what?; for what purpose, reason, cause, or end, why?; on which account, for which reason, and therefore; (archaic) because of which, in consequence or as a result of which.

wheresŏĕ′ver (-ârs-) *adv.* (emphat.) Wherever.

wherĕ′ver (-âr-) *adv.* At or to whatever place etc.

wherewitha′l (-ârwĭdhawl) *adv.* (archaic) Wherewith. **wher′ewithal** *n.* (colloq.) Means (esp. pecuniary).

whĕ′rry *n.* Light rowing-boat for carrying passengers and goods, esp. formerly on rivers; large light type of barge or lighter, esp. with single sail. **whĕ′rryman** *n.*

whĕt *n.* Sharpening; something that whets the appetite, esp. small draught of liquor as appetizer. *~ v.t.* Sharpen; make (interest, wits, appetite, etc.) (more) acute, keen, or eager; *whe'tstone,* shaped stone, natural or artificial, for giving sharp edge to cutting tools; any hard fine-grained rock from which whetstones are made.

whĕ′ther (-dh-) *conj.* Introducing dependent question or its equivalent expressing doubt, choice, etc., between alternations, or, freq. as ordinary sign of indirect interrogation *(if). ~ pron.* & *adj.* (archaic) Which of the two.

whew (hwū or whistle-like sound) *int.* Exclamation of astonishment, consternation, etc.

whey (-ā) *n.* Serum or watery part remaining after separation of curd from milk, esp. in cheesemaking.

which *adj.* & *pron.* 1. (interrog.) What one(s) of a stated or implied set of person, things, or alternatives. 2. (rel.) Relative adj. and pron., introducing additional statement about the antecedent, = 'and that (it, they, etc.),' 'that'.

whichĕ′ver *adj.* & *pron.* Any or either (of definite set of persons or things) that . . . ; no matter which.

whichsŏĕ′ver *adj.* & *pron.* (emphat.) Whichever.

whi′dah, whȳ- (-da) *n.* (also *~-bird*) African weaver-bird of genus *Vidua,* males of which have prevailingly black plumage with white or buff markings, and very long drooping tail-feathers. [orig. widow-bird, f. colour of plumage, altered by assoc. with *Whidah* (now Ouidah), town in Dahomey]

whiff *n.* 1. Puff, waft, of air, smoke, odour, etc. 2. Light narrow outrigged boat for one sculler, used on Thames. *~ v.* Blow or puff lightly.

whi′ffle *v.* 1. Puff lightly; move as if blown by puff of air. 2. Make light whistling sound. *~ n.* Slight movement of air.

Whig *adj.* & *n.* (Member) of the political party in Great Britain that, after the Revolution of 1688, aimed at subordinating the power of the Crown to that of Parliament and the upper classes, passed the Reform Bill, and in the 19th c. was succeeded by the Liberal party (opp. TORY). **Whi′ggery, Whi′ggism** *ns.* **Whi′ggish** *adj.* **Whi′ggishly** *adv.* **Whi′ggishness** *n.* [used earlier of Scotch Covenanters, prob. short for *whiggamer,* -*more,* of uncertain origin]

while *n.* Space of time, esp. time spent in doing something (now only in *worth (one's) ~, worth doing, advantageous); a ~,* (colloq.) a considerable time, some time; *all the, this, ~,* during the whole time (that). *~ conj.* During the time that, for as long as, at

the same time as; when on the contrary, whereas, although; and at the same time, besides that. ~ v.t. Pass (time etc.) away in leisurely manner or without wearisomeness. **whiles** (-lz) *conj.* (archaic) While.
whi′lom *adv. & adj.* (archaic) (That existed, or was such) at some past time; former(ly).
whilst *adv. & conj.* = WHILE.
whim *n.* Sudden fancy, caprice, freakish notion.
whi′mbrel *n.* Small curlew, esp. the European *Numenius phaeopus.*
whi′mper *v.i.* Cry querulously, whine softly. ~ *n.* Feeble whining broken cry.
whi′msical (*or* -z-) *adj.* Capricious, fanciful, characterized by whims. **whi′msically** *adv.*
whimsica′lity *n.*
whi′msy (-zĭ) *n.* Crotchet, whim.
whin[1] *n.* Gorse; *whi′nchat,* small European bird, *Saxicola rubetra,* allied to stonechat, with brownish mottled plumage and sweet song.
whin[2], **whi′nsill, whi′nstone** *ns.* (Boulder or slab of) very hard dark-coloured esp. basaltic rock or stone, used for road-metal and in building.
whi′nberry *n.* Bilberry.
whine *n.* Long-drawn complaining cry (as) of dog; suppressed nasal tone; feeble, mean, or undignified complaint. ~ *v.* Utter whine(s); utter, complain, whiningly.
whi′nny *v.i.* Neigh gently or joyfully. ~ *n.* Whinnying sound.
whinsill, whinstone: see WHIN[2].
whip *n.* 1. Instrument for flogging or beating, or for urging on horse etc., consisting usu. of lash attached to short or long stick. 2. (also *whipper-in*) Official responsible to huntsman for managing hounds and seeing that they do not stray from pack; hence, in British and some other Parliaments, official appointed to maintain discipline among members of his party in House of Parliament, give them necessary information, and secure their attendance esp. at divisions; also, written notice issued by him requesting attendance on particular occasion; *three-line* ~, such notice underlined 3 times to indicate its importance. 3. Whipping or lashing motion, esp. slight bending movement produced by sudden strain. 4. Simple kind of tackle for hoisting light objects, consisting of block with rope rove through it (*single* ~) or of standing block and running block with fall of former attached to latter (*double* ~, ~ *on* ~). 5. *whi′pcord,* thin tough kind of hempen cord for whip-lashes etc.; close-woven worsted fabric with fine close diagonal ribs, used for riding-breeches etc.; ~-*hand,* hand in which whip is held; (fig.) upper hand, control (*of*), advantage; ~-*lash,* lash of whip; object resembling this; ~-*saw,* saw with very long narrow tapering blade; ~-*scorpion,* arachnid resembling scorpion but without sting and usu. with lash-like organ at end of body; ~-*snake,* any of various slender snakes; ~-*stitch,* (sew with) whipping stitch. ~ *v.* 1. Move suddenly or briskly, snatch, dart; make *up* quickly or hastily. 2. Beat, drive or urge on, (as) with whip; lash, flog; beat up (eggs, cream, etc.) into froth; (angling) throw line or bait on water with movement like stroke of whip; (colloq.) overcome, defeat, 'lick'; ~ *in,* drive (hounds) with whip back into pack. 3. Bind round (rope, stick, etc.) with close covering of twine, thread, etc.; sew over and over, overcast, esp. hem, or gather (fabric) by overcasting rolled edge with fine stitches. 4. ~-*graft,* (make) graft with slit in end of both scion and stock, tongue of each being inserted in slit of the other; ~-*round,* appeal to number of persons for contribution to fund etc.
whi′pper *n.* (esp.) ~-*in:* see WHIP *n.* 2; ~-*snapper,* small child; young and insignificant but impertinent person.
whi′ppet *n.* Small dog like greyhound used for racing and coursing, and orig. bred (19th c.) in north of England from cross between greyhound and terrier or spaniel.
whi′pping *n.* (esp.) Overcasting of hem (ill. STITCH); ~-*boy,* (hist.) boy educated with young prince and chastised in his stead (also fig.); ~-*post,* post to which offenders were tied to be whipped; ~-*top,* top kept spinning by strokes of lash.
whi′ppoorwill *n.* Nightjar (*Caprimulgus vociferus*) of eastern U.S. and Canada. [f. its cry]
Whi′psnāde. Park in the Chiltern Hills, Bedfordshire, a reserve for the breeding and exhibition of wild animals, maintained by the Zoological Society of London.
whirl *v.* Swing round and round, revolve rapidly; send, travel, swiftly in orbit or curve; convey, go, rapidly in wheeled conveyance; (of brain, senses, etc.) be giddy, seem to spin round; *whir′lpool,* part of river, sea, etc., where water is in constant and usu. rapid circular motion; *whir′lwind,* mass of air whirling rapidly round and round and moving progressively over surface of land or water (also fig. of violent motion). ~ *n.* Whirling, swift, or violent movement; disturbance, commotion; distracted or dizzy state.
whir′ligig (-g-) *n.* Spinning toy like sails of windmill revolving on stick; merry-go-round; revolving motion.
whirr *n. & v.i.* (Make) continuous buzzing or vibratory sound, as of bird's rapidly fluttering wings, swiftly turning wheel, etc.
whisk *n.* 1. Bunch of twigs, grass, hair, bristles, etc., for brushing or dusting; instrument for beating up eggs, cream, etc., into a froth; slender hair-like part or appendage, as on tails of certain insects etc.; panicle of certain plants, esp. common millet. 2. Quick sweeping movement (as) of whisk, animal's tail, etc. ~ *v.* Convey, go, move with light rapid sweeping motion; brush or sweep lightly and rapidly from surface; beat up (eggs, cream, etc.), esp. with whisk.
whi′sker *n.* 1. (usu. pl.) Hair on cheeks or sides of face of adult man. 2. Each of set of projecting hairs or bristles on upper lip or about mouth of cat or other animals, birds, etc. **whi′skered** (-erd), **whi′skery** *adjs.*
whi′skў, whi′skey *ns.* (the spelling *whiskey* is now used to distinguish the Irish kind). Spirit distilled, orig. in Scotland and Ireland, but now also in U.S., Canada, and Australia, from malted barley, rye, maize, potatoes, or other cereals; ~-*toddy,* hot water and whisky usu. flavoured with lemon and sugar. [Gael. *uisge*(*beatha*) water (of life)]
whi′sper *n.* Speech or vocal sound without vibration of vocal cords; remark uttered thus; soft rustling sound; insinuation, rumour, hint. ~ *v.* Utter in whisper, esp. for sake of secrecy; communicate etc. quietly or confidentially; (of leaves etc.) make soft rustling sound; *Whispering Gallery,* circular gallery below dome of St. Paul's Cathedral, London, where a whisper can be heard from one side to the other; similar gallery elsewhere.
whist *n.* Game of cards, played (usu.) by 2 pairs of opponents with pack of 52 cards, in which one suit is trumps and tricks are taken by highest card of suit led or highest trump; *progressive* ~: see PROGRESSIVE; ~-*drive,* social function at which progressive whist is played, usu. for prizes.
whi′stle (-sl) *n.* 1. Tubular wind instrument of wood, metal, etc., producing shrill tone by forcing air or steam against a sharp edge or into a bell and causing it to vibrate, used for giving signal or alarm; also as musical toy, usu. of tin and pierced with six holes; (joc., colloq.) mouth or throat (esp. in *wet one's* ~, take a drink); ~ *stop,* (U.S.) pause of train at station to allow electioneer to make speech (from practice of announcing stop at country place by sounding train-whistle). 2. Whistling, clear shrill

sound produced by forcing breath through lips contracted to narrow opening; similar sound made by whistle or pipe; clear shrill note of bird; any similar sound, as of wind blowing through trees or missile flying through air. ~ v. Make sound of whistle with mouth, esp. as call or signal, expression of derision, contempt, astonishment, etc.; utter, produce, clear shrill sound or note; blow whistle; produce, utter, by whistling; call, send, (*away, off, up*) by whistling; ~ *for*, (colloq.) seek or expect in vain, go without.

whi′stler[1] (-sl-) *n.* One who whistles; (local) any of various whistling birds; large marmot of mountainous parts of N. America.

Whi′stler[2] (-sl-), James Abbott McNeill (1834–1903). American-born painter and etcher, active chiefly in England.

whit[1] *n.* (chiefly with neg.) Particle, least possible amount.

Whit[2] *adj.* Of Whitsuntide; ~ *Monday, Tuesday*, etc., days following ~ *Sunday* (= white Sunday), 7th Sunday after Easter, commemorating the descent of the Holy Spirit upon the disciples on the day of Pentecost (Acts 2), so called because white robes were worn on it; ~ *week*, that containing Whit Sunday.

white *adj.* Of the colour of snow or milk, of colour produced by reflection or transmission of all kinds of light in proportions in which they exist in complete visible spectrum, without sensible absorption; of some colour approaching this, pale, less dark than other things of the same kind; (fig.) innocent, unstained, harmless; (politics) of royalist, counter-revolutionary, or reactionary tendency (opp. RED); ~ *ant*, termite; *whi′tebait*, small silvery-white fish (fry of various fishes, chiefly herring and sprat) caught in large numbers in Thames Estuary and elsewhere, and esteemed as delicacy; other small fish resembling this and used as food; *whi′tebeam*, small tree (*Sorbus aris*) with large leaves having white silky hairs on underside; ~ *bear*, polar bear; *whi′tecap*, bird with light-coloured patch on head, esp. male redstart; white-crested wave; ~-*collar*, engaged in, being, non-manual work; ~ *corpuscle*, leucocyte; ~ *currant*, variety of *Ribes* with white berries; ~ *dwarf*, one of class of small stars of great density radiating white light; ~-*eye*, Old World passerine bird (family Zosteropidae) with white ring round eye; ~ *elephant*, Indian elephant with pale-coloured skin, venerated as rarity in Siam etc.; (fig.) burdensome or useless possession (from story that kings of Siam made presents of these animals to those whom they wished to ruin by cost of their maintenance); ~ *feather*, symbol or emblem of cowardice (from white feather in gamecock's tail, held to show that he is not purebred); *whi′tefish*, any light-coloured or silvery fish, as cod, haddock, whiting, etc.; lake-fish of *Coregonus* and allied genera, resembling salmon and valued as food; *W*~ *Friar*, Carmelite; ~ *frost*: see FROST; ~ *gold*, white-coloured alloy of gold, esp. alloy with nickel and zinc, resembling platinum; ~-*haired* (or -*headed*) *boy*, favourite; ~-*heart* (*cherry*), yellowish-white cultivated cherry; ~ *heat*, degree of temperature (higher than *red heat*) at which body radiates white light (freq. fig. of passions etc.); *W*~ *Horse*, figure of a horse cut on the face of the chalk downs near Wantage, Oxon., pop. supposed to be the national symbol of the Saxons; similar figure elsewhere; ~ *horses*, white-crested waves; ~-*hot*, at white heat; *W*~ *House*, official residence of U.S. President, at Washington, D.C.; ~ *lead*, basic lead carbonate, a heavy white powder, used as white pigment; ~ *lie*, innocent, harmless, or trivial lie, fib; ~-*livered*, cowardly, dastardly; ~ *man*, member of a people with light-coloured skin or complexion, esp. of European extraction; (colloq.) honourable, trustworthy, person; ~ *meat*, light-coloured meat, as poultry, veal, pork; ~ *metal*, white or silver-coloured alloy, esp. one which is easily fusible and so suitable for lining high-speed bearings; *W*~ *Monk*, Cistercian; *W*~ *Nile*: see NILE; ~ *paper*, parliamentary report, usu. less extensive than BLUE *book*; *W*~ *Russia*, Belorussia; *W*~ *Russian*, (native, language) of White Russia; ~ *sapphire*, colourless variety of sapphire; ~ *sauce*, sauce of flour or cornflour, milk, and butter, variously flavoured; *W*~ *Sea*, gulf of Arctic Ocean in U.S.S.R.; ~ *slave*, woman held unwillingly for purpose of prostitution, esp. one transported from one State or country to another; ~ *slaver*, *slavery* (*ns.*); *whi′tesmith*, tinsmith; polisher or finisher of metal goods (dist. from forger); ~ *spirit*, petroleum fraction used as a solvent and in paints etc.; ~ *staff*, white rod or wand carried as symbol of office by Lord High Treasurer of England, Lord Steward of Household, etc.; *whi′tethorn*, hawthorn; *whi′tethroat*, species of warbler, esp. *Sylvia communis*; N. Amer. brown bunting (*Zonotrichia albicollis*) with white patch on throat, also called ~-*throated sparrow*; *whi′tewash*, liquid composition of lime and water or whiting, size, and water, for whitening walls, ceilings, etc.; (fig.) glossing over person's faults; *whi′tewash* (*v.*) apply whitewash to (lit. & fig.); ~ *witch*, witch whose purposes are beneficent. **whi′telў** *adv.* **whi′teness** *n.* **whi′tish** *adj.* **white** *n.* White or light-coloured part of anything; white or nearly white colour; white pigment; white clothes or material; translucent viscid fluid surrounding yolk of egg, becoming white when coagulated; sclerotic coat, white part of eyeball surrounding coloured iris; white man; white butterfly, pigeon, pig, etc.; member of political party called 'white', reactionary, legitimist, extreme conservative; player having white (or light-coloured) pieces in chess etc.

Whi′techăpel (-t-ch-). District of London, E. of the City; ~ *cart*, light two-wheeled spring-cart.

Whi′tefield(-tf-), George(1714–70). English religious reformer, one of the founders of METHODISM, who engaged in evangelical preaching in N. America, adopted Calvinistic views, and formed a party of Calvinistic Methodists.

Whi′tehall(-t-hawl).Thoroughfare in the City of Westminster, London, bordered by government offices; hence, British Government or its policy. [f. *White Hall*, palace built by Wolsey which stood N. of Westminster Abbey]

whi′ten *v.* Make, become, white or whiter. **whi′tening** *n.* = WHITING[1].

whi′ther (-dh-) *adv.* (archaic) To where.

whi′ting[1] *n.* Preparation of finely powdered chalk used for whitewashing, cleaning plate, etc.

whi′ting[2] *n.* Common European small gadoid fish (*Merlangus merlangus*) with pearly white flesh, used as food; fish resembling this.

whi′tleather (-lĕdh-) *n.* Tawed leather; light-coloured soft pliant leather dressed with alum and salt.

Whi′tley Cou′ncil (-sl) One of a number of boards representing both employers and staff, set up (first in 1917) to settle wages, conditions of work, etc., in certain industries (where they are usu. known as Joint Industrial Councils) and in the civil service and local government service. [J. H. *Whitley*, chairman of committee recommending the councils]

whi′tlow (-ō) *n.* Inflammation, usu. with suppuration, on finger or toe, esp. about nail.

Whi′tman, Walt (1819–92). American poet, author of poems on moral, social, and political questions, written in an unconventional form between rhythmical prose and verse.

Whi′tsun *n.* Whit Sunday; Whitsuntide; *Whitsunday*′, Scottish quarter-day (15 May); *Whi′tsuntide*, week-end or week containing Whit Sunday.

Whi′ttier, John Greenleaf (1807–92). American Quaker poet.

Whi′ttington, Sir Richard (d. 1423). Lord Mayor of London three times (1397, 1406, 1419);

hero of the popular legend of Dick Whittington and his cat.
whi′ttle v. Dress, pare, with knife; cut thin slices or shavings from surface of, make or shape thus; (fig.) reduce amount or effect of by successive abstractions, pare *down*, take *away* by degrees.
whi′tÿ adj. Whitish (chiefly in ~-*brown*).
whĭz, whĭzz v. (Cause to) make sound as of body rushing through air; move swiftly (as) with such sound; ~-*bang*, (slang) kind of small high-velocity shell whose passing through the air can be heard before the report of the gun that fired it. ~ n. Act, sound, of whizzing.
W.H.O. abbrev. World Health Organization.
who (hoo) pron. 1. (interrog.) What or which person(s); what sort of person(s) in regard to origin, position, authority, etc.; *Who's Who*, title of reference book of contemporary biography (first issued 1849) and of similar works. 2. (rel.) (Person or persons) that; and, but, he (she, they); (archaic) the or any person(s) that.
whoa (wō′a) int. Word of command to horse etc. to stop or stand still.
whodŭ′nĭt (hoo-) n. (slang) Detective or mystery story.
whoĕ′ver (hoo-) pron. Whatever person(s), any(one) who; no matter who.
whole (hōl) adj. In sound condition, uninjured, not broken or divided, intact; integral, without fractions; undiminished, without subtraction; all, all of; *with one's ~ heart*, heartily, with concentrated effort, etc., whence ~-*hearted*, -*heartedly*, -*heartedness*; *go the ~ hog*, go to the utmost limit; act etc. without reservation; ~-*hogger*, one who goes the whole hog; *who′lemeal*, meal or flour made from whole grain of wheat (sometimes including bran); ~ *note*, (U.S.) semibreve; ~ *plate*, photographic plate or film 16·5 × 21·6 cm (6½ × 8½in.). ~ n. Full, complete, or total amount (*of*); complete thing; organic unity, complex system, total made up of parts.
who′lesāle (hōls-) n. Selling of articles in large quantities to be retailed by others. ~ adj. Selling by wholesale; pertaining to sale in gross; unlimited, indiscriminate; doing, done, largely or profusely. ~ adv. In large quantities, in gross; in abundance, extensively, indiscriminately. **whō′lesaler** n. One who sells wholesale.
who′lesome (hōls-) adj. Promoting, conducive to, health or well-being; beneficial, salutary, salubrious; not morbid, healthy. **whō′lesomelÿ** adv. **whō′lesomenèss** n.
whŏlly (hō′l-lĭ) adv. Entirely, completely, to the full extent, altogether; exclusively.

whom (hoom) pron. Objective (accus., dat.) case of WHO.
whoop (hoop) int. Cry expressing excitement, exultation, etc. (used esp. in hunting by N. Amer. Indians as signal or war-cry). ~ n. Cry of 'whoop'; characteristic drawing-in of breath after coughing in whooping-cough. ~ v.i. Utter whoop; *whoo′pingcough*, infectious disease, esp. of children, with violent convulsive cough followed by whoop, caused by a bacillus, *Haemophilus pertussis*.
whoō′pee int. Exclamation of exuberant joy. ~ n. Cry of 'whoopee'; *make* ~, (slang) rejoice noisily or hilariously, have a good time.
whŏp v.t. (slang) Thrash, defeat, overcome. **whŏ′pping** adj. Very large or great. **whŏ′pper** n. Very large thing; monstrous falsehood.
whōre (h-) n. Prostitute; ~ *of Babylon*, (see Rev. 17: 1, 5 etc.) abusively applied to Church of Rome, esp. in 17th c. **whōr′edom** n. Fornication. **whōr′emonger** (-mŭ-) n. Fornicator. **whōre** v.i. Have to do with whore(s), fornicate; (fig., archaic, after Deut. 31: 16) *go a-whoring after strange gods* etc., practise idolatry or iniquity.
whōrl n. Small flywheel or pulley on spindle to steady its motion (ill. SPINNING); convolution, coil, something suggesting whirling movement, esp. (of fingerprint) complete circle formed by central papillary ridges; each turn of spiral shell or any spiral structure; (bot.) ring of leaves, flowers, etc., springing from stem or axis at same level.
whor′tleberrÿ (wērtlb-) n. Bilberry.
whose (hooz) pron. Possessive case of WHO.
whosoĕ′ver (hoo-) pron. (emphat.) Whoever.
why adv. 1. (interrog.) On what ground, for what reason, with what purpose. 2. (rel.) On account of which. ~ n. Reason, cause, explanation, esp. in ~(s) *and wherefore*(s). ~ int. Exclamation expressing (esp. mild or slight) surprise, slight protest, etc., or emphasizing or calling attention to following statement, in opposition to possible doubt or objection.
whydah: see WIDAH.
W.I. abbrev. West Indies; Women's Institute.
wi′bble v.t. (eng.) = END-mill.
wick[1] n. Bundle of fibre, now usu. loosely twisted or woven cotton, immersed at one end in oil or grease of lamp, candle, etc., and drawing it up to maintain flame at other end.
wick[2] n. (obs. except in place-names or other compounds) Town, village, hamlet.
wi′ckėd adj. Sinful, iniquitous, vicious, morally depraved; (colloq.,

usu. joc.) very or excessively bad, malicious, mischievous, roguish; *W~ Bible*, English edition of 1632 with 'not' omitted in 7th commandment. **wi′ckėdlÿ** adv. **wi′ckėdnėss** n.
wi′cker n. Plaited pliant twigs or osiers as material of baskets, chairs, mats, etc.; *wi′ckerwork*, things made of wicker; craft of making them.
wi′ckėt n. 1. (also ~-*gate*) Small gate or door, esp. one made in or placed beside large one. 2. (cricket) Set of three stumps fixed upright in ground and surmounted by two bails, forming structure (71·1 × 22·9 cm) to be defended by batsman from balls aimed by bowler (ill. CRICKET); time during which batsman is or might be in; ground between and about wickets, pitch; *keep* ~, be wicket-keeper; *lose a* ~, (of batting side) have one batsman out; *take a* ~, (of bowler) put batsman out; *win by 4* (etc.) ~*s*, win having lost only 6 wickets in the last innings; ~-*keeper*, fieldsman stationed behind wicket to stop ball if it passes by, and if possible get batsman out by stumping or catching (ill. CRICKET).
Wi′cklow (-ō). Maritime county and city of Leinster, Ireland.
wi′ddershĭns (-z), **wĭth-** (-dh-) adv. (dial.) In direction contrary to apparent course of sun (considered as unlucky or disastrous). [MLG *wider-* against, *sin* direction]
wide adj. 1. Measuring much from side to side; broad, not narrow; in width (as *20 ft* ~). 2. Extending far, embracing much, of great extent; not tight, close, or restricted; loose, free, liberal, unprejudiced, general. 3. Open to full extent. 4. At considerable distance from point or mark, not within reasonable distance *of*. 5. (slang) Shrewd, skilled in sharp practice. 6. ~-*angle*, (of lens) having short focus and field extending through wide angle; ~ *ball*, = wide (n.); ~-*eyed*, with eyes wide open, gazing intently; (fig.) wondering, naïve. **wi′delÿ** adv. **wide** adv. Over or through large space or region, far abroad (now only in *far and* ~); at wide interval(s), far apart; with wide opening, to full extent, at a distance to one side, so as to miss mark or way, astray, esp. (cricket) out of reach of batsman; ~ *awake*, fully awake; (colloq.) on the alert, fully aware of what is going on, sharp-witted, knowing; ~-*awake*, (n.) soft wide-brimmed felt hat; *wi′despread*, widely disseminated or diffused. ~ n. (cricket) Ball bowled wide of wicket out of batsman's range and counting one run to his side.
wi′den v. Make, become, wide or wider.
widgeon: see WIGEON.
wi′dow (-ō) n. Woman who

[992]

has lost her husband by death and not married again; ~-*bird*, WHIDAH; ~'*s cruse*, small supply that seems inexhaustible (see 1 Kings 17: 10–16, 2 Kings 4: 1–7; ~'*s mite*: see MITE¹; ~'*s peak*, V-shaped growth of hair in centre of forehead. **wi'dowhood** (-ō-h-) *n*. **wi'dow** *v.t.* Make widow or widower of (usu. in past part.); bereave, deprive *of*.

wi'dower (-ōer) *n*. Man who has lost his wife by death and not married again.

width *n*. Distance or measurement from side to side; large extent; piece of material of same width as when woven, esp. one of such pieces sewn together to make garment etc.

Wie'land (v-), Christoph Martin (1733–1813). German poet and writer of verse romances; translated some of Shakespeare's plays into German.

wield *v.t.* Control, sway, hold and use, manage.

wife *n*. (pl. *wives*). 1. Married woman esp. in relation to her husband. 2. Woman, esp. one who is old and rustic or uneducated (now rare exc. in *old wives' tale*, foolish or superstitious tradition). **wi'fehood** *n*. **wi'fely** *adj*.

wig *n*. Artificial head of hair worn esp. to conceal baldness, or as part of professional, ceremonial, or fashionable costume; coarse hair on shoulders of full-grown male fur-seal; ~*s on the green*, (colloq., orig. Irish) coming to blows, sharp altercation.

wi'geon, widg- (-jon) *n*. Wild duck, esp. *Anas penelope* of Europe and N. Asia and *A. americana* of N. America.

wi'gging (-g-) *n*. (colloq.) Severe rebuke, scolding.

wi'ggle *v.t.* (colloq.) (Cause to) move from side to side.

wight¹ (wit) *n*. (archaic) Person. **Wight²**, Isle of: see ISLE OF WIGHT.

Wigorn. *abbrev.* (Bishop) of Worcester, replacing surname in his signature.

Wi'gtownshire (-tun-). Former county of SW. Scotland, since May 1975 part of the region of Dumfries and Galloway.

wi'gwag *v*. (colloq.) Wag, esp. wave flag or other object to and fro in signalling.

wi'gwam (*or* -ŏm) *n*. Tent or cabin of N. Amer. Indian tribes of region of Great Lakes and eastward, formed of bark, matting, or hides stretched over frame of converging poles.

Wi'lberforce. *William* ~ (1759–1833), English M.P.; devoted himself to the cause of the abolition of the slave-trade and slavery; *Samuel* ~ (1805–73), his son, successively bishop of Oxford and Winchester, and initiator of revision of A.V.

wi'lco *int*. Response used in oral communication by radio etc. to indicate that directions received will be carried out. [abbrev. of *wil*l *co*mply]

Wi'lcŏx, Mrs Ella Wheeler (1850–1919). Amer. poet and journalist.

wild *adj*. 1. Living or growing in state of nature, not domesticated, tame, or cultivated. 2. Uncivilized, barbarous. 3. Rebellious, lawless; not under control or restraint; tempestuous; rash, random. 4. Violently excited or agitated; passionately desirous (*to do*); elated, enthusiastic; haphazard, reckless, extravagant. 5. ~ *cat*, European wild species of cat (*Felis sylvestris*), larger and stronger than domestic cat and similar in colour and marking to tabby; (orig. U.S. colloq.) unsound or risky enterprise (freq. attrib.); ~-*cat strike*, unofficial strike; *wi'ldfire*, highly inflammable composition very difficult to extinguish, formerly used in warfare etc. (now chiefly in *spread like wildfire*, spread with immense rapidity); phosphorescent light; *wi'ldfowl*, wild birds, esp. wild game; ~ *goose*, any undomesticated goose, in England usu. greylag, in N. America the Canada goose; ~ *goose chase*, foolish, fruitless, or hopeless quest; ~ *man*, savage; ~ *man (of the woods)*, orang-utan; ~ *oats*, wild grass of genus *Avena*, resembling oats; *sow one's* ~ *oats*, indulge in youthful indiscretions and escapades; *W*~ *West*, western States of U.S. at period when they were lawless frontier districts; *wi'ldwood*, (chiefly poet.) uncultivated or unfrequented wood. **wi'ldly** *adv*. **wi'ldness** *n*. **wild** *n*. (usu. pl.) Desert, wild tract.

Wilde, Oscar Fingal O'Flahertie Wills (1854–1900). Irish-born writer of comedies, novels, and verse, a wit and aesthete.

wildebeest (vī'ldebāst) *n*. Gnu. [S. Afr. Du., = 'wild beast']

wi'lderness *n*. Desert, uncultivated and uninhabited land or tract; part of garden left looking uncultivated; mingled, confused, or vast assemblage *of*; *in the* ~, (of political party, with ref. to Num. 14: 33) out of office.

wi'lding *n*. Wild plant, esp. wild crab-apple; fruit of such plant.

wile *n*. Trick, cunning procedure, artifice. ~ *v.t.* Lure.

Wi'lfrid, Wi'lfrith, St. (634–700). Bishop of York, instrumental in winning over King Oswy of Northumbria to the Roman, as opposed to the Columban, Church.

wi'lful *adj*. Asserting or disposed to assert one's own will against instruction, persuasion, etc. obstinately self-willed; deliberate, intentional, showing perversity or self-will. **wi'lfully** *adv*. **wi'lfulness** *n*.

WIGS
A. PERIWIG OR PERUKE, *c* 1680. B. FULL-BOTTOMED, 1766. C. BAG-WIG, *c* 1725. D. RAMILLIES, EARLY 18TH C. E. BARRISTER'S WIG, 20TH C. (DATING FROM 17TH C.)
1. Cravat. 2. Cocked Hat. 3. Queue

[993]

Wilhelmstrasse (vĭ'lhĕlmshtrahse). Street in Berlin where Foreign Ministry and other government buildings were formerly situated; hence, (hist.) German Foreign Ministry.

Wilkes (-ks), John (1727–97). English Radical M.P., journalist, and agitator, several times expelled from the House of Commons.

Wĭ'lkie, Sir David (1785–1841). Scottish painter.

will[1] *n.* 1. Faculty or function which is directed to conscious and intentional action; act, action, of willing; intention or determination that something shall be done or happen; desire, wish, inclination (*to* do); (archaic or poet.) what one desires; *against one's* ~, unwillingly; *at* ~, according to one's volition or choice, as one will; *at the command or disposal (of);* (of estate etc.) held during owner's pleasure, (of tenant) that may be ousted at any time; *with a* ~, resolutely, determinedly, energetically; ~-*power*, (strength of) will, esp. power to control one's own actions etc. 2. Person's formal declaration, usu. in writing, of his intention as to disposal of his property etc. after his death; document in which this is expressed. ~ *v.* 1. Determine by the will, choose or decide to do something or that something shall be done; exercise the will; bring, get, (*into* etc.) by exercise of will; control (person), induce (another) *to do*, by exercise of one's will. 2. Direct by will or testament; dispose of by will, bequeath.

will[2] *v.t.* (past & conditional *would* pr. wood). Desire (thing; archaic); want, desire, choose, to; wish that; consent, be prevailed on, to; intend unconditionally; be accustomed, be observed from time to time, to; be likely to. ~ *v. aux.* Forming compound tenses or moods expressing (in 2nd and 3rd pers.) plain future or conditional statement or question, (in 1st pers.) future or conditional statement expressing speaker's will or intention.

wĭ'llĕt *n.* Large N. Amer. shore-bird of snipe family (*Catotrophorus semipalmatus*).

Wĭ'lliam[1] (-yam). Name of four kings of England: *William I* (*c* 1027–87), 'the Conqueror', Duke of Normandy, claimed the English throne, invaded England and defeated Harold at the Battle of Hastings (1066); reigned 1066–87; *William II* (1056–1100), 'Rufus', son of William I; reigned 1087–1100; *William III* (1650–1702), Prince of Orange, married Mary, daughter of James II, and reigned jointly with her 1689–94, and alone (after her death) until 1702; *William IV* (1765–1837), 3rd son of George III, succeeded his brother, George IV, in 1830.

Wĭ'lliam[2] (-yam). Name of three princes of Orange; *William I* (1533–84), 'the Silent', led the insurrection of the Netherlands against Spain and became (1580) the 1st stadholder of the United Provinces of the Netherlands; *William II* (1626–50); *William III* = William III of England (see WILLIAM[1]).

Wĭ'lliam[3] (-yam). Anglicized form of name (*Wilhelm*) of two German emperors and kings of Prussia; *William I* (1797–1888), king of Prussia 1861–88, 1st German emperor 1871–88; *William II* (1859–1941), 'the Kaiser', grandson of William I, succeeded his father, Frederick III, 1888, abdicated 1918 after the defeat of Germany, and fled to Holland.

Wĭ'lliam[4] (-yam). Anglicized form of name (*Willem*) of three kings of the Netherlands; *William I* (1772–1843) became 1st king of the Netherlands after the defeat of Napoleon, 1815, abdicated 1840 in favour of his son, *William II* (1792–1849), 2nd king of the Netherlands 1840–9; *William III* (1817–90), son of William II, whom he succeeded 1849.

Wĭ'lliam and Mār'y Cŏ'llĕge (-yam). College at Williamsburg, Virginia, founded 1693 by Dr James Blair.

wĭ'lling *adj.* Consenting, disposed (*to* do); ready to be of use or service; given, rendered, performed, etc., willingly. **wĭ'llĭnglў** *adv.* **wĭ'llĭngnĕss** *n.*

will-o'-the-wisp *n.* = IGNIS FATUUS; (fig.) person or thing that deludes or misleads by fugitive appearances. [orig. *Will with the wisp* (= handful of lighted tow etc.)]

Wĭ'lloŭghby (-lobĭ), Sir Hugh (d. 1553). English navigator; perished on the way to Russia, which was reached, via the White Sea, by other members of his expedition.

wĭ'llow (-ō) *n.* Tree or shrub of genus *Salix*, widely distributed in temperate and cold regions, usu. growing by water and with pliant branches and long narrow drooping leaves, grown for ornament or as furnishing osiers, light smooth soft wood, or medicinal astringent bark; cricket- or baseball-bat (made of willow-wood); *wear the (green)* ~, grieve for loss of loved one; ~-*herb*, plant of *Epilobium* and related genera, esp. *E. angustifolium*, with narrow willow-like leaves and showy purplish-pink flowers, a common weed in all parts of North Temperate zone; ~ *pattern*, blue pattern, of Chinese origin, on white china, introduced into England in late 18th c. by Thomas Turner, and including willow-tree etc.; ~-*tree*, willow; ~-*warbler*, -*wren*, small European song-bird, *Phylloscopus trochilus*; other bird of this and related genera. **wĭ'll'owў** *adj.* 1. Abounding in willows, bordered or shaded with willows. 2. Lithe and slender.

Will Scăr'lĕt. (in legend) One of the companions of Robin Hood.

Will's Cŏ'ffee House (-lz). Coffee-house (named after its proprietor William Unwin) formerly at corner of Bow St. and Russell St., London, frequented by wits, poets, and gamesters in Queen Anne's reign.

wĭ'llў-nĭ'llў *adv. & adj.* With or against the will of the persons concerned, whether one will or no, willing(ly) or unwilling(ly).

Wĭ'lson[1], Sir Harold (1916–), British Labour statesman; prime minister 1964–70, 1974–6.

Wĭ'lson[2], John (1785–1854). 'Christopher North', professor at Edinburgh University and notable literary critic.

Wĭ'lson[3], Thomas Woodrow (1856–1924). 28th president of U.S., 1913–21; U.S. representative at the peace treaty negotiations after the war of 1914–18 and sponsor of the Covenant of the League of Nations.

wilt *v.* (Cause to) fade, droop, become limp.

Wĭ'lton. Town in S. Wiltshire, noted since 16th c. for manufacture of carpets; ~ *carpet*, woollen or worsted carpet with short thick pile, resembling Brussels carpet, first made at Wilton.

Wilts. *abbrev.* Wiltshire.

Wĭ'ltshire. County of SW. England; hence, breed of sheep, kind of smoked bacon, variety of Cheddar cheese, as produced in Wiltshire.

wĭ'lў *adj.* Full of wiles, crafty, cunning. **wĭ'lĭlў** *adv.* **wĭ'linĕss** *n.*

Wĭ'mbledon (-bld-). Suburb of London, scene of international lawn tennis championships and matches.

wĭ'mple *n.* Cloth of linen or silk so folded as to cover head, chin, sides of face, and neck, formerly worn by women and retained in dress of nuns (ill. KIRTLE). ~ *v.* Envelop in wimple, veil; fall in folds.

win *v.* (past t. & past part. *won* pr. wŭn). Be victorious in (game, battle, race, law action, etc.); gain victory; get, gain, secure, esp. by effort or competition, as price or reward, by merit, or in

WILLOW PATTERN

[994]

WINCE

gaming or betting; gain affection or allegiance of, bring *over* to one's party or cause; make one's way to, make one's way *to*, *through*, etc.; get (coal, stone, or other mineral) from mine, pit, etc.; ~ *out* (colloq.), *through*, gain one's end, be successful. **wi′nner** *n*. **win** *n*. (colloq.) Victory in game or contest; (pl.) winnings.
wince *v.i.* Make involuntary shrinking movement, start, with pain, in alarm, etc., flinch. ~ *n*. Such movement.
wi′ncey *n*. Durable fabric with usu. linen warp and woollen weft.
winceye′tte *n*. Fabric resembling wincey with cotton warp.
winch *n*. Crank of wheel or axle; hoisting or hauling apparatus consisting essentially of revolving horizontal drum worked by a crank.
Wi′nchèster. Cathedral city in Hampshire; once the capital of Wessex and later of the Anglo-Saxon kingdom; ~ *College*, public school situated there, founded 1382 by William of Wykeham; ~ *quart*, (bottle containing) half a gallon, so called because standard measures were formerly deposited at Winchester.
Wi′nckelmănn (v-), Johann Joachim (1717–68). German writer on Greek art and antiquities.
wind[1] (*poet. also* wī-) *n*. 1. Air in motion, current of air of any degree of force perceptible to senses occurring naturally in atmosphere; this in reference to direction from which it blows or (naut.) its direction or position in

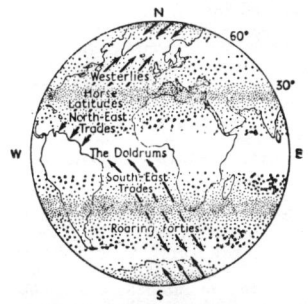

THE DIRECTIONS OF THE PREVAILING WINDS IN THE ATLANTIC

relation to ship; air artificially put in motion by passage of missile, action of bellows, etc.; scent, esp. of person or animal in hunting etc., conveyed on wind; *get ~ of*, (fig.) begin to suspect, hear rumour of; *in the ~*, happening or ready to happen, astir, afoot; *like the ~*, swiftly; *raise the ~*, (fig., colloq.) obtain money needed; *sail etc. close to the ~*, (fig.) come very near indecency or dishonesty; *take ~ out of person's sails*, (fig.) put him at a disadvantage, esp. by anticipating his arguments etc.

2. Gas in stomach or intestines; *break ~*, release it by anus; *get, have, put, the ~ up*, (slang) be, make, apprehensive. 3. Breath as needed in exertion, power of drawing breath without difficulty while running etc.; part of body in front of stomach, blow on which checks action of diaphragm and takes away breath; *second ~*, regular breathing regained after breathlessness during continued exertion (also fig.). 4. Breath as used in speaking, esp. (fig.) empty talk. 5. Breath or air as used for sounding musical instrument, as horn, flute, organ-pipe; (players of) wind instruments of orchestra collectively. 6. *~-bag*, wordy talker; *~-bound*, kept from sailing by adverse winds; *~ brace*, strengthening timber of roof (ill. ROOF); *wi′ndbreak*, something, esp. row of trees, used to break force of wind or as protection against it; *~-cheater*, windproof jacket fitting closely at waist and wrists; *~-chest*, chest in organ etc. filled with wind from bellows and admitting it to pipes or reeds (ill. ORGAN); *~-cone*, piece of cloth shaped like truncated cone, held open at larger end by ring of wire and used to indicate direction of wind, drogue; *~ egg*, soft-shelled egg; *wi′ndfall*, something blown down by wind, esp. fruit; (fig.) piece of unexpected good fortune, esp. legacy; *wi′ndflower*, anemone; *wi′ndgall*, soft tumour on horse's leg just above fetlock; fragment of rainbow or prismatic halo, supposed to presage windy weather; *wi′ndhover*, kestrel; *~ instrument*, musical instrument in which sound is produced by current of air, esp. by breath; *wi′ndjammer*, (colloq.) sailing-ship; *~ machine*, machine used in theatre etc. for producing blast of air or sound of wind; *wi′ndpipe*, air passage between throat and bronchi or lungs, trachea; *wi′ndproof*, affording protection from wind; *wi′ndrow*, row of mown grass or hay raked up to dry before being made into cocks, similar row of peats, corn-sheaves, etc.; *wi′ndscreen*, screen to keep off wind, esp. sheet of glass, etc., in front of driver of motor vehicle etc. (ill. MOTOR); *~-shake*, flaw or crack in timber supposed to be caused by wind; *wi′ndshield*, (U.S.) windscreen; *~-sleeve, -sock*, wind-cone; *~-swept*, swept by winds, exposed; *~-tight*, constructed so as to keep out wind; *~ tunnel*, enclosed chamber through which wind may be blown at known velocities, for testing (models of) aircraft etc.; *wi′ndward*, (region) lying in direction from which wind blows, facing the wind. **wi′ndless** *adj*. wind *v*. 1. (wī-) Sound (horn or bugle) by blowing; blow (note, call, etc.) on horn etc. 2. (wī-) Detect presence of by scent. 3. (wī-) Deprive of breath, make out of breath.

WINDOW

wind[2] *v*. (past t. & past part. *wound*). Move, traverse, in curved or sinuous course; coil, wrap closely, around something or upon itself, encircle or enclose thus; haul or hoist by turning windlass etc.; tighten (*up*) coiled spring of (clock etc.), or (fig.) tension, intensity, or efficiency of; ~ *up*, bring or come to conclusion, conclude; arrange and adjust affairs of (company, business concern) on its dissolution; *winding-sheet*, shroud; drippings of candle-grease clinging to side of candle. **wi′nder** *n*. Person, thing, that winds; winding step in staircase (ill. STAIR).
Wi′ndermēre. Largest lake in England, in the Lake District; town situated above its E. shore.
Windhoek (vĭ′nthŏŏk). Capital city of South West Africa.
wi′ndlass *n*. Mechanical contrivance for hauling or hoisting,

WINDLASS
1. Pawl. 2. Ratchet

consisting essentially of horizontal roller or beam on supports, with rope or chain wound round. ~ *v.t.* Hoist or haul with windlass.
wi′ndmill (*or* -nm-) *n*. Mill worked by action of wind on sails (*illustration, p. 969*); toy consisting of stick with shaped card or other light substance fixed to its end and revolving when moved through air; *fight, tilt at, ~s*, expend energy contending against imaginary opponents or difficulties (in allusion to story of Don Quixote's tilting at windmills under the delusion that they were giants).
wi′ndow (-ō) *n*. Opening, usu. filled with glass, in wall or roof of building, ship, car, train, etc., to admit light or air and afford view of what is outside or inside (*illustration, p. 970*); window space or opening, esp. used for display of goods, advertisements, etc., in shop etc.; any opening resembling window in shape or function; *~-box*, box placed outside window for cultivating (esp. ornamental) plants; *~-dresser*, one who arranges display in shop window etc.; *~-dressing*, art of arranging such display, (fig.) adroit presentation of facts etc. to give falsely favourable impression; *~-envelope*, envelope with opening or transparent panel

[995]

WINDSOR

through which address inside is visible; ~-*seat*, seat below window, usu. in recess or bay; ~-*shopping*, looking at shop displays without buying; ~-*sill*, sill of window; ~-*tax*, tax levied on all windows of a house after a certain number, enforced in England from 1695 to 1851.

Wi′ndsor (-nzer). Town in Berkshire on right bank of Thames, site of royal residence ~ *Castle*; surname assumed by English royal house in 1917; *Knights of* ~, small body of military officers who have pensions and apartments in Windsor Castle; *Duke of* ~, title conferred on Edward VIII on his abdication in 1936; ~ *chair*, kind of wooden chair with back formed of upright rod-like pieces surmounted by freq. curved or hoop-shaped cross-piece (ill. CHAIR); ~ (*soap*), kind of usu. brown or white scented toilet-soap.

Wi′ndward I′slands (ilandz). 1. Group of islands in the West Indies consisting of Grenada, St. Vincent, St. Lucia, and Dominica, with their dependencies. 2. Group of islands in southern part of Lesser Antilles, including British and French territories.

wi′ndy *adj.* Wind-swept; exposed to, blown upon or through, by wind; in which wind is frequent or prevalent, accompanied by (much) wind; generating, characterized by, flatulence; verbose, empty; (slang) frightened. **wi′ndily** *adv.* **wi′ndiness** *n.*

wine *n.* 1. Fermented grape-juice for drinking, varying in colour from *red* (usu. a purplish crimson) to *white* (pale gold); *dessert* ~, wine for drinking with dessert or after meal; *fortified* ~, wine (esp. port and sherry) to which brandy is added during manufacture; *table* ~, wine for drinking at meal. 2. Fermented drink more or less resembling wine, made from juice of other fruits or flowers or root vegetables. 3. (pharm., obs.) Solution of specified medicinal substance in wine. 4. Colour of red wine; ~-*red* (*adj.*). 5. ~-*apple*, large red apple with winy flavour; ~-*bibber*, tippler; ~-*biscuit*, light usu. sweet biscuit served with wine; biscuit flavoured with wine; ~-*cellar*, cellar used for storing wine; contents of this; ~-*cooler*, vessel in which bottles of wine are cooled with ice; ~-*glass*, small drinking-glass, usu. with stem and foot, for wine; (as measure) usu. = sherry-glass, about 4 tablespoons; ~-*press*, press in which grape-juice is extracted for making wine; ~-*red*: see sense 4; ~-*sap*, large red Amer. winter apple; ~-*skin*, skin of goat etc. sewn together to make primitive wine-vessel; ~-*sour*, small acid variety of plum; ~-*stone*, deposit of crude tartar in wine-casks; ~-*vault*, cellar for storing wine; bar, shop, etc., where wine is retailed. **wi′ny** *adj.* **wine** *v.* Drink wine; entertain with wine.

wing *n.* 1. Organ of flight of any flying animal, in birds a specially modified forelimb, in bats, extension of skin attached to modified parts of forelimb, in insects membranous expansions attached to thorax in addition to limbs. 2. Power or means of flight, flying. 3. Anything resembling wing in form or function, esp. one of the main supporting surfaces (planes) of aircraft (ill. AEROPLANE). 4. Lateral part or appendage, esp. curved side-piece over wheel of motor-car etc. as protection against mud. 5. Either of two divisions on each side of main body of army or fleet in

WINK

battle. 6. (footb. etc.) Position, player, on outside of forward line. 7. Section of political party etc. holding views deviating from centre: see RIGHT ~, LEFT ~. 8. Subordinate part of building on one side of main or central part. 9. Each of side-scenes on stage, (usu. pl.) space at side of stage where these stand (ill. THEATRE). 10. (anat., bot.) Lateral part or projection of some organ or structure, as lateral cartilage of nose, thin membranous appendage of seed or fruit serving for its dispersal by wind, etc. 11. Division of air force, in R.A.F. usu. comprising three squadrons, in U.S., three groups. 12. (pl.) Representation of pair of bird's wings worn as badge by those who have passed flying tests. 13. ~ *attack*, *defence*, (position of) netball player near opponents', own team's, goal (ill. NETBALL); ~-*case*, horny covering of functional wings in certain insects (ill. BEETLE[2]); ~-*chair*, chair with side-pieces projecting forwards at top of high back, for protection from draughts (ill. CHAIR); ~-*collar*, man's stiff collar with upper corners turned down; *W*~ *Commander*, officer of R.A.F. of rank between Group Captain and Squadron Leader; ~-*covert*: see COVERT; ~-*flap*, FLAP of aircraft; ~-*load(ing)*, total weight of loaded aircraft divided by area of supporting surfaces; ~-*nut*, nut with projections for thumb and fingers to turn it by (ill. SCREW); ~-*rib*, end rib of loin of beef (ill. MEAT); ~-*span*, -*spread*, extreme measurement between tips of wings of bird or aircraft; ~-*tip*, outer end or tip of wing of bird, aircraft, etc. ~ *v.* Equip with wings; enable to fly or mount; send in flight, lend speed to; travel, traverse, on wings; wound (esp. game bird) in the wing.

winged (-ngd, *poet. also* wi′ngid) *adj.* Having wings; swift, rapid, flying; (of speech) conveying its message swiftly and effectively; ~ *elm*, small N. Amer. elm (*Ulmus alata*) with corky winged branches; *W*~ *Horse*, Pegasus; ~ *pea*, S. European annual herb (*Lotus Tetragonolobus*) with 4-winged pods; *W*~ *Victory*, statue of Nike, Greek goddess of victory, with wings, esp. Hellenistic statue found in Samothrace, preserved in Louvre.

wi′ngless *adj.* Having no wings; (of birds) having rudimentary wings not used for flight.

wink *v.* Blink; close one eye momentarily in flippant or frivolous manner; close (an eye, eyes) for a moment; move swiftly, (cause to) flicker like an eyelid, twinkle; give (signal, message, etc.) by flashing lights; ~ *at*, shut one's eyes to, connive at; *like winking*, in a flash, in a twinkling. ~ *n.* Act of winking, esp. as signal; *not a* ~

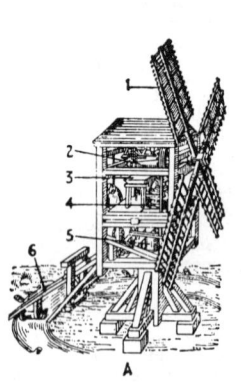

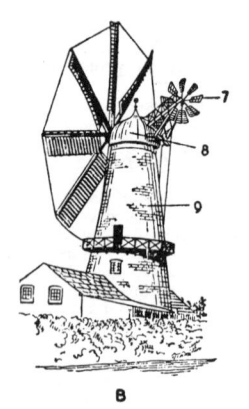

WINDMILLS

A. POST MILL FOR GRINDING CORN.   B. TOWER MILL FOR RAISING WATER

1. Sails. 2. Shaft on which sails are mounted. 3. Hopper. 4. Millstones. 5. Post on which mill turns. 6. Tail-pole for turning mill into the wind. 7. Fan. 8. Movable cap. 9. Fixed tower

WINKLE

(*of sleep*), no sleep at all; *tip*, *give the* ~, give signal or intimation.
wi'nkle *n.* Periwinkle, edible sea snail. ~ *v.t.* ~ *out*, extract or eject (as a winkle from its shell with a pin).
wi'nning *adj.* That wins; charming, attractive. ~ *n.* (esp.) 1. ~*-post*, post marking end of racecourse. 2. (pl.) Money won by gaming or betting.
Wi'nnipĕg. Capital city of Manitoba, Canada; *Lake* ~, lake in Manitoba.

WINNIPEG

WINDOWS

A. LANCET, EARLY 13TH C. (INTERIOR). B. PLATE TRACERY, EARLY 13TH C. C. GEOMETRIC BAR TRACERY, LATE 13TH C   D. DECORATED CURVILINEAR TRACERY WITH OGEE ARCH, 14TH C. E. PERPENDICULAR TRACERY, 15TH C. F. ROSE WINDOW, 14TH C. G. ORIEL WINDOW, 15TH C. H. BAY WINDOW, 15TH C. I. MULLION WINDOW, 16TH C. J. DORMER WINDOW. K. VENETIAN OR PALLADIAN WINDOW, 18TH C. L. SASH WINDOW, 18TH C. M. SASH WINDOW, 18TH C. (INTERIOR). N. FRENCH WINDOW, EARLY 19TH C.

1. Embrasure or splay. 2. Rear-arch. 3. Rear-vault. 4. Hoodmould, label, or dripstone. 5. Quatrefoil. 6. Iron stanchion. 7. Cusp. 8. Foil. 9. Mullion. 10. Transom. 11. Light. 12. Casement window with leaded quarries. 13. Lintel. 14. Architrave. 15. Glazing bar. 16. Pane. 17. Sill. 18. Pelmet. 19. Curtain. 20. Window-seat. 21. Shutter in reveal. 22. Balcony

wi′nnow (-ō) *v.t.* Fan (grain) free of chaff etc., fan (chaff) *away, out, from*; sift, separate, clear of worthless or inferior element, extract, select (*out*) thus.
wi′nsome *adj.* Attractive, charming. **wi′nsomely̆** *adv.* **wi′nsomenèss** *n.*
wi′nter *n.* 1. Coldest season of year, popularly reckoned in N. hemisphere as comprising December, January, and February, but astronomically as lasting from winter solstice (21 or 22 Dec.) to vernal equinox (20 or 21 Mar.). 2. (*attrib.* or *adj.*) Of, characteristic of, winter; occurring, used, etc., in, lasting for, winter; (of fruit) ripening late or keeping well until or during winter; ~ *aconite*, small perennial herb (*Eranthis hyemalis*) producing bright-yellow starry flowers in winter; ~*-fallow*, (land) lying fallow during winter; ~ *garden*, conservatory in which plants are kept flourishing in winter; *wi′ntergreen*, any of various creeping or low shrubby plants with leaves remaining green in winter, esp. N. Amer. *Gaultheria procumbens*, with drooping white flowers, edible scarlet berries, and aromatic leaves yielding oil used in medicine and for flavouring; *W~ Palace*, former royal residence on River Neva in Leningrad (St. Petersburg), later used as museum and art gallery; ~ *solstice*: see SOLSTICE; ~ *sports*, open-air sports, as skiing, skating, practised on snow or ice; ~ *wheat* (*oats* etc.), wheat (oats etc.) sown in autumn and remaining in ground all winter. ~ *v.* Spend winter (*at, in*); keep, feed, during winter.
Winton. *abbrev.* (Bishop) of Winchester (replacing surname in his signature).
wi′ntry̆ *adj.* Characteristic of winter, having the temperature, storminess, etc., appropriate to winter, cold, windy, cheerless; (of smile, greeting, etc.) devoid of warmth, dreary, chilly. **wi′ntrinèss** *n.*
wipe *v.* Clean or dry surface of by rubbing with cloth etc.; clear away (moisture, dust, etc.) thus; apply soft or liquid substance over surface by rubbing it on, esp., (plumbing) apply solder to (joint) thus; ~ *out*, destroy, annihilate, exterminate; ~ *the floor with*, (slang) humiliate (person) by defeat or correction. ~ *n.* Act of wiping.
wi′per *n.* (esp., also (*wind*)*screen* ~) Mechanical device that wipes windscreen of motor vehicle (ill. MOTOR).
wire *n.* (Piece of) metal drawn into slender flexible rod or thread; length or line of this used for various purposes, esp. for fencing, as conductor of electric current, etc.; wire-netting, framework of wire; snare of wire etc.; (pl.) lines by which puppets are worked

(chiefly fig., in *pull* (*the*) ~*s*); (colloq.) telegram; ~ *cloth*, fabric woven from wire; ~*-cutter*, tool for cutting wire; *wir′edraw* (*v.*) draw out into wire; elongate, attenuate; ~*-drawn* (*adj.*) fine-spun, elaborately subtle or refined; ~*-edge*, turned-over strip of metal sometimes produced on edge of tool etc. by faulty sharpening; ~ *entanglement*, entanglement of barbed wire stretched over ground to impede enemy's advance; ~ *gauge*, gauge for measuring diameter of wire etc.; standard series of sizes to which wire etc. is made; ~*-gauze*, gauze-like fabric of wire; ~*-haired*, (of dogs, esp. terriers) having rough hard wiry coat; ~*-mark*, faint line in paper made by wires of mould; ~ *nail*, nail of circular section, pointed but not tapering; ~*-netting*, netting made of wire; ~*-puller*, politician etc. who privately influences others; ~*-walker*, acrobat performing feats on wire rope; ~ *wool*, very fine wire used for scouring kitchen utensils etc.; *wir′eworm*, slender yellow larva of any click beetle destructive to plants; (also) millepede which destroys plant roots; ~*-wove paper*, fine smooth paper made in wire-gauze frame, used esp. for letter-writing. ~ *v.* Furnish, support, stiffen, secure, with wires; snare with wire; (colloq.) telegraph.
wīr′elèss (wīrl-) *adj.* Without wire(s), esp. (of telegraphy, telephony) with no connecting wire between transmitting and receiving stations; = RADIO; ~ *set*, radio receiver. ~ *n.* Radio receiver or transmitter; wireless telegraphy or telephony. ~ *v.* Send (message etc.), inform, by wireless.
wīr′y̆ *adj.* Made of wire; tough and flexible like wire; (of persons) tough, sinewy, untiring. **wīr′ily̆** *adv.* **wīr′inèss** *n.*
Wis. *abbrev.* Wisconsin.
Wiscŏ′nsĭn. State in northeastern U.S., admitted to Union in 1848; capital, Madison.
Wisd. *abbrev.* Wisdom (of Solomon; Apocr.).
wi′sdom (-z-) *n.* Being wise; soundness of judgement in matters relating to life and conduct; knowledge, enlightenment, learning; *W~ of Solomon*, book of the Apocrypha; ~ *of Jesus the son of Sirach*, Ecclesiasticus; *W~ literature*, biblical books of Job, Proverbs, Ecclesiastes, Wisdom of Solomon, Ecclesiasticus, and Epistle of James; ~ *tooth*, hindmost molar tooth on each side of upper and lower jaws in humans, usu. appearing about age of twenty (ill. TOOTH).
wise[1] (-z) *n.* (archaic) Way, manner, guise.
wise[2] (-z) *adj.* Having, exercising, proceeding from, indicating, sound judgement resulting from experience and knowledge; saga-

cious, prudent, sensible; having knowledge (*of*); (archaic) skilled in magic or occult arts; *be, get,* ~ *to*, (U.S. colloq.) be, become, aware of; *put* ~ (*to*), inform (of); *wi′secrack*, smart remark, witticism; (*v.i*) make wisecracks; ~ *guy*, (U.S. slang) cocksure person; ~ *man*, man of good judgement or discernment; (archaic) one skilled in magic, wizard, esp. one of the Magi; ~ *woman*, witch, female soothsayer, esp. harmless or beneficent one. **wī′sely̆** *adv.*
-wise (-z) *suffix.* In (specified) manner, way, or respect. [f. WISE[1]]
wī′seacre (-zāker) *n.* Sententious dullard. [MDu. *wijsseggher* soothsayer]
wish *n.* (Expression of) desire or aspiration; request; (pl.) expression of desire for another's welfare, success, etc.; *wi′shbone*, forked bone between neck and breast of cooked bird (because when two persons have pulled it apart the holder of the larger piece is entitled to the magical fulfilment of a wish); ~*-fulfilment*, (psychol.) alleged tendency of wishes, esp. when unconscious, to seek gratification in reality or fantasy. ~ *v.* Have, feel, express, a wish for; express desire or aspiration *for*; want (*to* do, person *to* do); request; (esp. in expressions of goodwill, greeting, etc.) desire (something, esp. something good) for a person etc.; *wishing-cap*, *-gate, -well*, etc., cap, well, etc., supposed to assure fulfilment of wishes.
wi′shful *adj.* Wishing, desirous; ~ *thinking*, believing a thing to be so because it is desired or desirable. **wi′shfully̆** *adv.* **wi′shfulnèss** *n.*
wi′shy̆-wa′shy̆ (-wŏ-) *adj.* Thin, sloppy; feeble or poor in quality or character.
wisp *n.* Small bundle or twist of straw, hay, etc.; thin, narrow, filmy, or slight piece or scrap (*of*). **wi′spy̆** *adj.*
wistār′ĭa, -ēr′ĭa *n.* Leguminous plant of genus *Wistaria* of N. Amer., Japanese, and Chinese hardy climbing deciduous shrubs with pendulous racemes of blue-lilac, purple, or white papilionaceous flowers. [Caspar *Wistar* or *Wister*, Amer. anatomist (1761–1818)]
wi′stful *adj.* Yearningly or mournfully expectant or eager. **wi′stfully̆** *adv.* **wi′stfulnèss** *n.*
wĭt[1] *n.* 1. (sing. or pl.) Intelligence, understanding; *at one's* ~*'s end*, utterly perplexed; *five* ~*s*, the five senses; *have one's* ~*s about one*, be mentally alert; *live by one's* ~*s*, get one's living by clever or crafty devices, without any settled occupation; *out of one's* ~*s*, mad, distracted. 2. Unexpected combining or contrasting of previously unconnected ideas or expressions; power of causing surprise and

[998]

delight by this; capacity for making brilliant observations in an amusing way. 3. Person with this capacity; (archaic) person of great mental ability, man of talent.
wit² v. (archaic) Know; to ~, that is to say, namely.
witch¹ n. Sorceress, woman supposed to have dealings with devil or evil spirits; (fig.) fascinating or bewitching woman; old ~, (colloq.) malevolent or ugly old woman; ~ ball, coloured glass ball of kind formerly hung up to keep away witches; wi'tchcraft, sorcery; ~-doctor, tribal magician of primitive people; witches' sabbath, midnight meeting of demons, sorcerers, and witches, presided over by the Devil, supposed in medieval times to have been held annually as orgy or festival; ~-hunt, -hunting, searching out and persecution of supposed witches, persons suspected of unpopular or unorthodox political views, etc.; ~'s broom, twiggy growth on trees, esp. birch, caused by mites. ~ v.t. Bewitch; (fig.) fascinate, charm; witching time (of night), (after 'Hamlet', III. ii. 406) time when witches are active, midnight. wi'tchery n.
witch² n. Flat-fish (Glyptocephalus cynoglossus) resembling lemon sole, used for food. [prob. f. WITCH¹, from its uncanny appearance]
witch³, wȳch ns. In name of various trees with pliant branches: ~-alder, shrub of genus Fothergilla, with alder-like leaves; ~-elm, species of elm (Ulmus glabra) with broader leaves and more spreading branches than common elm; ~-hazel, N. Amer. shrub (Hamamelis virginiana) with hazel-like leaves and yellow flowers; astringent extract of bark of this used as remedy for bruises, sprains, etc., and in cosmetics.
wi'tenagemō't (-g-) n. (hist.) National assembly of the Anglo-Saxons. [OE, = 'assembly of wise men' (wita wise man, gemot meeting, moot)]
with (-dh) prep. 1. (of conflict, rivalry, etc.) Against, in opposition to. 2. In or into company of or relation to, among, beside. 3. Agreeably or in harmonious relations to. 4. Having, carrying, possessed of, characterized by; ~ child, young, pregnant. 5. In the care, charge, or possession of. 6. By use of as instrument or means, by addition or supply of, by operation of, owing to. 7. In same way, direction, degree, at same time, as. 8. In regard to, concerning, in the mind or view of. 9. So as to be separated from. 10. Despite, notwithstanding, the presence of. 11. ~. it, (colloq.) up-to-the-minute, (capable of) understanding new ideas etc.
witha'l (-dhawl) adv. & prep. (archaic) With (it); in addition,

moreover, as well, at the same time.
withdraw' (widh-) v. (past t. -drew, past part. -drawn). 1. Pull aside or back; take away, remove; retract. 2. Retire from presence or place, go aside or apart. withdraw'al n.
withe (-dh; or wi'dhi), wi'thy (-dhi) ns. (pl. -thes pr. -dhiz, or -ths). Tough flexible twig or branch esp. of willow or osier used for binding bundles, making baskets, etc.
wi'ther (-dh-) v. Make, become, dry or shrivelled (up); deprive of or lose vigour, vitality, freshness, importance; decline, languish, decay; blight, paralyse (with look of scorn etc.). wi'thering adj. wi'theringly adv.
wi'thers (-dherz) n.pl. Ridge between shoulder-blades of horse and some other animals (ill. HORSE). [named as part that takes strain of collar, f. OE wither against]
withershins: see WIDDERSHINS.
withhō'ld (-dh-h-) v.t. (past t. & past part. -hēld). Hold back, restrain; refuse to give, grant, or allow.
withi'n (-dh-) adv. Inside, internally, inwardly; indoors; (theatr.) behind the scenes. ~ prep. To, on, in, the inside of; enclosed by; in the limits of; not beyond, above, outside, or farther than the extent of; in the scope or sphere of action of.
withou't (-dh-) adv. (literary or archaic) Outside, externally. ~ prep. 1. (archaic) Outside of. 2. Not having, not with; devoid of; lacking; free from. ~ conj. (archaic or illiterate) Unless.
withstä'nd (-dh-) v.t. (past t. & past part. -stood). Resist, oppose.
withy: see WITHE.
wi'tless adj. (archaic & literary) Lacking in wits, senseless; lacking wit. wi'tlessness n.
wi'tness n. 1. Testimony, evidence; confirmation. 2. Person giving sworn testimony in lawcourt or for legal purpose; person attesting execution of document by adding his signature; thing or person whose existence, position, etc., is testimony to or proof of; person present as spectator or auditor; ~-box, enclosed space from which witness gives evidence; ~-stand, (U.S.) stand from which witness gives evidence. ~ v. State in evidence (archaic); give evidence, serve as evidence; indicate, serve as evidence of; see, be spectator of; sign (document) as witness.
Wi'ttelsbach (v-, -ax). Princely house ruling in Bavaria from 1806 to 1918.
Wi'ttenberg (v-). German university town on the Elbe, famous as the place where Luther taught.
wi'tticism n. Witty saying, piece of wit; esp. jeer, witty sarcasm. [coined by Dryden from WITTY, after criticism]

wi'tting adj. Knowing or intending, conscious. wi'ttingly adv. [f. WIT²]
wi'tty adj. Capable of, given to, saying or writing brilliantly or sparklingly amusing things; full of wit. wi'ttily adv.
wi'zard n. Magician, sorcerer, male witch; person who effects seeming impossibilities. wi'zardry n. wi'zard adj. (colloq.) Marvellous, wonderful.
wi'zen, wi'zened (-zn, -znd) adjs. Of shrivelled or dried-up appearance.
W/L abbrev. Wavelength.
W.L.A. abbrev. Women's Land Army.
Wm abbrev. William.
W.M.O. abbrev. World Meteorological Organization.
WNW. abbrev. West-north-west.
wō int. = WHOA.
W.O. abbrev. War Office; Warrant Officer.
woad¹ n. European biennial plant Isatis tinctoria; blue, black, or green dye-stuff obtained from this, used before the introduction of indigo and afterwards in conjunction with it.
wŏ'bble v.i. Move unsteadily or with uncertain direction from side to side or backwards and forwards; shake, rock, quiver; (fig.) vacillate, hesitate, waver. ~ n. Wobbling motion. wŏ'bblȳ adj.
Wo'dehouse (wŏŏd-h-), Sir Pelham Granville (1881–1975). English-born novelist and humorist.
Wō'den. (Scand. myth.) = ODIN.
woe n. (chiefly poet. or joc.) Affliction, bitter grief, distress; (pl.) calamities, troubles; ~ is me! alas!; ~ be to, betide, a curse upon; ~ betide you if, you will be in trouble if; woe'begŏne, dismal-looking. woe'ful adj. woe'fully adv.
wŏg n. (slang, contempt.) Native of Middle East.
woken: see WAKE¹.
wōld n. Elevated tract of open uncultivated country or moorland; rolling uplands.
wolf¹ (wŏŏ-) n. (pl. -ves). 1. Any of various largish mammals of dog tribe (Canis, esp. C. lupus) of Europe, Asia, and N. America, with harsh grey or brownish-grey fur, erect pointed ears, and bushy tail, noted for fierceness and rapacity; rapacious or greedy person; (slang) man who pursues women; cry ~, raise false alarm; keep ~ from the door, ward off hunger or starvation; ~ in sheep's clothing, person concealing malicious intentions under guise of friendliness etc. 2. (mus.) Harsh howling sound of certain chords on keyed instruments, esp. organ, tuned by unequal temperament. 3. ~-cub, young wolf; W~ Cub: see CUB, 3; ~-dog, wo'lfhound, any of various large varieties of

[999]

WOLF

dog kept for hunting wolves; ~'s-bane, aconite, esp. European *Aconitum vulparia*, with dull-yellow flowers; ~ *whistle*, expressive whistle uttered by man at woman as indication of sexual attraction. **wo'lfish** *adj.* **wo'lfishly** *adv.* **wo'lfishness** *n.*
wolf *v.t.* Devour ravenously.
Wŏlf² (v-), Hugo (1860–1903). Austrian composer, esp. of songs.
Wolfe (wŏŏ-), James (1727–59). English general; commanded the British forces at the siege of Quebec, in which he was killed.
Wŏlff¹ (v-), Christian (1679–1754). German rationalist philosopher.
Wŏlff² (v-), Kaspar Friedrich (1733–94). German embryologist. **Wŏ'lffian** *adj.* ~ *body*, one of two renal organs of vertebrate embryos, becoming the kidneys in fishes and amphibians.
wo'lfram (wŏŏ-) *n.* Ore (FeWO₄) yielding tungsten.
Wŏ'lfram vŏn E'schenbăch (v-, ě-, -χ) (early 13th c.). German epic poet, whose chief work was 'Parzival'.
Wo'llaston (wŏŏ-), William Hyde (1766–1822). English chemist, discoverer of palladium and rhodium.
Wolsey (wŏŏ'lzĭ), Thomas (*c* 1475–1530). Archbishop of York, cardinal and statesman; chancellor under Henry VIII 1515–29.
wo'lverine (wŏŏ-, -ēn), **-ēne** *n.* = GLUTTON, 2, esp. of N. America.
wo'man (wŏŏ-) *n.* (pl. *women* pr. wi'min). Adult human female; female servant or attendant; (without article) the average or typical woman, the female sex; (attrib.) female, as ~ *doctor*, ~ *friend*; *wo'mankind*, women in general; *Women's Institute*, organization (now world-wide) founded in Ontario, Canada (1895), and Britain (1915), whose institutes are centres where women in rural areas may meet and work together, in crafts, social work, etc.; *Women's Lib*, movement urging liberation of women from domestic duties and subservient status; *women's rights*, rights claimed for women of equal privileges and opportunities with men; *Women's Royal Voluntary Service*, organization of women performing social and welfare work, orig. formed (1938) to help with A.R.P. services. **wo'manhŏŏd** *n.* State of being a woman; womanliness; womankind.
wo'manish (wŏŏ-) *adj.* Characteristic of woman as opp. to man; (of man) effeminate. **wo'manishly** *adv.* **wo'manishness** *n.*
wo'manīze (wŏŏ-) *v.* Make womanish; (of men) philander. **wo'manīzer** *n.*
wo'manlīke (wŏŏ-) *adj.* Like a woman.
wo'manly (wŏŏ-) *adj.* Having the qualities or bearing of a woman; befitting a woman. **wo'manliness** *n.*
womb (wŏŏm) *n.* Uterus (ill. PELVIS); (fig.) place where anything is generated or produced.
wo'mbăt *n.* Burrowing herbivorous marsupial, esp. of genus

WOMBAT
1 m long

Phascolomis, native to S. Australia and Tasmania, with thick heavy body, short legs, rudimentary tail, and general resemblance to small bear.
wo'mĕnfŏlk (wĭ-, -ōk) *n.* Women collectively, esp. of family or community.
wŏn¹: see WIN.
wŏn² (wŭn) *n.* Principal monetary unit of North and South Korea; = 100 jeon.
wo'nder (wŭ-) *n.* 1. Marvel, miracle, prodigy; astonishing thing, deed, event, occurrence, etc.; *for a ~*, as instance of surprising or exceptional fact or happening; *no ~*, (it is) not surprising; *Seven Wonders of the World*: see SEVEN. 2. Emotion excited by something novel and unexpected, or inexplicable; astonishment mixed with perplexity, bewildered curiosity, or admiration. 3. *wo'nderland*, imaginary realm of wonders, fairyland; *~-worker*, one who performs wonders or miracles. ~ *v.* 1. Be affected with wonder, marvel; *I shouldn't ~*, (colloq.) I should not be surprised. 2. Feel some doubt or curiosity, be desirous to know or learn.
wo'nderful (wŭ-) *adj.* Marvellous, surprising; surprisingly large, fine, excellent, etc. **wo'nderfully** *adv.* **wo'nderfulness** *n.*
wo'ndrous (wŭ-) *adj. & adv.* (poet., rhet.) Wonderful(ly). **wo'ndrously** *adv.*
wŏ'nky *adj.* (slang) Shaky, unsound.
wŏnt *adj.* (archaic) Accustomed, used (*to* do). ~ *n.* Custom; habit. **wŏ'ntĕd** *adj.* Habitual.
wŏn't. (colloq.) = Will not. ~ *n.* (usu. pl.) Refusal.
wŏŏ *v.* = COURT. **wŏŏ'er** *n.*
wŏŏd¹ *n.* 1. Collection of trees growing more or less thickly together, of considerable extent; piece of ground covered with trees; (now rare) wooded country, woodland; *out of the ~* (U.S. ~s), clear of a difficulty, danger, etc. 2. Hard compact fibrous substance making up trunks and branches of

WOOD

trees and shrubs between bark and pith, whether growing or cut down ready for use in arts and crafts, for fuel, etc.; particular kind of wood; (gardening) branch-wood. 3. Something made of wood, esp. cask in which wine etc. is stored, each bowl in the game of bowls, (mus.) wooden wind instruments, wood-wind. 4. ~ *alcohol*, methyl alcohol; ~ *anemone*, any of various common wild anemones, abundant in woods and flowering in early spring; *woo'dbind, woo'dbine*, any of various climbing plants, now esp. common wild fragrant yellow-flowered honeysuckle, (U.S.) Virginia creeper; *~-block*, block of wood, e.g. for paving or esp. with design for printing from; *woo'dcock*, common European migratory bird, *Scolopax rusticola*, allied to snipe, with long bill, large eyes, and mottled plumage, esteemed as food; similar but smaller N. Amer. *Philohela minor*; *woo'dcraft*, knowledge of and skill in forest conditions applied to hunting, maintaining oneself, making one's way, etc.; *woo'dcut*, print obtained from design cut in relief on block of wood (usu. sawn along the grain); this art; *woo'dcutter*, one who fells or lops trees for timber or fuel; ~ *engraving*, print obtained from design engraved on block of wood (usu. sawn across grain); this art; *woo'dland*, wooded country, woods; (attrib.) of, in, growing or dwelling in, consisting of, etc., woodland; *woo'dlark*, small European species of lark (*Lullula arborea*) which perches on trees, with shorter tail and more variegated plumage than skylark and different song; *woo'dlouse*, small terrestrial isopod crustacean of *Oniscus* or related genera, esp. *O. asellus*, found in old wood, under stones, etc.; *woo'dman*, forester, wood-cutter; *~-nymph*, nymph of the woods, dryad; *woo'dpecker*, any bird of numerous genera and species of family Picidae, found in most parts of world, with plumage usu. bright-coloured and variegated, characterized by habit of pecking holes in trunks and branches of trees to find insect food or make cavities for laying eggs; *~-pigeon*: see PIGEON¹; *~-pulp*, pulp made by mechanical or chemical disintegration of wood-fibre, used for making paper etc.; *woo'druff*, low-growing European woodland herb (*Asperula odorata*) with clusters of small white flowers and whorls of strongly sweet-scented leaves; *woo'dsman*, (chiefly U.S.) man living in or frequenting woods, one skilled in woodcraft; *~-sorrel*, low-growing spring-flowering woodland plant (*Oxalis acetosella*) with delicate trifoliate leaves and small white flowers streaked with purple; other species of *Oxalis*; *~-spirit*, methyl alcohol; *~-tar*, tar obtained in dry

[1000]

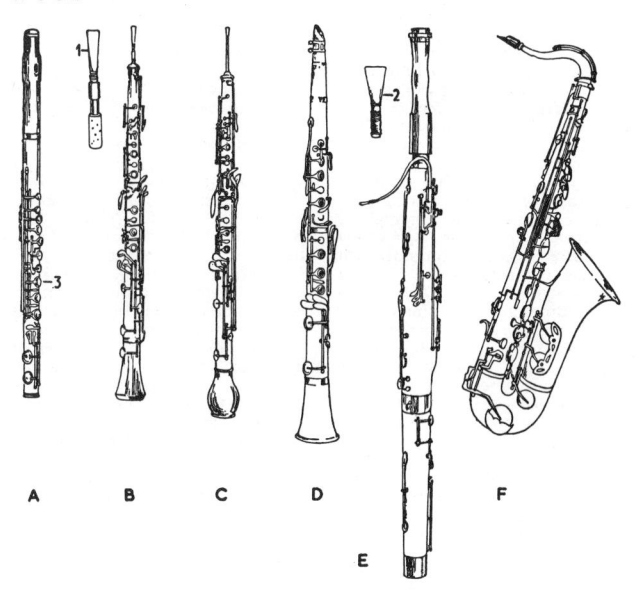

WOOD-WIND INSTRUMENTS
A. FLUTE. B. OBOE. C. COR ANGLAIS. D. CLARINET. E. BASSOON. F. SAXOPHONE
1. Double-reed mouthpiece of oboe. 2. Double-reed mouthpiece of bassoon. 3. Key

distillation of wood; ~-wind, wooden wind instruments of orchestra; *woo'dwork*, work done in wood, as carpentry; work in wood, wooden part *of* anything, esp. wooden interior parts of building; *woo'dworm*, wood-boring larva of a furniture beetle *Anobium punctatum*. **woo'dėd** *adj.* Covered with growing trees; abounding in woods.

Wōod², Sir Henry Joseph (1869–1944). English musical composer and conductor of promenade concerts at Queen's Hall, London.

Woo'dbŭrў, Walter Bentley (1834–85). English photographer and inventor; ~-*type*, process in which a design on a film of gelatine, obtained from a photographic negative, is transferred by heavy pressure to a metal plate from which it may be printed; print thus produced.

woo'dchŭck *n.* Thick-bodied reddish-brown marmot (*Marmota monax*) of north-eastern U.S. and Canada. [f. Amer. Ind. name, cf. Cree *vuchak, otchock*]

woo'den *adj.* Made, consisting, of wood; resembling wood, dull or dead like sound of wood when struck, dull and inert, stiff and lifeless, inexpressive; ~ *head*, blockhead; ~-*headed*; *W~ Horse*, wooden figure of a horse made by Greeks in TROJAN War; ~ *spoon*, (esp.) spoon made of wood traditionally presented at Cambridge to candidate placed lowest in Mathematical Tripos; (person taking) this position; ~ *walls*, (hist.) ships,

shipping, as defensive force. **woo'denlў** *adv.* **woo'dennėss** (-n-n-) *n.*

woo'dў *adj.* Covered with trees, abounding in woods, well-wooded; of the nature of, consisting of, wood; resembling (that of) wood; (of plant) forming wood, having woody stems and branches; ~ *nightshade*: see NIGHTSHADE.

woof *n.* (archaic & poet.) Weft.

wool *n.* Fine soft curly hair forming fleecy coat of domesticated sheep and similar animals, characterized by imbricated surface of the filaments, to which is due its property of felting, and used chiefly in prepared state for making cloth; twisted woollen yarn used for knitting etc.; woollen garment or cloth; short soft underhair or down of some animals; something resembling wool, esp. downy substance found on some plants, Negro's short crisp curly hair; any fine fibrous substance naturally or artificially produced; *dyed in the ~*, dyed before spinning; (fig.) thoroughgoing, out-and-out; *pull the ~ over* person's *eyes*, hoodwink; ~-*gathering*, gathering fragments of wool torn from sheep by bushes etc.; absent-minded-(ness), indulging or indulgence in idle imagining; ~-*pack*, (bag holding) large quantity of wool or fleeces; rounded cumulus cloud with horizontal base; *woo'lsack*, large package or bale of wool; large wool-stuffed cushion forming usual seat of Lord Chancellor in House of Lords (said to have been adopted in Edward III's reign as reminder to lords of importance of wool trade; ill. PARLIAMENT); hence, lord chancellorship; ~-*staple*, market appointed for sale of wool; *woo'lwork*, wool embroidery, esp. on canvas. ~ *adj.* (commerc.) Made of wool throughout (cf. WOOLLEN).

woo'len *adj.* & *n.* (U.S.) = WOOLLEN.

Woolf, Virginia (1882–1941). English novelist and critic.

woo'llen *adj.* & *n.* (Fabric, esp. coarse or loosely woven) made of wool or (commerc.) made of yarns which contain wool fibres.

woo'llў *adj.* Bearing, naturally covered with, wool or wool-like hair; resembling or suggesting wool in softness, texture, etc.; confused, blurred, hazy; (of thought) lacking clarity; (of plants) pubescent, downy; *wild and ~*, barbarous, lacking culture (orig. applied to West of U.S. in frontier days); ~ *bear*, (colloq.) large hairy caterpillar, esp. larva of tiger-moth. ~ *n.* Woollen, esp. knitted, garment.

Woo'lwich (-li-; *or* -lij). Metropolitan borough of London, site of the Royal Arsenal, and formerly of the Royal Military Academy (see SANDHURST).

wŏp *n.* (slang, contempt.) Italian or other S. European, esp. immigrant into U.S.

Worcester¹ (woo'ster). Cathedral city in county of Hereford and Worcester; scene of battle (1651) in which Cromwell defeated the Scottish army with Charles II; ~ *china, Royal ~*, porcelain made at Worcester in factory founded 1751; ~ *sauce*, pungent condiment consisting of soy, vinegar, etc., first made at Worcester.

Worcester² (woo'ster). City of Massachusetts.

Worcestershire (woo'st-). Former W. midland county of England, since April 1974 part of Hereford and Worcester.

Worcs. *abbrev.* Worcestershire.

word (werd) *n.* 1. Vocal sound or combination of sounds, or written or printed symbols of these, constituting minimal element of speech having a meaning as such and capable of independent grammatical use; ~ *for ~*, verbatim, exact(ly); *last ~*, final utterance in conversation or esp. dispute; (pl.) last utterance before death; final or conclusive statement, latest thing. 2. Thing(s) said, speech, utterance (usu. pl.); (pl.) text of song, actor's part, etc.; verbal expression contrasted with action or thought; (pl.) contentious or violent talk, altercation; (with negative etc.) anything at all (said or written); watchword, password; report, tidings, information; command, order; promise, undertaking; declaration, assurance; *the W~ (of God)*, the Bible or some part of it; second person of Trinity;

[1001]

man of his ~, one who keeps his promises. 3. ~-*blind*, unable as result of brain injury or disease to understand written or printed words; so ~-*deaf*, unable to understand speech though capable of hearing the sounds; ~-*painting*, vivid descriptive writing; ~-*perfect* knowing perfectly every word of lesson, theatrical part, etc.; ~-*square*, series of words so arranged as to read the same vertically and horizontally, puzzle of which solution is such a series. **wor′dless** *adj.* **wor′dlĕssly̆** *adv.* **word** *v.t.* Put into words, phrase, select words to express. **wor′ding** *n.* (esp.) Form of words used, phrasing.

Wordsworth (wer̄′dzwerth), William (1770–1850). English Romantic lyric poet, one of the Lake poets (see LAKE[1]); poet laureate from 1843.

wor′dy̆ (wer̄-) *adj.* Verbose; in, consisting of, words. **wor′dily̆** *adv.* **wor′diness** *n.*

work (werk) *n.* 1. Action involving effort or exertion, esp. as means of gaining livelihood; labour done in making something, as dist. from materials used; (phys. etc.) operation of a force in producing movement or other physical change, esp. as measurable quantity; something to do or to be done, employment, business, function; act, deed, proceeding, (pl.) doings; (theol., pl.) moral action considered in relation to justification; *at* ~, engaged in work, working, operating; *in* ~, in regular occupation, gainfully employed; *out of* ~, without work to do, unemployed; *set to* ~, set (person), apply oneself, to a task, or to do something; *the* ~ *of* . . ., a proceeding occupying (a stated time). 2. Product of labour, thing(s) made; result of action; (pl.) architectural or engineering operations; (mil.) fortified building, defensive structure, fortification; literary or musical composition, product of any fine art, as statue, picture, etc., (pl. or collect. sing.) person's writings, compositions, paintings, etc., as a whole; sewing, embroidery, knitting, etc. 3. (pl.) Establishment, building with machinery, etc., where industrial process, esp. manufacture, is carried on; (pl.) internal mechanism, moving parts of piece of machinery, etc., esp. clock or watch. 4. ~-*bag*, -*basket*, -*box*, bag etc. holding materials and implements for needlework; *wor′kday*, day on which work is ordinarily performed, weekday; *wor′khardened*, (of some metals) rendered brittle or otherwise altered by repeated bending, hammering, etc.; *wor′khouse*, (hist.) public institution for maintenance of paupers, in which able-bodied were set to work; ~-*in*, takeover by workers of factory etc. threatened with closure; *wor′kload*, amount of work that can be performed, considered as a unit; *wor′kman*, man hired to do work or (usu.) manual labour, esp. skilled labour; craftsman; one who works in specified manner; *wor′kmanlike*, characteristic of a good workman, efficient; *wor′kmanship*, skill as a workman, craftsmanship exhibited in piece of work; *wor′kpeople*, people employed in manual or industrial labour for wages; ~*s committee*, *council*, committee of workers in factory etc. or their representatives; *wor′kshop*, room or building in which manual or industrial work is carried on; *wor′kshy*, disinclined for work, lazy; ~-*table*, table for holding working-implements; *wor′kwoman*, female worker or operative. **wor′kless** *adj. & n.* **work** *v.* 1. Engage, be engaged, in bodily or mental work; carry on operations; make efforts; be craftsman (*in* some material); (of machine, plan, etc.) operate, act, (of person) put or keep (machine etc.) in operation; keep (person, machine, etc.) at work or going, exact toil from; purchase (*passage* etc.) with labour instead of money. 2. Carry on, manage, control; have influence or effect, exercise influence on; bring about, effect, accomplish, produce as result. 3. Be in motion, be agitated; cause agitation; ferment. 4. (Cause to) make way, make (way etc.), slowly or with difficulty or by shifting motions; gradually become (tight, free, etc.) by motion. 5. Knead, hammer, fashion, into shape or desired consistency; artificially and gradually excite (person) *into* (a rage etc.). 6. Do, make by, needlework or the like. 7. Solve (sum) by mathematical processes. 8. ~ *off*, get rid of, free oneself from; finish working at; pass off, palm off; ~ *out*, find (amount etc.), solve (sum) by calculation, (of amount etc.) be calculated (*at*); exhaust (mine etc.) by working; accomplish, attain, with difficulty; develop, elaborate, plan or provide for details of; discharge (debt, obligation), pay for, by labour instead of money; (of athlete, team, etc.) box, play, etc., for practice not in contest; ~-*out*, practice game, bout, run, etc.; ~ *up*, bring gradually to efficient state; elaborate in description; advance gradually *to* (climax); excite, incite, stir up, arouse (*to*); stir up, make up (materials), compose, produce, construct; study (subject) carefully and in detail.

wor′kable (wer̄-) *adj.* That can be worked, fashioned, manipulated, managed, conducted, etc. **wor′kably̆** *adv.* **workabi′lity̆** *n.*

wor′kaday (wer̄-) *adj.* Of, characteristic of, workday or its occupations; of ordinary humdrum everyday life.

wor′ker (wer̄-) *n.* (esp.) 1. One employed for a wage, esp. in manual or industrial work; one who works either with hand or brain (opp. CAPITALIST). 2. Neuter or undeveloped female of certain social hymenopterous and other insects, as ants and bees, which supplies food and performs other services for community (ill. BEE).

wor′king (wer̄-) *n.* (esp.) Way thing works, result of its working; action, operation; (chiefly pl.) place in which mineral is or has been extracted, excavation(s) made in quarrying, mining, tunnelling, etc.; ~ *capital*, capital used in actual conduct of business, not invested in buildings, machinery, etc.; ~ *day*, workday, number of hours of work entitling workman to day's pay, portion of day devoted to work; ~ *drawing(s)*, scale drawing(s) from which workmen carry out construction; ~ *order*, condition in which machine, system, etc., works (well, badly, etc.). ~ *adj.* (esp.) Engaged in manual or industrial work; ~ *class(es)*, grade(s) of society comprising those employed for wages, esp. in manual or industrial occupations; ~-*class*, of, for, the working class; ~-*man*, man of working class; ~ *model*, model of machine etc. capable of doing work on small scale, or of being operated; ~ *party*, (1) (mil.) party of men detailed for special work outside usual duties; (2) committee (orig. representing workers and management) appointed by government to report on the policies necessary to secure efficiency in any industry; any committee appointed to investigate and report on a question.

world (wer̄-) *n.* 1. Human existence, (also *this* ~) present life; pursuits and interests, affairs and conditions of life; secular or lay life and interests; *better*, *next*, *other*, ~, life after death; ~ *without end*, endlessly, eternally. 2. Earth and all created things upon it; planet or other heavenly body, esp. one viewed as inhabited; material universe as ordered system, system of created things; everything, all phenomena; countries of the earth and their inhabitants, all people; human society; particular section of this, esp. high or fashionable society; sphere of interest, action, or thought; (freq. pl.) great quantity, vast or infinite amount or extent; *for all the* ~, in every respect (like); *man, woman, of the* ~, one knowing the ways of society; *not for (all) the* ~, *not for* ~*s*, not on any account; ~*'s end*, farthest attainable limit. 3. ~ *history*, history embracing events of whole world; ~ *language*, artificial language intended for universal use; ~ *politics*, international politics, politics based upon considerations affecting whole world; ~ *power*, State or nation dominating world politics; ~ *war*, war affecting (most of) the world; *First W~ War*, that of 1914–18, *Second W~ War*, that of 1939–45; ~*-weary*, weary of (the life of) the world; ~*-wide*, spread over the world, known or found everywhere, universal.

wor'ldling (wēr-) *n.* Worldly person.

wor'ldly (wēr-) *adj.* Temporal, earthly; exclusively or predominantly concerned with or devoted to affairs of this life, esp. to pursuit of wealth or pleasure; ~ *goods*, *property*; ~*-minded*, intent on worldly things; ~ *wisdom*, esp. prudence in advancing one's own interests; ~*-wise*, having worldly wisdom. **wor'ldliness** *n.*

worm (wērm) *n.* 1. Slender burrowing invertebrate animal esp. of genus *Lumbricus*, usu. brown or reddish with soft body divided into segments, earthworm; any annelid (*ringed* or *segmented* ~), nematode (*round-*~), or platyhelminth (*flatworm*); platyhelminth or nematode living as parasite in intestine of man or other animal, (pl.) disorder characterized by presence of these; larva of insect, maggot, grub, esp. one feeding on or destructive to fruit, leaves, timber, paper, flesh, etc.; maggot supposed to eat dead bodies in the grave; SHIP-worm. 2. Abject, miserable, or contemptible person. 3. (fig.) Grief or passion that preys stealthily on the heart or torments the conscience. 4. Natural or artificial object resembling earthworm; small worm-shaped ligament in dog's tongue; any of various spiral implements, esp. spiral of screw, (also ~*-gear*) endless or tangent screw whose thread gears with teeth of toothed wheel etc. (ill. GEAR); long spiral or coiled tube connected to head of still, in which vapour is condensed. 5. ~*-cast*, convoluted mass of mould voided by earthworm and left on surface of ground; ~*-eaten*, eaten into by worm(s), full of wormholes; decayed, decrepit, antiquated; ~*-gear*, see sense 4; worm-wheel; ~*-hole*, hole in wood, fruit, book, etc., made by burrowing insect larva; ~*-wheel*, toothed wheel gearing with worm.

wor'my *adj.* worm *v.* 1. Hunt for worms; rid (plants etc.) of worms or grubs; extract worm from tongue of (dog) as supposed safeguard against madness. 2. Progress or move sinuously; make one's way insidiously, insinuate *oneself*, *into* (person's confidence, secrets, etc.); ~ *out*, extract (secret etc.) by insidious questioning.

wor'mwood (wēr-) *n.* European woody herb (*Artemisia absinthium*) with bitter aromatic taste, yielding dark-green oil, and formerly used as tonic and vermifuge, as protection against moths and fleas, etc., and now for making vermouth and

absinthe; (fig.) bitter humiliation or its cause.

Worms (vōrmz), Diet of: see DIET[1].

worn *adj.*: see WEAR[1]; (esp.) impaired by use, exposure, or wear; enfeebled, exhausted, by toil, age, anxiety, etc.; ~*-out*, no longer of use or service; utterly wasted in strength or vitality; stale, trite.

wo'rry (wŭ-) *n.* Harassing anxiety or solicitude; cause of this, matter for anxiety, (pl.) cares, troubles; ~ *beads*, loop of loosely threaded beads for fingering. ~ *v.* 1. Seize by throat with teeth and tear or lacerate, kill or injure by biting and shaking (of dog etc.); (fig.) harass, work at, get *along* or *through* with persistent aggression or dogged effort or struggle; vex or distress by inconsiderate or importunate behaviour, pester with repeated demands, requests, etc. 2. Make anxious and ill at ease; give way to anxiety or mental disquietude.

worse (wērs) *adj. & adv.* Used as comparative of *bad*, *evil*, *badly*, *ill*, or as opposite of *better*. ~ *n.* Worse thing(s); worse condition.

wor'sen *v.* Make or become worse, deteriorate.

wor'ship (wēr-) *n.* 1. Reverence paid to being or power regarded as divine; acts, rites, or ceremonies displaying this; adoration or devotion comparable to this felt or shown to person or principle; *public* ~, church service. 2. Respectful form of address to or mention of certain magistrates in court, also (formerly) persons of high rank etc. ~ *v.* Adore as divine, pay religious homage to; idolize, regard with adoration; attend public worship; be full of adoration. **wor'shipper** *n.*

wor'shipful (wēr-) *adj.* 1. Entitled to honour or respect (archaic); as honorific title, now restricted to justices of the peace, aldermen, recorders, London City companies, and freemasons' lodges and their masters; *right* ~, title applied to mayors and the sheriffs, aldermen, and recorder of London. 2. (archaic) Imbued with spirit of veneration; worthy of worship. **wor'shipfully** *adv.* **wor'shipfulness** *n.*

worst (wērs-) *adj. & adv.* Used as superlative of *bad*, *evil*, *badly*, *ill*; least good or well. ~ *n.* Worst part, feature, state, event, possible issue, action, etc.; *at (the)* ~, in the most evil or undesirable possible state; even on the most unfavourable view or surmise; *do one's* ~, do the utmost evil or harm possible; *get* (etc.) *the* ~ *of*, be worsted in; *if the* ~ *come(s) to the* ~, if things fall out as badly as possible or conceivable. ~ *v.t.* Get the better of, defeat, outdo.

wor'sted (woos-) *n.* Fine smooth-surfaced yarn spun from long-staple wool which has been combed so that fibres lie parallel; fabric woven from this. ~ *adj.* Made of worsted. [f. *Worste(a)d* in Norfolk]

wort[1] (wērt) *n.* Plant or herb used for food or medicine (archaic exc. as second element of plantnames).

wort[2] (wērt) *n.* Infusion of malt or other grain which after fermentation becomes beer.

worth (wērth) *predic. adj.* Of the value of (a specified amount or sum); of specified or certain value in other than material respects; sufficiently valuable or important to be equivalent or good return for (something); possessed of, owning; deserving or worthy of (something); ~ *while*, worth the time or effort spent; *wor'thwhile*, that is worth time or effort expended. **wor'thless** *adj.* **wor'thlessly** *adv.* **wor'thlessness** *n.* **worth** *n.* What a thing is worth, value; equivalent *of* specified sum or amount.

worthy (wēr'dhi) *adj.* Estimable; having high moral standard; of sufficient worth, value, desert, or merit (*to*), deserving (*of*). ~ *n.* Distinguished, eminent, or famous person, esp. hero of antiquity; *the Nine Worthies*, famous personages of ancient and medieval history and legend, 3 Jews (Joshua, David, Judas Maccabaeus), 3 Gentiles (Hector, Alexander, Julius Caesar), and 3 Christians (Arthur, Charlemagne, Godfrey of Bouillon).

would (wood): see WILL[2]; ~*-be* (*adj.*) desiring or professing to be, posing as.

wound[1] (woo-) *n.* Injury done by cutting, stabbing, lacerating, etc., animal or vegetable tissues with hard or sharp instrument, bullet, etc. (freq. fig.); *wou'ndwort*, plant used for healing or dressing wounds, esp. species of *Stachys*, golden-rod, comfrey, kidney-vetch, etc. ~ *v.* Inflict wound (on); inflict pain or hurt on, pain, grieve deeply.

wound[2]: see WIND[2].

wōve *adj.*: see WEAVE; (esp., of paper) made on mould of closely woven wire.

woven: see WEAVE.

wow[1] *n.* (U.S. slang) A striking success.

wow[2] *n.* (sound engin.) Waver, tremolo, in reproduced sound, due to fluctuations in record-speed.

wow'ser (-z-) *n.* (Austral.) Puritanical fanatic.

W.P. *abbrev.* Weather permitting.

W.P.B. *abbrev.* Waste-paper basket.

W.R.A.C. *abbrev.* Women's Royal Army Corps.

wrăck (r-) *n.* Seaweed or other marine vegetation cast up or growing on tidal beaches, and used for manure etc.

W.R.A.F. *abbrev.* Women's Royal Air Force.

wraith (r-) *n.* Apparition, ghost, of dead person; spectral appearance of living person supposed to portend his death.

wrangle (ră'nggl) *n. & v.i.* Brawl; (engage in) noisy, vehement, or contentious argument or quarrel.

wrăng'ler (răngg-) *n.* One who wrangles, quarrelsome person; (Camb. Univ.) candidate placed in first class in mathematical tripos (f. obs. sense of person who disputes publicly on a thesis); senior ~, first in first class when it was arranged in order of merit. **wră'nglership** *n.*

wrăp (r-) *v.* Enfold, enclose, pack, swathe, (freq. *up*) in garment or folded or soft encircling material; form wrap or covering for; involve, enfold, *in* something obscuring or disguising; fold, wind, draw (covering, garment, etc.) *about*, *round*, etc.; ~ *over*, overlap; ~ *up*, put on wraps; *wrapped up*, (esp.) engrossed, centred, absorbed, *in*; bound up with, involved *in*. ~ *n.* Wrapper, covering; blanket, rug, etc., (usu. pl.) additional outer garment worn as defence against wind and weather; woman's shawl, scarf, or the like.

wră'pper (r-) *n.* (esp.) Protective covering for parcel etc.; paper enclosing newspaper etc. for posting; paper cover of pamphlet or periodical; detachable outer paper cover of book; loose enveloping robe or gown; tobacco-leaf of superior grade used for outer cover of cigar.

wră'pping (r-) *n.* (esp., pl.) Wraps, enveloping garments; ~-*paper*, strong paper for packing or wrapping up parcels.

wrăsse (r-) *n.* Any species of family Labridae of spiny-finned, usu. brilliant-coloured, marine fishes.

wrath (rawth, U.S. rahth) *n.* (chiefly poet. or rhet.) Anger, indignation. **wra'thful** *adj.* **wra'thfully** *adv.* **wra'thfulness** *n.*

wreak (r-) *v.t.* Gratify (anger etc.), inflict (vengeance etc.), *on*.

wreath (r-) *n.* (pl. pr. -dhz or -ths). Flowers or leaves strung or woven or wound together into ring for wearing on head or for decorating statue, building, coffin, etc.; carved imitation of this; similar ring of soft twisted material, as silk; curl of smoke, circular or curved band of cloud, light drifting mass of sand, snow, etc.

wreathe (rēdh) *v.* Encircle as (or with, or as with) a wreath; form into wreath; entwine; wind, turn (flexible object) round or over something; (of smoke etc.) move in wreath-like shape.

wrĕck (r-) *n.* Disabling, destruction, ruin, overthrow, esp. of ship; ship that has suffered wreck; what remains *of* thing or person that has suffered ruin, waste, disablement, dilapidation, etc., anything broken down or ruined, person of undermined or shattered constitution; (law) goods etc. cast up by sea, piece of wreckage. ~ *v.* Cause wreck of (ship, train, person's constitution, undertaking, etc.); suffer wreck.

wrĕ'ckage (r-) *n.* Fragments or remains of wrecked or shattered vessel, structure, etc.; (fig.) act or process of wrecking.

wrĕ'cker (r-) *n.* (esp.) One who tries from shore to bring about shipwreck in order to plunder or profit by wreckage; one who steals wreckage; person employed in recovering wrecked ship or its contents; one who obstructs undertaking etc.

wrĕn[1] (r-) *n.* Any of numerous species of genus *Troglodytes* of small, usu. brown, passerine songbirds, esp. the common European wren, *T. troglodytes*, a very small dark-brown mottled bird with short erect tail; any of various other small birds of similar appearance or habits.

Wrĕn[2] (r-) *n.* Member of Women's Royal Naval Service. [f. initials]

Wrĕn[3] (r-), Sir Christopher (1632–1723). English architect; designer of St. Paul's Cathedral and many other London churches and buildings after Great Fire of 1666.

wrĕnch (r-) *n.* 1. Violent twist, turn, or pull; (fig.) pain or anguish caused by parting. 2. Instrument or tool of various forms for gripping or turning bolt-head, nut, etc., consisting essentially of metal bars with (freq. adjustable) jaws; adjustable spanner (ill. SPANNER). ~ *v.* Twist, turn; pull round or sideways, violently or with effort; pull *away*, *off*, *out*, thus; injure, pain, by straining or stretching.

wrĕst (r-) *v.* Twist, deflect, distort, pervert; force or wrench away from person's grasp. ~ *n.* Tuning-key of wire-stringed instrument, as harp, piano; ~-*block*, part of piano holding ~-*pins* to which strings are attached.

wrestle (rĕ'sl) *n.* Wrestling-match; hard struggle. ~ *v.* Strive to overpower and throw to the ground another, esp. in contest governed by fixed rules, by grappling with him and tripping or overbalancing him; have wrestling-match with; contend, grapple, struggle, *with* thing, difficulties, feelings, forces, etc.; (western U.S.) throw (cattle) for branding. **wrĕ'stler, wrĕ'stling** *ns.*

wrĕtch (r-) *n.* Miserable, unhappy, or unfortunate person; contemptible or vile person, one without conscience or shame (freq. as term of playful abuse).

wrĕ'tchĕd (r-) *adj.* Miserable, unhappy, afflicted; inferior, of poor quality, of no merit; contemptible; unsatisfactory; causing discontent, discomfort, or nuisance. **wrĕ'tchĕdlў** *adv.* **wrĕ'tchĕdnĕss** *n.*

wri'ggle (r-) *n.* Wriggling movement. ~ *v.* Twist or turn body about with short writhing movements; (fig.) be slippery, practise evasion; move (oneself, part of body, etc.) with wriggling motion, make (*way*) by wriggling.

wright[1] (rit) *n.* Artificer, handicraftsman, maker (now rare exc. in compounds).

Wright[2] (rit), Orville (1871–1948) and Wilbur (1867–1912). Two brothers, American technicians, who built and flew (1903) the first heavier-than-air motor-driven flying machine.

wring (r-) *v.t.* (past t. & past part. *wrŭng*). Press, squeeze, or twist, with hands or machine, esp. so as to drain or make dry, strain (moisture etc.) by squeezing or torsion from moist or wet thing; twist forcibly, break by twisting, torture, distress, rack; extort, get (money, concession, etc.) *out of* or *from* by exaction or importunity; press or clasp (person's *hand*) forcibly or with emotion; ~ *one's hands*, clasp and twist them together in distress or pain; *wringing* (*wet*), so wet that moisture may be wrung out. ~ *n.* Squeeze, act of wringing.

wri'nger (r-) *n.* (esp.) Device for wringing water from laundered clothes etc., usu. consisting essentially of two rollers between which article is squeezed.

wri'nkle (r-) *n.* 1. Furrow-like crease, depression or ridge in skin (esp. of kind produced by age, care, etc.) or other flexible surface. 2. (colloq.) Useful hint; clever expedient. **wri'nklў** *adj.* **wri'nkle** *v.* Acquire or assume wrinkles; produce wrinkles in.

wrist (r-) *n.* Joint in man connecting hand with forearm, carpus (ill. HAND); analogous joint in other animals; part of garment covering wrist; ~-*band*, band of sleeve covering or fastening about wrist; wristlet; ~-*bone*, a carpal bone; ~-*guard*, device protecting wrist esp. of archer; ~-*watch*, small watch worn on strap or bracelet round wrist.

wri'stlĕt (r-) *n.* Band, bracelet, strap, worn on wrist to strengthen or guard it, as ornament, to hold watch, etc.; handcuff.

writ (r-) *n.* 1. Holy, Sacred, *W*~, sacred writings collectively, esp. the Bible. 2. Formal written order issued by court in name of sovereign, State, etc., directing person(s) to whom it is addressed to do or refrain from doing specified act; document issued by Crown summoning spiritual or temporal lord to attend Parliament or directing sheriff to hold election of member(s) of Parliament.

write (r-) *v.* (past t. *wrōte*, past part. *wri'ttĕn*). Form symbols representing letter(s) or word(s) esp. on paper, parchment, etc.,

[1004]

with pen, pencil, brush, etc., form (such symbols), set (words etc.) down in writing, express in writing; chronicle, make record or account of; convey (message, information, etc.) by letter; engage in writing or authorship; produce writing; ~ *down*, set down in writing; write in disparagement or depreciation of; reduce (total, assets, etc.) to lower amount; ~ *off*, record cancelling of (bad debt, depreciated stock, etc.); reckon as lost or worthless; ~-*off* (*n.*) something that must be regarded as total loss or wreck, failure; ~ *out*, make written copy of; transcribe in full or detail; ~ *up*, write full account or record of; give full or elaborate description of; commend by appreciative writing, praise in writing; ~-*up* (*n.*) review or report.

wri′ter (r-) *n.* One who writes; person writing books, articles, etc., esp. as profession; clerk, esp. in government offices, Royal Navy, etc.; (Sc.) law-clerk, legal practitioner; *W*~ *to the Signet*, (abbrev. W.S.) one of ancient Scottish society of law-agents conducting cases before Court of Session and having exclusive privilege of preparing Crown writs, charters, etc.; solicitor in Scotland; ~'s *cramp*, painful spasmodic cramp affecting muscles of hand and fingers used in writing, and resulting from excessive writing. wri′tership *n.*

writhe (rīdh) *v.* Twist or roll oneself about (as) in acute pain, squirm; twist (*body* etc.) about, contort. ~ *n.* Act of writhing.

wri′ting (r-) *n.* (esp.) Written document; (piece of) literary work; personal script, handwriting; *put in* ~, write down; *the Writings*, *i.q.* is HAGIOGRAPHA; ~-*case*, case holding writing materials; ~-*desk*, desk; ~-*master*, instructor in penmanship; the yellow-hammer (from marks like scribbling on eggs); ~-*paper*, paper for writing on with ink, esp. note-paper; ~-*table*, desk.

wri′tten (r-) *adj.*: see WRITE; (esp.) that is in writing, esp. opp. *oral* or *printed*.

W.R.N.S. *abbrev.* Women's Royal Naval Service.

wrŏng (r-) *adj.* 1. Not morally right or equitable, unjust; doing or prone to do evil; not correct or proper; not true, mistaken; judging, acting, etc., contrary to facts, in error; ~-*headed*, perversely or obstinately wrong, characterized by perversity of judgement; *wronghea′dedness* (*n.*) 2. Not in good order or condition, amiss; not what is required or intended, unsuitable, inappropriate; (of way etc.) leading in, tending to, direction other than what is intended, desired, or expected; ~ *end*, end or limit less adapted or suitable for particular purpose; *get hold of the* ~ *end of the stick*, (fig.) be mistaken in judgement etc.; ~ *side*, side (of fabric etc.) not meant for use or show; *on the* ~ *side of*, older than (specified age); under a person's disapproval or disfavour; *get up, out of bed, on the* ~ *side*, be in irritable mood; ~ *side out*, (fig.) in bad temper, irritable, peevish; ~-'*un*, (colloq.) person of bad character; (*the*) ~ *way*, in contrary or opposite way to proper or usual one. wrŏ′nglў *adv.* wrŏ′ngnèss *n.* wrŏng *adv.* Amiss, in wrong course or direction; mistakenly, erroneously; in improper or unfitting manner; *go* ~, go astray; happen amiss or unfortunately; get out of gear or working order; take to bad ways. ~ *n.* What is morally wrong; wrong action; unjust action or treatment; being wrong in attitude, procedure, or belief (freq. *in the* ~); *wro′ngdo′ing*, transgression against moral or established law. ~ *v.t.* Treat unjustly, do wrong to; do injustice to by statement, opinion, etc.; dishonour by word or thought.

wrŏ′ngful (r-) *adj.* Marked by wrong, unfairness, injustice, etc.; contrary to law, etc., unlawful, illegal; (of persons) holding office, possession, etc., unlawfully or without legitimacy or right. wrŏ′ngfullў *adv.* wrŏ′ngfulnèss *n.*

wrote: see WRITE.

wrŏth (r-) *pred. adj.* (poet. & rhet.) Angry, stirred to wrath.

wrought (rawt) *adj.* Worked, processed, manufactured, worked into shape; (of metals) beaten out or shaped with hammer etc.; ~ *iron*: see IRON; ~-*up*, stirred up, excited or agitated.

wrung: see WRING.

W.R.V.S. *abbrev.* Women's Royal Voluntary Service.

wrў (rī) *adj.* Distorted, turned to one side; temporarily twisted or contorted in disgust, disrelish, etc.; *wry′bill*, New Zealand plover (*Anarhynchus frontalis*) with bill deflected to one side; *wry′mouth*, any of numerous large fish of family Stichaeidae, of blenny kind, the ghost-fish of northern Atlantic coasts of N. America; *wry′neck*, deformity with contortion of neck and face and lateral inclination of head, torticollis; species of genus *Jynx* of small migratory birds allied to woodpeckers, esp. *J. torquilla* of Europe and Asia, with peculiar manner of writhing neck and head. wrў′lў *adv.* wrў′nèss *n.*

W.S. *abbrev.* Writer to the Signet.

WSW. *abbrev.* West-southwest.

W/T *abbrev.* Wireless telegraphy, telephony.

wt *abbrev.* Weight.

Wu′lfīla (voō-) (*c* 311–83). Gothic bishop who translated the New Testament into Gothic.

Wundt (voŏnt), Wilhelm (1832–1920). German philosopher and psychologist.

Wür′ttemberg (vūr-). Former State of SW. Germany, now part of Baden-Württemberg, a province of West Germany.

W. Va. *abbrev.* West Virginia.

Wў′andŏtte *n.* 1. Member of tribe of N. Amer. Indians. 2. Domestic fowl of medium-sized breed, orig. white laced with black but now bred in various colours.

wych: see WITCH[3].

Wў′cherley, William (1640–1716). English writer of Restoration comedies.

Wў′clif, -liffe, John (*c* 1320–84). English religious reformer; attacked the papacy and asserted the right of every man to examine the Bible for himself; instituted the first translation into English of the whole Bible, himself translating the Gospels and probably other parts; his doctrines were taken up by the Lollards.

Wў′keham (-kam), William of (1324–1408). Bishop of Winchester and founder of Winchester College (1382) and New College, Oxford (1379). Wў′kehamist *n.* (Former) pupil of Winchester College.

wynd *n.* (Sc.) Narrow street or passage off main thoroughfare; narrow cross-street, lane, or alley.

Wyo. *abbrev.* Wyoming.

Wў̄ō′ming. State of northwestern U.S., admitted to the Union in 1890; capital, Cheyenne.

wў′vern *n.* (her.) Winged dragon with two feet like eagle's and barbed tail. [OF *wyvre* viper]

X

X, x (ĕks). 1. 24th letter of modern English and 21st of ancient Roman alphabet, adopted from the Greek alphabet introduced into Italy, with the value (ks) which it usually has in modern English except when occurring initially in words chiefly of Greek origin, when it is pronounced z. 2. Roman numeral symbol for ten; *X*, (U.S. slang) ten-dollar note. 3. (alg. etc.) Symbol for (esp. 1st)

XANTHATE

unknown or variable quantity; hence, incalculable or unknown factor or influence. 4. In designation of brands of ale etc. **XX** or double **X** = medium quality, **XXX** or treble **X**, strongest quality. **5.** *X*, symbol for Christ, representing the chi in Greek ΧΡΙΣΤΟΣ, used in abbreviations, e.g. Xmas (= Christmas). **6.** Representing *ex* as word or syllable; *X's*, (slang) expenses; *x-cp.*, *xd* etc., *x-i*: see entries. **7.** *X*, designation of cinema film for exhibition only to persons over 18 years. **8.** *x-height*, height of an x, height of body of letter (ill. TYPE). **9.** Object etc. shaped like X.
xă'nthāte (z-) *n*. (chem.) Salt of xanthic acid.
xă'nthēin (z-) *n*. (chem.) Yellow colouring matter found in plants.
Xă'nthǐan Măr'bles (z-, -lz). Collection of sculptures, now in the British Museum, discovered (1838) by Sir Charles Fellows in the ruins of Xanthus, an ancient city of Asia Minor.
xă'nthǐc (z-) *adj*. (chem. etc.) Yellow; of xanthin; ~ *acid*, complex acid ($C_3H_6OS_2$), many of whose salts are yellow.
xă'nthīne (z-) *n*. (chem.) Substance ($C_5H_4N_4O_2$) related to uric acid and found in animal secretions.
Xanthi'ppe (zănti-). Wife of Socrates, reputed to be a shrew; hence, shrewish woman or wife.
xănthō'ma (z-) *n*. (path.) Skin disease characterized by irregular yellowish patches on eyelids, neck, etc.
xă'nthophȳll (z-) *n*. Dark-brown crystalline compound found in plants, usu. associated with chlorophyll, and forming yellow colouring-matter of autumn leaves.
xă'nthous (z-) *adj*. (of a people) Having yellow(ish) or red(dish) hair; having yellow skin.
Xă'vier (z-), St. Francis (1506–52). Spanish Jesuit, one of the founders of the Society of Jesus, and a missionary in the Far East, commemorated 3 Dec.
xd, x-d., x-div. *abbrevs*. Ex dividend.
xě'běc (z-) *n*. Small three-masted Mediterranean vessel, usu. lateen rigged with some square sails, formerly used as ship of war.
Xěnō'crătēs (z-, -z). Greek Platonic philosopher (396–314 B.C.).

xě'nolǐth (z-) *n*. (geol.) Stone or rock occurring in a system to which it does not belong.
xě'non (z-) *n*. (chem.) Heavy inert gaseous element present in minute quantity in the atmosphere; symbol Xe, at. no. 54, at. wt 131·30. [Gk *xenos* strange]
Xěnō'phanēs (z-, -z) (*c* 570–490 B.C.). Greek philosopher and poet.
xěnophō'bǐa (z-) *n*. Morbid dislike or fear of foreigners, foreign customs, etc. **xě'nophōbe** *n*. Person showing xenophobia.
Xě'nophon (z-) (*c* 428–354 B.C.). Athenian historian and philosopher; pupil of Socrates, about whom he wrote in the 'Memorabilia' and the 'Symposium'; described in the 'Anabasis' the expedition of Cyrus against Artaxerxes (401–399 B.C.) in which he led the Greek mercenaries in their retreat to the Black Sea after they had been left in a dangerous situation between the Tigris and Euphrates.
Xeres. Old spelling of JEREZ.
xērŏ'graphy (z-) *n*. Dry printing process in which coloured resin adheres to those areas of the surface of paper which have been sensitized with a charge of static electricity.
xērŏ'phagȳ (z-) *n*. Strictest form of fast, practised in Eastern Church esp. during Lent or Holy Week, and forbidding meat, fish, cheese, milk, butter, oil, wine, and all seasonings except salt.
xērŏ'phǐlous (z-) *adj*. (bot.) Adapted to extremely dry conditions.
xērophthă'lmǐa (z-) *n*. (path.) Inflammation of the conjunctiva with abnormal dryness and corrugation.
xēr'ophȳte (z-) *n*. Plant adapted to very dry conditions, desert plant.
Xēr'ŏx (z-) *n*. Process of reproduction by xerography. **xēr'ŏx** *v.t.* Reproduce by Xerox. [tradename]
Xēr'xēs (z-, -z). King of Persia 486–465 B.C., son of Darius; invaded Greece and overcame the resistance of Leonidas and the Spartans at Thermopylae, but was defeated at Salamis 480 B.C.; called Ahasuerus in the Book of Esther.
xi (ksī, gzī, *or* zī) *n*. 15th (later 14th) letter of Greek alphabet (Ξ, ξ), corresponding to *x*.

x-i. *abbrev*. Ex interest.
Ximenes (hēmā'näth; pop. zī'-minēz): Jiménes de CISNEROS.
Xī'phǐăs (z-) *n*. (astron.) Southern constellation, also called Dorado. [Gk *xiphos* sword]
xiphistěr'num (z-) *n*. Xiphoid process.
xī'phoid (z-) *adj*. Sword-shaped; ~ *process*, cartilaginous or bony process at lower or posterior end of sternum in man and other animals (ill. SKELETON).
Xmas *abbrev*. Christmas (see X, x, 5).
xō'anon (z-) *n*. (pl. *-ana*). (Gk antiq.) Primitive usu. wooden image of deity, supposed to have fallen from heaven.
X-ray (ěks-) *n*. Electromagnetic radiation of very short wavelength emitted by electrons whose velocity is suddenly reduced, capable of passing through an extensive thickness of any body, whether transparent or not, of acting on photographic plates, and of ionizing gases; (also ~ *photograph*) shadow-photograph, esp. of bodies impervious to light, made with X-rays. ~ *v.t.* Photograph, examine, with X-rays; treat (disease, patient) with X-rays. [Ger. *X-strahlen*, name given by their discoverer, RÖNTGEN, to indicate that their essential nature was unknown]
Xt, Xtian *abbrevs*. Christ, Christian (see X, x, 5).
xu (sōō) *n*. (pl. same). $\frac{1}{100}$ of a North Vietnam dong.
xȳ'lěm (z-) *n*. (bot.) Woody tissue including vessels and fibres forming harder part of fibrovascular tissues of plant (opp. PHLOEM; ill. STEM[1]).
xȳ'lēne (z-) *n*. (chem.) One of three colourless, oily, isomeric hydrocarbons, derivatives of benzene, obtained from wood, tar, etc.
xȳ'logrăph (z-; *or* -ahf) *n*. Woodcut, esp. of early period.
xȳ'lonīte (z-) *n*. = CELLULOID.
xȳlŏ'phagous (z-) *adj*. (of insects) Feeding on, boring into, wood.
xȳ'lophōne (z-) *n*. Musical instrument consisting of a series of flat wooden bars, graduated in length to sound the musical scale, resting on strips of straw or felt, and played by striking with small wooden hammer(s).

Y

Y, y (wī). **1.** 25th letter of modern English and 23rd of ancient Roman alphabet, representing ultimately Υ, Y, of Greek alphabet, a differentiated form of primitive V (see U, V), first adopted in Latin alphabet as V, and later readopted in form Y to represent Y of borrowed Greek words; as a vowel, representing in English all the sounds (except ē) commonly spelt with *i*, and used as the normal spelling (*a*) for final *i*-sounds, (*b*) in words of Greek origin, representing upsilon, (*c*) before *i* in inflexional forms of verbs ending in *-y* or *-ie*, (*d*) in plural of nouns ending in *-y*

[1006]

Y.

preceded by another vowel; as a consonant, representing a voiced palatal spirant. 2. (alg. etc.) Symbol of 2nd of series of unknown or variable quantities (cf. *x*). 3. Object etc. shaped like Y; *Y-branch*, piece of piping with branch at acute angle to main.
Y. *abbrev.* Yeomanry.
y- *prefix.* Used esp. with past participles, still found in a few archaic forms, as *yclad* clad, *yclept* called, *ywis* surely.
yacht (yŏt) *n.* Light sailing-vessel kept, and usu. specially built, for racing; vessel propelled

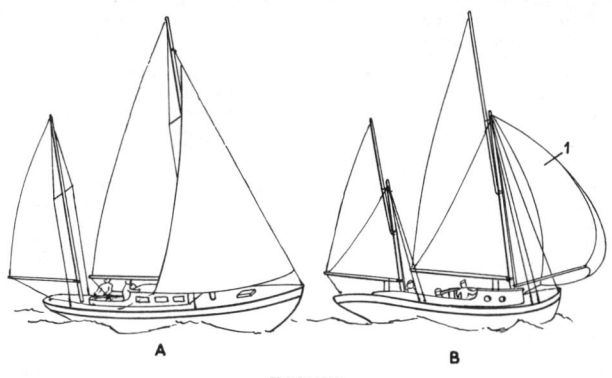

YACHTS
A. BERMUDA-RIGGED YAWL. B. GUNTER-RIGGED KETCH
1. Spinnaker

by sails, steam, or any motive power other than oars, and used for private pleasure excursions, cruising, travel, etc.; ~ *club*, club esp. for yacht-racing; *ya′chtsman*, person who yachts. ~ *v.i.* Race or cruise in yacht. [early mod. Du. *jaght(e)*, = *jaghtschip* (*jagen* to hunt); named f. its speed]
yă′ffle *n.* (dial.) Green woodpecker. [imit. of bird's laughing cry]
yah *int.* Exclamation of disgust, defiance, or derision.
yahoo′ *n.* In Swift's 'Gulliver's Travels', race of brutes in human shape; hence, degraded or bestial human being.
Yah′weh, -veh (-wā, -vā). (also *Jahweh, -veh*). Name of God in O.T., transliteration of the Tetragrammaton which is rendered JEHOVAH in the Authorized Version etc. **Yah′wist** *n.* Author(s) of those parts of the Hexateuch where God is referred to as *Yahweh* rather than *Elohim*. **Yahwi′stic** *adj.*
yăk *n.* Large humped bovine mammal (*Bos grunniens*) with long silky hair on sides, tail, etc., found wild and domesticated in Tibet and other high regions of central Asia, used as a beast of burden. [Tibetan *gyag*]
Yāle[1] *n.* Type of cylinder lock for doors etc. [trade-name, f. Linus *Yale* (1821–68), Amer. locksmith]
Yāle[2]. University at New Haven, Conn., orig. founded (1701) as a school at Saybrook, Conn.; transferred to New Haven in 1718, and called Yale College in consequence of benefactions received from Elihu Yale (1648–1721), a native of Boston, Mass., who entered the service of the East India Company and became governor of Madras; it received a charter 1745, and assumed the name of Yale University in 1887.
Yă′lta. Seaport in S. Ukraine on the Black Sea, scene of wartime conference (Feb. 1945) of Churchill, Roosevelt, and Stalin.
yăm *n.* Starchy tuberous root, largely replacing potato as a staple food in many tropical and subtropical countries, of various species of *Dioscorea*, twining herbs or shrubs with spikes of small inconspicuous flowers; any of these plants.
Ya′ma(yah-). (Hinduism) Ruler of the world of the dead.
Yă′ngtzĕ. (also ~ *Kiang*) Principal river of China; rises in Tibet and flows through central China to E. China Sea.
yănk[1] *n. & v.* (U.S. & slang) (Pull with) sudden sharp tug or jerk.
Yănk[2] *n.* (colloq.) Yankee.
Yă′nkee *n.* Native or inhabitant of New England or of northern States of U.S. generally; (applied by non-Americans to) any inhabitant of U.S.; (*attrib.*) of Yankees; that is a Yankee; ~ *Doodle*, popular U.S. song considered characteristically national; a Yankee. [perh. f. Du. *Janke* dim. of *Jan* John used derisively; or f. *Jengees* Indian pronunciation of *English*]
ya′ourt (yah-oort) *n.* = YOGHURT.
yăp *n. & v.i.* (Utter) shrill or fussy bark, yelp. [imit.]
yăpp *n.* Kind of bookbinding in limp leather with overlapping edges or flaps (ill. BOOK). [name of London bookseller for whom this style of binding was first made *c* 1860]

YAWN

yăr′borough (-boro) *n.* (cards) Whist- or bridge-hand with no card above a 9. [from an Earl of Yarborough who used to bet against its occurrence]
yărd[1] *n.* Piece of enclosed ground, esp. one surrounded by or attached to building(s) or used for some manufacturing or other purpose; prison-yard, shipyard, dockyard, stockyard, etc.; farmyard; garden (now chiefly U.S.); ground near railway station where rolling-stock is kept, trains made up, etc.; *the Y~*, SCOTLAND YARD; *~-master*, manager of railway-yard. **yăr′dage**[1] *n.* Fees payable for use of stockyard. **yărd** *v.t.* Enclose (cattle etc.) in yard.
yărd[2] *n.* 1. Unit of long measure, equal to 3 feet or 36 inches; measure of area (*square* ~), or of solidity (*cubic* ~), as in *~ of gravel, lime*, etc.; yard-length of material; ~-*measure*, rod, tape, etc., a yard long, usu. marked in feet and inches; ~ *of clay*, long clay pipe; ~ *of tin*, coachman's horn; *yar′dstick*, stick as yard-measure; (fig.) standard, criterion. 2. (naut.) Long usu. cylindrical spar, tapering to each end, slung (usu. at its centre for square sail) from mast, to support and extend sail (ill. SAIL[1]); ~-*arm*, either end of yard of square-rigged vessel. **yăr′dage**[2] *n.* Number of yards of material etc.
Yăr′mouth (-muth). Fishing-town on coast of Norfolk, England; ~ *bloater*, slightly salted and smoked herring.
yărn *n.* 1. Fibre, as of cotton, wool, silk, flax, spun and prepared for use in weaving, knitting, etc. 2. (colloq., orig.´ naut.) Story, tale; *spin a* ~, tell (usu. long) tale. ~ *v.i.* (colloq.) Tell yarn(s).
yă′rrow (-rō) *n.* Herb of genus *Achillea*, esp. *A. millefolium*, common on roadsides, dry meadows, and waste ground, with tough greyish stem, finely divided bipinnate leaves, and dull-white or pinkish flower-heads in close flat clusters.
yă′shmăk *n.* Double veil concealing face below eyes, worn by Muslim women of some countries in public.
yă′taghan (-găn) *n.* Short sword of Muslim countries with slight reverse curve (ill. SWORD).
yaw *v.i. & n.* (naut., aeron.) (Make) deviation from straight course owing to action of heavy sea or strong winds.
yawl *n.* Ship's boat like small pinnace, with 4 or 6 oars; 2-masted fore-and-aft sailing-boat with after mast much smaller than mainmast and placed far aft (ill. YACHT); small sailing-boat with stem and stern alike used for fishing etc.
yawn *v.* Breathe in involuntarily with mouth wide open, as from drowsiness, fatigue, boredom, etc.; utter or say with yawn; (of

[1007]

chasm etc.) gape, have wide opening. ~ n. Act of yawning.
yaws (-z) n.pl. Framboesia, contagious skin disease with raspberry-like tubercles or excrescences on skin, prevalent among tropical native populations and having many analogies with syphilis.
yclĕ′pt adj. (archaic or joc.) Called (so-and-so).
yd abbrev. Yard.
yĕ¹ pron. 2nd person pl. pronoun (archaic, dial. or poet.) = YOU.
yᵉ, ye² abbrev. (pr. yē). The (now only pseudo-archaic or joc.; the y is a survival of the obs. letter þ, = th).
yea (yā) adv. & n. (archaic) Yes.
yean v. (archaic) Bring forth (lamb, kid, etc.), bring forth young, as sheep, goat, etc.
yea′nling n. (archaic) Young lamb or kid.
year (or yẽr) n. 1. Time occupied by the earth in one revolution round the sun (also astronomical, equinoctial, natural, solar, tropical, ~; = 365 days, 5 hours, 48 minutes, 46 seconds) or by the sun in recovering its previous apparent relation to the fixed stars (astral or sidereal year, longer by 20 minutes, 23 seconds). 2. Period of days (esp. common ~ of 365 days reckoned from 1 Jan. or leap- or bissextile ~ of 366) used by community for dating or other purposes commencing on a certain day, usu. divided into 12 months, and corresponding more or less exactly in length to the astronomical year (also called calendar, civil, or legal ~). 3. Such space of time with limits not necessarily coinciding with those of civil year, used in reckoning age, period of office, occupation, etc., or for special purpose, as taxation, payment of dividends, etc. 4. (pl.) Age (of person); (pl.) period, times, a very long time. 5. ~ in, ~ out, right through the year, continuously; ~-book, annual publication containing information for the year.
year′ling (or yẽr-) n. & adj. (Animal, esp. sheep, calf, or foal) a year old; (racing) colt one year old from 1 Jan. of year of foaling.
year′ly (or yẽr-) adj. & adv. (Occurring, observed, done, etc.) once a year or every year; annual(ly).
yearn (yẽrn) v.i. Long; be moved with compassion or tender feelings. **year′ning** n.
yeast n. Minute unicellular fungus esp. of family Saccharomycetaceae; greyish-yellow substance produced as froth or sediment during alcoholic fermentation of malt infusions and other saccharine fluids, consisting of aggregations of minute fungi and used in manufacture of beer, to leaven bread, etc.; dried form of this substance prepared in cakes or granules. **yea′sty** adj. Frothy like yeast; in a ferment, working like yeast; made with yeast. **yea′stiness** n.

Yeats (yāts), William Butler (1865–1939). Irish lyric poet and dramatist; assisted in the creation of an Irish national theatre.

yĕgg n. (U.S. slang, also ye′ggman) Burglar, esp. one who breaks open safes. [said to be name of Amer. safe-breaker]

yĕll n. Sharp loud outcry of strong and sudden emotion, as rage, horror, agony; (U.S.) set of words or syllables shouted as an organized cheer, as by Amer. college students. ~ v. Make, utter with, yell.

yĕ′llow (-ō) adj. Of the colour of buttercup or lemon or sulphur or gold, most luminous of the primary colours, occurring in spectrum between green and orange; having a yellow skin or complexion, as the Mongolian peoples; (orig. U.S., of newspaper etc.) recklessly or unscrupulously sensational; (orig. U.S.) cowardly, craven; ye′llowback, cheap (esp. French) novel in yellow paper cover or yellow paper boards; ~ belly, (contempt.) Mexican; half-caste; Y~ Book, English illustrated quarterly (1894–7), with contributions from Aubrey Beardsley, Max Beerbohm, Henry James, Walter Sickert, and many other distinguished writers and artists; ~ fever, highly fatal febrile disease of hot climates, characterized by jaundice, vomiting, haemorrhages, etc., and transmitted by a mosquito; ye′llowhammer, common European species of bunting (Emberiza citrinella), the male of which has bright-yellow head, throat, and under-parts; ~ jack, yellow fever; quarantine flag; ~ ochre: see OCHRE; ~ peril, danger that the yellow peoples may overwhelm the white or dominate the world; Y~ River, most northerly of China's great rivers, known as 'China's Sorrow' because of its uncontrollable floods; Y~ Sea, arm of Pacific between China and Korea, into which the Yellow River formerly flowed; ~ soap, common household soap of tallow, rosin, and soda; ~ spot, point of acutest vision in retina; Ye′llowstone National Park, area of about 3,458 sq. miles, chiefly in Wyoming, reserved since 1872 for public uses, named after the Yellowstone River, a tributary of the Missouri, which rises there. ~ n. Yellow colour, pigment, fabric, etc.; yellow species or variety of bird, butterfly, moth, flower, etc. ~ v. Turn yellow.

yĕlp n. & v.i. (Utter) sharp shrill bark or cry (as) of dog in pain, excitement, etc.

Yĕ′men. Name of two republics in the Arabian peninsula: ~ Arab Republic, a republic since 1962 (kingdom 1934–62) of SW. Arabia, the Arabia Felix of the ancients, freed from Turkish rule in 1918; capital, Sana'a; People's Democratic Republic of ~, a republic since 1967 in S. Arabia bordering on the Yemen Arab Republic; capital, Aden. **Yĕ′meni, Yĕ′menīte** adjs. & ns.

yĕn¹ n. (pl. same). Monetary unit of Japan. [Jap., f. Chin. yüan round, dollar]

yĕn² n. (colloq., orig. U.S.) Passionate or impelling desire or longing. [Chin. yen smoke, opium]

Yeo., Yeom. abbrevs. Yeomanry.

yeo′man (yō-) n. (pl. -men). 1. Small landowner, person of middle class engaged in agriculture (esp. attrib., as ~ farmer); (hist.) person qualified by possessing free land of 40s. annual value to serve on juries, vote for knight of shire, etc. 2. (hist.) Servant and attendant in royal or noble household of rank between sergeant and groom or squire and page; Y~ of the Guard, member of bodyguard of English sovereign, first appointed by Henry VII, and now acting chiefly as warders of Tower of London. 3. (U.S. Navy) Petty officer performing clerical duties on board ship; ~ of the signals, (Royal Navy) petty officer in branch concerned with visual signalling. 4. Member of yeomanry force; ~('s) service, help in need; efficient service. **yeo′manly** adj. Of, befitting, a yeoman or yeomen.

yeo′manry (yō-) n. 1. Yeomen collectively. 2. (hist.) Volunteer cavalry force in British Army, orig. formed in 18th c. for home defence, merged in the Territorial Force in 1907.

yĕp adv. (dial., esp. U.S.) = YES.

yẽr′ba maté: see MATÉ. [Span., f. L herba grass, herb, and native mati]

yĕs adv. Particle expressing affirmative reply to request, question, etc. ~ n. Word, answer, 'yes'; ~-man, (colloq.) person who agrees uncritically with everything that is said to him, esp. by a superior.

yĕ′sterday n. & adv. (On) the day immediately preceding today; (in) time not long past.

yĕ′ster-year n. Last year (poet.). [coined by D. G. Rossetti to translate Fr. antan, f. L ante annum]

yĕt adv. 1. In addition or continuation, besides, also (archaic); (with comparative) even, still; nor ~, and also not. 2. Up to this or that time, till now, till then; at some time in the future, hereafter (though not hitherto), henceforth, even now (though not till now); not ~, still not, not by this (or that) time; as ~, hitherto. ~ adj. That is still such, still continuing. ~ conj. In spite of that, nevertheless, notwithstanding.

yĕ′ti n. (pop. the 'Abominable Snowman') Either of two unidentified animals occas. seen on high slopes of Himalayas, the one being prob. the red bear (*Ursus arctos isabellinus*) and the other possibly the langur monkey (*Presbytis entellus achilles*). [Tibetan *yeh* rocky area, *teh* animal]

yĕtt *n.* (in Scotland) Gate or portcullis with interlocking bands.

yew *n.* Tree (also ~-*tree*) of coniferous genus *Taxus*, widely distributed in north temperate zone, esp. common European *T. baccata*, with heavy elastic wood and dense dark-green foliage, freq. planted in churchyards and regarded as symbol of sadness; wood of this, formerly used for making bows.

YEW
1. Fruit. 2. Aril

Ygerne: see IGRAINE.

Y'ggdrasil (ĭg-). (Scand. myth.) The world tree, an ash; its roots and branches connect heaven, earth, and hell, and the Norns sit beneath it. [ON, app. f. *Yggr* name of Odin + *drasill* horse]

Y.H.A. *abbrev.* Youth Hostels Association.

Yĭd *n.* (slang, contempt.) Jew.

Yi'ddish *adj.* & *n.* (Of) the language used by Jews in Europe and America, a German dialect (orig. from Middle Rhine area) with an admixture of Hebrew elements and of words borrowed from several modern languages. [Ger. *jüdisch* Jewish]

yield *v.* 1. Produce or return as fruit, profit, or result. 2. Surrender or make submission (*to*); concede; give way *to* persuasion, entreaty, etc., give consent; be inferior *to*; (of vehicle or traffic) give right of way (*to*); ~ *to*, give way under, be affected by, physical action or agent, as pressure, heat, etc. ~ *n.* Amount yielded or produced, output, return.

y'lăng-y'lăng (ēl-, -ēl-) *n.* Tree (*Cananga odorata*) of Malaya, Philippines, etc., with fragrant greenish-yellow flowers; perfume distilled from these.

Y.M.C.A. *abbrev.* YOUNG Men's Christian Association.

Y'mir (ē-). (Scand. myth.) Primeval giant from whose body the gods created the world.

yŏb *n.* (slang, contempt.) Boy, lout.

yō'del *v.* Sing or warble with interchange of ordinary and falsetto voice in manner of Swiss and Tyrolese mountaineers. ~ *n.* Yodelling cry; yodelling-match.

Yō'ga *n.* Hindu system of ascetic practice, abstract meditation, and mental concentration as means of attaining union with Supreme Spirit. [Sansk. *yoga* union]

yŏ'ghurt, yŏ'gurt (-gert) *n.* Semi-solid junket-like or curdlike food prepared from milk fermented by addition of *Lactobacillus bulgaricus*. [Turk. *yoğurt*]

yō'gi (-gī) *n.* Devotee of YOGA.

yō-heave-hō *int.* Exclamation expressing effort of pulling or heaving, formerly used by sailors hauling at rope or capstan etc.

yō-hō *int.* (orig. naut.) Exclamation used to attract attention, accompanying effort, etc.

yoicks *int.* Exclamation used in fox-hunting to urge on hounds.

yōke *n.* 1. Contrivance, usu. curved or hollowed piece of wood over animals' necks, fastened at centre to chain or trace by which plough or vehicle is drawn, used from ancient times for coupling two animals, esp. oxen, for drawing vehicle etc. 2. Pair *of* oxen etc. 3. Piece of wood shaped to fit person's shoulders and support pail etc. at each end. 4. (Rom. hist.) Uplifted yoke, or arch of three spears symbolizing it, under which defeated enemy was made to march; (fig.) sway, dominion, servitude; (fig.) bond of union, esp. marriage tie. 5. Upper part of bodice; upper part of garment, from which the rest hangs. 6. Object resembling a yoke in shape, esp. cross-bar on which bell swings; cross-bar of rudder to whose ends steering lines are fastened, coupling-piece of two pipes discharging into one; kinds of coupling or controlling piece in machinery. ~ *v.t.* Put yoke upon; harness (draught-animal) *to* vehicle or plough; (fig.) couple, unite, join, link (*together*).

yō'kel *n.* (contempt.) Country bumpkin.

Yōkoha'ma (-hah-). Seaport of Tokyo, Japan.

yolk (yōk) *n.* Yellow(ish) internal part of egg, containing vitellin and other proteins, surrounded by white and serving as nourishment for young before hatching; (biol.) corresponding part in any animal ovum, serving for nutrition of embryo; substance from which embryo is developed (ill. EMBRYO). **yolked** (yōkt) *adj.*

Yōm Ki'ppur. (Jewish religion) The Day of Atonement, falling on the 10th day of the month Tishri (approx. October) and observed as a solemn fast day acc. to the rites described in Lev. 16.

yŏn, yŏ'nder *adjs.* & *advs.* (archaic or dial.) (Situated) over there, at some distance (but within sight).

yōre *n.* *of* ~, in or of time long past, former(ly).

yŏrk[1] *v.t.* Bowl with yorker.

York[2]. City and county town of North Yorkshire and seat of archbishop and primate of England; university, 1963.

York[3]. Name of English royal dynasty, descending from Edmund of Langley (1341–1402), 5th son of Edward III and (from 1385) 1st Duke of York, including Edward IV, Edward V, and Richard III; party of the white rose in the Wars of the Roses (see ROSE, 2); united with the House of Lancaster when Henry VII married the eldest daughter of Edward IV (1486).

yōr'ker *n.* (cricket) Ball so bowled as to pitch inside crease or just beneath bat. [prob. f. YORK[2]]

Yōr'kist *n.* & *adj.* (Adherent) of the house of YORK[3], esp. in the Wars of the Roses (see ROSE, 2).

Yorks. *abbrev.* Yorkshire.

Yōr'kshire. Former county of NE. England, since April 1974 divided among Humberside, North Yorkshire, South Yorkshire, and West Yorkshire; ~ *pudding*, baked batter, usu. eaten with meat, esp. roast beef; ~ *terrier*, small, longhaired terrier.

Yōr'ktown. Town on the shore of Chesapeake Bay, where, in 1781, the British army under Lord Cornwallis was blockaded by the American army and the French fleet.

Yō'ruba *n.* Member, language, of a Negro people of the West African coast.

Yose'mĭtė. U.S. National Park in E. California, named after the Yosemite River which traverses it.

you (yōō, *unstressed* yŏŏ) *pron.* 2nd person sing. and pl. pronoun denoting person(s) or thing(s) addressed; (in general statements freq. =) one, anyone, everyone, a person.

young[1] (yŭ-) *adj.* That has lived, existed, etc., a relatively short time; lately begun, formed, introduced, etc., recent, new; of young person(s) or youth; youthful, esp. having freshness or vigour of youth; *Y~ Chevalier, Y~ Pretender*: see PRETENDER; *Y~ Men's Christian Association*, association (founded 1844 in England) for promoting spiritual, intellectual, and physical welfare of young men (abbrev. Y.M.C.A.); *Y~ Women's Christian Association*, similar association for young women founded 1855 (abbrev. Y.W.C.A.); *Y~ Turks*, Turkish party which in 1908 forced Sultan Abdul Hamid II to proclaim liberal constitution and in 1909 deposed him in favour of his brother, Muhammad V. ~ *n.* Young people; young ones, offspring, of animals; *with* ~, pregnant.

Young[2] (yŭ-), Arthur (1741–1820). English writer of books on agriculture and travel, famous esp. for his 'Travels in France' (1792).

Young[3] (yŭ-), Brigham (1801–77). MORMON leader; headed the

Mormon migration to Utah (1847), founded Salt Lake City, and was appointed governor of Utah (1851).
Young[4] (yŭ-), Edward (1683–1765). English poet, chiefly remembered for his didactic poem, 'Night Thoughts on Life, Death, and Immortality' (1742–5).
you'ngster (yŭ-) *n.* Young person, esp. young man; child, esp. boy.
your (ūr *or* yŏr) *poss. pron.* Possessive case of YOU used as attrib. adj., belonging to, affecting, you; (archaic, now usu. derog.) that you know of, familiar.
yours (ūrz *or* yŏrz) *poss. pron.* Abs. and pred. form of YOUR; used in conventional ending to letter (~ *sincerely*, *truly*, etc.); ~ *truly*, (also, joc.) I; *what's* ~?, what will you drink?
yourse'lf (ūr- *or* yŏr-) *pron.* (pl. *-selves*). Emphatic and reflexive form corresponding to YOU.
youth (yōō-) *n.* 1. Being young; early part of life, esp. adolescence; quality or condition characteristic of the young. 2. Young people collectively; ~ *hostel*, cheap lodging, usu. provided by an association (in the British Isles, the *Y*~ *Hostels Association*) where young travellers put up for the night. 3. Young person, esp. young man between boyhood and maturity. **you'thful** *adj.* **you'thfullў** *adv.* **you'thfulness** *n.*

yowl *n.* & *v.* (Utter) loud wailing cry (as) of dog in distress, pain, etc., howl.
yō'-yō *n.* Kind of toy, small roughly spherical object with string attached to and wound round a deep central groove, made to fall and rise as its weight causes the string to unroll rapidly and roll up again. [trade-name]
Ypres (ēpr,*joc.* wī'perz). Belgian cloth-manufacturing town in W. Flanders, completely destroyed during the war of 1914–18 and subsequently rebuilt.
yr, yrs *abbrevs.* Year(s); your(s).
y[t] (usu. read 'that') *abbrev.* That (conj.): cf. Y[E].
ўtte̅r'bium *n.* (chem.) Metallic element of rare-earth group; symbol Yb, at. no. 70, at. wt 173·04. [f. *Ytterby* in Sweden]
ў'ttrium *n.* (chem.) Metallic element closely resembling ytterbium and found with it in gadolinite and other minerals; symbol Y, at. no. 39, at. wt 88·9059.
yüan[1] (yōōah'n) *n.* Principal monetary unit of China, = 10 jiao or 100 fen.
Yüan[2] (yōōah'n). Name of dynasty which ruled in China 1260–1368.
Yucatan. Var. of YUKATAN.
yŭ'cca *n.* Liliaceous plant of genus *Y*~, native to Central America, Mexico, etc., with woody stem, a crown of usu. rigid narrow pointed leaves, and upright cluster of white bell-shaped flowers.
Yugoslav (yōō'goslahv) *n.* & *adj.* 1. (Native, inhabitant) of Yugoslavia. 2. (Member) of the southern group of Slavic peoples, comprising Serbs, Croats, and Slovenes. 3. (Branch) of the Slavonic languages spoken in Yugoslavia, Serbo-Croatian.
Yugosla'via (yōōgoslah-). State in the Balkans; formed under a monarchy in Dec. 1918 by the union of Bosnia, Croatia, Dalmatia, Montenegro, Serbia, and Slovenia, proclaimed a republic in Nov. 1945; capital, Belgrade. [f. Serbian, = 'South Slav']
Yukatan (yōōkatah'n). Peninsula in SE. Mexico between the Gulf of Mexico and the Gulf of Honduras.
Yu'kon (yōō-). 1. Territory of NW. Canada, constituted a separate political unit in 1898 with its capital at Dawson. 2. River of Canada flowing into the Bering Sea.
yule (yōōl) *n.* (also ~-*tide*) Christmas season or festival; ~-*log*, large log burnt on hearth at Christmas.
Yü'nnăn. Province of SW. China; capital, Kunming.
Yves, St.: see IVES.
Y.W.C.A. *abbrev.* YOUNG Women's Christian Association.

Z

Z, z (zĕd, U.S. zē). 1. 26th and last letter of modern English and 23rd of later Roman alphabet, derived through Latin and Greek from Phoenician and ancient Hebrew, ⊥, Ζ, Ζ, and representing the voiced form of *s*, especially in loan-words; *from A to Z*, from beginning to end, all through. 2. (alg. etc.) Symbol of 3rd of series of unknown or variable quantities (cf. *x, y*). 3. Object etc. shaped like Z.
zăbăglione (-ălyō'nă) *n.* Dessert consisting of a mixture of egg yolks, sugar, and Marsala. [It.]
Zaire[1] (zah-ēr'). Republic of central Africa; independent since 1960; capital, Kinshasa. **Zair'ean** *adj.* & *n.*
zaire[2] (zah-ēr') *n.* Principal monetary unit of Zaire, = 100 makuta.
Zămbe'zĭ. African river, rising in Zambia and flowing into the Indian Ocean; on its course are the Victoria Falls.
Ză'mbia. Republic of central Africa; member State of the Commonwealth, independent since 1964; capital, Lusaka.
ză'nў *n.* Buffoon, simpleton;

(hist.) attendant on clown or acrobat awkwardly imitating his master's acts. [Fr. or It. *zani* servants acting as clowns in 'Commedia dell' Arte' (Venetian form of *Gianni* = *Giovanni* John)]
Zănzĭba̅r'. Island off east coast of Africa, formerly (with Pemba and some adjacent islets) a sultanate and British protectorate; since 1963 forming, with Tanganyika, the republic of TANZANIA. **Zănzĭba̅r'ĭ** *n.* Native, inhabitant, of Zanzibar.
Zărathŭ'stra. Old Iranian form of ZOROASTER.
zare'ba, -ri'ba (-rē-) *n.* Fence, stockade, usu. of thorn-bushes, for defence of camp, village, etc., in Sudan etc. [Arab. *zarība*(h) cattle-pen]
zeal *n.* Ardour, eagerness, enthusiasm, in pursuit of some end or in favour of person or cause.
zea'lous (zĕl-) *adj.* **zea'louslў** *adv.*
Zea'land (zēl-). (Dan. *Sjoelland*) Group of islands in E. Denmark; largest island of this group, on which Copenhagen is situated.
zea'lot (zĕl-) *n.* 1. Zealous person, fanatical enthusiast. 2. Z~,

(hist.) member of Jewish sect which aimed at Jewish theocracy over the world and fiercely resisted Romans until fall of Jerusalem in A.D. 70. **zea'lotrў** *n.*
Ze̅'bedee. Father of the Apostles James and John.
ze̅'bra *n.* African equine mammal of genus *Equus*, related to horse and ass, covered with black or brownish stripes on whitish or buff ground; ~ *crossing*, striped street-crossing where pedestrians have precedence over traffic; ~-*wood*, (ornamentally striped wood of) any of various trees and shrubs.
ze̅'bū *n.* Humped species of ox (*Bos indicus*), domesticated in India, China, Japan, and parts of Africa.
Ze̅'bŭlun. Hebrew patriarch, son of Jacob and Leah (Gen. 30: 20); tribe of Israel, traditionally descended from him.
Zech. *abbrev.* Zechariah (O.T.).
Zĕchari'ah (-k-, -a). Hebrew minor prophet; book of O.T. containing his prophecies.
zĕd *n.* The letter Z, z.
Zĕde̅kī'ah (-a). Son of Josiah, and the last king of Judah; he rebelled against Nebuchadnezzar

and was carried off to Babylon into captivity (2 Kings 24-5, 2 Chron. 26).

zee *n.* (U.S.) Letter Z, z.

Zee'land (*or* zā-). Maritime province of the Netherlands, consisting of six islands in the Scheldt estuary.

Zeitgeist (tsī'tgīst) *n.* Spirit of the times; characteristic trend of thought, culture, etc., of period. [Ger. *zeit* time, *geist* spirit]

zĕmī'ndār *n.* (hist., in India, esp. Bengal) Person holding land for which he paid land-tax to British Government. [Hind. f. Pers. *zemīndār* landholder]

zĕ'mstvŏ *n.* (hist.) Russian elective district or provincial council for local government, established by Alexander II (1864), and superseded after 1917 by soviets. [Russ. *zemlya* land]

zĕna'na (-ahna) *n.* (in India and Iran) Part of house reserved for women. [Hind., f. Pers. *zanāna* (*zan* woman)]

Zĕnd *n.* 1. Pahlavi translation and exposition of the Avesta. 2. (archaic, erron.) Avestan. [f. ZEND-AVESTA, because Zend was erron. thought to denote the language of the books]

Zĕnd-Avĕ'sta *n.* Avesta together with the Zend. [properly *Avestava-Zend*, text with interpretation]

zĕ'nĭth *n.* Point of sky directly overhead (ill. CELESTIAL); (fig.) highest point or state, culmination, acme. **zĕ'nĭthal** *adj.* ~ *projection*, projection of a portion of the globe upon a plane tangent to it at its centre, ensuring that all points have their true compass directions from the centre of the map (ill. PROJECTION). [Arab. *samt* (*ar-rās*) way (*over* the head)]

Zē'nō¹ (335-263 B.C.). Greek philosopher born at Citium, Cyprus, founder of STOIC School.

Zē'nō² (*c* 490-*c* 430 B.C.). Greek philosopher, pupil and friend of PARMENIDES.

Zeph. *abbrev.* Zephaniah (O.T.).

Zĕphanī'ah (-*a*) (7th c. B.C.). Hebrew minor prophet; book of O.T. containing his prophecies.

zĕ'phyr (-*er*) *n.* 1. West wind, esp. personified; soft mild gentle wind or breeze. 2. Fine very thin woollen material; garment made from this.

Zĕ'ppĕlin *n.* Cigar-shaped rigid dirigible airship of the type constructed by Count Ferdinand von Zeppelin in 1900, used in air raids against Britain in the war of 1914-18.

zēr'ō *n.* Figure 0, cipher (now chiefly U.S.); point or line marked o on graduated scale, esp. in thermometer or other measuring instrument; temperature corresponding to zero of thermometer, degree of heat reckoned as 0° (in Celsius and Réaumur scales, freezing-point of water; in Fahrenheit scale, 32° below this); (fig.) lowest point, bottom of scale, nullity, nonentity; zero hour; *absolute* ~, lowest possible temperature; temperature (approx. −273·1 °C) at which all substances have lost their heat and can be cooled no further; ~ *hour*, (orig. & esp. mil.?) hour at which any planned operation is timed to begin. ~ *v.t.* Adjust (instrument etc.) to a zero point. [Arab *çifr* cipher]

zĕst *n.* Piquancy, stimulating flavour; keen enjoyment or interest, relish, gusto. [Fr. *zeste* orange- or lemon-peel]

zē'ta *n.* 7th (later 6th) letter of Greek alphabet (Z, ζ), corresponding to z.

Zē'tland: = SHETLAND.

zeu'gma *n.* (gram.) Figure of speech in which single word is made to apply to two or more words in sentence while failing to give sense with one of these, e.g. *with weeping eyes and hearts* (where sense requires *bleeding hearts*); freq. (loosely) = SYLLEPSIS [Gk, = 'yoking']

Zeus. (Gk myth.) Supreme god, son of Cronos, whom he overthrew and succeeded. Zeus and his brothers divided the universe by casting lots, Zeus obtaining heaven, Poseidon the sea, and Pluto the underworld; he was regarded as the king and father of gods and men, with powers over all other deities save the Fates, as the dispenser of good and evil, giver of laws and defender of house and hearth; identified by the Romans with Jupiter.

Zeu'xis (5th c. B.C.). Greek painter; his most famous work was a picture of Helen of Troy.

zi'bĕt *n.* Asiatic or Indian civet cat (*Viverra zibetha*).

zi'ggurăt *n.* Pyramidal tower in ancient Mesopotamia, surmounted by a temple and with stages or a continuous ramp to the summit.

zi'gzăg *n.* Series of short lines inclined at angles in alternate directions; something having such lines or sharp turns. ~ *adj.* Having form of zigzag; with abrupt alternate left and right turns. ~ *adv.* In zigzag manner or course. ~ *v.i.* Move in zigzag course.

zinc *n.* (chem.) Hard bluish-white metallic element, brittle at subnormal temperatures and above 200 °C., but malleable between 100° and 150 °C., used for roofing, galvanizing sheet-iron, to make alloys, esp. brass, and in voltaic cells etc.; symbol Zn, at. no. 30, at. wt 65·37; ~ *ointment*, white unguent made from zinc oxide; ~ *oxide*, antiseptic astringent powder used for skin affections. ~ *v.t.* Treat, coat, with zinc.

Zī'ngarō (-ngg-) *n.* (pl. *-rī*; fem. *Zingara*, pl. *-rē*). Gipsy.

zi'nnia *n.* Tropical Amer. composite plant with showy flowers, esp. *Z*~ *elegans*, the common garden species. [J. G. *Zinn* (1727-59), German professor of medicine]

Zī'on. One of the hills of Jerusalem, on which the city of David was built, and which became the centre of Jewish life and worship; hence, the house of God, the Jewish religion, the Christian Church, the Heavenly Jerusalem or kingdom of God, a Christian (esp. nonconformist) place of worship. **Zī'onĭsm** *n.* Movement among modern Jews founded 1897 by Theodor HERZL, which resulted in the re-establishment of a Jewish nation in the land of Israel. **Zī'onĭst** *n.* & *adj.* (Adherent) of Zionism. [Heb. *Tsīyōn* hill]

zip *n.* (Movement accompanied by) light sharp sound as of tearing canvas, flying bullet, etc.; (fig.) energy, force, impetus; ~ *fastener*, fastening device consisting of two flexible strips with interlocking metal or plastic projections which can be closed or opened by a sliding clip pulled along them. ~ *v.* 1. Move or go with sound of zip or with great force or rapidity. 2. Close or fasten (*up*) with zip fastener. [imit.]

zi'pper *n.* Zip fastener. [orig., trade-name for kind of boot with sliding fastener]

zĭr'con *n.* (min.) Zirconium silicate, occurring usu. in variously coloured tetragonal crystals, of which translucent varieties are used as gems, esp. red or brownish kinds called HYACINTH. [Arab. *zarqūn*]

zĭrcō'nĭum *n.* (chem.) Metallic element obtained from zircon etc. as black powder or greyish crystalline substance; symbol Zr, at. no. 40, at. wt 91·22.

Zī'ska (*or* shĭsh-), Jan (1360-1424). Bohemian nobleman who became leader of the Hussites and gained many victories over the Imperialists.

zī'ther (-dh-) *n.* Musical instrument somewhat like dulcimer with flat sound-box and numerous strings (up to 40), held horizontally and played with fingers and plectrum.

zlŏ'tў *n.* (pl. same). Principal monetary unit of Poland, = 100 groszy. [Pol., = 'golden']

zō'dĭac *n.* Belt of the heavens limited by lines about 8° from the ecliptic on each side, including all apparent positions of the sun and planets as known to the ancient astronomers, and divided into 12 equal parts (*signs of the* ~: ARIES, TAURUS, GEMINI, CANCER, LEO, VIRGO, LIBRA, SCORPIO, SAGITTARIUS, CAPRICORN, AQUARIUS, PISCES) each formerly containing the similarly named constellation but now by precession of equinoxes coinciding with the constellation that bears the name of the preceding sign (e.g. the constellation Aries is now in Taurus). [Gk

[1011]

ZODIACAL

zodiakos (*kuklos*) (circle) of figures, f. *zōdion* dim. of *zōon* animal]
zōdī'acal *adj*. Of, in, the zodiac; ~ *light*, luminous tract of sky shaped like tall triangle occas. seen in east before sunrise or in west after sunset esp. in tropics.
zō'ėtrōpe *n*. Mechanical toy with series of images representing successive positions of moving object, so arranged on inner surface of cylinder that when it is rapidly rotated the object appears to be in motion. [Gk *zoē* life, *tropos* turn]
Zŏ'ffanў, John (1733–1810). German painter who came to England in 1758; famous for his pictures of stage scenes.
Zōla, Émile (1840–1902). French naturalistic novelist, author of 'Thérèse Raquin' (1867) and the Rougon-Macquart series of novels dealing with 19th-c. French life.
Zō'laism *n*. Excessively realistic treatment of the grosser sides of human nature, as in Zola's novels.
Zö'llner (tsĕr-), Johann Karl Friedrich (1834–82). German physicist; ~'s *lines*, parallel lines made

ZÖLLNER'S LINES

to appear to converge or diverge by series of short lines parallel to each other and intersecting each of them obliquely.
zollverein (tsŏ'lferin) *n*. Union of States having common customs tariff against outsiders and usu. free trade with each other; specif., customs union formed (1834) among the German States under the leadership of Prussia. [Ger.]
zŏ'mbie *n*. 1. (in voodoo) Supernatural force or spirit reanimating and controlling corpse; corpse so reanimated. 2. Person thought to resemble zombie; mindless or will-less automaton.
zōne *n*. 1. (archaic) Girdle or belt; band or ring, esp. one of series of concentric or alternate stripes of colour, light or shade, etc. 2. Each of five encircling regions, distinguished by differences of climate, into which surface of earth is divided by tropics of Cancer and Capricorn and polar circles (ill. EARTH). 3. Area enclosed between two concentric circles; any well-defined tract or region of more or less belt-like form; ~ *time*, standard time in a TIME zone. 4. (geol.) = HORIZON, 2. 5. Any part of a town or region divided off from other parts for a particular purpose (esp. in town and country planning). 6. (math.) Part of surface of sphere enclosed between two parallel planes, or of surface of any solid of revolution contained between two planes perpendicular to the axis. 7. (crystal.) Series of faces in crys-

tal having their lines of intersection parallel. **zō'nal** *adj*.
zō'nallў *adv*. **zōne** *v.t*. Mark, encircle, with a zone, divide into, assign to, zones (esp. in town and country planning). [f. L *zona*, f. Gr. *zōnē* girdle]
zōō *n*. ZOOLOGICAL Gardens.
zōōgĕŏ'graphў *n*. (Study of) the geographical distribution of animals. **zōōgĕŏ'grapher** *n*. **zōōgēŏgrăˈphical** *adj*.
zōō'graphў *n*. Descriptive zoology. **zōō'grapher** *n*. **zōōgrăˈphical** *adj*.
zō'oid *n*. Individual member of a colony of animals joined together.
zōō'latrў *n*. Worship of animals.
zōō'logў *n*. Branch of biology dealing with the animal kingdom and the physiology, classification, habits, etc., of its members. **zōō'logist** *n*. **zōōlŏ'gical** *adj*. Z~ *Gardens*, orig. gardens of London Zoological Society in Regent's Park, housing the society's collection of wild animals; any garden or park in which wild animals are kept for public exhibition.
zōōm *v*. 1. Make loud low-pitched buzzing sound. 2. (of aircraft) Climb for short time at high speed and very steep angle; make (aircraft) climb thus. 3. (cinemat.) Cause (image) to seem to approach or recede from viewer. ~ *n*. Act of zooming; ~ *lens*, (photog.) lens which by variation of focal length enables continuous alteration from long shot to close-up. [imit.]
zōōmōr'phic *adj*. Representing or imitating animal forms; having form of an animal; attributing form or nature of animal to something, esp. deity.
zō'ophyte *n*. Any of various animals of low organization, usu. fixed, and freq. resembling plants or flowers in having branched or radiating structure, as crinoids, sea-anemones, corals, sponges, etc. **zōōphў'tic** *adj*.
zō'ospore *n*. Spore occurring in certain algae, fungi, etc., having power of locomotion.
Zōr'ndŏrf (ts-). Place in Brandenburg where Frederick the Great defeated the Russians in 1758.
Zŏrōă'ster. (also *Zarathustra*) Persian believed to have lived in the 6th c. B.C., founder of the dualistic religious system of the Magi and ancient Persia which survives among the Parsees; its scriptures, the ZEND-AVESTA, teach that Ormazd, lord of goodness and light and creator of mankind, is ceaselessly at war with Ahriman and the evil spirits of darkness. **Zŏrōă'strian** *adj*. & *n*. **Zŏrōă'strianism** *n*.
Zouave (zōō'ahv) *n*. 1. Member of French light infantry corps orig. recruited from Zouaoua tribe of Algiers, distinguished for physique and dash, wearing uni-

ZYMURGY

form of bright-coloured baggy trousers, short open-fronted embroidered jacket, wide sash, and turban or tasselled cap. 2. (hist.) Member of any corps adopting similar dress, esp. in Amer. Civil War.
zounds (zŏōndz) *int*. (archaic) Exclamation used in oaths and asseverations. [shortening of (*by*) *God's wounds*]
zucchĕ'ttō (tsōōk-) *n*. Small round skull-cap worn by R.C. ecclesiastics, the pope's being white, a cardinal's red, a bishop's violet, that of others black.
Zui'der Zee (zi-). Large shallow inlet of the North Sea in the Netherlands, the reclamation of which was begun in 1924 for the purpose of forming a new province. [Du., = 'southern sea']
Zulu (zōō'lōō) *n*. & *adj*. (Member, language) of a South African Bantu people inhabiting NE. part of Natal. **Zu'lulănd**. Region inhabited by Zulus, annexed to Natal in 1897.
Zūr'ich (-k). (Ger. *Zürich*) Canton of N. Switzerland; the capital of the canton, situated on Lake ~.
Zwi'ngli (-ngg-), Ulrich (1484–1531). Swiss religious reformer; his doctrines, which contain elements of Reformed as distinguished from Lutheran doctrine, led to civil war between the Swiss cantons, in which he was killed. **Zwi'nglian** *adj*. & *n*. (Follower) of Zwingli. **Zwi'nglianism** *n*.
zỹgodă'ctyl *adj*. & *n*. (Bird) with toes arranged in pairs, two before and two behind, e.g. parrot.
zỹgō'ma *n*. Bony arch on each side of skull of vertebrates, joining cranial and facial bones, and consisting of cheek-bone and its connections (ill. HEAD). **zỹgomă'tic** *adj*.
zỹgomōr'phic *adj*. Having one plane of symmetry (esp. of flowers).
zỹ'gospore *n*. (in some algae and fungi) Spore or germ-cell arising from fusion of two similar cells.
zỹ'gōte *n*. (biol.) Cell arising from union of two reproductive cells or gametes, fertilized ovum (ill. ALGA). **zỹgō'tic** *adj*.
zỹ'māse *n*. (biochem.) Any of a group of enzymes converting glucose and a few other carbohydrates, in the presence of oxygen, into carbon dioxide and water, or, in the absence of oxygen, into alcohol and carbon dioxide, or into lactic acid.
zỹmŏ'lўsis *n*. Action of enzymes, changes produced by this. **zỹmolў'tic** *adj*.
zỹmŏ'sis *n*. Fermentation; zymotic disease. **zỹmŏ'tic** *adj*. Of fermentation.
zỹ'mūrgў *n*. Branch of applied chemistry dealing with science of wine-making, brewing, and distilling.

[1012]

ADDENDA

Callaghan (kă'lahan), (Leonard) James (1912–). British Labour statesman; prime minister 1976–9.
John Paul II (Karol Wojtyla 1920–), pope 1978– .
Thă'tcher, Margaret Hilda (1925–). British Conservative statesman; prime minister 1979– .

بَعُدَ الْمَدْيَنُ كَمَا بَعِدَتْ ثَمُودُ ۞ وَلَقَدْ أَرْسَلْنَا مُوسَىٰ بِآيَاتِنَا وَسُلْطَانٍ مُبِينٍ
إِلَىٰ فِرْعَوْنَ وَمَلَإِيْهِ فَاتَّبَعُوا أَمْرَ فِرْعَوْنَ وَمَا أَمْرُ فِرْعَوْنَ بِرَشِيدٍ ۞ يَقْدُمُ قَوْ
مَهُ يَوْمَ الْقِيَامَةِ فَأَوْرَدَهُمُ النَّارَ وَبِئْسَ الْوِرْدُ الْمَوْرُودُ ۞ وَأُتْبِعُوا فِي هَـٰذِهِ
لَعْنَةً وَيَوْمَ الْقِيَامَةِ بِئْسَ الرِّفْدُ الْمَرْفُودُ ۞ ذَٰلِكَ مِنْ أَنْبَاءِ الْقُرَىٰ نَقُصُّهُ
عَلَيْكَ مِنْهَا قَائِمٌ وَحَصِيدٌ ۞ وَمَا ظَلَمْنَاهُمْ وَلَـٰكِن ظَلَمُوا أَنفُسَهُمْ فَمَا
أَغْنَتْ عَنْهُمْ آلِهَتُهُمُ الَّتِي يَدْعُونَ مِن دُونِ اللَّهِ مِن شَيْءٍ لَّمَّا جَاءَ أَمْرُ رَبِّكَ وَمَا
زَادُوهُمْ غَيْرَ تَتْبِيبٍ ۞ وَكَذَٰلِكَ أَخْذُ رَبِّكَ إِذَا أَخَذَ الْقُرَىٰ وَهِيَ ظَالِمَةٌ
إِنَّ أَخْذَهُ أَلِيمٌ شَدِيدٌ ۞ إِنَّ فِي ذَٰلِكَ لَآيَةً لِّمَنْ خَافَ عَذَابَ الْآخِرَةِ ذَٰلِكَ
يَوْمٌ مَّجْمُوعٌ لَّهُ النَّاسُ وَذَٰلِكَ يَوْمٌ مَّشْهُودٌ ۞ وَمَا نُؤَخِّرُهُ إِلَّا لِأَجَلٍ مَّعْدُودٍ
يَوْمَ يَأْتِ لَا تَكَلَّمُ نَفْسٌ إِلَّا بِإِذْنِهِ فَمِنْهُمْ شَقِيٌّ وَسَعِيدٌ ۞ فَأَمَّا الَّذِينَ شَقُوا
فَفِي النَّارِ لَهُمْ فِيهَا زَفِيرٌ وَشَهِيقٌ خَالِدِينَ فِيهَا مَا دَامَتِ السَّمَاوَاتُ وَالْأَرْضُ

ARABIC WRITING: Alphabet in which vowel sounds are indicated by signs above or below the consonants. (A page of the Koran, the Mohammedan sacred book: 13th c.)